August 2022

For Ethan—
With love to
my favorite son.
Dad

WEST ACADEMIC PUBLISHING'S LAW SCHOOL ADVISORY BOARD

PRODUCTS LIABILITY LAW

Fourth Edition

David G. Owen
Carolina Distinguished Professor of Law Emeritus
University of South Carolina

HORNBOOK SERIES®

WEST ACADEMIC PUBLISHING

444 Cedar Street, Suite 700
St. Paul, MN 55101
1-877-888-1330

Printed in the United States of America

ISBN: 978-1-64708-714-2

For Joan, Wendy, Ethan, and Megan

Preface

The fourth edition of this book continues the exploration of products liability law in America, from its inception long ago to the present. From about 1960, modern products liability law was born, matured, and "reformed" by legislatures and courts across the nation. Various aspects of products liability law remain in flux, but its major features have sharpened, and many of its doctrinal disputes have been resolved. This book traces the evolution of products liability law in America, examines how courts and legislatures have defined and applied this field of law, and explores an array of issues on which courts and commentators still disagree.

In recent decades, tumultuous litigations have arisen over the proper allocation of responsibility for harm caused by various dangerous products—asbestos, cigarettes, handguns, automotive vehicles, prescription drugs, and contaminated foods, to name just a few products frequently involved in causing human harm. Litigations involving such products raise a host of procedural issues, as in MDLs and class actions, but those are only touched on here. Focusing on substantive issues of liability and defense, this work centers on the responsibility of makers and sellers of goods for product injuries.

For more than a century, commentators have chronicled and critiqued developing principles of products liability law propounded by courts and legislatures in the United States, and, more recently, abroad. Cobbling together many of these developments, this volume seeks to bring some order to the mélange of common law decisions and statutory provisions, tort and contract, which combine to create this tumultuous field of law that for so long appeared out of focus, as if viewed through air currents shimmering over a baking summer road.

The grist for almost any scholar, as others have also mused, is the scholarship of those who came before. Particularly in a work that seeks principally to organize and explain, little room remains for designing new pathways of development. Credit belongs to William Prosser for observing that such chroniclers essentially are packrats, "unblushingly" collecting and assembling bits and pieces from other scholars, judicial and academic.*

Even as products liability law in so many ways has begun to settle down, perfection in such a work, like proximate cause, remains as elusive as a butterfly. So, in an effort to move the next edition at least a bit in that direction, I invite corrections, suggestions, and comments on any aspect of this work: owen@sc.edu.

DAVID G. OWEN

Aiken, South Carolina
May 2022

---

* See W. Prosser, The Law of Torts (4th ed. 1971), preface, at xi. Or, "dwarfs perched on the shoulders of giants," to borrow a twelfth-century metaphor of Bernard of Chartres. See Jacques Le Goff, Intellectuals in the Middle Ages 12 (1957, 1985) (Teresa Lavender Fagan trans., Blackwell, 1993), citing Stephen C. Ferrulolo, The Origins of the University: The Schools of Paris and Their Critics, 1100–1215, at 154 (Stanford 1985).

Acknowledgments

Recognition is due to many persons whose contributions made this book possible. The largest share of credit and my profound gratitude go to Karen A. Miller, my dedicated and accomplished Research Associate, who expertly researched, edited, and adroitly managed production of the last three editions of this work, especially, this fourth edition.

Generations of student research and editorial assistants labored skillfully on earlier editions of this work and its progenitor treatise from which many of the chapters draw. I reiterate my appreciation for the excellent assistance of them all: including, on the third edition, Jonathan Asbill, Renee Ballew, Joseph Bowman, Jessica Cochran, Kimberly Cochran, Marshall Crane, Jacob Fling, Abigail Forrester, Christopher Jones, Kevin Malloy, Brooks Miller, William Mills, Soroush Moghaddassi, Mark Nash, Jessica Peters, Amanda Pickens, Andrew Powell, Jennie Rischbieter, Douglas Rushton, Danielle Salerno, Sara Svedberg, Olesya Vaskevich, Matthew Vlasman, and Andrew Walker. And many thanks again for the excellent labors, on the first two editions of this work and its progenitor treatise, to Jay A'Hearn, Van Anderson, Thomas Andrews, Angela Atanasov, Amanda Bailey, Kristen Baylis, John Bell, Denise Bessellieu, Justin Bice, Stephanie Borsanyi, Julie Brown, James Burns, Natalie Byars, James Callahan, Sara Centioni, Rangeley Bailey Chewning, Breana Burkett Collier, Huntley Crouch, Donald Cummings, Racheal Dain, Jason Dennis, Michael Dirnbauer, Julia Ebert, Danielle Evans, Sarah Berry Fellona, Carrie Fisher, Kathryn Flowers, Marilyn Gartley, Mary Gruenhagen, Stephen Hall, John Harper, Holly Harrington, John Harvey, Emily Howard, David Hoyle, Scott Johnson, William Jordan, Anne Kearse, Candy Kern-Fuller, Trent Kirk, David Kusa, Jeff Lack, Robert Lack, Taylor Lacy, René LeBlanc-Allman, Adam Lee, Nikki Lee, Jeff Little, David Marshall, James Mayberry, Steven McFarland, Jeremy Melville, Valerie Metrakos, Richard Miller, William Mills, Amy Neuschafer, Forrest Norvell, Catherine Noyes, Suzanne Guitar Odom, Rochelle Oldfield, Dana Pagän, Matthew Richardson, Anne Ross, David Scott, Ross Shealy, Dave Smith, Dayton Stout, Scott Taylor, Emma Thomas, Eric Tonnsen, Terri Vincent, David Watkins, Cathy Weaver, Sarah Dixon Wendell, Thad Westbrook, Adam Whitsett, Tod Williams, Jennifer Young, and Eric Zaiser. The first edition was brought to press by a particularly dedicated team of managing editors, Aaron Dias, Amy Neuschafer, and, especially, Alyson Campbell who devoted enormous work and skill to the first edition. And Robert Hill lent his keen talents to several chapters of the first edition, for which I am grateful.

Most of my work on earlier editions of this book took place at the University of South Carolina, and I owe an enormous debt to the unremitting encouragement and support of John Montgomery, now Dean Emeritus, over many years. Thanks also are due to Associate Dean Emeritus and Interim Dean Emeritus Philip Lacy for his enthusiastic and creative support of the project in untold ways. I also contributed considerable labor on earlier editions during visits to other universities—the Universities of Michigan, Texas, Indiana, Nebraska, Alabama, the University of Oxford (Corpus Christi and University Colleges) in England, and Santa Anna University in Pisa, Italy; I thank my friends at all these universities for their good support.

Various scholars lent valuable advice on this and previous editions, including Richard Ausness, Richard Cupp, Mary Davis, Jim Gash, Michael Green, Nicholas Wittner, and John Lopatka. Thanks also to my coauthors of various other books from which this work draws, including Mary Davis, Mike Green, Page Keeton, Robert Keeton, Stuart Madden, John Montgomery, and William Prosser. The early products liability scholarship of Deans Prosser and Keeton, together with that of Dix Noel, Fleming James, John Wade, and others, tilled this field of law with skillful inspiration, providing fertile groundwork for its explosive development in modern times. Thanks to James Boyd White for pointing me to Franklin's prudential algebra letter.

My appreciation goes to West and Thomson Reuters, for allowing me to place early versions of many chapters intended eventually for this work in Owen & Davis on Products Liability and, earlier, in Madden & Owen on Products Liability. And I thank West Academic for reciprocating. In addition, many passages in this volume began as passages in journal articles I published elsewhere over the decades, and I thank those journals for the return of my prior musings.

Abroad, several scholars stand out for special thanks. Richard Goldberg, Geraint Howells, John Miller, and Jane Stapleton provided me (as others) with a discerning body of scholarship on comparative products liability law, which has helped to shrink the globe. They also deserve special thanks for providing helpful comments on the section on foreign law. I am particularly in debt to Jane Stapleton, Peter Kane, and Martin Matthews, for their support at the University of Oxford, which gave me the opportunity to explore the moral foundations of this field of law, its sources in British law, and its comparisons to European law. My thanks also go to Giovanni Comandé of Santa Anna University, Pisa, Italy; Erwin Deutsch of the University of Göttingen, Germany; and Jean-Sebastien Borghetti, of the Université Panthéon-Sorbonne (Paris I), for providing portals for my inquiries into the products liability law of mainland Europe. To Akio Morishima of Nagoya University, and Michitaro Urakawa of Waseda University, I am grateful for a first-hand view of Japan's march into modern products liability law.

Closer to home, for many years of discussions on the vagaries of products liability law and theory, I am indebted to John Montgomery, Bob Felix (who also lent his wisdom on choice of law), and, for his patient efforts to guide me in the rudiments of how economic theory applies to tort law, John Lopatka, who now resides too far away. And my thanks continue to Pat Hubbard for his example in searching always for the groundwork of law, and for pointing me to the metaphor of the butterfly.

Particular thanks go to West Publishing, later West Group, then Thomson/West, later Thomson Reuters, now West Academic, for their patience while the first edition of this hornbook project was deferred as I explored the philosophical foundations of tort and products liability law, then directed my efforts to the Products Liability Restatement project, and then worked on the multi-volume predecessor of this book. In particular, I remain in debt to Roger Noreen who, with his characteristically gracious enthusiasm, endorsed the project of a then-young commentator in this then-new field of law; to John Hodson, whose persistent prodding was instrumental in keeping this project's first stage moving forward; and, finally, to Doug Powell, who, with genial encouragement, helped nurture the project of a weary commentator to its eventual completion. Thanks also for encouragement and support over many years by Louis Higgins, Pamela Siege Chandler, Pat Sparks, James Cahoy, and Mac Soto; and for creative production contributions by Roxanne Birkel, Greg Olson, Laura Holle, Megan Hoffman, and Staci Herr.

These acknowledgments would be incomplete without recognition of the many able judges, commentators, legislators, and lawyers, now global, whose swelling body of work on all aspects of products liability law has defined and enriched this field of law—a field that, after more than half a century of modern ferment, is beginning broadly to settle into a fair and coherent set of principles and rules. In particular, this field of law owes an enormous debt to Jim Henderson and Aaron Twerski—not only for their prodigious scholarship, but for their monumental *Restatement (Third) of Torts: Products Liability*, a project that consumed a major share of their labors for much of the 1990s. The Reporters' vision of how products liability law should be structured and conceived, inescapably controversial, reformulated this field of law sensibly for the new millennium.

My largest debt is to my family, Joan, Wendy, Ethan, Megan, Baron, and Blue, and to my friend, Don Brasher, all of whom long and graciously provided me with this project's vital ingredient—time. Finally, I am grateful for the many opportunities afforded to me by my parents and by living in this country.

Summary of Contents

Page

PART V. SPECIAL DEFENDANTS, TRANSACTIONS, AND PRODUCTS

Table of Contents

Page

PART III. CAUSATION

PART IV. DEFENSES

PART V. SPECIAL DEFENDANTS, TRANSACTIONS, AND PRODUCTS

Abbreviated Citations

Am. Law Prod. Liab. 3d

American Law of Products Liability 3d

Crockett, Product Warranties

Matt Crockett, The Law of Product Warranties (2022 ed.) (formerly Barkley Clark and Christopher Smith, The Law of Product Warranties (2d ed. 2002))

Dobbs, Law of Torts

Dan B. Dobbs, The Law of Torts (2000)

Frumer, Friedman, and Sklaren, Products Liability

Louis R. Frumer, Melvin I. Friedman, and Cary S. Sklaren, Products Liability (rev. ed. 2008)

Harper, James, and Gray on Torts

Fowler V. Harper, Fleming James, Jr., and Oscar S. Gray, The Law of Torts (3d ed. 2006)

Hawkland, UCC Series

William D. Hawkland, Uniform Commercial Code Series (CBC)

Lawrence's Anderson on the UCC

Lary Lawrence, Lawrence's Anderson on the Uniform Commercial Code (3d ed. 2001–2021 rev. ed.)

McCormick on Evidence

McCormick on Evidence (Kenneth S. Broun ed., 8th ed. 2020)

Owen & Davis on Products Liability

David G. Owen and Mary J. Davis, Owen & Davis on Products Liability (4th ed. 2014)

Products Liability Restatement

Restatement (Third) of Torts: Products Liability (1998)

Prosser and Keeton on Torts

W. Page Keeton, Dan B. Dobbs, Robert E. Keeton, and David G. Owen, Prosser and Keeton on the Law of Torts (5th ed. 1984)

White and Summers, UCC

James J. White and Robert S. Summers, Uniform Commercial Code (5th and 6th Pract. ed. 2010–2012) and (6th student ed. 2010)

PRODUCTS LIABILITY LAW

Fourth Edition

Chapter 1

INTRODUCTION

Table of Sections

§ 1.1 PRODUCTS LIABILITY LAW

Products liability law governs liability for the sale or other commercial transfer of a product that causes physical harm because it is defective or its properties are falsely represented. Accidental injuries and illnesses attributable to products are a massive, costly problem in the modern world. Americans suffer upwards of 200 million product injuries, illnesses, and deaths each year, at a national cost approaching $10 trillion.[1] Not all such harm is fairly attributable to product defects or safety misrepresentations, of course, but much of it is.

While the definition of "products liability law"[2] offered above might be thought too narrow, it captures the great bulk of cases normally viewed as falling under the "products liability" umbrella, and not too many more. Perhaps the largest category of cases excluded from this definition are those involving pure economic loss, excluded by the limitation to cases involving "physical harm," which includes only accidents resulting in personal injury, death, and property damage. Some lawyers view this field of law as including cases with purely commercial losses—such as profits lost by an industrial enterprise when a defect in a punch press halts production.[3] But most American lawyers view cases involving pure economic loss as commercial contractual disputes rather than "products liability" cases. And no doubt the definition here is too narrow for excluding other types of cases that arguably belong within this legal category, just as it surely is too broad for covering some cases that may be thought to lie outside this legal realm. But the field of products liability law is still developing, with borders still somewhat in flux, so the definition here is good enough for now.

Product Safety Law Distinguished

What products liability law is *not* is "product *safety*" law. "Products liability" and "product safety" are both terms conventionally used in America to describe law that

---

[1] These estimates of the annual number and cost of product accidents and illnesses in America are rough extrapolations from data and estimates in Ruttenberg, Cardi, and Fenton, The Taxpayers' Burden from Product-Related Harm, 21 Kan. J.L. & Pub. Pol'y 121 (2011–2012), a study discussed in § 1.3, below.

[2] Contrary to prevailing American usage, most courts and scholars in most other nations use the term *product* liability law, as do defense counsel (and some courts and scholars) in this nation.

[3] At least one prominent products liability scholar, Jane Stapleton, thinks the definition of products liability law should include the recovery *vel non* of pure economic loss. See Stapleton, Book Review, 122 Law Q. Rev. 695 (2006) (reviewing the first edition of this book).

addresses covers product-related dangers, accidents, and illnesses. A central issue in both products *liability* law and product *safety* law is establishing how products should be classified as "excessively" or "unduly" hazardous, "unreasonably" dangerous, or "defective." Both fields of law seek to reduce the toll of accidents from such hazards to improve product safety. But there they begin to diverge.

Product Safety Law

The law of product safety is *regulatory* law—the systems of rules established by legislatures and administrative agencies of federal, state, and occasionally municipal governments to regulate the safety of products sold to or used by the public. Product safety law operates *ex ante*, seeking to prevent product-caused accidents and diseases before they occur.

Municipal authorities regulate the safety of certain building products through building codes and prohibit the sale of various types of dangerous products. At the state level, departments of health and employment safety, fire boards, consumer protection, and other agencies administer safety laws on a wide diversity of products, such as glue, architectural glass, industrial tools and machinery, amusement rides, fireworks, mattresses, refrigerators, household chemicals, life preservers, power tools, toys, elevators, BB guns, slingshots, unvented gas heaters, food and drugs, blood, plastic bags and, in Connecticut (until some time ago), used hats.[4] These state and local laws, described as "a hodgepodge of tragedy-inspired responses" to the product safety problem, generally are characterized by "narrow scope, diffuse jurisdiction, minuscule budgets, absence of enforcement, mild sanctions, and casual administration."[5]

Product safety law at the federal level is more significant, with various federal regulatory agencies exerting considerable control over product safety on a national scale. The Consumer Product Safety Commission (CPSC) has broad jurisdiction to regulate consumer product safety under the Consumer Product Safety Act[6] and various other federal product safety statutes.[7] Congress vested authority for regulating the safety of other types of products in the National Highway Traffic Safety Administration (NHTSA) of the Department of Transportation,[8] the Food and Drug Administration (FDA) of the Department of Health and Human Services,[9] the Occupational Safety and Health

---

4 Conn. Gen. Stat. Ann. § 19–425 (repealed 1981).

5 Final Report, National Commission on Product Safety 2, 81–88 (1970). Municipal laws of these types often are administered more through education than enforcement. Id.

6 15 U.S.C. §§ 2051 et seq., originally enacted in 1972. See Southland Mower Co. v. Consumer Prod. Safety Comm'n, 619 F.2d 499 (5th Cir. 1980) (upholding CPSC design requirement for walk-behind power lawn mowers). The CPSA was substantially amended by the Consumer Product Safety Improvement Act of 2008, Pub. L. 110–314, 122 Stat. 1306, codified in scattered sections of 15 U.S.C. Manufacturers, distributors, and retailers of consumer products must "immediately" report defects creating a "substantial product hazard" or "an unreasonable risk of serious injury or death" to the Product Safety Commission. 15 U.S.C. § 2064(b). Other nations have similar product safety regulatory laws that often include reporting requirements. See 1 Owen & Davis on Products Liability §§ 1:20 et seq.

7 See, e.g., the Federal Hazardous Substances Act, 15 U.S.C. §§ 1261 et seq.; the Poison Prevention Packaging Act, 15 U.S.C. §§ 1471 et seq.; the Flammable Fabrics Act, 15 U.S.C. §§ 1191 et seq.; and the Refrigerator Safety Act, 15 U.S.C. §§ 1211 et seq.

8 This agency administers the National Traffic and Motor Vehicle Safety Act of 1966, 15 U.S.C. §§ 1381 et seq., re-codified at § 49 U.S.C. §§ 301 et seq.

9 This agency administers the Federal Food, Drug, and Cosmetic Act, 21 U.S.C. §§ 301 et seq. The 2009 Family Smoking Prevention and Tobacco Control Act (FSPTCA) extended FDA authority to tobacco products. See 21 U.S.C. § 387a. See also Nicopure Labs, LLC v. Food & Drug Admin., 266 F. Supp. 3d 360

Administration (OSHA) of the Department of Labor,[10] the Federal Aviation Administration (FAA) of the Department of Transportation,[11] and the Environmental Protection Agency (EPA).[12] These and other federal agencies also regulate the safety of pesticides, fungicides, foods, agricultural products, railroad appliances, firearms, cigarette labeling, and boats. While product safety regulatory law falls mostly outside the scope of products liability law, governmental safety regulation influences products liability law in a number of ways considered at various points in this book.

Products Liability Law

In contrast to product safety law, products liability law governs the private *litigation* of damages for product accidents—which inflict an enormous toll on our nation, as on other large nations as well. Studies reveal that roughly 200 million people in America alone suffer significant product-related harm each year, at an annual social cost of about $10 *trillion* per year.[13] Operating *ex post*, after a product accident has occurred, the rules of products liability law define the responsibility of commercial suppliers of products for physical harm from product defects and misrepresentations about a product's safety or performance capabilities.

A typical products liability case involves a claim for damages against the manufacturer or retailer of a product by a person injured while using the product. The plaintiff seeks to prove that the injury was caused by some deficiency in the way the product was made or marketed—that the product was in some manner "defective" or falsely described. In addition, the plaintiff will attempt to demonstrate that he or she was using the product properly or at least foreseeably. Typically, damage claims include medical expenses, disability and disfigurement, pain and suffering, lost earnings and earning capacity, sometimes emotional harm, and possibly some kind of property damage, perhaps to the product itself. The defendant usually attempts to show that the product was *not* defective—that it was in fact reasonably designed, correctly made, and properly marketed. Further, the defendant often seeks to establish that the plaintiff's injuries arose from improper use of the product by the plaintiff or someone else, or that something other than the product caused the harm. These are the central issues in a typical products liability case.

Some products liability cases involve transactions other than a sale. Products are sometimes leased, licensed, or commercially bailed. Or the injury-producing "product" may be something other than a typical, mass-produced chattel—for example, it may be a house,[14] a burial plot, a toxic substance, a recipe, electricity, a truckload of sand, an internet game, transfused blood, or a poisonous spider in a pair of pants.[15] Or the defendant may be a wholesaler, a component part manufacturer, a successor corporation, an employer, a publisher, a dentist, a trademark owner, or a plumber. All of these

(D.D.C. 2017) (holding FDA acted within its authority when extending cigarette regulations to electronic cigarettes and e-cigarette components of tobacco products), aff'd, 944 F.3d 267 (D.C. Cir. 2019).

[10] This agency administers the Occupational Safety and Health Act of 1970, 29 U.S.C. §§ 651 et seq.

[11] This agency administers the safety provisions of the Federal Aviation Act of 1958, 49 U.S.C. §§ 1301 et seq., re-codified at 49 U.S.C. §§ 40101 et seq.

[12] This agency administers the Toxic Substances Control Act, 15 U.S.C. §§ 2601 et seq.; the Federal Insecticide, Fungicide, and Rodenticide Act, 7 U.S.C. §§ 136 et seq.; and the Clean Air Act, particularly the regulation of asbestos removal in 42 U.S.C. § 7412.

[13] See note 1 and accompanying text, above.

[14] Blagg v. Fred Hunt Co., 612 S.W.2d 321, 324 (Ark. 1981).

[15] Flippo v. Mode O'Day Frock Shops of Hollywood, 449 S.W.2d 692 (Ark. 1970).

examples raise questions about the outer boundaries of products liability law—how to define a "product"; how to decide what kinds of transactions, defendants, and products should be covered by products liability principles; and how to draw lines between products liability and such overlapping fields of law as professional malpractice, environmental law, and workers' compensation.[16]

Other questions have emerged as technologies and products have changed over time: Should Amazon be strictly liable for harm from a defective product offered on its website by a third-party seller?[17] Should a chocolate candy manufacturer be held liable for not disclosing their suppliers' child or slave labor practices?[18] Or should a car manufacturer be liable for the consequences of a hack of its wireless systems?[19] And how might products liability law apply to 3D-printed[20] or cannabis-infused[21] products?

These are some of the issues of products liability law, the topic of this book.

Mixed Sources of Products Liability Law

Products liability law is full of mixtures. It is a mixture of tort law—negligence, strict liability in tort, and deceit—and of the contract law of sales—mostly warranty. It is a mixture of common law, now mostly on its tort side, and statutory law, generally on its contract side—notably sales law under Article 2 of the Uniform Commercial Code. In addition, many state legislatures (and Congress, to a lesser extent) have enacted products liability "reform" acts which address various products liability matters, often functionally apart from tort and contract. Because of these hybrid characteristics of products liability law, plaintiffs often have a variety of available claims. Negligence, breach of implied warranty, and strict liability in tort are all based on the notion that something was wrong with the product, that it was unduly dangerous or "defective." Remedies for breach of express warranty and fraud (and possibly other forms of tortious misrepresentation) may be available when a product is more dangerous than it was said to be, even if it was not defective or unfit by standards of negligence, implied warranty, or strict liability in tort.

As seen throughout this work, many of the most difficult issues in modern products liability law spring from the doctrinal mixture of tort and contract. Just to name a few of the many issues of this type, the clash of tort and contract doctrines has generated perplexing questions about the standard of liability, the test for design defectiveness, defenses, statutes of limitations, and recoverable damages.

The "Field" of Products Liability Law

The discussion so far has assumed that products liability is a proper field of law. Yet, the fact that products liability law involves a blend of tort and contract doctrines raises a question of whether it really is a field of law at all, or whether products liability

[16] As discussed below, the difficulty of drawing boundaries of this type has led some scholars to question whether "products liability" really defines a field of law at all. Outside scholarly debate, whether a problem on the border of products liability law truly is a "products liability" matter has a variety of real-world practical consequences in, for example, a manufacturer's coverage dispute with a liability insurance carrier, or its eligibility for a tax loss carryback under I.R.C. § 172(f) (allowing a 10-year carry back of losses "attributable to product liability").

[17] See § 15.2, below.

[18] See, e.g., Hodsdon v. Mars, Inc., 891 F.3d 857 (9th Cir. 2018) (Cal. law).

[19] See, e.g., Flynn v. FCA US LLC, 2020 WL 1492687, at *5 (S.D. Ill. 2020).

[20] See § 16.7, below.

[21] See § 16.10, below.

might best be viewed merely as a hodgepodge category that borrows principles from true fields of law (like tort and contract), and applies them to problems involving the sale of defective and falsely represented chattels that cause harm. A number of respected scholars have made the claim, mostly some time ago, that products liability is only one of many types of litigation existing inside tort (and warranty) law—that it is not a separate field of law, and that efforts to make it so should be abandoned.[22]

Much power resides in this argument, and determining when a subfield in fact becomes its own field of law, or when it *should* be viewed as having achieved this status, is a complex project. It certainly is true that products liability law could have developed perfectly well within the law of obligations that has quite comfortably contained both tort and warranty law for at least two thousand years.[23] There is no good reason why negligence doctrine from the law of torts, and (if less comfortably) implied warranty principles from the law of contracts, cannot handle design and warning cases with perfect ease. Nor do strong reasons exist why warranty and strict liability in tort cannot smoothly continue to regulate the law on manufacturing defects, nor why tortious misrepresentation, together with express warranty, cannot well manage the treatment of misstatements of product safety. But the substantial overlap of tort and contract rules in all these areas continues to stir up problems, and the doctrinal niceties of the two proud branches of the law of obligations—niceties that deserve respect—continue in products liability cases to be cast aside by attempts to force products liability issues into the tort or contract tents where such matters sometimes do not fit. For these reasons, many courts, scholars, state legislatures, and the American Law Institute in the *Restatement (Third) of Torts: Products Liability* all have begun a major shift away from conceptualizing products liability problems as "tort" or "contract" and toward viewing these problems as functionally distinct.[24]

---

[22] One of the first challenges to products liability as a field of law was made by a warranty law scholar, Richard Speidel, who critically reviewed W.P. Keeton, D. Owen, and J. Montgomery, Products Liability and Safety—Cases and Materials (1980), in Book Review, 33 Vand. L. Rev. 813, 822 (1980) (questioning whether products liability is a legitimate topic for a law school course, and concluding that "[t]he common law string in products cases barely holds its own weight and is in danger of breaking"). One of the first tort law scholars in the modern era to raise serious questions about the viability of products liability as a legitimate legal category was William Powers. See Powers, A Modest Proposal to Abandon Strict Products Liability, 1991 U. Ill. L. Rev. 639 (1991). Jane Stapleton has most vigorously articulated this thesis. See J. Stapleton, Product Liability ch. 13, at 341 et seq. (Butterworths 1994); Stapleton, Bugs in Anglo-American Products Liability, 53 S.C. L. Rev. 1225, 1254–55 (2002) (questioning "why in the Restatement Third and the Directive we tolerate a special tort rule for injuries that happened to have been caused by commercially supplied products," observing that "there does not seem to be any particular moral, economic, or social reason why the victims of such injuries should have been accorded any more special treatment than the victims of medical misadventures or environmental disasters," and concluding that "the creation of special rules for injuries associated with commercially supplied products warps our laws of obligation for little if any benefit and blinkers us to important common themes that run through all personal injury cases generally"). See also Bernstein, Restatement Redux, 48 Vand. L. Rev. 1663, 1681 (1995) (in reviewing Stapleton's Product Liability, sympathetically acknowledging Professor Stapleton's criticisms of the incoherence of the products liability topic, and observing that even "the Third Restatement lacks a conception of products liability as a discrete area of the law"). *But see* Bernstein, How Can a Product Be Liable?, 45 Duke L.J. 1, 3, 83 (1995) (drawn to the criticism of products liability as a legal category, but ultimately, powerfully, rejecting such criticism). See note 24, below.

[23] See § 1.2, below.

[24] See, e.g., Bernstein, How Can a Product Be Liable?, 45 Duke L.J. 1 (1995) (acknowledging, but rejecting, the argument that products liability is not a proper, discrete field of law, and arguing that how we make and what we do with products define ourselves and our cultures in a manner that gives content to this field of law): "Too limber for the Procrustean beds that commentators build, products liability continually reasserts its autonomy. Once acknowledged to be an independent doctrine, products liability can enlighten and provoke." Id. at 83. See also Owen, The Moral Foundations of Products Liability Law: Toward First Principles, 68 Notre Dame L. Rev. 427 (1993). See generally Reimann, Liability for Defective Products at the Beginning

An enormous amount of products liability law has accumulated in recent years, just in terms of published case decisions—over 42,000 products liability decisions of some significance reported in the United States through December 2021.[25] While the sheer number of cases alone ought not determine whether an independent field of law truly has emerged (thousands of vehicular traffic accidents do not a true "field" make), the mushrooming complexity of products liability principles and rules; the increasingly distinctive "products liability" way of thinking about the goals, principles, and doctrine for resolving cases of this type; and the increasing number of products liability statutes enacted by the states, all combine with the enormous amount of litigation on these sets of products liability issues to suggest that this area of the law might appropriately be called a "field." In addition, beginning in the 1960s, scholars and practitioners increasingly began to view products liability as a separate field of law and practice. Further, while including it under the "tort" umbrella, the American Law Institute in 1998 certified the independence of products liability law by giving it a *Restatement* of its own—the *Restatement (Third) of Torts: Products Liability*.[26] Finally, this area of the law has become codified and internationalized. Many American states, and many nations,[27] have enacted legislation recognizing products liability disputes as raising distinctive problems that require specialized treatment, such that products liability law "as a subject in its own right has spread throughout the world."[28]

---

of the Twenty-First Century: Emergence of a Worldwide Standard?, 51 Am. J. Comp. L. 751, 753 n.3 (2003) (noting "the vast and fast-growing mass of products liability literature").

The impetus to unify products liability law under a separate umbrella of its own was initiated by a comprehensive study of the field by the Interagency Task Force on Product Liability in the mid- to late-1970s which was tasked with finding reasons for and solutions to the substantial increases in products liability litigation and resulting insurance premiums then rampant. The Task Force, directed by Professor Victor Schwartz out of the Department of Commerce, published its results in 1977 and 1978 and proposed restructuring products liability law along the lines proposed in § 3 of its Model Uniform Product Liability Act and as it has now evolved. See Owen, Restructuring Products Liability Law, 16 Trial 49 (Nov. 1980) (recommending this approach). Selected results of the Task Force Study are set forth in § 1.3, below.

[25] The basis of the approximation here rests on our analysis of published decisions contained in Westlaw's products liability databases to January 1, 2022. This estimate assumes that 40% of the decisions in those databases were "significant products liability cases," based on research methodology explained in Owen, Products Liability Law § 1.1, note 16, at 6 (2d ed. 2008). That study revealed that most decisions reported in those databases concerned other fields or were procedural rulings resolved without analysis of substantive products liability issues, such as rulings on jurisdictional issues, sanctions, and motions to remand and to extend time limits. In 2014, we refined the methodology by using a series of shorter chronological searches for significant products liability case decisions in the Westlaw databases, with these results: 15,500 such reported cases as of July 1, 2004; 5,500 cases from July 1, 2004 through July 1, 2007; 5,900 cases from July 1, 2007 to July 1, 2012; 1,100 cases from July 1, 2012 to July 1, 2013; and 1,600 cases from July 1, 2013 to July 1, 2014. Based on the revised data, we estimated that 29,600 significant products liability cases had been reported in the Westlaw products liability databases to July 1, 2014, and we expected approximately 1,500 additional cases per year to be reported over the next several years. That expectation was validated when we found an average of 1,579 cases per year between 2014 and 2021 while retaining the assumption that 40% of the decisions in the Westlaw Edge products liability database were "significant products liability cases."

See also Robbins, Products Liability Cases, 12 AMJUR Trials 1 (2022 update) ("Products liability is today one of the most dynamic fields of law in the United States. Each year hundreds of appellate decisions are reported from every jurisdiction [and products liability cases] account for many of the country's largest personal injury verdicts."). A 2018 study concluded that products liability cases comprised 90% of the multidistrict litigations that filled 50% of federal civil dockets. See Foundations in Products Liability Law, 12 Bus. & Com. Litig. Fed. Cts. § 128:18 (5th ed. 2022 update).

[26] See § 6.5, below.

[27] Nations in the European Union are required to enact legislation conforming to the EC Product Liability Directive. See § 1.4, below.

[28] Reimann, Liability for Defective Products at the Beginning of the Twenty-First Century: Emergence of a Worldwide Standard?, 51 Am. J. Comp. L. 751, 756–57 (2003) (concluding that products liability is a separate area of private law because of specialized legislation governing it and recognition of it by scholars and

There simply is no arguing that products liability draws heavily from tort, contract, and other fields of law. Yet, its separate treatment by courts, academics, practitioners, and legislatures around the world dispels the view that modern products liability simply is bits and pieces of other fields of law—that it has no separate identity of its own. Academics may argue this point until the cows come home, but products liability is a field of law distinct unto itself.

The Moral Foundations of Products Liability Law

Products liability law lies at the center of the modern world. To a large extent, persons accomplish their individual and collective objectives, and relate to one another, through the products of science and technology—automobiles, punch presses, drain cleaners, tractors, prescription drugs, frozen dinners, smart phones, tennis rackets, perfumes, computers, and airplanes (civilian and military).[29] Matters concerning the creation and exchange of such products of science and technology are addressed by the law of property, patents, contracts, and commerce. Products liability law instead concerns the consequences of modern science and technology gone awry—when products, or the interactions between people and their products, fail.

But products liability law deals with matters of much greater import than merely the relationship between people and their machines. This rather sterile conception of the subject matter has dominated the thinking about products liability law since it arose in modern form in the middle of the last century. When a person is injured by a product, the principal question of interest in products liability law is whether the product was too dangerous according to some standard of product safety. This focus of modern products liability law on the products—both the one that caused the injury, and some hypothetical one of proper safety—thus tends to direct the liability issue into a barren, technologically-based determination.

Yet the most essential question in any products liability case is not whether certain engineering, production, or informational psychology standards were met or breached. Rather, the relationship between the maker of a product and the victim of a product accident implicates fundamental issues of moral philosophy. By choosing to expose product users and others to certain types and degrees of risk, manufacturers appropriate to themselves certain interests in safety and bodily integrity that may belong to those other persons. Similarly, by choosing to purchase products with certain inherent risks or by choosing to use such products in certain risky ways, and then by choosing to make claims against manufacturers for harm resulting from such risks or uses, victims of product accidents seek to appropriate to themselves economic interests that may belong to manufacturers and other consumers. Both situations involve important questions of how people should treat one another. Ethical and political theory thus have much to say about whether responsibility for product accidents should lie (in part or in whole) with

---

practitioners "as a particular field with (at least) its own rules and principles"). For a debate on the value of this field of law, see Polinsky and Shavell, The Uneasy Case for Product Liability, 123 Harv. L. Rev. 1437 (2010) (challenging the value of the field); Goldberg and Zipursky, The Easy Case for Products Liability Law: A Response to Professors Polinsky and Shavell, 123 Harv. L. Rev. 1919 (2010) (defending the field); and Polinsky and Shavell, A Skeptical Attitude About Product Liability Is Justified: A Reply to Professors Goldberg and Zipursky, 123 Harv. L. Rev. 1949 (2010). This debate misses the central, moral value of products liability law, addressed briefly immediately below.

[29] See Owen, Products Liability: Principles of Justice for the 21st Century, 11 Pace L. Rev. 63, 64–66 (1990).

the manufacturer, the retailer, the user, or the victim. At bottom, product accidents are moral—not technological—events.[30]

Products Liability Resources

Many works have been written on products liability law, and much of the most useful scholarship resides in law journals. Following are some of the most helpful general reference works in this field of law.

American Law

Frumer, Friedman, and Sklaren, Products Liability. Any discussion of products liability resources must begin with Louis Frumer, Melvin Friedman, and Cary Sklaren's classic treatise on products liability law, published by Matthew Bender. First published in 1960, *Frumer and Friedman* originally was structured around the law of negligence (and, to a lesser extent, warranty law). As products liability was redefined by strict liability in tort and other modern principles during the 1960s and 1970s, the organization of this treatise hindered its development. But Cary Sklaren took on the editorship during the 1980s, and the treatise since that time has been rewritten and reinvigorated. Now containing 11 volumes, *Frumer, Friedman, and Sklaren* has regained its place as the leading large treatise in the field. It explores products liability law and litigation widely, in great depth, and with sensitivity, such that courts and lawyers ignore this treatise at their peril.

American Law of Products Liability 3d. This comprehensive treatise on products liability law has some helpful, often exhaustive, treatments of a vast range of products liability topics. The American Law of Products Liability 3d, which now contains 21 core volumes, is published by Thomson Reuters. Many topics are addressed in encyclopedic fashion, and the discussions on some subjects are more complete and useful than those in other treatises. The American Law of Products Liability 3d is available on Westlaw Edge.

Owen & Davis on Products Liability (4th ed. 2014). This is the successor to *Madden & Owen on Products Liability* (3d ed. 2000). Published by Thomson Reuters, and authored by Dean Mary Davis and myself, *Owen & Davis* provides a short treatise treatment of a wide range of products liability and litigation topics. This superb four-volume treatise, annually updated, contains an invaluable discussion of the law and collects the most important products liability statutes, the *Restatements*, and similar resource materials in its Appendices. *Owen & Davis* is available on Westlaw Edge.

Shapo, Shapo on the Law of Products Liability (7th ed. 2017). This scholarly four-volume work by Marshall Shapo, published by Edward Elgar, examines the body of products liability jurisprudence through the distinctive lens of America's senior academic statesman in this field. Often more theoretical than the other treatises, it presents a cultural window on how society addresses product accidents that provides insightful, academic perspectives on this field of law.

---

[30] These observations are adapted from Owen, The Moral Foundations of Products Liability Law: Toward First Principles, 68 Notre Dame L. Rev. 427, 429–30 (1993). See also Watts, Fairness and Utility in Products Liability: Balancing Individual Rights and Social Welfare, 38 Fla. St. U. L. Rev. 597 (2011); Bernstein, How Can a Product Be Liable?, 45 Duke L.J. 1 (1995); Kuklin, The Asymmetrical Conditions of Legal Responsibility in the Marketplace, 44 U. Miami L. Rev. 893 (1990); Attanasio, The Principle of Aggregate Autonomy and the Calabresian Approach to Products Liability, 74 Va. L. Rev. 677 (1988).

Restatement (Third) of Torts: Products Liability (1998). This invaluable digest and restatement of the principles of modern American products liability law was written by two of the field's preeminent scholars, James Henderson and Aaron Twerski. Their Reporters' Notes contain a wealth of scholarship on major issues in the field. Though viewed by some as driven by a "reform" agenda, the *Products Liability Restatement* in fact was located close to the center of the evolving law in this field. The *Restatement*'s various provisions and commentaries have been frequently quoted, often adopted, sometimes rejected, and regularly addressed in numerous decisions since its publication. This monumental work, published by the American Law Institute in 1998 after five years of intense debate, is a signally important resource in this field.

Products Liability Reporter (CCH). This reporter contains short summaries of the law and collects full reports of most important products liability cases and statutes. Prior to Westlaw's development of online research, this reporter was an invaluable resource for a products liability lawyer. Because it provides full and timely reports of important cases online, this Reporter remains a helpful resource for those specializing in this field.

Product Liability & Toxics Law News. This news service from Bloomberg Law summarizes some of the most important judicial decisions, product safety agency regulatory developments, and product safety statutes. Always a helpful way to stay current on product safety as well as products liability law, this service's usefulness is enhanced by its availability online.

Casebooks. The American casebooks are David Owen and Mary Davis, Products Liability and Safety (Foundation Press 8th ed. 2020); David Fischer, Michael Green, William Powers, and Joseph Sanders, Products Liability (West 5th ed. 2014); Tim Kaye, Products Liability Law (American Bar Association 2015); James Henderson, Aaron Twerski, and Douglas Kysar, Products Liability (Aspen 9th ed. 2021); Jerry Phillips, Nicolas Terry, Frank Vandall, and Ellen Wertheimer, Products Liability (Matthew Bender 2d ed. 2002).

Other Books. Earlier works of significance include A. Weinstein, A. Twerski, H. Piehler, and W. Donaher, Products Liability and the Reasonably Safe Product (John Wiley 1978); R. Epstein, Modern Products Liability Law (Quorum 1980); P. Sherman, Products Liability (Shepard's/McGraw-Hill 1981); and F. Vandall, Strict Liability (Greenwood 1989). More recently, see M. Krauss, Principles of Products Liability (West 3d ed. 2019); B. Ottley, R. Lasso, and T. Kiely, Understanding Products Liability Law (LexisNexis 2d ed. 2013); R. Eades, Mastering Products Liability (Carolina Academic Press 2008); D. Dobbs, P. Hayden, and E. Bublick, Hornbook on Torts ch. 33 (West Hornbook 2d ed. 2016); and 5 F. Harper, F. James, and O. Gray, Harper, James and Gray on Torts ch. 28 (Aspen, 3d ed. 2008, annual updates). Many other books provide a more focused look at various aspects of products liability law, litigation, governmental regulation of product safety, and the science and engineering of product safety.

A number of state-specific books on products liability and litigation are an important resource for lawyers practicing products liability law in such states—R. Draim, Products Liability (Virginia Practice Series) (Thomson Reuters 2021–2022); R. Eades, Kentucky Products Liability Law (Harrison 2021–2022); M. Steenson, S. Anderson, and J. Prince, Products Liability Law (Vol 27, Minnesota Practice Series (Thomson Reuters 2021); J. Neal and C. Payne, Georgia Products Liability, 4th (Harrison 2012, annual updates); D. King and M. Murray, Missouri Products Liability,

2d (West 2002); J. McGoldrick and F. Smith, New Jersey Product Liability Law (N.J. L.J. 1997); W. Powers, Texas Products Liability Law (Butterworths 2d ed. 1992); M. Weinberger, New York Products Liability, 2d (Lawyers Coop. 1982). For a general overview, see Product Liability Desk Reference—A Fifty State Compendium (M. Daller, N. Daller eds., Wolters Kluwer, 2022).

D. Owen, Products Liability in a Nutshell (West Academic, 10th ed. 2023), a substantially abridged version of this book, provides a concise overview of the field. M. Geistfeld, Principles of Products Liability (Foundation Press, 3d ed. 2020), helpfully illuminates many aspects of products liability law.

Foreign Law

Stapleton, Product Liability (1994). This is Jane Stapleton's scholarly study of products liability law and policy, published by Butterworths. Written by one of the world's preeminent scholars of products liability law, this remains an insightful, critical, theoretical inquiry into this field of law.

Fairgrieve and Goldberg, Product Liability (3d ed. 2020). This comprehensive and enormously useful one-volume treatise (successor to the second edition by C. John Miller and Richard Goldberg) is written by two of England's leading products liability scholars, Duncan Fairgrieve and Richard Goldberg. Published by Oxford, this excellent book emphasizes British law, examines developing law in the EU states, particularly France, and provides helpful comparisons with American law.

Howells, ed., The Law of Product Liability (2d ed. 2007). This collection of essays on various aspects of the law, litigation, and regulation of products liability and product safety is edited by Geraint Howells, one of Europe's leading comparative law experts on products liability and consumer law. The essays in this useful volume, published by Lexis-Nexis Butterworths, extend beyond substantive products liability law to jurisdiction, choice of law, class actions, and the regulation of product safety.

Fairgrieve, ed., Product Liability in Comparative Perspective (2005). Some essays in this valuable collection, published by Cambridge and edited by Duncan Fairgrieve of the British Institute on International and Comparative Law, examine products liability law in particular European nations and Japan, whilst others approach products liability law issues from a comparativist approach.

Whittaker, Liability for Products: English Law, French Law, and European Harmonization (2005). This book, published by Oxford and written by Simon Whittaker, one of Oxford University's leading comparativists, focuses on English and French law and how the law of these two nations has adjusted to the European Directives on product liability and product safety.

European Law. In addition to the above, a researcher of European law is directed to Application of the EC Product Liability Directive—Quinquennial Reports to the Council.[31] A vast portal into European case and statutory law is available electronically to members, in English, at the BIICL Product Liability and Product Safety Database: www.biicl.org/plf.

---

[31] See European Commission: Enterprise and Industry-Liability for Defective Products, ec.europa.eu/growth/single-market/goods/free-movement-sectors/liability-defective-products_en#.

Canadian Law. Canadian products liability resources include S. Waddams, Products Liability (Thomson-Reuters 5th ed. 2012); L. Theall et al., Product Liability: Canadian Law and Practice (Canada Law Book, 2011); and D. Edgell, Product Liability Law in Canada (LexisNexis Canada 2000).

Foreign Law—Generally. An informative comparative law inquiry is Andrew McClurg, Adem Koyuncu, and Luis Sprovieri, Practical Global Tort Litigation: United States, Germany and Argentina (Carolina Academic Press 2007). Many other sources of foreign products liability law are cited below.[32]

§ 1.2 EARLY LAW

Products liability law, as a broad and coherent set of legal principles for the recovery of product-caused harm, is of recent origin. As late as 1955, one commentator remarked: "Products liability does not yet rank as a term of art in the courts of law."[33] With the exception of a few cases involving fraud and the sale of defective medicines and food, the appearance of products liability cases in the law reports coincides with the rise of the Industrial Revolution in the late 1800s. By 1900, such cases had begun to appear with some frequency. Despite its recency in Anglo-American law, the roots of modern products liability law reach deep into history, before the law of ancient Rome,[34] at least to the law of Mesopotamia.[35] The early origins of products liability law are mostly located in the tort-contract hybrid warranties of quality, both express and implied, although there are early signs of seller liability in negligence as well.

Roman Law

The products liability law of ancient Rome lies shrouded in the mists of history.[36] Neither the law of tort (*delict*) nor the law of sales (*emptio venditio*) provided much assistance to the disappointed purchaser under the early classical law as set forth in the Twelve Tables of 450 B.C.: "The original principle [although not the maxim] of the civil law was *caveat emptor* . . . [let the buyer beware]. The seller was not liable for any defects in the thing unless he had by *stipulation* expressly undertaken such liability."[37] Beginning roughly 300–200 B.C., however, basic principles of seller responsibility for certain aspects of particular types of sales began to emerge, and the law of sales

---

[32] See § 1.4, below. See also Ass'n Corporate Counsel, International Comparative Legal Guide Series, Product Liability 2021 (Global Legal Group 19th ed. 2021).

[33] Wilson, Products Liability (pt. 1), 43 Cal. L. Rev. 614 (1955).

[34] For pertinent texts of Roman law, the British Sales of Goods Act, and the Uniform Sales Act, see F. de Zulueta, The Roman Law of Sale—Introduction and Select Texts 61–222 (reprint from corr. 1st ed. 1966) (1945).

[35] See, e.g., C.H.W. Johns, Babylonian and Assyrian Laws, Contracts and Letters 234 (1904) (explaining how a standard provision in contracts for the sale of slaves frequently included a clause allowing rescission within a period of time which "really amount[ed] to demanding a guarantee from the seller that the slave was free from disease or other undisclosed weakness").

[36] Attempting to piece together a Roman law of products liability is fraught with difficulty. Especially for early Roman law, legal sources are few, incomplete, ambiguous, and sometimes unreliable. Roman law scholars disagree on various aspects of the nature and extent of liability for losses associated with defective products. One scholarly inquiry illustrating the necessary guesswork in attempting to unravel the nature and scope of recovery for defective products under the various Roman law forms of action is Honoré, The History of the Aedilitian Actions from Roman to Roman-Dutch Law, in Studies in the Roman Law of Sale 132 (D. Daube ed., reprint 1977) (1959). Helpful summaries of the Roman law of sales are J. A. C. Thomas, Textbook of Roman Law 15, 16, 286–88 (1976), and de Zulueta, above note 34, at 46–51. See also W. Buckland, A Text-Book of Roman Law from Augustus to Justinian 491–94 (3d ed. Stein rev. 1966); R. Lee, The Elements of Roman Law 13, 15, 314–16 (4th ed. 1956).

[37] B. Nicholas, An Introduction to Roman Law 181 (1962).

continued to develop, albeit haltingly, through its flowering in Justinian's *Digest* in 533 A.D.

The law of tort was quite undeveloped in early Roman law and appears to have afforded little, if any, protection to a person injured by a defective product. By the time of Justinian in the sixth century A.D., however, product sellers were being held responsible for certain losses attributable to their failure to exercise the greatest of care.[38] The standard of care for sellers as it eventually developed was quite rigorous: "[N]egligence due to the absence of the greatest care is a failure to observe such diligence as a good man of business or a very prudent man would exercise."[39] A person who held himself out as an expert in his occupation was deemed to be culpably negligent if he failed to use such skill.[40] Liability in negligence, in Roman law, was offset by the victim's own contributory negligence.[41]

The Roman law of fraud (*dolus*), in addition to covering express statements known to be false, broadly included the mere failure to disclose to the buyer such latent defects as the seller knew the product to possess.[42] Apart from fraud, the seller was also responsible for a product's failure to conform to express promises of quality that were innocently made, whether by formal stipulation (*stipulatio*) or by other description of the product.[43] Liability for express misrepresentations was limited to factual assertions, however, and sellers were not responsible for "puffing" the quality of their wares.[44]

The developing law of an implied warranty of quality—akin to the modern notion of strict products liability for the sale of a defective product—is perhaps the most interesting aspect of the Roman law of products liability. From 367 B.C., the *curule aediles* were magistrates charged with policing the public markets. From the Edict of the Aediles,[45] which regulated the public sale of slaves and certain livestock, the *aediles* required that the seller warrant the soundness of the subject of the sale.[46] If the seller

---

[38] See C. Sherman, 2 Roman Law in the Modern World 345 (2d ed., reprint 1994) (1922).

[39] Id. at 299 (citing Digest Book 19, Tit. 2, Lex 25, § 7 and Digest 18, 6, 13). The extra-high standard of care for sellers in Roman law may be a remote origin of the modern doctrine that a product seller is bound to exercise the care of an expert in the field. This doctrine appears in modern American products liability law in both negligence, see, e.g., § 2.2, below, and "strict" products liability. See, e.g., Farrell v. Johnson & Johnson, 238 A.3d 698, 708 (Conn. 2020) ("manufacturers are 'held to the knowledge of an expert in its field . . . and therefore [have] a duty "to keep abreast of scientific knowledge, discoveries, and advances and is presumed to know what is imparted thereby" ' ").

[40] " 'Want of skill is reckoned as negligence,' is the Roman jurist Gaius' famous interpretation of negligence." Sherman, above note 38, at 382 (quoting Digest 50, 17, 132; Digest 9, 2, 8).

[41] Id. at 383 (citing Digest 50, 17, 203; Digest 9, 2, 9, § 4; J. Inst. 4, 3, § 5; W. Hunter, Roman Law 246–47 (4th ed. 1903)).

[42] "[D]uring the last century of the Republic the notion of *dolus* was extended to cover both the statement by the seller that the thing sold possessed or did not possess some quality when he knew this was untrue and also the case when the seller knowingly concealed a defect." Honoré, above note 36, at 135. See also Rogerson, Implied Warranty Against Latent Defects in Roman and English Law, in Studies in the Roman Law of Sale 112, 113 (D. Daube ed., reprint 1977) (1959).

[43] See Rogerson, above note 42.

[44] See, e.g., Honoré, above note 36, at 141 (liability was restricted to "such statements or promises . . . which it is right to enforce as opposed to mere puffs or commendations for which it would be inappropriate to impose legal liability"). Justinian's *Digest* provides:

> What a seller says in order to puff his wares is to be considered neither as a statement nor as a promise. But if it was said in order to deceive the buyer, it must be held that, though here too there is no action for contravention of a statement or a promise, there is the action *de dolo*.

Digest 4, 3, 37, reprinted in de Zulueta, above note 34, at 158.

[45] The Aedilician Edict may have been promulgated in 199 B.C. See Honoré, above note 36, at 134.

[46] See Thomas, above note 36, at 287.

did not expressly so warrant, he was liable for defects in any event, whether or not he was aware of them.[47] The extent to which this implied warranty of quality was extended beyond the sale of slaves and livestock prior to Justinian is unclear.[48] Nevertheless, Justinian in his *Digest* announces a basic implied warranty of quality applicable to the sale of all products: "All sellers of all sorts of thing[s] are liable for defects."[49] This is a general rule of strict liability for the sale of a defective product,[50] for "liability exists independently of the seller's knowledge of the defect and in Justinian's law extends to sales of all kinds of things."[51]

Responsibility for obvious defects in a product lay with the buyer, not with the seller. This was true even with respect to the seller's express assertions of product quality that might otherwise be interpreted as denying the existence of the defect.[52] Moreover, the parties could negate all warranty responsibility by express agreement.[53]

Damages at Roman law depended upon the basis of liability. If a buyer could establish fraud (*dolus*), which included the seller's failure to disclose a latent defect known to the seller, the buyer was entitled to full recovery of his consequential damages. Under the strict liability rule of breach of the implied warranty of quality, however, the buyer's remedies were more restricted[54]—to rescind the sale, within six months

---

[47] See Sherman, above note 38, at 347 (citing Digest, 21, 1, 1, 1).

[48] "[T]he civil law was developing its own implied warranty of quality, outside, though in all probability influenced by the example of, the Edictal developments. The texts deal mainly with sales of land or its accessories, but there are others on movables. There is not a great deal of authority, and perhaps there was not any great need for a general warranty of quality." Rogerson, above note 42, at 117–18. Compare Sherman, above note 38, at 347 n.55 (edictal provisions spread from slaves and cattle to all products in first century A.D.) with Honoré, above note 36, at 139–40 (textual evidence for such surmise is thin).

[49] Rogerson, above note 42, at 115 (footnotes omitted) (relying on Digest 21, 1, 1, which provides in part: "Labeo writes that the edict of the curule aediles applies as well to sales of land as to sales of chattels inanimate or animate.").

Digest 21, 1, 1, 2 explains why sellers should be responsible for defects in their wares:

> The motive for the proposition of this edict is to defeat the artifices of sellers and to assist buyers whenever they are cheated by sellers. It is, however, to be understood that a seller, even though he was unaware of the existence of faults, . . . must nevertheless be held liable. Nor is this unfair; for the seller was in a position to inform himself on these matters, while to the buyer it makes no difference whether his deception is due to the seller's ignorance or to his guile.

Digest 21, 1, 1, 2, reprinted in de Zulueta, above note 34, at 139–40. Consider also Digest 21, 1, 63: "It should be understood that this edict relates only to sales, though to sales not of slaves only, but of everything else." de Zulueta at 147.

[50] "I have not found in the texts any discussion whether a seller who could not reasonably discover the existence of the defect is excused. It seems to be universally thought that he was not. . . . [I]t may be thought that, by a gradual development, a seller became liable for defects whether he could have discovered them or not, a form of strict liability familiar in the case of a stipulation." Honoré, above note 36, at 136 (footnote omitted).

[51] Rogerson, above note 42, at 113.

[52] "[P]atent defects, as in modern legal systems, were taken to be accepted by the buyer and even express warranties were deemed not to cover them—if, for instance, a one-eyed dog was sold as sound, it was as a sound one-eyed dog." Thomas, above note 36, at 286.

[53] de Zulueta, above note 34, at 51.

[54] "The bases of Justinian's law seem to be [that t]here is fault, though not as serious as *dolus*, in not knowing the thing one sells. The buyer wants and is entitled to a thing as free from faults as it appears to be. The seller does not perform his side of the contract by supplying a faulty thing. The compilers, wishing for these reasons to create a general implied warranty against defects, did so by extending the principle of the Edict to cover all sales and effected a fusion of these principles with civil law fraud liability and the much more meager civil law liability in the absence of fraud, making the award of consequential damages the feature differentiating between the liability of the fraudulent and the non-fraudulent seller." Rogerson, above note 42, at 129–30.

thereafter, or, within twelve months, to adjust the price to the actual value of the defective thing.[55]

Early English Law

From the laws of Justinian to early medieval English law, the legal system degenerated from a moderately sophisticated system of sales law to one that was crude at best. Indeed, private law, under which an aggrieved purchaser might sue the seller for damages caused by defective goods, was largely unknown in early England.[56] In time, guilds of the various crafts developed an elaborate system of localized criminal regulation of product quality by statutes that often developed into ordinances of the town. But such local statutes were designed principally to protect the public more from being cheated than from being injured. The late Roman law's insistence on the fair quality of goods sold was largely absent from the rustic local law of medieval England, but certain aspects of Justinian's law wended their way to a limited extent into early English law through the dominant role in society of the church, whose scholars were trained in the civil law.

In the thirteenth century, Thomas Aquinas (1225?–1274 A.D.) in his *Summa Theologica*[57] outlined the basic mercantile obligations consistent with those expressed by Justinian in his *Digest*. Thus, the seller was bound to disclose secret flaws: it was sin and fraud to sell a product containing a latent defect known to the seller but not the buyer, and the sale was void. If the seller was unaware of the defect, the sale was not a sin, but the seller was obligated to return to the buyer any excess in the price attributable to the defect.[58] The buyer was responsible for obvious defects, according to Aquinas, so that the seller was not bound to disclose such defects from "any duty of justice," but to do so would reflect "the more exuberant virtue."[59]

Despite the virtues of the ecclesiastical doctrine of seller responsibility for defective products, the early English common law over time developed the opposite notion of *caveat emptor*, or "let the buyer beware." The buyer's duty to protect himself against

---

[55] See, e.g., Rogerson, above note 42, at 123; Thomas, above note 36, at 287. The distinction in damages available for the innocent sale of a defective product and fraudulent nondisclosure of a defect is described in Digest 19, 1, 13:

> In the matter of damages in the action *ex empto* [*actio empti*] Julian, book 15, distinguishes between one who has sold with knowledge and one who has sold in ignorance. For, he says, the unwitting seller of a diseased herd or of unsound timber will have to make good in the action *ex empto* only the amount by which the price would have been reduced had the buyer known the truth, whereas, if the seller knew, but was silent and so deceived the buyer, he will have to make good to the buyer all losses that have fallen on him in consequence of the purchase: thus, if a house has collapsed owing to the unsound timber, he must make good the value of the house, or if the buyer's beasts have perished through being infected by the diseased herd, the damage sustained.

de Zulueta, above note 34, at 124 (footnote omitted).

[56] On early products liability law in England and America, see, e.g., Bohlen, The Basis of Affirmative Obligations in the Law of Tort (pts. 2 & 3), 53 U. Pa. L. Rev. 273, 337 (1905); Hamilton, The Ancient Maxim Caveat Emptor, 40 Yale L.J. 1133 (1931); Llewellyn, On Warranty of Quality, and Society (pts. 1 & 2), 36 Colum. L. Rev. 699 (1936), 37 Colum. L. Rev. 341 (1937); Prosser, The Implied Warranty of Merchantable Quality, 27 Minn. L. Rev. 117, 118–22 (1943); Murphy, Medieval Theory and Products Liability, 3 B.C. Indus. & Com. L. Rev. 29 (1961); Wade, Strict Tort Liability for Products: Past, Present and Future, 13 Cap. U. L. Rev. 335 (1984) (describing 19th and early 20th century English and American cases).

[57] T. Aquinas, Summa Theologica, Ethicus, II, II at question 77, arts. 1–4 (Fathers of the English Dominican Province trans., 2d rev. ed. 1920).

[58] See generally Hamilton, above note 56, at 1136–64.

[59] Id. at 1138 (quoting T. Aquinas, Summa Theologica, Ethicus, II, II at question 77, art. 4 (Rickaby trans., 2d ed. 1896)).

obvious defects was extended to embrace an obligation to protect himself against hidden defects as well, and any lingering notion of an implied warranty of quality from late Roman law withered away into oblivion in English law. In 1562, "[a]n ordinance of Lancaster, relating to the purchase of malt, ignored the distinction between obvious and latent defects and restated an old proverb, 'let their eye be their chapman.' "[60] By 1600, the basic notion that the risk of product defects lay on the buyer had become well established in English law. A much-quoted passage attributed to Coke on Littleton (1633) noted: "[B]y the civil law every man is bound to warrant the thing he selleth or conveyeth, albeit there be no express warranty, either in deed or in law; but the common law bindeth him not, for *caveat emptor*."[61]

The maxim of *caveat emptor* first appears in the law reports in the early 1600s.[62] In 1603, the judges and barons of the Exchequer Chamber decided the celebrated case of the bezoar stone,[63] *Chandelor v. Lopus*.[64] The plaintiff alleged that the defendant goldsmith sold him a stone "which he affirmed to Lopus to be a bezar-stone . . . for one hundred pounds; *ubi revera* it was not a bezoar-stone: the defendant pleaded not guilty, and verdict was given and judgment entered for the plaintiff in the King's Bench." Holding the declaration deficient, the Exchequer Chamber reversed, writing: "[T]he bare affirmation that it was a bezar-stone, without warranting it to be so, is no cause of action: and although he knew it to be no bezar-stone, it is not material; for every one in selling his wares will affirm that his wares are good, or the horse which he sells is sound; yet if he does not warrant them to be so, it is no cause of action. . . ."[65]

As *Chandelor v. Lopus* came to be interpreted, it announced a simple rule governing the rights of the buyer of inferior goods:

> He had a cause of action if he had exacted an express warranty at the time of the sale from a seller who knew his representations to be false. An affirmation, no matter how many holy saints were invoked, fell short of a warranty; latent defects, however impervious to ordinary vision, were the purchaser's own lookout. When in time writs were accommodated more sharply to specific complaints . . . the buyer had the alternative of a suit in assumpsit on express warranty or in deceit by proving a *scienter*. The exactions of a ceremonial were set down as an injunction to the buyer to look to himself for protection.[66]

---

[60] Id. at 1164. "It was proverbial in France, 'qui n'ouvre pas yeux doit ouvrir la bourse.' " Id. at n.208 (quoting 2 Borough Customs 183 (Mary Bateson ed., 1906)).

[61] Id. at 1165.

[62] See Moore v. Hussey, 80 Eng. Rep. 243 (K.B. 1601 or 1609).

[63] Analogous to pearls, bezoar stones were valuable "stones" created in the digestive tracts of goats, llamas, and certain other animals by the layering of biological matter around some foreign object. See Oxford English Dictionary 163 (2d ed. 1989). These stones were thought to possess mystical medicinal powers, particularly in combating the effects of poison or venom. Webster's New International Dictionary 261 (2d ed. 1936). In addition to such curative uses, the stones are said to have been used by royalty to detect (by changing color) and counteract arsenic and other poisons in wine; and by natives of Borneo, as an aphrodisiac. See https://en.wikipedia.org/wiki/Bezoar. Due to their rarity and unique features, bezoar stones have long been highly valued, a value that continues to increase: one gold-encased bezoar stone, salvaged from a shipwreck, was advertised for sale some years ago for $6.8 million. www.rareends.com/html/atocha (site now defunct). As of 2007, a bezoar stone in a gold pendant from a shipwreck (perhaps the same stone) was offered for $475,000. See www.melfisher.com (Treasure Sales, Collectors Treasures) (reference no longer available).

[64] (1603) 79 Eng. Rep. 3 (K.B.).

[65] Id. at 4.

[66] Hamilton, above note 56, at 1168–69.

For the next two centuries, except for cases of fraud and breach of express warranty, the doctrine of *caveat emptor* ruled supreme.

In 1810, the English courts finally replaced the *caveat emptor* rule—that the buyer takes the risks of hidden product defects—with its opposite doctrine, the implied warranty of quality—that the seller impliedly warrants that its products contain no hidden defects.[67] Five years later, in the leading case of *Gardiner v. Gray*,[68] Lord Ellenborough explained the fundamental notion of the implied warranty of merchantable quality:

> [T]he purchaser has a right to expect a saleable article answering the description in the contract. Without any particular warranty, this is an implied term in every such contract. Where there is no opportunity to inspect the commodity, the maxim of *caveat emptor* does not apply. He cannot without a warranty insist that it shall be of any particular quality or fineness, but the intention of both parties must be taken to be, that it shall be saleable in the market under the denomination mentioned in the contract between them. The purchaser cannot be supposed to buy goods to lay them on a dunghill.[69]

Subsequent cases established that this basic warranty of quality requires "not only that the goods delivered must be genuine according to the name, kind or description specified, but that they must be of a quality to pass in the market under that description, and this in turn to mean that they must be reasonably fit for the ordinary uses to which such goods are put."[70] In short, the implied warranty of merchantable quality reflected the view that sellers should be held accountable, as a matter of law rather than of the seller's intent, for defects in the products that they sold.[71] In 1893, Parliament eventually codified the common-law implied warranty of merchantability in the Sale of Goods Act.[72]

The other major development in English products liability law in the nineteenth century was the application of the privity-of-contract defense to negligence claims, which shielded remote sellers from negligence liability for making or selling defective products that cause harm. It was in 1842 that the Exchequer Chamber decided the celebrated case of *Winterbottom v. Wright*,[73] which held that an injury victim could not maintain a negligence action against a seller in the absence of privity of contract. The defendant, Wright, a manufacturer and repairer of stagecoaches, supplied a stagecoach to the Postmaster General under a contract to keep it in good repair. The coach subsequently broke down and overturned, injuring the driver, Winterbottom, who sued for damages.

---

67 See Holcombe v. Hewson, (1810) 170 Eng. Rep. 1194 (N.P.).

68 (1815) 171 Eng. Rep. 46 (K.B.). See also Laing v. Fidgeon, (1815) 128 Eng. Rep. 974 (C.P.).

69 *Gardiner*, 171 Eng. Rep. at 47.

70 Prosser, above note 56, at 121 (footnotes omitted). Whereas the implied warranty of merchantability was grounded on a product's fitness for its *ordinary* purposes, the implied warranty of fitness for a *particular* purpose evolved as a separate and independent implied warranty. See Jones v. Bright, (1829) 130 Eng. Rep. 1167 (C.P.); Randall v. Newson, (1877) 2 Q.B.D. 102. The developed common law of implied warranty at the time was usefully summarized in Jones v. Just, (1868) 3 L.R.Q.B. 197.

71 Perhaps the development of the implied warranty of merchantable quality reflected "the development of modern notions of policy, based upon the increasing practice of reputable sellers to assume responsibility for defective good[s] sold, together with the feeling that such responsibility is best placed upon the seller as a cost of his business, which he may distribute to the public at large as a part of the price. As a result, it is often said that implied warranties of quality arise by operation of law and are independent of any intention to agree upon their terms as a matter of fact . . . ." Prosser, above note 56, at 122 (footnotes omitted).

72 Sale of Goods Act, 1893, 56 & 57 Vict., c. 71, § 14(2).

73 (1842) 152 Eng. Rep. 402 (Exch. Div.).

The court gave judgment for the defendant. In an opinion reflecting the views of the other judges, Lord Abinger, C.B., remarked that to allow such claims would open up "an infinity of actions. . . . Unless we confine the operation of such contracts as this to the parties who entered into them, the most absurd and outrageous consequences, to which I can see no limit, would ensue."[74] It was not until 1932 that England finally abolished the privity-of-contract defense to negligence claims, in *Donoghue v. Stevenson*,[75] in which the plaintiff was sickened by consuming the decomposed remains of a snail in a bottle of ginger beer purchased by a friend.[76]

Early American Law

Warranty

Caveat emptor. The English doctrine of *caveat emptor* was widely embraced in the American colonies.[77] In 1804, Chancellor Kent of New York proclaimed that the doctrine of *caveat emptor* applied to latent defects in the sale of goods,[78] and other early nineteenth century American courts latched onto the rule with a gusto reflecting the new nation's devotion to individualism and free enterprise.[79] In 1870, a dissenting justice in *Barnard v. Kellogg*[80] summarized the American view of the *caveat emptor* doctrine:

> No principle of the common law has been better established, or more often affirmed, both in this country and in England, than that in sales of personal property, in the absence of express warranty, where the buyer has an opportunity to inspect the commodity, and the seller is guilty of no fraud, and is neither the manufacturer nor grower of the article he sells, the maxim of *caveat emptor* applies. Such a rule, requiring the purchaser to take care of his own interests, has been found best adapted to the wants of trade in the business transactions of life. And there is no hardship in it, because if the purchaser distrusts his judgment he can require of the seller a warranty that the quality or condition of the goods he desires to buy corresponds with the sample exhibited. . . . Of such universal acceptance is the doctrine of *caveat emptor* in

---

74 Id. at 404–05.

75 [1932] A.C. 562 (H.L.) (appeal taken from Scot.) (U.K.). On *Donoghue*, see D. Fairgrieve and R. Goldberg, Product Liability §§ 1.18–.23, 14.01–.08 (3d ed. 2020); G. Howells and S. Weatherill, Consumer Protection Law 453 (Ashgate 2d ed. 2005); J. Stapleton, Product Liability 20 (Butterworths 1994); G. Howells, Comparative Product Liability 69–72 (Dartmouth 1993).

76 *Donoghue* was preceded by George v. Skivington, (1869) 5 L.R. Exch. 1, in which a pharmacist was held liable to a buyer's wife for defective shampoo, and Heaven v. Pender, (1883) 11 Q.B.D. 503, in which a dry-dock owner was held liable for injuries to a worker injured by defective staging that broke. *Donoghue* was followed by Grant v. Australian Knitting Mills, Ltd., [1936] A.C. 85 (P.C. 1935) (appeal taken from Austl.), which extended the principle of *Donoghue* beyond food to products generally. See Fairgrieve and Goldberg, above, §§ 17.58–60; Howells, above, at 69–72.

77 For articles on early products liability in England and America, see note 56, above.

78 Seixas v. Woods, 2 Cai. 48 (N.Y. Sup. Ct. 1804).

79 Conventional historical wisdom holds that the doctrine of *caveat emptor* was the prevailing legal ethic during the seventeenth and eighteenth centuries. See, e.g., Prosser, above note 56. At least in the eighteenth and early nineteenth centuries, however, there is evidence of some pockets of resistance to the doctrine in the form of support for an implied warranty of quality in a few American jurisdictions and possibly in England, perhaps reflecting aberrational mercantile customs in certain areas. Yet once the nineteenth century was well under way, apparently all American jurisdictions except South Carolina adhered to the principle of *caveat emptor*. See generally M. Horwitz, The Transformation of American Law, 1780–1860, at 167, 180, 330 n.106 (1977) (asserting, however, that a "sound price" rule *generally* prevailed during the seventeenth and eighteenth century and that the *caveat emptor* notion did not take hold until about 1800).

80 77 U.S. 383 (1870).

> this country, that the courts of all the States in the Union where the common law prevails, with one exception (South Carolina), sanction it.[81]

Even as some courts began to impose an implied warranty of quality on manufacturers (and growers) as the nineteenth century progressed, the *caveat emptor* principle persisted in many states (especially in retailer cases) into the twentieth century.[82]

Toward the end of the nineteenth century, more and more states followed the lead of South Carolina and England and abandoned the *caveat emptor* doctrine in favor of an implied warranty of merchantable quality. Under the rule of *caveat venditor*, a sale "raises an implied warranty (against latent defects) from the fairness and fullness of the price paid, upon this clear and reasonable ground, that in the contract of sale, the purchaser is not supposed to part with his money, but in expectation of an adequate advantage, or recompense. . . . Selling for a sound price raises an implied warranty that the thing sold is free from defects, known and unknown (to the seller)."[83] By the turn of the twentieth century, enough American states had adopted a common-law implied warranty of quality that the doctrine was reduced to statutory form in the Uniform Sales Act of 1906,[84] patterned after the British Sales of Goods Act of 1893.[85]

Privity of contract. As courts began imposing implied warranties of quality on manufacturers in the latter part of the nineteenth century, manufacturers increasingly were handing over the retail function to third-party dealers. This meant that the typical consumer began to deal contractually only with the retailer. Thus, manufacturers sued in warranty by consumers of defective products in the late 1800s could assert the absence of privity of contract—a defense that was proving its effectiveness in actions brought in negligence. But the harshness of this defense in consumer injury cases was readily apparent, and courts began to riddle it with exceptions at an early date.[86]

The first cases to abolish outright the manufacturer's no-privity defense to implied warranty claims were decided at the turn of the twentieth century and involved defective

---

81 Id. at 388–89.

82 See, e.g., National Oil Co. v. Rankin, 75 P. 1013, 1014 (Kan. 1904) (stating general rule of *caveat emptor*).

83 Lane v. Trenholm Bldg. Co., 229 S.E.2d 728, 730 (S.C. 1976) (quoting Champneys v. Johnson, 4 S.C.L. (2 Brev.) 268, 273 (1809), and Southern Iron & Equip. Co. v. Bamberg E & W Ry. Co., 149 S.E. 271, 278 (S.C. 1929)).

84 Promulgated in 1906, the American Uniform Sales Act (predecessor to the UCC Article 2) provided, in § 15(2), for an implied warranty of merchantability in sales by description:

> Where the goods are bought by description from a seller who deals in goods of that description (whether he be the grower or manufacturer or not), there is an implied warranty that the goods shall be of merchantable quality.

See Unif. Sales Act § 15(2), 1 U.L.A. 7 (1950). The Uniform Commercial Code (UCC) restated the implied warranty of merchantability in § 2–314. See § 4.3, below.

85 Section 15(2) of the Uniform Sales Act adopted, almost verbatim, section 14(2) of the English Sale of Goods Act, which provided:

> Where goods are bought by description from a seller who deals in goods of that description (whether he be the manufacturer or not), there is an implied condition that the goods shall be of merchantable quality; provided that if the buyer has examined the goods, there shall be no implied condition as regards defects which such examination ought to have revealed.

Sale of Goods Act, 1893, 56 & 57 Vict., Ch. 71, § 14(2).

86 See Gillam, Products Liability in a Nutshell, 37 Or. L. Rev. 119, 153–55 (1958) (listing 29 such exceptions).

foodstuffs.[87] The court in *Jacob E. Decker & Sons, Inc. v. Capps*[88] explained that liability in such cases is based on "the broad principle of the public policy to protect human health and life." Producers place food products in the channels of commerce "with the intention that they shall pass from hand to hand until they are finally used by some remote consumer" who is ill-equipped to determine whether such food is fit to eat. When it is not in fact fit for human consumption, "there is such an utter failure of the purpose for which the food is sold, and the consequences of eating unsound food are so disastrous to human health and life, that the law imposes a warranty of purity in favor of the ultimate consumer as a matter of public policy."[89]

The breakdown of the remote seller's privity defense in implied warranty cases spread in the 1950s from human food to animal food and products for intimate bodily use, such as soap, hair dye, and permanent wave solution. Then, in the late 1950s and early 1960s, several courts in rapid succession extended nonprivity recovery to durable goods. The year was 1960, and the case was *Henningsen v. Bloomfield Motors, Inc.*,[90] in which the privity bar was decisively repudiated in a landmark implied warranty case involving injuries from a defective automobile. Justice Francis spoke for the New Jersey Supreme Court: "We see no rational doctrinal basis for differentiating between a fly in a bottle of beverage and a defective automobile. The unwholesome beverage may bring illness to one person, the defective car, with its great potentiality for harm to the driver, occupants, and others, demands even less adherence to the narrow barrier of privity."[91] In the words of William Prosser, *Henningsen* marked the "fall of the citadel of privity."[92]

The privity-of-contract requirement also presented a stumbling block for plaintiffs seeking recovery for breach of *express* warranty. Because sellers affirmatively create such warranties to induce remote consumers to purchase their goods, policy arguments against a privity defense to such claims were even stronger than for implied warranty. The 1958 Ohio Supreme Court decision of *Rogers v. Toni Home Permanent Co.*[93] is the landmark case abolishing the privity bar in express warranty cases. Noting that the

---

[87] See Mazetti v. Armour & Co., 135 P. 633 (Wash. 1913); Parks v. G.C. Yost Pie Co., 144 P. 202 (Kan. 1914). See also Jackson Coca-Cola Bottling Co. v. Chapman, 64 So. 791, 791 (Miss. 1914): "A 'sma' mousie' caused the trouble in this case. The 'wee, sleekit, cow'rin', tim'rous beastie' drowned in a bottle of coca-cola. . . . [The consumer] did not get joy from the anticipated refreshing drink. He was in the frame of mind to approve the poet's [Robert Burns'] words:

'The best-laid schemes o' mice an' men
Gang aft aglay
An' lea'e us nought but grief an' pain
For promis'd joy!' "

However, other courts continued to deny warranty recovery to users injured by food products they had not bought themselves. E.g., Chysky v. Drake Bros. Co., 139 N.E. 576 (N.Y. 1923). In *Chysky*, a waitress bit into a nail baked into a cake her employer had purchased from the defendant. The court denied recovery: "If there were an implied warranty which inured to the benefit of the plaintiff it must be because there was some contractual relation between her and the defendant, and there was no such contract. . . . [U]nless there be privity of contract, there can be no implied warranty." Id. at 577–78. Especially with food purchased for other family members, some courts employed agency principles to circumvent the privity problem and allow recovery. See, e.g., Greenberg v. Lorenz, 173 N.E.2d 773 (N.Y. 1961) (presumption that father purchased food for all members of household).

[88] 164 S.W.2d 828 (Tex. 1942).

[89] Id. at 829.

[90] 161 A.2d 69 (N.J. 1960).

[91] Id. at 83.

[92] Prosser, The Fall of the Citadel (Strict Liability to the Consumer), 50 Minn. L. Rev. 79 (1966).

[93] 147 N.E.2d 612 (Ohio 1958). *Rogers* is noted in 58 Colum. L. Rev. 1092 (1958); 19 Ohio St. L.J. 733 (1958); 44 Iowa L. Rev. 229 (1958); 11 Vand. L. Rev. 1459 (1958); 44 Va. L. Rev. 1002 (1958).

express warranty action derived originally from tort (deceit) rather than contract,[94] the *Rogers* court relied upon *Baxter v. Ford Motor Co.*[95] in extending the privity exception recognized in food cases to products generally, reasoning that it is only proper to permit consumers to recover for false advertising statements "aimed squarely" at them.[96] Today, express (as well as implied) warranties are widely held to run directly to the purchaser, despite the absence of privity of contract.[97]

Negligence and the Privity Obstacle

As manufacturing and retailing functions separated in the 1800s during the course of industrialization, American courts borrowed England's formidable obstacle to consumer recovery for injuries from defective products: the doctrine of *Winterbottom v. Wright,* previously discussed, that prohibited negligence actions against "remote" manufacturers—parties with whom injured plaintiffs had no "privity of contract." The privity requirement was an effective instrument of social policy for a nation bent on promoting the development of its infant industries. As explained by the Supreme Court of Pennsylvania, if a manufacturer of a boiler, machine, or steamship "owes a duty to the whole world" that the product contains no hidden defects, "it is difficult to measure the extent of his responsibility, and no prudent man would engage in such occupations upon such conditions. It is safer and wiser to confine such liabilities to the parties immediately concerned."[98] Despite occasional rumblings of discontent,[99] other American courts in the late nineteenth and early twentieth centuries, widely agreeing with the sentiment expressed by the Pennsylvania Supreme Court, staunchly applied the privity-of-contract doctrine to bar negligence claims in defective product cases.[100]

---

[94] *Rogers*, 147 N.E.2d at 614. On this point, see generally Ames, History of Assumpsit, 2 Harv. L. Rev. 1, 8 (1888); Prosser, The Assault Upon the Citadel (Strict Liability to the Consumer), 69 Yale L.J. 1099, 1126 (1960); Prosser, above note 56, at 118–25; 1 T. Street, Foundations of Legal Liability 377 (1906); 2 Williston on Sales § 15–1 (5th ed. 1995).

[95] 12 P.2d 409 (Wash. 1932). *Baxter* is discussed in § 3.4, below.

[96] *Rogers*, 147 N.E.2d at 615–16 ("The warranties made by the manufacturer in his advertisements and by the labels on his products are inducements to the ultimate consumers, and the manufacturer ought to be held to strict accountability to any consumer who buys the product in reliance on such representations and later suffers injury [as a result].").

[97] Holding that express warranties run directly to remote purchasers, see, e.g., Reid v. Volkswagen of Am., Inc., 512 F.2d 1294 (6th Cir. 1975) (Mich. law); Hauter v. Zogarts, 534 P.2d 377 (Cal. 1975); Hamon v. Digliani, 174 A.2d 294 (Conn. 1961); Kinlaw v. Long Mfg. N.C., Inc., 259 S.E.2d 552 (N.C. 1979). *Contra* Compex Int'l Co. v. Taylor, 209 S.W.3d 462 (Ky. 2006).

Third party beneficiaries of warranties, as most warranty law, now is addressed by the Uniform Commercial Code. See § 4.5, below.

[98] Curtain v. Somerset, 21 A. 244, 245 (Pa. 1891).

[99] At least one early scholar disagreed with the privity-of-contract doctrine: "To encourage commerce and industry by removing all duty and incentive to protect the public is to invite wholesale sacrifice of individual rights on the altar of commercial greed. . . . [I]t cannot be to the interest of any community to encourage carelessness and disregard of human life and property therein." Bohlen, above note 56, at 355.

[100] E.g., Loop v. Litchfield, 42 N.Y. 351 (1870); Lebourdais v. Vitrified Wheel Co., 80 N.E. 482 (Mass. 1907).

For historical studies of the privity defense to products liability claims brought in negligence, see Bohlen, The Basis of Affirmative Obligations in the Law of Tort (pts. 2 & 3), 53 U. Pa. L. Rev. 273, 337 (1905); Feezer, Tort Liability of Manufacturers and Vendors, 10 Minn. L. Rev. 1 (1925); Bohlen, Liability of Manufacturers to Persons Other than Their Immediate Vendees, 45 Law Q. Rev. 343 (1929); Russell, Manufacturers' Liability to the Ultimate Consumer, 21 Ky. L.J. 388 (1933); Gillam, Products Liability in a Nutshell, 37 Or. L. Rev. 119, 131 (1958).

By 1900, dissatisfaction with the privity bar had generated certain exceptions, summarized in *Huset v. J.I. Case Threshing Machine Co.*:[101] (1) "an act of negligence of a manufacturer or vendor which is imminently dangerous to the life or health of mankind [in preparing] an article intended to preserve, destroy, or affect human life"; (2) a property owner's negligence that injures a person invited "to use his defective appliance upon the owner's premises"; and (3) providing an article known to be "imminently dangerous to life or limb to another without notice of its qualities."[102] Despite minor variations in how courts formulated them, the three *Huset* exceptions were widely accepted at the time. To recover against a negligent manufacturer or other remote vendor, a plaintiff had to squeeze his case into one of the three exceptions—which usually was quite hard to do, since most courts at the time interpreted the exceptions narrowly. Clearly the most important exceptions were the first and third, which involved the sale of "imminently" or "inherently" dangerous products. Yet, when *Huset* was decided in 1903, courts confined these exceptions to products like poisons, drugs, guns, explosives, and foodstuffs.

Seven years after *Huset* was decided, Donald MacPherson, a stone cutter and gravestone dealer from a small village near Saratoga Springs, New York, purchased a new Buick runabout from the local automobile dealer. In late July 1911, while Mr. MacPherson was driving a sick neighbor to the hospital, the wooden spokes on his Buick's left rear wheel broke, causing the wheel to collapse and the car to go out of control and crash into a ditch, pinning Mr. MacPherson under the axle. The dealer probably did not have sufficient assets to pay MacPherson's damages claim, so MacPherson's lawyer decided to sue Buick Motor Company and fight the privity doctrine head on. Though MacPherson lacked privity of contract with Buick, the trial judge refused to bar the claim, and the jury returned a verdict of $5,000 for MacPherson. The intermediate appellate court affirmed,[103] and Buick appealed to the New York Court of Appeals.

In a case that lay the foundation for the modern era of products liability law, *MacPherson v. Buick Motor Co.*,[104] the New York Court of Appeals affirmed the decision for the plaintiff. Judge Benjamin Cardozo, writing for the majority, concluded that the imminent danger rule was not limited to poisons, explosives, and other products which "in their normal operation are implements of destruction. If the nature of a thing is such that it is reasonably certain to place life and limb in peril when negligently made, it is then a thing of danger. Its nature gives warning of the consequences to be expected."[105] If the manufacturer of such a foreseeably dangerous product knows that it "will be used by persons other than the purchaser, and used without new tests, then, irrespective of contract, the manufacturer of this thing of danger is under a duty to make it carefully." Announcing the liberation of tort law from the law of contracts, Judge Cardozo

---

[101] 120 F. 865 (8th Cir. 1903) (Sanborn, J.).

[102] Id. at 870–71.

[103] MacPherson v. Buick Motor Co., 145 N.Y.S. 462 (App. Div. 1914).

[104] 111 N.E. 1050 (N.Y. 1916). On *MacPherson*, see D. Peck, Decision at Law 40 et seq. (Greenwood Press 1961); Henderson, MacPherson v. Buick Motor Company: Simplifying the Facts While Reshaping the Law, in Torts Stories 41 (R. Rabin and S. Sugarman eds., Foundation Press 2003); Clarke, Unmanageable Risks: MacPherson v. Buick and the Emergence of a Mass Consumer Market, 23 Law & Hist. Rev. 1 (2005); Probert, Applied Jurisprudence: A Case Study in MacPherson v. Buick and Its Precedents, 21 U.C. Davis L. Rev. 789 (1988); Notes, 29 Harv. L. Rev. 866 (1916), 25 Yale L.J. 679 (1916).

England's *MacPherson* was Donoghue v. Stevenson, [1932] A.C. 562 (H.L.) (appeal taken from Scot.) (U.K.). See note 75, above.

[105] *MacPherson*, 111 N.E. at 1053.

proclaimed: "We have put aside the notion that the duty to safeguard life and limb, when the consequences of negligence may be foreseen, grows out of contract and nothing else. We have put the source of the obligation where it ought to be. We have put its source in the law."[106]

While many courts quickly followed *MacPherson*, others did not, and by 1933 the case law on the scope of the "imminently dangerous" exception was in a state of utter confusion.[107] One by one, however, courts swung over to *MacPherson*.[108] By 1955, Professor Fleming James could write that "[t]he citadel of privity has crumbled, and today the ordinary tests of duty, negligence and liability are applied widely to the man who supplies a chattel for the use of another."[109] Lingering in some states longer than others, the privity requirement in negligence actions was finally abolished in the last state, Maine, in 1982.[110] "This trend was responsive to ever-growing pressure for protection of the consumer coupled with a realization that liability would not unduly inhibit the enterprise of manufacturers and that they were well placed both to profit from its lessons and to distribute its burdens."[111] The *MacPherson* rule has been extended to property damage; to non-purchasers, including mere bystanders; to non-manufacturer suppliers; and even to repairmen and building contractors. In the words of Dean Prosser: "It has become, in short, a general rule imposing negligence liability upon any supplier, for remuneration, of any chattel."[112]

§ 1.3 Modern American Law

Once *MacPherson v. Buick Motor Co.*[113] gave birth to negligence claims against manufacturers in the early 1900s, products liability claims spread slowly across America.[114] By the 1950s, courts were beginning to apply warranty claims to manufacturers of defective food, cosmetics, and similar products. Truly modern products liability law in America began in 1960 with *Henningsen v. Bloomfield Motors*,[115] previously discussed, which allowed a non-purchaser injured in an accident caused by a defective automobile to maintain a breach of warranty action against the manufacturer despite the absence of privity of contract and notwithstanding a contractual disclaimer that barred such claims. Three years later, in 1963, the Supreme Court of California

---

[106] Id. "Subtle distinctions are drawn by the defendant between things inherently dangerous and things imminently dangerous, but the case does not turn upon these verbal niceties. If danger was to be expected as reasonably certain, there was a duty of vigilance, and this whether you call the danger inherent or imminent." Id. at 1054–55. Chief Justice Bartlett dissented.

[107] See Russell, Manufacturers' Liability to the Ultimate Consumer, 21 Ky. L.J. 388, 397–99 (1933).

[108] See, e.g., Carter v. Yardley & Co., 64 N.E.2d 693, 700 (Mass. 1946) ("The doctrine of the MacPherson case is now generally accepted. . . . [It] caused the exception to swallow the asserted general rule of nonliability, leaving nothing upon which that rule could operate."). See generally Peairs, The God in the Machine, 29 B.U. L. Rev. 37 (1949).

[109] James, Products Liability (pt. 1), 34 Tex. L. Rev. 44 (1955).

[110] Adams v. Buffalo Forge Co., 443 A.2d 932 (Me. 1982).

[111] James, above note 109, at 44.

[112] Prosser, The Assault Upon the Citadel (Strict Liability to the Consumer), 69 Yale L.J. 1099, 1102 (1960). See also Prosser, The Fall of the Citadel (Strict Liability to the Consumer), 50 Minn. L. Rev. 791 (1966). "Probably no other case has been as frequently cited in following decisions or has made as great an impact on industry." D. Peck, Decision at Law 69 (Greenwood Press 1961).

[113] 111 N.E. 1050 (N.Y. 1916).

[114] See § 1.2, above.

[115] 161 A.2d 69 (N.J. 1960).

decided *Greenman v. Yuba Power Products, Inc.*,[116] which declared that manufacturers of defective products are strictly liable in tort to persons injured by such products, irrespective of any contract limitations that might inhere in the law of warranty. In 1964, the American Law Institute memorialized the rule of strict products liability in tort in § 402A of the *Restatement (Second) of Torts*, officially promulgated in 1965. For the rest of the 1960s, the doctrine of strict products liability in tort, together with a miscellany of secondary principles, spread like wildfire across the nation. This was the birth of modern products liability law in America.

Yet the products liability law that prevails in the United States today is a much different creature than the simple story just related might suggest. Since those early days of the 1960s, products liability law has become far more complex, having evolved and transmogrified in myriad diffuse directions in some forty thousand reported cases and a proliferation of state statutes "reforming" products liability law in a variety of important ways.[117] After the expansionary days of the 1960s and 1970s, the decades of the 1980s and 1990s were marked by a fundamental shift in the central ethic of this field of law—from a concern for protecting and *expanding* the rights of persons injured by dangerous products to a concern for *limiting* those rights in an effort to protect makers and other sellers of products from burdens increasingly viewed as unfair and inefficient. At this point in the evolution of its modern principles, products liability law in America has broadly regained a footing in reason, and an essential balance—between too little liability on producers and other sellers, on the one hand, and too much liability, on the other. Today, as lawyers for victims of product accidents file products liability actions across the nation each year,[118] products liability prevention and litigation management figure prominently in the daily decisions of manufacturers, retailers, insurers, and law firms across America.

Reform

From the time manufacturers and insurers in the 1960s and 1970s first began to feel the impact of modern products liability law in practice, they began to push for its "reform," arguing that the products liability system had developed various excesses that unfairly increased liability at the expense of everyone except plaintiffs and their lawyers. Beginning in the late 1970s, products liability reform efforts took center stage in the United States Congress, many state legislatures, the courts, federal regulatory agencies (like the FDA), and the American Law Institute. In 1996, President Clinton vetoed an act of Congress[119] that would have significantly altered major aspects of this area of the law. In 1998, after several years of development and debate, the ALI provided products liability with its own *Restatement*—the *Restatement (Third) of Torts: Products Liability*.

---

[116] 377 P.2d 897 (Cal. 1963) (examined in § 5.2, below).

[117] See notes 25, above, and 120, below.

[118] Some portion of products liability litigation is funded by third-party investors: "the litigation finance industry is a $5 billion market in the United States." Levitt and Brown, Third Party Litigation Funding: Civil Justice and the Need for Transparency 1 (DRI Center for Law & Public Policy 2018). See, e.g., Strom, Nobody Knows Litigation Finance Size, but It's Not $85 Billion, Prod. Liab. & Toxics L. News (June 11, 2020); Gershman, Lawsuit Funding, Once Hidden in the Shadows, Faces Calls for More Sunlight, Wall St. J.com (Mar. 21, 2018); Randazzo, Litigation Funding Moves into Mainstream: Startups Like LexShares, Trial Funder Attract Investors with Promises of Double-digit Returns, Wall. St. J.com (Aug. 4, 2016). At least two states require parties to disclose third-party financing agreements. See W. Va. Code Ann. §§ 46A–6N–1 et seq.; Wis. Stat. Ann. § 804.01(2)(bg). See also Maslowski v. Prospect Funding Partners LLC, 944 N.W.2d 235, 241 (Minn. 2020) (abolishing Minnesota's common-law prohibition against champerty).

[119] See Common Sense Product Liability Legal Reform Act of 1996, H.R. 956, 104th Cong. (1996).

Since that time, courts and occasional state legislatures continue to reform this field of law.

Most legislative reform has been in the states, several of which have enacted broad products liability statutes that codify the basic principles of products liability law. Topics subject to statutory reform have included theories of liability and definitions of defects in manufacture, design, and warnings; defenses, including the effect of a user's fault, assumption of risk, obvious dangers, product alteration and misuse, state of the art, compliance with custom, compliance with statutes and regulations, and statutes of limitation and repose; retailer liability; pleading requirements for compensatory damages; standards for and limitations on punitive damages; and special rules governing certain specific topics, such as the effect of not using seatbelts and child restraint devices, and rules governing various types of products, such as tobacco, alcohol, guns, asbestos, prescription drugs, and breast implants.[120]

Anatomy of Modern Products Liability Litigation

Several studies provide useful empirical information on products liability law in action. The following statistics are gathered from a 1976–78 study by the federal Interagency Task Force on Product Liability, a 1985–86 insurance industry report, a 2005 report by a jury research firm, and a 2008 Department of Justice study. An important 2011 study by academics presents background data on the number and cost of particular product-related injuries, illnesses, and deaths in America each year. The final studies, from 2018–2021, present more recent litigation data.

Interagency Task Force Study—1976–78

The federal Interagency Task Force on Product Liability conducted an in-depth study of products liability law in the mid-1970s,[121] revealing the following statistics

---

[120] The broadest state statutes are Ariz. Rev. Stat. Ann. §§ 12–681 et seq.; Conn. Gen. Stat. Ann. §§ 52–572*l*, 52–572m et seq.; Ind. Code Ann. §§ 34–20–1–1 et seq.; Kan. Stat. Ann. §§ 60–3301 et seq.; La. Rev. Stat. Ann. §§ 9:2800.51 et seq.; Mich. Comp. Laws Ann. §§ 600.2945 et seq.; Miss. Code Ann. §§ 11–1–63 et seq.; N.J. Stat. Ann. §§ 2A:58C–1 et seq.; N.C. Gen. Stat. Ann. §§ 99B–1 et seq.; Ohio Rev. Code Ann. §§ 2307.71 et seq.; Tenn. Code Ann. §§ 29–28–101 et seq.; Tex. Civ. Prac. & Rem. Code Ann. §§ 82.001 et seq.; Utah Code Ann. §§ 78B–6–701 et seq.; Wash. Rev. Code Ann. §§ 7.72.010 et seq.; and Wis. Stat. Ann. §§ 895.046 to .047.

More narrow statutes include Ala. Code §§ 6–5–500 et seq.; Ark. Code Ann. §§ 16–116–202 et seq.; Colo. Rev. Stat. Ann. §§ 13–21–401 et seq.; Ga. Code Ann. §§ 51–1–11 et seq.; Idaho Code Ann. §§ 6–1401 et seq.; Ky. Rev. Stat. Ann. §§ 411.300 et seq.; Me. Rev. Stat. Ann. tit. 14, §§ 221 et seq. (essentially adopting § 402A); Mo. Ann. Stat. §§ 537.760 et seq.; Mont. Code Ann. § 27–1–719 (essentially adopting § 402A); Neb. Rev. Stat. §§ 25–21,180 et seq.; N.D. Cent. Code §§ 28–01.3–01 et seq.; Or. Rev. Stat. Ann. §§ 30.900 et seq.; S.C. Code Ann. §§ 15–73–10 et seq. (adopting § 402A); and S.D. Codified Laws §§ 29–9–9 et seq.

Some states have very narrow legislation, directed at only one or two issues. See, e.g., Cal. Health & Safety Code § 1714.4 (defectiveness of guns and ammunition), § 1714.45 (defectiveness of tobacco, alcohol, and sugar); Del. Code Ann. tit. 18, § 7001 (sealed container defense); D.C. Code §§ 6–2381 et seq. (firearms), §§ 6–2391 et seq. (assault rifles); Fla. Stat. Ann. §§ 774.201 et seq. (asbestos and silica claims); Iowa Code Ann. § 613.18 and § 668.12 (defenses); Minn. Stat. Ann. § 544.41 (retailer protection from strict liability in tort); R.I. Gen. Laws § 9–1–13 (10-year period of repose), § 9–1–32 (effect of alteration or modification).

Almost all states have "blood shield" statutes, shielding blood suppliers from strict products liability, a number have statutes of repose for products liability actions, and various states have special statutes governing certain aspects of a wide variety of products liability issues, such as asbestos and breast implant litigation. Products liability statutes are compiled in volumes 3 and 4 of Owen & Davis on Products Liability.

[121] A comprehensive study of products liability litigation was conducted under the auspices of the Interagency Task Force on Product Liability, formed in 1976 to examine the increase in products liability litigation and resulting insurance premiums. Under the direction of Professor Victor Schwartz, working out of The Department of Commerce, the Task Force analyzed hundreds of products liability decisions from 1965–76. The statistics here are from Product Liability: Final Report of the Legal Study, vol. 3 (Interagency Task

about products liability litigation at that time. Although the data now are dated, they present a useful picture of modern products liability law in its first decade.

The Forum—78% of the cases were tried in state court, 22% in federal court. Suit usually was brought in the state where the injury occurred, usually *not* where the product was manufactured, and almost always in the plaintiff's home state. Juries heard 86% of the cases tried.

Increase in Cases—The number of products liability cases reported in eight states doubled from 1965–70 to 1971–76.

Type of Product—About 1/3 of the cases involved automobiles, followed in frequency by industrial machinery.

Parties—Manufacturers were defendants in 79% of the cases, retailers in 33%, wholesalers in 5%, manufacturers' suppliers in 5%, employers in 4%, lessors in 3%, and installers in 5%. Manufacturers were third-party plaintiffs in 15% of the cases in which they were original defendants. Manufacturers were third-party defendants in about 10% of the cases; employers in 8%.

Age of Product—About 10% of the products were over 20 years old. Excluding automobiles, 21% of the products were over 20 years old.

Industrial Products—In 1971–76, 50% of the cases involved work-related injuries from machinery and tools.

Type of Defect—The bases of liability asserted were manufacturing (and inadequate inspection) defects in 42% of the cases, design defects in 39%, and warning defects in 21%.[122] Most automotive and container cases alleged defective manufacture, most machinery and recreational product cases alleged defective design, and most chemical cases alleged inadequate warnings.

Prevailing Party—Plaintiffs prevailed in 50% of all cases, defendants in 50%.[123] Of cases decided on the merits, plaintiffs prevailed 41% of the time in Arizona, 44% in Illinois, 58% in California, and 63% in Texas. Plaintiffs won 60% of jury trials but only 44% of non-jury trials. From 1965–70 to 1971–76, the rate of successful plaintiff cases rose 4%.

Damages—The average damage award in cases in which the plaintiff ultimately prevailed rose from $104,000 in 1965–70 to $222,000 in 1971–76. By state, average damage awards for the entire period were as follows: California ($272,000), Texas ($221,000), New York ($170,000), Pennsylvania ($137,000), and Illinois ($119,000). Much of the increase in awards between the two periods was attributable to inflation, especially the cost of medical care, which is often the largest component of products liability claims.

Force on Product Liability: U.S. Dep't of Com., 1977), summarized in id., vol. 1, at 17–18. In addition to the Final Report, see also Selected Papers, Interagency Task Force on Product Liability (1978).

[122] By comparison, a 1973 survey indicated the following breakdown of 222 cases brought in strict tort: manufacturing defects—28%; design defects—46%; warning defects—25%; and misrepresentation—1%.

[123] A comprehensive insurance industry survey in 1977 found that less than 4% of all products liability claims went all the way to verdict and, in contrast to the findings of the Task Force, fewer than 25% of the defendants in these cases were found liable. Highlights, Insurance Services Office Product Liability Closed Claim Survey: A Technical Analysis of Survey Results 6 (1977).

Insurance Industry Study—1985–86

The following statistics are from an insurance industry study of large (in excess of $100,000) products liability claims closed in 1985.[124] While such claims represent only 1–2% of all products liability claims, they account for 50–60% of insurer payments.

Payments at Various Stages of Litigation—In the 4% of large claims where no suit was filed, the average payment was $232,000. In the 71% of claims where suit was filed, but where settlement was reached before trial, payments averaged $441,000. Where settlement was reached during trial (14% of the cases), payments averaged $649,000. In cases that went to verdict (11%), payments averaged $532,000.

Theory of Liability—Strict liability was the only theory alleged in 22% of the claims; only negligence in 15%; and only breach of warranty in 3%. All three theories of liability were alleged in 30% of the claims. Strict liability was the main theory relied upon in settlement in 60% of the cases, negligence in 31%, and warranty in 8%.

Type of Defect—Where strict liability was the main liability theory, defective design was the applicable theory in 75% of the claims, and warning defects in 18%.

Punitive Damages—Punitive damages were demanded in 18% of the incidents; separate payments for such damages were awarded by a jury or paid for in settlement in 1% of the cases. Yet the threat of such damages probably increased the size of other settlements.

Number of Defendants—There was only one defendant in 56% of the cases. There were two defendants in 22%, three defendants in 9%, four defendants in 6%, and more than four in 7%.

Miscellaneous Issues—In the opinion of the claim reviewers, the question of product defect was too technical for the jury to understand and decide in 17% of the incidents; alteration, modification, or misuse was a cause of the accident in 34% of the incidents; and 12% of the products failed to comply with governmental safety standards.[125]

Jury Verdict Research Study—2005

In 2005, Jury Verdict Research published a study on products liability verdicts and settlements.[126]

Products Liability Cases of All Types—Probability of plaintiff recovery, 46%; median award, $1 million; awards of $1 million or greater, 52%.

Industrial, Construction, Commercial, and Farm Products—Probability of plaintiff recovery, 54%; median award, $1 million; awards of $1 million or greater, 52%.

Transportation Products—Probability of plaintiff recovery, 43%; median award, $2.68 million; awards of $1 million or greater, 70%.

---

[124] See L. Soular, A Study of Large Product Liability Claims Closed in 1985 (1986), a joint study of the Alliance of American Insurers and the American Insurance Association.

[125] Another study, based on cases from the late 1970s, found that 19% of products liability claims filed were dropped, and 95% of the remainder were settled. Of the 5% that went to verdict, plaintiffs won 37% and lost 63%. Viscusi, The Determinants of the Disposition of Product Liability Claims and Compensation for Bodily Injury, 15 J. Legal Stud. 321 (1986).

[126] See Product Liability Claims: An Overview of Jury Awards and Settlements (Jury Verdict Research, B. Doran ed., 2005).

General Consumer Products—Probability of plaintiff recovery, 39%; median award, $216,269; awards of $1 million or greater, 31%.

Medical Products—Probability of plaintiff recovery, 46%; median award, $987,500; awards of $1 million or greater, 51%.

One should be cautious in interpreting these data, not only because of the vagaries of statistics and the partisan nature of this field of law, but also because of changes over time. Products liability studies covering the late 1980s and most of the 1990s showed moderation and, in some instances, declines in case filings (at least in non-asbestos cases), verdicts, and plaintiff success rates.[127] But products liability costs and insurance tend to move in waves, sometimes up and sometimes down. A 2001 study revealed that during the 1990s fewer products liability cases were filed but the size of awards substantially increased—from about $500,000 in 1993 to over $1.8 million in 1999—and that the rate of increase in the amount of such awards was accelerating.[128] This study suggested that the plaintiff's bar was increasingly limiting its clients to those with serious injuries and a greater likelihood of success, and that it was refining its litigation techniques and skills, including the effective use of expert witnesses.

Department of Justice Study—2008

In 2008, the Bureau of Justice Statistics of the U.S. Department of Justice released a new study of tort, contract, and real property civil bench and jury trials in state courts during 2005. The study examined two types of products liability cases: 268 *ordinary* product cases and 87 involving *asbestos.*[129]

Proportion of Total—Ordinary products liability cases represented 1% of the total civil cases, down from 3% of the total fourteen years earlier; *asbestos* product cases 0.3%, down from the toxic substance total of 2.4% in the early 1990s. (By comparison, auto cases were 35% of the total, premises liability 6.9%, and medical malpractice 9.1%.)

Time to Verdict—Average periods from filing of a civil complaint to verdict were as follows: *Jury trials*—average time, 26 months; *Bench trials*—average time, 20 months.

Plaintiff Success Rates—Plaintiffs won 19.6% of *ordinary* product cases, 54.9% of *asbestos* cases.

Size of Awards, Generally—The size of the awards, including punitive damages, after adjusting for contributory negligence, prior settlement, and damages caps were as follows: *Ordinary* products—median, $500,000; *Asbestos*—median, $682,000. Of awards won by plaintiffs, 36.5% involving ordinary products exceeded $1 million as did 25.5% of those involving asbestos. Whereas inflation-adjusted damages awarded in all types of

---

[127] See, e.g., Message from the Chair, ABA TIPS Newsletter 1 (Spring/Summer 1995) (noting that products liability filings in federal court, apart from asbestos cases, declined 36% between 1985 and 1991); Hunter, Product Liability Insurance—Report of the Insurance Group of Consumer Federation of America (June 1998) (showing products liability insurance costs "minute" and declining, from 25¢ per $100 of retail product sales in 1985 to 16¢ in 1996).

[128] See Winter, Jury Awards Soar as Lawsuits Decline on Defective Goods, NY Times.com (Jan. 30, 2001) (reporting study of 2,751 products liability verdicts by LRP Publications, reputedly a nonpartisan organization that collects data on products liability case outcomes in several states).

[129] See Langton and Cohen, Civil Justice Survey of State Courts, 2005—Civil Bench and Jury Trials in State Courts, 2005, NCJ–223851 (October 2008).

tort jury trials from 1992 to 2005 declined by about 50%, median verdicts in products liability trials increased by about 500%, from $154,000 in 1992 to $749,000 in 2005.[130]

Ruttenberg, Cardi, and Fenton Study—2011

In 2011, Ruth Ruttenberg, Jonathan Cardi, and Estye Fenton published an empirical study that examined existing data on the extent of product-related harm in America each year.[131] Their estimates of "non-trivial" product injuries, illnesses, and deaths, presented in the table below, show a total annual number of reported product-related harms of 130 million. Three prior studies used by the authors of this study estimate the resulting annual cost to the nation at $4 trillion to $8 trillion.

Estimates of Annual Product-Related Fatalities, Injuries & Illnesses

Product	Fatalities	Injuries & Illnesses
CPSC-Regulated Products	28,200	33,600,000
Pesticides/Fungicides/Rodenticides	57	90,029 reported exposures, 4,236 hospitalizations
Workplace Product-Related Fatalities & Injuries	2,180	1,000,294
Firearms	30,386	62,086
Food	5,194	76,000,000
Prescription and Over-the-Counter Drugs	106,000	8,110,000
Medical Devices	418	453,965
Tobacco—smoking	443,000	8,860,000
Alcohol	23,199	N.A.
Asbestos	10,098	21,000
Airborne Products	97,789	N.A.
Boats	701	3,493
Aviation	606	866
Automobiles	33,808	2,217,000
TOTAL	***781,636***	***130,422,969***

As enormous as these numbers may be, they substantially understate the problem because a large proportion of product-related injuries, illnesses, and even deaths go chronically under-reported.[132] For example, a former OSHA head has estimated that

[130] The 2019 average and median products liability personal injury jury awards were $7.4 million and $2 million, respectively. See Insurance Information Institute, Facts + Statistics: Product Liability, https://www.iii.org/fact-statistic/facts-statistics-product-liability (last visited Mar. 1, 2022). From 2015 to 2019, federal court products liability punitive awards exceeded $1.2 billion and class action settlements neared $744 million. See Belle Isle, Lex Machina Releases 2020 Product Liability Report, LegalReader.com (June 1, 2020).

[131] Ruttenberg, Cardi, and Fenton, The Taxpayers' Burden from Product-Related Harm, 21 Kan. J.L. & Pub. Pol'y 121 (2011–2012) (footnotes omitted).

[132] See id. at 172 (discussing "the chronic problems of underreporting" and stating that the authors in this study did not correct for this recognized phenomenon); id. at 181 (stating that "nearly every product category draws from data that under-represent the number of fatalities and injuries").

40% of workplace deaths go unreported. Another example of under-reporting concerns the many thousands of nonfatal diseases and injuries attributable to alcohol consumption and resulting behavior (including violence) on which reliable data is unavailable and therefore not included in the study at all. For many such reasons, the study's authors were unable to obtain data on a considerable portion of product-related injuries and deaths, or on *most* product-related *illnesses* (including product-related harm from cancer, heart failure, and lung failure). Further, in the tradition of sound empirical scholarship, the authors studiously rendered conservative estimates (as for annual increases in health care costs). Because of these frailties in the data, the authors appropriately characterize their estimates, variously, as "conservative," "very conservative," and "extremely conservative"—an admirable approach to empirical scholarship that does not hamper my own estimates below, which are intended to be realistic. And of course the study's estimates, dated 2009, must be multiplied by an inflation factor to bring them up to date.

All told, a fair extrapolation of the figures in this study suggests that in the early 2020s Americans suffer upwards of 200 million non-trivial product-related injuries, illnesses, and deaths each year, at an annual cost to the nation of roughly $15–20 trillion. But it is important to highlight here that most of these product-related harms are principally caused by users or third parties who improperly use products that otherwise are reasonably safe—such as a slip in the bathtub; a drunken driver who crashes a car into a tree, injuring a passenger and himself; or a factory worker who spills a can of acid he knows is dangerous on another worker, or on his own ungloved hand. Such untoward product-related harms normally lie outside the system of products liability law. But there is also a substantial set of cases involving product-related harms from dangerous conditions in products that manufacturers reasonably should have taken steps to avoid. It is this latter set of cases that is the realm of products liability law.

Legal Analytics and Products Liability Litigation—2018–2021

Legal analytics, which apply machine learning algorithms and statistical methodologies, may be used to provide information on litigation trends, outcomes, venues, judges, experts, and other factors. A Thomson Reuters' Westlaw Edge Litigation Analytics query of federal products liability filings through February 2022 revealed that 45% ended in uncontested dismissal, 20% were docketed elsewhere (including assignment to MDL proceedings), 15% were settled, 6% ended in dispositive motions (including motions to dismiss, summary judgments, or default judgments), and 1% ended in a jury verdict.[133]

In 2018, LexisNexis' Lex Machina Legal Analytics® analyzed over 400,000 U.S. District Court product liability cases filed between January 1, 2009 and December 31, 2017. This study revealed, in part, that:

1) medical device and pharmaceutical cases dominated all products liability filings;

2) multidistrict litigation (MDL) comprised over 97% of medical device and pharmaceutical cases;

[133] Thomson Reuters Westlaw Edge, Litigation Analytics (product liability case type), https://1.next.westlaw.com/ (last visited Mar. 01, 2021) (St. David's Day).

3) asbestos cases declined from thousands to hundreds of annual filings beginning in 2012;

4) nearly all medical device or pharmaceutical cases were either settled or resolved procedurally, largely through summary judgment findings; and

5) "defendants prevail[ed] about 90% of the time" in the relatively few medical device/pharmaceutical cases decided on the merits.[134]

Theories of Recovery

Negligence

Negligence is the classic claim in American products liability law, and it remains a fundamentally important theory of recovery. Although the doctrinal significance of negligence slipped into the shadows as various "strict" theories of manufacturer liability developed during the 1960s, 1970s, and early 1980s, negligence remained the dominant theory of recovery in several states that chose not to adopt the new doctrine of strict products liability in tort. More broadly, negligence principles in recent decades have experienced a resurgence as courts and state legislatures across the land increasingly have returned to principles of negligence (though often still under the rubric of "strict liability") in many products liability contexts, highlighted by the explicit recognition of such principles in the *Restatement (Third) of Torts: Products Liability* as the foundation for several of its most important provisions.

Negligence may occur at any stage of the design, manufacturing, and marketing processes. To prove any products liability claim sounding in negligence—whether negligent design, negligent manufacture, or negligent failure to provide adequate warnings or instructions—a plaintiff must establish that: (1) the seller owed a duty to the plaintiff; (2) the seller breached that duty; (3) the breach was a cause in fact of the plaintiff's injury; (4) the cause in fact was a proximate cause of the injury; and (5) the particular type of harm is recoverable in negligence. In any case, the standard of care to which a manufacturer must conform is the standard of reasonable care of an expert manufacturer of such a product. A manufacturer's responsibility in negligence is limited to such risks, uses, and persons as are reasonably foreseeable at the time a product is made and sold.

Sometimes the negligence standard of care—reasonable care under the circumstances—may inhere in a statute or agency regulation, in which case a defendant's breach thereof may amount to negligence per se. Other times, an industry code or standard may be a good gauge of reasonable care, but rarely is industry custom strictly the measure of that care. And sometimes the breach of the standard of care, and causation, suggest themselves circumstantially by the way in which an accident occurs, which may activate the doctrine of res ipsa loquitur. Yet, ordinarily, negligence is determined by balancing the burden ("costs") of feasible yet untaken safety precautions against the safety benefits such precautions appeared likely to achieve. That is, the type and amount of care normally required is a function of the type, likelihood, and amount of harm (together viewed as the risk) that particular precautions may be expected to prevent. If the risk posed by the sale and use of a product in a certain condition is great, due care requires that great precautions be taken to avert the risk; if the risk is small,

---

[134] Lex Machina, Lex Machina's Inaugural Product Liability Litigation Report Focuses on Burgeoning Medical Device and Pharmaceutical Product Case Filings (Apr. 2, 2018). See also Belle Isle, Lex Machina Releases 2020 Product Liability Report, LegalReader.com (June 1, 2020).

reasonable care requires only small precautionary measures in response. Stated simply, a manufacturer in the exercise of due care is obligated to exercise an amount of care proportionate to the expected risk.

This principle of balance, sometimes referred to as the "calculus of risk," was expressed in a celebrated formulation by Judge Learned Hand in *United States v. Carroll Towing Co.*[135] There, Judge Hand reasoned that a determination of the degree of care appropriate to an occasion often reflects a calculus of three factors: the burden of taking precautions to avoid a risk of harm, on the one side, balanced against the likelihood that the actor's proposed conduct will produce the harm multiplied by the seriousness of the harm, on the other. Expressed algebraically, negligence is suggested if $B < P \times L$, where B is the burden (cost) of adopting a precaution to avoid accidental loss that foreseeably may result if B is not undertaken, P is the increase in probability of loss if B is not undertaken, and L is the probable magnitude (expected cost) of such loss. This calculus, the so-called "Hand formula," more fully reads: $B < P \times L \Rightarrow N$: that is, if the costs of taking a particular safety precaution (B) are less than the precaution's expected safety benefits ($P \times L$), then the manufacturer's failure to adopt the precaution implies its negligence ($\Rightarrow N$). Thus, in making and marketing its products, a manufacturer must exercise care proportionate to the foreseeable risks of harm.

Tortious Misrepresentation

Misrepresentation is the communication of false or misleading information to another. A tortious misrepresentation claim may arise in a products liability context if a manufacturer or other seller makes a false and material assertion about a product to a person who is physically harmed by reasonably relying on the truth of the assertion. For example, a manufacturer may claim that its cranes can lift 20,000 pounds of weight, whereas lifting that amount of weight will actually break the crane's boom, causing the load to fall on workers underneath; or a drug manufacturer may promote a medication as free of dangerous side effects, when it actually does cause such side effects in many people. Tortious misrepresentation claims therefore require no "defect" in the product but are based on the communication of false information that causes physical harm.

Three separate claims for tortious misrepresentation may arise at common law—bases of liability that differ principally according to the defendant's state of mind in making the representation. The elements of intentional misrepresentation ("fraud" or "deceit") are expressed many ways but almost always include some version of the following elements: (1) a representation; (2) its falsity; (3) its materiality; (4) the speaker's knowledge of its falsity or ignorance of its truth; (5) the speaker's intent that the hearer will believe and act in reliance on the representation; (6) the hearer's ignorance of its falsity; (7) the hearer's reliance on its truth; (8) the justifiability of that reliance; and (9) the hearer's consequent and proximate harm.

In place of the defendant's *scienter* (that the speaker knew the matter represented to be false and intended it to mislead the plaintiff), negligent misrepresentation substitutes a defendant's negligence in not knowing the falsity of a representation, or, less commonly, communicating it in a negligent manner. Finally, under *Restatement (Second) of Torts* § 402B a handful of jurisdictions allow claims of strict liability in tort

[135] 159 F.2d 169, 173 (2d Cir. 1947) (Hand, J.).

for innocent public misrepresentations about a product's safety, notwithstanding the seller's exercise of all due care and belief that the representations are true.

Breach of Warranty

Like tortious misrepresentation, warranty law concerns obligations that arise from representations connected with transactions. In the products liability context, the law of warranty prescribes the legal effect of assertions associated with the transfer of a product for value, usually through a sale. Such representations about a product may be express, through a seller's affirmative communications concerning the product's attributes, or they may be implied by the nature of the sales transaction.

Most products liability law today is based in tort, and warranty law is ordinarily conceived as part of the modern law of contract because the relevant representations arise out of the sale and purchase of a product. Several states that never did adopt the doctrine of strict liability in tort for the sale of defective products—notably Delaware, Massachusetts, Michigan, Virginia, and, to a lesser extent, North Carolina—constructed modern products liability jurisprudence largely upon an implied warranty of quality.

The modern source of most products liability warranty law is the article on sales law in the Uniform Commercial Code, Article 2, which prescribes how warranties arise and are defined, to whom they extend, and remedies for their breach.[136] Article 2 defines three types of warranties applicable to products liability litigation: express warranties, under UCC § 2–313; implied warranties of merchantability, under UCC § 2–314; and implied warranties of fitness for particular purpose, under UCC § 2–315. Claims for breach of express warranty are similar in many respects to strict liability claims for misrepresentation under *Restatement (Second) of Torts* § 402B, except that an express warranty claim requires that the buyer, rather than proving reliance on the representation, prove that the representation was part of the basis of the bargain. Claims for breach of an implied warranty of merchantability in products liability cases normally are based on a product's failure to be fit for the ordinary purposes of such products—as when the brakes on a new car fail, causing it to leave the highway and hit a tree. The essential basis of liability in such cases is that the product was not reasonably safe—that it was defective—which makes the basis for breach of the merchantability warranty essentially the same as the basis of liability for strict liability in tort under § 402A of the *Restatement (Second) of Torts*. An implied warranty of fitness for particular purpose, which only infrequently arises in products liability litigation, is something of a hybrid, lying part way between an express warranty and an implied warranty of merchantability. This warranty is most likely to arise in the products liability setting in a retail transaction when a seller has reason to know that a buyer is relying on the seller's skill or judgment to select a product for the buyer that will serve the buyer's special needs.

Various contractual doctrines limit the availability of breach of warranty claims under Article 2. If a person claiming breach of warranty was not the purchaser, then the plaintiff will not be in privity of contract with the seller and so must qualify as a third-party beneficiary under UCC § 2–318, which identifies parties other than buyers who may benefit from a seller's breach of warranty. Moreover, a buyer may not sue for breach

[136] In 2003, the National Conference of Commissioners on Uniform State Laws (NCCUSL) and the American Law Institute (ALI) completed a joint revision project on Article 2 and its sister on leases, Article 2A, and promulgated substantial amendments to both articles. Industry opposed some of the amendments, state legislatures ignored them, and in 2011 the two sponsoring bodies withdrew the amendments.

of warranty unless he or she has promptly notified the seller, under UCC § 2–607, of the supposed breach. But the most powerful limitation on warranty claims in Article 2 is the seller's ability to avoid warranty responsibility by contractual disclaimers, under UCC § 2–316, and to limit damages for breach of warranty, under UCC § 2–719. While the law restricts a seller's ability to disclaim responsibility[137] or limit damages for breach of warranty,[138] these limitations on warranty responsibility remain important obstacles to recovery in many situations.

Strict Liability in Tort

The doctrine of strict liability in tort has long been widely viewed as the predominant theory of recovery in modern products liability law. Indeed, the development and growth of the doctrine of strict products liability in tort was the centerpiece around which the rest of modern products liability law was constructed. In the 1960 case of *Henningsen v. Bloomfield Motors, Inc.*,[139] the New Jersey Supreme Court held the manufacturer of a defective car strictly liable for injuries to a driver, nominally on the basis of the manufacturer's breach of its implied warranty of quality, but without regard to the purchase contract's warranty exclusions or remedy limitations, and despite the fact that the injured driver had no "privity of contract" with the manufacturer.

On the footings of *Henningsen*, the Supreme Court of California in 1963 constructed a new theory of strict products liability in tort in *Greenman v. Yuba Power Products, Inc.*[140] The next year, Dean William Prosser, Reporter for the *Restatement (Second) of Torts*, included this new liability principle in § 402A of that *Restatement*, which the American Law Institute approved that year and promulgated the following year, in 1965. With a gusto unparalleled by any prior development in the law of torts, the new doctrine swept across the face of America during the late 1960s and 1970s as many courts and a few legislatures embraced § 402A and the bold new doctrine that it proclaimed—"strict" liability in tort for physical harm caused by the sale of defective products.

Liability for harm from product defects under § 402A was "strict" because it rested on the frustration of consumer expectations of product safety, rather than on the seller's fault, when a latent defect causes harm. Yet, as more and more courts during the 1970s and 1980s broadly extended the new principle beyond manufacturing flaws to design and warning defects, the truly strict consumer expectations test increasingly gave way to principles of foreseeability and risk-utility balancing that underlie the law of negligence. While courts continued to assert that they were applying "strict" liability, and while such liability indeed is strict when applied to manufacturing defects (and a retailer's liability for most hidden defects), it became increasingly clear that the principles governing liability in design and warning cases were truly based on fault.

In 1992, the American Law Institute began work on a new *Restatement (Third) of Torts* on the specific topic of products liability law, approving the new *Restatement* in 1997 and publishing it in 1998 as the *Restatement (Third) of Torts: Products Liability*. While the *Third Restatement* continues to base liability for manufacturing defects in

---

[137] Particularly under the Magnuson-Moss Federal Warranty Act, 15 U.S.C. §§ 2301 et seq. See § 4.9, below.

[138] Particularly with respect to personal injuries in the case of consumer goods. See UCC § 2–719(3).

[139] 161 A.2d 69 (N.J. 1960) (Francis, J.).

[140] 377 P.2d 897 (Cal. 1963) (Traynor, J.).

terms that are strict, it abandons any pretense of "strict" responsibility for design and warning defects, liability for which it grounds explicitly in principles of negligence.

Notwithstanding the *Third Restatement*, modern products liability law in most states still draws upon the "strict liability" language of § 402A. Thus, while an increasing number of courts have adopted certain key provisions of the *Products Liability Restatement*, and while many courts acknowledge that the principles they apply to design and warning cases are similar to negligence, most courts continue to parrot traditional § 402A jurisprudence that broadly calls modern products liability law "strict." In this way, many (perhaps most) modern courts have created a disjunction between what they say and what they do. Be that as it may, the principle of inertia suggests that many courts for many years will continue to apply principles of negligence to design and warning defect issues while purporting to apply their "strict" liability jurisprudence quite long ago spawned by § 402A.

Product Defectiveness

In General

In the great bulk of products liability cases, a plaintiff must prove that the defendant's product contained an unnecessary hazard that caused the harm.[141] All products are dangerous to some extent, at least when put to certain uses. But many product dangers—such as a knife's sharp blade—are impractical, if not impossible, to avoid. For such inherent product risks, *users* rather than makers or suppliers should avoid and may insure against the possibility of injury. But sometimes products carry foreseeably excessive risks that users and consumers should not have to bear, usually because they do not expect such risks and always because manufacturers can cost-effectively and practicably avoid them. In such cases, manufacturers properly bear responsibility for excessive harm their products cause to users and third parties. Products that carry excessive risk are called "defective."

While most jurisdictions still require plaintiffs in most cases to construct their cases under the traditional causes of action (negligence, breach of implied warranty, and/or strict liability in tort), a developing trend subordinates the formal doctrine of these traditional liability theories to a *functional* consideration of whether a product was "defective." Virtually every American jurisdiction now divides product defects into three categories, as further developed below:

(1) ***manufacturing defects***—hazards from production flaws;

(2) ***design defects***—hazards that reasonable design improvements would avoid; and

(3) ***warning defects***—hazards that reasonable warnings or instructions would avoid.

These three types of defect, and a manufacturer's obligations to avoid them, are principally separate and distinct.

Conceptualizing product defects and proving them are two very different things. The key to proof of a product defect rests necessarily on the effective use of experts to explain just how a product is defective (how its dangers are excessive), how these excessive dangers reasonably could have been removed, and how their presence caused

---

[141] This puts aside cases where a defendant's false statements cause the harm.

the plaintiff's harm. Particularly since the Supreme Court sought to rid the law of "junk science" in *Daubert v. Merrell Dow Pharmaceuticals, Inc.*,[142] which placed on courts a "gatekeeping" responsibility to evaluate the reliability and relevance of scientific expert testimony offered by the parties before allowing it in evidence, courts and lawyers have been striving to figure out how science and engineering properly help determine whether a product is defective and, if so, whether the defect caused the plaintiff's harm.

Various evidentiary doctrines affect proof of product defect and causation in modern products liability litigation. For example, if the cause of a product accident is a mystery, but its circumstances suggest the probability that the product was defective, then the "malfunction doctrine" (a close cousin to res ipsa loquitur) may establish the product's defectiveness. In other cases, proof that a product violated or complied with a safety standard adopted by industry or the government may help establish whether the product was or was not defective. Sometimes a product's defectiveness may be proved in part by similar failures of the same kind of product, while at other times a long safe history may help to show that a product was not defective. Finally, to avoid discouraging safety improvements, most courts apply the "repair doctrine" to exclude evidence that a manufacturer adopted remedial measures to improve a product's safety after an accident has occurred.

The Products Liability Restatement

In 1998, after several years of drafting and vigorous debate, the American Law Institute published the *Restatement (Third) of Torts: Products Liability*. As a guide to courts (not a statute), the *Third Restatement* is designed to replace the *Second Restatement*'s treatment of products liability law in § 402A and certain other sections. The *Products Liability Restatement* provides that liability should be imposed on manufacturers, retailers, and other commercial suppliers for harm resulting from their sale of products that are defective, in one of the three ways mentioned earlier, and for misrepresenting a product's safety. A product contains a *manufacturing defect* under *Products Liability Restatement* § 2(a) if it "departs from its intended design even though all possible care was exercised in the preparation and marketing of the product." A product contains a *design defect* under § 2(b) if a hazard could have been reduced by some "reasonable alternative design," meaning that the danger could have been designed away cost-effectively without unduly diminishing the product's usefulness. A product contains a *warning or instruction defect* under § 2(c) if the product was not, but reasonably should have been, accompanied by an adequate warning of foreseeable product hazards or instructions on how to avoid them. Other provisions govern special products, transactions, defendants, and duties, such as food, used products, prescription drugs, successor corporations, and post-sale duties to warn or recall.

Product Defects in Modern Law

Although plaintiffs' lawyers widely viewed the *Third Restatement* as a conservative reformation of products liability law, and while it did abandon the *Second Restatement*'s idea in § 402A of applying one general principle of "strict" liability to product defects of all types, the *Third Restatement* largely mirrors the paths many American courts and legislatures began to tread in the 1980s and 1990s as their understanding of products liability issues matured and as their commitment to the expansionary liability principles of the 1960s and 1970s began to wane. Today, while recovery for product accidents in

[142] 509 U.S. 579 (1993).

most states is still formally based on the underlying theories of recovery—negligence, breach of the implied warranty of merchantability, and strict liability in tort—liability largely rests on proof that the plaintiff's injury was caused by a defect in a product's manufacture, design, or warning.

Manufacturing defects. Manufacturers and other suppliers normally are liable for injuries caused by manufacturing defects in products that they sell. When strict liability principles are applied to defects of this type, liability is *truly* strict, based on proof of some error in production that caused the product to contain an unintended flaw. Most litigation over defectively manufactured goods concerns questions of causation rather than the defectiveness *vel non* of the accident product. If a product allegedly malfunctions in a manner that causes an accident, as when a vehicle's steering locks, causing it to leave the road and crash into a tree, the steering mechanism may be damaged in the accident. In such a case, it may be difficult or impossible to determine specifically why the steering failed, if it really did at all. When a product is damaged or destroyed in the accident, or lost thereafter, the "malfunction doctrine" may help a plaintiff who is unable to identify a specific defect. Quite like res ipsa loquitur, the malfunction doctrine comes into play when the circumstances of an accident suggest that it probably was caused by some defect in the product, and the plaintiff's evidence eliminates other normal causes of such accidents, such as an errant mechanic or driver error.

Defective food cases present the most unappetizing type of manufacturing defect cases, where mice turn up in soft drinks, glass in cans of spinach, clam shells in clam chowder, and maggots in dried pea soup. Today, food is considered defective in its "manufacture" if it contains a hazard the consumer did not reasonably expect, and a food supplier is strictly liable for resulting injuries.

Design defects. Manufacturers and other suppliers are subject to liability for unreasonable design hazards that injure users and other persons. Because users may put any type of product to dangerous use, no matter how safely it is designed, the law needs a definition of design defect that divides products designed with reasonable safety from those that are not. In the 1960s and 1970s, courts broadly applied § 402A's definition of "defective condition unreasonably dangerous"—whether a product was more dangerous than an ordinary consumer would contemplate (the "consumer expectations" test)—to all types of product dangers, including hazardous designs. In recent decades, however, courts have increasingly abandoned the consumer expectations standard because it fails to provide a meaningful test for complex designs and, also, because it shields manufacturers from responsibility for obvious dangers of design. Today, most courts use some form of cost-benefit analysis, often referred to as a "risk-utility" or "risk-benefit" test of liability, to make design defect determinations.

When courts apply cost-benefit principles to design defect decisions, they often assert that they are using a standard of "strict" liability. Yet the risk-utility test courts employ in such cases is nothing more or less than the risk-utility test applied in negligence, based on Judge Hand's formula in *Carroll Towing*, discussed in the negligence summary, above. That formula, it will be recalled, is $B < P \times L \Rightarrow N$. In modern products liability law, courts have substituted "defect" for "negligence" (D for N), which adapts the test to the purportedly "strict" products liability task of determining design defectiveness. So reformulated, the defectiveness "equation" becomes:

$$B < P \times L \Rightarrow D$$

This formula may be restated in cost-benefit terms as:

$$\text{(Precaution) Costs} < \text{(Safety) Benefits} \Rightarrow \text{Defect}$$

Stated otherwise:

$$\text{Defect} \Rightarrow \text{if a Precaution's Benefits} > \text{its Costs}$$

If we translate these cost-benefit terms into symbols, such that Defect = D, an Untaken Precaution = UP, its Safety Benefits = SB, and its Costs = C, then:

$$D \Rightarrow \text{if UP's SB} > C$$

In ordinary language, this means that a product's design may be considered defective if the costs of improving its safety (including dollar costs and any lost utility or increased dangers of other types) are less than the safety benefits expected to result. This risk-utility test for design defectiveness, which ties the measure of precaution to the measure of risk, grounds design safety determinations in fairness and utility.

A number of secondary design issues create special problems, such as whether a manufacturer may offer safety devices as optional equipment or must install them as a mandatory part of every product. The decisions are split on this perplexing issue, but the result usually turns on the extent to which the safety device will interfere with the product's usefulness and whether the buyer is in a better position than the manufacturer to evaluate the costs and benefits of adapting the device to the buyer's particular situation. Automobiles and pharmaceuticals present special design issues addressed below.

Warning defects. A product is defective if the manufacturer fails to provide adequate information about its hidden dangers (warnings) and how to avoid them (instructions). Warnings and instructions must be adequate not only in their substance or content, but also in the effectiveness of the means by which they are communicated to users and consumers. If a hazard is substantial, prudence may require that the warning be placed directly on the product rather than in product literature that may become separated from the product. Sometimes foreign language warnings or symbols usefully help communicate warning information, but American courts usually do not condition a warning's adequacy on such special ways to warn. If a supplier may expect its product to cause serious allergic reactions in many persons, it must disclose such risks of which consumers are not commonly aware.

The "sophisticated purchaser" and "bulk supplier" doctrines sometimes exempt manufacturers from their normal obligation to provide warnings of product hazards directly to users and consumers. Thus, when selling a product (like a chemical) to a "sophisticated user" (like a large manufacturing enterprise), or selling the product in bulk (like transporting chemicals by truck or railroad tanker car), these doctrines often relieve the seller of its duties to warn the product's end users—typically employees of the purchasing enterprise that itself may fully understand the product's risks and be better positioned than the seller to warn users of the hazards. Pharmaceuticals present special warning issues addressed below.

Limitations on Defectiveness

Although a product may be hazardous, various considerations may cut against classifying it as "defective" and so may shield a manufacturer from responsibility for accidental harm. The obviousness of a product hazard does not relieve a manufacturer from taking reasonable steps to design the danger out of the product, as by adopting an inexpensive safety device that does not reduce the product's usefulness. But almost all courts hold that there is no duty to *warn* of obvious or widely known product hazards—that sharp knives cut, that cigarettes are addictive, that alcohol causes intoxication, that guns can kill, and that fast food causes obesity—because little good is served by telling people what they already know. Not only are the hazards of such products obvious, but they also are inherent, meaning they cannot be designed away without harming the product's utility. Thus, while manufacturers of such inherently dangerous products are responsible for production errors and for warning of any hidden dangers, such products are not defective in design for their obvious, inherent risks.

When § 402A of the *Restatement (Second) of Torts* was being widely adopted during the 1960s and 1970s, many believed that "strict" products liability in tort meant that manufacturers were subject to liability even if a risk was unforeseeable or otherwise could not reasonably be prevented. This was the holding in *Beshada v. Johns-Manville Products Corp.*[143] in which the New Jersey Supreme Court in 1982 held that asbestos products were defective for not bearing a warning against an unforeseeable risk. A storm of academic protest led the court to reverse its position two years later in *Feldman v. Lederle Laboratories*,[144] where it ruled that manufacturers must warn only of risks they reasonably can foresee—dangers within the "state of the art" at the time they sell a product. Together, these two cases marked the pivotal point in modern American products liability law when courts began to shift away from imposing liability standards on manufacturers that were truly strict toward standards of responsibility to which manufacturers reasonably might conform. Today, no matter how dangerous a product may turn out to be, it is not "defective" (in all but a very few states) if its manufacturer could not reasonably have foreseen its hazards at the time of sale, nor is it defective if there was no reasonable way to remove its hazards. A manufacturer's sole design and warning duty, in other words, is only to assure that its products are as safe as reasonably appears possible under the prevailing "state of the art." These two propositions—that manufacturers must guard against risks only if they are *foreseeable*, and that manufacturers must guard against those risks only with precautions that are *reasonable*—are the two major pillars of modern products liability law in America.

Prenatal and preconception harm caused by drugs and chemicals, the effects of which can ripple through generations of offspring, raise challenging issues of foreseeability and the proper reach of tort law. Manufacturers of such products bear responsibility, of course, for failing to provide reasonable warnings of foreseeable risks of harm, even if that harm is caused prenatally—and possibly even if the harm is caused before conception, as when a chemical damages a woman's reproductive system which later injures a child who was not yet conceived when the mother's injuries were sustained. Several courts, reasoning that liability must stop somewhere, have applied no-duty rules (such as no duty to third-generation plaintiffs) to serve as bright-line

[143] 447 A.2d 539 (N.J. 1982).

[144] 479 A.2d 374 (N.J. 1984).

liability boundaries for the remote effects of prenatal harm to future generations from chemicals in pharmaceuticals and other toxic substances.

Another limitation on a manufacturer's responsibility for making its products safe reflects the fact that all products, like all lawyers and judges, eventually wear out. Courts widely hold that dangers arising from a product's natural deterioration normally do not render the product defective (except possibly for lacking a warning of resulting dangers), particularly if the dangers arise out of the dismantling and disposal of the product (perhaps releasing dangerous chemicals) at the end of its life.

The law regarding a manufacturer's post-sale responsibilities for product safety, once it learns that its products are causing injuries not expected when the product first was sold, has long been in a muddle. Thanks in part to the *Third Restatement*, at least the issues now are fairly clear. While federal product safety agencies may require manufacturers to recall products to remedy unreasonable dangers, there normally is no common-law duty to recall and fix a product. But courts increasingly are imposing a post-sale duty of reasonable care on manufacturers to provide whatever *warnings* may be reasonable in the circumstances when they discover undue hazards in products already in consumers' hands.

Causation

Causation, or "proximate causation," is comprised of two separate issues: (1) cause in fact, and (2) proximate cause. Courts sometimes confuse the matter by referring to a *factual* causation issue as one involving "proximate cause," so a reader of the law reports must cautiously study decisions on these topics to be certain which of these distinct issues is truly involved in the particular case.

Cause in Fact

In products liability cases, cause in fact is the actual connection between a product defect (or misrepresentation) and the plaintiff's harm. Although this physical (or metaphysical) nexus is not controverted in most cases, a plaintiff must always link his or her injury or disease to a defect in (or misrepresentation about) a product which the manufacturer made and sold. Thus, the first causal requirement in every case is to show that the challenged product was manufactured or sold by the defendant. Establishing the identity of the manufacturer of many durable products (like toasters, punch presses, SUVs, and butane lighters) usually is a simple task. Yet, after a serious accident, sometimes butane lighters and other products burn up or otherwise disappear, and memories fade. Many other kinds of products (like cleaning solvents, dish towels, and industrial chemicals) may have come from sources not remembered or quite unknown. And so a plaintiff's first, important causation task is to prove that it was the defendant, and not some other party, who made or sold the subject product.

Causally connecting a plaintiff's injury to a product defect involves the same hypothetical, causal inquiry involved in other tort law contexts, based on the same "but-for" test of cause in fact. A product defect thus may be a cause in fact of the plaintiff's harm if the defect was a *sine qua non* of the harm—a necessary antecedent without which the harm would not have occurred. Though California some time ago purported to substitute the "substantial-factor" test for the but-for test, subsequent decisions have recognized that even the substantial-factor test must usually contain the but-for test at its core. Most states more clearly reserve the substantial-factor test for situations where multiple products (such as several chemicals) combine to cause an injury that would have occurred even if one of them were removed. In such cases, a defendant's product will be considered a cause in fact of the plaintiff's harm so long as it was a substantial factor in producing it.

Toxic-substance cases present plaintiffs with a variety of causation problems, and the substantial-factor test helps in only some cases of this type. Tracing harmful consequences to asbestos fibers, drugs, and other kinds of chemicals often involves perplexing causation problems both in science and the law. Science itself often does not fully understand the biological mechanisms involved in disease causation, rendering it especially difficult for the law to be confident of evidence that a plaintiff's cancer or other condition was caused by his or her exposure to a particular product. While the but-for test remains at the center of the causal inquiry, and while the substantial-factor test assists in some respects, plaintiffs in toxic-substance cases normally must provide certain special types of proofs to establish factual causation: (1) *exposure*—that the plaintiff was exposed to the toxic substance; (2) *general causation*—that the substance is capable of causing the particular condition in humans; and (3) *specific causation*—that the substance probably caused the condition in the plaintiff. General causation sometimes is hotly contested, as was true for many years with harms suspected to be caused by Bendectin, silicone-gel breast implants, and even cell phones. Yet, for many diseases, exposure and general causation will be clear, in which case causal inquiries will revolve around the plaintiff's proof of specific causation. In asbestos cases, for example, where the connections between asbestos and certain lung diseases now are well established, a "frequency, regularity, and proximity" standard is often used to prove that a particular defendant's asbestos product was a cause of a plaintiff's lung disease.

A special kind of multiple-defendant causation problem arises when a plaintiff who is injured by a fungible product, such as a generic drug taken long ago, is unable to identify the manufacturer. The most distinctive products liability theory developed for cases of this type is the "market share" approach for establishing causation, whereby each manufacturer of the fungible product must contribute a proportion of the plaintiff's damages equal to its market share.[145] While courts in a number of major states adopted versions of this doctrine in the 1980s for use in cases involving a drug called DES, many courts have rejected this causation theory altogether, and most courts that have applied market share liability to DES have refused to extend it to other types of products. Plaintiffs have tried to induce the courts to adopt a number of other theories of collective responsibility on most or all members of an industry for harms that cannot be traced to particular manufacturers—alternative liability, enterprise liability, concert of action, and civil conspiracy—but these theories have mostly failed.

Warning claims present special causation problems. Whether an untaken durable precaution (like a guard on a machine) probably would have prevented the plaintiff's injury usually can be sensibly determined, even if it requires hypothetical deductions. Yet, trying to decide if a plaintiff (or someone responsible for the plaintiff's interests) would even have seen an adequate warning and, if so, whether he or she would have acted in a way to avoid the harm, raises questions that often are barely justiciable. By forcing plaintiffs to provide self-serving hypothetical testimony, causal inquiries in this context place speculation at the heart of every defective warning case. To avoid this problem, most courts have adopted a "heeding presumption" by which the law rebuttably

[145] See Sindell v. Abbott Labs., 607 P.2d 924 (Cal. 1980).

presumes (if dubiously) that, had the defendant provided an adequate warning, the plaintiff would have read and heeded it.

Proximate Cause

Proximate cause is a reasonably close connection between the plaintiff's injury and a product defect, a connection that is not "remote." Proximate causation principles applicable to tort law generally apply to products liability cases also, including the central limitation of responsibility to *foreseeable* types of risks. Normal principles of superseding causation apply to products liability cases when third parties deliberately put products to unfair, possibly criminal, use. When an employer unbolts a machine guard (that the manufacturer arguably should have welded permanently to the machine) to accelerate production, injuring a worker, or an assailant attacks the driver of a vehicle stranded in the wilderness due to a defective tire, whether the manufacturer's responsibility for the harm is broken by the intervening force depends on whether the type of intervention was a reasonably foreseeable consequence of the product defect, or whether instead legal responsibility more fairly rests entirely on the intervening agency.

Defenses

Conduct Defenses

If a product accident is caused in whole or in part by a user's behavior that was improper, or that was informed and voluntary, the manufacturer may avoid responsibility for some or all of the resulting damage even if the product was defective and the manufacturer was negligent. This is because manufacturers are properly responsible for injuries proximately caused by defects in their products, not for injuries caused by a user's improper or deliberately risky product use. While the role of contributory negligence is diminished in certain strict tort contexts, this doctrine remains a powerful defense to many products liability claims. This is so even in comparative fault states, most of which bar recovery for that portion of a plaintiff's injuries attributable to his or her fault, and for *all* damages when the plaintiff's fault exceeds the defendant's. Although the assumption of risk doctrine is dwindling to some extent, this defense still bars recovery entirely in many states. In other states, its merger into comparative fault has converted the plaintiff's deliberate and voluntary risk encounter into a damages-reducing factor. Product misuse widely bars recovery altogether, provided the misuse was unforeseeable.

The law is quite confused as to the application of tort law conduct defenses to warranty claims, and generalizations on this issue are not much help. Since warranty claims lie in contract, one might think that their defenses should derive from contract as well. Article 2 of the UCC indeed makes some scattered comments on the effect of a buyer's conduct—for example, stating that, when a buyer purchases or uses a product knowing it to contain a dangerous defect, any resulting injuries may be the proximate result of the plaintiff's use rather than of any unmerchantable condition in the product. But many courts apply the standard tort law conduct defenses of contributory (and comparative) negligence, assumption of risk, and product misuse to claims for breach of implied warranty, just as they do to claims for negligence and strict liability in tort. In fraud and other tortious misrepresentation actions, the basic misconduct issue is whether the plaintiff's reliance was "justifiable" or "reasonable," to wit, whether the plaintiff had a "right to rely" (based on reasonableness principles) on the particular representation.

Special Defenses

Several special defenses are sometimes available to products liability claims. One, the "contract specification defense," protects a manufacturer from design defect claims for merely fabricating a product according to design specifications provided by another enterprise, unless the defect was obvious to the fabricator. A special application of this principle is the "government contractor defense," which normally bars defective design claims against contractors who build products according to designs provided or approved by the government.

Another defense, sometimes called the "regulatory compliance defense," is based on a manufacturer's compliance with statutory or, more commonly, regulatory standards. Most courts hold that products liability claims are not barred ipso facto by proof of such compliance, but that the trier of fact may consider a product's conformance to government safety standards as evidence of nondefectiveness and non-negligence. Yet, the doctrine of "federal preemption," if applicable, will bar a products liability claim if the safety issue, such as the "adequacy" of warnings on cigarettes or a prescription drug, has already been resolved by Congress or a federal agency.

Finally, every state has statutes of limitations for tort claims, and some for products liability claims in particular, requiring that such actions be filed within some specified period—from one to six years, typically two or three—from the date the plaintiff reasonably should have discovered the injury, and perhaps its cause. Under UCC Article 2, warranty claims must be brought within four years from when a product first is sold. Some states have statutes of "repose," designed to put products liability claims ultimately to rest, whether they have been discovered or not, within some fairly long period of time. Most such statutes terminate claims after a specified period of time, anywhere from six to fifteen years (often ten years) after the date of sale. The time periods of a few repose statutes are more vague, based on a product's "useful life." Some states have realty-improvement statutes of repose, ranging from five to twenty years in length, which apply to products liability claims involving buildings and other products attached to realty.

Special Defendants, Transactions, Products, and Litigation

Most products liability principles are directed primarily at manufacturers who design, manufacture, and sell new chattels and who often are in the best position to provide warnings and instructions to users and consumers. When this classic products liability paradigm weakens, there may or may not be reason to apply products liability principles to special types of defendants, special types of transactions, and special types of products. Negligence principles usually apply in each of these special situations, and sometimes warranty principles as well, so that a recurring issue in these cases is whether the doctrine of strict products liability in tort applies to these special types of defendants, products, and transactions.

Special Defendants

When the defendant in a products liability case is not a manufacturer, it ordinarily has less control over product safety than does the enterprise that produced the product, raising the question of whether it is logical or fair to hold a non-manufacturing supplier strictly responsible for injuries from defects in the products it sells.

Retailers. Although most retailers usually play no role in a product's design or manufacture, or in providing warnings and instructions, they normally are subject to strict liability in both warranty and tort. In recent decades, however, some states have enacted statutes protecting retailers from suit if the manufacturer is solvent and within the jurisdiction of the court, but subjecting retailers to strict liability if no solvent manufacturer is available to the plaintiff. An important recent issue, on which courts presently disagree, is whether internet retailers such as Amazon.com should be subject to liability for "selling" defective products sold on their sites by third parties.

Raw material and component part suppliers. Suppliers of products of these types are subject to liability for injuries caused by defects in the materials or components they provide, but they generally are not responsible for defects in the design of the finished product unless they substantially participate in that design.

Parent corporations. Parent corporations normally are not responsible for harm caused by defective products manufactured by their subsidiaries because of fundamental principles of corporate law shielding shareholders from the debts of the corporation they own. Yet a court may allow a parent's "corporate veil" to be "pierced" on certain limited grounds, including agency and apparent agency, apparent manufacturer, concerted tortious action, and, most importantly, alter ego.

Trademark owners and franchisers. Consumers often suppose that defects in products bearing a trademark name or sold by a franchisee are the responsibility of the company that owns the trademark or the franchise. But trademark owners and franchisers are accountable for a defective product manufactured by a trademark licensee or franchisee only if the trademark owner or franchiser had substantial control over the product's safety.

Successor corporations. When one company (the successor) purchases the assets of another (the predecessor), the successor normally is not responsible, under general corporate law principles, for the predecessor's debts, including products liability claims after the sale of assets has occurred. Yet, courts widely recognize four exceptions to this rule, situations in which a successor corporation is responsible for the liabilities of its predecessor: (1) when the purchasing company expressly or impliedly assumes such liability; (2) when the transaction amounts to a consolidation or merger of the two companies; (3) when the successor is a mere continuation of the predecessor; and (4) when the transaction is a fraudulent attempt to avoid liability. Several states have broadened this list with one or two new exceptions: (5) when the successor continues the predecessor's product line; and (6) when there is a continuity of enterprise after the transaction.

Employers. Sometimes employers manufacture machinery and other products for use in their own enterprises, and sometimes employees are injured by defects in such products. Normally, the "exclusive remedy" principle of workers' compensation law precludes employees in this situation from suing their employers as manufacturers of defective products. While early cases in California and Ohio allowed such products liability claims under the "dual capacity" doctrine, this doctrine was rejected in other jurisdictions and now is dead as well in the two states that gave it life for several years.

Special Transactions and Products

In addition to being centered on manufacturers, the products liability paradigm rests on sales of new chattels. But some products liability litigation involves transactions at the border or outside this paradigm, which raises the question of whether principles of strict products liability should be extended from the new chattel sale situation to other transactional contexts in which other policies and principles may predominate.

Leased, bailed, and licensed products. Products may be leased, loaned, or licensed rather than sold outright. Courts have viewed commercial leases of rental cars and other leased products as involving largely the same policy issues as commercial sales and so have applied strict liability in tort (and warranty) doctrine to such leases. Courts have had more trouble determining whether to apply strict liability principles to commercial bailments or licenses for use of a product for a short time—such as ice skates at a rink, a go-cart at a fair, a grocery cart at a supermarket, a washing machine at a laundromat, or a wine glass at a restaurant. Only if the licensed or bailed product is necessary or "integral" to the sale of some other product (as a wine glass for the sale of wine), in which case it becomes a "tie-in" product, do most courts hold that it may be subject to strict liability in tort.

Sales-service transactions. A doctor who uses a hypodermic needle to inject serum into a patient's arm will probably include as part of the medical fee a charge for the hypodermic needle and the serum. If a defective needle breaks while in the patient's arm, or if the serum is defective, a patient who is thereby injured may wish to make a products liability claim against the doctor for "selling" a defective product that caused an injury. Sales-service transactions also arise with architects, engineers, building contractors, plumbers, and electricians who may purchase, install, and "sell" a defective water heater for use in a home. In sales-service hybrid cases of this type, most courts search for the "essence" of the transaction, to ascertain whether the sale or service aspect predominates, and then apply strict liability principles only if the entire transaction was more in the nature of a sale than a service.

Repaired, refurbished, reconditioned, rebuilt, and remanufactured products. In deciding whether to apply strict liability principles to these different product-improvement situations, courts generally apply some rough form of the essence-of-the-transaction or predominant-factor test mentioned above. This issue often resolves to whether the product that comes out from service is essentially the one that went into the process, in which case only negligence principles apply, or whether an essentially different product emerges, which then is introduced into the stream of commerce, in which case strict liability principles may well apply.

Used products. On whether strict liability principles should apply to used products, the courts are widely split. The majority view is that strict liability in tort ordinarily does *not* apply to the sale of used products, but a substantial minority of courts rule the other way.

Real estate. Most courts refuse to apply the doctrine of strict products liability in tort to claims involving defects in land, houses, and other structures attached to the land, reasoning that products liability law properly applies only to *products*, which are chattels or personal property, not *real* property. But many courts have applied such principles to component fixtures installed in houses and other structures, and a handful of early decisions applied strict liability in tort to builder-vendors of mass-produced residential homes and to manufacturers of prefabricated homes and structures.

Publications. Claims are sometimes made against publishers for injuries attributable to the content of books, magazine articles, films, records, computer games, websites, and aeronautical charts. Except for aeronautical charts containing false information, courts refuse to apply strict liability to the provision of information, reasoning that the message (as distinct from its packaging) is not a "product," and often mentioning but avoiding difficult First Amendment issues such claims would raise. A question awaiting future courts is whether publishers of CAD files or blueprints for 3D-printed products with defects that cause harm should bear responsibility for such harm.

Electronic technology. Most courts hold that electricity is a "product" that may subject its suppliers, electrical utility companies, to strict liability in tort for selling it in a defective condition once it passes through a customer's meter and thus is sold into the stream of commerce. Such cases typically involve power surges, causing personal injury or property damage by the excessive flow of electricity into a building. Yet many other courts refuse to apply strict liability to such cases, reasoning that the provision of electricity is a service rather than the sale of a product.

Courts have rejected a number of claims against manufacturers of video games and other visual entertainment products, often concluding that products liability principles do not apply to them because they simply are not "products." The Communications Decency Act of 1996 broadly immunizes interactive website providers from liability for harmful consequences of communications from third parties.

Whether manufacturers of computer software should be subject to products liability for personal injuries caused by defective software is an intriguing question. While commentators widely favor the application of products liability theories in such situations, the case law so far is limited to commercial contexts involving claims for economic loss without physical harm.

Blood and other biologics. Infected blood and blood products can cause AIDS or hepatitis, but almost all states have enacted "blood shield statutes" that protect blood banks and other suppliers from strict liability in tort or warranty, leaving victims to their proof of negligence in how the blood was gathered or tested for disease. In the few cases involving claims of infected human tissue other than blood, courts have applied similar rules to those applied in cases involving blood, to wit, holding that the supply of human tissue is a service, and that human tissue is not a "product" for purposes of products liability law.

Animals. Courts split on whether strict liability in tort applies to animals, most courts holding that living things are not "products" within the scope of the strict tort doctrine because an animal's nature is not fixed when it leaves the seller's control. Courts have been particularly reluctant to hold sellers subject to strict liability for an animal's natural proclivities, such as the tendency of some horses to buck and some dogs to bite.

Special Litigation

Special product litigation. Litigation has become quite specialized for various types of products—cigarettes, guns, asbestos, pharmaceuticals, and automobiles are good examples—where procedural considerations (such as rules on consolidation and class actions) often dominate litigation. These products often are inherently hazardous, requiring special thought as to whether and how normal principles of design and warning defects may need to be adjusted. Otherwise, the fundamental principles of liability and defense in these cases are largely the same as those applied in other types of products liability litigation. While it would be useful to isolate and separately examine recurring doctrinal and litigation issues related to these and other specific types of products, only automotive vehicles and prescription drugs (and medical devices) are separately considered here.

Motor vehicles. Automotive manufacturers must produce their vehicles free of manufacturing defects (in steering and braking systems, for example) and must provide users with reasonable warnings of hidden dangers, such as the possibility that an airbag might explosively inflate with sufficient force to kill a child seated in a particular position. In addition to these normal responsibilities applicable to manufacturers of most types of products, certain special liability principles govern automotive products liability litigation. A special rule of this type is the principle of "crashworthiness"—that automotive manufacturers must anticipate the possibility that their vehicles may crash and so must design them with reasonable safety for the crash environment. A manufacturer thus is subject to liability for "enhanced injuries" to occupants caused by uncrashworthy aspects of its vehicle designs—injuries over and above those that would have occurred in a crash anyway had the vehicle in fact been designed with reasonable safety for such accidents. If an occupant suffers indivisible injuries (such as paralysis or death) in a vehicular accident, apportioning the harm between the uncrashworthy aspect of the vehicle and the crash itself may be difficult, if not impossible. While some courts require plaintiffs to apportion damages in such situations, which often as a practical matter precludes recovery, a growing majority of courts hold manufacturers of uncrashworthy vehicles responsible for indivisible injuries.

Ordinary principles of user misconduct govern most aspects of automotive products liability litigation, but some special issues of driver fault arise in cases of this type. A difficult issue on which courts are sharply split is whether a driver's fault in causing an accident may be considered (as a matter of proximate cause or comparative fault) in apportioning damages for enhanced injuries in cases where the driver challenges the vehicle's crashworthiness. Some courts hold that a plaintiff's fault in causing the first collision (such as driving while intoxicated or running a red light) simply is irrelevant to a manufacturer's duty to protect occupants against unreasonable "second-collision" risks in a vehicle's design (such as sharp protrusions on a dashboard, a propensity to roll over, or a flimsy frame), since automotive collisions from one source or another are the very risk that manufacturers must reasonably attempt to avoid under the crashworthiness doctrine. Other courts reason that a plaintiff's contributions to an accident logically deserve the same treatment in crashworthiness cases as in any other context.

Car manufacturers often assert the "seatbelt defense" in an attempt to establish that a plaintiff is responsible for injuries a seatbelt would have prevented. But the law concerning this defense is fragmented, largely because the states have enacted various types of statutes that govern the effect of seatbelt nonuse in civil litigation—some permitting and others prohibiting nonuse evidence to reduce a plaintiff's damages, while some states leave the matter to the courts.

Pharmaceuticals. A considerable amount of products liability litigation concerns prescription drugs and medical devices. Aside from questions of federal preemption in these closely regulated products, many principles of products liability law are applicable to these products as any others, such as the rules on manufacturing defects. So, a pharmaceutical company is responsible for injuries caused by its dangerously contaminated drugs, and a device manufacturer is responsible for injuries caused by its pacemakers that are miswired during assembly.

Yet, the normal rules of design and warning defects fit awkwardly when applied to pharmaceutical products. Because of the importance of drugs in the preservation and enhancement of life, together with their potential for great harm, prescription drugs and devices are regulated more heavily than any other type of product—beginning with their availability only by prescription of physicians. Most products are not considered defectively designed, as previously noted, unless they reasonably should have been designed differently, on account of the greater safety benefits of some alternative design than the resulting costs. Yet, most drugs by their very nature cannot be redesigned, because their chemical formulations carry *inherent* dangers, risks that cannot be avoided without altering a drug's chemical structures in ways that destroy its health benefits as well as its risks. Moreover, before a drug can be marketed at all, the FDA is significantly involved in evaluating the balance of benefits and dangers of its design, and in approving appropriate warnings. For this reason, many courts are reluctant to allow this expert agency to be second-guessed in courtrooms by subjecting drug designs to judicial review.

Further, manufacturers of prescription drugs and medical devices have an important duty to provide warnings of a drug's or device's risks. Unlike other products, however, a manufacturer's duty is only to warn the prescribing doctor or other health professional, and *not* the ultimate consumer, because doctors stand as "learned intermediaries" between the drug supply and patients, with a responsibility to exercise their professional judgment to connect appropriate drugs and devices to appropriate patients. Such professional health care providers are uniquely situated to pass along whatever information may be important and otherwise appropriate for particular patients to know.

Finally, pharmacists are located at a vital position between doctors and patients, which raises important questions about their role in providing pharmaceuticals safely to patients. For various reasons, pharmacists generally are bound only to dispense drugs accurately according to the terms of valid prescriptions and, subject to certain fairly minimal exceptions that may slowly be expanding, they have no independent duty to warn their customers of dangers in the drugs they sell.

§ 1.4 FOREIGN LAW

Until the 1980s, other nations around the globe had not experienced the major legal jolt felt in America during the 1960s and early 1970s with the rapid adoption of strict liability in tort and other modern products liability doctrines. Thereafter, however, modern products liability law and litigation began to spread its wings around the world. Put differently, America no longer has a corner on the market of modern products liability law, and the resolution of products liability problems in the years ahead increasingly will be facilitated by a comparative law approach. For some time now, scholars have been comparing the products liability law of the U.S., the U.K., Europe, and other nations.[146] In 1985, the European Community organized the products liability

[146] Early treatments of comparative products liability include J. Stapleton, Product Liability (Butterworths 1994) (comparing the law of Europe, the United Kingdom, and the U.S.), and G. Howells, Comparative Product Liability (Dartmouth 1993) (Europe, the U.K., France, Germany, Scandinavia, the U.S., Canada, Australia, and New Zealand). More recent works include D. Fairgrieve and R. Goldberg, Product Liability (Oxford 3d ed. 2020) (U.K., U.S., Australia, New Zealand, Canada, France, Germany, and the EU); H. Koziol, M. Greene, M. Lunney, K. Oliphant, and Y. Lixwn, Product Liability: Fundamental Questions in a Comparative Perspective (De Gruyter 2017) (reports from Asia, Russia, Europe, North America, and the "Rest of World"); S. Whittaker, The Development of Product Liability (Cambridge 2014) (UK, France, Germany, Netherlands, Italy, and Spain); R. Goldberg, Medicinal Product Liability and Regulation (Oxford, Hart

law of EU nations under an overarching *Products Liability Directive*,[147] a statutory framework subsequently followed by many nations outside the EU. Modern principles of products liability law also have been developing elsewhere around the globe, which is touched on briefly below. Studying products liability from a truly global perspective is an enormous task that has only recently begun,[148] yet it is a perspective that soon may predominate in a world where products are manufactured, distributed, fail, and injure human beings without regard to the boundaries of nation states.

The topic of products liability law outside the United States is now far too broad to describe in any detail in a book like this devoted to products liability law in America. Yet products liability problems share similarities wherever they may arise, and so a lawyer, judge, scholar, or student examining a products liability problem in the United States should be aware that the legislatures and courts of Europe and elsewhere may have addressed and perhaps resolved the same or a similar issue. All that can be done here is to sketch out the framework of European products liability law and alert the reader to the existence of "the vast and fast-growing mass of products liability literature"[149] that is sprouting up around the world.

Before addressing foreign products liability law, a note of caution is in order. In considering the law of other nations, it is important to remember that the substantive legal rules are only as effective as allowed by the rules of procedure, damages, and law practice (including methods for funding litigation), all of which reflect the cultural tradition of a particular nation and its legal system.[150] Japan, for example, in 1995 enacted a products liability law patterned closely after Europe's *Product Liability Directive*.[151] Yet Japan has few lawyers in general, and even fewer plaintiffs' lawyers, in

---

Publishing 2013); International Product Liability (C. Campbell and D. Campbell eds., Juris. 2d ed. 2011); M. Tulibacka, Product Liability Law in Transition: A Central European Perspective (Ashgate 2009) (Czech Republic, Hungary, and Poland), reviewed, Stapleton, 126 Law Q. Rev. 487 (2010); A. McClurg, A. Koyuncu, and L. Sprovieri, Practical Global Tort Litigation—United States, Germany and Argentina (Carolina Academic Press 2007); Nottage and Kellam, Europeanisation of Product Liability in the Asia-Pacific Region: A Preliminary Empirical Benchmark, Sydney Law School Research Paper No. 07/30 (2007); Product Liability in Comparative Perspective (D. Fairgrieve ed., Cambridge 2005) (Spain, Italy, France, Germany, Holland, England, EU, America, and Japan); S. Whittaker, Liability for Products—English law, French Law, and European Harmonization (Oxford 2005); J.-S. Borghetti, La Responsabilité du Fait des Produits—Étude de Droit Comparé (LGDJ 2005) (U.S., England, France, and Europe); J. Kellam, The Contract-Tort Dichotomy and Theoretical Framework for Product Liability Law: A Comparison of the Elements of Liability in Australia, France and Germany (Baden-Baden, Nomoes 2000).

The British Institute of International and Comparative Law (BIICL) has a valuable database on the developing case and statutory products liability law of separate European nations. See www.biicl.org/plf. While the BIICL data base is available to members only, scholars may apply online to the Director of the Product Liability Forum for honorary memberships.

147 For current developments in European products liability law, see International Product Liability Review (Hogan Lovells, London), www.hoganlovells.com/en/knowledge (search "Publications"); Product Liability Laws and Regulations (A. Williams and T. Fox eds., 2021), https://iclg.com/practice-areas/product-liability-laws-and-regulations.

148 Most notably by Mathias Reimann. See Reimann, Liability for Defective Products at the Beginning of the Twenty-First Century: Emergence of a Worldwide Standard?, 51 Am. J. Comp. L. 751, 836–38 (2003); Reimann, Product Liability in a Global Context: The Hollow Victory of the European Model, 11 Eur. Rev. Priv. L. 128 (2003). See also Howells and Owen, Products Liability Law in America and Europe, in Handbook of International Consumer Law and Policy (G. Howells, I. Ramsey, and R. Wilhelmsson eds., Edward Elgar 2d ed. 2018). See also note 146, above.

149 Reimann, 51 Am. J. Comp. L., at 753 n.3.

150 Id. at 836–38.

151 See, e.g., Nottage, A Decade of Strict-Liability Litigation under Japan's Product Liability Law of 1994, 16 Australian Prod. Liab. Rptr. 65 (2005); L. Nottage, Product Safety and Liability Law in Japan: From

particular, and products liability litigation conflicts in various ways with Japanese cultural traditions and confronts numerous structural and procedural hurdles.[152] Europe may be somewhat more comfortable with litigation than Japan, but it views *ex ante* governmental regulation as a preferable way to achieve product safety and deter product accidents than litigation *ex post*.[153] Moreover, public health care in much of Europe reduces the need for victims to employ litigation to cover costs of medical treatment occasioned by product accidents.[154] In short, other nations are less dependent than America on the twin pillars of tort law policy in this nation—deterrence and compensation. For these reasons, even though the laws of Europe, Japan, Australia, and most other developed and some developing nations now declare the availability of remedies for harm caused by defective products, procedural and damages restrictions, together with rules on attorneys' fees (loser pays), substantially diminish the practical rights of injured persons in many nations to recover for their injuries. It is easy for American lawyers to forget that the products liability law in action in other nations may be much less useful than the law in theory,[155] and there is some real question whether recent products liability developments around the globe have accomplished much at all.[156] As so well put by one of the world's leading scholars on the subject: "Comparative products liability law is a dangerous business."[157]

Minamata to Mad Cows 126 (RoutledgeCurzon 2004); Kobayashi and Furuta, Products Liability Act and Transnational Litigation in Japan, 34 Tex. Int'l L.J. 93, 99–100 (1999).

[152] See, e.g., Ramseyer, Liability for Defective Products: Comparative Hypotheses and Evidence from Japan, 61 Am. J. Comp. L. 617 (2013); Marcuse, Why Japan's New Products Liability Law Isn't, 5 Pac. Rim L. & Pol'y J. 365 (1996) (explaining structural and procedural barriers to suit); Behrens and Raddock, Japan's New Product Liability Law: The Citadel of Strict Liability Falls, But Access to Recovery is Limited by Formidable Barriers, 16 U. Pa. J. Int'l Bus. L. 669 (1995) (cultural and legal barriers).

[153] See Council Directive 2001/95/EC, General Product Safety, 2002 O.J. (L 11/4). See generally Howells and Wilhelmsson, EC Consumer Law: Has It Come of Age?, 28 Eur. L. Rev. 370 (2003); Howells, The Relationship Between Product Liability and Product Safety—Understanding a Necessary Element in a European Product Liability Through a Comparison with the U.S. Position, 39 Washburn L.J. 305, 308 (2000) (explaining "the European commitment to regulation rather than litigation as a means of promoting product safety"); G. Howells and S. Weatherill, Consumer Protection Law ch. 10 (Ashgate 2d ed. 2005).

[154] See, e.g., Howells, The Relationship Between Product Liability and Product Safety—Understanding a Necessary Element in European Product Liability Comparison with the U.S. Position, 39 Washburn L.J. 305, 307 (2000) ("Litigation in the U.S. is widely recognized as a surrogate for the European welfare state."); Howells and Mildred, Is European Products Liability More Protective Than the Restatement (Third) of Torts: Products Liability?, 65 Tenn. L. Rev. 985, 992–93 (1998).

[155] See Reimann, Product Liability in a Global Context: The Hollow Victory of the European Model, 11 Eur. Rev. Priv. L. 128 (2003) (notant la "disparité entre l'influence de la Directive en théorie et son inefficacité en pratique"); Reimann, Liability for Defective Products at the Beginning of the Twenty-First Century: Emergence of a Worldwide Standard?, 51 Am. J. Comp. L. 751, 838 (2003) (concluding that "the United States is still the only country where product liability really matters on a grand scale").

[156] "After decades of reform and heroic rhetoric about 'strict' liability and the advancement of consumer rights against manufacturers, the humiliating truth for the United Kingdom and Continental consumer lobbyists and law reform bodies alike is that, were a new Thalidomide disaster to occur today, the victims would have no stronger remedies against the manufacturers than were present in the 1960s." Stapleton, The Conceptual Imprecision of "Strict" Product Liability, 6 Torts L.J. 260, 275 (1998).

[157] Stapleton, Products Liability in the United Kingdom: The Myths of Reform, 34 Tex. Int'l L.J. 45, 46 (1999). See also G. Howells, Comparative Product Liability vii (1993) (noting the risk of embarrassment from revealing incomplete knowledge of foreign legal systems).

Europe

Pre-Directive Law

Prior to 1985, products liability law in Europe varied from nation to nation, but it was largely based on negligence and warranty law,[158] as was true in many non-European nations.[159] In the United Kingdom,[160] the 1932 House of Lords abandoned the privity-of-contract bar to negligence claims in *Donoghue v. Stevenson*,[161] the celebrated case of a snail in a bottle of ginger beer,[162] and it later applied principles of circumstantial evidence, not unlike res ipsa loquitur, to facilitate recovery in products liability cases.[163] In the 1960s and early 1970s, tort law's failure satisfactorily to address the consequences of a major drug tragedy—in which thousands of women who took the drug Thalidomide during pregnancy gave birth to severely deformed children[164]—led to the creation of three commissions, each of which recommended the adoption of strict manufacturer responsibility for harm from defective products. England also had a Sales of Goods Act, which created warranties of quality for buyers that amounted to a form of strict liability.[165] During this time, products liability law in Germany also was developing in a pro-consumer direction.[166] In 1968, the German Supreme Court reversed the burden of proof, in the *Chicken-Pest* case,[167] and the law in practice thereafter began to approach a principle of liability without fault. The Thalidomide experience led the German Parliament to enact a Pharmaceutical Act, holding manufacturers strictly liable for harm caused by defective pharmaceuticals. The law of Ireland, the Netherlands, and Denmark[168] evolved in a similar fashion, drifting in various ways toward strict manufacturer liability.

Products liability law in France, Belgium, and Luxembourg at this time rested on a statutory framework based on the *Code Civil* of 1804.[169] This system allowed products

---

[158] Much of this subsection draws from Taschner, Harmonization of Product Liability Law in the European Community, 34 Tex. Int'l L.J. 21, 25–28 (1999). Dr. Taschner played a prominent role in drafting and promoting Europe's Product Liability Directive.

[159] See, e.g., Waddams, The Canadian Law of Products Liability, 34 Tex. Int'l L.J. 119 (1999); S. Waddams, Products Liability (Carswell 5th ed. 2011).

[160] See, e.g., Stapleton, Products Liability in the United Kingdom: The Myths of Reform, 34 Tex. Int'l L.J. 45, 48–51 (1999).

[161] [1932] A.C. 562 (H.L.) (appeal taken from Scot.) (U.K.).

[162] On *Donoghue*, see note 75, above.

[163] Grant v. Australian Knitting Mills, Ltd., [1936] A.C. 85 (P.C.) (appeal taken from Austl.). See D. Fairgrieve and R. Goldberg, Product Liability §§ 17.58–.60 (3d ed. 2020).

[164] Thalidomide, a drug used as a sleeping aid and for morning sickness throughout the world in the 1950s and 1960s, caused limb deformities in children born to women who took the drug while pregnant. The FDA's protracted review of the drug saved most Americans from this terrible tragedy. See Sanders, The Bendectin Litigation: A Case Study in the Life Cycle of Mass Torts, 43 Hastings L.J. 301, 313–14 (1992) (characterizing Thalidomide as "one of the most potent human teratogens ever found"). See also A. Bernstein, Formed by Thalidomide: Mass Torts as a False Cure for Toxic Exposure, 97 Colum. L. Rev. 2153 (1997).

[165] On sales law in the U.K., see D. Fairgrieve and R. Goldberg, Product Liability ch. 4 (Oxford 3d ed. 2020); Benjamin's Sale of Goods (M. Bridge ed., Sweet and Maxwell 11th ed. 2020).

[166] See Wandt, German Approaches to Products Liability, 34 Tex. Int'l L.J. 71 (1999). See also Möllers, European Directives on Civil Law—Shaping a New German Civil Code, 18 Tul. Eur. & Civ. L.F. 1 (2003) (effect on German law of EC directives, including Product Liability Directive (Produkthaftungsgesetz)).

[167] BGHZ 51, 91 (1968), in 2 B. Markesinis, The German Law of Obligations—The Law of Torts: A Comparative Introduction 493 (Clarendon Oxford 3d ed. 1997).

[168] See Hansen, Product Liability Legislation in Denmark—A Danish Lawyer Looks at the Directive, Prod. Liab. Int'l 146 (Oct. 1986).

[169] See J.-S. Borghetti, La Responsabilité du Fait des Produits—Étude de Droit Comparé (2004).

liability claims in both warranty and tort. While the basic tort provision of the *Code Civil* requires fault, courts began to apply other doctrines such as *garantie des vices cachés*, *garde de la structure*,[170] et *manquement à l'obligation de sécurité*,[171] in a manner that amounted to strict liability for sellers of defective products. Products liability law in Italy,[172] Greece, Spain,[173] and Portugal, although formally derived from the French *Code Civil*, was less generous to victims of accidents caused by product defects; if such persons were unable to prove the seller's fault, they generally were left without a remedy.

The Directive

Spurred by the Thalidomide tragedy in Europe and the widespread adoption of § 402A of the *Restatement (Second) of Torts* in America,[174] and after nearly a decade of study, debate, and raw political horse-trading, the European Economic Community (the EEC or Common Market) in 1985 adopted a *Directive on Liability for Defective Products*.[175] The *Product Liability Directive* sought to harmonize the laws of member states that governed liability for defective products in order to facilitate free trade within the Common Market.[176] Each member state in the Economic Community, now including all 27 members of the European Union,[177] is obligated to have national legislation "approximating" EC Directives, though member states are free to choose the "form and methods" of implementation.[178] What this means, of course, is that the wording and interpretation of the various states' national legislation differs in some respects from the *Directive*,[179] a problem that occasionally leads to challenges of national laws in the European Court of Justice.[180]

The bedrock premise of the *Directive* is that "liability without fault on the part of the producer is the sole means of adequately [protecting] the consumer against damage

---

170 See Reimann, Liability for Defective Products at the Beginning of the Twenty-First Century: Emergence of a Worldwide Standard?, 51 Am. J. Comp. L. 751, 758 (2003).

171 See J.-S. Borghetti, La Responsabilité du Fait des Produits—Étude de Droit Comparé (2004).

172 See Rajneri, Interaction Between the European Directive on Product Liability and the Former Liability Regime in Italy, 4 Global Jurist Topics (2004); Dreyfuss, The Italian Law on Strict Products Liability, 17 N.Y.L. Sch. J. Int'l & Comp. L. 37 (1997); Bernstein and Fanning, Heirs of Leonardo: Cultural Obstacles to Strict Products Liability in Italy, 27 Vand. J. Transnat'l L. 1 (1994).

173 See Sánchez, Products Liability in Spain, 32 Tex. Tech L. Rev. 979 (2001).

174 See Howells and Mildred, Is European Products Liability More Protective Than the Restatement (Third) of Torts: Products Liability?, 65 Tenn. L. Rev. 985, 992–93 (1998).

175 Council Directive 85/374/EEC of 25 July 1985 on the Approximation of the Laws, Regulations and Administrative Provisions of the Member States Concerning Liability for Defective Products, 1985 O.J. (L 210) 29.

176 See Taschner, Harmonization of Product Liability Law in the European Community, 34 Tex. Int'l L.J. 21, 22–25 (1999).

177 The United Kingdom exited the European Union on January 31, 2020.

178 See Taschner, above note 176.

179 See C. van Dam, European Tort Law § 1502–2 (2005) ("Substantial differences remain because of the options in the Directive, the remaining differences in the national laws of damages and the application of pre-existing liability regimes next to the Directive."); Infantino, Making European Tort Law: The Game and Its Players, 18 Cardozo J. Int'l & Comp. L. 45, 58 (2010) (noting differences between French, German, Italian, and United Kingdom interpretations of the Directive).

180 See, e.g., Case C–300/95, Commission v. United Kingdom, 1997 E.C.R. I–2649, discussed in Stapleton, Bugs in Anglo-American Products Liability, 53 S.C. L. Rev. 1225, 1246–52 (2002); Taschner, Harmonization of Product Liability Law in the European Community, 34 Tex. Int'l L.J. 21, 33–34 (1999); G. Howells and S. Weatherill, Consumer Protection Law § 4.2.4.3, at 234 (2d ed. 2004). See also Case C–183/00, Sánchez v. Medicina Asturiana SA, 2002 E.C.R. I–3901 (Spain); Case C–52/00, Commission v. France, 2002 E.C.R. I–3827; Case C–154/00, Commission v. Greece, 2002 E.C.R. I–3879; Case C–203/99, Veedfald v. Arhus Amtskommune, 2001 E.C.R. I–3569 (Danish organ transplant solution case).

caused by a defective product."[181] Flowing therefrom, Article 1 provides: "The producer shall be liable for damage caused by a defect in his product." Articles 2 and 3 define "product" and "producer"; Article 4 places the burden of proof on plaintiffs to establish damage, defect, and causation; and Article 5 endorses the principle of joint and several liability when two or more producers are liable for the same damage.[182]

"Defective." The heart of the *Directive* is Article 6, which states when a product will be deemed "defective" and hence subject its producer to liability:

Article 6

1. A product is defective when it does not provide the safety which a person is entitled to expect, taking all circumstances into account, including:

   (a) the presentation of the product;

   (b) the use to which it could reasonably be expected that the product would be put;

   (c) the time when the product was put into circulation.

2. A product shall not be considered defective for the sole reason that a better product is subsequently put into circulation.

So defining defectiveness, in terms of "the safety which a person is entitled to expect," opens a host of interpretative questions.[183] At first glance, Europe's consumer-expectation-entitlement test suggests a strong resemblance to the consumer expectations test of § 402A of the *Restatement (Second) of Torts*,[184] America's original, if now faded, standard for product defectiveness.[185] But this interpretation may be too facile and is probably incorrect. While there is not yet much European case law developing the meaning of product defectiveness, the standard is one of consumer "entitlement" rather than consumer "expectations." While America's original test of defectiveness, as set forth in the comments to § 402A of the *Second Restatement*, plainly defines the product safety norm in terms of the *actual* expectations of consumers,[186] the European *Directive* in Article 6 just as plainly rests liability on the level of safety people are *entitled* to expect. Under the Article 6 standard, the actual expectations of consumers are necessarily secondary to the ultimate question of what safety norm, under all the circumstances, is *appropriate*—a norm that surely is informed by actual consumer expectations, but that also fairly respects a manufacturer's reasonable efforts to balance product safety against a product's cost and utility within the practical confines of science, technology, manufacturing, and marketing.

---

[181] Preamble to the Directive.

[182] For a helpful overview of the United Kingdom's version of the Directive, the Consumer Protection Act of 1987, see G. Howells and S. Weatherill, Consumer Protection Law § 4.2.4.3 (2d ed. 2005). Valuable early critiques of the Directive include Stapleton, Products Liability Reform—Real or Illusory?, 6 Oxford J. Legal Stud. 392, 405 (1986); J. Stapleton, Product Liability 236–42 (1994).

[183] See D. Fairgrieve and R. Goldberg, Product Liability chs. 10–12 (3d ed. 2020).

[184] For such an interpretation, see, e.g., Henderson and Twerski, What Europe, Japan, and Other Countries Can Learn from the New American Restatement of Products Liability, 34 Tex. Int'l L.J. 1 (1999).

[185] On the consumer expectations test, see §§ 5.6 and 8.3, below.

[186] See Rest. (2d) Torts § 402A cmt. *g* (defining "defective condition" as "a condition not contemplated by the ultimate consumer, which will be unreasonably dangerous to him"), and cmt. *i* (defining "unreasonably dangerous" as "dangerous to an extent beyond that which would be contemplated by the ordinary consumer who purchases it, with the ordinary knowledge common to the community as to its characteristics").

One should be cautious in predicting how European law will develop on this important issue, but one may reasonably expect, supported by a European Commission Report,[187] that European courts in the long run will be drawn to interpret the consumer-entitlement standard as involving, at least in cases involving durable goods,[188] a cost-benefit evaluation of a product's safety.[189] Whether looked at normatively, from the view that consumers are "entitled" to expect no more safety than manufacturers reasonably can deliver, or textually, from the fact that Article 6 requires "taking all circumstances into account," including the use to which the product "could reasonably be expected" to be put[190] "at the time when the product was put into circulation,"[191] Article 6 appears to lead naturally to a risk-utility balancing test in conventional product cases involving defects in design.[192]

Development risks. The other central provision of the *Directive*, Article 7, sets forth defenses to products liability claims.[193] Of greatest interest to American lawyers,

---

[187] See the EC's third 5-year report on the Directive, 14 September 2006, acknowledging the advantages of risk-benefit analysis in design defect litigation recognized by U.S. courts (https://eur-lex.europa.eu/legal-content/EN/TXT/?uri=CELEX%3A52006DC0496&qid=1630416840107). See also Hibbert and Lenze, European Commission's Third Report on the Product Liability Directive, Eur. Prod. Liab. Rev. 2, 4–5 (No. 25, Dec. 2006). For the fourth (2011) report, see https://eur-lex.europa.eu/legal-content/EN/ALL/?uri=CELEX:52011DC0547.

[188] A U.K. decision applied an absolute, rather than risk-utility, standard to infected blood. See A v. National Blood Auth., [2001] 3 All E.R. 289 (Q.B.). As discussed below, cases involving such special products as blood, drugs, food, and toxic chemicals will surely receive the particularized treatment they deserve.

[189] This is the firm position of a leading scholar on European and Anglo-American products liability law, Professor Jane Stapleton. See, e.g., Stapleton, Bugs in Anglo-American Products Liability, 53 S.C. L. Rev. 1225 (2002); Stapleton, Products Liability in the United Kingdom: The Myths of Reform, 34 Tex. Int'l L.J. 45, 53–54 (1999) ("Despite the lack of a definition of defect, it seems most likely that the approach European judges will take will be the sort of broad balancing of costs and benefits which underlies the judicial resolution of the standard of care in negligence."); Stapleton, Products Liability Reform—Real or Illusory?, 6 Oxford J. Legal Stud. 392, 405 (1986); J. Stapleton, Product Liability 236 (1994). See also Stapleton, The Restatement (Third) of Torts: Products Liability, An Anglo-Australian Perspective, 39 Washburn L.J. 363, 376–79 (2000) (the interpretation of the "entitled to expect" standard as a consumer expectations test is "both widespread and dangerous," but "it is highly unlikely that European and Australian courts will interpret these provisions as mandating the consumer expectations test"); Owen, Strict Products Liability in America and Europe, in Festschrift für Erwin Deutsch 305, 309–10 (1999); Lord Griffiths, De Val, and Dormer, Developments in English Product Liability Law: A Comparison with the American System, 62 Tul. L. Rev. 353, 382 (1988).

[190] Article 6(b).

[191] Id.

[192] See authorities cited above and §§ 5.7 and 8.4, below.

[193] In full, this section of the *Product Liability Directive* provides:

Article 7

The producer shall not be liable as a result of this Directive if he proves:

(a) that he did not put the product into circulation; or

(b) that, having regard to the circumstances, it is probable that the defect which caused the damage did not exist at the time when the product was put into circulation by him or that this defect came into being afterwards; or

(c) that the product was neither manufactured by him for sale or any form of distribution for economic purpose nor manufactured or distributed by him in the course of his business; or

(d) that the defect is due to compliance of the product with mandatory regulations issued by the public authorities; or

(e) that the state of scientific and technical knowledge at the time when he put the product into circulation was not such as to enable the existence of the defect to be discovered; or

(f) in the case of a manufacturer of a component, that the defect is attributable to the design of the product in which the component has been fitted or to the instructions given by the manufacturer of the product.

from a conceptual point of view, is the "development risk" defense in Article 7(e), adopted in nearly all European nations.[194] Not unlike the state-of-the-art defense in America,[195] the development risk defense of Article 7(e) shields a producer from liability if "the state of scientific and technical knowledge at the time when he put the product into circulation was not such as to enable the existence of the defect to be discovered." Exactly what this means is difficult to say, for this provision has spawned a diversity of results: a Dutch court has ruled that the development risk defense protects sellers of HIV-infected blood;[196] an English court has held that the defense does not protect suppliers of infected blood, while it does apply to manufacturing defects—but only until a risk is actually discovered;[197] a German court has concluded that the defense does not apply to manufacturing defects;[198] and the European Court of Justice has ruled that the defense applies even if knowledge of the defect exists but is not "accessible."[199] Decisions in France and Italy concur that this defense, or something like it, operates in defective drug and HIV-contaminated blood cases where the defendant is unable to discover the risk.[200]

Directions in European Law

The future path of European products liability law, intertwined with European developments in product safety,[201] remains uncertain.[202] Yet, in 2021, the European

---

[194] Article 15(1)(b) permits member states to opt out of this provision. Of the 27 EU members as of 2021, only Luxembourg and Finland appear to have opted, under Article 15(1)(b), to omit this defense entirely. Spain excludes from this defense liability for the sale of defective medicines and food, Germany and Hungary for pharmaceuticals, and France for products (like blood) derived from the human body.

[195] Some commentators on European law distinguish the development risk defense from the state-of-the-art defense. See, e.g., Taschner, Harmonization of Product Liability Law in the European Community, 34 Tex. Int'l L.J. 21, 31 (1999); G. Howells and S. Weatherill, Consumer Protection Law § 4.1.3, at 201 (Ashgate 2d ed. 2005). Others appear to equate the two. See Wandt, German Approaches to Product Liability, 34 Tex. Int'l L.J. 71 (1999). See generally Howells and Mildred, Infected Blood: Defect and Discoverability—A First Exposition of the EC Product Liability Directive, 65 Mod. L. Rev. 95, 98 (2002); Stapleton, Bugs in Anglo-American Products Liability, 53 S.C. L. Rev. 1225, 1243–52 (2002); Stapleton, Products Liability in the United Kingdom: The Myths of Reform, 34 Tex. Int'l L.J. 45, 53–61 (1999); Newdick, Risk, Uncertainty and "Knowledge" in the Development Risk Defence, 20 Anglo-Am. L. Rev. 309 (1991); D. Fairgrieve and R. Goldberg, Product Liability ch. 13 (Oxford 3d ed. 2020); J. Stapleton, Product Liability 236–42 (Butterworths 1994).

[196] Scholten v. Foundation Sanquin of Blood Supply, Amsterdam, Feb. 3, 1999, NJ 621 (ann. DJV), discussed in Stapleton, Bugs in Anglo-American Products Liability, 53 S.C. L. Rev. 1225, 1252–53 (2002).

[197] A v. National Blood Auth., [2001] 3 All E.R. 289 (Q.B.). See Howells and Mildred, Infected Blood: Defect and Discoverability—A First Exposition of the EC Product Liability Directive, 65 Mod. L. Rev. 95, 98 (2002). See generally Feldman, Blood Justice: Courts, Conflicts, and Compensation in Japan, France, and the United States, 34 Law & Soc'y Rev. 651 (2000).

[198] BGHZ 129, 353, discussed in Hodges, The Case of the Exploding Bottle of Water, 18 Prod. Liab. Int'l 73 (1996).

[199] As, perhaps, where it resides only in a remote Manchurian scientific journal. See Case C–300/95, Commission v. United Kingdom, 1997 E.C.R. I–2649. Compare the decision of an Australian court, interpreting a similar provision, which ruled that the development risk defense applies where the general risk is known but its discovery in a particular product is impossible to detect. See Ryan v. Great Lakes Council (1999) 78 F.C.R. 309 (hepatitis-infected oysters), on appeal, Graham Barclay Oysters Party v. Ryan (2000) 102 F.C.R. 307, on further appeal on other grounds, (2002) 211 C.L.R. 540.

[200] See Hibbert and Lenze, European Commission's Third Report on the Product Liability Directive, Eur. Prod. Liab. Rev. 2, 5–6 (No. 25, Dec. 2006).

[201] For example, in 2020, the EC amended the Regulation on the Registration, Evaluation, Authorisation and Restriction of Chemicals ("REACH"), effective January 1, 2021. Commission Regulation 2020/878, 2020 OJ (L203/28) (amending 1907/2006, 2006 O.J. (L 396/1)). See also Raine, REACH Annex II Updates Came into Force in January 2021, NCEC.com (Jan. 1, 2021).

[202] After a Green Paper, a White Paper, a major research study, and the EC's Fourth Report on the Directive, the EC appeared content to leave the Directive in its present form, and calls for further European harmonization of products liability law (as by negating the effect of separate national laws on sales and other

Commission launched a civil liability *Initiative* for "Adapting product liability rules to the digital age, and circular economy," including damage from a product's intangible digital components and artificial intelligence, and provided a detailed Inception Impact Assessment therefor, which strongly suggests that the Commission is preparing the way for eventual modifications to the Directive.[203]

Hazarding a prediction on how European products liability law will develop, such as how European courts may define "defect" in any type of case, should make sensible American lawyers tremble. And attempting to predict how a court in any European nation will apply the development risk defense in cases involving special types of product dangers—such as toxic chemicals, artificial intelligence, natural food hazards, electrical surges, infected blood, and side effects in drugs—would be sheer folly. Neither the *Directive* nor the *Initiative* gives a hint at how such special issues should be resolved, and both Europe's and America's experience with quagmires such as these suggest that the underlying tensions in these special contexts will be resolved according to the varying cultural influences (and quite likely the economics) in particular European states.[204]

---

branches of products liability law) abated. See Liability for Defective Products: Green Paper from the European Commission, COM (1999) 396 final; Commission Report on the Application of Directive 85/374 on Liability for Defective Products, COM (2000) 893 final (Jan. 31, 2001, the "White Paper"); Product Liability in the European Union (Lovells, Feb. 2003) (the major research study); EC Third Report on Product Liability Directive (14 September 2006); Report From the Commission to the European Parliament, the Council and the European Economic and Social Committee, COM (2011) 547 final (Aug. 9, 2011). See generally Hibbert and Lenze, European Commission's Third Report on the Product Liability Directive, Eur. Prod. Liab. Rev. 2, 4–5 (No. 25, Dec. 2006); Stapleton, Bugs in Anglo-American Products Liability, 53 S.C. L. Rev. 1225, 1226–27 (2002); Stapleton, Products Liability in the United Kingdom: The Myths of Reform, 34 Tex. Int'l L.J. 45, 67–70 (1999) (predicting the future course of products liability law in the UK and the EU); G. Howells and S. Weatherill, Consumer Protection Law § 4.2.5, at 240 (Ashgate 2d ed. 2004).

The Directive was reevaluated in 2017 for correspondence to stakeholders' needs; coherence with, and added value to, other EU actions; and fitness for technological changes, including the Internet of Things and autonomous systems. The evaluation confirmed the Directive's effectiveness, coherence, and added value. While the Directive was found to be generally efficient in the context of producer costs and benefits, concerns were raised regarding the costs to consumers of bearing the burden of proof. See Evaluation of Council Directive 85/374/EEC on the Approximation of Laws, Regulations and Administrative Provisions of the Member States Concerning Liability for Defective Products: Final Report 94–98 (2018). Yet the Final Report highlighted uncertainties on the relevance of the Directive to emerging technologies:

> [The relevance of the Directive] is not confirmed with regard [to] new technological developments (cloud technologies, artificial intelligence and robots, 3D printers). This is especially the case with regard to specific provisions (e.g. no reference to the concept of service nor distinction between products and services) and definitions of the Product Liability Directive (such as articles 2, 3, 6, 7, and 9), which seem no longer . . . apt in guaranteeing the same level of protection.

Id. at 97. Most public consultation respondents recommended that the Directive be adapted to emerging technologies. See Luzak, A Broken Notion: Impact of Modern Technologies on Product Liability, 11 Eur. J. Risk Reg. 630 (2020); Fairgrieve, Reforming the European Product Liability Directive: plus ça change, plus c'est la même chose?, 1 J. Pers. Inj. 33 (2019); P. Machnikowski, European Product Liability: An Analysis of the State of the Art in the Era of New Technologies (Principles of European Tort Law) (Intersentia 2016).

[203] The *Initiative* encompasses liability for products recycled to meet sustainability goals and compensation obstacles presented by complex products. See European Commission, Inception Impact Assessment: Adapting Liability Rules to the Digital Age and Circular Economy (June 30, 2021) (the comment period ended in January 2022 and further action is expected in late 2022).

[204] Consider, for example, variations in interpretation of the development risk defense, above. For other variations in the newer, post-socialist EU states in Eastern Europe, see M. Tulibacka, Product Liability Law in Transition: A Central European Perspective (Ashgate 2009) (addressing the law of the Czech Republic, Hungary, and Poland), reviewed, J. Stapleton, 126 Law Q Rev. 487 (2010); Gheorghiu-Testa and Radocea, An Overview of Product Liability in Romania, Eur. Prod. Liab. Rev. 2 (No. 26, Mar. 2007); Gödölle, Being Liable for Your Product: Central and Eastern Europe, 26 Int'l Bus. Law 73 (1998).

Other Nations

In recent years, other nations have begun to address products liability law in a serious manner. Put otherwise, products liability law has gone global.[205] At least Turkey,[206] Japan,[207] Australia,[208] Taiwan, Israel,[209] and Brazil,[210] among others, have enacted (or introduced) "clones" of the *European Directive*, a products liability code that rapidly is becoming the worldwide model for products liability legislation outside the United States.[211] And many other nations in recent years have adopted various types of products liability laws, sometimes as independent products liability statutes, other times as portions of consumer protection acts, and still other times as part of the torts or sales law chapters of a civil code.[212] Such other nations with significant products liability

---

[205] See Reimann, Liability for Defective Products at the Beginning of the Twenty-First Century: Emergence of a Worldwide Standard?, 51 Am. J. Comp. L. 751, 836–38 (2003); Reimann, Product Liability in a Global Context: The Hollow Victory of the European Model, 11 Eur. Rev. Priv. L. 128 (2003). For a tri-continental, comparative law perspective, see A. McClurg, A. Koyuncu, and L. Sprovien, Practical Global Tort Litigation: United States, Germany and Argentina (Carolina Academic Press 2007).

[206] See Atamer and Micklitz, The Implementation of the EU Consumer Protection Directives in Turkey, 27 Penn St. Int'l L. Rev. 551, 573–76 (2009). Turkey still remains a candidate for membership in the EU.

[207] See, e.g., Ramseyer, Liability for Defective Products: Comparative Hypotheses and Evidence from Japan, 61 Am. J. Comp. L. 617 (2013); Kelemen and Sibbitt, The Americanization of Japanese Law, 23 U. Pa. J. Int'l Econ. L. 269 (2002); Rothenberg, Japan's New Product Liability Law: Achieving Modest Success, 31 Law & Pol'y Int'l Bus. 453 (2000); Easton, The Path for Japan?: An Examination of Product Liability Laws in the United States, The United Kingdom, and Japan, 23 B.C. Int'l & Comp. L. Rev. 311 (2000); Nottage, The Present and Future of Product Liability Dispute Resolution in Japan, 27 Wm. Mitchell L. Rev. 215 (2000); Kobayashi and Furuta, Products Liability Act and Transnational Litigation in Japan, 34 Tex. Int'l L.J. 93 (1999); L. Nottage, Product Safety and Liability Law in Japan: From Minamata to Mad Cows (RoutledgeCurzon 2004). See also Levin, Puffing Precedents: The Impact of the Who FCTC on Tobacco Product Liability Litigation in Japan, 11 Asian J. WTO & Int'l Health L. & Pol'y 19 (2016).

[208] See, e.g., C. Bozzi, Product Liability in Australian Commercial Law ch. 10 (D. Thampapillai, C. Bozzi, V. Tan, & A, Matthew, eds., Cambridge 2015); K. Barker et al., The Law of Torts in Australia ch. 13 (5th ed. 2012); E. Beerworth, Product Liability Australia (Butterworths 2001); Stapleton, Restatement (Third) of Torts: Products Liability, an Anglo-Australian Perspective, 39 Washburn L. J. 363 (2000); Kellam and Arste, Current Trends and Future Directions in Product Liability in Australia, 27 Wm. Mitchell L. Rev. 141 (2000).

[209] See Westermann, Product Liability in Germany and Israel Against the Background of European Standardization, 13 Tel Aviv U. Stud. in Law 205 (1997). Compare Billauer, Primacy in Products Liability: A Comparison of Israeli and American Law, 51 Tort Trial & Ins. Prac. L.J. 943, 955–56 (2016) (arguing that Israeli products liability law predates the *European Directive*).

[210] See Brüggemeier, European Civil Liability Law Outside Europe: The Example Of The Big Three: China, Brazil, Russia, 26 Tul. Eur. & Civ. L.F. 99 (2011).

[211] See Reimann, Product Liability in a Global Context: The Hollow Victory of the European Model, 11 Eur. Rev. Priv. L. 128 (2003) (observing that, as products liability law spread to the four corners of the globe in the previous two decades, the European Directive, rather than the American model, had become the blueprint for new laws, but also noting that these new products liability laws have had little real-world effect). See also Reimann, Liability for Defective Products at the Beginning of the Twenty-First Century: Emergence of a Worldwide Standard?, 51 Am. J. Comp. L. 751 (2003) (same).

[212] See, e.g., ASEAN Product Liability and Consumer Product Safety Law (L. Nottage, S. Thanitcul, and A. Nicholas, eds., Winyuchon, 2016) (reviewing products liability laws in Brunei, Cambodia, Indonesia, Loas, Malaysia, Myanmar, the Philippines, Singapore, and Vietnam); N. Amin, Product liability in Malaysia (Sweet & Maxwell Asia, 2007); Iturraspe, General Trends in South American Product Liability Law: An Overview, 20 Ariz. J. Int'l & Comp. L. 115 (2003); Maestroni, Overview of the Study Undertaken by the National Law Center for Inter-American Free Trade, 20 Ariz. J. Int'l & Comp. L. 1 (2003) (brief comparative overview of Latin American products liability doctrine in Argentina, Brazil, Chile, Uruguay, Mexico, Costa Rica, and Colombia); Velazquez, Preview of Problems in Product Liability: U.S. and Mexico, 8 U.S.-Mex. L.J. 117 (2000); Van Eeden and Van Wyk, Product Liability in South Africa, 26 Int'l Bus. Law. 63 (1998); Miller, Products Liability Law in Argentina, 33 Am. J. Comp. L. 611 (1985).

legislation include Korea,[213] Russia,[214] Poland,[215] Argentina,[216] Peru,[217] China,[218] India, Malaysia,[219] Philippines,[220] Taiwan,[221] and also the province of Québec.[222] And the law of products liability in Canada, while mostly common law, is quite developed.[223]

The literature on products liability law in other nations around the world is so vast, and is expanding so explosively, that a reader interested in finding resources on the products liability law of a particular foreign nation is best directed to a library or the internet.

---

[213] See Kim, The Korean Product Liability Act, 33 Korean J. Int'l & Comp. L. 47 (2005).

[214] Brüggemeier, European Civil Liability Law Outside Europe: The Example Of The Big Three: China, Brazil, Russia, 26 Tul. Eur. & Civ. L.F. 99 (2011).

[215] M. Tulibacka, Product Liability Law in Transition: A Central European Perspective (Ashgate 2009) (Czech Republic, Hungary, and Poland).

[216] See A. McClurg, A. Koyuncu, and L. Sprovieri, Practical Global Tort Litigation: United States, Germany and Argentina (Carolina Academic Press 2007).

[217] See Olenka Woolcott Oyague, Univ. de Lima-Peru, La Responsabilidad del Productor (Pontificia Univ. Católica del Perú 2003).

[218] See, e.g., C. Dong, Comparative Study on Product Defect Law of China and America (Law Press, China 2010); Thomas, The Product Liability System in China: Recent Changes and Prospects, 63 Int'l & Comp. L.Q. 755 (2014); Brüggemeier, European Civil Liability Law Outside Europe: The Example Of The Big Three: China, Brazil, Russia, 26 Tul. Eur. & Civ. L.F. 99 (2011); Li Han, The Product Quality Law in China: A Proper Balance Between Consumers and Producers?, 6 J. Chinese & Comp. L. 1 (2003); Zhao, Chinese Product Liability Law: Can China Build Another Great Wall to Protect Its Consumers?, 1 Wash. U. Global Stud. L. Rev. 581 (2002); Jansson and Riley, Product Liability in China, 10 I.C.C.L.R. 129 (1999); Hongjie, The Legal System of Product Liability in the People's Republic of China, 6 Consumer L.J. 213 (1998).

[219] See N. Amin, Product Liability in Malaysia (Sweet & Maxwell Asia, 2007).

[220] See International Product Liability (C. Campbell and D. Campbell eds., 2d ed. 2011); J. Kellam, Product Liability in the Asia-Pacific (2d ed. 1999).

[221] See Juang, The Taiwan Consumer Protection Law: Attempt to Protect Consumers Proves Ineffective, 6 Pac. Rim L. & Pol'y J. 219 (1997).

[222] See Gibbens, Overview of Québec Product Liability Law: Basic Principles under the Québec Civil Code and Consumer Protection Law (2003).

[223] See, e.g., S. Waddams, Product Liability (Carswell 5th ed. 2012); D. Edgell, Product Liability Law in Canada (LexisNexis Canada 2000); Morritt and Bjorkquist, Product Liability in Canada: Principles and Practice North of the Border, 27 Wm. Mitchell L. Rev. 177 (2000); Waddams, The Canadian Law of Products Liability, 34 Tex. Int'l L.J. 119 (1999).

Part I

THEORIES OF RECOVERY

Chapter 2

NEGLIGENCE

Table of Sections

§ 2.1 NEGLIGENCE—GENERALLY

Negligence is the classic products liability claim in American law. For the first half of the twentieth century, negligence was the principal basis of recovery in products liability cases. Even as its doctrinal significance slipped into the shadows as various "strict" theories of manufacturer liability pushed to center stage during the 1960s and 1970s, negligence retained a prominent place in the developing law of modern products liability. In most of the five states that refused to adopt the theory of strict products liability in tort,[1] negligence always remained the principal theory of recovery. In the great majority of other states, plaintiffs often have good reasons to emphasize a manufacturer's fault and so to base recovery at least in part on negligence. Tactically, perhaps because the rhetoric of negligence is "hotter" than strict liability, juries are more likely to find for plaintiffs, and in higher amounts, on negligence rather than strict liability claims.[2] In terms of evidence, some jurisdictions bar certain types of proof in strict liability in tort that may be allowed in negligence, such as evidence that a manufacturer failed to follow an industry safety standard.[3] In at least one state, a negligence or other fault-based claim is necessary to support a punitive damages claim,[4]

[1] Delaware, Massachusetts, Michigan, North Carolina, and Virginia. See, e.g., White v. APP Pharms., LLC, 2011 WL 2176151, at *2 (Del. Super. Ct. 2011); Sharp v. Hylas Yachts, Inc., 962 F. Supp. 2d 361 (D. Mass. 2013); Baye v. HBI Branded Apparel Enters., 2012 WL 6049656, at *5 (E.D. Mich. 2012); N.C. Gen. Stat. Ann. § 99B–1.1; Sears, Roebuck & Co. v. Tyco Fire Prods. LP, 833 F. Supp. 2d 892, 901 (N.D. Ill. 2011) (Va. law).

[2] See, e.g., Straub v. Cherne Indus., 880 A.2d 561 (Pa. 2005) (upholding verdict for defendant on strict liability claim and $4.5 million award to plaintiffs on negligence claim); Trull v. Volkswagen of Am., Inc., 320 F.3d 1 (1st Cir. 2002) (N.H. law) (affirming jury verdicts in crashworthiness case for defendant on strict liability claim and $9 million for plaintiff on negligence claim). See generally Cupp and Polage, The Rhetoric of Strict Products Liability Versus Negligence: An Empirical Analysis, 77 N.Y.U. L. Rev. 874, 924 (2002) (important empirical study finding that "jurors respond more favorably to negligence language than to strict liability language"); Rheingold, The Expanding Liability of the Product Supplier: A Primer, 2 Hofstra L. Rev. 521, 531–32 (1974) (prominent trial lawyer's similar experience).

[3] See § 2.3, below.

[4] See, e.g., Barnwell v. Barber-Colman Co., 393 S.E.2d 162 (S.C. 1989) (3–2 decision).

and, although unusual, a negligence claim may be available in some states when a strict tort claim is not.[5]

Since about 1980, there has been a growing movement in American law to return to negligence as the basis of liability in design, warning, and other types of cases, leading some state legislatures, courts, and the *Restatement (Third) of Torts: Products Liability*[6] to reassert the central role of negligence principles, and in some cases negligence doctrine, in a variety of products liability contexts.[7] For these and other reasons, the negligence cause of action is a vital theory of recovery in products liability litigation.[8]

Negligence may occur at any stage of the design, manufacturing, or marketing process. To prove any products liability claim sounding in negligence—whether negligent design, negligent manufacture, or a negligent failure to provide adequate warnings or instructions—a plaintiff must establish: (1) that the seller owed a duty to the plaintiff;[9] (2) that the seller breached that duty; (3) that the breach of duty was a cause in fact of the plaintiff's injury;[10] (4) that the cause in fact was a proximate cause of the injury;[11] and (5) that damages for the harm suffered are recoverable in negligence.[12] The plaintiff has the burden of proof on each element of the negligence cause of action.[13]

Duty

The first element in every negligence claim is the defendant's duty of care to protect the plaintiff from harm.[14] Because choices are improper under the law of negligence only if they breach a preexisting obligation to avoid and repair carelessly inflicted harms to others, duty gives definitional coherence to the negligence inquiry.[15] Whether the law

---

5 See, e.g., In re Vioxx Prods. Liab. Litig., 523 F. Supp. 2d 471, 473 (E.D. La. 2007) (S.C. law) (jury finding of negligent failure to warn not fully inconsistent with its finding of no liability on strict liability claim); Blue v. Environmental Eng'g, Inc., 828 N.E.2d 1128, 1133 (Ill. 2005) (statutes of limitations and repose precluded strict liability claim but not negligence claim); Tillman v. R.J. Reynolds Tobacco Co., 871 So.2d 28 (Ala. 2003) (cigarette smoker could not recover under strict liability in tort, but might in negligence); Phillips v. Cricket Lighters, 841 A.2d 1000, 1010 (Pa. 2003) (design of non-childproof disposable butane cigarette lighter used by 2-year-old child to start fire did not give rise to strict liability in tort because lighter was not unsafe for its *intended* users, adults, whereas negligent design claim was sufficient because children were *foreseeable* users); High v. Westinghouse Elec. Corp., 610 So.2d 1259 (Fla. 1992) (no strict liability in tort because dismantling of transformers containing PCBs substantially altered product, but manufacturer has post-sale duty to warn in negligence of subsequently discovered risks). See § 5.9, below.

6 See § 6.5, below.

7 See § 2.6, below.

8 For a comparison of negligence to strict liability, see § 5.9, below.

9 Various duty issues are examined in ch. 10, below.

10 Cause in fact is examined in ch. 11, below.

11 Proximate cause is examined in ch. 12, below.

12 See Owen, The Five Elements of Negligence, 35 Hofstra L. Rev. 1671 (2007).

13 See, e.g., Jablonski v. Ford Motor Co., 955 N.E.2d 1138, 1153–54 (Ill. 2011); Ford Motor Co. v. Rushford, 868 N.E.2d 806, 810 (Ind. 2007).

14 See, e.g., McClain v. Brainerd Chem. Co., 436 P.3d 752, 758 (Okla. Civ. App. 2019) ("An essential element to recovery [in negligence] is that the defendant owed the plaintiff a duty of care . . . ."); Modisette v. Apple Inc., 241 Cal. Rptr. 3d 209 (Ct. App. 2018) ("an essential element"); Gourdine v. Crews, 955 A.2d 769, 782 (Md. 2008) ("an essential element"; failure to warn of insulin side effects); Satterfield v. Breeding Insulation Co., 266 S.W.3d 347, 355 (Tenn. 2008) ("an essential element of all negligence claims"). See generally Goldberg and Zipursky, The Restatement (Third) and the Place of Duty in Negligence Law, 54 Vand. L. Rev. 657 (2001); Owen, Duty Rules, 54 Vand. L. Rev. 767 (2001); Rabin, The Duty Concept in Negligence Law, 54 Vand. L. Rev. 787 (2001).

15 See Owen, The Five Elements of Negligence, 35 Hofstra L. Rev. 1671, 1674–76 (2007); Owen, Duty Rules, 54 Vand. L. Rev. 767, 767–79 (2001).

imposes an obligation of reasonable care on one type of person to protect another type of person from a particular type of harm involves a host of factors.[16] Serving in this manner as the foundational element of a negligence claim, duty provides the front door to recovery for the principal cause of action in the law of torts: Every negligence claim must pass through the "duty portal" that bounds the scope of tort recovery for accidental harm.

Broadly stated, manufacturers have a duty to exercise reasonable care to refrain from selling products that contain unreasonable risks of harm. As American courts replaced the limited-duty rule of *Winterbottom v. Wright*[17] with the broader doctrine of *MacPherson v. Buick*[18] and its progeny, as previously discussed,[19] the duty of manufacturers was revealed to extend to foreseeable risks and foreseeable victims. That is, in the design, manufacture, and marketing of products, manufacturers have a duty of reasonable care to protect foreseeable victims from foreseeable risks of harm.

Due care in the *design* of a product requires that a manufacturer exercise reasonable care in a variety of different design tasks: that it carefully formulate the product's overall design for safety in its foreseeable uses and abuses;[20] that it carefully select and assemble appropriate materials and components into the finished product;[21] that it include appropriate safety devices for the product's expected uses;[22] and that it subject design prototypes to the most rugged forms of use and misuse the product foreseeably might have to endure.[23] Due care in a product's *manufacture* requires manufacturers to

---

[16] See, e.g., Erickson v. U-Haul Int'l, Inc., 738 N.W.2d 453, 460 (Neb. 2007) ("When determining whether a legal duty exists for actionable negligence, a court considers (1) the magnitude of the risk, (2) the relationship of the parties, (3) the nature of the attendant risk, (4) the opportunity and ability to exercise care, (5) the foreseeability of the harm, and (6) the policy interest in the proposed solution."); Phillips v. Cricket Lighters, 841 A.2d 1000, 1008 (Pa. 2003) (characterizing duty as the "primary" element and noting that duty rests on a balance of (1) the parties' relationship; (2) the social utility of the defendant's conduct; (3) the nature of the risk and foreseeability of the harm; (4) the consequences of imposing a duty in the circumstances; and (5) the public interest in imposing a duty on the defendant). See also note 31, below.

[17] (1842) 152 Eng. Rep. 402 (Exch. Div.).

[18] 111 N.E. 1050 (N.Y. 1916).

[19] See § 1.2, above.

[20] See, e.g., Blue v. Environmental Eng'g, Inc., 803 N.E.2d 187, 194 (Ill. App. Ct. 2003) ("it is generally the duty of the manufacturer 'to design a product so that it will be reasonably safe for its intended use and for any reasonably foreseeable use' "), aff'd, 828 N.E.2d 1128 (Ill. 2005); Rest. (2d) Torts § 398.

[21] See Champion v. Panel Era Mfg. Co., 410 So.2d 1230, 1241–42 (La. Ct. App. 1982) (manufacturer must use due care in selecting materials and components, assessing their design, "and have sufficient technical knowledge to form a reasonably accurate judgment as to whether these are such as to secure a safe finished product") (citing Rest. (2d) Torts § 395).

[22] See, e.g., Pittway Corp. v. Collins, 973 A.2d 771, 778 (Md. 2009) (claim that hard-wired smoke detector should have had safety battery back-up); Phillips v. Cricket Lighters, 841 A.2d 1000 (Pa. 2003) (claim that disposable butane lighter should have had child-resistant safety feature).

[23] See, e.g., Burton v. R.J. Reynolds Tobacco Co., 397 F.3d 906, 919–20 (10th Cir. 2005) (Kan. law) (tobacco manufacturer negligent; failed to test for peripheral vascular disease); Banks v. Koehring Co., 538 F.2d 176, 179 (8th Cir. 1976) (Iowa law).

A claim that a manufacturer negligently failed to test or inspect must include proof that the test likely would have revealed a defect that caused the plaintiff's harm, without which the claim will fail. See, e.g., Oxford v. Foster Wheeler LLC, 99 Cal. Rptr. 3d 418, 435 (Ct. App. 2009) (negligent testing claim fails in absence of product defect). Compare Dupere v. Ethicon, Inc., 2022 WL 523604, at *5 (S.D.N.Y. 2022) (N.Y. does not recognize a "separate cause of action for a failure to test"); Sardis v. Overhead Door Corp., 446 F. Supp. 3d 47, 54 (E.D. Va. 2020) ("Virginia law . . . does not recognize a ' "failure to test" theory as a viable claim' "; the duty to test "is subsumed within the general duty of the manufacturer to avoid acting in a negligent manner"). See also Houtz v. Encore Med. Corp., 2014 WL 6982767, at *3 (M.D. Pa. 2014) ("Pennsylvania courts have explicitly stated that negligent failure to test is not a viable cause of action, and '[they] have found no "duty to test" that would be the basis of such a claim.' "). On testing prototypes as part of due care in design, see § 2.2, below. On insufficient quality control supporting a negligence claim, but not a strict liability claim, see § 7.1, below.

exercise reasonable care in a product's assembly.[24] This duty requires manufacturers to exercise appropriate caution in at least two distinct stages of the manufacturing process: (1) the production process, as raw materials and component parts are assembled into the final product;[25] and (2) post-production, in applying quality control ("quality assurance") procedures reasonably designed to catch production flaws so as to limit the sale of defective products to the lowest reasonable level.[26] Finally, a manufacturer must exercise reasonable care to *instruct* consumers on how to use its products safely and to *warn* them of hidden dangers the products may contain.[27]

In considering the scope of a manufacturer's duty under negligence law, it is important not to substitute the notion of duty for negligence itself.[28] Though duty operates at a category level, it shares with breach the limiting principles of foreseeability, cost-effectiveness, and balance.[29] Rather than being absolute, as would a truly "strict" theory of liability, the duty under negligence law is limited to requiring only *reasonable* care—not perfect care; to protecting only persons *foreseeably* placed at risk—not all persons; and to avoiding only risks that are *foreseeable*—not all risks. In short, the duty imposed by negligence law is one of reasonableness, not perfection.

In addition to defining the scope of a manufacturer's obligations in general terms to persons foreseeably put at risk by unreasonable product dangers, duty serves another, sharper role of limitation. As a threshold issue of law in every negligence case,[30] the duty element provides courts with an effective screening device for dividing cases into two broad categories—those properly embraced by the negligence system and those properly excluded. Drawing from a broad range of considerations of fairness, justice, and social policy,[31] the duty issue provides courts an opportunity to consider the appropriateness

---

[24] Rest. (2d) Torts § 395.

[25] See, e.g., Jenkins v. General Motors Corp., 446 F.2d 377 (5th Cir. 1971) (Ga. law) (jury could find that GM assembly line worker had improperly torqued nut on bolt in suspension system causing nut to work loose, bolt to drop out, wheel to cant out, and loss of steering).

[26] See, e.g., Ford Motor Co. v. Zahn, 265 F.2d 729, 731 (8th Cir. 1959) (Minn. law) (jury could find negligent quality control where jagged burr on ash tray penetrated passenger's eye during sudden stop):

> [T]here is imposed upon the manufacturer of an article for sale or use the duty to exercise reasonable care to prevent defective conditions caused by a miscarriage in the manufacturing process. This duty requires reasonable skill and care in the process of manufacture and reasonable inspection or tests to discover defects.

Id. See Annot., 6 A.L.R.3d 91 (1966) (manufacturer's duty to test or inspect).

[27] See, e.g., Braaten v. Saberhagen Holdings, 198 P.3d 493, 498 (Wash. 2008) ("[a] product may be faultlessly manufactured and designed, yet still not be reasonably safe when placed in the hands of the ultimate user without first giving an adequate warning concerning the manner in which to safely use the product"); First Nat'l Bank & Trust Corp. v. American Eurocopter Corp., 378 F.3d 682, 691 (7th Cir. 2004) (Ind. law) (pursuant to statute, manufacturers and other sellers have duty of reasonable care to provide reasonable warnings of danger and instructions on proper use of products they sell). Rest. (2d) Torts § 388, Chattel Known to Be Dangerous for Intended Use, provides that sellers who have reason to know their products are dangerous in ways users may not recognize have a duty of reasonable care to inform users of those dangers.

[28] See Goldberg and Zipursky, The Restatement (Third) and the Place of Duty in Negligence Law, 54 Vand. L. Rev. 657 (2001).

[29] See Rest. (3d) Torts: Liability for Physical and Emotional Harm § 7 and comments thereto.

[30] Whether a duty exists is a question of law for the court. See, e.g., Maynard v. Snapchat, Inc., 870 S.E.2d 739, 744 (Ga. 2022); Morris v. Giant Four Corners, Inc., 498 P.3d 238, 242 (N.M. 2021) ("determination of whether a duty exists is a matter of law"); Oliver v. Narragansett Bay Ins. Co., 205 A.3d 445, 450 (R.I. 2019); Quisenberry v. Huntington Ingalls Inc., 818 S.E.2d 805, 808–09 (Va. 2018); Kesner v. Superior Court, 384 P.3d 283, 289 (Cal. 2016). See generally Keeton, Dobbs, Keeton, and Owen, Prosser and Keeton on the Law of Torts § 37 at 236; Dobbs, Law of Torts § 226.

[31] See, e.g., Maynard v. Snapchat, Inc., 870 S.E.2d 739, 747 (Ga. 2022) (Snapchat had duty to design Speed Filter to prevent driver's reckless speeding while trying to record a picture of the speedometer at 100

of applying negligence law to various types of claims at a category level.[32] For example, courts have employed no-duty rationales in denying claims against fast-food retailers for selling fattening foods to customers who get fat;[33] against manufacturers of brand-name drugs for failing to provide adequate warnings of side-effects endangering consumers of generic versions of the same drug;[34] against pharmacists for failing to warn clients of side effects of prescription drugs;[35] against manufacturers for failing to equip all their products with safety features sold as optional,[36] failing to warn of obvious dangers,[37] and failing to recall dangerous products;[38] and against manufacturers and retailers for selling alcohol to persons who get ill or cause an accident,[39] selling products that may be dangerous when disposed of or dismantled,[40] selling drugs that cause birth defects in the grandchild of the drug's recipient,[41] and for selling handguns in such quantities and locations as to facilitate handgun crime.[42]

Breach

In addition to duty, a plaintiff must also prove its breach. Breach of duty implies the preexistence of a standard of proper behavior to avoid imposing undue risks of harm to other persons and their property, which circles back to duty.[43] Simply stated, a breach of duty is established by proving that a manufacturer or other product seller failed to conform to the standard of reasonable care that defines the duty. The standard of care required varies with the risk and other circumstances, as examined more fully below.[44] Normally, however, manufacturers and other sellers are bound to act with *reasonable* care, often referred to as "due care," for the safety of consumers and others who

---

m.p.h. or higher using the mobile app, ending in a crash); Whelan v. Armstrong Int'l Inc., 231 A.3d 640, 656 (N.J. 2020) ("Typically, in determining whether one party owes a duty to another, we weigh 'several factors—the relationship of the parties, the nature of the attendant risk, the opportunity and ability to exercise care, and the public interest in the proposed solution.' In addition, 'foreseeability of harm is a significant consideration' in determining whether to impose a duty.") (strict liability); Modisette v. Apple Inc., 241 Cal. Rptr. 3d 209, 216 (Ct. App. 2018) (public policy concerns); Hamilton v. Beretta U.S.A. Corp., 750 N.E.2d 1055, 1060 (N.Y. 2001). See also Prosser and Keeton on Torts § 53, at 359 (duty includes such factors as "convenience of administration, capacity of the parties to bear the loss, a policy of preventing future injuries, the moral blame attached to the wrongdoer, and many others"). See also note 16, above.

[32] "The foreseeability of a particular kind of harm plays a very significant role in this calculus, but a court's task—in determining 'duty'—is not to decide whether a particular plaintiff's injury was reasonably foreseeable in light of a particular defendant's conduct, but rather to evaluate more generally whether the category of negligent conduct at issue is sufficiently likely to result in the kind of harm experienced that liability may appropriately be imposed on the negligent party." Friedman v. Merck & Co., 131 Cal. Rptr. 2d 885, 891 (Ct. App. 2003). Although the factors relevant to duty substantially overlap those relevant to both negligence and proximate cause, the fact that duty is decided at the category level distinguishes it from the other two elements which involve fact-specific inquiries into the propriety of applying negligence doctrine to particular claims. See, e.g., Kesner v. Superior Ct., 384 P.3d 283, 300 (Cal. 2016) (duty to prevent take-home asbestos exposure limited by policy considerations to a discrete category, namely, members of a worker's household); Rest. (3d) Torts: Liability for Physical and Emotional Harm § 7 and comments thereto.

[33] See § 10.3, below.

[34] See § 18.3, below.

[35] See § 18.4, below.

[36] See § 8.9, below.

[37] See § 10.2, below.

[38] See § 10.8, below.

[39] See § 10.3, below.

[40] See § 10.7, below.

[41] See § 10.5, below.

[42] See § 10.3, below.

[43] See Owen, The Five Elements of Negligence, 35 Hofstra L. Rev. 1671, 1676–79 (2007).

[44] See § 2.2, below.

foreseeably may be affected by unreasonable product hazards. A manufacturer that acts carelessly—*un*reasonably, without *due* care—*breaches* the duty of care, and such conduct is characterized as "negligent."

It is important to remember that duty in negligence law is limited to a duty of *reasonable* care, not a duty to produce goods without defects. Even the most careful manufacturers, those who follow all tenets of good manufacturing practices, sometimes produce products that are defective. Thus, because the duty under negligence law is only to act with reasonable care not to produce defective products, the mere fact that a particular product is defective ordinarily will not establish breach. Indeed, in order to establish breach, the plaintiff in a negligence case generally must prove both defect *and* negligence—that is, (1) that the product was defective (in its design, manufacture, or marketing), and (2) that the manufacturer was negligent in some manner in making or selling the product in that defective condition.[45] While it is readily apparent that a negligence claim requires establishing this second aspect of breach (negligence),[46] the first aspect of breach (defectiveness) is not so widely understood to be required in negligence as it is in strict liability in tort. Yet, except in certain limited contexts,[47] it is perfectly clear that a manufacturer or other seller cannot be negligent for making or selling a product that is good.[48]

Cause in Fact

Cause in fact is a necessary element in products liability claims brought in negligence,[49] as it is in negligence law more generally.[50] Thus, a plaintiff ordinarily must prove that the breach of duty of which he or she complains was a necessary antecedent to the harm at issue—that the harm would not have occurred but for the breach of duty. However, it is important to note that the breach need only be shown to have been one cause among others, that it was "a" cause of the harm, not "the" cause of the harm. So long as the breach is shown to have been a substantial contributing factor to the

---

[45] See, e.g., Merrill v. Navegar, Inc., 28 P.3d 116, 124 (Cal. 2001) (under both negligence and strict liability, plaintiff must prove a defect caused the injury and, under negligence, plaintiff must also prove "an additional element, namely, that the defect in the product was due to negligence of the defendant") (citing Prosser, Strict Liability to the Consumer, 18 Hastings L.J. 9, 50–51 (1966)); Oanes v. Westgo, Inc., 476 N.W.2d 248, 253 (N.D. 1991) ("In negligent design claims it is well established that a manufacturer or seller is not liable in the absence of proof that a product is defective. . . . Thus, [a plaintiff in such cases must prove two elements:] [1] that the defendants failed to use reasonable care in designing the [product] and [2] that such failure resulted in a defective product."). See also Garrett v. Hamilton Standard Controls, Inc., 850 F.2d 253, 257 (5th Cir. 1988) (Tex. law) ("a manufacturer logically cannot be held liable for failing to exercise ordinary care when producing a product that is not defective because . . . if a product is not unreasonably dangerous because of the way it was manufactured, it was not negligent to manufacture it that way"). See § 5.9, below.

[46] Note, however, that the proof of negligence in manufacturing flaw cases often may be inferred from defectiveness, as discussed in §§ 2.2 and 2.5, below.

[47] The principal exceptions are misrepresentation and negligent entrustment. See ch. 3 and § 15.2, below.

[48] See, e.g., Burton v. E.I. du Pont de Nemours & Co., Inc., 994 F.3d 791, 818 (7th Cir. 2021) (Wis. law) (negligence claims require proof of product defect); Toshiba Int'l Corp. v. Henry, 152 S.W.3d 774, 784–85 (Tex. App. 2004) ("[I]t is not logical for a manufacturer to be held liable for failing to exercise ordinary care when producing a product that is not defective. . . . Before a negligence theory can be utilized in a products liability case, there must be proof of a defect in the product."). See § 5.9, below.

[49] See, e.g., One Beacon Ins. Co. v. Electrolux, 436 F. Supp. 2d 291, 294–95 (D. Mass. 2006) (cause in fact is a necessary element of negligence claim); Lear Siegler, Inc. v. Perez, 819 S.W.2d 470 (Tex. 1991).

[50] See Prosser and Keeton on Torts § 41.

plaintiff's injury, this element generally will be established. These and other causation issues are examined in depth below.[51]

Proximate Cause

In addition to establishing a factual connection between the plaintiff's harm and the manufacturer's breach of duty, the plaintiff must also establish that the connection was reasonably close—that it was "proximate." This means that the harm must have resulted from one of the risks that the defendant negligently failed to prevent, and that the risk and the plaintiff were both of a reasonably foreseeable type.[52] In addition, for the harm to result proximately from the defendant's negligence, it must flow from the breach without any unforeseeable, intervening interruptions.[53] These and other principles of proximate cause are also treated later.[54]

Damage

Requiring a defendant to compensate a plaintiff for harm improperly inflicted by the defendant is the underlying, restitutionary (and deterrent) objective of the negligence cause of action.[55] That is, as much as money damages can do so, the law requires a negligent tortfeasor to restore what the plaintiff lost as a proximate result of the defendant's wrong. Yet a plaintiff in a products liability action brought in negligence must establish that the damage proximately caused by the manufacturer's breach of duty was a type of harm for which the law of negligence provides relief. Thus, most courts hold that only presently provable harm is recoverable, not for medical monitoring of an uncertain risk of future harm.[56] In addition, certain plaintiffs may recover in negligence for certain types of pure emotional harm, whereas other plaintiffs may not.[57] And, particularly in products liability actions that implicate the law of contracts, negligence law generally does not provide recovery for pure economic loss.[58] Yet punitive damages may be recoverable in products liability cases brought in negligence, provided that the plaintiff introduces additional evidence showing aggravated fault. Principles of compensatory and punitive damages law are treated elsewhere in depth.[59]

---

[51] See ch. 11, below.

[52] See, e.g., Jones v. Amazing Prods., Inc., 231 F. Supp. 2d 1228, 1241 (N.D. Ga. 2002) (foreseeable that consumer might transfer sulfuric acid drain cleaner to container that could melt; foreseeability "means that which would be foreseeably probable or objectively reasonable to expect, not merely what might occur").

[53] See, e.g., Johnson v. Wal-Mart Stores, Inc., 588 F.3d 439, 444 (7th Cir. 2009) (Ill. law) (suicide is "an independent intervening event that breaks the chain of causation, even after an illicit gun sale"); Stahlecker v. Ford Motor Co., 667 N.W.2d 244, 257 (Neb. 2003) (rape and murder of motorist stranded when tire failed due to alleged negligence of manufacturers of vehicle and tires; *held*, criminal assault was "an efficient intervening cause" that precludes negligence from being the proximate cause of the harm).

[54] See ch. 12, below.

[55] See Owen, The Five Elements of Negligence, 35 Hofstra L. Rev. 1671, 1685–86 (2007).

[56] See, e.g., Dougan v. Sikorsky Aircraft Corp., 251 A.3d 583, 598 (Conn. 2020) (plaintiffs' expert did not demonstrate need for medical monitoring of plaintiffs allegedly exposed to asbestos during demolition work); Paz v. Brush Engineered Materials, Inc., 555 F.3d 383, 392–98 (5th Cir. 2009) (Miss. law) (medical monitoring claims: affirming summary judgment for defendant where beryllium-sensitized plaintiffs lacked proof of present injury); Lowe v. Philip Morris USA, Inc., 183 P.3d 181 (Or. 2008) (dismissing smoker class action seeking medical monitoring damages for increased risk of future lung cancer, because negligence requires proof of present physical injury).

[57] See Frumer, Friedman, and Sklaren, Products Liability § 13.03[9].

[58] See id. at § 13.07[1].

[59] See Owen & Davis on Products Liability chs. 25 & 26; Frumer, Friedman, and Sklaren, Products Liability chs. 13–15; D. Fairgrieve and R. Goldberg, Product Liability ch. 16 (3d ed. 2020).

§ 2.2 THE STANDARD OF CARE

Most courts apply ordinary negligence parlance in defining the standard of care applicable to negligence claims in products liability cases. When courts do define the standard, they generally go no further than to state that the duty is one of "reasonable," "ordinary," or "due" care.[60] Sometimes a court will be more explicit, such as: "[N]egligence is the doing of something that a person of ordinary prudence would not have done in the same or similar circumstances or a failure to do something that a person of ordinary prudence would have done in the same or similar circumstances."[61] And some courts tailor these principles to the products liability context by comparing the defendant's conduct to that of a mythical "manufacturer of ordinary prudence in the exercise of ordinary care."[62] Finally, courts sometimes focus on the particular industry of the defendant and apply the standard prevailing in that particular business,[63] such as "a press manufacturer of ordinary prudence."[64] This kind of particularized focus is helpful to juries applying the general standard of care to a particular industry context where the technical knowledge and skill fairly expected of reasonable manufacturers may be specific to the industry.

Manufacturers Held to Standard of "Expert in the Field"

One of the most fundamental propositions of negligence law in the products liability context is that a manufacturer is held to the level of an expert in its field.[65] That is, because the manufacturer designs, produces, and markets its products for purchase and use, it is presumed to know the field in which it has chosen to do business. As such, its conduct is fairly measured against that of a reasonable manufacturer who knows how such product should be made.[66] Thus, a manufacturer is charged with the duty of design,

---

[60] See, e.g., Morris v. Giant Four Corners, Inc., 498 P.3d 238, 243 (N.M. 2021) ("reasonable care"); Quisenberry v. Huntington Ingalls Inc., 818 S.E.2d 805, 814 (Va. 2018) ("ordinary care and skill"); Croskey v. BMW of N. Am., Inc., 532 F.3d 511, 515 (6th Cir. 2008) (Mich. law) ("whether the manufacturer's conduct was reasonable under the circumstances").

[61] Rhoads v. Service Mach. Co., 329 F. Supp. 367, 373 (E.D. Ark. 1971). See also T & M Jewelry, Inc. v. Hicks, 189 S.W.3d 526, 530 (Ky. 2006) ("Ordinary care is the same degree of care as a prudent person engaged in a similar or like business would exercise under the circumstances.").

[62] *Rhoads*, 329 F. Supp. at 376.

[63] See, e.g., Townsend v. Sears, Roebuck & Co., 879 N.E.2d 893, 899 (Ill. 2007) (in negligence, "the standard of care is established by other manufacturers in the industry"); Alcala v. Emhart Indus., 495 F.3d 360, 364 (7th Cir. 2007) (Ill. law) ("the jury may presume that the manufacturer has the skill and knowledge that other manufacturers at the time possessed").

[64] *Rhoads*, 329 F. Supp. at 377.

[65] See, e.g., Farrell v. Johnson & Johnson, 238 A.3d 698, 708 (Conn. 2020) ("manufacturers are 'held to the knowledge of an expert in its field . . . and therefore [have] a duty "to keep abreast of scientific knowledge, discoveries, and advances and is presumed to know what is imparted thereby" ' "); Galinis v. Bayer Corp., 2019 WL 2716480, at *10 (N.D. Cal. 2019) ("the manufacturer is held to the knowledge and skill of an expert in the field; it is obliged to keep abreast of any scientific discoveries and is presumed to know the results of all such advances"). See generally 5 Harper, James, and Gray, Law of Torts 350–51:

> [A manufacturer] will be held to the skill of an expert in that business and to an expert's knowledge of the arts, materials, and processes. Thus manufacturers must keep reasonably abreast of scientific knowledge and discoveries touching their products and of techniques and devices used by practical people in their trade.

See also Noel, Manufacturer's Negligence of Design or Directions for Use of a Product, 71 Yale L.J. 816, 847 (1962) ("anyone who enters a special field of manufacturing will be held to possess the knowledge and skill of an expert in that field").

[66] See, e.g., Boyd v. Lincoln Elec. Co., 902 N.E.2d 1023, 1028 (Ohio Ct. App. 2008) (welding rod manufacturer); Burton v. R.J. Reynolds Tobacco Co., 397 F.3d 906, 917 (10th Cir. 2005) (Kan. law) (cigarette manufacturer); Trull v. Volkswagen of Am., Inc., 320 F.3d 1, 8 (1st Cir. 2002) (N.H. law) (auto manufacturer).

manufacture, and warnings with an expert's awareness of special dangers within the particular product's foreseeable environments of use.[67] For example, the manufacturer of a weed killer made of arsenic will be deemed to know of its long-lasting nature, invisibility, and toxic risk to a homeowner who, sometime after applying the poison in her yard, forgets several days later to protect herself against its insidious dangers.[68]

Large and experienced manufacturers normally are the true experts in their fields, so holding them to this standard amounts to nothing more than ordinary care. However, holding smaller and newer manufacturers to such a standard may amount to a kind of strict liability, for it establishes a standard of knowledge and responsibility that small and inexperienced manufacturers may be incapable of meeting even if they exercise "all due care," as it ordinarily is defined. Now that products liability doctrines that look more like negligence than "strict" liability have spread across the land,[69] courts might choose to rethink the logic and fairness of the "expert in the field" doctrine that sometimes unfairly stretches negligence law beyond its natural boundaries.

Responsibility Limited by Reasonable Foreseeability

One of the most basic tenets of all negligence law is that an actor's responsibility is limited to risks and victims foreseeably threatened by the conduct.[70] In other words, if a type of risk or victim lies outside the realm of reasonable foreseeability, the manufacturer or other actor cannot be faulted for failing to take steps to avert the risk or protect the victim.[71]

Especially before the advent of strict products liability in tort, courts sometimes stretched the concept of foresight to risks and persons lying at the outer edges of reasonable foreseeability. One strategy for this type of foreseeability expansion is the doctrine that a manufacturer is held to the knowledge and skill of an expert in the field, as just discussed.[72] Another way foreseeability doctrine expansively defines the scope of negligence liability is to include within the ambit of responsibility those risks and victims of which the actor knew *or should have known*. This is the concept of "constructive knowledge,"[73] which holds that a risk (or victim) is deemed foreseeable if a manufacturer

---

[67] See, e.g., Huggins v. Stryker Corp., 932 F. Supp. 2d 972, 987 n.14 (D. Minn. 2013); Strothkamp v. Chesebrough-Pond's, Inc., 1993 WL 79239, at *7 (Mo. Ct. App. 1993) (manufacturer should have warned of risk that child could be injured by placing cotton swab too far inside ear). See Comment, Foreseeability in Product Design and Duty to Warn Cases—Distinctions and Misconceptions, 1968 Wis. L. Rev. 228.

[68] Boyl v. California Chem. Co., 221 F. Supp. 669, 674 (D. Or. 1963) (toxic chemical manufacturers must warn users of its long-lasting dangers arising out of use, storage, and disposal).

[69] See §§ 2.6 and 5.10, below.

[70] See, e.g., T & M Jewelry, Inc. v. Hicks, 189 S.W.3d 526, 530–31 (Ky. 2006). See Owen, Figuring Foreseeability, 44 Wake Forest L. Rev. 1277 (2009).

[71] See, e.g., Sternhagen v. Dow Co., 935 P.2d 1139 (Mont. 1997) (cancer from herbicide exposure). *Sternhagen* is examined in § 10.4, below.

[72] See notes 65–68, above.

[73] See, e.g., Love v. Weecoo™, 774 Fed. Appx. 519, 521 (11th Cir. 2019) (Ga. law) ("A seller of a product may be liable under a negligent failure-to-warn theory 'if, at the time of the sale, it had actual or constructive knowledge that its product created a danger for the consumer.' "). While the conventional "should have known" formulation of constructive knowledge may stretch the scope of negligence responsibility, it does not suffer from the unfair strictness that sometimes attends the "expert in the field" doctrine, since the "should have known" standard views foreseeability from the perspective of an enterprise in the same or similar circumstances as the defendant, a standard to which a cautious manufacturer should be able to conform, whereas the "expert in the field" standard measures the defendant against a standard of knowledge and expertise that may well exceed its capabilities.

in the same position acting reasonably would have foreseen the risk (or victim).[74] In such cases, a court simply implies ("constructs") the knowledge based on the reasonable foreseeability of the risk.[75]

The *Second* and *Third Restatements of Torts* both reveal the prominent role foreseeability plays in defining the scope of negligence responsibility. Section 395 of the *Restatement (Second) of Torts* employs foreseeability as a limit on a manufacturer's responsibility for harm caused by its negligent mistakes in various ways. First, in order to be "unreasonable," a *risk* of harm from a product must be foreseeable.[76] Second, a manufacturer is subject to negligence liability only if the *use* to which the article was put was foreseeable.[77] Finally, the plaintiff must fall within the class of *persons* foreseeably placed at risk by the manufacturer's negligence.[78] These basic foreseeability limitations are carried forward into the *Restatement (Third) of Torts*.[79]

In negligence, therefore, a manufacturer is required to exercise reasonable care to make its products safe only if, and to the extent that, it is foreseeable that a failure to do so will create an unreasonable risk of physical harm to a person, or class of persons, foreseeably at risk. Liability does not require that a manufacturer divine the precise *manner* in which an accident may occur; it only requires that a defendant should have foreseen the general type of risk that caused the accident.[80] For example, in an exploding soda bottle case, the plaintiff's injury did not occur directly from the exploding glass, but from his fall as he attempted to clean up the resulting spill. The court ruled that a manufacturer of a defective bottle of liquid under pressure that explodes should foresee not only broken glass and a spill but also normal efforts to clean it up.[81] Establishing whether foreseeability of a particular type of harm should limit liability is troublesome, to say the least. How far any court will follow the chain of consequences in any case is a function of the particular facts, the particular court's view of fairness, and policy implications in the circumstances.[82]

---

[74] "Foreseeability often relates to practical considerations concerning the actor's ability to anticipate future events or to understand dangerous conditions that already exist. In such cases, what is foreseeable concerns what the actor 'should have known.'" Rest. (3d) of Torts: Liability for Physical and Emotional Harm § 3 cmt. *g*.

[75] "'Constructive knowledge' refers to knowledge that one has the opportunity to possess by the exercise of ordinary care." First Nat'l Bank v. Nor-Am Agric. Prods., Inc., 537 P.2d 682, 690 (N.M. Ct. App. 1975).

[76] A manufacturer's responsibility rests in part on "the foreseeability of harm if proper care is not used." Rest. (2d) Torts § 395 cmt. *b*.

[77] Liability does not extend to "unforeseeable use or manner of use." Id. cmt. *j*. See also id. cmt. *k*.

[78] Liability extends to users and "those whom [the manufacturer] should expect to be endangered by its probable use." Id. See also id. cmts. *h*, *i*, and *j*.

[79] "To establish the actor's negligence, it is not enough that there be a likelihood of harm; the likelihood must be foreseeable to the actor at the time of conduct." Rest. (3d) Torts: Liability for Physical and Emotional Harm § 3 cmt. *g*. See also Products Liability Rest. § 2(b) and (c), defining defective design and warning, respectively, in terms of foreseeable risks and foreseeable uses. See id. cmt. *m*. These "functional" definitions of product defect are applicable to negligence claims. See id. cmt. *n*.

[80] See, e.g., T & M Jewelry, Inc. v. Hicks, 189 S.W.3d 526, 531 (Ky. 2006); Moran v. Faberge, Inc., 332 A.2d 11 (Md. 1975) (although cologne manufacturer could not foresee specific risk that teenage girls would attempt to scent lit candle with cologne, it should have foreseen general risk that cologne might come in contact with some ignition source, such as a match to light a cigarette, or a candle on a vanity).

[81] Wallace v. Owens-Illinois, Inc., 389 S.E.2d 155 (S.C. Ct. App. 1989) (Bell, J.).

[82] On proximate cause, see ch. 12, below.

If a product's use or misuse is not reasonably foreseeable, the manufacturer has no responsibility to protect persons against it.[83] But a manufacturer's duty to anticipate harm may extend to risks from product misuse—use in a way or for a purpose for which it was not designed, built, or sold. Many products are commonly used for purposes for which they are not sold. For instance, the manufacturer of a chair may be required to anticipate that it will be stood as well as sat upon.[84] Where it is reasonably foreseeable that a product will be used for some purpose other than that for which it is sold, the manufacturer will be required to use due care to make it reasonably safe for that purpose; and where it is reasonably foreseeable that the product will be misused, the manufacturer is generally required to reduce the risk consistent with principles of reasonable foreseeability and reasonable care.[85]

Finally, it should be stressed that foreseeability is a principle of liability *limitation*, not a basis of liability in itself. From the premise that liability in negligence may be imposed only for harm the risk of which was reasonably foreseeable, it does not follow that negligence liability should be assigned for *all* risks that are foreseeable. As is true in tort law generally, foreseeability is a necessary but not sufficient criterion for negligence liability in products liability cases. Such liability may be imposed only when the defendant created a risk that, in addition to being reasonably foreseeable, was also unreasonable.[86]

Determining Due Care—Cost-Benefit Analysis

Whether a risk the defendant created was reasonable or unreasonable—whether the defendant conformed to or breached the standard of reasonable care—ordinarily may be determined by balancing the burdens ("costs") of safety precautions the defendant failed to adopt against the safety benefits the precautions would have achieved. That is, the type and amount of care that reason requires are generally a function of the type, likelihood, and degree of harm (together viewed as the magnitude of the risk) that precautions (of a particular cost) may be expected to prevent.[87] If the risk posed by the

---

[83] See, e.g., Magoffe v. JLG Indus., 375 Fed. Appx. 848, 856–59 (10th Cir. 2010) (N.M. law) (manufacturer not subject to liability for injuries from unforeseeable modification of safety mechanism on portable elevator); Jones v. Amazing Prods., Inc., 231 F. Supp. 2d 1228, 1240–41 (N.D. Ga. 2002) (manufacturers not liable for injuries from abnormal, unforeseeable use of product); Wolfe v. Stork RMS-Protecon Inc., 683 N.E.2d 264, 268 (Ind. Ct. App. 1997) (manufacturer not liable for damages caused by employer's unforeseeable alteration of product); Romito v. Red Plastic Co., 44 Cal. Rptr. 2d 834 (Ct. App. 1995) (manufacturer of skylight did not have duty to make it durable enough to withstand falling person).

[84] See, e.g., Phillips v. Ogle Aluminum Furniture, Inc., 235 P.2d 857 (Cal. Ct. App. 1951).

[85] See, e.g., Sobczak v. General Motors Corp., 871 N.E.2d 82, 87, 94–95 (Ill. App. Ct. 2007) (foreseeable that repeated attempts to start engine would overheat exhaust system and cause fire); Hiner v. Deere & Co., 340 F.3d 1190, 1199 (10th Cir. 2003) (Kan. law) (alteration of tractor front-end loader was reasonably foreseeable); In re September 11 Litig., 280 F. Supp. 2d 279, 313 (S.D.N.Y. 2003) (Va. law) (airplane manufacturer had duty to design secure cockpit because hijacking was a foreseeable risk). See generally § 13.5 (*Misuse*), below.

[86] "In order that an act may be negligent it is necessary that the actor should realize that it involves a risk of causing harm to some interest of another, such as the interest in bodily security, which is protected against unintended invasion. But this is not of itself sufficient to make the act negligent. Not only must the act involve a risk which the actor realizes or should realize, but the risk which is realized or should be realized must be unreasonable." Rest. (2d) Torts § 289 cmt. *b*. See also Prosser and Keeton on Torts 170 ("In the light of the recognizable risk, the conduct, to be negligent, must be unreasonable.").

[87] Section 3 of the Restatement (3d) Torts: Liability for Physical and Emotional Harm formulates negligence in cost-benefit terms:

> A person acts with negligence if the person does not exercise reasonable care under all the circumstances. Primary factors to consider in ascertaining whether the person's conduct lacks reasonable care are the foreseeable likelihood that it will result in harm, the foreseeable severity

sale and use of a product in a certain condition is great, reasonable care normally requires that great precautions be taken to avert the risk; if the risk is small, reasonable care ordinarily requires only small precautionary measures in response.

For example, if the risk at issue concerns the possible failure of an automobile's steering, brakes, or tires at highway speeds, or the possibility that a punch press ram may unexpectedly descend upon an operator's hand, "reasonable" care will demand the utmost precautions by the manufacturer to avert the risk. Yet, if the foreseeable risk is relatively minimal, reasonably appearing to involve a risk at most of minor harm to person or property—a minor bruise, a fabric tear, or a harmless product malfunction—then a manufacturer has little reason to devote more than a modest amount of attention, expense, or other resources to reduce such a trivial risk of harm. This principle of balance, inherent in tort law generally and negligence law in particular, is sometimes referred to as the "calculus of risk."

The most celebrated formulation of the calculus-of-risk approach for evaluating conduct under the negligence standard of care was offered by Judge Learned Hand in *United States v. Carroll Towing Co.*[88] In *Carroll Towing*, Judge Hand reasoned that the degree of care appropriate to an occasion reflects a calculus of three factors: the burden of taking precautions to avoid a risk of harm, on the one side, balanced against the likelihood that the actor's conduct will produce the harm multiplied by the seriousness of that harm, on the other. Negligence is implied if an actor fails to adopt a burden of precaution of less magnitude than the harm the precaution is likely to prevent. Judge Hand expressed this concept algebraically: Negligence is suggested if $B < P \times L$, where B is the burden (cost) of avoiding accidental loss that foreseeably may result if B is not undertaken, P is the increased probability of loss if B is not undertaken, and L is the probable magnitude of such loss, the failure to incur B is negligence.[89] This is the so-called "Hand formula." If the formula is augmented with a sign for the implication of negligence ($\Rightarrow N$), the full formula[90] reads:

$$B < P \times L \Rightarrow N$$

of the harm that may ensue, and the burden that would be borne by the person and others if the person takes precautions that eliminate or reduce the possibility of harm.

88 159 F.2d 169, 173 (2d Cir. 1947) (N.Y. law). Judge Hand first employed this approach in Conway v. O'Brien, 111 F.2d 611 (2d Cir. 1940) (Vt. law), rev'd on other grounds, 312 U.S. 492 (1941), and reexamined the approach in Moisan v. Loftus, 178 F.2d 148, 149 (2d Cir. 1949) (Vt. law). On *Carroll Towing*, see Gilles, United States v. Carroll Towing Co.: The Hand Formula's Home Port, in Torts Stories 11 (R. Rabin and S. Sugarman eds., Foundation Press 2003).

89 See Mesman v. Crane Pro Servs., 512 F.3d 352, 354–57 (7th Cir. 2008) (Ind. law) (Posner, J.):

> [I]n a negligence case the risk of injury has to be weighed against the cost of averting it. In Judge Learned Hand's negligence formula, failure to take a precaution is negligent only if the cost of the precaution (what Judge Hand called the "burden" of avoiding the accident) is less than the probability of the accident that the precaution would have prevented multiplied by the loss that the accident if it occurred would cause. *United States v. Carroll Towing Co.*, 159 F.2d 169, 173 (2d Cir. 1947) (i.e., $B < PL$). . . . [T]he cheaper the precaution, the greater the risk of accident[, and] the greater the harm caused by the accident, the likelier it is that the failure to take the precaution was negligent.
>
> * * *
>
> . . . Suppose the probability (*P* in Hand's formula) were .001, the loss if the accident occurred (*L*) $1 million, and the cost of avoiding the accident (*B*, for burden of precaution) $500. Then because $500 is less than $1 million × .001 (=$1,000), the injurer would be adjudged negligent.

90 The formula may be further refined by explicitly indicating the *change* (Δ) and *foreseeability* (*f*) of the risk that B is expected to reduce. So enhanced, the formula reads:

$$B < \Delta\,(f)\,(P \times L) \Rightarrow N$$

The Hand formula may helpfully be explained in cost-benefit terms as follows: if the expected costs of an untaken precaution (B) are less than its foreseeable safety benefits (accidents avoided or P × L), a manufacturer's failure to adopt the precaution implies its negligence (⇒ N).[91] In such cost-benefit terms, the formula states:

(Untaken Precaution) Costs < (Safety) Benefits ⇒ Negligence

Stated otherwise:

N ⇒ if an untaken Precaution's Benefits > its Costs

If we translate the symbols into cost-benefit terms, such that UP = Untaken Precaution, SB = Safety Benefits, and C = Costs, then:

N ⇒ if UP's SB > C

The Hand formula expresses algebraically the commonsense idea that people are fairly required to evaluate the possible consequences of important actions before so acting. That is, nearly all reasoned decisions involve a weighing of the costs and benefits expected to flow from a contemplated course of action,[92] and the decisions of product manufacturers are no different.[93] In making particular design, production, and marketing decisions, manufacturers of course may properly consider product usefulness, consumer cost, and profitability. But the point of the Hand calculus-of-risk formula is that manufacturers acting reasonably are also duty-bound to include in the balance a properly proportionate consideration of the various risks of harm to others that fairly may be expected to result when the product is put to real-world use.

In sum, due care requires a manufacturer to exercise an amount of care proportionate to an expected risk of harm. This simple yet fundamental principle of reasonableness, which ties the measure of care to the measure of risk, grounds the manufacturer's duty of care. And, after an accident, the Hand formula provides an

---

where B is the cost of taking a precaution that is expected to reduce by a certain extent (Δ) a foreseeable (*f*) risk of harm (P × L). A failure to take a precaution implies negligence if its cost is less than its expected safety benefit (that is, reduction in risk).

91 See Mark Grady's perceptive analysis in Grady, Untaken Precautions, 18 J. Legal Stud. 139 (1989); Grady, A New Positive Economic Theory of Negligence, 92 Yale L.J. 799, 815, 814–17 (1983).

92 See, e.g., Benjamin Franklin, Letter (Sept. 19, 1772), reproduced in E. Gramlich, Benefit-Cost Analysis of Government Programs 1–2 (1981) (suggesting, as an aid to rendering difficult decisions, that one list and consider "all the reasons pro and con" and contemplate "where the balance lies"):

> [T]hough the weight of reasons cannot be taken with the precision of algebraic quantities, yet when each is thus considered, separately and comparatively, and the whole lies before me, I think I can judge better, and am less liable to make a rash step, and in fact I have found great advantage from this kind of equation, in what may be called moral or prudential algebra.

Consider also Oliver W. Holmes, The Path of Law, 10 Harv. L. Rev. 457, 474 (1897) ("for everything[,] we have to give up something else, and we [must] set the advantage we gain against the other advantage we lose"). The moral foundation of the Hand formula is explained in Owen, Philosophical Foundations of Fault in Tort Law, in Philosophical Foundations of Tort Law 201, 214–15 (D. Owen ed., Oxford 1995).

93 For the Hand formula's relevance to products liability law, see generally Green, Negligence = Economic Efficiency: Doubts, 75 Tex. L. Rev. 1605 (1997); Owen, Toward a Proper Test for Design Defectiveness: "Micro-Balancing" Costs and Benefits, 75 Tex. L. Rev. 1661 (1997); Green, The Schizophrenia of Risk-Benefit Analysis in Design Defect Litigation, 48 Vand. L. Rev. 609, 615–16 (1995); Gilles, The Invisible Hand Formula, 80 Va. L. Rev. 1015, 1025 (1994); Owen, The Moral Foundations of Products Liability Law: Toward First Principles, 68 Notre Dame L. Rev. 427, 479 (1993); Miller, Design Defect Litigation in Iowa: The Myths of Strict Liability, 40 Drake L. Rev. 465, 476 (1991); White, Risk-Utility Analysis and the Learned Hand Formula: A Hand that Helps or a Hand that Hides?, 32 Ariz. L. Rev. 77 (1990); Viscusi, Wading Through the Muddle of Risk-Utility Analysis, 39 Am. U. L. Rev. 573 (1990); Epstein, The Risks of Risk/Utility, 48 Ohio St. L.J. 469 (1987). See also R. Posner, Economic Analysis of Law §§ 6.1 and 6.6 (9th ed. 2014).

appropriate and convenient method for a court and jury to evaluate a manufacturer's failure to employ a particular safety feature the plaintiff claims should have been adopted. These important calculus-of-risk principles are applicable to each of the three contexts (production, design, and marketing) where a manufacturer's failure to consider product risks adequately may unreasonably endanger the safety of consumers and others.

Due Care in Manufacture

Manufacturers sometimes make negligent mistakes at some stage of the production process, and such mistakes occasionally cause harm to consumers and other persons foreseeably placed at risk.[94] Beginning with the careful selection, inspection, and testing of raw materials and component parts, the manufacturing process involves all aspects of the maker's construction, assembly, and preparation of the product for distribution. The manufacturer is bound to exercise reasonable care at each step to reduce the risk of dangerous defects in its products. Even when a manufacturer exercises the utmost care in production, it is inevitable that some small percentage of products—from time to time and for one reason or another—will contain manufacturing flaws of one type or another that are dangerous to users or third parties. For this reason, manufacturers must exercise reasonable care after production to catch such defects by designing and implementing quality control ("quality assurance") systems appropriate to the nature and degree of risk. Due care in the manufacturing process therefore often requires the sampling and testing of products off the assembly line, for "[p]ernicious products should be scrapped in the factory rather than dodged in the home."[95] In short, manufacturers must exercise reasonable prudence in all aspects of the production and preparation of products for commercial distribution.

The proportionality principles of the Hand formula previously discussed are helpful in resolving the issue of negligence in the manufacture of a defective product. The *Restatement (Second) of Torts* § 395, Negligent Manufacture of Chattel Dangerous Unless Carefully Made, provides:

> A manufacturer who fails to exercise reasonable care in the manufacture of a chattel which, unless carefully made, he should recognize as involving an unreasonable risk of causing physical harm . . . is subject to liability for physical harm caused . . . by its lawful use in a manner and for a purpose for which it is supplied.

How a manufacturer (or jury) is to determine how much care is "reasonable" in particular cases is described in comment *g*, which provides that "the amount of care which the manufacturer must exercise is proportionate to the extent of the risk involved in using the article if manufactured without the exercise of these precautions." So, "[w]here, as in the case of an automobile or high speed machinery or high voltage electrical devices, there is danger of serious bodily harm or death unless the article is substantially perfect, it is reasonable to require the manufacturer to exercise almost meticulous precautions

---

[94] See, e.g., Soufflas v. Zimmer, Inc., 474 F. Supp. 2d 737 (E.D. Pa. 2007) (defective polyethylene knee replacement broke); Johnson Controls Battery Grp., Inc. v. Runnels, 2003 WL 21191063 (Tex. App. 2003) (defective battery exploded); McGuire v. Davidson Mfg. Corp., 258 F. Supp. 2d 945 (N.D. Iowa 2003) (defective ladder broke), aff'd, 398 F.3d 1005 (8th Cir. 2005).

[95] Morris, Negligence in Tort Law—With Emphasis on Automobile Accidents and Unsound Products, 53 Va. L. Rev. 899, 909 (1967).

. . . in order to secure substantial perfection."[96] However, "it would be ridiculous to demand equal care of the manufacturer of an article which, no matter how imperfect, is unlikely to do more than . . . trivial harm."[97]

Yet, with infrequent exceptions,[98] courts are rarely explicit in applying calculus-of-risk principles to negligent manufacturing cases. Instead, once an accident is proved to have been caused by a manufacturing defect, courts routinely seem to assume (or allow a jury to conclude) that the manufacturer was negligent for making and selling the product in a defective condition.[99] In such cases, courts seem essentially to be applying the doctrine of res ipsa loquitur, but they are doing so *sub silentio*. Instead, courts normally should apply the res ipsa doctrine explicitly if ordinary proofs fail to explain how the accident occurred and the doctrine otherwise is appropriate on the facts.[100] If, without resort to res ipsa, the evidence in fact reveals why the product failed, the normal calculus-of-risk principles of reasonableness and balance ordinarily should be applied to determine whether the manufacturer was negligent in allowing the defect to occur. These and other aspects of a manufacturer's obligations to market products free of manufacturing defects are explored below in a chapter on this topic.[101]

Due Care in Design

For many decades, courts routinely have examined the reasonableness of the design of products involved in accidents.[102] Indeed, a manufacturer's primary safety function is conceiving the essential idea of what a product will be—its purpose, its shape, its materials, and how those materials are joined together. It is at this crucial initial stage that a manufacturer makes decisions that will affect the safety of the entire product line: decisions concerning the types and strengths of raw materials and component parts, the manner in which they are combined into the finished product, whether safety devices are included, the overall product concept, and the type and extent of prototype testing to

---

[96] Rest. (2d) Torts § 395, cmt. *g*. Comment *d* to § 395 refers the "unreasonableness" of risk determination to § 291, which provides:

> § 291. Unreasonableness; How Determined; Magnitude of Risk and Utility of Conduct
>
> Where an act is one which a reasonable man would recognize as involving a risk of harm to another, the risk is unreasonable and the act is negligent if the risk is of such magnitude as to outweigh what the law regards as the utility of the act or of the particular manner in which it is done.

[97] Rest. (2d) Torts § 395, cmt. *g*.

[98] See, e.g., Clifford v. Crop Prod. Servs., 627 F.3d 268, 272–73 (7th Cir. 2010) (Ill. law); Burley v. Kytec Innovative Sports Equip., Inc., 737 N.W.2d 397, 407 (S.D. 2007); Ford Motor Co. v. Zahn, 265 F.2d 729 (8th Cir. 1959) (Minn. law).

[99] See, e.g., Klinke v. Mitsubishi Motors Corp., 556 N.W.2d 528 (Mich. Ct. App. 1996) (negligent manufacture; fracture of automobile steering knuckle); Pouncey v. Ford Motor Co., 464 F.2d 957 (5th Cir. 1972) (Ala. law) (negligent manufacture and design; automobile fan blade broke); Jenkins v. General Motors Corp., 446 F.2d 377 (5th Cir. 1971) (Ga. law) (negligent manufacture and inspection of automobile rear suspension system).

[100] See § 2.5, below.

[101] See ch. 7, below.

[102] See, e.g., Jablonski v. Ford Motor Co., 955 N.E.2d 1138, 1154 (Ill. 2011) ("the key question in a negligent-design case is whether the manufacturer exercised reasonable care in designing the product," but reversing jury finding of negligent design of defendant's fuel system); Mesman v. Crane Pro Servs., a Div. of Konecranes, Inc., 409 F.3d 846, 852 (7th Cir. 2005) (Ind. law) (Posner, J.) (evidence of negligent design of renovated crane sufficient to grant new trial); Jones v. Amazing Prods., Inc., 231 F. Supp. 2d 1228, 1240 (N.D. Ga. 2002) (evidence sufficient to establish negligent design of drain cleaner container).

ensure that the product works safely when put to use.[103] A judicial determination of whether the design of any particular product was "adequately" safe—or was, instead, "unreasonably" hazardous—is often a difficult task, particularly since the process usually involves second-guessing (with the benefit of hindsight) the defendant's design engineers. Yet, "mistakes" of this type sometimes are made, and resulting injuries are sometimes traceable to the manufacturer's failure to exercise reasonable care in designing its products.[104]

The usefulness of the Hand cost-benefit formula is most evident in design cases. Here, design engineers regularly evaluate various trade-offs between product usefulness, cost, and safety. Normally, designing more safety into a product decreases its usefulness and/or affordability. That is, safety generally comes at a cost in terms of utility, price, or both—safety devices may interfere with a product's functioning and usually add to its monetary costs. Thus, in making the often difficult decisions of how much safety should be designed into any particular product, the duty of due care ordinarily requires that a manufacturer's engineers are guided by the Hand formula's principles of proportionality: the greater the foreseeable risk of harm, the greater the precautions should be to avoid the harm. In this manner, the Hand formula, based on cost-benefit principles of reasonableness, optimality, and balance, is especially useful in determining whether a particular design decision was reasonable or unreasonable—whether the manufacturer, in adopting the design, was negligent or not.[105]

A case in which the court explicitly applied these Hand principles of balance is *Griggs v. BIC Corp.*,[106] which involved a negligent design claim for injuries in a fire

---

[103] Just as there is a duty to test and inspect products for manufacturing flaws, so too does the manufacturer have a duty of reasonable care to test a product prototype for hidden dangers in design. Consider Dalehite v. United States, 346 U.S. 15, 51–52 (1953) (Jackson, J., dissenting):

> This is a day of synthetic living, when to an ever-increasing extent our population is dependent upon mass producers for its food and drink, its cures and complexions, its apparel and gadgets. These no longer are natural or simple products but complex ones whose compositions and qualities are often secret. Such a dependent society must exact greater care than in more simple days and must require from manufacturers or producers increased integrity and caution as the only protection of its safety and well-being. Purchasers cannot try out drugs to determine whether they kill or cure. Consumers cannot test the youngster's cowboy suit or the wife's sweater to see if they are apt to burst into fatal flames. Carriers, by land or by sea, cannot experiment with the combustibility of goods in transit. Where experiment or research is necessary to determine the presence or the degree of danger, the product must not be tried out on the public, nor must the public be expected to possess the facilities or the technical knowledge to learn for itself of inherent but latent dangers.

See also Banks v. Koehring Co., 538 F.2d 176, 179 (8th Cir. 1976) (Iowa law) ("When a manufacturer offers a machine or equipment to the public . . ., the user is entitled to presume that the manufacturer has fully tested the mechanism.").

[104] Rest. (2d) Torts § 398, Chattel Made Under Dangerous Plan or Design, provides:

> A manufacturer of a chattel made under a plan or design which makes it dangerous for the uses for which it is manufactured is subject to liability to others whom he should expect to use the chattel or to be endangered by its probable use for physical harm caused by his failure to exercise reasonable care in the adoption of a safe plan or design.

Section 398 is "a special application of the rule stated in § 395," id. cmt. *a*, such that it adopts the proportionality principles of § 395 cmt. *g*.

[105] "A risk-utility balancing test invites the trier of fact to consider the alternatives and risks faced by the manufacturer in designing the product and to determine whether in light of certain factors 'the manufacturer exercised reasonable care in making the design choices it made.' " Croskey v. BMW of N. Am., Inc., 532 F.3d 511, 516 (6th Cir. 2008) (Mich. law). See Mesman v. Crane Pro Servs., 409 F.3d 846 (7th Cir. 2005) (Ind. law) (Posner, J.); Mesman v. Crane Pro Servs., 512 F.3d 352 (7th Cir. 2008) (Ind. law) (Posner, J.).

[106] 981 F.2d 1429, 1436–37 (3d Cir. 1992) (Pa. law).

started by a 3-year-old boy who used a BIC disposable butane cigarette lighter that did not contain the kind of childproof design now required by the Consumer Product Safety Commission (CPSC). The CPSC estimated that, in the early 1980s, 120 people were killed and 750 persons injured each year in residential fires started by children playing with lighters, for a national cost of lighter fires of $300–$375 million. This amounted to an accident cost of $.60–$.75 per lighter, which at the time cost less than $1.00 apiece. The district court gave summary judgment to BIC on the plaintiff's negligent design claim, but the Court of Appeals reversed, remarking: "As the gravity of the possible harm increases, the apparent likelihood of its occurrence need be correspondingly less to generate a duty of precaution." The appeals court reasoned that a jury could find that the lighter's injury costs without a childproof design were unreasonable because of "the high social value placed on the safety of people and property threatened by childplay fires, the high gravity of risk, the considerable probability of risk, and the likelihood [that] a reasonably available [safer] alternative [design feature] may outweigh BIC's interest in producing its lighters without childproofing features."[107] While specific evidence on the components of the negligence calculus of risk may rarely be available to this degree,[108] *Griggs* nevertheless is helpful in illustrating how the injury costs may be balanced against injury-prevention costs in negligent design cases.

Proof of negligence in a design case usually centers on the availability of a feasible alternative design that would have prevented the accident and would have been safer overall.[109] As a general proposition, if there is no reasonable way to design a particular danger out of a product, the manufacturer cannot be held negligent for the product's design. This and other aspects of a manufacturer's design responsibilities are examined in depth below in a chapter devoted to that topic.[110]

Due Care in Warnings and Instructions

A product may be designed and produced exactly as its manufacturer intended yet still be unduly hazardous to consumers who do not appreciate its dangerous characteristics. This is increasingly true as consumers confront a burgeoning array of mechanical, chemical, and electrical products of ever-increasing complexity. Thus, consumers are increasingly dependent on expert manufacturers to supply them with information on product dangers and how to avoid them. In order to "apprise a party of a danger of which he is not aware, and thus enable him to protect himself against it,"[111] due care may require a manufacturer "to speak out if the product is capable of harm and does not itself carry a message of danger."[112] Thus, in passing along a finished product

---

[107] See id. at 1437.

[108] More typical is Metzgar v. Playskool Inc., 30 F.3d 459, 461 (3d Cir. 1994) (Pa. law), where on less specific information on the costs of injury and its prevention a jury was permitted to find that the defendant manufacturer had negligently designed a toy block of a "size and shape which made the block susceptible of being swallowed and causing a child to choke."

[109] Compare Richards v. Michelin Tire Corp., 21 F.3d 1048 (11th Cir. 1994) (Ala. law) (plaintiff's alternative design might have decreased overall safety: *not negligent*), and Garst v. General Motors Corp., 484 P.2d 47 (Kan. 1971) (design of 40-ton earthmover that could neither be turned nor braked quickly: *not negligent*), with South Austin Drive-In Theatre v. Thomison, 421 S.W.2d 933 (Tex. App. 1967) (failure to provide $3 shield to cover rear of power mower: *negligent*), and Calkins v. Sandven, 129 N.W.2d 1 (Iowa 1964) (absence of simple, inexpensive shield over exposed conveyor mechanism on power farm wagon, where shield would not interfere with operation: *negligent*). See § 8.5, below.

[110] See ch. 8, below.

[111] Jonescue v. Jewel Home Shopping Serv., 306 N.E.2d 312, 316 (Ill. App. Ct. 1973).

[112] Dillard and Hart, Product Liability: Directions for Use and the Duty to Warn, 41 Va. L. Rev. 145, 147 (1955).

to the ultimate consumer, a prudent manufacturer must provide whatever information reasonably appears necessary to permit the consumer to use the product with reasonable safety. A manufacturer consequently may be negligent if it fails to provide consumers with adequate *warnings* of dangers in its product or *instructions* on methods for its safe use.[113] The duty to warn and instruct is independent of the manufacturer's duty to design and manufacture its products safely.[114]

The cost-benefit principles of the Hand formula apply in an interesting way to the duty to warn, and courts occasionally are quite explicit in applying this form of analysis to warning cases. In an early case involving the manufacturer's failure to warn of skin irritation from a herbicide, the court remarked: "In determining the duty of care required of defendant in the case at hand, the likelihood of harm, and the gravity of harm if it happens, must be weighed against the burden of precaution which would be effective to avoid the harm."[115] One clear application of the Hand formula to the negligent warning context is *Moran v. Faberge, Inc.*,[116] where the defendant failed to warn that its perfume was flammable:

> [A] manufacturer's duty to produce a safe product, with appropriate warnings and instructions when necessary, is no different from the responsibility each of us bears to exercise due care to avoid unreasonable risks of harm to others. Whether any such unreasonable risk exists in a given situation depends on balancing the probability and seriousness of harm, if care is not exercised, against the costs of taking appropriate precautions. [Yet] the cost of giving an adequate warning is usually so minimal, amounting only to the expense of adding some more printing to a label, that this balancing process will almost always weigh in favor of an obligation to warn of latent dangers, if the manufacturer is otherwise required to do so.

Despite the clarity of the *Moran* court's reasoning, it should be noted that its explicit discussion of cost-benefit principles is unusual in a negligent warning case. Instead, as in cases involving claims of negligent manufacture, courts more often appear simply to assume that a manufacturer is negligent for failing to provide adequate warnings of a significant hidden danger.[117] These and many other aspects of a manufacturer's warning obligations are explored below in a chapter on that topic.[118]

---

[113] See, e.g., Michaels v. Mr. Heater, Inc., 411 F. Supp. 2d 992, 1007 (W.D. Wis. 2006) (danger that propane heater could leak and cause explosion); Hunter v. Werner Co., 574 S.E.2d 426 (Ga. Ct. App. 2002) (danger of improperly transporting fiberglass ladder); Jones v. Amazing Prods., Inc., 231 F. Supp. 2d 1228, 1240 (N.D. Ga. 2002) (dangers of transferring "Liquid Fire" drain cleaner to another container).

[114] "It is not necessary that the product be negligently designed or manufactured; the failure to warn of hazards associated with foreseeable uses of a product is itself negligence, and if that negligence proximately results in a plaintiff's injuries, the plaintiff may recover." Laaperi v. Sears, Roebuck & Co., 787 F.2d 726, 729 (1st Cir. 1986) (Mass. law). See also Loredo v. Solvay Am., Inc., 212 P.3d 614, 632 (Wyo. 2009) (duty to warn of danger even if product is "flawlessly manufactured"). See § 6.2, below.

[115] Holladay v. Chicago, Burlington & Quincy R.R., 255 F. Supp. 879, 884 (S.D. Iowa 1966). See also Jonescue v. Jewel Home Shopping Serv., 306 N.E.2d 312 (Ill. App. Ct. 1973) (child drank all-purpose cleaner); Boyl v. California Chem. Co., 221 F. Supp. 669 (D. Or. 1963) (no warning of long-lasting toxicity of weed killer; plaintiff sunbathed on treated area).

[116] 332 A.2d 11, 15 (Md. 1975).

[117] See Rest. (2d) Torts § 388, Chattel Known to Be Dangerous for Intended Use, which addresses a manufacturer's responsibility for negligent failure to warn. Except for cmt. *n* (warnings to third persons), which is firmly grounded in calculus-of-risk principles, section 388 contains little discussion of cost-benefit concepts.

[118] See ch. 9, below. See also Ausness, Tort Liability for the Sale of Non-Defective Products: An Analysis and Critique of the Concept of Negligent Marketing, 53 S.C. L. Rev. 907 (2002).

§ 2.3 PROOF OF NEGLIGENCE—INDUSTRY STANDARDS

Proving negligence in a products liability case requires evidence that a product supplier failed to exercise reasonable care for the plaintiff's safety. More specifically, if the defendant is a manufacturer, such proof ordinarily involves evidence that the defendant acted unreasonably in developing, producing, or marketing a defective product. Evidence of this type normally entails, directly or circumstantially, the components of the negligence calculus—the nature, magnitude, and likelihood of a foreseeable risk of harm, on the one hand, weighed against the various costs and practicality of mitigating the risk, on the other.[119]

Many aspects of proving negligence are similar or identical to proving other types of products liability claims and so are treated in other chapters that focus on the common features of such types of proof. For example, expert testimony, as important to proving negligence as it is to proving strict products liability in tort and breach of implied warranty, is addressed in the context of proving defectiveness;[120] proof of other similar accidents and subsequent remedial measures, relevant to other types of claims as well as negligence, is also treated in that context;[121] proof in cases involving defective food and drink[122] and automotive crashworthiness[123] remains essentially the same regardless of the cause of action, and so is examined in those contexts; and proof of compliance with a statute or regulation, while relevant to negligence, spans all theories of products liability and so is examined principally as a special defense,[124] though it is touched on briefly here as well.

This and the next two sections address three major forms of proof that may be especially germane to a negligence claim: industry custom, safety statutes and regulations, and res ipsa loquitur.[125] A plaintiff's negligence claim ordinarily is enhanced by proof that a defendant violated a customary safety standard or one set more formally by industry in a code or by the government in a statute or regulation, whereas a defendant's defense to such a claim typically is strengthened by proof that it complied with all industry and governmental safety standards. In cases where a plaintiff is unable to prove precisely how an accident happened, the doctrine of res ipsa loquitur may provide a method for the plaintiff to establish the defendant's negligence by circumstantial evidence.

Industry Standards as Custom—in General

Custom—how a community addresses particular situations according to prevailing social norms—is one of the most rudimentary and powerful sources of law.[126] Because the standard of reasonable behavior in negligence law is grounded in community

---

119 See § 2.2, above.

120 See § 6.3, below.

121 See § 6.4, below.

122 See § 7.5, below.

123 See § 17.3, below.

124 See § 14.4, below. Violation of statute, as proof of negligence or product defect, is considered in §§ 2.4 (negligence) and 6.4 (defect), below.

125 The discussion on proof here draws from Owen, Proving Negligence in Modern Products Liability Litigation, 36 Ariz. St. L.J. 1003 (2004).

126 See Symposia, The Legal Construction of Norms, 86 Va. L. Rev. 1577 (2000); Social Norms, Social Meaning, and the Economic Analysis of Law, 27 J. Legal Stud. 537 (1998); Law, Economics, & Norms, 144 U. Pa. L. Rev. 1643 (1996).

norms,[127] whether an actor who has caused harm to another acted or failed to act as similar actors customarily behave in the same situation goes to the heart of negligence determinations. Thus, one traditional definition of negligence is a failure to exercise "ordinary" care.[128] This definition reflects a thought that most actors usually strive to act in a sensible, prudent manner, reasonably balancing the costs and benefits of contemplated action to other persons as well as to themselves. And in attempting to make rational choices about how to act in given situations, actors necessarily frame those decisions against a backdrop of the expected environment of their actions, including the customary behavior of others.[129]

Yet people tend to be self-centered and imperfect, and actors in a complex world often are so focused on accomplishing their personal interests that they fail to adequately consider risks to others that may emanate from their efforts to advance their own goals. In such situations, it is not uncommon for people to devote less care and attention to protecting others from the risks of their activities than warranted by ordinary prudence. In such a case, a person would be negligent for *failing* to conform to the customary level of care. In many other situations, the converse may be true: the community over time may allow the ordinary level of care for protecting others to fall below the level of care that a reasonable prudent person would provide. Here, an actor would be negligent for *conforming* to the customary level of care. In short, while the standard of customary prudence often is the standard of reasonable prudence, sometimes it is not. In the famous *T.J. Hooper* case, Judge Learned Hand articulated the rule, by then well established,[130] that industry practice or custom is important evidence of the reasonableness of its members' conduct but that, generally, it is not conclusive on due care, since the industry as a whole may have been derelict in failing to adopt precautionary measures dictated by reasonable prudence.[131] This conclusion leads to the universal rule[132] in negligence law that a defendant's conformance to or violation of applicable customary standards of care is some evidence, though rarely conclusive, of whether a particular defendant in fact exercised due care in a particular situation.[133]

---

[127] See, e.g., Prosser and Keeton on Torts § 33, at 193 et seq.

[128] The person of "ordinary" prudence standard in negligence law can be traced to Vaughn v. Menlove, (1837) 132 Eng. Rep. 490 (C.P.). More recently, see, e.g., Smith v. Central Mine Equip. Co., 876 F. Supp. 2d 1261, 1268–69 (W.D. Okla. 2012) ("ordinary care"). See generally Prosser and Keeton on Torts § 32, at 174.

[129] See Owen, Expectations in Tort, 43 Ariz. St. L.J. 1287 (2011).

[130] Judge Hand drew from Texas & Pac. Ry. Co. v. Behymer, 189 U.S. 468, 470 (1903), in which Oliver Wendell Holmes, Jr. observed, "What usually is done may be evidence of what ought to be done, but what ought to be done is fixed by a standard of reasonable prudence, whether it usually is complied with or not."

[131] See The T.J. Hooper v. Northern Barge Corp., 60 F.2d 737, 740 (2d Cir. 1932) (N.Y. law) (L. Hand, C.J.) ("[I]n most cases reasonable prudence is in fact common prudence; but strictly it is never its measure; a whole calling may have unduly lagged in the adoption of new and available devices. It never may set its own tests, however persuasive be its usages. Courts must in the end say what is required; there are precautions so imperative that even their universal disregard will not excuse their omission.").

[132] See Rest. (3d) Torts: Liability for Physical and Emotional Harm § 13, Custom, which provides:

> (a) An actor's compliance with the custom of the community, or of others in like circumstances, is evidence that the actor's conduct is not negligent but does not preclude a finding of negligence.
>
> (b) An actor's departure from the custom of the community, or of others in like circumstances, in a way that increases risk is evidence of the actor's negligence . . . .

On the role of evidence of custom in negligence law, there is no minority view. See id. Reporters' Note to cmt. *b*.

[133] See Abraham, Custom, Noncustomary Practice, and Negligence, 109 Colum. L. Rev. 1784 (2009); Hetcher, Creating Safe Social Norms in a Dangerous World, 73 S. Cal. L. Rev. 1 (1999); Epstein, The Path to The T.J. Hooper: The Theory and History of Custom in the Law of Tort, 21 J. Legal Stud. 1 (1992); Morris,

Industry Standards in Products Liability Law

These negligence law principles concerning evidence of custom[134] apply to negligence claims in products liability litigation.[135] That is, evidence that a defendant failed to or did adopt a standard for a product's design, warning, or manufacture customarily used by manufacturers of similar products normally is relevant evidence that, if otherwise admissible,[136] the defendant was or was not negligent with respect to the customary matter. Either way, evidence of applicable customs may tend to show the foreseeability of the risk as well as the cost, feasibility, utility, and acceptability among consumers of the particular safety measures the plaintiff asserts the defendant negligently failed to adopt. While a jury thus may normally consider evidence of customary safety standards as bearing on the standard of care and whether it was breached, such evidence is usually only part of the package of evidence offered by the parties on the particularities of the case.

In addition to evidence of custom, a plaintiff generally will want to introduce specific evidence on the foreseeability and magnitude of the risk, its hidden nature, and the feasibility, utility, and cost-effectiveness of a means to avoid it. A manufacturer, on the other hand, will seek to show the opposite: that the risk was remote, open and obvious, and impracticable and costly to remove. Evidence of custom, then, usually will

---

Custom and Negligence, 42 Colum. L. Rev. 1145 (1942) (classic article); Prosser and Keeton on Torts § 33, at 193–96; Rest. (3d) Torts: Liability for Physical and Emotional Harm § 13; Rest. (2d) Torts § 295.

[134] The terms "custom" and "state of the art" are sometimes interchanged and often confused. See Products Liability Rest. § 2 Reporters' Note to cmt. *c*, at 81–84; Boyd and Ingberman, Should "Relative Safety" Be a Test of Product Liability?, 26 J. Legal Stud. 433 (1997). "Custom" is customarily used to mean the prevailing practices in an industry. See, e.g., Carter v. Massey-Ferguson, Inc., 716 F.2d 344, 347 (5th Cir. 1983) (Tex. law) (custom means "the usual practice of the manufacturer, that is, what is done"); Chown v. USM Corp., 297 N.W.2d 218, 221 (Iowa 1980) (custom means "what was being done in the industry"). While "state of the art" may mean largely the same thing as custom to business managers and engineers, the latter phrase, although variously defined, has evolved into a term of art in products liability law that essentially means the best science or technology reasonably available at the time of manufacture, in contrast to the customary, prevailing use of science or technology. See, e.g., Kim v. Toyota Motor Corp., 424 P.3d 290, 296 (Cal. 2018) (industry custom is "what is done" while state of the art is " 'what can be done' under present technological capacity") (strict products liability); Potter v. Chicago Pneumatic Tool Co., 694 A.2d 1319, 1347 (Conn. 1997) ("state of the art refers to what is technologically feasible, rather than merely industry custom"). Compare Lohrmann v. Pittsburgh Corning Corp., 782 F.2d 1156, 1164 (4th Cir. 1986) (Md. law):

> Industry standards are the practices common to a given industry . . . often set forth in some type of code, such as a building code or electrical code, or they may be adopted by the trade organization of a given industry. State of the art is a higher standard because scientific knowledge expands much more rapidly than industry can assimilate the knowledge and adopt it as a standard.

On state of the art, see § 10.4, below.

[135] See Frumer, Friedman, and Sklaren, Products Liability § 18.04[1]; Owen & Davis on Products Liability § 2:15; Am. Law. Prod. Liab. § 30:47; Products Liability Rest. § 2, cmt. *d*. On the very similar rules applied in most jurisdictions to strict liability in tort, see Comment, Custom's Proper Role in Strict Product Liability Actions Based on Design Defect, 38 UCLA L. Rev. 439 (1990); § 6.4, below.

[136] To avoid the rule against hearsay and otherwise be admissible, Federal Rule of Evidence 803(18) requires that published industry standards be reliable, meaning deemed trustworthy by other professionals in the field, and be called to the attention of or relied upon by an expert who can assist the factfinder by explaining the standards. See 2 McCormick on Evidence § 321. See generally Brown v. Clark Equip. Co., 618 P.2d 267, 275–76 (Haw. 1980) (discussing hearsay problem); Comment, 37 Tenn. L. Rev. 581, 582 (1970) (same); Annot., 58 A.L.R.3d 148 (1974) (admissibility of safety codes and standards). Additionally, evidence meeting these requirements may still be excluded under Federal Rule of Evidence 403 if its probative value is substantially outweighed by its prejudicial impact or likelihood of confusing or misleading the jury.

supplement these more basic types of proof as to how and why the defendant was or was not negligent in terms of the various components of the calculus of risk.[137]

Industry customs often are developed over time and informally as a matter of trial and error by engineers working in the field. Yet many formal product safety standards are promulgated by standard-setting organizations, such as the American National Standards Institute (ANSI),[138] the American Standards Association (ASA),[139] the National Safety Council (NSC),[140] Underwriters Laboratories (UL),[141] the Society of Automotive Engineers (SAE),[142] the National Fire Protection Association,[143] and other specialized organizations, such as the National Spa and Pool Institute,[144] the Scaffolding and Shoring Institute,[145] the Industrial Stapling and Nailing Technical Association,[146] the American Conference of Governmental and Industrial Hygienists,[147] and many others.[148] Such organizations typically work closely with industry to ensure that the safety standards they establish—safety "codes"—are practicable as well as useful. While some of these organizations are more independent than others,[149] safety standards contained in the codes of such organizations normally represent the industry's consensus on the most appropriate balance of safety, practicality, and cost.[150] And because

[137] Jablonski v. Ford Motor Co., 955 N.E.2d 1138, 1156 (Ill. 2011) ("conformance to industry standards is relevant, but not dispositive on the issue of negligence"); Rest. (3d) Torts: Liability for Physical and Emotional Harm § 13 Reporters' Note to cmt. *b* ("standing alone [proof of compliance with custom] does not justify a directed verdict on behalf of the actor").

[138] See, e.g., Evans v. Nacco Materials Handling Grp., Inc., 810 S.E.2d 462, 470 (Va. 2018) (adjustable brake on commercial lift truck); Binning v. Louisville Ladder, Inc., 2014 WL 4249667, at *5 (E.D. Cal. 2014) (ladders); Furlan v. Schindler Elevator Corp., 864 F. Supp. 2d 291, 300–01 (E.D. Pa. 2012) (escalators).

[139] See, e.g., G.W.M. v. Flink Co., 2009 WL 2337117, at *3 (E.D. Mo. 2009) (machine guarding standards for salt spreader); Thomas v. Mallett, 701 N.W.2d 523, 544 (Wis. 2005) (standard limiting content of lead in interior paint); Poches v. J. J. Newberry Co., 549 F.2d 1166 (8th Cir. 1977) (S.D. law) (specifications for speed and angle of power mower blade).

[140] See, e.g., Whitmire v. Terex Telelect, Inc., 390 F. Supp. 2d 540, 552–53 (E.D. Tex. 2005) (standards for heavy equipment); Hutchison v. Urschel Labs., Inc., 157 F.3d 613, 615 (8th Cir. 1998) (Mo. law) (guarding standards for chicken dicer).

[141] See, e.g., Kay v. Sunbeam Prods., Inc., 2010 WL 2178506, at *2 (W.D. Mo. 2010) (safety standard for electrically heated blanket); McKinnon v. Skil Corp., 638 F.2d 270, 276–77 (1st Cir. 1981) (Mass. law) (lower-blade guard standards for power saw).

[142] See, e.g., Lawson v. FCA US, LLC, 2021 WL 3727236, at *4 (W.D. Va. 2021) (keyless ignition control alerts); Linden v. CNH Am., LLC, 673 F.3d 829, 838 (8th Cir. 2012) (Iowa law) (belt standards); Kagan v. Harley Davidson, Inc., 2008 WL 3874824, at *14 n.31 (E.D. Pa. 2008) (motorcycle kickstand standards).

[143] See Lightolier, a Div. of Genlyte Thomas Grp., LLC v. Hoon, 876 A.2d 100, 104–05 (Md. 2005) (National Electric Code; electrical device installation safety standards); Soproni v. Polygon Apartment Partners, 971 P.2d 500, 505–06 (Wash. 1999) (window standards).

[144] See Duffy v. Togher, 887 N.E.2d 535, 550 (Ill. App. Ct. 2008) (pool liner standards); Ryan v. KDI Sylvan Pools, Inc., 579 A.2d 1241, 1243–44 (N.J. 1990) (pool depth standards).

[145] See McNeal v. Hi-Lo Powered Scaffolding, Inc., 836 F.2d 637, 642–43 (D.C. Cir. 1988) (standards for scaffolding clips).

[146] See Baier v. Bostitch, 611 N.E.2d 1103 (Ill. App. Ct. 1993) (contact trip on nailer should prevent tool from discharging under its own weight).

[147] See Potter v. Chicago Pneumatic Tool Co., 694 A.2d 1319 (Conn. 1997) (vibration limits for tools). These and other standards-setting organizations are described in Frumer, Friedman, and Sklaren, Products Liability § 76.03.

[148] See Frumer, Friedman, and Sklaren, Products Liability § 76.03.

[149] See, e.g., Thomas v. Mallett, 701 N.W.2d 523, 544 (Wis. 2005) (ASA is "a voluntary group comprised of representatives from a variety of medical, public health and industry groups"); Fayerweather v. Menard, Inc., 659 N.W.2d 506 (Wis. Ct. App. 2003) (ANSI's ladder committee membership from industry, users, and chosen from CPSC, OSHA, labor organizations, and "outside specialists").

[150] See Allenbrand v. Louisville Ladder Grp., L.L.C., 2007 WL 120805, at *1 (D. Kan. 2007) (OSHA "views ANSI Section A14 as the 'national consensus standard' pertaining to ladders"); Hansen v. Abrasive

organizations that issue such standards and codes may be heavily influenced (if not entirely controlled) by industry, courts generally treat the admissibility of such standards the same as any other industry standards.[151] Yet the formal way in which such standards may be developed and formulated into specific codes and industry's commensurate reliance upon them suggest that they sometimes should be accorded greater weight.[152]

As proof of the negligence of a manufacturer's product design, courts have admitted evidence of a defendant's failure to meet industry standards governing the design of such products as a toy action figure,[153] a tire,[154] a meat grinder,[155] a vehicle such as a front-end loader,[156] a cigarette lighter,[157] and various machinery and equipment that is unguarded[158] or not equipped with an emergency stop device.[159] So, too, have courts admitted as proof of due care a manufacturer's *compliance* with design standards for a grinder, a tractor, a press, a treadmill, and a car.[160]

In negligence claims alleging that a manufacturer has failed to provide adequate warnings or instructions, courts have allowed plaintiffs to introduce evidence that the defendant failed to conform to industry practices governing appropriate warnings or instructions with respect to the assembly of a floor lamp[161] and the location of warnings

---

Eng'g & Mfg., 856 P.2d 625, 628 (Or. 1993) (ANSI standards help determine negligence because they represent a consensus as to what reasonable industry member would do).

[151] Yet, because some standards-setting groups contain members from outside the industry, and because their standards are voluntary guidelines of minimum safety, such standards might not be equated with "industry custom," as such. See Fayerweather v. Menard, Inc., 659 N.W.2d 506 (Wis. Ct. App. 2003) (because some ANSI ladder standards committee members came from outside industry, "the standards are not evidence of 'custom and usage' within an industry as contemplated" by standard jury instruction, so that trial court's failure to give it was not error).

[152] See Vermett v. Fred Christen & Sons Co., 741 N.E.2d 954, 971 (Ohio Ct. App. 2000) ("compliance with ANSI is a compelling factor").

[153] See Lugo v. LJN Toys, Ltd., 552 N.E.2d 162 (N.Y. 1990) (plaintiff's eye injured when 8-pointed detachable star from Voltron-Defender of the Universe was thrown just as on TV; expert's testimony, based on customs and standards in toy safety community, that detachable star rendered design defective because Voltron would throw his star on TV, was sufficient to create question for jury and withstand defendant's summary judgment motion).

[154] See Morden v. Continental A.G., 611 N.W.2d 659, 675–76 (Wis. 2000).

[155] See De Pree v. Nutone, Inc., 422 F.2d 534, 535–36 (6th Cir. 1970) (Mich. law) (U.L. standards for cutter plate).

[156] See Brown v. Clark Equip. Co., 618 P.2d 267, 275–76 (Haw. 1980) (National Safety Council standards).

[157] See Glover v. BIC Corp., 6 F.3d 1318, 1325 (9th Cir. 1993) (en banc) (Or. law) (ASTM standards for extinguishment).

[158] See, e.g., Cigna Ins. Co. v. Oy Saunatec, Ltd., 241 F.3d 1, 12 (1st Cir. 2001) (Mass. law); Cacevic v. Simplimatic Eng'g Co., 645 N.W.2d 287, 291–92 (Mich. Ct. App. 2001) (ANSI standards for guarding palletizer); Wallner v. Kitchens of Sara Lee, Inc., 419 F.2d 1028, 1032 (7th Cir. 1970) (Ill. law) (American Safety Standards Institute standards for guarding conveyor).

[159] See Malen v. MTD Prods., Inc., 628 F.3d 296, 304 (7th Cir. 2010) (Ill. law) (ANSI standards for stopping riding mower blade within 5 seconds after dismount); Almazan v. CTB, Inc., 2000 WL 33348244, at *10 (W.D. Tex. 2000) (ASME standards).

[160] See Clarke v. LR Sys., 219 F. Supp. 2d 323, 334 (E.D.N.Y. 2002) (ANSI guarding standard for grinders); Spieker v. Westgo, Inc., 479 N.W.2d 837, 843–44 (N.D. 1992) (tractor's power take-off driveline); Vermett v. Fred Christen & Sons Co., 741 N.E.2d 954, 971 (Ohio Ct. App. 2000) (ANSI safeguards for press); Palmer v. Lakeside Wellness Ctr., 798 N.W.2d 845, 851 (Neb. 2011) (American Society for Testing and Materials' specifications for motorized treadmills); Hasson v. Ford Motor Co., 650 P.2d 1171, 1182–83 (Cal. 1982) (SAE standards for automotive brakes).

[161] See Creadore v. Shades of Light, 2003 WL 152003, at *3 (S.D.N.Y. 2003) (UL guidelines).

on containers holding explosive materials.[162] Similarly, as evidence of due care, courts have allowed defendants to show their compliance with the customary types of warnings or instructions used for a trampoline[163] and asbestos products.[164] While most of the cases involving evidence of industry safety standards pertain to a product's design, and occasionally to a product's warnings or instructions, as just discussed, such evidence may also bear on a product's defective manufacture.[165]

Evidence of compliance or noncompliance with an industry standard of care is almost always admissible evidence on whether the defendant exercised due care,[166] assuming the standard is applicable to the dangerous aspect of the product in question,[167] but it rarely is conclusive of a defendant's negligence.[168] Nevertheless, some courts view certain industry safety codes as particularly persuasive on whether a manufacturer was negligent,[169] and an argument may be made for holding compliance or noncompliance with clear and important industry standards to be dispositive of negligence or defect in special situations.[170]

---

[162] See Beadling v. William Bowman Assocs., 809 A.2d 188, 191 (N.J. Super. Ct. App. Div. 2002).

[163] See Anderson v. Hedstrom Corp., 76 F. Supp. 2d 422, 450 (S.D.N.Y. 1999).

[164] See Horne v. Owens-Corning Fiberglas Corp., 4 F.3d 276, 281–82 (4th Cir. 1993) (N.C. law).

[165] See, e.g., Holder v. Keller Indus., 2000 WL 141070 (Tex. App. 2000) (ladder that broke constructed of low-density wood in violation of ANSI standards). See also Doe v. American Nat'l Red Cross, 848 F. Supp. 1228, 1233 (S.D. W. Va. 1994) (whether Red Cross met collection standards of blood-banking industry to protect against risk that donor might have AIDS). One of the earliest cases concerning manufacturing defect claims was Grant v. Graham Chero-Cola Bottling Co., 97 S.E. 27, 28 (N.C. 1918) (bottle of ginger ale exploded because it was too highly charged or bottle was defective; evidence that bottles of beverages sold by other bottling plants also frequently exploded during bottling, transportation, and use by consumers "was not evidence that they were reasonable and prudent men, but, on the contrary, that they were as careless and negligent in their duty to the public and [consumers] as this defendant").

[166] See, e.g., Reis v. Volvo Cars of N. Am., 18 N.E.3d 383 (N.Y. 2014); Cekic v. Royal-Pak Sys., Inc., 874 N.Y.S.2d 178, 179 (App. Div. 2009) (ANSI trash compactor standards should have been admitted into evidence); Kent Vill. Assocs. Joint Venture v. Smith, 657 A.2d 330, 337 (Md. Ct. Spec. App. 1995) ("where relevant to the case and upon a proper evidentiary foundation, safety standards promulgated by organizations such as ANSI may be admitted to show an accepted standard of care, the violation of which may be regarded as evidence of negligence"); Mich. Comp. Laws Ann. § 600.2946(1) (evidence of compliance admissible); Wash. Rev. Code Ann. § 7.72.050 (compliance or noncompliance). See generally Frumer, Friedman, and Sklaren, Products Liability § 18.04[1] ("almost every jurisdiction").

[167] See, e.g., Fidalgo v. Columbus McKinnon Corp., 775 N.E.2d 803, 809 (Mass. App. Ct. 2002).

[168] See, e.g., Evans v. Nacco Materials Handling Grp., Inc., 810 S.E.2d 462, 469 (Va. 2018) ("Governmental safety standards and industry practices are highly relevant on the question of whether the manufacturer's design was negligent because they permit an inference that the manufacturer exercised (or failed to exercise) ordinary prudence. . . . Governmental regulations and industry standards and practices are not dispositive, however."); Cruz v. Kumho Tire Co., 2015 WL 2193796, at *16 (N.D.N.Y. 2015) (compliance with regulatory testing requirements not determinative of due care); Howard v. Omni Hotels Mgmt. Corp., 136 Cal. Rptr. 3d 739, 752 (Ct. App. 2012) (manufacturer's "compliance with regulations, directives or trade custom does not necessarily eliminate negligence but instead simply constitutes evidence for jury consideration with other facts and circumstances"); Taylor v. Smithkline Beecham Corp., 658 N.W.2d 127, 130 (Mich. 2003).

In Kentucky, compliance with customary industry standards results in a rebuttable presumption that the product was not defectively designed or manufactured, applicable to any products liability action. See Ky. Rev. Stat. Ann. § 411.310(2).

[169] See, e.g., Vermett v. Fred Christen & Sons Co., 741 N.E.2d 954, 971 (Ohio Ct. App. 2000) ("compliance with ANSI is a compelling factor").

[170] See, e.g., Lamb v. Kysor Indus. Corp., 759 N.Y.S.2d 266 (App. Div. 2003) (that saw guard met industry standards proved product was not defective as a matter of law); Wilder v. Toyota Motor Sales, U.S.A., Inc., 23 Fed. Appx. 155, 157 (4th Cir. 2001) (Va. law) (while conformity with industry custom does not absolve a defendant from liability, compliance may be conclusive if no evidence shows product was not reasonably safe). Compare Henderson and Twerski, Achieving Consensus on Defective Product Design, 83 Cornell L. Rev. 867 (1998) (arguing that defendant's violation of clear industry standard should be conclusive proof of product's defectiveness).

§ 2.4 PROOF OF NEGLIGENCE—VIOLATION OF STATUTE

The standard of care applied in negligence actions is usually the common-law standard of reasonable care and prudence in the circumstances of the particular case. Products liability claims for negligence are usually adjudicated in this manner. Yet legislatures sometimes specify by statute, and regulatory agencies sometimes specify by regulation, particular safety measures required in certain situations and particular dangerous conditions prohibited in others. Such statutes (or regulations) may provide explicitly for civil damages arising from their breach.[171] More typically, however, safety statutes[172] provide criminal or quasi-criminal penalties for their violation. If a manufacturer, retailer, or other products liability defendant violates such a safety statute in a manner that harms a plaintiff, the doctrine of negligence per se may permit the plaintiff to establish the defendant's duty of care and breach thereof by proving the statutory violation.[173] In such situations, a court borrows the specific standard of conduct set forth in the statute,[174] deferring to the legislative determination of proper behavior in substitution for a judicial determination of the standard of reasonable care.[175]

---

[171] On civil damages acts, see 3 Harper, James, and Gray, Law of Torts § 17.5.

[172] "By 'statute' is meant both state and federal legislative and administrative enactments." Lukaszewicz v. Ortho Pharm. Corp., 510 F. Supp. 961, 964 (E.D. Wis. 1981).

[173] "[T]he violation of a statute, or regulation having the force of statute, enacted for the safety of others is negligence in law or negligence per se." Price v. Blood Bank of Del., Inc., 790 A.2d 1203, 1212–13 (Del. 2002). See generally Frumer, Friedman, and Sklaren, Products Liability §§ 10.03, 55.02[3]; Am. Law Prod. Liab. §§ 12:10–:38; D'Angelo, Effect of Compliance or Noncompliance with Applicable Governmental Product Safety Regulations on a Determination of Product Defect, 36 S. Tex. L. Rev. 453 (1995); Wheeler, The Use of Criminal Statutes to Regulate Product Safety, 13 J. Legal Stud. 593 (1984); Note, Products Liability Based Upon Violation of Statutory Standards, 64 Mich. L. Rev. 1388 (1966) (classic treatment); Products Liability Rest. § 4(a).

More generally, see Prosser and Keeton on Torts § 36; Dobbs, Law of Torts §§ 133–42; 3 Harper, James, and Gray, Law of Torts § 17.6; Rest. (3d) Torts: Liability for Physical and Emotional Harm § 14; Morris, The Role of Criminal Statutes in Negligence Actions, 49 Colum. L. Rev. 21 (1949); Lowndes, Civil Liability Created by Criminal Legislation, 16 Minn. L. Rev. 361 (1932); Thayer, Public Wrong and Private Action, 27 Harv. L. Rev. 317 (1914).

The effect of violation of statute or compliance therewith on proving a product's defectiveness or nondefectiveness, is a closely related issue examined in §§ 6.4 (violation) and 14.4 (compliance), below.

[174] If a statutory standard is not specific, but merely restates a general safety principle of tort law, the statute will have borrowed from the common law, in which case there is no reason for a court to borrow the standard back again. Thus, the doctrine of negligence per se applies only to safety standards that are specific rather than vague and general. See, e.g., Sikora v. Wenzel, 727 N.E.2d 1277, 1280 (Ohio 2000); Shanks v. Upjohn Co., 835 P.2d 1189, 1201 (Alaska 1992). *But see* Howard v. Zimmer, Inc., 299 P.3d 463 (Okla. 2013) (6–3 decision) (allowing negligence per se claim, for failure of knee replacement due to oily residue left on implant, for violation of FDA Good Manufacturing Practices regulation requiring manufacturers to remove deleterious manufacturing materials from a device, notwithstanding general and non-device-specific nature of regulation).

[175] "Negligence per se 'is merely a negligence claim with a statutory standard of care substituted for the common law standard of care.' " Sims v. Atrium Med. Corp., 349 F. Supp. 3d 628, 641 (W.D. Ky. 2018). "When the doctrine of negligence per se applies, the general standard of a reasonable man is replaced by a specific rule of conduct established in a statute or regulation." Dougherty v. Santa Fe Marine, Inc., 698 F.2d 232, 234 (5th Cir. 1983) (La. law). See Strong v. American Cyanamid Co., 261 S.W.3d 493, 516 (Mo. Ct. App. 2007) ("Negligence *per se* arises when the legislature pronounces in a statute what the conduct of a reasonable person must be, whether or not the common law would require similar conduct, and the court then adopts the statutory standard of care to define the standard of conduct of [a] reasonable person."); Anderson v. State, Dep't of Natural Res., 693 N.W.2d 181, 189–90 (Minn. 2005) ("A per se negligence rule substitutes a statutory standard of care for the ordinary prudent person standard of care, such that a violation of a statute is conclusive evidence of duty and breach.").

If relevant statutes and regulations are numerous and complex, a plaintiff may need expert testimony to explain their meaning and how they are applicable to the litigation. See, e.g., McNeil Pharm. v. Hawkins, 686 A.2d 567, 580–85 (D.C. 1996).

Negligence Per Se—the Two-Pronged Test

All safety rules, whether statutory, regulatory, or common law, are adopted to protect certain types of persons from certain types of risk of harm, and the reach of all such rules is limited to this extent.[176] Accordingly, most courts will adopt a standard of behavior set by a statute or regulation for use in a negligence action only if they determine that: (1) the plaintiff was injured by a type of risk[177] the statute (or regulation) intended to prevent, and (2) the plaintiff was in the class of persons the statute (or regulation) intended to protect.[178] This is the classic two-pronged test for deciding whether a criminal safety statute[179] may properly be used as the standard of care[180] in a negligence action under the doctrine of negligence per se.

Risks Prevented

As for the types of risk sought to be prevented, courts have ruled that the National Traffic and Motor Vehicle Safety Act, enacted to reduce traffic accidents and deaths, sought to prevent deaths in an accident caused by a manufacturer's deficient recall of a car with defective steering in violation of the Act's recall provisions;[181] that an FDA regulation requiring drug manufacturers to report adverse reactions to the agency was intended to prevent just such reactions;[182] and that a state housing standards act was designed to protect against the risks of unsafe construction and installation of mobile homes, including failing to anchor them to the ground.[183] On the other hand, a statute requiring motor vehicles to be equipped with turn signals does not apply to a road grader which is statutorily exempted therefrom;[184] a statute prohibiting the sale of cars

---

[176] See Hill v. Lundin & Assocs., Inc., 256 So.2d 620 (La. 1972); Malone, Ruminations on Cause-In-Fact, 9 Stan. L. Rev. 60, 73 (1956); Rest. (3d) Torts: Liability for Physical and Emotional Harm § 14 (comments).

[177] Courts and commentators often use the term "harm" for "risk of harm." See, e.g., Prosser and Keeton on Torts § 36. The Third Restatement changes "type of harm" to "type of accident." Rest. (3d) Torts: Liability for Physical and Emotional Harm § 14.

[178] See, e.g., Wing v. U-Haul Int'l, Inc., 2020 WL 773474, at *3 (Ariz. Ct. App. 2020) (If "a 'statute's purpose is in part to protect a class of persons that includes the plaintiff from 'the type of harm that occurred,' a court may adopt the statute as the relevant standard of care in a negligence action."). Rest. (3d) Torts: Liability for Physical and Emotional Harm § 14, Statutory Violations as Negligence Per Se, provides:

> An actor is negligent if, without excuse, the actor violates a statute that is designed to protect against the type of accident the actor's conduct causes, and if the accident victim is within the class of persons the statute is designed to protect.

Rest. (2d) Torts § 286 formulates the doctrine in a four-part test, including class of persons, interest, harm, and hazard.

[179] Sims v. Atrium Med. Corp., 349 F. Supp. 3d 628, 641 (W.D. Ky. 2018) ("to state a plausible negligence per se claim, a plaintiff must show that . . . the statute is penal in nature and provides no civil remedy").

[180] The two-part test of negligence per se focuses on duty and the standard of care. More fully, it might be said that there are four elements in a negligence per se claim: (1) violation; (2) plaintiff in class intended to be protected; (3) risk of type statute designed to prevent; and (4) violation proximately caused injury. Steele v. Evenflo Co., 178 S.W.3d 715, 718 (Mo. Ct. App. 2005).

Most courts and commentators state the two-pronged test in reverse order to how it is stated here in the text, asking first if the plaintiff is included in the protected class. Yet, because the class of plaintiffs a statute seeks to protect is largely a subset of the hazards the statute seeks to prevent, the Third Restatement's ordering is preferable in beginning the analysis with an inquiry into the risks prevented, from which the class of protected victims easily tumbles.

[181] See Lowe v. General Motors Corp., 624 F.2d 1373, 1380 (5th Cir. 1980) (Ala. law) (violation of NHTSA regulations governing automotive recalls).

[182] See Stanton v. Astra Pharm. Prods., Inc., 718 F.2d 553, 564 (3d Cir. 1983) (Pa. law) (Becker, J.) (drug manufacturer failed to file adverse reaction reports required by FDA regulation).

[183] See Gem Homes, Inc. v. Contreras, 861 S.W.2d 449, 453 (Tex. App. 1993) (home rolled over in storm).

[184] See Cook v. Caterpillar, Inc., 849 S.W.2d 434 (Tex. App. 1993).

equipped with hood ornaments that protrude beyond the face of the radiator grill applies only to the hazard of hood ornaments on moving cars piercing people, not the risk of people piercing themselves on the hood ornament of a car at rest;[185] a statute requiring that gasoline be dispensed only into safe containers is intended to prevent the risk of leaks, not the risk that gasoline bought in a cup might be thrown on a person to facilitate catching her on fire;[186] a statute that prohibits false statements to the government[187] is a "truth" statute, not a "safety statute" protecting users against risks from prescription drugs;[188] and an act requiring insurers of total-loss vehicles to send their titles and plates to the Department of Revenue is an "anti-theft" act, not a safety statute designed to prevent such vehicles from being defectively rebuilt and thereafter causing accidents.[189]

Plaintiffs Protected

As for the class of plaintiffs sought to be protected, the federal Motor Vehicle Safety Act, enacted to reduce traffic accidents and deaths, is intended to protect the driver and passenger in a car that was dangerously defective in violation of the Act;[190] an FDA regulation prohibiting the use of sulfites on raw fruits and vegetables seeks to protect sulfite-sensitive individuals from consuming food so treated;[191] a state statute requiring manufacturers of toxic products to supply purchasers with a material safety data sheet (MSDS) is designed to protect users of the product, often the purchaser's employees;[192] and a statute prohibiting the use of "any pesticide in a manner inconsistent with its labeling" is designed to protect the public, including residential consumers, from injuries caused by toxic chemicals not intended for interior household use.[193] But an act requiring insurers to return titles and licenses of total-loss vehicles to the Department of Revenue seeks to protect owners of vehicles from thefts, not pedestrians injured by runaway vehicles defectively rebuilt;[194] a driving permit requiring paraplegic drivers to be accompanied by co-drivers is intended to protect persons on the highways, not the paraplegic driver himself while using a defective wheelchair lift on a vehicle at rest;[195] and a state statute barring hood ornaments from protruding beyond the front hood is intended to protect persons who might be struck by moving cars, not those who impale themselves on such an ornament on a car at rest.[196]

Other Negligence Per Se Requirements

An essential element of every negligence per se action is that the defendant actually *violated* the pertinent statute or regulation—proof that the safety standard contained

---

185 See Hatch v. Ford Motor Co., 329 P.2d 605, 608 (Cal. Ct. App. 1958).

186 See Walcott v. Total Petroleum, Inc., 964 P.2d 609, 613 (Colo. App. 1998).

187 "Whoever . . . knowingly and wilfully . . . falsifies . . . a material fact [or] makes any materially false, fictitious, or fraudulent statement or representation . . . shall be [in violation of this statute]." 18 U.S.C. § 1001.

188 See McNeil Pharm. v. Hawkins, 686 A.2d 567, 580 (D.C. 1996) (action on behalf of patient who died of severe liver failure following administration of defendant's pharmaceutical).

189 See Treadwell Ford, Inc. v. Campbell, 485 So.2d 312, 317–18 (Ala. 1986).

190 See Lowe v. General Motors Corp., 624 F.2d 1373, 1380 (5th Cir. 1980) (Ala. law).

191 See Allen v. Delchamps, Inc., 624 So.2d 1065 (Ala. 1993) (sale of celery hearts treated with sodium bisulfite in violation of FDA regulation).

192 Byrne v. SCM Corp., 538 N.E.2d 796, 813 (Ill. App. Ct. 1989).

193 See Kaltman v. All Am. Pest Control, Inc., 706 S.E.2d 864, 871–73 (Va. 2011).

194 See Treadwell Ford, Inc. v. Campbell, 485 So.2d 312, 317–18 (Ala. 1986).

195 See Keegan v. Joytech Int'l, Inc., 2002 WL 982643, at *5 (Cal. Ct. App. 2002).

196 See Hatch v. Ford Motor Co., 329 P.2d 605, 608 (Cal. Ct. App. 1958).

therein was breached.[197] Indeed, a court confronting a negligence per se claim sometimes may choose to reverse the normal duty-breach order of decisionmaking by first considering the issue of breach. If the statute was not breached, there is no reason to proceed to the sometimes more elusive task of applying the two-pronged duty test. Further, even if a plaintiff establishes that a statute was breached and meets the two-pronged test, so that it may be used to set the standard of care, the plaintiff still must also prove each of the other elements of a negligence claim.[198] So, a court will not apply a statutory standard if the violation was not a cause in fact,[199] or not a proximate cause,[200] of the plaintiff's harm. Moreover, application of the negligence per se doctrine to any particular case is discretionary, and a court usually should decline to adopt a statutory standard that is obsolete, arcane, trivial, amounts to little more than a general common-law rule of reasonable care, is otherwise vague and of little help to courts setting a standard of care in a particular situation,[201] or "if sufficient policy considerations militate against it."[202]

Licensing Statutes

Whether on grounds of proximate causation or scope of risk, a defendant's violation of a licensing statute generally does not amount to negligence per se.[203] Thus, a restaurant's failure to obtain an operating license from the health department, a drug manufacturer's failure to obtain proper FDA approval of a new drug or medical device,[204]

[197] See, e.g., Schmidt v. International Playthings LLC, 536 F. Supp. 3d 856, 918 (D.N.M. 2021) (Calico Critters Yellow Labrador Twins toy violated federal regulation banning toys with small parts that could choke young children); QashQeesh v. Monster Beverage Corp., 2020 WL 6544246, at *2 (S.D. Ohio 2020) (dead rodent in energy drink violated Ohio's Pure Food and Drug Law; negligence per se claim not abrogated by Ohio Product Liability Act); In re Meridia Prods. Liab. Litig., 328 F. Supp. 2d 791 (N.D. Ohio 2004).

[198] See, e.g., Gaines-Tabb v. ICI Explosives, USA, Inc., 160 F.3d 613, 622 (10th Cir. 1998) (Okla. law) ("The violation of a statute constitutes negligence per se only if the other elements of negligence are present.").

[199] See, e.g., Hughes v. Boston Scientific Corp., 631 F.3d 762, 776 (5th Cir. 2011) (Miss. law) (a "negligence claim, including one relying on the rule of negligence per se, can only succeed if the plaintiff can prove that the defendant's violation of a statute or regulation caused the plaintiff's injury"); Johnson v. Honeywell Int'l, Inc., 101 Cal. Rptr. 3d 726, 732 (Ct. App. 2009) (under negligence per se, "[t]he plaintiff still has the burden of proving causation"); Alexander v. Smith & Nephew, P.L.C., 98 F. Supp. 2d 1310, 1319–20 (N.D. Okla. 2000) (negligence per se claim failed in part on causation grounds because plaintiff's orthopedic surgeon knew that medical device had not been approved for inserting bone screws in vertebral pedicles but relied on his own judgment in recommending the surgery).

[200] See, e.g., Walcott v. Total Petroleum, Inc., 964 P.2d 609, 611–13 (Colo. App. 1998) (gas station's sale of gasoline in paper cup to customer not proximate cause of injuries to person on whom customer threw gasoline to set on fire); Gaines-Tabb v. ICI Explosives, USA, Inc., 160 F.3d 613, 623 (10th Cir. 1998) (Okla. law) (defendants' manufacture and sale of ammonium nitrate used by terrorists to bomb federal building in Oklahoma City was not the proximate cause of the injuries because of "the intervention of a supervening cause—the unforeseeable, nearly unprecedented, criminal bombing of the Murrah Building. Absent proximate cause there can be no negligence, *per se* or otherwise.").

[201] See, e.g., In re Shigellosis Litig., 647 N.W.2d 1 (Minn. Ct. App. 2002) (no negligence per se in food poisoning case for violation of federal Food, Drug, and Cosmetic Act prohibition against sale of adulterated food because act fails to particularize any affirmative standard of care); Jones v. GMRI, Inc., 551 S.E.2d 867, 873 (N.C. Ct. App. 2001) (same—metal in meatball; state pure food act); Sikora v. Wenzel, 727 N.E.2d 1277, 1280 (Ohio 2000) (negligence per se applies where statute sets out a "positive and definite standard of care" but not where it "contains a general, abstract description of a duty").

[202] McNeil Pharm. v. Hawkins, 686 A.2d 567, 579 (D.C. 1996).

[203] See Prosser and Keeton on Torts § 36, at 226; Gregory, Breach of Criminal Licensing Statutes in Civil Litigation, 36 Cornell L.Q. 622, 630–42 (1951).

[204] See, e.g., King v. Danek Med., Inc., 37 S.W.3d 429, 453–60 (Tenn. Ct. App. 2000) (pedicle screws sold for unapproved purposes; FDA pre-marketing approval regulations are administrative in nature and do not establish a standard of care or quality). See generally Beck and Valentine, Challenging the Viability of FDCA-Based Causes of Action in the Tort Context: The Orthopedic Bone Screw Experience, 55 Food & Drug L.J. 389 (2000).

or an aircraft manufacturer's failure to obtain proper certification from the FAA for a new airplane, each may subject the manufacturer to administrative penalty, but none of these violations converts the defendant into an outlaw subject to absolute liability. Food sold by an unlicensed restaurant may be just as tasty and pure as food sold by a restaurant that licensing officials grade as "A"; a drug or medical device may be reasonably safe without approval for use by the FDA; and an uncertified plane may be entirely airworthy and equally as safe as one approved by the FAA. In such cases, a plaintiff may not rest upon the defendant's violation of a certification rule but must prove the defendant's negligence another way.[205]

Excuses

Treating a defendant's violation of a statute as a breach of duty amounts to a form of "strict" liability: liability flows merely from the defendant's breach of statute rather than from particularized proof of how the defendant was at fault. That is, a plaintiff may establish a breach of the duty of care without specific evidence showing how the defendant's actions were unreasonable—how they foreseeably exposed the plaintiff to an undue risk of harm.[206] Yet this strictness in the basis of liability usually is fleeting, for courts normally set liability back on a fault foundation by providing a broad range of excuses covering most situations in which a defendant could not reasonably have avoided the violation or the harm.[207] Many courts accept the list of statutory violation excuses set forth in the *Restatement (Second) of Torts*, which relieves a defendant of liability in negligence for violating a statute or administrative regulation if the violation is due to the defendant's incapacity, unawareness of a need for compliance,[208] inability to comply,[209] an emergency not due to the defendant's own misconduct, or if compliance would have presented a greater risk of harm than violation.[210] While these traditional negligence per se excuses may not be relevant to most products liability litigation,[211]

Breaches of federal statutes and regulations also raise issues of federal preemption. See § 14.5, below.

[205] See, e.g., *King*, above note 204; Keegan v. Joytech Int'l, Inc., 2002 WL 982643 (Cal. Ct. App. 2002) (paraplegic truck driver's violation of special licensing statute).

[206] See, e.g., Adamany v. Cub Cadet Corp., 2005 WL 1167913, at *4 (W.D. Wis. 2005) ("In strict liability, or negligence per se, the plaintiff need not prove fault; '[t]he focus in negligence per se is on the condition of the product, i.e., on the results of the defendant's actions.' "); Ross Labs. v. Thies, 725 P.2d 1076, 1081 (Alaska 1986) (retailer's unknowing violation of misbranding provisions of state food, drug, and cosmetic act: "the basis for the retailer's liability perhaps could as aptly be called strict liability per se"). See also Elliott v. City of N.Y., 747 N.E.2d 760, 762 (N.Y. 2001) (observing that violation of statute that creates specific duty "constitutes negligence per se, or may even create absolute liability").

[207] See Wing v. U-Haul Int'l, Inc., 2020 WL 773474, at *4–5 (Ariz. Ct. App. 2020); Sikora v. Wenzel, 727 N.E.2d 1277, 1281 (Ohio 2000); Prosser and Keeton on Torts § 36, at 227–29; Dobbs, Law of Torts §§ 140 and 141. And sometimes courts simply refuse to apply negligence per se.

[208] See, e.g., Sikora v. Wenzel, 727 N.E.2d 1277, 1280 (Ohio 2000). Compare In re: 3M Combat Arms Earplug Prods. Liab. Litig., 2021 WL 2186831, at *2 (N.D. Fla. 2021) (granting plaintiff JMOL on defendants' "excuse" defense to negligence per se claim; no evidence defendants should not have known that EPA regulations or the Noise Control Act applied to combat earplugs); Dura Corp. v. Harned, 703 P.2d 396 (Alaska 1985) (manufacturer's ignorance of standards of nationally recognized safety code no excuse).

[209] See, e.g., Roth v. I & M Rail Link, L.L.C., 179 F. Supp. 2d 1054, 1063 (S.D. Iowa 2001) (impossibility of compliance, meaning "not reasonably practicable").

[210] See Rest. (2d) Torts § 288A.

[211] See Products Liability Rest. § 4, cmt. *d*.

they sometimes are germane,[212] in which case they should be available as in any other context.[213]

Procedural Effect

Jurisdictions vary in the procedural effect they accord to a statutory or regulatory violation.[214] Some courts, possibly a majority,[215] hold that such a violation conclusively establishes the defendant's negligence—that an unexcused violation of a statute or regulation is negligence in itself, or negligence "per se."[216] While such a procedural effect powerfully stamps the violation as a breach of duty as a matter of law, it nevertheless leaves open all other issues involved in negligence claims, such as cause in fact, proximate cause, the plaintiff's damage, and any affirmative defenses that might apply.[217] Many other jurisdictions treat a violation merely as evidence of negligence,[218] perhaps the best approach,[219] which the trier of fact may accept or reject as it sees fit.[220] In a small number of jurisdictions, by common law or statute, a violation of a safety statute or regulation creates a rebuttable presumption of negligence.[221] And some jurisdictions that give conclusive status to violations of a legislature's statutes give a

---

[212] As when a drug's or other chemical's risk is unforeseeable.

[213] See D'Angelo, Effect of Compliance or Noncompliance with Applicable Governmental Product Safety Regulations on a Determination of Product Defect, 36 S. Tex. L. Rev. 453 (1995).

[214] See Prosser and Keeton on Torts § 36, at 229–31.

[215] Commentators long have asserted that the conclusive effect proclaimed by Judge Cardozo in Martin v. Herzog, 126 N.E. 814, 815 (N.Y. 1920), that "jurors have no . . . power . . . [to] relax" the standard set by the legislature, is the majority rule. See, e.g., Note, Products Liability Based Upon Violation of Statutory Standards, 64 Mich. L. Rev. 1388, 1393–94 (1966) (citing sources mostly prior to 1950). See also Rest. (3d) Torts: Liability for Physical and Emotional Harm § 14 Reporters' Note to cmt. *c* (*Martin*'s conclusive effect approach is "the strong majority rule"). Yet, because of the different meanings of the phrase "negligence per se," and because many of the more recent cases treat statutory violations as mere evidence of negligence, it is unclear whether most jurisdictions still treat the violation of statute as conclusive of negligence.

[216] See, e.g., RLI Ins. Co. v. Union Pac. R.R., 463 F. Supp. 2d 646, 650 n.2 (S.D. Tex. 2006) ("Negligence per se is the unexcused violation of a penal statute designed to protect the class of persons to which the injured party belongs, establishing negligence as a matter of law.") (dictum); Stanton v. Astra Pharm. Prods., Inc., 718 F.2d 553, 564–65 (3d Cir. 1983) (Pa. law) (Becker, J.); Harned v. Dura Corp., 665 P.2d 5, 12–13 (Alaska 1983) (failure of tank to conform to ASME standards, incorporated into state law, was negligence per se). This is the rule of Rest. (2d) Torts § 288B.

[217] See Anchundia v. Northeast Utils. Serv. Co., 2010 WL 2400154, at *4 (E.D.N.Y. 2010) ("Under Connecticut law, negligence per se . . . enables plaintiffs to establish as a matter of law that the defendant's conduct constituted a breach of duty, so that only causation and damages need be proved."); Solo v. Trus Joist MacMillan, 2004 WL 524898, at *6 n.8 (D. Minn. 2004) (" '[N]egligence per se, however, is not liability per se. There remain (the defenses of) assumption of risk, contributory negligence and proximate cause. . . .' "); Prosser and Keeton on Torts § 36, at 229–31.

[218] See, e.g., Berish v. Bornstein, 770 N.E.2d 961, 979 (Mass. 2002); King v. Danek Med., Inc., 37 S.W.3d 429 (Tenn. Ct. App. 2000); Horstmeyer v. Golden Eagle Fireworks, 534 N.W.2d 835 (N.D. 1995).

[219] According a breach of statute any greater weight confronts a number of theoretical obstacles. See Prosser and Keeton on Torts § 36, at 220–22.

[220] Compare Bausch v. Stryker Corp., 630 F.3d 546, 553 (7th Cir. 2010) (Ill. law) ("Illinois treats a violation of a statute or ordinance designed to protect human life or property as prima facie evidence of negligence, though the violation may not always be conclusive on the issue of negligence.").

[221] See, e.g., Ramirez v. Plough, Inc., 863 P.2d 167, 172 (Cal. 1993) (dictum; citing evidence code); Klanseck v. Anderson Sales & Serv., Inc., 393 N.W.2d 356 (Mich. 1986). Or "prima facie" evidence thereof, raising such a presumption but allowing an excuse. See, e.g., Magna Trust Co. v. Illinois Cent. R.R. Co., 728 N.E.2d 797, 804–05 (Ill. App. Ct. 2000) ("Since the violation is only *prima facie* evidence of negligence, a defendant may prevail by showing that he acted reasonably under the circumstances."); Bacon v. Lascelles, 678 A.2d 902 (Vt. 1996). See also Colo. Rev. Stat. Ann. § 13–21–403(2) (rebuttable presumption); Kan. Stat. Ann. § 60–3304(b) (product deemed defective unless manufacturer shows violation was reasonably prudent action). The rebuttable presumption approach is further discussed at § 14.4, below.

lesser, mere-evidence effect to violations of a city's ordinances[222] or regulations of administrative agencies,[223] both considered "subordinate rule-making bod[ies]."[224]

Federal Law and Federal Courts

Negligence per se claims, being creatures of state tort law, must be distinguished from the federal doctrine prescribing when a private cause of action may be implied in a federal statute.[225] More narrow than negligence per se, the federal implication doctrine allows private claims only when Congress clearly so intended.[226] While the federal implication doctrine may be its cousin, negligence per se is an independent, substantive doctrine of state tort law applicable in both state courts[227] and federal diversity actions[228]

---

[222] See, e.g., Elliott v. City of N.Y., 747 N.E.2d 760 (N.Y. 2001).

[223] See, e.g., Montalvo v. Rheem Textile Sys., Inc., 1991 WL 52777 (S.D.N.Y. 1991) (violation of state workplace safety agency regulation requiring that presses be equipped with, and operable by, two separate push-buttons was merely evidence of negligent design; not conclusive).

[224] See Elliott v. City of N.Y., 747 N.E.2d 760, 762 (N.Y. 2001) (citing, *inter alia*, Martin v. Herzog, 126 N.E. 814 (N.Y. 1920)). See generally Prosser and Keeton on Torts § 36, at 231.

[225] See Sherman, Use of Federal Statutes in State Negligence Per Se Actions, 13 Whittier L. Rev. 831 (1992).

[226] "Like substantive federal law itself, private rights of action to enforce federal law must be created by Congress. The judicial task is to interpret the statute Congress has passed to determine whether it displays an intent to create not just a private right but also a private remedy. Statutory intent on this latter point is determinative. Without it, a cause of action does not exist and courts may not create one, no matter how desirable that might be as a policy matter, or how compatible with the statute." Alexander v. Sandoval, 532 U.S. 275, 286–87 (2001) (describing how implication doctrine narrowed from J.I. Case Co. v. Borak, 377 U.S. 426, 433 (1964), to Cort v. Ash, 422 U.S. 66, 78 (1975), to 2001). *Cort*'s four-factor test has effectively been conflated back into the one determinative factor of Congressional intent. See Jackson v. Birmingham Bd. of Educ., 309 F.3d 1333, 1338 n.5 (11th Cir. 2002), rev'd and remanded on other grounds, 544 U.S. 167 (2005).

See, e.g., In re Cook Med., Inc., IVC Filters Mktg., Sales Practices & Prod. Liab. Litig., 2017 WL 6816861, at *1 (S.D. Ind. 2017) (negligence per se claim failed; no private right of action under the Food, Drug, and Cosmetic Act); Martin v. Ortho Pharm., Corp., 661 N.E.2d 352 (Ill. 1996) (disallowing claim for violation of FDA consumer warnings regulation on risk of birth limb reductions from pills used in first trimester of pregnancy). Compare Swenson v. Emerson Elec. Co., 374 N.W.2d 690 (Minn. 1985) (allowing private claim for violation of CPSC's substantial product hazard reporting regulations), with Drake v. Honeywell, Inc., 797 F.2d 603 (8th Cir. 1986) (*contra*). See Comment, 70 Minn. L. Rev. 955 (1986) (private claims under reporting rules of CPSC). See also National Bank of Commerce v. Kimberly-Clark Corp., 38 F.3d 988 (8th Cir. 1994) (allowing warning defect claim under Medical Device Amendments for woman's death by toxic shock syndrome).

[227] See, e.g., Mize v. Mentor Worldwide LLC, 265 Cal. Rptr. 3d 468, 481 (Cal. Ct. App. 2020) ("Federal statutes, such as the FDCA or MDA, and federal regulations, such as those imposed by the FDA, may provide the applicable state standard of care . . . ."); Howard v. Zimmer, Inc., 299 P.3d 463 (Okla. 2013) (allowing negligence per se claim for violation of FDA regulation under Medical Device Amendments to FDCA); Nissan Motor Co. v. Armstrong, 32 S.W.3d 701, 711 (Tex. App. 2000) (car manufacturer's failure to report safety defect under federal law; dictum), rev'd on other grounds, 145 S.W.3d 131 (Tex. 2004); Wallace v. Parks Corp., 629 N.Y.S.2d 570, 575–76 (App. Div. 1995) (notwithstanding federal preemption of inadequate warning claims, negligence claim allowed for violating labeling requirements of Federal Hazardous Substances Act).

[228] Milanese v. Rust-Oleum Corp., 244 F.3d 104, 109–10 (2d Cir. 2001) (N.Y. law) (allowing negligent "misbranding" claim for violating labeling requirements of Federal Hazardous Substances Act, although federal preemption precluded claim that manufacturer should have provided warnings additional to those required by Act); Loewy v. Stuart Drug & Surgical Supply, Inc., 1999 WL 216656 (S.D.N.Y. 1999) (pedicle screw case; violation of Medical Device Amendments to Federal Food, Drug, and Cosmetic Act); Stanton v. Astra Pharm. Prods., Inc., 718 F.2d 553, 564 (3d Cir. 1983) (Pa. law) (Becker, J.) (failure to file adverse reaction reports required by FDA regulation).

Many courts disagree, mistakenly believing that to allow such state law claims, even in a diversity action, is somehow inconsistent with a ruling that the statute does not allow a private right of action under the implication doctrine as a matter of federal law. See, e.g., Rimbert v. Eli Lilly & Co., 577 F. Supp. 2d 1174, 1239–40 (D.N.M. 2008) (granting summary judgment to defendant on negligence per se claim for alleged FDCA violation); Hackett v. G.D. Searle & Co., 246 F. Supp. 2d 591, 594 (W.D. Tex. 2002) (because FDCA does not provide for private claims, many courts hold plaintiffs cannot enforce act via negligence per se claims); Rodriguez v. American Cyanamid Co., 858 F. Supp. 127, 129–31 (D. Ariz. 1994) (exploding bug bombs; failure to comply with adverse incidents reporting requirements of FIFRA; negligence per se claim disallowed for not

for violations of both state[229] and federal[230] statutes and regulations, regardless of whether the implication doctrine would also allow a private claim.[231] If the negligence per se issue concerns a federal statute or regulation, an important additional issue will be whether the federal law preempts the claim for negligence per se together with some or all of the plaintiff's other products liability claims.[232]

Compatibility with Ordinary Negligence Claims

Finally, it is important to note that, while negligence per se and ordinary negligence claims are separate and independent, the two are quite compatible. Indeed, plaintiffs typically and properly include counts for both ordinary negligence and negligence per se in the same complaint, and a plaintiff may prevail by establishing the defendant's breach of its duty of care on either form of negligence claim.[233]

---

meeting standards for implying cause of action into statute). See generally Beck and Valentine, Challenging the Viability of FDCA-Based Causes of Action in the Tort Context: The Orthopedic Bone Screw Experience, 55 Food & Drug L.J. 389 (2000).

These courts and commentators miss the point: that negligence per se, as a matter of state common-law doctrine, borrows the standard of proper behavior from a state or federal statute, not because the legislature intended to create a private cause of action for breach of the statute, but because the more specific standard of behavior specified in a statute may provide a better standard of conduct for a court to employ in a negligence case than the general tort law standard of reasonable prudence. See, e.g., Lowe v. General Motors Corp., 624 F.2d 1373, 1381 (5th Cir. 1980) (Ala. law) (violation of federal automotive safety statute in diversity action was negligence per se; because no private right of action or federal question was involved, "*Cort v. Ash* was not at all at issue in this case").

The case law on this point is split and decidedly confused. For lists of state court decisions allowing and disallowing negligence per se claims for violations of FDCA provisions and FDA regulations, see In re Allergan Biocell Textured Breast Implant Prods. Liab. Litig., 537 F. Supp. 3d 679, 714–15 (D.N.J. 2021) . See generally James, Statutory Standards and Negligence in Accident Cases, 11 La. L. Rev. 95, 106 (1950–51); Thayer, Public Wrong and Private Action, 27 Harv. L. Rev. 317, 322 (1913).

[229] See, e.g., Gaines-Tabb v. ICI Explosives, USA, Inc., 160 F.3d 613, 623 (10th Cir. 1998) (Okla. law) (state statute and regulations governing sale of explosives; by implication); Montalvo v. Rheem Textile Sys., Inc., 1991 WL 52777 (S.D.N.Y. 1991) (state workplace safety agency regulation requiring presses to be equipped with, and operable by, two separate push-buttons).

[230] See, e.g., Schmidt v. Int'l Playthings LLC, 536 F. Supp. 3d 856, 918 (D.N.M. 2021) (manufacturer violated CPSC regulation banning toys with small parts that could choke young children); Howard v. Zimmer, Inc., 299 P.3d 463 (Okla. 2013) (FDA regulation under Medical Device Amendments); Sharp v. Artifex, Ltd., 110 F. Supp. 2d 388 (W.D. Pa. 1999) (violations of FDCA and MDA by pedicle screw manufacturer).

[231] "The mere fact that the law which evidences negligence is Federal while the negligence action itself is brought under State common law does not mean that the state law claim metamorphoses into a private right of action under Federal regulatory law." Lowe v. General Motors Corp., 624 F.2d 1373, 1379 (5th Cir. 1980) (Ala. law) (violation of Motor Vehicle Safety Act provisions governing automotive recalls). See also In re StarLink Corn Prods. Liab. Litig., 212 F. Supp. 2d 828, 836 (N.D. Ill. 2002) (violation of FIFRA labeling requirements could support negligence per se claims even though there is no federal private right of action under statute).

[232] The doctrine of federal preemption is examined in § 14.5, below. Negligence per se damages claims for breach of federal statutes and regulations may be entirely proper "parallel claims" under federal preemption law. See, e.g., In re Allergan Biocell Textured Breast Implant Prods. Liab. Litig., 537 F. Supp. 3d 679, 715 (D.N.J. 2021) ("[T]he FDCA and the FDA regulations may set the basis for Plaintiffs' negligence *per se* claims. Because Plaintiffs' negligence *per se* claims 'invoke the statutory violations to prove defendants' liability for a separate underlying tort,' instead of 'contending the violations themselves form a cause of action,' they are not impliedly preempted.") (citing cases in accord and contra) (emphasis in original). *But see* Heath v. C.R. Bard Inc., 2021 WL 3172315, at *10 (M.D. Tenn. 2021) (a "number of courts . . . have held that [21 U.S.C. § 337] impliedly preempts state-law negligence per se claims based on FDCA violations").

[233] Because a court may deny a negligence per se claim or find an applicable excuse, a plaintiff's lawyer normally should also include an additional claim for ordinary negligence in the complaint.

Compliance with Statutory Standards—Evidence of Due Care

Since a manufacturer or other product seller may be found negligent per se if it *violates* an applicable product safety statute or regulation, such a defendant might fairly ask to be shielded from negligence liability if it *complies* with an applicable safety statute or regulation.[234] Yet, because "the lawmaking process can sometimes be insufficiently attentive to the interests of potential victims,"[235] a product seller's compliance with a statutory or regulatory safety standard in a negligence action is proper evidence of reasonable care but is not conclusive of that issue.[236] In very unusual situations, where no special circumstances suggest the need for greater caution, a court may rule that a defendant's conformity to a statutory or regulatory safety standard amounts to due care as a matter of law.[237] A few state products liability reform statutes provide that compliance with a statute or regulation raises a rebuttable presumption that a manufacturer was not negligent.[238] In the great majority of cases, however, because legislatures and regulatory agencies normally set criminal safety standards at minimally acceptable levels, a jury is free to find that a manufacturer was negligent for failing to take further steps to improve a product's design,[239] manufacture,[240] or warnings[241] beyond the level of safety prescribed by a legislature or by an administrative

---

[234] See Tobias, FDA Regulatory Compliance Reconsidered, 93 Cornell L. Rev. 1003, 1025–27 (2008) (listing states that have adopted some form of regulatory compliance defense); Symposium, Regulatory Compliance as a Defense to Products Liability, 88 Geo. L.J. 2049 (2000); Ausness, The Case for a "Strong" Regulatory Compliance Defense, 55 Md. L. Rev. 1210, 1241–47 (1996); D'Angelo, Effect of Compliance and Noncompliance with Applicable Governmental Product Safety Regulations on a Determination of Product Defect, 36 S. Tex. L. Rev. 453 (1995).

[235] Rest. (3d) Torts: Liability for Physical and Emotional Harm § 16 cmt. *b*. See Schwartz, The Role of Federal Safety Regulations in Products Liability Actions, 41 Vand. L. Rev. 1121 (1988).

[236] "[C]ompliance with a statutory standard is evidence of due care, [but] it is not conclusive on the issue. Such a standard is no more than a minimum, and it does not necessarily preclude a finding that the actor was negligent in failing to take additional precautions." Prosser and Keeton on Torts § 36, at 233; Rest. (3d) Torts: Liability for Physical and Emotional Harm § 16 cmt. *b* ("compliance is evidence of non-negligence but is not conclusive"). "In modern years, the rule has been frequently applied in products-liability cases where the defendant has complied with a federal regulatory standard." Rest. (3d) Torts: Liability for Physical and Emotional Harm § 16 Reporters' Note to cmt. *b*.

[237] See, e.g., Ramirez v. Plough, Inc., 863 P.2d 167, 172, 176–77 (Cal. 1993) (compliance with FDA's English-language-only warning requirement shielded drug manufacturer from also having to warn in Spanish that giving aspirin to children suffering flu might cause Reyes Syndrome); Beatty v. Trailmaster Prods., Inc., 625 A.2d 1005 (Md. 1993) (compliance with bumper height statute was complete defense). See Rest. (3d) Torts: Liability for Physical and Emotional Harm § 16 cmt. *e* (in "unusual situations," statutory or regulatory compliance may be conclusive).

[238] See, e.g., Colo. Rev. Stat. Ann. § 13–21–403(1); Ind. Code Ann. § 34–20–5–1. Compare Utah Code Ann. § 78B–6–703(2) (presumption of nondefectiveness).

[239] See, e.g., Kagan v. Harley Davidson, Inc., 2008 WL 3874824, at *14 n.31 (E.D. Pa. 2008) ("compliance with motor vehicle safety standards does not eliminate common law liability"); Brooks v. Beech Aircraft Corp., 902 P.2d 54, 63 (N.M. 1995) (crashworthiness of aircraft design; evidence of defendant's compliance with applicable government regulations is relevant to whether it was negligent but does not conclusively establish its non-negligence).

[240] Cf. Reiter v. Zimmer Inc., 897 F. Supp. 154 (S.D.N.Y. 1995) (manufacturing procedures for prosthesis implant cement allegedly failed to meet FDA "good manufacturing processes").

[241] See, e.g., Caraker v. Sandoz Pharms. Corp., 172 F. Supp. 2d 1018, 1033 (S.D. Ill. 2001) ("the FDA's drug labeling decisions impose only 'minimum' standards that are open to supplementation by state law through a jury's verdict enforcing a manufacturer's common law duty to warn"); Ferebee v. Chevron Chem. Co., 736 F.2d 1529 (D.C. Cir. 1984) (Md. law) (EPA-approved label for paraquat herbicide, under Federal Insecticide, Fungicide, and Rodenticide Act); Burch v. Amsterdam Corp., 366 A.2d 1079 (D.C. 1976) (Federal Hazardous Substances Act labeling requirements); Stevens v. Parke, Davis & Co., 507 P.2d 653, 661 (Cal. 1973) (FDA warning requirements).

agency. The *Third Restatement of Torts* is in accord.[242] The general topic of compliance with governmental safety statutes and regulations is addressed later in depth as a matter of special defense.[243] Also examined later is the special defense of federal preemption,[244] a cousin to the compliance-with-statute defense.

§ 2.5 PROOF OF NEGLIGENCE—RES IPSA LOQUITUR

To establish a defendant's negligence, the plaintiff usually must prove, with specificity, the manner in which the defendant was negligent in making or selling the product that injured the plaintiff. Proof merely that a product malfunctioned and caused an accident usually does not suffice.[245] Thus, a plaintiff normally cannot make out a prima facie case if he or she fails to establish just *how* the defendant was negligent in making or selling a product, and just *how* that negligence caused the harm. Yet evidence of the defendant's negligence and causation may be unavailable through no fault of the plaintiff, as when the plaintiff encounters a bug[246] or a mouse[247] in his Coke or a toe in his chewing tobacco,[248] where circumstantial evidence surrounding the misadventure nevertheless may quite strongly suggest that the product's defective condition resulted from some negligent act or omission of the manufacturer or other supplier.[249] In situations like these, negligence law contains a doctrine of circumstantial evidence that allows a plaintiff to establish a prima facie case without direct evidence of how specifically the product failed or how the defendant may have been negligent—"res ipsa loquitur."

---

[242] Section 4(b) of the Products Liability Restatement provides that, in connection with liability for defective design and warning, "a product's compliance with an applicable product safety statute or administrative regulation is properly considered in determining whether the product is defective with respect to the risks sought to be reduced by the statute or regulation, but such compliance does not preclude as a matter of law a finding of product defect." While this provision is framed in terms of product defects, it draws from and embraces negligence claims as well. See § 4 cmt. *e* and Reporters' Note thereto.

Rest. (3d) Torts: Liability for Physical and Emotional Harm § 16(a), Statutory Compliance, provides:

> An actor's compliance with a pertinent statute, while evidence of nonnegligence, does not preclude a finding that the actor is negligent under § 3 for failing to adopt precautions in addition to those mandated by the statute.

[243] See § 14.4, below.

[244] See § 14.5, below.

[245] See Prosser and Keeton on Torts § 32, at 242; Dobbs, Law of Torts § 154, at 370.

[246] See, e.g., Oklahoma Coca-Cola Bottling Co. v. Newton, 237 P.2d 627 (Okla. 1951) (fly).

[247] See, e.g., Harris v. Coca-Cola Bottling Co., 183 N.E.2d 56 (Ill. App. Ct. 1962); Trembley v. Coca-Cola Bottling Co., 138 N.Y.S.2d 332 (App. Div. 1955); Moss v. Coca-Cola Bottling Co., 229 P.2d 802 (Cal. Ct. App. 1951). See generally Annot., 52 A.L.R.2d 117 (1957).

[248] "We can imagine no reason why, with ordinary care, human toes could not be left out of chewing tobacco, and if toes are found in chewing tobacco, it seems to us that somebody has been very careless." Pillars v. R.J. Reynolds Tobacco Co., 78 So. 365, 366 (Miss. 1918).

[249] "Some circumstantial evidence is very strong, as when you find a trout in the milk." Henry David Thoreau, in The Writings of Henry David Thoreau, Journal II 1850—September 18, 1851, 94 (Bradford Torrey ed., Houghton Mifflin & Co. 1906) (Nov. 1850 journal entry; where a trout in a can of milk indirectly but compellingly suggests that the dairy farmer diluted the milk by dipping the can into a trout stream, a recurring problem in the 1800s).

Res ipsa loquitur ("res ipsa") is an established doctrine of circumstantial evidence,[250] applied by name in nearly every state,[251] that may assist a plaintiff in proving a negligence claim in a products liability case, as in any other type of case.[252] The doctrine originated from a casual remark by Chief Baron Pollock during argument with counsel in *Byrne v. Boadle*,[253] where a pedestrian, hit on the head by a barrel of flour that rolled out of a second-story window over the defendant's shop beside the street where the plaintiff was walking, sought recovery from the defendant without introducing affirmative proof of how and why the barrel fell from the window. To the defendant's argument that the plaintiff's case must be dismissed because he failed to prove specifically how the defendant was negligent in allowing the barrel to tumble from the window, Chief Baron Pollock remarked, "res ipsa loquitur," the thing speaks for itself, and allowed the plaintiff's verdict. This remark promptly evolved into a full-blown doctrine[254]—that a plaintiff may establish a defendant's breach of duty indirectly, in situations where an accident's specific cause is unknown but where the circumstances indicate that some negligent act or omission by the defendant probably was its cause—a doctrine that was warmly embraced by the Anglo-American law of negligence.

Two years after *Byrne v. Boadle*, another English judge described the doctrine: "There must be reasonable evidence of negligence; but where the thing is shown to be under the management of the defendant or his servants, and the accident is such as in the ordinary course of things does not happen if those who have the management use proper care, it affords reasonable evidence, in the absence of explanation by the defendants, that the accident arose from want of care."[255] Plausible as this principle surely is, it has resulted in over a century and a half of complexity and confusion.[256]

Especially prior to development of the strict liability theories of products liability law in the 1960s, res ipsa served in certain cases as an important mechanism for unburdening plaintiffs from having to establish specifically how a manufacturer or other

---

[250] "The doctrine of res ipsa loquitur is neither procedural nor substantive, but 'only a shorthand expression for circumstantial proof of negligence—a rule of evidence.' " Waering v. BASF Corp., 146 F. Supp. 2d 675, 687 (M.D. Pa. 2001). See, e.g., Cambers v. Bureau Veritas N. Am., Inc., 2022 WL 198812, at *4 (D. Kan. 2022) (res ipsa "does not provide a basis for a separate cause of action, but rather it provides a method of proving a negligence claim"); Stagg-Shehadeh v. LPM Mfg., Inc., 2021 WL 2405605, at *13 (S.D. Tex. 2021) ("Res ipsa loquitur is not a rule of substantive law but a rule of evidence."). See Prosser and Keeton on Torts §§ 39 and 40; Dobbs, Law of Torts §§ 154–61; 4 Harper, James, and Gray, Law of Torts § 19.5–.12; Cal. Evid. Code § 646; Rest. (2d) Torts § 328D. See also 9 Wigmore, Evidence § 2509 (3d ed. 1940); 2 McCormick on Evidence § 342.

[251] South Carolina prides itself in eschewing the doctrine by name while applying similar principles of circumstantial evidence. Compare Legette v. Smith, 220 S.E.2d 429 (S.C. 1975) (rejecting doctrine), with McQuillen v. Dobbs, 204 S.E.2d 732 (S.C. 1974) (applying similar circumstantial evidence principles).

[252] See generally Kahn and Lopatka, Res Ipsa Loquitur: Reducing Confusion or Creating Bias?, 108 Ky. L.J. 239 (2020); Hoffman, Res Ipsa Loquitur And Indeterminate Product Defects: If They Speak For Themselves, What Are They Saying?, 36 S. Tex. L. Rev. 353 (1995); Frumer, Friedman, and Sklaren, Products Liability § 10.04; Am. Law Prod. Liab. §§ 15:01 et seq. For a discussion of the "malfunction doctrine" (perhaps "*defect* ipsa loquitur"), a parallel theory of proof in strict products liability, see § 7.4, below.

[253] (1863) 159 Eng. Rep. 299 (Exch. Div.). See also Prosser and Keeton on Torts § 39, at 243; Dobbs, Law of Torts § 154, at 372.

[254] *But see* Jackson v. Millar, 1 S.C.R. 225, 235–36 (Can. 1975) (not a "doctrine"); Ballard v. North British Ry. Co., 1923 S.L.T. 2197 (Scot. 1923) (Lord Shaw) ("If that phrase had not been in Latin, nobody would have called it a principle.").

[255] Scott v. London & St. Katherine Docks Co., (1865) 159 Eng. Rep. 665, 667 (Exch. Div.) (Erle, C.J.).

[256] Res ipsa loquitur is "a thing of fearful and wonderful complexity and ramifications, and the problems of its application and effect have filled the courts of all our states with a multitude of decisions, baffling and perplexing alike to students, attorneys and judges." Prosser, Res Ipsa Loquitur in California, 37 Cal. L. Rev. 183, 183 (1949).

supplier had been negligent in the production or sale of a defective product. Particularly where an obviously bad product caused injury, res ipsa provided a bridge between the difficulties of proving negligence by direct evidence and modern products liability claims based on product defect that relieve a plaintiff (at least in theory) from having to prove a manufacturer's fault. A prime example is *Escola v. Coca Cola Bottling Co.*,[257] a negligence case against the bottler by a waitress injured when a bottle of Coke exploded in her hand. Today, *Escola* is remembered for Justice Traynor's renowned concurring opinion in which he outlined the various reasons for favoring a rule of "absolute liability" for manufacturers of defective products,[258] reasons that provided a foundation for his opinion for the court in *Greenman v. Yuba Power Products, Inc.*,[259] nearly two decades later.[260] Now largely forgotten is the fact that the *Escola* majority, on the basis of res ipsa loquitur, upheld a judgment for the waitress despite her inability to prove specifically how the defendant bottler may have been negligent.[261] With the advent of strict products liability in tort and warranty, and strict liability's parallel "malfunction doctrine" in particular,[262] the importance of res ipsa in products liability law has diminished considerably. Nevertheless, res ipsa loquitur remains a valid doctrine that plaintiffs continue to plead and with which they continue to win products liability claims.

Limitations

Certain attributes of res ipsa limit its applicability. First, the doctrine applies only when the circumstances of an accident are mysterious and unknown. That is, there is neither need nor room for a doctrine of circumstantial evidence designed to allow plausible guesses as to how an accident occurred where direct evidence reveals with specificity all pertinent facts—to wit, how the product was defective, how the defendant was blameworthy in allowing the defect to occur, and how the defect caused the plaintiff's injury. So, though many courts allow a plaintiff to rely on res ipsa even when the plaintiff pleads and offers specific evidence on negligence and causation—particularized proof on how and why a product accident occurred[263]—the need for res ipsa vanishes, like a bat in the light, once a plaintiff's evidence specifically and fully explains how the product failed and particularizes reasonable steps the defendant could have taken to prevent the failure.[264] Frequently, however, a plaintiff's proof of how an accident occurred will not be specific and complete, in which case the plaintiff should be entitled to rely upon res ipsa in addition to more specific proof.[265]

---

[257] 150 P.2d 436 (Cal. 1944).

[258] Id. at 440.

[259] 377 P.2d 897 (Cal. 1963).

[260] See § 5.2, below.

[261] See 150 P.2d at 438.

[262] See § 7.4, below.

[263] See, e.g., Weyerhaeuser Co. v. Thermogas Co., 620 N.W.2d 819, 831 (Iowa 2000). See generally Frumer, Friedman, and Sklaren, Products Liability § 10.04[4].

[264] See, e.g., White v. Mazda Motor of Am., Inc., 313 Conn. 610, 99 A.3d 1079, 1091 (Conn. 2014) (a "res ipsa loquitur instruction is not appropriate [when] the plaintiff is not relying solely on circumstantial evidence, but instead alleges and introduces into evidence specific acts of negligence by the defendant"); Stahlecker v. Ford Motor Co., 667 N.W.2d 244, 252 (Neb. 2003) ("if specific acts of negligence are alleged or there is direct evidence of the precise cause of the accident, . . . res ipsa loquitur is not applicable"); Dover Elevator Co. v. Swann, 638 A.2d 762 (Md. 1994) (res ipsa inapplicable where plaintiff's expert fully explained why elevator misleveled). See Prosser and Keeton on Torts at 260; Dobbs, Law of Torts at 372 and 387.

[265] See, e.g., Weyerhaeuser Co. v. Thermogas Co., 620 N.W.2d 819, 830 (Iowa 2000) (specific negligence and res ipsa may be pleaded and submitted to jury in the alternative).

Second, it should be stressed that res ipsa loquitur normally is little more than an application of ordinary principles of circumstantial evidence to the accident law context, albeit in crystallized form tailored to the law of negligence.[266] The principal benefit of res ipsa is to supply the plaintiff a method of circumstantial proof from which a jury may infer the defendant's breach of duty. While causation also is frequently established by the res ipsa inferences,[267] a plaintiff relying on the doctrine still has the burden of proving, in a large majority of states, *all* the elements of a negligence case—the defendant's duty, breach, cause in fact, proximate cause, and damage.[268] That is, as discussed below, the procedural effect of res ipsa in most jurisdictions is merely to provide evidence of one or two elements of negligence—breach of duty and possibly cause in fact—which a jury may accept or reject as it sees fit.

Third, one should remember that res ipsa loquitur is a rule of *negligence*, not strict products liability, such that the inferences (or presumptions) must point to a probability that defendant was *negligent* in allowing a product to become defective, not merely that the product was defective.[269] So, the doctrine may establish both defect and causation in addition to negligence when a product's failure destroys evidence of its cause—as when a fire in a new car's engine compartment burns up all the wires and electrical equipment. And the doctrine will operate just as well when it establishes negligence alone because the product's defect is crystal clear but the origin of the defect is a matter of conjecture—as when a mouse shows up in a bottle of Coke.[270] In either case, what must be inferred is the defendant's *negligence* in allowing the defect into the product and in selling it in that condition. And proof of a product defect alone simply will not suffice.[271]

Elements

Although res ipsa loquitur is not a cause of action but merely a method of proof, it nevertheless has two or three definite elements. Most traditional formulations of res ipsa in America derive from the first edition of *Wigmore on Evidence*, which divided the doctrine into three elements:

> (1) the event must be of a kind which ordinarily does not occur in the absence of someone's negligence; (2) it must be caused by an agency or instrumentality within the exclusive control of the defendant; and (3) it must not have been due to any voluntary action or contribution on the part of the plaintiff.[272]

---

[266] See, e.g., Waering v. BASF Corp., 146 F. Supp. 2d 675, 687 (M.D. Pa. 2001); Weyerhaeuser Co. v. Thermogas Co., 620 N.W.2d 819, 831 (Iowa 2000). See generally Prosser and Keeton on Torts § 39.

[267] See, e.g., Knight v. Just Born, Inc., 2000 WL 924624, at *13 (D. Or. 2000) (allowing res ipsa for both negligence and causation); Dover Elevator Co. v. Swann, 638 A.2d 762, 765 (Md. 1994) ("Res ipsa loquitur is 'merely a short way of saying that the circumstances attendant upon an accident are themselves of such a character as to justify a [court or] jury in inferring negligence as the cause of that accident.' "). See generally Prosser and Keeton on Torts § 39, 247–48.

[268] See, e.g., Dover Elevator Co. v. Swann, 638 A.2d 762, 765 (Md. 1994); Rest. (2d) Torts § 328D(1) and cmt. *e*.

[269] See, e.g., Olshansky v. Rehrig Int'l, 872 A.2d 282 (R.I. 2005). *But see* Lawson v. Mitsubishi Motor Sales of Am., Inc., 938 So.2d 35, 46–49 (La. 2006); Parsons v. Ford Motor Co., 85 S.W.3d 323, 331 (Tex. App. 2002) ("The doctrine of res ipsa loquitur can apply to both negligence and strict liability cases to provide a presumption of product defect and causation.").

[270] See note 247, above.

[271] A closely similar principle of circumstantial evidence, tailored to proof of *strict* products liability, which might well be called *defect* ipsa loquitur, is often labeled the "malfunction doctrine." See § 7.4, below.

[272] See 4 Wigmore, Evidence § 2509 (1st ed. 1905), quoted in Prosser and Keeton on Torts 244. See also 9 Wigmore, Evidence § 2509 (3d ed. 1940); 2 McCormick on Evidence § 342.

In order, these elements raise inferences (1) that *someone* was negligent; (2) that the someone was the *defendant*; and (3) that the someone was *not* the *plaintiff*. In combination, these elements mean that a plaintiff may rely on res ipsa where the circumstances suggest that an accident probably resulted from the defendant's negligence, and not from the actions of the plaintiff or another.

Recently, however, prompted by the widespread adoption of comparative fault, many courts have eliminated the third element—an element that suggests an absence of the plaintiff's contributory fault. Thus, though many courts continue to define the doctrine in terms of the traditional three elements,[273] sounder formulations of res ipsa today limit the essential elements to the first two, as discussed below. In terms of inferences, these elements establish that the accident probably resulted from someone's negligence, and that the negligent actor probably was the defendant.[274] Whether the elements of res ipsa loquitur are established in any given case, and whether the doctrine otherwise applies to the facts, are said to be questions of law for the court.[275]

It is sometimes said that res ipsa, which provides an incentive for a defendant to come forward with evidence of how an accident occurred, cannot be applied unless the plaintiff shows that the evidence is more accessible to the defendant than to the plaintiff.[276] It is true enough that providing such an incentive to defendants is one secondary function of the doctrine.[277] Yet few courts today explicitly treat this secondary purpose as a formal requirement, for to do so would confusingly erect a "cardboard defense"[278] that does little more than parrot the second element's requirement that the plaintiff show that the defendant controlled the instrumentality that caused the harm.

Accident of Type That Normally Results Only from Negligence

The purpose of the first res ipsa element, that the accident was a type that ordinarily does not occur without someone's negligence, is to determine if the accident was probably caused by a negligent act or omission. For example, it may be that the negligence of someone is most likely the cause of a mouse or bug in a Coke,[279] a toe in chewing tobacco,[280] a trout in the milk,[281] a candy so hot that it burns one's mouth,[282] a

---

[273] See below (*Plaintiff's Noninvolvement*).

[274] See, e.g., Turbines, Inc. v. Dardis, 1 S.W.3d 726, 741 (Tex. App. 1999) ("The first factor is necessary to support the inference of negligence and the second to support the inference that the defendant was the negligent party."). See generally Dobbs, Law of Torts § 154, at 370–71.

[275] See, e.g., Barretta v. Otis Elevator Co., 698 A.2d 810, 811 (Conn. 1997).

[276] See Prosser and Keeton on Torts § 39, at 254; Dobbs, Law of Torts § 160.

[277] See, e.g., Turbines, Inc. v. Dardis, 1 S.W.3d 726, 740 (Tex. App. 1999) ("The purpose of res ipsa loquitur is to relieve the plaintiff of the burden of proving a specific act of negligence by the defendant when it is impossible for the plaintiff to determine the sequence of events, or when the defendant has superior knowledge or means of information to determine the cause of the accident.").

[278] Professor Dan Dobbs must be credited with this apt metaphor. See Dobbs, Law of Torts § 160, at 386.

[279] See, e.g., Harris v. Coca-Cola Bottling Co., 183 N.E.2d 56 (Ill. App. Ct. 1962) (mouse); Oklahoma Coca-Cola Bottling Co. v. Newton, 237 P.2d 627 (Okla. 1951) (fly).

[280] See Pillars v. R.J. Reynolds Tobacco Co., 78 So. 365 (Miss. 1918).

[281] "Some circumstantial evidence is very strong, as when you find a trout in the milk." Henry David Thoreau, in The Writings of Henry David Thoreau, Journal II 1850—September 18, 1851, 94 (Bradford Torrey ed., Houghton Mifflin & Co. 1906) (Nov. 1850 journal entry; alluding to indirect but compelling evidence, such as the presence of a trout in a can of milk strongly suggesting that the dairy farmer diluted the milk with water from a trout stream, a recurring problem in the 1800s).

[282] See Knight v. Just Born, Inc., 2000 WL 924624 (D. Or. 2000) (so hot it felt on fire).

new motor home that catches fire,[283] a hand grenade that explodes too quickly,[284] or the steering[285] or brakes[286] of an automobile that suddenly fail.

Looked at from the other direction, limiting the res ipsa doctrine's operation to situations in which someone probably was negligent properly excludes from coverage true accidents most likely caused by no one's fault.[287] While many product misadventures are attributable to someone's failure to exercise reasonable care—the manufacturer, the user, or someone else—many others are an inevitable result of imperfect humans using imperfect machines in an uncertain world. Thus, it may be most likely that a product accident is attributable to no one's negligence when injury results from a motor home that catches fire,[288] a vehicle that goes off a slippery highway,[289] an escalator that malfunctions,[290] an airbag that fails to deploy,[291] or an underground gas tank that springs a leak.[292] In cases such as these, because the product might well have failed for reasons other than someone's negligent act or omission, a court may well conclude that res ipsa does not apply.

Defendant's Exclusive Control

In general. No matter how clearly the plaintiff establishes the first element, that someone was negligent in making or handling the product, a res ipsa case will fail unless the plaintiff further shows that the defendant is most likely the particular party who was negligent. Traditionally, and quite roughly, this inference is established by showing that the manufacturer or other defendant had exclusive control of the instrumentality that caused the accidental harm—the product in question—at the relevant time. That is, the "exclusive control" requirement ensures that the injury probably was caused by the defendant.[293]

In products liability cases, the exclusive control requirement helpfully protects manufacturers from responsibility for harm caused by the user or other parties. For example, a manufacturer of cardboard boxes, transported in flattened bundles, should

---

[283] See Hinckley v. La Mesa R.V. Ctr., Inc., 205 Cal. Rptr. 22 (Ct. App. 1984).

[284] See McGonigal v. Gearhart Indus., 788 F.2d 321 (5th Cir. 1986) (Tex. law) (visible defects).

[285] See General Motors Corp. v. Dillon, 367 A.2d 1020 (Del. 1976).

[286] See, e.g., Holman v. Ford Motor Co., 239 So.2d 40 (Fla. Dist. Ct. App. 1970).

[287] "The world in which we live is an imperfect one, one in which accidents will happen due to no one's negligence. . . . The growing tendency of the victims of accidents and their attorneys to always attempt to find a reason to blame someone else to obtain compensation is disturbing where any reasonable person should recognize that the injury was not another person's fault. It seems that injuries from incidents that regularly happen at home and would be considered as accidents as a matter of course become full blown negligence actions when a solvent defendant is involved. Our society will benefit if this type of thinking is eliminated. No one benefits from the prosecution of cases involving accidents which, while with hindsight may have been avoided, are unquestionably not the result of any unreasonable behavior." Triche v. McDonald's Corp., 164 So.3d 253, 259 (La. Ct. App. 2014).

[288] See Rocky Mountain Fire & Cas. Co. v. Biddulph Oldsmobile, 640 P.2d 851 (Ariz. 1982).

[289] See, e.g., Beatty v. Ford Motor Co., 574 S.E.2d 803, 807–08 (W. Va. 2002). But, with an old vehicle, not without proof eliminating other causes. See, e.g., Cruz v. DaimlerChrysler Motors Corp., 66 A.3d 446, 451–53 (R.I. 2013).

[290] See, e.g., Ellis v. Sears Roebuck & Co., 388 S.E.2d 920 (Ga. Ct. App. 1989).

[291] See Batiste v. General Motors Corp., 802 So.2d 686 (La. Ct. App. 2001).

[292] See Mitchell v. Suburban Propane Gas Corp., 581 N.Y.S.2d 927 (App. Div. 1992).

[293] See Depositors Ins. Co. v. Wal-Mart Stores, Inc., 506 F.3d 1092, 1096 (8th Cir. 2007) (Iowa law); Prosser and Keeton on Torts § 39, at 248. "Exclusive control is merely one fact which establishes the responsibility of the defendant; and if it can be established otherwise, exclusive control is not essential to a res ipsa loquitur case." Rest. (2d) Torts § 328D cmt. *g*.

not be responsible for the death of the driver of a truck trailer into which the bundles were loaded under supervision by the trucker, when the driver is later struck by an unstable bundle that falls from the trailer when he opens its doors to unload the bundles after transporting them to a storage warehouse.[294] Yet the exclusive control requirement poses unnecessary difficulties in many products liability situations where a manufacturer's negligence and a resulting accident are typically separated by considerable time and distance. In such cases, it is of utmost importance to decide whether the relevant *time* of exclusive control over the instrumentality is the time of the *accident*, on the one hand, or the time of the probable *negligence*, on the other.[295]

Basing res ipsa on the defendant's control at the time of the accident makes good sense in many conventional types of negligence cases, such as a passenger's claim against the driver where a car leaves the highway and goes into a ditch—a type of case where common sense suggests that the operator of the vehicle at the time of the accident was most likely responsible for the car's misadventure. But asking who had control of the instrumentality at the time of the accident makes no sense in many products liability cases where manufacturers typically relinquish control of a product to a retail dealer or someone else long before a product accident occurs. Indeed, plaintiffs themselves often are in control of products at the time they are injured. So, if a car-in-a-ditch case is brought by the driver's estate against the manufacturer of the car, and the plaintiff proves that the car was new, the weather was clear, the roadway was empty, and the driver was awake, sober, and driving properly, the relevant time of control logically would seem to be the time when the product was designed and manufactured, not the time of the accident. To take another example, a person drinking a bottle of Coke who suddenly encounters a bug or a mouse surely has control of the product at the time of the misadventure. But the circumstantial evidence in such a case is very strong that the relevant negligence was that of the bottler who had exclusive control of the product at the time of bottling, the time of the probable negligence, and who just as surely had not a whit of control at the time of consumption.[296]

Thus, if a court were to apply the exclusive control element in a products liability case mechanically to mean control-at-the-time-of-injury, res ipsa almost never would be applied in this type of litigation.[297] For many years, however, a trend has been afoot to interpret the exclusive control element in a way that promotes its purpose in identifying the party most likely responsible for the negligence inferred by element number one.[298]

---

[294] Vargo-Schaper v. Weyerhaeuser Co., 619 F.3d 845, 850–51 (8th Cir. 2010) (Minn. law) (manufacturer was not in exclusive control after bundles were loaded on truck).

[295] See Prosser and Keeton on Torts § 39, at 250; Dobbs, Law of Torts § 157.

[296] See, e.g., Bickham v. Coca Cola Refreshments USA, Inc., 2015 WL 7301078, at *6–7 (S.D.N.Y. 2015) (plaintiff's testimony that he "popped [the Coke can] open" before swallowing a dried, brittle mass was "sufficient evidence for a jury to hold defendant liable for negligence under a res ipsa loquitur theory").

[297] See, e.g., Smoot v. Mazda Motors of Am., Inc., 469 F.3d 675, 679 (7th Cir. 2006) (Wis. law) (making this point). A few courts still do apply the exclusive control test narrowly in this manner. See, e.g., Harris v. General Motors Corp., 34 Fed. Appx. 487 (7th Cir. 2002) (Ill. law) (late deployment of airbag on 1-year-old car; res ipsa inapplicable because defendant did not have exclusive control); McConchie v. Samsung Elec. Am., Inc., 2000 WL 1513777 (D.N.H. 2000) (res ipsa inapplicable to 6½-month-old microwave that caught fire because it was installed in plaintiffs' kitchen and so was not under defendant's exclusive control); Darms v. Bunce Rental, Inc., 2000 WL 1174548, at *6 (Wash. Ct. App. 2000) (plaintiff operating lift at time of accident).

[298] See, e.g., Allstate Lloyds Co. v. Marvin Lumber & Cedar Co., 2006 WL 2506776, at *5 (Tex. App. 2006) ("Control, as it applies to *res ipsa loquitur,* does not mean exclusive control or even control at the time of the accident [but only] that the plaintiff 'so reduce' the likelihood of other causes that 'the jury can reasonably find by a preponderance of the evidence that the negligence, if any, lies at the defendant's door.' "); Pavon v.

As early as *Escola v. Coca Cola Bottling Co.*,[299] discussed above, many courts construed the control test more logically as being determined properly *at the time of the probable negligence*, rather than at the time of the accident.[300] Many other courts have similarly interpreted the time of control in this commonsense fashion.[301]

The probability that a defect is attributable to the manufacturer, retailer, or other supplier diminishes over time as the product suffers ordinary wear and tear, deterioration from the elements, abuse by users and mechanics, repairs, accidents, and other misadventures.[302] By the same token, as such post-sale incidents mount over the life of a product, the likelihood increases that a defect causing a product malfunction is attributable to such an event rather than to an original defect present at the time of sale. Thus, the longer a product is out and about in the hurly-burly world, the more likely it is that a product failure cannot be traced to the doorstep of the original product suppliers. In such cases, once it becomes more likely than not that causes other than the defendant supplier's original negligence were responsible for a product's failure, the exclusive control element shields the defendant from the rigors of res ipsa. Hence, courts have refused to apply res ipsa to a high-mileage vehicle that malfunctioned,[303] tires that blew out,[304] an old ladder that buckled,[305] a car[306] or tractor[307] that caught fire, a folding chair that collapsed,[308] and to many other cases where causes outside of the defendant's control best explained a product mishap.[309]

Rudin, 679 N.Y.S.2d 27, 30 (App. Div. 1998). See generally Frumer, Friedman, and Sklaren, Products Liability § 10.04[3][a]; Rest. (2d) Torts § 328D cmt. *g*.

[299] 150 P.2d 436 (Cal. 1944).

[300] See id. at 438: "Many authorities state that the happening of the accident does not speak for itself where it took place sometime after defendant had relinquished control of the instrumentality causing the injury. Under the more logical view, however, the doctrine may be applied upon the theory that defendant had control at the time of the alleged negligent act, although not at the time of the accident, provided plaintiff first proves that the condition of the instrumentality had not been changed after it left the defendant's possession."

[301] See, e.g., Blasius v. Angel Auto., Inc., 839 F.3d 639, 650 (7th Cir. 2016) (Ind. law) ("a defendant need not be in control of the causative instrumentality at the exact moment of injury, provided the defendant was the last person in control"); Cruz v. DaimlerChrysler Motors Corp., 66 A.3d 446, 451–53 (R.I. 2013). See also Prosser and Keeton on Torts § 39, at 250 ("there is now quite general agreement" to this effect).

[302] See § 10.6, below.

[303] See, e.g., Beatty v. Ford Motor Co., 574 S.E.2d 803, 808 (W. Va. 2002) (alleged steering failure on van driven 110,000 miles: "[O]ther responsible causes, including the conduct of the appellant and third persons, [were] not sufficiently eliminated by the evidence. [I]t was not clear how the van had been operated or maintained over the many miles that the van had accumulated, suggesting that the conduct of unknown third persons could have caused the accident."). See also Mosesian v. Ford Motor Co., 2002 WL 31009208, at *4 (Cal. Ct. App. 2002) (fire in 7-year-old car, during which time it had "a series of repairs, both major and minor, some of which involved the electrical system," including an electrical malfunction leading to its repair 3 days before the fire: no evidence linked "fire to the original condition of the car or rebut[ed] the possibility that the problem arose from a modification of the motor or electrical system or from a faulty repair by a third party. [T]he requirement of exclusive control would be rendered meaningless if it could be applied to the present case.").

[304] See Goodyear Tire & Rubber Co. v. Hughes Supply, Inc., 358 So.2d 1339 (Fla. 1978).

[305] See Crawford v. Sears Roebuck & Co., 295 F.3d 884 (8th Cir. 2002) (Ark. law) (ladder was 20 to 28 years old).

[306] See Parsons v. Ford Motor Co., 85 S.W.3d 323 (Tex. App. 2002) (ignition switch had been replaced before fire).

[307] See United States Fid. & Guar. Co. v. J. I. Case Co., 432 S.E.2d 654 (Ga. Ct. App. 1993) (drivers used tractor for 300 hours without following instruction manual on cooling engine down).

[308] See Rivera-Emerling v. M. Fortunoff of Westbury Corp., 721 N.Y.S.2d 653 (App. Div. 2001) (chair had been on sales floor to which innumerable shoppers had access).

[309] See, e.g., Sherwood Forest Mobile Home Park v. Champion Home Builders Co., 199 S.W.3d 707, 710 (Ark. Ct. App. 2004) (mobile home fire might have been caused by rough transportation which loosened electrical connections rather than by manufacturing defect).

Multiple defendants. The exclusive control element is problematic for plaintiffs in cases with multiple defendants.[310] If more than one defendant handles a product in a way that could cause the injury, no one defendant will have had exclusive control over the product and a res ipsa case ordinarily will fail.[311] To make out a res ipsa case against any one defendant in such a successive control situation, a plaintiff usually will have to show that the probable negligence was attributable to a particular defendant and not the others—by evidence that implicates the particular defendant, exonerates the other parties, or some combination of the two.[312] But a number of courts, in varying situations, have allowed plaintiffs to rely on res ipsa against multiple defendants who separately or jointly controlled the product before it caused the injury.[313]

Plaintiff's Noninvolvement

The third traditional res ipsa element is that the plaintiff did not participate in causing the accident. Of course, this requirement makes sense if the plaintiff himself may just as likely have caused an injury he is attempting to foist on a manufacturing defendant.[314] However, like the exclusive-control requirement, if the plaintiff noninvolvement element were applied literally, a plaintiff using a product at the time it malfunctions could never recover under the res ipsa doctrine. Such a result would sap res ipsa of much of its proper power. While some courts and commentators have viewed the third element as a surrogate for disproving contributory negligence (albeit as part of the plaintiff's case in chief), the third conventional element may more logically be viewed as a subset of and check on the second element. That is, if the defendant at the relevant time had *exclusive* control of the product, then the plaintiff must have had none and so could not have participated in causing the accident.[315] From either perspective, the third element (as is true with the second) bears a distinctly antiquarian appearance of a search for an accident's sole responsible cause.[316] Yet modern principles of joint causation and comparative fault have decisively discarded the notion that a plaintiff's case against a

---

[310] See Frumer, Friedman, and Sklaren, Products Liability § 10.04[3][c]; Prosser and Keeton on Torts § 39, at 251.

[311] See, e.g., Waering v. BASF Corp., 146 F. Supp. 2d 675, 687 (M.D. Pa. 2001) ("res ipsa loquitur is problematic where, as here, there are several defendants who had successive control over the harm-causing instrumentality and there is no reason to believe that more than one defendant is responsible for the harm [because each of] the other defendants are 'other responsible causes' that must be sufficiently eliminated in order for it to be more likely than not that the remaining defendant is responsible for the harm").

[312] See id. (evidence of prior negligent packaging by manufacturer of hazardous chemical, with no evidence of negligent shipping or handling by transporter or warehouser, sufficed to implicate manufacturer and exonerate the transporter and warehouser).

[313] See, e.g., Moore v. Anesthesia Servs., P.A., 966 A.2d 830, 841–42 (Del. Super. Ct. 2008) (defective surgical suture or medical malpractice; court would give a "conditional" res ipsa instruction directing jury first to consider medical malpractice claim, and then, if no malpractice, to consider application of res ipsa to negligent manufacturing claim); National Union Fire Ins. Co. v. Harrington, 854 So.2d 880, 891–92 (La. Ct. App. 2003) (manufacturer or operator of vehicle, where former controlled vehicle when it was manufactured and latter controlled it at time it caught fire); Knight v. Just Born, Inc., 2000 WL 924624 (D. Or. 2000) (defective candy—manufacturer and retail seller); Samansky v. Rush-Presbyterian-St. Luke's Med. Ctr., 567 N.E.2d 386 (Ill. 1990) (catheter line broke in plaintiff's body during bypass surgery—manufacturer, hospital, and doctors all had "consecutive" control); Ruiz v. Otis Elevator, 703 P.2d 1247 (Ariz. Ct. App. 1985) (elevator that squashed plaintiff—owner or party who manufactured, installed, and maintained it).

[314] See, e.g., Vargo-Schaper v. Weyerhaeuser Co., 619 F.3d 845, 851 (8th Cir. 2010) (Minn. law) (cargo bundle, which defendant manufacturer loaded into plaintiff truck driver's trailer, fell on driver after transport when he opened trailer doors: "[plaintiff] may have shifted the bundle [while driving], or he may have dislodged the bundle upon opening the trailer door in some fashion").

[315] See Dobbs, Law of Torts § 159.

[316] See Prosser and Keeton on Torts § 38.

negligent defendant is demolished if the plaintiff in some minor way contributed to the accident's causation.[317]

Today, while many courts continue to recite the "absence of voluntary action by the plaintiff" as part of the conventional three-element res ipsa rule,[318] many other courts have dropped the third Wigmorian element, as previously discussed, reducing res ipsa to its two principal elements: (1) the accident being of a type that normally results only from negligence, and (2) the defendant's exclusive control.[319] Perhaps because they believe that the plaintiff-noninvolvement element may be logically subsumed by the exclusive-control element, some courts rely upon the latter element in barring res ipsa claims where the plaintiff was using the product at the time of injury.[320]

Procedural Effect

The importance of res ipsa loquitur lies in its procedural or evidentiary effect. First, application of the doctrine may well protect the plaintiff from the normal requirements of proving defect and causation by expert testimony.[321] As for the procedural effect of res ipsa, a large majority of courts hold that res ipsa provides nothing more than an inference that the defendant was negligent—an inference the jury is free to accept or reject, as is true with other types of circumstantial evidence.[322] In such mere-inference

---

[317] See, e.g., McGuire v. Davidson Mfg. Corp., 398 F.3d 1005, 1008 (8th Cir. 2005) (Iowa law) (most states considering issue have ruled that "voluntary action rule" no longer applies after adoption of comparative fault, citing cases from Ariz., Colo., Conn., Ill., N.M., and Wis.); Montgomery Elevator Co. v. Gordon, 619 P.2d 66, 70 (Colo. 1980) (the no-plaintiff-contribution element is "in direct contravention to the concept of comparative negligence" because "[a] plaintiff who . . . had to rely on res ipsa and who was only slightly negligent would be barred from recovery since his contributory negligence would deny him the application of the res ipsa loquitur doctrine"). See generally Dobbs, Law of Torts § 159. See also ch. 13, below.

[318] See, e.g., Genaw v. Garage Equip. Supply Co., 856 Fed. Appx. 23, 30 (6th Cir. 2021) (Batchelder, J., concurring) (Mich. law); Lyles v. Medtronic Sofamor Danek, USA, Inc., 871 F.3d 305, 312 (5th Cir. 2017) (La. law); Szanto v. Target Corp., 2010 WL 346297, at *9 (Minn. Ct. App. 2010); Olshansky v. Rehrig Int'l, 872 A.2d 282, 288 (R.I. 2005); Mosesian v. Ford Motor Co., 2002 WL 31009208, at *3 (Cal. Ct. App. 2002); Searle v. Suburban Propane Div. of Quantum Chem. Corp., 700 N.Y.S.2d 588, 592 (App. Div. 2000) (including a fourth element: "evidence as to the true explanation of the event must be more readily accessible to the defendant than the plaintiff").

[319] See, e.g., Parks v. Steak & Ale of Texas, Inc., 2006 WL 66428, at *2 (Tex. App. 2006) (for res ipsa, "a plaintiff must show (1) that the character of the injury is such that it would not have ordinarily occurred without negligence and (2) that the instrumentality causing the injury was under the management and control of the defendant"); Weyerhaeuser Co. v. Thermogas Co., 620 N.W.2d 819, 831 (Iowa 2000); Giles v. New Haven, 636 A.2d 1335 (Conn. 1994). Some courts add a duty element. See, e.g., Waering v. BASF Corp., 146 F. Supp. 2d 675 (M.D. Pa. 2001) (negligence in question must be within defendant's scope of duty to plaintiff).

[320] See, e.g., Beatty v. Ford Motor Co., 574 S.E.2d 803, 808 (W. Va. 2002) ("[T]here is a substantial possibility that the rain-soaked highway and/or the appellant's carelessness in operating the van may have been, at the very least, a contributing factor to the accident. Accordingly, the appellant has not shown that the accident was of a kind that ordinarily would not have occurred in the absence of the [defendant's] negligence.").

[321] See, e.g., McMahon v. Robert Bosch Tool Corp., 5 F.4th 900, 906 (8th Cir. 2021) (Mo. law) ("under a res ipsa [loquitur]-type theory . . . some product liability claims may be submitted to juries without expert testimony that identifies specific product defects"); Laspesa v. Arrow Int'l, Inc., 2009 WL 5217030, at *9 (D. Mass. 2009) ("the failure to provide expert testimony does not end the case . . . as long as [the plaintiff] prevails on the res ipsa loquitur theory"). See also McDaid v. Aztec W. Condo. Ass'n, 189 A.3d 321, 330–31 (N.J. 2018) (expert testimony not required in "complex instrumentality cases" for res ipsa inference; "an elevator door that closes onto and injures a passenger is an occurrence bespeaking negligence that falls within the common knowledge of judges and jurors").

[322] See, e.g., Matthews v. Yoplait USA, Inc., 835 S.E.2d 393, 397 (Ga. Ct. App. 2019) ("Res ipsa loquitur 'allow[s] the jury to decide the case and to make or reject the inference authorized as it sees fit—it does not create a presumption to that effect for the defendant to overcome.' "; sharp metal fragments in strawberry yogurt); Smoot v. Mazda Motors of Am., Inc., 469 F.3d 675, 679 (7th Cir. 2006) (Wis. law) (Posner, J.) (res ipsa gives rise to a permissible inference of negligence); Barretta v. Otis Elevator Co., 698 A.2d 810, 812 (Conn. 1997) ("The doctrine permits, but does not compel, such an inference. The doctrine has no evidential force, does

states, a defendant confronted with res ipsa may choose to introduce no evidence at all, and simply argue that the plaintiff's circumstantial evidence is insufficient to make a case. Yet, even a mere inference may be exceedingly important to a plaintiff deprived by circumstances of direct proof of negligence and causation, saving him or her from summary judgment or a directed verdict for the defendant.[323] In a few states, res ipsa provides the plaintiff with a "presumption" of negligence, or makes out a prima facie case, which shifts the burden of going forward with the evidence (or the "burden of proof") to the defendant, who thereupon must produce some evidence that it was not negligent or lose the case.[324] Few terms are more slippery than "presumption" and "burden of proof,"[325] and a lawyer must look closely and skeptically at res ipsa opinions using those words to be certain precisely what procedural effect the court has in mind.[326]

§ 2.6 THE RESURGENCE OF NEGLIGENCE

Beginning in the 1980s, negligence began a resurgence in American products liability law. This development, visible in some American states more than others, still appears to be largely resisted in Europe and elsewhere in the world.[327] The shift away from strict products liability back to negligence has occurred, albeit sporadically, in both courts and state legislatures—a development observed and encouraged by some commentators[328] while lamented by others.[329]

---

not shift the burden of proof and does not give rise to a presumption. It is but a specific application of the general principle that negligence can be proved by circumstantial evidence.").

[323] See, e.g., Moore v. Anesthesia Servs., P.A., 966 A.2d 830, 841 (Del. Super. Ct. 2008); Parks v. Steak & Ale of Texas, Inc., 2006 WL 66428, at *2 (Tex. App. 2006) ("a plaintiff who successfully invokes the doctrine of res ipsa loquitur can survive a no-evidence challenge on the issue of negligence because some evidence of negligence has been presented to the jury"); Jurls v. Ford Motor Co., 752 So.2d 260 (La. Ct. App. 2000) (reversing directed verdict).

[324] See, e.g., Lyles v. Medtronic Sofamor Danek, USA, Inc., 871 F.3d 305, 312 (5th Cir. 2017) (La. law) ("res ipsa loquitur can be applied in products liability actions and used to 'shift the burden of proof to the defendant-manufacturer' "); Stalter v. Coca-Cola Bottling Co. of Ark., 669 S.W.2d 460, 462 (Ark. 1984) ("the burden shifts to the defendant to go forward with evidence to offset the inference of negligence").

[325] When courts say that res ipsa shifts the "burden of proof," they usually mean only that the doctrine shifts to the defendant the burden of producing evidence, not the ultimate burden of persuasion. See 2 McCormick on Evidence § 342.

[326] See, e.g., National Union Fire Ins. Co. v. Harrington, 854 So.2d 880, 892 (La. Ct. App. 2003) (variously describing res ipsa as allowing factfinder to "infer negligence," as creating a "presumption of negligence," and as requiring defendant to "rebut an inference of negligence"); McGuire v. Davidson Mfg. Corp., 258 F. Supp. 2d 945, 952 (N.D. Iowa 2003) (res ipsa doctrine permits "inference of negligence," yet defendant must present "rebutting evidence"), aff'd, 398 F.3d 1005 (8th Cir. 2005). See 2 McCormick on Evidence § 342.

[327] Europe, Japan, and other nations, which began their modern development of products liability law systems more recently than America, still appear to be attempting to ground this field of law largely on a truly "strict" liability foundation. See § 1.4, above.

[328] See, e.g., Owen, The Evolution of Products Liability Law, 26 Rev. Litig. 955 (2007); Twerski, Chasing the Illusory Pot of Gold at the End of the Rainbow: Negligence and Strict Liability in Design Defect Litigation, 90 Marq. L. Rev. 7 (2006); Cupp and Polage, The Rhetoric of Strict Products Liability Versus Negligence: An Empirical Analysis, 77 N.Y.U. L. Rev. 874 (2002); Owen, Defectiveness Restated: Exploding the "Strict" Products Liability Myth, 1996 U. Ill. L. Rev. 743; Owen, The Moral Foundations of Products Liability Law: Toward First Principles, 68 Notre Dame L. Rev. 427 (1993); Henderson and Twerski, A Proposed Revision of Section 402A of the Restatement (Second) of Torts, 77 Cornell L. Rev. 1512 (1992); Powers, A Modest Proposal to Abandon Strict Products Liability, 1991 U. Ill. L. Rev. 639, 639; Birnbaum, Unmasking the Test for Design Defect: From Negligence [to Warranty] to Strict Liability to Negligence, 33 Vand. L. Rev. 593 (1980); Epstein, Products Liability: The Search for the Middle Ground, 56 N.C. L. Rev. 643 (1976).

[329] See, e.g., Phillips, Consumer Expectations, 53 S.C. L. Rev. 1047 (2002); Shapo, In Search of the Law of Products Liability: The ALI Restatement Project, 48 Vand. L. Rev. 631 (1995); Vandall, The Restatement (Third) of Torts: Products Liability Section 2(b): The Reasonable Alternative Design Requirement, 61 Tenn. L. Rev. 1407 (1994); Corboy, The Not-So-Quiet Revolution—Rebuilding Barriers to Jury Trial in the Proposed

Resurgence in the Courts

In most jurisdictions, the doctrine of strict liability in tort never fully displaced principles of negligence in products liability cases. In adopting strict liability in tort during the 1960s and 1970s, many courts stated or suggested that the new strict products liability doctrine eliminated the need for a separate theory of liability in negligence. But as courts applied the new "strict" liability doctrine in an expanding array of contexts, they increasingly recognized that liability for design and warning defects is best defined in terms of negligence principles, centered on a balance of foreseeable risk, cost, utility, reasonableness, and optimality.[330] This resurgence of negligence principles is widely evident in the evolving law on defects in both design and warnings.

As for defects in design,[331] the now-dominant risk-utility test for determining liability in design defect cases is usually little or nothing more than the Learned Hand negligence calculus discussed above.[332] Many courts have acknowledged this close similarity, or "functional equivalence," of negligence and "strict" liability in the design context, and a small number boldly apply negligence principles explicitly, rather than those of "strict" liability, in design defect cases.[333] But most courts so far have refused to take the final step to acknowledge that negligence doctrine should displace "strict" liability as the single, proper liability standard for rendering risk-utility determinations in design defect cases.[334]

Many courts have most forthrightly admitted the central role of negligence principles in so-called "strict" liability claims involving the duty to warn. In the words of Justice Mosk of the California Supreme Court: "In no area of strict products liability has the impact of

---

Restatement (Third) of Torts: Products Liability, 61 Tenn. L. Rev. 1043 (1994); Wertheimer, Unknowable Dangers and the Death of Strict Products Liability: The Empire Strikes Back, 60 U. Cin. L. Rev. 1183, 1206–41 (1992).

330 See Owen, Defectiveness Restated: Exploding the "Strict" Products Liability Myth, 1996 U. Ill. L. Rev. 743.

331 As discussed below, in §§ 5.7 and 8.4.

332 "The risk-utility balancing test is merely a detailed version of Judge Learned Hand's negligence calculus. See United States v. Carroll Towing Co., 159 F.2d 169, 173 (2d Cir. 1947). "As Dean Prosser has pointed out, the liability of the manufacturer rests 'upon a departure from proper standards of care, so that the tort is essentially a matter of negligence.' " Prentis v. Yale Mfg. Co., 365 N.W.2d 176, 184 (Mich. 1984) (negligence only proper basis for liability in design defect cases). See § 2.2, above.

333 Two good examples are Branham v. Ford Motor Co., 701 S.E.2d 5, 13–17 (S.C. 2010) (explicitly replacing § 402A consumer expectation test with Third Rest. § 2(b) negligence-based risk-utility test), and Wright v. Brooke Grp. Ltd., 652 N.W.2d 159 (Iowa 2002) (same). The best early example is Prentis v. Yale Mfg. Co., 365 N.W.2d 176, 185–86 (Mich. 1984). Refusing to apply the strict liability principles of implied warranty doctrine to design defect cases, *Prentis* concluded: "Imposing a negligence standard for design defect litigation is only to define in a coherent fashion what our litigants in this case are in fact arguing and what our jurors are in essence analyzing. Thus we adopt, forthrightly, a pure negligence, risk-utility test in products liability actions against manufacturers of products, where liability is predicated upon defective design."

334 Banks v. ICI Ams., Inc., 450 S.E.2d 671, 674 n.3 (Ga. 1994), is typical:

> While we recognize that the determination of whether a product was defective (involving the reasonableness of a manufacturer's design decisions), which is a basic inquiry for strict liability purposes, generally will overlap the determination of whether the manufacturer's conduct was reasonable, which is a basic inquiry for negligence purposes, we cannot agree that the use of negligence principles to determine whether the design of a product was "defective" necessarily obliterates under every conceivable factual scenario the distinction Georgia law has long recognized between negligence and strict liability theories of liability. Hence, we see no reason to conclude definitively that the two theories merge in design defect cases.

See also Smith v. Alza Corp., 948 A.2d 686, 799 (N.J. Super. Ct. App. Div. 2008).

principles of negligence become more pronounced than in failure-to-warn cases."[335] Courts increasingly agree with the Supreme Court of Ohio's assertion in *Crislip v. TCH Liquidating Co.*[336] that "the standard imposed upon the defendant in a strict liability claim grounded upon an inadequate warning is the same as that imposed in a negligence claim based upon inadequate warning."[337] In *Olson v. Prosoco, Inc.*,[338] the Supreme Court of Iowa took the final step of recognizing that, because negligence is indeed a better doctrine than strict liability in product warning cases, negligence should formally displace the doctrine of strict liability in tort in this context.[339]

Nevertheless, even while acknowledging that "strict" liability in design and warning cases is really nothing more than negligence, most courts continue to pretend that it really is something more. Thus, even in the warning context, most courts still call liability "strict." *Crislip* is one case in point. The Ohio Supreme Court took care to explain that "[w]e do not mean to suggest that a cause of action for negligent failure to warn or warn adequately is identical to one brought under strict liability."[340] *Anderson v. Owens-Corning Fiberglas Corp.*[341] is another example of a court struggling to apply negligence principles under the guise of "strict" liability. In deciding that a defendant in a warning case may present evidence on state of the art, the majority of the California Supreme Court noted that, "while a manufacturing or design defect can be evaluated without reference to the conduct of the manufacturer, the giving of a warning cannot."[342] Nevertheless, the majority also asserted (but failed convincingly to explain)[343] that

---

[335] Anderson v. Owens-Corning Fiberglas Corp., 810 P.2d 549, 561 (Cal. 1991) (Mosk, J., concurring and dissenting).

[336] 556 N.E.2d 1177 (Ohio 1990) (failure to instruct on strict liability failure to warn claim was harmless error).

[337] Id. at 1183. See also Gourdine v. Crews, 955 A.2d 769, 782 (Md. 2008) (noting that negligence and strict liability have "morphed together" in failure to warn cases); McConnell v. Cosco, Inc., 238 F. Supp. 2d 970, 976 (S.D. Ohio 2003) ("the same standard applies for both strict liability and negligence claims for inadequate warning").

[338] 522 N.W.2d 284 (Iowa 1994).

[339] The court remarked, at 289–90:

> [T]he correct submission of instructions regarding a failure to warn claim for damages is under a theory of negligence and the claim should not be submitted as a theory of strict liability. In testing the defendant's liability for negligence in failing to warn, the defendant should be held to the standard of care of an expert in its field. The relevant inquiry therefore is whether the reasonable manufacturer knew or should have known of the danger, in light of the generally recognized and prevailing best scientific knowledge, yet failed to provide adequate warning to users or consumers.

[340] *Crislip*, 556 N.E.2d at 1183 (explaining that the claims are not identical principally because plaintiff's comparative fault may not reduce damages in strict liability in Ohio).

[341] 810 P.2d 549 (Cal. 1991).

[342] Id. at 558.

[343] The frailty of the majority's efforts to explain the supposed differences between negligence and strict tort liability in the warning context rang hollow in the ears of Justice Stanley Mosk, a member of the California Supreme Court since 1964 who personally helped develop "[t]he pure concepts of products liability so pridefully fashioned and nurtured" by that court in the 1960s and 1970s. *Anderson*, 810 P.2d at 561. Nevertheless, Justice Mosk rebelled against continuing the subterfuge. Noting that the strict liability focus "has become blurred through the years," he observed that "our past acquiescence in this muddled state of affairs does not justify making matters worse. Misconception compounded cannot result in authenticity." Id. He concluded that the court "should consider the possibility of holding that failure-to-warn actions lie solely on a negligence theory." Id. at 563. (Mosk, J., concurring and dissenting). When the court was later so asked, it refused. See Carlin v. Superior Court, 920 P.2d 1347 (Cal. 1996) (strict liability in tort proper theory for warning claim in prescription drug case).

"despite its roots in negligence, failure to warn in strict liability differs markedly from failure to warn in the negligence context."[344]

Thus, American courts rendering products liability decisions increasingly recognize that negligence *principles* properly control determinations in both design and warning cases. While most courts have not yet explicitly repudiated "strict" liability *doctrine* in favor of negligence law in these two contexts, more courts in the years ahead may be expected to see the merits of such a forthright approach to legal doctrine.

Resurgence in the *Restatement*

These developments in the courts are mirrored by the *Restatement (Third) of Torts: Products Liability*, which, although defining liability in terms of "defect," acknowledges that liability for both design and warning defects is based on principles of negligence. In § 2(b), design defectiveness is defined as follows:

> [A product] is defective in design when the foreseeable risks of harm posed by the product could have been reduced or avoided by the adoption of a reasonable alternative design . . . and the omission of the alternative design renders the product not reasonably safe.

Comment *d* recognizes that the liability standard is essentially negligence because it "adopts a reasonableness ('risk-utility balancing') test as the standard for judging the defectiveness of product designs. More specifically, the test is whether a reasonable alternative design would, at reasonable cost, have reduced the foreseeable risks of harm posed by the product and, if so, whether the omission of the alternative design rendered the product not reasonably safe." The necessary "comparison between an alternative design and the product design that caused the injury [is] undertaken from the viewpoint of a reasonable person. That standard is also used in administering the traditional reasonableness standard in negligence."[345]

Section 2(c) similarly limits *warning* defects to "foreseeable risks of harm" that a manufacturer could have avoided with "reasonable instructions or warnings." Comment *i* observes that this liability standard "adopts a reasonableness test for judging the adequacy of product instructions and warnings [and so] parallels Subsection (b)."[346] In sum, the *Third Restatement* definitions of both design and warning defects are grounded in negligence principles.

Resurgence in Reform Statutes

Negligence principles also figure prominently in products liability reform legislation enacted in a number of states. A prominent feature of many such statutes is the definition of liability in negligence terms. Several of the statutes define design defectiveness in classic risk-utility language, which, as discussed above, is simply an application in the product design context of Judge Learned Hand's negligence formula in the *Carroll Towing* case.[347] In addition, many of the statutes define the liability standard for warning and instruction defects in conventional negligence terms.

---

[344] *Anderson*, 810 P.2d at 558.

[345] Products Liability Rest. § 2 cmt. *d*.

[346] Products Liability Rest. § 2(c) cmt. *i*.

[347] United States v. Carroll Towing Co., 159 F.2d 169 (2d Cir. 1947). See § 2.2, above.

A few state statutes have quite explicitly reapplied negligence doctrine to both design and warning cases. Indiana, in 1978, adopted strict products liability in tort legislatively by codifying § 402A of the *Restatement (Second) of Torts* essentially verbatim. On its face, it is clear that § 402A imposes liability that purports to be truly strict, rejecting any intimation that a manufacturer or other seller may defend on the ground that it exercised all due care in the preparation or sale of the product. In 1996, however, the Indiana legislature amended its § 402A statute by adding the following proviso: "However, in an action based on an alleged design [or warning defect], the [plaintiff] must establish that the manufacturer or seller failed to exercise reasonable care under the circumstance in designing the product or in providing the warnings or instructions."[348] Washington's reform statute similarly declares in part that "[a] product manufacturer is subject to liability to a claimant if the claimant's harm was proximately caused by the negligence of the manufacturer in that the product was not reasonably safe as designed or not reasonably safe because adequate warnings or instructions were not provided."[349] And North Carolina's statute elegantly reaffirms its rejection of the strict products liability in tort doctrine[350] and provides that a manufacturer is not subject to liability for design defects unless it is proved to have "acted unreasonably in designing or formulating the product . . . ."[351]

Other reform statutes, while not so explicitly redefining liability in negligence *doctrine*, redefine the standard of liability in negligence *terms*. Thus, a number of state reform statutes quite clearly use negligence calculus-of-risk principles in defining liability for defects in *design*. Louisiana's statute, for example, formulates its standard for design defect liability largely in terms of whether "[t]he likelihood that the product's design would cause the claimant damage and the gravity of that damage outweighed the burden on the manufacturer of adopting [an] alternative design and the adverse effect, if any, of such alternative design on the utility of the product."[352]

So, too, in warning defect cases, an even larger number of state legislatures, mirroring the common-law development in the courts, have turned quite explicitly to negligence doctrine to define a manufacturer's liability. In addition to the Indiana and Washington reform act provisions mentioned previously, the Louisiana statute provides that "[a] product is unreasonably dangerous [if] the product possessed a characteristic that may cause damage and the manufacturer failed to use reasonable care to provide an adequate warning of such characteristic and its danger to users and handlers of the product."[353] Mississippi's statute provides that "[a]n adequate product warning or instruction is one that a reasonably prudent person in the same or similar circumstances would have provided."[354] New Jersey's statutory return to negligence

---

[348] Ind. Code Ann. § 34–20–2–2, recodifying Ind. Code Ann. § 33–1–1.5–3(b)(2). See also Gunter v. Weston Brands, LLC, 2020 WL 3104376, at *3 (S.D. Ind. 2020) (plaintiff's common law negligence claims against manufacturer of allegedly defective meat grinder were subsumed in the Indiana Product Liability Act).

[349] Wash. Rev. Code Ann. § 7.72.030(1). But note that the statute ambiguously adds, in subsection (3): "In determining whether a product was not reasonably safe under this section, the trier of fact shall consider whether the product was unsafe to an extent beyond that which would be contemplated by the ordinary consumer." By including consumer expectations as a factor in the "reasonably safe" calculus, this statutory definition of design defect mirrors that of the Third Rest. in § 2(b). See § 8.8, below.

[350] N.C. Gen. Stat. Ann. § 99B–1.1 ("There shall be no strict liability in tort in product liability actions.").

[351] Id. at § 99B–6(a).

[352] La. Rev. Stat. Ann. § 9:2800.56(2).

[353] La. Rev. Stat. Ann. § 9:2800.57(A).

[354] Miss. Code Ann. § 11–1–63(c)(ii).

principles in warning cases is similarly clear, providing that "[a]n adequate product warning or instruction is one that a reasonably prudent person in the same or similar circumstances would have provided."[355] A manufacturer or other seller is liable in a warning case in North Carolina only if the defendant "acted unreasonably in failing to provide [a] warning or instruction."[356] And Ohio limits recovery in warning cases to circumstances where the manufacturer knew or should have known of a risk and "failed to provide the warning or instruction that a manufacturer exercising reasonable care would have provided."[357]

Thus, in an increasing number of states, negligence principles are returning to the law of products liability as the dominant (and sometimes exclusive) tort law standard of liability in design and warning cases, a development endorsed and hastened by the *Restatement (Third) of Torts: Products Liability*.[358] This important reversal in basic tort law principles of products liability law to where they stood in the 1950s and early 1960s—back from strict liability to negligence[359]—is a powerful trend, building sound doctrine on sound policy,[360] that assuredly will continue in courts and legislatures in the years ahead.

---

[355] N.J. Stat. Ann. § 2A:58C–4.

[356] N.C. Gen. Stat. Ann. § 99B–5.

[357] Ohio Rev. Code Ann. § 2307.76(A)(1)(b).

[358] See § 6.5, below.

[359] See Green, The Unappreciated Congruity of the Second and Third Torts Restatements on Design Defects, 74 Brooklyn L. Rev. 807, 837 (2009) ("the *Third Restatement* brings us very close to where we were when section 402A was adopted"), so elegantly penned perhaps after reading Owen, The Evolution of Products Liability Law, 26 Rev. Litig. 955, 989 (2007):

> Quite remarkably, products liability law in America has returned to roost not too far from where it was a half century in the past .... [M]anufacturers are responsible for harm caused by their misrepresentations, manufacturing mistakes, and failures to take reasonable precautions to avoid harm from design and insufficient warning dangers in their products.... For the last half century, untold toil and turmoil have been expended in an effort to find some flaw in these simple principles of responsibility, some way to make them new. It is hard to know why this nation struggled with such intensity to evolve commonsense, self-evident principles of fairness and justice that we knew so long ago, before the wonders of microwave ovens, computers, cell phones, or SUVs. Yet the enduring values of products liability law are the same today as they were before, though we see them a bit more clearly now.

See generally § 5.10, below.

[360] Policy and ethical reasons supporting the use of negligence principles in design and warning cases are explained in Owen, The Moral Foundations of Products Liability Law: Toward First Principles, 68 Notre Dame L. Rev. 427 (1993).

Chapter 3

TORTIOUS MISREPRESENTATION

Table of Sections

§ 3.1 MISREPRESENTATION—GENERALLY

Misrepresentation, it will be recalled,[1] is one of two ways that informational failures may give rise to products liability claims in tort. A failure to provide adequate warnings of product dangers is the other form of informational failure,[2] whereas misrepresentation is an affirmative communication of false or misleading information to another. Three separate claims for tortious misrepresentation exist at common law[3]—distinct theories of liability that differ principally as to the defendant's state of mind in making the representation.[4] The classic tortious misrepresentation claim, "deceit" (now more commonly, if roughly, called "fraud"), requires a showing of *scienter*—that the defendant knew the matter represented to be false and intended it to mislead the plaintiff,[5] or some similar state of mind. Negligent misrepresentation requires proof only that the defendant was negligent in not knowing the falsity of a representation, or, less commonly, that the defendant communicated it in a negligent manner. Finally, a few jurisdictions allow claims of strict liability in tort for innocently making public misrepresentations about a product's safety, notwithstanding the seller's belief that the representations are true, the seller's good faith, and the seller's exercise of all due care.

---

1 See § 1.1, above.

2 See ch. 9 (*Warning Defects*), below.

3 Liability for *contractual* misrepresentation lies in UCC § 2–313 (Express Warranty). See § 4.2, below.

4 See, e.g., In re Tobacco Cases II, 113 Cal. Rptr. 2d 120, 130 (Ct. App. 2001) ("intentional fraud and negligent misrepresentation . . . involve fundamentally different state of mind requirements"); Cummings v. HPG Int'l, Inc., 244 F.3d 16, 22–23 (1st Cir. 2001) (Mass. law) (hypothesizing that the confusion in knowledge required for deceit claims may derive from failure of courts to distinguish between intentional and negligent misrepresentation).

Section 9 of the Products Liability Restatement, entitled "Liability of Commercial Product Seller or Distributor for Harm Caused by Misrepresentation," provides:

> One engaged in the business of selling or otherwise distributing products who, in connection with the sale of a product, makes a fraudulent, negligent, or innocent misrepresentation of material fact concerning the product is subject to liability for harm to persons or property caused by the misrepresentation.

See § 6.5, below. An early, classic article on the topic is Bohlen, Misrepresentation as Deceit, Negligence, or Warranty, 42 Harv. L. Rev. 733 (1929). More recent treatments of tortious misrepresentation include Dobbs, Law of Torts ch. 35; 2 Harper, James, and Gray on Torts ch. 7; Keeton, Dobbs, Keeton, and Owen, Prosser and Keeton on the Law of Torts ch. 18.

5 "Scienter" is Latin for "knowingly"; here, with an intent to deceive. See, e.g., In re Neurontin Mktg., Sales Practices & Prods. Liab. Litig., 618 F. Supp. 2d 96, 113 (D. Mass. 2009) (for scienter, a "fraud claim generally requires plaintiff to establish that defendant made a false representation which was knowingly 'false or was recklessly indifferent to its truth or falsity,' with the intention to defraud").

Other differences between these three separate theories of recovery are considered below.

Products liability claims of misrepresentation generally are grounded in a manufacturer's or other seller's communication of false and material information about a product to a plaintiff who is harmed by reasonably relying on that information.[6] Such claims therefore require no "defect" in the product—only the communication of words that are false. Hinging in this manner upon particular words written or spoken by the defendant, misrepresentation claims require the precise identification and close scrutiny of the particular, offending language. Thus, a lawyer or judge addressing a misrepresentation claim must first and foremost isolate the exact words challenged, framed by the particular context in which they were communicated, in order to assess whether they properly give rise to a misrepresentation claim.[7]

§ 3.2 FRAUD

The action of fraudulent misrepresentation or "deceit," often referred to as "fraud" or "intentional misrepresentation," may be traced in old English law to the writ of deceit, dating at least to 1201,[8] which most likely evolved from the action of *dolus* (fraud) in Roman law.[9] One of the earliest reported English cases allowing recovery for personal injuries in a products liability case was grounded on fraud,[10] and such claims continue to figure prominently (if somewhat infrequently) in modern American products liability litigation.[11] Depending on the jurisdiction, proof of fraud may advantage a plaintiff's case

---

[6] The classic study of how misrepresentation broadly shapes products liability is Shapo, A Representational Theory of Consumer Protection: Doctrine, Function and Legal Liability for Product Disappointment, 60 Va. L. Rev. 1109 (1974). See also Ausness, "The Disorderly Conduct of Words": Civil Liability for Injuries Caused by the Dissemination of False or Inaccurate Information, 65 S.C. L. Rev. 131 (2013); Craswell, Taking Information Seriously: Misrepresentation and Nondisclosure in Contract Law and Elsewhere, 92 Va. L. Rev. 565 (2006); Phillips, Product Misrepresentation and the Doctrine of Causation, 2 Hofstra L. Rev. 561 (1974); Frumer, Friedman, and Sklaren, Products Liability § 2.05; Annot., 93 A.L.R.5th 103 (2001) (advertising statements as affecting liability for product injury).

[7] See, e.g., Wang v. Tesla, Inc., 2021 WL 3023088, at *3–4 (E.D.N.Y. 2021) (plaintiffs' fraud claims failed without allegations of the specific website or showroom misrepresentations they relied on about Tesla's Autopilot technology); Ludy v. Eli Lilly & Co., 2020 WL 3510811, at *6 (S.D. Ind. 2020) (fraud and negligent misrepresentation claims dismissed; complaint failed to identify a specific false or fraudulent statement or representation); Rowan Cnty. Bd. of Educ. v. United States Gypsum Co., 418 S.E.2d 648, 659 (N.C. 1992) (requiring proof of a specific representation helps courts distinguish "mere puffing, guesses, or assertions of opinions from representations of material facts.").

But see Bullock v. Philip Morris USA, Inc., 71 Cal. Rptr. 3d 775, 791–92 (Ct. App. 2008) (reliance established by evidence of manufacturer's advertising, press releases, publications, and "other means" of misleading "the public about the adverse health effects of smoking cigarettes"); Boeken v. Philip Morris, Inc., 26 Cal. Rptr. 3d 638, 655 (Ct. App. 2005) (plaintiff's memory of Marlboro advertising themes was sufficient proof of reliance).

[8] See 1 T. Street, The Foundations of Legal Liability 374–77 (1906).

[9] See id.; J. Thomas, Textbook of Roman Law 288–90 (1976).

[10] Langridge v. Levy, (1837) 150 Eng. Rep. 863 (Exch. Div.), aff'd, (1838) 150 Eng. Rep. 1458 (Exch. Div.).

[11] By way of example, fraud claims have figured prominently in litigation against cigarette manufacturers. See, e.g., Bullock v. Philip Morris USA, Inc., 71 Cal. Rptr. 3d 775 (Ct. App. 2008); In re Simon II Litig., 211 F.R.D. 86, 139 (E.D.N.Y. 2002) (Weinstein, J.) (certifying national tobacco class action seeking punitive damages for fraud: "The ingenuity of humanity in devising frauds, and the need to deter them, has led to the creation of a common law and statutory net sufficiently wide to ensnare an enormous and ever-expanding universe of frauds."), vacated, 407 F.3d 125 (2d Cir. 2005) (decertifying class). See generally Motley and Player, Issues in "Crime-Fraud" Practice and Procedure: The Tobacco Litigation Experience, 49 S.C. L. Rev. 187 (1998).

with respect to privity,[12] federal preemption, a statute of limitations, the effect of a disclaimer, contributory negligence, and, possibly, punitive damages. In some jurisdictions, however, fraud claims do not survive the death of a party.[13]

The contemporary cause of action for intentional or fraudulent misrepresentation requires a plaintiff to establish each of a number of elements, which together comprise the intentional tort of fraud, or deceit. Although the manner in which the elements are specified varies somewhat from jurisdiction to jurisdiction, most courts agree in substance that a plaintiff must establish each of the following kinds of requirements in order to prevail on a claim for fraud:

> (1) a representation; (2) its falsity; (3) its materiality; (4) the speaker's knowledge of its falsity or ignorance of its truth; (5) his intent that it should be acted on by the person and in the manner reasonably contemplated; (6) the hearer's ignorance of its falsity; (7) his reliance on its truth; (8) his right to rely thereon; (9) and his consequent and proximate injury.[14]

In formulating these requirements for the tort of deceit, some courts condense them into three,[15] four,[16] five,[17] or six[18] elements. For example, elements (7) and (8) in the above formulation may be combined into a single element designated "justifiable reliance." In contrast, other courts splinter the various requirements into as many as eleven elements[19]—for example, by pulling apart "misrepresentation," often stated as the first element, into some combination of its separate components of "false," "representation,"

---

[12] See Wright v. Brooke Grp., Ltd., 652 N.W.2d 159, 175–76 (Iowa 2002) (privity of contract unnecessary to fraud claim).

[13] See, e.g., Faircloth v. Finesod, 938 F.2d 513 (4th Cir. 1991) (S.C. law) (*held*, constitutional).

[14] Estate of Schwarz v. Philip Morris Inc., 135 P.3d 409, 422–23 (Or. Ct. App. 2006).

[15] See, e.g., Cummings v. HPG Int'l, Inc., 244 F.3d 16, 22 (1st Cir. 2001) (Mass. law) ("a plaintiff must show that the defendant: [1] made a false representation of material fact; [2] for the purpose of inducing reliance; and [3] that plaintiff relied upon the representation to his or her detriment").

[16] See, e.g., Wang v. Tesla, Inc., 2021 WL 3023088, at *3 (E.D.N.Y. 2021) ("[1] a misrepresentation or a material omission of fact which was false and known to be false by defendant, [2] made for the purpose of inducing the other party to rely upon it, [3] justifiable reliance of the other party on the misrepresentation or material omission, and [4] injury"); Batoh v. McNeil-PPC, Inc., 167 F. Supp. 3d 296, 315–16 (D. Conn. 2016) ("(1) that a false representation was made as a statement of fact; (2) that it was untrue and known to be untrue by the party making it; (3) that it was made to induce the other party to act on it; and (4) that the latter did so act on it to his injury").

[17] See, e.g., Lemley v. Red Bull N. Am., Inc., 2017 WL 2126595, at *2 (S.D. Ga. 2017) ("(1) that the defendant made representations; (2) that at the time he knew they were false; (3) that he made them with the intention and purpose of deceiving the plaintiff; (4) that the plaintiff relied on the representations; and (5) that the plaintiff sustained the alleged loss and damage as the proximate result of their having been made"); Valspar Refinish, Inc. v. Gaylord's, Inc., 764 N.W.2d 359, 368 (Minn. 2009) ("(1) a false representation by [defendant] of a past or existing material fact susceptible of knowledge; (2) made with knowledge of the falsity of the representation or made without knowing whether it was true or false; (3) with the intention to induce [plaintiff] to act in reliance thereon; (4) that the representation caused [plaintiff] to act in reliance thereon; and (5) that [plaintiff] suffered pecuniary damages as a result of the reliance"); Gourdine v. Crews, 955 A.2d 769, 791 (Md. 2008).

[18] See, e.g., Corder v. Ethicon, Inc., 473 F. Supp. 3d 749, 762 (E.D. Ky. 2020) ("a) material representation b) which is false c) known to be false or made recklessly d) made with inducement to be acted upon e) acted in reliance thereon and f) causing injury").

[19] See, e.g., Yost v. Millhouse, 373 N.W.2d 826, 829–30 (Minn. Ct. App. 1985): (1) a representation; (2) that is false; (3) concerning a past or present fact; (4) which is material; (5) and susceptible of knowledge; (6) that the representer knows to be false (or, in the alternative, that he asserts as of his own knowledge without knowing whether it is true or false; (7) on which the representer intends to induce the other person to act, or on which be justified in acting; (8) that the other person is so induced to act or so justified in acting; (9) that the other person's action is in reliance upon the representation; (10) that the other person suffers damage; (11) that such representation proximately causes such damage.

"existing," and "fact." Regardless of how the elements are divided, courts widely agree that a plaintiff must prove the substance of each of these components to establish a claim for fraudulent misrepresentation.[20]

Fraud claims are bounded by certain restrictive principles of pleading and proof. In many states,[21] and under the Federal Rules of Civil Procedure,[22] a plaintiff must plead "with particularity" the facts constituting a fraud. Moreover, supposedly because of the accompanying stigma associated with the commission of a fraud,[23] many jurisdictions apply a "clear and convincing evidence" standard of proof to claims of fraudulent misrepresentation.[24] The plaintiff's burden of proof applies to each element of fraudulent misrepresentation, and such a claim will fail unless the plaintiff establishes each one of the separate elements. For these reasons, recovery on fraudulent misrepresentation

---

[20] Compare, for example, Minnesota's enumeration of 11 elements in *Yost*, above, with the five element list in *Valspar Refinish*, note 17.

[21] **Pleading.** See, e.g., Board of Educ. of Chi. v. A, C & S, Inc., 546 N.E.2d 580, 593–94 (Ill. 1989):

> The facts which constitute an alleged fraud must be pleaded with sufficient specificity, particularity and certainty to apprise the opposing party of what he is called upon to answer. . . . The pleadings must contain specific allegations of facts from which fraud is the necessary or probable inference. . . . Even under the more lenient Federal rules . . . a plaintiff must at least plead with sufficient particularity facts establishing the elements of fraud, including what misrepresentations were made, when they were made, who made [them] and to whom they were made.

Note that most states have now adopted rules of civil procedure patterned on the federal rules.

[22] **Fed. R. Civ. P. 9(b).** This special pleading rule provides in part: "In alleging fraud or mistake, a party must state with particularity the circumstances constituting fraud or mistake." See, e.g., Dupere v. Ethicon, Inc., 2022 WL 523604, at *6 (S.D.N.Y. 2022) ("to meet Rule 9(b)'s heightened pleading standard in a claim for actual or constructive fraud, the complaint must (1) detail the events giving rise to the fraud, such as the statement or omission that is alleged to be fraudulent, the identity of the speaker, the location of the fraud, and the reason the statement is fraudulent and (2) allege facts 'that give rise to a strong inference of fraudulent intent' "); Ludy v. Eli Lilly & Co., 2020 WL 3510811, at *6 (S.D. Ind. 2020) (plaintiff's fraud and negligent misrepresentation claims dismissed; complaint did not identify "a specific statement or other representation [or the] when, where, by whom, or to whom those representations were made"); Gray v. Abbott Labs., Inc., 2011 WL 3022274, at *5 (N.D. Ill. 2011); Rash v. Stryker Corp., 589 F. Supp. 2d 733, 737 (W.D. Va. 2008) ("The requirements of Rule 9(b) have been analogized to the goal of a good newspaper lead—who, what, when, where, and how."); Tuosto v. Phillip Morris USA Inc., 2007 WL 2398507, at *8 (S.D.N.Y. 2007) ("These heightened pleading standards facilitate three goals: '(1) to provide a defendant with fair notice of the plaintiff's claim, (2) to protect a defendant from harm to his or her reputation or goodwill, and (3) to reduce the number of strike suits.' ").

***Iqbal* and *Twombly*.** In addition to Fed. R. Civ. P. 9(b), lawyers pleading in federal court must be cognizant of the Supreme Court's requirement that pleading under Fed. R. Civ. P. 8(a)(2) be specific, rather than conclusory. See Bell Atl. Corp. v. Twombly, 550 U.S. 544 (2007), and Ashcroft v. Iqbal, 556 U.S. 662 (2009). This heightened pleading requirement applies broadly to *all* federal products liability cases, not just cases for fraud. See, e.g., Manuel v. Wichita Hotel Partners, 2010 WL 4025607 (D. Kan. 2010) (dismissing conclusory claim of strict liability for misrepresentation under Rest. (2d) of Torts § 402B); Brooks v. Mentor Worldwide LLC, 985 F.3d 1272, 1281 (10th Cir. 2021) (plaintiffs failed to adequately plead their manufacturing defect claim under the *Iqbal/Twombly* standard; "[a]n allegation is conclusory where it states an inference without stating underlying facts or is devoid of any factual enhancement").

[23] "[I]n civil cases involving . . . fraud or some other quasi-criminal wrongdoing by the defendant[,] [t]he interests at stake . . . are . . . more substantial than mere loss of money[,] and some jurisdictions accordingly reduce the risk to the defendant of having his reputation tarnished erroneously by increasing plaintiff's burden of proof." Rodriguez v. Suzuki Motor Corp., 936 S.W.2d 104, 110 (Mo. 1996) (en banc).

[24] See, e.g., Gourdine v. Crews, 955 A.2d 769, 791 (Md. 2008) (each element must be so proven); Boeken v. Philip Morris, Inc., 26 Cal. Rptr. 3d 638, 675 (Ct. App. 2005); Goldstein v. Phillip Morris, Inc., 854 A.2d 585, 590–91 (Pa. Super. Ct. 2004).

Examining the nature and origins of the clear and convincing standard of proof in this context, see Riley Hill Gen. Contractor v. Tandy Corp., 737 P.2d 595, 605 (Or. 1987) (detailing how the clear and convincing standard of proof means that "the evidence must be free from confusion, fully intelligible, distinct and establish to the jury that the defendant intended to deceive the plaintiff or did so with a reckless disregard for the truth [and that] the truth of the facts asserted must be highly probable").

claims can be particularly difficult,[25] and plaintiffs often shy away from this tort if relief appears available on some other theory of recovery with fewer elements and less stringent requirements of proof.[26]

Representation; Fraudulent Concealment

First and foremost, the notion of a misrepresentation rests on an actor's communication of information to the plaintiff or another. As previously discussed, the plaintiff in a fraudulent misrepresentation case must identify with specificity a particular representation, and the failure to do so will result in dismissal of the claim. Information usually is communicated by spoken or written word, but it may also be conveyed pictorially or by conduct. Hence, a manufacturer or other seller may be liable in deceit for showing a picture of the product performing tasks it cannot safely perform,[27] or by covering a defect with paint or grease, making the product look safer than it actually is.[28]

More difficult conceptually is the question of whether a defendant may be liable in fraud for mere silence—for *failing* to communicate information about some hidden defect or danger lurking in a product.[29] This issue also may be phrased as whether the law of deceit imposes on suppliers a "duty of disclosure"—whether liability may attach for *non*disclosure—with respect to hidden dangers in products that they sell. The converse of the duty to warn (which rests on a supplier's affirmative duty to provide others with beneficial safety information),[30] an actor's passive duty in misrepresentation cases is to refrain from providing others with dangerously false information. Because the tort of fraudulent misrepresentation thus rests fundamentally on a defendant's affirmative act of communicating harmful information to another, the general rule long has been that the mere failure to provide information does not give rise to an action of deceit. So, proof only that a defendant *failed* to communicate information about dangers ordinarily does not satisfy the "representation" element of a claim for fraud.[31] This general rule is eminently sound, of course, for otherwise any failure to warn would amount ipso facto to a misrepresentation, an entirely different legal claim.

---

[25] "Of all civil liabilities fraud is the most difficult to establish." Dobbin v. Pacific Coast Coal Co., 170 P.2d 642, 648 (Wash. 1946) (distributor of defective furnace not liable in fraud).

[26] Assuming no problems with privity, disclaimers, or notice, probably the easiest misrepresentation theory on which to recover is breach of express warranty under Article 2 of the UCC, a doctrine available in every state. See § 4.2, below.

[27] For example, promotional literature for a tent or kerosene lantern picturing use of such a lantern inside a tent, since carbon dioxide fumes from such lanterns can be deadly.

[28] See Kuelling v. Roderick Lean Mfg. Co., 75 N.E. 1098, 1099 (N.Y. 1905), where the beam on a farm machine was made of unfit, cross-grained wood with a knothole. "[D]efendant concealed this knothole with a plug of soft wood nailed in, and then the knot, the plug, the hole, the cross-grain of the wood, and the kind of wood used were covered up and concealed by the defendant with putty and paint . . . ." This amounted to "an affirmative representation that the [beam] was sound . . . ." Id. at 1101. See also Woodward v. Miller & Karwisch, 46 S.E. 847 (Ga. 1904) (large crack in axle of buggy covered over with grease). See generally W. P. Keeton, Fraud—Concealment and Non-disclosure, 15 Tex. L. Rev. 1 (1936).

[29] See Craswell, Taking Information Seriously: Misrepresentation and Nondisclosure in Contract Law and Elsewhere, 92 Va. L. Rev. 565 (2006).

[30] The duty to warn is examined in chapter 9, below.

[31] "It has commonly been stated as a general rule, particularly in the older cases, that the action will not lie for such tacit nondisclosure." Prosser and Keeton on Torts § 106, at 737. "When the parties to a transaction deal with each other at arm's length, with no confidential relationship, no obligation to disclose information arises when the information is not requested." Mason v. Chrysler Corp., 653 So.2d 951, 954–55 (Ala. 1995).

Since a simple no-duty-to-disclose rule is sometimes harsh in application, courts from an early date found it necessary to create exceptions to the general rule for certain limited situations.[32] When such special situations are present, the failure affirmatively to provide information is sometimes called "fraudulent concealment."[33] While one might frame such an exception[34] as giving rise to "a duty to speak whenever justice, equity, and fair dealing demand it,"[35] a formulation flexible enough to accommodate any special situation, such a formulation would be too broad and vague for principled application in specific cases.[36] For this reason, the courts have particularized, with some degree of specificity, exceptions that give rise to an affirmative duty to speak in certain limited situations.

One such exception applicable to the products liability context is for "half-truths," where a representation that is literally true implies facts that are false, in which case the speaker must disclose whatever additional facts are necessary to cure the misconception.[37] "[A] statement which is technically true as far as it goes may nevertheless be fraudulent, where it is misleading because it does not state matters which materially qualify the statement as made. In other words, a half-truth is sometimes more misleading than an outright lie."[38]

---

[32] See W.P. Keeton, Fraud—Concealment and Non-disclosure, 15 Tex. L. Rev. 1 (1936); Note, Silence as Fraudulent Concealment—Vendor and Purchaser—Duty to Disclose, 36 Wash. L. Rev. 202 (1961).

[33] See, e.g., In re Toyota Motor Corp. Unintended Acceleration Mktg., Sales Practices, & Prods. Liab. Litig., 754 F. Supp. 2d 1145, 1189–90 (C.D. Cal. 2010) ("fraudulent concealment"; "A plaintiff may demonstrate a duty to disclose in four circumstances: '(1) when the defendant is in a fiduciary relationship with the plaintiff; (2) when the defendant had exclusive knowledge of material facts not known to the plaintiff; (3) when the defendant actively conceals a material fact from the plaintiff; and (4) when the defendant makes partial representations but also suppresses some material fact.' "); Tuosto v. Phillip Morris USA Inc., 672 F. Supp. 2d 350, 362–63 (S.D.N.Y. 2009) ("fraudulent concealment"; "A duty to disclose will arise if parties are in a fiduciary relationship; if one party has made a partial or ambiguous statement that only complete disclosure of facts will elucidate fully; or if a party possesses superior knowledge, not available to the other party, knowing that the other party is acting on the basis of mistaken knowledge."). See also note 44, below.

[34] For example, a defendant may have a duty to speak if the plaintiff requests particular information from the defendant. See Mason v. Chrysler Corp., 653 So.2d 951, 954 (Ala. 1995). See also University Sys. of N.H. v. United States Gypsum Co., 756 F. Supp. 640, 651 (D.N.H. 1991) (duty to disclose arises when seller knows of concealed defect, dangerous to life or property, that is unknown to and not capable of detection by buyer). While seemingly fair, the problem with such a dangerous-defect exception is that it appears to embrace every instance where there is a duty to warn and so is overly broad as a description of the circumstances giving rise to a duty to speak under the law of fraud.

[35] W.P. Keeton, Fraud—Concealment and Non-disclosure, 15 Tex. L. Rev. 1, 31 (1936). See Loughridge v. Goodyear Tire & Rubber Co., 192 F. Supp. 2d 1175, 1184 (D. Colo. 2002) ("concealment of a material existing fact that in equity and good conscience should be disclosed").

[36] See Note, Silence as Fraudulent Concealment—Vendor and Purchaser—Duty to Disclose, 36 Wash. L. Rev. 202, 204 (1961) ("a somewhat nebulous standard, praiseworthy as looking toward more stringent business ethics, but possibly difficult of practical application").

[37] "The most obvious [exception] is that if the defendant does speak, he must disclose enough to prevent his words from being misleading, and that there is fraud in a statement [when he does not do so]. In other words, half of the truth may obviously amount to a lie, if it is understood to be the whole." Prosser and Keeton on Torts § 106, at 738. See, e.g., Boeken v. Philip Morris, Inc., 26 Cal. Rptr. 3d 638, 653 (Ct. App. 2005) ("Philip Morris concedes that a duty to speak may arise when necessary to clarify misleading 'half-truths' "). *But see* Jowers v. BOC Grp., Inc., 2009 WL 995613, at *7 (S.D. Miss. 2009) (Mississippi does not recognize the "half-truth" exception), aff'd in part, vacated in part, remanded on other grounds sub nom. Jowers v. Lincoln Elec. Co., 617 F.3d 346 (5th Cir. 2010). See also Wright v. Brooke Grp. Ltd., 652 N.W.2d 159, 175 (Iowa 2002) ("a manufacturer has a duty to a consumer under Rest. (2d) Torts § 551(2)(b) to disclose 'matters known to [the manufacturer] that [it] knows to be necessary to prevent [its] partial or ambiguous statement of the facts from being misleading' and under section 551(2)(c) to disclose subsequently acquired information that would prevent a prior statement from being false or misleading").

[38] St. Joseph Hosp. v. Corbetta Constr. Co., 316 N.E.2d 51, 71 (Ill. App. Ct. 1974). General Electric's Textolite wall paneling failed the UL flame spread fire tunnel test, scoring 255. UL refused to rate Textolite

Another exception to the no-duty-to-disclose general rule, sometimes applicable to products liability cases, is the duty to correct information believed by the speaker to be true at the time it was communicated, but which the speaker subsequently discovers to be false. "[W]here one has made a statement which at that time is true but subsequently acquires new information which makes it untrue or misleading, he must disclose such information to anyone whom he knows to be acting on the basis of the original statement—or be guilty of fraud or deceit."[39]

A third exception, occasionally mentioned in products liability cases, applies to fiduciary or confidential relationships. These relations may impose an affirmative duty on a person entrusted with a special position of power and trust over another party's interests to provide the dependent party with such information as may be necessary to protect that party's interests.[40] But the normal relationship between manufacturers and consumers can hardly be characterized as fiduciary or confidential,[41] no matter how shoddy or dangerous the products sold may be,[42] so that some other exception to the general no-duty-to-disclose rule must be found to support a tortious misrepresentation claim[43] for failing to disclose defects in goods that are sold.

---

because it considered any product testing in excess of 200 dangerously flammable. In selling Textolite to a contractor constructing a hospital in Chicago, which by code required paneling be rated no higher than 15, GE stated the paneling did not have a flame spread rating. Yet, GE failed to mention that the reason it was not rated was that, if it were, its rating would be 17 times the maximum permitted by the city. *Held*, GE's nondisclosure of the true full facts was fraudulent, despite the literal truth of "no-flame-spread-rating," which was intended as a "gross deception" to "cover[ ] up the real truth namely that GE was proposing for installation in this hospital a material [it] actually knew was utterly unfit for use in such an institution."

[39] *St. Joseph Hosp.*, 316 N.E.2d at 71. See Prosser and Keeton on Torts § 106, at 738. See also Wright, 652 N.W.2d at 175 (Iowa 2002).

[40] See Prosser and Keeton on Torts § 106, at 738.

[41] See, e.g., Grisham v. Philip Morris, Inc., 670 F. Supp. 2d 1014, 1043 (C.D. Cal. 2009) (no fiduciary relationship between smoker and tobacco company: "Commercial, arms-length relationships are not fiduciary relationships."); Taylor v. Ford Motor Co., 2006 WL 2228973, at *5 (D. Me. 2006) ("To infuse the law of fiduciary relations into personal injuries resulting from the use of consumer products, such as an automobile, would largely displace well-developed concepts of tort, contract, and strict liability law with narrowly-drawn and ill-fitting principles of trust law."); Wells v. Radiator Specialty Co., 413 F. Supp. 2d 778, 783 (S.D. Miss. 2006) ("since silence, in the absence of a duty to speak, is not actionable, plaintiffs' claims for misrepresentation by omission are dependent on the existence of a duty of disclosure, which would arise if a fiduciary relationship existed"; *held*, no fraudulent concealment because no duty to disclose toxic nature of product in absence of fiduciary duty); Burton v. R.J. Reynolds Tobacco Co., 397 F.3d 906, 912–13 (10th Cir. 2005) (Kan. law) ("the relationship between a product buyer and seller is not fiduciary in nature"; excellent discussion).

[42] See, e.g., Wright v. Brooke Grp. Ltd., 652 N.W.2d 159, 177 (Iowa 2002) ("[A] manufacturer's failure to warn or to disclose material information does not give rise to a fraud claim when the relationship between a plaintiff and a defendant is solely that of a customer/buyer and manufacturer with two exceptions[—]where the manufacturer (1) has made misleading statements of fact intended to influence consumers, or (2) has made true statements of fact designed to influence consumers and subsequently acquires information rendering the prior statements untrue or misleading."). See also Estate of White v. R.J. Reynolds Tobacco Co., 109 F. Supp. 2d 424, 431 (D. Md. 2000) (no duty to disclose based on mere relationship of manufacturer and buyer); Connick v. Suzuki Motor Co., 675 N.E.2d 584, 593 (Ill. 1996) (owners of Suzuki Samurais prone to roll over could not maintain fraudulent concealment claim against manufacturer with whom they had no fiduciary or confidential relationship); Mason v. Chrysler Corp., 653 So.2d 951 (Ala. 1995) (sale of shoddily manufactured car does not give rise to fiduciary or other special relationship, on the part of either manufacturer or dealer, sufficient to give rise to duty to speak; nor does the dealer's repair of the car on several occasions alter this conclusion). *A fortiori*, a manufacturer has no duty to disclose information to third parties who buy a competitor's products. See, e.g., Flynn v. American Home Prods. Corp., 627 N.W.2d 342, 350 (Minn. Ct. App. 2001) (manufacturer of brand-name phen-fen weight loss drug had no duty to disclose risks to purchasers of generic drug: "there is no fiduciary relationship here").

[43] Independent of tortious misrepresentation, manufacturers have an affirmative duty to warn consumers of dangerous defects their products may contain. See ch. 9, below.

Many courts[44] and a few legislatures[45] characterize claims based on a duty to disclose (that is, claims where there is some exception to the general rule of *no* duty to disclose) as claims for "fraudulent concealment,"[46] as previously mentioned. Unfortunately, judicial discussions of fraudulent concealment often are ambiguous and otherwise confused, failing to distinguish clearly between a supplier's truly affirmative act of concealment, on the one hand, and its mere failure to disclose facts about a hidden product danger, on the other. In situations of the latter type, the information may well be important to users and consumers,[47] but the law of most states properly characterizes a supplier's failure to provide it merely as a failure to warn, not as fraudulent.[48] The sort

---

[44] **"Fraudulent concealment."** Quite a few jurisdictions unambiguously allow claims for fraudulent concealment with elements of its own. See, e.g., McAuliffe v. Microport Orthopedics, Inc., 2021 WL 3930365, at *3 (N.D. Ill. 2021) ("(1) the concealment of a material fact; (2) that the concealment was intended to induce a false belief, under circumstances creating a duty to speak; (3) that the innocent party could not have discovered the truth through a reasonable inquiry or inspection, or was prevented from making a reasonable inquiry or inspection, and relied upon the silence as a representation that the fact did not exist; (4) that the concealed information was such that the injured party would have acted differently had he been aware of it; and (5) that reliance by the person from whom the fact was concealed led to his injury"); Andrews v. R.J. Reynolds Tobacco Co., 2021 WL 3472504, at *5 (E.D. Mo. 2021) ("(1) the fact was not within the fair and reasonable reach of the plaintiff; (2) the plaintiff was unable to discover the concealed information; and (3) plaintiff exercised reasonable diligence"). See also Frankson v. Brown & Williamson Tobacco Corp., 886 N.Y.S.2d 714, 717, 722 (App. Div. 2009) (upholding compensatory award against tobacco company for fraudulently concealing health risks of smoking before 1969); In re Neurontin Mktg., Sales Practices & Prods. Liab. Litig., 618 F. Supp. 2d 96, 112–14 (D. Mass. 2009) (allowing fraudulent concealment claims against drug company for failure of sales reps to warn doctors of depressive and suicidal side effects); Pinney v. Nokia, Inc., 402 F.3d 430, 445 (4th Cir. 2005) (Ga., Md., N.Y., and Pa. law) ("Concealment of a material fact, with intent to deceive, satisfies the false representation element of fraud."); Nicolet, Inc. v. Nutt, 525 A.2d 146, 149 (Del. 1987) (allowing fraudulent concealment claim against asbestos manufacturers for (1) knowingly and falsely asserting that it was safe to work in close proximity to asbestos materials, and (2) suppressing from the workers medical and scientific data on potential health hazards of asbestos inhalation); note 33, above.

Pleading. Because fraudulent concealment claims rest on a defendant's *failure* to communicate, rather than affirmatively *making* false statements, the heightened pleading standard of Fed. R. Civ. P. 9(b) logically should be relaxed, if it applies at all. See, e.g., Clark v. American Honda Motor Co., 528 F. Supp. 3d 1108, 1122–23 (C.D. Cal. 2021) ("When a claim rests on allegations of fraudulent omission . . . the Rule 9(b) standard is somewhat relaxed because 'a plaintiff cannot plead either the specific time of [an] omission or the place, as he is not alleging an act, but a failure to act.' "); Belville v. Ford Motor Co., 60 F. Supp. 3d 690, 697 (S.D. W. Va. 2014) ("a more relaxed standard under Rule 9(b) should apply in omission cases because a plaintiff cannot be required to specifically identify the precise time, place, and content of an event that did not occur"). See also Harju v. Johnson & Johnson, 2021 WL 3929232, at *4 (W.D. Wash. 2021) (plaintiffs' allegations that "Defendants knowingly, falsely, and actively misrepresented that the [mesh implant] products did not cause chronic injuries . . . with actual knowledge that these representations were false" satisfied Rule 9(b) pleading for fraud by omission).

[45] For example, Cal. Civ. Code § 1710 provides that a deceit includes "[t]he suppression of a fact, by one who is bound to disclose it." See also Holmes v. Wegman Oil Co., 492 N.W.2d 107, 114 (S.D. 1992), in which the manufacturer of a thermostatic control for gas water heaters discovered a dangerous design defect in the control five years after it first marketed the control. Once the company learned of the problem, it began to develop a safer design for the control and eventually replaced the dangerous design with the safe design. Although the company thereupon destroyed its inventory of defective valves and implemented a recall campaign to replace them, the company failed to warn customers of the risk prior to the recall and failed to implement the recall as vigorously as it might have. *Held*, evidence supported finding of "fraudulent concealment" under a statute which provides that deceit may be established by "the suppression of a fact by one who is bound to disclose it."

[46] Or "fraudulent suppression." Mason v. Chrysler Corp., 653 So.2d 951, 954–55 (Ala. 1995). Or "silent fraud." McEldowney v. Air Prods. & Chems., Inc., 2007 WL 1576390, at *5 (Mich. Ct. App. 2007).

[47] See, e.g., Smith v. DaimlerChrysler Corp., 2002 WL 31814534, at *6 (Del. Super. Ct. 2002) (failure to warn miniature-sized persons of special hazards they confront from airbags).

[48] In cigarette litigation, plaintiffs often allege that the defendants "fraudulently concealed" the industry's increasing awareness of the addictiveness and other health risks of cigarettes. Claims of this type, often amounting to little more than claims of failure to warn, aim at a loophole in Cipollone v. Liggett Grp., Inc., 505 U.S. 504 (1992), where the Supreme Court ruled that federal preemption bars warning claims but *not* most claims of fraud/fraudulent concealment. But the transparency of merely changing the label from "failure

of "concealment" appropriately characterized as "fraudulent" involves a defendant's truly affirmative action designed to hide information about a product danger from a plaintiff who not only needs it but is otherwise entitled to it, such as where a supplier acts affirmatively to frustrate a plaintiff's investigation of a product's condition by altering its appearance to hide some flaw, as by painting over a crack,[49] or by otherwise affirmatively obstructing a plaintiff's rightful access to facts that may reveal a product's dangerous condition.[50]

While courts for some time have applied the "fraudulent concealment" term to situations that give rise to a duty to speak under the traditional exceptions to the no-duty-to-disclose rule,[51] it seems better to avoid altogether using such a polemical and confusing term. Instead, courts would do well to begin analysis in silence-as-representation cases with the general principle of no-duty-to-disclose and then proceed to address whatever half-truth, subsequently-acquired information, or other limited exception may (or may not) give rise to the duty to speak in the particular situation. Loose talk about "fraudulent concealment" tends to frustrate sound analysis of the issues in a complicated context where such analysis is especially needed.[52] If courts find that they must use this confusing term, they could at least reduce confusion by carefully distinguishing "fraudulent concealment" from the simple duty to warn, restricting the former term to its traditional, narrow meaning of a defendant's affirmative action to hide facts about a product's dangers from a buyer or other person specially entitled to that information.[53]

Fact

To support a fraud claim, a representation must be of an existing *fact*. The fact represented must exist at the time of the representation, such that fraudulent misrepresentation claims will not lie with respect to predictions of future conditions or events,[54] unless such predictions falsely imply the existence of facts that presently

---

to warn" to "fraudulent concealment" is not lost on many courts. See, e.g., Burton v. R.J. Reynolds Tobacco Co., 397 F.3d 906, 913 (10th Cir. 2005) (Kan. law) (sales of cigarettes do not create fiduciary relationships; holding otherwise would convert all duty to warn claims into fraud claims); In re Kings Cnty. Tobacco Litig., 727 N.Y.S.2d 241, 245 n.8 (Sup. Ct. 2000). *But see* Prentice v. R.J. Reynolds Tobacco Co., 2022 WL 805951, at *6 (Fla. 2022) (fraudulent concealment claim requires proof that plaintiff relied on a statement "that concealed or omitted material information about the health effects or addictiveness of smoking cigarettes"); Clinton v. Brown & Williamson Holdings, Inc., 498 F. Supp. 2d 639, 645 (S.D.N.Y. 2007).

[49] See note 28, above.

[50] See, e.g., Nicolet, Inc. v. Nutt, 525 A.2d 146, 149 (Del. 1987), where the court characterizes "concealment" as sufficient to establish a prima facie case of intentional misrepresentation where plaintiff proves (1) deliberate concealment by defendant of material fact, or silence in the face of a duty to speak; (2) defendant acted with scienter; (3) defendant had an intent to induce plaintiff's reliance on the concealment; (4) causation; and (5) damages from the concealment.

[51] See, e.g., Cheney Bros. v. Batesville Casket Co., 47 F.3d 111, 115 (4th Cir. 1995) (S.C. law); Zimmerman v. Northfield Real Estate, Inc., 510 N.E.2d 409, 413 (Ill. App. Ct. 1987).

[52] See, e.g., In re Neurontin Mktg., Sales Practices & Prods. Liab. Litig., 618 F. Supp. 2d 96, 112–14 (D. Mass. 2009) ("caselaw does not always draw clear lines" between failure to warn and fraudulent concealment claims; surveying cases, recognizing confusion, but allowing such claims on facts of case); Roney v. Gencorp, 431 F. Supp. 2d 622, 637 (S.D. W. Va. 2006) (confusingly conflating fraudulent concealment and duty to warn). Compare James v. Stryker Corp., 2011 WL 292240, at *2–3 (M.D. Pa. 2011).

[53] See, e.g., Lloyd v. General Motors Corp., 916 A.2d 257, 274 (Md. 2007) (helpfully distinguishing duty to warn from fraudulent concealment, and defining the latter narrowly as "any statement or other conduct which prevents another from acquiring knowledge of a fact, such as diverting the attention of a prospective buyer from a defect which otherwise, he would have observed").

[54] See, e.g., Valspar Refinish, Inc. v. Gaylord's, Inc., 764 N.W.2d 359, 368–69 (Minn. 2009) (fraudulent misrepresentation claim failed because representations that production problems would be resolved were

exist.[55] A promise of future performance made with no present intention of keeping it constitutes a misstatement of an existing fact.[56]

The misrepresentation must concern a *fact* as opposed to an *opinion*.[57] That is, the matter misrepresented must be specific and capable of objective determination. Interpretation of a representation as fact or opinion may depend on the expertise of the manufacturer: "Where the party making the representations has superior knowledge regarding the subject matter of his representations, and the other party is so situated that he may reasonably rely on such supposed superior knowledge or special information, the representations may be construed as fact and not opinion."[58]

By definition, a "puff" is not a representation of fact. A seller's expressions of subjective beliefs concerning the value or quality of a product, including general commendatory characterizations—such as "good," "excellent," "high quality,"[59] or "terrific"—are universally considered to be mere "sales talk" or "puffery," not intended or taken to be factual assertions, and so ordinarily are insufficient to support an action for fraud.[60] Normally, the more specific the assertion, the more likely that it fairly may be regarded as factual, and the more general it is, the more likely that it should be

"predictions of future results" rather than statements "about a past or existing material fact susceptible of knowledge"); Champion Home Builders Co. v. ADT Sec. Servs., Inc., 179 F. Supp. 2d 16, 23 (N.D.N.Y. 2001), as amended (2002); Mason v. Chrysler Corp., 653 So.2d 951, 953–54 (Ala. 1995) ("predictions as to events to occur in the future are not statements concerning material facts upon which individuals have a right to act and, therefore, will not support a fraud claim").

55 See, e.g., Cummings v. HPG Int'l, Inc., 244 F.3d 16, 22 (1st Cir. 2001) (Mass. law) (manufacturer's assertion that roof would last 20 years implied that manufacturer "knew facts to justify its statement").

56 See Valspar Refinish, Inc. v. Gaylord's, Inc., 764 N.W.2d 359, 369 (Minn. 2009); Estate of Schwarz v. Philip Morris Inc., 135 P.3d 409, 422–23 (Or. Ct. App. 2006) (in Tobacco Institute's 1962 "Frank Statement" and otherwise, defendant represented to public that it would research tobacco safety and disclose the results to the public, a promise it did not then intend to keep; fraud includes "a promise made with the knowledge that it will not be performed or with reckless disregard about whether it will be performed").

57 See, e.g., Crowther v. Guidone, 441 A.2d 11, 13 (Conn. 1981) (court should focus on "whether, under the circumstances surrounding the statement, the representation was intended and understood as one of fact distinguished from one of opinion").

58 Toole v. Richardson-Merrell Inc., 60 Cal. Rptr. 398, 411 (Ct. App. 1967) (drug that produced serious eye damage to defendant's test animals, and later to humans, was advertised as "virtually non-toxic," "safe," and free of "significant side effects"). See W.P. Keeton, Fraud: Misrepresentations of Opinion, 21 Minn. L. Rev. 643 (1937).

59 See Tatum v. Cordis Corp., 758 F. Supp. 457, 463 (M.D. Tenn. 1991) (pacemaker was produced with "the highest degree of dedication and skill").

60 See, e.g., Stearns v. Select Comfort Retail Corp., 2009 WL 1635931, at *10 (N.D. Cal. 2009) (bed advertisements stating "Your Sleep Number is key to a perfect night's sleep," that they "provide 'an ideal level of bed comfort, firmness and support,' and promises that a user would never have 'a better nights [sic] sleep' " were "mere puffery"); Champion Home Builders Co. v. ADT Sec. Servs., Inc., 179 F. Supp. 2d 16, 23–25 (N.D.N.Y. 2001), as amended (2002) (fire alarm provider was "industry leader"); Holley v. Central Auto Parts, 347 S.W.2d 341 (Tex. App. 1961) (tire rim was "a good one"); Lambert v. Sistrunk, 58 So.2d 434 (Fla. 1952) (stepladder would "last a lifetime" and customer would "never break it"); Mason v. Chrysler Corp., 653 So.2d 951, 953–54 (Ala. 1995) (buyers of new car assured that it was "a smooth-riding, luxury car" comparable to Cadillacs and Lincolns but "much less expensive," its warranty was "the best," buyers "were making a good deal," and "couldn't get a better deal any place." *Held*, summary judgment for Chrysler and dealer affirmed: "[S]tatements of opinion amounting to 'puffery' [are not statements of] material facts upon which individuals have a right to act and, therefore, will not support a fraud claim." These assertions "were statements commonly made in the course of selling cars and do not amount to misstatements of a material fact."). Compare Wang v. Tesla, Inc., 2021 WL 3023088, at *3 (E.D.N.Y. 2021) (showroom agent's comment that driver could "close his eyes and relax" when using Autopilot was insufficient to "meet the elements of fraud").

characterized as opinion.[61] Thus, to say that a crane is "capable of safely lifting 40,000 pounds" is a statement of fact, but to say that it is "a mighty strong crane" is a statement of opinion. In the final analysis, whether a statement is factual depends on whether it is capable of objective determination.[62]

Falsity

In any misrepresentation claim, the plaintiff must prove that a fact represented was false. Interpreting particular words as true or false is crucially important to the analysis of a misrepresentation claim, and interpretation of falsity is typically the threshold step in determining the viability of such a claim. In ascertaining a representation's truth or falsity, its fair meaning must first be established. The second step is to ascertain whether that meaning deviates substantially from the truth—from the actual facts concerning the matter represented. In order to determine whether a representation should be considered substantially true or false, the words should be construed in the total context surrounding their utterance by the defendant and their communication to the plaintiff. As previously discussed, a statement may be considered false if it is a "half-truth"—a statement that, though literally true, misleads others by implying facts that are themselves untrue.[63]

Materiality

To support a claim for fraud, the misrepresentation must be *material*, as distinguished from trivial or irrelevant.[64] One is not likely to rely, nor does one have a right to rely, on information that is truly insignificant to a transaction. "There are misstatements which are so trivial, or so far unrelated to anything of real importance in the transaction, that the plaintiff will not be heard to say that they substantially affected his decision."[65] In the words of the *Restatement (Second) of Torts*, "[r]eliance upon a fraudulent misrepresentation is not justifiable unless the matter misrepresented is material."[66] The *Restatement* classifies a fact as "material" either if a reasonable person would consider it important *or* if the speaker expects the recipient to so consider it.[67]

---

[61] See, e.g., Cummings v. HPG Int'l, Inc., 244 F.3d 16, 22 (1st Cir. 2001) (Mass. law) (manufacturer's assertion that roof would last 20 years "was specific and verifiable, not a mere expression of opinion or estimate," and implied that manufacturer "knew facts to justify its statement").

[62] This definition draws from a variety of contexts. See, e.g., Vaughn v. General Foods Corp., 797 F.2d 1403, 1411 (7th Cir. 1986) (Ind. law) (fraud; "A statement may be characterized as one of fact if the content of the statement is susceptible of 'exact knowledge' at the time the statement is made."). See also SAIF Corp. v. Ramirez, 161 P.3d 326, 327–28 (Or. Ct. App. 2007) (workers' comp.: whether impairment is capable of being verified as true or false by empirical facts); Z-Tel Commc'ns, Inc. v. SBC Commc'ns, Inc., 331 F. Supp. 2d 513, 565–66 (E.D. Tex. 2004) (Lanham Act § 43(a) false advertising claim must be based on factual statements that are "specific" and "capable of being . . . 'adjudged true or false in a way that (2) admits of empirical verification' "); Milkovich v. Lorain Journal Co., 497 U.S. 1, 21 (1990) (defamatory statements of "opinion" may support defamation claim if "sufficiently factual to be susceptible of being proved true or false").

[63] See text at notes 37–38, above.

[64] "Where the fact represented would not influence the reasonable person, either because of its triviality or because of its irrelevance to the subject dealt with, the law will ordinarily regard that fact as immaterial and reliance on it unjustified." 2 Harper, James, and Gray on Torts 516–17.

[65] Prosser and Keeton on Torts, at 753.

[66] Rest. (2d) Torts § 538.

[67] A fact is material if: "(a) a reasonable man would attach importance to its existence or nonexistence in determining his choice of action in the transaction in question; or (b) the maker of the representation knows or has reason to know that its recipient regards or is likely to regard the matter as important in determining his choice of action, although a reasonable man would not so regard it." Id.

"Scienter"—Knowledge of Falsity and Intent to Deceive

The central elements of the tort of fraud or deceit, distinguishing it from negligent and innocent misrepresentation, are a defendant's *knowledge* that its representation is false and its *intent* to deceive the plaintiff thereby. Because of the difficulties in proving this guilty state of mind, plaintiffs in fraud cases often have difficulty establishing this important "scienter" component to an intentional misrepresentation claim.[68]

Many courts have stretched the scienter requirement in cases of fraud, some ruling that "deliberate deception or scienter is not a necessary element of the cause of action for fraud . . . . It is sufficient if the speaker makes the statement as of his own knowledge without knowing whether it is true or false."[69] Thus, while such a defendant may not *know* that what he says is false, he *does* know that he does *not* know whether the assertion is true or false.[70] In such a case, the "[d]efendant has lied about the extent of his knowledge of the facts in question; he has in effect represented that he knew a thing to be true when he knew that he only believed or surmised it to be true,"[71] or when he knew that he had no idea whether it was true or not. In short, " 'fraud' includes pretense of knowledge, where there is no knowledge."[72] While some courts squeeze this type of state of mind into the "intent" mold, others classify it merely as "recklessness."[73] Characterized either way, such a state of mind normally is considered adequate scienter to support a claim for fraud.

Justifiable Reliance

The plaintiff, or someone acting on the plaintiff's behalf (such as a parent, employer, physician, or the operator of a dangerous product in the plaintiff's vicinity),[74] must in

---

[68] **Proof of scienter.** See, e.g., In re Fosamax Prods. Liab. Litig., 807 F. Supp. 2d 168, 188–89 (S.D.N.Y. 2011) (granting defendant's summary judgment motion because plaintiff failed to show that defendant "willfully defrauded" plaintiff's doctor); Limited Flying Club, Inc. v. Wood, 632 F.2d 51, 55 (8th Cir. 1980) (Iowa law) (scienter and intent to deceive were not established by statements that airplane was "airworthy" and a "good little airplane," although the defendant was aware of prior damage and repairs and failed to report repairs in logbook).

Pleading scienter. Note, however, that the standard for *pleading* scienter, as distinguished from proving it at trial, may be less rigorous than for pleading other aspects of a fraudulent representation, because Fed. R. Civ. P. 9(b) "states that 'malice, intent, knowledge, and other condition of mind of a person may be averred generally.' " Oestreicher v. Alienware Corp., 544 F. Supp. 2d 964, 968 (N.D. Cal. 2008).

[69] Clements Auto Co. v. Service Bureau Corp., 298 F. Supp. 115, 126 (D. Minn. 1969), rev'd in part on other grounds, 444 F.2d 169 (8th Cir. 1971).

[70] See, e.g., Cummings v. HPG Int'l, Inc., 244 F.3d 16, 23 (1st Cir. 2001) (Mass. law) (reciting Rest. (2d) Torts § 526):

> A misrepresentation is fraudulent if the maker (a) knows or believes that the matter is not as he represents it to be, (b) does not have the confidence in the accuracy of his representation that he states or implies, or (c) knows that he does not have the basis for his representation that he states or implies.

[71] 2 Harper, James, and Gray on Torts § 7.3, at 463.

[72] Sgarlata v. Carioto, 201 N.Y.S.2d 384, 385 (Albany City Ct. 1960). See also Cooper v. R.J. Reynolds Tobacco Co., 234 F.2d 170, 174–75 (1st Cir. 1956) (Mass. law) (Magruder, J., concurring) (lung cancer from Camel cigarettes advertised as "healthful" and "harmless to the respiratory system"). See generally W.P. Keeton, Fraud: The Necessity for an Intent to Deceive, 5 UCLA L. Rev. 583 (1958).

[73] See, e.g., Guiggey v. Bombardier, 615 A.2d 1169, 1173 (Me. 1992) (no recovery for intentional misrepresentation unless plaintiff establishes that "statements were made with knowledge of falsity or reckless disregard of truth or falsity"); Limited Flying Club, Inc. v. Wood, 632 F.2d 51, 54–55 (8th Cir. 1980) (Iowa law) (scienter requires at least a showing that misrepresentations were made "in reckless disregard of their truth or falsity").

[74] Ordinarily, reliance by a person responsible for the plaintiff's safety should satisfy the reliance requirement. See, e.g., In re 3M Combat Arms Earplug Prods. Liab. Litig., 2021 WL 2605971, at *4 (N.D. Fla. 2021) (Wash. law) (misrepresentations made to military that earplug would protect soldiers' hearing); Wyeth,

fact learn about and then act somehow in *reliance* on the misrepresentation—as by purchasing the product, using it in a particular manner, or failing to take certain precautions. If a plaintiff fails to establish such reliance on the defendant's misrepresentation, the case will fail.[75]

A plaintiff's reliance normally provides the crucial causal link between the defendant's wrongful act and the plaintiff's harm, establishing that the wrong somehow generated the harmful consequences for which recovery is sought.[76] Thus, a person who takes no action on account of a misrepresentation usually is not harmed by it. Typically, causation is embedded in reliance, and proof of the former often establishes the latter.[77] The converse is also widely true: a plaintiff's proof of reliance on a misrepresentation often establishes a causal link between the defendant's misrepresentation and the plaintiff's harm.[78] But this connection does not always exist, and reliance on a misrepresentation does not uniformly prove causation.[79] For example, a long-time smoker seriously considering stopping may continue smoking because he sees, believes, and relies upon particular fraudulent advertisements of a cigarette manufacturer; but,

---

Inc. v. Weeks, 159 So.3d 649, 692 (Ala. 2014) (dissenting opinion of Murdock, J.) (doctor serves as patient's agent for purposes of reliance on drug representations); Tetuan v. A.H. Robins Co., 738 P.2d 1210, 1228 (Kan. 1987) (physician). Compare In re Bard IVC Filters Prods. Liab. Litig., 2018 WL 3586404, at *10 (D. Ariz. 2018) (plaintiffs' fraud claims failed absent evidence physician relied on information provided by the inferior vena cava filter manufacturer, sales force, or other sources). See also Rest. (3d) Torts: Products Liability § 9 Reporters' Note to cmt. *b*(2), at 190. *Contra* Ex parte DaimlerChrysler Corp., 952 So.2d 1082, 1090–91 (Ala. 2006) (teenager killed in rollover of Jeep Wrangler his mother purchased 6 years earlier when, in response to her query, salesman said roll bar provided protection in rollover accidents. But, *held*, fraud claim for son failed without proof he personally relied on the assertion).

[75] See, e.g., Renaissance Leasing, LLC v. Vermeer Mfg. Co., 322 S.W.3d 112, 132–33 (Mo. 2010) (en banc) (subject to three exceptions, reliance vitiated by plaintiff's independent investigation, as by observation of terrain leveler machine during two-month demonstration at a quarry); Scelta v. Boehringer Ingelheim Pharms., Inc., 404 Fed. Appx. 92, 94–95 (8th Cir. 2010) (Minn. law) (plaintiff failed to show he or his physician relied on alleged misrepresentation); Hoffman v. Hampshire Labs, Inc., 963 A.2d 849, 855 (N.J. Super. Ct. App. Div. 2009) (Herculex, an erectile dysfunction drug, was "guaranteed" to "induce the biggest erections of your life"; "a harder, stiffer, more rigid erection"; "one erection after another"; and "cause female partners to experience spine-quaking orgasms"; fraud claim conditionally dismissed because plaintiff failed to plead detrimental reliance); Fitzgerald v. Liberty Safe & Sec. Prods., Inc., 80 Fed. Appx. 897, 898–89 (5th Cir. 2003) (Miss. law) (fraud claim as to ability of safe to withstand fire not sustainable where plaintiff bought safe for protection from burglaries, not fire). On justifiable reliance and other defenses to misrepresentation claims, see § 13.7, below.

[76] "Justifiable reliance exists when the misrepresentation or nondisclosure was an immediate cause of the plaintiff's conduct which alters his legal relations, and when without such misrepresentation or nondisclosure he would not, in all reasonable probability, have entered into the contract or other transaction." Pritchett v. Avon Prods., Inc., 2002 WL 31547045, at *8 (Cal. Ct. App. 2002).

[77] See, e.g., Tetuan v. A.H. Robins Co., 738 P.2d 1210, 1230–31 (Kan. 1987):

> [T]he magic word "reliance" was not used, but the effect was the same: the jury was required to find that Robins' misrepresentations caused Dr. Pfuetze to use the Dalkon Shield which, in turn, caused [the plaintiff's] injuries. The jury was thus required to find reliance . . . .

See also Learjet Corp. v. Spenlinhauer, 901 F.2d 198, 200 (1st Cir. 1990) (Kan. law) ("If the aircraft would not have been put into commerce without the FAA certificate of airworthiness, it follows that a purchaser necessarily relied on the certificate, since a sale could not have occurred but for the FAA certificate.").

[78] Indeed, there typically is no explicit reference to causation in misrepresentation cases because the causal work usually rests on the shoulders of reliance.

[79] See, e.g., Dillon v. Zeneca Corp., 42 P.3d 598, 603 (Ariz. Ct. App. 2002) (plaintiffs relied on manufacturer's statement that herbicide effectively controlled weeds, but plaintiff's reliance on that representation, even if false, did not cause damage resulting from herbicide's killing crops); Small v. Lorillard Tobacco Co., 679 N.Y.S.2d 593, 601 (App. Div. 1998) (noting absence of evidence of "reliance and causation elements," suggesting their independence), aff'd, 698 N.Y.S.2d 615 (N.Y. 1999).

if the smoker dies from lung cancer soon after first seeing the advertisements, his death is most probably not causally attributable to his reliance on those ads.[80]

A plaintiff who does not hear or see a misrepresentation at all generally will be unable to establish reliance upon it.[81] Nor do most courts allow reliance by other buyers to suffice, the so-called fraud-on-the-market theory of reliance.[82] Yet, the reliance need not be by the plaintiff personally, so long as it is by someone acting on his or her behalf.[83] Thus, where a manufacturer knowingly provides dangerously false information about its product's dangers in a manual it gives to a purchasing employer, an employee's "indirect reliance" on his supervisor's assurances of safety gleaned from the manual should satisfy the reliance requirement.[84] So, too, "where a patient relies on a physician for treatment or advice as to an ethical or prescription device, justifiable reliance by the physician . . . constitutes justifiable reliance by the patient."[85]

Formerly, courts applied the same principle to situations where a manufacturer made fraudulent representations to a government agency, such as the FDA or the FAA, to get approval to market a new product, such as a new prescription drug or a new model aircraft. In such cases, while the fraud is aimed at the government agency, the

---

80 Cf. Cooper v. R.J. Reynolds Tobacco Co., 256 F.2d 464, 466 (1st Cir. 1958) (Mass. law).

81 See, e.g., Canady v. Ortho-McNeil Pharm., Inc., 2014 WL 4930675, at *5 (N.D. Ohio 2014) (no evidence that plaintiffs relied on any alleged false representations made by defendants; plaintiffs "never read the detailed patient labeling, saw any advertisements, or read anything about the Ortho Evra® birth control patch" and relied on physician for information); DeLuca v. Liggett & Myers, Inc., 2003 WL 1798940, at *5 (N.D. Ill. 2003) ("There is no evidence that [plaintiff] saw or much less relied on the 'Frank Statement.' There is also no evidence that he was aware of the 1994 testimony [by the defendants' CEOs, before Congress, that they did not believe nicotine was addictive] let alone that it affected his actions in any way."); Miller v. Pfizer Inc. (Roerig Div.), 196 F. Supp. 2d 1095, 1100 (D. Kan. 2002) (no reliance where patient's doctor never read the representations), aff'd on point, 356 F.3d 1326 (10th Cir. 2004).

82 **"Fraud on the Market."** A plaintiff who personally did not see and rely on a misrepresentation normally cannot establish reliance by proving reliance by other consumers—the so-called "fraud-on-the-market" theory drawn from securities law. See, e.g., Brown v. Philip Morris Inc., 228 F. Supp. 2d 506, 518–20 (D.N.J. 2002) (rejecting fraud-on-the-market theory where no proof deceased smoker ever saw defendant's ads). *But see* Bullock v. Philip Morris USA, Inc., 71 Cal. Rptr. 3d 775, 792 (Ct. App. 2008); Williams v. Philip Morris Inc., 48 P.3d 824, 830–31 (Or. Ct. App. 2002) (allowing fraud claim against cigarette manufacturer despite plaintiff's inability to identify particular statements on which he relied, based on defendant's claim over many years of advertising to the effect that there was a legitimate controversy over the safety of cigarette smoking; rejecting defendant's argument that claim was based on a "fraud on the American public" similar to "fraud on the market"), vacated on other grounds, Philip Morris USA Inc. v. Williams ("Williams II"), 540 U.S. 801 (2003). See also Goldberg and Zipursky, The Fraud-on-the-Market Tort, 66 Vand. L. Rev. 1755 (2013).

83 See, e.g., Miller v. Pfizer Inc. (Roerig Div.), 196 F. Supp. 2d 1095 (D. Kan. 2002) (doctor, by implication), aff'd, 356 F.3d 1326 (10th Cir. 2004). *But see* Ernst & Young, L.L.P. v. Pacific Mut. Life Ins. Co., 51 S.W.3d 573, 580 (Tex. 2001) (representations as to quality of TMJ jaw implant made to medical community at large, rather than specifically to injured patient, could not support misrepresentation claim: "For a misrepresentation to be actionable, the maker must intend to influence the very person to whom he makes the representation."); Wilson v. Dryvit Sys., Inc., 206 F. Supp. 2d 749 (E.D.N.C. 2002) (homeowners could not base fraud claim on fraudulent statements made by manufacturer of building materials to such "third parties" as builders, trade associations, and government entities), aff'd, 71 Fed. Appx. 960 (4th Cir. 2003). See generally Phillips, Product Misrepresentation and the Doctrine of Causation, 2 Hofstra L. Rev. 561 (1974); Owen, The Highly Blameworthy Manufacturer: Implications on Rules of Liability and Defense in Products Liability Actions, 10 Ind. L. Rev. 769, 781–84 (1977).

84 See Jowers v. BOC Grp., Inc., 2009 WL 995613, at *7 (S.D. Miss. 2009) (assertion in manual that welding fumes are "innocuous"; such indirect reliance suffices for fraudulent misrepresentation, citing Rest. (2d) Torts §§ 310 and 311), aff'd in part, vacated in part, remanded on other grounds sub nom. Jowers v. Lincoln Elec. Co., 617 F.3d 346 (5th Cir. 2010).

85 Tetuan v. A.H. Robins Co., 738 P.2d 1210, 1228 (Kan. 1987) (upholding awards of $1.7 million compensatory and $7.5 million punitive damages for fraudulently marketing dangerous Dalkon Shield IUD). See also Albertson v. Richardson-Merrell, Inc., 441 So.2d 1146, 1149–51 (Fla. Dist. Ct. App. 1983); Wechsler v. Hoffman-La Roche, Inc., 99 N.Y.S.2d 588, 590 (Sup. Ct. 1950).

fraudfeasor knows full well that its harmful effects may come to rest on the consuming public, which itself relies upon the integrity of the approval process administered by the agency. So, where the purchaser of an airplane relies upon an FAA airworthiness certificate the manufacturer procured by means of fraudulent representations to the FAA, a fraud claim brought by the purchaser against the manufacturer logically should rest upon the FAA's reliance on the misrepresentations made to it by the manufacturer.[86] Notwithstanding the soundness of this general principle, the Supreme Court has dubiously declared that such "fraud-on-the-agency" claims violate the principles of federal preemption.[87]

In contrast to the entirely subjective nature of reliance itself, involving as it does the issue of whether the plaintiff or other representee subjectively believed the representation and took action (at least in part) as a result thereof, the *justifiability* of the reliance rests on an *objective* standard of reasonableness in all the circumstances.[88] Thus, for a fraud to be actionable, a plaintiff must not only rely on the misrepresentation, but the reliance must be justifiable or reasonable. Yet, since justifiability is an element of a claim for *intentional* misrepresentation, courts often are understandably reluctant to allow a plaintiff's careless trust on a defendant's calculated fraud to bar a claim for this intentional tort.[89] In the end, however, a plaintiff must have had a "right to rely" on the defendant's misrepresentation, and a case for fraud will fail if the plaintiff cannot prove the justifiability of his or her reliance.[90]

Bound together with this broad issue of the reasonableness or justifiability of a plaintiff's reliance—whether the plaintiff had a "right to rely"—are the more specific issues involving the fact/opinion distinction and the element of materiality,[91] both

---

86 See, e.g., Learjet Corp. v. Spenlinhauer, 901 F.2d 198, 201–03 (1st Cir. 1990) (Kan. law). See also Toole v. Richardson-Merrell Inc., 60 Cal. Rptr. 398, 410–12 (Ct. App. 1967) (misrepresentations of drug's safety made to FDA to obtain approval to market new drug).

87 Buckman Co. v. Plaintiffs' Legal Comm., 531 U.S. 341, 352–53 (2001) (fraud-on-the-FDA claim federally preempted). Federal preemption is addressed in § 14.5, below.

88 Courts often define "justifiability" or "right to rely" in terms of reasonableness. See, e.g., In re Simon II Litig., 211 F.R.D. 86, 139 (E.D.N.Y. 2002) (Weinstein, J.) (restating element (4) of fraud, "plaintiff justifiably relied on the misrepresentation," as "reasonable reliance"), vacated on other grounds, 407 F.3d 125 (2d Cir. 2005); Pollmann v. Belle Plaine Livestock Auction, Inc., 567 N.W.2d 405, 410 (Iowa 1997) ("Reliance is justified when a reasonably careful person would be justified in relying on the information supplied. Reliance is not justified if the person receiving the information knows or in the exercise of ordinary care should know that the information is false."). *But see* Wright v. Brooke Grp. Ltd., 114 F. Supp. 2d 797, 821 (N.D. Iowa 2000) (stating that Iowa standard is subjective). See § 13.7, below.

89 On the tendency of courts to push justifiability toward a more subjective approach in cases involving true fraud, see § 13.7, below.

90 See, e.g., Soliman v. Philip Morris Inc., 311 F.3d 966, 975 (9th Cir. 2002) (Cal. law) ("A necessary element of a fraud claim is justifiable reliance on the defendant's misrepresentation or omission. . . . California law presumes a plaintiff's awareness that smoking causes addiction and other health problems. . . . Purported reliance on the industry's failure to disclose those facts is therefore not justifiable. Fraud that 'should be apparent even to the plaintiff[ ]' is not actionable.").

91 See 2 Harper, James, and Gray on Torts §§ 7.8 and 7.9; Prosser and Keeton on Torts §§ 108 and 109. For a helpful discussion of justifiability factors, see Sippy v. Cristich, 609 P.2d 204 (Kan. Ct. App. 1980):

> "[Such factors include] the intelligence, education, business experience and relative situation of the parties; the general information and experience of the persons involved as to the nature and use of the property; the habits and methods of those in the industry or profession involved; the opportunity for both parties to make an independent investigation as well as the nature, extent, and result of any investigation so made; and any contract the parties knowingly and understandingly entered into." . . . " 'A recipient of a fraudulent misrepresentation is justified in relying upon its truth without investigation, unless he knows or has reason to know of facts which make his reliance unreasonable.' . . . [T]he test is whether the recipient has 'information which

examined earlier. In making significant purchase decisions, buyers ordinarily do not accept as factual truth a seller's general commendations of its product or general assurances of the product's great value or extraordinary usefulness. Representations of this sort properly are viewed merely as the seller's opinion rather than as statements of fact. Nor do buyers ordinarily make important purchase decisions on the basis of the seller's assurances concerning matters that are trivial.

At bottom, it makes little difference whether one views puffs, and irrelevant and trivial representations, from an objective viewpoint that buyers have no *right* to rely on such representations in making important decisions, or, instead, from a subjective perspective that buyers in such cases most likely do not in *fact* rely on such representations. In either case, the law should not provide an injured buyer with an easy way to escape responsibility for an injury principally caused by his or her own careless decision to buy a product or use it in a particular way rather than by some insignificant misstatement that played little or no role in either the buyer's purchase or use decision. Thus, a plaintiff must establish that the reliance was "justifiable" not because a fraudfeasor should be shielded from accountability by the plaintiff's gullibility or contributory negligence[92] but because such proof provides additional, objective assurance that the plaintiff probably did in fact rely on the particular representation.

Resulting Damage

A plaintiff may recover damages that result from relying upon a defendant's fraudulent misrepresentation. While the type, scope, and measure of damages for fraud present special considerations beyond the scope of this text,[93] it should be noted here that a claim for deceit is completed by proof of this final element—actual damages causally resulting from the misrepresentation. Without sufficient proof of present

---

> would serve as a danger signal and a red light to any normal person of his intelligence and experience.' "

Id. at 208 (quoting from, *inter alia*, Rest. (2d) Torts § 540 and comments thereto).

[92] In misrepresentation claims by individuals against institutions, most modern courts no longer hold plaintiffs to a duty of care to investigate the truth of a defendant's representation. See, e.g., Kavarco v. T.J.E., Inc., 478 A.2d 257, 262 (Conn. App. Ct. 1984) (plaintiff not required to "make an independent investigation which would have revealed that the representation upon which he relied was false"), overruled on other grounds by Kaczynski v. Kaczynski, 981 A.2d 1068 (Conn. 2009). This development would seem especially apt in a typical personal injury products liability case against a manufacturer. The softening of the justifiability element in cases of fraudulent misrepresentation is examined in § 13.7, below.

In claims between business enterprises dealing with one another at arm's length, however, the requirement of justifiability of reliance still properly has considerable force. See, e.g., Valspar Refinish, Inc. v. Gaylord's, Inc., 764 N.W.2d 359, 369 (Minn. 2009) (plaintiff could not "demonstrate that it reasonably relied" on defendant's representations; the parties "were sophisticated business equals operating in a commercial setting, and [plaintiff] conducted an investigation and experimentation regarding the quality and application of [defendant's] paint product").

[93] **Pure economic loss: no recovery.** This rule may bar certain fraud claims for pure economic loss, including diminished value of products of inferior quality that do not work properly. See, e.g., Milan Supply Chain Sols., Inc. v. Navistar, Inc., 627 S.W.3d 125, 129 (Tenn. 2021) (economic loss rule applies when "a fraud claim seeks recovery of only economic losses and is premised solely on misrepresentations or nondisclosures about the quality of goods that are the subject of a contract between sophisticated commercial parties"). *But see* Robinson Helicopter Co. v. Dana Corp., 102 P.3d 268 (Cal. 2004) (economic loss rule does not bar fraud claim that is independent of breach of contract). Note that the UCC remedies for breach of warranty are available for fraudulent breach. UCC § 2–721.

Wrongful death. As previously mentioned, fraud claims may not survive the death of a party. See, e.g., Faircloth v. Finesod, 938 F.2d 513 (4th Cir. 1991) (SC law; denial of such claims is constitutional).

Punitive damages. For the role of fraud in recovering punitive damages, see Owen & Davis on Products Liability § 26:13.

damages (in addition to causation, discussed earlier in connection with reliance), an intentional misrepresentation claim normally will fail.[94]

Other Issues

State Statutes—Deceptive Trade Practices Acts

In addition to traditional common law (and, in some code states, statutory) fraud claims, all states have consumer protection statutes that variously prohibit false, misleading, unfair, or deceptive trade practices.[95] As further discussed below, these laws commonly provide for treble damages and attorney's fees. Generally brought as class actions,[96] claims under these statutes often seek injunctive relief.[97] Yet, because the principal goal of such statutes is to discourage commercial parties from engaging in unfair and deceptive trade practices, and to protect consumers from the economic consequences of such conduct, remedies provided by these statutes generally are not available to persons suffering *physical* injuries from products deceptively promoted in apparent violation of statutes of this type.[98]

Mislabeling claims against manufacturers of food and other consumer products frequently allege violations of consumer protection statutes. So, manufacturers may not

---

[94] **No-injury claims.** When a manufacturer falsely represents a product as safe, the public's subsequent discovery of the concealed defect diminishes the value of all such products that are more dangerous than consumers had thought. Whether owners not physically injured by such a product have claims in tort or warranty is a difficult question that involves a host of complex matters. In addition to the economic loss rule, such cases implicate knotty issues concerning standing and class actions. See, e.g., In re Toyota Motor Corp. Unintended Acceleration Mktg., Sales Practices, & Prods. Liab. Litig., 2013 WL 3224585 (C.D. Cal. 2013) (preliminary approval of $1.4 billion class action settlement of diminished value claims by owners of Toyotas allegedly subject to sudden unintended acceleration); In re Ford Motor Co. E-350 Van Prods. Liab. Litig. (No. II), 2012 WL 379944 (D.N.J. 2012). *But see* Wallis v. Ford Motor Co., 208 S.W.3d 153, 159 (Ark. 2005) ("no-injury" claim: "[While] some jurisdictions have concluded that the 'diminution in value' of a product alone is enough to succeed on a common-law fraud claim, we decline to adopt this principle [and adhere] to our well-settled case law [that] common-law fraud claims not resulting in injury are not actionable"); Frank v. DaimlerChrysler Corp., 741 N.Y.S.2d 9, 16 (App. Div. 2002) (same; "public policy": "it would be manifestly unfair to require a manufacturer to become, in essence, an indemnifier for a loss that may never occur"). See White, Reverberations from the Collision of Tort and Warranty, 53 S.C. L. Rev. 1067 (2002) (viability of tort and warranty claims for "inchoate injury").

[95] Common names for such statutes include "Consumer Protection Acts, Consumer Fraud Acts, Deceptive Trade Practices Acts, 'little FTCs,' or some combination thereof." Sweeney and Englund, The Class Action Fairness Act's Impact on State Consumer Protection Laws, 72 Def. Couns. J. 233, 235 (2005). See, e.g., In re Philips/Magnavox Television Litig., 2010 WL 3522787, at *6 (D.N.J. 2010) ("[a]lthough these statutes have different substantive requirements, collectively, they are intended to broadly prohibit unconscionable or immoral commercial practices, and fraud and deception through misrepresentations or intentional omissions of material facts"; consumer fraud claims against manufacturers of allegedly defective flat screen televisions, brought under Ark., Cal., Fla., Ill., Mich., N.J., Ohio, Tex., and Wash. statutes).

[96] See, e.g., Downing v. Keurig Green Mountain, Inc., 2021 WL 2403811 (D. Mass. 2021) (retaining Massachusetts claims that coffee pods were falsely advertised as recyclable but dismissing nationwide class); Lee v. Conagra Brands, Inc., 958 F.3d 70 (1st Cir. 2020) (reversing dismissal of class action claims that "100% Natural" label on cooking oil containing genetically modified organisms violated Massachusetts law prohibiting unfair and deceptive trade practices); Langan v. Johnson & Johnson Consumer Cos., 2017 WL 985640 (D. Conn. 2017) (class action alleging "natural" sunscreen, baby shampoo, and baby bath products contained chemicals). See also Ramey, The Case for Plain Vanilla Gets Its Day in Court, Wall St. J., Feb. 7, 2021, at A1 (describing numerous class actions against numerous defendants alleging misrepresentation of artificial flavoring as "natural" vanilla).

[97] See, e.g., Schoonover v. Iovate Health Scis. U.S.A. Inc., 2020 WL 5015269, at *2 (C.D. Cal. 2020) (non-functional slack-filled packaging of powdered nutritional supplement "pre-workout" products); Sotelo v. Rawlings Sporting Goods Co., 2019 WL 3240098, at *4 (C.D. Cal. 2019) (mislabeled weights on Youth 5150 USA baseball bats).

[98] See notes 112–113 and accompanying text, below.

claim that their products are "natural,"[99] made of "whole grain,"[100] contain no "artificial" ingredients,[101] nor that they are "rapid release,"[102] unless such assertions are factually correct. While these statutes forbid *making* false and misleading assertions of fact about the nature of one's products, this does not mean that a manufacturer must affirmatively *disclose* every untoward detail of how its products are produced, such as any sordid aspects of its supply chains not affecting the quality of its products.[103]

Another common type of consumer protection act claim alleges that a manufacturer deliberately underfills its product's containers, so that the container size misrepresents the amount of the product carried within. Claims that such oversized "slack fill" packaging is fraudulent thus rest on there being an appreciable nonfunctional difference between a container's practicable capacity and the product volume it actually contains.[104]

A key feature of unfair competition/false and fraudulent business act/deceptive advertising/consumer protection statutes is how widely they differ from state to state—e.g., some requiring proof of fraud; others requiring merely negligent misrepresentation; and some requiring no fault at all by a seller in making a claim about a product that is false or misleading. Such statutes also differ importantly in what type of proof is required on reliance.

Because such state statutes vary considerably in how they describe the conduct they prohibit and what they otherwise require a plaintiff to prove to establish a claim,[105] a lawyer must study an applicable statute carefully to determine its elements,[106] including

---

[99] See, e.g., Lee v. Conagra Brands, Inc., 958 F.3d 70 (1st Cir. 2020) (reversing dismissal of plaintiff's claims that "100% Natural" label on cooking oil containing genetically modified organisms violated Massachusetts law prohibiting unfair and deceptive trade practices); Langan v. Johnson & Johnson Consumer Cos., 2017 WL 985640 (D. Conn. 2017) (class action alleging "natural" sunscreen, baby shampoo, and baby bath products contained chemicals); Briseno v. ConAgra Foods, Inc., 844 F.3d 1121 (9th Cir. 2017) (class action alleging "100% Natural" cooking oil was made from genetically-modified organisms). See also Ramey, The Case for Plain Vanilla Gets Its Day in Court, Wall St. J., Feb. 7, 2021, at A1 (describing numerous class actions against numerous defendants alleging misrepresentation of artificial flavoring as "natural" vanilla).

[100] See Mantikas v. Kellogg Co., 910 F.3d 633 (2d Cir. 2018) (Cal. and N.Y. law).

[101] See Clark v. Hershey Co., 2019 WL 2288041 (N.D. Cal. 2019) (class action alleging chocolate-covered candy balls with "no artificial flavors, no artificial colors" were flavored by malic acid).

[102] See Bailey v. Rite Aid Corp., 2019 WL 4260394, at *6 (N.D. Cal. 2019) (study revealed that Rite Aid's higher-priced "Rite Aid Rapid Release" acetaminophen caplets dissolve at a slower rate than its lower-priced Rite Aid non-rapid release caplets).

[103] See Hodsdon v. Mars, Inc., 891 F.3d 857, 860 (9th Cir. 2018) (Cal. law) (that defendant used cocoa beans, the raw ingredient for chocolate, from the Ivory Coast, where some cocoa farms used child and slave labor; "California consumer protection laws do not obligate [defendants] to label their goods as possibly being produced by child or slave labor. In the absence of any affirmative misrepresentations by the manufacturer, we hold that the manufacturers do not have a duty to disclose the labor practices in question, even though they are reprehensible, because they are not physical defects that affect the central function of the chocolate products.").

[104] See, e.g., Schoonover v. Iovate Health Scis. U.S.A. Inc., 2020 WL 5015269, at *2 (C.D. Cal. 2020) (claims of non-functional slack fill of powdered nutritional supplement "pre-workout" products sufficiently pled for standing for injunctive relief and to avoid summary judgment); Kennard v. Lamb Weston Holdings, Inc., 2019 WL 1586022, at *8–9 (N.D. Cal. 2019) (nonfunctional slack fill claims that frozen sweet potato fries package contained 50% empty space sufficiently pled to avoid summary judgment); Daniel v. Tootsie Roll Indus., LLC, 2018 WL 3650015, at *11 (S.D.N.Y. 2018) (claims that Junior Mints boxes contained "non-functional slack fill" failed; boxes clearly displayed candy weight and serving size).

[105] See In re Philips/Magnavox Television Litig., 2010 WL 3522787, at *6 (D.N.J. 2010) (Ark., Cal., Fla., Ill., Mich., N.J., Ohio, Tex., and Wash. consumer fraud statutes "have different substantive requirements").

[106] See, e.g., In re Nat'l Prescription Opiate Litig., 452 F. Supp. 3d 745, 776 (N.D. Ohio 2020) (Florida's Deceptive and Unfair Trade Practices Act has 3 elements: "(1) a deceptive act or unfair practice in the course of trade or commerce; (2) causation; and (3) actual damages"); De Bouse v. Bayer A.G., 922 N.E.2d 309, 313

particularly whether and how a plaintiff may prove a private right of action.[107] Iowa's consumer fraud act, for example, is enforceable only by the attorney general,[108] and claims under Minnesota's unfair trade practices, consumer fraud, and false advertising acts may be pursued by private parties only indirectly, under that state's private attorney general statute, and only then if the private lawsuit can be shown to provide a public benefit.[109]

As with the federal odometer tampering statute,[110] which provides redress for a particular form of fraudulent behavior, deceptive trade practices laws often provide for treble damages and attorneys' fees.[111] Yet, it bears repeating that state legislatures enacted such statutes principally to discourage and remedy economic losses,[112] not physical injuries, such that their robust statutory remedies are generally unavailable in products liability personal injury cases.[113] How consumer fraud statutes, products liability statutes, Article 2 of the UCC, and the common law interrelate raises questions of state-specific interpretation of particular statutory language and purpose.[114]

(Ill. 2009) (Illinois' Consumer Fraud Act claims: (1) defendant's deceptive act or practice; (2) defendant's intent that plaintiff rely on the deception; (3) such deception "in a course of conduct involving trade or commerce"; (4) plaintiff's actual damage; (5) resulting from the deception).

[107] See, e.g., Newman v. Axiom Worldwide, 2010 WL 2265227, at *4 (D.N.J. 2010) ("The Consumer Fraud Act ('CFA') vests private citizens with a cause of action under defined circumstances: Any person who suffers any ascertainable loss of moneys or property, real or personal, as a result of the use or employment by another person of any method, act, or practice declared unlawful under this act may bring an action in any court of competent jurisdiction. N.J. Stat. Ann. § 56:8–19."); Robinson v. Bristol-Myers Squibb Co., 2009 WL 5206126, at *5 (D.N.J. 2009) (Md. law).

[108] See Iowa Code Ann. § 714.16.

[109] See In re Levaquin Prods. Liab. Litig., 752 F. Supp. 2d 1071, 1079 (D. Minn. 2010) (allowing, under such acts, inadequate warning claims against manufacturer of dangerous drug marketed to public because the "lawsuit may indirectly cause defendants to redress a public safety hazard, a result of obvious benefit to the public under the Private AG Statute").

[110] 49 U.S.C. § 32710.

[111] See, e.g., Cooper v. Samsung Elecs. Am., Inc., 374 Fed. Appx. 250, 256 (3d Cir. 2010) (Ambro, J., dissenting) (N.J. law) ("While one purpose of the New Jersey Consumer Fraud Act is to compensate defrauded consumers, it 'serves as a deterrent' by awarding successful plaintiffs 'treble damages, attorneys' fees, filing fees, and costs.' ").

[112] See, e.g., In re Ford Motor Co. E-350 Van Prods. Liab. Litig. (No. II), 2008 WL 4126264, at *29 (D.N.J. 2008) (consumer fraud statute allows consumers right to recover economic losses); Tex. Bus. & Com. Code Ann § 17.50(b)(1) (economic damages and damages for mental anguish if intentional); Am. Law Prod. Liab. 3d § 25:7. *But see* Murphy v. Proctor & Gamble, Co., 695 F. Supp. 2d 600, 606 n.3 (E.D. Mich. 2010) (citing cases where economic loss doctrine "precludes fraud claim" under state consumer protection statutes).

[113] See generally Boswell, Stagg, and Myers, Deceptive Trade Practice—Consumer Protection Acts and Their Effect on Product Liability Litigation, 15 Forum 716 (Spring 1980). *But see* Sun Chemical Corp. v. Fike Corp., 235 A.3d 145, 156 (N.J. 2020) ("A [Consumer Fraud Act] claim alleging express or affirmative misrepresentations—deceptive, fraudulent, misleading, and other unconscionable commercial practices—may proceed in separate counts of the same pleading as a [Products Liability Act] claim alleging product design, manufacturing, or warning defects."; answering certified question); Maldonado v. Nutri/System, Inc., 776 F. Supp. 278 (E.D. Va. 1991) ("loss" under such a statute included loss of gall bladder caused by defendant's weight loss food advertised as safe).

[114] For example, compare Sinclair v. Merck & Co., 948 A.2d 587, 595–96 (N.J. 2008) (plaintiffs' medical monitoring claim under consumer fraud act failed to circumvent products liability statute requirement of present injury), with Crouch v. Johnson & Johnson Consumer Cos., 2010 WL 1530152, at *9 (D.N.J. 2010) (Kan. law) (unlike New Jersey, "the expansive reach of the Kentucky CPA appears to encompass and allow for the assertion of products liability/personal injury tort claims"). See also Norman v. Xytex Corp., 848 S.E.2d 835, 844 (Ga. 2020) (affirming dismissal of non-cognizable wrongful birth products liability claims against sperm bank for providing sperm from donor # 9623, whose hospitalizations for mental health issues and criminal background went undiscovered, while reversing dismissal of claims for consumer protection violations, misrepresentation, and other claims "not predicated on life as an injury"); Doe 1 v. Xytex Corporation, 2017 WL 1112996, at *8 (N.D. Cal. 2017) (retaining wrongful birth, negligence, false advertising,

Federal Statutes

The federal odometer tampering statute just mentioned is a rare federal statute authorizing claims and providing damages remedies for fraud.[115] More commonly, under the doctrine of federal preemption,[116] federal regulatory safety statutes *bar* a victim's efforts to recover damages for a fraud. Sometimes, when federal preemption of state products liability law is an issue, as in litigation over injuries from cigarettes,[117] and certain other products,[118] fraud claims may avoid preemption if the fraud falls outside the realm of conduct addressed by Congress. Yet, depending on the particular federal statute, even fraud claims sometimes do not escape the grasp of federal preemption.[119]

Mail or wire fraud (including fraud by telephone, television, and radio) that establishes a "pattern of racketeering activity" may give rise to treble damages and attorney's fees under the Racketeer Influenced and Corrupt Organizations Act ("RICO"), enacted by Congress in 1970.[120] The Supreme Court has interpreted the RICO statute restrictively, however, and courts now hold that it applies only to massive and ongoing schemes perpetrated by repeated and intensive use of the mail and wires.[121] Moreover, RICO claims are unavailable in ordinary products liability actions for personal injuries, since the statute provides that civil damages are available only for injuries to a person's "business or property."[122] But such claims may be available for third-party healthcare

---

and unfair business practices claims against sperm bank providing sperm from donor # 9623, while dismissing strict products liability, breach of warranty, and battery claims).

[115] 49 U.S.C. § 32710.

[116] See § 14.5, below.

[117] Most of plaintiff's fraud claims escaped preemption in Cipollone v. Liggett Grp., Inc., 505 U.S. 504, 528–31 (1992), and such claims continued thereafter to figure prominently in litigation against the tobacco industry. See, e.g., Altria Grp., Inc. v. Good, 555 U.S. 70, 76–90 (2008) (fraudulent misrepresentation claims under Maine Unfair Trade Practices Act (MUTPA) against manufacturer of "light" cigarettes not preempted by Federal Cigarette Labeling and Advertising Act (FCLAA)).

[118] See, e.g., Fabian v. Fulmer Helmets, Inc., 628 F.3d 278, 281–83 (6th Cir. 2010) (Tenn. law) (fraud and negligent misrepresentation claims against motorcycle helmet manufacturer not preempted by NHTSA regulations).

[119] See, e.g., Buckman Co. v. Plaintiffs' Legal Comm., 531 U.S. 341, 348 (2001) (fraud-on-the-FDA claims federally preempted). See also DJ Coleman, Inc. v. Nufarm Ams., Inc., 693 F. Supp. 2d 1055, 1080–81 (D.N.D. 2010) (misbranding claim under North Dakota Consumer Fraud Act preempted by FIFRA). On federal preemption, see § 14.5, below.

[120] 18 U.S.C. §§ 1961 et seq.

[121] See, e.g., H.J. Inc. v. Northwestern Bell Tel. Co., 492 U.S. 229 (1989); cf. Reves v. Ernst & Young, 507 U.S. 170 (1993), noted, 108 Harv. L. Rev. 1405 (1995).

[122] See 18 U.S.C. § 1964(c). On RICO civil damages actions, see Pierson, Rico Trends: From Gangsters to Class Actions, 65 S.C. L. Rev. 213 (2013); Grell, Exorcising RICO from Product Litigation, 24 Wm. Mitchell L. Rev. 1089 (1998); Marple, "Pattern" Requirement Renders RICO Inapplicable to Ordinary Business Disputes, 14 Rev. Litig. 343 (1995); Camp, Dual Construction of RICO: The Road Not Taken in Reves, 51 Wash. & Lee L. Rev. 61 (1994); Annots., 96 A.L.R. Fed. 881 (1990) (recovery for personal injuries under RICO), 70 A.L.R. Fed. 538 (1984) (civil damage actions under RICO).

Fraudulent corporate behavior may also be discouraged by assessing civil fines, penalties, and even criminal charges. See, e.g., Andazzo, Purdue Pharma Reaches $8.34 Billion Settlement Over Opioid Probes, Wall St. J.com (Oct. 21, 2020) (in settlement with justice Department, Purdue Pharma LP also to plead guilty to three felonies for its conduct in marketing and distributing OxyContin); Fisk and Raphael, VW Exec Gets Seven Years in Prison for Role in Diesel Scam, 45 Prod. Safety & Liab. Rep. (BNA) 1199 (Dec. 11, 2017); Fisk and Butters, Takata to Pay $1B in U.S. Air Bag Probe; Execs Charged, 45 Prod. Safety & Liab. Rep. (BNA) 89 (Jan. 23, 2017).

providers, and possibly claims by other institutional defendants, who suffer loss from fraudulent schemes by drug companies and other manufacturers.[123]

Statutes of Limitations

Fraud claims ordinarily are governed by their own statutes of limitations,[124] rather than by the contract statute of limitations contained in the Uniform Commercial Code,[125] at least where the claim for fraud is separately cognizable.[126]

Disclaimers

Because fraud and deceit claims are grounded in conduct that normally is intentionally harmful, the law attempts to discourage persons from devising ways to engage in this type of antisocial behavior without legal accountability. Accordingly, contractual waivers and disclaimers against liability for fraud normally are held to be void as against public policy.[127]

§ 3.3 NEGLIGENT MISREPRESENTATION

If a person injured as a result of a misrepresentation is unable to prove fraud for lack of scienter,[128] the injured party nevertheless may be able to establish a claim for negligent misrepresentation.[129] A negligent misrepresentation claim resembles a claim for intentional misrepresentation except that the elements of duty and negligence in claims for negligent misrepresentation[130] replace the elements of knowledge of falsity

---

[123] See, e.g., City of Bos. v. Purdue Pharma, L.P., 2020 WL 977056, at *6 (Mass. Super. Ct. 2020) (fraud claims against opioid distributors); In re Neurontin Mktg. & Sales Practices Litig., 712 F.3d 21 (1st Cir. 2013) (federal and Cal. law) (successful RICO and unfair business practices claims against drug company, for fraudulently pushing Neurontin to healthcare providers for off-label conditions for which it was ineffective).

[124] See, e.g., Lynch v. Jack in the Box, 2007 WL 2274838, at *3 (Tex. App. 2007) (4-year limitations period for fraud); County of Santa Clara v. Atlantic Richfield Co., 40 Cal. Rptr. 3d 313, 345 (Ct. App. 2006) (3-year limitations period for fraud).

[125] See UCC § 2–725 (four years); § 14.6, below.

[126] That is, where the fraud claim is distinct from a claim for fraudulent nonperformance of the contract. See Triangle Underwriters, Inc. v. Honeywell, Inc., 604 F.2d 737, 747–48 (2d Cir. 1979) (N.Y. law).

[127] See, e.g., Cummings v. HPG Int'l, Inc., 244 F.3d 16, 21 (1st Cir. 2001) (Mass. law); First Nat'l Bank of Louisville v. Brooks Farms, 1990 WL 6386 (Tenn. Ct. App. 1990) (good discussion), aff'd on this point, 821 S.W.2d 925 (Tenn. 1991). Compare Champion Home Builders Co. v. ADT Sec. Servs., Inc., 179 F. Supp. 2d 16, 25 (N.D.N.Y. 2001), as amended (2002) (fire alarm company's exculpatory clause enforceable on grounds of public policy in absence of gross negligence or fraudulent inducement; even if false, contractual assertions are not fraudulent unless defendant intended not to perform them at the time of contract).

[128] "Scienter" refers to the defendant's knowledge of falsity and intent to deceive. See §§ 3.1 and 3.2, above.

[129] See Frumer, Friedman, and Sklaren, Products Liability § 2.05[3]; Rest. (3d) of Torts: Products Liability § 9.

[130] See, e.g., McClarty v. C.R. Bard, Inc., 2020 WL 6075520, at *9–10 (E.D. Mich. 2020) ("In addition to reliance, . . . the elements of negligent misrepresentation are: (1) the defendant made a material misrepresentation; (2) the representation was false; (3) the defendant was negligent in making the misrepresentation; and (4) the plaintiff suffered damages as a result."); Great Northern Ins. Co. v. Amazon.com, Inc., 2019 WL 3935038, at *3 (N.D. Ill. 2019) (Illinois law: "(1) a false statement of material fact; (2) carelessness or negligence in ascertaining the truth of the statement by the party making it; (3) an intention to induce the other party to act; (4) action by the other party in reliance on the truth of the statement; (5) damage to the other party resulting from such reliance; and (6) a duty on the party making the statement to communicate accurate information.' "); First American Specialty Ins. Co. v. Carmax Auto Superstores Cal., LLC, 2017 WL 5235646, at *4 (N.D. Cal. 2017) ("a plaintiff must show that the defendant (1) asserted a material fact, (2) which was untrue, (3) without a reasonable grounds for believing it to be true, (4) with the intent that plaintiff would rely upon the assertion, (5) that the plaintiff justifiably relied upon the representation, and (6) as a result was harmed"); Fagan v. AmerisourceBergen Corp., 356 F. Supp. 2d 198, 219 (E.D.N.Y. 2004) ((1) duty, from special relationship, to provide plaintiff with correct information; (2) false representation defendant should have known was incorrect; (3) defendant knew plaintiff desired information

and intent to deceive in claims for fraud.[131] Thus, negligent misrepresentation partakes of two quite different torts—negligence and deceit—a union that can inject confusion into the contours of this particular type of claim.[132] Although negligent misrepresentation claims are not allowed by all states for all types of harm,[133] this basis of recovery is widely available in a products liability case involving physical harm if its elements are properly pleaded[134] and established.[135]

As with claims for fraudulent misrepresentation, a plaintiff claiming negligent misrepresentation must prove each of the non-scienter elements of deceit—including that the defendant made a false representation of material fact on which the plaintiff, or

---

for serious purpose; (4) plaintiff intended to rely and act on information; and (5) plaintiff reasonably relied on information to his or her detriment). See also Lloyd v. General Motors Corp., 916 A.2d 257, 273 (Md. 2007), stating the elements of negligent misrepresentation:

(1) the defendant, owing a duty of care to the plaintiff, negligently asserts a false statement;

(2) the defendant intends that his statement will be acted upon by the plaintiff;

(3) the defendant has knowledge that the plaintiff will probably rely on the statement, which, if erroneous, will cause loss or injury;

(4) the plaintiff, justifiably, takes action in reliance on the statement; and

(5) the plaintiff suffers damage proximately caused by the defendant's negligence.

[131] See, e.g., Snelten v. Schmidt Implement Co., 647 N.E.2d 1071, 1076 (Ill. App. Ct. 1995):

> To state a cause of action for negligent misrepresentation, the complaint must again allege a duty to plaintiff, a breach of the duty and injury proximately resulting from such breach. . . . Restatement (Second) of Torts § 311 (1965) provides there may be liability for negligently giving false information to another if the information causes some physical harm to the person who justifiably relies on the information. . . . [T]he elements of a cause of action for negligent misrepresentation are essentially the same as those for fraudulent misrepresentation except the defendant need not know or believe the statement to be false; instead, the plaintiff need only allege the defendant was careless or negligent in ascertaining the truth of the statement made.

See also Strong, "But He Told Me It Was Safe": The Expanding Tort of Negligent Misrepresentation, 40 U. Mem. L. Rev. 105, 142 (2009).

[132] Compare Cummings v. HPG Int'l, Inc., 244 F.3d 16, 25 (1st Cir. 2001) (Mass. law) ("Massachusetts courts treat negligent misrepresentation claims more as negligence actions than deceit actions, focusing on the degree of care exercised by the speaker in making the statement"), with In re Tobacco Cases II, 113 Cal. Rptr. 2d 120, 129–31 (Ct. App. 2001) (negligent misrepresentation claims normally are viewed in California as a form of fraud, but they are subject to negligence law's remoteness doctrine).

[133] See, e.g., Cotton v. Ethicon, Inc., 2021 WL 736211, at *7 (N.D. Ind. 2021) (declining to extend negligent misrepresentation to sale of implanted medical device; "the Seventh Circuit has recognized the law of negligent misrepresentation in Indiana to be 'relative chaos' "); Barnhill v. Iowa Dist. Ct. for Polk Cnty., 765 N.W.2d 267, 274 (Iowa 2009) (negligent misrepresentation claims for pecuniary loss not allowed "against product manufacturers or product sellers who supply information about the product in connection with its sale"); Valspar Refinish, Inc. v. Gaylord's Inc., 764 N.W.2d 359, 369–71 (Minn. 2009) (same, under state statute); Driver v. Burlington Aviation, Inc., 430 S.E.2d 476, 480–81 (N.C. Ct. App. 1993) (passenger injured in aircraft that crashed due to carburetor icing denied recovery for negligent misrepresentation; such claims available in North Carolina only for pecuniary loss, not for personal injury). On the economic loss rule, see § 5.3 (*Types of Damages*), below. See also Farrell v. Johnson & Johnson, 238 A.3d 698, 715–16 (Conn. 2020) (no strict liability for innocent misrepresentations for medical services).

[134] **Pleading.** See, e.g., Stearns v. Select Comfort Retail Corp., 2009 WL 1635931, at *12 (N.D. Cal. 2009) (negligent misrepresentation is based in fraud and so subject to the heightened pleading requirements of Fed. R. Civ. P. 9(b)). On its face, Rule 9(b) applies to allegations of fraud or mistake. Whether or not it properly applies as well to averments of mere *negligent* misrepresentation, the heightened pleading requirements of Bell Atl. Corp. v. Twombly, 550 U.S. 544 (2007), and Ashcroft v. Iqbal, 556 U.S. 662 (2009), apply broadly to *all* tortious misrepresentation (as other) averments in federal court, not just those alleging fraud. See, e.g., Holland v. Ethicon, Inc., 2021 WL 3432833, at *2 (M.D. Ala. 2021) (dismissing negligent misrepresentation claim; plaintiffs' "general allegations [did] not detail the 'precise' negligent misrepresentations made nor [did] they shed light on 'the time, place, and person responsible' "); Teal v. Argon Med. Devices, Inc., 533 F. Supp. 3d 535, 554 (E.D. Mich. 2021) (dismissing negligent misrepresentation claim for failing to specify "where and when" alleged misrepresentations were made). Rule 9(b), *Twombly*, and *Iqbal* are briefly addressed in § 3.2 note 22, above.

[135] See Frumer, Friedman, and Sklaren, Products Liability § 2.05[3].

someone acting on the plaintiff's behalf,[136] justifiably and detrimentally relied.[137] Thus, a negligent misrepresentation claim will fail if there is no representation,[138] if the representation cannot fairly be construed as an affirmation of fact,[139] if the representation is not material,[140] or if the representation is more a prediction of the product's future performance than a representation of existing fact.[141] Also, a claim for negligent misrepresentation cannot be sustained if the plaintiff fails to rely upon the defendant's representation[142] or does so without justification,[143] or if the plaintiff's reliance on the representation did not cause the plaintiff's harm.[144]

Courts often assert that a negligent misrepresentation claimant must show an additional element—that the defendant owed a *duty* to the claimant to impart accurate information,[145] the scope of which depends upon the kind of harm risked by the defendant and suffered by the plaintiff. With respect to risks of personal injury and property damage, the duty to refrain from negligent misrepresentation normally is

---

[136] See, e.g., McClarty v. C.R. Bard, Inc., 2020 WL 6075520, at *11–12 (E.D. Mich. 2020) (claim failed; no evidence that deceased surgeon or other medical provider relied on allegedly inadequate inferior vena cava filter warnings). Some courts limit negligent misrepresentation claims to persons to whom the representation was made, or to those in privity with the defendant. See, e.g., Soule v. Norton, 750 N.Y.S.2d 692, 695 (App. Div. 2002) (patients could not maintain negligent misrepresentation claim against manufacturer of surgical laser because they did not have "actual privity of contract . . . or a relationship so close as to approach that of privity"). See also Great N. Ins. Co. v. Amazon.com, Inc., 524 F. Supp. 3d 852, 858–59 (N.D. Ill. 2021) (internet marketplace provider not liable for third-party's negligent misrepresentations under both Illinois law and § 230 of the Communications Decency Act).

[137] "To establish a claim for both negligent misrepresentation and strict responsibility for misrepresentation the plaintiff must show that the defendant made a representation of fact, that the representation was untrue, and that the plaintiff believed the representation and relied upon it to his or her detriment." Consolidated Papers, Inc. v. Dorr-Oliver, Inc., 451 N.W.2d 456, 459 (Wis. Ct. App. 1989).

[138] See, e.g., Riggins v. Ortho McNeil Pharm., Inc., 51 F. Supp. 3d 708, 712 (N.D. Ohio 2014) (no evidence of defendant's misrepresentation of birth control patch risks); Forslund v. Stryker Corp., 2010 WL 3905854, at *5 (D. Minn. 2010); Krueger Assocs., Inc. v. American Dist. Tel. Co., 247 F.3d 61, 67 (3d Cir. 2001) (Pa. law).

[139] See, e.g., Maneely v. General Motors Corp., 108 F.3d 1176, 1181 (9th Cir. 1997) (Cal. law) (plaintiffs riding in cargo bed of pickup truck paralyzed when truck crashed into palm tree; advertisements showing people in cargo bed of defendant's pick-up trucks "do not make any affirmations of fact or promises regarding the safety of riding in the cargo bed").

[140] See, e.g., Ward Dev. Co. v. Ingrao, 493 A.2d 421, 426 (Md. Ct. Spec. App. 1985).

[141] See, e.g., Pacnet Network Ltd. v. KDDI Corp., 912 N.Y.S.2d 178, 180 (App. Div. 2010) (affirming dismissal of negligent representation claim; representations were "statements of prediction or expectation"); Champion Home Builders Co. v. ADT Sec. Servs., Inc., 179 F. Supp. 2d 16 (N.D.N.Y. 2001) (no negligent misrepresentation claim for statements of future intent).

[142] See, e.g., Great N. Ins. Co. v. Amazon.com, Inc., 524 F. Supp. 3d 852, 860 (N.D. Ill. 2021) (no evidence hoverboard purchaser relied on the false assertion the product had Samsung batteries); Evans v. Toyota Motor Corp., 2005 WL 2001141, at *5–6 (S.D. Tex. 2005) (no evidence plaintiffs read owner's manual or relied on advertisements); Cadlo v. Owens-Illinois, Inc., 23 Cal. Rptr. 3d 1, 6 (Ct. App. 2004) (no evidence of plaintiff's reliance). A plaintiff's failure to rely on false advertisements normally precludes a causal link between the defendant's wrong and plaintiff's harm, which is fatal to the claim). See Lowe v. Sporicidin Int'l, 47 F.3d 124, 131 (4th Cir. 1995) (Md. law) ("She never alleged that she relied on the advertisements and that this reliance caused her to use [the product] and so resulted in her injuries.").

[143] See, e.g., Village of Cross Keys, Inc. v. U.S. Gypsum Co., 556 A.2d 1126, 1135 (Md. 1989); Board of Educ. of Chi. v. A, C & S, Inc., 546 N.E.2d 580 (Ill. 1989). On justifiable reliance and other defenses to misrepresentation claims, see § 13.7, below.

[144] See, e.g., Daye v. General Motors Corp., 720 So.2d 654, 660 (La. 1998) (driver's high speed driving and imprudent application of brakes were sole causes of accident, not his reliance on promotional information); Foster v. American Home Prods. Corp., 29 F.3d 165, 168 (4th Cir. 1994) (Md. law) (causation necessary to negligent misrepresentation claim).

[145] Foster v. American Home Prods. Corp., 29 F.3d 165, 171 (4th Cir. 1994) (Md. law) (no negligent misrepresentation action without duty); Board of Educ. of Chi. v. A, C & S, Inc., 546 N.E.2d 580, 591 (Ill. 1989) (same; claim by school districts against suppliers of asbestos materials for costs of removal).

limited at least to foreseeable types of risks and types of plaintiffs,[146] and the duty to protect against the risk of pure economic loss, if allowed at all, is even more narrowly limited.[147] Nor will a manufacturer have a duty to plaintiffs who otherwise are too remote,[148] such as many courts hold consumers of generic drugs to be from manufacturers of the corresponding brand-name drugs.[149]

In place of the element of fraudulent intent or scienter, a plaintiff asserting a negligent misrepresentation claim must prove that the defendant was somehow negligent in making the representation.[150] In such claims, negligence ordinarily is established by proof that the defendant communicated the matter represented without possessing a reasonable basis to ascertain the truth or falsity of the matter,[151] but a

---

[146] See, e.g., Nichols v. General Motors Corp., 1999 WL 33292839, at *4 (N.H. Super. Ct. 1999) (no duty to subsequent purchasers). See also In re Rezulin Prods. Liab. Litig., 2002 WL 31852826, at *3 (S.D.N.Y. 2002) (Mississippi law requires a misrepresentation made to plaintiffs, "as opposed to others").

[147] See, e.g., Thompson v. Procter & Gamble Co., 2018 WL 5113052, at *1, 3–4 (S.D. Fla. 2018) (economic loss rule barred plaintiffs' negligent misrepresentation claim against manufacturer for advertising Ivory soap containing chemical that adversely affected "2–10% of the population" as " 'trusted,' 'mild,' and 'gentle on the hand' "); Moore Excavating, Inc. v. Consolidated Supply Co., 63 P.3d 592, 597–98 (Or. Ct. App. 2003) (no requisite special relationship to base negligent misrepresentation claim); Board of Educ. of Chi. v. A, C & S, Inc., 546 N.E.2d 580, 591–93 (Ill. 1989) (allowing negligent misrepresentation claim by school districts against suppliers of asbestos materials for costs of removal and repair; court characterized school district's damages as property damage rather than economic loss, noting narrower ambit of duty for negligently caused pecuniary loss, under Rest. (2d) Torts § 552, than for negligently caused personal injury and property loss, under Rest. (2d) Torts § 311).

[148] See, e.g., Soule v. Norton, 750 N.Y.S.2d 692, 695 (App. Div. 2002) (patients could not maintain negligent representation claim against manufacturer of surgical laser because they did not have "actual privity of contract . . . or a relationship so close as to approach that of privity"); In re Tobacco Cases II, 113 Cal. Rptr. 2d 120, 131–32 (Ct. App. 2001) (medical expenses paid by union too remote to be recoverable under negligent misrepresentation).

[149] See, e.g., McNair v. Johnson & Johnson, 818 S.E.2d 852, 863 (W. Va. 2018) (declining "to extend the duty of brand manufacturers to those allegedly injured by a competitor's product"; "The vast majority of courts that have addressed this issue have also declined to extend liability to brand manufacturers."); In re Zofran (Ondansetron) Prods. Liab. Litig., 261 F. Supp. 3d 62, 71 (D. Mass. 2017) ("The overwhelming majority of courts [hold] that the manufacturer of a brand-name drug [is not] liable for injuries caused by ingest[ing] its generic equivalent, regardless of the theory of liability."); In re Darvocet, Darvon, & Propoxyphene Prods, Liab. Litig., 756 F.3d 917, 938–39 (6th Cir. 2014) ("the highest courts in each of the 22 implicated states would not recognize [generic consumers'] misrepresentation claims" against brand-name manufacturers; surveying cases). *But see* T.H. v. Novartis Pharms. Corp., 407 P.3d 18, 29 (Cal. 2017) ("a brand-name drug manufacturer has the duty under California law to warn of the risks about which it knew or reasonably should have known, regardless of whether the consumer is prescribed the brand-name drug or its generic 'bioequivalent' "); Kellogg v. Wyeth, 762 F. Supp. 2d 694, 706–09 (D. Vt. 2010) (summarizing cases).

In Wyeth, Inc. v. Weeks, 159 So.3d 649, 676 (Ala. 2014) (6–3 opinion), the Alabama Supreme Court held that a brand-name drug manufacturer may be liable for fraud or misrepresentation to a plaintiff physically injured by a generic drug. In response, the Alabama legislature enacted Ala. Code § 6–5–530, which prohibits claims by generic drug users against brand-name manufacturers. Nor do generic drug consumers have misrepresentation claims against the generic drug manufacturers under federal preemption "impossibility" principles. See PLIVA, Inc. v. Mensing, 564 U.S. 604 (2011). See §§ 14.5 and 18.3, below.

[150] See Fahey v. R.J. Reynolds Tobacco Co., 1995 WL 809837, at *5 (Mass. Super. Ct. 1995) (for "negligent misrepresentation, plaintiffs must show that the defendants made false statements about important facts without using the amount of care a reasonable person would use in those circumstances to see what s/he said was true [and] need not prove an actual intent to deceive").

[151] See, e.g., In re Wright Med. Tech. Inc., Conserve Hip Implant Prods. Liab. Litig., 178 F. Supp. 3d 1321, 1359 (N.D. Ga. 2016) (Utah law) ("Defendant's representations about the efficacy of the hip replacement device for active patients, and the reduced metal ion release, were made without sufficient knowledge to support these claims and thus were made, at least, negligently."); M & H Enters. v. Tri-State Delta Chems., Inc., 35 S.W.3d 899, 904 (Mo. Ct. App. 2001) (negligent misrepresentation claims premised on idea that speaker believed information was correct, "but was negligent in so believing"); Board of Educ. of Chi. v. A, C & S, Inc., 546 N.E.2d 580, 591 (Ill. 1989). Thus, a negligent misrepresentation claim will fail without proof that, in making the representation, the defendant failed to exercise reasonable care. See, e.g., Cummings v. HPG Int'l, Inc., 244 F.3d 16, 25 (1st Cir. 2001) (Mass. law).

negligent misrepresentation claim may also lie for the communication of information in some negligent manner.[152]

Most of the older products liability cases based on negligent misrepresentation involve retailers.[153] However, manufacturers have also been held responsible for negligent misrepresentation, usually in connection with representations on a product's label or in advertising.[154] On occasion, certifiers of product quality are held subject to liability for negligent misrepresentation. The most prominent case of this type was *Hanberry v. Hearst Corp.*,[155] an early California case against the publisher of Good Housekeeping magazine brought by the purchaser of slippery shoes that the magazine accorded the "Good Housekeeping's Consumers' Guaranty Seal." The court ruled that a product endorser "may be liable to a purchaser who, relying on the endorsement, buys the product and is injured because it is defective and not as represented in the endorsement."[156] Reasoning that the very purpose of the seal is to induce consumers to rely upon its assertions of quality, the court held that negligent misrepresentation, but not implied warranty or strict liability in tort, was the appropriate remedy for a consumer injured by reliance upon such an endorsement.[157] In similar situations, Underwriters Laboratories has also been held liable for negligent misrepresentation.[158]

---

[152] See, e.g., Cummings v. HPG Int'l, Inc., 244 F.3d 16, 24 (1st Cir. 2001) (Mass. law) (plaintiff must show that defendant "failed to exercise reasonable care . . . in obtaining or communicating the information"). See generally Rest. (2d) Torts § 552, cmt. *e* (same).

[153] A defendant's negligence in retailer cases usually consists of its failure to exercise reasonable care to ascertain the accuracy of its representation. Used car cases long have provided grist for this particular type of claim. See, e.g., Boos v. Claude, 9 N.W.2d 262, 263, 265 (S.D. 1943) (car with defective steering said to be in "perfect mechanical condition," yet "defendants had not used reasonable care in making tests for the purpose of ascertaining defects"); Flies v. Fox Bros. Buick Co., 218 N.W. 855, 856–57, 860 (Wis. 1928) (Owen, J.) (dealer who represented car, restored after wreck, to be "in proper operating condition" was negligent in not discovering defective brakes). The type of products liability case allowing negligent misrepresentation claims referred to here involve personal injuries or death, rather than only pecuniary loss which raises problems previously discussed.

[154] In early cases, manufacturers not infrequently labeled or advertised products as "safe" or "harmless" when in fact the products contained hidden dangers. A manufacturer's failure to disclose the danger in such cases often supported claims for both negligent failure to warn and negligent misrepresentation. See, e.g., Crist v. Art Metal Works, 243 N.Y.S. 496, 497 (App. Div. 1930) (toy revolver, advertised as "absolutely harmless," ignited boy's Santa Claus beard and costume during demonstration of product in department store window), aff'd, 175 N.E. 341 (N.Y. 1931); Henry v. Crook, 195 N.Y.S. 642 (App. Div. 1922) (sparklers advertised as "[a] harmless and delightful amusement for children" ignited 7-year-old plaintiff's dress).

[155] 81 Cal. Rptr. 519 (Ct. App. 1969).

[156] Id. at 521.

[157] The defendant permitted sellers of products approved by the magazine to advertise the fact of that approval and to use the defendant's seal in such ads: "Implicit in the seal and certification is the representation that respondent has taken reasonable steps to make an independent examination of the product endorsed, with some degree of expertise, and found it satisfactory. . . . [T]he very purpose of respondent's seal and certification is to induce consumers to purchase products so endorsed . . . ." Because the defendant "loaned its reputation" to market such products, reasoned the court, it had a duty to exercise reasonable care in the issuance of its seal of approval and certification of quality. Id. at 522.

[158] See, e.g., United States Lighting Serv., Inc. v. Llerrad Corp., 800 F. Supp. 1513, 1517 (N.D. Ohio 1992) (defective lighting equipment approved by Underwriters Laboratories (UL), a nonprofit testing organization, which was negligent in applying its own internal testing procedures): "The raison d'etre of the UL mark is to show that a product has met safety standards. By offering its mark to manufacturers, UL has placed itself into the stream of commerce. . . . The UL seal does not guarantee that a manufacturer has acted with ordinary care but sound public policy requires that UL act with ordinary care in the conduct of its own business—the certification process." The court emphasized, however, that liability against an endorser is limited to negligence and does not extend to strict liability. In 807 F. Supp. 439 (N.D. Ohio 1992), the *Llerrad* court vacated its earlier opinion, presumably because the case was settled. See also Hempstead v. General Fire Extinguisher Corp., 269 F. Supp. 109, 118 (D. Del. 1967), where UL allowed the use of its inspection and testing label on a manufacturer's fire extinguishers. *Held*, UL could be subject to liability for injuries from the

A typical negligent misrepresentation case against a retail seller was *Pabon v. Hackensack Auto Sales, Inc.*,[159] where the plaintiff was injured when the steering on his new automobile locked, causing the car to crash. He had noticed a "clicking" and "chopping" sensation in the steering that he had told the defendant's service manager about on three occasions prior to the accident. Each time, without checking the problem, the service manager said something like, "It's a new car. Don't worry about it. It'll wear out." The court held that a jury could find the defendant car dealer liable for negligent misrepresentation on these facts because the service manager made positive assertions without a reasonable basis to know them to be true.[160]

Negligent misrepresentation claims possibly may escape federal preemption,[161] although one must be cautious in generalizing rules in this complex and statute-specific context of products liability law.[162] Also complex is the issue of whether a defendant may contractually disclaim responsibility for damages arising out of negligent misrepresentations. Some courts in some contexts allow contractual clauses that disclaim responsibility for negligent misrepresentation,[163] but this issue is multi-layered and fact-specific, and other courts in other contexts invalidate clauses seeking to avoid responsibility for negligent misrepresentation.[164]

Misrepresentation as a Violation of Statute—Negligence Per Se

If a defendant's misrepresentation violates a statute or administrative regulation designed to protect consumers from harm, a consumer injured as a result may have a claim against the defendant based on the violation. If the statute or regulation itself provides for civil redress,[165] the consumer will have a claim directly under the statute or regulation. If the statute or regulation is in the nature of a quasi-criminal safety measure, however, with no damages provision for persons harmed by its violation, an injured consumer may have a claim against the defendant under the common-law doctrine of negligence per se.[166] Thus, false labeling or advertising concerning a product's

---

explosion of an extinguisher carrying its label, for negligent approval of its design. *Hanberry*, and claims against product certifiers and endorsers, are addressed in § 15.7, below.

[159] 164 A.2d 773 (N.J. Super. Ct. App. Div. 1960).

[160] See id. at 784.

[161] See, e.g., Fabian v. Fulmer Helmets, Inc., 628 F.3d 278, 282–83 (6th Cir. 2010) (Tenn. law) (negligent misrepresentation claim not preempted by National Traffic and Motor Vehicle Safety Act of 1966). See also Goeb v. Tharaldson, 615 N.W.2d 800 (Minn. 2000) (Federal Insecticide, Fungicide, and Rodenticide Act (FIFRA) preempts claim for label warnings, but not a negligent misrepresentation claim against insecticide manufacturer for hotline assurances made directly to consumer). *But see* M & H Enters. v. Tri-State Delta Chems., Inc., 35 S.W.3d 899 (Mo. Ct. App. 2001) (claim preempted under FIFRA).

[162] On federal preemption, see § 14.5, below.

[163] At least with respect to misrepresentations other than those inducing the plaintiff to enter into the contract containing the disclaimer. See, e.g., Houghland v. Security Alarms & Servs., Inc., 755 S.W.2d 769, 773 (Tenn. 1988) (exculpatory provisions by burglary and fire alarm service providers normally upheld in absence of fraud). *But see* Agristor Leasing v. A.O. Smith Harvestore Prods., Inc., 869 F.2d 264, 268 (6th Cir. 1989) ("Tennessee law . . . gives no effect to disclaimers in the presence of fraud or negligent misrepresentations.").

[164] See, e.g., Snelten v. Schmidt Implement Co., 647 N.E.2d 1071 (Ill. App. Ct. 1995), arising out of injuries to the plaintiff who was run over by his newly purchased used tractor that he started while it was in gear. The purchase order, which included an "as is" clause, also represented that the tractor had been serviced, adjusted, and inspected according to specific representations, and that it had not been modified or altered. "[W]hen a written contract contains a specific, written, affirmative representation, the inclusion of general 'as is,' 'with all faults' or like language does not, in and of itself, relieve the party making the statement of a duty arising from the statement." Id. at 1075.

[165] As does, for example, the Federal Odometer Tampering Act, 49 U.S.C. § 32710.

[166] See § 2.4, above.

safety that contravenes a misbranding, false advertising, or unfair and deceptive trade practices act may[167] (or may not)[168] support a claim for damages either directly under the statute or under the common-law doctrine of negligence per se.

An early, prominent decision allowing recovery for breach of such a statute was *Wright v. Carter Products, Inc.*[169] In this case, although the defendant manufacturer had received over 373 complaints of skin irritation over a 4-year period, it continued to advertise its deodorant, Arrid, as "safe" and "harmless," and that it "does not irritate the skin." Suffering a skin disorder from using Arrid, the plaintiff alleged that the defendant had misrepresented and falsely advertised its product. Applying conventional negligence per se principles, the court allowed the claim, observing that "a statutory violation may be the basis for civil liability if the injured person is a member of the class for whose express benefit the statute was enacted and the harm resulting from the violation is of the type that the statute was designed to prevent."[170]

Subsequent decisions also have allowed negligence per se claims for misrepresentations that result in violations of state statutes.[171] In limited situations, courts sometimes permit a claim for statutory violation by implying a private cause of action into the statute.[172] Negligence per se claims may possibly also be maintained, as a matter of state law, for violation of a federal safety statute or regulation, though some courts disagree.[173]

§ 3.4 STRICT LIABILITY FOR MISREPRESENTATION

A manufacturer or other seller who innocently makes a false statement about a product's quality or safety that results in harm is not subject to liability for deceit or negligent misrepresentation, but such a defendant may be subject to liability in contract for breach of an express warranty.[174] Some states provide an additional claim for such

---

167 See, e.g., Soule v. Norton, 750 N.Y.S.2d 692, 695 (App. Div. 2002) (party injured by violation of act prohibiting "deceptive practices," under General Business Law § 349(a), may recover damages if defendant engaged in "consumer oriented" conduct that is deceptive or misleading in a material way that caused injury to the plaintiff). See also In re Medtronic, Inc., Implantable Defibrillators Litig., 465 F. Supp. 2d 886, 898–900 (D. Minn. 2006) (claims for violation of false advertising, deceptive trade practice, and consumer protection statutes not preempted by Medical Device Amendments to FDCA).

168 See, e.g., In re Meridia Prods. Liab. Litig., 328 F. Supp. 2d 791, 823–24 (N.D. Ohio 2004) (denying claim, describing the variety of such statutes, and quoting First Circuit's characterization of the Massachusetts unfair and deceptive practices act as including practices that "attain a level of rascality that would raise an eyebrow of someone inured to the rough and tumble of the world of commerce"), aff'd, 447 F.3d 861 (6th Cir. 2006); Barrow v. Bristol-Myers Squibb, 1998 WL 812318, at *46 (M.D. Fla. 1998) (ruling that Florida's deceptive trade practices act does not apply to claims for personal injury or death).

169 244 F.2d 53 (2d Cir. 1957) (Mass. law).

170 Id. at 61.

171 See, e.g., Tetuan v. A.H. Robins Co., 738 P.2d 1210, 1233–34 (Kan. 1987) (false advertising of dangerous Dalkon Shield IUD).

172 See, e.g., Bob Godfrey Pontiac, Inc. v. Roloff, 630 P.2d 840, 844–47 (Or. 1981) (excellent analysis).

173 On the applicability of negligence per se doctrine to violations of federal statutes, see § 2.4, above.

Material misrepresentations knowingly made to a federal agency are criminalized by 18 U.S.C. § 1001: "[W]hoever . . . knowingly and wilfully . . . falsifies . . . a material fact [or] makes any materially false, fictitious or fraudulent statement or representation [violates this statute]." However, this statute may be viewed more of a "truth" rather than a "safety" statute, such that its violation may not amount to a breach of a standard of care sufficient to trigger the doctrine of negligence per se. See McNeil Pharm. v. Hawkins, 686 A.2d 567, 580 (D.C. 1996) (in deceased patient's claim against drug manufacturer for death from severe liver failure, false-claims statute did not establish manufacturer's standard of care).

174 On express warranty, including a comparison of it with strict liability in tort for misrepresentation, see § 4.2, below.

strict or no-fault liability for misrepresentation under a parallel cause of action in tort. The modern claim for strict products liability in tort for misrepresentation is formulated in *Restatement (Second) Torts* § 402B.[175] This section provides as follows:

§ 402B. Misrepresentation by Seller of Chattels to Consumer

> One engaged in the business of selling chattels who, by advertising, labels, or otherwise, makes to the public a misrepresentation of a material fact concerning the character or quality of a chattel sold by him is subject to liability for physical harm to a consumer of the chattel caused by justifiable reliance upon the misrepresentation, even though
>
> (a) it is not made fraudulently or negligently, and
>
> (b) the consumer has not bought the chattel from or entered into any contractual relation with the seller.

Section 402B was developed as a kind of "non-contractual 'express warranty' made to the consumer in the form of the representation to the public upon which he relies."[176] But liability is grounded in principles of the law of tort, not contract.[177] Probably because it trespasses deeply into express warranty domain that is statutorily defined today in UCC Article 2,[178] and notwithstanding its solid foundation in moral theory,[179] judicial support for § 402B has been narrow and weak.[180] The courts of most states have never adopted or applied the doctrine at all,[181] and case authority for the doctrine in states in which the doctrine at one time or another has been cited or discussed is generally sparse and often dated. Nevertheless, this section of the *Restatement (Second) of Torts* was reaffirmed by the *Restatement (Third) of Torts: Products Liability* with little fanfare, analysis, or debate.[182] Because the doctrine still might have a twitch of life—if rarely

[175] On § 402B, see Sales, The Innocent Misrepresentation Doctrine: Strict Tort Liability Under Section 402B, 16 Hous. L. Rev. 239 (1979); Green, Strict Liability Under Sections 402A and 402B: A Decade of Litigation, 54 Tex. L. Rev. 1185 (1976); Shapo, A Representational Theory of Consumer Protection: Doctrine, Function and Legal Liability for Product Disappointment, 60 Va. L. Rev. 1109 (1974); Comment, Interpreting the Restatement of Torts Section 402B After the Changes to Section 402A, 28 Cumb. L. Rev. 177 (1997–1998).

[176] Rest. (2d) Torts § 402B cmt. *d*.

[177] Id.

[178] See, e.g., Hauter v. Zogarts, 534 P.2d 377, 388 (Cal. 1975) (Clark, J., concurring).

[179] See Owen, The Moral Foundations of Products Liability Law, 68 Notre Dame L. Rev. 427, 463–64 (1993) (explaining how powerful reasons based on autonomy, truth, equality, and utility support a rule of strict liability for accidental harm from innocent but false assertions of product quality).

[180] Appendices to Rest. (2d) Torts § 402B digest state court opinions that appear to apply § 402B in Arizona, California, Colorado, Illinois, Pennsylvania, Tennessee, Texas, and Washington, and opinions from several other states (including Nebraska, New Jersey, and Wyoming) that appear to refer favorably to this doctrine. A law journal student comment cites cases thought to show support for the doctrine in eighteen states: Ariz., Cal., Colo., Ill., Kan., Md., Miss., N.M., N.J., N.Y., N.D., Ohio, Or., Pa., Tenn., Tex., Wash., and Wyo. See Comment, 28 Cumb. L. Rev. 177, 178 n.5 (1997–1998). Actual support for the doctrine in some of these states is dubious. See, e.g., Manuel v. Wichita Hotel Partners, 2010 WL 4025607, at *3 (D. Kan. 2010) (conclusory § 402B claim dismissed; "the Second Restatement of Torts has been superseded by Section 9 of the Third Restatement of Torts, Product Liability"); Freeman v. Hoffman-La Roche, Inc., 618 N.W.2d 827, 844–46 (Neb. 2000).

[181] See, e.g., Bougopoulos v. Altria Grp., Inc., 954 F. Supp. 2d 54 (D.N.H. 2013) (dismissing § 402B claim); DiBartolo v. Abbott Labs., 914 F. Supp. 2d 601 (S.D.N.Y. 2012) (New York has never adopted § 402B).

[182] Section 9 of the Rest. (3d) of Torts: Products Liability, entitled "Liability of Commercial Product Seller or Distributor for Harm Caused by Misrepresentation," provides:

> One engaged in the business of selling or otherwise distributing products who, in connection with the sale of a product, makes a fraudulent, negligent, or innocent misrepresentation of material fact concerning the product is subject to liability for harm to persons or property caused by the misrepresentation.

used—in such major jurisdictions as California, Illinois, Ohio, Pennsylvania, and Texas,[183] it may be a bit premature to consign it to the scrapheap of dead doctrines.

Background

Like so much modern products liability law, the doctrine of strict products liability in tort for misrepresentation grew out of the law's impatience with the limitation on claims imposed by the doctrine of privity of contract, applied in this context to the express warranty cause of action in cases involving personal injuries.[184] The classic case widely credited with paternity of the doctrine of strict products liability in tort for misrepresentation is *Baxter v. Ford Motor Co.*,[185] decided by the Supreme Court of Washington in 1932. While the plaintiff was driving his Model A Ford, a pebble from a passing car struck his windshield, causing small pieces of glass to fly into his eye, which he lost as a result. The plaintiff sued Ford Motor Co. for misrepresenting the windshield's safety characteristics in its advertising catalogues, which stated: "Triplex Shatter-Proof Glass Windshield. All of the new Ford cars have a Triplex shatter-proof glass windshield—so made that it will not fly or shatter under the hardest impact. . . . Its extra margin of safety is something that every motorist should look for in the purchase of a car—especially where there are women and children."[186] Ford defended on the basis that there could be no claim for "express warranty" in the absence of privity of contract, but the Supreme Court of Washington rejected such a narrow, doctrinal perspective:

> The rule in such cases does not rest upon contractual obligations, but rather on the principle that the original act of delivering an article is wrong, when, because of the lack of those qualities which the manufacturer represented it as having, the absence of which could not be readily detected by the consumer, the article is not safe for the purposes for which the consumer would ordinarily use it.[187]

The court reasoned that it should not allow a manufacturer to create consumer demand for its products by means of false statements in mass advertising and then to hide behind the privity-of-contract defense when consumers, induced by the false statements to

---

Rather than "restating" § 402B in a black-letter section of its own, section 9 reaffirms the misrepresentation principles of the Second Restatement, including § 402B in comment *b*: "The rules governing liability for innocent product misrepresentation are stated in the Restatement, Second, of Torts § 402B." Products Liability Rest. § 9 cmt. *b*.

[183] See, e.g., Gawloski v. Miller Brewing Co., 644 N.E.2d 731, 734 (Ohio Ct. App. 1994) (§ 402B adopted via Ohio Rev. Code Ann. § 2307.77); Hollenbeck v. Selectone Corp., 476 N.E.2d 746, 747–48 (Ill. App. Ct. 1985); Klages v. General Ordnance Equip. Corp., 367 A.2d 304, 310–11 (Pa. Super. Ct. 1976); Hauter v. Zogarts, 534 P.2d 377, 380–81 (Cal. 1975); Crocker v. Winthrop Labs., 514 S.W.2d 429, 431–32 (Tex. 1974). *But see* Hawkins v. Medtronic, Inc., 62 F. Supp. 3d 1144, 1162 (E.D. Cal. 2014) (dismissing plaintiff's strict products liability misrepresentation claim against bone graft device's manufacturer; "[N]o California court has determined the viability of (and this Court's own research has yielded no California case where damages were awarded for) a claim based on innocent misrepresentation by a manufacturer in the last 20 years.").

The Tennessee courts endorsed § 402B in an important early decision, Ford Motor Co. v. Lonon, 398 S.W.2d 240, 250 (Tenn. 1966), and subsequently reaffirmed the doctrine. See Ritter v. Custom Chemicides, Inc., 912 S.W.2d 128, 131–32 (Tenn. 1995); Ladd v. Honda Motor Co., 939 S.W.2d 83, 97–99 (Tenn. Ct. App. 1996) (extensive analysis of doctrine's history and application).

[184] See Sales, The Innocent Misrepresentation Doctrine: Strict Tort Liability Under Section 402B, 16 Hous. L. Rev. 239 (1979) (excellent historical discussion). See also American Safety Equip. Corp. v. Winkler, 640 P.2d 216, 219–20 (Colo. 1982).

[185] 12 P.2d 409 (Wash. 1932).

[186] Id. at 411.

[187] Id. at 411–12.

purchase the products, are injured as a result.[188] Affirming a verdict for the plaintiff on second appeal, the court ruled that the seller's belief in the truth of its representations and proof that the windshield was as good as any then made were irrelevant.[189]

Baxter thus held that liability for misrepresentation was truly strict, like liability for express warranty, yet unburdened by the warranty law rules concerning privity of contract and other contractual limitations. Scholars at the time astutely observed that, in *Baxter*, they were witnessing the birth of a new tort.[190] Prior to the inclusion of § 402B in the *Restatement (Second) of Torts* in 1965, at least a couple of decisions followed the lead of *Baxter* by allowing recovery for personal injuries on similar principles.[191]

Nature of Liability

It is fundamental that the § 402B action presaged in *Baxter* is not dependent on culpable conduct by the seller. Material representations concerning the character or quality of a product are made to the public at a seller's peril: if the representations are false, and if injury follows from justifiable reliance thereon, the seller is liable.[192] Liability under § 402B, therefore, is truly "strict"—liability may attach regardless of the seller's total inability to discover that its representations are false.[193] Thus, the § 402B claim defined in the *Restatement (Second) of Torts* eliminates the difficulties in proving scienter and fault that inhere in actions for deceit and negligent misrepresentation. Unlike liability under § 402A, however, section 402B bases recovery on an improper communication. Accordingly, liability under § 402B is grounded in a defendant's communication of false information that physically harms the plaintiff, and so it does

188 "Radio, billboards, and the products of the printing press [are used to create] a large part of the demand that causes goods to depart from factories to the ultimate consumer. It would be unjust to recognize a rule that would permit manufacturers of goods to create a demand for their products by representing that they possess qualities which they, in fact, do not possess, and then, because there is no privity of contract existing between the consumer and the manufacturer, deny the consumer the right to recover if damages result from the absence of those qualities, when such absence is not readily noticeable." Id. at 412.

189 "I[f] a person states as true material facts susceptible of knowledge to one who relies and acts thereon to his injury, if the representations are false, it is immaterial that he did not know they were false, or that he believed them to be true." Baxter v. Ford Motor Co., 35 P.2d 1090, 1092 (Wash. 1934).

190 "As to this general field—negligence, deceit, warranty, or whatever the *Baxter* case may really involve—I take it we are feeling our way. . . . Perhaps we are actually witnessing the birth of a new type of tort liability." Leidy, Another New Tort?, 38 Mich. L. Rev. 964, 986 (1940). See also Feezer, Manufacturer's Liability for Injuries Caused by His Products: Defective Automobiles, 37 Mich. L. Rev. 1, 26 (1938).

191 See Worley v. Proctor & Gamble Mfg. Co., 253 S.W.2d 532 (Mo. Ct. App. 1952), in which the defendant manufacturer represented that "Tide is kind to your hands." *Held,* representation could support non-contractual warranty action imposing strict liability for its breach on manufacturer despite absence of privity. See also Rogers v. Toni Home Permanent Co., 147 N.E.2d 612 (Ohio 1958). The plaintiff suffered hair loss and severe scalp irritation after using defendant's product, which was labeled "safe" and "harmless." Reiterating *Baxter*'s rationales, the court imposed strict liability for misrepresentation: "The warranties made by the manufacturer in his advertisements and by the labels on his products are inducements to the ultimate consumers, and the manufacturer ought to be held to strict accountability to any consumer who buys the product in reliance on such representations . . . ." Id. at 615–16.

192 Section 402B makes this point clear in black letter. See § 402B(a).

193 See Crocker v. Winthrop Labs., 514 S.W.2d 429, 433 (Tex. 1974), where the decedent became addicted to a drug the defendant manufacturer had represented as nonaddictive:

> Whatever the danger and state of medical knowledge, and however rare the susceptibility of the user, when the drug company positively and specifically represents its product to be free and safe from all dangers of addiction, and when the treating physician relies upon that representation, the drug company is liable when the representation proves to be false and harm results.

not require that the product contain a "defect" unless the manufacturer falsely states that the product is free thereof.[194]

Apart from the absence of seller fault, the elements of a § 402B claim for innocent misrepresentation closely track those of deceit[195]—elements that must be pleaded in sufficient detail to meet current standards of particularity.[196] Thus, as in deceit, a plaintiff must prove that the defendant affirmatively communicated information bearing on the product's safety,[197] such that a buyer's reliance on the manufacturer's good name alone will not suffice. The plaintiff also must prove, of course, that the representation was *false*, so that if it fairly may be interpreted as true, or at least as not being false with respect to the relevant facts, then no misrepresentation claim will lie. Consequently, it is vital that the particular words be fairly interpreted, and read together with any warnings, to determine if the alleged misrepresentation was actually true or false.[198]

For example, in *General Motors Corp. v. Howard*,[199] the plaintiff truck driver sustained injuries to his head and chest when another truck hit the side of his vehicle, thrusting him against the steering wheel. Plaintiff claimed that the steering column, which had been advertised as "telescopic," failed to telescope adequately, contrary to the representation. Noting that the column would have telescoped more had the collision been head-on, and that it had telescoped somewhat even though plaintiff had been hit at an angle, the court concluded that the representation was not false: "The statement

---

[194] See Products Liability Rest. § 9 cmt. *d*. Cf. Freeman v. Hoffman-La Roche, Inc., 618 N.W.2d 827, 844 (Neb. 2000) (citing comment *d* on this point but declining to adopt § 9).

[195] See, e.g., Baughn v. Honda Motor Co., 727 P.2d 655, 667 (Wash. 1986):

> Three requirements must be met in order to establish a prima facie case under § 402B: (1) there must be a misrepresentation of a material fact concerning the character or quality of a chattel; (2) the misrepresentation must be made to the public; and (3) physical harm must have resulted to a consumer from justifiable reliance upon the misrepresentation.

See also Ladd v. Honda Motor Co., 939 S.W.2d 83, 97 (Tenn. Ct. App. 1996) (liability under § 402B requires a misrepresentation of material fact, made to the public about the character and quality of a product, which is false and upon which the consumer is expected to justifiably rely; "[t]he representations must be more than mere statements of opinion or the kind of loose general sales talk commonly referred to as 'puffing' ").

While § 402B claims are basically no-fault versions of the fault-based causes of action for misrepresentation, strict liability claims for "public" misrepresentation are narrower than deceit and negligent misrepresentation claims in certain respects. As discussed below, the strict liability claim probably precludes recovery for misrepresentations made privately to the plaintiff, and for those that cause pure economic loss. Moreover, at least in some jurisdictions, innocent misrepresentation claims may be available to a smaller class of plaintiffs than are the fault-based claims.

[196] **Pleading.** Although Fed. R. Civ. P. 9(b) may not apply to strict liability claims for public misrepresentations, lawyers pleading in federal court must be cognizant of the heightened pleading requirements of Fed. R. Civ. P. 8(a)(2) that preclude conclusory pleading. See Bell Atl. Corp. v. Twombly, 550 U.S. 544, 555 (2007), and Ashcroft v. Iqbal, 556 U.S. 662, 679 (2009). See, e.g., Manuel v. Wichita Hotel Partners, 2010 WL 4025607, at *4 (D. Kan. 2010) (dismissing strict liability for misrepresentation claim under Rest. (2d) Torts § 402B as conclusory). See also Deskevich v. Spirit Fabs, Inc., 2021 WL 2290820, at *3 (M.D. Pa. 2021) (plaintiff's § 402B claim dismissed for failure to adequately plead that defendant was a "seller" of the mispresented metal sheeting). Particularized pleading of fraudulent and negligent misrepresentation claims are addressed respectively in § 3.2 note 22 and § 3.3 note 134, above.

[197] See Willis v. Buffalo Pumps Inc., 34 F. Supp. 3d 1117, 1128–30 (S.D. Cal. 2014) (§ 402B claim failed; plaintiff did not prove defendant made affirmative statement misrepresenting safety of asbestos exposure); Eiser v. Brown & Williamson Tobacco Corp., 2005 WL 1323030, at * 4 (Pa. Ct. Com. Pl. 2005) (§ 402B claim failed; no evidence of express statement of fact about product), aff'd, 897 A.2d 524 (Pa. Super. Ct. 2006).

[198] See, e.g., Chandler v. Gene Messer Ford, Inc., 81 S.W.3d 493, 500 (Tex. App. 2002) (general advertisements showing children riding in front seat should be interpreted together with warnings about dangers of airbags to children in front seat and instruction to restrain them in rear seat if possible).

[199] 244 So.2d 726 (Miss. 1971), overruled on other grounds by Toliver v. General Motors Corp., 482 So.2d 213 (Miss. 1986) .

of appellant . . . never asserted that the steering column would telescope under any and all circumstances and conditions."[200]

If a manufacturer advertises its products generally as possessing certain characteristics, then the failure of any model to possess such characteristics may be found to render the advertisement false.[201] But an advertisement that a particular model possesses certain traits may not necessarily be construed as meaning that other models of the product possess those same features.[202] And if the product is claimed to possess a certain trait—even the most important general trait of being "safe"—when used in a particular manner or under other specified conditions, then its failure to possess the trait in the absence of those conditions simply may not be false.[203]

The matter misrepresented must be *factual*, and the § 402B doctrine "does not apply to statements of opinion, and, in particular, it does not apply to the kind of loose general praise of wares sold which . . . is considered to be 'sales talk,' and is commonly called 'puffing.' "[204] So, representations that a helicopter is "easy to fly" for beginners,[205] or that a truck's braking device offers "unprecedented safety,"[206] or that "You meet the nicest people on a Honda" mini-trail bike,[207] or advertising "to protect your dreams" and showing children riding in a vehicle's front seat,[208] are all such vague and general commendations that they are properly interpreted as "puffs" rather than assertions of fact.[209] In contrast, a representation that a golfing practice device is "completely safe—ball will not hit player" is the kind of specific assurance of an ascertainable safety characteristic that may reasonably be construed as fact rather than as opinion.[210] No better test has been devised for fact *versus* opinion than whether the assertion is capable of objective determination.[211]

In addition to being factual, a misrepresentation must be material, which means that it would be important to a normal purchaser, who therefore would be justified in relying upon it in buying or using the product.[212]

---

[200] Id. at 729.

[201] See, e.g., Ladd v. Honda Motor Co., 939 S.W.2d 83 (Tenn. Ct. App. 1996) (advertisements showing young children using all-terrain vehicles).

[202] See Haynes v. American Motors Corp., 691 F.2d 1268, 1270–71 (8th Cir. 1982) (Ark. law) (excluding plaintiff's evidence of Jeep advertisements that involved a different model than that driven by plaintiffs, and where the advertisements portrayed off-road settings whereas plaintiffs' vehicle slid off rain-slick pavement); American Safety Equip. Corp. v. Winkler, 640 P.2d 216, 223 (Colo. 1982) (4–3 decision) (§ 402B claim failed where based on different model of motorcycle helmet from plaintiff's).

[203] See, e.g., Baughn v. Honda Motor Co., 727 P.2d 655 (Wash. 1986) (representation of safety of mini-trail bike, sold only for off-road use, inapplicable to use of bike on road).

[204] Rest. (2d) Torts § 402B cmt. *g* (entitled "*Material fact*").

[205] Berkebile v. Brantly Helicopter Corp., 337 A.2d 893, 903 (Pa. 1975). See also Hittle v. Scripto-Tokai Corp., 166 F. Supp. 2d 142, 159 (M.D. Pa. 2001).

[206] Hoffman v. A.B. Chance Co., 339 F. Supp. 1385, 1388 (M.D. Pa. 1972).

[207] Baughn v. Honda Motor Co., 727 P.2d 655, 668 (Wash. 1986).

[208] Chandler v. Gene Messer Ford, Inc., 81 S.W.3d 493, 500 (Tex. App. 2002).

[209] See id. (salesman's assertion that dual airbags made Ford Aspire safer than a Geo Metro—opinion, not statement of fact).

[210] Hauter v. Zogarts, 534 P.2d 377, 381–83 (Cal. 1975) (the celebrated case of the "Golfing Gizmo").

[211] See discussion and authorities on "Fact" in § 3.2, above.

[212] Restatement (2d) Torts § 402B cmt. *g*. Cf. Chandler v. Gene Messer Ford, Inc., 81 S.W.3d 493, 500 (Tex. App. 2002) (fact that Aspire, sold by Ford with a "Ford" warranty, was actually made by Kia, could not support § 402B claim).

As with other tortious misrepresentation claims, those based on innocent misrepresentations require that the plaintiff prove a causal link between the wrong (the misrepresentation) and the injury.[213] That is, no matter how factual, false, and material a statement may be, a claim for misrepresentation will fail if the statement does not have some untoward effect—if it does not in some manner cause the plaintiff's harm. It is the element of *reliance* that usually (but not always) establishes this imperative causal connection.[214] Thus, the strict liability for misrepresentation doctrine does not apply if the representation is never seen, or otherwise learned about, and acted upon by the plaintiff or someone acting on the plaintiff's behalf.[215] As with express warranty, the necessary reliance is often established by proof that the plaintiff (or another) decided to purchase the product because of the quality misrepresented, at least in part.[216] But, because the misrepresentation claim lies in tort, the harm need not be linked to the purchase decision if it can be sufficiently connected to a decision (by the plaintiff or another) as to how the product may be used.[217] Nor does it matter, also because the action lies in tort, whether the reliance is by the purchaser, user, or third person injured by the product, provided that the requisite causal linkage is established.[218] Thus, a prescribing doctor's reliance on misrepresentations by a pharmaceutical company that its drug is nonaddictive will support a claim by the doctor's patient who becomes addicted to the drug;[219] a mother's decision to purchase a product advertised as "completely safe" will support her child's claim for injuries;[220] an adult's decision to loan his ATV to his friend's young son, on the strength of advertisements showing young children safely riding such vehicles, may establish reliance for a claim on behalf of the injured boy;[221] the reliance of a retailer on a manufacturer's representations will support a claim by a customer;[222]

---

[213] In addition to the more typically relevant issue of cause in fact, proximate cause must also be established. See Hollenbeck v. Selectone Corp., 476 N.E.2d 746, 747–48 (Ill. App. Ct. 1985) (police officer's pager failed when he sought to use it to summon assistance; *held*, criminal attack was not unforeseeable risk that would break causal connection between pager manufacturer's representations and officer's injuries). See also § 12.3, below.

[214] See Baker v. Danek Med., 35 F. Supp. 2d 875, 878 (N.D. Fla. 1998) (noting that a defendant is subject to liability under § 402B for harm caused by reliance on a representation).

[215] The rule "does not apply where the misrepresentation is not known, or there is indifference to it, and it does not influence the purchase or subsequent conduct. . . . Since the liability here is for misrepresentation, the rules as to what will constitute justifiable reliance [for the action of deceit] are applicable to this Section, so far as they are pertinent." Restatement (2d) Torts § 402B cmt. *j*. See, e.g., Wolfe v. McNeil-PPC, Inc., 773 F. Supp. 2d 561, 573 (E.D. Pa. 2011) (strict liability misrepresentation claim failed; no evidence that plaintiff, her mother, or anyone else relied on the representation when product purchased or consumed); Miller v. Pfizer Inc. (Roerig Div.), 196 F. Supp. 2d 1095, 1123 (D. Kan. 2002) (no reliance because prescribing doctor never read and would simply throw away promotional materials containing misrepresentations), aff'd, 356 F.3d 1326 (10th Cir. 2004).

[216] Comment *j* to § 402B notes that "the misrepresentation need not be the sole inducement to purchase, or to use the chattel, and it is sufficient that it has been a substantial factor in that inducement."

[217] Comment *j* to § 402B (entitled "*Justifiable reliance*") requires that the misrepresentation either "influence the purchase *or* subsequent conduct" (emphasis added). See, e.g., Ladd v. Honda Motor Co., 939 S.W.2d 83 (Tenn. Ct. App. 1996).

[218] "[The reliance] may be that of the ultimate purchaser of the chattel, who because of such reliance passes it on to the consumer who is in fact injured, but is ignorant of the misrepresentation." Restatement (2d) Torts § 402B cmt. *j*.

[219] See, e.g., Crocker v. Winthrop Labs., 514 S.W.2d 429, 433 (Tex. 1974).

[220] Cf. Hauter v. Zogarts, 534 P.2d 377 (Cal. 1975) (the "Golfing Gizmo" case).

[221] See Ladd v. Honda Motor Co., 939 S.W.2d 83, 100–01 (Tenn. Ct. App. 1996).

[222] See, e.g., Westlye v. Look Sports, Inc., 22 Cal. Rptr. 2d 781, 802 (Ct. App. 1993); Baughn v. Honda Motor Co., 727 P.2d 655 (Wash. 1986) (en banc).

and an employer's decision to purchase equipment on the strength of a manufacturer's misrepresentations should support an employee's claim against the manufacturer.

Even the strongest reliance, of course, must also be *justified*, and the principles concerning the plaintiff's (or another's) right to rely on a representation applicable to deceit claims are also applicable to claims for innocent misrepresentation.[223] So, if the plaintiff relies on obvious puffs, clearly dubious assertions, representations he has reason to doubt are true, or those that do not fairly apply to his particular model, then the reliance may not be justifiable and a claim under § 402B will not lie.[224]

Although the *Restatement* explicitly takes no position on whether the strict liability doctrine should apply to private misrepresentations,[225] the rule is formulated explicitly in terms of *public* misrepresentations—and that is how the courts have applied it.[226] Thus, the misrepresentation must be made "by public advertising in newspapers or television, by literature distributed to the public through dealers, by labels on the product sold, or leaflets accompanying it," or by any other public means of communication.[227]

Damage

Section 402B provides for "liability for physical harm to a consumer," and the *Second Restatement* defines "physical harm" to mean "physical impairment of the human body, or of land or chattels."[228] While this general *Restatement* definition suggests an intent to include liability for property damage as well as personal injury, all the cases cited in the comments and all four illustrations involve personal injuries. Moreover, when § 402B's damages language is compared with that of § 402A,[229] a persuasive argument may be made that the American Law Institute intended to restrict § 402B to cases involving personal injury or death. There is a paucity of judicial authority on

[223] See § 402B cmt. *j*. See, e.g., Gawloski v. Miller Brewing Co., 644 N.E.2d 731, 736 (Ohio Ct. App. 1994), a claim by incarcerated criminals that their criminal behavior resulted from their addiction to Miller beer the defendant had misrepresented as safe, negating any defense based on the common knowledge of dangers from alcohol consumption. *Held*, the plaintiffs' reliance was not justified; judgment on pleadings for manufacturer affirmed. On justifiable reliance and other defenses to misrepresentation claims, see § 13.7, below.

[224] See, e.g., Herzog v. Arthrocare Corp., 2003 WL 1785795, at *9–10 (D. Me. 2003) (summary judgment for seller of surgical tool because plaintiff was physician who, due to his medical knowledge, could not have justifiably relied on defendant's assertions); American Safety Equip. Corp. v. Winkler, 640 P.2d 216, 223 (Colo. 1982) (4–3 decision) ("Justifiable reliance contemplates the reasonable exercise of knowledge and intelligence in assessing the represented facts. Unsupportable subjective reliance is inadequate.").

[225] Restatement (2d) Torts § 402B Caveat (1). Compare Products Liability Restatement § 9 cmt. *b* ("This question remains open.").

[226] See, e.g., Chandler v. Gene Messer Ford, Inc., 81 S.W.3d 493, 499 (Tex. App. 2002) (salesman's private representations not covered by § 402B); Freeman v. Hoffman-La Roche, Inc., 618 N.W.2d 827, 844–45 (Neb. 2000). Indeed, at least one court has included the public nature of the misrepresentation as an element of this tort. See Baughn v. Honda Motor Co., 727 P.2d 655, 667 (Wash. 1986).

[227] Rest. (2d) Torts § 402B cmt. *h* (entitled "*To the public*"). Notwithstanding Caveat (1), which provides that the ALI takes no position on whether the rule may apply "where the representation is not made to the public, but to an individual," comment *h* plainly states that the doctrine "is limited to misrepresentations which are made by the seller to the public at large."

[228] Rest. (2d) Torts § 7(3). Compare Rest. (3d) Torts: Liability for Physical and Emotional Harm § 4 ("physical harm" includes harm to human body or to property, whereas emotional harm is distinct; see cmt. *a*).

[229] In contrast to § 402B's language of "physical harm to a consumer," section 402A speaks in terms of "physical harm thereby caused to the ultimate user or consumer, or to his property." Rest. (2d) Torts § 402A.

whether the section supports recovery for property damage. At least one case reads § 402B restrictively, though not unreasonably, as excluding recovery for such losses.[230]

As for recovery of pure economic loss under § 402B, the law is much more clear. An early, prominent Tennessee decision, *Ford Motor Co. v. Lonon*,[231] did allow recovery for pure economic loss on a claim of strict liability in tort for misrepresentation on the basis of § 402B and its reference, in comment *a*, to a draft parallel rule applicable to pecuniary loss in a then-proposed § 552D.[232] But the ALI never adopted the proposed § 552D, and Tennessee long stood as the solitary state allowing recovery in such cases for pure economic loss. In time, the Tennessee Supreme Court[233] repudiated the *Lonon* holding.[234] Apart from *Lonon* and its progeny in Tennessee,[235] the courts have universally rejected claims for pure economic loss based on § 402B.[236]

[230] See Fischbach & Moore Int'l Corp. v. Crane Barge R-14, 632 F.2d 1123, 1127 (4th Cir. 1980) (Md. law) ("Section 402B, in contrast to § 402A, provides liability for misrepresentation . . . for physical harm to the consumer, not for property damage."). *But see* Ritter v. Custom Chemicides, Inc., 912 S.W.2d 128, 131–33 (Tenn. 1995); Westric Battery Co. v. Standard Elec. Co., 482 F.2d 1307, 1315–16 (10th Cir. 1973) (Colo. law).

[231] 398 S.W.2d 240 (Tenn. 1966).

[232] The proposed provision, entitled "Misrepresentation by Seller of Chattels to Public," mirrored the language of § 402B, except that it rendered the defendant "subject to liability for pecuniary loss caused to another . . . ." Rest. (2d) Torts, Council Draft No. 17, p. 76, quoted in *Lonon*, 398 S.W.2d at 246–47.

[233] With some help by the legislature. See Tenn. Code Ann. §§ 29–28–101 et seq.

[234] First Nat'l Bank of Louisville v. Brooks Farms, 821 S.W.2d 925, 929–31 (Tenn. 1991). See also Ritter v. Custom Chemicides, Inc., 912 S.W.2d 128, 132–33 (Tenn. 1995).

[235] See, e.g., Vicon, Inc. v. CMI Corp., 657 F.2d 768, 775 (5th Cir. 1981) (Tenn. law).

[236] See, e.g., Rice v. Bell Tel. Co., 524 A.2d 522, 523–24 (Pa. Super. Ct. 1987); Roxalana Hills, Ltd. v. Masonite Corp., 627 F. Supp. 1194, 1198 (S.D. W. Va. 1986), aff'd, 813 F.2d 1228 (4th Cir. 1987).

Chapter 4

WARRANTY

Table of Sections

§ 4.1 WARRANTY—GENERALLY

Warranty law concerns the legal obligations arising from promises and other assertions connected with sales and related transactions.[1] In products liability cases, the law of warranty prescribes the legal effect of assertions associated with the transfer of a product for value, usually through a sale, and it provides liability for breach of warranty if a product's failure to conform to a warranty proximately causes harm.[2] Assertions about a product may be express,[3] from a seller's affirmative communications about the product's attributes, or they may be implied by the nature of a particular transaction.[4] The roots of warranty law reach deep into history, at least to the law of ancient Rome.[5]

In contrast to most products liability law, which today generally is based in tort, products liability claims in warranty address promises arising out of sales transactions and so ordinarily is viewed as part of modern contract law. In fact, however, warranty

---

[1] Helpful general treatments on the law of warranty under the Uniform Commercial Code include D. Frisch, Lawrence's Anderson on the Uniform Commercial Code (3d ed. 2001–2002 rev. ed., annual updates); J. White and R. Summers, Uniform Commercial Code (6th pract. ed., annual updates) and (6th hornbook ed. 2010); UCC Case Digest (Callaghan, West 2022 update); M. Crockett, The Law of Product Warranties (2022 ed.) (formerly by B. Clark and C. Smith); R. Nordstrom, Law of Sales (1970); O. Harris and A. Squillante, Warranty Law in Tort and Contract Actions (1989); C. Bjerre, Hawkland's Uniform Commercial Code Series (2000 rev. ed., annual updates); and P. Fonseca and J. Fonseca, 2 and 3 Williston on Sales (rev. 5th ed. 2005–2006, annual updates). Useful shorter works include C. Gillette and S. Walt, Sales Law (3d ed. 2016); and W. Henning, W. Lawrence, and H. Gabriel, Understanding Sales and Leases of Goods (3d ed. 2016). See also Frumer, Friedman, and Sklaren, Products Liability ch. 9; Am. Law Prod. Liab. 3d chs. 18–24; D. Fairgrieve and R. Goldberg, Product Liability chs. 2–6 (Oxford 3d ed. 2020) (British law).

[2] See, e.g., Daigle v. Ford Motor Co., 713 F. Supp. 2d 822, 825 (D. Minn. 2010) ("To establish a warranty claim the plaintiff must basically prove: the existence of a warranty, a breach, and a causal link between the breach and the alleged harm.").

[3] Uniform Commercial Code (UCC) § 2–313; see § 4.2, below.

[4] Uniform Commercial Code (UCC) §§ 2–314 (merchantability) and 2–315 (fitness for particular purpose); see §§ 4.3 and 4.4, below.

[5] For an historical overview of warranty law in the products liability context, see § 4.3, below.

law sprang from the law of torts,[6] and it was the direct progenitor of the doctrine of strict products liability in tort.[7] A small number of states that never did adopt the doctrine of strict liability in tort for the sale of defective products (notably Delaware, Massachusetts, and Virginia) constructed much of their modern products liability jurisprudence upon an implied warranty of quality.[8] Yet much of the common-law "warranty" doctrine of such states was patterned after the developed tort law jurisprudence of negligence and the *Restatement (Second) of Torts* § 402A[9] and so in essence (if not fully in doctrine) is part of the larger law of tort.[10]

Statutory Basis of Modern Warranty Law

Warranty law governing the sale of chattels, which first evolved as a matter of common law in both England and America, was codified by the Sale of Goods Act of 1893 in Great Britain[11] on which the United States patterned its Uniform Sales Act of 1906.[12] Article 2 (Sales) of the Uniform Commercial Code (UCC), promulgated in the 1950s and adopted by state legislatures across the United States during the late 1950s and 1960s, supplanted the Uniform Sales Act.[13] Thus, the modern products liability law of warranty

---

6 See Ames, The History of Assumpsit, 2 Harv. L. Rev. 1, 8 (1888); Prosser, The Implied Warranty of Merchantable Quality, 27 Minn. L. Rev. 117, 118–22 (1943); Prosser, The Assault Upon the Citadel (Strict Liability to the Consumer), 69 Yale L.J. 1099, 1103–10, 1124–27 (1960). See note 136, below.

7 See § 5.2, below.

8 Michigan and North Carolina, the other states that always rejected strict products liability in tort, each have had a controlling statute for some time. See § 5.3, below.

9 See, e.g., Evans v. Lorillard Tobacco Co., 990 N.E.2d 997, 1013 (Mass. 2013) (restating that the "Massachusetts law of warranty [is] congruent in nearly all respects with the principles expressed in Restatement (Second) of Torts § 402A," but acknowledging that the law now embraces the principles of the Third Restatement); Jeld-Wen, Inc. v. Gamble, 501 S.E.2d 393, 396 (Va. 1998) (level of required safety "is essentially the same whether the theory of liability is labeled warranty or negligence," both requiring proof that the product was "unreasonably dangerous" for a foreseeable use); Gregory v. Cincinnati Inc., 538 N.W.2d 325, 329–30 (Mich. 1995).

10 The law of warranty, which in early English times appears to have arisen out of the tort law action of deceit, preceded the development of assumpsit and contract law. See Ames, The History of Assumpsit, 2 Harv. L. Rev. 1, 8 (1888). Beginning with Stuart v. Wilkins, (1778) 99 Eng. Rep. 15 (K.B.), warranty law was increasingly absorbed into the branch of contract law dealing with the law of sales. See Prosser, The Implied Warranty of Merchantable Quality, 27 Minn. L. Rev. 117, 118–22 (1943). Nevertheless, some courts throughout the nineteenth and into the twentieth centuries continued to apply a special, tort-like warranty of quality to the sale of food. See, e.g., Van Bracklin v. Fonda, 12 Johns. 468, 468 (N.Y. 1815) (Blackstone states that, in sales of foodstuffs, "it is always implied that they are wholesome; and if they are not, case lies to recover damages for the deceit"); Jacob E. Decker & Sons, Inc. v. Capps, 164 S.W.2d 828, 829 (Tex. 1942). See generally Prosser, The Assault Upon the Citadel (Strict Liability to the Consumer), 69 Yale L.J. 1099, 1103–10 (1960). Several courts in the late 1950s expanded the "tort" food warranty to sales of pet food and products for intimate bodily use, and this development laid the foundation for the extension of the tort warranty to durable products and its transformation in the early 1960s into the doctrine of strict products liability in tort. See § 5.2, below. On the early history of the law of deceit, warranty, and other products liability law principles, see § 1.2, above.

11 On sales law in the U.K., see Benjamin's Sale of Goods (M. Bridge, ed., Sweet and Maxwell, 11th ed. 2020); D. Fairgrieve and R. Goldberg, Product Liability ch. 4 (3d ed. 2020).

12 The Uniform Sales Act, patterned after the British Sales of Goods Act, was written by Samuel Williston. P. Fonseca, and J. Fonseca, 1 Williston on Sales § 1:5, at 6 (rev. 5th ed. 2005, annual updates) [hereinafter 1 Williston on Sales]. Pertinent provisions of both acts, together with their sources in Justinian's Digest, are set forth in F. de Zulueta, The Roman Law of Sale—Introduction and Select Texts, pt. II at 61 et seq. (corr. 1st ed. 1945). Both were based on principles of law and commerce of the 1800s, and, to some extent, even the 1700s. See Wiseman, The Limits of Vision: Karl Llewellyn and the Merchant Rules, 100 Harv. L. Rev. 465, 475 (1987); C. Reitz, Consumer Protection Under the Magnuson-Moss Warranty Act 14 (1978).

13 In 1940, the idea of a uniform commercial code was conceived, overseen by a joint Editorial Board of the National Conference of Commissioners on Uniform State Laws and the American Law Institute. Judge Herbert Goodrich (Chairman), Professor Karl Llewellyn (Chief Reporter), Professor Soia Mentschikoff (Associate Chief Reporter), and numerous committees began work on the Code, unofficially in 1942 and officially in 1945. A final first draft appeared four years later, the "1949 Official Text," comprised of nine

generally concerns the interpretation and application of various sections of UCC Article 2. Yet lawyers should beware that some state legislatures, when adopting Article 2, altered some of its provisions; that courts in various jurisdictions have interpreted Article 2's "uniform" provisions in differing ways; that other legislation in many states overlaps or supersedes Article 2 (typically, consumer protection or products liability reform acts);[14] and that conflicting federal law preempts inconsistent provisions of Article 2.[15]

In 2003, the National Conference of Commissioners on Uniform State Laws (NCCUSL) and the American Law Institute (ALI) completed a joint revision project on Article 2 and its sister provision governing leases, Article 2A,[16] which beneficially amended key sections in these two Articles.[17] Industry opposed the promulgated amendments (particularly certain e-commerce amendments), state legislatures correspondingly ignored them, and in 2011 the amendments were withdrawn, leaving these two articles unchanged.[18]

---

articles with notes and comments. This draft was substantially critiqued and debated, resulting in a revised 1952 edition, enacted by Pennsylvania in 1953 to take effect in 1954. The several other states into whose legislatures this version of the Code was introduced referred it to study commissions, notably the New York Law Review Commission. The Editorial Board studied the critiques of various state commissions and offered a new version of the Code in late 1956, the "1957 Official Text," which was enacted by Massachusetts in 1957 and Kentucky in 1958, after which a further revised "1958 Official Text" was successively enacted in Connecticut, New Hampshire, Rhode Island, Wyoming, Arkansas, New Mexico, Ohio, Oregon, Oklahoma, Illinois, New Jersey, Georgia, Alaska, New York, Michigan, and Pennsylvania (which substituted the 1958 text for the 1952 version it had earlier enacted). Thereafter, because of the large number of individual state amendments, a newly constituted Permanent Editorial Board promulgated a revised "1962 Official Text," the version (as amended in 1966) which the other states subsequently enacted. See generally 1 Uniform Laws Annotated xv–xl (2004); 1 Williston on Sales § 1:5. The UCC was last adopted by Arizona and Idaho in 1967 and Louisiana (selected articles, *not* including Article 2) in 1974. See 1A Uniform Laws Annotated, Uniform Commercial Code 1 (master ed. cum. ann. pocket pt.).

[14] Some state legislatures adopted non-uniform versions of certain sections of Article 2, and unfair and deceptive practices acts and other consumer-protective legislation in many states may complement or supersede certain warranty provisions in Article 2. See, e.g., Allen v. Hyland's, Inc., 2021 WL 718295, at *1 (C.D. Cal. 2021) (original claims against homeopathic products manufacturers included California's Unfair Competition Law and Consumer Legal Remedies Acts, warranty, and the Magnuson-Moss Warranty Act); Wynn v. Topco Assocs., LLC, 2021 WL 168541 (S.D.N.Y. 2021) (addressing and denying plaintiffs' implied and express warranty, deceptive business practices, false advertising, and Magnuson-Moss warranty Act claims, among others, against almond milk manufacturer with leave to amend). Moreover, judicial interpretations and applications of Article 2 provisions can vary considerably among jurisdictions. See, e.g., Arons v. Rite Aid Corp., 2005 WL 975462, at *22–23 (N.J. Super. Ct. Law. Div. 2005) (notwithstanding the "rubric" of the UCC, "the law that has emerged thereunder is not pristinely uniform[;] it is sometimes tangled and contradictory between jurisdictions, and in some instances clear expressions of the law notwithstanding the statutory language have not emerged," on such issues as the need for vertical privity and for reliance in express warranty). See generally Owen & Davis on Products Liability, Appendix J1 (*Non-Uniform UCC Modifications*). Note, as well, that comparative fault acts, statutes of limitations, and a number of products liability reform acts, as well as certain federal statutes, may supersede UCC Article 2.

[15] On federal preemption, see § 14.5, below.

[16] On lease transactions, see § 16.2, below.

[17] For a description of the revisions (called "amendments"), see Rusch, Is the Saga of the Uniform Commercial Code Article 2 Revisions Over? A Brief Look at What NCCUSL Finally Approved, 6 De. L. Rev. 41 (2003). For a summary of the most important of these amendments applicable to products liability law, see the final subsections in §§ 4.2 (express warranty), 4.3 (implied warranty of merchantability), and 4.7 (disclaimers) in Owen, Products Liability Law ch. 4 (2d ed. 2008) (summarizing the most important changes pertinent to products liability law). For one commentator's concerns about some amendments, see Braucher, Under the Surrounding Circumstances: Amended Article 2's Redundant (or Worse) Electronic Commerce Provisions, 68 Ohio State L.J. 115 (2007).

[18] In 2010, "[r]ecognizing that the prospects for enactment of the 2003 amendments are bleak, the [UCC Permanent Editorial Board (PEB)] concluded that no purpose was served by retaining those amendments in the Official Text of the Uniform Commercial Code, which would represent the law of no state either now or in

The Structure of Article 2

Understanding UCC Article 2 requires, as a preliminary but essential matter, examining its structure and organization. As seen later in this chapter, the warranties generally at issue in products liability litigation are UCC § 2–313 (express warranties), UCC § 2–314 (implied warranties of merchantability), and, infrequently, UCC § 2–315 (implied warranties of fitness for particular purpose). Products liability warranty litigation thus normally focuses on Part 3 of this article, its centerpiece, which includes these three principal sections.[19] But these particular warranty provisions cannot be fully understood without reference to other portions of Article 2 and, more generally, of the UCC—beginning with Article 1, which sets forth general provisions applicable to commercial transactions, including certain definitions, such as "conspicuous,"[20] a crucial requirement of certain disclaimers in § 2–316(2).[21] In Article 2 itself, Part 3 (obligation and construction) describes (among other things) how warranties are created, interrelate, and whom they benefit—*not*, explicitly, how they are breached, nor the kind of damages recoverable for breach, nor the extent to which a seller may limit damages, nor various other requirements for recovering on a breach of warranty claim.

For answers to these and other secondary questions, a lawyer must turn to various other sections of Part 3, and other parts of Article 2, such as: Part 1 (general), which contains additional definitions especially pertinent to sales transactions; Part 2 (form), which details important formal requirements of sales contracts, such as the statute of frauds, the parol evidence rule, and rules on modification, rescission, and waiver; other sections in Part 3, which address such topics as how an unconscionable clause may affect a sales contract,[22] how warranties may be disclaimed,[23] how separate types of warranties interrelate,[24] and to whom they flow;[25] Part 6 (breach), which addresses a buyer's obligation promptly to notify the seller of breach,[26] and how a buyer may revoke (rescind) acceptance of a purchased product;[27] and Part 7 (remedies), which describes a buyer's

---

the foreseeable future. Accordingly, . . . the PEB unanimously decided to recommend amending the Official Text of the Uniform Commercial Code to revert to the prior text of Articles 2 and 2A, as amended in conjunction with the 2003 revision of Article 7. . . . The recommendation was approved by the ULC Executive Committee on January 8, 2011." Memorandum, UCC Permanent Editorial Board (2011). The ALI approved this recommendation at its annual meeting in May 2011.

Although the Article 2 revisions were never enacted by state legislatures and were eventually withdrawn by NCCUSL and the ALI, the revisions contain interpretive significance in that they reduced to proposed uniform, statutory form the revisers' view of the best evolved law on sales warranties. Hence, these provisions, together with their comments and underlying research, are significant research artifacts. that sometimes are well be worth examining. See note 17, above.

[19] For examples of cases reviewing the applicability of each of these three warranties, see, e.g., Westfield Ins. Co. v. Amazon.com Inc., 2021 WL 877684, at *2 (D. Del. 2021) (reviewing the elements of the three warranties and dismissing those claims as insufficiently pled); O'Neil v. Argon Med. Devices, Inc., 2020 WL 1149904, at *7–10 (N.D.N.Y. 2020) (reviewing the elements of the three warranties and dismissing the express warranty and implied warranty of fitness for particular purpose claims as inadequately pled).

[20] See UCC § 1–201(b)(10).

[21] See § 4.7, below.

[22] See UCC § 2–302.

[23] See UCC § 2–316.

[24] See UCC § 2–317.

[25] See UCC § 2–318.

[26] See UCC § 2–607(3)(a).

[27] See UCC § 2–608.

other remedies for breach,[28] such as the types of damages available,[29] how a sales contract may limit damages,[30] and the statute of limitations for breach of warranty claims.[31]

One should note that Article 2 addresses a seller's *breach* of warranty only obliquely in Part 3, which focuses instead on whether or not a warranty of some type was *created*, and its scope, in the first place, and whether it inures to an injured plaintiff's benefit, in the second. Part 6 of Article 2 deals with certain matters secondarily related to breach, and Part 7 addresses damages available for breach, where breach is treated as a product's failure to *conform* to the warranty. Indeed, the Code largely equates the two terms—"breach" and "non-conformity."[32] And so a products liability lawyer normally should consider "breach" to mean a product's failure to conform to an applicable warranty (to wit, the product's deviation therefrom) that proximately causes allowable damages to a buyer or other appropriate plaintiff.

Finally, it is important to recognize that Article 2 connects breach of warranty with damages by the two notions of cause in fact and proximate cause, important elements in claims for negligence and strict liability in tort as well.[33] This conjunctive requirement for breach of warranty claims—that a plaintiff's damages proximately resulted from the defendant's breach of warranty—is most explicitly iterated in § 2–715(2)(b), which specifically authorizes damages for "injury to person or property proximately resulting from any breach of warranty."[34]

Warranty and Tort Claims Compared

There is substantial overlap, but also considerable difference, between products liability law in tort and products liability law in warranty under the UCC.[35] Claims for breach of express warranty under UCC § 2–313 are similar in many respects to strict liability claims for product misrepresentation under *Restatement (Second) of Torts* § 402B.[36] Also, claims for breach of the implied warranty of merchantability under UCC § 2–314 are cousin claims to those for negligence,[37] and sister claims to those for defective products under § 402A of the *Second Restatement*, and § 2 of the *Third Restatement*.[38] Because of fundamental similarities in these separate claims under the UCC and in tort, a plaintiff's lawyer contemplating the applicability of one such products liability theory of recovery almost invariably should examine the possible applicability of the others, at least as a matter of initial consideration.

---

28 See UCC § 2–711.

29 See UCC §§ 2–714 and 2–715.

30 See UCC § 2–719.

31 See UCC § 2–725.

32 For example, UCC § 2–714, entitled a "Buyer's Damages for *Breach* . . .," provides in subsection (1) that a buyer may recover "damages for any *non-conformity* . . . the loss resulting . . . from the seller's *breach* . . . ." See also subsection (2), defining damages for *breach* of warranty in terms of damages from *non-conformity*, to wit, from the failure of the goods to be "as warranted."

33 See chs. 11 (cause in fact) and 12 (proximate cause), below.

34 Section 2–715(2)(b) expands upon the general authorization of consequential damages in § 2–714(3).

35 For a comparison of UCC § 2–313 and Rest. (2d) Torts § 402B, see § 4.2, below.

36 See § 3.4, above.

37 Warranty "liability . . . has much . . . in common with negligence liability . . . ." White and Summers, UCC § 10–1, at 447.

38 See §§ 5.3 and 6.5, below.

Tort and warranty claims, however, possess a variety of important distinctions. Warranty claims often are restricted by contract law limitations, such as privity, disclaimers, limitations on remedies, and notice.[39] But the Code's uniform statute of limitations is a generous four years (normally from the date of sale),[40] which often is longer than typical tort statutes of limitations of two or three (or, as in California, one) years (normally from the date when the injury or claim should have been discovered).[41] In addition, as discussed below, § 402B is drafted more narrowly in certain respects than UCC § 2–313,[42] and, at least in New York, an implied warranty of merchantability claim may lie in circumstances where a § 402A claim does not.[43] And negligence claims, of course, explicitly require proof that the defendant was somehow at fault in how it made or sold a product.[44] Finally, defenses based on user conduct (and, to a lesser extent, third-party conduct) may vary between actions brought in tort and those brought in contract under Article 2 of the UCC.[45]

Topics Covered

This chapter separately examines the major topics of Article 2 of the Uniform Commercial Code applicable to products liability law. First considered are each of the three applicable warranties—express warranties, under UCC § 2–313; implied warranties of merchantability, under UCC § 2–314; and implied warranties of fitness for particular purpose, under UCC § 2–315. Next examined is the issue of privity of contract, under UCC § 2–318, addressing the question of which parties other than the buyer may benefit from a seller's breach of warranty. The buyer's obligation to promptly notify the seller of a breach of warranty, under UCC § 2–607, is then briefly explored. Next considered is the seller's ability contractually to avoid warranty responsibility by disclaimers, under UCC § 2–316, and to limit damages for breach of warranty, under UCC § 2–719. Last examined are the various warranty reform measures designed to protect consumers from unfair and unbargained-for disclaimers—both under state law and the federal Magnuson-Moss Warranty Act.

---

[39] **Class actions.** Some limitations on warranty claims (like privity, notice, and reliance), based on an individual buyer's advertence and conduct, can undercut class action certification of warranty claims. See, e.g., Brown v. Electrolux Home Prods., Inc., 817 F.3d 1225, 1238 (11th Cir. 2016) (Cal. and Tex. law) (remanding for determination whether state law notice, opportunity to cure, and defect manifestation requirements defeated class certification of warranty claims); Oscar v. BMW of N. Am., LLC, 274 F.R.D. 498, 509 (S.D.N.Y. 2011) (denying certification of national class action due to individualized issues, noting that "numerous courts have recognized that there are significant variances among the interpretation of the elements of an implied warranty of merchantability claim among the states"); Powers v. Lycoming Engines, 272 F.R.D. 414, 428 (E.D. Pa. 2011) (denying motion to certify class due to variations in state laws on privity, disclaimers, and notice).

[40] UCC § 2–725. The limitations period may exceed four years if the warranty "explicitly extends" to future performance, in which case the claim accrues when the breach is or should have been discovered. See, e.g., LTL Acres Ltd. P'ship v. Butler Mfg. Co., 136 A.3d 682, 688 (Del. 2016) (building cladding materials); Noll v. Apex Surgical, LLC, 2010 WL 2813430, at *3–4 (W.D. Okla. 2010) (hip implant). Compare Harrison v. Porsche Cars N. Am., Inc., 2016 WL 1455864, at *4 (W. Va. 2016) (4-year limitation period barred warranty claim; no explicit extension to future performance); Zaremba v. Marvin Lumber & Cedar Co., 458 F. Supp. 2d 545, 551 (N.D. Ohio 2006) (warranty limited to repair and replacement did not extend to future performance; hence, normal 4-year period applied). See also § 14.6 (*Warranty law statutes*), below.

[41] Statutes of limitations are considered in § 14.6, below.

[42] See § 4.2, below.

[43] Denny v. Ford Motor Co., 662 N.E.2d 730, 738–39 (N.Y. 1995) (manufacturer of SUV not strictly liable in tort where design necessary for vehicle's off-road capability increased its tendency to roll over during highway use, but manufacturer did breach implied warranty of merchantability where vehicle was advertised for general highway and family use). *Denny* is examined in § 5.9, below.

[44] See ch. 2, above.

[45] See ch. 13, below.

§ 4.2 Express Warranty

Express warranties in products liability law are affirmative assertions, made by a seller in connection with a sales transaction, that a product possesses certain characteristics of quality, construction, performance capability, durability, or safety. This form of warranty springs from a seller's words or other form of communication rather than from any inherent characteristic of the product itself. Hence, as with tortious misrepresentation,[46] claims for breach of express warranty rest on the falsity of such asserted information rather than on a deficiency in the product itself. Stated otherwise, a plaintiff need not prove that a product was "defective," or that the seller was at fault, to prove that the seller made and breached an express warranty.[47]

Such warranties may be written, oral,[48] or communicated by some other means, and they generally must precede or accompany the sale, as discussed below. Legal responsibility follows from breach of an express warranty because a manufacturer or other seller[49] is deemed to have assumed responsibility for the harmful consequences of false representations made to consumers in an effort to sell a product.[50] For centuries, law and custom have provided a remedy if a seller fractures a buyer's "frame of reference" and equal freedom interests by making a false claim of product quality that causes injury to the buyer.[51]

---

46 See § 3.1, above.

47 See, e.g., In re Valsartan, Losartan, & Irbesartan Prods. Liab. Litig., 2021 WL 222776, at *10 (D.N.J. 2021) ("Claims for breach of express warranty depend on neither deficiency in the product nor falsity of seller's asserted information, which relieves plaintiff from pleading product 'defect' or seller's fault."); Forbes v. General Motors Corp., 935 So.2d 869, 876 (Miss. 2006) ("An express warranty is any affirmation of fact or promise which concerns the product and becomes part of the basis for the purchase of such a product. Fault does not need to be shown to establish a breach. The plaintiff need only show that the product did not live up to its warranty."); Bell Sports, Inc. v. Yarusso, 759 A.2d 582, 594 (Del. 2000) (jury could find motorcycle helmet manufacturer made and breached express warranty while also finding that helmet was not defective and manufacturer was not negligent).

Courts sometimes loosely refer to breach of express warranty as a kind of "defect," an infelicitous linguistic practice. See, e.g., Genetti v. Caterpillar, Inc., 621 N.W.2d 529, 541 (Neb. 2001) (for breach of express warranty plaintiff "must show, among other things, that 'the goods did not comply with the warranty, that is, that they were defective' ").

48 See, e.g., Paper Mfrs. Co. v. Rescuers, Inc., 60 F. Supp. 2d 869, 882–83 (N.D. Ind. 1999) (that ink was suitable for use on label of container of bone cement powder); Crothers v. Cohen, 384 N.W.2d 562 (Minn. Ct. App. 1986) (that used car, which next day went out of control and crashed into tree, was a "good runner").

49 In addition to bearing responsibility for its own express warranties, a retail seller may also bear responsibility for those of the manufacturer which the retailer "adopts." This principle is treated in § 15.2, below.

50 See Huebert v. Federal Pac. Elec. Co., 494 P.2d 1210, 1214–15 (Kan. 1972) (advertising claims may assure buyers "that the product will operate in a manner on which the purchaser can rely and no injury will occur"):

> A manufacturer may b[y] express warranty assume responsibility in connection with its products which extends beyond liability for defects. . . . [D]efects in the product may be immaterial if the manufacturer warrants that a product will perform in a certain manner and the product fails to perform in that manner. [T]he approach to liability is the failure of the product to operate or perform in the manner warranted by the manufacturer.

51 On the history of express warranty law, see § 1.2, above. On its grounding in moral theory, see Owen, The Moral Foundations of Products Liability Law: Toward First Principles, 68 Notre Dame L. Rev. 427, 463–65 (1993). Compare Craswell, Taking Information Seriously: Misrepresentation and Nondisclosure in Contract Law and Elsewhere, 92 Va. L. Rev. 565 (2006).

Uniform Commercial Code § 2–313

Today, whether an assertion made in connection with a chattel-sale transaction gives rise to an express warranty is governed by § 2–313 of the Uniform Commercial Code, which provides:

> **§ 2–313. Express Warranties by Affirmation, Promise, Description, Sample**
>
> (1) Express warranties by the seller are created as follows:
>
> (a) Any affirmation of fact or promise made by the seller to the buyer which relates to the goods and becomes part of the basis of the bargain creates an express warranty that the goods shall conform to the affirmation or promise.
>
> (b) Any description of the goods which is made part of the basis of the bargain creates an express warranty that the goods shall conform to the description.
>
> (c) Any sample or model which is made part of the basis of the bargain creates an express warranty that the whole of the goods shall conform to the sample or model.
>
> (2) It is not necessary to the creation of an express warranty that the seller use formal words such as "warrant" or "guarantee" or that he have a specific intention to make a warranty, but an affirmation merely of the value of the goods or a statement purporting to be merely the seller's opinion or commendation of the goods does not create a warranty.

Note that § 2–313 explicitly describes how an express sales warranty is *created*, not how it is breached. Article 2 buries the concept of breach within the notion of non-conformity, which it addresses only impliedly in § 2–313 and treats more directly in the damages provisions.[52] So, a seller *breaches* an express warranty by selling a product that fails to conform to the warranty and the buyer or another is proximately injured as a result. The central idea of non-conformity to a contractual warranty means quite simply that the seller made an affirmation about its product that was false.[53]

An express warranty claim in a products liability case thus requires an injured plaintiff to show that (1) the plaintiff bought a product from the seller or was a third-party beneficiary of any accompanying warranty; (2) the seller made a factual assertion about the product; (3) the assertion was false; (4) the assertion was part of the basis of the bargain; and (5) the assertion's falsity proximately caused the plaintiff harm.[54]

---

[52] In UCC §§ 2–714 and 2–715. See § 4.1, above.

[53] To establish an express warranty claim in Missouri, a plaintiff must show that:

> (1) the defendant sold goods to the plaintiff; (2) the seller made a statement of fact about the kind or quality of those goods; (3) the statement of fact was a material factor inducing the buyer to purchase the goods; (4) the goods did not conform to that statement of fact; (5) the nonconformity injured the buyer; and (6) the buyer notified the seller of the nonconformity in a timely fashion."

Renaissance Leasing, LLC v. Vermeer Mfg. Co., 322 S.W.3d 112, 122 (Mo. 2010) (en banc).

[54] Claims for breach of express warranty thus are embraced by more general descriptions of breach of warranty. See, e.g., TreeHouse Foods, Inc. v. SunOpta Grains & Foods Inc., 463 F. Supp. 3d 802, 814 (N.D. Ill. 2020) ("To establish a breach of warranty claim, a plaintiff must prove: 'the existence of a warranty, a breach, and a causal link between the breach and the alleged harm.' "); Daigle v. Ford Motor Co., 713 F. Supp. 2d 822, 825 (D. Minn. 2010) ("To establish a warranty claim the plaintiff must basically prove: the existence of a warranty, a breach, and a causal link between the breach and the alleged harm.").

Compared to Strict Liability in Tort for Misrepresentation

A claim for breach of express warranty under UCC § 2–313 is similar to that for misrepresentation under *Restatement (Second) of Torts* § 402B.[55] A seller makes an express warranty under UCC § 2–313 by "[a]ny affirmation of fact or promise" or by "[a]ny description of the goods." Such a warranty is breached if it is untrue and that falsity proximately harms a buyer or other appropriate plaintiff. *Restatement (Second) of Torts* § 402B similarly bases liability on "a misrepresentation of a material fact concerning the character or quality" of a product that proximately harms the plaintiff. Both types of claims provide relief to plaintiffs injured as a result of false representations about a product, and both impose a form of "strict" liability upon sellers that requires no showing of fault.[56] Also like claims of tortious misrepresentation, express warranty claims require a close focus on particular words asserted to constitute the warranty and to be false.[57]

Express warranty claims under the Code do differ in certain material respects from misrepresentation claims under § 402B of the *Restatement (Second) of Torts*, which is drawn more narrowly in certain respects than UCC § 2–313. Under § 402B, a plaintiff must establish actual reliance by himself or someone else,[58] whereas an express warranty claimant under the Code may be entitled to a presumption that he relied upon a seller's representations that became "part of the basis of the bargain."[59] Section 402B is generally deemed to apply only to public forms of representation, as in advertisements and manuals accompanying a product, whereas UCC § 2–313 express warranties apply as well to private misrepresentations between individual sales clerks and customers. Further, § 402B by its terms applies only to merchants "engaged in the business of selling chattels," whereas UCC § 2–313 (in contrast to UCC § 2–314) applies more widely to merchant and non-merchant sellers alike. In addition, § 402B applies only to representations of "material" fact, whereas UCC § 2–313 claimants in some situations might be able to show that ordinarily trivial words became part of the basis of a particular bargain. Moreover, UCC § 2–313 allows recovery of all types of damages available under Article 2, including pure economic loss,[60] whereas § 402B provides recovery only for "physical harm." Finally, it is important to note that warranty claims under the Uniform Commercial Code are controlled by a very different set of doctrines involving a large variety of secondary issues, such as the requirements of privity of contract and notice of breach, statutes of limitations, special defenses based on disclaimers and limitations of remedy, user conduct, and the non-availability of punitive damages, to name some of the more prominent warranty distinctions.

---

[55] Strict liability in tort for product misrepresentation, under Rest. (2d) Torts § 402B, is treated in § 3.4, above.

[56] It is axiomatic that breach of express warranty requires no showing of fault and thus is truly "strict" liability. Moreover, "no 'defect' other than a failure to conform to the warrantor's representations need be shown in order to establish a breach of an express warranty." McCarty v. E.J. Korvette, Inc., 347 A.2d 253, 264 (Md. Ct. Spec. App. 1975) (tire guaranteed against blowouts). See also Voelkel v. General Motors Corp., 846 F. Supp. 1468, 1476 (D. Kan. 1994) (seatbelt buckle described as "trouble-free, safe").

[57] See § 3.1, above.

[58] Section 402B states explicitly that the claimed harm must have been caused by "justifiable reliance."

[59] See UCC § 2–313 cmt. 3 ("no particular reliance on such statements need be shown in order to weave them into the fabric of the agreement"). One must be cautious, however, to recognize the controversial nature of reliance in § 2–313. The "basis of the bargain" requirement in UCC § 2–313, and the relevance of reliance to that issue, is further discussed below.

[60] See UCC §§ 2–714 and 2–715.

Manner of Communication

There is no fixed manner by which an express warranty must be created,[61] and such a warranty may arise from any affirmative means by which information is conveyed. Thus, an express warranty may arise from a seller's assurances to a buyer's pilots that a used plane is "ready to go,"[62] a sales clerk's assertion that a pressure cooker will not explode,[63] a label on a can stating "Boned Chicken" and newspaper advertisements stating that the chicken contains "No Bones,"[64] or an "off" designation for a control handle on an electrical panel that is alive with current.[65] Such warranties may be created by language and other representations in various places, such as on a product's label,[66] packaging,[67] or tags,[68] and in advertisements,[69] circulars,[70] catalogues,[71] brochures,[72] pamphlets,[73] product literature,[74] owners' manuals,[75] specification sheets,[76] promotional videos,[77] and on a seller's website.[78]

---

[61] In particular, the formation of an express warranty does not require the use of magic words such as "warranty" or "guarantee." UCC § 2–313(2). See Rite Aid Corp. v. Levy-Gray, 894 A.2d 563, 576 (Md. 2006).

[62] Husky Spray Serv., Inc. v. Patzer, 471 N.W.2d 146 (S.D. 1991).

[63] Joseph v. Sears Roebuck & Co., 77 S.E.2d 583 (S.C. 1953).

[64] Lane v. C.A. Swanson & Sons, 278 P.2d 723 (Cal. Ct. App. 1955).

[65] Huebert v. Federal Pac. Elec. Co., 494 P.2d 1210 (Kan. 1972).

[66] See, e.g., Klingenberg v. Vulcan Ladder USA, 936 F.3d 824, 832–33 (8th Cir. 2019) (Iowa law) (label on extension ladder that "Working Load" is "300 lbs.").

[67] See, e.g., Penikila v. Sergeant's Pet Care Prod., LLC, 442 F. Supp. 3d 1212, 1215 (N.D. Cal. 2020) (statement on packaging that flea medicine was "Safe For Use Around Children and Pets"); Snyder v. Farnam Cos., 792 F. Supp. 2d 712, 722–23 (D.N.J. 2011) (statements on product boxes).

[68] See, e.g., Pegasus Helicopters, Inc. v. United Techs. Corp., 35 F.3d 507 (10th Cir. 1994) (Colo. law) (aircraft part repaired by manufacturer carried tag stating that part conformed to original specifications).

[69] See, e.g., Jones v. WFM-Wo, Inc., 265 F. Supp. 3d 775, 781–82 (M.D. Tenn. 2017) (Whole Foods' signage identifying pizza as "Vegan Garden Pizza" and listing its ingredients created an express warranty that the pizza did not contain nuts or nut products); Lane v. C.A. Swanson & Sons, 278 P.2d 723 (Cal. Ct. App. 1955). *But see* Flores v. FCA US LLC, 2021 WL 1122216, at *7 (E.D. Mich. 2021) (Cal., Mich., N.J., N.Y., Nev., S.C., and Va. law) (statements in advertising or other marketing materials that were not included in written warranty booklets strangely did not create express warranties).

[70] See, e.g., Limbach Co. v. Owens-Corning Fiberglas Corp., 1987 WL 46869 (D.N.H. 1987); Lindroth v. Walgreen Co., 87 N.E.2d 307 (Ill. App. Ct. 1949) (baby in snuggle bunny burned in fire caused by vaporizer packed with circular stating "No danger from flame").

[71] See, e.g., Morgan v. Cabela's Inc., 788 F. Supp. 2d 552, 555–57 (E.D. Ky. 2011) (statements in catalog may be puffs, but express warranty claim based on such statements survives defendant's summary judgment motion).

[72] See, e.g., Duvall v. Bristol-Myers-Squibb Co., 103 F.3d 324 (4th Cir. 1996) (Md. law) (advertising brochure for penile prosthesis).

[73] See, e.g., Rite Aid Corp. v. Levy-Gray, 894 A.2d 563, 576 (Md. 2006).

[74] See, e.g., Imperia v. Marvin Windows of N.Y., Inc., 747 N.Y.S.2d 35, 37 (App. Div. 2002) (product literature).

[75] See, e.g., Forbes v. General Motors Corp., 935 So.2d 869, 875 (Miss. 2006); Caboni v. General Motors Corp., 398 F.3d 357, 360 (5th Cir. 2005) (La. law); Bell Sports, Inc. v. Yarusso, 759 A.2d 582 (Del. 2000) (express warranty claim allowed for motorcyclist's neck injury and resulting paraplegia where motorcycle helmet manual stated that liner was designed to reduce harmful effects of a blow to the head).

[76] See, e.g., Huebert v. Federal Pac. Elec. Co., 494 P.2d 1210 (Kan. 1972) (electrician's action against manufacturer of electrical panel boards).

[77] See, e.g., McLaughlin v. Denharco, Inc., 129 F. Supp. 2d 32, 39 (D. Me. 2001).

[78] See, e.g., Legal Aid of Nebraska, Inc. v. Chaina Wholesale, Inc., 2020 WL 42471, at *4 (D. Neb. 2020) (space heater description posted on Amazon website); Snyder v. Farnam Cos., 792 F. Supp. 2d 712, 722–23 (D.N.J. 2011) (statements on manufacturer's website and product boxes).

In addition, statements contained in promotional literature provided to doctors,[79] package inserts,[80] drug advice pamphlets provided by pharmacies to patients,[81] and even an assurance that a blood provider had exercised "utmost care" in donor selection on a container[82] have all been held to create express warranties. In short, a seller may be responsible for factual assertions it may make regardless of the means of communication.[83]

Express warranties normally are created by written assertions about a product's safety, performance, or other qualities, and, without such specific words, promises or statements, an express warranty claim usually will fail.[84] Yet express representations need not always be in words, for a description of an article may be pictorial,[85] or presented by blueprint, technical specifications,[86] samples, models, or even by past deliveries which have set a standard that fairly may be considered a description of the article.[87]

General representations of safety may support an express warranty action,[88] as may generalized guarantees.[89] But a claim for breach of express warranty asserts a communicative wrong, such that it requires a plaintiff to plead and prove that the defendant affirmatively conveyed information by words or other express form of affirmation, without which such a claim collapses and will be dismissed.[90]

---

79 See, e.g., Friedman v. Medtronic, Inc., 345 N.Y.S.2d 637 (App. Div. 1973). Expert testimony may be necessary to establish whether assertions directed at physicians amount to express warranties. See § 6.3, below.

80 See, e.g., Rosci v. AcroMed, Inc., 669 A.2d 959 (Pa. Super. Ct. 1995).

81 See Rite Aid Corp. v. Levy-Gray, 894 A.2d 563, 576 (Md. 2006).

82 See Jackson v. Muhlenberg Hosp., 232 A.2d 879 (N.J. Super. Ct. Law Div. 1967) (despite a statement that expressly rejected any warranty against the danger of infection), rev'd on other grounds, 249 A.2d 65 (N.J. 1969).

83 See generally Connick v. Suzuki Motor Co., 656 N.E.2d 170, 177 (Ill. App. Ct. 1995) (documents, brochures, and advertisements), rev'd in part on other grounds, 675 N.E.2d 584 (Ill. 1996).

84 See, e.g., Morrison v. Hoffmann-La Roche, Inc., 2016 WL 5678546, at *10 (E.D.N.Y. 2016). See also note 90, below.

85 See, e.g., Sylvestri v. Warner & Swasey Co., 398 F.2d 598, 602 (2d Cir. 1968) (N.Y. law). *But see* Maneely v. General Motors Corp., 108 F.3d 1176, 1181 (9th Cir. 1997) (Cal. law) (television and print ads showing young people standing and sitting in open cargo bed of pickup trucks, where most portrayals were of stationary trucks without a driver, did not create express warranty that it was safe to ride in trucks in this manner).

86 See, e.g., Sullivan v. Young Bros. & Co., 91 F.3d 242 (1st Cir. 1996) (Me. law) (express warranty created by manufacturer's product specification sheet accompanying fiberglass tubing used in lobster boat's exhaust system).

87 See UCC § 2–313 cmt. 5; Unicomp, Inc. v. Elementis Pigments, Inc., 1999 WL 1995400, at *15 (D. Me. 1999) ("Past deliveries may set the description of quality, either expressly or impliedly by course of dealing.").

88 See, e.g., Carlin v. Superior Ct., 38 Cal. Rptr. 2d 576 (Ct. App. 1995), aff'd, 920 P.2d 1347 (Cal. 1996); Cipollone v. Liggett Grp., Inc., 893 F.2d 541 (3d Cir. 1990) (N.J. law) (advertisements that long-term smoking of defendant's cigarettes would not endanger smoker's health), rev'd in part on other grounds, 505 U.S. 504 (1992); Drayton v. Jiffee Chem. Corp., 395 F. Supp. 1081 (N.D. Ohio 1975) (advertising claims that particularly caustic drain cleaner was safe for household use), modified on other grounds, 591 F.2d 352 (6th Cir. 1978).

89 See, e.g., Jones v. Cranman's Sporting Goods, 237 S.E.2d 402 (Ga. Ct. App. 1977) (explosion of "fully guaranteed" rifle).

90 See, e.g., Reynolds v. Bordelon, 172 So.3d 607, 615 (La. 2015) (plaintiff alluded to general expectations rather than a specifically stated warranty); In re Bisphenol-A (BPA) Polycarbonate Plastic Prods. Liab. Litig., 687 F. Supp. 2d 897, 905–06 (W.D. Mo. 2009) (plaintiffs failed to identify any assertions by defendants); Pulte Home Corp. v. Parex, Inc., 579 S.E.2d 188, 190–91 (Va. 2003); Schneidman v. Whitaker Co., 758 N.Y.S.2d 142 (App. Div. 2003) (express warranty claim properly dismissed because plaintiff failed to present evidence that defendant made any specific statement of fact); Anthony v. Country Life Mfg., LLC, 70

Breach—Falsity and Interpretation

An express warranty is breached only if an assertion is *false*.[91] As in tortious misrepresentation,[92] the truth or falsity of an assertion rests upon its fair interpretation in light of the context of the particular transaction. Questions of interpretation—the essential meaning and scope of a particular assertion, and whether it was true or false—are generally factual questions to be determined by the trier of fact.[93]

Two examples illustrate the inherently factual nature of interpreting the meaning of communications to ascertain whether they are true or false. In *Sylvestri v. Warner & Swasey Co.*,[94] the plaintiff was thrown from the operator's seat of a backhoe manufactured by the defendant. The vehicle tipped when its stabilizing outriggers shifted while it was being used to lift boulders and swing them around to different locations. An advertising brochure showed the backhoe lifting a length of pipe and stated that the "hydraulic system provides powerful lift force for material handling."[95] Upholding a verdict for the plaintiff for breach of express warranty, the court remarked: "While Sylvestri apparently did not attach the rock to the backhoe in exactly the same manner that the pipe was attached in the brochure picture, and while lifting rock may in some way be different from lifting pipe, [the jury was properly left to] determine . . . whether the brochure picture and statements as a whole represented an affirmation of fact or promise that the machine could be used as Sylvestri used it. It is the 'essential idea' conveyed by the advertising representations which is relevant . . . ."[96]

In contrast to *Sylvestri* is *Salk v. Alpine Ski Shop, Inc.*,[97] where the court denied the plaintiff's express warranty claim. There, a skier who broke his leg when his ski bindings failed to release sued the bindings manufacturer for breach of express warranty for

---

Fed. Appx. 379, 383 (7th Cir. 2003) (Ill. law) ("While an express warranty need not be formed by words, there must nonetheless be some affirmation."). See also note 84, above.

[91] See, e.g., Caboni v. General Motors Corp., 398 F.3d 357, 360 (5th Cir. 2005) (La. law) (express warranty was untrue because airbag failed to perform as described in owner's manual).

Breach, of course, also requires that the false aspect of an assertion proximately harms an appropriate plaintiff. See § 4.1, above.

[92] See §§ 3.2 and 3.4, above.

[93] See, e.g., Klingenberg v. Vulcan Ladder USA, 936 F.3d 824, 832–33 (8th Cir. 2019) (Iowa law) (label on extension ladder from which worker fell stated separately that "Working Load" is "300 lbs." and that it was manufactured to "OSHA ANSI A 14.2 SPECIFICATIONS"; jury could find that "300 lbs." statement was independent assertion so that neither compliance with OSHA standards nor lack of design defect undercut independent "300 lbs." breach of express warranty claim); Bell Sports, Inc. v. Yarusso, 759 A.2d 582, 593 (Del. 2000) (jury properly could conclude that statements that motorcycle helmet was designed "to reduce the harmful effects of a blow to the head" and to absorb and spread the force of a blow to the head as much as possible were express warranty to motorcyclist who suffered neck injury and paralysis from blow to helmet, notwithstanding warning that helmets cannot protect against all impacts); Yuzwak v. Dygert, 534 N.Y.S.2d 35 (App. Div. 1988) (representation that horse, which kicked plaintiff's daughter in face while she was leading it to barn, was good for children).

If a term is susceptible of two meanings, its interpretation ordinarily is a question for the finder of fact. See McLaughlin v. Denharco, Inc., 129 F. Supp. 2d 32, 38 (D. Me. 2001) (whether ambiguous affirmation was express warranty was for jury). In Bud Wolf Chevrolet, Inc. v. Robertson, 496 N.E.2d 771, 775–76 (Ind. Ct. App. 1986), modified on other grounds, 508 N.E.2d 567 (Ind. Ct. App. 1987), vacated in part on other grounds, 519 N.E.2d 135 (Ind. 1988), a truck sold as "new" had been previously damaged on the lot. "Although . . . the evidence was susceptible to reasonably differing interpretations, the jury could have inferred that the truck . . . was not 'new,' as the term is commonly understood by the general public . . . ." Id. at 775–76.

[94] 398 F.2d 598 (2d Cir. 1968) (N.Y. law).

[95] Id. at 602.

[96] Id.

[97] 342 A.2d 622 (R.I. 1975).

advertisements that stated: "Cubco is the precise binding . . . that releases when it's supposed to. . . . Both heel and toe release at the exact tension you set. And release whichever way you fall."[98] For liability here, reasoned the court, Cubco would have had to assert that its bindings "would release in every situation presenting a danger to the user's limbs," and the defendant's advertising here fell short of such a "blanket guarantee."[99] Trial had revealed that the Cubco multi-directional release bindings could be adjusted to release at varying tensions and that any binding set to release during slow falls would also sometimes release during normal skiing maneuvers. The court thus concluded that the advertisements did no more than affirm these uncontroverted facts.[100]

Many other cases similarly demonstrate the preliminary importance in express warranty litigation of properly interpreting the meaning and scope of a defendant's representations alleged to constitute a warranty in order to determine whether those assertions were true or false.[101] This factual inquiry into the meaning of an express warranty in all cases requires a full and careful consideration of all the facts and circumstances surrounding the particular words; the particular type of product; the circumstances of its use; the nature of the purchase and sales transaction; and, ultimately, how persons in both the seller's and plaintiff's positions fairly and probably would have interpreted the meaning of the particular assertions in relation to the situation that gives rise to the claim.[102] In short, *context* is often the key to unraveling the true meaning of assertions claimed to be express warranties.

Interpretation—Fact *vs.* Opinion ("Puffs")

To create an express warranty, a seller's affirmation ordinarily must be one of *fact*, meaning that such a statement must convey more information than simply the seller's opinion of the product's safety or other worth. In attempting to sell products to consumers, sellers often make exaggerated statements of opinion heralding their products' virtues—a form of salesmanship consumers are accustomed to treat as devoid of content. Such embellished claims of product value have long and widely been dubbed mere "puffing." Even to the extent that such hollow commendations of value and quality may be true, they ordinarily contain no content other than, at best, an expression of the seller's subjective and inflated perception of the product's worth. Reasonable buyers

---

98 Id. at 626.

99 Id.

100 Id.

101 See, e.g., Lambert v. Dollar Gen. Corp., 2017 WL 2619142, at *4 (N.D. Ill. 2017) (statements on Aloe Gel packaging that it contained "aloe barbadensis leaf extract" and was "made with aloe vera" were not true); Nationwide Mut. Ins. Co. v. Barton Solvents, Inc., 855 N.W.2d 145, 153 (S.D. 2014) (plaintiff "failed to identify evidence suggesting that the defendants' warnings were an affirmative description, instruction, or illustration that constituted an express warranty of heptane that was untrue"); Sherman v. Sunsong Am., Inc., 485 F. Supp. 2d 1070, 1088 (D. Neb. 2007) (warning label that misuse of fireworks "may result in injury or fire" was not an express affirmation that "proper use will not result in injury"); Kolarik v. Cory Int'l Corp., 721 N.W.2d 159, 164 (Iowa 2006) ("stuffed" on label of jar of olives did not warrant that olives contained no pits or pit fragments); Whitmer v. Schneble, 331 N.E.2d 115, 118 (Ill. App. Ct. 1975) (female Doberman Pinscher, represented by sellers to be "docile," bit child viewing dog's new puppies 2½ years after sale; *held*, no recovery: "Even a docile dog is known and expected to bite under certain circumstances"; moreover, statement pertained to dog's personality at time of sale and did not mean that its personality could not change); Whittington v. Eli Lilly & Co., 333 F. Supp. 98, 100 (S.D. W. Va. 1971) (birth control pills said to "offer virtually 100% protection" in fact offered 98.1% protection; *held*, no promise of *absolute* protection).

102 See, e.g., Huebert v. Federal Pac. Elec. Co., 494 P.2d 1210, 1215 (Kan. 1972) ("All express warranties must be reasonably construed taking into consideration the nature of the product, the situation of the parties, and surrounding circumstances.").

generally understand such puffs as mere sales pitches, designed to bend the buyer's will and encourage a sale.[103] A representation is likely to be construed as fact, on the other hand, when it describes specific traits of quality, construction, performance capability, durability, or safety possessed by the product—information of a type likely to be known by a seller but not a buyer, which communicates a message of real value on which a prospective buyer may justifiably be expected to rely.[104]

Section 2–313(1)(a) of the Uniform Commercial Code states broadly that express warranties are created by "[a]ny affirmation of fact." Section 2–313(2) further provides that "an affirmation merely of the value of the goods or a statement purporting to be merely the seller's opinion or commendation of the goods does not create a warranty." However, the "purporting to be" language suggests that the fact/opinion distinction in § 2–313 is intended to be read narrowly, such that commendations that purport to have some factual basis may be made part of the basis of a bargain, a suggestion reinforced by comment 8 to this section.[105]

If a seller's assertion is specific, technically based, clearly important to the buyer, and its truth is capable of objective determination ("this crane can support loads of 20,000 pounds") or if, by contrast, it is vague praise ("this used car is terrific"), one may conclude with some confidence that the statement should be deemed a fact (as in the first example) or an opinion (as in the second). But many cases involve assertions much closer to the middle, where it is exceedingly difficult to isolate clear principles for determining whether a particular representation should be classified as fact or opinion. In such cases, the fact/opinion determination rests not only on the words at issue but also on a host of other considerations concerning the parties, including their corporate or personal identities, the nature of any pre-existing relationship they may have had, their respective power, their knowledge of and ability to discover information related to the matter asserted, their likely expectations, their actions and other statements surrounding the transaction, and many other factors.[106]

---

[103] See, e.g., Clark v. American Honda Motor Co., 528 F. Supp. 3d 1108, 1119 (C.D. Cal. 2021) (sales brochure statements were "non-actionable puffery"); Chic Promotion, Inc. v. Middletown Sec. Sys., Inc., 688 N.E.2d 278, 282 (Ohio Ct. App. 1996) (general assertions in sales brochure "did not cross the line from puffing to warranty"; brochure was deemed a pre-sale inducement "which is the very purpose of advertising"). See also Learned Hand's classic exposition on this point in Vulcan Metals Co. v. Simmons Mfg. Co., 248 F. 853, 856 (2d Cir. 1918):

> There are some kinds of talk which no sensible man takes seriously, and if he does he suffers from his credulity. If we were all scrupulously honest, it would not be so; but, as it is, neither party usually believes what the seller says about his own opinions, and each knows it. Such statements, like the claims of campaign managers before election, are rather designed to allay the suspicion which would attend their absence than to be understood as having any relation to objective truth.

[104] See, e.g., Scott v. Illinois Tool Works, Inc., 550 N.W.2d 809, 813–14 (Mich. Ct. App. 1996) (statement that average breaking strength of polyester strapping was 800 pounds).

[105] UCC § 2–313 cmt. 8 provides in part:

> Concerning affirmations of value or a seller's opinion or commendation under subsection (2), the basic question remains the same: What statements of the seller have in the circumstances and in objective judgment become part of the basis of the bargain? As indicated above, all of the statements of the seller do so unless good reason is shown to the contrary. The provisions of subsection (2) are included, however, since common experience discloses that some statements or predictions cannot fairly be viewed as entering into the bargain.

[106] "Certainly the specificity of the statement is important" and "[c]ertainly a written statement is less likely to pass as a puff than an oral one, and a written statement in the contract of the parties is less likely to pass as a puff than a written statement in an advertisement." White and Summers, UCC § 10–4, at 454–55. All aspects of the "context" in which the words are spoken are important, such as the reasonableness of the

Seller representations that are specific and unambiguous, particularly if they concern the safety of a product, are likely to be construed as factual. Thus, express warranties have been found to be created by an "off" designation on a high-voltage electrical panel switch;[107] an advertisement that a skin cream was "safe";[108] a tire manufacturer's advertisement, "If it only saves your life once, it's a bargain," where plaintiff's decedent was killed when his tire blew out;[109] a booklet accompanying a steam vaporizer stating that it was safe to be used all night and featuring a picture of the appliance in use near a baby's crib, where a toddler was badly burned when the vaporizer overturned;[110] representations that a tree hunting stand was "probably the safest one on the market" and "there is no way [one] can fall" from it, where the plaintiff did;[111] a nightclub server's statement that the club's special drink that night was "good," where the plaintiffs were mistakenly served glasses of dishwashing liquid containing highly toxic lye;[112] statements in the owner's manual for an off-road motorcycle helmet that "the primary function of a helmet is to reduce the harmful effects of a blow to the head," where a rider's neck was injured when he was thrown from his motorcycle and struck his head;[113] and a representation that a Golfing Gizmo training device was "Completely Safe—Ball Will Not Hit Player," where a boy hit beneath the ball, catching the attached cord and causing the ball to fly back and hit him in the head—as opposed to another statement by the manufacturer that practice with the Gizmo would permit the user to challenge Jack Nicklaus.[114]

In contrast to such specific factual assertions, a seller's vague and general representations that appear merely to express the seller's personal views on a product's characteristics, worth, or quality, do not ordinarily constitute material facts. Such statements of seller opinion are known as "puffs." An illustrative case in which a sales clerk's statements were held to be only her opinion of the product's virtues, and so insufficient to create an express warranty, is *Carpenter v. Alberto Culver Co.*,[115] where the plaintiff suffered an adverse skin reaction from hair dye purchased from a store. The selling clerk had assured the plaintiff that she, the clerk, had used the same product; that her own hair came out "very nice" and "very natural"; and that the plaintiff "would get very fine results."[116] Concluding that the sales clerk's commendation was mere puffery and not a representation of fact creating an express warranty, the court noted the importance of considering whether the seller "assumes to assert a fact of which the buyer is ignorant, or merely states an opinion or judgment upon a matter of which the

---

plaintiff's reliance and whether the seller hedges in making the representation. Id. at 455–56. See Federal Signal Corp. v. Safety Factors, Inc., 886 P.2d 172, 178–79 (Wash. 1994) (outlining relevant factors).

107 Huebert v. Federal Pac. Elec. Co., 494 P.2d 1210 (Kan. 1972).

108 Spiegel v. Saks 34th St., 252 N.Y.S.2d 852 (Sup. Ct. 1964) ("the warranty was *express*, that the [skin cream] was 'safe' for anyone who purchased it; the warranty in effect stated that . . . there would be no allergic reaction"), aff'd, 272 N.Y.S.2d 972 (App. Div. 1966).

109 Collins v. Uniroyal, Inc., 315 A.2d 16 (N.J. 1974).

110 McCormack v. Hankscraft Co., 154 N.W.2d 488 (Minn. 1967).

111 Moore v. Berry, 458 S.E.2d 879, 880 (Ga. Ct. App. 1995) (question of fact for jury).

112 Cott v. Peppermint Twist Mgmt. Co., 856 P.2d 906 (Kan. 1993).

113 Bell Sports, Inc. v. Yarusso, 759 A.2d 582, 593 (Del. 2000).

114 Hauter v. Zogarts, 534 P.2d 377, 379 (Cal. 1975).

115 184 N.W.2d 547 (Mich. Ct. App. 1970).

116 Id. at 548.

seller has no special knowledge, and on which the buyer may be expected also to have an opinion and to exercise his judgment."[117]

A seller's commendations of a product's worth ordinarily are mere puffs intended to enhance the product's attractiveness for prospective buyers rather than to assert a fact on which buyers may justifiably rely. So, statements that a Suzuki Samurai "never lets you down," has "fun written all over it," and is "nifty,"[118] are the kind of loose and general "sales talk" that should be viewed as puffing rather than as affirmations of fact that the vehicle was not prone to roll over.[119] Other examples of statements held to be mere puffery rather than factual include claims that a truck, the roof of which collapsed after it fell nearly 30 feet, was "rock-solid" and its roof was "strong";[120] that an automotive manufacturer believed that "Quality is job one";[121] that a used car was in good shape;[122] that a fondue pot, which tipped over and burned a young child caught in its cord, was the "finest product of its kind available" and was "engineered to give [an] extra measure of satisfaction";[123] that computer modeling and laboratory tests resulted in "great road cars," including the plaintiff's that contained a defective seatbelt;[124] that a defective gas heater, which burned down the plaintiffs' house, was from "America's most complete line of reliable, economical gas heating appliances";[125] that heavy equipment tires were good and had been used successfully on prior occasions;[126] that a bungee cord was of "premium quality";[127] that a helmet worn during all-terrain vehicle driving was "top rated";[128] and that "You meet the nicest people on a Honda and a Honda bike is a good one for children."[129]

Ascertaining whether a particular assertion is a statement of fact, such that it may create an express warranty, or whether instead it is merely an opinion and puff, is often highly fact-specific and so peculiarly suited for juries to resolve.[130] In such a murky sea,[131] predicting whether a jury or court will construe a particular assertion in a

---

[117] Id. at 549.

[118] Connick v. Suzuki Motor Co., 656 N.E.2d 170, 183 (Ill. App. Ct. 1995) (" 'the Samurai never lets you down. . . . Nothing else comes close to giving you a better run for your money'; [it is a] 'funmobile,' with 'fun written all over it,' and 'a million laughs' "), rev'd in part on other grounds, 675 N.E.2d 584 (Ill. 1996).

[119] Although the *Connick* court addressed the fact/opinion distinction in the specific context of fraud, the case involved various misrepresentation claims, including breach of express warranty, to which the fact/opinion discussion would be relevant as well.

[120] Jordan v. Paccar, Inc., 37 F.3d 1181, 1185 (6th Cir. 1994) (Ohio law).

[121] Martin v. Ford Motor Co., 914 F. Supp. 1449, 1456 (S.D. Tex. 1996).

[122] Jenkins v. Landmark Chevrolet, Inc., 575 So.2d 1157, 1161 (Ala. Civ. App. 1991).

[123] Rock v. Oster Corp., 810 F. Supp. 665, 667 (D. Md. 1991).

[124] Voelkel v. General Motors Corp., 846 F. Supp. 1482, 1484–85 (D. Kan. 1994).

[125] Warzynski v. Empire Comfort Sys., Inc., 401 S.E.2d 801, 803 (N.C. Ct. App. 1991).

[126] McLaughlin v. Michelin Tire Corp., 778 P.2d 59, 65 (Wyo. 1989).

[127] Anderson v. Bungee Int'l Mfg. Corp., 44 F. Supp. 2d 534, 541 (S.D.N.Y. 1999) ("statements that the Bungee cords are of premium or superior quality are generalized statements of salesmanship and [hence] puffery [rather than] descriptions of particular characteristics of the goods").

[128] Wojcik v. Borough of Manville, 2010 WL 322893, at *3 (N.J. Super. Ct. App. Div. 2010).

[129] Federal Signal Corp. v. Safety Factors, Inc., 886 P.2d 172, 179 (Wash. 1994) (citing Baughn v. Honda Motor Co., 727 P.2d 655 (Wash. 1986)).

[130] See, e.g., In re Second Chance Body Armor, Inc., 417 B.R. 750, 755–57 (W.D. Mich. 2009); Bussian v. DaimlerChrysler Corp., 411 F. Supp. 2d 614, 620 (M.D.N.C. 2006); Yuzwak v. Dygert, 534 N.Y.S.2d 35 (App. Div. 1988) (horse that kicked plaintiff's daughter in face was said to be good for children; whether statement was fact or opinion was for jury).

[131] See, e.g., Metcalfe v. Biomet, Inc., 2019 WL 192902, at *5–6 (D.N.J. 2019) ("Some courts note that puffery determinations may be reserved for the jury 'except in clear cases. . . .' This is a clear case."; holding

particular context as fact or opinion is risky business, to say the least, particularly now that many jurors and courts seem to be demanding greater personal responsibility and may be less concerned about protecting consumer rights. These factors lead warranty law experts to conclude: "Only a foolish lawyer will be quick to label a seller's statement as puffs or not puffs, and only a reckless one will label a seller's statement at all without carefully examining such factors as the nature of the defect (was it obvious or not) and the buyer's and seller's relative knowledge."[132]

Basis of the Bargain; Reliance

For a seller's affirmation of fact to become an express warranty under Uniform Commercial Code § 2–313(1), the affirmation must become "part of the basis of the bargain."[133] Replacing the "reliance" requirement contained in its predecessor, § 12 of the Uniform Sales Act,[134] § 2–313 thus appears quite plainly to abandon reliance as a requirement in express warranty cases. Yet, the law on what, if any, continuing role reliance may have under § 2–313 is in quite a muddle.[135]

Nature of the Reliance Debate

During the nineteenth century, warranty law migrated into contract law from the tort law misrepresentation action of "deceit."[136] Tortious misrepresentation has always

---

hip replacement system's marketing brochure statement "offers optimal joint mechanical restoration": puff, "offers . . . ultra low-wear rates [sic] in vivo": fact); Bussian v. DaimlerChrysler Corp., 411 F. Supp. 2d 614, 620 (M.D.N.C. 2006) (courts' characterization of fact/opinion nether land was "hazy").

[132] White and Summers, UCC § 10–4, at 455. See also R. Nordstrom, The Law of Sales 219 (1970) ("In one sense, every statement made by a seller is nothing more than his opinion as to the goods or how the goods will operate; yet at some point he makes his statement in a manner and under such conditions that the buyer does not understand that *only* this seller's opinion is involved."). Compare Carney v. Sears, Roebuck & Co., 309 F.2d 300, 302 (4th Cir. 1962) (Va. law) ("good quality ladder"; *held,* opinion), with Turner v. Central Hardware Co., 186 S.W.2d 603, 606 (Mo. 1945) (ladder "mighty strong and durable"; *held,* fact: "the seller's protection lies in the fact that his is the choice of language and action"). Compare also Jenkins v. Landmark Chevrolet, Inc., 575 So.2d 1157, 1161 (Ala. Civ. App. 1991) (used car "in good shape" was a puff), with Jones v. Kellner, 451 N.E.2d 548, 550 (Ohio Ct. App. 1982) (used car "mechanically A-1"; *held,* fact: "although it was unclear how long this warranty would have lasted, it should have lasted at least long enough for the appellee to get the car home").

[133] See, e.g., Swanstrom v. Teledyne Cont'l Motors, Inc., 43 So.3d 564, 587 (Ala. 2009) (neither statement in marketing executive's letter nor advertisements constituted a "basis of the bargain" for aircraft purchase); Rite Aid Corp. v. Levy-Gray, 894 A.2d 563, 573 (Md. 2006). On basis of the bargain and reliance under UCC § 2–313, see White, Freeing the Tortious Soul of Express Warranty Law, 72 Tul. L. Rev. 2089 (1998) (thorough review, analysis, and classification of all cases decided between 1965 and 1998).

[134] USA § 12 stated in part: "Any affirmation of fact or any promise by the seller relating to the goods is an express warranty if the natural tendency of such affirmation or promise is to induce the buyer to purchase the goods, and if the buyer purchases the goods relying thereon."

[135] See Michael v. Wyeth, LLC, 2011 WL 2150112, at *8 (S.D. W. Va. 2011) ("there is considerable divergence as to whether reliance is an element of a breach of warranty claim under U.C.C. § 2–313"; canvassing case law across the nation); Kelleher v. Marvin Lumber & Cedar Co., 891 A.2d 477, 500–01 (N.H. 2005) (same); 1 White and Summers, UCC § 10–14 (6th pract. ed. 2012); Frumer, Friedman, and Sklaren, Products Liability § 9.02[2].

[136] Although now frequently forgotten, tort law's paternity of warranty law has long been acknowledged by scholars of contract and commercial law. See S. Williston, The Law Governing Sales of Goods at Common Law and Under the Uniform Sales Act 251 (1909): "[T]he action upon a warranty was in its origin a pure action of tort . . . [and its tortious character] was recognized by Blackstone, [a perspective that] has been lost sight of by some courts. . . ." See also White, note 133, above, at 2090, noting that "[w]arranty law started as tort but progressively, from sometime in the nineteenth century, has moved step-by-step from tort to contract," deducing from the decided cases "that there is an irrepressible minimum of tort buried in express warranty," and concluding properly, and boldly for a scholar of contract and commercial law, that "we should let it out."

required the plaintiff to prove reliance on the defendant's misrepresentation as a causal link between the defendant's false statement and the plaintiff's harm.[137] By contrast, under traditional contract-law doctrine, a contracting party was bound to the terms of a contract whether or not the other party had relied upon them.[138] As express warranty law was absorbed over time into the law of contracts, first into the common law and then into § 12 of the Uniform Sales Act, it carried with it the tort-law element of reliance. Karl Llewyllen and other contract law scholars who drafted Article 2 of the UCC, vexed that a major section of sales law was anchored by a concept that belonged to tort,[139] sought to move express warranty doctrine more fully into contract law by rejecting "reliance" as a formal element. But the novel phrase selected to replace reliance, "[part of the] basis of the bargain," has proved infelicitous, to say the least.[140] Just how the drafters intended the new concept to be interpreted, and the extent to which reliance still might play a role, was left quite unclear.[141] Thus, the basic issue in ascertaining the meaning of "basis of the bargain" in UCC § 2–313 is to determine how that contract-based standard may differ, in varying contexts, from the tort-based notion of reliance.

There are basically two approaches to interpreting the "basis of the bargain" requirement of § 2–313.[142] The first, "strong," interpretation assumes that drafters of Article 2, in switching to the "basis of the bargain" language from "reliance," intended to make a significant shift in warranty law, redirecting the focus away from the deal the buyer thought he or she was getting to the deal the seller's affirmations reasonably and objectively appeared to make.[143] This view finds support in comment 4 to UCC § 2–313, which provides: "In view of the principle that the whole purpose of the law of warranty is to determine what it is that the seller has in essence agreed to sell, the policy is adopted of those cases which refuse except in unusual circumstances to recognize a material deletion of the seller's obligation. Thus, a contract is normally a contract for a sale of something describable and described."[144] Simply put, if the seller makes a factual

---

Tort scholars, of course, have long concurred. See, e.g., Prosser, The Implied Warranty of Merchantable Quality, 27 Minn. L. Rev. 117, 118–19 (1943):

> In its inception, breach of warranty was a tort. The action was upon the case, for breach of an assumed duty, and the wrong was conceived to be a form of misrepresentation, in the nature of deceit. . . . Warranty has never entirely lost this tort character which . . . may have important consequences at the present day.

137 See the discussion of reliance in fraud and deceit, § 3.2, above. For a case suggesting that "basis of the bargain" in § 2–313 serves the same causal-linkage function in express warranty as reliance in tortious misrepresentation, see Lowe v. Sporicidin Int'l, 47 F.3d 124, 131–32 (4th Cir. 1995) (Md. law) (plaintiff's misrepresentation and express warranty claims both failed because she failed to allege reliance on defendant's advertisements or other representations).

138 See 1 T. Murray, J. Perillo, Corbin on Contracts § 1.1 (2021 rev. ed).

139 And distraught, perhaps, by the fundamental superiority of tort law to the law of contracts.

140 See White, above note 133, at 2094–95, 2106–07.

141 In his UCC study for the N. Y. Law Revision Commission, Professor Honnold noted the novelty of the "basis of the bargain" language, opined that its meaning was "less than clear," and suggested that "for lack of any other meaningful standard, courts must employ the test of whether buyer relied on the affirmation or promise, the test presently employed in Section 12 of the Uniform Sales Act." Study of Uniform Commercial Code: Article 2—Sales, reprinted in 1 State of New York Report of The Law Revision Commission for 1955, Study of the Uniform Commercial Code, at 355, 392, as cited in White, above note 133, at 2095 n.20.

142 Both well summarized in Hauter v. Zogarts, 534 P.2d 377, 383–84 (Cal. 1975) (the Golfing Gizmo case), from which the textual discussion draws.

143 See, e.g., Note, 34 U. Pitt. L. Rev. 145, 150 (1972); R. Nordstrom, Law of Sales §§ 66–68 (1970).

144 Comment 8 to § 2–313 states that "the basic question remains the same: What statements of the seller have in the circumstances and in objective judgment become part of the basis of the bargain? As indicated above, all of the statements of the seller do so unless good reason is shown to the contrary."

statement about the product, the statement becomes part of the deal purchased by the buyer, and the seller must stand behind the statement.[145]

The second, "weak," interpretation of "basis of the bargain" postulates that reliance remains an important consideration, although its absence now must be proven by the seller. This conception of § 2–313, that it merely shifts the burden of proving non-reliance to the seller,[146] finds support in comment 3 to UCC § 2–313, which provides that "no particular reliance . . . need be shown in order to weave [the seller's affirmations of fact] into the fabric of the agreement. Rather, any fact which is to take such affirmations, once made, out of the agreement requires clear affirmative proof."

Courts and commentators have struggled mightily in deciding between these two views.[147] Many courts steer clear of any explicit use of the traditional reliance requirement whatsoever. Perhaps on the theory that the drafters of § 2–313 would not have altered the language of such a fundamental element of express warranty law without a purpose, such courts and commentators might plausibly reason that requiring an affirmation of fact to be part of the basis of a bargain, which sounds in contract, must somehow appreciably differ from requiring the buyer to rely on such an affirmation, which sounds in tort. Abandoning the reliance requirement altogether has some logical appeal, for it holds a seller to the deal the seller thought it was making—a deal that, viewed broadly, might reasonably be deemed to include whatever promises the seller made in an effort to merchandise its product.[148] From this perspective, in pricing its product, a seller might fairly be expected to include as a reserved expense the cost of fulfilling its claims of product description, quality, and performance. So, whether or not the buyer relies upon or even knows about a particular warranty, and regardless of whether it was made specifically to him or to the public at large, the buyer arguably has paid for and bought it as part of the sales transaction.[149] Moreover, the seller might fairly

---

[145] "[T]he seller must show by clear affirmative proof either that the statement was retracted by him before the deal was closed or that the parties understood that the goods would not conform to the affirmation or description. [T]he affirmation, once made, is a part of the agreement, and lack of reliance by the buyer is not a fact which would take the affirmation out of the agreement." Note, "Basis of the Bargain"—What Role Reliance?, 34 U. Pitt. L. Rev. 145, 151 (1972).

[146] See, e.g., Boyd, Representing Consumers—The Uniform Commercial Code and Beyond, 9 Ariz. L. Rev. 372, 385 (1968). On this view, Article 2 relegates "the metaphysical 'buyer's reliance' requirement to secondary status, where it properly belongs." Ezer, The Impact of the Uniform Commercial Code on the California Law of Sales Warranties, 8 UCLA L. Rev. 281, 285 (1961). Ezer also notes: "The Code's implicit premise is that buyer's reliance is prima facie established from the fact that he made the purchase. If the seller can establish that the buyer in fact did not rely on the seller, that the affirmation or promise was not the 'basis of the bargain,' to use the Code language, then there is no express warranty." Id. at 285 n.30. For more recent discussion, see, e.g., Frumer, Friedman, and Sklaren, Products Liability § 9.02[2]; Lawrence's Anderson on the UCC § 2–313:56.

[147] For thorough analysis, see White, above note 133, and Cipollone v. Liggett Grp., Inc., 893 F.2d 541, 563–70 (3d Cir. 1990) (N.J. law) (Becker, J.), rev'd in part on other grounds, 505 U.S. 504 (1992). See Professor Honnold's analysis for the New York Law Revision Commission, shortly after the Code was promulgated, in White and Summers, UCC § 10–5, at 457–58.

[148] See R. Nordstrom, Law of Sales 209 (1970) ("The 'basis of the bargain' includes the dickered terms, but is not limited to them. The 'basis of the bargain' is also the item purchased, and a part of that bargain includes the statements which the seller made about what he sold.").

[149] See id. See also White and Summers, The Law of Sales 282 (1972) ("Cases . . . which hold that the unread advertisement may constitute a warranty reach the preferable result—and the result which is more consistent with the intention of the Code."); Lewis, Toward a Theory of Strict "Claim" Liability: Warranty Relief for Advertising Representations, 47 Ohio St. L.J. 671 (1986). Jerry Phillips also adhered to this view. See Phillips, Product Misrepresentation and the Doctrine of Causation, 2 Hofstra L. Rev. 571 (1974). While this wide view of basis-of-the-bargain has merit, one might question whether buyers actually or fairly expect

be estopped from denying that the total product package sold and purchased included the seller's promises about the product, even if the injured buyer did not rely upon (or even know about) those promises. For these reasons and others, many courts have held that a plaintiff need not establish reliance in order to recover for breach of express warranty under UCC § 2–313.[150]

Many other courts and some commentators, unable to disengage themselves from an intuitive attraction to the deeply ingrained requirement of reliance, have refused to abandon it as a central component in express warranty responsibility, at least in certain contexts.[151] Such an approach is based in part on the apparent unfairness of allowing a buyer to obtain redress for damage that in a real sense did not result from the seller's misstatement. Allowing a buyer who did not rely upon a warranty to recover damages on account of its breach might be seen as holding the seller as a kind of outlaw, responsible for any harm to anyone who bought and suffered damage from the seller's goods, and as providing a windfall to the buyer who has no true cause to charge the seller for his loss. "Why should one who has not relied on the seller's statement have the right to sue? That plaintiff is asking for greater protection than he would get under the warranty of merchantability, far more than he bargained for."[152] Thus, many courts indicate that the plaintiff's reliance is an implicit or explicit element in express warranty litigation under § 2–313, often by asserting or implying that the plaintiff's awareness of and reliance on the seller's representation may or must be established to show that a representation was part of the "basis of the bargain" and amounted to a warranty.[153]

---

that, in addition to the product, they are purchasing an accident insurance policy for harmful consequences if unknown representations by the seller prove false.

[150] See, e.g., Weng v. Allison, 678 N.E.2d 1254, 1256 (Ill. App. Ct. 1997) (trial court erred in ruling that seller's statements could not have been part of basis of bargain because no reasonable person could have relied on statements; seller has burden to offer clear proof that affirmations were not basis of bargain); Martin v. American Med. Sys., Inc., 116 F.3d 102, 105 (4th Cir. 1997) (Va. law); Lutz Farms v. Asgrow Seed Co., 948 F.2d 638, 645 (10th Cir. 1991) (Colo. law) (asserting that most jurisdictions no longer require proof of reliance, citing cases); Keith v. Buchanan, 220 Cal. Rptr. 392 (Ct. App. 1985). See also White, above note 133, at 2099 n.30 (collecting cases which assert that reliance is not a condition of express warranty recovery).

[151] See, e.g., Jarrett v. Duro-Med Indus., 2008 WL 89932, at *9 (E.D. Ky. 2008); Kelleher v. Marvin Lumber & Cedar Co., 891 A.2d 477, 500 (N.H. 2005) ("A majority of jurisdictions continues to find that reliance is an essential element of an express warranty claim."). One must be cautious about counting jurisdictions on most legal issues, particularly issues like this that are fuzzy at best. *Kelleher* relies on Frumer, Friedman, and Sklaren, Products Liability § 9.02[2] that, listing authorities both ways, suggests that a substantial majority of courts deciding the issue require reliance for § 2–313. But In re General Motors Corp. Dex-Cool Prods. Liab. Litig., 241 F.R.D. 305, 319 (S.D. Ill. 2007), citing many cases, states that "a large number of states in the class, possibly a majority, hold that reliance is not an element of an express warranty claim." Lawrence's Anderson on the UCC §§ 2–313:55–:58 suggests that the cases on either side of the split are roughly equivalent.

Citing a number of cases, *Kelleher* adopts what it calls "an intermediate third approach," based on comment 3, that a rebuttable presumption (that a representation becomes part of the basis of a bargain) arises if a plaintiff, during negotiations, becomes aware of a representation of a type that naturally would give rise to purchasing the good. 891 A.2d at 501–02. See also Michael v. Wyeth, LLC, 2011 WL 2150112, at *7–9 (S.D. W. Va. 2011) (examining all three approaches, and predicting that West Virginia would adopt the intermediate approach); In re General Motors Corp. Dex-Cool Prods. Liab. Litig., 241 F.R.D. 305, 320 (S.D. Ill. 2007) (citing cases following rebuttable presumption approach).

[152] White and Summers, UCC § 10–5, at 463.

[153] Though divided, courts "are loath to give up the reliance requirement and continue it via the 'basis of the bargain' test of 2–313(1)." 1 White and Summers, UCC § 10–5, at 459 n.3. See, e.g., Forbes v. General Motors Corp., 935 So.2d 869, 875 (Miss. 2006) (plaintiff must show justifiable reliance); PPG Indus. v. JMB/Houston Ctrs. Partners Ltd. P'ship, 146 S.W.3d 79, 99 (Tex. 2004) ("The basis-of-the-bargain requirement 'loosely reflects the common-law express warranty requirement of reliance . . . .' "); Sprague v. Upjohn Co., 1995 WL 376934, at *3 (D. Mass. 1994) ("in an express warranty claim, plaintiff must show reliance on such warranty"); Wendt v. Beardmore Suburban Chevrolet, Inc., 366 N.W.2d 424, 428 (Neb. 1985) ("Since an express warranty must have been 'made part of the basis of the bargain,' it is essential that the plaintiffs prove reliance

Contextualizing Reliance

After canvassing all basis-of-the-bargain cases decided during the last part of the twentieth century, Professor James White concluded that the best solution to the question of whether reliance should be required for express warranty claims under the Code is to "unbundle" the issue, along the lines described above, by acknowledging that different considerations at play in different contexts call for different doctrine.[154] Thus, he proposes that reliance not be required for representations and promises that are truly part of the contract, such as terms in a written contract and oral terms that were part of a negotiated deal, nor that reliance be required in writings closely connected to the contract, such as product labels, the owner's manual, and other literature delivered with the product. Professor White further argues that reliance should in fact be required in the case of representations far removed from the actual deal, such as most advertisements and post-sale representations and promises.[155] Such a decoupling of representational situations, which widely span the contract/tort horizon and therefore raise quite different problems, goes a long way toward resolving the basis-of-the-bargain/ reliance conundrum that has confounded courts and commentators for so long.

Advertisements and brochures. Probably the strongest case for requiring reliance may be made for assertions in advertisements, brochures, and the like that a particular buyer may never read or even see before the bargain is completed, or even before the product accident. Such statements are typically far removed from the time and place of the actual contract, and including them therein stretches the contract notion to great lengths. In such cases, many courts understandably take the view that unread and unheard statements simply cannot form the basis for an express warranty claim, whether on "basis of the bargain" or "reliance" grounds.[156]

Post-sale statements. Like advertisements, post-sale statements—promises or representations made after a sales transaction is concluded—present an especially

---

upon the warranty."); Scaringe v. Holstein, 477 N.Y.S.2d 903, 904 (App. Div. 1984) ("A necessary element in the creation of an express warranty is the buyer's reliance upon the seller's affirmations or promises.").

[154] "[N]ot all warranty claims are the same; some are contract plain and simple; some are special and some really are tort or, in the words of Williston, quasi-tort. I believe that the law will be more certain, more predictable, and subject to smaller manipulation if we unbundle these liabilities." White, above note 133, at 2110.

[155] See id. at 2110–11.

[156] See, e.g., Judge Becker's scholarly analysis in Cipollone v. Liggett Grp., Inc., 893 F.2d 541, 567–68 (3d Cir. 1990) (N.J. law), rev'd in part on other grounds, 505 U.S. 504 (1992), in which he reconciles the reliance/ basis-of-the-bargain debate by ruling that a plaintiff must prove:

> [T]hat she read, heard, saw or knew of the advertisement containing the affirmation of fact or promise. Such proof will suffice "to weave" the affirmation of fact or promise "into the fabric of the agreement," U.C.C. Comment 3, and thus make it part of the basis of the bargain. [O]nce the buyer has become aware of the affirmation of fact or promise, the statements are presumed to be part of the "basis of the bargain" unless the defendant, by "clear affirmative proof," shows that the buyer knew that the affirmation of fact or promise was untrue.

See also Hope v. Nissan N. Am., Inc., 353 S.W.3d 68, 86 (Mo. Ct. App. 2011) ("while a brochure, catalog, or advertisement may constitute part of an express warranty, that catalog, advertisement, or brochure must have *at least* been read by the party claiming the express warranty."); In re Toyota Motor Corp. Unintended Acceleration Mktg., Sales Practices, & Prods. Liab. Litig., 754 F. Supp. 2d 1145, 1182–83 (C.D. Cal. 2010) (same; car owners had no class-action express warranty claim without allegations that they were exposed to the pertinent statements); Kelleher v. Marvin Lumber & Cedar Co., 891 A.2d 477, 502 (N.H. 2005) ("a plaintiff claiming breach of express warranty based upon a representation in a catalog or brochure would have to prove, at a minimum, that he or she read, heard, saw or was otherwise aware of the representation"). See generally White, above note 133, at 2106–11 (many cases support the sound proposition that reliance is required for advertisements and post-sale representations and promises).

strong case for requiring reliance. One might reasonably conclude that a seller's post-sale statements about a product, generally unsupported by consideration, should not be viewed as part of the bargain or as something on which the buyer relied in making a deal. For this reason, some commentators on Article 2 sensibly argue that reliance should be required in such cases where a representation is distanced from the sale transaction.[157] But assurances and other statements made shortly after a deal is formally concluded, while it is still "warm," involve a limited class of cases in which the buyer possesses certain equities. Comment 7 to § 2–313 states that the "precise time" when a statement is made is unimportant, and that what matters is only whether the statement is "fairly to be regarded as part of the contract," such that assurances by a seller made shortly after a sales transaction formally is concluded often may properly be viewed as part of that transaction.[158]

Appearing to ignore the explicit language of comment 7, at least one early decision refused to allow recovery for such a post-sale statement. In *Stang v. Hertz Corp.*,[159] a tire blew out on a car rented by a nun, killing another nun who was a passenger. Plaintiffs made express warranty claims against the rental agency, Hertz, for two statements: (1) the rental agreement's provision that the vehicle was in good mechanical condition, and (2) the rental agent's comment that "you have got good tires." Upholding a directed verdict for Hertz, the court reasoned that there was "no evidence that any of the nuns relied on, or in any way considered, the terms of the rental agreement before agreeing to the rental [and the] comment concerning 'good tires' was made after the car had been rented."[160] Despite some cases of this sort, the plain language of comment 7 states that a seller's statements made shortly after a transaction formally is completed may be considered part of the basis of the broader bargain—if they fairly may be considered part of the contract.[161] Similarly, representations made in an owner's manual tucked in a glove compartment,[162] or in a brochure buried inside a product's packaging[163] (so-called "warranties in a box") are properly considered part of the basis of the bargain.

---

[157] See White and Summers, UCC § 10–5, at 462–63, arguing that such post-sale statements made once the deal is no longer warm should require reliance unless they can be established as modifications under § 2–209; White, above note 133, at 2106–11.

[158] Comment 7 provides as follows:

> The precise time when words of description or affirmation are made or samples are shown is not material. The sole question is whether the language or samples or models are fairly to be regarded as part of the contract. If language is used after the closing of the deal (as when the buyer when taking delivery asks and receives an additional assurance), the warranty becomes a modification, and need not be supported by consideration if it is otherwise reasonable and in order (Section 2–209).

Note, however, that the comment concludes by limiting such post-sale warranties to those that are "in order" under the rather strict modification and waiver principles of § 2–209.

[159] 490 P.2d 475 (N.M. Ct. App. 1971), rev'd on other grounds, 497 P.2d 732 (N.M. 1972).

[160] Id. at 477.

[161] See White and Summers, UCC § 10–5; R. Nordstrom, Law of Sales 205–07 (1970).

[162] See, e.g., Forbes v. General Motors Corp., 935 So.2d 869, 875 (Miss. 2006) ("It would be quite unusual for a consumer to read an owner's manual before buying a car. Even more unusual would be for a consumer to insist upon reading the manual before buying the automobile and requiring that an understanding of the manual be a condition precedent to purchasing the car.").

[163] See Rite Aid Corp. v. Levy-Gray, 894 A.2d 563, 573–77 (Md. 2006) (drug advice pamphlet provided by pharmacist at time of sale; "[E]xpress warranties may be formed prior to the completion of the sale or even after the sale has been consummated. What is paramount is the relationship between the sale of the goods and the affirmations made by the seller.").

Bargaining statements. Proof of reliance is least necessary with representations made in written contracts and oral representations made while the contract is being negotiated, as suggested by comment 3 to § 2–313. This is because both parties fairly should be able to rely on the truth of the bargaining promises of the other—representations made "during a bargain."[164] Comment 3 comes close to saying, and reasonably may be interpreted to mean, that affirmations of a seller in a bargaining context may rebuttably be presumed to be part of the deal, part of the "basis of the buyer's bargain."[165] Quite often, buyers do in fact rely upon such representations, and such statements ordinarily are so clearly part of the contract that it makes little sense to require the tort-based notion of reliance in this express warranty context.[166] And so, even the staunchest advocates of retaining the reliance requirement in express warranty doctrine agree that reliance may be presumed, rebuttably,[167] in the case of statements made in written contracts and oral contract negotiations.[168]

Trend Toward Requiring Buyer's Awareness

The debate over the role of reliance in a benefit-of-the-bargain world continues to vex many lawyers and judges alike, and confusion about this issue continues to abound. As mentioned earlier, many courts continue to resolve the issue in clear-cut terms one way or the other, declaring that reliance *is* required under § 2–313, or that it is *not*. Other courts recognize the confusion and split of opinion but side-step the issue to avoid taking a position on what remains a legal conundrum.[169] The best course is surely some kind of contextual approach to the problem, as previously discussed, which recognizes that a buyer's reliance fairly should be required in some contexts (such as commercials never seen by the buyer), but not in others (such as a seller's statements that are explicitly negotiated or expressed in writings attached to the product).

But a trend may be discerned that serves as a partial proxy for a contextual approach: requiring a buyer to show that, at the time of purchase, he knew about the warranty terms he claims the seller breached. That is, courts increasingly appear to be requiring that a plaintiff must establish his or her own *scienter*: that he or she read or

---

164 Comment 3 to UCC § 2–313 provides in full:

> The present section deals with affirmations of fact by the seller, descriptions of the goods or exhibitions of samples, exactly as any other part of a negotiation which ends in a contract is dealt with. No specific intention to make a warranty is necessary if any of these factors is made part of the basis of the bargain. In actual practice affirmations of fact made by the seller about the goods during a bargain are regarded as part of the description of those goods; hence no particular reliance on such statements need be shown in order to weave them into the fabric of the agreement. Rather, any fact which is to take such affirmations, once made, out of the agreement requires clear affirmative proof. The issue normally is one of fact.

165 Judge Becker explains the rebuttable presumption view in Cipollone v. Liggett Grp., Inc., 893 F.2d 541, 563–71 (3d Cir. 1990) (N.J. law), rev'd in part on other grounds, 505 U.S. 504 (1992).

166 As part of the contract-based law of sales in UCC Article 2, one might think that situations such as this, that involve purely contractual analysis, should be resolved using purely contractual doctrine.

167 Reliance may be rebutted if the buyer admits that he already believed in the truth of the matter represented and so was not affected by the representation. Compare Putensen v. Clay Adams, Inc., 91 Cal. Rptr. 319 (Ct. App. 1970) (whether representation was "part of the basis of the bargain" was jury question), with Ball v. Mallinkrodt Chem. Works, 381 S.W.2d 563 (Tenn. Ct. App. 1964) (no reliance on representation if buyer possesses independent knowledge of matter represented).

168 See White and Summers, UCC § 10–5, at 459. To this short list, Professor White adds manuals, labels, and the like attached to or delivered with the goods. White, above note 133, at 2106–11 (1998).

169 See, e.g., Daigle v. Ford Motor Co., 713 F. Supp. 2d 822, 825–26 (D. Minn. 2010).

otherwise knew about a seller's representation for it to be part of a purchase "bargain."[170] This buyer-awareness requirement is admittedly rigorous, and it hardly resolves all reliance/basis-of-the-bargain questions in this misty land, but it embraces assertions and tends to help resolve many other problems by a simple, intuitively fair standard. Of course, buyers always may fairly urge that sellers be bound by the written terms of a sales transaction, but sellers often may fairly urge that they normally should not be bound by their advertisements and other assertions unknown to the plaintiff and, hence, usually playing no causal role in either the purchase or the accident.[171]

§ 4.3 IMPLIED WARRANTY OF MERCHANTABILITY

The basic implied warranty of quality in the sale of goods, now referred to as the implied warranty of "merchantability," revealed early sprouts thousands of years ago in the ancient law of Babylonia and Assyria, and began to blossom in late Roman law.[172] Over the centuries, after a long period of stagnation during the dark ages,[173] this warranty slowly began to see signs of life in English law, and later in American common law, first in cases involving defective foodstuffs[174] and much later (during the nineteenth century) as a broad repudiation of the long-entrenched doctrine of *caveat emptor*.[175] The renewed notion of *caveat venditor* required a seller to take responsibility for harm caused by any latent defects in goods sold, on the theory that fair dealing implied a fundamental guarantee of fair quality in the sale of a product—a guarantee that the product would conform to the general description under which it was sold.[176] Fair quality of the "good" received in time became a legal quid pro quo for a fair price paid. In the colorful words

[170] See, e.g., Morgan v. Cabela's Inc., 788 F. Supp. 2d 552, 556–57 (E.D. Ky. 2011); In re Bisphenol-A (BPA) Polycarbonate Plastic Prods. Liab. Litig., 687 F. Supp. 2d 897, 906–07 (W.D. Mo. 2009) ("For a representation to be part of the bargain, it must be known to all parties to that bargain."; collecting many cases). Compare In re 3M Combat Arms Earplug Prods. Liab. Litig., 2021 WL 2605971, at *4 (N.D. Fla. 2021) (plaintiff's description of the information card in the earplug's packaging sufficiently identified the express warranties upon which he relied).

[171] "For a warranty to become the basis of the bargain, the plaintiff must show that he or she actually read the warranty before making the purchase in question." Morgan v. Cabela's Inc., 788 F. Supp. 2d 552, 556–57 (E.D. Ky. 2011) (quoting prior case to effect that "[a] warranty is the basis of the bargain if it has been relied upon as one of the inducements for purchasing the product," yet allowing claim to go to the jury on flimsy reliance assertions). See also Porcell v. Lincoln Wood Prods., Inc., 713 F. Supp. 2d 1305, 1318 (D.N.M. 2010) ("proof that a statement was made in a Lincoln catalog or brochure or on its website must at a minimum be coupled with proof that a particular class member saw the statement in order for it to become part of the basis of that class member's bargain with Lincoln").

[172] See § 1.2, above.

[173] Except in early Church law, as reported by Aquinas, which recognized such warranties. Id.

[174] See §§ 5.2 and 7.5, below.

[175] "It has been said that the concept of implied warranty rests upon the foundation of business ethics and constitutes an exception to the maxim 'let the buyer beware,' itself encompassing the idea that there is no warranty implied with respect to the quality of the goods being sold." Lambert v. Sistrunk, 58 So.2d 434, 434–35 (Fla. 1952). On the development of the implied warranty of merchantability, see Prosser, The Assault Upon the Citadel (Strict Liability to the Consumer), 69 Yale L.J. 1099, 1103–10, 1124–27 (1960); Prosser, The Implied Warranty of Merchantable Quality, 27 Minn. L. Rev. 117, 118–22 (1943); Llewellyn, On Warranty of Quality, and Society (pts. 1 and 2), 36 Colum. L. Rev. 699 (1936), 37 Colum. L. Rev. 341 (1937).

[176] See Lane v. Trenholm Bldg. Co., 229 S.E.2d 728, 730 (S.C. 1976): "Under the rule of *caveat venditor*, a sale 'raises an implied warranty (against latent defects) from the fairness and fullness of the price paid, upon this clear and reasonable ground, that in the contract of sale, the purchaser is not supposed to part with his money, but in expectation of an adequate advantage, or recompense.' Champneys v. Johnson, [4 S.C.L. (2 Brev.) 268, 272 (1809)]. 'Selling for a sound price raises an implied warranty that the thing sold is free from defects, known and unknown (to the seller).' "

of Lord Ellenborough: "The purchaser cannot be supposed to buy goods to lay them on a dunghill."[177]

Thus, the implied warranty of merchantability is an assurance, imposed by law upon the seller, that a product is reasonably suitable for the general uses for which it is bought and sold.[178] This warranty of basic quality does not arise out of any express agreement or intention between the buyer and the seller but is created instead, at the point of sale, by operation of law. Its foundation lies in public policy, in order to promote fair dealing by sellers of chattels, and to protect fair expectations of buyers of goods.

The implied warranty of merchantability is the central and most important warranty in UCC Article 2, and a claim for its breach is often a central claim in many products liability cases.[179] Because liability for breach of such a warranty generally is based merely on a product's deficient condition without regard to the seller's fault, it truly is a form of "strict" liability. Consequently, proof of a seller's negligence is not only unnecessary but also irrelevant to such claims.[180] Generally, proof that a product is "defective" under strict liability in tort will establish that a product is not merchantable, and vice versa.[181] In this fundamental way, these two bases of products liability law—one contract, the other tort—are essentially the same.[182]

So, courts often recognize that a claim for a breach of the merchantability warranty will lie for injuries caused by manufacturing defects,[183] inadequate warnings,[184] or defective design.[185] But some courts, for varying purposes, distinguish between the two

[177] Gardiner v. Gray, (1815) 171 Eng. Rep. 46, 47 (K.B.). See Prosser, The Implied Warranty of Merchantable Quality, 27 Minn. L. Rev. 117 (1943).

[178] See, e.g., McCabe v. L.K. Liggett Drug Co., 112 N.E.2d 254, 256 (Mass. 1953).

[179] "The implied warranty of merchantability in 2–314 is an important warranty. It is a first cousin to strict tort liability, and 'products liability' cases are often tried under the merchantability banner." White and Summers, UCC § 10–11, at 480.

[180] See, e.g., McGinty v. Grand Casinos of Miss., Inc.-Biloxi, 245 So.3d 444, 449–50 (Miss. 2018) (ruling that plaintiffs failed to make a prima facie case for negligence against the defendant for serving bad pork but allowing breach of implied warranty of merchantability claim to go to jury). *But see* Curry v. Meijer, Inc., 780 N.W.2d 603 (Mich. Ct. App. 2009) (under Michigan reform act, plaintiff must establish the seller's negligence and proximate cause to recover for breach of implied warranty). Yet, note that reform statutes in some states shield retailers and other non-manufacturing sellers from liability unless, typically, they are negligent, make and breach an *express* warranty, or the manufacturer of a defective product is bankrupt or beyond the jurisdiction of the state courts. See § 15.2, below.

[181] See, e.g., Michael v. Wyeth, LLC, 2011 WL 2150112, at *4 (S.D. W. Va. 2011) (implied warranty claim for inadequate warning of increased breast cancer risk from hormone replacement drug; "claims for strict liability and breach of the implied warranty of merchantability are essentially coextensive in products liability actions"); Depositors Ins. Co. v. Wal-Mart Stores, Inc., 506 F.3d 1092, 1095 (8th Cir. 2007) (Iowa law) (implied warranty liability "requires proof of a product defect as defined in Products Restatement section 2"); Ford Motor Co. v. General Accident Ins. Co., 779 A.2d 362, 369 (Md. 2001) ("a plaintiff must prove the existence of a defect at the time the product leaves the manufacturer to recover on an implied warranty claim as well as with regard to strict liability and negligence claims"). See also Freeman v. Hoffman-La Roche, Inc., 618 N.W.2d 827, 842–44 (Neb. 2000) (merging implied warranty into design and manufacturing defect claims). Compare Branham v. Ford Motor Co., 701 S.E.2d 5, 8 (S.C. 2010) (on any theory of recovery, plaintiffs in products liability actions must prove: (1) that plaintiff was injured by a product; (2) that was unchanged from when it left defendant; and (3) that the injury was caused by a defective condition unreasonably dangerous to the plaintiff). See also note 192, below. See generally § 5.9, below.

[182] See, e.g., Kirkbride v. Terex USA, LLC, 798 F.3d 1343, 1353–55 (10th Cir. 2015) (Utah law).

[183] Elliott v. Kraft Foods N. Am., Inc., 118 S.W.3d 50 (Tex. App. 2003) (consumer bit into rock in cereal).

[184] See, e.g., DeWitt v. Eveready Battery Co., 550 S.E.2d 511, 517 (N.C. Ct. App. 2001), aff'd, 565 S.E.2d 140 (N.C. 2002) (injuries from leaky car battery; "[inadequate] warnings of a product's dangerous propensities may render a product unmerchantable under section 25–2–314").

[185] See, e.g., Evans v. Lorillard Tobacco Co., 990 N.E.2d 997, 1010 (Mass. 2013) (design of cigarettes).

liability theories. The New York Court of Appeals may be the sole high court to rule, questionably if quite long ago, that breach of the merchantability warranty, unlike strict liability in tort, does not require proof that a product is "defective."[186] But the two claims have differences other than the central basis of liability. So, claims for breach of implied warranty of merchantability lie for pure economic loss,[187] unlike tort actions, and warranty claims have different (often longer) statutes of limitations than claims for negligence or strict liability in tort.[188] Consequently, injured plaintiffs sometimes can recover for breach of the implied warranty of merchantability where relief is unavailable under the law of tort. In short, while claims for breach of implied warranty normally lie somewhat off-center in most products liability litigation, they sometimes provide powerful support to a products liability complaint.

Uniform Commercial Code § 2–314

The implied warranty of merchantability was first "codified" in America in § 15(2) of the Uniform Sales Act, which provided, "Where the goods are bought by description from a seller who deals in goods of that description (whether he be the grower or manufacturer or not), there is an implied warranty that the goods shall be of merchantable quality." In the 1950s, this warranty was rewritten into § 2–314 of the Uniform Commercial Code as follows:

> **§ 2–314. Implied Warranty: Merchantability; Usage of Trade**
>
> (1) Unless excluded or modified (Section 2–316), a warranty that the goods shall be merchantable is implied in a contract for their sale if the seller is a merchant with respect to goods of that kind. Under this section the serving for value of food or drink to be consumed either on the premises or elsewhere is a sale.
>
> (2) Goods to be merchantable must be at least such as
>
> (a) pass without objection in the trade under the contract description; and
>
> (b) in the case of fungible goods, are of fair average quality within the description; and

[186] See Denny v. Ford Motor Co., 662 N.E.2d 730 (N.Y. 1995) (rollover case involving Ford Bronco II; *held*, cause of action for breach of implied warranty of merchantability may support design deficiency claim where strict liability in tort did not). See, e.g., Fahey v. A.O. Smith Corp., 908 N.Y.S.2d 719, 725 (App. Div. 2010) ("The 'defect' element in a breach of implied warranty claim under the UCC is premised on contract principles and focuses on the purchaser's disappointed expectations, while the 'defect' element in a strict products liability claim is based upon tort principles concerned with social policy and risk allocation."). See generally Lawrence's Anderson on the UCC § 2–314:165. *Denny* is critically examined in § 5.9, below, and in White, Reverberations from the Collision of Tort and Warranty, 53 S.C. L. Rev. 1067, 1072–73 (2002) (noting "the need to draw the line between injury to life, limb and property—the domain of both tort and warranty—and injury that is purely economic, the exclusive domain of warranty").

[187] See 1 Crockett, Product Warranties 2d ch. 7. See, e.g., In re Toyota Motor Corp. Unintended Acceleration Mktg., Sales Practices, & Prods. Liab. Litig., 754 F. Supp. 2d 1145, 1183–86 (C.D. Cal. 2010) (allowing breach of implied warranty claim in class action alleging diminished vehicle value due to sudden unintended acceleration); Lloyd v. General Motors Corp., 916 A.2d 257, 290–91 (Md. 2007) (allowing breach of warranty of merchantability claim in class action by owners of automobiles with dangerously defective seatbacks, though plaintiffs had suffered no physical injury: "Unlike general tort claims . . . the measure of injury in breach of contract claims is not bodily harm, nor is a consumer required to wait for a malfunction to occur as a result of a product defect in order to assert an articulable injury.").

[188] Under UCC § 2–725 the statute of limitations is 4 years from the date of sale. In most states, the statute of limitations for tort claims is 2 or 3 years from the date of discovery. See § 14.6, below.

(c) are fit for the ordinary purposes for which such goods are used; and

(d) run, within the variations permitted by the agreement, of even kind, quality and quantity within each unit and among all units involved; and

(e) are adequately contained, packaged, and labeled as the agreement may require; and

(f) conform to the promises or affirmations of fact made on the container or label if any.

(3) Unless excluded or modified (Section 2–316) other implied warranties may arise from course of dealing or usage of trade.

Official Comments to § 2–314 point out the importance of custom and usage to a determination of merchantability. Comment 6 states that the listing of merchantability standards in subsection (2) "does not purport to exhaust the meaning of 'merchantable' nor to negate any of its attributes . . . arising by usage of trade or through case law" and explains that "the intention is to leave open other possible attributes of merchantability." This section of the Code applies only to sales by "merchants," that is, persons in the business of selling products of that kind.[189] It does not apply to isolated sales made by persons not fitting that description, "isolated sales" being such as occur infrequently in a seller's business.

Subsection (2) particularizes a concept that often is expressed more simply. To many courts, "merchantability" simply means reasonable fitness for the general purposes for which an article is sold and used. It does not imply absolute perfection of any type, and certainly not perfect safety; it does not require the seller to provide an article that will not wear out; it does not even imply high quality. The fitness need not, in other words, be absolute, and the warranty is met when an article is free of major imperfections; conforms to ordinary standards; and is of the average grade, quality, and value of similar goods sold commercially.[190] As with all warranties, the breach of this warranty does not require that the manufacturer or other seller have been negligent, nor did it traditionally require that the product was "defective" or "unreasonably dangerous" by the standards of the law of tort.[191] Yet it is difficult to untangle merchantability from defectiveness,

---

[189] See UCC § 2–104.

[190] See, e.g., Phillips v. Cricket Lighters, 852 A.2d 365, 370–71 (Pa. Super. Ct. 2004) ("The concept of 'merchantability' does not require that the goods be the best quality, or the best obtainable, but it does require that they have an inherent soundness which makes them suitable for the purpose for which they are designed, that they be free from significant defects, that they perform in the way that goods of that kind should perform, and that they be of reasonable quality within expected variations and for the ordinary purpose for which they are used."), rev'd in part on other grounds, 883 A.2d 439, 444 (Pa. 2005) (but agreeing that "merchantability" does not require that goods be the best quality, but only that they "have an inherent soundness which makes them suitable for the purpose for which they are designed").

[191] See, e.g., *Phillips*, 852 A.2d at 371 ("a product need not be defective, for purposes of strict products liability, in order to be unfit for ordinary purposes" under implied warranty of merchantability), rev'd in part on other grounds, 883 A.2d 439, 445 (Pa. 2005) (refusing to conflate distinct claims for breach of implied warranty of merchantability and strict liability in tort or to hold that they are coterminous); Denny v. Ford Motor Co., 662 N.E.2d 730 (N.Y. 1995) (claims for strict tort liability and breach of implied warranty of merchantability not identical); Lawrence's Anderson on the UCC § 2–314:654 (a plaintiff needs to prove only breach of warranty "and is not required to prove that the warranty was breached by a defect that made the product dangerously defective").

and at least in products liability cases involving personal injuries, the concepts of "unmerchantable" and "defective" are virtually congruent.[192]

Requirements of "Merchant" and "Sale"

In contrast to warranty claims under §§ 2–313 and 2–315, claims for breach of implied warranty of merchantability under UCC § 2–314 require that the seller be a "merchant" of such products in the ordinary course of trade.[193] An isolated sale of a product does not render a person a merchant for purposes of the Code.[194] Accordingly, it has been held that volunteer parent organizations providing food at school functions are not merchants as that term is used in UCC § 2–314,[195] nor are persons engaged in isolated sales of a fishing boat,[196] a used airplane,[197] a used car,[198] or an entire business including its machinery.[199] However, for § 2–314 to apply, a seller need not deal regularly in the particular type of good sold if the seller in the regular course of business deals in goods of the same general type.[200] But the defendant must be a merchant with respect to the type of goods sold to the plaintiff.[201] So, a bank that sells a repossessed boat to a plaintiff in an isolated transaction, may well not be a "merchant" with respect to such a product for purposes of § 2–314.[202]

---

[192] See, e.g., Kirkbride v. Terex USA, LLC, 798 F.3d 1343, 1353–55 (10th Cir. 2015) (Utah law); Keffer v. Wyeth, 791 F. Supp. 2d 539, 545 (S.D. W. Va. 2011) ("courts have recognized that claims for strict liability and breach of the implied warranty of merchantability are essentially coextensive in products liability actions"); Rodriguez v. Stryker Corp., 2011 WL 31462, at *11 (M.D. Tenn. 2011) ("[a] finding that a product was not defective or unreasonably dangerous forecloses an implied warranty claim" under Tennessee Products Liability Act); Solo v. Trus Joist MacMillan, 2004 WL 524898, at *14 (D. Minn. 2004) ("This warranty is breached when the product is defective to a normal buyer making ordinary use of the product."); Foster v. Ford Motor Co., 621 F.2d 715, 719 (5th Cir. 1980) (Tex. law) ("The negative implication of the warranty requirement that goods be 'fit for the ordinary purposes for which such goods are used' is that the goods not be unreasonably dangerous"). "For a product to flunk the merchantability test, it must contain an inherent defect." 1 Crockett, Product Warranties § 5:5 (stating that "the courts find goods to be unfit for their ordinary purposes when they can identify one of three general types of defects: manufacturing defects, design defects, and failure to give the buyer proper instructions with respect to the goods" and noting that the test for unmerchantability is essentially the same as under strict liability in tort except that unmerchantability does not require a product to be "unreasonably dangerous"). See also note 181, above. See generally § 5.9, below.

Though now formally withdrawn, see § 4.1, at n.17, above, Amended § 2–314 explicitly adopted this latter view by providing that "merchantability" be defined in personal injury cases by the products liability tort law of the state. See Amended UCC § 2–314 cmt. 7.

[193] UCC § 2–314(1). See UCC § 2–104(1) ("merchant" defined).

[194] See cmt. 3 to § 2–314: "A person making an isolated sale of goods is not a 'merchant' within the meaning of the full scope of this section . . . ."

[195] See Samson v. Riesing, 215 N.W.2d 662 (Wis. 1974) (salmonella food poisoning from turkey salad).

[196] See Prince v. LeVan, 486 P.2d 959 (Alaska 1971).

[197] See Downs v. Shouse, 501 P.2d 401 (Ariz. Ct. App. 1972) (Piper Cherokee 235).

[198] See Ballou v. Trahan, 334 A.2d 409 (Vt. 1975) (a sale of used Porsche by private person was an "isolated sale").

[199] See Olson v. U.S. Indus., 649 F. Supp. 1511, 1514 (D. Kan. 1986).

[200] See, e.g., McHugh v. Carlton, 369 F. Supp. 1271 (D.S.C. 1974) (service station operator with stock of new and used tires was a merchant with respect to recapped tires, though he did not keep stock of recapped tires and ordered them only on specific request). See also Stachurski v. K-Mart Corp., 447 N.W.2d 830 (Mich. Ct. App. 1989) (issue for jury).

[201] See, e.g., Gavula v. ARA Serv., Inc., 756 A.2d 17, 21 (Pa. Super. Ct. 2000) (company sold corporate assets, including van from which plaintiff was thrown); Siemen v. Alden, 341 N.E.2d 713 (Ill. App. Ct. 1975) (sawmill operator that sold used power saw to plaintiff after replacing it with new one was not merchant with respect to goods of that kind).

[202] Donald v. City Nat'l Bank of Dothan, 329 So.2d 92 (Ala. 1976). See Annot., 91 A.L.R.3d 876 (1979) (UCC § 2–314 "merchant" defined).

As is true of all warranty claims under UCC Article 2,[203] breach of the implied warranty of merchantability generally requires there to be a product "sale." Thus, some courts hold that Article 2 warranties do not apply where a product is merely leased, as is the case with a rental car,[204] or where the plaintiff is merely a bailee of the product.[205] Many other courts, however, have applied the Code principles directly, or by analogy, to lease transactions.[206] The general application of warranties (including the implied warranty of merchantability) to lease transactions is now routine, inasmuch as almost all states have adopted UCC Article 2A ("Leases"), promulgated in 1987 and amended in 1990.[207] Article 2A's warranty provisions closely mimic those on Sales in Article 2.

The precise moment in time when a sale occurs and an implied warranty of merchantability attaches has been litigated in the context of shopper injuries occurring after a shopper takes a product from the shelf, but prior to payment and a technical sale at the checkout counter. Typical are cases involving beverage bottles that explode in a shopper's hands, or in a shopping cart. Noting that comment 1 to § 2–314 provides that "[t]he seller's obligation applies to present sales *as well as to contracts to sell*,"[208] many courts conclude that the merchant's placement of the product on the shelf constitutes an offer of sale, and the buyer's removal of the product from the shelf constitutes an acceptance, creating a contract sufficient for application of UCC § 2–314.[209] In such cases, the bottle and the contents are both covered by the merchantability warranty.[210]

Fitness for Ordinary Purpose

As seen above, Uniform Commercial Code § 2–314(2) provides a long and nonexclusive list of merchantability tests.[211] Yet the heart of the merchantability warranty, as provided in subsection (c), is that a product is warranted to be "fit" for its "ordinary purposes," a notion that has deep roots in the law. A classic example of a court applying the merchantability concept to the products liability context involved a new coffee maker that exploded, injuring the plaintiff.[212] Ruling for the plaintiff, the court remarked: "If the coffee maker was so imperfect in design that it could not be used

---

[203] Article 2, of course, is entitled "Sales."

[204] See, e.g., Bechtel v. Paul Clark, Inc., 412 N.E.2d 143 (Mass. App. Ct. 1980) (car overturned due to brake defect).

[205] Watford v. Jack LaLanne Long Island, Inc., 542 N.Y.S.2d 765, 767 (App. Div. 1989) (rowing machine at health club; no merchantability warranty claim). Compare Levondosky v. Marina Assocs., 731 F. Supp. 1210 (D.N.J. 1990) (casino's provision of complimentary drink; merchantability claim allowed); Hurley v. Larry's Water Ski Sch., 762 F.2d 925 (11th Cir. 1985) (Fla. law) (wooden tow handle on water ski boat; merchantability but not strict tort claim allowed).

[206] See, e.g., Januse v. U-Haul Co., 399 So.2d 402 (Fla. Dist. Ct. App. 1981) (steering defect caused truck to overturn). See generally White and Summers, UCC § 10–2.

[207] For the 2003 Amendments to Article 2A, and their withdrawal, see § 4.1 notes 17 and 18, above.

[208] Emphasis added.

[209] See Giant Food, Inc. v. Washington Coca-Cola Bottling Co., 332 A.2d 1 (Md. 1975). In Fender v. Colonial Stores, Inc., 225 S.E.2d 691 (Ga. Ct. App. 1976), plaintiff was injured when a bottle of Coca-Cola exploded as she was placing it on the defendant grocer's check-out counter. *Held*, defendant offered the beverage for sale by placing it on shelf; plaintiff accepted offer by taking physical possession of item; and § 2–314 was thereafter applicable.

[210] See Sheeskin v. Giant Food, Inc., 318 A.2d 874 (Md. Ct. Spec. App. 1974), aff'd sub nom. Giant Food, Inc. v. Washington Coca-Cola Bottling Co., 332 A.2d 1 (Md. 1975) .

[211] So, for example, a product may be unmerchantable if it is not adequately contained under UCC § 2–314(2)(e). See, e.g., Keaton v. A.B.C. Drug Co., 467 S.E.2d 558, 560 (Ga. 1996) (plaintiff's eye injured from bleach spilled from container as she sought to remove it from high shelf in store: "bleach which spills via a loose cap is not adequately contained or packaged").

[212] McCabe v. L.K. Liggett Drug Co., 112 N.E.2d 254, 257 (Mass. 1953).

without the likelihood of an explosion it could be found that the appliance was not reasonably fit for making coffee and therefore not merchantable." The important message of this and many other cases is that "merchantability" and "fitness for ordinary purposes" in the products liability context mean that products are *reasonably safe* for their *ordinary* uses.[213] "The warranty of merchantability is broader than that the goods will do the ordinary job for which they were made. They must [also] do the job safely."[214]

For example, shoes reasonably may be expected to have their heels firmly attached so they will not fall off in normal use;[215] a ladder may be expected not to collapse;[216] hair lotion may be expected not to burn the user's scalp;[217] a cookie may be expected to be free of maggots and foreign objects;[218] and an SUV marketed for ordinary driving may be expected to be reasonably stable and not roll over in normal highway use.[219] Similarly, insulation that emits noxious fumes is not merchantable,[220] nor is a clothes dryer[221] or refrigerator[222] that overheats and catches fire, nor a flash cube,[223] coffee maker,[224] or stove[225] that explodes in the user's face.

On the other hand, insignificant flaws or irregularities do not render a product unmerchantable. "Merchantable," in other words, does not mean perfect, flawless, completely satisfactory, nor that the product will precisely fulfill all the buyer's expectations.[226] It follows, therefore, that the presence of one small bone in a fish filet

---

[213] See, e.g., In re September 11 Litig., 280 F. Supp. 2d 279, 306 (S.D.N.Y. 2003) (Va. law) (a merchantability warranty "guarantees that a product 'was reasonably safe for its intended use' "). See generally 1 Crockett, Product Warranties § 5:4 ("not reasonably safe").

[214] R. Nordstrom, Law of Sales § 76, at 236 (1970). *But see* Haffner v. Stryker Corp., 2014 WL 4821107, at *6 (D. Colo. 2014) ("An item can be fit for the ordinary purposes for which it is used—here as a knee-replacement device—without being safe for every possible user."); Wolfe v. McNeil-PPC, Inc., 773 F. Supp. 2d 561, 574 (E.D. Pa. 2011) ("seller is not . . . required to guarantee against every possible harm that results from the use of its products"; no implied warranty claim for "an extremely rare disease [occurring] six or fewer times per million people per year"); Whitson v. Safeskin Corp., 313 F. Supp. 2d 473, 480 (M.D. Pa. 2004) ("ordinary purpose" of latex gloves was to protect health care workers from transmitting or being exposed to blood-borne pathogens, so that merchantability warranty did not protect against latex allergies caused by gloves).

[215] Chairaluce v. Stanley Warner Mgmt. Corp., 236 F. Supp. 385 (D. Conn. 1964).

[216] Lariviere v. Dayton Safety Ladder Co., 525 A.2d 892 (R.I. 1987).

[217] Newmark v. Gimbel's, Inc., 258 A.2d 697 (N.J. 1969).

[218] See, e.g., Young v. Kraft Foods Global, Inc., 2011 WL 2177247 (Conn. Super. Ct. 2011) (maggots in Oreo cookies package); Otis Spunkmeyer, Inc. v. Blakely, 30 S.W.3d 678 (Tex. App. 2000) (hardened herbaceous stem in oatmeal-raisin cookie).

[219] Denny v. Ford Motor Co., 662 N.E.2d 730 (N.Y. 1995). Conversely, a vehicle marketed as safe for off-road use will fail of its ordinary purpose if a defect makes it unsuitable for that use. See, e.g., Flores v. FCA US LLC, 2021 WL 1122216, at *10 (E.D. Mich. 2021) (plaintiffs adequately alleged their "vehicles are not fit for the ordinary purpose of providing safe and reliable transportation on public roads and are not suitable for the purpose of off-roading due to the Sway Bar Defect and their inability to withstand water").

[220] Shooshanian v. Wagner, 672 P.2d 455, 461–62 (Alaska 1983).

[221] Crandell v. Larkin & Jones Appliance Co., 334 N.W.2d 31 (S.D. 1983).

[222] Bradley v. Earl B. Feiden, Inc., 864 N.E.2d 600, 604–05 (N.Y. 2007).

[223] Maybank v. S.S. Kresge Co., 266 S.E.2d 409 (N.C. Ct. App. 1980), modified on other grounds and affirmed, 273 S.E.2d 681 (N.C. 1981).

[224] McCabe v. L.K. Liggett Drug Co., 112 N.E.2d 254 (Mass. 1953).

[225] Logan v. Montgomery Ward & Co., 219 S.E.2d 685 (Va. 1975).

[226] " '[M]erchantable' is not synonymous with 'perfect.' Likewise, fitness for ordinary purposes does not mean that the product will fulfill buyer's every expectation." White and Summers, UCC § 10–12, at 491. See also Ferraro v. Hewlett-Packard Corp., 2012 WL 394256, at *12 (N.D. Ill. 2012) (laptop power adapter performed its ordinary function of charging computer's battery despite allegedly burning arm of purchaser who fell asleep on product); Rasheed v. Church & Dwight Co., Inc., 2012 WL 262619, at *1, 5 (E.D. Tex. 2012) (insufficient evidence that Trojan premium lubricant condoms or its chemicals, which allegedly caused plaintiff's severe blisters from head to foot and "cooked [his] Penis and testes," were "either defective or unfit

may not breach an implied warranty of merchantability,[227] nor will slight damage to a new car that does not affect the vehicle's "usefulness or drivability."[228] Similarly, the merchantability warranty is not breached where minor repairs will make the product fit for normal use, and the seller has offered to undertake such repairs.[229]

Likewise, if a product characteristic is "open and obvious," posing risks apparent to the ordinary consumer, the product generally will not be considered unfit for its ordinary purposes.[230] Article 2 addresses the obviousness issue in the section on disclaimers, § 2–316(3)(b), which provides that a buyer who examines goods prior to purchase (or who refuses to so examine them) obtains "no implied warranty with regard to defects which an examination ought in the circumstances to have revealed to him." That is, the implied warranty of merchantability normally extends only to defects that are latent;[231] conversely, there is no implied warranty of merchantability with respect to defects that are obvious, whether the buyer discovers them or not.[232]

The implied warranty of merchantability may be breached only if a product failure or mishap occurs during the product's "ordinary" use.[233] Consistent with this requirement, there is no breach of the merchantability warranty when safety glasses fail after being subjected to force exceeding what they reasonably should be expected to endure,[234] or when sliding glass doors leak upon exposure to unusual wind and spray conditions at an ocean-front property.[235] Determining whether a particular product use that causes harm is or is not "ordinary" sometimes is quite simple. A beer bottle thrown against a telephone pole for the very purpose of smashing it is not an ordinary use of the

---

for the ordinary purpose for which they are normally used"); Johnson v. Unifirst Corp., 935 N.Y.S.2d 763, 765 (App. Div. 2011) (welder's uniform that ignited was "fit and reasonably safe for the ordinary purposes for which it was to be used"); Chandler v. Gene Messer Ford, 81 S.W.3d 493, 503 (Tex. App. 2002) (child injured by front-seat airbag: a product that "performs its ordinary function adequately does not breach the implied warranty of merchantability merely because it does not function as the buyer would prefer").

[227] Ex parte Morrison's Cafeteria of Montgomery, Inc., 431 So.2d 975, 979 (Ala. 1983) ("undisputed that, in light of the process used to mass produce fillets, it was commercially impractical to remove all bones").

[228] Horne v. Claude Ray Ford Sales, Inc., 290 S.E.2d 497, 499 (Ga. Ct. App. 1982).

[229] Hannon v. Original Gunite Aquatech Pools, Inc., 434 N.E.2d 611 (Mass. 1982).

[230] See, e.g., In re Bisphenol-A (BPA) Polycarbonate Plastic Prods. Liab. Litig., 2011 WL 6740338, at *2 (W.D. Mo. 2011) (plaintiffs who knew about the presence and dangers of BPA in plastic baby bottles have no claim for implied warranty of merchantability); Darrell Wood v. Bass Pro Shops, Inc., 462 S.E.2d 101, 103 (Va. 1995) ("a plaintiff may not recover damages for breach of an implied warranty if the purported defect . . . was 'known, visible or obvious' to him"); Toney v. Kawasaki Heavy Indus., 975 F.2d 162 (5th Cir. 1992) (Miss. law) (absence of leg protection on motorcycle; not unfit for ordinary purpose because ordinary rider would appreciate risk of leg injury in side collision with automobile).

[231] See, e.g., Driscoll v. Standard Hardware, Inc., 785 N.W.2d 805, 816–17 (Minn. Ct. App. 2010) (industrial drill jacks that tended to crack).

[232] "A failure to notice defects which are obvious cannot excuse the buyer." UCC § 2–316 cmt. 8. See, e.g., American Tobacco Co. v. Grinnell, 951 S.W.2d 420 (Tex. 1997) (common knowledge of health risks of cigarette smoking is defense barring claim for breach of implied warranty).

Whether defects are latent or obvious may be a question of fact for the jury. See, e.g., Cannon Techs., Inc. v. Sensus Metering Sys., Inc., 734 F. Supp. 2d 753, 765 (D. Minn. 2010) (electromechanical meter).

[233] A seller's liability for injuries from the foreseeable misuse of a product has not enjoyed the development in warranty that is seen in negligence and strict liability. On misuse generally, see § 13.5, below.

[234] American Optical Co. v. Weidenhamer, 457 N.E.2d 181 (Ind. 1983).

[235] Festa v. Closure Co., 436 N.E.2d 977 (Mass. App. Ct. 1982).

bottle.[236] And a plaintiff's failure to follow instructions in using a product, assuming the danger of nonobservance is warned about or obvious, is not an ordinary use.[237]

But characterizing uses as "ordinary" requires careful consideration within each separate context of how the seller and user fairly might expect the product to perform in each particular situation.[238] Thus, the manufacturer of paint used for submerged murals on the walls of swimming pools may not breach an implied warranty of merchantability when the variegated coloring of the walls hampers detection of a drowning person.[239] Nor may the manufacturer of a toy ball breach a merchantability warranty when a child dies from choking on the ball,[240] or the manufacturer of a disposable butane cigarette lighter when a toddler uses it to set fire to his apartment.[241] Yet, when a child sprays flammable hair spray on her dress and hair because of the pleasant fragrance, a jury might be permitted to find that such a use could be expected and so was "ordinary."[242] Such decisions, rooted in the fair expectations of the parties, are multi-faceted, fact specific, and peculiarly suited for jury determination.[243]

In a typical case involving a claim for breach of implied warranty of merchantability, the plaintiff will attempt to establish the precise manner in which the product failed. However, sometimes a product is destroyed in an accident, or proof of how the product failed to operate safely will otherwise be unavailable. In such "malfunction" cases, the plaintiff still may rely on the merchantability warranty and need not necessarily show with particularity the precise nature of the defect or the precise physical mechanism that caused the product to fail.[244] For example, if a new car's steering suddenly fails, causing the car to smash at high speed into a tree with such force that the steering mechanism is damaged so badly that the cause of the steering failure cannot be determined, the plaintiff should still prevail. It is sufficient in such a case for the plaintiff merely to show

---

[236] Venezia v. Miller Brewing Co., 626 F.2d 188, 190–91 (1st Cir. 1980) (Mass. law) (fitness for ordinary purposes rests on "reasonable consumer expectations. . . . No reasonable consumer would expect anything but that a glass beer bottle, apparently well suited for its immediate intended use, would fail to safely withstand the type of purposeful abuse involved here [hurling it against a telephone pole].").

[237] See, e.g., Watson v. Uniden Corp. of Am., 775 F.2d 1514 (11th Cir. 1985) (Ga. law) (dismissing warranty claims for plaintiff's failure to follow phone's instructions and warnings, but jury issue existed on adequacy of warning for negligence and strict liability in tort claims).

[238] See, e.g., Moss v. Batesville Casket Co., 935 So.2d 393, 401 (Miss. 2006) (though cherry-wood casket had cracked and separated during 2 ½ years before exhumation, ordinary use of casket was to "house the remains of the departed until interment," not to "preserve the remains for an indefinite period of time"). For other "ordinary purpose" cases, see note 226, above.

[239] Kelly v. Koppers Co., 293 So.2d 763 (Fla. Dist. Ct. App. 1974).

[240] Brazier v. Hasbro, Inc., 2004 WL 515536, at *4 (S.D.N.Y. 2004).

[241] Phillips v. Cricket Lighters, 883 A.2d 439, 444 (Pa. 2005) ("[T]he ordinary purpose of the Cricket lighter was to allow an adult to produce a flame . . . not to be a two year old child's plaything.").

[242] See Hardman v. Helene Curtis Indus., 198 N.E.2d 681, 691 (Ill. App. Ct. 1964) ("essential question" is "whether the product failed to safely and adequately satisfy the uses to which such products are ordinarily put").

[243] "Merchantability" is generally recognized to be a question of fact. See Lawrence's Anderson on the UCC § 2–314:679.

[244] See, e.g., Bradley v. Earl B. Feiden, Inc., 864 N.E.2d 600, 604 (N.Y. 2007) (fire appeared to have started in refrigerator/freezer; implied warranty claims "may be sustainable solely on circumstantial evidence"); Genetti v. Caterpillar, Inc., 621 N.W.2d 529, 541 (Neb. 2001); Alvarez v. American Isuzu Motors, 749 N.E.2d 16, 22–23 (Ill. App. Ct. 2001); Red Hill Hosiery Mill, Inc. v. Magnetek, Inc., 530 S.E.2d 321, 327 (N.C. Ct. App. 2000) (whether "tort or warranty, a product defect may be inferred from evidence of the product's malfunction, if there is evidence the product had been put to its ordinary use").

the malfunction, regardless of its specific cause.[245] As expressed by one court: "When machinery 'malfunctions,' it obviously lacks fitness regardless of the cause of the malfunction. Under the theory of warranty, the 'sin' is the lack of fitness as evidenced by the malfunction itself rather than some specific dereliction by the manufacturer in constructing or designing the machinery."[246]

§ 4.4 IMPLIED WARRANTY OF FITNESS FOR PARTICULAR PURPOSE

The implied warranty of fitness for particular purpose is a narrow and somewhat peculiar warranty,[247] sandwiched conceptually between express warranty and the implied warranty of merchantability. Some courts and commentators refer to the implied warranty as the implied warranty of "fitness of purpose" or, simply, of "fitness." The precise designation perhaps should be of little consequence, except that some courts occasionally confuse the matter by referring to the implied warranty of *merchantability* misleadingly as the "fitness" warranty—probably because of the central definition of the merchantability warranty as "fitness" for ordinary purposes.[248] Although these two separate implied warranties (and express warranties) may sometimes overlap,[249] they are defined entirely differently and are conceptually distinct from each other.

In its essence, the implied warranty of fitness is an implied promise by a seller that a product sold will meet the buyer's *particular* needs. It shares some similarities with express warranty, in that it is premised on a kind of representation by the seller—a representation that the product is suitable for some special purposes of the buyer made known to the seller. More specifically, the seller's implicit representation in this context is that the seller is aware of and promises to respect the buyer's trust that the seller has special skills or judgment which the seller will apply in selecting a particular product that will promote the buyer's satisfaction of a particular, unusual type. The fitness warranty is therefore quite different from the merchantability warranty, which is based on the seller's implicit representation that the product will safely and effectively perform the *normal* functions for which that type of product is ordinarily bought and sold. The fitness warranty typically arises in a one-on-one dealing between a buyer and seller calculated to create quite explicit expectations in the buyer that a particular product selected by the seller should accomplish the buyer's particular task—and safely so, in a products liability context. Yet the fitness warranty (like the merchantability warranty) does not depend on nor is precluded by an express seller affirmation, such that the fitness warranty (also like the merchantability warranty) truly is *implied*.

---

[245] This assumes, of course, that evidence suggests the accident probably was *not* caused by the plaintiff, a third party, or ordinary wear and tear, leaving a defect in the product as the probable cause. On the malfunction doctrine, see § 7.4. below.

[246] Greco v. Bucciconi Eng'g Co., 283 F. Supp. 978, 982 (W.D. Pa. 1967), aff'd, 407 F.2d 87 (3d Cir. 1969). See also Legal Aid of Neb., Inc. v. Chaina Wholesale, Inc., 2020 WL 42471, at *5 (D. Neb. 2020) ("a space heater that under normal use causes a fire, is not a good fit for the ordinary purposes for which it would be used"); DeWitt v. Eveready Battery Co., 565 S.E.2d 140, 150 (N.C. 2002) (battery leaked fluid); Collins v. Sears, Roebuck & Co., 583 N.E.2d 873 (Mass. App. Ct. 1992) (dryer's electrical system caught fire); Lawrence's Anderson on the Uniform Commercial Code § 2–314:167 (breach of implied warranty of merchantability "may be shown by circumstantial evidence of a failure of the goods to function properly, even though the buyer fails to establish the specific defect that made it malfunction").

[247] On the implied warranty of fitness for particular purpose, see generally Annot., 83 A.L.R.3d 669 (1978) ("particular purpose" defined for UCC § 2–315).

[248] UCC § 2–314(2)(c).

[249] See UCC § 2–317 (*Cumulation and Conflict of Warranties Express or Implied*).

The distinction between the implied warranties of fitness and merchantability is explained well in comment 2 to Uniform Commercial Code § 2–315:

> A "particular purpose" differs from the ordinary purpose for which the goods are used in that it envisages a specific use by the buyer which is peculiar to the nature of his business whereas the ordinary purposes for which goods are used are those envisaged in the concept of merchantability and go to uses which are customarily made of the goods in question. For example, shoes are generally used for the purpose of walking upon ordinary ground, but a seller may know that a particular pair was selected to be used for climbing mountains.

Although the implied warranty of fitness for a particular purpose is invoked only infrequently in products liability litigation,[250] occasionally this special warranty is especially appropriate in this context. For example, a buyer may ask a hardware store salesman for a chain saw to cut out tree stumps below the level of the soil, requiring the saw to endure frequent encounters with dirt and rocks. If the salesman, after selecting the saw from several in stock, plunks it down on the counter saying, "That will be two hundred dollars," the implied warranty of fitness likely will have been made; and, if the saw's chain breaks from this particularly taxing use, the fitness warranty likely will have been breached. If, as occurs more frequently in such face-to-face encounters, the salesman were to add, "Oh, sure; this one will work just fine," he will have made an express warranty as well. Thus, express warranties often co-exist with implied warranties of fitness for a particular purpose.[251]

Uniform Commercial Code § 2–315

Article 2 of the Uniform Commercial Code describes fitness warranties:

§ 2–315. Implied Warranty: Fitness for Particular Purpose

> Where the seller at the time of contracting has reason to know any particular purpose for which the goods are required and that the buyer is relying on the seller's skill or judgment to select or furnish suitable goods, there is unless excluded or modified under the next section an implied warranty that the goods shall be fit for such purpose.

So, for *breach* of the fitness warranty, a plaintiff must establish that:

(1) *Buyer's Particular Purpose.* The buyer bought a product intending to use it for a purpose that is special, to wit, out of the ordinary;

(2) *Buyer's Reliance.* The buyer relied on the seller's skill or judgment to select an appropriate product for this special purpose;

---

[250] See White and Summers, UCC § 10–14, at 499.

[251] On the overlap between express and implied warranties of fitness for particular purpose, see, e.g., Klein v. Sears Roebuck & Co., 773 F.2d 1421, 1424–25 (4th Cir. 1985) (Md. law), discussed in the text below. See also Filler v. Rayex Corp., 435 F.2d 336, 338 (7th Cir. 1970) (Ind. law) (sunglasses advertised as "Baseball Sunglasses," which splintered when hit by baseball, "not fit for baseball playing, the particular purpose for which they were sold"). See generally UCC § 2–317; Annot., 83 A.L.R.3d 656 (1978) (overlap of UCC express and implied warranties). Compare Brain, The Unnecessary Implied Warranty of Fitness for a Particular Purpose, 23 Chap. L. Rev. 163 (2020) (arguing that fitness claims best fall under the UCC's express warranty provisions).

(3) *Seller's Knowledge.* The seller had reason to know (a) the special purpose, and that (b) the buyer was relying on his skill or judgment to select an appropriate product;

(4) *Unfitness for Purpose.* The product was not fit for the particular purpose; and

(5) *Causation and Harm.* The product's unfitness for this purpose caused the plaintiff harm.

From these elements for breach of the fitness warranty, the first three (which together determine whether such a warranty arose) often predominate in importance: (1) the particularity of the buyer's purpose for the product; (2) the buyer's reliance on the seller's skill or judgment to select an appropriate product for this purpose; and (3) the seller's reason to know both the buyer's special purpose and reliance on his special selection skills. The fourth element—unfitness—is the central issue of breach that often is uncontroverted in cases of substantial personal injury.[252] The issues contained in the fifth element, causation and harm, embedded in breach, are considered later.[253]

An example of a products liability case where the plaintiffs proved each element of their implied warranty of fitness claim is *Klein v. Sears Roebuck & Co.*[254] In that case, the plaintiffs bought a particular model riding lawnmower upon the recommendation of the defendant's salesman for use on their hilly property, subject to the salesman's inspection of the property to confirm that the mower was appropriate. When the salesman delivered the mower, he inspected the property and pronounced the mower suitable, provided it was driven vertically up the steepest hills. While the plaintiff husband was mowing vertically up one of the steeper slopes, the mower tipped over backwards, injuring him. On these facts, the court affirmed a verdict for the plaintiff husband for breach of an implied warranty of fitness in addition to breach of express warranty.

A plaintiff, of course, has the burden of proof on each element of his or her claim, and an implied warranty of fitness case will fail in the absence of sufficient proof of any element. *Rynders v. E.I. DuPont de Nemours & Co.*[255] was one of many actions against DuPont for selling Teflon to a small manufacturer, Vitek, which used Teflon to manufacture jaw implants marketed to help alleviate wearing of the jaw caused by TMJ syndrome. DuPont advised Vitek of studies suggesting the unsuitability of Teflon for human implants, but Vitek wrote DuPont that later studies showed solutions to the earlier problems and accepted responsibility for using Teflon in its implants. Teflon turned out to be drastically unsuited for this use, thousands of people suffered resulting injuries, Vitek went bankrupt, and its founder fled the country. There had been no breach of the implied warranty of merchantability, of course, because Teflon was a perfectly safe and reliable product for most uses. As for the fitness warranty, the court

---

[252] This is because a products liability claim for breach of the fitness warranty arises only if a product is dangerously unsuited for a particular purpose, which often is self-evident from the injury.

[253] Causation issues are examined in chapters 11 and 12, below, and damages are addressed by UCC §§ 2–714 and 2–715.

[254] 773 F.2d 1421 (4th Cir. 1985) (Md. law).

[255] 21 F.3d 835 (8th Cir. 1994) (S.D. law).

held that (1) DuPont had no reason to suspect that Vitek was relying on DuPont's skill or judgment, and (2) Vitek did not in fact so rely.[256]

Buyer's Particular Purpose

For this special fitness warranty to arise, a plaintiff must of course establish that his or her purpose was *particular*—that is, different from the ordinary purposes for which such goods ordinarily are used.[257] While some courts hold that a fitness warranty may arise simultaneously with an ordinary-purpose merchantability warranty when a buyer communicates to the seller his or her anticipated use for the product, most courts disagree, ruling instead that the class of purposes contemplated by § 2–315's "*particular* purpose" notion is necessarily distinct from the merchantability notion of uses such products *ordinarily* serve.[258]

Buyer's Reliance

As discussed above, the fitness warranty partakes of some aspects of express warranty. As is true generally for misrepresentation claims, including those based on express warranty, the buyer's reliance is a fundamental aspect of the claim.[259] The fitness warranty arises when, in dealings between a seller and a buyer, the seller renders an implicit assurance that a particular product selected by the seller will fulfill a specific need designated by the buyer. Even in the absence of an express representation to this effect, such dealings can create the same kinds of expectations of specific satisfaction. Yet, if the buyer fails to rely on such an implicit assurance of suitability, any harm suffered by the buyer probably resulted from something other than the product's failure to conform to the assurance. Thus, implied warranty of fitness claims require the buyer's reliance to provide a causal link between the seller's misconduct (the false message) and the buyer's harm.

A plaintiff's reliance or non-reliance on the seller's skill and judgment is sometimes very clear. Examples of self-evident reliance include a beauty shop customer who relies on the beautician to select an appropriate permanent wave solution, not one that will cause injuries to her scalp and loss of hair,[260] and purchasers of a casket and vault who rely on a funeral home to select a casket that will fit in the vault.[261] The reliance may be made by a prior party in the distributive chain, so that a patient in whom a prosthetic device is implanted may take the benefit of the hospital's reliance on the skill and judgment of the manufacturer of the device.[262] Sometimes evidence on the reliance issue points clearly the other way—that the buyer made an independent decision to buy and

---

[256] See also Kalinowski v. E.I. Du Pont de Nemours & Co., 851 F. Supp. 149 (E.D. Pa. 1994).

[257] See, e.g., Presnell v. Snap-On Securecorp, Inc., 2022 WL 295917, at *9 (M.D.N.C. 2022) (hammer); Miller v. DePuy Synthes Sales, Inc., 2019 WL 4016207, at *6 (D. Nev. 2019) (orthopedic implant; "there is no particular purpose on which the Plaintiff could conceivably rely—his use was ordinary"); Marcus v. Apple Inc., 2015 WL 151489, at *9 (N.D. Cal. 2015) (laptops; no particular purpose alleged); Tyree v. Boston Scientific Corp., 2014 WL 5359008, at *7 (S.D. W. Va. 2014) (transvaginal mesh system; same).

[258] See discussion at note 281, below.

[259] The reliance element in express warranty is now cast in terms of "basis of the bargain" in § 2–313, but the basic concept is similar.

[260] Newmark v. Gimbel's, Inc., 246 A.2d 11 (N.J. Super. Ct. App. Div. 1968), aff'd, 258 A.2d 697 (N.J. 1969).

[261] Caldwell v. Brown Serv. Funeral Home, 345 So.2d 1341 (Ala. 1977).

[262] Perfetti v. McGhan Med., 662 P.2d 646 (N.M. Ct. App. 1983).

put a product to a particular use.[263] So, if a buyer purchases a lawnmower of a particular type because his neighbor has one, and he fails to seek advice from or discuss the purchase decision with anyone, the absence of reliance on the seller will defeat a warranty of fitness claim.[264]

Certain situations suggest the absence of reliance. In early sales law, various specific rules were designed to ensure the buyer's reliance and to weed out cases where it did not exist. For example, a buyer's inspection of a product, or in some jurisdictions even his or her opportunity to inspect, negated both the implied warranties of fitness and merchantability. Section 15(3) of the Uniform Sales Act restricted this exclusion to actual examinations and defects that ought to have been revealed thereby, a restriction that continued in UCC § 2–316(3)(b).

A buyer's reliance was also ensured by another rule that precluded implied warranties of fitness for particular purpose in the case of articles that were "known, described and definite."[265] One application of this restriction was the more specific provision of Uniform Sales Act § 15(4) that precluded such warranties "[i]n the case of a contract to sell or a sale of a specified article under its patent or other trade name."[266] Today, a buyer's designation of a product by name is only one factor to be considered on the ultimate factual issue of reliance.[267] Finally, where the buyer rather than the seller prepares specifications for a product, it is well established that a product made to those specifications carries no warranty of fitness for a particular purpose, even when that purpose is known to the seller.[268]

A buyer who inspects a product, or otherwise participates in its selection, may have some difficulty in establishing reliance on the seller's judgment in selecting the product. So, where a plaintiff looked over various stepladders and chose the one recommended by

---

[263] As in Rynders v. E.I. DuPont de Nemours & Co., 21 F.3d 835 (8th Cir. 1994) (S.D. law), discussed at notes 255 and 256, above. See also Crandall v. Seagate Tech., 2011 WL 280990, at *7 (D. Idaho 2011) (even though salesperson told buyer that computer hard drives buyer had asked store to hold for him were "perfect" for plaintiff's needs, no fitness warranty arose where plaintiff had decided to purchase the drives before he even went to the store).

[264] Freeman v. Case Corp., 924 F. Supp. 1456 (W.D. Va. 1996), rev'd on other grounds, 118 F.3d 1011 (4th Cir. 1997).

[265] 1 Williston on Sales § 235, at 607 (1948 rev. ed.).

[266] See id. at §§ 234–36a.

[267] Compare UCC § 2–315 cmt. 5:

> The elimination of the "patent or other trade name" exception constitutes the major extension of the warranty of fitness . . . . [T]he existence of a patent or other trade name and the designation of the article by that name, or indeed in any other definite manner, is only one of the facts to be considered on the question of whether the buyer actually relied on the seller, but it is not of itself decisive of the issue. If the buyer himself is insisting on a particular brand he is not relying on the seller's skill and judgment and so no warranty results. But the mere fact that the article purchased has a particular patent or trade name is not sufficient to indicate nonreliance if the article has been recommended by the seller as adequate for the buyer's purposes.

Thus, in a riding mower purchase situation like *Klein*, above, a fitness warranty might well have arisen even if the buyer had asked the seller to select the best model International Harvester mower, among six models available, for his hilly yard. Yet no such warranty would arise, even if the seller knew the hilly nature of the buyer's yard, if the buyer saw that only one model of IH mower was available and simply told the seller that he would like to buy it.

[268] See, e.g., Stephens v. Paris Cleaners, Inc., 885 A.2d 59, 72 (Pa. Super. Ct. 2005) (buyer designed product and "allowed no exception or alterations to his design"); Singleton v. L.P. Anderson Supply Co., 943 P.2d 968 (Mont. 1997) (buyer ordered exact item of particular size); Fisher v. Monsanto Co., 863 F. Supp. 285 (W.D. Va. 1994) (buyer's specifications). See also Jacobs v. E.I. du Pont de Nemours & Co., 67 F.3d 1219 (6th Cir. 1995) (Tenn. law) (no implied warranty of fitness where buyer merely orders specified goods).

a salesman, the court held that a fitness warranty did not arise because the selection was not "exclusively within the control of" the salesman and the buyer's "discretion and judgment played a major part in the selection."[269] Generally, however, a buyer's inspection should not conclusively establish non-reliance. In *Peters v. Lyons*,[270] the buyer asked for a dog chain strong enough to restrain his 100- to 120-pound German shepherd. The saleswoman selected the strongest chain, which she and the buyer both inspected and agreed would be sufficient. It was not, and the plaintiff was attacked and injured by the dog. The court held that the buyer had established his reliance on the seller's skill and judgment: "The buyer's reliance on the seller need not be total reliance. The buyer may rely on his own judgment as to some matters and on the seller's skill and judgment as to others."[271]

Seller's Knowledge

In order for the fitness warranty to arise, a seller must *have reason to know* that a buyer plans to put a product to some *special* use known to the seller, a use that is different from the ordinary uses for which the product usually is sold. The seller must further have reason to know that the buyer is relying on the seller's skill or judgment to select a product appropriate for this special purpose. The requirement that a seller be aware of these facts is a necessary predicate for the seller's (implicit) representation that the goods are suitable for a special use; a seller can hardly make a specific promise about something of which it has no reason to know.

A seller's knowledge of a buyer's particular use and of the buyer's reliance on the seller's skill or judgment sometimes is very clear, as when an ordinary consumer requests a product with sophisticated characteristics from a dealer in such products who purports to have expertise in the product's special characteristics. So, when a prospective buyer of a riding lawnmower seeks and obtains an assurance from the selling dealer that a particular type and model lawnmower will be suited safely to mow the uphill slopes inspected by the dealer, as in the *Klein* case discussed above, the dealer will know full well that the buyer is relying for his safety on the dealer's skill and judgment in the selection of a proper mower.[272]

The source of the seller's knowledge is unimportant, so long as it in fact exists. Although buyers commonly inform sellers of their intended use of products, a verbal communication that a buyer aims directly at the seller is unnecessary if the seller acquires the information from some other source, including the context of the particular transaction.[273]

An implied warranty of fitness claim will fail if the plaintiff is unable to prove any aspect of the seller's required knowledge.[274] Thus, the fitness warranty will not apply to the sale of a stove, if the distributor is unaware of the buyer's particular heating needs;[275] or of retreaded tires for a pickup truck, if the seller is unaware that the truck will be

---

[269] See Carney v. Sears, Roebuck & Co., 309 F.2d 300 (4th Cir. 1962) (Va. law).

[270] 168 N.W.2d 759 (Iowa 1969).

[271] Id. at 764.

[272] See *Klein*, 773 F.2d at 1424–25.

[273] See cmt. 1 to UCC § 2–315. See, e.g., Miller v. Andy Burger Motors, Inc., 370 S.W.2d 654 (Mo. Ct. App. 1963) (sale of automobile).

[274] See Cal. Civ. Code §§ 1792.1–.2.

[275] See Dalton v. Stanley Solar & Stove, Inc., 629 A.2d 794 (N.H. 1993).

used in the buyer's construction business;[276] or of a truck cab chassis, if the manufacturer does not know it will be put to use as a tow truck;[277] or of diesel fuel, if the seller is unaware that it will be used to manufacture road asphalt.[278]

Compared to Implied Warranty of Merchantability

Unlike the implied warranty of merchantability in UCC § 2–314, which requires that the seller be a "merchant" of such goods, UCC § 2–315 applies to any seller.[279] While buyers normally rely for selection advice on knowledgeable merchants, a warranty under UCC § 2–315 "can arise as to nonmerchants where this is justified by the particular circumstances."[280]

Another important distinction between these two implied warranties concerns the issue of reliance. Reliance is a critically important element of the fitness warranty, as discussed above. But reliance is simply not an issue with respect to the implied warranty of merchantability—the warranty of basic quality for *ordinary* uses, which arises solely from the product's sale.

More fundamentally, as noted earlier, the fitness warranty is entirely distinct and independent from the implied warranty of merchantability. As lucidly explained in comment 2 to § 2–315, above, this distinction is so perfectly clear that one might reasonably conclude that an "ordinary" use by definition must be separate and distinct from a purpose that is "particular" to a buyer. Indeed, most courts logically have so concluded, ruling that an ordinary use cannot also be a special use.[281] For example, in *Miles v. Ford Motor Co.*,[282] the passenger in a Ford Ranger pickup truck was paralyzed in an accident by a defectively designed shoulder harness. Noting that all of the state's previous fitness warranty cases had involved evidence that the seller was aware of "peculiar or extraordinary uses to which the buyer intended to put the product that were at least somewhat out of the ordinary," the court concluded that "the better rule is that a particular purpose must be a particular nonordinary purpose."[283] Thus, the sale of an

[276] See Jones v. Marcus, 457 S.E.2d 271 (Ga. Ct. App. 1995).

[277] See Ford Motor Co. v. General Accident Ins. Co., 779 A.2d 362, 374–79 (Md. 2001) (implied warranty of fitness for particular purpose claim against manufacturer failed because no proof that manufacturer knew that cab chassis would be converted to tow truck).

[278] See Ace Am. Ins. v. Allison Oil Co., 2006 WL 1365927, at *1–2 (S.D. Miss. 2006).

[279] In the predecessor Uniform Sales Act, this warranty applied to a seller "whether he be the grower or the manufacturer or not." See UCC § 2–315 cmt. 4.

[280] Id. See, e.g., Barb v. Wallace, 412 A.2d 1314 (Md. Ct. Spec. App. 1980) (sale of old lawnmower motor for use in go-cart).

[281] See, e.g., Security Nat. Bank of Sioux City, Iowa v. Abbott Labs., 2012 WL 327863, at *18 (N.D. Iowa 2012) (no fitness warranty since Similac baby formula was used for its ordinary, customary purpose, "i.e., feeding babies"); Michael v. Wyeth, LLC, 2011 WL 2150112, at *6 (S.D. W. Va. 2011) (no fitness warranty where use of hormone replacement therapy for treatment of menopausal symptoms was "the ordinary, rather than particular, purpose for which the drugs were used"); Crane v. Bagge & Son, Inc., 2005 WL 1576544, at * 6 (Cal. Ct. App. 2005) ("A 'particular purpose' means something other than the ordinary purpose . . . a specific use by the buyer which is peculiar to the nature of his business."); Coghlan v. Aquasport Marine Corp., 73 F. Supp. 2d 769, 774 (S.D. Tex. 1999) ("the particular purpose must be some unusual, out of the ordinary purpose peculiar to the needs of an individual buyer"), aff'd, 240 F.3d 449 (5th Cir. 2001); Stones v. Sears, Roebuck & Co., 558 N.W.2d 540 (Neb. 1997) (ordinary, not particular, purpose of propane grill was to grill).

[282] 922 S.W.2d 572 (Tex. App. 1996), rev'd in part on other grounds, 967 S.W.2d 377 (Tex. 1998).

[283] Id. at 587.

ordinary pickup truck did not include a warranty of fitness for the particular purpose of carrying passengers, since this was one of the ordinary purposes of such trucks.[284]

Notwithstanding the logic of this view, some courts remain confused.[285] Perhaps led astray by comment 2 to § 2–315,[286] a few courts have ruled that an ordinary use under § 2–314 can also amount to a particular purpose under § 2–315.[287] "Such confusion under the Code is inexcusable. Sections 2–314 and 2–315 make plain that the warranty of fitness for a particular purpose is narrower, more specific, and more precise."[288] It is true, of course, that a product's unmerchantability may also render it unfit for some particular purpose for which it was specially warranted. In such a case, however, a claim for breach of implied warranty of fitness for a particular purpose will lie only if the buyer establishes each aspect of the fitness claim, including the special, *un*common nature of the purpose for which the product allegedly was warranted.[289]

The converse is also true: the implied warranty of fitness for a particular purpose may be breached (as may an express warranty) even if the product is entirely merchantable and "nondefective." While a product sold in breach of the fitness warranty may sometimes be "defective" or unmerchantable for its ordinary uses, too, many products that normally are entirely safe may be dangerous and entirely unfit when put to other uses for which those products were not designed. The point is that the fitness warranty has no concern with a product's safety when put to its *general* uses, but only when put to such *particular* uses as the buyer and seller make part of their special deal. Thus, the fitness warranty may be breached when a seller selects a product that is perfectly safe for its normal purposes but that is dangerously unsuited to the special purposes both parties know lie at the center of their particular sales transaction.[290]

§ 4.5 PRIVITY OF CONTRACT AND THIRD-PARTY BENEFICIARIES

The privity of contract issue was examined earlier from the perspective of its availability as a defense to *negligence* claims, as established in *Winterbottom v. Wright*.[291] In repudiating the privity defense for negligence claims, *MacPherson v. Buick*[292] emphasized the irrelevance of contractual relationships to the independent obligations imposed on sellers by the law of torts. In the words of Judge Cardozo:

---

[284] "Even if [the buyer] had expressly told either Ford or the dealership that he intended to carry passengers in his truck, that is the ordinary purpose of a passenger truck, rather than a particular purpose." Id. See also American Suzuki Motor Corp. v. Superior Ct., 44 Cal. Rptr. 2d 526 (Ct. App. 1995) (consumer's purpose for buying automobile was not a *particular* purpose).

[285] See, e.g., South Side Trust & Savings Bank v. Mitsubishi Heavy Indus., Ltd., 927 N.E.2d 179, 191–92 (Ill. App. Ct. 2010) (ruling that the "particular purpose for the aircraft is obvious: to fly it and travel safely in it"); Frisby-Cadillo v. Mylan, Inc., 2010 WL 1838729, at *3–4 (N.D. Cal. 2010); Lariviere v. Dayton Safety Ladder Co., 525 A.2d 892 (R.I. 1987).

[286] Comment 2 states in part, "A contract may of course include both a warranty of merchantability and one of fitness for a particular purpose."

[287] See, e.g., Soaper v. Hope Indus., 424 S.E.2d 493, 495 (S.C. 1992) (the two implied warranties may "merge and are cumulative, such that a plaintiff may proceed upon either theory"); Great Dane Trailer Sales, Inc. v. Malvern Pulpwood, Inc., 785 S.W.2d 13, 17 (Ark. 1990) (the two implied warranties merge "[i]f the particular purpose for which goods are to be used coincides with their general functional use").

[288] White and Summers, UCC § 10–14, at 495.

[289] Compare Bimini Boat Sales, Inc. v. Luhrs Corp., 892 N.Y.S.2d 548, 550 (App. Div. 2010) (boat's unmerchantability rendered it unfit for particular purpose of resale).

[290] See, e.g., McLaughlin v. Michelin Tire Corp., 778 P.2d 59, 66 (Wyo. 1989) (affirming proposition).

[291] (1842) 152 Eng. Rep. 402 (Exch. Div.).

[292] 111 N.E. 1050 (N.Y. 1916). *MacPherson* and *Winterbottom* are discussed in § 1.2, above.

> We have put aside the notion that the duty to safeguard life and limb, when the consequences of negligence may be foreseen, grows out of contract and nothing else. We have put the source of the obligation where it ought to be. We have put its source in the law.[293]

It was at this place and time, New York in 1916, that tort law took one of its most important detours away from the law of contract, especially in products liability actions, by stripping away the privity defense from actions that lay in negligence. In explaining the elemental difference between tort and contract law in respect to privity, Judge Cardozo indirectly revealed the logical power of the defense of privity in its own domain—contract cases involving claims for breach of warranty. That is, while a contractual relationship between a seller and a victim of a product accident may be irrelevant to a negligence (or other tort law) claim, such a relationship is fundamental to whether the victim has a claim for breach of a contractual warranty.

In the early part of the twentieth century, the law of contracts quite firmly restricted the enforcement of contractual undertakings to the contracting parties themselves. In denying recovery to a person claiming as a contract beneficiary in one early case, Lord Haldane remarked: "[I]n the law of England certain principles are fundamental. One is that only a person who is a party to a contract can sue on it."[294] Contractual rights were extended to nonparties to the contract ("third-party beneficiaries") only in limited situations where the contracting parties clearly intended to confer benefits on such other persons "remote" from the contract.[295] So, it is evident that the absence of a contractual relationship between the parties (the absence of "privity of contract") is logically a significant obstacle to a breach of warranty or other *contract* claim.

For products liability claims brought in warranty, the privity-of-contract issue may helpfully be divided into the separate notions of "vertical" and "horizontal" privity. Both issues involve a determination of the proper parties to breach-of-warranty actions: What types of sellers are bound by warranties, in other words, and what types of injured parties obtain their benefits?

"Vertical privity" refers to the contractual relationship between the parties up and down the chain of product distribution, from suppliers of raw materials and component parts, at the top, to manufacturers, distributors, wholesalers, retailers, and, at the bottom of the chain, purchasers of products. A vertical privity requirement limits buyers to warranty law recourse only against their immediate sellers—those with whom they had a contract of purchase and sale and, hence a relation of "privity" of contract. Up and down the chain of distribution, the vertical privity issue may be framed as: *Who can be sued?*

"Horizontal privity," on the other hand, concerns the reach of contractual protection to non-purchasers who may be harmed by a product and who seek to stand in the purchaser's shoes to obtain the remedial benefits of whatever warranties flowed to the purchaser by virtue of his or her contract of purchase. Such non-purchasers, extending horizontally away from the purchaser in diminishing order of affinity, include the purchaser's family, members of the purchaser's household and household guests, the

[293] Id. at 1051. By "law," Judge Cardozo meant "tort law," the obligations toward other persons imposed by law on every person regardless of consent, as distinguished from the law of contracts which enforces private agreements that people consensually undertake.

[294] Dunlop Pneumatic Tyre Co. v. Selfridge & Co., [1915] A.C. 847, 853 (H.L.) (U.K.).

[295] See J. Perillo, Calamari and Perillo on Contracts ch. 17 (6th ed. 2009).

purchaser's employees, and other, more remote defendants often referred to as "(mere) bystanders." The horizontal privity issue may be framed as: *Who can sue?*[296]

Vertical Privity

Until the industrial revolution, consumers often bought their basic products—lamps, guns, leather goods, and garden and dairy produce—directly from the parties who made or grew them—the smiths, farmers, and butchers who produced the goods.[297] Yet, just as many American courts began to impose implied warranties of quality on manufacturers during the latter part of the nineteenth century, manufacturers increasingly were spinning off the retail function to third-party dealers. This meant that consumers typically began to deal contractually only with retailers. Of course, if a retail dealer were an agent of the manufacturer, the buyer could satisfy the privity requirement in a claim against the manufacturer. But during the early twentieth century, the growing contractual remoteness of manufacturers from consumers, who typically were separated at least by a retailer (and often by a wholesaler or other distributor), meant that consumers and manufacturers were no longer in "privity of contract" with one another. Even in negligence actions, this vertical privity defense was proving its effectiveness, at least until the anti-privity principles of *MacPherson v. Buick Motor Co.*[298] spread slowly across the nation during the first half of the twentieth century.[299] The harshness of this defense in cases of consumer injury was readily apparent, and courts began to riddle it with exceptions from an early date.[300]

The first cases to abolish outright the manufacturer's privity defense in implied warranty personal injury cases were decided early in the twentieth century and involved defective foodstuffs.[301] By mid-century, the weakening of the privity defense in implied

---

[296] On the distinction between vertical and horizontal privity, see Hyundai Motor Am., Inc. v. Goodin, 822 N.E.2d 947, 952 (Ind. 2005) (explaining and distinguishing vertical from horizontal privity); Szajna v. General Motors Corp., 503 N.E.2d 760, 762–70 (Ill. 1986) (same); Dalton v. Stanley Solar & Stove, Inc., 629 A.2d 794, 796–97 (N.H. 1993):

> The term vertical privity describes the relationship between adjoining parties in a marketing chain. *See* Hawkland, 1 UCC Series § 2–218:01, at 421 (1984). Vertical privity exists, for example, between a wholesaler and retailer, and between a retailer and the ultimate buyer, but not between a wholesaler and the ultimate buyer. Vertical privity is readily distinguishable from horizontal privity, which denotes the relationship between the retailer and one who uses or consumes the goods. Where a dealer sells goods to a buyer, and a third party is injured due to a defect in the goods, whether the third party can sue the dealer is an issue of horizontal privity.

[297] "In earlier times the one who made the article generally sold it directly to the ultimate user, and thus the consumer, being in privity of contract with the manufacturer, was allowed to recover on the usual warranties for losses caused by defective workmanship." Jeanblanc, Manufacturers' Liability to Persons Other Than Their Immediate Vendees, 24 Va. L. Rev. 134, 134 (1937).

[298] 111 N.E. 1050 (N.Y. 1916).

[299] See § 1.2, above.

[300] See Gillam, Products Liability in a Nutshell, 37 Or. L. Rev. 119, 152–55 (1958) (listing 29 such exceptions).

[301] See Mazetti v. Armour & Co., 135 P. 633 (Wash. 1913); Parks v. G.C. Yost Pie Co., 144 P. 202 (Kan. 1914); Jackson Coca-Cola Bottling Co. v. Chapman, 64 So. 791 (Miss. 1914); Jacob E. Decker & Sons, Inc. v. Capps, 164 S.W.2d 828 (Tex. 1942):

> Liability in such case is [based] on the broad principle of the public policy to protect human health and life. [A]rticles of food are manufactured and placed in the channels of commerce, with the intention that they shall pass from hand to hand until they are finally used by some remote customer. It is usually impracticable, if not impossible, for the ultimate customer to analyze the food and ascertain whether or not it is suitable for human consumption. . . . [W]here food products sold for human consumption are unfit for that purpose, there is such an utter failure of the purpose for which the food is sold, and the consequences of eating unsound food are so disastrous to human

warranty cases began to spread to products for intimate bodily use such as soap, hair dye, and permanent wave solution.[302] Then, in the late 1950s and early 1960s, several courts in rapid succession extended the idea to durable goods. In 1960, in *Henningsen v. Bloomfield Motors, Inc.*,[303] the privity bar was emphatically repudiated in a landmark implied warranty case involving injuries from a defective automobile manufactured by defendant, Chrysler Corporation, and sold to a dealer, Bloomfield Motors, which sold it to Mr. Henningsen. The car had a steering defect, and Mr. Henningsen's wife was injured ten days after purchase when the car went off the road. Speaking for the New Jersey Supreme Court, Justice Francis explained why the demise of the privity defense in food and drink cases compelled its demise in a case involving a defective car: "We see no rational doctrinal basis for differentiating between a fly in a bottle of beverage and a defective automobile. The unwholesome beverage may bring illness to one person, the defective car, with its great potentiality for harm to the driver, occupants, and others, demands even less adherence to the narrow barrier of privity."[304]

In the view of Dean William Prosser, *Henningsen* marked the end of the privity defense in products liability claims brought in implied warranty—the "fall of the citadel of privity."[305] Finding the vertical privity requirement for implied warranty claims outmoded and bad policy, many courts have now abandoned it in cases of personal injury,[306] some in cases of property damage,[307] and a few even for economic loss.[308] Nevertheless, because implied warranty claims lie in contract, many courts still require

health and life, that the law imposes a warranty of purity in favor of the ultimate consumer as a matter of public policy.

[302] The breakdown of the privity defense is recounted in Prosser, The Assault Upon the Citadel (Strict Liability to the Consumer), 69 Yale L.J. 1099 (1960). See also E. Levi, Introduction to Legal Reasoning (1949).

[303] 161 A.2d 69 (N.J. 1960). *Henningsen*'s role in the development of strict liability in tort is examined at § 5.2, below.

[304] Id. at 83. For further discussion of the court's rejection of the privity defense, see § 5.2, below.

[305] Prosser, The Fall of the Citadel (Strict Liability to the Consumer), 50 Minn. L. Rev. 791, 791 (1966).

[306] See, e.g., AgGrow Oils, L.L.C. v. National Union Fire Ins. Co. of Pittsburgh, 276 F. Supp. 2d 999, 1014 (D.N.D. 2003) (dictum, distinguishing economic loss cases), aff'd, 420 F.3d 751 (8th Cir. 2005); Colon v. BIC USA, Inc., 199 F. Supp. 2d 53, 95 (S.D.N.Y. 2001) ("No showing of privity is required in a personal injury action for breach of express or implied warranty."); Bouverette v. Westinghouse Elec. Corp., 628 N.W.2d 86, 91 (Mich. Ct. App. 2001) (privity unnecessary for injured bystanders suing manufacturer for breach of warranty or negligence); R.R. Donnelley & Sons Co. v. North Tex. Steel Co., 752 N.E.2d 112, 124–25 (Ind. Ct. App. 2001); Berry v. G.D. Searle & Co., 309 N.E.2d 550 (Ill. 1974) (implied warranty of fitness).

Massachusetts, never having adopted the doctrine of strict products liability in tort, accomplishes the same result through its implied warranty of merchantability. See, e.g., Haglund v. Philip Morris, Inc., 847 N.E.2d 315, 321 (Mass. 2006); § 5.3, below. As other states do in strict tort cases, Massachusetts discards privity as a requirement in products liability cases. See, e.g., DaSilva v. Toyota Motor Corp., 474 F. Supp. 3d 448, 456 (D. Mass. 2020) ("Massachusetts has long rejected contractual privity as an essential element for recovery in a case seeking recovery for damages suffered by reason of a defective product.").

[307] See, e.g., Kassab v. Central Soya, 246 A.2d 848 (Pa. 1968) (property damage), overruled on other grounds by AM/PM Franchise Ass'n v. Atlantic Richfield Co., 584 A.2d 915 (Pa. 1990).

[308] See, e.g., Hyundai Motor Am., Inc. v. Goodin, 822 N.E.2d 947, 951–59 (Ind. 2005) (thorough discussion).

vertical privity for implied warranty claims for economic loss,[309] and some (because of the availability of tort law claims) even in cases involving personal injuries.[310]

The vertical privity issue long presented a stumbling block for plaintiffs relying on *express* warranties, especially in earlier years. Yet, where a seller affirmatively creates such warranties in an effort to induce consumers to purchase the seller's goods, the fairness and policy arguments supporting a privity defense are especially weak.[311] That is, warranty law reasonably might hold a manufacturer responsible for harmful consequences of false advertisements directed at consumers to convince them to buy its products.[312] Although a consumer injured by relying on such a warranty will almost never have contracted in a formal sense directly with the manufacturer, the very purpose of a manufacturer's marketing efforts is to link itself contractually, albeit through a retail intermediary, with consumers who buy the product because they believe the warranties to be true.

Rogers v. Toni Home Permanent Co.[313] is the landmark case abolishing the privity defense in express warranty cases.[314] Noting that the express warranty action derived originally from tort (deceit) rather than from contract, the court relied upon *Baxter v. Ford Motor Co.*[315] to extend the privity exception recognized in food cases to products generally, reasoning that basic fairness requires that such claims be allowed.[316] It now

---

309 See, e.g., Boddison v. General Motors LLC, 2021 WL 2435388, at *5 (M.D. Fla. 2021) (malfunctioning in-dash infotainment system; "privity of contract is an essential element of a claim for breach of implied warranty"); Buckeye Resources, Inc. v. Duratech Indus. Int'l, Inc., 2011 WL 5190787, at *4 (S.D. Ohio 2011) (privity required for recovery of lost sales and expenses); Powers v. Lycoming Engines, 272 F.R.D. 414, 420–21 (E.D. Pa. 2011) (surveying states); Jordan v. Four Winds Int'l, Inc., 2010 WL 1337691, at *7 (W.D. Pa. 2010) (N.Y. law) (economic loss implied warranty claims require privity); Szajna v. General Motors Corp., 503 N.E.2d 760, 762–70 (Ill. 1986) (thorough analysis).

310 See, e.g., Elkins v. Extreme Prod. Grp., LLC, 2022 WL 409694, at *3 (E.D. Ky. 2022) (manufacturer of defective inversion table was not in privity with injured buyer; "privity of contract [is required] to bring a breach of warranty claim under Kentucky state law"); Xavier v. Philip Morris USA Inc., 787 F. Supp. 2d 1075, 1082 (N.D. Cal. 2011) (dismissing breach of implied warranty claim for medical monitoring in putative class action by heavy smokers, because "they bought Marlboro cigarettes only from retailers, such as liquor stores, and not directly from Philip Morris itself").

311 Policy and fairness considerations may point the other way, in favor of requiring privity, if a component part manufacturer makes an express warranty to an assembler who then sells the finished product to consumers who themselves never see (or rely upon) the warranty. See, e.g., Goodman v. PPG Indus., 849 A.2d 1239, 1245–46 (Pa. Super. Ct. 2004).

312 See, e.g., Dravo Equip. Co. v. German, 698 P.2d 63, 65 (Or. Ct. App. 1985) ("A seller, as the master of a warranty's destiny, is free to make it as broad or as narrow as it chooses. Express warranties can be limited in effect, duration and transferability. Because the seller is free to create an express warranty in any fashion it chooses, there is no reason why the warranty should not extend to remote purchasers when it is not so limited.").

313 147 N.E.2d 612 (Ohio 1958). *Rogers* is noted in 58 Colum. L. Rev. 1092 (1958); 19 Ohio St. L.J. 733 (1958); 44 Iowa L. Rev. 229 (1958); 11 Vand. L. Rev. 1459 (1958); 44 Va. L. Rev. 1002 (1958); Annots., 93 A.L.R.5th 103 (2001); 75 A.L.R.2d 112 (1961).

314 Other important early cases were Silverman v. Samuel Mallinger Co., 100 A.2d 715 (Pa. 1953), and Hamon v. Digliani, 174 A.2d 294 (Conn. 1961). Note that the issue in these cases, how no privity affects *express* warranty claims, is to be distinguished from the issue of how no privity affects *implied* warranty claims (the issue in *Henningsen*).

315 12 P.2d 409 (Wash. 1932). *Baxter* is considered in § 3.4, above.

316 See *Rogers*, 147 N.E.2d at 615–16:

> The consuming public ordinarily relies exclusively on the representations of the manufacturer in his advertisements. What sensible or sound reason then exists as to why, when the goods purchased by the ultimate consumer on the strength of the advertisements aimed squarely at him do not possess their described qualities and goodness and cause him harm, he should not be permitted to move against the manufacturer to recoup his loss. [W]arranties made by the manufacturer in his advertisements and by the labels on his products are inducements to

is widely accepted that express warranties arising from advertisements, labels, brochures, and owner's manuals run with the goods directly to "remote" purchasers who in reliance on the truth of such assertions thereby suffer harm, especially consumers who suffer personal injury,[317] but sometimes also remote consumers who suffer only economic loss.[318]

It is important to note, however, that many states which have abolished the requirement of vertical privity in *express* warranty cases have retained it in cases of *implied* warranties, such that the absence of privity may bar an implied warranty claim in the same case in which an express warranty claim is allowed.[319] For example, *Connick v. Suzuki Motor Co.*[320] involved a claim for economic loss by purchasers against the manufacturer of Suzuki Samurai sport utility vehicles based on the tendency of the vehicles to roll over. Having bought their vehicles from dealers who were not agents of the manufacturer, the purchasers were not in privity with the manufacturer. Allowing the express warranty claim because "a manufacturer which extends a written warranty to a consumer establishes privity between it and the consumer,"[321] the court nevertheless dismissed one group of plaintiffs' merchantability and fitness implied warranty claims for want of vertical privity.[322]

California requires vertical privity of contract in warranty products liability claims, but it allows some exceptions. *Clemens v. DaimlerChrysler Corp.*[323] was a class action against an automotive manufacturer in which the plaintiff, among other claims, alleged for the class that the defendant had breached the implied warranty of merchantability by selling cars with defective head gaskets. Affirming dismissal of this warranty claim, the Ninth Circuit summarized California law on vertical privity in such actions, explaining that normally vertical privity is required, and that none of the exceptions—for express assertions or in cases involving foodstuffs, pesticides, pharmaceuticals, or employees—applied in the case.[324]

---

the ultimate consumers, and the manufacturer ought to be held to strict accountability to any consumer who buys the product in reliance on [them and later is injured as a result].

317 See, e.g., Anderson v. Olmsted Util. Equip., Inc., 573 N.E.2d 626 (Ohio 1991); Whitman v. Consolidated Aluminum Corp., 637 S.W.2d 405 (Mo. Ct. App. 1982); Kinlaw v. Long Mfg. N.C., Inc., 259 S.E.2d 552 (N.C. 1979); Reid v. Volkswagen of Am., Inc., 512 F.2d 1294 (6th Cir. 1975) (Mich. law); Hauter v. Zogarts, 534 P.2d 377 (Cal. 1975). *Contra* Oats v. Nissan Motor Corp., 879 P.2d 1095, 1102 (Idaho 1994).

318 See, e.g., Kinlaw v. Long Mfg. N.C., Inc., 259 S.E.2d 552 (N.C. 1979) (absence of privity of contract between purchasing farmer and manufacturer of tractor no bar to farmer's claim for economic losses due to tractor's continual breaking down, where farmer relied on statements in owner's manual). Many courts allow such claims brought by non-privity corporations. See, e.g., Larrison v. Moving Floors, Inc., 873 P.2d 1092 (Or. Ct. App. 1994); Fullerton Aircraft Sales & Rentals, Inc. v. Beech Aircraft Corp., 842 F.2d 717 (4th Cir. 1988) (Kan. law); Prairie Prod., Inc. v. Agchem Div.-Pennwalt Corp., 514 N.E.2d 1299 (Ind. Ct. App. 1987). Yet, some courts still require privity in pure economic loss cases even for express warranty claims. See, e.g., Carcone v. Gordon Heating & Air Conditioning Co., 623 N.Y.S.2d 679 (App. Div. 1995). Compare Vermont Plastics, Inc. v. Brine, Inc., 79 F.3d 272 (2d Cir. 1996) (Vt. law) (vertical privity unnecessary in express warranty cases involving personal injury, property damage, or Magnuson-Moss Federal Warranty Act claims by consumers).

319 See, e.g., Evraets v. Intermedics Intraocular, Inc., 34 Cal. Rptr. 2d 852 (Ct. App. 1994).

320 656 N.E.2d 170 (Ill. App. Ct. 1995), rev'd in part on other grounds, 675 N.E.2d 584 (Ill. 1996).

321 Id. at 177.

322 Id. at 180.

323 534 F.3d 1017 (9th Cir. 2008) (Cal. law).

324 See id. at 1023. See also Warnshuis v. Bausch Health U.S., 2020 WL 7239588, at *3 (E.D. Cal. 2020) ("In California, vertical privity is generally required for both express and implied warranty claims. . . . For express warranties, advertising materials or labeling on a package may be sufficient to excuse the privity requirement with respect to the manufacturer. For the implied warranty of merchantability, the vertical privity requirement is excused with respect to manufacturers of foodstuffs and 'medicines.' "). In Izzetov v.

In addition to the many state court decisions that have abolished the privity defense in various contexts involving warranty claims by purchasers against remote sellers, a few state legislatures have taken hold of the vertical privity requirement and expressly abolished it without regard to the type of injury suffered by the plaintiff.[325] Moreover, some courts and commentators have taken the position that the federal Magnuson-Moss Warranty Act,[326] in cases where a manufacturer issues an express warranty and the Act otherwise applies, effectively abolishes the vertical privity bar to consumers seeking to maintain implied warranty claims against remote manufacturers.[327] A close reading of the Act, however, suggests that courts reasoning to the contrary are correct in concluding that the Act leaves state privity rules intact.[328]

Finally, it should be noted that a state's abolition of the *vertical* privity defense, involving the issue of whether the actual purchaser in the stream of distribution may maintain a warranty action upstream against a remote seller (usually the manufacturer), does not affect the separate question of whether a non-purchaser who is injured—such as a family member, an employee, or a bystander—may have a valid warranty claim against the retail or other final seller.[329] This latter question involves the issue of *horizontal* privity, which now is addressed statutorily in most states under § 2–318 of the UCC.[330]

Horizontal Privity—Third-Party Beneficiaries Under § 2–318

Due to the doctrine of privity of contract, early cases denied warranty recovery to persons injured by products purchased by others.[331] Especially in cases of food purchases

Tesla Inc., 2020 WL 1677333 (N.D. Cal. 2020), a child's finger was trapped in a partially retracted "ice breaker" mechanism designed to assist the electric motor in opening a Tesla Model X front door. The plaintiffs' implied warranty claim failed under California law for lack of vertical privity with Tesla, since the car had been purchased by the plaintiffs' agent from a retailer in Prague, Czech Republic. Nor did the express warranty exception to California's vertical privity requirement apply to the plaintiffs' claims.

[325] See, e.g., Virginia's "anti-privity" statute, a non-uniform version of UCC § 2–318. Va. Code Ann. § 8.2–318. Similar legislation exists in Maine, Massachusetts, and New Hampshire. At least Virginia's statute does not apply to consequential damages, however, because UCC § 2–715(2)(a) suggests that such damages are available only to parties in privity of contract. See Pulte Home Corp. v. Parex, Inc., 579 S.E.2d 188 (Va. 2003).

At least a couple of states have held that UCC § 2–318 Alternative B by its terms eliminates vertical as well as horizontal privity. See Bishop v. Sales, 336 So.2d 1340 (Ala. 1976). See also Gasque v. Eagle Mach. Co., 243 S.E.2d 831 (S.C. 1978). New Hampshire's enactment of a provision similar to Alternative C "removed both horizontal and vertical privity as defenses to implied warranty claims." Dalton v. Stanley Solar & Stove, Inc., 629 A.2d 794, 797 (N.H. 1993).

[326] Enacted in 1975, the Act is codified at 15 U.S.C. §§ 2301 et seq. See § 4.9, below.

[327] See, e.g., Szajna v. General Motors Corp., 503 N.E.2d 760, 769 (Ill. 1986) ("[I]f a Magnuson-Moss written warranty (either 'full' or 'limited') is given . . ., the nonprivity 'consumer' should be permitted to maintain an action on an implied warranty against the 'warrantor.' ").

[328] See, e.g., Hyundai Motor Am., Inc. v. Goodin, 822 N.E.2d 947, 951 (Ind. 2005); Walsh v. Ford Motor Co., 588 F. Supp. 1513, 1524–27 (D.D.C. 1984): Because the Act defines "implied warranty" as "an implied warranty arising under State law," it must respect the state law's privity rules which help determine whether it arises under state law, quoting Feinstein v. Firestone Tire & Rubber Co., 535 F. Supp. 595, 606 n.13 (S.D.N.Y. 1982) ("[I]f state law requires vertical privity to enforce an implied warranty and there is none, then, like the yeastless souffle, the warranty does not 'arise.' ").

[329] The distinction between the two different forms of privity is considered in a number of decisions. See note 296, above.

[330] Choosing to omit § 2–318 from its adoption of Article 2, California continued to require privity of contract in warranty actions. Virginia and other states went the other direction, broadly rejecting the privity defense to warranty claims against manufacturers and other sellers. See note 325, above.

[331] See, e.g., Chysky v. Drake Bros. Co., 139 N.E. 576 (N.Y. 1923) (waitress bit into nail baked into cake purchased by her employer from defendant).

for other family members, some courts employed agency principles to avoid the privity problem and allow recovery.[332] In 1960, the New Jersey Supreme Court rendered its landmark opinion in *Henningsen v. Bloomfield Motors, Inc.*,[333] which held that the wife of a purchaser of a defective automobile, injured while driving the car, could recover against both the retailer and the manufacturer notwithstanding her lack of privity with the defendants. At about the same time, Article 2 addressed the issue of horizontal privity (and, perhaps, vertical privity to some extent) in § 2–318 of the Uniform Commercial Code, entitled "Third Party Beneficiaries of Warranties Express or Implied." By the mid-1960s, as the pro-consumer movement gained momentum across the nation, substantial differences appeared in the common-law development of the privity doctrine among the states.

Accordingly, in 1966, § 2–318 was amended to provide three alternative approaches to the privity issue, which allowed each state to choose the form that best conformed to its own law and public policy on a matter that had become a fast-moving and controversial issue—the reach of strict products liability law in warranty.[334]

The three alternatives of § 2–318 are as follows:

Alternative A

> A seller's warranty whether express or implied extends to any natural person who is in the family or household of his buyer or who is a guest in his home if it is reasonable to expect that such person may use, consume or be affected by the goods and who is injured in person by breach of the warranty. A seller may not exclude or limit the operation of this section.

Alternative B

> A seller's warranty whether express or implied extends to any natural person who may reasonably be expected to use, consume or be affected by the goods and who is injured in person by breach of the warranty. A seller may not exclude or limit the operation of this section.

---

[332] See, e.g., Greenberg v. Lorenz, 173 N.E.2d 773 (N.Y. 1961) (presumption that food purchase by father was made for all members of household).

[333] 161 A.2d 69 (N.J. 1960). See §§ 1.2, above, and notes 303–304, above.

[334] Commentary to § 2–318 explains the rationale for amending the section and offering it in alternative form:

> This section as drawn in 1950 was substantially in the form of the new Alternative B. The form shown as Alternative A was substituted in 1951, limiting beneficiaries to the family, household and guests of the buyer. Beyond this, according to Comment 3, the section was neutral and was not intended to enlarge or restrict "the developing case law." The section was criticized in California as "a step backward," and was omitted from the Code as enacted in California and in Utah. Nonuniform versions were enacted in ten states, and proposals for amendment have been made elsewhere. There appears to be no national consensus as to the scope of warranty protection which is proper, but the promulgation of alternatives may prevent further proliferation of separate variations in state after state. Alternative B is therefore promulgated in substantially the 1950 form, and Alternative C is drawn to reflect the trend of more recent decisions as indicated by Restatement of Torts 2d § 402A (Tentative Draft No. 10, 1965) extending the rule beyond personal injuries.
>
> [Conforming changes were made in paras. 2 and 3 of the Comment, infra, in 1966].

2 Hawkland UCC Series § 2–318 (C. Bjerre ed. 2022 update).

Alternative C

A seller's warranty whether express or implied extends to any person who may reasonably be expected to use, consume or be affected by the goods and who is injured by breach of the warranty. A seller may not exclude or limit the operation of this section with respect to injury to the person of an individual to whom the warranty extends.

Each alternative describes how far warranty protection extends beyond the purchaser in sales transactions.[335] As stated in comment 2, the broad purpose of § 2–318 "is to give certain beneficiaries the benefit of the same warranty which the buyer received in the contract of sale, thereby freeing any such beneficiaries from any technical rules as to 'privity.' "[336] Accordingly, "any beneficiary of a warranty may bring a direct action for breach of warranty against the seller whose warranty extends to him."[337] The requirement of vertical privity had begun to crumble in the pre-Code law, as discussed above, and § 2–318 was directed principally at the horizontal privity question[338] in implied warranty cases[339] as to what types of persons obtain the benefits of warranties received by the purchaser.[340]

Alternatives A and B conclude with the sentence, "A seller may not exclude or limit the operation of this section," to which Alternative C adds "with respect to injury to the person of an individual to whom the warranty extends." As discussed below in connection with disclaimers,[341] this language extends all warranties received by the purchaser to third-party beneficiaries under this section.[342]

Most American jurisdictions, including half the states, adopted Alternative A, or something similar.[343] Six and a half jurisdictions adopted Alternative B, or a close

[335] See generally Hyundai Motor Am., Inc. v. Goodin, 822 N.E.2d 947, 954–59 (Ind. 2005) (thoroughly discussing development of § 2–318 and describing each alternative); Camero, Two Too Many: Third Party Beneficiaries of Warranties Under the Uniform Commercial Code, 86 St. John's L. Rev. 1 (2012).

[336] See, e.g., Rynders v. E.I. Du Pont De Nemours & Co., 21 F.3d 835 (8th Cir. 1994) (S.D. law) (third-party beneficiaries who can be reasonably anticipated are placed in shoes of buyer for purposes of enforcing express and implied warranties made by seller).

[337] UCC § 2–318 cmt. 2.

[338] For authority that at least Alternative A of UCC § 2–318 is directed to the issue of horizontal privity alone, not to vertical privity, and that vertical privity therefore still may be required, see, e.g., Thomaston v. Fort Wayne Pools, Inc., 352 S.E.2d 794, 796 (Ga. Ct. App. 1987) ("Nothing contained in [UCC § 2–318, Alternative A], which extends the seller's warranties to family members and guests in the buyer's home who may reasonably be expected to use the product and who are injured thereby, eliminates the requirement that the buyer and the defendant be in privity.").

[339] Section 2–318 rests "primarily upon the merchant-seller's warranty under this Article that the goods sold are merchantable and fit for the ordinary purposes for which such goods are used." UCC § 2–318 cmt. 2. As discussed in connection with the *Rogers* case, note 313, above, the privity defense finds little support in modern cases involving express warranty claims based on public advertising, labels, and brochures.

[340] See, e.g., Flory v. Silvercrest Indus., 633 P.2d 383, 387 (Ariz. 1981) (Alternative A "eliminates the necessity of horizontal privity as to certain personally injured plaintiffs, but not the necessity of vertical privity, or privity in the chain of distribution").

[341] See § 4.7, below.

[342] This provision is well explained in comment 1 to § 2–318.

[343] Alternative A or a similar provision was adopted in Alaska, Arizona, Connecticut, District of Columbia, Florida, Georgia, Idaho, Illinois, Indiana, Kentucky, Michigan, Missouri, Montana, Nebraska, Nevada, New Jersey, New Mexico, North Carolina, Ohio, Oklahoma, Oregon, Pennsylvania, Tennessee, Washington, West Virginia, and Wisconsin.

approximation,[344] and fourteen and a half adopted Alternative C, or a close equivalent.[345] California omitted § 2–318 from its version of the UCC and requires privity in implied warranty cases as a matter of common law.[346] Texas also leaves the matter to its courts,[347] Louisiana never did adopt Article 2, and several states have nonuniform provisions on privity.[348] At least Virginia and Tennessee prohibit the privity defense to warranty claims.

Alternative A, which was the sole provision of § 2–318 from 1951 until 1966, is the most restrictive of the three alternatives. Most importantly, Alternative A limits recovery to a person who "is in the family or household of his buyer or who is a guest in his home," whereas Alternatives B and C broadly extend the benefits of a purchaser's warranties to a "person who may reasonably be expected to use, consume or be affected by the goods," an extension that appears to embrace all persons who foreseeably might be harmed by a warranty's breach.[349] Alternatives A and B are limited to "natural" or human persons whereas Alternative C, by extending warranty protection to "any person," includes "legal" persons such as business enterprises.[350] Similar to Alternatives B and C, even the narrow categories of persons designated in Alternative A may recover only "if it is reasonable to expect that such person may use, consume or be affected by the goods." Finally, Alternatives A and B both limit recovery to cases where a plaintiff

---

[344] Alternative B or a similar provision was adopted in Alabama, Delaware, Kansas, Maryland, New York, and Vermont. South Carolina adopted a hybrid lying between B and C.

[345] Alternative C or a similar provision was adopted in Arkansas, Colorado, Hawaii, Iowa, Maine, Massachusetts, Minnesota, New Hampshire, North Dakota, Rhode Island, South Dakota, Utah, Virgin Islands, and Wyoming. South Carolina adopted a hybrid lying between B and C.

[346] See, e.g., Evraets v. Intermedics Intraocular, Inc., 34 Cal. Rptr. 2d 852 (Ct. App. 1994) (injuries from intraocular lens surgically implanted in eye; absence of privity barred warranty claim); In re Air Crash Disaster at Sioux City Iowa, 760 F. Supp. 1283 (N.D. Ill. 1991). But California has an exception for warranty claims arising out of the sale of food and drugs, where privity is not required. See, e.g., Arnold v. Dow Chem. Co., 110 Cal. Rptr. 2d 722, 739 (Ct. App. 2001) (extending exception to pesticides).

[347] By statute. Tex. Bus. & Com. Code Ann. § 2.318. See, e.g., Hou-Tex, Inc. v. Landmark Graphics, 26 S.W.3d 103 (Tex. App. 2000); Garcia v. Texas Instruments, Inc., 610 S.W.2d 456 (Tex. 1980).

[348] Nonuniform provisions on privity and third-party beneficiary warranty claims were adopted in Mississippi, Texas, and Virginia. Maine, New Hampshire, and Rhode Island adopted provisions similar in effect to Alternative C. Several states made less significant modifications to the language in the various alternatives. See 1B Uniform Laws Annotated, Uniform Commercial Code (master ed. 2004) (classifying states under the three Alternatives). Classification errors in the ULA are corrected in the jurisdictional lists set forth above. The Virginia anti-privity act prohibited a privity defense in all warranty actions. Compare Tenn. Code Ann. § 29–34–104, which provides: "In all causes of action for personal injury or property damage brought on account of negligence, strict liability, or breach of warranty . . . privity shall not be a requirement to maintain said action." The Virginia anti-privity act more broadly provides: "Lack of privity between plaintiff and defendant shall be no defense in any action brought against the manufacturer or seller of goods to recover damages for breach of warranty, express or implied, or for negligence, although the plaintiff did not purchase the goods from the defendant, if the plaintiff was a person whom the manufacturer or seller might reasonably have expected to use, consume, or be affected by the goods . . . ." Va. Code Ann. § 8.2–318.

[349] This assumes that the Code's notion of reasonable expectations, reflecting the nature and reach of contract law, see Hadley v. Baxendale, 156 Eng. Rep. 145 (Ex. 1854), is a rough equivalent of tort law's concept of reasonable foreseeability. Thus, Alternative C covers employees injured by defective business equipment purchased by their employers. See, e.g., Mills v. Allegiance Healthcare Corp., 178 F. Supp. 2d 1, 7 (D. Mass. 2001) (seller should have foreseen and expected nurse employee of purchasing hospitals to use latex gloves); Lariviere v. Dayton Safety Ladder Co., 525 A.2d 892 (R.I. 1987).

Manufacturers of brand-name drugs cannot be expected to anticipate risks to consumers of generic copy-cat drugs who may be indirectly influenced by the brand-name manufacturer's labeling or advertising. See, e.g., Mosley v. Wyeth, Inc., 719 F. Supp. 2d 1340, 1351 (S.D. Ala. 2010) (declining to extend Alternative B to purchasers of generic brand drugs). On special problems concerning generic drugs, see ch. 18, below.

[350] See, e.g., TCF Bank & Sav., F.A. v. Marshall Truss Sys., Inc., 466 N.W.2d 49 (Minn. Ct. App. 1991), overruled on other grounds by Lloyd F. Smith Co. v. Den-Tal-Ez, Inc., 491 N.W.2d 11 (Minn. 1992) .

"is injured in person," a limitation that should preclude claims solely for property damages[351] or economic loss,[352] at least where privity has not otherwise been abolished.

Alternative A Categories

In General. Deciding what types of plaintiffs fall into a purchaser's "family," "household," or "guest[s] in his home," the categories specified in Alternative A, has generated considerable litigation. With some exceptions, courts have interpreted such categories in a commonsense manner. So, a mother who does not live with her married daughter may not be in her daughter's "family";[353] a church member, trapped inside the church's walk-in freezer, is not a member of the church's "family," nor in its "household," nor a guest in its "home";[354] a customer injured by a patio chair on display in a store is not in the store's "family," nor in its "household," nor a "guest" in its home;[355] passengers in automobiles,[356] boats,[357] and airplanes[358] are not "guests" in the vehicle buyer's "home;" parents of children injured when an uncrashworthy school bus crashed are not in the "family" of the purchasing school board;[359] a patron in a shop is not a "guest in the home";[360] and a maid, whose finger was amputated by her employer's garage door, "simply does not fall into the category of persons benefitting from" Alternative A.[361]

Other persons excluded from warranty recovery under Alternative A include bystanders, such as a school girl struck in the eye by a rock thrown by a rotary lawnmower through an open classroom window;[362] a driver killed when his car collided with a defective truck stalled on a freeway;[363] business invitees who are injured on escalators in department stores and shopping malls;[364] a tenant injured by a defective table purchased by the landlord;[365] and patients injured by defective drugs or medical products provided by their doctors or hospitals—one who suffered side effects from a

---

[351] See, e.g., Wellcraft Marine v. Zarzour, 577 So.2d 414 (Ala. 1990) (no implied warranty claim against manufacturer for property damage without privity of contract).

[352] See, e.g., Hyundai Motor Am., Inc. v. Goodin, 822 N.E.2d 947, 955 (Ind. 2005) (allowing recovery for economic loss notwithstanding Alternative A). See generally Lawrence's Anderson on the UCC § 2–318:24.

[353] See Lane v. Barringer, 407 N.E.2d 1173 (Ind. Ct. App. 1980).

[354] Crews v. W.A. Brown & Son, Inc., 416 S.E.2d 924 (N.C. Ct. App. 1992).

[355] Denton v. Sam Blount, Inc., 669 So.2d 951 (Ala. Civ. App. 1995) (N.C. law).

[356] Thomas v. Ford Motor Co., 2006 WL 1423501, at *1 (N.D. Ohio 2006); Thompson v. Reedman, 199 F. Supp. 120, 121 (E.D. Pa. 1961) ("It is too much of a leap, it seems, to classify a guest passenger in an automobile as a guest in the *home*"; warranty nevertheless ran to plaintiff under "the developing case law" of Pennsylvania).

[357] Smith v. Mitlof, 198 F. Supp. 2d 492, 506–07 (S.D.N.Y. 2002) (Conn. law); Curlee v. Mock Enters., Inc., 327 S.E.2d 736 (Ga. Ct. App. 1985) (even though boat owner and passenger had made preparations in owner's home to go to boat where passenger was injured by defective gun).

[358] Driver v. Burlington Aviation, Inc., 430 S.E.2d 476 (N.C. Ct. App. 1993) (passengers in private plane, manual of which failed to alert pilot to risk of carburetor icing); Alexander v. Beech Aircraft Corp., 952 F.2d 1215 (10th Cir. 1991) (Ind. law).

[359] Jones by & through Jones v. IC Bus, LLC, 626 S.W.3d 661, 684–85 (Ky. Ct. App. 2020).

[360] Miller v. Sears, Roebuck & Co., 500 N.E.2d 557 (Ill. App. Ct. 1986), overruled in part by Whitaker v. Lian Feng Mach. Co., 509 N.E.2d 591 (Ill. App. Ct. 1987) .

[361] Verddier v. Neal Blun Co., 196 S.E.2d 469, 470 (Ga. Ct. App. 1973).

[362] Stovall & Co. v. Tate, 184 S.E.2d 834 (Ga. Ct. App. 1971).

[363] General Motors Corp. v. Davis, 233 S.E.2d 825 (Ga. Ct. App. 1977).

[364] See, e.g., Hayes v. Otis Elevator Co., 946 F.2d 1272, 1276 n.5 (7th Cir. 1991) (Ill. law) (woman not warned of necessity for egress fell at intermediate stop); Westinghouse Corp. v. Ruiz, 537 So.2d 596 (Fla. Dist. Ct. App. 1988) (4-year-old child caught hand in escalator).

[365] Barry v. Ivarson Inc., 249 So.2d 44 (Fla. Dist. Ct. App. 1971).

drug sample provided by her doctor,[366] another who contracted polio from a vaccine,[367] and another who had a defective surgical nail implanted in his femur.[368]

Yet, other courts have stretched the interpretation of the "family," "household," and "guest in his home" categories to include certain persons who are not literally within those designations. For example, a guest *outside* the home may be considered a guest "*in* the home";[369] and a niece not living in the household nevertheless may be in the buyer's "family,"[370] as may the nephew of the purchaser of a vaporizer-humidifier that shoots boiling water on the nephew.[371] In addition, courts that have not felt restricted by the specifically designated categories have extended coverage under Alternative A to various types of other persons.[372]

Employees. Courts are split on whether an employee injured by a defective product purchased by his or her employer may maintain a warranty claim under Alternative A against the supplier of the defective product.[373] Probably most courts preclude such claims, ruling that employees fit within none of the specifically designated categories, namely, a purchaser's "family," "household," and "guest[s] in [the] home."[374] Other courts, as in *Whitaker v. Lian Feng Machine Co.*,[375] reason that the categories of included beneficiaries are merely statutory *minima* that do not prevent a court from allowing other persons lacking privity to take the benefit of a seller's warranties to its buyers.[376] Such courts rely upon comment 3 to § 2–318, which provides in part:

> The first alternative [Alternative A] expressly includes as beneficiaries within its provisions the family, household, and guests of the purchaser. Beyond this, the section in this form is neutral and is not intended to enlarge

---

[366] Bryant v. Hoffmann-La Roche, Inc., 585 S.E.2d 723 (Ga. Ct. App. 2003) (patient who did not purchase drug from manufacturer but obtained sample from doctor could not sue under Alternative A).

[367] Snawder v. Cohen, 749 F. Supp. 1473 (W.D. Ky. 1990).

[368] Munn v. Pfizer Hosp. Prods. Grp., Inc., 750 F. Supp. 244 (W.D. Ky. 1990). By contrast, a patient who receives a defective implant in an Alternative C state has no such problem. See, e.g., Larsen v. Pacesetter Sys., Inc., 837 P.2d 1273 (Haw. 1992) (pacemaker), amended in part on reconsideration, 843 P.2d 144 (Haw. 1992).

[369] Handrigan v. Apex Warwick, Inc., 275 A.2d 262, 266 (R.I. 1971) (plaintiff, friend of purchaser of ladder, fell while helping paint friend's house).

[370] See Wolfe v. Ford Motor Co., 376 N.E.2d 143, 149 (Mass. App. Ct. 1978) (niece, not in household, was within buyer's family; "family" interpreted broadly to include persons of common progenitor to help distinguish word from "household"). Accord Chastain v. Fuqua Indus., 275 S.E.2d 679 (Ga. Ct. App. 1980).

[371] Miller v. Preitz, 221 A.2d 320 (Pa. 1966), overruled on other grounds by Kassab v. Central Soya, 246 A.2d 848 (Pa. 1968) .

[372] See, e.g., Reed v. City of Chi., 263 F. Supp. 2d 1123 (N.D. Ill. 2003) (prison inmate, known to be suicidal, who hanged himself with paper isolation gown that failed to tear away, was proper beneficiary of seller's warranty).

[373] Employees of course may maintain such warranty claims in states that have adopted the broader Alternatives B and C. See, e.g., Atkinson v. Ormont Mach. Co., 423 N.Y.S.2d 577 (Sup. Ct. Spec. Term 1979).

[374] Halderman v. Sanderson Forklifts Co., 818 S.W.2d 270, 273 (Ky. Ct. App. 1991). See, e.g., Hester v. Purex Corp., 534 P.2d 1306, 1308 (Okla. 1975).

[375] 509 N.E.2d 591 (Ill. App. Ct. 1987) (employee's breach of warranties claims were not barred by lack of privity; legislature "left it for the courts to decide . . . whether warranty coverage should [extend beyond Alternative A] to any other non-purchasing users of a product").

[376] See, e.g., Salvador v. Atlantic Steel Boiler Co., 319 A.2d 903 (Pa. 1974). McNally v. Nicholson Mfg. Co., 313 A.2d 913, 920 (Me. 1973), held that employees are in the "business family" of their employers for purposes of Alternative A. With uncommon clarity of expression, *McNally* explained why employees are proper beneficiaries of Code warranties although they do not fall in any of the categories of Alternative A: "The literal specifications of Section 2–318 are the guideposts of a fundamental course of policy flow adaptable to encompass other relationships which, policy-wise, may be fairly regarded as functionally equivalent to those textually designated." Webber, J., sat at argument but retired before the decision was rendered.

or restrict the developing case law on whether the seller's warranties, given to his buyer who resells, extend to other persons in the distributive chain.

Emphasizing the beginning of the second sentence, "Beyond this, the section in this form is neutral and is not intended to enlarge or restrict the developing case law . . .,"[377] the *Whitaker* court reasoned that the legislature thereby left the judiciary free to determine whether to expand the class of beneficiaries specifically designated. The problem with this interpretation is that it ignores the remainder of the second sentence, which modifies the type of developing case law that remains permissible: ". . . on whether the seller's warranties, given to the buyer who resells, extend to other persons in the distributive chain."[378] This second half of the sentence may be paraphrased as: "on whether *vertical* privity should or should not remain a requirement."

Hence, this sentence in comment 3 most probably means that a legislature adopting Alternative A authorizes courts to continue to erode the doctrine of *vertical* privity,[379] but that the legislature itself has defined (with exclusive particularity) the only categories of third-party beneficiaries for whom the *horizontal* privity requirement is relaxed.[380] The *Whitaker* court also relied on the third sentence of comment 3, which begins, "The second alternative [Alternative B] is designed for states where the case law has already developed further. . . ."[381] However, this sentence continues, ". . . and for those that desire to expand the class of beneficiaries." This latter phrase suggests that state legislatures which did *not* wish to expand the beneficiary categories would opt for Alternative A, where the categories are specifically and exclusively set forth.[382]

While some small interpretative room may reside in comment 3 for a court to reason that the legislature left the judiciary power to expand the categories of non-privity plaintiffs beyond those listed in Alternative A, such an interpretation is quite strained.[383] More fundamentally, in construing a state statute enacted in 1961 (as it was in Illinois), it might be better to ignore an "Official Comment" rewritten by national law revision entities[384] five years later. To the extent that the actual intent of state legislators is relevant, one might reasonably conclude that those who actually considered this particular section before voting on enactment probably interpreted the language of Alternative A as it reads, which appears to describe the *only* categories of non-privity plaintiffs allowed to take the benefits of a buyer's warranties.

---

[377] *Whitaker*, 509 N.E.2d at 594.

[378] Id.

[379] See, e.g., Hyundai Motor Am., Inc. v. Goodin, 822 N.E.2d 947, 954–56 (Ind. 2005).

[380] This interpretation reflects an Illinois Supreme Court decision rendered several months prior to *Whitaker*, Szajna v. General Motors Corp., 503 N.E.2d 760 (Ill. 1986), in which the court retained the *vertical* privity requirement in economic loss cases. Stating that "in Illinois section 2–318 . . . is concerned only with horizontal privity," the court observed that comment 3 "professes neutrality insofar as vertical privity and developing case law in that area are concerned." Id. at 766.

[381] *Whitaker*, 509 N.E.2d at 594.

[382] This was the reasoning of the court in Miller v. Sears, Roebuck & Co., 500 N.E.2d 557 (Ill. App. Ct. 1986), overruled by Whitaker v. Lian Feng Mach. Co., 509 N.E.2d 591 (Ill. App. Ct. 1987), in concluding that Alternative A did not extend protection to business customers of a purchaser.

[383] Illinois courts have been reluctant to expand *Whitaker*, ruling that non-employee truck drivers and other service providers of purchasers are too remote to fall inside Alternative A. See, e.g., Frank v. Edward Hines Lumber Co., 761 N.E.2d 1257 (Ill. App. Ct. 2001); Lukwinski v. Stone Container Corp., 726 N.E.2d 665 (Ill. App. Ct. 2000).

[384] The American Law Institute and the National Conference of Commissioners on Uniform State Laws.

Damage Claims Available

Considerable litigation surrounds the issue of whether non-privity plaintiffs should be permitted to recover damages for particular types of harm—personal injury, property damage, direct economic loss (such as loss of bargain, where a product's defects diminish its value, and the cost of repair or replacement), or consequential economic loss (such as lost profits, goodwill, and business reputation).[385] As previously discussed, Alternative A extends the buyer's warranty claims only to persons in the designated categories who are "injured in person." A spouse who loses the consortium of his or her spouse should probably be considered "injured in person."[386] Yet, courts may be more reluctant to allow non-privity warranty claims for ordinary emotional distress, independent of an underlying physical injury.[387] Even more clearly, neither property damage[388] nor pure economic loss[389] is an injury to the plaintiff's "person," and so neither should be recoverable to non-privity plaintiffs under Alternative A or Alternative B. By contrast, there are no restrictions on types of compensatory damages recoverable to non-privity plaintiffs under Alternative C.[390]

At the opposite end of the damages spectrum from consumers suffering personal injuries lie commercial enterprises suffering consequential economic loss. The privity-of-contract restriction, in terms of logic and equity, is most at home in this context. Especially with respect to consequential damages, the arguments are cogent for precluding plaintiff firms in most such cases from exploiting other parties' bargains to recover such damages from firms with whom they had no contractual relations.[391] By way of example, warranty claims against manufacturers have been denied for lack of vertical privity in the case of a swimming pool contractor who purchased allegedly defective paint from a third-party paint supplier and sought recovery against the supplier for the cost of repainting a customer's pool;[392] a roofing contractor who purchased defective roofing materials from an intermediary seller;[393] a shopkeeper who purchased atrium doors through a retailer but sought to recover damages for

---

385 See White and Summers, UCC ch. 12.

386 See Phipps v. General Motors Corp., 363 A.2d 955 (Md. 1976) (recovery allowed under Alternative A).

387 See Carcone v. Gordon Heating & Air Conditioning Co., 623 N.Y.S.2d 679, 680 (App. Div. 1995) ("extreme emotional and mental trauma" from breakdown or nonperformance of product).

388 See, e.g., Wellcraft Marine v. Zarzour, 577 So.2d 414 (Ala. 1990) (no implied warranty claim against manufacturer for property damage without privity of contract).

389 See, e.g., Morris v. Osmose Wood Preserving, 667 A.2d 624 (Md. 1995); Rhodes v. General Motors Corp., 621 So.2d 945 (Ala. 1993). *Contra* Hyundai Motor Am., Inc. v. Goodin, 822 N.E.2d 947, 954–59 (Ind. 2005) (abolishing vertical privity under Alternative A in consumer actions for economic loss).

390 See Dalton v. Stanley Solar & Stove, Inc., 629 A.2d 794 (N.H. 1993), where the court noted that the New Hampshire legislature had removed both horizontal and vertical privity as defenses to implied warranty claims by its enactment of a version of § 2–318 that resembles Alternative C. See also In re Conagra Peanut Butter Prods. Liab. Litig., 251 F.R.D. 689, 696–97 (N.D. Ga. 2008) ("Alternative C of § 2–318 eliminates the need for privity of contract in breach of warranty actions whenever the claim is simply for 'injury.' "); Jacobs v. Yamaha Motor Corp. U.S.A., 649 N.E.2d 758 (Mass. 1995) (manufacturer liable to buyer of defective motorcycle that could not be repaired; statutory provision similar to Alternative C).

391 For a cogent summary of arguments against non-privity claims for such damages between business enterprises, see White and Summers, UCC § 12–6, at 551–52. See generally Speidel, Products Liability, Economic Loss and the UCC, 40 Tenn. L. Rev. 309 (1973). For one court's criticism of the effort to distinguish between direct and consequential economic loss for purposes of privity, see Szajna v. General Motors Corp., 503 N.E.2d 760, 767 (Ill. 1986).

392 McCrary v. Kelly Tech. Coatings, Inc., 1985 WL 75663, at *4 (Tenn. Ct. App. 1985) .

393 GAF Corp. v. Zack Co., 445 So.2d 350 (Fla. Dist. Ct. App. 1984).

deterioration of the doors and water damage to flooring from the manufacturer;[394] a cattle feeder who purchased an ineffective growth hormone from veterinarians instead of from the manufacturer;[395] and a subcontractor, required to replace plumbing fittings installed in a number of new homes, who purchased the fittings from intermediate suppliers rather than from the manufacturers.[396]

Yet, not all courts agree. In *Spring Motors Distributors, Inc. v. Ford Motor Co.*,[397] the New Jersey Supreme Court held that a commercial buyer seeking economic loss sustained from the purchase of defective goods may recover for breach of warranty from the remote seller as well as from the immediate seller. Other courts, sometimes under the authority of Alternative C, have similarly permitted commercial buyers to bring warranty claims against remote sellers where the damage is purely economic. For example, where a subcontractor manufactured and sold wooden trusses to a general contractor to support a canopy over a drive-through window at a savings and loan, and the canopy collapsed, the successor bank was permitted to maintain a breach of warranty claim for the costs of redesign and repair of the facility against the subcontractor, notwithstanding the absence of privity between the bank and the subcontractor.[398] Similarly, courts have allowed warranty claims against remote manufacturers for economic losses to a purchaser of a defective paving machine[399] and to a buyer of numerical controls.[400] Even under Alternative C, however, some courts refuse to allow recovery for economic loss, because they interpret "injury" in that Alternative as inconsistent with economic loss[401] or where a plaintiff did not use or consume the product so that its economic losses are simply too remote.[402]

In jurisdictions where the out-of-privity buyer suffering economic loss might be denied warranty recovery, resourceful parties may be able to prevail by showing that the manufacturer was aware of the particular purpose to be made of the product yet proceeded nevertheless to provide a product unsuited to that use. It has been held, therefore, that when a remote manufacturer knows "the identity, purpose, and requirements of a dealer's customer and manufactured or delivered the goods specifically to meet those requirements," recovery of economic losses should be permitted even absent privity.[403]

---

[394] Gregory v. Atrium Door & Window Co., 415 S.E.2d 574 (N.C. Ct. App. 1992).

[395] Tomka v. Hoechst Celanese Corp., 528 N.W.2d 103 (Iowa 1995) (consequential economic loss).

[396] Beard Plumbing & Heating, Inc. v. Thompson Plastics, Inc., 491 S.E.2d 731 (Va. 1997).

[397] 489 A.2d 660, 677 (N.J. 1985).

[398] TCF Bank & Sav., F.A. v. Marshall Truss Sys., Inc., 466 N.W.2d 49 (Minn. Ct. App. 1991) (Alternative C).

[399] Moscatiello v. Pittsburgh Contractors Equip. Co., 595 A.2d 1198 (Pa. Super. Ct. 1991).

[400] Patty Precision Prods. Co. v. Brown & Sharpe Mfg. Co., 846 F.2d 1247, 1254 (10th Cir. 1988) (Okla. law) (Oklahoma has "rejected the majority view that a 'vertical' non-privity plaintiff . . . cannot maintain an action for breach of implied warranty").

[401] Nebraska Innkeepers, Inc. v. Pittsburgh-Des Moines Corp., 345 N.W.2d 124, 129 (Iowa 1984) (Alternative C's reference to a person "injured" suggests physical harm to plaintiff or his property, not economic loss).

[402] See Coverstar, Inc. v. Cooley, Inc., 2006 WL 1579620 (D. Utah 2006); Minnesota Mining & Mfg. Co. v. Nishika Ltd., 565 N.W.2d 16 (Minn. 1997).

[403] Crest Container Corp. v. R.H. Bishop, Co., 445 N.E.2d 19, 25 (Ill. App. Ct. 1982).

In products liability cases, recovery of damages for pure economic loss is a complicated issue that is treated elsewhere extensively.[404] Commercial disputes involving only economic loss, which often involve complex issues of commercial law, are covered in treatises that address in detail the interrelationships between privity of contract, various types of economic loss, and related problems from a specialized, commercial-law perspective.[405]

Punitive damages, touched on very briefly in § 5.3, are explicitly unavailable for breach of warranty under UCC Article 2.[406]

§ 4.6 NOTICE OF BREACH

After purchase and acceptance of a product, a buyer who is injured by breach of warranty—a defect in the goods or the falsity of a representation—must promptly notify the seller of the breach. Prompt notification of breach has long been an established requirement for breach of warranty claims in sales law, and such a requirement was included in the Uniform Sales Act.[407] Today, notice is required by Uniform Commercial Code § 2–607(3), which provides:

> Where a tender has been accepted
>
> (a) the buyer must within a reasonable time after he discovers or should have discovered any breach notify the seller of breach or be barred from any remedy . . . .[408]

Because the consequence of a failure to comply with the notice requirement is severe—the buyer is barred from any recovery for breach of warranty[409]—and because many courts hold that the provision of timely notice must be pleaded as an element of or condition precedent to maintaining a warranty claim,[410] a lawyer representing a products liability claimant should focus closely on this requirement at the outset of

---

404 See Frumer, Friedman, and Sklaren, Products Liability § 13.07; Am. Law Prod. Liab. 3d §§ 60:45–60:47, 60:71–:72.

405 See, e.g., J. Feinman, Economic Negligence ch. 13 (1995); White and Summers, UCC §§ 12–5 (privity and direct economic loss), 12–6 (privity and consequential economic loss); 1 Crockett, Product Warranties §§ 10:10–:21.

406 UCC § 1–106(1) provides: "[N]either consequential or special nor penal damages may be had except as specifically provided in this Act or by any other rule of law."

407 Uniform Sales Act § 49 provided: "[I]f . . . the buyer fail[s] to give notice to the seller of the breach of any promise or warranty within a reasonable time after the buyer knows, or ought to know of such breach, the seller shall not be liable therefor." See also USA § 69(3) (rescission conditioned on notice within reasonable time).

408 See Reitz, Against Notice: A Proposal to Restrict the Notice of Claims Rule in U.C.C. § 2–607(3)(a), 73 Cornell L. Rev. 534 (1988).

409 Amended UCC § 2–607(3)(a) would have relaxed this provision, barring a buyer's claim only if and to the extent that the seller is prejudiced by the buyer's failure to give timely notice. For the fate of the amendments, see § 4.1, at notes 17 and 18, above.

410 See, e.g., Hunter v. Shanghai Huangzhou Elec. Appliance Mfg. Co., 505 F. Supp. 3d 137, 158–60 (N.D.N.Y. 2020) (warranty claim failed where notice not pleaded); Langner v. Bos. Sci. Corp., 492 F. Supp. 3d 925, 936 (D. Neb. 2020) (same); Stanley v. Central Garden & Pet Corp., 891 F. Supp. 2d 757, 772 (D. Md. 2012) (breach of implied warranty; "a lawsuit cannot constitute notice of a breach under §§ 2–607, 2–608"); Powers v. Lycoming Engines, 272 F.R.D. 414, 428–29 (E.D. Pa. 2011) (differing notice and other warranty rules in various states rendered class action unmanageable); Hays v. General Elec. Co., 151 F. Supp. 2d 1001, 1010 (N.D. Ill. 2001) (notice is not affirmative defense but an element on which plaintiff bears burden of proof). As discussed below, however, this rule of pleading does not apply in many jurisdictions that allow a personal injury victim to satisfy the notice requirement by filing a timely complaint.

representation. For example, in *Buford v. Toys R' Us, Inc.*,[411] a boy was seriously injured when a defective weld caused the steer tube on his bicycle to separate from the front fork, throwing him to the pavement. His parents sued the retailer of the defective bicycle for strict liability in tort, negligence, and breach of the implied warranty of merchantability. The trial court granted summary judgment to the retailer on all three claims, which was affirmed on appeal. The appellate court ruled that there was no claim for strict liability in tort because the state products liability statute provides that such liability applies only to manufacturers, not retailers. Because the defective weld had been painted over during the course of manufacture, the retailer could not have been negligent in failing to discover it. As for the implied warranty of merchantability, which surely was breached by the retailer's sale of a dangerously defective bike, the court ruled that the parents' failure to notify the seller of the claim until it filed a complaint two years after the accident was "unreasonable" as a matter of law, which barred the one claim against the retailer that surely would have succeeded on the merits.

A general warranty-law requirement that a buyer notify the seller promptly that a product defect (or false assertion) caused an injury promotes several goals.[412] First, prompt notice permits the seller to act quickly to try to correct or "cure" the problem to minimize resulting losses for the buyer and damages for the seller.[413] Moreover, if a product contains a design or warning problem, or if an express warranty is dangerously misleading, early notification of the problem permits the seller to remedy the danger promptly and thus minimize the risk of loss to others. Further, prompt notice of defect and injury allows a seller to gather information about the product defect or representational problem, which should promote fairness, efficiency, and justice by increasing the probability of informed settlement or principled litigation based on facts that are true and complete.[414] Finally, requiring prompt notice promotes the expeditious resolution of controversies and so serves the several goals of finality, much like statutes of limitations.[415]

Although certain policies behind the notice requirement are applicable to consumers and bystanders physically injured in product accidents, others are not, and the notice requirement can become a "booby trap for the unwary," as colorfully expressed by Dean Prosser.[416] Indeed, the notice requirement was one of the "big three" warranty defenses[417] that long frustrated products liability claimants and led in the 1960s to the

[411] 458 S.E.2d 373 (Ga. Ct. App. 1995).

[412] See, e.g., Langner v. Bos. Sci. Corp., 492 F. Supp. 3d 925, 935 (D. Neb. 2020) (requirement to plead notice "serves three purposes: (1) to provide the seller with an opportunity to cure the breach of warranty issue, (2) to aid the seller in preparation for negotiation and litigation, and (3) to protect against stale claims"); Richards v. Johnson & Johnson, Inc., 2018 WL 6573332, at *1 (N.D.N.Y. 2018) ("The policies underlying the notice requirement include: (1) facilitating settlement through negotiation; (2) giving the seller access to the facts to investigate the claim; (3) allowing the seller to avoid future defects; and (4) protecting the seller from stale claims.").

[413] See, e.g., Brame v. General Motors LLC, 535 F. Supp. 3d 832, 839 (E.D. Wis. 2021) (requiring pre-suit notice "makes sense, as one of the purposes of the notice requirement is to enable the seller to take corrective action and avoid litigation"). The notice requirement "can be described as offering 'the seller an opportunity to cure.'" Cauley v. Sabic Innovative Plastics, U.S., L.L.C., 2012 WL 192303, at *5 (S.D. Miss. 2012).

[414] Sufficient notice "opens the way for normal settlement through negotiation." UCC § 2–607 cmt. 4.

[415] See § 14.6, below.

[416] See Keeton, Dobbs, Keeton, and Owen, Prosser and Keeton on the Law of Torts § 97, at 691.

[417] The other two big warranty defenses were the requirement of privity of contract, discussed in § 4.5, above, and contractual disclaimers, discussed in § 4.7, below.

adoption of the doctrine of strict products liability in tort.[418] In fact, two states have amended their versions of the UCC to ban the notice requirement in personal injury cases.[419] While the notice doctrine may appear strangely out of place to a personal injury lawyer who usually fishes in the waters of tort law,[420] a number of its policies designed to promote a sound functioning of commerce may also have some relevance, if diminished, to warranty claims brought by victims of product accidents.[421]

"Reasonable" Time

In recognition of a proper but reduced role for the notice requirement in personal injury products liability litigation, the comments to UCC § 2–607 state that the notification rule *does* apply to victims of product accidents but that the allowable "reasonable" time for notification is *stretched* for consumers[422] and bystanders[423] beyond that which normally would apply to merchant buyers. By so extending the notice time period for such persons, § 2–607 eases the burden for persons whose injuries may limit for some time their ability to focus on the cause of their accidents and legal responsibility therefor.

Assessing how long a delay is reasonable in a particular case depends on the balance of reasons for the delay and the equities in allowing the plaintiff to pursue a possibly meritorious claim, on the one hand, against the reasons for shielding the defendant (and the court) from having to litigate a claim on faded evidence that may be insufficient to permit principled adjudication, on the other. "Reasonableness" in this context rests peculiarly on the particular facts and equities of each case, and so it normally is a question of fact for the jury to resolve.[424] As with any question of fact, however, a court

---

[418] See, e.g., Henningsen v. Bloomfield Motors, Inc., 161 A.2d 69 (N.J. 1960) (court bypassed privity and disclaimer defenses to warranty claims); Greenman v. Yuba Power Prods., Inc., 377 P.2d 897 (Cal. 1963) (court bypassed notice defense to warranty claims by adopting doctrine of strict liability in tort). See §§ 5.2 and 5.3, below.

[419] Maine's version of § 2–607(7) provides that § 2–607(3)(a) "shall not apply where the remedy is for personal injury resulting from any breach." Me. Rev. Stat. Ann. tit. 11, § 2–607(7). South Carolina's addition to § 2–607(3)(a) provides: "however, no notice of injury to the person in the case of consumer goods shall be required." S.C. Code Ann. § 36–2–607(3)(a).

[420] But many states impose similar, and often very short, notice obligations on accident victims contemplating suits against local and state governments. See Prosser and Keeton on Torts § 131, at 1045–46 (discussing notice-of-claim statutes).

[421] See comments 4 and 5 to § 2–607, below.

[422] Comment 4 provides in part:

> The time of notification is to be determined by applying commercial standards to a merchant buyer. "A reasonable time" for notification from a retail consumer is to be judged by different standards so that in his case it will be extended, for the rule of requiring notification is designed to defeat commercial bad faith, not to deprive a good faith consumer of his remedy.

[423] Comment 5 provides:

> Under this Article various beneficiaries are given rights for injuries sustained by them because of the seller's breach of warranty. Such a beneficiary does not fall within the reason of the present section in regard to discovery of defects and the giving of notice within a reasonable time after acceptance, since he has nothing to do with acceptance. However, the reason of this section does extend to requiring the beneficiary to notify the seller that an injury has occurred. What is said above, with regard to the extended time for reasonable notification from the lay consumer after the injury is also applicable here; but even a beneficiary can be properly held to the use of good faith in notifying, once he has had time to become aware of the legal situation.

[424] See, e.g., Nathan v. Whirlpool Corporation, 492 F. Supp. 3d 747, 757 (S.D. Ohio 2020) (question for jury whether 16 and 10 months were unreasonable delays in plaintiffs' notice; "average consumer lacks experience estimating [whether] horsepower . . . . in the Blender pitchers [matches] horsepower advertised on the box"); Precourt v. Fairbank Reconstruction Corp., 856 F. Supp. 2d 327, 341 (D.N.H. 2012) (sufficiency of

may rule on the reasonableness of a delay in notice when the time period was clearly adequate or clearly inadequate, such that the jury can properly come to only one conclusion.[425]

Most courts are appropriately lenient in deciding what is a "reasonable" time for plaintiffs physically injured by defective products to give notice.[426] Reflecting the balance of fairness between a plaintiff and defendant discussed above, courts ruling that a plaintiff's delay in notice was reasonable often point to the lack of prejudice to the defendant from the delay.[427] Courts have allowed warranty claims for personal injuries when the delay in notice (after an accident or discovery of harm) amounted to two days,[428] four months,[429] ten months;[430] and two,[431] three,[432] and nearly four years.[433]

However, in a number of cases, courts have barred warranty claims of product accident victims for delays of one to twenty-eight years.[434] As illustrated below, the usual

---

notice is a jury question; letter sent to defendant roughly nine months after injury involving contaminated ground beef was not within a reasonable time).

See also Bryant v. Adams, 448 S.E.2d 832, 844 (N.C. Ct. App. 1994) (reasonableness of 3-year delay from date 14-year-old boy fell from trampoline and was rendered quadriplegic was jury issue:

> Whether a prima facie showing that the notice was given "within a reasonable time" has been made can be determined only by examining the particular facts and circumstances of each case and the policies behind the notice requirement. If plaintiff's evidence shows that the policies behind the requirement have not been frustrated and, instead, have been fulfilled, the evidence is sufficient to withstand a directed verdict motion.

[425] See, e.g., Bassaw v. United Indus. Corp., 482 F. Supp. 3d 80, 87 (S.D.N.Y. 2020) (3 years is "plainly unreasonable as a matter of law"); Heath v. Tristar Prods., Inc., 2019 WL 4738004, at *8 (D. Nev. 2019) (plaintiff's letter to pressure cooker manufacturer three months after her injury and six months before filing satisfied notice requirement as a matter of law); Paper Mfrs. Co. v. Rescuers, Inc., 60 F. Supp. 2d 869, 882 (N.D. Ind. 1999) (plaintiff sent manufacturer letter describing problems with ink about four months after ink contaminated plaintiff's product; time reasonable as matter of law); Hebron v. American Isuzu Motors, Inc., 60 F.3d 1095 (4th Cir. 1995) (Va. law) (2-year delay unreasonable as a matter of law where plaintiff failed to preserve evidence); Lariviere v. Dayton Safety Ladder Co., 525 A.2d 892 (R.I. 1987) (letter plaintiff's attorney sent to manufacturer, one month after worker fell from stepladder, was timely).

[426] See, e.g., Richards v. Johnson & Johnson, Inc., 2018 WL 6573332, at *4 (N.D.N.Y. 2018) (because sufficiency of notice is normally a jury issue, and because of authority declining to apply the notice requirement in personal injury actions, court refused to dismiss express warranty claim for lack of presuit notice before trial); Ho v. Michelin N. Am., Inc., 2011 WL 3241466, at *16–17 (D. Kan. 2011) (discussing cases where courts relieved injured persons from pre-suit notice requirement; consumers, particularly those who suffer personal injuries, need not provide pre-suit notice of breach; dictum). Noting comment 4 to § 2–607, White & Summers, UCC § 12–10, at 565 observe: "Not only the drafters but also the commentators and the courts seem to disfavor the lack of notice defense when invoked against an injured consumer."

[427] See, e.g., Wal-Mart Stores, Inc. v. Wheeler, 586 S.E.2d 83, 85 (Ga. Ct. App. 2003); Chapman v. Bernard's, Inc., 167 F. Supp. 2d 406, 415–16 (D. Mass. 2001); Maldonado v. Creative Woodworking Concepts, Inc., 694 N.E.2d 1021 (Ill. App. Ct. 1998); Maybank v. S. S. Kresge Co., 273 S.E.2d 681 (N.C. 1981).

[428] Bailey v. Jordan Marsh Co., 6 Mass. App. Dec. 17 (1953) (after collapse of ladder).

[429] Bonker v. Ingersoll Prods. Corp., 132 F. Supp. 5 (D. Mass. 1955) (plaintiff, who swallowed bone from can of boneless chicken fricassee, had several operations before giving notice).

[430] See, e.g., Pritchard v. Liggett & Myers Tobacco Co., 295 F.2d 292 (3d Cir. 1961) (Pa. law) (letter sent to manufacturer 10 months after plaintiff's cancerous lung removed).

[431] Palmer v. A.H. Robins Co., 684 P.2d 187 (Colo. 1984).

[432] Maybank v. S. S. Kresge Co., 273 S.E.2d 681 (N.C. 1981).

[433] Maldonado v. Creative Woodworking Concepts, Inc., 694 N.E.2d 1021 (Ill. App. Ct. 1998).

[434] See, e.g., Leeper v. Banks, 487 S.W.2d 58 (Ky. 1972) (1 year); Castro v. Stanley Works, 864 F.2d 961 (1st Cir. 1989) (Mass. law) (1 ⅔ years); Hearn v. R.J. Reynolds Tobacco Co., 279 F. Supp. 2d 1096, 1116 (D. Ariz. 2003) (almost 2 years); Hebron v. American Isuzu Motors, Inc., 60 F.3d 1095 (4th Cir. 1995) (Va. law) (2 years); Buford v. Toys R' Us, Inc., 458 S.E.2d 373, 375 (Ga. Ct. App. 1995) (2 years; no notice until complaint served on seller of defective bicycle); Wagmeister v. A.H. Robins Co., 382 N.E.2d 23 (Ill. App. Ct. 1978) (2 ½ years; plaintiff learned IUD failed on Oct. 31, 1972, delivered stillborn baby on February 19, 1973, gave notice of breach on September 26, 1975); Sacramona v. Bridgestone/Firestone, Inc., 106 F.3d 444 (1st Cir. 1997)

basis for barring a claim for the unreasonableness of a delay in providing notice is *prejudice*—that the time lapse has unfairly disadvantaged the defendant seller by occasioning the loss, deterioration, or destruction of physical evidence, often the product itself.[435] Sometimes, however, courts hold that a delay in notice bars a warranty claim simply because it has caused the claim to grow stale.

Hebron v. American Isuzu Motors, Inc.[436] barred a warranty claim because of the unfairness in forcing the defendant to defend a case when the delay resulted in the loss of crucial evidence. The court ruled that a two-year delay after an accident was unreasonable where the plaintiff truck owner failed to take pictures, had no inspection conducted, and disposed of the truck before notifying the manufacturer of the dispute. Thus, the manufacturer was prejudiced by the delay because it was unable to inspect the truck to determine the cause of the accident. The court further noted that prompt notice also would have promoted settlement of the claim.

Sacramona v. Bridgestone/Firestone, Inc.[437] is another loss-of-evidence case. The plaintiff gas station worker was injured by the explosion of a 16-inch tire he was attempting to inflate, which he had mounted on a 16- or 16½-inch wheel of a van to replace a leaking tire. After the accident, the wheel and tire were stored outside in the van owner's yard for three months before the plaintiff's attorney collected them. They were subsequently sent to a consulting engineer, who extensively cleaned the wheel, which rendered it impossible for the defendants to check for markings that might have revealed whether the original leaking tire had been mismatched on a larger wheel. Later, the plaintiff's expert subjected the wheel to a "somewhat destructive" examination. Three years after the accident, the worker finally filed a breach of warranty claim against the manufacturers of the tire and wheel, asserting that both should have been designed to avoid the risk of mismatching tires and wheels. Sometime previously, the gas station had been sold and the original leaking tire, the mounting machine, and various safety and equipment manuals were lost. Affirming summary judgment for the defendants, the court ruled that the delay prejudiced the defendants and was unreasonable.[438]

An example of a case based on the staleness of the claim rather than deterioration or loss of the product is *Williams v. Mozark Fire Extinguisher Co.*[439] In this case, the plaintiff restaurant owner sued the manufacturer of an allegedly defective fire extinguisher system for fire damage to her restaurant, amending her complaint five years after the fire (with no prior notice of breach) to add a warranty claim to her claims

---

(Mass. law) (3 years); Ratkovich v. Smithkline, 711 F. Supp. 436, 438 (N.D. Ill. 1989) (28 years; plaintiff allegedly suffered brain damage from drug, Dexadrine, ingested by mother during pregnancy; in dismissing warranty claims, court remarked that it was "virtually impossible to believe that plaintiff's parents were unaware of the possibility of Smithkline's breach of its implied warranties until 28 years after plaintiff was born with brain damage [and that the] parents must have been considering the various possible causes of plaintiff's injury from the moment she was born").

[435] See, e.g., Smith v. Robertshaw Controls Co., 410 F.3d 29, 36 (1st Cir. 2005) (Mass. law) (affirming summary judgment for defendant prejudiced by 3-year delay in notice by which time crucial evidence under plaintiff's control had been lost).

[436] 60 F.3d 1095 (4th Cir. 1995) (Va. law).

[437] 106 F.3d 444 (1st Cir. 1997) (Mass. law).

[438] "[T]he requirement of prompt notice allows the defendant to gather evidence in timely fashion; without such notice, a defendant could easily be surprised by a lawsuit many years after selling its products." Id. at 449.

[439] 888 S.W.2d 303 (Ark. 1994).

in tort. Holding that the warranty claim was insufficient for failure to provide timely notice, the court pointed to two goals of the notice requirement: (1) giving the seller an opportunity to minimize damages, by correcting the defect, and (2) protecting the seller from stale claims. While the time delay did not diminish the manufacturer's ability to minimize its damages, because the fire extinguisher system had been destroyed in the fire, the manufacturer was entitled to be protected from stale claims.

Bystanders and Other Non-Purchasers; Sellers to Whom Notice Should Be Given

A common question is whether the notice requirements of § 2–607 apply beyond the actual buyer to those who take the benefits of the buyer's warranties under § 2–318.[440] As mentioned earlier, a comment to § 2–607 provides quite clearly that the notice requirement applies to bystanders and other non-purchasers as well as to purchasing consumers;[441] and occasionally courts have barred warranty claims brought by such third parties for failure to provide timely notice.[442] But most courts take the position that third-party consumers *physically* injured by defective products are not bound by the notice requirement of § 2–607,[443] frequently reasoning that the black-letter language of § 2–607 explicitly pertains to "buyers" and no one else, and that comments 4 and 5 to this section explain that the notification requirement should be relaxed for injured plaintiffs who are retail consumers or third-party beneficiaries.[444]

In business litigation, courts split over whether a commercial buyer seeking recovery against a remote manufacturer must provide prompt notice to that seller as well as to the immediate seller.[445] But when the plaintiff is personally injured in a

---

[440] See Stallworth, An Analysis of Warranty Claims Instituted by Non-Privity Plaintiffs in Jurisdictions that Have Adopted Uniform Commercial Code Section 2–318 (Alternative A), 20 Pepp. L. Rev. 1215 (1993); Prince, Overprotecting the Consumer? Section 2–607(3)(a) Notice of Breach in Nonprivity Contexts, 66 N.C. L. Rev. 107 (1987).

[441] Comment 5 to § 2–607 provides in pertinent part that "the reason of this section does extend to requiring the [third-party] beneficiary [of a warranty under § 2–318] to notify the seller that an injury has occurred [because] even a beneficiary can be properly held to the use of good faith in notifying, once he has had time to become aware of the legal situation." See note 423, above.

[442] Compare Sacramona v. Bridgestone/Firestone, Inc., 106 F.3d 444 (1st Cir. 1997) (Mass. law) (gas station manager, inflating tire for van owner, injured by explosion of allegedly defective tire he had mounted on allegedly defective wheel). *Sacramona* should be viewed cautiously because the non-uniform Massachusetts version of UCC § 2–318 includes the following sentence: "Failure to give notice shall not bar recovery under this section unless the defendant proves that he was prejudiced thereby." See Cameo Curtains, Inc. v. Philip Carey Corp., 416 N.E.2d 995, 998 (Mass. App. Ct. 1981).

[443] See, e.g., Ho v. Michelin N. Am., Inc., 2011 WL 3241466, at *15–17 (D. Kan. 2011) (car with allegedly defective tire crashed into plaintiff's car; notwithstanding Official Comment 5 to § 2–607(3), consumers, particularly those who suffer personal injuries, need not provide pre-suit notice of breach; dictum); Kolarik v. Cory Int'l Corp., 721 N.W.2d 159, 163 (Iowa 2006) (remote buyers who are extended beneficiaries under UCC § 2–318 "are not required to give the notice to seller that is otherwise required"); Morgan v. Sears, Roebuck & Co., 700 F. Supp. 1574 (N.D. Ga. 1988) (third-party burn victim who did not buy garment); Carlson v. Armstrong World Indus., 693 F. Supp. 1073 (S.D. Fla. 1987) (painter who did not buy paint). See also Cole v. Keller Indus., 132 F.3d 1044, 1048 (4th Cir. 1998) (Va. law) (asserting that all but one case rule that personally injured non-purchasers are not bound by warranty notice requirements of § 2–607).

[444] See, e.g., Ho v. Michelin N. Am., Inc., 2011 WL 3241466, at *15–17 (D. Kan. 2011); Yates v. Pitman Mfg., Inc., 514 S.E.2d 605, 607 (Va. 1999) (laborer injured by crane; "only buyers . . . must give notice of breach of warranty to the seller as a prerequisite to recovery"); Carlson v. Armstrong World Indus., 693 F. Supp. 1073 (S.D. Fla. 1987); McKnelly v. Sperry Corp., 642 F.2d 1101 (8th Cir. 1981) (Iowa law); Simmons v. Clemco Indus., 368 So.2d 509 (Ala. 1979); Frericks v. General Motors Corp., 363 A.2d 460 (Md. 1976) (criticizing cmt. 5). For comments 4 and 5, see notes 422 and 423, above.

[445] See Cooley v. Big Horn Harvestore Sys., Inc., 813 P.2d 736, 742 (Colo. 1991), discussing the split and holding that even a commercial buyer "is not required to give notice of such injury to a remote manufacturer prior to initiating litigation against such manufacturer."

product accident, he or she may give notice to the retailer or other immediate seller who is then expected to pass it along upstream to the manufacturer.[446] In *Palmer v. A.H. Robins Co.*,[447] for example, a woman injured by a defective IUD was able to pursue her warranty claim against the manufacturer even though before the litigation she had only informed her immediate seller, the doctor. The court ruled that her notice to this party was sufficient to support her claim against the manufacturer.[448]

Method and Form of Notice; Filing of Complaint

In General

Comment 4 to § 2–607 provides that notification need not specify the buyer's objections to the goods nor that the buyer is making, or intends to make, a claim for damages. Instead, "[t]he content of the notification need merely be sufficient to let the seller know that the transaction is still troublesome and must be watched [and to inform] the seller that the transaction is claimed to involve a breach, and thus opens the way for normal settlement through negotiation."[449] Oral notification may be sufficient,[450] and an attorney's letter stating that he is representing a person injured by the manufacturer's faulty product provides the defendant with adequate notice.[451] There is, in short, no magic form in which notice must be made.

Further, if a defendant is already aware of the general product deficiency that caused the plaintiff's injury from other lawsuits or otherwise,[452] some courts hold that the notice requirement is satisfied or unnecessary. Yet, courts are divided on how particular this type of indirect notice must be. In a split decision, a majority of the Illinois Supreme Court held that a vehicle manufacturer's generalized knowledge of a possible rollover problem—from newspaper reports, magazines, and lawsuits brought by attorneys general of several states and by a consumer group—does not satisfy the notice requirements of § 2–607, which contemplates that the manufacturer be apprised of the trouble with a particular product of a particular buyer.[453] On this authority, a lower Illinois court subsequently ruled that car buyers are not excused from the notice requirement by the manufacturer's issuance of a federally mandated recall notice and accompanying press releases.[454]

---

[446] See, e.g., Ragland Mills, Inc. v. General Motors Corp., 763 S.W.2d 357 (Mo. Ct. App. 1989); Firestone Tire & Rubber Co. v. Cannon, 452 A.2d 192 (Md. Ct. Spec. App. 1982), aff'd on opinion below, 456 A.2d 930 (Md. 1983); Goldstein v. G. D. Searle & Co., 378 N.E.2d 1083 (Ill. App. Ct. 1978).

[447] 684 P.2d 187 (Colo. 1984).

[448] "[A]s long as the buyer has given notice of the defect to his or her immediate seller, no further notification to those distributors beyond the immediate seller is required." Id. at 206.

[449] UCC § 2–607 cmt. 4.

[450] See, e.g., Atwood v. Southeast Bedding Co., 485 S.E.2d 217 (Ga. Ct. App. 1997); Bennett v. United Auto Parts, Inc., 315 So.2d 579 (Ala. 1975); Sullivan v. H.P. Hood & Sons, Inc., 168 N.E.2d 80 (Mass. 1960) (son told president of milk supplier that mother should bring suit because she encountered dead mouse while drinking milk from container).

[451] Lariviere v. Dayton Safety Ladder Co., 525 A.2d 892 (R.I. 1987).

[452] See, e.g., Ragland Mills, Inc. v. General Motors Corp., 763 S.W.2d 357 (Mo. Ct. App. 1989) (buyer had car technically examined on immediate seller's premises after wreck); Malawy v. Richards Mfg. Co., 501 N.E.2d 376 (Ill. App. Ct. 1986) (employees of hospital vendor of metal bone plate learned plate had broken when they removed it from plaintiff's broken leg); Palmer v. A.H. Robins Co., 684 P.2d 187 (Colo. 1984) (prior lawsuits over same problem with IUD; no prejudice by delay).

[453] Connick v. Suzuki Motor Co., 675 N.E.2d 584 (Ill. 1996).

[454] Perona v. Volkswagen of Am., Inc., 684 N.E.2d 859 (Ill. App. Ct. 1997).

Filing of Complaint

An issue in products liability cases is whether a plaintiff, to comply with § 2–607, must provide the seller with a separate notification of breach prior to instituting the lawsuit, or whether the complaint itself, if otherwise timely, will suffice. Put otherwise, must the buyer provide notice to the seller prior and as a pre-condition to filing a lawsuit?

When consumers sue for personal injuries, courts commonly hold that the complaint alone satisfies the § 2–607 notice requirements,[455] particularly where the policies behind the notice rule have not been frustrated by the delay.[456] When consumers make claim for economic loss,[457] and even in personal injury cases where the delay is substantial, courts sometimes hold that the complaint itself may not suffice.[458]

When plaintiffs are commercial parties who seek damages for pure economic losses in business litigation, probably most courts hold that the filing of a complaint does not satisfy the notice requirement, so that a prior, separate notice is required.[459] More complicated are consumer class actions seeking damages for pure economic loss, where the law is quite unsettled on whether the filing of a complaint provides sufficient notice under § 2–607.[460] In this consumer economic-loss context, many courts apply normal, commercial law rules requiring a plaintiff to provide the seller with separate notice of an alleged breach prior to filing suit.[461]

---

[455] See, e.g., Richards v. Johnson & Johnson, Inc., 2018 WL 6573332, at *4 (N.D.N.Y. 2018) (because sufficiency of notice is normally a jury issue, and because of authority declining to apply the notice requirement in personal injury actions, court refused to dismiss express warranty claim for lack of presuit notice before trial). Compare Collins v. Pfizer Inc., 2009 WL 126913, at *2–4 (S.D. Ind. 2009) (discussing arguments both ways, but refusing to rule prematurely on whether pre-suit notice was necessary in death action in part because Indiana law unclear on point).

[456] See, e.g., Johnson v. Eisai, Inc., 2022 WL 704581, at *6 (N.D. Ohio 2022) ("[a]ny pre-litigation notice here would have been 'wholly futile' because it would not have provided Defendant an opportunity to cure the defect. [The weight-loss product's] defect is that it causes cancer."); Ho v. Michelin N. Am., Inc., 2011 WL 3241466, at *15–17 (D. Kan. 2011) (car with allegedly defective tire crashed into plaintiff's car; notwithstanding Official Comment 5 to § 2–607(3), consumers, particularly those who suffer personal injuries, need not provide pre-suit notice of breach; dictum); Bryant v. Adams, 448 S.E.2d 832 (N.C. Ct. App. 1994) (complaint filed 3 years after trampoline accident; because warranty claim was based on failure to warn, which did not require visual inspection of particular trampoline, reasonableness of delay left to jury).

[457] See, e.g., Brame v. General Motors LLC, 535 F. Supp. 3d 832, 840 (E.D. Wis. 2021) (claims that vehicles consume excessive oil).

[458] See, e.g., Cauley v. Sabic Innovative Plastics, U.S., L.L.C., 2012 WL 192303, at *5 (S.D. Miss. 2012) (implied warranty claim failed without proof of notice); see also note 434, above. Compare Stanley v. Central Garden & Pet Corp., 891 F. Supp. 2d 757, 772 (D. Md. 2012) (class action against manufacturer of dog toys for intestinal injuries to dogs; "This notification is a prerequisite for claims of breach of implied warranty; a lawsuit cannot constitute notice of a breach under §§ 2–607, 2–608.").

[459] See, e.g., Armco Steel Corp. v. Isaacson Structural Steel Co., 611 P.2d 507 (Alaska 1980). The law here, too, is quite unsettled. See, e.g., In re Ford Motor Co. E-350 Van Prods. Liab. Litig., 2010 WL 2813788, at *39–40, 53, 64–65, 78 (D.N.J. 2010) (*Texas law*: filing a complaint does not satisfy notice; *Massachusetts law*: unclear if filing a complaint is sufficient notice, jury must conclude defendant was not prejudiced; *Michigan law*: filing a complaint is sufficient notice; *Pennsylvania law*: filing a complaint is sufficient notice, but reasonableness of time to give notice is question of fact).

[460] See, e.g., Porcell v. Lincoln Wood Prods., 713 F. Supp. 2d 1305, 1316 (D.N.M. 2010) ("Whether the filing of a lawsuit that was never certified as a class action can constitute sufficient individual notice . . . presents an unsettled question of law.").

Differing warranty rules among the states, including differing notice requirements, may render a putative class action unmanageable. See, e.g., Powers v. Lycoming Engines, 272 F.R.D. 414, 428–29 (E.D. Pa. 2011) (so concluding).

[461] See, e.g., Daigle v. Ford Motor Co., 713 F. Supp. 2d 822, 827 (D. Minn. 2010) (dismissing warranty claims in putative class action for defective transmissions because plaintiffs failed to allege notice to Ford or its dealers prior to filing suit, which "deprived Ford of the opportunity to cure the alleged defect or otherwise

§ 4.7 DISCLAIMERS

A free market contemplates that buyers and sellers normally may strike whatever deals they choose—that they may define the terms of their transactions however they decide. If parties to a sales transaction choose to exchange a certain amount of cash for a particular product containing certain limitations and flaws (perhaps old furniture or a used car), for a price reflecting their mutual view of the product's worth in that condition, they generally may do so. This approach to sales law suggests that buyers and sellers should be able to decide who between them will be responsible for unknown problems in the product and, if the seller is the one responsible, the type and extent of remedy for breach the buyer will receive. Allowing buyers and sellers to so define all aspects of their transactions, unfettered by legal control, is grounded in two fundamental assumptions: (1) that they both have reasonable access to information about the product (including its flaws), and (2) that they both can bargain effectively to protect their respective interests.

In the real world, of course, product manufacturers and other sellers usually know much more about the general characteristics of their products than buyers do, and power to define transaction terms usually is skewed heavily toward the top of the chain of distribution. This is particularly true, of course, in the case of consumer transactions where buyers generally know much less than manufacturers about the nature and extent of dangers in complex products[462] and usually have no power to bargain for more or less safety in particular products. Manufacturers and other sellers often are motivated to increase revenues by making consumers believe that products are safer and that warranties are broader (that both are more valuable) than they are in fact. Correspondingly, sellers are motivated to decrease expenses by cutting quality (increasing hazards) and avoiding responsibility for product accidents by excluding warranties or limiting remedies for their breach in sales contracts. Such contractual avoidance provisions, if allowed, can be especially effective in consumer transactions where consumers of new products typically hold major negotiating disadvantages—they know little about a product's dangers, have minimal power to bargain for more safety, and possess few skills on how to value warranties, their exclusion, or limitations on remedies for their breach. If permitted, sellers benefit most from providing disclaimers (and remedy limitations) in a way that buyers do not see or understand.[463]

In the interest of free markets, but in recognition of the shortcomings of actual markets, Article 2 of the Uniform Commercial Code establishes a framework for parties to structure their deals freely within certain guidelines. Article 2 works most fairly and efficiently in transactions between merchant buyers and sellers—the types of actors most likely to be informed and capable of bargaining effectively. But the Code also

---

negotiate the claim"). Even in consumer class actions, a court may require pre-litigation notice unless plaintiffs allege personal injuries. See Connick v. Suzuki Motor Co., 675 N.E.2d 584 (Ill. 1996) (Ill. and Pa. law), where plaintiffs, for purposes of notice, were divided into three categories: merchant buyers, consumer buyers who did not suffer personal injuries, and consumer buyers who did suffer personal injuries. Only plaintiffs in the last category could satisfy the notice requirement by filing a complaint against the seller.

[462] However, consumers often do have more information than product sellers about how products may perform in particular settings when put to particularly risky uses. See Priest, The Current Insurance Crisis and Modern Tort Law, 96 Yale L.J. 1521 (1987); Priest, Theory of the Consumer Product Warranty, 90 Yale L.J. 1297, 1311 (1981).

[463] Henningsen v. Bloomfield Motors, Inc., 161 A.2d 69, 97 (N.J. 1960). See § 4.9, below. *Henningsen*'s role in the development of strict liability in tort is examined at § 5.2, below.

contemplates and allows for, if in a plainly secondary fashion, certain frailties in markets for consumer goods.[464]

Article 2 provides two principal means for sellers to avoid or limit responsibility for the consequences of product defects and false warranties: (1) disclaimers of warranties, in § 2–316, and (2) limitations on remedies for breach of warranty, in §§ 2–718 and 2–719.[465] While disclaimers and remedy limitations may abstractly serve the same seller objective of avoiding responsibility for damages caused by defective products and false warranties, these two contractual techniques operate independently and are conceptually distinct.[466] Section 2–316 allows sellers to disclaim responsibility for express and implied warranties, and §§ 2–718 and 2–719 allow sellers to define and limit the type of remedy and amount of damages a buyer will receive in the event a warranty is breached. An effective disclaimer under § 2–316 prevents a warranty from ever arising, so that there is nothing for the seller to breach. By contrast, §§ 2–718 and 2–719, which assume that a valid warranty exists and has been breached, concern only the nature and extent of remedy for the breach. An effective damages limitation under § 2–718 "liquidates" the buyer's damages at a predetermined, set amount; an effective limitation under § 2–719 typically limits the buyer's recovery for breach to repair or replacement of the product and allows no recovery for the buyer's incidental or consequential damages.

While Article 2 generally allows buyers and sellers to agree to shift the normal responsibility for breach of warranty from the seller to the buyer, and so to reintroduce the doctrine of *caveat emptor* into a sales contract, the Code seeks to ensure that such changes in the normal allocation of responsibility are made apparent to the buyer. Comment 1 to § 2–316 explains this point:

---

[464] In certain important respects, Amended UCC § 2–316 would have provided consumers with further protection from unfair and unbargained-for reductions in warranty protection. For the fate of Article 2 amendments, see § 4.1, notes 17 and 18, above.

[465] See § 2–316(4) which prescribes these alternative approaches for a seller to avoid liability. See, e.g., McCarty v. E.J. Korvette, Inc., 347 A.2d 253 (Md. Ct. Spec. App. 1975):

> [UCC] § 2–316 specifically recognizes a right on the part of the warrantor to negate, modify or limit an express or implied warranty under certain circumstances. It also implicitly recognizes that warranties may be limited in two different ways-one by 'disclaiming' the warranty or a part of the warranty itself in the manner prescribed by subsections (1)–(3), and the other by 'limiting the remedy' available upon breach (subsection (4)) in the manner prescribed by [UCC] §§ 2–718 and 2–719.

Id. at 259 (quoting White and Summers: "A disclaimer clause is a device used to exclude or limit the seller's warranties; it attempts to control the seller's liability, by reducing the number of situations in which the seller can be in breach. An exclusionary clause (limitation of remedies), on the other hand, restricts the remedies available to one or both parties once a breach is established." White and Summers, UCC § 12–11, at 383–84 (1st ed., 1972)).

Despite their similarity in providing sellers with contractual means of protection against warranty liability, their differences require close attention. As discussed below, for example, the Code does not permit a seller to limit a buyer's *remedy* so far as to avoid *all* warranty responsibility. See § 2–719 cmt. 1. For a discussion of the horse-and-buggy nature of §§ 2–316 and 2–719, see § 4.8, text at notes 596–603, below.

[466] See, e.g., Fleming Farms v. Dixie Ag Supply, Inc., 631 So.2d 922, 925 n.4 (Ala. 1994) ("A disclaimer of warranties and a limitation of remedies are in substance the same, although they are conceptually different. A disclaimer of warranties reduces the circumstances in which the seller would be liable for breach of contract; a limitation of remedies restricts the remedies available once a breach is established."). On their similarity of purpose, see § 2–316(4) (referencing §§ 2–718 and 2–719) and § 2–719 cmt. 3 (noting that consequential damages may be excluded, but not in an unconscionable manner, and that a seller in all cases can avoid all warranty responsibility per § 2–316).

> This section is designed principally to deal with those frequent clauses in sales contracts which seek to exclude "all warranties, express or implied." It seeks to protect a buyer from unexpected and unbargained language of disclaimer by denying effect to such language when inconsistent with language of express warranty and permitting the exclusion of implied warranties only by conspicuous language or other circumstances which protect the buyer from surprise.

Thus, the Code's goal is to ensure that buyers know when a product does not in fact carry a warranty that ordinarily would attach to such a sales transaction. In this way, the Code seeks to mandate that sales transactions, as much as reasonably possible, reflect consensual "bargains" between the parties.

Third-Party Beneficiaries—Limiting Rights by Disclaimer or Limitation

A plaintiff not in privity with a seller may sometimes step into the shoes of the buyer under § 2–318, as previously discussed.[467] Because of the derivative nature of such a person's warranty claims, he or she has no greater right than the buyer to recover on a warranty.[468] Accordingly, limitations on and exclusions of warranties, and limitations on remedies for breach of warranty, logically carry over from the buyer to third-party beneficiaries.[469] For example, an express warranty's time limitation will apply to third-party beneficiaries as well as to the buyer.[470] And if the buyer never received a warranty in the first place, because it was effectively disclaimed in the sales contract between the seller and the buyer, then a third party harmed by a defect in the product will have no warranty upon which to base a claim for breach.[471]

While a third-party beneficiary logically may take no *greater* warranty rights than the buyer, may he or she be given any *less*? In an effort to cut liability costs, a seller may wish to provide certain warranties only to the purchaser and to cut off responsibility at that point, excluding warranties (and remedies for breach of warranty) for all third-party beneficiaries. A split disclaimer or limitation arrangement of this type may also please the buyer who personally receives warranty protection and may pay a lower price reflecting the seller's lower warranty costs. This temptation of sellers and buyers to conspire to deprive third-party beneficiaries of warranty protection for personal injuries is specifically precluded by the last sentence to each of the three Alternative provisions of § 2–318, which all provide: "A seller may not exclude or limit the operation of this section."[472] Comment 1 to § 2–318 explains:

---

[467] See § 4.5, above.

[468] See Lawrence's Anderson on the UCC §§ 2–318:14 et seq.

[469] See id. §§ 2–316:146 et seq.

[470] See, e.g., Ford Motor Co. v. Moulton, 511 S.W.2d 690 (Tenn. 1974).

[471] See, e.g., Brooks v. GAF Materials Corp., 284 F.R.D. 352, 358–59 (D.S.C. 2012) (third party beneficiaries get no greater warranty rights than buyer, even if they never see disclaimer); Budnick Converting, Inc. v. Nebula Glass Int'l, 866 F. Supp. 2d 976, 1001 (S.D. Ill. 2012) (third party beneficiary "must take the contract as the original parties made it [and] cannot take those parts of the contract which favor him and reject those parts which distress him"); Buettner v. R.W. Martin & Sons, Inc., 47 F.3d 116 (4th Cir. 1995) (Va. law) (valid "as is" disclaimer in employer's purchase contract also bound employee). *Contra* Wright v. Dow Chem. U.S.A., 845 F. Supp. 503, 511 (M.D. Tenn. 1993) (homeowners injured by pesticide applied by pest control company not bound by label disclaimers they never saw).

[472] Alternative C further adds to the end of this sentence: "with respect to injury to the person of an individual to whom the warranty extends."

> To the extent that the contract of sale contains provisions under which warranties are excluded or modified, or remedies for breach are limited, such provisions are equally operative against beneficiaries of warranties under this section. What this last sentence forbids is exclusion of liability by the seller to the persons to whom the warranties which he has made to his buyer would extend under this section.

Attempts to split disclaimers and remedy limitations in this manner are quite unusual, and they should be denied effect under this provision of § 2–318.[473]

Disclaimers of Express Warranties

In General

The very notion of a disclaimer of an *express* warranty appears unprincipled. Why should a seller be permitted to avoid responsibility for making a promise for which the buyer paid, on which the buyer relied, and which constituted part of the basis of the buyer's bargain? Perhaps for this reason, South Carolina simply prohibits the disclaimer of express warranties.[474] In states that do permit express warranties to be disclaimed, such disclaimers are sometimes said to be disfavored by the courts.[475]

Yet, Article 2 of the Code explicitly *permits* such disclaimers in a limited way, which makes good sense. Section 2–316(1) provides:

> Words or conduct relevant to the creation of an express warranty and words or conduct tending to negate or limit warranty shall be construed wherever reasonable as consistent with each other; but subject to the provisions of this Article on parol or extrinsic evidence (Section 2–202) negation or limitation is inoperative to the extent that such construction is unreasonable.

The first clause of § 2–316(1), which permits "consistent" express warranty limitations, is designed to permit sellers to define express warranties with specificity. All express warranties, of course, logically must have *some* definitional borders, some scope, for dividing product failures that fall within the warranty from those that fall without.[476] So, a manufacturer of a new tire may expressly warrant it against "blowouts." But any such warranty will have some limitations to its scope—for time (3 years),[477]

---

[473] See, e.g., Hydra-Mac, Inc. v. Onan Corp., 430 N.W.2d 846 (Minn. Ct. App. 1988), rev'd in part on other grounds, 450 N.W.2d 913 (Minn. 1990). *But cf.* Marshall v. Wellcraft Marine, 103 F. Supp. 2d 1099, 1113–14 (S.D. Ind. 1999) (Fla. law) (express warranty limited to first retail purchaser of boat; absence of privity barred recovery).

[474] See S.C. Code Ann. § 36–2–316(1): "If the agreement creates an express warranty words disclaiming it are inoperative."

[475] See, e.g., Woodruff v. Clark Cnty. Farm Bureau Coop. Ass'n, 286 N.E.2d 188, 200 (Ind. Ct. App. 1972) (noting the "judicial aversion to negation of express warranties"). On disclaimers of express warranties, see generally Lawrence's Anderson on the UCC §§ 2–316:90 et seq.

[476] See, e.g., Boddison v. General Motors LLC, 2021 WL 2435388, at *4 (M.D. Fla. 2021) (dismissing express warranty claims; express warranty disclaimed software errors, including "connectivity to, from, or through the vehicles" by its "plain terms").

[477] See, e.g., Hahn v. Ford Motor Co., 434 N.E.2d 943 (Ind. Ct. App. 1982) (durational limitation effective). Although such "time warranties" occasionally have been invalidated as unreasonable, e.g., Community Television Servs., Inc. v. Dresser Indus., 435 F. Supp. 214 (D.S.D. 1977), aff'd, 586 F.2d 637 (8th Cir. 1978), they are a standard method for defining the scope of a seller's responsibility, which buyers understand. Accordingly, assuming compliance with the Magnuson-Moss Federal Warranty Act, discussed in § 4.9, below, such time limitations generally should be viewed as permissible under § 2–316. See generally 1 Crockett, Product Warranties § 8:4; 1 White and Summers, UCC § 13–12, at 1076, n.6 (6th pract. ed. 2012).

mileage (36,000 miles), type of use (normal, non-commercial passenger car road and highway driving), and manner of use or hazard (no coverage for tires run flat or damaged from off-road driving, fire, collision, vandalism, misalignment, mechanical defects in the vehicle, or deliberate misuse).[478] Surely sellers must be permitted to define the scope of their express warranties in this manner—whether by defining the scope of warranty under § 2–313 or, alternatively, by limiting its scope or excluding it altogether under § 2–316. By their nature, definitional borders serve to exclude as well as to include.

If a disclaimer cannot reasonably be construed as consistent with an express warranty, the disclaimer is void.[479] This is the basic purpose of the second clause in § 2–316(1), which invalidates attempts to limit or disclaim an express warranty where the disclaimer contradicts an essential aspect of the warranty, involving such basic features as a product's safety,[480] or its express description[481] as new,[482] or the descriptions and pictures in advertisements and brochures.[483] *Realmuto v. Straub Motors, Inc.*[484] illustrates the operation of § 2–316's unreasonable construction clause. Plaintiff was injured when the accelerator-carburetor linkage malfunctioned on the used car he had purchased six days earlier from the defendant dealer. The salesman had written "30 day warranty" on the face of the purchase agreement. A printed clause on the back provided in part: "It is expressly agreed that there are no warranties, express or implied, made by either the selling dealer or the manufacturer . . . ."[485] Citing § 2–316(1), the court ruled that "[t]his attempted disclaimer of any express warranties is inoperative since to give effect to the disclaimer would be unreasonable in view of the writing on the face."[486]

A disclaimer of an express warranty is ineffectual if it does not become part of the basis of the bargain. Thus, if a disclaimer is printed in a writing not provided to the buyer until after the time of sale, it will have no effect.[487] For example, if a seller attempts to condition an express warranty on the return of a "warranty registration card" by a writing located inside a product's packaging,[488] or to limit or exclude express

[478] See McCarty v. E.J. Korvette, Inc., 347 A.2d 253, 259 (Md. Ct. Spec. App. 1975).

[479] See, e.g., Security Nat. Bank of Sioux City, Iowa v. Abbott Labs., 2012 WL 327863, at *17 (N.D. Iowa 2012); Snelten v. Schmidt Implement Co., 647 N.E.2d 1071 (Ill. App. Ct. 1995).

[480] See, e.g., Bell Sports, Inc. v. Yarusso, 759 A.2d 582, 593 (Del. 2000) (disclaimer stating that bike helmet could not guard against all injuries dubiously held to be ineffective where it also stated that its primary function was to reduce harmful effects of a blow to the head); Schlenz v. John Deere Co., 511 F. Supp. 224, 229 (D. Mont. 1981) (disclaimer was "ineffective to destroy the express warranty of safety made in the operator's manual").

[481] See Fundin v. Chicago Pneumatic Tool Co., 199 Cal. Rptr. 789, 794–95 (Ct. App. 1984) (disclaimer construed so as not to disclaim express description that could not reasonably be disclaimed); H. G. Fischer X-Ray Co. v. Meredith, 433 A.2d 1306 (N.H. 1981) (description prevailed over disclaimer). If a description is mere puffing or not otherwise part of the basis of the bargain, of course, it does not amount to an express warranty, so there is nothing to disclaim. See, e.g., Cuthbertson v. Clark Equip. Co., 448 A.2d 315 (Me. 1982) (holding that various descriptions were not part of basis of bargain).

[482] See, e.g., Rivers v. BMW of N. Am., Inc., 449 S.E.2d 337 (Ga. Ct. App. 1994); Century Dodge, Inc. v. Mobley, 272 S.E.2d 502 (Ga. Ct. App. 1980) (express warranty, describing car as new, could not reasonably be negated by disclaimer).

[483] See Grady, Inadvertent Creation of Express Warranties: Caveats for Pictorial Product Representations, 15 UCC L.J. 268 (1983).

[484] 322 A.2d 440 (N.J. 1974).

[485] Id. at 442 n.2.

[486] Id. See also Woodruff v. Clark Cnty. Farm Bureau Coop. Ass'n, 286 N.E.2d 188, 200 (Ind. Ct. App. 1972) (noting "judicial aversion to negation of express warranties").

[487] See, e.g., Dorman v. International Harvester Co., 120 Cal. Rptr. 516, 522 (Ct. App. 1975).

[488] Of course, if the parties' original agreement specifically conditions an express warranty on the return of a warranty registration card, such a condition may be valid. See 1 Crockett, Product Warranties § 8:4. But

warranties by a form placed inside the glove compartment of a new car delivered after execution of the sales contract, neither post-sale attempt at a disclaimer will be part of the original agreement and so neither will be effective.[489]

Disclaimers of Oral Warranties

What has been said so far concerns a seller's attempts to disclaim express *written* warranties. But a buyer may assert that a salesperson *orally* promised that a product would perform in a certain manner, or that it could be used safely under certain specified conditions. After the fact, such claims of oral warranties raise obvious problems of proof, depending as they do on the veracity of both the buyer and the seller, and on memories that tend to fade and evolve into one's subjective recollection of a negotiation that often looks quite different from opposite sides of a sales transaction, especially one that transpired long ago. In pre-sale negotiations, a salesperson may well overstate a product's virtues, and a buyer may well misinterpret the seller's comments about a product and so mistakenly conclude that the product is stronger or otherwise safer than it truly is. After the fact, when a product failure causes injury, the buyer's claim of an oral warranty can be quite nettlesome to a retail seller.

The Code addresses oral express warranties indirectly in § 2–316(1)'s reference to "parol or extrinsic evidence": "The seller is protected under this Article against false allegations of oral warranties by its provisions on parol and extrinsic evidence and against unauthorized representations by the customary 'lack of authority' clauses."[490] Probably a seller's most effective defense to oral warranties is to insert a merger clause in the contract of sale, stating that any oral representations made about the product during negotiations have no effect and are merged into the written contract, which is the complete, exclusive, and final expression of the parties' agreement. If properly drafted, conspicuously presented, and acknowledged by the buyer's signature, such an agreement may serve effectively to disclaim express oral warranties, possibly even when a buyer has a claim for personal injuries, and so to prevent misunderstanding and litigation.[491]

Disclaimers of Implied Warranties

In General

Implied warranties, obligations that arise merely from the sale of goods, are generally easier to disclaim than express warranties that a seller makes as part of a specific sales agreement. In the context of commercial transactions, the parties normally should be permitted to shape the nature of the deal as they desire. The difficulties consumers have in evaluating and negotiating the content of warranties accompanying the sale of new products were discussed above. In this context, permitting a seller to exclude the implied warranty of merchantability, the basic warranty of product quality

---

such a condition may be invalidated if it is principally a marketing information tool. See Van Den Broeke v. Bellanca Aircraft Corp., 576 F.2d 582 (5th Cir. 1978) (Miss. law). Or it may be proscribed by statute. See, e.g., Cal. Com. Code § 2801 (preventing seller from voiding warranty solely for failure to complete and return form to manufacturer or retail seller).

On the treatment of warranty registration cards under the Magnuson-Moss Warranty Act, see 2 Crockett, Product Warranties § 17:16; C. Reitz, Consumer Protection Under the Magnuson-Moss Warranty Act 33 (ALI 1978 and rev. ed. 1987); § 4.9, below.

[489] Post-sale disclaimers are more extensively examined below.

[490] UCC § 2–316 cmt. 2.

[491] On oral warranties and merger clauses, and for an example of a clear and complete merger clause, see White and Summers, UCC § 13–4.

and safety, seems singularly inappropriate. For this reason, there are a number of restrictions on such disclaimers. Section 2–316 of the Uniform Commercial Code attaches certain requirements to such disclaimers, and a number of state statutes and the federal Magnuson-Moss Warranty Act prohibit or substantially restrict the ability of manufacturers and other sellers to disclaim implied warranties or to limit damages for breach of warranty in sales of consumer products, as discussed below.[492] Where state law permits the complete exclusion of implied warranties under § 2–316, as most states do,[493] courts tend to disfavor such disclaimers and interpret them narrowly in favor of consumers.[494]

Notwithstanding the general oppressiveness of implied warranty disclaimers in sales of new consumer goods, however, most states long ago adopted the uniform version of § 2–316, which allows manufacturers and other sellers to disclaim completely both types of implied warranties: the implied warranty of merchantability, which otherwise would arise under § 2–314, and the implied warranty of fitness for particular purpose, which otherwise might arise under § 2–315. Accordingly, a disclaimer drafted to comport with the requirements of § 2–316 operates under the Code to prevent a consumer from recovering damages against a manufacturer or other seller for breach of warranty even if the consumer is killed or seriously injured by a dangerously defective product.[495]

For example, in *Ford Motor Co. v. Moulton*,[496] the plaintiff was severely injured when a steering defect in his 14-month-old car caused it to veer off a bridge and fall to the street below. His 12-month/12,000-mile express warranty had expired, and the contract of sale disclaimed the implied warranty of merchantability in accordance with § 2–316(2). The plaintiff's tort law claims were barred by a one-year statute of limitations, and the court ruled that the properly-drawn disclaimer barred his claim for breach of the warranty of merchantability. In short, the law provided no redress to a consumer severely injured by a dangerous defect in a car that was nearly new.

Implied warranties may be disclaimed in several ways under § 2–316. Subsection (2) provides a fail-safe disclaimer method—a "safe harbor"—for manufacturers and other sellers of new products:

> Subject to subsection (3), to exclude or modify the implied warranty of merchantability or any part of it the language must mention merchantability and in case of a writing must be conspicuous, and to exclude or modify any implied warranty of fitness the exclusion must be by a writing and conspicuous. Language to exclude all implied warranties of fitness is sufficient if it states, for example, that "There are no warranties which extend beyond the description on the face hereof."

Subsection (2), it should be noted, is subordinate to subsection (3). As discussed below, subsection (3) permits alternative methods by which implied warranties may be

---

[492] See § 4.9, below.

[493] See Powers v. Lycoming Engines, 272 F.R.D. 414, 428 (E.D. Pa. 2011) (addressing variations in validity of implied warranty disclaimers in survey of state law; motion to certify class action denied).

[494] "The courts do not look with great favor on disclaimers; unless every *i* is dotted and every *t* crossed, the disclaimer will be nullified." 1 Crockett, Product Warranties § 8:6. See Lawrence's Anderson on the UCC §§ 2–316:12 to :13, :34 to :39.

[495] See, e.g., Hollman v. Taser Int'l Inc., 928 F. Supp. 2d 657 (E.D.N.Y. 2013) (arrestee killed by defendant's taser; warranty claims effectively disclaimed).

[496] 511 S.W.2d 690 (Tenn. 1974).

disclaimed. That said, sellers of new products usually employ subsection (2) to disclaim implied warranties. Under this approach, a disclaimer of the implied warranty of merchantability must specifically mention the word "merchantability."[497] To exclude implied warranties of fitness, the seller may use general language,[498] such as "no warranties of any kind accompany the sale of this product."

In addition, disclaimers of both types of implied warranties must be *conspicuous*. Disclaimers of implied warranties also must be written rather than oral—the fitness warranty, as explicitly required by § 2–316(2), and the merchantability warranty as a practical matter in most cases involving the sale of new consumer goods, especially those that prove dangerously defective.[499]

Conspicuousness

In general. Disclaimers of implied warranties generally must be conspicuous to ensure as much as possible that a buyer will know that a product is being sold "naked," without any implied warranties of quality or performance.[500] If such warranties are effectively disclaimed, the risk that a product may contain latent defects is shifted from the seller to the buyer, a significant reversal of the risk-of-loss rule of *caveat venditor* that normally governs the sale of goods today. Thus, to help assure that a buyer understands that a particular purchase transaction does *not* include the implied warranties that normally arise, Uniform Commercial Code § 2–316(2) requires that such disclaimers be conspicuous.[501]

"Conspicuous" is defined in UCC § 1–201(10):

> "Conspicuous": A term or clause is conspicuous when it is so written that a reasonable person against whom it is to operate ought to have noticed it. A printed heading in capitals (as: NON-NEGOTIABLE BILL OF LADING) is conspicuous. Language in the body of a form is "conspicuous" if it is in larger or other contrasting type or color. . . . Whether a term or clause is "conspicuous" or not is for decision by the court.

Thus, an exclusion of an implied warranty must be made to stand out from the rest of the sales contract, by means of larger, bolder, or different color or style of typeface; by a heading, such as **DISCLAIMER OF IMPLIED WARRANTIES**, that specifically calls the buyer's attention to the fact of the disclaimer; by location of the disclaimer in a prominent place in the agreement—as immediately above the principal signature line for the buyer, or with a separate buyer signature or initial line accompanying the

[497] See UCC § 2–316 cmt. 3.

[498] See UCC § 2–316 cmt. 4.

[499] By conflicting with the text of § 2–316, the assertion in the text—that merchantability disclaimers must be written in most sales of new consumer goods—admittedly is bold. But it probably is an accurate statement of how most modern courts see the issue, perhaps on grounds of conscionability, particularly in the case of defects in new products physically injuring consumers. By contrast, retail sellers of *used* products sometimes might plausibly attempt to disclaim such warranties in oral rather than written form. See White and Summers, UCC § 12–5. Even in the used product context, however, it is difficult to imagine that a court would rule that, by (clearly) uttering the words "this car comes with no warranty of merchantability," a used car dealer effectively protects itself against responsibility for injuries caused shortly after the sale by a latent defect in the car's steering that the seller unreasonably chose not to repair. Amended UCC § 2–316(2) and § 2–316(3), see § 4.1 notes 17 and 18, above, would have required all merchantability disclaimers of consumer goods to be in writing and conspicuous.

[500] See Lawrence's Anderson on the UCC §§ 2–316:105 et seq.

[501] See UCC § 2–316 cmt. 1.

disclaimer and asserting that the buyer has read and understands the resulting forfeiture of rights; and by any other method that helps ensure that a buyer will be protected from "unexpected and unbargained language of disclaimer."[502]

While a seller should include as many features of conspicuousness mentioned in § 1–201(10) as feasible, § 2–316(2) does not require sellers to adopt each and every one of these separate techniques so long as, taken as a whole, the disclaimer is prominently displayed and likely to draw the attention of a reasonable person.[503] In addition to comprehensibility, discussed below, a seller drafting a warranty normally should focus particularly upon three elements of prominence: *font* (size, style, color, italics, or bold type face), *heading*, and *location*.[504] If a seller fails to make a disclaimer conspicuous, the result is clear: it will be void and of no effect, and a buyer's claim for breach of warranty will be unaffected by the purported words of disclaimer.[505]

A case illustrating how an implied warranty of merchantability disclaimer may fail on conspicuousness grounds is *Dorman v. International Harvester Co.*[506] There, a tractor manufacturer's form contract provided that "no other warranties, express or implied, including without limitation, the implied warranties of *merchantability and fitness for a particular purpose shall apply*." In deciding whether this attempted disclaimer met the conspicuousness requirement under § 2–316, the court acknowledged that the language was located near the buyer's signature line, that it was printed in slightly larger type than the preceding paragraph, and that it was printed partially in italics. However, citing § 1–201(10), the court reasoned that the language was not conspicuous because it was not presented "in clear and distinct language and prominently set forth in large, bold print in such position as to compel notice."[507] In concluding that the disclaimer was not conspicuous, the court also noted the form's failure to carry a prominent

---

[502] Id.

[503] See, e.g., Haft v. Haier US Appliance Sols., Inc., 2022 WL 62181, at *5 (S.D.N.Y. 2022) (warranty limitation, in 15-page manual entitled in large bold letters "GE Electric Range Warranty," in subsection titled "EXCLUSION OF IMPLIED WARRANTIES" on p. 4 was conspicuous, where table of contents listed "Warranty" in bold and directed readers to p. 4, and no claim manual not available prior to purchase); Taylor v. Taser Int'l, Inc., 2019 WL 1434213, at *13 (S.D. Tex. 2019) (TASER X26E disclaimers, "conspicuous as a matter of law," printed in bold typeface); Cullen v. Premier Baths, Inc., 2012 WL 3638466, at *2 (N.D. Ill. 2012) (disclaimer on interior page was otherwise conspicuous); Hartford v. Lyndon-DFS Warranty Servs., Inc., 2010 WL 2220443, at *11–12 (Tex. App. 2010) (disclaimer "set out" from surrounding text using capital letters and bold font was conspicuous); Rochester-Genesee Reg'l Transp. Auth. v. Cummins Inc., 2010 WL 2998768, at *5–6 (W.D.N.Y. 2010) (disclaimer was conspicuous in clearly labeling separate section written in large, bold font, and capital letters). See generally Special Project, Article Two Warranties in Commercial Transactions: An Update, 72 Cornell L. Rev. 1159 (1987) [hereinafter Cornell II].

[504] Cornell II, at 1269, suggests the following general guidelines: "Disclaimers should be written in large, noticeable print, set off from the rest of the page, and placed below a heading that clearly indicates that a *disclaimer* follows; sellers should ensure that the disclaimer or a noticeable reference to it appears near the buyer's signature."

[505] See, e.g., Benedict v. Hankook Tire Co. Ltd., 295 F. Supp. 3d 632, 656–60 (E.D. Va. 2018) (inconspicuous; thorough application of "holistic" view of conspicuity); American Aerial Servs., Inc. v. Terex USA, LLC, 39 F. Supp. 3d 95, 108 (D. Me. 2014) (inconspicuous; disclaimer "does not appear in capital letters; does not appear in type that is larger than the surrounding text; does not mention merchantability; and does not appear in a contrasting font or color compared to the surrounding text"); Paper Mfrs. Co. v. Rescuers, Inc., 60 F. Supp. 2d 869, 879–80 (N.D. Ind. 1999) (disclaimer in small type and difficult to read was not conspicuous); Basic Adhesives, Inc. v. Robert Matzkin Co., 420 N.Y.S.2d 983, 987 (City Civ. Ct. 1979) ("considering all factors—the size, prominence and contrast of the capitalized words—the disclaimer on the label was sufficiently conspicuous"), aff'd as modified, 1980 WL 98464 (N.Y. App. Div. 1980) (but "microscopic print" disclaimer was inconspicuous and ineffective); Dorman v. International Harvester Co., 120 Cal. Rptr. 516 (Ct. App. 1975) (disclaimer in contract was neither conspicuous nor comprehensible).

[506] 120 Cal. Rptr. 516 (Ct. App. 1975).

[507] Id. at 522.

"DISCLAIMER OF WARRANTIES" heading to call the buyer's attention to the content of this important clause.[508]

The *Dorman* court provided an important, additional reason for invalidating the seller's attempted disclaimer—that the phrasing and partial italics rendered it ambiguous and, hence, difficult to comprehend. Indeed, the court observed that the emphasized portion of the disclaimer—"*merchantability and fitness for a particular purpose shall apply*"—actually suggested that the contract was *including* such warranties rather than the other way around. Thus, the fact of disclaimer was not comprehensibly conveyed: its meaning was not clear, definite, or specific. Although the court did not refer to the comprehensibility issue as one of "conspicuousness," and while strictly speaking it probably is not,[509] the Code's stated purpose of conspicuousness is to prevent the reasonable buyer's surprise at an unexpected bargain.[510] For this reason alone, stated the court, the attempted disclaimer was ineffective.

Back-side ("buried") disclaimers. Disclaimers appearing on the back side or an interior page of a sales contract form are particularly suspect. In *Koellmer v. Chrysler Motors Corp.*,[511] the buyer of a new Dodge truck sued the dealer and manufacturer for breach of the implied warranty of merchantability. The plaintiff had signed a purchase order form on the back of which was a disclaimer in the seventh of ten separate paragraphs, printed in the same size and style type, in the same color, totaling over 800 words, and with nothing characteristic about the disclaimer clause to distinguish it from the other paragraphs. On these facts, the court ruled that the disclaimer clause did not satisfy the conspicuousness requirement of § 2–316(2). As explained by another court,[512] "it is the policy of the law to look with disfavor upon semi-concealed or obscured self-protective provisions of a contract prepared by one party, which the other is not likely to notice."[513] Yet, a disclaimer located other than on the front page of a sales agreement is not invalid per se, provided that the buyer's attention is effectively directed to the clause and the clause is otherwise prominently displayed.[514]

Disclaimers known to buyer. A particularly thorny issue is whether an inconspicuous disclaimer should be invalidated even if the buyer admits that he or she read or otherwise knew about it at the time of contracting.[515] Comment 1 to § 2–316 states that the conspicuousness requirement is designed to prevent sellers from

---

[508] Id.

[509] In § 1–102(10), "conspicuous" is defined in terms of physical prominence, not comprehensibility. See Cornell II, at 1269–70 (arguing that the conspicuous notion should not include the notion of "understandable," despite some authority for so broadening the concept).

[510] See cmt. 1 to § 2–316. Compare the *Dorman* court's reliance on authority requiring such language to be "clear" in order to effectuate the parties' intent. *Dorman*, 120 Cal. Rptr. at 521.

[511] 276 A.2d 807 (Conn. App. Ct. 1970).

[512] Christopher v. Larson Ford Sales, Inc., 557 P.2d 1009, 1012 (Utah 1976) (such a disclaimer should not bind a buyer "unless it is shown that the provision [on the back of the form] was actually called to his attention").

[513] Id. See also Ressallat v. Burglar & Fire Alarms, Inc., 606 N.E.2d 1001 (Ohio Ct. App. 1992).

[514] See, e.g., Brown v. Range Rover of N. Am., Inc., 24 UCC Rep. Serv. 2d 418 (Va. Cir. Ct. 1993); Houck v. DeBonis, 379 A.2d 765, 773 (Md. Ct. Spec. App. 1977), where a reverse-side disclaimer was held conspicuous: "The face of the contract mentions in two separate places that additional terms and conditions are contained on its reverse side. Furthermore, the disclaimer language is separately underscored in Item No. 7, and a heading in capital letters ['DISCLAIMER OF IMPLIED WARRANTY'] demarcates the section." See also Collins Radio Co. v. Bell, 623 P.2d 1039 (Okla. Ct. App. 1980), discussed approvingly in Cornell II, at 1268–69. See Lawrence's Anderson on the UCC §§ 2–316:110–:112.

[515] See Lawrence's Anderson on the UCC § 2–316:113.

sneaking unbargained-for disclaimers into agreements that may surprise a buyer. This suggests that the ultimate question behind the conspicuousness requirement is the subjective issue of the buyer's knowledge. If so, then perhaps a court should enforce an inconspicuous disclaimer if a particular buyer at the time of purchase is in fact aware that the product carries no implied warranties. On the other hand, the "conspicuous" definition in § 1–201(10) is crafted in terms that are plainly objective: "A term or clause is conspicuous when *so written* that a *reasonable* person against whom it is to operate *ought to have* noticed it."[516]

Courts and commentators have split over the effect of a buyer's pre-sale knowledge of a disclaimer that is inconspicuous. Some courts, supported by some commentators,[517] hold that at least commercial buyers aware of such disclaimers should be bound to the deal they believe exists.[518] Other courts, supported by other commentators,[519] hold to the contrary that an inconspicuous disclaimer should have no effect even if the buyer knows it exists.[520] In the case of ordinary products liability litigation involving personal injuries, courts would do well to hold sellers strictly to the conspicuousness requirement in § 2–316(2). Allowing sellers to disclaim the basic warranty of reasonable quality in new consumer products is almost always contrary to the true expectations of most consumers and is hence unjust.[521] In such a context, there simply is no good reason to shield a seller from the plain meaning of § 2–316(2)'s admonition that such disclaimers "must be conspicuous" nor to protect a seller from the plainly objective definition of "conspicuous" in § 1–201(10).

Post-Sale Disclaimers

Sellers frequently include disclaimers in owners' manuals, postcards, and invoices; inside product packaging; on information delivered with a product; or otherwise in a manner inaccessible to buyers until after purchase.[522] Such disclaimers bear a practically insurmountable obstacle to validity if they purport to affect contracts of sale that have already been formed.[523] "In all of these cases, it is as though the seller were determined that the buyer not see the disclaimer until after the fact. Given this seller perversity, it is not surprising that the courts generally nullify such post-contract disclaimers."[524]

---

[516] Emphasis added.

[517] See, e.g., White and Summers, UCC § 13–5, at 579–80; Weintraub, Disclaimer of Warranties and Limitation of Damages for Breach of Warranty Under the UCC, 53 Tex. L. Rev. 60 (1974).

[518] See, e.g., Imperial Stamp & Engraving Co. v. Bailey, 403 N.E.2d 294 (Ill. App. Ct. 1980).

[519] See, e.g., Cornell II, at 1271 ("Courts should abide by [§ 2–316(2)'s] language and only enforce disclaimers that are objectively conspicuous.").

[520] See, e.g., Rehurek v. Chrysler Credit Corp., 262 So.2d 452 (Fla. Dist. Ct. App. 1972).

[521] The difficulty for consumers in acquiring and properly evaluating information on the risk of product defects is an important fact of life that the law should acknowledge. See C. Gillette and S. Walt, Sales Law 266–67, 271–72 (1999).

[522] See, e.g., Virgin Valley Water Dist. v. Vanguard Piping Sys. (Canada), Inc., 2011 WL 830083, at *2 (D. Nev. 2011) (no evidence that seller gave or buyer received the disclaimer). See generally Lawrence's Anderson on the UCC §§ 2–316:45 et seq.

[523] See, e.g., G.W. White & Son, Inc. v. Gosier, 632 N.Y.S.2d 910 (App. Div. 1995) (no effect unless parties agree to modification of sales contract). See generally White and Summers, UCC § 13–5(d); Cornell II, at 1273.

[524] 1 Crockett, Product Warranties § 8:8. See, e.g., Nationwide Agribusiness Ins. Co. v. SMA Elevator Const. Inc., 816 F. Supp. 2d 631, 674 n.12 (N.D. Iowa 2011) (post-sale disclaimers invalid); Hartford Fire Ins. Co. v. Roadtec, Inc., 2010 WL 4967979, at *4 (S.D.N.Y. 2010) (warranty disclaimers first appearing when product is delivered, rather than during bargain, are invalid in New York); Dorman v. International Harvester

Courts hold such disclaimers invalid for a number of reasons.[525] Some courts reason that such a disclaimer should not be viewed as "conspicuous" under UCC § 1–201(10) because it is "not so written that a reasonable person against whom it is to operate ought to have noticed it," at least not at the time of contracting.[526] A more basic and perhaps preferable reason for invalidating post-sale disclaimers is that they are not part of the contract agreed to by the parties.[527] For this reason, to validate such a disclaimer, a seller generally will have to satisfy the modification conditions of § 2–209, which require the seller's good faith, the buyer's agreement to the modification, and possibly the buyer's signature thereon.[528] It seems inconceivable that a seller could satisfy each of these requirements in a typical consumer sales transaction, so that it appears virtually impossible for sellers to bind consumers to post-sale disclaimers in such transactions. Thus, a post-sale disclaimer normally has no effect on a warranty claim by a consumer personally injured by a defective product.[529]

"As Is" and Other Language

In general. Uniform Commercial Code § 2–316(3) provides three alternative methods for eliminating implied warranties that a seller may use in lieu of the safe-harbor techniques provided in UCC § 2–316(2). Comment 6 to § 2–316 provides in part:

> The exceptions to the general rule set forth in paragraphs (a), (b) and (c) of subsection (3) are common factual situations in which the circumstances surrounding the transaction are in themselves sufficient to call the buyer's attention to the fact that no implied warranties are made or that a certain implied warranty is being excluded.

Section 2–316 establishes the relative priority of subsection (3) by making subsection (2) "[s]ubject to subsection (3)" and by beginning subsection (3) with the phrase, "Notwithstanding subsection (2), ..." What this prioritization means is that the safe-harbor approach to disclaimer nullification in subsection (2) is optional, that disclaimers may be drafted in other ways that work as well, provided they effectively communicate the fact that the buyer takes the risk of product defects. Thus, if a merchantability disclaimer satisfies subsection (3), it need not mention "merchantability." Nevertheless, many courts have construed subsection (3) narrowly to prevent its "exceptions" from swallowing the more specific procedures of subsection (2), an approach applauded by some commentators,[530] albeit contrary to the plain language of § 2–316.

Co., 120 Cal. Rptr. 516, 522 (Ct. App. 1975) ("A disclaimer of warranties must be specifically bargained for so that a disclaimer in a warranty given to the buyer *after* he signs the contract is *not* binding.").

[525] See 1 Crockett, Product Warranties § 8:8.

[526] See, e.g., Uganski v. Little Giant Crane & Shovel, Inc., 192 N.W.2d 580 (Mich. Ct. App. 1971).

[527] See, e.g., Paper Mfrs. Co. v. Rescuers, Inc., 60 F. Supp. 2d 869, 880 (N.D. Ind. 1999) (post-sale disclaimers represent a "unilateral attempt by the seller to avoid warranty obligations that have already arisen").

[528] See UCC § 2–209. "Thus, a warranty booklet stuffed in a glove compartment of a new car would not be binding on a buyer who receives the car three days after signing the sales agreement—unless the buyer 'agreed' to the modification." White and Summers, UCC § 13–5, at 583.

[529] *But see* Temple v. Velcro USA, Inc., 196 Cal. Rptr. 531, 533 (Ct. App. 1983), which involved the crash of a hot-air balloon after the manufacturer of a hook and loop closure issued warnings against the use of its product to hold in place the deflation panels on such balloons: "If the warning was adequate it certainly would be a proper disclaimer to any express or implied warranties . . . ." The court offered no analysis for this conclusion.

[530] See, e.g., Cornell II, at 1278 ("We continue to urge courts to read section 2–316(3)(a) narrowly.").

Subsection (3)(a) permits a seller to disclaim implied warranties by using "as is"[531] or similar language:[532]

> [U]nless the circumstances indicate otherwise, all implied warranties are excluded by expressions like "as is," "with all faults" or other language which in common understanding calls the buyer's attention to the exclusion of warranties and makes plain that there is no implied warranty.

The thrust of this subsection is to permit a product seller to exclude implied warranties by making it clear to the buyer, without using the safe-harbor language of "merchantability" required in subsection (2), that no such warranties accompany the sale. The common expression "as is," and other language which plainly states that the buyer takes the risk that a product may contain latent defects, thus excludes any implied warranties from the sales transaction. As discussed below, however, subsection (3) contains an important initial caveat that will invalidate "as is" and similar disclaimers if "the circumstances indicate otherwise."

Type of buyer and type of product. In commercial sales transactions involving buyers who are knowledgeable business enterprises, "as is" and similar language of disclaimer generally serve effectively to exclude implied warranties, even if the buyer's employee is injured by a defect in the product.[533] However, even in this context, "as is" disclaimers ordinarily may be expected only for sales of goods which are *used*,[534] so that a court may refuse to enforce such a disclaimer where the goods sold are *new*.[535] Moreover, while subsection (3)(a) may properly be applied in many consumer transactions involving used products, courts may conclude that "the circumstances indicate otherwise" in particular consumer sale situations.[536]

Commentators disagree on the proper effect of "as is" disclaimers in consumer sales transactions, some arguing that such disclaimers should effectively exclude implied warranties even in the consumer context,[537] others suggesting to the contrary that such disclaimers should be valid only in commercial sales,[538] and some taking a middle view dependent on the circumstances of the particular case.[539] One reasonable middle view

---

[531] See Lawrence's Anderson on the UCC §§ 2–316:141 to :156.

[532] See id. §§ 2–316:174 to :181.

[533] See, e.g., Buettner v. Super Laundry Mach., 857 F. Supp. 471 (E.D. Va. 1994) ("as is" disclaimer not unconscionable toward injured employee because employer was sophisticated business buyer), aff'd sub nom. Buettner v. R.W. Martin & Sons, Inc., 47 F.3d 116 (4th Cir. 1995).

[534] See, e.g., Pelc v. Simmons, 620 N.E.2d 12 (Ill. App. Ct. 1993) (used car; "as is" effective disclaimer).

[535] See, e.g., Gindy Mfg. Corp. v. Cardinale Trucking Corp., 268 A.2d 345 (N.J. Super. Ct. Law Div. 1970).

[536] See, e.g., Knipp v. Weinbaum, 351 So.2d 1081, 1084 (Fla. Dist. Ct. App. 1977) ("the clause 'unless the circumstances indicate otherwise' . . . precludes a finding that automatic absolution can be achieved in the sale of used consumer goods merely by the inclusion in a bill of sale of the magic words 'as is' ").

[537] See, e.g., Honnold, 1 N.Y. State Law Revision Comm'n, 1955 Report 409, referenced in White and Summers, UCC § 13–6, at 585 n.6; Cornell II, at 1278 (backtracking from the consumer-friendly view of Special Project, Article Two Warranties in Commercial Transactions, 64 Cornell L. Rev. 30, 195–96 (1978) [hereinafter Cornell I]); 1 Crockett, Product Warranties § 8:10:

> If the seller uses the buzz phrases set out in the statute, the court should not inquire into the characteristics of the buyer. . . . Otherwise, the courts are drawn into ticklish questions of fact with great resulting uncertainty. [T]here is simply no justification in the statute for such line-drawing.

[538] See, e.g., Cornell I, at 195–96.

[539] Although Professors White and Summers appear to lean toward universal enforcement of such clauses, they may be read to be equivocal on the consumer issue for which they might favor some middle-road approach. See White and Summers, UCC § 13–6, at 584–86.

might be to protect consumers generally from "as is" and similar disclaimers in new product cases, but to hold them to such disclaimers in used goods cases, with the result in either situation being rebuttable upon clear proof that the circumstances of the particular transaction call for other treatment.

An "as is" disclaimer will not shield a seller from fraud,[540] or from obligations arising from a service contract[541] or an express warranty,[542] but most courts hold in the absence of such circumstances that sellers of used cars may effectively exclude implied warranties by means of such disclaimers.[543] Most of the used car cases, however, involve claims for repair costs for unexpected mechanical problems, and a court confronted with a personal injury claim excluded by an "as is" disclaimer is likely to scrutinize quite closely the "circumstances" of the particular case to see if they might "indicate otherwise."[544]

Conspicuousness. One perplexing issue is whether "as is" and similar subsection (3)(a) disclaimers must be conspicuous. The explicit requirement of conspicuousness in subsection (2) and its omission in (3)(a) strongly suggest that the drafters of § 2–316 did *not* intend to require that subsection (3)(a) disclaimers be conspicuous to be effective. A few courts take this view.[545] Alternatively, perhaps the drafters believed that the language "unless the circumstances indicate otherwise" should be used to invalidate inconspicuous subsection (3)(a) disclaimers, especially in consumer transactions, unless the buyer was aware of the provision.[546] Troubled by the anomaly of requiring conspicuousness for subsection (2) but not (3)(a) disclaimers, and influenced by § 2–316's underlying goal of preventing buyers from surprise, probably most courts hold that "as is" disclaimers must be conspicuous.[547] Except, perhaps, when a particular buyer truly is aware of and understands the consequences of such exclusionary language, requiring

---

[540] See, e.g., Adeli v. Silverstar Auto., Inc., 960 F.3d 452, 464 (8th Cir. 2020) (Ark. law) (dealer fraudulently concealed used Ferrari's cracked exhaust headers that could have caused fire); Oakwood Mobile Homes, Inc. v. Cabler, 73 S.W.3d 363, 371–72 (Tex. App. 2002); Danley v. Murphy, 658 So.2d 483 (Ala. Civ. App. 1994) (used car dealer said car that had been totaled had been "smacked" in front).

[541] Patton v. McHone, 822 S.W.2d 608 (Tenn. Ct. App. 1991).

[542] See, e.g., Safadi v. Thompson, 487 S.E.2d 457 (Ga. Ct. App. 1997) ("as is" language does not disclaim express warranty that car had not been wrecked); Barksdale v. Van's Auto Sales, Inc., 577 N.E.2d 426 (Ohio Ct. App. 1989). However, courts occasionally assert that "as is" disclaimers *do* exclude liability for express as well as implied warranties, at least between commercial parties. See, e.g., Welch Sand & Gravel, Inc. v. O & K Trojan, Inc., 668 N.E.2d 529 (Ohio Ct. App. 1995). See generally Lawrence's Anderson on the UCC § 2–316:150.

[543] See, e.g., Scaffidi v. United Nissan, 425 F. Supp. 2d 1172, 1185–87 (D. Nev. 2005) ("as is" disclaimer negated both implied warranties of merchantability and fitness); Richardson v. Mast, 560 N.W.2d 488 (Neb. 1997); David [not Owen] v. Davenport, 656 So.2d 952 (Fla. Dist. Ct. App. 1995); Jenkins v. Landmark Chevrolet, Inc., 575 So.2d 1157 (Ala. Civ. App. 1991); DeVoe Chevrolet-Cadillac, Inc. v. Cartwright, 526 N.E.2d 1237 (Ind. Ct. App. 1988).

[544] *But see* Wilke v. Woodhouse Ford, Inc., 774 N.W.2d 370, 378–79 (Neb. 2009) (failure of brake pedal safety mechanism on used van allowed child accidentally to shift out of park, injuring mother while trying to rescue child; although a safety defect was involved, court ruled "as is" disclaimer permitted by § 2–316 was not against public policy).

[545] See, e.g., Auburn Ford, Lincoln Mercury, Inc. v. Norred, 541 So.2d 1077, 1080 (Ala. 1989).

[546] Comment 1 to § 2–316 suggests that an inconspicuous "as is" disclaimer read by a buyer should render the disclaimer valid and enforceable: "This section . . . seeks to protect a buyer from unexpected and unbargained language of disclaimer by . . . permitting the exclusion of implied warranties only by conspicuous language *or other circumstances which protect the buyer from surprise*." (emphasis added.)

[547] See, e.g., Basselen v. General Motors Corp., 792 N.E.2d 498, 508 (Ill. App. Ct. 2003) (by implication); Lumber Mut. Ins. Co. v. Clarklift of Detroit, Inc., 569 N.W.2d 681 (Mich. Ct. App. 1997).

"as is" disclaimers to be conspicuous in consumer products liability cases may be the better view.[548]

Prior Inspection

Implied warranties may be disclaimed by the buyer's prior inspection, or the seller's demand that the buyer conduct such an inspection, of a product.[549] Uniform Commercial Code § 2–316(3)(b) provides:

> [W]hen the buyer before entering into the contract has examined the goods or the sample or model as fully as he desired or has refused to examine the goods there is no implied warranty with regard to defects which an examination ought in the circumstances to have revealed to him . . . .

This provision specifies two separate ways in which implied warranties may be disclaimed: (1) by the buyer's *actual* inspection of a product, and (2) by the buyer's *refusal* of the seller's *demand* that the buyer inspect a product.[550] In the first situation, the buyer is deemed to have discovered any obvious flaws in the product and so to understand that there is no implied assurance that such flaws do not exist.[551] As previously discussed,[552] obvious dangers are excluded from the scope of the condition that is warranted, whether the buyer actually discovers them or not—that is, the obvious nature of a danger effectively disclaims any implied promise that the danger does not exist.[553] In the second situation, by refusing a seller's demand, the buyer simply takes the risk of such flaws: "The seller by the demand puts the buyer on notice that he is assuming the risk of defects which the examination ought to reveal."[554]

Subsection (3)(b) disclaimers apply only to "defects which an examination ought in the circumstances to have revealed." Thus, in most cases, only defects that are truly obvious are covered by this form of disclaimer, for a buyer cannot be expected to uncover latent defects in an ordinary examination.[555] For example, if a used car dealer tells a prospective purchaser to examine a car carefully before buying it, the buyer's refusal to so inspect the car, or his inspection that fails to reveal that the tires are worn completely through to the fabric, probably will amount to a disclaimer of an implied warranty of the tires' obviously unmerchantable condition.[556] Similarly, if a diver were to ask a seller for

---

[548] See 1 Crockett, Product Warranties § 8:11. Though now withdrawn, see § 4.1 notes 17 and 18, above, Amended § 2–316(3)(a) would have required disclaimers of fitness warranties to be in writing in consumer contracts.

[549] See Lawrence's Anderson on the UCC §§ 2–316:177 to :192.

[550] A refusal-to-examine-the-goods disclaimer arises under subsection (3)(b) only if the seller explicitly "demand[s] that the buyer examine the goods fully." UCC § 2–316 cmt. 8.

[551] See, e.g., Darrell Wood v. Bass Pro Shops, Inc., 462 S.E.2d 101, 103 (Va. 1995) (no implied warranty case if purported defect was "known, visible or obvious" to plaintiff); Toney v. Kawasaki Heavy Indus., 975 F.2d 162 (5th Cir. 1992) (Miss. law) (absence of leg protection on motorcycle did not render it unfit for ordinary purpose because normal rider would appreciate risk of leg injury in side collision with auto).

[552] See § 4.3, above.

[553] UCC § 2–316 cmt. 8 (buyer's failure to notice obvious defects no excuse).

[554] UCC § 2–316 cmt. 8. See Hays v. General Elec. Co., 151 F. Supp. 2d 1001, 1013–14 (N.D. Ill. 2001) (buyers held to objective standard of what a buyer of particular product in the field should know).

[555] See, e.g., Driscoll v. Standard Hardware, Inc., 785 N.W.2d 805, 816–17 (Minn. Ct. App. 2010) (implied warranty not disclaimed by prior inspection; latent defect causing cracks in drill jacks "could not have been discovered by routine examination," even by sophisticated purchaser). See also In re Subaru Battery Drain Prods. Liab. Litig., 2021 WL 1207791, at *21 (D.N.J. 2021) (declining to dismiss plaintiffs' implied warranty claim; latent defect exception applied).

[556] However limited the warranty in this situation might be. See UCC § 2–314 cmt. 3.

a water-resistant watch good to 100 meters and, while examining the watch handed to him in response, notices "30m" printed on its face, any implied warranty of fitness to 100 meters might well be disclaimed under § 2–316(3)(b). But neither warranty would be disclaimed if the defect were latent: if, in the first situation, the car's frame were dangerously defective,[557] or if, in the second, no depth indication were printed anywhere on the watch. Consumers generally will be responsible for discovering only the most glaring flaws.[558] Sophisticated commercial buyers who know precisely what to look for and how to conduct an effective examination of a particular type of product are held to a higher standard of discovery,[559] but even they are protected against defects that a professional investigation would not reveal.[560]

Course of Dealing

The third and final alternative method by which a disclaimer may arise is described in UCC § 2–316(3)(c):

> [A]n implied warranty can also be excluded or modified by course of dealing or course of performance or usage of trade.[561]

The Code defines "course of dealing" as a "sequence of previous conduct between the parties to a particular transaction which is fairly to be regarded as establishing a common basis of understanding for interpreting their expressions and other conduct."[562] It defines "usage of trade" as "any practice or method of dealing having such regularity of observance in a place, vocation or trade as to justify an expectation that it will be observed with respect to the transaction in question."[563]

Subsection (3)(c) warranty exclusions are rarely litigated in the products liability context, but they can arise. For example, such exclusions might arise when a manufacturer of dangerous chemicals or machinery regularly supplies an industrial company with its products. These two parties may have an arrangement whereby the manufacturer sells the product "raw" to the buying company, with no warnings or guards, because the buying company adds such safety enhancements to the product in a way best suited to the peculiarities of each setting and, hence, is most efficient and effective in protecting the safety of its employees. While a manufacturer's duty to warn and to provide safety devices sometimes may be nondelegable,[564] a course of dealing like the one described normally should serve to exclude any implied warranty that the product could be safely used as sold.

---

[557] See Twin Lakes Mfg. v. Coffey, 281 S.E.2d 864, 867 (Va. 1981), involving defects in the frame of a mobile home: "[The] defects . . . did not become apparent, even to experienced workmen, until pressure was applied to join the two sections [of the house]. Such latent defects are not those contemplated by [subsection (3)(b)]," such that the buyer's inspection did not waive implied warranties concerning those defects.

[558] See 1 Crockett, Product Warranties § 8:13: "If the buyer is a consumer without any special knowledge of the goods, the court will not find a disclaimer by inspection unless the defect reaches out and bites the buyer. This is particularly the case where automobiles are involved."

[559] See UCC § 2–316 cmt. 8 (distinguishing between professional and lay buyers).

[560] See, e.g., Driscoll v. Standard Hardware, Inc., 785 N.W.2d 805, 816–17 (Minn. Ct. App. 2010) (implied warranty not disclaimed by prior inspection; latent defect causing cracks in drill jacks "could not have been discovered by routine examination," even by sophisticated purchaser).

[561] See Lawrence's Anderson on the UCC §§ 2–316:61 et seq.

[562] UCC § 1–205(1).

[563] UCC § 1–205(2).

[564] See §§ 8.9 (design) and 9.5 (warning), below.

Consumer transactions involving dangerously defective products only infrequently are affected by implied warranty exclusions under § 2–316(3)(c), but such exclusions can occur in this context, too. Suppose, for example, that a farmer regularly buys used tractor tires from a tire dealer who keeps a large pile of such tires behind his shop. The first time they do business, the tire dealer may inform the farmer that he has no idea which of the used tires may be good or bad, and that he sells these tires for $20 each on condition that the buyer personally inspect the tire and bear the entire risk that it may be defective. Thereafter, the dealer may sell many such tires to the farmer over the years while never uttering these words again,[565] and the farmer may simply discard and replace any such tires that after purchase turn out to be bad. If one day the farmer is injured when one such tire blows out, he might sue the dealer for breach of an implied warranty. In a case like this, a court may well hold that subsection (3)(c) excludes any implied warranties from arising in this situation because of the parties' "course of dealing." Furthermore, if tire dealers and farmers commonly address the risk of loss from defective used tractor tires in this same manner, implied warranties might also be excluded by "usage of trade."

Unconscionability

A question that has long vexed courts and commentators is whether a disclaimer drafted in compliance with Uniform Commercial Code § 2–316 can ever be struck down for being "unconscionable."[566] More specifically, may a disclaimer of the implied warranty of merchantability that is properly drafted under § 2–316(2) (by conspicuously mentioning merchantability) or § 2–316(3) (by conspicuously stating "as is") ever be invalidated as unconscionable under the Code? Those who reason that the Code's unconscionability principles do apply to disclaimers draw upon one or two sections of Article 2: (1) the general provision on unconscionability in § 2–302, and (2) the specific application of unconscionability doctrine to consequential damages limitations in § 2–719(3).[567]

Section 2–302

Article 2's general unconscionability provision, § 2–302, provides as follows:

§ 2–302. Unconscionable Contract or Clause

(1) If the court as a matter of law finds the contract or any clause of the contract to have been unconscionable at the time it was made the court may refuse to enforce the contract, or it may enforce the remainder of the contract without the unconscionable clause, or it may so limit the application of any unconscionable clause as to avoid any unconscionable result.

---

[565] The dealer's argument would be even stronger, of course, if the dealer frequently had reminded the buyer of the disclaimer. See Tolmie Farms, Inc. v. J.R. Simplot Co., 862 P.2d 299 (Idaho 1993).

[566] The classic article arguing that the Code's unconscionability provisions do not apply to § 2–316 disclaimers is Leff, Unconscionability and the Code—The Emperor's New Clause, 115 U. Pa. L. Rev. 485, 516–28 (1967) [hereinafter Leff, Unconscionability and the Code]. This conclusion is supported by 1 N.Y. State Law Revision Comm'n, 1955 Report 586 (1955). For early statements of the opposite view, see, e.g., Ellinghaus, In Defense of Unconscionability, 78 Yale L.J. 757 (1969); Weintraub, Disclaimer of Warranties and Limitation of Damages for Breach of Warranty Under the UCC, 53 Tex. L. Rev. 60, 75–83 (1974). Modern commentators conclude that the exclusion of warranties is not per se unconscionable but recognize that some courts will apply § 2–302 to invalidate disclaimers in particular cases where they appear one-sided and oppressive. See Lawrence's Anderson on the UCC §§ 2–316:72 to :80; White and Summers, UCC § 12–11, at 848 (splitting on propriety of this result).

[567] See Annot., 38 A.L.R.4th 25 (1985) (unconscionability of disclaimers and limitations).

Despite the prominence of the important concept of "unconscionability" in § 2–302 and various other sections, Article 2 never really defines the term. Whether this is because the notion is too vague or perhaps too complicated to permit a meaningful definition, courts and commentators have spilled considerable ink over the years wrestling with the meaning and effect of unconscionability in contract law, generally, and sales law under Article 2 of the UCC in particular. Comment 1 to § 2–302 provides at best a hint of what the term might mean, referring to unconscionable clauses as being particularly "one-sided" and to the goal of § 2–302 as "the prevention of oppression and unfair surprise," but *not* the disturbance of "allocation of risks" arising from "superior bargaining power."[568] Many courts, usually outside the products liability context,[569] have defined and applied the term more fully in a wide variety of situations.[570]

---

[568] Comment 1 provides more fully:

> The basic test is whether, in the light of the general commercial background and the commercial needs of the particular trade or case, the clauses involved are so one-sided as to be unconscionable under the circumstances existing at the time of the making of the contract. . . . The principle is one of the prevention of oppression and unfair surprise . . . and not of disturbance of allocation of risks because of superior bargaining power.

[569] The most significant products liability case, of course, was Henningsen v. Bloomfield Motors, Inc., 161 A.2d 69, 97 (N.J. 1960) (Francis, J.), involving a claim for personal injuries caused by a steering defect in a new Chrysler, where the court concluded that a disclaimer of the implied warranty of merchantability and a limitation of remedy to repair or replacement in a standardized form sales contract were "violative of public policy and void." *Henningsen* was decided the year before New Jersey adopted the UCC. On *Henningsen*, see § 4.9, below.

[570] See, e.g., Brunsman v. DeKalb Swine Breeders, Inc., 952 F. Supp. 628, 633 (N.D. Iowa 1996) (bargain unconscionable if "such as no person in his senses and not under delusion would make on the one hand, and as no honest and fair person would accept on the other"; relevant factors include "assent, unfair surprise, notice, disparity of bargaining power, and substantive unfairness"), aff'd, 138 F.3d 358 (8th Cir. 1998). See also Auto-Owners Ins. Co. v. Toole, 947 F. Supp. 1557 (M.D. Ala. 1996) (also defining in no-man-in-his-senses-and-not-under-delusion terms, and considering the following factors: whether one party was uneducated or unsophisticated; whether one party had no meaningful choice; whether terms unreasonably favored one party; whether there was unequal bargaining power; and whether the contract contained oppressive, one-sided, or patently unfair terms).

Consider Wayman v. Amoco Oil Co., 923 F. Supp. 1322, 1341 (D. Kan. 1996), aff'd, 145 F.3d 1347 (10th Cir. 1998), in which the court noted that the doctrines of both unconscionability and adhesion "are concerned with unfairness and one-sidedness in a contract as a result of unequal bargaining power":

> An adhesion contract is a "[s]tandardized contract form offered to consumers of goods and services on essentially 'take it or leave it' basis without affording consumer realistic opportunity to bargain and under such conditions that consumer cannot obtain desired product or services except by acquiescing in form contract."

Quoting the "basic test" of unconscionability in cmt. 1 to § 2–302 set forth in the text above, the court referred to other Kansas courts' formulation of this issue as whether a provision is "so outrageous and unfair in its wording or its application that it shocks the conscience or offends the sensibilities of the court," involving such considerations as: use of printed boilerplate drafted by stronger party; excessive price; denial of basic rights and remedies to consumers; penalty clauses; circumstances of contract execution and effect; hiding disadvantageous clauses in inconspicuous location or in mass of fine-print trivia; phrasing language incomprehensibly or misleadingly; imbalance of bargain's rights and responsibilities; exploitation of the unsophisticated and uneducated; and unequal bargaining power. Id. at 1342.

See Professor Leff's classic distinction between "substantive" and "procedural" unconscionability in Leff, Unconscionability and the Code, 115 U. Pa. L. Rev., at 487, above. See, e.g., Walker v. American Cyanamid Co., 948 P.2d 1123 (Idaho 1997) (invalidating disclaimer on both substantive and procedural grounds); Nelson v. McGoldrick, 896 P.2d 1258, 1262 (Wash. 1995) ("substantive unconscionability"—terms are one-sided or "monstrously harsh"; "procedural unconscionability"—one party's lack of meaningful choice, as from inability to discover or understand terms). See also Allan v. Snow Summit, Inc., 59 Cal. Rptr. 2d 813, 825 (Ct. App. 1996) ("substantive inadequacy" not only one-sided result, but also absence of justification for that result, or unreasonable or unexpected reallocation of risks of bargain). The court defined "procedural unconscionability" as based either on (1) *oppression*, from unequal bargaining power precluding negotiation and choice; or (2) *surprise*, from supposedly agreed-upon terms being hidden in a prolix printed form.

Whether a disclaimer should be invalidated as unconscionable is particularly important in products liability cases in which manufacturers frequently attempt by contract to define the full extent of their legal responsibility for product accidents and to exclude as much responsibility as possible for implied warranties. Although much has been changed by state reform statutes[571] and the federal Magnuson-Moss Warranty Act,[572] manufacturers of automobiles and many other types of products conventionally attempted to disclaim *all* implied warranties, especially the merchantability warranty, by mentioning "merchantability" conspicuously in the contract of sale. This return to the now-discredited doctrine of *caveat emptor* raises the question, answered powerfully in favor of consumers in *Henningsen v. Bloomfield Motors*,[573] whether such complete disclaimers of the basic warranty of safety can ever be conscionable in the context of the sale of new consumer products.

The issue that confronts a court adjudicating a claim for breach of warranty under Article 2 of the Uniform Commercial Code is one of statutory interpretation: Is § 2–316 entirely independent and self-contained, so that the validity of a disclaimer can be tested solely by whether it meets the requirements of this one section, which thus may be seen to "preempt" § 2–302? This might be called the "preemption" view. Alternatively, must disclaimers jump through *two* separate validity hoops: (1) § 2–316's specific disclaimer requirements, *and* (2) § 2–302's general policing filter, which requires that contract terms be conscionable? This latter approach might be called the "two-hoop" view.[574]

Strong arguments support both views.[575] Proponents of the preemption view argue, first, that § 2–316 clearly and specifically authorizes disclaimers and nowhere, in the text or comments, makes any mention of unconscionability. By contrast, § 2–316's cousin section that addresses limitations of consequential damages, § 2–719(3), specifically conditions such limitations on their conscionability.[576] Indeed, comment 3 to § 2–719 distinguishes that section from § 2–316 on the ground that, unlike § 2–719(3), "[t]he seller in *all* cases is free to disclaim warranties in the manner provided in Section 2–316."[577] Further, the principal purpose of § 2–316 is to protect buyers from "unbargained language of disclaimer" and "surprise," a policy that overlaps § 2–302's own goals of preventing "oppression and unfair surprise."[578] This suggests that § 2–316 contains within itself as much internal policing of the fairness of disclaimers as useful, such that it can do without assistance from the general policing provisions of § 2–302.

Proponents of the two-hoop view observe that § 2–302 by its terms applies to "any clause of the contract,"[579] and nowhere does it suggest that disclaimers under § 2–316 are somehow out of bounds. Moreover, seven of the ten illustrative cases in comment 1 to § 2–302 involve disclaimers denied full effect. And while § 2–316 may protect buyers from "surprise," it does not protect them from one-sided contractual "oppression" of the

---

[571] See § 4.9, below.

[572] See id.

[573] 161 A.2d 69 (N.J. 1960).

[574] See 1 Crockett, Product Warranties § 8:12.

[575] Both sets of arguments are well summarized in Crockett, above, and White and Summers, UCC § 13–11.

[576] See § 4.8, below.

[577] UCC § 2–719 cmt. 3 (emphasis added).

[578] UCC § 2–302 cmt. 1.

[579] UCC § 2–302(1) (emphasis added).

type that the automotive industry imposed on consumers in *Henningsen v. Bloomfield Motors, Inc.*[580]

Like the commentators, the courts are split on whether § 2–316 disclaimers may be found unconscionable under § 2–302. There is clear judicial support for the preemption view that § 2–316 disclaimers simply may not be declared unconscionable.[581] Yet, a number of cases suggest[582] that § 2–302 may invalidate disclaimers that comply with § 2–316.[583]

Section 2–719(3)

Rather than invoke the general unconscionability provision of § 2–302, some plaintiffs ask courts to nullify § 2–316 disclaimers under the remedy limitation provision, § 2–719(3), which provides:

> Consequential damages may be limited or excluded unless the limitation or exclusion is unconscionable. Limitation of consequential damages for injury to the person in the case of consumer goods is prima facie unconscionable but limitation of damages where the loss is commercial is not.

The argument is that if a disclaimer drafted in compliance with § 2–316 operates so as to deny a plaintiff the right to consequential damages for injury to person, it is (prima facie) invalid on grounds of unconscionability under § 2–719.[584]

While a couple of courts have accepted this kind of "reasoning,"[585] it squarely contradicts the structure and wording of Article 2. In comments to both § 2–316 and § 2–719, the Code makes clear as a bell that § 2–316, which addresses whether a warranty's creation was nullified *ab initio* by a disclaimer, is independent of the entirely separate issue in § 2–719(3) of whether a seller may limit personal injury damages recoverable for breach of a warranty that has *not* been nullified under § 2–316.

In particular, comment 2 to § 2–316 provides:

> This Article treats the limitation or avoidance of consequential damages as a matter of limiting remedies for breach, separate from the matter of creation of liability under a warranty. *If no warranty exists, there is of course no problem of limiting remedies for breach of warranty.* Under [§ 2–316(4)] the question of limitation of remedy is governed by [§ 2–719 and related sections] rather than by this section.[586]

---

[580] 161 A.2d 69 (N.J. 1960). Professor Weintraub favored applying § 2–302 to certain disclaimers valid under § 2–316; it "seems consistent with Code policy that section 2–302 be used to police against unconscionable warranty disclaimers, even those that have meticulously adhered to the formal requirements of section 2–316." Weintraub, above note 566, at 83 (suggesting relevance to unconscionability determination of such factors as (1) type of remedy excluded—lost profits *vs.* personal injury, (2) advertence—whether the buyer understood the disclaimer's meaning and practical consequences, and (3) adhesion—whether the buyer could bargain for better terms).

[581] See, e.g., Ford Motor Co. v. Moulton, 511 S.W.2d 690 (Tenn. 1974).

[582] However, finding a case that actually *holds* a disclaimer invalid on this basis may be difficult. See White and Summers, UCC § 13–11, at 614.

[583] See, e.g., Murray v. Holiday Rambler, Inc., 265 N.W.2d 513 (Wis. 1978); Hiigel v. General Motors Corp., 544 P.2d 983 (Colo. 1975), as modified (1976). Cf. Henningsen v. Bloomfield Motors, Inc., 161 A.2d 69 (N.J. 1960) (new automobile; pre-Code case).

[584] UCC § 2–719 is more fully examined in § 4.8, below.

[585] See, e.g., Ford Motor Co. v. Tritt, 430 S.W.2d 778 (Ark. 1968).

[586] Emphasis added.

Professors White and Summers succinctly explain the incontrovertible meaning of this comment:

> The comment's reasoning is elementary: there can be no consequential damages if there is no breach; there can be no breach of warranty if there is no warranty; there can be no warranty if the seller has disclaimed them pursuant to 2–316. Although a particular warranty may be unconscionable under 2–302, it seems clear that the scheme of the Code does not permit a court to disregard that disclaimer on the basis that it operates to exclude consequential damages that could not be excluded under 2–719(3).[587]

Not only does comment 2 to § 2–316 make entirely clear that § 2–719(3)'s unconscionability provision cannot be used to invalidate a warranty disclaimer that is good under § 2–316, but this point is underscored by comment 3 to § 2–719. After recognizing that unconscionability constrains the extent to which a seller may limit damages, the comment proceeds to declare that a seller "in *all* cases is free to disclaim warranties" under § 2–316.[588] Surely this must mean that § 2–316 disclaimers in all cases are free from the unconscionability constraints of § 2–719(3).[589]

The independence of § 2–316 and § 2–719(3) from each other, and the resulting impropriety of applying § 2–719(3) to invalidate disclaimers that are properly drawn under § 2–316, thus seem evident, as some courts have held.[590] Curiously, a small number of courts,[591] and even some commentators,[592] have disagreed. The explanation for such an apparent breach of the Code's integrity in several of the cases appears to spring from confusion as to how the Code is structured.[593] Another explanation for why a few courts have mistakenly applied the § 2–719 unconscionability provision to § 2–316 disclaimers may be an effort to ameliorate the harshness of denying any remedy to a consumer who is physically injured by a defective product.[594]

While a court might well be tempted to adopt a chancellor mantle to render justice in such cases, it would seem that a state legislature's adoption of meticulously structured and precisely drafted sections of a commercial code should be respected. Creative justice in products liability judging appears more appropriately directed to the realm of tort law where judicial doctrines of tortious misrepresentation, negligence, and strict liability in tort provide courts in most cases ample room to protect deserving persons injured by defective products. And in cases where tort law closes its doors on such persons, perhaps because of a short tort law statute of limitations, a court faced with an oppressive

---

[587] White and Summers, UCC § 13–12, at 618.

[588] "Subsection (3) recognizes the validity of clauses limiting or excluding consequential damages but makes it clear that they may not operate in an unconscionable manner. Actually such terms are merely an allocation of unknown or undeterminable risks. *The seller in all cases is free to disclaim warranties in the manner provided in Section 2–316.*" UCC § 2–719 cmt. 3 (emphasis added).

[589] White and Summers capture this point: "The last sentence [of comment 3] seems to be telling the seller, 'If you really want to limit your liability, why don't you disclaim all warranties? Then you won't have to worry about limiting damages.' " White and Summers, UCC § 13–12, at 618.

[590] See, e.g., Ford Motor Co. v. Moulton, 511 S.W.2d 690 (Tenn. 1974).

[591] See Walsh v. Ford Motor Co., 298 N.Y.S.2d 538 (Sup. Ct. 1969); Ford Motor Co. v. Tritt, 430 S.W.2d 778 (Ark. 1968).

[592] See, e.g., Note, 63 Va. L. Rev. 791 (1977).

[593] See, e.g., Ford Motor Co. v. Tritt, 430 S.W.2d 778 (Ark. 1968).

[594] See White and Summers, UCC § 13–12, at 619.

disclaimer of a warranty claim might turn in good conscience to the general unconscionability provisions of § 2–302.[595]

§ 4.8 LIMITATIONS OF REMEDY

As with any damages claim, a products liability action consists of two major components: (1) a breach of legal duty, and (2) resulting damage. In warranty law, a seller breaches a legal duty by making and breaching a warranty. As previously discussed, a disclaimer is an explicit means by which a seller may contractually avoid making warranties, particularly implied warranties, that otherwise would arise from the sale of a product.[596] One might view disclaimers as a seller's front-door method for avoiding warranty responsibility for product accidents.

A second method by which a seller may contractually avoid some or all responsibility for breach of warranty is to exclude or limit a buyer's remedies for breach.[597] In a world of perfect freedom of contract, a buyer and seller might agree to a sale in which (1) the product carries various (undisclaimed) express and implied warranties, but (2) the buyer's only remedy for breach, no matter how great the actual damages, would be $100.[598] More plausibly, a dealer might sell a used car with a 30-day express warranty against mechanical defects but with an exclusion of damages for personal injuries and a limitation of the buyer's remedy to repair or replacement of defective parts. This type of limitation-of-remedy provision in sales contracts might be viewed as a seller's back-door method for avoiding substantial warranty responsibility for product accidents.

As examined earlier, UCC § 2–316, located in the "General Obligation" portion of Article 2,[599] authorizes and imposes various controls on a seller's efforts to avoid *creating* warranties via *disclaimers* of their existence.[600] Section 2–719, located in the "Remedies" portion of Article 2,[601] authorizes and controls the *limitations* a seller may place on a buyer's *remedies* for breach of warranty. While proclaiming the separate and independent status of these two provisions, the Code suggests the tandem nature of how they may interrelate in sales transactions. The Code's warranty-disclaimer section, in § 2–316(4), cross-references the Code's remedy-limitation provisions:

> Remedies for breach of warranty can be limited in accordance with the provisions of this Article on liquidation or limitation of damages and on contractual modification of remedy (Sections 2–718 and 2–719).

---

[595] Amended UCC § 2–316 would have improved consumer protection against unbargained-for disclaimers of implied warranties in a number of ways. For its fate, see § 4.1 notes 17 and 18, above.

[596] See § 4.7, above.

[597] See id., text at notes 462–470, and particularly note 465, for a discussion of how disclaimers and limitations provide sellers with alternative methods for avoiding responsibility for product defects and false warranties.

[598] Depending on the circumstances, this kind of agreement may well be forbidden by UCC § 2–719's premise that "it is of the very essence of a sales contract that at least minimum adequate remedies be available. If the parties intend to conclude a contract for sale within this Article they must accept the legal consequence that there be at least a fair quantum of remedy for breach of the obligations or duties outlined in the contract." UCC § 2–719 cmt. 1.

[599] Part 3, General Obligation and Construction of Contract, begins with § 2–301.

[600] See § 4.7, above.

[601] Part 7, Remedies, begins with § 2–701.

Correspondingly, comment 3 to Article 2's remedy-limitation section, § 2–719, recognizes disclaimers as an alternative method by which sellers may avoid warranty responsibility by contractually allocating risk to buyers:

> [Terms that limit or exclude consequential damages are allowable if not unconscionable.] Actually such terms are merely an allocation of unknown or undeterminable risks. *The seller in all cases is free to disclaim warranties in the manner provided in Section 2–316.*[602]

Thus, while operating independently, disclaimers and limitations form the horse and buggy of a product seller's responsibility-avoidance measures.[603]

The predicates to the § 2–719 limitations-of-remedy provisions are the Code's provisions defining a buyer's allowable damages for breach of warranty in §§ 2–714 and 2–715. Section 2–714(3) authorizes awards of "consequential damages" for breach of warranty, and § 2–715(2)(b) defines such damages to include "injury to person or property proximately resulting from any breach of warranty."

As with many other provisions in Article 2,[604] §§ 2–714 and 2–715 operate principally as "default" provisions—rules that take effect only if the parties' contract does not otherwise address the issue. That is, if a buyer and seller fail to specify in their agreement what damages will be available for breach of warranty, a buyer may recover the types of damages prescribed in §§ 2–714 and 2–715. Operating within a framework of freedom of contract, such default provisions serve to "fill in" contracts that fail to specify an important term with the kind of term most parties normally would agree to if they freely bargained and were informed.[605]

Thus, § 2–719 authorizes and conditions the *alteration* of a buyer's *remedies* otherwise available under §§ 2–714 and 2–715. Consistent with Article 2's objective of allowing parties to a sales transaction to shape their particular deals as they may agree, subject only to controls to help ensure that their decisions are informed and free, the purpose of § 2–719 is to allow sellers and buyers to frame remedy provisions in their sales contracts consistent with informed free choice.[606] Each of the three subsections to § 2–719 reflects these general principles.

---

[602] UCC § 2–719 cmt. 3 (emphasis added).

[603] See § 4.7, note 465, above.

[604] Other notable default provisions in Article 2 are those on implied warranties in §§ 2–314 and 2–315. These two provisions may arise by default in sales contracts that do not explicitly create or exclude them.

[605] Subject to certain special protections, the UCC broadly attempts to implement the parties' agreement. See UCC § 1–102(3): "The effect of provisions of this Act may be varied by agreement, except as otherwise provided in this Act and except that the obligations of good faith, diligence, reasonableness and care prescribed by this Act may not be disclaimed by agreement . . . ."

[606] Comment 1 to § 2–719 explains:

> Under this section parties are left free to shape their remedies to their particular requirements and reasonable agreements limiting or modifying remedies are to be given effect.
>
> However, it is of the very essence of a sales contract that at least minimum adequate remedies be available. If the parties intend to conclude a contract for sale within this Article they must accept the legal consequence that there be at least a fair quantum of remedy for breach of the obligations or duties outlined in the contract. Thus any clause purporting to modify or limit the remedial provisions of this Article in an unconscionable manner is subject to deletion and in that event the remedies made available by this Article are applicable as if the stricken clause had never existed. Similarly, under subsection (2), where an apparently fair and reasonable clause because of circumstances fails in its purpose or operates to deprive either party of the substantial value of the bargain, it must give way to the general remedy provisions of this Article.

Limitation of Remedies Generally; Repair or Replacement

Section 2–719(1) provides:

> (1) Subject to the provisions of subsections (2) and (3) of this section and of the preceding section on liquidation and limitation of damages,
>
> > (a) the agreement may provide for remedies in addition to or in substitution for those provided in this Article and may limit or alter the measure of damages recoverable under this Article, as by limiting the buyer's remedies to return of the goods and repayment of the price or to repair and replacement of non-conforming goods or parts; and
> >
> > (b) resort to a remedy as provided is optional unless the remedy is expressly agreed to be exclusive, in which case it is the sole remedy.

Subsection (1) generally allows a seller to limit a buyer's remedies to repair or replacement of the goods or defective parts, and otherwise to alter the types and amounts of damages normally available for breach, provided the contract makes clear that the limited or modified remedy is the sole and exclusive remedy available to the buyer.[607] If the exclusivity of an attempted limitation-of-remedy provision is at all ambiguous, the remedy provided will be deemed to *supplement*, rather than displace, the Article 2 general remedy provisions.[608] Thus, a contract that purports to limit a seller's "warranties," "obligations," or "liability," rather than the buyer's "remedies," may well be interpreted to be an invalid disclaimer of liability rather than a valid limitation of remedies.[609]

Failure of Essential Purpose

Section 2–719(2) provides:

> (2) Where circumstances cause an exclusive or limited remedy to fail of its essential purpose, remedy may be had as provided in this Act.

Courts generally apply this failure-of-essential-purpose provision to cases involving products that are "lemons," *not* to ordinary personal injury claims. The paradigm subsection (2) case involves a car with many recurring defects the seller cannot or will not repair within a reasonable period of time, thereby indefinitely depriving the owner of its full and effective use. In such a case, a limitation of the buyer's remedy to "repair or replacement of defective parts" fails its essential purpose of guaranteeing (in essence) that the seller will, within a reasonable period of time, cure the defects (by repair or replacement) and thereby put the product into workable condition.[610] Thus,

---

See generally Powers v. Lycoming Engines, 272 F.R.D. 414, 429 (E.D. Pa. 2011) (surveying limitation of remedies provisions in various states).

[607] "If the parties intend the term to describe the sole remedy under the contract, this must be clearly expressed." UCC § 2–719 cmt. 2.

[608] "Subsection (1)(b) creates a presumption that clauses prescribing remedies are cumulative rather than exclusive." UCC § 2–719 cmt. 2.

[609] See, e.g., Stream v. Sportscar Salon, Ltd., 397 N.Y.S.2d 677 (City Civ. Ct. 1977); Ford Motor Co. v. Reid, 465 S.W.2d 80 (Ark. 1971).

[610] See, e.g., Pack v. Damon Corp., 434 F.3d 810, 817 (6th Cir. 2006) (Mich. law) (motor home out of service for 162 days during first year of ownership; warranty likely failed of its essential purpose); Bailey v. Skipperliner Indus., 278 F. Supp. 2d 945 (N.D. Ind. 2003) (defendant made several unsuccessful attempts to fix boat engine; jury could reasonably conclude that limited warranty failed its essential purpose); Trgo v. Chrysler Corp., 34 F. Supp. 2d 581, 590 (N.D. Ohio 1998) ("If, after repeated repairs, a vehicle fails 'to operate as should a new vehicle,' the repair remedy fails of its essential purpose."); King v. Taylor Chrysler-Plymouth,

notwithstanding a seller's effort to limit remedies to repair or replacement, the buyer of such a lemon product may be entitled to revoke acceptance of the product under UCC § 2–608 if its defects "substantially impair" its value.[611]

Riley v. Ford Motor Co.[612] is an early example of this type of irreparable new car case, where an exclusive repair or replacement provision was held to deprive the buyer of the "substantial value of the bargain."[613] There, the car had over 14 defects in the first few weeks that the dealer did not satisfactorily repair. Another example is *Ex parte Miller*,[614] where the seller, over a 21-month period, attempted to repair a large variety of different problems in a new tractor-type vehicle. Striking an exclusive repair-or-replacement clause on failure-of-essential-purpose grounds, the court observed that "the seller does not have an unlimited time" to cure defects in the products that it sells.[615]

Whether a particular limited remedy fails of its essential purpose is a question of fact for the jury.[616] The problems of irreparable products and inadequate warranty remedies are now also addressed by the federal Magnuson-Moss Warranty Act[617] and various state "lemon laws."[618]

Personal Injury Damage Exclusions—Unconscionability

In General

Far and away the most important aspect of § 2–719 for personal injury products liability litigation is § 2–719(3), particularly the second sentence thereof:

> Consequential damages may be limited or excluded unless the limitation or exclusion is unconscionable. Limitation of consequential damages for injury to the person in the case of consumer goods is prima facie unconscionable but limitation of damages where the loss is commercial is not.

Inc., 457 N.W.2d 42 (Mich. Ct. App. 1990) (purchaser took car to dealer to repair stalling problems seven times over nine months of unsuccessful repairs).

[611] See, e.g., Sheehan v. Monaco Coach Corp., 2006 WL 208689, at *7–9 (E.D. Wis. 2006) (Fla. law). On revocation of acceptance under § 2–608, see generally 1 Crockett, Product Warranties § 7:9; White and Summers, UCC § 9–4.

[612] 442 F.2d 670 (5th Cir. 1971) (Ala. law).

[613] UCC § 2–719 cmt. 1.

[614] 693 So.2d 1372 (Ala. 1997).

[615] Id. at 1378. "[A]t some point after the purchase of a new [product], the same should be put in good running condition, that is, the seller does not have an unlimited time for the performance of the obligation to replace and repair parts. . . . [a]t some point in time, it must become obvious to all people that a particular [product] cannot be repaired or parts replaced so that the same is made free from defect." Id.

[616] See, e.g., Norcold, Inc. v. Gateway Supply Co., 2010 WL 3385797, at *4–6 (Ohio Ct. App. 2010); Kraft v. Staten Island Boat Sales, Inc., 715 F. Supp. 2d 464, 475–76 (S.D.N.Y. 2010).

[617] See § 4.9, below.

[618] Almost all states now have automobile "lemon laws," first enacted in 1982, that typically permit buyers of new cars to receive a replacement of the car or a refund of the purchase price (less the value of its use) after the dealer has made three or four unsuccessful attempts to repair a substantial defect ("impairment") within one or (as in New York) two years after purchase. A few states, notably California (the Song-Beverly Consumer Warranty Act), but also Kansas and Minnesota, apply various warranty protections to consumer products more generally. See Cal. Civ. Code §§ 1790 et seq.; Kan. Stat. Ann. §§ 50–623 et seq. (Kansas Consumer Protection Act); Minn. Stat. Ann. ch. 325F (Consumer Protection; Products and Sales).

On lemon laws, see, e.g., 1 Crockett, Product Warranties § 7:19; Honigman, The New "Lemon Laws" Expanding U.C.C. Remedies, 17 UCC L.J. 116 (1984); Kegley and Hiller, "Emerging" Lemon Car Laws, 24 Am. Bus. L.J. 87 (1986); Reitz, What You Should Know About State "Lemon Laws," 34 Prac. Law. 83 (1988); Consumer Product Warranty Acts, 17 Am. Jur. 2d Consumer Prod. Warranty Acts §§ 49–57 (1990); Annot., 88 A.L.R.5th 301 (2001) (auto lemon laws).

Because subsection (3) takes priority over subsection (1),[619] the second sentence of § 2–719(3) means that sellers of consumer goods may not contractually limit damages for personal injuries, to repair or replacement or otherwise, unless the seller can show that such a limitation is not "unconscionable."[620] At the very least, such showings—that an exclusion of personal injury damages in consumer contracts is *not* unconscionable—will be rare,[621] and it is safe to say that limitations on personal injury damages in consumer goods cases will be held unconscionable and void in almost every case.[622]

Nevertheless, one may imagine situations where a seller might reasonably and fairly attempt to limit its responsibility for personal injuries, such as where a seller

---

[619] UCC § 2–719(1) begins: "Subject to the provisions of subsections (2) and (3) . . . ."

[620] As with disclaimers, see § 4.7, note 570, above, unconscionability analyses of § 2–719(3), per § 2–302, sometimes note a distinction between so-called *procedural* unconscionability—which subverts a buyer's awareness of a contractual limitation, and *substantive* unconscionability—which denotes a one-sided provision that unreasonably favors the seller. See, e.g., Santos v. SANYO Mfg. Corp., 2013 WL 1868268, at *3 (D. Mass. 2013) ("A party claiming unconscionability must prove both procedural and substantive unconscionability, that is, that there was an absence of meaningful choice on the part of one of the parties, together with contract terms which are unreasonably favorable to the other party."); In re Porsche Cars North America, Inc., 880 F. Supp. 2d 801, 821–22 (S.D. Ohio 2012).

Some courts consider a potpourri of factors relevant to both types of unconscionability determinations. See, e.g., NEC Techs., Inc. v. Nelson, 478 S.E.2d 769 (Ga. 1996) ("unconscionability" under § 2–302 is a flexible doctrine that embraces a variety of factors rather than a formulaic concept). Observing that procedural unconscionability addresses "the process of making the contract," whereas substantive unconscionability focuses on "the contractual terms themselves," the *NEC* court offered a "non-inclusive" list of procedural unconscionability factors, including "age, education, intelligence, business acumen and experience of the parties, their relative bargaining power, the conspicuousness and comprehensibility of the contract language, the oppressiveness of the terms, and the presence or absence of a meaningful choice." Substantive unconscionability, on the other hand, focuses on such matters as "the commercial reasonableness of the contract terms, the purpose and effect of the terms, the allocation of the risks between the parties, and similar public policy concerns." Id. at 771–72. Holding that the exclusion of consequential damages for property loss in the sale of a television set was not unconscionable, the *NEC* court, id. at 774, adopted the analysis of Fotomat Corp. of Fla. v. Chanda, 464 So.2d 626, 630 (Fla. Dist. Ct. App. 1985):

> People should be entitled to contract on their own terms without the indulgence of paternalism by courts in the alleviation of one side or another from the effects of a bad bargain. Also, they should be permitted to enter into contracts that actually may be unreasonable or which may lead to hardship on one side. It is only where it turns out that one side or the other is to be penalized by the enforcement of the terms *of a contract so unconscionable that no decent, fairminded person would view the ensuing result without being possessed of a profound sense of injustice*, that equity will deny the use of its good offices in the enforcement of such unconscionability.

See also Razor v. Hyundai Motor America, 854 N.E.2d 607, 622 (Ill. 2006) (excellent discussion; "A determination of whether a contractual clause is unconscionable is a matter of law, to be decided by the court.").

[621] An unusual case that did enforce a contractual avoidance of a personal injury claim under § 2–719 is Mullan v. Quickie Aircraft Corp., 797 F.2d 845 (10th Cir. 1986) (Colo. law), which involved the sale of a home-built aircraft kit that included a contractual waiver of claims arising from defects in or safety of the aircraft. The plane crashed on take-off, and the pilot purchaser of the kit sued the manufacturer for his injuries. Upholding the waiver of such claims against a charge of prima facie unconscionability under § 2–719, the court reasoned that the "disclaimer provision" was not unconscionable in view of the plaintiff's expertise with respect to aircraft and woodworking, his thorough investigation of the aircraft before ordering it, his modification of the sales agreement and "other circumstances surrounding the formation of the contract." Id. at 852. Note, however, that *Mullan*, while purporting to interpret § 2–719, involved a general waiver clause that looked as much like a disclaimer of warranties as a limitation of remedies.

[622] "[I]t is virtually impossible to imagine what the disclaiming party can do or show to overcome the 'prima facie' language. In effect we probably have an absolute bar in section 2–719." Franklin, When Worlds Collide: Liability Theories and Disclaimers in Defective-Product Cases, 18 Stan. L. Rev. 974, 1013 (1966). See also Lawrence's Anderson on the UCC § 2–719:102.

For examples of personal injury damages exclusions ruled unconscionable, see, e.g., Ruzzo v. LaRose Enters., 748 A.2d 261, 269 (R.I. 2000) (leased plumbing tool; UCC § 2A–719(3)); Larsen v. Pacesetter Sys., Inc., 837 P.2d 1273 (Haw. 1992) (heart pacemaker), amended by 843 P.2d 144 (Haw. 1992); McCarty v. E.J. Korvette, Inc., 347 A.2d 253 (Md. Ct. Spec. App. 1975) (express warranty against tire blowouts); Matthews v. Ford Motor Co., 479 F.2d 399 (4th Cir. 1973) (Va. law) (defective car).

provides consumers with an *extra* warranty over and above the kind of coverage against defects that other sellers normally provide consumers. For example, assume that most tire manufacturers warrant tires of a certain type and price against defects in materials and workmanship for 36 months/36,000 miles. During this warranty period, consumers injured in accidents caused by tire defects may recover personal injury damages under § 2–715, and any attempt by tire sellers to limit damages to repair or replacement in such cases would be void under § 2–719(3).

Now, suppose that Acme Tire Co. wishes to offer consumers an extra, broader warranty that covers not only all damages caused by *defects* but that also provides a limited remedy for damages from non-defect sources of failure, as from road hazards like nails and glass. Acme will be responsible, of course, for personal injuries caused by tire defects during the warranty period, but it may be willing to broaden the warranty beyond defects to include all-hazard coverage only if it can limit its remedy for such *extra* coverage to repair or replacement of the nondefective tire. Assuming that this remedy limitation on the extra warranty is made entirely clear in the sales agreement, there appears to be no good reason why a seller should be discouraged from offering, and consumers precluded from receiving, this kind of extra benefit.

The argument for allowing personal injury damages limitations for such "extra" warranties was made by the dissenting judge in *Collins v. Uniroyal, Inc.*,[623] a warranty case involving the failure of a nondefective tire, and its logic was endorsed in a prominent law review commentary.[624] But the dissent's reasoning failed to impress the *Collins* majority, which held such a limitation to be "patently unconscionable."[625] While the *Collins* dissent had the better argument, courts in personal injury cases involving consumer goods commonly refuse to penetrate the thicket of conscionability in ruling on attempted exclusions of responsibility for personal injuries.[626]

Consumer Goods

A vital limitation on the scope of the unconscionability provision in § 2–719(3) bears special attention: it applies only to *consumer* goods. This restriction to consumer goods means that sellers of *commercial* products *may* exclude responsibility for consequential damages, including personal injuries to a buyer's workers, without such exclusions being held prima facie unconscionable under § 2–719(3).

---

[623] 315 A.2d 16 (N.J. 1974). In *Collins*, the purchaser of a tire manufactured by the defendant and guaranteed against blowouts was killed when the tire blew out. Since the warranty guaranteed against blowouts from external causes as well as from defects in the tires, and since no defect was shown in this case, Judge Clifford argued in dissent that the manufacturer's limitation of remedy to repair or replacement should be enforced: "The drafters presumably had something in mind when they chose the expression 'prima facie unconscionable' instead of 'per se unconscionable' or simply 'unconscionable' . . . ." Id. at 20. Judge Clifford concluded that "where the express warranty goes beyond what is required by the Code and the common law of this state, and where the product is found to be free from defect, the prima facie unconscionability contemplated by the Code has been overcome. I would so hold. I emphasize that I would limit this holding to the 'extra' guarantee case." Id. at 21.

[624] See Note, 50 N.Y.U. L. Rev. 148, 174–75 (1975) (limitation of remedies for *nondefective* failures might be viewed as *not* prima facie unconscionable because "such limitations simply do not seem to be unfair if the consumer is given an understanding of their operation and effect").

[625] *Collins*, 315 A.2d at 18.

[626] One unusual exception is Mullan v. Quickie Aircraft Corp., 797 F.2d 845 (10th Cir. 1986) (Colo. law), discussed in note 621, above.

For example, *Reibold v. Simon Aerials, Inc.*[627] involved a claim by a mechanic, Reibold, employed by Hertz Equipment, a lessor of industrial and construction equipment, for injuries to his hand, which was struck by an unshielded engine cooling fan on an aerial lift manufactured by the defendant. Hertz had purchased the lift from the defendant manufacturer with a warranty that excluded liability for consequential damages, including injury to person. In response to Reibold's warranty claim, the defendant asserted the damages exclusion in its sales contract with Hertz Equipment, Reibold's employer. Reibold contended that the exclusion was unconscionable and void under § 2–719(3). Granting summary judgment for the defendant on the plaintiff's warranty claim (but denying summary judgment on the tort claims), Judge Doumar reasoned persuasively that commercial parties are free to apportion the risk of loss from commercial products as they see fit. Moreover, because unconscionability "can only be examined with reference to the original parties to the bargain[, no] agreement can possibly be unconscionable with regard to a third party who may benefit from the agreement but who was not a party to the agreement in the first place."[628] Noting that employers are responsible under the workers' compensation laws for on-the-job injuries to their employees caused by third parties, the court persuasively concluded that it should not interfere with allocation-of-risk bargains struck by employers and the suppliers of their machinery.[629]

"Consumer goods" are defined in the Code as goods "used or bought for use primarily for personal, family or household purposes."[630] This definition may suggest a subjective test based on the buyer's intended or actual use,[631] which is sometimes problematic. Under a subjective definition, a real estate broker's car, were it to crash due to a steering defect during a family drive to the beach, would *not* be a consumer good if the broker had bought and used the car principally for driving clients around town. At least in this context, it would be more reasonable to interpret the phrase "consumer goods" in § 2–719 *objectively* in terms of the primary use to which people generally put this type of product, that is, whether it is "normally used for personal, family, or household purposes."[632] Viewed this way, because most people buy and use most cars primarily as consumer products, a salesperson's car reasonably would be considered a "consumer good." An objective definition of consumer products avoids the anomaly of basing responsibility for identical products solely on the fortuity of a particular buyer's predominant use of a product, which often has little relation to the logic or fairness of allowing a damages exclusion.[633]

---

627 859 F. Supp. 193 (E.D. Va. 1994).

628 Id. at 199.

629 Id. at 200:

> [I]t makes good policy sense to allow employer-purchasers to negotiate warranties with manufacturers, because the employer is in an excellent position to measure and control the risks of employees injuring themselves while using such goods. Especially in a case such as this one, where Hertz maintains its own mechanics and engages in extensive company-wide safety training, it makes sense for Hertz to bear the risks of employee injuries in exchange for a cut in the price from the manufacturer. In any case, where two sophisticated and relatively equal parties enter such bargains—whether the bargain appears to make sense or not after the fact—it is not for the court or for juries to second-guess and rewrite such bargains.

630 UCC § 9–102(23). This definition applies to Article 2. See UCC § 2–103(3).

631 See, for example, the pick-up truck example in White and Summers, UCC § 13–11, at 610–11.

632 See Magnuson-Moss Federal Warranty Act, 15 U.S.C. § 2301(1) ("consumer product").

633 Note, however, that an objective definition of "consumer goods" hinders the case of a consumer who buys for personal use a pick-up truck of a type normally used by contractors. But the hindrance of such actions,

Property Damage

Courts have split on whether limitations and exclusions of consequential damages should be stricken as unconscionable in consumer cases if the damages claim is for *property* loss. A few courts have held such limitations unconscionable,[634] particularly if the limitations are part of a broad exclusion of all consequential damages including personal injuries.[635]

Because § 2–719(3) classifies limitations on remedies as *prima facie* unconscionable only with respect to personal injury damages, probably most courts hold that limitations and exclusions of property damage, though possibly unconscionable on particular facts, are generally allowable under this section of the Code.[636]

Arbitration *vs.* Judicial Resolution

Clauses requiring the resolution of claims through individual arbitration are increasingly included in product warranties.[637] These clauses limit judicial remedies available to consumers, including the right to join class action proceedings.[638] For

---

arising out of the general commercial nature of such products, is more justified than the kind of unpredictable and haphazard product differentiations that would result from a subjective definition. Moreover, applying an objective definition to all cases—consumer purchasers of commercial goods as well as commercial purchasers of consumer goods—is consistent with the Code's characterization of specially-protected sales situations as involving consumer "goods" rather than consumer "transactions."

[634] See, e.g., WEL Cos. v. Haldex Brake Prods. Corp., 467 F. Supp. 3d 545, 567–68 (S.D. Ohio 2020) (commercial truck brake chamber warranty limited to replacement or a credit was substantively and procedurally unconscionable where defendant had prior knowledge of defect and the risk of extensive damage from explosions and fires); DJ Coleman, Inc. v. Nufarm Ams., Inc., 693 F. Supp. 2d 1055, 1069–74 (D.N.D. 2010) (herbicide that damaged sunflower crop contained preprinted label limiting damages to refund or replacement that was ruled procedurally and substantively unconscionable; surveying chemical agriculture cases).

[635] See, e.g., Fischer v. General Elec. Hotpoint, 438 N.Y.S.2d 690 (Dist. Ct. 1981); McCarty v. E.J. Korvette, Inc., 347 A.2d 253 (Md. Ct. Spec. App. 1975) (breach of express tire warranty against blowouts caused damage to car as well as personal injury).

[636] See, e.g., Zaremba v. Marvin Lumber & Cedar Co., 458 F. Supp. 2d 545, 549 (N.D. Ohio 2006) (repair or replacement limitation was *not* unconscionable: "a warranty in which the party disclaiming warranties or remedies assumes some form of responsibility for the performance or maintenance of the product in issue is not unconscionable"); NEC Techs., Inc. v. Nelson, 478 S.E.2d 769, 771 (Ga. 1996) (property damage to house from fire caused by television set; upholding trial court's partial summary judgment for manufacturer on warranty claim because exclusion of all incidental and consequential damages was not unconscionable; "[t]he Legislature could have provided that a limitation on consequential property damages in the case of consumer goods is prima facie unconscionable, as it did with consequential damages for personal injuries, but it chose not to do so"); Gladden v. Cadillac Motor Car Div., Gen. Motors Corp., 416 A.2d 394 (N.J. 1980).

[637] See Lewis and Dow, Searching for Clarity Amid Confusion: An Examination of the Standards for Determining Waiver and Revival of the Right to Arbitrate, 67 U. Kan. L. Rev. 327, 327–28 (2018) ("In the United States, arbitration is increasingly used to resolve disputes in many diverse areas, including those involving consumer . . . law. This growth was fueled in part by U.S. Supreme Court decisions beginning in 1983 that amplified the scope and impact of the Federal Arbitration Act (FAA)."); Silver-Greenberg and Corkery, Beware the Fine Print: In Arbitration, "A Privatization of the Justice System" (Part II) N.Y. Times Online (Nov. 1, 2015) ("Over the last 10 years, thousands of businesses across the country—from big corporations to storefront shops—have used arbitration to create an alternate system of justice."); Silver-Greenberg and Gebeloff, Beware the Fine Print: Arbitration Everywhere, Stacking the Deck of Justice N.Y. Times Online (Oct. 31, 2015).

[638] Silver-Greenburg and Corkery, above ("the allure of arbitration grew after [AT&T Mobility LLC v. Concepcion, 563 U.S. 333 (2011)] cleared the way for [arbitration] clauses to quash class-action lawsuits"); Silver-Greenburg and Gebeloff, above ("By inserting individual arbitration clauses into a soaring number of consumer and employment contracts, companies . . . devised a way to circumvent the courts and bar people from joining together in class-action lawsuits, realistically the only tool citizens have to fight illegal or deceitful business practices.").

example, in *Payne v. Amazon.com, Inc.*,[639] the plaintiffs brought class action negligence and consumer fraud claims against Amazon for eye injuries from allegedly defective eclipse glasses purchased on the Amazon website. The court held that Amazon's individual arbitration agreement, disclosed through the link "By placing your order, you agree to Amazon.com's privacy notice and conditions of use," positioned just above the "place your order" button, was enforceable.[640] Note, however, that plaintiffs have had some success in defeating defendants' motions to compel arbitration where the arbitration agreement was inconspicuously included in a booklet offering product and warranty information.[641]

§ 4.9 ANTI-DISCLAIMER AND OTHER WARRANTY REFORM STATUTES

Disclaimers of warranties and limitations of remedies for personal injuries in sales transactions involving new consumer products are, in general, inherently perverse. Manufacturers and other sellers normally should not be permitted to shield themselves from warranty responsibility for personal injuries resulting from explicit or implicit misrepresentations concerning the essential quality and safety of new consumer products. Particularly if a seller seeks to avoid such responsibility by burying fine-print legalese deep inside a standard form sales contract, such provisions should be considered contrary to public policy and void.

In the landmark case of *Henningsen v. Bloomfield Motors, Inc.*,[642] decided in 1960, the New Jersey Supreme Court reached this eminently sensible conclusion. Although more than half a century now has passed, *Henningsen* still powerfully illuminates the reasons for disallowing boilerplate disclaimers and limitations of remedies in consumer sales transactions. While Mrs. Henningsen was driving a new 1955 Plymouth sedan her husband had purchased ten days earlier from Bloomfield Motors, the car's steering failed due to a mechanical defect, whereupon the car veered sharply off the highway and crashed into a brick wall, injuring Mrs. Henningsen. Mr. and Mrs. Henningsen sued the dealer and manufacturer, Chrysler Corporation, for breach of the implied warranty of merchantability, and the defendants offered the language of disclaimer and remedy limitation in the purchase order in defense.

Included among the ten fine-print paragraphs called "Conditions" on the reverse side of the sales contract was number 7, which Mr. Henningsen testified he did not read. Paragraph 7 provided that the manufacturer warranted the car against defects in

---

[639] 2018 WL 4489275 (D.S.C. 2018) (Wash. law).

[640] Id. at *5, 8. See also Nicosia v. Amazon.com, Inc., 815 Fed. Appx. 612, 614 (2d Cir. 2020) (Wash. law) (plaintiff purchased weight loss product at least 27 times after Amazon filed motion to compel arbitration; "a reasonable person would understand [that those purchases would] constitute assent" to arbitration); Annot., 95 A.L.R.6th 57, § 5 (2014) (discussing *Nicosia*). Effective mid-2021, Amazon revised its customer terms of service, moving claims resolution from arbitration to litigation. See, e.g., Randazzo, Amazon Faced 75,000 Arbitration Demands. Now It Says: Fine, Sue Us—The retail giant is no longer steering customers away from the court system, as companies scramble to find ways to avoid lawyers who file mass-arbitration claims, Wall St. J.com (June 1, 2021).

[641] See, e.g., Samsung Elecs. Am., Inc. v. Ramirez, 777 Fed. Appx. 243, 243 (9th Cir. 2019) (Cal. law) ("the inaptly titled booklet containing the terms and conditions and the smartphone packaging's vague reference to terms and conditions are insufficient to put a reasonable consumer (or a reasonably prudent smartphone user) on notice of the arbitration provision that Samsung seeks to enforce"); Noble v. Samsung Elecs. Am., Inc., 682 Fed. Appx. 113, 118 (3d Cir. 2017) (N.J. law) (arbitration clause appearing on the 97th page of the "Health and Safety and Warranty Guide" without other "notice of something claiming to be a binding bilateral agreement and waiver of legal rights [was] not a valid contractual term").

[642] 161 A.2d 69 (N.J. 1960).

materials or workmanship for 90 days or 4,000 miles; that the company's only responsibility was to repair or replace defective parts; and that this warranty was "expressly in lieu of all other warranties expressed or implied, and all other obligations or liabilities . . . ."[643]

The *Henningsen* jury returned verdicts in favor of the plaintiffs against both defendants, who appealed. In one of America's classic judicial decisions, Justice Francis affirmed the plaintiffs' verdicts for a unanimous court. He observed that the carefully crafted "warranty" was "a sad commentary upon the automobile manufacturers' marketing practices" by converting a "warranty," developed as a protective measure for consumers, into an instrument of oppression to abolish consumer rights.[644] The standardized fine-print form imposed on all car buyers, a one-sided contract of adhesion reflecting the "gross inequality of bargaining position" of consumers, was "inimical to the public welfare."[645] Even had Mr. Henningsen read the fine print, it did not explain that he was surrendering all warranty claims for personal injury damages if his car proved defective, thereby consigning him to negligence law's formidable challenges of having to prove the seller's fault in making or selling the car in a defective condition.[646] In its adoption of the Uniform Sales Act, the New Jersey legislature long before had declared that sales of all goods, including automobiles, would carry implied warranties of merchantability as a form of economic protection for consumers against the risk of injuries from defective products, and Chrysler's disclaimer and remedy limitation revealed "a studied effort to frustrate that protection."[647] In sum, Chrysler's attempts in

---

[643] Id. at 74.

[644] The court observed:

> The terms of the warranty are a sad commentary upon the automobile manufacturers' marketing practices. Warranties developed in the law in the interest of and to protect the ordinary consumer who cannot be expected to have the knowledge or capacity or even the opportunity to make adequate inspection of mechanical instrumentalities, like automobiles, and to decide for himself whether they are reasonably fit for the designed purpose. But the ingenuity of the Automobile Manufacturers Association, by means of its standardized form, has metamorphosed the warranty into a device to limit the maker's liability.

Id. at 78. "The language gave little and withdrew much. In return for the delusive remedy of replacement of defective parts at the factory, the buyer is said to have accepted the exclusion of the maker's liability for personal injuries arising from the breach of the warranty . . . ." Id. at 85.

[645] Id. at 87. "The warranty before us is a standardized form designed for mass use. It is imposed upon the automobile consumer. He takes it or leaves it, and he must take it to buy an automobile. No bargaining is engaged in with respect to it." Id.

[646] The court, id. at 92–93, further remarked:

> [The disclaimer and limitation were hidden in the fine print on the back of the form, but there is more than this. Even had Mr. Henningsen read the language,] can it be said that an ordinary layman would realize what he was relinquishing in return for what he was being granted? Under the law, breach of warranty against defective parts or workmanship which caused personal injuries would entitle a buyer to damages even if due care were used in the manufacturing process. Because of the great potential for harm if the vehicle was defective, that right is the most important and fundamental one arising from the relationship. Difficulties so frequently encountered in establishing negligence in manufacture in the ordinary case make this manifest. . . . [O]nly the abandonment of all sense of justice would permit us to hold that, as a matter of law, the phrase "its obligation under this warranty being limited to making good at its factory any part or parts thereof" signifies to an ordinary reasonable person that he is relinquishing any personal injury claim that might flow from the use of a defective automobile.

[647] More fully, id. at 95, the court explained:

> [The legislature] has imposed an implied warranty of merchantability as a general incident of sale of an automobile by description. The warranty does not depend upon the affirmative intention of the parties. It is a child of the law; it annexes itself to the contract because of the very nature of the transaction. The judicial process has recognized a right to recover damages for personal injuries arising from a breach of that warranty. The disclaimer of the implied warranty

the sales contract to exclude the implied warranty of merchantability and to exclude responsibility for personal injury damages were unconscionable, "violative of public policy and void."[648]

On its appearance in 1960, *Henningsen* was widely hailed for its logic, fairness, and the brilliant light it cast into dark corners of sharp commercial practices that undercut basic consumer rights. Yet *Henningsen* ran headlong into the Uniform Commercial Code, which had begun to be adopted around America about this time.[649] Although the practice of burying ambiguous disclaimers in pages of fine print was invalidated by the conspicuousness requirement of UCC § 2–316(2), that same section explicitly allowed conspicuous disclaimers of the implied warranty of merchantability that did little more than mention "merchantability."[650] And as the Uniform Commercial Code (including § 2–316) was adopted by one state legislature after another in the early 1960s, the brightness of the *Henningsen* beacon of judicial protection for consumers dimmed steadily into oblivion.

From the inception of Article 2 of the Uniform Commercial Code, many commentators observed that its disclaimer provisions were unsatisfactory for consumer transactions.[651] This should have come as no surprise, for Article 2 was based to a large extent on the Uniform Sales Act of 1906, which itself drew from sales law principles of the 1800s,[652] to some extent from principles of the 1700s,[653] and even somewhat from the law of ancient Rome.[654] As interest in consumer rights spread across America during the 1960s and early 1970s, so too did criticism of the Code's treatment of disclaimers. In the words of one commentator, the disclaimer section was "the most controversial and ambiguous" section in all of Article 2. Although the Code claimed an interest in protecting buyers from unexpected and unbargained-for language of disclaimer, "its requirement that any disclaimer must mention 'merchantability' almost ensures failure of this purpose because the term conveys so little information to the average consumer."[655] Indeed, § 2–316(2) empowers merchants "to continue shifting the risk of loss back to consumers while camouflaging their action with legal jargon."[656]

---

and exclusion of all obligations except those specifically assumed by the express warranty signify a studied effort to frustrate that protection.

[648] Id. at 97.

[649] See § 4.1, above.

[650] See § 4.7, above. Consider, for example, Marshall v. Murray Oldsmobile Co., 154 S.E.2d 140 (Va. 1967), where the Virginia Supreme Court explicitly rejected the *Henningsen* approach. Pointing to the legislative approval of disclaimers in § 2–316 of the Uniform Commercial Code, adopted in Virginia in 1966 after the case sub judice had arisen, the court reaffirmed its commitment to the principles of freedom of contract.

[651] See, e.g., Peters, Remedies for Breach of Contracts Relating to the Sale of Goods Under the Uniform Commercial Code: A Roadmap for Article Two, 73 Yale L.J. 199, 282–83 (1963).

[652] "The warranty provisions in Article 2 of the U.C.C. largely reenact the principles that Chalmers had found in nineteenth-century common law and codified in the British Sale of Goods Act of 1893." C. Reitz, Consumer Protection Under the Magnuson-Moss Warranty Act 14 (1978).

[653] See Wiseman, The Limits of Vision: Karl Llewellyn and the Merchant Rules, 100 Harv. L. Rev. 465, 475 (1987) (noting that the Uniform Sales Act "was based on the English Sales of Goods Act of 1893, which itself was based on the nineteenth-century English sales law that reflected the organization of nineteenth and even eighteenth-century commerce").

[654] See § 1.2, above.

[655] Rothschild, The Magnuson-Moss Warranty Act: Does It Balance Warrantor and Consumer Interests?, 44 Geo. Wash. L. Rev. 335, 343–44 (1976) (also arguing that the "unconscionability" restriction on remedy limitations in § 2–719(3) is too vague to offer consumers much protection).

[656] Id.

Targeting the specific problem of disclaimers in consumer sales transactions, some state legislatures and Congress eventually passed legislation that effectively curtailed the widespread manipulation of consumer warranty rights by manufacturers and other product sellers. Tipping the fairness scales significantly toward consumers, several states enacted legislation that completely prohibited the disclaimer of implied warranties (and some that prohibited the limitation of remedies) in consumer sales transactions. As part of a broad effort to strengthen consumer warranties, the United States Congress in 1976 enacted the federal Magnuson-Moss Warranty Act, which sharply limited a seller's ability to disclaim implied warranties in most significant consumer sales transactions.

State Anti-Disclaimer Statutes

At least sixteen states and the District of Columbia have enacted legislation prohibiting or restricting disclaimers and/or limitations of remedy in sales transactions involving consumer products.[657] Most states have achieved this result by amending their versions of UCC §§ 2–316 or 2–719, but others have included such provisions in broader consumer warranty statutes.

The first variety of legislation, amending a state's version of § 2–316, § 2–719, or both, is illustrated by Connecticut's addition of a fifth subsection to its version of § 2–316:

> (5) The provisions of subsections (2), (3) and (4) shall not apply to sales of new or unused consumer goods, except for those goods clearly marked "irregular," "factory seconds" or "damaged." Any language, oral or written, used by a seller or manufacturer of consumer goods, which attempts to exclude or modify any implied warranties of merchantability and fitness for a particular purpose or to exclude or modify the consumer's remedies for breach of those warranties, shall be unenforceable.[658]

In addition to Connecticut, several other jurisdictions have amended one or both of their commercial codes' disclaimer or remedy limitation provisions, as discussed below.

Alabama adds a subsection (5) to § 2–316: "Nothing in subsection (2) or subsection (3)(a) or in [the succeeding section] shall be construed so as to limit or exclude the seller's liability for damages for injury to the person in the case of consumer goods."[659]

The District of Columbia adds a § 2–316.01, which excludes consumer goods from § 2–316, and substitutes new provisions that prohibit disclaimers of warranties in sales of consumer goods except for conspicuous notations of particular defects.[660]

---

[657] See 1 Crockett, Product Warranties § 8:34 (listing twelve states that have enacted anti-disclaimer legislation); Clark and Davis, Beefing Up Product Warranties: A New Dimension in Consumer Protection, 23 U. Kan. L. Rev. 567 (1975). See especially Professor Donald Clifford's informative overview and analysis of the state provisions in Clifford, Non-UCC Statutory Provisions Affecting Warranty Disclaimers and Remedies in Sales of Goods, 71 N.C. L. Rev. 1011 (1993).

[658] Conn. Gen. Stat. Ann. § 42a–2–316(5).

[659] Ala. Code § 7–2–316(5). Alabama also adds a subsection (4) to Ala. Code § 7–2–719: "Nothing in this section or in [the preceding section] shall be construed so as to limit the seller's liability for damages for injury to the person in the case of consumer goods."

[660] D.C. Code § 28:2–316.01.

Maine adds a subsection (5) to § 2–316 that provides in part that subsections (2), (3), and (4) "do not apply to sales of consumer goods or services."[661]

Maryland excludes consumer goods from § 2–316 and substitutes new provisions that prohibit disclaimers of warranties in sales of consumer goods, except for sales of certain old cars if the buyer is properly notified.[662]

Massachusetts excludes consumer goods from § 2–316 and adds new provisions that prohibit disclaimers of warranties in sales of consumer goods.[663]

New Hampshire renumbers § 2–316(4) as § 2–316(5) and adds a new subsection (4) that nullifies disclaimers of implied warranties with respect to personal, family, and household goods unless the seller provides the buyer with a clear, simple, concise, and conspicuous writing, signed by the buyer, informing the buyer, before or at the time of the sale, (a) that the goods are sold "as is" or "with all faults"; (b) that the entire risk as to quality and performance of the goods is with the buyer; and (c) that, if the goods are defective, the buyer assumes the entire cost of repair.[664]

Rhode Island,[665] Vermont,[666] and Washington[667] have also enacted similar consumer-protective amendments to their versions of UCC Article 2.

In addition to these states that have curtailed disclaimer and remedy-limitation abuses by amending their commercial codes, at least California, Kansas, Maryland, Minnesota, Oregon, and West Virginia have special warranty protection legislation outside the commercial code that offers consumers broad protection in sales transactions and (except for Maryland) specifically curtails the ability of product sellers to disclaim implied warranties in such transactions.[668]

---

[661] Me. Rev. Stat. Ann. tit. 11, § 2–316(5).

[662] Md. Code Ann. Com. Law § 2–316.1.

[663] Mass. Gen. Laws Ann. ch. 106, § 2–316A.

[664] N.H. Rev. Stat. Ann. § 382–A:2–316(4).

[665] Rhode Island adds a § 2–329(2), which provides that every "consumer sale" is accompanied by an implied warranty of merchantability and, if the circumstances warrant, a fitness warranty; that disclaimers of implied warranties in "as is" and "with all faults" consumer sales are effective only if a conspicuous writing clearly informs the buyer, prior to the sale, in simple and concise language that the goods are sold on such a basis and that the entire risk as to quality and performance lies with the buyer; and that express warranties in the sale of new consumer goods cannot disclaim implied warranties. R.I. Gen. Laws § 6A–2–329(2) to (3)(a).

[666] Vermont adds a subsection (5) to § 2–316, which provides that subsections (2), (3), and (4) do not apply to sales of new consumer goods and that any attempts to disclaim implied warranties and limit remedies for breach of such warranties are unenforceable. Vt. Stat. Ann. tit. 9A, § 2–316(5).

[667] Washington substitutes a subsection (4) in § 2–316, which provides that "where goods are purchased primarily for personal, family or household use and not for commercial or business use, disclaimers of the warranty of merchantability or fitness for particular purpose shall not be effective to limit the liability of merchant sellers except insofar as the disclaimer sets forth with particularity the qualities and characteristics which are not being warranted. Remedies for breach of warranty can be limited in accordance with [UCC §§ 2–718 and 2–719]." Wash. Rev. Code Ann. § 62A.2–316(4).

[668] See Cal. Civ. Code §§ 1790 et seq. (Song-Beverly Consumer Warranty Act); Kan. Stat. Ann. §§ 50–623 et seq. (Consumer Protection Act) and § 50–639 (anti-disclaimer provision); Md. Code Ann. Com. Law §§ 14–401 et seq. (Consumer Products Guaranty Act) and §§ 13–101 et seq. (Consumer Protection Act); Minn. Stat. Ann. ch. 325F (Consumer Protection; Products and Sales) and Minn. Stat. Ann. §§ 325G.17 et seq. (anti-disclaimer provisions); Or. Rev. Stat. Ann. §§ 72.8010 et seq. (Consumer Warranty Act) and Or. Rev. Stat. Ann. § 72.8050 (anti-disclaimer provision); R.I. Gen. Laws § 6A–2–329 (various consumer warranty protections, including prohibition of disclaimers, included in commercial code); W. Va. Code Ann. ch. 46A (Consumer Credit and Protection Act) and W. Va. Code Ann. § 46A–6–107 (anti-disclaimer provision).

The Federal Magnuson-Moss Warranty Act

In General

In an effort to improve the truth, strength, and clarity of consumer product warranties, Congress enacted the Magnuson-Moss Warranty—Federal Trade Commission Improvement Act of 1975.[669] The Act does not require product sellers to issue warranties but imposes certain obligations on suppliers who do provide written warranties[670] to consumers buying consumer products[671] costing more than $10 or $15.[672] Written warranties must be labeled either "full (statement of duration) warranty," requiring the warrantor to provide consumers with a designated spectrum of warranty rights, or "limited warranty," which requires full, clear, and non-deceptive presale disclosure of the warranty's terms, prohibits tie-in conditions, and protects consumers from unfair and unexpected disclaimers.[673] Written warranties for covered products must disclose fully, conspicuously, clearly, and without deception the warranty's terms and conditions;[674] warranty terms must be disclosed to consumers before purchase;[675] warrantors ordinarily may not condition warranties on the

---

[669] 15 U.S.C. §§ 2301 et seq. On the Magnuson-Moss Warranty Act, see, e.g., Squillante, Remedies Provided by the Magnuson-Moss Warranty Act, 92 Com. L.J. 366 (1987); Miller and Kanter, Litigation Under Magnuson-Moss: New Opportunities in Private Actions, 13 UCC L.J. 10 (1980); Roberts and Mann, The Magnuson-Moss Federal Warranty Act and Uniform Commercial Code Section 2–719: Further Reflections and Recent Developments, 1979 Ariz. St. L.J. 765 (1979); Schroeder, Private Actions under the Magnuson-Moss Warranty Act, 66 Cal. L. Rev. 1 (1978); Eddy, Effects of the Magnuson-Moss Act Upon Consumer Product Warranties, 55 N.C. L. Rev. 835 (1977); Denicola, The Magnuson-Moss Warranty Act: Making Consumer Product Warranty a Federal Case, 44 Fordham L. Rev. 273 (1975); 2 Crockett, Product Warranties chs. 14–21; C. Reitz, Consumer Protection Under the Magnuson-Moss Warranty Act (1978); C. Reitz, Consumer Product Warranties Under Federal and State Laws (2d ed. 1987); Jovanovic, Consumer Product Warranty Acts, 17 Am. Jur. 2d §§ 1 et seq. (1990); Annot., 59 A.L.R. Fed. 461 (Magnuson-Moss Act claims in federal court).

[670] Or if the seller provides a service contract. 15 U.S.C. § 2308(a).

[671] The Warranty Act applies only to *consumer* products, defined as products "normally used for personal, family, or household purposes" in § 2301(1); 16 CFR § 700.1. See, e.g., Bennett v. CMH Homes, Inc., 770 F.3d 511, 515 (6th Cir. 2014) (manufactured home not a "consumer product" under the MMWA); Kelly v. Georgia-Pacific LLC, 671 F. Supp. 2d 785, 800–01 (E.D.N.C. 2009) (building material that was integrated into the structure of a dwelling at the time of construction was not a "consumer product" under the MMA); Essex Ins. Co. v. Blount, Inc., 72 F. Supp. 2d 722, 723 (E.D. Tex. 1999) (heavy timber equipment not consumer product, precluding protection under Act). Compare Chrysler Fin. Co. v. Flynn, 88 S.W.3d 142 (Mo. Ct. App. 2002) (whether dump truck, used by farmer for household purposes, was consumer product was question of fact for jury).

The Warranty Act protects only consumers who *buy* consumer products. 15 U.S.C. § 2301(3). See Parrot v. DaimlerChrysler Corp., 130 P.3d 530, 536 (Ariz. 2006) (car lessee not a protected consumer). *But see* Friedberg v. Maserati N. Am., Inc., 2018 WL 3642277, at *3 (E.D. Pa. 2018) (lessee could make a claim under the Magnuson-Moss Warranty Act against a manufacturer that "sold the vehicle to the dealer with a warranty [and] the dealer then leased the car to [the plaintiff] with the warranty").

[672] Notwithstanding a $5 trigger in 15 U.S.C. § 2302(e), FTC regulations governing disclosure of warranty terms, 16 CFR §§ 701 et seq., and presale availability of warranty information, id. at §§ 7:02 et seq., apply only to products costing more than $15. See 2 Crockett, Product Warranties § 17:3. The designations of warranties as "full" or "limited" apply to consumer products costing more than $10. 15 U.S.C. § 2303(d). See 16 CFR § 700.6.

[673] Warranties must be labeled "full" or "limited." 15 U.S.C. § 2303(a). The minimum requirements for warranties designated as "full" are set forth in 15 U.S.C. § 2304.

[674] See 15 U.S.C. § 2302. Particular disclosure requirements are mandated by FTC rules. See 16 CFR § 701. On the Act's disclosure requirements, see 2 Crockett, Product Warranties ch. 17. The Act defines and prohibits "deceptive warranties" in 15 U.S.C. § 2310(c). Internet retailers are not exempt. See Assam, FTC Letters Remind Internet Retailers to Give Consumers Warranty Information, 41 Prod. Safety & Liab. Rep. (BNA) 1449 (2013).

[675] 15 U.S.C. § 2302(b)(1)(A). On the Act's requirements for presale disclosure of written warranty terms, see generally 2 Crockett, Product Warranties ch. 18. Note that the E-Warranty Act of 2015 (S. 1359) amended the Magnuson-Moss Warranty Act to provide for electronic warranties. 15 U.S.C. § 2302(b)(4).

consumer's use of any other product or service;[676] disclaimers of implied warranties under UCC § 2–316 are severely restricted;[677] and providers of full warranties must provide consumers with prompt and effective procedures for repairing or replacing defective products or provide a refund of the purchase price.[678] Thus, the Magnuson-Moss Act is a consumer protection statute designed (1) to improve the truthfulness, strength, and comprehensibility of warranties that accompany consumer products, and (2) to provide consumers of products that carry "full" warranties with effective mechanisms for resolving warranty complaints. Importantly, the Act does *not* provide new remedies for injured plaintiffs to use in ordinary products liability litigation.[679]

Restrictions on Disclaimers

The Magnuson-Moss Warranty Act contains one provision that profoundly alters warranty responsibility for product accidents: § 108 of the Act effectively outlaws implied warranty disclaimers in sales of major consumer goods. For consumer products costing more than $10[680] for which a written warranty is provided,[681] the Act nullifies implied warranty disclaimers,[682] notwithstanding the fact that such disclaimers are authorized by state law in UCC § 2–316.[683] While the Act prohibits all implied warranty limitations for products carrying "full" warranties,[684] it does permit a supplier who provides a "limited" warranty to restrict the *duration* of implied warranties to the period of the

---

If a warranty is conditioned on the consumer's return of a warranty registration card, that fact must be disclosed. While such a condition is permissible for "limited" warranties, the FTC has ruled that it is an unreasonable duty and, hence, impermissible for "full" warranties. See 16 CFR at § 700.7; 2 Crockett, Product Warranties §§ 17:16 et seq.; C. Reitz, Consumer Protection Under the Magnuson-Moss Warranty Act 33 (1978); § 4.7, above.

[676] 15 U.S.C. § 2302(c). For example, a manufacturer of a new car ordinarily may not condition the car's warranty on the buyer's use of the manufacturer's own brand of oil or repair parts.

[677] As discussed below, the Act prohibits complete disclaimers of implied warranties. Id. at § 2308(a).

[678] Id. at § 2304(a)(4).

[679] Except for its restrictions on disclaimers, the Magnuson-Moss Warranty Act leaves most state warranty law unaffected, such that plaintiffs ordinarily must satisfy the requirements of state warranty law as a predicate to establishing a federal law claim. "If state law requires vertical privity to enforce an implied warranty and there is none, then, like the yeastless souffle, the warranty does not 'arise.'" Feinstein v. Firestone Tire & Rubber Co., 535 F. Supp. 595, 605 n.13 (S.D.N.Y. 1982). See also Cardenas v. Toyota Motor Corp., 418 F. Supp. 3d 1090, 1110–11 (S.D. Fla. 2019) ("To state a claim under the Magnuson-Moss Warranty Act, though, a plaintiff must also state a valid breach of warranty claim."); Tait v. BSH Home Appliances Corp., 2011 WL 1832941, at *5 (C.D. Cal. 2011) (because Magnuson-Moss Act claims derive from state warranty law, "[a] viable MMWA claim requires a plaintiff to successfully plead a violation of state warranty law"); David v. American Suzuki Motor Corp., 629 F. Supp. 2d 1309, 1323–24 (S.D. Fla. 2009) (implied warranty claim brought under Magnuson-Moss does not circumvent Florida's vertical privity bar). See generally 2 Crockett, Product Warranties ch. 16 and § 20:39.

But at least a couple decisions hold that a warranty claim brought under Magnuson-Moss *may* circumvent a state's vertical privity bar. See Borchardt v. Mako Marine Int'l, Inc., 2011 WL 2084177, at *4–5 (S.D. Fla. 2011) (an express warranty claim is cognizable under Magnuson-Moss Act even though plaintiff could not establish privity and basis-of-the-bargain requirements of state warranty law); Rothe v. Maloney Cadillac, Inc., 518 N.E.2d 1028, 1031 (Ill. 1988). *But see* Jamison v. Summer Infant (USA), Inc., 778 F. Supp. 2d 900, 913–14 (N.D. Ill. 2011) (implied warranty claim under MMWA dismissed for lack of privity, distinguishing *Rothe*).

[680] The FTC's cost threshold is set forth in 16 C.F.R. § 700.6.

[681] Or for which a service contract is provided. 15 U.S.C. § 2308(a).

[682] Id.

[683] See § 4.7, above. Thus, by virtue of the Supremacy Clause, Congress has rewritten state disclaimer law to this extent.

[684] See 15 U.S.C. § 2304(a)(2). See also § 2308(a), which prohibits disclaimers of implied warranties, and § 2308(b), which allows certain duration limitations on implied warranties unless a full warranty has been provided.

written warranty, provided that this restriction is reasonable, conscionable, and clearly communicated to consumers on the face of the warranty.[685]

The Magnuson-Moss Warranty Act's disclaimer provisions are set forth in § 108 of the Act, in title 15 of the United States Code:

> **§ 2308. Implied warranties**
>
> (a) Restrictions on disclaimers or modifications
>
> No supplier may disclaim or modify (except as provided in subsection (b) of this section) any implied warranty to a consumer with respect to such consumer product if (1) such supplier makes any written warranty to the consumer with respect to such consumer product, or (2) at the time of sale, or within 90 days thereafter, such supplier enters into a service contract with the consumer which applies to such consumer product.
>
> (b) Limitation on duration
>
> For purposes of this chapter (other than section 2304(a)(2) of this title), implied warranties may be limited in duration to the duration of a written warranty of reasonable duration, if such limitation is conscionable and is set forth in clear and unmistakable language and prominently displayed on the face of the warranty.
>
> (c) Effectiveness of disclaimers, modifications, or limitations
>
> A disclaimer, modification, or limitation made in violation of this section shall be ineffective for purposes of this chapter and State law.

Although the Act does not directly address products liability litigation, it does indirectly affect such litigation in several important ways. First and foremost, by nullifying complete disclaimers otherwise allowable under UCC § 2–316 in most substantial consumer product cases,[686] the Magnuson-Moss Warranty Act removes the most deadly arrow from the product seller's quiver of contractual defenses in products liability warranty litigation. Also important for products liability plaintiffs is the Act's requirement that limitations on an implied warranty's *duration* meet a rigorous fourfold test.[687] Any such durational limitation must be (1) reasonable in length, (2) conscionable, (3) set forth in clear and unmistakable language, and (4) prominently displayed on the face of the warranty.[688] A limitation that violates any of these requirements is void and of no effect.[689]

---

[685] 15 U.S.C. § 2308(b).

[686] Section 108 disclaimer restrictions do *not* apply to (1) non-consumer products, (2) products for which no written warranty (or service contract) has been provided, or (3) products which cost $10 or less. See 16 CFR § 700.6 (cost threshold).

[687] 15 U.S.C. § 2308(b).

[688] Id. On whether a car manufacturer's limitation of implied warranties to the duration of its two/three-year 24,000/36,000-mile express warranties was "reasonable" and "conscionable," in a class action over defective diesel engines which gave out after the warranted period, see Carlson v. General Motors Corp., 883 F.2d 287 (4th Cir. 1989). Compare Abraham v. Volkswagen of Am., Inc., 795 F.2d 238 (2d Cir. 1986); Hahn v. Ford Motor Co., 434 N.E.2d 943, 947 (Ind. Ct. App. 1982) (upholding 12-month/12,000-mile limitation on implied warranty).

[689] 15 U.S.C. § 2308(c).

Private Claims Under the Act; Jurisdiction and Attorneys' Fees

The Magnuson-Moss Act appears to provide that any breach of warranty, express or implied, is a violation of the Act, which seemingly would give rise to federal jurisdiction and the possibility of attorneys' fees in most serious products liability cases.[690] The Act states that a consumer damaged by a supplier's failure "to comply with any obligation under this chapter, or under a written warranty, implied warranty, or service contract," may (1) sue for damages in state court or, if the amount in controversy is at least $50,000, in federal court; and (2) recover attorneys' fees if he finally prevails.[691] Early commentators reasonably read this section of the Act to federalize products liability warranty claims: "[C]onsumers suddenly have a federal forum, as well as the prospect of recovering their attorneys' fees, for a violation of UCC section 2–314! In many respects, this 'muscling up' of the UCC could be one of the most important aspects of the Federal Act."[692] But the Act suffers from serious ambiguity on its applicability to products liability plaintiffs with personal injuries, for it elsewhere provides (with certain exceptions) that it does not "affect the liability of, or impose liability on, any person for personal injury."[693]

Boelens v. Redman Homes, Inc.[694] involved a claim under state law and the Magnuson-Moss Warranty Act against the retailer and manufacturer of a mobile home for chemical hepatitis and other injuries caused by formaldehyde fumes from materials used to construct the home. Plaintiffs did not allege a breach of any substantive provision of the Federal Warranty Act, such as the prohibition against disclaiming implied warranties, but instead based their claim under the Act solely upon the defendants' breach of warranty under state law.[695] The jury awarded the plaintiffs substantial compensatory and punitive damages, the federal district judge awarded the plaintiffs $237,000 in attorneys' fees and other litigation expenses, and the defendants appealed to the United States Court of Appeals. The issue before the Fifth Circuit was whether a personal injury claim arising from a product supplier's breach of state warranty law may be brought under the Magnuson-Moss Act in the absence of a separate and independent violation of the Act.

Vacating the plaintiffs' judgment, the Fifth Circuit ruled that personal injury claims based on breach of warranty are *not* cognizable under the Magnuson-Moss Warranty Act

---

[690] On private claims under the Act, see 2 Crockett, Product Warranties ch. 20; Miller and Kanter, Litigation Under Magnuson-Moss: New Opportunities in Private Actions, 13 UCC L.J. 10 (1980). See also Parasharami, Ranlett, and Noveck, Are Claims Under the Magnuson-Moss Warranty Act Exempt from Arbitration?, 40 Prod. Safety & Liab. Rep. (BNA) 451 (2012).

[691] 15 U.S.C. § 2310(d). Virchow v. University Homes, Inc., 699 N.W.2d 499, 507 (S.D. 2005) (in the discretion of the court, "consistent with the purpose and goals of the Act"). See also Hyundai Motor Am., Inc. v. Goodin, 822 N.E.2d 947, 951–59 (Ind. 2005) (attorneys' fees awarded in economic loss claims for breach of merchantability warranty).

[692] Clark and Davis, Beefing Up Product Warranties: A New Dimension in Consumer Protection, 23 Kan. L. Rev. 567, 616 (1975).

[693] 15 U.S.C. § 2311(b)(2) provides:

> Nothing in this chapter (other than sections 2308 and 2304(a)(2) and (4) of this title) shall (A) affect the liability of, or impose liability on, any person for personal injury, or (B) supersede any provision of State law regarding consequential damages for injury to the person or other injury.

Note that the reference to subsection 2304(a)(4) was probably a mistaken drafting attempt to refer to subsection (a)(3). See Boelens v. Redman Homes, Inc., 748 F.2d 1058, 1065 n.10 (5th Cir. 1984) (Tex. law).

[694] 748 F.2d 1058 (5th Cir. 1984) (Tex. law) (Wisdom, J.).

[695] Both under the state UCC and a state deceptive practices act.

unless the supplier also violated an important substantive provision of the Act.[696] Carefully reviewing the history and purposes of the Act, Judge Wisdom observed that permitting ordinary warranty claims under the Act "would allow virtually any state products liability action for personal injury damages . . . into federal court, subject only to the amount-in-controversy requirement."[697] To the contrary, reasoned Judge Wisdom: "Congress was content to let the question of personal injury products liability remain a matter of state-law causes of action, except to the extent that certain substantive provisions in the Magnuson-Moss Act overrule contrary state laws relating to the warrantor's ability to disclaim personal injury liability."[698] Thus, the court concluded that § 2311(b)(2) of the Act "prohibits claims arising from personal injury based solely on a breach of warranty, express or implied," but that a plaintiff might recover personal injury damages for the violation of a substantive provision of § 2308 (that prohibits all warrantors from completely disclaiming implied warranties) and § 2304(a) (that prohibits full warrantors from limiting the duration of implied warranties and from excluding or limiting consequential damages without conspicuously so stating on the face of the warranty).[699]

Other courts have agreed that "an action for personal injury may be maintained only for substantive violations of §§ 2308 and 2304(a)(2) and (3)."[700] These sections of the Act (1) restrict disclaimers of implied warranties; and (2) regulate (a) limitations on the duration of implied warranties, and (b) exclusions or limitations of consequential damages for breach of warranty.[701] In sum, the Act appears to say that a consumer of a covered product may bring an action under the Act to recover personal injuries caused by a breach of warranty under state law only if the product supplier violated the Act's disclaimer or consequential damages rules.

While the Act may be read in this manner to allow personal injury claims if a seller violates a substantive disclaimer provision, such claims are peculiar because there appears to be no requirement of a causal connection between such a violation and the

---

696 *Boelens*, 748 F.2d at 1060, 1071.

697 Id. at 1067. The Federal Warranty Act specifies that, for federal court jurisdiction, the amount in controversy be at least $50,000. 15 U.S.C. § 2310(d)(3)(B). See Grant v. Cavalier Mfg. Inc., 229 F. Supp. 2d 1332, 1334 (M.D. Ala. 2002) (in determining amount in controversy, courts should consider only actual claim brought under the Act).

698 *Boelens*, 748 F.2d at 1068 (quoting Gorman v. Saf-T-Mate, Inc., 513 F. Supp. 1028, 1035 (N.D. Ind. 1981)).

699 Id.

700 Voelkel v. General Motors Corp., 846 F. Supp. 1468, 1474 (D. Kan. 1994). "In short, § 2311(b)(2) does not directly impose personal injury liability but may have the effect of creating the same under state law in the event that a warranty disclaimer or modification or limitation is struck down." Id. at 1474 n.2. See also Oliver v. Homes of Legend, Inc., 2000 WL 1092130 (M.D. Ala. 2000) (no claim for emotional distress damages); Santarelli v. BP Am., 913 F. Supp. 324, 333 (M.D. Pa. 1996) (injuries from eating contaminated salmon: "The Act does not create a private, independent cause of action for personal injuries which are otherwise state law claims for breach of warranty."). *But see* Hughes v. Segal Enters., Inc., 627 F. Supp. 1231, 1237 (W.D. Ark. 1986) (acknowledging *Boelens* rule, but allowing class action under Magnuson-Moss for personal injury and economic loss claims for mobile home seller's failure to conspicuously label warranted homes as "full" or "limited") (sharply criticized in 2 Crockett, Product Warranties § 20:31).

701 Note that exclusions and limitations of consequential damages are only regulated, not prohibited, by § 108 of the Act. Indeed, such exclusions and limitations are specifically permitted by § 104(a)(3) of the Act, so long as the "exclusion or limitation conspicuously appears on the face of the warranty." In the case of personal injuries, however, the drafters quite clearly intended to leave UCC § 2–719(3) intact. See § 111(b) of the Act, 15 U.S.C. § 2311(b). Consequently, the Act does not address attempts by sellers to exclude responsibility for personal injuries arising from breach of warranty which are still essentially prohibited by UCC § 2–719(3). See § 4.8, above.

plaintiff's personal injury claim.[702] Arguably, personal injury claims should simply be prohibited under the Act even where a supplier has breached the Act's disclaimer requirements.[703] Nevertheless, allowing personal injury claims in such cases might be justified on the ground that the Act's disclaimer provisions are so important that they should offer as much federal protection for personal injury claims as for economic loss claims.

Although attorneys' fees and other costs of litigation theoretically are available to a prevailing plaintiff in the discretion of the court, one might expect many courts to exercise this discretion narrowly in personal injury cases.[704] The Magnuson-Moss Act was designed to protect consumers from sharp warranty practices that diminish the value of consumer products, not to provide attorneys' fees to plaintiffs injured by defective products, as Judge Wisdom noted in his decision in the *Boelens* case, discussed above. Accordingly, even a physically injured consumer who can prove a technical breach of a relevant substantive provision on disclaimers or remedy limitations should expect a cold judicial shoulder to a Magnuson-Moss claim for attorneys' fees in the absence of convincing proof that the defendant supplier deliberately and blatantly flouted an important disclaimer prohibition or other important provision of the Act.[705]

---

[702] See 2 Crockett, Product Warranties 2d § 20:31 ("there is no real connection between a personal injury claim and unrelated violations of Magnuson-Moss in the sales documentation").

[703] See id. (noting that one might well "conclude that Section 2311 excludes personal injury claims from the scope of Magnuson-Moss, even if a substantive violation of the federal statute is involved").

[704] See, e.g., Rubin v. Marshall Field & Co., 597 N.E.2d 688 (Ill. App. Ct. 1992) (no attorneys' fees for Magnuson-Moss warranty claim for injuries from eye makeup remover). A court that does allow attorneys' fees may limit them to recorded time specifically attributable to the narrow Magnuson-Moss Act issues. Such a limitation would exclude recovery for the great bulk of a plaintiff's counsel's time spent in preparing and trying the many state law issues of law and fact involved in a normal (warranty law) products liability action. Compare Hibbs v. Jeep Corp., 666 S.W.2d 792 (Mo. Ct. App. 1984) (attorneys' fees disallowed where billings did not clearly differentiate between Magnuson-Moss and other work on case), with Drouin v. Fleetwood Enters., 209 Cal. Rptr. 623 (Ct. App. 1985) (fees allowed; apportionment not required where plaintiff's claims arise from common core of facts or involve related legal theories).

[705] A plaintiff should expect the same cold reception for punitive damages in products liability claims somehow brought under the Magnuson-Moss Act. Although punitive damages are unavailable for breach of warranty under UCC § 1–106(1), some jurisdictions allow such damage claims in contract actions when they accompany substantive claims in tort. But combining a tort claim with a breach of warranty claim will not help a plaintiff reach the $50,000 jurisdictional amount to support a claim under the Magnuson-Moss Act. Consider Van Alfen v. Toyota Motor Sales, USA, Inc., 2011 WL 4633986, at *10 (C.D. Cal. 2011) ("Although punitive damages may be available in Utah for breach of warranty claims sounding in tort, because danger to person or property must first be involved, any punitive damages stemming therefrom are rooted in personal injury, and must necessarily by excluded from consideration under an MMWA claim.").

Chapter 5

STRICT LIABILITY IN TORT

Table of Sections

§ 5.1 STRICT LIABILITY IN TORT—GENERALLY

Strict products liability in tort, from the 1970s into the early 2000s, was widely considered the principal basis of recovery in modern products liability law—as it still is thought to be in many American states today. Indeed, lawyers, judges, and even some law professors untutored in the finer points of products liability law sometimes mistakenly exchange the terms "strict liability" and "products liability," confusing one term for the other.[1] Such usage is imprecise and should be avoided because it equates a single theory of liability with an entire field of law that embraces various types of claims other than strict tort liability.[2] But there can be no doubt that the development and growth of the doctrine of strict liability in tort was the centerpiece around which the rest of modern products liability law was formed and evolved during the latter part of the twentieth century, continuing in many respects today.

---

1 See, e.g., Schall v. Suzuki Motor of Am., Inc., 450 F. Supp. 3d 771, 778 (W.D. Ky. 2020) ("products liability focuses on the strict liability of a defendant for inadequacies in the quality of the product, whereas negligence liability focuses on the conduct of the actor"); Patch v. Hillerich & Bradsby Co., 257 P.3d 383, 386 n.1 (Mont. 2011) (plaintiffs "asserted negligence, products liability, and breach of warranty claims"). Even Stanford and Harvard law professors are not immune. See Polinsky and Shavell, The Uneasy Case for Product Liability, 123 Harv. L. Rev. 1437 (2010) (falling into this linguistic trap). At least one Harvard and one Fordham professor know better. See Goldberg and Zipursky, The Easy Case for Products Liability Law: A Response to Professors Polinsky and Shavell, 123 Harv. L. Rev. 1919, 1923–25 (2010) (noting if all too charitably tolerating this ignorant blunder).

2 While the most common type of products liability claim, "strict liability in tort," is merely one of several causes of action in "products liability" law. See, e.g., McNair v. Johnson & Johnson, 818 S.E.2d 852, 859 (W. Va. 2018) (" 'Product liability actions may be premised on three independent theories—strict liability, negligence, and warranty. Each theory contains different elements which plaintiffs must prove in order to recover.' "). See also Smith v. Ethicon, Inc., 2021 WL 4098408, at *3 (E.D. Ky. 2021); Cofresi v. Medtronic, Inc., 450 F. Supp. 3d 759, 765 (W.D. Tex. 2020).

On the multiplicity of products liability claims, see ch. 1, above. Claims for negligence, tortious misrepresentation, and breach of warranty (express or implied), are addressed, respectively, in chapters 2, 3, and 4, above.

This chapter examines the central aspects of the doctrine of strict products liability in tort—its origins, evolution, nature, rationales, tests, and characteristics—that distinguish it from other theories of liability for harm from product accidents. In particular, the discussion here describes the development and explores the interior of § 402A of the *Restatement (Second) of Torts*, published in 1965. A final section describes the decline of strict liability in tort as negligence principles began to regain their prominence during the 1980s and accelerated in subsequent decades.

Consideration of the *Restatement (Third) of Torts: Products Liability*, published in 1998, is deferred to the next chapter because it explicitly abandons the doctrine of "strict" products liability for design and warning defects, which comprise the bulk of products liability litigation.[3] The many particulars of modern products liability law are addressed in depth in subsequent chapters.

After more than a century of slow and tortured growth in warranty, culminating in 1960 in *Henningsen v. Bloomfield Motors, Inc.*,[4] strict manufacturer liability for harm from defective products swept like a storm into the American law of torts during the 1960s.[5] On the footings of *Henningsen*, as detailed below, Judge Traynor in 1963 constructed a new doctrine of strict products liability in tort in *Greenman v. Yuba Power Products, Inc.*;[6] in 1964, Dean Prosser, Reporter for the *Second Restatement*, proposed that the American Law Institute (ALI) endorse this principle in § 402A of the *Restatement (Second) of Torts*, which the Institute thereupon endorsed, and then published the following year; and a flood of American jurisdictions rapidly thereafter adopted the new tort law doctrine of strict liability for selling defective products that cause physical harm.[7]

Liability under § 402A is "strict" because it is based not on a supplier's fault in producing or selling a defective product, but on the frustration of consumer expectations of safety when a latent defect in a product causes physical harm. However, as more and more courts during the 1970s and 1980s broadly extended the new principle to design and warning cases,[8] the truly strict consumer expectations liability standard increasingly gave way to principles of foreseeability and risk-utility balancing that underlie the law of negligence.[9] While courts widely continued to claim that they were applying liability that was "strict," it became increasingly clear that the liability standards most courts were applying in warning and design cases were truly based on fault.[10]

---

3 See § 1.3, above. The Products Liability Restatement is examined in § 6.5, below.

4 161 A.2d 69 (N.J. 1960).

5 See § 5.2, below.

6 377 P.2d 897 (Cal. 1963).

7 See § 5.3, below.

8 Some courts had begun in earnest to examine manufacturers' design and warning choices during the 1950s, but the cases were based on negligence or warranty. See, e.g., Matthews v. Lawnlite Co., 88 So.2d 299, 301 (Fla. 1956) (unguarded mechanism under arm rest of aluminum lounge chair's handle clipped off plaintiff's finger "with the ease that one clips a choice flower with pruning shears"; negligent design). See generally Noel, Manufacturer's Negligence of Design or Directions for Use of a Product, 71 Yale L.J. 816 (1962); Noel, Recent Trends in Manufacturer's Negligence as to Design, Instructions or Warnings, 19 Sw. L.J. 43 (1965).

9 See § 5.7, below.

10 See Owen, Defectiveness Restated: Exploding the "Strict" Products Liability Myth, 1996 U. Ill. L. Rev. 743. The path *away* from strict liability is addressed in § 5.10, below.

In 1992 the ALI began work on a new *Restatement of Torts* on the specific topic of products liability law, approving the new *Restatement* in 1997 and publishing it in 1998 as the *Restatement (Third) of Torts: Products Liability*.[11] While the *Third Restatement* continued to base liability for manufacturing defects in terms that are truly strict, it abandoned any pretense of "strict" responsibility for design and warning defects, which it grounded explicitly (though buried in its comments rather than located in black letter) in principles of negligence.[12]

During the 1990s, the *Third Restatement* (the "*Products Liability Restatement*") was carefully conceived, constructed, debated, approved, and published in 1998.[13] Since that time, an increasing number of courts[14] (and at least a couple of legislatures)[15] have adopted some of its key provisions. Yet modern products liability doctrine and rhetoric in most states was constructed squarely on § 402A of the *Second Restatement* which, in various important respects, the *Third Restatement* largely dismantles.[16] For this reason of precedent,[17] and to avoid a hot-button political issue, courts widely have declined so far to "adopt" the product defect liability formulations of the *Third Restatement*.[18] And it seems increasingly likely that most courts will never explicitly jettison their evolved § 402A jurisprudence for the liability standards articulated in the *Third Restatement*. Accordingly, much jurisprudence of "strict" products liability in tort spawned by § 402A may be expected formally to control products liability litigation in many jurisdictions for years to come.

---

11 The Restatement (Third) of Torts: Products Liability is fully examined in § 6.5, below.

12 See id. and § 5.9, below. Though explicit, this foundational shift from § 402A's basis in strict liability, is buried in its comments. Id.

13 See Owen, Products Liability Law Restated, 49 S.C. L. Rev. 273 (1998).

14 See, e.g., Davis v. UHP Projects, Inc., 2021 WL 1293858, at *3 (V.I. 2021) (adopting § 2, and § 3 by implication, note 3); Great Northern Insurance Co. v. Honeywell Int'l, Inc., 911 N.W.2d 510, 520 (Minn. 2018) ((post-sale duty to warn, § 10); Olivero v. Trek Bicycle Corp., 291 F. Supp. 3d 1209, 1223 (D. Colo. 2017) (predicting that Colorado would adopt malfunction doctrine, § 3); Metropolitan Prop. & Cas. Ins. Co. v. Deere & Co., 25 A.3d 571, 581 (Conn. 2011) (malfunction doctrine, § 3); Dobrovolny v. Ford Motor Co., 793 N.W.2d 445, 449 (Neb. 2011) (economic loss rule, § 21); Branham v. Ford Motor Co., 701 S.E.2d 5, 14 (S.C. 2010) (design defect, § 2(b)); Gudmundson v. Del Ozone, 232 P.3d 1059, 1072–73 (Utah 2010) (component parts doctrine, § 5); Larkin v. Pfizer, Inc., 153 S.W.3d 758, 770 (Ky. 2004) (learned intermediary doctrine, § 6(d)); Wright v. Brooke Grp. Ltd., 652 N.W.2d 159 (Iowa 2002) (§§ 1 and 2). Compare Normandy v. American Med. Sys., Inc., 262 A.3d 698, 705 n.6 (Conn. 2021) (deeming Restatement Third "instructive" when "the issue presented . . . does not require . . . a significant shift from the analysis of the Restatement (Second)").

15 See Wis. Stat. Ann. § 895.047(1)(a) (adopting defect definitions of Third Rest. § 2). See also Ohio Rev. Code Ann. §§ 2307.74 to 2307.76 (expanding upon defect definitions of Third Rest. § 2); Tex. Civ. Prac. & Rem. Code Ann. § 82.005 (expanding upon design defect definition of Rest. § 2(b); Wash. Rev. Code Ann. § 7.72.030 (expanding upon defect definitions of Rest. § 2).

16 See note 10, above.

17 And surely to avoid the resulting political fallout.

18 See, e.g., Ford Motor Co. v. Trejo, 402 P.3d 649, 658 (Nev. 2017) (declining to adopt § 2(b)); Bifolck v. Philip Morris, Inc., 152 A.3d 1183, 1196 (Conn. 2016) (same); Aubin v. Union Carbide Corp., 177 So.3d 489, 512 (Fla. 2015) (§ 2); Malcolm v. Evenflo Co., 217 P.3d 514, 522 (Mont. 2009) (regulatory compliance defense, § 5); Mikolajczyk v. Ford Motor Co., 901 N.E.2d 329, 352 (Ill. 2008) (§ 2, but formulation of the risk-utility test "instructive"); TRW Vehicle Safety Sys., Inc. v. Moore, 936 N.E.2d 201, 209 n.2 (Ind. 2010) (§ 2(b) reasonable alternative design standard inconsistent with Indiana Product Liability Act); Braaten v. Saberhagen Holdings, 198 P.3d 493, 497 n.5 (Wash. 2008) (en banc) (§ 2(c), failure to warn, dictum); Halliday v. Sturm, Ruger & Co., 792 A.2d 1145 (Md. 2002) (design defect, § 2(b)); Vautour v. Body Masters Sports Indus., 784 A.2d 1178, 1182–84 (N.H. 2001) (§ 2(b), design defect).

§ 5.2 THE PATH TO STRICT LIABILITY IN TORT

The path to strict products liability in tort was tortured, tortuous, and tortious only in part.[19] This lengthy journey involved the intertwining of parts of two major branches of the law of obligations that have evolved over thousands of years: tort law and contract law.[20] Each field of law separately contributed a central feature to the development of strict manufacturer liability for harm caused by defective products, and they combined to contribute a third. Tort law's major contribution, launched in 1916 by *MacPherson v. Buick Motor Co.*,[21] was its rejection of the privity-of-contract requirement in tort law claims. In so doing, tort law championed the view that manufacturers are obligated to "remote" consumers by a public duty, independent of any private contractual obligations that may exist between them. To this, contract law contributed the idea that liability should be "strict," contrary to the general tort law notion that breach of duty generally must be based on a supplier's negligence or other fault. Tort and contract law conjoined in warranty to generate the doctrine of strict manufacturer liability in tort. Though warranty law today is largely viewed as part of the law of sales, a branch of the law of contracts, it developed out of the tort action of deceit and remained a tort-type action, particularly in food cases, until quite recently.[22] Even modern courts occasionally have turned to common-law warranties in tort for products liability and other types of claims.[23]

The story of the origins of strict products liability in tort is largely a tale of warranty law that traces its history at least to ancient Mesopotamia and Rome in the development of principles of sales law, warranty, and deceit.[24] It suffices here, however, to consider more recent developments in American law over the last couple of centuries. The brief

---

[19] "Tortured," "tortuous," and "tort," the latter from the French for injury or wrong, all derive from the Latin *tortus*, meaning twisted or crooked. See Keeton, Dobbs, Keeton, and Owen, Prosser and Keeton on the Law of Torts § 1, at 2. See also Birks, The Concept of a Civil Wrong, in Philosophical Foundations of Tort Law 39 (D. Owen ed., Oxford 1995) (citing The Oxford Dictionary of English Etymology, C. Onions ed., 1966): " 'Wrong' and 'tort', like 'crook' and 'bent', play on the same metaphor which contrasts to 'right' and 'straight'. Wrong conduct, or, using the French word, 'tort', is twisted, a metaphor for condemned or disapproved."

[20] For early commentary on the path to strict products liability, see, e.g., James, Products Liability (pts. 1 and 2), 34 Tex. L. Rev. 44, 192 (1955); James, General Products—Should Manufacturers Be Liable Without Negligence?, 24 Tenn. L. Rev. 923 (1957); Noel, Manufacturers of Products—The Drift Toward Strict Liability, 24 Tenn. L. Rev. 963 (1957); Gillam, Products Liability in a Nutshell, 37 Or. L. Rev. 119 (1958); Prosser, The Assault Upon the Citadel (Strict Liability to the Consumer), 69 Yale L.J. 1099 (1960); Keeton, Products Liability: Liability Without Fault and the Requirement of a Defect, 41 Tex. L. Rev. 855 (1963); Keeton, Products Liability—The Nature and Extent of Strict Liability, 1964 U. Ill. L.F. 693; Wilson, Products Liability (pts. 1 and 2), 43 Cal. L. Rev. 614, 809 (1965); Traynor, The Ways and Meanings of Defective Products and Strict Liability, 32 Tenn. L. Rev. 363 (1965); Wade, Strict Tort Liability of Manufacturers, 19 Sw. L.J. 5 (1965); Prosser, The Fall of the Citadel (Strict Liability to the Consumer), 50 Minn. L. Rev. 791 (1966); Wade, On the Nature of Strict Tort Liability for Products, 44 Miss. L.J. 825 (1973); Rest. (2d) Torts § 402A cmt. *b* (brief historical sketch). Commentary on the theoretical paths to strict products liability is collected in § 5.4, below.

[21] 111 N.E. 1050 (N.Y. 1916).

[22] See Ames, The History of Assumpsit, 2 Harv. L. Rev. 1, 8 (1888); Prosser, The Implied Warranty of Merchantable Quality, 27 Minn. L. Rev. 117, 118–22 (1943); Prosser, The Assault Upon the Citadel (Strict Liability to the Consumer), 69 Yale L.J. 1099, 1103–10, 1124–27 (1960).

[23] See, e.g., Goldberg v. Kollsman Instrument Corp., 191 N.E.2d 81, 82 (N.Y. 1963) ("[a] breach of warranty, it is now clear, is not only a violation of the sales contract out of which the warranty arises but is a tortious wrong suable by a noncontracting party"). See also Payne v. Soft Sheen Prods., Inc., 486 A.2d 712, 719–21 (D.C. 1985) (tort-like warranty claim essentially was claim for strict liability in tort); Lonzrick v. Republic Steel Corp., 218 N.E.2d 185 (Ohio 1966) (applying "implied warranty in tort" to products liability claim); Temple v. Wean United, Inc., 364 N.E.2d 267 (Ohio 1977) (moving from "implied warranty in tort theory" to § 402A). See also W. Prosser, Handbook of the Law of Torts § 95, at 635 (4th ed. 1971); § 4.1, above.

[24] See § 1.2, above.

narration below describes how certain limbs of warranty and tort law increasingly grew toward one another for a century or so and then, in the early 1960s, suddenly and spectacularly fused to beget the radical new doctrine of strict products liability in tort.

The tort law action of deceit, with its ancient heritage,[25] spawned the law of warranty long before the law of assumpsit or contract was even born.[26] Yet, beginning with a late eighteenth century English case,[27] warranty in Anglo-American law gradually evolved during the nineteenth century into the branch of contract law dealing with the law of sales.[28] Well into the twentieth century, however, a particular pocket of warranty law remained protected, shielded from contract law's predatory clutch—in cases involving unwholesome food and drink, American courts continued persistently to apply the ancient tort-like warranty of quality.[29]

Throughout the history of Anglo-American law, food suppliers have always been held closely accountable for the wholesomeness of their provisions.[30] A series of early English statutes, beginning in 1266, criminalized the sale of "corrupt" food and drink for immediate consumption, and, as of 1431, "[a] taverner or vintner was bound as such to sell wholesome food and drink."[31] Whether this special duty amounted to a common-law warranty of the wholesomeness of food is uncertain,[32] but American courts from an early date assumed that it was, holding sellers of food strictly liable for harm to their direct consumers.[33] As early as 1815, a New York court, relying on Blackstone, noted that a warranty of quality is always implied into the sale of foodstuffs because "the preservation of health and life" requires the seller to be "bound to know that they are sound and

---

[25] See §§ 1.2 and 3.2, above.

[26] See Ames, The History of Assumpsit, 2 Harv. L. Rev. 1, 8 (1888); Prosser, The Implied Warranty of Merchantable Quality, 27 Minn. L. Rev. 117, 118–22 (1943).

[27] Stuart v. Wilkins, (1778) 99 Eng. Rep. 15 (K.B.). While Stuart v. Wilkins appears to have been the first judicial pronouncement that assumpsit would lie for breach of warranty if it were express (but not yet if it were implied), the court's opinion may merely have certified the understanding and practice among lawyers from 1750 or shortly thereafter. See Prosser, The Implied Warranty of Merchantable Quality, 27 Minn. L. Rev. 117, 119–20 (1943).

[28] See Prosser, The Implied Warranty of Merchantable Quality, 27 Minn. L. Rev. 117, 118–22 (1943).

[29] See, e.g., Jacob E. Decker & Sons, Inc. v. Capps, 164 S.W.2d 828, 831–32 (Tex. 1942) (noting that the warranty in food cases was not the modern contractual warranty but the tort law warranty derived from the action of deceit which is "not dependent on any provision of the contract").

[30] On the evolution of the tort-like warranty applied to food cases in Anglo-American law, see H. Melick, The Sale of Food and Drink (1936); R. Dickerson, Products Liability and the Food Consumer (1951); Perkins, Unwholesome Food as a Source of Liability (pts. 1 and 2), 5 Iowa L. Bull. 6, 86 (1919–1920); Waite, Retail Responsibility and Judicial Law Making, 34 Mich. L. Rev. 494 (1936); Brown, The Liability of Retail Dealers for Defective Food Products, 23 Minn. L. Rev. 585 (1939). See especially Prosser, The Assault Upon the Citadel (Strict Liability to the Consumer), 69 Yale L.J. 1099, 1103–10 (1960), from which much of this discussion is drawn.

[31] Ames, The History of Assumpsit, 2 Harv. L. Rev. 1, 9 (1888). See U.S. v. Park, 421 U.S. 658, 672 (1975), which affirmed a criminal conviction of the president of a large national retail food store chain under the Federal Food, Drug, and Cosmetic Act, for allowing shipment in interstate commerce of adulterated food. Noting that "the Act imposes not only a positive duty to seek out and remedy violations when they occur but also, and primarily, a duty to implement measures that will insure that violations will not occur," the Court explained: "The requirements of foresight and vigilance imposed on responsible corporate agents are beyond question demanding, and perhaps onerous, but they are no more stringent than the public has a right to expect of those who voluntarily assume positions of authority in business enterprises whose services and products affect the health and well-being of the public that supports them." Cf. Wasserstrom, Strict Liability in the Criminal Law, 12 Stan. L. Rev. 731, 741–45 (1960).

[32] Compare H. Melick, The Sale of Food and Drink 10 (1936) (yes), with Perkins, Unwholesome Food as a Source of Liability, 5 Iowa L. Bull. 6, 8–9 (1919) (uncertain).

[33] See Van Bracklin v. Fonda, 12 Johns. 468 (N.Y. 1815) (seller knew but failed to disclose that beef cow was diseased prior to slaughter).

wholesome at his peril."[34] A century later, the New York Court of Appeals reaffirmed the necessity of a strict liability rule for harm from the sale of food, stating that such a rule was necessary to the public health and welfare.[35]

From at least 1913,[36] courts in food cases began to extend the strict liability rule to third persons.[37] Toward the middle of the twentieth century, although the courts were divided,[38] many jurisdictions enforced a special food warranty running to remote consumers that lay outside of contract law and hence was one of tort. In a 1942 case from Texas, *Jacob E. Decker & Sons v. Capps*,[39] a producer sold contaminated sausage to a retail merchant, who sold it to Mr. Capps. The Capps family consumed the sausage, which killed one of the children and seriously sickened the rest of the family.

In an action against the producer, the court noted that the food manufacturer's duty to consumers rested on "the broad principle of the public policy to protect human health and life."[40] The court observed that food items are placed in the channels of commerce with the intention that they pass from hand to hand until they find their way to some remote consumer who usually is unable to analyze the food to determine if it is safe. So, in the case of defective food, "there is such an utter failure of the purpose for which the food is sold, and the consequences of eating unsound food are so disastrous to human health and life, that the law imposes a warranty of purity in favor of the ultimate consumer as a matter of public policy."[41]

For products other than food, the path to strict products liability in tort took much longer. Over the first half of the twentieth century, tort law moved slowly in expanding a manufacturer's responsibility for product-caused harm to remote consumers. In particular, the *MacPherson* doctrine, which banished the no-privity-of-contract defense from negligence actions against manufacturers,[42] took decades to spread across the nation[43] and did nothing to relieve an injured consumer of the burden of proving the supplier's fault.

---

[34] Id.

[35] Race v. Krum, 118 N.E. 853, 854 (N.Y. 1918) ("This rule is based upon the high regard which the law has for human life. The consequences to the consumer resulting from consumption of articles of food sold for immediate use may be so disastrous that an obligation is placed upon the seller to see to it, at his peril, that the articles sold are fit for the purpose for which they are intended. The rule is an onerous one, but public policy, as well as the public health, demand such obligation should be imposed.").

[36] Prosser reports that the first third-party case was Mazetti v. Armour & Co., 135 P. 633 (Wash. 1913), Prosser, The Assault Upon the Citadel (Strict Liability to the Consumer), 69 Yale L.J. 1099, 1106 (1960), yet *Mazetti* relies on earlier cases, which suggests an even earlier origin of this principle.

[37] For a more expansive discussion of all of these developments, see Prosser, The Assault Upon the Citadel (Strict Liability to the Consumer), 69 Yale L.J. 1099, 1103–10 (1960).

[38] In the first edition of his treatise, though noting a trend in the opposite direction, Prosser observed that "[t]he majority of the courts still refuse to find a strict liability even as to food." W. Prosser, Handbook of the Law of Torts § 83, at 692 (1941).

[39] 164 S.W.2d 828 (Tex. 1942).

[40] Id. at 829.

[41] Id.

[42] See § 1.2, above.

[43] As late as 1937, commenting on *MacPherson*, Francis Bohlen remarked: "Admirable as is the result, convincing as is the reasoning, the doctrine in that case has not gained the acceptance which its merits deserve." Bohlen, Fifty Years of Torts (pts. 1 and 2), 50 Harv. L. Rev. 725, 1225, 1234 (1937).

Escola

In the first edition of his celebrated tort law treatise in 1941, Professor William Prosser[44] succinctly catalogued a variety of arguments favoring strict liability for injuries caused by remote sellers of defective products and why that liability should lie in tort.[45] Three years later, in *Escola v. Coca Cola Bottling Co.*,[46] the Supreme Court of California upheld a res ipsa loquitur verdict for a waitress injured when a Coke bottle exploded in her hand. In perhaps the most renowned concurring opinion in all American tort law, Justice Roger Traynor elegantly elaborated each of Prosser's arguments for strict products liability in tort.[47] Reasoning that "the manufacturer's negligence should no longer be singled out as the basis of a plaintiff's right to recover in cases like the present one," Traynor concluded that "it should now be recognized that a manufacturer incurs an absolute liability when an article that he has placed on the market, knowing that it is to be used without inspection, proves to have a defect that causes injury to human beings." Regardless of fault, "public policy demands that responsibility be fixed wherever it will most effectively reduce the hazards to life and health inherent in defective products that reach the market." Manufacturers can test their products for defects in ways that consumers cannot, and the economic consequences of an injury from a defective product "may be an overwhelming misfortune to the person injured, and a needless one, for the risk of injury can be insured by the manufacturer and distributed among the public as a cost of doing business." Moreover, manufacturers rather than consumers are best situated to provide the most effective public protection against the "menace" of defective products.[48]

Further, Justice Traynor explained that a rule imposing strict liability without privity on manufacturers of defective products would result in judicial economies since manufacturers were already indirectly subject to strict liability to remote consumers for selling defective products—an injured consumer could sue the retailer for breach of the implied warranty of merchantability; the retailer could then recover against the wholesaler for selling an unmerchantable product; and the wholesaler could in turn recover back against the manufacturer. But such a tortuous path "is needlessly circuitous and engenders wasteful litigation. Much would be gained if the injured person could base his action directly on the manufacturer's warranty."[49]

Observing that manufacturers of defective foods are held to a warranty of quality running to remote consumers, and that the rights of such persons to legal protection do not depend "upon the intricacies of the law of sales," Justice Traynor asserted that the same protection should be extended to consumers of all types of defective products:

---

[44] Technically, Prosser was no longer a professor when he published his hornbook in 1941, since he had resigned his professorship at Minnesota Law School the previous year to become that state's counsel for the U.S. Office of Price Administration. Yet he wrote most of his book while still on the Minnesota law faculty, and he returned permanently to academia in 1947 when he taught law for a year at Harvard before taking on the deanship of Berkeley Law.

[45] W. Prosser, Handbook of the Law of Torts 688–93 (1941) (summarized in § 5.4, note 276, below). For one study of Dean Prosser's contributions to the development of strict products liability in tort, see G. White, Tort Law in America—An Intellectual History 168–73, 198–200 (expanded ed. 2003).

[46] 150 P.2d 436 (Cal. 1944). On *Escola*, see M. Geistfeld, *Escola v. Coca Cola Bottling Co.*: Strict Products Liability Unbounded, in Torts Stories 229 (R. Rabin and S. Sugarman eds., Foundation Press 2003).

[47] See G. White, Tort Law in America—An Intellectual History 198–200 (expanded ed. 2003) (detailed comparison of arguments in Prosser's hornbook and Traynor's opinion).

[48] *Escola*, 150 P.2d at 440–41.

[49] Id. at 442.

"Dangers to life and health inhere in other consumers' goods that are defective and there is no reason to differentiate them from the dangers of defective food products."[50] Nor would courts have to resort to the kinds of fictions they created in food product cases to rationalize extending the manufacturer's warranty to remote consumers "if the warranty is severed from the contract of sale between the dealer and the consumer and based on the law of torts as a strict liability."[51]

Justice Traynor explained that a doctrine of strict products liability in tort was necessary to adjust the law to the vast changes in how products are manufactured and merchandised in the modern world. "As handicrafts have been replaced by mass production with its great markets and transportation facilities, the close relationship between the producer and consumer of a product has been altered." In marketing complex machines and chemicals, modern manufacturers urge remote consumers to trust in the safety of such products and to relinquish the consumer's historical self-protective role in evaluating a product's safety prior to purchase and use.[52] For these many reasons, Justice Traynor concluded that manufacturers should be strictly responsible for injuries their defective products cause consumers.

Justice Traynor's *Escola* opinion attracted a bit of notoriety,[53] but it received only passing notice[54] for a number of years.[55] During the 1950s, a number of courts expanded the "tort" food warranty to sales of dog and fish food,[56] and to products for intimate bodily use,[57] as scholars increasingly argued for a general principle of strict manufacturer liability for physical harm from defective products.[58]

---

[50] Id.

[51] Id. at 442–43 (citing Jacob E. Decker & Sons, Inc. v. Capps, 164 S.W.2d 828 (Tex. 1942)); W. Prosser, Handbook of the Law of Torts 689 (1941).

[52] *Escola*, 150 P.2d at 443–44.

[53] Compare Dean Prosser's brief but favorable reference to Justice Traynor's *Escola* opinion, in Prosser, Res Ipsa Loquitur in California, 37 Cal. L. Rev. 183, 224 n.235 (1949), with Dean Pound's extensive criticism of the opinion for expressing sentiments Pound viewed to be Marxist. See R. Pound, New Paths of the Law 45 (1950), and Law in the Service State: Freedom v. Equality, 36 A.B.A. J. 977, 981 (1950). *But see* Pound, The Problem of the Exploding Bottle, 40 B.U. L. Rev. 167, 180–81, 185–86 (1960), by which time Pound had converted to Traynor's views.

[54] See, e.g., James, Accident Liability: Some Wartime Developments, 55 Yale L.J. 365 n.4 (1946) (Traynor's opinion given a "*cf.*" cite in article's introductory paragraph). In the 1955 edition of his treatise, Prosser merely cited but did not discuss Traynor's concurring opinion in *Escola*. See W. Prosser, Handbook of the Law of Torts 19 n.47, 506 n.1 (2d ed. 1955). While he quoted from Traynor's *Escola* opinion five years later in his "Assault" article, Prosser there remarked that "the question remains whether our courts, our legislators, and public sentiment in general, are yet ready to adopt so sweeping a legal philosophy, and to impose so heavy a burden abruptly and all at once upon all producers." Prosser, The Assault Upon the Citadel (Strict Liability to the Consumer), 69 Yale L.J. 1099, 1120 (1960).

[55] See Priest, The Invention of Enterprise Liability: A Critical History of the Intellectual Foundations of Modern Tort Law, 14 J. Legal Stud. 461, 498–99 (1985).

[56] See McAfee v. Cargill, Inc., 121 F. Supp. 5 (S.D. Cal. 1954) (dog food); Midwest Game Co. v. M.F.A. Milling Co., 320 S.W.2d 547 (Mo. 1959) (fish food). Both "apparently on the bald theory that food is food." Prosser, The Assault Upon the Citadel (Strict Liability to the Consumer), 69 Yale L.J. 1099, 1111 (1960).

[57] See Worley v. Proctor & Gamble Mfg. Co., 253 S.W.2d 532 (Mo. Ct. App. 1952) (detergent; dictum); Kruper v. Proctor & Gamble Co., 113 N.E.2d 605 (Ohio Ct. App. 1953) (soap), rev'd on other grounds, 117 N.E.2d 7 (Ohio 1954); Graham v. Bottenfield's, Inc., 269 P.2d 413 (Kan. 1954) (hair dye); Rogers v. Toni Home Permanent Co., 147 N.E.2d 612 (Ohio 1958) (permanent wave); Markovich v. McKesson & Robbins, Inc., 149 N.E.2d 181 (Ohio Ct. App. 1958) (same); Ross v. Philip Morris Co., 164 F. Supp. 683 (W.D. Mo. 1958) (cigarettes). All are chronicled in Prosser, The Assault Upon the Citadel (Strict Liability to the Consumer), 69 Yale L.J. 1099, 1110–14 (1960), and W. Prosser, Handbook on the Law of Torts 510 (2d ed. 1955). See also Dean Prosser's Notes to the Rest. (2d) Torts § 402A at 9–14 (Tent. Draft No. 7, April 16, 1962).

[58] See § 5.4, below.

Henningsen

This was the legal landscape in 1960 when the New Jersey Supreme Court was asked to decide *Henningsen v. Bloomfield Motors, Inc.*[59] Ten days after Bloomfield Motors sold a new 1955 Plymouth sedan, the buyer's wife was injured when a defect in the car's steering caused the car to veer off the highway and crash into a brick wall. In Mr. and Mrs. Henningsen's suit for breach of the implied warranty of merchantability against the dealer and manufacturer, Chrysler Corporation, Chrysler defended on the grounds that it was not in privity of contract with the plaintiffs and that, in the purchase order, it had effectively disclaimed responsibility and limited its damages to repair or replacement of any defective parts. The jury returned verdicts in favor of the plaintiffs. On appeal to the New Jersey Supreme Court, the defendants claimed that the case should have been dismissed on grounds of lack of privity of contract and because of the disclaimer of implied warranties and limitations of remedies in the sales contract Mr. Henningsen had signed.

In a unanimous opinion, the court affirmed the plaintiffs' verdicts. Drawing from the reasoning of the food warranty cases, Dean Prosser's treatise, and Justice Traynor's concurrence in *Escola*, Justice Francis observed that implied warranties are a necessary protection for consumers unable effectively to inspect products for latent defects. "Warranties developed in the law in the interest of and to protect the ordinary consumer who cannot be expected to have the knowledge or capacity or even the opportunity to make adequate inspection of mechanical instrumentalities, like automobiles, and to decide for himself whether they are reasonably fit for the designed purpose."[60] Building from the right of consumers of defective food to recover from manufacturers despite the absence of privity of contract, Justice Francis saw "no rational doctrinal basis for differentiating between a fly in a bottle of beverage and a defective automobile. The unwholesome beverage may bring illness to one person, the defective car, with its great potentiality for harm to the driver, occupants, and others, demands even less adherence to the narrow barrier of privity."[61] And thus, in the immortal words of Dean Prosser, *Henningsen* marked the "fall of the citadel" of privity.[62]

Nor did the court have much use for Chrysler's defenses based on clauses in its purchase order that purported to disclaim the implied warranty of merchantability and to limit remedies for breach of warranty to repair or replacement of defective parts. Reasoning that the disclaimer and remedy limitation clauses in the fine-print form were oppressive, one-sided, and rested on the "gross inequality of bargaining position" of consumers, the court concluded that Chrysler's purchase order was an unconscionable contract of adhesion. In short, Chrysler's effort to disclaim and limit its responsibility for personal injuries flowing from its basic warranty obligations was "inimical to the public welfare,"[63] and thus "violative of public policy and void."[64]

---

[59] 161 A.2d 69 (N.J. 1960). *Henningsen* was examined in the warranty law context at §§ 4.5 and 4.7, above.

[60] Id. at 78.

[61] Id. at 83. Compare the observation of Professor Fleming James, three years earlier: "Surely greater danger lurks in a defective automobile wheel than in a pebble in a can of beans." James, General Products—Should Manufacturers Be Liable Without Negligence?, 24 Tenn. L. Rev. 923, 926 (1957).

[62] Prosser, The Fall of the Citadel (Strict Liability to the Consumer), 50 Minn. L. Rev. 791 (1966).

[63] *Henningsen*, 161 A.2d at 87.

[64] Id. at 97. The court's treatment of the disclaimer provisions is more fully addressed in § 4.9, above.

Remarkably,[65] just a few weeks after *Henningsen* was handed down,[66] Dean Prosser published his seminal article, "The Assault Upon the Citadel,"[67] arguing for and predicting precisely such a result. Tracing the development of a manufacturer's warranty responsibility to consumers for injuries caused by defective products, Prosser related the variety of ingenious methods devised by courts to avoid contract law obstacles to recovery, such as privity, disclaimers, and the requirement that a buyer promptly notify the seller of a breach. Prosser argued that the "warranty" rule of strict liability should be extended beyond cases of unwholesome food and other products for bodily use. "The public interest in the safety of products which the public must buy certainly extends to a great many other things. The wedge has entered, and we are on our way. . . . Ultimately, . . . we may arrive at a 'general rule' of strict liability for all products."[68] Such would be the correct rule, but the "warranty" label was wrong. "If there is to be strict liability in tort," contended Prosser, "let there be strict liability in tort, declared outright, without an illusory contract mask."[69]

Now that a few courts,[70] supported by leading tort law scholars,[71] were urging a generalized doctrine of strict manufacturer liability for selling defective products, the stage was set for judicial adoption of a doctrine of strict products liability that lay explicitly in tort. When Dean Prosser wrote his "Assault Upon the Citadel" article in 1960, however, he erred in one prediction: that the courts were not then ready for so novel a theory that, he opined, might take until the year 2010 before it was accepted.[72]

Greenman

Quite the contrary, it was a scant three years later, in 1963, that the California Supreme Court handed down its landmark decision in *Greenman v. Yuba Power Products, Inc.*[73] While using his combination power tool as a lathe, Mr. Greenman was injured when the tailstock of the lathe vibrated loose and the piece of wood he was shaping flew out and struck him on the head. He sued the manufacturer and retailer for negligence and breach of warranty, and he received a verdict and judgment against the manufacturer on his express warranty claim, which the manufacturer challenged on appeal, arguing that the plaintiff had failed to provide timely notice of breach.[74]

Justice Traynor, who in 1944 had offered an eloquent, lone voice for strict products liability in tort in his concurring opinion in *Escola v. Coca Cola Bottling Co.*,[75] authored

---

65 "This simultaneity of prediction and confirmation is extraordinary and is unknown even in scientific work." Priest, The Invention of Enterprise Liability: A Critical History of the Intellectual Foundations of Modern Tort Law, 14 J. Legal Stud. 461, 507 (1985).

66 George Priest notes that *Henningsen* was announced on May 9, 1960, and Dean Prosser's "Assault" article was published in the June 1960 issue of the Yale Law Journal. Priest, above note 65, at 506 n.292.

67 Prosser, The Assault Upon the Citadel (Strict Liability to the Consumer), 69 Yale L.J. 1099 (1960).

68 Id. at 1140.

69 Id. at 1134.

70 In addition to *Henningsen*, see, e.g., Picker X-Ray Corp. v. General Motors Corp., 185 A.2d 919 (D.C. 1962).

71 Dean Prosser was by no means alone. See § 5.4, below.

72 "Thus far there has been relatively little indication that the time is yet ripe for what may very possibly be the law of fifty years ahead." Prosser, The Assault Upon the Citadel (Strict Liability to the Consumer), 69 Yale L.J. 1099, 1120 (1960).

73 377 P.2d 897 (Cal. 1963).

74 For a discussion of the buyer's duty to provide the seller with timely notice of breach of warranty under UCC § 2–607, see § 4.6, above.

75 150 P.2d 436, 440–44 (Cal. 1944), previously discussed.

an opinion in *Greenman*, too; but this time he spoke for a unanimous court. Affirming the plaintiff's judgment, *Greenman* ruled that the commercial code's requirement of prompt notice was inappropriate in cases involving injured consumers,[76] such that even an untimely notice would not bar a consumer's express warranty claim. But Justice Traynor did not stop there. "Moreover, to impose strict liability on the manufacturer under the circumstances of this case, it was not necessary for plaintiff to establish an express warranty [under the commercial code]. *A manufacturer is strictly liable in tort when an article he places on the market*, knowing that it is to be used without inspection for defects, *proves to have a defect that causes injury to a human being*."[77] Tracing the development of the strict products liability doctrine under the warranty umbrella—from the food cases through products for intimate bodily use, to durable products such as the car in *Henningsen*—Justice Traynor explained that the rejection of the requirement of privity of contract, "the recognition that the liability is not assumed by agreement but imposed by law, and the refusal to permit the manufacturer to define the scope of its own responsibility for defective products[,] make clear that the liability is not one governed by the law of contract warranties but by the law of strict liability in tort."[78]

There was no reason to "recanvass the reasons for imposing strict liability on the manufacturer" that had already been "fully articulated,"[79] declared Traynor, citing his concurring opinion in *Escola*,[80] Prosser's "Assault Upon the Citadel" article,[81] and the Harper and James torts treatise:[82] "The purpose of such liability is to insure that the costs of injuries resulting from defective products are borne by the manufacturers that put such products on the market rather than by the injured persons who are powerless to protect themselves. Sales warranties serve this purpose fitfully at best."[83] For example, in the present case, the plaintiff could rely on an express warranty only because he happened to have read and relied on representations of the Shopsmith's ruggedness in the manufacturer's brochure. "Implicit in the machine's presence on the market, however, was a representation that it would safely do the jobs for which it was built." Thus, "it should not be controlling whether plaintiff selected the machine because of the statements in the brochure, or because of the machine's own appearance of excellence that belied the defect lurking beneath the surface, or because he merely assumed that it would safely do the jobs it was built to do."[84]

In *Greenman*, the path to strict manufacturer liability for defective products led home to the law of tort.[85]

---

[76] See § 4.6, above.

[77] *Greenman*, 377 P.2d at 900. (emphasis added.)

[78] Id. at 901.

[79] Id.

[80] Escola v. Coca Cola Bottling Co., 150 P.2d 436, 440 (Cal. 1944).

[81] Prosser, The Assault Upon the Citadel (Strict Liability to the Consumer), 69 Yale L.J. 1099 (1960); *Greenman*, 377 P.2d at 901.

[82] 2 F. Harper and F. James, Law of Torts §§ 28.15–28.16, at 1569–74; *Greenman*, 377 P.2d at 901.

[83] *Greenman*, 377 P.2d at 901 (citing Prosser, The Assault Upon the Citadel (Strict Liability to the Consumer), 69 Yale L.J. 1099, 1124–34 (1960)).

[84] Id. Nor should it matter if an implied warranty arose, because " '[t]he remedies of injured consumers ought not to be made to depend upon the intricacies of the law of sales.' Ketterer v. Armour & Co., 200 F. 322, 323 (S.D.N.Y. 1912). To establish the manufacturer's liability it was sufficient that plaintiff proved that he was injured while using the Shopsmith in a way it was intended to be used as a result of a defect in design and manufacture of which plaintiff was not aware that made the Shopsmith unsafe for its intended use."

[85] The path *away* from strict liability is described in § 5.10, below.

§ 5.3 RESTATEMENT (SECOND) OF TORTS § 402A

In the 1950s and 1960s, the American Law Institute was in the midst of a quarter-century revision of the *Restatement of Torts,* originally promulgated in the 1930s. The Reporter for the new *Restatement (Second) of Torts* was none other than Dean William Prosser of the University of California at Berkeley. In the late 1950s, prior to *Henningsen v. Bloomfield Motors, Inc.*,[86] Dean Prosser began to revise chapter 14 of the first *Restatement,* which encompassed rules of negligence law governing the liability of product suppliers.[87] Revising the negligence sections in conventional form, he then turned to the special tort-like warranty that had been evolving for some time in the context of the sale of food.[88] Crafting a special section, new § 402A, to serve as a vehicle for the specialized development of "strict" tort liability for the sale of food "in a dangerous condition to the consumer," Prosser included a draft of his proposed new food provision in a *Preliminary Draft* of the new *Restatement* in 1958,[89] and subsequently in a *Council Draft* in 1960.[90] And so began the journey of § 402A, quite modestly at the start, which propagated and mushroomed as it progressed.[91]

After initially sprouting in 1958 and 1960, § 402A proceeded in 1961 to a *Tentative Draft* which set forth a principle of strict liability for the sale of "food for human consumption."[92] Judicial developments were moving rapidly and, the next year, Dean Prosser expanded coverage of § 402A to include "products intended for intimate bodily use," including "products intended for external application or contact" where it was "of an intimate character," such as chewing gum, chewing tobacco, snuff, cigarettes, drugs, clothing, soap, cosmetics, liniments, hair dye, and permanent wave solutions.[93] With the *Greenman* decision in 1963,[94] even this broadened version became obsolete, and the American Law Institute the next year approved Prosser's final draft of § 402A which made the strict liability rule applicable to all products.[95]

The ALI published § 402A the following year, 1965, in volume 2 of the *Restatement (Second) of Torts*:

> **§ 402A. Special Liability of Seller of Product for Physical Harm to User or Consumer**
>
> (1) One who sells any product in a defective condition unreasonably dangerous to the user or consumer or to his property is subject to liability for physical harm thereby caused to the ultimate user or consumer, or to his property, if

---

86 161 A.2d 69 (N.J. 1960).

87 In both the First and Second Restatements of Torts, chapter 14 (beginning with § 388, which concerns a supplier's duty to warn third parties of certain risks) is entitled "Liability of Persons Supplying Chattels for the Use of Others."

88 See § 5.2, above.

89 Rest. (2d) Torts § 402A (Prelim. Draft No. 6, 1958).

90 Rest. (2d) Torts § 402A (Council Draft No. 8, 1960).

91 For a discussion of how early drafts of § 402A applied only to food, drugs, and other inherently dangerous products, see § 6.2, below.

92 Rest. (2d) Torts § 402A (Tentative Draft No. 6, 1961).

93 Rest. (2d) Torts § 402A (Tentative Draft No. 7, 1962).

94 See § 5.2, above.

95 See Putman v. Erie City Mfg. Co., 338 F.2d 911, 918–19 (5th Cir. 1964) (Tex. law) (reciting evolution of § 402A drafts).

(a) the seller is engaged in the business of selling such a product, and

(b) it is expected to and does reach the user or consumer without substantial change in the condition in which it is sold.

(2) The rule stated in Subsection (1) applies although

(a) the seller has exercised all possible care in the preparation and sale of his product, and

(b) the user or consumer has not bought the product from or entered into any contractual relation with the seller.

Stripped of its prolixity, the liability principle of § 402A is short and simple—manufacturers and other sellers are subject to strict liability in tort for physical harm caused by defects in products they sell.

Nature of Strict Products Liability in Tort

"Strict" Liability

Section 402A provides that manufacturers and other product sellers are subject to liability for selling products containing defects that proximately cause physical harm.[96] Liability is "strict" because a seller is liable even if it was not negligent, even if it exercised all due care. "The rule is one of strict liability, making the seller subject to liability to the user or consumer even though he has exercised all possible care in the preparation and sale of the product."[97]

Yet, all courts agree that the doctrine of strict products liability in tort is constrained by certain definite limitations[98]—that liability is not absolute, that manufacturers are not insurers of their products' safety,[99] nor are they required to provide only the very safest of products[100] that represent the "ultimate in safety"[101] or are accident-proof.[102] The obligation imposed on manufacturers and other product sellers

---

[96] See discussion of the elements of strict products liability in tort, below.

[97] Rest. (2d) Torts § 402A cmt. *a.* "The rule stated in Subsection (1) applies although (a) the seller has exercised all possible care in the preparation and sale of his product." § 402A(2).

[98] See, e.g., Spieker v. Westgo, Inc., 479 N.W.2d 837, 845 (N.D. 1992), approving the following instruction, though characterizing it as "argumentative":

> 1) manufacturers are not insurers of the safety of persons who use the product, 2) manufacturers are under no duty to make an accident-proof or fool-proof product, 3) manufacturers are not required by law to guarantee their products cannot be used in such a way to cause injury, 4) so long as a product is reasonably safe for its intended use, manufacturers have done all that the law requires, even though other possible designs might be safer, and 5) manufacturers have no legal duty to produce products incorporating only the ultimate in safety.

[99] See, e.g., Nikirk v. ConducTV Brands, 2021 WL 391621, at *6 (N.J. Super. Ct. App. Div. 2021) ("Strict liability requires [proof of] a defect in the product, which distinguishes strict liability from absolute liability and prevents a party sued under a products liability claim from becoming an 'insurer' of the product."); In re Zantac (Ranitidine) Prods. Liab. Litig., 510 F. Supp. 3d 1234, 1248 (S.D. Fla. 2020); Kim v. Toyota Motor Corp., 424 P.3d 290, 296 (Cal. 2018). See generally Traynor, The Ways and Meanings of Defective Products and Strict Liability, 32 Tenn. L. Rev. 363, 366–67 (1965).

[100] See, e.g., Osorio v. One World Techs. Inc., 659 F.3d 81, 89 (1st Cir. 2011) (Mass. law) (a manufacturer is "not obliged to market only one version of a product, that being the very safest design possible"); Salerno v. Innovative Surveillance Tech., Inc., 932 N.E.2d 101, 111 (Ill. App. Ct. 2010) (a product need not "reflect the safest design possible or be incapable of causing injury").

[101] See, e.g., Wielgus v. Ryobi Techs., Inc., 893 F. Supp. 2d 920, 925 (N.D. Ill. 2012) (manufacturers not required to produce a product representing "the ultimate in safety").

[102] See, e.g., Pierre v. Intuitive Surgical, Inc., 476 F. Supp. 3d 1260, 1269 (S.D. Fla. 2020); Holiday Motor Corp. v. Walters, 790 S.E.2d 447 (Va. 2016) ("[t]he manufacturer is not an insurer and is not required to design

under § 402A is to provide products that are not "unreasonably dangerous" or "defective," rather than to provide products that are perfectly safe.[103] This means, of course, that plaintiffs must show more than that a product's safety could have been improved.[104] Instead, something must be *wrong* with a product before a court will hold a seller responsible for harm.[105] Just how the law should make this determination, and how the standard of "defectiveness" should be defined, are complex questions that require appropriate liability tests, as examined at length below.[106]

Elements of a Strict Tort Claim

There usually is little need to state the "elements" of a claim for strict products liability in tort, since the nature of such claims is so clear and simple. Courts do vary in how they define this cause of action, but the formulations share a common core. Stated simply, the rule in almost every state is that manufacturers and other commercial suppliers are subject to strict liability in tort for physical harm proximately caused by defects in new products that they sell.[107] Although variously expressed (often in multiple elements),[108] all courts require a plaintiff to prove two central propositions: (1) that the defendant sold a defective product; (2) that proximately caused the plaintiff's harm.[109] These two elements imply a third: (3) that the product was defective at the time of sale—when it left the defendant's control—a requirement many courts make explicit in formulating the elements of this tort.[110]

Despite the clarity and simplicity of a strict tort products liability claim, some courts do get entangled, understandably, in the prolix language of § 402A, which imposes strict liability for selling an injury-producing product in a "defective condition unreasonably dangerous" to the user or consumer. The history of this clumsy phrase is just one part of

---

and market an accident-proof product"); Bouher v. Aramark Servs., Inc., 910 N.E.2d 40, 43 (Ohio Ct. App. 2009) ("A manufacturer need not make its product accident-proof or foolproof.' ").

103 On the intellectual movement away from "absolute" toward a limited "strict" liability, see § 5.5, below.

104 Branham v. Ford Motor Co., 701 S.E.2d 5, 16 (S.C. 2010) ("a product is not in a defective condition unreasonably dangerous merely because it 'can be made more safe' ").

105 See, e.g., Smith v. ZOLL Med. Corp., 505 F. Supp. 3d 787, 795 (W.D. Tenn. 2020) (a plaintiff "must show that there was something wrong with the product, and trace [his] injury to the specific defect"). "There has to be something wrong with the product." 38 ALI Proceedings 88 (1961) (remarks of Reporter for Rest. (2d) Torts, Dean William Prosser, on § 402A draft).

106 See §§ 5.5–5.8, below.

107 The general rule is stated in terms of new product sales by manufacturers—the paradigm products liability case. While many principles of strict products liability in tort apply more broadly, other defendants and transactions are treated in chs. 15–18, below.

108 Compare Flores v. Merck & Co., 2022 WL 798374, at *5 (D. Nev. 2022) (in strict liability, a plaintiff must prove " '(1) the product had a defect which rendered it unreasonably dangerous, (2) the defect existed at the time the product left the manufacturer, and (3) the defect caused the plaintiff's injury.' "); Frost v. Ippolito Int'l, L.P., 2021 WL 412276, at *2 (W.D. Mo. 2021) (" '(1) the defendant sold a product in the course of its business; (2) the product was then in a defective condition, unreasonably dangerous when put to a reasonably anticipated use; (3) the product was used in a manner reasonably anticipated; and (4) the plaintiff was damaged as a direct result of such defective condition as existed when the product was sold' ").

109 As used here, "proximate cause" embraces factual causation and also limits a seller's responsibility for harmful consequences from use of a product to those a seller should have foreseen as naturally arising from sale of the product in a dangerously defective condition. On both aspects of causation, see chs. 11 & 12, below.

110 See, e.g., Reeves v. Scott's Co., LLC, 2021 WL 799313, at *3 (W.D. Tex. 2021) ("a plaintiff must prove that the product was defective when it left the hands of the manufacturer"); Gencarelli v. Coca-Cola Co., 2020 WL 2561258, at *4 (N.D.N.Y. 2020) (same). See note 120, below.

§ 402A's tortuous path from conception to completion,[111] and this bulky characterization of a product's condition continues to mislead many courts into concluding that there is a two-fold liability standard—that a product must be *both* defective *and* unreasonably dangerous, that its defective condition must *render* its condition unreasonably dangerous. So, some courts nominally divide § 402A's "defective condition unreasonably dangerous" language into two separate elements, "defective" and "unreasonably dangerous."[112] And some state products liability acts similarly state or suggest a two-pronged liability standard.[113] Yet rarely does a court explicitly address the differences between the two elements, perhaps because the comments to § 402A define both phrases congruently, as dangerous beyond a consumer's expectation[114]—or perhaps because the underlying liability concept is so clearly a unitary notion.

Fortunately, most courts (and almost all commentators) recognize that the § 402A liability standard truly means just one thing—that the product is more dangerous than it properly should be—a single concept fully captured in a single term, such as "defective" *or* "unreasonably dangerous."[115] Several state products liability statutes similarly ground liability in a single term, whether that be "defective," "unreasonably dangerous," or some other single term unburdened by a second prong.[116] Even courts in some jurisdictions whose legislatures adopted § 402A statutorily[117] have avoided the trap of dividing the "defective condition unreasonably dangerous" phrase into two separate

---

[111] The phrase resulted from Dean Prosser's response (overreaction?) to the ALI Council's complaint that the "dangerous condition" language he initially proposed was over-broad. See § 5.8, below.

[112] Some jurisdictions do so quite explicitly. See, e.g., Reeves v. Scott's Co., LLC, 2021 WL 799313, at *2 (W.D. Tex. 2021) (strict liability requires proof that "(1) a product is defective; (2) the defect rendered the product unreasonably dangerous; . . ."); Tosseth v. Remington Arms Co., LLC, 483 F. Supp. 3d 659, 670 (D.N.D. 2020) (same); Gaumer v. Rossville Truck & Tractor Co., 257 P.3d 292, 301 (Kan. 2011) ("a plaintiff must show that the product was both defective and unreasonably dangerous.").

[113] See, e.g., Ark. Code Ann. § 16–116–101(a)(2) ("the product was supplied . . . in a defective condition that rendered it unreasonably dangerous"); Miss. Code Ann. § 11–1–63(a)(ii) (same); N.D. Cent. Code § 28–01.3–06 ("a defect or defective condition in the product which made the product unreasonably dangerous"); Wis. Stat. Ann. § 895.047(1)(b) ("[t]hat the defective condition rendered the product unreasonably dangerous"). Indiana's curious statute adopts the "defective condition unreasonably dangerous" language of § 402A, Ind. Code Ann. § 34–20–2–1, and then defines "defective condition" as a condition (1) not contemplated by consumers, and (2) that is "unreasonably dangerous." Ind. Code Ann. § 34–20–4–1. Compare Tenn. Code Ann. § 29–28–105(a): "A manufacturer or seller of a product shall not be liable for any injury to a person or property caused by the product unless the product is determined to be in a defective condition *or* unreasonably dangerous at the time it left the control of the manufacturer or seller" (emphasis added).

[114] See, e.g., Schall v. Suzuki Motor of Am., Inc., 450 F. Supp. 3d 771, 779 (W.D. Ky. 2020).

[115] See, e.g., Gillespie v. Edmier, 182 N.E.3d 54, 58 (Ill. 2020) ("unreasonably dangerous"); McAlpine v. Rhone-Poulenc Ag Co., 16 P.3d 1054, 1058 (Mont. 2000), quoting Dean W. Page Keeton of Texas, one of the ALI Advisers for the Second Restatement:

> It is unfortunate perhaps that Section 402A of the *Restatement (Second) of Torts* provides that as a basis for recovery it must be found that the product was both "defective" and "unreasonably dangerous" when as a matter of fact the term "unreasonably dangerous" was meant only as a definition of defect. The phrase was not intended as setting forth two requirements but only one.

Keeton, Product Liability and the Meaning of Defect, 5 St. Mary's L.J. 30, 32 (1973). *McAlpine* held that the trial court erred in instructing the jury that liability depended on the product having been in a "defective condition unreasonably dangerous," rather than only in a "defective condition," because the full Restatement phrase could mislead. While "defective" is the conventional term, the term "unreasonably dangerous" by itself captures the concept equally well.

[116] See, e.g., La. Rev. Stat. Ann. § 9:2800.54 ("unreasonably dangerous"); N.J. Stat. Ann. § 2A:58C–2 ("designed in a defective manner"); Ohio Rev. Code Ann. § 2307.73(A)(1) ("defective"); Tex. Civ. Prac. & Rem. Code Ann. § 82.001(2) ("defective"); Wash. Rev. Code Ann. § 7.72.030(2) ("not reasonably safe").

[117] See, e.g., Me. Rev. Stat. Ann. tit. 14, § 221; Mont. Code Ann. § 27–1–719; Or. Rev. Stat. Ann. § 30.920; S.C. Code Ann. § 15–73–10.

elements,[118] and there simply is no good reason to perpetuate a linguistic error grounded in a *Restatement* that now has been superseded.[119]

Time When Defect Must Exist

Section 402A(1)(b) conditions liability on proof that the product "is expected to and does reach the user or consumer without substantial change in the condition in which it is sold." Thus, the plaintiff must establish not only that a defect caused his or her harm, but also that the product contained the defect at the time the product left the defendant's control.[120] As earlier discussed, this requirement, usually applicable only to manufacturing defects,[121] is often stated as an explicit element of a strict tort claim. Elaborating on this requirement, comment *g* to § 402A observes that the strict liability rule "applies only where the product is, at the time it leaves the seller's hands, in a condition not contemplated by the ultimate consumer, which will be unreasonably dangerous to him." Put otherwise, a seller is not responsible if a product is safe at the time it sells a product that thereafter is rendered defective due to the actions of a downstream seller or other subsequent events. Moreover, the burden of proof that the product was defective at the time the defendant sold it rests upon the injured plaintiff.[122]

Comment *g* also makes clear that, if a manufacturer fails to take adequate precautions to insure that its products remain in a safe condition for a reasonable length of time, the manufacturer will not be relieved of liability simply because its product was not actively dangerous at the time it left his possession.[123] A manufacturer, in other words, must take reasonable steps to protect users from a product's dangerously

---

[118] See, e.g., Nobles v. DePuy Synthes Sales, Inc., 471 F. Supp. 3d 717, 724 (D.S.C. 2020) (liability required expert proof that particular design rendered product "defective"); McAlpine v. Rhone-Poulenc Ag Co., 16 P.3d 1054, 1058 (Mont. 2000) ("a plaintiff is not required to show that a product is defective and also that it is unreasonably dangerous because establishing that a product is unreasonably dangerous is merely a means of proving that it is defective"). See also McCathern v. Toyota Motor Corp., 23 P.3d 320, 329–32 (Or. 2001) (statutory consumer expectations test is sole standard for assessing whether product is in a "defective condition unreasonably dangerous" to user).

[119] Section 402A of the Second Restatement is superseded by the Products Liability Restatement. See § 6.5, below. The history and conundrum of § 402A's apparently two-headed liability definition is further addressed in §§ 5.6 and 5.8, below.

Regrettably, the *Third Restatement* succumbed again to an ambiguous liability standard in § 2(b) and (c) which declare that a product's design or warning is "defective" if the absence of a "reasonable" alternative design or warning that would have prevented an accident rendered the product "not reasonably safe." See Owen, Defectiveness Restated: Exploding the "Strict" Products Liability Myth, 1996 U. Ill. L. Rev. 743, 766–76. Not unexpectedly, this inapt phasing again has misled some courts into thinking that liability is two-headed. See, e.g., Karst v. Shur-Co., 878 N.W.2d 604, 610 (S.D. 2016) ("both the Restatement (Second) and Restatement (Third) rules contemplate a causal relationship between two elements: a defect must 'make' or 'render' a product unreasonably dangerous (not reasonably safe). As we have previously said, '[s]trict liability requires that the product be defective *and* unreasonably dangerous.' ").

[120] Numerous cases are in accord. See, e.g., Meidinger v. Zoetis, Inc., 2022 WL 614867, at *3 n.4 (D.N.D. 2022) ("the plaintiff must show. . . the defect existed when the product left the manufacturer"); Hauck v. Wabash Nat'l Corp., 2021 WL 621213, at *2 (D.N.M. 2021) ("a plaintiff must demonstrate that: (1) 'the product was defective;' (2) 'the product was defective when it left the hands of the defendant and was substantially unchanged when it reached the user or consumer; . . .' "); York v. American Med. Sys., Inc., 166 F.3d 1216 (6th Cir. 1998) (Ohio law) (no proof that pinpoint hole in cylinder of inflatable penile prosthesis was caused by manufacturer). See note 110, above.

[121] The principle could apply to a design or warning defect if a third party forcibly removed a securely attached guard or warning tag from the product after it had left the defendant's control.

[122] Rest. (2d) Torts § 402A cmt. *g*.

[123] "Safe condition at the time of delivery . . . will, however, include proper . . . precautions required to permit the product to remain safe for a normal length of time when handled in a normal manner." Id.

unexpected deterioration.[124] Thus, a producer must ensure that its product is safe—that its food is pure, that its vehicles steer properly, and that its other products are free of untoward danger—not only at the time of sale but also for a reasonable period of time thereafter, perhaps for many years. This requirement, identical to that long employed in negligence law,[125] is not an exception to the rule that a defect must exist at the time the product leaves the defendant's hands, for it recognizes that a product may be defective at the time of sale if it then harbors a latent danger that eventually may erupt into harm.[126]

Types of Defendants and Transactions

Strict products liability in tort applies to all parties in the commercial chain of a product's distribution,[127] from manufacturers,[128] through intermediate dealers,[129] to retailers.[130] While the strict liability rule generally applies to a commercial business that provides products incidental to its principal business, such as a movie theater that sells popcorn,[131] and while it may apply to the sale by a specialty shop of a custom-designed product in the ordinary course of business,[132] it does not apply to the occasional private seller, such as a private individual who sells his or her used car.[133]

---

[124] Thus, if deterioration is likely to cause a product eventually to fail without warning in a dangerous manner, the manufacturer has a duty at least to warn users of this fact. See, e.g., Strauch v. Gates Rubber Co., 879 F.2d 1282 (5th Cir. 1989) (La. law). See § 10.6, below.

[125] See, e.g., Mickle v. Blackmon, 166 S.E.2d 173, 188–90 (S.C. 1969) (Ford responsible for injuries to passenger impaled on gearshift lever in collision when white plastic knob cover over lever shattered due to weakening from exposure to sunlight that Ford knew black knob would have prevented).

[126] On product deterioration, see § 10.6, below.

[127] See Rest. (2d) Torts § 402A cmt. *f* ("The rule stated in this Section applies to any person engaged in the business of selling products for use or consumption. It therefore applies to any manufacturer of such a product, to any wholesale or retail dealer or distributor, and to the operator of a restaurant.").

[128] Manufacturers, who usually are responsible for causing products to be defective, are the paradigmatic defendants in products liability cases, including a large majority of those cited in this volume.

[129] See ch. 15, below.

[130] Note, however, that some states now have special statutes protecting retailers from strict products liability unless the manufacturer is bankrupt or outside the jurisdiction of the court. See § 15.2, below.

[131] See Rest. (2d) Torts § 402A cmt. *f* ("It is not necessary that the seller be engaged solely in the business of selling such products. Thus the rule applies to the owner of a motion picture theatre who sells popcorn or ice cream, either for consumption on the premises or in packages to be taken home."). Verily, products liability jurisprudence truly *does* include a popcorn case. See Tombank v. National Amusements, Inc., 1996 WL 240445, at *2 (Conn. Super. Ct. 1996).

[132] See Sprung v. MTR Ravensburg, Inc., 788 N.E.2d 620, 623 (N.Y. 2003) (while " 'casual' or 'occasional' sales are not subject to claims of strict liability," custom fabricator of retractable floor sold in ordinary course of business subject to strict liability).

[133] See Rest. (2d) Torts § 402A cmt. *f*:

> The rule does not . . . apply to the occasional seller of food or other such products who is not engaged in that activity as a part of his business. Thus it does not apply to the housewife who, on one occasion, sells to her neighbor a jar of jam or a pound of sugar. Nor does it apply to the owner of an automobile who, on one occasion, sells it to his neighbor, or even sells it to a dealer in used cars, and this even though he is fully aware that the dealer plans to resell it. The basis for the rule is the ancient one of the special responsibility for the safety of the public undertaken by one who enters into the business of supplying human beings with products which may endanger the safety of their persons and property, and the forced reliance upon that undertaking on the part of those who purchase such goods. This basis is lacking in the case of the ordinary individual who makes the isolated sale, and he is not liable to a third person, or even to his buyer, in the absence of his negligence.

See, e.g., Griffin Indus. v. Jones, 975 S.W.2d 100 (Ky. 1998). Compare Products Liability Rest. § 1 cmt. *c* (defect rule applies to manufacturers and other commercial sellers and distributors engaged in the business of

Because the question of whether manufacturers of defective *component parts* should be subject to strict products liability was an open question at the time § 402A was drafted and promulgated during the late 1950s and early 1960s,[134] the ALI explicitly left this issue unresolved in a caveat.[135] However, modern courts have uniformly held component part makers strictly liable in tort where a risk is foreseeable and an intermediate assembler merely includes a defective component into a larger product.[136] But the case is otherwise where an assembler merges a non-defective component into a larger product in a manner that creates an unreasonable danger to consumers.[137]

Many cases have examined the suitability of the doctrine of strict liability in tort under § 402A for particular types of defendants engaged in a miscellany of sales and non-sales transactions involving a diversity of products. For example, courts have ruled on whether § 402A liability should be applied to retailers and internet providers, raw material and component suppliers, successor corporations, employers, financiers, product lease transactions, bailments, licenses, franchises, services (including medical) where products are provided incidentally, repaired and used products, real estate, publications of dangerous information, electricity, electronics, blood and other human tissue, diseased or dangerous animals, automotive vehicles, drugs, and medical devices. Whether strict products liability should be allowed in each of these distinct situations requires examination of factors that are specific to each particular context, and each is separately considered below.[138]

Types of Plaintiffs—Bystanders and Others

Section 402A makes clear that liability in no way depends on privity of contract between a plaintiff and the product supplier, as discussed above.[139] A passive user or consumer, such as a passenger in a defective automobile or a customer in a beauty shop whose hair is treated with a dangerously defective solution, is covered by the doctrine.[140] Yet, whether § 402A covers non-users and non-consumers, such as a person injured by a buyer's exploding soft drink bottle or a pedestrian hit by a defective car, is another question.[141] While "users" and "consumers" are defined broadly in comment *l*, the

---

distributing the type of product that harmed the plaintiff, including movie theater's sale of popcorn, but not to "casual sales").

[134] See Goldberg v. Kollsman Instrument Corp., 191 N.E.2d 81 (N.Y. 1963) (assembler-manufacturer of airplane, but not supplier of defective component, an altimeter, held liable for crash).

[135] See Rest. (2d) Torts § 402A caveat (3). But cmt. *q* remarks: "It is no doubt to be expected that where there is no change in the component part itself, but it is merely incorporated into something larger, the strict liability will be found to carry through to the ultimate user or consumer."

[136] See § 15.3, below, which discusses the liability of such defendants under both the Second and Third Restatements.

[137] See id.

[138] See chapters 15–18, below. The responsibility of miscellaneous types of defendants is treated contextually in various places throughout this book, such as the warning duties of pharmacists and manufacturers of prescription drugs and medical devices, in §§ 18.3 and 18.4, below.

[139] See Rest. (2d) Torts § 402A(2)(b). Comment *l* to that section explains that "it is not necessary that the ultimate user or consumer have acquired the product directly from the seller, although the rule applies equally if he does so. He may have acquired it through one or more intermediate dealers. It is not even necessary that the consumer have purchased the product at all. He may be a member of the family of the final purchaser, or his employee, or a guest at his table, or a mere donee from the purchaser."

[140] Id.

[141] On early extensions of strict products liability in tort to bystanders, see, e.g., Haumersen v. Ford Motor Co., 257 N.W.2d 7 (Iowa 1977) (car went out of control in school yard and ran over child); Passwaters v. General Motors Corp., 454 F.2d 1270 (8th Cir. 1972) (Iowa law) (motorcycle passenger's leg lacerated by Ben-Hur-type ornamental wheel cover protrusions on car manufactured by defendant); Howes v. Hansen, 201

question of whether liability under § 402A extends to "innocent bystanders" (persons who are *not* "users" or "consumers") is a question that caveat (1) expressly left unresolved.[142]

While case decisions prior to § 402A had not extended strict products liability in tort to bystanders,[143] subsequent decisions have almost unanimously allowed recovery to foreseeable bystanders,[144] including rescuers,[145] for injuries caused by defective products.[146] Because bystanders have no choice in selecting products (and hence have no control over whether safety or price should be preferred in choosing among products), nor any control over inspecting products (no opportunity to "kick the tires") or the manner of their use, courts from an early date have reasoned that such plaintiffs deserve protection at least as much as users and consumers.[147] The extension of strict tort liability to bystanders normally does not burden manufacturers with additional precautions "for the reason that the same precautions required to protect the buyer or

---

N.W.2d 825 (Wis. 1972). See generally Watts, Fairness and Utility in Products Liability: Balancing Individual Rights and Social Welfare, 38 Fla. St. U. L. Rev. 597, 638–44 (2011); Cochran, Dangerous Products and Injured Bystanders, 81 Ky. L.J. 687, 725 (1993); Note, 38 U. Chi. L. Rev. 625 (1971); Annot., 33 A.L.R.3d 415 (1970).

[142] This is explained in Rest. (2d) Torts § 402A cmt. *o*, which provides in part:

> There may be no essential reason why such plaintiffs should not be brought within the scope of the protection afforded, other than that they do not have the same reasons for expecting such protection as the consumer who buys a marketed product; but the social pressure which has been largely responsible for the development of the rule stated has been a consumers' pressure, and there is not the same demand for the protection of casual strangers.

[143] See Rest. (2d) Torts § 402A cmt. *o*, which provides in part:

> Thus far the courts, in applying the rule stated in this Section, have not gone beyond allowing recovery to users and consumers . . . . Casual bystanders . . . have been denied recovery.

[144] See, e.g., Dubas v. Clark Equip. Co., 532 F. Supp. 3d 819, 825–27 (D. Neb. 2021); Mayor & City Council of Baltimore v. Monsanto Co., 2020 WL 1529014, at *11 (D. Md. 2020); Mestas v. Air & Liquid Sys. Corp., 2019 WL 1967129, at *6 (D. Colo. 2019); Lawing v. Trinity Mfg., Inc., 749 S.E.2d 126, 136–38 (S.C. Ct. App. 2013) (Few, J.) (brilliant decision); Clair v. Monsanto Co., 412 S.W.3d 295 (Mo. Ct. App. 2013) (Cal. law); Patch v. Hillerich & Bradsby Co., 257 P.3d 383, 387 (Mont. 2011) (18-year-old pitcher struck in head and killed by ball hit with aluminum baseball bat manufactured by defendant; to deny failure to warn claims for bystanders would be contrary to § 402A as codified in Montana and "incongruent with this Court's products liability jurisprudence"); Horst v. Deere & Co., 769 N.W.2d 536, 544, 554 (Wis. 2009) (affirming judgment on jury verdict where father backed riding mower over 2-year-old son; acknowledging strict liability protection is afforded to injured bystanders, but declining to adopt plaintiffs' proposed "bystander contemplation test"); Lunsford v. Saberhagen Holdings, Inc., 106 P.3d 808, 811 (Wash. Ct. App. 2005) (child exposed to asbestos dust on father's clothing developed mesothelioma; "Policy considerations . . . support an expansion of [strict liability] coverage to include bystanders and other persons that the manufacturer could reasonably foresee would come into contact with its product."); Stegemoller v. ACandS, Inc., 767 N.E.2d 974 (Ind. 2002) (spouse who developed disease due to exposure to asbestos residue on husband's clothing was domestic bystander with standing to sue asbestos manufacturers). For warning duties to bystanders, see § 9.4, below. On bystander emotional distress, see note 158, below.

[145] See, e.g., Baldonado v. El Paso Natural Gas Co., 176 P.3d 277 (N.M. 2007) (fire fighters); Holloway v. Midland Risk Ins. Co., 832 So.2d 1004 (La. Ct. App. 2002) (professional rescuer's doctrine not applicable to firefighter suing manufacturer of rescue equipment for injuries from failure of equipment); McKernan v. General Motors Corp., 3 P.3d 1261 (Kan. 2000) (policy reasons for "firefighter rule," precluding recovery by firemen against person whose negligence caused fire, do not apply in products liability context); McCoy v. American Suzuki Motor Corp., 961 P.2d 952 (Wash. 1998) (en banc) (motorist, struck by hit-and-run driver while stopped to help passengers in defectively designed vehicle that overturned on highway, could maintain products liability claim under rescue doctrine).

[146] One curious exception is Pennsylvania, where § 402A operates only if a product is unsafe for its *intended* users, *not* for its *foreseeable* victims. Hence, the doctrine does not protect victims of fires started by young children with disposable butane cigarette lighters, not equipped with a childproof design, intended only for adults. See Phillips v. Cricket Lighters, 841 A.2d 1000 (Pa. 2003). Since that time, the law on bystanders in Pennsylvania has been evolving but remains quite unclear. Bystander recovery still may not be allowed. See D'Antonio v. FMC Techs., Inc., 2016 WL 7324151, at *1 (W.D. Pa. 2016).

[147] See, e.g., Elmore v. American Motors Corp., 451 P.2d 84 (Cal. 1969).

user would generally do the same for the bystander."[148] Unless the risk to bystanders falls outside the scope of reasonable prevision,[149] the doctrine of strict liability in tort logically and fairly extends to such persons. Put simply, "[t]he price of dangerous products should include the losses that they cause to bystanders."[150] Similarly, responsibility extends to other types of users, consumers, and other persons foreseeably placed at risk by a product defect.[151]

Types of Damages

Physical Harm. By its terms, § 402A provides that a seller of a defective product "is subject to liability for physical harm thereby caused to the ultimate user or consumer, or to his property . . . ."[152] All courts thus allow recovery under this doctrine for personal injury and death,[153] and the widely prevailing view is that recovery is allowable under strict products liability in tort for property damage alone.[154] Claims for suffering only an increased *risk* of injury or disease generally have failed.[155]

Emotional Distress. The law on damages under § 402A for emotional distress is complex. Courts in some products liability contexts have denied claims for such damages,

---

[148] Giberson v. Ford Motor Co., 504 S.W.2d 8, 12 (Mo. 1974) (court permitted strict tort suit by occupants of car involved in pile-up that occurred when engine in police car manufactured by defendant exploded in traffic, creating dense smoke that obscured vision).

[149] See, e.g., Kirk v. Michael Reese Hosp. & Med. Ctr., 513 N.E.2d 387, 394 (Ill. 1987) (passenger injured when driver, who consumed alcohol after taking prescription drugs, lost control of car; *held*, on inadequate warning claim, that manufacturers "[could not] have reasonably foreseen that their drugs would be dispensed without warnings by the physicians, that the patient would be discharged from the hospital, drink alcohol, drive a car, lose control of his car, hit a tree, and injure the passenger [all] on the same day").

[150] Cochran, Dangerous Products and Injured Bystanders, 81 Ky. L.J. 687, 725 (1993).

[151] See, e.g., Dubas v. Clark Equip. Co., 532 F. Supp. 3d 819, 828 (D. Neb. 2021) (denying dismissal of bystander's strict liability claim; plaintiff was cleaning cattle pen with leaf blower when a Bobcat steer loader driven in reverse severely injured his leg); Mayor & City Council of Balt. v. Monsanto Co., 2020 WL 1529014, at *11 (D. Md. 2020) (it was foreseeable under the consumer expectations test that defectively designed and manufactured PCBs would contaminate the city's waterways; strict liability recovery for design defects not limited to a product's ultimate users); Martinez v. Cont'l Tire Americas, LLC, 476 F. Supp. 3d 1137, 1143 (D.N.M. 2020) (undocumented immigrant); Levey v. Yamaha Motor Corp., 825 A.2d 554 (N.J. Super. Ct. App. Div. 2003) (dealer's salesmen expected to demonstrate jet boat's operation to prospective customers); Jones v. NordicTrack, Inc., 550 S.E.2d 101 (Ga. 2001) (plaintiff who tripped over exercise machine was owed duty as one who might use, consume, or reasonably be affected by it).

[152] Rest. (2d) Torts § 402A(1).

[153] On damages for personal injury and death in products liability actions, see Owen & Davis on Products Liability ch. 25.

[154] See, e.g., Dehring v. Keystone Shipping Co., 2013 WL 3879619 (E.D. Mich. 2013); Wyman v. Ayer Props., LLC, 979 N.E.2d 782, 788 (Mass. App. Ct. 2012) ("injury or damage must occur to person or property beyond the defective product or structure itself"); Dobrovolny v. Ford Motor Co., 793 N.W.2d 445, 446 (Neb. 2011) ("a plaintiff cannot recover under strict liability . . . without any claim of personal injury or damage to other property"); Jimenez v. Superior Ct., 58 P.3d 450, 451 (Cal. 2002) ("a manufacturer, distributor, or retailer of a defective product is strictly liable in tort for any resulting harm to a person or to property other than the product itself"). See also Seely v. White Motor Co., 403 P.2d 145, 152 (Cal. 1965) (Traynor, C.J.) ("Physical injury to property is so akin to personal injury that there is no reason for distinguishing them."). On damages for property damage in products liability actions, see Frumer, Friedman, and Sklaren, Products Liability § 13.02; Am. Law Prod. Liab. 3d § 60:18.

[155] See, e.g., Berry v. City of Chicago, 181 N.E.3d 679, 689 (Ill. 2020) ("increased risk of harm [from lead water pipes is not] a cognizable injury"); Kahn v. Shiley Inc., 266 Cal. Rptr 106 (Ct. App. 1990) (mechanical heart valve was defective but had not yet malfunctioned); Payton v. Abbott Labs, 437 N.E.2d 171, 181 (Mass. 1982) (DES daughters, not yet suffering vaginal cancer, could not recover for emotional distress from increased likelihood that they might incur such cancer in the future). See generally Klein, A Model for Enhanced Risk Recovery in Tort, 56 Wash. & Lee L. Rev. 1173 (1999).

in strict liability as well as negligence,[156] but many other courts have allowed recovery, to both direct victims[157] and bystanders,[158] in strict liability under rules similar to those applied under the law of negligence.[159] Fear of cancer ("cancerphobia") or other disease, from contact with a harmful substance, is a special variety of claim for emotional distress,[160] and recovery for medical monitoring is sometimes sought, and occasionally permitted, in such cases.[161] Courts allow recovery for lost consortium to spouses (and in

---

[156] See, e.g., Colbert v. Moomba Sports, Inc., 176 P.3d 497, 506–07 (Wash. 2008) (en banc) (father could not recover against boat manufacturer for negligent infliction of emotional distress because he did not witness daughter's drowning caused by inhalation of carbon monoxide); Gu v. BMW of N. Am., LLC, 33 Cal. Rptr. 3d 617, 627–28 (Ct. App. 2005) (BMW had no duty to avoid negligently causing emotional distress to owners who lend vehicles to close family members who are injured out of the owner's presence while using defective vehicle); Blackmon v. American Home Prods. Corp., 267 F. Supp. 2d 667, 676–77 (S.D. Tex. 2003) (parents could not recover emotional distress damages against vaccine manufacturers for children's serious neurological injuries from mercury used as preservative in vaccines; no recovery of emotional distress as bystanders because distress did not result from "shocking accident" but from "routine vaccination").

[157] Accordingly, most courts require a plaintiff to establish that the emotional distress was caused by—or that *it* caused—some impact, injury, illness or other physical condition. See, e.g., Schmidt v. Boardman Co., 11 A.3d 924 (Pa. 2011); Zeigler v. Fisher-Price, Inc., 261 F. Supp. 2d 1047, 1053 (N.D. Iowa 2003) (homeowner could not recover emotional distress damages from manufacturer of defective toy that caused home to catch on fire where homeowner not injured in fire); Slaton v. Vansickle, 872 P.2d 929 (Okla. 1994) (owner of defective gun could not recover for emotional distress from accidentally killing person while handling gun because owner suffered no injury).

[158] See, e.g., Schmidt v. Boardman Co., 11 A.3d 924, 953 (Pa. 2011) (strict liability claim brought by family members of children either killed or seriously injured when fire hose broke loose from moving fire engine; evenly divided Supreme Court affirmed award of damages for emotional distress); Pearsall v. Emhart Indus., 599 F. Supp. 207 (E.D. Pa. 1984) (mother-wife allowed to recover in strict tort against manufacturer of defective smoke alarm for distress at discovering smoldering bodies of two children and husband shortly after their deaths in burning house). Compare Bray v. Marathon Corp., 588 S.E.2d 93, 95–96 (S.C. 2003) (worker at controls of trash compactor that crushed co-worker to death could not recover as a bystander but was a direct victim who might recover, as a "user," for physical injuries from her own fright at crushing co-worker in machine).

[159] At least one court has held that damages for emotional distress are not recoverable in strict liability because such damages are based on fault. See Pasquale v. Speed Prods. Eng'g, 654 N.E.2d 1365 (Ill. 1995) (parts of race-car clutch burst through defective bellhousing and flew into crowd of spectators, partially decapitating plaintiff's wife, revealing interior of her head including backs of her eyeballs, and spewing bone marrow, blood, and brain matter on plaintiff's face with such force as to leave marks for weeks; *held*, no recovery in strict tort for emotional distress). On damages for emotional distress in products liability actions, see Frumer, Friedman, and Sklaren, Products Liability § 13.03[9]; Am. Law Prod. Liab. 3d §§ 60:28 to :40.

[160] See, e.g., Lavelle v. Owens-Corning Fiberglas Corp., 507 N.E.2d 476 (Ohio Com. Pl. 1987) (allowing claim by asbestosis-afflicted plaintiff for increased fear of cancer); Payton v. Abbott Labs, 437 N.E.2d 171, 181 (Mass. 1982) (DES daughters, not yet suffering vaginal cancer, could not recover for emotional distress from increased likelihood that they might incur such cancer in the future). See also Potter v. Firestone Tire & Rubber Co., 863 P.2d 795, 816 (Cal. 1993) (cancerphobia claims allowable "only if the plaintiff pleads and proves that (1) as a result of the defendant's negligent breach of a duty owed to the plaintiff, the plaintiff is exposed to a toxic substance which threatens cancer; *and* (2) the plaintiff's fear stems from a knowledge, corroborated by reliable medical or scientific opinion, that it is more likely than not that the plaintiff will develop the cancer in the future due to the toxic exposure"). See generally Rabin, Harms from Exposure to Toxic Substances: The Limits of Liability Law, 38 Pepp. L. Rev. 419 (2011); Klein, Fear of Disease and the Puzzle of Futures Cases in Tort, 35 U.C. Davis L. Rev. 965 (2002); Henderson and Twerski, Asbestos Litigation Gone Mad: Exposure-Based Recovery for Increased Risk, Mental Distress, and Medical Monitoring, 53 S.C. L. Rev. 815, 823 (2002); Dworkin, Fear of Disease and Delayed Manifestation Injuries: A Solution or a Pandora's Box?, 53 Fordham L. Rev. 527, 576 (1984).

[161] See generally Caronia v. Philip Morris USA, Inc., 715 F.3d 417 (2d Cir. 2013) (N.Y. law) (thoroughly reviewing cases in New York and other states on cancerphobia and medical monitoring, and certifying question to N.Y. Court of Appeals as to viability of independent claim for medical monitoring by heavy smoker for diseases such as cancer). Answering question, in Caronia v. Philip Morris USA, Inc., 5 N.E.3d 11, 18 (N.Y. 2013), the New York court concluded that "policy reasons . . . militate against a judicially-created independent cause of action for medical monitoring." See also In re Bard IVC Filters Prods. Liab. Litig., 2019 WL 4233758, at *24 (D. Ariz. 2019) ("only" 16 states permit claims for medical monitoring); Norwood v. Raytheon Co., 414 F. Supp. 2d 659, 668 (W.D. Tex. 2006) (predicting Texas courts would not recognize this claim). See notes 171–173, below.

one case a quasi-spouse) of victims harmed by defective products.[162] While many courts refuse, in this context as in others, to permit claims by parents or children for the loss of companionship of the other,[163] an increasing number of states allow such damages.[164]

Pure Economic Loss. Since the inception of § 402A, a minor debate has swirled around the issue of whether recovery in strict liability in tort should be allowed for pure economic loss,[165] including damage a defective product causes to itself.[166] In time, spearheaded by a decision of the United States Supreme Court,[167] a great majority of courts (and some legislatures, in products liability reform acts) have applied the "economic loss rule" to such claims, denying recovery in strict tort liability (or negligence) for pure economic loss—that is, for pecuniary losses a defective product causes other than those growing out of personal injuries or out of damage it causes to "other property,"

---

[162] See, e.g., Kilgore v. Bos. Sci. Corp., 2015 WL 5838513, at *6 (S.D. W. Va. 2015) (allowing husband's claim for loss of consortium for defective transvaginal surgical mesh implanted in wife); Mealy v. B-Mobile, Inc., 124 Cal. Rptr. 3d 804 (Ct. App. 2011) (husband allowed damages for loss of consortium, but not for severe emotional distress from observing wife fracture hip when she fell from a motorized sling lift that moved her between wheelchair and bed); Mikloajczyk v. Ford Motor Co., 870 N.E.2d 885, 890 (Ill. App. Ct. 2007) (strict liability design defect claim; jury award to widow of $25 million for "loss of society and sexual relations" remanded for remittitur), rev'd on other grounds, 901 N.E.2d 329 (2008); Knight v. Just Born, Inc., 2000 WL 924624, at *15 (D. Or. 2000) (husband's mouth burned by defective candy); Timms v. Verson Allsteel Press Co., 520 F. Supp. 1147 (N.D. Ga. 1981) (husband's fingers crushed in press). The quasi-spouse case is Ratcliff v. Good Times Rests., Inc., 2019 WL 2774217, at *3 (D. Colo. 2019) (live-in boyfriend prior to marriage; "While claims for loss of consortium between unmarried cohabitants are infrequent, the movement toward allowing them to make the claim aligns with the increase of unmarried cohabitants in the United States.").

[163] See, e.g., Cambron v. Ford Motor Co., 2012 WL 34233, at *1 n.1 (Cal. Ct. App. 2012) (noting that loss of consortium claims are not available in California in parent-child situation); Trevino v. Blitz U.S.A., Inc., 2011 WL 1458725, at *1 (M.D. Tenn. 2011) (Tennessee does not recognize loss of filial consortium claim for personal injury); Robinson v. Hartzell Propeller Inc., 276 F. Supp. 2d 412, 415 (E.D. Pa. 2003) (predicting that Pennsylvania Supreme Court would not allow claim by children for loss of parental consortium).

[164] See, e.g., Hyman & Armstrong, P.S.C. v. Gunderson, 279 S.W.3d 93, 116 (Ky. 2008) (addressing availability of loss of parental consortium and loss of child's consortium); General Motors Corp. v. Burry, 203 S.W.3d 514 (Tex. App. 2006) (allowing three children about $1 million each for loss of consortium with severely brain-damaged mother); Higgins v. Intex Recreation Corp., 99 P.3d 421 (Wash. Ct. App. 2004) (allowing stepchild's claim for loss of parental consortium); Owens v. American Home Prods. Corp., 203 F. Supp. 2d 748, 757 (S.D. Tex. 2002) (allowing parents' claims for loss of consortium of children injured by mercury-contaminated vaccines).

[165] Peri & Sons Farms, Inc. v. Jain Irrigation, Inc., 933 F. Supp. 2d 1279, 1283–85 (D. Nev. 2013) (nonrecoverable pure economic loss is "the loss of the benefit of the user's bargain [including] pecuniary damage for inadequate value, the cost of repair and replacement of the defective product, or consequent loss of profits, without any claim of personal injury or damage to other property"); Cooperative Power Ass'n v. Westinghouse Elec. Corp., 493 N.W.2d 661, 663 n.5 (N.D. 1992) (in products liability cases, such a loss is "pecuniary damage that occurs through loss of value or use of the goods sold or the cost of repair together with consequential lost profits when there has been no claim of personal injury or damage to other property"). On damages for economic loss in products liability actions, see, e.g., Rusch, Products Liability Trapped by History: Our Choices of Rules Our Choices, 76 Temp. L. Rev. 739 (2003); Frumer, Friedman, and Sklaren, Products Liability §§ 9.05[1][c], 13.07 [1]; Am. Law Prod. Liab. 3d §§ 60:45 to :69; White and Summers, UCC § 11–5.

[166] See, e.g., Sapp v. Ford Motor Co., 687 S.E.2d 47, 49 (S.C. 2009) ("there is no tort liability for a product defect if the damage suffered by the plaintiff is only to the product itself"); Tennessee Farmers Mut. Ins. Co. v. Ford Motor Co., 2002 WL 1332492 (Tenn. Ct. App. 2002) (no strict products liability recovery where spontaneous combustion destroyed vehicle but did not cause personal injuries nor damage to other property). Compare the classic cases both ways, Santor v. A & M Karagheusian, Inc., 207 A.2d 305 (N.J. 1965) (recoverable), with Seely v. White Motor Co., 403 P.2d 145 (Cal. 1965) (Traynor, C.J.) (not recoverable). See generally Annot., 72 A.L.R.4th 12 (1989) (recovery in strict tort for damages to product alone).

[167] East River S.S. Corp. v. Transamerica Delaval, Inc., 476 U.S. 858, 870 (1986): "Even when the harm to the product itself occurs through an abrupt, accident-like event, the resulting loss due to repair costs, decreased value, and lost profits is essentially the failure of the purchaser to receive the benefit of its bargain—traditionally the core concern of contract law."

that is, apart from any damage a defective product may cause to itself.[168] This is the position of the *Products Liability Restatement* which excludes liability for pure economic loss.[169] While many courts follow this no-duty rule without exception, some courts allow pecuniary damages caused by dangerous defects that are hazardous to property or human safety—such as the costs of repairing a dangerous condition in a car, or of removing asbestos from school buildings.[170]

Courts have confronted a couple of special types of claims for economic losses in recent years. One seeks recovery for the costs of "medical monitoring"[171] of victims exposed to some toxic substance or defective medical device (previously mentioned in connection with emotional distress), where future harm is possible but difficult to detect.[172] Most courts have denied such claims without proof of some type of present

---

[168] See, e.g., Des Moines Flying Serv., Inc. v. Aerial Servs. Inc., 880 N.W.2d 212, 218 (Iowa 2016) ("a plaintiff cannot recover [purely economic damages] in tort. . . . whether that loss arose out of negligence or strict liability"); Tiara Condo. Ass'n, Inc. v. Marsh & Mclennan Cos., 110 So.3d 399, 404 (Fla. 2013) (manufacturers have no duty, in negligence or strict liability in tort, "to prevent a product from injuring itself"); Dobrovolny v. Ford Motor Co., 793 N.W.2d 445 (Neb. 2011) (no recovery for value of truck in either negligence or strict liability in tort for destruction of parked pickup truck that caught fire; adopting majority view of economic loss rule that disallows tort recovery when damages are to product alone, following both Restatement (Third) of Torts and *East River*); Jimenez v. Superior Court, 58 P.3d 450, 456 (Cal. 2002) (economic loss not recoverable under strict products liability). On the economic loss rule generally, see Rusch, Products Liability Trapped by History: Our Choice of Rules Our Choices, 76 Temp. L. Rev. 739 (2003); Symposium, Dan B. Dobbs Conference on Economic Tort Law, 48 Ariz. L. Rev. 687 (2006).

Some products liability statutes explicitly exclude recovery for economic loss. See, e.g., Cincinnati v. Beretta U.S.A. Corp., 768 N.E.2d 1136, 1146 (Ohio 2002) (applying Ohio Rev. Code Ann. § 2307.71(M), excluding economic loss from definition of "product liability claim"); Wash. Rev. Code Ann. § 7.72.010(6) (economic loss excluded from definition of recoverable "harm").

[169] Products Liability Rest. § 21 provides that damages for "harm to persons or property," allowable under § 1, includes economic loss only if it results from harm the product causes to person or "property other than the defective product itself."

[170] See, e.g., Tuscumbia City Sch. Sys. v. Pharmacia Corp., 871 F. Supp. 2d 1241, 1288 (N.D. Ala. 2012) (putative class action for PCBs in ballasts for fluorescent light fixtures; forecasting that Alabama "will join that growing number of jurisdictions which have embraced the 'dangerous-nondangerous' distinction [that allows recovery] for *all* losses if the defective product causes—*or creates a substantial and unreasonable risk of causing*—personal injury or damage to property other than the defective product," and explaining that "the 'dangerous-nondangerous' distinction appears to be the best approach . . . for separating contract/warranty actions from tort cases") (emphasis in original); Lloyd v. General Motors Corp., 916 A.2d 257, 266 (Md. 2007) (class action for cost of repairing cars with dangerously defective seat backs; recognizing and applying "increasingly popular" exception to general rule barring recovery for pure economic loss when plaintiff alleges "facts that demonstrate that the product at issue creates a *dangerous condition*, one that gives rise to a *clear danger of death or personal injury*") (emphasis in original); Tioga Pub. Sch. Dist. No. 15 v. United States Gypsum Co., 984 F.2d 915 (8th Cir. 1993) (N.D. law) (recovery of asbestos abatement costs allowed). See generally Ausness, Tort Liability for Asbestos Removal Costs, 73 Or. L. Rev. 505 (1994).

[171] **Medical monitoring.** In "medical monitoring" claims, plaintiffs "seek to recover the anticipated costs of long-term diagnostic testing necessary to detect latent diseases that may develop as a result of tortious exposure." In re: Zantac (Ranitidine) Prods. Liab. Litig., 2021 WL 4593943, at *2 (S.D. Fla. 2021) (stating elements of such claims). See also Gallacher, Medical Monitoring of Medical Devices: An Industry-Based Solution Provides the Best Results, 10 Loy. Consumer L. Rev. 239, 239–40 (1998).

[172] On medical monitoring claims, see, e.g., Glasenapp, Judicially Sanctioned Environmental Injustice: Making the Case for Medical Monitoring, 49 N.M. L. Rev. 59 (2019); Schwartz and Silverman, The Rise of "Empty Suit" Litigation™: Where Should Tort Law Draw the Line?, 80 Brook. L. Rev. 599, 612–28 (2015); Scheuerman, The NFL Concussion Litigation: A Critical Assessment of Class Certification, 8 Fla. Int'l U. L. Rev. 81, 101–05 (2012) (class actions for medical monitoring claims); Rabin, Harms from Exposure to Toxic Substances: The Limits of Liability Law, 38 Pepp. L. Rev. 419 (2011); Schwartz, Lorber, and Laird, Medical Monitoring: The Right Way and the Wrong Way, 70 Mo. L. Rev. 349 (2005); Guzelian, Hillner, and Guzelian, A Quantitative Methodology for Determining the Need for Exposure-Prompted Medical Monitoring, 79 Ind. L.J. 57 (2004); Henderson and Twerski, Asbestos Litigation Gone Mad: Exposure-Based Recovery for Increased Risk, Mental Distress, and Medical Monitoring, 53 S.C. L. Rev. 815, 836 (2002); Abraham, Liability for Medical Monitoring and the Problem of Limits, 88 Va. L. Rev. 1975 (2002); Geistfeld, The Analytics of Duty: Medical Monitoring and Related Forms of Economic Loss, 88 Va. L. Rev. 1921 (2002); Goldberg and Zipursky,

injury.[173] In addition, the economic loss rule has been an obstacle to a recent form of class action that seeks recovery for the reduction in value of a product because it contains a dangerous condition, such as a particular type of tire likely to blow out, an SUV likely to roll over, or a car that may suddenly accelerate without warning. Most courts have been largely unreceptive to such "no-injury" claims, whether grounded in strict liability in tort or other theory of recovery.[174] Yet this type of claim has some intuitive appeal, particularly if the damages sought are to repair a dangerously defective condition, and it has shown some success in at least a couple of litigations.[175]

Unrealized Torts, 88 Va. L. Rev. 1625 (2002); Schwartz et al., Medical Monitoring: Should Tort Law Say Yes?, 34 Wake Forest L. Rev. 1057 (1999). See note 161, above.

[173] See, e.g., Dougan v. Sikorsky Aircraft Corp., 251 A.3d 583, 599 (Conn. 2020) (plaintiffs' expert's conclusory statements failed to demonstrate a "reasonable need" for medically monitoring plaintiffs allegedly exposed to asbestos during demolition work; reviewing cases that both allowed and rejected medical monitoring claims in the absence of physical injury); Berry v. City of Chicago, 181 N.E.3d 679, 689 (Ill. 2020) ("increased risk of harm [from lead water pipes is not] a cognizable injury"); Caronia v. Philip Morris USA, Inc., 5 N.E.3d 11, 18 (N.Y. 2013) ("policy reasons . . . militate against a judicially-created independent cause of action for medical monitoring"); Slemmer v. McGlaughlin Spray Foam Insulation, Inc., 955 F. Supp. 2d 452, 465 (E.D. Pa. 2013) (dismissing claim for medical monitoring: "Plaintiffs have failed to identify . . . a serious latent disease which requires monitoring"); Paz v. Brush Engineered Materials, Inc., 555 F.3d 383, 391–99 (5th Cir. 2009) (Miss. law) (citing Paz v. Brush Engineered Materials Inc., 949 So.2d 1 (Miss. 2007) (4–3 decision) (denying medical monitoring claim based on exposure alone without proof that exposure caused current physical or emotional injury; citing decisions from other jurisdictions that require, and those that do not require, proof of present injury to support such claims); Sinclair v. Merck & Co., 948 A.2d 587, 589 (N.J. 2008) (Vioxx class action medical monitoring claim failed without proof of present, manifest injury); Lowe v. Philip Morris USA, Inc., 183 P.3d 181, 186 (Or. 2008) (smoker's "cost of medical monitoring—is not sufficient to give rise to a negligence claim").

[174] See, e.g., Tiara Condo. Ass'n, Inc. v. Marsh & McLennan Cos., 110 So.3d 399, 404 (Fla. 2013) (claiming that "extending strict products liability to cover economic damage would result in 'contract law drown[ing] in a sea of tort,' " while failing to recognize the excellence of that result); Frank v. DaimlerChrysler Corp., 741 N.Y.S.2d 9, 16 (App. Div. 2002) (rejecting "no-injury" claims based on strict liability and other causes of action because "it would be manifestly unfair to require a manufacturer to become, in essence, an indemnifier for a loss that may never occur"). See also Wallis v. Ford Motor Co., 208 S.W.3d 153, 158 (Ark. 2005) (denying class action claims for diminution in value of Ford Explorer SUVs with alleged tendency to roll over, noting that the no-injury approach had been rejected in various decisions, and observing that "[t]he striking feature of a typical no-injury class is that the plaintiffs have either not yet experienced a malfunction because of the alleged defect or . . . not been harmed by it" and so "have not suffered any physical harm or out-of-pocket economic loss"); Ziegelmann v. DaimlerChrysler Corp., 649 N.W.2d 556, 565 (N.D. 2002) (in negligence, fraud, and deceit, diminution-in-value damages for vehicle design hazard that might cause future injury are "simply too speculative to constitute a legally cognizable tort injury"); In re Bridgestone/Firestone, Inc. Tires Prods. Liab. Litig., 155 F. Supp. 2d 1069, 1087 (S.D. Ind. 2001) (plaintiffs could not recover for emotional distress from possibility that their defective tires might suffer future tread separations causing their vehicles to roll over, nor for the resulting lower resale price they might one day receive for their vehicles, because "[t]hese simply are not cognizable tort injuries"). On no-injury claims, see generally White, Reverberations from the Collision of Tort and Warranty, 53 S.C. L. Rev. 1067 (2002) (brilliant exegesis).

[175] See In re Toyota Motor Corp. Unintended Acceleration Mktg., Sales Practices, and Prods. Liab. Litig., 2013 WL 3224585 (C.D. Cal. 2013) (preliminary approval of settlement valued at about $1.6 billion, including separate funds valued at $250 million for diminished value of vehicles, $400 million for costs of installing brake override systems (BOS) on affected vehicles, $250 million for cash payments in lieu of BOS, $478 million for extended warranty program, and $200 million for attorney fees, all on behalf of class of Toyota owners over about a decade whose vehicles, equipped with electronic throttle control systems, allegedly were subject to sudden unintended acceleration from phantom electronic defect that NHSTA, NASA, and the National Research Council's Transportation Research Board all concluded was nonexistent and essentially a phantom substitute for defective users—drivers pressing inadvertently on accelerators instead of brakes).

In Lloyd v. General Motors Corp., 916 A.2d 257, 257 (Md. 2007), a no-injury class action, the court allowed a variety of claims against car manufacturers for "the cost to repair defective seatbacks, which allegedly have a tendency to collapse in rear-impact collisions, causing, in some cases, serious bodily injury or death to drivers and/or passengers in the class vehicles," including negligence, strict liability in tort, fraudulent concealment, negligent misrepresentation, breach of the implied warranty of merchantability, and breach of a consumer protection statute. "[A] consumer should not have to wait until injury or death has occurred to assert a claim when the likelihood of injury or death is great . . . ." Id. at 272. For an excellent critique of *Lloyd*, see Korzec,

Punitive Damages. Intriguing damages questions in products liability litigation surround the availability and measurement of punitive damages. Such damages first appeared in scattered products liability cases during the late 1960s and the 1970s,[176] and punitive damages have been awarded from time to time thereafter (on average, in roughly 2% of all products liability cases, often involving asbestos or tobacco).[177] Punitive damages are recoverable on underlying claims of negligence, fraud, or strict liability in tort (but not breach of warranty), on proof that a manufacturer flagrantly disregarded consumer safety in selling a defective product.

Examples of such gross misconduct include fraudulently marketing unsafe products, or selling a product known to contain a serious hidden hazard without disclosing it to consumers, in order to promote the product's sale. Such damages may be assessed (1) to punish such manufacturers and thereby provide retribution to victims and society; (2) to deter the knowing or reckless sale of dangerously defective products; (3) to help enforce the common-law rules of product safety; (4) to educate manufacturers on the importance of product safety; and (5) to ensure that consumers injured by flagrantly improper conduct by manufacturers are roughly compensated for all their injuries, and thereby provided full restitution for their flagrantly inflicted harm, including their amorphous but very real injuries and the costs of litigation.

Punitive damages are subject to criticism on various fronts, including the vagueness of the standards for their recovery and for determining their amount. In an effort to impose some control on awards of punitive damages, courts in recent decades have focused closely on such damage claims and awards in an effort to curtail their abuse in products liability litigation, and many states have adopted one or more statutory reforms—the most common being an increase in the standard of proof from "preponderance of the evidence" to "clear and convincing" proof.

Beginning with *Pacific Mutual Life Insurance Co. v. Haslip*[178] in 1991, the Supreme Court rendered a series of decisions imposing due process constraints on punitive damages.[179] These decisions require that trial courts instruct juries properly on the functions of punitive damages, that trial and appellate courts review such awards with studied care to ensure that they are awarded on rational grounds, that punitive awards are not assessed for conduct outside the state that may be legal elsewhere, and that the ratio of punitive to compensatory awards be reasonable (not unduly large). The Supreme Court decisions have had a marked effect, for courts in recent years have reduced or reversed punitive damage awards in many products liability cases on the due process principles laid down in these decisions.

Lloyd v. General Motors Corp.: An Unfortunate Detour in Maryland Products Liability Law, 38 U. Balt. L.F. 127, 149 (2008) (arguing that claims for "unmanifested defects" should be denied).

[176] See Owen, Punitive Damages in Products Liability Litigation, 74 Mich. L. Rev. 1257 (1976).

[177] See Owen & Davis on Products Liability § 26:4, at nn.16–17 (arriving at this estimate based on numerous empirical studies).

[178] 499 U.S. 1 (1991).

[179] After *Haslip*, the decisions addressing due process limitations on punitive damages were TXO Prod. Corp. v. Alliance Res. Corp., 509 U.S. 443 (1993); Honda Motor Co. v. Oberg, 512 U.S. 415 (1994); BMW of N. Am. v. Gore, 517 U.S. 559 (1996); Cooper Indus. v. Leatherman Tool Group, 532 U.S. 424 (2001); State Farm Mutual Auto. Ins. Co. v. Campbell, 538 U.S. 408 (2003); Philip Morris USA Inc. v. Williams ("Williams I"), 540 U.S. 801 (2003); and Philip Morris USA v. Williams ("Williams II"), 549 U.S. 346 (2007).

While these and other important issues concerning the availability of punitive damages in products liability litigation are beyond the scope of this book, they are fully addressed in the treatise expansion of this work.[180]

Adoption of § 402A

The American Law Institute approved *Restatement (Second) of Torts* § 402A at its annual meeting in 1964[181] and published it the following year in volume 2 of the *Second Restatement*. With a gusto unmatched in the annals of *Restatements of the Law*,[182] the new doctrine swept across the face of America as courts and legislatures embraced § 402A and the bold new doctrine that it proclaimed: "strict" liability in tort for physical harm caused by defective products.[183] Tort law has probably never witnessed such a rapid, widespread, and altogether explosive change in a rule and theory of legal responsibility.[184]

Connecticut, Illinois, Kentucky, and New Jersey all adopted the principles of § 402A in 1965.[185] In 1966, four more states embraced the doctrine—Mississippi, Ohio, Pennsylvania, and Tennessee[186]—as did four more in 1967—Minnesota, Oregon, Texas, and Wisconsin.[187] By the time of Dean Prosser's death in 1971, twenty-eight states had adopted the doctrine, and, by the mid-1970s, over forty states had embraced the principle of strict manufacturer liability in tort for physical harm caused by the sale of defective products.[188] The last state to adopt the doctrine was Wyoming, in 1986,[189] by which time a total of forty-five states, the District of Columbia, Puerto Rico, and the Virgin Islands

---

[180] See Owen & Davis on Products Liability ch. 26.

[181] The ALI Reporter, Dean Prosser, presented this section for consideration by the Institute in Rest. (2d) of Torts, Tentative Draft No. 10, April 20, 1964.

[182] At the June 8, 1993 meeting of the Consultative Group on the Products Liability Restatement, Professor Geoffrey Hazard, then Director of the ALI, reported that § 402A had been cited in judicial opinions more than any other section of any Restatement.

[183] In 1963, of course, California had already adopted strict products liability in tort in *Greenman*, and New York had more or less followed suit in Goldberg v. Kollsman Instrument Corp., 191 N.E.2d 81, 83 (N.Y. 1963) (4–3 decision), decided three and a half months after *Greenman*. Leaning heavily on *Greenman* for support, the New York Court of Appeals in *Goldberg* held an aircraft manufacturer strictly liable to a passenger killed in a crash due to a defective altimeter in the plane. Basing its decision on breach of implied warranty in *tort*, the court held that privity of contract was not required.

[184] See, e.g., Prosser, The Fall of the Citadel (Strict Liability to the Consumer), 50 Minn. L. Rev. 791, 793–94 (1966) (characterizing the adoption of strict products liability in the early 1960s as "the most rapid and altogether spectacular overturn of an established rule in the entire history of the law of torts"). See also V. Nolan and E. Ursin, Understanding Enterprise Liability 105 (1995) (characterizing the spread of § 402A doctrine as "the strict products liability 'revolution,' the most spectacular episode of judicial creativity in the history of American tort law"); Bird and Smythe, Social Network Analysis and the Diffusion of the Strict Liability Rule for Manufacturing Defects, 37 L. & Soc. Inquiry 565 (2012) (tracing the proliferation of the doctrine from federal courts to state law).

[185] In order of adoption, see Santor v. A. & M. Karagheusian, Inc., 207 A.2d 305 (N.J. 1965); Suvada v. White Motor Co., 210 N.E.2d 182, 187 (Ill. 1965); Dealers Transp. Co. v. Battery Distrib. Co., 402 S.W.2d 441, 446–47 (Ky. Ct. App. 1965), as modified (1966); Garthwait v. Burgio, 216 A.2d 189 (Conn. 1965).

[186] See State Stove Mfg. Co. v. Hodges, 189 So.2d 113, 119 (Miss. 1966); Lonzrick v. Republic Steel Corp., 218 N.E.2d 185, 192–93 (Ohio 1966); Webb v. Zern, 220 A.2d 853 (Pa. 1966); Ford Motor Co. v. Lonon, 398 S.W.2d 240 (Tenn. 1966).

[187] See McCormack v. Hankscraft Co., 154 N.W.2d 488, 501 (Minn. 1967) (dictum); Heaton v. Ford Motor Co., 435 P.2d 806, 808 (Or. 1967); McKisson v. Sales Affiliates, Inc., 416 S.W.2d 787 (Tex. 1967); Dippel v. Sciano, 155 N.W.2d 55 (Wis. 1967).

[188] See Priest, The Invention of Enterprise Liability: A Critical History of the Intellectual Foundations of Modern Tort Law, 14 J. Legal Stud. 461, 518 (1985).

[189] In Ogle v. Caterpillar Tractor Co., 716 P.2d 334 (Wyo. 1986).

had all adopted a doctrine of strict products liability in tort.[190] The only states that never did formally accept the doctrine of strict products liability in tort are Delaware, Massachusetts, Michigan, North Carolina, and Virginia, as discussed below. Although these states refused to join the official strict tort bandwagon, each applies the bulk of modern products liability jurisprudence as it has evolved across the nation, either by reform statute or through the law of warranty or the law of negligence, to sellers of defective products.

In Delaware, the court refused to adopt § 402A in *Cline v. Prowler Industries of Maryland, Inc.*,[191] reasoning that the legislature's adoption of Article 2 of the Uniform Commercial Code preempted the products liability issue. Yet, by basing warranty liability in products liability cases on tort-law standards of ordinary and reasonable prudence and care, Delaware courts have developed products liability law concepts of design and warning responsibility markedly like those that other jurisdictions apply not

[190] The adopting decisions and statutes were as follows: *Alabama*: Casrell v. Altec Indus., 335 So.2d 128 (Ala. 1976), and Atkins v. American Motors Corp., 335 So.2d 134 (Ala. 1976); *Alaska*: Clary v. Fifth Ave. Chrysler Ctr., Inc., 454 P.2d 244 (Alaska 1969); *Arizona*: O.S. Stapley Co. v. Miller, 447 P.2d 248 (Ariz. 1968), and also Shannon v. Butler Homes, Inc., 428 P.2d 990, 993 (Ariz. 1967) (en banc) (dictum); *Arkansas*: Ark. Code. Ann. § 4–86–102 (1973), subsequently recodified at § 16–116–101 (2016); *California*: Greenman v. Yuba Power Prods., Inc., 377 P.2d 897 (Cal. 1963); *Colorado*: Hiigel v. General Motors Corp., 544 P.2d 983 (Colo. 1975); *Connecticut*: Garthwait v. Burgio, 216 A.2d 189 (Conn. 1965); *District of Columbia*: The early tangled case law on strict liability in tort in the District of Columbia never expressly adopts the doctrine, but it surely exists by 1985: Picker X-Ray Corp. v. General Motors Corp., 185 A.2d 919 (D.C. 1962), Cottom v. McGuire Funeral Serv., Inc., 262 A.2d 807 (D.C. 1970) (dictum), and Payne v. Soft Sheen Prods., Inc., 486 A.2d 712 (D.C. 1985); *Florida*: West v. Caterpillar Tractor Co., 336 So.2d 80, 87 (Fla. 1976); *Georgia*: Ga. Code Ann. § 105–106 (1968), subsequently recodified at § 51–1–11 (1975); *Hawaii*: Stewart v. Budget Rent-A-Car Corp., 470 P.2d 240 (Haw. 1970); *Idaho*: Shields v. Morton Chem. Co., 518 P.2d 857 (Idaho 1974); *Illinois*: Suvada v. White Motor Co., 210 N.E.2d 182 (Ill. 1965); *Indiana*: Cornette v. Searjeant Metal Prods., Inc., 258 N.E.2d 652 (Ind. Ct. App. 1970); *Iowa*: Hawkeye-Security Ins. Co. v. Ford Motor Co., 174 N.W.2d 672 (Iowa 1970); *Kansas*: Brooks v. Dietz, 545 P.2d 1104 (Kan. 1976); *Kentucky*: Dealers Transp. Co. v. Battery Distrib. Co., 402 S.W.2d 441 (Ky. Ct. App. 1965), as modified (1966); *Louisiana*: Weber v. Fidelity & Cas. Ins. Co., 250 So.2d 754 (La. 1971); *Maine*: Me. Rev. Stat. Ann. tit. 14, § 221 (1973); *Maryland*: Phipps v. General Motors Corp., 363 A.2d 955 (Md. 1976); *Minnesota*: McCormack v. Hankscraft Co., 154 N.W.2d 488 (Minn. 1967); *Mississippi*: State Stove Mfg. Co. v. Hodges, 189 So.2d 113 (Miss. 1966); *Missouri*: Keener v. Dayton Elec. Mfg. Co., 445 S.W.2d 362 (Mo. 1969); *Montana*: Brandenburger v. Toyota Motor Sales, U.S.A., Inc., 513 P.2d 268 (Mont. 1973); *Nebraska*: Kohler v. Ford Motor Co., 191 N.W.2d 601 (Neb. 1971); *Nevada*: Shoshone Coca-Cola Bottling Co. v. Dolinski, 420 P.2d 855 (Nev. 1966); *New Hampshire*: Buttrick v. Arthur Lessard & Sons, 260 A.2d 111 (N.H. 1969); *New Jersey*: Santor v. A & M Karagheusian, Inc., 207 A.2d 305 (N.J. 1965); *New Mexico*: Stang v. Hertz Corp., 497 P.2d 732 (N.M. 1972); *New York*: Codling v. Paglia, 298 N.E.2d 622 (N.Y. 1973); *North Dakota*: Johnson v. American Motors Corp., 225 N.W.2d 57 (N.D. 1974); *Ohio*: Lonzrick v. Republic Steel Corp., 218 N.E.2d 185 (Ohio 1966); *Oklahoma*: Marathon Battery Co. v. Kilpatrick, 418 P.2d 900 (Okla. 1965); *Oregon*: Heaton v. Ford Motor Co., 435 P.2d 806 (Or. 1967); *Pennsylvania*: Webb v. Zern, 220 A.2d 853 (Pa. 1966); *Puerto Rico*: Mendoza v. Cerveceria Corona, Inc., 97 D.P.R. 499 (1969); *Rhode Island*: Ritter v. Narragansett Elec. Co., 283 A.2d 255 (R.I. 1971); *South Carolina*: S.C. Code Ann. §§ 15–73–10 et seq. (1974); *South Dakota*: Engberg v. Ford Motor Co., 205 N.W.2d 104 (S.D. 1973); *Tennessee*: Ford Motor Co. v. Lonon, 398 S.W.2d 240 (Tenn. 1966); *Texas*: McKisson v. Sales Affiliates, Inc., 416 S.W.2d 787 (Tex. 1967); *Utah*: Ernest W. Hahn, Inc. v. Armco Steel Co., 601 P.2d 152 (Utah 1979); *Vermont*: Zaleskie v. Joyce, 333 A.2d 110 (Vt. 1975); *Virgin Islands*: Gumbs v. International Harvester, Inc., 718 F.2d 88 (3d Cir. 1983) (V.I. law); *Washington*: Ulmer v. Ford Motor Co., 452 P.2d 729, 735 (Wash. 1969); *West Virginia*: Morningstar v. Black & Decker Mfg. Co., 253 S.E.2d 666 (W. Va. 1979); *Wisconsin*: Dippel v. Sciano, 155 N.W.2d 55 (Wis. 1967); *Wyoming*: Ogle v. Caterpillar Tractor Co., 716 P.2d 334 (Wyo. 1986).

[191] 418 A.2d 968 (Del. 1980). This remains the law today. See Katz v. Tractor Supply Co., Inc., 2020 WL 1287754, at *4 (Del. Super. Ct. 2020) (granting defendant's motion for summary judgement on strict products liability claim, citing *Cline*). In 2008, the Delaware Superior Court extended this reasoning to deny a strict liability claim against a lessor, stating that adoption of UCC Article 2A precluded the claim. Middlesex Mut. Assurance Co. v. Delaware Elec. Signal Co., 2008 WL 4216145, at *5 (Del. Super. Ct. 2008).

only in negligence but also under the developed jurisprudence of *Restatement (Second) of Torts* § 402A.[192]

In Massachusetts, courts formally apply Article 2 of the Uniform Commercial Code to products liability cases,[193] but they have long used § 402A cases for guidance, if not authority. "Warranty liability is 'fully as comprehensive as the strict liability theory of recovery that has been adopted by a great many other jurisdictions . . . and 'congruent in nearly all respects with the principles expressed in Restatement (Second) of Torts § 402A (1965).' "[194] So, for many years, "[a]ctions under Massachusetts law for breach of the implied warranty of merchantability [were] the functional equivalent of strict liability in other jurisdictions."[195] At least for warning cases, however, the Massachusetts Supreme Judicial Court in the late 1990s firmly rejected the strict liability principles of § 402A, in *Vassallo v. Baxter Healthcare Corp.*,[196] in favor of the negligence principles in that context expressed by the *Restatement (Third) of Torts: Products Liability* § 2(c).

In Michigan,[197] early products liability decisions emphasized the practical congruence between negligence, warranty, and strict products liability in tort.[198] In *Owens v. Allis-Chalmers Corp.*,[199] for example, the court remarked that "the requisite elements for a cause of action based upon strict liability in tort are congruent to those for breach of warranty." More recently, however, Michigan courts have highlighted the distinction between strict liability and negligence, and declared unequivocally that "Michigan does not recognize strict liability as a theory of recovery in product liability actions."[200] Since this also has been the direction of most states in design and warning cases, Michigan remains in the mainstream of modern products liability law.

The North Carolina courts never did adopt § 402A or anything resembling it, and they probably never will. In the height of tort reform in the mid-1990s, a coalition of medical and other enterprises, quietly funded in part by the tobacco industry, steered an elegantly drafted reform bill through the legislature that, among other things, precluded North Carolina courts from adopting the doctrine of strict liability in tort. In no

---

192 See Graham v. Pittsburgh Corning Corp., 593 A.2d 567, 571 (Del. Super. Ct. 1990) (warning; duty based on conduct of manufacturer of reasonable prudence); Nacci v. Volkswagen of Am., Inc., 325 A.2d 617, 620 (Del. Super. Ct. 1974) (defective design; reasonable fitness determined by whether ordinarily prudent manufacturer would have adopted alternative design).

193 See, e.g., Carrozza v. CVS Pharmacy, Inc., 992 F.3d 44, 59 (1st Cir. 2021) ("there is no independent claim of 'strict liability in tort' [for a defective product] under Massachusetts law, and the sole remedy for strict liability is provided under the UCC").

194 Haglund v. Philip Morris, Inc., 847 N.E.2d 315, 321 (Mass. 2006).

195 Id.

196 696 N.E.2d 909 (Mass. 1998). On *Vassallo*, see § 10.4, below.

197 In 1995, Michigan enacted a products liability reform act, Mich. Comp. L. Ann. §§ 600.2945 et seq.

198 See Owens v. Allis-Chalmers Corp., 268 N.W.2d 291, 293 (Mich. Ct. App. 1978), aff'd, 326 N.W.2d 372 (Mich. 1982). See also Smith v. E.R. Squibb & Sons, Inc., 273 N.W.2d 476 (Mich. 1979) (issue of warning adequacy identical under implied warranty and negligence). *But cf.* Lagalo v. Allied Corp., 577 N.W.2d 462 (Mich. 1998) (noting differences between negligence and implied warranty).

199 268 N.W.2d 291, 293 (Mich. Ct. App. 1978).

200 Rodger v. Ford Motor Co., 2008 WL 4646140, at *6 (Mich. Ct. App. 2008). See also Mich. Comp. L. Ann. § 600.2948(3), applicable to claims of defective warnings and instructions, providing that a plaintiff must prove "that the manufacturer knew or should have known about the risk of harm [based on the state of art at the time of sale]." Yet Michigan's implied warranty, negligence, and statutory "approach is consistent with the traditional understanding of common law product liability, which is a form of strict liability in which a plaintiff need only prove the defective nature of the product when it left the manufacturer's hands and that the defect caused the plaintiff's injuries." Patel v. Reinalt-Thomas Corp., 2018 WL 5305098, at *8 (Mich. Ct. App. 2018).

uncertain terms, the statute declares that "[t]here shall be no strict liability in tort in product liability actions."[201] Yet, the North Carolina statute, which provides a fairly comprehensive set of rules governing products liability law, adopts a number of plaintiff-protective principles of modern products liability law put in place by courts from other states that operate under the strict tort umbrella.[202] Moreover, because the statute makes no effort to displace warranty law under the state's commercial code,[203] North Carolina's composite products liability law in action may well develop not far removed from the evolving law of other jurisdictions.

In Virginia, early decisions appeared to equate the negligence basis of liability with that of warranty, in terms that sounded like strict products liability in tort under § 402A. In *Jeld-Wen, Inc. v. Gamble*,[204] for example, the court observed that "the standard of safety of goods imposed on . . . the manufacturer of a product is essentially the same whether the theory of liability is labeled warranty or negligence." Under both theories of recovery, the state supreme court declared, "a plaintiff must show (1) that the [product was] unreasonably dangerous either for the use to which [it] would ordinarily be put or for some other reasonably foreseeable purpose, and (2) that the unreasonably dangerous condition existed when the goods left the manufacturer's hands."[205] Subsequently, the Virginia courts returned to negligence principles in both warning cases and design cases,[206] similar to the trend of products law across the nation, if under the rubric of "strict liability."

Many courts have pointed to the functional equivalence of strict tort liability and negligence in design and warning cases,[207] and, at least the Iowa Supreme Court has followed the *Third Restatement*'s approach of abandoning reference to such doctrinal

---

[201] See N.C. Gen. Stat. Ann. § 99B–1.1.

[202] For example, the statute imposes a post-sale duty on manufacturers to warn consumers of defects discovered in their products after initial distribution. See N.C. Gen. Stat. Ann. § 99B–5(a)(2). The duty is one of due care, the standard of responsibility normally adopted even in "strict" tort states that impose such a post-sale duty. See Products Liability Rest. § 10(a) (sellers have a post-sale duty to warn when a reasonable seller would do so).

[203] See N.C. Gen. Stat. Ann. § 99B–1.2.

[204] 501 S.E.2d 393 (Va. 1998).

[205] Id. at 396 (quoting Morgen Indus. v. Vaughan, 471 S.E.2d 489 (Va. 1996)). In *Morgen Industries*, the court observed that a product may be "unreasonably dangerous if it is defective in assembly or manufacture, unreasonably dangerous in design, or unaccompanied by adequate warnings concerning its hazardous properties." 471 S.E.2d at 492.

[206] See, Funkhouser v. Ford Motor Co., 736 S.E.2d 309, 316, 319 (Va. 2013) (concurring and dissenting opinion) (inadequate warning claim): "The cause of action for failure to warn is not a theory of strict liability. The plaintiff must prove that the product was dangerous, that the defendant knew or had reason to know of this dangerous condition, and that the defendant had no reason to believe the plaintiff would realize the dangerous condition. Furthermore, the plaintiff must prove that the defendant failed to exercise reasonable care to warn of the dangerous condition of the product it supplied to the plaintiff and that its failure to exercise such care caused plaintiff's damages." See also Simmons v. MTD Prods., Inc., 2008 WL 6744128, at *9 (Va. Cir. Ct. 2008) (riding mower design; "[S]trict liability [is] a doctrine that is not recognized in Virginia.").

[207] See, e.g., Nemes v. Dick's Sporting Goods, Inc., 521 F. Supp. 3d 328, 340 (S.D.N.Y. 2021) ("Although strict liability and negligence are distinct theories, courts often analyze strict liability and negligence claims together on the theory that they are 'functionally equivalent.' "; plaintiff's failure to prove a feasible alternative design doomed both his negligence and strict liability claims); Carter v. Ethicon, Inc., 2021 WL 1226531, at *3–4 (D. Nev. 2021) (because plaintiff's negligence and strict liability warning claims were "duplicative of and subsumed by the strict liability claims," court granted defendant's summary judgment motion on plaintiff's negligence claims); Webb v. Special Elec. Co., 370 P.3d 1022, 1035 (Cal. 2016) (" 'there is little functional difference between the two theories in the failure to warn context").

categories and speaking solely in terms of design or warning defect claims.[208] In most states, in design and warning cases alike, both the process and results of litigation are generally unaffected by whether the basis of tort liability is formally called "negligence" or "strict."[209] The same may be said with respect to implied warranty of merchantability as the basis of products liability recovery—except, of course, for important secondary issues such as privity, disclaimers, notice, and statutes of limitation.[210] This all suggests, despite some real variations in secondary doctrine in both warranty and tort,[211] that the fundamentals of modern products liability law and litigation should continue broadly to evolve in quite similar respects across America, even in the five renegade states—which now might be viewed as having been prescient—that formally refused to follow that aspect of the products liability revolution that classified the basis of all products liability in tort law as "strict."

It is true, of course, that the *Third Restatement of Torts* officially abandoned the strict liability principles of *Restatement (Second) of Torts* § 402A in design and warning defect cases, as discussed throughout the remaining chapters.[212] While the *Third Restatement* does explicitly reject the idea of "strict" liability in design and warning cases, it should be noted that it fairly did "restate" the law as courts and some legislatures were increasingly defining and applying it across America when the *Third Restatement* was debated and eventually approved during the 1990s—and as the law continues to this day. Moreover, whether courts persist in nominally following § 402A of the *Second Restatement* or explicitly switch instead to the *Third Restatement*, the actual jurisprudence of the law in action will continue to apply to design and warning defect cases the negligence-like principles of balance, reasonableness, and foreseeable risk about which courts have come to a virtual consensus across the nation.[213]

Variations on § 402A

Judicial Variations

Most states embraced the theory of strict products liability in tort by judicial "adoption" of § 402A.[214] Since the time of its initial adoption, however, the products liability jurisprudence of America has moved far beyond the original formulation of the

---

[208] See Wright v. Brooke Grp. Ltd., 652 N.W.2d 159, 164–69 (Iowa 2002) (design defect claims stand on their own apart from strict liability in tort or negligence); Olson v. Prosoco, Inc., 522 N.W.2d 284, 289 (Iowa 1994) ("any posited distinction between strict liability and negligence principles is illusory"; warning claims lie in negligence, not strict liability in tort).

[209] See § 5.9, below. Formerly, a major difference between the two theories was that a plaintiff's simple contributory negligence barred recovery in negligence but not in strict liability in tort. In most jurisdictions today, however, comparative fault operates equally on both types of claim. See ch. 13, below.

[210] See § 5.9, below.

[211] One state supreme court judge characterized products liability law in the U.S. as "the peculiarly American system of fifty uncoordinated, separate schemes of tort law coexisting within one industrial nation." Blankenship v. General Motors Corp., 406 S.E.2d 781, 785 (W. Va. 1991) (Neely, J.).

[212] See especially § 6.5, below.

[213] See § 5.10, below.

[214] See, e.g., Heaton v. Ford Motor Co., 435 P.2d 806, 808 (Or. 1967) ("we now adopt Section 402A"); Hawkeye-Security Ins. Co. v. Ford Motor Co., 174 N.W.2d 672, 684 (Iowa 1970) ("[w]e now adopt the principles found in Restatement, Second, Torts § 402A"); Ritter v. Narragansett Elec. Co., 283 A.2d 255, 261 (R.I. 1971) ("the adoption of § 402A will well serve to promote the cause of justice"); Phipps v. General Motors Corp., 363 A.2d 955, 963 (Md. 1976) ("we adopt the theory of strict liability as expressed in § 402A of the Restatement (Second) of Torts [which a]lmost all of the courts of our sister states have adopted").

doctrine described in § 402A and its comments,[215] and the American Law Institute in 1998 replaced it entirely with the *Restatement (Third) of Torts: Products Liability*.[216]

A number of states took a rather independent route from the start of modern products liability law, refusing simply to "adopt" § 402A yet adhering to the general principles of the developing jurisprudence of strict products liability in tort. One such state was Oklahoma where, in *Kirkland v. General Motors Corp.*,[217] the state supreme court adopted an extensively described theory of strict products liability in tort, called "Manufacturers' Products Liability."[218] Alabama also followed an independent path, in *Casrell v. Altec Industries, Inc.*[219] and *Atkins v. American Motors Corp.*,[220] by adopting a strict products liability in tort doctrine labeled the "Alabama Extended Manufacturer's Liability Doctrine (AEMLD)," likening the doctrine to negligence per se. In *Halphen v. Johns-Manville Sales Corp.*,[221] Louisiana adopted separate classifications of unreasonably dangerous products, although this development was promptly overruled by the legislature's subsequent adoption of a comprehensive products liability reform statute in 1988.[222]

New York, which was at the forefront of the charge toward strict manufacturer liability to remote consumers in its *Goldberg v. Kollsman Instrument Corp.*[223] decision in 1963, did not formally adopt the doctrine of strict products liability,[224] nor make it clear that liability lay in tort, until 1973.[225] From the start, the New York decisions wove a somewhat distinctive pattern to the texture of strict products liability in tort—a singularity that has continued to mark the decisions of that state's high court.[226]

The California Supreme Court, which in 1963 gave birth to strict products liability in tort in *Greenman v. Yuba Power Products, Inc.*,[227] seemed to adopt § 402A in 1970, in *Pike v. Frank G. Hough Co.*[228] However, in 1972, the California high court repudiated the *Restatement* formulation of the liability standard, "defective condition unreasonably dangerous," and reaffirmed the *Greenman* characterization of the basis of liability as merely "defective," in *Cronin v. J.B.E. Olson Corp.*[229]

---

[215] For the diversity of approaches at an early date, see J. Beasley, Products Liability and the Unreasonably Dangerous Requirement 23 (1981): "Prosser's apprehension that the strict liability section would soon become outmoded was well-founded. Today, it is grossly out-of-date. Despite his constant effort in the first half of the 1960s to keep pace with new developments in the case law, strict tort liability has gone well beyond the confines, however flexibly they were written, of Section 402A."

[216] See §§ 5.10 and 6.5, below.

[217] 521 P.2d 1353 (Okla. 1974).

[218] See McNichols, The Kirkland v. General Motors Manufacturers' Products Liability Doctrine—What's in a Name?, 27 Okla. L. Rev. 347 (1974).

[219] 335 So.2d 128 (Ala. 1976).

[220] 335 So.2d 134 (Ala. 1976).

[221] 484 So.2d 110 (La. 1986).

[222] Louisiana Products Liability Act, La. Rev. Stat. Ann. §§ 9:2800.51 et seq.

[223] 191 N.E.2d 81 (N.Y. 1963) (assembler-manufacturer of airplane, but not supplier of defective component, an altimeter, held strictly liable to passenger killed in crash).

[224] See Codling v. Paglia, 298 N.E.2d 622 (N.Y. 1973).

[225] See Velez v. Craine & Clark Lumber Corp., 305 N.E.2d 750, 754 (N.Y. 1973).

[226] See, e.g., Denny v. Ford Motor Co., 662 N.E.2d 730 (N.Y. 1995). *Denny* is examined in § 5.9, below.

[227] 377 P.2d 897 (Cal. 1963).

[228] 467 P.2d 229 (Cal. 1970).

[229] 501 P.2d 1153 (Cal. 1972). *Cronin* and other California developments are examined in § 5.8, below.

Pennsylvania took the most adventurous (indeed, twisted) route after adopting § 402A. While beginning its 402A jurisprudence with all normalcy,[230] the Pennsylvania Supreme Court subsequently veered off the common pathways for defining and administering liability for product defects into a doctrinal thicket that long ensnared whoever attempted to understand that state's products liability doctrine.[231] Finally, the Pennsylvania high court decided *Tincher v. Omega Flex, Inc.*,[232] which retained strict liability as the nominal basis of liability and adopted a two-pronged standard similar to that in California's *Barker v. Lull Engineering Co.*,[233] permitting plaintiffs in design defect cases to pursue claims on either the consumer expectations or risk-utility approach. But the Pennsylvania court deferred a decision on the burden of proof in the risk-utility test, and it recognized but did not fully endorse California's subsequent decision in *Soule v. General Motors Corp.*,[234] which limited the consumer expectations test to cases involving simple designs.[235]

Florida also hovered for a while between the two *Restatements*. The Third District of that state adopted at least sections 2 and 5 of the *Third Restatement* in 2005 and 2010 decisions, reaffirmed in a 2012 decision.[236] In 2015, the Florida Supreme Court finally resolved the issue in an extensive opinion that reaffirmed its commitment to § 402A of the *Second Restatement*, approved consumer expectations as a proper test for design defect liability (together with risk-utility), and reaffirmed its endorsement of the traditional rationales supporting strict products liability in tort.[237]

Products Liability Reform Statutes

Several state legislatures enacted the doctrine of strict products liability in tort statutorily. Statutes enacted in Indiana, Maine, Montana, Oregon, and South Carolina, at least initially, were nearly verbatim restatements of § 402A.[238] Arkansas and Georgia also enacted statutes adopting versions of strict products liability.[239] Many states have

---

[230] See Webb v. Zern, 220 A.2d 853 (Pa. 1966) (adopting § 402A).

[231] In Azzarello v. Black Bros. Co., 391 A.2d 1020 (Pa. 1978). See Beard v. Johnson & Johnson, Inc., 41 A.3d 823, 836 (Pa. 2012) ("we again recognize the continuing state of disrepair in the arena of Pennsylvania strict-liability design defect law"). Pennsylvania's early tortured path was well examined in Thomas, Defining "Design Defect" in Pennsylvania: Reconciling *Azzarello* and the *Restatement (Third) of Torts*, 71 Temp. L. Rev. 217 (1998). *Azzarello* is examined in § 5.8, below.

[232] 104 A.3d 328 (Pa. 2014), summarized in Dunlap v. Federal Signal Corp., 194 A.3d 1067, 1070 (Pa. Super. Ct. 2018).

[233] 573 P.2d 443 (Cal. 1978).

[234] 882 P.2d 298 (Cal. 1994).

[235] See §§ 5.8 (Combining Tests—Consumer Expectations and Risk-Utility) and 8.6. For an explanation of why consumer expectations work poorly as a liability standard in most cases, see Owen, Expectations in Tort, 43 Ariz. St. L.J. 1287 (2011).

[236] Union Carbide Corp. v. Aubin, 97 So.3d 886 (Fla. Dist. Ct. App. 2012).

[237] Aubin v. Union Carbide Corp., 177 So.3d 489, 512 (Fla. 2015); In re Standard Jury Instructions in Civil Cases—Report No. 13–01 (Products Liability), 160 So.3d 869 (Fla. 2015) (mem.) (approving both consumer expectations and risk-utility as proper liability tests in design defect cases). See also Cavanaugh v. Stryker Corp., 308 So.3d 149, 155 (Fla. Dist. Ct. App. 2020) (distinguishing *Aubin*, "we hold that the consumer expectations test cannot be logically applied here, where the product in question is a complex medical device available to an ordinary consumer only as an incident to a medical procedure"; trial court did not err in refusing to instruct the jury on consumer expectation test).

[238] See Ind. Code Ann. § 33–1–1.5–3 (superseded by Ind. Code Ann. §§ 34–20–2–1 et seq., which limits strict liability in tort to manufacturers and precisely redefines the basis of a manufacturer's liability); Me. Rev. Stat. Ann. tit. 14, § 221; Mont. Code Ann. § 27–1–719; Or. Rev. Stat. Ann. § 30.920; S.C. Code Ann. §§ 15–73–10 et seq.

[239] See Ark. Code Ann. § 16–116–101; Ga. Code Ann. § 51–1–11 (manufacturers of new chattels strictly liable for injuries from unmerchantable products).

enacted various reform statutes that modify particular aspects of products liability law and litigation,[240] sometimes detailing the bases of recovery in different contexts, defenses, available damages, and various procedural aspects of such litigation.

States with substantial products liability reform statutes currently include Alabama,[241] Arizona,[242] Colorado,[243] Connecticut,[244] Idaho,[245] Kansas,[246] Kentucky,[247] Louisiana,[248] Michigan,[249] Mississippi,[250] Missouri,[251] Nebraska,[252] New Jersey,[253] North Carolina,[254] North Dakota,[255] Ohio,[256] South Dakota,[257] Tennessee,[258] Texas,[259] Utah,[260] Washington,[261] and Wisconsin.[262]

The Wisconsin Supreme Court historically was one of the most liberal courts in interpreting and applying § 402A in a way it thought favored consumers—stubbornly sticking, for example, to the consumer expectations test long after most other courts had abandoned it and despite spirited objections by dissenting justices.[263] In 2011, however, the Wisconsin legislature put an end to the judicial wrangling by adopting the product defect definitions of the *Third Restatement*,[264] thereby effectively overturning § 402A and much of its underlying jurisprudence.

The Illinois legislature enacted a comprehensive products liability statute,[265] but that state's Supreme Court struck down the statute in 1997 as unconstitutional,[266] the

---

240 The statutes are cited in section § 1.3, note 120, above.

241 See Ala. Code §§ 6–5–500 et seq.

242 See Ariz. Rev. Stat. Ann. §§ 12–681 et seq.

243 See Colo. Rev. Stat. Ann. §§ 13–21–401 et seq.

244 See Conn. Gen. Stat. Ann. §§ 52–572*l* et seq.

245 See Idaho Code Ann. §§ 6–1401 et seq.

246 See Kan. Stat. Ann. §§ 60–3301 et seq.

247 See Ky. Rev. Stat. Ann. §§ 411.300 et seq.

248 See La. Rev. Stat. Ann. §§ 9:2800.51 et seq.

249 See Mich. Comp. Laws Ann. §§ 600.2945 et seq.

250 See Miss. Code Ann. §§ 11–1–63 et seq.

251 See Mo. Ann. Stat. §§ 537.760 et seq.

252 See Neb. Rev. Stat. §§ 25–21,180 et seq.

253 See N.J. Stat. Ann. §§ 2A:58C–1 et seq.

254 See N.C. Gen. Stat. Ann. §§ 99B–1 et seq.

255 See N.D. Cent. Code §§ 28–01.3–01 et seq.

256 See Ohio Rev. Code Ann. ch. 2307 (Product Liability Claims). Ohio's Supreme Court declared a major products liability reform statute unconstitutional in State ex rel. Ohio Academy of Trial Lawyers v. Sheward, 715 N.E.2d 1062 (1999), and the legislature enacted a number of subsequent statutes as late as 2007. See Abaray, Déjà Vu All Over Again Ohio's 2005 Tort Reform Act Cannot Survive a Rational Basis Challenge, 31 U. Dayton L. Rev. 141 (2006); Werber, Ohio: A Microcosm of Tort Reform Versus State Constitutional Mandates, 32 Rutgers L.J. 1045 (2001).

257 See S.D. Codified Laws §§ 20–9–9 et seq.

258 See Tenn. Code Ann. §§ 29–28–101 et seq.

259 See Tex. Civ. Prac. & Rem. Code Ann. §§ 82.001 et seq.

260 See Utah Code Ann. §§ 78B–6–701 to –707.

261 See Wash. Rev. Code Ann. §§ 7.72.010 et seq.

262 See Wis. Stat. Ann §§ 895.046 to .047.

263 See, e.g., Green v. Smith & Nephew AHP, Inc., 629 N.W.2d 727 (Wis. 2001), where the court applied the consumer expectations test to allow recovery for damage from an allegedly unforeseeable risk.

264 In Wis. Stat. Ann. § 895.047(1)(a). See also Nelson v. Johnson & Johnson, 428 F. Supp. 3d 1, 9 (E.D. Wis. 2019) (holding Wis. Stat. Ann. § 895.047 unconstitutional as retroactively applied).

265 See 735 Ill. Comp. Stat. Ann. 5/2–621 et seq.

266 Best v. Taylor Mach. Works, 689 N.E.2d 1057 (Ill. 1997).

same fate that met New Hampshire's products liability statute fourteen years earlier.[267] North Carolina's elegantly drafted reform statute,[268] while expressly rejecting the doctrine of strict liability in tort, broadly adopts many of the secondary liability principles of modern products liability law. Many other states have enacted products liability reform statutes covering a miscellany of topics: "state of the art" defenses and statutes of repose; shields for sellers of fattening foods and manufacturers of guns and ammunition; protections for retailers (entirely or conditionally) from strict liability; and a host of other limitations.[269] These and many other topics, including a general account of the path away from strict products liability in tort,[270] are explored later in this work.

§ 5.4 POLICIES AND RATIONALES

For half a century before the doctrine of strict manufacturer liability in tort burst forth in American courts during the 1960s, scholars had been examining the general question of whether enterprises should be strictly liable for injuries caused by their operations.[271] More particularly, several decades prior to § 402A, commentators began to explain and justify (usually in the warranty law context, often arguing against the privity doctrine) why manufacturers of defective products should be liable for injuries to consumers.[272] Conceptual explorations into strict manufacturer liability are discernible in America as early as the 1920s with one commentator's call for a seller's implied warranty—"insurer's liability" based on "risk-bearing."[273] The rationalization of such liability developed more fully in the 1930s, especially in writings by warranty law scholar Karl Llewellyn, who argued that the law should impose strict liability on large manufacturers (and large retailers) who are "equipped to spread, and indeed to reduce, risks" to consumers from defective products that they sell.[274]

---

[267] See Heath v. Sears, Roebuck & Co., 464 A.2d 288 (N.H. 1983).

[268] See N.C. Gen. Stat. Ann. §§ 99B–1 et seq.

[269] The statutes are collected in Appendices I and J of Owen & Davis on Products Liability.

[270] See § 5.10, below.

[271] In the early 1900s, the scholarship centered on an employer's strict liability for injury to its employees under the new workers' compensation statutes that swept the nation in the first two decades of the century. This particular literature is discussed generally in the commentary cited in the following note.

[272] There is now a rich literature on the evolution of the theoretical underpinnings to a rule of strict liability for manufacturers of defective products. See, e.g., Kysar, The Expectations of Consumers, 103 Colum. L. Rev. 1700, 1708 (2003) (collecting the literature); Witt, Speedy Fred Taylor and the Ironies of Enterprise Liability, 103 Colum. L. Rev. 1 (2003); Keating, The Theory of Enterprise Liability and Common Law Strict Liability, 54 Vand. L. Rev. 1285 (2001); Hackney, Jr., The Intellectual Origins of American Strict Products Liability: A Case Study in American Pragmatic Instrumentalism, 29 Am. J. Legal Hist. 443 (1995) (describing its origins in pragmatism, institutional economics, and legal realism, collectively referred to as "pragmatic instrumentalism"); Gray, Reflections on the Historical Context of Section 402A, 10 Touro L. Rev. 75 (1993); Priest, The Invention of Enterprise Liability: A Critical History of the Intellectual Foundations of Modern Tort Law, 14 J. Legal Stud. 461 (1985); V. Nolan and E. Ursin, Understanding Enterprise Liability (1995); M. Rahdert, Covering Accident Costs (1995); G. White, Tort Law in America—An Intellectual History (expanded ed. 2003).

[273] See, e.g., Patterson, The Apportionment of Business Risks Through Legal Devices, 24 Colum. L. Rev. 333, 358 (1924).

[274] See, e.g., Llewellyn, On Warranty of Quality, and Society (pt. 1), 36 Colum. L. Rev. 699, 704 n.14 (1936). In his celebrated casebook, he argued that manufacturers of defective products should be strictly liable to injured consumers "to shift the immediate incidence of the hazard of life in an industrial society away from the individual over to a group which can distribute the loss; and to place the loss where the most pressure will be exerted to keep down future losses." K. Llewellyn, Cases and Materials on the Law of Sales 341 (1930).

> The consumer, barring his own fault in use, should have no negligence to prove; that the article was not up to its normal character should be enough. . . . Under such an ideal system of law the

In 1941, as previously recounted,[275] William Prosser catalogued the reasons for strict manufacturer liability in the first edition of his torts treatise,[276] and Judge Traynor elaborated upon those reasons in his famous concurring opinion in *Escola v. Coca Cola Bottling Co.* in 1944.[277] These were burgeoning versions of the same rationales drawn on by scholars in the 1950s, as the march toward strict manufacturer accountability to remote consumers accelerated.[278] In the 1960s,[279] notably in Dean Prosser's "Assault Upon the Citadel" article in 1960, and comment *c* to § 402A of the *Restatement (Second) of Torts*, published in 1965, for which Prosser was Reporter,[280] these same rationales were cogently combined to justify the new legal doctrine that exploded upon the tort law landscape over the latter half of that decade. In comment *c*, Prosser summarized the rationales for strict products liability in tort as then conceived—that manufacturers assume a "special responsibility" toward consumers who may be injured by their products; that consumers properly expect reputable sellers to stand behind their goods; that the economic burden of injuries from product accidents should be borne by sellers and treated as a cost of production that may be insured against by liability insurance; and that consumers are "entitled to the maximum of protection at the hands of someone, and the proper persons to afford it are those who market the products."

> loss would lie ultimately where it belongs, on the consumers of the article concerned *en masse*, in competition with other articles each carrying its own true costs in human life and effort. . . .

Id. at 341–42. On Llewellyn's influence, see generally Clutterbuck, Karl Llewellyn and the Intellectual Foundations of Enterprise Liability Theory, 97 Yale L.J. 1131 (1987); Wiseman, The Limits of Vision: Karl Llewellyn and the Merchant Rules, 100 Harv. L. Rev. 465 (1987). See also Feezer, Manufacturer's Liability for Injuries Caused by His Products: Defective Automobiles, 37 Mich. L. Rev. 1, 5–6, 22 n.58 (1938) (quoting from Llewellyn's casebook, and arguing in products liability cases for warranty without privity "as a basis for shifting the burden where it can be distributed and so can best be borne").

[275] See § 5.2, above.

[276] In W. Prosser, Handbook of the Law of Torts § 83, at 688–89 (1941), Prosser described the increased impetus "to find some ground for strict liability which would make [the manufacturer] in effect a guarantor of his product, even though he had exercised all reasonable care," a development fueled by "an increased feeling that social policy demands that the burden of accidental injuries caused by defective chattels be placed upon the producer, since he is best able to distribute the risk to the general public by means of prices and insurance." In addition, Prosser observed, was "the difficulty of proving negligence in many cases where it exists, even with the aid of res ipsa loquitur, together with the wastefulness and uncertainty of a series of warranty actions carrying liability back through retailer and jobber to the original maker, the practice of reputable manufacturers to stand behind their goods as good business policy, and a recognition that the intermediate seller is usually a mere conduit to market the product. There is an obvious argument that in the public interest the consumer is entitled to the maximum of protection at the hands of some one, and that the producer, practically and morally, is the one to provide it."

[277] 150 P.2d 436, 440 (Cal. 1944). On *Escola*, see § 5.2, above.

[278] See, e.g., James, General Products—Should Manufacturers Be Liable Without Negligence?, 24 Tenn. L. Rev. 923 (1957); Noel, Manufacturers of Defective Products—The Drift Toward Strict Liability, 24 Tenn. L. Rev. 963 (1957); James, Products Liability (pt. 2), 34 Tex. L. Rev. 192 (1955); Wilson, Products Liability (pts. 1 and 2), 43 Cal. L. Rev. 614, 809 (1955).

A number of leading scholars during this time expounded more broadly upon the benefits of enterprise responsibility for accidental harm based on broad loss distribution objectives. See, e.g., Ehrenzweig, Negligence Without Fault (1951), reprinted in 54 Cal. L. Rev. 1422 (1966); Morris, Hazardous Enterprises and Risk Bearing Capacity, 61 Yale L.J. 1172 (1952); Ehrenzwieg, A Psychoanalysis of Negligence, 47 Nw. U. L. Rev. 855 (1953); L. Green, The Individual's Protection Under Negligence Law: Risk Sharing, 47 Nw. U. L. Rev. 751 (1953). See generally G. Schwartz, The Beginning and the Possible End of the Rise of Modern American Tort Law, 26 Ga. L. Rev. 601, 635 (1992).

[279] See, e.g., Pound, The Problem of the Exploding Bottle, 40 B.U. L. Rev. 167, 180–81, 185–86 (1960) (embracing the *Escola* concurrence rationales).

[280] In his celebrated article, The Assault Upon the Citadel (Strict Liability to the Consumer), 69 Yale L.J. 1099 (1960), Dean Prosser disparaged both the insurance (risk-spreading) and deterrence rationales.

Rationales—in General

Early courts and commentators offered a variety of these rationales for a manufacturer's strict products liability, generally predicating such liability on the increasing intricacy and danger of modern products comprised of complex mechanical and chemical substances. In contrast to simple products of previous generations, modern consumers often have no practical way to evaluate the safety of such products.[281]

Consumer Expectations

The complex-product premise was often drawn upon to support a fundamental rationale for holding manufacturers strictly liable to consumers: to protect a consumer's fair expectations of safety in goods mass merchandised by manufacturers.[282] Tort law borrowed this particular justification from warranty law which, by the middle of the twentieth century, was generally considered a branch of contract law grounded in the protection of the parties' reasonable expectations.[283] As examined below, the law's jealous protection of this cardinal foundation—a footing for interpersonal transactions that transcends the law of contract and tort[284]—evolved into an important early standard or "test" of strict products liability in tort.[285]

Probable Negligence

Some commentators also reasoned that defective products usually result from a manufacturer's negligence, such that holding a manufacturer strictly liable would serve as a proxy for the doctrine of res ipsa loquitur in the many cases in which the

---

[281] See, e.g., Escola v. Coca Cola Bottling Co., 150 P.2d 436, 443 (Cal. 1944) (Traynor, J., concurring):

> As handicrafts have been replaced by mass production with its great markets and transportation facilities, the close relationship between the producer and consumer of a product has been altered. Manufacturing processes, frequently valuable secrets, are ordinarily either inaccessible to or beyond the ken of the general public. The consumer no longer has means or skill enough to investigate for himself the soundness of a product, even when it is not contained in a sealed package, and his erstwhile vigilance has been lulled by the steady efforts of manufacturers to build up confidence by advertising and marketing devices such as trade-marks. Consumers no longer approach products warily but accept them on faith, relying on the reputation of the manufacturer or the trade mark.

On how humans today regularly depend on myriad complex products, see Owen, Products Liability: Principles of Justice for the 21st Century, 11 Pace L. Rev. 63, 64–66 (1990).

[282] See, e.g., Jacob E. Decker & Sons v. Capps, 164 S.W.2d 828, 832–33 (Tex. 1942) (noting that the modern manufacturer "uses the newspapers, magazines, billboards, and the radio to build up the psychology to buy and consume his products [and thereby acts to] create a demand for his products by inducing a belief that they are suitable for human consumption"). See also Prosser, The Assault Upon the Citadel (Strict Liability to the Consumer), 69 Yale L.J. 1099, 1123 (1960):

> The supplier, by placing the goods upon the market, represents to the public that they are suitable and safe for use; and by packaging, advertising or otherwise, he does everything that he can to induce that belief. He intends and expects that the product will be purchased and used in reliance upon this assurance of safety; and it is in fact so purchased and used.

For an early discussion of this rationale, see Prosser, The Implied Warranty of Merchantable Quality, 27 Minn. L. Rev. 117, 122–25 (1943). For a rich exploration of this basis of products liability, see the monumental inquiry by Professor Marshall Shapo, A Representational Theory of Consumer Protection: Doctrine, Function and Legal Liability for Product Disappointment, 60 Va. L. Rev. 1109 (1974).

[283] See, e.g., R. Pound, Social Control Through Law 114 (reprint 1968) (1942) ("[i]n civilized society men must be able to assume that [others] will make good reasonable expectations which their promises or other conduct reasonably create"); 1 J. Perillo, Corbin on Contracts § 1, at 2 (rev. ed. 1993) (the "main underlying purpose" of contract law is to enforce "the realization of reasonable expectations that have been induced by the making of a promise").

[284] On why the law broadly seeks to protect justified expectations, see generally Owen, Expectations in Tort, 44 Ariz. St. L. Rev. 1287 (2011).

[285] See § 5.6, below.

manufacturer probably was negligent in producing a defective product but where proof of negligence is practicably unavailable to a person injured by the defect.[286] In the words of one court adopting § 402A, "the requirement of proof of a defect rendering a product unreasonably dangerous is a sufficient showing of fault on the part of the seller to impose liability without placing an often impossible burden on the plaintiff of proving specific acts of negligence."[287]

Judicial Efficiency

A further argument for holding manufacturers strictly liable to consumers for product accidents, perhaps best viewed as a procedural rather than substantive justification, was the promotion of judicial efficiency: retailers were strictly liable to consumers anyway, via the implied warranty of merchantability: retailers held liable would obtain indemnity for their litigation losses from their suppliers, and those suppliers would themselves recover from the manufacturer. To avoid this type of wasteful, repetitive litigation, went the argument, consumers injured by defective products should simply be allowed to skip over retailers (and other intermediate sellers) and maintain strict liability actions directly against manufacturers.[288]

Cost Internalization

Early arguments for strict manufacturer liability to consumers centered on the propriety of relieving individual consumers of the economic consequences of injuries caused by defective products by shifting such losses to the enterprises that manufactured those products. Holding manufacturers liable for losses caused by defects in their products would force such firms to "internalize" these accident costs just as they must absorb other costs of production—materials, labor, and capital.[289] Manufacturers would then "spread" these costs, as a kind of third-party insurer, by "passing them on" to those

---

[286] See Cowan, Some Policy Bases of Products Liability, 17 Stan. L. Rev. 1077, 1087 (1965), observing that courts recognize "the great expense that plaintiffs would have to undergo to prove negligent manufacture of one out of a million products of the defendant [and] that if plaintiff were sufficiently well-heeled he would probably succeed in a surprisingly large number of cases in proving that the manufacturer was indeed negligent in the ordinary sense of the word." Thus, "implied warranty becomes 'presumed negligence.' Needless to say, this is really not very far from *res ipsa loquitur*. It merely extends its use." Compare Dean Wade's early, undeveloped idea that the sale of a defective product is akin to negligence per se. See Wade, Strict Tort Liability of Manufactures, 19 Sw. L.J. 5, 14 (1965).

[287] Phipps v. General Motors Corp., 363 A.2d 955, 958 (Md. 1976).

[288] See, e.g., Escola v. Coca Cola Bottling Co., 150 P.2d 436, 442 (Cal. 1944) ("Such a procedure, however, is needlessly circuitous and engenders wasteful litigation. Much would be gained if the injured person could base his action directly on the manufacturer's warranty."). Prosser explained: "It is already possible to enforce strict liability by resort to a series of actions, in which the retailer is first held liable on a warranty to his purchaser, and indemnity on a warranty is then sought successively from other suppliers, until the manufacturer finally pays the damages, with the added costs of repeated litigation." Thus, "[w]hat is needed is a blanket rule which makes any supplier in the chain liable directly to the ultimate user, and so short-circuits the whole unwieldy process." Prosser, The Assault Upon the Citadel (Strict Liability to the Consumer) 69 Yale L.J. 1099, 1123–24 (1960).

[289] Important early articles promoting the general concept of cost internalization include Smith, Sequel to Workmen's Compensation Acts (pts. 1 and 2), 27 Harv. L. Rev. 235, 344 (1914); Thayer, Liability Without Fault, 29 Harv. L. Rev. 801 (1916); Green, The Duty Problem in Negligence Cases, 28 Colum. L. Rev. 1014 (1928); Morris, Rough Justice and Some Utopian Ideas, 24 Ill. L. Rev. 730 (1930); Feezer, Capacity to Bear Loss as a Factor in the Decision in Certain Types of Tort Cases (pt. 1), 78 U. Pa. L. Rev. 805 (1930), (pt. 2), 79 U. Pa. L. Rev. 742 (1931); Bohlen, Fifty Years of Torts, 50 Harv. L. Rev. 1225 (1937). An important later work is Cowan, Some Policy Bases of Products Liability, 17 Stan. L. Rev. 1077 (1965). See generally Priest, The Invention of Enterprise Liability: A Critical History of the Intellectual Foundations of Modern Tort Law, 14 J. Legal Stud. 461, 481 (1985).

who benefit from the enterprise[290]—the owners (through lower profits) and consumers (through higher prices).[291] An important additional aspect of this cost-internalization process is that it motivates manufacturers to eliminate defects in their products, in an effort to minimize accident costs which otherwise they must at least partially absorb, thus promoting public safety.[292]

Deterrence (Safety) and Risk-Spreading

Although courts and commentators offered a host of justifications for the doctrine of strict manufacturer liability in tort for harm caused by defective products, both before[293] and after[294] the promulgation of § 402A, it is important to highlight the two major goals that lay behind and motivated the cost-internalization rationale and which

---

[290] Thus, the "benefit theory" of tort liability, prevalent during the first part of the twentieth century, provides important theoretical support to cost-internalization and risk-spreading. The leading exponent of this theory was Francis Bohlen. See Bohlen, The Basis of Affirmative Obligations in the Law of Torts (pts. 1–3), 53 Am. L. Reg. 209, 273, 337 (1905). See generally Priest, The Invention of Enterprise Liability: A Critical History of the Intellectual Foundations of Modern Tort Law, 14 J. Legal Stud. 461, 465–70 (1985).

[291] See, e.g., Escola v. Coca Cola Bottling Co., 150 P.2d 436, 441 (Cal. 1944) ("The cost of an injury and the loss of time or health may be an overwhelming misfortune to the person injured, and a needless one, for the risk of injury can be insured by the manufacturer and distributed among the public as a cost of doing business."). Influential early treatments of the risk-spreading rationale were Thayer, Liability Without Fault, 29 Harv. L. Rev. 801 (1916); Douglas, Vicarious Liability and Administration of Risk (pts. 1 and 2), 38 Yale L.J. 534, 720 (1929); Feezer, Capacity to Bear Loss as a Factor in the Decision in Certain Types of Tort Cases (pt. 1), 78 U. Pa. L. Rev. 805 (1930); James, Contribution Among Joint Tort Feasors: A Pragmatic Criticism, 54 Harv. L. Rev. 1156, 1157 (1941) (a rule which can "effect loss distribution over a large segment of society [generally should predominate over] a rule which will bring about a less effective distribution"); Prosser, The Implied Warranty of Merchantable Quality, 27 Minn. L. Rev. 117, 122–25 (1943); Friedmann, Social Insurance and the Principles of Tort Liability, 63 Harv. L. Rev. 241 (1949); Morris, Hazardous Enterprises and Risk Bearing Capacity, 61 Yale L.J. 1172 (1952); Green, The Individual's Protection Under Negligence Law: Risk Sharing, 47 Nw. U. L. Rev. 751 (1953).

[292] See, e.g., Escola v. Coca Cola Bottling Co., 150 P.2d 436, 440–41 (Cal. 1944) (Judge Traynor remarked that even without negligence, "public policy demands that responsibility be fixed wherever it will most effectively reduce the hazards to life and health inherent in defective products that reach the market," and that "[i]t is to the public interest to discourage the marketing of products having defects that are a menace to the public").

[293] See especially the cataloguing of rationales by Dean Prosser, in his treatise, note 276, above, and their elaboration by Justice Traynor, in *Greenman*, discussed in § 5.2, above.

[294] See, e.g., Brandenburger v. Toyota Motor Sales, U.S.A., Inc., 513 P.2d 268 (Mont. 1973). The various rationales for § 402A liability were summarized in Montgomery and Owen, Reflections on the Theory and Administration of Strict Tort Liability for Defective Products, 27 S.C. L. Rev. 803, 809–10 (1976):

> (1) Manufacturers convey to the public a general sense of product quality through the use of mass advertising and merchandising practices, causing consumers to rely for their protection upon the skill and expertise of the manufacturing community.
>
> (2) Consumers no longer have the ability to protect themselves adequately from defective products due to the vast number and complexity of products which must be "consumed" in order to function in modern society.
>
> (3) Sellers are often in a better position than consumers to identify the potential product risks, to determine the acceptable levels of such risks, and to confine the risks within those levels.
>
> (4) A majority of product accidents not caused by product abuse are probably attributable to the negligent acts or omissions of manufacturers at some stage of the manufacturing or marketing process, yet the difficulties of discovering and proving this negligence are often practicably insurmountable.
>
> (5) Negligence liability is generally insufficient to induce manufacturers to market adequately safe products.
>
> (6) Sellers almost invariably are in a better position than consumers to absorb or spread the costs of product accidents.
>
> (7) The costs of injuries flowing from typical risks inherent in products can fairly be put upon the enterprises marketing the products as a cost of their doing business, thus assuring that these enterprises will fully "pay their way" in the society from which they derive their profits.

most energized the rise of strict products liability in tort: (1) *Deterrence* (sometimes called "safety"), and (2) *Risk-Spreading* (also called "cost-spreading," "loss distribution," or "insurance").[295] Some courts and commentators emphasized deterrence, and others emphasized risk-spreading, but these two rationales predominated during the rise of modern products liability law, and both continue to be widely cited in support of holding manufacturers of defective products responsible for consumer injuries.

Deterrence

The case for deterrence seemed clear to most. Although there has been no shortage of skeptics,[296] many courts[297] and commentators[298] long have argued that raising the

---

[295] See Owen, The Moral Foundations of Products Liability Law: Toward First Principles, 68 Notre Dame L. Rev. 427, 430–31 (1993):

> During the 1960s and 1970s, as modern products liability doctrine first swept across the land, most of the theorizing that sought to justify and explain these developments [invoked two rationales]: (1) the need to provide compensation to injured consumers, through the mechanism of risk-spreading, by means of a third-party accident insurance system imposed on manufacturers by the courts, and (2) the need to improve product safety and restrain the power of manufacturers through rules designed to deter the production of dangerous products.

For earlier musings on tort law's "Siamese twin functions" of punishment and deterrence, on the one hand, and compensation and risk-spreading, on the other, see Morris, Rough Justice and Some Utopian Ideas, 24 U. Ill. L. Rev. 730 (1930).

For a more modern, Canadian perspective, see Trebilcock, The Social Insurance-Deterrence Dilemma of Modern North American Tort Law: A Canadian Perspective of the Liability Insurance Crisis, 24 San Diego L. Rev. 929 (1987).

[296] A considerable body of literature questions whether a move from negligence to a strict basis of products liability in fact improves product safety. See, e.g., Williams, Second Best: The Soft Underbelly of Deterrence Theory in Tort, 106 Harv. L. Rev. 932 (1993) (economic critique of deterrence rationale); Posner, Strict Liability: A Comment, 2 J. Legal Stud. 205, 211–12 (1973) ("whether a general substitution of strict for negligence liability would improve efficiency seems at this stage hopelessly conjectural; the question is at bottom empirical and the empirical work has not been done"). Compare Gifford, The Peculiar Challenges Posed by Latent Diseases Resulting from Mass Products, 64 Md. L. Rev. 613 (2005) (arguing that tort liability generally has little deterrent impact on manufacturers of toxic substances that cause latent diseases); Sugarman, Doing Away With Tort Law, 73 Cal. L. Rev. 555, 566 (1985) (citing 1983 Rand study by Eads and Reuter which found that some manufacturers treat specific case outcomes as "random noise"). See generally Products Liability Rest. § 2 cmt. *a* and Reporters' Note thereto.

Defense lawyers formerly argued that the standard of a design defect was too *vague* to be a meaningful deterrent and was often simply ignored. See Raleigh, The "State of the Art" in Product Liability: A New Look at an Old "Defense," 4 Ohio N.U. L. Rev. 249, 250–52 (1977) (General Motors' chief products liability lawyer's criticism of the then-prevailing rules of products liability). Others argued that manufacturers are generally as careful as reasonably possible anyway, regardless of the theory of liability, in order to safeguard their valuable reputations. See Plant, Strict Liability of Manufacturers for Injuries Caused by Defects in Products—An Opposing View, 24 Tenn. L. Rev. 938 (1957).

[297] See, e.g., Flagstaff Affordable Hous. Ltd. P'ship v. Design Alliance, Inc., 223 P.3d 664, 667 (Ariz. 2010) (en banc) ("[s]trict liability promotes product safety"); Horst v. Deere & Co., 769 N.W.2d 536, 542–43 (Wis. 2009); Calles v. Scripto-Tokai Corp., 864 N.E.2d 249, 262–63 (Ill. 2007); Larsen v. Pacesetter Sys., Inc., 837 P.2d 1273, 1287 (Haw. 1992) ("imposing liability on Pacesetter will promote product safety by encouraging manufacturers to anticipate and test for foreseeable defects likely to cause severe injury"). See generally Geistfeld, The Coherence of Compensation-Deterrence Theory in Tort Law, 61 DePaul L. Rev. 383, 392–93 (2012) ("the difficulty of proving negligence liability can substantially reduce its deterrence capabilities, a problem that courts have relied upon to justify rules of strict liability, including the critically important rule of strict liability governing the commercial distribution of defective products").

[298] See, e.g., Shavell, Strict Liability v. Negligence, 9 J. Legal Stud. 1 (1980); Tietz, Strict Products Liability, Design Defects and Corporate Decision-Making: Greater Deterrence Through Stricter Process, 38 Vill. L. Rev. 1361, 1365 (1993) ("Courts and commentators generally agree that strict products liability creates incentives for manufacturers to ensure greater product safety."); Stewart, Strict Liability for Defective Product Design: The Quest for a Well-Ordered Regime, 74 Brook. L. Rev. 1039, 1046 (2009) ("Deterrence of unsafe practices, whether in a manufacturing or design context, is even more important now in an era of rapidly changing technology, deregulation, and underfunding of regulatory agencies than it was in the 1960s."). On

standard of liability for manufacturers from negligence to strict liability will improve product safety.[299] To them, it seemed self-evident that forcing producers to internalize the accident costs resulting from defects in their products would force producers to take such costs into account and, hence, induce them to reduce or eliminate defects as much as reasonably possible. Safety, so important to the public, should thereby be improved.

In an early case example,[300] Mr. Huckleby fed his hogs grain that had been treated with a chemical seed disinfectant that contained mercury. The Huckleby family ate one of the hogs that had eaten the treated grain, and the children suffered blindness and paralysis from mercury poisoning. In approving a claim under § 402A against the disinfectant manufacturer for inadequately warning of the danger, the court of appeals remarked that "[p]ublic interest in human life, health and safety requires that the law give consumers maximum protection against dangerous product defects."[301] The court reasoned that allowing plaintiffs to proceed on the basis of strict liability in tort, without being required to prove negligence, "will cause manufacturers to take cautionary steps to prevent the marketing of dangerously defective products."[302]

Risk-Spreading

The other major rationale—risk-spreading—has also been instrumental in the development of strict products liability in tort.[303] If forced to absorb the costs of product accidents, manufacturers will strive to pass them along as much as possible to consumers through increased prices. In the process, manufacturers will relieve individual

---

deterrence generally, see G. Schwartz, Reality in the Economic Analysis of Tort Law: Does Tort Law Really Deter?, 42 UCLA L. Rev. 377 (1994).

[299] It appears quite clear that the increasing impact of products liability has caused many manufacturers to devote more attention, personnel, and money to product safety, and that products are generally safer today as a result. See Final Report, Interagency Task Force on Product Liability VI-47 (1977); N. Weber, Product Liability: The Corporate Response (Conference Bd. 1987); The Benefits of the Modernization of the Tort Law in the Context of the Social Movement for Improved Safety and Quality in the National Economy (Consumer Fed. of Am. Sept. 1987); Fuchsgruber v. Custom Accessories, Inc., 628 N.W.2d 833, 839 (Wis. 2001). See also Barton, Tort Reform, Innovation, and Playground Design, 58 Fla. L. Rev. 265 (2006) (products liability has radically improved the safety of playgrounds in recent decades).

[300] First Nat'l Bank v. Nor-Am Agric. Prods., Inc., 537 P.2d 682 (N.M. Ct. App. 1975).

[301] Id. at 695.

[302] Id., quoting Phillips v. Kimwood Mach. Co., 525 P.2d 1033, 1042 (Or. 1974), to the effect that "in the final analysis, the imposition of liability has a beneficial effect on manufacturers of defective products both in the care they take and in the warning they give." Note, however, that the *First Nat'l Bank* court takes the *Phillips* court's remarks somewhat out of context.

[303] See, e.g., Keeton, Products Liability—The Nature and Extent of Strict Liability, 1964 U. Ill. L.F. 693, 695 (1964):

> The principal reason that has now gained undisputed acceptance for shifting losses from users and consumers to manufacturers is the capacity of those engaged in the manufacturing enterprise to distribute the losses of the few to the many who purchase the products. Thus, the assumption is that the greater part of these losses suffered by the few victims will be shifted to the many consumers by way of higher prices for the products.

Even the Supreme Court of Michigan, which never did adopt § 402A, acknowledged the widespread acceptance of the risk-spreading rationale. See Prentis v. Yale Mfg. Co., 365 N.W.2d 176, 181 (Mich. 1984) (courts "have agreed that manufacturers can most effectively distribute the costs of injuries"). On the risk-spreading function of modern products liability law, see generally M. Rahdert, Covering Accident Costs—Insurance, Liability, and Tort Reform (1995). Compare Priest, The Invention of Enterprise Liability: A Critical History of the Intellectual Foundations of Modern Tort Law, 14 J. Legal Stud. 461 (1985) (risk-distribution rationale played decisive role in development of strict products liability in tort), with G. Schwartz, The Beginning and the Possible End of the Rise of Modern American Tort Law, 26 Ga. L. Rev. 601, 634–47 (1992) (loss-distribution rationale played important, but not decisive, role in development of strict products liability in tort). Quite possibly the most discerning article ever written on this subject was by then Assistant Professor Guido Calabresi, Some Thoughts on Risk Distribution and the Law of Torts, 70 Yale L.J. 499 (1961).

consumers of possibly crushing financial burdens of personal injuries and, at the same time, spread such losses widely among the consuming public. Because modern science and technology benefit society as a whole, the argument goes, all consumers fairly may be asked to pay slightly higher prices as premiums for insurance against the risk of often random, sometimes crushing harm when science and technology go awry. By spreading the costs of resulting product accidents in this manner, manufacturers thus provide all consumers, albeit indirectly, with mandatory accident insurance for harm from product defects. Moreover, because competition often prevents manufacturers from raising prices significantly, some portion of the accident costs will be spread, not unfairly, to the owners of the enterprises that made and sold the defective products.

Recent Theoretical Developments

Most courts and commentators in the 1960s and 1970s uncritically embraced deterrence, risk-spreading, and the other rationales for the doctrine of strict liability in tort for defective products,[304] frequently overlooking the doctrine's important limitations.[305] Even from the start, however, some judges[306] and commentators[307] found

---

[304] As for the courts, see, e.g., Santor v. A & M Karagheusian, Inc., 207 A.2d 305, 311 (N.J. 1965); McCormack v. Hankscraft Co., 154 N.W.2d 488 (Minn. 1967); Phillips v. Kimwood Mach. Co., 525 P.2d 1033 (Or. 1974); First Nat'l Bank v. Nor-Am Agric. Prods., Inc., 537 P.2d 682, 695 (N.M. Ct. App. 1975); Phipps v. General Motors Corp., 363 A.2d 955, 958 (Md. 1976).

As for the commentators, see, e.g., Keeton, Products Liability—The Nature and Extent of Strict Liability, 1964 Ill. L.F. 693 (1964); Traynor, The Ways and Meanings of Defective Products and Strict Liability, 32 Tenn. L. Rev. 363 (1965); Wade, Strict Tort Liability of Manufacturers, 19 Sw. L.J. 5 (1965); Keeton, Products Liability—Some Observations About Allocation of Risks, 64 Mich. L. Rev. 1329 (1966); Wade, On the Nature of Strict Tort Liability for Products, 44 Miss. L.J. 825 (1973); Vetri, Products Liability: The Developing Framework for Analysis, 54 Or. L. Rev. 293 (1975); Montgomery and Owen, Reflections on the Theory and Administration of Strict Tort Liability for Defective Products, 27 S.C. L. Rev. 803, 810 (1976) ("In combination, [the articulated rationales] present a compelling case for basing the liability of product sellers on some foundation other than fault.").

[305] Forgotten now by most courts and commentators was the conjunctive link, in early products liability theorizing by tort law scholars, between the expansion of a manufacturer's *liability* and a commensurate reduction of tort law *damages*. In 1955, Fleming James urged the adoption of "a rational scheme of strict liability for injurious products." James, Products Liability (pt. 2), 34 Tex. L. Rev. 192, 228 (1959). Yet such an enterprise liability scheme would have to be funded, which in James' view meant that victims might have to surrender their common-law right to damages for pain and suffering, which he considered predicated on a defendant having been a true "wrongdoer." James, Damages in Accident Cases, 41 Cornell L.Q. 582, 583 (1956). Further, a rational enterprise liability scheme might require victims to surrender compensation even for some of their *pecuniary* losses, because "accidents bring a net pecuniary loss to society . . . so that if the victim is made entirely whole, he will fare better than society and will not himself share the economic burden he is asking society to distribute." Id. at 584. The idea of limiting pain and suffering damages was shared by other scholars of the day, including such notables as Albert Ehrenzweig, Louis Jaffe, Leon Green, Marcus Plant, Clarence Morris, and Roger Traynor. See also Prosser, The Assault Upon the Citadel (Strict Liability to the Consumer), 69 Yale L.J. 1099, 1121 (1960). See generally V. Nolan and E. Ursin, Understanding Enterprise Liability ch. 15 (1995).

[306] See, e.g., Bailey v. Montgomery Ward & Co., 431 P.2d 108, 119 (Ariz. Ct. App. 1967) (Molloy, J., discerningly dissenting) ("The all-inclusive ring of 'strict liability' will cause an overextension (as here) of what is conceived by its progenitors to be a limited concept."); Markle v. Mulholland's Inc., 509 P.2d 529, 546 (Or. 1973) (Bryson, J., dissenting) ("I am not willing to place the court in a position of adopting a law based on a socialistic theory."); Cline v. Prowler Indus., 418 A.2d 968 (Del. 1980).

[307] See, e.g., Speidel, The Virginia "Anti-Privity" Statute: Strict Products Liability Under the Uniform Commercial Code, 51 Va. L. Rev. 804 (1965); Smyser, Products Liability and the American Law Institute: A Petition for Rehearing, 42 U. Det. L.J. 343 (1965); Lange, Compensation of Victims—A Pious and Misleading Platitude, 54 Cal. L. Rev. 1559 (1966). See generally Titus, Restatement (Second) of Torts Section 402A and The Uniform Commercial Code, 22 Stan. L. Rev. 713, 714–15 (1970) (summarizing criticisms). At least a couple of commentators saw the doctrine coming, and opposed it before it arrived. See, e.g., Peairs, The God in the Machine—A Study in Precedent, 29 B.U. L. Rev. 37 (1949); Plant, Strict Liability of Manufacturers for Injuries Caused by Defects in Products—An Opposing View, 24 Tenn. L. Rev. 938, 946 (1957) ("what is sometimes

fault with the new strict products liability in tort doctrine and its underlying rationales,[308] and, as the initial flush of excitement over the new strict liability doctrine subsided, commentators increasingly questioned the wisdom and logic of the doctrine's rationales. But the conventional justifications for a broad doctrine of strict manufacturer liability have not yet been consigned to the trash heap. Indeed, a fair number of courts[309] and commentators,[310] sometimes with a modern theoretical spin,[311] still cling tenaciously to the traditional rationales.[312]

---

euphemistically called 'social engineering' . . . frequently turns out to be crass expediency seeking its ends without any particular regard for basic principles").

[308] See, e.g., A. Schwartz, Products Liability and Judicial Wealth Redistribution, 51 Ind. L.J. 558 (1976); Epstein, Products Liability: The Search for the Middle Ground, 56 N.C. L. Rev. 643, 661 (1978) ("[t]o allow loss spreading issues covertly to dominate the structure of the tort law will only produce unsound results and bad general principles [and] will only bring the law into disrepute as the courts say one thing and do yet another"); R. Epstein, Modern Products Liability Law ch. 4 (1980); Owen, Rethinking the Policies of Strict Products Liability, 33 Vand. L. Rev. 681, 703–07 (1980); Epstein, Products Liability as an Insurance Market, 14 J. Legal Stud. 645 (1985); Priest, The Invention of Enterprise Liability: A Critical History of the Intellectual Foundations of Modern Tort Law, 14 J. Legal Stud. 461 (1985); Weinrib, The Insurance Justification and Private Law, 14 J. Legal Stud. 681 (1985); Huber, Safety and the Second Best: The Hazards of Public Risk Management in the Courts, 85 Colum. L. Rev. 277 (1985); Epstein, The Unintended Revolution in Product Liability Law, 10 Cardozo L. Rev. 2193, 2202 (1989) ("the anticontractual bias of both *Henningsen* and *Greenman* has proved to have devastating long-term consequences for the soundness of the product liability system"); Owen, Products Liability: Principles of Justice for the 21st Century, 11 Pace L. Rev. 63 (1990); Powers, A Modest Proposal to Abandon Strict Products Liability, 1991 U. Ill. L. Rev. 639, 639 (1991); Owen, The Moral Foundations of Products Liability Law: Toward First Principles, 68 Notre Dame L. Rev. 427, 484–93 (1993); Owen, Defectiveness Restated: Exploding the "Strict" Products Liability Myth, 1996 U. Ill. L. Rev. 743, 754–55; Feldman, Harm and Money: Against the Insurance Theory of Tort Compensation, 75 Tex. L. Rev. 1567 (1997); Ausness, An Insurance-Based Compensation System for Product-Related Injuries, 58 U. Pitt. L. Rev. 669 (1997); Ausness, Replacing Strict Liability with a Contract-Based Products Liability Regime, 71 Temp. L. Rev. 171 (1998); Henderson, Why Negligence Dominates Tort, 50 UCLA L. Rev. 377 (2002); Henderson, Echoes of Enterprise Liability in Product Design and Marketing Litigation, 87 Cornell L. Rev. 958 (2002); Twerski, Chasing the Illusory Pot of Gold at the End of the Rainbow: Negligence and Strict Liability in Design Defect Litigation, 90 Marq. L. Rev. 7 (2006); Watts, Fairness and Utility in Products Liability: Balancing Individual Rights and Social Welfare, 38 Fla. St. U. L. Rev. 597 (2011). See also Gerhart, The Death of Strict Liability, 56 Buff. L. Rev. 245 (2008); note 562, below. For problems with the risk-spreading rationale, see § 8.4, below.

[309] See, e.g., Cassidy v. China Vitamins, LLC, 120 N.E.3d 959, 968 (Ill. 2018), reaffirming the threefold rationales it offered in 1975: "(1) the public interest in human life and safety demands broad protection against the sale of defective products; (2) the manufacturer solicits and invites the use of his products by representing that they are safe and suitable for use; and (3) the losses caused by defectively dangerous products should be borne by those who have created the risks and reaped the profits by placing the products into commerce." See also Gaumer v. Rossville Truck & Tractor Co., 257 P.3d 292, 303–05 (Kan. 2011) (protection of injured party, deterrence, expectations protection); Flagstaff Affordable Hous. Ltd. P'ship v. Design Alliance, Inc., 223 P.3d 664, 667 (Ariz. 2010) (en banc); Sternhagen v. Dow Co., 935 P.2d 1139, 1145–46 (Mont. 1997).

[310] See, e.g., Conk, Punctuated Equilibrium: Why Section 402A Flourished and the *Third Restatement* Languished, 26 Rev. Litig. 799 (2007); Phillips, The Unreasonably Unsafe Product and Strict Liability, 72 Tenn. L. Rev. 833, 842 (2005); Wertheimer, The Biter Bit: Unknowable Dangers, The Third Restatement, and the Reinstatement of Liability Without Fault, 70 Brook. L. Rev. 889 (2005); Vandall, Constricting Products Liability: Reforms in Theory and Procedure, 48 Vill. L. Rev. 843, 858 (2003); Korzec, Dashing Consumer Hopes: Strict Products Liability and the Demise of the Consumer Expectations Test, 20 B.C. Int'l & Comp. L. Rev. 227 (1997); Prentice and Roszkowski, "Tort Reform" and the Liability "Revolution": Defending Strict Liability in Tort for Defective Products, 27 Gonz. L. Rev. 251 (1991–1992).

[311] See, e.g., Kysar, The Expectations of Consumers, 103 Colum. L. Rev. 1700, 1790 (2003); Keating, The Theory of Enterprise Liability and Common Law Strict Liability, 54 Vand. L. Rev. 1285 (2001); Keating, The Idea of Fairness in the Law of Enterprise Liability, 95 Mich. L. Rev. 1266 (1997); Croley and Hanson, Rescuing the Revolution: The Revived Case for Enterprise Liability, 91 Mich. L. Rev. 683 (1993); Hanson and Logue, The First Party Insurance Externality: An Economic Justification for Enterprise Liability, 76 Cornell L. Rev. 129 (1990); Attanasio, The Principle of Aggregate Autonomy and the Calabresian Approach to Products Liability, 74 Va. L. Rev. 677 (1988).

[312] For sensitive evaluations of the conventional rationales, see V. Nolan and E. Ursin, Understanding Enterprise Liability (1995); M. Rahdert, Covering Accident Costs—Insurance, Liability, and Tort Reform

§ 5.5 LIABILITY TESTS

"Strict" liability may tend to connote responsibility that is absolute, liability for which there is no excuse. Indeed, in tort law theorizing during the early decades of the twentieth century, long before *Greenman v. Yuba Power Products, Inc.*[313] and *Restatement (Second) of Torts* § 402A burst into the limelight in the 1960s, the terms "strict" and "absolute" were frequently interchanged in general discussions of enterprise liability for causing harm.[314] For example, in his famous concurring opinion in *Escola v. Coca Cola Bottling Co.*,[315] Justice Traynor remarked: "In my opinion it should now be recognized that a manufacturer incurs an absolute liability when an article that he has placed on the market, knowing that it is to be used without inspection, proves to have a defect that causes injury to human beings."[316] In truth, however, tort law provides no home for a ground of liability so extreme as to be truly "absolute."[317] Modern tort law understands that absolute safety is normally an impossible technological goal; and that, even when perfect safety is possible, it almost invariably is too expensive.[318] Risk, that is, inheres in life.[319]

Although some theorists in the 1950s still archaically equated liability without fault and "absolute" liability,[320] most tort law commentators by that time had begun to distinguish "strict" from "absolute" liability.[321] While absolute liability implies the complete absence of excuse, strict liability properly suggests only that responsibility is predicated on some basis other than an actor's fault, thus permitting defenses on such grounds as the victim's contributory fault or assumption of risk, the absence of proximate causation, and possibly even the actor's inability to prevent the harm.[322] "Manufacturers," it was understood by the 1950s, "are not expected to subsidize every act of carelessness on the part of consumers, nor compensate for every injury remotely connected with the use of a product."[323]

(1995); G. Schwartz, Mixed Theories of Tort Law: Affirming Both Deterrence and Corrective Justice, 75 Tex. L. Rev. 1801 (1997). See also Wright, The Principles of Product Liability, 26 Rev. of Litig. 1068 (2007).

313 377 P.2d 897 (Cal. 1963) (Traynor, J.).

314 See the discussion in Ehrenzweig, Negligence Without Fault (1951), reprinted, 54 Cal. L. Rev. 1422, 1450 n.1 (1966).

315 150 P.2d 436, 440 (Cal. 1944).

316 Id.

317 See Winfield, The Myth of Absolute Liability, 42 L.Q. Rev. 37 (1926). By the time he authored *Greenman* in 1963, Judge Traynor had come to appreciate the necessity of stating the liability standard in limited "strict" rather than "absolute" liability terms. See Traynor, The Ways and Meanings of Defective Products and Strict Liability, 32 Tenn. L. Rev. 363, 366 (1965) (liability requires that something be wrong with a product, that it be defective).

318 See Owen, Defectiveness Restated: Exploding the "Strict" Products Liability Myth, 1996 U. Ill. L. Rev. 743, 754–55; Huber, Safety and the Second Best: The Hazards of Public Risk Management in the Courts, 85 Colum. L. Rev. 277 (1985); G. Calabresi, The Costs of Accidents 17–18 (1970). For explanations in moral theory, see Owen, Philosophical Foundations of Fault in Tort Law, in Philosophical Foundations of Tort Law 201 (D. Owen ed., Oxford 1995); Owen, The Moral Foundations of Products Liability Law: Toward First Principles, 68 Notre Dame L. Rev. 427 (1993).

319 "Creating mere risks to the interests of others is an inherent and unavoidable consequence of every action, for every action entails harm (at least contingently) to others." Owen, Philosophical Foundations of Fault in Tort Law, in Philosophical Foundations of Tort Law 226 (D. Owen ed., Oxford 1995). On inherent product hazards, see § 10.3, below.

320 See, e.g., Gregory, Trespass to Negligence to Absolute Liability, 37 Va. L. Rev. 359 (1951).

321 See Ehrenzweig, Negligence Without Fault (1951), reprinted, 54 Cal. L. Rev. 1422, 1450 n.1 (1966).

322 See Winfield, The Myth of Absolute Liability, 42 Law Q. Rev. 37 (1926).

323 Wilson, Products Liability (pt. 2), 43 Cal. L. Rev. 809, 809 (1955).

"Strict" products liability in tort, indisputably, is *not* absolute liability. The doctrine of strict products liability in tort does not require manufacturers to ensure perfect product safety nor guarantee that consumers are never injured by their products, as discussed above.[324] Since absolute safety is not to be the rule, the task is normally one of line drawing between degrees of safety—of deciding how to separate products that are unacceptably dangerous from those that are safe enough. In designing products, manufacturers are properly required only to make reasonable trade-offs between safety, utility, and cost; once a product causes harm, courts do not demand safety perfection but merely assess the soundness of the manufacturer's trade-offs to ascertain whether they were reasonable. In short, the central liability question in most products liability cases can often be reduced to: "How safe is safe enough?"

The *Restatement (Second) of Torts* § 402A presents this cardinal issue of products liability law in terms of whether a product was sold in a "defective condition unreasonably dangerous" to the user or consumer. In litigation under § 402A, therefore, the question of whether a particular injury-producing product was too dangerous, or instead was safe enough, depends upon the meaning of the phrase "defective condition unreasonably dangerous." One of the most insightful early products liability decisions attempting to decode this central liability phrase in § 402A was *Phillips v. Kimwood Machine Co.*,[325] where the court noted that "courts continue to flounder while attempting to determine how one decides whether a product is 'in a defective condition unreasonably dangerous to the user.' " Observing that "[t]he problem with strict liability of products has been one of limitation," the court remarked: "No one wants absolute liability where all the article has to do is to cause injury. To impose liability there has to be something about the article which makes it dangerously defective without regard to whether the manufacturer was or was not at fault for such condition. A test for unreasonable danger is therefore vital."[326] And so the courts began to search for an appropriate yardstick or "test" of liability, a standard to apply to particular injury-producing products to determine if their level of safety was adequate or, instead, if they were sold in a "defective condition unreasonably dangerous" to persons foreseeably put at risk.

As liability under § 402A was beginning to be worked out in the 1960s and 1970s, courts and commentators generally sought a unitary liability standard or defect test—a single, general test that could determine defectiveness in every type of case. However, as products liability law and litigation matured in the 1980s and 1990s, and as its complexities were better understood, it became increasingly clear that liability standards should be contextually based, that is, that an appropriate test of liability depended upon the particular manner in which a product was unsafe. In recent decades, therefore, courts have moved toward using separate liability tests for manufacturing defects, design defects, and warning defects. As seen below, it has been the search for a proper definition of *design* defectiveness that has most confounded courts and commentators, and the evolution of strict tort liability tests has centered on judging the adequacy of a product's design.

The next three sections of this chapter examine the progression of liability tests for strict products liability in tort, from the early 1960s, under *Greenman v. Yuba Power Products, Inc.* and § 402A of the *Restatement (Second) of Torts*, through the late 1990s

---

[324] See § 5.3, above.

[325] 525 P.2d 1033 (Or. 1974).

[326] Id. at 1035–36.

when the *Restatement (Third) of Torts: Products Liability* reformulated those tests, to the present time. Section 5.6 first explores the development, meaning, and problems of the "consumer expectations" test, the first principal test of products liability. Section 5.7 examines the "risk-utility" test, which in design and warning cases has displaced the consumer expectations test in many states. The last liability test section in this chapter, § 5.8, investigates a variety of alternative liability tests that courts have used as modern products liability law has evolved and matured. This last section considers various alterations in § 402A's verbal standard of "defective condition unreasonably dangerous," examines various ways in which some courts have combined the two principal tests (consumer expectations and risk-utility), and considers the movement toward defect-specific liability tests. The discussion of these tests in this chapter offers an overview of each of these tests. Detailed treatments of the tests as courts increasingly apply them in the particular contexts of defects in manufacture, design, and warnings are left to the chapters on those particular topics.[327] The liability standards in the *Third Restatement* are treated in § 6.5 and in the chapters addressing particular types of defect.[328]

§ 5.6 THE CONSUMER EXPECTATIONS TEST

In attempting to ascertain the meaning of § 402A's liability standard—"defective condition unreasonably dangerous"—the first place courts and commentators looked for guidance was the Reporter's Comments that Dean William Prosser wrote to that section of the *Restatement (Second) of Torts*. There, in comments *g* and *i*, lies the basis for the first important liability test for establishing strict products liability in tort—the consumer expectations test.[329] Comment *g* to § 402A, entitled "defective condition," states in part as follows:

> The rule stated in this Section applies only where the product is, at the time it leaves the seller's hands, *in a condition not contemplated by the ultimate consumer*, which will be unreasonably dangerous to him.[330]

---

[327] See chs. 7 (manufacturing defects), 8 (design defects), and 9 (warning defects), below.

[328] See id.

[329] On this test, see Wertheimer, The Biter Bit Unknowable Dangers, the Third Restatement, and the Reinstatement of Liability Without Fault, 70 Brook. L. Rev. 889 (2005), critiqued in Henderson and Twerski, A Fictional Tale of Unintended Consequences: A Response to Professor Wertheimer, 70 Brook. L. Rev. 939 (2005); Kysar, The Expectations of Consumers, 103 Colum. L. Rev. 1700, 1790 (2003); Phillips, Consumer Expectations, 53 S.C. L. Rev. 1047 (2002); Korzec, Dashing Consumer Hopes: Strict Products Liability and the Demise of the Consumer Expectations Test, 20 B.C. Int'l & Comp. L. Rev. 227 (1997); Little, The Place of Consumer Expectations in Product Strict Liability Actions for Defectively Designed Products, 61 Tenn. L. Rev. 1189 (1994); Kennedy, The Role of the Consumer Expectations Test Under Louisiana's Products Liability Tort Doctrine, 69 Tul. L. Rev. 117, 162 (1994); Bernacchi, A Behavioral Model for Imposing Strict Liability in Tort: The Importance of Analyzing Product Performance in Relation to Consumer Expectation and Frustration, 47 U. Cinn. L. Rev. 43 (1978); Hubbard, Reasonable *Human* Expectations: A Normative Model For Imposing Strict Liability for Defective Products, 29 Mercer L. Rev. 465 (1978); Fischer, Products Liability—The Meaning of Defect, 39 Mo. L. Rev. 339, 348–52 (1974); Shapo, A Representational Theory of Consumer Protection: Doctrine, Function and Legal Liability for Product Disappointment, 60 Va. L. Rev. 1109 (1974); Dickerson, Products Liability: How Good Does a Product Have to Be?, 42 Ind. L.J. 301 (1967); Rheingold, What Are the Consumer's "Reasonable Expectations"?, 22 Bus. Law. 589 (1967).

Compare Masterman and Viscusi, The Specific Consumer Expectations Test for Product Defects, 95 Ind. L.J. 183 (2020) (proposing limiting the consumer expectations test to specific instances where a consumer expects a product to reduce a particular risk or provide a particular benefit and the product instead increases risk or harms rather than benefits the consumer); Comment, The Resurrection of the Consumer Expectations Test: A Regression in American Products Liability, 26 U. Miami Int'l & Comp. L. Rev. 525 (2019).

[330] Rest. (2d) Torts § 402A cmt. *g* (emphasis added).

Thus, according to this Comment, the term "defective condition" in § 402A means "a condition not contemplated by the ultimate consumer, which will be unreasonably dangerous to him." Comment *i*, entitled "unreasonably dangerous," explains the meaning of the latter phrase:

> The rule stated in this Section applies only where the defective condition of the product makes it unreasonably dangerous to the user or consumer. Many products cannot possibly be made entirely safe. . . . That is not what is meant by "unreasonably dangerous" in this Section. The article sold must be *dangerous to an extent beyond that which would be contemplated by the ordinary consumer who purchases it*, with the ordinary knowledge common to the community as to its characteristics.[331]

In short, to be "unreasonably dangerous" under § 402A, as well as "defective," a product must be more dangerous than an ordinary consumer would expect.

Yet how these two terms—"defective condition" and "unreasonably dangerous"—interrelate is problematic. The last phrase of the comment *g* definition and the first sentence in comment *i*, both set out above, suggest that the terms "defective condition" and "unreasonably dangerous" mean different things, and that a plaintiff must separately prove each in order to prevail. Indeed, the compound black-letter phrase, "defective condition unreasonably dangerous," itself suggests such a two-part interpretation, as an array of courts,[332] at least one state statute,[333] and a number of leading products liability lawyers[334] have suggested.

But the view that § 402A's liability test requires two separate showings, as elsewhere explained,[335] is decidedly problematic, if not downright wrong. Quite plainly, the "unreasonably dangerous" definition in comment *i* is virtually identical to the "defective condition" definition in comment *g*: both halves of § 402A's "defective condition unreasonably dangerous" liability standard ultimately are defined in terms of *dangerous beyond a consumer's contemplations*. For this reason, many courts interpreting § 402A in the 1960s and 1970s concluded that the full definitional phrase established a *single* test of liability based on a single standard of product safety measured by "consumer expectations."[336] This is surely the sounder view.

---

[331] Id. cmt. *i* (emphasis added).

[332] See § 5.3 notes 112 and 113, above.

[333] See Ark. Code Ann. § 16–116–101(a)(2) (strict liability for harm from sale of product "in a defective condition which rendered it unreasonably dangerous"). Compare Tenn. Code Ann. § 29–28–105 (product must be "in a defective condition or unreasonably dangerous").

[334] That some products liability lawyers so interpret § 402A is seen in a products liability anthology of state-by-state descriptions of products liability law written by practitioners from each state. See Product Liability Desk Reference: A Fifty-State Compendium (M. Daller and N. Daller, eds., 2022 ed.) (*Colorado*: a plaintiff must prove a product is in a defective condition and unreasonably dangerous; *Idaho*: which has adopted § 402A, a plaintiff must prove the product is defective and unreasonably dangerous; *Maryland*: proof of a design defect requires that a product is both in a defective condition and unreasonably dangerous).

[335] See § 5.3 (*Elements*), above, and § 5.8, below.

[336] Many early courts defined "defective condition unreasonably dangerous" according to a single consumer expectations standard, drawing from comments *g* and *i*. See, e.g., Heaton v. Ford Motor Co., 435 P.2d 806, 808 (Or. 1967); Dunham v. Vaughan & Bushnell Mfg. Co., 247 N.E.2d 401 (Ill. 1969); Lunt v. Brady Mfg. Corp., 475 P.2d 964 (Ariz. Ct. App. 1970); Vincer v. Esther Williams All-Aluminum Swimming Pool Co., 230 N.W.2d 794 (Wis. 1975).

Basis of the Consumer Expectations Test

Consumer expectation protection was a logical initial foundation for strict products liability under § 402A. It will be recalled that modern products liability law, and § 402A in particular, evolved out of the law of warranty which by the twentieth century had been absorbed into the law of sales and contracts.[337] One of the most basic goals of law in general,[338] and the most fundamental pillar of contract law,[339] is the protection of the expectations—the *reasonable* expectations—of the contracting parties. Warranty law is based upon a manufacturer's explicit and implicit representations made to consumers in sales transactions, and the law reasonably protects consumer expectations predictably generated from such representations.[340] Because the warranty law cases that paved the way for § 402A aimed to protect a consumer's ordinary or reasonable expectations, this was the natural liability test for the new tort doctrine.[341]

Powerful reasons support protection of a consumer's expectations of product safety that arise from the safety representations of a manufacturer or other seller, whether

---

[337] See § 5.2, above.

[338] See R. Pound, Social Control Through Law 114 (1942, 1968 reprint):

> In civilized society men must be able to assume that those with whom they deal in the general intercourse of society will act in good faith and hence
>
> (a) will make good reasonable expectations which their promises or other conduct reasonably create; [and]
>
> (b) will carry out their undertakings according to the expectations which the moral sentiment of the community attaches thereto. . . .

See also Owen, Expectations in Tort, 43 Ariz. St. L.J. 1287, 1295 (2011):

> A person's ability to control his or her life, to live effectively within a dynamic world, . . . depends upon the extent to which the person's vision of the world is true. When the world operates in a manner contrary to what people expect, they are vulnerable to both intentionally and accidentally inflicted harm. Truth—expectation fulfillment—is thus fundamentally important to the freedom that humans need to protect themselves from harm, and fault for harm is often rooted in how and why the expectations of an actor and a victim departed from the truth.

[339] See 1 J. Perillo, Corbin on Contracts § 1.1 (rev. ed. 1993):

> § 1.1 The Main Purpose of Contract Law is the Realization of Reasonable Expectations Induced by Promises
>
> The underlying purpose of law and government is human happiness and contentment, to be brought about by the satisfaction of human desires in the highest practicable degree. . . .
>
> That portion of the field of law that is classified and described as the law of contracts attempts the realization of reasonable expectations that have been induced by the making of a promise. . . .
>
> The law does not attempt the realization of every expectation that has been induced by a promise; the expectation must be a reasonable one. . . .

[340] See, e.g., Markle v. Mulholland's Inc., 509 P.2d 529, 532 (Or. 1973), where the majority remarked that consumer expectations are "the result of the manufacturer's or seller's placing the article in the stream of commerce with the intention that it be purchased. This expectation is given legal sanction by the law through an assumption that the seller, by so placing the article in the stream of commerce, has represented that the article is not unreasonably dangerous if put to its intended use." Further, "[o]ne can only determine what a purchaser had a right to expect by the implications express or inherent in the sale to him. These implications are analogous to those underlying a representation of merchantable quality." Id. at 534. Consider also the powerful analysis of Marshall Shapo, A Representational Theory of Consumer Protection: Doctrine, Function and Legal Liability for Product Disappointment, 60 Va. L. Rev. 1109, 1370 (1974) ("liability . . . should center initially and principally on the portrayal of the product which is made, caused to be made or permitted by the seller. . . . viewed in the context of the impression reasonably received by the consumer from . . . advertising, [the product's appearance, its usual functions, and] other ways in which the product projects an image on the mind of the consumer").

[341] See Fischer, Products Liability—The Meaning of Defect, 39 Mo. L. Rev. 339, 348 (1974). Judge Roger Traynor perceptively observed that the consumer contemplation test reflected the "surprise element of danger." Traynor, The Ways and Meanings of Defective Products and Strict Liability, 32 Tenn. L. Rev. 363, 370 (1965).

those representations be express or implied.[342] When making safety "promises" in an effort to sell its products, a manufacturer seeks to convince potential buyers that its affirmations are valuable because they are true. Safety information is valuable to users because it provides a "frame of reference" that permits a user to shift his or her limited cognitive and other resources away from self-protection toward the pursuit of other goals—which in turn shifts responsibility for protecting the user to the manufacturer. In this manner, true safety information adds value to a product by enhancing the user's autonomy, for which value the consumer fairly pays a price. So, if the information is not true but false, the purchaser loses significant autonomy as well as the benefit of the bargain. Since an important purpose of the law is to promote autonomy, and the equality of the buyer's and seller's interests as reflected in their deal, the law fairly may demand that the seller rectify the underlying falsity and resulting inequality in the exchange transaction if harm results.

Like most other standards of tort law, the consumer expectations test is an *objective* test: it is based on the average, normal, or "ordinary" expectations of a reasonable person.[343] This follows from § 402A's grounding in warranty and contract law, where the law protects only the "reasonable" or "justified" expectations of the contracting parties, as previously mentioned, and not those that arise from idiosyncratic fits of fancy. An objective standard is plainly necessary,[344] because a manufacturer in its design decisions is bound to "legislate" an amount of safety that is optimal for all consumers as a class, and it cannot be expected to design products separately for every user's secret preferences.[345]

An early example of a court seizing on the consumer expectations test as the liability test for § 402A is *Vincer v. Esther Williams All-Aluminum Swimming Pool Co.*[346] There, a 2-year-old child climbed up the ladder of an above-ground swimming pool, fell in, and suffered brain damage in the water. In the strict tort claim against the manufacturer of the pool, the plaintiff claimed that the design of the pool was defective because the manufacturer failed to take the simple step of adding a self-closing and self-latching gate at the top of the ladder to prevent small children from entering the pool. On appeal from a dismissal of the plaintiff's claim, the Wisconsin Supreme Court, relying on the portions of comments *g* and *i* set out above, remarked that "the test in Wisconsin of whether a product contains an unreasonably dangerous defect depends upon the reasonable expectations of the ordinary consumer concerning the characteristics of this type of

---

[342] See Shapo, A Representational Theory of Consumer Protection: Doctrine, Function and Legal Liability for Product Disappointment, 60 Va. L. Rev. 1109 (1974); Owen, Expectations in Tort, 43 Ariz. St. L.J. 1287 (2011).

[343] Rest. (2d) Torts § 402A comment *i* is phrased in terms of the "ordinary" consumer "with the ordinary knowledge common to the community." See, e.g., Sigler v. American Honda Motor Co., 532 F.3d 469, 483–84 (6th Cir. 2008) (Tenn. law) ("ordinary consumer having ordinary, 'common knowledge' "); Liggett Grp. Inc. v. Davis, 973 So.2d 467, 475 (Fla. Dist. Ct. App. 2007) (defect "issue is based on an objective standard and not the viewpoint of any particular consumer"); Benjamin v. Wal-Mart Stores, Inc., 61 P.3d 257, 268 (Or. Ct. App. 2002) ("The relevant question is not what consumers *should* expect or how a product *should* perform; rather, the jury is to determine 'the basically factual question of what reasonable consumers *do* expect from the product.' ").

[344] *But see* L. Green, Strict Liability Under Sections 402A and 402B: A Decade of Litigation, 54 Tex. L. Rev. 1185, 1211 (1976) ("[Are] not the expectations of the specific injured consumer enough? He must be given credit for expecting a product that was reasonably safe. He certainly did not expect an unreasonably dangerous product.").

[345] See Owen, The Moral Foundations of Products Liability Law: Toward First Principles, 68 Notre Dame L. Rev. 427, 468–84 (1993).

[346] 230 N.W.2d 794 (Wis. 1975).

product. If the average consumer would reasonably anticipate the dangerous condition of the product and fully appreciate the attendant risk of injury, it would not be unreasonably dangerous and defective."[347] Noting that "[t]his is an objective test and is not dependent upon the knowledge of the particular injured consumer,"[348] the court affirmed dismissal of the plaintiff's claim. The pool was not defective, reasoned the court, because an average consumer could not help but comprehend the danger to young children from the obvious absence of a self-latching gate.[349]

During the 1960s and 1970s, the consumer expectations test was the dominant standard of defectiveness used by the courts, despite a growing number that rejected it as the sole or principal test of strict products liability.[350] And despite the drawbacks of using consumer expectations as a liability standard, many courts, sometimes pursuant to legislation,[351] still use this standard today, either by itself or combined in some fashion with risk-utility.[352]

---

[347] Id. at 798.

[348] Id. (also noting that a consumer's personal knowledge might bear on contributory negligence).

[349] Id. at 799.

[350] See Fischer, Products Liability—The Meaning of Defect, 39 Mo. L. Rev. 339, 348–52 (1974) (noting that its use as the sole test of defectiveness involves "serious drawbacks" and, "[a]s a consequence, an increasing number of courts . . . have rejected this test in a number of situations").

[351] See, e.g., Ind. Code Ann. § 34–20–4–1 (a product is defective if its condition is "not contemplated by reasonable persons"); Tenn. Code Ann. § 29–28–102(8) ("unreasonably dangerous" means dangerous beyond ordinary consumer's expectations); Utah Code Ann. § 78B–6–702 (" '[U]nreasonably dangerous' means that the product was dangerous to an extent beyond which would be contemplated by the ordinary and prudent buyer, consumer, or user of that product in that community considering the product's characteristics . . . together with any actual knowledge, training, or experience possessed by that particular buyer, user, or consumer.").

[352] See, e.g., Flaherty v. E-Go Bike, LLC, 2022 WL 445428, at *4 (M.D. Fla. 2022) (electric bike stopping suddenly, throwing plaintiff over handlebars onto concrete, causing severe injuries, showed that bike "failed to perform as safely as an ordinary consumer would expect"); Pilliod v. Monsanto Co., 282 Cal. Rptr. 3d 679, 704 (Ct. App. 2021) (consumer expectations test appropriate where advertisements portrayed Roundup as harmful only to plants, not people or pets, and safe to use without protective gear or other precautions; "[O]rdinary consumers do have expectations about whether they will develop cancer as a result of using widely sold and advertised herbicides. Their expectation is they will not."); Ford Motor Co. v. Trejo, 402 P.3d 649, 658 (Nev. 2017) (crushed Ford Excursion's roof "failed to perform in a manner reasonably expected in light of its nature and intended function and was more dangerous than would be contemplated by the ordinary user having the ordinary knowledge available in the community"; declining to adopt Rest. 3d § 2(b)); Bradley v. Ameristep, Inc., 800 F.3d 205, 211 (6th Cir. 2015) (Tenn. law) ("ordinary consumer would not expect [hunting treestand] ratchet straps to catastrophically fail after only a few months of exposure to the elements"; after improperly excluding plaintiffs' expert witness, district court further erred by not proceeding under consumer expectation test with lay testimony); Wilson Sporting Goods Co. v. Hickox, 59 A.3d 1267, 1275 (D.C. 2013); Gaumer v. Rossville Truck and Tractor Co., Inc., 257 P.3d 292, 303 (Kan. 2011); Horst v. Deere & Co., 769 N.W.2d 536, 550 (Wis. 2009) ("consumer contemplation test is the proper standard for all strict products liability cases") (yet, in Wis. Stat. Ann. § 895.047(1)(a), the legislature replaced the consumer expectations standard with the Third Restatement's risk-utility standard); Mikolajczyk v. Ford Motor Co., 901 N.E.2d 329, 352–53 (Ill. 2008) (both consumer-expectation and risk utility tests "have their place in our law . . . . If the evidence . . . implicate[s] the risk-utility test, the broader test, which incorporates . . . consumer expectations, is to be applied . . . ."); Allison v. Merck & Co., 878 P.2d 948, 952 (Nev. 1994) (measles, mumps, and rubella vaccine that caused blindness, deafness, and mental retardation did not perform as reasonably expected); Jarke v. Jackson Prods., 631 N.E.2d 233 (Ill. App. Ct. 1994) (side rim of welding mask funneled molten welding slag into ear); Lester v. Magic Chef, Inc., 641 P.2d 353 (Kan. 1982).

The Reporters for the Products Liability Restatement listed Alaska, Arkansas, Hawaii, Nebraska, Oklahoma, and Wisconsin as states then still having an undiluted, independent consumer expectations basis for products liability in tort. See Products Liability Rest. § 2(b), Reporters' Notes on cmt. *d*, § II(D), at 76. This conclusion was challenged by John Vargo, who concluded that the consumer expectations test was then applied in some manner in half the states. Vargo, The Emperor's New Clothes: The American Law Institute Adorns a "New Cloth" for Section 402A Products Liability Design Defects—A Survey of the States Reveals a Different Weave, 26 U. Mem. L. Rev. 493, 556 & 951 (1996) (index 2). For the Reporters' more recent tally of the states, see Henderson and Twerski, Manufacturers' Liability for Defective Product Designs: The Triumph of Risk-

Problems with the Consumer Expectations Test

Despite the strength of consumer expectation protection as a theoretical foundation of products liability law, a number of serious, practical obstacles interfere with attempting to use consumer expectations as the primary test of strict liability in tort across products liability law.[353]

Obvious Dangers

First, the consumer expectations test undesirably bars consumers from recovery in virtually every case in which a danger was obvious, even if the manufacturer could easily and cheaply have removed a serious danger.[354] As illustrated by *Vincer*, the above-ground swimming-pool case discussed above, obvious product dangers are ipso facto "contemplated" by consumers. Put another way, because consumers' safety expectations are almost never frustrated by obvious product dangers, the expectancy test almost always precludes liability in such cases.

For example, in *Hartman v. Miller Hydro Co.*,[355] the defendant manufactured and sold a bottle-washing machine with an unguarded drive shaft to the plaintiff's employer, the Pepsi Cola Bottling Company. The plaintiff, an assistant manager responsible for plant safety, leaned over the revolving shaft to set up some fallen bottles and was injured when his trousers were pulled into the machine. Applying the expectancy test of comment *i*, the court upheld a judgment for the defendant on the plaintiff's § 402A claim. Dismissing the plaintiff's testimony that he did not comprehend the danger in leaning against the exposed drive shaft, the court noted that another employee had previously been caught in the same shaft. "Thus, it cannot be said that a danger existed which was beyond contemplation of an ordinary user. The danger was obvious."[356] Many other cases similarly have denied recovery under the consumer expectations test to plaintiffs injured by obvious product dangers.[357]

Utility, 74 Brooklyn L. Rev. 1061 (2009). See also Branham v. Ford Motor Co., 701 S.E.2d 5, 14–15 & n.14 (S.C. 2010) (adopting risk-utility balancing in design defects cases; surveying cases and identifying ten jurisdictions then still employing consumer expectations as the exclusive liability standard (Idaho, Ind., Kan., Neb., Nev., Okla., R.I., Vt., Wis., and Wyo.)). At least Wisconsin should be removed from the consumer expectations list since its legislature adopted the Restatement definitions of products liability in 2011. Wis. Stat. Ann. § 895.047(1)(a). Yet classifying jurisdictions by defect standards is a perilous task because design defect liability standards (and warning defect standards, to a lesser extent) across the nation have long been moving, often in jagged steps, away from consumer expectations and toward risk-utility balancing. In addition, many jurisdictions apply a consumer expectations standard to certain limited types of products, such as food and drink, see § 7.5, below, and used products, see § 16.5, below.

[353] See Owen, Expectations in Tort, 43 Ariz. St. L.J. 1287 (2011); Davis, Design Defect Liability: In Search of a Standard of Responsibility, 39 Wayne L. Rev. 1217, 1236–37 (1993).

[354] This is conventionally recognized as an inherent weakness in this test. See Prosser and Keeton on Torts § 99, at 698 ("Under this test, a victim could never recover for harm suffered as a result of a design hazard that was open or obvious or one with respect to which the purchaser was adequately informed."). *But see* Phillips, Consumer Expectations, 53 S.C. L. Rev. 1047, 1049 (2002) (characterizing as "semantic" the consumer expectations test's foreclosure of relief to persons injured by obvious dangers).

[355] 499 F.2d 191 (10th Cir. 1974) (Kan. law).

[356] Id. at 194.

[357] See, e.g., Calles v. Scripto-Tokai Corp., 864 N.E.2d 249, 257 (Ill. 2007) (utility lighter "performed as an ordinary consumer would expect"); Crosswhite v. Jumpking, Inc., 411 F. Supp. 2d 1228, 1231 (D. Or. 2006) ("an ordinary consumer buys and uses a trampoline to jump on it, and a design that allows for such activity is exactly that which is contemplated by an ordinary consumer or user of a trampoline"); Ahrens v. Ford Motor Co., 340 F.3d 1142 (10th Cir. 2003) (Okla. law) (absence of seatbelt on tractor from which decedent was thrown); Halliday v. Sturm, Ruger & Co., 792 A.2d 1145, 1158 (Md. 2002) (death by self-inflicted gunshot wound: "There was no malfunction of the gun; regrettably, it worked exactly as it was designed and intended to work and as any ordinary consumer would have expected it to work."); Bruner v. Anheuser-Busch, Inc., 153

Whose Expectations?

While the consumer expectations test may work satisfactorily in some cases where the accident victim bought the product, it often fails to provide meaningful guidance in cases involving other victims of product accidents. The first question in this regard concerns whether the pertinent expectations are those of the purchaser or of the ultimate consumer, if the two are different. Under the law of contracts, the relevant expectations, of course, are those of the purchaser, a contracting party, which is the standard set forth in § 402A comment *i*.[358] But, even though § 402A grew out of the law of warranty, it sets forth a liability standard for the law of *torts*, not contracts, and tort law duties normally extend to all foreseeable victims, as suggested by comment *g*.[359]

When accident victims are persons whose safety is the responsibility of others—children, patients, employees, or innocent bystanders—the consumer expectations standard poses particular problems. The issue in such cases is whether the expectations of the victim (the child, patient, employee, or bystander) or those of the buyer (the parent, doctor, employer, or user) should govern. Where the safety custodian, but not the ward, can best evaluate and control the risk, as often is the case with parents, doctors, adult users, and sometimes employers, courts generally have applied the expectations of the custodian, rather than the ward whose safety expectations are usually vague or nonexistent.[360] This often may be a proper result in such cases, since responsibility in tort frequently and properly is placed on those responsible for controlling risk.[361] Yet, if custodians generally are aware of hazards that manufacturers easily can eliminate, using a custodian's rather than ward's expectations might often unfairly bar recovery.

A good example of the parent-child context is *Bellotte v. Zayre Corp.*,[362] in which a 5-year-old child was burned when his cotton pajama top ignited while he was playing with matches. In deciding whether the pajamas were "unreasonably dangerous to the user or consumer" because the fabric had not been treated with an effective fire-retardant substance, the court addressed the question of whether the safety characteristics of the pajamas should be measured according to the expectations of the "consuming" child or the "purchasing" parent. Plaintiffs contended that "the test should be whether they were dangerous to an extent beyond that which would be contemplated by the ordinary five-year-old child." The court did not agree: "Children of that age do not contemplate even the unavoidable dangers of cotton pajamas and their flammable

---

F. Supp. 2d 1358 (S.D. Fla. 2001) (harm from over-consumption of beer; because dangers of alcohol abuse are common knowledge, Budweiser beer is not dangerous beyond consumer's expectations); Menard v. Newhall, 373 A.2d 505, 507 (Vt. 1977) (plaintiff's eye put out in BB gun fight: "A BB gun which is neither defectively designed nor manufactured is not dangerous beyond that which would be contemplated by the ordinary consumer. . . . A warning by the defendant Daisy that a BB gun, if fired at a person, could injure an eye, is nothing that even a 7-year-old child does not already know.").

On obvious dangers, see § 10.2, below.

[358] Comment *i* to § 402A states: "The article sold must be dangerous to an extent beyond that which would be contemplated by *the ordinary consumer who purchases it* . . . ." (emphasis added).

[359] Comment *g* to § 402A refers to "a condition not contemplated by *the ultimate consumer*" (emphasis added).

[360] The user-bystander situation presents analogous issues. See, e.g., Horst v. Deere & Co., 769 N.W.2d 536, 550 (Wis. 2009) (rejecting adoption of a "bystander contemplation test"); Ewen v. McLean Trucking Co., 706 P.2d 929 (Or. 1985) (pedestrian, struck by truck, could not recover as "consumer" under comment *i*); Cornelius v. Bay Motors Inc., 484 P.2d 299 (Or. 1971). See § 5.3 (*Types of Plaintiffs*), above.

[361] See, e.g., Owen, Rethinking the Policies of Strict Products Liability, 33 Vand. L. Rev. 681, 711–13 (1980).

[362] 352 A.2d 723 (N.H. 1976) (Grimes, J.).

characteristics. There would therefore be no base from which to determine unreasonableness and the seller would become an insurer."[363] Thus, in injuries to young children, the parent or other buyer's (or user's) expectations ordinarily should control.[364]

In the doctor-patient situation, the expectations issue is likely to be more complicated and often depends on the type of product that fails and the reason for its failure. If a surgical needle breaks while being inserted into a patient's body, the relevant expectations surely are the doctor's, not the patient's: it is the doctor (together with the manufacturer) who controls the risk; and it is the doctor, not the patient, who knows about the strength of such needles and what forces they fairly should be expected to withstand.[365] But if a patient is injured by the failure of a medical device or implant, such as a pacemaker or breast implant, the expectations issue is not so clear. Assuming that the doctor fully apprised the patient of all material risks and benefits of the medical device, the informed patient's reasonable expectations of the device's limitations seemingly should control.[366] But real-world medical care often differs quite materially from this model of ideal counseling, and in cases where the doctor, not the patient, makes the informed choice of risks and benefits, probably the doctor's expectations should be determinative. Not unfairly, in such a case, a patient may properly look solely to the doctor for proper counseling and recovery under the medical malpractice doctrine of informed consent.[367]

Employer-employee cases present other problems. While employees are in many respects dependent on employers to maintain workplaces that are safe, including the selection of safe industrial machinery and chemicals, manufacturers sometimes can best provide protection by warning employees directly of a risk. For example, in *Jackson v. Coast Paint & Lacquer Co.*,[368] the plaintiff, injured while spray-painting the inside of a tank car when the accumulated paint fumes ignited unexpectedly, sued the paint manufacturer for failing to warn of this risk. The defendant contended that no warning was necessary since plaintiff's employer knew of the risk, even if plaintiff did not. Holding for the plaintiff, the court reasoned that warnings could have been placed effectively on the paint container labels. The "community" whose expectations were

---

[363] Id. at 725.

[364] See also Horst v. Deere & Co., 769 N.W.2d 536, 553–54 n.24 (Wis. 2009) (surveying cases; courts "resoundingly" reject arguments that "the expectations of an ordinary child . . . should govern[; instead] it is the ordinary consumer or user's expectations that govern"); Calles v. Scripto-Tokai Corp., 864 N.E.2d 249, 256 (Ill. 2007) (child died after using lighter to start a fire; since ordinary consumer of lighter is adult, use and safety expectations "must be viewed from the point of view of the adult consumer"); Welch v. Scripto-Tokai Corp., 651 N.E.2d 810 (Ind. Ct. App. 1995) (3-year-old ignited his pajamas with disposable butane cigarette lighter; *held*, ordinary consumer is adult, and adults expect lighters to generate a flame); Brawner v. Liberty Indus., 573 S.W.2d 376 (Mo. Ct. App. 1978) (gasoline container lacking child-proof lid not unreasonably dangerous beyond the expectations of the ordinary consumer, because it was designed for adult use only).

[365] See Ethicon, Inc. v. Parten, 520 S.W.2d 527, 533 (Tex. Civ. App. 1975) (surgical needle broke in patient's body).

[366] See V. Mueller & Co. v. Corley, 570 S.W.2d 140, 145 (Tex. Civ. App. 1978) (silicone breast implant broke in patient's body; "The defective condition in the prosthesis in question rendered it unreasonably dangerous to Mrs. Corley, not to her physician, Dr. Leeves. The appropriate question for the jury, therefore, was whether the defective condition was one which was not contemplated by the user, the 'ultimate consumer' [such that the] trial court properly keyed its instructions to the mind of the person who would be injured by the dangerous condition of the product.").

[367] See Prosser and Keeton on Torts § 32, at 189–93.

[368] 499 F.2d 809, 812 (9th Cir. 1974) (Mont. law).

relevant, under comment *i*, consisted of the painters who would be exposed to the danger, not the employers who bought the paint.[369]

Vagueness

A third and especially problematic aspect of the consumer expectations test lies in the vagueness of consumer expectations in many contexts.[370] Particularly in considering the design adequacy of a complex product—such as an automobile, a pharmaceutical drug, or other chemical product—consumers often have no meaningful idea how safely the product really ought to perform in various situations.[371] How can an ordinary consumer possibly know the extent of crash protection or injury fairly to expect when an automobile crashes into a tree at 20, 30, or even 40 miles per hour?[372] Or how hard and far might a user reasonably expect a power lawn mower to eject a piece of plastic or a rock toward a person sitting on a stoop or in a classroom with an open window?[373]

Indeed, "an attempt to determine the consumer's reasonable expectations of safety concerning a technologically complex product may well be an exercise in futility, for the consumer may have at most only a generalized expectancy—perhaps more accurately only an unconscious hope—that the product will not harm him if he treats it with a reasonable amount of care."[374] And so, lurking at the heart of the consumer expectations test, the vagueness problem undermines the test in many of the most complex cases where a reliable standard of liability is needed most.[375]

---

[369] Note, however, that trained, experienced, professional workers will be held to understand the need to read and follow instructions with respect to products marketed for such professional purposes, and defectiveness will be determined according to such informed, professional expectations. See, e.g., Hutchins v. Silicone Specialties, Inc., 881 P.2d 64 (Okla. 1993). On when a manufacturer must warn employees directly, see § 9.4, below.

[370] See Prosser and Keeton on Torts at 699:

> In a sense the ordinary purchaser cannot reasonably expect anything more than that reasonable care in the exercise of the skill and knowledge available to design engineers has been exercised. The test can be utilized to explain most any result that a court or jury chooses to reach. The application of such a vague concept in many situations does not provide much guidance for a jury.

[371] This problem springs from a variety of factors: "(1) humans lack the data necessary to form expectations; (2) humans are psychologically unable to contemplate injury to themselves and thus underestimate the importance of such injury in making decisions; and (3) people overvalue short-term gains and losses and undervalue long-range considerations." Hubbard, Reasonable *Human* Expectations: A Normative Model for Imposing Strict Liability for Defective Products, 29 Mercer L. Rev. 465, 475 (1978).

[372] Or when a 5- to 6-inch rock strikes the wheel of a 4-wheel-drive pickup truck at normal highway speed. See Heaton v. Ford Motor Co., 435 P.2d 806 (Or. 1967). See Dickerson, Products Liability: How Good Does a Product Have To Be?, 42 Ind. L.J. 301, 307 (1967): "The most troublesome situations are those in which consumer attitudes have not sufficiently crystallized to define an expected standard of performance. What, for instance, should the law do about tractors that overturn, surgical implants that break, and rear-engined automobiles that tend to swerve at high speeds?" See also Rest. (3d) Torts § 2(b) cmt. *d*, Reporters' Notes, § III(A), at 79.

[373] See, e.g., Dugan v. Sears, Roebuck & Co., 454 N.E.2d 64 (Ill. App. Ct. 1983) (boy, sitting on house's front stoop, hit in eye by pierce of plastic ejected by power mower ten feet away); Stovall & Co. v. Tate, 184 S.E.2d 834 (Ga. Ct. App. 1971) (school girl struck in the eye by a rock thrown by a rotary lawnmower through an open classroom window).

[374] Montgomery and Owen, Reflections on the Theory and Administration of Strict Tort Liability for Defective Products, 27 S.C. L. Rev. 803, 823 (1976).

[375] On problems with the consumer expectations test, see Davis, Design Defect Liability: In Search of a Standard of Responsibility, 39 Wayne L. Rev. 1217, 1236–37 (1993); Fischer, Products Liability—The Meaning of Defect, 39 Mo. L. Rev. 339, 348–52 (1974). For a totally new perspective, see Geistfeld, Strict Products Liability 2.0: The Triumph of Judicial Reasoning over Mainstream Tort Theory, 14 J. Tort L. 403, 464 (2021) (arguing for a tort law implied warranty of quality that "obligat[es] the seller to supply the amount of product safety that well-informed consumers would choose," via a risk-utility test from the consumer's perspective).

Decline of the Consumer Expectations Test

For these and other reasons, courts[376] and legislatures[377] increasingly are abandoning consumer expectations as the sole means for determining defectiveness in most cases. Some courts, troubled at abandoning consumer expectations, do so furtively, by defining consumer expectations in risk-utility terms. One of the first such decisions was *Seattle-First National Bank v. Tabert*,[378] which finessed the consumer expectations test's inability to resolve complex design issues in an automotive liability case by converting this test to one of risk-utility: "In determining the reasonable expectations of the ordinary consumer, a number of factors must be considered [including t]he relative cost of the product, the gravity of the potential harm from the claimed defect and the cost and feasibility of eliminating or minimizing the risk . . . ."[379]

The European Community's *Product Liability Directive* defines "defect" in terms of consumer expectations.[380] Yet, the European liability standard is phrased in terms of what consumers are "entitled" to expect. Thus, consumers may be entitled to expect their products to be free of manufacturing flaws, and they probably are entitled to expect that the designs of most types of products are reasonably safe, not absolutely safe or accident-proof. Hence, the "entitled-to-expect" standard may require risk-utility analysis in most situations to determine how safe a manufacturer reasonably could have designed a product in lieu of fashioning a test from the actual contemplations of consumers.[381]

Although the consumer expectations test is withering as the true, sole test for strict products liability in tort, it remains an important consideration in many products liability cases. As previously discussed, it remains the principal, or only, test of liability in a number (if dwindling) of states;[382] in others, even if considered only as a factor in the risk-utility balance, it may be determinative in certain situations;[383] and in a small set of special product cases it remains the central liability consideration.[384]

---

[376] For movements from consumer expectations to risk-utility, see, e.g., Nichols v. Union Underwear Co., 602 S.W.2d 429 (Ky. 1980); St. Germain v. Husqvarna Corp., 544 A.2d 1283, 1286 (Me. 1988); Banks v. ICI Ams., Inc., 450 S.E.2d 671 (Ga. 1994). In Sperry-New Holland v. Prestage, 617 So.2d 248, 255–56 (Miss. 1993), the court followed "the trend in most federal and state jurisdictions" by moving from consumer expectations to risk-utility because the latter "best protects both the manufacturer and the consumer." In Branham v. Ford Motor Co., 701 S.E.2d 5, 15–17 (S.C. 2010), the court switched from consumer expectations to risk-utility for design defects, asserting that the risk-utility test is used by "35 of the 46 states that recognize strict products liability."

[377] See Wis. Stat. Ann. § 895.047(1)(a), where the legislature in 2011 replaced the consumer expectations standard with the Third Restatement's risk-utility standard.

[378] 542 P.2d 774 (Wash. 1975). See §§ 5.8 and 8.6, below.

[379] 542 P.2d at 779.

[380] Article 6(1) of the 1985 European Community Directive "Concerning Liability for Defective Products" provides that "[a] product is defective when it does not provide the safety which a person is entitled to expect, taking all circumstances into account, including: (a) the presentation of the product; (b) the use to which it could reasonably be expected that the product would be put; and (c) the time when the product was put into circulation." See § 1.4, above.

[381] Professor Jane Stapleton has lucidly explained this point. See, e.g., Stapleton, Products Liability in the United Kingdom: The Myths of Reform, 34 Tex. Int'l L.J. 45 (1999); Stapleton, Products Liability Reform—Real or Illusory?, 6 Oxford J. Legal Stud. 392, 405 (1986). See also Owen, Strict Products Liability in America and Europe, in Festschrift für Erwin Deutsch 305, 309–10 (1999). See generally D. Fairgrieve and R. Goldberg, Product Liability (3d ed. Oxford 2020).

[382] See Products Liability Rest. § 2(b), Reporters' Notes on cmt. *d*, § II(D), at 76.

[383] See Products Liability Rest. § 2 cmt. *g*.

[384] Id. at cmt. *h*: "With regard to two special product categories consumer expectations play a special role in determining product defect. See § 7 (food products) and § 8 (used products)."

§ 5.7 THE RISK-UTILITY TEST

Most courts, dissatisfied with the consumer expectations test and recognizing the advantages of the calculus-of-risk principles of negligence law,[385] use some form of "risk-utility" ("risk-benefit" or "cost-benefit") test for strict products liability in tort.[386] Borrowed from the law of negligence, this test was converted to the realm of strict products liability in tort at an early date.[387] For example, in *Helicoid Gage Division of American Chain & Cable Co. v. Howell*,[388] a pressure gauge manufactured by the defendant burst, throwing a piece of the gauge lens into the plaintiff's eye. The jury rendered a verdict for the plaintiff, which the appellate court affirmed. "To determine whether a product is unreasonably dangerous," said the court, "it is necessary to weigh the risk of harm against the utility of the product, considering whether safety devices would unreasonably raise the cost or diminish the utility of the product."[389] The evidence revealed that shatterproof glass, which would have prevented the injury, would have increased the cost of each gauge by only one dollar without reducing its utility at all. Moreover, an "inexpensive" safety shield, which would not have diminished the utility of the gauge, could have been added for about $2.50.

In another early case, *Dorsey v. Yoder Co.*,[390] the operator's hand and arm were caught and drawn into an unguarded metal slitter machine. On the defendant's motion for judgment notwithstanding the verdict after a verdict for the plaintiff, the court observed that "a guard would not eliminate the machine's usefulness, nor would the cost of $200 to $500 on an $8,000 machine be unreasonable. Moreover, the seriousness of the potential harm was great. Ultimately, all of these facts were questions to be weighed by the jury in making their ultimate determination as to whether, under all of the circumstances, the machine was 'defective.' " Observing that the jury found that "the

---

[385] "It is necessary to remember that whether the doctrine of negligence . . . or strict liability is being used to impose liability, the same process is going on in each instance, i.e., weighing the utility of the article against the risk of its use." Phillips v. Kimwood Mach. Co., 525 P.2d 1033, 1039 (Or. 1974). See § 2.2 (cost-benefit analysis in negligence), above.

[386] On the risk-utility test, see Gilles, United States v. Carroll Towing Co.: The Hand Formula's Home Port, in Torts Stories 11 (R. Rabin and S. Sugarman eds., Foundation Press 2003); Miller, Myth Surrenders to Reality: Design Defect Litigation in Iowa, 51 Drake L. Rev. 459 (2003); Owen, Toward a Proper Test for Design Defectiveness: "Micro-Balancing" Costs and Benefits, 75 Tex. L. Rev. 1661 (1997); Owen, Risk-Utility Balancing in Design Defect Cases, 30 U. Mich. J.L. Reform 239 (1997); M. Green, The Schizophrenia of Risk-Benefit Analysis in Design Defect Litigation, 48 Vand. L. Rev. 609 (1995); Miller, Design Defect Litigation in Iowa: The Myths of Strict Liability, 40 Drake L. Rev. 465 (1991); White, Risk-Utility Analysis and the Learned Hand Formula: A Hand That Helps or a Hand That Hides?, 32 Ariz. L. Rev. 77 (1990); Epstein, The Risks of Risk/Utility, 48 Ohio St. L.J. 469 (1987). For a useful practitioner perspective, see Rheingold, The Risk/Utility Test in Product Cases, 18 Trial Law. Q. 49 (1987).

For economic perspectives on risk-utility ("cost-benefit") analysis, see, e.g., R. Posner, Economic Analysis of Law §§ 6.1, 6.6 (9th ed. 2014); Gilles, The Invisible Hand Formula, 80 Va. L. Rev. 1015, 1025 (1994); W. Viscusi, Reforming Products Liability ch. 4 (1991); Viscusi, Wading Through the Muddle of Risk-Utility Analysis, 39 Am. U. L. Rev. 573 (1990); Schwartz, Proposals for Products Liability Reform: A Theoretical Synthesis, 97 Yale L.J. 353, 384–88 (1988); Epstein, The Risks of Risk/Utility, 48 Ohio St. L.J. 469 (1987); Comment, 84 Colum. L. Rev. 2045 (1984); Note, 73 Cornell L. Rev. 606 (1988).

[387] See, e.g., Roach v. Kononen, 525 P.2d 125 (Or. 1974), an action against Ford Motor Co. for injuries from a crash occurring when the hood on a Ford automobile suddenly flew up and blocked the driver's vision. Experts testified that the hood could have been designed to permit substantially better visibility in such situations; that Ford was aware of six or seven inadvertent hood openings over a seven or eight year period; and that the proposed design would require adding certain reinforcements to the hood and its hinges that would cost $5–$10 per car. *Held*, jury verdict for defendant affirmed.

[388] 511 S.W.2d 573 (Tex. Civ. App. 1974).

[389] Id. at 577.

[390] 331 F. Supp. 753 (E.D. Pa. 1971), aff'd, 474 F.2d 1339 (3d Cir. 1973).

balance tipped in favor of plaintiff," the court remarked that it "could not possibly rule otherwise."[391]

As judicial experience during the 1970s progressed, a number of products liability law scholars began to call for a shift away from § 402A's consumer expectations test toward a cost-benefit test, particularly in design defect cases.[392] An early study of products liability law by a group of law and engineering professors reflects the beginnings of the shift toward evaluating product hazards in terms of the costs and benefits of remedying those hazards. "It is time to abandon the perspective of the reasonable consumer," they proclaimed, in order to "formulate the strict liability question for what it is. The issue in every products case is whether the product *qua* product meets society's standards of acceptability. The unreasonable danger question, then, is posed in terms of whether, given the risks and benefits of and possible alternatives to the product, we as a society will live with it in its existing state or will require an altered, less dangerous form." In short, "the question is whether the product is a reasonable one given the reality of its use in contemporary society."[393] As more and more courts turned to some form of risk-benefit test in the 1980s and 1990s, and with the *Third Restatement*'s adoption of the risk-utility test for design and warning cases,[394] cost-benefit evaluation became, and remains, the predominant liability standard in products liability law.[395]

Nature of the Risk-Utility Test

The basic "risk-benefit," "cost-benefit," "risk-utility," or "calculus-of-risk" approach to products liability decisionmaking was explained in the context of negligence, above.[396] Although the fundamentals of this approach are identical in the strict liability context,[397] they are worth restating here. "The basic notion of cost-benefit assessment is not new. Any individual decision is usually the consequence of the actor's assessment of the advantages (benefits) and disadvantages (costs) of the action."[398] As phrased in one early design case, a determination of whether a design hazard is "unreasonable" involves "a

---

[391] Id. at 760.

[392] See particularly Henderson, Judicial Review of Manufacturers' Conscious Design Choices: The Limits of Adjudication, 73 Colum. L. Rev. 1631 (1973).

[393] Donaher, Piehler, Twerski, and Weinstein, The Technological Expert in Products Liability Litigation, 52 Tex. L. Rev. 1303, 1307 (1974).

[394] See §§ 6.5 and 8.8, below.

[395] See a wide collection of authority to this effect by the Reporters for the Third Restatement, in § 2, Reporters' Notes to cmt. *d*. For a contrary view, canvassing the law of every state, see Vargo, The Emperor's New Clothes: The American Law Institute Adorns a "New Cloth" for Section 402A Products Liability Design Defects—A Survey of the States Reveals a Different Weave, 26 U. Mem. L. Rev. 493 (1996).

[396] See § 2.2, above.

[397] With the lingering exception of the *foreseeability* of the costs and benefits, which many early courts and commentators believed distinguished strict from negligence-based liability. Because a large majority of courts and commentators now believe that a plaintiff must establish foreseeability in "strict" tort actions as well as in negligence, cost-benefit or risk-utility analysis should normally be identical in both contexts. Foreseeability, which implicates the so-called Wade-Keeton test and often is examined under the "state of the art" umbrella, is addressed in §§ 8.7 and 10.4, below. See also § 12.2 (foreseeability in proximate cause), below.

[398] H. Green, Cost-Risk-Benefit Assessment and the Law: Introduction and Perspective, 45 Geo. Wash. L. Rev. 901, 903–04 (1977). Consider also Merrill, Risk-Benefit Decisionmaking by the Food and Drug Administration, 45 Geo. Wash. L. Rev. 994, 996 (1977) (" 'Risk-benefit' . . . includes any technique for making choices that explicitly or implicitly attempts to measure the potential adverse consequences of an activity and to predict its benefits. In its most refined form, such an analysis may make use of refined mathematical methods for calculating risks and benefits, attempting to assign uniform values, usually in dollars, to all factors, including human lives.").

balancing of the probability and seriousness of harm against the costs of taking precautions. Relevant factors to be considered include the availability of alternative designs, the cost and feasibility of adopting alternative designs, and the frequency or infrequency of injury resulting from the design."[399] In short, a product is considered "defective" under a risk-utility test if the costs of eliminating a particular hazard are less than the resulting safety benefits.[400]

The cost-benefit or risk-utility test, which balances a particular risk of harm against the burden ("costs") of avoiding that risk, is most useful for ascertaining the safety or defectiveness of a product's design.[401] Thus, the type and amount of safety required is generally a function of the type, likelihood, and amount of expected harm (together viewed as the magnitude of the risk) that design precautions (of a particular cost) may be expected to prevent. If the risk posed by the sale and use of a product in a certain condition is great, substantial precautions must be taken to avert the risk; if the risk is small, precautions may be small as well. Thus, if the risk at issue concerns the possible failure of an automobile's steering, brakes, or tires at highway speeds, or the possibility that a punch press ram may unexpectedly depress upon an operator's hand, the manufacturer must employ the utmost precautions to avert the risk. Yet, if the risk is relatively minimal, reasonably appearing to involve at most the risk of minor harm to person or property—scratches, fabric stains, or the harmless malfunction of the product—then a manufacturer need apply only minimal precautions to reduce such risks. This principle of balance that inheres in tort law generally is sometimes referred to as the "calculus of risk."[402]

The Hand Formula in the Strict Liability Context

The most celebrated formulation of the risk-benefit test, albeit in the context of negligence rather than "strict" products liability, was provided by Judge Learned Hand in the case of *United States v. Carroll Towing Co.*,[403] discussed above.[404] In *Carroll Towing*, Judge Hand reasoned that a determination of precautions appropriate to an occasion generally reflects a calculus of three factors: the burden of taking precautions to avoid a risk of harm, on the one side, balanced against the likelihood that the actor's conduct will produce the harm multiplied by the seriousness of the harm, on the other. Negligence is implied if an actor fails to adopt a burden of precaution of less magnitude

---

[399] Raney v. Honeywell, Inc., 540 F.2d 932, 935 (8th Cir. 1976) (Iowa law).

[400] See Owen, Toward a Proper Test for Design Defectiveness: "Micro-Balancing" Costs and Benefits, 75 Tex. L. Rev. 1661, 1686–90 (1997).

[401] Courts find the risk-benefit test most helpful in making design defectiveness determinations and only marginally helpful in warning cases. See ch. 8 (design defects) and ch. 9 (warning defects), below. In manufacturing flaw cases decided in strict tort, where courts have sought to apply a truly "strict" basis of liability, cost-benefit analysis is properly ignored. See ch. 7, below.

[402] See, e.g., Hurd and Moore, Negligence in the Air (pt. I), 3 Theoretical Inquires L. 333, 359 (2002); Feldman, Science and Uncertainty in Mass Exposure Litigation, 74 Tex. L. Rev. 1, 37–38 (1995). This phrase is derived from the "calculus" of the Hand formula. See, e.g., Nelson, The Moral Perversity of the Hand Calculus, 45 St. Louis U. L.J. 759, 766 (2001).

[403] 159 F.2d 169, 173 (2d Cir. 1947). Hand first used this approach in Conway v. O'Brien, 111 F.2d 611 (2d Cir. 1940), rev'd on other grounds, 312 U.S. 492 (1941), and later reexamined it in Moisan v. Loftus, 178 F.2d 148, 149 (2d Cir. 1949).

[404] The *Carroll Towing* case and the Hand formula are examined in the negligence context in § 2.2, above, and the design defect context, in § 8.4, below. Particularly helpful accounts of both *Carroll Towing* and the Hand formula are Gilles, United States v. Carroll Towing Co.: The Hand Formula's Home Port, in Torts Stories 11 (R. Rabin and S. Sugarman eds., Foundation Press 2003), and Gilles, The Invisible Hand Formula, 80 Va. L. Rev. 1015, 1025 (1994). For other treatments, see note 386, above.

than the harm it is likely to prevent. Judge Hand expressed this concept algebraically: Negligence is suggested if $B < P \times L$, where B is the burden (cost) of avoiding accidental loss expected to result if B is not undertaken, P is the increase in the probability of loss if B is not undertaken, and L is the probable magnitude (expected cost) of such loss if it does occur. This is the so-called "Hand formula." If the formula is supplemented with a symbol for the implication of negligence ($\Rightarrow N$), the full formula reads: $B < P \times L \Rightarrow N$. Thus, conceived and applied to negligence determinations in the products liability context, the Hand formula may be explained as follows: if the cost of adopting a particular safety precaution (B) is less than the safety gains expected to result therefrom ($P \times L$), the manufacturer's failure to adopt the precaution implies its negligence ($\Rightarrow N$).

By substituting "defect" for "negligence" (D for N), the Hand formula converts comfortably to the "strict" products liability task of determining defectiveness. So reformulated, the defectiveness "equation" looks like this:

$$B < P \times L \Rightarrow D$$

In cost-benefit terms, the formula states:

$$\text{(Untaken Precaution) Costs} < \text{(Safety) Benefits} \Rightarrow \text{Defect}$$

Stated otherwise:

$$\text{Defect} \Rightarrow \text{if an untaken Precaution's Benefits} > \text{its Costs}$$

That is, if D = Defect, UP = an Untaken Precaution, SB = its Safety Benefits, and C = Costs, then:

$$D \Rightarrow \text{if UP's SB} > C$$

Thus, a product defect is suggested if the safety benefits of an untaken precaution[405] foreseeably exceed the resulting costs, including any diminished usefulness or diminished safety.[406]

Early courts, following earlier commentators, unhelpfully formulated the risk-utility test in broader terms, by weighing a *product*'s risks against the *product*'s benefits or utility.[407] Yet the formulation above (the Hand formula in cost-benefit terms) describes the test as lawyers and judges properly put it to use in trial courtrooms around the nation.[408] That is, the issue properly litigated almost always concerns the narrow "*micro*-balance" of pros and cons of a manufacturer's failure to adopt some particular design feature the plaintiff claims would have prevented the plaintiff's harm—whether the marginal costs of *changing* the overall design in some particular (micro) manner were worth the foreseeable safety benefits.[409] This more narrow formulation of the test,

[405] For Mark Grady's helpful analysis of untaken precautions, see Grady, Untaken Precautions, 18 J. Legal Stud. 139 (1989). See also Grady, A New Positive Economic Theory of Negligence, 92 Yale L.J. 799, 814–17 (1983).

[406] See Owen, Toward a Proper Test for Design Defectiveness: "Micro-Balancing" Costs and Benefits, 75 Tex. L. Rev. 1661, 1690 (1997).

[407] See Owen, Risk-Utility Balancing in Design Defect Cases, 30 U. Mich. J.L. Reform 239 (1997) (surveying risk-utility tests among the states); § 8.4, below. All too frequently, the persistence of precedent leads unwary courts back into the macro-balance trap. See, e.g., Yun Tung Chow v. Reckitt & Colman, Inc., 950 N.E.2d 113, 116 (N.Y. 2011) ("[i]f the 'utility' of a product 'does not outweigh the danger inherent in its [sale],' then the product is defectively designed").

[408] See Owen, *Risk-Utility Balancing*, at 242.

[409] The more narrow formulation of the test reflects how courts and lawyers actually proceed in assessing liability under the Hand formula. See, e.g., R. Heafey and D. Kennedy, Product Liability: Winning Strategies and Techniques §§ 4.04, 4.05, and pp. 4–9 (1994) (characterizing the manufacturer's choice to forego

which evaluates the marginal costs and benefits of a specific untaken precaution, avoids the problems inherent in the flawed *macro*-balance way of defining the risk-utility test.[410]

The Hand defectiveness formula succinctly captures the commonsense idea that products are unacceptably dangerous if they contain dangers that might cost-effectively (and practicably) be removed. A premise of the formula is that manufacturers may fairly be required to contemplate the consequences to consumers of foreseeable dangers in their products before they place those products on the market. So, in its design and marketing decisions, a responsible manufacturer should consider the risks of injury to consumers and bystanders and should weigh the interests of those parties equally to its own interest in maximizing profits. Manufacturers, of course, may also properly consider such factors as a product's usefulness, its cost, and profitability. But the point of the Hand formula is that manufacturers are also duty-bound to include in the balance a properly proportionate consideration of the various risks of harm that may be expected to result from the product when put to real-world use.

Thus, the risk-utility test demands manufacturers adopt precautions proportionate to the magnitude of the expected risk. This simple yet fundamental principle of defectiveness, which ties the measure of precaution to the measure of risk, grounds the safety obligations of manufacturers in "strict" liability as well as in negligence.

Because this method for ascertaining responsibility is identical in both negligence and strict liability, many courts and commentators have recognized the "functional" equivalence of the two liability theories in design and warning cases,[411] causing the Iowa Supreme Court first to repeal its doctrine of strict products liability in tort in warning cases in favor of plain negligence,[412] and later to abandon liability theory labels altogether in design defect cases.[413] The virtual identity of the two liability doctrines in

---

a reasonable alternative design as "the heart of the plaintiff's case"). See also Rheingold, The Risk/Utility Test in Product Cases, 18 Trial Law. Q. 49, 50 (1987) ("The usual and proper approach for a plaintiff in a design defect case is to present evidence on an alternative design which the jury can find should have been adopted for the product in question.").

> The attorney for the plaintiff will try to find some act which, if the defendant had taken it, would have significantly reduced the probability of the accident at low cost [such] that the increment in the expected loss was greater than the cost of avoidance . . . . The defendant will try to respond that the expected benefits of the proposed act were, in fact, less than the costs of undertaking it. [The decision-maker is then] asked to compare the incremental expected benefits with the incremental costs.

Brown, Toward An Economic Theory of Liability, 2 J. Legal Stud. 323, 334–35 (1973).

[410] See Brown, above; Owen, Risk-Utility Balancing in Design Defect Cases, 30 U. Mich. J.L. Reform 239 (1997). This definitional issue is examined further in § 8.4, below.

[411] See, e.g., Argonaut Ins. Co. v. Samsung Heavy Indus. Co., 929 F. Supp. 2d 159, 177 (N.D.N.Y. 2013) (in both design and warning defect cases, New York courts view negligence and strict liability as "functionally synonymous"); Nunnally v. R.J. Reynolds Tobacco Co., 869 So.2d 373, 381 (Miss. 2004) (the "risk-utility balancing test is merely a detailed version of Judge Learned Hand's negligence calculus"); Mayor & City Council of Balt. v. Utica Mut. Ins. Co., 802 A.2d 1070, 1089 (Md. Ct. Spec. App. 2002) ("these two theories—negligence and strict liability failure to warn—have been described as nearly identical"); Jones v. NordicTrack, Inc., 550 S.E.2d 101, 103 n.5 (Ga. 2001) (*design:* "no significant distinction between negligence and strict liability for purposes of the risk-utility analysis"); Olson v. Prosoco, Inc., 522 N.W.2d 284, 289 (Iowa 1994) (*warnings:* "we believe any posited distinction between strict liability and negligence principles is illusory").

[412] See Olson v. Prosoco, Inc., 522 N.W.2d 284, 289 (Iowa 1994) ("[i]nevitably the conduct of the defendant in a failure to warn case becomes the issue").

[413] See Wright v. Brooke Grp. Ltd., 652 N.W.2d 159, 169 (Iowa 2002) ("We question the need for or usefulness of any traditional doctrinal label in design defect cases because . . . a negligence claim and a strict

design and warning cases, in jurisdictions that rely on the risk-utility test, is examined further in this chapter[414] and in the chapters on defective designs and warnings.[415]

Risk-Utility Theory

The risk-utility test is constructed on solid theoretical footings.[416] While the consumer expectations test seeks to promote the autonomy of potential product victims, the goal of the risk-utility test is to maximize the common good. By judging the sufficiency of a product's safety according to a balance of the costs and benefits of improving its safety in a particular manner, the test provides a powerful standard of responsibility: failure to adopt a safety feature is wrongful if the untaken feature should have been expected to produce more good than harm, and such a failure is justified if the costs of adopting such a feature should have been expected to exceed its benefits. This standard derives from utilitarian theory, which itself is grounded in the moral ideals of both freedom and equality. By judging a manufacturer's safety decision in terms of its expected costs and benefits, whether it would likely augment or diminish net communal welfare, the standard requires manufacturers to provide fair respect to the freedom interests of persons endangered by its products by according a respect to those interests equal to that accorded the interests of other purchasers and users, and its shareholders.

By attempting to channel a manufacturer's decisions in a cost-effective direction, the risk-utility test also helps to protect society's scarce resources and minimize waste, which generally advances social welfare. While the operation of a risk-utility rule in practice may only crudely assist the goal of optimizing product safety,[417] the test at least may help achieve a roughly efficient allocation of resources by discouraging manufacturers from making and selling products that contain excessive accident costs. In addition, higher prices resulting from liability judgments and settlements should beneficially reduce consumption of excessively hazardous products. Finally, judicial use of an efficiency-based standard of liability provides important symbolic value in publicly condemning the wasteful (unjustified) sacrifice of human life and limb.

Problems with the Risk-Utility Test

Despite the risk-utility test's solid theoretical foundation, and its effectiveness as a test of liability in design cases in particular, it has some weaknesses. Because many courts purport to balance a large miscellany of factors,[418] much broader than the direct costs and benefits discussed above, some critics charge that this type of balancing test is too indeterminate (and thus arguably unprincipled) to be of any use.[419] Other critics

---

liability claim . . . rest on an identical risk-utility evaluation."). See generally Miller, Myth Surrenders to Reality: Design Defect Litigation in Iowa, 51 Drake L. Rev. 549 (2003).

[414] See § 5.9, below.

[415] See chs. 8 (design) and 9 (warning), below.

[416] Its moral footings are examined in Owen, The Moral Foundations of Products Liability Law: Toward First Principles, 68 Notre Dame L. Rev. 427 (1993). Its economic footings are explained in Judge Posner's classic essay, A Theory of Negligence, 1 J. Legal Stud. 29 (1972), and sources cited in note 386, above.

[417] See Calabresi, Optimal Deterrence and Accidents, 84 Yale L.J. 656 (1975); Calabresi and Hirschoff, Toward a Test for Strict Liability in Torts, 81 Yale L.J. 1055 (1972).

[418] Courts often draw on Dean John Wade's famous factors. See Wade, On the Nature of Strict Tort Liability for Products, 44 Miss. L.J. 825 (1973). The Wade factors are critiqued in the chapter on defects in design. See § 8.4, below.

[419] See, e.g., Epstein, The Risks of Risk/Utility, 48 Ohio St. L. J. 469, 475–76 (1987) ("There is nothing in the disorganized array of [factors such as Wade's] that prevents a single headstrong jury from making fundamental decisions about what may be marketed and what may not be sold at all."). Professor Epstein argues: "With variables so numerous, the ingenuity of lawyers should never be doubted when the stakes in

complain that risk-utility decisionmaking, supposedly based on stark economic efficiency, suffers from a lack of richness and humanism,[420] and even basic justice.[421]

There is, no doubt, some real truth to both of these challenges, but they fail to squarely hit the mark. Indeterminacy is a real problem for courts that try to balance a wide array of diverse factors. But the narrowly focused cost-benefit formulation of the test outlined above escapes this problem to a large extent. Arguments that cost-benefit determinations lack humanism and justice miss a couple of important points as well. Manufacturers simply are unable to bargain with consumers individually; if such individualization were practicable, it would ideally permit each consumer to maximize (or optimize) his or her own preferences. Yet manufacturers have no choice but to "legislate" safety decisions for consumers as a group. Arguably, manufacturers should give extra weight to the safety side of the scales, since they are forcing a collective cost-benefit tradeoff on all consumers, whether it meets their personal preferences or not.[422] Yet, a manufacturer that conscientiously applies cost-benefit analysis to safety decisions by that very process accords proper, equal respect to the safety rights of consumers as a group. Rather than undercutting consumer safety, therefore, the risk-utility method of decisionmaking promotes the rights of all foreseeably affected parties in equal measure.[423]

Because of the risk-utility test's special importance in judging the adequacy of safety in design, other aspects of this test, such as Dean Wade's seven factors and the requirement that the plaintiff prove a feasible design alternative, are considered in the chapter on that topic.[424]

§ 5.8 ALTERNATIVE TESTS

The discussion of strict products liability in tort to this point has been based on *Restatement (Second) of Torts* § 402A's "defective condition unreasonably dangerous" formulation of the liability standard, and the discussion has addressed the two principal tests of liability, consumer expectations and risk-utility, as largely warring standards. This section explores various alternative approaches that some courts have applied to

---

litigation are very high and discovery underregulated. The test is couched in an offhand way that makes difficult matters [look simple]. It is a utilitarian nightmare. What starts out as a faithful application of the utilitarian calculus ends up as an unprincipled battle of the experts. Everything is admissible; nothing is quantifiable; nothing is dispositive." Id. at 476.

420 See, e.g., Klemme, The Enterprise Liability Theory of Torts, 47 U. Colo. L. Rev. 153, 190 n.106 (1976). Professor Balkin, in Too Good to Be True: The Positive Economic Theory of Law, 87 Colum. L. Rev. 1447, 1475–76 (1987), faults efficiency tests for being incomplete: "Human values and goals may take wealth maximization into account, but they may not be exclusively or even primarily concerned with it. Human action and human decision may rest only in part on [efficiency analysis. Thus,] the greatest problem with wealth maximization as a theory of human practical reason may be that it is insufficiently rich." See also Hubbard, Reasonable *Human* Expectations: A Normative Model for Imposing Strict Liability for Defective Products, 29 Mercer L. Rev. 465, 468–69 (1978) (human expectation should prevail over efficiency because we can afford some inefficiency, whereas a denial of expectations, negating a person's right to be viewed as an end rather than as a means, is fundamentally offensive).

421 Compare Wright, Hand, Posner, and the Myth of the "Hand Formula," 4 Theoretical Inquiries L. 145, 201–02, 270 (2003) (arguing that risk-utility liability standards usually contravene principles of justice, but appearing to recognize an exception for products liability cases).

422 See Geistfeld, Reconciling Cost-Benefit Analysis with the Principle that Safety Matters More Than Money, 76 N.Y.U. L. Rev. 114 (2001).

423 Owen, Expectations in Tort, 44 Ariz. St. L. Rev. 1287 (2011); Owen, The Moral Foundations of Products Liability Law: Toward First Principles, 68 Notre Dame L. Rev. 427 (1993).

424 See ch. 8, below.

both the terminological and substantive standards of liability, including the trend toward associating the two conventional standards in some conciliatory manner.

Terminological Standards

The awkward "defective condition unreasonably dangerous" liability standard in § 402A resulted from pressure by the ALI Council on Dean William Prosser, the *Restatement* Reporter, to make clear that "strict" products liability has inherent limitations—that something must truly be *wrong* with a product before liability may be imposed.[425] Dean Prosser's early drafts of § 402A (in 1958[426] and 1960[427]), when the section still narrowly covered only food, defined the liability standard in terms of "a condition dangerous to the consumer." Responding to Council concerns that the "dangerous" "condition" phrasing of the standard was over-broad, Dean Prosser overreacted by modifying both "dangerous" with "unreasonably" and "condition" with "defective," thus setting § 402A's liability standard in its final form: "*defective condition unreasonably dangerous*."[428] When § 402A was first debated on the floor of the American Law Institute in 1961, its double-headed definition of the liability standard in the black letter was uniformly criticized as confusing, "gilding the lily," and likely to cause mischief[429]—all of which proved true.

The "defective condition unreasonably dangerous" standard appears to have two poles, "defective condition" and "unreasonably dangerous," such that the full phrase appears to establish a two-pronged test of liability.[430] This appearance is accentuated by

---

[425] The objective was to foreclose the possibility that a manufacturer of such inherently dangerous products as butter, drugs, whiskey, cigarettes, and automobiles would become "automatically responsible for all the harm that such things do in the world." Prosser, Strict Liability to the Consumer in California, 18 Hastings L.J. 9, 23 (1966). The history of § 402A with respect to this objective is detailed in § 6.2, below. See, e.g., Buckingham v. R.J. Reynolds Tobacco Co., 713 A.2d 381, 384 (N.H. 1998) ("When the plaintiff cannot allege that something is 'wrong' with the product, strict liability should not be used as a tool of social engineering to mandate that manufacturers bear the entire risk and costs of injuries caused by their products."). See also § 10.3 (liability for inherently dangerous products).

[426] See Rest. (2d) Torts § 402A (Prelim. Draft No. 6, 1958).

[427] See Rest. (2d) Torts § 402A (Council Draft No. 8, 1960).

[428] Prosser explained this point to the ALI membership at the 1961 meeting at which Tentative Draft No. 6 was reviewed. Noting the Council's objection to his original "dangerous" "condition" formulation (in fact, he mistakenly asserted that his initial drafts had read "*unreasonably* dangerous"), Dean Prosser remarked:

> The Council then proceeded to raise the question of a number of products which, even though not defective, are in fact dangerous to the consumer—whiskey, for example [laughter]; cigarettes, which cause lung cancer; various types of drugs which can be administered with safety up to a point but may be dangerous if carried beyond that—and they raised the question whether "unreasonably dangerous" was sufficient to protect the defendant against possible liability in such cases.
>
> Therefore, they suggested that there must be something wrong with the product itself, and hence the word "defective" was put in; but the fact that the product itself is dangerous, or even unreasonably dangerous, to people who consume it is not enough. There has to be something wrong with the product.

38 ALI Proceedings 86–89 (1961). Earlier in the discussion Dean Prosser had indicated that the "*unreasonably* dangerous" language also had been added "to head off liability for a product which is sold where there is nothing wrong with the product as a product, but nevertheless it is going to injure some people. A good many individuals are allergic to strawberries and eggs. That doesn't mean that there is anything wrong with the food. There is something wrong with the individual. 'Defective condition' and 'unreasonably dangerous' are deliberately designed to protect the defendant against undue liability." Id. at 55. See Viscusi, Wading Through the Muddle of Risk-Utility Analysis, 39 Am. U. L. Rev. 573 (1990); Wade, On the Nature of Strict Tort Liability for Products, 44 Miss. L.J. 825, 830 (1973).

[429] See 38 ALI Proceedings 86–89 (1961).

[430] See §§ 5.3 and 5.6, above.

the fact that the two sub-phrases are separately treated in different comments to the section—at least until one realizes, however, that both sub-phrases are defined in nearly identical consumer-contemplation terms,[431] as discussed above.[432] But one is left to wonder whether the section's liability standard requires proof of one element or two, and, if two, how the elements may differ. Such linguistic confusion is regrettable, and it brings to mind the definition of a (two-humped) camel.[433] From the very start, and for many years, courts and commentators struggled valiantly with the meaning of this centrally important language.

The great definitional debate came to a head in 1972 in *Cronin v. J.B.E. Olson Corp.*[434] where the California Supreme Court was asked to decide "whether the injured plaintiff seeking recovery upon the theory of strict liability in tort must establish, among other facts, not only that the product contained a defect which proximately caused his injuries but also that such defective condition made the product unreasonably dangerous to the user or consumer."[435] The court reviewed the development of the strict tort doctrine in California, particularly its 1963 decision in *Greenman v. Yuba Power Products, Inc.*,[436] which held that "[a] manufacturer is strictly liable in tort when an article he places on the market, knowing that it is to be used without inspection for defects, proves to have a defect that causes injury to a human being."[437] The court contrasted *Greenman*'s characterization of the requisite condition merely as a "defect" to § 402A's "defective condition unreasonably dangerous" basis of liability. Acknowledging that the "unreasonably dangerous" phrase had been added to *Greenman*'s "defect" formulation as a limitation on a supplier's responsibility for harm from inherent product dangers, the *Cronin* court observed that this limitation worked not only to prevent sellers from becoming insurers of any harm caused by their products but also "has burdened the injured plaintiff with proof of an element which rings of negligence." Noting "the susceptibility of Restatement section 402A to a literal reading that requires a fact finder to conclude that a product is, first, defective and, second, unreasonably dangerous,"[438] the court observed that "[a] bifurcated standard is of necessity more difficult to prove than a unitary one. But merely proclaiming that the phrase 'defective condition unreasonably dangerous' requires only a single finding would not purge that phrase of its negligence complexion." Reasoning that "a requirement that a plaintiff also prove that the defect made the product 'unreasonably dangerous' places upon him a significantly increased burden and represents a step backward in the area pioneered by this court," *Cronin* decisively banished the "unreasonably dangerous" language from California's strict products liability in tort jurisprudence.[439]

---

[431] "Defective condition," in § 402A cmt. *g* and "unreasonably dangerous," in § 402A cmt. *i*.

[432] See §§ 5.3 and 5.6, above.

[433] As a horse (defectively) designed by a committee.

[434] 501 P.2d 1153 (Cal. 1972).

[435] Id. at 1155.

[436] 377 P.2d 897 (Cal. 1963). On *Greenman*, see § 5.2, notes 73–85, above.

[437] Id. at 900.

[438] Citing Note, 55 Geo. L.J. 286, 296 (1966).

[439] *Cronin*, 501 P.2d at 1161–63. "[T]o require an injured plaintiff to prove not only that the product contained a defect but also that such defect made the product unreasonably dangerous to the user or consumer would place a considerably greater burden upon him than that articulated in *Greenman*. . . . [T]he *Greenman* formulation is consonant with the rationale and development of products liability law in California because it provides a clear and simple test for determining whether the injured plaintiff is entitled to recovery." Id. at 1163.

The *Cronin* court's concern that the full "defective condition unreasonably dangerous" phrase might lead courts to require proof of two separate elements was not misplaced. Many early decisions,[440] at least three statutes,[441] and many courts still today[442] define the liability rule of § 402A in such a two-step way.

The California Supreme Court in *Cronin* was surely wise to select a single term to characterize "bad" products, and the single word "defective" is now used by most courts and commentators as a short-hand way of signifying that a product's excessive dangers render the seller liable for resulting harm. That is, "defective" signifies a legal conclusion that a product is unacceptably dangerous, rather than providing a test for arriving at that conclusion.[443] However, while a few courts followed *Cronin* in banishing the "unreasonably dangerous" phrase from the formal liability standard,[444] most did not.[445] Most courts simply ignored the *Cronin* decision and stuck with § 402A's "defective condition unreasonably dangerous" phraseology as the formal liability standard, despite its awkwardness. Other courts, while agreeing with the *Cronin* court's decision to select a single test of liability, viewed the word "defective" as too narrow and mechanical to embrace the variety of complex issues which a liability test must address. While the word "defective" quite well describes the simple concept of a manufacturing flaw, it fails to capture the sensitive balance of usefulness, risk, and cost that lies at the heart of design adjudication.[446] For this reason, a few early courts[447] and the Louisiana legislature[448] took an opposite approach to *Cronin*, banishing "defective" from the formal standard and

---

[440] See, e.g., Phipps v. General Motors Corp., 363 A.2d 955, 958 (Md. 1976) ("For recovery, it must be established that (1) the product was in a defective condition [and] (2) that it was unreasonably dangerous."); Early-Gary, Inc. v. Walters, 294 So.2d 181, 186 (Miss. 1974) (one of § 402A's three elements is that "the injury resulted from a defect in the product which rendered it unreasonably dangerous").

[441] See Ark. Code Ann. § 16–116–101(a)(2) (plaintiff must prove product was sold "in a defective condition that rendered it unreasonably dangerous"); Miss. Code Ann. § 11–1–63(a)(i)–(ii) (plaintiff must establish that product was defective and that "[t]he defective condition rendered the product unreasonably dangerous"). Tennessee permits a plaintiff to recover if a product was in a defective condition *or* unreasonably dangerous. Tenn. Code Ann. § 29–28–105.

[442] See § 5.3 (*Elements*), above.

[443] See Armentrout v. FMC Corp., 842 P.2d 175, 186 (Colo. 1992).

[444] See, e.g., Glass v. Ford Motor Co., 304 A.2d 562 (N.J. Super. Ct. Law Div. 1973); Butaud v. Suburban Marine & Sporting Goods, Inc., 543 P.2d 209 (Alaska 1975); Berkebile v. Brantly Helicopter Corp., 337 A.2d 893 (Pa. 1975).

[445] Noting that "Cronin has been widely criticized as providing no useful definition of an actionable defect, particularly in relation to a case of a product of unsafe design," the Supreme Court of New Jersey repudiated *Glass*, above, note 444, on this point in Cepeda v. Cumberland Eng'g Co., 386 A.2d 816, 829 (N.J. 1978), overruled on other grounds by Suter v. San Angelo Foundry & Mach. Co., 406 A.2d 140 (N.J. 1979). Like *Cepeda*, most courts that considered the question rejected the *Cronin* approach. See, e.g., Byrns v. Riddell, Inc., 550 P.2d 1065 (Ariz. 1976); Heldt v. Nicholson Mfg. Co., 240 N.W.2d 154 (Wis. 1976). Law review commentary on *Cronin* was generally critical. See, e.g., Fischer, Products Liability—The Meaning of Defect, 39 Mo. L. Rev. 339 (1974); Keeton, Product Liability and the Meaning of Defect, 5 St. Mary's L.J. 30 (1973); Wade, On the Nature of Strict Tort Liability for Products, 44 Miss. L.J. 825 (1973).

[446] See, e.g., Cepeda v. Cumberland Eng'g Co., 386 A.2d 816 (N.J. 1978), overruled on other grounds by Suter v. San Angelo Foundry & Mach. Co., 406 A.2d 140 (N.J. 1979). See generally Owen, Defectiveness Restated: Exploding the "Strict" Products Liability Myth, 1996 U. Ill. L. Rev. 743, 754 ("the goal of both design engineers and the law should be to promote in products an ideal balance of product usefulness, cost, and safety").

[447] See Ross v. Up-Right, Inc., 402 F.2d 943, 947 (5th Cir. 1968) (Tex. law) (Wisdom, J.) ("[T]o speak in terms of 'defect' only causes confusion. . . . The key, then, is whether the product is 'unreasonably dangerous.' "); Suvada v. White Motor Co., 210 N.E.2d 182 (Ill. 1965). Compare Lietz v. Snyder Mfg. Co., 475 S.W.2d 105, 109 (Mo. 1972) (once a product is shown to be unreasonably dangerous, it is "deemed" to be defective).

[448] See La. Rev. Stat. Ann. §§ 9:2800.51 et seq.

selecting "unreasonably dangerous" as the better phrase to describe the balance and optimality concepts that frame design and warning cases in particular.

Eventually, most courts came to understand that the full *Restatement* phrase, "defective condition unreasonably dangerous," signifies a unitary concept that may be dubbed "defective"—convenient for general discussion but unhelpful as a liability "test" for ascertaining whether a particular product is or was adequately safe. Yet, many courts (and some statutes) continue to employ the full *Restatement* phrase, which unfortunately continues to lead some courts (and probably some juries) to the false conclusion that the phrase must mean two things.[449]

Other courts from time to time have experimented with a variety of other definitional phrases, such as "not reasonably safe," "unduly unsafe," "not reasonably fit, suitable and safe," and "dangerously defective." In *Azzarello v. Black Bros. Co.*,[450] the Pennsylvania Supreme Court endorsed the following standard jury instruction:

> The [supplier] of a product is the guarantor of its safety. The product must, therefore, be provided with every element necessary to make it safe for [its intended] use, and without any condition that makes it unsafe for [its intended] use. If you find that the product, at the time it left the defendant's control, lacked any element necessary to make it safe for [its intended] use or contained any condition that made it unsafe for [its intended] use, then the product was defective, and the defendant is liable for all harm caused by such defect.

This standard, that the supplier is a "guarantor" of product safety, has frightening implications, and it has been soundly rejected as too extreme and as running counter to the universally accepted notion, even in Pennsylvania, that a manufacturer is not an "insurer" of the safety of its products.[451] After many years of confusion, the Pennsylvania Supreme Court, in *Tincher v. Omega Flex, Inc.*, finally overruled *Azzarello*.[452]

Combining Tests—Consumer Expectations and Risk-Utility

The discussion to this point of the consumer expectations and risk-utility tests, which has examined their pros and cons as discrete and independent tests, has shown that both tests have much merit in moral theory: the consumer expectancy test of contract law protects vital interests of buyers and sellers who strike "private" contractual bargains involving certain implied assurances of quality and safety; and the risk-utility test of tort law protects the general public by requiring product sellers to accord proper respect to the safety interests of persons foreseeably put at risk by defective products.

---

449 The trial court appears to have been so misled in Stinson v. E.I. DuPont de Nemours & Co., 904 S.W.2d 428 (Mo. Ct. App. 1995) (by implication). Compare McAlpine v. Rhone-Poulenc Ag Co., 16 P.3d 1054 (Mont. 2000) (jury verdict overturned because "defective condition unreasonably dangerous" language in jury instructions created vague and imprecise dual test). See Owen, Defectiveness Restated: Exploding the "Strict" Products Liability Myth, 1996 U. Ill. L. Rev. 743, 776–77.

450 391 A.2d 1020, 1027 n.12 (Pa. 1978).

451 See, e.g., Bugosh v. I.U. N. Am., Inc., 971 A.2d 1228, 1230 n.3 (Pa. 2009) (Saylor, J., dissenting) ("it was never the intention of the Second Restatement to render manufacturers insurers of their products, responsible for any and all harm caused from their use, regardless of the products' utility and relative safety"). See Thomas, Defining "Design Defect" in Pennsylvania: Reconciling *Azzarello* and the *Restatement (Third) of Torts*, 71 Temp. L. Rev. 217 (1998) (critical of *Azzarello*'s rash language, but reconciling decision with mainstream law); Wertheimer, Azzarello Agonistes: Bucking the Strict Products Liability Tide, 66 Temp. L. Rev. 419 (1993) (favoring *Azzarello*); Notes, 81 Dick. L. Rev. 374 (1977), 21 Vill. L. Rev. 794 (1976). For a brief consideration of Pennsylvania's confused approach, see § 5.3, above.

452 104 A.3d 328 (Pa. 2014) (thoroughly reviewing developments in products liability law and theory and adopting a combined theory of consumer expectations and risk-utility for design defects).

Recognizing the validity of both of these goals and the dual origins of strict products liability in warranty and tort, the Supreme Court of California embraced *both* such tests in an important decision decided in 1978. In *Barker v. Lull Engineering Co.*,[453] discussed in detail below in the chapter on design defects,[454] the California high court, reasoning that a proper test of strict products liability should reflect its dual origins, *combined* the consumer expectations and risk-utility tests into a single, two-pronged test, and shifted the burden of proof on risk-utility to manufacturers:

> [A] trial judge may properly instruct the jury that a product is defective in design (1) if the plaintiff demonstrates that the product failed to perform as safely as an ordinary consumer would expect when used in an intended or reasonably foreseeable manner, or (2) if the plaintiff proves that the product's design proximately caused his injury and the defendant fails to prove, in light of the relevant factors [the gravity of the danger, the likelihood of harm, the feasibility of altering the design to eliminate the danger, and the cost and other adverse effects of so altering the design], that on balance the benefits of the challenged design outweigh the risk of danger inherent in such design.[455]

A handful of courts explicitly followed *Barker*'s two-pronged definition of product defect,[456] but generally not its shift in the burden of proof,[457] and at least a couple of courts explicitly rejected the *Barker* test.[458] A few courts danced around the issue, seemingly adopting the *Barker* two-pronged approach, but without saying so explicitly.[459] A number of courts seemingly followed a *de facto Barker* approach, variously applying the consumer expectations and risk-utility tests, often without explaining why one test was applied in one situation and the other test in some other.[460] While these

---

[453] 573 P.2d 443 (Cal. 1978).

[454] See ch. 8, below.

[455] *Barker*, 573 P.2d at 457–58. See also Merrill v. Navegar, Inc., 28 P.3d 116, 125 (Cal. 2001).

[456] See Caterpillar Tractor Co. v. Beck, 593 P.2d 871 (Alaska 1979); Knitz v. Minster Mach. Co., 432 N.E.2d 814 (Ohio 1982); Ontai v. Straub Clinic & Hosp., Inc., 659 P.2d 734 (Haw. 1983); Dart v. Wiebe Mfg., Inc., 709 P.2d 876 (Ariz. 1985); Lamkin v. Towner, 563 N.E.2d 449 (Ill. 1990).

[457] Except for *Beck* (Alaska), and *Lamkin* (Illinois), note 456, above, courts rejected *Barker*'s second-prong shift in the burden of proof, and Illinois eventually rejected it. See, e.g., Calles v. Scripto-Tokai Corp., 864 N.E.2d 249, 257 (Ill. 2007); Armentrout v. FMC Corp., 842 P.2d 175 (Colo. 1992) (overruling prior case on point); Kallio v. Ford Motor Co., 407 N.W.2d 92 (Minn. 1987); Hayes v. Ariens Co., 462 N.E.2d 273 (Mass. 1984); Ontai v. Straub Clinic & Hosp., Inc., 659 P.2d 734 (Haw. 1983); Cremeans v. International Harvester Co., 452 N.E.2d 1281 (Ohio 1983); Wilson v. Piper Aircraft Corp., 579 P.2d 1287 (Or. 1978) (on rehearing). Commentators were critical of *Barker*'s shift in the burden of proof:

> The rule places an enormous burden on the concept of a "product design that proximately causes injury," a burden which the concept seems ill-equipped to handle. . . . People fall off ladders all the time, and the fact that ladders are both high and in some general way unstable enables these falls to occur. Does it or doesn't it follow that in every case of a person's falling off a ladder, the ladder's design proximately causes the fall?

Schwartz, Foreword: Understanding Products Liability, 67 Cal. L. Rev. 435, 466–67 (1979). See also Prosser and Keeton on Torts 702; Wade, On Product "Design Defects" and Their Actionability, 33 Vand. L. Rev. 551, 573 (1980).

[458] See, e.g., Kallio v. Ford Motor Co., 407 N.W.2d 92, 95 (Minn. 1987); Lester v. Magic Chef, Inc., 641 P.2d 353 (Kan. 1982).

[459] See, e.g., Soproni v. Polygon Apt. Partners, 971 P.2d 500, 504 (Wash. 1999); Ortho Pharm. Corp. v. Heath, 722 P.2d 410 (Colo. 1986) (by implication), overruled in part on other grounds by Armentrout v. FMC Corp., 842 P.2d 175 (Colo. 1992).

[460] See, e.g., Yun Tung Chow v. Reckitt & Colman, Inc., 950 N.E.2d 113, 116 (N.Y. 2011); Halliday v. Sturm, Ruger & Co., 792 A.2d 1145 (Md. 2002); Bragg v. Hi-Ranger, Inc., 462 S.E.2d 321, 328 (S.C. Ct. App. 1995). Cf. Haglund v. Philip Morris, Inc., 847 N.E.2d 315, 322–23 (Mass. 2006) (defectiveness in warranty (lack

decisions may be faulted for failing clearly to specify when and how the two separate tests should be applied, many courts were feeling their way and, in time, may be expected to explicate how the two tests fit together.[461] At bottom, much may be said for a liability regime that logically blends, in one way or another, both standards of liability.[462]

Two other developments, examined further in the design defect chapter,[463] are also worthy of note. First was a redefinition of consumer expectations in risk-utility terms, at least in certain types of cases,[464] based on the idea that consumers should be able to expect manufacturers to make their products as safe as reasonably possible in view of the relevant costs and benefits.[465] A second development was the movement toward applying the consumer expectations test in design cases of a *simple* mechanism, such as a fan with unguarded metal blades, but a risk-utility test to a product with a *complex* design, such as the structure of a car. Although earlier cases had so held,[466] the California Supreme Court adopted such a test in an automobile crashworthiness case in 1994.

In *Soule v. General Motors Corp.*,[467] the California court restricted *Barker*'s consumer expectations prong to simple product cases where consumers from everyday experience are able to acquire meaningful expectations about the product's performance and safety characteristics, especially in cases where expert testimony is for this reason unnecessary and perhaps improper: "[T]he consumer expectations test is reserved for cases in which the *everyday experience* of the product's users permits a conclusion that the product's design violated minimum safety assumptions, and is thus defective

---

of "fitness") primarily determined by consumer expectations, but design defectiveness determined by risk-utility).

Note that a court effectively applies a *de facto Barker* approach when it allows a merchantability warranty claim for design defect based on consumer expectations, together with a strict tort claim based on risk-utility, for the same design defect. See Denny v. Ford Motor Co., 662 N.E.2d 730 (N.Y. 1995), § 5.9, below.

[461] A good example is South Carolina, whose courts in design defect cases first applied the consumer expectations test and, later, a risk-utility test cloaked in consumer expectations clothing. Eventually, this state's Supreme Court adopted Products Liability Rest. § 2(b), which intelligently includes consumer expectations as a factor in the risk-utility test, quite probably the best of all blended approaches for defining a design defect. See Branham v. Ford Motor Co., 701 S.E.2d 5 (S.C. 2010). Compare Mikolajczyk v. Ford Motor Co., 901 N.E.2d 329 (Ill. 2008), essentially adopting the Restatement's 2(b) risk-utility test while asserting that it declined to do so (reflecting tort reform politics in action).

[462] See, e.g., Long v. TRW Vehicle Safety Sys., Inc., 796 F. Supp. 2d 1005 (D. Ariz. 2011) ("two models may be used to determine whether a product was defectively designed: the consumer expectation test and risk/benefit analysis"); Kirkland v. Emhart Glass S.A., 805 F. Supp. 2d 1072, 1076 (W.D. Wash. 2011) (under Washington Product Liability Act, plaintiff may use either consumer expectations or risk-utility test for design defect and failure to warn claims); Kennedy, The Role of the Consumer Expectations Test Under Louisiana's Products Liability Tort Doctrine, 69 Tul. L. Rev. 117, 162–63 (1994) ("[I]t will be prudent in some cases to employ the consumer expectation test in conjunction with the risk-utility balancing test in the form of a 'risk-utility consumer expectation test.' Fusing the test often will make good sense given the complexity of products and products liability tort litigation today; the moral, social, economic, and jurisprudential values sought to be advanced by tort liability; and the superiority of the risk-utility balancing test in serving these interests and in resolving many of the tough issues presented in most products liability disputes.").

[463] See § 8.6, below.

[464] Notably complex cases, as next discussed.

[465] See, e.g., McCathern v. Toyota Motor Corp., 23 P.3d 320, 331 (Or. 2001); Vautour v. Body Masters Sports Indus., 784 A.2d 1178, 1182 (N.H. 2001) (unreasonably dangerous defined in terms of consumer expectations defined in terms of risk-utility); Potter v. Chicago Pneumatic Tool Co., 694 A.2d 1319 (Conn. 1997). See also Seattle-First Nat'l Bank v. Tabert, 542 P.2d 774 (Wash. 1975), discussed in § 5.6, above.

[466] See, e.g., Scoby v. Vulcan-Hart Corp., 569 N.E.2d 1147 (Ill. App. Ct. 1991) (only the consumer expectations test should be applied when a mechanism is simple and the danger is obvious), disapproved, Calles v. Scripto-Tokai Corp., 864 N.E.2d 249, 257–60 (Ill. 2007).

[467] 882 P.2d 298 (Cal. 1994).

regardless of expert opinion about the merits of the design."[468] A number of courts and commentators have moved in this direction,[469] which may put both of the traditional tests to their highest use,[470] provided that courts do not employ the consumer expectation test in simple-product situations as an obvious-danger bar in disguise.[471]

Defect-Specific Tests

A major development in products liability defect tests in recent decades has been the trend toward using separate tests for separate types of defect.[472] Except in food cases,[473] there has been little need to define the nature of a production flaw (a "manufacturing defect"), because the fact of "defectiveness" and the resulting violation of a consumer's expectations are both generally self-evident in such cases. Accordingly, early courts rarely bothered to define this form of defect.[474] More recently, however, many courts and state legislatures have been defining manufacturing defects in terms of a deviation or departure from the manufacturer's intended design.[475] This is the liability standard articulated by the *Third Restatement*,[476] which makes such good sense, and is so noncontroversial, that it should continue to spread widely across the nation.

Neither the consumer expectations nor risk-utility test is generally very helpful in determining whether a particular danger warrants a warning or whether a particular warning adequately conveys information about the risk. A product with an inadequate warning of danger quite obviously violates a consumer's expectations, and the safety

---

[468] Id. at 308 (emphasis in original). See also Pruitt v. General Motors Corp., 86 Cal. Rptr. 2d 4 (Ct. App. 1999) (consumer expectations test did not apply to defective design of airbag claim).

[469] *But see* Calles v. Scripto-Tokai Corp., 864 N.E.2d 249, 264 (Ill. 2007) (concluding that "there is no per se rule excepting application of the risk-utility test where a product is deemed simple and its dangers are open and obvious").

[470] See, e.g., Walker v. Ford Motor Co., 406 P.3d 845, 851 (Colo. 2017) ("'exclusive reliance upon consumer expectations' is 'particularly inappropriate' where both the dangerousness of the design and 'the efficacy of alternative designs . . . must be defined primarily by technical, scientific information'"); Delaney v. Deere & Co., 999 P.2d 930, 944 (Kan. 2000) ("recogniz[ing] the validity of risk/utility analysis as a guide in determining the expectations of consumers in complex cases"); Potter v. Chicago Pneumatic Tool Co., 694 A.2d 1319 (Conn. 1997). See also McCathern v. Toyota Motor Corp., 23 P.3d 320, 331 (Or. 2001); Kennedy, The Role of the Consumer Expectations Test Under Louisiana's Products Liability Tort Doctrine, 69 Tul. L. Rev. 117 (1994).

[471] See Calles v. Scripto-Tokai Corp., 864 N.E.2d 249, 259 (Ill. 2007) (majority rejected use of consumer expectations test in simple-product situations, after careful analysis, because "adoption of a 'simple product' exception is nothing more than the adoption of a general rule that a manufacturer will not be liable for open and obvious dangers").

[472] See §§ 6.2 and 6.5, below.

[473] See § 7.5, below.

[474] The more typical litigation problem in manufacturing defect cases concerns the problem of *proving* that the *cause* of a product malfunction was a production defect rather than something else. The malfunction theory of recovery addresses this problem, as discussed below. See § 7.4, below.

[475] See, e.g., Grant v. Ford Motor Co., 89 So.3d 655, 675–76 (Miss. Ct. App. 2012) (reform statute states that a product contains a manufacturing defect if it "deviated in a material way from the manufacturer's specifications or from otherwise identical units manufactured to the same manufacturing specifications"); Godoy v. E.I. du Pont de Nemours & Co., 768 N.W.2d 674, 683–84 (Wis. 2009); Cooper Tire & Rubber Co. v. Mendez, 204 S.W.3d 797, 800 (Tex. 2006) ("when a product deviates, in its construction or quality, from the specifications or planned output in a manner that renders it unreasonably dangerous"); Allstate Ins. Co. v. Ford Motor Co., 772 So.2d 339, 344 (La. Ct. App. 2000) (La. Code: if "product deviated in a material way from the manufacturer's specifications or performance standards for the product or from otherwise identical products manufactured by the same manufacturer"). See § 7.2, below.

[476] See Products Liability Rest. § 2(a). See § 6.5, below.

benefits of adding a sufficient warning virtually always exceed its monetary costs.[477] For this reason, the warning defect issue is generally posited merely in terms of the sufficiency ("adequacy") of the information provided and of the method by which it was conveyed.[478] The implicit assumption here is that people commonly understand that, to be "adequate," a warning must meaningfully alert consumers to all significant latent dangers and, also, how a user might reasonably avoid them.[479] Most courts have turned to general negligence principles for guidance in warning cases,[480] and at least one court has abolished the warning claim for strict tort liability in such cases and returned outright to the claim for negligence.[481]

At the inception of strict products liability in tort, most courts defined design defects in terms of consumer expectations. However, with the maturity of products liability law and litigation, most courts have shifted to the risk-utility test for resolving design defectiveness, sometimes combining this test with some form of consumer expectancy analysis. The use of these tests for design defect determinations, previously discussed,[482] is examined in further detail in the chapter on defects in design.[483]

The trend toward separately defining the liability standard by type of defect was validated by the *Third Restatement* which, while formulating design and warning defects in similar risk-utility terms, trifurcates defectiveness into the three separate types of defect, each with its own separate definition.[484] The defect-specific standards for strict products liability in tort are provided separate treatment below in the respective defect chapters.[485]

§ 5.9 COMPARISON WITH OTHER LIABILITY THEORIES

The doctrine of strict products liability in tort for physical harm from selling defective products[486] may usefully be compared to the other two principal theories of products liability law, negligence and warranty, in two respects: (1) how the underlying theories of liability compare and contrast, and (2) how secondary aspects of such claims—

---

477 See, e.g., Moran v. Faberge, Inc., 332 A.2d 11, 15 (Md. 1975) (observing that a risk almost always exceeds the small expense of a warning). See § 2.2, above. But other safety costs arise from over-warning, sometimes referred to as "warnings pollution," which also should be considered. See § 9.3, below.

478 See, e.g., Stanley v. Central Garden & Pet Corp., 891 F. Supp. 2d 757, 763 (D. Md. 2012); Braaten v. Saberhagen Holdings, 198 P.3d 493, 498 (Wash. 2008) (en banc) (a hazard may require manufacturer to give "an adequate warning concerning the manner in which to safely use the product"); Lightolier, a Div. of Genlyte Thomas Grp., LLC v. Hoon, 876 A.2d 100, 110 (Md. 2005) (manufacturer may avoid liability by giving "adequate warnings or instructions," which will render product not defective); Lewis v. Sea Ray Boats, Inc., 65 P.3d 245, 249 (Nev. 2003) ("strict liability may be imposed even though the product is faultlessly made if it was unreasonably dangerous to place the product in the hands of the user without suitable and adequate warning concerning safe and proper use"). See § 9.3, below.

479 On warnings adequacy, see § 9.3, below.

480 See, e.g., Anderson v. Owens-Corning Fiberglas Corp., 810 P.2d 549, 561 (Cal. 1991) (Mosk, J., concurring and dissenting); Crislip v. TCH Liquidating Co., 556 N.E.2d 1177, 1183 (Ohio 1990). See also § 9.2, below.

481 See Olson v. Prosoco, Inc., 522 N.W.2d 284 (Iowa 1994). Note also that some states have achieved this result by legislation. See § 9.2, below.

482 Most defect-test cases examined earlier in this section concerned dangers of design.

483 See ch. 8, below.

484 See §§ 6.2 and 6.5, below.

485 See ch. 7 (manufacturing defects), ch. 8 (design defects), and ch. 9 (warning and instruction defects), below.

486 Strict products liability in tort for misrepresentation and express warranty are compared and contrasted in chapters on those topics. See §§ 3.4 and 4.1, above.

such as causation, damages, defenses, and statutes of limitations—correspond and differ. The first comparison, between the respective theories of liability, is treated here. How different liability theories affect other aspects of a products liability action is detailed in subsequent chapters devoted to those special topics. The future of such differing liability theories is addressed at the end of the next and final section of this chapter. Before strict products liability in tort is compared to negligence and warranty, it may be helpful to contrast it to the other major strict liability in tort doctrine: strict liability for abnormally dangerous activities.

Strict Products Liability *vs.* Strict Liability for Abnormally Dangerous Activities

One might think that the two major strict liability in tort doctrines—one for selling a dangerously defective product and the other for conducting an abnormally dangerous activity—might have much in common. In fact, however, the two doctrines are fundamentally distinct.[487] Strict products liability in tort concerns the responsibility of a supplier for selling a product containing a reasonably avoidable and often unexpected danger—such as the manufacturer of a car with defective brakes—which causes physical harm to the user or someone else. By contrast, strict liability for an abnormally dangerous activity involves the responsibility of an actor, such as a contractor who sets off a large charge of dynamite in a city, for the harmful consequences of introducing a substantial, unavoidable danger into a setting where the hazard is largely out of place.

In the products liability context, strict liability follows the creation and sale of a product that is unreasonably dangerous because it was made improperly or bears insufficient warning of its dangers, such that the hazard could and reasonably should have been avoided—so that it should not have been *sold* in that condition at all. By contrast, strict liability for an abnormally dangerous activity arises out of an actor's inappropriate *use* of a product or other activity whose dangers, though substantial, are reasonable when the activity is conducted in an appropriate location where the hazard may be properly contained.[488] Such an actor is strictly liable for creating an excessive ("abnormal") danger by using a product in a manner and context where the danger is substantial, unavoidable, and out of place.[489]

With almost no exceptions, courts have steadfastly kept these two theories of strict tort liability separate and distinct. In refusing to extend the abnormally dangerous or ultrahazardous activity doctrine to the products liability context, courts have emphasized that product defect cases rarely satisfy the abnormally dangerous activity doctrine's basic requirements that the hazard be both unavoidable and uncommon,

[487] See, e.g., Cantu, Distinguishing the Concept of Strict Liability for Ultra-Hazardous Activities from Strict Products Liability Under Section 402A of the Restatement (Second) of Torts: Two Parallel Lines of Reasoning that Should Never Meet, 35 Akron L. Rev. 31, 56 (2001) ("the concept of strict liability for ultra-hazardous activities is entirely different from strict liability under Section 402A"); Montgomery and Owen, Reflections on the Theory and Administration of Strict Tort Liability for Defective Products, 27 S.C. L. Rev. 803, 825–28 (1976).

[488] See United States v. Union Corp., 277 F. Supp. 2d 478, 494 (E.D. Pa. 2003) ("abnormal dangerousness in the context of sections 519 and 520 of the Restatement (Second) of Torts is a property of *activities* and not of substances").

[489] See Rest. (3d) Torts: Liability for Physical and Emotional Harm § 20 (strict liability for abnormally dangerous activities whose risks are "highly significant," foreseeable, unavoidable, and uncommon).

conditions which strongly suggest that this particular version of strict tort liability has no role to play in products liability litigation.[490]

Strict Liability *vs.* Negligence

In General

How strict liability differs from fault-based liability, and which is preferable, may be the most fundamental issue in all of tort law.[491] It is elemental that the very basis of negligence liability, whether in products liability or another tort law context, is grounded in fault.[492] In contrast, the essence of strict products liability in tort is the supplier's responsibility for harm caused by product defects *regardless* of fault. Thus, *Restatement (Second) of Torts* § 402A "applies although (a) the seller has exercised all possible care in the preparation and sale of his product."[493] Liability is called "strict" because the basis of responsibility for sellers of defective products is "no-fault" liability, meaning that liability is assessed without regard to the seller's fault. Unlike negligence, as has been said many times, strict products liability focuses on the condition of the product rather than the conduct of the manufacturer.[494]

The fundamental divide between negligence and strict liability in tort is manifest in manufacturing flaw cases, where even the most careful supplier is subject to liability under § 402A for injuries caused by a stone in a can of peas, an air bubble in a tire, or a crossed wire in the electrical system of a punch press.[495] Even in these cases, however, once the plaintiff proves the existence of a defect, establishing an inference of negligence requires very little proof,[496] and courts in such cases often presume that the

[490] See, e.g., Parker v. Brush Wellman, Inc., 377 F. Supp. 2d 1290, 1304 (N.D. Ga. 2005) (defendant's *use* of beryllium-containing products at its plant "takes this controversy outside of the 'pure' manufacturing cases . . . and puts in issue whether Defendants actually engaged in an *activity* (*i.e.*, use of beryllium) that was itself abnormally dangerous"), aff'd, 230 Fed. Appx. 878 (11th Cir. 2007); United States v. Union Corp., 277 F. Supp. 2d 478, 495 (E.D. Pa. 2003) ("manufacture and sale of PCBs is not an abnormally dangerous activity"); Ehlis v. Shire Richwood, Inc., 233 F. Supp. 2d 1189, 1191–93 (D.N.D. 2002) (strict liability for abnormally dangerous or ultrahazardous activity doctrine does not apply to sale of prescription drugs), aff'd, 367 F.3d 1013 (8th Cir. 2004); Merrill v. Navegar, Inc., 89 Cal. Rptr. 2d 146, 190–92 (Ct. App. 1999) (same: sale of guns), superseded on other grounds, 991 P.2d 755 (Cal. 2000); Gaines-Tabb v. ICI Explosives USA, Inc., 995 F. Supp. 1304 (W.D. Okla. 1996) (same: ammonium nitrate, labeled as fertilizer, used as explosive). On guns, see McNicholas and McNicholas, Ultrahazardous Products Liability: Providing Victims of Well-Made Firearm Ammunition to Fire Back at Gun Manufacturers, 30 Loy. L.A. L. Rev. 1557, 1599 (1997) (proposing theory of "ultrahazardous products liability" that would hold manufacturers of certain assault rifles liable for all damages caused by their products).

[491] See Owen, Philosophical Foundations of Fault in Tort Law, in Philosophical Foundations of Tort Law 201 (D. Owen ed., Oxford 1995). On the differences and parallels between negligence and strict liability in tort in products liability law, see Am. Law Prod. Liab. 3d § 28:14.

[492] See § 2.1, above.

[493] Rest. (2d) Torts § 402A(2).

[494] See, e.g., Elkharroubi v. Six Flags Am., LP, 2022 WL 152416, at *2 (4th Cir. 2022) (Md. law) ("The relevant inquiry in a strict liability action focuses not on the conduct of the manufacturer but rather on the product itself."); Johnson v. Auto Handling Corp., 523 S.W.3d 452, 466 (Mo. 2017) (en banc) ("The focus [of strict liability in tort] is on the product and its condition when sold, not on the manufacturer's conduct . . . . By contrast, proving negligent failure to warn—and by analogy negligent design defect—'focuses on what the manufacturer knew rather than on the product.' "); Calles v. Scripto-Tokai Corp., 864 N.E.2d 249, 263–64 (Ill. 2007).

[495] See § 7.2, below.

[496] Dean Prosser thought that proof that a defect was a result of the manufacturer's negligence "is by far the easiest" of the plaintiff's tasks, "and it is one in which the plaintiff almost never fails." Prosser, The Assault Upon the Citadel (Strict Liability to the Consumer), 69 Yale L.J. 1099, 1114 (1960).

manufacturer's failure to detect or remove the defect was a result of negligence.[497] For this reason, Dean Prosser supposed in such cases that "there is not one case in a hundred in which strict liability would result in recovery where negligence does not."[498]

When the issue shifts away from manufacturing defects to dangers in a product's design or inadequate warnings and instructions, there can be little difference between negligence and strict liability because the plaintiff in each such case is required to show effectively the same thing—that the product contained a danger that was *unreasonable.* If the question of whether a particular danger was unreasonable is determined by the consumer expectations test,[499] the results may vary from a determination under principles of negligence. But as courts turn increasingly to the risk-utility test, which balances the costs and benefits of avoiding the danger, the method for determining "defect" or "unreasonable danger" is the same as that for establishing the supplier's fault in negligence law, as discussed above.[500]

At an early date, perceptive products liability scholars recognized the necessity for evaluating design and (to a lesser extent) warning defect claims by means of a "negligence" cost-benefit approach. In an article written in 1957, as the push toward strict products liability of manufacturers was beginning to accelerate, Professor Leon Green observed that the rule of negligence, rather than strict liability, was best suited to such cases.[501] "Negligence law here," he reasoned, "is in its ancestral environment."[502] Products liability theorizing was in its infancy at the time, and so the essence of his observation may fairly be distilled. What he really meant of course, was that cost-benefit analysis, inherent in negligence law, is the basic analytical tool used by engineers in designing products, and so it is the method by which the "reasonableness" of those decisions fairly and logically should be judged.[503]

Together with the commentators, many courts have come to appreciate the substantial equivalence of negligence and strict liability in tort in design and warning cases. In one early case, the court perceptively observed that "the distinction between the so-called strict liability principle and negligence is of no practical significance so far as the standard of conduct required of the defendant is concerned. In either event the standard required is reasonable care."[504] While most early judges did not appreciate this important point about liability in most product defect cases, and while a few stubborn holdouts remain, modern courts increasingly recognize that the basis of liability in both

---

[497] Courts make the inference or presumption either formally, under the doctrine of res ipsa loquitur, or informally, as needing no discussion. See, e.g., Pouncey v. Ford Motor Co., 464 F.2d 957 (5th Cir. 1972) (Ala. law); Jenkins v. General Motors Corp., 446 F.2d 377 (5th Cir. 1971) (Ga. law). See generally § 2.5 (res ipsa), above.

[498] Prosser, The Assault Upon the Citadel (Strict Liability to the Consumer), 69 Yale L.J. 1099, 1114 (1960).

[499] This test is examined in § 5.6, above.

[500] See § 5.7, above.

[501] Although addressing only "mechanical products," as distinguished from food and chemical products where he thought a rule of strict liability was proper, Professor Green's case examples indicate that he was envisaging design and warning problems with such mechanical machines. See Green, Should the Manufacturer of General Products Be Liable Without Negligence?, 24 Tenn. L. Rev. 928 (1957).

[502] Id. at 934.

[503] See Donaher, Piehler, Twerski, and Weinstein, The Technological Expert in Products Liability Litigation, 52 Tex. L. Rev. 1303 (1974).

[504] Jones v. Hutchinson Mfg., Inc., 502 S.W.2d 66, 69–70 (Ky. 1973).

design[505] and warning cases[506] is virtually, or completely, equivalent in negligence and strict liability in tort. This recognition has finally reached the point that a few courts, usually indirectly but sometimes explicitly, have ruled that the equivalence of strict tort liability and negligence in design and warning cases supports a single cause of action. In an insightful splash of candor, the Iowa Supreme Court, in *Olson v. Prosoco, Inc.*,[507] boldly repealed its rule of "strict" liability for warning cases, returning to a formal rule of negligence. In a later case, the same court adopted the *Third Restatement*'s application of cost-benefit analysis to design defect determinations and its abandonment in such cases of doctrinal labels and distinctions between negligence and strict liability.[508] Certainly most courts, however, still cling tenaciously to the view that the doctrines of negligence and strict liability in tort are and must be kept conceptually distinct.[509]

Juries, Strategy, and Inconsistent Verdicts

The near or complete equivalence of the basis of liability in design and warning cases of negligence and strict liability in tort raises a couple of important trial issues, one strategic and the other theoretical. One aspect of the strategic issue concerns whether a plaintiff's lawyer should plead both theories, covering all bases, but risk confusing the jury which may, unless precisely guided by court and counsel, mistakenly believe that liability requires a finding of all the elements of both types of claims. If, on the other hand, plaintiff's counsel chooses to use a rifle shot approach by providing the jury with a single claim, which should it be, negligence or strict liability? Logic might seem to suggest that a plaintiff's lawyer simply abandon the negligence claim for the simpler and easier-to-prove claim of strict liability in tort, and that it would almost be malpractice to assert a negligence claim alone. Yet seasoned plaintiff's counsel[510] and an

---

505 See, e.g., Baker v. Cottrell, Inc., 2017 WL 6730572, at *8 n.8 (E.D. Cal. 2017) ("The analysis of whether a [defectively designed] product caused a plaintiff's injury is identical under both negligence and strict liability theories. That is, if a defendant is found liable in a products liability case on a theory of negligence, it will necessarily also be liable on a strict liability theory because the latter claim is fully contained within the negligence claim."); Forslund v. Stryker Corp., 2010 WL 3905854, at *2 (D. Minn. 2010) ("strict liability and negligence theories [merge] under a single products liability theory [that] analyzes design defect claims under the reasonable-care balancing test"). See also Reichmann v. Whirlpool Corp., 2020 WL 207749, at *5 (E.D.N.Y. 2020) ("While design defect claims for strict product liability are distinguishable from those based in negligence, . . . for purposes of establishing a prima facie case in the summary judgment context, the claims are 'functionally equivalent.' . . . Accordingly, in the summary judgment context, the claims are often analyzed together.").

506 See, e.g., Whelan v. Armstrong Int'l Inc., 231 A.3d 640, 653 n.7 (N.J. 2020) (citing authorities on functional equivalence of negligence and strict liability for warnings claims); McIntyre v. Bradford White Corp., 130 N.Y.S.3d 632, at *4 (Sup. Ct. 2020) (table) ("[F]ailure-to-warn claims grounded in strict liability and negligence are functionally equivalent, as both forms of a failure-to-warn claim depend on the principles of reasonableness and public policy at the heart of any traditional negligence action."); Wedgewood v. U.S. Filter/Whittier, Inc., 2011 WL 2150102, at *13 (Neb. Ct. App. 2011) (citing authorities for notion that negligence and strict liability are functionally equivalent for warnings claims); Gourdine v. Crews, 955 A.2d 769, 782 (Md. 2008) ("negligence concepts and those of strict liability have 'morphed together' . . . in failure to warn cases"). See § 2.6, above.

507 522 N.W.2d 284 (Iowa 1994).

508 Wright v. Brooke Grp. Ltd., 652 N.W.2d 159, 169 (Iowa 2002) ("We question the need for or usefulness of any traditional doctrinal label in design defect cases because . . . a negligence claim and a strict liability claim . . . rest on an identical risk-utility evaluation.").

509 See, e.g., Pennsylvania Dep't of Gen. Servs. v. United States Mineral Prods. Co., 898 A.2d 590, 602 (Pa. 2006) ("negligence concepts have no place in strict liability doctrine").

510 See Rheingold, The Expanding Liability of the Product Supplier: A Primer, 2 Hofstra L. Rev. 521, 531–32 (1974) (plaintiff's counsel would prefer to argue in "hot" negligence terms that a drug company concealed side effects from consumers than that the warning label was inadequate).

important empirical jury study[511] conclude that juries respond far more favorably to plaintiffs—in both verdict likelihood and size of awards—on the "hot" rhetoric of negligence than on the "cold" logic of strict liability.

The theoretical issue arising from the overlapping of negligence and strict liability concerns a thorny problem involving inconsistent jury verdicts.[512] Suppose that a court submits a case to the jury on both negligence and strict liability in tort claims, and, by special interrogatories, the jury decides for the plaintiff on the negligence claim but for the defendant on the strict liability claim. The problem, of course, is that the two verdicts are logically inconsistent. A strict liability ruling requires a finding that the product is defective; and a negligence ruling requires two implicit findings: (1) that the product is "bad" (defective), and (2) that the defendant was at fault in supplying the product in that condition.[513] A manufacturer or other supplier can hardly be faulted for supplying consumers with a "good" product—one that is *not* defective. So, a finding that a product is not defective for purposes of strict liability in tort logically precludes a finding that the manufacturer or other supplier was negligent in making or selling it in that condition.[514] An early Minnesota decision succinctly captured the essence of this point: "If a product is not . . . defective . . ., it is not negligence to manufacture it that way."[515] Hence, the two findings—that a product is not defective but that the defendant was negligent in making or selling it—are normally contradictory and simply cannot be harmonized or reconciled.[516]

Despite a curiously large number of decisions to the contrary,[517] most courts convincingly reason that a negligence finding is necessarily inconsistent with a finding

511 See Cupp and Polage, The Rhetoric of Strict Products Liability Versus Negligence: An Empirical Analysis, 77 N.Y.U. L. Rev. 874, 936–37 (2002) (in mock trials of same case, 26% of jurors in strict liability trial awarded damages whereas 38% of jurors in negligence trial awarded damages; jurors on average awarded damages nearly twice as large in negligence than in strict liability).

512 See Blydenburgh, Analyzing Inconsistent Verdicts in Products Liability Cases, 73 Def. Couns. J. 46 (2006).

513 See, e.g., Kosmynka v. Polaris Indus., 462 F.3d 74, 86 (2d Cir. 2006) (N.Y. law) (both strict liability and negligence "entail a showing that a product defect caused the injury; but to show negligence, the plaintiff must also prove that the injury caused by the defect could have been reasonably foreseen by the manufacturer"); Merrill v. Navegar, Inc., 28 P.3d 116, 124 (Cal. 2001) (under both negligence and strict liability, plaintiff must prove a defect caused the injury and, under negligence, plaintiff must also prove "an additional element, namely, that the defect in the product was due to negligence of the defendant") (quoting Prosser, Strict Liability to the Consumer in California, 18 Hastings L.J. 9, 50–51 (1966)).

The Third Restatement makes this point: "Negligence rests on a showing of fault leading to product defect. Strict liability rests merely on a showing of product defect." Products Liability Rest. § 2 cmt. *n*. See generally § 2.1 (*Breach*), above.

514 "Ordinarily, strict liability, which was developed to ease a claimant's burden of proof, requires proof of fewer elements than negligence, making a positive verdict on the latter difficult to explain if strict liability cannot be found." Annot., 41 A.L.R.4th 9, § 2[A] (1985) (inconsistent products liability verdicts).

515 Halvorson v. American Hoist & Derrick Co., 240 N.W.2d 303, 307 (Minn. 1976).

516 See Annot., 41 A.L.R.4th 9, § 2[A] (1985) (inconsistent products liability verdicts; "if the alleged faults underlying the negligence and strict liability claims are clearly the same, the courts have commonly ruled that a finding of negligence but no strict liability cannot be sustained").

517 See, e.g., Bayes v. Biomet, Inc., 2021 WL 3329294, at *4 (E.D. Mo. 2021) (defendant not liable under strict liability but liable under negligence; "juries considering strict-liability and negligent-design claims do not have to reach verdicts in favor of the same party"); In re Bard IVC Filters Prods. Liab. Litig., 2018 WL 3037161, at *9 (D. Ariz. 2018) (defendants liable under negligence but not liable under strict liability for failure to warn of inferior vena cava risks; harmonizing the verdicts: "jury could have found, consistent with the instructions and the evidence, that the warning provided with the G2 filter when it was sold was not inadequate, but that Bard was negligent in failing to warn about later-acquired information"), aff'd on other grounds, 969 F.3d 1067 (9th Cir. 2020); Moeller v. Garlock Sealing Techs., LLC, 2009 WL 1208179, at *3 (W.D. Ky. 2009) (defendant not liable under strict liability but liable for negligence; "Since the [jury] instructions are

that a product was not defective.[518] In such a case, a jury's rendering of two fatally inconsistent findings normally invalidates the verdict, requiring that the verdict be vacated and a new trial granted.[519]

It is difficult to understand why a jury might return inconsistent findings of this type. It may simply be because the jury does not fully understand the true meaning of the legal term of art, "defective": a jury may believe that even an inadequately designed product, or one carrying inadequate warning, is not "defective" if it contains no loose screws or broken parts.[520] Or it may be because the phrase "unreasonably dangerous" may sound to the jury "as if the requisite proof for a product defect is some form of 'extraordinary' danger."[521] In addition to such confusion, it may be, as suggested by one court, that such inconsistencies reflect a jury's desire to be lenient with the plaintiff or to effect a kind of compromise between the parties.[522] But, whatever the reason, such findings logically make no sense, are offensive to sound jurisprudence, and ordinarily should not be tolerated.

Verdicts are inconsistent, of course, only when the two claims pertain to the same particular fault or defect in the product. Thus, there is nothing inconsistent in a jury finding that a product was negligently designed, but that its warnings were sufficient; or that the manufacturer negligently failed to provide an adequate instruction or warning, but that the design itself, perhaps burdened with an unavoidable latent

---

not duplicative, the different responses are not inherently inconsistent."), rev'd on other grounds, 660 F.3d 950 (6th Cir. 2011); Phillips v. Cricket Lighters, 841 A.2d 1000, 1008–10 (Pa. 2003) (because the elements of the two torts are distinct, it would be "illogical" to reject a negligence claim solely because of the failure of the claim for strict liability in tort); Connelly v. Hyundai Motor Co., 351 F.3d 535 (1st Cir. 2003) (N.H. law) (no inconsistency in jury's finding of no defective design but negligence in testing or design); Sharp v. Case Corp., 595 N.W.2d 380, 387 (Wis. 1999); Brown v. Yamaha Motor Corp., 691 P.2d 577 (Wash. Ct. App. 1984); Robertson v. General Tire & Rubber Co., 462 N.E.2d 706 (Ill. App. Ct. 1984); Randall v. Warnaco, Inc., 677 F.2d 1226 (8th Cir. 1982) (N.D. law).

[518] See, e.g., Trejo v. Johnson & Johnson, 220 Cal. Rptr. 3d 127, 149 (Ct. App. 2017) (jury's verdict against manufacturer on negligent failure to warn of dangers of rare skin disease from taking over-the-counter Motrin was fatally inconsistent with its verdict for manufacturer on strict liability failure to warn); Branham v. Ford Motor Co., 701 S.E.2d 5, 8–9 (S.C. 2010) (design); Oxford v. Foster Wheeler LLC, 99 Cal. Rptr. 3d 418, 436 (Ct. App. 2009) (because record disclosed "no explanation of how the jury might have found defendant negligent for failure to warn while also finding that the product was not defective with respect to its warnings," it was "hopelessly inconsistent" and, hence, "against the law"); Kosmynka v. Polaris Indus., 462 F.3d 74, 86 (2d Cir. 2006) (N.Y. law) ("a manufacturer whose defective product causes injury can be held strictly liable even if not negligent, but not the reverse"); Lecy v. Bayliner Marine Corp., 973 P.2d 1110, 1113 (Wash. Ct. App. 1999) ("Federal and state case law in other jurisdictions [generally holds] that a jury's rejection of strict liability for design defect precludes a finding of negligent design.").

[519] See, e.g., In re Testosterone Replacement Therapy Prods. Liab. Litig. Coordination Pretrial Proc., 2018 WL 3303269, at *10 (N.D. Ill. 2018) (appropriate remedy for inconsistent verdicts on strict liability and negligence claims is new trial on all claims); Coba v. Tricam Indus., Inc., 164 So.3d 637, 644 (Fla. 2015) ("If a party timely objects to an inconsistent verdict and the trial court erroneously denies the objection and discharges the jury, the correct remedy is to grant a new trial."); *Oxford*, 99 Cal. Rptr. 3d at 436 ("irreconcilable inconsistency in the verdicts" requires new trial); *Kosmynka*, 462 F.3d at 87 (trial court "failed to remedy the inconsistent verdict"; vacated and remanded for new trial); *Lecy*, 973 P.2d at 1117 (inconsistent verdict requires new trial; otherwise, judge's judgment is substituted for jury's); Witt v. Norfe, Inc., 725 F.2d 1277 (11th Cir. 1984) (Fla. law). *But see* Eagle-Picher Indus. v. Balbos, 578 A.2d 228 (Md. Ct. Spec. App. 1990) (because inconsistent verdict may reflect lenity, mistake, or compromise, new trial would interfere with jury's decisional role), rev'd in part on other grounds, 604 A.2d 445 (Md. 1992). See also Mack Trucks, Inc. v. Coates, 2018 WL 2175932, at *8 (Md. Ct. Spec. App. 2018) (defendants' failure to object to inconsistent verdict before jury was discharged invalidated their post-trial motion for new trial on the issue).

[520] Cf. Rinker v. Ford Motor Co., 567 S.W.2d 655, 659–60 (Mo. Ct. App. 1978).

[521] Twerski, From Defect to Cause to Comparative Fault—Rethinking Some Product Liability Concepts, 60 Marq. L. Rev. 297, 334 (1977).

[522] See *Eagle-Picher Indus.*, 578 A.2d 228, note 519, above.

danger, was reasonably safe.[523] In such cases, the separate findings may be harmonized, and the plaintiff's verdict should be sustained.[524]

One solution to the inconsistent verdict problem would be to require the plaintiff to elect a single theory, strict liability or negligence, upon which to submit the case to the jury. While most courts do not require such a choice,[525] a few courts have withdrawn the negligence count from the jury on grounds that it would be "superfluous and would tend to confuse the jurors" if included with a count for strict liability in tort.[526] A few other courts have gone the other way, ruling that juries should be instructed only on negligence, and not on strict liability in tort.[527] Or a court could avoid the problem altogether by adopting the *Third Restatement*'s approach of abandoning distinctions between negligence and strict liability and submitting cases to juries according to the type of proof required for the type of defect plaintiff has alleged.[528]

Strict Liability in Tort *vs.* Warranty

In General

Many courts and commentators in the 1960s agreed with Dean Prosser's view that the merger of warranty and tort into a new tort doctrine of strict products liability was a legal inevitability.[529] But a substantial segment of the legal academy was always troubled by the overlap between the two strict products liability doctrines—the one doctrine standing proudly in tort while the other cowers shamelessly in contract, disparate branches of the law competing for coverage of a single social problem.[530] As both tort and contract law during the 1960s tried to stamp their brands on strict manufacturer liability for product accidents, scholars from different sides of the academy viewed the matter from quite different windows.

One leading commercial law scholar, Richard Speidel, argued that "nagging doubts about the propriety of a judicial imposition of strict products liability, recurring attacks upon the bases of liability itself, the complexity of the underlying problems of cost allocation among the various enterprises and individuals involved, and a suspicion that in a zealous attempt to protect the consumer interest the courts may have created more problems than they can solve all dictate against the type of 'unrealistic absolutism'

[523] On the independence of the three separate types of defect, see § 6.2, below.

[524] See, e.g., Hakim v. Safariland, LLC, 2022 WL 1136552, at *5 (N.D. Ill. 2022); In re Vioxx Prods. Liab. Litig., 523 F. Supp. 2d 471, 474 (E.D. La. 2007) (S.C. law); Perry v. Red Wing Shoe Co., 597 So.2d 821 (Fla. Dist. Ct. App. 1992); Peterson v. Little-Giant Glencoe Portable Elevator Div. of Dynamics Corp. of Am., 349 N.W.2d 280 (Minn. Ct. App. 1984) (jury findings of negligence but not strict liability were consistent when based on claims of separate conduct), rev'd in part on other grounds, 366 N.W.2d 111 (Minn. 1985). See generally Annot., 41 A.L.R.4th 9 (1985) (inconsistent products liability verdicts).

[525] Hansen v. Cessna Aircraft Co., 578 F.2d 679 (7th Cir. 1978) (Wis. law); Howes v. Deere & Co., 238 N.W.2d 76 (Wis. 1976). Compare § 402A cmt. *a*.

[526] See, e.g., Mather v. Caterpillar Tractor Corp., 533 P.2d 717, 719 (Ariz. Ct. App. 1975). The cases are collected in Annot., 52 A.L.R.3d 101 (1974) (necessity and propriety of instructing on alternative theories in products liability cases). See generally Slattery, Terschan, and Griffin, Product Liability Verdict Formulation in Wisconsin, 61 Marq. L. Rev. 381 (1978).

[527] See, e.g., Olson v. Prosoco, Inc., 522 N.W.2d 284, 289 (Iowa 1994) (warning defect).

[528] See, e.g., Wright v. Brooke Grp. Ltd., 652 N.W.2d 159, 169 (Iowa 2002) (design defect).

[529] See §§ 5.2–5.4, above.

[530] See, e.g., Owen, Defectiveness Restated: Exploding the "Strict" Products Liability Myth, 1996 U. Ill. L. Rev. 743, 756 (observing that, in modern design defect theory, "the utilitarian, fault-based negligence principles of tort law and the expectational, strict liability principles of the law of contracts are conjoined" and opining that "[w]hether this conjunction is proper may well be doubted, for the separate spheres of tort and contract law serve distinct functions and derive from disparate policies and ethics").

displayed in Section 402A of the *Restatement of Torts, Second*."[531] Professor Speidel opined that warranty principles, under a contract law umbrella, allow individuals to make whatever purchase and sales transactions suit their particular needs and preferences and so are preferable to "the treacherous uncertainties of strict products liability" in tort.[532] Tort law scholars broadly disagreed. For example, Mark Franklin, a leading tort law scholar, was "left with regret that the Code, devoted so extensively to dealings within the business community, decided to try its hand at the products liability problem. That it did so is clear. That it should have is much less clear. The considerations involved in the products cases are so different from traditional commercial dealings that the Code's insistence on covering all of an abstract 'commercial' area may unfortunately lead to similar treatment for dissimilar problems."[533]

Such arguments fail sufficiently to embrace the important historical fact that the doctrine of strict products liability in tort sprang from the law of warranty, as previously discussed.[534] Yet, once the decisions in *Henningsen v. Bloomfield Motors, Inc.*[535] and *Greenman v. Yuba Power Products, Inc.*[536] stripped the implied warranty claim of its traditional contract law defenses, what remained, in all its naked glory, was a doctrine of strict products liability in tort,[537] as aptly noted by some courts.[538] Despite the different manner in which the tort and implied warranty liability standards are phrased—"defective condition unreasonably dangerous"[539] *versus* "fit for the ordinary purposes for which such goods are used"[540]—courts often recite the virtual or complete equivalence of the two standards of liability, holding that they require the same types of proof.[541] Thus, most courts today properly view the notion of unmerchantability to be the equivalent of the defect concept in both negligence and strict products liability in tort.[542]

That strict liability in tort derived largely from warranty law's inability to provide injured consumers with an effective mode of recovery—due to the restrictions of privity,

---

[531] Speidel, The Virginia "Anti-Privity" Statute: Strict Products Liability Under The Uniform Commercial Code, 51 Va. L. Rev. 804, 851 (1965).

[532] See id. ("Until an ultimate legislative solution to the problem is formulated and enacted into law, the treacherous uncertainties of strict products liability imposed by courts can be reduced by at least one firm anchor to the traditional values of freedom of contract.")

[533] Franklin, When Worlds Collide: Liability Theories and Disclaimers in Defective-Product Cases, 18 Stan. L. Rev. 974, 1019–20 (1966).

[534] See § 5.2, above.

[535] 161 A.2d 69 (N.J. 1960).

[536] 377 P.2d 897 (Cal. 1963).

[537] See § 5.2, above.

[538] See, e.g., Nave v. Rainbo Tire Serv., Inc., 462 N.E.2d 620, 625 (Ill. App. Ct. 1984) (strict liability in tort "is essentially the liability of implied warranty divested of the contract doctrines of privity, disclaimer and notice").

[539] Rest. (2d) Torts § 402A.

[540] UCC § 2–314(2)(c).

[541] To recover on either implied warranty or strict liability, a plaintiff in a products liability case must establish three facts: "(1) the existence of a defect, (2) the attribution of the defect to the seller, and (3) a causal relation between the defect and the injury." Lloyd v. General Motors Corp., 916 A.2d 257, 286 (Md. 2007).

[542] See, e.g., In re Davol, Inc./C.R. Bard, Inc., Polypropylene Hernia Mesh Prods. Liab. Litig., 2020 WL 5223363, at *22 (S.D. Ohio 2020) (Utah law) ("the elements of breach of an implied warranty and products liability are essentially the same"); Kirkbride v. Terex USA, LLC, 798 F.3d 1343, 1354–55 (10th Cir. 2015) (Utah law); Haglund v. Philip Morris, Inc., 847 N.E.2d 315, 321–22 (Mass. 2006).

See also Baird v. Wernerco Servs., Inc., 2019 WL 3753694, at *3 (S.D. Tex. 2019) (products liability statute subsumes personal injury implied warranty claims); Bergeron v. Pacific Food, Inc., 2011 WL 1017872, at *3 n.7 (Conn. Super. Ct. 2011) (claims under product statue " shall be in lieu of all other claims against product sellers, including actions of negligence, strict liability and warranty, for harm caused by a product").

disclaimer, and notice—raises an interesting question of whether courts can properly "legislate" around carefully crafted warranty law principles enacted by state legislatures which have adopted Article 2 of the Uniform Commercial Code. Thus, in *Cline v. Prowler Industries of Maryland, Inc.*,[543] the Delaware Supreme Court refused to adopt § 402A as the law of that state because of the legislature's then-recent enactment of the UCC. "[T]he General Assembly did not intend to permit the adoption of a competing theory of liability in cases involving the sales of goods and, thus, preempted the field."[544] But most courts were little concerned with the argument that strict products liability in tort might impermissibly invade a field preempted by the UCC, and the issue is now of little more than modest historical interest.[545]

Inconsistent Jury Verdicts—Denny v. Ford Motor Co.

The virtual or complete identity between the concept of defectiveness under § 402A and the notion of unmerchantability under UCC § 2–314 has led some courts to hold that conflicting jury verdicts on the two theories must be irreconcilable and, hence, the basis for reversal. On such reasoning, for example, an extension cord found *not* to be defective can hardly also be found to be unmerchantable.[546] Further, if the two claims are in fact redundant, a court may properly refuse to instruct a jury on both doctrines.[547]

For many years, the inconsistency of jury verdicts was little more than a footnote to the developing body of products liability jurisprudence. In 1995, however, the New York Court of Appeals decided *Denny v. Ford Motor Co.*[548] in which it ruled that claims of strict products liability in tort and breach of implied warranty are not always coextensive. Nancy Denny was injured when she slammed on the brakes of her Ford Bronco II SUV to avoid hitting a deer and the vehicle rolled over, injuring her. Ms. Denny sued Ford in federal court, challenging the vehicle's design for rolling over too easily due to its relatively narrow track width, high center of gravity, short wheelbase and suspension system, and Ford's failure to warn of the vehicle's propensity to roll over. While the design of the Bronco II made the vehicle less stable for the normal kind of suburban highway driving for which Ford marketed the car, it made the vehicle more useful for driving over irregular off-road terrain, a supposed purpose of such a "sport utility vehicle."

Plaintiff asserted the same design and failure to warn claims in separate counts of (1) strict liability in tort, for selling a product in a defective condition, and (2) breach of the implied warranty of merchantability, for marketing a car that was not fit for its ordinary purposes. Despite the defendant's objections that the claims were identical, the

---

[543] 418 A.2d 968 (Del. 1980).

[544] Id. at 980. Compare Middlesex Mut. Assurance Co. v. Delaware Elec. Signal Co., 2008 WL 4216145, at *5 (Del. Super. Ct. 2008) (adoption of UCC Article 2A "preempts the application of strict liability in the lease context").

[545] Arguing that the preemption view was wrong, Dean John Wade had the last word in a decade-long debate with Professor Reed Dickerson on whether tort law had improperly invaded the field of warranty and contract. See Wade, Tort Liability for Products Causing Physical Injury and Article 2 of the U.C.C., 48 Mo. L. Rev. 1 (1983) (arguing that tort law properly applies to this field of law). Though eventually withdrawn, Amended § 2–314 attempted to put the matter to rest by defining "merchantability" in personal injury cases by the products liability tort law of the state. See Amended UCC § 2–314 cmt. 7. See § 4.3 note 192, above.

[546] See State Farm Fire & Cas. Co. v. Miller Elec. Co., 562 N.E.2d 589 (Ill. App. Ct. 1990). See also Gumbs v. International Harvester, Inc., 718 F.2d 88 (3d Cir. 1983) (V.I. law). *Contra* Malawy v. Richards Mfg. Co., 501 N.E.2d 376 (Ill. App. Ct. 1986) (distinguishing the two theories).

[547] See, e.g., Goblirsch v. Western Land Roller Co., 246 N.W.2d 687, 690 (Minn. 1976).

[548] 662 N.E.2d 730 (N.Y. 1995).

district court submitted the case to the jury on both claims. Without objection, the court instructed the jury that the tort law claim required the plaintiff to prove that the vehicle was "defective" or "not reasonably safe," determinable by a risk-utility evaluation of the costs and benefits of designing out the danger. The court further explained that the implied warranty claim required the plaintiff to prove that the vehicle was not "reasonably fit for the ordinary purposes for which it was intended."[549]

The jury returned a split verdict, concluding that (1) the Bronco was *not* "defective," so that Ford was not liable for strict products liability in tort, but that (2) Ford *had* breached an implied warranty of merchantability and so was liable on that basis for plaintiff's injuries.[550] On defendant's appeal, the Second Circuit Court of Appeals certified certain questions to the New York high court, asking whether the two claims were identical, and, if not, whether the jury's finding of no defect was reconcilable with its finding of a breach of warranty. Answering the question, the New York court ruled that the claims are *not* identical and, on the facts, the jury's findings *were* reconcilable. Defectiveness in strict liability in tort, reasoned the court, contains a "negligence-like risk/benefit component," which rests on the manufacturer's reasonableness in not adopting feasible alternative designs, whereas the implied warranty of merchantability rests on whether a product is "fit for ordinary purposes," measured by consumer expectations of how the product should operate in foreseeable situations.[551] The court stated that the jury reasonably could have concluded that the Bronco II was not "defective" for tort law purposes because its utility as an off-road vehicle outweighed the risk of rollovers, while also concluding that the vehicle was *not* safe under warranty law for the "ordinary purpose" of everyday on-road driving for which it was marketed and sold. Thus, the jury could have concluded simultaneously that the strict products liability claim failed but that the defendant had breached its implied warranty of merchantability of "fitness" for "ordinary purpose." The case was distinctive, thought the court, because the "ordinary purpose" for which the product was marketed and sold, the basis for the implied warranty claim, was different from the utility against which the risk was weighed, which underlay the tort claim.[552]

In a subsequent federal opinion applying New York law, the Second Circuit characterized *Denny* as adopting a doctrine that "can aptly be called the 'dual purpose'

---

[549] Id. at 732.

[550] Id. at 733.

[551] See id. at 736:

It is [the] negligence-like risk/benefit component of the defect element that differentiates strict products liability claims from UCC-based breach of implied warranty claims in cases involving design defects. While the strict products concept of a product that is "not reasonably safe" requires a weighing of the product's dangers against its over-all advantages, the UCC's concept of a "defective" product requires an inquiry only into whether the product in question was "fit for the ordinary purposes for which such goods are used" (UCC § 2–314[2][c]). The latter inquiry focuses on the expectations for the performance of the product when used in the customary, usual and reasonably foreseeable manners. The cause of action is one involving true "strict" liability, since recovery may be had upon a showing that the product was not minimally safe for its expected purpose—without regard to the feasibility of alternative designs or the manufacturer's "reasonableness" in marketing it in that unsafe condition.

[552] Id. at 738–39.

requirement."[553] The *Denny* dual-purpose rationale is a clever, *Barker*-like approach,[554] that sometimes, albeit infrequently, may improve the fairness of a particular result.[555] Yet, by opening up a whole new representational doctrine that skirts around conventional rules of tortious misrepresentation and express warranty, and that applies to only a tiny subset of cases, *Denny* may have concocted a cannon to kill a fly. Commentators have not been kind to *Denny*,[556] it contravenes a strong majority rule,[557] and it has been rejected by the American Law Institute in the *Products Liability Restatement*.[558]

§ 5.10 THE PATH AWAY FROM STRICT LIABILITY IN TORT

Strict liability in tort, by definition, imposes liability on a seller for physical harm caused by product defects even if the seller was not negligent in any way, even if it exercised all due care.[559] Liability is "strict" because it rests solely on the defective condition of a product without regard to the seller's fault in making or selling the product in that condition. For about two decades, from the mid-1960s to the mid-1980s, strict liability in tort under *Restatement (Second) of Torts* § 402A spread from state to state, as one court after another (and an occasional state legislature) adopted the new doctrine.[560] By about 1980, the rule of strict products liability in tort appeared entrenched in American law.

As courts applied the new principle across the nation, however, it began to develop various troubling fissures, weaknesses largely dormant at its inception, which began to cast pallor over the very idea of "strict" products liability in tort. Surely the dominant concern was the idea of holding manufacturers responsible for harm that was not their fault—rendering them subject to liability even if they could not have foreseen the hazard nor were otherwise incapable of preventing it. As previously discussed, a small minority of states and commentators never did accept the new rule, viewing its rationales as contrary to traditional principles of fairness and efficiency that strongly supported fault

---

[553] Castro v. QVC Network, Inc., 139 F.3d 114, 118 (2d Cir. 1998) (N.Y. law) (Calabresi, J.) (following *Denny:* "in *Denny,* the Court of Appeals pointed out that the fact that a product's overall benefits might outweigh its overall risks does not preclude the possibility that consumers may have been misled into using the product in a context in which it was dangerously unsafe. . . . even though the benefits in other uses might make the product sufficiently reasonable so that it passed the risk/utility test"). On the *Denny* "dual purpose" test, see Ausili, Ramifications of Denny v. Ford Motor Co., 15 Touro L. Rev. 735 (1999).

[554] See § 5.8, above.

[555] In addition to *Denny* itself, see also Bradley v. Earl B. Feiden, Inc., 864 N.E.2d 600 (N.Y. 2007) (refrigerator was unmerchantable though defrost timer was not defective).

[556] See, e.g., White, Reverberations from the Collision of Tort and Warranty, 53 S.C. L. Rev. 1067, 1072–75 (2002); Ausili, Ramifications of Denny v. Ford Motor Co., 15 Touro L. Rev. 735 (1999); Schwartz and Behrens, An Unhappy Return to Confusion in the Common Law of Products Liability—Denny v. Ford Motor Company Should Be Overturned, 17 Pace L. Rev. 359, 377 (1997) ("the Court should overrule *Denny* and the Court's opinion should be ignored by courts of other states"); Note, 62 Mo. L. Rev. 381 (1997).

[557] See, e.g., Hyundai Motor Co. v. Rodriguez, 995 S.W.2d 661 (Tex. 1999). For additional citations, see Ausili, Ramifications of Denny v. Ford Motor Co., 15 Touro L. Rev. 735 (1999).

[558] Products Liability Rest. § 2 cmt. *n*, at 34–35 ("two or more factually identical defective-design claims or two or more factually identical failure-to-warn claims should not be submitted to the trier of fact in the same case under different doctrinal labels"). And the Institute also rejected *Denny* in approving Amended Article 2 of the UCC, see Amended UCC § 2–314 cmt. 7, although the Institute subsequently rescinded its approval of Article 2 on other grounds.

[559] Rest. (2d) Torts § 402A cmt. *m* (1965). This point is made in black letter: "The rule stated in Subsection (1) applies although (a) the seller has exercised all possible care in the preparation and sale of his product." Rest. (2d) Torts § 402A(2).

[560] This development is traced in § 5.3, above.

as the basis of negligence liability. As legal scholars increasingly highlighted conceptual frailties in the new tort doctrine—beginning as early as the 1950s,[561] and following the birth of § 402A nearly a decade later[562]—courts and state legislatures in the 1970s and 1980s began to move the basis of a seller's liability for physical harm from defective products away from truly "strict" liability and back to principles of fault.

This movement back to negligence principles may be attributed to a series of overlapping judicial and legislative developments in products liability law beginning in the 1970s and accelerating during the 1980s and 1990s: (1) the decline of a duty to warn of unknowable dangers, reflecting a commensurate revitalization of foreseeability of risk; (2) the decline of the two strict liability standards or liability "tests"—(a) the Wade-Keeton test, and (b) the consumer expectations test; (3) the rise of a state-of-the-art defense; and (4) the promulgation of the *Third Restatement of Torts* on products liability law. Each of these developments sprang from a powerful, general conception that actors (including manufacturers) ought not be held accountable for risks they cannot control—

561 See Plant, Strict Liability of Manufacturers for Injuries Caused by Defects in Products—An Opposing View, 24 Tenn. L. Rev. 938, 940 (1957) ("the proposed rule is completely out of accord with modem concepts of justice and legal policy").

562 Early critiques included Speidel, The Virginia "Anti-Privity" Statute: Strict Products Liability Under The Uniform Commercial Code, 51 Va. L. Rev. 804, 851 (1965) ("[N]agging doubts about the propriety of a judicial imposition of strict products liability, recurring attacks upon the bases of liability itself, the complexity of the underlying problems of cost allocation . . ., and a suspicion that in a zealous attempt to protect the consumer interest the courts may have created more problems than they can solve all dictate against the type of 'unrealistic absolutism' displayed in Section 402A of the *Restatement of Torts, Second*."); Henderson, Judicial Review of Manufacturers' Conscious Design Choices: The Limits of Adjudication, 73 Colum. L. Rev. 1531, 1534 (1973) ("courts are not suited to the task of establishing specific product safety standards in the course of applying general reasonableness tests to determine the adequacy of allegedly defective products brought before them"); Klemme, The Enterprise Liability Theory of Torts, 47 U. Colo. L. Rev. 153, 174 (1976) ("The theory of strict or absolute tort liability is not, I would suggest, a theory at all. It does not provide any general unifying criteria or rationale which can be used to account for why the tort law has developed any of its various rules of liability and nonliability. Strict liability does nothing more than describe a result in certain limited cases."); Hoenig, Products Liability Problems and Proposed Reforms, 1977 Ins. L.J. 213, 215 (1977) ("Whatever may be the appropriate label, it is apparent that the current strict liability-oriented system of resolving products claims may actually be creating problems greater than those it was supposed to solve."); Epstein, The Search for a Middle Ground, 56 N.C. L. Rev. 643, 652 (1978) ("modern design litigation . . . is an invitation to the kind of standardless adjudication that reduces a lawsuit to a glorious, if expensive, game of chance"); O'Donnell, Design Litigation and Strict Liability: The Problem of Jury Instructions Which Do Not Instruct, 56 U. Det. J. Urb. L. 1051, 1061 (1979) ("the decisions of judge and jury often are mere exercises of power, so arbitrary as to be akin to a lottery"); Birnbaum, Unmasking the Test for Design Defect: From Negligence (to Warranty) to Strict Liability to Negligence, 33 Vand. L. Rev. 593, 601 (1980) ("The courts, in attempting to avoid both the notion of fault implicit in negligence and the harshness of no-fault implicit in absolute liability, have focused the jury's attention on the condition of the product rather than on the manufacturer's conduct. By so doing, some courts have engaged in semantic gymnastics that confuse juries, who must ultimately apply understandable guidelines if they are justly to adjudicate the rights and duties of all parties."); Owen, Rethinking the Policies of Strict Products Liability, 33 Vand. L. Rev. 681, 683 (1980) (opining that "[m]ushy notions of consumer welfarism [that] dominated much of the thinking of the 1960s . . . spawned a hasty and large-scale reconstitution of this entire field of law within a very few years," and calling for a reconsideration of strict products liability in tort); Twerski, Weinstein, Donaher, and Piehler, Shifting Perspectives in Products Liability: From Quality to Process Standards, 55 N.Y.U. L. Rev. 347, 348 (1980) ("The explosion of design defect litigation during the last two decades has failed to develop products liability into a cohesive and workable body of law."); Wade, On Product "Design Defects" and Their Actionability, 33 Vand. L. Rev. 551, 557 (1980) ("the orderly flow of development has turned into a swampy quagmire and threatens to split into several different streams with diverse destinations."); note 308, above. See also the variety of critiques of modern products liability law in the momentous study directed by Professor Victor Schwartz, Product Liability: Final Report of the Legal Study, vol. 3 (Interagency Task Force on Product Liability: U.S. Dep't of Comm., 1977).

the essential principle of fault that has long provided foundational support to negligence as the cornerstone of accident law in America and across the globe.[563]

The Decline of a Duty to Warn of Unknowable Dangers

By the early 1980s, the reach of strict products liability in tort was expanding ever wider, so that few were much surprised when the New Jersey Supreme Court announced, in *Beshada v. Johns-Manville Products Corp.*,[564] that its strict liability rule was truly "strict." In this asbestos case, the court ruled that a product sold without a warning of its hidden dangers was defective, subjecting the manufacturer to liability for resulting harm, even if the risk was unforeseeable.[565] The manufacturer, in other words, was held to have a duty to warn of hidden dangers, whether knowable or not, or pay the consequences.[566]

Beshada was the first products liability decision rendered by a major court in which the outcome of the case explicitly depended on the principle of strict liability, where the manufacturer's inability to foresee or guard against the danger was held to make no difference. This decision proved to be the high-water mark of modern strict liability law for defective products. Despite the internal plausibility of the *Beshada* court's reasoning, the commentators railed against the absurdity of a duty to warn of the unknowable, to say nothing of its apparent unfairness and untoward policy implications.[567] The New Jersey Supreme Court appears to have listened to the critical commentary for, remarkably, it entirely changed its mind a scant two years later, in *Feldman v. Lederle Laboratories*,[568] a case involving a prescription drug, in which it effectively overruled *Beshada*.

Feldman marked the beginning of the decline of strict liability in warning cases—the point at which American law turned away from a lock-step march toward strict liability, back toward principles of foreseeability and fault.[569] Lest *Feldman* have been interpreted as a fluke, the California Supreme Court certified its rectitude in another prescription drug case in 1988, *Brown v. Superior Court*,[570] and then announced a broad rejection of strict liability principles in defective warning cases three years later, in *Anderson v. Owens-Corning Fiberglas Corp.*,[571] although it later waffled once again.[572]

---

[563] The core of products liability law, where principles of fault control, concerns design and warning defects. This leaves some room at the edges of products liability law for strict liability in less-common situations, principally involving misrepresentations and manufacturing defects. See chs. 3 and 7, respectively.

[564] 447 A.2d 539 (N.J. 1982).

[565] The risk was to workers of contracting asbestosis, mesothelioma, and other illnesses from asbestos insulation products.

[566] This discussion draws from Owen, The Evolution of Products Liability Law, 26 Rev. Litig. 955, 987–89 (2007). See also § 10.4, below.

[567] Or "rubbish," in English English. Much of the immediate scholarly criticism was contained in a symposium published by the New York University Law Review in 1983. See Symposium, The Passage of Time: The Implications for Product Liability, 58 N.Y.U. L. Rev. 734 (1983). *Feldman* itself cites several articles critical of *Beshada*. *See* Feldman v. Lederle Labs., 479 A.2d 374, 388 (N.J. 1984).

[568] 479 A.2d 374 (N.J. 1984).

[569] On the importance of these two notions in products liability law, see Owen, Bending Nature, Bending Law, 62 Fla. L. Rev. 569 (2010). On their importance in tort law generally, see Owen, Figuring Foreseeability, 44 Wake Forest L. Rev. 1277 (2009).

[570] 751 P.2d 470 (Cal. 1988).

[571] 810 P.2d 549 (Cal. 1991) (asbestos).

[572] In Carlin v. Superior Ct., 920 P.2d 1347 (Cal. 1996), the court curiously ruled that "strict liability" defective warning claims are still viable in that state, even if controlled by the principle that manufacturers need warn only of foreseeable risks. "[A]lthough *Anderson*, following *Brown*, incorporated certain negligence

The significance of *Feldman* and *Brown* in the development of modern American products liability law—in revitalizing the foreseeability of risk as a critical element of responsibility for harm—cannot be overstated. These two decisions in the 1980s signaled the beginning of a national repudiation of the doctrine of strict manufacturer liability in tort by the very two courts that had led the products liability revolution during the 1960s and 1970s. In addition to these two decisions, the structural underpinnings of strict products liability law began to falter in other ways during the 1980s and 1990s.

The Decline of the Wade-Keeton Test

Another development that undercut the strictness of products liability in the 1980s and 1990s was the decline of the so-called Wade-Keeton test for strict liability in tort. In fixing responsibility on manufacturers for defects in design, courts and commentators have always sought to avoid absolute liability, recognizing that the concepts of design safety and design danger are matters of degree involving trade-offs between a product's usefulness, cost, and safety. The idea of a design defect, in other words, has long been understood to rest on the idea of reasonable balance.[573] Because negligence itself is grounded on reasonableness and balance, one is led to inquire whether and how negligence and strict liability may differ in design defect litigation. Accordingly, in the 1960s and 1970s, products liability scholars searched for a way to define strict liability for selling products defective in design or warnings that would distinguish strict liability from mere negligence.

In particular, Dean Page Keeton of the University of Texas and Dean John Wade of Vanderbilt University articulated separate versions of a similar definition of defectiveness that distinguished negligence-based responsibility from liability called "strict" in a fundamental way. Their test, which others dubbed the "Wade-Keeton" test,[574] quite simply was a negligence test stripped of scienter.[575] That is, both defined defectiveness in terms of whether a manufacturer or other seller *with full knowledge of a product's dangerous condition* would be *negligent* in selling it in that condition. By requiring a seller to know its product's risks, commensurately relieving an injured plaintiff of the burden of proving the foreseeability of those risks, this test imposed on sellers "constructive knowledge" of any dangers their products might contain.[576] A number of courts picked up quite early on this Wade-Keeton "hindsight" test as a way to distinguish strict liability design claims (and warning claims) from those in negligence.[577]

---

concepts into the standard of strict liability for failure to warn, it did not thereby adopt a simple negligence test." Id. at 1351.

[573] See, e.g., Owen, Defectiveness Restated: Exploding the "Strict" Products Liability Myth, 1996 U. Ill. L. Rev. 743.

[574] See, e.g., Privette v. CSX Transp., Inc., 79 Fed. Appx. 879, 889 (6th Cir. 2003) (Tenn. law) (referring to this liability standard more fully as "the Wade-Keeton prudent manufacturer test"); Brooks v. Beech Aircraft Corp., 902 P.2d 54, 63 (N.M. 1995); Cupp and Polage, The Rhetoric of Strict Liability Versus Negligence: An Empirical Analysis, 77 N.Y.U. L. Rev. 874, 884 (2002). The rise and fall of the Wade-Keeton test is explored more fully in §§ 8.7 and 10.4, below.

[575] See, e.g., Wade, On the Nature of Strict Tort Liability for Products, 44 Miss. L.J. 825, 834–35 (1973).

[576] See, e.g., Phillips v. Kimwood Mach. Co., 525 P.2d 1033 (Or. 1974).

[577] See, e.g., Dorsey v. Yoder, 331 F. Supp. 753, 759–60 (E.D. Pa. 1971) (stating test for strict products liability in tort as "whether a reasonable manufacturer would continue to market his product in the same condition as he sold it to the plaintiff with knowledge of the potential dangerous consequences the trial just revealed"); Phillips v. Kimwood Mach. Co., 525 P.2d 1033, 1036 (Or. 1974) (A product is defective if "a reasonable person would not put into the stream of commerce *if he had knowledge of its harmful character*. The test, therefore, is whether the seller would be negligent if he sold the article *knowing of the risk involved*.

By the early 1980s, however, some courts and commentators had begun to question the fairness and logic of strict liability's elimination of foreseeability from design defect decisions; and the only other truly strict test of products liability, the consumer expectations test, had already begun its decline. In time recognizing their mistake, Dean Wade and Dean Keeton both repudiated the test that bore their names: Dean Wade because he never meant what he had said,[578] and Dean Keeton because he no longer believed what he had said.[579] The *Products Liability Restatement*, adopting a negligence-like risk-utility standard of liability, based on foreseeable risks at the time of sale, explicitly rejected the Wade-Keeton test, observing that "[t]he idea has not worn well with time."[580] Almost all courts focusing on the issue in recent years have agreed, rejecting the hindsight test and limiting a manufacturer's responsibility to risks that are foreseeable.[581]

The Decline of the Consumer Expectations Test

Another development that slowed the growth and eventually hastened the fall of strict products liability in tort was the decline of its principal early liability standard, especially in design defect cases—the consumer expectations test. Problems with this test—in cases involving obvious dangers, victims whose expectations are ignored by the test, and its inherent vagueness—were considered earlier.[582] Because of the frailties of this particular method for gauging design defects, lawyers, judges, and juries widely preferred evaluating the safety of particular designs on the kind of cost-benefit decisional calculus that manufacturers and their engineers are supposed to apply in practice—including, of course, a due concern for consumer safety. Because the application of cost-benefit analysis seemed a more logical, fair, and orderly method for assessing the safety adequacy of products charged with being defective in their designs or warnings, the so-called "risk-utility" standard gradually supplanted consumer expectations as the principal liability test, as we have seen.[583] But this form of analysis simply circled back to negligence, which courts, legislatures, commentators, and lawyers increasingly recognized. In formal terms, the switchover in American products liability law during the 1980s and 1990s, from a truly strict consumer expectations test to a fault-based cost-benefit standard, hastened the decline of "strict" liability under § 402A.

The Rise of the State of the Art Defense

While increasing case law in America weakened the *liability* foundations of "strict" manufacturer liability for product accidents from the front, another powerful development in modern products liability law assaulted strict products liability law as a *defense* from the rear. This development was most clearly revealed by judicial decisions and state reform statutes that forthrightly allowed a defense to products liability claims based on a manufacturer's compliance with the state of the scientific and technological

---

Strict liability imposes what amounts to constructive knowledge of the condition of the product.") (emphasis in original).

[578] See Wade, On the Effect in Product Liability of Knowledge Unavailable Prior to Marketing, Postscript, 58 N.Y.U. L. Rev. 734, 761 (1983).

[579] See Prosser and Keeton on Torts 697–98 n.21 (5th ed. 1984).

[580] See Rest. (3d) Torts: Products Liability Reporters' Note to § 2 cmt. *m*.

[581] A prominent example is the Supreme Judicial Court of Massachusetts, in Vassallo v. Baxter Healthcare Corp., 696 N.E.2d 909 (Mass. 1998). While the Wade-Keeton test sometimes arises in design defect cases, it more often arises in the warning context. See § 10.4, below.

[582] See § 5.6, above. These and other problems with this test are further examined in § 8.3, below.

[583] For the inevitability of this result, see Owen, Expectations in Tort, 44 Ariz. St. L. Rev. 1287 (2011).

art—often dubbed a "state of the art" defense—at the time a product was made and sold.[584]

While manufacturers of most products are at least generally aware of the kinds of hazards that lurk within their products before they are sold to consumers and cause harm, dangers are sometimes simply unknowable before a product is sold and put to use. Blood infected with serum hepatitis, formerly undetectable before transfusion into a person,[585] was a prime example in earlier times, as was the AIDS virus in blood products prior to the development of reliable tests during the early 1980s.[586] Similarly, pharmaceutical drugs, chemicals, and other substances—such as asbestos products in former times, and nanotech products today—may only be discovered to have toxic effects long after such products are marketed and harm consumers, sometimes generations later. If such dangers prove to have been foreseeable, discoverable with appropriate pre-market testing or analysis, and if the hazards were avoidable by appropriate warning, processing, or redesign, then manufacturers of such products may be held responsible for the harmful consequences of failing to discover or avoid those risks under ordinary principles of negligence, warranty, and strict liability in tort. But if the risks were in fact unforeseeable ("unknowable") or otherwise unavoidable before consumers began to suffer harm, the question of a supplier's responsibility for failing to warn about (or otherwise address) such risks is more complicated.[587]

As science and technology evolve over time, and as new and improved methods for discovering and eliminating hazards are developed, public attitudes toward risk and responsibility also evolve. Now that we are well into the twenty-first century, people expect much more safety in machine guarding, automotive crash protection, and fabric flammability than they did in 1900, or even in 1950.[588] Yet it is difficult to know what the safety expectations of consumers are (or should be) with respect to food, biologics, and other products whose most basic properties have been fundamentally, microscopically created or reconfigured by new scientific techniques such as nanotechnology, genetic manipulation, or three-dimensional printing in ways that generate unknown risks that even scientists and engineers cannot contemplate.

In the early 1960s, before section 402A of the *Restatement (Second) of Torts* was promulgated and adopted by the courts, the few courts considering the issue held that a manufacturer had to warn only of such risks "the manufacturer knew, or by the application of reasonable developed human skill and foresight should have known."[589] And then, in 1965, came the strict liability standard of section 402A that appeared to

---

[584] For the role of state of the art in products liability law, see § 10.4, below.

[585] See, e.g., Cunningham v. MacNeal Mem'l Hosp., 266 N.E.2d 897, 902 (Ill. 1970) (rejecting state-of-the-art defense). While various screening and testing approaches in recent years have substantially reduced this risk, an undiscoverable residuum remains. See Centers for Disease Control and Prevention, Recommendations for Prevention and Control of Hepatitis C Virus (HCV) Infection and HCV-Related Chronic Disease (1998) (noting that the CDC hepatitis surveillance system had not detected a transfusion-related hepatitis transmission since 1994).

[586] See § 16.9, below.

[587] This discussion draws from Owen, Bending Nature, Bending Law, 62 Fla. L. Rev. 569 (2010).

[588] "A consumer would not expect a Model T to have the safety features which are incorporated in automobiles made today." Bruce v. Martin-Marietta Corp., 544 F.2d 442, 447 (10th Cir. 1976) (Okla. law). See Henderson, Jr., Coping with the Time Dimension in Products Liability, 69 Cal. L. Rev. 919 (1981).

[589] See, e.g., Howard v. Avon Prods., Inc., 395 P.2d 1007, 1011 (Colo. 1964) (unforeseeable risk from cosmetic). This was true in both negligence and implied warranty. See, e.g., id. (both claims); Ross v. Philip Morris & Co., 328 F.2d 3 (8th Cir. 1964) (Mo. law) (both claims); Cudmore v. Richardson-Merrell, Inc., 398 S.W.2d 640, 644 (Tex. App. 1965) (implied warranty).

preclude any possibility of a "state of the art" defense based on the unforeseeability of a product risk.

As the risk-utility test for design defects increasingly displaced the consumer expectations standard around the nation,[590] and as the Wade-Keeton constructive knowledge test fell into desuetude, the relevance of state-of-the-art evidence became increasingly clear. In balancing the costs and benefits of a design feature that would have prevented a plaintiff's injury, courts widely came to recognize the salience of state-of-the-art evidence on the issue of the defectiveness of a product's design.[591] In warning cases involving "unknowable" risks of harm, state-of-the-art evidence played an even more critical role. Despite a few early decisions,[592] most courts,[593] even on strict liability claims and often under a state-of-the-art umbrella, eventually recognized the need to shield manufacturers from a duty to compensate consumers injured by hidden risks not warned about if those risks at the time were unknowable[594]—a critical development in the crumbling of the pantheon of strict products liability in tort.[595]

The *Restatement (Third) of Torts: Products Liability*

When Dean Prosser crafted § 402A of the *Second Restatement of Torts* in the early 1960s, products liability law was in its infancy. At this very early stage in the development of the law, the defect concept was roughly conceptualized as a unitary concept: products were either too dangerous (defective) or safe enough (nondefective). As courts in the 1960s and 1970s applied the principles of § 402A to an ever-widening array of products in an ever-widening range of contexts, the disparities among the various forms of product dangers increasingly revealed themselves.

By the late 1980s and early 1990s, many courts and commentators had come to recognize the need to apply different doctrinal approaches to three very different forms of product defect: (1) manufacturing flaws, (2) design inadequacies, and (3) insufficient warnings of danger and instructions on safe use.[596] By then, virtually all agreed that manufacturers should be strictly responsible for harm from manufacturing defects. Yet, in the many more cases involving claims of design defects, courts and state legislatures increasingly replaced the contract-based, truly strict consumer-expectations test with a cost-benefit ("risk-utility") test based on principles of foreseeability and balance that

---

590 This development was just discussed. See also Owen, The Evolution of Products Liability Law, 26 Rev. Litig. 955, 987–89 (2007), from which this discussion draws.

591 See, e.g., Boatland of Houston, Inc. v. Bailey, 609 S.W.2d 743 (Tex. 1980) (evidence on feasibility of alternative designs admissible); Potter v. Chicago Pneumatic Tool Co., 694 A.2d 1319, 1347 (Conn. 1997) (such evidence is "relevant and assists the jury in determining whether a product is defective and unreasonably dangerous"); LaBelle v. Philip Morris, Inc., 243 F. Supp. 2d 508, 517–22 (D.S.C. 2001) (no design defect if plaintiff unable to prove availability of technology to make safer cigarette); Kaufman v. Wyeth, LLC, 2011 WL 10483576, at *6 (S.D. Fla. 2011) (under state-of-the-art statute, manufacturer may show product's design was not defective per "scientific and technical knowledge at time of manufacture").

592 Most notably, Beshada v. Johns-Manville Prods. Corp., 447 A.2d 539 (N.J. 1982), discussed above.

593 Most notably, Feldman v. Lederle Labs., 479 A.2d 374 (N.J. 1984), discussed above.

594 See, e.g., Powers v. Taser Int'l, Inc., 174 P.3d 777, 779–84 (Ariz. Ct. App. 2008) (declining to extend Arizona's hindsight test from defective design to warning defect cases, and holding by implication that the duty to warn extends only to foreseeable risks); Tucker v. Wright Med. Tech., Inc., 2013 WL 1149717, at *12 (N.D. Cal. 2013) (recovery in defective warning cases now depends on proof that the relevant risks "were known or knowable at the time of manufacture or distribution, or sale").

595 See § 10.4, below.

596 On the now-conventional nature of this tripartite classification, see Rest. (3d) Torts: Products Liability § 1 cmt. *a*, Reporters' Note, and § 2. See also § 6.2, below.

underlie the law of negligence.[597] In addition, many courts and state reform acts were following the *Feldman* view that there should be no duty to warn of unforeseeable product hazards, but that the duty to warn should extend only to latent dangers that a manufacturer reasonably should have foreseen within the state of existing science and technology.

Reflecting the increasing social and political conservatism of the 1980s, judicial and legislative enthusiasm for section 402A's "pro-consumer" doctrine went into serious decline. So, while nearly all states continued to embrace a doctrine of products liability in tort that they still nominally called "strict," a growing number of courts, legislatures, and commentators had begun by the 1990s to question the legitimacy of strict liability in tort as a liability standard for evaluating the safety of a product's design and warnings. By then, judicial and scholarly attention had widely shifted away from examining why and how products liability doctrine should be *expanded* to why and how the doctrine should be *curtailed*,[598] putting the doctrine of strict products liability in tort seriously on the run.

It was about this time, when the *Restatement (Second) of Torts* was about a quarter century old, that the American Law Institute decided to "restate" the law of torts once again. Because tort law had grown so large and cumbersome, the ALI decided to subdivide it into various components. Due to the enormous expansion of products liability law after promulgation of § 402A of the *Second Restatement* in 1965, the Institute announced in 1991 that products liability would be the first of the new tort law *Restatements*. In 1992, Professor James Henderson and Professor Aaron Twerski were appointed Reporters for the project, and so began the process of converting a single section of the *Second Restatement*, § 402A, into an entire *Restatement* of its own. Over about five years, the Reporters issued a series of drafts critiqued by ALI Advisers and many other groups, and in 1997 the ALI voted to adopt a Proposed Final Draft, which it published the following year as the *Restatement (Third) of Torts: Products Liability*.[599]

Probably the most salient feature of the entire *Products Liability Restatement* is that it grounds the liability standards for physical harm from design and warning defects—the great majority of products liability claims—in the reasonableness and balancing concepts in which negligence law has long been anchored.[600] Particularly in the context of design dangers, most courts had come to employ a "risk-utility" test for ascertaining whether such dangers are excessive or acceptable, as previously discussed.[601] In most cases, this determination is based on a cost-benefit analysis of the manufacturer's choice to forego a safety improvement the plaintiff claims was necessary to render the design reasonably safe.[602] This reasonable-safer-design concept lies at the

[597] Two fairly early examples are Sperry-New Holland v. Prestage, 617 So.2d 248, 254–56 (Miss. 1993); Banks v. ICI Ams., Inc., 450 S.E.2d 671, 674 (Ga. 1994). More recently, see, e.g., Branham v. Ford Motor Co., 701 S.E.2d 5 (S.C. 2010) (adopting the negligence-based risk-utility test of Products Liability Rest. § 2(b)); Wis. Stat. Ann. § 895.047(1)(a) (2011) (same).

[598] As chronicled in Schwartz, The Beginning and Possible End of the Rise of Modern American Tort Law, 26 Ga. L. Rev. 601, 683–99 (1992), and Owen, The Fault Pit, 26 Ga. L. Rev. 703, 705–10 (1992).

[599] For a more thorough summary of the Products Liability Restatement, see § 6.5, below.

[600] The moral propriety of these principles is explained elsewhere. See Owen, Philosophical Foundations of Fault in Tort Law, in Philosophical Foundations of Tort Law 201 (D. Owen ed., Oxford 1995); Owen, The Moral Foundations of Products Liability Law: Toward First Principles, 68 Notre Dame L. Rev. 427 (1993).

[601] See also ch. 8, below.

[602] See Owen, Toward a Proper Test for Design Defectiveness: "Micro-Balancing" Costs and Benefits, 75 Tex. L. Rev. 1661 (1997).

heart of the *Third Restatement*'s definition of design defects in subsection 2(b), and a similar negligence-grounded definition supports the *Third Restatement*'s formulation of warning and instruction defects in subsection 2(c).[603]

For some years it had been an open secret that most courts, while purporting to apply "strict" liability doctrine to design and warning cases, in fact were applying principles that looked remarkably like negligence.[604] That is, courts and juries widely based defect determinations in both design and warning cases on the risk-utility principles of balance, reasonableness, and foreseeability. Except in manufacturing defect cases and certain other limited contexts, courts and state legislatures rejected efforts to make manufacturers guarantors of product safety, requiring only that manufacturers (1) make their products as safe as they reasonably are able to do; and (2) warn of foreseeable, material risks, by methods that are reasonably available and reasonably likely to be effective.[605] This is negligence, pure and simple, in fact if not in name. So, by grounding liability for design and warning defects in the principles of negligence, the new *Restatement* truly "restated" most products liability law—the law addressing design and warning defects—on principles of negligence, far away from strict liability in tort.[606]

Whither Strict Liability?

Quite remarkably, American products liability law in the twenty-first century has returned to roost not far from where it was a half century in the past, and where it rested long before.[607] While the web of products liability doctrine and methods of its practice have matured and mushroomed in complexity in myriad diverse ways, the foundations of a manufacturer's responsibility remain largely as they long have stood, in both tort and warranty—manufacturers remain strictly responsible for harm caused by their manufacturing mistakes and misrepresentations, yet they need answer only for their failures to take reasonable precautions to avoid harm from design dangers and warning inadequacies in their products.

---

[603] See section 6.5, below.

[604] See Davis, Design Defect Liability: In Search of a Standard of Responsibility, 39 Wayne L. Rev. 1217, 1238–48 (1993); Powers, A Modest Proposal to Abandon Strict Products Liability, 1991 U. Ill. L. Rev. 639; Henderson and Twerski, Doctrinal Collapse in Products Liability: The Empty Shell of Failure to Warn, 65 N.Y.U. L. Rev. 265, 277–78 (1990); Birnbaum, Unmasking the Test for Design Defect: From Negligence [to Warranty] to Strict Liability to Negligence, 33 Vand. L. Rev. 593, 601 (1980). This divergence between illusory strict liability doctrine and actual liability principles is diagrammatically portrayed in Owen, The Fault Pit, 26 Ga. L. Rev. 703, 706 (1992).

[605] In addition, of course, manufacturers must not affirmatively misrepresent the safety of their products.

[606] At least Iowa has followed the Third Restatement's lead in defining design defectiveness functionally and ignoring traditional theories of recovery such as negligence, warranty, or strict liability in tort. See Wright v. Brooke Grp. Ltd., 652 N.W.2d 159, 169 (Iowa 2002) (adopting sections one and two of the Products Liability Rest.).

[607] See Owen, The Evolution of Products Liability Law, 26 Rev. Litig. 955, 989 (2007). See also Green, The Unappreciated Congruity of the Second and Third Torts Restatements on Design Defects, 74 Brook. L. Rev. 807, 837 (2009). Staunchly rebuffing this trend, however, and still tenaciously clinging to the rationale and doctrine of § 402A, are Bifolck v. Philip Morris, Inc., 152 A.3d 1183 (Conn. 2016), and Tincher v. Omega Flex, Inc., 104 A.3d 328 (Pa. 2014), both of which retained strict liability as the nominal basis of liability and adopted two-pronged standards similar to that in California's Barker v. Lull Eng'g Co., 573 P.2d 443 (Cal. 1978), permitting plaintiffs in design defect cases to pursue claims on either the consumer expectations or risk-utility approach, and Aubin v. Union Carbide Corp., 177 So.3d 489, 512 (Fla. 2015), reaffirming § 402A of the Second Restatement, approving consumer expectations as a proper test of design defect liability (together with risk-utility, and endorsing the traditional rationales supporting strict products liability in tort. See also Ford Motor Co. v. Trejo, 402 P.3d 649, 657 (Nev. 2017) ("risk-utility analysis inserts negligence standards into claims of design defect, contrary to the public policy supporting the adoption of strict liability in Nevada").

For the last half century, American law has devoted untold toil and turmoil in an effort to find some flaw in these simple principles of responsibility, some way to make them better—by calling liability in all such cases "strict." It is hard to know why the law struggled with such intensity to repackage commonsense, self-evident principles of fairness and justice we long have understood, before the wonders of computers, smart phones, 3D printing, nanotechnology, and SUVs. Yet the enduring principles and values of products liability law are the same today as they were before, though we see them a bit more clearly now.

Whither Traditional Bases of Recovery for Harm from Product Defects?

Overarching all products liability law is a slow but important movement displacing *all* traditional bases of recovery—negligence, warranty, and strict liability in tort—with claims grounded in the three particular types of defect, together with one for misrepresentation in tort. This was the approach taken in the late 1970s in §§ 103 and 104 of the *Model Uniform Product Liability Act*, spearheaded by Victor Schwartz from the U.S. Department of Commerce.[608] The idea of replacing conventional tort and warranty claims with independent, particularized product defect (and misrepresentation) claims, garnered a bit of insightful academic support,[609] and it slowly but eventually found its way into a number of state products liability reform statutes[610] and into the "functional" approach to liability definitions in §§ 1 and 2 of the *Third Restatement*, and its misrepresentation provision in § 9.[611] Now that products liability has achieved status as an independent legal field,[612] the internal reconstitution of its principal bases of liability according to types of product defect and misrepresentation is a natural development whose continuing spread across the land should surely help reduce confusion and improve clarity throughout this field of law.

---

[608] See § 1.3, above. The Model Act is reproduced in Owen & Davis on Products Liability Appendix H.

[609] See, e.g., Owen, Restructuring Products Liability Law, 16 Trial 58, 60–61 (Nov. 1980).

[610] A few states by statute have merged negligence, warranty, and strict liability claims into a single "product liability" claim. See, e.g., Conn. Gen. Stat. Ann. §§ 52–572m, 52–572n; Ind. Code Ann. § 34–6–2–115; La. Rev. Stat. Ann. § 9:2800.52; N.J. Stat. Ann. § 2A:58C–1(b)(3); Wash. Rev. Code Ann. § 7.72.010(4). See also Wright v. Brooke Grp. Ltd., 652 N.W.2d 159, 167 (Iowa 2002) (same: design defects); Olson v. Prosoco, Inc., 522 N.W.2d 284 (Iowa 1994) (same: warning defects).

[611] "Rather than perpetuating confusion spawned by existing doctrinal categories [negligence, warranty, and strict liability in tort], §§ 1 and 2 define the liability for each form of defect in terms directly affecting the various forms of defects." Products Liability Rest. § 1 cmt. *a*. See also id. § 2 cmt. *n*. The Restatement is discussed in § 6.5, below.

[612] See § 1.1, above.

Part II

PRODUCT DEFECTIVENESS

Chapter 6

NATURE AND PROOF OF DEFECTIVENESS

Table of Sections

§ 6.1 DEFECTIVENESS—GENERALLY

Defectiveness lies at the center of products liability law. Merely making and selling a product that causes accidental harm fails to provide a sufficient basis for moral or legal responsibility.[1] Instead, the essence of accountability in products liability law is that the defendant supplied a product that was *deficient* in some respect, that the product was "defective." In Roman law, responsibility for product harm rested to a large extent on the notion of product defect, as it did under medieval ecclesiastical law and the law of early America.[2] Defectiveness continues to provide the core concept of modern products liability law around the world.[3]

Since the rise of modern products liability law in America during the 1960s, determining how product defectiveness should be conceived, defined,[4] and proved[5] has preoccupied the courts (and some legislatures), commentators, and products liability lawyers. Apart from special types of claims (such as those involving misrepresentation,[6] negligent entrustment,[7] and certain others[8]), every products liability claim requires proof that the injury was caused by an unnecessary hazard in the defendant's product. Regardless of the underlying cause of action, plaintiffs in products liability cases normally must establish that something was *wrong* with the product. Every product, when put to certain uses, is dangerous in some manner and to some extent. But most

---

1 "The fact that a manufacturer makes and sells products, which generally are good, is an insufficient reason for requiring a manufacturer to compensate a victim of a product accident. . . . [M]oral philosophy requires more than action, related in some manner to another's harm, for the actor to be held accountable for the harm." Owen, The Moral Foundations of Products Liability Law: Toward First Principles, 68 Notre Dame L. Rev. 427, 461 (1993).

2 For an overview of products liability history, see §§ 1.2 and 5.2, above.

3 For an overview of modern products liability law in other nations, see § 1.4, above.

4 See § 4.3 (implied warranty), and §§ 5.5–5.10 (strict liability in tort), above, and §§ 7.2 (manufacturing defects), 8.2 (design defects), and 9.2 (warning defects), below.

5 See §§ 6.3 and 6.4, below.

6 See ch. 3, above.

7 See § 15.2, below.

8 Such as those based on the implied warranty of fitness for particular purpose, under UCC § 2–315, or possibly on the violation of a product safety statute, such as a prohibition on the sale of fireworks to children or unlicensed persons (a species of unlawful entrustment). Yet many products liability statutes, such as pure food acts, are designed to prevent the sale of defective products. See § 2.4 (proof of negligence, violation of statute), above; § 6.4 (proof of defect, recurring issues), and § 7.5 (food and drink), below.

such dangers are a simple fact of physics, chemistry, or biology, which there is no reasonable way to avoid. For such natural risks of life, product users rather than product suppliers properly bear responsibility for avoiding and insuring against injuries that may result.[9] But some products carry excessive risk that users and consumers should not fairly be required to shoulder, sometimes because the risks are unexpected by consumers and almost always because they are reasonably avoidable by manufacturers or other product suppliers. So, before the law shifts a risk of loss from a product accident to a manufacturer or other seller, it properly requires that the type or level of danger in the product is *excessive*. The label the law attaches to products carrying such excessive risk is "defective."[10]

At least implicitly, each of the three major causes of action in products liability law requires that a product be defective. Negligence claims are predicated on the defectiveness of a product, because its supplier ordinarily cannot be faulted for selling a product that is good (i.e., not defective).[11] Breach of the implied warranty of merchantability typically is based on the idea that a product is "unfit" for ordinary use, usually meaning the same thing as "defective."[12] And strict liability in tort, of course, explicitly rests on the sale of a defective product.[13] The centrality of the concept of defectiveness to products liability law is reflected in the *Second* and *Third Restatements of Torts*, both of which ground liability on the notion of product defect.[14] Quite simply, product defectiveness is the heart of products liability law.

Chapters 6–10 explore in depth various specialized issues of product defects. The present chapter addresses recurring issues concerning defects of all types, such as how the three separate forms of defect relate to one another, special rules governing expert testimony on defectiveness and causation, and other recurring issues of proof of defect. The chapter ends with an overview of the *Products Liability Restatement*, which itself centers on the concept of product defect. Chapter 7 examines manufacturing defects, including the applicable liability tests[15] and the special issues involved in defective food and drink.[16] Chapter 8 considers design defects, including the twisted evolution of defect tests in this context[17] and the special issue of optional safety devices.[18] Chapter 9 explores the topic of warning defects, including defect tests,[19] the notion of a warning's

---

9 See Owen, The Moral Foundations of Products Liability Law: Toward First Principles, 68 Notre Dame L. Rev. 427 (1993).

10 See, e.g., Prentis v. Yale Mfg. Co., 365 N.W.2d 176, 181–82 (Mich. 1984) ("the plaintiff must, *in every case, in every jurisdiction*, show that the product was defective") (emphasis in original); Phillips v. Kimwood Mach. Co., 525 P.2d 1033, 1036 (Or. 1974) ("To impose liability there has to be something about the article which makes it dangerously defective . . . ."). See also Products Liability Rest. § 1 (liability for harm from commercial sale of "defective" product).

11 See §§ 2.1 and 5.9, above.

12 See, e.g., Mills v. Ethicon, Inc., 406 F. Supp. 3d 363, 381–83 (D.N.J. 2019); Scott v. Dorel Juvenile Grp., Inc., 456 Fed. Appx. 450, 456 (5th Cir. 2012) (Tex. law) ("To recover damages for breach of an implied warranty of merchantability, a plaintiff must prove there was some defect in the product . . . that renders them unfit for the ordinary purpose for which they are used"). See §§ 4.3 and 5.9, above.

13 See ch. 5, above.

14 See Rest. (2d) Torts § 402A; Products Liability Rest. §§ 1 and 2.

15 See §§ 7.2–7.4, below.

16 See § 7.5, below.

17 See §§ 8.2–8.8, below.

18 See § 8.9, below.

19 See § 9.2, below.

adequacy,[20] and the parties to whom warnings must be provided.[21] Finally, Chapter 10 examines a wide range of limited duty doctrines on the defect concept, including the role of obvious dangers,[22] inherent risks and product category liability,[23] the many strands of state of the art,[24] liability for prenatal harm,[25] product deterioration,[26] disposal and salvage,[27] and the developing law on post-sale duties to warn or recall.[28] Defect issues applicable to special types of defendants, transactions, and products are addressed in later chapters on those special topics.

§ 6.2 THE THREE TYPES OF DEFECT

Both the *Second* and *Third Restatements of Torts* base liability on the concept of product defect. Section 402A of the *Second Restatement* provides that sellers are subject to liability for selling a product in a "defective condition unreasonably dangerous"[29] and § 1 of the *Third Restatement* provides that commercial sellers are subject to liability for selling "a defective product." Notwithstanding this common grounding of liability on the basis of a "defective" product, the two *Restatements* treat the defect concept in vastly different ways.

When Dean Prosser crafted § 402A of the *Second Restatement* in the late 1950s and early 1960s, products liability law was in its infancy.[30] At this very early stage in the development of this field of law, the defect concept was only roughly understood and conceived of, quite naively, as a unitary concept: products were either too dangerous (defective) or safe enough (nondefective).[31] As courts in the 1960s and 1970s applied the principles of § 402A to an ever-widening array of products in an ever-widening range of contexts, the disparities among the various forms of product dangers increasingly revealed themselves. Over time, courts and commentators came to understand the fundamental distinctions between three very different forms of product defect: (1) manufacturing flaws—unintended physical irregularities that can occur during the production process;[32] (2) design inadequacies—hazards lurking in a product's engineering or scientific conception that can and reasonably should be avoided by a different design or formula;[33] and (3) insufficient warnings of danger or instructions for safe use—the absence of information needed by users to avoid product hazards.[34]

---

20 See § 9.3, below.

21 See §§ 9.4 and 9.5, below.

22 See §§ 10.2 and 10.3 (*Fast Foods*), below.

23 See § 10.3, below.

24 See § 10.4, below.

25 See § 10.5, below.

26 See § 10.6, below.

27 See § 10.7, below.

28 See § 10.8, below.

29 Rest. (2d) Torts § 402A.

30 See §§ 5.2 and 5.3, above. For an earlier version of the discussion here, see Owen, The Puzzle of Comment *j*, 55 Hastings L.J. 1377 (2004).

31 See §§ 5.3 and 5.5, above.

32 See ch. 7, below.

33 See ch. 8, below.

34 See ch. 9, below.

Misrepresentation, the fourth principal basis of products liability, is not generally classified as a product "defect."[35]

Over the many decades since § 402A first roughly sketched a general doctrine of strict products liability in tort, the need to accord separate treatment to the liability issues distinctive to each of these very different defect concepts has become a well-accepted axiom. Today, while warnings may well be relevant to risk reduction (and hence to the need *vel non* to improve the safety of a design),[36] that these three separate types of defect create independent sets of obligations is axiomatic in American products liability law.[37]

Section 402A of the *Second Restatement*, as seen above, provides a single rule of liability for physical harm from the sale of defective products.[38] Because the *Third Restatement* in § 1 begins quite similarly in providing that a seller of a "defective product" is subject to liability for such harm,[39] it might at first glance appear to restate the *Second Restatement*'s no-fault doctrine of "strict liability" that has dominated products liability doctrine since the 1960s. But § 2 of the *Third Restatement* radically departs from § 402A by splintering the defect notion into its three separate forms—defects in manufacture,[40] design,[41] and instructions or warnings[42]—each with separate doctrines of its own.[43] By so trifurcating defectiveness, § 2 affords separate vessels for separate liability standards: § 2(a) defines liability for manufacturing defects in terms of a product's departure from its intended design, whereas § 2(b) and (c) define liability for design and warning defects in the foreseeable risk-utility terms of fault-based liability.[44] Liability in § 2 of the *Third Restatement* thus is truly "strict" for defects in

---

[35] By convention, although it would be as logical to attach the "defective" description to products carrying safety misrepresentations as to products carrying insufficient safety information. At least Ohio does so, imposing liability if a product "was defective because it did not conform to a representation made by its manufacturer." Ohio Rev. Code Ann. § 2307.73(A)(1). See id. at § 2307.77. See also Phillips, The Unreasonably Unsafe Product and Strict Liability, 72 Tenn. L. Rev. 833, 842 (2005) ("a fourth and very significant category of product defectiveness arises from misrepresentation").

[36] The interconnection of design and warning defects was recognized by some early courts and commentators who classified defects into two categories—defects of manufacture or design—and conceived of the duty to warn as a subcategory of the duty to design. See, e.g., LaGorga v. Kroger Co., 275 F. Supp. 373, 380 (W.D. Pa. 1967); Schuh v. Fox River Tractor Co., 218 N.W.2d 279, 284 (Wis. 1974). Compare Glover v. BIC Corp., 6 F.3d 1318, 1323 (9th Cir. 1993) (Or. law) (warnings are part of the duty of safe design; Or. Rev. Stat. Ann. §§ 30.900 to .920). See also Wade, On the Effect in Products Liability of Knowledge Unavailable Prior to Marketing, 58 N.Y.U. L. Rev. 734, 740 (1983) ("although 'failure to warn' usually is treated as a separate basis for finding a product actionable, 'failure to warn' cases may properly be viewed as 'defective design' cases").

[37] See, e.g., Seguin v. Remington Arms Co., 22 F.4th 492 (Owen, C.J.), 500–01 (5th Cir. 2022) (Dennis, J., dissenting) (La. law); McDougall v. CRC Indus., Inc., 523 F. Supp. 3d 1061 (D. Minn. 2021); Kaiser v. Johnson & Johnson, 947 F.3d 996, 1007 (7th Cir. 2020) (Ind. law) (a "product may be defective . . . if it is defectively designed, if it has a manufacturing flaw, or if it lacks adequate warnings"); Moultrie v. Coloplast Corp., 2020 WL 1249354, at *7 (W.D. Pa. 2020) ("Pennsylvania recognizes three types of defective conditions that can give rise to strict liability: design defect, manufacturing defect, and failure to warn."); Sherer-Smith v. C.R. Bard, Inc., 2020 WL 1470962, at *3 (W.D. Wis. 2020) (same); Chavez v. Glock, Inc., 144 Cal. Rptr. 3d 326, 342 (Ct. App. 2012) (same). See Products Liability Rest. § 1 Reporters' Note to cmt. *a*, and § 2 cmt. *a*.

[38] See § 5.3, above.

[39] "One engaged in the business of selling or otherwise distributing products who sells or distributes a defective product is subject to liability for harm to persons or property caused by the defect." Products Liability Rest. § 1.

[40] See Products Liability Rest. § 2(a).

[41] See Products Liability Rest. § 2(b).

[42] See Products Liability Rest. § 2(c).

[43] See note 37, above.

[44] Notwithstanding the strict-sounding language of "defectiveness" in which the definitions are cast. See Products Liability Rest. § 1 cmt. *a*, § 2 cmts. *a*, *c*, *d*, *i*, and *m*. Note that the Third Restatement describes

manufacture but is based on negligence for defects in design and warnings.[45] As will be explained below, the *Restatement (Third) of Torts: Products Liability* is premised on the substantial independence of these three forms of defect, not only in the tripartite division of defectiveness in § 2, but also in various provisions governing a product seller's obligations in different contexts.[46]

While variations among the liability standards may be the most fundamental distinction between the separate types of defects, other important consequences flow from the particular type of defect alleged and proved. By way of illustration, the obviousness of a danger normally precludes, as a matter of law, a finding of a warning defect, but not a design defect.[47] Also, certain types of evidence may be proper in proving one type of defect but not another. In addition, some jurisdictions provide for special defenses tailored to particular types of defect.[48]

Thus, the three different types of product defect generate three separate, independent sets of obligations for product suppliers.

The Puzzle of Comment *j*

That the three types of defect beget distinct and largely independent obligations would seem to be beyond dispute. Yet, from time to time, this fundamental principle of products liability law escapes an unwary court. Often, this confusion springs from a curious puzzle that lies at the heart of § 402A of the *Restatement (Second) of Torts*, the fountainhead of modern products liability law. The puzzle is this: § 402A, crafted by Dean Prosser, generated the expansive, plaintiff-protective doctrine of strict liability in tort for the sale of products that are defective in any of three very different ways—in manufacturing, warning, or design. Yet one sentence in a comment to § 402A, comment *j*, can be read quite literally to mean that a manufacturer who provides a warning—*any* type of warning, no matter how deficient—eludes altogether the vital duty of safe design. If this were true, if a warning were indeed to trump design responsibility as a number of courts mistakenly have held, then § 402A is a much weaker doctrine than widely believed. This interpretation of comment *j* would mean that Prosser, in a single sentence of a single comment to a single section of the *Restatement*, had robbed strict products liability in tort—subtly and implausibly—of much of its intrinsic power.

---

liability rules applicable to products generally in §§ 1–4, after which it addresses liability standards applicable to special defendants, such as sellers of component parts (§ 5), prescription drugs (§ 6), food (§ 7), and used products (§ 8).

[45] See Owen, Defectiveness Restated: Exploding the "Strict" Products Liability Myth, 1996 U. Ill. L. Rev. 743.

[46] See, e.g., Products Liability Rest. § 6 (sellers of prescription drugs and medical devices subject to differing standards for manufacturing defects, design defects, and warning defects).

[47] See § 10.2, below.

[48] See, e.g., Cacciola v. Selco Balers, Inc., 127 F. Supp. 2d 175, 185–88 (E.D.N.Y. 2001) (substantial modification defense may preclude liability for design, but not warning, defect); N.J. Stat. Ann. § 2A:58C–3(a)(1) (certain state-of-the-art defenses apply only to design dangers).

Comment *j* sets forth, in a largely noncontroversial manner, a product seller's duty to warn of foreseeable hazards.[49] However, the comment concludes with the following "unfortunate language":[50]

> Where warning is given, the seller may reasonably assume that it will be read and heeded; and a product bearing such a warning, which is safe for use if it is followed, is not in [a] defective condition, nor is it unreasonably dangerous.

This language is indeed "unfortunate" because its ambiguity permits it to be interpreted in any number of significantly different ways. For example, it may be read as meaning that *any* warning, no matter how inadequate, satisfies the informational obligations addressed in comment *j*; or that a warning *if adequate* satisfies those obligations; or that *any* warning, no matter how inadequate, satisfies *every* duty of whatever type owed by the seller to the user; or that an *adequate* warning will satisfy *every* duty of whatever type owed by the seller to the user.

Most courts and commentators, perplexed by the comment's enigmatic message about the relationship between a manufacturer's duty to warn and its duty of safe design, have side-stepped the interpretative problem simply by ignoring comment *j* altogether.[51] And commentators who have studied the comment closely, including the Reporters for the *Third Restatement of Torts*, for the most part have read it to mean what it perversely seems to say—that a manufacturer's warnings somehow cancel out its duty of safe design.[52] But all of these interpretations are wrong. In fact, the riddle of comment *j* has

---

[49] Comment *j* to § 402A provides in full:

j. Directions or warning. In order to prevent the product from being unreasonably dangerous, the seller may be required to give directions or warning, on the container, as to its use. The seller may reasonably assume that those with common allergies, as for example to eggs or strawberries, will be aware of them, and he is not required to warn against them. Where, however, the product contains an ingredient to which a substantial number of the population are allergic, and the ingredient is one whose danger is not generally known, or if known is one which the consumer would reasonably not expect to find in the product, the seller is required to give warning against it, if he has knowledge, or by the application of reasonable, developed human skill and foresight should have knowledge, of the presence of the ingredient and the danger. Likewise in the case of poisonous drugs, or those unduly dangerous for other reasons, warning as to use may be required.

But a seller is not required to warn with respect to products, or ingredients in them, which are only dangerous, or potentially so, when consumed in excessive quantity, or over a long period of time, when the danger, or potentiality of danger, is generally known and recognized. Again the dangers of alcoholic beverages are an example, as are also those of foods containing such substances as saturated fats, which may over a period of time have a deleterious effect upon the human heart.

Where warning is given, the seller may reasonably assume that it will be read and heeded; and a product bearing such a warning, which is safe for use if it is followed, is not in defective condition, nor is it unreasonably dangerous.

[50] This is the characterization by the Reporters for the Third Restatement. See Products Liability Rest. § 2 Reporters' Note to cmt. *j*.

[51] Ignoring this confounding language makes good sense. After all, this problem resides in a single sentence of a single comment to a single section in a *Restatement* that now has been superseded. Among the various interpretations offered above, other than the correct one explained below, the best is that a manufacturer satisfies its duty to provide safety information to purchasers and users—and only this duty—by providing them with warnings and instructions adequately explaining the risks of hidden dangers and how to avoid them. Yet, even this interpretation falsely assumes that comment *j* applies to the effect of warnings on the general duty to design any type of product, whereas comments *i*, *j*, and *k* in fact apply only to products possessing inherent, *unavoidable* dangers, those that cannot be designed away.

[52] See, e.g., Products Liability Rest. § 2 cmt. *l*; Henderson and Twerski, The Politics of the Products Liability Restatement, 26 Hofstra L. Rev. 667, 689 (1998); Latin, "Good" Warnings, Bad Products, and

a key that really is quite simple, discoverable from examining the history of § 402A within the context of the times, consistent with the way products liability law evolved since its modern inception many decades in the past.[53]

The true meaning of comment *j*'s curious last sentence, as explained below, is the narrow proposition that sellers of a very small category of products, those that are *inherently* dangerous—like food, alcohol, tobacco, and drugs—have more limited safety obligations than sellers of ordinary products.[54] That is, sellers of inherently dangerous products, in addition to avoiding impurities and misrepresentations of safety, need only warn consumers of the unavoidable, latent dangers such products intrinsically contain. That is, because this limited category of products by hypothesis cannot be *designed* more safely, their sellers' principal remaining duty (putting aside producing them without flaws and not misrepresenting their safety) is to provide adequate warnings of danger and instructions on safe use. Understanding why this narrow interpretation is correct requires reading comment *j* in the context of its neighboring comments; examining the "legislative history" of these comments; considering the relevant policies; and reviewing related products liability developments over time.

The Context of Comment j

In attempting to unravel the inscrutable meaning of this clause of comment *j*, one needs to read it in context by considering the comments surrounding it and the narrow subject matter these comments in fact addressed. In examining this context, it must be remembered that the *Restatement* Reporter, Dean William Prosser, researched and first drafted comment *j* in the late 1950s and early 1960s to accompany a narrow draft of § 402A of the *Second Restatement* limited to defective food and related products—such as drugs, alcoholic beverages, and tobacco—several years before a general doctrine of strict liability in tort applicable to all products ever saw the light of day.

A close reading of comments *i*, *j*, and *k* to the *Restatement (Second) of Torts* § 402A, together with their "legislative history," reveals that these comments were directed exclusively to a narrow set of issues pertinent to a limited class of products, to wit, the liability (and limits of liability) of sellers of certain types of products—food, drugs, whiskey, cigarettes, and similar products that contain inherent hazards, dangers that by nature are unavoidable. While the titles to comments *i* ("*Unreasonably dangerous*") and *j* ("*Directions or warning*") unfortunately suggest that they might have general application to *all* products, these comments, together with comment *k* ("*Unavoidably unsafe products*"), in fact were drafted solely to address a single narrow topic—the responsibility of sellers of products like food, alcoholic beverages, tobacco, and drugs containing inherent product dangers that cannot be designed away.

The premise of each of these three comments is that strict liability under § 402A does not apply unless a manufacturer has a reasonable way to eliminate a product's hazards. Based on this premise, the main point of these three comments is that the principal duty of manufacturers of food, whiskey, cigarettes, drugs, and similar products containing inherent dangers (assuming they are not contaminated) is to warn consumers of hidden dangers. The comments thus explain that this limited class of products,

---

Cognitive Limitations, 41 UCLA L. Rev. 1193, 1294–95 (1994); Priest, Strict Products Liability: The Original Intent, 10 Cardozo L. Rev. 2301, 2303 (1989).

[53] See the incalculably insightful analysis in Owen, The Puzzle of Comment *j*, 55 Hastings L.J. 1377 (2004), from which much of this discussion draws.

[54] Inherent product hazards are examined in § 10.3, below.

accompanied by proper warnings, are not in a "defective condition unreasonably dangerous" with respect to the unavoidable dangers that are inherent in all products of this type.

Comment *i*. Comment *i* explains why the American Law Institute (ALI) added the phrase "defective condition" to modify the "(unreasonably) dangerous" term used in an earlier, preliminary draft of § 402A. Dean Prosser added the "defective condition" language (at the urging of the ALI Council) to make clear that the new "strict" liability in tort would *not* give rise to design liability for the sale of products like whiskey, cigarettes, and butter that contain inherent dangers that cannot be eliminated.[55] Comment *i* thus makes the single point that the strict liability principle of § 402A is inappropriate for some products that are widely known to be inherently dangerous such that consumers who choose to use such products are deemed to accept those inherent risks.[56]

Comment *j*. Comment *j*, first attached to the 1961 draft of § 402A that applied only to food and similar products, also discusses and applies only to dangerous foods, alcoholic beverages, and drugs—products that by their nature cannot be rendered safe except by warning. This comment makes three points: first, continuing the reasoning of the previous comment, sellers of food, tobacco, alcohol, drugs, and similar products widely known to be inherently dangerous are *not* generally subject to strict liability for such inherent dangers because consumers understand that products of these types necessarily include such risks; second, that sellers of such products *do* have a duty to warn consumers of any latent risks of which consumers generally are unaware; and third, because there simply is no way other than by warning that sellers of such products can minimize their inherent risks, the *only* duty for manufacturers of such products is to warn consumers of any hidden dangers.[57]

The premise here is that sellers of *inherently dangerous products* may trust[58] that users, properly informed of any hidden dangers, will read and heed any (adequate) warning and take responsibility for such inherent risks. Thus, properly interpreted, comment *j*'s concluding sentence actually means:

> Where [adequate] warning [of hidden dangers] is given, the seller [of inherently dangerous products like food, drugs, alcoholic beverages, and cigarettes] may reasonably assume that [the warning] will be read and heeded [because there is nothing else the manufacturer can do to avoid the danger]; and [such] a product bearing such a warning, which is safe for use if it is followed, is not in [a] defective condition, nor is it unreasonably dangerous.

Thus, comment *j* in fact addresses only the narrow issue of a seller's duties with respect to food, tobacco, drugs, alcoholic beverages, and similar products containing inherent, unavoidable risks that cannot be designed away.[59] Conversely, comment *j* simply does

---

55 See 38 A.L.I. Proc. 87–89 (1961).

56 "Many products cannot possibly be made entirely safe . . . ." Rest. (2d) Torts § 402A cmt. *i*.

57 Putting aside, of course, the duties to produce a product without manufacturing defects and not to misrepresent a product's safety.

58 Indeed, manufacturers *must* trust in the good sense of users of such products, for there is nothing else to be done.

59 This interpretation of comment *j* is further supported by its direction that any required warnings be placed on the product's "container," surely the best place to warn of inherent dangers in packaged food, drugs, whiskey, and cigarettes, but nonsensical when applied to the vast array of durable products that come without containers—tools, clothing, power mowers, automobiles, vacuum cleaners, and punch presses—for which the

not address how warnings affect the duty of safe design for *other* types of products whose dangers *can* reasonably be designed away.[60]

Comment *k*. Reiterating the overarching theme of all three comments—that a limited class of inherently and unavoidably dangerous products should be exempt from any design obligations of the § 402A strict liability rule—comment *k* explains how, in particular, the principles of comments *i* and *j* apply to prescription drugs. In the context of this special type of unavoidably dangerous product, comment *k* makes the dual points that a seller does have a duty to provide proper warnings but that it is not otherwise liable for any inherent risks that the manufacturer cannot eliminate.[61]

In sum, a careful reading of comments *i*, *j*, and *k* makes clear that they were addressed *only* to the narrow unavoidable danger issue with respect to inherently dangerous products like foods, cigarettes, whiskey, and drugs.[62] Everything in the comments points to their limited applicability to unavoidably dangerous products of this type, and nothing[63] suggests that they were intended to limit a seller's duty to design its products safely if there is a reasonable way to do so.[64]

Comment j's "Legislative History"

The above contextual interpretation of comment *j* is confirmed by an examination of the evolution of § 402A drafts from 1961 through 1964, together with the contemporaneous scholarship of Dean Prosser and several key *Restatement* Advisers. Preceded by at least a couple of committee drafts,[65] § 402A was formally presented to the ALI three times, beginning with Tentative Draft No. 6 in 1961. In this draft, § 402A imposed strict liability in tort upon sellers of "food in a defective condition unreasonably dangerous to consumers." In three small paragraphs, a single comment f (entitled

law requires that warnings against significant hidden dangers be located in the most appropriate place. See ch. 9, below.

60 Dangers that *can* reasonably be designed out of products are by definition neither "inherent" nor "unavoidable."

61 Comment *k* provides in pertinent part:

> There are some products which, in the present state of human knowledge, are quite incapable of being made safe for their intended and ordinary use. . . . The seller of such products [particularly drugs], again with the qualification that they are properly prepared and marketed, and proper warning is given, where the situation calls for it, is not to be held to strict liability for unfortunate consequences [from] a known but apparently reasonable risk.

62 The *only* examples in comments *i*, *j*, and *k* are, in order: sugar (diabetes), castor oil (used by Mussolini for torture), whiskey (drunkenness), tobacco (cancer), butter (cholesterol and heart attacks), eggs (allergies), strawberries (allergies), alcohol (drunkenness), fatty foods (heart attacks), Pasteur rabies vaccine (allergic reactions), and other drugs and vaccines (side effects).

63 Except possibly for the unfortunate generality of their titles, left over from early tentative drafts of § 402A that applied only to food, and then food, drug, and bodily use products. Once Greenman v. Yuba Power Prods., Inc., 377 P.2d 897 (Cal. 1963), was decided, Dean Prosser promptly expanded the black letter of § 402A from food and products for "intimate bodily use" to *all* products. In his haste to revise the draft in this manner, as discussed below, Prosser neglected to adapt many of the comments to their now much broader scope, leaving many of them in the form in which they had originally been drafted with a much more limited type of product in mind. Had he had more time, no doubt he would have added a major heading over comments *i*, *j*, and *k*, entitled "UNAVOIDABLY UNSAFE PRODUCTS" (or, perhaps, "INHERENTLY DANGEROUS PRODUCTS") and then changed the title of comment *k* to "*Prescription drugs*."

64 Comment *i* includes butter, which can lead to obesity and heart attacks, as an example of a product not susceptible to design safety enhancement. To capture this idea, one adroit plaintiff's counsel, John Kassel, observed that you can't put a safety device on a stick of butter.

65 See Preliminary Draft No. 6, for review by the Advisory Committee (Jan. 3, 1958), and Council Draft No. 8 (Nov. 1, 1960). These early versions contained no direct reference to the unavoidable danger issues eventually addressed in comments *i*, *j*, and *k*.

"*Unreasonably dangerous*") contained the entire discussion of the issues that in the final, published version eventually spanned three comments—*i*, *j*, and *k*. Although the § 402A black letter in this first draft spoke only in terms of "food," comment *c* defined that word to embrace "all products intended for internal human consumption," including beverages, candy, chewing gum, chewing tobacco, snuff, unground coffee beans, and drugs. In order to embrace these non-food items more comfortably, Prosser in the next draft expanded the black letter of § 402A to cover, in addition to food, "other products for intimate bodily use."[66] In this draft, the discussions in comment f of the previous draft were expanded upon and divided into comments *i*, *j*, and *k*. After Justice Traynor's landmark 1963 ruling in *Greenman v. Yuba Power Products, Inc.*,[67] Dean Prosser expanded the black letter of § 402A once again, this time to broaden the applicability of strict liability in tort to the sale of *all* products in a "defective condition unreasonably dangerous to the user or consumer."[68] In this final draft, which Dean Prosser hurriedly rewrote to accommodate *Greenman*,[69] comments *i*, *j*, and *k* (all three of which sprang from comment f which he had first written to accompany the "food" draft of 1961)[70] remained essentially unchanged[71]—suggesting that he was too rushed to think through how these comments (written to apply only to inherently dangerous products) might be incorrectly thought to apply to *all* products, including those that a manufacturer reasonably should have designed differently to eliminate unreasonable risks.

Contemporary Scholarship

The contemporaneous scholarship of William Prosser and key ALI Advisers, at the time § 402A was being conceived and debated, also suggests that comment *j* was intended only to address the narrow unavoidable danger issue in foods, drugs, cigarettes, whiskey, and other potentially toxic substances. In the only three products liability articles Dean Prosser published after the ALI promulgated § 402A in 1965,[72] and in the

---

66 See Tentative Draft No. 7 (Apr. 16, 1962).

67 377 P.2d 897 (Cal. 1963).

68 Tentative Draft No. 10, approved by the ALI in 1964 and promulgated in final, published form the next year.

69 Once *Greenman* was rendered in 1963, Dean Prosser had to scramble to convert § 402A from its prior, narrow coverage to *all* products. Apart from his many other duties as Torts Restatement Reporter, dean, and professor, he had to prepare Tentative Draft No. 10 for circulation, first, to the Advisers, then to the Council, and finally to the whole ALI membership in time for the May 1964 annual meeting.

70 And which he had fleshed out in the 1962 draft to accommodate other products for intimate bodily use.

71 Apart from the addition of a butter example to comment *i*, and corrections of technical errors throughout, the comments in Tentative Drafts 7 and 10 are substantially the same.

There is only sparse discussion of the comment *j* issue in the Restatement debates, but nothing there suggests that Dean Prosser or anyone else contemplated that limiting a seller's responsibility to a duty to warn extended beyond the inherently dangerous food-type products then being considered; certainly there is no intimation that this limited duty might apply to manufacturers of durable goods whose dangers may reasonably be designed away. In discussing a manufacturer's duty to warn, Dean Prosser noted: "It is not correct to say that [the manufacturer] can always avoid liability by giving reasonable notice." 38 A.L.I. Proc. 68 (1961). While the meaning of this sentence is somewhat unclear in its context, Dean Prosser's general remarks do make clear that the last sentence of then comment f (now comment *j*) only addressed the kinds of inherent, unavoidable risks dealt with in the food and drug examples covered by then comment f (now comments *i*, *j*, and *k*).

72 Prosser, Products Liability in Perspective, 5 Gonz. L. Rev. 157, 164 et seq. (1970); Prosser, The Fall of the Citadel (Strict Liability to the Consumer), 50 Minn. L. Rev. 791, 807 et seq. (1966); Prosser, Strict Liability to the Consumer in California, 18 Hastings L.J. 9 et seq. (1966).

next (and final) edition of his hornbook,[73] he examined the unavoidable danger issue, using the same examples and reasoning he had used in comments *i*, *j*, and *k*. The only salient difference of his treatment of these issues in his scholarship[74] (distinguished from the comments) is that he reverted in his scholarship to lumping the inherent danger issues all together, under a single "unavoidable danger" umbrella, as he had originally done in comment f to § 402A in Tentative Draft No. 6.[75] This suggests that Dean Prosser, as Reporter for § 402A, intended the narrow, contextual interpretation of comment *j* explained above. Although it appears that Prosser never closely focused on the availability of design defect claims under § 402A for failing to adopt a reasonable alternative design, his writings suggest that he believed § 402A properly applied to such cases without regard to whether the danger was obvious or a warning had been given.[76]

The scholarship of at least four key ALI Advisers, Professor Fleming James, Deans Page Keeton and John Wade, and Justice Roger Traynor,[77] confirms that the duty of safe design is largely independent of the duty to warn. A decade prior to § 402A, Professor James wrote: "[T]he risk that warning will not be heeded, and the danger likely to ensue if it is not, may be so great as to call for some safety device or even for abandonment of the process or the product if its utility is outweighed by the danger. Surely an automobile manufacturer would be negligent in marketing cars without brakes, even if that fact were known to all the world."[78] Dean Keeton's scholarship reveals that the principal concern of tort scholars at the time was whether strict liability should be applied broadly to manufacturing defects and, more controversially, to inherently dangerous products such as food, drugs, cosmetics, whiskey, and tobacco.[79] As for more usual kinds of products, Dean Keeton rejected the view that a manufacturer's duty of safe design somehow vanishes if the danger is obvious or the user otherwise (as by a warning) is aware of the danger.[80] Dean Wade, just as Professor James, was more explicit, explaining

---

73 W. Prosser, Handbook of the Law of Torts § 99, at 660 (4th ed. 1971) (beginning: "The second, and more important, question concerns [whether 402A should apply to] products that in the present state of human skill and knowledge are unavoidably dangerous, and cannot be made safe.").

74 In his last (and least formal) article, Dean Prosser explained that sellers of food, drugs, and other useful products containing unavoidable dangers are subject only to duties to warn and keep their products pure: "You cannot impose strict liability upon a man who sells what appears to be a perfectly reputable product and is actually extremely beneficial to the human race; you cannot make him strictly liable because once in a while something goes wrong with it in a way which he cannot prevent." Prosser, Products Liability in Perspective, 5 Gonz. L. Rev. 157, 166 (1970).

75 In all three articles and his hornbook, Prosser states that the question of whether § 402A should apply to unavoidably dangerous products is one of the two or three most important issues on the proper reach of strict liability, and he organizes this discussion (that the final draft of § 402A splintered into comments *i*, *j*, and *k*) under the general heading, "Type of Product" (in the articles) and "Unsafe Products" (in the hornbook).

76 This is explained in Owen, The Puzzle of Comment *j*, 55 Hastings L.J. 1377, 1386–87 (2004).

77 Professor Fleming James (Harper, James, and Gray on Torts) of Yale, Dean W. Page Keeton (Prosser and Keeton on Torts) of Texas, and Dean John W. Wade (Prosser, Wade, and Schwartz on Torts) of Vanderbilt were prominent tort law scholars of the day. Chief Justice Roger Traynor authored the principal judicial authority for § 402A, Greenman v. Yuba Power Prods., Inc., 377 P.2d 897 (Cal. 1963), theoretically grounded in his concurring opinion in Escola v. Coca Cola Bottling Co., 150 P.2d 436, 439 (Cal. 1944).

78 James, Products Liability, 34 Tex. L. Rev. 44, 58 (1955).

79 See Keeton, Products Liability—Liability Without Fault and the Requirement of a Defect, 41 Tex. L. Rev. 855 (1963). See generally Priest, Strict Products Liability: The Original Intent, 10 Cardozo L. Rev. 2301, 2303 (1989). Cf. Wade, Strict Tort Liability of Manufacturers, 19 Sw. L.J. 5, 22 (1965).

80 "[T]he proposition that the user's knowledge of a particular hazard involved in the use of a product should necessarily preclude recovery by him if victimized by that hazard is rejected . . . ." Keeton, Products Liability—Inadequacy of Information, 48 Tex. L. Rev. 398, 401 (1970) (also rejecting an economic argument "that a consumer and others who are injured through the use of a product do not have any right to be secure

that "a warning will not always be sufficient."[81] Chief Justice Traynor, an ALI Adviser for § 402A as well as the author of *Greenman*, addressed this issue head-on in an article published the same year as § 402A. Observing that the last sentence of comment *j* was directed solely at inherently dangerous products such as poison and cigarettes, products with dangers that cannot be designed away,[82] he specifically noted that comment *j* in no way insulates manufacturers who provide warnings from liability for the other two types of product defects: manufacturing defects and defects in design. That is, manufacturers cannot use warnings to shift responsibility to consumers for these other, independent types of defects.[83]

It is evident that the comments to § 402A were not provided as a complete products liability "code" but in fact addressed only certain limited aspects of the new doctrine of strict products liability in tort. The comments do not directly address, outside of the narrow context of unavoidably dangerous products, the broader issue of the relationship between the general duties of warning and safe design. As seen above, however, contemporaneous scholarship of Dean Prosser and his key ALI Advisers quite firmly suggests that comments *i*, *j*, and *k* were intended to address only the narrow issue of the limited manner in which the new strict liability section applied to unavoidably dangerous products whose inherent risks cannot be designed away. Their scholarship suggests, and the comments to § 402A imply, that the new strict liability doctrine in fact requires manufacturers to physically remove substantial dangers—even if they are warned about, obvious, or generally known—if there is a reasonable way to do so.[84]

---

from harm from dangerous products apart from a right to be informed or apart from safety legislation") (emphasis omitted).

[81] Wade, On the Nature of Strict Tort Liability for Products, 44 Miss. L.J. 825, 842 (1973). Dean Wade provided some examples: "An electrical appliance with uninsulated wires would not be made duly safe by attaching a warning to look out for the danger of electric shock." Id. n.56. "A rotary lawn mower, for example, which had no housing to protect a user from the whirling blade would not be treated as duly safe, despite the obvious character of the danger." Id. at 843. He also notes the similarity of issues in cases where a danger is *warned* about and where it is *obvious*. Id.

[82] See Traynor, The Ways and Meanings of Defective Products and Strict Liability, 32 Tenn. L. Rev. 363, 367–73 (1965) (examining the cases on food, drugs, tobacco, and similar products). "Some dangers are generic to the goods, so that people regard the goods as fit for ordinary use even with such qualities. The manufacturer would not be liable, under the *Restatement* test, for harm caused by generic dangers." Id. at 370 (referring to comment *i*). See also id. at 367 (§ 402A "would impose no strict liability for what are classified as 'unavoidably unsafe products' ") (citing comment *k*); id. at 372 (warnings "cannot be used, however, to mask a disclaimer of responsibility that would shift the risk to the consumer") (referring to comment *j*).

[83] See id. at 372:

> What is the effect of warning or notice? The *Restatement* provides: "Where proper warning is given, the seller may reasonably assume that it will be read and heeded; and a product bearing such a warning which is safe for use if the warning is heeded, is not in a defective condition. . . ." [citing comment *j*.] Example: poison. A warning or notice cannot be used, however, to mask a disclaimer of responsibility that would shift the risk to the consumer. Thus, a notice by a manufacturer of soft drinks listing the possible foreign substances that might be contained in a bottle of its beverage, or a notice by an automobile manufacturer listing possible difficulties that might be encountered by the user of the car, would not preclude liability.

[84] Research on § 402A reveals that the Reporter, the Advisers, and the ALI were focused at the time on the narrow issue of liability for injuries from products containing inherent, unavoidable dangers (such as food and drugs), *not* on the general duties of manufacturers of ordinary products to design them safely and warn of hidden dangers. See Owen, The Puzzle of Comment j, 55 Hastings L.J. 1377, 1386–87 (2004); Schwartz, Considering the Proper Federal Role in American Tort Law, 38 Ariz. L. Rev. 917, 947 & n.185 (1996). See also Priest, Strict Products Liability: The Original Intent, 10 Cardozo L. Rev. 2301 (1989).

Policy

It makes good sense to interpret comment *j* narrowly, as limiting the duties of sellers of inherently dangerous products like drugs, cigarettes, and alcoholic beverages to providing products that are uncontaminated and possess adequate warning of hidden dangers. Because there is no way (other than by providing warnings) that manufacturers of such products can minimize the inherent dangers of such products without also destroying their utility, there is no good reason in corrective justice or economics to force manufacturers to insure consumers against risks of harm they have chosen to accept by purchasing products with inherent risks of which they are fully aware. But if a product contains substantial risks that *can* reasonably be designed away, then a manufacturer that does not do so should be faulted, in both fairness and economics, for failing to respect the rights of consumers to reasonable product safety. These fundamental precepts, explored elsewhere in greater depth,[85] support the logic and fairness of keeping the manufacturer's duty of safe design largely independent of the duty to warn. To hold that warnings immunize manufacturers from the duty of safe design (or the duty of safe manufacture) would obliquely, unfairly, and implausibly subordinate the interests of consumers to the interests of manufacturers.[86]

No rule, of course, provides that fulfilling *one* of several independent tort law duties fulfills them *all*. Surely a driver has a duty of reasonable care to give warning, by honking the horn, to all pedestrians endangered by the car's approach, even if they are at fault for being in the roadway and failing to pay attention to oncoming traffic. But a driver also has duties to maintain a proper lookout, to operate the car soberly and with reasonable skill, to brake as appropriate, to obey traffic signals, and not to speed. It would make no sense to relieve a driver of all responsibilities to pedestrians so long as the driver, though violating all the other duties, simply honked the horn. Similarly, it makes no sense to relieve a manufacturer of all its other duties—notably its duties to design and manufacture its products safely—simply because it places a warning on its products. Such a rule would allow a manufacturer of household fans to put a simple warning on the base of its fans—"Metal blades may cut off fingers"—in lieu of surrounding the blades with a protective cage; it would allow a manufacturer of power

---

[85] See Owen, The Moral Foundations of Products Liability Law: Toward First Principles, 68 Notre Dame L. Rev. 427 (1993).

[86] See Latin, "Good" Warnings, Bad Products, and Cognitive Limitations, 41 UCLA L. Rev. 1193, 1294–95 (1994) (thoroughly critiquing interpretation of comment *j* as meaning that warnings trump manufacturer's duty of safe design):

> [T]he comment j presumption is unrealistic from a behavioral perspective, inefficient from an accident-prevention perspective, and inequitable from a normative perspective. . . . Good product warnings may be useful, indeed necessary, in many accident-prevention settings but their value is inherently limited and they consequently should not be treated as legally acceptable alternatives to safer product designs and marketing strategies.

See also Henderson and Twerski, A Proposed Revision of Section 402A of the Restatement (Second) of Torts, 77 Cornell L. Rev. 1512, 1538 (1992) ("Product warnings cannot bear the full burden of ensuring that products will be used safely. If a sensible design alternative can significantly reduce risk, the law will demand that the manufacturer design out the risk rather than merely warn against it."). See generally § 10.2 (Obvious Dangers), below.

The issue was debated by Professors Phillips and Ausness. Compare Phillips, Products Liability: Beyond Warnings, 26 N. Ky. L. Rev. 595, 602 (1999) ("It seems too late . . . to return to an unbridled doctrine of laissez faire or caveat emptor, in the modern-day of complex products, advertising blandishments, and clearly foreseeable human frailty."), with Ausness, When Warnings Alone Won't Do: A Reply to Professor Phillips, 26 N. Ky. L. Rev. 627, 646 (1999) (Professor Phillips "rightly criticizes" comment *j*, but the Third Restatement's approach in comment *l* to § 2 goes too far the other way). See also Weissman, A "Comment J" Parry to Howard Latin's "Good" Warnings, Bad Products, and Cognitive Limitations, 70 St. John's L. Rev. 629 (1996).

mowers to leave off a protective housing around the blade if it warned on the handle "Rotating blade can cut off toes and fingers"; and it would permit a manufacturer of industrial machinery a warning escape hatch—"Keep hands away from all moving parts of all machines"—that would nullify its basic duty to equip dangerous industrial machinery with simple guards and other safety devices reasonably necessary to avoid substantial risks of serious harm.

The Evolving Products Liability Jurisprudence

Comment *j*, as previously explained, was intended to address only the limited issue of a seller's responsibility under § 402A for harm caused by unavoidable dangers inherent in a narrow class of products. Reading comment *j* more broadly, as according warnings the power of a shield against the duty of safe design applicable to products generally, conflicts not only with its intended scope but also with sound policy, as just discussed. Such an approach also contrasts starkly with products liability law over the past half century. When Prosser researched and initially drafted comment *j* in 1959 and 1960, products liability law was still dominated by many strictures from the early 1900s: liability was infrequently imposed for a manufacturer's conscious design choices;[87] the patent danger doctrine still limited a manufacturer's design responsibility to latent dangers;[88] consumer expectations were the only gauge of strict products liability (in warranty and, later, under § 402A);[89] consumer carelessness in any degree, even in the face of an egregiously dangerous product design, served to bar recovery altogether;[90] and the intended use doctrine barred liability for most forms of consumer misuse ("abnormal use"), including the failure to follow a seller's instructions, on the ground that it superseded the manufacturer's responsibility.[91] Yet, soon after § 402A (with its comments, including comment *j*) was published in 1965, the law took several sharp turns the other way. By the 1970s, courts began with a gusto to apply judicial oversight to a manufacturer's design choices;[92] the patent danger doctrine began a precipitous decline into virtual extinction;[93] the risk-utility standard began to swallow up the consumer expectations test for evaluating the safety of a product's design;[94] the total bar for user carelessness rapidly gave way to damages apportionment based on comparative fault;[95] and the scope of a manufacturer's responsibility for product safety was widening broadly from intended uses to all foreseeable uses.[96]

In the twenty-first century, the most sensible way to interpret comment *j*'s ambiguous last sentence is according to its original intent—that it applies only to the narrow category of inherently dangerous products with unavoidable dangers like food, drugs, alcoholic beverages, tobacco, and a small category of other products that are

---

87 See § 8.1, below.

88 See § 10.2, below.

89 See §§ 5.6, above, and 8.3, below.

90 See § 13.2, below.

91 See § 13.5, below; Prosser on Torts § 102, at 669 (4th ed. 1971); Prosser, The Fall of the Citadel (Strict Liability to the Consumer), 50 Minn. L. Rev. 791, 824–26 (1966).

92 See § 8.1, below.

93 See § 10.2, below.

94 See §§ 5.6–5.7, above, and 8.2–8.8, below.

95 See § 13.3, below.

96 See § 13.5, below.

inherently (unavoidably) dangerous.[97] If for some reason a court feels impelled to interpret this sentence more broadly, as applicable to *all* types of products, then the sentence should be interpreted as meaning nothing more than that a manufacturer may fulfill its informational obligations to consumers by providing adequate warnings and instructions.[98] According any greater import to comment *j*, as meaning that a warning cancels the fundamental duty of manufacturers of ordinary products to take reasonable steps to design away serious hazards, would elevate consumer responsibility for accidents to the archaic position it has not occupied for more than half a century,[99] and it would revive a host of discredited doctrines that long ago were properly put to rest.[100]

Present Status of Comment j

With the exception of a handful of decisions that have misinterpreted comment *j* as negating the general duty of safe design,[101] a great majority of courts, many implicitly but some explicitly rejecting comment *j* on this point,[102] hold that the separate forms of

---

[97] Like trampolines. See, e.g., Parish v. Jumpking, Inc., 719 N.W.2d 540 (Iowa 2006) (trampoline with adequate warnings not defective in design; relying on Third Restatement); Crosswhite v. Jumpking, Inc., 411 F. Supp. 2d 1228, 1233 (D. Or. 2006) (same; relying in part on comment *j*).

[98] See, e.g., Moulton v. Rival Co., 116 F.3d 22, 28 (1st Cir. 1997) (Me. law) (comment *j* restricted to cases involving only duty to warn). See also Evridge v. American Honda Motor Co., 685 S.W.2d 632, 636 (Tenn. 1985).

[99] Imposing absolute responsibility on consumers ignores real-world limitations on human cognition:

> The Comment *j* presumption embodies the behavioral assumption that "reasonable" users can be expected to receive, correctly interpret, and obey every comprehensible warning accompanying every product they use or encounter. Yet, people are exposed each day to innumerable risks created by appliances that may malfunction or be mishandled; by potentially toxic pollutants, food additives, and other chemical substances; by cosmetics, drugs, and cleansing agents that may be improperly applied and are inherently dangerous for some sensitive individuals; by machine tools, presses, and other industrial or occupational equipment; and by hazardous transportation and recreation devices. Indeed, almost all products present substantial risks if improperly manufactured, designed, or used. People would have to read, understand, remember, and follow innumerable product warnings to protect themselves from all product-related risks they may confront.

Latin, "Good" Warnings, Bad Products, and Cognitive Limitations, 41 UCLA L. Rev. 1193, 1206 (1994) (cognitive theory shows that warnings should only be used to supplement reasonable designs, not to substitute therefore). See also Twerski et al., The Use and Abuse of Warnings in Products Liability: Design Defect Comes of Age, 61 Cornell L. Rev. 495, 506 (1976); Products Liability Rest. § 2 Reporters' Note to cmt. *l*.

[100] Defense lawyers, who naturally prefer defendant-protective rules, argue that comment *j* should be interpreted to mean that a manufacturer that provides a warning should be relieved of its duty of safe design. See, e.g., Silvergate, The Restatement (Third) of Torts: Products Liability—The Tension Between Product Design and Product Warnings, 75-DEC Fla. B.J. 10, 11 (2001); Morrison, Warning v. Design in Products Litigation: Third Time's Not Always a Charm, 10 Kan. J.L. & Pub. Pol'y 86 (2000). Compare Schwartz, See No Evil, Hear No Evil: When Clear and Adequate Warnings Do Not Prevent the Imposition of Product Liability, 68 U. Cin. L. Rev. 47, 59–60 (1999) (recognizing the Third Restatement's "legitimate concern" that people may not read and heed all warnings, cautioning that "courts could 'over-read' Comment *j* . . . to mean that a manufacturer who warns about a risk is not liable," as with a power lawnmower, where a warning to stay away from an unguarded blade would not displace the duty to guard). Although I disagree with the thrust of Steve Morrison's article above, he was an exceptional lawyer to whose memory this section of the book is dedicated.

[101] Interpreting comment *j* to mean that a warning eliminates the manufacturer's duty to provide a safe design, see, e.g., Lightolier, a Div. of Genlyte Thomas Grp., LLC v. Hoon, 876 A.2d 100, 110–11 (Md. 2005), criticized in Recent Decision, 65 Md. L. Rev. 1303 (2006); Curcio v. Caterpillar, Inc., 543 S.E.2d 264 (S.C. Ct. App. 2001), rev'd on other grounds, 585 S.E.2d 272 (S.C. 2003); Ferguson v. F.R. Winkler GMBH & Co. KG, 79 F.3d 1221 (D.C. Cir. 1996); Freas v. Prater Constr. Corp., 573 N.E.2d 27 (Ohio 1991); Simpson v. Standard Container Co., 527 A.2d 1337 (Md. Ct. Spec. App. 1987). Compare Wagoner v. Exxon Mobil Corp., 813 F. Supp. 2d 771, 788–89 (E.D. La. 2011) (Ala. law) (adequate warning precludes claim based on design defect).

[102] That is, rejecting the conventional misinterpretation of comment *j* as meaning that warnings insulate manufacturers from their duty of safe design. Prior to the Third Restatement, most courts ignored the curious statement in comment *j*, and thereby avoided addressing the relationship between the separate duties of warning and design. The Third Restatement's explicit rejection of this assertion in the Second Restatement's

defect give rise to separate obligations that may independently support a products liability claim.[103] Thus, except in certain limited contexts,[104] it is abundantly clear that a manufacturer is subject to liability for a product's *manufacturing* defects, no matter how clear the product's warnings or how perfect its design;[105] for *warning* defects, no matter how perfect the product's manufacture or how impeccable its design;[106] and for *design* defects, no matter the precision of its manufacture or the abundance of its warnings.[107] This latter point may be the most significant, because of the lingering, perverse effects of comment *j*'s long tentacles of misinterpretation in a number of jurisdictions.[108]

---

comment *j*, however, focused courts and lawyers specifically on this point. For examples of cases explicitly rejecting the warnings-trump-design interpretation of comment *j*, see, e.g., Delaney v. Deere & Co., 999 P.2d 930, 942 (Kan. 2000) ("just because there is a warning on a piece of equipment, the warning does not prevent the equipment from being dangerous"); Uniroyal Goodrich Tire Co. v. Martinez, 977 S.W.2d 328, 335–37 (Tex. 1998); Rogers v. Ingersoll-Rand Co., 144 F.3d 841, 844 (D.C. Cir. 1998). See also Ryle v. NES Rentals, 2006 WL 931862, at *3 n.2 (M.D. Pa. 2006) (noting the rejection of cmt. *j* in the context of design cases by courts, commentators, and the Products Liability Restatement); Leaf v. Goodyear Tire & Rubber Co., 590 N.W.2d 525, 529 (Iowa 1999) (dictum critical of cmt. *j*).

[103] Even critics of the Third Restatement's rejection of the warnings-trump-design approach acknowledge that the Third Restatement position is widely embraced by the courts. See, e.g., Ausness, When Warnings Alone Won't Do: A Reply to Professor Phillips, 26 N. Ky. L. Rev. 627, 638 (1999).

[104] Particularly in the case of drugs and other inherently dangerous products containing unavoidable dangers, where warnings normally are the only way to eliminate dangers in design. See Rest. (2d) Torts § 402A cmt. *k*. On inherent risks and unavoidable dangers, see §§ 10.3 and 10.4, below.

[105] See, e.g., Falada v. Trinity Indus., 642 N.W.2d 247, 251 (Iowa 2002) ("defective design and defective workmanship are separate concepts"); Chapman v. Maytag Corp., 297 F.3d 682, 689 (7th Cir. 2002) (Ind. law) (" 'adequate warnings will not render a product with a manufacturing defect non-defective,' regardless of whether compliance with the warnings would have rendered the product safe"); Glover v. BIC Corp., 987 F.2d 1410, 1416 (9th Cir. 1993) (Or. law) (same).

[106] See, e.g., Flores v. Merck & Co., 2022 WL 798374, at *5 (D. Nev. 2022) ("Strict liability may be imposed even where the product is faultlessly made, if it was unreasonably dangerous to place the product in the hands of the consumer without adequate warnings concerning its safe and proper use."); Hakim v. Safariland, LLC, 2022 WL 1136552, at *5 (N.D. Ill. 2022); Burton v. E.I. du Pont de Nemours & Co., Inc., 994 F.3d 791, 822 (7th Cir. 2021) (Wis. law) ("A properly designed and manufactured product may still be defective if 'an intended use of the product is dangerous, but the manufacturer did not provide sufficient warning or instruction.' "); Evans v. Nacco Materials Handling Grp., Inc., 810 S.E.2d 462, 472 (Va. 2018) ("A product may be as safe as engineering will permit, and suffer from no design defect, but nevertheless require a warning to consumers about a hidden danger."); Moore v. Ford Motor Co., 332 S.W.3d 749, 757 (Mo. 2011) (en banc) (although "a product may be designed and manufactured properly, the lack of an adequate warning, in itself, may render a product defective or unreasonably dangerous"); Lewis v. Sea Ray Boats, Inc., 65 P.3d 245, 249 (Nev. 2003) ("strict liability may be imposed even though the product is faultlessly made if it was unreasonably dangerous to place the product in the hands of the user without suitable and adequate warning concerning safe and proper use").

[107] See, e.g., Eskridge v. Pacific Cycle, Inc., 556 Fed. Appx. 182, 189 (4th Cir. 2014) (W. Va. law) (even good warnings and instructions do not supplant the duty of safe design); Delaney v. Deere & Co., 999 P.2d 930, 942 (Kan. 2000) ("just because there is a warning on a piece of equipment, the warning does not prevent the equipment from being dangerous"); White v. ABCO Eng'g Corp., 221 F.3d 293, 305–06 (2d Cir. 2000) (N.J. law) (despite clearly adequate warnings, conveyor manufacturer was subject to liability for failing to provide side guarding); Lewis v. American Cyanamid Co., 715 A.2d 967, 977 (N.J. 1998); Rogers v. Ingersoll-Rand Co., 144 F.3d 841, 844 (D.C. Cir. 1998); Crow v. Manitex, Inc., 550 N.W.2d 175 (Iowa Ct. App. 1996) (manufacturer of improperly used crane, contrary to adequate warnings and instructions that would have prevented accident if heeded, subject to liability for failing to design crane so as to prevent the accident); Glittenberg v. Doughboy Recreational Indus., 491 N.W.2d 208, 216 (Mich. 1992); Robinson v. G.G.C., Inc., 808 P.2d 522, 525 (Nev. 1991) ("a warning is not an adequate replacement when a safety device will eliminate the need for the warning"); Uloth v. City Tank Corp., 384 N.E.2d 1188, 1192 (Mass. 1978) ("If a slight change in design would prevent serious, perhaps fatal, injury, the designer may not avoid liability by simply warning of the possible injury."). For early recognition that a manufacturer has a duty of safe design independent of any warnings, see, e.g., James, Products Liability (pt. 1), 34 Tex. L. Rev. 44, 49, 58–59 (1955).

[108] If comment *j* retains any beneficial vitality in the modern world, it is as a source of consumer protection on an entirely separate issue. Indeed, most courts addressing the last paragraph of comment *j* have

"Decisively" repudiating the "primitive" interpretation of comment *j* that would accord warnings the power to override a manufacturer's other safety responsibilities,[109] the *Third Restatement* declares in no uncertain terms that the law does not permit a manufacturer to hide behind a warning in an attempt to insulate itself from its independent duty of safe design:

> In general, when a safer design can reasonably be implemented and risks can reasonably be designed out of a product, adoption of the safer design is required over a warning that leaves a significant residuum of such risks. . . . Warnings are not . . . a substitute for the provision of a reasonably safe design.[110]

The courts have quite colorfully expressed the same idea. For example, the Michigan Supreme Court has observed that "[a] warning is not a Band-Aid to cover a gaping wound, and a product is not safe simply because it carries a warning."[111] And the Court of Appeals for the District of Columbia Circuit has ruled that "[i]t is thus not correct that a manufacturer may . . . merely slap a warning onto its dangerous product, and absolve itself of any obligation to do more."[112] More succinctly, warnings do not trump design.[113]

Overlap of Safety Obligations

Proper Role of Warnings in Design Defect Determinations

While the three forms of defect generate independent safety obligations, such that the satisfaction of one obligation does not ipso facto satisfy the others, fulfilling one duty sometimes helps to satisfy another. This overlap of safety responsibilities is clearest in the areas of design and warnings. The safer a manufacturer *designs* its products, the fewer dangers there will be about which to *warn*. As seen above, however, the issue usually is posed the other way: how may a *warning* affect a manufacturer's duty of safe *design*? Although warnings will only rarely satisfy a manufacturer's duty of safe design, as previously explained, warnings sometimes are the only practical way to reduce a risk,

---

applied it in a consumer-*friendly* way—ruling, in cases where adequate warnings are not provided, that comment *j* supports the creation of a presumption in favor of consumers that, had the manufacturer provided an adequate warning, the plaintiff (or someone acting on his behalf) would have read and heeded it. Courts widely use this "heeding presumption" to satisfy the consumer's burden of proof on cause in fact. See, e.g., Coffman v. Keene Corp., 628 A.2d 710 (N.J. 1993). After *Coffman*, a manufacturer that had warned of a danger asked the New Jersey court to apply comment *j* in *its* favor to bar the plaintiff's design defect claim. The court would not allow this nonsense: "Allowing such a warning to defeat a design-defect claim . . . would frustrate the imposition of liability when a product's design fails to take into account an injured party's objectively foreseeable misuse of the product." On the heeding presumption and cause in fact, see § 11.4, below.

[109] The Restatement Reporters frequently have castigated this interpretation of comment *j*: "The Products Restatement rejects this primitive notion decisively." Henderson and Twerski, The Politics of the Products Liability Restatement, 26 Hofstra L. Rev. 667, 689 (1998).

[110] Products Liability Rest. § 2 cmt. *l*. See Twerski, In Defense of the Products Liability Restatement: Part I, 8 Kan. J.L. & Pub. Pol'y 27, 29 (1998) ("[C]omment j took the position that a product whose dangers are warned against, is not defective. We took the position in section 2 comment 1 of the Restatement (Third) of Torts that one cannot warn one's way out of a design defect case. If there is a reasonable design which would make the product safer, the mere fact that one warned against it does not insulate the seller from liability. . . . We vehemently disagree with the *Second Restatement*."); Henderson and Twerski, The Politics of the Products Liability Restatement, 26 Hofstra L. Rev. 667, 689 (1998).

See, e.g., Richetta v. Stanley Fastening Sys., L.P., 661 F. Supp. 2d 500, 510 (E.D. Pa. 2009) (allowing defective design claim for nail gun with warnings but no trigger lock; following comment *l* of section 2 of Third Restatement and rejecting literal meaning of comment *j* of Second Restatement).

[111] Glittenberg v. Doughboy Recreational Indus., 491 N.W.2d 208, 216 (Mich. 1992).

[112] Rogers v. Ingersoll-Rand Co., 144 F.3d 841, 844 (D.C. Cir. 1998).

[113] See Owen, Warnings Don't Trump Design: The Rise and Fall of § 402A Comment *j*, 153 Products Liability Advisory 1 (Nov. 2001). Thanks to John Kassel for this apt characterization.

particularly in the case of pharmaceutical drugs and other chemical and inherently toxic products.[114]

For example, a furniture polish that is very harmful if swallowed by young children would clearly be defective if sold without child-proof tops and adequate warnings of the danger.[115] Assuming there is no way to change the chemical formulation of the polish to reduce the risk without sacrificing its effectiveness, a manufacturer who warns of such an unavoidable hazard has no duty to design the polish differently, for there is no duty to do the impossible, to design away an unavoidable risk.[116] Even with a strong warning of the hazard, of course, the manufacturer of such a toxic substance would have a duty to ensure that its *container* was child-proof in design. So, cases like this are properly viewed as involving purely a duty to warn and not a duty to design away a danger inherent in the product.

Because warnings and instructions may in fact serve to reduce design hazards,[117] at least to some extent, the provision of such information may have *some* bearing on design defectiveness. Just as the obviousness of a hazard reduces the likelihood of resulting harm,[118] so, too, do warnings and instructions.[119] Thus, because warnings reduce the risk of injury from design hazards, the presence of a warning is one factor—sometimes an important one—to be balanced in the calculus of considerations involved in a determination of design defectiveness. That is, in balancing the risk factors relevant to design defectiveness, a trier of fact should consider, among other factors, whether the design hazard was obvious, warned about, or generally known.[120]

Compatibility of Separate Defect Claims

While the three types of defect are conceptually distinct, separate claims for each often are compatible. Thus, in an appropriate case, the plaintiff may claim that a product was defective because of two, or (if infrequently) all three different types of defect.[121] That is, the different types of defect claims are not mutually exclusive.[122] Indeed, design and warning defect claims regarding the same danger are commonly asserted and

---

114 This is especially so with many inherent product risks, as discussed in comment *j*. See § 10.3, below.

115 See, e.g., Spruill v. Boyle-Midway, Inc., 308 F.2d 79 (4th Cir. 1962) (Va. law).

116 See §§ 10.3 and 10.4, below.

117 See § 9.1, below.

118 See § 10.2, below.

119 See § 9.1, below.

120 See §§ 8.8 and 10.3, below. The Third Restatement makes this point in describing the "broad range of factors" that may be relevant to the defectiveness of a product's design, including "the magnitude and probability of the foreseeable risks of harm, the instructions and warnings accompanying the product, and the nature and strength of consumer expectations regarding the product . . . ." Products Liability Rest. § 2 cmt. *f*.

121 See, e.g., Pilliod v. Monsanto Co., 282 Cal. Rptr. 3d 679, 705 (Ct. App. 2021) (2–1 decision) (allowing plaintiffs' verdict on separate design and warning defect claims); Kaiser v. Johnson & Johnson, 947 F.3d 996 (7th Cir. 2020) (Ind. law) (same); Ozbun v. Rite-Hite Corp., 2012 WL 3777206, at *3 (D. Mont. 2012) (allowing plaintiff's design, warning, and manufacturing defect claims, and noting that warning defect claims are "separate and distinct" from design defect claims); Anaya v. Town Sports Int'l, Inc., 843 N.Y.S.2d 599 (App. Div. 2007) (allowing claims of design and warning defects against manufacturer of rock-climbing safety harness); Anderson v. Owens-Corning Fiberglas Corp., 810 P.2d 549, 553 n.7 (Cal. 1991) ("In most instances, as here, the plaintiff alleges both design and warning defects."). Yet, the facts of particular cases often preclude the assertion of particular defect claims. See, e.g., Dierks v. Mitsubishi Motors Corp., 256 Cal. Rptr. 230, 231 (Ct. App. 1989) (where plaintiff tried auto rollover case as a design case, claiming that the roof collapsed too easily, trial court properly refused to instruct jury on manufacturing defect claim: "A defect in manufacture is, of course, quite different from a defect in design.").

122 See, e.g., Caterpillar Tractor Co. v. Beck, 593 P.2d 871, 878 n.15 (Alaska 1979) ("Manufacturing defects and design errors are not mutually exclusive . . .").

properly allowed in cases where a manufacturer allegedly failed to warn of a significant hidden danger that reasonably could have been designed away.[123] For example, an SUV that rolls over too easily on particular steering maneuvers may be defective in design, because its center of gravity is too high and its track width too narrow, and it may also be defective because of the absence of a warning of this tendency.[124]

And while manufacturing defect claims often stand alone, they may be combined with design and even warning defect claims on appropriate facts. So, if an occasional flashcube explodes when defectively manufactured, the seller may well have a duty to warn of this tendency.[125] Sometimes the evidence is quite unclear as to whether a product was defective in manufacture or design,[126] and a plaintiff with credible evidence should be allowed to try to make out a case on both.[127] For example, a product's wires or cables may be dangerously crossed during manufacture because the engineers did not design a sufficient separation to minimize this production risk. And if the engineers should have foreseen this hazard, perhaps they also should have warned about the resulting danger. Malfunction cases are another example of how defect theories fairly may overlap: while the circumstances of a product malfunction may usually suggest a production defect, sometimes a design defect may just as likely be the culprit.[128]

§ 6.3 PROOF OF DEFECT—EXPERT TESTIMONY

Proof of defectiveness and causation often requires scientific and technical experts to explain the relevant science and engineering of product safety and accidents to a lay jury and the court.[129] Understanding various aspects of the design, manufacture, and labeling of products normally involves a host of complex considerations requiring

---

[123] See, e.g., Anderson v. Owens-Corning Fiberglas Corp., 810 P.2d 549, 553 n.7 (Cal. 1991) ("In most instances, as here, the plaintiff alleges both design and warning defects."); Evridge v. American Honda Motor Co., 685 S.W.2d 632, 636 (Tenn. 1985) (interpreting comment *j* to allow simultaneous warning and design defect claims).

[124] See, e.g., Bericochea-Cartagena v. Suzuki Motor Co., 7 F. Supp. 2d 109 (D.P.R. 1998) (Suzuki Sidekick); Purvis v. American Motors Corp., 538 So.2d 1015 (La. Ct. App. 1988) (Jeep CJ-5).

[125] See Maybank v. S.S. Kresge Co., 266 S.E.2d 409 (N.C. Ct. App. 1980), modified on other grounds and aff'd, 273 S.E.2d 681 (N.C. 1981).

[126] See, e.g., Stazenski v. Tennant Co., 617 So.2d 344 (Fla. Dist. Ct. App. 1993) (worker cut on sharp edge of industrial sweeper).

[127] See, e.g., Richcreek v. General Motors Corp., 908 S.W.2d 772, 777 (Mo. Ct. App. 1995), where a car's seat hinge pin may have been too short and needed welding rather than pounding into place, may have been pounded improperly: Here, there is "a very fine line between design and manufacturing defects under strict liability. To limit a plaintiff to one theory where no inconsistency exists with others is too restrictive."

[128] See, e.g., Morden v. Continental A.G., 611 N.W.2d 659, 664 (Wis. 2000) (upholding verdict for plaintiff finding that tire manufacturer was negligent in design *or* manufacture of tires); Smith v. Ford Motor Co., 215 F.3d 713, 716 (7th Cir. 2000) (Ind. law) (reversing dismissal of plaintiff's claim, although plaintiff's expert, who concluded that steering failed due to defect in van's steering gearbox, was unable to determine whether defect was due to design or manufacture). On the malfunction doctrine, see § 7.4, below.

[129] See, e.g., Kuhar v. Petzl Co., 2022 WL 1101580, at *3 (3d Cir. 2022) (N.J. law) ("where a factfinder must employ 'scientific, technical, or other specialized knowledge' use of expert testimony is required"); Emerson Electric Co. v. Johnson, 627 S.W.3d 197, 207 (Tex. 2021) (expert causation testimony is required when "an issue involves matters beyond jurors' common understanding"); Pitts v. Genie Indus., Inc., 921 N.W.2d 597, 609 (Neb. 2019) (affirming summary judgment for defendant where plaintiffs' expert's causation evidence was speculative; "Findings of fact as to technical matters beyond the scope of ordinary experience are not warranted in the absence of expert testimony supporting such findings. . . . [T]he mechanical functioning of an aerial lift, its component parts, and its electrical circuitry [were] technical matters well outside the scope of ordinary experience" and so required expert testimony); Torres v. Skil Corp., 2013 WL 3105815 (D. Mass. 2018) (plaintiff's fingers injured by power circular saw when its blade guard allegedly failed to snap down promptly when he released saw's trigger; because "the mechanical components of the saw's blade guard are beyond the common knowledge of a layperson," expert testimony was required on defect and causation).

specialized expertise. Mechanical, chemical, and materials engineers, chemists, physicists, pharmacologists, epidemiologists, and other technical specialists are often necessary to help the factfinder comprehend how a product was made, how it was supposed to operate, whether and how it may have malfunctioned or otherwise caused an accident, and how it could have been made differently to avoid accidents of that type. Thus, involving as it does the inner workings of science and technology, products liability litigation often resolves into a "battle of the experts."[130]

The Significance of Expert Testimony

Expert testimony has special significance in products liability litigation for several reasons. Most fundamentally, it is the means by which juries and judges in most products liability cases obtain the analytical tools to decide whether a particular product was "defective" and whether that product defect caused the plaintiff's injury. Some products, and some product failures, are quite simple to understand, such as the explosion of a thermos bottle[131] or the presence of a cockroach in a sandwich.[132] In such cases, there is little "beyond the ken" of the judge or jury on which expert counsel is required.[133] But the mechanisms of most product failures are more complex. In such cases, courts and juries generally are dependent on the information and opinions provided by scientific and technical specialists on the technical issues that typically lie at the heart of a products liability case.[134] In this respect, judges and juries, who by hypothesis are incapable of understanding without assistance the technical aspects of such a case, are at the mercy of the experts. In addition, the law of evidence gives experts especially wide latitude to offer opinions not available to ordinary witnesses.[135] For these reasons, expert testimony can be particularly powerful, and it has a particular power to

[130] See, e.g., Simmons v. Ford Motor Co., 2022 WL 168540, at * (S.D. Fla. 2022) ("The proper course [when a] court is faced with this 'battle of the experts,' is to submit the question to the factfinder."); In re Toyota Motor Corp. Unintended Acceleration Marketing, Sales Practices, & Prods. Liab. Litig., 978 F. Supp. 2d 1053, 1070 (C.D. Cal. 2013) (conflicting expert opinions on driver's abilities and behavior prior to crash "create[d] a 'battle of the experts'" properly resolved by the jury); Warnke v. Warner-Lambert Co., 799 N.Y.S.2d 666, 669 (App. Div. 2005) ("[a]s in most strict products liability cases, the trial herein was essentially a battle of experts"); Jenkins v. General Motors Corp., 446 F.2d 377, 380 (5th Cir. 1971) ("It all boils down to a battle of experts . . ."). This simple fact of products liability litigation has long been true. See D. Peck, Decision at Law 40–64 (1961) (detailing expert testimony on hickory grain of spoke, nature of break, and tests and inspections of broken automobile wheel involved in MacPherson v. Buick Motor Co., 111 N.E. 1050 (N.Y. 1916)). For an earlier version of the discussion here, see Owen, A Decade of *Daubert,* 80 Denv. U. L. Rev. 345 (2002).

[131] See, e.g., Virgil v. "Kash N' Karry" Serv. Corp., 484 A.2d 652, 656 (Md. Ct. Spec. App. 1984) ("The general rule is well established that expert testimony is only required when the subject of the inference is so particularly related to some science or profession that it is beyond the ken of the average layman.").

[132] See Bullara v. Checker's Drive-In Rest., Inc., 736 So.2d 936 (La. Ct. App. 1999) (chili dog).

[133] See, e.g., Faryniarz v. Nike, Inc., 2002 WL 530997 (S.D.N.Y. 2002) (expert testimony unnecessary for jury to find running shoes defectively designed because excessively long laces could get caught on pull-tab).

[134] See, e.g., Kubicki v. Medtronic, Inc., 293 F. Supp. 3d 129, 156 (D.D.C. 2018) (expert testimony ordinarily indispensable on causation in complex medical product liability cases); Hughes v. Stryker Sales Corp., 2010 WL 1961051, at *5 (S.D. Ala. 2010) ("The interaction between a complex and technical medical device and the unique physiological and medical circumstances of the patient in which it is implanted is a subject on which no ordinary juror could rationally be expected to have knowledge. The net result is that, without the benefit of expert testimony, a reasonable jury could not possibly make a determination on this summary judgment record that Hughes' injuries were caused by a manufacturing or design defect in the prosthetic hip."); Air Reduction Co. v. Philadelphia Storage Battery Co., 14 F.2d 734, 740 (3d Cir. 1926) (case involving explosion of drilled-steel manifold involved "highly technical subject matter" that generated a "compelling necessity of scientific information to enable the court and jurors to understand . . . the character of materials used [and] the dangers incident to their use . . . which [information] enabled court and jury . . . to intelligently understand and fairly decide the case").

[135] See Fed. R. Evid. 701–03, 705, and similar state evidentiary rules.

mislead.[136] While the rules governing the admissibility of expert testimony on science and technology are treated extensively elsewhere,[137] the topic is so centrally important to products liability litigation that it deserves special treatment here.

Expert testimony is often necessary to establish a defect in manufacture, design, and warnings and instructions. As mentioned earlier, juries normally need the guidance of expert testimony to understand the technical aspects of both defectiveness and causation. Without such testimony, juries would be left to assumption, conjecture, and speculation on these central elements of every case. Thus, a products liability case usually will fail without an expert's proof of defect[138] by expert testimony.[139]

---

[136] "Judge Weinstein has explained: 'Expert evidence can be both powerful and quite misleading because of the difficulty in evaluating it' " (citation omitted). Daubert v. Merrell Dow Pharms., Inc., 509 U.S. 579, 595 (1993). See also In re C.R. Bard, Inc., 948 F. Supp. 2d 589, 601 (S.D. W. Va. 2013) ("expert witnesses have the potential to be both powerful and quite misleading"); Betz v. Pneumo Abex, LLC, 44 A.3d 27, 53 (Pa. 2012) (recognizing "the influential nature of expert testimony on complex subjects, and the potential that distortions have to mislead laypersons"); Mendez, Expert Testimony and the Opinion Rule: Conforming the Evidence Code to the Federal Rules, 37 U.S.F. L. Rev. 411, 411 (2003) (noting a concern "that testimony by experts with impressive credentials will overwhelm the jurors"); A. Schwartz, A "Dogma of Empiricism" Revisited: *Daubert v. Merrell Dow Pharmaceuticals, Inc.* and the Need to Resurrect the Philosophical Insight of *Frye v. United States*, 10 Harv. J.L. & Tech. 149, 196–98 (1997); Black et al., Science and the Law in the Wake of *Daubert*: A New Search for Scientific Knowledge, 72 Tex. L. Rev. 715, 789 (1994) ("[M]ost commentators believe ostensibly scientific testimony may sway a jury even when as science it is palpably wrong. Science can be greatly distorted by the pressures of litigation, but once it is admitted into evidence, it has an imprimatur of legitimacy and validity, and cross-examination often will not expose its flaws.").

[137] See, e.g., D. Faigman, D. Kaye, M. Saks, and J. Sanders, Science in the Law—Standards, Statistics and Research Issues (2002) (in-depth coverage of admissibility, nature of expertise, ethical issues, scientific method, statistical proof, survey research, epidemiology, and toxicology); Reference Manual on Scientific Evidence (Federal Judicial Center 3d ed. 2011); Weinstein's Federal Evidence ch. 702 (2d ed. 2002); 1 McCormick on Evidence §§ 10–18; Frumer, Friedman, and Sklaren, Products Liability ch. 18A; R. Park, D. Leonard, and S. Goldberg, Evidence Law ch. 14 (3d ed. 2011).

There are hundreds of articles on this topic. See, e.g., Faigman, Slobogin, and Monahan, Gatekeeping Science: Using the Structure of Scientific Research to Distinguish Between Admissibility and Weight in Expert Testimony, 110 Nw. U. L. Rev. 859 (2016); Helland and Klick, Does Anyone Get Stopped at the Gate? An Empirical Assessment of the *Daubert* Trilogy in the States, 20 Sup. Ct. Econ. Rev. 1 (2012); Imwinkelried, Serendipitous Timing: The Coincidental Emergence of the New Brain Science and the Advent of an Epistemological Approach to Determining the Admissibility of Expert Testimony, 62 Mercer L. Rev. 959 (2011); Jurs, Judicial Analysis of Complex & Cutting-Edge Science In the *Daubert* Era: Epidemiologic Risk Assessment as a Test Case for Reform Strategies, 42 Conn. L. Rev. 49 (2009); Bernstein, Expert Witnesses, Adversarial Bias, and the (Partial) Failure of the Daubert Revolution, 93 Iowa L. Rev. 451 (2008); Cheng, Independent Judicial Research in the *Daubert* Age, 56 Duke L.J. 1263 (2007); Cheng and Yoon, Does *Frye* or *Daubert* Matter: A Study of Scientific Admissibility Standards, 91 Va. L. Rev. 471 (2005); Owen, A Decade of *Daubert*, 80 Denv. U. L. Rev. 345 (2002); Saks, The Aftermath of Daubert: An Evolving Jurisprudence of Expert Evidence, 40 Jurimetrics J. 229 (2000); Capra, The Daubert Puzzle, 32 Ga. L. Rev. 699 (1998); Green, Expert Witnesses and Sufficiency of Evidence in Toxic Substances Litigation: The Legacy of Agent Orange and Bendectin Litigation, 86 Nw. U. L. Rev. 643, 661 (1992); Annot., 177 A.L.R. Fed. 77 (2002) (Supreme Court cases on expert testimony).

[138] In addition to more general testimony, an expert may testify that a product is "defective" under Fed. R. Evid. 704 and similar state evidence rules that now permit expert opinions on the "ultimate issue" in a case. See, e.g., In re Guidant Corp. Implantable Defibrillators Prods. Liab. Litig., 2007 WL 1964337, at *2 (D. Minn. 2007) ("Rule 704 provides that 'testimony . . . otherwise admissible is not objectionable because it embraces an ultimate issue to be decided by the trier of fact.' Fed. R. Evid. 704."); Vaughn v. Daniels Co., 841 N.E.2d 1133, 1137 (Ind. 2006) (Indiana Evidence Rule 704 permits opinions to embrace ultimate issues to be decided by the trier of fact, but prohibits opinions as to legal conclusions). See Fed. R. Evid. 704.

[139] See, e.g., Wells v. Kawasaki Motors Corp., U.S.A., 854 Fed. Appx. 242, 248 (10th Cir. 2021) (affirming summary judgment for jet ski manufacturer; trial court did not abuse discretion in excluding plaintiff's experts' testimony); Hunt v. CNH Am. LLC, 857 F. Supp. 2d 320, 348 (W.D.N.Y. 2012) (granting manufacturer's motion for summary judgment because plaintiff failed to provide admissible expert testimony); Watson v. Ford Motor Co., 699 S.E.2d 169, 177–79 (S.C. 2010) (reversing jury verdict for plaintiffs; expert's testimony failed "any indicia of reliability," so plaintiffs "lacked admissible evidence in the record to support their products liability claim"); McCreless v. Global Upholstery Co., 500 F. Supp. 2d 1350, 1358–59 (N.D. Ala. 2007) (chair collapse:

Manufacturing defects are sometimes so self-evident that expert proof will not be required,[140] but expert testimony ordinarily will be necessary to establish that the manufacturer was negligent[141] or that an accident product deviated from the manufacturer's design specifications.[142] And while reliance on the malfunction doctrine can sometimes assist a plaintiff when the precise cause of a product failure cannot be shown,[143] expert proof is often necessary even under this theory of recovery to rule out other possible causes of the accident.[144]

Simple warning issues sometimes are entirely comprehensible by a jury and thus may not be appropriate for expert testimony.[145] But the science of how to communicate danger and safety information most effectively is evolving in sophistication such that expert testimony on warnings and instructions is often helpful, and sometimes mandatory, as in many cases involving the labeling of dangerous machinery,[146] pharmaceutical drugs,[147] and in other specialized labeling situations.[148]

Most jurisdictions define design defectiveness in terms of risk-utility analysis, an analytical approach that requires an evaluation of the feasibility, costs, and benefits of altering a design to avoid an injury.[149] Such claims almost always require expert proof,[150]

---

defendants' motion for summary judgment granted because plaintiff had no expert testimony on defect in design or manufacture or on proximate cause); Brooks v. Colonial Chevrolet-Buick, Inc., 579 So.2d 1328, 1332 (Ala. 1991) ("because of the complex and technical nature of the product and in order to present evidence from which a lay jury may reasonably infer that a defective condition of the product was the cause of the product's failure and the cause of the resultant injury to the plaintiff, expert testimony is *usually* essential and, therefore, usually required"). See also Weisgram v. Marley Co., 528 U.S. 440 (2000), discussed in note 222, below.

140 See, e.g., O'Shea v. Zimmer Biomet Holdings, Inc., 342 F. Supp. 3d 1354, 1362–63 (N.D. Ga. 2018) (complaint form, completed by manufacturer's employee, was admission that replacement knee "malfunctioned or failed to perform as intended" in the absence of "contributing conditions"; sufficient circumstantial evidence to defeat defendant's summary judgment motion on plaintiff's manufacturing defect claim).

141 See, e.g., Miller v. Ford Motor Co., 653 S.E.2d 82, 84 (Ga. Ct. App. 2007) (claim that seatbelt and airbag were defectively manufactured failed without expert testimony).

142 See, e.g., Williams v. Kawasaki Motors Corp., U.S.A., 30 F.4th 66, 70 (1st Cir. 2022) (expert's testimony that motorcycle's right-side frame weld's deviation from specifications caused the fire after a crash was excluded as "too large an analytical leap"). See § 7.3, below.

143 See § 7.4, below.

144 See id.

145 See, e.g., Robertson v. Norton Co., 148 F.3d 905 (8th Cir. 1998) (Ark. law) (noting issue).

146 A sophisticated system is described in Product Safety Sign and Label System (FMC Corp. 1993).

147 See, e.g., J.C. v. Pfizer, Inc., 814 S.E.2d 234, 246 (W. Va. 2018) (plaintiffs failed to provide expert evidence that the 2003 Zoloft label inadequately warned of the risk of birth defects if drug ingested during pregnancy; "the complex issues [of] what should and should not be included in a drug label demonstrates that this is a case where expert testimony is necessary"); Handbook of Nonprescription Drugs (D. Krinsky ed., 17th ed. 2012) (U.S.); Patient Information in Medicine (R. Mann ed., 1991) (Europe). *But cf.* Stahl v. Novartis Pharms. Corp., 283 F.3d 254, 265 (5th Cir. 2002) (holding that a treating physician's testimony that certain drug warnings were adequate is not "expert testimony" and thus need not meet *Daubert* standards).

148 Such as how tires should be labeled. See, e.g., Goodyear Tire & Rubber Co. v. Rios, 143 S.W.3d 107, 118 (Tex. App. 2004) ("A jury could not have determined, without the benefit of expert testimony, which, among many, warnings and instructions should be printed on a sidewall."). See also Weatherspoon v. Nissan N. Am., Inc., 2010 WL 606561, at *10 (S.D. Miss. 2010) (expert testimony that pictorial warning not to travel with a car seat in the reclining position should "not have been relegated to the owner's manual and should have appeared in the compartment"). See generally ch. 9, below. On applying *Daubert* to warning-label testimony, see Note, 76 Ind. L.J. 465 (2001).

149 See ch. 8, below.

150 See, e.g., Quiles v. Bradford-White Corp., 2012 WL 1355262 (N.D.N.Y. 2012) (design defect claims require expert testimony on feasibility and efficacy of alternative designs unless a reasonable alternative design is obvious and understandable by layperson; claims for design defect in water heater dismissed because fire origin experts who investigated cause of explosion not qualified as experts on alternative design theory—

sometimes on the mechanisms of how the accident occurred and almost always on how the design hazard that led to the accident feasibly could have been eliminated.[151] However, if design defectiveness is defined purely in consumer-expectation terms,[152] whether expert testimony is appropriate may depend on the type of product under scrutiny. A jury might well need expert guidance on the safety expectations of users of industrial, professional, or other products designed for use by specialists in a field.[153] But consumer goods, particularly simple ones, are another matter: it is difficult to see how the opinion of a technical or other expert on ordinary consumer expectations about the safety of a simple consumer product could assist a jury, which would seem to preclude expert testimony on defectiveness in such cases.[154]

Regardless of the type of defect, expert testimony often is necessary to prove causation, the link that connects a product defect to a plaintiff's harm.[155] Causation is typically at issue in pharmaceutical drug and other toxic substance cases, where expert testimony on causation (and defectiveness) almost invariably is necessary and often poses a major problem for plaintiffs.[156] Although plaintiffs often fail to prove causation in such cases (often on *Daubert* grounds),[157] sometimes they prevail. One such case was

---

that pilot light should have been located 18 inches from floor, which required explanation of chemical properties of flammable vapors at various heights from floor and of feasibility of locating tank at that height); Bass v. Air Prods. & Chems., Inc., 2006 WL 1419375, at *12 (N.J. Super. Ct. App. Div. 2006) (summary judgment for manufacturers proper; expert testimony normally is required on risk-utility balance and design defectiveness).

[151] See § 8.5, below.

[152] See § 8.3, below.

[153] See, e.g., Kirk v. Clark Equip. Co., 991 F.3d 865, 878–79 (7th Cir. 2021) (Ill. law) (plaintiffs' strict liability design defect claims against manufacturer of front-end loader failed under both the consumer expectations and risk-utility tests without expert testimony).

[154] See, e.g., Rogers v. K2 Sports, LLC, 348 F. Supp. 3d 892, 904 (W.D. Wis. 2018) (expert testimony not required to explain ski helmet fitting instructions written in plain language; denying summary judgment for defendant on plaintiffs' defective instructions claim); Jenks v. New Hampshire Motor Speedway, 2012 WL 405479, at *5 (D.N.H. 2012) ("A statement of the obvious which is within the ken of a lay jury is not the proper subject of expert testimony."); Sub-Zero, Inc. v. General Elec. Co., 2010 WL 3584427, at *3–4 (W.D. Wis. 2010) (expert testimony not necessary because whether a light bulb that burst and caused a fire was defectively dangerous is within the "realm of ordinary experience"); United States v. Zajanckauskas, 441 F.3d 32, 39 (1st Cir. 2006) ("Expert testimony does not assist where the [trier of fact] has no need for an opinion because it easily can be derived from common sense, common experience, the [trier of fact's] own perceptions, or simple logic."); Faryniarz v. Nike, Inc., 2002 WL 530997 (S.D.N.Y. 2002) (expert testimony unnecessary for jury to find running shoes defectively designed because excessively long laces could get caught on pull-tab). See also Soule v. General Motors Corp., 882 P.2d 298, 308 (Cal. 1994) ("[W]here the minimum safety of a product is within the common knowledge of lay jurors, expert witnesses may not be used to demonstrate what an ordinary consumer would or should expect. Use of expert testimony for that purpose would invade the jury's function . . . .").

[155] On proof of causation, including the need for expert testimony, see ch. 11, below.

[156] See Zellars v. NexTech Northeast, LLC, 895 F. Supp. 2d 734, 752 (E.D. Va. 2012) ("Reliable and relevant expert testimony is generally required to prove both general and specific causation, *i.e.*, (1) 'that a particular chemical is harmful to humans generally,' and (2) 'that exposure to the potentially harmful agent actually caused [the plaintiff's harm].' "). "Courts in the toxic tort arena have been struggling for two decades with the task, imposed by *Daubert v. Merrell Dow Pharmaceuticals, Inc.*, of determining which expert causation opinions meet the reliability standard imposed by *Daubert*." M. Green, Pessimism About *Milward*, 3 Wake Forest J.L. & Pol'y 41 (2013) (discussing history of Rest. (3d) of Torts § 28(a) cmt. *c*). See generally Note, 10 Rev. Litig. 117, 119–23 (1990) (expert witness problems in toxic substance cases). Causation in toxic substance litigation is considered generally at § 11.2, below.

[157] See, e.g., Lanzo v. Cyprus Amax Mins. Co., 254 A.3d 691, 712 (N.J. Super. Ct. App. Div. 2021) (reversing $117 million compensatory and punitive damages awards for long-time talc user suffering from mesothelioma; trial court erred in allowing plaintiffs' experts to present unreliable theories that non-asbestiform cleavage fragments can cause an asbestos disease); Mallozzi v. EcoSMART Techs., Inc., 2013 WL 2415677 (E.D.N.Y. 2013) (insufficient testimony from plaintiff's experts on general and specific causation that plaintiff's inhalation of peppermint oil fumes from liquid pesticide caused his GERD or LPR); Parmentier v.

Milward v. Acuity Specialty Products Group, Inc.,[158] which addressed the admissibility of expert opinion testimony on general causation in a toxic substance case. The district court excluded the plaintiff's expert opinion testimony that exposure to benzene can cause leukemia, an opinion the expert arrived at by a form of analysis called "reasoning-to-the-best-inference" methodology. The Court of Appeals concluded that the district court's exclusion of the expert's testimony was erroneous because it failed to recognize the validity of the expert's reasoning-to-the-best-inference methodology and, further, because the trial court had itself weighed the evidence, rather than properly leaving that task to the jury.[159]

Even in cases involving durable goods, where proofs of defectiveness and causation are often linked closely together, expert evidence on how the defect caused the harm usually is necessary to a plaintiff's case.[160] To give but a few examples, judges and juries surely will need expert tutelage on defectiveness if the issue in dispute is whether the speed control mechanism for a paver should have been in the form of a lever rather than a rotary dial;[161] whether a sport utility vehicle should have been equipped with a barrier between the seats and cargo area, together with a warning, to make it safe for occupants in the rear;[162] whether the strength of a corn chip rendered it unreasonably dangerous;[163] whether and how the steering gearbox in a vehicle may have been improperly assembled or designed;[164] whether the operator compartment on a forklift should have been equipped with a door[165] or wire mesh;[166] whether cigarettes could have been made more safely;[167] whether a hay baler should have had a guard;[168] or whether a lift truck should have had operator restraints and a protected cockpit.[169]

On causation, expert testimony similarly will almost certainly be necessary if the parties disagree on whether a product defect caused the plaintiff's harm—such as whether a causal link exists between a plaintiff's ingestion of Viagra and his heart

Novartis Pharm. Corp., 2012 WL 2324502 (E.D. Mo. 2012) (plaintiff's case failed once court excluded expert testimony on specific causation, that cancer drugs caused decedent's osteonecrosis of jaw); Butler v. Union Carbide Corp., 712 S.E.2d 537 (Ga. Ct. App. 2011) (unreliable expert testimony that decedent's exposure to very small amounts of asbestos from defendant's products caused his mesothelioma); Parker v. Mobil Oil Corp., 857 N.E.2d 1114, 1121–22 (N.Y. 2006) (plaintiff's experts failed to offer sufficient evidence that exposure to benzene in gasoline caused gas station attendant's leukemia).

[158] 639 F.3d 11 (1st Cir. 2011) (Mass. law).

[159] Id. at 20. See also In re Blair Hugger Forced Air Warming Devices Prods. Liab. Litig., 9 F.4th 768, 789 (8th Cir. 2021) (reversing summary judgment for manufacturer of forced-air patient-warming device based on erroneous inadmissibility decisions regarding plaintiffs' experts' general causation testimony); Schultz v. Akzo Nobel Paints, LLC, 721 F.3d 426, 434 (7th Cir. 2013) (Wis. law) (same: benzene). See generally Green, Pessimism about *Milward*, 3 Wake Forest J. L. & Pol'y 41 (2013). On "reasoning to the best inference," see note 263, below.

[160] See, e.g., Romo v. Ford Motor Co., 798 F. Supp. 2d 798, 809–10 (S.D. Tex. 2011) (even with expert evidence establishing a defect, plaintiffs' cases fail if they do not prove cause in fact); Auto Club Grp. Ins. Co. v. All-Glass Aquarium Co., 716 F. Supp. 2d 686, 691–94 (E.D. Mich. 2010) (cause of home fire); Mack Trucks, Inc. v. Tamez, 206 S.W.3d 572, 583 (Tex. 2006) (cause of fatal petroleum tanker truck fire).

[161] See Alfred v. Caterpillar, Inc., 262 F.3d 1083 (10th Cir. 2001).

[162] See Bowersfield v. Suzuki Motor Corp., 151 F. Supp. 2d 625 (E.D. Pa. 2001).

[163] See Grady v. Frito-Lay, Inc., 839 A.2d 1038 (Pa. 2003).

[164] See Smith v. Ford Motor Co., 215 F.3d 713 (7th Cir. 2000).

[165] See, e.g., Dhillon v. Crown Controls Corp., 269 F.3d 865 (7th Cir. 2001); Berry v. Crown Equip. Corp., 108 F. Supp. 2d 743 (E.D. Mich. 2000).

[166] See Bourelle v. Crown Equip. Corp., 220 F.3d 532 (7th Cir. 2000).

[167] See LaBelle v. Philip Morris, Inc., 243 F. Supp. 2d 508 (D.S.C. 2001).

[168] See Masters v. Hesston Corp., 2001 WL 567736 (N.D. Ill. 2001), aff'd, 291 F.3d 985 (7th Cir. 2002).

[169] See Anderson v. Raymond Corp., 340 F.3d 520 (8th Cir. 2003) (Ark. law).

attack;[170] an allegedly defective product and a house fire that starts nearby;[171] the absence of a kill switch on an outboard motor and injuries to the plaintiff's hand;[172] an anti-depressant drug taken by a teenager and his suicide;[173] a spinal rod implanted in the plaintiff's back to eliminate a painful condition and his quite similar post-operative pain;[174] a mother's failure to wake up from an alarm on her baby's heart-rate monitor and the baby's death;[175] or exposure to innumerable drug, chemical, and other toxic substances and sundry illnesses and disease.[176] In short—on both defect and causation—experts are usually crucial to the prosecution and defense of a products liability case.

Qualifications and Sources of Expert Witnesses

To serve as an expert witness, a person first must be *qualified*—"by knowledge, skill, experience, training, or education"[177]—to offer opinions on a matter for which his or her expertise is relevant and helpful. No matter how qualified an expert is in one field, he or she may not offer opinion testimony on matters outside that person's expertise.[178] The bulk of qualified specialists in most fields of product design, manufacturing, and labeling are employed by private industry, often by the manufacturing enterprises who

---

170 See Brumley v. Pfizer, Inc., 200 F.R.D. 596 (S.D. Tex. 2001).

171 See, e.g., Whirlpool Corp. v. Camacho, 251 S.W.3d 88 (Tex. App. 2008) (clothes dryer); Booth v. Black & Decker, Inc., 166 F. Supp. 2d 215 (E.D. Pa. 2001) (fire allegedly caused by toaster oven); Travelers Prop. & Cas. Corp. v. General Elec. Co., 150 F. Supp. 2d 360 (D. Conn. 2001) (clothes dryers); Weisgram v. Marley Co., 528 U.S. 440 (2000) (electric baseboard heater); Pride v. BIC Corp., 218 F.3d 566 (6th Cir. 2000) (cigarette lighter); Pappas v. Sony Elec., Inc., 136 F. Supp. 2d 413 (W.D. Pa. 2000) (television).

172 See Brooks v. Outboard Marine Corp., 234 F.3d 89, 92 (2d Cir. 2000).

173 See Miller v. Pfizer Inc., 196 F. Supp. 2d 1062, 1085 (D. Kan. 2002) (Zoloft; excluding the testimony of plaintiff's expert, a psychopharmacologist, on specific and general causation, noting that "the flaws in Dr. Healy's methodology . . . are glaring, overwhelming and unexplained"), aff'd, 356 F.3d 1326 (10th Cir. 2004).

174 See Alexander v. Smith & Nephew, P.L.C., 98 F. Supp. 2d 1310 (N.D. Okla. 2000).

175 Graves v. CAS Med. Sys., Inc., 735 S.E.2d 650 (S.C. 2012) (wrongful death claim for infant subject to dismissal without sufficient expert testimony that software defect caused failure of monitor that tracked breathing and heart rate of premature baby; claim involved complex issues of computer design and software beyond understanding of laymen).

176 "Causation is an essential element of a toxic tort case, and proof of causation in such cases 'generally requires reliable expert testimony.' " Butler v. Union Carbide Corp., 712 S.E.2d 537, 540 (Ga. Ct. App. 2011) (whether decedent's exposure to tiny percentage of asbestos from defendant's molding compound, compared to other sources, was a contributing cause of decedent's mesothelioma; disregarding testimony by plaintiff's toxicologist, a "quintessential expert for hire"). See also Vargas v. Ortho-McNeil Pharm., Inc., 2013 WL 3776628 (N.D. Ohio 2013) (no expert testimony on whether contraceptive patch injured plaintiff's ovaries; "When the central issue in a products liability case is a medical question, expert testimony is required to establish causation."); Johnson v. Arkema, Inc., 685 F.3d 452 (5th Cir. 2012) (whether workplace chemicals caused plaintiff's lung diseases); Rink v. Cheminova, Inc., 400 F.3d 1286 (11th Cir. 2005) (Fla. law) (whether Mediterranean fruit fly pesticide caused plaintiff's disease).

177 Fed. R. Evid. 702. See, e.g., Clark v. Safety-Kleen Corp., 845 A.2d 587 (N.J. 2004) (on the basis of education, training, or experience, chemist was qualified to testify on medical causation of plaintiff's injury).

178 See, e.g., Curry v. Royal Oak Enters., LLC, 2013 WL 3196390, at *5 (E.D. Pa. 2013) (plaintiff's proffered expert chemist not qualified to testify on labeling nor hence on adequacy of warning labels); Pooshs v. Philip Morris USA, Inc., 904 F. Supp. 2d 1009, 1023 (N.D. Cal. 2012) (plaintiff's proffered expert, former Director of Applied Research at Philip Morris, with a Ph.D. in physical chemistry and author of over 80 published papers, not qualified to testify on cigarette design, nicotine pharmacology, addiction, or cancer causation); Swanstrom v. Teledyne Cont'l Motors, Inc., 43 So.3d 564, 579–82 (Ala. 2009) (accident investigator without background in fire safety, fire investigation, and fire pattern standards not qualified to testify about causes of in-flight fire or emission of toxic gases from the fire); Bryant v. Hoffmann-La Roche, Inc., 585 S.E.2d 723 (Ga. Ct. App. 2003) (doctors not qualified to testify on adequacy of manufacturer's testing and evaluation of heart drug with respect to whether FDA should have approved the drug); Alexander v. Smith & Nephew, P.L.C., 98 F. Supp. 2d 1310, 1315 (N.D. Okla. 2000) (board-certified doctor of family medicine: "The simple possession of a medical degree is insufficient to qualify a physician to testify as to the advantages of a spinal fixation device, the medical causation of spine-related ailments, or the mechanical functioning of an orthopedic implantation device.").

are defendants in products liability litigation. Thus, because such persons are already in its employ, a manufacturer usually has little difficulty in finding appropriate engineering and other technical experts to help defend a products liability case. Indeed, such experts may include the very persons who designed the accident product, devised the product's warnings and instructions, or designed and supervised the assembly process by which the product was produced. Plaintiffs' lawyers, on the other hand, generally are limited to two principal resource pools for expert witness talent—universities and private consulting expert firms.[179]

The Rise of the "Professional" Expert Witness; the Problem of "Junk Science"

As products liability litigation began to mushroom in the late 1960s and the 1970s, so too did the plaintiff's need for experts to battle a manufacturer's engineers over defectiveness and causation—in expert reports, depositions, and ultimately at trial. Straining the then-existing pool of forensic technical talent, a surge in demand for expert testimony in the 1970s and 1980s spawned a whole new industry of "professional" expert engineers and other specialists who mostly, but not exclusively,[180] testified for the plaintiff's bar. Many such experts were of course entirely competent to testify on the issues they agreed to evaluate. But others advertised a willingness to testify, for a fee, on the defectiveness of (and even the propriety of punitive damages for) just about anything,[181] "from toys to airplanes."[182]

The very idea of a *professional* expert witness is problematic. "Expertise" in any field requires substantial time to stay abreast of current developments—by reading, experimenting, writing, perhaps teaching, and otherwise pursuing knowledge in a specialized field of study. The problem is that much of a professional expert's time is spent in courtrooms and preparing for trial rather than in pursuing expertise. Moreover, because many "professional" experts become economically dependent on being retained by lawyers to testify that particular products are (or are not) defective and caused (or

---

[179] Sources traditionally included books and specialized organizations—i.e., L. Atkinson, H. Philo, and H. Philo, Jr., Lawyers Desk Reference: Technical Sources for Conducting a Personal Injury Action (9th ed. 2001); the American Association for Justice (AAJ, formerly ATLA) Experts Exchange at www.atlanet.org; and Technical Advisory Service for Attorneys ("TASA"), an expert referral service at www.tasanet.com. Among the many engineering and other expert consulting firms are Triodyne Inc. at www.triodyne.com and Engineering Design & Testing Corp. at www.edtengineers.com. Now, the internet provides a plentiful source of experts and expert-finding services, including Thomson Reuters Expert Witnesses Services. See generally Solomon, Insight: What Makes a Great Expert Witness? Look for the Four C's. Bloomberg L. (Apr. 10, 2019); Cade and Dilenschneider, Finding Experts: Top 10 Tips for Researching Experts Online, 37 Prod. Safety & Liab. Rep. (BNA) 1266 (Dec. 14, 2009).

If only a few experts dominate a new or arcane field, counsel may be tempted to tie them up before the opposition can find a qualified expert. But sharing confidential information with a potential expert principally to disqualify or prevent the opposition from using that expert may violate Rules of Professional Conduct. See Texas P.R. Op. 676 (Aug. 2018); Rattan, Lawyer Can't Talk to Experts Just So Adversary Can't Use Them, U.S. Law Week (Sept. 4, 2018).

[180] While manufacturers rely substantially on their own in-house technical experts, they frequently use outside consultants for accident reconstruction and the development of other proofs for trial. One such firm of engineering and scientific consultants drawn upon by defendants, at least in automotive products liability litigation, is Exponent at www.exponent.com.

[181] See, e.g., Huber, Safety and the Second Best: The Hazards of Public Risk Management in the Courts, 85 Colum. L. Rev. 277, 333 (1985) ("a Ph.D. can be found to swear to almost any 'expert' proposition, no matter how false or foolish"). See generally Note, 10 Rev. Litig. 117, 119–23 (1990) (examining seamy side of expert witness business).

[182] One "system safety and human factors enginee[r]" listed in an early expert directory advertised as having testified "in over 100 cases with products ranging from toys to airplanes." Products Liability and Transportation Directory 196 (1983). On problems with professional expert witnesses, see Richmond, The "Professional Expert" Witness: Doctor Lichtor, I Presume?, 17 J. Prod. & Toxics Liab. 197, 223 (1995).

did not cause) particular injuries, they have a natural bias to arrive at conclusions that favor their employers. Without a steady moral compass, grounded in a personal reservoir of knowledge, judgment, professional conviction, and an alternative source of income, a professional witness will be tempted to tell the employing lawyer what the expert thinks the lawyer *wants* to hear, rather than what he or she *needs* to hear. Whether working for the plaintiff or defense, this temptation for professional witnesses to mold their findings and conclusions to make the case for their employer is persistent and strong; and it is insidious, in part because such experts may hide weaknesses in their testimony from their own employer.

The kind of twisted testimony[183] that too easily results from a hired expert's natural bias provides one explanation of why professional witnesses sometimes contradict themselves in different cases, a strategic Achilles heel that an opposing attorney may discover by diligent research. If an opposing attorney discovers such conflicting testimony, both the expert and the employing attorney may find themselves at trial in the dreadful predicament of scrambling to explain the contradiction on the spot. On occasion, professional witnesses provide knowingly false, perjurious testimony that, if discovered, will likely devastate the party's entire case.[184]

The explosion of expert testimony in products liability litigation during the 1970s and 1980s, fueled by an expanding plaintiffs' bar fed by contingent fees, quite naturally led to a rather rapid increase in products liability lawsuits based on novel, untested, abstract, and occasionally quite fantastic theories of science and technology propounded by "experts" who sometimes were dubiously qualified to testify on issues on which they claimed expertise. As products liability litigation during this period marched along,

[183] For one expert's primer on how to mislead a jury, see Sanchez v. Black Bros. Co., 423 N.E.2d 1309 (Ill. App. Ct. 1981) (excerpting speech by defendant's witness to engineers on how to manipulate juries and obfuscate answers on cross-examination).

[184] See, e.g., Jones v. Lincoln Elec. Co., 188 F.3d 709 (7th Cir. 1999); Harre v. A.H. Robins Co., 750 F.2d 1501 (11th Cir. 1985) (judgment for defendant reversed and remanded since verdict based in part on perjured testimony by defense expert). See also Antolovich v. Brown Grp. Retail, Inc., 183 P.3d 582, 607 (Colo. App. 2007) (new trial for perjury granted only for "willful fabrication of evidence bearing on a material issue"); Chewning v. Ford Motor Co., 579 S.E.2d 605 (S.C. 2003) (judgment may be set aside for fraud upon court only if extrinsic fraud thereafter proved by clear and convincing evidence); Jenkins v. General Motors Corp., 446 F.2d 377 (5th Cir. 1971) (trial court properly excluded plaintiff's expert who was under indictment for perjury).

courts[185] and commentators,[186] always skeptical of this form of witness,[187] increasingly decried a perceived growth in abuses of expert testimony—of "junk science" run amok.[188]

Early Limitations on Expert Testimony—*Frye*

At early common law,[189] the only real limitation on expert testimony was that the person proffered as an expert must be *qualified* as an expert in the field. Courts generally allowed such experts to provide testimony about technical matters without restriction: once a person was qualified as an expert, the judge simply admitted his or her relevant testimony into evidence as a matter of course.[190] This liberal approach to expert testimony reflected the thought that a reliable test of the quality of expertise is the market from which an expert makes a living.[191] While the marketplace test generally may have worked satisfactorily to determine the expertise of a carriage maker or pharmacist, this test was unhelpful when applied to expert opinions about *new* science or technology where an existing market for such expertise did not yet exist.

---

185 See, e.g., Lamon v. McDonnell Douglas Corp., 576 P.2d 426, 435 (Wash. Ct. App. 1978) (Anderson, J., dissenting), aff'd, 588 P.2d 1346 (Wash. 1979). More recently, see Rivera Pomales v. Bridgestone Firestone, Inc., 217 F.R.D. 290, 295 (D.P.R. 2003) ("[T]he use of professional expert witnesses has become rampant. . . . [I]nstead of utilizing professionals that work in a specific field to comment and give learned opinions on certain subjects, attorneys turn to 'guns for hire' whose main job or means of living is generated from giving expert testimony [which can result] in supposed experts not utilizing scientific methods to render an opinion but rather by twisting scientific methods to produce a result that will support the case of those footing the bill.").

186 The "junk science" term and concept was popularized by Peter W. Huber who worked for the Manhattan Institute, a conservative think-tank. See, e.g., P. Huber, Galileo's Revenge: Junk Science in the Courtroom (1991); P. Huber, Liability: The Legal Revolution and Its Consequences (1988); Huber, Safety and the Second Best: The Hazards of Public Risk Management in the Courts, 85 Colum. L. Rev. 277, 333 (1985). For a powerful rebuttal, see Chesebro, Galileo's Retort: Peter Huber's Junk Scholarship, 42 Am. U. L. Rev. 1637 (1993).

187 See, e.g., Ferguson v. Hubbell, 97 N.Y. 507, 514 (1884) (expert witnesses' views "cannot fail generally to be warped by a desire to promote the cause in which they are enlisted"); Friedman, Expert Testimony, Its Abuse and Reformation, 19 Yale L.J. 247, 247 (1910) (noting "a constant complaining and mistrust on the part of judges, juries and lawyers of the expert witness"). More recently, see, e.g., Williams v. Michelin N. Am., Inc., 381 F. Supp. 2d 1351, 1362 (M.D. Fla. 2005) (limiting testimony of plaintiff's expert: "Dr. Milner is a professional advocate, dressed in scientific garb.").

188 See P. Huber, Galileo's Revenge: Junk Science in the Courtroom 3 (1991):

> Junk science cuts across chemistry and pharmacology, medicine and engineering. . . . It is a catalog of every conceivable kind of error: data dredging, wishful thinking, truculent dogmatism, and, now and again, outright fraud.
>
> On the legal side [is] a speculative theory that expects lawyers, judges, and juries to search for causes at the far fringes of science and beyond. The legal establishment has adjusted rules of evidence accordingly, so that almost any self-styled scientist, no matter how strange or iconoclastic his views, will be welcome to testify in court. The same scientific questions are litigated again and again, in one courtroom after the next, so that error is almost inevitable.
>
> Junk science is impelled through our courts by a mix of opportunity and incentive. "Let-it-all-in" legal theory creates the opportunity. The incentive is money: the prospect that the Midas-like touch of a credulous jury will now and again transform scientific dust into gold.

See generally Black, A Unified Theory of Scientific Evidence, 56 Fordham L. Rev. 595, 597–98 nn.1–3 (1988).

189 On early discussions of expert testimony, see Chapin, Experts and Expert Testimony, 22 Alb. L.J. 365 (1880); Learned Hand, Historical and Practical Considerations Regarding Expert Testimony, 15 Harv. L. Rev. 40 (1901). See also Landsman, Of Witches, Madmen, and Products Liability: An Historical Survey of the Use of Expert Testimony, 13 Behav. Sci. & L. 131 (1995); Rosen, Expert Testimony in the Social Sciences: A Historical Overview of Contemporary Issues, 38 Law & Hist. Rev. 123 (2020).

190 See D. Faigman, D. Kaye, M. Saks, and J. Sanders, Science in the Law: Standards, Statistics, and Research Issues 3–5 (2002).

191 "The assurance of expertise was implied by the expert's success in an occupation or profession that embraced that knowledge. . . . In effect, the marketplace determined whether valid knowledge existed by endowing it with commercial value." Id. at 4.

This was the situation confronting the court in *Frye v. United States*[192] in which the defendant in a murder case offered the results of an early polygraph test to show his innocence. In passing on the merits of testimony on a new form of science or technology, ruled the court, the test is whether it is "sufficiently established to have gained general acceptance in the particular field in which it belongs."[193] Shifting the fulcrum of decision from the expert to the expertise,[194] the *Frye* "general acceptance" test tended to exclude testimony on cutting-edge science and technology since new ideas become accepted wisdom only over time. During the next half century, *Frye*'s general acceptance standard, although increasingly criticized,[195] evolved into the prevailing test for admissibility of expert testimony.[196]

As modern products liability and other technical litigation expanded in the late 1960s and early 1970s, coincident with the debate over the newly proposed Federal Rules of Evidence then under consideration, the *Frye* test suddenly became quite "trendy."[197] In 1975, the Federal Rules of Evidence were adopted, including Rule 702 which provides for the admission of scientific and technical evidence by a qualified expert only if such testimony will "assist the trier of fact"—if it is helpful to the jury,[198] and Rule 703, which allows an expert to rely on facts and data "reasonably relied upon by experts" in the field.[199] Neither Rule 702 nor the Advisory Committee's comment on it made any reference to the *Frye* test, but most jurisdictions interpreted this rule to incorporate *Frye*'s general acceptance standard.[200]

During the 1980s and early 1990s, the logic and fairness of *Frye*'s general acceptance test came under ever more scrutiny as courts increasingly debated whether and to what extent this test made sense and whether it was truly consistent with Rule 702.[201] During this period, courts struggled to find a balance between the need to open courtrooms to new science, on the one hand, with the problems of allowing experts to

---

[192] 293 F. 1013 (D.C. Cir. 1923).

[193] Id. at 1014.

[194] See Faigman, Porter, and Saks, Check Your Crystal Ball at the Courthouse Door, Please: Exploring the Present, and Worrying About the Future of Scientific Evidence, 15 Cardozo L. Rev. 1799, 1805–09 (1994).

[195] See, e.g., McCormick on Evidence § 203.4 ("General scientific acceptance is a proper condition for taking judicial notice of scientific facts, but it is not suitable as a determinant of the admissibility of scientific evidence."). Criticisms often centered on its conservatism and its vagueness. See, e.g., D. Faigman, D. Kaye, M. Saks, and J. Sanders, Science in the Law: Standards, Statistics, and Research Issues 7–10 (2002) (examining criticisms of the *Frye* test). See also Note, 78 Chi.-Kent L. Rev. 861, 886–95 (2003) (criticizing *Frye* and urging Illinois to adopt *Daubert* or Federal Rule of Evidence 702).

[196] See Giannelli, The Admissibility of Novel Scientific Evidence: *Frye v. United States*, a Half-Century Later, 80 Colum. L. Rev. 1197, 1204 (1980); Comment, 29 Hous. L. Rev. 1029, 1034 (1992).

[197] Faigman, Porter, and Saks, above, note 194, at 1808.

[198] Fed. R. Evid. 702 at the time provided:

> If scientific, technical, or other specialized knowledge will assist the trier of fact to understand the evidence or to determine a fact in issue, a witness qualified as an expert by knowledge, skill, experience, training, or education, may testify thereto in the form of an opinion or otherwise.

As discussed below, Rule 702 was amended in 2000 to reflect the holding in *Daubert*.

[199] Fed. R. Evid. 703 provided:

> The facts or data in the particular case upon which an expert bases an opinion or inference may be those perceived by or made known to him at or before the hearing. If a type reasonably relied upon by experts in the particular field in forming opinions or inferences upon the subject, the facts or data need not be admissible in evidence.

[200] See Faigman, Porter, and Saks, above, at 1803–09.

[201] See Comment, Liars, Damn Liars, and Expert Witnesses: Unhelpful Approaches to Unreliable Scientific Testimony in the Third and Fifth Circuits, 29 Hous. L. Rev. 1029 (1992).

propound bad science, on the other. Increasingly, courts began to strike this balance by partially shifting the focus away from whether the science was "generally accepted," the *Frye* approach, to evaluating the methodology by which the expert reached his or her conclusion.[202]

Daubert and Its Progeny

Daubert

In *Daubert v. Merrell Dow Pharmaceuticals*,[203] after several years of avoiding the issue,[204] the Supreme Court in 1993 finally decided to examine the admissibility of expert testimony on novel scientific theories and the relationship of the *Frye* test to Rule 702. *Daubert* involved the drug Bendectin, an anti-nausea medicine that, from 1956 until 1983, was widely prescribed to pregnant women for morning sickness.[205] From the first Bendectin case filed in 1979, which claimed that the drug had caused the plaintiff's missing and malformed fingers, nearly 2,000 cases eventually were filed claiming damages for birth defects from the drug. In *Daubert,* filed late in the life cycle of the litigation, the plaintiffs claimed that their birth defects were caused by Bendectin administered to their mothers during pregnancy. The defendant manufacturer moved for summary judgment, arguing that there was no causal link between Bendectin and birth defects. In affidavits from its expert scientists, the defendant showed that none of the thirty-eight epidemiological studies of Bendectin published by that time had found a causal connection between birth defects and the drug.[206] In opposition, plaintiffs offered affidavits from eight expert witnesses who concluded—on the basis of chemical structure analyses, *in vitro* (test tube) studies of animal cells, *in vivo* (live) animal studies, and a "reanalysis" of the previous epidemiological studies—that Bendectin can in fact cause birth defects. Concluding that the plaintiffs' proffered expert evidence did not meet

---

[202] See, e.g., United States v. Downing, 753 F.2d 1224, 1237 (3d Cir. 1985); Brock v. Merrell Dow Pharms., Inc., 874 F.2d 307, 310 (5th Cir. 1989) (difficult questions such as whether Bendectin caused birth defects compel courts to "critically evaluate the reasoning process by which the experts connect data to their conclusions in order . . . to consistently and rationally resolve the disputes before them"), modified, 884 F.2d 166 (5th Cir. 1989); Christophersen v. Allied-Signal Corp., 939 F.2d 1106, 1110 (5th Cir. 1990) (en banc) (for an expert's scientific conclusions to be admissible, they must, *inter alia,* be based on "a well-founded methodology").

[203] 509 U.S. 579 (1993).

[204] See, e.g., Justice White's dissents to the denial of certiorari in Mustafa v. United States, 479 U.S. 953, 953–54 (1986), and Christophersen v. Allied-Signal Corp., 503 U.S. 912, 912 (1992).

[205] See Green, Expert Witnesses and Sufficiency of Evidence in Toxic Substances Litigation: The Legacy of Agent Orange and Bendectin Litigation, 86 Nw. U. L. Rev. 643, 661 (1992) (prescribed, during the 1960s and 1970s, to upwards of 25% of all pregnant women in the U.S.). On the Bendectin litigation, see generally J. Sanders, Bendectin on Trial: A Study of Mass Tort Litigation (1998); Green, Bendectin and Birth Defects: The Challenges of Mass Toxic Substances Litigation (1996); Sanders, From Science to Evidence: The Testimony on Causation in the Bendectin Cases, 46 Stan. L. Rev. 1 (1993); Sanders, The Bendectin Litigation: A Case Study in the Life Cycle of Mass Torts, 43 Hastings L.J. 301 (1992); Gross, Substance and Form in Scientific Evidence: What *Daubert* Didn't Do, in Reforming the Civil Justice System 234–44 (L. Kramer ed., 1996) (summarizing the Bendectin litigation).

[206] Four types of scientific studies commonly are used to determine the toxicity of a substance—(1) *chemical structure* analyses of the substance comparing it to known toxins; (2) *in vitro* tests on how the substance affects human or animal cells in the lab; (3) *in vivo* studies on how the substance affects live animals in the lab; and (4) *epidemiological* studies that examine its effects on human beings. Scientists normally consider epidemiological studies on large populations of humans the best test of a substance's toxicity. See Gross, above note 205, at 238–39.

Frye's "general acceptance" standard of admissibility, the district court granted the defendant's summary judgment motion, and the Ninth Circuit affirmed.[207]

In the Supreme Court, the petitioning plaintiffs argued that the *Frye* "general acceptance" standard had been superseded by the Federal Rules of Evidence. Vacating and remanding, the Supreme Court agreed that the Rules do not allow a court to use the degree of acceptance of a subject of scientific testimony as the sole determinant of admissibility.[208] Because Rule 702 allows qualified experts to testify about "scientific . . . knowledge," the Court reasoned that a trial judge must determine that proposed expert testimony is both "scientific" and "knowledge"—that the subject of the testimony is "ground[ed] in the methods and procedures of science," that it be "derived by the scientific method." An expert's proposed testimony must be "supported by appropriate validation—i.e., 'good grounds'. . . ." That is, expert testimony must be *reliable*.[209] In addition to requiring that expert testimony be reliable, the Court further reasoned that Rule 702 requires that such testimony be *relevant,* since the rule allows expert scientific or technical testimony only if it will "assist the trier of fact to understand the evidence or to determine a fact in issue." This is the "helpfulness" requirement of Rule 702, requiring that expert testimony be sufficiently related to disputed facts to help the jury resolve facts or issues in dispute, a requirement the Court characterized simply as "fit."[210] Thus, when a party proffers expert scientific testimony, the trial court must make a preliminary, "gatekeeping" determination of both the (1) *reliability* (validity), and (2) *relevance* (fit) of the expert's reasoning or methodology underlying the testimony proposed.[211]

Among the factors a court may usefully employ in assessing the validity of an expert's proffered testimony on scientific evidence, the Court noted four:[212]

(1) ***Testability***: whether the theory or technique is testable and has been tested—its ability to withstand objective, verifiable challenge and scientific trial;[213]

(2) ***Control***: whether its operation has been subjected to appropriate control standards with an acceptable rate of error;

(3) ***Peer review***: whether it has been published or otherwise subjected to peer review;[214] and

---

[207] Daubert v. Merrell Dow Pharms., 951 F.2d 1128 (9th Cir. 1991), aff'g 727 F. Supp. 570 (S.D. Cal. 1989).

[208] *Daubert,* 509 U.S. at 587–89.

[209] Id. at 589–90.

[210] Id. at 591–92.

[211] Id. at 592–93. That is, "a trial judge must evaluate the proffered testimony to assure that it is at least minimally reliable; concerns about expert testimony cannot simply be referred to the jury as a question of weight." Capra, The *Daubert* Puzzle, 32 Ga. L. Rev. 699, 701–02 (1998).

[212] See *Daubert,* 509 U.S. at 593–94. See also the five-factor list in Capra, The *Daubert* Puzzle, 32 Ga. L. Rev. 699, 702 (1998), which is the basis for the formulation in Federal Rule of Evidence 702, Advisory Committee Note to 2000 Amendment. Headings are added here, and the factors are reordered for logical flow.

[213] The Advisory Committee Note explains this factor more fully: "whether the expert's theory or technique can be or has been tested—that is, whether the expert's theory can be challenged in some objective sense, or whether it is instead simply a subjective, conclusory approach that cannot reasonably be assessed for reliability." Id.

[214] On peer review, see Childs, The Overlapping Magisteria of Law and Science: When Litigation and Science Collide, 85 Neb. L. Rev. 643 (2007); Haack, Peer Review and Publication: Lessons for Lawyers, 36 Stetson L. Rev. 789 (2007).

(4) ***General acceptance***: whether it is widely accepted in the relevant scientific community.

These are *Daubert*'s now-familiar reliability factors. In determining the admissibility of expert testimony under Rule 702, the Court emphasized that the inquiry into pertinent reliability considerations should be flexible, and that the focus of inquiry "must be solely on principles and methodology, not on the conclusions that they generate."[215] Because the lower courts had based their decisions in this case almost exclusively on *Frye*'s general acceptance standard, rather than on the broader reliability and fit requirements of Federal Rule of Evidence 702, the Supreme Court remanded the case to the Court of Appeals.[216]

Supreme Court Progeny

After *Daubert*, the Supreme Court revisited the expert testimony issue several times. In *General Electric Co. v. Joiner*,[217] a district court applied *Daubert* to exclude expert testimony that purported to link the plaintiff's exposure to PCBs to his lung cancer, and the court of appeals reversed. Reinstating the district court's ruling, the Supreme Court emphasized that federal trial courts have wide discretion to exclude expert testimony, holding that such determinations are subject only to a permissive "abuse of discretion" review. The Court further noted that *Daubert*'s direction that courts focus on an expert's *methodology* did not preclude a trial judge from scrutinizing the quality of an expert's *conclusions*.[218]

Next came *Kumho Tire Co. v. Carmichael*,[219] a tire blowout case involving a worn tire containing at least two punctures that previously had been inadequately repaired. In a suit against the tire manufacturer, the plaintiffs relied on the deposition testimony of an expert in tire failure analysis to support their claim that the blowout had been caused by a defect in the tire rather than abuse. Although the expert's testimony might have been viewed as "technical" rather than "scientific," the trial court applied the gatekeeping principles of *Daubert*, closely scrutinizing the reliability of the expert's hypotheses, methodology, and conclusions. Concluding that they failed each of the *Daubert* factors, and that their reliability had not been established on any other ground, the district court excluded the expert's testimony and granted the defendant's motion for summary judgment. The circuit court reversed, ruling that *Daubert* applied only to experts relying on "scientific" principles rather than on the kind of skill-based or experience-based observations of the type relied on by plaintiff's expert. Reversing the circuit court, the Supreme Court held that Rule 702's broad reference to expert testimony on "scientific, technical, or other specialized knowledge" means that the *Daubert*

---

[215] *Daubert*, 509 U.S. at 593–95.

[216] On remand, applying the *Daubert* analysis, the Ninth Circuit ruled again that the district court had properly excluded the plaintiffs' expert testimony, reasoning that the testimony of one of the plaintiffs' experts was not reliable and that the testimony of the others was not relevant because they would only testify that Bendectin is "capable of causing" birth defects, not that the drug *in fact* (more likely than not) caused the plaintiffs' birth defects. Daubert v. Merrell Dow Pharms., Inc., 43 F.3d 1311, 1321 (9th Cir. 1995).

[217] 522 U.S. 136 (1997).

[218] The Court remarked: "[C]onclusions and methodology are not entirely distinct from one another. Trained experts commonly extrapolate from existing data. But nothing in either *Daubert* or the Federal Rules of Evidence requires a district court to admit opinion evidence that is connected to existing data only by the *ipse dixit* of the expert. A court may conclude that there is simply too great an analytical gap between the data and the opinion proffered." Id. at 146.

[219] 526 U.S. 137 (1999).

gatekeeping principles apply to *all* expert testimony.[220] Further, the Court reaffirmed the flexibility of the reliability inquiry and noted that the trial court has wide latitude, subject to review only for abuse of discretion, to determine what reliability factors are appropriate to the particular expert testimony under examination.[221]

The final Supreme Court decision on expert testimony so far is *Weisgram v. Marley Co.*,[222] a wrongful death action against the manufacturer of a heater arising out of a house fire. On testimony by three experts that the heater was defective and that the defect caused the fire, the plaintiffs obtained a judgment on a jury verdict, over the defendant's objection that the testimony was unreliable and therefore inadmissible under Rule 702 and *Daubert*. The circuit court reversed, agreeing with the defendant that the plaintiffs' expert testimony offered mere speculation as to the heater's defectiveness, making it scientifically unsound. Rather than remanding for a retrial, and reasoning that the plaintiffs had had a fair opportunity to prove their claim and so did not deserve a second chance, the circuit court directed judgment for the defendant manufacturer. The Supreme Court affirmed. Rejecting an argument that a plaintiff might hold certain expert testimony in reserve to shore up the claim if the proffered expert testimony were to be found insufficient, the Court noted that *Daubert* put parties relying on expert evidence on notice of "the exacting standards of reliability" demanded of such evidence. "It is implausible to suggest, post-*Daubert*, that parties will initially present less than their best expert evidence in the expectation of a second chance should their first try fail."[223] Reminding parties (usually plaintiffs) that they may well not get a second chance, *Weisgram* underscores *Daubert*'s basic message: expert testimony must be rigorously grounded in good science and technology and relevant to the particular issues in the case.

Amendments to Federal Rule of Evidence 702

2000 Amendment. In 2000,[224] the Supreme Court approved certain amendments to the Rules of Evidence on opinion evidence and expert testimony to conform them to the principles of *Daubert* and its progeny.[225] In addition to making certain minor changes to Rules 701 and 703, the 2000 amendments added an important proviso to Rule 702 that permits expert testimony only if such testimony is (a) grounded on "sufficient facts and data," is (b) the result of "reliable principles and methods," and (c) which the expert has reliably applied to the facts of the case.[226] The Advisory Committee's helpful Note to the 2000 amendment to Rule 702 requires only that the data, principles, and methods used by an expert are reliable and reliably applied, and it observes that the quality of expert testimony is still largely to be tested by cross-examination and the other

---

[220] Id. at 147–49.

[221] Id. at 149–53.

[222] 528 U.S. 440 (2000).

[223] Id. at 455–56.

[224] The amendments were effective December 1, 2000, a quarter century after the Rules were first adopted in 1975.

[225] See Fed. R. Evid. 702 Advisory Committee's Note (2000 amendment).

[226] With the added language italicized here, the 2000 Federal Rule of Evidence 702 provided in full:

> If scientific, technical, or other specialized knowledge will assist the trier of fact to understand the evidence or to determine a fact in issue, a witness qualified as an expert by knowledge, skill, experience, training, or education, may testify thereto in the form of an opinion or otherwise, *if (1) the testimony is based on sufficient facts and data, (2) the testimony is the product of reliable principles and methods, and (3) the witness has applied the principles and methods reliably to the facts of the case.*

safeguards of the adversary system. Observing that "[a] review of the caselaw after *Daubert* shows that the rejection of expert testimony is the exception rather than the rule," the Committee Note adds that the amendment "is not intended to provide an excuse for an automatic challenge to the testimony of every expert."[227]

As for *Daubert's* reliability factors, the Advisory Committee's Note reiterates *Daubert's* factor list set forth above (which it converts to five factors) and further enumerates several additional factors courts have found useful in varying contexts:

(1) Whether experts are "proposing to testify about matters growing naturally and directly out of research they have conducted independent of the litigation, or whether they have developed their opinions expressly for purposes of testifying."

(2) Whether the expert has unjustifiably extrapolated from an accepted premise to an unfounded conclusion.

(3) Whether the expert has adequately accounted for obvious alternative explanations.

(4) Whether the expert "is being as careful as he would be in his regular professional work outside his paid litigation consulting."

(5) Whether the field of expertise claimed by the expert is known to reach reliable results for the type of opinion the expert would give.[228]

While recognizing the importance of these and the original *Daubert* factors, the Committee observed that the amendment makes no attempt to "codify" the factors, which the Supreme Court has emphasized are not exclusive. Instead, the new standards added to Rule 702 are "broad enough to require consideration of any or all of the specific *Daubert* factors where appropriate." In sum, the amendment (including the Committee Note) to Federal Rule of Evidence 702 does not provide a necessary roadmap for each specific aspect of expert testimony, but it does provide helpful guidance on the fundamental *Daubert* reliability principles.[229]

2011 Stylistic Amendment. Rule 702 was stylistically revised in 2011 with "no intent to change any result in any ruling on evidence admissibility."[230] Federal Rule of Evidence 702 now provides in full:

---

[227] Fed. R. Evid. 702 Advisory Committee's Note (2000 amendment).

[228] Citations omitted.

[229] Pointing to the Supreme Court's admonition that *Daubert's* reliability factors are not exclusive, the Advisory Committee Note observes that the amendments do not attempt to "codify" the factors but instead set forth standards that are "broad enough to require consideration of any or all of the specific *Daubert* factors where appropriate."

In 2021, the federal judiciary's Advisory Committee on Evidence Rules proposed two changes to Rule 702 that are expected to be approved by the Supreme Court in late 2022. The first change establishes a "preponderance of evidence" standard for courts when applying the Rule's reliability-based requirements in their gatekeeping role: "A witness who is qualified as an expert by knowledge, skill, experience, training, or education may testify in the form of an opinion or otherwise if the proponent has demonstrated by a preponderance of the evidence . . . ." The second change clarifies the reliability requirement of Rule 702(d): "the expert's opinion reflects a reliable application of the principles and methods to the facts of the case." Fed. R. Evid. 702 Advisory Committee Preliminary Draft (Aug. 2021). See also Bernard, Say Goodbye to '*Daubert* motion,' Hello to New Rule 702, Prod. Liab. & Toxics L. (Mar. 10, 2022).

[230] Fed. R. Evid. 702 Advisory Committee's Note (2011 amendment).

Rule 702. Testimony by Expert Witnesses

A witness who is qualified as an expert by knowledge, skill, experience, training, or education may testify in the form of an opinion or otherwise if:

(a) the expert's scientific, technical, or other specialized knowledge will help the trier of fact to understand the evidence or to determine a fact in issue;

(b) the testimony is based on sufficient facts or data;

(c) the testimony is the product of reliable principles and methods; and

(d) the expert has reliably applied the principles and methods to the facts of the case.

Daubert *in the Lower Federal Courts*

Daubert had its intended effect of pushing courts to examine expert testimony more closely. Since *Daubert*, federal district courts, exercising their appointed "gatekeeper" function, have heightened their scrutiny of expert testimony, often holding rigorous pre-trial "*Daubert* hearings"—frequently outcome-determinative—to decide the admissibility of proffered expert testimony.[231] But heightened judicial scrutiny of expert testimony does not mean that a court will necessarily exclude a plaintiff's expert even if the testimony is unusual. The circuit courts sometimes affirm plaintiff verdicts in novel contexts in which traditional scientific indicia of defectiveness or causation is marginal at best,[232] and they sometimes reverse district courts for excluding a plaintiff's expert testimony with excessive zeal.[233]

---

[231] See, e.g., In re Johnson & Johnson Talcum Powder Prod. Mktg., Sales Pracs. & Prod. Litig., 509 F. Supp. 3d 116, 128 (D.N.J. 2020) (selecting 5 plaintiffs' and 3 defendants' experts from 35 experts, the court's *Daubert* hearing limited the plaintiffs' experts' testimony and denied exclusion of the defendants' experts); Rink v. Cheminova, Inc., 400 F.3d 1286, 1290–91 (11th Cir. 2005) (testimony of the plaintiffs' expert witness on causation was excluded after a five day pre-trial *Daubert* hearing, resulting in summary judgment for defendant); Rudlin, The Judge as Gatekeeper: What Hath *Daubert-Joiner-Kumho* Wrought?, 29 Prod. Safety & Liab. Rep. (BNA) 329 (Apr. 2, 2001):

> [T]he *Daubert* hearing and ruling have effectively become virtually as case outcome determinative as a class certification hearing and ruling: once decided, a case either shrivels up and goes away, or becomes more dangerous to try. *Daubert* hearings are often every bit as case dispositive, practically speaking, as a summary judgment hearing. Thus, practitioners whose cases rely in any material way on expert testimony must [be] prepared for a full-blown "*trial within a trial*" that the *Daubert* hearing often becomes.

Pennsylvania has not yet adopted *Daubert*, but its courts can in appropriate cases hold *Frye* hearings to test the validity of an expert's theories. See, e.g., Betz v. Pneumo Abex, LLC, 44 A.3d 27, 53 (Pa. 2012) (approving trial court's rejection, after *Frye* hearing, of plaintiff's pathologist proffering any-exposure theory of mesothelioma causation by asbestos).

On the effects of *Daubert* motions, see Cooper, Information and Settlement: Empirical Evidence on *Daubert* Rulings and Settlement Rates, 51 Int'l Rev. L. & Econ. 1 (2017); Cooper, Timing and Disposition of *Daubert* Motions in Federal District Courts: An Empirical Examination (2015) (from a sample of 2,127 *Daubert* motions, 47% resulted in some limitation on expert testimony; courts struck expert testimony entirely in only 23% of the motions; and 50% of defendants had at least part of their *Daubert* motion granted versus 40% of plaintiffs), www.masonlec.org/timing-disposition-daubert-motions-federal-district-courts/.

[232] See, e.g., Bonner v. ISP Techs., Inc., 259 F.3d 924 (8th Cir. 2001) (affirming award for assembly line worker, exposed to defendant's organic solvent, who suffered psychological injuries, cognitive impairment, and Parkinsonian symptoms).

[233] See, e.g., Bensenberg v. FCA US LLC, 31 F.4th 529, 540 (7th Cir. 2022) (Ill. law) (reversing summary judgment for defendant; plaintiff's expert made out a prima facie case of a non-specific defect in airbag system); In re Bair Hugger Forced Air Warming Devices Prods. Liab. Litig., 9 F.4th 768, 788 (8th Cir. 2021) (reversing exclusion of plaintiffs' general causation experts for "too great an analytical gap" between literature and their opinions and reversing in part the exclusion of their engineering expert); Bradley v. Ameristep, Inc., 800 F.3d 205, 209 (6th Cir. 2015) (abuse of discretion to exclude plaintiffs' expert as a metallurgist unqualified to testify

But *Daubert* decisions usually go the other way, by excluding a plaintiff's expert testimony as unreliable or irrelevant. Thus, lower federal courts have disallowed expert testimony on *Daubert* grounds because the expert proposed to testify on a novel causal theory, not generally accepted or subjected to peer review, that was developed only for the litigation;[234] relied too heavily on the temporal proximity of harm to its alleged cause;[235] failed sufficiently to inspect or test the accident product or a proposed alternative design;[236] failed faithfully to reconstruct the circumstances of the accident;[237]

---

about hunting treestand ratchet straps; expert had "thirty-five years of experience analyzing the forces and conditions that lead to product failures[,] served as an instructor in materials analysis and microscopic analysis for university students, professional organizations, and state agencies[,] conducted materials failure analysis on 'all types of polymer materials,' and on five or six occasions . . . specifically analyzed failures of polymer straps or webbing in 'load-bearing applications' "); Smith v. BMW N. Am., Inc., 308 F.3d 913 (8th Cir. 2002) (rejecting testimony from forensic pathologist for being outside pathologist's field is abuse of discretion where other information in his field supported opinion that allegedly defective airbag caused the death); Smith v. Ford Motor Co., 215 F.3d 713 (7th Cir. 2000) (rejecting expert testimony on single ground of lack of peer review is abuse of discretion; no single factor is conclusive in determining reliability of expert's methodology).

[234] See, e.g., In re Mirena IUD Prods. Liab. Litig., 713 Fed. Appx. 11, 15 (2d Cir. 2017) (experts' theories not generally accepted and developed for the litigation); Wilden v. Laury Transp., LLC, 2016 WL 4522670, at *4 (W.D. Ky. 2016) (experts' alternative trailer side guard concept not generally accepted and was conceived after start of litigation); Johnson v. Manitowoc Boom Trucks, 484 F.3d 426, 435 (6th Cir. 2007) (plaintiff's expert was "quintessential expert for hire" whose "opinions were conceived, executed, and invented solely" for the litigation); Wagner v. Hesston Corp., 450 F.3d 756, 759 (8th Cir. 2006) (one expert's alternative hay baler guard designs were largely "built in connection with [the] litigation" and another's test of his alternative design was performed "for the sole purpose of [the] litigation" with no showing of peer review or general acceptance of the theory).

But see In re Bair Hugger Forced Air Warming Devices Prods. Liab. Litig., 9 F.4th 768, 783 (8th Cir. 2021) ("where a 'hired gun' expert's work has been peer reviewed and published, and the developed-for-litigation concern is the only remaining reason for excluding the testimony—we conclude that lingering questions of reliability and objectivity go to weight rather than admissibility"); In re Viagra (Sildenafil Citrate) & Cialis (Tadalafil) Prods. Liab. Litig., 424 F. Supp. 3d 781, 791 (N.D. Cal. 2020) (plaintiffs' experts "reached their conclusions only in the context of this litigation and only from a review of the work of others [weighed] slightly against a finding of sufficient reliability [but] does not tip the balance in favor of exclusion").

[235] See, e.g., Lowery v. Sanofi-Aventis LLC, 2021 WL 872620, at *14 (N.D. Ala. 2021) (plaintiff's expert's opinion, based on temporal proximity between injection of medical device and onset of septic arthritis, was inadmissible; "temporal proximity is not a reliable indicator of causation but 'leads to the blunder of the post hoc ergo propter hoc fallacy' "); Altmeyer v. Secretary of Dep't of Health & Human Servs., 2013 WL 5316926, at *10 (Fed. Cl. 2013) (dismissing claim under Vaccine Act; "merely showing a proximate temporal connection between a vaccination and an injury is insufficient, standing alone, to establish causation"). But the immediacy of acute symptoms to exposure may buttress the reliability of an expert's causation hypothesis. See, e.g., Bonner v. ISP Techs., Inc., 259 F.3d 924, 931 (8th Cir. 2001) (strong temporal connection is sometimes powerful evidence of causation); Westberry v. Gislaved Gummi AB, 178 F.3d 257 (4th Cir. 1999) (same; temporal relationship between exposure to talcum powder, and sinus infection).

[236] See, e.g., Ruggiero v. Yamaha Motor Corp., U.S.A., 778 Fed. Appx. 88, 93 (3d Cir. 2019) (plaintiff's expert's warning label opinions were untested, "mere speculation, not based on any reliable methodology"); Timm v. Goodyear Dunlop Tires N. Am., Ltd., 932 F.3d 986, 994 (7th Cir. 2019) (expert "had not done any testing to validate his opinion, was unaware of any relevant tests conducted by others, and knew of no way others could objectively replicate his approach"); Karavitis v. Makita U.S.A., Inc., 722 Fed. Appx. 53, 55 (2d Cir. 2018) (no evidence from tests or published studies "that the omission of a riving knife rendered the circular saw at issue unreasonably dangerous"); Wilden v. Laury Transp., LLC, 901 F.3d 644, 654 (6th Cir. 2018) (experts failed to build or test prototype of telescoping trailer side guard); Buck v. Ford Motor Co., 810 F. Supp. 2d 815, 825 (N.D. Ohio 2011) ("Though the *Daubert* standard is flexible, that Armstrong failed to verify his theory [that EMI can cause a vehicle to accelerate] through testing weighs against finding his opinion reliable."); Berry v. Crown Equip. Corp., 108 F. Supp. 2d 743, 754 (E.D. Mich. 2000) ("courts interpreting *Daubert* have considered testability of the expert's theory to be the most important of the four factors, and this is especially true in cases involving allegations of defect in product design").

[237] See, e.g., Hinken v. Sears Roebuck and Co., 2015 WL 165027, at *6 (E.D. Ky. 2015) (plaintiff's expert failed to perform any tests of the tractor mower or exemplars; the court was "unpersuaded" that accident reconstruction was not feasible); Dunn v. Nexgrill Indus., 636 F.3d 1049, 1055–57 (8th Cir. 2011); Rose v. Truck Ctrs., Inc., 388 Fed. Appx. 528, 535 (6th Cir. 2010).

failed to provide a theory of causation supported by sufficient confirmatory studies;[238] failed to conduct a differential diagnosis to rule out alternative potential causes,[239] or applied such an approach improperly;[240] failed to show the relevance ("fit") of accepted principles to the plaintiff's case;[241] or otherwise failed to proffer reliable and relevant

---

[238] See, e.g., Kesse v. Ford Motor Co., 2020 WL 832363, at *8 (N.D. Ill. 2020) (plaintiff's expert's theory that electro-magnetic interference caused sudden acceleration was not supported by peer review or widespread acceptance and was rebutted by NHTSA investigations of similar unintended acceleration claims); Wells v. Kawasaki Motors Corp., U.S.A., 2019 WL 5842921, at *4 (D. Utah 2019) (plaintiff's experts' causation theories were unsupported by peer review and were not generally accepted within the appropriate technical community); In re Mirena Ius Levonorgestrel-Related Prods. Liab. Litig. (No. II), 341 F. Supp. 3d 213, 247 (S.D.N.Y. 2018) (plaintiffs' expert epidemiologist's theories were not generally accepted or supported by outside scholarship); Norris v. Baxter Healthcare Corp., 397 F.3d 878, 885–86 (10th Cir. 2005) (expert's conclusion that silicone gel breast implants cause systemic disease was "flatly contrary to *all* of the available epidemiological evidence").

However, courts generally hold that epidemiological studies are not required to prove causation. See, e.g., In re Tylenol (Acetaminophen) Marketing, Sales Practices, & Prods. Liab. Litig., 198 F. Supp. 3d 446, 456 (E.D. Pa. 2016) (epidemiological studies can be valuable evidence of causation, but they are not necessary); Monroe v. Zimmer U.S. Inc., 766 F. Supp. 2d 1012, 1027 (E.D. Cal. 2011) (allowing expert testimony of causation based on associational study; non-epidemiological sources are frequently used by experts in their scientific opinions and, under *Daubert*, should be considered by court assessing reliability).

Meta-analysis of studies. In forming causation opinions, experts sometimes use a meta-analysis of multiple studies, a statistical technique that combines the results of multiple epidemiological and other studies to enhance their findings. See, e.g., Deutsch v. Novartis Pharms. Corp., 768 F. Supp. 2d 420, 452 (E.D.N.Y. 2011) (meta-analysis of cohort studies indicating use of intravenous bisphosphonate drugs in cancer patients increased risk of jaw osteonecrosis); In re Gadolinium-Based Contrast Agents Prods. Liab. Litig., 2010 WL 1796334, at *22–24 (N.D. Ohio 2010) (meta-analysis linking Nephrogenic Systemic Fibrosis disease to contrast agent in magnetic resonance scans). *But see* In re Zoloft (Sertraline Hydrochloride) Prods. Liab. Litig., 858 F.3d 787, 797 (3d Cir. 2017) (meta-analysis and other statistical techniques generally reliable, but expert's use thereof was unreliable); Miller v. Pfizer, Inc., 196 F. Supp. 2d 1062, 1077–81 (D. Kan. 2002) (meta-analysis is a "generally accepted methodology," but expert's use thereof was flawed), aff'd, 356 F.3d 1326 (10th Cir. 2004).

[239] **Differential diagnosis.** Another well-accepted scientific method for establishing causation in certain circumstances is "differential diagnosis," or, perhaps more precisely, "differential etiology." "[D]ifferential diagnosis is 'a patient-specific process of elimination that medical practitioners use to identify the "most likely" cause of a set of signs and symptoms from a list of possible causes.' " Ruggiero v. Warner-Lambert Co., 424 F.3d 249, 254 (2d Cir. 2005). First, the cause for which a defendant is responsible must be *ruled in*, and differential diagnosis ordinarily cannot rule in a cause by principles of general causation. That is, differential diagnosis normally *assumes*, and cannot establish, general causation. See id; In re Rezulin Prods., 2004 WL 2884327, at *3–4 (S.D.N.Y. 2004). Hence, differential diagnosis will not defeat a defendant's motion for summary judgment if its results are "flatly contrary to *all* of the available epidemiological evidence." Norris v. Baxter Healthcare Corp., 397 F.3d 878, 885–86 (10th Cir. 2005) ("Plaintiff's experts' differential diagnoses and case studies are scientifically unreliable because they assume what science has largely shown does not exist—a causal connection between silicone breast implants and disease.").

In some situations, an expert's *failure* to apply this diagnostic approach will undercut the validity of his or her conclusions. See, e.g., N.K. v. Abbott Labs., 731 Fed. Appx. 24, 27 (2d Cir. 2018) (each of plaintiffs' experts failed to conduct an independent differential diagnosis to eliminate genetic defects as the cause of infant's birth defects); Turner v. Iowa Fire Equip. Co., 229 F.3d 1202 (8th Cir. 2000) (expert made no attempt to exclude possible causes of respiratory problems, allegedly caused by accidental discharge of substance from fire suppression equipment, until only one remained). See also note 263 and § 11.2 (proof of causation), below.

[240] See, e.g., Arevalo v. Coloplast Corp., 2021 WL 2148771, at *4 (N.D. Fla. 2021) (expert failed to explain his procedure for ruling out alternative causes of plaintiff's injury); Milward v. Rust-Oleum Corp., 820 F.3d 469, 476 (1st Cir. 2016) (upholding exclusion of expert witness who conducted "scientifically unreliable" differential analysis); Hines v. Wyeth, 2011 WL 2792436, at *4 (S.D. W. Va. 2011) ("It appearing that Dr. Burns did not 'systematically and scientifically' rule in and rule out specific causes until a final cause remained, the court concludes that Dr. Burns' differential diagnosis does not satisfy the *Daubert* reliability standard."). See Sanders and Machal-Fulks, The Admissibility of Differential Diagnosis Testimony to Prove Causation in Toxic Tort Cases: The Interplay of Adjective and Substantive Law, 64 Law & Contemp. Probs. 107 (2001).

[241] See, e.g., Macy v. Whirlpool Corp., 613 Fed. Appx. 340, 344 (5th Cir. 2015) (plaintiffs' expert failed to show relevance of two studies linking low levels of carbon monoxide exposure and serious health effects to the facts of the case); Phillips v. American Honda Motor Co., 238 Fed. Appx. 537, 540 n.2 (11th Cir. 2007) (expert failed to link temperature reading from a dummy foot on an ATV to "his extrapolations about Plaintiff's injuries," making those readings "not directly relevant" and illustrative of the problem of "fit"); Benkwith v.

testimony—supported by reliable data, methods, and conclusions—that was likely to be helpful to the trier of fact.[242] Quite often, an expert's testimony will fail *Daubert* scrutiny for many of these reasons.[243]

It may well be that the experts in each such case in which the testimony was excluded propounded bad science; or perhaps plaintiffs' counsel failed to prepare their experts adequately on the *Daubert* requirements before trial; or perhaps counsel failed at trial (or at a *Daubert* hearing) to provide a sufficient offer of proof. Be that as it may, the cases reveal that *Daubert* provides federal trial judges with a powerful operating manual for excluding expert testimony that, in the court's sound discretion, does not meet prevailing criteria for "good science."[244] There is indeed some logic to the view, suggested by the Supreme Court itself in *Daubert*,[245] that its ruling is balanced in its effect: while closing the door to testimony based on unreliable theories and methodologies, it opens the door to expert testimony on cutting-edge science and technology.[246] But the fact remains that only infrequently is *Daubert* invoked to exclude

Matrixx Initiatives, Inc., 467 F. Supp. 2d 1316, 1325 (M.D. Ala. 2006) (expert's test of nasal spray on cadavers did not "fit" the facts of the case, which "involve the nose of a living human"); Daubert v. Merrell Dow Pharms., Inc., 43 F.3d 1311 (9th Cir. 1995) (on remand from Supreme Court, Bendectin birth defect case dismissed because plaintiff's experts could not testify that relative risk was more than the 2.0 necessary to show probability of causal connection).

[242] See, e.g., Elward v. Electrolux Home Products, Inc., 2020 WL 2850982, at *15 (N.D. Ill. 2020) (plaintiffs' expert's testimony failed to "set forth a reliable, testable, or helpful theory"); Prall v. Ford Motor Co., 2017 WL 361545, at *3 (D. Nev. 2017) (expert's opinion based on circumstantial evidence would not help the jury, "who may draw these inferences on their own"); Conklin v. Novartis Pharmas Corp., 2012 WL 4127301, at *4 (E.D. Tex. 2012) (expert's opinion regarding a lower dose regimen of Zometa "not helpful"); Ervin v. Johnson & Johnson, 492 F.3d 901, 903–05 (7th Cir. 2007) (expert's opinion based on temporal proximity and an internet Google search "had no reliable basis"); Cacciola v. Selco Balers, Inc., 127 F. Supp. 2d 175, 183 (E.D.N.Y. 2001) (having neither inspected machine itself nor interviewed injured worker, engineer's deposition testimony that machine's safety interlock switch was too accessible, based on photographs alone, "rests upon unsubstantiated generalizations, speculative hypotheses and subjective evaluation that are based neither upon any professional study or experience-based observation").

[243] See, e.g., Bury v. Harbor Freight Tools USA, Inc., 2021 WL 3828449, at *2 (W.D. Ark. 2021) (expert's report failed to explain his testing methodology or offer evidence that his theory of material failure in the stepstool was generally accepted or supported by peer review); Fateri v. Ducati N. Am., Inc., 2021 WL 797390, at *1 (S.D. Tex. 2021) (plaintiff's expert's opinion that motorcycle's fuel tank was vulnerable to punctures during collisions was "speculative, conclusory, and failed to consider or disprove alternative causes"); Walker v. Louisville Ladder, Inc., 2009 WL 307786, at *4 (E.D. Tenn. 2009) (expert's methodology did "not satisfy any of the *Daubert* factors"); Chapman v. Maytag Corp., 297 F.3d 682, 688 (7th Cir. 2002) (expert's testimony that kitchen range was defectively designed failed all reliability factors, where his opinions "amount[ed] to nothing more than unverified statements unsupported by scientific methodology" or by any article, text, study, scientific literature, or data produced by others in the field); Oddi v. Ford Motor Co., 234 F.3d 136, 156 (3d Cir. 2000) (the "haphazard, intuitive inquiry" of plaintiff's expert engineer, who conducted no tests nor calculated forces involved in vehicle accident, failed each of eight reliability factors).

[244] See, e.g., Daniels-Feasel v. Forest Pharms., Inc., 2021 WL 4037820, at *7 (S.D.N.Y. 2021) (plaintiffs' expert's opinion was not generally accepted; "no regulatory agency, professional organization, peer-review study, or medical treatise concludes that Lexapro causes [autism spectrum disorder], and the FDA has approved its prescription to pregnant women"); Brooks v. Outboard Marine Corp., 234 F.3d 89 (2d Cir. 2000) (expert testimony that outboard motor, propeller of which injured plaintiff's hand, should have been equipped with kill switch was inadmissible because plaintiff's expert had never seen boat or motor, either in person or in photographs; did not know boat's configuration or dimensions; had not spoken to boys involved in accident nor otherwise knew precisely how accident happened; nor attempted to reconstruct the accident to test his theory that a lanyard-activated kill switch would have disengaged motor under circumstances of accident). Compare Brasher v. Sandoz Pharms. Corp., 160 F. Supp. 2d 1291, 1295 n.12 (N.D. Ala. 2001) (noting a busy trial court's temptation to apply *Daubert* "heavy-handedly" to lighten a heavy caseload, "as a party stripped of its expert often must dismiss the claims or settle the lawsuit").

[245] See *Daubert*, 509 U.S. at 595–97.

[246] "[T]he first several victims of a new toxic tort should not be barred from having their day in court simply because the medical literature, which will eventually show the connection between the victims' condition and the toxic substance, has not yet been completed." Bonner v. ISP Techs., Inc., 259 F.3d 924, 928

Because *Daubert* requires exclusion only of evidence that is invalid or irrelevant, even a rigorous application of its principles does not compel the exclusion of expert testimony that is merely inconclusive or otherwise only marginally helpful to the trier of fact. Many product accidents leave few and ambiguous clues of accident causation (especially if the product is severely damaged in the accident or lost thereafter),[256] where proof of design defectiveness and causation is by nature vague and indeterminate.[257] In such cases, courts should allow plausible expert hypotheses, provided they are based on sound methodology and reasoning, that attempt to reconstruct the causal origins of an accident and how it might have been prevented.

Rudd v. General Motors Corp.[258] is an example of a case that *allowed* a plaintiff's expert testimony after rigorous *Daubert* scrutiny. The plaintiff was injured when a fan blade on his pickup truck broke loose and struck him while he stood in front of the truck's open hood twisting the distributor housing to adjust the engine's timing. He sued the vehicle manufacturer, claiming that the fan blade had been made of defective metal, based largely on the testimony of his expert, Edmondson, a mechanical engineer with extensive experience in failure analysis. GM moved for summary judgment, arguing that the plaintiff had offered no admissible evidence of a manufacturing defect.

Choosing not to hold a *Daubert* hearing,[259] the district court ruled on the admissibility of Edmondson's testimony on the basis of his expert report and deposition testimony. Edmondson found no direct evidence of a physical flaw in the fan blade but arrived at his conclusion circumstantially by excluding other possible explanations of how the fan blade might have broken. Preliminarily, he determined that the plaintiff's use of the vehicle at the time the fan blade broke was entirely proper: the plaintiff's technique in adjusting the timing, while running the engine at 1,200 to 1,500 rpms, was entirely normal and specifically recommended by GM's tune-up manuals. Next, based on visual examination, "total indicator reading" measurements of the accident fan and fan assembly, and background reading, Edmondson determined that prior to the accident the fan blade had not been bent at the site of the fracture origin (or elsewhere) and that there was no visible damage to the blade that might have caused the fatigue fracture and break.[260] Had the fan blade been subjected to a sudden trauma during operation, Edmondson testified that it would have left physical indicia, such as broken paint,

[256] On the malfunction theory, see § 7.4, below.

[257] On design defectiveness, see ch. 8, below.

[258] 127 F. Supp. 2d 1330 (M.D. Ala. 2001).

[259] Normally, a decision whether to hold a *Daubert*/Rule 702 hearing is discretionary with the trial court. There may be no need for such a hearing if the parties have developed an extensive pre-trial evidentiary record, including expert reports, depositions, and literature that supports the expert opinions, and assuming that the issues are well briefed. See, e.g., id. at 1334, n.3 (citing authorities); In re Cessna 208 Series Aircraft Prods. Liab. Litig., 2009 WL 3756980, at *1 n.2 (D. Kan. 2009) (declining to hold a *Daubert* hearing: "the experts' methodology does not involve new scientific theory or new and novel testing methodologies; their reports are self-explanatory and the parties have filed comprehensive and thorough briefs"); Miller v. Baker Implement Co., 439 F.3d 407, 413 (8th Cir. 2006) (trial court declined to hold a *Daubert* hearing: "A district court's *Daubert* inquiry need not take any specific form, and its sua sponte consideration of the admissibility of expert testimony is permissible so long as the court has an adequate record on which to base its ruling."); McClain v. Metabolife Int'l, Inc., 401 F.3d 1233, 1239 n.5 (11th Cir. 2005) ("the trial court does not need to waste time with a *Daubert* hearing" if unnecessary). As with any discretionary matter, however, a trial court's failure to hold a *Daubert*/Rule 702 hearing in particular circumstances, whether or not requested by the losing party, may be an abuse of discretion, particularly if the admissibility issue turns on factual issues and will be determinative of summary judgment. See, e.g., Hoffman v. Ford Motor Co., 493 Fed. Appx. 962, 973–74, n.18 (10th Cir. 2012).

[260] *Rudd*, 127 F. Supp. 2d at 1340.

scarring, or denting, none of which were visible. The absence of any indications that the fan had been subjected to abnormal forces during operation led him to conclude that its break was due to a metal-fatigue fracture resulting from a microscopic manufacturing defect, such as a scratch, grind mark, gas bubble, or an inclusion. The court concluded that Edmondson's systematic elimination of alternative causes led to circumstantial proof of defectiveness that was *relevant* to a jury's determination of that issue.[261]

Further, as to the *reliability* of Edmondson's expert testimony, the court ruled that it satisfied each of the three specific reliability standards of amended Rule 702—that it was based on (1) sufficient data, (2) reliable principles and methods, and (3) reliable application of the methods to the facts. First, the factual basis of Edmondson's testimony was sufficient—based on his visual inspection of the accident fan blade and other fans, his account of the use history of the truck and fan blade, his "total indicator reading" measurements, his reliance on two failure-analysis publications (which included a case study of a car fan fatigue fracture) and GM tune-up manuals, and his background and training analyzing metal fractures,[262] including automotive fan fatigue fractures. Second, the court ascertained that Edmondson's method for determining the cause of the fatigue fracture—by eliminating ("ruling out") other possible causes—is a well-established and reliable scientific method for determining causation.[263] Moreover, because a specialty publication had employed the process-of-elimination method in a failure analysis model, which included a case history of a fatigue fracture in an automobile fan, this method further satisfied *Daubert*'s reliability factors on publication and acceptance within a relevant community of experts. Third, and finally, the court found that Edmondson reliably applied this method to the accident fan—by determining that the fan's history showed no improper operation and by closely inspecting the fan blade metal for physical indicia of other causes. Noting that Edmondson could not fairly be expected to assign a particular error rate to his techniques, the court concluded that his testimony was reliable, and hence admissible, "because he provides a step-by-step and transparent account" of "reasoning processes and data sources" on which he relies, "the physical indicia he associates with each possible alternative cause, and his reasons

---

[261] Id. at 1342.

[262] The court quoted the Advisory Committee Note to Rule 702 to the effect that an expert's *experience* (alone or in conjunction with other knowledge, skill, training or education) may provide a sufficient foundation for the expert's testimony if the witness explains "how that experience leads to the conclusion reached, why that experience is a sufficient basis for the opinion, and how that experience is reliably applied to the facts." Id. at 1336.

[263] **Differential diagnosis.** Particularly in the medical context, experts quite often apply this well-accepted method for determining causation, called "differential diagnosis" (or "differential etiology"). See, e.g., Guinn v. AstraZeneca Pharm. LP, 602 F.3d 1245, 1252–54 (11th Cir. 2010) (differential diagnosis is a "scientifically accepted methodology"; but expert failed to "adequately consider possible alternative causes of [plaintiff's] weight gain and diabetes"); Ervin v. Johnson & Johnson, Inc., 2006 WL 1529582, at *5 (S.D. Ind. 2006) ("the majority of the courts of appeals has recognized the technique as valid and reliable"; but finding application of method unreliable in this case); Castillo v. E.I. Du Pont De Nemours & Co., 854 So.2d 1264, 1270–71 (Fla. 2003) (expert's use of differential diagnosis, to prove causal link between agricultural fungicide and birth defect, is generally accepted method in the relevant community under *Frye* test for admissibility).

This type of analysis by ruling out alternative causes is sometimes characterized as a process of "reasoning to the best inference." See also Bitler v. A.O. Smith Corp., 400 F.3d 1227, 1236–37 (10th Cir. 2004) (experts tracing explosion to defect in water heater by process of eliminating other possible causes, used reasoning process like differential diagnosis that might be "more aptly characterized as a process of reasoning to the best inference"). See generally Sanders and Machal-Fulks, The Admissibility of Differential Diagnosis Testimony to Prove Causation in Toxic Tort Cases: The Interplay of Adjective and Substantive Law, 64 Law & Contemp. Probs. 107 (2001). Also on differential diagnosis, see notes 239–240, above.

for excluding each of the alternative causes."[264] By fully revealing the grounds of his opinions, Edmondson's testimony thus supplied the defendant with a fair basis to challenge his opinions by cross-examination and the presentation of contrary evidence, the fundamental tools of the adversary process.[265]

Daubert in the State Courts

Because *Daubert* interprets Federal Rule of Evidence 702, it applies by its terms only to the federal courts. For this and other reasons, quite a few state courts, trusting in *Frye*, cross-examination, and other conventional rules governing the admissibility of expert testimony, still refuse to adopt *Daubert* as a formal matter.[266] Yet, prior to the Supreme Court's decision in *Daubert* in 1993, many state courts had already adopted reliability principles quite similar to *Daubert*'s,[267] and an increasing number of states have rejected *Frye* and swung over to the *Daubert* point of view.[268] Although most states still have not adopted the 2000 amendment to Rule 702 that expressly articulates the *Daubert* holding, some have.[269] And the evidence codes in a large majority of states are patterned on the Federal Rules of Evidence, including the original Rule 702 on which *Daubert* was based.[270] Moreover, to the extent that *Daubert*'s precepts are grounded in

---

[264] *Rudd*, 127 F. Supp. 2d at 1344.

[265] Id.

[266] As of early 2022, at least seven states still purport to follow *Frye*, or at least to reject *Daubert* (Cal., Ill., Minn., N.Y., N.D., Pa., and Wash.). See, e.g., O'Neill v. Novartis Consumer Health, Inc., 55 Cal. Rptr. 3d 551, 559 n.7 (Ct. App. 2007); Parker v. Mobil Oil Corp., 857 N.E.2d 1114, 1120 n.3 (N.Y. 2006) (reaffirming *Frye*); Grady v. Frito-Lay, Inc., 839 A.2d 1038 (Pa. 2003) (rejecting *Daubert*; in applying *Frye*, proponent must prove that expert's *methodology* is generally accepted as a method for reaching a conclusion, not that the conclusion itself is generally accepted); Goeb v. Tharaldson, 615 N.W.2d 800 (Minn. 2000) (same; thoroughly examining policy issues). See also In re Accutane Litig., 191 A.3d 560, 594–95 (N.J. 2018) ("In adopting use of the Daubert factors, we stop short of declaring ourselves a '*Daubert* jurisdiction.' Like several other states, we find the factors useful, but hesitate to embrace the full body of *Daubert* case law as applied by state and federal courts."); Howe v. Microsoft Corp., 656 N.W.2d 285, 295 n.1 (N.D. 2003) ("Admission of expert evidence at trial is governed by N.D. R. Evid. 702, and the trial court has broad discretion to determine whether the witness is qualified as an expert and whether the evidence will assist the trier of fact."); Donaldson v. Central Ill. Pub. Serv. Co., 767 N.E.2d 314 (Ill. 2002); Santosa v. Chrysler Corp., 2002 WL 31045305 (Wash. Ct. App. 2002); Mercer v. Pittway Corp., 616 N.W.2d 602, 628 (Iowa 2000) (while not required to apply *Daubert*, "trial courts may find it helpful in complex cases to use one or more of the relevant *Daubert* 'considerations' in assessing the reliability of expert testimony"). An Arizona statute codifying *Daubert* and adopting the *Daubert* trilogy (Ariz. Rev. Stat. Ann. § 12–2203 (2010)) was declared unconstitutional in Lear v. Fields, 245 P.3d 911, 918 (Ariz. Ct. App. 2011). But the Arizona Supreme Court denied review of *Lear* in 2011 and adopted the 2011 Amendments to Fed. R. Evid. 702 effective January 1, 2012. The Kansas legislature adopted the *Daubert* evidence standard in 2014. See Kan. Stat. Ann. § 60–456(b). See generally Lepore, On Evidence: Proving *Frye* As a Matter of Law, Science, and History, 124 Yale L.J. 1092 (2015); Bernstein and Jackson, The *Daubert* Trilogy in the States, 44 Jurimetrics J. 351 (2004); States Move to *Daubert*, Even When They Say They're Stuck on *Frye*, 2 Expert Evid. Rep. 161 (BNA Mar. 18, 2002).

[267] See Howerton v. Arai Helmet, Ltd., 597 S.E.2d 674, 689 (N.C. 2004) ("our focus on reliability in this context had been developing under North Carolina case law for many years prior to *Daubert*"); Hamilton, The Movement from *Frye* to *Daubert*: Where Do the States Stand?, 38 Jurimetrics J. 201, 210–13 (1998) (listing twenty-one such states).

[268] By 2005, Cheng and Yoon had counted twenty-two states that had adopted *Daubert*. Cheng and Yoon, Does *Frye* or *Daubert* Matter: A Study of Scientific Admissibility Standards, 91 Va. L. Rev. 471, 473 (2005). See also Bernstein and Jackson, The *Daubert* Trilogy in the States, 44 Jurimetrics J. 351, 357–63 (2004) (same). Since that time, other states have joined the *Daubert* bandwagon. See note 269, below.

[269] As of 2022, more than one-fourth of the states, including at least Ariz., Del., Fla., Ga., Kan., Ky., Mich., Miss., Mo., N.C., N.H., Okla., S.D., Vt., and Wyo., have so amended their rules of evidence. The Massachusetts rule is based on the amended federal rule, but allows the judge to satisfy the gatekeeper duty through the *Frye* or *Daubert-Lanigan* analysis. See MA Guide to Evidence § 702.

[270] See, e.g., Baker Valley Lumber, Inc. v. Ingersoll-Rand Co., 813 A.2d 409, 415 (N.H. 2002) (noting, in adopting *Daubert*, that that state's Rule 702 was identical to Fed. R. Evid. 702 when *Daubert* was decided). See also Ga. Code Ann. § 24–7–702(f).

reasoned principles of logic and fair play for adjudicating disputes involving principles of science and technology,[271] those precepts have a persuasive power that is difficult for state courts to ignore—but which a vigilant court can sometimes apply, albeit more awkwardly, through *Frye*.[272] For these reasons, a growing majority of states have now adopted *Daubert* (or somewhat similar) principles of reliability and relevance for expert testimony.[273]

The Legacy of Daubert

In *Daubert* and its progeny, the Supreme Court attempted to bridge the yawning gap between how reality is perceived and described, and how problems are resolved, in science, on the one hand, and in the law, on the other.[274] In particular, the Court sought to improve the legitimacy of judicial determinations involving science and technology by requiring courts to rigorously scrutinize the foundations of an expert's scientific or technological opinions. This is a messy task that requires both courts and lawyers to do the kind of rigorous science they may have entered law to avoid.[275]

Abandoning *Frye*'s "general acceptance" standard, which was based on the precept that courts should defer to scientific communities to decide for themselves whether a particular type of scientific approach should be recognized as useful, *Daubert* switched legal responsibility for making such decisions to the courts, a shift that on balance may make good sense. It is hard to gainsay the Court's decision that trial judges should serve as "gatekeepers" for expert testimony, as preliminary decision-makers of whether a

---

[271] Note, however, that *Daubert* remains controversial. See, e.g., Schroeder, Toward A More Apparent Approach to Considering the Admission of Expert Testimony, 95 Notre Dame L. Rev. 2039 (2020); Haack, Mind the Analytical Gap! Tracing A Fault Line in *Daubert*, 61 Wayne L. Rev. 653 (2016); Allen, Daubert and Its Discontents, 76 Brook. L. Rev. 131 (2010); Heinzerling, Doubting *Daubert*, 14 J.L. & Pol'y 65 (2006); Cranor, The Dual Legacy of *Daubert v. Merrell-Dow Pharmaceutical*: Trading Junk Science for Insidious Science, in Rescuing Science from Politics (W. Wagner and R. Steinzor eds., 2006); A. Schwartz, A "Dogma of Empiricism" Revisited: *Daubert v. Merrell Dow Pharmaceuticals, Inc.* and the Need to Resurrect the Philosophical Insight of *Frye v. United States*, 10 Harv. J.L. & Tech. 149 (1997); Note, Flexible Standards, Deferential Review: *Daubert*'s Legacy of Confusion, 29 Harv. J.L. Pub. Pol'y 1085 (2006).

[272] See, e.g., Chesson v. Montgomery Mut. Ins. Co., 75 A.3d 932 (Md. 2013) (rejecting expert's theory that mold in building caused workers' various illnesses); Betz v. Pneumo Abex, LLC, 44 A.3d 27, 53 (Pa. 2012) (approving trial court's rejection, after *Frye* hearing, of plaintiff's pathologist proffering any-exposure theory of mesothelioma causation by asbestos).

[273] See, e.g., Hyundai Motor Am. v. Hutton, 328 So.3d 592, 607–08 (Miss. 2021) (reversing $2 million jury verdict; plaintiffs' experts' testimony, "which was based on their subjective beliefs and unsupported speculation, fail[ed] to satisfy Rule 702 and *Daubert* and should have been excluded"); Rochkind v. Stevenson, 236 A.3d 630, 645 (Md. 2020) (4–3 decision) (adopting *Daubert* and remanding childhood lead paint exposure case for interpretation of Md. R. 5–702 under the *Daubert* standard); In re Amendments to Florida Evidence Code, 278 So.3d 551 (Fla. 2019) (adopting amended Fla. Stat. Ann. § 90.702 (2013) that incorporated the Daubert standard in the Florida Rules of Evidence); Motorola Inc. v. Murray, 147 A.3d 751, 758–59 (D.C. 2016) (adopting Fed. R. Evid. 702).

[274] For a smattering of cerebration on the baffling borderland between law and science, see, e.g., Faigman, The *Daubert* Revolution and the Birth of Modernity: Managing Scientific Evidence in the Age of Science, 46 U.C. Davis L. Rev. 893 (2013); Imwinkelried, Serendipitous Timing: The Coincidental Emergence of the New Brain Science and the Advent of an Epistemological Approach to Determining the Admissibility of Expert Testimony, 62 Mercer L. Rev. 959 (2011); Jurs, Judicial Analysis of Complex & Cutting-Edge Science In the *Daubert* Era: Epidemiologic Risk Assessment as a Test Case for Reform Strategies, 42 Conn. L. Rev. 49 (2009); Feldman, Science and Uncertainty in Mass Exposure Litigation, 74 Tex. L. Rev. 1 (1995); Brennan, Causal Chains and Statistical Links: The Role of Scientific Uncertainty in Hazardous-Substances Litigation, 73 Cornell L. Rev. 469 (1988); see also A. Porat and A. Stein, Tort Liability Under Uncertainty (2001).

[275] See Beecher-Monas, The Heuristics of Intellectual Due Process: A Primer for Triers of Science, 75 N.Y.U. L. Rev. 1563 (2000) (questioning courts' ability to comprehend genuine scientific inquiry); Comment, Proposals for Reform in the Evaluation of Expert Testimony in Pharmaceutical Mass Tort Cases, 13 Alb. L.J. Sci. & Tech. 517, 542 (2003) ("the *Daubert* standard . . . is flawed in vesting additional authority to evaluate science in a nonscientific judiciary").

qualified expert witness has devoted as much rigor, and has applied the same exacting methodologies, to the matter before the court as the expert devotes to his or her own professional projects.[276] But courts must sedulously avoid using this important gatekeeping function to bar evidence that, though novel, actually may be sound.[277]

Daubert requires trial courts to look seriously at the quality of the science or technology used by a witness proffered as an expert. Courts no longer can simply pass along to juries the principal task of determining the validity of expert testimony on difficult questions of science and engineering. Yet, as door-closing rules governing the admissibility of expert testimony, the *Daubert* principles are capable of being applied oppressively to smother the full airing of legitimate disputes.[278]

Instead, courts need to apply the principles even-handedly—excluding expert testimony that is insufficiently grounded in sound methodology while allowing such testimony that reasonably, if boldly, reaches into uncharted waters of evolving knowledge.[279] By requiring "experts" to provide reasoned bases for their opinions, and by requiring that such opinions be grounded in reliable methodology and relevant to the legal issues in a case, *Daubert*'s principles, used properly, provide a firm foundation for the fair and rational resolution of the scientific and technological issues that lie at the heart of products liability adjudication.

§ 6.4 Proof of Defect—Recurring Evidentiary Issues

In most products liability cases, the plaintiff's basic claim is that a defect in a product sold by the defendant proximately caused his harm. The plaintiff has the burden of proof on each element of such a case, including of course the product defect.[280] Sometimes the reasons for a product accident will be a mystery but its circumstances may logically suggest that the product probably was defective, and perhaps that the manufacturer was negligent in selling it in that condition. In such cases, the doctrines of res ipsa loquitur[281] or product malfunction[282] may help the plaintiff establish product defect or the defendant's negligence. In other cases, a plaintiff may introduce evidence that a product violated a safety standard—adopted by industry or the government—to establish a product defect[283] and possibly the manufacturer's negligence.[284] Similarly,

[276] See *Kumho*, 526 U.S. at 152; Fed. R. Evid. 702 Adv. Comm. Note, additional reliability factor (4).

[277] "Courts must be especially careful not to hobble the jury system by excluding potential evidence. Prematurely cutting off the flow of evidence to the jury generally favors defendants, who do not have the burden of proof on most issues, leading not only to a violation of the Constitution, but a tilting of the scales of justice." In re Simon II Litig., 211 F.R.D. 86, 156 (E.D.N.Y. 2002) (Weinstein, J.), vacated on other grounds, 407 F.3d 125 (2d Cir. 2005).

[278] See, e.g., 985 Assocs., Ltd. v. Daewoo Elecs. Am., Inc., 945 A.2d 381, 385 (Vt. 2008) (trial court's *Daubert* inquiry unreasonably intruded into substantive merits of case); Schafersman v. Agland Coop., 631 N.W.2d 862 (Neb. 2001). See also Capra, The *Daubert* Puzzle, 32 Ga. L. Rev. 699 (1998); Graham, The *Daubert* Dilemma—At Last a Viable Solution, 179 F.R.D. 1 (1998).

[279] Moreover, trial judges must conduct their *Daubert* duties impartially and avoid giving an appearance that they disbelieve a party's expert witnesses. See, e.g., Price v. Blood Bank of Del., Inc., 790 A.2d 1203 (Del. 2002).

[280] See Products Liability Rest. § 2 cmts. *c* (manufacturing defects), *d* and *f* (design defects), and *i* (instruction and warning defects).

[281] See § 2.5, above.

[282] See § 7.4, below.

[283] See discussion below.

[284] The effect on a negligence claim of proof that a defendant violated a safety statute or regulation, often referred to as the doctrine of negligence per se, is addressed in § 2.4, above.

although often with a different procedural effect, a defendant may rely on its *compliance* with such safety standards as evidence of a product's *non*defectiveness.[285] In proving defectiveness, sometimes a plaintiff may rely in part on similar failures of other, similar products made by the defendant, and sometimes a defendant may prove the *absence* of similar accidents (the product's record of safe performance) to help prove the converse. Finally, a plaintiff may try to prove a product defect or the defendant's negligence by showing that the defendant acknowledged the problem, and the feasibility of its cure, by remedying the hazard after the plaintiff's injury. These recurring issues of proof are covered here.

Safety Standards

Proof that a product violates or conforms to certain safety standards pertaining to the risk that caused the plaintiff's harm may be probative that the product was or was not defective. Such standards may be adopted by industry itself, perhaps through a standards-setting organization such as the American National Standards Institute (ANSI), the National Safety Council (NSC), or the Society of Automotive Engineers (SAE). Or safety standards may be promulgated by the government, by statute or regulation of some governmental product safety agency, such as the federal food and drug agency (the FDA) or the federal automotive safety agency (NHTSA). In general, evidence that a products liability defendant violated or complied with an applicable safety standard is admissible on the issue of product defect. The role of such evidence in proving or disproving defectiveness derives from and normally parallels the law governing its use in proving and disproving negligence, a topic examined earlier.[286]

Industry Standards—Custom

A common type of evidence introduced to show that a product is or is not defective is the industry's prevailing safety standards with respect to the particular issue in dispute.[287] A plaintiff may seek to show, in an effort to prove a product's defectiveness, that other manufacturers in the industry regularly use a safer design or warning that the defendant failed to adopt. Conversely, in an effort to show that its product is *not* defective, a defendant manufacturer may seek to introduce evidence that other manufacturers customarily use the same design or warning approach followed by the defendant for the type of product on trial in the case. The admissibility of evidence on customary standards in an industry, to help determine whether a product is or is not defective, grew out of and draws heavily from the use of this type of evidence in nearly two centuries of negligence law—a good place to begin in attempting to unravel an evidence-of-custom conundrum in the context of strict liability in tort.[288]

Industry safety standards for products often develop informally over time, as a matter of custom, as engineers and other technical experts around the nation (and the world) migrate between companies and exchange ideas in papers, at conferences, and

[285] Or to help disprove the defendant's negligence. See § 2.4, above.

[286] See §§ 2.3 and 2.4, above. For the minority view, see note 313, below.

[287] See Abraham, Custom, Noncustomary Practice, and Negligence, 109 Colum. L. Rev. 1784 (2009); Hetcher, Creating Safe Social Norms in a Dangerous World, 73 S. Cal. L. Rev. 1 (1999); Boyd and Ingberman, Should "Relative Safety" Be a Test of Products Liability?, 26 J. Legal Stud. 433 (1997); Comment, Custom's Proper Role in Strict Products Liability Actions Based on Design Defect, 38 UCLA L. Rev. 439 (1990); Frumer, Friedman, and Sklaren, Products Liability § 18.04[1]; Am. Law. Prod. Liab. § 30:47; Products Liability Rest. § 2 cmt. *d*.

[288] See § 2.3, above.

otherwise. Many industry safety provisions are spawned more formally by standards-setting organizations that specialize in developing practicable standards of efficacy and safety, including the American National Standards Institute (ANSI),[289] the American Standards Association (ASA),[290] the National Safety Council (NSC),[291] Underwriters Laboratories (UL),[292] the Society of Automotive Engineers (SAE),[293] and a host of more arcane and specialized organizations, such as the American Society of Agricultural and Biological Engineers,[294] the National Spa and Pool Institute,[295] the Scaffolding and Shoring Institute,[296] the Industrial Stapling and Nailing Technical Association,[297] and the American Conference of Governmental and Industrial Hygienists.[298] Although sometimes referred to as "quasi-public," these are actually private organizations, many of which derive from and are basically controlled by the industries they serve. Thus, while some of these organizations can be quite independent,[299] the standards of others are little more than formalized industry standards. Though industry may rely on this type of standard as setting proper types and levels of safety,[300] most courts treat evidence

---

[289] See, e.g., Davis v. Little Giant Ladder Sys., LLC, 2022 WL 657062 (M.D. Fla. 2022) (ladder standards); Myrick v. Husqvarna Prof'l Prod., Inc., 508 F. Supp. 3d 846, 858 (D. Kan. 2020) (mower standards); Adams v. Genie Indus., 929 N.E.2d 380, 385 (N.Y. 2010) (outrigger standards for personnel lift); Hare v. Hoveround Corp., 2009 WL 3086404, at *5 (N.D.N.Y. 2009) (power wheel chair standards); Arnoldy v. Forklift L.P., 927 A.2d 257, 265–66 (Pa. Super. Ct. 2007) (warning device standard for trucks and tractors).

[290] See, e.g., G.W.M. v. Flink Co., 2009 WL 2337117, at *3 (E.D. Mo. 2009) (machine guard standards; salt spreader); Thomas v. Mallett, 701 N.W.2d 523, 544 (Wis. 2005) (standard limiting lead content in interior paint); Poches v. J. J. Newberry Co., 549 F.2d 1166, 1167 (8th Cir. 1977) (S.D. law) (specifications for speed and angle of power mower blade).

[291] See, e.g., G.W.M. v. Flink Co., 2009 WL 2337117, at *3 (E.D. Mo. 2009) (machine guard standards; salt spreader); Whitmire v. Terex Telelect, Inc., 390 F. Supp. 2d 540, 552–53 (E.D. Tex. 2005) (standards for heavy equipment); Hutchison v. Urschel Labs., Inc., 157 F.3d 613, 615 (8th Cir. 1998) (Mo. law) (guarding standards for chicken dicer).

[292] See, e.g., Kay v. Sunbeam Prods., Inc., 2010 WL 2178506, at *2 (W.D. Mo. 2010) (safety standard for electrically heated blanket); Lightolier, a Div. of Genlyte Thomas Grp., LLC v. Hoon, 876 A.2d 100, 104 n.1 (Md. 2005) (electric light marking standards).

[293] See, e.g., Baley v. Federal Signal Corp., 982 N.E.2d 776, 800 (Ill. App. Ct. 2012) (siren decibel level standards); Linden v. CNH Am., LLC, 673 F.3d 829, 838 (8th Cir. 2012) (Iowa law) (off-road seat belt standards); Kagan v. Harley Davidson, Inc., 2008 WL 3874824, at *14 n.31 (E.D. Pa. 2008) (motorcycle kickstand standards).

[294] See Myrick v. Husqvarna Prof'l Prod., Inc., 508 F. Supp. 3d 846, 860 (D. Kan. 2020) (mower warning standards for operating on a slope); Masters v. Hesston Corp., 291 F.3d 985, 991 (7th Cir. 2002) (Ill. law) (hay baler safety standards).

[295] See, e.g., Duffy v. Togher, 887 N.E.2d 535, 549–50 (Ill. App. Ct. 2008) (pool liner standards); Ryan v. KDI Sylvan Pools, Inc., 579 A.2d 1241, 1243–44 (N.J. 1990) (pool depth standards).

[296] See McNeal v. Hi-Lo Powered Scaffolding, Inc., 836 F.2d 637, 642–43 (D.C. Cir. 1988) (standards for scaffolding clips).

[297] See Baier v. Bostitch, 611 N.E.2d 1103, 1106 (Ill. App. Ct. 1993) (contact trip on nailer should prevent tool from discharging under its own weight).

[298] See Potter v. Chicago Pneumatic Tool Co., 694 A.2d 1319, 1326 (Conn. 1997) (vibration limits for tools). These and other standards-setting organizations are examined in Frumer, Friedman, and Sklaren, Products Liability § 76.03.

[299] See, e.g., Thomas v. Mallett, 701 N.W.2d 523, 544 (Wis. 2005) (ASA is "a voluntary group comprised of representatives from a variety of medical, public health and industry groups"); Fayerweather v. Menard, Inc., 659 N.W.2d 506, 506 (Wis. Ct. App. 2003) (ANSI's ladder committee membership: from industry, users, and chosen from CPSC, OSHA, labor organizations, and "outside specialists").

[300] See, e.g., Allenbrand v. Louisville Ladder Grp., L.L.C., 2007 WL 120805, at *1 (D. Kan. 2007) ("The Occupational Safety and Health Administration views ANSI Section A14 as the 'national consensus standard' pertaining to ladders."); Del Cid v. Beloit Corp., 901 F. Supp. 539, 545 (E.D.N.Y. 1995) ("ANSI standards are relied upon by the manufacturers of machinery and by experts in various fields to conduct evaluations of the safety of machinery and processes.").

of such standards largely the same as less formal types of customary industry standards.[301]

Admissibility. A great majority of courts allow applicable evidence of industry custom.[302] To be applicable, a standard normally must have existed at the time the defendant manufactured the product[303] and must otherwise be directed to the particular aspect of the particular type of product involved in the dispute.[304] Thus, to prove a design defect, a plaintiff may introduce that the defendant manufacturer failed to comply with an applicable industry standard for the design of a speed control mechanism on an asphalt paver,[305] aircraft actuators that could be installed backwards by mistake,[306] a grader back-up alarm that was not tamper-proof,[307] power tools that vibrated excessively,[308] or the guarding of pinch points on industrial machinery.[309] Similarly, in seeking to prove a warning defect, a plaintiff may show that a product's warnings are inadequate for failing to comply with industry warning standards with respect to a risk that a crane operator might be shocked if the crane were to hit electrical wires,[310] that a kitchen floor cleaning chemical might cause severe burns,[311] or that a winch should use a safety-latched hook.[312] Notwithstanding the widespread admissibility of such evidence on the issue of product defect, a few courts refuse altogether to allow evidence of industry custom in actions based on strict liability in tort, reasoning that evidence of the customary behavior of manufacturers with respect to safety issues improperly injects into a strict liability case issues of conduct and due care that have no relevance to the legal standard of product defectiveness, whether measured by consumer expectations or something else.[313] As an outmoded holdover from early, misguided efforts to distinguish

---

[301] However, because some standards-setting groups are comprised of members outside the industry, and because their standards are voluntary guidelines of minimum safety, they are not to be equated with "industry custom" as such. See Fayerweather v. Menard, Inc., 659 N.W.2d 506, 506 (Wis. Ct. App. 2003) (because ⅔ of ANSI ladder standards committee members came from outside industry, "the standards are not evidence of 'custom and usage' within an industry as contemplated" by standard jury instruction, so that court's failure to give it was not error).

[302] See Frumer, Friedman, and Sklaren, Products Liability § 18.04. Industry "custom," meaning prevailing use of technology, differs from "state of the art," meaning the best technology reasonably available at the time, a higher standard. See § 2.3, above, and § 10.4, below. For the minority view, see note 313, below.

[303] See, e.g., Hutchison v. Urschel Labs., Inc., 157 F.3d 613, 615 (8th Cir. 1998) (Mo. law); Bottignoli v. Ariens Co., 560 A.2d 1261, 1266 (N.J. Super. Ct. App. Div. 1989).

[304] See, e.g., Chapman v. Bernard's Inc., 167 F. Supp. 2d 406, 422 (D. Mass. 2001) (industry standards plaintiff sought to use as evidence pertained to cribs, toddler beds, and bunk beds, not day beds like the one causing baby's death when he slipped between its mattress and side rail).

[305] See Alfred v. Caterpillar, Inc., 262 F.3d 1083 (10th Cir. 2001) (Okla. law) (SAE standards called for such a control to be a lever rather than a rotary dial; operator backed up, squashing plaintiff against tree, rather than proceeding forward as operator intended).

[306] See Nesselrode v. Executive Beechcraft, Inc., 707 S.W.2d 371, 379 (Mo. 1986).

[307] See Bohnstedt v. Robscon Leasing L.L.C., 993 P.2d 135, 136 (Okla. Civ. App. 1999) (testimony that other manufacturers use tamper-resistant screws).

[308] See Potter v. Chicago Pneumatic Tool Co., 694 A.2d 1319, 1326 (Conn. 1997).

[309] See, e.g., Masters v. Hesston Corp., 291 F.3d 985, 991 (7th Cir. 2002) (Ill. law) (hay baler); Del Cid v. Beloit Corp., 901 F. Supp. 539, 545–49 (E.D.N.Y. 1995) (plastic injection molding machine).

[310] See Evanoff v. Grove Mfg. Co., 650 N.E.2d 914, 919 (Ohio Ct. App. 1994).

[311] See Westley v. Ecolab, Inc., 2004 WL 1068805, at *10 (E.D. Pa. 2004).

[312] See Beneway v. Superwinch, Inc., 216 F. Supp. 2d 24, 30 (N.D.N.Y. 2002).

[313] See, e.g., Sullivan v. Werner Co., 253 A.3d 730, 747–48 (Pa. Super. Ct. 2021) (trial court did not err in excluding defendant's evidence of ANSI scaffolding standard; "evidence of industry standards may be excluded because those standards do not go to the safety of the product itself"); Green v. Schutt Sports Mfg. Co., 369 Fed. Appx. 630, 636–37 (5th Cir. 2010) (Tex. law) (industry standard inadmissible unless offered to rebut plaintiff's alternative design); Malcolm v. Evenflo Co., 217 P.3d 514, 522 (Mont. 2009) (declining to adopt

strict liability from negligence, the few courts still clinging to the minority view may be expected to swing over in time to the more logical majority perspective.[314]

By the same token, a manufacturer seeking to establish that its product's *design* is reasonably safe, that it is not defective for failing to meet the safety standard of some alternative design,[315] may show that its product complied with applicable industry standards for a stepladder,[316] a chair,[317] the fuel system of a pickup truck,[318] or the protective guard of a log skidder[319] or a grinder;[320] or, in an attempt to refute a defective *warning* claim, that its compliance with industry standards for warnings and instructions was adequate for the product, such as a hot water heater[321] or a trampoline;[322] or, that its product was free of manufacturing defects.[323]

Products Liability Rest. § 4; evidence of compliance with a regulation "would inject into strict products liability analysis the manufacturer's reasonableness and level of care—concepts that are . . . irrelevant on the issue of design defect liability"); Lewis v. Coffing Hoist Div., Duff-Norton Co., 528 A.2d 590, 594 (Pa. 1987) (evidence of customary design of control box for hoist inadmissible in strict liability action because such evidence introduces concepts of negligence and focuses on manufacturer's conduct rather than condition of product, thus distracting jury; concurring judge, id. at 595, remarked that "a manufacturer cannot avoid liability to its consumers that it injures or maims through its defective designs by showing that 'the other guys do it too' "; dissents argued that evidence that 90% of industry used similar switch should be allowed to show, not conclusively, that product was safe, and that courts should follow negligence approach allowing such evidence to help illuminate environment in which products are made and used).

[314] In Kim v. Toyota Motor Corp., 424 P.3d 290, 301 (Cal. 2018), disapproving earlier cases, the California Supreme Court held that evidence of industry custom and practices, although not dispositive, may be admissible in a strict liability design defect risk-benefit determination "if it sheds light on whether, objectively speaking, the product was designed as safely as it should have been, given 'the complexity of, and trade-offs implicit in, the design process.' " New York for some time could not make up its mind, but now allows evidence of industry standards. See, e.g., Pacy v. Cowen Holdings, Inc., 50 N.Y.S.3d 745, 746 (App. Div. 2017) ("washing machine complied with industrial and safety standards [and] was reviewed and certified by several national safety organizations").

[315] Comment *d* to Products Liability Rest. § 2(b) explains the relevance of industry custom to the feasibility requirement of design defect determinations:

> [A] design is defective if the product could have been made safer by the adoption of a reasonable alternative design. . . . When a defendant demonstrates that its product design was the safest in use at the time of sale, it may be difficult for the plaintiff to prove that an alternative design could have been practically adopted. The defendant is thus allowed to introduce evidence with regard to industry practice that bears on whether an alternative design was practicable. Industry practice may also be relevant to whether the omission of an alternative design rendered the product not reasonably safe. While such evidence is admissible, it is not necessarily dispositive. If the plaintiff introduces expert testimony to establish that a reasonable alternative design could practically have been adopted, a trier of fact may conclude that the product was defective notwithstanding that such a design was not adopted by any manufacturer, or even considered for commercial use, at the time of sale.

[316] See, e.g., Allenbrand v. Louisville Ladder Grp., L.L.C., 2007 WL 120805, at *1 (D. Kan. 2007) (8-foot ladder passed all tests for compliance with ANSI standards; summary judgment for manufacturer); DiCarlo v. Keller Ladders, Inc., 211 F.3d 465, 468 (8th Cir. 2000) (Mo. law) (ANSI standards; affirming judgment on verdict for manufacturer).

[317] See Delery v. Prudential Ins. Co. of Am., 643 So.2d 807, 813 (La. Ct. App. 1994) (ANSI standards).

[318] See Ake v. General Motors Corp., 942 F. Supp. 869, 874 (W.D.N.Y. 1996).

[319] See Westfall v. Caterpillar, Inc., 821 P.2d 973, 976 (Idaho 1991).

[320] See Clarke v. LR Sys., 219 F. Supp. 2d 323, 334 (E.D.N.Y. 2002) (ANSI guarding standard for grinders).

[321] See Moore v. Mississippi Valley Gas Co., 863 So.2d 43, 46 (Miss. 2003) (scald warnings, American Gas Association and ANSI standards).

[322] See Ford v. Nairn, 717 N.E.2d 525, 530 (Ill. App. Ct. 1999) (ASTM Standard F381–84; summary judgment for defendant affirmed); Anderson v. Hedstrom Corp., 76 F. Supp. 2d 422, 450 (S.D.N.Y. 1999).

[323] See, e.g., Emody v. Medtronic, Inc., 238 F. Supp. 2d 1291, 1294 (N.D. Ala. 2003) (rod in spinal fusion device met ASTM standards for chemistry, hardness, and microstructure).

Evidentiary effect. A large majority of jurisdictions maintain that a manufacturer's compliance or noncompliance with custom is some evidence that the product was[324] or was not[325] defective,[326] while an occasional court appears to give such evidence somewhat greater weight.[327] A couple of state products liability reform statutes address the topic, at least one providing that evidence of industry custom and nongovernmental standards is admissible,[328] while another accords a presumption of nondefectiveness to products that "conformed to the generally recognized and prevailing standards."[329] Finally, courts in strict tort cases, borrowing from negligence law's *T.J. Hooper* rule,[330] almost universally hold that evidence of a defendant's compliance[331] or noncompliance[332] with industry safety standards does not alone conclusively establish whether a product is defective.[333] Yet, in unusual cases, proof of a defendant's

---

[324] See, e.g., Williams v. MD Cowan, Inc., 2011 WL 4527361, at *2 (E.D. Ark. 2011); Alfred v. Caterpillar, Inc., 262 F.3d 1083, 1088 (10th Cir. 2001) (Okla. law).

[325] See, e.g., Williams v. MD Cowan, Inc., 2011 WL 4527361, at *2 (E.D. Ark. 2011) ("The ANSI and API standards, however, are not the law; they are voluntary standards. Any violation of ANSI or API standards is only evidence of defect; it does not establish that the rig was defective as a matter of law."); Holst v. KCI Konecranes Int'l Corp., 699 S.E.2d 715, 721 (S.C. Ct. App. 2010); Ake v. General Motors Corp., 942 F. Supp. 869, 874 (W.D.N.Y. 1996); Wash. Rev. Code Ann. § 7.72.050.

[326] See Frumer, Friedman, and Sklaren, Products Liability § 18.04[1] ("almost every jurisdiction").

[327] See, e.g., Vermett v. Fred Christen & Sons Co., 741 N.E.2d 954, 971 (Ohio Ct. App. 2000) ("compliance with ANSI is a compelling factor"); Jordan v. Massey-Ferguson, Inc., 100 F.3d 956, 956 (6th Cir. 1996) (table) (Ky. law) ("a manufacturer rarely 'will be held liable for failing to do what no one in his position has ever done before' "); Del Cid v. Beloit Corp., 901 F. Supp. 539, 545–49 (E.D.N.Y. 1995); Mears v. General Motors Corp., 896 F. Supp. 548, 552 (E.D. Va. 1995) (while compliance with industry practices does not conclusively establish product's safety, manufacturer seldom will be liable for failing to adopt safety measures no other member of industry employs). See also Products Liability Rest. § 2(b) cmt. *d*, at 20: "When a defendant demonstrates that its product design was the safest in use at the time of sale, it may be difficult for the plaintiff to prove that an alternative design [required for a finding of design defect] could have been practically adopted."

[328] See Wash. Rev. Code Ann. § 7.72.050(1) (trier of fact may consider such evidence with respect to design, warning, or manufacturing defects).

[329] Ky. Rev. Stat. Ann. § 411.310(2).

[330] See The T.J. Hooper v. Northern Barge Corp., 60 F.2d 737, 740 (2d Cir. 1932), discussed at § 2.3, above.

[331] See, e.g., Clarke v. LR Sys., 219 F. Supp. 2d 323, 334–35 (E.D.N.Y. 2002) (compliance with ANSI standard not dispositive of design defect issue and other evidence on design and safety of machine may be considered); Brooks v. Beech Aircraft Corp., 902 P.2d 54, 64 (N.M. 1995).

[332] See, e.g., Williams v. MD Cowan, Inc., 2011 WL 4527361, at *2 (E.D. Ark. 2011) (as voluntary standards, a violation of ANSI or API standards is only evidence of defectiveness); Rupolo v. Oshkosh Truck Corp., 749 F. Supp. 2d 31, 43 (E.D.N.Y. 2010) ("lack of compliance" with ANSI and OSHA standards "is not dispositive of the issue of a design defect").

[333] See, e.g., Howard v. Omni Hotels Mgmt. Corp., 136 Cal. Rptr. 3d 739, 756–60 (Ct. App. 2012) (evidence of compliance is one factor to be considered; "industry standards alone would not be dispositive"); Linden v. CNH Am., LLC, 673 F.3d 829, 838 (8th Cir. 2012) (Iowa law) (jury may consider defendant's compliance with SAE off-road seat belt standards); Mathis-Kay v. McNeilus Truck & Mfg., Inc., 2011 WL 4498386, at *6 (W.D.N.Y. 2011) ("conformity with industry standards is but one of several factors for a jury to consider in determining whether a design is reasonably safe"). See generally Frumer, Friedman, and Sklaren, Products Liability § 18.04[1]. *But see* Blue v. Environmental Eng'g, Inc., 828 N.E.2d 1128, 1141–42 (Ill. 2005) (where, oddly, the court suggests that compliance with industry standards may be an absolute defense in negligence), critiqued in Twerski, Chasing the Illusory Pot of Gold at the End of the Rainbow: Negligence and Strict Liability in Design Defect Litigation, 90 Marq. L. Rev. 7 (2006).

Recall the more stringent minority view that compliance with customary safety standards is not even relevant to strict liability in tort. See note 313, above.

compliance[334] or noncompliance[335] with a clear and vital industry custom conceivably may be a proper basis for a dispositive determination of a product's defectiveness.

Governmental Standards—Statutes and Regulations

Violation. The effect of a manufacturer's violation of a safety statute or regulation on a negligence determination was examined earlier in connection with the doctrine of negligence per se. It was there seen that a defendant's breach of an applicable statute or regulation—one addressing the type of risk that harmed the plaintiff to a person like the plaintiff—is at least evidence (and possibly conclusive) of the negligence issue.[336] The question examined here is whether the law recognizes an equivalent method of proving product defectiveness for purposes of strict products liability in tort,[337] a doctrine that might be labeled "defectiveness per se."

It is useful to remember that a finding of product defect is normally a kind of "lesser included offense" in a negligence determination, which normally requires a conclusion that the defendant negligently made or sold a product that was defective in some respect.[338] Stated otherwise, a finding of negligence (whether by normal proofs or negligence per se) usually implies a finding of defectiveness. So, if a plaintiff establishes negligence per se—that a product was in violation of a safety statute or regulation that sought to protect persons like the plaintiff from risks like those that caused the plaintiff's harm—then the plaintiff logically has also made a case that the product was defective.[339] This is the premise of the *Products Liability Restatement*, which states a defectiveness per se principle in traditional negligence per se terms.[340] Section 4(a) of the *Restatement* provides that "a product's noncompliance with an applicable product safety statute or administrative regulation renders the product defective with respect to the risks sought to be reduced by the statute or regulation."[341] Observing that the rule derives from the doctrine of negligence per se,[342] the *Restatement* extends the principle across products liability theories to strict liability theories based on defectiveness as well as traditional negligence.[343]

---

334 See Wilder v. Toyota Motor Sales, U.S.A., Inc., 23 Fed. Appx. 155, 157 (4th Cir. 2001) (Va. law) ("While conformity with industry custom does not absolve a manufacturer or seller of a product from liability, such compliance may be conclusive when there is no evidence to show that the product was not reasonably safe.").

335 See Henderson and Twerski, Achieving Consensus on Defective Product Design, 83 Cornell L. Rev. 867 (1998) (arguing that a defendant's violation of a clear industry standard should be conclusive proof of a product's defectiveness).

336 See § 2.4, above.

337 See Frumer, Friedman, and Sklaren, Products Liability §§ 10.03, § 55.02[3]; Am. Law Prod. Liab. §§ 12:8–:15; D'Angelo, Effect of Compliance with Applicable Governmental Product Safety Regulations on a Determination of Product Defect, 36 S. Tex. L. Rev. 453 (1995); Wheeler, The Use of Criminal Statutes to Regulate Product Safety, 13 J. Legal Stud. 593 (1984); Note, Products Liability Based Upon Violation of Statutory Standards, 64 Mich. L. Rev. 1388 (1966) (classic treatment); Products Liability Rest. § 4(a).

338 See §§ 2.1 and 5.9, above, and § 15.2, below.

339 See Elsworth v. Beech Aircraft Corp., 691 P.2d 630, 632 (Cal. 1984) (applying negligence per se doctrine to find defective design).

340 The formulation is traditional except that it conflates the conventional two-pronged test, see § 2.4, above, into a single scope-of-risk prong.

341 Products Liability Rest. § 4(a).

342 See id. Reporters' Note to cmt. *d*.

343 Treating products liability doctrine broadly, without regard to distinctions between the traditional claims (negligence, implied warranty, and strict liability in tort), is consistent with the Third Restatement's "functional" approach to products liability which seeks to transcend the different causes of action, reducing them to simple products liability claims. See Products Liability Rest. §§ 1–4. See § 6.5, below.

While a doctrine of defectiveness per se might appear logically embedded in the concept of negligence per se, as just discussed, the underlying rationale of *any* type of per se liability in tort for breach of statute is unclear. Negligence per se itself has always been theoretically suspect,[344] and just why a statutory or regulatory violation should be deemed to establish a product defect, if intuitively appealing, is not logically evident. The idea may be that governmental product safety standards necessarily take into account consumer expectations and the costs and benefits of alternative safety approaches, thereby resting on implicit determinations of product defectiveness; or perhaps it is the other way around, that consumers can reasonably expect that manufacturers will obey the law, and can reasonably expect no more.[345] But rationales like these seem contrived to make a point. The *Restatement*'s purported "policy" explanation for the rule[346] is tautological, which may reflect the fact that most courts that have applied the per se principle to proof of defectiveness in strict liability have borrowed this approach from negligence law without critical consideration.[347] Case law on the issue is sparse, and most of the few courts that apply the doctrine are federal courts sitting in diversity, sometimes drawing support dubiously from one another. In short, the doctrine of defectiveness per se, by which a violation of a safety statute or regulation establishes that a product is defective, rests on a slender case-law reed. But a couple of state statutes,[348] a large handful of scattered opinions,[349] and the *Products Liability Restatement* do support this type of proof of product defect. In the final analysis, and for whatever reason, a product's failure to meet minimal government safety rules does indeed seem somehow relevant—perhaps very relevant—to a defectiveness determination.[350]

To be admissible on the issue of product defect, a statutory violation must be *relevant* to that issue, which is another way of saying that the plaintiff must have been injured by the risk the statute sought to prevent.[351] Probably the most contentious issue in this regard concerns OSHA regulations for the guarding of machinery and a myriad

---

[344] See, e.g., Keeton, Dobbs, Keeton, and Owen, Prosser and Keeton on the Law of Torts § 36, at 220–22.

[345] Cf. Soproni v. Polygon Apartment Partners, 971 P.2d 500, 505–06 (Wash. 1999) (regulatory compliance *vel non* "is merely relevant evidence that may be considered by the trier of fact [together with the availability of feasible alternative designs, in determining] if the product was unsafe to an extent beyond that which would be expected by an ordinary consumer").

[346] "The rule in [§ 4(a)] is based on the policy judgment that designs and warnings that fail to comply with applicable safety standards established by statute or regulations are . . . defective." Products Liability Rest. § 4(a) cmt. *d*.

[347] The courts are not alone in simply assuming that the per se principle for breach of statute may be transferred from negligence law to strict products liability. See, e.g., Rabin, Reassessing Regulatory Compliance, 88 Geo. L.J. 2049, 2051 (2000) ("If, in fact, a regulation is taken to set a minimum standard of safety, a violation can surely be taken to import responsibility as a matter of law.").

[348] See Colo. Rev. Stat. Ann. § 13–21–403(2) (violation creates rebuttable presumption of defectiveness); Kan. Stat. Ann. § 60–3304(b) (violation renders product defective unless manufacturer establishes that violation was appropriate).

[349] See, e.g., Stanton v. Astra Pharm. Prods., Inc., 718 F.2d 553, 558–65 (3d Cir. 1983) (Pa. law) (Xylocaine manufacturer negligent per se for failing to file adverse reaction reports required by FDA regulation; violation also rendered drug defective under § 402A, since FDA was unable to ensure that warnings of adverse reactions were disseminated to doctors); Lukaszewicz v. Ortho Pharm. Corp., 510 F. Supp. 961, 962–65 (E.D. Wis. 1981) (manufacturer of Ortho-Novum birth control pills negligent per se, and liable under § 402A, for failure to warn user directly of side effects pursuant to FDA regulation, 21 C.F.R. § 310.501).

[350] "Indeed, it seems anomalous to accord such a standard of conduct, promulgated by the community through its elected representatives, anything less than the force of law . . . in the context of a civil suit." Note, 64 Mich. L. Rev. 1388, 1391 (1966).

[351] See, e.g., Hagan v. Gemstate Mfg., Inc., 982 P.2d 1108, 1112–13 (Or. 1999).

other workplace safety matters.[352] OSHA's machine guarding regulations focus exclusively on the obligations of *employers*, rendering the admissibility of such regulations in actions against *manufacturers* immediately suspect in the halls of relevance.[353] Nevertheless, both plaintiffs and defendants may seek to have such standards admitted into evidence in a products liability case. A plaintiff quite naturally will want to show that a manufacturer failed to adopt whatever guarding or other pertinent standards OSHA has required. Because machine guarding and most other OSHA safety regulations are directed at employers rather than manufacturers,[354] their breach (by employers) cannot establish a manufacturer's liability per se. Yet, because such standards prescribe the types of safety devices the federal workplace safety agency deems minimally appropriate for the safety of particular machinery, these standards help plaintiffs define the standard of acceptable safety practices—the prevailing custom—in the industry of machinery manufacturers.[355]

Manufacturers themselves sometimes seek to introduce OSHA safety standards.[356] While standing behind a shield that it cannot violate a safety regulation that applies only to employers, a manufacturer of industrial machinery may nevertheless seek to use such a regulation to inform the jury, if indirectly, of a couple important points: (1) that the employer, which is not a party in a products liability action,[357] owed and breached a duty under federal law to protect the worker and so in a sense was primarily responsible for the accident;[358] and (2) that the injured worker is already being compensated by workers' compensation benefits and so will not be left destitute if the jury finds the product not defective.

Deciding how best to mesh workers' compensation and products liability law is exceedingly complex,[359] but violations of OSHA regulations applicable only to employers simply cannot establish product defectiveness per se.[360] Some courts bar the admission

---

[352] See Frumer, Friedman, and Sklaren, Products Liability § 18.05[3].

[353] See, e.g., Gray v. Navistar Int'l Corp., 630 N.Y.S.2d 596, 598 (App. Div. 1995) (truck not equipped with back-up beeping device; OSHA standards inadmissible); Jemmott v. Rockwell Mfg. Co., 628 N.Y.S.2d 184, 185 (App. Div. 1995) (press guarding; OSHA standards inadmissible).

[354] Note that other OSHA regulations, such as the OSHA Hazard Communication Standard, 29 C.F.R. § 1910.1200(g)(6)(I), requiring manufacturers and importers of chemicals to supply purchasers with Safety Data Sheets, are indeed directed at employers. See, e.g., Messer v. Amway Corp., 210 F. Supp. 2d 1217, 1230 (D. Kan. 2002), aff'd 106 Fed. Appx. 678 (10th Cir. 2004).

[355] See, e.g., Gillespie v. Edmier, 182 N.E.3d 54, 59 (Ill. 2020) (plaintiffs' expert's testimony that dump trailer's steps and side rails conflicted with OSHA and other industry guidelines created a "genuine issue of material fact as to whether the dump trailer was unreasonably dangerous"); Couch v. Astec Indus., 53 P.3d 398, 403–04 (N.M. Ct. App. 2002) (OSHA standards admissible on this ground). Compare 29 U.S.C. § 653(b)(4), providing that the OSHA statute does not affect the common law "rights, duties, or liabilities of employers and employees." See generally Dobbs, Law of Torts § 133, at 313.

[356] See, e.g., Sweitzer v. Oxmaster, Inc., 2010 WL 5257226, at *10–11 (E.D. Pa. 2010); Sims v. Washex Mach. Corp., 932 S.W.2d 559, 565 (Tex. App. 1995) (machine's compliance with OSHA regulations was "strong evidence" that it was not defective).

[357] Due to the workers' compensation statutes which protect employers from tort suits by employees in exchange for workers' compensation insurance benefits. See § 15.6, below.

[358] See, e.g., Brodsky v. Mile High Equip. Co., 69 Fed. Appx. 53, 56–57 (3d Cir. 2003) (Pa. law) (evidence that OSHA imposed fines upon decedent's employer for failing to properly train employee was admissible to show that employer's intervening negligence was a superseding cause of employee's death); Porchia v. Design Equip. Co., 113 F.3d 877, 881 (8th Cir. 1997) (Ark. law) (admissible on whether employer's actions were sole proximate cause of injury). *Contra* Colegrove v. Cameron Mach. Co., 172 F. Supp. 2d 611, 617 (W.D. Pa. 2001) (irrelevant and inadmissible).

[359] See § 15.6, below.

[360] See, e.g., Jemmott v. Rockwell Mfg. Co., 628 N.Y.S.2d 184, 185 (App. Div. 1995) (OSHA press guarding standards inadmissible). See also Wingard v. Nutro Corp., 2007 WL 675456 (Mich. Ct. App. 2007)

of such evidence, as being irrelevant[361] or as introducing more confusion into a products liability case than it is worth,[362] while others allow it against manufacturers as helping to draw a full and accurate portrayal of the environment into which industrial machines are sold and used.[363] A manufacturer's compliance with OSHA standards is examined later, in connection with the regulatory compliance defense.[364]

Most strict liability in tort cases involving noncompliance with safety statutes and regulations concern claims of defects in a product's design[365] or warnings,[366] and the *Products Liability Restatement* limits the per se principle to such cases. But a safety statute or regulation may pertain to manufacturing defects, as by prescribing the maximum level of contamination or flaws allowable in products such as food,[367] drugs,[368] or lumber,[369] or proper manufacturing processes for a medical material,[370] in which context the defectiveness per se principle would seem to apply with equal force and logic.

Jurisdictions vary in the procedural effect they accord a finding of noncompliance with a governmental safety standard. Most of the few opinions on point treat the violation of a safety statute or regulation as evidence of the product's defectiveness.[371]

(court's exclusion of state's OSHA standards, which apply only to employers and employees, was not abuse of discretion).

[361] See, e.g., Forrest v. Beloit Corp., 424 F.3d 344, 352 (3d Cir. 2005) (Pa. law) (manufacturer cannot invoke OSHA standards to show employer's responsibility where state imposes non-delegable safety duty on manufacturer); Colegrove v. Cameron Mach. Co., 172 F. Supp. 2d 611, 617 (W.D. Pa. 2001).

[362] See, e.g., Perez v. Townsend Eng'g Co., 562 F. Supp. 2d 647, 649–50 (M.D. Pa. 2008) (inadmissible; "such evidence shifts jury's focus from existence of defect to reasonableness of manufacturer's conduct"); Byrne v. Liquid Asphalt Sys., Inc., 238 F. Supp. 2d 491, 492–93 (E.D.N.Y. 2002) (inadmissible; OSHA standards not intended to impose duties upon manufacturers and they would likely mislead or confuse jury).

[363] See, e.g., Salvatore v. Viking Sports Cruisers, Inc., 2012 WL 1067864, at *4 (D.N.J. 2012) (negligence claim; "violations of OSHA are to be considered with other 'fairness' factors in determining the existence of a duty and the duty's scope"); Waters v. NMC-Wollard, Inc., 2009 WL 51313, at *8 (E.D. Pa. 2009) ("At most, [OSHA non-compliance] is evidence that the product carries certain risks"); Hagan v. Gemstate Mfg., Inc., 982 P.2d 1108, 1112 (Or. 1999).

[364] For a discussion of a manufacturer's use of OSHA standards against plaintiffs, see § 14.4, below.

[365] See, e.g., Bennett v. PRC Pub. Sector, Inc., 931 F. Supp. 484, 501 (S.D. Tex. 1996) (NIOSH standards on design of work station that caused repetitive motion disorders); Brooks v. Beech Aircraft Corp., 902 P.2d 54, 64 (N.M. 1995) (absence of shoulder harnesses in private airplane allegedly rendered it uncrashworthy); Hall v. Fairmont Homes, Inc., 664 N.E.2d 546, 556 (Ohio Ct. App. 1995) (whether levels of formaldehyde fumes from by mobile home construction materials exceeded HUD regulations).

[366] See, e.g., Stanton v. Astra Pharm. Prods., Inc., 718 F.2d 553, 565 (3d Cir. 1983) (Pa. law) (manufacturer of Xylocaine anesthetic failed to file adverse reaction reports required by FDA regulation rendering drug defective under § 402A, since FDA was unable to ensure that warnings of adverse reactions were disseminated to doctors); Lukaszewicz v. Ortho Pharm. Corp., 510 F. Supp. 961 (E.D. Wis. 1981) (manufacturer of Ortho-Novum birth control pills negligent per se, and liable under § 402A, for failure to warn user directly of side effects pursuant to FDA regulation, 21 C.F.R. § 310.501).

[367] Cf. Kolarik v. Cory Int'l Corp., 721 N.W.2d 159 (Iowa 2006) (tooth fractured on olive pit; USDA standards for pitted olives permitted 1.3 pits or pit parts per 100 olives); Coffer v. Standard Brands, Inc., 226 S.E.2d 534, 538 (N.C. Ct. App. 1976) (tooth injury on unshelled nut from bottle of shelled nuts; statute and regulation allowed for 1.00% to 2.50% unshelled peanuts per unit of shelled peanuts).

[368] Cf. St. Louis Univ. v. United States, 182 F. Supp. 2d 494 (D. Md. 2002) (polio vaccine did not meet federal "neurovirulence" standards), rev'd on other grounds, 336 F.3d 294 (4th Cir. 2003).

[369] See, e.g., Holder v. Keller Indus., 2000 WL 141070, at *8 (Tex. App. 2000) (low density wood may have violated ANSI standards).

[370] Cf. Reiter v. Zimmer Inc., 897 F. Supp. 154, 163 (S.D.N.Y. 1995) (blending times for loads of prosthesis implant cement allegedly failed to meet FDA "good manufacturing practices").

[371] See, e.g., Gibson v. Wal-Mart Stores, Inc., 189 F. Supp. 2d 443, 447 (W.D. Va. 2002); Quay v. Crawford, 788 So.2d 76, 84–85 (Miss. Ct. App. 2001) (federal trucking regulation requiring effective rear-underride guard); Hall v. Fairmont Homes, Inc., 664 N.E.2d 546, 551 (Ohio Ct. App. 1995) (formaldehyde

In a few states, such a violation gives rise to a presumption of defectiveness that may shift the burden of proof.[372] At least one or two courts hold that breach of such a provision conclusively establishes that a product is defective,[373] a position endorsed by the *Products Liability Restatement*[374] which parallels what was conventionally said to be the majority rule in negligence per se.[375] But the *Restatement* further provides that a products liability defendant generally may not avail itself of the array of excuses or justifications allowed in negligence law for violating a statute or regulation,[376] reasoning that excuses are not applicable to most products liability situations where a manufacturer has occasion to know the facts and the law, and has time to conform its behavior to the safety standard's provisions.[377] It is true that valid justifications for violating safety statutes and regulations will arise less frequently in the products liability context than in ordinary accident situations where emergencies and reasonable mistakes more commonly occur. But case authority for the *Restatement*'s dual position—holding such violations to be conclusive on defectiveness, yet allowing no excuses—is ephemeral, to say the least,[378] and courts might well be leery of adopting a truly "strict" form of liability for design and warning cases without allowing in some manner for truly justifiable violations.[379]

In sum, the doctrine of "defectiveness per se," if such there be, is undeveloped and ethereal, with little real law or policy to give it legs. To the extent that this doctrine does exist, the cases suggest that a defendant's noncompliance with an applicable product safety statute or regulation may be considered evidence, though not dispositive, that a product was defective.

Compliance. The rule as to a manufacturer's compliance with a governmental safety standard set forth in a statute or regulation largely mimics the rule on violation: compliance with a regulated safety standard, such as a mandated warning, is widely considered proper evidence of a product's nondefectiveness but is not conclusive of that

---

emissions from materials used in mobile home exceeded HUD standards; by implication). See also Wash. Rev. Code Ann. § 7.72.050(1).

[372] See, e.g., McGee v. Cessna Aircraft Co., 188 Cal. Rptr. 542 (Ct. App. 1983) (FAA specification that aircraft firewalls between engine and passenger compartment resist flame penetration for at least fifteen minutes); Colo. Rev. Stat. Ann. § 13–21–403(2) (rebuttable presumption); Kan. Stat. Ann. § 60–3304(b) (product deemed defective unless manufacturer shows that violation was reasonably prudent action). The rebuttable presumption approach is discussed later, in the context of the regulatory compliance defense. See § 14.4, below.

[373] See Stanton v. Astra Pharm. Prods., Inc., 718 F.2d 553, 569–71 (3d Cir. 1983) (Pa. law) (Becker, J.) (Xylocaine manufacturer's failure to file adverse reaction reports required by FDA regulation rendered drug defective under § 402A). See also note 378, below.

[374] See Products Liability Rest. § 4(a).

[375] See § 2.4, above. Most assertions to this effect draw their support from sources from the 1940s, 1930s, or earlier. Research has uncovered no recent jurisdictional tally.

[376] See Products Liability Rest. § 4 cmt. *d*.

[377] Id.

[378] See D'Angelo, Effect of Compliance or Noncompliance with Applicable Governmental Product Safety Regulations on a Determination of Product Defect, 36 S. Tex. L. Rev. 453, 469 (1995) (asserting that only one state, Alaska, accords such violations conclusive effect). The Reporters cite Bachner v. Rich, 554 P.2d 430 (Alaska 1976), but this is a workplace safety action against a contractor in which the court acknowledges the general availability of excuses to negligence per se but finds them inapplicable to the facts.

[379] Cf. St. Louis Univ. v. United States, 182 F. Supp. 2d 494 (D. Md. 2002) (some of nation's best scientists, employed by NIH to enforce polio vaccine "neurovirulence" standards, approved vaccine that did not comply with such standards because they believed the standards, subsequently abolished, were unreasonably high), rev'd on other grounds, 336 F.3d 294 (4th Cir. 2003).

issue.[380] Notwithstanding such compliance, a jury normally is free to find a complying design or warning "defective" because governmental safety requirements generally are set at levels minimally acceptable for regulatory purposes.[381] Section 4(b) of the *Products Liability Restatement* follows these general principles, providing that, for design and warning defect purposes, "a product's compliance with an applicable product safety statute or administrative regulation is properly considered in determining whether the product is defective with respect to the risks sought to be reduced by the statute or regulation, but such compliance does not preclude as a matter of law a finding of product defect." Some states go further, providing that a manufacturer's compliance with an applicable statute or regulation raises a rebuttable presumption that the product is not defective.[382] In very unusual situations, where no special circumstances suggest the need for greater caution, a court may rule that a defendant's conformity to a statutory or regulatory safety standard amounts to due care as a matter of law,[383] and this principle of special applicability very probably applies to claims for strict liability in tort as well.

The topic of compliance with governmental safety statutes and regulations is addressed later in depth as a matter of special defense.[384] Also examined later is the special defense of federal preemption,[385] a distant cousin to the defense of compliance with statute.

---

[380] See, e.g., Covell v. Bell Sports, Inc., 651 F.3d 357, 366 (3d Cir. 2011) (Pa. law) (compliance with CPSC's Safety Standard for Bicycle Helmets (16 C.F.R. § 1203) was not conclusive but was relevant); O'Neill v. Novartis Consumer Health, Inc., 55 Cal. Rptr. 3d 551, 558 (Ct. App. 2007) (FDA standards "do not immunize a drug manufacturer from liability," but they are "entitled to 'serious consideration' on the issue" of safety); Soproni v. Polygon Apartment Partners, 971 P.2d 500, 505–06 (Wash. 1999) (design of window, through which child fell, that complied with building and fire codes; compliance merely evidence of nondefectiveness); Contini v. Hyundai Motor Co., 840 F. Supp. 22, 23 (S.D.N.Y. 1993) (compliance with NHTSA seatbelt regulations). Compliance with government statutes and regulations is a popular subject of statutory reform. See, e.g., Wash. Rev. Code Ann. § 7.72.050(1) (admissible evidence).

[381] See, e.g., Broyles v. Kasper Mach. Co., 865 F. Supp. 2d 887, 896 (S.D. Ohio 2012) (following "majority of states [holding that] standards and regulations create minimum thresholds, adherence to which does not foreclose liability, but which may be considered by a jury in determining reasonableness"); Riani v. Louisville Ladder, Inc., 2010 WL 2802040, at *2–3 (D. Mass. 2010) (allowing plaintiff's expert's testimony that ANSI ladder standards adopted by OSHA in 29 C.F.R. § 1926.1053 "should be considered at best minimum requirements"). Perhaps the classic instance of extraordinarily minimal standards are the flammability standards in the Flammable Fabrics Act. See, e.g., Needham v. Coordinated Apparel Grp., Inc., 811 A.2d 124, 131 (Vt. 2002); Gryc v. Dayton-Hudson Corp., 297 N.W.2d 727, 733–35 (Minn. 1980); Raymond v. Riegel Textile Corp., 484 F.2d 1025 (1st Cir. 1973) (N.H. law).

[382] See, e.g., Egbert v. Nissan N. Am., Inc., 167 P.3d 1058, 1062 (Utah 2007); Schultz v. Ford Motor Co., 857 N.E.2d 977, 987 (Ind. 2006); BIC Pen Corp. v. Carter, 171 S.W.3d 657, 667 (Tex. App. 2005), rev'd on other grounds, 251 S.W.3d 500 (Tex. 2008); Cansler v. Mills, 765 N.E.2d 698 (Ind. Ct. App. 2002) (presumption of nondefectiveness rebutted; summary judgment for manufacturer reversed); Colo. Rev. Stat. Ann. § 13–21–403(1); Fla. Stat. Ann. § 768.1256; Ind. Code Ann. § 34–20–5–1; Kan. Stat. Ann. § 60–3304(a); Tenn. Code Ann. § 29–28–104(a); Tex. Civ. Prac. & Rem. Code Ann. § 82.008(a); Utah Code Ann. § 78B–6–703(2).

[383] See, e.g., Ramirez v. Plough, Inc., 863 P.2d 167, 172, 176–77 (Cal. 1993) (compliance with FDA's English language only warning requirement shielded drug manufacturer from also having to warn in Spanish that giving aspirin to children suffering flu might cause Reye's Syndrome); Beatty v. Trailmaster Prods., Inc., 625 A.2d 1005, 1014 (Md. 1993) (compliance with bumper height statute was complete defense). See Products Liability Rest. § 4 cmt. *e* (in "unusual situations," statutory or regulatory compliance may be conclusive). Cf. Taylor v. Smithkline Beecham Corp., 658 N.W.2d 127, 131 (Mich. 2003) (upholding as constitutional Michigan statute shielding drug manufacturers from liability if their drugs comply with FDA regulations).

[384] See § 14.4, below.

[385] See § 14.5, below.

Other Similar Accidents

A common and often quite persuasive form of proof in products liability litigation is proof of other similar accidents.[386] Plaintiffs commonly offer evidence of other similar accidents to help prove, circumstantially, a product's dangerous or defective condition, the defendant's notice of it, or that it caused the plaintiff's injury. Less commonly, defendants offer converse evidence of this type (the *absence* of other similar accidents) in an attempt to prove the contrary—that a product's condition was *not* especially dangerous, that the defendant had no reason to know about it, or that it did *not* cause the plaintiff's harm. In addition, such evidence is sometimes allowed to rebut or impeach the other party's witness.[387] Plaintiffs' attorneys consider other-accident evidence to be an especially powerful form of proof,[388] while defense attorneys often view it as largely, if not entirely, irrelevant and prejudicial to the fair and rational adjudication of a products liability case.[389]

Relevance

Other-accident evidence may be relevant to one or more of three basic factual matters commonly in dispute in products liability litigation: (1) the nature and extent of a product's dangerous condition,[390] (2) the defendant's awareness of that condition,[391] and (3) the causal relationship between the condition and the plaintiff's harm. Each of these matters might be controverted, for example, in an action against the manufacturer

---

[386] See Nissan Motor Co. v. Armstrong, 145 S.W.3d 131, 138–40 (2004) (good summary of principles). See generally 1 McCormick on Evidence § 200; 2 Weinstein's Federal Evidence § 401.08[2] (2d ed. 2002); C. Wright and K. Graham, Jr., 22 Fed. Prac. & Proc. § 5170 (2001) (cases on admissibility of similar incident evidence in state of hopeless disorder); G. Lilly, An Introduction to the Law of Evidence § 5.17 (4th ed. 1996); 2 J. Wigmore on Evidence § 458 (J. Chadbourn rev. ed., 1979); Frumer, Friedman, and Sklaren, Products Liability § 18.02; Am. Law Prod. Liab. 3d § 14:28–:37; Morris, Proof of Safety History in Negligence Cases, 61 Harv. L. Rev. 205 (1948); Annot., 51 A.L.R.4th 1186 (1987).

[387] See, e.g., Samuel v. Ford Motor Co., 112 F. Supp. 2d 460, 465 (D. Md. 2000), aff'd, 95 Fed. Appx. 520 (4th Cir. 2004); Hale v. Firestone Tire & Rubber Co., 820 F.2d 928, 934–35 (8th Cir. 1987) (evidence of other explosions of identical multi-piece tire rims allowed to impeach defendant's expert), critically noted, 53 Mo. L. Rev. 547 (1988).

[388] See, e.g., Hare, Admissibility of Evidence Concerning Other Similar Incidents in a Defective Design Product Case: Courts Should Determine "Similarity" by Reference to the Defect Involved, 21 Am. J. Trial Advoc. 491 (1998); Turner, Proving Design Defects with Other Similar Incidents Evidence, 35 Trial 42 (1999) (techniques for finding and using such evidence in auto cases).

[389] See, e.g., Reynolds and Kirschman, The Ten Myths of Product Liability, 27 Wm. Mitchell L. Rev. 551 (2000) (other-accident evidence peculiarly subject to misuse by jury; discussing limiting instructions and strategy for exclusion); Carlson, Is Revised Expert Witness Rule 703 a Critical Modernization for the New Century?, 52 Fla. L. Rev. 715 (2000); Sachs, "Other Accident" Evidence in Product Liability Actions: Highly Probative or an Accident Waiting to Happen?, 49 Okla. L. Rev. 257 (1996).

An analogous evidentiary issue concerns "comparative risk" evidence. Defense attorneys in ATV and other high-risk product cases may attempt to introduce comparative risk studies comparing the risks of ATVs to other off-road recreational vehicles, such as snowmobiles, minibikes, and trail bikes, and sometimes to such dissimilar activities as flying, skydiving, scuba diving, swimming, skiing, boating, bicycling, and horseback riding. At least two courts have allowed such evidence for some purposes. See, e.g., Kava v. American Honda Motor Co., 48 P.3d 1170, 1173–76 (Alaska 2002); Bittner v. American Honda Motor Co., 533 N.W.2d 476, 479–87 (Wis. 1995).

But see Jaramillo v. Ford Motor Co., 116 Fed. Appx. 76 (9th Cir. 2004) (reversing judgment for defendant; trial court erroneously permitted defendant's comparative risk evidence on the basis that plaintiff's evidence had "opened the door" to such evidence). See generally Frumer, Friedman, and Sklaren, Products Liability § 18.02.

[390] These factors comprise the P × L side of the Hand risk-utility formula for negligence and defectiveness, examined in §§ 2.2 and 5.7, above, and § 8.4, below.

[391] More particularly, this is the issue of "notice," actual or constructive (that defendant knew or should have known), the latter of which includes foreseeability.

of a sport utility vehicle for injuries in a rollover that occurred during a particular steering maneuver on a particular grade at a particular speed.[392] Evidence that there have been 100 serious accidents involving the same model SUV under similar circumstances might tend to show all three facts: (1) that this model SUV is especially prone to rolling over under these particular conditions; (2) that the manufacturer, because of the large number of similar accidents, had likely become informed of this danger in the vehicle; and (3) that certain aspects of the vehicle's design (and perhaps the absence of adequate warnings or instructions) may have contributed to cause the accidents. In short, other-accident evidence may be probative of a product's dangerous condition,[393] notice,[394] or causation.[395] In addition, because punitive damages may be based upon a defendant's failure to take simple steps to address a serious hazard of which it is aware,[396] evidence of other similar accidents may be relevant to the defendant's culpability on this special damages issue.[397]

---

[392] Compare McCathern v. Toyota Motor Corp., 23 P.3d 320 (Or. 2001) (Toyota 4Runner rollover; fact of 15 other substantially similar incidents relevant to understanding expert's opinion).

[393] See, e.g., Branham v. Ford Motor Co., 701 S.E.2d 5, 19–21 (S.C. 2010) (evidence of pre-manufacture rollover accident rates was relevant to issue of defectiveness, but evidence of similar accidents occurring post-manufacture was inadmissible); Shipler v. General Motors Corp., 710 N.W.2d 807, 835 (Neb. 2006) (evidence of other accidents allowed to show defectiveness of vehicle's roof design); Lovick v. Wil-Rich, 588 N.W.2d 688 (Iowa 1999) (cultivator wing fell on plaintiff after he removed a pin; evidence of other accidents showing collapse of wing on workers showed dangerousness of location of wing lock bracket subjecting operator to risk from collapse); Santos v. Chrysler Corp., 715 N.E.2d 47 (Mass. 1999) (rear of minivan skidded when brakes applied hard; relevant to dangerousness, defect, and notice).

[394] See, e.g., Specter v. Texas Turbine Conversions, Inc., 2020 WL 7360146, at *6 (D. Alaska 2020) (allowing evidence of four other crashes involving the same aircraft engine modifications that were probative of whether defendants were on notice of the problem; excluding evidence of a fifth crash in a plane lacking the engine modification); Chrysler Group, LLC v. Walden, 792 S.E.2d 754, 762 (Ga. Ct. App. 2016) ("evidence of other incidents involving the product is admissible . . . and relevant to the issue . . . of notice of a defect . . . provided there is a showing of substantial similarity"); Wielgus v. Ryobi Techs., Inc., 2012 WL 3614642, at *10 (N.D. Ill. 2012) (evidence of prior table saw accidents "put the defendants on notice of a potential defect," foreseeable injury, and "that flesh-detection technology would have mitigated or prevented" injury); Waddill v. Anchor Hocking, Inc., 27 P.3d 1092 (Or. Ct. App. 2001) (notice that fish bowl might shatter in one's hands; failure to warn of necessity to inspect fish bowl for dings and cracks); Toole v. Baxter Healthcare Corp., 235 F.3d 1307 (11th Cir. 2000) (92 breast implant complaints relevant to fragility of product, although only 13 resulted from rupture by closed capsulotomy).

[395] See, e.g., Blumer v. Ford Motor Co., 20 A.3d 1222, 1230–32 (Pa. Super. Ct. 2011) (no error in admission of 25 reports of substantially similar parking brake accidents as circumstantial evidence of defect, cause, and notice of defect; strict products liability claim brought under product malfunction theory); Arabian Agric. Servs. Co. v. Chief Indus., 309 F.3d 479, 485 (8th Cir. 2002) (Neb. law) (allowing evidence that other silos of manufacturer also collapsed; "[e]vidence of similar incidents may be relevant to prove the defendant's notice of defects, the defendant's ability to correct known defects, the magnitude of the danger, the product's lack of safety for intended uses, or causation"); Newman v. Ford Motor Co., 975 S.W.2d 147, 152 (Mo. 1998) (evidence of five other rear-end collisions properly admitted, in case involving ejection from seat that collapsed despite passenger's wearing seatbelt, with limiting instruction that jury consider the evidence only for determining effect of seatbelt in restraining occupants in rear-impact crash, not for deciding whether seat was defective).

[396] See § 5.3, above.

[397] See, e.g., McClure v. Walgreen Co., 613 N.W.2d 225, 234 (Iowa 2000) (34 incident reports of misfilled prescriptions over 3-year period admissible for punitive damages to show notice of problem without effort to cure it); Preston v. Montana Eighteenth Jud. Dist. Ct., 936 P.2d 814 (Mont. 1997). *But see* Kopczick v. Hobart Corp., 721 N.E.2d 769 (Ill. App. Ct. 1999) (reversing $20 million punitive damages verdict against manufacturer of meat saw; while notice of prior accidents relevant to punitive damages, 30 prior accidents not sufficient to put manufacturer of widely used, inherently dangerous product on notice that it was unreasonably dangerous).

Sometimes courts admit other-accident evidence as proof of a product's *defectiveness* or the manufacturer's *negligence*.[398] While this form of evidence may indeed help to prove part of defectiveness or negligence, other-accident evidence logically establishes (in addition to foreseeability or notice) only the type and level of danger in those other products.[399] To the extent that the products and other circumstances involved in the other accidents were similar to those involved in the plaintiff's lawsuit, such evidence at best provides circumstantial evidence that a particular design feature or absence of warning shared in common by the products (including the one that harmed the plaintiff) was *dangerous*, and that the danger was a common *cause* of the accidents.

But to prevail in a strict products liability action, a plaintiff must prove more than that a product that injured him was dangerous—he or she must also prove that the product's design (or absence of warning) was *defective*. And in a negligence action, the plaintiff must further prove that the defendant, by selling the product in such a dangerous condition, was negligent.[400] In addition to evidence that a product's condition was dangerous, both negligence and strict liability in tort generally require additional proof that the dangerous condition was both (1) foreseeable, and (2) reasonably preventable.[401] Other-accident evidence may help to establish the first requirement, foreseeability, because a manufacturer is likely to learn about such accidents and their cause, particularly if numerous and severe. Indeed, the more numerous and serious the similar accidents caused by a product, the more likely it is that the manufacturer did or should have become aware of the product's danger—providing the manufacturer with "notice" of the danger, actual or constructive.[402] But other-accident evidence in no way helps establish the second requirement—the availability of a reasonable alternative design (or warning) that could have prevented the plaintiff's accident. For this, the plaintiff must rely upon other types of proof.[403]

Substantial Similarity

The most fundamental requirement of other-accident evidence is that the other accidents be "substantially similar" to the plaintiff's accident.[404] First, of course, the

---

[398] See, e.g., Carballo Rodriguez v. Clark Equip. Co., 147 F. Supp. 2d 66 (D.P.R. 2001) (design defect, warning defect, negligence, and notice); Smith v. Ingersoll-Rand Co., 214 F.3d 1235 (10th Cir. 2000) (N.M. law) (defectiveness); Santos v. Chrysler Corp., 715 N.E.2d 47 (Mass. 1999) (defectiveness).

[399] See, e.g., Bullock v. Daimler Trucks N. Am., LLC, 2011 WL 4501923 (D. Colo. 2011) (evidence of a separate truck rollover accident admissible to prove the general mechanics and physics of a tractor-trailer rollover); Melton v. Deere & Co., 887 F.2d 1241, 1245 (5th Cir. 1989) (Miss. law) (relevant to both danger and consumer expectations").

[400] See ch. 2, above.

[401] See chs. 2 and 5, above, and § 10.4, below.

[402] See, e.g., Love v. Weecoo™, 774 Fed. Appx. 519, 521 (11th Cir. 2019) (Ga. law) (reversing summary judgment for Amazon.com; plaintiff's allegations of prior hoverboard fires "alleged enough facts to state plausibly that Amazon had actual or constructive knowledge that the Hoverboard posed a risk of fire at the time of Plaintiff's purchase").

[403] In particular, proof by expert testimony that a reasonable alternative design (or warning) was available when the product was made and sold. See §§ 8.5 and 9.2, below.

[404] Steede v. General Motors, LLC, 2013 WL 142484, at *9 (W.D. Tenn. 2013):

> [T]he substantial similarity doctrine [provides] that evidence of prior accidents is admissible to prove a defect so long as the prior accidents involved the same model, design, and defect, and occurred under similar circumstances [which] 'does not require identical products [but only] substantial similarity among the variables relevant to the plaintiff's theory of defect.' The plaintiff has the burden to establish the substantial similarity of [the two products], and the court's task is to undertake a fact-specific [determination of] whether the two are indeed substantially similar.

products involved in the other accidents, including the specific, allegedly defective aspect of the design or warning, must be the same as, or similar to, the one claimed to have injured the plaintiff.[405] But the relevance of such evidence also rests on a similarity between the principal causative facts and circumstances involved in the other accidents and those in the plaintiff's case.[406]

Accordingly, evidence of other accidents generally is admissible if the plaintiff establishes the substantial similarity of their circumstances to the plaintiff's accident,[407] and it will be excluded in the absence of such proof.[408] But "similar" does not mean identical,[409] and evidence of other accidents is admissible if the facts and circumstances surrounding the other accidents are shown to be reasonably similar to those surrounding the plaintiff's case,[410] and the jury may consider any dissimilarities in evaluating the

---

See also Cooper Tire & Rubber Co. v. Crosby, 543 S.E.2d 21, 23 (Ga. 2001); Lovick v. Wil-Rich, 588 N.W.2d 688, 697 (Iowa 1999).

405 See note 408, below.

406 See, e.g., Funkhouser v. Ford Motor Co., 736 S.E.2d 309 (Va. 2013) (proffered evidence of fires in seven other vehicles failed substantially similar test in failure to warn case for death of child; although incidents occurred under substantially similar circumstances, no proof that other fires were caused by the same or similar defects); Watson v. Ford Motor Co., 699 S.E.2d 169, 179 (S.C. 2010) (alleged sudden acceleration incidents not substantially similar because other Ford Explorers were made in different years from accident vehicle, different models, and cause of malfunctions not shown to be similar); Gable v. Village of Gates Mills, 784 N.E.2d 739, 744–45 (Ohio Ct. App. 2003) (airbag injuries to be similar must involve victim of similar size, gender, and position in same seat; evidence of previous airbag injury involved female driver rather than male passenger).

407 **Allowed:** Suzuki Motor of Am., Inc. v. Johns, 830 S.E.2d 549, 559 (Ga. Ct. App. 2019) (no abuse of discretion to allow evidence of similar accidents; "the motorcycles shared a common defect and . . . those defects shared a common causation"); Cruz v. Mathenge, 2019 WL 926498 (Cal. Ct. App. 2019) (trial court did not abuse discretion to allow evidence of accidents involving identical diagnostic trouble code and brake pedals going to the floor); Adams v. Toyota Motor Corp., 867 F.3d 903, 914 (8th Cir. 2017) (Minn. law) (like plaintiff's 1996 Camry, each of the three similar incident vehicles were 1996 Camrys driven over 100,000 miles, each accelerated or maintained speed when gas pedal was not depressed, and brakes were ineffective in slowing or stopping each of the vehicles).

408 **Excluded:** Susman v. Goodyear Tire & Rubber Co., 2020 WL 1065179, at *2 (D. Neb. 2020) (similar accident evidence excluded unless the accident "(1) involved an LT235/85R16 Goodyear Wrangler HT tire manufactured between 1992 and 1998; (2) that experienced a partial or complete tread separation; (3) on a vehicle that was traveling between 70 and 80 miles per hour"); Parr v. Ford Motor Co., 109 A.3d 682, 700 (Pa. Super. Ct. 2014) (plaintiffs' statistical compilations failed to meet substantial similarity test and were properly excluded); Funkhouser v. Ford Motor Co., 736 S.E.2d 309, 315 (Va. 2013) (evidence of similar accidents was properly excluded; negligent failure to warn); Graves v. CAS Med. Sys., Inc., 735 S.E.2d 650, 657 (S.C. 2012) (no evidence that failures of similar SIDS monitor alarms were caused by a similar software defect); Chism v. CNH Am. LLC, 638 F.3d 637, 641–42 (8th Cir. 2011) (Ark. law) (no abuse of discretion in excluding evidence of other accidents from different baler models and injuries occurring while standing on baler tires instead of on platform). Compare In re General Motors LLC Ignition Switch Litig., 2017 WL 4417693, at *7 (S.D.N.Y. 2017) (evidence of 58 incidents admissible to prove notice, but plaintiff prohibited from introducing evidence of those incidents (most of which involved "different vehicle platforms, with different ignition switches and systems") as proof of defect or causation).

409 See, e.g., Williams v. Manitowoc Cranes, L.L.C., 898 F.3d 607, 626 (5th Cir. 2018) (Miss. law) (no abuse of discretion for trial court to allow evidence of two accidents involving different crane models equipped with similarly positioned, identical counterweights that fell unsecured toward cab when cranes tipped over); Smith v. Ingersoll-Rand Co., 214 F.3d 1235, 1248 (10th Cir. 2000) (N.M. law) (different models, but same design problem: "The substantial similarity rule does not require identical products; nor does it require us to compare the products in their entireties [but only as to] variables relevant to the plaintiff's theory of defect.").

410 See, e.g., Ulm v. Ford Motor Co., 750 A.2d 981 (Vt. 2000) (breakage of steering gear sector shaft on Bronco caused loss of steering control; Ford's engineering investigations into complaints of accidents alleging loss of steering control relevant under business record exception of hearsay rule); Lovick v. Wil-Rich, 588 N.W.2d 688, 697–98 (Iowa 1999) (several prior instances of farm cultivator wings falling on farm workers); Moulton v. Rival Co., 116 F.3d 22, 26–27 (1st Cir. 1997) (Me. law) (reports to potpourri pot manufacturer of previous burns to young children admissible despite differences in circumstances).

weight of the evidence.[411] It is sometimes noted that the substantial similarity requirement is heightened if other incidents are offered to prove defectiveness or causation, and relaxed if such evidence is offered to show merely the defendant's notice of the possibility that its product is dangerous or defective.[412]

The question of substantial similarity is a matter for the sound discretion of the trial court, reversible only for abuse of discretion.[413] As with other forms of evidence, a court should exclude other-accident evidence, even if relevant, "if its probative value is substantially outweighed by a danger of one or more of the following: unfair prejudice, confusing the issues, misleading the jury, undue delay, wasting time, or needlessly presenting cumulative evidence."[414] In balancing probative value against the various disadvantages of this form of evidence, a court properly may allow evidence of those other accidents deemed most similar and exclude the rest.[415]

Absence of Other Accidents

Because plaintiffs normally are permitted to use other-accident evidence to prove dangerousness, notice, and causation, it seems only fair and logical to allow defendants to use the *absence* of such evidence to prove the opposite,[416] when reliable evidence of this type is offered.[417] Accordingly, defendants generally may introduce evidence of the

---

[411] Santos v. Chrysler Corp., 715 N.E.2d 47, 53 (Mass. 1999).

[412] See, e.g., Harris v. General Motors Corp., 2007 WL 622226, at *9–10 (N.J. Super. Ct. App. Div. 2007) (clear and convincing evidence standard); Smith v. Ingersoll-Rand Co., 214 F.3d 1235 (10th Cir. 2000) (N.M. law); Weir v. Crown Equip. Corp., 217 F.3d 453 (7th Cir. 2000) (Ind. law). See generally 2 Weinstein's Federal Evidence § 401.08[2] (2d ed. 2002) (less similarity required for notice, while very high degree of similarity necessary to prove product was unreasonably dangerous); 1 McCormick on Evidence § 200.

[413] See, e.g., In re Daimler Trucks N. Am. LLC, 2020 WL 7251471, at *4 (Tex. App. 2020) (trial court abused discretion by ordering overbroad discovery of documents from a different lawsuit in West Virginia that included documents from twenty-two post-collision engine fires, many of which involved different truck models with dissimilar defects); Stokes v. Ford Motor Co., 300 P.3d 648 (Mont. 2013) (no abuse of discretion in excluding evidence assembled by personal representative of vehicle driver's estate of 3,000 rollover accidents involving Ford Explorers, in wrongful death claim arising out of rollover of Ford Explorer, where plaintiff's counsel failed to demonstrate substantial similarity of the other vehicles and accident circumstances to those involved in action); Funkhouser v. Ford Motor Co., 736 S.E.2d 309, 313 (Va. 2013) (no abuse of discretion in refusing to admit proffered evidence of fires in seven other Windstar vans for lack of substantial similarity).

[414] Fed. R. Evid. 403. See, e.g., McMahon v. Yamaha Motor Corp., U.S.A., 95 So.3d 769, 774–55 (Ala. 2012) (trial court did not abuse discretion where prejudicial impact of excluded evidence "substantially outweigh[ed] the probative value"); Stokes v. National Presto Indus., 168 S.W.3d 481 (Mo. Ct. App. 2005) (photographs of injuries from other deep fryer accidents and allegations from complaints in other lawsuits against the manufacturer "could be unduly prejudicial and cause confusion by becoming the proverbial 'sideshow taking over the circus' "); Brooks v. Chrysler Corp., 786 F.2d 1191, 1198 (D.C. Cir. 1986) (affirming trial court's exclusion of evidence of consumer complaints because of minimal probative value and substantial delay: "Chrysler would have attempted to rebut the substance of *each* of the 330 complaints or to distinguish the nature of the complaints contained therein from the alleged defect in this case.").

[415] See, e.g., Sobolik v. Briggs & Stratton Power Prods. Grp., LLC, 2011 WL 1258503, at *3 (D. Minn. 2011) (limiting evidence of similar lawn tractor accidents to a weight class of under 850 pounds, eliminating admission of all but one incident from plaintiff's spreadsheet); Jones v. Ford Motor Co., 559 S.E.2d 592, 601–02 (Va. 2002).

[416] See, e.g., Croskey v. BMW of N. Am., Inc., 532 F.3d 511, 518 (6th Cir. 2008) ("A positive safety history may be admissible under certain conditions. See McCormick On Evidence § 200"); Schaefer v. Cedar Fair, L.P., 791 A.2d 1056 (N.J. Super. Ct. App. Div. 2002).

[417] See, e.g., Sappington v. Skyjack, Inc., 512 F.3d 440, 447 (8th Cir. 2008) (Mo. law) (evidence of the absence of other accidents "has been held relevant and admissible in a product liability case," but defendants failed to produce such evidence); Forrest v. Beloit Corp., 424 F.3d 344, 353–62 (3d Cir. 2005) (reversing judgment for manufacturer because such evidence and argument was allowed despite manufacturer's failure to maintain safety records). See also McNeal v. Genie Indus., Inc., 2020 WL 6036835, at *6 (Wash. Ct. App. 2020) (no abuse of discretion to exclude evidence that defendant's employee had no knowledge of similar accidents where there was no system for tracking accidents); In re Yasmin & Yaz (Drospirenone) Mktg., Sales

absence of other accidents to help establish that a product was not dangerous or defective, that the defendant had no notice of a danger or defect, or the absence of causation.[418] This reverse type of other-accident evidence—product *safe*-use evidence—also requires a proper foundation of substantial similarity: the defendant must show the regular safe use[419] of the same type of product under substantially similar conditions to those of the plaintiff's accident.[420]

It may be that evidence of the absence of prior accidents is less probative than evidence of the existence of prior accidents since proof of the absence of accidents only really shows that none have been discovered, not that they did not occur.[421] It thus has been asserted "that proving a negative by the lack of accidents is 'more complex' than proving the happening of an accident."[422] While case law on the admissibility of the absence of accidents is sparse, a number of cases have allowed evidence of a product's good safety history to help refute a plaintiff's other-accident evidence,[423] or to help disprove dangerousness,[424] causation,[425] or notice.[426] But evidence of the absence of other accidents normally is relevant only in cases involving design and warning defects and so generally should be excluded in manufacturing defect cases.[427]

Practices & Relevant Prods. Liab. Litig., 2011 WL 2650948, at *1 (S.D. Ill. 2011) (declining to allow manufacturer's employees or employees' families to testify of safe use of the oral contraceptive; such testimony was irrelevant, had no probative value, and would be highly prejudicial).

[418] See, e.g., Estate of Thompson v. Kawasaki Heavy Indus., 933 F. Supp. 2d 1111, 1144–46 (N.D. Iowa 2013) (denying plaintiff's motion in limine to exclude defendant's evidence of no or low number of other claims of wobble/weave incidents involving 2007 Ninja ZX-10R equipped with the OEM Ohlins steering damper, to show not defective; thorough discussion of absence-of-prior-claims rule in products liability litigation); Varano v. Jabar, 197 F.3d 1, 5 (1st Cir. 1999) (causation). See generally McCormick on Evidence § 200; Ross, A Good Accident Reporting System Can Help in Defending Product Liability Cases, 7 Prod. Liab. L. & Strategy 1 (2000) (admissibility may be dependent on existence of effective accident reporting system); Morris, Proof of Safety History in Negligence Cases, 61 Harv. L. Rev. 205 (1948); Annot., 51 A.L.R.4th 1186 (1987) (admissibility of absence of other product accidents).

[419] The reliability of this kind of evidence requires similar use by a large number of other persons. See, e.g., Watkins v. Toro Co., 901 S.W.2d 917, 920 (Mo. Ct. App. 1995).

[420] See, e.g., Harold v. Black & Decker U.S., Inc., 295 Fed. Appx. 530, 531 (3d Cir. 2008) (N.J. law) (vacating and remanding for new trial; evidence of lack of prior accidents in thousands of "functionally identical" rotary hammers from two electronic databases, 13-month record of every call to customer complaint hotline, and 12-year record of every claim filed should have been admitted); Pandit v. American Honda Motor Co., 82 F.3d 376, 380–81 (10th Cir. 1996).

[421] See 1 McCormick on Evidence § 200; G. Lilly, An Introduction to the Law of Evidence § 5.17 (3d ed. 1996).

[422] Schaefer v. Cedar Fair, L.P., 791 A.2d 1056, 1064 (N.J. Super. Ct. App. Div. 2002) (discussing the distinction between other-accident and no-accident evidence).

[423] See id.; Estate of Thompson v. Kawasaki Heavy Indus., 933 F. Supp. 2d 1111, 1144–46 (N.D. Iowa 2013).

[424] See, e.g., Tran v. Toyota Motor Corp., 420 F.3d 1310, 1316 (11th Cir. 2005) (manufacturer's study of other accidents allowed to show restraint system's effectiveness in various types of accidents); Espeaignnette v. Gene Tierney Co., 43 F.3d 1 (1st Cir. 1994); Emerson Elec. Co. v. Garcia, 623 So.2d 523, 524 (Fla. Dist. Ct. App. 1993).

[425] See Varano v. Jabar, 197 F.3d 1, 4–5 (1st Cir. 1999); Spino v. John S. Tilley Ladder Co., 696 A.2d 1169, 1173 (Pa. 1997).

[426] See, e.g., Hargett v. Snap-On Inc., 2009 WL 5030708, at *3–4 (D. Md. 2009) (defendant had no prior notification of similar problem from over 1,200 same model tire changers in daily use and sold over 10-year period); Jimenez v. Sears, Roebuck & Co., 885 P.2d 120, 122–23 (Ariz. Ct. App. 1994) (defendant's detailed offer of proof on company's thorough accident-information gathering system satisfied rigorous admissibility test).

[427] See, e.g., McKenzie v. S K Hand Tool Corp., 650 N.E.2d 612, 619–20 (Ill. App. Ct. 1995) (in case involving alleged manufacturing defect of ratchet wrench, trial court erred in admitting evidence of absence of

Subsequent Accidents

Most other-accident evidence admitted in products liability litigation involves accidents that occur prior to a plaintiff's accident. Some courts hold that other-accident evidence should be limited to such incidents, particularly in view of the wide-spread modern view that responsibility for product accidents, whether in negligence or strict liability, must be limited to risks that are foreseeable at the time a product is designed, manufactured, marketed, and sold.[428] A number of courts go further, however, and allow evidence of other accidents that occurred *after* the defendant's product was involved in the accident that injured the plaintiff.[429] These courts reason that the probative force of such evidence to show a product's dangerous (or defective) condition, or causation, in no way depends on when the other accidents occurred. It is clear, however, that evidence of subsequent accidents can have no relevance to the issue of notice,[430] and the relevance of subsequent-accident evidence rests upon the substantial similarity of such accidents to the plaintiff's accident.[431] At least one jurisdiction allows evidence of subsequent similar accidents to show a defendant's culpability for purposes of punitive damages.[432]

Subsequent Remedial Measures

The longer a product is on the market, the more a manufacturer learns about its hazards and how best to eliminate them. Thus, as the years progress, a manufacturer with due concern for product safety will tend to improve its manufacturing processes, enhance the design safety of its products, and provide consumers with better information on product dangers and how to avoid them. This natural evolution of product safety over time gives rise to an important evidentiary issue as to the admissibility of evidence that a manufacturer, after making and selling a product that injured the plaintiff, improved the product's safety in a manner that would have prevented the injury.

The fact that a manufacturer has eliminated the very danger responsible for a plaintiff's injury can be powerful evidence that the particular safety enhancement was

---

other accidents); Jones v. Pak-Mor Mfg. Co., 700 P.2d 819, 826 (Ariz. 1985) (safety history of entire line of products irrelevant to whether accident product was mismanufactured).

However, the safety history of the *particular* product unit claimed to have injured the plaintiff may be relevant to a manufacturing defect claim. See Stanley v. Schiavi Mobile Homes, Inc., 462 A.2d 1144, 1149 (Me. 1983) (absence of prior reports of stumbling by people going through mobile home).

[428] See, e.g., Branham v. Ford Motor Co., 701 S.E.2d 5, 20 (S.C. 2010) (allowing plaintiff's "voluminous evidence of post-manufacture rollover data" was error, even if "substantially similar" threshold met, because post-manufacture evidence of similar incidents inadmissible on liability: "for the liability system to be fair and efficient, the balancing of risks and benefits in judging product design . . . must be done in light of the knowledge of risks and risk-avoidance techniques reasonably attainable at the time of distribution," quoting Products Liability Rest. cmt. *a*); Mercer v. Pittway Corp., 616 N.W.2d 602, 615 (Iowa 2000) (similar incident evidence rule generally limited to prior incidents).

[429] See, e.g., Herbst v. L.B.O. Holding, Inc., 783 F. Supp. 2d 262, 269–71 (D.N.H. 2011) (alpine slide; warnings); Van Slyke v. Sunterra Corp., 2001 WL 543419 (Va. Cir. Ct. 2001) (showerhead; causation); Carballo-Rodriguez v. Clark Equip. Co., 147 F. Supp. 2d 66 (D.P.R. 2001) (latching defect in crane; notice and negligent design).

[430] See, e.g., Smith v. Ingersoll-Rand Co., 214 F.3d 1235, 1248 (10th Cir. 2000) (N.M. law).

[431] Compare Crowston v. Goodyear Tire & Rubber Co., 521 N.W.2d 401, 411–12 (N.D. 1994) (upholding exclusion of evidence of subsequent accidents not shown to be substantially similar to plaintiff's accident), with Nelson v. Stanley Works, 2004 WL 2094374 (Minn. Ct. App. 2004) (allowing evidence of a second tool breaking after plaintiff was injured by the first; the two were purchased at the same time and used in the same manner); Gowler v. Ferrell-Ross Co., 563 N.E.2d 773, 777–78 (Ill. App. Ct. 1990) (allowing such evidence where subsequent accidents were similar, though not identical).

[432] See Smith v. Ingersoll-Rand Co., 214 F.3d 1235, 1249 (10th Cir. 2000) (N.M. law). *Contra* Burke v. Deere & Co., 6 F.3d 497, 507–09 (8th Cir. 1993) (Iowa law).

both practicable and otherwise reasonable at the time the safety change was made. So, by improving a product's design safety or by providing additional warnings or instructions, a manufacturer acknowledges that, at least at that time, the benefits of the safety improvement exceed their costs. Absent a technological breakthrough between the time the accident product is manufactured (or when the plaintiff is injured) and the time the product's safety is improved, evidence of such a product safety enhancement may well suggest that prior to its improvement the product was defective and possibly that the manufacturer was negligent. Normally, therefore, evidence that a manufacturer adopted a subsequent remedial measure would appear to be relevant to liability and, hence, presumptively admissible in a products liability case.[433]

Common-Law Development of the "Repair Doctrine"

Although evidence that an actor cured a dangerous condition after it injured a plaintiff may generally be relevant to the condition's defectiveness and the actor's negligence, such evidence does not by itself establish either, and it may unjustly punish actors for their care and prudence. Moreover, allowing subsequent repair evidence actually may serve to diminish safety by providing parties in control of dangerous conditions with a disincentive to reduce or cure such hazards for fear that their repairs may be used against them in subsequent litigation.[434] For these reasons, courts at an early date developed a special rule of relevancy called the "repair doctrine,"[435] barring evidence of a defendant's post-accident repairs to show the defendant's negligence. Spreading from Britain[436] to America,[437] the doctrine was announced by the United States Supreme Court in 1892 in a case in which the Court explained that "it is now settled [that post-accident repair] evidence is incompetent, because the taking of such precautions against the future is not to be construed as an admission of responsibility for the past, has no legitimate tendency to prove that the defendant had been negligent before the accident happened, and is calculated to distract the minds of the jury from the real issue, and to create a prejudice against the defendant."[438]

Today, the rule barring evidence of subsequent remedial measures to prove negligence is the law in almost every state[439] by common law or formal rule of

---

[433] See Fed. R. Evid. 402 ("Relevant evidence is admissible . . . .").

[434] A post-accident repair "afford[s] no legitimate basis for construing such an act as an admission of previous neglect of duty. A person may have exercised all the care which the law required, and yet in the light of his new experience, . . . may adopt additional safeguards. The more careful a person is . . . the more likely he would be to do so; and it would seem unjust that he could not do so without being liable to have such acts construed as an admission of prior negligence." Morse v. Minneapolis & St. L. Ry. Co., 16 N.W. 358, 359 (Minn. 1883).

[435] Also known as the "subsequent repair," "subsequent remedial measure," and "post-accident corrective measure" rule or doctrine.

[436] In Hart v. Lincolnshire & Yorkshire Ry., 21 L.T.R. 261, 263 (Exch. 1869), Lord Bramwell of the court of the exchequer explained that it would be "barbarous . . . to hold that because the world gets wiser as it gets older, therefore it was foolish before."

[437] See, e.g., Terre Haute & Indianapolis R.R. v. Clem, 23 N.E. 965 (Ind. 1890).

[438] Columbia & Puget Sound R.R. v. Hawthorne, 144 U.S. 202, 207 (1892).

[439] Rhode Island appears to be the only state that broadly allows the admission of evidence of subsequent remedial measures. See R.I. R. Evid., R. 407.

evidence.[440] It is a controversial rule, as much for the breadth of its exceptions,[441] which can operate to swallow the general rule of exclusion, as for the logic of its premises, the ambiguity of its formulation, and its economic and other policy implications.[442] The repair doctrine applies to products liability litigation, barring evidence of subsequent safety improvements to prove negligence and, in some jurisdictions, product defectiveness.[443]

Federal Rule of Evidence 407

The general rule prohibiting evidence of post-accident repairs to prove negligence was adopted in Federal Rule of Evidence 407, "Subsequent Remedial Measures," which originally provided:

> When, after an event, measures are taken which, if taken previously, would have made the event less likely to occur, evidence of the subsequent measures is not admissible to prove negligence or culpable conduct in connection with the event. This rule does not require the exclusion of evidence of subsequent measures when offered for another purpose, such as proving ownership, control, or feasibility of precautionary measures, if controverted, or impeachment.

In this original iteration, Rule 407 generated interpretative problems concerning (1) whether the rule barred evidence of subsequent remedial measures in strict products liability cases, or whether instead its exclusionary principle was limited to negligence claims;[444] and (2) whether, regardless of the theory of recovery, the rule applied to safety measures a manufacturer adopted after the date of manufacture and sale of the accident product but before the plaintiff was injured, or whether it applied only to measures adopted after the plaintiff's injury.

---

[440] See, e.g., Ray v. American Nat'l Red Cross, 685 A.2d 411 (D.C. 1996) (evidence that, after plaintiff contracted HIV, Red Cross began to screen donors by questioning them directly was not admissible to prove negligence); Fernandez v. Higdon Elevator Co., 632 N.Y.S.2d 546 (App. Div. 1995) (such evidence "is never admissible as proof of admission of negligence").

See generally C. Wright and K. Graham, 23 Fed. Prac. & Proc. Evid. § 5282 (2002); McCormick on Evidence § 267; 2 Wigmore on Evidence § 283 (J. Chadbourn rev. ed., 1979); 2 J. Weinstein and M. Berger, Weinstein's Federal Evidence ch. 407 (J. McLaughlin, 2d ed. 2002); G. Lilly, An Introduction to the Law of Evidence § 5.18 (3d ed. 1996); D. Leonard, The New Wigmore, A Treatise on Evidence, Selected Rules of Limited Admissibility ch. 2 (rev. ed. 2002); Annot., 158 A.L.R. Fed. 609 (1999) (Fed. R. Evid. 407); Annot., 15 A.L.R.5th 119 (1993) (repair doctrine—modern state cases).

[441] See, e.g., 1 M. Graham, Modern State and Federal Evidence: A Comprehensive Reference Text 480 (1989) ("The opportunities for admissibility may fairly be said to come close to swallowing up the rule [of exclusion]").

[442] See, e.g., C. Wright and K. Graham, 23 Fed. Prac. & Proc. Evid. § 5282 (2002) (challenging Rule 407's justifications); J. Weinstein and M. Berger, Weinstein's Evidence Manual § 7.04[1] (2d ed. 2002) (same); Carver, Subsequent Remedial Measures 2000 and Beyond, 27 Wm. Mitchell L. Rev. 583, 587 (2000) (criticizing the rule on all these grounds and characterizing the current rule as "a post hoc litigation artifice for clever lawyers to use to their client's advantage").

[443] See Frumer, Friedman, and Sklaren, Products Liability § 18.06; Am. Law. Prod. Liab. 3d §§ 14:53 et seq., 54:11–:12; Stephenson, Alone and Out of Excuses: The Tenth Circuit's Refusal To Apply Federal Rule of Evidence 407 To Product Liability Actions, 36 N.M. L. Rev. 391 (2006); Carver, Subsequent Remedial Measures 2000 and Beyond, 27 Wm. Mitchell L. Rev. 583, 585 n.5 (2000) (citing the large body of literature); Stewart and Andreas, Subsequent Remedial Measures: An Analytical Model for Product Liability Cases, 26 Tort & Ins. L.J. 74 (1990); Annots., 38 A.L.R.4th 583 (1985) (admissibility of post-injury warnings), 84 A.L.R.3d 1220 (1978) (recall letters), 74 A.L.R.3d 1001 (1976) (admissibility in products liability cases, generally). The admissibility of subsequent remedial measure evidence often involves issues on the admissibility of evidence on recall campaigns. On product recalls, see § 10.8, below.

[444] The interpretive question was whether "culpable conduct" included strict products liability.

To resolve these questions, the first sentence of Rule 407 was amended in 1997 to read:

> When, after an injury or harm allegedly caused by an event, measures are taken that, if taken previously, would have made the injury or harm less likely to occur, evidence of the subsequent measures is not admissible to prove negligence, culpable conduct, a defect in a product, a defect in a product's design, or a need for a warning or instruction.

The amended rule thus makes clear that, in federal court:[445] (1) the rule applies and so bars evidence of a defendant's safety improvements[446] in strict products liability as well as negligence, and that it applies to all three types of defect;[447] and (2) the rule excludes only evidence of safety improvements adopted after the plaintiff's *injury*, leaving the admissibility of safety improvements made after manufacture but before the plaintiff's injury to the general rules of relevancy and prejudice.[448] While a large number of other issues remain unresolved,[449] the 1997 amendments to Fed. R. Evid. 407 considerably clarified how the repair doctrine applies to products liability cases under federal law.

In 2011, Rule 407 was amended again, in a manner "intended to be stylistic only."[450] The rule now provides in full:

Federal Rule of Evidence 407. Subsequent Remedial Measures

> When measures are taken that would have made an earlier injury or harm less likely to occur, evidence of the subsequent measures is not admissible to prove:
>
> - negligence;
> - culpable conduct;
> - a defect in a product or its design; or
> - a need for a warning or instruction.

---

[445] Most federal courts hold that the federal rule applies, rather than state law, in diversity cases. The Tenth Circuit was an exception, although that may have changed. See Sims v. Great Am. Life Ins. Co., 469 F.3d 870, 880 (10th Cir. 2006) (Okla. law) (characterizing as "dicta" its prior discussion of the application of state law rather than Rule 407, and stating that "we are persuaded that *Erie* is inapplicable to the Federal Rules of Evidence"). See generally Frumer, Friedman, and Sklaren, Products Liability § 18.06[3][g]; Stephenson, Alone and Out of Excuses: The Tenth Circuit's Refusal To Apply Federal Rule of Evidence 407 To Product Liability Actions, 36 N.M. L. Rev. 391 (2006); Casenote, 71 U. Colo. L. Rev. 757, 779–86 (2000) (excellent discussion).

[446] It may also apply to the admissibility of safety improvements made by *others* as well. See Hayes v. MTD Prods., Inc., 2008 WL 2859223 (W.D. Ky. 2008) (evidence of *other* manufacturers' subsequent remedial measures were inadmissible to prove "dangerousness" of lawnmower under Rule 407).

[447] See, e.g., Stahl v. Novartis Pharms. Corp., 283 F.3d 254, 270 n.10 (5th Cir. 2002) (warning added to package insert after plaintiff's injury not admissible to show that earlier warning was defective); J.B. Hunt Transp., Inc. v. General Motors Corp., 243 F.3d 441, 445 (8th Cir. 2001) (GM's subsequent design safety improvements in seat integrity inadmissible).

[448] See, e.g., Caraballo Rodriguez v. Clark Equip. Co., 147 F. Supp. 2d 66, 77 (D.P.R. 2001) (evidence of pre-accident service bulletin and warning decal on crane not barred by Rule 407). Compare United States Fid. & Guar. Co. v. Baker Material Handling Corp., 62 F.3d 24, 27 (1st Cir. 1995) (although evidence of pre-accident design change subject to Rule 403, Rule 407 did not apply). See generally Advisory Committee Note to the 1997 Amendments: "Evidence of subsequent measures that is not barred by Rule 407 may still be subject to exclusion on Rule 403 grounds when the dangers of prejudice or confusion substantially outweigh the probative value of the evidence."

[449] On Fed. R. Evid. 407, see Annot., 158 A.L.R. Fed. 609 (1999).

[450] Fed. R. Evid. 407 Advisory Committee's Note (2011 amendment).

> But the court may admit this evidence for another purpose, such as impeachment or—if disputed—proving ownership, control, or the feasibility of precautionary measures.

Strict Liability Claims Under State Law

While several states have adopted the 1997 clarifications of the federal rule,[451] the evidence codes and common law of most states still track the repair doctrine's traditional formulation in terms of negligence and culpability.[452] Courts agree that the repair doctrine applies to products liability claims based on negligence, but they split on whether the rule should be limited to such claims or instead should be expanded to shield manufacturers against strict products liability claims. Many states, by formal rule of evidence[453] or judicial opinion,[454] limit the exclusionary rule to negligence claims and so *allow* a plaintiff to introduce evidence of subsequent remedial measures in products liability cases based on strict liability. The classic case adopting this view is *Ault v. International Harvester Co.*,[455] which rejected the empirical assumptions underlying the rule in the modern products liability context:

> The contemporary corporate mass producer of goods, the normal products liability defendant, manufactures tens of thousands of units of goods; it is manifestly unrealistic to suggest that such a producer will forego making improvements in its product, and risk innumerable additional lawsuits and the attendant adverse effect upon its public image, simply because evidence of adoption of such improvement may be admitted in an action founded on strict liability for recovery on an injury that preceded the improvement.[456]

Yet, many other states have opted instead to broaden the rule beyond its traditional negligence basis so as to *exclude* evidence of subsequent remedial measures in the strict liability context as well.[457]

Courts that favor the exclusion of such evidence reason that the policies which support excluding such evidence in negligence cases—the questionable relevance of safety measures taken subsequent to a product's manufacture, the undesirability of

---

[451] See Ala. R. Evid. 407; Ariz. R. Evid. 407; Conn. Code Evid. § 4–7; Del. R. Evid. 407; Fla. Stat. Ann. § 90.407 (but omitting "defect in product's design, or a need for a warning or instruction"); Idaho R. Evid, 407; Ind. R. Evid. 407; Ky. R. Evid. 407; Me. R. Evid. 407; Miss. R. Evid. 407; Mont. R. Evid. 407; N.H. R. Evid. 407; N.D. R. Evid. 407; N.M. R. Evid. 11–407; Okla. Stat. Ann. tit. 12, § 2407; Pa. R. Evid. 407; S.D. Codified Laws § 19–19–407; Tex. R. Evid. 407; Utah R. Evid. 407; Vt. R. Evid. 407; W. Va. R. Evid. 407.

[452] Although many states have some version of the Federal Rules of Evidence, including Rule 407, many legislatures have not yet amended their rules to conform to more recent changes to Federal Rule 407 that explicitly applies to strict products liability claims.

[453] See, e.g., Alaska R. Evid., R. 407; Conn. Code Evid. § 4–7; Haw. Rev. Stat. § 626–1, R. 407; Iowa R. Evid., R. 5.407; Wyo. R. Evid. 407.

[454] See, e.g., Green v. Smith & Nephew AHP, Inc., 617 N.W.2d 881, 892–93 (Wis. Ct. App. 2000), aff'd, 629 N.W.2d 727 (Wis. 2001); Forma Scientific, Inc. v. Biosera, Inc., 960 P.2d 108, 111 (Colo. 1998) (rule 407 inapplicable to strict liability design defect claim); Wagner v. Clark Equip. Co., 700 A.2d 38 (Conn. 1997); McFarland v. Bruno Mach. Corp., 626 N.E.2d 659, 664 (Ohio 1994).

[455] 528 P.2d 1148 (Cal. 1974).

[456] Id. at 1152.

[457] See, e.g., Mohammad v. Toyota Motor Sales, U.S.A., Inc., 947 A.2d 598, 613–14 (Md. Ct. Spec. App. 2008) (recall notice inadmissible under Md. Rule 5–407(a)); First Premier Bank v. Kolcraft Enters., Inc., 686 N.W.2d 430, 449–52 (S.D. 2004) (overturning prior rulings); Duchess v. Langston Corp., 769 A.2d 1131, 1132–50 (Pa. 2001) (5–2 decision) (but allowing such evidence under both feasibility and impeachment exceptions); Hyjek v. Anthony Indus., 944 P.2d 1036, 1038 (Wash. 1997); Smith v. Black & Decker (U.S.), Inc., 650 N.E.2d 1108, 1113 (Ill. App. Ct. 1995) (noting "potential chilling effect on safety improvements").

discouraging safety improvements, and the risk of juror confusion—are as applicable to products liability claims that rest on strict liability as those that rest on negligence.[458] New York quite oddly straddles the issue, excluding evidence of subsequent remedial measures in strict products liability cases involving design and warning defects (unless feasibility is contested) while allowing such evidence in the much less typical context of manufacturing defects.[459]

Feasibility, Impeachment, and Other Limitations

The repair doctrine, which as a general rule excludes evidence of post-accident repairs, is subject to various exceptions that allow a plaintiff to present evidence of a manufacturer's subsequent remedial measures in certain situations. That is, the post-accident repair rule bars the use of such evidence only for the purpose of proving the defendant's negligence, culpability, or, in many jurisdictions, the product's defectiveness. By its terms, the doctrine does not affect the admissibility of post-accident repair evidence when offered "for another purpose."[460] In particular, the rule does *not* require the exclusion of evidence of subsequent remedial measures to prove "if disputed . . . the feasibility of precautionary measures,"[461] or to impeach a witness,[462] exceptions which often overlap.[463]

The significance of the "feasibility" and "impeachment" exceptions depends on how narrowly or widely they are interpreted and applied, and the integrity of this evidentiary rule depends on the exceptions not being applied so widely as to swallow the general rule of exclusion. A manufacturer, of course, controverts feasibility if it denies the *technological possibility* of a safety measure it subsequently adopts, even if it does so only implicitly, as by asserting that the product that injured the plaintiff was the safest possible.[464] So, too, a manufacturer "controverts" the "feasibility" of a safety measure if it explicitly denies that fact.[465] By the same token, if a manufacturer explicitly *admits* the feasibility of precautionary measures, proof that it subsequently adopted them normally should be excluded.[466]

---

[458] See, e.g., Duchess v. Langston Corp., 769 A.2d 1131, 1138–50 (Pa. 2001) (5–2 decision) (thoroughly examining applicability of traditional rationales to strict products liability).

[459] See Demirovski v. Skil Corp., 610 N.Y.S.2d 551, 552 (App. Div. 1994); Cover v. Cohen, 461 N.E.2d 864, 868 (N.Y. 1984).

[460] Fed. R. Evid. 407.

[461] Id. Note that the question of the *feasibility* of a safety improvement may raise another evidentiary issue—the admissibility of state-of-the-art evidence. In cases where technology has advanced from the time a product was manufactured to when the manufacturer adopted a safety improvement, the state-of-the-art doctrine is likely to bar evidence of the safety enhancement if it was practicably unavailable at the time of manufacture. See, e.g., Griffin v. Suzuki Motor Corp., 124 P.3d 57, 69 (Kan. 2005) (interpreting Kan. Stat. Ann. § 60–3307(a)(1)); Patton v. Hutchinson Wil-Rich Mfg. Co., 861 P.2d 1299, 1312–13 (Kan. 1993). On state of the art, see § 10.4, below.

[462] See, e.g., McCarthy v. 390 Tower Assocs., LLC, 800 N.Y.S.2d 875, 881–82 (App. Div. 2005); Wilson Foods Corp. v. Turner, 460 S.E.2d 532, 535 (Ga. Ct. App. 1995); Traylor v. Husqvarna Motor, 988 F.2d 729, 733–34 (7th Cir. 1993) (Ind. law).

[463] The overlap is most pronounced when a manufacturer's witness denies the feasibility of a safety measure it adopted shortly after the plaintiff's accident.

[464] See Frumer, Friedman, and Sklaren, Products Liability § 18.06[1][g].

[465] See, e.g., Reese v. Mercury Marine Div. of Brunswick Corp., 793 F.2d 1416, 1428 (5th Cir. 1986) (defendant denied feasibility of warnings subsequently added to instruction manual); Dixon v. International Harvester Co., 754 F.2d 573, 584 (5th Cir. 1985) (defendant's witness asserted that alternative design was not feasible because it would block tractor operator's view).

[466] See, e.g., Hathcock v. Hankook Tire Am. Corp., 330 S.W.3d 733, 742–43 (Tex. App. 2010) (defendant testified that alternative tire design was feasible at a cost of 30 to 50 cents per tire, but "would have made no

More difficult is the question of whether a manufacturer "controverts feasibility" of safety measures (or may have its witnesses impeached) because it defends the "safety," "reasonableness," or "acceptability" of its earlier design or warning. While a defendant's general arguments along these lines arguably might open the admissibility door under one or both exceptions, most courts have construed the exceptions more narrowly to prevent their swallowing the general rule of exclusion.[467]

The repair doctrine rests on the premise that a defendant normally should be allowed to assert that its product and actions both were safe and reasonable at the time of manufacture without having to contend with proof that it decided to improve the product at some later time. This suggests that the exceptions should not be interpreted so broadly as to allow a plaintiff to use a back-door exception to introduce evidence of a type and for a purpose that the general rule bars at the front—that the controverting-feasibility and impeachment exceptions should not be used to let in evidence of post-accident safety improvements to prove that a product was defective or the defendant was negligent.

So, if a manufacturer in fact concedes the economic and technological feasibility of a particular safety enhancement that it eventually adopted, it still may fairly argue that "the safety problem was not great enough to warrant the trade-off of consumer frustration, increased complexity of the product, and risk of consumer efforts to disconnect the safety device" without opening the door to proof that it adopted the enhancement under the feasibility or impeachment exception.[468] Thus, the feasibility and impeachment exceptions normally should be applied, and evidence of a subsequent corrective measure admitted, only if a manufacturer asserts that the measure was at least impracticable at the time.[469]

A variety of other issues lurk within the subsequent repair doctrine that may restrict or expand its use, and the resolution of such issues in state court may rest upon the particular state's formulation of the repair doctrine. While a great majority of the subsequent repair cases involve design or warning defects, the doctrine may also apply to defects in a product's manufacture.[470] One important issue that still divides the states

---

difference in the non-speed-rated tire"; feasibility of precautionary measure not controverted and plaintiff not entitled to the "exception to the subsequent remedial measure rule"); J.B. Hunt Transp., Inc. v. General Motors Corp., 243 F.3d 441, 445 n.3 (8th Cir. 2001) (defendant stipulated feasibility of stiffer seats by admitting that it had "tested proposed seating systems that were both stronger and not as strong as the seating system in the 1991 Camaro"); Kallio v. Ford Motor Co., 407 N.W.2d 92, 98 (Minn. 1987) (defendant conceded feasibility).

But a manufacturer may be too clever in first admitting "feasibility" and then attempting to limit its definition to technological possibility. See Duchess v. Langston Corp., 769 A.2d 1131, 1145–50 (Pa. 2001) (rejecting defendant's effort to avoid evidence of subsequent safety measure by admitting its feasibility, but only in terms of technological possibility, and arguing that its use would preclude the product from functioning properly).

[467] See Duchess v. Langston Corp., 769 A.2d 1131, 1145–50 (Pa. 2001); Frumer, Friedman, and Sklaren, Products Liability § 18.06[1][f].

[468] See, e.g., Gauthier v. AMF, Inc., 788 F.2d 634, 638 (9th Cir. 1986) (admission of evidence of subsequent remedial measures improper in view of manufacturer's concession of feasibility).

[469] Compare Duchess v. Langston Corp., 769 A.2d 1131, 1145–50 (Pa. 2001) (applying both exceptions and holding that trial court erred in excluding evidence of subsequently adopted interlock safety device where defendant challenged practicability of that device), with Keating v. United Instruments, Inc., 742 A.2d 128, 130–31 (N.H. 1999) (trial court properly excluded evidence of subsequent safety measure in aircraft altimeter because measure did not "directly" impeach defendant's expert).

[470] See, e.g., Rix v. General Motors Corp., 723 P.2d 195, 202 (Mont. 1986). See also Fed. R. Evid. 407, barring admission of subsequent remedial measures to prove, *inter alia*, "*a defect in a product* or its design; or

is *when* the exclusionary period begins—for remedial measures taken after the plaintiff's *accident or injury*, as the revised federal rule and some state courts hold,[471] or whether instead the rule should more broadly exclude evidence of any safety improvements made after the date a product is *manufactured or sold*.[472] The latter would seem to be the sounder view—to encourage safety enhancements at the earliest possible time.

Another question is whether the repair rule applies to safety measures taken by a third party, such as an employer who adds a safety feature to a product after an employee is injured; most courts hold that the doctrine is limited to defendant manufacturers and so does not bar evidence of safety improvements by third parties, which seems to make good sense, since employers have their own incentives to reduce injuries in order to keep workers compensation insurance rates low. Nevertheless, at least a couple of courts appear not to have thought the issue through and so rotely extend the exclusionary rule beyond manufacturers to remedial measures adopted by other parties.[473]

A further issue on which courts are split is whether the repair rule should apply to remedial measures required by the government, such as mandatory safety improvements ordered by NHTSA or another federal agency in charge of safety regulation, since here the safety-disincentive rationale disappears.[474] Moreover, such situations normally suggest strongly that such safety improvements were needed earlier and so should have been earlier adopted by the manufacturers of such products, which probably were dangerously defective without the safety improvements.

§ 6.5 RESTATEMENT (THIRD) OF TORTS: PRODUCTS LIABILITY

For most of the late twentieth century, § 402A of the *Restatement (Second) of Torts*, the fountainhead of modern products liability law, ruled supreme. With approval by the

---

a need for a warning or instruction" (emphasis added). For an early example, see Foley v. Coca-Cola Bottling Co., 215 S.W.2d 314, 317 (Mo. Ct. App. 1948) (tacks in soft drink; implied warranty).

[471] **Date of accident.** See, e.g., Blumer v. Ford Motor Co., 20 A.3d 1222, 1228 (Pa. Super. Ct. 2011) (no abuse of discretion in allowing testimony of "alternative braking systems contemplated by [defendant] prior to the accident at issue"); Myers v. Hearth Techs., Inc., 621 N.W.2d 787, 792 (Minn. Ct. App. 2001) (rule did not apply to, and so did not bar admission of, safety enhancement made before accident); Tucker v. Caterpillar, Inc., 564 N.W.2d 410 (Iowa 1997) (same).

[472] **Date of manufacture or sale.** See, e.g., Ariz. Rev. Stat. Ann. § 12–686(2) (rule applies to corrective measures adopted after sale); McCarthy v. 390 Tower Assocs., LLC, 800 N.Y.S.2d 875, 881 (App. Div. 2005) (evidence of remedial measures taken after sale of product inadmissible in negligent manufacturing case); Brown v. Ford Motor Co., 714 N.E.2d 556, 559 (Ill. App. Ct. 1999) (after sale or manufacture; same policy considerations apply); Cover v. Cohen, 461 N.E.2d 864, 868 (N.Y. 1984) (after manufacture).

[473] Compare Ford Motor Co. v. Nuckolls, 894 S.W.2d 897, 900 (Ark. 1995) (evidence that employer improved product's safety after accident was properly admitted), and Wagner v. Clark Equip. Co., 700 A.2d 38, 51 (Conn. 1997) (same), with Torrens v. Delta Int'l Mach. Corp., 696 N.Y.S.2d 230, 231 (App. Div. 1999) (evidence that employer, subsequent to accident, fashioned safety guard that would have prevented injury was properly excluded). See generally Annot., 64 A.L.R.5th 119 (1998) (admissibility of evidence of subsequent repairs by non-defendant third party).

[474] See Annot., 158 A.L.R.Fed. 609, at § 5 (1999) (citing cases both ways on whether there is a "superior authority" exception to Rule 407); Note, 1991 U. Ill. L. Rev. 843.

On product recalls, see § 10.8, below.

American Law Institute[475] of the *Restatement (Third) of Torts: Products Liability*[476] in 1997, § 402A of the *Second Restatement* was effectively repealed.[477] In its place now sits an entire *Restatement* dedicated solely to the topic of products liability law.[478] This section describes the process by which the ALI "restated" the law in this area, outlines the structure of the *Products Liability Restatement*, and summarizes its provisions.

Development

With the termination of a dubious "enterprise responsibility" project in 1991,[479] the American Law Institute turned to restating the law of torts in more conventional form. Because tort law had grown so large and cumbersome, the ALI decided for *Restatement* purposes to subdivide the law on this topic into various components. Due to the explosive expansion of products liability law after the promulgation of § 402A in the *Second Restatement of Torts* in 1965, the ALI announced in 1991 that the first of the new tort law *Restatements* would be the *Restatement (Third) of Torts: Products Liability*. In 1992, Professors James Henderson and Aaron Twerski were appointed Reporters for the

---

475 The American Law Institute (the "ALI" or "Institute") was formed in 1923 to clarify, simplify, and improve the common law of this nation. See W. D. Lewis, How We Did It, in ALI, Restatement in the Courts: History of the American Law Institute and the First Restatement of the Law 1 (perm. ed. 1945). With an elected membership of roughly 3,000 of the nation's 1.1 million judges, law professors, and practicing lawyers, the ALI's "Restatements" of various fields of law command broad respect.

For commentary on the ALI and the Restatement process, see, e.g., Rapp, Torts 2.0: The Restatement 3rd and the Architecture of Participation in American Tort Law, 37 Wm. Mitchell L. Rev. 1582, 1582 (2011); M. Green, The Unappreciated Congruity of the Second and Third Torts Restatements on Design Defects, 74 Brook. L. Rev. 807, 832 (2009); Adams, Blaming the Mirror: The Restatements and the Common Law, 40 Ind. L. Rev. 205 (2007); Symposium on the American Law Institute: Process, Partisanship, and the Restatements of Law, 26 Hofstra L. Rev. 567 (1998); Frank, The American Law Institute, 1923–1998, 26 Hofstra L. Rev. 615 (1998); Henderson and Twerski, The Politics of the Products Liability Restatement, 26 Hofstra L. Rev. 667 (1998); Schwartz, The Restatement (Third) of Torts: Products Liability—The American Law Institute's Process of Democracy and Deliberation, 26 Hofstra L. Rev. 743 (1998); Howells and Mildred, Is European Products Liability More Protective than the *Restatement (Third) of Torts: Products Liability*?, 65 Tenn. L. Rev. 985 (1998); Shapo, In Search of the Law of Products Liability: The ALI Restatement Project, 48 Vand. L. Rev. 631 (1995); Linde, Courts and Torts: "Public Policy" Without Public Politics?, 28 Val. U. L. Rev. 821, 840, 844 (1994); Wechsler, Restatements and Legal Change: Problems of Policy in the Restatement Work of the American Law Institute, 13 St. Louis U. L.J. 185 (1968); L. Green, The Torts Restatement, 29 Ill. L. Rev. 582, 591–92 (1935).

Among the several state treatments of the Restatement (3d) of Torts: Products Liability, see Steenson, A Comparative Analysis of Minnesota Products Liability Law and the Restatement (Third) of Torts: Products Liability, 24 Wm. Mitchell L. Rev. 1 (1998); Dreier, The *Restatement (Third) of Torts*: Products Liability and New Jersey Law—Not Quite Perfect Together, 50 Rutgers L. Rev. 2059 (1998); Thomas, Defining "Design Defect" in Pennsylvania: Reconciling *Azzarello* and the *Restatement (Third) of Torts*, 71 Temp. L. Rev. 217 (1998); Note, 101 W. Va. L. Rev. 285 (1998) (West Virginia).

476 In conformity with its standard practice, the ALI titled the new Restatement the "Restatement of the Law Third, Torts: Products Liability," which here is often cited as the "Products Liability Restatement."

477 The development of the Restatement (2d) Torts § 402A, is chronicled in § 5.3, above. For a summary analysis of the highlights of the Third Restatement, see Owen, Products Liability Law Restated, 49 S.C. L. Rev. 273 (1998).

478 At its annual meeting in Washington, D.C., on May 20, 1997, the ALI membership voted to adopt the Proposed Final Draft of the Products Liability Restatement, subject to editorial revision and amendments approved at the meeting.

479 Initially entitled "Compensation and Liability for Product and Process Injuries," the Enterprise Responsibility for Personal Injury Project results were published in 1991 in the form of a "Reporters' Study," which was never submitted to the ALI membership for approval. See ALI, Reporters' Study: Enterprise Responsibility for Personal Injury (1991). The project suffered from a variety of defects on which numerous observers, sometimes not unfairly, heaped their scorn. See, e.g., Phillips, Comments on the Reporters' Study of Enterprise Responsibility for Personal Injury, 30 San Diego L. Rev. 241 (1993).

project, and so began the conversion of a single section of the *Second Restatement*, § 402A, into an entire *Restatement* of its own.

Throughout the *Products Liability Restatement* project, the Reporters regularly met with and were advised by the ALI Council,[480] the ALI Advisers,[481] and the ALI Consultative Group comprised of interested members of the Institute.[482] In addition, the Reporters periodically met with and obtained advice from other groups and persons interested in the *Restatement* project, including various interest groups representing a wide variety of claimant, defense, academic, and other interests. Over the course of the project, beginning with Preliminary Draft No. 1 in 1993, the Institute circulated drafts of various portions of the *Restatement* to these special interest groups for comment and critique.[483] Beginning with Tentative Draft No. 1 in 1994, the full ALI membership[484] debated and voted on Tentative Drafts of various provisions at each of its annual meetings until the Institute's final debate and adoption of the Proposed Final Draft in May 1997. Although debates on each successive draft at these four ALI meetings were vigorous and occasionally contentious, the membership's final vote to adopt the Proposed Final Draft was unanimous.

Once the ALI voted to adopt the Proposed Final Draft in 1997, the Reporters folded in amendments from the final meeting,[485] and the *Restatement* as finally revised was reviewed for technical correctness and stylistic consistency.[486] To ensure that the final amendatory revisions remained faithful to the approval vote of the ALI membership, the final revisions were reviewed by several designated members of the Institute. In 1998, the Institute published the *Restatement (Third) of Torts: Products Liability*.

Structure

The *Products Liability Restatement* is comprised of four broad chapters, some of which are divided into sub-topics, for a total of 21 black-letter sections. The centerpiece of this *Restatement* is Chapter 1, Topic 1, entitled "Liability Rules Applicable to Products Generally." Topic 1, comprising §§ 1–4, contains basic liability standards and methods of proof. The first two sections within Topic 1 set forth the basic principles of liability,

---

[480] Roughly sixty lawyers, judges, and law professors comprise the ALI Council.

[481] Nineteen lawyers, judges, and law professors comprised the basic Adviser group and one especially clever law professor served as Editorial Adviser.

[482] Roughly three hundred lawyers, judges, and law professors who are members of the ALI comprised the Consultative Group.

[483] Prior to publication of the final version of the Products Liability Restatement in 1998, the ALI published a total of twelve drafts of various portions of the work: Preliminary Draft No. 1 (April 20, 1993); Council Draft No. 1 (September 17, 1993); Council Draft No. 1A (January 4, 1994); Tentative Draft No. 1 (April 12, 1994); Preliminary Draft No. 2 (May 19, 1994); Council Draft No. 2 (September 2, 1994); Tentative Draft No. 2 (Mar. 13, 1995); Preliminary Draft No. 3 (May 18, 1995); Council Draft No. 3 (November 15, 1995); Tentative Draft No. 3 (April 5, 1996); Proposed Final Draft (Preliminary Version), Volumes I and II (October 18, 1996); and the Proposed Final Draft (April 1, 1997).

[484] The ALI holds annual meetings in May for the principal purpose of debating and voting on drafts of Institute projects, including the various Restatements of the Law. Several hundred members attended the annual meetings from 1994 through 1997 at which the Products Liability Restatement drafts were considered and, typically, some 300 members were present and voted on issues put to the membership. Each year the Institute publishes an edited transcript of the annual meeting proceedings.

[485] During final debate on the Products Liability Restatement at the 1997 annual ALI meeting, the Proposed Final Draft was amended in various relatively minor respects. Some amendments were by formal vote while others were agreed to by the Reporters or specified by the Director to resolve problematic phraseology, mostly in the comments.

[486] Final technical proofing was conducted by the Reporters, the Editorial Adviser, and Deputy Directors of the Institute.

based on the concept of defectiveness, that apply to products generally. Section 1 provides the *Restatement*'s foundational rule—that commercial suppliers are subject to liability for physical harm caused by defects in products that they sell. Section 2, which contains definitions for defects in manufacture, design, and warnings and instructions, is the heart of the *Third Restatement*. Section 3 describes a circumstantial evidence doctrine, akin to the doctrine of res ipsa loquitur, for establishing defectiveness when the circumstances of an accident render it likely that it was caused by a product defect. Section 4, the final section in Topic 1, describes the effect of a product's violation of, or compliance with, governmental standards of product safety.

The second topic in Chapter 1, Liability Rules Applicable to Special Products or Product Markets, contains §§ 5–8. These sections set forth principles governing the liability of sellers of particular types of products: component parts, prescription drugs, food, and used products.

Chapters 2 (Liability of Commercial Product Sellers Not Based on Product Defects at Time of Sale) and 3 (Liability of Successors and Apparent Manufacturers), which include §§ 9–14, address other special duty issues: misrepresentation, post-sale duties to warn and recall, and the responsibilities of successor enterprises and apparent manufacturers. Chapter 4 (Provisions of General Applicability) first addresses, in §§ 15–18, causation issues and affirmative defenses based on user misconduct and contractual disclaimers. The final sections in Chapter 4, §§ 19–21, define "product," "seller," and "harm."

The most significant structural feature of the *Products Liability Restatement* is that its most important liability provisions, mostly contained in § 2, are configured in "functional" rather than "doctrinal" form. Rules, of course, may be formulated as they are *stated* by the courts ("doctrinal" form) or they may be restated as the courts in fact *apply* them ("functional" form). From the birth of § 402A of the *Second Restatement* in 1963–65, the hallmark of modern products liability law has been that liability is "strict." Yet the rhetoric of "strictness" proved so unrelenting that it hampered the reasoned evolution of doctrine over time. Products liability law-in-action continued to develop, but the language of the law (its doctrine) failed to keep pace.

The most prominent example of how doctrine lagged behind function concerns the definition of liability for design and warning dangers. Courts quickly discovered that they had no choice but to apply principles of reasonableness to resolve the difficult issues of balance between product usefulness, safety, cost, practicality, and information dissemination inherent in such cases. Whether one calls this method for determining liability "strict" or "popcorn," it is at bottom negligence. And, once one recognizes that responsibility in such cases must be limited by principles of foreseeability, as most courts have done,[487] then the liability standard is plainly one of negligence, and nothing more.[488] Increasingly, in other words, whatever "strictness" there ever was in a manufacturer's design and warning responsibility has drained away. Yet most courts,

[487] This development arose from the evolution of two doctrines in particular, both of which are addressed in later chapters: (1) the decline of the Wade-Keeton liability test, which presumes that a manufacturer knew at the time of manufacture the nature and extent of its product's hazards, and (2) the rise of the state-of-the-art defense. See §§ 8.7 and 10.4, below. The evolution of both doctrines is summarized in § 5.10, above.

[488] See Owen, Defectiveness Restated: Exploding the "Strict" Products Liability Myth, 1996 U. Ill. L. Rev. 743.

while often acknowledging the application of negligence principles in such cases, continued to insist on calling liability "strict," on calling a pig a mule.[489]

Many observers would have preferred that the *Third Restatement* preserve the form and language of the *Second Restatement*'s "strict" products liability doctrine as echoed by the courts in thousands of courtrooms and written decisions for three decades.[490] Others thought that doctrine should follow practice, suggesting that the liability rule in design and warning cases formally be returned to the law of negligence.[491] Perhaps not unwisely, in view of the undiluted passion of the warring camps, the Reporters decided to ignore the conventional doctrinal labels of "strict liability" and "negligence" and, instead, to define liability functionally according to the required proof.[492]

Basic Liability Provisions

Sections 1 and 2 define the fundamental rules of defectiveness theory and proof applicable to most products liability cases.[493] Grounding the *Restatement*, § 1 provides the overarching general principle of modern products liability law—that commercial enterprises are liable for harm caused by defects in products that they sell:

> **§ 1. Liability of Commercial Seller or Distributor for Harm Caused by Defective Products**
>
> One engaged in the business of selling or otherwise distributing products who sells or distributes a defective product is subject to liability for harm to persons or property caused by the defect.

Basing liability on whether a product is "defective," § 1 is bound together with § 2, which defines the three ways in which a defect may occur:

---

[489] See id. at 749.

[490] See, e.g., Shapo, A New Legislation: Remarks on the Draft Restatement of Products Liability, 30 U. Mich. J.L. Reform 215 (1997); Vandall, Constructing a Roof Before the Foundation Is Prepared: The *Restatement (Third) of Torts: Products Liability* Section 2(b) Design Defect, 30 U. Mich. J.L. Reform 261 (1997); Vargo, The Emperor's New Clothes: The American Law Institute Adorns a "New Cloth" for Section 402A Products Liability Design Defects—A Survey of the States Reveals a Different Weave, 26 U. Mem. L. Rev. 493, 557 (1996); Shapo, In Search of the Law of Products Liability: The ALI Restatement Project, 48 Vand. L. Rev. 631 (1995); Phillips, Achilles' Heel, 61 Tenn. L. Rev. 1265 (1994); Note, Just What You'd Expect: Professor Henderson's Redesign of Products Liability, 111 Harv. L. Rev. 2366 (1998).

[491] See, e.g., Owen, Products Liability Law Restated, 49 S.C. L. Rev. 273 (1998); Owen, Defectiveness Restated: Exploding the "Strict" Products Liability Myth, 1996 U. Ill. L. Rev. 743; Owen, The Graying of Products Liability Law: Paths Taken and Untaken in the New *Restatement*, 61 Tenn. L. Rev. 1241 (1994). Much of the following discussion draws from these articles.

[492] See Products Liability Rest. § 2 cmt. *n* (because design and warning claims rest on a risk-utility assessment regardless of doctrinal label, courts should not risk inconsistent verdicts by submitting such claims to juries on different causes of action, whether negligence, implied warranty, or strict liability in tort). At least one state supreme court agrees. See Wright v. Brooke Grp. Ltd., 652 N.W.2d 159, 169 (Iowa 2002) ("We question the need for or usefulness of *any* traditional doctrinal label in design defect cases because, as comment *n* points out, a court should not submit both a negligence claim and a strict liability claim based on the same design defect since both claims rest on an identical risk-utility evaluation. Moreover, to persist in using two names for the same claim only continues the dysfunction engendered by section 402A. Therefore, we prefer to label a claim based on a defective product design as a design defect claim without reference to strict liability or negligence.").

[493] Commentary on the great bulk of products liability law is loaded into the official Comments and Reporters' Notes to these two initial sections, particularly section 2.

§ 2. Categories of Product Defect

A product is defective when, at the time of sale or distribution, it contains a manufacturing defect, is defective in design, or is defective because of inadequate instructions or warnings. A product:

(a) contains a manufacturing defect when the product departs from its intended design even though all possible care was exercised in the preparation and marketing of the product;

(b) is defective in design when the foreseeable risks of harm posed by the product could have been reduced or avoided by the adoption of a reasonable alternative design by the seller or other distributor, or a predecessor in the commercial chain of distribution, and the omission of the alternative design renders the product not reasonably safe;

(c) is defective because of inadequate instructions or warnings when the foreseeable risks of harm posed by the product could have been reduced or avoided by the provision of reasonable instructions or warnings by the seller or other distributor, or a predecessor in the commercial chain of distribution, and the omission of the instructions or warnings renders the product not reasonably safe.[494]

The three liability standards in § 2 provide the foundation for most modern products liability law.[495]

Distinguishing the Separate Types of Defect

When Dean William Prosser crafted § 402A of the *Second Restatement of Torts* in the early 1960s, products liability law was in its infancy. At this very early stage in the development of the law, the defect concept was only roughly understood and conceived of quite naively as a unitary concept: products were either too dangerous (defective) or safe enough (nondefective). As courts in the 1960s and 1970s applied the principles of § 402A to an ever-widening array of products in an ever-widening range of contexts, the disparities among the various forms of product dangers increasingly revealed themselves. Today, most courts and commentators accept as axiomatic the fundamental distinctions between three very different forms of product defect: (1) manufacturing flaws, (2) design inadequacies, and (3) insufficient warnings of danger and instructions on safe use.[496] Over the decades since § 402A was adopted by the ALI, the need to develop different doctrinal approaches to the problems in these three very different contexts had become a well-accepted premise of products liability law.

Although § 1 of the *Products Liability Restatement* sets the doctrinal stage somewhat deceptively, by establishing a single principle of liability for harm from selling "defective" products, § 2 decisively splinters the notion into the three separate forms of defect.[497] Because the general principle of § 1 is rooted in the notion of a "defective

---

[494] Id. at § 2.

[495] The Comments to § 2 canvass most central issues in products liability law, and the Reporters' Note to this section in particular provides a wealth of case, statutory, and secondary authority on these issues.

[496] On the now-conventional nature of this tripartite classification, see Products Liability Rest. § 1 cmt. *a*, Reporters' Note. See also § 6.2, above.

[497] The Restatement continues this form of segregation by type of defect in various contexts, as in § 6 which separately defines the various duties of sellers of prescription drugs and medical devices by type of defect.

product" rather than fault, it might appear simply to restate the no-fault doctrine of "strict liability" that dominated products liability doctrine from the 1960s. However, apart from cases involving manufacturing flaws, the language of defectiveness is merely a cloak for a standard of design and warning "defect" liability that is grounded in fault. Indeed, the primary reason for trifurcating defectiveness in § 2 is to provide separate vessels for separate liability standards: subsection 2(a) defines liability for manufacturing defects in terms that are truly "strict," whereas subsections 2(b) and (c) define liability for design and warning defects largely in terms of negligence principles, notwithstanding the strict-sounding language of "defectiveness" in which the definitions are cast.[498] In short, liability in § 2 of the *Third Restatement* truly is strict for manufacturing defects but rests on negligence for design and warning defects.[499]

Manufacturing Defects

The *Third Restatement* defines the standard of liability for manufacturing defects in the strict liability manner of the law of contract. Thus, as seen above, a product is deemed defective in manufacture under § 2(a) "when the product departs from its intended design even though all possible care was exercised in the preparation and marketing of the product."[500] Although only a small number of courts have explicitly used this type of deviation-from-blueprints form of definition, it plainly is implied by the word "defective" when applied to the manufacturing flaw context. Seeing no need to define the straightforward notion of a manufacturing defect, most courts have seemed simply to assume this kind of commonsense definition.

The *Restatement*'s standard of liability for manufacturing defects, quite explicitly stated to be strict, was noncontroversial during the ALI debates on the *Restatement* and for nearly two decades of debate in Congress over scores of products liability bills. Because of the special significance of the user's expectation interests in manufacturing flaw cases, grounded in philosophic principles of equal freedom,[501] the strict-liability principle of contract law has long been recognized as appropriate in this context. Quite simply, true strict liability in this context is both logical and fair.

Design and Warning Defects

The *Third Restatement*'s liability standards for design and warning (and instruction) defects are formulated in parallel fashion in § 2, as seen above. Neither liability standard is stated in traditional strict liability or negligence terms. Instead, § 2

---

[498] The reasoning behind this move is explained in § 1, comment *a*. See Owen, Defectiveness Restated: Exploding the "Strict" Products Liability Myth, 1996 U. Ill. L. Rev. 743, 747–51. See also § 5.10, above, at notes 607–612.

[499] Comment *a* to § 2 provides in part: "The rules set forth in this Section establish separate standards of liability for manufacturing defects, design defects, and defects based on inadequate instructions or warnings." The comment explains that subsection (a) imposes "[s]trict liability without fault," and further provides:

> Subsections (b) and (c), which impose liability for products that are defectively designed or sold without adequate warnings or instructions and are thus not reasonably safe, achieve the same general objectives as does liability predicated on negligence.

It is important to note, however, that a retailer's liability under subsections 2(b) and 2(c), in contrast to the liability of a manufacturer, is truly strict. See Products Liability Rest. § 1 cmt. *e* and § 2 cmt. *o*. See § 15.2 (liability of retailers), below.

[500] Products Liability Rest. § 2(a).

[501] The policy reasons supporting strict liability in this context are summarized in Products Liability Rest. § 2 cmt. *a*. The reasons in moral theory are developed in Owen, The Moral Foundations of Products Liability Law: Toward First Principles, 68 Notre Dame L. Rev. 427, 467–68 (1993).

defines both design and warning defects in terms of the availability of a "reasonable alternative" design or warning. The Reporters selected this kind of "functional"[502] method for refashioning the basic liability tests because of the schizophrenic nature of design and warning liability law which, in doctrine, speaks the language of "strict" liability but which, in practice, bespeaks the law of negligence.[503] Products liability judicial opinions were simply stuck in a no-man's-land somewhere between negligence and true strict liability.

As a way around this doctrinal dilemma, the Reporters focused on the type of proof courts require to establish a design or warning defect case. What their research revealed, although hotly contested,[504] was that courts in these cases generally require a plaintiff to establish that the defendant reasonably could have adopted some alternative design or warning that would have prevented the plaintiff's harm.[505] Thus, in both design and warning cases, the *Products Liability Restatement* defines liability functionally in terms of whether the manufacturer reasonably could have provided a safer product. Stripping the rather cumbersome *Restatement* language to its essentials, the standard of liability under subsections 2(b) and (c) for design and warning defects may be translated[506] as follows:

> A product is defective if its foreseeable risks of harm could have been reduced by the adoption of a reasonable alternative design (or warning), the omission of which renders the product not reasonably safe.

Converted to the active voice, the *Restatement's* liability standard for design and warning defects reduces essentially to this:

> A product is defective if the seller failed to reduce its foreseeable risks of harm by adopting a reasonable alternative design (or warning), the omission of which renders the product not reasonably safe.

The requirements of "foreseeability" and "reasonableness" in subsections 2(b) and 2(c) effectively return the products liability standard for these types of cases to one of negligence—a rather remarkable retreat from § 402A's explicitly "strict" standard of liability of the *Second Restatement* that most courts for decades boldly purported to apply to design and warning cases. Thus, while reaffirming the doctrine of strict tort liability for manufacturing defects in subsection 2(a), subsections 2(b) and 2(c) of the *Third*

---

502 The Reporters aptly characterize their definitional approach as "functional," and cite widespread authority therefor. See § 1 cmt. *a* and § 2 cmt. *n*, and the Reporters' Note thereto.

503 See Owen, Defectiveness Restated: Exploding the "Strict" Products Liability Myth, 1996 U. Ill. L. Rev. 743, 747–51.

504 See, e.g., Vargo, The Emperor's New Clothes: The American Law Institute Adorns a "New Cloth" for Section 402A Products Liability Design Defects—A Survey of the States Reveals a Different Weave, 26 U. Mem. L. Rev. 493 (1996) (comprehensive survey of the states); Klemme, Comments to the Reporters and Selected Members of the Consultative Group, *Restatement of Torts (Third): Products Liability*, 61 Tenn. L. Rev. 1173 (1994); Vandall, The *Restatement (Third) of Torts: Products Liability* Section 2(b): The Reasonable Alternative Design Requirement, 61 Tenn. L. Rev. 1407, 1413–18 (1994).

505 For an extended discussion of this point, see the Products Liability Rest. Reporters' Note to § 2 cmt. *d*.

506 The Restatement's liability formulations are linguistically deconstructed in Owen, Defectiveness Restated, above, at 766–76.

Restatement abandon strict liability and apply negligence principles to design and warning cases.[507] This point is clearly made in comment *a* to § 1:

> [The strict liability] rule developed for manufacturing defects is inappropriate for [design and warnings claims]. These latter categories of cases require determinations that the product could have reasonably been made safer by a better design or instruction or warning. . . . [The definitions of defect in these cases] rely on a reasonableness test traditionally used in determining whether an actor has been negligent.[508]

Thus, the *Products Liability Restatement* grounds liability for design and warning defects in the reasonableness-balancing-negligence concepts that properly dominate the law of tort.[509] Particularly in the context of design dangers, most courts have come to employ a "risk-utility" test for ascertaining whether such dangers are excessive or acceptable.[510] In most cases, this determination is based upon a cost-benefit analysis of the manufacturer's choice to forego a safety improvement that the plaintiff claims was necessary to render the design reasonably safe.[511] This reasonable-safer-design concept lies at the heart of the *Third Restatement*'s definition of design defectiveness in subsection 2(b).

Consumer expectations remain entitled to important respect in evaluating design and warning defect claims,[512] but the comments to § 2 unceremoniously relieve consumer expectations of their elevated status as the test of liability under § 402A. Instead, the *Third Restatement*, following the approach of most courts,[513] relegates consumer expectations to the balancing calculus.[514] Some commentators vociferously complained of these definitional changes to the basic liability tests made by subsections 2(b) and (c) (and related comments), fearful that these provisions in the *Products Liability*

---

[507] Design and warning claims comprise the bulk of products liability causes of action. Together, such claims were asserted in 60% of products liability claims in one early study, and 71% of strict liability in tort claims in another. In a later study of large claims (in excess of $100,000) in which strict liability was the main theory of liability, defective design was the theory in 75% of the claims, and warning defects was the theory in 18%. See § 1.3, above.

[508] Products Liability Rest. § 1 cmt. *a*.

[509] The grounding of these principles in moral theory is explained elsewhere. See Owen, Philosophical Foundations of Fault in Tort Law, in Philosophical Foundations of Tort Law 201 (D. Owen ed., Oxford, 1995); Owen, The Moral Foundations of Products Liability Law: Toward First Principles, 68 Notre Dame L. Rev. 427, 467–68 (1993).

[510] For surveys of how different states define the risk-utility test, see the Products Liability Rest. Reporters' Note to § 2 cmt. *d* (concluding that most courts use a risk-utility test), Owen, Risk-Utility Balancing in Design Defect Cases, 30 U. Mich. J.L. Reform 239 (1997) (same), and Vargo, 26 U. Mem. L. Rev. 493 (1996) (querulously challenging this conclusion).

[511] How the cost-benefit test is and should be formulated is closely examined in Owen, Risk-Utility Balancing in Design Defect Cases, 30 U. Mich. J.L. Reform 239 (1997), and Owen, Toward a Proper Test for Design Defectiveness: "Micro-Balancing" Costs and Benefits, 75 Tex. L. Rev. 1661 (1997).

[512] "[A]lthough consumer expectations do not constitute an independent standard for judging the defectiveness of product designs, they may substantially influence or even be ultimately determinative on risk-utility balancing in judging whether the omission of a proposed alternative design renders the product not reasonably safe." Products Liability Rest. § 2 cmt. *g*.

[513] Compare Potter v. Chicago Pneumatic Tool Co., 694 A.2d 1319 (Conn. 1997) (retaining consumer expectations test in name, but redefining it in cost-benefit terms), discussed at § 8.6, below.

[514] See Products Liability Rest. § 2 cmt. *f*. Risk-utility balancing normally is used only in design cases. While it applies in some respects to warning cases, such cases are by their nature more fundamentally based on the frustration of expectations. Nevertheless, for a variety of good reasons, negligence principles properly govern warning cases, too. See Owen, The Moral Foundations of Products Liability Law: Toward First Principles, 68 Notre Dame L. Rev. 427, 465–66 (1993).

Restatement would jettison decades of consumer protection progress in this area of the law.[515] Yet, by shifting from "strict" liability to negligence principles, the *Third Restatement* merely "restates" what most courts had long been doing if rarely saying.

It has been an open secret for many years that while purporting to apply "strict" liability doctrine to design and warning cases, courts in fact have been applying principles that look remarkably like negligence.[516] That is, most courts in most contexts have based the defective determination in both design and warning cases on risk-utility principles of balance, reasonableness, and foreseeability. Except in certain very limited contexts, courts have rejected efforts to make manufacturers guarantors of product safety, requiring only that manufacturers (1) design their products as safe as they are reasonably able to do; and (2) warn of foreseeably material risks, by methods that are reasonably available and reasonably likely to be effective.[517] This is negligence, pure and simple, in fact if not in name. Consequently, by grounding liability for design and warning defects in principles of negligence, the *Third Restatement* truly "restates" the law—no doubt quite differently from how most courts stated the law to be, but in fact quite closely to how most courts functionally applied the law in litigation.[518]

The Basic Limitations on Liability—in General

In the jurisprudence of products liability law, the basic limitations on liability have proved at least as significant, and their contours have been litigated at least as frequently, as the basic definitions of defectiveness. A review of the basic liability principles would be incomplete without at least a mention of four of the most important boundary issues of products liability law: obvious dangers, inherent product dangers, foreseeability, and product misuse and alteration.

Obvious Dangers

Courts hold that manufacturers should be protected, at least to some extent, from responsibility for accidents attributable to dangers that are obvious.[519] Almost all courts agree that manufacturers have no duty to warn of obvious dangers for the simple reason that there is no need to inform people further of dangers that a product on its face already displays.[520] Yet, the proper role of a danger's obviousness in determining design defects is more difficult and subtle. Although the old no-duty rule for obvious dangers in this context is now properly defunct as an independent doctrine in almost all jurisdictions,

---

515 See, e.g., Little, The Place of Consumer Expectations in Product Strict Liability Actions for Defectively Designed Products, 61 Tenn. L. Rev. 1189 (1994).

516 See, e.g., Owen, Defectiveness Restated: Exploding the "Strict" Products Liability Myth, 1996 U. Ill. L. Rev. 743; Davis, Design Defect Liability: In Search of a Standard of Responsibility, 39 Wayne L. Rev. 1217, 1238–48 (1993); Powers, Jr., A Modest Proposal to Abandon Strict Products Liability, 1991 U. Ill. L. Rev. 639; Henderson and Twerski, Doctrinal Collapse in Products Liability: The Empty Shell of Failure to Warn, 65 N.Y.U. L. Rev. 265, 277–78 (1990); Birnbaum, Unmasking the Test for Design Defect: From Negligence (to Warranty) to Strict Liability to Negligence, 33 Vand. L. Rev. 593, 601 (1980). This divergence between illusory strict liability doctrine and actual liability principles is diagrammatically portrayed in Owen, The Fault Pit, 26 Ga. L. Rev. 703, 706 (1992).

517 In addition, of course, manufacturers must not misrepresent the safety of their products.

518 At least one state supreme court has followed the Third Restatement's lead in defining design defectiveness functionally and ignoring traditional theories of recovery. See Wright v. Brooke Grp. Ltd., 652 N.W.2d 159, 169 (Iowa 2002).

519 See Products Liability Rest. § 2 cmt. *j*. In addition to dangers that are obvious, most of the same limiting principles apply to dangers that generally are known. See § 10.2, below.

520 "When a risk is obvious or generally known, the prospective addressee of a warning will or should already know of its existence." Products Liability Rest. § 2 cmt. *j*.

courts that test a product's design defectiveness according to consumer expectations are logically compelled to shield manufacturers from design liability in cases where the danger is apparent on the product's face. As discussed above, however, most courts now ascertain a design's defectiveness according to some form of risk-utility balancing of the costs and benefits of failing to adopt a proposed alternative design. Within this calculus, obviousness of danger is properly considered to be an important—but not necessarily decisive—factor in the ultimate balance that determines design defectiveness. The *Third Restatement* reaffirms these widely accepted limitations that courts place on recovery for injuries from dangers that are obvious.[521]

Inherent Product Dangers

A perplexing issue in the law of products liability is whether manufacturers should be held responsible for injuries resulting from inherent product hazards that are incapable of being designed or warned away.[522] Many products, from simple kitchen knives and matches to complex chemicals and aircraft, may be classified as possessing such inherent dangers. In most such cases, however, the product's benefits so clearly outweigh its risks that liability for the product's general inherent risk is never litigated. Some courts and commentators, however, have questioned whether manufacturers of certain unavoidably dangerous products should be subject to liability—or, instead, should be *immune* from liability—for the harm such products inevitably cause. Surely the most notorious product of this type today is the cigarette, but alcoholic beverages, cheap handguns, and certain other products all might be viewed as inherently defective because they arguably cause more social harm than good.

Producers of such generically dangerous products argue that they are merely providing lawful goods consumers demand and, accordingly, that they should not be held accountable for harm from danger that is unavoidably part and parcel of the demanded product design. Some consumer advocates argue to the contrary that, while products of this type (say, cigarettes or cheap handguns) may be "demanded" by consumers, such "goods" are inherently bad (defective) if the aggregate social harm they cause exceeds their aggregate benefit. At bottom, this debate involves fundamental questions of separation of powers between the legislative and judicial branches of government, for arguably the decision of whether the harm from cigarettes should be paid for by cigarette manufacturers is properly a legislative rather than judicial decision, if properly a governmental decision at all. Attitudes and the law are still in flux on responsibility for cigarette-caused harm,[523] but the courts historically have almost universally shut their doors to design defect claims arising from generic product dangers which unavoidably inhere in a product's design.[524] On this intriguing issue, the *Restatement* adopts the

---

[521] For the warning context, see Products Liability Rest. § 2 cmt. *j*, which provides in part: "In general, a product seller is not subject to liability for failing to warn or instruct regarding risks and risk avoidance measures that should be obvious to, or generally known by, foreseeable product users." For the design context, see id. § 2 cmt. *d*, which provides in part: "Subsection (b) does not recognize the obviousness of a design-related risk as precluding a finding of defectiveness. The fact that a danger is open and obvious is relevant to the issue of defectiveness, but does not necessarily preclude a plaintiff from establishing that a reasonable alternative design should have been adopted that would have reduced or prevented injury to the plaintiff."

[522] On inherent product hazards, see § 10.3, below.

[523] See § 10.3, below.

[524] In rare instances where courts have allowed liability in these cases, legislatures generally have overturned the judicial decisions. See Products Liability Rest. § 2 cmt. *d*, Reporters' Note.

prevailing view that, except in extreme cases,[525] and putting aside the special case of cigarettes, the courts have no business legislating the overall desirability of necessarily dangerous but widely-consumed products.

Foreseeability

Whether manufacturers should or should not be responsible in "strict" products liability for unforeseeable risks is an issue that long divided courts and commentators.[526] Prior to the mid-1980s, courts and commentators widely assumed that the "strictness" of liability under § 402A precluded a defense based on the unforeseeability of the risk.[527] But two decisions in the mid-1980s, the first in New Jersey[528] and the second in California,[529] boldly renounced the illogic and unfairness of holding pharmaceutical manufacturers liable for harm they could neither anticipate nor prevent, and the California court subsequently expanded this fault-based principle to producers generally.[530] In recent years, while an occasional court still clings tenaciously to the notion that strict liability for defective design and warning should not depend upon the foreseeability of the risk,[531] most courts squarely confronting the issue have shielded manufacturers from liability for harm caused by unforeseeable product risks.[532] The *Third Restatement*'s explicit limitation of liability to foreseeable risks of harm in § 2, in addition to being based on logic and fairness, thus in fact restates the law applied by most courts.[533]

---

[525] Extreme cases involve products of "manifestly unreasonable design." Products Liability Rest. § 2 cmt. *e*. Such a product may be ruled defective because "the extremely high degree of danger posed by its use or consumption so substantially outweighs its negligible social utility that no rational, reasonable person, fully aware of the relevant facts, would choose to use, or to allow children to use, the product." Id.

[526] This was the central feature of the Wade-Keeton liability test, and this issue variously has been posed in terms of "undiscoverable dangers" or of whether the discoverability of the risk was within the "state of the art." See §§ 8.7 and 10.4, below.

[527] From the initial adoption of the doctrine of strict products liability in tort during the mid-1960s, courts routinely made this point. But, in cases where liability was established, negligence or warranty doctrine typically was sufficient for liability on the facts, for there were usually fairly simple steps that the manufacturer reasonably could have taken to prevent the harm. The first noteworthy decision to emphasize and explain the "strictness" of strict tort liability for selling defective products, on facts where liability turned on the foreseeability of the risk, was Beshada v. Johns-Manville Prods. Corp., 447 A.2d 539 (N.J. 1982). For the rise and fall of *Beshada*, see § 10.4, below.

[528] Feldman v. Lederle Labs., 479 A.2d 374, 388 (N.J. 1984) (restricting *Beshada*, 447 A.2d 539, an asbestos case, to its facts).

[529] Brown v. Superior Ct., 751 P.2d 470 (Cal. 1988). To some extent, the California court backtracked doctrinally from *Brown* in Carlin v. Superior Court, 920 P.2d 1347 (Cal. 1996).

[530] The California Supreme Court extended its rejection of true strict liability beyond prescription drugs to other products in Anderson v. Owens-Corning Fiberglas Corp., 810 P.2d 549 (Cal. 1991) (asbestos). *But cf. Carlin*, 920 P.2d 1347 (reaffirming the "strict liability" label).

[531] See, e.g., Golonka v. General Motors Corp., 65 P.3d 956, 963 (Ariz. Ct. App. 2003); Green v. Smith & Nephew AHP, Inc., 629 N.W.2d 727 (Wis. 2001); Sternhagen v. Dow Co., 935 P.2d 1139, 1142–45 (Mont. 1997) (knowledge of danger, whether or not discoverable, is to be imputed to manufacturer; state-of-the-art evidence is not admissible to show that manufacturer could not have known of danger). See § 10.4, below.

[532] Even the California decision that reaffirmed the applicability of "strict" products liability to drug warning cases, Carlin v. Superior Ct., 920 P.2d 1347 (Cal. 1996), limits liability to risks that are foreseeable.

[533] Comment *a* to § 2 provides in part: "Most courts agree that, for the liability system to be fair and efficient, the balancing of risks and benefits in judging product design and marketing must be done in light of the knowledge of risks and risk-avoidance techniques reasonably attainable at the time of distribution. . . . [M]anufacturers may persuasively ask to be judged by a normative behavior standard to which it is reasonably possible for manufacturers to conform. For these reasons, Subsections (b) and (c) speak of products being defective only when risks are reasonably foreseeable." Products Liability Rest. § 2 cmt. *a*. Cf. id. § 2 cmt. *m*. For the propriety of this approach in moral theory, see Owen, The Moral Foundations of Products Liability Law: Toward First Principles, 68 Notre Dame L. Rev. 427, 465–67, 483–84, and 490–92 (1993).

Product Misuse and Alteration

When people choose to use and abuse products in ways that are unforeseeable and unreasonable, courts generally relieve manufacturers of at least partial responsibility for resulting harm.[534] Products can hardly be designed to do all things safely for all people, and so product misuse and alteration provide important limitations on liability for the sale of defective products. While courts widely hold that manufacturers have a duty to adopt reasonable precautions against uses, misuses, and alterations that in fact are reasonably foreseeable, manufacturers generally have no duty to protect against uses and abuses that are not foreseeable. The "defense" of misuse by a user,[535] and proximate cause in cases of third-party misuse,[536] bar liability altogether if a misuse was unforeseeable, and the principles of comparative responsibility generally reduce the responsibility of a manufacturer proportionate to the user's own fault for putting a product to an improper type or extent of use.[537] The *Products Liability Restatement* adopts these widespread views on the role of product alteration and misuse.[538]

Circumstantial Proof of Defect

Section 3 provides a method for establishing product defect when the specific kind of proof contemplated by the § 2 definitions has been destroyed in an accident or is otherwise practicably unavailable. While plaintiffs ordinarily must prove their cases under the § 2 defect provisions, § 3 provides a mechanism for establishing liability by circumstantial evidence in special cases where logic and fairness suggest that a plaintiff's inability to establish a specific defect according to conventional proof requirements should not preclude the claim. In such cases, proof of defect under § 3 is allowed when the very circumstances of the accident themselves suggest, more probably than not, that the accident was caused by a product defect rather than something else:

> **§ 3. Circumstantial Evidence Supporting Inference of Product Defect**
>
> It may be inferred that the harm sustained by the plaintiff was caused by a product defect existing at the time of sale or distribution, without proof of a specific defect, when the incident that harmed the plaintiff:
>
> (a) was of a kind that ordinarily occurs as a result of product defect; and
>
> (b) was not, in the particular case, solely the result of causes other than product defect existing at the time of sale or distribution.[539]

Section 3, roughly adapted from the res ipsa loquitur provision of the *Second Restatement of Torts*,[540] might fairly be termed a principle of "defect ipsa loquitur." This section adopts the so-called "malfunction doctrine" which a number of states have

---

[534] "Product sellers . . . are not required to foresee and take precautions against every conceivable mode of use and abuse to which their products might be put. Increasing the costs of designing and marketing products in order to avoid the consequences of unreasonable modes of use is not required." Products Liability Rest. § 2 cmt. *m*. See ch. 13, below.

[535] See § 13.5, below.

[536] See § 12.3, below.

[537] See Products Liability Rest. § 2 cmt. *p*. See also § 13.3, below.

[538] See id. § 2 cmts. *m* (foreseeability of risk), *p* (misuse, modification, and alteration); id. § 15 (legal causation); id. § 17 (apportionment of responsibility). Damages apportionment, treated generally in § 17 as an issue of comparative responsibility, is addressed thoroughly in its own Restatement. See Rest. (3d) Torts: Apportionment of Liability.

[539] Products Liability Rest. § 3.

[540] The Reporters drew § 3 from § 328D of the Rest. (2d) Torts. See Products Liability Rest. § 3 cmt. *a*.

explicitly adopted, and which most implicitly apply, to accommodate problems of proof that plague plaintiffs when events conspire to eliminate direct evidence of a specific defect but where circumstances suggest that the product's failure most probably resulted from a defect. For example, if a new electric coffee maker spontaneously ignites, burning its electrical components beyond recognition in the resulting fire, one may reasonably assume that the fire was caused by some defect in its electrical mechanism. This is true even though, because of the nature of the product accident, direct proof of defect from an examination of the product itself is simply unavailable.

Product Safety Statutes and Regulations

The final basic liability provision in the *Third Restatement*, § 4, addresses how a product's compliance or noncompliance with statutory or regulatory rules of product safety affects defectiveness.[541] Subsection 4(a) provides that a product is defective if its design, warning, or instruction violates a product safety statute or safety regulation and a person is injured by the risk which the statute or regulation attempts to reduce. This section effectively converts the widespread, conventional doctrine of "negligence per se" into a new doctrine of "defectiveness per se."

Subsection (b) addresses the opposite issue, whether a manufacturer may successfully *defend* a case if the product's design, warning, or instruction *conforms* to some safety statute or regulation. Following the approach of virtually all courts, the *Third Restatement* provides that compliance with such safety provisions is merely some evidence that a product is not defective, so that a defect determination is still possible in many cases.

The reasoning for this limited role for compliance with safety statutes and regulations is that such provisions normally prescribe minimum levels of acceptable safety, below which a manufacturer's conduct is criminalized. Because such safety provisions usually do not reach a higher level of safety contemplated by the law of negligence and "strict" products liability, a product's design or warning may comport with the minimum required by the criminal safety statute or regulation yet still be unacceptably dangerous under notions of cost-effectiveness and reasonableness inherent in the principles of products liability law, a branch of common law developed and applied by the courts independent of statutory and regulatory law. Section 4 provides:

> **§ 4. Noncompliance and Compliance with Product Safety Statutes or Regulations**
>
> In connection with liability for defective design or inadequate instructions or warnings:
>
> (a) a product's noncompliance with an applicable product safety statute or administrative regulation renders the product defective with respect to the risks sought to be reduced by the statute or regulation; and
>
> (b) a product's compliance with an applicable product safety statute or administrative regulation is properly considered in determining whether the product is defective with respect to the risks sought to be reduced by the statute or regulation, but such compliance does not preclude as a matter of law a finding of product defect.

---

[541] See §§ 2.4 and 6.4, above, and § 14.4, below.

In sum, §§ 1 through 4 of the *Products Liability Restatement* together comprise a framework of principles that resolve the great bulk of liability issues in ordinary products liability litigation.

Component Parts and Raw Materials

Courts have had a difficult time determining just when the supplier of a raw material (such as iron ore or asbestos) or a component part (such as a motor in an industrial machine) should bear responsibility for injuries from a defective product into which the material or component is integrated by an assembling manufacturer.[542] The *Products Liability Restatement* takes a commonsense approach to this problem, holding a supplier liable if: (1) the material or component is itself defective, or (2) the component supplier so substantially participates in integrating the component into the assembled design of the integrated product that the component's supplier becomes in essence a co-designer of that final product. Section 5 provides:

> **§ 5. Liability of Commercial Seller or Distributor of Product Components for Harm Caused by Products Into Which Components Are Integrated**
>
> One engaged in the business of selling or otherwise distributing product components who sells or distributes a component is subject to liability for harm to persons or property caused by a product into which the component is integrated if:
>
> (a) the component is defective in itself, as defined in this Chapter, and the defect causes the harm; or
>
> (b)(1) the seller or distributor of the component substantially participates in the integration of the component into the design of the product; and
>
> (2) the integration of the component causes the product to be defective, as defined in this Chapter; and
>
> (3) the defect in the product causes the harm.

Defective Drugs and Medical Devices

Consistent with the developing law, sellers of prescription drugs (and medical devices, such as pacemakers) are accorded special protection in § 6 of the *Third Restatement*. Manufacturers of such products are subject to true strict liability for manufacturing defects in their products, just as sellers of other types of products. But, because the safety (and efficacy) of prescription drugs and medical devices are heavily regulated by a powerful governmental agency, the Food and Drug Administration (the FDA), which scrutinizes and regulates the "design" of prescription drugs and medical devices and the warnings and instructions that accompany such products, courts have tended to treat manufacturers of such products somewhat differently than producers of other types of products.[543]

Only infrequently have courts held prescription drug manufacturers liable for *design* defects, and the *Products Liability Restatement* mirrors this perspective by

---

542 See § 15.3, below.

543 See ch. 18, below.

strictly limiting design liability in § 6(c) to cases where a drug is shown to have no net value for *any* class of patient. Section 6(d) restates the "learned intermediary" doctrine for warning cases, which usually obligates prescription drug manufacturers to warn only the prescribing physician, not the patient. Finally, § 6(e) provides that pharmacists and other retail sellers are subject only to negligence liability for selling such products containing design or warning defects. Section 6 provides:

§ 6. Liability of Commercial Seller or Distributor for Harm Caused by Defective Prescription Drugs and Medical Devices

(a) A manufacturer of a prescription drug or medical device who sells or otherwise distributes a defective drug or medical device is subject to liability for harm to persons caused by the defect. A prescription drug or medical device is one that may be legally sold or otherwise distributed only pursuant to a health-care provider's prescription.

(b) For purposes of liability under Subsection (a), a prescription drug or medical device is defective if at the time of sale or other distribution the drug or medical device:

(1) contains a manufacturing defect as defined in § 2(a); or

(2) is not reasonably safe due to defective design as defined in Subsection (c); or

(3) is not reasonably safe due to inadequate instructions or warnings as defined in Subsection (d).

(c) A prescription drug or medical device is not reasonably safe due to defective design if the foreseeable risks of harm posed by the drug or medical device are sufficiently great in relation to its foreseeable therapeutic benefits that reasonable health-care providers, knowing of such foreseeable risks and therapeutic benefits, would not prescribe the drug or medical device for any class of patients.

(d) A prescription drug or medical device is not reasonably safe due to inadequate instructions or warnings if reasonable instructions or warnings regarding foreseeable risks of harm are not provided to:

(1) prescribing and other health-care providers who are in a position to reduce the risks of harm in accordance with the instructions or warnings; or

(2) the patient when the manufacturer knows or has reason to know that health-care providers will not be in a position to reduce the risks of harm in accordance with the instructions or warnings.

(e) A retail seller or other distributor of a prescription drug or medical device is subject to liability for harm caused by the drug or device if:

(1) at the time of sale or other distribution the drug or medical device contains a manufacturing defect as defined in § 2(a); or

(2) at or before the time of sale or other distribution of the drug or medical device the retail seller or other distributor fails to exercise reasonable care and such failure causes harm to persons.

Food

The principal feature of § 7, the special section on food products, is its explicit adoption of the so-called "consumer expectations" test of liability for food containing injurious matter, such as the proverbial mouse in a bottle of Coke, or a nail or fish bone in a can of fish soup.[544] Some states formerly applied the "foreign-natural" test, which held the seller liable only if the injurious substance was "foreign" to the food item, as a nail in fish soup. By the same token, if a substance "naturally" occurred in the product, such as a fish bone in fish soup, then consumers might fairly be on the lookout for it, so that consumers should be responsible for any resulting harm. Although this "foreign-natural" test often worked efficiently, fairly, and consistently with reasonable consumer expectations, sometimes it did not. Accordingly, courts have largely switched to the more functional, and more flexible, consumer expectations test in food cases of this type. Thus, the *Restatement*'s adoption of this test is consistent with the developed law on liability for the sale of defective food products. Section 7 provides:

> **§ 7. Liability of Commercial Seller or Distributor for Harm Caused by Defective Food Products**
>
> One engaged in the business of selling or otherwise distributing food products who sells or distributes a food product that is defective under § 2, § 3, or § 4 is subject to liability for harm to persons or property caused by the defect. Under § 2(a), a harm-causing ingredient of the food product constitutes a defect if a reasonable consumer would not expect the food product to contain that ingredient.

Used Products

Retail sellers of used products often are far less able than manufacturers of new products to eliminate defects in their products, especially defects in design. Moreover, buyers of used automobiles and other products usually do not expect the product to have the same level of safety in all respects as such products when they were new. Accordingly, courts often treat sellers of used products more leniently in products liability cases than manufacturers of new products.[545] Reflecting this perspective, § 8(a) provides that sellers of used products generally are liable only if they are negligent, with the following limited exceptions: where consumers fairly *do* expect the same degree of safety as a new product (such as the buyer of an automobile used only for one week), § 8(b); where products are sold as "remanufactured," § 8(c); and where a consumer's injuries are attributable to the seller's violation of an applicable safety statute or regulation, § 8(d). Section 8 provides:

> **§ 8. Liability of Commercial Seller or Distributor of Defective Used Products**
>
> One engaged in the business of selling or otherwise distributing used products who sells or distributes a defective used product is subject to liability for harm to persons or property caused by the defect if the defect:
>
> (a) arises from the seller's failure to exercise reasonable care; or

[544] See § 7.5, below.

[545] See § 16.5, below.

(b) is a manufacturing defect under § 2(a) or a defect that may be inferred under § 3 and the seller's marketing of the product would cause a reasonable person in the position of the buyer to expect the used product to present no greater risk of defect than if the product were new; or

(c) is a defect under § 2 or § 3 in a used product remanufactured by the seller or a predecessor in the commercial chain of distribution of the used product; or

(d) arises from a used product's noncompliance under § 4 with a product safety statute or regulation applicable to the used product.

A used product is a product that, prior to the time of sale or other distribution referred to in this Section, is commercially sold or otherwise distributed to a buyer not in the commercial chain of distribution and used for some period of time.

Misrepresentation

Section 9 concerns the liability of suppliers for misrepresentation.[546] This section of the *Products Liability Restatement* broadly provides that the general principles of tortious misrepresentation apply to products liability cases. All states agree that a product seller is liable in tort for harm from wrongful misrepresentation, that is, for fraudulent (intentional) and negligent misrepresentation. And all states, under Uniform Commercial Code § 2–313 on express warranties, hold sellers liable in *contract* for damages caused by misrepresentation without regard to fault. What is more questionable is whether a seller should also be liable in *tort* for misrepresentation in the absence of the seller's fault—that is, whether product sellers should be strictly liable in tort for misrepresentation.

The *Restatement (Second) of Torts*, in § 402B, promulgated by the ALI in 1965, did provide for such a strict liability rule for a seller's public misrepresentations. Courts in a few states, notably in California, Texas, and Pennsylvania, and Ohio's legislature, adopted § 402B, but most states have not. Instead, most states have left the doctrine of strict seller liability for misrepresentations to the law of contract and, in particular, to UCC § 2–313. So, while perhaps noncontroversial at a substantive level (almost everyone agrees that sellers should be strictly liable for physical harm from misrepresentations), § 9 of the *Third Restatement* "restates" tort law logically but more boldly than it actually exists in most states. Section 9 will require courts to confront anew the issue of whether the doctrine of product seller responsibility for misrepresentation without fault should be left exclusively to the law of contract or whether instead the law of torts should be broadened to embrace the doctrine as well. Section 9 provides:

§ 9. Liability of Commercial Product Seller or Distributor for Harm Caused by Misrepresentation

One engaged in the business of selling or otherwise distributing products who, in connection with the sale of a product, makes a fraudulent, negligent, or innocent misrepresentation of material fact concerning the product is subject to liability for harm to persons or property caused by the misrepresentation.

[546] See chapter 3, above.

Post-Sale Duty to Warn

The liability of sellers for defects that become known after a product is placed on the market is covered in §§ 10 and 11. Once a product already is on the market and in the hands of consumers, a manufacturer who discovers a defective condition in the product can do only one of two things to remedy the danger: (1) it can attempt to provide a warning to consumers who own the product, and/or (2) it can recall the product, to fix the defect or destroy the product.[547]

Section 10 concerns the liability of a supplier for failing to warn of a danger discovered after a product is sold. Responsibility for failing to provide post-sale warnings, in § 10(a), is controlled by rules of negligence: a seller must warn in situations where it is "reasonable" to do so. However, rather than leave the issue of reasonableness in this context open-ended, the *Restatement* in § 10(b) follows a number of well-reasoned judicial opinions which particularize when the duty to warn will arise in this context according to a balance of certain prescribed factual issues: the existence of a substantial danger of which the seller is or should be aware, the probability that consumers will be unaware of the danger, and the feasibility of identifying and providing warnings to persons who possess the product. Section 10 provides:

> **§ 10. Liability of Commercial Product Seller or Distributor for Harm Caused by Post-Sale Failure to Warn**
>
> (a) One engaged in the business of selling or otherwise distributing products is subject to liability for harm to persons or property caused by the seller's failure to provide a warning after the time of sale or distribution of a product if a reasonable person in the seller's position would provide such a warning.
>
> (b) A reasonable person in the seller's position would provide a warning after the time of sale if:
>
> (1) the seller knows or reasonably should know that the product poses a substantial risk of harm to persons or property; and
>
> (2) those to whom a warning might be provided can be identified and can reasonably be assumed to be unaware of the risk of harm; and
>
> (3) a warning can be effectively communicated to and acted on by those to whom a warning might be provided; and
>
> (4) the risk of harm is sufficiently great to justify the burden of providing a warning.

Post-Sale Duty to Recall

Section 11 concerns a supplier's liability for failing to recall a product to remedy a defect. Although a couple of early decisions imposed a duty to recall on manufacturers of defective products under principles of negligence, there is very little judicial support for any duty to recall in the absence of a governmental order to do so. The *Products Liability Restatement* conforms to the majority view of those few states that have ruled on this issue, holding that a manufacturer's only duty to recall is when an administrative agency specifically requires the recall, as occurs from time to time and probably most frequently

---

[547] See § 10.8, below.

in the automotive industry regulated by the National Highway Traffic Safety Administration. The Food and Drug Administration and the Consumer Product Safety Commission also occasionally require manufacturers to recall defective products. Thus, the *Restatement* narrowly provides that a seller is subject to liability for failing to recall a product if (1) the government orders the seller to recall the product, or (2) the seller recalls the product but does so negligently. Section 11 provides:

§ 11. Liability of Commercial Product Seller or Distributor for Harm Caused by Post-Sale Failure to Recall Product

One engaged in the business of selling or otherwise distributing products is subject to liability for harm to persons or property caused by the seller's failure to recall a product after the time of sale or distribution if:

(a)(1) a governmental directive issued pursuant to a statute or administrative regulation specifically requires the seller or distributor to recall the product; or

(2) the seller or distributor, in the absence of a recall requirement under Subsection (a)(1), undertakes to recall the product; and

(b) the seller or distributor fails to act as a reasonable person in recalling the product.

Liability of Successor Corporations

Sections 12 and 13 concern the liability of a successor corporation for injuries caused by products sold by a predecessor company.[548] Section 12 restates the widely accepted rule that a successor company that has merely purchased the assets of the predecessor (as opposed to merging or consolidating with it) is generally *not* liable for defects in products sold by the predecessor, subject to four conventional exceptions. Section 12 provides:

§ 12. Liability of Successor for Harm Caused by Defective Products Sold Commercially by Predecessor

A successor corporation or other business entity that acquires assets of a predecessor corporation or other business entity is subject to liability for harm to persons or property caused by a defective product sold or otherwise distributed commercially by the predecessor if the acquisition:

(a) is accompanied by an agreement for the successor to assume such liability; or

(b) results from a fraudulent conveyance to escape liability for the debts or liabilities of the predecessor; or

(c) constitutes a consolidation or merger with the predecessor; or

(d) results in the successor becoming a continuation of the predecessor.

Successor Post-Sale Duty to Warn

Section 13 addresses the limited situation in which a successor manufacturer has a duty to warn persons who possess products manufactured and sold by a predecessor corporation. If the successor corporation services its predecessor's products or otherwise

[548] See § 15.5, below.

undertakes some responsibility with respect to those products, then it fairly may be expected to act with reasonable care. Thus, the successor company in such a situation is obligated, under § 13, to act reasonably to warn according to the same principles as in § 10(b).

Section 13 provides:

§ 13. Liability of Successor for Harm Caused by Successor's Own Post-Sale Failure to Warn

(a) A successor corporation or other business entity that acquires assets of a predecessor corporation or other business entity, whether or not liable under the rule stated in § 12, is subject to liability for harm to persons or property caused by the successor's failure to warn of a risk created by a product sold or distributed by the predecessor if:

(1) the successor undertakes or agrees to provide services for maintenance or repair of the product or enters into a similar relationship with purchasers of the predecessor's products giving rise to actual or potential economic advantage to the successor, and

(2) a reasonable person in the position of the successor would provide a warning.

(b) A reasonable person in the position of the successor would provide a warning if:

(1) the successor knows or reasonably should know that the product poses a substantial risk of harm to persons or property; and

(2) those to whom a warning might be provided can be identified and can reasonably be assumed to be unaware of the risk of harm; and

(3) a warning can be effectively communicated to and acted on by those to whom a warning might be provided; and

(4) the risk of harm is sufficiently great to justify the burden of providing a warning.

Product Sponsorship

Section 14 concerns the liability of a supplier of a product made by another under the supplier's name.[549] This section adopts the principle of § 400 of the *Restatement (Second) of Torts* that sellers (such as large retailers) who market under their own names products manufactured by others are liable as if they were the manufacturer. Although trademark licensors are not liable under this provision, they are liable for injuries from defects in products sold under their trademarks or logos if such licensors substantially participate in the design, manufacture, or distribution of the product.

The reasoning underlying these principles is that a product carrying a particular company's name, trademark, or logo represents that the indicated company is responsible in some manner for the product's quality.

[549] See § 15.4, below.

Section 14 provides:

§ 14. Selling or Distributing as One's Own a Product Manufactured by Another

One engaged in the business of selling or otherwise distributing products who sells or distributes as its own a product manufactured by another is subject to the same liability as though the seller or distributor were the product's manufacturer.

Causation in General

Section 15 merely provides, in general terms, that causation between a product defect and the plaintiff's harm is an important element necessary to any products liability claim.[550] The *Products Liability Restatement* does not address most specific issues of causation because those issues are treated in detail in separate *Restatements (Third) of Torts* on *Apportionment* and on *Liability for Physical and Emotional Harm*. Section 15 provides:

§ 15. General Rule Governing Causal Connection Between Product Defect and Harm

Whether a product defect caused harm to persons or property is determined by the prevailing rules and principles governing causation in tort.

Causation of Additional Harm

Section 16 concerns a manufacturer's responsibility for increased harm ("enhanced injuries") caused by a product defect, the one particular causation topic addressed by the *Products Liability Restatement*. Arising most frequently in vehicular products liability cases (including cars, tractors, snowmobiles, etc.), the enhanced injury issue typically concerns the liability of a vehicle manufacturer (and retailer) for injuries attributable to a so-called "second collision."[551] For example, consider an intersectional collision where an otherwise nondefective automobile is rammed on the side of the driver's door by a truck (the first collision), causing the automobile to roll over. Assume further that the driver's left arm is broken by the force of the collision and his neck is broken when the roof collapses on his head in the rollover (the *second* collision, between the occupant and the interior of the vehicle). The truck driver, of course, may be liable for all such foreseeable damages under ordinary principles of tort law. Section 16 addresses the separate issue of the liability of the automobile manufacturer, who may share responsibility with the truck driver.

Section 16(a) states the general rule that manufacturers may be liable for certain enhanced injuries in such situations. Section 16(b) provides that the automobile manufacturer in the situation above may (or may not) be responsible for the broken neck injuries, depending on whether (or not) the roof was designed with adequate strength for rollovers under ordinary principles of design defectiveness in § 2(b). However, even if the roof design is defective under § 2(b), the roof design did not cause the broken arm, and so § 16(b) provides that the manufacturer is not liable for that particular "divisible" injury. Section 16(c) addresses the situation where the evidence establishes that the defectively designed roof was probably a substantial factor in causing the roof to collapse

---

550 See chapters 11 and 12, below.

551 See § 17.3, below.

as hard as it did on the plaintiff's head, breaking his neck, but where the evidence further shows that a properly designed roof also would have collapsed somewhat, so that the driver's head or neck would have been injured to some extent anyway. In such a case, where causation of the neck injury by the initial collision and the defect is "indivisible," § 16(c) provides that the manufacturer responsible for the defect is fully liable for the indivisible (broken neck) harm.

Finally, § 16(d) provides that a manufacturer liable under the principles of §§ 16(b) or 16(c) is jointly and severally liable, or severally liable, under the jurisdiction's prevailing rules on joint and several liability. Thus, the truck driver, but not the automobile manufacturer, would be subject to liability for the divisible injury of the broken arm. If the roof design is proven defective, and if this defect is proven to be a substantial cause of the plaintiff's broken neck, then the automobile manufacturer, depending on the jurisdiction's rule on joint and several liability, would be jointly and severally liable, or severally liable, with the truck driver for the plaintiff's broken neck. Section 16 provides:

§ 16. Increased Harm Due to Product Defect

(a) When a product is defective at the time of commercial sale or other distribution and the defect is a substantial factor in increasing the plaintiff's harm beyond that which would have resulted from other causes, the product seller is subject to liability for the increased harm.

(b) If proof supports a determination of the harm that would have resulted from other causes in the absence of the product defect, the product seller's liability is limited to the increased harm attributable solely to the product defect.

(c) If proof does not support a determination under Subsection (b) of the harm that would have resulted in the absence of the product defect, the product seller is liable for all of the plaintiff's harm attributable to the defect and other causes.

(d) A seller of a defective product that is held liable for part of the harm suffered by the plaintiff under Subsection (b), or all of the harm suffered by the plaintiff under Subsection (c), is jointly and severally liable or severally liable with other parties who bear legal responsibility for causing the harm, determined by applicable rules of joint and several liability.

Apportionment of Damages

Section 17, which concerns the apportionment of damages between the plaintiff, defendant, and others, adopts the comparative fault rule by which a plaintiff's damages are reduced proportionate to fault.[552] This principle is consistent with the law in all but a handful of jurisdictions. Because the question of how damages are to be apportioned between multiple parties is treated in depth in the *Restatement (Third) of Torts: Apportionment*, the specifics of apportionment (and the doctrine of assumption of risk) are not addressed in the *Products Liability Restatement*.

---

[552] See § 13.3, below.

Section 17 provides:

§ 17. Apportionment of Responsibility Between or Among Plaintiff, Sellers and Distributors of Defective Products, and Others

(a) A plaintiff's recovery of damages for harm caused by a product defect may be reduced if the conduct of the plaintiff combines with the product defect to cause the harm and the plaintiff's conduct fails to conform to generally applicable rules establishing appropriate standards of care.

(b) The manner and extent of the reduction under Subsection (a) and the apportionment of plaintiff's recovery among multiple defendants are governed by generally applicable rules apportioning responsibility.

Contractual Disclaimers

Section 18 restates the prevailing rule applied to strict products liability cases in tort that contractual disclaimers and limitations of remedy have no effect on claims brought by plaintiffs injured in person by defective products.[553] Because this section is limited to injury to persons, who have limited bargaining power, corporate plaintiffs who bring claims for property damage may still be bound by such contractual provisions. Section 18 provides:

§ 18. Disclaimers, Limitations, Waivers, and Other Contractual Exculpations as Defenses to Products Liability Claims for Harm to Persons

Disclaimers and limitations of remedies by product sellers or other distributors, waivers by product purchasers, and other similar contractual exculpations, oral or written, do not bar or reduce otherwise valid products liability claims against sellers or other distributors of new products for harm to persons.

"Product" Defined

In the concluding definitional sections, §§ 19–21, the *Products Liability Restatement* defines its borders and, hence, who and what are subject to its provisions.[554] Thus, in § 19, the word "product" is defined, consistent with the developed case law, to include most movable personal property, but to exclude services (such as a doctor's implantation of a defective pacemaker), blood, and human tissue. The *Restatement* leaves products such as real property (for example, a defectively designed swimming pool) and electricity, to which some courts have applied products liability rules in certain contexts, to case-by-case treatment depending on the context. Section 19 provides:

§ 19. Definition of "Product"

For purposes of this Restatement:

(a) A product is tangible personal property distributed commercially for use or consumption. Other items, such as real property and electricity, are products when the context of their distribution and use is sufficiently analogous to the distribution and use of tangible personal property that it is appropriate to apply the rules stated in this Restatement.

---

[553] See § 5.3, above.

[554] See chapters 16 (transactions and products), 17 (autos), and 18 (drugs and medical devices), below.

(b) Services, even when provided commercially, are not products.

(c) Human blood and human tissue, even when provided commercially, are not subject to the rules of this Restatement.

Sellers and Distributors

Section 20 applies the *Restatement* to manufacturers, wholesalers, retailers, and other commercial transferors of products for ultimate consumption.[555] It covers commercial lessors (such as rental car companies) and commercial bailors (such as laundromats charging a fee for the use of washing machines). The *Restatement* does not apply to a supermarket which provides shopping carts merely as a convenience to its customers, nor institutions (such as banks) that merely provide financing for product purchases, nor to product advertisers or auctioneers.

Section 20 provides:

§ 20. Definition of "One Who Sells or Otherwise Distributes"

For purposes of this Restatement:

(a) One sells a product when, in a commercial context, one transfers ownership thereto either for use or consumption or for resale leading to ultimate use or consumption. Commercial product sellers include, but are not limited to, manufacturers, wholesalers, and retailers.

(b) One otherwise distributes a product when, in a commercial transaction other than a sale, one provides the product to another either for use or consumption or as a preliminary step leading to ultimate use or consumption. Commercial nonsale product distributors include, but are not limited to, lessors, bailors, and those who provide products to others as a means of promoting either the use or consumption of such products or some other commercial activity.

(c) One also sells or otherwise distributes a product when, in a commercial transaction, one provides a combination of products and services and either the transaction taken as a whole, or the product component thereof, satisfies the criteria in Subsection (a) or (b).

Economic Loss

The final section of the *Products Liability Restatement*, § 21, addresses the responsibility of a supplier for economic loss.[556] Courts have routinely permitted recovery in products liability tort actions for personal injury, property loss, and any accompanying economic loss (most typically, lost earnings) resulting from the injury. Increasingly, courts have also permitted spouses, and sometimes parents or children, to recover damages for harm to their relationship ("consortium") with the injured person. Courts also permit punitive damages in appropriate cases, but those damages lie outside the scope of the *Products Liability Restatement*.

In the early years of products liability in America, in the 1960s and 1970s, courts were split on whether the *Restatement (Second) of Torts* § 402A should apply to "pure" economic loss, as when a manufacturing company suffered production losses due to a

---

[555] See chapter 15 (defendants), below.

[556] See § 5.3, above.

defect in an industrial machine purchased from the manufacturer of such machines. Over time, courts have moved strongly toward the position that strict products liability in tort should *not* apply to such pure economic losses that, instead, should be addressed by the law of contract. Adopting this majority position, the *Products Liability Restatement* provides for the recovery of compensatory damages for personal injury, consortium losses to family members, property damage, and economic loss flowing therefrom, but not for pure economic loss. Section 21 provides:

§ 21. Definition of "Harm to Persons or Property": Recovery for Economic Loss

For purposes of this Restatement, harm to persons or property includes economic loss if caused by harm to:

(a) the plaintiff's person; or

(b) the person of another when harm to the other interferes with an interest of the plaintiff protected by tort law; or

(c) the plaintiff's property other than the defective product itself.

Conclusion

The *Restatement (Third) of Torts: Products Liability* provides an encyclopedia of products liability law in America as it stood at the threshold of the twenty-first century. The black-letter provisions set forth above provide a skeleton of the law that is elaborated in copious comments and reporters' notes. While no one fairly can expect to be perfectly satisfied with each of its provisions, the *Third Restatement* faithfully captures the essence of American products liability law that "strikes both a fair and reasonable balance between individual justice and social utility."[557] No study of a products liability law problem is complete without careful consideration of the *Products Liability Restatement*.

[557] Watts, Fairness and Utility in Products Liability: Balancing Individual Rights and Social Welfare, 38 Fla. St. U. L. Rev. 597, 651 (2011) (although insufficiently protecting bystanders in design defect cases).

Chapter 7

MANUFACTURING DEFECTS

Table of Sections

§ 7.1 MANUFACTURING DEFECTS—GENERALLY

Manufacturing defects, flaws or irregularities in products arising from errors in production,[1] give rise to the most basic type of products liability claim. For example, the misalignment of a punch press may result in a jagged burr along a product's metal edge;[2] the mis-position of a nut on a bolt may interfere with a device's operation;[3] and the failure to prevent foreign matter from entering food or drink may cause its contamination.[4] Accidents from tire failures caused by manufacturing defects are a classic form of products liability case.[5] When the manufacturing process goes awry, the resulting products may fail to meet the manufacturer's own design specifications. If such a product escapes the manufacturer's quality controls, its flawed condition may lead to its failure during use, to an accident, to an injury to the user or another, and to a products liability claim for a manufacturing defect.[6]

---

1 See, e.g., Catalano v. MarineMax, 2022 WL 715465, at *12 (E.D.N.Y. 2022) ("when the unit in question deviates in quality and other performance standards from all of the other identical units"); Sharp v. St. Jude Medical, S.C., Inc., 838 Fed. Appx. 462, 466 (11th Cir. 2020) (Ga. law) ("a departure from the manufacturer's specifications"); Colon v. BIC USA, Inc., 199 F. Supp. 2d 53, 85 (S.D.N.Y. 2001) (" 'some mishap in the manufacturing process itself, improper workmanship, or because defective materials were used in construction' [that is] when the unit in question deviates in quality and other performance standards"); Wood v. Old Trapper Taxi, 952 P.2d 1375, 1379–80 (Mont. 1997) (when "the product is flawed due to improper construction [causing] imperfections that inevitably occur in a typically small percentage of products of a given design as a result of the fallibility of the manufacturing process").

2 See, e.g., Ford Motor Co. v. Zahn, 265 F.2d 729 (8th Cir. 1959) (Minn. law) (jagged burr on car's dashboard ashtray).

3 See, e.g., Jenkins v. General Motors Corp., 446 F.2d 377 (5th Cir. 1971) (Ga. law) (inadequately torqued nut on bolt in suspension system that resulted in bolt falling out and loss of steering).

4 See, e.g., Matthews v. Yoplait USA, Inc., 835 S.E.2d 393, 397 (Ga. Ct. App. 2019) (sharp metal fragments in strawberry yogurt); Dellatorre v. Buca, Inc., 211 So.3d 272 (Fla. Dist. Ct. App. 2017) (broken mussel shell in pasta dish); Langan v. BJ's Wholesale Club, Inc., 2006 WL 2524178, at *1 (D.N.J. 2006) (Owen ate E. coli-infected beef); Cooper v. Borden, Inc., 709 So.2d 878 (La. Ct. App. 1998) (penicillin in milk).

5 See, e.g., Griffith v. Goodyear Dunlop Tires N. Am. Ltd., 2018 WL 4658721, at *3 (W.D.N.Y. 2018) (tire had "poor bonding between the tire's polyester cord and rubber skim stock . . . caused by a lack of adhesive dip on large portions of the ply"); Cone v. Hankook Tire Co., Ltd., 2017 WL 342003 (W.D. Tenn. 2017) ("the tire's tread separation was caused by distorted belt cords, insufficient gauge of the belt skim coat, reduced component adhesion, and substantial belt misalignments"); Hewitt v. B.F. Goodrich Co., 732 F.2d 1554 (11th Cir. 1984) (Fla. law) (tire bead bundle broke during manufacturing process); Am. Law Prod. Liab. 3d § 98.

6 See, e.g., Cosh v. Atrium Med. Corp., 2021 WL 1177770, at *3 (S.D.N.Y. 2021) ("to plead and prove a manufacturing flaw under either negligence or strict liability, the plaintiff must show that a specific product

Responsibility for manufacturing defects is the most fundamental obligation of product manufacturers. The law governing production errors is now quite settled, and it fairly may be viewed as the first pillar of modern products liability law.[7] In general, manufacturers and other suppliers are liable for injuries caused by manufacturing defects in products that they sell.[8]

Keeler v. Richards Manufacturing Co.,[9] which involved a surgical compression screw, is an illustrative manufacturing defect case. The screw broke several months after a surgeon inserted it into the plaintiff's broken hip to assist the healing process. In the plaintiff's action against the manufacturer, her experts testified that the screw had four irregularities they considered manufacturing defects, any one of which could have caused the failure by increasing stress concentrations that led to fatigue failure in the screw: (1) the screw's internal threads were longer (1.1875 inches) than the maximum length (1.125 inches) specified in the blueprint specifications; (2) the screw contained excessive metal debris that could have interfered with the surgeon's ability to compress the screw properly, leading to excess movement of the bones; (3) its radius was shorter than the exemplar screw furnished by the manufacturer; and (4) it failed to comply with the 35% ductility standard of the American Society of Testing and Materials. The jury concluded that the screw was defectively manufactured, and the court upheld this determination on appeal.

In former times, from ancient Rome through medieval England and into early American law of the nineteenth and early twentieth centuries, the incipient law of products liability was largely comprised of cases involving physical flaws or defects.[10] With the advent of modern products liability law during the mid-1900s,[11] manufacturing defect cases began to occupy a decreasing proportion of products liability litigation as the plaintiffs' bar increasingly challenged the sufficiency of product designs and warnings.[12] This proportional decline in manufacturing defect cases in part reflects

---

unit was defective as a result of 'some mishap in the manufacturing process itself, improper workmanship, or because defective materials were used in construction,' and that the defect was the cause of plaintiff's injury").

[7] Owen, The Moral Foundations of Products Liability Law: Toward First Principles, 68 Notre Dame L. Rev. 427, 467–68, 473–74, 502–03 (1993).

[8] On liability for manufacturing defects, see Frumer, Friedman, and Sklaren, Products Liability § 11.02; Am. Law Prod. Liab. § 31; D. Fairgrieve and R. Goldberg, Product Liability ch. 11 (Oxford, 3d ed. 2020) (British law); Products Liability Rest. §§ 2(a); Owen, Manufacturing Defects, 53 S.C. L. Rev. 851 (2002).

[9] 817 F.2d 1197 (5th Cir. 1987) (Tex. law).

[10] See, e.g., Van Bracklin v. Fonda, 12 Johns. 468 (N.Y. 1815) (contaminated beef); Langridge v. Levy, (1837) 150 Eng. Rep. 863 (Exch. Div.), aff'd, (1838) 150 Eng. Rep. 1458 (Exch. Div.) (defective gun fraudulently represented as safe); Devlin v. Smith, 89 N.Y. 470 (1882) (planks on painter's scaffold nailed rather than lashed down); Schubert v. J.R. Clark Co., 51 N.W. 1103 (Minn. 1892) (stepladder constructed of cross-grained and decaying lumber). On early law generally, see § 1.2, above. The development of warranty law liability for selling defective foodstuffs is examined in § 5.2, above. See also § 7.5, below.

In the twentieth century, the classic products liability cases involved manufacturing defects. See, e.g., MacPherson v. Buick Motor Co., 111 N.E. 1050 (N.Y. 1916) (collapse of car's wheel made of defective wood—negligence); Henningsen v. Bloomfield Motors, Inc., 161 A.2d 69 (N.J. 1960) (defect in car's steering system—implied warranty). In Greenman v. Yuba Power Prods., Inc., 377 P.2d 897 (Cal. 1963), it is unclear whether the set screws were "inadequate" because of a defect in manufacture or design.

[11] Even in the 1950s, manufacturing defects still dominated products liability litigation. See Wilson, Products Liability (pt. 1): The Protection of the Injured Person, 43 Cal. L. Rev. 614, 636 (1955).

[12] See Priest, Strict Products Liability: The Original Intent, 10 Cardozo L. Rev. 2301 (1989); Twerski, Weinstein, Donaher and Piehler, The Use and Abuse of Warnings in Products Liability: Design Defect Comes of Age, 61 Cornell L. Rev. 495 (1976); Henderson, Judicial Review of Manufacturers' Conscious Design Choices: The Limits of Adjudication, 73 Colum. L. Rev. 1531 (1973); Noel, Manufacturer's Negligence of Design or Directions for Use of a Product, 71 Yale L.J. 816 (1962).

improvements in the technology of production engineering, including enhancements in quality assurance. Also, because the liability standards governing manufacturing flaw cases are generally clear and noncontroversial, there usually is little debate on whether a physically flawed product is "defective." Thus, manufacturing flaw cases are more likely to settle than design and warning defect cases, which by nature involve normative judgments of safety sufficiency. Manufacturing defect cases usually involve disputes over the sufficiency of evidence of causation—whether the product in fact contained a manufacturing flaw, whether any such flaw was attributable to the manufacturer, and whether that flaw caused the plaintiff's harm.[13] Such factual determinations are peculiarly committed to jury determination and usually are upheld on appeal.[14]

Manufacturing defect claims possess certain advantages for plaintiffs over claims involving design and warning defects. First, manufacturing defect claims are normally much less expensive to pursue because they challenge only a single product unit rather than a company's entire line of products.[15] In addition, quite unlike design and warning cases, the liability standards for manufacturing defects—departure from intended design[16] and product malfunction[17]—are conceptually simple and truly "strict."[18] Moreover, manufacturing defect claims may be immune from certain types of requirements, limitations, or defenses applicable to other types of claims.[19] Nor can it be doubted that moral imperatives normally favor recovery for plaintiffs injured by physical flaws in the products they buy and use. Manufacturers deliberatively set the level of manufacturing flaws in their products by the level of investment they choose to make in the quality of their production and quality control processes.[20] For this reason, and because buyers reasonably expect that new products they purchase will be free of dangerous defects, principles of fairness, truth, and restitution all suggest that manufacturers should compensate persons injured by production defects.[21]

---

13 On causation issues, see ch. 11, below.

14 See, e.g., Jenkins v. General Motors Corp., 446 F.2d 377 (5th Cir. 1971) (Ga. law) (upholding jury's determination that crash was caused by defective suspension system rather than by driver inattention); Shoshone Coca-Cola Bottling Co. v. Dolinski, 420 P.2d 855 (Nev. 1966) (upholding jury's rejection of bottler's theory that third-party tamperer put mouse in bottle of Squirt).

15 This difference gives rise to a rule in some jurisdictions exempting manufacturing defect claims from the rule that prohibits evidence of subsequent improvements in design. See, e.g., Cover v. Cohen, 461 N.E.2d 864 (N.Y. 1984) (evidence of subsequent modifications admissible in strict liability manufacturing defect claims); R. Barker and V. Alexander, Evidence in New York State and Federal Courts (Vol. 5 New York Practice Series) § 4:52 (Thomson West 2013).

16 See § 7.3, below.

17 See § 7.4, below.

18 See §§ 6.2 and 6.5, above.

19 See, e.g., In re: Allergan Biocell Textured Breast Implant Prods. Liab. Litig., 537 F. Supp. 3d 679, 712 (D.N.J. 2021) ("manufacturing defects, when properly alleged, may not be expressly or impliedly preempted"); Rodriguez v. General Dynamics Armament & Tech. Prods., Inc., 2010 WL 1507979, at *1 (D. Hawai'i 2010) (government contractor defense inapplicable to manufacturing defect claim for explosion of mortar shell); Reed v. Smith & Nephew, Inc., 527 F. Supp. 2d 1336, 1354–55 (W.D. Okla. 2007) ("unavoidably unsafe product" defense inapplicable to manufacturing defect claims); Bearden v. Wyeth, 482 F. Supp. 2d 614, 618 n.5 (E.D. Pa. 2006) (comment *k* defense inapplicable to manufacturing defect claims in some states, such as Arkansas); Falada v. Trinity Indus., 642 N.W.2d 247 (Iowa 2002) (state of the art was no defense to manufacturing defect claim that an ammonia tank was welded improperly); N.J. Stat. Ann. § 2A:58C–3 (certain state-of-the-art defenses apply only to design dangers).

20 See Cowan, Some Policy Bases of Products Liability, 17 Stan. L. Rev. 1077, 1086–92 (1965).

21 See Owen, The Moral Foundations of Products Liability Law: Toward First Principles, 68 Notre Dame L. Rev. 427, 467–68, 473–74, 502–03 (1993).

For all these reasons, and to avoid the cost and publicity of litigation with a low probability of success, a manufacturer persuaded that a physical flaw in one of its products injured a claimant normally will be amenable to settling the case. But a manufacturer is likely to litigate a case involving a physically flawed product if it believes that (1) the product was not in fact defective;[22] (2) even if the product was defective, the plaintiff's harm was caused by something other than the defect;[23] (3) even if a product defect caused the plaintiff's harm, someone or something other than the manufacturer caused the defect after the product left the manufacturer's control;[24] or (4) the amount of plaintiff's damage claim is unreasonable.[25]

A manufacturer may breach its duty to manufacture nondefective products in various ways. First, the raw materials or components used to construct the product may contain physical flaws. For example, the materials used to make the product—such as the defective wooden spoke of the car wheel in *MacPherson v. Buick Motor Co.*[26]—may contain weaknesses or impurities.[27] Similarly, a product's components may be manufactured incorrectly,[28] damaged,[29] or contaminated[30] during production. Third,

---

[22] See cases in note 45, below.

[23] See, e.g., iLight Techs. Inc. v. Clutch City Sports & Ent., L.P., 414 S.W.3d 842 (Tex. App. 2013); Johnson v. Bauer Corp., 898 N.Y.S.2d 397 (App. Div. 2010). Compare Church v. Martin-Baker Aircraft Co., 643 F. Supp. 499 (E.D. Mo. 1986) (death of fighter pilot who ejected from plane could have been caused by defective ejection seat or by external wind blasts); Price v. Ashby's Inc., 354 P.2d 1064, 1065 (Utah 1960) (hole in airlift line caused auto to tilt, but there was no proof that this defect—rather than driver error—caused car to continue straight at bend in road: "With two or more possible causes such as an inattentive driver and a mechanical defect . . . proof that it may have been either is not proof that it was in fact either.").

[24] See, e.g., Cincinnati Cos. v. Ford Motor Co., 2001 WL 227362 (Ohio Ct. App. 2001) (electrical short-circuit in car caused fire; summary judgment for defendant affirmed as to manufacturing defect because plaintiff failed to show that defect existed when car left manufacturer's control); Maher v. General Motors Corp., 346 N.E.2d 833 (Mass. 1976) (steering suddenly locking failed to establish defect at time of sale since steering had been serviced on three occasions). See also note 47, below.

[25] There is little other explanation for many of the cases, often involving defective foodstuffs, where proof of a true manufacturing defect causing plaintiff's harm (including emotional distress) is clear. See, e.g., Brayman v. 99 W., Inc., 116 F. Supp. 2d 225 (D. Mass. 2000) (piece of glass in mashed potatoes; court rejected excessiveness challenge, with respect to verdict of $25,000, for cut in diner's throat), aff'd, 26 Fed Appx. 24 (1st Cir. 2002); Kroger Co. v. Beck, 375 N.E.2d 640 (Ind. Ct. App. 1978) (hypodermic needle in beef; $2700 not excessive, despite absence of resulting physical injury, for prick in housewife's throat).

[26] 111 N.E. 1050 (N.Y. 1916). Compare Bell v. T.R. Miller Mill Co., 768 So.2d 953 (Ala. 2000) (telephone pole that broke, causing accident, was made of wood containing pre-manufacture decay and bursts).

[27] See, e.g., Pugh v. Louisville Ladder, Inc., 361 Fed. Appx. 448, 450 (4th Cir. 2010) (N.C. law) ("micro-cracks" in aluminum ladder); Benitez v. Synthes, Inc., 199 F. Supp. 2d 1339 (M.D. Fla. 2002) (surgical rod had fractures and cracks); Rudd v. General Motors Corp., 127 F. Supp. 2d 1330 (M.D. Ala. 2001) (defective steel in vehicle's fan blade); Pouncey v. Ford Motor Co., 464 F.2d 957 (5th Cir. 1972) (Ala. law) (same).

[28] See, e.g., Currier v. Stryker Corp., 2012 WL 1037940, at *3 (E.D. Cal. 2012) (weak spot in composite femoral stem that caused it to break in plaintiff's body); Air Reduction Co. v. Philadelphia Storage Battery Co., 14 F.2d 734, 736–37 (3d Cir. 1926) (Pa. law) (sloppy drilling of manifold, leaving "rough places, fins or splinters" that increased risk of combustion, explosion, and fire).

[29] See, e.g., Fillebrown v. Steelcase, Inc., 63 Fed. Appx. 54 (3d Cir. 2003) (N.J. law) (machining marks on metal spindle connecting base of chair to seat); Chapman v. Maytag Corp., 2000 WL 1038183 (S.D. Ind. 2000) (pinched wire in stove), aff'd, 297 F.3d 682 (7th Cir. 2002); Simon v. Coppola, 876 P.2d 10 (Colo. App. 1993) (crimp in hot tub thermostat actuator allowed water to overheat); Hewitt v. B.F. Goodrich Co., 732 F.2d 1554 (11th Cir. 1984) (Fla. law) (tire bead bundle broke during manufacturing process).

[30] See, e.g., Flagstar Enters., Inc. v. Davis, 709 So.2d 1132 (Ala. 1997) (human blood in biscuit and gravy); Glover v. BIC Corp., 6 F.3d 1318 (9th Cir. 1993) (Or. law) (brass chips left in disposable lighter could cause it to fail to extinguish); Williams v. Volkswagenwerk A.G., 226 Cal. Rptr. 306 (Ct. App. 1986) (foreign substance cluster in metal near break point); Simpson v. Logan Motor Co., 192 A.2d 122 (D.C. 1963) (foreign substance in hydraulic fluid); Trowbridge v. Abrasive Co. of Phila., 190 F.2d 825 (3d Cir. 1951) (Pa. law) (abrasive wheel disintegrated due to trapped gases that caused internal fissures and cracks).

although a product's components individually may be free of flaws, a mistake may be made in how they are assembled into final form. This is the most common type of manufacturing defect case. Thus, the ingredients in a particular batch may deviate from the specified formulation;[31] the rivets, welds, screws, bolts, or nuts used to hold components together may be improperly made, applied, inserted, attached, or combined, weakening the product's assembly;[32] or the product's components may otherwise be assembled improperly.[33] Fourth, after assembly, an otherwise properly produced product may not be finished sufficiently, leaving its edges too rough, too sharp, or otherwise hazardous.[34] Finally, a properly assembled and finished product may be rendered defective because of a dangerous flaw in its package or container.[35]

The quality control process is designed to catch such manufacturing mistakes, but sometimes it fails to do so. And while insufficient quality assurance may provide the basis for a claim of negligence,[36] a manufacturer's failure to adequately inspect or test

---

Yet impurities alone do not automatically render a product legally defective. "[T]he concept of defect is not self-defining when a product contains a flaw. Since all products are flawed at some technological level, the decision must still be made as to when a flaw emerges as a defect. In order to make this decision, some judgmental standard must be utilized." Weinstein, Twerski, Piehler, and Donaher, Product Liability: An Interaction of Law and Technology, 12 Duq. L. Rev. 425, 430–31 (1974). "To a metallurgist all metallic structures contain flaws or irregularities at some size level. They range from dislocations at the atomic size level to cracks visible to the naked eye. . . . Since these flaws [unfortunately sometimes called *defects* by metallurgists] can be identified in all products, the critical question to be asked is when can these deviations from structural perfection really lead to a conclusion of [legal] defect." Id. at 430 n.11. "Materials processing and fabrication are thus based upon flaw or irregularity control to achieve an economically feasible trade-off among all the properties of the material which, together with proper design, serve to achieve a given performance requirement. . . . [Thus], the mere presence of an identifiable irregularity or flaw in a metallic structure is in and of itself an insufficient basis for the establishment of defect." Id. at 432 n.11(4).

[31] See, e.g., Reiter v. Zimmer Inc., 897 F. Supp. 154 (S.D.N.Y. 1995) (improper proportion of ingredients in batch of bone cement).

[32] See, e.g., Dieker v. Case Corp., 73 P.3d 133 (Kan. 2003) (failure to fully tighten nut on combine's hydraulic valve caused fire); Benson v. Tennessee Valley Elec. Coop., 868 S.W.2d 630 (Tenn. Ct. App. 1993) (repair weld in aerial boom failed because it was too weak); Harley-Davidson Motor Co. v. Wisniewski, 437 A.2d 700 (Md. Ct. Spec. App. 1981) (cross-threaded screw on throttle clamp fractured); Jenkins v. General Motors Corp., 446 F.2d 377 (5th Cir. 1971) (Ga. law) (improperly tightened nut on bolt caused suspension assembly to fail); O'Donnell v. Geneva Metal Wheel Co., 183 F.2d 733 (6th Cir. 1950) (Ohio law) (wheelbarrow tire exploded because metal rivets holding rim together were weakened during assembly by pressing the metal too thin which generated visible radial cracks).

[33] See, e.g., Caterpillar Inc. v. Trinity Indus., 134 P.3d 881, 884 (Okla. Civ. App. 2005) (improper assembly of hinge bracket caused 1,500-pound door to fall on workers); Yamaha Motor Co. v. Thornton, 579 So.2d 619 (Ala. 1991) (motorcycle speed reduction plate left out in manufacture); Gasque v. Heublein, Inc., 315 S.E.2d 556 (S.C. Ct. App. 1984) (wire hood attached improperly to stopper in bottle of sparkling wine); Horne v. Liberty Furniture Co., 452 So.2d 204 (La. Ct. App. 1984) (chair parts improperly glued together); Willis v. Floyd Brace Co., 309 S.E.2d 295 (S.C. Ct. App. 1983) (parts improperly aligned); Hall v. Chrysler Corp., 526 F.2d 350 (5th Cir. 1976) (La. law) (misrouted transmission cable lay against exhaust manifold which melted cable).

[34] See, e.g., Stazenski v. Tennant Co., 617 So.2d 344 (Fla. Dist. Ct. App. 1993) (worker cut on sharp edge of industrial sweeper); McBurnette v. Playground Equip. Corp., 130 So.2d 117 (Fla. Dist. Ct. App. 1960) (child's finger cut off by sharp edge of swing), rev'd in part on other grounds, 137 So.2d 563 (Fla. 1962); Ford Motor Co. v. Zahn, 265 F.2d 729 (8th Cir. 1959) (Minn. law) (driver braked suddenly, throwing passenger's face into dashboard where sharp metal burr protruding from ashtray impaled his eye, squirting eye juice all around car).

[35] See, e.g., DeWitt v. Eveready Battery Co., 565 S.E.2d 140 (N.C. 2002) (acid leaked from battery case onto plaintiff); Helm v. Pepsi-Cola Bottling Co. of St. Louis, Inc., 723 S.W.2d 465 (Mo. Ct. App. 1986) (bottles fell through cardboard carton, and exploding glass injured plaintiff). See also Ebenhoech v. Koppers Indus., 239 F. Supp. 2d 455, 475 (D.N.J. 2002) (tank car is the "packaging" for hazardous chemical that left slippery residue on top of tank car from which plaintiff fell).

[36] Because quality control procedures are an important aspect of production, used to catch defectively manufactured products before they are sold, evidence of inadequate quality control may be especially relevant to negligent manufacturing claims. See, e.g., Lancenese v. Vanderlans & Sons, Inc., 2007 WL 1521121, at *5

its products is not itself a strict products liability claim.[37] A manufacturer's evidence of *good* quality control might seem to be logically irrelevant to a strict products liability claim, because the issue in such cases is the defectiveness of the product and not the manufacturer's conduct in allowing the defect to arise.[38] Nevertheless, especially in cases involving allegations of foreign objects or contamination in foodstuffs, such evidence may be admissible, even in strict liability in tort or breach of warranty cases,[39] if it tends to show that the manufacturer is not responsible for causing the defect, to wit, that the defect (if any) probably arose after the product left the manufacturer's control.[40]

Causation issues, rather than the product's defectiveness, typically dominate cases based on claims of manufacturing defects. Especially if the product accident destroys direct evidence of why an accident occurred, the crucial issue is often whether the plaintiff's proof sufficiently establishes that the accident was attributable to a manufacturing defect as opposed to some other plausible cause—such as normal wear and tear[41] or the conduct of the user or someone else. In general, a plaintiff must plead and establish, by a reasonable probability, that the product contained a defect attributable to the manufacturer and that such hypothesis is more likely than any other suggested by the evidence.[42]

If a product dangerously malfunctions, but the plaintiff is unable to prove the existence of a specific defect, the malfunction doctrine may provide relief if the plaintiff can eliminate other normal causes of such malfunctions, as discussed below.[43] Yet an

---

(E.D. Pa. 2007) (sufficient evidence of inadequate quality control for negligent manufacturing claim to survive summary judgment); Ford Motor Co. v. Zahn, 265 F.2d 729, 731 (8th Cir. 1959) (Minn. law). See § 2.2, above.

[37] There is no separate strict liability claim for defective quality control. See, e.g., Burley v. Kytec Innovative Sports Equip., Inc., 737 N.W.2d 397, 408 (S.D. 2007) ("A manufacturer's duty to test and inspect traditionally does not give rise to an independent cause of action for products liability."); Valentine v. Baxter Healthcare Corp., 81 Cal. Rptr. 2d 252, 264 (Ct. App. 1999). Yet, defective quality control may support a negligence claim for a manufacturing defect. See § 2.2, above, and § 7.2, below.

[38] See, e.g., Nave v. Rainbo Tire Serv., Inc., 462 N.E.2d 620 (Ill. App. Ct. 1984).

[39] "In an action based on breach of warranty, it is of course necessary to show not only the existence of the warranty but the fact that the warranty was broken and that the breach of warranty was the proximate cause of the loss sustained.... [E]vidence indicating that the seller exercised care in the manufacture, processing or selection of the goods is relevant to the issue of whether the warranty was in fact broken." UCC § 2–314 cmt. 13.

[40] See, e.g., Preston v. Peter Luger Enters., Inc., 858 N.Y.S.2d 828, 831 (App. Div. 2008) (steak sauce bottles inspected and tested for flaws); Hazelton v. Safeway Stores, Inc., 745 P.2d 309 (Kan. Ct. App. 1987) (needle in baked bread; baker's evidence that it tested for metal contamination was proper); Johnesee v. Stop & Shop Cos., 416 A.2d 956, 960 (N.J. Super. Ct. App. Div. 1980) (quality control evidence proper in case of possibly contaminated soup, going to improbability it was defective); Brown v. General Foods Corp., 573 P.2d 930, 934 (Ariz. Ct. App. 1978) (manufacturer's quality control procedures admissible on improbability that banana peel entered cereal box during production).

[41] See, e.g., Michelin N. Am., Inc. v. Deal, 381 P.3d 641 (Nev. 2012) (no error in court's instruction that a tire failing due to wear cannot be "defective"); Dykes v. Husqvarna Outdoor Prods., N.A., Inc., 869 F. Supp. 2d 749, 758–59 (S.D. Miss. 2012) (plaintiff failed to eliminate normal wear and tear as possible cause of malfunction); Barnish v. KWI Bldg. Co., 916 A.2d 642, 648 (Pa. Super. Ct. 2007) (plaintiffs failed to present a case "free of reasonable, secondary causes, *e.g.*, wear and tear from prolonged use"), aff'd, 980 A.2d 535 (Pa. 2009).

[42] See, e.g., Metropolitan Prop. & Cas. Ins. Co. v. Deere & Co., 25 A.3d 571, 583–84 (Conn. 2011); Tluczek v. Prestige BMW, 2009 WL 2601625, at *2 (N.J. Super. Ct. App. Div. 2009); Estate of Triplett v. General Elec. Co., 954 F. Supp. 149, 151 (W.D. Mich. 1996) ("the plaintiff must provide direct or circumstantial evidence that 'adequately supports a reasonable inference that the accident was probably caused by a defect attributable to the manufacturer' ").

[43] See § 7.4, below.

allegation of a manufacturing defect is properly dismissed if the plaintiff fails to plead[44] and prove, one way or another, that the product contained a defect[45] which caused the harm,[46] and that the defect was in the product when it left the manufacturer's control.[47] In many manufacturing defect cases, as in products liability litigation generally, the plaintiff may,[48] and often must,[49] establish his case by competent expert testimony.

---

[44] See, e.g., Crowther v. Wright Med. Tech., Inc., 2019 WL 1059966, at *4 (D. Utah 2019) ("Crowther's claim that the metal acetabular cup and metal ball head implanted in him differed from the manufacturer's specifications, and specifically that the clearance levels differed from the manufacturers' specifications, is plausible and has a reasonable likelihood of being proven through available evidentiary means. The allegation is specific enough to allow Wright Medical to identify the specific claimed defect."). Compare Brooks v. Mentor Worldwide LLC, 985 F.3d 1272, 1281 (10th Cir. 2021) (plaintiffs failed to adequately plead their manufacturing defect claim under the *Iqbal/Twombly* standard; "[a]n allegation is conclusory where it states an inference without stating underlying facts").

[45] See, e.g., Dalton v. Animas Corp., 913 F. Supp. 2d 370, 375 (W.D. Ky. 2012) (insufficient evidence that manufacturing defect caused stuck key in insulin pump); Wright v. Brooke Grp. Ltd., 652 N.W.2d 159 (Iowa 2002) (cigarettes not manufactured defectively where they were in condition intended by manufacturer); In re Coordinated Latex Glove Litig., 121 Cal. Rptr. 2d 301, 314–15 (Ct. App. 2002) (claim that excessive protein levels in latex gloves were manufacturing defect failed absent evidence of design standard for protein levels); Prohaska v. Sofamor, S.N.C., 138 F. Supp. 2d 422, 444 (W.D.N.Y. 2001) (insufficient proof that defendant's pedicle bone screws were manufactured with "inadequate materials of construction, inadequate quality control in machining of critical components and poor finishing processes"); Holder v. Keller Indus., 2000 WL 141070 (Tex. App. 2000) (insufficient proof that ladder was defectively manufactured).

[46] See, e.g., BIC Pen Corp. v. Carter, 346 S.W.3d 533 (Tex. 2011) (insufficient proof that child would have been prevented from igniting lighter if each of its child-resistant force specifications had been met during production); Booth v. Black & Decker, Inc., 166 F. Supp. 2d 215 (E.D. Pa. 2001) (insufficient proof that manufacturing defect in toaster caused fire that burned down house); Stewart v. Von Solbrig Hosp., Inc., 321 N.E.2d 428, 432 (Ill. App. Ct. 1974) (defective stainless steel surgical pin implanted in plaintiff's leg not designed to withstand weight of person; plaintiff walked on leg contrary to doctor's orders, breaking pin; pin would have broken even if it had not contained manufacturing defects that reduced its strength by one third). On causation generally, see ch. 11, below.

[47] See, e.g., Miller v. Ford Motor Co., 653 S.E.2d 82, 84 (Ga. Ct. App. 2007) ("mere failure of automobile equipment" does not itself prove that manufacturer caused defect "since the failure can be the result of myriad causes not related to its manufacture"); Barnish v. KWI Bldg. Co., 916 A.2d 642, 647–48 (Pa. Super. Ct. 2007) (jury could not reasonably infer defect in sensors manufactured ten years prior to malfunction); Hamilton v. Emerson Elec. Co., 133 F. Supp. 2d 360 (M.D. Pa. 2001) (plaintiff failed to prove that defect in miter saw's braking device existed when saw left manufacturer); Cincinnati Cos. v. Ford Motor Co., 2001 WL 227362 (Ohio Ct. App. 2001) (electrical short-circuit in car); York v. American Med. Sys., Inc., 166 F.3d 1216 (6th Cir. 1998) (Ohio law) (no proof that manufacturer responsible for pinpoint hole in cylinder of inflatable penile prosthesis).

See Rest. (2d) Torts § 402A cmt. *g*:

> The rule . . . applies only where the product is, at the time it leaves the seller's hands, in a [defective condition] . . . . The burden of proof [on this point] is upon the injured plaintiff; and unless evidence can be produced which will support the conclusion that it was then defective, the burden is not sustained.

[48] See, e.g., Pugh v. Louisville Ladder, Inc., 361 Fed. Appx. 448, 455–56 (4th Cir. 2010) (N.C. law) (allowing expert testimony on aluminum ladder micro-cracks); Benitez v. Synthes, Inc., 199 F. Supp. 2d 1339 (M.D. Fla. 2002) (allowing expert testimony on machining process to establish that surgical rod contained fractures and cracks).

[49] See, e.g., iLight Techs., Inc. v. Cutch City Sports & Entm't, L.P., 414 S.W.3d 842, 850–53 (Tex. App. 2013) (reversing verdict for plaintiff whose experts failed to establish that sign deviated from specifications); Dalton v. Animas Corp., 913 F. Supp. 2d 370, 375 (W.D. Ky. 2012) (insufficient evidence of manufacturing defect in insulin pump where expert failed to recreate "stuck button"); Cooper Tire & Rubber Co. v. Mendez, 204 S.W.3d 797, 807 (Tex. 2006); Emody v. Medtronic, Inc., 238 F. Supp. 2d 1291 (N.D. Ala. 2003) (summary judgment appropriate where expert's criticism of spinal fusion rod was based solely on visual inspection and rod passed all objective tests); Cantrell v. Weber-Stephen Prods. Co., 38 Fed. Appx. 921, 923 (4th Cir. 2002) (Md. law) (plaintiff failed to provide expert testimony on why gas grill exploded; without such testimony, "a jury could only infer the presence of a defect in the grill by engaging in 'surmise, conjecture, or speculation' "); Moisenko v. Volkswagenwerk A.G., 100 F. Supp. 2d 489, 493 (W.D. Mich. 2000) (granting defendant's motion for summary judgment for manufacturing defect claims; "it is well-settled that such a claim cannot be proven without expert testimony"). On expert testimony generally, see § 6.3, above.

§ 7.2 THEORIES AND TESTS OF LIABILITY

Manufacturing defects may generate any number of products liability claims. For example, a manufacturer may misrepresent the purity of its products,[50] or a supplier of contaminated food or drink may be negligent per se for violating a pure food statute.[51] More commonly, however, a seller of a defectively manufactured product is subject to liability under one or more of the three primary products liability theories of recovery—negligence, breach of implied warranty, and strict liability in tort.

Negligence

In earlier times, most products liability cases for manufacturing defects were brought in negligence.[52] A prominent case in point is *MacPherson v. Buick Motor Co.*,[53] which involved the crash of an automobile due to a defective wooden spoke in its wheel. Indeed, until the development of the doctrine of strict products liability in tort in the 1960s, most products liability cases were manufacturing defect cases brought in negligence.[54] Because negligence is more difficult to prove than strict liability in manufacturing defect cases,[55] negligence claims in such cases are less common today than formerly. Nevertheless, negligent manufacturing (including negligent testing and quality control) remains a viable basis of products liability recovery in almost every state.[56]

Negligence, it will be recalled,[57] is unreasonable conduct, as measured against the conduct of a reasonable, prudent manufacturer in the same or similar circumstances.[58] Ordinarily, reasonable care is ascertained according to a calculus of risk, balancing the burden or costs of improving safety against the foreseeable safety benefits of so doing. If the foreseeable risks from an occasional flaw are simply that a person may suffer a scratch or may snag an article of clothing, then minimal quality control generally is

---

[50] On tortious misrepresentation, see ch. 3, above. On breach of express warranty, see § 4.2, above.

[51] See § 7.5, below.

[52] One small category of cases which most commonly asserted breach of warranty involved defective foodstuff claims against retailers. See F. R. Dickerson, Products Liability and the Food Consumer 69–70 (1951). In very early times, most claims lay in warranty. See § 1.2, above.

[53] 111 N.E. 1050 (N.Y. 1916). *MacPherson* is discussed in § 1.2, above.

[54] See, e.g., Wilson, Products Liability (pt. 1), 43 Cal. L. Rev. 614, 636 (1955).

[55] Price v. Wilson Sporting Goods Co., 2005 WL 1677512, at *5–7 (D. Colo. 2005) (pitching wedge head broke off when golfer teed off on ninth hole, striking plaintiff in the head; plaintiff met burden of proof for summary judgment on strict liability manufacturing defect claim but not on negligent manufacturing claim).

[56] A negligence claim is logically superfluous to a claim for strict liability in tort, since the former requires proof of all elements of the latter plus fault. See, e.g., Guilbeault v. R.J. Reynolds Tobacco Co., 84 F. Supp. 2d 263, 280 (D.R.I. 2000) ("it is unclear to this Court why plaintiff would include a negligent manufacturing claim in this Complaint since strict liability will lie due to a manufacturing defect without . . . the additional requirement that defendant knew or should have known of the defect"). *But see* Barnes v. Medtronic, Inc., 2021 WL 3742436, at *3 (N.D. Ga. 2021) (denying defendants' motions to dismiss manufacturing defect claims brought under both strict products liability and negligence). See § 5.9, above. In addition, a few states by statute have merged negligence, warranty, and strict liability claims into a single "product liability" claim. See, e.g., Conn. Gen. Stat. Ann. §§ 52–572m, 52–572n; Ind. Code Ann. § 34–6–2–115; La. Rev. Stat. Ann. § 9:2800.52; N.J. Stat. Ann. § 2A:58C–1(b)(3); Wash. Rev. Code Ann. § 7.72.010(4). See also Wright v. Brooke Grp. Ltd., 652 N.W.2d 159, 167 (Iowa 2002) (same: design defects); Olson v. Prosoco, Inc., 522 N.W.2d 284 (Iowa 1994) (same: warning defects).

[57] Negligence claims are addressed generally in chapter 2, above.

[58] See, e.g., Holder v. Keller Indus., 2000 WL 141070, at *6 (Tex. App. 2000) (defendant ladder manufacturer's conduct must be measured against "standard of a reasonably prudent manufacturer . . . of ladders rather than an ordinary prudent person").

sufficient.[59] Yet, if the foreseeable risks from a manufacturing flaw are substantial, as with defects in a punch press or the steering or braking mechanisms of a car, then due care requires that a manufacturer devote considerable resources to preventing such errors during production and to catching resulting flaws thereafter in an effective quality control system.[60]

Because of the difficulties that commonly exist in discovering and proving the specific manufacturing mistake that caused a production flaw in an accident product, together with the likelihood that any such mistake was the result of the manufacturer's negligence, courts commonly allow juries to infer negligence from proof of a manufacturing flaw alone.[61]

Strict Liability Generally

Even if manufacturers exercise due care, however, they generally are strictly liable—in warranty and in tort—for injuries caused by production defects in products they make and sell.[62] The very essence of an ordinary exchange transaction involving a new product is the notion that the buyer is paying appropriate value for a certain type of "good" comprised of various utility and safety characteristics common to each unit of that type produced by the maker according to a single design. Both the manufacturer and the buyer contemplate (and hence contract for) an exchange of a standard, uniform monetary value for a standard, uniform package of utility and safety. At some level of abstract awareness most consumers know, of course, that manufacturers sometimes make mistakes and that the cost of perfect production for many types of products would be exorbitant, if possible at all. Yet, while consumers may abstractly comprehend the practical necessity of allowing imperfect production, their actual expectation when purchasing a new product is that its important attributes, including safety, will match those of other similar units.[63] When a purchaser pays full value for a product that appears to be the same as every other, only to receive a product with a dangerous hidden flaw, the product's price and appearance both generate false expectations of safety in the buyer. Buyers do not intend to pay fair value for a mismanufactured product only to be

---

[59] See Ford Motor Co. v. Zahn, 265 F.2d 729 (8th Cir. 1959) (Minn. law) (rejecting this argument).

[60] "The obligation to inspect must vary with the nature of the thing to be inspected. The more probable the danger, the greater the need of caution." MacPherson v. Buick Motor Co., 111 N.E. 1050, 1055 (N.Y. 1916) (Cardozo, J.). See Rest. (2d) Torts § 395 cmt. *e*:

> A garment maker is not required to subject the finished garment to anything like so minute an inspection for the purpose of discovering whether a basting needle has not been left in a seam as is required of the maker of an automobile or of high speed machinery or of electrical devices, in which the slightest inaccuracy may involve danger of death.

[61] See, e.g., Klinke v. Mitsubishi Motors Corp., 556 N.W.2d 528 (Mich. Ct. App. 1996) (car's steering knuckle fractured), aff'd, 581 N.W.2d 272 (Mich. 1998); Pouncey v. Ford Motor Co., 464 F.2d 957, 961 (5th Cir. 1972) (Ala. law) (automobile fan blade made of dirty steel); Jenkins v. General Motors Corp., 446 F.2d 377 (5th Cir. 1971) (Ga. law) (improper tightening of nut on bolt in rear suspension system). See also Schall v. Suzuki Motor of Am., Inc., 450 F. Supp. 3d 771, 785 (W.D. Ky. 2020) (the corrosion and hydrogen gas within a brake's master cylinder was sufficient circumstantial evidence of negligent manufacturing to defeat defendants' summary judgment motion). On the doctrine of res ipsa loquitur, see § 2.5, above.

[62] Similarly, retailers and other suppliers downstream from the manufacturer ordinarily are also strictly liable for harm from manufacturing defects in products they supply. See Products Liability Rest. § 1 cmt. *e*, and § 2 cmt. *c*. See generally § 15.2, below.

[63] See, e.g., Dico Tire, Inc. v. Cisneros, 953 S.W.2d 776, 783 (Tex. App. 1997) (due to defective bead bundle, tire exploded during repair; jury verdict for plaintiff affirmed; "The manufacturing defect theory is based upon a consumer expectancy that a mass-produced product will not differ from its counterparts in a manner which makes it more dangerous than the others.").

maimed or killed.[64] Nor, in the modern world, can a manufacturer reasonably expect to be relieved of responsibility for such harm from hidden production defects.[65] Thus, the expectations of the parties, buttressed by principles of fairness and restitution, support the maker's strict responsibility for harm from latent manufacturing defects.[66] For all these reasons, courts and legislatures widely provide that strict liability is an appropriate standard of liability for injuries resulting from manufacturing defects.[67]

Warranty

The earliest approach the modern law employed to enforce production quality, now in effect for about two centuries,[68] was to imply into the exchange transaction a promise or warranty by the seller of the basic soundness—safety, in this context—of its goods. Today, the implied warranty of merchantability provides buyers a general guarantee, enforceable under Article 2 of the Uniform Commercial Code, against manufacturing defects in the goods they buy.[69] In addition, the sale of a defectively manufactured product may breach an express warranty[70] or the implied warranty of fitness for particular purpose.[71] While strict liability in tort in most states normally may be a preferable theory of recovery for personal injury and property damage, the implied warranty of merchantability also offers a strict basis of liability for those same damages in almost all states, a fact of particular importance in the few states that never did adopt the doctrine of strict products liability in tort;[72] it provides a basis for recovering pure economic losses in the many states that preclude recovery of such damages in tort;[73] and it offers a miscellany of other advantages in various situations.[74]

---

[64] In the leading English case explaining this notion of implied warranty, Lord Ellenborough colorfully explained the concept: "[T]he intention of both parties must be taken to be, that [the product] shall be saleable in the market under the denomination mentioned in the contract between them. The purchaser cannot be supposed to buy goods to lay them on a dunghill." Gardiner v. Gray, 171 Eng. Rep. 46, 47 (K.B. 1815).

[65] If the defect is obvious, there is no untruth within the transaction to generate false safety expectations in the consumer nor, hence, to support a claim against the manufacturer on expectations grounds.

[66] For the policies underlying strict liability for manufacturing defects, see Products Liability Rest. § 2 cmt. *a*. For the ethical bases of strict liability in this context, see Owen, The Moral Foundations of Products Liability Law: Toward First Principles, 68 Notre Dame L. Rev. 427, 467–74 (1993).

[67] By defining liability for manufacturing defects in terms of departure from design specifications, courts and legislatures are employing a basis of liability that is truly strict. See § 7.3, below.

[68] It has been in effect longer in England than in most American states. See Prosser, The Implied Warranty of Merchantable Quality, 27 Minn. L. Rev. 117 (1943). For its roots in ancient law, see § 1.2, above.

[69] UCC § 2–314; see § 4.3, above.

[70] UCC § 2–313; see § 4.2, above.

[71] UCC § 2–315; see § 4.4, above.

[72] Del., Mass., Mich., N.C., and Va. See, e.g., DeWitt v. Eveready Battery Co., 565 S.E.2d 140 (N.C. 2002) (battery leaked acid—implied warranty of merchantability); Estate of Triplett v. General Elec. Co., 954 F. Supp. 149 (W.D. Mich. 1996) (defect in fluorescent light caused fire; common law implied warranty). And of course the merchantability warranty is available in other states. See, e.g., Kline v. Zimmer Holdings, Inc., 2013 WL 3279797, at *7 (W.D. Pa. 2013) (merchantability claim supported defect in hip implant).

[73] See, e.g., Pulte Home Corp. v. Parex, Inc., 923 A.2d 971, 1010 (Md. Ct. Spec. App. 2007) (manufacturing defect causing economic loss actionable in warranty but probably not strict tort), aff'd, 942 A.2d 722 (Md. 2008); Dieker v. Case Corp., 73 P.3d 133 (Kan. 2003) (economic loss doctrine barred negligence and strict liability in tort claims, but plaintiff could recover for manufacturing defect in implied warranty of merchantability)). On the economic loss doctrine, see § 5.3, above.

[74] One important advantage is the 4-year statute of limitations (from date of sale) under UCC § 2–725, compared to the 2- or 3-year statute of limitations normally provided in tort. See § 14.6, below.

Strict Liability in Tort

The doctrine of strict products liability in tort, which evolved out of warranty cases involving manufacturing defects,[75] is particularly well-suited to claims for injuries caused by manufacturing defects.[76] A majority of the earliest cases adopting § 402A of the *Restatement (Second) of Torts* in the mid-1960s involved manufacturing defects,[77] and strict liability in tort remains the preferred basis of recovery in manufacturing defect cases generally[78] and under § 2(a) of the *Restatement (Third) of Torts: Products Liability* in particular.[79]

Whether a product is in a "defective condition unreasonably dangerous" under § 402A, according to the Reporter's comments, depends upon whether it is dangerous beyond the safety expectations of ordinary consumers.[80] For this reason, and because the protection of reasonable consumer expectations is a basic rationale for imposing strict liability on sellers of defectively manufactured products, many of the earlier strict liability decisions involving manufacturing defects explained liability in terms of protecting consumer expectations.[81] Some strict liability decisions have not only explained but purported to apply consumer expectations as a test of liability,[82] sometimes straining because of the vagueness of this test in certain situations.[83]

---

[75] See § 5.2, above.

[76] "Commentators and courts agree that the manufacturing defect case presents the clearest and strongest case for applying both strict liability in tort and the consumer expectations test." Korzec, Dashing Consumer Hopes: Strict Products Liability and the Demise of the Consumer Expectations Test, 20 B.C. Int'l & Comp. L. Rev. 227, 243 n.120 (1997). See also Westerbeke, The Sources of Controversy in the New Restatement of Products Liability: Strict Liability Versus Products Liability, 8 Kan. J.L. & Pub. Pol'y 1 (1998); § 5.1, above. This point has long been acknowledged. See, e.g., Fischer, Products Liability—The Meaning of Defect, 39 Mo. L. Rev. 339 (1974).

[77] Of the first eight cases adopting § 402A, all in 1965 and 1966, six appear to have involved manufacturing defect claims. See § 5.3, above.

[78] See, e.g., Doughtery v. C.R. Bard, Inc., 2012 WL 2940727, at *2–6 (E.D. Pa. 2012) (Pennsylvania law allows strict liability claim for manufacturing defects, though not for design or warning defects, in medical devices); Riley v. De'Longhi Corp., 238 F.3d 414 (4th Cir. 2000) (Md. law).

[79] See, e.g., Estate of Thompson v. Kawasaki Heavy Indus., 922 F. Supp. 2d 780, 786 (N.D. Iowa 2013) ("The Third Products Restatement recognizes that 'strict liability is appropriate in manufacturing defect cases, but negligence principles are more suitable for other defective product cases.' "); Depositors Ins. Co. v. Wal-Mart Stores, Inc., 506 F.3d 1092, 1095 (8th Cir. 2007) (Iowa law). See generally Products Liability Rest. § 1 cmt. *a*, and § 2 cmt. *a*. Special types of manufacturing defect cases may also be decided under the malfunction doctrine. See Products Liability Rest. § 3; see generally § 7.4, below.

[80] See Rest. (2d) Torts § 402A cmts. *g* and *i*. See generally § 5.6 (in general), above and § 8.3 (design defectiveness), below; Annot., Products Liability: Consumer Expectations Test, 73 A.L.R.5th 75 (1999).

[81] See, e.g., State Stove Mfg. Co. v. Hodges, 189 So.2d 113 (Miss. 1966); Ford Motor Co. v. Darryl, 432 S.W.2d 569 (Tex. App. 1968); Phipps v. General Motors Corp., 363 A.2d 955 (Md. 1976); Cassisi v. Maytag Co., 396 So.2d 1140 (Fla. Dist. Ct. App. 1981).

[82] See, e.g., Flaherty v. E-Go Bike, LLC, 2022 WL 445428, at *4 (M.D. Fla. 2022) (denying dismissal of manufacturing defect claim under the consumer expectations test; bike "failed to perform as safely as an ordinary consumer would expect"); Salerno v. Innovative Surveillance Tech., Inc., 932 N.E.2d 101, 109 (Ill. App. Ct. 2010) ("When proceeding under a manufacturing defect theory, we apply the consumer-expectation test to determine whether the product is unreasonably dangerous."); Boy v. I.T.T. Grinnell Corp., 724 P.2d 612, 620 (Ariz. Ct. App. 1986) ("If something goes wrong in the manufacturing process, the result is a product which the manufacturer did not intend and which could hardly be contemplated by the consumer."). See also Branham v. Ford Motor Co., 701 S.E.2d 5, 14 (S.C. 2010) ("the consumer expectations test fits well in manufacturing defect cases").

[83] See, e.g., Chapman v. Maytag Corp., 2000 WL 1038183 (S.D. Ind. 2000), aff'd, 297 F.3d 682 (7th Cir. 2002); Bhagvandoss v. Beiersdorf, Inc., 723 S.W.2d 392, 395–96 (Mo. 1987) (users of non-sterile bandage could not expect it to be free of microorganisms); Fitzgerald Marine Sales v. LeUnes, 659 S.W.2d 917 (Tex. App. 1983). On the vagueness of the consumer expectations test, see § 5.6, above.

Many other courts, apparently understanding that *rationales* for liability theories often serve poorly as liability *tests*,[84] have tended to avoid using consumer expectations as a formal liability standard in manufacturing defect cases,[85] except in certain limited contexts where the consumer expectations test is particularly appropriate.[86] Recognizing that the risk-utility test is entirely inappropriate in a context which properly requires a strict liability standard,[87] many courts in the 1980s and early 1990s simply left manufacturing defect undefined without a liability "test" of its own.

Spurred in the 1990s by the liability definitions for manufacturing defects in the *Products Liability Restatement*, courts in recent years have increasingly based liability for manufacturing defects in two quite different ways. As a formal definition of manufacturing defect, recent decisions have often turned to the *Products Liability Restatement*'s liability standard, "departure from intended design."[88] And in cases involving a product malfunction, where evidence of a specific defect is unavailable but the accident circumstances suggest a product defect, many courts have applied the "malfunction doctrine," a principle of circumstantial evidence allowing recovery on evidence of this type.[89] These two bases of strict liability, examined in the following two sections, are now the principal liability tests for manufacturing defects in most cases. The final section addresses the special case of defective food and drink.[90]

§ 7.3 DEPARTURE FROM DESIGN SPECIFICATIONS

For many years, both courts and commentators considered the meaning of the "manufacturing defect" concept so self-evident as to be self-defining. A defect in manufacture meant simply that through some mistake in the production process a product was produced improperly and, therefore, was "defective."[91] Thus, until quite recently, judicial decisions involving this form of defect generally failed to provide a definitional "test" of liability for such defects.[92] If a plaintiff establishes a manufacturing defect from a commonsense perspective, and further proves that the manufacturer was responsible for the defect and that the defect injured the plaintiff, defendants usually have no reason to contest the plaintiff's conception of a "manufacturing defect."

---

84 See Owen, Expectations in Tort, 44 Ariz. St. L. Rev. 1287, 1306 (2011).

85 See, e.g., Dico Tire, Inc. v. Cisneros, 953 S.W.2d 776 (Tex. App. 1997). However, if a statute defines defectiveness in consumer expectation terms, a court is bound to use that standard in manufacturing defect as in other cases. See, e.g., Chapman v. Maytag Corp., 2000 WL 1038183, at *4 (S.D. Ind. 2000) (Ind. statute; wire pinched between parts of stove during assembly), aff'd, 297 F.3d 682 (7th Cir. 2002).

86 See § 7.5 (*Food and Drink*), and § 16.5 (*Used Products*) below.

87 "The risk-utility analysis applies to design defects case[s], not manufacturing defect cases." Leverette v. Louisville Ladder Co., 183 F.3d 339, 342 (5th Cir. 1999) (Miss. law). For a rare exception to this nearly universal principle of strict products liability, see Controlled Atmosphere, Inc. v. Branom Instrument Co., 748 P.2d 686 (Wash. Ct. App. 1988).

88 See Products Liability Rest. § 2(a). See generally § 7.3, below.

89 See Products Liability Rest. § 3. See generally § 7.4, below.

90 See § 7.5, below.

91 See, e.g., Wade, Strict Tort Liability of Manufacturers, 19 Sw. L.J. 5, 14 (1965) ("[A] defective condition is easily understandable [when] a particular article has something wrong with it. Because of a mistake in the manufacturing process, for example, the product was adulterated or one of its parts was broken or weakened or not properly attached . . . ."); Wilson, Products Liability (pt. 2), 43 Cal. L. Rev. 809, 810 (1955).

92 See, e.g., Bell v. T.R. Miller Mill Co., 768 So.2d 953 (Ala. 2000) (telephone pole made of rotten wood); Sanders v. Hartville Milling Co., 14 S.W.3d 188, 200 (Mo. Ct. App. 2000) (toxins in animal feed); Hewitt v. B.F. Goodrich Co., 732 F.2d 1554 (11th Cir. 1984) (Fla. law) (tire bead bundle broke during manufacturing process); Hall v. Chrysler Corp., 526 F.2d 350 (5th Cir. 1976) (Mich. law) (misrouted transmission cable on truck).

Development of the Departure-from-Design Test

During the 1960s, although little attention was devoted to the issue, products liability scholars began to define the manufacturing defect concept in a manner that evolved into a departure from the manufacturer's intended design standards—a deviation, as it were, from the maker's "blueprint" specifications.[93] Manufacturing defects were so defined in a prominent law review article by James Henderson in 1973,[94] and, over the next couple of decades, a scattering of courts picked up and repeated variations of this formulation,[95] a number of them relying on Professor Henderson's article for authority.[96]

From the first draft of the first sections of the *Products Liability Restatement* in 1993,[97] a manufacturing defect was defined in terms of "a departure from the product's intended design," and § 2 of the *Restatement* as eventually published in 1998 provides:

> A product: (a) contains a manufacturing defect when the product departs from its intended design even though all possible care was exercised in the preparation and marketing of the product . . . .

Since the American Law Institute's adoption of the departure-from-intended-design definition in the early 1990s, an increasing number of courts have used some form of this standard for defining manufacturing defects,[98] some expressly relying on § 2(a) of the

---

[93] See, e.g., Nader and Page, Automobile Design and the Judicial Process, 55 Cal. L. Rev. 645, 649 (1967); Traynor, The Ways and Meanings of Defective Products and Strict Liability, 32 Tenn. L. Rev. 363, 367 (1965) ("A defective product may be defined as one that fails to match the average quality of like products, and the manufacturer is then liable for injuries resulting from deviations from the norm. . . . If a normal sample of defendant's product would not have injured plaintiff, but the peculiarities of the particular product did cause harm, the manufacturer is liable for injuries caused by this deviation."); W.P. Keeton, Products Liability—Liability Without Fault and the Requirement of a Defect, 41 Tex. L. Rev. 855, 859 (1963) ("a miscarriage in the manufacturing process" that made the product different from what "it was intended to be").

On the departure-from-design-specification standard for defining manufacturing defects, see Frumer, Friedman, and Sklaren, Products Liability § 11.02[3][b]; Am. Law Prod. Liab. 3d § 31:3; Products Liability Rest. § 2(a).

[94] Henderson, Judicial Review of Manufacturers' Conscious Design Choices: The Limits of Adjudication, 73 Colum. L. Rev. 1531, 1543 (1973):

> Manufacturing flaws are imperfections that inevitably occur in a typically small percentage of products of a given design as a result of the fallibility of the manufacturing process. A flawed product does not conform in some significant aspect to the intended design, nor does it conform to the great majority of products manufactured in accordance with that design.

[95] The cases almost all involved design defects where the manufacturing defect definition was dictum. See, e.g., Barker v. Lull Eng'g Co., 573 P.2d 443, 454 (Cal. 1978) (a "manufacturing or production defect is readily identifiable because [the product] differs from the manufacturer's intended result or . . . other ostensibly identical units"); Back v. Wickes Corp., 378 N.E.2d 964, 970 (Mass. 1978); Caterpillar Tractor Co. v. Beck, 593 P.2d 871, 881 (Alaska 1979) (under deviation from norm test, a product is defective if it fails to "match the quality of most similar products"); Prentis v. Yale Mfg. Co., 365 N.W.2d 176, 182 (Mich. 1984).

[96] See, e.g., Thibault v. Sears, Roebuck & Co., 395 A.2d 843, 846 (N.H. 1978) (Douglas, J.).

[97] Products Liability Rest. § 101(2)(a), at 7 (Prelim. Draft No. 1, 1993).

[98] See, e.g., Catalano v. MarineMax, 2022 WL 715465, at *12 (E.D.N.Y. 2022) (a unit "deviates in quality and other performance standards from all of the other identical units," so that such a claim that does not allege "that a particular unit differed [from] others in the same product line will be dismissed"); Engren v. Johnson & Johnson, Inc., 2021 WL 4255296, at *2 (D. Mass. 2021) ("a 'deviation from the design [that] rendered the product unreasonably dangerous and therefore unfit for its ordinary purposes' "); Lim v. Ethicon, Inc., 519 F. Supp. 3d 380, 384 (S.D. Miss. 2021) (a "product 'deviated in a material way from the manufacturer's or designer's specifications or from otherwise identical units manufactured to the same manufacturing specifications' "); Sharp v. St. Jude Medical, S.C., Inc., 838 Fed. Appx. 462, 466 (11th Cir. 2020) (Ga. law) ("a deviation from some objective standard or a departure from the manufacturer's [design] specifications"); BIC Pen Corp. v. Carter, 346 S.W.3d 533, 540 (Tex. 2011); Carson v. Depuy Spine, Inc., 365 Fed. Appx. 812, 814 (9th Cir. 2010) (Cal. law).

Restatement.[99] In addition, beginning with Washington in 1981,[100] several states have enacted reform statutes defining manufacturing defects by some formulation of the departure-from-design theme.[101] Mississippi's statute is a good example, providing for liability if a product was "defective because it deviated in a material way from the manufacturer's or designer's specifications or from otherwise identical units manufactured to the same manufacturing specifications."[102]

One of the few early reported decisions explicitly applying a deviation-from-design-specifications standard is *McKenzie v. S K Hand Tool Corp*.[103] While using a ¾-inch ratchet wrench, the parts of which were held together by a snap ring, the plaintiff was injured when the wrench came apart, causing him to fall upon the floor. In an action for his injuries against the wrench manufacturer, the plaintiff's expert theorized that the snap ring failed because of defective manufacture in both (1) the hardness of the snap ring, and (2) the diameter of the wrench handle groove in which the ring was seated. The manufacturer's blueprints contained specifications for the sizes of each component of the wrench together with specific tolerances (upper and lower limits) for each measurement. Each particular wrench was considered acceptable if its particular measurements fit within the tolerance limits, and if any measurement fell outside the upper or lower limits, the machinist knew that the part was unacceptable. As for the ring's hardness, the specifications called for a 48–52 measurement on the Rockwell C scale, whereas the accident-wrench ring ranged (in various places) from 45–51. As for the diameter of the handle groove, the specifications called for 2.290 inches, with a tolerance of .005 inches, providing an acceptable range of 2.285–2.295 inches. Yet the diameter of the groove on the accident wrench measured appreciably larger, between 2.3125–2.3130 inches. Concluding that this evidence was relevant to defectiveness and causation, and that the trial court's exclusion of it therefore was erroneous, the *McKenzie* court ruled that the plaintiff had established a prima facie case of a manufacturing defect.

There are many slight variations in how courts and legislatures define the deviation-from-specification liability standard, although all mean essentially the same thing.[104] A benefit of the *Products Liability Restatement* formulation in departure-from-intended-design terms is that it provides a sound basis upon which formulations of the liability test have already begun to settle.[105] Of course, any such standard must allow

---

[99] See, e.g., Davis v. UHP Projects, Inc., 2021 WL 1293858, at *3 (V.I. 2021); Estate of Thompson v. Kawasaki Heavy Indus., 922 F. Supp. 2d 780, 788–89 (N.D. Iowa 2013); Warren v. K-Mart Corp., 765 So.2d 235 (Fla. Dist. Ct. App. 2000); Myrlak v. Port Auth., 723 A.2d 45 (N.J. 1999) (also relying on state statute).

[100] Wash. Rev. Code Ann. § 7.72.030(2)(a) provides: "A product is not reasonably safe in construction if, when the product left the control of the manufacturer, the product deviated in some material way from the design specifications or performance standards of the manufacturer, or deviated in some material way from otherwise identical units of the same product line."

[101] See La. Rev. Stat. Ann. § 9:2800.55; Miss. Code Ann. § 11–1–63(a)(i)(1); N.J. Stat. Ann. § 2A:58C–2; Ohio Rev. Code Ann. § 2307.74.

[102] Miss. Code Ann. § 11–1–63(a)(i)(1).

[103] 650 N.E.2d 612 (Ill. App. Ct. 1995).

[104] Definitions vary over time even in the same jurisdiction. Compare BIC Pen Corp. v. Carter, 346 S.W.3d 533, 540 (Tex. 2011) ("A manufacturing defect exists 'when a product deviates, in its construction or quality, from the specifications or planned output in a manner that renders it unreasonably dangerous.' "), with Dico Tire, Inc. v. Cisneros, 953 S.W.2d 776, 783 (Tex. App. 1997) ("A manufacturing defect exists when a product does not conform to the design standards and blueprints of the manufacturer and the flaw makes the product more dangerous and therefore unfit for its intended or foreseeable uses.").

[105] The adoption of the standard by a number of courts suggests that this process has begun. Yet the Restatement itself appears unconcerned with uniformity of terminology. See Products Liability Rest. § 2(a)

for tolerances within which a product may be considered nondefective, as the tolerances mentioned above in *McKenzie* illustrate, since absolute perfection is not possible (because of limitations of science and technology), nor desirable (because of cost), nor necessary (for accident prevention).

A straightforward departure-from-design definition sometimes may fail to capture a product hazard that properly should be considered a manufacturing defect, such that the normal shorthand definition sometimes will need to be supplemented in some respect. One way several states embellish the normal deviation-from-design-specs liability standard is to add deviations from "performance standards" or from "intended performance" to their liability definitions,[106] an approach other courts reject.[107] This broadening of a state's formulation of the general liability standard appears intended to cover situations where a product suddenly fails without apparent reason, cases normally handled perfectly well via the malfunction doctrine.[108] Indeed, in appropriate cases, most courts will certainly want to allow such manufacturing defects to be established by the malfunction doctrine and possibly by other forms of proof.[109] Yet deviation from a product's specifications is a cleaner, less ambiguous way to cover the great bulk of manufacturing defect cases. This suggests that most courts likely will continue to define manufacturing defects principally in terms of departure from a product's design.

Methods of Proof; Ethical Implications

The statutes and several judicial decisions mentioned above explicitly provide a two-pronged definition of manufacturing defect that allows a plaintiff to establish defectiveness by either of two alternative methods of proof: comparing the accident-product unit to the manufacturer's formal design specifications *or* to the dimensions and other parameters of some otherwise identical product. The result of either form of proof

cmt. c, restating § 2(a) as meaning "a manufacturing defect is a departure from a product unit's design specifications."

106 Ohio, N.J., La., Wash. (all by statute), and courts in at least N.Y. and Okla. all include deviation from "performance standards" in their formal liability definitions for manufacturing defects. For example, N.J. Stat. Ann. § 2A:58C–2 provides: "A manufacturer or seller of a product shall be liable in a product liability action only if the claimant proves by a preponderance of the evidence that the product causing the harm was not reasonably fit, suitable or safe for its intended purpose because it: a. deviated from the design specifications, formulae, or performance standards of the manufacturer or from otherwise identical units manufactured to the same manufacturing specifications or formulae . . . ." See, e.g., Stich v. Smith & Nephew, Inc., 2021 WL 1997411, at *5 (D.N.J. 2021); Miller v. C. R. Bard, Inc., 2021 WL 1063800, *3 (W.D. Okla. 2021) ("When a defect is alleged to stem from the manufacture of the product, the plaintiff must show that the product 'deviates in some material way from its design or performance standards.' "); Tomlin v. Smith & Nephew, Inc., 2020 WL 5230830, at *5 (S.D. Ohio 2020); Gambardella v. Tricam Indus., Inc., 2020 WL 5548825, at *7 (S.D.N.Y. 2020) ("a manufacturing flaw exists when the unit in question deviates in quality and other performance standards from all of the other identical units"); La. Rev. Stat. Ann. § 9:2800.55.

107 See Norman v. Bodum USA, Inc., 2021 WL 2292808, at *8 (W.D. Tex. 2021) ("Texas law . . . does not permit a plaintiff to rely on deviation from performance standards to establish a manufacturing defect."). See also Zetz v. Bos. Sci. Corp., 398 F. Supp. 3d 700, 709 (E.D. Cal. 2019) ("Plaintiffs' allegations that the Product degraded and fragmented and failed to perform as designed and intended after being implanted into Ms. Zetz do not demonstrate, let alone plead, a manufacturing defect.").

108 See, e.g., Metropolitan Prop. & Cas. Ins. Co. v. Deere & Co., 25 A.3d 571, 584–85 (Conn. 2011) (citing Third Rest. § 3); Shaun T. Mian Corp. v. Hewlett-Packard Co., 237 S.W.3d 851, 858 (Tex. App. 2007); Jurls v. Ford Motor Co., 752 So.2d 260, 265–66 (La. Ct. App. 2000) (3–2 decision). On the malfunction doctrine generally, see § 7.4, below.

109 See Magnuson v. Kelsey-Hayes Co., 844 S.W.2d 448, 455 (Mo. Ct. App. 1992) ("a showing of non-conformity to design . . . is illustrative of one form of proof which may be presented"). See also Gonzalez v. Autoliv ASP, Inc., 64 Cal. Rptr. 3d 908, 918 (Ct. App. 2007) (a manufacturing defect "is often demonstrated by showing [that] the product performed differently from other ostensibly identical units of the same product line").

should be essentially the same, for the two approaches provide alternative routes to the same destination—a determination of whether the product in question was produced or assembled in a manner contrary to the manufacturer's intentions.

Permitting a plaintiff to establish an accident-product's defectiveness simply by comparing its characteristics to those of a like product unit found on a retailer's shelf[110] has interesting practical and ethical implications. As a practical matter, this liability standard means that a plaintiff's lawyer often may easily be able to determine the defectiveness of an accident product prior to filing a lawsuit. The plaintiff's expert, after locating another product unit of the same make and model, may simply compare and contrast the two products to ascertain whether the accident is fairly traceable to some physical difference between the two product units resulting from some variation in the production process.[111] In some cases, no doubt, an expert will be unable reliably to determine defectiveness or causation simply by comparing two product units.[112] Often, however, a simple comparative analysis will provide a firm basis for determining whether a product accident in fact was caused by a flaw in manufacture.

Certain strategic and ethical implications spring from this ready availability of a relatively simple test of manufacturing defectiveness. In particular, it would seem that plaintiffs' attorneys handling manufacturing defect cases must seek to obtain such comparative analyses prior to filing suit.[113] Similarly, once defense counsel gain access to accident products in manufacturing defect cases, they must compare those product units to the manufacturer's design specifications and conform the defense of such cases to the results of those comparisons.[114]

What all this ordinarily means, of course, is that a plaintiff's counsel may not ethically pursue a manufacturing defect claim, nor may a defense counsel ethically contest such a claim, once the manufacturing defect issue[115] is resolved simply by the physical evidence.

§ 7.4 PRODUCT MALFUNCTION

In modern products liability litigation, it is axiomatic that a plaintiff normally must prove that a product was defective, that the product contained the defect when it left the defendant's control, and that the defect proximately caused the plaintiff's harm.[116] A plaintiff who fails to establish each of these elements by a preponderance of the evidence

---

[110] Literally or metaphorically.

[111] See, e.g., In re Mentor Corp. Obtape Transobturator Sling Prods. Liab. Litig., 2015 WL 5139616, at *2 (M.D. Ga. 2015) (unable to examine the implanted defective product, plaintiff's expert's testimony that Obtape samples tested for earlier litigation contained closed-end pores and pores smaller than 40 microns—departures from specifications requiring pore sizes of 40 to 100 microns—was sufficient to defeat the manufacturer's summary judgment motion).

[112] For example, in the *McKenzie* case discussed above, the measurements were so precise that a reliable defectiveness determination may have been possible only because the experts were able to compare the measurements of the accident product against the measurements and tolerances actually specified by the manufacturer. *McKenzie*, 650 N.E.2d at 614–15.

[113] See Fed. R. Civ. P. 11.

[114] Id.

[115] Causation, of course, is another matter.

[116] See Keeton, Dobbs, Keeton, and Owen, Prosser and Keeton on the Law of Torts § 103, at 712–13.

fails to make a prima facie case.[117] If a manufacturing defect causes a product accident, usually the plaintiff can prove the defect and its causal relation to both the manufacturer and the accident largely by direct evidence—as by testimony from an expert that the product contained an identifiable production flaw, a deviation from design specifications, that caused the product to fail in a particular manner.[118]

Sometimes, however, a product may malfunction under circumstances suggesting a manufacturing defect (or possibly a design defect)[119] but without leaving any direct physical evidence as to how or why, specifically, the product failed to operate properly. In such cases, the absence of direct evidence of product defectiveness and causation hampers a plaintiff's efforts to establish a prima facie products liability case.

In negligence law, if the specific cause of a product malfunction is unknown, the doctrine of res ipsa loquitur allows a jury to infer a manufacturer's negligence when the circumstances of the accident suggest that a product was negligently manufactured or designed, or it contained inadequate warnings or instructions. However, because the res ipsa doctrine is designed to establish a defendant's *negligence* rather than a product's *defectiveness*, most courts consider the res ipsa doctrine technically inapplicable to strict liability in tort or breach of implied warranty, both of which are unconcerned with a defendant's conduct.[120] Although not entirely necessary,[121] the courts, in an effort to maintain a fundamental distinction between negligence and strict liability, began at an early date to tailor principles similar to those that underlie res ipsa loquitur[122] into a

---

117 This is certainly true for strict liability in tort. See § 5.3, above. It is generally true as well for negligence and breach of the implied warranty of merchantability. See, e.g., Riley v. De'Longhi Corp., 238 F.3d 414 (4th Cir. 2000) (Md. law) (requirements apply to strict liability, negligence, and breach of warranty).

118 See §§ 6.3 and 7.3, above.

119 See, e.g., Genaw v. Garage Equip. Supply Co., 856 Fed. Appx. 23, 27 (6th Cir. 2021) (Mich. law) ("The fact that simply driving a vehicle onto the lift caused it to slide suddenly and with enough force to fatally wound a person standing nearby is enough to raise a reasonable inference that Garage Equipment manufactured a defective lift."); Gambardella v. Tricam Indus., Inc., 2020 WL 5548825, at *8 (S.D.N.Y. 2020) (plaintiff's testimony that she heard a snapping sound before she fell from footstool "raised a genuine issue of material fact as to whether the stepstool had a manufacturing defect such that her stepstool was defective"). See also Rudd v. General Motors Corp., 127 F. Supp. 2d 1330, 1340 (M.D. Ala. 2001) (pickup truck's fan blade broke due to fatigue fracture that might have resulted from low-strength alloy used to make fan); Products Liability Rest. § 3 cmt. *b*.

120 See, e.g., Olshansky v. Rehrig Int'l, 872 A.2d 282 (R.I. 2005); Myrlak v. Port Auth., 723 A.2d 45, 53 (N.J. 1999) ("*Res ipsa loquitur* is a doctrine created under the fault theory of negligence as a means of circumstantially proving a defendant's lack of due care. Strict products liability, on the other hand, is a theory of liability based upon allocating responsibility regardless of a defendant's unreasonableness, negligence, or fault."). This is the majority rule. See also O'Connor v. General Motors Corp., 1997 WL 792996, at *3 (Conn. Super. Ct. 1997) ("Res ipsa loquitur relates to cases involving negligence and has no application to cases where a strict liability theory is advanced."); Tresham v. Ford Motor Co., 79 Cal. Rptr. 883, 886 (Ct. App. 1969) ("When a party relies on the rule of *strict* liability the requirement of showing a defect cannot be satisfied by reliance on the doctrine of res ipsa loquitur."). On the relationship between res ipsa loquitur and the malfunction doctrine, see, e.g., Metropolitan Prop. & Cas. Ins. Co. v. Deere & Co., 25 A.3d 571, 581 n.7 (Conn. 2011).

A couple of courts allow plaintiffs to use res ipsa to establish defectiveness for purposes of strict products liability. See, e.g., Parsons v. Ford Motor Co. 85 S.W.3d 323, 331 (Tex. App. 2002) (res ipsa available in both negligence and strict liability to provide presumption of product defect and causation); Jurls v. Ford Motor Co., 752 So.2d 260 (La. Ct. App. 2000) (res ipsa may be used to establish liability under statute defining manufacturing defect as a deviation from manufacturer's design specifications).

121 Unnecessary because a negligence claim requires proof of each element of a strict products liability claim, including defectiveness, plus the additional element of fault. See §§ 2.1 and 5.9, above. Thus, proof of a manufacturer's negligence under res ipsa logically includes within itself proof that the product was defective.

122 "Strictly speaking, since proof of negligence is not in issue, res ipsa loquitur has no application to strict liability; but the inferences which are the core of the doctrine remain, and are no less applicable." W. Prosser, Law of Torts § 103, at 672–73 (4th ed. 1971). On res ipsa, see § 2.5, above.

separate doctrine for proving claims in strict products liability.[123] Aptly dubbed the "malfunction theory"[124]—or sometimes the "indeterminate defect" or "general defect" theory[125]—these special principles of circumstantial evidence now provide a widely accepted means for proving, when direct evidence of a product's defectiveness is unavailable, that a product's failure was most likely attributable to a defect.[126]

Under the malfunction doctrine, a plaintiff may establish a prima facie case of product defect by proving circumstantially that the product failed in normal use under circumstances suggesting that a product defect probably caused the failure. Put otherwise, a product defect may be inferred by evidence that: (1) the product malfunctioned, (2) the malfunction occurred during proper use, and (3) the product had not been altered or misused in a manner that may plausibly have caused the malfunction. More generally, the malfunction doctrine holds that a plaintiff need not identify a *specific* defect that caused an accident if that is not feasible and if circumstantial evidence permits an inference that the product, in one way or another, probably was defective.[127]

Since normal products liability doctrine requires a plaintiff to establish that a product was defective and that the defect caused his or her harm, requiring a plaintiff to prove that a specific defect caused the accident normally makes good sense. But the very purpose of the malfunction doctrine is to allow a plaintiff to prove a case by circumstantial evidence when a product clearly fails but there simply is no direct evidence of precisely how or why it did so. Sometimes the specific cause of a malfunction disappears in the accident when the product blows up, burns up, is otherwise severely

---

[123] Early examples of the doctrine in nascent form include Marathon Battery Co. v. Kilpatrick, 418 P.2d 900 (Okla. 1965); Greco v. Bucciconi Eng'g Co., 283 F. Supp. 978, 982 (W.D. Pa. 1967), aff'd, 407 F.2d 87 (3d Cir. 1969); MacDougall v. Ford Motor Co., 257 A.2d 676 (Pa. Super. Ct. 1969). For the doctrine's even earlier warranty law basis, see W. Prosser, Law of Torts § 103 (4th ed. 1971).

[124] Or the "malfunction doctrine." It is called one or the other in several jurisdictions, including Pennsylvania, which (together with New Jersey) has the most developed jurisprudence on this doctrine. See, e.g., Beard v. Johnson & Johnson, Inc., 41 A.3d 823, 825 (Pa. 2012); Barnish v. KWI Bldg. Co., 916 A.2d 642, 646–48 (Pa. Super. Ct. 2007); Ducko v. Chrysler Motors Corp., 639 A.2d 1204 (Pa. Super. Ct. 1994); Rogers v. Johnson & Johnson Prods., Inc., 565 A.2d 751 (Pa. 1989); Kuisis v. Baldwin-Lima-Hamilton Corp., 319 A.2d 914 (Pa. 1974). See generally Metropolitan Prop. & Cas. Ins. Co. v. Deere & Co., 25 A.3d 571, 581–83 (Conn. 2011) (fully describing the malfunction doctrine).

[125] The *indeterminate* and *general* defect terms reflect the doctrine's application when circumstances surrounding an accident suggest a product defect but no direct evidence of any *specific* defect is available. See, e.g., Bensenberg v. FCA US LLC, 31 F.4th 529, 540 (7th Cir. 2022) (Ill. law) ("non-specific defect" theory; airbag failure to deploy); Roskop Dairy, L.L.C. v. GEA Farm Techs., Inc., 871 N.W.2d 776, 796 (Neb. 2015) ("indeterminate"); Assurance Co. of Am. v. York Int'l, Inc., 305 Fed. Appx. 916, 921 (4th Cir. 2009) (Md. law) (same); Myrlak v. Port Auth., 723 A.2d 45, 55 (N.J. 1999) (same); Corcoran v. General Motors Corp., 81 F. Supp. 2d 55, 66 (D.D.C. 2000) ("general"); Hall v. General Motors Corp., 8 F.3d 27 (9th Cir. 1993) (Or. law) (same). See also McManus v. Barnegat Operating Co., L.P., 828 Fed. Appx. 846, 849 (3d Cir. 2020) (N.J. law). To distinguish this doctrine of strict liability, one might label it "defect ipsa loquitur." Without assigning a particular name to the doctrine, most courts refer to "it" simply as a principle of circumstantial evidence.

[126] See Frumer, Friedman, and Sklaren, Products Liability § 8.06 (in general) and § 22.09[8] (automobiles); Am. Law Prod. Liab. §§ 3:13, 17:66, & 31:21–31:28; Marks, Determining the Indeterminate Defect, 36 St. Mary's L.J. 237 (2005); Hoffman, Res Ipsa Loquitur and Indeterminate Product Defects: If They Speak for Themselves, What Are They Saying?, 36 S. Tex. L. Rev. 353 (1995); Schwartz, New Products, Old Products, Evolving Law, Retroactive Law, 58 N.Y.U. L. Rev. 796, 828 (1983); Note, Rolling the "Barrel" a Little Further: Allowing Res Ipsa Loquitur to Assist in Proving Strict Liability in Tort Manufacturing Defects, 38 Wm. & Mary L. Rev. 1197 (1997); Annot., 65 A.L.R.4th 346 (1988) (malfunction doctrine); Prod. Liab. Rep. (CCH) ¶ 1740; Products Liability Rest. § 3.

[127] Products Liability Rest. § 3, cmt. *c*, provides: "The inference of defect may be drawn under this Section without proof of the specific defect. Furthermore, quite apart from the question of what type of defect was involved, the plaintiff need not explain specifically what constituent part of the product failed."

damaged, or is thereafter discarded[128] or simply lost.[129] Yet sometimes products simply malfunction, inexplicably, leaving no tangible trace of how or why they failed. In such "mystery malfunction" situations, provided that circumstantial evidence sufficiently replaces direct evidence that is plausibly unavailable, courts often properly refuse to require a plaintiff to prove what specific defect caused a product to malfunction.

Because the malfunction doctrine is merely a principle of circumstantial evidence rather than a formal definition of what constitutes a manufacturing defect, the doctrine is logically compatible with a definition of manufacturing defect in terms of a departure from the manufacturer's design specifications.[130]

Applicability

The malfunction doctrine is frequently applied to cases involving cars and other automotive vehicles. In *Ducko v. Chrysler Motors Corp.*,[131] for example, the plaintiff was driving a new Chrysler Fifth Avenue[132] on a dry road at 55 mph when the car suddenly jerked to the right, the steering locked, and the brakes failed to respond. The car crashed, and the plaintiff broke her back. No specific defect in the vehicle could be found. The plaintiffs' expert concluded that the accident was caused by a transient malfunction of the power system for the steering and brakes, whereas Chrysler's expert postulated that the accident resulted from driver error. Because the plaintiff could not prove the specific defect that caused the crash, the trial court entered summary judgment for the defendant. Based on the malfunction doctrine, the superior court reversed and remanded for trial, holding that a plaintiff need not establish a specific defect to prove a manufacturing defect but may establish a case-in-chief by proving (1) that the product malfunctioned, and (2) the absence of likely causes other than product defect.[133] Because circumstantial evidence of this type would permit a jury to infer that the product probably was defective at the time of sale,[134] the trial court's grant of summary judgment to Chrysler improperly precluded the jury from determining the cause of the accident—

---

[128] See, e.g., DiCosolo v. Janssen Pharms., Inc., 951 N.E.2d 1238, 1244 (Ill. App. Ct. 2011) (plaintiff discarded the product); Fallon v. Matworks, 918 A.2d 1067, 1074–76 (Conn. Super. Ct. 2007) (after plaintiff fell on carpet tile, when its rubber backing delaminated, carpet was taken up and discarded; explaining malfunction doctrine, court denied seller's motion for summary judgment).

[129] **Spoliation of evidence.** The loss of a product that is the subject of a products liability action raises issues of "spoliation" of evidence. See, e.g., Schaeger v. Universal Scaffolding & Equip., LLC, 839 F.3d 599, 610–12 (7th Cir. 2016) (Ill. law) (reversing dismissal of plaintiffs' spoliation claim); Wallace v. Ford Motor Co., 2013 WL 3288435, at *7 (S.D. Miss. 2013) (allowing evidence and argument on whether vehicle was lost by plaintiff's attorney through "bad conduct"); Martin v. Keeley & Sons, Inc., 979 N.E.2d 22, 30–33 (Ill. 2012) (summary judgment for defendant on spoliation of evidence claims); Arch Ins. Co. v. Broan-NuTone, LLC, 509 Fed. Appx. 453, 457 (6th Cir. 2012) (Ky. law) (plaintiff sanctioned for spoliation of evidence); Flynn v. Metalcraft, 2007 WL 1464578, at *3–4 (D.S.C. 2007) (denying defendant's summary judgment motion for spoliation); Rizzuto v. Davidson Ladders, Inc., 905 A.2d 1165 (Conn. 2006) (recognizing intentional spoliation of evidence as independent tort, contrary to most courts). *But see* Reynolds v. Bordelon, 172 So.3d 589 (La. 2015) (declining to recognize negligent spoliation tort). See generally 2 McCormick on Evidence § 265; 2 Wigmore on Evidence §§ 277–81, 291 (1979).

[130] See Jurls v. Ford Motor Co., 752 So.2d 260, 265–66 (La. Ct. App. 2000) (3–2 decision) (under deviation-from-specifications statutory definition of manufacturing defect, proof of product malfunction entitled plaintiff to jury determination of manufacturing defect on basis of res ipsa).

[131] 639 A.2d 1204 (Pa. Super. Ct. 1994).

[132] The car had been driven 1,655 miles since its purchase less than two months earlier. Id. at 1205.

[133] The Pennsylvania courts characterize such alternative likely causes as "abnormal use or reasonable, secondary causes for the malfunction." See *Ducko*, 639 A.2d at 1205 (citing Rogers v. Johnson & Johnson Prods., Inc., 565 A.2d 751, 754 (Pa. 1989)).

[134] *Ducko*, 639 A.2d at 1205.

whether driver error or, based on the plaintiff's testimony of steering and braking problems, some defect in the car.[135]

In addition to cases like *Ducko* that involve the sudden failure of a vehicle's steering[136] or brakes,[137] courts have applied the malfunction doctrine to other automotive cases in which a vehicle inexplicably accelerates,[138] changes gears,[139] catches fire,[140] or rolls over;[141] in which a tire fails;[142] or in which an airbag fails to deploy,[143] deploys improperly,[144] or spews acid on an occupant.[145] In addition to automobiles, courts have applied the doctrine to malfunctions of a wide range of other products, as when a bottle of ketchup,[146] jar of peanuts,[147] an automatic coffee maker's glass carafe,[148] or a silicone breast implant[149] breaks apart; a bottle of soda pop,[150] gas grill,[151] glass baby bottle,[152]

---

[135] "Mrs. Ducko's testimony of the erratic performance of the vehicle's steering and braking systems, under the circumstances of this case, was sufficient to make out a prima facie case of a manufacturing defect in the vehicle. The issue of strict liability, therefore, was a disputed issue for the jury. Although a jury, after considering the testimony of appellee's expert witnesses, may find that the vehicle was not defective and that the accident was caused by operator error, it was improper for the trial court to make such a determination summarily and as a matter of law." Id. at 1207.

[136] See, e.g., Stackiewicz v. Nissan Motor Corp. in U.S.A., 686 P.2d 925 (Nev. 1984) (steering on automobile with 2,400 total miles suddenly locked; routine maintenance performed at 1,000 miles); Millette v. Radosta, 404 N.E.2d 823 (Ill. App. Ct. 1980) (11,000 miles); Caprara v. Chrysler Corp., 423 N.Y.S.2d 694 (App. Div. 1979), aff'd on other grounds, 417 N.E.2d 545 (N.Y. 1981); Stewart v. Ford Motor Co., 553 F.2d 130 (D.C. Cir. 1977) (12 days old; 1,400 miles).

[137] See, e.g., Strzelczyk v. Palumbo, 958 N.Y.S.2d 245, 246–47 (App. Div. 2012) (antilock brake); Vernon v. Stash, 532 A.2d 441 (Pa. Super. Ct. 1987) (parking brake); Tweedy v. Wright Ford Sales, Inc., 357 N.E.2d 449 (Ill. 1976) (7,500 miles); Darryl v. Ford Motor Co., 440 S.W.2d 630 (Tex. 1969) (truck: 600–700 miles).

[138] See, e.g., Wakabayashi v. Hertz Corp., 660 P.2d 1309 (Haw. 1983) (1½ years old; 22,577 miles); Phipps v. General Motors Corp., 363 A.2d 955 (Md. 1976). See also Hill v. Kia Motors Am., Inc., 2022 WL 557823, at *9–10 (6th Cir. 2022) (Tenn. law) (unintended acceleration resulted in three fatalities); Jurls v. Ford Motor Co., 752 So.2d 260 (La. Ct. App. 2000) (cruise control apparently failed to disengage).

[139] See, e.g., Harrell Motors, Inc. v. Flanery, 612 S.W.2d 727 (Ark. 1981); Williams v. Deere & Co., 598 S.W.2d 609 (Mo. App. 1980) (tractor: 2 years old).

[140] See, e.g., TNT Road Co. v. Sterling Truck Corp., 2004 WL 1626254 (D. Me. 2004); Cincinnati Ins. Co. v. Volkswagen of Am., Inc., 502 N.E.2d 651 (Ohio App. 1985); Hinckley v. La Mesa R.V. Ctr., Inc., 205 Cal. Rptr. 22 (Ct. App. 1984).

[141] See, e.g., Perkins v. Trailco Mfg. & Sales Co., 613 S.W.2d 855 (Ky. 1981) (new dump truck, properly used and maintained, overturned).

[142] See Taylor v. Cooper Tire & Rubber Co., 130 F.3d 1395 (10th Cir. 1997) (Utah law); Colboch v. Uniroyal Tire Co., 670 N.E.2d 1366 (Ohio Ct. App. 1996).

[143] See, e.g., Silvestri v. General Motors Corp., 210 F.3d 240 (4th Cir. 2000) (N.Y. law).

[144] See Perez-Trujillo v. Volvo Car Corp., 137 F.3d 50, 51 (1st Cir. 1998) (P.R. law).

[145] See McEneaney v. Haywood, 687 N.Y.S.2d 547 (App. Div. 1999).

[146] See Powers v. Hunt-Wesson Foods, Inc., 219 N.W.2d 393 (Wis. 1974).

[147] See Welge v. Planters Lifesavers Co., 17 F.3d 209, 210 (7th Cir. 1994) (Ill. law) (Posner, C.J.).

[148] See, e.g., Rizzo v. Corning Inc., 105 F.3d 338, 343 (7th Cir. 1997) (Ill. law) (Posner, C.J.) ("A carafe designed to be used for years, not months, breaks in half without being dropped or banged or cleaned with abrasive cleansers or damaged in a flood or fire. In these unusual circumstances the accident itself is sufficient evidence of a defect to permit, though of course not compel, the jury to infer a defect. Whether these *were* the circumstances of the accident was a jury question."); Mondido v. Cory Corp., 483 F. Supp. 26 (E.D.N.Y. 1979).

[149] See Baxter Healthcare Corp. v. Grimes, 1998 WL 548729 (Tex. App. 1998).

[150] See, e.g., Dansak v. Cameron Coca-Cola Bottling Co., 703 A.2d 489 (Pa. Super. Ct. 1997); Robertson v. Gulf S. Beverage, Inc., 421 So.2d 877 (La. 1982); Embs v. Pepsi-Cola Bottling Co., 528 S.W.2d 703 (Ky. Ct. App. 1975); Lee v. Crookston Coca-Cola Bottling Co., 188 N.W.2d 426 (Minn. 1971).

[151] See Adkins v. K-Mart Corp., 511 S.E.2d 840 (W. Va. 1998).

[152] See Patterson v. Foster Forbes Glass Co., 674 S.W.2d 599 (Mo. Ct. App. 1984).

transformer,[153] propane fuel canister,[154] an aerosol can of paint,[155] or an oxygen tank's glass humidifier[156] explodes; a television,[157] clothes dryer,[158] dishwasher,[159] portable heater,[160] combine,[161] refrigerator,[162] lawn tractor,[163] or an electric blanket[164] catches fire; a crutch,[165] grain auger,[166] football helmet,[167] or ladder collapses;[168] a crane brake fails and the crane drops a load;[169] the blade guard of a power circular saw fails to close;[170] a staple gun misfires a staple;[171] a winch cable snaps;[172] and many other situations in which products have inexplicably malfunctioned.[173] Without other plausible explanations for such misadventures, such products are as plainly and palpably unfit for use—"defective"—as the proverbial "trout in the milk."[174]

Limitations and Effect

While courts have applied the malfunction doctrine in many cases to help plaintiffs get to the jury when evidence of a specific defect is unavailable, plaintiffs have lost many other cases in which they have relied unreasonably upon this type of circumstantial

---

[153] See Bich v. General Elec. Co., 614 P.2d 1323 (Wash. Ct. App. 1980).

[154] See Eaton Corp. v. Wright, 375 A.2d 1122 (Md. 1977).

[155] See Van Zee v. Bayview Hardware Store, 74 Cal. Rptr. 21 (Ct. App. 1968).

[156] See James v. Keefe & Keefe, Inc., 377 N.Y.S.2d 991 (App. Div. 1975).

[157] See, e.g., Rone v. Sharp Elecs. Corp., 2000 WL 133822 (D. Kan. 2000); Union Ins. Co. v. RCA Corp., 724 P.2d 80 (Colo. App. 1986).

[158] See United Fire & Cas. Co. v. Whirlpool Corp., 704 F.3d 1338, 1343 (11th Cir. 2013) (Fla. law); Weir v. Federal Ins. Co., 811 F.2d 1387 (10th Cir. 1987) (Colo. law); Cassisi v. Maytag Co., 396 So.2d 1140 (Fla. Dist. Ct. App. 1981) (thorough analysis of doctrine).

[159] See McCoy v. Whirlpool Corp., 2003 WL 21554950 (D. Kan. 2003).

[160] See Riley v. De'Longhi Corp., 238 F.3d 414 (4th Cir. 2000) (Md. law); Pearson Constr. Corp. v. Intertherm, Inc., 566 P.2d 575 (Wash. Ct. App. 1977).

[161] See Dieker v. Case Corp., 73 P.3d 133 (Kan. 2003).

[162] See Speller v. Sears, Roebuck & Co., 790 N.E.2d 252 (N.Y. 2003).

[163] See Metropolitan Prop. & Cas. Ins. Co. v. Deere & Co., 25 A.3d 571, 584–85 (Conn. 2011) (citing Third Rest. § 3).

[164] See, e.g., Henderson v. Sunbeam Corp., 46 F.3d 1151 (10th Cir. 1995) (Okla. law); Watson v. Sunbeam Corp., 816 F. Supp. 384 (D. Md. 1993).

[165] See Varady v. Guardian Co., 506 N.E.2d 708 (Ill. App. Ct. 1987).

[166] See Thudium v. Allied Prods. Corp., 36 F.3d 767 (8th Cir. 1994) (Mo. law).

[167] See Rawlings Sporting Goods Co. v. Daniels, 619 S.W.2d 435 (Tex. Civ. App. 1981).

[168] See, e.g., Gillespie v. R.D. Werner Co., 375 N.E.2d 1294 (Ill. 1978).

[169] See Kuisis v. Baldwin-Lima-Hamilton Corp., 319 A.2d 914 (Pa. 1974).

[170] See, e.g., Skil Corp. v. Lugsdin, 309 S.E.2d 921 (Ga. Ct. App. 1983); Agostino v. Rockwell Mfg. Co., 345 A.2d 735 (Pa. Super. Ct. 1975).

[171] See Senco Prods., Inc. v. Riley, 434 N.E.2d 561 (Ind. Ct. App. 1982).

[172] See Lachney v. Motor Parts & Bearing Supply, Inc., 357 So.2d 1277 (La. Ct. App. 1978).

[173] See, e.g., Gambardella v. Tricam Indus., Inc., 2020 WL 5548825, at *8 (S.D.N.Y. 2020) (plaintiff's testimony that she heard a snapping sound before she fell from footstool "raised a genuine issue of material fact as to whether the stepstool had a manufacturing defect such that her stepstool was defective"); Fallon v. Matworks, 918 A.2d 1067 (Conn. Super. Ct. 2007) (plaintiff fell when rubber backing delaminated from carpet tile); Dietz v. Waller, 685 P.2d 744, 748 (Ariz. 1984) (new speed boat "disintegrated" at high speed during normal operation).

[174] "Some circumstantial evidence is very strong, as when you find a trout in the milk." Henry David Thoreau, in The Writings of Henry David Thoreau, Journal II 1850—September 18, 1851, 94 (Bradford Torrey ed., Houghton Mifflin & Co. 1906) (Nov. 1850 journal entry). When Thoreau penned this adage in the mid-1800s, dairymen sometimes watered down their milk from trout streams. See, e.g., Watson v. Roof Brothers Wine & Spirits, Inc., 2017 WL 1102996, at *4 n.15 (Ky. Ct. App. 2017); Harper v. Barge Air Conditioning, Inc., 686 S.E.2d 668, 672 (Ga. Ct. App. 2009).

proof.[175] The doctrine presents a seductive but faulty shelter for plaintiffs with insufficient proof of defect and causation, and the law reports brim with decisions that recite the propriety of the doctrine as a general proposition but hold it inapplicable to the facts.[176] The opinions in such cases frequently recite that, while the malfunction doctrine provides a method for plaintiffs in proper cases to establish defectiveness and causation, the law will not allow plaintiffs or juries to rely on guess, conjecture, or speculation.[177]

Although the malfunction doctrine may come to a plaintiff's rescue when circumstances fairly suggest that a product defect caused an accident, it is hornbook law that proof of a product *accident* alone proves neither defectiveness nor causation.[178] Nor does further proof that the accident was *caused by a malfunction* suffice to prove these elements.[179] The crucial additional showing required of a plaintiff in a malfunction case is the *negation of other causes* for the malfunction apart from a product defect. If a plaintiff fails to provide sufficient proof negating alternative causes (most particularly his or her own conduct), a malfunction case will also fail.[180] A fortiori, if a plaintiff seeks to prove alternative causes for the accident rather than negating them, this may serve to undercut an opportunity to rely upon the malfunction theory.[181]

---

[175] Cases both ways are collected in Annot., 65 A.L.R.4th 346 (1988).

[176] See id.

[177] See, e.g., Michelin N. Am., Inc. v. Deal, 381 P.3d 641 (Nev. 2012); Fallon v. Matworks, 918 A.2d 1067, 1076 (Conn. Super. Ct. 2007); Woodin v. J.C. Penney Co., 629 A.2d 974, 976–77 (Pa. Super. Ct. 1993); Willard v. BIC Corp., 788 F. Supp. 1059, 1064 (W.D. Mo. 1991); State Farm Fire & Cas. Co. v. Chrysler Corp., 523 N.E.2d 489, 496–97 (Ohio 1988); Thomas v. Amway Corp., 488 A.2d 716 (R.I. 1985) (irritation, red splotches, rash, and bleeding may have been caused by soap, but cause of condition could not be left to jury speculation).

[178] Including, of course, this hornbook. See, e.g., Black v. DJO Global, Inc., 488 P.3d 1283, 1288 (Idaho 2021) (plaintiff's lower back burns were known to occur during interferential current therapy, which precluded "a jury from inferring that 'an injury would not have occurred . . . had there not been a defect attributable to the manufacturer' "); Michelin N. Am., Inc. v. Deal, 381 P.3d 641 (Nev. 2012); Shaun T. Mian Corp. v. Hewlett-Packard Co., 237 S.W.3d 851, 858 (Tex. App. 2007) (mere fact of product-related accident does not give rise to inference of defect); Bennett v. ASCO Servs., Inc., 621 S.E.2d 710, 717 (W. Va. 2005) (a product defect cannot be presumed solely from accident). See generally W. Prosser, Law of Torts § 103, at 673 (4th ed. 1971); Annot., 65 A.L.R.4th 346, at § 4 (1988) (collecting cases).

[179] Rohde v. Smiths Med., 165 P.3d 433, 438 (Wyo. 2007) ("mere proof" of product malfunction insufficient to create inference of product defect); Williams v. Smart Chevrolet Co., 730 S.W.2d 479 (Ark. 1987) (car door suddenly swinging open while car in motion does not alone prove car was defective; directed verdict for defendant affirmed).

[180] In Ramos v. Howard Indus., 885 N.E.2d 176, 178–79 (N.Y. 2008), the Court of Appeals held that the trial court should have granted summary judgment for the defendant:

> It is well settled that a products liability cause of action may be proven by circumstantial evidence, and thus, a plaintiff need not identify a specific product defect. "In order to proceed in the absence of evidence identifying a specific flaw, a plaintiff must prove that the product did not perform as intended and exclude all other causes for the product's failure that are not attributable to defendants" . . . .
>
> Plaintiff failed to present evidence excluding all other causes for the transformer's malfunction not attributable to defendant such that a reasonable jury could find that the transformer was defective in the absence of evidence of a specific defect. Although a plaintiff is not required to identify a specific defect in a circumstantial case, plaintiff's theory here—that the explosion resulted from a manufacturing defect in the form of an "internal electrical fault"—is pure speculation. Furthermore, . . . plaintiff's expert failed to exclude the possibility presented by defendant's expert that the transformer exploded because it was improperly rewired or rebuilt by Niagara Mohawk employees after leaving defendant's possession. In sum, based on plaintiff's proof, a reasonable jury could not conclude that all other causes of the transformer explosion were excluded, and thus, plaintiff's manufacturing defect claim fails as a matter of law.

[181] See Pitts v. Genie Indus., Inc., 921 N.W.2d 597, 614–15 (Neb. 2019) ("[T]he Pittses have pointed to evidence of specific design defects in the lift that possibly caused an electrical malfunction; but, later, in an

While malfunctions are sometimes caused by defects for which the manufacturer is responsible, product failures also result from improper treatment of products by users and repairers, and many products eventually simply wear out from a long and possibly rugged life.[182] Tires, for example, when worn enough, will eventually blow out. Thus, if the plaintiff fails to show that he used the product properly;[183] or does not show that the product was not misused or tampered with by other parties (such as prior users and repairers) who had access to the product;[184] or that it was properly maintained;[185] or does not establish that the product failed during a normal life span of safe use;[186] then a malfunction case will fail.

So, too, the malfunction doctrine will not help a plaintiff injured when her butane lighter causes an explosion if she lights a cigarette while surrounded by gas fumes in a boat her husband has just fueled up;[187] nor will the doctrine assist a plaintiff injured when his grinding disc explodes if he does not show that the prior user had not abused it;[188] nor will it assist the owner of a used pickup truck that catches fire, where the truck

---

effort to forward his manufacturing defect theory, relied on the malfunction theory by generally asserting that a flaw in the lift's circuitry caused this electrical malfunction. For this reason, the malfunction theory is inapplicable in this case and the district court did not err in refusing to apply it.").

182 On the effect of product deterioration on a products liability case, see § 10.6, below.

183 See, e.g., Corcoran v. General Motors Corp., 81 F. Supp. 2d 55, 69 (D.D.C. 2000) (alleged brake failure; because other evidence suggested driver error, summary judgment for defendant); Saieva v. Budget Rent-A-Car of Rockford, 591 N.E.2d 507, 516 (Ill. App. Ct. 1992) (summary judgment for defendant affirmed where record supported inference that plaintiff was speeding over dark, wet, and bumpy rural highway and simply lost control of van); Cohen v. General Motors Corp., 427 So.2d 389 (Fla. Dist. Ct. App. 1983) (while car was on an incline in reverse gear, plaintiff reached inside and released parking brake, causing car to back over his leg).

184 See, e.g., Parsons v. Ford Motor Co., 85 S.W.3d 323 (Tex. App. 2002) (malfunction doctrine did not apply where dealer's intervening replacement and repair of allegedly defective ignition switch negated inference of a defect); Yielding v. Chrysler Motor Co., 783 S.W.2d 353 (Ark. 1990) (repairers); Farmer v. Ford Motor Co., 316 So.2d 140 (La. Ct. App. 1975) (use of car by prior owner); Scanlon v. General Motors Corp., 326 A.2d 673 (N.J. 1974) (dealer repairer and wife as other driver); Elliott v. Lachance, 256 A.2d 153 (N.H. 1969) (hair loss from permanent solution could result if beautician left solution on hair too long).

185 See, e.g., Schlier v. Milwaukee Elec. Tool Corp., 835 F. Supp. 839, 842 (E.D. Pa. 1993) (blade of power circular saw was dull and saw was dirty).

186 See, e.g., Greco v. Broan-NuTone LLC, 2020 WL 1044002, at *13 (D. Conn. 2020) (bathroom exhaust fan regularly used for seven years without incident; "no reasonable juror could attribute a defect in the product to Defendants."); Kourim v. Emerson Elec. Co., 2004 WL 1391747, at *4 (N.D. Tex. 2004) (where refrigerator leaked and caused damage, "any circumstantial evidence created merely by the valve's malfunction is rebutted by Defendants' evidence that the age of the filter . . . could have caused the failure"); Corcoran v. General Motors Corp., 81 F. Supp. 2d 55, 69 (D.D.C. 2000) ("although brake failure in a new car gives rise to the inference that a defect existed when the car entered the stream of commerce, this inference is unavailable to the plaintiff, whose complaint involves a 7½-year-old car which he drove approximately 23,000 miles without incident"); Woodin v. J.C. Penney Co., 629 A.2d 974 (Pa. Super. Ct. 1993) (no evidence of defect in cord of freezer that had functioned flawlessly for 8 years of continuous operation); Mullen v. General Motors Corp., 336 N.E.2d 338 (Ill. App. Ct. 1975) (28-month-old tire driven 24,000 miles, possibly driven on while underinflated). See generally Prosser and Keeton on Torts § 99, at 696 ("[t]he older the product, the less likely it is that evidence of malfunctioning will suffice as an inference of a construction flaw").

However, even if the product has had a long and full life, "[w]here a failure is caused by a defect in a relatively inaccessible part integral to the structure of the automobile not generally required to be repaired, replaced or maintained, it may be reasonable, absent misuse, to infer that the defect is attributable to the manufacturer." Holloway v. General Motors Corp., 271 N.W.2d 777, 782 (Mich. 1978) (4-year-old car, driven 47,000 miles, suddenly left highway and hit a utility pole; directed verdict for manufacturer reversed).

187 Willard v. Bic Corp., 788 F. Supp. 1059 (W.D. Mo. 1991).

188 See Jakubowski v. Minnesota Mining & Mfg., 199 A.2d 826, 831 (N.J. 1964) (plaintiff failed to show that grinding disc's failure was more likely caused by defect than by wearing out or misuse):

> There is no hint in the record as to the manner and extent of use of the disc prior to plaintiff's use of it. Plaintiff failed to produce as a witness the workman he succeeded or to introduce other evidence which would exclude prior mishandling or overuse of the disc as a cause of the break. It

had been driven over 50,000 miles by two prior owners, one of whom had installed a spotlight on the door frame;[189] nor can homeowners rely upon the doctrine when their toaster-oven catches fire and burns down their home if the toaster-oven may well have lived out its useful life.[190] But a plaintiff must negate only the most likely alternative causes of malfunction, and only by a preponderance of the evidence, so that a plaintiff need not conclusively disprove every conceivable alternative theory of how the malfunction may possibly have occurred.[191]

By nature, the malfunction doctrine often permits a plaintiff to establish a prima facie case—proof of a malfunction together with the absence of plausible causes other than the product's defectiveness—without resort to expert testimony.[192] But if the testimony of the parties and lay witnesses, together with common sense, do not remove the probability of other causes of a malfunction, then a plaintiff fairly may be required to exclude such other causes by expert testimony.[193]

When a plaintiff successfully invokes the malfunction doctrine, a permissible inference arises that a defect caused the malfunction—an inference that the defendant has no obligation (and frequently has no evidence) to rebut.[194] The plaintiff still has the

---

is quite possible that a weakness in the backing was created by inexpert or careless use during the preceding operation, causing the disc to break when plaintiff subsequently used it.

[189] Ford Motor Co. v. Ridgway, 135 S.W.3d 598, 600 (Tex. 2004) (plaintiff's expert "suspected" an electrical system malfunction caused the fire but could not rule out other causes).

[190] Walker v. General Elec. Co., 968 F.2d 116 (1st Cir. 1992) (Me. law) (plaintiffs' expert admitted that shut-off mechanisms on toaster-ovens sometimes wear out and need to be replaced; plaintiffs' toaster-oven used daily for over six years).

[191] In Welge v. Planters Lifesavers Co., 17 F.3d 209 (7th Cir. 1994) (Ill. law) (Posner, C.J.), the plaintiff was injured when a bottle of peanuts shattered as he attempted to replace the lid. The plaintiff testified that he did not mishandle the bottle, but the defendants asserted that the plaintiff had failed to exclude causes for the shattering apart from the bottle's defectiveness. "Elves may have played ninepins with the jar of peanuts while Welge and Godfrey were sleeping. . . . The plaintiff in a products liability suit is not required to exclude every possibility, however fantastic or remote, that the defect which led to the accident was caused by someone other than one of the defendants." Id. at 211. "Normal people do not lock up their jars and cans lest something happen to damage these containers while no one is looking. The probability of such damage is too remote. It is not only too remote to make a rational person take measures to prevent it; it is too remote to defeat a products liability suit should a container prove dangerously defective." Id. at 211–12. See also Bennett v. ASCO Servs., Inc., 621 S.E.2d 710, 717–18 (W. Va. 2005); W. Prosser, Law of Torts § 103, at 673 (4th ed. 1971) ("The plaintiff is not required to eliminate all other possibilities, and so prove his case beyond a reasonable doubt. . . . [I]t is enough that he makes out a preponderance of probability.").

[192] See, e.g., DiCosolo v. Janssen Pharms., Inc., 951 N.E.2d 1238, 1243 (Ill. App. Ct. 2011) (plaintiff not required to provide expert testimony that product contained a specific defect); Sundberg v. Keller Ladder, 189 F. Supp. 2d 671 (E.D. Mich. 2002) (plaintiff need not proffer expert testimony to show that ladder which collapsed was defectively manufactured); Colon v. BIC USA, Inc., 199 F. Supp. 2d 53, 94 (S.D.N.Y. 2001) (plaintiff and other lay witnesses' account of event was sufficient for jury to decide if particular butane lighter was a "lemon"); Perez-Trujillo v. Volvo Car Corp. (Swed.), 137 F.3d 50, 55–56 (1st Cir. 1998) (P.R. law).

[193] See, e.g., Perez v. Toyota Motor Sales U.S.A., Inc., 2013 WL 3540508 (D. Conn. 2013) (Eginton, J.) (alleged unintended acceleration of 8-year-old used Tacoma; malfunction claim failed due to lack of expert testimony excluding alternative causes); McCreless v. Global Upholstery Co., 500 F. Supp. 2d 1350 (N.D. Ala. 2007) (summary judgment for manufacturers of one-year-old chair that collapsed; plaintiff's case depended on engineering expert whose testimony failed *Daubert* standards of reliability by not explaining basis for conclusions that collapse was due to manufacturing and design defects); Cantrell v. Weber-Stephen Prods. Co., 38 Fed. Appx. 921, 923 (4th Cir. 2002) (Md. law) (summary judgment for defendant proper where plaintiff failed to provide expert testimony on why gas grill exploded; without such testimony, "a jury could only infer the presence of a defect in the grill by engaging in 'surmise, conjecture, or speculation' "); Clark v. Bohn Ford, Inc., 213 F. Supp. 2d 957 (S.D. Ind. 2002) (dismissing claim that tire had manufacturing defect for lack of expert testimony because tire failure is not such an unusual event that a defect can be inferred solely from fact that accident occurred).

[194] "[T]he circumstantial evidence rules established in these malfunction theory cases merely establish a prima facie case and permit but do not require a finding for the plaintiff even in the absence of contrary

burden to prove both defectiveness and causation by a preponderance of the evidence; the doctrine merely provides a circumstantial method by which these elements may be proved in the limited class of cases in which direct evidence is unavailable for some good reason.[195] "The plaintiff still must satisfy the burden of proving that a defect is the most likely cause of the accident, and therefore must negate the likelihood of other reasonable causes."[196] Indeed, because of the vagueness of this ephemeral form of evidence built on circumstantial inferences, the plaintiff's burden of proof is especially important in malfunction cases to protect defendants from unfounded liability. Thus, a plaintiff must establish such a case by the *probabilities*, not just the possibilities,[197] and where there is an equal probability that an accident occurred for reasons other than a defect attributable to the defendant, the plaintiff's case will fail.[198]

Acceptance

Having spread across the nation with little fanfare over the last half century, the malfunction doctrine has become a well-established precept of modern products liability law.[199] A substantial and growing majority of American jurisdictions[200] (usually without the "malfunction doctrine" label) now accept this principle of circumstantial evidence for proving defectiveness in strict products liability.[201] Certifying the propriety of the

---

evidence. Thus a defendant need not come forward with rebuttal evidence to avoid a directed verdict. . . . [T]he burden of production does not shift . . . ." O'Connor v. General Motors Corp., 1997 WL 792996, at *3 (Conn. Super. Ct. 1997). See also Cassisi v. Maytag Co., 396 So.2d 1140, 1151 (Fla. Dist. Ct. App. 1981). *But cf.* Graham v. Walter S. Pratt & Sons Inc., 706 N.Y.S.2d 242, 243 (App. Div. 2000) (the inference of defectiveness (and causation) raised by a product malfunction serves effectively to shift to the defendant the burden of coming forward with the evidence (the "burden of production")).

[195] See, e.g., Walker v. General Elec. Co., 968 F.2d 116 (1st Cir. 1992) (Me. law); Ocean Barge Transp. Co. v. Hess Oil Virgin Islands Corp., 726 F.2d 121, 124–25 (3d Cir. 1984) (V.I. law).

[196] *Ocean Barge Transp.*, 726 F.2d at 125. "A party relying on circumstantial evidence [must] eliminate all other potential causes of their injury." Burgett v. Troy-Bilt LLC, 970 F. Supp. 2d 676, 684 (E.D. Ky. 2013).

[197] "For circumstantial evidence to make out a prima facie case, it must tend to negate other reasonable causes, or there must be an expert opinion that the product was defective. Because liability in a products liability action cannot be based on mere speculation, guess or conjecture, the circumstances shown must justify an inference of probability as distinguished from mere possibility." Mateika v. LaSalle Thermogas Co., 418 N.E.2d 503, 505 (Ill. App. Ct. 1981). See also Henry v. Bridgestone/Firestone Inc., 63 Fed. Appx. 953 (7th Cir. 2003) (Okla. law) (plaintiff need not produce the allegedly defective product to succeed on a manufacturing defect claim but must produce circumstantial evidence that tends to support the theory with reasonable certainty and probability).

[198] See Willard v. Bic Corp., 788 F. Supp. 1059, 1064 (W.D. Mo. 1991) (evidence pointing "equally to a cause for which the defendants are responsible and to one for which the defendants are not responsible" will not support submitting a strict liability in tort case to a jury); State Farm Fire & Cas. Co. v. Chrysler Corp., 523 N.E.2d 489, 496–97 (Ohio 1988); Mays v. Ciba-Geigy Corp., 661 P.2d 348 (Kan. 1983) (pipeline explosion).

[199] See Products Liability Rest. § 3, Reporters' Note to cmt. *b* ("A huge body of case law supports this proposition."). For the older case authority, see W. Prosser, Law of Torts § 103 (4th ed. 1971).

[200] Many of the older cases are collected in Annot., 65 A.L.R.4th 346 (1988). Frumer, Friedman, and Sklaren, Products Liability § 8.06[3] lists the following jurisdictions as adhering to some version of the malfunction theory under whatever name: Ala., Ariz., Ark., Colo., Conn., D.C., Fla., Idaho, Ill., Ind., Kan., Ky., La., Me., Md., Mass, Mich., Mo., Neb., Nev., N.H., N.J., N.Y., N.C., Ohio, Pa., S.D., Texas, W. Va., and Wyo. To this list should be added at least Cal., Ga., Haw., Iowa, Minn., Mont., Okla., Or., P.R., R.I., Utah, V.I., Wash., and Wis. Particularly helpful decisions include Metropolitan Prop. & Cas. Ins. Co. v. Deere & Co., 25 A.3d 571 (Conn. 2011), and Myrlak v. Port Auth., 723 A.2d 45 (N.J. 1999). While most case decisions in this list of states were much less explicit and detailed than those cited from Connecticut and New Jersey, at least one decision in each such jurisdiction acknowledges the malfunction method of proof by circumstantial evidence for use in appropriate products liability cases.

[201] Because strict liability in tort is still the principal claim in modern products liability litigation, most applications of the malfunction doctrine have been in this context. See, e.g., Pitts v. Genie Indus., Inc., 921 N.W.2d 597, 614 (Neb. 2019) (holding that "the malfunction theory is applicable in a strict liability manufacturing defect claim"). But the malfunction theory is also especially applicable to claims for breach of the implied warranty of merchantability based on a product's being "unfit" for the ordinary purposes for which

doctrine's widespread acceptance, the American Law Institute in 1998 endorsed the principle in the *Products Liability Restatement* § 3.[202]

It is important for courts and juries to apply the malfunction doctrine sparingly, limiting its use to situations where, first, the circumstances of the case conspire to prevent the plaintiff from establishing defectiveness and causation by ordinary methods of proof, and, second, where circumstantial evidence in the case points fairly to a likelihood that some defect attributable to the manufacturer caused the accident.[203] In a proper case,[204] however, it is difficult to see how any jurisdiction could reject some

---

such goods are used. See UCC § 2–314(2)(c). In Greco v. Bucciconi Eng'g Co., 283 F. Supp. 978, 982 (W.D. Pa. 1967), aff'd, 407 F.2d 87 (3d Cir. 1969), the court explained:

> When machinery "malfunctions", it obviously lacks fitness regardless of the cause of the malfunction. Under the theory of warranty, the "sin" is the lack of fitness as evidenced by the malfunction itself rather than some specific dereliction by the manufacturer in constructing or designing the machinery.

See also Crawford-Sachs v. Goodyear Tire & Rubber Co., 2007 WL 948688, at *1 (Mich. Ct. App. 2007) (to prove breach of warranty, a plaintiff must prove defect, and "[a] demonstrable malfunction is generally clear evidence of a defect"); DeWitt v. Eveready Battery Co., 565 S.E.2d 140 (N.C. 2002); Genetti v. Caterpillar, Inc., 621 N.W.2d 529 (Neb. 2001) (thorough analysis); Sipes v. General Motors Corp., 946 S.W.2d 143, 158 (Tex. App. 1997) (airbag failed to deploy); Collins v. Sears, Roebuck & Co., 583 N.E.2d 873 (Mass. App. Ct. 1992) (fire in dryer's electrical system).

[202] Rest. (3d) of Torts: Products Liability § 3, "Circumstantial Evidence Supporting Inference of Product Defect," provides:

> It may be inferred that the harm sustained by the plaintiff was caused by a product defect existing at the time of sale or distribution, without proof of a specific defect, when the incident that harmed the plaintiff:
>
> (a) was of a kind that ordinarily occurs as a result of product defect; and
>
> (b) was not, in the particular case, solely the result of causes other than product defect existing at the time of sale or distribution.

See Myrlak v. Port Auth., 723 A.2d 45 (N.J. 1999) (adopting § 3). See also Olivero v. Trek Bicycle Corp., 291 F. Supp. 3d 1209, 1221, 1224 (D. Colo. 2017) (predicting Colorado Supreme Court would likely adopt § 3; plaintiffs were "entitled to a jury instruction consistent with Restatement § 3 [whether] a manufacturing defect of unknown nature caused the [bicycle] fork to fail").

[203] See Products Liability Rest. § 3 cmt. *b*; Henderson and Twerski, Intuition and Technology in Product Design Litigation: An Essay on Proximate Causation, 88 Geo. L.J. 659, 672 (2000) (malfunction cases "constitute a relatively narrow subset of products liability cases"); Hoffman, Res Ipsa Loquitur and Indeterminate Product Defects: If They Speak for Themselves, What Are They Saying?, 36 S. Tex. L. Rev. 353, 380 (1995) ("it will be up to the courts to ensure that [§ 3 of the Restatement] is appropriately limited to cases in which circumstantial evidence truly supports a reasonable inference that a defect existed in the product at the time it left the manufacturer's hands and is not simply a 'catchall' for cases in which plaintiffs are unable to sustain their burden of proof of a specific manufacturing or design defect").

[204] Such as when a new appliance explodes or catches fire. See, e.g., Cassisi v. Maytag Co., 396 So.2d 1140, 1151–52 (Fla. Dist. Ct. App. 1981) (strength of inference of defectiveness from malfunction depends on particular type of product; stronger inference of defect arises from dangerous malfunction in self-operating products like televisions and dryers than in products, like cars leaving highway, whose dangers are to a large extent under driver's control).

properly formulated version[205] of such a well-established,[206] fair,[207] and logical[208] principle of proof. In short, the manifest merits of this simple canon of circumstantial evidence—called perhaps "defect ipsa loquitur"—suggest that its acceptance should soon be universal.

§ 7.5 FOOD AND DRINK

From early times, people have relied on the skill and care of others to catch, gather, grow, preserve, prepare, and provide much of the food and drink indispensable to survival. Whether paid for with a beaver pelt, a copper coin, or a dollar, food has always been the single most important product bought and sold by human beings. Both king and pauper live by food and drink, just as both may die by food or drink gone bad. And this essential fact of human life is as true today as it was a thousand years ago. Because pure food is necessary to survival, rendering humans elementally dependent for their health, safety, and very lives on the care and skill of food providers, the rules that govern liability for selling defective food and drink have long stood apart from those concerning other types of products.[209]

Defective food and drink can harm people in myriad ways. The types of defects in different types of foods span the gamut of spoiled meat;[210] particles of glass in ice cream;[211] ptomaine poison in a can of pork and beans;[212] a piece of metal in a meatball;[213] arsenic in biscuit flour;[214] tacks or wire in a loaf of bread;[215] clam shells in a bowl of

---

[205] The Restatement's statement of the doctrine is not ideal, which reflects the difficulty of constructing a concise, general statement of the principle. A formulation of the malfunction doctrine like the following seems preferable:

> If proof of a specific product defect is unavailable through no fault of the plaintiff, the factfinder may infer that a product which malfunctioned was defective at the time of sale if the plaintiff establishes that (1) the malfunction was of a kind that ordinarily does not occur unless the product is defective, and (2) any defect in the product was most likely attributable to the manufacturer and not to the plaintiff, a third party, normal wear and tear, or other causes.

Consider also the commonsense formulation by Chief Judge Richard Posner: "If it is the kind of accident that would not have occurred but for a defect in the product, and if it is reasonably plain that the defect was not introduced after the product was sold, the accident is evidence that the product was defective when sold." Welge v. Planters Lifesavers Co., 17 F.3d 209, 211 (7th Cir. 1994) (Ill. law).

[206] See W. Prosser, Law of Torts § 103 (4th ed. 1971).

[207] When a product "is lost or destroyed in the accident, direct evidence of specific defect may not be available" in which case the malfunction doctrine "may offer the plaintiff the only fair opportunity to recover." Products Liability Rest. § 3 cmt. *b*.

[208] "When the jury reasonably can find that the product is unchanged from the condition it was in when sold and the unusual behavior of the product is not due to any conduct on the part of the plaintiff or anyone else who has a connection with the product, logic dictates that it is a distinct possibility that there is some defect in the product." Brownell v. White Motor Corp., 490 P.2d 184, 187 (Or. 1971).

[209] "No man can justify selling corrupt victual, but an action on the case lies against the seller, whether the victual was warranted to be good or not. But if a man sells me cloth or other thing, [he must] know the cloth to be bad [to] be punished by writ on the case." Keilway's Report (Frowike) 91, 72 Eng. Rep. 254 (1507), quoted in F. R. Dickerson, Products Liability and the Food Consumer 20 (1951).

[210] See, e.g., Prejean v. Great Atl. & Pac. Tea Co., 457 So.2d 60, 61 (La. Ct. App. 1984) (rotten roast was "green as grass"); Swift & Co. v. Wells, 110 S.E.2d 203 (Va. 1959) (food poisoning from pork shoulder containing staphylococci organisms); Salmon v. Libby, McNeill & Libby, 76 N.E. 573 (Ill. 1905).

[211] See Minutilla v. Providence Ice Cream Co., 144 A. 884 (R.I. 1929). See also Davila v. Goya Foods, Inc., 2007 WL 415147, at *1 (S.D.N.Y. 2007) (glass fragments in can of octopus).

[212] See Davis v. Van Camp Packing Co., 176 N.W. 382 (Iowa 1920).

[213] See Jones v. GMRI, Inc., 551 S.E.2d 867 (N.C. Ct. App. 2001).

[214] See Ballard & Ballard Co. v. Jones, 21 So.2d 327 (Ala. 1945).

[215] See Collins Baking Co. v. Savage, 150 So. 336 (Ala. 1933).

chowder[216] and in fried clam strips;[217] a crustaceous creature in a can of mackerel;[218] strychnine in a box of candy;[219] a metal screw in chewing gum;[220] and glass, dead flies, worms, condoms, and mice in Coca-Cola and other soft drinks,[221] not to mention contaminated water[222] and soft drink bottles that explode.[223] But the prize for the most repulsive "food" item sold to a consumer probably should be awarded to the can of chewing tobacco that contained a human toe.[224]

A large majority of the cases involve claims that foodstuffs contained "manufacturing" defects—hazardous objects, contaminants, mice or bugs, and other departures from the safe and wholesome condition intended by the seller and expected by the buyer.[225] Less frequently, foodstuff cases involve claims of defects in design or warning, as from coffee served at too high a temperature with insufficient warning of the risks,[226] or from failing to warn consumers of health risks in certain types of food.[227]

---

216 See Koperwas v. Publix Supermarkets, Inc., 534 So.2d 872 (Fla. Dist. Ct. App. 1988).

217 See Mitchell v. T.G.I. Friday's, 748 N.E.2d 89, 90 (Ohio Ct. App. 2000).

218 See Johnson v. Epstein, 1998 WL 166805 (N.D.N.Y. 1998).

219 See Whitethorn v. Nash-Finch Co., 293 N.W. 859 (S.D. 1940).

220 See Hickman v. William Wrigley, Jr. Co., 768 So.2d 812 (La. Ct. App. 2000).

221 See Watson v. Augusta Brewing Co., 52 S.E. 152 (Ga. 1905) (glass); Floyd v. Florence Nehi Bottling Co., 198 S.E. 161 (S.C. 1938) (dead fly); Norfolk Coca-Cola Bottling Works v. Land, 52 S.E.2d 85 (Va. 1949) (worm); Hagan v. Coca-Cola Bottling Co., 804 So.2d 1234 (Fla. 2001) (condom); Eisenbeiss v. Payne, 25 P.2d 162 (Ariz. 1933) (mouse).

222 See Gash, Beyond Erin Brockovich and a Civil Action: Should Strict Products Liability Be the Next Frontier for Water Contamination Lawsuits?, 80 Wash. U. L.Q. 51 (2002).

223 See, e.g., Escola v. Coca Cola Bottling Co., 150 P.2d 436 (Cal. 1944). Because these cases do not involve risks from consuming the beverage itself, they are treated elsewhere. See generally Frumer, Friedman, and Sklaren, Products Liability § 48.24; Spangenberg, Exploding Bottles, 24 Ohio St. L.J. 516 (1963) (also examining bottle cases, including mice-in-bottle cases); § 7.4, above.

224 See Pillars v. R.J. Reynolds Tobacco Co., 78 So. 365 (Miss. 1918).

225 See, e.g., Young v. Kraft Foods Global, Inc., 2011 WL 2177247 (Conn. Super. Ct. 2011) (maggots in package of Oreo cookies); Mills v. Giant of Md., LLC, 508 F.3d 11, 14 n.1 (D.C. Cir. 2007) (a pebble in a can of peas is a manufacturing defect) (citing Products Liability Rest. § 7 cmt. *a*); Davila v. Goya Foods, Inc., 2007 WL 415147 (S.D.N.Y. 2007) (glass in can of octopus); Phillips v. Restaurant Mgmt. of Carolina, L.P., 552 S.E.2d 686 (N.C. Ct. App. 2001) (employee's saliva in nacho chips bought at Taco Bell); Hickman v. William Wrigley, Jr. Co., 768 So.2d 812 (La. Ct. App. 2000) (screw in gum).

226 The hot coffee cases normally involve claims of defective design (too high a temperature) or warning (failure to warn adequately of the high temperature and its capacity to burn), rather than manufacturing defects. See, e.g., Kessel v. Stansfield Vending, Inc., 714 N.W.2d 206 (Wis. Ct. App. 2006) (hot chocolate); McCroy v. Coastal Mart, Inc., 207 F. Supp. 2d 1265 (D. Kan. 2002) (no duty to warn about severity of potential burns from hot chocolate; extensive review of hot beverage cases); Olliver v. Heavenly Bagels, Inc., 729 N.Y.S.2d 611 (Sup. Ct. 2001) (summary judgment for defendants; discussing other cases). Liability in such cases thus depends on rules that govern these other types of defects, discussed in chapters 8 and 9, below. See Products Liability Rest. § 7 and cmt. *a*. See generally Note, 10 Loy. Consumer L. Rev. 310 (1998) (discussing split in hot coffee burn cases); § 10.3, below. On punitive damages for coffee burns, see Owen & Davis on Products Liability § 26:5.

227 Some courts impose at least a duty to warn of the risk of a serious, possibly deadly, infection from contaminated oysters; the risk normally is only to persons with cirrhosis of the liver, hepatitis, diabetes, high iron content, or suppressed immune systems, which conditions diminish the ability of the body to destroy the bacteria. See, e.g., Woeste v. Washington Platform Saloon & Rest., 836 N.E.2d 52, 55–57 (Ohio Ct. App. 2005) (affirming summary judgment for defendant; warning printed on menu below all oyster entrees was adequate as a matter of law); Simeon v. Doe, 618 So.2d 848 (La. 1993) (no strict liability, but may be duty in negligence to warn); Kilpatrick v. Superior Court, 11 Cal. Rptr. 2d 323 (Ct. App. 1992); Cain v. Sheraton Perimeter Park S. Hotel, 592 So.2d 218 (Ala. 1991) (jury might find oyster eater did not reasonably expect contamination that could cause hepatitis).

A seller's duty to warn of hidden, inherent risks is examined in § 10.3, below.

This section examines recurring issues that arise in the more typical manufacturing defect cases involving food and drink.[228]

Early Law

Early law provided both criminal penalties and civil remedies for the sale of defective food and drink. Beginning in 1266, a series of early English statutes criminalized the sale of "corrupt" food and drink for immediate consumption,[229] and by 1431 the civil law held purveyors of foodstuffs strictly accountable for the wholesomeness of their provisions.[230] Whether this special duty amounted to a common law warranty of the wholesomeness of food is uncertain,[231] but American courts from an early date assumed that it did. In an 1815 New York decision, *Van Bracklin v. Fonda*,[232] a seller of beef was held strictly liable for failing to disclose that the cow had been diseased prior to slaughter. Relying on Blackstone, the court observed that a warranty of quality is always implied into the sale of foodstuffs because "the preservation of health and life" requires the seller to be "bound to know that they are sound and wholesome, at his peril."[233] A century later, recognizing the special vulnerability of food consumers, the

---

[228] For early treatments of the liability of purveyors of food and drink, see, e.g., Perkins, Unwholesome Food as a Source of Liability (pts. 1 and 2), 5 Iowa L. Bull. 6, 86 (1919, 1920); H. Melnick, The Sale of Food and Drink at Common Law and Under the Uniform Sales Act (1936), reviewed in 50 Harv. L. Rev. 553 (1937); Guiher and Morris, Handling Food Products Liability Cases, 1 Food Drug Cosmetic L.Q. 109 (1946); Mintener, Product Liability Law, 5 Food Drug Cosm. L.J. 168 (1950); F. R. Dickerson, Products Liability and the Food Consumer (1951); Note, 92 U. Pa. L. Rev. 306 (1944).

For more recent treatments, see T. Lytton, Outbreak: Foodborne Illness and the Struggle for Food Safety (University of Chicago Press 2019); Alexandre, Justice Kagan's Presidential Administration and Bioengineered Foods: Making the Case for Congressional Guidance as a Check to Presidential Policy Setting, 46 Ind. L. Rev. 265 (2013); Goldberg, Dangerous Drinks, 49 Trial 28 (Mar. 2013); Roses, Food Allergen Law and the Food Allergen Labeling and Consumer Protection Act of 2004: Falling Short of True Protection for Food Allergy Sufferers, 66 Food & Drug L.J. 225 (2011); Noah, One Decade of Food and Drug Law Scholarship: A Selected Bibliography, 55 Food Drug Cosm. L.J. 641 (2000); Annots., 2 A.L.R.5th 1 (1992) (liability for spoiled or contaminated food), 2 A.L.R.5th 189 (1992) (liability for object related to but not intended to be in food). See generally Frumer, Friedman, and Sklaren, Products Liability § 48; Prod. Liab. Rep. (CCH) ¶¶ 30,002H, 30,007; Products Liability Rest. § 7. On English, Irish, and E.U. law, see, e.g., R. O'Rourke, Food Safety and Product Liability (Palladian 2000); R. O'Rourke, European Food Law (Sweet & Maxwell, 3d ed. 2005); D. Jukes, Food Legislation of the UK (Butterworths-Heinemann 1997).

[229] See F. R. Dickerson, Products Liability and the Food Consumer 20 (1951).

[230] "A taverner or vintner was bound as such to sell wholesome food and drink." Ames, The History of Assumpsit, 2 Harv. L. Rev. 1, 9 (1888). The case decided in 1431 provided: "[I]f I come into a tavern to eat and the taverner gives and sells me beer or food which is corrupt, by which I am put to great suffering, I shall clearly have an action against the taverner on the case even though he makes no warranty to me." Year Book, 9 Hen. VI, f. 53B, pl.37 (1431), quoted in F. R. Dickerson, Products Liability and the Food Consumer 20 (1951).

On the evolution of the tort-like warranty applied to food cases, see F. R. Dickerson, Products Liability and the Food Consumer (1951); Prosser, The Assault on the Citadel (Strict Liability to the Consumer), 69 Yale L.J. 1099, 1103–10 (1960) (from which much of this historical discussion is derived).

[231] Compare H. Melick, The Sale of Food and Drink at Common Law and Under the Uniform Sales Act 9 n.10 (1936) (yes), with Perkins, Unwholesome Food as a Source of Liability, 5 Iowa L. Bull. 6, 8–9 (1919) (no).

[232] 12 Johns. 468 (N.Y. 1815).

[233] More fully, the court remarked: "In 3 Black. Com. 165, it is stated as a sound and elementary proposition, that in contracts for provisions, it is always implied that they are wholesome; and if they are not, case lies to recover damages for the deceit. In the sale of provisions for domestic use, the vendor is bound to know that they are sound and wholesome, at his peril. This is a principle, not only salutary, but necessary to the preservation of health and life. [Here,] the concealment of the fact that the animal was diseased, is equivalent to the suggestion of a falsehood that she was sound." Id.

New York high court reaffirmed the view that the special importance of food safety fully justifies imposing strict liability on sellers of defective food and drink.[234]

Although American courts from an early date applied the ancient tort-like warranty of quality to sales of foodstuffs made directly to consumers,[235] the absence of privity of contract often obstructed recovery.[236] However, from the early 1900s,[237] some courts, often intermingling theories of negligence and implied warranty, began breaking through the privity barrier to hold food purveyors liable to third parties. By the middle of the twentieth century, many jurisdictions had abandoned the requirement of privity in food cases by enforcing a special food warranty in tort that ran to remote consumers.[238]

One such case was *Jacob E. Decker & Sons v. Capps*,[239] where a producer sold contaminated sausage to a retail merchant who sold it to Mr. Capps. The Capps family consumed the sausage, killing one of the children and seriously sickening the remainder of the family. In an action against the remote producer, the court imposed an implied warranty in tort into the sale of food and drink running to those injured by the defective meat, reasoning that this kind of strict liability to remote food consumers is necessary as a deterrent to protect human health and life; that remote providers intend that the food they sell to intermediaries eventually will be consumed by someone; that most consumers, lacking the tools, skills, and time necessary to inspect their food for hazards, are unable to protect themselves effectively against dangerous defects in the foods they eat; and that incentives for improving food safety are best placed on food suppliers.[240] Yet, it should be noted that *Capps* was in the vanguard of developing doctrine on the privity issue, and most jurisdictions continued for some time to prohibit warranty actions

---

[234] Race v. Krum, 118 N.E. 853, 854 (N.Y. 1918):

> This rule is based upon the high regard which the law has for human life. The consequences to the consumer resulting from consumption of articles of food sold for immediate use may be so disastrous that an obligation is placed upon the seller to see to it, at his peril, that the articles sold are fit for the purpose for which they are intended. The rule is an onerous one, but public policy, as well as the public health, demand such obligation should be imposed.

[235] See, e.g., Van Bracklin v. Fonda, 12 Johns. 468 (N.Y. 1815) (implication of fraudulent concealment of contamination, and possibly an express representation that the beef was edible). See generally Jacob E. Decker & Sons, Inc. v. Capps, 164 S.W.2d 828, 831–32 (Tex. 1942) (noting that the warranty in food cases was not the modern contractual warranty but the separate tort law warranty derived from the action of deceit).

[236] **Claims against retailers.** See, e.g., Prinsen v. Russos, 215 N.W. 905 (Wis. 1927) (guest—trichinae in ham sandwich); Shepard v. Beck Bros., 225 N.Y.S. 438, 440 (City Ct. 1927) (grandson—nail in coffee cake); Bourcheix v. Willow Brook Dairy, 196 N.E. 617 (N.Y. 1935) (chauffeur—glass in milk); Hazelton v. First Nat'l Stores, 190 A. 280 (N.H. 1937) (wife and two children—trichinosis); Borucki v. MacKenzie Bros. Co., 3 A.2d 224 (Conn. 1938) (purchaser's child—glass in liverwurst).

Claims against manufacturers. See, e.g., Nelson v. Armour Packing Co., 90 S.W. 288 (Ark. 1905); Chysky v. Drake Bros. Co., 139 N.E. 576 (N.Y. 1923). See F. R. Dickerson, Products Liability and the Food Consumer §§ 1.22 (retailers and restaurants), 2.1–2.6 (manufacturers) (1951).

[237] And possibly before. See, e.g., Tomlinson v. Armour & Co., 70 A. 314 (N.J. Ct. Err. & App. 1908), and Mazetti v. Armour & Co., 135 P. 633 (Wash. 1913) (both citing earlier cases). See generally Prosser, The Assault Upon the Citadel (Strict Liability to the Consumer), 69 Yale L.J. 1099, 1106 (1960).

[238] But many courts still refused. Although noting a trend in favor of liability, Prosser in 1941 observed that "[t]he majority of courts still refuse to find a strict liability even as to food." W. Prosser, Handbook of the Law of Torts § 83, at 692 (1941).

[239] 164 S.W.2d 828 (Tex. 1942).

[240] "[W]here food products sold for human consumption are unfit for that purpose, there is such an utter failure of the purpose for which the food is sold, and the consequences of eating unsound food are so disastrous to human health and life, that the law imposes a warranty of purity in favor of the ultimate consumer as a matter of public policy." Id. at 829.

in the absence of privity, leaving negligence for some time as the only form of relief in cases of this type.[241]

Theories of Recovery

Negligence

Although most jurisdictions continued to require privity of contract in most negligence claims well into the twentieth century,[242] courts long have made an exception for products that were "imminently dangerous," initially as to a product's inherent condition[243] and later as to its condition if defective.[244] Food products were so classified from an early date, such that the absence of privity dropped away in state after state as an obstacle to negligence claims.[245]

Because of society's special concern for food safety, some early negligence decisions held purveyors of food and drink to a standard of extraordinary or utmost care.[246] Today, however, consistent with the widespread repudiation of special levels of care,[247] modern courts hold sellers of food and drink, like sellers of other types of products, to the normal standard of reasonable care.[248]

Sometimes, the easiest way for a plaintiff to establish negligence in a bad food case is by proof of a violation of a pure food act, which in many states amounts to negligence per se.[249] But before a court may rule that a pure food act provides a basis for negligence per se, the defendant must have violated the statute, which typically requires a finding

---

[241] See Prosser, The Assault Upon the Citadel (Strict Liability to the Consumer), 69 Yale L.J. 1099, 1103–10 (1960).

[242] Until rejected by MacPherson v. Buick Motor Co., 111 N.E. 1050 (N.Y. 1916), and its progeny.

[243] Such products include poisons, guns, and explosives. See Huset v. J.I. Case Threshing Mach. Co., 120 F. 865, 865, 871 (8th Cir. 1903) (Minn. law).

[244] See MacPherson v. Buick Motor Co., 111 N.E. 1050 (N.Y. 1916).

[245] See, e.g., Freeman v. Schults Bread Co., 163 N.Y.S. 396, 397 (City of N.Y. Mun. Ct. 1916); Minutilla v. Providence Ice Cream Co., 144 A. 884 (R.I. 1929) (good summary). See also Drury v. Armour & Co., 216 S.W. 40 (Ark. 1919); Comment, 4 Fordham L. Rev. 295, 296 n.7 (1935) (collecting cases).

[246] See, e.g., Eisenbeiss v. Payne, 25 P.2d 162 (Ariz. 1933) (the "highest duty known to the law"); Linker v. Quaker Oats Co., 11 F. Supp. 794 (D. Okla. 1935) (very high degree of care).

[247] See Prosser and Keeton on Torts § 34.

[248] See, e.g., Rudloff v. Wendy's Rest. of Rochester, Inc., 821 N.Y.S.2d 358, 361 (City Ct. 2006) ("ordinary care"); Hyde v. Schlotzsky's, Inc., 561 S.E.2d 876 (Ga. Ct. App. 2002) (franchisor not liable in negligence to patrons who contracted Hepatitis A from eating tainted food at franchisee's restaurant where franchisor lacked the ability to control restaurant's day-to-day operations); Jones v. GMRI, Inc., 551 S.E.2d 867 (N.C. Ct. App. 2001); Porteous v. St. Ann's Cafe & Deli, 713 So.2d 454, 457–58 (La. 1998); Flagstar Enters., Inc. v. Davis, 709 So.2d 1132, 1139–41 (Ala. 1997).

[249] See, e.g., QashQeesh v. Monster Beverage Corp., 2020 WL 6544246, at *2 (S.D. Ohio 2020) (dead rodent in energy drink violated Ohio's Pure Food and Drug Law; negligence per se claim was not abrogated by Ohio Product Liability Act); Chambley v. Apple Rests., Inc., 504 S.E.2d 551 (Ga. Ct. App. 1998) (condom in chicken salad); Allen v. Delchamps, Inc., 624 So.2d 1065 (Ala. 1993) (prepackaged celery hearts treated with sulfites in violation of FDA regulations banning their use on fresh produce; asthmatic customer suffered anaphylactic reaction); Koster v. Scotch Assocs., 640 A.2d 1225 (N.J. Super. Ct. Law Div. 1993) (salmonella from Smuggler's Cove); Coward v. Borden Foods, Inc., 229 S.E.2d 262 (S.C. 1976) (hard object in Cracker Jack popcorn). *Contra*, Jones v. GMRI, Inc., 551 S.E.2d 867 (N.C. Ct. App. 2001) (negligence per se doctrine inapplicable to food case).

On negligence per se, see § 2.4, above.

that the particular foodstuff was "adulterated"[250] and which may allow a defense for good faith efforts to comply.[251]

Without the assistance of a pure food act, a plaintiff may have difficulty proving the negligence of the purveyor of defective food.[252] This is particularly true in the case of a food product retailer who purchases the food and then resells it in a sealed container, a situation that deprives the seller of any opportunity to inspect for defects.[253] But, in other cases, the seller's fault is clear.[254] Also, some courts allow juries to infer the negligence of a manufacturer or other seller merely from the presence of a defect in the food.[255]

In cases where direct evidence of responsibility and fault is unavailable, but circumstantial evidence points to the defendant's probable negligence for defective food, plaintiffs in most jurisdictions can invoke the doctrine of res ipsa loquitur.[256] Speaking to this very point, Henry David Thoreau long ago declared, "some circumstantial evidence is very strong, as when you find a trout in the milk."[257] In such cases, the circumstantial evidence surrounding the accident leads to inferences that the food would not have been defective without the negligence of someone, that the defendant's exclusive control over the foodstuff at the time of preparation suggests the negligence was that of the defendant, and that the plaintiff did not contribute to the injury.[258]

Such inferences may be quite strong in cases in which the consumer is injured by a foreign object in food or drink, particularly if it is found in a package, can, or other

---

[250] See, e.g., Jones v. GMRI, Inc., 551 S.E.2d 867 (N.C. Ct. App. 2001); Goodman v. Wenco Foods, Inc., 423 S.E.2d 444 (N.C. 1992) (small bone sliver in ground beef not "adulteration"); Allen v. Grafton, 164 N.E.2d 167 (Ohio 1960) (oysters with shell were not adulterated); Norris v. Pig'n Whistle Sandwich Shop, 53 S.E.2d 718 (Ga. Ct. App. 1949) (barbecued pork sandwich containing piece of pig bone not adulterated).

[251] For example, a criminal pure food act may provide an exception if the seller has acted in good faith, as by obtaining a guarantee of wholesomeness from its own supplier. See F. R. Dickerson, Products Liability and the Food Consumer 282 (1951).

[252] See, e.g., Jones v. GMRI, Inc., 551 S.E.2d 867 (N.C. Ct. App. 2001) (affirming directed verdict for restaurateur on negligence claim for serving meatball with a piece of metal lodged inside); Livingston v. Marie Callender's, Inc., 85 Cal. Rptr. 2d 528 (Ct. App. 1999) (affirming judgment for defendant on negligence, but reversing on strict liability in tort, for not warning of possible allergic reaction to MSG in soup); Cain v. Winn-Dixie La., Inc., 757 So.2d 712 (La. Ct. App. 1999) (no proof that grocery store's bakery was negligent in allowing hair to get into baked cake); Porteous v. St. Ann's Cafe & Deli, 713 So.2d 454 (La. 1998) (reversing judgment for plaintiff on claim of restaurant's negligence for failing to find and remove pearl in oyster po-boy sandwich).

[253] See, e.g., McCauley v. Manda Bros. Provisions Co., 211 So.2d 637 (La. 1968). On the sealed-container (or "original-package") doctrine or defense, see § 15.2, below.

[254] See, e.g., Bullara v. Checker's Drive-In Rest., Inc., 736 So.2d 936 (La. Ct. App. 1999) (allowing cockroach to enter chili dog, failing to discover roach lurking in dog prior to sale, and making sale to customer of roach-infested dog); Flagstar Enters., Inc. v. Davis, 709 So.2d 1132 (Ala. 1997) (allowing blood from unbandaged cut to spill into take-out order of biscuit and gravy).

[255] See, e.g., Bullara v. Checker's Drive-In Rest., Inc., 736 So.2d 936 (La. Ct. App. 1999) (by implication); Vamos v. Coca-Cola Bottling Co., 627 N.Y.S.2d 265, 270 (Civ. Ct. 1995) ("it has long been the rule that a prima facie case of negligence is made out merely [on proof of] a foreign substance . . . sold in a sealed container"); Cohen v. Allendale Coca-Cola Bottling Co., 351 S.E.2d 897, 899 (S.C. Ct. App. 1986) (Bell, J.).

[256] See, e.g., Matthews v. Yoplait USA, Inc., 835 S.E.2d 393, 397 (Ga. Ct. App. 2019) (sharp metal fragments in strawberry yogurt); Knight v. Just Born, Inc., 2000 WL 924624 (D. Or. 2000) (severe chemical burns to mouth from eating Hot Tamale candy); Giant Food, Inc. v. Washington Coca-Cola Bottling Co., 332 A.2d 1 (Md. 1975). *Contra* Jones v. GMRI, Inc., 551 S.E.2d 867, 873 (N.C. Ct. App. 2001) ("*res ipsa loquitur* does not apply in a case involving an injury from the ingestion of an adulterated food product"). See generally Frumer, Friedman, and Sklaren, Products Liability §§ 48.08[3], 48.10[2].

On res ipsa loquitur, see § 2.5, above. On the related malfunction doctrine, see § 7.4, above.

[257] Henry David Thoreau, Nov. 11, 1850, in 2 The Journal of Henry David Thoreau 94 (B. Torry and F. Allen eds., 1984). For explanation, see § 7.4, note 174.

[258] See cases cited note 256, above.

container sealed at the defendant's place of business.[259] In an early case of this type, in which the plaintiff encountered a human toe in a can of chewing tobacco, the court had little difficulty in finding an inference of negligence: "We can imagine no reason why, with ordinary care, human toes could not be left out of chewing tobacco, and if toes are found in chewing tobacco, it seems to us that somebody has been very careless."[260]

Warranty

In cases involving foodstuffs, as with any type of product, warranty claims have a distinct advantage over negligence in that proof of the defendant's fault is not necessary.[261] Although express warranty actions are unusual in foodstuff cases, occasionally they do arise.[262] Thus, when a seller of canned chicken advertises its product as "boned chicken" that contains "no bones," a consumer injured by a bone sliver lurking in the chicken may recover for the seller's false affirmations of fact.[263] Much more typical in food cases are claims for breach of the implied warranty of quality or wholesomeness.[264] This latter form of warranty, now encompassed by the implied warranty of merchantability, provides a strict, no-fault basis for liability under Article 2 of the Uniform Commercial Code.[265] While the sealed-container doctrine,[266] privity,[267] and other sales law restrictions may sometimes limit the reach of warranty law claims,

---

[259] Res ipsa has long been applied in this situation. See, e.g., Richenbacher v. California Packing Corp., 145 N.E. 281 (Mass. 1924); Dryden v. Continental Baking Co., 77 P.2d 833 (Cal. 1938).

[260] Pillars v. R.J. Reynolds Tobacco Co., 78 So. 365, 366 (Miss. 1918).

[261] See §§ 4.1, 4.3, and 5.9, above.

[262] See, e.g., Cott v. Peppermint Twist Mgmt. Co., 856 P.2d 906 (Kan. 1993) (night club waitress told patrons that drink was "good" whereas it was dishwashing detergent containing lye).

[263] See Lane v. C.A. Swanson & Sons, 278 P.2d 723 (Cal. Ct. App. 1955).

[264] See, e.g., McGinty v. Grand Casinos of Miss., Inc.-Biloxi, 245 So.3d 444, 449–50 (Miss. 2018) (allowing breach of implied warranty of merchantability claim to go to jury on "evidence that (1) the pork chop 'tasted funny,' (2) a doctor opined that the illness was 'related to food or drink,' (3) the McGintys drank only water between eating the pork chop and becoming ill, (4) the McGintys both ate the same food and both became sick around the same time, and (5) the time between ingesting the pork chops and their illnesses was short in duration"); Williams v. O'Charley's, Inc., 728 S.E.2d 19, 22 (N.C. Ct. App. 2012) (affirming judgment on verdict for plaintiff hospitalized for seven days after eating chicken that "had a bad aftertaste, stuck to the plate, and was dry"); Phillips v. Restaurant Mgmt. of Carolina, L.P., 552 S.E.2d 686, 689 (N.C. Ct. App. 2001) (state trooper ate food from Taco Bell that contained saliva from employee who spit in food because he thought that trooper might be officer who had previously "harassed" him for skateboarding); Elliot v. Kraft Foods N. Am., Inc., 118 S.W.3d 50 (Tex. App. 2003) (rocks in Grape Nuts cereal breached implied warranty of merchantability); CEF Enters., Inc. v. Betts, 838 So.2d 999 (Miss. Ct. App. 2003) (insect in biscuit from Burger King breached implied warranty of merchantability).

[265] See UCC § 2–314; § 4.3, above.

[266] This doctrine may preclude warranty claims against retailers. See, e.g., Porrazzo v. Bumble Bee Foods, LLC, 822 F. Supp. 2d 406, 422 (S.D.N.Y. 2011) (mercury in canned tuna; retail seller not liable for breach of implied warranty for defect it could not discover through ordinary inspection); Jones v. GMRI, Inc., 551 S.E.2d 867, 870–71 (N.C. Ct. App. 2001) (sealed container defense protected restaurant from implied warranty claim); *Contra* Gentry v. Hershey Co., 687 F. Supp. 2d 711, 721 (M.D. Tenn. 2010) (sealed container doctrine does *not* apply to breach of warranty actions, express or implied); Sparks v. Total Body Essential Nutrition, Inc., 27 So.3d 489, 496 (Ala. 2009); Bonenberger v. Pittsburgh Mercantile Co., 28 A.2d 913 (Pa. 1942) (3–2 decision) (consumer may recover from retail dealer for breach of implied warranty of wholesomeness, even if food sold in sealed container).

On the sealed-container (or "original-package") doctrine or defense, see § 15.2, below.

[267] This doctrine may preclude warranty claims against remote sellers. See, e.g., Barnett v. Leiserv, Inc., 968 F. Supp. 690 (N.D. Ga. 1997) (warranty action brought by child, burned by hot coffee purchased and spilled by family friend in restaurant, barred by lack of privity); Minutilla v. Providence Ice Cream, 144 A. 884, 885 (R.I. 1929) ("there can be no warranty without privity of contract").

courts have long and widely used the law of warranty to provide relief to persons injured by defective food and drink.[268]

Strict Liability in Tort

With the rise of the doctrine of strict products liability in tort in America during the 1960s and 1970s, problems of establishing negligence and satisfying the technical rules of warranty law fell away in cases involving foodstuffs as with other types of products.[269] Negligence and warranty claims are still often asserted in foodstuff cases,[270] but various advantages of strict liability in tort[271] make this doctrine a preferred theory of recovery in most such cases. Thus, purveyors of food or drink have been held subject to strict tort liability for injuries from mice and cigarettes in soft drink bottles, contaminated oysters, a metal screw in a stick of chewing gum, a pebble in a biscuit, MSG in soup, human blood in a biscuit and gravy, and many other cases of defective food and drink.[272]

Regardless of the particular cause of action, two issues of proof frequently predominate in foodstuff cases: defectiveness and causation. The burden of proof on both issues, of course, resides on the plaintiff.[273]

Proving Defectiveness—in General

To recover for injuries from ingesting food or drink, a plaintiff must establish that the food contained some dangerous element that rendered it unwholesome or "defective."[274] Thus, a food or beverage item generally is defective, and a seller generally is subject to liability, if the food product's condition is dangerous in a manner neither

---

[268] See, e.g., Young v. Kraft Foods Global, Inc., 2011 WL 2177247, at *2 (Conn. Super. Ct. 2011) (maggots in package of Oreo cookies); Otis Spunkmeyer, Inc. v. Blakely, 30 S.W.3d 678 (Tex. App. 2000) (hardened herbaceous stem in oatmeal-raisin cookie); Cott v. Peppermint Twist Mgmt. Co., 856 P.2d 906 (Kan. 1993). See generally Frumer, Friedman, and Sklaren, Products Liability §§ 48.15–.19; F. R. Dickerson, Products Liability and the Food Consumer 19–170 (1951); ch. 4, above.

[269] See § 5.2, above.

[270] See, e.g., Williams v. O'Charley's, Inc., 728 S.E.2d 19, 22 (N.C. Ct. App. 2012) (implied warranty); Kolarik v. Cory Int'l Corp., 721 N.W.2d 159 (Iowa 2006) (negligence, strict tort, express and implied warranty); Otis Spunkmeyer, Inc. v. Blakely, 30 S.W.3d 678 (Tex. App. 2000) (implied warranty and strict tort).

[271] See § 5.9, above.

[272] See Davila v. Goya Foods, Inc., 2007 WL 415147, at *6 (S.D.N.Y. 2007) (glass fragments in octopus); Almquist v. The Finley Sch. Dist. No. 53, 57 P.3d 1191 (Wash. Ct. App. 2002) (tacos tainted with E. coli bacteria); Hickman v. William Wrigley, Jr. Co., 768 So.2d 812 (La. Ct. App. 2000) (screw in chewing gum); Knight v. Just Born, Inc., 2000 WL 924624 (D. Or. 2000) (chemical burns to mouth from piece of Hot Tamale cinnamon candy with concentrated cinnamon oil); Livingston v. Marie Callender's, Inc., 85 Cal. Rptr. 2d 528 (Ct. App. 1999) (MSG in soup); Creach v. Sara Lee Corp., 502 S.E.2d 923 (S.C. Ct. App. 1998) (pebble in biscuit); Flagstar Enters., Inc. v. Davis, 709 So.2d 1132 (Ala. 1997) (blood in biscuit and gravy); Kilpatrick v. Superior Court, 277 Cal. Rptr. 230 (Ct. App. 1991) (contaminated oysters); Shoshone Coca-Cola Bottling Co. v. Dolinski, 420 P.2d 855 (Nev. 1966) (mouse in Coke); Pulley v. Pacific Coca-Cola Bottling Co., 415 P.2d 636 (Wash. 1966) (cigarette in Coke). See generally Annots., 2 A.L.R.5th 1 (1992) (liability for spoiled or contaminated food), 2 A.L.R.5th 189 (1992) (liability for object related to but not intended to be in food).

But strict liability does not apply to naturally contaminated shrimp in Puerto Rico. See Gonzalez Caban v. JR Seafood, 2017 WL 6612724 (P.R. 2017) (*held*, 5–4, that the sale of a shrimp contaminated with saxitoxin is not subject to strict liability because it was not a manufactured product). See also Gonzalez Caban v. JR Seafood, 2019 WL 1399315 (D.P.R. 2019) (dismissing negligence claims).

[273] See, e.g., Cooper v. Borden, Inc., 709 So.2d 878, 881 (La. Ct. App. 1998) (to establish manufacturer's liability for harm from food consumption, plaintiff must prove: (1) defendant's product contained deleterious substance, (2) plaintiff consumed it, and (3) the consumption caused plaintiff's injury); Valenti v. Great Atl. & Pac. Tea Co., 615 N.Y.S.2d 84, 85 (App. Div. 1994).

[274] See, e.g., Anderson v. Piccadilly Cafeteria, Inc., 804 So.2d 75 (La. Ct. App. 2001) (plaintiff's testimony that fruit salad was discolored, malodorous, and made her nauseous insufficient to prove fruit salad was defective); Mann v. D.L. Lee & Sons, Inc., 537 S.E.2d 683 (Ga. Ct. App. 2000).

intended by the seller nor expected by the consumer. As with any other type of product, a person injured by food or drink must establish its defectiveness—in this context, that it was unwholesome, unfit for human consumption, adulterated,[275] or contained a foreign or otherwise dangerous substance of a type that consumers do not expect.[276]

Sometimes the defectiveness of a food or drink product is very clear, as when a soft drink contains slivers of glass,[277] a condom,[278] a slimy substance,[279] a moth,[280] or a mouse;[281] a meatball contains a piece of metal;[282] a can of pork and beans contains a condom;[283] a can of spinach,[284] a bowl of soup,[285] or a candy bar[286] is infested with worms; or a chili dog contains a cockroach.[287] Where a food's defectiveness is clear, unless the danger was so obvious that it should have been apparent to the consumer,[288] its manifest deficiency renders it unwholesome, unfit, and defective by any standard.[289] In such cases, unless causation is in doubt, food suppliers generally should want to avoid litigation unless the plaintiff's settlement demand is excessive. In other cases, whether a foodstuff's hazard is a "defect" may be in doubt. In the hot coffee cases, for example, most

[275] See, e.g., Sowell v. Hyatt Corp., 623 A.2d 1221 (D.C. 1993) (worm in rice; unwholesome); Slonsky v. Phoenix Coca-Cola Bottling Co., 499 P.2d 741 (Ariz. Ct. App. 1972) (metallic filings in bottle of Coke; same); Johnson v. Epstein, 1998 WL 166805, at *2 (N.D.N.Y. 1998) ("foreign substance that was revolting or unfit for human consumption"). "Adulterated" commonly describes food that may not be sold under pure food acts. See, e.g., Chambley v. Apple Rests., Inc., 504 S.E.2d 551 (Ga. Ct. App. 1998) (condom in chicken salad).

[276] See discussions of the foreign/natural and consumer expectations tests, below.

[277] See Peryea v. Coca-Cola Bottling Co. of New England, 286 A.2d 877 (R.I. 1972). See also Ratcliff v. Good Times Rests., Inc., 2019 WL 2774217 (D. Colo. 2019) (shards of broken glass in milkshake).

[278] See Hagan v. Coca-Cola Bottling Co., 804 So.2d 1234 (Fla. 2001).

[279] See Cernes v. Pittsburg Coca Cola Bottling Co., 332 P.2d 258, 262 (Kan. 1958) (jelly substance in beverage, "slimy like serum, mud or a bug").

[280] See Simmons v. Baton Rouge Coca-Cola Bottling Co., 282 So.2d 827 (La. Ct. App. 1973) (decomposed moth in bottle of Tab).

[281] Early soft drink intruder cases were collected in Bishop, Trouble in a Bottle, 16 Baylor L. Rev. 337 (1964), which classified the cases. Glass was the most frequent intruder into beverage bottles, followed by mice in the following conditions and numbers: dead—16; dead, fur oozing Coca-Cola—1; dead and putrid—2; dead, badly battered—1; decayed—2; decomposed—14; decomposed and swollen—1; skeleton only—1; small—1; unspecified—9. Flies, spiders, worms, and cockroaches also appeared with some frequency. Led by Louisiana, the "top" eight states (by number of reported cases) all were in the South.

[282] See Jones v. GMRI, Inc., 551 S.E.2d 867 (N.C. Ct. App. 2001).

[283] See Gentry v. Stokely-Van Camp, Prod. Liab. Rep. (CCH) ¶ 9259 (Tenn. Ct. App. 1982).

[284] See Food Fair Stores of Fla., Inc. v. Macurda, 93 So.2d 860 (Fla. 1957).

[285] See Campbell Soup Co. v. Gates, 889 S.W.2d 750 (Ark. 1994).

[286] See Kassouf v. Lee Bros., 26 Cal. Rptr. 276, 277 (Ct. App. 1962). After eating part of a Mr. Goodbar, plaintiff "bit into a mushy worm. When she looked at the bar, she saw that it was covered with worms and webbing; worms were crawling out of the chocolate and the webbing had little eggs 'hanging onto it.' "

[287] See Bullara v. Checker's Drive-In Rest., Inc., 736 So.2d 936 (La. Ct. App. 1999) (customer bit into cockroach in chili dog).

[288] In Harris-Teeter, Inc. v. Burroughs, 399 S.E.2d 801, 802 (Va. 1991), the plaintiff's daughter-in-law went to the grocery store and bought a birthday cake decorated with two white plastic birds resting on white "clouds" which were part of the cake's design. Plaintiff ate a piece of the cake, white bird and all, swallowing it whole without chewing. Quite soon she realized that she had a problem, and the bird was surgically removed from her colon. Applying the plain view doctrine, the court held that there was no negligence in supplying a cake ornament the same color as the icing.

[289] **Reporting food problems.** Rather than filing lawsuits, consumers of disgusting food or drink may wish to register their complaints in nonlitigious ways. After suffering food poisoning from a bacon-lettuce-tomato wrap, an enterprising ex-banker developed a crowd-sourced website to track customer complaints against restaurant chains (iwaspoisoned.com). See Kochkodin, How Ex-Banker's Food Poisoning Led to the Latest Chipotle Plunge, 45 Prod. Safety & Liab. Rep. (BNA) 748 (July 31, 2017). The FDA invites consumers to file their complaints about food, cosmetics, and other products on the MedWatch Online Voluntary Reporting Form, available at www.accessdata.fda.gov/scripts/medwatch/index.cfm?action=reporting.home.

courts rule as a matter of law that the propensity of a hot drink to burn is not a defective condition but an obvious risk that must be borne by those who drink hot beverages.[290] Also, a food's defectiveness may be subject to challenge if the hazard naturally occurs in that food, such as a chicken bone in chicken soup, an issue examined below.

A plaintiff must establish that the complained-of food product really did contain a foreign or other deleterious substance, a crucial fact that the plaintiff's testimony may establish.[291] But the plaintiff's uncorroborated testimony that he or she swallowed a bug is not the strongest type of evidence, and so a plaintiff who swallows or otherwise disposes of the objectionable item, such as a cockroach in a dish of beans and rice[292] or a piece of metal or other hard object in a meatball,[293] may find the lawsuit traveling a route quite similar.[294] Yet, even if the plaintiff has no direct evidence of a defect in the food, defectiveness properly may be established by circumstantial evidence and credible expert testimony that the defendant's food probably was defective.[295]

The Foreign/Natural and Consumer Expectations Tests

Defectiveness is clear enough, as mentioned earlier, when food or drink contains a foreign object, such as glass, steel, or bugs, or when the food is spoiled[296] or otherwise contaminated.[297] Yet the parties' expectations and legal responsibility may be quite different with respect to hazards that are natural to certain types of food, such as clamshells in clam chowder, cherry pits in cherry pies, and fish bones in fish fillets. To the extent such naturally occurring objects are dangerous, food purveyors ordinarily try to keep them out of the food and drink they sell. But sometimes their efforts are unsuccessful and a food consumer is injured by a naturally occurring object of this type.

---

[290] See, e.g., Maneri v. Starbucks Corp. Store #1527, 2019 WL 5626650, at *7 (E.D. Pa. 2019) ("the fact that a hot beverage such as tea is hot enough to cause second degree burns, should be obvious"); McCroy v. Coastal Mart, Inc., 207 F. Supp. 2d 1265 (D. Kan. 2002) (hot chocolate; no duty to warn about severity of potential burns; extensive review of hot beverage cases); Olliver v. Heavenly Bagels, Inc., 729 N.Y.S.2d 611 (Sup. Ct. 2001) (summary judgment for defendants; discussing other cases). On hot beverages as inherent risks, see § 10.3, below.

[291] See, e.g., Johnson v. Epstein, 1998 WL 166805 (N.D.N.Y. 1998) (crustacean attached to mackerel in can shown to others).

[292] See Wimberly v. B.P. Newman Invs., Inc., 805 So.2d 239 (La. Ct. App. 2001) (plaintiff's testimony that he was served beans and rice containing fully-intact cockroach was inconceivable given manner in which the beans and rice were prepared and served by Popeye's).

[293] See Jones v. GMRI, Inc., 551 S.E.2d 867 (N.C. Ct. App. 2001).

[294] See, e.g., Farroux v. Denny's Rests., Inc., 962 S.W.2d 108 (Tex. App. 1997) (restaurant patron allegedly sickened from undercooked eggs; insufficient evidence where plaintiff's affidavit conflicted with his own deposition and his medical records contained no evidence of food poisoning but only showed that he suffered from obesity and gout); Valenti v. Great Atl. & Pac. Tea Co., 615 N.Y.S.2d 84, 85 (App. Div. 1994) (flu-like symptoms after eating beans allegedly containing worm, where no mention of worm during visit to doctor the next day).

[295] See, e.g., Williams v. O'Charley's, Inc., 728 S.E.2d 19, 23 (N.C. Ct. App. 2012) (expert medical testimony that "it was more likely than not that defendant's food was the cause of plaintiff's injuries"); Schafer v. JLC Food Sys., Inc., 695 N.W.2d 570 (Minn. 2005) (plaintiff's throat cut from eating pumpkin muffin; even if object is swallowed and disappears, prima facie case that food was defective can be established by circumstantial evidence); Trapnell v. John Hogan Interests, Inc., 809 S.W.2d 606, 610 (Tex. App. 1991) (expert testimony, based on reasonable medical probability, permitted conclusion that fatal allergic reaction was triggered by sulfite potato whiteners); Gant v. Lucy Ho's Bamboo Garden, Inc., 460 So.2d 499, 502 (Fla. Dist. Ct. App. 1984) (food poisoning from egg rolls; doctor testified that the bacteria involved is usually transmitted from fecal matter of infected person, and that the egg rolls were the probable source).

[296] See, e.g., Prejean v. Great Atl. & Pac. Tea Co., 457 So.2d 60 (La. Ct. App. 1984) (rotten roast); Swift & Co. v. Wells, 110 S.E.2d 203 (Va. 1959) (staphylococci organisms in pork shoulder).

[297] See, e.g., Cooper v. Borden, Inc., 709 So.2d 878, 881 (La. Ct. App. 1998) (penicillin in milk); Claxton Coca-Cola Bottling Co. v. Coleman, 22 S.E.2d 768 (Ga. Ct. App. 1942) (kerosene in Coke).

The question here is whether the food may be viewed as "defective" or whether consumers should expect and guard against such naturally occurring objects and so bear responsibility for any harm.[298]

The Rise of the Foreign/Natural Doctrine

In *Mix v. Ingersoll Candy Co.*,[299] the plaintiff was injured from swallowing a fragment of a chicken bone contained in a chicken pie sold and served by the defendant restaurant to the plaintiff. The plaintiff sued the restaurant for negligence and breach of implied warranty, alleging that the food was not reasonably fit to eat. The trial court dismissed the claims, and the plaintiff appealed. Stating that the defendant's obligation in warranty was only to sell food that was *reasonably* fit, not perfect, the California Supreme Court upheld the dismissal of the complaint. While the court acknowledged that even slight deviations from perfection may sometimes cause a food to be legally unfit, it reasoned that "in certain instances a deviation from perfection, particularly if it is of such a nature as in common knowledge could be reasonably anticipated and guarded against by the consumer, may not be such a defect as to result in the food being not reasonably fit for human consumption."

Observing that the warranty cases holding food unfit involved foreign substances such as glass, stones, wires, or nails, or foods that were tainted, decayed, diseased, or infected, the court remarked that warranty law could not hold restaurateurs liable for serving a fish dish with a fish bone, a cherry pie with a cherry stone, or T-bone steaks or beef stew with bones "natural to the type of meat served." Hence, "[b]ones which are natural to the type of meat served cannot legitimately be called a foreign substance, and a consumer who eats meat dishes ought to anticipate and be on his guard against the presence of such bones." Thus, because such naturally occurring risks are to be expected by the food consumer, neither implied warranty[300] nor negligence compels a restaurant to ensure that its chicken pies are perfectly free of chicken bones.[301]

The *Mix* approach to liability for naturally occurring hazards in food and drink—which came to be known as the "foreign/natural" test or doctrine—held that sellers are subject to liability for injuries from objects that are "foreign" to a food's ingredients, but that consumers should expect and thereby bear the risks of hazards that are in some way "natural" to the food. At a time when rules of law were an accepted judicial method for avoiding jury trials in recurring situations where responsibility ordinarily is clear,[302] the foreign/natural doctrine appeared to be a sensible way for courts to short-circuit needlessly repetitive litigation. As time went by, a number of jurisdictions adopted the doctrine and applied it to such perils as bones and bone slivers in dressing served with

---

[298] See Annot., 2 A.L.R.5th 189 (1992) (liability for object related to but not intended to be in food); Products Liability Rest. § 7.

[299] 59 P.2d 144 (Cal. 1936), overruled by Mexicali Rose v. Superior Court, 822 P.2d 1292, 1304 (Cal. 1992).

[300] The result is different under express warranty if the seller affirms that the product is "boned chicken" which has "no bones." See Lane v. C.A. Swanson & Sons, 278 P.2d 723, 726 (Cal. Ct. App. 1955).

[301] *Mix*, 59 P.2d at 148.

[302] See Prosser and Keeton on Torts § 35; Dobbs, Law of Torts § 132.

a roast turkey dinner,[303] a pork chop,[304] creamed chicken,[305] barbecue pork sausage,[306] and fish chowder;[307] a piece of broken prune pit in a jar of prune butter;[308] a crystallized grain of corn in a box of Corn Flakes;[309] and an unshelled filbert in a jar of shelled nuts.[310]

The Shift to a Consumer Expectations Test

Although a number of courts applied the foreign/natural doctrine as a method for determining the defectiveness of food in certain types of cases, this test never was adopted in more than a handful of jurisdictions. In 1951, America's leading food law scholar, Professor Reed Dickerson, argued that the foreign/natural inquiry should be rejected in favor of a determination of consumer expectations.[311] And during the 1950s, courts began to manifest their discontent with the doctrine's applicability to processed foods by refocusing the inquiry away from whether the offending object naturally and initially occurred in some ingredient of the food to whether it was appropriate to the food as it ultimately was served. This analytical shift narrowed the foreign/natural doctrine into oblivion by allowing claims for bones in chicken soup,[312] sausage,[313] and canned chicken labeled "boned."[314] Moreover, at least a couple of fairly early decisions rejected the foreign/natural test outright, reasoning that the decisive issue should not be whether an ingredient was natural or foreign to the food at some stage of preparation, but whether the consumer might reasonably expect to find such a substance in the type of food involved.[315]

As modern principles of products liability law established a foothold in the 1960s and 1970s, criticism of the foreign/natural doctrine accelerated.[316] During this period, courts and commentators began to recognize the inconsistency between the *caveat emptor* principles inherent in this doctrine and the consumer protection objectives of

---

[303] Silva v. F.W. Woolworth Co., 83 P.2d 76 (Cal. Ct. App. 1938).

[304] Brown v. Nebiker, 296 N.W. 366 (Iowa 1941).

[305] Goodwin v. Country Club of Peoria, 54 N.E.2d 612 (Ill. App. Ct. 1944), abrogated by Jackson v. Nestle-Beich, Inc., 589 N.E.2d 547 (Ill. 1992).

[306] Norris v. Pig'n Whistle Sandwich Shop, 53 S.E.2d 718 (Ga. Ct. App. 1949).

[307] Webster v. Blue Ship Tea Room, Inc., 198 N.E.2d 309, 312 (Mass. 1964) (offering a history of, and several recipes for, New England chowder (a "gustatory adventure") and observing: "We should be prepared to cope with the hazards of fish bones, the occasional presence of which in chowders is, it seems to us, to be anticipated, and which, in the light of a hallowed tradition, do not impair their fitness or merchantability.").

[308] Courter v. Dilbert Bros., 186 N.Y.S.2d 334 (Sup. Ct. 1959).

[309] Adams v. Great Atl. & Pac. Tea Co., 112 S.E.2d 92 (N.C. 1960), abrogated by Goodman v. Wenco Foods, Inc., 423 S.E.2d 444 (N.C. 1992).

[310] See Coffer v. Standard Brands, Inc., 226 S.E.2d 534 (N.C. Ct. App. 1976).

[311] "The better test of what is legally defective appears to be what consumers customarily expect and guard against. Canned foods are expected to be found already washed, cleaned, and trimmed, while the same foods in fresh form normally call for work of that sort by the consumer." F. R. Dickerson, Products Liability and the Food Consumer 185 (1951).

[312] Even if chicken bones were necessary to the preparation of chicken soup, "the question is not whether the substance may have been natural or proper at some time in the early stages of preparation of this kind of soup, but whether the presence of such substance, if it is harmful and makes the food unfit for human consumption, is natural and ordinarily expected to be in the final product which is impliedly represented as fit for human consumption." Wood v. Waldorf Sys., Inc., 83 A.2d 90, 93 (R.I. 1951).

[313] Lore v. De Simone Bros., 172 N.Y.S.2d 829 (Sup. Ct. 1958).

[314] Bryer v. Rath Packing Co., 156 A.2d 442 (Md. 1959).

[315] See, e.g., Bonenberger v. Pittsburgh Mercantile Co., 28 A.2d 913 (Pa. 1942) (oyster shell in can of oysters—though plaintiff's name suggests a different problem); Betehia v. Cape Cod Corp., 103 N.W.2d 64, 67 (Wis. 1960) (chicken bone in chicken sandwich).

[316] See, e.g., Hunt v. Ferguson-Paulus Enters., 415 P.2d 13 (Or. 1966) (cherry pit in pie; court noted criticism of foreign/natural rule, but avoided issue by deferring to jury).

modern products liability law.[317] As time progressed, courts from the 1980s forward increasingly adopted a reasonable[318] consumer expectations standard, often explicitly rejecting the foreign/natural doctrine, for determining the defectiveness of food.[319] Typical of these decisions was *Jackson v. Nestle-Beich, Inc.*,[320] a carefully reasoned decision of the Illinois Supreme Court that adopted a reasonable consumer expectations test. There, the court rebuffed the defendant's invitation to adopt Louisiana's then-existing middle-of-the-road approach that shielded food sellers from strict liability, but not negligence, for dangers naturally occurring in food products.[321]

In the mid-1990s,[322] the propriety of the shift from the foreign/natural doctrine to a consumer expectations test was certified by the American Law Institute in the *Products Liability Restatement*.[323] In recent years, courts have rarely applied the foreign/natural

---

[317] See, e.g., Zabner v. Howard Johnson's, Inc., 201 So.2d 824, 826 (Fla. Dist. Ct. App. 1967) (walnut shell in maple walnut ice cream: "Naturalness of the substance to any ingredients in the food served is important only in determining whether the consumer may reasonably expect to find such substance in the particular type of dish or style of food served."); Hochberg v. O'Donnell's Rest., Inc., 272 A.2d 846, 848–49 (D.C. 1971) (pit in olive); Stark v. Chock Full O'Nuts, 356 N.Y.S.2d 403, 404 (App. Term 1974) (walnut shell in nutted cheese sandwich); Williams v. Braum Ice Cream Stores, Inc., 534 P.2d 700 (Okla. Ct. App. 1974) (cherry seed or pit in cherry-pecan ice cream); Jim Dandy Fast Foods, Inc. v. Carpenter, 535 S.W.2d 786, 790 (Tex. Civ. App. 1976) (piece of bone in chicken meat). See Annot., 2 A.L.R.5th 189 (1992).

[318] The standard is framed in terms of a *reasonable* consumer's expectations, an objective test. See, e.g., Phillips v. Town of W. Springfield, 540 N.E.2d 1331 (Mass. 1989).

[319] See, e.g., Ex parte Morrison's Cafeteria of Montgomery, Inc., 431 So.2d 975, 978 (Ala. 1983); Gates v. Standard Brands Inc., 719 P.2d 130, 134 (Wash. Ct. App. 1986) (adopting "buyer oriented" consumer expectations test); Yong Cha Hong v. Marriott Corp., 656 F. Supp. 445, 448–49 (D. Md. 1987) (noting that reasonable expectations test "has largely displaced the natural/foreign test"); Phillips v. Town of W. Springfield, 540 N.E.2d 1331, 1332–33 (Mass. 1989); Goodman v. Wenco Foods Inc., 423 S.E.2d 444, 451 (N.C. 1992) (thorough discussion); Jackson v. Nestle-Beich, Inc., 589 N.E.2d 547, 549 (Ill. 1992) (foreign/natural test is an "outdated and discredited doctrine"); Langiulli v. Bumble Bee Seafood, Inc., 604 N.Y.S.2d 1020, 1021 (Sup. Ct. 1993). Legal commentators unanimously approved this development. See, e.g., F. R. Dickerson, Products Liability and the Food Consumer, §§ 4.2 and 4.3, at 184–90 (1951); Spak, Bone of Contention: The Foreign-Natural Test and the Implied Warranty of Merchantability for Food Products, 12 J.L. & Com. 23 (1992); Dobbs, Law of Torts, § 356, at 981; W. Prosser, Law of Torts, § 99, at 660, n.76 (4th ed. 1971).

[320] 589 N.E.2d 547 (Ill. 1992).

[321] See, e.g., Title v. Pontchartrain Hotel, 449 So.2d 677 (La. Ct. App. 1984) (restaurant not liable for allowing pearl to remain in fried oyster); Musso v. Picadilly Cafeterias, Inc., 178 So.2d 421 (La. Ct. App. 1965) (restaurant not negligent in failing to remove every pit in cherry pie). Louisiana abandoned this hybrid approach in Porteous v. St. Ann's Cafe & Deli, 713 So.2d 454 (La. 1998), which shifted to a negligence analysis that weighs the naturalness of an item's presence with consumer expectations. In Mexicali Rose v. Superior Court, 822 P.2d 1292, 1303 (Cal. 1992) (chicken bone in enchilada), California adopted a similar approach, by replacing its *Mix* foreign/natural test with a hybrid negligence-but-not-strict liability-for-natural hazards approach. See note 299, above.

[322] In 1995, Tentative Draft No. 2 of the Products Liability Rest., comment *g* to § 2, suggested that the consumer expectations test was the majority rule. The far more decisive rejection of the foreign/natural test in favor of the consumer expectations test first appeared as a separate section in the Proposed Final Draft in 1997, and the Restatement was published in final form in 1998.

[323] Products Liability Rest. § 7, "Liability of Commercial Seller or Distributor for Harm Caused by Defective Food Products," provides:

> One engaged in the business of selling or otherwise distributing food products who sells or distributes a food product that is defective under § 2, § 3, or § 4 is subject to liability for harm to persons or property caused by the defect. Under § 2(a), a harm-causing ingredient of the food product constitutes a defect if a reasonable consumer would not expect the food product to contain that ingredient.

In comment *b*, the Reporters note: "A consumer expectations test in this context relies upon culturally defined, widely shared standards that food products ought to meet."

doctrine as a liability determinative rule,[324] and the judicial march toward a reasonable consumer expectations test appears inexorable.[325]

In short, modern courts have rejected the foreign/natural distinction as too rigid a rule of law for assessing the defectiveness of food. While restricting liability for natural hazards to appropriate negligence claims[326] arguably strikes a nuanced balance between consumer and seller obligations, most courts today prefer the blunter but simpler consumer expectation protection approach of the type adopted by the *Products Liability Restatement*. Absent from most discussions of the battle between these two food defect tests is a recognition of the specially high protection the law historically has afforded food consumers, as previously discussed.

Perhaps the disappearance from common discourse of the high priority of food safety reflects the fact that consumers today confront a host of deadly dangers—mechanical, chemical, biological, and electronic—which may suggest that foods no longer deserve an elevated level of protection. Yet, even within the kind of broader human safety plan the law must now embrace, food safety remains an elemental social goal that undoubtedly is better protected by the reasonable consumer expectations test, plainly now the prevailing legal doctrine,[327] than the wooden foreign/natural doctrine that fittingly is on the run.

Court and Jury

Even with the decline of the foreign/natural test, which is nearing extinction as a general test of liability, the "naturalness" of a dangerous item's presence in a food necessarily lingers on as an important sub-issue in assessing reasonable expectations in particular contexts—that is, in determining just what types of dangers consumers justifiably *should* be required to expect in certain types of foods.[328] While the task of ascertaining such expectations normally is peculiarly well suited for jury resolution,[329] reasonable consumer expectations sometimes are so clear that a court should take the issue from the jury. For example, in an early case that essentially rejected the foreign/natural test and embraced the consumer expectations test as the liability

---

[324] For remnants of the foreign/natural doctrine, see, e.g., Harris v. Costco Wholesale Corp., 2011 WL 198154, at *1 (N.D. Cal. 2011) (fatal choking on large meat sample served at grocery store; "size and configuration of the meat were natural to the preparation of the food sample"); Zumpe v. Zara's Little Giant Super Mkt., 35 So.3d 1158, 1161 (La. Ct. App. 2010) ("an olive pit is a naturally occurring substance in olives"); Lewis v. Handel's Homemade Ice Cream & Yogurt, 2003 WL 21509258, at *3 (Ohio Ct. App. 2003) ("common sense dictates that the presence of a pistachio shell in a pistachio nut ice cream cone is a natural occurrence that appellant reasonably should have anticipated and guarded against"); Mitchell v. T.G.I. Friday's, 748 N.E.2d 89 (Ohio Ct. App. 2000) (schizophrenically applying both tests per Ohio's equivocal approach).

[325] See, e.g., Estate of Pinkham v. Cargill, Inc., 55 A.3d 1, 8 (Me. 2012) (adopting Third Restatement's reasonable expectations test); Kolarik v. Cory Int'l Corp., 721 N.W.2d 159 (Iowa 2006) (same); Schafer v. JLC Food Sys., Inc., 695 N.W.2d 570 (Minn. 2005) (same).

[326] This is the former rule in Louisiana that now is applied in California. See note 321, above.

[327] See Products Liability Rest. § 7, Reporters' Note 1 to cmt. *b* ("strong majority of courts").

[328] Reasonable expectations are also used in determinations of how carefully a consumer should chew. See, e.g., Hochberg v. O'Donnell's Rest., Inc., 272 A.2d 846 (D.C. 1971) (restaurant patron broke tooth on pit in olive served in vodka martini).

[329] See, e.g., Rudloff v. Wendy's Rest. of Rochester, Inc., 821 N.Y.S.2d 358, 361 (City Ct. 2006) ("except in the rarest of cases [consumer expectations] should not be decided as a matter of law"); Phillips v. Town of W. Springfield, 540 N.E.2d 1331 (Mass. 1989) (trier of fact determines reasonable expectations); Yong Cha Hong v. Marriott Corp., 656 F. Supp. 445, 448–49 (D. Md. 1987).

standard, the court nevertheless ruled as a matter of law that the consumer should have expected to find an oyster shell in a serving of fried oysters.[330]

More recently, courts have held as a matter of law that consumers should expect that a fish fillet might contain a 1-centimeter bone,[331] that a can of clam chowder[332] or a fried clam strip[333] might contain a piece of clam shell, that a raw clam served in a restaurant might contain harmful bacteria,[334] that a pistachio shell might reside in a pistachio nut ice cream cone,[335] and that a cake might contain a strand of human hair.[336] The contrary is also true: courts should rule as a matter of law for injured food consumers who have no reason to expect a particular food hazard, such as a lethally sharp sliver of bone in a fried strip of chicken, "natural" though it might be.

Modern courts assert their control over juries in a variety of ways,[337] and the decline of the foreign/natural doctrine in favor of a consumer expectations test should not be viewed as a wholesale shift of power from judge to jury. Instead, the battle lines for judicial rulings in foodstuff cases have simply shifted—away from classifying food hazards as "foreign" versus "natural," to case-specific judicial rulings on when consumers, as a matter of law, should be required to expect to find natural hazards in the foodstuffs that they eat.

Proving Causation

Even if a plaintiff can establish that a food or drink ingested was dangerously defective, the plaintiff still must connect the defect both to the defendant and to the plaintiff's injury or illness.[338]

Linking Foodstuff to Defendant

It is fundamental, of course, that a seller is responsible for an injury only if the seller was responsible for the defect—that is, only if the defect was in the product when it left the seller's control.[339] Thus, even if the plaintiff proves that a Baby Ruth candy bar contained a pin, the plaintiff still may be unable to meet his burden of proving that the

---

[330] Allen v. Grafton, 164 N.E.2d 167 (Ohio 1960) (4–3 decision). See also Mitchell v. T.G.I. Friday's, 748 N.E.2d 89 (Ohio Ct. App. 2000) (fried clams); Mathews v. Maysville Seafoods, Inc., 602 N.E.2d 764, 765–66 (Ohio Ct. App. 1991) (plaintiff's case failed under either test since "consumer must reasonably anticipate and guard against the presence of a fish bone in a fish fillet").

[331] Ex parte Morrison's Cafeteria of Montgomery, Inc., 431 So.2d 975 (Ala. 1983). See also Ruvolo v. Homovich, 778 N.E.2d 661 (Ohio Ct. App. 2002) (customer should reasonably expect that chicken sandwich may contain chicken bone).

[332] See Koperwas v. Publix Supermarkets, Inc., 534 So.2d 872 (Fla. Dist. Ct. App. 1988).

[333] See Mitchell v. T.G.I. Friday's, 748 N.E.2d 89 (Ohio Ct. App. 2000).

[334] See Clime v. Dewey Beach Enters., Inc., 831 F. Supp. 341 (D. Del. 1993). *But see* Ayala v. Bartolome, 940 S.W.2d 727 (Tex. App. 1997) (whether ordinary consumer would expect raw oysters to be contaminated with bacteria fatal to persons with liver disease is fact issue for jury).

[335] See Lewis v. Handel's Homemade Ice Cream & Yogurt, 2003 WL 21509258 (Ohio Ct. App. 2003).

[336] See Cain v. Winn-Dixie La., Inc., 757 So.2d 712 (La. Ct. App. 1999).

[337] See Powers, Judge and Jury in the Texas Supreme Court, 75 Tex. L. Rev. 1699 (1997).

[338] See, e.g., Meyer v. Super Disc. Mkts., Inc., 501 S.E.2d 2 (Ga. Ct. App. 1998); Cooper v. Borden, Inc., 709 So.2d 878, 881 (La. Ct. App. 1998).

[339] See, e.g., Gentry v. Hershey Co., 687 F. Supp. 2d 711, 718 (M.D. Tenn. 2010) (no proof that York Peppermint Pattie was defective when it left manufacturer); Mears v. H.J. Heinz Co., 1995 WL 37344 (Tenn. Ct. App. 1995) (sliver of tin plate in bowl of soup could have come from sources other than defendant; expert testified 90% of all tin plate is used to make tin cans).

For the requirement that a product must contain the alleged defect at time of the defendant's sale, see § 5.3, above.

pin was in the candy bar when it left the defendant's candy factory if the manufacturer introduces evidence of rigorous quality control procedures at its plant.[340] Often, time is of the essence in establishing causation of this type. If a plaintiff discovers maggots, "[l]ittle bitty worms with a black head," floating and squiggling in chicken-flavored soup made from a dry mix sold by the defendant manufacturer six weeks prior to the plaintiff's purchase, she cannot recover if the larvae might reasonably have entered the soup between the time when the defendant sold it and when her mother bought and prepared it.[341]

But a plaintiff need not prove the defendant's responsibility for the defect beyond all doubt; the plaintiff may recover if the evidence, including reasonable inferences from any circumstantial evidence, suggests the likelihood that the defect was in the product at the time the defendant sold it.[342] Thus, a plaintiff may recover if she bites into a cockroach in a chili dog she purchased if she establishes that she ate the dog shortly after she got home and before her own household roaches had time to crawl inside.[343] And while a jokester conceivably may cram a mouse into a soft drink bottle after it leaves the bottling plant, a jury may reasonably interpret dark fecal stains at the bottom of the bottle as suggesting that the mouse resided in the bottle long before that point.[344]

Linking Foodstuff to Plaintiff's Harm

To link an injury or illness to a defective foodstuff, a plaintiff first must connect the injury or illness to food the defendant sold, and further show that that food item—rather than some other food the plaintiff may have eaten—was bad.[345] When a person becomes ill shortly after eating, the natural tendency is to associate the illness with the foods or beverages the person recently consumed. Often, any food remaining unconsumed is discarded, which means that no samples are available for testing to ascertain whether the food was good or bad. In such cases, courts properly allow plaintiffs to go to the jury if they offer reasonable circumstantial evidence of defectiveness, such as that a particular food item smelled or tasted strange.[346] Yet, without credible evidence that a food item probably was defective, a plaintiff's case quite properly will fail.[347]

---

[340] See Tardella v. RJR Nabisco, Inc., 576 N.Y.S.2d 965 (App. Div. 1991) (pin in Baby Ruth candy bar; in view of defendant's detailed evidence of rigorous quality control procedures, plaintiff failed to meet burden of proof that pin was in candy bar when it left defendant's plant).

[341] Campbell Soup Co. v. Gates, 889 S.W.2d 750 (Ark. 1994).

[342] See, e.g., Cooper v. Borden, Inc., 709 So.2d 878, 881 (La. Ct. App. 1998) (penicillin in milk); Flagstar Enters., Inc. v. Davis, 709 So.2d 1132 (Ala. 1997) (blood in take-out order of biscuit and gravy); Cohen v. Allendale Coca-Cola Bottling Co., 351 S.E.2d 897, 899 (S.C. Ct. App. 1986) (Bell, J.) (plaintiff's testimony that the bug was lying on the bottom of the bottle, that it might have been partially decomposed, and that no bugs were flying around his office that day was sufficient circumstantial evidence that bug entered bottle at defendant's plant).

[343] See Bullara v. Checker's Drive-In Rest., 736 So.2d 936 (La. Ct. App. 1999) (by implication).

[344] See Shoshone Coca-Cola Bottling Co. v. Dolinski, 420 P.2d 855 (Nev. 1966).

[345] See § 11.1, below.

[346] See, e.g., McGinty v. Grand Casinos of Miss., Inc.-Biloxi, 245 So.3d 444, 449–50 (Miss. 2018) (pork chop " 'tasted funny," the illness occurred shortly after eating, no other food had been ingested, and doctor attributed the illness to food or drink); Schafer v. JLC Food Sys., Inc., 695 N.W.2d 570, 576–78 (Minn. 2005) (reversing summary judgment for defendant; circumstantial evidence that sharp object in pumpkin muffin caused cut in plaintiff's throat raised jury question); Croteau v. Denny's Rest., Inc., 2002 Mass. App. Div. 81 (Dist. Ct. 2002) (salmonella poisoning; evidence that symptoms occurred during incubation period and that restaurant had been cited for violations of sanitary code sufficient to establish causation).

[347] "A person claiming injury from consuming allegedly unwholesome food must show a causal link between that food and the resulting illness." Mann v. D.L. Lee & Sons, Inc., 537 S.E.2d 683, 684 (Ga. Ct. App. 2000) (although plaintiffs probably suffered food poisoning, insufficient evidence that defendant's ham was

In addition to showing that a particular food item was defective, a plaintiff must also link the defective food product to his or her injury or illness. In many cases, the causal link between defective foodstuff and a plaintiff's harm is undisputed, as when the plaintiff immediately is injured or sickened from consuming food that clearly is defective, as a sirloin steak containing the tip end of a hypodermic needle,[348] or a chili dog containing a cockroach.[349] But if the connection between defective food or drink and a person's illness is unclear, as often is the case, reliable[350] expert testimony may be required to establish the causal link between the defect and the harm.[351]

A plaintiff who proves all three elements—(1) that an item of food or drink was defective, (2) that the defendant seller was responsible for the defect, and (3) that the defect proximately caused the harm[352]—may recover damages for the harm.[353] If a plaintiff bites off the head of a mouse[354] or a cockroach[355] hiding in a sandwich, the plaintiff normally can recover damages for emotional distress.[356] Even if nothing is eaten of the intruder or even of the foodstuff, the plaintiff still may establish causation in most jurisdictions by proving that he or she was sickened by observing, touching, or smelling

defective: "Given that no laboratory test performed on the Manns revealed any pathogen responsible for their symptoms, that the Manns consumed other foods at the same time they ate the ham, and that the ham itself was not available for testing but had not looked, smelled, or tasted bad, the Manns could not carry their burden of excluding every other reasonable hypothesis as to the cause of their illness."). See also Velazquez v. Abbott Labs., 901 F. Supp. 2d 279, 294 (D.P.R. 2012) (plaintiffs failed to raise genuine dispute that warehouse beetles in infant formula caused illness); Anderson v. Piccadilly Cafeteria, Inc., 804 So.2d 75 (La. Ct. App. 2001) (plaintiff's testimony that fruit salad was discolored, malodorous, and made her nauseous was insufficient by itself to prove fruit salad was defective); Fuggins v. Burger King, 760 So.2d 605 (La. Ct. App. 2000) (evidence insufficient to establish that plaintiff's illness was food poisoning and, if so, whether it was caused by defendant's hamburger); Meyer v. Super Disc. Mkts., 501 S.E.2d 2, 4 (Ga. Ct. App. 1998) ("a mere showing that a person became sick subsequent to eating food is insufficient").

348 See Kroger Co. v. Beck, 375 N.E.2d 640 (Ind. Ct. App. 1978) (prick in throat made plaintiff vomit).

349 See Bullara v. Checker's Drive-In Rest., 736 So.2d 936 (La. Ct. App. 1999). See also CEF Enters., Inc. v. Betts, 838 So.2d 999 (Miss. Ct. App. 2003) (expert testimony not necessary to show that eating a biscuit containing an insect makes one ill).

350 See, e.g., Wilson v. Pinnacle Foods Inc., 2022 WL 419595, at *12 (W.D. Ky. 2022) (expert's testimony linking plaintiff's illness to Listeria in frozen dinner was unreliable and based on speculation); Lassiegne v. Taco Bell Corp., 202 F. Supp. 2d 512 (E.D. La. 2002) (unreliable expert testimony that chicken bone caused eater's migraine headaches, post-traumatic stress, and impotency).

351 See, e.g., Arbourgh v. Sweet Basil Bistro, Inc., 740 So.2d 186 (La. Ct. App. 1999) (doctor's testimony that food poisoning probably was caused by raw chicken eaten at defendant restaurant sufficiently established causation).

352 On proximate cause, see, e.g., Shih v. Starbucks Corp., 267 Cal. Rptr. 3d 919, 925 (Ct. App. 2020) (hot tea was filled to the brim and served without a sleeve, but neither factor was proximate cause of plaintiff's spilling tea when she scooted out her chair, lost her balance, and knocked over tea when she grabbed the table).

353 See, e.g., Cooper v. Borden, Inc., 709 So.2d 878, 881 (La. Ct. App. 1998).

354 Plaintiff bought a barbecue sandwich from a vending machine, heated it in a microwave oven, and took a bite. She heard "an awful crunch," opened the sandwich and discovered a small mouse with a small tail, but no head. She sued, and the jury awarded damages of $10,000. Greenville News (S.C.), Feb. 24 & 25, 1993.

355 Bullara v. Checker's Drive-In Rest., Inc., 736 So.2d 936 (La. Ct. App. 1999) (customer bit into cockroach in chili dog).

356 See, e.g., Brayman v. 99 W., Inc., 116 F. Supp. 2d 225, 233–34 (D. Mass. 2000) (plaintiff, cut in throat by piece of glass hidden in mashed potatoes, could recover for past and future pain and suffering, emotional distress, anxiety, mental anguish, embarrassment, and loss of enjoyment of life), aff'd, 26 Fed. Appx. 24 (1st Cir. 2002); Way v. Tampa Coca Cola Bottling Co., 260 So.2d 288, 289 (Fla. Dist. Ct. App. 1972) (while sucking the partially frozen contents out of a bottle of Coke, plaintiff encountered a "rat with the hair sucked off"; damages for emotional distress allowed). The distress must be reasonable. See, e.g., Coca-Cola Bottling Co. v. Hagan, 813 So.2d 167 (Fla. Dist. Ct. App. 2002) (plaintiffs who drank from a bottle that they thought contained a used condom could not recover for fear of AIDS absent basis for this fear; citing fear-of-AIDS cases).

(and thinking about) the mouse, bug, spoilage, or other offending condition.[357] As with other types of products, damages for distress from observing injuries to others,[358] and damages for lost consortium,[359] may be available on proper proofs.

[357] See, e.g., Chambley v. Apple Rests., Inc., 504 S.E.2d 551 (Ga. Ct. App. 1998) (condom in chicken salad); Sowell v. Hyatt Corp., 623 A.2d 1221 (D.C. 1993) (worm in rice plaintiff almost ate); Prejean v. Great Atl. & Pac. Tea Co., 457 So.2d 60 (La. Ct. App. 1984) (rotten roast that was "green as grass"); Wallace v. Coca-Cola Bottling Plants, Inc., 269 A.2d 117 (Me. 1970) (unpackaged prophylactic in Coke). To recover for emotional distress, most states require plaintiff to prove the distress caused, or was caused by, some injury, illness, or other physical condition. See, e.g., Ellington v. Coca Cola Bottling Co. of Tulsa, Inc., 717 P.2d 109 (Okla. 1986) (plaintiff could recover for emotional distress from observing piece of Good-n-Plenty candy she thought was a worm in her bottle of Coke because her distress caused nausea, diarrhea, dehydration, kidney infection, and fever). At least Florida and Maine have abolished the physical injury requirement for such distress from consuming contaminated food. See Hagan v. Coca-Cola Bottling Co., 804 So.2d 1234 (Fla. 2001); Culbert v. Sampson's Supermarkets Inc., 444 A.2d 433 (Me. 1982).

[358] See, e.g., Culbert v. Sampson's Supermarkets Inc., 444 A.2d 433 (Me. 1982) (mother could recover for her distress from observing infant son gag and choke on foreign substance in jar of baby food).

[359] See, e.g., Ratcliff v. Good Times Rests., Inc., 2019 WL 2774217, at *3 (D. Colo. 2019) (consortium claim allowed for injury to live-in boyfriend); Bullara v. Checker's Drive-In Rest., 736 So.2d 936 (La. Ct. App. 1999) (after biting cockroach in chili dog, wife not in the mood for sex and husband had to cook and eat alone).

Chapter 8

DESIGN DEFECTS

Table of Sections

§ 8.1 DESIGN DEFECTS—GENERALLY

The concept of design defectiveness lies at the heart of products liability law. A product's design predetermines the extent to which use of the product will result in human injury, and modern products liability law rests foundationally on the premise that manufacturers are fairly held to answer in the courts for the basic safety of their products' designs. Yet judicial oversight of a manufacturer's design choices is a relatively new phenomenon. Design defect claims under any theory of liability were infrequently entertained by courts early in the twentieth century,[1] and only in the last several decades have courts with any frequency begun to adjudicate the reasonableness of product designs in accident litigation.

Finding an acceptable definition for what constitutes a "defective" design is a difficult task. Elusive as an elf, the true meaning of "design defect" largely escaped capture by court or commentator until quite recently, and the search therefor has led inexorably to consternation and confusion. The quest for understanding design

1 For a small handful of early examples, see James, Products Liability (pt. 1), 34 Tex. L. Rev. 44, 50 (1955).

defectiveness perennially vexes courts[2] and accomplished products liability lawyers[3] attempting to unravel design defect problems; delights law clerks,[4] young associates,[5] and law students[6] furnished an occasion for displaying their erudition; and provides

---

[2] For the views of Chief Justice Roger Traynor, who argued for, adopted, and explained strict products liability in tort, see Escola v. Coca Cola Bottling Co., 150 P.2d 436 (Cal. 1944) (concurring opinion), Greenman v. Yuba Power Prods., Inc., 377 P.2d 897 (Cal. 1963), and Traynor, The Ways and Meanings of Defective Products and Strict Liability, 32 Tenn. L. Rev. 363 (1965). Judicial confusion over design defectiveness was not just a phenomenon of early products liability law. From the 1970s, see, e.g., Phillips v. Kimwood Mach. Co., 525 P.2d 1033, 1035 (Or. 1974) ("courts continue to flounder while attempting to determine how one decides whether a product is 'in a defective condition unreasonably dangerous to the user' "). From the 1980s, see, e.g., Prentis v. Yale Mfg. Co., 365 N.W.2d 176, 182 (Mich. 1984) ("questions related to 'design defects' . . . appear to be the most agitated and controversial issues before the courts in the field of products liability"). From the 1990s, see, e.g., Denny v. Ford Motor Co., 662 N.E.2d 730, 739, 740 (N.Y. 1995) (Simons, J., dissenting) ("the word 'defect' has no clear legal meaning"). From the 2000s, see, e.g., Pritchett v. Cottrell, Inc., 512 F.3d 1057, 1063 (8th Cir. 2008) (Kan. and Mo. law) (" 'when a product is actionable because of the nature of its design' " is one of " 'the most agitated controversial question[s]' that courts face"). From the 2010s, see, e.g., Bifolck v. Philip Morris, Inc., 152 A.3d 1183, 1200 (Conn. 2016). And in the 2020s, confusion still abounds. See, e.g., Purdy v. Deere & Co., 492 P.3d 99 (Or. Ct. App. 2021) (reversing judgment for erroneous instructions; confused discussion of confused lines of precedent); Crawford v. ITW Food Equip. Grp., LLC, 977 F.3d 1331, 1343 n.5 (11th Cir. 2020) (Fla. law) (" 'the definition of a 'design defect' is in a 'state of flux in Florida' [and] 'in "the byzantine world of products liability" it is unsettled' ").

[3] For a small sampling of the large literature on design defects by the practicing bar, see, e.g., Emison, Don't Overlook A Product Defect, Trial, October 2020, at 42; Bugay, Tincher v. Omega Flex, Inc.: A Lightning Strike on Pennsylvania Products Liability Law, 85 Pa. B.A. Q. 39 (2014); Combs and Cooke, Modern Products Liability Law in West Virginia, 113 W. Va. L. Rev. 417 (2011); White, Products Liability Law for Design Defects in South Carolina: The Aftermath of Branham v. Ford Motor Co., 62 S.C. L. Rev. 781 (2011); Fisher, Connecticut's Jury Instruction on Design Defect is Defective: A Second Look at Potter v. Chicago Pneumatic Tool, 84 Conn. B.J. 325 (2010); Stewart, Strict Liability for Defective Product Design: The Quest for a Well-Ordered Regime, 74 Brook. L. Rev. 1039 (2009); Rheingold, What are the Consumer's "Reasonable Expectations"?, 22 Bus. Law. 589 (1967).

[4] See, e.g., Vandall and J. Vandall, A Call for an Accurate *Restatement (Third) of Torts: Design Defect*, 33 U. Mem. L. Rev. 909 (2003) (J. Vandall law clerk); Ausili, Ramifications of Denny v. Ford Motor Co., 15 Touro L. Rev. 735 (1999); Thompson, The Arkansas Products Liability Statute: What Does "Unreasonably Dangerous" Mean in Arkansas?, 50 Ark. L. Rev. 663 (1998) (law clerk to Eighth Circuit Court of Appeals Chief Judge Arnold).

[5] See, e.g., Wilmot, Baseball Bats in the High Tech Era: A Products Liability Look at New Technology, Aluminum Bats, and Manufacturer Liability, 16 Marq. Sports L. Rev. 353 (2006); V. Schwartz and Tedesco, The Re-Emergence of "Super Strict" Liability: Slaying the Dragon Again, 71 U. Cin. L. Rev. 917 (2003).

[6] The law reviews are filled with hundreds of student commentaries on the meaning of a product defect. See, e.g., Notes, 74 Vand. L. Rev. 187 (2021); 44 N.M. L. Rev. 207 (2014). Perhaps the most valuable student work was a two-part article, an LL.M. thesis by Richard Wilson under the supervision of Dean William Prosser and Professor Albert Ehrenzweig at the University of California, Berkeley. See Wilson, Products Liability (pts. 1 and 2), 43 Cal. L. Rev. 614, 809, 810–35 (1955) (exploring the meaning of product defectiveness).

fertile grist for law professors[7] aspiring for the renown thought to follow discovery of the key to any riddle wrapped in a mystery inside an enigma.[8]

Just as strict liability in tort is still the dominant liability doctrine in major products liability litigation, design defectiveness remains the dominant claim in most major products liability cases.[9] Manufacturer design determinations involve a multitude of safety-related choices, including decisions on the types and strengths of raw materials and component parts, the manner in which such materials and parts are shaped and combined, whether safety devices will be included, and the overall product concept. A frequent design defect claim is the absence of some type of adequate safety device, such as a sufficient housing surrounding a power lawnmower,[10] a mechanical guard or

---

[7] For early excursions by the law professors into the quagmire of design defectiveness, see, e.g., Keeton, Products Liability—Current Developments, 40 Tex. L. Rev. 193, 210 (1961); Keeton, Products Liability: Liability Without Fault and the Requirement of a Defect, 41 Tex. L. Rev. 855 (1963); Wade, Strict Tort Liability of Manufacturers, 19 Sw. L.J. 5 (1965); Dickerson, Products Liability: How Good Does a Product Have To Be?, 42 Ind. L.J. 301 (1967); Wade, On the Nature of Strict Tort Liability for Products, 44 Miss. L.J. 825, 837–38 (1973) (setting forth his famous seven factors); Henderson, Judicial Review of Manufacturers' Conscious Design Choices: The Limits of Adjudication, 73 Colum. L. Rev. 1531, 1534, 1538 (1973). At a very early date, Professor Karl Llewellyn referred to design defects in defining "defect" in Revised Uniform Sales Act § 1(b), cmt. *b*, at 125 (2d draft 1941), cited in Wilson, Products Liability (pt. 2), 43 Cal. L. Rev. 809, 810 n.7 (1955).

For a sampling of more recent expositions on design defects from academics, see, e.g., Twerski, An Essay on the Quieting of Products Liability Law, 105 Cornell L. Rev. 1211 (2020); Masterman and Viscusi, The Specific Consumer Expectations Test for Product Defects, 95 Ind. L.J. 183 (2020); Ausness, "Fasten your Seat Belt, Orville!": Exploring the Relationship Between State-of-the-Art, Technological and Commercial Feasibility, and the *Restatement*'s Reasonable Alternative Design Requirement, 45 Ind. L. Rev. 669 (2012); Green, The Unappreciated Congruity of the Second and Third Torts Restatements on Design Defect, 74 Brook. L. Rev. 807 (2009); Owen, Design Defect Ghosts, 74 Brook L. Rev. 927 (2009); Vetri, Order Out of Chaos: Products Liability Design-Defect Law, 43 U. Rich. L. Rev. 1373 (2009); Owen, Design Defects, 73 Mo. L. Rev. 291 (2008) (drawing from an earlier version of this chapter); Wright, The Principles of Product Liability, 26 Rev. Litig. 1067 (2007); Twerski, Chasing the Illusory Pot of Gold at the End of the Rainbow: Negligence and Strict Liability in Design Defect Litigation, 90 Marq. L. Rev. 7 (2006); Phillips, The Unreasonably Unsafe Product and Strict Liability, 72 Tenn. L. Rev. 833 (2005), reprinting 72 Chi.-Kent L. Rev. 129 (1996); Kysar, The Expectations of Consumers, 103 Colum. L. Rev. 1700 (2003); Miller, Myth Surrenders to Reality: Design Defect Litigation in Iowa, 51 Drake L. Rev. 549 (2003); Vandall and J. Vandall, A Call for An Accurate *Restatement (Third) of Torts: Design Defect*, 33 U. Mem. L. Rev. 909 (2003); Owen, Toward a Proper Test for Design Defectiveness: "Micro-Balancing" Costs and Benefits, 75 Tex. L. Rev. 1661 (1997); Owen, Risk-Utility Balancing in Design Defect Cases, 30 U. Mich. J.L. Reform 239 (1997); Owen, Defectiveness Restated: Exploding the "Strict" Products Liability Myth, 1996 U. Ill. L. Rev. 743; Vandall, The Restatement (Third) of Torts, Products Liability, Section 2(b): Design Defect, 68 Temp. L. Rev. 167 (1995); Green, The Schizophrenia of Risk-Benefit Analysis in Design Defect Litigation, 48 Vand. L. Rev. 609 (1995); Davis, Design Defect Liability: In Search of a Standard of Responsibility, 39 Wayne L. Rev. 1217 (1993); D. Fairgrieve and R. Goldberg, Product Liability ch. 11 (Oxford 3d ed. 2020) (British law).

[8] Design defectiveness in the 2020s is surely less inscrutable than was Russia in the late 1930s, but Winston Churchill's inimitable characterization nevertheless seems apt.

[9] An insurance industry study of large claims (in excess of $100,000) some time ago revealed that strict liability design defect was the principal claim in 75% of such cases. See A Study of Large Product Liability Claims Closed in 1985, summarized in § 1.3, above.

[10] See, e.g., Thibault v. Sears, Roebuck & Co., 395 A.2d 843 (N.H. 1978) (lack of rear trailing guard on rotary lawn mower). See also Berrier v. Simplicity Mfg., Inc., 563 F.3d 38, 65–66 (3d Cir. 2009) (Pa. law) (lack of roller barrier on back of riding mower).

electrical interlock cut-off device on a dangerous machine,[11] or a "safety" on a gun.[12] Much automotive products liability litigation challenges the design of motor vehicles, notably the extent to which their designs are sufficiently "crashworthy" to provide their occupants adequate protection in the event of a crash.[13] In addition to such typical design danger claims, numerous other forms of product hazards may give rise to claims of design defectiveness—such as combat earplugs that cause hearing loss and tinnitus, fire sirens so loud they can damage firefighters' hearing, bathtubs in which a person can slip while taking a shower, drain cleaners comprised of unnecessarily caustic chemicals, hormone replacement drugs that may cause breast cancer, asbestos products comprised of toxic fibers, allergenic latex gloves, fabrics not treated with flame-retardant chemicals, tampons that are too absorbent, coffee that is too hot, and tell-tale mechanical heart valves that emit excessive noise.[14]

The discussion of defects in the chapter on strict liability in tort[15] focused on the quest by courts for a general definition of "defectiveness," commonly viewed in early products liability excursions as embracing a single principle applicable to any type of

---

[11] See, e.g., Hargis v. Wellspeak Enters., Inc., 2012 WL 3144962 (S.D. Ind. 2012) (no guard on conveyor intake rollers); Miles v. DESA Heating LLC, 2012 WL 1038677 (D.S.C. 2012) (insufficient guard on heater to keep clothing from instantly igniting); Brochtrup v. Mercury Marine, 426 Fed. Appx. 335 (5th Cir. 2011) (Tex. law) (no guard on spinning boat propeller that mangled plaintiff's leg); Lent v. Signature Truck Sys., Inc., 2011 WL 4575312, at *8 (W.D.N.Y. 2011) (no guard on truck's power take-off (PTO) drive shaft); Gould v. Rexon Indus. Corp., 2006 WL 2301852, at *3 (N.D.N.Y. 2006) (removable guard on table saw blade); Knitz v. Minster Mach. Co., 1987 WL 6486 (Ohio Ct. App. 1987) (no interlock gate guard on press ram that descended on operator's hand).

[12] See, e.g., Halliday v. Sturm, Ruger & Co., 792 A.2d 1145 (Md. 2002); Sturm, Ruger & Co. v. Day, 594 P.2d 38 (Alaska 1979), modified on other grounds, 615 P.2d 621 (Alaska 1980). *But see* Nelson v. Original Smith & Wesson Business Entities and/or Corporations, 449 Fed. Appx. 581 (9th Cir. 2011) (Alaska law) (gun manufacturer had no duty to include a safety lock on revolver).

[13] See § 17.3, below.

[14] See, e.g., In re 3M Combat Arms Earplug Prods. Liab. Litig., 2021 WL 2605971, at *3 (N.D. Fla. 2021) (combat earplugs); Baley v. Federal Signal Corp., 982 N.E.2d 776 (Ill. App. Ct. 2012) (fire sirens too loud); Howard v. Omni Hotels Mgmt. Corp., 136 Cal. Rptr. 3d 739, 745 (Ct. App. 2012) (denying design defect claim brought against tub manufacturer by plaintiff who slipped and "zip," "flew out of" the tub that met industry standards for coefficient of friction and surface coverage of anti-slip coating); Yun Tung Chow v. Reckitt & Colman, Inc., 950 N.E.2d 113 (N.Y. 2011) (lye drain cleaner); Keffer v. Wyeth, 791 F. Supp. 2d 539 (S.D. W. Va. 2011) (hormone replacement therapy medication for menopausal symptoms that may have caused breast cancer); Saller v. Crown Cork & Seal Co., 115 Cal. Rptr. 3d 151 (Ct. App. 2010) (asbestos-containing insulation); Green v. Smith & Nephew AHP, Inc., 629 N.W.2d 727 (Wis. 2001) (allergic reactions to latex gloves with excessive proteins and other toxic chemical substances); Nadel v. Burger King Corp., 695 N.E.2d 1185 (Ohio Ct. App. 1997) (175° coffee caused second-degree burns); Bravman v. Baxter Healthcare Corp., 984 F.2d 71 (2d Cir. 1993) (N.Y. law) (noisy mechanical heart valve); Apels v. Murjani Int'l Ltd., 1986 WL 122176 (D. Kan. 1986) (blouse fabric, 80% cotton and 20% polyester, excessively flammable); West v. Johnson & Johnson Prods., Inc., 220 Cal. Rptr. 437 (Ct. App. 1985) (extra-high absorbency tampons caused toxic shock syndrome). See also Strothkamp v. Chesebrough-Pond's, Inc., 1993 WL 79239 (Mo. Ct. App. 1993) (box of cotton swabs not childproofed); Toner v. Lederle Labs., 828 F.2d 510 (9th Cir. 1987) (Idaho law) (DPT vaccine not formulated in safer manner); Boyer v. Empiregas, Inc. of Chillicothe, 734 S.W.2d 828 (Mo. Ct. App. 1987) (inadequately odorized propane gas exploded); Hilliard v. A.H. Robins Co., 196 Cal. Rptr. 117 (Ct. App. 1983) (Dalkon Shield IUD, with multifilament tail string, facilitated migration of bacteria into uterus); Drayton v. Jiffee Chem. Corp., 395 F. Supp. 1081 (N.D. Ohio 1975) (formulation of drain cleaner, 26% lye, unnecessarily caustic), modified, 591 F.2d 352 (6th Cir. 1978).

[15] See ch. 5, above.

case.[16] As products liability law matured,[17] however, most courts[18] and commentators[19] came to understand that meaningful evaluation of the acceptability of a product's dangers logically turns on considerations that vary contextually depending on whether the problem was one of manufacture, design, or the absence of sufficient warnings.[20] And early in the evolution of products liability law, observers recognized that determining how and why a design danger should or should not be characterized as "defective" was at once the most important and the most baffling problem in this entire field of law.[21] For this reason, much of the search for a general definition of "product defect," examined earlier,[22] was in fact a search for the meaning of defectiveness in design, as further discussed below.

Evaluating the acceptability of a product's design is difficult in part because a product's design is the essence of what its maker decides to create and sell. A manufacturing defect is truly a mistake, one that results from some fault in the production process whereby a particular product deviates from the manufacturer's own "blueprint" specifications of the intended design. Quite to the contrary, a charge that a product is defective in *design* challenges those very specifications on the ground that the design engineers, in their conceptual rendition of the product, failed to take safety into adequate account. Consequently, challenging a product's design challenges the decision of the manufacturer's engineers and managers to develop and sell a product containing a particular type and level of utility and danger. Thus, unlike a manufacturing defect claim, which implicates merely a single product unit, a design defect claim challenges the integrity of the very product concept and so pierces to the core of its maker's enterprise. For this reason, design defect claims are of greatest concern to manufacturers, since a judicial declaration that the design of a particular product is "defective" condemns the entire product line.[23]

Judicial evaluations of manufacturer design decisions encounter other difficulties, too. Far more than in manufacturing and warning defect cases, design cases require courts to second-guess a manufacturer's analyses of consumer market preferences. Some commentators have challenged the propriety of courts displacing multi-faceted

16 Some early commentators recognized that design and manufacturing defects were conceptually distinct (and warning defects to a lesser extent, because such defects were sometimes viewed as a subset of design defects), but they generally viewed the classification as having little or no doctrinal significance. See, e.g., James, Products Liability, 34 Tex. L. Rev. 44, 49 (1955). See generally § 6.2, above.

17 Although the distinctive nature of design, manufacturing, and warning defects was overlooked by many during the burst of excitement surrounding the adoption of strict products liability in tort, both the First and the Second Restatements of Torts so divided the cases in the law of negligence. See Rest. (2d) Torts §§ 388 (duty to warn), 395 (manufacturing flaws), and 398 (dangerous design).

18 Some courts still miss this point. See, e.g., Urena v. Biro Mfg. Co., 114 F.3d 359, 365 (2d Cir. 1997) (N.Y. law) (Plaintiff's evidence that "design was unreasonably dangerous because it lacks adequate warnings and instructions was unrebutted. He therefore survives summary judgment on his design defect claim.").

19 Some writers also miss this point. See, e.g., Shapo, In Search of the Law of Products Liability: The ALI Restatement Project, 48 Vand. L. Rev. 631, 659 (1995); Corboy, The Not-So-Quiet Revolution: Rebuilding Barriers to Jury Trial in the Proposed *Restatement (Third) of Torts: Products Liability*, 61 Tenn. L. Rev. 1043, 1089 (1994); Phillips, Achilles' Heel, 61 Tenn. L. Rev. 1265, 1267 (1994); Price, Toward a Unified Theory of Products Liability: Reviving the Causative Concept of Legal Fault, 61 Tenn. L. Rev. 1277, 1319 (1994).

20 See §§ 5.10, 6.2, and 6.5, above.

21 For law journal discussions of this point, see note 7, above.

22 See ch. 5, above.

23 See, e.g., Sluis v. Ethicon, Inc., 529 F. Supp. 3d 1004, 1019 (D.S.D. 2021); Beard v. Johnson & Johnson, Inc., 41 A.3d 823, 837 n.16 (Pa. 2012) ("a verdict for a plaintiff in a design-defect case is tantamount to a determination that the entire product line is defective").

engineering and managerial determinations of this type with judicial fiats rendered in the litigation arena.[24] Be that as it may, courts around the nation have come to adjudicate the sufficiency of product designs on a regular basis.

This chapter examines the tests of design defectiveness developed by the courts, particularly in applying the doctrine of *Restatement (Second) of Torts* § 402A. Although these tests were examined preliminarily in the chapter on strict liability in tort, their application to design defect cases, as well as the *Third Restatement*'s definition of design defectiveness and a manufacturer's liability for equipping its products with optional, rather than mandatory, safety features are explored in greater depth in this chapter.

Other topics of special interest in design defect litigation are examined elsewhere, such as how a warning may affect a manufacturer's duty of safe design;[25] proof of defect,[26] including the use of expert witnesses;[27] product misuse;[28] certain limitations on liability affecting design defect determinations, such as obvious dangers, generic risks, state of the art, and product deterioration;[29] automotive crashworthiness;[30] and the liability of pharmaceutical manufacturers for the design of prescription drugs and medical devices.[31]

§ 8.2 THEORIES AND TESTS OF LIABILITY

Manufacturers and other sellers[32] are subject to liability for defective design under each of the major theories of liability. Thus, as is true as well for other types of defects, product suppliers are subject to liability in negligence, for negligently making and selling products that are defectively designed;[33] in implied warranty, for selling products that are not fit for their ordinary purposes (and hence "unmerchantable") because they are defectively designed;[34] and in strict liability in tort for simply selling products that are defective in design.[35]

---

[24] See, e.g., Henderson, Judicial Review of Manufacturers' Conscious Design Choices: The Limits of Adjudication, 73 Colum. L. Rev. 1531, 1534, 1538 (1973) (characterizing such decisions by manufacturers as "polycentric" and "managerial"); Huber, Safety and the Second Best: The Hazards of Public Risk Management in the Courts, 85 Colum. L. Rev. 277 (1985); Epstein, The Risks of Risk/Utility, 48 Ohio St. L.J. 469 (1987).

[25] See § 6.2, above.

[26] See § 6.4, above.

[27] See § 6.3, above.

[28] See § 13.5, below.

[29] See ch. 10, below.

[30] See § 17.3, below.

[31] See § 18.2, below.

[32] Some jurisdictions partially immunize retailers and other non-manufacturers from liability for design defects and other forms of strict liability. See § 15.2, below.

[33] See, e.g., Crawford v. ITW Food Equip. Grp., LLC, 977 F.3d 1331, 1343–45 (11th Cir. 2020) (Fla. law) (jury properly found that FEG did not use reasonable care, failing the risk-utility test, in designing its meat saw with an adjustable, rather than auto-deploying, blade guard); Calles v. Scripto-Tokai Corp., 864 N.E.2d 249, 263–64 (Ill. 2007) (design of utility lighter that was not child-resistant); Shipler v. General Motors Corp., 710 N.W.2d 807 (Neb. 2006) (negligent design of roof structure that collapsed in rollover accident).

[34] See, e.g., Haglund v. Philip Morris, Inc., 847 N.E.2d 315, 322–23 (Mass. 2006) (cigarettes); Smith v. DaimlerChrysler Corp., 2002 WL 31814534 (Del. Super. Ct. 2002) (automobile); Denny v. Ford Motor Co., 662 N.E.2d 730 (N.Y. 1995) (Bronco II SUV).

[35] See, e.g., Baley v. Federal Signal Corp., 982 N.E.2d 776 (Ill. App. Ct. 2012) (fire sirens too loud); Calles v. Scripto-Tokai Corp., 864 N.E.2d 249, 263–64 (Ill. 2007) (utility lighter not child-resistant); Vautour v. Body Masters Sports Indus., 784 A.2d 1178 (N.H. 2001) (leg press machine with fixed stops); McCathern v. Toyota Motor Corp., 23 P.3d 320 (Or. 2001) (SUV rollover).

Regardless of the theory of liability, whether a design is "defective" is typically the central issue in litigation associated with a product's design. Indeed, the *Products Liability Restatement* proposes that liability in such cases be grounded solely on the notion of product defect rather than on traditional theories of liability such as negligence and strict liability in tort.[36] Strict liability in tort, of course, is defined principally in terms of a product's "defectiveness."[37] Yet proof of a defect in a product's design is just as important in cases brought in negligence inasmuch as a manufacturer hardly can be at fault for selling a product with a *safe* design—a design that is *not* defective.[38] Moreover, in the great majority of states, and even in most cases brought in the Empire State,[39] proving that a product design is dangerously unmerchantable under UCC § 2–314 amounts to virtually the same thing as proving that the product is "defective" (or "unreasonably dangerous") under *Restatement (Second) of Torts* § 402A.[40]

In considering the concept of design defectiveness, it is crucial to remember that a manufacturer's liability for harm from a product's design characteristics, even if labeled "strict," is not absolute. As the strict manufacturer liability principles of *Greenman v. Yuba Power Products, Inc.*[41] and *Restatement (Second) of Torts* § 402A spread across the nation in the 1960s and 1970s,[42] courts and commentators searched mightily for standards or "tests" of liability that would stop liability well short of absolute.[43] Although

---

[36] See Products Liability Rest. § 2 cmt. *n* (because design defect claims rest on a risk-utility assessment regardless of doctrinal label, courts should not risk inconsistent verdicts by submitting such claims to juries on different causes of action, whether negligence, implied warranty, or strict liability in tort). At least one state supreme court agrees. See Wright v. Brooke Grp. Ltd., 652 N.W.2d 159, 169 (Iowa 2002) ("We question the need for or usefulness of *any* traditional doctrinal label in design defect cases because, as comment *n* points out, a court should not submit both a negligence claim and a strict liability claim based on the same design defect since both claims rest on an identical risk-utility evaluation. Moreover, to persist in using two names for the same claim only continues the dysfunction engendered by section 402A. Therefore, we prefer to label a claim based on a defective product design as a design defect claim without reference to strict liability or negligence."). Reform statutes in several other states similarly ground liability on definitions of design defect rather than on negligence, implied warranty, or strict liability in tort. See, e.g., Conn. Gen. Stat. Ann. §§ 52–572m, 52–572n; Ind. Code Ann. § 34–6–2–115; La. Rev. Stat. Ann. § 9:2800.52; N.J. Stat. Ann. § 2A:58C–1(b)(3); Wash. Rev. Code Ann. § 7.72.010(4).

[37] See § 5.3, above.

[38] See §§ 2.1 and 5.9, above.

[39] Denny v. Ford Motor Co., 662 N.E.2d 730 (N.Y. 1995), held that a product not defectively designed for purposes of strict products liability in tort could nevertheless be unmerchantable under UCC § 2–314(2). Yet even *Denny* recognized that the two standards in most cases will produce precisely the same result: "As a practical matter, the distinction between the defect concepts in tort law and in implied warranty theory may have little or no effect in most cases." Id. at 738. On *Denny*, see § 5.9, above.

[40] Or under the Third Restatement § 2(b). See § 8.8, below. Courts often recite the virtual or complete equivalence of warranty and tort liability standards: "[T]o bring an action in implied warranty for personal injury a plaintiff is required to show product unmerchantability sufficient to avoid summary judgment on the issue of defectiveness in a tort strict products liability suit." Larsen v. Pacesetter Sys., Inc., 837 P.2d 1273, 1284–85 (Haw. 1992), as amended, 843 P.2d 144 (Haw. 1992). See also Musick v. Dorel Juvenile Group, Inc., 847 F. Supp. 2d 887, 901 (W.D. Va. 2012) (design defect claims are "essentially the same" in warranty and negligence, both of which require a defect that renders product "unreasonably dangerous" for foreseeable use); Virgil v. Kash N' Karry Serv. Corp., 484 A.2d 652, 656 (Md. Ct. Spec. App. 1984):

> To recover on either theory—implied warranty or strict liability—the plaintiff in a products liability case must satisfy three basics . . .: (1) the existence of a defect, (2) the attribution of the defect to the seller, and (3) a causal relation between the defect and the injury.

See also §§ 4.3 and 5.9, above.

[41] 377 P.2d 897 (Cal. 1963) (Traynor, J.).

[42] See §§ 5.2 et seq., above.

[43] See § 5.3, above. Phillips v. Kimwood Mach. Co., 525 P.2d 1033, 1035–36 (Or. 1974), may have said it best. Noting that the "courts continue to flounder while attempting to determine how one decides whether a product is 'in a defective condition unreasonably dangerous to the user,' " the court observed:

early test formulations generally failed to distinguish between the various forms of defect, most of the early cases struggling with the meaning of defectiveness involved dangers in design.[44] Consequently, the evolution of early strict liability tests examined in chapter 5—the consumer expectations test, the risk-utility test, combinations thereof, and alternative tests—generally involved a search for appropriate methods for separating product designs that were adequately safe from those that were not.

All courts judge the adequacy of a product's design upon one of two basic standards, or some combination thereof: (1) the "consumer expectations" test—whether the design meets the safety expectations of users and consumers, and/or (2) the "risk-utility" test—whether the safety benefits of designing away a foreseeable danger exceed the resulting costs. Section 8.3 reconsiders § 402A's original standard—the consumer expectations test. The fundamentals of the risk-utility test, first explored in § 2.2, above, are then reassessed in § 8.4, which considers appropriate factors weighed in a risk-utility balance. Section 8.5 next considers the critical role of feasible design alternatives in risk-utility decisionmaking. Section 8.6 investigates the blending by some courts of the consumer expectations and risk-utility tests; § 8.7 examines the Wade-Keeton prudent-seller hindsight test, based on constructive knowledge of a product's design dangers; § 8.8 explores the *Products Liability Restatement* treatment of the concept of design defect; and § 8.9 considers design adequacy when safety devices are optional.

§ 8.3 THE CONSUMER EXPECTATIONS TEST

Roughly two centuries in the past, warranty law broke away from the tort law action of deceit and migrated to the law of contracts,[45] a field of law that seeks at bottom to protect the reasonable expectations of the contracting parties.[46] Warranty law sensibly protects consumer expectations predictably generated by a manufacturer's representations about its products, both express and implied.[47] When the Reporter for the *Restatement (Second) of Torts*, William Prosser, was drafting § 402A in the late 1950s and early 1960s,[48] virtually all of the scant case authority for strict manufacturer liability for injuries to remote consumers from defective products had been decided under the law of warranty.[49] The strongest authority for the new tort doctrine was a long line of food and drink cases, a context where the law has long protected consumer expectations with special vigilance.[50] So, it was only natural for Dean Prosser to define

---

> The problem with strict liability of products has been one of limitation. No one wants absolute liability where all the article has to do is to cause injury. To impose liability there has to be something about the article which makes it dangerously defective without regard to whether the manufacturer was or was not at fault for such condition. A test for unreasonable danger is therefore vital.

[44] See, e.g., id.

[45] See § 5.2, above.

[46] See 1 A. Corbin, Corbin on Contracts 2 (1993 rev. ed.) ("the law of contracts attempts the realization of reasonable expectations"). On the elemental importance of human expectations, and how expectation protection grounds tort law, see Owen, Expectations in Tort, 43 Ariz. St. L.J. 1287 (2011).

[47] See, e.g., Denny v. Ford Motor Co., 662 N.E.2d 730, 736 (N.Y. 1995) (warranty law, originating in the law of contracts, "directs its attention to the purchaser's disappointed expectations"); Markle v. Mulholland's Inc., 509 P.2d 529, 532, 534 (Or. 1973). See generally Owen, The Moral Foundations of Products Liability Law, 68 Notre Dame L. Rev. 427, 462–65 (1993); Shapo, A Representational Theory of Consumer Protection: Doctrine, Function and Legal Liability for Product Disappointment, 60 Va. L. Rev. 1109, 1370 (1974). On warranty law under the Uniform Commercial Code, see ch. 4, above.

[48] See §§ 5.2–5.6, above.

[49] On the warranty law background of strict products liability in tort, see § 5.2, above.

[50] Id.

strict products liability in the *Second Restatement*, first drafted to cover dangerous food products,[51] in the same consumer expectations terms that supported the warranty cases that provided authority for the new strict tort doctrine.

Restatement (Second) of Torts § 402A, of course, provides in black letter that sellers are strictly liable in tort for physical harm resulting from the sale of products "in a defective condition unreasonably dangerous" to users, consumers, or their property.[52] Its comments explain the meaning of both halves of this new standard of liability. Comment *g* defines "*defective condition*" as follows:

> The rule stated in this Section applies only where the product is, at the time it leaves the seller's hands, in *a condition not contemplated by the ultimate consumer*, which will be unreasonably dangerous to him.

Comment *i* defines the other half of the liability standard, "*unreasonably dangerous*":

> The article sold must be *dangerous to an extent beyond that which would be contemplated by the ordinary consumer who purchases it,* with the ordinary knowledge common to the community as to its characteristics.

Because "defective condition" and "unreasonably dangerous" both are defined as dangerous beyond a consumer's contemplations, most courts applying § 402A in the 1960s and 1970s understandably concluded that design defects under § 402A should be proven according to a standard of product safety gauged by "consumer expectations."[53]

Modern Application of the Test

Most modern courts have abandoned consumer expectations as the sole test for design defectiveness due to its inherent weaknesses,[54] explored again below. Yet many modern courts still apply the consumer expectations test in design defect cases, in one way or another,[55] and some version of the test is statutory in a small number of states.[56]

---

[51] See §§ 5.2 and 5.3, above.

[52] See § 5.3, above. Emphasis is added in the text of both comments following this note.

[53] See id. For examples of early decisions defining § 402A's "defective condition unreasonably dangerous" in the consumer expectations terms of comments *g* and *i*, see, e.g., Rossignol v. Danbury Sch. of Aeronautics, Inc., 227 A.2d 418 (Conn. 1967); Dunham v. Vaughan & Bushnell Mfg. Co., 247 N.E.2d 401 (Ill. 1969); Lunt v. Brady Mfg. Corp., 475 P.2d 964 (Ariz. Ct. App. 1970); Vincer v. Esther Williams All-Aluminum Swimming Pool Co., 230 N.W.2d 794 (Wis. 1975).

[54] See also § 5.6, above.

[55] See, e.g., Flaherty v. E-Go Bike, LLC, 2022 WL 445428, at *4 (M.D. Fla. 2022) (electric bike that stopped suddenly, throwing plaintiff over the handlebars onto the concrete, "failed to perform as safely as an ordinary consumer would expect"); Pilliod v. Monsanto Co., 282 Cal. Rptr. 3d 679, 704 (Ct. App. 2021) (2–1 decision) (rejecting defendant's arguments that the consumer expectations test was inappropriately applied; "[O]rdinary consumers do have expectations about whether they will develop cancer as a result of using widely sold and advertised herbicides. Their expectation is they will not."); Kirk v. Clark Equip. Co., 991 F.3d 865, 878 (7th Cir. 2021) (Ill. law) ("a plaintiff may establish a design defect through two different approaches: 'the consumer-expectations test and the risk-utility test' "); Ford Motor Co. v. Trejo, 402 P.3d 649, 655 (Nev. 2017) ("even in cases of complex or technical products, a lay jury is sufficiently equipped to determine whether a product performs in a manner to be reasonably expected under certain circumstances, pursuant to the consumer-expectation test"); Evans v. Lorillard Tobacco Co., 990 N.E.2d 997 (Mass. 2013) (jury permitted but not bound to consider consumer expectations as to safety of cigarettes as one factor in risk-utility test); Wilson Sporting Goods Co. v. Hickox, 59 A.3d 1267, 1275 (D.C. 2013) (impact of foul ball striking major league catcher's mask equipped with newly designed throat guard, that angled forward instead of straight down, caused concussion and damaged joint in plaintiff's inner ear; approving instruction that "[a] design is defective if the product fails to perform as safely as an ordinary customer would expect when [the product is] used in an intended or reasonably foreseeable manner").

[56] A North Dakota statute, N.D. Cent. Code § 28–01.3–01(4), explicitly defines "unreasonably dangerous" in consumer contemplation terms, as does one in Utah, although the latter is more robust, defining

Although the consumer expectations standard was conventionally viewed as more protective of plaintiffs than the risk-utility standard,[57] it now is clear that courts have used the consumer expectations test most frequently to *deny* recovery to plaintiffs in the many cases involving obvious design hazards.[58]

One of the relatively few cases applying the consumer expectations standard to *allow* a design defect claim is *Jarke v. Jackson Products*,[59] which involved a welder's claim against the manufacturer of a welding mask. The plaintiff was injured while squatting beneath an object he was welding overhead, with his head cocked to one side, when some molten metal dropped from above onto his mask, rolled down to the mask's side rim, which channeled it into his ear. The complaint alleged that the mask was defectively designed without ear guards and because the its overall configuration could channel molten metal into a user's ears. Reasoning that the danger to a user's ears was obvious, the trial court granted the defendant manufacturer's motion for summary judgment, and the plaintiff appealed. Although the appellate court agreed that the obvious absence of an ear guard precluded a finding of design defectiveness under the consumer expectations test on that particular ground, it reversed and remanded on the issue of whether an ordinary person would understand that the mask's overall design created the means for molten slag to be channeled into a user's ear.[60]

---

the term as "dangerous to an extent beyond which would be contemplated by the ordinary and prudent buyer, consumer, or user in that community considering the product's characteristics, propensities, risks, dangers, and uses together with any actual knowledge, training, or experience possessed by that particular buyer, user, or consumer." Utah Code Ann. § 78B–6–702. Two statutes, Or. Rev. Stat. Ann. § 30.920 and S.C. Code Ann. § 15–73–30, embrace the consumer contemplations standard indirectly by incorporating into the statute the comments to § 402A, including comment *g* and *i*. The South Carolina court decided to ignore the statute and apply a risk-utility test in design defect cases in Branham v. Ford Motor Co., 701 S.E.2d 5, 14 (S.C. 2010), stating that the consumer expectations test "is ill-suited in design defect cases" and ruling that "the exclusive test in a products liability design case is the risk-utility test with its requirement of showing a feasible alternative design." A Tennessee statute defines "unreasonably dangerous" alternatively in both consumer contemplations and prudent manufacturer terms. See Tenn. Code Ann. § 29–28–102(8); Ray v. BIC Corp., 925 S.W.2d 527, 529 (Tenn. 1996).

[57] See, e.g., Shapo, In Search of the Law of Products Liability: The ALI Restatement Project, 48 Vand. L. Rev. 631 (1995); Phillips, Achilles' Heel, 61 Tenn. L. Rev. 1265 (1994). Yet some scholars vigilantly protective of plaintiff interests recognized the weaknesses in the consumer expectations test. See, e.g., Vandall, The *Restatement (Third) of Torts: Products Liability* Section 2(b): The Reasonable Alternative Design Requirement, 61 Tenn. L. Rev. 1407 (1994).

[58] As discussed in § 5.6, above. See, e.g., Farkas v. Addition Mfg. Techs., LLC, 952 F.3d 944, 950 (8th Cir. 2020) (Mo. law) ("danger of a tube forming machine to the user's hand was . . . 'open, obvious, and apparent' "); Chavez v. Glock, Inc., 144 Cal. Rptr. 3d 326, 350 (Ct. App. 2012) (no reasonable consumer "would expect an unlockable and loaded weapon, left in ready-to-fire condition in a location accessible to a child or other unauthorized users, not to accidentally discharge"); Johnson v. Cricket Co., 2010 WL 4599044, at *6 (Cal. Ct. App. 2010) (cosmetologist should have expected that particularly sharp point of scissors might injure her if she stuck her wrist with it); Bourne v. Marty Gilman, Inc., 452 F.3d 632 (7th Cir. 2006) (Ind. law) (risk that aluminum goalpost might snap and fall dangerously when Ball State students rushed on field and climbed on post to celebrate football victory); Crosswhite v. Jumpking, Inc., 411 F. Supp. 2d 1228, 1231 (D. Or. 2006) (jumping on trampolines is their purpose, which ordinary user would contemplate); Brown v. Sears, Roebuck & Co., 328 F.3d 1274, 1282–83 (10th Cir. 2003) (Utah law) (ordinary and prudent user would expect danger to toddler standing behind riding mower operated in reverse); Menard v. Newhall, 373 A.2d 505, 507 (Vt. 1977) (that plaintiff's eye might be put out in BB gun fight). See also note 67 in § 10.2, below.

[59] 631 N.E.2d 233 (Ill. App. Ct. 1994).

[60] Id. at 239. A factually analogous case is Wilson Sporting Goods Co. v. Hickox, 59 A.3d 1267 (D.C. 2013), which approved use of the consumer expectations test to allow recovery by a catcher using a mask equipped with a newly designed throat guard. When a foul ball struck the mask, the force was so great that the catcher suffered a concussion and damage to his inner ear.

Problems with the Test

Third-Party Victims

It will be recalled that the consumer expectations test is an *objective* test based on the average, normal, or "ordinary" expectations of an ordinary, reasonable user or consumer.[61] Usually that person, whether a user or consumer, will be the person placed at risk by the product's danger in design.[62] Yet purchasers and users sometimes control product risks to *other* persons, as previously discussed. In such cases, when one person (such as a parent or a doctor) uses a product with particular dangers in a manner that injures a person under his or her control (such as the parent's child or the doctor's patient), the law normally looks to the expectations of the risk controller rather than to those of the victim.[63]

The bystander problem with the consumer expectations test is illustrated by a Wisconsin case, *Horst v. Deere & Co.*[64] While driving his riding lawn mower in reverse, the operator rode over and severed the feet of his two-year-old son hidden behind the mower. Although a simple design alteration would have precluded the riding mower from operating in reverse, Wisconsin law at the time based strict products liability in tort solely on consumer safety expectations. The trial court thus instructed the jury that "A product is said to be defective when it is in a condition not contemplated by the ordinary user or consumer . . .,"[65] and the jury returned a verdict for the defendant manufacturer. Affirming judgment for the defendant, and rejecting the plaintiff's request to adopt a "*bystander* contemplation" test, Justice Gableman for the majority acknowledged the inability of a consumer expectations test to assist bystanders but, nevertheless, reaffirmed consumer expectations as a coherent and appropriate standard for all products liability cases.[66]

Obvious Dangers

The utility of the consumer expectations test is severely compromised when design dangers are obvious, as mentioned above.[67] Because consumers acquire their safety and

---

61 Comment *i* is phrased in terms of the "ordinary" consumer "with the ordinary knowledge common to the community." Yet, many modern courts read "ordinary" to mean "reasonable." See, e.g., Mansur v. Ford Motor Co., 129 Cal. Rptr. 3d 200, 208 (Ct. App. 2011) ("The test is that of a hypothetical reasonable consumer, not the expectation of the particular plaintiff in the case."); Calles v. Scripto-Tokai Corp., 864 N.E.2d 249, 255 (Ill. 2007) ("Under the consumer-expectation test, a plaintiff must establish what an ordinary consumer purchasing the product would expect about the product and its safety. This is an objective standard based on the average, normal, or ordinary expectations of the reasonable person; it is not dependent upon the subjective expectation of a particular consumer or user."). Compare Mason v. Mitcham, 382 S.W.3d 717, 720 (Ark. Ct. App. 2011) (describing "a subjective approach" based on "the expectations of the actual plaintiff sitting in the courtroom"). See generally § 5.6, above.

62 See § 5.6, above.

63 See, e.g., Calles v. Scripto-Tokai Corp., 864 N.E.2d 249, 256 (Ill. 2007) (plaintiff's 3-year-old daughter used utility lighter to start fire in which she died; because ordinary consumer of a lighter is an adult, the safety expectations about such a product must be viewed from perspective of an adult consumer). Compare Colgate v. JUUL Labs, Inc., 402 F. Supp. 3d 728, 754 (N.D. Cal. 2019) (class action against manufacturer of flavored e-cigarettes legally sold only to adults; because minors are unable "to fully appreciate the risks of using JUUL's ENDS, the products are defective under the consumer expectations test").

64 769 N.W.2d 536, 550–51 (Wis. 2009).

65 Id. at 540.

66 See id. at 550–54. For an excellent discussion of how bystanders are inadequately protected by modern products liability law, see Watts, Fairness and Utility in Products Liability: Balancing Individual Rights and Social Welfare, 38 Fla. St. U. L. Rev. 597 (2011).

67 On obvious dangers, see § 10.2, below.

danger expectations most directly from a product's appearance, obvious dangers—such as the risk to human limbs from an unguarded power mower or industrial machine—are virtually always contemplated or expected by the user or consumer, who thereby is necessarily unprotected by the consumer expectations test, no matter how probable and severe the likely danger nor how easy and cheap the means of avoiding it. In such cases, the buyer gets what he or she paid for, or the user engaged a danger that he or she expected, so that the risk of injury shifts to the buyer or user who chose to accept it,[68] or to a third-party victim who had no say in the matter at all.[69]

Thus, while the consumer expectations test protects the autonomy of buyers and users by shielding them from unexpected harm, the flip side of this test requires users and consumers to be ever vigilant and take responsibility for the harmful consequences of their choices about risk. And a dire consequence of the consumer expectations test, unless its plain consequences are baldly ignored,[70] is that it perversely rewards manufacturers for failing to adopt cost-effective measures to remedy glaring dangers to human life and limb.[71] The failure of the consumer expectations test to deal adequately with the obvious danger problem profoundly weakens the usefulness of this test and effectively disqualifies it for principled use[72] as the sole basis for determining defects in design.[73]

Vagueness

Another significant limitation on the usefulness of consumer expectations as a liability standard in design cases concerns the vagueness of a consumer's expectations

---

[68] Such as a teenager paralyzed from attempting a flip on a trampoline. See Crosswhite v. Jumpking, Inc., 411 F. Supp. 2d 1228, 1231 (D. Or. 2006). Yet using the expectations of younger users is problematic. See, e.g., Bunch v. Hoffinger Indus., 20 Cal. Rptr. 3d 780, 796 (Ct. App. 2004) (affirming jury award of $12 million to child rendered quadriplegic after diving into shallow above-ground pool; "the danger of diving into a shallow aboveground pool is not open and obvious to an 11 year old as a matter of law").

[69] Such as a toddler run over by a riding lawn mower. See Brown v. Sears, Roebuck & Co., 328 F.3d 1274, 1282–83 (10th Cir. 2003) (Utah law).

[70] See Chaney v. Hobart Int'l, Inc., 54 F. Supp. 2d 677, 681 (E.D. La. 1999) ("As dangerous as the meat grinder may have been without a feed pan guard, it was clearly 'not dangerous to an extent beyond that which would be contemplated by the ordinary user.' The possibility of injury is glaring."). On occasion, some courts do baldly ignore the logically inescapable impact of an obvious design danger on the consumer expectations test. See, e.g., Hansen v. New Holland N. Am., Inc., 574 N.W.2d 250, 254 (Wis. Ct. App. 1997), where the plaintiff's hand was caught and injured in the mechanism of a hay baler while he was trying to cut away a buildup of hay on the rollers with a jackknife. The trial court dismissed the plaintiff's design defect claim on the ground that the danger of placing one's hands near the moving mechanism presented an obvious danger which precluded recovery under the consumer expectations test. *Held*, reversing and remanding, jury question presented on whether an average user would have fully appreciated the risk: "[F]ocusing solely on the user's conduct will frustrate public policy considerations underlying product liability law. A danger that is open and obvious to a consumer is equally apparent to the manufacturer."

[71] See, e.g., Hansen v. New Holland N. Am., Inc., 574 N.W.2d at 254 (Wis. Ct. App. 1997) (The test "creates an incentive for manufacturers to ensure that hazards are in fact open and obvious, possibly minimizing needed safeguards and exposure to liability for designing dangerous products.").

[72] True, this test may be distorted to avoid the harsh results of its principled application. See Phillips, Consumer Expectations, 53 S.C. L. Rev. 1047, 1049 (2002) (characterizing as "semantic" the consumer expectations test's foreclosure of relief to persons injured by obvious dangers). While I am unsympathetic to Jerry Phillips' unwavering devotion to the consumer expectations test, his contributions to tort and products liability scholarship were enormous. I dedicate this section to his memory.

[73] See id. In switching from the consumer expectations test to the risk-utility standard in 1993, the Mississippi Supreme Court noted that its conversion to risk-utility permitted it to reject the patent danger rule that inhered in the consumer expectations test. Sperry-New Holland v. Prestage, 617 So.2d 248, 256 n.4 (Miss. 1993), superseded by statute as recognized in Wolf v. Stanley Works, 757 So.2d 316 (Miss. 2000).

concerning most complex designs.[74] For example, consumers comprehend that automobiles are not completely crash proof, but they have no meaningful expectations as to the extent to which a vehicle may be compromised in the event of a collision or rollover at substantial speeds. The consumer expectations test thus was held to be an invalid gauge of design defectiveness in one case where a large rock hit the wheel of a vehicle traveling on the highway;[75] in another where the driver's airbag deployed and broke her jaw in a low-speed collision;[76] in one where an SUV rolled over, crushing its roof;[77] and in another where the passenger compartment collapsed in upon the driver's feet in a near head-on collision.[78] In such cases, the ordinary user of a vehicle "simply has 'no idea' how it should perform in all [such] situations."[79] For this reason, some courts that use the consumer expectations test limit the applicability of the test to cases involving simple, rather than complex, product designs and accident mechanisms, as examined in detail below.[80]

Some courts[81] and legislatures[82] more generally blend the consumer expectations test with the risk-utility standard,[83] or replace consumer expectations with risk-utility altogether, for determining design defectiveness.[84] Even in a risk-utility regime, however, consumer expectations may be considered together with the other evaluative factors[85] and occasionally can even be conclusive of design defect determinations.[86] In addition, the consumer expectations standard is still widely accepted as the most

---

74 See Keeton, Dobbs, Keeton, and Owen, Prosser and Keeton on the Law of Torts § 99, at 699. *But see* Phillips, Consumer Expectations, 53 S.C. L. Rev. 1047, 1052–61 (2002) (consumer expectations can be based on risk-utility, informed by experts, as in the *Potter* case, discussed in § 8.6, below).

75 Heaton v. Ford Motor Co., 435 P.2d 806 (Or. 1967).

76 Pruitt v. General Motors Corp., 86 Cal. Rptr. 2d 4 (Ct. App. 1999).

77 Edwards v. Ford Motor Co., 683 Fed. Appx. 610, 611 (9th Cir. 2017) (Cal. law) ("Drivers' everyday experiences do not allow for the formation of reasonable expectations as to the degree that a [Ford Explorer's] roof should crush during a rollover.").

78 Soule v. General Motors Corp., 882 P.2d 298 (Cal. 1994).

79 Id. at 308.

80 See § 8.6, below.

81 See, e.g., McCathern v. Toyota Motor Corp., 23 P.3d 320, 330–32 (Or. 2001) (risk-utility evidence may be required to prove consumer expectations); Vautour v. Body Masters Sports Indus., 784 A.2d 1178 (N.H. 2001) (consumer expectations defined in terms of risk-utility); Potter v. Chicago Pneumatic Tool Co., 694 A.2d 1319 (Conn. 1997) (same); Seattle-First Nat'l Bank v. Tabert, 542 P.2d 774, 779 (Wash. 1975).

82 For example, in Tennessee (as formerly in Ohio), liability is alternatively defined in both consumer expectations and risk-utility terms. See Tenn. Code Ann. § 29–28–102(8). A Washington statute blends the consumer expectations and risk-utility tests by providing (1) that a design is not reasonably safe if it fails the risk-utility test, and (2) that the trier of fact shall also consider whether the product's dangers exceeded the contemplations of the ordinary consumer. See Wash. Rev. Code Ann. § 7.72.030(1)(a) and (3). Miss. Code Ann. § 11–1–63(f)(ii) requires that a plaintiff alleging defective design must prove that "[t]he product failed to function as expected and there existed a feasible design alternative" that would have prevented the harm.

83 See § 8.6, below.

84 See §§ 5.6 and 5.7, above, and §§ 8.4–8.6, below.

85 See, e.g., Evans v. Lorillard Tobacco Co., 990 N.E.2d 997 (Mass. 2013) (jury permitted but not bound to consider consumer expectations as to safety of cigarettes as one factor in risk-utility test); Mikolajczyk v. Ford Motor Co., 901 N.E.2d 329, 352 (Ill. 2008) (adopting a formulation of the risk-utility test in which "consumer expectations are included within the scope of the broader risk-utility test"); Nichols v. Union Underwear Co., 602 S.W.2d 429 (Ky. 1980); Products Liability Rest. § 2 cmt. *g*.

86 "Such expectations are often influenced by how products are portrayed and marketed and can have a significant impact on consumer behavior. Thus, although consumer expectations do not constitute an independent standard for judging the defectiveness of product designs, they may substantially influence or even be ultimately determinative on risk-utility balancing . . . ." Id. § 2(b) cmt. *g*.

appropriate test for certain limited types of cases.[87] Finally, the consumer expectations test still plays some role as a liability standard for design defectiveness in roughly half of all the American states,[88] and a related standard, at least in name, exists in Europe.[89]

§ 8.4 THE RISK-UTILITY TEST

The risk-utility test is the principal modern standard for judging the safety or defectiveness of a product's design.[90] While liability for design defects was more commonly based on the consumer expectations test in the 1960s and early 1970s, even during those early years some courts saw the wisdom of assessing design defectiveness according to whether the safety benefits of remedying a design danger were worth the costs.[91] As courts and legislatures over the decades have turned away from the consumer

---

[87] Most notably in cases involving contaminated food and defects in used products. See Products Liability Rest. § 2 cmt. *h*, § 7 (food products), and § 8 (used products). See, e.g., Foor v. Amici's East Coast Pizzeria, 2011 WL 3854818, at *6 (Cal. Ct. App. 2011) (broken tooth on olive pit in antipasto salad); Porrazzo v. Bumble Bee Foods, LLC, 822 F. Supp. 2d 406 (S.D.N.Y. 2011) (mercury poisoning from canned tuna); Gaumer v. Rossville Truck & Tractor Co., 257 P.3d 292, 303 (Kan. 2011) (holding that Kansas law, informed partly by policy to "protect consumer expectations," permits strict liability actions against sellers of used products). Note, however, that food-product cases often involve "manufacturing" rather than design defects, and that used-product cases often do as well. On defects in food and drink, see § 7.5, above.

[88] See § 5.6, above.

[89] See the EC Directive "Concerning Liability for Defective Products," adopted in 1985, which provides in art. 6(1) as follows: "A product is defective when it does not provide the safety which a person is entitled to expect. . . ." See generally J. Stapleton, Product Liability, ch. 10 (Butterworths 1994); G. Howells, Comparative Product Liability, ch. 3 (Dartmouth 1993). Note, however, that because this provision addresses the degree of safety a person is *entitled* to expect, the standard may be applied in risk-utility fashion. See Stapleton, Products Liability in the United Kingdom: The Myths of Reform, 34 Tex. Int'l L.J. 45 (1999); Stapleton, Products Liability Reform—Real or Illusory?, 6 Oxford J. Legal Stud. 392, 405 (1986). See § 1.4, above.

[90] On the risk-utility test, see Green, The Unappreciated Congruity of the Second and Third Torts Restatements on Design Defects, 74 Brook. L. Rev. 807 (2009); Owen, Design Defect Ghosts, 74 Brook. L. Rev. 927 (2009); Twerski and Henderson, Manufacturers' Liability for Defective Product Designs: The Triumph of Risk-Utility, 74 Brook. L. Rev. 1061 (2009); Owen, Design Defects, 72 Mo. L. Rev. 291 (2008); Twerski, Chasing the Illusory Pot of Gold at the End of the Rainbow: Negligence and Strict Liability in Design Defect Litigation, 90 Marq. L. Rev. 7 (2006); Miller, Myth Surrenders to Reality: Design Defect Litigation in Iowa, 51 Drake L. Rev. 549 (2003); Owen, Toward a Proper Test for Design Defectiveness: "Micro-Balancing" Costs and Benefits, 75 Tex. L. Rev. 1661 (1997); Owen, Risk-Utility Balancing in Design Defect Cases, 30 U. Mich. J.L. Reform 239 (1997); Green, The Schizophrenia of Risk-Benefit Analysis in Design Defect Litigation, 48 Vand. L. Rev. 609 (1995); Miller, Design Defect Litigation in Iowa: The Myths of Strict Liability, 40 Drake L. Rev. 465 (1991); White, Risk-Utility Analysis and the Learned Hand Formula: A Hand That Helps or a Hand That Hides?, 32 Ariz. L. Rev. 77 (1990). For a useful practitioner perspective, see Rheingold, The Risk/Utility Test in Product Cases, 18 Trial Law. Q. 49 (Summer/Fall 1987). See also Gilles, United States v. Carroll Towing Co.: The Hand Formula's Home Port, in Torts Stories 11 (R. Rabin and S. Sugarman eds., Foundation Press 2003).

For economic perspectives on risk-utility analysis, see, e.g., Hylton, The Law and Economics of Products Liability, 88 Notre Dame L. Rev. 2457 (2013); Geistfeld, Reconciling Cost-Benefit Analysis with the Principle that Safety Matters More Than Money, 76 N.Y.U. L. Rev. 114 (2001); Gilles, The Invisible Hand Formula, 80 Va. L. Rev. 1015, 1025 (1994); Viscusi, Wading Through the Muddle of Risk-Utility Analysis, 39 Am. U. L. Rev. 573 (1990); A. Schwartz, Proposals for Products Liability Reform: A Theoretical Synthesis, 97 Yale L.J. 353, 384–88 (1988); Epstein, The Risks of Risk/Utility, 48 Ohio St. L.J. 469 (1987); R. Posner, Economic Analysis of Law §§ 6.1 and 6.6 (9th ed. 2014); W. Viscusi, Reforming Products Liability ch. 4 (1991).

For discussions of the risk-utility test in negligence and strict liability in tort, see § 2.2 and § 5.7, above.

[91] See, e.g., Helicoid Gage Div. of Am. Chain & Cable Co. v. Howell, 511 S.W.2d 573, 577 (Tex. App. 1974) (affirming verdict for plaintiff, where $2.50 safety shield could have prevented burst pressure gauge from throwing piece of lens into plaintiff's eye):

> To determine whether a product is unreasonably dangerous, . . . it is necessary to weigh the risk of harm against the utility of the product, considering whether safety devices would unreasonably raise the cost or diminish the utility of the product. The evidence at trial showed that shatterproof glass would have increased the cost of each gage by approximately one dollar and would not have reduced the gage's utility. Further, there was testimony that this injury would not have occurred had shatterproof glass been used.

expectations test in design danger cases,[92] they have substituted some form of cost-benefit ("risk-utility," "risk-benefit," or "benefit-risk") standard of liability, which is the liability standard for design defects in the *Restatement (Third) of Torts: Products Liability*.[93] In the new millennium, despite the tenacity of consumer expectations in a decreasing (yet still large) number of jurisdictions,[94] risk-utility has become America's preferred test for design defectiveness.[95]

See also Dorsey v. Yoder Co., 331 F. Supp. 753 (E.D. Pa. 1971) (jury properly found that $8,000 machine was defective for not being equipped with $200 to $500 guard that would have protected operator's hand and arm from being caught and drawn into metal slitter machine), aff'd, 474 F.2d 1339 (3d Cir. 1973); McCormack v. Hankscraft Co., 154 N.W.2d 488 (Minn. 1967) (jury could find that vaporizer top could have been threaded cheaply, without diminishing its utility, so that it could have been screwed onto top of glass container of hot water that tipped over and scalded infant plaintiff when top fell off). Compare Roach v. Kononen, 525 P.2d 125 (Or. 1974) (though car, which crashed when hood flew up and blocked driver's vision, could have been designed with substantially better visibility in such situations by adding hinge reinforcements costing $5–$10 per car, jury reasonably could find for Ford which was aware of only six or seven inadvertent hood openings over a seven- to eight-year period).

[92] Movements away from consumer expectations toward risk-utility include Davis v. UHP Projects, Inc., 2021 WL 1293858, at *3 (V.I. 2021) (adopting Products Liability Rest. § 2); Branham v. Ford Motor Co., 701 S.E.2d 5, 14 (S.C. 2010) (holding that the consumer expectation test "is ill-suited in design defect cases [and that] the exclusive test in a products liability design case is the risk-utility test with its requirement of showing a feasible alternative design"); Hickey v. Otis Elevator Co., 840 N.E.2d 637, 640 n.1 (Ohio Ct. App. 2005) (noting legislature's repeal of consumer expectations test earlier that year); McCathern v. Toyota Motor Corp., 23 P.3d 320, 330–32 (Or. 2001) (risk-utility evidence may be required to prove consumer expectations); Vautour v. Body Masters Sports Indus., 784 A.2d 1178 (N.H. 2001) (consumer expectations defined in risk-utility terms); Delaney v. Deere & Co., 999 P.2d 930, 944 (Kan. 2000) (recognizing "the validity of risk/utility analysis as a guide in determining the expectations of consumers in complex cases"); Potter v. Chicago Pneumatic Tool Co., 694 A.2d 1319 (Conn. 1997) (redefining consumer expectations in risk-utility terms); Banks v. ICI Ams., Inc., 450 S.E.2d 671 (Ga. 1994) (switching from consumer expectations to risk-utility); Nichols v. Union Underwear Co., 602 S.W.2d 429 (Ky. 1980); Seattle-First Nat'l Bank v. Tabert, 542 P.2d 774, 779 (Wash. 1975). In 2011, Wisconsin switched away from a consumer expectations standard to risk-utility in Wis. Stat. Ann. § 895.047(1)(a).

[93] For the prevalence of the risk-utility test in design defect cases, see Products Liability Rest. § 2, Reporters' Notes to cmt. *d*, which the Reporters updated in Henderson and Twerski, Manufacturers' Liability for Defective Product Designs: The Triumph of Risk-Utility, 74 Brook. L. Rev. 1061, 1079–93 (2009). On the Third Restatement definition, see § 8.8, below.

[94] See Kysar, The Expectations of Consumers, 103 Colum. L. Rev. 1700, 1701 (2003) (characterizing the consumer expectations test as "stubbornly and inexplicably persistent"). See also Phillips, Consumer Expectations, 53 S.C. L. Rev. 1047 (2002); § 5.6 note 352, above.

[95] See, e.g., In re: Ethicon Physiomesh Flexible Composite Hernia Mesh Prods. Liab. Litig. v. Ethicon, Inc., 2020 WL 9887565, at *8 (N.D. Ga. 2020) ("[d]rawing upon the Third Restatement of Torts, many other states rely upon some form of risk-utility analysis"); Branham v. Ford Motor Co., 701 S.E.2d 5, 14 & n.11 (S.C. 2010) ("an overwhelming majority" of states use some form of a risk-utility test); Bass v. Air Prods. & Chems., Inc., 2006 WL 1419375, at *11 (N.J. Super. Ct. App. Div. 2006) (the risk-utility test "has gained prominence in common law design defect claims"); Wright v. Brooke Grp. Ltd., 652 N.W.2d 159 (Iowa 2002) (adopting Products Liability Rest. § 2(b)); In re Methyl Tertiary Butyl Ether ("MTBE") Prods. Liab. Litig., 175 F. Supp. 2d 593, 623 (S.D.N.Y. 2001) (Cal., Fla., Ill., and N.Y. law) ("Courts have generally utilized the 'risk-utility balancing' test to determine whether a product is defectively designed."); Ford Motor Co. v. Miles, 967 S.W.2d 377, 386 (Tex. 1998) (Owen, J., concurring) (instruction conflicted with "the risk versus utility analysis that lies at the core of products liability design defect law"); Warner Fruehauf Trailer Co. v. Boston, 654 A.2d 1272, 1276 (D.C. 1995) (most states use a risk-utility test in design defect cases); Sperry-New Holland v. Prestage, 617 So.2d 248, 255 (Miss. 1993) ("[r]isk-utility has become the trend"). The dominance of the risk-utility test for determining design defectiveness has been clear for some time. See Foley v. Clark Equip. Co., 523 A.2d 379, 388 (Pa. Super. Ct. 1987) (most courts use a risk-utility balancing test for design defects). Compare In re Valsartan, Losartan, & Irbesartan Prods. Liab. Litig., 2021 WL 307486, at *18 (D.N.J. 2021) (where the court misread the count of states: "Most . . . [use] the consumer expectation test, others the risk-utility analysis, and a few apply both or a hybrid of the two."). Some states have legislated a risk-utility design defect test. See, e.g., Ohio Rev. Code Ann. § 2307.75; Wis. Stat. Ann. § 895.047(1)(a).

Fundamentals of Cost-Benefit Analysis; the Hand Formula

Risk-utility (cost-benefit) analysis is widely used to define liability for design defectives in both negligence[96] and strict liability in tort,[97] and it may helpfully be reviewed here, too. An analytical technique explicitly relied upon by Benjamin Franklin and Oliver Wendell Holmes,[98] cost-benefit analysis is as old as rational thought. All deliberative decisions involve a weighing of the advantages (benefits) and disadvantages (costs) of a contemplated course of action.[99] Whether a particular design danger is properly classified as "unreasonable" (that is, "defective") involves "a balancing of the probability and seriousness of harm against the costs of taking precautions. Relevant considerations include the availability of alternative designs, the cost and feasibility of adopting alternative designs, and the frequency or infrequency of injury resulting from the design."[100] Moreover, because a product's warnings and instructions serve to reduce the risks of many designs (similar to the obviousness of a hazard), the provision of such information is often an important factor in design defect risk-utility analysis.[101]

A product's design is "defective" under a risk-utility test if the costs of avoiding a particular hazard are foreseeably less than the resulting safety benefits. In other words, if the costs of a precaution are foreseeably less than the precaution's safety benefits, a product designed without the precaution is defective under the cost-benefit ("risk-

---

[96] See § 2.2, above.

[97] See § 5.7, above.

[98] See, e.g., Letter, Benjamin Franklin (Sept. 19, 1772) (suggesting, as aid to rendering difficult decisions, that one list and consider "all the reasons pro and con" and contemplate "where the balance lies"), reprinted in Edward M. Gramlich, Benefit-Cost Analysis of Government Programs 1–2 (1981). Franklin said:

> [T]hough the weight of reasons cannot be taken with the precision of algebraic quantities, yet when each is thus considered, separately and comparatively, and the whole lies before me, I think I can judge better, and am less liable to make a rash step, and in fact I have found great advantage from this kind of equation, in what may be called moral or prudential algebra.

Id. at 2 (emphasis omitted). Consider also Oliver Wendell Holmes, Jr., The Path of the Law, 10 Harv. L. Rev. 457, 474 (1897) (advising that "for everything we have to give up something else, and we are taught to set the advantage we gain against the other advantage we lose").

[99] See Green, Cost-Risk-Benefit Assessment and the Law: Introduction and Perspective, 45 Geo. Wash. L. Rev. 901, 903–04 (1977). Consider also Merrill, Risk-Benefit Decisionmaking by the Food and Drug Administration, 45 Geo. Wash. L. Rev. 994, 996 (1977) ("Risk-benefit analysis . . . includes any technique for making choices that explicitly or implicitly attempts to measure the potential adverse consequences of an activity and to predict its benefits. In its most refined form, such analysis may make use of refined mathematical methods for calculating risks and benefits, attempting to assign uniform values, usually in dollars, to all factors, including human lives.").

[100] Raney v. Honeywell, Inc., 540 F.2d 932, 935 (8th Cir. 1976) (Iowa law).

[101] See Hansen v. Sunnyside Prods., Inc., 65 Cal. Rptr. 2d 266 (Ct. App. 1997) (design defectiveness of household cleaner):

> We do not think that the risk to the consumer of the design of many household products can be rationally evaluated without considering the product's warnings. [W]hat is the risk of the design of a power saw, or other power tools or equipment, without considering the product's directions and warnings? We dare say that the risk would be astronomically, and irrationally, high. The same could be said about common garden pesticides, or even the household microwave oven. [W]ere we to ask jurors to evaluate the risks of the design of many household products without considering their directions or warnings, the practical result would be the withdrawal from the market of many useful products that are dangerous in the abstract but safe when used as directed.

Id. at 278 (noting that Dean John Wade "expressly lists consideration of warnings or instructions as a factor relevant to the determination of whether a product is unreasonably dangerous," id. at 276 n.9, referring to Dean Wade's factor number six, discussed below). See generally Products Liability Rest. § 2(b) cmt. *f* (among "broad range of factors" relevant to design defectiveness are "the instructions and warnings accompanying the product"), and id. cmt. *l*. See also § 6.2, notes 114–120, above. On the effect of a danger's obviousness on risk-utility determinations, see § 10.2, below.

utility") standard of liability.[102] Costs and benefits should be limited to those that are foreseeable,[103] and both should be calculated for the entire product line[104] for some substantial period of time.[105] The risk-utility test for design defectiveness is unaffected by whether the underlying theory of recovery is negligence,[106] strict liability in tort,[107] or even implied warranty,[108] because the appropriate balance between a particular design feature's safety, costs, and effect on product utility remains the same.[109]

The cost-benefit test,[110] in balancing the safety benefits of avoiding a particular risk against the avoidance costs ("burdens"), is especially well suited to establishing the safety or defectiveness of a product design.[111] The type and degree of design safety required in any situation depends upon the type, likelihood, and amount of harm (viewed together as the magnitude of the risk) that a particular burden of precaution (of a particular cost) may be expected to prevent.[112] If the risk posed by the design of a product

---

[102] See, e.g., Warner Fruehauf Trailer Co. v. Boston, 654 A.2d 1272, 1276 (D.C. 1995) (plaintiff must show "that the magnitude of the danger from the product outweighed the costs of avoiding the danger"). On how to formulate such a test, see Owen, Toward a Proper Test for Design Defectiveness: "Micro-Balancing" Costs and Benefits, 75 Tex. L. Rev. 1661, 1686–90 (1997).

[103] See, e.g., Coleman v. Cintas Sales Corp., 40 S.W.3d 544, 549 (Tex. App. 2001) (employee uniforms need not be flame retarded when there is no foreseeable risk that they will be exposed to fire); Products Liability Rest. § 2(b) and cmt. *a* (design may be defective "only when risks are reasonably foreseeable").

[104] Courts should guard against the tendency of juries to narrowly compare the individuated costs of precaution and safety benefits of the particular accident in the case at hand which, of course, is never the proper form of cost-benefit calculation for establishing design defectiveness.

[105] The period selected, whether one year or the projected lifetime of the product line, generally should not matter provided it is large enough to establish a standard rate and that both costs and benefits are measured over the same period.

[106] See § 2.2, above.

[107] See, e.g., Frazier v. Mylan Inc., 911 F. Supp. 2d 1285, 1299 (N.D. Ga. 2012) (negligent design and strict liability for design defect claims "both . . . use the same risk-utility analysis, and therefore, will be treated as one claim"); Jablonski v. Ford Motor Co., 955 N.E.2d 1138, 1155 (Ill. 2011) (balancing test for strict liability design defects and negligent design are "essentially identical," and "any distinction is mere semantics") (citing Twerski, Chasing the Illusory Pot of Gold at the End of the Rainbow: Negligence and Strict Liability in Design Defect Litigation, 90 Marq. L. Rev. 7, 12 (2006)).

Note, however, that many courts formerly distinguished strict liability from negligence on the basis of the *foreseeability* of the costs and benefits of improving the product's design safety, and a few still do. See, e.g., Blue v. Environmental Eng'g, Inc., 828 N.E.2d 1128, 1152–53 (Ill. 2005) (Fitzgerald, J., concurring) ("In negligence, foreseeability of harm is a fact question, whereas, in strict liability, a product's propensity to inflict harm is assumed."). Because most courts and commentators now believe that a plaintiff must establish the foreseeability of harm (manufacturers rarely challenge the foreseeability of precautionary costs) in "strict" tort actions as well as in negligence, cost-benefit (risk-utility) analysis should normally be identical in both contexts. The foreseeability issue is addressed in connection with the Wade-Keeton constructive knowledge test in § 8.7, below, and is further examined in the "state of the art" context in § 10.4, below.

[108] See, e.g., Gregory v. Cincinnati Inc., 538 N.W.2d 325, 329 (Mich. 1995).

[109] Yet, a manufacturer's safety representations may raise specific consumer expectations protectable in warranty. See, e.g., Denny v. Ford Motor Co., 662 N.E.2d 730 (N.Y. 1995) (rollover of Bronco II); Leichtamer v. American Motors Corp., 424 N.E.2d 568 (Ohio 1981) (pitch-over of Jeep). See generally Shapo, A Representational Theory of Consumer Protection: Doctrine, Function and Legal Liability for Product Disappointment, 60 Va. L. Rev. 1109 (1974).

[110] Although the "risk-utility" term gained ground in recent years over the more traditional "risk-benefit" phraseology, "cost-benefit" is the preferable term. See Owen, Toward a Proper Test for Design Defectiveness: "Micro-Balancing" Costs and Benefits, 75 Tex. L. Rev. 1661, 1692 (1997). The terms are used interchangeably here.

[111] Courts have found cost-benefit analysis most helpful in making design defectiveness determinations and only marginally helpful in warning cases. In manufacturing flaw cases decided in strict tort, this method of analysis has been virtually ignored.

[112] For example, if the risk at issue concerns the possible failure of an automobile's steering, brakes, or tires at highway speeds, or the possibility that a punch press ram may unexpectedly depress upon an operator's hand, the manufacturer must employ the utmost precautions to avert the risk. Yet, if the risk is relatively

in a certain manner is great, greater precautions must be taken to avert the risk; if the risk is small, less precaution is required. This principle of balance, inherent in tort law generally, is sometimes referred to as the "calculus of risk."

The most celebrated formulation of the risk-benefit test was provided by Judge Learned Hand in *United States v. Carroll Towing Co.*,[113] previously discussed.[114] In *Carroll Towing*, Judge Hand reasoned that ascertaining an appropriate level of precaution may be viewed as a function of three factors: the burden of taking precautions to avoid a risk of harm, on the one side, balanced against the likelihood of harm of a particular magnitude, on the other. Negligence is implied if an actor fails to adopt a precaution of less magnitude than the harm it is likely to prevent.

Judge Hand expressed this concept algebraically: Negligence is suggested if $B < P \times L$, where B is the burden or cost of adopting precautions against accidental loss that foreseeably might result if B is not undertaken, P is the increased probability of loss if B is not undertaken, and L is the probable magnitude (expected cost) of such loss if it does occur. This is the so-called "Hand formula."[115] If the formula is supplemented with a symbol for the implication of negligence ($\Rightarrow N$), the full formula becomes: $B < P \times L \Rightarrow N$. Applied to negligence determinations in the products liability context, the Hand formula may be explained as follows: if the cost of adopting a particular safety precaution (B) is less than the safety gains expected to result therefrom ($P \times L$), the manufacturer's failure to adopt the precaution implies its negligence ($\Rightarrow N$).

By substituting "defect" for "negligence" (D for N), the Hand formula converts comfortably to the "strict" products liability task of determining design defect, as discussed above.[116] So reformulated, the defectiveness "equation" may be stated as follows:

$$B < P \times L \Rightarrow D$$

In cost-benefit terms, the formula looks like this:

$$\text{(Untaken Precaution) Costs} < \text{(Safety) Benefits} \Rightarrow \text{Defect}$$

Stated otherwise:

$$\text{Defect} \Rightarrow \text{if an Untaken Precaution's Benefits} > \text{its Costs}$$

If we translate these cost-benefit terms into symbols, such that Design Defect = DD, an Untaken Precaution = UP, its Safety Benefits = SB, and its Costs = C, then:

$$DD \Rightarrow \text{if } UP\text{'s } SB > C$$

minimal, reasonably appearing to involve at most the risk of minor harm to person or property—scratches, stains, or the harmless malfunction of the product—then a manufacturer need apply only minimal precautions to reduce such risks.

[113] 159 F.2d 169, 173 (2d Cir. 1947). Judge Hand first employed this approach in Conway v. O'Brien, 111 F.2d 611 (2d Cir. 1940), rev'd on other grounds, 312 U.S. 492 (1941), and later reexamined it in Moisan v. Loftus, 178 F.2d 148, 149 (2d Cir. 1949).

[114] *Carroll Towing* is examined in the negligence context in § 2.2, and the strict liability in tort context in § 5.7, above.

[115] Helpful accounts of *Carroll Towing* and the Hand formula are Gilles, United States v. Carroll Towing Co.: The Hand Formula's Home Port, in Torts Stories 11 (R. Rabin and S. Sugarman eds., 2003, and Gilles, The Invisible Hand Formula, 80 Va. L. Rev. 1015 (1994). For other treatments, see note 90, above.

[116] See § 5.7, above. See generally Owen, Toward a Proper Test for Design Defectiveness: "Micro-Balancing" Costs and Benefits, 75 Tex. L. Rev. 1661, 1684–86 (1997).

In short, a product's design is defective if the safety benefits of an untaken design precaution[117] foreseeably exceed the precaution's costs.[118]

Based on certain imprecise language in some early scholarly explorations into a possible meaning of product defectiveness,[119] most appellate courts formulate the risk-utility test more broadly in terms of whether a *product's* risks are greater than the *product's* benefits or utility.[120] While such a formulation may appear harmless at first glance, it is logically misleading and in fact conflicts with how the law actually is applied. As discussed below,[121] the proper issue almost always properly litigated in trial courtrooms is the narrow "*micro*-balance" of pros and cons of a manufacturer's failure to adopt some particular design *feature* that would have prevented the plaintiff's harm—that is, whether the marginal costs of *changing* the design in some particular ("micro") manner would have been worth the resulting safety benefits.[122] Courts could avoid considerable confusion by formulating the risk-utility standard according to the proper cost-benefit terms of the Hand formula.[123]

The Hand defectiveness formula succinctly captures the commonsense idea that a product's design is unacceptably dangerous if it contains a danger that might cost-effectively (and practicably) be removed. More basically, the Hand formula requires manufacturers, in designing products, to consider risks of injury to consumers and bystanders and weigh the interests of those parties fairly in relation to their own interest in maximizing profits.[124] In designing products in particular ways, manufacturers properly consider such factors as their usefulness, dollar costs, and profitability. Yet the Hand formula provides a legal incentive for manufacturers, when they legislate for consumers the mix of costs and benefits of various design alternatives, to include in the recipe a proportionate consideration of the various hazards in a product's chosen design. That is, the Hand cost-benefit formula demands only that a manufacturer adopt safety

[117] For Mark Grady's insightful analysis of untaken precautions, see Grady, Untaken Precautions, 18 J. Legal Stud. 139 (1989).

[118] In addition to dollar costs, "costs" here broadly includes any diminished usefulness or diminished safety that may result from the particular precaution. Owen, Toward a Proper Test for Design Defectiveness: "Micro-Balancing" Costs and Benefits, 75 Tex. L. Rev. 1661, 1690 (1997).

[119] Notably, Keeton, Products Liability—Current Developments, 40 Tex. L. Rev. 193, 210 (1961); Wade, On the Nature of Strict Tort Liability for Products, 44 Miss. L.J. 825, 837 (1973) (first two factors framed in global terms). See generally Owen, Toward a Proper Test for Design Defectiveness: "Micro-Balancing" Costs and Benefits, 75 Tex. L. Rev. 1661, 1683 n.74 (1997).

[120] See Owen, Risk-Utility Balancing in Design Defect Cases, 30 U. Mich. J.L. Reform 239 (1997) (surveying risk-utility tests among states). Some courts still use this parlance. See, e.g., Nemes v. Dick's Sporting Goods, Inc., 521 F. Supp. 3d 328, 342 (S.D.N.Y. 2021) ("a defect 'requires a weighing of the product's dangers against its over-all advantages' "); Emerson Elec. Co. v. Johnson, 627 S.W.3d 197 (Tex. 2021).

[121] See § 8.5, below.

[122] Brown, Toward an Economic Theory of Liability, 2 J. Legal Stud. 323, 342 (1973); R. Heafey and D. Kennedy, Product Liability: Winning Strategies and Techniques §§ 4.04–4.05, and at 4–9 (1994) (characterizing the manufacturer's choice to forego a reasonable alternative design as "the heart of the plaintiff's case"). See also Rheingold, The Risk/Utility Test in Product Cases, 18 Trial Law. Q. 49, 50 (Spring/Fall 1987) ("The usual and proper approach for a plaintiff in a design defect case is to present evidence on an alternative design which the jury can find should have been adopted for the product in question.").

[123] See Owen, Risk-Utility Balancing, 30 U. Mich. J.L. Reform at 242.

[124] See Owen, Philosophical Foundations of Fault in Tort Law, in Philosophical Foundations of Tort Law 201, 214–15 (D. Owen ed., Oxford 1995); Owen, The Moral Foundations of Products Liability Law: Toward First Principles, 68 Notre Dame L. Rev. 427 (1993). The basic economics of this perspective are explained in Judge Posner's classic essay, A Theory of Negligence, 1 J. Legal Stud. 29 (1972).

precautions proportionate to the magnitude of the expected risk.[125] This simple yet fundamental principle of defectiveness, which ties the measure of precaution to the measure of risk, thus grounds the design safety obligations of a manufacturer in both fairness and utility.

Costs, Benefits, Burdens, and Utility

The major categories of costs, benefits, burdens, and utility weighed by manufacturers (in making the many trade-off decisions involved in any product's design) and courts (in evaluating design decisions after a product accident) are a product's usefulness (utility), its pecuniary costs, and its safety. Thus, when designing a product, manufacturers attempt to maximize its utility and safety and minimize its costs—that is, they seek to maximize a product's utility and minimize its dangers and other costs. Yet, it is important to realize that managers of manufacturing firms naturally view cost-benefit analysis from the perspective of their own firms (often measured by short-term profits), rather than from the broader social perspective contemplated by the Hand formula. This differing perspective sometimes results in a major disjunction between the two.

After an accident has occurred, it is a plaintiff's responsibility to prove that the manufacturer omitted a design feature that would have prevented the accident and whose safety benefits foreseeably would have exceeded its costs.[126] From a Hand formula perspective, safety "benefits" are the injuries (P × L) avoided by a particular precaution of certain "costs," viewed broadly. A large component of a design feature's costs, of course, are its dollar costs (or "expense"). But other "costs" of an untaken safety feature may be important, too—particularly diminished utility, and sometimes increased hazards of other types. In addition to monetary costs (of labor and materials), adding a safety feature may make a product bulkier or otherwise less useful, and it may make it less attractive or otherwise less desirable.

The blades of power lawn mowers, for example, now are surrounded by guards, which improve their safety by helping keep out stray feet and hands. But these guards also add to a mower's weight and expense; they can hang up on tree roots and get caught in ivy; and they widen mowers by at least a couple inches, requiring more room to store them in garages and less able to fit between some trees. In short, power mowers with guards today are more expensive, and less useful, than they would be without guards. These negative attributes of power mowers equipped with guards are very real costs of safety. Another example of the costs of enhancing a product's safety are automotive air bags, which vehicle manufacturers began installing for front seat passengers in the 1990s. In addition to the safety provided to front seat adults in serious frontal collisions, air bags of course add substantially to the expense of manufacturing such vehicles. In addition, an air bag's activation added a new automotive danger—from the explosive force of their activation, resulting sometimes in broken noses, arms, and wrists—and much more serious dangers to children and small adults sitting in front seats. This added danger also diminishes the utility of motor vehicles, because small adults and children

[125] It may be that manufacturers should give safety a greater weight than cold cost-benefit analysis might suggest, since individual consumers have little voice in the collective tradeoffs forced upon them. See Geistfeld, Reconciling Cost-Benefit Analysis with the Principle that Safety Matters More Than Money, 76 N.Y.U. L. Rev. 114 (2001). Yet, the risk-utility test has the elasticity to absorb refinements of this type.

[126] Except in California and a small number of its followers, where a defendant has the burden to prove that all design decisions concerning an accident product were correct. See § 8.6, below.

now can only ride safely in the rear. Moreover, the location of front airbags behind the dashboard takes up room that otherwise might be devoted to glove compartments, engine instruments, electronics, and other items.

Manufacturers confront other costs (or "burdens") of adding safety features, too, including added maintenance, diminished convenience, and, sometimes, diminished aesthetics. For example, hood ornaments and tail fins graced automobiles in the 1950s and 1960s, until their danger to pedestrians (and changing consumer tastes) led to their removal.[127] While a product's aesthetics may seem like a trivial, abstract value, especially when compared to human safety, we need to remember that aesthetics and other intangible values can be an important part of human satisfaction, the fulfillment of which ultimately is the purpose of all products—things demanded by (and supplied to) consumers to satisfy their large variety of needs and wants.[128] While safety is a vital good, it cannot be viewed as an absolute value that invariably trumps other goods—including utility, aesthetics, durability, or other goods.[129] Thus, whether aesthetics are viewed as a "cost" that a safety enhancement might sacrifice, or positively as part of a design feature's "utility," this value and other forms of intangible satisfaction are important dimensions of life that manufacturers properly consider in designing products, and which courts and juries also should fairly evaluate in judging the quality of a manufacturer's design decisions.

While cost-benefit analysis of untaken design precautions thus needs broadly to consider various factors, this form of analysis needs to be disciplined. A few appellate courts have opened a Pandora's Box by formulating the risk-utility calculus too widely, which renders it unwieldy.[130] For example, in adopting a risk-benefit test for design defect determinations, the Georgia Supreme Court in *Banks v. ICI Americas, Inc.*[131] remarked: "[N]o finite set of factors can be considered comprehensive or applicable under every factual circumstance, since such matters must necessarily vary according to the unique facts of each case. Such diverse matters as competing cost trade-offs, tactical market decisions, product development and research/testing demands, the idiosyncrasies of individual corporate management styles, and federal and other regulatory restrictions" can properly enter into a determination of the "reasonableness" of the manufacturer's design determination.[132] The court offered the following "non-exhaustive list of general factors," beginning with these considerations:

> [T]he usefulness of the product; the gravity and severity of the danger; . . . the likelihood of that danger; the avoidability of the danger, i.e., the user's knowledge of the product, publicity surrounding the danger, or the efficacy of warnings, as well as common knowledge and the expectation of danger; the

---

[127] See, e.g., Hatch v. Ford Motor Co., 329 P.2d 605, 606 (Cal. Ct. App. 1958) (boy walked into car's hood ornament that pierced his eye).

[128] See § 8.5 note 214, below.

[129] See Bell v. Bayerische Motoren Werke Ak., 105 Cal. Rptr. 3d 485, 504 (Cal. Ct. App. 2010):

> Plaintiffs contend aesthetics is not a proper consideration in the risk-benefit analysis . . . . We disagree. [M]uch of the perceived benefit of a car lies in its appearance. A car is not a strictly utilitarian product. We believe that a jury properly may consider aesthetics in balancing the benefits of a challenged design against the risk of danger inherent in the design.

See also Products Liability Rest. § 2 cmt. *f* (including "aesthetics" in list of considerations properly considered in cost-benefit determinations of defects *vel non* of designs).

[130] See authorities in § 8.1 note 24, above.

[131] 450 S.E.2d 671 (Ga. 1994).

[132] Id. at 675.

user's ability to avoid danger; the state of the art . . .; the ability to eliminate danger without impairing the usefulness of the product or making it too expensive; and the feasibility of spreading the loss in the setting of the product's price or by purchasing insurance.[133]

The court then listed the "[a]lternative safe design factors" also pertinent to the design defect calculus: "the feasibility of an alternative design; the availability of an effective substitute for the product which meets the same need but is safer; the financial cost of the improved design; and the adverse effects from the alternative."[134] Finally, the court set forth "benefit factors" that may also be considered in the balancing test: "the appearance and aesthetic attractiveness of the product; its utility for multiple uses; the convenience and extent of its use, especially in light of the period of time it could be used [safely]; and the collateral safety of a feature other than the one that harmed the plaintiff."[135]

No doubt many (perhaps most) of the factors from *Banks*' long list[136] should be considered by a manufacturer's engineers making fully informed design decisions about their products. And most of the listed factors will surely be legitimate issues in different kinds of design cases courts confront over time. Indeed, the Georgia court's "alternative safe design" factors *usually* will be important for both manufacturers making design decisions and courts adjudicating the safety or defectiveness of particular designs after product accidents have occurred, as discussed below.[137] But such a wide and open-ended catalogue of factors provides little help for adjudicating the design defect issue in particular cases,[138] and a practicable "test" for design defects must be formulated far more narrowly in terms of the particular types of costs and benefits normally at issue in typical design defect cases.

The Wade Factors

Over-broad formulations of risk-utility analysis for design defect decisionmaking are traceable to a widely quoted set of liability factors proposed in an early, influential article written by Dean John Wade,[139] *On the Nature of Strict Tort Liability for Products*.[140] Dean Wade proposed that a court[141] consider the following list of factors:

---

[133] Id. at 675 n.6. Compare the Wade factors, below.

[134] Id.

[135] Id.

[136] Thirty-three, by my count. See also Jablonski v. Ford Motor Co., 955 N.E.2d 1138, 1155 (Ill. 2011) ("There are a myriad of factors that may be relevant to the balance [in a risk-utility analysis], and they may vary depending upon the unique facts and circumstances of each case. In applying the balancing test, the court must initially balance factors it finds relevant to determine if the case is a proper one to submit to the jury.").

[137] See § 8.5, below.

[138] For an effort, see Moore v. ECI Mgmt., 542 S.E.2d 115 (Ga. Ct. App. 2000) (applying multi-factor risk-utility test to washer/dryer design defect claim).

[139] Indeed, the *Banks* court's first list of factors, the risk factors, was largely a restatement of Dean Wade's seven factors.

[140] 44 Miss. L.J. 825, 837–38 (1973). See also Keeton, Products Liability—Current Developments, 40 Tex., L. Rev. 193 (1961).

[141] But Dean Wade believed that a court should *not* instruct the jury on the factors. Id. at 840. Courts largely have agreed. See, e.g., Fiorino v. Sears Roebuck & Co., 707 A.2d 1053, 1057–58 (N.J. Super. Ct. App. Div. 1998) (including factor seven in jury instruction is reversible error because it improperly introduces insurance into case). *But see* Potter v. Chicago Pneumatic Tool Co., 694 A.2d 1319 (Conn. 1997) (in risk-utility balancing, jury may consider Wade factors among others).

(1) The usefulness and desirability of the product—its utility to the user and to the public as a whole.

(2) The safety aspects of the product—the likelihood that it will cause injury, and the probable seriousness of the injury.

(3) The availability of a substitute product which would meet the same need and not be as unsafe.

(4) The manufacturer's ability to eliminate the unsafe character of the product without impairing its usefulness or making it too expensive to maintain its utility.

(5) The user's ability to avoid danger by the exercise of care in the use of the product.

(6) The user's anticipated awareness of the dangers inherent in the product and their avoidability, because of general public knowledge of the obvious condition of the product, or of the existence of suitable warnings or instructions.

(7) The feasibility, on the part of the manufacturer, of spreading the loss by setting the price of the product or carrying liability insurance.

Searching for direction in the murky sea of design defectiveness, early appellate courts quickly grasped onto the Wade factors for use in ascertaining defects in design,[142] saying that these factors were somehow relevant to design defect cases.[143] However, while courts across the continent have authoritatively *quoted* these six or seven[144] factors for decades, only infrequently do courts actually try to *apply* the factors in assessing whether a particular product was defective in design. Even more rarely has an application of these factors actually *helped* a court determine design defectiveness;[145] more typically, a court attempting to apply the factors has become ensnared in one of their many traps.[146]

---

[142] See, e.g., Roach v. Kononen, 525 P.2d 125, 129 (Or. 1974) ("We agree that these factors should be considered by a court before submitting a design defect case to the jury. Also, proof of these factors bears on the jury's determination of whether or not a given design is defective."); Cepeda v. Cumberland Eng'g Co., 386 A.2d 816, 826–27 (N.J. 1978). For an inspired reduction of the Wade and other factors, see Montgomery and Owen, Reflections on the Theory and Administration of Strict Tort Liability for Defective Products, 27 S.C. L. Rev. 803, 818 (1976) (proposing four elegantly crafted factors).

[143] More recent recitations of the Wade factors include Purdy v. Deere & Co., 492 P.3d 99, 104 n.4 (Or. Ct. App. 2021) (reciting Wade factors); Smith v. NMC Wollard, Inc., 2021 WL 3128674, at *6 (E.D. Pa. 2021) (same); Sullivan v. Werner Co., 253 A.3d 730, 742 (Pa. Super. Ct. 2021) (same); Thompson v. Ethicon, Inc., 2020 WL 3893253, at *4 (D. Md. 2020) (same); Vandegrift v. BIC USA Inc., 2020 WL 3468196 (D.N.J. 2020) (same); Fasolas v. Bobcat of N.Y., Inc., 128 N.E.3d 627, 633 (N.Y. 2019) (factors somewhat reworded).

[144] Many courts have omitted the seventh factor, loss-spreading, as discussed below.

[145] Monahan v. Toro Co., 856 F. Supp. 955 (E.D. Pa. 1994) (astute application of factors).

[146] See, e.g., Johansen v. Makita U.S.A., Inc., 607 A.2d 637, 645 (N.J. 1992) (court should have instructed jury not to consider evidence of plaintiff's lack of care in deciding question of product defect, because fifth factor pertained only to users generally, not to particular plaintiff's conduct). Compare Murphy v. Playtex Family Prods. Corp., 176 F. Supp. 2d 473, 490–91 (D. Md. 2001), where the court valiantly tried to apply the factors, yet ended up basing its determination on the reasonableness of the defendant's actions, aff'd, 69 Fed. Appx. 140 (4th Cir. 2003).

Despite some early favorable commentary on the Wade factor approach,[147] commentators now view the Wade factors as largely problematic.[148] The first factor, the utility of the product, has been criticized on political grounds for allowing courts to second-guess the market as to the desirability of different kinds of products. In particular, this factor seems to reflect "the fallacy that 'essentials' provide utility whereas 'luxuries' do not."[149] Factor two, on the other hand, which embraces the P × L (risk of harm) side of the Hand formula discussed above, is vital to intelligent cost-benefit decisionmaking.[150]

The third factor, the availability of a substitute product, is difficult to interpret. If it is read narrowly to mean the availability of a substitute design *feature*, then it properly introduces the necessarily central question in design defect analysis of the availability of a feasible and otherwise reasonable alternative design feature—a crucial issue discussed below.[151] If, on the other hand, this factor is interpreted literally, as Dean Wade probably intended it,[152] the availability of substitute "products" falls victim to the flaw infecting the first factor by inviting a judge or jury to engage in social engineering of the highest (and most dubious) order. Factor four, the manufacturer's ability to eliminate the risk without unduly sacrificing price or utility, properly raises the relevant issues of the costs and benefits of altering the chosen design to eliminate the risk. Indeed, factors two and four together form the heart of proper cost-benefit analysis in design defect litigation.

Factor five, the user's ability to avoid the risk, importantly introduces the issue of consumer responsibility into the matrix. Its only fault lies in its tendency to mislead courts, and especially juries, into confusing the proper issue of how users generally may act, on the one hand, with whether a particular plaintiff behaved inappropriately in using a particular product in a manner that led to an accident, on the other.[153] The sixth factor, the user's awareness of the danger and avoidance techniques, is problematic. Its most reasonable interpretation appears to be subjective, which then introduces the plaintiff's conduct into the prima facie case of design defectiveness, rather than leaving it as an affirmative defense where it more properly belongs. If, on the other hand, this factor is interpreted with some strain as a broader inquiry into the extent to which consumers generally may be expected to comprehend a product's dangers, it would fit nicely with (although should precede) factor five, which in combination would present

[147] See, e.g., Montgomery and Owen, Reflections on the Theory and Administration of Strict Tort Liability for Defective Products, 27 S.C. L. Rev. 803 (1976) (attributable to untutored, youthful enthusiasm and uncritical reliance on the wisdom of a giant in the field).

[148] See, e.g., Green, The Schizophrenia of Risk-Benefit Analysis in Design Defect Litigation, 48 Vand. L. Rev. 609, 615–16 (1995); Viscusi, Wading Through the Muddle of Risk-Utility Analysis, 39 Am. U. L. Rev. 573 (1990); Epstein, The Risks of Risk/Utility, 48 Ohio St. L.J. 469 (1987); R. Epstein, Simple Rules for a Complex World 239–45 (1995); W. Viscusi, Reforming Products Liability 62–86 (1991).

[149] Viscusi, Wading Through the Muddle of Risk-Utility Analysis, 39 Am. U. L. Rev. 573, 582 (1990).

[150] See id. at 583.

[151] See § 8.5, below.

[152] This interpretation springs from the need to differentiate factor three from factor four, which appears to cover the feasible alternative design issue. See Smith v. NMC Wollard, Inc., 2021 WL 3128674, at *6 (E.D. Pa. 2021) (defendant's use of airplane belt loaders with single rather than double guardrails "goes toward the burden and cost of taking such a precaution—as embodied in the third and fourth [Wade] factors . . . but it is not the *sine qua non* of the risk-utility analysis.).

[153] See, e.g., Johansen v. Makita U.S.A., Inc., 607 A.2d 637, 645–46 (N.J. 1992) (court should have instructed jury not to consider evidence of plaintiff's lack of care in deciding the question of product defect, because the fifth factor pertained only to users generally, not to particular plaintiff's conduct). While irrelevant to breach of duty, a particular user's conduct is relevant to the conduct defenses. See ch. 13, below.

the important issues on the proper allocation of responsibility for product accidents between manufacturers and users.

The final Wade factor, number seven, is especially problematic as a factor for design liability decisionmaking. As a rationale for a generalized doctrine of strict tort liability for manufacturers, "loss-spreading" ("insurance" by another name) has been viewed in recent decades with increasing skepticism.[154] If the strict products liability litigation system were to serve as a substitute for private and social insurance, it would force people to buy types and levels of insurance that many neither need nor want, and at excessive cost. By so requiring consumers to pay higher prices for products as a form of product accident insurance, loss-spreading may be seen as both unfair[155] and inefficient.[156] Poor people pay regressively unfair premiums (or "taxes," when the tort system substitutes for social welfare insurance) for this form of insurance,[157] and the litigation method for determining whether particular accidents are covered by the system (whether a product is "defective," whether jurisdiction is proper, whether any defenses apply, etc.) is exceedingly time-consuming, enervating, and expensive. For the most serious accidents, where a victim's compensation needs are immediate and immense, it will likely take several years to complete the litigation compensation process. And in the end, the victim may lose the case and end up with no compensation whatsoever. In short, design defect liability is a poor means for society to spread the losses that result from product accidents.

As a factor for helping assess whether *particular* products are defective, loss-spreading is even more seriously flawed, because it will *always* point toward liability: a finding of design defectiveness resulting in a judgment for the plaintiff will always spread the plaintiff's loss, at least among the shareholders of the manufacturer.[158] But the rationale for properly limiting a manufacturer's liability to designs that are defective is to distinguish between products whose design dangers are acceptable from those that are not,[159] as previously discussed. Including loss-spreading, or any other factor that always weighs on the same side of the scales, can only subvert the process of fair and rational adjudication of design defects.[160] As a result, courts occasionally have excluded as inappropriate this seventh, loss-spreading consideration from the list of factors.[161]

---

[154] On the nature and problems of loss-spreading as a products liability rationale, see § 5.4, above.

[155] See, e.g., Owen, The Moral Foundations of Products Liability Law: Toward First Principles, 68 Notre Dame L. Rev. 427, 484–93 (1993).

[156] See, e.g., Viscusi, Wading Through the Muddle of Risk-Utility Analysis, 39 Am. U. L. Rev. 573, 584–91 (1990); Priest, The Current Insurance Crisis and Modern Tort Law, 96 Yale L.J. 1521 (1987).

[157] George Priest observed that the level of insurance "premiums" manufacturers add to product prices regressively penalizes the poor who stand to gain far less in damages for lost earnings than wealthy victims who pay the same premium for much higher coverage. See, e.g., Priest, The Current Insurance Crisis and Modern Tort Law, 96 Yale L.J. 1521, 1558–60 (1987).

[158] See Owen, Products Liability: Principles of Justice for the 21st Century, 11 Pace L. Rev. 63, 71–72 (1990); G. Schwartz, Understanding Products Liability, 67 Cal. L. Rev. 435, 445 (1979) (explaining how the loss-spreading rationale dictates that accident victims *always* should be compensated, whereas tort law at bottom seeks to be selective and, hence, fashion liability rules to "exclude recovery for some accident victims while permitting recovery for others").

[159] See James Henderson's classic rock-tub metaphor, in Henderson, Should a "Process Defense" Be Recognized in Product Design Cases?, 56 N.Y.U. L. Rev. 585, 601–03 (1981).

[160] See Owen, The Moral Foundations of Products Liability Law: Toward First Principles, 68 Notre Dame L. Rev. 427, 492–93 (1993); Owen, Rethinking the Policies of Strict Products Liability, 33 Vand. L. Rev. 681, 703–07 (1980).

[161] See, e.g., Nunnally v. R.J. Reynolds Tobacco Co., 869 So.2d 373, 380 (Miss. 2004).

It is understandable that in the early days of modern products liability law courts looked for guidance to the Wade factors which had an aura of logic, fairness, and commonsense. Indeed, modern products liability law has absorbed many of Dean Wade's factors in a variety of ways. But modern design defect jurisprudence has moved far beyond the place it was when Dean Wade conceived it at the time § 402A was just getting off the ground. Indeed, modern courts rarely do little more than pay lip service to the Wade factors, which are now well past their prime. Typically, a court will recite the factors and then move on to a far narrower, appropriate cost-benefit analysis of some particular design feature offered by the plaintiff as a safer and preferred alternative design, or to some other topic altogether.[162] In short, the design defect bus long ago left the "catalogue of factors" station and now rides comfortably on the wheels of costs and benefits of alternative designs.[163]

The *Products Liability Restatement*

The *Products Liability Restatement* explicitly adopts risk-utility balancing as the test for design defectiveness, as previously discussed.[164] In essence, § 2(b) of the *Third Restatement* classifies a design as defective if the plaintiff suffered a foreseeable injury that probably would have been prevented by a reasonable alternative design.[165] Section 2(b) thus "adopts a reasonableness ('risk-utility balancing') test as the standard for judging the defectiveness of product designs."[166] Numerous factors may be relevant to "whether an alternative design is reasonable and whether its omission renders a product not reasonably safe" under § 2(b), including the likelihood and seriousness of foreseeable harm from the chosen design, warnings accompanying the product,[167] and the relative costs and benefits of the alternative design relative to the chosen design.[168] Finally, it is important to note that while the *Restatement* rejects consumer expectations as an independent basis for ascertaining the defectiveness of product designs, it includes consumer expectations as a factor in the calculus of risk-utility considerations.[169] The *Third Restatement*'s treatment of these and other aspects of design defectiveness is explored in greater depth below.[170]

---

[162] See, e.g., Vandegrift v. BIC USA Inc., 2020 WL 3468196 (D.N.J. 2020) (reciting Wade factors, and then summarily dismissing plaintiff's design defect claim); Fasolas v. Bobcat of New York, Inc., 128 N.E.3d 627, 633 (N.Y. 2019) (reciting the Wade factors, and then granting new trial to correct error in jury instruction on optional safety device); Estate of Popolizio v. Ford Motor Co., 2013 WL 2459878 (D.N.J. 2013) (quoting Wade factors, and then summarily granting summary judgment for defendant due to lack of plaintiff's expert testimony); Cantrell v. Wirtgen Am., Inc., 2011 WL 915324, at *8 (D. Md. 2011).

[163] See § 8.5, below.

[164] See § 6.5, above.

[165] See id. The Restatement addresses the special, narrow category of generically dangerous products that may possess a manifestly unreasonable design in cmt. *e*. See § 10.3, below.

[166] Products Liability Rest. § 2(b), cmt. *d*.

[167] Id. cmt. *f*.

[168] Including the effects the alternative design feature would likely have on production costs, product longevity, maintenance, repair, aesthetics, and "the range of consumer choice." Id.

[169] See id. cmt. *g*.

[170] See § 8.8, below.

§ 8.5 PROOF OF A REASONABLE ALTERNATIVE DESIGN

Just as design defectiveness lies at the center of products liability law,[171] cost-benefit analysis of an alternative design lies at the heart of design defectiveness.[172] As examined earlier,[173] design defectiveness is usually best resolved by risk-utility analysis, the purpose of which is to determine "whether the risk of injury might have been reduced or avoided if the manufacturer had used a feasible alternative design."[174] In the words of a leading tort law scholar, "one simply cannot talk meaningfully about a risk-benefit defect in a product design until and unless one has identified some design alternative (including any design omission) that can serve as the basis for a risk-benefit analysis."[175]

Throughout the twentieth century, a great majority of design defect cases involved proof by the plaintiff of a feasible alternative design—proof of some practicable, cost-effective, untaken design precaution that would have prevented the plaintiff's harm.[176] Early cases included a manifold that exploded, where the resulting fire could have been contained by chamber walls made of copper or brass, instead of steel;[177] a commercial coffee urn that exploded, where the explosion could have been prevented by a simple reducing valve;[178] a tractor steering wheel made of rubber and fiber that broke in the driver's hands, causing him to fall into the path of the tractor, where a rim made of wood or metal would not have broken;[179] a vaporizer that overheated and caught fire when the water boiled away, where the fire could have been prevented by a simple cutoff device;[180]

---

[171] See § 8.1, above.

[172] See, e.g., Jones v. NordicTrack, Inc., 550 S.E.2d 101, 103 (Ga. 2001) ("The 'heart' of a design defect case is the reasonableness of selecting from among alternative product designs and adopting the safest feasible one. [Hence, the question in such cases is] whether the defendant failed to adopt a reasonable alternative design which would have reduced the foreseeable risks of harm presented by the product."). See also Ford Motor Co. v. Miles, 967 S.W.2d 377, 386 (Tex. 1998) (Owen, J., concurring) (examining "the risk versus utility analysis that lies at the core of products liability design defect law"). See generally Ausness, "Fasten your Seat Belt, Orville!": Exploring the Relationship Between State-of-the-Art, Technological and Commercial Feasibility, and the *Restatement*'s Reasonable Alternative Design Requirement, 45 Ind. L. Rev. 669 (2012).

[173] See § 8.4, above. See also Products Liability Rest. § 1 cmt. *a*; § 2(b) cmt. *d*. The Third Restatement approach to design defectiveness, which requires the plaintiff in design defect cases to prove that a "reasonable alternative design" would have prevented the injury, is examined in § 6.5, above, and § 8.8, below.

[174] McCarthy v. Olin Corp., 119 F.3d 148, 155 (2d Cir. 1997) (N.Y. law). See Vetri, Order Out of Chaos: Products Liability Design-Defect Law, 43 U. Rich. L. Rev. 1373, 1385 (2009) ("To establish the dangerously defective nature of the product, proof is usually required of an actual or potential alternative design that is safer, feasible, cost-effective, and does not impair the utility of the product.").

[175] G. Schwartz, Foreword: Understanding Products Liability, 67 Cal. L. Rev. 435, 468 (1979). A prominent tort law scholar in the late twentieth century, Gary Schwartz was a professor at UCLA, an adviser for the Products Liability Restatement, and the initial Reporter for the Restatement (Third) of Torts: Liability for Physical and Emotional Harm. Other commentators widely agree with Professor Schwartz's assertion quoted in the text. See, e.g., Owen, Defectiveness Restated: Exploding the "Strict" Products Liability Myth, 1996 U. Ill. L. Rev. 743, 774–75; Green, The Schizophrenia of Risk-Benefit Analysis in Design Defect Litigation, 48 Vand. L. Rev. 609 (1995); Henderson and Twerski, Closing the American Products Liability Frontier: The Rejection of Liability Without Defect, 66 N.Y.U. L. Rev. 1263 (1991). This section is dedicated to Gary's memory.

[176] See Noel, Manufacturer's Negligence of Design or Directions for Use of a Product, 71 Yale L.J. 816, 820 (1962).

[177] Air Reduction Co. v. Philadelphia Storage Battery Co., 14 F.2d 734, 736–37 (3d Cir. 1926).

[178] Muller v. Kirschbaum Co., 148 A. 851 (Pa. 1930).

[179] Goullon v. Ford Motor Co., 44 F.2d 310 (6th Cir. 1930) (Ky. law).

[180] Lindroth v. Walgreen Co., 87 N.E.2d 307 (Ill. App. Ct. 1949), aff'd, 94 N.E.2d 847 (Ill. 1950).

a moving metal mechanism under the arm-rest of a lawn chair that amputated a user's finger, where a simple housing could have shielded the mechanism.[181]

As modern products liability developed after the promulgation of *Restatement (Second) of Torts* § 402A, courts and commentators alike increasingly recognized the logical and practical necessity in most design defect cases that plaintiffs prove their harm would have been prevented if the manufacturer had adopted some alternative design.[182] As science and technology advanced, toward the end of the twentieth century and into the twenty-first, the requisite alternative designs, though sometimes quite simple, sometimes were quite complex and so often required expert testimony.[183] Illustrative are cases involving a drain cleaner comprised of chemicals that were highly corrosive to human skin, where a change in the chemical formulation would have made it much safer and actually improved its efficacy at cleaning drains;[184] a Dalkon Shield IUD that had a multi-filament tail string, facilitating migration of bacteria into the uterus, where a single filament would have minimized the risk;[185] an industrial machine with a sharp edge that cut a worker, where the sharp edge served no purpose and could easily have been rounded smooth;[186] a small Playskool play block that asphyxiated a baby, where slightly increasing the size of the cylindrical block would have made it too big to swallow;[187] a truck lift gate equipped with a single hydraulic cylinder that was prone to collapse unexpectedly, where the addition of a second cylinder would have eliminated the risk;[188] and a car's power window, which lacked an auto-reverse feature that would have protected a child's head and neck.[189]

Without affirmative proof of a feasible design alternative, a plaintiff usually cannot establish that a product's design is defective. Put otherwise, there typically is nothing wrong with a product that simply possesses inherent dangers that cannot reasonably be designed away.[190] For example, in *Blissenbach v. Yanko*,[191] a child was injured by scalding water from a hot water vaporizer when it tipped over, causing the lid to fall off the top of the container. The plaintiff alleged that the manufacturer's failure to secure the lid to the container was a negligent design, but the manufacturer defended on the ground that the lid was left unattached in order to provide a "natural safety valve" for the release of steam if the aperture for discharging medicated vapor became clogged.[192] In part because the plaintiff made no proof of a feasible alternative design method for

---

[181] Matthews v. Lawnlite Co., 88 So.2d 299 (Fla. 1956).

[182] See, e.g., Sutkowski v. Universal Marion Corp., 281 N.E.2d 749, 753 (Ill. App. Ct. 1972); Phillips, The Standard for Determining Defectiveness in Products Liability, 46 U. Cin. L. Rev. 101, 104 n.18 (1977) ("[D]esign alternatives [should be] considered whether reasonable care is the basis of liability or where liability is predicated upon strict tort liability. . . . 'The possible existence of alternate designs introduces the feature of feasibility since a manufacturer's product can hardly be faulted if safer alternatives are not feasible.' ").

[183] See § 6.3, above.

[184] Drayton v. Jiffee Chem. Corp., 395 F. Supp. 1081 (N.D. Ohio 1975), judgment modified on other grounds, 591 F.2d 352 (6th Cir. 1978).

[185] Hilliard v. A.H. Robins Co., 196 Cal. Rptr. 117 (Ct. App. 1983).

[186] Stazenski v. Tennant Co., 617 So.2d 344 (Fla. Dist. Ct. App. 1993).

[187] Metzgar v. Playskool Inc., 30 F.3d 459 (3d Cir. 1994) (Pa. law).

[188] Warner Fruehauf Trailer Co. v. Boston, 654 A.2d 1272 (D.C. 1995).

[189] Perez v. FCA USA LLC, 2021 WL 2139334, at *2 (E.D. Mich. 2021).

[190] See § 6.2, above, and § 10.3, below.

[191] 107 N.E.2d 409 (Ohio Ct. App. 1951).

[192] Id. at 411.

releasing steam, the plaintiff's verdict was reversed on appeal.[193] *McCormack v. Hankscraft Co.*[194] was another vaporizer tip-over case decided on similar facts except that the plaintiff's experts explained that the danger "could have been eradicated by the adoption of any one of several practical and inexpensive alternative designs which utilized simple and well known techniques to secure the top to the jar [to] the inside of the plastic top so it could screw onto the jar and the putting of two or three small holes in the top, which would take care of any danger that steam would build up inside the jar." Based on proof of such feasible alternative designs, the *McCormack* court affirmed a verdict for the plaintiff.

Recognizing the central role of an alternative design to design defectiveness, many jurisdictions, probably most,[195] now require proof of a feasible design alternative in most design defect cases. That is, to prove a design defect in many states, a plaintiff must prove the existence of a safer, practical, alternative design available to the manufacturer that would have prevented the harm.[196] Many courts continue to assert that alternative

---

[193] See Noel, Manufacturer's Negligence of Design or Directions for Use of a Product, 71 Yale L.J. 816, 823 (1962).

[194] 154 N.W.2d 488, 495 (Minn. 1967).

[195] See Hernandez v. Tokai Corp., 2 S.W.3d 251 (Tex. 1999), asserting that most states make proof of a reasonable alternative design a prerequisite to a determination of design defectiveness. See generally Vetri, Order Out of Chaos: Products Liability Design-Defect Law, 43 U. Rich. L. Rev. 1373 (2009).

For an encyclopedic tally of states on this issue by the Restatement Reporters, see Henderson and Twerski, Manufacturers' Liability for Defective Product Designs: The Triumph of Risk-Utility, 74 Brook. L. Rev. 1061, 1079–93 (2009) (subsection entitled "Reasonable Alternative Design Is the Strong Majority Rule for Classic Design Defect Cases," which details statutes and cases by state that effectively require such proof, including five state statutes and twenty states whose common law holds or suggests the requirement of such proof to prove a defective design). The Reporters explain how a close reading of the common law of many of the other states reveals the practical requirement of alternative design proof in design defect litigation, and conclude that plaintiffs "live or die by their ability to establish a reasonable alternative design." Id. at 1108. See also Twerski, An Essay on the Quieting of Products Liability Law, 105 Cornell L. Rev. 1211, 1217 (2020) ("[R]egardless of the theory that a state follows[,] the plaintiff almost invariably introduces a RAD into evidence. It is rare to find a design case where the plaintiff did not do so. . . . If a RAD is not required de jure, it is de facto a staple in almost all design cases.").

[196] See, e.g., Emerson Elec. Co. v. Johnson, 627 S.W.3d 197, 203 (Tex. 2021); Smith v. Ethicon, Inc., 2021 WL 4098408, at *3 (E.D. Ky. 2021); Villarreal v. Navistar, Inc., 2021 WL 1894700, at *1 (N.D. Tex. 2021); Willet v. Johnson & Johnson, 465 F. Supp. 3d 895, 904 (S.D. Iowa 2020) (citing Products Liability Rest. § 2(b)); Halsey v. AGCO Corp., 755 Fed. Appx. 524, 531 (6th Cir. 2018) (Ky. law) (in design defect cases, "the plaintiff must offer 'proof of a feasible alternative design' "); Branham v. Ford Motor Co., 701 S.E.2d 5, 16 (S.C. 2010) (same; "a reasonable alternative design"); Clinton v. Brown & Williamson Holdings, Inc., 498 F. Supp. 2d 639, 646 (S.D.N.Y. 2007) (same; "a feasible alternative design"); Parish v. Jumpking, Inc., 719 N.W.2d 540, 543 (Iowa 2006); Bagley v. Mazda Motor Corp., 864 So.2d 301 (Ala. 2003); Wankier v. Crown Equip. Corp., 353 F.3d 862 (10th Cir. 2003) (Utah law) (trial court's failure to instruct jury on plaintiff's duty to establish safer alternative design was reversible error).

For an exhaustive state-by-state list of design defect cases in the early 1990s on the feasible alternative design requirement, see Products Liability Rest. § 2(b) Reporters' Note to cmt. *d*, revealing widespread support, either expressly or by implication, for this requirement. Yet, when the Reporters first put forward their initial draft of § 2(b) in the early 1990s, case decisions on alternative design proof were jumbled and inconsistent, and some commentators interpreted them quite differently from the Reporters—as generally *not* requiring such proof. See, e.g., Vargo, The Emperor's New Clothes: The American Law Institute Adorns a "New Cloth" for Section 402A Products Liability Design Defects—A Survey of the States Reveals a Different Weave, 26 U. Mem. L. Rev. 493 (1996); Shapo, In Search of the Law of Products Liability: The ALI Restatement Project, 48 Vand. L. Rev. 631, 668–71 (1995); Klemme, Comments to the Reporters and Selected Members of the Consultative Group, *Restatement of Torts (Third): Products Liability*, 61 Tenn. L. Rev. 1173 (1994); Vandall, The *Restatement (Third) of Torts: Products Liability* Section 2(b): The Reasonable Alternative Design Requirement, 61 Tenn. L. Rev. 1407 (1994). Fifteen years later, a prominent member of the plaintiffs' bar remained skeptical of the claim that the Third Restatement's § 2(b) risk-utility rule, "including proof of an alternative design, constituted the majority rule in the United States" when offered by the Reporters in the

design proof is allowable on risk-utility, but not required,[197] as discussed below.[198] Most courts properly hold that the plaintiff has the burden of proof on this issue,[199] and if a plaintiff fails to present sufficient evidence on this point, a design defect claim in most states ordinarily will fail.[200]

In some states, statutes require plaintiffs to prove a feasible alternative design, either in every case or with some limited exceptions.[201] Other states that employ a risk-utility test implicitly require such proof in most design defect cases.[202] And a number of jurisdictions—sometimes noting the value of proof of a feasible alternative design, other times observing how difficult and costly a requirement of such proof would be for

early 1990s. See Stewart, Strict Liability for Defective Product Design: The Quest for a Well-Ordered Regime, 74 Brook. L. Rev. 1039, 1045 (2009).

As a matter of practical jurisprudence, the Reporters may well have been correct in their view at the time that plaintiffs typically (and appropriately) faced a likelihood of dismissal or directed verdict in most normal design defect cases without proof of a feasible alternative design. More recently, the Reporters updated their tally in another exhaustive study, which makes a strong case (enhanced by subsequent judicial and legislative developments) that proof of an alternative design is now required in ordinary design defect cases in a true majority of American jurisdictions. See note 195, above.

[197] See, e.g., Bifolck v. Philip Morris, Inc., 152 A.3d 1183, 1201 (Conn. 2016) ("risk-utility test permits a plaintiff to elect whether to proffer evidence of a reasonable alternative design"); Aubin v. Union Carbide Corp., 177 So.3d 489, 512 (Fla. 2015) ("parties may . . . present evidence that a reasonable alternative design existed and argue whether the benefit of the product's design outweighed any risks of injury or death caused by the design"); Baley v. Federal Signal Corp., 982 N.E.2d 776, 796 (Ill. App. Ct. 2012) ("a feasible alternative design is not a required showing but instead is merely one factor for a jury to consider").

[198] See note 203, below.

[199] See, e.g., Paul v. Henri-Line Mach. Tools, Inc., 938 F. Supp. 2d 691, 697 (E.D. Mich. 2013). Despite a contrary rule in California and a small number of other states, the plaintiff logically and fairly has the burden of proof on the feasibility and cost-effectiveness of the alternative design. See Products Liability Rest. § 2(b) cmt. *f*; Prosser and Keeton on Torts § 99, at 702; Wade, On Product "Design Defects" and Their Actionability, 33 Vand. L. Rev. 551, 573 (1980) (criticizing cases that shift the burden of proof to the defendant); G. Schwartz, Foreword: Understanding Products Liability, 67 Cal. L. Rev. 435, 466–67 (1979).

[200] "Since plaintiff failed to present evidence that there was a safe and reasonably feasible alternative to defendants' product, the trial court properly concluded that there was no issue of design defect for the jury to determine." Macri v. Ames McDonough Co., 512 A.2d 548, 551 (N.J. Super. Ct. App. Div. 1986) (hammer that chipped). See also Petersen v. Raymond Corp., 994 F.3d 1224, 1230 (10th Cir. 2021) (Utah law) (plaintiff's strict liability claims against forklift manufacturer failed without expert proof of a safer, feasible alternative design); Nemes v. Dick's Sporting Goods, Inc., 521 F. Supp. 3d 328, 339 (S.D.N.Y. 2021) (without expert testimony on the availability of a reasonable alternative design, plaintiffs' design defect claims failed); Dunlap v. Federal Signal Corp., 194 A.3d 1067, 1073 (Pa. Super. Ct. 2018) (2–1 decision) (plaintiff failed to prove that alternative design of fire truck siren effectively warned people in the vicinity); Wilson v. Piper Aircraft Corp., 577 P.2d 1322, 1326–27 (Or. 1978).

[201] Statutes in at least eight states require proof of a feasible (or reasonable) alternative design to establish liability in all or most design defect cases. See La. Rev. Stat. Ann. § 9:2800.56; Miss. Code Ann. § 11–1–63(f)(ii); N.J. Stat. Ann. § 2A:58C–3(a)(1); N.C. Gen. Stat. Ann. § 99B–6(a)(1); Ohio Rev. Code Ann. § 2307.75(F) (2001 reenactment); Tex. Civ. Prac. & Rem. Code Ann. § 82.005(a)(1); Wash. Rev. Code Ann. § 7.72.030(1)(a); Wis. Stat. Ann. § 895.047(1)(a). Washington's statute ambiguously provides for the jury to consider such proof together with a consumer's safety contemplations. Statutes in New Jersey and North Carolina make exceptions for cases involving egregiously dangerous products. Illinois had such a provision that was part of a broad tort reform act that was held unconstitutional. See Best v. Taylor Mach. Works, 689 N.E.2d 1057 (Ill. 1997).

The Products Liability Restatement Reporters note three major exceptions to the alternative design proof requirement: product malfunctions, products whose design violates explicit safety standards, and egregiously dangerous products. See, e.g., Parish v. Jumpking, Inc., 719 N.W.2d 540, 543–45 (Iowa 2006) (rejecting plaintiff's argument that trampoline was a "manifestly unreasonable" product; and, so, rejecting design defect claim for failing the alternative-design requirement).

[202] See, e.g., Products Liability Rest. § 2(b), Reporters' Notes to cmt. *d*.

plaintiffs—explicitly reject any idea that proof of an alternative design is a necessary element of a plaintiff's design defect case.[203]

Risk-Utility Analysis of an Alternative Design

Although the risk-utility issue in design defect cases is frequently framed vaguely in terms of a balance between the risks and benefits of the "product," as mentioned earlier and discussed further below, the cost-benefit issue properly litigated in almost every case involves a much narrower, *marginal* determination—whether the safety benefits of *altering* the product's design in a particular manner would have foreseeably exceeded the costs of the alteration.[204] Risk-utility analysis is focused, in other words, on the costs and benefits of the specific alternative design feature proposed by the plaintiff.

The relevant *benefits* of a proposed alternative design are limited to the aggregate safety benefits to people suffering injury and property damage from hazards of a similar type to that which harmed the plaintiff.[205] The *costs* of an alternative design feature more diversely may include: (1) the monetary costs of adopting the alternative design for all such products—its *expense*; (2) any loss of usefulness of the product the design change may cause—its *reduced utility*; and (3) any additional hazards the design feature may introduce—its *new dangers*.

Expense

The risk-utility (cost-benefit) issue often is conceptually quite simple: whether the aggregate dollar costs of adding some safety feature proposed by the plaintiff is or is not outweighed by the aggregate safety benefit of preventing foreseeable accidents like that which injured the plaintiff. So, if a safety feature would be expensive to adopt, and if it would be unlikely to produce substantial safety benefits, it is not required.[206] But a manufacturer will fail the risk-utility test if it does not adopt a relatively inexpensive safety feature that could appreciably improve a product's safety, such as incorporating a child-resistant feature in a utility lighter for less than 5¢ per lighter;[207] installing a $2.50 shield made of shatterproof glass over a pressure gauge to protect a person's eyes;[208]

---

203 See, e.g., Tucker v. Ethicon, Inc., 2021 WL 3910768, at *10 (E.D. Mo. 2021) (proof of an alternative design not required as part of prima facie case for design defect); Leonard v. General Motors L.L.C., 504 F. Supp. 3d 73, 96 (D. Conn. 2020) (same); Kaiser v. Johnson & Johnson, 947 F.3d 996, 1013 (7th Cir. 2020) (Ind. law) (evidence of a reasonable alternative design not required but allowed); Mikolajczyk v. Ford Motor Co., 901 N.E.2d 329, 347 (Ill. 2008) ("the existence of a feasible alternative design and the balancing of risks and benefits are relevant considerations in a strict product liability design defect case, but they are not elements of the claim that the plaintiff is required to plead and prove in every case"); Potter v. Ford Motor Co., 213 S.W.3d 264, 269–70 (Tenn. Ct. App. 2006) ("highly relevant and probative" of defectiveness, but not required); Potter v. Chicago Pneumatic Tool Co., 694 A.2d 1319, 1334 (Conn. 1997). See also note 197, above. See generally Note, Just What You'd Expect: Professor Henderson's Redesign of Products Liability, 111 Harv. L. Rev. 2366, 2373 (1998) (requiring alternative design proof places a " 'potentially insurmountable stumbling block' in the way of those injured by badly designed products").

204 See Owen, Toward a Proper Test for Design Defectiveness: "Micro-Balancing" Costs and Benefits, 75 Tex. L. Rev. 1661, 1690 (1997); § 8.4, at notes 119–123, above.

205 Thus, a manufacturer may *not* introduce evidence of the collateral social benefits from cigarette production, such as profits, employment, benefits to suppliers of goods and services, tax revenues paid, and charitable contributions made to the community. See Wright, The Principles of Product Liability, 26 Rev. Litig. 1067, 1081 (2007); Cipollone v. Liggett Grp., Inc., 644 F. Supp. 283, 286 (D.N.J. 1986); Products Liability Rest. § 2(b) cmt. *f*; Note, 73 Cornell L. Rev. 606, 616–19 (1988).

206 See Products Liability Rest. § 2(b) cmt. *f* (noting that a court should consider "the likely effects of the alternative design on production costs").

207 Flock v. Scripto-Tokai Corp., 319 F.3d 231, 240 (5th Cir. 2003) (Tex. law) (at a total cost to the company of $500,000).

208 Helicoid Gage Div. of Am. Chain & Cable Co. v. Howell, 511 S.W.2d 573 (Tex. App. 1974).

including a $3 shield to cover the rear of a power mower;[209] adding a $25 switch to a $10,000 aerial lift to automatically lower the bucket if pressure changes on a stabilizing outrigger;[210] or adding an automatic shut-off feature that might cost as little as $5 to a water heater in case it overheats.[211]

Because the cost of a safety improvement is weighed against the risk of harm it should prevent, even safety features that substantially raise a product's cost and price will sometimes be required. So, if a guard costing $200 to $500 will protect an operator against a substantial risk of losing a hand and arm in an $8,000 machine, the cost of safety may be worth the benefit.[212] And even if adding a child-proof device to a disposable butane cigarette lighter increases its cost by as much as 60%–75%, raising its price to that extent may be worth the benefit of substantially reducing the massive accident costs repeatedly caused by children playing with lighters not equipped with such devices.[213]

Reduced Utility

In addition to the actual dollar costs of enhancing a product's safety, risk-utility analysis of a plaintiff's proposed alternative design requires consideration of another significant cost—any reduction in the product's usefulness. Adding a guard to a punch press may help to keep out hands, but it may preclude the operator from feeding large sheets of metal into the press and may slow down production. Child-proofing tops of medicines and household cleansers will reduce the number of small children poisoned by such products, but childproof designs may make such products useless to older persons whose hands are weakened by arthritis. Adding flame-repellant chemicals to fabrics used for clothing will protect against fabric fire injuries, but such chemicals may decrease a fabric's comfort and durability, may make it more difficult to wash out odors, and may make the fabric more prone to wrinkle and more difficult to dry. Many hazards are serious enough that sacrificing a little product usefulness in exchange for greater safety makes good sense. But people buy and use products to help them with their labors and to give them satisfaction,[214] so that sacrifices in a product's utility are important

---

[209] South Austin Drive-In Theatre v. Thomison, 421 S.W.2d 933 (Tex. App. 1967).

[210] Genie Indus. v. Matak, 462 S.W.3d 80, 87 (Tex. App. 2012) (the cost-effective alternative design increased the utility and safety of the aerial lift; expert proposed a total of four feasible, cost-effective alternative designs).

[211] A.O. Smith Corp. v. Settlement Inv. Mgmt., 2006 WL 176815, at *3 (Tex. App. 2006) ($9,000 commercial water heater overheated and caused fire).

[212] See Dorsey v. Yoder Co., 331 F. Supp. 753 (E.D. Pa. 1971), aff'd, 474 F.2d 1339 (3d Cir. 1973). See also *A.O. Smith Corp.*, above (shut-off feature might have cost as much as $200).

[213] See Griggs v. BIC Corp., 981 F.2d 1429 (3d Cir. 1992) (Pa. law) (in early 1980s, increase of 60¢ to 75¢ per lighter then costing under $1 apiece; 120 people killed and 750 persons injured in such fires at annual national cost of $300–$375 million). Compare Todd v. Societe BIC, S.A. (*Todd II*), 9 F.3d 1216, 1221 n.† (7th Cir. 1993) (Ill. law) (Easterbrook, J.) (noting CPSC estimates that childproofing lighters would raise their unit market price by only 15¢ to 20¢, but also noting the elusiveness of such statistics).

[214] Satisfaction may come from a pleasurable taste, smell, or touch: a motorcyclist's pleasure of rushing air through an open design of a motorcycle helmet might be worth the slightly increased dangers. And satisfaction may be aesthetic, such as the pleasure experienced by an owner of an especially sleek, small sports car that may be far more dangerous than larger cars. Assuming in both situations that the additional risks are evident, or fully disclosed to buyers, one might well conclude that the benefits of such a design may well exceed the commensurate risks. Indeed, in a free society, one may question whether courts and juries should be allowed to second-guess consumer choices on the types and amount of inherent product design risks they personally choose to accept. See § 8.4 note 130, above, and § 10.3, below.

costs that must be carefully evaluated in assessing the costs and benefits of an alternative design.[215]

New Dangers

Another important (though less common) cost in the risk-utility evaluation of a plaintiff's proposed alternative design is the possibility that it may introduce *new* dangers into the product. That is, in eliminating one set of dangers, the change in design proposed by a plaintiff may create new types of dangers not present in the manufacturer's chosen design. For example, seatbelts and airbags of various designs protect the safety of many occupants in certain collisions, but in other situations both seatbelts and airbags may cause more harm than good.[216] Guarding motorboat propellers presents another example. *Fitzpatrick v. Madonna*[217] was one of a number of cases involving claims by swimmers injured or killed by motorboat propellers alleging that the propeller should have been shrouded with a guard. The benefit of such guards would be the large number of swimmers saved from propeller injuries. But such devices are not without cost—including reduced speed, fuel efficiency, and maneuverability. In addition to hazards created by the loss of speed and maneuverability, propeller guards introduce a number of other new risks—such as the larger size of the guarded propeller that is more likely to hit swimmers and its creation of a trap where human limbs can become wedged.[218] Any new dangers in a proposed alternative design are important safety costs that, together with expense and reduced utility, must be balanced against an alternative design's safety benefits.[219]

Costs and benefits of differing alternative designs vary considerably with the type of product, type of danger, and available methods for reducing risk. But the basic risk-utility issue remains the same: whether the product reasonably could have been designed more safely so as to prevent the plaintiff's harm without unduly increasing the product's cost, decreasing its utility, or introducing other hazards. The *Products Liability*

---

[215] See, e.g., Products Liability Rest. § 2(b) cmt. *f* ("evidence of the magnitude and probability of foreseeable harm may be offset by evidence that the proposed alternative design would reduce the efficiency and the utility of the product"). See, e.g., BIC Pen Corp. v. Carter, 171 S.W.3d 657, 672 (Tex. App. 2005) (concluding, however, that a few complaints of reduced utility do not rise to the level of "substantial" impairment required under statute to overcome benefits of child-proof lighter's safer alternative design), rev'd on other grounds, 251 S.W.3d 500 (Tex. 2008).

[216] Cf. Connelly v. Hyundai Motor Co., 351 F.3d 535, 541 (1st Cir. 2003) (N.H. law) (jury entitled to find aggressive front seat airbag was not defective because "on balance, the benefit to the public of including the overly aggressive airbag system in the Sonata outweighed the danger caused by the airbag system (because the system saved many more lives than it took)").

[217] 623 A.2d 322 (Pa. Super. Ct. 1993).

[218] Id. at 325.

[219] See, e.g., Taillard v. Rooto Corp., 787 Fed. Appx. 281, 284 (6th Cir. 2019) (Mich. law) (insufficient proof that alternative design would be safer overall and was equally convenient); Newbern v. Ford Motor Co., 833 S.E.2d 861, 866 (S.C. Ct. App. 2019) (plaintiffs' airbag system alternative designs "could result in a more dangerous product rather than a less dangerous product"); Evans v. Nacco Materials Handling Grp., Inc., 810 S.E.2d 462, 472 (Va. 2018) (while jury could have concluded that plaintiff's proposed redesign would reduce or prevent risk of the type of accident in this case, there was no evidence that the proposed redesign would make the product safer overall; while it might, in fact it may increase the overall risks to operators and bystanders); A.O. Smith Corp. v. Settlement Inv. Mgmt., 2006 WL 176815, at *4 (Tex. App. 2006) ("the alternative design also must not impose an equal or greater risk of harm under other circumstances"). See cmt. *f* to § 2(b) of the Products Liability Rest.:

> When evaluating the reasonableness of a design alternative, the overall safety of the product must be considered. It is not sufficient that the alternative design would have reduced or prevented the harm suffered by the plaintiff if it would also have introduced into the product other dangers of equal or greater magnitude.

Restatement addresses the relevant balance of costs and benefits in ascertaining a product's design defectiveness in terms of whether an alternative design is "reasonable"—whether the safety advantages of the alternative design are on balance worth its costs and other disadvantages.[220]

The "Product"

Finally, an alternative design must not fundamentally change the nature of the "product," making it safer but changing its functions and characteristics in fundamental ways. This issue is similar to "reduced utility," above, but an alternative design might actually be *more* useful to some people for various purposes, yet end up being a materially different "product" from what it was meant to be. For example, in *Niedner v. Ortho-McNeil Pharm., Inc.*,[221] a sexually active 17-year-old coed died of a pulmonary embolism caused by a blood clot likely attributable to a hormonal birth control skin patch manufactured by the defendant. The product warned that the risk of deadly clots from the more convenient patch might be twice as high as the risk from birth control pills. Affirming dismissal of the plaintiff's design defect claim, the court addressed the requirement of a safer alternative design:

> Here, Niedner contends that oral contraceptives, which are taken daily, are a feasible and safer alternative design to the patch, which is applied once per week for three weeks, with the fourth week being patch-free. While both products are hormonal contraceptives that prevent pregnancy, the difference in the drug delivery method, each of which has its own advantages and disadvantages, makes the pill fundamentally different from the patch.[222] As such, one cannot serve as a safer alternative for the other.

Other courts similarly hold that acceptable alternative designs may not substantially change the nature of the product being challenged.[223]

The "Feasibility" of an Alternative Design

An "alternative" design implies a reasonable choice between available designs. That is, a safety feature that a plaintiff claims a product should have carried can fairly be considered a design "alternative" only if there was a practical means by which a manufacturer reasonably could have adopted such a safety feature at the time the product was designed. Thus, the plaintiff must prove that the alternative design, offered to show that the manufacturer's chosen design was defective, was "feasible."[224] Because

---

[220] See Products Liability Rest. § 2(b) and cmt. *f* thereto.

[221] 58 N.E.3d 1080 (Mass. App. Ct. 2016).

[222] Id. at 1087 (citing Products Liability Rest. § 2 illustration 9, at 26–27 (1998)).

[223] See, e.g., Isaac v. C. R. Bard, Inc., 2021 WL 1177882, at *6–7 (W.D. Tex. 2021) (question of fact whether permanent inferior vena cava filter was "substantially different" from the defective optionally retrievable filter implanted in plaintiff; an "alternative device cannot be a 'substantially different product' ").

[224] See, e.g., Gillespie v. Edmier, 182 N.E.3d 54, 58 (Ill. 2020) ("Evidence of an alternative design introduces the question of feasibility because a manufacturer's product cannot be faulted when safer alternatives are not feasible."); Burgett v. Troy-Bilt LLC, 579 Fed. Appx. 372, 378 (6th Cir. 2014) (Ky. law) ("design defect liability requires proof of a feasible alternative design"; no evidence plaintiffs' expert's hypothetical alternative pull-cord starter would work with battery-powered riding mowers); Morritt v. Stryker Corp., 2011 WL 3876960, at *8 (E.D.N.Y. 2011) ("With no evidence of a feasible, alternative design, however, plaintiffs are unable to make out a prima facie case in strict products liability for design defects."); Malen v. MTD Prods., Inc., 628 F.3d 296, 308 (7th Cir. 2010) (Ill. law) ("A design defect is established by evidence of a practical, cost-effective alternative that was technologically feasible and would have prevented [plaintiff's] injury."); Croskey v. BMW of N. Am., Inc., 532 F.3d 511, 516 (6th Cir. 2008) (Mich. law) (reasonable alternative design must be "available" and "practicable"). See also Tex. Civ. Prac. & Rem. Code § 82.005(a), (b) (to prove a

the feasibility of an alternative design suggests that the design feature proposed by a plaintiff was technically and commercially practical, feasibility is often bound up in the issue of "state of the art."[225] Feasibility requires at least technological capability,[226] but it helpfully may be viewed more broadly to include cost, commercial practicability (including practical availability of materials and components),[227] and the likelihood of consumer acceptance.[228] Viewed in this expanded fashion, "feasible" really means "reasonable," as reflected in the *Products Liability Restatement* definition of a design

---

design defect, plaintiff must prove that a safer alternative design that would have prevented the accident "was economically and technologically feasible at the time the product left the control of the manufacturer or seller by the application of existing or reasonably achievable scientific knowledge").

On feasibility, plaintiff has the burden of proof. Wielgus v. Ryobi Techs., Inc., 2012 WL 3643682, at *7 (N.D. Ill. 2012) ("A products-liability plaintiff is not required to offer evidence of an alternative design in order to prevail under the risk-utility method, but if the plaintiff chooses to put forth an alternative design, the cases suggest that it is the plaintiff—not the defendant—who must show that it is economically, technically, and practically feasible.").

[225] See, e.g., Cavanaugh v. Skil Corp., 751 A.2d 518, 523 (N.J. 2000) (absence of practical and technically feasible alternative device necessary to state-of-the-art defense); Potter v. Chicago Pneumatic Tool Co., 694 A.2d 1319, 1344–49 (Conn. 1997); Boatland of Houston, Inc. v. Bailey, 609 S.W.2d 743, 748 (Tex. 1980) (state-of-the-art evidence "important in determining whether a safer design was feasible"); Lancaster Silo & Block Co. v. Northern Propane Gas Co., 427 N.Y.S.2d 1009, 1016 (App. Div. 1980) ("state of the art sets the parameters of feasibility"). On state of the art, see § 10.4, below.

[226] See, e.g., Martin v. Michelin N. Am., Inc., 92 F. Supp. 2d 745, 754 (E.D. Tenn. 2000) (feasibility defined in terms of what manufacturer could have known under existing state of technological and scientific art at the time of manufacture).

[227] See, e.g., Quiles v. Bradford-White Corp., 2012 WL 1355262, at *4–5 (N.D.N.Y. 2012) (alternative design must have been safer, "feasible, practical, economical, and safe"); Malen v. MTD Prods., Inc., 628 F.3d 296, 308 (7th Cir. 2010) (Ill. law) (requiring proof of "a practical, cost-effective alternative that was technologically feasible"); Croskey v. BMW of N. Am., Inc., 532 F.3d 511, 516 (6th Cir. 2008) (Mich. law) (reasonable alternative design must be "available" and "practicable"); Glover v. BIC Corp., 6 F.3d 1318 (9th Cir. 1993) (Or. law) (practicability means economic feasibility in terms of cost, overall design, and operation); Rix v. General Motors Corp., 723 P.2d 195 (Mont. 1986); Troja v. Black & Decker Mfg. Co., 488 A.2d 516 (Md. Ct. Spec. App. 1985); Oberst v. International Harvester Co., 640 F.2d 863 (7th Cir. 1980) (Ill. law).

[228] Consumer acceptability is the pillar that supports feasibility in an alternative design, since products have no value (hence, no market) if they fail to satisfy consumer demand—either by relieving consumers of work or providing them with pleasure or other satisfaction. While cigarettes may be an unpalatable example, they make the point, since many people continued to smoke regular cigarettes, rather than switching to "lights," when the latter were marketed and generally thought to be safer than the former. In Rose v. Brown & Williamson Tobacco Corp., 855 N.Y.S.2d 119, 122 (App. Div. 2008), after smoking the defendants' cigarettes for nearly fifty years, the plaintiff eventually contracted lung cancer and died. A jury awarded her damages for negligent design but the appellate division reversed, ruling that "consumer acceptability is the only way to demonstrate the feasibility of light cigarettes as an alternative to regular cigarettes." Acknowledging the irony in ruling in favor of cigarette companies, the court remarked: "It is, of course, incongruous to speak of a toxic product, which offers only fleeting sensual pleasure while sickening, disabling and killing multitudes each year, as serving a 'function,' or having 'utility,' for the consumer. Nonetheless, cigarettes plainly serve some subjective function or utility for smokers; if this were not true, the tobacco companies would quickly go out of business. Thus, an affirmance of the judgment holding defendants liable for the severe health effects of regular cigarettes, regardless of plaintiffs' failure to prove that any alternative product design would feasibly serve the same function, would essentially outlaw the satisfaction of the demand for any product serving that function." Id. at 125.

In Adamo v. Brown & Williamson Tobacco Corp., 900 N.E.2d 966, 968 (N.Y. 2008), the Court of Appeals affirmed: "Plaintiffs made no attempt to prove that smokers find light cigarettes as satisfying as regular cigarettes—indeed, it is virtually uncontested that they do not. Both regular and light cigarettes are available on the market, and the enhanced dangers that come from smoking regular cigarettes are well known, but large numbers of consumers continue to prefer regular cigarettes." The court concluded: "It is not necessary in every product liability case that the plaintiff show the safer product is as acceptable to consumers as the one the defendant sold; but such a showing is necessary where, as here, satisfying the consumer is the only function the product has." Id. See also Olson v. Brenntag N. Am., Inc., 2020 WL 6603580, at *13 (N.Y. Sup. Ct. 2020) (jury could properly find that safer "cornstarch-based baby powder was equally acceptable to consumers, and thus a safer design alternative to talcum powder for design-defect purposes").

defect in terms of the availability of a "reasonable alternative design."[229] All significant disadvantages of a proposed alternative design are properly embraced within the feasibility concept, including any increased cost, decreased utility (including consumer acceptance), and increased dangers of other types.[230] And while a plaintiff has the burden to prove the practical feasibility of making the product in a safer alternative way,[231] the feasibility requirement does not mean that a plaintiff's expert must construct a prototype in every case, since that enterprise itself often is unfeasible—as with the nautical or aeronautical dynamics of an ocean liner that capsizes or a jet liner that crashes.[232]

An early case that viewed feasibility in this broader sense was *Wilson v. Piper Aircraft Corp.*[233] *Wilson* involved the crash of a small plane, possibly due to carburetor icing, a condition that could not have occurred if the plane's engine had been equipped with a fuel-injection rather than carburetor system. Although fuel injection systems were available at the time, some 80%–90% of small airplanes used carbureted engines that had various advantages and were approved by the FAA. Reversing jury verdicts for the plaintiffs, the court observed that the plaintiff in a design defect case must establish the availability of an "alternative, safer design, practicable under the circumstances," meaning that the alternative design must be feasible "in terms of cost, practicality and technological possibility."[234] The appellate court concluded that the trial court should not submit a design case to a jury unless the jury reasonably may find that the proposed alternative design is "not only technically feasible but also practicable in terms of cost and the over-all design and operation of the product."[235]

The cost-benefit approach for evaluating proposed alternative designs may be logical and fair, but the balancing of a variety of intangible considerations involved in safety, cost, and utility trade-offs involves a complex conceptual balance that is as much politics and art as it is "facts." Accordingly, the risk-utility balance determination,

---

[229] "A product . . . is defective in design when the foreseeable risks of harm posed by the product could have been reduced or avoided by the adoption of a reasonable alternative design . . . and the omission of the alternative design renders the product not reasonably safe." Products Liability Rest. § 2(b). See Miranda C. v. Nissan Motor Co., 741 S.E.2d 34, 39–40 (S.C. Ct. App. 2013) (emphasizing that alternative designs must be "feasible" or "reasonable," and interchanging the two terms).

[230] See, e.g., Cappellano v. Wright Med. Grp., Inc., 838 F. Supp. 2d 816, 832 (C.D. Ill. 2012) (granting summary judgment to defendant on design defect claim; plaintiff failed to present a basis for comparing the risks and benefits of the feasible alternative design to the allegedly defective hip prosthesis); Caterpillar, Inc. v. Shears, 911 S.W.2d 379 (Tex. 1995) (front-end loader equipped with detachable rather than permanent rollover protective structure (ROPS) was not defective; permanent structure was not "feasible" because it would have destroyed multi-purpose nature of loader); Monahan v. Toro Co., 856 F. Supp. 955 (E.D. Pa. 1994) (lawn tractor rolled over on steep slope; adding roll-bar and altering center of gravity might diminish utility).

[231] An expert witness's mere concept of an alternative design, if it has never been developed in the real world, may not satisfy the feasibility requirement. See, e.g., Quiles v. Bradford-White Corp., 2012 WL 1355262, at *5 (N.D.N.Y. 2012) (while there is no specific evidence a plaintiff must introduce, the plaintiff's expert should show that an alternative design is already in use or should demonstrate its feasibility "through testing and construction of a prototype"); Ballarini v. Clark Equip. Co., 841 F. Supp. 662 (E.D. Pa. 1993) (interlock device that would disable forklift when operator forgets to apply parking brake before dismounting); Allen v. Minnstar, Inc., 8 F.3d 1470 (10th Cir. 1993) (Utah law) (speculative prototype for motorboat propeller guard does not satisfy requirement that alternative design be practicable and available).

[232] See, e.g., Nelson v. Sunbeam Prods., Inc., 2022 WL 79838, at *7 (E.D. Tex. 2022) (prototype not required, but plaintiff "must prove that the alternative design is capable of being developed"); Baley v. Federal Signal Corp., 982 N.E.2d 776, 796 (Ill. App. Ct. 2012) ("[T]he feasible alternative design factor does not require actually building the alternative design; the factor is called a '*feasible* alternative design' and not an '*actual* alternative design.' Feasibility includes the '*technological possibilities* viewed in the present state of the art.' ").

[233] 577 P.2d 1322 (Or. 1978).

[234] Id. at 1326.

[235] Id. at 1327.

assuming the plaintiff has offered credible evidence for an alternative balance, almost always raises an issue of fact for jury determination.[236]

Focusing the Risk-Utility Test on the Proposed Alternative Design

A particularly nettlesome aspect of defining the risk-utility standard for design defectiveness is deciding precisely what to balance against what. Many courts have purported to lean heavily on Dean Wade's famous seven factors, as discussed in the previous section, and some of the problems with relying on such an open-ended catalogue of possibly relevant considerations were there examined. A related problem, also previously noted, arises out of the overly broad way in which many courts phrase the risk-utility balance for design defectiveness—in terms of weighing the risks and utility of the "product."[237] Design defect litigation would be rendered more comprehensible if courts would explicitly formulate the risk-utility test more narrowly to correspond to the issues actually litigated in courtrooms across the nation.[238] Sometimes, the widespread, confused expression of the liability test in appellate decisions produces confused results.[239] Even though many courts (and commentators who should know better)

---

[236] See id. at 1327 nn.3 & 5. See also McClarty v. C.R. Bard, Inc., 2020 WL 6075520, at *5 (E.D. Mich. 2020); Great N. Ins. Co. v. BMW of N. Am. LLC, 84 F. Supp. 3d 630, 657 (S.D. Ohio 2015) (question of fact for the jury whether plaintiff's alternative design for stiffener plate to prevent squirrel's nest debris that caused fire was "practical, technically feasible, and [whether it] substantially impairs the usefulness or intended purpose of the vehicle"); Lloyd v. General Motors Corp., 275 F.R.D. 224, 229 (D. Md. 2011) (jury must "decide whether alternative designs posited by the Plaintiffs would have been preferable and feasible"); Osorio v. One World Techs. Inc., 659 F.3d 81 (1st Cir. 2011) (Mass. law) (affirming jury verdict for construction worker whose hand was injured when it slipped into the blade of a table saw). In *Osorio*, plaintiff's expert, the inventor of "SawStop" technology that would sense and stop a blade on contact with human flesh, proposed such technology as an alternative design. The court concluded that "[i]t is the province of the jury to determine whether the relevant factors, properly balanced, suggest that a product's design is unreasonable, including such factors as "the added cost [allegedly less than $150] or increased weight of Osorio's proposed alternative design," weighing such factors as increased price, increased weight, and "mechanical feasibility," all of which the jury was entitled to weigh under Massachusetts' "multi-factored design defect test." Id. at 85–87.

[237] See, e.g., Stollings v. Ryobi Techs., Inc., 725 F.3d 753, 767 (7th Cir. 2013) (a product's "utility to the public as a whole" is balanced against the "costs the product imposes on society as well as the benefits to society"); Sansom v. Crown Equip. Corp., 880 F. Supp. 2d 648, 660 (W.D. Pa. 2012) ("If the risks of the product outweigh its utility to the public under the facts alleged, then the suit proceeds to the jury . . . ."); Halliday v. Sturm, Ruger & Co., 792 A.2d 1145, 1150 (Md. 2002) ("a product [is] defective and unreasonably dangerous . . . if the danger presented by the product outweighs its utility"); Roberts v. Rich Foods, Inc., 654 A.2d 1365, 1371 (N.J. 1995) (a product is defective in design if "its risks outweighed its utility"); Denny v. Ford Motor Co., 662 N.E.2d 730, 735–36 (N.Y. 1995) (design defect test "weigh[s] the product's benefits against its risks" and "the product's dangers against its over-all advantages"); Caterpillar, Inc. v. Shears, 911 S.W.2d 379, 384 (Tex. 1995) ("balancing the utility of the product against [its]risks").

Courts in at least a couple of states, most notably New Jersey, appear to believe in the propriety of both broad and narrow forms of risk-utility balancing in design defect cases. See, e.g., Lewis v. American Cyanamid Co., 715 A.2d 967, 980 (N.J. 1998) ("A plaintiff must prove either that the product's risks outweighed its utility or that the product could have been designed in an alternative manner so as to minimize or eliminate the risk of harm. Plaintiffs who assert that the product could have been designed more safely must prove under a risk-utility analysis the existence of an alternative design that is both practical and feasible."). New Jersey's statutory exception to the feasible alternative design requirement, for "egregiously unsafe or ultrahazardous" products and those with "little or no usefulness," suggests approval of broad risk-utility balancing in this narrow class of cases. See N.J. Stat. Ann. § 2A:58C–3(b).

[238] One example of a court focusing more closely on a proper comparison of the marginal costs and safety benefits of a particular design feature is Colon v. BIC USA, Inc., 199 F. Supp. 2d 53, 91 n.32 (S.D.N.Y. 2001) (test of lighters defective in design because of their bright color is whether "the risk of bright color outweighs the utility of using a bright color compared to the risk versus utility of using a dull color"). The proper balance is explained in Owen, Toward a Proper Test for Design Defectiveness: "Micro-Balancing" Costs and Benefits, 75 Tex. L. Rev. 1661 (1997); Owen, Risk-Utility Balancing in Design Defect Cases, 30 U. Mich. J. L. Reform 239 (1997).

[239] For a decision that got it totally backwards, see Wielgus v. Ryobi Techs., Inc., 2012 WL 3643682, at *13 (N.D. Ill. 2012) (faulting plaintiff's expert's correct use of marginal cost-benefit analysis of an alternative

continue stubbornly to express the risk-utility liability standard incorrectly in terms of balancing the risks and utility of an accident *product*, both judges and lawyers seem to understand the true meaning of such boilerplate formulations of the risk-utility test, a balance that properly compares the marginal costs and benefits of a particular, untaken design *feature*.

Another way to understand the role of the marginal costs and benefits of an alternative design feature in design defect cases is to focus on two separate designs, both of which are evaluated at trial: (1) the manufacturer's chosen design, and (2) the alternative design proposed by the plaintiff that allegedly would reasonably have prevented the plaintiff's harm. The propriety of the first (chosen) design would seem to be the more important issue in such a case, and to a real extent it is: the "defectiveness" (*vel non*) of the chosen design remains the ultimate issue in the trial. Yet, the propriety of a chosen design is no more than that—the ultimate legal determination that merely characterizes, but provides no guidelines for establishing, the outcome of a case. What is central to the adjudication process is the second, alternative, *untaken* design—more specifically, the reasons for and against the manufacturer's failure to adopt it. This is the narrow design decision normally and properly at issue in the trial which lies at the heart of nearly every design defect case, requiring particularized cost-benefit proof by the parties and evaluative processing by the judge and jury. Although the propriety of the manufacturer's chosen design remains of ultimate consequential interest in terms of legal outcome, the propriety of that design ordinarily is determinable only indirectly by evaluating the costs and benefits of the untaken design precaution proposed by the plaintiff.

Thus, regardless of how broadly appellate courts may formulate the risk-utility test, design defect litigation almost invariably focuses on the costs and benefits related directly to a solution of the particular design problem asserted by the plaintiff. That is, the design defect issue properly litigated is a *micro*-balance of the pros and cons of the manufacturer's *failure* to adopt some design feature that would have prevented the plaintiff's harm—the balance of the safety benefits from changing the design in some particular manner weighed against the various costs of adopting the safety feature.[240] Most simply, the risk-utility balance truly at issue in design defect litigation is *whether the safety benefits of an alternative design feature would have been worth the resulting costs*.[241] More fully formulated, a product's design is defective if the safety benefits of the

---

design safety feature, SawStop technology—where the expert properly compared the costs and safety benefits of the untaken feature, the court (drawing on verbiage from a high court case) erroneously ruled that the expert should have assessed "the usefulness and desirability" of the accident table saw to "the public as a whole").

[240] See, e.g., R. Heafey and D. Kennedy, Product Liability: Winning Strategies and Techniques § 4.04, at 4–9 (1994) (characterizing the manufacturer's choice to forego a reasonable alternative design as "the heart of the plaintiff's case"). See also Rheingold, The Risk/Utility Test in Product Cases, 18 Trial Law. Q. 49, 50 (Summer/Fall 1987) ("The usual and proper approach for a plaintiff in a design defect case is to present evidence on an alternative design which the jury can find should have been adopted for the product in question."). This is how design defects are defined in Products Liability Rest. § 2 comments *d* and *f*, and it reflects how courts and lawyers actually proceed in assessing liability under the Hand formula. One scholar states that a plaintiff's attorney will "try to find some act which, if the defendant had taken it, would have significantly reduced the probability of the accident at low cost [such] that the increment in the expected loss was greater than the cost of avoidance [and the defendant's attorney tries to show] that the expected benefits of the proposed act were, in fact, less than the costs of undertaking it. [The decision maker is then] asked to compare the incremental expected benefits with the incremental costs." Brown, Toward an Economic Theory of Liability, 2 J. Legal Stud. 323, 334–35 (1973).

[241] "In sum, an alternative design is reasonable if its marginal benefits exceed its marginal costs." Products Liability Rest. § 2(b), Reporters' Note to cmt. *f*.

plaintiff's proposed alternative design features foreseeably would have exceeded its resulting costs, including any diminished usefulness and diminished safety.[242]

When the risk-utility test is properly defined in terms of the costs and benefits of the alternative design feature proposed by plaintiff, it does fail to catch a very limited class of design dangers—those that are *unavoidably* dangerous—such as those in exploding cigars, lawn darts that are deadly sharp, and arguably guns, cigarettes, and alcohol whose inherent dangers cannot be designed away and which on balance arguably cause more social harm than good. The difficult problem here is whether the law properly may impose this type of product category liability for inherently dangerous products,[243] an important issue examined in a later chapter.[244] A number of courts,[245] at least two state legislatures,[246] and the *Products Liability Restatement*,[247] all require plaintiffs in design cases to prove a feasible alternative design as a general rule but provide a special exception for a very small category of egregiously dangerous products which possess little redeeming value, a quite reasonable approach to a difficult problem.

§ 8.6 COMBINING CONSUMER EXPECTATIONS AND RISK-UTILITY

Evolving separately from the law of warranty and the law of negligence, the consumer expectations and risk-utility tests for design defects developed respectively as rival liability standards. Thus, for much of modern products liability law, most courts determined design defectiveness exclusively by one test and refused to recognize the validity of the other. More recently, however, reflecting the combined warranty-tort heritage of products liability law, and because of shortcomings in consumer expectations as an exclusive standard,[248] many courts have blended the two tests in one way or another. The two principal approaches for blending the two standards are: (1) defining

---

[242] See Owen, Toward a Proper Test for Design Defectiveness: "Micro-Balancing" Costs and Benefits, 75 Tex. L. Rev. 1661, 1690 (1997).

[243] As mentioned in the text, the classic examples are cigarettes, certain guns, and alcoholic beverages. See also Products Liability Rest. § 2 cmts. *d* and *e*, and illus. 5 (exploding cigar). For a range of views on the appropriateness of using broad-based risk-utility analysis to find cigarettes defectively designed, see the three separate opinions, each concurring and dissenting, in Horton v. American Tobacco Co., 667 So.2d 1289 (Miss. 1995) (compare opinion of Hawkins, C.J., arguing that risk-utility analysis is inappropriate in such cases and noting that liability has been denied by every prior decision, with the opinions of Lee, P.J., and McRae, J., arguing that cigarette manufacturers properly may be held liable under a risk-utility test). For a case holding that the absence of an alternative design to hollow-point bullets, used in a shooting spree on a passenger train, precluded a finding of a design defect under the risk-utility test because the purpose of the hollow points is to make the bullets kill especially effectively, see McCarthy v. Olin Corp., 119 F.3d 148 (2d Cir. 1997) (N.Y. law) (2–1 decision, Calabresi, J., dissenting).

[244] See § 10.3, below.

[245] See, e.g., Parish v. Jumpking, Inc., 719 N.W.2d 540 (Iowa 2006); Armentrout v. FMC Corp., 842 P.2d 175, 185 n.8 (Colo. 1992) (en banc); Kallio v. Ford Motor Co., 407 N.W.2d 92, 97 n.8 (Minn. 1987); Rix v. General Motors Corp., 723 P.2d 195, 201 (Mont. 1986); Wilson v. Piper Aircraft Corp., 577 P.2d 1322, 1328 n.5 (Or. 1978).

[246] New Jersey's statute provides that the plaintiff must prove a feasible alternative design or that the product was especially hazardous or practically useless. See N.J. Stat. Ann. § 2A:58C–3(b). North Carolina's statute provides that the plaintiff must prove a feasible alternative design or "that a reasonable person, aware of the relevant facts, would not use or consume a product of this design." See N.C. Gen. Stat. Ann. § 99B–6(a)(2).

[247] See Products Liability Rest. § 2(b) cmt. *e*, entitled "Design defects: possibility of manifestly unreasonable design," which notes that a court might choose to abandon the alternative design requirement in special cases where "the extremely high degree of danger posed by [a product's] use or consumption so substantially outweighs its negligible social utility that no rational, reasonable person, fully aware of the relevant facts, would choose to use, or to allow children to use, the product."

[248] See Schwartz, Foreword: Understanding Products Liability, 67 Cal. L. Rev. 435, 471–82 (1979); § 8.3, above.

one test in terms of the other; or (2) establishing each as separate liability "prongs,"[249] either one of which may independently support a design defect finding. Some jurisdictions that embrace the two-pronged approach have narrowed the applicability of the consumer expectations prong to product design hazards viewed as "simple."

Defining One Test in Terms of the Other—the *Tabert-Potter* Approach

Quite early in the development of modern products liability law, Judge Minor Wisdom recognized how the two basic liability tests might be viewed as partners in evaluating product dangers. In *Welch v. Outboard Marine Corp.*,[250] the operator of a power lawn mower was injured when a piece of wire was thrown back from the mower, injuring his ankle. Plaintiff sued, asserting that the mower was defectively designed because it lacked a guard plate hinged to the back. The trial court instructed the jury that it could find the mower defectively designed if "a reasonable man would not sell the product if he knew the risks involved. To put it another way, a product is unreasonably dangerous if it is dangerous to an extent beyond which would be contemplated by the ordinary consumer."[251] The jury gave a verdict for the defendant, and the plaintiff appealed, complaining that the instruction confused the jury by giving them two contradictory definitions of the liability standard.

Affirming a judgment on the verdict, Judge Wisdom observed no inconsistency between the reasonable seller and reasonable buyer tests, which he viewed as merely "two sides of the same standard."[252] Although this two-sides-of-the-same-coin perspective failed initially to achieve much of a judicial following, it was recognized by some early courts and commentators as a novel but logical approach that appropriately reflected the hybrid evolution of strict manufacturer liability from warranty and tort.[253] Developing Judge Wisdom's concept further, commentators recommended interpreting the *Welch* definition not as a single liability "coin" or standard, but as a bifurcated test that would provide recovery *either* if a product failed a risk-benefit test *or* if the product's dangers exceeded consumer expectations.[254]

One year later, in 1974, the Supreme Court of Oregon entered the search for a design defect test in *Phillips v. Kimwood Machine Co.*,[255] a case involving the design of an industrial sanding machine that ejected a piece of fiberboard back at the operator.[256] Although the Oregon court had previously adopted the consumer expectations test for ascertaining design defectiveness, in *Heaton v. Ford Motor Co.*,[257] it had been troubled in that case with the vagueness of a consumer's safety expectations in view of the kinds

---

[249] In Barker v. Lull Eng'g Co., 573 P.2d 443, 456 (Cal. 1978), the court aptly referred to the use of two alternative bases of liability as the "two-pronged definition of design defect." See Schwartz, Foreword: Understanding Products Liability, 67 Cal. L. Rev. 435, 436 (1979).

[250] 481 F.2d 252 (5th Cir. 1973) (La. law).

[251] Id. at 253–54.

[252] "A product is defective and unreasonably dangerous when a reasonable seller would not sell the product if he knew of the risks involved or if the risks are greater than a reasonable buyer would expect." Id. at 254.

[253] See, e.g., Phillips v. Kimwood Mach. Co., 525 P.2d 1033, 1036–37 (Or. 1974); Montgomery and Owen, Reflections on the Theory and Administration of Strict Tort Liability for Defective Products, 27 S.C. L. Rev. 803, 843–45 (1976).

[254] Montgomery and Owen, above, at 845 n.147.

[255] 525 P.2d 1033 (Or. 1974).

[256] The claimed design defect was the absence of teeth on the machine that could have prevented regurgitation of the boards. Id. at 1035.

[257] 435 P.2d 806 (Or. 1967).

of engineering tradeoffs between costs and benefits unknown to consumers that inhere in design decisionmaking.[258] In the process of switching from a consumer expectations test to risk-utility,[259] the *Phillips* court reiterated Judge Wisdom's view in *Welch* that the two tests may be the same "because a seller acting reasonably would be selling the same product which a reasonable consumer believes he is purchasing."[260] The Oregon court's assertion that buyers and sellers have the same safety expectations ignores its important criticism in *Heaton* that consumer expectations fail to provide a meaningful safety gauge for complex designs; but the court may have repeated the equivalency of the two tests as window-dressing for its switch away from the problematic consumer expectations test to the more felicitous risk-utility standard for design defect determinations. Be that as it may, collapsing consumer expectations into risk-utility, *Phillips* abandoned the consumer expectations test in favor of risk-utility.

The following year, the Supreme Court of Washington decided *Seattle-First National Bank v. Tabert*,[261] a crashworthiness case involving the structural integrity of a snub-nosed Volkswagen van. A husband and wife were killed when the front of their van collapsed back upon them after it struck the rear of a flatbed truck. Reversing a summary judgment for the defendants, the court defined design defect liability under § 402A in terms of an ordinary consumer's reasonable safety expectations.[262] Observing that an ordinary consumer "evaluates a product in terms of safety, recognizing that virtually no product is or can be made absolutely safe,"[263] the *Tabert* court expressly folded the consumer expectations test into risk-utility analysis, stating that the reasonable expectations of ordinary consumers include the cost and feasibility of avoiding the risk.[264] Because the plaintiff's expert in his affidavit properly applied risk-utility analysis to the weakness of the vehicle's forward structure, the plaintiff had presented a question of fact for the jury.[265]

By defining the design defect test in terms of consumer expectations, and then "determining" consumer expectations in terms of the costs and benefits of eliminating or minimizing the danger, the *Tabert* court blended the two tests of design defectiveness. But how the blend should operate is not made clear. While the court states that risk-utility factors are determinants of consumer expectations, it retains consumer expectations as the formal test of liability. At this early stage in the development of design defect theory, the court was feeling its way and so could only have had a rough conception of how the two standards might relate to one another. It may be that the court

---

[258] See id. at 809.

[259] *Phillips*, 525 P.2d at 1036.

[260] Id. at 1037. The court continued: "That is to say, a manufacturer who would be negligent in marketing a given product, considering its risks, would necessarily be marketing a product which fell below the reasonable expectations of consumers who purchase it. The foreseeable uses to which a product could be put would be the same in the minds of both the seller and the buyer unless one of the parties was not acting reasonably." Id. Note, however, the *Phillips* court also curiously remarked that the two tests "are not necessarily different standards." Id. at 1036.

[261] 542 P.2d 774 (Wash. 1975).

[262] Id. at 779.

[263] Id.

[264] Observing that "[t]he purchaser of a Volkswagen cannot reasonably expect the same degree of safety as would the buyer of the much more expensive Cadillac," the court remarked that a number of factors must be considered in determining an ordinary consumer's reasonable expectations: "The relative cost of the product, the gravity of the potential harm from the claimed defect and the cost and feasibility of eliminating or minimizing the risk may be relevant in a particular case." Id.

[265] See id. at 779–80.

was thinking that in crashworthiness and other complex design cases consumers only have a right to expect that a vehicle be reasonably designed according to the cost-benefit calculations of reasonable engineers. Yet, by leaving room for "other factors" in other situations, the court implicitly left open the possibility of applying a pure consumer expectations test in other contexts, perhaps in cases involving simple designs.

Whatever the *Tabert* court may actually have had in mind, the Washington state legislature several years later enacted a statute ambiguously basing liability for design dangers on the costs and benefits of a feasible alternative design *and* on the safety contemplations of an ordinary consumer.[266] A subsequent Washington decision interpreted the statute to mean that a plaintiff could prevail on *either* basis, which amounts to a two-pronged approach for defining design defects[267]—a dubious statutory interpretation (regardless of its merits as a liability standard) that narrowly avoided being overruled in a 1999 en banc decision.[268]

At the time, courts in most other jurisdictions largely ignored the *Welch* and *Tabert* approach that combined the consumer expectations and risk-utility tests in some amorphous manner,[269] and the idea of mixing the two approaches to design defectiveness (or finding them equivalent) lay dormant during the 1980s[270] as the consumer expectations test gradually lost ground to risk-utility in their battle for supremacy as independent tests of design defectiveness. Then, as if awakening Rip Van Winkle from a lengthy slumber, courts in a small number of states in the late 1990s and early 2000s resurrected the nearly defunct idea that the two independent design defect standards are equivalent,[271] merely representing "two sides of the same coin."[272]

---

[266] See Couch v. Mine Safety Appliances Co., 728 P.2d 585 (Wash. 1986); Wash. Rev. Code Ann. § 7.72.030(1)(a) and (3).

[267] Falk v. Keene Corp., 782 P.2d 974, 977–80 (Wash. 1989). *Falk*'s interpretation of the statutory standard converts it into a *Barker* standard, discussed below.

[268] Soproni v. Polygon Apt. Partners, 971 P.2d 500 (Wash. 1999) (5–4 decision). Compare Eriksen v. Mobay Corp., 41 P.3d 488, 494 (Wash. Ct. App. 2002) (asserting unequivocally that a plaintiff may establish design defect liability by statute on either risk-utility or consumer expectations).

[269] *But see* McCathern v. Toyota Motor Corp., 985 P.2d 804 (Or. Ct. App. 1999), aff'd, 23 P.3d 320, 330–32 (Or. 2001); Potter v. Chicago Pneumatic Tool Co., 694 A.2d 1319 (Conn. 1997), discussed below.

[270] Or nearly dormant. Robinson v. Reed-Prentice Div. of Package Mach. Co., 403 N.E.2d 440, 443 (N.Y. 1980) ("a defectively designed product is one which, at the time it leaves the seller's hands, is in a condition not reasonably contemplated by the ultimate consumer and is unreasonably dangerous for its intended use; that is one whose utility does not outweigh the danger inherent in its introduction into the stream of commerce").

[271] In Ray v. BIC Corp., 925 S.W.2d 527, 531 (Tenn. 1996), noting the error in viewing the two tests as equivalent, the court "decline[d] to weave the two tests into one." Even Oregon, which asserted in *Phillips* the equivalence of the two tests, now understands the naivete of that view. See McCathern v. Toyota Motor Corp., 23 P.3d 320, 330–32 (Or. 2001). Yet the fact that the equivalency notion is now largely discredited does not mean that courts do not occasionally muddle the developing products liability jurisprudence by dragging this obsolete notion from obscurity. See, e.g., Jackson v. Bomag GmbH, 638 N.Y.S.2d 819, 821 (App. Div. 1996).

[272] The quote is from Ray v. BIC Corp., 925 S.W.2d 527, 530 (Tenn. 1996), which was quoting Estate of Ryder v. Kelly-Springfield Tire Co., 587 P.2d 160, 164 (Wash. 1978). However, the Tennessee court merely noted this approach and criticized it as incorrect and obsolete. *Ray*, 925 S.W.2d at 531. Subsequent decisions resting on the idea include Potter v. Chicago Pneumatic Tool Co., 694 A.2d 1319 (Conn. 1997), and Bragg v. Hi-Ranger, Inc., 462 S.E.2d 321, 328 (S.C. Ct. App. 1995) ("[W]e balance the utility of the risk inherent in the design of the product with the magnitude of the risk to determine the reasonableness of the manufacturer's action in designing the product. This 'balancing act' is also relevant to the determination that the product, as designed, is unreasonably dangerous in its failure to conform to the ordinary user's expectations."). See also Flemister v. General Motors Corp., 723 So.2d 25 (Ala. 1998), where consumer expectations are redefined in risk-utility terms, and risk-utility appears to trump consumer expectations. See also note 81, above.

The most notable decision in the 1990s to embrace the equivalency notion is *Potter v. Chicago Pneumatic Tool Co.*,[273] decided by the Supreme Court of Connecticut in 1997. This case was brought by shipyard workers against manufacturers of pneumatic hand tools for injuries from excessive vibration of the tools. Although the consumer expectations test was "well established in Connecticut strict products liability decisions,"[274] the court was nevertheless troubled by the vagueness problem in consumer expectations about the safety of complex designs. Following jurisdictions like Washington "that have modified their formulation of the consumer expectation test by incorporating risk-utility factors into the ordinary consumer expectation analysis,"[275] *Potter* adopted *Tabert*'s reformulation of the consumer expectations test in risk-utility terms for complex designs,[276] as further discussed below. The *Potter* court observed that this "modified formulation" of the consumer expectations test "would establish the product's risk and utility, and the inquiry would then be whether a reasonable consumer would consider the product design unreasonably dangerous."[277]

Other courts, also moving the liability standard from consumer expectations to a balance of costs and benefits, have followed *Potter*'s approach of redefining the consumer expectations test in risk-utility terms, at least in cases involving complex designs. The *Potter* court and others following its approach of defining consumer expectations in risk-utility terms are obviously conflicted about abandoning consumer expectations altogether in favor of risk-utility as the basis for design defect liability, often because they succumb to the now-suspect view that the consumer expectations test protects consumer interests better than the risk-utility test.[278] These courts have recognized, if reluctantly, the need to turn to a true risk-utility test for evaluating the safety of complex designs in order to provide a determinate standard for liability decisions. As discussed below, however, much may be said for completely breaking with consumer expectations as an independent test for evaluating the safety of product designs, particularly complex ones, and switching to risk-utility as the exclusive liability standard for most such cases.[279]

Two Liability "Prongs"—the *Barker* Approach

A more forthright and intelligible approach for design defects, which accommodates both the warranty and tort law foundations of strict manufacturer liability, and which acknowledges the separate value of each, recognizes two independent bases or "prongs" of liability. By such a "two-pronged," alternative approach to design defectiveness, an injured plaintiff may establish a design defect if the product's design fails *either* (1) a consumer expectations test, *or* (2) a risk-utility test. This approach has logical appeal because it formally protects the essential interests furthered by each test: contract law's protection of the expectations of buyers and sellers in their private bargains, and tort

---

[273] 694 A.2d 1319 (Conn. 1997).

[274] Id. at 1330.

[275] Id. at 1333.

[276] Id.

[277] Id. In determining what a consumer reasonably would expect, the court noted that a jury should consider most of the Wade risk-utility factors. Id. at n.15. See § 8.4, above.

[278] For difficulties the consumer expectations test causes plaintiffs, see § 8.3, above.

[279] The consumer expectations standard still may be a useful liability test for simple product failures, discussed below, and it serves well in certain other specialized contexts. See Products Liability Rest. § 2 cmt. *h*, § 7 (food) and § 8(b) (used products).

law's protection of potential victims by requiring sellers to accord due respect to the safety interests of persons foreseeably endangered by defective products.[280]

Barker v. Lull Engineering Co.,[281] decided by the California Supreme Court in 1978, was the first judicial formulation of an explicitly two-pronged definition of design defects. The plaintiff, while operating a high-lift loader manufactured by the defendant, was struck by a piece of lumber when he leaped from the vehicle as his load began to shift. His strict liability in tort claim alleged that the loader's design was deficient because it was not equipped with stabilizing outriggers, a seatbelt, a roll bar, or an automatic locking device on the leveling lever, and was deficient in certain other respects as well. The trial court instructed the jury that strict liability for defective design is "based on a finding that the product was unreasonably dangerous," the jury found for the defendant, and the plaintiff appealed. Reversing because of errors in the design defect instruction, the Supreme Court of California adopted a two-pronged test for defects in design:

> [A] trial judge may properly instruct the jury that a product is defective in design (1) if the plaintiff demonstrates that the product failed to perform as safely as an ordinary consumer would expect when used in an intended or reasonably foreseeable manner, or (2) if the plaintiff proves that the product's design proximately caused his injury and the defendant fails to prove, in light of the relevant factors, . . . that on balance the benefits of the challenged design outweigh the risk of danger inherent in such design.[282]

Among other factors relevant to the risk-utility prong of this test, the court listed the likelihood and gravity of danger posed by the challenged design, "the mechanical feasibility of a safer alternative design, the financial cost of an improved design, and the adverse consequences to the product and to the consumer that would result from an alternative design."[283]

As for the burden of proof, the *Barker* court left it on the plaintiff for the consumer expectations prong but shifted it to the manufacturer for the risk-utility prong.[284] Observing that the doctrine of strict manufacturer liability in tort was designed to relieve injured plaintiffs of "the onerous evidentiary burdens" of proving a manufacturer's negligence, the court explained the shift in the burden of proof by noting that most risk-benefit evidence on the feasibility and cost of alternative designs involves "technical matters peculiarly within the knowledge of the manufacturer."[285]

While at least a couple of courts explicitly rejected *Barker*'s two-pronged definition of design defect,[286] a handful of states now explicitly follow this alternative form of

---

[280] The explicitly two-pronged approach may have originated in Montgomery and Owen, Reflections on the Theory and Administration of Strict Tort Liability for Defective Products, 27 S.C. L. Rev. 803, 843–45 (1976), which was inspired by *Welch*, note 250, above.

[281] 573 P.2d 443 (Cal. 1978).

[282] Id. at 457–58.

[283] Id. at 455.

[284] Id. ("once the plaintiff makes a prima facie showing that the injury was proximately caused by the product's design, the burden should appropriately shift to the defendant to prove, in light of the relevant factors, that the product is not defective"). See also id. at 456.

[285] Id. at 455.

[286] See, e.g., Kallio v. Ford Motor Co., 407 N.W.2d 92, 95 (Minn. 1987); Lester v. Magic Chef, Inc., 641 P.2d 353 (Kan. 1982). While the Kansas court flatly rejected the *Barker* two-pronged approach in favor of the consumer expectations test in *Lester*, risk-utility evidence crept back into that state's method for determining

definition.[287] One such state is Pennsylvania, which in a 2014 Supreme Court decision adopted a two-pronged standard similar to *Barker*'s, permitting plaintiffs to pursue design defect claims on either the consumer expectations or risk-utility approach.[288] But the Pennsylvania court deferred a decision on the burden of proof.[289] Another state that followed this approach is Washington, which has a confusing statutory definition of design defectiveness. The statute separately provides that a product design may be considered defective on a finding of the cost-effectiveness of a feasible alternative design and for violating the safety contemplations of an ordinary consumer, but the statute fails to state whether the two design defect standards are independent or whether one will trump the other.[290] As mentioned earlier, the Washington Supreme Court interpreted this statute as establishing a two-pronged standard[291]—a questionable interpretation that narrowly escaped reversal a decade later.[292] Unlike Washington's ambiguous legislation, statutes enacted in Tennessee[293] and Ohio[294] clearly provided *Barker*-like, two-pronged standards for design defectiveness, though Ohio subsequently abandoned the two-pronged standard in favor of a multifaceted risk-utility approach.[295]

A few courts danced around the issue, seemingly adopting the *Barker* two-pronged approach, but without saying so explicitly.[296] A number of jurisdictions adopted a *de facto Barker* approach, variously applying the consumer expectations and risk-utility tests in

---

defects in design. See Delaney v. Deere & Co., 999 P.2d 930, 944 (Kan. 2000) (recognizing "the validity of risk/utility analysis as a guide in determining the expectations of consumers in complex cases").

[287] See, e.g., Gillespie v. Edmier, 182 N.E.3d 54, 58 (Ill. 2020) ("Plaintiffs may demonstrate that a product was defectively designed by presenting evidence that the product fails to satisfy the 'consumer-expectation test' or the 'risk-utility test.' "); Rivera Pomales v. Bridgestone Firestone, Inc., 217 F.R.D. 290, 295 (D.P.R. 2003); Ontai v. Straub Clinic & Hosp., Inc., 659 P.2d 734 (Haw. 1983); Knitz v. Minster Mach. Co., 432 N.E.2d 814 (Ohio 1982), superseded by statute, Ohio Rev. Code Ann. § 2307.75(B)(5).

[288] In Tincher v. Omega Flex, Inc., 104 A.3d 328 (Pa. 2014). *Tincher* is discussed in § 5.3, above.

[289] *Tincher*, 104 A.3d at 431. And the court recognized without entirely endorsing California's subsequent decision in *Soule v. General Motors Corp.*, discussed below.

[290] On this issue, see Wash. Rev. Code Ann. § 7.72.030(1)(a) and (3).

[291] See Falk v. Keene Corp., 782 P.2d 974, 977–80 (Wash. 1989). See also Bruns v. PACCAR, Inc., 890 P.2d 469 (Wash. Ct. App. 1995).

[292] See Soproni v. Polygon Apt. Partners, 971 P.2d 500 (Wash. 1999) (5–4 decision). See also Spokane Sch. Dist. No. 81 v. Northwest Bldg. Sys., Inc., 2006 WL 696282, at *9 (E.D. Wash. 2006) ("Two alternative tests may be used to establish that a product was not reasonably safe as designed: the risk-utility test and the consumer expectations test.").

[293] See Tenn. Code Ann. § 29–28–102(8), defining an "unreasonably dangerous" product as "a product [that] is dangerous to an extent beyond that which would be contemplated by the ordinary consumer who purchases it, [or a product that] because of its dangerous condition would not be put on the market by a reasonably prudent manufacturer or seller, assuming that [the manufacturer or seller] knew of its dangerous condition." See, e.g., Ray v. BIC Corp., 925 S.W.2d 527 (Tenn. 1996) (declining to weave the two standards into one, and holding that the prudent manufacturer prong requires risk-utility analysis).

[294] Ohio Rev. Code Ann. § 2307.75(A) (as reenacted in 2001).

[295] Ohio adopted *Barker*'s two-pronged definition of design defectiveness judicially in the 1980s and legislatively in the 1990s, but a 2004 statute (effective 2005) adopted a multi-factor risk-utility test for design defectiveness that deleted consumer expectations as a separate basis of liability but included it as one factor in the risk-utility determination. See Ohio Rev. Code Ann. § 2307.75(B)(5).

[296] See, e.g., Brinkley v. Pfizer, Inc., 772 F.3d 1133, 1140 (8th Cir. 2014) (Mo. law) (plaintiffs may present "evidence that the utility of a design outweighs its risks, or that consumer expectations were violated, or any other theory of unreasonable dangerousness supported by the evidence"); Dart v. Wiebe Mfg., Inc., 709 P.2d 876 (Ariz. 1985) (jumping past *Barker* to an approach similar to Soule v. General Motors Corp., 882 P.2d 298 (Cal. 1994), examined below); Baughn v. Honda Motor Co., 727 P.2d 655, 660 (Wash. 1986) (applying "consumer expectations test with a risk-utility base"). Colorado courts also now appear to have jumped past *Barker* to a *Soule* approach. See Walker v. Ford Motor Co., 406 P.3d 845, 851 (Colo. 2017) (only the risk-benefit test, not consumer expectations, can be used to assess whether a product's design was defective when that issue is "defined primarily by technical, scientific information").

different situations,[297] sometimes without a satisfactory explanation as to why one test is applied in one situation and the other test in some other.[298] And the *Potter* approach discussed above and further below, which conflates consumer expectations and risk-utility, is itself a variation on the *Barker* two-pronged standard. While some of these decisions may be faulted for failing clearly to specify when and how the two separate tests should be applied, most courts still are feeling their way in the seemingly never-ending search for an ideal test for design defectiveness. And it certainly was reasonable to conclude, at this point in the evolution of design defect jurisprudence, that there might be real value in the idea of intelligently combining, in some manner or another, both standards of liability.[299]

A small number of jurisdictions adopting *Barker*'s two-pronged design-defect approach also followed that decision's reversal of the normal burden of proof.[300] However, most courts adopting a two-pronged approach rejected this change in the balance of litigation responsibility and continue to require the plaintiff to prove the feasibility and cost-effectiveness of the alternative design, together with other components of the risk-utility analysis.[301] At a superficial level, *Barker*'s shift in the burden of proof seems fair and reasonable because at least some information on cost-benefit tradeoffs is likely to reside in the defendant's files. Yet it hardly seems unfair to require the plaintiff challenging a product's design as "defective" to offer and prove a hypothesis as to how, specifically, it ought to have been more safely designed. And, requiring a defendant to prove why it did not adopt any of an infinite number of potential alternative designs

---

[297] See, e.g., Halliday v. Sturm, Ruger & Co., 792 A.2d 1145, 1153 (Md. 2002) (consumer expectations test applies to design cases unless product malfunctions, in which case risk-utility test applies).

[298] See, e.g., Bragg v. Hi-Ranger, Inc., 462 S.E.2d 321, 328 (S.C. Ct. App. 1995); Warner Fruehauf Trailer Co. v. Boston, 654 A.2d 1272, 1276 (D.C. 1995) (truck liftgate suddenly collapsed because it had only one, rather than two, hydraulic cylinders). In *Warner*, following what it said was the majority approach, the court used a risk-utility test for the design defect determination in the case before it, "[g]iven the type of product," but observed that consumer expectations test is also frequently used. Id. Compare Pritchett v. Cottrell, Inc., 512 F.3d 1057, 1064 (8th Cir. 2008) (Mo. law) (allowing plaintiffs to argue "that the utility of a design outweighs its risks, or that consumer expectations were violated, or any other theory of unreasonable dangerousness supported by the evidence").

[299] See, e.g., Kennedy, The Role of the Consumer Expectation Test Under Louisiana's Products Liability Tort Doctrine, 69 Tul. L. Rev. 117, 162–63 (1994) ("[I]t will be prudent in some cases to employ the consumer expectation test in conjunction with the risk-utility balancing test in the form of a 'risk-utility consumer expectation test.' . . . given the complexity of products and products liability tort litigation today; the moral, social, economic, and jurisprudential values sought to be advanced by tort liability; and the superiority of the risk-utility balancing test in serving these interests and in resolving many of the tough issues presented in most products liability disputes.").

[300] See, e.g., Quintana-Ruiz v. Hyundai Motor Corp., 303 F.3d 62 (1st Cir. 2002) (P.R. law); Lamkin v. Towner, 563 N.E.2d 449 (Ill. 1990); Ortho Pharm. Corp. v. Heath, 722 P.2d 410 (Colo. 1986), overruled on other grounds by Armentrout v. FMC Corp., 842 P.2d 175 (Colo. 1992); Ontai v. Straub Clinic & Hosp., Inc., 659 P.2d 734 (Haw. 1983); Caterpillar Tractor Co. v. Beck, 593 P.2d 871 (Alaska 1979). Colorado and Illinois both eventually recanted and rejected the burden shift. See Armentrout v. FMC Corp., 842 P.2d 175, 183 (Colo. 1992); Blue v. Environmental Eng'g, Inc., 828 N.E.2d 1128, 1142–44 (Ill. 2005). In Soule v. General Motors Corp., 882 P.2d 298, 311 n.8 (Cal. 1994), the California Supreme Court revisited and reaffirmed *Barker*'s shift in the burden of proof.

[301] Except for Alaska, Hawaii, and Puerto Rico, courts in other states rejected California's second-prong shift in the burden of proof, initially or in time. See, e.g., Blue v. Environmental Eng'g, Inc., 828 N.E.2d 1128, 1142–44 (Ill. 2005) (disapproving prior case); Armentrout v. FMC Corp., 842 P.2d 175 (Colo. 1992) (overruling prior case); Kallio v. Ford Motor Co., 407 N.W.2d 92 (Minn. 1987); Hayes v. Ariens Co., 462 N.E.2d 273 (Mass. 1984), overruled in part on other grounds by Vassallo v. Baxter Healthcare Corp., 696 N.E.2d 909 (Mass. 1998); Cremeans v. International Harvester Co., 452 N.E.2d 1281 (Ohio 1983). See also Ray v. BIC Corp., 925 S.W.2d 527, 532 (Tenn. 1996) (labeling *Barker*'s shift in the burden of proof "aberrant"); Dart v. Wiebe Mfg., Inc., 709 P.2d 876 (Ariz. 1985) (en banc) (by implication).

unfairly requires it to prove a negative. For these and other reasons, leading tort law scholars viewed *Barker*'s shift in the burden of proof as plainly wrong.[302]

Putting aside the troublesome shift in the burden of proof on the risk-utility prong, *Barker*'s basic two-pronged approach to defining design defects makes good sense in many respects. And it is far more forthright and intelligible than artful definitions of consumer expectations and risk-utility in terms of one another. In addition to simple clarity, an advantage of the two-pronged approach is that each test shores up the weaknesses of the other. When used independently as the exclusive test of design defectiveness, both the consumer expectations and risk-utility tests must be expanded past their fair limits to provide liability in some cases where it is appropriate. Thus, plaintiffs are helped by the two-pronged approach, because they get to bite the apple on both sides. But this test also provides benefits for defendants and the courts. Defendants may be advantaged by the paring down of both tests to their leanest forms, where the proofs may be clearer and results more predictable from each test. And courts may benefit in the same respect from the improvement in logic and clarity from narrowing down the tests to permit them to establish proper norms of responsibility for their own particular realms. Despite the benefits of such a lean, two-pronged definitional approach, however, such a standard must be shaped carefully around the inherent weaknesses of the consumer expectations test—its derogation of the interests of bystanders, its indeterminacy in evaluating complex designs, and its bar to claims involving obvious dangers that could easily have been designed away.

Complex *vs.* Simple Designs—the *Soule* Approach

From the very earliest days of modern products liability law, courts and commentators turned to the risk-utility test to avoid applying the consumer expectations test to cases involving vague expectations concerning complex designs.[303] In one early case, *Heaton v. Ford Motor Co.*,[304] the driver of a pickup hit a 5- or 6-inch rock, damaging the wheel, which caused the truck to leave the road and tip over. In making a claim for design defectiveness under § 402A, the plaintiff introduced no risk-utility evidence of the costs or feasibility of designing a stronger wheel but relied exclusively on the consumer expectations test to prove his case. Affirming a nonsuit against the plaintiff, the Oregon Supreme Court ruled that, without evidence on the costs and benefits of designing the wheel more strongly, the jury did not have the necessary tools to render a principled decision: without such data, it could only speculate on the reasonableness of the wheel's design.[305] Put otherwise, the complexity of the engineering trade-offs involved in the

---

[302] "The rule places an enormous burden on the concept of a 'product design that proximately causes injury,' a burden which the concept seems ill-equipped to handle. . . . People fall off ladders all the time, and the fact that ladders are both high and in some general way unstable enables these falls to occur. Does it or doesn't it follow that in every case of a person's falling off a ladder, the ladder's design proximately causes the fall?" G. Schwartz, Foreword: Understanding Products Liability, 67 Cal. L. Rev. 435, 466–67 (1979). See also Prosser and Keeton on Torts § 99 at 702; Wade, On Product "Design Defects" and Their Actionability, 33 Vand. L. Rev. 551, 573 (1980).

[303] See, e.g., Wade, On the Nature of Strict Tort Liability for Products, 44 Miss. L.J. 825, 829 (1973) (criticizing use of consumer expectations test in cases where "the consumer would not know what to expect, because he would have no idea how safe the product could be made").

[304] 435 P.2d 806 (Or. 1967).

[305] "Where the jury has no experiential basis for knowing this, the record must supply such a basis. In the absence of either common experience or evidence, any verdict would, in effect, be the jury's opinion of how strong the product *should* be. Such an opinion by the jury would be formed without the benefit of data concerning the cost or feasibility of designing and building stronger products. Without reference to relevant factual data, the jury has no special qualifications for deciding what is reasonable." Id. at 809.

wheel's design rendered consumer expectations unsuitable as a test of its adequacy. Instead, the risk-utility test's factors of feasibility, costs, and benefits were needed to ascertain the sufficiency of the design. Several years later, the Oregon courts took the final plunge by abandoning the consumer expectations test in favor of a risk-utility test requiring proof of a feasible alternative design.[306]

After the California Supreme Court decided *Barker v. Lull Engineering Co.* in 1978,[307] other courts began to view consumer expectations and risk-utility as compatible rather than mutually exclusive ways to define a design defect.[308] Some courts that followed *Barker* in adopting a two-pronged test for design defects began to limit the consumer expectations prong to cases where consumers have meaningful expectations on a product's safety. For example, rather than abandoning the consumer expectations test altogether, the Supreme Court of Arizona, in a 1985 decision that adopted the *Barker* two-pronged approach, limited the consumer expectations test to cases where such expectations are well-defined, requiring the risk-utility test in cases where consumer expectations are vague.[309] The next year, the Supreme Court of Colorado adopted the *Barker* two-pronged test,[310] observing the following year that the consumer expectations test was inappropriate for judging the adequacy of complex designs.[311]

By the 1990s, it had become quite clear that the consumer expectations test was a poor gauge for ascertaining the adequacy of complex designs. In 1994 the California Supreme Court, in *Soule v. General Motors Corp.*,[312] squarely confronted the vagueness problem inherent in *Barker*'s consumer expectations prong. The plaintiff's ankles were fractured when the Chevrolet Camaro she was driving collided with another vehicle at a closing speed of 50–60 miles per hour. She sued the manufacturer, asserting that the design of her automobile was defective because its left front wheel broke free, collapsed rearward, and smashed the toe pan and floorboard into her feet. In particular, she claimed that the configuration of the car's frame, and the bracket attaching the wheel assembly to it, were defectively designed because they did not limit the wheel's rearward travel in the event the bracket should fail. At trial, the parties disagreed on the angle and force of the impact and the extent to which the toe pan had actually deformed.

---

[306] See, e.g., Roach v. Kononen, 525 P.2d 125 (Or. 1974); Phillips v. Kimwood Mach. Co., 525 P.2d 1033 (Or. 1974); Wilson v. Piper Aircraft Corp., 577 P.2d 1322 (Or. 1978); Willamette Essential Oils, Inc. v. Herrold & Jensen Implement Co., 683 P.2d 1374 (Or. Ct. App. 1984); Wood v. Ford Motor Co., 691 P.2d 495 (Or. Ct. App. 1984). In 1979, the Oregon legislature essentially adopted Rest. (2d) Torts § 402A, including its comments defining "defective" and "unreasonably dangerous" in consumer contemplation terms. See Or. Rev. Stat. Ann. § 30.920(3). While at least one Oregon court interpreted the statute to require use of the consumer expectations test alone, Burns v. General Motors Corp., 891 P.2d 1354 (Or. Ct. App. 1995), the resiliency of the risk-utility test was illustrated by subsequent decisions reintroducing risk-utility analysis as a basis for design defectiveness in complex cases. See, e.g., McCathern v. Toyota Motor Corp., 23 P.3d 320, 330–32 (Or. 2001) (risk-utility evidence may be required to prove consumer expectations).

[307] 573 P.2d 443 (Cal. 1978).

[308] See, e.g., Biosera, Inc. v. Forma Scientific, Inc., 941 P.2d 284, 287 (Colo. App. 1996) (The two tests "are not mutually exclusive. Rather, a court should review each to determine if it is an appropriate standard for judging the dangerous nature of the product at issue."), aff'd on other grounds, 960 P.2d 108 (Colo. 1998).

[309] Dart v. Wiebe Mfg., Inc., 709 P.2d 876 (Ariz. 1985).

[310] Ortho Pharm. Corp. v. Heath, 722 P.2d 410 (Colo. 1986) (by implication), overruled on other grounds by Armentrout v. FMC Corp., 842 P.2d 175 (Colo. 1992).

[311] See Camacho v. Honda Motor Co., 741 P.2d 1240, 1246–47 (Colo. 1987) ("exclusive reliance upon consumer expectations is a particularly inappropriate means of determining [defectiveness] where both the unreasonableness of the danger in the design defect and the efficacy of alternative designs in achieving a reasonable degree of safety must be defined primarily by technical, scientific information").

[312] 882 P.2d 298 (Cal. 1994).

Design defectiveness and causation both were addressed by numerous experts on biomechanics, metallurgy, orthopedics, design engineering, crash-test simulation, and other matters. Plaintiff's experts, relying on crash tests, metallurgical analysis, and other evidence, explained how the damage to her car would have been minimized had it been properly designed. Defendant's experts attempted to refute these claims by explaining how plaintiff's ankle injuries were caused by the force of the collision and her failure to wear a seatbelt rather than any defect in the car. The trial court instructed the jury on the consumer expectations test, and the jury returned a verdict for the plaintiff.

On appeal, an important question in *Soule* was whether the trial court had erred in instructing the jury on the consumer expectations test in a case in which the common experience of product users does not provide a basis for determining how safely the product should have performed. The intermediate appellate court affirmed the judgment for the plaintiff, and the defendant appealed to the California Supreme Court. The Supreme Court held that the trial court had erred in instructing the jury on the consumer expectations test on the facts of the case.[313] The court noted that it previously had explained, in *Barker v. Lull Engineering Co.*,[314] that a proper assessment of the costs, benefits, and practicality inherent in appropriate design defect determinations requires risk-utility balancing rather than a gauge of consumer expectations.[315] The court there had cited automotive crashworthiness litigation as an example of the kind of complex case in which the feasibility, costs, and benefits of particular designs are "implicit" in an evaluation of the quality of the manufacturer's design decision.[316] Distinguishing a prior decision, *Campbell v. General Motors Corp.*,[317] in which it had held that consumer expectations were a proper gauge for judging the design adequacy of a bus without a "grab bar" within easy reach of the plaintiff's seat, the *Soule* court reasoned that the safety issue in that case was a matter of common understanding. In such situations, where simple product safety issues about which consumers and jurors have a common understanding of widely accepted minimum safety expectations, and where expert testimony on defectiveness normally would invade the province of the jury, the consumer expectations test of *Barker*'s first prong is appropriate.[318]

Courts should apply the risk-utility test alone to accidents involving complex risk tradeoffs requiring expert engineering or scientific explanation, *Soule* explained, because such accident situations ordinarily do not intelligibly engage the reasonable minimum safety expectations of consumers.[319] Thus, in automotive crashworthiness situations, consumers typically have "no idea" how safely their vehicles should have performed in the particular circumstances of a crash. In such cases, "the jury must consider the manufacturer's evidence of competing design considerations, and the issue of design defect cannot fairly be resolved by standardless reference to the 'expectations'

---

313 Id. at 307–08. But the error was harmless. See note 322, below.

314 573 P.2d 443 (Cal. 1978).

315 *Soule*, 882 P.2d at 305.

316 *Barker*, 573 P.2d at 456.

317 649 P.2d 224 (Cal. 1982).

318 So, the consumer expectations test of *Barker*'s first prong is reserved "for cases in which the *everyday experience* of the product's users permits a conclusion that the product's design violated minimum safety assumptions, and is thus defective *regardless of expert opinion about the merits of the design*." *Soule*, 882 P.2d at 308 (emphasis in original).

319 Id.

of an 'ordinary consumer.' "[320] Because safety performance mechanisms in such cases typically are complex, and consumer safety expectations are commensurably vague, juries must turn to "the balancing of risks and benefits required by the second prong of *Barker*."[321] The *Soule* court thus concluded that the jury should *not* have been instructed on the consumer expectations test because the plaintiff's design defect theory involved complex technical and mechanical issues.[322]

Soule's allocation of the consumer expectations and risk-utility tests to their best uses—the former to designs involving simple safety issues (where expert testimony may be improper) and the latter to designs involving complex cost-benefit tradeoffs (where expert testimony is required)—makes basically very good sense.[323] For this reason, many courts have adopted *Soule*'s approach of applying design defect tests based on the complexity or simplicity of a product's design, or risk mechanisms,[324] while others have rejected the complex *vs.* simple product approach outright.[325]

Yet, selecting defect tests on the basis of whether a product is "simple" or "complex" can result in serious mischief if it is used to deprive plaintiffs of a right to employ the risk-utility test in cases where a simple risk is obvious, such as a lighter not equipped with a simple child-proof design.[326] Courts dividing design defect tests along *Soule* lines

---

[320] Id.

[321] Id. at 308–09.

[322] An ordinary car buyer "cannot reasonably expect that a car's frame, suspension, or interior will be designed to remain intact in any and all accidents. Nor would ordinary experience and understanding inform such a consumer how safely [a car's] design should perform under the esoteric circumstances of the collision at issue here. Indeed, both parties assumed that quite complicated design considerations were at issue, and that expert testimony was necessary to illuminate these matters. Therefore, injection of ordinary consumer expectations into the design defect equation was improper." Id. at 310. Nevertheless, because of the voluminous evidence presented on the costs and benefits of the Camaro's design, the court saw no reason to believe that the jury ignored the risk-utility issue and only relied on the consumer expectations test. [Thus], the court held that the trial court's error in instructing the jury on the consumer expectations prong was harmless. Id. at 311.

[323] See Kennedy, The Role of the Consumer Expectation Test Under Louisiana's Products Liability Tort Doctrine, 69 Tul. L. Rev. 117 (1994).

[324] See, e.g., Verrazono v. Gehl Co., 263 Cal. Rptr. 3d 663, 670 (Ct. App. 2020) (consumer expectations test inapplicable to plaintiff's defect theory that "seeks to examine the behavior of 'obscure components under complex circumstances' outside the ordinary experience of the consumer" such that the defect may only be proved by risk-benefit analysis); Walker v. Ford Motor Co., 406 P.3d 845, 851 (Colo. 2017) (only the risk-benefit test can be used to assess whether a product's design was defective when that issue is "defined primarily by technical, scientific information"); Force v. Ford Motor Co., 879 So.2d 103, 110 (Fla. Dist. Ct. App. 2004) (some products may be "too complex for a logical application of the consumer-expectation standard"); Quintana-Ruiz v. Hyundai Motor Corp., 303 F.3d 62, 77 (1st Cir. 2002) (P.R. law) (the rule against using consumer expectations in a case with "complex technical matters" precludes its use in airbag design defect case); Morson v. Superior Ct., 109 Cal. Rptr. 2d 343, 350–51 (Ct. App. 2001) (consumer expectations test inappropriate to determine design defectiveness of latex gloves that could trigger harmful allergic reactions in certain persons). See also cases cited in note 81, above.

[325] See, e.g., Calles v. Scripto-Tokai Corp., 864 N.E.2d 249, 259 (Ill. 2007) (rejecting "simple product" exception to risk-utility test where 3-year-old killed in fire she started with utility lighter not equipped with child-resistant safety device, and noting that the effect of such an exception would be to relieve manufacturers of design responsibility for obvious dangers); Jackson v. General Motors Corp., 60 S.W.3d 800 (Tenn. 2001) (refusing to limit consumer expectations prong of two-pronged statutory design defect standard to simple product designs).

[326] Compare Todd v. Societe BIC, S.A., 21 F.3d 1402 (7th Cir. 1994) (Ill. law) (holding that Illinois would use consumer expectations prong of its two-pronged test in judging design of simple products with obvious risks; thus, a disposable butane cigarette lighter, not equipped with a child-proof design, is not defective because consumers expect it to ignite when activated), with Robins v. Kroger Co., 80 S.W.3d 641 (Tex. App. 2002) (seller of lighter without child-proof design not entitled to summary judgment on risk-utility test that included consumer expectations as one factor in the balance).

Courts in Michigan, and formerly Illinois, sometimes slipped into this beastly trap. See, e.g., Bates v. Richland Sales Corp., 803 N.E.2d 977 (Ill. App. Ct. 2004) (risk from removing loader's roll bar); Miles v. S.C.

will need to make cautious allowances for these types of cases to avoid resurrecting the patent danger rule, which now is properly defunct.[327]

It will be recalled that *Soule*'s primary example of a "simple product" case appropriate for the consumer expectations test was *Campbell v. General Motors Corp.*, where a bus passenger was thrown from her seat during a sharp turn.[328] The court there held that the consumer expectations test properly allowed a design defect claim without expert testimony, based on the absence of a grab bar in easy reach of the injured passenger's seat, because jurors could decide the issue from common experience.[329] This is true, of course, but the case could have been decided just as easily, and on a more principled risk-utility basis, had the plaintiff introduced evidence of where and how, precisely, grab bars could and should have been installed on this particular model bus.

The *Soule* court's other examples of "simple" risk cases appropriate only for consumer expectations include cars that "explode while idling at stoplights," that "roll over and catch fire in two-mile-per-hour collisions," or new cars that suffer steering or brake failures.[330] Putting aside the implausibility of these hypotheticals, and acknowledging that the consumer expectations test could indeed reasonably resolve such simple product cases, that test is hardly necessary for this purpose in the great majority of states that have the malfunction doctrine previously discussed.[331] Thus, while the *Soule* court nicely explains why the risk-utility test is the only practical and principled way to resolve design defect problems in complex design cases,[332] such as the automotive crashworthiness issues there involved, it fails to make a convincing case for retaining *Barker*'s consumer expectations prong for use in simple risk situations.

Probably the most serious flaw in *Soule*'s relegation of simple product design cases to the consumer expectations test is that it unreasonably dooms plaintiffs to lose most such cases because the dangers in such "simple" cases typically are *obvious* to—and so *expected* by—consumers, a problem previously addressed. This was the conclusion of the Illinois Supreme Court in *Calles v. Scripto-Tokai Corp.*,[333] decided in 2007, which addressed the *Soule* simple-product refinement of *Barker* in a case where a young child used a utility lighter, an Aim 'n Flame, to set a deadly fire. The trial court in *Calles* granted summary judgment to the lighter's manufacturer on the defendant's argument that a lighter without a child-proof safety mechanism was a simple product, restricting the plaintiff to the consumer expectations test which required a ruling for the defendant.[334] Reversing, the intermediate court of appeal held that the lighter was not "the kind of especially simple device" that rendered risk-utility balancing "too obvious

---

Johnson & Son, Inc., 2002 WL 1303131 (N.D. Ill. 2002) (obvious danger to young child who eats crystal Drano drain cleaner). Compare Mills v. Curioni, Inc., 238 F. Supp. 2d 876, 892 (E.D. Mich. 2002) ("It is only when a 'simple tool' is involved that the 'open and obvious danger' rule will relieve a manufacturer of liability on a design defect claim."), with Cacevic v. Simplimatic Eng'g Co., 617 N.W.2d 386, 392 (Mich. Ct. App. 2000) ("the open and obvious danger doctrine [does not] obviate a manufacturer's duty in a case alleging defective design of a simple product"), vacated in part on other grounds, 625 N.W.2d 784 (Mich. 2001) (table).

[327] See § 10.2, below.

[328] 649 P.2d 224, 225 (Cal. 1982).

[329] Id. at 232–33.

[330] *Soule*, 882 P.2d at 308 n.3.

[331] See § 7.4, above.

[332] *Soule*, 882 P.2d at 309.

[333] 864 N.E.2d 249, 256–57 (Ill. 2007).

[334] Id. at 254.

for trial."[335] Affirming, the Illinois Supreme Court refused to limit its *Barker*-like two-pronged design defect test by *Soule*'s mandated use of the consumer expectations prong in simple-product cases because of the perverse effect of such a result in many obvious danger situations.[336] Instead, the *Calles* court ruled that, even in simple risk cases, the risk-utility test remained an available standard, and the obvious nature of the danger was just one consideration in the multi-factor evaluation of a dangerous design.[337]

The next year, the Illinois Supreme Court exhaustively reevaluated its design defect jurisprudence in *Mikolajczyk v. Ford Motor Co.*[338] While declining to adopt the *Third Restatement*'s § 2(b) definition of design defects, the court nevertheless did adopt the *Restatement*'s broadly inclusive risk-utility formulation, a liability standard that includes consumer expectations along with other relevant factors.[339] Read together, *Calles* and *Mikolajczyk* suggest that Illinois skipped over *Soule* and jumped to the essence of the *Third Restatement*'s design defect approach in § 2(b), examined later.[340]

While restricting plaintiffs to the consumer expectations test in simple-product cases may be justified in abstract autonomy terms of promoting personal responsibility, courts unanimously crossed that policy bridge years ago by rejecting the patent danger rule in design defect cases in favor of social utility.[341] The California Supreme Court should be credited with substantially advancing the search for an ideal design defect liability standard in moving away from a consumer expectations standard toward risk-utility, first in *Barker* and further in *Soule*—a progression that leaves this court just a single step from recognizing the virtue in the *Third Restatement*'s evaluation of design defectiveness by a unitary risk-utility standard that felicitously folds consumer expectations into a wide family of flexible factors.[342]

Courts that have defined consumer expectations in terms of risk-utility, the *Tabert-Potter* approach discussed above,[343] have effectively chosen to follow the *Barker-Soule* approach, if by a crooked path. The Connecticut Supreme Court's experience in *Potter v. Chicago Pneumatic Tool Co.*,[344] previously discussed, illustrates this point nicely. There, reasoning that "a consumer's expectations may be viewed in light of various factors that balance the utility of the product's design with the magnitude of its risks,"[345] the court ruled that this risk-utility formulation (that it dubbed a "*modified* consumer expectation test") should be used for complex design cases. Following *Soule*, the *Potter* court further concluded that the "*ordinary* consumer expectation test" should be reserved for use

---

335 832 N.E.2d 409, 416 (Ill. App. Ct. 2005).

336 "[T]he dangers associated with a product that is deemed 'simple' are, by their very nature, open and obvious. . . . [The] adoption of a 'simple product' exception is nothing more than the adoption of a general rule that a manufacturer will not be liable for open and obvious dangers." *Calles*, 864 N.E.2d at 258–59.

337 Id. at 260.

338 901 N.E.2d 329 (Ill. 2008).

339 Id. at 352 (adopting a formulation of the risk-utility test in which "consumer expectations are included within the scope of the broader risk-utility test"). Compare Kirk v. Clark Equip. Co., 991 F.3d 865, 878 (7th Cir. 2021) (Ill. law) ("if the evidence before the court implicates the risk-utility test, it is the one that the court should use, 'because the latter [i.e., the consumer-expectations test] is incorporated into the former and is but one factor among many for the jury to consider' ") (citing *Mikolajczyk*, 901 N.E.2d at 352).

340 See § 8.8, below.

341 See § 10.2, below.

342 The Restatement approach is examined in § 8.8, below.

343 See note 81, above.

344 694 A.2d 1319 (Conn. 1997).

345 Id. at 1333.

"when the everyday experience of the particular product's users permits the inference that the product did not meet minimum safety expectations."[346] In so doing, *Potter* established its own version of a two-pronged *Barker-Soule* test—with the first prong being an "ordinary" consumer expectations test, limited to simple design cases, and the second prong being a risk-utility test (window-dressed as a "modified" consumer expectation test), for application in complex cases. *Potter*'s basic result is sound, but tying the risk-utility prong to consumer expectations sows seeds of confusion for future design defect litigation. Yet *Potter* also contains an important insight: that risk-utility analysis should be turned to when "ordinary" consumer expectations fail to provide a rational basis for recovery.[347] Two decades after *Potter*, in *Bifolck v. Philip Morris, Inc.*,[348] the Connecticut Supreme Court fully reconsidered its design defect tests, renaming its "modified consumer expectations test" the "risk-utility test." In a comprehensive analysis of the issues, the court announced a two-pronged, combined design defect definition that drew from both § 402A of the *Second Restatement* and the *Third Restatement*.

As cost-benefit analysis gathers strength around the globe as the dominant method for judging whether a product's design is adequately safe,[349] courts and legislatures continue to search for ways to accommodate consumer expectations without banishing it altogether from design defect determinations.[350] Even the *Products Liability Restatement*, though assigning consumer expectations to a secondary position as a mere factor in the risk-utility balance, recognizes that consumer expectations may play an important—sometimes decisive—role in assessing design defectiveness.[351] The approach of some courts in defining consumer expectations and risk-utility in terms of one another may accommodate both perspectives, but does so through a sleight of hand that muddies products liability jurisprudence. The *Barker* two-pronged test for design defectiveness achieves the same objectives, more clearly and intelligibly, but the burden of proof should be left on plaintiffs for both prongs. Moreover, the consumer expectations prong should be limited to simple design dangers, as in *Soule* and *Potter*, yet, with one vital enhancement—that the risk-utility prong be retained for use in simple design cases where the risks are widely known or obvious, or imposed on bystanders. Combining the consumer expectations and risk-utility tests along these lines may provide an optimal standard for judging design defectiveness.[352]

---

[346] Id. (emphasis added).

[347] As, presumably, in obvious danger cases. *Potter* emphasized that only the risk-utility test (dubbed the "*modified* consumer expectations test"), not the ("ordinary") consumer expectation test, should be used in cases where the consumer expectations test does not provide relief. Id. at 1334.

[348] 152 A.3d 1183, 1202–03 (Conn. 2016).

[349] This trend is not limited to the United States. See § 1.4, above.

[350] See, e.g., Ferraro v. Hewlett-Packard Co., 721 F.3d 842, 848 (7th Cir. 2013) (Ill. law) ("Where the two tests yield conflicting results, . . . the risk-utility test 'trumps,' and the product is deemed not unreasonably dangerous (notwithstanding consumers' expectations that the product would be safer)."); Pritchett v. Cottrell, Inc., 512 F.3d 1057, 1063–64 (8th Cir. 2008) (Mo. law) (though Missouri formally follows the consumer expectations test, the ultimate issue is whether a product is "unreasonably dangerous," so that litigants may argue "that the utility of a design outweighs its risks, or that consumer expectations were violated, or any other theory of unreasonable dangerousness supported by the evidence"); Mikolajczyk v. Ford Motor Co., 901 N.E.2d 329, 352 (Ill. 2008) (rejecting Third Restatement's definition of design defect, but adopting a formulation of the risk-utility test in which "consumer expectations are included within the scope of the broader risk-utility test"); Glenn v. Overhead Door Corp., 935 So.2d 1074, 1081 (Miss. Ct. App. 2006) ("the Products Liability Act requires the manufacturer's product to pass both the risk-utility and the consumer expectations tests"); Miss. Code Ann. § 11–1–63(b).

[351] See § 8.8, below.

[352] Such a test might look something like the following:

§ 8.7 CONSTRUCTIVE KNOWLEDGE—THE WADE-KEETON TEST

In holding manufacturers responsible for defects in design, courts and commentators have always sought to avoid absolute liability, recognizing that the concepts of design safety and design danger are matters of degree involving trade-offs between a product's usefulness, cost, and safety.[353] The idea of a design defect, in other words, has long been understood to rest on the idea of reasonable balance.[354] Because negligence itself is grounded on both reasonableness and balance, one is led to inquire whether and how negligence and strict liability may differ in design defect litigation. Accordingly, in the 1960s, products liability scholars began to search for a way to define strict liability for selling products with defects in design (and warning) in a manner that distinguished the strict liability standard from mere negligence.

Other than Dean Prosser, the two most prominent tort law scholars in the 1960s who shared a special interest in products liability law were Dean Page Keeton of the University of Texas and Dean John Wade of Vanderbilt University. As modern products liability law was just beginning to emerge in the 1960s, the two deans, both advisers to the American Law Institute's *Restatement (Second) of Torts* that was then in progress, offered separate versions of a similar definition of product defectiveness that distinguished negligence-based responsibility from liability called "strict" in a fundamental way.

At this time, courts and commentators were just beginning to feel their way around the new precept of holding manufacturers of defective products "strictly" accountable for injuries to remote consumers.[355] Little thought was being devoted to how the new field might be divided up, for purposes of the standard of liability, according to different types of defect.[356] Thus, as with most other scholars of the day, the search by Deans Keeton and Wade for an appropriate "test" of strict liability was a search for a single liability standard that alone would embrace most products liability problems of the day.[357]

> A simple product design is defective if it fails to perform as safely as an ordinary consumer fairly would expect, and any design is defective if it reasonably should have been designed more safely. A product reasonably should have been designed more safely if the foreseeable safety benefits of an untaken design precaution clearly would have exceeded its foreseeable costs, including any diminished usefulness or safety.

The liability standard suggested here limits design defect determinations to situations where a manufacturer's cost-benefit decisions are "clearly" wrong in order to maximize product diversity and, hence, consumer choice among a wide range of products with differing, yet acceptable, balances of cost, utility, and safety.

[353] See ch. 5, above.

[354] See, e.g., Owen, Defectiveness Restated: Exploding the "Strict" Products Liability Myth, 1996 U. Ill. L. Rev. 743, 754–61.

[355] See §§ 5.3 and 5.4, above.

[356] See § 6.2, above. This is not to say that certain scholars of the day did not perceive a great divide between manufacturing and design defects, for they did. See, e.g., Keeton, Products Liability—Liability Without Fault and the Requirement of a Defect, 41 Tex. L. Rev. 855, 859 (1963).

[357] Especially in the 1960s, the case law was quite limited, and, like other scholars of the time, both Deans Keeton and Wade drew on various examples of defects in manufacturing, design, and warnings.

The test developed by Deans Keeton and Wade, which in time became known as the "Wade-Keeton" test,[358] quite simply was a negligence test stripped of scienter.[359] That is, both scholars proposed defining defectiveness in terms of whether a manufacturer or other seller with full knowledge of its product's dangerous condition would be negligent in selling it in that condition. By requiring a seller to know its product's risks, commensurately relieving an injured plaintiff of the burden of proving the foreseeability of those risks, this test imposes on the seller "constructive knowledge" of any dangers its products may possess.[360]

In 1961, two years before Judge Roger Traynor penned his opinion in *Greenman v. Yuba Power Products, Inc.*,[361] three years before Dean William Prosser submitted to the ALI his draft of *Restatement (Second) of Torts* § 402A applicable to products generally,[362] and four years before Dean Wade first offered a similar proposal, Dean Page Keeton authored a little article in the Texas Law Review in which he first articulated a liability test for product defects that was truly strict. At the conclusion of the article in which he examined the various techniques by which courts were holding manufacturers accountable for injuries from defective products, in both tort and warranty,[363] Dean Keeton proposed that a product should *not* be considered defective "if a reasonable man with full knowledge of all the properties and the danger therein, would continue to market the product because the utility of its use outweighs the danger."[364]

Two years later, Dean Keeton hinted at this test in another article in the Texas Law Review,[365] and then, in 1964, in an article exploring the nature of strict products liability,[366] he explained that courts had imposed strict manufacturer liability when "the product was so dangerous to the user in the condition that it was in that a reasonable man would not have sold it in such condition with knowledge of such a condition and appreciation of the danger. The manufacturer would have been negligent except for his excusable ignorance of the danger."[367]

In numerous other articles, from 1966 to at least 1980, Dean Keeton recommended and refined his test of design defectiveness. In his later articles, he emphasized that a design's risks should be determined at the date of trial, which of course imposes constructive knowledge on the manufacturer at the time of first design and sale: "A

[358] See, e.g., Privette v. CSX Transp., Inc., 79 Fed. Appx. 879, 889 (6th Cir. 2003) (Tenn. law) (referring to this standard more fully as "the Wade-Keeton prudent manufacturer test"); Brooks v. Beech Aircraft Corp., 902 P.2d 54, 63 (N.M. 1995); Cupp and Polage, The Rhetoric of Strict Liability Versus Negligence: An Empirical Analysis, 77 N.Y.U. L. Rev. 874, 884 (2002).

[359] See, e.g., Wade, On the Nature of Strict Tort Liability for Products, 44 Miss. L.J. 825, 834–35 (1973). The Wade-Keeton test is examined from a state-of-the-art perspective in § 10.4, below.

[360] See, e.g., Phillips v. Kimwood Mach. Co., 525 P.2d 1033 (Or. 1974).

[361] 377 P.2d 897 (Cal. 1963).

[362] The ALI approved § 402A when Dean Prosser presented it in final form, applicable to products generally, in 1964. See § 5.3, above.

[363] Keeton, Products Liability—Current Developments, 40 Tex. L. Rev. 193 (1961).

[364] Id. at 210. "This is close to a negligence test but not the same [because] excusable ignorance of a defect or the properties of a product is immaterial. . . ." Id. In his full discussion, Dean Keeton mistakenly confuses the negative and positive formulations of the standard.

[365] Keeton, Products Liability—Liability Without Fault and the Requirement of a Defect, 41 Tex. L. Rev. 855, 867–68 (1963).

[366] Keeton, Products Liability—The Nature and Extent of Strict Liability, 1964 U. Ill. L.F. 693, 702.

[367] Id.

product is defectively designed [if] the magnitude of the danger in fact of the design as it is proved to be at the trial outweighs the utility of the design."[368]

In 1965, in an article[369] in which he cited both of Dean Keeton's Texas articles,[370] Dean John Wade offered a nearly identical strict liability test for ascertaining whether a product is unreasonably dangerous: "assuming that the defendant had knowledge of the condition of the product, would he then have been acting unreasonably in placing it on the market?"[371] Further, Dean Wade remarked: "If the test is equivalent to that of whether a reasonable prudent man would put it on the market if he knew of the dangers of this particular article, then the elements for determining negligence are relevant. We have here again the problem of balancing the utility of the risk against the magnitude of the risk."[372]

In his famous 1973 article in the Mississippi Law Journal,[373] Dean Wade restated his version of the test:

> The simplest and easiest way [to define defectiveness] is to assume that the defendant knew of the dangerous condition of the product and ask whether he was then negligent in putting it on the market or supplying it to someone else. In other words, the scienter is supplied as a matter of law, and there is no need for the plaintiff to prove its existence as a matter of fact. Once given this notice of the dangerous condition of the chattel, the question then becomes whether the defendant was negligent. . . . Another way of saying this is to ask whether the magnitude of the risk created by the dangerous condition of the product was outweighed by the social utility attained by putting it out in this fashion.[374]

Just why the "Wade-Keeton" test was labeled precisely as it was is shrouded in the mists of time,[375] but its name is surely backwards. Not only does it appear to have been

---

[368] Keeton, Products Liability—Design Hazards and the Meaning of Defect, 10 Cumb. L. Rev. 293, 314–15 (1979). In this article, Dean Keeton noted that his test "differs from negligence primarily because, as proposed, the danger in fact as proven at trial determines whether a product is good or bad. . . . When the negligence of the defendant is in issue, it is perceivable danger at the time the product was designed that is the basis for weighing danger against utility. Therefore, a clear difference between proof of negligence and proof of defect as a basis for recovery is apparent." Id. at 314–15.

In a footnote, Dean Keeton pointed out that the difference between the two tests was the requirement for negligence that the danger be foreseeable, whereas, under his "strict" liability test, "it is irrelevant that the defendant did not know or had no reason to know of the danger." Id. at 315 n.87.

[369] Wade, Strict Tort Liability of Manufacturers, 19 Sw. L.J. 5 (1965). The article arose out of a products liability symposium the year before in Dallas, Texas where both deans presented papers.

[370] Id. at 12, 13 n.45.

[371] Id. at 15.

[372] Id. at 17.

[373] Wade, On the Nature of Strict Tort Liability for Products, 44 Miss. L.J. 825 (1973).

[374] Id. at 834–35. Dean Wade also recommended how the jury might be instructed on this test:

> A [product] is not duly safe if it is so likely to be harmful to person [or property] that a reasonable prudent manufacturer [supplier], who had actual knowledge of its harmful character would not place it on the market. It is not necessary to find that this defendant had knowledge of the harmful character of the [product] in order to determine that it was not duly safe.

Id. at 839–40.

[375] The dual origins of the test were noted at least as early as 1974, see Phillips v. Kimwood Mach. Co., 525 P.2d 1033, 1036 n.6 (Or. 1974), and the "Wade-Keeton" moniker appeared in print no later than 1978. See Cepeda v. Cumberland Eng'g Co., 386 A.2d 816, 829 (N.J. 1978). See also Birnbaum, Unmasking the Test for Design Defect: From Negligence [to Warranty] to Strict Liability to Negligence, 33 Vand. L. Rev. 593, 619 n.125 (1980).

invented by Dean Keeton in 1961,[376] four years before Dean Wade first proposed it, but Dean Keeton spread the theory far and wide. Dean Wade, who appears to have borrowed the idea for the test from Dean Keeton,[377] may have offered the test in the law journals merely twice, in 1965 and 1973.[378] By contrast, Dean Keeton proposed and explained the test in law journals and his products liability casebook at least a dozen times, from 1961 at least to 1980.[379]

Be that as it may, a number of courts, themselves searching for a basis by which to distinguish strict liability design claims (and warning claims) from those in negligence, picked up quite early on the Wade-Keeton hindsight test (sometimes referred to as the prudent-manufacturer test).[380] Perhaps the first such case was *Dorsey v. Yoder*,[381] where the court stated that the proper test for strict products liability in tort is "whether a reasonable manufacturer would continue to market his product in the same condition as he sold it to the plaintiff with knowledge of the potential dangerous consequences the trial just revealed."[382]

More prominently, in *Phillips v. Kimwood Machine Co.*,[383] the Supreme Court of Oregon embraced the test in 1974. A worker injured when a commercial sanding machine ejected a fiberboard sheet sued the manufacturer for failing either to warn of the danger or equip the machine with an inexpensive line of metal teeth that would have prevented the expulsion without interfering with the functioning of the machine. Reversing a summary judgment for the manufacturer, the court formulated the test in the following terms:

> A dangerously defective article would be one which a reasonable person would not put into the stream of commerce *if he had knowledge of its harmful character*. The test, therefore, is whether the seller would be negligent if he

---

376 In Keeton, Products Liability—Current Developments, 40 Tex. L. Rev. 193, 210 (1961).

377 It should be noted that Dean Wade reported that, at the time he wrote his Southwestern Law Journal article in 1964–65, he had not even read Dean Keeton's 1961 Texas article. Wade, On the Effect in Product Liability of Knowledge Unavailable Prior to Marketing, 58 N.Y.U. L. Rev. 734, 761 (1983) ("Postscript: An Excursus on the 'Wade-Keeton' Approach"). By 1983, Dean Wade appears to have forgotten that he cited both of Dean Keeton's 1961 and 1962 Texas articles in his own article in the Southwestern Law Journal. See Wade, Strict Tort Liability of Manufacturers, 19 Sw. L.J. 5, 12, 13 n.45 (1965).

378 My research on this point was not exhaustive and may have missed Dean Wade's endorsement of the test somewhere else.

379 In addition to Dean Keeton's articles cited elsewhere in this section, see, e.g., W.P. Keeton, D. Owen, and J. Montgomery, Products Liability and Safety 245 n.1 (1980); Keeton, The Meaning of Defect in Products Liability Law—A Review of Basic Principles, 45 Mo. L. Rev. 579, 592 (1980); Keeton, Product Liability and the Meaning of Defect, 5 St. Mary's L.J. 30, 37–38 (1973); Keeton, Products Liability—Drugs and Cosmetics, 25 Vand. L. Rev. 131, 144 (1972); Keeton, Product Liability—Inadequacy of Information, 48 Tex. L. Rev. 398, 402–03 (1970); Keeton, Manufacturer's Liability: The Meaning of "Defect" in the Manufacture and Design of Products, 20 Syracuse L. Rev. 559, 568 (1969); Keeton, Some Observations About the Strict Liability of the Maker of Prescription Drugs: The Aftermath of MER/29, 56 Cal. L. Rev. 149, 158 (1968); Keeton, Products Liability—Some Observations About Allocation of Risks, 64 Mich. L. Rev. 1329, 1336 (1966).

380 Early examples include Dorsey v. Yoder Co., 331 F. Supp. 753, 759–60 (E.D. Pa. 1971), aff'd, 474 F.2d 1339 (3d Cir. 1973); Phillips v. Kimwood Mach. Co., 525 P.2d 1033, 1036 (Or. 1974); Cepeda v. Cumberland Eng'g Co., 386 A.2d 816, 829 (N.J. 1978). See generally Dart v. Wiebe Mfg., Inc., 709 P.2d 876 (Ariz. 1985).

381 331 F. Supp. 753 (E.D. Pa. 1971).

382 Id. at 759–60 (emphasis omitted) (citing Keeton, Manufacturer's Liability: The Meaning of "Defect" in the Manufacture and Design of Products, 20 Syracuse L. Rev. 559, 568 (1969)).

383 525 P.2d 1033 (Or. 1974).

sold the article *knowing of the risk involved.* Strict liability imposes what amounts to constructive knowledge of the condition of the product.[384]

In the 1980s, however, courts and commentators began to question the fairness and logic of imposing strict liability for design defectiveness,[385] and the only other truly strict test of products liability, the consumer expectations test, had already begun its decline.[386] Recognizing the problems in forcing truly strict liability on manufacturers for dangers in design, Dean Wade and Dean Keeton, in the early 1980s, both repudiated the test that bore their names: Dean Wade asserted that he never meant what he had said,[387] and Dean Keeton admitted that he no longer believed what he had said.[388] The *Products Liability Restatement*, adopting a negligence-like risk-utility standard of liability, based explicitly on risks that are foreseeable at the time of sale, candidly rejects the Wade-Keeton test and notes with pith: "The idea has not worn well with time."[389] Most courts focusing on the state-of-the-art issue have agreed, rejecting the hindsight test and limiting a manufacturer's responsibility to risks that are foreseeable.[390]

Despite the rejection of the Wade-Keeton test by the scholars who gave it birth, some courts continued to adopt the test after its "official" demise in the early 1980s,[391]

---

[384] Id. at 1036 (emphasis in original). "The advantage of describing a dangerous defect in the manner of Wade and Keeton is that it preserves the use of familiar terms and thought processes with which courts, lawyers, and jurors customarily deal." Id. at 1037. Moreover, "[w]hile apparently judging the seller's conduct, the test set out above would actually be a characterization of the product by a jury. If the manufacturer was not acting reasonably in selling the product, knowing of the risks involved, then the product would be dangerously defective when sold and the manufacturer would be subject to liability." Id. See also Vetri, Products Liability: The Developing Framework for Analysis, 54 Or. L. Rev. 293, 299 (1975).

[385] See §§ 5.4, 8.1, and 8.4, above.

[386] See §§ 5.4, 5.6, 8.3, and 8.4, above.

[387] See Wade, On the Effect in Product Liability of Knowledge Unavailable Prior to Marketing, Postscript, 58 N.Y.U. L. Rev. 734, 761 (1983).

[388] See Prosser and Keeton on Torts § 99 at 697–98 n.21 (5th ed. 1984).

[389] See Reporters' Note to § 2 cmt. m.

[390] The Wade-Keeton test was traditionally used in both design and warning defect cases, but it most frequently arises as a factual issue in toxic substance cases involving claims of inadequate warnings of hidden danger. For examples of the rejection of a hindsight approach in both contexts, see, e.g., D'Agnese v. Novartis Pharms. Corp., 952 F. Supp. 2d 880 (D. Ariz. 2013) (dismissing failure to warn case where risk was unforeseeable, since hindsight test inapplicable to such cases); Georgia Pac., LLC v. Farrar, 69 A.3d 1028 (Md. 2013) (asbestos manufacturer had no duty to warn in 1968–69 of risk to granddaughter who contracted mesothelioma from asbestos dust on grandfather's work clothes that she regularly washed):

> [U]nder § 402A . . . "[a] manufacturer cannot warn of dangers that were not known to it or knowable in light of the *generally recognized and prevailing* scientific and technical knowledge available at the time of manufacture and distribution." As the . . . courts have pointed out, any other rule would make the manufacturer not just *strictly,* but *absolutely* liable—an insurer of the product's safety—and that is not the law.

Id. at 1036. See also Mack v. Stryker Corp., 893 F. Supp. 2d 976, 988 (D. Minn. 2012) (granting defendant's motion for summary judgment; "The Court will not subject Stryker to liability based on speculation and hindsight."); Williams v. Wal-Mart Stores E., L.P., 99 So.3d 112, 118 n.6 (Miss. 2012) (same; "the foreseeability inquiry is not governed by hindsight"); Branham v. Ford Motor Co., 701 S.E.2d 5, 17 (S.C. 2010); Vassallo v. Baxter Healthcare Corp., 696 N.E.2d 909 (Mass. 1998); Wagner v. Roche Labs., 671 N.E.2d 252, 256 (Ohio 1996); Anderson v. Owens-Corning Fiberglas Corp., 810 P.2d 549 (Cal. 1991) (asbestos); Brown v. Superior Ct., 751 P.2d 470 (Cal. 1988) (DES); Feldman v. Lederle Labs., 479 A.2d 374 (N.J. 1984) (tetracycline drug). See § 10.4, below. On the moral foundations of the foreseeability limitation in tort law, see Owen, Figuring Foreseeability, 44 Wake Forest L. Rev. 1277 (2009).

[391] See, e.g., Sternhagen v. Dow Co., 935 P.2d 1139, 1147 (Mont. 1997) (adopting Wade-Keeton constructive knowledge test for strict products liability, and holding that "knowledge of any undiscovered or undiscoverable dangers should be imputed to the manufacturer").

others continue rotely to restate the test,[392] some seemingly still apply it,[393] and one even proudly reaffirmed allegiance to it while knowing it had died.[394] While one state legislature reversed the judicial adoption of the Wade-Keeton test,[395] another appears to have affirmatively adopted it.[396] One must wonder at its staying power in scattered decisions (and at least one statute) across the nation. The time of the Wade-Keeton test has come and gone, yet its ghost continues to haunt judicial halls.[397]

§ 8.8 DESIGN DEFECTS IN THE THIRD RESTATEMENT

Largely repudiating § 402A of the *Restatement (Second) of Torts*, the *Restatement (Third) of Torts: Products Liability* substantially restructured the principles of responsibility for selling products containing defects in design.[398] Rather than using

[392] See, e.g., Jones v. Medtronic Inc., 411 F. Supp. 3d 521, 532 (D. Ariz. 2019) ("the fact-finder employs a ' "hindsight" test to decide whether it was reasonable for a manufacturer . . . to have put the product on the market' "), aff'd sub nom. Jones v. Medtronic, 830 Fed. Appx. 925 (9th Cir. 2020); Sadler v. Advanced Bionics, Inc., 929 F. Supp. 2d 670, 684 (W.D. Ky. 2013); Sobolik v. Briggs & Stratton Power Prods. Grp., LLC, 2011 WL 1258503, at *1 (D. Minn. 2011) ("The distinction between strict liability and negligence in design-defect and failure-to-warn cases is that in strict liability, knowledge of the condition of the product and the risks involved in that condition will be imputed to the manufacturer, whereas in negligence these elements must be proven."); Sternhagen v. Dow Co., 935 P.2d 1139, 1144 (Mont. 1997) ("Strict liability imposes what amounts to constructive knowledge of the condition of the product.").

Courts in California and New York that continue to parrot boilerplate from old decisions may be the worst offenders. See, e.g., City of Pomona v. SQM N. Am. Corp., 801 Fed. Appx. 488, 490 (9th Cir. 2020) (Cal. law) ("the jury must determine 'through hindsight' whether 'the risk of danger inherent in the challenged design outweighs the benefits of such design' "); Reis v. Volvo Cars of N. Am., 18 N.E.3d 383 (N.Y. 2014). It remains unclear if the high court of either state would apply the hindsight test today if faced squarely with the issue.

[393] See, e.g., Monroe v. Zimmer U.S. Inc., 766 F. Supp. 2d 1012, 1038 (E.D. Cal. 2011) (denying defendant's motion for summary judgment, because plaintiff's evidence might show that, "in hindsight, ZAP's design carries with it a risk of inherent danger that outweighs the benefits of its design"); Golonka v. General Motors Corp., 65 P.3d 956, 963–64 (Ariz. Ct. App. 2003). In City of Pomona v. SQM N. Am. Corp., 801 Fed. Appx. 488, 490 (9th Cir. 2020) (2–1 decision) (Cal. law). Dissenting, Lee, J., noted that California courts have not held defendants liable for dangers unknowable at the time of injury for decades. Id at 492.

[394] See Brooks v. Beech Aircraft Corp., 902 P.2d 54, 63 (N.M. 1995), recognizing that the Wade-Keeton test had become a misnomer, but reaffirming it where the facts did not show a true advancement in the technological state of the art:

> [I]n those hypothetical instances in which technology known at the time of trial and technology knowable at the time of distribution differ—and outside of academic rationale we find little to suggest the existence in practice of unknowable design considerations—it is more fair that the manufacturers and suppliers who have profited from the sale of the product bear the risk of loss.

The standard New Mexico jury instruction adopted the Wade-Keeton test from Keeton, Product Liability and the Meaning of Defect, 5 St. Mary's L.J. 30, 37–38 (1973). See *Brooks*, 902 P.2d at 62. The Wade-Keeton test still appears to be the rule in New Mexico. See NMRA, Civ. UJI 13–1407.

[395] In 1979, the Oregon legislature abolished the Wade-Keeton test, that its high court had adopted in Phillips v. Kimwood Mach. Co., 525 P.2d 1033 (Or. 1974), by enacting Rest. (2d) Torts § 402A, including its comments which define defect in consumer contemplation terms. See Or. Rev. Stat. Ann. § 30.920; Burns v. General Motors Corp., 891 P.2d 1354 (Or. Ct. App. 1995) (statute inconsistent with instruction on *Phillips*' reasonable manufacturer test).

[396] See Tenn. Code Ann. § 29–28–102(8). *But see* id. at § 29–28–105. See generally Griffin v. Navistar Inc., 2010 WL 2734043 (W.D. Tenn. 2010) (purporting to apply the test); Brown v. Crown Equip., 181 S.W.3d 268, 281–82 (Tenn. 2005) (same); Irion v. Sun Lighting, Inc., 2004 WL 746823 (Tenn. Ct. App. 2004) (same).

[397] See, e.g., Sobolik v. Briggs & Stratton Power Prods. Grp., LLC, 2011 WL 1258503, at *1 (D. Minn. 2011) (noting that, in strict liability design and warning cases, "knowledge of the condition of the product and the risks involved in that condition will be imputed to the manufacturer"); Bugosh v. I.U. N. Am., Inc., 971 A.2d 1228, Appendix A, at 1246 (Pa. 2009) (Saylor, J., dissenting) (acknowledging view of one court and commentator that time of Wade-Keeton test has come and gone, but recognizing the issue as open in Pennsylvania). See generally Owen, Design Defect Ghosts, 74 Brook. L. Rev. 927 (2009).

[398] For a review of the entire Products Liability Restatement, see § 6.5, above. For views on design defects and the Restatement's liability standard in § 2(b), ten years after its formal promulgation, see Geistfeld,

doctrinal labels of "strict" liability or "negligence," the *Products Liability Restatement* provides separate "functional" definitions of liability for each of the three forms of defect, including defects in design. Sections 1 and 2 set forth the basic principles of a seller's liability for design defectiveness. Section 3 provides a special rule of circumstantial evidence for proof of product defect in cases where direct evidence of the cause of an accident is unavailable but where circumstances suggest the probability that a product defect caused the harm;[399] and § 4 addresses the effect on liability of compliance or noncompliance with product safety statutes and regulations.[400] Design defects in prescription drug and medical device cases receive separate treatment both in the *Third Restatement* and in this work.[401]

Design Defects in §§ 1 and 2

Products Liability Restatement § 1 establishes the basic liability principle of products liability: one who sells "a defective product is subject to liability for harm to persons or property caused by the defect." Section 2, basing liability on the three separate types of defect, provides in subsection (b) that a product "is defective in design when the foreseeable risks of harm posed by the product could have been reduced or avoided by the adoption of a reasonable alternative design by the seller or other distributor, or a predecessor in the commercial chain of distribution, and the omission of the alternative design renders the product not reasonably safe." Stripped to its essence, § 2(b) provides:

> [A product] is defective in design when the foreseeable risks of harm posed by the product could have been reduced or avoided by the adoption of a reasonable alternative design . . . and the omission of the alternative design renders the product not reasonably safe.

Paraphrased, § 2(b) provides:

> A product is defective in design if its foreseeable risks could have been avoided by a reasonable alternative design, the omission of which renders the product not reasonably safe.

Converted to the active voice, § 2(b) means:

> A product is defective in design if the seller could have reduced the foreseeable risk that harmed the plaintiff by adopting a reasonable alternative design, the omission of which renders the product not reasonably safe.[402]

The Value of Consumer Choice in Product Liability, 74 Brook. L. Rev. 781 (2009); Green, The Unappreciated Congruity of the Second and Third Torts Restatements on Design Defects, 74 Brook. L. Rev. 807 (2009); Owen, Design Defect Ghosts, 74 Brook. L. Rev. 927 (2009); Stewart, Strict Liability for Defective Product Design: The Quest for a Well-Ordered Regime, 74 Brook. L. Rev. 1039 (2009); Twerski and Henderson, Manufacturers' Liability for Defective Product Designs: The Triumph of Risk-Utility, 74 Brook. L. Rev. 1061 (2009).

[399] While § 3 usually applies to manufacturing defects, it may also apply to design defects. See Estate of Edward W. Knoster v. Ford Motor Co., 200 Fed. Appx. 106, 113–14 (3d Cir. 2006) (N.J. law) (sudden acceleration accident; New Jersey recognizes the application of § 3 to design defect cases); Rudd v. General Motors Corp., 127 F. Supp. 2d 1330, 1340 (M.D. Ala. 2001) (pickup truck's fan blade broke from fatigue fracture that might result from low-strength alloy used in fan); Products Liability Rest. § 3 cmt. *b*. Restatement § 3 and the "malfunction theory" are addressed in § 7.4, above.

[400] Compliance and noncompliance with safety statutes and regulations are addressed in § 14.4 (compliance), below, and §§ 2.4 (noncompliance, negligence) and 6.4 (noncompliance, strict liability), above.

[401] See Products Liability Rest. § 6(c). Design defects in prescription drugs and medical devices are examined in § 18.2, below.

[402] For a more complete linguistic deconstruction of § 2(b), see Owen, Defectiveness Restated: Exploding the "Strict" Products Liability Myth, 1996 U. Ill. L. Rev. 743, 766–77.

By requiring that an alternative design be "reasonable," and basing a manufacturer's liability on its failure to adopt such an alternative design only if it renders the product "not reasonably safe," the *Third Restatement* rejects absolute safety in favor of optimality: "Society does not benefit from products that are excessively safe . . . any more than it benefits from products that are too risky. Society benefits most when the right, or optimal, amount of product safety is achieved."[403] The risk-utility balance of § 2(b) for design defect determinations ordinarily resolves into a negligence-style[404] evaluation of the foreseeable[405] costs and benefits of the manufacturer's decision to forego an alternative design:

> Subsection (b) adopts a reasonableness ("risk-utility balancing") test as the standard for judging the defectiveness of product designs. More specifically, the test is whether a reasonable alternative design would, at reasonable cost, have reduced the foreseeable risks of harm posed by the product and, if so, whether [its] omission . . . rendered the product not reasonably safe.[406]

In making the relevant cost-benefit assessment, "[a] broad range of factors may be considered in determining whether an alternative design is reasonable and whether its omission renders a product not reasonably safe."[407] The balance includes a variety of design considerations that often conflict with one another: the foreseeable risks of harm, consumer expectations, usefulness, cost, longevity, responsibility for maintenance, aesthetics, marketability, and other advantages and disadvantages of the chosen and alternative designs.[408] A judge or jury must evaluate these factors for the design of both the accident product and the alternative design feature put forward by the plaintiff. A product's design is "not reasonably safe," and hence "defective," if a comparison between the accident product *without* the plaintiff's proposed safety feature and the alternative product *with* the proposed safety feature demonstrates that the balance of costs and benefits of the alternative design is better than the balance of these same factors in the

---

[403] Products Liability Rest. § 2 cmt. *a*. "Some sort of independent assessment of advantages and disadvantages, to which some attach the label 'risk-utility balancing,' is necessary. [T]he various trade-offs need to be considered in determining whether accident costs are more fairly and efficiently borne by accident victims, on the one hand, or, on the other hand, by consumers generally through the mechanism of higher product prices attributable to liability costs imposed by courts on product sellers."

[404] "Assessment of a product design in most instances requires a comparison between an alternative design and the product design that caused the injury, undertaken from the viewpoint of a reasonable person. That approach is also used in administering the traditional reasonableness standard in negligence. See Rest. (2d) Torts § 283, cmt. *c*. The policy reasons that support use of a reasonable-person perspective in connection with the general negligence standard also support its use in the products liability context." Id. cmt. *d*. See also id. § 1 cmt. *a*.

[405] In the black-letter definition of a design defect in § 2(b), above, the Third Restatement limits a seller's responsibility to risks that are "foreseeable," an important limitation explained in comment *a*:

> Most courts agree that, for the liability system to be fair and efficient, the balancing of risks and benefits in judging product design and marketing must be done in light of the knowledge of risks and risk-avoidance techniques reasonably attainable at the time of distribution. To hold a manufacturer liable for a risk that was not foreseeable when the product was marketed might foster increased manufacturer investment in safety. But such investment by definition would be a matter of guesswork. Furthermore, manufacturers may persuasively ask to be judged by a normative behavior standard to which it is reasonably possible for manufacturers to conform. For these reasons, Subsections (b) and (c) speak of products being defective only when risks are reasonably foreseeable.

[406] Id. cmt. *d*.

[407] Id. cmt. *f*.

[408] See id.

chosen design that resulted in the accident.[409] And the converse is also true: if the balance of competing design considerations in the accident product without the proposed safety feature was as good as or better than the balance in the proposed alternative design, then the accident product's design will be deemed "reasonably safe" and "nondefective."[410]

In short, "the requirement of Subsection (b) that a product is defective in design if the foreseeable risks of harm could have been reduced by a reasonable alternative design is based on the common-sense notion that liability for harm caused by product designs should attach only when harm is reasonably preventable."[411]

Consumer Expectations

One of the most controversial aspects of the *Third Restatement*'s definition of design defect concerned the elimination of consumer expectations as an independent liability *test* and the relegation of those expectations to mere "factor" status in the list of risk-utility considerations.[412] Section 2 comment *g* declares: "Under Subsection (b), consumer expectations do not constitute an independent standard for judging the defectiveness of product designs."[413] Although not determinative in most cases, if consumer safety expectations are implicated by a particular design, they factor into an evaluation of whether the manufacturer should have adopted a reasonable alternative design.[414] Moreover, the *Third Restatement* makes clear that manufacturers and other sellers may not use consumer expectations as a defense when a product contains substantial hazards, even if obvious, which may reasonably be designed away.[415]

---

[409] The plaintiff, of course, must also prove causation—that the alternative product would have prevented or reduced his harm. See id. § 1; § 2, cmts. *f* and *q*; and § 15. Causation is treated generally in id. §§ 15 and 16. See also ch. 11, below.

[410] A "better balance" definition of defective design is proposed in Owen, Defectiveness Restated: Exploding the "Strict" Products Liability Myth, 1996 U. Ill. L. Rev. 743, 775.

[411] Products Liability Rest. § 2 cmt. *f*.

[412] See, e.g., Shapo, A New Legislation: Remarks on the Draft *Restatement* of Products Liability, 30 U. Mich. J.L. Reform 215 (1997); Vandall, Constructing a Roof Before the Foundation Is Prepared: The *Restatement (Third) of Torts: Products Liability* Design Defect, 30 U. Mich. J.L. Reform 261 (1997); Vargo, The Emperor's New Clothes: The American Law Institute Adorns a "New Cloth" for Section 402A Products Liability Design Defects—A Survey of the States Reveals a Different Weave, 26 U. Mem. L. Rev. 493, 557 (1996); Phillips, Achilles' Heel, 61 Tenn. L. Rev. 1265 (1994).

[413] Products Liability Rest. § 2 cmt. *g*.

[414] See id.:

> [C]onsumer expectations do not play a determinative role in determining defectiveness. See Comment *h*. Consumer expectations, standing alone, do not take into account whether the proposed alternative design could be implemented at reasonable cost, or whether an alternative design would provide greater overall safety. Nevertheless, consumer expectations about product performance and the dangers attendant to product use affect how risks are perceived and relate to foreseeability and frequency of the risks of harm, both of which are relevant under Subsection (b). See Comment *f*. Such expectations are often influenced by how products are portrayed and marketed and can have a significant impact on consumer behavior. Thus, although consumer expectations do not constitute an independent standard for judging the defectiveness of product designs, they may substantially influence or even be ultimately determinative on risk-utility balancing in judging whether the omission of a proposed alternative design renders the product not reasonably safe.

[415] "Subsection (b) likewise rejects conformance to consumer expectations as a defense. The mere fact that a risk presented by a product design is open and obvious, or generally known, and that the product thus satisfies expectations, does not prevent a finding that the design is defective. . . . [W]hile disappointment of consumer expectations may not serve as an independent basis for allowing recovery under Subsection (b), neither may conformance with consumer expectations serve as an independent basis for denying recovery. Such expectations may be relevant in both contexts, but in neither are they controlling." Id. See § 10.2, below.

As previously seen, many courts use some or all of the design-defect approach of § 2(b),[416] particularly its requirement that a plaintiff establish a reasonable alternative design under a risk-utility standard.[417] Yet a fair number of courts have pointedly refused to replace *Restatement (2d) of Torts* § 402A with the *Third Restatement*—often reasoning that the alternative design requirement renders proof of design defects too expensive and otherwise unfairly disadvantages plaintiffs, and reaffirming their allegiance to the consumer expectations test and underlying principles (and often doctrine) of § 402A.[418] In short, how courts and legislatures define design defects across the American continent remains somewhat in a muddle.[419]

Special Design Defect Issues

Inherently Dangerous Products

While proof of a reasonable alternative design is normally required to establish a design defect under § 2(b), inherent risks in certain products by their very nature cannot be designed away. Ordinarily, there can be no recovery for injuries from the "design" of such products because the plaintiff cannot prove the availability of a reasonable alternative design.[420] The *Second Restatement* immunized sellers of such products from design defect liability, listing as examples ordinary sugar (which can cause diabetes), castor oil (used by Mussolini as an instrument of torture), "good whiskey," "good tobacco," "good butter" (containing cholesterol which can lead to heart attacks), eggs and strawberries (to which some people are allergic), and prescription drugs, such as the Pasteur vaccine for rabies (which sometimes causes severe adverse reactions).[421] As examined elsewhere,[422] the *Third Restatement* takes a similar position, providing that "[c]ommon and widely distributed products such as alcoholic beverages, firearms, and

---

[416] "Follow the approach" includes courts that the Third Restatement itself followed, as well as courts that have followed the Third Restatement—that is, courts that today follow that approach.

[417] See, e.g., Emerson Elec. Co. v. Johnson, 627 S.W.3d 197, 206 (Tex. 2021) (plaintiffs in design defect cases must prove the existence of a safer alternative design where "the cost, feasibility, and availability of the alternative design relative to the claimed danger [demonstrates] that the danger present in the product was unreasonable in light of the product's intended use"); Davis v. UHP Projects, Inc., 2021 WL 1293858, at *3 (V.I. 2021) (adopting Products Liability Rest. § 2); Branham v. Ford Motor Co., 701 S.E.2d 5, 14 (S.C. 2010). Many such cases are cited in Twerski, An Essay on the Quieting of Products Liability Law, 105 Cornell L. Rev. 1211 (2020); Twerski and Henderson, Manufacturers' Liability for Defective Product Designs: The Triumph of Risk-Utility, 74 Brook. L. Rev. 1061 (2009).

[418] More recent cases include Ford Motor Co. v. Trejo, 402 P.3d 649, 657 (Nev. 2017); Bifolck v. Philip Morris, Inc., 152 A.3d 1183, 1199 (Conn. 2016) (seeing the good sense of the Third Restatement, yet politically unable to endorse it, *Bifolck* rejects the new Restatement yet then constructs its own elaborate design-defect approach resting largely on its views); Aubin v. Union Carbide Corp., 177 So.3d 489, 510 (Fla. 2015) (observing that "the Third Restatement's new approach is inconsistent with the rationale behind the adoption of strict products liability"); Tincher v. Omega Flex, Inc., 104 A.3d 328 (Pa. 2014).

[419] See, e.g., Purdy v. Deere & Co., 492 P.3d 99 (Or. Ct. App. 2021) (reversing judgment for erroneous instructions on how risk-utility balancing may be used in rendering design defect decisions based on consumer expectations; confused discussion of confused lines of precedent); Crawford v. ITW Food Equip. Grp., LLC, 977 F.3d 1331, 1343 n.5 (11th Cir. 2020) (Fla. law) (" 'the definition of a 'design defect' is in a 'state of flux in Florida' [and] 'in "the byzantine world of products liability" it is unsettled whether the consumer-expectation test, risk-utility test or both should be applied in evaluating an alleged defect' ").

[420] Id. cmt. *d*.

[421] See Rest. (2d) Torts § 402A cmts. *i*, *j*, and *k*. For an extended discussion of inherent product risks, see § 6.2, above, and § 10.3, below.

[422] See id.

above-ground swimming pools may be found to be defective" in design only if the plaintiff proves a reasonable alternative design under subsection 2(b).[423]

Noticeably absent in the *Third Restatement* from the special list of generically dangerous products protected from judicial scrutiny are tobacco products (cigarettes, in particular), which just narrowly missed the boat. "Tobacco" was on the list of protected products in the *Proposed Final Draft* of the *Third Restatement*, sandwiched between alcoholic beverages and firearms. At the final meeting of the American Law Institute on the *Third Restatement*, after five years of intense debate over thousands of particulars, during the closing moments of final discussion a member moved from the floor to strike "tobacco" from the short list of examples of protected products. Noting the increasing crescendo of legal and political attacks against cigarette manufacturers then in progress, he argued that the ALI should not go on record as providing favored treatment for this product. The unscheduled motion caught almost everyone by surprise, and, after a brief debate in which the Reporters explained again that court decisions to date supported leaving tobacco within the protected category,[424] the motion to strike "tobacco" carried by a whisker. Thus, the *Products Liability Restatement* takes no explicit position on whether sellers should be liable for the inherent dangers contained in tobacco products.

Comment *e* to § 2 of the *Third Restatement* addresses the related, controversial issue of whether courts should hold manufacturers liable for selling products with inherent risks so serious that they may be viewed as possessing "manifestly unreasonable

---

[423] Products Liability Rest. § 2 cmt. *d.* In the absence of normal proof of a design or other defect, the comment notes that "courts have not imposed liability for categories of products that are generally available and widely used and consumed, even if they pose substantial risks of harm. Instead, courts generally have concluded that legislatures and administrative agencies can, more appropriately than courts, consider the desirability of commercial distribution of some categories of widely used and consumed, but nevertheless dangerous, products." Id.

[424] Most courts still consider cigarettes inherently, unavoidably dangerous and so largely immune from challenge for being defectively designed. See, e.g., Fabiano v. Philip Morris Inc., 909 N.Y.S.2d 314, 320 (Sup. Ct. 2010) ("What Plaintiffs suggest is that what constitutes this object known as a cigarette should be devoid of all of its major properties. Yet that would no longer be a cigarette, and this Court [cannot] ban cigarettes."); Rose v. Brown & Williamson Tobacco Corp., 855 N.Y.S.2d 119, 125 (App. Div. 2008) ("holding defendants liable for the severe health effects of regular cigarettes, regardless of plaintiffs' failure to prove that any alternative product design would feasibly serve the same function, would essentially outlaw the satisfaction of the demand for any product serving that function"), aff'd sub nom., Adamo v. Brown & Williamson Tobacco Corp., 900 N.E.2d 966 (N.Y. 2008); Clinton v. Brown & Williamson Holdings, Inc., 498 F. Supp. 2d 639, 648 (S.D.N.Y. 2007) (cigarette design defect claims are "exactly the type of claim that [the] alternative feasible design requirement was meant to disallow").

But see Izzarelli v. R.J. Reynolds Tobacco Co., 136 A.3d 1232, 1249–53 (Conn. 2016) (under the modified consumer expectations test, design defect claim could proceed "if the plaintiff identifies some defect specific to the cigarette brand(s) at issue and/or a reasonably safer alternative"; "ordinary consumer's awareness of the product's potential danger [does not] preclude recovery as a matter of law"); Evans v. Lorillard Tobacco Co., 990 N.E.2d 997, 1018–19 (Mass. 2013) (evidence could support jury finding "that low tar, low nicotine cigarettes are a safer, reasonable alternative design to the design [of] Newport cigarettes" for the "subclass of cigarette consumers who are not yet addicted but [not] for the subclass of consumers who are already addicted").

"Although courts generally reject claims based on the inherent risks of tobacco products, they recognize design defect claims based on a specific defect such as [adding] 'excessive nicotine' to the cigarettes to increase addiction." Robinson v. Philip Morris USA, Inc., 2019 WL 1787637, at *6 (E.D. Pa. 2019). See also Anderson v. R.J. Reynolds Tobacco Co., 2021 WL 3525165, at *3 (E.D. Mo. 2021) (denying defendant's motion to dismiss design defect claim; plaintiff adequately alleged "that RJR's cigarettes contained filters that were ineffective in removing cancerous components, that RJR 'manipulated the levels of nicotine' in its cigarettes, and that it 'manipulated the potency of the nicotine' by adding ammonia or diammonium phosphate to their tobacco"); Colgate v. JUUL Labs, Inc., 402 F. Supp. 3d 728, 753 (N.D. Cal. 2019) (denying dismissal of class's design defect claims; "JUUL's products are more addictive than necessary to provide an alternative to combustible cigarettes . . . the risk of higher levels of addiction [does] not outweigh the benefits of a nicotine formulation that the body absorbs at twice the rate of a pack of combustible cigarettes with the same amount of nicotine").

designs."[425] Such products fortunately now are rare, but, in former times, lawn darts, highly flammable hula skirts, and similarly hazardous products containing substantial threats to safety but little social utility were no strangers to the market. There is a paucity of court decisions on the topic of whether courts should second-guess the market with respect to such manifestly unreasonable designs,[426] but comment *e* adopts dicta from a small number of cases suggesting that a manufacturer might properly be subject to liability for harm from selling a product if "the extremely high degree of danger posed by its use or consumption so substantially outweighs its negligible social utility that no rational, reasonable person, fully aware of the relevant facts, would choose to use, or to allow children to use, the product."[427] The broader issue of products with inherent risks is examined elsewhere in this work in greater depth.[428]

Obvious Dangers and Misuse

Certain other issues of design defectiveness involve whether a product should be characterized as defectively designed if its dangers are obvious or result from product misuse or alteration. On these important issues, treated extensively below,[429] the *Products Liability Restatement* follows well-accepted judicial norms. The obviousness of a danger is relevant to design defectiveness because the obvious nature of the danger gives warning to persons who confront it so that they are likely to act to protect themselves.[430] But the *Third Restatement* summarily rejects the long-discredited patent danger rule which barred recovery altogether in such cases.[431]

When people use and abuse products unreasonably and unforeseeably, courts generally relieve sellers of at least partial responsibility for resulting harm.[432] No product can be designed to be perfectly safe for every use, and so the doctrines of product misuse and alteration provide important limitations on liability for product design defects. In general, manufacturers and other sellers have no duty to design against unintended uses, misuses, and alterations that cannot be foreseen, but the converse is also true: sellers must adopt reasonable design precautions against product uses and abuses that they reasonably should foresee.[433] Further, third-party misuse raises issues of intervening and superseding causation that may bar liability altogether if a misuse was unforeseeable,[434] and principles of comparative fault generally reduce a seller's responsibility proportionately to the user's fault in putting a product to an improper type

---

[425] This issue lies closely beside the problem of design defect liability for alcohol, certain types of guns, and cigarettes, but the Restatement segregates those products (except tobacco) in comment *d* and separately classifies this topic in comment *e*.

[426] Products Liability Rest. § 2 Reporters' Note to cmt. *e*.

[427] Products Liability Rest. § 2 cmt. *e*.

[428] See § 6.2, above, and § 10.3, below.

[429] The issue of a seller's liability for obvious dangers is examined in § 10.2, below; the role of product misuse is treated in § 13.5, below; and product alteration is treated in § 12.3, below.

[430] Products Liability Rest. § 2 cmt. *d*.

[431] Id.

[432] "Product sellers . . . are not required to foresee and take precautions against every conceivable mode of use and abuse to which their products might be put. Increasing the costs of designing and marketing products in order to avoid the consequences of unreasonable modes of use is not required." Products Liability Rest. § 2 cmt. *m*.

[433] See §§ 12.3 and 13.5, below.

[434] See § 12.3 (*Intervening and Superseding Causes*), below.

or extent of use.[435] The *Third Restatement* adopts these widespread principles on the role of product alteration and misuse,[436] topics separately addressed below.[437]

§ 8.9 OPTIONAL SAFETY DEVICES

Sometimes manufacturers offer safety devices only as optional add-ons to their products rather than installing them as mandatory features of every product unit sold. For example, a manufacturer may sell a chain saw with an optional, rather than a mandatory, chain brake;[438] a radial arm saw with an optional, non-mandatory lower blade guard;[439] a forklift,[440] tractor,[441] loader,[442] mine roof-bolting machine,[443] or tractor loader,[444] with an optional rather than mandatory overhead guard; a truck chassis and cab,[445] forklift,[446] or bus[447] with an optional back-up alarm; a concrete mixer truck with an optional platform guardrail;[448] an industrial machine with an optional point-of-operation guard[449] or an optional start-up warning horn;[450] a high-speed transit train without a better, optional type of horn;[451] or a motorcycle, with or without leg-protective crash bars at the option of the buyer.[452] If a purchaser rejects an optional safety device, and someone is subsequently injured in a manner that the safety device would have prevented, the accident victim may seek recovery against the manufacturer for failing to incorporate the safety device as a standard feature of the product. Whether such a claim may lie is a question that has confounded courts and commentators.[453]

---

[435] See § 13.5 (*Misuse*), below.

[436] See Products Liability Rest. § 2 cmts. *m* (foreseeability of risk) and *p* (misuse, modification, and alteration); § 15 (legal causation); § 17 (apportionment of responsibility). Damages apportionment, treated generally in § 17 as an issue of comparative responsibility, is addressed thoroughly in its own Restatement. See Rest. (3d) of Torts: Apportionment of Liability (2000). On user conduct defenses, see ch. 13, below.

[437] See § 12.3 (*Intervening and Superseding Causes*) and ch. 13 (*User Conduct Defenses*), below.

[438] See, e.g., Nettles v. Electrolux Motor AB, 784 F.2d 1574 (11th Cir. 1986) (Ala. law).

[439] See, e.g., Sears, Roebuck & Co. v. Kunze, 996 S.W.2d 416 (Tex. App. 1999).

[440] See, e.g., Geddes v. Crown Equip. Corp., 709 N.Y.S.2d 770 (App. Div. 2000); Christopherson v. Hyster Co., 374 N.E.2d 858 (Ill. App. Ct. 1978).

[441] See, e.g., Austin v. Clark Equip. Co., 48 F.3d 833 (4th Cir. 1995) (Va. law); Morrison v. Kubota Tractor Corp., 891 S.W.2d 422 (Mo. Ct. App. 1994); Davis v. Caterpillar Tractor Co., 719 P.2d 324 (Colo. App. 1985).

[442] See, e.g., Fasolas v. Bobcat of N.Y., Inc., 128 N.E.3d 627, 633 (N.Y. 2019) (rented loader); Biss v. Tenneco, Inc., 409 N.Y.S.2d 874 (App. Div. 1978).

[443] See Loredo v. Solvay Am., Inc., 212 P.3d 614, 635 (Wyo. 2009).

[444] See, e.g., Pahuta v. Massey-Ferguson, Inc., 170 F.3d 125 (2d Cir. 1999) (N.Y. law).

[445] See, e.g., Ogletree v. Navistar Int'l Transp. Corp., 535 S.E.2d 545 (Ga. Ct. App. 2000); Verge v. Ford Motor Co., 581 F.2d 384 (3d Cir. 1978) (V.I. law).

[446] See, e.g., Cordani v. Thompson & Johnson Equip. Co., 792 N.Y.S.2d 675 (App. Div. 2005); Euclides Campos v. Crown Equip. Corp., 35 Fed. Appx. 31 (2d Cir. 2002) (N.Y. law); Dean v. Toyota Indus. Equip. Mfg., 540 S.E.2d 233 (Ga. Ct. App. 2000); Patane v. Thompson & Johnson Equip. Co., 649 N.Y.S.2d 547 (App. Div. 1996); Austin v. Clark Equip. Co., 48 F.3d 833 (4th Cir. 1995) (Va. law).

[447] See, e.g., Scarangella v. Thomas Built Buses, Inc., 717 N.E.2d 679 (N.Y. 1999).

[448] See, e.g., Pigliavento v. Tyler Equip. Corp., 669 N.Y.S.2d 747 (App. Div. 1998).

[449] See, e.g., Mustafa v. Halkin Tool, Ltd., 2007 WL 959704, at *15 (E.D.N.Y. 2007).

[450] See, e.g., Davidson v. Besser Co., 70 F. Supp. 2d 1020 (E.D. Mo. 1999).

[451] See Nna v. American Standard, Inc., 630 F. Supp. 2d 115, 119 (D. Mass. 2009).

[452] See, e.g., Rainbow v. Albert Elia Bldg. Co., 436 N.Y.S.2d 480 (App. Div. 1981).

[453] See generally Henderson and Twerski, Optional Safety Devices: Delegating Product Design Responsibility to the Market, 45 Ariz. St. L.J. 1399 (2013); Ausness, Risky Business: Liability of Product Sellers Who Offer Safety Devices as Optional Equipment, 39 Hofstra L. Rev. 807, 828–40 (2011); Powell, Products Liability and Optional Safety Equipment—Who Knows More?, 73 Neb. L. Rev. 843, 866–67 (1994); Annot., 99 A.L.R.3d 693 (1980) (supplier's duty to supply/recommend safety devices for industrial equipment).

Cases involving the liability of a manufacturer for providing optional rather than mandatory safety devices raise issues of duty,[454] defectiveness (or negligence),[455] actual and proximate causation,[456] and the responsibility of manufacturers of component parts.[457] More deeply, they raise fundamental questions of how far manufacturers should be required to design safety features into their products, raising their costs and diminishing their utility, which many purchasers do not want but which reduce the risks of certain types of injuries. In addition, whether the law prescribes a no-duty rule in certain optional safety device cases raises significant issues of allocation of power between courts and juries.

Whether a manufacturer is subject to liability for allowing buyers to decide whether a product should be equipped with a particular safety feature is part of the broader issue of design defectiveness, or the scope of a manufacturer's design responsibilities, previously discussed. As a general proposition, if the safety of a product can be substantially enhanced by adding a practical, relatively inexpensive safety device that does not appreciably diminish the product's usefulness, then the manufacturer is obligated to add the feature, and to make it mandatory.[458] Thus, even if a manufacturer were to offer such a feature as optional equipment, a court normally would conclude that a product sold without such a feasible, safety-enhancing, inexpensive safety feature is defective[459] and the manufacturer is negligent for failing to equip the product with the feature as a standard part of the design.[460]

For example, most courts would agree that a pressure gauge equipped with a lucite lens that foreseeably fractures, injuring a worker's eye, is defective, even if a safer, shatterproof lens is offered as an option at a slightly greater cost.[461] And the converse is also true: because some safety features may not be particularly effective, practical, or

---

454 Compare Bexiga v. Havir Mfg. Corp., 290 A.2d 281 (N.J. 1972) (general duty to supply safety devices), with Loredo v. Solvay Am., Inc., 212 P.3d 614, 634 (Wyo. 2009) (no duty to provide roof bolter machine with overhead canopy where it was offered to and declined by knowledgeable buyer who did not intend to use it in unsupported roof areas); Beemer v. Deere & Co., 794 N.Y.S.2d 253 (App. Div. 2005) (no duty to supply safety device where buyer is knowledgeable about product, its uses, and availability of the safety device; where there are circumstances in which product can be used safely without the device; and where buyer is in a position to conduct a risk-benefit analysis); Coleman v. Cintas Sales Corp., 40 S.W.3d 544 (Tex. App. 2001) (when seller offers buyers option of flame-retardant uniforms or flammable uniforms, depending on whether employees will be exposed to ignition sources, seller not liable for selling employer cheaper and more comfortable flammable uniforms).

455 See, e.g., Parker v. Raymond Corp., 911 N.Y.S.2d 694 (Sup. Ct. 2010) (forklift without rear foot guard not defective); Cordani v. Thompson & Johnson Equip. Co., 792 N.Y.S.2d 675 (App. Div. 2005) (forklift without reverse beeper not defective); Rife v. Hitachi Const. Mach. Co., 609 S.E.2d 565, 571 (S.C. Ct. App. 2005) (that optional seat belt would make excavator safer was insufficient proof of defectiveness); Tannebaum v. Yale Materials Handling Corp., 38 F. Supp. 2d 425 (D. Md. 1999) (summary judgment for defendant; not defective as matter of law); Fernandez v. Ford Motor Co., 879 P.2d 101 (N.M. Ct. App. 1994) (reversing summary judgment for defendant; unreasonably dangerous issue for jury).

456 See, e.g., Ogletree v. Navistar Int'l Transp. Corp., 535 S.E.2d 545 (Ga. Ct. App. 2000) (no cause in fact or proximate causation as matter of law); Davidson v. Besser Co., 70 F. Supp. 2d 1020, 1027 (E.D. Mo. 1999) ("in the face of the literature sent by the defendant," whether employer's failure to install purchased safety device was superseding cause of accident was question of fact for jury).

457 See, e.g., Brewer v. PACCAR, Inc., 124 N.E.3d 616, 620 (Ind. 2019) (semi-truck, with 40' blind spot in rear, backed over supervisor; because truck had only one use, jury should decide whether component parts seller reasonably should have at least offered final manufacturer various safety features, such as a rear-view window, a backup alarm, a backup camera, or backup flashers); § 15.3, below.

458 This conclusion is based on simple cost-benefit analysis, examined in § 8.4, above.

459 See id.

460 See § 2.2, above.

461 See Helicoid Gage Div. of Am. Chain & Cable Co. v. Howell, 511 S.W.2d 573 (Tex. App. 1974).

cost-effective, and may even increase various dangers, a product may *not* be defective for failing to include such a safety device as standard equipment.[462] Thus, although adding a rear door to the back opening of a forklift may reduce a very small risk that an operator may be ejected through the opening, a forklift without such a standard design feature is not defective because such a feature would diminish the convenience and safety of the forklift by eliminating a useful egress.[463]

Although manufacturers sometimes fail to incorporate safety devices into their products simply to maximize sales and improve their competitive position[464] without regard to safety, manufacturers generally provide safety devices on an optional rather than mandatory basis in order to make a product more adaptable for a variety of uses. Overhead guards on forklifts, for example, are important safety enhancements for most purposes, but they may render such vehicles unusable for passing under low doorways;[465] motorcycle leg guards undoubtedly enhance safety for many uses, but they may diminish safety for others;[466] point-of-operation guards add vital safety to industrial presses put to certain uses, but they may interfere, possibly dangerously, with certain other functions;[467] and while rollover protection structures (ROPS) add an important safety dimension to tractors used on hilly farms, they offer little protection, and add unnecessary cost and inconvenience, when used on flat terrain.[468] In short, safety features that are feasible, cost-effective, and vitally important in some contexts may be unnecessary, inconvenient, and even dangerous in others. Just as consumers want and need vehicles and other products that come in varying size, shape, power, and even color, depending on their special needs and preferences, the type and amount of safety individual consumers may need and want also varies according to their special needs and preferences. One safety size, in short, may not fit all.

It often is asserted that there are two lines of conflicting authority on the optional safety device issue: one holding that a manufacturer simply may not delegate important safety decisions to consumers, and another holding that a manufacturer has no duty to equip its products with mandatory safety features if consumers are informed of the availability of such devices as optional equipment.[469] While this classification has some value, it glosses over variations in the decisions and ignores the frequent overlap

---

[462] See, e.g., Banzhaf v. ADT Sec. Sys. Sw., Inc., 28 S.W.3d 180 (Tex. App. 2000) (court refused to second-guess convenience store's decision not to add distress feature to security system for fear that it might endanger employees). See also Bates v. Richland Sales Corp., 803 N.E.2d 977 (Ill. App. Ct. 2004) (optional, removable roll bar on loader would have prevented death of operator; permanent roll bar had been removed to allow better access); Berczyk v. Emerson Tool Co., 291 F. Supp. 2d 1004, 1007 (D. Minn. 2003) (optional lower blade guard for radial saw could increase risks).

[463] See Tannebaum v. Yale Materials Handling Corp., 38 F. Supp. 2d 425 (D. Md. 1999) (forklift not defective under risk-utility test as matter of law; manufacturer's motion for summary judgment granted).

[464] See, e.g., Derrick v. Yoder Co., 410 N.E.2d 1030, 1038–39 (Ill. App. Ct. 1980).

[465] See, e.g., Bates v. Richland Sales Corp., 803 N.E.2d 977 (Ill. App. Ct. 2004) (optional, removable roll bar on loader would have prevented death of operator; permanent roll bar had been removed to allow better access); Christopherson v. Hyster Co., 374 N.E.2d 858 (Ill. App. Ct. 1978) (but duty to supply guards was nondelegable, notwithstanding buyer's insistence that forklift not have guards to permit its use in low-clearance areas, because of evidence that retractable overhead guards were then available).

[466] Rainbow v. Albert Elia Bldg. Co., 436 N.Y.S.2d 480, 483 (App. Div. 1981).

[467] See, e.g., Bexiga v. Havir Mfg. Corp., 290 A.2d 281 (N.J. 1972) (but two-button control would not so interfere).

[468] See, e.g., Morrison v. Kubota Tractor Corp., 891 S.W.2d 422 (Mo. Ct. App. 1994).

[469] See, e.g., Powell, Products Liability and Optional Safety Equipment—Who Knows More?, 73 Neb. L. Rev. 843, 866–67 (1994). See generally Ausness, Risky Business: Liability of Product Sellers Who Offer Safety Devices as Optional Equipment, 39 Hofstra L. Rev. 807, 822–28 (2011) (examining three categories of cases).

between the two approaches that undermines meaningful analysis of the cases. In truth, it is difficult to classify the cases on optional safety devices with clarity because the law in this area is muddled and quite sparse.

The debate over whether a manufacturer should be subject to design defect liability for offering consumers safety features on an optional rather than mandatory basis finds its origins in *Bexiga v. Havir Manufacturing Corp.*,[470] an important, early case examining the general duty of manufacturers to equip machinery with safety devices.[471] The plaintiff was injured while adjusting a piece of metal beneath the ram of an unguarded punch press when he mistakenly depressed the foot control, activating the ram. The trial and intermediate appellate courts held that the plaintiff could not maintain a design defect claim against the manufacturer of the press for failing to guard the machine because, by custom and state statute, responsibility for guarding industrial machinery lay with the employer-purchasers of such machinery rather than with the manufacturer.[472] Reversing, the Supreme Court of New Jersey ruled that the manufacturer was in a better position than the employer to install feasible safety devices on industrial machinery. The court reasoned that manufacturers can make the best decisions about what types of safety devices are reasonably necessary on such machinery, and that the law should place responsibility for such devices on manufacturers rather than leaving such critical decisions about design safety to "the haphazard conduct" of buyers.[473]

Bexiga did not directly involve the issue of optional safety devices, but its holding that manufacturers may not delegate design safety decisions to purchasers lay the foundation for the optional safety device debate. Quickly becoming a benchmark for the "nondelegable duty doctrine,"[474] *Bexiga* provided a beacon for the view that manufacturers, even if they have a reasonable basis for believing that purchasers normally will add appropriate safety devices to their products, should nevertheless bear ultimate responsibility for harm caused by a buyer's failure to add such design features as may be necessary to make the product reasonably safe. Sometimes citing *Bexiga*,[475] but often not,[476] a number of courts have ruled that a manufacturer may not delegate its safe-design responsibility by offering as optional equipment a safety device necessary to a product's safety.

---

[470] 290 A.2d 281 (N.J. 1972).

[471] For an earlier case arriving at the same conclusion, see Rhoads v. Service Mach. Co., 329 F. Supp. 367 (E.D. Ark. 1971).

[472] *Bexiga*, 290 A.2d at 283–84.

[473] See id. at 285:

> Where a manufacturer [makes and sells a product] which should be provided with safety devices because without such it creates an unreasonable risk of harm, and where such safety devices can feasibly be installed by the manufacturer, the fact that he expects that someone else will install such devices should not immunize him. The public interest in assuring that safety devices are installed demands more from the manufacturer than to permit him to leave such a critical phase of his manufacturing process to the haphazard conduct of the ultimate purchaser. The only way to be certain that such devices will be installed on all machines—which clearly the public interest requires—is to place the duty on the manufacturer where it is feasible for him to do so.

[474] See, e.g., Note, 86 Harv. L. Rev. 923 (1973) (noting *Bexiga*).

[475] See, e.g., Fernandez v. Ford Motor Co., 879 P.2d 101, 111–12 (N.M. Ct. App. 1994) (thorough discussion, citing numerous cases both ways); Bilotta v. Kelley Co., 346 N.W.2d 616 (Minn. 1984).

[476] See, e.g., Sears, Roebuck & Co. v. Kunze, 996 S.W.2d 416 (Tex. App. 1999); Nettles v. Electrolux Motor AB, 784 F.2d 1574 (11th Cir. 1986) (Ala. law); Caterpillar Tractor Co. v. Ford, 406 So.2d 854 (Ala. 1981); Helicoid Gage Div. of Am. Chain & Cable Co. v. Howell, 511 S.W.2d 573 (Tex. App. 1974).

Six years after *Bexiga*, two cases were decided quite the other way, shielding manufacturers from liability for delegating the choice of appropriate safety devices to purchasers down the chain of distribution. In the first, *Verge v. Ford Motor Co.*,[477] a garbage truck without a back-up buzzer backed into and squashed a garbage man against a garbage can. The garbage truck had been assembled by a company that installed a compactor unit on a multi-purpose flat-bed truck cab and chassis it had purchased from Ford Motor Company. In an action against Ford and the garbage truck assembler for failing to equip the vehicle with a back-up buzzer, the Third Circuit ruled that Ford had no duty to install the alarm. Reversing judgment on a verdict for the plaintiff, the Court of Appeals reasoned that (1) trade custom, (2) the relative expertise of the parties,[478] and (3) feasibility mandated that the assembler alone should bear responsibility for the selection and installation of appropriate safety equipment on the final truck.[479]

Three months after *Verge*, a New York appellate court decided *Biss v. Tenneco, Inc.*,[480] which involved a multi-use loader that slid off a road, tipped over, and squashed the operator between the loader and a pole. A design defect claim was instituted against the manufacturer for failing to build into the vehicle a rollover protective structure (ROPS), which might have saved the plaintiff's life, rather than offering it merely as optional equipment. When the plaintiff's employer purchased the loader for use in its logging operations, it knew that the ROPS was available as an option from the manufacturer. Affirming a dismissal of the plaintiff's claim, the New York court reasoned that the manufacturer's only duty was to ensure that appropriate safety devices were made known and available to the purchaser because the danger of a rollover varies with the nature of particular job sites where particular buyers use the loader, an issue on which buyers have better information than the manufacturer. Consequently, a buyer informed of an available safety option like a ROPS is in a better position than the manufacturer to make an informed cost-benefit decision on whether the machine should be equipped with such a safety device.[481] Other courts, particularly in New York,[482] have followed the *Verge-Biss* approach of not holding manufacturers to an unwavering duty to equip their products with standard safety features if such features are available to purchasers as optional equipment.[483]

---

[477] 581 F.2d 384 (3d Cir. 1978) (V.I. law).

[478] Nna v. American Standard, Inc., 630 F. Supp. 2d 115, 119 (D. Mass. 2009) (manufacturer may have been in better position than buyer to make a risk-utility assessment).

[479] *Verge*, 581 F.2d at 387–90. Compare *Nna*, note 478, above.

[480] 409 N.Y.S.2d 874 (App. Div. 1978).

[481] Id. at 876–77.

[482] The landmark case is Scarangella v. Thomas Built Buses, Inc., 717 N.E.2d 679, 683 (N.Y. 1999). Affirming summary judgment for the defendant, the New York Court of Appeals held that a product is not defectively designed where the evidence reveals that: (1) the buyer is thoroughly knowledgeable about the product, its use, and the availability of the safety feature; (2) the product is safe for some normal use without the optional equipment; and (3) "the buyer is in a position, given the range of uses of the product, to balance the benefits and the risks of not having the safety device in the specifically contemplated circumstances of *the buyer's* use of the product." Id. at 683. Compare Cordani v. Thompson & Johnson Equip. Co., 792 N.Y.S.2d 675 (App. Div. 2005) (defendant met all three factors; summary judgment for defendant affirmed), with Passante v. Agway Consumer Prods., Inc., 909 N.E.2d 563 (N.Y. 2009) (4–3 opinion) (defendant failed to prove all prongs of the *Scarangella* test). See also Fasolas v. Bobcat of New York, Inc., 128 N.E.3d 627, 635–36 (N.Y. 2019) (rejecting a "rental market" exception to the *Scarangella* defense).

[483] See, e.g., Parks v. Ariens Co., 829 F.3d 655, 661 (8th Cir. 2016) (Iowa law) (predicting state would adopt "the optional equipment doctrine"; defendant fulfilled duty to plaintiff by providing information on ROPS as optional feature for mower); Loredo v. Solvay Am., Inc., 212 P.3d 614, 634 (Wyo. 2009) (no duty to provide

While the *Bexiga* nondelegable duty doctrine and the *Verge-Biss* no-duty to supply safety devices as standard equipment doctrine may be contrasted as "radically different point[s] of view"[484] if formulated in bluntest fashion, all three cases contain caveats that diminish their differences and lead toward middle ground. In *Bexiga*, for example, the New Jersey court carefully limited its holding in two respects: (1) to cases where it was "feasible" to install a particular safety device "on all machines," and (2) to those where "the device would [not] render the machine unusable for its intended purposes."[485] Thus, *Bexiga* "does not imply automatic manufacturers' liability" and is consistent with the view that the nondelegable duty applies only when no single safety device can be employed effectively for all the product's uses.[486] By the terms of *Bexiga* itself, it is not "feasible" for a manufacturer to install a one-size-fits-all safety device as standard equipment on a multi-purpose product if the device makes the product "unusable" for one of its functions.[487] Thus, even under *Bexiga*, a manufacturer does not have a duty to provide a guard that sacrifices a product's "multi-functional nature."[488] Since *Biss* itself involved a multi-purpose vehicle, the *Biss-Verge* doctrines may be seen as converging into a single sub-doctrine that manufacturers ordinarily may offer safety features as optional rather than standard equipment on multi-functional products if there is no standard safety feature that will allow each function to operate unimpeded.

Apart from whether a product has one or multiple uses, and whether or not a reasonable safety feature exists that is compatible with each use, courts have pointed to other factors relevant to whether a manufacturer may satisfy its design obligations by supplying safety features as optional (rather than as standard) equipment. Such factors include the relative expertise of the parties,[489] which party could more feasibly have installed the safety device,[490] the dangerousness of the product without the safety device,[491] the obviousness of the danger,[492] the cost of the safety feature,[493] industry custom,[494] and the sophistication of purchasers of the particular type of product.[495] Buyer sophistication is an especially important factor, since the justification for allowing manufacturers to delegate some portion of design safety responsibility to purchasers is the assumption that buyers can make better cost-benefit analyses of whether particular

---

roof bolter machine with overhead canopy where it was offered to and declined by knowledgeable buyer who did not intend to use it in unsupported roof areas). See also cases cited at note 455, above.

484 See Powell, Products Liability and Optional Safety Equipment—Who Knows More?, 73 Neb. L. Rev. 843, 876 (1994).

485 Id.

486 Westbrock v. Marshalltown Mfg. Co., 473 N.W.2d 352, 357 (Minn. Ct. App. 1991).

487 Id. at 358. An earlier Minnesota decision, Bilotta v. Kelley Co., 346 N.W.2d 616, 624 (Minn. 1984), which adopted the *Bexiga* nondelegable duty doctrine, observed this limitation on the doctrine, noting that the *Biss* no-duty doctrine "can be justified only where multi-use equipment is involved and the optional device would impair the equipment's utility" for certain uses.

488 While *Bexiga* itself involved a multi-purpose press, the safety device at issue there, a two-button control mechanism, was consistent with all functions of the press.

489 See, e.g., Verge v. Ford Motor Co., 581 F.2d 384 (3d Cir. 1978) (V.I. law).

490 See, e.g., id.

491 See Annot., 99 A.L.R.3d 693, § 2 (1980).

492 See, e.g., Price v. Niagara Mach. & Tool Works, 136 Cal. Rptr. 535 (Ct. App. 1977).

493 See, e.g., Bilotta v. Kelley Co., 346 N.W.2d 616 (Minn. 1984); Helicoid Gage Div. of Am. Chain & Cable Co. v. Howell, 511 S.W.2d 573 (Tex. App. 1974).

494 See, e.g., Verge v. Ford Motor Co., 581 F.2d 384 (3d Cir. 1978) (V.I. law).

495 See, e.g., Noonan v. Texaco, Inc., 713 P.2d 160, 163 (Wyo. 1986); Rainbow v. Albert Elia Bldg. Co., 436 N.Y.S.2d 480, 483 (App. Div. 1981).

safety features are appropriate for their own particular needs.[496] For this reason, most of the cases protecting manufacturers from liability for offering optional safety devices involve industrial machines purchased by sophisticated commercial enterprises. But there are also contexts where human buyers are likely to be well-informed about the risks and benefits of particular types of guards that may interfere with some ways in which a product may be used, such as complex wood-working saws. There would appear to be no good reason to force all woodworkers to buy a guard that interferes with a normal operation of such a machine. At least a couple of decisions support this view, one holding that a manufacturer may sell a motorcycle with optional leg-protection crash bars to a buyer who is an experienced motorcycle enthusiast,[497] and another allowing a manufacturer to sell a tractor with an optional rollover protection system to an experienced farmer.[498] Both reasoned that the plaintiff, not the manufacturer, "was in the best position to exercise an intelligent judgment in making the trade-off between cost and function" in order to decide whether the particular safety devices were reasonably necessary for the buyer's particular purposes.[499]

Perhaps the most significant distinction between the two "conflicting" doctrines on optional safety devices is whether the issue presents a duty question of law for courts or a factual question for juries. But even here, there are cases in jurisdictions following the *Bexiga* approach holding that a manufacturer has no duty to offer safety features only as standard equipment,[500] and cases in *Biss-Verge* jurisdictions holding that the matter is for the jury.[501] Indeed, the New York courts may be retreating from the no-duty aspect of the *Biss* line of cases.[502] Nor does the no-duty approach address the fact that the question of how responsibility over safety devices should be allocated between courts and juries is peculiarly fact-sensitive and hence appropriate for factual distinctions. Moreover, while the no-duty approach often appears to make most sense, it fails to recognize a purchasing employer's natural tendency to prefer an uncertain future risk to its employees, who bear substantial responsibility for their own safety and are covered by workers' compensation, over having to absorb a certain and immediate expense in purchasing an optional safety feature. Nor does the no-duty approach recognize the fact that the uses of construction equipment, punch presses, and other heavy machinery that

---

[496] See, e.g., Davis v. Caterpillar Tractor Co., 719 P.2d 324, 327 (Colo. App. 1985). See also Wagner v. International Harvester Co., 611 F.2d 224, 231 (8th Cir. 1979) (Ill. law) (appropriate safety device not offered to purchasers on facts of case, but protecting sellers who offer optional safety devices is "basically sound"):

> [T]he purchaser of multi-use equipment knows best the dangers associated with its particular use, and so it should determine the degree of safety provided. [T]he purchaser may be in the best position to make the cost-benefit analysis implicit in the principles of general negligence. Imposing liability on such a purchaser would result in minimizing the sum of accident and preventive costs.

Id. at 231. See generally Powell, Products Liability and Optional Safety Equipment—Who Knows More?, 73 Neb. L. Rev. 843, 881–82 (1994) (endorsing "sophisticated consumer" approach).

[497] "[P]laintiff was an experienced motorcyclist [who] was familiar with crash bars and their availability and . . . had removed crash bars mounted on a previously owned motorcycle, finding them dangerous for his needs." Rainbow v. Albert Elia Bldg. Co., 436 N.Y.S.2d 480, 483 (App. Div. 1981).

[498] Morrison v. Kubota Tractor Corp., 891 S.W.2d 422 (Mo. Ct. App. 1994).

[499] Rainbow v. Albert Elia Bldg. Co., 436 N.Y.S.2d 480, 483 (App. Div. 1981). See also *Morrison*, 891 S.W.2d at 428.

[500] See, e.g., Westbrock v. Marshalltown Mfg. Co., 473 N.W.2d 352, 358 (Minn. Ct. App. 1991).

[501] Pahuta v. Massey-Ferguson, Inc., 170 F.3d 125 (2d Cir. 1999) (N.Y. law).

[502] See Scarangella v. Thomas Built Buses, Inc., 717 N.E.2d 679 (N.Y. 1999); Pahuta v. Massey-Ferguson, Inc., 170 F.3d 125 (2d Cir. 1999) (N.Y. law).

may last for decades change over time, and a safety device that is unnecessary for a machine's immediate intended uses may be necessary for its uses of tomorrow.

If an important safety feature can reasonably be integrated as a standard feature without diminishing a product's utility, a manufacturer ordinarily should not be permitted to delegate the decision of whether to include the safety feature to purchasers likely to make improper cost-benefit safety decisions. But whether safety devices should be added to certain products, especially when those devices interfere with important functions of a multi-use product, is a decision that sometimes is better assessed by purchasers than manufacturers, particularly if the consumer group is generally well-informed. If purchasers as a group are likely to have special needs or wants for which a standard safety feature may be unnecessary or inappropriate, and as long as they have access to appropriate safety features and understand the safety tradeoffs those features represent, courts generally should permit manufacturers to delegate to individual purchasers the decision of what, if any, safety features may best fit their special needs.[503] A no-duty rule appears most appropriate in such cases, despite its rigor, particularly when safety features are relatively expensive and may interfere substantially with a product's utility. The nondelegable duty principle works poorly in such cases, and juries normally should not be asked to decide these cases as questions of fact. In optional safety device cases of this type, the law should step aside and leave decisions to individual product purchasers.

[503] See Ausness, Risky Business: Liability of Product Sellers Who Offer Safety Devices as Optional Equipment, 39 Hofstra L. Rev. 807, 856 (2011) (manufacturers should not be subject to liability for design defect claims "if the buyer is familiar with the product's general characteristics and inherent risks, is actually aware the safety feature in question is available, and is in a position to balance the risks and benefits of purchasing or declining to purchase the safety feature").

Chapter 9

WARNING DEFECTS

Table of Sections

§ 9.1 WARNING DEFECTS—GENERALLY

Manufacturers and other sellers have a duty to provide consumers with warnings of hidden product dangers and instructions on how products may be safely used.[1] Products that fail to carry sufficient informational "software" of this type are deemed "defective." If a user or consumer is injured as a result of a warning defect,[2] because such danger or safety information was not provided, the manufacturer is subject to liability for the harm.[3]

---

1 Retail sellers as well as manufacturers and other product suppliers also may have a duty to warn buyers of product hazards. See, e.g., Crawfordsville Town & Country Home Ctr., Inc. v. Cordova, 119 N.E.3d 119, 128 (Ind. Ct. App. 2019) (duty to warn may be satisfied by passing along manufacturer's warnings); Bylsma v. R.C. Willey, 416 P.3d 595, 629–32 (Utah 2017). Because warning defects normally originate with the manufacturer, this chapter addresses the law on warning defects principally in relation to manufacturers. For special rules applicable to retailers, see § 15.2, below.

2 The term "warning defects" is often used as an umbrella term to include instruction defects, too, as discussed below. In Texas, warning defects are referred to as "marketing defects." See, e.g., Emerson Elec. Co. v. Johnson, 627 S.W.3d 197, 210 (Tex. 2021); Ranger Conveying & Supply Co. v. Davis, 254 S.W.3d 471, 480 (Tex. App. 2007). In West Virginia, sometimes they are referred to as "use defects." See, e.g., Eskridge v. Pacific Cycle, Inc., 556 Fed. Appx. 182, 186–87 (4th Cir. 2014) (W.Va. law).

3 On warnings generally, see Twerski and Henderson, Fixing Failure to Warn, 90 Ind. L.J. 237 (2015); Todd, A Rhetoric of Warning Defects, 54 S. Tex. L. Rev. 343 (2012); Twerski and Cohen, Resolving the Dilemma of Nonjusticiable Causation in Failure-To-Warn Litigation, 84 S. Cal. L. Rev. 125 (2010); Schwartz and Appel, Effective Communication of Warnings in the Workplace: Avoiding Injuries in Working with Industrial Materials, 73 Mo. L. Rev. 1 (2008); Korzec, Restating the Obvious in Maryland Products Liability Law: The Restatement (Third) of Torts: Products Liability and Failure to Warn Defenses, 30 U. Balt. L. Rev. 341 (2001); Bowbeer, Lumish, and Cohen, Warning! Failure to Read This Article May Be Hazardous to Your Failure to Warn Defense, 27 Wm. Mitchell L. Rev. 439 (2000) (all caps in title removed); Viscusi, Using Warnings to Extend the Boundaries of Consumer Sovereignty, 23 Harv. J.L. & Pub. Pol'y 211 (1999); Geistfeld, Inadequate Product Warnings and Causation, 30 U. Mich. J.L. Reform 309 (1997); Rheingold and Feinglass, Risk-Utility Analysis in the Failure to Warn Context, 30 U. Mich. J.L. Reform 353 (1997); R. Keeton, Warning Defect: Origins, Policies, and Directions, 30 U. Mich. J.L. Reform 367 (1997); Latin, Good Warnings, Bad Products, and Cognitive Limitations, 41 UCLA L. Rev. 1193 (1994); Noah, The Imperative to Warn: Disentangling the "Right to Know" from the "Need to Know" About Consumer Product Hazards, 11 Yale J. on Reg. 293 (1994); Pittenger, Reformulating the Strict Liability Failure to Warn, 49 Wash. & Lee L. Rev. 1509 (1992); Jacobs, Toward a Process Based Approach to Failure-to-Warn Law, 71 N.C. L. Rev. 121 (1992); Henderson and Twerski, Doctrinal Collapse in Products Liability: The Empty Shell of Failure to Warn, 65 N.Y.U. L. Rev. 265 (1990); Madden, The Duty to Warn in Products Liability: Contours and Criticism, 89 W. Va. L. Rev. 221 (1987); Twerski, Weinstein, Donaher, and Piehler, The Use and Abuse of Warnings in Products Liability—Design Defect Litigation Comes of Age, 61 Cornell L. Rev. 495 (1976); W.P. Keeton, Products Liability—Inadequacy of Information, 48 Tex. L. Rev. 398 (1970); Noel, Manufacturer's Negligence of Design or Directions for Use of a Product, 71 Yale L.J. 816 (1962); Dillard and Hart, Product Liability: Directions for Use and the Duty to

History

A manufacturer's duty to warn of hidden dangers in its products is ancient, with roots reaching back at least to Roman sales law. Under Roman law, a seller aware of hidden defects in its products who failed to disclose them to its buyers was guilty of fraud (*dolus*).[4] Later, Justinian pronounced that "if the seller knew, but was silent and so deceived the buyer, he will have to make good to the buyer all losses that have fallen on him in consequence of the purchase."[5] In the thirteenth century, Thomas Aquinas[6] outlined the responsibilities of merchants in the *Summa Theologica*,[7] consistent with Justinian principles in the *Digest*. A seller was bound to disclose any secret flaws a product might possess: it was a sin and fraud to sell a product containing a latent defect known to the seller but not the buyer, and such a sale was void. If the seller was unaware of the defect, the sale was not a sin, but the seller nevertheless had to return any excess price attributable to the defect.[8] A seller was not bound to disclose obvious defects from "any duty of justice," but to do so would reflect "the more exuberant virtue."[9]

In America, products liability claims based on a seller's failure to provide adequate warnings or instructions arose during the 1800s, although claims for failure to warn, as products liability claims more generally, were uncommon until the 1900s.[10] The earliest warning claims grew out of and intermingled notions of false representations and deceit,[11] with the courts following the ancient approach of considering a merchant's failure to disclose a known defect to be fraudulent.[12] On this basis, early courts held

Warn, 41 Va. L. Rev. 145 (1955); Owen & Davis on Products Liability ch. 9; Frumer, Friedman, and Sklaren, Products Liability ch. 12; Am. Law Prod. Liab. 3d chs. 32–34; D. Fairgrieve and R. Goldberg, Product Liability ch. 12 (Oxford 3d ed. 2020) (British and European law); S. Pape, Warnings and Product Liability: Lessons Learned from Cognitive Psychology and Ergonomics (Hague 2011) (European law). See also B. Peters, The Warnings Compendium (2015).

4 See J. Thomas, Textbook of Roman Law 286 (1976) ("The concern is with latent or hidden defects. . . . [I]f the vendor was aware of the defect and did not disclose it, he was guilty of *dolus* and would be liable in the *actio empti* . . . ."); Honoré, The History of the Aedilitian Actions from Roman to Roman-Dutch Law, in Studies in the Roman Law of Sale 132, 135 (D. Daube ed., reprint 1977) (1959) ("during the last century of the Republic the notion of *dolus* was extended to cover both the statement by the seller that the thing sold possessed or did not possess some quality when he knew this was untrue and also the case when the seller knowingly concealed a defect"). See also Rogerson, Implied Warranty Against Latent Defects in Roman and English Law, in Studies in the Roman Law of Sale 112, 113 (D. Daube ed., reprint 1977) (1959).

5 Justinian's Digest, Book 19, Tit. 1, Lex 13 (533 A.D.).

6 1225?–1274 A.D.

7 Thomas Aquinas, Summa Theologica, Ethicus, II, II at Q. 77, arts. 2–4 (Fathers of the English Dominican Province trans., 2d rev. ed. 1920).

8 See Hamilton, The Ancient Maxim Caveat Emptor, 40 Yale L.J. 1133 (1931).

9 Id. at 1138 (quoting Aquinas, Summa Theologica, Ethicus, II, II at Q. 77, Art. 4 (Rickaby trans., 2d ed. 1896)).

10 See Bohlen, The Basis of Affirmative Obligations in the Law of Tort, 53 U. Pa. L. Rev. 273 (1905); Dillard and Hart, Product Liability: Directions for Use and the Duty to Warn, 41 Va. L. Rev. 145 (1955) (thorough historical review of duty to warn); Noel, Manufacturer's Negligence of Design or Directions for Use of a Product, 71 Yale L.J. 816 (1962).

11 Notably Langridge v. Levy, (1837) 150 Eng. Rep. 863 (Exch. Div.), aff'd, (1838) 150 Eng. Rep. 1458 (Exch. Div.) (retailer subject to liability in tort for misrepresenting that poorly made gun, an inherently dangerous instrument, was made by a good manufacturer and was safe), and Thomas v. Winchester, 6 N.Y. 397 (1852) (medicine seller who falsely labels belladonna as extract of dandelion liable for resulting injuries) (citing *Langridge v. Levy*).

12 *But see* Bohlen, The Basis of Affirmative Obligations in the Law of Tort, 53 U. Pa. L. Rev. 273 (1905) (mentioning vendor's positive duty to disclose known dangers to a buyer and distinguishing it from vendor's negative duty not to misrepresent).

sellers liable for failing to warn that sheep were diseased;[13] that lead paint had been spilled on hay sold for cow feed which killed the cow;[14] and that a painted step-ladder was made of defective wood.[15] A plaintiff seeking recovery on a warning claim against a remote seller could be barred by the absence of privity of contract with the defendant,[16] and sometimes on the basis that the seller was not aware of the danger,[17] or that the plaintiff was.[18] But a number of early decisions permitted claims by remote parties, on principles made famous in *Huset v. J.I. Case Threshing Machine Co.*,[19] where the defendant sold "an article which he knows to be imminently dangerous to life or limb to another without notice of its qualities."[20]

Early cases alleged that a manufacturer or other seller had failed to provide adequate warnings about a variety of dangers—that naphtha sold for lamp oil could explode;[21] that a pull-out bed frame might fall if the legs were not secured;[22] that stove polish might ignite;[23] that coal oil sold for use in starting fires was mixed with gasoline and might explode;[24] that a car crank might kick back and break an arm;[25] that dye in a coat's fur collar might cause allergies;[26] that a can of paint stain might ignite;[27] and that dehydrated milk might go bad.[28] While most of these early warning claims remained partially rooted in deceit, by the middle of the twentieth century warning claims stood solidly on their own.[29]

Nature of Duty to Warn

The "duty to warn" is an umbrella term for describing a manufacturer's informational obligations to those who purchase and use its products. This duty actually is comprised of two quite separate obligations: the duty to *warn*—to inform buyers and users of hidden dangers in a product; and the duty to *instruct*—to inform buyers on how

---

13 Jeffrey v. Bigelow & Tracy, 13 Wend. 518 (N.Y. Sup. Ct. 1835) (citing Evans' Pothier, pt. 1, ch. 2, art. 3, pl. 166).

14 French v. Vining, 102 Mass. 132 (1869) (if the defendant knew the hay was "dangerous or poisonous, it would plainly be a violation of good faith, and an illegal act, to sell it to the plaintiff without disclosing its condition") (citing *Thomas v. Winchester* and *Langridge v. Levy*, note 11).

15 Schubert v. J.R. Clark Co., 51 N.W. 1103 (Minn. 1892) (cites *Thomas v. Winchester* and holds that the defendant had a duty to warn of the latent defect).

16 See § 1.2, above.

17 See, e.g., Peaslee-Gaulbert Co. v. McMath's Adm'r, 146 S.W. 770 (Ky. 1912) (sellers unaware of risk that painters would put candle close to can of paint, causing can to explode).

18 Leavitt v. Fiberloid Co., 82 N.E. 682 (Mass. 1907) (flammability of "fiberloid" used to make combs).

19 120 F. 865 (8th Cir. 1903) (Minn. law), discussed in § 1.2, above. See, e.g., Wellington v. Downer Kerosene Oil Co., 104 Mass. 64 (1870); Schubert v. J.R. Clark Co., 51 N.W. 1103 (Minn. 1892). See also Heizer v. Kingsland & Douglass Mfg. Co., 19 S.W. 630, 633 (Mo. 1892) (dictum); Olds Motor Works v. Shaffer, 140 S.W. 1047, 1051 (Ky. 1911) (defective rumble seat on which plaintiff was sitting fell off car; dictum).

20 *Huset*, 120 F. at 871.

21 Wellington v. Downer Kerosene Oil Co., 104 Mass. 64 (1870).

22 Lewis v. Terry, 43 P. 398 (Cal. 1896).

23 Clement v. Crosby & Co., 111 N.W. 745 (Mich. 1907).

24 Waters-Pierce Oil Co. v. Deselms, 212 U.S. 159 (1909).

25 Martin v. Maxwell-Brisco Motor Vehicle Co., 138 S.W. 65 (Mo. 1911).

26 Gerkin v. Brown & Sehler Co., 143 N.W. 48 (Mich. 1913).

27 Thornhill v. Carpenter-Morton Co., 108 N.E. 474 (Mass. 1915).

28 Rosenbusch v. Ambrosia Milk Corp., 168 N.Y.S. 505 (App. Div. 1917).

29 See, e.g., Orr v. Shell Oil Co., 177 S.W.2d 608 (Mo. 1943) (worker could maintain claim for failing to warn that contact with chemical could cause damage to kidneys and other injuries) (citing Rest. (2d) of Torts § 388); Dillard and Hart, Product Liability: Directions for Use and the Duty to Warn, 41 Va. L. Rev. 145 (1955) (citing *Orr* as illustration of modern approach to duty to warn).

to *avoid* a product's dangers in order to use it safely.[30] Together, these duties require that important information on product hazards and product safety are transferred from manufacturers, who possess the information, to buyers and users of products, who need it.[31]

From a manufacturer's perspective, it usually is less costly to warn of a danger than to improve manufacturing processes, quality assurance, or to design the problem entirely out of the product. Courts sometimes assume that supplying warnings and instructions is an easy and inexpensive way for manufacturers to fulfill their obligation to make their products reasonably safe. And injured plaintiffs often reinforce this view, frequently adding warning defect claims indiscriminately to cases where they have no business, since proving that a warning is "defective" often appears to be a far easier (and less expensive) task than successfully attacking a product's design.[32] Yet many courts look skeptically at warning claims and do not lightly impose a duty to warn on manufacturers.[33]

The direct economic costs of providing warnings and instructions typically are minimal, but less obvious costs raise subtle and important issues. One is the danger of providing too *much* information—the risk of over-warning or "warnings pollution."[34] Moreover, the decision on how much and what types of information a manufacturer should provide with a product can only be answered intelligibly if the goals sought to be achieved by the legal requirements are fully understood. Probably the most generally accepted goal of products liability law is deterrence—risk reduction—predicated on the view that a consumer informed about product dangers and methods of safe use will use that information for self-protection. And deterrence rests on the more complex goal of economic efficiency, which seeks to maximize social resources by minimizing wasteful injuries.[35] There can be no doubt that warnings and instructions often are an efficient way to help protect consumers from latent product hazards.[36]

Another reason for requiring warnings and instructions, grounded in a more fundamental human value, is the promotion of individual autonomy—by shifting cost-benefit decisionmaking on product hazards from manufacturers to individual consumers.[37] A consumer who is fully informed of a product's dangers and how to avoid

---

[30] See, e.g., Ontai v. Straub Clinic & Hosp., Inc., 659 P.2d 734, 743 (Haw. 1983).

[31] Warnings and instructions are distinguished in § 9.3, below.

[32] See, e.g., Richmond, Renewed Look at the Duty to Warn and Affirmative Defenses, 61 Def. Couns. J. 205 (1994) ("failure to warn claims are not technical and are relatively inexpensive to prosecute, unlike traditional design defect cases"). See also Funkhouser v. Ford Motor Co., 736 S.E.2d 309, 314 (Va. 2013) (plaintiff "amended his initial complaint from a design defect claim to a failure to warn claim because he realized that he could not definitively prove the specific defect that caused the fire").

[33] See, e.g., McCracken v. Ford Motor Co., 588 F. Supp. 2d 635, 642–43 (E.D. Pa. 2008) (plaintiff's failure to warn allegations that traveling at high speeds would increase radiation levels in vehicle leading to thyroid cancer were "too conclusory to support his claim"); Killeen v. Harmon Grain Prods., Inc., 413 N.E.2d 767, 770–71 (Mass. App. Ct. 1980) (manufacturer of cinnamon-flavored toothpicks had no duty to warn of danger to child falling during play while holding one in mouth: duty to warn not imposed as "a mindless ritual").

[34] See § 9.3, below.

[35] See § 5.4, above.

[36] See, e.g., Geistfeld, Inadequate Product Warnings and Causation, 30 U. Mich. J.L. Reform 309, 314 (1997). See also Kurns v. Railroad Friction Prods. Corp., 565 U.S. 625, 635 (2012) ("Reasonable designs and instructions or warnings both play important roles in the production and distribution of reasonably safe products.") (quoting Products Liability Rest. § 2 cmt. *l*).

[37] See Viscusi, Using Warnings to Extend the Boundaries of Consumer Sovereignty, 23 Harv. J.L. & Pub. Pol'y 211, 231 (1999) (noting that "there is typically substantial heterogeneity in individuals' willingness

them may choose to use the product in a particular, safer manner. Or the informed consumer may choose not to buy or use the product at all.[38] Unlike the risk-reduction rationale, which reflects a utilitarian perspective rooted in economic efficiency, this kind of informed consent value focuses on protecting a user's individual rights—specifically, the user's right of self-determination, the right "to determine his own fate."[39] The idea here is "that the user or consumer is entitled to make his own choice as to whether the product's utility or benefits justify exposing himself to the risks of harm. Thus, a true choice situation arises, and a duty to warn attaches, whenever a reasonable man would want to be informed of the risk in order to decide whether to expose himself to it."[40] In short, the purpose of a manufacturer's duty to warn of dangers and how to avoid them is to empower users and consumers to make informed decisions on whether to buy and use particular products (with particular benefits and detriments), and, if so, on how to use them safely.[41]

Lurking within the duty to warn lies a paradox: The duty to warn is at once the most essential, yet least effective, duty in the law of products liability. Its value lies in its grounding in the autonomy of consumers, as discussed above, together with its promotion of utility by helping to reduce the level of unnecessary product accidents, even if only modestly. Its ineffectiveness springs from how easy it is to assert a warning claim,[42] even if unjustified; how elusive such claims are to adjudicate rationally;[43] and what little impact warnings have on product safety—since mounting studies reveal that they often are ignored.[44] If this latter point is true, if most warnings and instructions truly are ignored, then a manufacturer's duty to warn and instruct may be mostly sound and fury, signifying little. So, warnings are powerful because they transfer important safety information and decisionmaking to consumers, yet they frequently make no

to bear risk and in the kinds of products they prefer" and that "[h]azard warnings enable consumers to make decentralized choices for the products that best promote their welfare").

[38] See Products Liability Rest. § 2(c) cmt. *i*.

[39] Pavlides v. Galveston Yacht Basin, Inc., 727 F.2d 330, 338 (5th Cir. 1984) (Tex. law).

[40] Borel v. Fibreboard Paper Prods. Corp., 493 F.2d 1076, 1089 (5th Cir. 1973) (Tex. law) (asbestos insulation worker, not warned of risks, contracted asbestosis and mesothelioma).

[41] Lawing v. Trinity Mfg., Inc., 749 S.E.2d 126, 138 (S.C. Ct. App. 2013) (Few, J.) (purpose of warnings is to permit people to "avoid the product altogether or avoid the danger by careful use"); Buckner v. Milwaukee Elec. Tool Corp., 166 Cal. Rptr. 3d 202, 211 (Ct. App. 2013) (purpose of warnings "is to permit the consumer to choose to refrain from using the product altogether or to avoid the danger by careful use").

[42] See, e.g., Richmond, Renewed Look at the Duty to Warn and Affirmative Defenses, 61 Def. Couns. J. 205 (1994); Priest, Products Liability Law and the Accident Rate, in Liability: Perspectives and Policy 217–20 (R. Litan and C. Winston eds., 1988); A. Schwartz, Proposals for Products Liability Reform: A Theoretical Synthesis, 97 Yale L.J. 353, 398 (1988); P. Huber, Liability: The Legal Revolution and Its Consequences 51–58 (1988); R. Epstein, Modern Products Liability Law 93 (1980).

[43] See, e.g., Henderson and Twerski, Doctrinal Collapse in Products Liability: The Empty Shell of Failure to Warn, 65 N.Y.U. L. Rev. 265 (1990).

[44] See, e.g., Sunstein, The Laws of Fear, 115 Harv. L. Rev. 1119, 1123 (2002) (reviewing P. Slovic, The Perception of Risk) ("ordinary people often deal poorly with the topic of risk"); Symposium: Rational Actors or Rational Fools? The Implications of Psychology for Products Liability, 6 Roger Williams U. L. Rev. 1 (2000); Hanson and Kysar, Taking Behavioralism Seriously: The Problem of Market Manipulation, 74 N.Y.U. L. Rev. 630, 724 (1999); Hanson and Kysar, Taking Behavioralism Seriously: Some Evidence of Market Manipulation, 112 Harv. L. Rev. 1420, 1425 (1999); Latin, Good Warnings, Bad Products, and Cognitive Limitations, 41 UCLA L. Rev. 1193 (1994). See also Food & Drug Administration, Experimental Evaluation of the Impact of Distraction on Consumer Understanding of the Risk and Benefit Information in Direct-to-Consumer Prescription Drug Television Advertisements: Executive Summary (June 2011). This matter is examined in the context of cause in fact. See § 11.4, below.

difference because consumers often fail to read, and often fail to process and rationally apply, safety information. This is the paradox of the duty to warn.

Relationship Between Duty to Warn and Duty of Safe Design

A fundamental aspect of the duty to warn is its relationship to the duty of safe design. The duty to warn is undoubtedly linked to a product's design, in that a warning or instruction provides information about hazards inherent in a product's design and how those design hazards may be avoided. For this reason, some early courts and commentators viewed the duty to warn as a subsidiary obligation of the duty of safe design.[45] Yet, while design defect and warning defect claims often go hand in hand,[46] almost all jurisdictions today view the duty to warn and the duty of safe design largely as distinct, independent obligations.[47] Thus, even if a product's design is as safe as it can be, the manufacturer still has a duty to warn of hidden dangers in the product.[48] And if a substantial danger can be designed out of a product practicably and at little cost, all but a few misguided courts hold that even an "adequate" warning does not insulate a manufacturer who fails to employ the safer design.[49] "A warning is not a Band-Aid to cover a gaping wound, and a product is not safe simply because it carries a warning."[50] This essential point was more fully developed above.[51]

---

[45] See Noel, Manufacturer's Negligence of Design or Directions for Use of a Product, 71 Yale L.J. 816 (1962). This thought still lingers in some minds. See, e.g., Gonzalez v. Autoliv ASP, Inc., 64 Cal. Rptr. 3d 908, 918 (Ct. App. 2007) ("The failure to warn may constitute a design defect."); Colegrove v. Cameron Mach. Co., 172 F. Supp. 2d 611, 635 (W.D. Pa. 2001) (trial court did not err in allowing engineer's testimony that absence of guard on foot switch of machine and lack of warning regarding the unguarded foot switch were both design defects).

[46] See, e.g., McConnell v. Cosco, Inc., 238 F. Supp. 2d 970 (S.D. Ohio 2003) (risk that infant, while trying to get out of highchair, could catch neck and be strangled on food tray supported claims for design defect and failure to warn); Watkins v. Ford Motor Co., 190 F.3d 1213 (11th Cir. 1999) (Ga. law) (valid claims that Bronco II, which had propensity to roll over, was designed defectively and that Ford should have warned of this condition).

[47] See § 6.2, above. See, e.g., Gillespie v. Edmier, 182 N.E.3d 54, 63 (Ill. 2020) (Karmeier, J. concurrence) ("the failure to warn claim is a separate method of liability that warrants a separate analysis"); Heckman v. Ryder Truck Rental, Inc., 962 F. Supp. 2d 792, 803 (D. Md. 2013) (unreasonableness of warning is an independent basis of liability).

[48] See, e.g., Burton v. E.I. du Pont de Nemours & Co., Inc., 994 F.3d 791, 822 (7th Cir. 2021) (Wis. law) ("A properly designed and manufactured product may still be defective if 'an intended use of the product is dangerous, but the manufacturer did not provide sufficient warning or instruction.' "); Evans v. Nacco Materials Handling Grp., Inc., 810 S.E.2d 462, 472 (Va. 2018) ("A product may be as safe as engineering will permit, and suffer from no design defect, but nevertheless require a warning to consumers about a hidden danger."); Kurns v. Railroad Friction Prods. Corp., 565 U.S. 625, 642 (2012) (Kagan, J., concurring) ("a product may be flawlessly designed and still subject its manufacturer or seller to liability for lack of adequate instructions or warnings"); Moore v. Ford Motor Co., 332 S.W.3d 749, 757 (Mo. 2011) (en banc) (although "a product may be designed and manufactured properly, the lack of an adequate warning, in itself, may render a product defective or unreasonably dangerous").

[49] See, e.g., Kleppel v. Hunter's Mfg. Co., 2018 WL 6436269, at *11 (S.D. Tex. 2018) ("*Warnings are not . . . a substitute for the provision of a reasonably safe design.*"; quoting Prods. Liab. Rest. § 2 cmt. *l*) (emphasis in original); Eskridge v. Pacific Cycle, Inc., 556 Fed. Appx. 182, 189 (4th Cir. 2014) (W. Va. law) (even good warnings and instructions do not supplant the duty of safe design); Delaney v. Deere & Co., 999 P.2d 930, 942 (Kan. 2000) ("just because there is a warning on a piece of equipment . . . does not prevent the equipment from being dangerous"); White v. ABCO Eng'g Corp., 221 F.3d 293, 305–06 (2d Cir. 2000) (N.J. law) (notwithstanding clearly adequate warning, conveyor manufacturer was subject to liability for failing to provide side guarding).

[50] Glittenberg v. Doughboy Recreational Indus., 491 N.W.2d 208, 216 (Mich. 1992). See Products Liability Rest. § 2 cmt. *l*.

[51] See § 6.2, above. See also § 10.2, below.

Variety of Warning Issues

This chapter considers the fundamental issues surrounding the duty to warn: what theories of recovery support the duty to warn, what types of information that duty requires manufacturers to convey, how that information must be communicated, and to whom it must be given. The chapter first addresses the theories and tests of liability in warning cases,[52] and the central issue of whether a manufacturer's warnings and instructions for a particular product are "adequate" given its likely environments of use.[53] The final inquiry in this chapter focuses on who, other than the purchaser, the manufacturer must warn,[54] an inquiry that includes consideration of the bulk supplier and sophisticated user doctrines.[55]

Many other important warning issues lie scattered throughout this book, as they are scattered widely throughout products liability law. Addressed in other contexts are the role of expert testimony in proving that a warning was defective and that the defect caused the plaintiff's harm;[56] the absence, in almost all jurisdictions, of a duty to warn of obvious and widely known dangers;[57] the fading idea of a duty to warn of unknowable dangers;[58] the spreading acceptance of a manufacturer's post-sale duty to warn;[59] the duty, accepted in virtually every jurisdiction, to warn against foreseeable product misuse;[60] the limited duty to warn consumers of dangers in a third-party's products;[61] the circumstances in which a manufacturer's common-law duty to warn may be preempted by a federal safety statute or regulation;[62] the duties to warn owed by non-manufacturing suppliers, such as retailers,[63] successor corporations,[64] and sellers of used products;[65] the duties of drug manufacturers and pharmacists to warn of dangers in prescription drugs and medical devices;[66] and circumstances in which a manufacturer's failure to warn of danger may result in punitive damages.[67]

§ 9.2 THEORIES AND TESTS OF LIABILITY

Warning defect claims may be brought in most jurisdictions on the basis of negligence, breach of the implied warranty of merchantability, and strict liability in tort. While plaintiffs often plead two or all three causes of action to support a warning claim in modern products liability litigation,[68] the negligence cause of action long has been

---

[52] See § 9.2, below.

[53] See § 9.3, below.

[54] See § 9.4, below.

[55] See § 9.5, below.

[56] See § 6.3, above.

[57] See § 10.2, below.

[58] See § 10.4, below.

[59] See § 10.8, below.

[60] See § 13.5, below.

[61] See §§ 9.4, 13.5, below.

[62] See § 14.5, below.

[63] See § 15.2, below.

[64] See § 15.5, below.

[65] See § 16.5, below.

[66] See §§ 18.3 and 18.4, below.

[67] See Owen & Davis on Products Liability § 26:17 (punitive damages for failing to warn of known dangers), and § 26:18 (for failing to warn or recall after sale) (4th ed. 2014).

[68] See, e.g., Camejo v. Angelini Pharma Inc., 2021 WL 141338, at *7 (Del. Super. Ct. 2021) (strict liability in tort, negligence, breach of express warranty, and breach of implied warranty claims were "grounded

viewed as the most natural basis for such claims.[69] To "apprise a party of a danger of which he is not aware, and thus enable him to protect himself against it,"[70] due care may require a manufacturer "to speak out if the product is capable of harm and does not itself carry a message of danger."[71] The law reports are filled with cases in which a warning claim is based, entirely or in part, on negligence.[72] With increasing evidence that plaintiffs fare better in products liability claims based on negligence than on strict liability, both for likelihood of success and size of verdict,[73] negligence surely will continue to be a favored cause of action for warning claims.

To recover on a warning claim in negligence, the plaintiff must establish that the manufacturer failed to exercise reasonable care to provide adequate information in a reasonable manner to an appropriate person about a foreseeable risk that was significant enough to justify the costs of providing the information.[74] How much care is reasonable, as previously discussed, reflects a balance of the expected safety benefits of a warning against its expected costs.[75] Courts infrequently engage explicitly in this type of cost-benefit analysis in any type of case, much less in negligence cases involving warning claims. But when they do, the conclusion appears inescapable that "the cost of giving an adequate warning is usually so minimal, amounting only to the expense of

---

in a purported inadequate warning"); Romero v. ITW Food Equip. Grp., LLC, 987 F. Supp. 2d 93, 99 (D.D.C. 2013) (negligence, implied warranty, and strict liability in tort); Moore v. Ford Motor Co., 332 S.W.3d 749 (Mo. 2011) (en banc) (negligence, strict liability); Larkin v. Pfizer, Inc., 153 S.W.3d 758 (Ky. 2004) (negligence, breach of warranty, and strict liability).

Reform acts in a few states replace common law claims of negligence, breach of implied warranty of merchantability, and strict liability in tort with simple products liability claims such as failure to warn. See, e.g., Bowles v. Novartis Pharms. Corp., 2013 WL 5297257, at *7–8 (S.D. Ohio 2013); Bergeron v. Pacific Food, Inc., 2011 WL 1017872, at *3 n.7 (Conn. Super. Ct. 2011); Tex. Civ. Prac. & Rem. Code Ann. § 82.001(2). Products Liability Rest. § 2 cmt. *n* recommends applying defective warning (as defective design) claims without resort to multiple theories of liability: "two or more factually identical failure-to-warn claims should not be submitted to the trier of fact in the same case under different doctrinal labels." Some courts recognize the superfluity of a negligence (and sometimes an implied warranty) claim when a strict liability in tort claim is asserted. See, e.g., *Romero*, above, 987 F. Supp. 2d at 99 (all three claims merge into strict liability in tort); Daughetee v. Chr. Hansen, Inc., 960 F. Supp. 2d 849, 875 (N.D. Iowa 2013) (recognizing logic of this approach but allowing warning claims of negligence and implied warranty as not redundant). See generally § 5.9, above.

[69] "[W]here directions for use and duty to warn are in the picture, as they are to an increasing extent nowadays, negligence has been, and still is, the favorite cause of action." Prosser, Products Liability in Perspective, 5 Gonz. L. Rev. 157, 158 (1970). See generally Henderson and Twerski, Doctrinal Collapse in Products Liability: The Empty Shell of Failure to Warn, 65 N.Y.U. L. Rev. 265, 269 (1990) (noting, if critiquing, the assumption "that the all-purpose negligence formula works well in failure-to-warn cases"); Noel, Manufacturer's Negligence of Design or Directions for Use of a Product, 71 Yale L.J. 816 (1962); Dillard and Hart, Product Liability: Directions for Use and the Duty to Warn, 41 Va. L. Rev. 145 (1955); Keeton, Dobbs, Keeton, and Owen, Prosser and Keeton on the Law of Torts § 99, at 697.

Deviations from this view, which found some favor prior to the mid-1980s, included the Wade-Keeton definition of liability, usually (but not always) applied to design defect cases, and early rejections of the state-of-the-art defense in warning cases. See W.P. Keeton, Products Liability—Inadequacy of Information, 48 Tex. L. Rev. 398 (1970); § 8.7 (the Wade-Keeton test), above, and § 10.4 (state of the art), below.

[70] Jonescue v. Jewel Home Shopping Serv., 306 N.E.2d 312, 316 (Ill. App. Ct. 1973).

[71] Dillard and Hart, Product Liability: Directions for Use and the Duty to Warn, 41 Va. L. Rev. 145, 147 (1955).

[72] See note 68, above.

[73] See Cupp and Polage, The Rhetoric of Strict Products Liability Versus Negligence: An Empirical Analysis, 77 N.Y.U. L. Rev. 874 (2002).

[74] See Rest. (Second) of Torts § 388. See generally § 2.2, above.

[75] See id. See also Vaskas v. Kenworth Truck Co., 2013 WL 1126022, at *2 (M.D. Pa. 2013) (discussing risk-utility balancing test of Products Liability Rest. § 2(c)); Stanley v. Central Garden & Pet Corp., 891 F. Supp. 2d 757, 763 (D. Md. 2012) ("To decide if a warning is adequate, Maryland courts ask if the benefits of a more detailed warning outweigh the costs of requiring the change.").

adding some more printing to a label, that this balancing process will almost always weigh in favor of an obligation to warn of latent dangers, if the manufacturer is otherwise required to do so."[76] Yet the values, policies, and justice considerations at play in negligence inquiries are more subtle and complex than such a simple weighing of economic costs and safety benefits implies,[77] and courts usually provide little explanation or justification of negligence determinations in defective warning cases.

Since the 1980s, there has been a significant resurgence in negligence reasoning in products liability law—in case law, state reform legislation, and in the *Products Liability Restatement*. These developments have been particularly pronounced with respect to warning claims, which so comfortably rest on the principles of negligence, as mentioned earlier. As has been pointed out for many years, claims for warning defects in negligence and strict liability in tort are nearly, or entirely, identical.[78] At least one state supreme court abandoned strict liability for negligence in warning cases,[79] as have several state statutes,[80] as examined elsewhere in greater detail.[81] Be that as it may, negligence is widely held to be a proper basis of liability for inadequate warning claims.[82]

Breach of implied warranty of merchantability is claimed less frequently than negligence in products liability litigation generally, and the same holds true in warning cases.[83] Yet breach of implied warranty, usually on the ground that a product was unfit for its ordinary purposes,[84] is an entirely sound basis of recovery for injuries attributable

---

[76] Moran v. Faberge, Inc., 332 A.2d 11, 15 (Md. 1975). See § 2.2, above.

[77] See, e.g., Wright, The Standards of Care in Negligence Law, in Philosophical Foundations of Tort Law 249 (D. Owen ed., Oxford 1995); Henderson and Twerski, Doctrinal Collapse in Products Liability: The Empty Shell of Failure to Warn, 65 N.Y.U. L. Rev. 265 (1990).

[78] See, e.g., Burton v. E.I. du Pont de Nemours & Co., Inc., 994 F.3d 791, 822 (7th Cir. 2021) (Wis. law) (the duty to warn is materially identical under negligence and strict liability in tort); Price v. One World Techs., Inc., 2020 WL 5821478, at *8 (N.D.N.Y. 2020) ("Where liability is predicated on a failure to warn, New York views negligence and strict liability claims as equivalent."); Romero v. ITW Food Equip. Grp., LLC, 987 F. Supp. 2d 93, 100 (D.D.C. 2013) ("negligence and strict liability are functionally the same" and "merge" into one another); Gourdine v. Crews, 955 A.2d 769, 782 (Md. 2008) ("negligence concepts and those of strict liability have 'morphed together' . . . in failure to warn cases"); Feldman v. Lederle Labs., 479 A.2d 374, 386 (N.J. 1984) ("functional equivalents"). See generally Anderson v. Owens-Corning Fiberglas Corp., 810 P.2d 549, 561 (Cal. 1991) (Mosk, J., concurring and dissenting) ("In no area of strict products liability has the impact of principles of negligence become more pronounced than in failure-to-warn cases."); Frumer, Friedman, and Sklaren, Products Liability § 12.02[1] (collecting cases). *But see* Shahbaz v. Johnson & Johnson, 2020 WL 5894590, at *11 (C.D. Cal. 2020) ("[F]ailure to warn in strict liability differs markedly from failure to warn in the negligence context. Negligence law in a failure-to-warn case requires a plaintiff to prove that a manufacturer or distributor did not warn of a particular risk for reasons which fell below the acceptable standard of care, i.e., what a reasonably prudent manufacturer would have known and warned about. Strict liability is not concerned with the standard of due care or the reasonableness of a manufacturer's conduct.").

[79] Olson v. Prosoco, Inc., 522 N.W.2d 284 (Iowa 1994). Subsequently, Iowa abandoned negligence claims as well. See Security Nat. Bank of Sioux City, Iowa v. Abbott Labs, 947 F. Supp. 2d 979, 997 (N.D. Iowa 2013) (Iowa no longer supports a distinction between strict liability and negligence claims in warning and design defect cases, so that "warning defect" claims are now so designated, pursuant to Products Liability Rest. § 2(c), without identifying them as "negligence" or "strict liability").

[80] At least Indiana, Louisiana, Mississippi, New Jersey, North Carolina (restating negligence principles for warning cases), Ohio, and Washington.

[81] See §§ 2.6 (negligence) and 5.9 (strict liability in tort), above.

[82] See, e.g., J.D.O. v. Gymboree Corp., 2013 WL 6196970, at *5–9 (D. Minn. 2013); R & R Insulation Servs., Inc. v. Royal Indem. Co., 705 S.E.2d 223, 233 (Ga. Ct. App. 2010) (sellers must exercise reasonable care to warn persons of dangers likely to make a product dangerous); Simonetta v. Viad Corp., 197 P.3d 127, 131 (Wash. 2008) (en banc) ("ordinary care includes a duty to warn of hazards involved in the use of a product, which are or should be known to the manufacturer").

[83] See § 4.3, above.

[84] See UCC § 2–314(2)(c). A defective warning claim may be supported by other subsections. See, e.g., Reid v. Eckerds Drugs, Inc., 253 S.E.2d 344 (N.C. Ct. App. 1979) (plaintiff liberally applied deodorant, lit a

to a manufacturer's failure to provide sufficient warnings or instructions.[85] After all, a product unequipped with the information necessary to make it reasonably safe is quite obviously "unfit" for its ordinary uses. More fundamentally, to the extent that the implied warranty of merchantability is grounded in protecting a purchaser's reasonable expectations of product safety,[86] a seller's failure to warn consumers of a product's hidden dangers assuredly subverts the buyer's safety expectations. In such a case, having paid full value for a product that contained less safety than expected, the buyer would be deprived of the benefit of the bargain.

Today, strict liability in tort, often paired with a negligence claim, is a prominent cause of action for defective warning claims. A product with inadequate information about product dangers and how to avoid them is "defective," plain and simple. In short, such claims are routine in modern products liability litigation and are widely held to be a proper basis of recovery.[87]

It will be recalled that the two principal liability tests for design defectiveness in strict liability in tort are the consumer expectations test and the risk-utility test,[88] both of which sometimes illuminate why information should be provided to users about a product's danger.[89] Yet neither test provides much guidance for distinguishing between dangers that should be warned about and those that should not, nor for determining whether a given warning adequately conveys information about a risk. If a product fails to have adequate warnings of a serious hidden danger, it plainly violates a consumer's expectations,[90] as the implied warranty discussion explains; and the safety benefits of

---

cigarette, and burst into blue flame; an inadequate warning of danger might render the product unmerchantable under UCC § 2–314(2) subsections (c), (e), and (f)).

[85] See, e.g., Ducat v. Ethicon, Inc., 534 F. Supp. 3d 152, 160 (D. Mass. 2021) ("Warranty liability may be based on failure to warn . . . ."); In re NuvaRing Prods. Liab. Litig., 2013 WL 3716389, at *8 (E.D. Mo. 2013) ("Under Section 2–314 of the UCC, a manufacturer may breach its implied warranty of merchantability, based on lack of fitness for ordinary purposes, by failing to provide adequate instructions or warnings."); Keffer v. Wyeth, 791 F. Supp. 2d 539, 546 (S.D. W. Va. 2011) (denying defendant's summary judgment motion on implied warranty of merchantability claim for inadequate drug labeling); Wright v. Brooke Grp. Ltd., 652 N.W.2d 159, 179–83 (Iowa 2002) (cigarettes); Hollister v. Dayton Hudson Corp., 201 F.3d 731, 740 (6th Cir. 2000) (Mich. law) (flammable shirt); Bly v. Otis Elevator Co., 713 F.2d 1040, 1045 (4th Cir. 1983) (Va. law). See generally Lawrence's Anderson on the UCC § 2–314:219 (product without warning of hidden danger, or with inadequate warning, may be unmerchantable).

[86] See § 4.3, above.

[87] See, e.g., Specter v. Texas Turbine Conversions, Inc., 2021 WL 218720, at *5 n.44 (D. Alaska 2021); Diew v. Amazon.com Servs., LLC, 2021 WL 2435265, at *3 (N.D. Cal. 2021) (strict products liability may arise from warning defects, "meaning, the defendant gave inadequate warnings or failed entirely to warn of defects"); Whyte v. Stanley Black & Decker, Inc., 514 F. Supp. 3d 684, 700 (W.D. Pa. 2021) (jury question whether inadequate warnings made hammer unreasonably dangerous); O'Neal v. Bumbo Int'l Trust, 959 F. Supp. 2d 972, 977 (S.D. Tex. 2013) (Ind. law) (baby fell from infant seat parents set on kitchen countertop; manufacturer subject to strict liability in tort if it fails to provide adequate instructions on safe use and adequate warnings of dangers from improper use); Moore v. Ford Motor Co., 332 S.W.3d 749, 769 (Mo. 2011) (en banc) (front seat of vehicle occupied by overweight person could collapse during collision); Leary v. Syracuse Model Neighborhood Corp., 799 N.Y.S.2d 867, 873–74 (Sup. Ct. 2005) (stove could tip); Lewis v. Sea Ray Boats, Inc., 65 P.3d 245 (Nev. 2003) (warning of danger of carbon monoxide exposure from engine exhaust caused by running boat's heater might not have adequately apprised users of risk of such poisoning from using air conditioner run by generator); McConnell v. Cosco, Inc., 238 F. Supp. 2d 970 (S.D. Ohio 2003) (failing to warn that infant, trying to get out of high chair, could get strangled if neck caught on tray); Benjamin v. Wal-Mart Stores, Inc., 61 P.3d 257 (Or. Ct. App. 2002) (risk of asphyxiation from using propane heater in tent).

[88] See chs. 5 and 8, above.

[89] Recall that the consumer expectations and risk-utility tests for product defect arose because they were the general tests for breach of warranty and negligence, respectively, which combined to generate strict liability in tort. See ch. 5, above.

[90] By paying fair value for products appearing to contain certain types and levels of risk, consumers expect to encounter those risks—not others, known to the seller but undisclosed, which frustrate the

proper warnings and instructions almost always exceed their monetary costs, as noted in the negligence discussion.[91]

Thus, when applied to warning cases, both design defect tests unhelpfully point toward liability in every case where a product supplier is charged with failing to provide reasonable warnings of material hidden risks. This frailty in the design defect tests has led courts largely to avoid them both and simply to apply commonsense, negligence-like concepts in assessing warning defects—to wit, if a product does not carry information about all foreseeable, hidden, and material dangers, and on how to avoid them, the product is defective if there was a reasonable way for the information to be conveyed to consumers. Put otherwise, a manufacturer has a duty to provide adequate warnings of all foreseeable, latent, and material dangers, and how to avoid them, and it will be subject to strict liability in tort for physical harm if it neglects to supply reasonable warnings and instructions about such hazards with the products that it sells.

Not surprisingly, this is essentially the standard juries and courts apply *sub silencio* in judging warning defects—that a product is defective if it does not have meaningful warnings of its material hidden risks. So, if a manufacturer can foresee that users and consumers will not recognize a material product hazard, the manufacturer must take reasonable steps to inform them about the risk; and such a product is defective if it does not carry such information. More concisely,[92] manufacturers have a duty to warn users and consumers of material product risks, and a manufacturer will breach that duty by failing to supply adequate warnings and instructions with products that it sells.[93]

Two important related issues treated elsewhere should be noted here. Perhaps the most fundamental issue, when a warning claim is brought in strict liability in tort, is whether the duty to warn is limited to foreseeable risks or whether the duty extends to risks that are unforeseeable, undiscoverable, or "unknowable" at the time the product is sold. In the developmental stages of modern products liability law, a few courts[94] and commentators[95] took the position that the move to "strict" liability must mean that the risks of unforeseeable hazards shifted from consumers to manufacturers, so that a product that did not carry a warning of unforeseeable risks would be "defective" for purposes of strict liability in tort. Over the last few decades, however, American courts and commentators have widely (if not quite universally) rejected this kind of "super-strict" liability on grounds of fairness, logic, and practicality. The various strands of this

---

consumers' reasonable expectations and deprive them of the fair value of their deals. See, e.g., Needham v. Coordinated Apparel Grp., Inc., 811 A.2d 124 (Vt. 2002) (jury could find that clothing fabric which ignites some distance from a fire, and burns explosively, is more dangerous than a consumer would expect).

91 See, e.g., Moran v. Faberge, Inc., 332 A.2d 11, 15 (Md. 1975) (flammability risk of perfume exceeded small expense of printing a warning). See ch. 2, above. But other safety costs arise from over-warning, sometimes referred to as "warnings pollution," which also should be considered.

92 Admittedly incomplete, this formulation is stated simply in a manner applicable to most cases. Two fundamental limitations on the duty to warn, implied in this formulation to keep it concise, are that the duty to warn extends only to risks that are (1) foreseeable, see § 10.4, below; and (2) latent, risks of which consumers generally are unaware. See § 10.2, below.

93 See Gershonowitz, The Strict Liability Duty to Warn, 44 Wash. & Lee L. Rev. 71 (1987) (proposing a similar standard). See also Note, 49 Wash. & Lee L. Rev. 1509 (1992) (proposing a more elaborate version of this standard).

94 See especially Beshada v. Johns-Manville Prods. Corp., 447 A.2d 539, 545 (N.J. 1982), examined in § 10.4, below.

95 See, e.g., W.P. Keeton, Products Liability—Inadequacy of Information, 48 Tex. L. Rev. 398 (1970).

important aspect of the duty to warn are examined later in the context of state of the art.[96]

The second issue is how, if at all, strict liability in tort claims for warning defects differ from claims in negligence. As mentioned earlier in this section, most courts now agree that these types of claims are nearly, or entirely, identical—that, in the words of the Ohio Supreme Court, "the standard imposed upon the defendant in a strict liability claim grounded upon an inadequate warning is the same as that imposed in a negligence claim based upon inadequate warning."[97] Nevertheless, even while acknowledging that "strict" liability in the warning context is really nothing more than negligence, many (perhaps still most) courts insist on pretending that it really is something more—that liability, perhaps because of differing defenses and other secondary rules, still is somehow "strict."[98]

The *Third Restatement* rejects doctrinal labels such as "negligence," "implied warranty," and "strict liability in tort" in defining a seller's liability for warning defects.[99] In § 2(c), a mirror image of the design defect definition in § 2(b),[100] the *Products Liability Restatement* bases liability in warning cases on principles of reasonableness:

> A product . . . is defective because of inadequate instructions or warnings when the foreseeable risks of harm posed by the product could have been reduced or avoided by the provision of reasonable instructions or warnings . . . and the omission of the instructions or warnings renders the product not reasonably safe.

While simplicity and elegance may be wanting,[101] this definition of a warning states a simple proposition: that a product without adequate ("reasonable") warnings or instructions (of foreseeable risks) is defective. Although resting on principles of negligence, the *Restatement* test for warning defects is compatible with the other two conventional causes of action (implied warranty and strict liability in tort) in requiring that a seller provide adequate ("reasonable") safety information with a product. In time, as a number of states have accomplished by reform statute, and one by judicial opinion, separate theories of liability for warning defects may eventually disappear.[102]

---

[96] See § 10.4, below.

[97] Crislip v. TCH Liquidating Co., 556 N.E.2d 1177, 1183 (Ohio 1990) (failure to instruct on strict liability failure to warn claim was harmless error).

[98] *Crislip* is a case in point, the court there explaining that "[w]e do not mean to suggest that a cause of action for negligent failure to warn or warn adequately is identical to one brought under strict liability," principally because a plaintiff's comparative fault may not reduce damages in a strict liability claim in Ohio. See also Anderson v. Owens-Corning Fiberglas Corp., 810 P.2d 549 (Cal. 1991) (unsuccessful attempt to distinguish strict liability in tort from negligence claims).

[99] See Products Liability Rest. § 2 cmt. *n*. And a few states by reform statute have merged negligence, warranty, and strict liability claims into a single "product liability" claim. See, e.g., Conn. Gen. Stat. Ann. §§ 52–572m, 52–572n; Ind. Code Ann. § 34–6–2–115; La. Rev. Stat. Ann. § 9:2800.52; N.J. Stat. Ann. § 2A:58C–1(b)(3); Wash. Rev. Code Ann. § 7.72.010(4).

[100] The "reasonableness test for judging the adequacy of product instructions and warnings . . . [parallels § 2(b)] which adopts a similar standard for judging the safety of product designs. Although the liability standard is formulated in identical terms[,] the defectiveness concept is more difficult to apply in the warnings context." Products Liability Rest. § 2(c) cmt. *i*.

[101] Only one reason for its prolixity is that it unnecessarily includes causation in the definition of a warning defect.

[102] For example, see Ohio's reform statute, discussed in Bowles v. Novartis Pharms. Corp., 2013 WL 5297257, at *7–8 (S.D. Ohio 2013). See also Security Nat. Bank of Sioux City, Iowa v. Abbott Labs., 947 F. Supp. 2d 979, 997 (N.D. Iowa 2013), note 79, above.

Thus, the duty to warn in negligence, implied warranty, and strict liability in tort, under the *Third Restatement*, and under state products liability reform statutes,[103] explicitly centers on one central issue: whether "adequate" warnings and instructions were provided with a product. If so, the product supplier has fulfilled its duty to warn; if not, it has breached its duty and is subject to liability. In short, the liability test for warning claims, regardless of the theory of liability, is "adequacy."

§ 9.3 ADEQUACY

At the center of the duty to warn lies "adequacy." Each theory of liability supporting a warning claim is premised on the defendant's failure to provide users and consumers adequate information about a product danger or how to avoid it, as just discussed.[104] Unless a plaintiff can prove that a warning was "inadequate," a defective warning claim will fail.[105]

"Adequacy" suggests a matter of degree, and most adequacy cases do involve products for which some warning of danger or instruction on safe use was provided. But the "adequacy" category also embraces situations where no warning is provided whatsoever. While the issues in many no-warning cases overlap with adequacy, such as whether the nature and appearance of a product adequately telegraphed its dangers,[106] no-warning cases often are more properly treated as "duty" cases—such as whether there is a duty to warn consumers that their clothing may ignite some distance from a fire, and burn explosively thereafter, or whether this hazard is only part of the flammability risk of which consumers generally are aware.[107]

Many courts have stated what makes a warning "adequate." One helpful formulation is from *Pavlides v. Galveston Yacht Basin, Inc.*,[108] where the court explained that, to be adequate, a warning "must provide 'a complete disclosure of the existence and extent of the risk involved.' A warning must (1) be designed so it can reasonably be expected to catch the attention of the consumer; (2) be comprehensible and give a fair indication of the specific risks involved with the product; and (3) be of an intensity

[103] See, e.g., La. Rev. Stat. Ann. § 9:2800.57; N.J. Stat. Ann. § 2A:58C–4; Ohio Rev. Code Ann. § 2307.76.

[104] See § 9.2, above.

[105] See, e.g., Crawfordsville Town & Country Home Ctr., Inc. v. Cordova, 119 N.E.3d 119, 121–23 (Ind. Ct. App. 2019) ("warnings and illustrations supplied adequate warnings of danger about the risks of electrocution when using the aerial lift"); Farias v. Mr. Heater, Inc., 684 F.3d 1231, 1234–36 (11th Cir. 2012) (Fla. law) (propane gas heater; product box contained operating instructions, "important safeguards," and written and pictorial examples of proper use, and instruction manual contained series of warnings against indoor use); Parish v. Jumpking, Inc., 719 N.W.2d 540, 545–46 (Iowa 2006) (trampoline; 3 warnings on pad, placards provided to place on trampoline, and combination of pictorial and written warnings together adequately warned of dangers); Austin v. Will-Burt Co., 361 F.3d 862 (5th Cir. 2004) (Miss. law) (news van worker killed when van's telescoping mast hit power lines; yellow labels on mast, with red and black lettering, stated: "DANGER! PLEASE READ INSTRUCTIONS BEFORE RAISING!—DANGER. WATCH FOR WIRES. YOU CAN BE KILLED IF THIS PRODUCT COMES NEAR ELECTRICAL POWER LINES").

[106] Compare Greene v. A.P. Prods., Ltd., 717 N.W.2d 855, 862 (Mich. 2006) (given list of natural and "unfamiliar ingredients" on label of hair oil, "a reasonably prudent product user would, or should be, loath to ingest it"; no duty to warn of risks from so doing), with Fralish v. A.O. Smith Corp., 2004 WL 1587559 (Pa. Super. Ct. 2004) (no warning on water heater of scalding risk; trial court improperly granted summary judgment for manufacturer).

[107] Compare Needham v. Coordinated Apparel Grp., Inc., 811 A.2d 124 (Vt. 2002) (duty to warn of cotton garment's explosive flammability), with Coleman v. Cintas Sales Corp., 100 S.W.3d 384 (Tex. App. 2002) (no duty to warn that non-flame retardant uniform would ignite when exposed to open flame and that flaming fabric would be difficult to extinguish). Duty issues associated with products containing obvious and commonly known hazards are addressed in § 10.2, below.

[108] 727 F.2d 330 (5th Cir. 1984) (admiralty law).

justified by the magnitude of the risk."[109] Another court observed that a warning's adequacy depends on a balance of many factors, including "the severity of the danger; the likelihood that the warning will catch the attention of those who will foreseeably use the product and convey the nature of the danger to them; the intensity and form of the warning; and the cost of improving the strength or mode of the warning."[110] The *Products Liability Restatement* states that determining a warning's adequacy requires focusing on its "content and comprehensibility, intensity of expression, and the characteristics of expected user groups," and it emphasizes that courts must be sensitive to a large range of considerations that inform adequacy determinations in different situations.[111] Put otherwise, to be adequate, a warning must provide information about a product's material hidden dangers and how to avoid them, in a manner and intensity justified by the risks and calculated to reach and be understood by those likely to need the information.[112]

The adequacy of a warning is often bound up with the issue of *who* should be warned, so that a warning ordinarily will not be adequate unless it warns persons foreseeably threatened by a product hazard or others in the best position (such as parents, employers, and doctors) to act on warnings to protect persons subject to the hazard.[113] This aspect of warning adequacy informs several issues examined in this section, such as whether warnings should be made in foreign languages (or by symbols) to alert persons who do not read English, and whether industrial machinery should be equipped with back-up bells or buzzers to warn bystanders whom operators do not see. While the issue of whom the manufacturer should warn is touched on indirectly in this

---

[109] Id. at 338. Other courts still rely on this formulation. See, e.g., Lewis v. Sea Ray Boats, Inc., 65 P.3d 245, 248 (Nev. 2003).

[110] Bloxom v. Bloxom, 512 So.2d 839, 844 (La. 1987). See also Feasel v. Tracker Marine, LLC, 496 P.3d 95, 100 (Utah 2021) (to be adequate, a warning must "(1) be designed so it can reasonably be expected to catch the attention of the consumer; (2) be comprehensible and give a fair indication of the specific risks involved with the product; and (3) be of an intensity justified by the magnitude of the risk"); Gray v. Badger Mining Corp., 676 N.W.2d 268, 274 (Minn. 2004) ("To be legally adequate, the warning should (1) attract the attention of those that the product could harm; (2) explain the mechanism and mode of injury; and (3) provide instructions on ways to safely use the product to avoid injury.").

[111] Products Liability Rest. § 2(c) cmt. *i.* Observing that warnings and instructions rarely can provide "all potentially relevant information" about product hazards, that there is no easy guideline for courts to turn to in assessing the adequacy of warnings and instructions, and that determining the appropriate level of detail in warnings is particularly problematic, the Restatement notes that courts should be sensitive to many factors, such as the possibility that "educated or experienced product users and consumers may benefit from inclusion of more information about the full spectrum of product risks, whereas less-educated or unskilled users may benefit from more concise warnings and instructions stressing only the most crucial risks and safe-handling practices," and that "products intended for special categories of users, such as children, may require more vivid and unambiguous warnings." Excessive detail in some cases may diminish a normal person's ability "to focus on the important aspects of the warnings," while "reasonably full disclosure" may be necessary in other cases "to enable informed, efficient choices by product users." Id.

> Product warnings and instructions can rarely communicate all potentially relevant information, and the ability of a plaintiff to imagine a hypothetical better warning in the aftermath of an accident does not establish that the warning actually accompanying the product was inadequate. No easy guideline exists for courts to adopt in assessing the adequacy of product warnings and instructions. In making their assessments, courts must focus on various factors, such as content and comprehensibility, intensity of expression, and the characteristics of expected user groups.

Id.

[112] This perfect formulation of an adequate "warning" of danger implicitly includes "instructions" on safe use. The first part mostly addresses *content* (its "substantive" adequacy), and the latter portion mostly concerns *form* of conveyance (its "procedural" adequacy).

[113] See Anderson v. Hedstrom Corp., 76 F. Supp. 2d 422, 440 (S.D.N.Y. 1999) ("The factual determination of whether an adequate warning was given is 'often interwoven with the question of whether the defendant manufacturer has a duty to warn, and if so, to whom that duty is owed.' ").

section, it is specifically addressed in later sections that inquire generally into the categories of persons to whom warnings should be given (including allergic users);[114] that consider the sophisticated user and bulk supplier doctrines most applicable to the workplace;[115] and that examine the learned intermediary doctrine applicable to warnings for prescription drugs and medical devices.[116]

Whether a manufacturer or other seller has provided sufficient information about a product's hazards is especially fact intensive, such that the adequacy of warnings and instructions normally, but not always,[117] is a factual question for the jury to decide.[118]

Depending on the nature of a product and its hazards, expert testimony may or may not be appropriate on the adequacy of a warning or instruction.[119] Expert testimony will not be allowed in a particular case if the jury has no need for expert guidance on the adequacy of a warning;[120] if the testimony is unreliable;[121] or, possibly, if adequacy is the ultimate issue in the case.[122] Yet courts often admit testimony on the adequacy of warnings by experts with various backgrounds, such as pharmacological labeling,

---

114 See § 9.4, below.

115 See § 9.5, below.

116 See § 18.3, below.

117 See, e.g., Dziedzic v. United Rentals, Inc., 2022 WL 854073, at *6 (M.D. Pa. 2022) (warning adequacy is a question of law for the trial judge); Cates v. Zeltiq Aesthetics, Inc., 535 F. Supp. 3d 1222, 1229 (M.D. Fla. 2021) (adequate as a matter of law); Nelson v. C.R. Bard, Inc., 553 F. Supp. 3d 343, 351 (S.D. Miss. 2021) (adequacy of warning usually for trier of fact, but a court may hold a warning adequate as a matter of law if the manufacturer specifically warned against the specific risk); Ludy v. Eli Lilly & Co., 2020 WL 3510811, at *5 (S.D. Ind. 2020) (detailed, clear, and unambiguous warnings of withdrawal side effects suffered by plaintiff were adequate as a matter of law); Calhoun v. Hoffman-La Roche, Inc., 768 So.2d 57, 61 (La. Ct. App. 2000) (adequacy is a question of law when the warning is "accurate, clear, and unambiguous"). See generally Frumer, Friedman, and Sklaren, Products Liability § 12.03[1][b].

118 See, e.g., In re Davol, Inc./C.R. Bard, Inc., Polypropylene Hernia Mesh Prods. Liab. Litig., 2021 WL 3929825, at *4 (S.D. Ohio 2021) ("whether the warning was adequate in the face of some risk is an issue of fact for the jury"); Kincaid v. Kubota Tractor Corp., 464 P.3d 43, at *6 (Kan. Ct. App. 2020) (table) ("Whether a manufacturer breached its duty to provide an adequate warning is normally a question of fact."); Repka v. Arctic Cat, Inc., 798 N.Y.S.2d 629, 631 (App. Div. 2005) (adequacy of warning is " a question of fact to be determined at trial."). See also LaScala v. QVC, 162 N.Y.S.3d 383, 388 (App. Div. 2022) (" 'Issues regarding the adequacy of instructions or warnings . . . are generally inappropriate for summary judgment relief.' "). See generally Frumer, Friedman, Sklaren, Products Liability § 12.03[1][b].

119 On expert testimony, see § 6.3, above.

120 See, e.g., Rogers v. K2 Sports, LLC, 348 F. Supp. 3d 892, 904 (W.D. Wis. 2018) (expert testimony not required to explain ski helmet fitting instructions written in plain language); Ferebee v. Chevron Chem. Co., 552 F. Supp. 1293, 1304 (D.D.C. 1982) ("[N]o question [is] more appropriately left to a common sense lay judgment than that of whether a written warning gets its message across to an average person. After all, it is to the layman that the warning is addressed, not to the expert on labeling."), aff'd, 736 F.2d 1529 (D.C. Cir. 1984).

121 See, e.g., Wells v. Kawasaki Motors Corp., U.S.A., 854 Fed. Appx. 242, 247 (10th Cir. 2021) (affirming exclusion of plaintiff's expert's unreliable warning label opinion); Medina v. Louisville Ladder, Inc., 496 F. Supp. 2d 1324, 1327–28 (M.D. Fla. 2007) (opinions on bilingual warnings and instructions unreliable); Worthington v. Wal-Mart Stores, Inc., 257 F. Supp. 2d 1339, 1344 (D. Kan. 2003) (testimony of plaintiff's human factors/ergonomics and labeling expert on need for flammability warning labels on flannel shirts properly excluded as unreliable); Kerrigan v. Maxon Indus., 223 F. Supp. 2d 626, 634 (E.D. Pa. 2002) (driver of cement truck injured when mixer unexpectedly raised and struck overpass; expert not qualified to testify on in-cab warning light or buzzer that would have informed driver that mixer was rising while vehicle was in motion; nor was expert's proposed testimony reliable, since he had prepared no plans, drawings, or data showing how feature would work); Meyerhoff v. Michelin Tire Corp., 852 F. Supp. 933 (D. Kan. 1994).

122 See, e.g., Worthington v. Wal-Mart Stores, Inc., 257 F. Supp. 2d 1339, 1343–44 (D. Kan. 2003) (plaintiff's expert could not testify on defendant's responsibility for failing to provide appropriate warning); Shell Oil Co. v. Gutierrez, 581 P.2d 271 (Ariz. Ct. App. 1978) (expert opinion admissible on the properties of chemicals, but not on adequacy of warning). Note, however, the decline of the traditional rule prohibiting experts from offering expert opinions on the ultimate issue in a case. See § 6.3, above.

communications psychology, human factors engineering, and others.[123] In cases involving complex hazards, such as those involving toxic substances and prescription drugs, expert testimony may be necessary to explain the technical or scientific mechanisms or effects that make a particular type of warning necessary.[124]

Content—"Substantive Adequacy"

Content—in General

To be adequate, warnings and instructions must inform consumers, users, and sometimes others of product dangers—an important form of product detriment—and how to avoid harm therefrom. The adequacy requirement of warnings is premised on the duty of manufacturers and other sellers to take reasonable steps to obtain and transmit such information to persons who need and expect it to allow them to make informed decisions on whether to buy a particular product and how to use or otherwise relate to it safely. First and foremost, then, adequacy means that the danger and safety concepts communicated by a warning message contain enough informational content to reasonably accomplish these informational goals. A written warning thus must clearly and comprehensibly describe both the nature and severity of a risk, and an instruction must provide similarly effective information on how to avoid harm from the risk.

Warnings vs. Instructions

A supplier's duty to "warn," it will be recalled,[125] is comprised of two separate duties: (1) the duty to *warn*, to provide information on hidden dangers in a product; and (2) the duty to *instruct*, to provide information on how to avoid those dangers and use the product safely.[126] Because these duties are largely independent—opposite sides of the same safety coin, fulfilling one normally does not fulfill the other. So, no matter how

---

[123] See, e.g., Hopkins v. Superior Metal Workings Sys., L.L.C., 203 P.3d 803, 805–06 (Mont. 2009) (reversing summary judgment for defendant; court's findings on insufficiency of plaintiff's engineering experts' opinions on adequacy of warnings was error); Burley v. Kytec Innovative Sports Equip., Inc., 737 N.W.2d 397 (S.D. 2007) (reversing exclusion of psychology professor's testimony and remanding for determination of reliability); Michaels v. Mr. Heater, Inc., 411 F. Supp. 2d 992 (W.D. Wis. 2006) (human factors expert's testimony on warning method admissible); Benjamin v. Wal-Mart Stores, Inc., 61 P.3d 257, 265 (Or. Ct. App. 2002) (mechanical engineering professor, specializing in human factors engineering, could explain how warning was inadequate: "A warning's adequacy is a proper subject of expert testimony."); Yamaha Motor Co., U.S.A. v. Arnoult, 955 P.2d 661, 668–69 (Nev. 1998) (industrial engineer specializing in human factors and ergonomics allowed to testify; *Daubert* did not apply); Surace v. Caterpillar, Inc., 1995 WL 303895 (E.D. Pa. 1995) (mechanical and safety engineer, and human factors psychologist, both could testify on adequacy of back-up alarm on pavement profiler); Prevatt v. Pennwalt Corp., 237 Cal. Rptr. 488 (Ct. App. 1987) (cognitive psychologist: labels failed to attract user's attention or to warn appropriately of the danger).

[124] See, e.g., Aguilar v. American Med. Sys., Inc., 2020 WL 6504323, at *4 (W.D. Wash. 2020) (plaintiff's experts' evidence of medical device's inadequate warnings raised causation issues of fact); Beadling v. William Bowman Assocs., 809 A.2d 188, 193–94 (N.J. Super. Ct. App. Div. 2002) (explosion of methanol vapor in empty 55 gallon drum when worker was welding nearby; expert testimony on warning inadequacy sufficient); Campagna v. American Cyanamid Co., 767 A.2d 996 (N.J. Super. Ct. App. Div. 2001) (how polio vaccine warning was inadequate; doctor's testimony sufficient to withstand summary judgment).

[125] See § 9.1, above.

[126] See, e.g., McDougall v. CRC Indus., Inc., 523 F. Supp. 3d 1061, 1073 (D. Minn. 2021) ("The duty to warn consists of two duties: '(1) The duty to give adequate instructions for safe use; and (2) the duty to warn of dangers inherent in improper usage.' "); Bensenberg v. FCA US LLC, 2020 WL 7029885, at *10 (C.D. Ill. 2020) ("There are two duties underlying failure to warn cases: a duty to warn of a foreseeable danger and a duty to provide adequate instructions for safe use."), rev'd on other grounds, 31 F.4th 529 (7th Cir. 2022). See also Products Liability Rest. § 2(c) cmt. *i*: "[S]ellers must provide reasonable instructions and warnings about risks of injury posed by products. Instructions inform persons how to use and consume products safely. Warnings alert users and consumers to the existence and nature of product risks so that they can prevent harm either by appropriate conduct during use or consumption or by choosing not to use or consume."

adequately a manufacturer may warn about a product's danger, consumers still may need instructions on how to use the product safely.[127] Thus, a telescope that may be used for viewing the sun must include not only warnings of the dangers of viewing the sun without a proper filter, but it must further provide clear and complete directions on how to install the sun filter in a manner that will protect against the danger; and other products may need to include information on the dangers of, and ways to avoid, installing parts upside-down.[128]

The converse is also true: instructions ordinarily do not satisfy the duty to warn. While manufacturers often argue that their instructions amount to warnings, sometimes luring an unwary court into this deceptive trap, even the best instruction will not usually satisfy a manufacturer's duty to warn if it does not alert users to specific dangers hidden in the product.[129] Yet, some instructions do imply a seriousness of danger, even if only indirectly, that in certain circumstances should sufficiently alert users to the risk.[130] So, if the label on a disposable butane cigarette lighter says, "Keep out of reach of children," it may just be that this is a sufficient "warning" of the risk that a young child might use the lighter to start a fire. On a small object such as a lighter, there is insufficient space to describe most dangers fully if at all. In such cases, particularly when adults already have a quite accurate impression of the risk, a "Keep out of reach of children" instruction should alone imply, sufficiently, that the product poses a serious risk to children that adults had better heed.[131]

Nature and Degree of Specific Risk

To be adequate, a warning must clearly and comprehensibly describe the nature and degree of a product's specific risks. This formulation conflates at least three ideas. First, warnings must be expressed in terms that are clear and *comprehensible*, meaning that they use language that effectively communicates information about a product's hazards. If warning language is unclear and confusing, so that readers cannot fully

---

[127] See, e.g., Myers v. Hoffman-La Roche, Inc., 170 P.3d 254, 265 (Ariz. Ct. App. 2007) ("Warnings of a product's possible harmful effects are not equivalent to adequate directions on how to safely use the product in order to avoid the identified harm.").

[128] See Midgley v. S.S. Kresge Co., 127 Cal. Rptr. 217 (Ct. App. 1976) (K-Mart telescope had inadequate written instructions, and no diagrammatic illustrations, on proper method of attaching sun filter); Nesselrode v. Executive Beechcraft, Inc., 707 S.W.2d 371 (Mo. 1986) (plane); Duford v. Sears, Roebuck & Co., 833 F.2d 407 (1st Cir. 1987) (N.H. law) (wood stove). See also Piper v. Bear Med. Sys., Inc., 883 P.2d 407 (Ariz. Ct. App. 1993) (respirator patient died when therapist, not having been warned of risk, attached one-way valve backwards); Downing v. Overhead Door Corp., 707 P.2d 1027 (Colo. App. 1985).

[129] "Instructions on the use of a product [do] not discharge a manufacturer's duty to warn." Shuras v. Integrated Project Servs., Inc., 190 F. Supp. 2d 194, 201 (D. Mass. 2002). Accord Schulz v. Medtronic, Inc., 2022 WL 503960, at *9 (D. Conn. 2022) (traceostomy tube instructions did not warn of "complication" that contributed to patient's death); McConnell v. Cosco, Inc., 238 F. Supp. 2d 970 (S.D. Ohio 2003) (highchair's instruction to "secure baby with safety straps" does not warn of risk of strangulation); Fuentes v. Shin Caterpillar Mitsubishi, Ltd., 2003 WL 22205665, at *4 (Cal. Ct. App. 2003) ("!WARNING Use self-attaching air chuck and stand behind tire tread while inflating" was really an instruction and was an inadequate warning that tire assembly or rim could explode when inflated, causing serious injury or death); Brown v. Glade & Grove Supply, Inc., 647 So.2d 1033 (Fla. Dist. Ct. App. 1994) (advising driver to operate tractor with lock-out pins in place is instruction, not warning); Meisner v. Patton Elec. Co., 781 F. Supp. 1432 (D. Neb. 1990) (instruction to plug space heater directly into wall outlet did not warn that extension cord could cause short circuit and fire).

[130] See, e.g., Broyles v. Kasper Mach. Co., 865 F. Supp. 2d 887, 897 (S.D. Ohio 2012) (supervisor fell from industrial automated molding line leaving him quadriplegic; "Instructions in a safety manual may satisfy a defendant's duty to warn.").

[131] See Todd v. Societe BIC, S.A. (*Todd II*), 9 F.3d 1216, 1218–19 (7th Cir. 1993) (Ill. law) (Easterbrook, J.).

understand its meaning, then the warning is inadequate.[132] Second, a warning should describe, with reasonable precision, the particular way in which a product is or may become dangerous, the *specific risks* from using or misusing it in different ways. A warning that describes these risks vaguely and too generally, or that describes a different risk from the one that harms a plaintiff, will likely be inadequate.[133] Third, a warning must effectively communicate the risk's *magnitude*—the likelihood and severity of injury the risk may cause. If serious injury of a particular type, or death, may be a consequence, those potentially severe consequences should be specified—with an intensity proportionate to the risk—or the warning will be inadequate.[134] A warning's strength, in other words, "must be commensurate with the dangers involved."[135]

An adequate warning should disclose all foreseeable, material risks from foreseeable ways in which a product may be used. To begin with, a manufacturer must provide adequate warning of all material risks that may arise from a product's normal, intended uses, including the risk of allergic reactions discussed in a later section.[136] But a manufacturer also must warn adequately of risks from unintended uses (which a manufacturer may call "misuses"), provided they are reasonably foreseeable.[137] And a

---

[132] See, e.g., Wilson v. Thompson/Center Arms Co., 2007 WL 2809991, at *8 (E.D. La. 2007) (confusing and misleading instructions on assembly of muzzleloader rifle); Benjamin v. Wal-Mart Stores, Inc., 61 P.3d 257 (Or. Ct. App. 2002) (juxtaposing warning not to use propane heater in unventilated area beside warning of the risk of fire might lead reader to believe that the heater posed a risk of fire in a tent, not that it would asphyxiate the occupants of the tent).

[133] See, e.g., Moore v. Ford Motor Co., 332 S.W.3d 749, 765 (Mo. 2011) (jury question whether adequate warning was given that front vehicle seats occupied by overweight people could collapse during rear-end collision); Wilson v. Thompson/Center Arms Co., 2007 WL 2809991, at *8 (E.D. La. 2007) (muzzleloader backfired violently, causing severe injuries, after plaintiff's reassembly of rifle; manual failed to state consequences of using wrong wrench); Lewis v. Sea Ray Boats, Inc., 65 P.3d 245 (Nev. 2003) (warning of carbon monoxide poisoning from using boat's engines to run heater does not warn of risk of such poisoning from using generator to run air-conditioning); Hayes v. Spartan Chem. Co., 622 So.2d 1352 (Fla. Dist. Ct. App. 1993) (warning of general risks of cleaning fluids inadequate without mentioning risks from one brief exposure); Ayers v. Johnson & Johnson Baby Prods. Co., 818 P.2d 1337 (Wash. 1991) (warning that baby may get diarrhea from ingesting "Baby Oil" does not warn of paralysis); General Chem. Corp. v. De La Lastra, 815 S.W.2d 750 (Tex. App. 1991) ("toxic" inadequately describes death), rev'd in part on other grounds, 852 S.W.2d 916 (Tex. 1993).

Compare Spillane v. Georgia Pac. Corp., 1995 WL 71183, at *3–4 (E.D. Pa. 1995), which involved a roofing compound that warned: "CAUTION, SLIPPERY WHEN WET. Do not walk on surface unless it is completely dry. Follow proper safety precautions, including using appropriate shoes and safety rope." Plaintiff, a roofer, slipped on the compound, fell off a roof, and sued the manufacturer for failing adequately to warn. *Held*, defendant's motion for summary judgment denied. Although the language "at first seems the epitome of unambiguous clarity," it failed to convey how "appallingly slick" the roof surface was. The court drew an analogy to warning "Beware of cat. Stay Away," which would fail adequately to warn a person "chomped" by "a full-grown, hungry cheetah . . . . The cheetah is the quickest land-animal in the world, and plaintiffs' papers suggest this was just about the slickest roof in the world."

But see Kelso v. Bayer Corp., 398 F.3d 640, 642–43 (7th Cir. 2005) (Ill. law) ("[f]requent or prolonged use may cause nasal congestion to recur or worsen" adequately warned plaintiff of permanent nasal tissue damage after continuous use for three years); Werckenthein v. Bucher Petrochemical Co., 618 N.E.2d 902 (Ill. App. Ct. 1993) (warning against "repeated exposure" to chemical adequately warned chemist who suffered cancer and stroke after using sniff test on chemicals for many years).

[134] See, e.g., Benjamin v. Wal-Mart Stores, Inc., 61 P.3d 257 (Or. Ct. App. 2002) (jury could find the given warning inadequate on a propane heater: "WARNING: FOR OUTDOOR USE ONLY. Never use inside house, camper, tent, vehicle or other unventilated or enclosed areas" because it did not warn that user could suffer "serious injury" or "death," or be "killed"); General Chem. Corp. v. De La Lastra, 815 S.W.2d 750 (Tex. App. 1991) ("toxic" inadequately describes death), rev'd in part on other grounds, 852 S.W.2d 916 (Tex. 1993).

[135] Shuras v. Integrated Project Servs., Inc., 190 F. Supp. 2d 194, 201 (D. Mass. 2002). Accord Farias v. Mr. Heater, Inc., 684 F.3d 1231, 1234–36 (11th Cir. 2012) (Fla. law) (see note 140, below).

[136] See § 9.4, below.

[137] See, e.g., Magadan v. Interlake Packaging Corp., 845 N.Y.S.2d 443, 445–46 (App. Div. 2007); Benjamin v. Wal-Mart Stores, Inc., 61 P.3d 257 (Or. Ct. App. 2002) (jury properly found that manufacturer

manufacturer must provide warnings and instructions on peripheral uses that reasonably may be expected, such as why a hazardous chemical may need to be disposed of safely, and how to do so.[138] Yet, there simply is no way to warn perfectly of every risk, and too much information presents dangers of its own—the "warnings pollution" problem discussed below.

Form—"Procedural Adequacy"

Form—in General

For a warning or instruction to be adequate, it must be conveyed in a manner likely to reach and be comprehended by those who buy or otherwise come in contact with the product. This type of adequacy, because it often deals with physical methods for delivering information, may be referred to as "procedural"—to distinguish it from the substantive content of information, which addresses its meaning. Procedural adequacy has various dimensions—the conspicuousness of written warnings, including their placement in prominent locations; the use of foreign languages; and nonverbal warnings (such as buzzers, beeps, and smells), when fairly called for in the circumstances.

Conspicuousness. Most warnings are conveyed in written form, and a recurring procedural adequacy issue for written warnings is whether they are "conspicuous." Conspicuousness typically depends on type size, its style or font, its color, whether it contrasts with other messages nearby, whether the warning carries a heading such as "WARNING!" or "CAUTION," and its location. Conspicuousness has long been a formal requirement of warranty disclaimers, as seen earlier, and considerations for determining whether a writing is conspicuous in that context translate well to cases involving the procedural adequacy of written warnings.[139] So, if a warning is written in yellow or red letters that are large and bold, and preceded by a large "WARNING!" heading,[140] it is

---

could foresee propane heater, marketed only for outdoor use because of its carbon monoxide fumes, might be used to heat a tent). A manufacturer has no duty to warn of unforeseeable uses. See § 13.5 (misuse), below.

[138] See, e.g., Tucci v. Bossert, 385 N.Y.S.2d 328 (App. Div. 1976) (partially used can of Drano placed in trash bag in front of house because manufacturer had inadequately warned of risks); Boyl v. California Chem. Co., 221 F. Supp. 669 (D. Or. 1963) (inadequate warning on how and why to safely rinse highly toxic residue from weed killer spray tank). On a maker's responsibility for dangers of disposal, see § 10.7, below.

[139] See § 4.7, above.

[140] See, e.g., Farias v. Mr. Heater, Inc., 684 F.3d 1231, 1234–36 (11th Cir. 2012) (Fla. law) (affirming summary judgment for propane gas heater manufacturer; "The warnings also adequately convey the message that misuse of the heater runs a serious risk of not only fire, but explosions, asphyxiation, carbon monoxide poisoning, electrical shock, and personal injury, loss of life and property damage. [The warnings are] in bold and capital letters and contain the headings 'WARNING.' We find these warnings to be 'of such intensity as to cause a reasonable man to exercise for his own safety caution commensurate with the potential danger' of fire that occurred due to Farias's misuse of the heater."); Crosswhite v. Jumpking, Inc., 411 F. Supp. 2d 1228 (D. Or. 2006) (trampoline warnings that provided multiple specific warnings against risks and how to avoid them, and that were preceded by "! WARNING" headings, were adequate as a matter of law); Austin v. Will-Burt Co., 361 F.3d 862 (5th Cir. 2004) (Miss. law) (dismissing inadequate warning claim for electrocution of news van worker killed when van's telescoping mast hit power lines; yellow labels on mast, with red and black lettering, stated: "DANGER! PLEASE READ INSTRUCTIONS BEFORE RAISING!—DANGER. WATCH FOR WIRES. YOU CAN BE KILLED IF THIS PRODUCT COMES NEAR ELECTRICAL POWER LINES.").

Compare Beadling v. William Bowman Assocs., 809 A.2d 188, 193–94 (N.J. Super. Ct. App. Div. 2002) (methanol vapor in empty 55-gallon drum exploded while worker was welding nearby; flammability warning label on top of drum, obscured by dark oily residue, should also have been placed on sides of drum and had plastic coating—ANSI standard provides that label should be protected from "damage, fading or visual obstruction" from abrasion, ultra-violet light, lubricants, chemical, or dirt).

more likely to be conspicuous than if the warning is black and white, small, and has no heading.[141]

Location. An important feature of conspicuousness is location. When warnings are set apart and located in a prominent position, they are most likely to be observed and absorbed. Thus, warnings are more likely to be conspicuous if they are printed by themselves on the front of the product or its label, rather than together with other information on a product's side or back.[142] Similarly, warnings are more likely to catch the attention of users if they are placed near the point of danger,[143] at eye level,[144] and at a place where the user normally focuses attention, such as near the controls and on the front of the product.[145] Warnings are less likely to be seen, and thus may be inconspicuous, if they are buried deep inside an operator's manual or instructions booklet.[146]

These principles of conspicuousness point to one of the most basic questions of location—whether a warning must be placed *directly on the product itself*, such as on its label, container, or body—or whether instead the warning may be included in a sheet, leaflet, manual, contract, or other form of conveyance intended to accompany the product. This adequacy issue is bound up with that of *who* must be warned of product hazards, since it often arises in the context of industrial products, such as punch presses

---

[141] See, e.g., Jones v. Amazing Prods., Inc., 231 F. Supp. 2d 1228, 1248 (N.D. Ga. 2002) (cautionary instruction on drain cleaner label in such small print, "buried in the middle of a long paragraph," that even judge, looking for this language, had to read label twice to find it; *held*, adequacy for jury); Jaurequi v. John Deere Co., 971 F. Supp. 416, 428 (E.D. Mo. 1997) (warnings on farm machine were inadequate: too small and located far from hazard); Spruill v. Boyle-Midway, Inc., 308 F.2d 79, 82 (4th Cir. 1962) (Va. law) (furniture polish ingested by small child; classic case in which warning printed in small, brown type was held inadequate).

[142] Compare Falkner v. Para Chem, 2003 WL 21396693, at *7 (Ohio Ct. App. 2003) (warning that carpet adhesive should not be used indoors because its vapors were flammable "could easily be missed" because it was located on side panel not read by carpet installers), with Mohney v. U.S. Hockey, Inc., 300 F. Supp. 2d 556 (N.D. Ohio 2004) (location, form, and method of display of warnings on hockey helmet were adequate). See also Delery v. Prudential Ins. Co. of Am., 643 So.2d 807, 814 (La. Ct. App. 1994) (warning that chair was unstable on carpeting, located beneath chair rather than in sales brochure or shipping box, was inadequate).

[143] See, e.g., Green Plains Otter Tail, LLC v. Pro-Env't, Inc., 953 F.3d 541, 548 (8th Cir. 2020) (Minn. law) (warning that failure to maintain accumulator in hydraulic pump unit could cause death, personal injury, or property damage was attached to accumulator; warning included instructions to follow maintenance procedures listed in manuals and on website address printed on warning); Manion v. General Elec. Co., 2007 WL 2565979, at *5–6 (N.D. Fla. 2007) (warning that range could tip from placing weight on oven door, located inside oven door and clearly visible when door was open, would adequately attract a user's attention); Jaurequi v. John Deere Co., 971 F. Supp. 416, 428 (E.D. Mo. 1997) (expert could testify that warnings on farm machine were inadequate because placed remote from hazard).

[144] See, e.g., Holst v. Konecranes Int'l Corp., 699 S.E.2d 715, 723 (S.C. Ct. App. 2010) ("Danger" and "Hanging Load" warning decals located at eye-level on crane); General Motors Corp. v. Saenz, 873 S.W.2d 353 (Tex. 1993) (warning against overloading truck, located on doorjamb at eye level, in accordance with custom and federal regulations, was adequate); Gordon v. Niagara Mach. & Tool Works, 574 F.2d 1182, 1194 (5th Cir. 1978) (Miss. law) (warning on press, "conspicuously displayed at eye level," would be more effective than words in a manual). See note 149, below.

[145] See, e.g., Vermett v. Fred Christen & Sons Co., 741 N.E.2d 954, 971 (Ohio Ct. App. 2000) (warnings adequate—on front of press, at eye level, directly in front of operator, and stating: "NEVER PLACE ANY PART OF YOUR BODY AT THE POINT OF OPERATION (UNDER THE RAM OR WITHIN THE DIE AREA)" and "NEVER OPERATE MACHINE WITHOUT PINCH POINTS GUARDED AND WITHOUT ADEQUATE POINT OF OPERATION SAFEGUARDING"). Compare Ruggiero v. Yamaha Motor Corp., U.S.A., 778 Fed. Appx. 88, 92 (3d Cir. 2019) (N.J. law) (personal watercraft warnings to wear protective clothing, posted below front handlebars and above rear boarding deck, with orange WARNING banners, were visible to injured passenger and adequately warned of danger), with Mizrahi v. Yamaha Motor Corp., U.S.A., 2019 WL 3890311, at *4 (S.D. Fla. 2019) (issue of fact for jury whether similar warnings were conspicuous to a passenger).

[146] See, e.g., Yazdani v. BMW of N. Am., LLC, 2016 WL 2755589, at *6–7 (E.D. Pa. 2016) (jury question whether warnings of fire risk from running motorcycle at standstill, included among 50 other warnings in 89-page owner's manual, should have been attached to motorcycle itself).

or cranes, where the manufacturer fails to place a warning label directly on the product but includes danger warnings in an "operator's manual" that the people who actually operate the machine may never see.[147] Whether adequacy requires in any given case that warnings be placed directly on a product involves a balance of the significance of the hazard, the user's need for the information, the availability of a feasible means to place the warnings on the product, and other factors in the calculus of risk.

If feasible, sometimes warnings of serious hazards should be placed on the product itself rather than in a pamphlet, booklet, or information sheet that can be damaged, lost, discarded, destroyed, or stuffed in a drawer.[148] Warnings often can quite easily be located on a container or its label, on a plate near the ram of a press or other danger point of a machine, etched into the product's body, or printed on a tag attached somewhere likely to be seen.[149] Yet, depending on the circumstances, a warning sometimes may be adequate even if located off the product in a manual, other writing, or on a website.[150]

Foreign Language Warnings

A special aspect of both form and comprehensibility is whether warnings must be provided in a foreign language. With the increasingly global marketplace for products manufactured in this nation, where Spanish is spoken on our southern borders, French on our northeastern borders, and Asian languages increasingly on the West Coast, one must wonder whether English-only warnings can possibly be adequate in the modern world. If manufacturers target markets in southern portions of Florida, Texas, New Mexico, Arizona, and California, or in Northern Vermont and Maine (adjacent to Québec), the question is whether the law should require such products to carry warnings in Spanish, French, Japanese, Korean, or Chinese as well as English. Another question is whether the choice of whether products should carry multi-lingual warnings should be left to manufacturers or should be mandated by the government. And, if it is thought the government should intervene, one must decide which branch or branches of government should make and enforce that determination—legislatures, administrative agencies, the courts, or some combination of the three. So far, each branch of government has played some role in making these decisions. Yet, there has been surprisingly little debate on this important issue, perhaps reflecting the deep English-only tradition that long has prevailed in America, which is geographically isolated from most other cultures. But the world is rapidly going global, as is the law of products liability,[151] and the various

---

[147] See §§ 9.4–9.5, 18.3, below.

[148] See Rest. (2d) of Torts § 402A cmt. *j* (a seller may be required to place warnings or instructions on a product's container).

[149] See, e.g., Mohr v. Yamaha Motor Co., 2013 WL 3762719, at *6 (N.J. Super. Ct. App. Div. 2013) (warning against lifting rear of running snowmobile should have been affixed to its back rather than only in owner's manual); Michaels v. Mr. Heater, Inc., 411 F. Supp. 2d 992, 999 (W.D. Wis. 2006) (warning tag should have been permanently affixed to heater, not a replaceable part); Fuentes v. Shin Caterpillar Mitsubishi, Ltd., 2003 WL 22205665, at *4 (Cal. Ct. App. 2003) (warning of risk that tire rim might explode while putting air in tire should have been stamped on wheel of loader); Griggs v. Firestone Tire & Rubber Co., 513 F.2d 851 (8th Cir. 1975) (Mo. law) (warning against mismatching multipiece tire rims to prevent violent explosions could have been stamped on rim components); West v. Broderick & Bascom Rope Co., 197 N.W.2d 202 (Iowa 1972) (metal tag with load limit could have been bonded to collar of metal rope or "sling" that broke). Compare Westry v. Bell Helmets, Inc., 487 N.W.2d 781 (Mich. Ct. App. 1992) (warning stickers sufficed; no duty to emboss warnings permanently on helmet). See notes 143–145, above.

[150] See, e.g., Herbert v. Titan Int'l, Inc., 778 Fed. Appx. 275, 278 (5th Cir. 2019) (jury could find that warnings on website and in catalogue were adequate without placing them on multi-piece wheel that exploded); Freas v. Prater Constr. Corp., 573 N.E.2d 27 (Ohio 1991) (crane manual adequately warned not to stand under boom, and warning need not have been placed on boom itself).

[151] See § 1.4, above.

branches of American government increasingly will need to focus on the multilingual question.

Only a handful of judicial decisions in America have examined whether a warning must be made in a foreign language to be adequate.[152] Several decisions have ruled that warnings are not to be held inadequate because they are written only in English. In *Ramirez v. Plough, Inc.*,[153] an infant contracted Reye's Syndrome after his Spanish-speaking mother gave him St. Joseph's Aspirin for Children to relieve his cold symptoms. The aspirin's label warned of the Reye's Syndrome risk in English but not in Spanish. Although the FDA specifically permitted English-only labeling, the plaintiff claimed that the label's failure to include a Spanish warning rendered it inadequate. The court reviewed a number of related factors, including the web of rules on foreign-language labeling requirements in various other contexts adopted by the California legislature; the FDA's quite specific rules governing foreign-language labeling that permitted, but did not require, such labeling; and a multiplicity of health, social, cost, and practicability considerations. Considering all these factors, the court concluded that foreign-language labeling requirements were better determined by legislatures and regulatory agencies than by the courts. Because other branches of government had determined that English-only warnings were sufficient, the court decided that it should apply the same rule to the case.[154]

On similar reasoning, a federal circuit court approved the English-only flammability warnings on a 55-gallon drum of chemicals that exploded when Spanish-speaking workers in Puerto Rico used a welding torch near the drum.[155] Because OSHA regulations only required employers to warn in English, allowing but not requiring them to warn in other languages, the court was strongly influenced by the administrative policy to leave decisions on multi-lingual warnings to the discretion of employers and, inferentially, to the discretion of manufacturers. Thus, even though the chemical product was sold for use in Spanish-speaking Puerto Rico, the English-only warnings were held sufficient.[156] More recently, at least four other courts have also refused to rule that English-only warnings are inadequate.[157]

---

152 See Richmond, When Plain English Isn't: Manufacturers' Duty to Warn in a Second Language, 29 Tort & Ins. L.J. 588 (1994); Notes, 25 Minn. J. Int'l L. 519 (2016), 47 Vand. L. Rev. 1107 (1994), 29 Ga. L. Rev. 197 (1994), 29 Ga. J. Int'l & Comp. L. 573 (1994), 15 J. Legal Med. 129 (1994); Annot., 27 A.L.R.5th 697 (1995).

153 863 P.2d 167 (Cal. 1993). *Ramirez* is also examined in § 14.4, below.

154 Noting that the FDA stresses the importance of "uniformity of presentation and clarity of message," the court concluded: "To preserve that uniformity and clarity, to avoid adverse impacts upon the warning requirements mandated by the federal regulatory scheme, and in deference to the superior technical and procedural lawmaking resources of legislative and administrative bodies, we adopt the legislative/regulatory standard of care that mandates nonprescription drug package warnings in English only." Id. at 177.

155 Torres-Rios v. LPS Labs., Inc., 152 F.3d 11, 13–14 (1st Cir. 1998) (P.R. law).

156 In addition to the warnings in English, the drum prominently displayed a pictorial of a flame, "a universal symbol of flammability," which "filled any language gap." Id.

157 See, e.g., Crawfordsville Town & Country Home Center, Inc. v. Cordova, 119 N.E.3d 119, 130 (Ind. Ct. App. 2019) (rental company did not owe duty to furnish additional warnings to Hispanic worker about the dangers of using an aerial lift near power lines); Farias v. Mr. Heater, Inc., 684 F.3d 1231, 1234–36 (11th Cir. 2012) (Fla. law) (affirming adequacy of English-only warnings and distinguishing *Stanley*, discussed in the text at note 159, below); Martinez v. Triad Controls, Inc., 593 F. Supp. 2d 741, 764–65 (E. D. Pa. 2009) (dismissing warnings claim alleging inadequacy of English-only warning and distinguishing *Stanley Industries*; there was no evidence that the power press manufactured and sold in Canada was intended for an Hispanic population); Medina v. Louisville Ladder, Inc., 496 F. Supp. 2d 1324, 1329–30 (M.D. Fla. 2007) (disagreeing with and declining to follow *Stanley*; summary judgment for defendant).

Other cases point the opposite direction, suggesting that foreign-language warnings sometimes might be necessary to make a warning adequate.[158] In *Stanley Industries, Inc. v. W. M. Barr & Co.*,[159] the defendant manufactured and sold linseed oil in a can that warned in English that rags soaked with the oil could spontaneously combust. Spanish-speaking workers used the rags, which ignited and caused a fire. Because the defendant marketed its product in an area with a substantial Spanish-speaking population, the trial court allowed the jury to decide if the warning was inadequate because it did not warn in Spanish.[160] In another case, a Spanish-speaking worker, who was not wearing safety goggles, was injured in the eye while using a pneumatic nailer.[161] The nailer's manual warned in English, but not Spanish, of the need for eye protection. Here, the court allowed a warning expert to testify that the warning was defective for being written only in English where labor statistics revealed that 51% of non-fatal injuries by nail guns were caused to Hispanics, and two of the defendant's competitors put dual-language warnings on their nailers.

Quite the opposite question was raised by *Fuentes v. Shin Caterpillar Mitsubishi, Ltd.*,[162] where a Spanish-speaking driver of a loader tractor in California was injured when the tractor's tire exploded as he was inflating it with air. His suit against the Japanese manufacturer alleged that the warnings were inadequate because they should have been in English, not just Japanese. While agreeing that warnings for products made for a foreign market should be written in the language of that market, the court dismissed the claim because the manufacturer had sold the tractor for use exclusively in Japan.[163]

Nonverbal Warnings—Pictures, Symbols, Bells, and Smells

General danger symbols—adults. A recurring (if secondary) theme in the foreign-language cases just discussed is that pictures or symbols may be a particularly effective way to convey information on product dangers to people who read only foreign languages, or who cannot read at all.[164] In perhaps the earliest case involving the adequacy of warnings on a product used by foreign workers, *Hubbard-Hall Chemical Co.*

---

[158] See, e.g., Arbaiza v. Delta Int'l Mach. Corp., 1998 WL 846773 (E.D.N.Y. 1998) (table saw warned in small print and English only; adequacy was jury question).

[159] 784 F. Supp. 1570 (S.D. Fla. 1992).

[160] "Given the advertising of defendants' product in the Hispanic media and the pervasive presence of foreign-tongued individuals in the Miami workforce, it is for the jury to decide whether a warning, to be adequate, must contain language other than English or pictorial warning symbols." Id. at 1576.

[161] Ortiz v. Stanley-Bostitch, Inc., 2000 WL 640645 (S.D.N.Y. 2000).

[162] 2003 WL 22205665 (Cal. Ct. App. 2003).

[163] "Determining whether a warning would be feasible and effective necessarily involves a consideration of the language in which a warning must be given. We certainly believe that if a Japanese manufacturer places a product in the stream of commerce, and it is reasonably foreseeable that the product will be used in United States, safety warnings regarding the risks of operation should be in English." However, plaintiff failed to prove manufacturer knew their product, made and sold in Japan, would be resold to a purchaser in U.S. Id. at *11.

[164] See also Campos v. Firestone Tire & Rubber Co., 485 A.2d 305, 310 (N.J. 1984) ("In view of the unskilled or semi-skilled nature of the work and the existence of many in the work force who do not read English, warnings in the form of symbols might have been appropriate, since the employee's 'ability to take care of himself' was limited."). For examples of adequate pictorial warnings, see, e.g., Crawfordsville Town & Country Home Center, Inc. v. Cordova, 119 N.E.3d 119, 121–23 (Ind. Ct. App. 2019) ("aerial lift had multiple warning labels with diagrams placed on the aerial lift by the manufacturer that directed users not to use the lift within ten feet of a high-voltage line"; diagrams reproduced in the opinion); Ruggiero v. Yamaha Motor Corp., U.S.A., 778 Fed. Appx. 88, 90 (3d Cir. 2019) (warning label on jet ski glovebox included an "illustration of a properly dressed rider wearing a wetsuit bottom").

v. Silverman,[165] two Spanish-speaking farm workers died from inhaling insecticide dust from bags that had English warnings only. After the jury was instructed that an adequate warning is one "calculated to bring home to a [reasonable user] the nature and extent of the danger of the product involved," it returned a verdict for the plaintiffs. The appellate court upheld the verdict, reasoning that the jury properly could have concluded that even the best of written warnings was inadequate because it was foreseeable that the insecticide would be used by illiterate farm workers who needed warnings conveyed by a skull and crossbones or other danger symbol.

The traditional skull and crossbones, like the one below, has long been viewed as an effective, if general, nonverbal way to communicate a danger.[166]

Empirical research confirms the inference that symbols, such as a skull and crossbones, often may be necessary to alert even literate adults to product dangers. Some studies suggest that it matters little how completely a written warning is worded, or even whether it is given at all, since few people will read or heed it anyway.[167] More recent and sophisticated behavioral studies confirm the conclusion that consumers process information irrationally.[168] For whatever reasons, people frequently fail to process verbal danger information in a manner that will avoid accidents.

General danger symbols—children. Research at the Pittsburgh Poison Center of the Children's Hospital of Pittsburgh in 1971 revealed that the traditional skull and crossbones symbol tended to *attract* rather than repel small children to hazardous substances so labeled. The children associated the symbol with cartoon pirates, adventure, excitement, and (at least in Pittsburgh) the Pittsburgh Pirates baseball team. So researchers sought a new symbol that would deter young children from playing with (or consuming) toxic substances in the home. Children at daycare centers were shown six bottles of mouthwash, separately labeled with different symbols, and asked to identify bottles they might not like to play with. The symbols included a red stop sign, a skull and crossbones, a scowling green face, and three others. The least popular was the

---

165 340 F.2d 402 (1st Cir. 1965) (Mass. law).

166 See, e.g., Mossrud v. Lee, 157 N.W. 758 (Wis. 1916) (jury could find that farm supplier was negligent for selling quack grass poison in containers that did not include skull and crossbones).

167 See, e.g., Goldhaber and deTurk, Effects of Consumers' Familiarity With a Product on Attention To and Compliance With Warnings, 11 J. Prod. Liab. 29 (1988); Dorris and Purswell, Warnings and Human Behavior: Implications for the Design of Product Warnings, 1 J. Prod. Liab. 254 (1977).

168 See, e.g., Symposium: Rational Actors or Rational Fools? The Implications of Psychology for Products Liability, 6 Roger Williams U. L. Rev. 1 (2000); Hanson and Kysar, Taking Behavioralism Seriously: The Problem of Market Manipulation, 74 N.Y.U. L. Rev. 630, 724 (1999); Hanson and Kysar, Taking Behavioralism Seriously: Some Evidence of Market Manipulation, 112 Harv. L. Rev. 1420, 1425 (1999). See generally Sunstein, The Laws of Fear, 115 Harv. L. Rev. 1119, 1123 (2002) (reviewing P. Slovic, The Perception of Risk (2000); "ordinary people often deal poorly with the topic of risk").

scowling face, which one of the youngsters said "looks yukky," which gave rise to the famous "Mr. Yuk":

Mr. Yuk

Green-faced Mr. Yuk stickers, for parents to affix to toxic substances around the home, are now widely available from poison control centers across the nation. He is a registered trademark and was copyrighted by the Children's Hospital of Pittsburgh. Mr. Yuk stickers are thought to be partially responsible for a substantial drop in child poisonings.[169]

Whether making Mr. Yuk look even more revolted and revolting would be more likely to scare children away from toxic substances, and hence be more effective, is difficult to know. The variation on Mr. Yuk shown below, is a registered New Zealand trademark of Quik Stik International:

A large field trial revealed that the super-revolted Mr. Yuk shown immediately above would *not* be effective in preventing child poisonings. Many of the parents believed the symbol actually attracted children to the labeled substances.[170] Perhaps explaining why plaintiffs have not based defective warning claims on a manufacturer's failure to use danger symbols on drain cleaners, furniture polish, and other toxic household products is the difficulty of establishing the efficacy of such symbols in averting consumption by young children.

Particularized danger symbols—adults. In an effort to increase attention to product warnings, both the government and private industry have explored the use of

---

[169] On the effectiveness of Mr. Yuk, see Strothkamp v. Chesebrough-Pond's, Inc., 1993 WL 79239, at *7 (Mo. Ct. App. 1993) (5-year-old child who injured his ear with a Q-Tip from box that did not have Mr. Yuk sticker testified that he would not touch anything marked with a Mr. Yuk sticker).

[170] See 5 Prod. Liab. Int'l 190 (Dec. 1983).

danger symbols to signify particular types and levels of particular product risks. A powerful anti-acne drug called Accutane, a synthetic derivative of Vitamin A, was found to cause birth defects in about 25% of children born to pregnant women taking the drug. Rather than totally banning the drug, the FDA required the manufacturer to provide emphatic written warnings and instructions, in both patient and physician information labeling, together with the following diagram on each page of the patient leaflet and on each side of the drug's packaging. In addition, the FDA directed that patient information labeling was to include a drawing of a deformed baby.[171]

While warning symbols often help convey danger information, symbols by themselves sometimes may not be adequate to fully convey a danger and how to avoid it.[172] In such cases, a reasonable warning may require supplementing the picture or symbol with written warnings or instructions. Several companies and industry associations have researched how to improve communications on product hazards in the workplace. The leader in this area has long been FMC Corporation, which some time ago developed a sophisticated industrial product warnings system that combines particularized danger symbols with written warnings and instructions.[173] Its Product Safety Sign and Label System uses pictorials, combined with words and colors, in formats designed to present hazard information to industrial workers as effectively as possible.[174] The system uses 3-paneled rectangular labels to communicate: (1) the level of hazard seriousness; (2) the nature of the hazard; (3) the consequence of interaction with the hazard; and (4) instructions on how to avoid the hazard.

As seen below, the top panel in each warning contains a signal word (DANGER, WARNING or CAUTION) that communicates the level of hazard seriousness. (DANGER is printed in white letters, against a red background; WARNING, in black on orange; and CAUTION, in black on yellow.) The center panel contains the pictorial which communicates the nature of the hazard, and the likely consequence of human interaction with the hazard. Some pictorials also depict a method for avoiding the hazard, such as wearing protection for the eyes. The third panel provides an instruction on how to avoid the hazard and may further describe the hazard and/or its consequences to the worker.

---

[171] See Willis, New Warning About Accutane and Birth Defects, FDA Consumer 27 (Oct. 1988).

[172] See Parish v. Jumpking, Inc., 719 N.W.2d 540, 545–46 (Iowa 2006) (warning symbols combined with written warnings adequately conveyed dangers of trampoline); Fyssakis v. Knight Equip. Corp., 826 P.2d 570 (Nev. 1992) (symbol for corrosiveness on soap dispenser inadequately warned that dishwashing soap could blind).

[173] See Product Safety Sign and Label System, © 1993 FMC Corporation.

[174] The communication system was designed to meet or exceed the requirements of American National Standard Z535.4–1991, Products Safety Signs and Labels.

Sometimes a separate box, entitled SAFETY INSTRUCTIONS (white letters on green), provides more information on safe use.

(E7580)

The United Nations developed the following "globally harmonized system (GHS)" for labeling chemicals,[175] which OSHA ordered applicable to American employers.[176]

175 The Globally Harmonized System of Classification and Labelling of Chemicals (GHS) 25, figure 4.9 (rev. 5th ed., United Nations, 2013).

176 29 C.F.R. § 1910.1200. Required by mid-2015, "[e]ach pictogram consists of a symbol on a white background framed within a red border and represents a distinct hazard(s). The pictogram on the label is determined by the chemical hazard classification." OSHA QuickCard: Hazard Communication Standard Pictogram, https://www.osha.gov/sites/default/files/publications/OSHA3491QuickCardPictogram.pdf (where the QuickCard contains OSHA's 2021 version of the classification and labeling system).

GHS Pictograms and Hazard Classes		

• Oxidizers	• Flammables • Self Reactives • Pyrophorics • Self-Heating • Emits Flammable Gas • Organic Peroxides	• Explosives • Self Reactives • Organic Peroxides

• Acute toxicity (severe)	• Corrosives	• Gases Under Pressure

• Carcinogen • Respiratory Sensitizer • Reproductive Toxicity • Target Organ Toxicity • Mutagenicity • Aspiration Toxicity	• Environmental Toxicity	• Irritant • Dermal Sensitizer • Acute toxicity (harmful) • Narcotic Effects • Respiratory Tract • Irritation

Such pictorial warnings are undoubtedly more effective, in general, than written warnings alone. But the absence of case law addressing whether products liability law *requires* such sophisticated warning systems suggests that safety labeling experts are still uncertain as to just how effective such pictorial warnings may be. Even more difficult would be establishing causation—whether such a warning, had it been provided in lieu of or in addition to a mere written warning, would have prevented a particular product accident.[177]

Other nonverbal warning methods. Apart from pictorial warnings, danger information may be communicated to users in other nonverbal ways—even in non-visual ways, relying on other senses. A needle gauge or warning light may helpfully inform an operator that a crane is about to tip, that fuel is low, that a parking brake is engaged, or that a rear mounted aircraft engine has stopped operating.[178] A buzzer, bell, rear-view mirror, or rear camera (with a viewing screen inside the vehicle's cabin) may warn operators or potential victims of the risks from vehicles operated in reverse.[179] Color may be added to a dangerous, clear, chemical fluid to distinguish it from water,[180] and odor may be added to propane gas to give notice of its presence.[181] And warnings may rely on the sense of touch, such as vibration in the seat of a crane about to tip over, or in the steering wheel of a car drifting out of its highway lane. There simply is no end to the kinds of creative ways warnings may be conveyed.

Nullifying Warnings with Safety Assurances—"Overpromotion"

An otherwise adequate warning may be nullified by assurances of safety. The classic case on this issue is *Maize v. Atlantic Refining Co.*,[182] where a woman died from inhaling tetrachloride fumes in a cleaning fluid she used to clean her rugs. The label on the can twice stated, "CAUTION: Do not inhale fumes. Use only in a well ventilated place." However, in letters that were several times larger, the cleaner's name—"Safety-Kleen"—was emblazoned around the container. Affirming judgments for the plaintiffs, the court observed that "the conspicuous display on each of the four sides of a can of the words 'Safety-Kleen' would naturally lull the user [into] a false sense of security [so] as to make the word 'Caution' and the admonition against inhaling fumes and as to use only in a well ventilated place seem of comparatively minor import."[183] Several other decisions have applied the "overpromotion" principle to nullify a manufacturer's product warnings,[184] including one in which warnings and instructions provided by the

---

[177] See, e.g., Mustafa v. Halkin Tool, Ltd., 2007 WL 959704, at *17 n.32 (E.D.N.Y. 2007) (Albanian machine operator, whose hands were severed in press, admitted that he paid no attention to the two pictorial warnings provided on ram).

[178] See, e.g., Hiser v. Bell Helicopter Textron Inc., 4 Cal. Rptr. 3d 249 (Ct. App. 2003) (helicopter's low-fuel warning light conflicted with fuel gauges); U.S. Xpress, Inc. v. Great N. Ins. Co. as Subrogee of N. Am. Commc'ns Res., Inc., 2003 WL 124021 (D. Minn. 2003) (rejecting claim that truck manufacturer's use of 1000-hour bulb instead of 5000-hour bulb in warning light was unreasonable); Kay v. Cessna Aircraft Co., 548 F.2d 1370 (9th Cir. 1977) (Cal. law) (warning light not necessary because engine gauges on Skymaster instrument panel would have indicated dead engine). See also Euclides Campos v. Crown Equip. Corp., 35 Fed. Appx. 31 (2d Cir. 2002) (N.Y. law) (forklift not defective for having backup alarm and warning lights as optional, rather than standard, equipment).

[179] See, e.g., Pike v. Frank G. Hough Co., 467 P.2d 229 (Cal. 1970).

[180] See, e.g., Hayes v. Kay Chem. Co., 482 N.E.2d 611 (Ill. App. Ct. 1985) (McDonald's employee wiped face with towel saturated with caustic grill cleaner).

[181] See, e.g., Donahue v. Phillips Petrol. Co., 866 F.2d 1008 (8th Cir. 1989) (Mo. law); Jones v. Hittle Serv., Inc., 549 P.2d 1383 (Kan. 1976) (odorized to smell like rotten eggs or dead mice).

[182] 41 A.2d 850 (Pa. 1945).

[183] Id. at 852.

[184] "Many states apply the overpromotion theory, under which a manufacturer can be liable for failure to warn even when the warnings were adequate if it engaged in an advertising campaign that in effect negated the warnings." In re Testosterone Replacement Therapy Prods. Liab. Litig. Coordinated Pretrial Proc., 2017 WL 1836435, at *16 (N.D. Ill. 2017). See also Incollingo v. Ewing, 282 A.2d 206 (Pa. 1971) (pharmaceutical

manufacturer of a jet boat were cancelled out by a salesman's demonstration of the boat in ways contrary to those warnings.[185] But overpromotion rulings are infrequent these days, perhaps because the doctrine has been absorbed into the general principle of a warning's adequacy.

Over-Warning—"Warnings Pollution"

Cutting across the ideal conception of adequacy, the risk of *over*-warning is an important real-world limitation. To be adequate, as noted previously, warnings ideally should provide precise information about all specific dangers from all foreseeable uses, and this information ideally should be conveyed to users in a form most likely to catch their attention, help them understand the true nature and extent of the hazard, and help them understand how to avoid it. For example, in *Burch v. Amsterdam Corp.*,[186] the plaintiff was badly burned in a flash fire and explosion that occurred while he was applying a floor tile mastic adhesive sold by the defendant. The label on the can of adhesive read, "DANGER! EXTREMELY FLAMMABLE—DO NOT USE NEAR FIRE OR FLAME—USE WITH ADEQUATE VENTILATION." The plaintiff read the instructions on the can label, opened the windows, and turned on his fans. He checked the area to be sure there were no flames but did not think about the pilot light on a gas stove in the kitchen where he was working. After he had applied a first coat of adhesive to the floor, the vapors reached the pilot light and exploded. The plaintiff heard a "whoosh," "had a sense of time being elongated, felt searing heat and saw the skin peeling from his body."

The trial court granted summary judgment for defendant on plaintiff's inadequate warnings claim, but the Court of Appeals reversed, reasoning that the defendant had failed to warn of the *specific* risk that the fumes might explode when they came in contact with a pilot light.[187] Chief Judge Reilly dissented, arguing that requiring a duty to warn about pilot lights in particular, other than about "fire and flame" in general, suggested

company's sales persons minimized drug's hazards and stressed its benefits and widespread acceptance). Compare Ayers v. Johnson & Johnson Baby Prods. Co., 818 P.2d 1337 (Wash. 1991) (warning of diarrhea, but not paralysis, from ingesting "pure and gentle" baby oil).

[185] See Levey v. Yamaha Motor Corp., 825 A.2d 554, 556 (N.J. Super. Ct. App. Div. 2003) (the "seller vitiated the effectiveness of the printed instructions and warnings accompanying its product by providing a demonstration of the product to intended users in which the seller violated its own safety warnings"). See also O'Neal v. Bumbo Int'l Trust, 959 F. Supp. 2d 972, 978–81 (S.D. Tex. 2013) (Ind. law) (warning that Bumbo infant seat was designed for use on floor only, with admonition never to put it on a raised surface, was contradicted by a picture on the product's box showing three infants sitting in such seats on top of birthday party table with no adult supervision).

[186] 366 A.2d 1079 (D.C. 1976).

[187] "[A]n ordinary user might not have realized that 'near fire or flame' included nearby pilot lights or that fumes and vapors, as well as the adhesive itself, were extremely flammable." Id. at 1087–88. At least one court went even further than the *Burch* majority, ruling that a similar warning that contained a specific warning to extinguish pilot lights was not enough. See Murray v. Wilson Oak Flooring Co., 475 F.2d 129, 130–33 (7th Cir. 1973) (Ill. law), where plaintiff was burned when the vapors from the mastic flooring adhesive he was applying were ignited by the pilot light of a water heater or stove. The label specifically warned, "KEEP AWAY From Fire, HEAT and OPEN flame LIGHTS—CAUTION: INFLAMMABLE MIXTURE—DO NOT USE NEAR FIRE OR FLAME—USE IN WELL VENTILATED AREA—Do not smoke—Extinguish flame—including pilot lights." In a negligent warning action against the manufacturer, the jury found for the plaintiff, the trial court granted the defendant's motion for j.n.o.v., and the Court of Appeals reversed, reinstating the plaintiff's verdict. Experts had agreed that the adhesive emits a heavy and highly explosive vapor that can travel for some distance along a floor, burn with explosive force when it comes in contact with a flame, and can transmit the flame back to the spread adhesive. The Court of Appeals concluded that it could not hold as a matter of law that "near" adequately informed the plaintiff that spreading the adhesive "within four feet of a pilot light *located behind a closed door* and within eight feet of stove pilot lights three feet off the floor exposed him to the risk of an explosion."

that a vendor would also have to warn about the risks from "lighted pipes, cigars and cigarettes, vigil lights, candles, sparks from an electric lamp switch, a running fan or motor, and the other myriad of things which could possibly ignite vapors. If this is what the law requires, big lettering would have to be discarded for smaller print enumerating details at such length that few users would bother to read it—the warning then lacking the requisite 'intensity.' "[188]

Burch was decided in the mid-1970s, at the height of products law's expansion when courts were beguiled by the thought that products liability law should be maximized to promote product safety incentives and loss-spreading principles.[189] As a single-minded pursuit of these goals has faded in recent decades, courts and commentators have begun to recognize that there is such a thing as *too much* information—that information, like everything, can be an evil in excess. By the 1980s, courts began to acknowledge the dangers of over-warning, "warnings pollution," that had concerned Chief Judge Reilly in his dissent in *Burch*. This simple idea is that product warnings ideally should contain *optimal* types and levels of danger and safety information, not maximum information.[190]

One of the first cases decided on warning pollution principles was *Cotton v. Buckeye Gas Products Co.*,[191] decided in 1988. Plaintiff, a night heater watcher for a construction company, monitored heaters used to cure concrete in cold weather and changed the propane cylinders supplied by the defendant when they ran low on gas. Polyethylene curtains draped the areas being cured to contain the heat. Despite warnings on the cylinders that they contained "flammable" gas and should not be used or stored in "living areas," plaintiff neglected to close the valves on the used cylinders and stored them near the active heaters within the polyethylene-enclosed areas. Gas escaping from the used cylinders ignited and severely burned the plaintiff. In his suit against the suppliers, the plaintiff claimed that the warning was inadequate because it failed (1) to warn that propane was not only flammable but "explosive"; (2) to instruct users to shut the valves on used cylinders; (3) to advise users not to use or store the cylinders in enclosed, unventilated areas; and (4) to warn that gas might escape from used cylinders believed to be empty. The jury agreed, but the trial court granted the defendant's motion for judgment notwithstanding the verdict, which the appellate court affirmed.

Debunking the assumption that keying warnings to every particular type of risk is "virtually cost free," the court noted that there is a real cost in the increased time and effort necessary to grasp the message. The court observed that each extra item included "dilutes the punch of every other item. Given short attention spans, items crowd each

---

[188] *Burch*, 366 A.2d at 1089.

[189] See §§ 5.3–5.5, above.

[190] See Twerski, Weinstein, Donaher, and Piehler, The Use and Abuse of Warnings in Products Liability—Design Defect Litigation Comes of Age, 61 Cornell L. Rev. 495, 514–16 (1976): "Warnings, in order to be effective, must be selective. . . . The warning process, in order to have impact, will have to select carefully the items which are to become part of the consumer's mental apparatus while using the product. Making the consumer account mentally for trivia or guard against risks that are not likely to occur imposes a very real societal cost. . . . In short, when calculating the burden of precaution which is part of the risk-utility calculus, it will be necessary to focus on costs other than the cost of label printing." See also Comment, 38 Ariz. St. L.J. 633 (2006).

Some commentators view warnings pollution claims skeptically. See Latin, Good Warnings, Bad Products, and Cognitive Limitations, 41 UCLA L. Rev. 1193 (1994); Grether, Schwartz, and Wilde, The Irrelevance of Information Overload: An Analysis of Search and Disclosure, 59 S. Cal. L. Rev. 277 (1986). See generally Symposium, Rational Actors or Rational Fools? The Implications of Psychology for Products Liability, 6 Roger Williams U. L. Rev. 1 (2000).

[191] 840 F.2d 935 (D.C. Cir. 1988).

other out; they get lost in fine print." The defendant's warning approach was reasonable, thought the court, in providing brief "flammability" warnings on the cylinders and more detailed warnings in the pamphlet provided to the purchaser, which included an admonition to close the valves. Nor was the court persuaded that the warnings were inadequate because they merely said "flammable" rather than "explosive," noting that the plaintiff's injuries exclusively were burns. And while the pamphlet did not explicitly warn that the valves should be closed on cylinders after they were "empty" (because they might still contain some propane), this was common sense. "[A] warning need not dot every i,"[192] and the warnings given were adequate on the whole: "warnings need not spell out [every] risk in intricate detail"[193] for "the list of foolish practices warned against would be so long, it would fill a volume."[194] Many other courts have agreed that warnings and instructions should be judicious and selective, that they need not—should not—provide information on the details of every product hazard.[195]

Another case that made the point that more numerous and more prominent warnings are not always better, and not always required, was *General Motors Corp. v. Saenz*,[196] which involved a claim that GM's warning against overloading a truck was not specific enough. The court held that it was, reasoning that just because the warning could have been more prominent did not prove that it was not prominent enough: "Every WARNING can always be made bigger, brighter and more obvious. GM could have placed the WARNING where it could not possibly have been overlooked, perhaps engraved upon the dashboard, or backlit on the instrument panel." But GM could not have placed every important warning on the dashboard, or any other place. Indeed, the more warnings and instructions located in one place—whether on the dashboard, a doorplate, or in the owner's manual—the less likely that users will notice any one. The court concluded that the issue was not whether GM should have put the overloading warning on a sticker near the gear shift, as the plaintiffs argued, but whether the warning that GM did provide offered "reasonable notice" against the risk of overloading.

Saenz is a good case with which to end, because it illustrates the important point that warnings, to be "adequate," need not be perfect, only "reasonable." This crucial

---

[192] Id. at 938.

[193] Id. at 939.

[194] Id. at 937–39 (quoting Kerr v. Koemm, 557 F. Supp. 283, 288 n.2 (S.D.N.Y. 1983)).

[195] See, e.g., Wu Jiang v. Ridge Tool Co., 764 Fed. Appx. 43, 46 (2d Cir. 2019) (N.Y. law) ("The lack of a specific warning concerning the dust created by sanding a wood floor treated with polyurethane did not render the vacuum's warning inadequate, as '[r]equiring too many warnings trivializes and undermines the entire purpose of the rule,' and 'would neutralize the effectiveness of warnings.' "); Aetna Cas. & Sur. Co. v. Ralph Wilson Plastics Co., 509 N.W.2d 520, 523 (Mich. Ct. App. 1993) (2–1 decision), where a glue maker warned of the extreme flammability of its solvents and instructed users to turn off pilot lights, stoves, heaters, flames and electric motors, and not to smoke. Plaintiff was injured when static electricity from a solvent clean-up sponge set off an explosion. *Held*, the warning was adequate. "A spark is a spark, and a possible source of ignition of a highly flammable compound irrespective of the means by which the spark was generated, whether by static electricity or otherwise." Id. at 523. The majority further noted that "excessive warnings on product labels may be counterproductive, causing 'sensory overload' which literally drowns crucial information in a sea of mind-numbing detail."

See also Todd v. Societe BIC, S.A. (*Todd II*), 9 F.3d 1216, 1218–19 (7th Cir. 1993) (Ill. law) (Easterbrook, J.) ("KEEP OUT OF REACH OF CHILDREN" was sufficient "warning" on BIC disposable butane lighter: among the problems with more extensive warning is that "the more text must be squeezed onto the product, the smaller the type, and the less likely is the consumer to read or remember any of it. Only pithy and bold warnings can be effective. Long passages in capital letters are next to illegible, and long passages in lower case letters are treated as boilerplate. Plaintiff wants a warning in such detail that a magnifying glass would be necessary to read it.").

[196] 873 S.W.2d 353 (Tex. 1993).

aspect of the law of warnings took courts some decades to appreciate, and it is a foundational pillar of the warning defect standard in the *Third Restatement*.[197]

§ 9.4 PERSONS TO BE WARNED

The duty to warn supposes that the warning will reach, be read by, and protect the safety interests of certain types of persons.[198] Deciding what categories of persons should be warned raises important questions of duty and adequacy. The selection of proper groups to warn is part of a lexical series of questions following a determination that a warning is needed: (1) whom the warning should protect; (2) who can best accomplish that protection; and (3) what type of warning will offer reasonable protection. The last question is one of adequacy, the factual question just examined.[199] Although the first two questions sometimes mix law and fact, they often involve basic duty issues for a court.

Whom a manufacturer has a duty to protect—who has a right to be protected—normally is clear: persons a product foreseeably puts at risk.[200] While a manufacturer's responsibility for product safety once was limited to purchasers,[201] and while transactional considerations to some extent still control the scope of obligations under the law of warranty,[202] privity of contract no longer binds the hands of duty in the law of tort.[203] So, the answer to the first question stated above is that the duty to warn is limited to users and other persons foreseeably endangered by a product's use.[204] Yet, foreseeability, constrained importantly by principles of reasonableness and fairness,[205] stretches only so far and comprises only one part of the much richer notion of duty, which "may call upon every possible reason of fairness, justice, and social policy."[206] For a variety of reasons, for example, many courts hold that manufacturers of asbestos products may have no duty to warn a worker's family of the risks of inhaling asbestos dust when washing the worker's clothing, even if those risks are foreseeable, as discussed below. And some other courts rule that manufacturers of valves and pumps made without asbestos may have no duty to warn buyers and users about the dangers of using

---

[197] See Products Liability Rest. § 2(c) and cmt. *i*. See also § 9.2, above.

[198] In the words of the Products Liability Restatement, warning of product dangers must be provided to users or consumers so "they can prevent harm either by appropriate conduct during use or consumption or by choosing not to use or consume." Section 2(c) cmt. *i*.

[199] See § 9.3, above.

[200] See ch. 5, above, and ch. 12, below.

[201] See § 1.2, above.

[202] See § 4.5, above.

[203] See §§ 1.2, 5.2, and 5.3, above.

[204] See, e.g., Patch v. Hillerich & Bradsby Co., 257 P.3d 383, 388 (Mont. 2011) (18-year-old pitcher killed when ball struck with aluminum bat hit his head; manufacturer's duty to warn of increased velocity of balls struck with aluminum bat owed not just to batters but to all players put at risk, all of whom were also "users and consumers" of the bat); Dozier Crane & Mach., Inc. v. Gibson, 644 S.E.2d 333, 336 (Ga. Ct. App. 2007) (temporary construction workers, helping guide rebar lifted by crane, electrocuted when crane hit power line; equipment dealer, who had removed warning signs when refurbishing crane, owed duty to third persons to warn of the foreseeable dangers of its refurbished equipment); Hanus v. Texas Utils. Co., 71 S.W.3d 874 (Tex. App. 2002) (homeowner, who struck defendant's buried power cable when he dug 3-foot hole, was a foreseeable victim).

[205] See §§ 12.2 (foreseeability in proximate cause) and 13.5 (foreseeability in misuse), below.

[206] Owen, Figuring Foreseeability, 44 Wake Forest L. Rev. 1277, 1301–02 (2009) (also explaining that "duty balances the interests of certain classes of potential victims in security from certain types of hazards and harm . . . against the interests of certain classes of actors in freedom of action").

asbestos insulation or replacement parts—even if that possibility is entirely foreseeable.[207]

The question remaining to be resolved is who should protect persons a product puts at risk? Normally, people can best protect themselves, assuming they recognize a hazard and can control it. Because users and consumers normally are the people threatened by a product's hazards, they are usually the ones best situated to decide how to protect themselves from harm. Even if real-world safety decisions of users and consumers often fall short on logic, giving them the opportunity to make product safety decisions that affect their welfare advances the ideal of self-determination.[208] Accordingly, even when a manufacturer sells its products to intermediaries, it normally should also provide warnings and instructions about product hazards directly to users and consumers if there is a reasonable way to do so.[209] One iteration of the warn-consumers-directly principle is the manufacturer's duty, previously discussed,[210] to place warnings directly on dangerous products, if feasible and otherwise reasonable. This principle rests on reason, rather than being absolute, because the form of some products precludes placing warnings on the body of the product, such as products that are tiny or liquid and gas sold in bulk. The bulk-supplier doctrine, discussed below,[211] addresses the latter point.

In other situations, where users and consumers rely on others for protection, warnings should be given to those other persons in addition to or, if appropriate, in lieu of users and consumers. Young children depend on parents and other adults to make informed safety decisions about their food, clothing, and toys; workers depend on supervisors to make informed safety decisions on what types of machinery to purchase and to develop safe procedures for operating and maintaining those machines; and patients depend on doctors to make informed decisions on prescription drugs and medical devices. These and other special categories of persons charged with protecting others often can make better use of product safety information than the ultimate users and consumers,[212] as discussed later. Two special categories of persons treated briefly

---

[207] See, e.g., Coffman v. Armstrong Int'l, Inc., 615 S.W.3d 888, 899 (Tenn. 2021) (4–1 decision) ("manufacturers have no duty to warn with respect to products manufactured and sold by others" under the Tennessee Products Liability Act; persuasive dissent); O'Neil v. Crane Co., 266 P.3d 987, 1004 (Cal. 2012) (There is no "duty to warn about dangers arising entirely from another manufacturer's product, even if it is foreseeable that the products will be used together. Were it otherwise, manufacturers of the saws used to cut insulation would become the next targets of asbestos lawsuits."); Braaten v. Saberhagen Holdings, 198 P.3d 493 (Wash. 2008) ("a manufacturer generally has no duty to warn of hazards associated with another manufacturer's products").

But see Whelan v. Armstrong Int'l Inc., 231 A.3d 640, 659–60 (N.J. 2020) ("As a matter of law, we hold that defendant manufacturers and distributors can be found strictly liable for the failure to warn of the dangers of their products, including their own asbestos-containing components and a third party's replacement components."); § 10.3 (*Asbestos—Peripheral parties; the "bare metal defense"*), below.

[208] See Products Liability Rest. § 2(c) cmt. *i*.

[209] See, e.g., Smith v. Brown & Williamson Tobacco Corp., 275 S.W.3d 748, 785 (Mo. Ct. App. 2008) ("Missouri has long recognized that a manufacturer has the duty to warn ultimate users of its products or articles which are inherently dangerous or are dangerous because of the use to which they are put."); Lee v. Martin, 45 S.W.3d 860, 865 (Ark. Ct. App. 2001) ("As a general rule, there is a duty to warn the ultimate user of a product of the risk of the product . . . under either a negligence theory or a strict-liability theory."). See also In re 3M Combat Arms Earplug Prods. Liab. Litig., 545 F. Supp. 3d 1239, 1244 (N.D. Fla. 2021) (Wash. law) (declining to extend Washington's sophisticated intermediary doctrine to combat earplugs that were "marketed and sold both to the military and directly to the general public").

[210] See § 9.3, above.

[211] See § 9.5, below.

[212] See Conn. Gen. Stat. Ann. § 52–572q(d) (seller must warn "the person best able to take or recommend precautions against the potential harm").

here are bystanders and persons who are allergic to certain products, both of whom may need special types of warnings.

Bystanders

Warnings play two different roles in protecting bystanders. Bystanders may be placed at risk when products are used dangerously by other people, as when a crane operator uses a crane in a dangerous manner that threatens workers underneath the load. In such cases, warnings necessary to the safe operation of the crane protect persons foreseeably placed at risk, including the operator's fellow workers ("bystanders") who may be standing beneath the crane. The manufacturer of such a crane has a duty to warn the operator and others foreseeably placed at risk, including bystanders, for the benefit of them all.[213] So, also, although the manufacturer of a car or plane normally has a duty to provide warnings and instructions concerning operational hazards only to the operator, not to passengers,[214] the breach of the duty to warn the operator will violate the safety rights of passengers and other bystanders injured as a result of the operator's failure to have such safety information.[215] This is the normal type of bystander case in which a manufacturer's duty to bystanders is largely governed by ordinary principles of reasonable foreseeability, in tort,[216] and by third-party beneficiary principles, in warranty.[217]

A type of bystander case mentioned earlier that has perplexed the courts is whether asbestos product manufacturers owed a duty, in addition to asbestos workers who inhaled asbestos dust on the job, to their family members who themselves were exposed to the dust in the home, as when washing their dust-laden work clothes. Courts have addressed similar asbestos "bystander" issues,[218] including whether *employers* (rather

---

213 See, e.g., Dozier Crane & Mach., Inc. v. Gibson, 644 S.E.2d 333, 336 (Ga. Ct. App. 2007) (crane dealer owed duty to construction workers guiding rebar who were electrocuted when crane lifting rebar hit power line).

214 See, e.g., Reichwaldt v. General Motors LLC, 304 F. Supp. 3d 1312, 1317 (N.D. Ga. 2018) (public policy argues against imposing "duty to warn reasonably foreseeable third-party victims of the dangerous fuel tank system" where duty had "almost no fixed scope" and "satisfying this duty would be nearly impossible"); Stevens v. Cessna Aircraft Co., 170 Cal. Rptr. 925, 926 (Ct. App. 1981) (4-seat airplane crashed, allegedly because it was overloaded with pilot and three passengers; manufacturer did not have duty to post notice in passenger compartment of plane's load capacity): "[T]he passenger necessarily depends upon the skill and judgment of the pilot to determine the load capacity of the airplane in light of the flying conditions to be encountered. Plaintiff's argument implies logically that numerous other bits of information should be posted in the passenger compartment to enable the passengers to second-guess the pilot on a myriad of flying decisions. It would be impossible ultimately to provide meaningful information to the passenger, and in the long run a rule requiring the manufacturer to provide such information directly to the passenger would not be in the interests of passenger safety." *But see* Bickram v. Case I.H., 712 F. Supp. 18, 22 (E.D.N.Y. 1989) (suggesting that bystanders might be entitled to effective written warnings).

215 See, e.g., Hisrich v. Volvo Cars of N. Am., Inc., 226 F.3d 445 (6th Cir. 2000) (Ohio law) (inadequate warning to operator that unbelted child passenger could be killed by airbag).

216 See, e.g., Lawing v. Trinity Mfg., Inc., 749 S.E.2d 126, 136–38 (S.C. Ct. App. 2013) (Few, J.) (brilliant decision); Bah v. Nordson Corp., 2005 WL 1813023, at *15 (S.D.N.Y. 2005) (though not a user of the defective machine, employee burned by hot glue from the machine could bring inadequate warnings claim against the manufacturer). *But see* Kirk v. Michael Reese Hosp. & Med. Ctr., 513 N.E.2d 387, 393 (Ill. 1987) (manufacturer's duty to warn doctors of risk of drinking alcohol while taking prescription drug might possibly extend to passengers in cars driven by persons who drank alcoholic beverages while on the drug, but such a combination of events was unforeseeable as a matter of law). See generally § 5.3, above.

217 See § 4.5, above.

218 See, e.g., Dixon v. Ford Motor Co., 70 A.3d 328 (Md. 2013) (allowing recovery for death of wife of garage mechanic who worked on brakes containing asbestos); Campbell v. Ford Motor Co., 141 Cal. Rptr. 3d 390 (Ct. App. 2012) (premises owners have no duty to protect a worker's family from "take-home" asbestos dust). Compare Ford Motor Co. v. Boomer, 736 S.E.2d 724, 734 (Va. 2013) (jury could find that Ford and Bendix

than manufacturers), whose employees worked around asbestos dust, owe such a duty to family members, an issue on which the courts have split[219]—some holding that an asbestos worker's household members are indeed foreseeable victims to whom an employer owes a duty,[220] others ruling that employers owe no such duty.[221] In products liability suits, manufacturers stand much further removed from the families of asbestos workers. So, while a few courts have broadened the protection of a manufacturer's duty to warn to include family members,[222] other courts have held that manufacturers could not foresee asbestos illness risks to such persons or, at least, that manufacturers were so far removed from worker families that they had no practical way to identify or warn them, even if manufacturers had wanted to do so.[223]

Sometimes, use of a product plainly puts bystanders at risk, a situation that may well entitle them to have warnings provided directly to themselves.[224] For example, cranes sometimes must move in reverse, and, even equipped with rear-view mirrors, a crane cab may make it impossible for an operator to see directly behind the crane. In this type of situation, a crane normally must be equipped with a back-up horn or buzzer, and also perhaps with flashing lights, to warn bystanders behind the crane that it is

---

should have foreseen inhalation and mesothelioma risk to state trooper who supervised automobile service where mechanics used compressed air to blow dust from brakes comprised of asbestos).

[219] See, e.g., In re Asbestos Prods. Liab. Litig. (No. VI), 2011 WL 6016081, at *1 (E.D. Pa. 2011) (surveying split on whether to allow "take-home asbestos exposure" claims against employers brought by family members of asbestos workers). See also § 2.1 note 32 and § 5.3 note 144, above, and § 10.3 notes 406 and 407, below.

[220] See, e.g., Mata v. Liberty Utilities (Park Water) Corp., 2020 WL 6792382, at *9 (Cal. Ct. App. 2020), noncitable (water company's negligence in exposing plaintiff to asbestos fibers on his father's work uniform was a substantial factor in causing plaintiff's mesothelioma); Mestas v. Air & Liquid Sys. Corp., 2019 WL 1253683, at *5 (D. Colo. 2019) (denying motion to dismiss "take home" asbestos exposure claims; "The social utility of failing to provide safe-handling instructions or warn users of products containing asbestos about the associated health risks is clearly outweighed by harmfulness of asbestos on human health. . . . Defendants owed Plaintiffs a duty of reasonable care."); Ramsey v. Georgia S. Univ. Advanced Dev. Ctr., 189 A.3d 1255, 1262 (Del. 2018) (overruling prior cases and holding "that a household member who regularly launders an employee's asbestos-covered clothing . . . may sue her spouse's employer for its failure to provide warnings and safe laundering instructions"); Quisenberry v. Huntington Ingalls Inc., 818 S.E.2d 805, 814 (Va. 2018).

[221] See, e.g., Jack v. DCo, LLC, 837 Fed. Appx. 421, 422 (9th Cir. 2021) (Wash. law) ("take-home exposure claim . . . fails on legal duty"); Certainteed Corp. v. Fletcher, 794 S.E.2d 641, 645 (Ga. 2016) (no duty to warn daughter who regularly washed father's asbestos-laden work clothing); Palmer v. 999 Quebec, Inc., 874 N.W.2d 303, 311 (N.D. 2016) (reviewing "take-home" asbestos cases; no duty to warn plaintiff of risks of exposure to asbestos from father's dusty work clothes); Price v. E.I. DuPont de Nemours & Co., 26 A.3d 162 (Del. Supr. 2011) (employer owed no duty to worker's wife); In re N.Y. City Asbestos Litig., 840 N.E.2d 115 (N.Y. 2005) (employer owed no duty to worker's wife who washed husband-employee's clothes).

[222] See, e.g., Mestas v. Air & Liquid Sys. Corp., 2019 WL 1253683, at *5 (D. Colo. 2019) (son); Stegemoller v. ACandS, Inc., 767 N.E.2d 974 (Ind. 2002) (duty—wife who washed clothes); Lunsford v. Saberhagen Holdings, Inc., 106 P.3d 808 (Wash. Ct. App. 2005) (son); Fuller-Austin Insulation Co. v. Bilder, 960 S.W.2d 914 (Tex. App. 1998) (step-daughter). See also Georgia-Pacific Corp. v. Pransky, 800 A.2d 722 (Md. 2002) (daughter, who suffered mesothelioma from exposure to asbestos dust from joint compound father used in renovating basement, was a foreseeable bystander).

[223] See, e.g., Jack v. DCo, LLC, 837 Fed. Appx. 421, 422 (9th Cir. 2021) (Wash. law) ("harm to workers' family members was not foreseeable"; "take-home exposure claim . . . fails on legal duty"); Gillen v. Boeing Co., 40 F. Supp. 3d 534 (E.D. Pa. 2014) (no duty to wife; to avoid threat of "infinite" liability); Georgia Pac., LLC v. Farrar, 69 A.3d 1028, 1037 (Md. 2013) (no duty; even if manufacturer should have foreseen that family members were in zone of danger, "there was no practical way that any warning given by it to any of the suggested intermediaries would or could have avoided that danger"); Riedel v. ICI Ams. Inc., 968 A.2d 17, 26 (Del. Super. Ct. 2009) (no duty to warn wife; asbestos on husband's work clothes); Rohrbaugh v. Owens-Corning Fiberglas Corp., 965 F.2d 844 (10th Cir. 1992) (Okla. law) (wife, no duty). See also Rodarmel v. Pneumo Abex, L.L.C., 957 N.E.2d 107 (Ill. Ct. App. 2011) (no duty to ex-wife to have warned of dangers of exposure in 1950s).

[224] See, e.g., Frumer, Friedman, and Sklaren, Products Liability § 12.06[2]; see also § 5.3, above.

being run in reverse by an operator with limited rear visibility.[225] While there once was some question of whether a manufacturer's duties of protection ran to bystanders,[226] courts have extended a warning duty to protect foreseeable bystanders in so many contexts[227] that this duty now is axiomatic.[228]

Allergic Persons

Some foods, drugs, cleansers, and lotions that are useful and entirely safe to a great majority of people can cause serious allergic reactions in other persons. Peanuts,[229] aspirin,[230] strawberries,[231] penicillin,[232] oysters,[233] crabs,[234] monosodium glutamate,[235] cosmetic removers,[236] and latex gloves[237] are examples of products many people eat or use but that can cause some people to become very sick or even die. The defect in such

---

225 See, e.g., Bohnstedt v. Robscon Leasing L.L.C., 993 P.2d 135 (Okla. Civ. App. 1999) (backup alarm on grader needed to be maintained to protect bystanders). *But see* Vickery v. Waste Mgmt. of Ga., Inc., 549 S.E.2d 482, 484 (Ga. Ct. App. 2001) (truck manufacturer had no duty to warn purchaser or bystander that truck was not equipped with backup alarm). Compare Dozier Crane & Mach., Inc. v. Gibson, 644 S.E.2d 333, 336 (Ga. Ct. App. 2007) (crane dealer owed duty to warn workers around crane of electrocution risk if crane hit power line).

226 See Rest. (2d) of Torts § 402A (leaving open a seller's responsibility to bystanders, in caveat 1, and stating in cmt. *o* that "bystanders . . . have been denied recovery").

227 See, e.g., Hakim v. Safariland, LLC, 2022 WL 1136552, at *5 (N.D. Ill. 2022) (duty to warn users of specialized shotgun ammo that fragments might ricochet off wood and strike persons on building's other floors) (by implication); Lawing v. Trinity Mfg., Inc., 749 S.E.2d 126, 136–38 (S.C. Ct. App. 2013) (Few, J.) (while using blow torches to cut pipes attached to plant's ceiling, workers injured when molten metal fell and hit bags of chemicals that explosively caught fire; workers were "users" of chemicals, protected by § 402A statute); Patch v. Hillerich & Bradsby Co., 257 P.3d 383, 391 (Mont. 2011) (defendant "is subject to liability to all [ball] players, including [plaintiff pitcher], for the physical harm caused by [aluminum] bat's increased exit speed"); Karns v. Emerson Elec. Co., 817 F.2d 1452, 1457 (10th Cir. 1987) (Okla. law) (hand-held "Weed Eater" brush-cutting device, with exposed 10-inch circular steel saw blade struck something near ground, causing machine to swing violently around and cut off arm of user's nephew standing 6–10 feet away); Hayes v. Kay Chem. Co., 482 N.E.2d 611 (Ill. App. Ct. 1985) (McDonald's employee wiped face with towel saturated with colorless, odorless, caustic grill cleaner used by another employee; duty extended beyond user to foreseeable persons and "nonusers"); Givens v. Lederle, 556 F.2d 1341 (5th Cir. 1977) (Fla. law) (mother contracted polio, possibly from contact with diapers of child recently administered defendant's vaccine).

228 On a manufacturer's duties to bystanders generally, see § 5.3, above.

229 See, e.g., Thompson v. East Pac. Enters., Inc., 2003 WL 352914, at *1 (Wash. Ct. App. 2003) (peanuts residue in chicken dish); Note, Suing for Peanuts, 75 Notre Dame L. Rev. 1269 (2000). See also Jones v. WFM-Wo, Inc., 265 F. Supp. 3d 775, 777 (M.D. Tenn. 2017) ("Vegan Garden Pizza" with nut products); Cline v. Publix Super Markets, Inc., 2015 WL 3650389, at *11 (M.D. Tenn. 2015) (tree nuts in cookie).

230 See Products Liability Rest. § 2 cmt. *k*, illus. 13.

231 See Rest. (2d) of Torts § 402A cmt. *j*.

232 See, e.g., Thompson v. East Pac. Enters., Inc., 2003 WL 352914 (Wash. Ct. App. 2003) (plaintiff was allergic to penicillin as well as peanuts and other substances).

233 See, e.g., Collier v. Bloom, 2016 WL 6078748, at *1 (Conn. Super. Ct. 2016); Woeste v. Washington Platform Saloon & Rest., 836 N.E.2d 52 (Ohio Ct. App. 2005) (restaurant's warning was adequate); Gregor v. Argenot Great Cent. Ins. Co., 851 So.2d 959 (La. 2003) (raw oysters and other marine filter feeders may contain vibrio vulnificus, a naturally occurring salt water organism not dangerous to most people but dangerous, possibly fatal, to persons with chronic health problems including gastric disorders, liver diseases, and immune disorders; restaurant posted mandatory warning in oyster bar but not in dining room where plaintiff ate raw oysters from which he died); Edwards v. Hop Sin, Inc., 140 S.W.3d 13 (Ky. Ct. App. 2003) (jury might find that a reasonable consumer would expect to be warned of such a serious risk).

234 See, e.g., Crawford v. Marriott Hotel Servs., Inc., 2021 WL 1990191, at *5 n.6 (N.D. Ga. 2021) (no duty to consumer of chicken with blue crab stuffing who failed to inform server of her allergy).

235 See, e.g., Livingston v. Marie Callender's, Inc., 85 Cal. Rptr. 2d 528 (Ct. App. 1999) (MSG in soup).

236 See, e.g., Potts v. Johnson & Johnson Consumer Inc., 2021 WL 2177386, at *9 (D.N.J. 2021).

237 See, e.g., Belanger v. Safeskin Corp., 2005 WL 2542936, at *3 (Mass. Super. Ct. 2005) (latex gloves used by nurse); Green v. Smith & Nephew AHP, Inc., 629 N.W.2d 727 (Wis. 2001) (latex gloves used by health workers).

situations arguably may be said to lie in the persons who incur idiosyncratic reactions, rather than in the product.[238] The issue in these situations is whether the producer has a duty to warn that its product may cause allergic reactions.[239]

If the population of allergic users is foreseeably quite large, and if such users are not generally aware of the risk,[240] then a manufacturer must provide adequate warnings of a product's allergenic tendencies.[241] If the risk is not foreseeable, then there can be no duty to warn about it,[242] except in a couple of jurisdictions.[243] If the group of allergic persons is small, the courts are split on whether the manufacturer has a duty to warn. Most courts require the manufacturer to warn only if it can foresee a risk of serious allergy to a *substantial* number of persons.[244] This was the position of the *Second Torts Restatement*,[245] and it is followed by the *Third Restatement*, which observes that what

---

[238] "The term *allergy* or *hypersensitivity* refers to the condition or state of an individual who reacts specifically and with unusual symptoms to the administration of, or to contact with, a substance which when given in similar amounts to the majority of all other individuals proves harmless or innocuous." It is not so clear, therefore, that there is anything "defective" about a product which generates an allergic reaction: "A person suffering an allergic reaction to a product is, by definition, abnormal or hypersensitive. The resulting harm, therefore, is arguably more fairly attributable to some 'defect' in the person's body rather than to a 'defect' in the product—a product that is entirely safe for all normal ('nondefective') people." Panel Discussion, Medico-Legal Aspects of Allergies, 24 Tenn. L. Rev. 840, 840–42 (1957).

See, e.g., Thompson v. East Pac. Enters., Inc., 2003 WL 352914, at *1 (Wash. Ct. App. 2003) (plaintiff allergic to peanut residue and penicillin, walnut, pine nut, sunflower seed, almond, soybean, pecan, hazelnut, brazil nut, sesame seed, and other substances); Henderson, Process Norms in Products Litigation: Liability for Allergic Reactions, 51 U. Pitt. L. Rev. 761, 804 (1990) ("[T]here is nothing defective about perfectly pure shampoo that happens to cause allergic reactions in a handful of abnormally sensitive individuals, assuming warnings describing the risks accompany the product. The consumer, rather than the product, is defective.").

[239] See Barrett, Latex Gloves, 22 J. Legal Med. 263 (2001); Henderson, above; Major, Manufacturer's Failure to Warn Consumer of Allergenic Nature of Product, 47 Am. Jur. Proof of Facts 2d 227 (1987); Note, Suing for Peanuts, 75 Notre Dame L. Rev. 1269 (2000); Prosser and Keeton on Torts § 96, at 687–88.

[240] "The ingredient that causes the allergic reaction must be one whose danger or whose presence in the product is not generally known to consumers. When both the presence of an allergenic ingredient in the product and the risks presented by such ingredient are widely known, instructions and warnings about that danger are unnecessary." Products Liability Rest. § 2 cmt. *k*. See, e.g., Mills v. Giant of Md., LLC, 508 F.3d 11 (D.C. Cir. 2007) (milk producers; no duty to warn of lactose intolerance); Pelman v. McDonald's Corp., 237 F. Supp. 2d 512, 536 (S.D.N.Y. 2003).

[241] See, e.g., Green v. Smith & Nephew AHP, Inc., 629 N.W.2d 727 (Wis. 2001) (duty to warn health care users, 5–17% of whom were allergic, that proteins in powdered latex gloves might cause allergies).

[242] See, e.g., Adelman-Tremblay v. Jewel Cos., 859 F.2d 517 (7th Cir. 1988) (Wis. law) (one million nail kits sold and plaintiff suffered first allergic reaction to glue in kit; state would follow general rule that sellers are not strictly liable for injuries from idiosyncratic or rare allergic reactions). See generally § 10.4, below.

[243] This duty exists in Montana, formerly in Wisconsin, and possibly one or two other states. See Green v. Smith & Nephew AHP, Inc., 629 N.W.2d 727 (Wis. 2001) (duty to warn users allergic to proteins in powdered latex gloves, even if risk was unforeseeable); § 10.4 (state of the art), below.

[244] See, e.g., Friedman v. Merck & Co., 131 Cal. Rptr. 2d 885, 894 (Ct. App. 2003) ("a TB test distributor's negligent failure to warn that the test contains animal products is not . . . sufficiently likely to result in *serious* harm to a sufficiently significant segment of the population" so as to impose a duty to so advise on defendants as a matter of law); *Green*, above note 241; Daley v. McNeil Consumer Prods. Co., 164 F. Supp. 2d 367 (S.D.N.Y. 2001) (Lactaid); Morris v. Pathmark Corp., 592 A.2d 331 (Pa. Super. Ct. 1991) (hair straightener); Griggs v. Combe, Inc., 456 So.2d 790 (Ala. 1984) (first known case of systemic illness from benzocaine in vaginal itch ointment); Kaempfe v. Lehn & Fink Prods. Corp., 249 N.Y.S.2d 840, 845–46 (App. Div. 1964) (dermatitis from aluminum sulphate in deodorant; no liability where manufacturer received only four sensitivity complaints in 600,000 sales), aff'd 231 N.E.2d 294 (N.Y. 1967).

[245] A seller may assume that persons with common allergies, like "eggs or strawberries, will be aware of them, and he is not required to warn against them. Where, however, the product contains an ingredient to which a substantial number of the population are allergic, and the ingredient is one whose danger is not generally known, or if known is one which the consumer would reasonably not expect to find in the product, the seller is required to give warning against it, if he [reasonably should know] of the presence of the ingredient and the danger." Rest. (2d) of Torts § 402A cmt. *j*. See also Rest. (2d) of Torts § 395 cmt. *k* ("the manufacturer may know, or may be under a duty to discover, that some possible users of the product are especially susceptible

passes as a "substantial number" logically should decrease as the risk of harm increases.[246]

Another line of cases rejects a strict no-duty approach for "insignificant" or "insubstantial" numbers of allergy victims and, instead, imposes a duty to warn of *any* foreseeable allergy that may be serious.[247] Assuming that the duty is restricted to allergic risks of which users generally are unaware, this latter formulation of the duty might be viewed as more fairly and flexibly tying the duty to warn to traditional tort law principles of reasonableness and foreseeability, rather than anchoring it to a wooden category of "substantial numbers," whatever that may mean. Yet the substantial or appreciable number of allergic persons requirement has the virtue of being somewhat less vague than the evanescent notion of "foreseeability,"[248] and it also contains a threshold of materiality that may be helpful in excluding trivial claims.[249]

If there *is* a duty to warn of an allergic reaction risk, the warning must be adequate.[250] This means that a manufacturer must warn not only of the possibility and type of allergic reaction that may occur, and identify the kinds of users who may be especially subject to the risk,[251]—assuming those facts are not widely known to persons with such allergies—but also of the relevant consequences, if they are not widely known as well.[252]

---

to harm from it, if it contains an ingredient to which any substantial percentage of the population are allergic or otherwise sensitive, and he fails to take reasonable precautions, by giving warning or otherwise, against harm to such persons").

[246] See Products Liability Rest. § 2 cmt. *k*, which provides in part: "The general rule in cases involving allergic reactions is that a warning is required when the harm-causing ingredient is one to which a substantial number of persons are allergic. The degree of substantiality is not precisely quantifiable. Clearly the plaintiff in most cases must show that the allergic predisposition is not unique to the plaintiff. In determining whether the plaintiff has carried the burden in this regard, however, the court may properly consider the severity of the plaintiff's harm. The more severe the harm, the more justified is a conclusion that the number of persons at risk need not be large to be considered 'substantial' so as to require a warning. Essentially, this reflects the same risk-utility balancing undertaken in warning cases generally. But courts explicitly impose the requirement of substantiality in cases involving adverse allergic reactions."

[247] See, e.g., Kehm v. Procter & Gamble Mfg. Co., 724 F.2d 613 (8th Cir. 1983) (Iowa law) (user of defendant's extra absorbent Rely tampon died from toxic shock syndrome): "[L]iability does not turn on whether the risk of harm runs to a substantial number of persons. Rather, in determining whether a manufacturer has a duty to warn, courts inquire whether the manufacturer knew that there were even a relatively few persons who could not use its product without serious injury, and whether a proper warning would have helped prevent harm to them." Id. at 620. Cf. Goldman v. Walco Tool & Eng'g, 614 N.E.2d 42 (Ill. App. Ct. 1993) (no duty to warn idiosyncratic users of risks from over-the-counter products, but rule does not apply to other types of products like dangerous chemicals in rust-preventative oil).

[248] For critiques of foreseeability on grounds of indeterminacy, see §§ 12.2 and 13.5, below.

[249] In this respect, consider Friedman v. Merck & Co., 131 Cal. Rptr. 2d 885, 894 (Ct. App. 2003), which used the "significant segment of the population" classification, together with the immateriality of the harm, to deny a claim against a TB test distributor for failing to warn that the test contained animal products that vegans would find objectionable.

[250] See, e.g., Mitchell v. VLI Corp., 786 F. Supp. 966 (M.D. Fla. 1992), where the package insert for nonprescription "Today" contraceptive sponges stated that approximately 2% of users in studies "discontinued use because of allergic reactions." Plaintiff suffered a severe allergic reaction that ultimately led to a hysterectomy. *Held*, because it was unclear whether lay person would understand "allergic reaction" to include a severe reaction requiring major surgery, the manufacturer's motion for summary judgment on warning claim was denied. See also Tongate v. Wyeth Labs., 580 N.E.2d 1220 (Ill. App. Ct. 1991) (jury question whether manufacturer's inserts for tetanus toxoid contained adequate warnings of potential neurologic complications).

[251] Such as when persons who are allergic to one substance, such as penicillin, are more likely to be allergic to another. See, e.g., Jacobs v. Dista Prods. Co., 693 F. Supp. 1029 (D. Wyo. 1988).

[252] "When the presence of the allergenic ingredient would not be anticipated by a reasonable user or consumer, warnings concerning its presence are required. Similarly, when the presence of the ingredient is

§ 9.5 SOPHISTICATED USERS AND BULK SUPPLIERS

Two doctrines that may exempt manufacturers from their normal obligation to provide end-users and consumers with warnings of product hazards are the "sophisticated user doctrine" and the "bulk supplier doctrine." Both doctrines relieve an upstream seller of the duty to warn a downstream purchaser or user in circumstances where the downstream purchaser already knows about the risk.[253] Because these two doctrines relieve manufacturers of the duty to warn in certain situations, they partake of a defense.[254] Yet, they more appropriately are seen as helping define the proper scope of a manufacturer's duty to warn in certain contexts, such that their application undermines the plaintiff's prima facie case.[255] Because both doctrines rest on hazard information possessed by downstream purchasers, the two doctrines sometimes are blended together into a single doctrine.[256] Yet, while they often overlap,[257] most courts properly view them as legal doctrines that are related but quite distinct.[258]

---

generally known to consumers, but its dangers are not, a warning of the dangers must be given." Products Liability Rest. § 2 cmt. *k*.

[253] See Sungaila and Mayer, Limiting Manufacturers' Duty to Warn: The Sophisticated User and Purchaser Doctrines, 76 Def. Couns. J. 196 (2009); Kemp and Alleman, The Bulk Supplier, Sophisticated User, and Learned Intermediary Doctrines Since the Adoption of the Restatement (Third) of Torts, 26 Rev. Litig. 927 (2007); Schwartz, Behrens, and Crouse, Getting the Sand Out of the Eyes of the Law: The Need for a Clear Rule for Sand Suppliers in Texas After Humble Sand & Gravel, Inc. v. Gomez, 37 St. Mary's L.J. 283 (2006); Korzec, Restating the Obvious in Maryland Products Liability Law: The Restatement (Third) of Torts: Products Liability and Failure to Warn Defenses, 30 U. Balt. L. Rev. 341 (2001); Madden, Liability of Suppliers of Natural Raw Materials and the Restatement (Third) of Torts: Products Liability—A First Step Toward Sound Public Policy, 30 U. Mich. J.L. Reform 281, 291–95 (1997); Mansfield, Reflection on Current Limits on Component and Raw Material Supplier Liability and the Proposed Third Restatement, 84 Ky. L.J. 221 (1996); Ausness, Learned Intermediaries and Sophisticated Users: Encouraging the Use of Intermediaries to Transmit Product Safety Information, 46 Syracuse L. Rev. 1185 (1996); Baker, Effects of Products Liability on Bulk Suppliers of Biomaterials, 50 Food & Drug L.J. 455 (1995); Owen & Davis on Products Liability §§ 9:28 (sophisticated users), 9:29 (bulk suppliers); Frumer, Friedman, and Sklaren, Products Liability § 12.06[4] and [5]; Am. Law Prod. Liab. 3d §§ 33:21 to :30.

[254] See, e.g., Cabasug v. Crane Co., 988 F. Supp. 2d 1216, 1219–24 (D. Hawai'i 2013) (sophisticated user defense); Riggs v. Asbestos Corp., 304 P.3d 61, 68–69 (Utah Ct. App. 2013) (bulk supplier defense); Kitzner v. Houghton Fluid Care, 2007 WL 127793, at *2–3 (Mich. Ct. App. 2007) (applying sophisticated user doctrine, an affirmative defense); Hoffman v. Houghton Chem. Corp., 751 N.E.2d 848, 852 (Mass. 2001) (adopting bulk supplier doctrine as affirmative defense); Higgins v. E.I. DuPont de Nemours & Co., 671 F. Supp. 1055 (D. Md. 1987) (applying "sophisticated user/bulk supplier defense"). See also Mich. Comp. Laws Ann. § 600.2947(4).

[255] See, e.g., Humble Sand & Gravel, Inc. v. Gomez, 146 S.W.3d 170, 194 (Tex. 2004) (sophisticated user doctrine is a question of duty, for the plaintiff to establish, rather than a defense).

[256] See, e.g., Higgens v. E.I. DuPont de Nemours & Co., 671 F. Supp. 1055 (D. Md. 1987), which applied a "sophisticated user/bulk supplier defense" to shield manufacturers of chemicals sold to DuPont for its use in making paint that allegedly was teratogenic: "There is no duty on product suppliers to warn ultimate users (whether employees or customers) of product-related hazards in products supplied in bulk to a knowledgeable user." Id. at 1061.

[257] See, e.g., Taylor v. American Chem. Council, 576 F.3d 16, 25–27 (1st Cir. 2009) (Mass. law) (examining both doctrines); Gray v. Badger Mining Corp., 676 N.W.2d 268, 280–81 (Minn. 2004) (same); In re Silicone Gel Breast Implants Prods. Liab. Litig., 996 F. Supp. 1110, 1113–14 (N.D. Ala. 1997) (referring to the "raw material supplier defense" or the "bulk sales/sophisticated purchaser rule," observing that these "doctrines, though conceptually distinct, overlap and tend to merge," and stating that the strongest case for exempting a supplier from its duty to warn end users is when the doctrines overlap, "namely, when a supplier sells to a knowledgeable manufacturer raw materials in bulk, which are not themselves inherently dangerous and which are substantially changed during the manufacturing process before resale to consumers, and when the supplier has little or no role in the design of the end product").

[258] See, e.g., Carrel v. National Cord & Braid Corp., 852 N.E.2d 100, 108–09 (Mass. 2006) (distinguishing bulk supplier defense from sophisticated user doctrine); Hoffman v. Houghton Chem. Corp., 751 N.E.2d 848, 854 (Mass. 2001).

Sophisticated User Doctrine

The "sophisticated user" or "sophisticated purchaser" doctrine[259] may arise if there is no *need* to warn, because of the expertise of the buyer or user.[260] Under this doctrine, a product supplier has no duty to warn employees of knowledgeable commercial buyers[261] about product hazards of which such buyers are aware.[262] Explained by the absence of a reason to provide buyers with warning information they should already possess, the sophisticated purchaser or user doctrine is a close cousin of the generally accepted principle that there is no duty to warn of obvious or commonly known dangers,[263] considered below.[264] The purpose of warnings, as seen above, is to inform buyers and users on hazards and safety information they do not know about—so they may choose to avoid the product altogether or avoid the danger by careful use.[265] There

---

Because the cases in which these doctrines arise often involve sand, chemicals, and other raw and component materials, cases in which these doctrines appear often implicate the special obligations of suppliers of raw materials and component parts. See § 15.3, below.

[259] Sometimes also called the "sophisticated intermediary" defense. See, e.g., Rickicki v. Borden Chem., 72 N.Y.S.3d 302 (App. Div. 2018) (similar doctrine called "knowledgeable user" doctrine); Webb v. Special Elec. Co., 370 P.3d 1022 (Cal. 2016) (jury could find that supplier of crocidolite asbestos did not reasonably rely on purchaser to warn downstream users; detailed discussion). Some courts confusingly refer to the sophisticated use doctrine as the "learned intermediary" doctrine. See, e.g., Specter v. Texas Turbine Conversions, Inc., 2021 WL 218720, at *9 (D. Alaska 2021) (noting that "some courts apply the learned intermediary and sophisticated user defenses interchangeably"); Hill v. Konecranes, Inc., 2020 WL 3259178, at *19 (S.D. Ga. 2020) (noting the distinction). In fact, the "learned intermediary doctrine" properly applies only to health care professionals who stand between drug manufacturers and patients. This latter doctrine holds that a drug manufacturer's duty is to warn only doctors, not patients, to avoid interfering with the doctor-patient relationship. See § 18.3, below.

[260] An early, landmark case explaining this point is Littlehale v. E.I. du Pont de Nemours & Co., 268 F. Supp. 791, 798–99 (S.D.N.Y. 1966), aff'd, 380 F.2d 274 (2d Cir. 1967): "There need be no warning to one in a particular trade or profession against a danger generally known to that trade or profession." Moreover, "[i]f no warning is required to be given by the manufacturer to a purchaser who is well aware of the inherent dangers of the product, there is no duty on the part of the manufacturer to warn an employee of that purchaser." Though normally applied to warning claims, at least one state holds that it also applies to design defect claims. See Brewer v. PACCAR, Inc., 124 N.E.3d 616 (Ind. 2019).

[261] Some jurisdictions apply similar principles to individual purchasers who themselves are sophisticated users. See, e.g., Smith v. Louisville Ladder Co., 237 F.3d 515, 521 (5th Cir. 2001) (Tex. law) (ladders were sold to individuals in the telecommunications industry who were familiar with the risk of ladder slides; "a supplier may rely on the professional expertise of the user in tailoring its warning"); Crook v. Kaneb Pipe Line Operating P'ship, 231 F.3d 1098 (8th Cir. 2000) (Neb. law) (manager of farmer's co-op killed in propane gas explosion could not recover against propane supplier because co-op stored large quantities of propane gas and manager had specialized knowledge of propane hazards).

[262] Goodbar v. Whitehead Bros., 591 F. Supp. 552, 559 (W.D. Va. 1984) ("there is no duty on product suppliers to warn employees of knowledgeable industrial purchasers as to product-related hazards"), aff'd sub nom. Beale v. Hardy, 769 F.2d 213 (4th Cir. 1985).

[263] See, e.g., Linden v. CNH Am., LLC, 673 F.3d 829, 836–37 (8th Cir. 2012) (Iowa law) (jury could consider whether plaintiff knew about dangers in his use of bulldozer); Johnson v. American Standard, Inc., 179 P.3d 905, 916 (Cal. 2008) ("Just as a manufacturer need not warn ordinary consumers about generally known dangers, a manufacturer need not warn members of a trade or profession (sophisticated users) about dangers generally known to that trade or profession."); Donald v. Shinn Fu Co. of Am., 2002 WL 32068351, at *8–10 (E.D.N.Y. 2002) ("knowledgeable user" doctrine barred failure to warn claim against manufacturer of fork lift jack by forklift operator who knew there was a risk of collapse from using jack without its stand).

[264] See § 10.2, below.

[265] See § 9.1, above. This point is well expressed in Dehring v. Keystone Shipping Co., 2013 WL 3879619, at *13 (E.D. Mich. 2013):

> The purpose of the duty to warn is to inform the audience of a product's non-obvious risks. What risks are non-obvious depends on the audience—risks that may not be obvious to a layman may be obvious to the skilled professional. The sophisticated user doctrine is thus not an exception to the duty to warn, but an application of it. . . . When the foreseeable users are skilled professionals in an industry instead of unsophisticated novices, the risks that are obvious will be different.

Accord Cabasug v. Crane Co., 988 F. Supp. 2d 1216, 1221 (D. Hawai'i 2013).

is thus no need to warn sophisticated users of dangers they already understand, and the absence of such warnings to such persons may not be a proximate cause of any harm resulting from those risks suffered by a sophisticated purchaser's employees or by others downstream. Because the sophisticated user doctrine substitutes the user's knowledge for a warning from the supplier, the scope of knowledge possessed by the sophisticate "must parallel the scope of the warning that would otherwise be required."[266]

Examples of the sophisticated user doctrine abound: a sheet metal supplier has no duty to warn a building contractor that the metal may be slippery, or to warn of the dangers in working with metal at heights;[267] a chimney manufacturer has no duty to warn an installer of the risk of carbon monoxide poisoning if the chimney is not kept clean;[268] and a seller of diving platforms need not warn a high school buyer of the danger if used for diving in shallow water.[269] More typically, the doctrine shields suppliers from liability for failing to warn employees of toxic substance buyers of the risks of breathing toxic fumes or dust, and how to avoid those risks.[270] For example, the doctrine shields a silica sand supplier from a duty to warn foundry workers that they can contract silicosis from breathing silica dust if the supplier has reason to believe that the purchasing foundry is a "sophisticated user" who already fully knows this risk and how to avoid it.[271]

But the doctrine has its limitations. For example, it may not relieve a supplier of its warning responsibilities if the purchaser's awareness is limited to a general risk that does not include a specific hazard that results in harm.[272] Thus, if a supplier of silica sand knows that disposable respirators are not effective in preventing silicosis, it has a duty to provide this specific safety information to a foundry that knows of the general risk of silicosis but does not specifically know that the type of respirators its workers use are ineffective.[273] Ultimately, as addressed in the *Restatement* discussion below, when a supplier sells a product to a sophisticated intermediate buyer, the supplier may rely on

---

[266] Buckner v. Milwaukee Elec. Tool Corp., 166 Cal. Rptr. 3d 202, 211–12 (Ct. App. 2013).

[267] See Contranchis v. Travelers Ins. Co., 839 So.2d 301, 304 (La. Ct. App. 2003) (no duty to warn sophisticated users of dangers they may be presumed to know because of their familiarity with product).

[268] See Gajewski v. Pavelo, 652 A.2d 509 (Conn. App. Ct. 1994).

[269] See Mohr v. St. Paul Fire & Marine Ins. Co., 674 N.W.2d 576 (Wis. Ct. App. 2003).

[270] See, e.g., Parker v. Schmeide Mach. & Tool Corp., 445 Fed. Appx. 231, 235 (11th Cir. 2011) (Ga. law) (Lockheed was a sophisticated user of beryllium, which generated respiratory particles, and served as a "learned intermediary between its employees and the manufacturers of beryllium products"); Taylor v. Airco, Inc., 503 F. Supp. 2d 432, 436 (D. Mass. 2007) (cancer from vinyl chloride fumes and contact; duty to warn employees fell on employer, Monsanto, rather than manufacturers), aff'd sub nom. Taylor v. American Chem. Council, 576 F.3d 16 (1st Cir. 2009); Irrer v. Milacron, Inc., 484 F. Supp. 2d 677 (E.D. Mich. 2007) (supplier of metalworking fluids to General Motors had no duty to warn GM employees of risks of respiratory illnesses).

[271] See, e.g., Haase v. Badger Mining Corp., 669 N.W.2d 737 (Wis. Ct. App. 2003) (silica sand supplier had no duty to warn foundry of risk that foundry workers might contract silicosis), aff'd on other grounds, 682 N.W.2d 389 (Wis. 2004) (manufacturer of silica sand was not subject to strict liability in tort because sand underwent substantial change by purchasing foundry that combined it with other materials to make molds for cast iron products like manhole covers, after which silica molds were broken off); Bergfeld v. Unimin Corp., 319 F.3d 350 (8th Cir. 2003) (Iowa law); Taylor v. Monsanto Co., 150 F.3d 806 (7th Cir. 1998) (Ind. law) (PCBs).

[272] See, e.g., Swope v. Columbian Chems. Co., 281 F.3d 185, 206 (5th Cir. 2002) (La. law) (sophisticated user defense does not apply unless user "already knew or reasonably should have been expected to know of the product's dangerous characteristics"). *But see* Taylor v. Monsanto Co., 150 F.3d 806, 808–09 (7th Cir. 1998) (Ind. law) (questioning "plaintiffs' attempt to fine-tune the 'sophisticated intermediary' doctrine to make it require Westinghouse to have specific expertise on human health and employee safety issues related to PCBs" and noting that "there is often no easy way to select the particular 'level of abstraction' that governs" such an inquiry), overruled on other grounds by Hill v. Tangherlini, 724 F.3d 965 (7th Cir 2013).

[273] Gray v. Badger Mining Corp., 676 N.W.2d 268 (Minn. 2004).

the intermediary to warn end-users of hidden dangers in the product with one important proviso—that the supplier's reliance is reasonable in the circumstances.[274]

Several states have statutes that bear, at least to some extent, on the sophisticated user doctrine. Michigan's statute is the most direct, specifically providing that a manufacturer or other seller, unless required to warn by statute or regulation, is not subject to liability for failure to warn "if the product is provided for use by a sophisticated user."[275] In addition, Connecticut's statute provides that a warning, to be adequate, must be provided to "the person best able to take or recommend precautions" to avoid harm;[276] Louisiana's statute states that a manufacturer need not warn of specific dangers of which the user already knows or should be expected to know;[277] and the Kansas statute eliminates the duty to warn of dangers and precautions of which the user or consumer should be aware.[278]

Bulk Supplier Doctrine

The bulk supplier doctrine may arise if there is no *way* to warn, because of the nature of the product and the form in which it is sold.[279] This doctrine normally applies to liquids, sand, minerals, gas, and other products provided in bulk to commercial purchasers by railroad car or tanker truck. The difficulty with imposing a duty to warn on such bulk suppliers is that there normally is no practical way to place a warning on such a product to alert end-users of its dangers. Moreover, the purchaser may itself repackage the chemical or other product in drums or other containers for subsequent transport and distribution to users or consumers, or it may simply use it as it arrives in bulk for some manufacturing process.[280] In either event, there typically is little practicable way for an upstream seller of such a product to provide warnings to the ultimate users or consumers of hazards the product may contain.[281] Accordingly, if the purchaser knows of the product's hazards, from warnings provided to it by the bulk

---

[274] See, e.g., Lawing v. Trinity Mfg., Inc., 749 S.E.2d 126, 132 (S.C. Ct. App. 2013) (Few, J.).

[275] Mich. Comp. Laws Ann. § 600.2947(4), applied in Bearup v. General Motors Corp., 2009 WL 249456, at *7–12 (Mich. Ct. App. 2009).

[276] See Conn. Gen. Stat. Ann. § 52–572q(d) (a "seller may not be considered to have provided adequate warnings or instructions unless they were devised to communicate with the person best able to take or recommend precautions against the potential harm"). See Gajewski v. Pavelo, 652 A.2d 509 (Conn. App. Ct. 1994).

[277] See La. Rev. Stat. Ann. § 9:2800.57(B)(2).

[278] See Kan. Stat. Ann. § 60–3305.

[279] This doctrine applies with extra force in many cases because the purchasers are knowledgeable users who usually do not need any warning, as discussed above. Because the doctrine applies to such materials as sand, chemicals, and other raw materials sold to other manufacturers, the doctrine sometimes is called the "raw material supplier" doctrine. See Frumer, Friedman, and Sklaren, Products Liability § 12.06[5].

Products Liability Rest. § 5, "Liability of Commercial Seller or Distributor of Product Components for Harm Caused by Products Into Which Components Are Integrated," provides that the supplier of a nondefective component (including a raw material) is subject to liability only if it "substantially participates in the integration of the component" into the integrated product, and the integration causes the product to be defective. Suppliers of "raw materials" do not have a duty to investigate or warn end uses. See id. cmt. *c*. On the special duties of suppliers of raw materials, see § 15.3, below.

[280] See, e.g., Gray v. Badger Mining Corp., 676 N.W.2d 268, 280–81 (Minn. 2004) (foundry used silica sand for making molds into which molten metal was poured, after which molds were knocked off castings, pulverizing sand into sub-micron sized particles of dust that workers could inhale unless protected by adequate respirators).

[281] *But see* Gryc v. Dayton-Hudson Corp., 297 N.W.2d 727, 731 (Minn. 1980) (manufacturer of flammable fabric sold to manufacturer of pajamas argued that any warnings it provided to garment manufacturers would not find their way to consumers; yet manufacturer used hang tags for marketing purposes, sent through the chain of commerce, that did reach consumers).

supplier or from general knowledge, the bulk supplier normally will have no duty to provide additional warnings to the ultimate user or consumer.[282] However, if the bulk supplier knows more about a product hazard or how to avoid it than its purchasers,[283] or if it has reason to suspect that its purchaser will not provide the necessary warnings,[284] it has a duty to provide this additional safety information at least to the purchaser, and possibly to the purchaser's employees or other end users, if there is some reasonable way to do so.

In *Purvis v. PPG Industries, Inc.*,[285] a dry cleaner employee was poisoned by a cleaning solvent manufactured by the defendant, PPG, which shipped the solvent in tank trucks to various distributors who then resold the solvent in drums to users such as the plaintiff's employer. PPG provided its distributors with warning labels and all relevant danger information in Material Safety Data Sheets.[286] The plaintiff sued PPG, claiming that the company should have provided the warnings directly to her. Affirming summary judgment for the defendant, the court held that PPG had no duty to provide warnings directly to the plaintiff. The court reasoned that sometimes manufacturers, like PPG, have no effective way to convey information directly to ultimate users or consumers about dangers of products sold in bulk.

Whether due to bulk sales, repackaging, or product combinations, upstream manufacturers sometimes may properly rely on downstream distributors to perform the warning function, provided there is a reasonable basis for the supplier to believe that the purchasing distributors will pass along appropriate warnings to their vendees.[287]

---

[282] See, e.g., Genereux v. American Beryllia Corp., 577 F.3d 350, 374 (1st Cir. 2009) (Mass. law) (when product is delivered in bulk, doctrine applies for two reasons: "[1] products delivered in bulk are often reformulated and repackaged by an intermediary, making it unlikely that the supplier could provide a warning that would reach end users; and [2] bulk supplies are often put to 'multitudinous commercial uses,' making it unduly burdensome to require the supplier to warn all foreseeable end users"); Wood v. Phillips Petrol. Co., 119 S.W.3d 870, 874 (Tex. App. 2003) (supplier of benzene to petrochemical company had no duty to warn purchaser on why and how to protect workers from its well-known toxic effects: "In some instances, a bulk supplier, who has no package of its own on which to place a label, may satisfy its duty to warn ultimate users . . . by proving that the intermediary to whom it sells the product is adequately trained and warned, familiar with the propensities of the product and its safe use, and capable of passing its knowledge on to users in a warning. . . . The question in any case is whether a bulk supplier has a reasonable assurance that its warning will reach those endangered by the use of its product."); In re TMJ Implants Prods. Liab. Litig., 872 F. Supp. 1019, 1029 (D. Minn. 1995) (because DuPont sold Teflon in bulk to knowledgeable medical device manufacturer to make jaw implants, it had no duty to warn ultimate consumers that Teflon might not be suited for human implants).

[283] See, e.g., Gray v. Badger Mining Corp., 676 N.W.2d 268 (Minn. 2004) (reversing summary judgment for supplier).

[284] See, e.g., Tilton v. Union Oil Co. of Cal., 831 N.E.2d 391 (Mass. App. Ct. 2005) (buyer's employee injured when nearly empty drum of chemical solvent exploded as he tried to remove lid with acetylene torch; jury could find that bulk supplier doctrine did not protect petroleum company that sold highly volatile solvent where it had delivered chemical to plaintiff's employer by pumping it into unlabeled drums).

[285] 502 So.2d 714 (Ala. 1987).

[286] The Hazard Communication Standard promulgated by OSHA requires manufacturers, distributors, and importers to label all containers of hazardous chemicals and to provide Safety Data Sheets (SDSs—formerly called "material safety data sheets," or MSDSs) to purchasing employers. In turn, employers must make SDS information available to employees, and must train their employees in the safe handling of such substances. OSHA required a uniform format for new SDSs effective June 1, 2015. 29 C.F.R. § 1910.1200 (2013); OSHA QuickCard: Hazard Communication Standard Pictogram, United States Department of Labor, Occupational Safety & Health Administration; § 9.3, notes 175–176, above (Globally Harmonized Hazard Communication Standard pictograms required under 29 C.F.R. § 1910.1200 effective June 1, 2015). See generally M. Green, When Toxic Worlds Collide: Regulatory and Common Law Prescriptions for Risk Communication, 13 Harv. Envt'l L. Rev. 209 (1989); O'Reilly, Risks of Assumptions: Impacts of Regulatory Label Warnings Upon Industrial Products Liability, 37 Cath. U. L. Rev. 85 (1987).

[287] *Purvis*, 502 So.2d at 722.

Hence, the bulk supplier doctrine may exempt manufacturers who sell in bulk from having to warn the ultimate user or consumer about the hazards in hydrogen peroxide sold to a hospital;[288] natural gas sold to a city;[289] propane sold to a transporter of propane;[290] asbestos sold to a manufacturer of joint compounds;[291] flammable chemicals sold to a manufacturer of ink;[292] or chemicals sold to a company that treated wood[293] or manufactured automobile seats.[294]

The *Restatements*

Both the bulk supplier and sophisticated user doctrines are offshoots of a general principle expressed in *Restatement (Second) of Torts* § 388, the basic provision on a chattel supplier's duty to warn under the law of negligence. Addressing a seller's duty to warn when it sells a product to an intermediate supplier, comment *n* to § 388 provides that a seller may rely on the intermediary to provide warnings to the end-user if that reliance is reasonable under the circumstances.[295] Such reliance is reasonable only if the seller has reason to believe that the intermediary will faithfully discharge this obligation, and, even then, the seller may have a duty to warn end users of particularly serious hazards if a feasible means of communication exists.[296] Section 388 often is relied on for the principle that a manufacturer may *not* always rely on an intermediary to pass along warnings of a product hazard.[297] But the other side of this coin—that a manufacturer *may* properly rely on an intermediary if there is a reasonable basis for such reliance—provides the basis for an exemption from the duty to warn for both the

---

[288] See Cook-Pizzi v. Van Waters & Rogers, Inc., 94 S.W.3d 636 (Tex. App. 2002).

[289] See Downs v. Panhandle E. Pipeline Co., 694 N.E.2d 1198 (Ind. Ct. App. 1998).

[290] See Stoffel v. Thermogas Co., 998 F. Supp. 1021 (N.D. Iowa 1997).

[291] Compare Robinson v. Union Carbide Corp., 2019 WL 3822531 (Del. Super. Ct. 2019) (Ohio law) (bulk supplier defense applied to supplier of asbestos pellets who warned sophisticated purchaser on whom it reasonably relied to pass on warnings to ultimate users), with Gibbs v. 84 Lumber Co., 2020 WL 5798072, at *7 (Del. Super. Ct. 2020) (S.C. law) (sophisticated user defense; supplier of bulk asbestos had no duty to warn end users of its customers' manufactured products).

[292] See Hoffman v. Houghton Chem. Corp., 751 N.E.2d 848 (Mass. 2001).

[293] Coffey v. Chemical Specialities, Inc., 4 F.3d 984 (4th Cir. 1993) (S.C. law).

[294] Adams v. Union Carbide Corp., 737 F.2d 1453 (6th Cir. 1984) (Ohio law).

[295] See, e.g., Persons v. Salmon N. Am., Inc., 265 Cal. Rptr. 773 (Ct. App. 1990).

[296] Comment *n* to § 388, entitled Warnings given to third person, provides in part:

> Chattels are often supplied for the use of others . . . . In all such cases the question may arise as to whether the person supplying the chattel is exercising that reasonable care, which he owes to those who are to use it, by informing the third person through whom the chattel is supplied of its actual character.
>
> Giving to the third person through whom the chattel is supplied all the information necessary to its safe use is not in all cases sufficient to relieve the supplier from liability. It is merely a means by which this information is to be conveyed to those who are to use the chattel. The question remains whether this method gives a reasonable assurance that the information will reach those whose safety depends upon their having it. . . .
>
> [I]f the danger involved in the ignorant use of a particular chattel is very great, it may be that the supplier does not exercise reasonable care in entrusting the communication of the necessary information even to a person whom he has good reason to believe to be careful. Many such articles can be made to carry their own message to the understanding of those who are likely to use them by the form in which they are put out, by the container in which they are supplied, or by a label or other device, indicating with a substantial sufficiency their dangerous character. Where the danger involved in the ignorant use of their true quality is great and such means of disclosure are practicable and not unduly burdensome, it may well be that the supplier should be required to adopt them.

[297] See, e.g., Tilton v. Union Oil Co. of Cal., 831 N.E.2d 391, 394–95 (Mass. App. Ct. 2005) (reliance not reasonable where supplier pumped its highly volatile chemical into purchaser's unlabeled drums).

sophisticated user and bulk supplier doctrines.[298] While § 388 of the *Restatement (Second) of Torts* addresses the obligations of a supplier to warn in the law of negligence, most courts also apply its principles to the duty to warn in strict products liability.[299]

Providing some amount of danger information to an intermediate buyer may not be enough if a reasonable supplier would provide the buyer with more or better information,[300] or would provide it directly to the ultimate users—considering the overall balance of costs and benefits, including the reliability of the intermediary, the magnitude of the hazard, and the feasibility of providing better or more direct warnings,[301] a principle well summarized in the *Third Restatement*.[302] Even if an upstream supplier had a reasonable basis for trusting an intermediate purchaser in the past, discovering

---

[298] See, e.g., Roney v. Gencorp, 654 F. Supp. 2d 501, 508 (S.D. W. Va. 2009) (predicting that West Virginia courts would adopt sophisticated user and bulk supplier defenses, per § 388 cmt. *n*); McGhee v. Oryx Energy Co., 657 So.2d 853 (Ala. 1995) (house exploded from propane gas leak not detected due to odor fade; producer, who sold gas through pipeline to distributors whom it warned, had no way to identify or warn individual consumers); Newson v. Monsanto Co., 869 F. Supp. 1255, 1262 (E.D. Mich. 1994) (suppliers of chemical to Ford Motor Co. used to make shatterproof windshields could reasonably assume that Ford had or would obtain information "abundantly available in the scientific literature").

[299] See, e.g., Lawing v. Trinity Mfg., Inc., 749 S.E.2d 126, 133 (S.C. Ct. App. 2013) (Few, J.) (implied warranty); Cabasug v. Crane Co., 988 F. Supp. 2d 1216 (D. Hawai'i 2013); Johnson v. American Standard, Inc., 179 P.3d 905, 916 (Cal. 2008) (adopting sophisticated user defense to failure to warn claims in negligence and strict liability); Carrel v. National Cord & Braid Corp., 852 N.E.2d 100, 109 (Mass. 2006) (adopting sophisticated user defense to failure to warn claims in negligence and breach of warranty); Humble Sand & Gravel, Inc. v. Gomez, 146 S.W.3d 170, 181 (Tex. 2004) (thorough review of comment *n* factors); Hoffman v. Houghton Chem. Corp., 751 N.E.2d 848 (Mass. 2001) (§ 388 applies to strict products liability duty to warn in implied warranty); Higgins v. E.I. DuPont de Nemours & Co., 671 F. Supp. 1055 (D. Md. 1987).

A few early decisions refused to apply the sophisticated user and bulk supplier doctrines as no-duty rules in strict liability in tort, holding that the duty to warn in strict tort is nondelegable as a matter of law so that suppliers must directly warn ultimate users. See, e.g., Menschik v. Mid-America Pipeline Co., 812 S.W.2d 861 (Mo. Ct. App. 1991). See also Hall v. Ashland Oil Co., 625 F. Supp. 1515 (D. Conn. 1986); Whitehead v. St. Joe Lead Co., 729 F.2d 238 (3d Cir. 1984) (N.J. law).

Some courts hold that whether there is a duty to provide warnings directly to ultimate users is a factual question for the jury, based on a balance of risk versus feasibility. See, e.g., Union Carbide Corp. v. Aubin, 97 So.3d 886, 901 (Fla. Dist. Ct. App. 2012) (bulk supplier of chrysotile asbestos; "Because the evidence was conflicting, and supported different reasonable inferences, the duty to warn issue was a question of fact [for] the jury."); Lambert v. B.P. Prods. N. Am., Inc., 2006 WL 924988, at *2–4 (S.D. Ill. 2006); Tilton v. Union Oil Co. of Cal., 831 N.E.2d 391 (Mass. App. Ct. 2005) (jury could find that bulk supplier doctrine did not apply because petroleum company that sold highly volatile solvent did not reasonably rely on purchaser to warn its employees); Bryant v. Technical Research Co., 654 F.2d 1337 (9th Cir. 1981) (Idaho law) (bulk supplier might have obtained distributor's customer list and directly warned end users); Shell Oil Co. v. Gutierrez, 581 P.2d 271 (Ariz. Ct. App. 1978).

[300] See, e.g., Union Carbide Corp. v. Kavanaugh, 879 So.2d 42, 45 (Fla. Dist. Ct. App. 2004) (asbestos supplier not protected by § 388 because, "although UCC provided information and some warning to Georgia-Pacific, it did not fully disclose the magnitude of the hazards then known to exist").

[301] See, e.g., Gray v. Badger Mining Corp., 676 N.W.2d 268 (Minn. 2004) (reversing summary judgment for supplier; provision of MSDS not necessarily enough); Little v. Liquid Air Corp., 939 F.2d 1293 (5th Cir. 1991) (Miss. law) (court should consider all aspects of the reasonableness of relying on a particular intermediate distributor in a particular situation; summary judgment for bulk supplier is improper solely on proof that it supplied its vendee with a MSDS containing the risk information).

[302] Products Liability Rest. § 2(c) cmt. *i* provides:

> There is no general rule as to whether one supplying a product for the use of others through an intermediary has a duty to warn the ultimate product user directly or may rely on the intermediary to relay warnings. The standard is one of reasonableness in the circumstances. Among the factors to be considered are the gravity of the risks posed by the product, the likelihood that the intermediary will convey the information to the ultimate user, and the feasibility and effectiveness of giving a warning directly to the user.

See also Products Liability Rest. § 5, which addresses the duties of suppliers of component parts and raw materials. Comment *c* thereto provides that raw material suppliers do not have a duty to warn end users. See § 15.3, below.

facts suggesting that the vendee is failing to pass on important warnings extinguishes the basis for relying on the vendee and restores the supplier's duty to provide warnings directly to end-users.[303] Moreover, when a product is a durable good (or is shipped in drums or other containers) on which a warning may be attached or embossed, the manufacturer usually has a ready means to provide warnings about serious hazards directly to end users—regardless of whether there is a knowledgeable or "sophisticated" employer or other intermediary involved.[304]

---

[303] See Lakeman v. Otis Elevator Co., 930 F.2d 1547 (11th Cir. 1991) (Ala. law) (where manufacturer sold chemical in bulk to repackager who resold it to industrial customers with some warnings, but not the most important ones, bulk supplier had duty to warn ultimate users once it became aware of intermediate seller's inadequate warning labels).

[304] "[W]hen the purchaser of machinery is the owner of a workplace who provides the machinery to employees for their use, and there is reason to doubt that the employer will pass warnings on to employees, the seller is required to reach the employees directly with necessary instructions and warnings if doing so is reasonably feasible." Products Liability Rest. § 2(c) cmt. *i.* See, e.g., Square D Co. v. Hayson, 621 So.2d 1373 (Fla. Dist. Ct. App. 1993) (manufacturer of electrical busway system should have placed label on system directly warning workers of backwards installation risks). *But see* Vines v. Beloit Corp., 631 So.2d 1003 (Ala. 1994) (manufacturer of machine discharged its duty toward users of machinery by warning sophisticated employer). See generally §§ 9.3 and 9.4, above.

Chapter 10

LIMITATIONS ON DEFECTIVENESS

Table of Sections

§ 10.1 LIMITATIONS ON DEFECTIVENESS—GENERALLY

The inquiry to this point has focused on when and why manufacturers *should* be held accountable for accidental harm caused by defective products. In this chapter, the focus reverses direction to a consideration of arguments and doctrine that *deny* a manufacturer's responsibility for harm from product accidents. While the underlying justifications for assigning or denying responsibility in such cases remain largely the same—feasibility, economic efficiency, manufacturer accountability, consumer choice, personal responsibility, and judicial competency—the issues explored in this chapter look past the preliminary conditions and justifications for imposing liability to certain salient circumstances that delimit the normal principles of responsibility for selling defective products. In short, this chapter considers various factors that tend to *limit* a manufacturer's responsibility for product hazards.

The remaining chapters examine additional types of limitation on the responsibility of a manufacturer or other seller for product accidents. The chapters on actual and proximate causation focus on limiting links between a defendant's wrongful conduct, or sale of a defective product, and the plaintiff's harm. The chapters on defenses consider limitations that have crystallized into formal defenses limiting the responsibility of sellers of defective products. One topic treated there, product misuse, might comfortably have been included in the present chapter since most courts view the extent to which manufacturers must protect users against their own misuse to be an issue that defines the outer boundaries of a manufacturer's scope of duty.[1] Subsequent chapters examine how the law limits and otherwise adjusts the normal liability principles to fit a variety of special types of defendants, transactions, and products.

This chapter first inquires into the extent to which manufacturers and other sellers are responsible for obvious and inherent product hazards. Both issues involve important

[1] But some courts, and those states that address product misuse statutorily, treat the issue as a matter of affirmative defense, similar to contributory and comparative negligence and assumption of risk. Because of the affinity between product misuse and these traditional (mis)conduct defenses, misuse is treated in the chapter on that topic. See § 13.5, below.

questions of personal choice, consumer expectations, social utility, and accountability for accidental injury.[2] The remaining sections consider how the passage of time in various situations tends to weaken a manufacturer's responsibility for product-related accidents, including developments in the "state of the art" that improve product safety; prenatal and preconception harm caused by drugs and other chemicals, the effects of which can ripple through generations; product deterioration over time; the special risks of product disposal and salvage; and the extent to which manufacturers may have post-sale duties to warn, repair, or recall when hazards are revealed by a product's recurring use and misuse by consumers in the field. The formal affirmative defenses arising out of the passage of time—statutes of limitations and repose—are treated in a later chapter on special defenses.[3]

§ 10.2 OBVIOUS DANGERS

Hidden ("latent") product dangers are the most pernicious, for they deprive buyers and users of the opportunity to choose how best to address a danger, or possibly even to avoid a dangerous product altogether, to avoid the risk of harm. In response, the law generally requires manufacturers and other sellers to provide purchasers and users with warnings of material hidden dangers and instructions on how to avoid them.[4] Yet merely supplying a warning of danger often is not enough: if providing such information does not substantially eliminate a material risk, manufacturers ordinarily must take all reasonable steps to design the hidden danger away. A manufacturer's duty to provide warnings and instructions, in other words, is largely independent of its duty of safe design.[5]

But products frequently contain "open and obvious" dangers, hazards plainly appearing on a product's face which are manifest to those who buy and use the product. For example, the hazards to human limbs from power saws, power lawn mowers, and punch presses are evident for all to see. This section examines how the obviousness of a danger may affect a manufacturer's responsibility to design away and warn against such obvious ("patent") hazards. In particular, the section reviews the rise and fall of the "open and obvious danger" doctrine, a no-duty doctrine that formerly shielded manufacturers from design defect responsibility for harm caused by obvious dangers in their products, often called the "patent danger" rule.[6]

---

[2] For explorations of the moral groundwork of these and other foundational issues in products liability, see, e.g., Watts, Fairness and Utility in Products Liability: Balancing Individual Rights and Social Welfare, 38 Fla. St. U. L. Rev. 597 (2011); Owen, Expectations in Tort, 44 Ariz. St. L. Rev. 1287 (2011); Wright, The Principles of Product Liability, 26 Rev. Litig. 1067 (2007); Owen, The Moral Foundations of Products Liability Law: Toward First Principles, 68 Notre Dame L. Rev. 427 (1993).

[3] See § 14.6, below.

[4] See ch. 9, above.

[5] See § 6.2, above.

[6] On the role of obviousness in products liability litigation, see cautiously Geistfeld, The Value of Consumer Choice in Products Liability, 74 Brook. L. Rev. 781, 791–92 (2009) (nicely explaining the virtues of autonomy protection, and the role of obvious dangers, in tort law; yet wrongly characterizing *the* clearly leading products liability work as merely "a" leading one; blithely ignoring the preeminent book's principal section on this particular topic, obviously entitled "obvious dangers"; intelligently quoting from the work, though carelessly quoting from the first edition whilst citing the second; annoyingly omitting vital qualifying analysis that reveals the treatise author's laudable dedication to autonomy protection; wrongly suggesting that the work defends a harsh but correct application of the pure consumer expectations test in obvious-danger cases—which, by contrast, the second edition explicitly calls a "dire consequence" of that test; and mistakenly (if amusingly) asserting that the book makes a mistaken assumption, when in fact it makes no mistakes of any kind). See generally Owen, Information Shields in Tort Law, in Exploring Tort Law 295 (S. Madden ed.,

The Rise and Fall of the Patent-Danger Doctrine

Design Defects

Ancient law had little sympathy for persons injured by obvious dangers in products they bought from others. By the time of Justinian's *Digest* in 533 A.D., responsibility in Roman law for obvious defects in products lay with the buyer, not the seller. This was true even with respect to a seller's express assertions of product quality which might otherwise be interpreted as denying the existence of the defect. "[P]atent defects, as in modern legal systems, were taken to be accepted by the buyer and even express warranties were deemed not to cover them—if, for instance, a one-eyed dog was sold as sound, it was as a sound one-eyed dog."[7] Not much had changed by the thirteenth century *Summa Theologica*,[8] where Thomas Aquinas (1225?–1274 A.D.) outlined basic mercantile obligations consistent with the *Digest*. In *Summa Theologica*, Aquinas makes clear that a seller must disclose secret flaws: it is sin and fraud for a person to sell a product he knows to contain a latent defect, but which the buyer does not, without disclosing the flaw to the buyer; and the sale is void. If the seller is himself unaware of the defect, the sale is not a sin, but the seller must return to the buyer any excess in price attributable to the defect.[9] The buyer is responsible for manifest defects, reasons Aquinas, such that a seller is not bound to disclose such defects from "any duty of justice," but to do so would reflect "the more exuberant virtue."[10]

Until quite recently, American law continued to protect sellers from the harmful consequences of manifest dangers in products they sold to others. Into the 1970s, the "patent-danger doctrine" widely barred claims against manufacturers and other sellers for harm from product dangers that were "open and obvious." The classic case was *Campo v. Scofield*,[11] decided by the New York Court of Appeals in 1950. The plaintiff, working on his son's farm, was dumping a crate of onions into an "onion topping" machine when his hands became caught in its revolving steel rollers and were so badly injured that they required amputation. He sued the manufacturers of the machine for negligently failing to equip it with a guard or stopping device. The trial court denied the defendants' motion to dismiss, the Appellate Division reversed, and the Court of Appeals affirmed the Appellate Division's order to dismiss. Ruling that the plaintiff's failure to allege that the danger was latent or unknown was fatal to the complaint, Judge Fuld spoke for a unanimous Court of Appeals:

> If a manufacturer does everything necessary to make the machine function properly for the purpose for which it is designed, if the machine is without any

---

Cambridge 2005); Bowbeer and Killoran, Liriano v. Hobart Corp.: Obvious Dangers, The Duty to Warn of Safer Alternatives, and the Heeding Presumption, 65 Brook. L. Rev. 717 (1999); Jacobs, Toward a Process-Based Approach to Failure-to-Warn Law, 71 N.C. L. Rev. 121, 128–37 (1992); Henderson and Twerski, Doctrinal Collapse in Products Liability: The Empty Shell of Failure To Warn, 65 N.Y.U. L. Rev. 265, 306 (1990); Phillips, Products Liability: Obviousness of Danger Revisited, 15 Ind. L. Rev. 797 (1982); Darling, The Patent Danger Rule: An Analysis and a Survey of Its Vitality, 29 Mercer L. Rev. 583 (1978); Marschall, An Obvious Wrong Does Not Make a Right: Manufacturers' Liability for Patently Dangerous Products, 48 N.Y.U. L. Rev. 1065 (1973); Annot., 35 A.L.R.4th 861 (1985) (status of patent danger liability rule).

7 J. A. C. Thomas, Textbook of Roman Law 286 (1976) (footnote omitted).

8 T. Aquinas, Summa Theologica, Ethicus, II, II at question 77, arts. 1–4 (Fathers of the English Dominican Province trans., 2d rev. ed. 1920).

9 See generally Hamilton, The Ancient Maxim Caveat Emptor, 40 Yale L.J. 1133, 1136–38 (1931).

10 Id. at 1138 (quoting T. Aquinas, Summa Theologica, Ethicus, II, II, question 77, art. 4 (Rickaby trans., 2d ed. 1896)).

11 95 N.E.2d 802 (N.Y. 1950).

> latent defect, and if its functioning creates no danger or peril that is not known to the user, then the manufacturer has satisfied the law's demands. We have not yet reached the state where a manufacturer is under the duty of making a machine accident proof or foolproof.[12]

A manufacturer simply has no duty to protect people against "a patent peril or from a source manifestly dangerous."[13] Otherwise, reasoned the court, the manufacturer of an axe, buzz saw, or airplane with an exposed propeller would be subject to liability to a user cut by the blade or propeller. "In such cases, the manufacturer has the right to expect that such persons will do everything necessary to avoid such contact, for the very nature of the article gives notice and warning of the consequences to be expected, of the injuries to be suffered. In other words, the manufacturer is under no duty to render a machine or other article 'more' safe—as long as the danger to be avoided is obvious and patent to all."[14]

Campo was by no means the first case so holding,[15] but it anchored the patent-danger doctrine like a rock. Its simple statement of individual responsibility for self-protection struck a responsive chord throughout the nation, and, following *Campo*, many courts adopted the doctrine, or reaffirmed it if they had relied on it before.[16] In the 1950s and early 1960s, the *Campo* obvious-danger rule was one of the most firmly entrenched doctrines in all products liability law. Professor Fleming James, ever critical of rules that limited recovery for injured persons,[17] derided the absolutist no-duty nature of the rule as "a vestigial carryover from pre-*MacPherson* days when deceit was needed for recovery."[18] Yet, even two decades after *Campo*, the Maryland Court of Appeals opted to align itself with other vestigial jurisdictions in adhering to the rule.[19]

Most design danger claims before the 1970s involved hidden or "latent" dangers,[20] and courts at the time exhibited little patience with claims involving design dangers that were obvious. For example, in *Bartkewich v. Billinger*,[21] decided in 1968, the hand of a glass-breaking machine operator was crushed when he reached into the machine to free a piece of glass that was jamming, and he thought damaging, the machine. Addressing the operator's design defect claim against the manufacturer for failing to provide guards or strategically located cut-off switches, the court held that the manufacturer had no

---

12 Id. at 804.

13 Id.

14 Id.

15 See, e.g., Stevens v. Allis-Chalmers Mfg. Co., 100 P.2d 723 (Kan. 1940); Yaun v. Allis-Chalmers Mfg. Co., 34 N.W.2d 853 (Wis. 1948).

16 See, e.g., Tyson v. Long Mfg. Co., 107 S.E.2d 170 (N.C. 1959); Stevens v. Durbin-Durco, Inc., 377 S.W.2d 343 (Mo. 1964); Parker v. Heasler Plumbing & Heating Co., 388 P.2d 516 (Wyo. 1964).

17 See V. Nolan and E. Ursin, Understanding Enterprise Liability (1995); Priest, The Invention of Enterprise Liability: A Critical History of the Intellectual Foundations of Modern Tort Law, 14 J. Legal Stud. 461 (1985).

18 James, Products Liability (pt. 1), 34 Tex. L. Rev. 44, 52 (1955). See also 2 F. Harper and F. James, The Law of Torts § 28.5, at 1544 (1956).

19 See Blankenship v. Morrison Mach. Co., 257 A.2d 430, 433 (Md. 1969). See also Halvorson v. American Hoist & Derrick Co., 240 N.W.2d 303 (Minn. 1976), overruled by Holm v. Sponco Mfg., Inc., 324 N.W.2d 207 (Minn. 1982) .

20 See Luque v. McLean, 501 P.2d 1163, 1168 (Cal. 1972) ("the great majority of reported decisions dealing with products liability have involved defects classifiable as latent").

21 247 A.2d 603 (Pa. 1968).

such duty: "If he thought the machine was being damaged, what did he think would happen to his hand?"[22]

But not all courts were unsympathetic to the plight of workers and others injured by obvious product dangers. As the consumer protectionist perspective of *Restatement (Second) of Torts* § 402A spread across America in the late 1960s and 1970s, judicial acceptance of the patent-danger rule began to crumble. Some courts, persuaded by the safety, representational, and risk-spreading rationales thought to support the new strict tort doctrine, began to reject the obvious-danger rule as outmoded and wrong-headed.[23]

One such case rejecting the patent-danger rule, *Pike v. Frank G. Hough Co.*,[24] involved a negligent design claim against the manufacturer of a large earth-moving machine, a paydozer, which backed over a worker. The paydozer had a large engine box in the rear that created a large blind spot behind the operator of the machine, but it was not equipped with rearview mirrors. Contending that the danger of being struck by the paydozer was obvious, the manufacturer claimed that it had no duty to install safety devices to protect against such a patent peril. Rejecting this defense, the California Supreme Court relied on criticism of the patent-danger doctrine and *Campo v. Scofield* by Professor James who had observed in his tort law treatise that "the bottom does not logically drop out of a negligence case against the maker when it is shown that the purchaser knew of the dangerous condition. Thus if the product is a carrot-topping machine with exposed moving parts,[25] or an electric clothes wringer dangerous to the limbs of the operator, and if it would be feasible for the maker of the product to install a guard or a safety release, it should be a question for the jury whether reasonable care demanded such a precaution, though its absence is obvious."[26] Reversing the nonsuit of the plaintiff, the *Pike* court concluded that "the obviousness of peril is relevant to the manufacturer's defenses, not to the issue of duty."[27]

Other courts also began to abandon the patent-danger doctrine as contrary to the policies of the day. In *Palmer v. Massey-Ferguson, Inc.*,[28] for example, a farmer sued the manufacturer of a hay baler for injuries to his hand caught in the mechanism of the machine. Observing that the patent-danger rule conflicted with the trend toward expanding manufacturer responsibility, the court thought that "a rule which excludes the manufacturer from liability if the defect in the design of his product is patent but applies the duty if such a defect is latent is somewhat anomalous. The manufacturer of the obviously defective product ought not to escape because the product was obviously a bad one. The law, we think, ought to discourage misdesign rather than encouraging it in its obvious form."[29]

---

[22] Id. at 605.

[23] See, e.g., Wright v. Massey-Harris, Inc., 215 N.E.2d 465 (Ill. App. Ct. 1966).

[24] 467 P.2d 229 (Cal. 1970).

[25] Citing *Campo*. The product in *Campo* in fact was an onion-topping machine.

[26] 467 P.2d at 235 (citing 2 F. Harper and F. James, The Law of Torts § 28.5, at 1542–43 (1956)). Fleming James first published his discussion of the obvious-danger doctrine in James, Products Liability (pt. 1), 34 Tex. L. Rev. 44, 51–54 (1955). *Pike* also relied on similar conclusions by Dix Noel, in Manufacturer's Negligence of Design or Directions for Use of a Product, 71 Yale L.J. 816, 838 (1962). See *Pike*, 467 P.2d at 235.

[27] 467 P.2d at 234.

[28] 476 P.2d 713 (Wash. Ct. App. 1970).

[29] Id. at 718–19. Surely a catchy phrase, but its fallacy is that it is the *danger* that is obvious, not the defect.

Once the 1970s were under way, the expansionary principles of modern products liability law quickly took hold, and courts increasingly reevaluated how the obviousness of a danger should affect design defectiveness. For example, in *Luque v. McLean*,[30] the California Supreme Court in 1972 reexamined the applicability of the patent-danger doctrine to design claims brought under § 402A in a case where the operator of a power lawn mower was injured when he slipped on wet grass and his hand slid through an unguarded area in the front of the machine. Relying on language in *Greenman v. Yuba Power Products, Inc.*,[31] which suggests that a plaintiff must establish that he was not aware of the product's defective condition,[32] the trial court so instructed the jury, which returned a verdict for the defendant. Reversing for error in this instruction, the California court repudiated the patent-danger rule in strict products liability.[33] And as the decade of the 1970s progressed, more and more courts rejected the patent-danger doctrine in design defect cases, holding that the obviousness of a danger is merely one factor in assessing the negligence or defectiveness of a product's design, not an absolute bar to liability.[34]

The landmark decision repudiating the obvious-danger doctrine was decided in New York, in 1976, by the same court that in 1950 had provided the doctrine's bedrock *Campo* decision. In *Micallef v. Miehle Co.*,[35] the New York Court of Appeals reconsidered the viability of its adamant adherence to the patent-danger rule. The plaintiff, who operated a huge photo-offset printing press, some 150 feet in length, discovered a foreign object on the printing plate which was rotating at high speed. In order to avoid stopping the machine (which took at least three hours to restart), the plaintiff lightly touched the revolving plate with an 8-inch-wide piece of plastic, called "chasing the hickie on the run." In the process, the plastic and the plaintiff's hand were drawn together into the machine. To prevent a user's hands from entering the machine, the plaintiff's expert engineer testified that the machine should have been equipped with guards, which would not have impeded the common practice of hickie chasing. The defendant countered that the absence of guards was an open and obvious condition which it had no duty to correct. The jury gave its verdict for the plaintiff, but the Appellate Division reversed, relying in part on *Campo*'s patent-danger doctrine.

Reversing the Appellate Division, the Court of Appeals left no doubt as to its conclusion, beginning its decision: "The time has come to depart from the patent-danger rule enunciated in *Campo v. Scofield* . . . ."[36] In support of its decision to overrule *Campo*, the court noted the "sustained attack" on that opinion, stemming from "the belief that, in our highly complex and technological society, we fall victim to the manufacturer who

---

[30] 501 P.2d 1163 (Cal. 1972).

[31] 377 P.2d 897 (Cal. 1963).

[32] "To establish the manufacturer's liability it was sufficient that plaintiff proved that he was injured while using the Shopsmith in a way it was intended to be used as a result of a defect in design and manufacture *of which plaintiff was not aware* that made the Shopsmith unsafe for its intended use." Id. at 901 (emphasis added).

[33] As the *Luque* court pointed out, it had repudiated the obvious-danger rule in the *negligent* design context in *Pike*. Other early cases rejecting the patent-danger doctrine in California are Thompson v. Package Mach. Co., 99 Cal. Rptr. 281 (Ct. App. 1971), and Buccery v. General Motors Corp., 132 Cal. Rptr. 605 (Ct. App. 1976).

[34] See, e.g., Byrns v. Riddell, Inc., 550 P.2d 1065 (Ariz. 1976); Micallef v. Miehle Co., 348 N.E.2d 571 (N.Y. 1976); Stenberg v. Beatrice Foods Co., 576 P.2d 725 (Mont. 1978); Auburn Mach. Works Co. v. Jones, 366 So.2d 1167 (Fla. 1979).

[35] 348 N.E.2d 571 (N.Y. 1976).

[36] Id. at 573.

holds himself out as an expert in his field." Further, the court pointed to charges that the patent-danger rule was little more than an assumption of risk defense as a matter of law; that it was anomalous to require manufacturers to develop reasonably safe products, on the one hand, while immunizing them from obvious dangers no matter how unreasonable, on the other; and that its rigidity produced harsh results for consumers who could not always recognize and appreciate obvious hazards. Accordingly, the court held that a manufacturer must design its products with reasonable care to avoid unreasonable risks of harm to persons who might be exposed to foreseeable dangers, based on "a balancing of the likelihood of harm, and the gravity of harm if it happens, against the burden of the precaution which would be effective to avoid the harm."[37] Thus, while the obviousness of a product danger often does reduce the likelihood of accidents, and so factors into the calculus of risk, and while a danger's obviousness might affect the issues of contributory negligence and assumption of risk,[38] "the patent-danger doctrine should not, in and of itself, prevent a plaintiff from establishing his case."[39]

Once the *Campo* patent-danger doctrine was repudiated in its own home state, the rule proceeded to collapse around the nation. One court after another, usually for claims in both negligence and strict liability in tort, abandoned the rule's absolute no-duty power and reduced the obviousness of danger to mere "factor" status in the cost-benefit evaluation of the safety of a product's design.[40] Courts in some states continued the obvious-danger design defect rule into the 1980s,[41] as did a few courts even into the 1990s, sometimes by bald applications of the rule in all its splendor,[42] other times by

---

37 Id. at 577–78.

38 See, e.g., Ford v. GACS, Inc., 265 F.3d 670, 676 (8th Cir. 2001) (Mo. law) (obviousness of design dangers goes to comparative fault, not to duty).

39 348 N.E.2d at 578. One fairly early case, Auburn Mach. Works Co. v. Jones, 366 So.2d 1167, 1170 (Fla. 1979), explained the rationale:

> The patent danger doctrine encourages manufacturers to be outrageous in their design, to eliminate safety devices, and to make hazards obvious. For example, if the cage which is placed on an electric fan as a safety device were left off and someone put his hand in the fan, under this doctrine there would be no duty on the manufacturer as a matter of law.

40 See, e.g., Genie Indus., Inc. v. Matak, 462 S.W.3d 1, 17 (Tex. 2015) (under a risk-utility analysis, "an 'open and obvious' and 'generally known' danger [in design] can give rise to liability"); Calles v. Scripto-Tokai Corp., 864 N.E.2d 249, 260 (Ill. 2007) ("the open and obvious danger of a product does not create a *per se* bar to a manufacturer's liability"); Thongchoom v. Graco Children's Prods., Inc., 71 P.3d 214 (Wash. Ct. App. 2003) (plaintiff may prove design defect with either consumer expectations test or risk-utility test; obviousness does not preclude liability under the risk-utility analysis); Hernandez v. Tokai Corp., 2 S.W.3d 251 (Tex. 1999); Perkins v. Wilkinson Sword, Inc., 700 N.E.2d 1247 (Ohio 1998); LeBlanc v. American Honda Motor Co., 688 A.2d 556 (N.H. 1997); Seymour v. Brunswick Corp., 655 So.2d 892 (Miss. 1995); Holm v. Sponco Mfg., Inc., 324 N.W.2d 207 (Minn. 1982). See also Owens v. Allis-Chalmers Corp., 326 N.W.2d 372 (Mich. 1982) (restricting patent-danger rule to cases involving simple tools and products).

41 See, e.g., Miller v. Dvornik, 501 N.E.2d 160 (Ill. App. Ct. 1986); Hedgepeth v. Fruehauf Corp., 634 F. Supp. 93 (S.D. Miss. 1986); Gray v. Manitowoc Co., 771 F.2d 866 (5th Cir. 1985) (Miss. law) (refusing to abandon patent-danger rule, despite fact that the rule had been the subject of much criticism); Coast Catamaran Corp. v. Mann, 321 S.E.2d 353 (Ga. Ct. App. 1984); Estrada v. Schmutz Mfg. Co., 734 F.2d 1218, 1220 (7th Cir. 1984) (Ind. law) (Posner, J.) (factory worker's hand caught while brushing ink on rollers: if you "go to the zoo and put your hand through the bars of the lion's cage, and the lion bites your hand off, . . . you do not have an action against the zoo").

42 "Despite criticism of the 'open and obvious' rule, it remains the law in this state." Vax v. Albany Lawn & Garden Ctr., 433 S.E.2d 364, 366 (Ga. Ct. App. 1993) (riding mower not equipped with smooth-start clutch or deadman control; "the fact that the defect was not latent but open and obvious constitutes an absolute legal defense"). See also Farkas v. Addition Mfg. Techs., LLC, 952 F.3d 944, 950 (8th Cir. 2020) (Mo. law) (affirming dismissal of plaintiff's negligence claim; "danger of a tube forming machine to the user's hand was . . . 'open, obvious, and apparent' "); Morrison v. Kubota Tractor Corp., 891 S.W.2d 422, 427–28 (Mo. Ct. App. 1994) (in *negligence*, tractor manufacturer owed "no duty to guard against the patent peril of injury in a roll over accident involving [a] ROPS-less tractor by installing a ROPS" when the tractor was manufactured). While this is still

virtue of some lingering offshoot of the doctrine that still showed some weak signs of life. Since that time, the doctrine has lost its remaining strongholds—Georgia[43] and Illinois[44]—leaving just Missouri[45] as the rule's single remaining holdout, applicable to negligent design cases alone.[46]

Despite the formal collapse of the patent-danger doctrine in design defect cases in recent decades, it is important to note that the obviousness of a product's risk still may combine with other risk-utility factors (including warnings) to bar recovery as a matter of law.[47] Even more pointedly, the obviousness of a danger may alone perversely bar liability, no matter how simply the danger may be corrected by redesign, under the guise of the consumer expectations test. This untoward result may also obtain in some jurisdictions in "simple-product" cases.[48] Yet, even with these caveats, the rise and fall of the patent-danger rule in design defect cases during the last half of the twentieth century remains one of the most fascinating tales of products liability law. Now entirely discredited as an absolute limitation on a manufacturer's duty of safe design in virtually every state, the patent-danger doctrine as an independent no-duty rule in design defect cases essentially is dead.[49]

---

the rule for negligent design claims in Missouri, manufacturers *are* subject to *strict* products liability for obvious dangers. See, e.g., Miller v. Varity Corp., 922 S.W.2d 821, 826–27 (Mo. Ct. App. 1996) (lack of ROPS); Sappington v. Skyjack, Inc., 512 F.3d 440, 447 (8th Cir. 2008) (Mo. law) (obviousness of danger not dispositive but only relevant to fault).

[43] In Ogletree v. Navistar Int'l Transp. Corp., 500 S.E.2d 570, 571–72 (Ga. 1998) ("The overwhelming majority of jurisdictions have held that the open and obvious nature of the danger does not preclude liability for design defects.").

[44] In Calles v. Scripto-Tokai Corp., 864 N.E.2d 249, 257–60 (Ill. 2007), where the court rejected Scoby v. Vulcan-Hart Corp., 569 N.E.2d 1147 (Ill. App. Ct. 1991), which excepted "simple" products with open and obvious dangers from the risk-utility test, leaving consumer expectations as the only test, where the latter test by nature barred liability for obvious dangers. "[T]he open and obvious danger of a product does not create a *per se* bar to a manufacturer's liability [but] is one factor that may be weighed in the risk-utility test." *Calles*, 864 N.E.2d at 260.

[45] In Missouri, the patent-danger doctrine does not apply to its statutory strict liability actions, but it still does apply to common law negligent design claims. See, e.g., Farkas v. Addition Mfg. Techs., LLC, 952 F.3d 944, 949–50 (8th Cir. 2020) (Mo. Law) (Missouri still holds that, in negligence, a manufacturer has no duty to reduce or eliminate product dangers that are "open, obvious, and apparent."). See note 42, above.

[46] Some time ago, Michigan law had a simple-product doctrine that muddied the jurisprudential waters in that state on the role of obvious dangers in design defect cases. See, e.g., Mallard v. Hoffinger Indus., 564 N.W.2d 74, 77 (Mich. Ct. App. 1997) (affirming summary judgment for manufacturer of above-ground swimming pool, which was a simple product, and therefore had no duty to users to design out obvious danger of hitting bottom of pool). But the simple-product doctrine in design defect cases now appears to have been laid to rest in Michigan. See, e.g., Dehring v. Keystone Shipping Co., 2013 WL 3879619, at *24 (E.D. Mich. 2013).

[47] See, e.g., Timpte Indus. v. Gish, 286 S.W.3d 306, 312 (Tex. 2009) (reinstating summary judgment for manufacturer of truck trailer from the top of which plaintiff fell while loading fertilizer; while "the obviousness of danger in and of itself is not an absolute bar" to design defect claims, "the obviousness of the claimed defect is 'an important consideration' " in rendering design defect determinations).

[48] Remaining offshoots of the patent-danger rule for obvious design dangers, such as the "simple-product" exception to the risk-utility test, still appear to exist in a state here and there. See notes 44 and 46, above. On the simple-product doctrine more generally, see § 8.6, above.

[49] This is the clear position of the Products Liability Restatement:

> Subsection (b) does not recognize the obviousness of a design-related risk as precluding a finding of defectiveness. The fact that a danger is open and obvious is relevant to the issue of defectiveness, but does not necessarily preclude a plaintiff from establishing that a reasonable alternative design should have been adopted that would have reduced or prevented injury to the plaintiff.

Products Liability Rest. § 2 cmt. *d*. See also id. Reporters' Note ("A strong majority of courts have rejected the 'open and obvious' or 'patent danger' rule as an absolute defense to a claim of design defect. The obviousness of the danger is one factor among many to consider as to whether a product design meets risk-utility norms.").

Warning Defects

In contrast to *design* defect cases, where the obviousness of a danger is now viewed as merely one of many factors in the risk-utility defect balance, courts widely hold that there simply is no duty to *warn* of dangers that are obvious. Put otherwise, while the patent-danger-no-duty rule has fallen into oblivion in design defect litigation, the open-and-obvious-danger rule is alive and well in warning cases where it properly precludes recovery in negligence,[50] implied warranty,[51] and strict liability in tort[52] for a defendant's failure to warn of dangers that are evident. Although a very small number of early decisions flatly disagreed,[53] virtually all modern courts hold,[54] and statutes in several states provide,[55] that manufacturers and other sellers simply have no duty to warn of dangers that are open, obvious, or commonly known.

Courts and commentators frequently observe that it is senseless to require warnings of dangers that are obvious.[56] A warning of a hidden danger provides useful

---

50 Liability for negligent failure to warn arises only if a seller "has no reason to believe that those for whose use the chattel is supplied will realize its dangerous condition." Rest. (2d) Torts § 388(b).

51 The "fit for the ordinary purposes" standard of the implied warranty of merchantability, UCC § 2–314(2)(c), is based on the satisfaction of an ordinary buyer's reasonable expectations of safety and other quality. See, e.g., Scheibe v. Fort James Corp., 276 F. Supp. 2d 246, 252 (D. Del. 2003) ("When a purchaser knows of the dangers of a product, or where that danger is obvious, . . . no implied warranty of merchantability arises."); American Tobacco Co. v. Grinnell, 951 S.W.2d 420, 435 (Tex. 1997). An implied warranty of merchantability does not arise with respect to dangers which the buyer observes before purchase, UCC § 2–316(3)(b) and cmt. 8, and the discovery of dangers after purchase bears on whether breach was a cause of any injury. UCC § 2–314 cmt. 13. See § 4.3, above.

52 See Rest. (2d) Torts § 402A cmts. *j* and *k*.

53 See, e.g., Armentrout v. FMC Corp., 842 P.2d 175, 181 (Colo. 1992); Harnischfeger Corp. v. Gleason Crane Rentals, Inc., 585 N.E.2d 166 (Ill. App. Ct. 1991); Campos v. Firestone Tire & Rubber Co., 485 A.2d 305 (N.J. 1984), superseded by statute as stated in Dewey v. R.J. Reynolds Tobacco Co., 577 A.2d 1239 (N.J. 1990). The duty to warn of obvious dangers rules in both Illinois and New Jersey subsequently were overturned. See more recent cases in next footnote, below.

54 See, e.g., Rardon v. Falcon Safety Prods., Inc., 2021 WL 2008923, at *9 (W.D. Mo. 2021) (no duty to warn of the open and obvious dangers of driving a car after inhaling Dust-Off to get high); Reichmann v. Whirlpool Corp., 2020 WL 207749, at *6 (E.D.N.Y. 2020) (dismissing any claim for failing to warn of a puddle of water from a known refrigerator leak); Kurzinsky v. Petzl Am., Inc., 794 Fed. Appx. 187, 190 (3d Cir. 2019) (Pa. law) (no duty to warn of obvious risk of travelling at high speed on a Tandem Speed Pulley on a zip line); Crawfordsville Town & Country Home Ctr., Inc. v. Cordova, 119 N.E.3d 119, 130 (Ind. Ct. App. 2019) (no duty to warn of obvious danger of using aerial lift near power lines); Knott v. AMFEC, Inc., 471 Fed. Appx. 561, 562 (8th Cir. 2012) (Minn. law); Farias v. Mr. Heater, Inc., 684 F.3d 1231, 1233 (11th Cir. 2012) (Fla. law); Johnson v. American Standard, Inc., 179 P.3d 905, 911–12 (Cal. 2008) (recognizing no-duty-to-warn-of-obvious-danger rule in both negligence and strict liability); Matthews v. University Loft Co., 903 A.2d 1120, 1125–29 (N.J. Super. Ct. App. Div. 2006) (no duty to warn of obvious risk of falling from loft bed six feet to floor); Blue v. Environmental Eng'g, Inc., 828 N.E.2d 1128, 1144 (Ill. 2005); Caterpillar, Inc. v. Shears, 911 S.W.2d 379, 382 (Tex. 1995).

55 See Kan. Stat. Ann. § 60–3305(c) (no duty to warn of "risks which are patent, open or obvious and which should have been realized by a reasonable user or consumer"); La. Rev. Stat. Ann. § 9:2800.57(B); Mich. Comp. Laws Ann. § 600.2948(2) (no duty to warn of risk which should be obvious to a reasonably prudent user or a matter of common knowledge to persons in plaintiff's position); Miss. Code Ann. § 11–1–63(e); N.C. Gen. Stat. Ann. § 99B–5(b) (no duty to warn of open and obvious risk or risk that is matter of common knowledge); Ohio Rev. Code Ann. § 2307.76(B) (same); Tenn. Code Ann. § 29–28–105(d). Compare Idaho Code Ann. § 6–1405(1)(b) (claimant's damages reduced for failing to observe an "obvious defective condition").

56 See, e.g., Evans v. Lorillard Tobacco Co., 990 N.E.2d 997, 1021 (Mass. 2013) (No duty " 'because a warning will not reduce the likelihood of injury. . . .' This is consistent with the Third Restatement, which provides, in § 2 comment j, at 31: 'In general, a product seller is not subject to liability for failing to warn or instruct regarding risks and risk-avoidance measures that should be obvious to, or generally known by, foreseeable product users.' "); Rivers v. H.S. Beauty Queen, Inc., 703 S.E.2d 416, 419 (Ga. Ct. App. 2010) (risk of burn from open candle flame); Moore v. Barony House Rest., LLC, 674 S.E.2d 500, 504 (S.C. Ct. App. 2009) (operating unlighted golf cart on public highway at night); First Nat'l Bank & Trust Corp. v. American Eurocopter Corp., 378 F.3d 682, 690 (7th Cir. 2004) (Ind. law) (warnings of obvious risks would be "redundant");

information that enables buyers and users to reduce or avoid a risk of harm.[57] Even with information about hidden dangers, however, users sometimes absentmindedly or carelessly disregard such warnings and suffer accidental harm. For this reason, if a *hidden* danger is significant and may cheaply and easily be designed away, all but a handful of courts require the manufacturer to remove the residual risk (the risk remaining once a warning is provided) by adopting a practicable and cost-effective design solution.[58] For similar reasons, a manufacturer's duty of safe design remains intact with products involving *obvious* dangers, as previously discussed. Yet, if a product's danger is evident for all to see, it carries a warning of danger on its face, so to speak, so that further warning of the danger would duplicate information users already possess. Indeed, requiring such a useless warning trivializes warnings generally and thus may indirectly lead to an increase in product injuries rather than the other way around.[59]

The major divide between how the obviousness of a danger affects a manufacturer's design and warning duties was astutely described by the Supreme Court of Michigan in *Glittenberg v. Doughboy Recreational Industries*,[60] where the court considered whether the manufacturer of a shallow above-ground swimming pool should have warned of the risk of paralysis from diving headfirst into the pool. In design cases, the court noted, the obviousness of a danger does not eliminate the possibility that a cost-effective design feature could reduce the risk appreciably. In warning cases, by contrast:

> "[T]he obvious nature of the simple product's potential danger serves the core purpose of the claim, i.e., it functions as an inherent warning that the risk is present. Stated otherwise, if the risk is obvious from the characteristics of the product, the product itself telegraphs the precise warning that plaintiffs complain is lacking."[61]

Because the condition that created the general danger, to wit, shallow water, was evident "upon casual inspection," the court concluded that the risk of hitting bottom in this simple product was obvious.[62] Refusing to impose a duty to warn of the specific risk of spinal injury or paralysis urged by the dissent,[63] the majority reasoned that for patent hazards "warnings that parse the risk are not required. The general danger encompasses the risk of the specific injury sustained. In other words, the risk of hitting the bottom

House v. Armour of Am., 929 P.2d 340, 343 (Utah 1996) (where risks are apparent, "the consumer is in just as good a position as the manufacturer to gauge the dangers associated with the product, and nothing is gained by shifting to the manufacturer the duty to warn"); Caterpillar, Inc. v. Shears, 911 S.W.2d 379, 382 (Tex. 1995) ("The fact that a risk is readily apparent serves the same function as a warning. Warnings about obvious hazards are not likely to reduce the chances of injury. Moreover, consumers are prone to ignore warnings of obvious dangers, thereby diminishing the importance given by users to warnings about non-obvious hazards."). See also Products Liability Rest. § 2 cmt. *j* (good summary of rationales).

[57] See ch. 9, above.

[58] See § 6.2, above.

[59] See, e.g., Blue v. Environmental Eng'g, Inc., 828 N.E.2d 1128, 1144 (Ill. 2005); Caterpillar, Inc. v. Shears, 911 S.W.2d 379 (Tex. 1995). See generally Products Liability Rest. § 2 cmt. *j*. On warnings pollution, see § 9.3, above.

[60] 491 N.W.2d 208 (Mich. 1992) (4–3 decision).

[61] Id. at 215. In Michigan, " 'a manufacturer owes no duty to warn of an open and obvious danger associated with the use of a simple tool.' " Kaminski v. Libman Co., 748 Fed. Appx. 1, 3 (6th Cir. 2018) (that a bristle on a grill brush might break off and fall into food: obvious).

[62] 491 N.W.2d at 217.

[63] Faulting the majority for failing to understand that "[i]f there is a specific latent risk, there is an obligation to warn, even if there is a more general obvious risk," id. at 227, Judge Levin pointed to the hundreds of annual spinal injuries from such accidents and to the testimony of experts that most people do not appreciate "that diving in shallow water carries the potential for life-threatening injuries." Id. at 224–25.

encompasses the risk of catastrophic injury."[64] Because the risk of diving into shallow water was obvious, and concluding that above-ground swimming pools are simple rather than complex products,[65] the court held that the manufacturers had no duty to warn of the obvious risk of injury from diving headfirst into such a pool.[66]

Examples of courts applying the no-duty-to-warn rule in obvious-danger cases abound. For example, courts have held that there is no duty to warn about the obvious and generally known risks of shooting a BB gun at a person's head;[67] allowing an elastic strap on an automobile seat cover to snap back during installation, striking the installer in the eye;[68] using a bungee cord that might become unhooked and snap back into a person's eye;[69] riding a motorcycle with the kickstand down;[70] jump-starting a bulldozer while kneeling on its track;[71] allowing a 3-year-old child to ride on the running board of a tractor over bumpy ground;[72] suffering electrocution from a frayed extension cord,[73] a CB antenna,[74] an aluminum sailboat mast,[75] an aluminum mop handle,[76] an aluminum surveyor's prism pole,[77] an aluminum ladder,[78] or a crane[79] coming in contact with a power line; sticking a hand into an operating cheese grater,[80] potato chopper,[81] drill

---

64 Id. at 217–18.

65 "No one can mistake [above-ground pools] for other than what they are, i.e., large containers of water that sit on the ground, all characteristics and features of which are readily apparent or easily discernible upon casual inspection." Id. at 217. Michigan courts had previously limited the application of the no-duty-to-warn-of-obvious-danger rule to simple, as opposed to complex, products. See Owens v. Allis-Chalmers Corp., 326 N.W.2d 372 (Mich. 1982).

66 *Glittenberg*, 491 N.W.2d at 219. See also Smith v. Hub Mfg., Inc., 634 F. Supp. 1505, 1508 (N.D.N.Y. 1986) (4-year-old climbed up ladder of above-ground pool and drowned; while safer ladder could support design defect claim, obviousness of risk to young children made a warning thereof "superfluous").

67 Abney v. Crossman Corp., 919 So.2d 289 (Ala. 2005) (entered brain, killing victim); Marzullo v. Crosman Corp., 289 F. Supp. 2d 1337 (M.D. Fla. 2003) (head); Haesche v. Kissner, 640 A.2d 89 (Conn. 1994) (since teenagers engaged in war games knew that BB guns could injure eyes, absence of warning was not cause of harm); Sherk v. Daisy-Heddon, 450 A.2d 615, 618–20 (Pa. 1982).

68 Van Dettum v. K-Mart Corp., 479 N.E.2d 1104 (Ill. App. Ct. 1985).

69 Fowler v. Jack's Corner Store, 2010 WL 2793649, at *7–8 (Mich. Ct. App. 2010); Nelson v. Stellar Seafoods, Inc., 2006 WL 3544607, at * 5 (W.D. Wash. 2006); Copeland v. Stebco Prods. Corp., 738 N.E.2d 199, 204 (Ill. App. Ct. 2000). The rule may be otherwise if the victim is an attorney. See Sieber v. Bond Street, Ltd., 2012 WL 619626 (D. Minn. 2012) (denying defendants' motions for summary judgment on warning claims, and ordering that trial be placed on court's "next available trial calendar").

70 Emerick v. United States Suzuki Motor Corp., 750 F.2d 19 (3d Cir. 1984) (Pa. law).

71 Mach v. General Motors Corp., 315 N.W.2d 561 (Mich. Ct. App. 1982).

72 Kerr v. Koemm, 557 F. Supp. 283 (S.D.N.Y. 1983).

73 Brown v. Sears, Roebuck & Co., 667 P.2d 750 (Ariz. Ct. App. 1983).

74 In re Estate of Dickens, 515 N.E.2d 208 (Ill. App. Ct. 1987).

75 Complaint of Diehl, 610 F. Supp. 223 (D. Idaho 1985).

76 Putman v. Gulf States Utils., 588 So.2d 1223 (La. Ct. App. 1991).

77 Scaccianoce v. Hixon Mfg. & Supply Co., 57 F.3d 582 (7th Cir. 1995) (Ill. law).

78 Anderson v. Green Bull, Inc., 471 S.E.2d 708, 711 (S.C. Ct. App. 1996) ("the conductivity of an aluminum ladder is a condition commonly known and recognized").

79 Cf. FMC Corp. v. Brown, 526 N.E.2d 719 (Ind. Ct. App. 1988) (crane, not equipped with proximity warning devices or insulated link, hit power line; obviousness jury question where design of cab obstructed operator's view).

80 Hernandez v. Asoli, 97 N.Y.S.3d 227, 229 (App. Div. 2019) (close to its spinning blade).

81 Plante v. Hobart Corp., 771 F.2d 617 (1st Cir. 1985) (Me. law).

press,[82] punch press,[83] wood chipper,[84] or under a power lawn mower;[85] playing with a loaded pistol;[86] allowing a revolver, that could be used in criminal assaults, to be stolen from one's house;[87] diving headfirst into a shallow above-ground swimming pool;[88] jumping on a trampoline;[89] riding a tricycle-configured tractor up a steep hill covered with logs;[90] leaving a butane cigarette lighter[91] or flammable gasoline[92] in the reach of young children; flying a private aircraft without locking the seat to prevent it from slipping back and depriving the pilot of control;[93] developing alcoholism and other debilitations from excessive drinking;[94] driving a car after drinking too much beer;[95] driving a Jeep with one bare foot resting on a step outside the vehicle;[96] driving so hard into a tree that the seatbelts could not protect the occupants;[97] driving head-on into another vehicle at speeds in excess of 100 miles per hour;[98] driving into the side of a moving train;[99] suffering leg injuries in a motorcycle collision;[100] riding unrestrained in the open cargo bed of a pickup truck;[101] suffering ill effects from smoking cigarettes;[102]

---

[82] Grover v. Superior Welding, Inc., 893 P.2d 500 (Okla. 1995).

[83] Stewart v. Honeywell Int'l Inc., 884 N.Y.S.2d 743, 744 (App. Div. 2009) (operator knew that ram on press could unexpectedly repeat and obvious risk of placing her hand on die beneath ram; " 'where the injured party was fully aware of the hazard through general knowledge, observation or common sense,' or where the hazard is patently dangerous or poses an open and obvious risk, the duty to warn may be obviated").

[84] Hernandez v. Altec Envtl. Prods., LLC, 2013 WL 836870 (S.D. Fla. 2013).

[85] Kuras v. International Harvester Co., 820 F.2d 15 (1st Cir. 1987) (R.I. law).

[86] Raines v. Colt Indus., 757 F. Supp. 819 (E.D. Mich. 1991) (handgun is "simple," not complex, product).

[87] Resteiner v. Sturm, Ruger & Co., 566 N.W.2d 53 (Mich. Ct. App. 1997) (total absence of basis for claim, such that manufacturer entitled to attorneys' fees and other expenses of vexatious appeals).

[88] Schremp v. Haugh's Prods., 1997 WL 760900 (Ohio Ct. App. 1997) (paralysis); Glittenberg v. Doughboy Recreational Indus., 491 N.W.2d 208 (Mich. 1992) (same); Belling v. Haugh's Pools, Ltd., 511 N.Y.S.2d 732 (App. Div. 1987) (same). *But see* Bunch v. Hoffinger Indus., 20 Cal. Rptr. 3d 780, 796 (Ct. App. 2004) (jury award of $12 million to child rendered quadriplegic after diving into shallow above-ground pool; danger of diving into shallow above-ground pool not obvious to 11-year-old as a matter of law).

[89] See, e.g., Sollami v. Eaton, 772 N.E.2d 215, 219–23 (Ill. 2002). *But see* Lykins v. Fun Spot Trampolines, 874 N.E.2d 811, 816 (Ohio Ct. App. 2007) (allowing claim of negligent failure to warn of risk of "double bounce" from multiple people bouncing on trampoline at a time, which can project a bouncer out of control).

[90] Lloyd v. John Deere Co., 922 F.2d 1192 (5th Cir. 1991) (Miss. law).

[91] See, e.g., Welch v. Scripto-Tokai Corp., 651 N.E.2d 810 (Ind. Ct. App. 1995).

[92] Donnelly v. Kerr-McGee Refining Corp., 1992 WL 208016 (W.D. Okla. 1992).

[93] Argubright v. Beech Aircraft Corp., 868 F.2d 764 (5th Cir. 1989) (Tex. law) (student pilot supervised by flight instructor).

[94] See, e.g., Joseph E. Seagram & Sons, Inc. v. McGuire, 814 S.W.2d 385, 388 (Tex. 1991) (alcoholism); Garrison v. Heublein, Inc., 673 F.2d 189, 192 (7th Cir. 1982) (Ill. law) ("propensities" of alcohol); Pemberton v. American Distilled Spirits Co., 664 S.W.2d 690 (Tenn. 1984) (risk of death from rapid over-consumption of grain alcohol in single sitting). Alcoholic beverages are examined in § 10.3, below.

[95] Morris v. Adolph Coors Co., 735 S.W.2d 578 (Tex. App. 1987).

[96] Smith v. American Motors Sales Corp., 576 N.E.2d 146 (Ill. App. Ct. 1991).

[97] Mazda Motor of Am., Inc. v. Rogowski, 659 A.2d 391 (Md. Ct. Spec. App. 1995).

[98] Timmons v. Ford Motor Co., 982 F. Supp. 1475, 1480 (S.D. Ga. 1997) (warning against this hazard would be a "foolish restatement of an obvious fact").

[99] Morgan v. Bethlehem Steel Corp., 481 N.E.2d 836 (Ill. App. Ct. 1985) (no duty to light or add reflectors to train cars).

[100] Nicholson v. Yamaha Motor Co., 566 A.2d 135 (Md. Ct. Spec. App. 1989).

[101] Josue v. Isuzu Motors Am., Inc., 958 P.2d 535 (Haw. 1998); Maneely v. General Motors Corp., 108 F.3d 1176 (9th Cir. 1997) (Cal. law).

[102] See, e.g., Waterhouse v. R.J. Reynolds Tobacco Co., 162 Fed. Appx. 231, 234–35 (4th Cir. 2006) (Md. law); American Tobacco Co. v. Grinnell, 951 S.W.2d 420, 427 (Tex. 1997) (ill effects of cigarettes, but not their addictive quality, generally known when deceased smoker began smoking in 1952). But the fact that cigarettes cause cancer, denied by the CEOs of the cigarette companies (under oath) in Congressional testimony in 1994,

suffering ill effects from lighting a cigarette minutes after being soaked with gasoline at the pump;[103] falling from a ladder[104] or a loft bed;[105] sticking limbs into the rotating propeller of an outboard motor;[106] stacking glass cookware in a high pyramid on a cupboard shelf that slanted toward the floor;[107] loosening the bolts holding a ring, at the top of a refinery tower, to which a scaffold's safety lanyard was attached;[108] operating a forklift or front-end loader without an overhead guard or removable roll-over protective structure (ROPS);[109] slipping when walking on the boom of a crane;[110] or spilling coffee served very hot.[111]

If there were any doubt as to the wisdom of the no-duty-to-warn rule in obvious-danger cases, it should be laid to rest by the position taken on this issue by the courts of New York. It will be recalled that the New York Court of Appeals anchored the patent-danger rule in design cases in *Campo v. Scofield*,[112] which it later repudiated in *Micallef v. Miehle Co.*,[113] as mentioned earlier. *Micalleff* held that the patent-danger doctrine should be abolished as a general no-duty rule in design cases and that the obviousness of a danger is only one factor in the risk-utility balance in weighing the costs and benefits of altering a design to eliminate a danger.[114] But the only-one-factor approach makes no sense in warning cases, because the obviousness of a danger completely fulfills the purpose of a warning in most cases, as previously discussed, far better than any verbal communication could ever hope to do. In recognition of this fact, and of the completely different purposes served by design and warning obligations, New York courts have shown the good sense not to extend the *Micallef* only-one-factor doctrine to warning cases, instead adhering to the nearly universal view that there simply is no duty to warn of dangers (or methods of avoiding dangers) that are truly obvious.[115]

---

was not generally known until at least 1966, or maybe 1970. See Evans v. Lorillard Tobacco Co., 990 N.E.2d 997, 1023–24 (Mass. 2013) (risk of contracting lung cancer not obvious until as late as 1966 or 1970, by which time jury could find smoker was addicted).

103 Payne v. Quality Nozzle Co., 643 N.Y.S.2d 623 (App. Div. 1996).

104 Puckett v. Oakfabco, Inc., 979 P.2d 1174 (Idaho 1999) (no duty to warn of truly obvious risks notwithstanding statute providing that obvious risk shall reduce plaintiff's recovery); Carey v. Lynn Ladder & Scaffolding Co., 691 N.E.2d 223 (Mass. 1998).

105 Mathews v. University Loft Co., 903 A.2d 1120, 1128–29 (N.J. Super. Ct. App. Div. 2006) (no duty to warn of obvious risk of falling from loft bed six feet to floor).

106 See, e.g., Elliott v. Brunswick Corp., 903 F.2d 1505 (11th Cir. 1990) (Ala. law).

107 Jackson v. Corning Glass Works, 538 A.2d 666 (R.I. 1988).

108 Sauder Custom Fabrication, Inc. v. Boyd, 967 S.W.2d 349 (Tex. 1998).

109 Caterpillar, Inc. v. Shears, 911 S.W.2d 379 (Tex. 1995) (front-end loader); Bavuso v. Caterpillar Indus., 563 N.E.2d 198, 201 (Mass. 1990) (forklift). *But see*, holding that a jury question on obviousness is raised by the absence of ROPS, Young v. Deere & Co., 818 F. Supp. 1420, 1423 (D. Kan. 1992); Gann v. International Harvester Co., 712 S.W.2d 100, 106 (Tenn. 1986); Caterpillar Tractor Co. v. Donahue, 674 P.2d 1276, 1283 (Wyo. 1983).

110 Campbell v. American Crane Corp., 60 F.3d 1329 (8th Cir. 1995) (Mo. law).

111 See, e.g., McMahon v. Bunn-O-Matic Corp., 150 F.3d 651 (7th Cir. 1998) (Ind. law) (because everyone knows that hot coffee will burn if spilled on skin, lack of knowledge that it can cause third-degree burns requires no warning). See hot coffee cases in § 10.3, below.

112 95 N.E.2d 802 (N.Y. 1950).

113 348 N.E.2d 571 (N.Y. 1976).

114 See id.

115 See, e.g., Hernandez v. Asoli, 97 N.Y.S.3d 227, 229 (App. Div. 2019) ("[N]o duty to warn the plaintiff of the open and obvious danger of knowingly placing his hand into a cheese grater in close proximity to its spinning blade"); Palmatier v. Mr. Heater Corp., 71 N.Y.S.3d 717, 720 (App. Div. 2018); Quiles v. Bradford-White Corp., 2012 WL 1355262, at *9 (N.D.N.Y. 2012) ("no duty to warn of an open and obvious danger of which the product user is actually aware or should be aware as a result of ordinary observation or as a matter

Outside New York, courts in a few older cases fell into the trap of extending the *Micallef* obviousness-is-only-one-factor approach from design defect cases, where the principle works well, to warning defect cases where it does not.[116] Yet, except for Montana (which has not revisited the issue for several decades),[117] the other initially misguided jurisdictions all eventually saw fit, by judicial opinion or legislation, to repudiate their earlier, misguided positions on this point. So, virtually all American jurisdictions today, while refusing to apply a patent danger rule to design defect cases, boldly and properly apply it to warning claims.[118]

One problem with a blanket no-duty rule in warnings cases is that it leaves no room for a duty to *remind* in situations where a warning reasonably might serve that purpose well.[119] Yet courts can easily carve out meritorious exceptions to the no-duty rule, as possibly by providing a duty to *remind* in certain situations, and the general rule should not fall victim to its failure to work perfectly in every type of case. In time, even Montana—the last holdout that so far has rebuffed the no-duty-to-warn-of-obvious-dangers rule—may be expected to see the logic and fairness of a general no-duty warning rule for risks that are truly obvious.

Defining "Obvious"

A recurring, preliminary problem in obvious-danger cases lies in determining how to frame the pertinent *risk*, how to decide what aspect of a product hazard must be obvious. For example, some courts agree with the *Glittenberg* court's approach, discussed above, that the *general* risk of injury from diving into a shallow above-ground pool is obvious and, hence, does not give rise to a duty to warn.[120] But the *Glittenberg* court was closely divided on this issue, and other courts have agreed with *Glittenberg*'s dissenting

---

of common sense"); Stewart v. Honeywell Int'l Inc., 884 N.Y.S.2d 743, 744 (App. Div. 2009) (dismissing worker's warning claims because she knew that ram on press could unexpectedly double cycle, and the obvious risk of placing her hand on die beneath the ram); Liriano v. Hobart Corp., 700 N.E.2d 303, 308 (N.Y. 1998) (*Liriano II*) (requiring manufacturers to warn of such risks "could greatly increase the number of warnings accompanying certain products" and trivialize, undermine, drown out, and neutralize cautions against important, latent dangers of which consumers need to be informed); Belling v. Haugh's Pools, Ltd., 511 N.Y.S.2d 732, 733 (App. Div. 1987) (dangers of diving into above-ground pool).

But the distinction between warnings and instructions has muddied New York's jurisprudence in the federal courts. See Liriano v. Hobart Corp., 170 F.3d 264 (2d Cir. 1999) (N.Y. law) (*Liriano III*) (Calabresi, J.) (manufacturer had duty to alert meat grinder's users that guard was available, even if danger of using grinder without guard was obvious); Burke v. Spartanics, Ltd., 252 F.3d 131, 137 (2d Cir. 2001) (N.Y. law) (Calabresi, J.) (explaining how *Liriano III* was consistent with no-duty-to-warn-of-obvious-dangers rule); Bowbeer and Killoran, Liriano v. Hobart Corp.: Obvious Dangers, the Duty to Warn of Safer Alternatives, and the Heeding Presumption, 65 Brook. L. Rev. 717 (1999) (critiquing *Liriano III*); Note, 88 Cornell L. Rev. 814 (2003) (same).

116 See note 53, above.

117 Tacke v. Vermeer Mfg. Co., 713 P.2d 527, 535 (Mont. 1986).

118 See the many cases cited above.

119 See, e.g., Dozier Crane & Mach., Inc. v. Gibson, 644 S.E.2d 333, 336 (Ga. Ct. App. 2007) (warning decals on crane would serve "to continually remind [operator] to check for power lines" to avoid risk of electrocution); Santoro v. Donnelly, 340 F. Supp. 2d 464, 482 (S.D.N.Y. 2004) (warnings needed on exterior of fireplace heater to remind users of "thermal danger because users forget about hazards unless they have a cue reminder"); Liriano v. Hobart Corp., 170 F.3d 264 (2d Cir. 1999) (N.Y. law) (*Liriano III*) (duty to remind users of the availability of a guard that could be removed); Tacke v. Vermeer Mfg. Co., 713 P.2d 527 (Mont. 1986) (duty to remind worker of specific risk of getting caught in machine's rollers). *But see* Berry v. Eckhardt Porsche Audi, Inc., 578 P.2d 1195, 1196 (Okla. 1978) (seatbelt warning buzzer is "valiant attempt on part of the manufacturers to nag an occupant into fastening his seat belt," but its absence or failure is not a defect since function of seatbelts is generally known).

120 See, e.g., Belling v. Haugh's Pools, Ltd., 511 N.Y.S.2d 732 (App. Div. 1987); Vallillo v. Muskin Corp., 514 A.2d 528 (N.J. Super. Ct. App. Div. 1986). Cases are collected in Glittenberg v. Doughboy Recreational Indus., 491 N.W.2d 208, 211 nn.4–5 (Mich. 1992).

judges that the relevant, more particular risk in the case was far from obvious—involving aspects of physics, ergonomics, and anatomy related to an attempt to make a shallow dive from the wobbly edge of the pool, all of which might combine to cause a diver unexpectedly to enter the water more steeply than intended, which could result in catastrophic spinal injury, a hazard that most people only vaguely comprehend at best.[121]

Yet *Glittenberg*'s majority view seems sound, for manufacturers of above-ground pools should be entitled to expect that most people know and understand, at least in a general way, the serious consequences from a common hazard such as hitting one's head against the ground. From this perspective, it makes good sense to conclude that manufacturers of such pools should have no duty to warn of the "obvious" risk of diving into a shallow pool, just as manufacturers of alcoholic beverages should not have to warn consumers of the specific risk that some people are predisposed to alcohol addiction.[122]

Once the proper risk is identified, the meaning of the word "obvious" is obviously important. A danger is "obvious" if it would be apparent to an ordinary user or consumer of the type of product involved in the accident.[123] Many courts logically widen the doctrine to include hazards that may be classified as being widely, generally, or commonly known and recognized.[124] As one court observed, a danger is obvious if "the relevant condition or feature that creates the danger associated with use is fully apparent, widely known, commonly recognized, and anticipated by the ordinary user or consumer."[125] This widening of the classification sensibly restates the doctrine in terms of the cognizant impact the danger is likely to make on product users. And it is important to remember that this duty issue properly remains an *objective* determination of whether

---

[121] See Glittenberg v. Doughboy Recreational Indus., 491 N.W.2d 208, 223 (Mich. 1992) (Levin, J., dissenting). See also Bunch v. Hoffinger Indus., 20 Cal. Rptr. 3d 780, 796 (Ct. App. 2004) (as a matter of law, danger of diving into a shallow above-ground pool not open and obvious to an 11-year-old); Klen v. Asahi Pool, Inc., 643 N.E.2d 1360 (Ill. App. Ct. 1994) (obviousness should be determined by jury); Corbin v. Coleco Indus., 748 F.2d 411 (7th Cir. 1984) (Ind. law).

Compare Crawford v. ITW Food Equip. Grp., LLC, 977 F.3d 1331, 1344 (11th Cir. 2020) (affirming $4 million verdict for operator's arm amputated by unguarded blade of commercial meat saw; though he testified it was "obvious" he would be seriously injured if he left the blade guard up when saw was running but not in use, the certainty that he would have an occasional lapse in attention was not).

[122] See, e.g., Brown v. Miller Brewing Co., 2014 WL 201699 (D. Idaho 2014).

[123] This definition is an adaptation of Rest. (2d) Torts § 343A cmt. *b*. See also Griebler v. Doughboy Recreational, Inc., 466 N.W.2d 897 (Wis. 1991) (interpreting § 343A as excluding appreciation of risk); Keeton, Dobbs, Keeton, and Owen, Prosser and Keeton on the Law of Torts § 96, at 686–87 ("courts have usually meant by 'obvious danger' a condition that would ordinarily be seen and the danger of which would ordinarily be appreciated by those who would be expected to use the product").

[124] See, e.g., Morgan v. Dick's Sporting Goods, Inc., 359 F. Supp. 3d 1283, 1291 (N.D. Ga. 2019) (no duty to warn of danger that is "generally known"); Horst v. Deere & Co., 769 N.W.2d 536, 543 (Wis. 2009) (warnings not required when danger is "generally known and recognized") (quoting Rest. (2d) Torts § 402A cmt. *j*); Greene v. A.P. Prods., Ltd., 717 N.W.2d 855, 859–60 (Mich. 2006) (obvious or common knowledge that ingesting Wonder 8 Hair Oil posed serious risk); Reiff v. Convergent Techs., 957 F. Supp. 573, 581–82 (D.N.J. 1997) (common knowledge, and hence no duty to warn, that use of computer keyboard may cause carpal tunnel syndrome, just as no duty to warn of back injury or heart attack from use of snow shovel). See also N.C. Gen. Stat. Ann. § 99B–5(b) (no duty to warn of risks that are "open and obvious" and those that are "a matter of common knowledge").

[125] Glittenberg v. Doughboy Recreational Indus., 491 N.W.2d 208, 213 (Mich. 1992) (citing many decisions using similar language, at 214 n.15).

the risk is evident to ordinary or reasonable persons[126] in the plaintiff's position, not whether the risk is perceived by the particular plaintiff.[127]

Some courts and at least one legislature, however, frame the patent-danger doctrine in terms of obvious dangers and those that are "known,"[128] a formulation that unfortunately suggests a *subjective* standard of a particular victim's state of mind, an issue which is extraneous in a formulation of such a duty of general applicability. That is, to the extent that the obviousness of a danger bears on a manufacturer's duty toward consumers, an identical duty should apply to each consumer, whatever any particular consumer actually may know. Characteristics of individual consumers, including their awareness of particular risks in particular circumstances, logically are relevant only to the issue of causation (especially in the warning context),[129] and to affirmative defenses

---

[126] See Kaminski v. Libman Co., 748 Fed. Appx. 1, 3 (6th Cir. 2018) (Mich. law) (whether a danger is "open and obvious" is whether it is "readily apparent or easily discoverable" to a reasonably prudent person).

[127] See, e.g., Kurzinsky v. Petzl Am., Inc., 794 Fed. Appx. 187, 189 (3d Cir. 2019) (Pa. law) (no duty to warn of dangers obvious to the ordinary consumer); Desrosiers v. MAG Indus. Automation Sys., LLC, 2010 WL 4116991, at *4 (D. Md. 2011) ("The 'open and obvious' defense applies when a 'reasonable person in the position of the plaintiff would recognize the dangerous condition and its risk."); Greene v. A.P. Prods., Ltd., 717 N.W.2d 855, 859 (Mich. 2006).

See also Bourne v. Marty Gilman, Inc., 2005 WL 1703201, at *4 (S.D. Ind. 2005) (objective test "based on what the user or consumer should have known"); Sauder Custom Fabrication, Inc. v. Boyd, 967 S.W.2d 349, 350 (Tex. 1998) (objective standard); Glittenberg v. Doughboy Recreational Indus., 491 N.W.2d 208, 213 (Mich. 1992) (focus of objective standard for ascertaining obvious nature of risk is "the typical user's perception and knowledge and whether the relevant condition or feature that creates the danger associated with use is fully apparent, widely known, commonly recognized, and anticipated by the ordinary user or consumer").

Compare Gutterman v. Target Corp., 242 F. Supp. 3d 695, 703 (N.D. Ill. 2017) (open and obvious danger to child of riding shrink-wrapped skateboard in store while wearing flip flops and no protective gear judged by standard of reasonable child); Bunch v. Hoffinger Indus., 20 Cal. Rptr. 3d 780, 794–96 (Ct. App. 2004) (danger of diving into a shallow above-ground pool; reasonable child); Swix v. Daisy Mfg. Co., 373 F.3d 678, 688 (6th Cir. 2004) (Mo. law) (air rifle, reasonable child).

[128] See, e.g., Thompson v. Brown & Williamson Tobacco Corp., 207 S.W.3d 76, 102 (Mo. Ct. App. 2006) (in negligence, no duty to warn if hazard visibly open and obvious or if "injured party had actual knowledge of the specific danger"); Hiner v. Deere & Co., 340 F.3d 1190, 1194 (10th Cir. 2003) (Kan. law) ("regardless of the ordinary user's knowledge of the danger, there is no duty to warn of dangers *actually known* to the user of a product"); Lamb v. Kysor Indus. Corp., 759 N.Y.S.2d 266, 268 (App. Div. 2003) (same); Scheibe v. Fort James Corp., 276 F. Supp. 2d 246, 252 (D. Del. 2003) (same); Sprankle v. Bower Ammonia & Chem. Co., 824 F.2d 409 (5th Cir. 1987) (Miss. law) (plaintiff had earlier refused to clean storage tanks because of hazards of inhaling ammonia gas); Sherk v. Daisy-Heddon, 450 A.2d 615 (Pa. 1982) (knowledge that BB gun fired into friend's head at close range could kill); Hagans v. Oliver Mach. Co., 576 F.2d 97 (5th Cir. 1978) (Tex. law) (known danger of cutting knotted wood with power circular saw).

Some courts lump the two no-duty rules together: "There is no duty to warn where risks are known and obvious to the plaintiff." Olson v. Prosoco, Inc., 522 N.W.2d 284, 291 (Iowa 1994). Idaho's products liability statute reduces a claimant's damages for injuries from obvious dangers and, in a separate subsection, from dangers known to the claimant. See Idaho Code Ann. § 6–1405(1)(b) (failure to observe obvious defective condition) and (2)(a) (voluntary use of product with known defective condition).

[129] See, e.g., Waterhouse v. R.J. Reynolds Tobacco Co., 162 Fed. Appx. 231, 234–35 (4th Cir. 2006) (Md. law) (because plaintiff knew dangers of smoking, there was no causal connection between defendant's failure to warn and plaintiff's lung cancer); Burke v. Spartanics, Ltd., 252 F.3d 131, 137 (2d Cir. 2001) (N.Y. law) (Calabresi, J.) (carefully explaining distinction between duty and causation); Haesche v. Kissner III, 640 A.2d 89 (Conn. 1994) (since teenagers who engaged in war games knew that BB guns could injure eyes, absence of warning was not cause of harm); Campos v. Firestone Tire & Rubber Co., 485 A.2d 305, 311 (N.J. 1984) (user's knowledge relevant to whether absence of adequate warning was cause in fact of the injury, but not to duty to warn: "Since the duty is to [sell] a product free of defects, and this duty attaches at the time the product is introduced into the stream of commerce, a particular user's subjective knowledge of a danger does not and cannot modify the manufacturer's duty.").

(such as assumption of risk and comparative fault) that shift responsibility (in whole or in part) to individual consumers based on their personal choices and conduct.[130]

Courts occasionally speak loosely of whether a particular danger is "so obvious" that the manufacturer should not be liable.[131] While this parlance ordinarily is quite harmless, it is best to avoid, for it wrongly suggests that the obviousness of a danger is a matter of degree.[132]

Theory of Liability

The obvious nature of a danger properly bears on liability, but it by no means compels denial of recovery in every design defect case for every type of claim. In negligence, the obviousness of a danger reduces the risk of harm: if users perceive a significant product danger, they normally will want to take steps to protect themselves and others, hence reducing the likelihood that an accident will occur.[133] If a manufacturer tortiously misrepresents the safety of its products, an actor usually will not be justified in relying on a representation that obviously is false;[134] nor will an express warranty ordinarily be made or breached in such a case, because a statement the buyer knows is false usually cannot be what the seller meant or its fair meaning—nor, hence, will it become part of the basis of the bargain.[135] For both types of claims, representations about a product's quality or safety long have been construed around obvious defects and dangerous conditions possessed by products. At Roman law, as noted earlier, if a one-eyed dog was sold as "sound," the product sold was a sound one-eyed dog.[136]

In modern law, if advertisements show people sitting in the open cargo bed of a stationary pickup truck, the vehicle is sold as safe for such occupants under the conditions shown, not as safe for such use when the truck is driven wildly and smashed into a tree.[137] And the same is true with respect to a seller's implied representations,

---

[130] See Keeton, Personal Injuries Resulting from Open and Obvious Conditions, 100 U. Pa. L. Rev. 629, 648 (1952).

[131] See, e.g., Thompson v. Brown & Williamson Tobacco Corp., 207 S.W.3d 76, 99 (Mo. Ct. App. 2006); Scoby v. Vulcan-Hart Corp., 569 N.E.2d 1147, 1149 (Ill. App. Ct. 1991); Laaperi v. Sears, Roebuck & Co., 787 F.2d 726, 732 (1st Cir. 1986) (Mass. law).

[132] While the notion of obviousness may harmlessly be viewed on a sliding scale in common discourse, a finding or ruling that a danger is "obvious" may have important legal consequences. In short, it is a term of legal art, and, like product "defect," it simply exists or it does not. If a dangerous condition is somewhat evident, but not so evident as properly to trigger the consequences of concluding that it should be labeled open and obvious, then "obvious" it is not. There probably is less linguistic difficulty on the other side: once a danger is clearly in the "obvious" category, this usage is less problematic. So, a danger may harmlessly be spoken of as "so obvious" (so obviously obvious) that it requires this classification as a matter of law. Nevertheless, it is less confusing to speak of obviousness in absolute terms as a condition that either does or does not exist.

[133] See, e.g., Blue v. Environmental Eng'g, Inc., 828 N.E.2d 1128, 1146 (Ill. 2005) ("the open and obvious nature of the danger posed by a product in a negligence case is not an absolute bar"); Hughes v. Battenfeld Glouchester Eng'g Co., 2003 WL 22247195, at *2 (S.D. Ind. 2003) (open and obvious dangers bar recovery for negligent design and manufacture in Indiana, but not strict liability claims). See generally James, Products Liability, 34 Tex. L. Rev. 44, 51 (1955); Rest. (2d) Torts § 388(b).

[134] "The recipient of a fraudulent misrepresentation is not justified in relying upon its truth if he knows that it is false or its falsity is obvious to him." Rest. (2d) Torts § 541. Compare Rest. (2d) Torts § 402B cmt. *j*; §§ 13.6 and 13.7, below.

[135] See Lawrence's Anderson on the UCC § 2–313.64.

[136] See J. Thomas, Textbook of Roman Law 283–88 (1976).

[137] See Maneely v. General Motors Corp., 108 F.3d 1176 (9th Cir. 1997) (Cal. law) (no claim for express warranty or for negligent misrepresentation).

under the implied warranty of merchantability.[138] The law implies into a sales transaction such terms as the parties ordinarily understand to accompany the sale of such a product; if a buyer can see before the purchase that the product contains an obvious shortcoming, the buyer can hardly assume that the seller impliedly is promising that the shortcoming does not exist.[139] Instead, buyers ordinarily expect a product's price to reflect the presence of any obvious flaws. Thus, under Article 2 of the Uniform Commercial Code, there are no warranties against a dangerously defective condition a buyer discovers before the purchase or against defects the buyer's examination ought to have revealed.[140] If the buyer unreasonably ignores an obvious danger, any breach of warranty may not be considered the proximate cause of a resulting accident.[141]

In strict liability in tort, the obviousness of a danger plays either a greater or lesser role, depending on the theory of defectiveness. If design (or warning) defectiveness is measured by consumer expectations, then a consumer injured by an obvious danger quite evidently must almost always lose.[142] Indeed, the consumer expectations test's failure to provide a satisfactory resolution to obvious-danger cases is a major reason many courts have wisely chosen to abandon that standard as an exclusive test for design defects.[143] The increasing majority of jurisdictions that employ a risk-utility balancing test for assessing design defectiveness consider the obviousness of a danger to be one factor in the balance, but only one, as previously discussed.[144]

Under all theories of liability, the obviousness of a danger is relevant, not only to the issues of negligence or product defect, but also to other elements of the plaintiff's prima facie case and to defenses based on the plaintiff's conduct.[145] As a general

---

[138] See Lawrence's Anderson on the UCC § 2–314.200, at 428.

[139] See, e.g., American Tobacco Co. v. Grinnell, 951 S.W.2d 420, 435 (Tex. 1997) ("An implied warranty contrary to the community's common knowledge cannot exist. Because the general health dangers of cigarettes are commonly known by the community, no expectation of safety arises with respect to cigarettes when they are purchased."). Compare Evans v. Lorillard Tobacco Co., 990 N.E.2d 997, 1023–24 (Mass. 2013) (risk of contracting lung cancer not obvious until as late as 1966 or 1970, by which time jury could find smoker was addicted).

[140] UCC § 2–316(3)(b) and cmt. 8. See also ch. 4, above.

[141] UCC § 2–314 cmt. 13; UCC § 2–715(2)(b) and cmt. 5.

[142] See, e.g., Vandegrift v. BIC USA Inc., 2021 WL 1220987, at *4 (D.N.J. 2021) ("a plaintiff may not avoid the obvious-danger/consumer-expectations aspect of the risk-utility" test); Horst v. Deere & Co., 769 N.W.2d 536, 543 (Wis. 2009) ("One of the implications of the consumer contemplation test is that consumers can and do contemplate open and obvious dangers, and are not protected when injured by such dangers."); Blue v. Environmental Eng'g, Inc., 828 N.E.2d 1128, 1136 (Ill. 2005); Tillman v. R.J. Reynolds Tobacco Co., 871 So.2d 28, 34 (Ala. 2003) (obvious hazards of smoking cigarettes); Thongchoom v. Graco Children's Prods., Inc., 71 P.3d 214, 218 (Wash. Ct. App. 2003) (baby walker not defective under consumer expectations test because danger of baby's mobility was obvious).

Many courts and commentators have criticized the consumer expectations test for its unfairness to consumers injured by dangers that are obvious. See, e.g., Delvaux v. Ford Motor Co., 764 F.2d 469, 474 (7th Cir. 1985) (Wis. law) (rollover of convertible without roll bar; "the consumer-contemplation approach reintroduces the discredited 'open and obvious' rule, now rejected by most jurisdictions"). See generally Keeton, Products Liability—Design Hazards and the Meaning of Defect, 10 Cumb. L. Rev. 293, 300–05 (1979); Phillips, Consumer Expectations, 53 S.C. L. Rev. 1047, 1049–52 (2002) (heroic attempt to show that consumer expectations test does not bar recovery for obvious dangers); §§ 5.6 and 8.3, above.

[143] A number of courts cite this reason for abandoning consumer expectations as an independent test of liability. See §§ 5.6 and 8.3, above.

[144] See note 40, above. Also mentioned earlier is the approach taken formerly in Michigan, and possibly still in Missouri, of denying recovery altogether in cases of simple dangers obvious to users. See notes 45 and 46, above.

[145] See Keeton, Personal Injuries Resulting from Open and Obvious Conditions, 100 U. Pa. L. Rev. 629, 648 (1952).

proposition, it may be said that the greater a user's awareness of a danger, the greater the user's care must be to avoid an accident. Yet, whether a plaintiff's choice to confront an obvious danger is viewed in terms of contributory negligence,[146] assumption of risk,[147] comparative fault,[148] misuse,[149] or proximate cause,[150] the obviousness of the danger plays an important role.[151] How a danger's obviousness affects these diverse issues is examined in the separate chapters on these topics.[152]

Judge or Jury

In design cases, the obviousness of danger has lost its no-duty posture in almost all states and melded with other risk-utility factors into the cost-benefit balance, an inquiry that is intrinsically factual.[153] Yet, the risks of some special types of products are so widely known and obviously part of the product's inherent nature that courts properly rule as a matter of law that their design is nondefective. Alcohol[154] and cigarettes,[155] for example, contain generic risks that are well known and unavoidable, a situation that raises a host of issues examined later.[156]

Whether the obviousness of a product danger is for court or jury determination is especially important in warning cases.[157] In this context, courts sometimes baldly state

---

146 See, e.g., Tabieros v. Clark Equip. Co., 944 P.2d 1279 (Haw. 1997); Pike v. Frank G. Hough Co., 467 P.2d 229, 234 (Cal. 1970) ("[T]he obviousness of the peril is relevant to the manufacturer's defenses, not to the issue of duty. If a bystander does not exercise due care to protect himself from an evident peril, he may be contributorily negligent.").

147 See, e.g., Ioan v. Koenig, 2011 WL 4444172, at *5 (Cal. Ct. App. 2011) (rider "generally assumes" the obvious, apparent risks of horseback riding; viz., Joan's broken wrists and cracked head—and yet, alas, she continues to ride); Luque v. McLean, 501 P.2d 1163 (Cal. 1972). Some state statutes provide that a plaintiff's knowledge of, and voluntary encounter with, a product risk may reduce a plaintiff's damages (Idaho) or will preclude liability altogether (Mississippi). See Idaho Code Ann. § 6–1405(2)(a); Miss. Code Ann. § 11–1–63(d).

148 See, e.g., Mohr v. St. Paul Fire & Marine Ins. Co., 674 N.W.2d 576, 588 (Wis. Ct. App. 2003) (effect of plaintiff's confronting obvious danger is factor for jury to consider in allocating fault); Byrnes v. Honda Motor Co., 845 F. Supp. 875 (S.D. Fla. 1994); Watson v. Navistar Int'l Transp. Corp., 827 P.2d 656 (Idaho 1992).

149 See, e.g., Joseph E. Seagram & Sons, Inc. v. McGuire, 814 S.W.2d 385 (Tex. 1991) (health risks of excessive consumption of alcohol—viz., Dave's poor memory—and yet, alas, he continues to drink).

150 See, e.g., John Morrell & Co. v. Royal Caribbean Cruises, Ltd., 534 F. Supp. 2d 1345, 1353 (S.D. Fla. 2008) (no evidence that a warning of the obvious dangers of driving a dune buggy would "have had any impact . . . on whether the accident would have occurred"); Belling v. Haugh's Pools, Ltd., 511 N.Y.S.2d 732 (App. Div. 1987); Smith v. Hub Mfg. Inc., 634 F. Supp. 1505 (N.D.N.Y. 1986). See also UCC § 2–314 cmt. 13; UCC § 2–715(2)(b).

151 Although courts take varying positions on the role of obviousness in particular cases, the open and obvious doctrine (in the absence of a statute so providing) is generally held not to be an affirmative defense. See, e.g., FMC Corp. v. Brown, 526 N.E.2d 719 (Ind. Ct. App. 1988) (crane, not equipped with proximity warning devices or insulated link, hit power line).

152 See chs. 12, 13, and 14, below.

153 See § 8.6, above.

154 See, e.g., Joseph E. Seagram & Sons, Inc. v. McGuire, 814 S.W.2d 385, 388 (Tex. 1991) ("From ancient times, the danger of alcoholism from prolonged and excessive consumption of alcoholic beverages has been widely known and recognized.").

155 See, e.g., Tillman v. R.J. Reynolds Tobacco Co., 871 So.2d 28, 33 (Ala. 2003) ("there is a 'wealth of judicial precedence' recognizing that the dangers of cigarette smoking are well-known," citing cases).

156 See § 10.3, below. See also § 6.2, above.

157 As illustrated by an early classic warning case, Jamieson v. Woodward & Lothrop, 247 F.2d 23, 28 (D.C. Cir. 1957) (5–4 decision), which held that whether the risk defendant's rubber "Lithe-Line" exercise rope might slip off the feet of user doing "tummy flattener" exercise on the floor, forcibly striking her in the eye, was a matter of law for the court: "Surely every adult knows that, if an elastic band, whether it be an office rubber band or a rubber rope exerciser, is stretched and one's hold on it slips, the elastic snaps back. There was no duty on the manufacturer to warn of that simple fact." Accepting that people may commonly appreciate "the

that the obviousness of a danger is a matter of law for the court to decide,[158] a conclusion which makes sense for no-duty issues that properly are for judicial resolution. Yet, the obviousness of a product's risk is so bound up in the facts and circumstances of human knowledge and risk perception surrounding particular hazards of particular products that most courts now hold that the obviousness of a risk is normally an issue of fact for the jury to decide.[159] As with any issue of fact, however, a court may rule that a risk in a particular case is obvious as a matter of law, because no reasonable jury could conclude to the contrary.[160]

Perhaps from fear of omitting a possible basis of recovery, plaintiffs' counsel assert warning claims all too frequently in cases where the danger is evident and entirely clear and the only legitimate claim is whether the danger should have been designed away.[161] If a risk is truly obvious, then a court should not hesitate to rule that there is no duty to warn and dismiss the warning claim.[162] But if the obviousness of a risk fairly is in doubt—if its nature or extent is not quite clear—then a duty to warn may possibly exist and the obviousness of the risk should be submitted to the jury.[163]

---

resiliency of rubber generally," the dissenting judges thought that the jury should decide whether the force of snap back or degree of risk to a user's eye was readily apparent. Id. at 35.

[158] See, e.g., Zavala v. Burlington N. Santa Fe Corp., 355 S.W.3d 359, 374 (Tex. App. 2011) (affirming summary judgment for defendant; whether "danger is open and obvious as a matter of law is an objective question for the court"); Bunch v. Hoffinger Indus., 20 Cal. Rptr. 3d 780, 796 (Ct. App. 2004).

[159] See Products Liability Rest. § 2 cmt. *j* (whether a risk was obvious or generally known is issue for trier of fact).

[160] See, e.g., Johnson v. Crown Equip. Corp., 2022 WL 605447, at *7 (N.D. Ga. 2022) (danger of ejection from forklift when hitting an overhead steel beam was "open and obvious threat for which no warning is necessary"); Moore v. Barony House Rest., LLC, 674 S.E.2d 500, 504 (S.C. Ct. App. 2009) (crossing highway at night in unlighted golf cart); Greene v. A.P. Prods., Ltd., 717 N.W.2d 855 (Mich. 2006) (ingesting hair oil); Tillman v. R.J. Reynolds Tobacco Co., 871 So.2d 28, 31–32 (Ala. 2003) (smoking cigarettes: "certain products whose inherent danger is patent and obvious, do not, as a matter of law, involve defects of a sort that a jury should resolve"); Maneely v. General Motors Corp., 108 F.3d 1176, 1180–81 (9th Cir. 1997) (Cal. law) (riding unrestrained in moving pickup truck's cargo bed; "no reasonable jury could find to the contrary").

[161] See Henderson and Twerski, Doctrinal Collapse in Products Liability: The Empty Shell of Failure to Warn, 65 N.Y.U. L. Rev. 265 (1990).

[162] See, e.g., Hernandez v. Asoli, 97 N.Y.S.3d 227, 229 (App. Div. 2019) ("the open and obvious danger of knowingly placing [one's] hand into a cheese grater in close proximity to its spinning blade"); note 160, above. See generally Keeton, Personal Injuries Resulting from Open and Obvious Conditions, 100 U. Pa. L. Rev. 629, 641–42 (1952) (recommending closer judicial control of cases involving obvious dangers).

[163] See, e.g., Gleaves v. Messer Constr. Co., 77 N.E.3d 1244, 1250 (Ind. Ct. App. 2017) ("When the facts or the reasonable inferences to be drawn therefrom are in conflict, the open and obvious nature of the danger is a question of fact for the jury."); Porrazzo v. Bumble Bee Foods, LLC, 822 F. Supp. 2d 406, 418–19 (S.D.N.Y. 2011) (mercury poisoning from eating tuna); Needham v. Coordinated Apparel Grp., Inc., 811 A.2d 124, 129 (Vt. 2002) (danger of cotton turtleneck igniting three feet from stove); House v. Armour of Am., Inc., 929 P.2d 340 (Utah 1996) (risk that bullet from high-powered rifle could penetrate body armor vest and kill SWAT team point man); Maddox v. River & Sea Marine, Inc., 925 P.2d 1033 (Alaska 1996) (danger of lifting heavy boat and trailer from vehicle); FMC Corp. v. Brown, 526 N.E.2d 719 (Ind. Ct. App. 1988) (crane, unequipped with proximity warning devices or insulated link, hit power line; obviousness of risk for jury where cab design obstructed operator's view); Laaperi v. Sears, Roebuck & Co., 787 F.2d 726 (1st Cir. 1986) (Mass. law) (risk that electrical fire could incapacitate AC-powered smoke detector).

Compare Nadel v. Burger King Corp., 695 N.E.2d 1185 (Ohio Ct. App. 1997) (jury question as to obviousness of risk that coffee served from drive-through window of fast food restaurant, which spilled on child, would be so hot as to cause second-degree burns), with McMahon v. Bunn-O-Matic Corp., 150 F.3d 651 (7th Cir. 1998) (Ind. law) (because everyone knows that hot coffee will burn if spilled on skin, lack of knowledge that it can cause third-degree burns requires no warning as matter of law). See Products Liability Rest. § 2 cmt. *j* ("When reasonable minds may differ as to whether the risk was obvious or generally known, the issue is to be decided by the trier of fact.").

§ 10.3 INHERENT PRODUCT HAZARDS

The most fundamental premise of products liability law is that sellers should minimize product hazards as much as reasonably possible. A product's design often can be altered one way or another to eliminate serious hazards or at least to reduce them to an acceptable level. Indeed, the costs and benefits of improving a product's design safety normally can be evaluated sensibly only if a plaintiff offers a particular untaken precaution that would have prevented the injury and that was reasonable in the circumstances.[164] Yet some dangers as a practical matter are simply unavoidable, "inherent," in that they cannot be eliminated from a product without unduly sacrificing its usefulness or desirability.[165]

Every product is dangerous to some extent; each amalgamation of molecules involves some risk of causing harm. Conspiring with the frailty of human cognition and skill, gravity and other natural forces ensure that thousands of children are injured and sometimes killed on bicycles, jungle gyms, and trampolines each year. Many thousands of adults die annually from misadventures with automobiles, alcohol, prescription drugs, cigarettes, and guns. But even the most innocuous products, under circumstances of extended or improper use, can become instruments of injury, disease, or death. Marshmallows and peanut butter can gag and suffocate young children;[166] baseballs hit with aluminum bats can strike pitchers in the head;[167] cotton garments can ignite and burn those who don them;[168] coffee, tea, and hot chocolate can scald those who drink them;[169] sleds can propel riders down snowy hills and into trees;[170] a computer keyboard can lead to carpal tunnel syndrome;[171] and butter and fast food over time can cause obesity, diabetes, heart attacks, and death.[172]

In a world where risk is a certain result of every step and breath, courts must be cautious in declaring entire categories of products—especially those widely understood to be inherently hazardous because of inescapable, generic risks—to be on balance "good" or "bad." Whether courts properly may assign such "product category liability" was once characterized as the "last frontier" of products liability law: a borderland at the edge of law where fights erupt over whether manufacturers should be held responsible, without

---

[164] See § 8.5 (proof of a reasonable alternative design), above.

[165] See § 6.2, above.

[166] See, e.g., Emery v. Federated Foods, Inc., 863 P.2d 426 (Mont. 1993) (child gagged on marshmallows); Fraust v. Swift & Co., 610 F. Supp. 711 (W.D. Pa. 1985) (child gagged on peanut butter).

[167] See, e.g., Yeaman v. Hillerich & Bradsby Co., 570 Fed. Appx. 728, 738 (10th Cir. 2014) (Okla. law) (detailed but insufficient expert testimony); Patch v. Hillerich & Bradsby Co., 257 P.3d 383, 386 (Mont. 2011) (young baseball pitcher fatally struck in head by ball hit with baseball bat made by defendant; upholding judgment on verdict on warning but not design claim). Compare Vincer v. Esther Williams All-Aluminum Swimming Pool Co., 230 N.W.2d 794, 799 (Wis. 1975) (dissent citing baseball bat as unavoidably unsafe product), with Sanchez v. Hillerich & Bradsby Co., 128 Cal. Rptr. 2d 529 (Ct. App. 2002) (allowing pitcher to pursue claim that bat was defectively designed).

[168] See, e.g., Ledbetter v. Blair Corp., 2012 WL 2464000, at *1 (M.D. Ala. 2012) (cotton chenille robe); Marchand v. JEM Sportwear, Inc., 147 P.3d 90 (Idaho 2006) (cotton t-shirt); Ellsworth v. Sherne Lingerie, Inc., 495 A.2d 348 (Md. 1985) (nightgown); Gryc v. Dayton-Hudson Corp., 297 N.W.2d 727 (Minn. 1980) (child's pjs). Compare Coleman v. Cintas Sales Corp., 100 S.W.3d 384 (Tex. App. 2002) (35% cotton and 65% polyester).

[169] See discussion of fast food, below.

[170] See, e.g., Jordon v. K-Mart Corp., 611 A.2d 1328 (Pa. Super. Ct. 1992).

[171] See, e.g., Reiff v. Convergent Techs., 957 F. Supp. 573 (D.N.J. 1997) (no duty to warn that physical manipulation inherent in use of certain objects can cause injuries to some persons in certain circumstances).

[172] See Rest. (2d) Torts § 402A cmt. *i* (butter); Pelman v. McDonald's Corp., 237 F. Supp. 2d 512 (S.D.N.Y. 2003) (fast food). See discussion of fast food, below.

the usual proofs of defect, for selling products adjudged by a court or jury to be more bad than good.[173]

In a legal regime where responsibility is formally based on fault, the scope of a manufacturer's liability for supplying products of whatever type or degree of danger is quite clear: the manufacturer must take all reasonable measures proportionate to the danger to reduce foreseeable risks of harm.[174] Normally this means that a manufacturer must exercise reasonable care to eliminate from its products all substantial dangers that reasonably can be designed away; to minimize dangerous flaws in manufacturing products; to warn consumers about all substantial, hidden dangers that remain; and to avoid misrepresenting a product's safety. If manufacturers exercise reasonable care in all these respects, consumers, under a negligence regime, must bear responsibility for any remaining dangers in the products used in daily life, whether those dangers are characterized as "defects" or "generic risks."

During the 1960s and 1970s, the basis of tort liability for product accidents in America nominally changed from fault to one called "strict."[175] At its inception, the doctrine of strict products liability in tort appeared to accomplish a broad-based shift of responsibility for injuries associated with the use of products away from consumers and onto product suppliers, particularly manufacturers, who were viewed as better risk bearers than the human victims of product accidents.[176] This far-reaching shift in the apparent basis of liability for product accidents, particularly when justified by insurance theory, raised fundamental questions of how far a manufacturer's liability should extend for the inevitably harmful results of inherently hazardous products like butter that causes high cholesterol and heart attacks; drugs that unavoidably may produce dangerous side-effects; cigarettes that cause lung disease; and alcohol that causes liver damage, violence, and car accidents. Indeed, when the nascent concept of strict products liability in tort was first debated and developed in the 1950s and 1960s, this very question of the proper scope of supplier responsibility for such inherent or "generic" risks

---

[173] See Henderson and Twerski, Closing the American Products Liability Frontier: The Rejection of Liability Without Defect, 66 N.Y.U. L. Rev. 1263 (1991) (criticizing generic liability and coining the "last frontier" metaphor). Also criticizing product category liability, see, e.g., Ausness, Product Category Liability: A Critical Analysis, 24 N. Ky. L. Rev. 423 (1997); Grossman, Categorical Liability: Why the Gates Should Be Kept Closed, 36 S. Tex. L. Rev. 385 (1995). Favoring product category liability, see, e.g., Bogus, War on the Common Law: The Struggle at the Center of Products Liability, 60 Mo. L. Rev. 1 (1995); Wertheimer, The Smoke Gets in Their Eyes: Product Category Liability and Alternative Feasible Designs in the Third Restatement, 61 Tenn. L. Rev. 1429, 1454 (1994). See also Schwartz and Silverman, Category Liability: Properly Precluding Claims That Propose an Alternative Product Rather Than an Alternative Design, 44 Prod. Safety & Liab. Rep. (BNA) 40 (Jan. 11, 2016). See generally Symposium on Generic Products Liability, 72 Chi.-Kent L. Rev. 3 (1996) (articles by Bogus, Bell, Page, Phillips, Powers, and Wertheimer). For additional articles, see discussions of specific product categories, below.

The notions of "generic risk" and "product category" liability, which surfaced in the products liability literature in the 1980s and 1990s, overlap notions of "unavoidable danger" and "state of the art," examined in § 10.4, below. The "generic risk" phrase may be traced to an article by Joseph Page, Generic Product Risks: The Case Against Comment K and for Strict Tort Liability, 58 N.Y.U. L. Rev. 853 (1983), the first explicit foray into a variety of the interrelated and knotty issues here involved. This book uses the term "inherent risk." The discussion in this section draws from Owen, Inherent Product Hazards, 93 Ky. L.J. 377, 422 (2005).

[174] See ch. 2, above.

[175] See § 5.2, above.

[176] See § 5.4, above.

in certain limited categories of products—food, drugs, whiskey, and cigarettes—was one of the central issues of concern to Dean Prosser and other scholars of the day.[177]

To the scholars who were crafting the doctrine of strict products liability in tort in the early 1960s, particularly as they molded and debated § 402A of the *Restatement (Second) of Torts*, it was clear that manufacturers of unavoidably hazardous products could only be expected to ensure that their products were free of production defects and contained warnings of hidden dangers they could foresee. To avoid the possibility that the new "strict liability" doctrine might be stretched further—that is, to prevent it from being misconstrued as permitting a challenge to the *design* of products possessing such inherent dangers—Dean Prosser and the ALI explicitly excluded such an obligation from the new strict tort regime. In comments *i*, *j*, and *k* to § 402A of the *Restatement (Second) of Torts*, they made clear that the only duties of manufacturers of inherently dangerous products (such as alcoholic beverages, prescription drugs, cigarettes, certain foods, and other products whose dangers cannot be designed away) are to avoid manufacturing defects and to warn consumers of hidden dangers. Put otherwise, because such products by hypothesis are unavoidably unsafe precisely because their dangers cannot be removed without destroying their utility, such products cannot be defective in design.[178]

Judicial Rejection of Design Liability for Inherent Hazards

In recent decades, the underlying debate over liability for inherent product risks has centered on whether a product can properly be viewed as legally "defective" because its overall social injury costs exceed its overall social benefits.[179] Two prominent, controversial examples are cheap handguns, used by criminals to maim and kill while possessing little positive value (even for self-defense), and cigarettes, that sicken and kill hundreds of thousands of Americans each year for the "benefit" of satisfying an

---

[177] See § 6.2 (discussing development of comments *i*, *j*, and *k* to § 402A on liability for inherent risks), above, and § 10.4 (discussing unavoidable dangers due to state of the art), below. See generally Owen, The Puzzle of Comment *j*, 55 Hastings L.J. 1377 (2004).

[178] See Dunlap v. Federal Signal Corp., 194 A.3d 1067, 1073 (Pa. Super. Ct. 2018) (2–1 decision) (maker of fire truck siren that directed loud sound forward not liable for firefighters' hearing loss without proof of alternative design that was similarly effective in warning motorists and pedestrians in the vicinity); Clinton v. Brown & Williamson Holdings, Inc., 498 F. Supp. 2d 639, 647–48 (S.D.N.Y. 2007). *But see* Evans v. Lorillard Tobacco Co., 990 N.E.2d 997, 1023–24 (Mass. 2013) (affirming judgments on verdicts for estate of smoker who died from lung cancer; jury could find that low tar, low nicotine cigarettes were a reasonable alternative design to ordinary cigarettes for subclass of persons not yet addicted but *not* for subclass of smokers already addicted).

[179] Professor Carl Bogus illuminated the essence of the "generic liability" debate:

> Generic liability, or product category liability as it is also called, involves products that remain unreasonably dangerous despite the best possible construction, design and warnings. Some argue that products liability should end at this point, that a manufacturer who has done everything feasible to make its product reasonably safe ought not be subject to strict liability. Others contend that a manufacturer has a duty not to put unreasonably dangerous products, *i.e.*, products that have a greater social cost than social benefit, into the stream of commerce, and that a manufacturer who cannot feasibly make his product reasonably safe can elect not to distribute his product at all [or, Bogus might say, pay for its accident costs]. To many, generic liability is a radical concept: it raises the specter of courts deciding which products may and may not be distributed, and they perceive it as a judicial usurpation of legislative authority.

Bogus, War on the Common Law: The Struggle at the Center of Products Liability, 60 Mo. L. Rev. 1, 8–9 (1995).

addiction.[180] A small handful of courts[181] and a number of commentators[182] have taken the position that a product can fail a risk-utility test applied to a product considered *as a whole,* as distinguished from the normal risk-utility test based on proof that the manufacturer's failure to adopt a particular safety feature rendered the product defectively designed.[183] In some cases, the argument goes, even though there is no practicable way to design away a product's inherent danger, the product may be adjudged defective at a global level if it fails a "macro-balance" of its social costs and

---

[180] See, e.g., *Clinton,* above; Rose v. Brown & Williamson Tobacco Corp., 855 N.Y.S.2d 119, 125 (App. Div. 2008) ("It is, of course, incongruous to speak of a toxic product, which offers only fleeting sensual pleasure while sickening, disabling and killing multitudes each year, as serving a 'function,' or having 'utility,' for the consumer.").

"Cigarette smoking is the most effective way of delivering nicotine, the world's most addictive substance, to the bloodstream. Once the drug reaches the brain, its molecules bind to receptor cells, kicking off a chemical cascade that gives the smoker a burst of feel-good pleasure." Conover, Talking Back to Chantix, Post & Courier, Nov. 26, 2007, at D1–2. Compare Wertheimer, The Smoke Gets In Their Eyes: Product Category Liability and Alternative Feasible Designs in the Third Restatement, 61 Tenn. L. Rev. 1429, 1443 (1994) ("a product which is dangerous, useless, and without feasible alternative design is the cigarette"), with G. Schwartz, Cigarette Litigation's Offspring: Assessing Tort Issues Related to Guns, Alcohol, & Other Controversial Products In Light of the Tobacco Wars, 27 Pepp. L. Rev. 751, 751 (2000) (noting such "undeniably significant benefits" of cigarettes as their flavor, ability to enhance concentration, and service as antidepressants and tranquilizers, to which one might add weight control—making them, "a kind of miracle drug [obtainable] without going through the costly intervention of any physician").

[181] The Products Liability Restatement Reporters note three such cases: Halphen v. Johns-Manville Sales Corp., 484 So.2d 110 (La. 1986) (asbestos manufacturer subject to strict liability for products that fail broad social risk-utility test); Kelley v. R.G. Indus., 497 A.2d 1143 (Md. 1985) (manufacturer of "Saturday Night Special" cheap handgun subject to liability for criminal use of gun where its overall danger exceeded its overall benefits); and O'Brien v. Muskin Corp., 463 A.2d 298, 306 (N.J. 1983) (slippery vinyl bottom of above-ground swimming pool rendered pool defective even if no way to avoid risk). Each of these cases was overruled by statute. See Products Liability Rest. § 2 Reporters' Note to cmt. *d* § IV(D). There are other cases. See notes 193 (lawn darts) and 194 (flammable clothing), below.

One case that articulates the global risk-utility ("macro-balancing") approach to design liability in dictum (since the case involved warning claims) and that distinguishes this approach from the conventional, narrower, micro-balance standard is Beshada v. Johns-Manville Prods. Corp., 447 A.2d 539, 545 (N.J. 1982) (asbestos):

> [W]e can distinguish two tests for determining whether a product is safe: (1) does its utility outweigh its risk? and (2) if so, has that risk been reduced to the greatest extent possible consistent with the product's utility? The first question looks to the product as it was in fact marketed. If that product caused more harm than good, it was not reasonably fit for its intended purposes. We can therefore impose strict liability for the injuries it caused without having to determine whether it could have been rendered safer. The second aspect of strict liability, however, requires that the risk from the product be reduced to the greatest extent possible without hindering its utility. Whether or not the product passes the initial risk-utility test, it is not reasonably safe if the same product could have been made or marketed more safely.

Also in dictum, other courts have opined that, in rare cases, a court may justifiably find that a product's overall dangers exceed its overall social benefits. See, e.g., Armentrout v. FMC Corp., 842 P.2d 175, 185 n.8 (Colo. 1992) (en banc); Kallio v. Ford Motor Co., 407 N.W.2d 92, 97 n.8 (Minn. 1987) ("Conceivably, rare cases may exist where the product may be judged unreasonably dangerous because it should be removed from the market rather than be redesigned."); Rix v. General Motors Corp., 723 P.2d 195, 201 (Mont. 1986); Wilson v. Piper Aircraft Corp., 577 P.2d 1322, 1328 n.5 (Or. 1978).

[182] See, e.g., Bogus, The Third Revolution in Products Liability, 72 Chi.-Kent L. Rev. 3 (1996); Bell, Children's Lives, Indonesians' Lives, and Generic Liability, 72 Chi.-Kent L. Rev. 21 (1996); Wertheimer, Unavoidably Unsafe Products: A Modest Proposal, 72 Chi.-Kent L. Rev. 189 (1996); Bogus, War on the Common Law: The Struggle at the Center of Products Liability, 60 Mo. L. Rev. 1, 8–9 (1995). See also Page, Liability for Unreasonably and Unavoidably Unsafe Products: Does Negligence Doctrine Have a Role to Play?, 72 Chi.-Kent L. Rev. 87 (1996).

[183] On the perils of judicial "macro-balancing," as contrasted to the properly more limited judicial task of "micro-balancing" the costs and benefits of particular design improvements, see Owen, Risk-Utility Balancing in Design Defect Cases, 30 U. Mich. L. Rev. 239 (1997); Owen, Toward a Proper Test for Design Defectiveness: "Micro-Balancing" Costs and Benefits, 75 Tex. L. Rev. 1661 (1997) (explaining that proper design defect determinations rest upon a balance of the marginal costs and benefits of particular alternative design features); Products Liability Rest. § 2 Reporters' Note to cmt. *f*; §§ 8.4 and 8.5, above.

benefits—if, on balance and in the aggregate, the product is simply "bad." Yet the vast majority of courts have been markedly unreceptive to the call to displace markets, legislatures, and governmental agencies by decreeing whole categories of products to be "outlaws."[184]

Both the *Second* and *Third Restatements of Torts* endorse this highly restrained judicial approach. The *Second Restatement* addresses unavoidably dangerous products—such as food, alcohol, cigarettes, and drugs—in comments *i*, *j*, and *k* to § 402A. These comments make clear that a manufacturer of such unavoidably dangerous products must avoid manufacturing defects (such as contamination) and must warn of hidden dangers. But the central message of these comments to § 402A—responding to the central concern of tort scholars at the time (the early 1960s) over the potentially over-broad scope of the new strict liability doctrine—was that a manufacturer of useful but unavoidably dangerous products was not to be held liable for making them available to a public that desired them while recognizing (and accepting) their inherent risks.[185]

The *Third Restatement* emphatically adheres to the principle that entire categories of products commonly understood to be inherently dangerous—such as alcoholic beverages, firearms, and above-ground swimming pools (but not cigarettes[186])—cannot as a general rule be judicially classified as "defective" in *design.* That is, the *Third Restatement* takes the position that plaintiffs in design defect cases generally must establish that the manufacturer failed to adopt a reasonable method for designing out the danger—an impossible task, of course, if a product's risks are, by hypothesis,

---

[184] See, e.g., Fabiano v. Philip Morris Inc., 909 N.Y.S.2d 314, 320 (Sup. Ct. 2010) ('the vast majority of courts have been markedly unreceptive to the call that they displace markets, legislatures, and governmental agencies by decreeing whole categories of products to be outlaws"); Rose v. Brown & Williamson Tobacco Corp., 855 N.Y.S.2d 119, 125 (App. Div. 2008) (courts should not effectively outlaw cigarettes that have "long been consciously tolerated—and taxed and regulated—by the political branches of government"); Parish v. Jumpking, Inc., 719 N.W.2d 540 (Iowa 2006) (trampoline); Jones v. Amazing Prods., Inc., 231 F. Supp. 2d 1228, 1248–51 (N.D. Ga. 2002) (drain cleaner containing 97% sulfuric acid). For individual products, see cases cited below. See generally Products Liability Rest. § 2(b) Reporters' Note to cmt. *d* § IV(D), at 87 et seq.; Gifford, Impersonating the Legislature: State Attorneys General and Parens Patriae Product Litigation, 49 B.C. L. Rev. 913 (2008); D. Gifford, Suing the Tobacco and Lead Pigment Industries: Government Litigation as Public Health Prescription (U. Mich. Press 2010).

Judicial decisions, of course, do not literally "outlaw" the sale of alcohol, cigarettes, cheap handguns, and other inherently dangerous products by holding their manufacturers liable for their resulting harm because manufacturers may continue to sell their products and pay tort judgments to persons injured by them. While a judicial policy that requires manufacturers to internalize the full injury costs of such products has a variety of fairness, efficiency, and other social benefits to commend it, see § 5.4, above, the resulting cost increases of such products might well price them off the market. As a practical matter, therefore, a rule of manufacturer liability for inherently dangerous products may be said to "outlaw" them. See Owen, Product Outlaws, 10 Kan. J. L. & Pub. Pol'y 126 (2000) (examining dwarf-tossing).

[185] See, e.g., Myers v. Philip Morris Cos., 50 P.3d 751, 755–56 (Cal. 2002). See also § 6.2, above, examining the Restatement debate and scholarship at the time.

[186] Products Liability Rest. § 2 cmt. *d*, at 21 (Proposed Final Draft, April 1, 1997) included tobacco among the small category of products immunized from judicial scrutiny. During the American Law Institute debate on final approval, Professor Dratler of the University of Hawaii moved to strike the word "tobacco" from the list, arguing that the then escalating assault on the tobacco industry made ALI sanctuary for tobacco inappropriate. Over objection by the Reporters, who reasoned that the law did not justify removing tobacco from its protected position, the ALI membership voted narrowly to strike tobacco from the list of examples of inherently dangerous products for which manufacturers are not subject to claims for defective design. See ALI Proceedings 209–10 (1997); Henderson and Twerski, Achieving Consensus on Defective Product Design, 83 Cornell L. Rev. 867 (1998); Givelber, Cigarette Law, 73 Ind. L.J. 867, 871 (1998); ALI Membership Grants Final Approval to Influential Product Liability Treatise, 25 Prod. Safety & Liab. Rep. (BNA) 21, at 509 (May 23, 1997); § 8.8, above. The cigarette litigation is briefly discussed later in this section.

"inherent" and unavoidable.[187] Similar to the *Second Restatement*, however, the *Third Restatement* proclaims that provisional immunity from design liability in no way immunizes manufacturers of inherently dangerous products from the duties to *manufacture* such products free of dangerous defects and to *warn* consumers of any foreseeable, hidden dangers the products may contain, for these are independent duties of manufacturers of every type of product.[188]

The *Third Restatement* further recognizes that some courts[189] have quite reasonably retained wiggle room for rare cases to conclude that an "egregiously unacceptable" product may be of "manifestly unreasonable design," even if there is no reasonable way to design the danger away—cases where "the extremely high degree of danger posed by its use or consumption so substantially outweighs its negligible social utility that no rational, reasonable person, fully aware of the relevant facts, would choose to use, or to allow children to use, the product."[190] This category of egregiously dangerous products is at once very narrow yet open-ended, and it might fairly include such products as toy guns that shoot hard pellets at high velocity,[191] exploding novelty cigars,[192] lawn darts,[193] and clothing made of highly flammable fabrics.[194] While it may well be that products like these should be banned altogether by legislatures or administrative safety agencies (as they sometimes are),[195] it also seems appropriate for courts to allow products liability claims by persons injured by products that in fact can be clearly proven to produce far more social harm than good.[196]

Yet the list of such products properly must be very short, including only products that courts can be confident possess far greater risk than utility, such that they almost certainly should not be sold at all. Moreover, courts should be wary of allowing inherent danger design defect claims to go to sympathetic juries and so, except in exceptional cases, should bar such claims as a matter of law.[197]

---

[187] See Clinton v. Brown & Williamson Holdings, Inc., 498 F. Supp. 2d 639, 646–48 (S.D.N.Y. 2007) (cigarettes: "This is exactly the type of claim [the] alternative feasible design requirement was meant to disallow."). See generally Products Liability Rest. § 2 cmt. *d* (recognizing that "courts generally have concluded that legislatures and administrative agencies can, more appropriately than courts, consider the desirability of commercial distribution of some categories of widely used and consumed, but nevertheless dangerous, products").

[188] See Products Liability Rest. § 2 cmt. *d*; § 6.2, above.

[189] See Products Liability Rest. § 2(b) Reporters' Note to comment *d*, IV(D), at 87 (entitled "Rejection by a Majority of Jurisdictions of Liability Based on Nondefective Products That Are Nevertheless Egregiously Dangerous").

[190] Id. cmt. *e*.

[191] See id.

[192] See id. illus. 5.

[193] See, e.g., Aimone v. Walgreen's Co., 601 F. Supp. 507 (N.D. Ill. 1985). Lawn darts long ago were banned by the Consumer Product Safety Commission.

[194] See, e.g., Chapman v. Brown, 198 F. Supp. 78 (D. Haw. 1961) (hula skirt); LaGorga v. Kroger Co., 275 F. Supp. 373 (W.D. Pa. 1967) (jacket); Carter v. Joseph Bancroft & Sons Co., 360 F. Supp. 1103 (E.D. Pa. 1973) (dress); Abels v. Murjani Int'l, Ltd., 1986 WL 122176 (D. Kan. 1986) (blouse). See generally Noel, Manufacturer's Negligence of Design or Directions for Use of a Product, 71 Yale L.J. 816, 844–45 (1962). Note, however, that flame retardants can reduce the flammability of some fabrics so that excessive flammability may not be an unavoidable hazard. See, e.g., Gryc v. Dayton-Hudson Corp., 297 N.W.2d 727 (Minn. 1980); *LaGorga*, 275 F. Supp. at 380.

[195] See note 193, above.

[196] See Owen, The Graying of Products Liability Law: Paths Taken and Untaken in the New Restatement, 61 Tenn. L. Rev. 1241, 1253–57 (1994).

[197] See, e.g., Jones v. Amazing Prods., Inc., 231 F. Supp. 2d 1228, 1248–51 (N.D. Ga. 2002) (sulfuric acid drain cleaner; manufacturer's motion for summary judgment granted on claim that product was too dangerous

Reform Legislation on Inherent Risks

A number of states and the federal government have enacted legislation addressing in one way or another the issue of products that contain substantial inherent risks.[198] Some state and federal statutes ban or regulate the sale of such dangerous products as fireworks, cigarettes,[199] alcohol, and controlled substances,[200] while other states have enacted products liability reform legislation that limits a manufacturer's liability for generic product risks. North Carolina's provision, for example, shields manufacturers from design defect claims arising out of "an inherent characteristic of the product that cannot be eliminated without substantially compromising the product's usefulness or desirability and that is recognized by the ordinary person with the ordinary knowledge common to the community."[201] Statutes of this type quite clearly contemplate products such as alcohol and cigarettes.

Other states have also enacted generic risk statutes, but often with important variations.[202] New Jersey's statute, for example, generally shields manufacturers of such products from design defect claims but allows such claims for industrial machinery and products whose design is "egregiously unsafe."[203] And California and Texas enacted nearly identical reform statutes adopting the safe harbor list of inherently dangerous products of comment *i* to § 402A of the *Restatement (Second) of Torts*, which shelters manufacturers of some such products from most products liability exposure.[204] In 1998, however, California's legislature deleted "tobacco" from the safe-harbor list of protected products and added new provisions specifically authorizing products liability suits against the tobacco industry.[205] Some statutory provisions are quite specific, such as a North Carolina provision that protects manufacturers of prescription drugs that are unavoidably unsafe if adequate warnings are provided.[206]

Congress and the states have enacted a number of reform statutes addressing inherent product dangers in various other significant ways. The discussions that follow address such reform legislation as it applies to particular products: alcoholic beverages, cigarettes, firearms, opioids, and fast foods. Such statutes are sometimes enacted to protect public safety, but sometimes to protect manufacturers from litigation over

---

to sell at all). *But see* Yun Tung Chow v. Reckitt & Colman, Inc., 950 N.E.2d 113, 116 (N.Y. 2011) (lye drain cleaner; reversing summary judgment for defendant).

198 The statutes are collected in Appendices I and J of Owen & Davis on Products Liability.

199 The 2009 Family Smoking Prevention and Tobacco Control Act (FSPTCA) provides the FDA with regulatory authority over most aspects of the design, manufacturing, and marketing of tobacco products. See 21 U.S.C. § 387a. See generally Carvajal, Clissold, and Shapiro, The Family Smoking Prevention and Tobacco Control Act: An Overview, 64 Food & Drug L.J. 717 (2009). Implementation of the FDA rule requiring graphic warning images on cigarette packages, see 85 FR 15,638 (2020), is expected in 2022. See Steinberg, In-Store Cigarette Warnings Delayed Again as Hearing Pushed Back, Prod. Liab. & Toxics L. (May 3, 2021).

200 In addition to banning the sale of dangerous products, legislatures sometimes address their disposal. See, e.g., 15 U.S.C. § 1211 (prohibiting the disposal of refrigerators without first removing their latching doors); 42 U.S.C. §§ 14321, 14322 (requiring recycling instructions on regulated batteries).

201 N.C. Gen. Stat. Ann. § 99B–6(c).

202 In addition to the North Carolina statute, see Cal. Civ. Code § 1714.45(a) and (b); Mich. Comp. Laws Ann. § 600.2947(5); Miss. Code Ann. § 11–1–63(b); N.J. Stat. Ann. § 2A:58C–3(a)(2); Tex. Civ. Prac. & Rem. Code Ann. § 82.004(a).

203 N.J. Stat. Ann. § 2A:58C–3(b)(1). Compare Products Liability Rest. § 2 cmt. *e*.

204 See Cal. Civ. Code § 1714.45(a) and (b). Tex. Civ. Prac. & Rem. Code Ann. § 82.004 ("Inherently Unsafe Products").

205 See Cal. Civ. Code § 1714.45(e), (f), and (g).

206 See N.C. Gen. Stat. Ann. § 99B–6(d).

inherent risks. The limiting effect of these and other federal statutes regulating hazardous products (such as pesticides, insecticides, drugs, medical devices, and automotive vehicles) on products liability litigation is considered through the lens of federal preemption in a later chapter.[207]

Particular Products

While commentators debate the desirability of a broad or narrow judicial role in cases involving design liability for inherent product risks, courts have been busy handling expanding dockets involving litigation over products containing substantial inherent dangers of various types. Alcohol, cigarettes, and firearms might be singled out as prototypical products containing inherent risks that victims have sought to shift judicially to manufacturers. Many other types of products might be classified as inherently dangerous, some of which have generated very little litigation—such as marshmallows, peanut butter, snow sleds, jungle gyms, baby walkers, bullet-proof vests, and aluminum baseball bats;[208] other types of products whose dangers are great enough to trigger sizable litigation—such as ladders,[209] power boat motor propellers,[210] and trampolines;[211] and some whose dangers are so serious and widespread as to spawn a multitude of lawsuits around the nation—such as automotive vehicles, various prescription drugs, asbestos, lead paint, and fast food.[212] Except for fast food, which some years ago briefly appeared on the judicial landscape,[213] a court or lawyer confronting litigation concerning inherently dangerous products of these latter types may draw from an enormous body of case law and commentary on these particular types of litigation.[214]

---

[207] See § 14.5, below.

[208] See, e.g., Patch v. Hillerich & Bradsby Co., 257 P.3d 383, 386 (Mont. 2011) (aluminum baseball bat); Winslow v. L.B.O. Holding, Inc., 2009 WL 3739657 (Conn. Super. Ct. 2009) (sled in Alpine slide ride); Thongchoom v. Graco Children's Prods., Inc., 71 P.3d 214 (Wash. Ct. App. 2003) (baby walker); Sanchez v. Hillerich & Bradsby Co., 128 Cal. Rptr. 2d 529 (Ct. App. 2002) (bat); Emery v. Federated Foods, Inc., 863 P.2d 426 (Mont. 1993) (marshmallow); Jordon v. K-Mart Corp., 611 A.2d 1328 (Pa. Super. Ct. 1992) (sled); Cozzi v. North Palos Elementary Sch. Dist., 597 N.E.2d 683 (Ill. App. Ct. 1992) (jungle gym); Linegar v. Armour of Am., Inc., 909 F.2d 1150 (8th Cir. 1990) (Mo. law) (bullet-resistant vest); Fraust v. Swift & Co., 610 F. Supp. 711 (W.D. Pa. 1985) (peanut butter). See also Greene v. A.P. Prods., Ltd., 717 N.W.2d 855 (Mich. 2006) (hair oil).

[209] See, e.g., Werner Co. v. DeVallee, 2021 WL 1134387 (Tex. App. 2021) (fall); Castles v. Tricam Indus., 2020 WL 4569209 (D.S.C. 2020) (same); Stuhlmacher v. Home Depot U.S.A., Inc., 774 F.3d 405 (7th Cir. 2014) (Ind. law) (same). See also Hoeft v. Louisville Ladder Co., 904 S.W.2d 298 (Mo. Ct. App. 1995) (aluminum ladder hit power line).

[210] See, e.g., Thatcher v. Dargel Boats, Inc., 2019 WL 2601819 (S.D. Tex. 2019); Hinton v. Outboard Marine Corp., 2012 WL 260033 (D. Me. 2012) (speedboat motor caught and injured plaintiff's leg); McGarrigle v. Mercury Marine, 838 F. Supp. 2d 282 (D.N.J. 2011); Sprietsma v. Mercury Marine, a Div. of Brunswick Corp., 537 U.S. 51 (2002) (boat passenger who fell from boat and was struck and killed by propeller blades of motor not equipped with propeller guard; federal preemption doctrine did not bar design defect claim).

[211] See, e.g., Fitness, Fun, & Freedom, Inc. v. Perdue, 2021 WL 653240 (W. Va. 2021); Paranto v. Piotrkowski, 2010 WL 4226765 (Conn. Super. Ct. 2010) (summary judgment for defendant); Parish v. Jumpking, Inc., 719 N.W.2d 540 (Iowa 2006) (design not "manifestly unreasonable" under cmt. *e* to § 2(b) of Third Rest.); Sollami v. Eaton, 772 N.E.2d 215 (Ill. 2002) (dangers open and obvious). *But see* Lykins v. Fun Spot Trampolines, 874 N.E.2d 811, 816 (Ohio Ct. App. 2007) (risk that multiple people bouncing on trampoline at same time could cause "double bounce" that can project an adjacent person out of control).

[212] For automotive vehicles, see ch. 17, below. For prescription drugs, see ch. 18, below. For asbestos, lead paint, and fast food, see discussions in this section, below.

[213] See discussion of Pelman v. McDonald's Corp., 237 F. Supp. 2d 512 (S.D.N.Y. 2003), and progeny in fast food discussion, below.

[214] Sources are compiled below by type of product. For a panoramic exploration of the growth of tort law culminating in the litigations over tobacco, handguns, and lead, see D. Gifford, Suing the Tobacco and Lead Pigment Industries: Government Litigation as Public Health Prescription (U. Mich. Press 2010).

Cases involving the liability of manufacturers of such inherently dangerous products as those described above involve a panoply of complex issues, substantive and procedural, and only rarely do they address the underlying social welfare question of whether such a product should be characterized as defective (in design) because its global injury costs exceed its global social benefits. Occasionally, however, courts do address issues of personal autonomy that lie close to the heart of these cases—concepts of free choice and individual responsibility—concepts which support the idea that consumers who choose to accept the benefits of an obviously and unavoidably dangerous product must accept responsibility for the product's risks as well. Sometimes this powerful ideal of personal accountability finds doctrinal expression in the consumer expectations test of product defectiveness, or in rules on assumption of risk or no duty to warn of commonly known dangers, but more often it lies hidden below discussions of unrelated legal doctrines. Embedded to some extent in the rules of products liability law,[215] the value of personal responsibility assuredly is the reason plaintiffs have had such little success in convincing courts and juries that cigarette manufacturers should pay for the hundreds of thousands of Americans who die from smoking each year.

Because every type of product is inherently dangerous in some respect, as mentioned at the outset, there is no end to the list of other types of products that might be included in this category.[216] But a small number of particular products may be mentioned here because of the serious and widespread nature of their inherent risks and the recurring nature of the resulting products liability litigation.

The following discussions highlight recurring issues arising in litigation on several types of products whose notoriety springs from the substantial hazards they inherently contain. As explained below, most litigation involving inherently dangerous products has been brought by private plaintiffs (individually and collectively), but some such claims also have been instituted by cities, states, and national governments.

Alcoholic Beverages

In general. Alcoholic beverages provide widespread pleasure and relaxation, but they also wreak widespread harm.[217] Alcoholism, liver and other diseases, birth defects, car accidents, violence, and family discord follow all too frequently as direct results of

---

[215] See Owen, The Moral Foundations of Products Liability Law: Toward First Principles, 68 Notre Dame L. Rev. 427 (1993).

[216] Silicone breast implants, for example, led to many thousands of claims against their manufacturers. Plaintiffs prevailed in some cases. See, e.g., Transue v. Aesthetech Corp., 341 F.3d 911, 919 (9th Cir. 2003) (Wash. law); Dow Chem. Co. v. Mahlum, 970 P.2d 98 (Nev. 1998); Baxter Healthcare Corp. v. Grimes, 1998 WL 548729 (Tex. App. 1998). See also In re Breast Implant Cases, 942 F. Supp. 958 (S.D.N.Y. 1996) (discussing possible transfer of thousands of cases). Defendants have prevailed in many others, often on federal preemption grounds, Sewell v. Mentor Worldwide, LLC, 847 Fed. Appx. 380 (9th Cir. 2021), or because the plaintiffs failed to prove causation. See, e.g., Jacob v. Mentor Worldwide, LLC, 393 F. Supp. 3d 912 (C.D. Cal. 2019), aff'd sub nom. Nunn v. Mentor Worldwide, LLC, 847 Fed. Appx. 373 (9th Cir. 2021); See Kolata, Company Making Case to Allow Breast Implants, NY Times.com (Oct. 11, 2003) (Institute of Medicine committee study in 2000 that reviewed epidemiological data found no evidence that breast implants cause any serious disease, including cancer, neurological diseases, autoimmune diseases like lupus, or connective tissue diseases like arthritis). As with asbestos, this massive litigation has bankrupted at least one manufacturer (Dow). See generally Wagner, When All Else Fails: Regulating Risky Products Through Tort Litigation, 95 Geo. L.J. 693, 714–20 (2007); Spanbauer, Breast Implants as Beauty Ritual: Woman's Sceptre and Prison, 9 Yale J.L. & Feminism 157 (1997); Stine, Silicone, Science and Settlements: Breast Implants and a Search for Truth, 63 Def. Couns. J. 491 (1996).

[217] "Alcohol, like tobacco, is the nation's leading cause of death." D. Barry, Dave Barry's Money Secrets 60 (2006).

alcohol consumption.[218] Put simply, "water is best."[219] One might plausibly argue that alcohol consumption causes society more harm than good—that its social costs exceed its social benefits—a conclusion of the American people more than a century ago when they adopted the 18th Amendment that launched the storied saga of Prohibition. But the courts and *Torts Restatements* reject this form of judicial macro-balance risk-utility reasoning in part because such major social decisions are appropriately made (if at all) by legislatures, not the courts.[220] In addition, the dangers of alcoholic beverages are inherent, unavoidable, widely known, and now generally accepted as a necessary cost of these beverages that people widely desire. Indeed, almost all adults know and understand, at least in a general way, the variety of serious risks that can result from excessive alcohol consumption. Accordingly, and because over-consumption is viewed commonly as a form of product misuse,[221] ordinary alcoholic beverages cannot reasonably be viewed as "defective."

The unavoidability of alcohol's inherent dangers—intoxication and disease—is highlighted in two comments to § 402A of the *Restatement (Second) of Torts*. Comment *i* uses alcoholic beverages as a prime example of how products that contain commonly known dangers cannot be classified as "unreasonably dangerous." Noting that "any food or drug necessarily involves some risk of harm, if only from over-consumption," comment *i* declares that the strict liability doctrine only applies to a product that is "dangerous to an extent beyond that which would be contemplated by the ordinary consumer who purchases it, with the ordinary knowledge common to the community as to its characteristics. Good whiskey is not unreasonably dangerous merely because it will make some people drunk, and is especially dangerous to alcoholics."

The *Third Restatement* continues this safe harbor for alcoholic beverages from defectiveness in design.[222] As for the duty to warn, except for a couple of rogue decisions in the late 1980s,[223] courts have been nearly unanimous in holding that manufacturers have no common-law duty to *warn* consumers of the dangers of drinking alcoholic

---

[218] See Cochran, From Cigarettes to Alcohol: The Next Step in Hedonic Product Liability?, 27 Pepp. L. Rev. 701 (2000); Cochran, "Good Whiskey," Drunk Driving, and Innocent Bystanders: The Responsibility of Manufactures of Alcohol and Other Dangerous Hedonic Products for Bystander Injury, 45 S.C. L. Rev. 269 (1994); LeBel, John Barleycorn Must Pay—Compensating the Victims of Drinking Drivers (1992); Annot., Products Liability: Alcoholic Beverages, 42 A.L.R.4th 253 (1985); Frumer, Friedman, and Sklaren, Products Liability § 12.07; Am. Law Prod. Liab. §§ 83:5 et seq.

[219] Pindar, Olympian Odes, cited in Note, 31 Wm. & Mary L. Rev. 157 n.1 (1989). *But see* Gash, Beyond Erin Brockovich and a Civil Action: Should Strict Products Liability be the Next Frontier for Water Contamination Lawsuits?, 80 Wash. U. L.Q. 51 (2002).

[220] See Products Liability Rest. § 2 cmt. *d* ("courts generally have concluded that legislatures and administrative agencies can, more appropriately than courts, consider the desirability of commercial distribution of some categories of widely used and consumed, but nevertheless dangerous, products"). The inappropriateness of the judicial branch forcing producers to bear all secondary costs of alcohol runs squarely into the 21st Amendment that repealed the 19th Amendment in 1933. See generally D. Gifford, Suing the Tobacco and Lead Pigment Industries: Government Litigation as Public Health Prescription (U. Mich. Press 2010) (thoroughly examining how such major social choices lie properly in the realm of legislatures, not courts).

[221] Although it is foreseeable and, so as a formal matter, falls outside of the conventional definition of this "defense." See § 13.5, below.

[222] See Products Liability Rest. § 2 cmt. *d* ("Common and widely distributed products such as alcoholic beverages . . . may be found to be defective only upon proof of the requisite conditions in Subsection (a), (b), or (c)."). See, e.g., Bruner v. Anheuser-Busch, Inc., 153 F. Supp. 2d 1358 (S.D. Fla. 2001), aff'd, 31 Fed. Appx. 932 (11th Cir. 2002) (table).

[223] See Hon v. Stroh Brewery Co., 835 F.2d 510 (3d Cir. 1987) (Pa. law) (risk of death from pancreatitis caused by long-term moderate beer consumption); Brune v. Brown Forman Corp., 758 S.W.2d 827 (Tex. App. 1988) (risk of death to co-ed from acute alcohol poisoning from chugging tequila).

beverages in excess, or drinking and driving, because these dangers already are widely known.[224]

In 1988, however, Congress altered the duty-to-warn field by mandating that suppliers place warning labels on alcoholic beverages, as further discussed below.[225] Now that the duty to warn is mandated by federal statute, most warning claims appear to be barred by the doctrine of federal preemption,[226] and they may also be precluded by an inherent-risk provision of a state reform act, both of which are discussed below. For all of these reasons, it now seems safe to conclude that beverage manufacturers, as a general proposition, are not subject to liability for injuries resulting from the consumption of unadulterated alcoholic beverages.[227]

Reform legislation. From the 1960s, and year after year during the 1970s and 1980s, the FDA, Senator Strom Thurmond of South Carolina, and other members of Congress pressed the alcoholic beverage industry to adopt a voluntary labeling program warning of the dangers of such beverages. One proposed statute would have required every alcoholic beverage container to be labeled, on a rotating basis, with warnings that alcohol consumption (1) during pregnancy can cause mental retardation and other birth defects to the baby; (2) impairs a person's ability to drive a car or operate machinery; (3) is particularly hazardous in combination with some drugs; (4) can increase the risk of developing hypertension, liver disease, and cancer; and (5) is a drug and may be addictive. One bill substituted for (5) a warning that its rapid consumption can cause immediate death.[228]

---

[224] See, e.g., Brown v. Miller Brewing Co., 2014 WL 201699 (D. Idaho 2014) (no duty to warn that some people are predisposed to alcoholism); Bruner v. Anheuser-Busch, Inc., 153 F. Supp. 2d 1358, 1360 (S.D. Fla. 2001) (noting "the universal recognition of all potential dangers associated with alcohol"), aff'd, 31 Fed. Appx. 932 (11th Cir. 2002) (table); Joseph E. Seagram & Sons, Inc. v. McGuire, 814 S.W.2d 385, 388 (Tex. 1991) (risk of alcoholism; "From ancient times, the danger of alcoholism from prolonged and excessive consumption of alcoholic beverages has been widely known and recognized."); Morris v. Adolph Coors Co., 735 S.W.2d 578, 583 (Tex. App. 1987) (car accident caused by driver drunk on beer; "The ordinary consumer in today's society . . . knows of the dangers of driving while intoxicated."); Garrison v. Heublein, Inc., 673 F.2d 189 (7th Cir. 1982) (Ill. law) (no liability for physical and mental injuries from consumption of Smirnoff vodka over 20 years). Compare Cook v. MillerCoors, LLC, 872 F. Supp. 2d 1346, 1352 (M.D. Fla. 2012) (dismissing claim by motorcycle passenger for injuries in crash).

[225] See 27 U.S.C. §§ 213 et seq. This statute and pertinent state statutes are examined in the discussion of reform legislation, at notes 228–232, below.

[226] See, e.g., Comment, 38 Emory L.J. 1189 (1989) (preempted). *But see* Note, 18 Hofstra L. Rev. 943 (1990). See also Cuevas v. United Brands Co., 2012 WL 760403 (S.D. Cal. 2012) (allowing economic loss class action claim against producer of alcoholic energy drink, called "Joose," for breach of deceptive practices acts and implied warranty for failing to disclose effects of caffeine and alcohol). See generally § 14.5, below.

[227] The proposition is limited to a general one to allow room for claims of contamination and fraudulent advertising. See Comment, 38 Emory L.J. 1189 (1989). Courts have been unreceptive to deceptive advertising claims based on conventional "good life" advertising. See, e.g., Bruner v. Anheuser-Busch, Inc., 153 F. Supp. 2d 1358 (S.D. Fla. 2001), aff'd, 31 Fed. Appx. 932 (11th Cir. 2002) (table); Overton v. Anheuser-Busch Co., 517 N.W.2d 308, 309 (Mich. Ct. App. 1994) (Bud Lite ads showing "fantasies coming to life, fantasies involving tropical settings, and beautiful women and men engaged in unrestricted merriment" were merely puffs, not false statements of fact); Joseph E. Seagram & Sons, Inc. v. McGuire, 814 S.W.2d 385, 388 (Tex. 1991).

Policy arguments are much stronger for allowing recovery to third parties injured or killed by a drunk driver. See Cochran, From Cigarettes To Alcohol: The Next Step in Hedonic Product Liability?, 27 Pepp. L. Rev. 701 (2000); Cochran, "Good Whiskey," Drunk Driving, and Innocent Bystanders: The Responsibility of Manufacturers of Alcohol and Other Hedonic Products for Bystander Injury, 45 S.C. L. Rev. 269 (1994); Watts, Fairness and Utility in Products Liability: Balancing Individual Rights and Social Welfare, 38 Fla. St. U. L. Rev. 597, 640–41 (2011) ("Cochran makes a compelling argument that the costs of these harms should be spread among alcohol consumers rather than the injured bystanders.").

[228] S. 2047, 100th Cong., 2d Sess. (1988).

By the late 1980s, proposed legislation of this type was widely debated in Congress, state legislatures, and the media. Bills were filed (and rejected) in at least Florida and California, and one passed the Massachusetts House of Representatives in 1987. More than 60 national health organizations supported the federal bill summarized above, and a Gallup poll found that nearly 80% of Americans favored the labeling of alcoholic beverages with health warnings. A national editorial contended: "Consumers need to be able to make informed choices about everything they eat or drink or take as medicine. Especially alcoholic beverages. They need to know what's in them. And to be alerted to any possible hazards."[229] Citing statistics that 100,000 Americans die from alcohol use each year, that thousands of children are born with alcohol-related birth defects, that "18 million Americans and their families are torn apart by addiction and related problems," and that the annual loss to the nation exceeds $100 billion, the House and Senate sponsors of the warning label legislation—Congressman Conyers and Senator Thurmond—repeatedly urged its passage.[230]

Finally, Congress enacted a compromise bill, the Alcoholic Beverage Labeling Act of 1988,[231] requiring that alcoholic beverages be labeled as follows:

> Government Warning: (1) According to the Surgeon General, women should not drink alcoholic beverages during pregnancy because of the risk of birth defects.
>
> (2) Consumption of alcoholic beverages impairs your ability to drive a car or operate machinery, and may cause health problems.

This legislation preempts products liability claims for warning inadequacies, at least on beverage containers.[232]

Cigarettes

In general. Few health hazards are as harmful as cigarette smoking.[233] Some 34 million (13.7% of) American adults presently are smokers, 480,000 of whom die each year

---

[229] Convers and Thurmond, We Can't Wait for Industry to Act, USA Today, April 8, 1988, at 10A, col. 1.

[230] Noting that they had "waited more than a decade for the industry to heed the Food and Drug Administration's call for warning labels," they concluded: "What the alcohol marketers fear is information. What the public needs is that information. If marketers will not act responsibly to educate consumers about the real risks and costs, then Congress should." Id. at col. 3.

[231] Codified at 27 U.S.C. §§ 213 et seq.

[232] 27 U.S.C. § 216, the act's preemption clause, provides that state law may not require any other warning to be placed on any alcoholic beverage container or package. Claims for adulteration and fraudulent misrepresentation quite probably survive the Act, but warning claims, even creative ones, are preempted. See Note, 99 Com. L.J. 108 (1994) (proposing implied warranty claims for allergic reaction). On federal preemption, see § 14.5, below.

A tragic footnote to this legislation concerns its Senatorial champion, Strom Thurmond, who fought for years for its enactment. In 1993, his daughter was struck and killed by a drunk driver.

[233] "Tobacco smoke . . . contains acetone, ammonia, arsenic, benzene, cadmium, carbon monoxide, formaldehyde, hydrogen cyanide, lead, toluene and more. Each puff of smoke contains more than fifty known or probable carcinogens. [The 2004 and 2006 Surgeon General's Reports reported, respectively,] that smoking causes diseases in nearly every organ of the body, and . . . that there is no known safe level of smoking or exposure to secondhand smoke." Banthin, Potentially Reduced Exposure Cigarettes: The Need for a Public Health Policy, 8 Minn. J. L. Sci. & Tech. 127, 129–30 (2007).

"Smoking is the nation's number one cause of cancer, emphysema, heart disease, death, [and] ugly . . . teeth, and generally smelling like a fire at a . . . factory. Also, many smokers—as a result of having to leave their smoke-free office buildings to go outside in the dead of winter [in order to smoke] are eaten by wolves." Barry, Dave Barry's Money Secrets 59 (2006) (characterizing smoking as "an unbelievably stupid, expensive, evil, deadly addiction that benefits [only] lawyers").

from lung cancer, heart disease, and other tobacco-caused illness,[234] as do roughly 8 million of the 1 billion smokers in other nations around the globe.[235] In the late 1990s and early 2000s, litigation against tobacco manufacturers—including the state health-care expense recoupment cases that resulted in a $246 billion settlement between the states and the tobacco industry,[236] and a $145 billion punitive damages verdict in a smoker class action in Florida,[237] later reversed[238]—figured among the most high-profile products liability litigation in America.[239]

During the early 1900s, when products liability was in its infancy, little thought was given to holding manufacturers of cigarettes liable for the illnesses they might cause. Indeed, during the 1930s, manufacturers advertised some cigarettes as "harmless" and even "healthful."[240] As the years progressed, however, knowledge about the harmful effects of smoking cigarettes mounted; by the 1950s, when about half of all American adults were smokers,[241] studies had begun to establish a clear link between cigarettes and disease.[242] Public disclosure of this connection promptly led to a ten percent drop in cigarette consumption over a two year period, spurring the industry to engage the services of a public relations firm to help it combat the growing concern over cigarettes and health.[243] The consultant's advice to the industry was to attack the health matter head-on by creating a supposedly independent organization, the Tobacco Industry Research Committee, for the purported purpose of studying the relationship of tobacco smoking and disease. Thereafter, the industry's message to smokers was united, plain, and unequivocal: cigarettes do not cause cancer.[244]

As products liability litigation began to accelerate during the 1960s, the cigarette industry sought legal cover. Two powerful developments in that decade served to construct a strong fortress around the tobacco industry for most of the remainder of the

---

[234] See CDC, Smoking & Tobacco Use: Fast Facts (June 2, 2021) (at current smoking rate, "5.6 million of today's Americans younger than 18 years of age are expected to die prematurely from a smoking-related illness"; "The tobacco epidemic is one of the biggest public health threats the world has ever faced, killing more than 8 million people a year around the world.").

[235] See World Health Organization, Tobacco: Key Facts (July 26, 2021).

[236] This litigation is discussed below.

[237] R.J. Reynolds Tobacco Co. v. Engle, 672 So.2d 39 (Fla. Dist. Ct. App. 1996) (upholding class certification); Engle v. RJ Reynolds Tobacco, 2000 WL 33534572 (Fla. Cir. Ct. 2000) (denying defendants' motions after two years of trial).

[238] Liggett Grp. Inc. v. Engle, 853 So.2d 434 (Fla. Dist. Ct. App. 2003), aff'd in part, quashed in part, Engle v. Liggett Grp., Inc., 945 So.2d 1246 (Fla. 2006) .

[239] On the Florida litigation, see, e.g., Reeder, Engle, State Farm, Florida Law, and Punitive Damages: Was the $145 Billion Punitive Award Truly Excessive?, 31 Nova L. Rev. 57 (2006); Finch, Giving Full Faith and Credit to Punitive Damages Awards: Will Florida Rule the Nation?, 86 Minn. L. Rev. 497 (2002); Gottlieb and Daynard, Will Big Tobacco Seek Bankruptcy Protection? A $145 Billion Verdict Poses the Question, 26 Wm. & Mary Envtl. L. & Pol'y Rev. 359 (2001); Wertheimer, Pandora's Humidor: Tobacco Producer Liability in Tort, 24 N. Ky. L. Rev. 397 (1997). Punitive damages aspects of *Engle* are addressed in Owen & Davis on Products Liability § 26.5.

On smoker litigation more generally, see articles cited in notes 247–248, below.

[240] See, e.g., Pritchard v. Liggett & Myers Tobacco Co., 295 F.2d 292, 296–97 (3d Cir. 1961) (Pa. law) (Chesterfields); Cooper v. R.J. Reynolds Tobacco Co., 234 F.2d 170, 174–75 (1st Cir. 1956) (Magruder, J., concurring), on reappeal 256 F.2d 464 (1st Cir. 1958) (Mass. law) (Camels).

[241] See, Rabin, The Third Wave of Tobacco Tort Litigation, in Regulating Tobacco 176 (R. Rabin and S. Sugarman eds., 2001).

[242] See Givelber, Cigarette Law, 73 Ind. L.J. 867, 889 (1998).

[243] See id.; Rabin, A Sociolegal History of the Tobacco Tort Litigation, 44 Stan. L. Rev. 853, 858, 875 n.130 (1992).

[244] Givelber, above, at 889.

twentieth century: (1) the inclusion of tobacco in a "safe harbor" provision in the *Restatement (Second) of Torts* in 1965 for certain inherently dangerous products,[245] and (2) two separate federal labeling statutes, enacted in 1965 and 1969, mandating that manufacturers place certain warnings by the Surgeon General about smoking hazards on cigarette packages—Acts of Congress that served at once to provide the industry with an iron-clad assumption of risk defense together with a defense to inadequate warning claims based on federal preemption.[246]

Smoker litigation. Tobacco litigation, the subject of unrelenting scholarly analysis,[247] has been divided into three waves: the first, from 1954 to the 1960s or early 1970s; the second, from the early 1980s to the early 1990s; and the third, beginning in the early to mid-1990s and continuing to the present.[248] Prior to the third wave, the tobacco industry was an "impenetrable fortress,"[249] litigating hard and boasting that it had never paid a dime in damages in the hundreds of lawsuits it had defended since the

---

[245] See discussion of Rest. (2d) Torts § 402A cmt. *i*, above.

[246] Givelber, above, at 889–90. This Congressional legislation, and the Supreme Court's holding on its preemptive effect on products liability litigation, is examined in § 14.5, below.

[247] See generally Engstrom and Rabin, Pursuing Public Health Through Litigation: Lessons from Tobacco and Opioids, 73 Stan. L. Rev. 285 (2021); Berman, Tobacco Litigation, E-Cigarettes, and the Cigarette Endgame, 13 Ne. U.L. Rev. 219 (2021); Blum, Tobacco Product Warnings in the Mist of Vaping: A Retrospective on the Public Health Cigarette Smoking Act, 23 Chap. L. Rev. 53 (2020); Berman, The Faltering Promise of FDA Tobacco Regulation, 12 St. Louis U.J. Health L. & Pol'y 145 (2018); Halabi, The Scope of Preemption Under the 2009 Family Smoking Prevention and Tobacco Control Act, 71 Food & Drug L.J. 300 (2016); Puig, Tobacco Litigation in International Courts, 57 Harv. Int'l L.J. 383 (2016); Luff, Regulating Tobacco Through Litigation, 47 Ariz. St. L.J. 125 (2015); Daynard, Regulatory Approaches To Ending Cigarette-Caused Death and Disease in The United States, 39 Am. J.L. & Med. 290 (2013); Henderson and Twerski, Reaching Equilibrium in Tobacco Litigation, 62 S.C. L. Rev. 67 (2010); Eggen, The Synergy Of Toxic Tort Law and Public Health: Lessons From a Century Of Cigarettes, 41 Conn. L. Rev. 561 (2008) (discussing the epidemiological studies on smoking in the context of their impact on toxic tort litigation); LeBel and Ausness, Toward Justice in Tobacco Policymaking: A Critique of Hanson and Logue and an Alternative Approach to the Costs of Cigarettes, 33 Ga. L. Rev. 693 (1999) (moral theory suggests imposing an excise tax on cigarettes and allowing industry immunity from tort liability except for fraud), critiquing Hanson and Logue, The Costs of Cigarettes: The Economic Case for Ex Post Incentive-Based Regulation, 107 Yale L.J. 1163 (1998) (economic theory suggests strict tort liability and an administrative smokers compensation program); Galligan, A Primer on Cigarette Litigation Under the Restatement (Third) of Torts: Products Liability, 27 Sw. U. L. Rev. 487 (1998); Vandall, The Legal Theory and the Visionaries That Led to the Proposed $368.5 Billion Tobacco Settlement, 27 Sw. U. L. Rev. 473, 473–76 (1998); Kelder and Daynard, The Role of Litigation in the Effective Control of the Sale and Use of Tobacco, 8 Stan. L. & Pol'y Rev. 63, 71 (1997); LeBel, "Of Deaths Put on by Cunning and Forced Cause": Reality Bites the Tobacco Industry, 38 Wm. & Mary L. Rev. 605 (1997); Annot., 36 A.L.R.5th 541 (1996) (cigarettes and other tobacco products); Frumer, Friedman, and Sklaren, Products Liability § 56; Am. Law Prod. Liab. 3d § 88:13. See generally A. M. Brandt, The Cigarette Century: The Rise, Fall, and Deadly Persistence Of the Product That Defined America (2007) (discussing the hold that the tobacco industry has had on the American public despite the many studies demonstrating the hazards of smoking). For tobacco litigation in other nations, see, e.g., Cupp, International Tobacco Litigation's Evolution as a United States Torts Law Export: To Canada and Beyond?, 38 Pepp. L. Rev. 283 (2011); G. Howells, The Tobacco Challenge: Legal Policy and Consumer Protection (Routledge 2016).

[248] Rabin, The Third Wave of Tobacco Tort Litigation, in Regulating Tobacco 176 (R. Rabin and S. Sugarman eds., 2001); Cupp, A Morality Play's Third Act: Revisiting Addiction, Fraud, and Consumer Choice in "Third Wave" Tobacco Litigation, 46 U. Kan. L. Rev. 465 (1998); Schwartz, Tobacco Liability in the Courts, in Smoking Policy: Law, Politics, and Culture (R. Rabin and S. Sugarman eds., 1992) (describing first and second waves); Rabin, A Sociolegal History of the Tobacco Tort Litigation, 44 Stan. L. Rev. 853, 874 (1992).

[249] Note, 14 J.L. & Health 297, 298 (1999–2000).

1950s.[250] In the first wave, the plaintiffs' claims for negligence, breach of warranty,[251] and deceit were burdened by the absence of substantial scientific evidence linking smoking to disease. Sparing no expense and tenaciously defending each case, the tobacco lawyers were consistently victorious.[252] In the second wave, the plaintiffs had considerably better scientific evidence on causation, but their strict liability in tort design and warning claims were encumbered by § 402A comment *i*'s safe haven for tobacco and by the freedom of choice argument that smokers knew that smoking could be dangerous yet voluntarily assumed the risk.[253] The tobacco lawyers relentlessly fought on, outspending every plaintiff's lawyer, and winning every case.[254]

In the third wave of tobacco litigation, spurred in part by new revelations of misleading and manipulative conduct by the tobacco industry, the cigarette industry's fortunes began to change. First, after several years in the lower courts, the Supreme Court in 1992 decided the carefully litigated case of *Cipollone v. Liggett Group, Inc.*[255] Although the Supreme Court ruled in *Cipollone* that the congressionally mandated cigarette warnings preempted the plaintiffs' inadequate warning claims, the Court ruled that certain other claims (such as design defectiveness, breach of express warranty, and fraud) lay outside the federal labeling act's preemptive reach.[256] In 1994, documents and testimony provided by two whistle-blowers from the tobacco industry, made public in the newspapers and in Congressional hearings on tobacco, revealed stark new evidence of the industry's conspiracy to deceive the public about the hazards of smoking and, in

---

[250] See Cupp, A Morality Play's Third Act: Revisiting Addiction, Fraud, and Consumer Choice in "Third Wave" Tobacco Litigation, 46 U. Kan. L. Rev. 465, 648 n.17 (1998) (industry by then had prevailed in over 800 lawsuits); Birnbrich, Forcing Round Classes Into Square Rules: Attempting Certification of Nicotine Addiction-as-Injury Class Actions Under Federal Rule of Civil Procedure 23(B)(3), 29 U. Tol. L. Rev. 699, 700 (1998) (not "a single dollar"); Rachlinski, Regulating in Foresight Versus Judging Liability in Hindsight: The Case of Tobacco, 33 Ga. L. Rev. 813, 813 (1999) (not "one dime"); Rabin, A Sociolegal History of the Tobacco Tort Litigation, 44 Stan. L. Rev. 853, 874 (1992) (not "a cent").

[251] On the implied warranty of merchantability in cigarette litigation, see Note, 63 Ohio St. L.J. 1165 (2002).

[252] See, e.g., Ross v. Philip Morris & Co., 328 F.2d 3 (8th Cir. 1964) (Mo. law). *But cf.* Cooper v. R.J. Reynolds Tobacco Co., 234 F.2d 170, 173–74 (1st Cir. 1956) (Mass. law) (all claims properly dismissed except that for deceit, based on ads asserting that "20,000 doctors say that Camel cigarettes are healthful" and that Camels are "harmless to the respiratory system"). On remand, plaintiff failed to produce the ads, and the deceit claim was dismissed. In fact, the defendant did so advertise. See Cooper v. R.J. Reynolds Tobacco Co., 256 F.2d 464 (1st Cir. 1958) (Mass. law).

[253] "[T]he most salient theme in the second wave litigation has been freedom of choice. . . . [T]obacco litigation is a last vestige of a perhaps idealized vision of nineteenth century tort law as an interpersonal morality play. The sophisticated tobacco plaintiffs' lawyers . . . counted on the advent of comparative fault, buttressed by their ability to depict a socially irresponsible industry overpromoting a highly dangerous product, to counter—or, at least, blunt—the personal choice argument. In doing so, . . . they simply failed to grasp how intensely most jurors would react to damage claims by individuals who were aware of the risks associated with smoking and nonetheless chose to continue the activity over a long time period." Rabin, A Sociolegal History of the Tobacco Tort Litigation, 44 Stan. L. Rev. 853, 870–71 (1992).

[254] See, e.g., Rogers v. R.J. Tobacco Co., 745 N.E.2d 793 (Ind. 2001) (affirming trial court judgment on verdict for defendant in case initiated in 1980s); Roysdon v. R.J. Reynolds Co., 849 F.2d 230 (6th Cir. 1988) (Tenn. law). See generally Birnbrich, above note 250, at 700; Rabin, A Sociolegal History of the Tobacco Tort Litigation, 44 Stan. L. Rev. 853, 867–68 (1992) (detailing tobacco industry's "no-holds-barred defense of every claim"). "As a tobacco industry lawyer would put it, . . . the industry's hardball tactics made the litigation 'extremely burdensome and expensive for plaintiffs' lawyers. . . . To paraphrase Gen. [George] Patton, the way we won these cases was not by spending all of Reynolds' money, but by making [the enemy] spend all his.' " Id. at 868.

[255] 505 U.S. 504 (1992).

[256] See § 14.5, below.

particular, the addictive qualities of nicotine.[257] As early as 1963, for example, one of the industry's top lawyers observed that "[w]e are, then, in the business of selling nicotine, an addictive product."[258] These revelations, combined with increasing public antipathy toward "Big Tobacco," prompted the plaintiffs' bar, newly enriched from the coffers of the (former) asbestos industry, to pool their resources and aggressively begin the third round of litigation that has continued to this day.

In the post-*Cipollone* world, plaintiffs continue to lose many cases altogether,[259] but other courts have allowed such claims as negligence, breach of implied warranty, design defectiveness, fraud, conspiracy, and failure to warn prior to the 1966 federal labeling act,[260] or possibly prior to the subsequent labeling act in 1969.[261] A recurring defense in the third wave litigation is that the dangers of smoking long have been common knowledge. This defense has known some success,[262] but it has been roundly rejected by

---

[257] Both whistleblowers had worked for Brown & Williamson—one a paralegal at the company's defense law firm, who copied internal documents prior to his dismissal, and the other the head of research and development for the company, fired after years of contention over the company's failure to address the perils of tobacco responsibly. See Rabin, The Third Wave of Tobacco Tort Litigation, in Regulating Tobacco, at 183–85 (R. Rabin and S. Sugarman eds., 2001).

[258] Rabin, A Sociolegal History of the Tobacco Tort Litigation, 44 Stan. L. Rev. 853, 870–71 (1992).

[259] See, e.g., McCracken v. R.J. Reynolds Tobacco, 821 Fed. Appx. 122, 127 (3d Cir. 2020) (Pa. law) (without causation evidence, pro se plaintiff's design defect and failure to warn claims failed); Adamo v. Brown & Williamson Tobacco Corp., 900 N.E.2d 966, 968–69 (N.Y. 2008) (plaintiffs failed to show that light cigarettes are equivalent to regular ones); Lowe v. Philip Morris USA, Inc., 183 P.3d 181, 187 (Or. 2008) (increased risk of cancer and medical monitoring did not give rise to negligence claims); Waterhouse v. R.J. Reynolds Tobacco Co., 162 Fed. Appx. 231, 234–35 (4th Cir. 2006) (Md. law) (smoking risks were obvious); Badon v. R.J. Reynolds Tobacco Co., 934 So.2d 927 (La. Ct. App. 2006) (defectiveness per se of cigarettes preempted by Congressional policy); Tillman v. R.J. Reynolds Tobacco Co., 871 So.2d 28 (Ala. 2003) (no liability under consumer expectations test); Brown v. Philip Morris Inc., 228 F. Supp. 2d 506, 521–25 (D.N.J. 2002) (statutory state-of-the-art defense); LaBelle v. Philip Morris, Inc., 243 F. Supp. 2d 508 (D.S.C. 2001) (Pa. law) (plaintiff failed to prove feasible alternative design); Hughes v. Tobacco Inst., Inc., 278 F.3d 417 (5th Cir. 2001) (applying Texas "inherently unsafe product" defense). See also § 8.5, note 228, above (consumer dissatisfaction with light cigarettes defeats their feasibility as alternative design).

[260] See, e.g., Perkins v. R.J. Reynolds Tobacco Co., 2021 WL 3557206, at *4 (E.D. Mo. 2021) (denying dismissal of strict liability design and failure to warn claims against manufacturer of Kool cigarettes smoked by plaintiff since 1962 when he was 13 years old); DeLisle v. Crane Co., 258 So.3d 1219, 1223, 1230 (Fla. 2018) (negligent and strict liability in tort failure to warn and design defect claims against manufacturer of Kent cigarettes containing crocidolite asbestos filters during the 1950s); Pooshs v. Phillip Morris USA, Inc., 2013 WL 2252471, at *12 (N.D. Cal. 2013) (allowing claims for fraud, negligent misrepresentation, and pre-1969 failure to warn, after dismissing many other claims); Bougopoulos v. Altria Grp., Inc., 954 F. Supp. 2d 54, 60 (D.N.H. 2013) (manipulation of nicotine is a design defect claim apart from claiming "that cigarettes as a whole are inherently dangerous"); Izzarelli v. R.J. Reynolds Tobacco Co., 806 F. Supp. 2d 516 (D. Conn. 2011) (denying defendant's post-trial motions after entering judgment for $28 million); Estate of Schwarz v. Philip Morris, 235 P.3d 668, 670 (Or. 2010) (low-tar cigarettes; negligence, strict product liability, and fraud). See note 267, below.

See also Naegele v. R.J. Reynolds Tobacco Co., 50 P.3d 769 (Cal. 2002) (immunity statute only barred claims for "inherent" risks in unadulterated cigarettes and so did not bar claim that companies fraudulently adulterated cigarettes by increasing their nicotine content); Myers v. Philip Morris Cos., 50 P.3d 751 (Cal. 2002) (state's tobacco immunity statute enacted in 1987 and repealed in 1997 does not bar claims with respect to tobacco company conduct before or after 10-year immunity period).

[261] See, e.g., Izzarelli v. R.J. Reynolds Tobacco Co., 2018 WL 6575458 (D. Conn. 2018) (Salem Kings smoker suffering from larynx cancer awarded $7.9 million compensatory damages and $8 million punitive damages); Evans v. Lorillard Tobacco Co., 990 N.E.2d 997, 1022 (Mass. 2013) (affirming judgment on verdict, as remitted to $10 million for son's loss of companionship and $25 million to estate of smoker who died from lung cancer; jury could find that the risk of lung cancer from smoking was not obvious until 1966 or even 1970).

[262] See, e.g., Caronia v. Philip Morris USA, Inc., 2010 WL 520558, at *8 (E.D.N.Y. 2010) ("In light of widespread knowledge of the risks of tobacco use, it is difficult to imagine that consumers failed to understand that the ordinary use of cigarettes entails a risk of contracting cancer."); Waterhouse v. R.J. Reynolds Tobacco Co., 162 Fed. Appx. 231, 234–35 (4th Cir. 2006) (Md. law); Tillman v. R.J. Reynolds Tobacco Co., 871 So.2d 28, 33–34 (Ala. 2003); Glassner v. R.J. Reynolds Tobacco Co., 223 F.3d 343 (6th Cir. 2000) (Ohio law); Insolia v. Philip Morris, Inc., 216 F.3d 596 (7th Cir. 2000) (Wis. law) (because most beginning adult smokers understood

other courts on a variety of grounds, such as "moral estoppel";[263] that knowing the general hazards of smoking does not amount to knowing that it can cause particular diseases or that it can be highly addictive;[264] and that common knowledge or the user's awareness of some risk from smoking is not dispositive of liability but is merely one factor for consideration in a risk-utility analysis of defectiveness.[265] For these reasons, many courts have ruled that judicial notice on this issue is improper.[266] On convincing evidence of fraud and conspiracy, a few juries have returned substantial verdicts, comprised mostly of punitive damages, with some favorable appellate results.[267]

---

health risks of smoking in 1935 and early 1950s, including fact that it is habit-forming, strict liability claims precluded under consumer expectations test); Sanchez v. Liggett & Myers, Inc., 187 F.3d 486 (5th Cir. 1999) (Tex. law).

[263] "If there were such a thing as moral estoppel, the outcome of this appeal would be plain. For decades tobacco companies have assured the public that there is nothing to fear from cigarettes, yet they now slough off lawsuits like this one by professing that everybody knew all along that smoking was risky." Insolia v. Philip Morris, Inc., 216 F.3d 596, 598 (7th Cir. 2000) (Wis. law).

[264] See, e.g., Tompkin v. American Brands, 219 F.3d 566, 572 (6th Cir. 2000) (Ohio law) ("The pertinent issue here is not whether the public knew that smoking was hazardous to health at some undifferentiated level, but whether it knew of the specific linkages between smoking and lung cancer. Public awareness of a broad-based and ambiguous risk that smoking might be tenuously connected to lung cancer does not suggest 'common knowledge' of the known scientific fact that cigarette smoking is a strong precipitant of lung cancer."); Wright v. Brooke Grp. Ltd., 114 F. Supp. 2d 797, 810–14 (N.D. Iowa 2000) (because "there is a considerable difference between knowing that smoking is bad and knowing that smoking is addictive," the risk of addiction is not a "lesser included risk" of the risks of smoking).

Levels of nicotine, which causes addiction to cigarettes, have continued to rise in recent years. See Kuiper et al., Trends in Manufacturer-Reported Nicotine Yields in Cigarettes Sold in the United States, 2013–2016, 17 CDC Original Research (Nov. 25, 2020) ("During 2013–2016, manufacturer-reported, sales-weighted nicotine yield in cigarettes increased, most notably for menthol cigarettes.").

[265] See, e.g., Evans v. Lorillard Tobacco Co., 990 N.E.2d 997, 1011–14 (Mass. 2013) (consumer expectations were just one of many factors pertinent to design defect determination); Henley v. Philip Morris, Inc., 9 Cal. Rptr. 3d 29 (Ct. App. 2004); Wright v. Brooke Grp. Ltd., 652 N.W.2d 159, 170–71 (Iowa 2002).

[266] See, e.g., Smith v. Brown & Williamson Tobacco Corp., 275 S.W.3d 748, 759 (Mo. Ct. App. 2008) (negligent failure to warn and strict liability design defect); Ferlanti v. Liggett Grp., Inc., 929 So.2d 1172, 1175 (Fla. Dist. Ct. App. 2006) (because "numerous factual issues" surrounded common knowledge of smoking risks, trial court erred in taking judicial notice of same).

[267] In a half century of litigation prior to the state settlements in the late 1990s, only three smokers had ever prevailed in cigarette litigation, two of whose cases were reversed on appeal. In the first four years following the settlement of state claims, individual smokers won nearly ten cases. See, e.g., R.J. Reynolds Tobacco Co. v. Kenyon, 856 So.2d 998 (Fla. Dist. Ct. App. 2003) (table) (affirming compensatory award); Henley v. Philip Morris Inc., 9 Cal. Rptr. 3d 29 (Ct. App. 2004) ($50 million award to smoker, remitted by trial judge to $25 million, further remitted by appellate court to $9 million), review granted, 88 P.3d 497 (Cal. 2004); Boeken v. Philip Morris, Inc., 26 Cal. Rptr. 3d 638 (Ct. App. 2005) (affirming punitive damages award but further reducing it to $50 million; trial court had reduced $3 billion verdict to $100 million).

Plaintiffs in some cases continue to win awards, sometimes very large. See, e.g., Laramie v. Philip Morris USA Inc., 173 N.E.3d 731 (Mass. 2021) (affirming jury award of $11 million compensatory and $10 million punitive damages to smoker's widow); Izzarelli v. R.J. Reynolds Tobacco Co., 2018 WL 6575458 (D. Conn. 2018) (Salem Kings smoker with larynx cancer awarded $7.9 million compensatory damages and $8 million punitive damages); Williams v. R.J. Reynolds, No. 2008 CA (Fla. Cir. Ct. July 19, 2014) (jury award of $16 million to widow, with $23 *billion* punitive damages, reported in Nesmith, Reynolds to Appeal $23B Verdict in Florida Widow's Tobacco Suit, 42 Prod. Safety & Liab. Rep. (BNA) 819 (July 20, 2013)); Evans v. Lorillard Tobacco Co., 990 N.E.2d 997 (Mass. 2013) (jury awarded $21 million to son, for lost companionship of mother, $50 million to estate of smoker who died of lung cancer, and assessed $81 million in punitive damages; Supreme Judicial Court affirmed remitted judgments of $10 million for son and $25 million for estate, but reversed and remanded for a new trial on punitive damages); Bullock v. Philip Morris USA, Inc., 131 Cal. Rptr. 3d 382, 406 (Ct. App. 2012) (affirming award of $850,000 compensatory and $13.8 million punitive damages); Estate of Schwartz v. Philip Morris, 235 P.3d 668, 678 (Or. 2010) (affirming award of $168,000 compensatory damages, vacating the remitted $100 million punitive damages award, and remanding for new punitive damages trial).

Class actions, despite some initial dramatic success, for the most part have failed. In *Castano v. American Tobacco Co.*,[268] plaintiffs in 1995 filed a national class action against seven cigarette manufacturers and the Tobacco Institute, Inc., which was certified by the trial court but reversed on appeal. Plaintiffs' counsel thereafter brought a large number of state class actions, almost all of which eventually were lost.[269] *R.J. Reynolds Tobacco Co. v. Engle*,[270] a smokers' class action brought in Florida, led to a spectacular verdict of $145 billion,[271] comprised mostly of punitive damages, but the District Court of Appeal reversed the judgment and decertified the class.[272] Affirming the reversal of punitive damages,[273] the Florida Supreme Court upheld the decertification of the class on various procedural grounds.[274] But the court did rule that members of the class could proceed individually and that findings in favor of the class at the earlier trial would have res judicata effect in subsequent trials between individual class members and the defendants filed within one year.[275] Plaintiffs' counsel thereupon filed approximately 9,000 individual "*Engle*-progeny" cases, many of which resulted in large jury verdicts,[276] and others of which had punitive damage claims barred by Florida's 12-year statute of repose for fraud.[277] And the *Engle*-progeny litigation continues to congest Florida's trial and appellate courts to this day.[278]

---

[268] 160 F.R.D. 544 (E.D. La. 1995), rev'd, 84 F.3d 734 (5th Cir. 1996) (decertifying class). See Rabin, The Third Wave of Tobacco Tort Litigation, in Regulating Tobacco 179–89 (R. Rabin and S. Sugarman eds., 2001).

[269] See, e.g., Estate of Mahoney v. R.J. Reynolds Tobacco Co., 204 F.R.D. 150 (S.D. Iowa 2001) (denying certification of class of Iowa smokers). *But see* Philip Morris Companies, Inc. v. Miner, 462 S.W.3d 313 (Ark. 2015) (affirming certification of class of Arkansas light cigarette smokers). See also Cooper, Marlboro Lights Smoker Class Status OK'd; Rare Certification Says Predominance No Bar, 43 Prod. Safety & Liab. Rep. (BNA) 291 (Mar. 9, 2015) (noting split between states that have certified such class actions—Cal., Mass., Mo., and Ill.—and the federal and state courts that have denied certification or decertified light cigarette class actions in Ohio, Haw., Wis., N.H., Cal., Ill., Me., and D.C.). See generally Rabin, note 268, above, at 188.

[270] 672 So.2d 39 (Fla. Dist. Ct. App. 1996) (upholding certification of more than one million Florida smokers suffering from tobacco diseases), review denied, 682 So.2d 1100 (Fla. 1996), noted in 18 T.M. Cooley L. Rev. 201 (2001).

[271] See Engle v. RJ Reynolds Tobacco, 2000 WL 33534572 (Fla. Cir. Ct. 2000) (denying defendants' motions after two years of trial).

[272] Liggett Grp. Inc. v. Engle, 853 So.2d 434 (Fla. Dist. Ct. App. 2003), aff'd in part, quashed in part, Engle v. Liggett Grp., Inc., 945 So.2d 1246 (Fla. 2006) .

[273] Engle v. Liggett Grp., Inc., 945 So.2d 1246, 1263–65 (Fla. 2006) (punitive damages could not be awarded to class prior to determining compensatory damages).

[274] Id. at 1277.

[275] Id. at 1254.

[276] See, e.g., Philip Morris USA, Inc. v. Naugle, 103 So.3d 944, 949 (Fla. Dist. Ct. App. 2012) (reversing damages awards after trial court remitted $58.2 million compensatory award to $9.8 million and $244 million punitive damages to $25.9 million, and remanding for new trial on damages); R.J. Reynolds Tobacco Co. v. Townsend, 90 So.3d 307, 312, 316 (Fla. Dist. Ct. App. 2012) (affirming $10.8 compensatory award, but reversing and remanding $40.8 million punitive damages for new trial or remitter); R.J. Reynolds Tobacco Co. v. Martin, 53 So.3d 1060, 1073 (Fla. Dist. Ct. App. 2010) (affirming court-reduced award to smoker's widow of $3.3 million compensatory and $25 million punitive damages), cert. denied, 566 U.S. 905 (2012). See generally Henderson and Twerski, Reaching Equilibrium in Tobacco Litigation, 62 S.C. L. Rev. 67, 100 (2010) (summarizing *Engle*-progeny cases tried to verdict through May 2010).

[277] See, e.g., Philip Morris USA, Inc. v. Kayton, 104 So.3d 1145, 1153 (Fla. Dist. Ct. App. 2012) (reversing and remanding $16 million punitive damages award, which the court will allow "to stand if on re-trial the plaintiff prevails on the statute of repose issue"). Subsequently, in Philip Morris USA, Inc. v. Douglas, 110 So.3d 419, 436 (Fla. 2013), the Florida Supreme Court affirmed that defendants' due process rights were not violated by the res judicata effect of the *Engle* Phase I liability findings.

[278] Many cases remain in progress. See, e.g., Prentice v. R.J. Reynolds Tobacco Co., 2022 WL 805951, at *6 (Fla. 2022) (resolving a split among Florida appellate courts; *Engle*-progeny plaintiffs must prove reliance "on a statement . . . that concealed or omitted material information about the health effects or addictiveness of smoking cigarettes" to succeed in their fraudulent concealment or concealment conspiracy claims); R.J. Reynolds Tobacco Co. v. Neff, 325 So.3d 872 (Fla. Dist. Ct. App. 2021) (reversing jury verdict for plaintiff and

A few class actions have been brought for second-hand smoke,[279] which have met with varying success.[280] And at least one proposed class action was filed on behalf of users of chewing tobacco who claimed to have suffered various cancers from the product.[281]

Class actions have sought a number of remedies other than conventional damages for personal injury and death. The court in at least one smoker class action allowed a claim for medical monitoring, and another court awarded a smoking cessation program to certain class members.[282] Lawyers have filed a number of other smoker class actions for economic losses. The most prominent case of this type, filed in Illinois, resulted in a verdict for $10.1 billion, which was upheld by the intermediate appellate court[283] but reversed in a split decision by the Supreme Court of Illinois.[284] A few such class actions for economic damages have survived,[285] while a few others have failed.[286] In 2002, Judge

remanding for new trial; plaintiff's attorney's improper closing arguments were harmful error and conspiracy charge jury verdict form questions were reversible errors); R.J. Reynolds Tobacco Co. v. Schlefstein, 284 So.3d 584 (Fla. Dist. Ct. App. 2019) ($41.8 million verdict in favor of the estate of a deceased smoker reversed and remanded for new trial; defenses improperly limited); R.J. Reynolds Tobacco Co. v. Ledo, 274 So.3d 416, 418 (Fla. Dist. Ct. App. 2019) (remanding for new trial to determine amount of punitive damages award). See also Burkhart v. R.J. Reynolds Tobacco Co. 884 F.3d 1068, 1093 (11th Cir. 2018) (Florida Supreme Court's "grant of preclusive weight to *Engle* progeny plaintiffs' concealment and conspiracy claims" did not offend the federal Due Process Clause); Philip Morris USA, Inc. v. Douglas, 110 So.3d 419 (Fla. 2013) (upholding and clarifying certain res judicata effects of *Engle*). As of 2019, the United States Supreme Court had denied due process review of *Engle*'s res judicata effects at least 27 times. Barash, Philip Morris, Other Tobacco Companies Rebuffed Again by SCOTUS, Prod. Liab. & Toxics L. (Feb. 25, 2019).

[279] See O'Neil, A Warning on Hazards of Smoke from Others, N.Y. Times, June 28, 2006, at A14 (the Surgeon General reports that "[t]he evidence is now 'indisputable' that secondhand smoke is an 'alarming' public health hazard, responsible for tens of thousands of premature deaths among nonsmokers each year").

[280] See, e.g., Broin v. Philip Morris Cos., 641 So.2d 888 (Fla. Dist. Ct. App. 1994) (approving class action of flight attendants who inhaled second-hand smoke); Badillo v. American Brands, Inc., 16 P.3d 435 (Nev. 2001) (class of smokers and non-smokers exposed to second-hand smoke; claim for medical monitoring costs denied).

[281] See Haggman, Tobacco Wars Are Going Smokeless, Nat'l L.J. A10 (Nov. 18, 2002).

[282] See Donovan v. Philip Morris USA, Inc., 914 N.E.2d 891, 898 (Mass. 2009) (allowing medical monitoring claim). *Contra* Caronia v. Philip Morris USA, Inc., 5 N.E.3d 11 (N.Y. 2013) (disallowing medical monitoring claim); Scott v. American Tobacco Co., Inc., 949 So.2d 1266, 1275–76, 1291 (La. Ct. App. 2007) (same, but establishing 10-year smoking cessation program funded by defendants and administered by the court).

[283] Price v. Philip Morris, Inc., 793 N.E.2d 942 (Ill. App. Ct. 2003) (on verdict of $7.1 billion compensatory damages, to recompense class for cost of purchased cigarettes, and $3 billion punitive damages award, trial court erred in reducing $12 billion appeal bond; state-wide class action for fraudulently marketing "light," "low tar," and "mild" cigarettes as safer than ordinary cigarettes, while knowing they did not lower the risk of lung cancer).

[284] Price v. Philip Morris, Inc., 848 N.E.2d 1 (Ill. 2005) (3–2 decision) (defendant's marketing practices in compliance with FTC consent orders exempted it from liability and barred smokers' claims), cert. denied, 549 U.S. 1054 (2006). An Illinois appellate court reinstated the $10.1 billion verdict for the plaintiffs, Price v. Philip Morris, Inc., 9 N.E.3d 599 (Ill. App. Ct. 2014), but the Illinois Supreme Court vacated the reinstatement. Price v. Philip Morris, Inc., 43 N.E.3d 53, 65–66 (Ill. 2015) (appeals court lacked authority to grant relief to the state supreme court's 2005 reversal of the circuit court's judgment).

[285] See, e.g., Philip Morris Cos., Inc. v. Miner, 462 S.W.3d 313 (Ark. 2015) (affirming certification of class of Arkansas "light" cigarette smokers against manufacturer for deceptive trade practices); In re Light Cigarettes Mktg. Sales Practices Litig., 751 F. Supp. 2d 196 (D. Me. 2010) (denying defendant's motion for summary judgment for lack of causation); In re Tobacco II Cases, 207 P.3d 20 (Cal 2009) (4–3 decision) (reversing decertification of class and allowing case to proceed); Aspinall v. Philip Morris, Inc., 902 N.E.2d 421, 416 (Mass. 2009) (class action, for deceptive trade practices against "light" cigarette manufacturers, not preempted); Good v. Altria Grp., Inc., 501 F.3d 29 (1st Cir. 2007) (Me. law) (vacating dismissal of action by Maine smokers of "light" cigarettes seeking class certification for fraudulent misrepresentation claims under Maine's Unfair Trade Practices Act; claims not preempted), aff'd, 555 U.S. 70 (2008).

[286] See, e.g., Pearson v. Philip Morris, Inc., 361 P.3d 3, 36 (Or. 2015) (trial court properly denied class certification to plaintiffs seeking economic damages for allegedly deceptive marketing of light cigarettes);

Weinstein certified a class action seeking punitive damages for fraud on behalf of most injured smokers in the United States,[287] but the court of appeals eventually vacated the certification order.[288]

Electronic cigarettes. E-cigarettes ("e-cigs" or "vapes") are devices used to produce an aerosol, usually including nicotine, that a user inhales into the lungs.[289] Often resembling cigarettes, such vaping devices come in various shapes and sizes. Typically, a user puffs on the device, activating a battery-powered heating device that vaporizes liquid in a cartridge, generating vapor for inhalation. E-cigs are often marketed as a way to help smokers stop smoking cigarettes, and some research suggests that they may be less harmful than ordinary cigarettes. Yet the FDA, working with the CDC, reports that these devices have caused thousands of lung illnesses and dozens of deaths. Popular among teenagers, vaping is the most common form of nicotine consumption by American youth today.[290]

In 2016, under the Family Smoking Prevention and Tobacco Control Act,[291] the FDA issued final rules extending the agency's regulatory authority to other tobacco products, including electronic cigarettes.[292] To curb the use of flavored electronic cigarettes among minors, the FDA announced plans in 2018 to limit the sales of most flavored electronic cigarettes to age-restricted outlets and to ban menthol in cigarettes and cigars.[293] By 2020, the FDA and CDC issued warnings linking e-cigarettes and vaping devices to severe lung disease, prompting further regulatory control,[294] including bans by various states and local governments of flavored tobacco products, which are perceived as particular threats to youth.[295] Alternative forms of electronic cigarette systems are now

---

Shaffer v. R.J. Reynolds Tobacco Co., 860 F. Supp. 2d 991 (D. Ariz. 2012) (denying plaintiff's motion for partial summary judgment in putative class action); McLaughlin v. American Tobacco Co., 522 F.3d 215 (2d Cir. 2008) (decertifying RICO class certified by Judge Jack Weinstein); Davies v. Philip Morris U.S.A., Inc., 2006 WL 1600067 (Wash. Super. Ct. 2006) (denying class certification); Marrone v. Philip Morris USA, Inc., 850 N.E.2d 31 (Ohio 2006) (reversing class certification under Ohio's Consumer Sales Practices Act for deceptively marketing cigarettes as "light").

[287] In re Simon II Litig., 211 F.R.D. 86 (E.D.N.Y. 2002) (Weinstein, J.) (certifying national tobacco class action seeking punitive damages for fraud).

[288] In re Simon II Litig., 407 F.3d 125 (2d Cir. 2005) (decertifying class).

[289] See Berman, Tobacco Litigation, E-Cigarettes, and the Cigarette Endgame, 13 Ne. U.L. Rev. 219 (2021); Blum, Tobacco Product Warnings in the Mist of Vaping: A Retrospective on the Public Health Cigarette Smoking Act, 23 Chap. L. Rev. 53 (2020); Comment, The Vaping Reaper: The Evali Crisis and Why FDA Regulation Is Needed to Prevent Further Issues, 17 J. Health & Biomedical L. 119 (2020).

[290] See, e.g., Lavito, Teen Vaping Craze Shows No Signs of Easing, U.S. Officials Say, Prod. Liab. & Tox. L. (Oct. 1, 2021) (2 million U.S. teenagers use e-cigs); NIH, Vaping Devices (Electronic Cigarettes) Drug Facts (Jan. 2020).

[291] Pub.L. 111–31, Div. A, Title II, §§ 201(a), 202(b), 206, June 22, 2009, 123 Stat. 1842, 1845, 1849.

[292] See 81 Fed. Reg. 28973–01 (2016). See generally Berman, Tobacco Litigation, E-Cigarettes, and the Cigarette Endgame, 13 Ne. U. L. Rev. 219 (2021). See also Cigar Ass'n of Am. v. United States Food & Drug Admin., 5 F.4th 68 (D.C. Cir. 2021) (affirming dismissal of plaintiffs' challenges to FDA's extension of cigarette regulation to other tobacco products).

[293] Gottlieb, Statement from FDA Commissioner Scott Gottlieb, M.D., on Proposed New Steps to Protect Youth by Preventing Access to Flavored Tobacco Products and Banning Menthol in Cigarettes (Nov. 15, 2018).

[294] See, e.g., Porter, Some Vaping Flavors Banned as FDA Seeks to Curb Teen Use, Prod. Liab. & Toxics L. (Jan. 2, 2020); Cortez, U.S. Advises Non-Smokers to Avoid e-Cigarettes Amid Outbreak, Prod. Liab. & Toxics L. (Aug. 30, 2019). In September 2021, the FDA issued marketing denial orders for over 946,000 flavored e-cigarette products, including the finding that any benefit of those products to adults was outweighed by health risks to teens. See FDA, FDA Makes Significant Progress in Science-Based Public Health Application Review, Taking Action on Over 90% of More Than 6.5 Million 'Deemed' New Tobacco Products Submitted (Sept. 9, 2021).

[295] Tobacco industry challenges to state and local bans on the sale of flavored tobacco products have met with mixed success. For successful challenges to such ordinances, see, e.g., Slis v. State, 956 N.W.2d 569 (Mich.

available. For example, in 2019, the FDA approved Philip Morris's IQOS, an alternative to electronic cigarettes, that heats tobacco without burning it.[296] As "vaping lung" illnesses spread across the nation,[297] the first wrongful death claim was filed in 2019.[298]

Cigarette litigation by states, nations, and insurers. Surely the most significant event in cigarette litigation was the tobacco industry's settlement of the health care reimbursement claims brought by the American states.[299] During the mid-1990s, beginning with Mississippi, the individual states sued the industry on a number of grounds, including public nuisance,[300] unjust enrichment, and restitution[301] to recoup their accumulated expenses for Medicaid health care expenditures resulting from

---

Ct. App. 2020), appeal denied, 948 N.W.2d 82 (Mich. 2020) (Court of Claims did not abuse discretion in granting a preliminary injunction against emergency rules prohibiting the sale and distribution of flavored nicotine vapor products in Michigan); Cigar Ass'n of Am. v. City of Philadelphia, 500 F. Supp. 3d 428 (E.D. Pa. 2020) (granting preliminary injunction; city ordinance banning sale of flavored tobacco products preempted by Pennsylvania law). *But see* R.J. Reynolds Tobacco Co. v. County of Los Angeles, 29 F.4th 542 (9th Cir. 2022) (ordinance banning sale of flavored tobacco products was not expressly or impliedly preempted under the federal Family Smoking Prevention and Tobacco Control Act); R.J. Reynolds Tobacco Co. v. City of Edina, 482 F. Supp. 3d 875 (D. Minn. 2020) (same). For litigation arising from flavored nicotine product marketing targeting youth, see, e.g., In re JUUL Labs, Inc., Mktg., Sales Pracs., & Prods. Liab. Litig., 497 F. Supp. 3d 552, 630, 650, 662, 677 (N.D. Cal. 2020) (denying dismissal of consumers' fraud, public entities' nuisance, and school districts' negligence claims against defendants who marketed their nicotine and electronic nicotine delivery systems to students; RICO claims dismissed with leave to amend); Colgate v. JUUL Labs, Inc., 402 F. Supp. 3d 728, 754 (N.D. Cal. 2019) (minor plaintiffs sufficiently alleged that e-cig products were defectively designed "to encourage use by minors by 'offering candy-like flavors; manipulating nicotine content to increase addictiveness and reduce "throat hit"; adding a light up "party mode" feature; and utilizing a sleek, stylish—and easily concealable—design popular with youth"); Abdel-Baqui and Maloney, Juul to Pay $40 Million to Settle Lawsuit Alleging It Targeted Teens: Suit brought by North Carolina is the first of many against e-cigarette maker set to go to trial, Wall St. J.com (June 28, 2021).

[296] Philip Morris Int'l, IQOS: Tobacco Meets Technology, www.pmi.com/smoke-free-products/iqos-our-tobacco-heating-system. See also LaVito, Philip Morris Allowed to Say IQOS Reduces Harmful Exposure, Prod. Liab. & Toxics L. (July 7, 2020); Kary, Du, and Sasso, Philip Morris Quietly Brings IQOS to U.S. Amid Vaping Uproar, Prod. Liab. & Toxics L. (Oct. 4, 2019); Kary, Philip Morris's By-the-Books E-Cig Approval Now Looks Smart, Prod. Liab. & Toxics L. (Sept. 26, 2019). It is predicted that other electronic cigarette alternatives may also clear FDA review. See, e.g., Kary and Stein, Reynolds Applies for FDA Clearance of Vuse as Vaping Fears Grow, Prod. Liab. & Toxics L. (Oct. 11, 2019).

[297] See Abbott, What We Know About Vaping-Related Lung Illness, Wall St. J.com (Nov. 10, 2019) ("more than 2,000 confirmed and probable cases of pulmonary illness in the U.S. related to vaping and e-cigarette products").

[298] Barash, Juul Hit with Suit Over Teen's Death from Respiratory Injury, Prod. Liab. & Toxics L. (Oct. 15, 2019) (complaint alleged claims for strict product liability, negligence, fraudulent concealment, conspiracy, and violation of California consumer-protection law, among others).

[299] See Gifford, Impersonating the Legislature: State Attorneys General and Paren Patriae Product Litigation, 49 B.C. L. Rev. 913 (2008); Ausness, Public Tort Litigation: Public Benefit or Public Nuisance?, 77 Temp. L. Rev. 825 (2004); Luka, The Tobacco Industry and the First Amendment: An Analysis of the 1998 Master Settlement Agreement, 14 J.L. & Health 297 (1999–2000); Ratliff, Parens Patriae: An Overview, 74 Tul. L. Rev. 1847 (2000); Rachlinski, Regulating in Foresight Versus Judging Liability in Hindsight: The Case of Tobacco, 33 Ga. L. Rev. 813 (1999); Galligan, A Primer on Cigarette Litigation Under the Restatement (Third) of Torts: Products Liability, 27 Sw. U. L. Rev. 487 (1998); Appendix III—Tobacco Settlement Summary, 2 J. Health Care L. & Pol'y 167 (1998); Rabin, The Third Wave of Tobacco Tort Litigation, in Regulating Tobacco (R. Rabin and S. Sugarman eds., 2001); Annot., 25 A.L.R.6th 435 (2007) (Master Settlement Agreement).

[300] See Schwartz and Goldberg, The Law of Public Nuisance: Maintaining Rational Boundaries on a Rational Tort, 45 Washburn L.J. 541, 554–55 (2006); Ausness, Public Tort Litigation: Public Benefit or Public Nuisance?, 77 Temp. L. Rev. 825 (2004). See also Lin, Dodging Public Nuisance, 11 UC Irvine L. Rev. 489, 498–99 (2020).

[301] Other claims include fraud, negligence, breach of warranty, strict liability in tort, and antitrust and consumer protection statutory violations.

tobacco use.[302] In 1998, after settling with Mississippi for $3.6 billion, Texas for $15.3 billion, Florida for $11.3 billion, and Minnesota for $7.1 billion,[303] all on the eve of or during trial, the tobacco industry saw the futility of continuing to fight the well-organized and well-funded state attorneys general and plaintiffs' lawyers and negotiated a global settlement with the states for a total of $246 billion, payable over 25 years.[304]

Following this extraordinarily successful litigation by the states, a number of health insurers, unions, hospitals, and others filed similar "me-too suits" seeking recompense of the costs they had incurred from smokers' health care expenses.[305] None of these claims were successful, the courts reasoning generally that the costs to these types of institutional plaintiffs were too remote to give them standing to complain.[306] In 1999, the United States Department of Justice filed its own suit against the tobacco industry seeking various relief, including a disgorgement of $289 billion in unlawful profits garnered by the tobacco industry over a half century of fraud and deceit.[307] In 2005, the Court of Appeals threw out the government's disgorgement claim.[308] After trial on the

---

[302] See, e.g., State v. Philip Morris Inc., 577 N.W.2d 401 (Iowa 1998) (claims too remote); State v. American Tobacco Co., 14 F. Supp. 2d 956 (E.D. Tex. 1997) (allowing most claims; not too remote); American Tobacco Co. v. Florida, 697 So.2d 1249 (Fla. Dist. Ct. App. 1997) (discovery matters).

[303] The total Minnesota recovery was comprised of $6.6 billion for the state and $469 million for Blue Cross-Blue Shield of Minnesota, which had joined in the suit.

[304] The figure of $246 billion is comprised of the four state settlements (also payable over 25 years) of roughly $40 billion together with a global settlement for the other 46 states plus the District of Columbia and four territories amounting to $206 billion, payable mostly from 2000 to 2025. See Ausness, Public Tort Litigation: Public Benefit or Public Nuisance?, 77 Temp. L. Rev. 825 (2004) (describing each state's litigation).

[305] See, e.g., A.O. Fox Mem'l Hosp. v. American Tobacco Co., 754 N.Y.S.2d 368, 370 (App. Div. 2003) (claims "too remote to permit recovery"); Regence Blueshield v. Philip Morris Inc., 5 Fed. Appx. 651, 653 (9th Cir. 2001) (Wash. law) (plaintiffs' damages were not proximately caused by tobacco firms' "unlawful conduct, but were instead derivative of the personal injuries of smokers afflicted by tobacco-related illnesses"); Service Emps. Int'l Union Health & Welfare Fund v. Philip Morris Inc., 249 F.3d 1068 (D.C. Cir. 2001) (claims too remote, not proximate, and employment health care funds lacked standing); Allegheny Gen. Hosp. v. Philip Morris, Inc., 228 F.3d 429 (3d Cir. 2000) (Pa. law); International Bhd. of Teamsters, Local 734 Health & Welfare Trust Fund v. Philip Morris Inc., 196 F.3d 818, 824 (7th Cir. 1999) (Ill. law); Steamfitters Local Union No. 420 Welfare Fund v. Philip Morris, Inc., 171 F.3d 912 (3d Cir. 1999) (Pa. law) (remoteness; proximate cause). See generally Gangarosa, Vandall, and Willis, Suits by Public Hospitals to Recover Expenditures for the Treatment of Disease, Injury and Disability Caused by Tobacco and Alcohol, 22 Fordham Urb. L.J. 81 (1994).

[306] Attempts to recover health care expenses from cigarette companies under the Medicare Secondary Payer (MSP) statute, 42 U.S.C. § 1395y, have also failed. See, e.g., United Seniors Ass'n v. Philip Morris USA, 500 F.3d 19 (1st Cir. 2007) (no standing to bring claim); Glover v. Liggett Grp., Inc., 459 F.3d 1304, 1309 (11th Cir. 2006) (private right of action under MSP only for persons responsible for paying a Medicare beneficiary's medical costs).

[307] United States v. Philip Morris Inc., 116 F. Supp. 2d 131 (D.D.C. 2000) (allowing RICO claim, but not others, to proceed). "[T]he Justice Department asserts . . . that the major cigarette companies are running what amounts to a criminal enterprise by manipulating nicotine levels, lying to their customers about the dangers of tobacco and directing their multibillion-dollar advertising campaigns at children." Lichtblau, U.S. Lawsuit Seeks Tobacco Profits, N.Y. Times, Mar. 18, 2003, at A1. The U.S. contended that the "defendants' scheme to defraud permeated and influenced all facets of defendants' conduct—research, product development, advertising, marketing, legal, public relations, and communications—in a manner that has resulted in extraordinary profits for the past half-century, but has had devastating consequences for the public's health." Id. A 1971 company research report purportedly refutes the industry's persistent denial of tobacco's addictive qualities by acknowledging the depression, irritability, and "neurotic symptoms" that can result from attempting to quit. The research report "mocked an antismoking commercial that depicted an exuberant couple leaping for joy after they quit smoking" since a "more appropriate commercial would show a restless, nervous, constipated husband bickering viciously with his bitchy wife who is nagging him about his slothful behavior and growing waistline." Id. See also Ausness, Conspiracy Theories: Is There a Place for Civil Conspiracy in Products Liability Litigation?, 74 Tenn. L. Rev. 383, 384–85 (2007).

[308] See U.S. v. Philip Morris, 396 F.3d 1190, 1202 (D.C. Cir. 2005).

remaining claims,[309] the district court denied the government's damages claims, concluding that the Court of Appeals' interpretation of RICO prevented the "backward-looking remedies" demanded by the government, such as monetary penalties and smoker cessation programs. While its hands were tied in this respect, the court did enjoin the defendants from future acts of racketeering and ordered them to make public corrective statements clarifying the risks of smoking, to disclose marketing data to the government, and not to transfer tobacco brands or businesses without the permission of the court.[310]

Several foreign nations also sued the tobacco industry for their health care costs from tobacco diseases, but the cases were dismissed on the ground that the plaintiffs' damages were too remote to satisfy the requirements of proximate cause and standing.[311] An entirely different type of litigation by foreign nations and the European Community[312] involved civil RICO[313] and tort law[314] claims that certain tobacco companies aided and abetted cigarette smuggling into their sovereign borders—black market operations typically bound up with money laundering, organized crime, and even terrorism.[315] Such operations are highly lucrative to tobacco manufacturers who can expand their markets by keeping the price of their cigarettes relatively low by avoiding the sometimes steep taxes imposed on cigarettes by foreign governments. Correspondingly, however, the plaintiff nations (and the EU) lose enormous tax revenues and must bear a variety of other costs, including the costs of maintaining anti-smuggling forces, and the economic and social costs of a sometimes violent criminal black market for cigarettes.[316]

In the first smuggling case to reach the courts, *Attorney General of Canada v. R.J. Reynolds Tobacco Holdings, Inc.*,[317] a federal district court dismissed Canada's case on

---

[309] During the course of the 9-month trial, the Justice Department reduced its demands from $280 billion in penalties to approximately "$14 billion for smoking-cessation programs and antismoking advertising." O'Connell, Anderson, and Fields, Cigarette Companies Escape Major Financial Penalty in Suit, Wall St. J.com (Aug. 18, 2006). See also Lichtblau, Lawyers Fought U.S. Move to Curb Tobacco Penalty, N.Y. Times, June 16, 2005, at A1; Janofsky and Johnston, Limit for Award in Tobacco Case Sets Off Protest, N.Y. Times, June 9, 2005, at A1.

[310] See United States v. Philip Morris USA, Inc., 449 F. Supp. 2d 1, 27–28, 938–45 (D.D.C. 2006) (court's opinion totaled 1,653 pages), order clarified, 477 F. Supp. 2d 191 (D.D.C. 2007), aff'd in part, vacated in part, U.S. v. Philip Morris USA Inc., 566 F.3d 1095 (D.C. Cir. 2009).

[311] See, e.g., State of São Paulo of the Federative Republic of Brazil v. American Tobacco Grp., 919 A.2d 1116, 1122 (Del. 2007) (no standing to sue as parens patriae; collecting cases); Service Emps. Int'l Union Health & Welfare Fund v. Philip Morris Inc., 249 F.3d 1068 (D.C. Cir. 2001) (claims by Guatemala, Nicaragua, and Ukraine were essentially derivative, too remote, damages were not proximate, and defendants lacked standing), aff'g Republic of Guatemala v. Tobacco Inst., Inc., 83 F. Supp. 2d 125 (D.D.C. 1999). See generally Note, 16 Am. U. Int'l L. Rev. 809 (2001) (parens patriae doctrine, unlike remoteness doctrine, would allow proper claims by foreign governments).

[312] See European Cmty. v. Japan Tobacco, Inc., 186 F. Supp. 2d 231 (E.D.N.Y. 2002), vacated in part, 355 F.3d 123 (2d Cir. 2004), vacated and remanded, 544 U.S. 1012 (2005), reinstated, 424 F.3d 175 (2d Cir. 2005).

[313] The claims brought under the Racketeer Influenced and Corrupt Organizations Act ("RICO"), 18 U.S.C. §§ 1961 et seq., alleged that the defendant tobacco companies engaged in and directed a pattern of racketeering activity in conducting cigarette smuggling and money laundering activities.

[314] The tort law claims alleged fraud, public nuisance, restitution for unjust enrichment, negligence, and negligent misrepresentation.

[315] See 147 Cong. Rec. S11028–29 (daily ed. Oct. 25, 2001) (remarks of Sen. Kerry: "Smuggling, money laundering, and fraud against our allies are an important part of the schemes by which terrorism is financed.").

[316] These harms are in addition to the evident health care problems from increased consumption due to the enhanced availability of cigarettes to price-sensitive consumers at lower black-market prices.

[317] 103 F. Supp. 2d 134 (N.D.N.Y. 2000) (dismissing complaint alleging civil RICO violations and common law fraud), aff'd, 268 F.3d 103 (2d Cir. 2001) (2–1 decision). In a powerful dissent, Judge Calabresi

the basis of the "revenue rule," and, in a split decision, the Court of Appeals affirmed. The revenue rule is an archaic doctrine first promulgated by the English courts in the 1700s for the purpose of protecting the lucrative smuggling trade that British merchants then controlled around the world under the protection of the British navy, which ruled the seven seas. In present form, the revenue rule has evolved into an abstention doctrine by which a court may choose whether or not to hear a tax claim brought by a foreign government seeking recovery on a tax debt under foreign law.[318] Parochially perverse from its inception, the revenue rule has been roundly and fairly criticized by modern courts[319] and commentators[320] as an unseemly blight on American jurisprudence in a shrinking global environment where nations must cooperate in deterring transnational criminal conspiracies hatched in, directed from, and carried out in different nations. Despite its serious flaws, the rule has been applied by some courts in order to steer clear of international disputes that may enmesh them, if only indirectly, in enforcing the tax laws of other nations.[321]

Although *Canada* (and its unfortunate progeny) was roundly and properly denounced by courts and commentators, as just mentioned, it led a couple of district judges to dismiss certain smuggling claims against tobacco companies, in one case brought by Ecuador[322] and another, more significant, consolidated action against certain cigarette manufacturers for smuggling, money laundering, and related tortious activities brought by most states of the Republic of Colombia, the European Community, and a majority of its member states.[323] After the district court dismissed most of the EC claims on the basis of *Canada*, the plaintiffs in *European Community* refiled with an emphasis on the defendants' money laundering, racketeering, and various tortious activities, but once again the case was dismissed, and the dismissal affirmed,[324] albeit with a small

reasoned: "It is manifest that the suit before us in no way requires our courts to enforce foreign judgments or claims; it simply is an action for damages provided for and brought under federal law." 268 F.3d at 135.

318 See, e.g., Milwaukee Cnty. v. M.E. White Co., 296 U.S. 268, 275 (1935).

319 See, e.g., European Cmty. v. Japan Tobacco, Inc., 186 F. Supp. 2d 231, 234 (E.D.N.Y. 2002) (noting criticism of rule), vacated in part, 355 F.3d 123 (2d Cir. 2004); European Cmty. v. RJR Nabisco, Inc., 150 F. Supp. 2d 456, 472–86 (E.D.N.Y. 2001) (thoroughly examining basis for, defects in, and applicability of the rule); Banco Frances e Brasileiro S.A. v. John Doe, 331 N.E.2d 502, 505 (N.Y. 1975) (Jasen, J.) (the revenue rule is "justifiable neither precedentially nor analytically").

320 See, e.g., Notes, 51 St. Louis U. L.J. 203 (2006) (characterizing the revenue rule as "archaic," "extremely nationalistic," and "isolationist"), 115 Harv. L. Rev. 2333, 2340 (2002), 77 Wash. L. Rev. 843, 844–45 (2002) (*Canada* "was wrongly decided"), 15 N.Y. Int'l L. Rev. 101 (2002) (*Canada* wrongly decided because it undercut goal of RICO to force wrongdoers to disgorge illicit profits). *But see* Dodge, Breaking the Public Law Taboo, 43 Harv. Int'l L.J. 161, 233–34 (2002) (revenue rule and *Canada* both correct because courts, unlike other branches of government, cannot ensure reciprocity in enforcement of foreign tax laws).

321 "The revenue rule is a longstanding common law doctrine providing that courts of one sovereign will not enforce final tax judgments or unadjudicated tax claims of other sovereigns. It has been defended on several grounds, including respect for sovereignty, concern for judicial role and competence, and separation of powers." *Canada*, 268 F.3d at 109. See also Republic of Ecuador v. Philip Morris Cos., 188 F. Supp. 2d 1359 (S.D. Fla. 2002) (quoting earlier American decisions approving revenue rule), aff'd on point, 341 F.3d 1253 (11th Cir. 2003). *But see* Milwaukee Cnty. v. M.E. White Co., 296 U.S. 268, 272–74 (1935); King of Spain v. Oliver, 14 F. Cas. 577 (C.C.D. Pa. 1810).

322 See Republic of Ecuador v. Philip Morris Cos., 188 F. Supp. 2d 1359 (S.D. Fla. 2002), aff'd on point, 341 F.3d 1253 (11th Cir. 2003).

323 See European Cmty. v. Japan Tobacco, Inc., 186 F. Supp. 2d 231 (E.D.N.Y. 2002) (holding that revenue rule required dismissal of smuggling claims seeking lost tax revenue but that money laundering claims seeking other types of damages might proceed), vacated in part, 355 F.3d 123 (2d Cir. 2004), vacated and remanded, European Cmty. v. RJR Nabisco, Inc., 544 U.S. 1012 (2005), on remand, 424 F.3d 175 (2d Cir. 2005) (reaffirming circuit court's dismissal of claims under revenue rule).

324 European Cmty. v. RJR Nabisco, Inc., 355 F.3d 123 (2d Cir. 2004), vacated and remanded, 544 U.S. 1012 (2005), dismissal reinstated, 424 F.3d 175 (2d Cir. 2005).

window for the plaintiffs to file another lawsuit on their money laundering claims.[325] Apparently the window was large enough, because one defendant settled with the EC soon thereafter for $1.25 billion.[326] It is difficult to predict how long the vilified revenue rule may continue to frustrate efforts in a global economy to halt smuggling and other commercial frauds that respect no borders. Yet, apparently for now, smugglers of cigarettes into foreign nations and those complicit have a curious immunity from the laws of the United States.

Firearms

Background. The criminal abuse of guns, particularly handguns but also various assault rifles, has spawned a morass of litigation and debate.[327] Each year, tens of thousands of Americans are killed by guns—roughly the same number as are killed in car accidents.[328] While initially startling, this statistic reflects the fact that there are substantially more firearms in this nation as people.[329] While some ninety-eight percent of all firearms are used lawfully,[330] the two to three million of those used illegally each year cause enormous injury and suffering.[331] Firearm injuries caused by defective

---

[325] See 355 F.3d at 138.

[326] See, e.g., EU Signs $1.25B Deal with Philip Morris, NY Times.com (AP, July 9, 2004).

[327] See Mullenix, Outgunned No More?: Reviving A Firearms Industry Mass Tort Litigation, 49 Sw. L. Rev. 390 (2021); Thomas and Alexander, Suing Guns Out of Existence?, 75 Wash. & Lee L. Rev. Online 175 (2019); Blower, Guns Don't Kill People, Although 30,000 Americans Each Year Would Disagree: An Analysis of Gun Manufacturer Liability, 7 Rutgers J. L. & Pub. Pol'y 187 (2010); Vandall, A Preliminary Consideration Of Issues Raised In The Firearms Sellers Immunity Bill, 38 Akron L. Rev. 113 (2005); Eggen and Culhane, Public Nuisance Claims Against Gun Sellers: New Insights and Challenges, 38 U. Mich. J.L. Reform 1 (2004); Ausness, Tort Liability for the Sale of Non-Defective Products: An Analysis and Critique of the Concept of Negligent Marketing, 53 S.C. L. Rev. 907 (2002); Eggen and Culhane, Gun Torts: Defining a Cause of Action for Victims in Suits Against Gun Manufacturers, 81 N.C. L. Rev. 115 (2002); Vandall, Economic and Causation Issues in City Suits Against Gun Manufacturers, 27 Pepp. L. Rev. 719 (2001); Lytton, Lawsuits Against the Gun Industry: A Comparative Institutional Analysis, 32 Conn. L. Rev. 1247 (2000); Lytton, Tort Claims Against Gun Manufacturers for Crime-Related Injuries: Defining a Suitable Role for the Tort System in Regulating the Firearms Industry, 65 Mo. L. Rev. 1 (2000); Twerski and Sebok, Liability Without Cause? Further Ruminations on Cause-in-Fact as Applied to Handgun Liability, 32 Conn. L. Rev. 1379 (2000); Kairys, Legal Claims of Cities Against the Manufacturers of Handguns, 71 Temp. L. Rev. 1 (1998); Bogus, Pistols, Politics and Products Liability, 59 U. Cin. L. Rev. 1103 (1991); Hardy, Product Liability and Weapons Manufacture, 20 Wake Forest L. Rev. 541 (1984); Suing the Gun Industry: A Battle at the Crossroads of Gun Control and Mass Torts (T. Lytton ed., 2005); Frumer, Friedman, and Sklaren, Products Liability §§ 3.05, 12.07. Compare 108 Harv. L. Rev. 1679 (1995) (proposing statute imposing absolute liability for manufacture of ammunition), with 97 Harv. L. Rev. 1912, 1928 (1984) (role of handguns in society is properly for legislatures to decide, and courts should not use products liability law to usurp control over issue of handgun control).

[328] With more Americans dying "of gun-related injuries . . . than in any other year on record," the 45,222 gun fatalities in 2020 divided as follows: 54% suicides, 43% homicides, and 3% other causes. While the total number of gun fatalities increased in 2020, the 13.6 deaths per 100,000 people—the highest rate since the 1990s—remained below the highest per capita rate of 16.3 deaths in the 1970s. Gramlich, What the Data Says About Gun Deaths in the U.S., Pew Research Center (Feb. 3, 2022). In addition, another 115,000 people are injured by guns each year. UC Davis Health, Facts and Figures (2022), https://health.ucdavis.edu/what-you-can-do/facts.html.

[329] "With about 121 firearms in circulation for every 100 residents, the United States is by far the most heavily armed society in the world . . . ." Sullivan, Explainer: More Guns Than People: Why Tighter U.S. Firearms Laws Are Unlikely, Reuters (Apr. 14, 2021). Additionally, 31% of households have firearms, and 22% of American adults own one or more firearms. UC Davis Health, Facts and Figures (2022), https://health.ucdavis.edu/what-you-can-do/facts.html.

[330] Barnes, Taking Aim: The Impetus Driving Suits Against Gun Manufacturers, 27 Pepp. L. Rev. 735, 736 (2000).

[331] Between 2003 and 2015, the U.S. firearm homicide rate was 24.9 times higher than the combined rate of other high-income countries; furthermore, the U.S. firearm death rate increased during the period while decreasing in other high-income countries. Grinshteyn and Hemenway, Violent Death Rates in the US Compared to Those of the Other High-Income Countries, 2015, 123 Preventive Med. 20 (2019).

firearms are just like any other kind of products liability case and so are simply noted here.[332] In addition to injuries caused by defective firearms, when retailers sell guns to youths, drunks, mental incompetents, or criminals, foreseeable victims may have claims for negligent entrustment[333] or negligence per se.[334] Much more controversial is whether products liability law should have anything to say about criminally inflicted gun injuries and deaths—an issue that was intensely litigated in courtrooms and debated in legislatures around the nation until Congress banned this type of litigation in 2005, as discussed below.

Injury victim litigation. A spate of decisions in the 1970s and 1980s, frequently pointing to the refusal of legislatures to ban handguns, were hostile to damages claims brought by shooting victims against handgun manufacturers alleging that such guns are inherently defective.[335] Two cases in the 1980s, however, were decided the other way. In the first case, *Richman v. Charter Arms Corp.*,[336] a federal district judge ruled that, while handguns are not defective under ordinary products liability principles, the sale of such a product might constitute an ultrahazardous activity. In the second case, *Kelley v. R.G. Industries, Inc.*,[337] an action against the manufacturer of the handgun used by a grocery store robber to shoot the assistant manager in the chest, the Maryland high court ruled that a manufacturer may be subject to strict liability for selling a general type of product

---

[332] See, e.g., Tosseth v. Remington Arms Co., LLC, 483 F. Supp. 3d 659, 679 (D.N.D. 2020) (denying dismissal of claims that pistol extractor mechanism design defect caused daughter's death); Palatka v. Savage Arms, Inc., 535 Fed. Appx. 448 (6th Cir. 2013) (Mich. law) (barrel of muzzle-loading rifle exploded allegedly due to manufacturing or design defect); Stage v. Stage, 2012 WL 443834 (D. Ariz. 2012) (allowing claim against seller for failing to warn not to use high velocity .45 Colt ammunition in "The Judge" revolver); Ellis v. Beemiller, Inc., 910 F. Supp. 2d 768 (W.D. Pa. 2012) (dismissing malfunction claim that handgun exploded in hand without pulling the trigger; expert testimony necessary to explain apparently impossible event).

[333] See, e.g., Shirley v. Glass, 308 P.3d 1 (Kan. 2013) (sale of gun to convicted felon); Noble v. Shawnee Gun Shop, Inc., 409 S.W.3d 476 (Mo. Ct. App. 2013) (denying claim by parents of murder victims against gun store where murderer purchased gun magazines with stolen credit card, as invalid negligent entrustment claim); Kitchen v. K-Mart Corp., 697 So.2d 1200 (Fla. 1997) (allowing girlfriend victim's negligent entrustment action against retailer for selling gun to her intoxicated boyfriend); Knight v. Wal-Mart Stores, Inc., 889 F. Supp. 1532, 1535 (S.D. Ga. 1995) (allowing negligent entrustment claim against retailer for selling rifle to "crazy" customer who shot and killed himself with rifle). On negligent entrustment, see generally § 15.2, below.

[334] See, e.g., Shirley v. Glass, 308 P.3d 1 (Kan. 2013) (sale of gun to convicted felon; dictum); Williams v. Wal-Mart Stores E., L.P., 99 So.3d 112, 116 (Miss. 2012) (violation of federal gun control act constitutes negligence per se but use of gun to murder mother's boyfriend was not a foreseeable consequence in this case). On negligence per se, see generally § 2.4, above.

[335] See, e.g., Patterson v. Rohm Gesellschaft, 608 F. Supp. 1206, 1209 n.5 (N.D. Tex. 1985) (rejecting plaintiff's risk-utility argument under conventional strict products liability in tort, citing many cases in accord):

> [D]espite this court's admiration for such a delightfully nonsensical claim: that a product which does not have a defect can nevertheless, under the law, be defective—the plaintiff's attorneys are simply wrong. Under Texas law, there can be no products liability recovery unless the product does have a defect. Without this essential predicate, that something is wrong with the product, the risk/utility balancing test does not even apply.

Id. at 1210–11. The court further noted that "the theory advanced by the plaintiff's attorneys perverts the very purpose of the 'risk/utility balancing test' [which] incorporates the idea that a defect is something that can be remedied or changed." Id. at 1212. See also Burkett v. Freedom Arms, Inc., 704 P.2d 118 (Or. 1985) (rejecting strict liability claim based on manufacturer's conducting abnormally dangerous activity); Martin v. Harrington & Richardson, Inc., 743 F.2d 1200 (7th Cir. 1984) (Ill. law) (rejecting theory of manufacturer's strict liability under ultrahazardous activity theory); Mavilia v. Stoeger Indus., 574 F. Supp. 107, 111 (D. Mass. 1983) (rejecting tort claim for marketing handguns and holding "as a matter of law that at least with regard to the .38 caliber Llama automatic pistol, the gun is not inherently defective").

[336] 571 F. Supp. 192 (E.D. La. 1983), summary judgment for one manufacturer aff'd, and summary judgment for other manufacturer ordered in consolidated appeal, Perkins v. F.I.E. Corp., 762 F.2d 1250 (5th Cir. 1985) (La. law) (Wisdom, J.).

[337] 497 A.2d 1143 (Md. 1985).

that on balance is bad for society. *Kelley* held that strict tort liability could be imposed on sellers of "Saturday Night Specials" for harm to victims from the use of such guns.[338] In response to the holding in *Kelley*, the National Rifle Association conducted a multimillion dollar campaign to have the decision overturned, first by the Maryland legislature, and then by the people in a referendum petition. In time, the gun lobby and gun control advocates agreed to compromise legislation that overturned *Kelley* but prohibited the sale of Saturday Night Specials in the state, and the voters, by referendum, approved the law.[339]

A number of subsequent handgun victim cases against manufacturers of handguns,[340] assault rifles,[341] and ammunition[342] have involved claims for design defect, negligent marketing, and strict liability for selling products that are abnormally dangerous.[343] While plaintiffs had some initial success in a number of cases in the lower courts, and occasionally in the appellate courts,[344] most of these gunshot victim cases were dismissed on such grounds as no duty, no defect (the guns or ammo did what they were designed to do), and because of the superseding intervention of criminals putting them to improper use (the abuse of the guns by people, not the guns themselves, are the proximate cause of harm).[345]

Municipality litigation. After the successful partnership of state attorneys general and major plaintiffs' law firms in the cigarette litigation, a number of municipalities filed claims against the gun industry for blanketing their cities with an oversupply of guns, particularly cheap handguns, that far exceeded the lawful market

---

[338] "Saturday Night Specials" are poorly made, cheap, small, inaccurate, and easily concealable handguns useful principally for criminal activity rather than self-protection or other legitimate activity.

[339] The referendum passed by a vote of 58% to 42%. See Bogus, Pistols, Politics and Products Liability, 59 U. Cin. L. Rev. 1103, 1145–48 (1991). See generally Halliday v. Sturm, Ruger & Co., 792 A.2d 1145 (Md. 2002) (child shot himself in head with father's gun; describing legislative developments and rejecting claim that gun was defective for failing to have child-proof design).

[340] See, e.g., Halliday v. Sturm, Ruger & Co., 792 A.2d 1145 (Md. 2002) (no design defect under consumer expectations test); Hamilton v. Beretta U.S.A. Corp., 750 N.E.2d 1055 (N.Y. 2001) (no duty), answering certified question from Hamilton v. Beretta U.S.A. Corp., 222 F.3d 36 (2d Cir. 2000). See also id., 264 F.3d 21 (2d Cir. 2001) (ordering that Weinstein, J., dismiss Hamilton v. Accu-Tek, 62 F. Supp. 2d 802 (E.D.N.Y. 1999)).

[341] See, e.g., Merrill v. Navegar, Inc., 28 P.3d 116 (Cal. 2001), rev'g 89 Cal. Rptr. 2d 146 (Ct. App. 1999). See also Kromke, California's Legislative Response to Merrill v. Navegar: An Analysis, 24 Whittier L. Rev. 833 (2003).

[342] See McCarthy v. Olin Corp., 119 F.3d 148 (2d Cir. 1997) (N.Y. law) (2–1 decision) (Black Talon hollow-point bullets not defectively designed; dissenting, Calabresi, J., reasoned that the bullets properly might be classified as egregiously unsafe and, hence, not immune from liability), aff'g McCarthy v. Sturm, Ruger & Co., 916 F. Supp. 366 (S.D.N.Y. 1996).

[343] See Benston and Vandall, Legal Control Over the Supply of Handguns: An Analysis of the Issues, With Particular Attention to the Law and Economics of the Hamilton v. Beretta Lawsuit Against Handgun Manufacturers, 26 Pace L. Rev. 305 (2006).

[344] See Ileto v. Glock Inc., 349 F.3d 1191 (9th Cir. 2003) (Cal. law) (2–1 decision) (allowing negligence and public nuisance claims, and noting legislature's actions to permit claims against gun manufacturers). But the case was dismissed on remand under the retroactive provision of the Protection of Lawful Commerce in Arms Act, discussed below. See Ileto v. Glock, Inc., 421 F. Supp. 2d 1274, 1304 (C.D. Cal. 2006), aff'd, 565 F.3d 1126 (9th Cir. 2009).

[345] The Products Liability Restatement includes firearms in its short list of inherently dangerous products that are not defective in design. See Products Liability Rest. § 2 cmt. *d*. On negligent marketing, see Ausness, Tort Liability for the Sale of Non-Defective Products: An Analysis and Critique of the Concept of Negligent Marketing, 53 S.C. L. Rev. 907, 962–64 (2002) (criticizing negligent marketing concept as paternalistic and elitist); McClurg, The Tortious Marketing of Handguns: Strict Liability Is Dead, Long Live Negligence, 19 Seton Hall Legis. J. 777, 806–18 (1996) (praising negligent marketing theory).

for firearms.[346] Following the first such suit by New Orleans in 1998, over 30 cities and counties instituted such "recoupment" lawsuits seeking to recover the various municipal costs associated with gun violence—such as the increased expenses of law enforcement, emergency rescue services, medical care for gunshot victims, prosecutorial and prison services, social services, and lost tax revenues. Such lawsuits typically made claims against gun manufacturers, distributors, trade associations, and major retailers for defective design because of the absence of safety features; failure to provide adequate warnings; negligent marketing and distribution; public nuisance; deceptive trade practices; and restitution for unjust enrichment. Most of these cases were dismissed,[347] but a number survived motions to dismiss and several withstood appeal.[348]

From the start, the municipality gun cases confronted a number of formidable doctrinal roadblocks. The large variety of obstacles to such litigation included standing, duty, proximate cause (or remoteness), the inappropriateness of public nuisance and restitution in this new type of litigation, and the persistent (if dubious) doctrine prohibiting public bodies from recovering the costs of emergency governmental services, called the "municipal cost recovery rule."[349] In time, a growing number of state statutes prohibited actions against gun manufacturers in general or, more narrowly, prohibited

[346] See Lin, Dodging Public Nuisance, 11 UC Irvine L. Rev. 489, 498–99 (2020); Wagner, When All Else Fails: Regulating Risky Products Through Tort Litigation, 95 Geo. L.J. 693, 720–27 (2007); Schwartz and Goldberg, The Law of Public Nuisance: Maintaining Rational Boundaries on a Rational Tort, 45 Washburn L.J. 541, 555–57 (2006); Ausness, Public Tort Litigation: Public Benefit or Public Nuisance?, 77 Temp. L. Rev. 825 (2004); Gifford, Public Nuisance as a Mass Products Liability Tort, 71 U. Cin. L. Rev. 743 (2003); Ausness, Tort Liability for the Sale of Non-Defective Products: An Analysis and Critique of the Concept of Negligent Marketing, 53 S.C. L. Rev. 907, 936 (2002); Kairys, The Origin and Development of the Governmental Handgun Cases, 32 Conn. L. Rev. 1163 (2000); Kairys, The Governmental Handgun Cases and the Elements and Underlying Policies of Public Nuisance, 32 Conn. L. Rev. 1175 (2000); D. Gifford, Suing the Tobacco and Lead Pigment Industries: Government Litigation as Public Health Prescription (U. Mich. Press 2010).

[347] See, e.g., District of Columbia v. Beretta U.S.A. Corp., 2002 WL 31811717 (D.C. Super. Ct. 2002) (no duty, proximate cause, and remoteness under Holmes v. Securities Investor Prot. Corp., 503 U.S. 258 (1992)), rev'd in part, 847 A.2d 1127 (D.C. 2004) (no duty or standing), vacated and superseded, 872 A.2d 633 (D.C. 2005) (en banc), judgment for defendant on pleadings as preempted under PLCAA, 2006 WL 1892023 (D.C. Super. Ct. 2006), aff'd, 940 A.2d 163 (D.C. 2008); Philadelphia v. Beretta U.S.A. Corp., 277 F.3d 415 (3d Cir. 2002) (no duty, no proximate cause, remoteness, and no standing); Baker v. Smith & Wesson Corp., 2002 WL 31741522 (Del. Super. Ct. 2002) (municipal cost recovery rule bars action). See also City of N.Y. v. Beretta U.S.A. Corp., 524 F.3d 384 (2d Cir. 2008) (ordering Judge Weinstein to dismiss nuisance claims as barred by the PLCAA), rev'g 401 F. Supp. 2d 244, 258–71 (E.D.N.Y. 2005).

[348] See, e.g., James v. Arms Tech., Inc., 820 A.2d 27 (N.J. Super. Ct. App. Div. 2003) (allowing negligence, public nuisance, and punitive damages claims); Cincinnati v. Beretta U.S.A. Corp., 768 N.E.2d 1136 (Ohio 2002) (rejecting defenses including municipal cost recovery rule); White v. Smith & Wesson, 97 F. Supp. 2d 816 (N.D. Ohio 2000) (Cleveland) (same); City of Boston v. Smith & Wesson Corp., 2000 WL 1473568 (Mass. Super. Ct. 2000) (same). See also District of Columbia v. Beretta, U.S.A., Corp., 872 A.2d 633 (D.C. 2005) (en banc) (allowing subrogated damages claims for medical expenses of named individuals together with claims by injured individuals).

[349] Also referred to as the "free public services doctrine." Compare City of Chi. v. Beretta U.S.A. Corp., 821 N.E.2d 1099, 1147 (Ill. 2004) (dismissing action; municipal cost recovery rule bars money damages), and Baker v. Smith & Wesson Corp., 2002 WL 31741522 (Del. Super. Ct. 2002) (applying doctrine and dismissing action), with James v. Arms Tech., Inc., 820 A.2d 27 (N.J. Super. Ct. App. Div. 2003) (rejecting doctrine and allowing action to proceed). See generally Lytton, Should Government Be Allowed to Recover the Costs of Public Services from Tortfeasors?: Tort Subsidies, the Limits of Loss Spreading, and the Free Public Services Doctrine, 76 Tul. L. Rev. 727, 728 (2002) (arguing for the rule's abrogation because it "shields industrial tortfeasors from liability[,] constitutes a tort subsidy to industry and functions as an insurance scheme for industrial accidents paid for by taxpayers"). See also Ausness, Public Tort Litigation: Public Benefit or Public Nuisance?, 77 Temp. L. Rev, 825, 892–95 (2004).

claims by local governments against manufacturers and other sellers for injuries caused by guns.[350]

Reform legislation. Beginning in the 1980s, a number of states enacted legislation seeking to protect makers and sellers of firearms and ammunition from products liability exposure for injury and death resulting from their improper use.[351] Many of the statutes bar the use of risk-benefit analysis for judging the defectiveness of guns and ammunition,[352] and some provide that it is the unlawful use of such products, not their lawful manufacture and sale, that is the proximate cause of most such harm.[353] The National Rifle Association lobbied vigorously for reform legislation along these lines, and many states enacted statutes of this general type.[354] At least two state statutes remove authority from localities to sue manufacturers and other sellers of firearms and ammunition for damages resulting from their lawful manufacture and sale, reserving the right to bring such actions to the state.[355] Pointing in the other direction, toward gun control, the District of Columbia enacted ordinances in the early 1990s providing that manufacturers and other sellers who knowingly engage in the illegal sale of a firearm,[356] including certain specified assault weapons,[357] are strictly liable in tort for injury or death resulting from the discharge of such a firearm in the District.

In 2005, Congress enacted The Protection of Lawful Commerce in Arms Act[358] that bars litigation against manufacturers for injuries arising out of the "criminal or unlawful misuse" of firearms or ammunition.[359] While the statute continues to allow conventional actions for firearm injuries (as for defective manufacture and negligent entrustment),[360] and while its "predicate exception" leaves open certain types of litigation,[361] the statute

---

[350] See Owen & Davis on Products Liability Appendix J (*Firearms*).

[351] See id.

[352] See, e.g., Cal. Civ. Code § 1714.4(a) (1983) ("no firearm or ammunition shall be deemed defective in design on the basis that the benefits of the product do not outweigh the risk of injury, damage, or death when discharged"), repealed in 2002.

[353] See, e.g., S.D. Codified Laws § 21–58–1 ("the unlawful use of firearms, rather than their lawful manufacture, distribution, or sale, is the proximate cause of any injury arising from their unlawful use").

[354] See Owen & Davis on Products Liability Appendix J (*Firearms*) (statutes in Alaska; Cal., repealed 2002; Colo.; Fla.; Id.; Ind.; La.; Mont.; Nev.; N.C.; S.C.; S.D.; Tenn.; Tex.; Wash). See, e.g., Seguin v. Remington Arms Co., 31 F.4th 311, 319 (5th Cir. 2022) (La. law) (reversing $500,000 judgment for injured plaintiff; held: La. Stat. Ann. § 9:2800.60 prohibits design defect claims against firearm manufacturers).

[355] See Me. Rev. Stat. Ann. tit. 30–A, § 2005; Tenn. Code Ann. § 39–17–1314.

[356] See D.C. Code §§ 7–2531.01 et seq.

[357] See id. §§ 7–2551.01 et seq.

[358] 15 U.S.C. §§ 7901 et seq.

[359] Id. § 7903(5)(A).

[360] The Act expressly allows "(ii) an action brought against a seller for negligent entrustment or negligence per se; . . . (iv) an action for breach of contract or warranty in connection with the purchase of the product; [or] (v) an action for death, physical injuries or property damage resulting directly from a defect in design or manufacture of the product, when used as intended or in a reasonably foreseeable manner, except that where the discharge of the product was caused by a volitional act that constituted a criminal offense. . . ." 15 U.S.C. § 7903(5)(A). See, e.g., Delana v. CED Sales, Inc., 486 S.W.3d 316, 326 (Mo. 2016) (en banc) (plaintiff's negligent entrustment claim was not preempted under the PLCAA). Compare In re Academy, Ltd., 625 S.W.3d 19, 31–32 (Tex. 2021) ("[N]o viable cause of action exists under Texas law for negligent entrustment based on a sale of chattel[, nor may the plaintiffs] rely on the negligent-entrustment exception to pursue their claims" against retailer that sold semi-automatic rifle used to kill 26 and injure 20 church attendees).

[361] The exception for predicate statutory violations allows claims if a defendant knowingly violates a state or federal statute "applicable to the sale or marketing of the product," possibly including state nuisance statutes. 15 U.S.C. § 7903(5)(A)(iii). See, e.g., Soto v. Bushmaster Firearms Int'l, LLC, 202 A.3d 262, 325 (Conn. 2019) (reversing dismissal of plaintiffs' wrongful marketing claims against manufacturer of rifle used to kill 26 children and adults at the Sandy Hook Elementary School in 2012; violation of the Connecticut Unfair

does put to rest the principal types of inherent risk litigation for damages caused by the unlawful use of non-defective guns that increasingly threatened firearm manufacturers during the late 1990s and early 2000s.[362]

Tasers. Stun guns ("tasers"), which are designed to disable rather than kill a victim, are now widely used by police departments across the nation. While these devices usually are a more humane way to stop criminals than ordinary guns, they nevertheless can be "overused" cruelly, and they occasionally may cause a victim's heart to fail. Accordingly, this form of "gun" has spawned debate and litigation. Yet, because the very purpose of tasers is to disable a victim, and because their manufacturer provides police department purchasers with comprehensive warnings of danger and instructions on proper use, litigation against TASER has quite widely failed.[363]

3D-printed guns. Beginning in the early 2010s, 3D printers made possible the personal manufacture at home of a controversial new type of handgun made of plastic. Such 3D-printed guns are a form of "ghost gun," meaning that they cannot be traced by a serial number or registration like ordinary guns.[364] To make such a gun, a person with

---

Trade Practices Act prohibiting "the unethical advertising of dangerous products for illegal purposes . . . qualifies as a predicate statute" under the PLCAA); Englund v. World Pawn Exchange, LLC, 2017 WL 7518923, at *6 (Or. Cir. Ct. 2017) (trial order) (claims against internet arms seller and pawn shop middleman for straw man gun sales to mother of convicted felon suffering from mental and drug addiction infirmities fell under Act's predicate exception); Williams v. Beemiller, Inc., 952 N.Y.S.2d 333, 339 (App. Div. 2012) (reversing dismissal; claims fell under the Act's predicate exception); City of N.Y. v. A-1 Jewelry & Pawn, Inc., 247 F.R.D. 296, 348–53 (E.D.N.Y. 2007) (public nuisance claims against out-of-state retailers fell under the Act's predicate exception); Smith & Wesson Corp. v. City of Gary, 875 N.E.2d 422, 434 (Ind. Ct. App. 2007) (public nuisance, negligence, and negligent design claims against firearm manufacturers, distributors, and retailers fell under Act's predicate exception). See also Adames v. Shehan, 909 N.E.2d 742, 741 (Ill. 2009) (holding that the Act barred design defect and failure to warn claims; child who accidentally shot and killed his friend committed "a volitional act constit[uting] a criminal offense"). See generally Rojas, Zraick, and Closson, Sandy Hook Families Settle With Gunmaker for $73 Million Over Massacre, N.Y. Times.com (Feb. 15, 2022); Mullenex, Outgunned No More?: Reviving A Firearms Industry Mass Tort Litigation, 49 Sw. L. Rev. 390 (2021) (exploring whether *Soto v. Bushmaster*, above, may fuel a new wave of firearm litigation).

In 2021, in reaction to gun violence, New York enacted legislation to hold "those responsible for the illegal or unreasonable sale, manufacture, distribution, importing or marketing of firearms . . . liable for the public nuisance caused by such activities." 2021 Sess. Law News of N.Y. Ch. 237 (S. 7196), codified as N.Y. Gen. Bus. Law §§ 898–a–e. Gun manufacturers challenged the nuisance law under the preemptive effect of the PLCAA. See, e.g., Barash, Gun Makers Challenge Addition of Firearms to N.Y. Nuisance Law, Prod. Liab. & Toxics L. (Dec. 16, 2021).

[362] See, e.g., Travieso v. Glock Inc., 526 F. Supp. 3d 533, 548–51 (D. Ariz. 2021) (14-year-old girl's accidental discharge of firearm that caused plaintiff's paraplegia was a criminal offense triggering the Act's preemption of products liability claims; Act was constitutional under the Fifth and Tenth Amendments to the U.S. Constitution); Prescott v. Slide Fire Solutions, LP, 341 F. Supp. 3d 1175, 1191 (D. Nev. 2018) (mass shooting victims' claims against bump stock manufacturer failed under the Act); Ileto v. Glock, Inc., 565 F.3d 1126 (9th Cir. 2009) (Act preempts ordinary state law claims in tort and nuisance), noted, 35 S. Ill. U. L.J. 573 (2011); City of N.Y. v. Beretta U.S.A. Corp., 524 F.3d 384, 404 (2d Cir. 2008) (Act prohibits city claims for injunctive relief).

[363] See, e.g., Mitchell v. City of Warren, 803 F.3d 223 (2015) (arrestee died from cardiac arrest after law enforcement officers stunned him; affirming summary judgment for manufacturer on failure to warn and negligence claims); Bachtel v. TASER Int'l, Inc., 747 F.3d 965 (8th Cir. 2014) (traffic stop detainee died after taser shot; affirming summary judgment for manufacturer on warning and design defect claims). See generally Eisler, Szep, Reid, and Smith, Shock Tactics: Inside the Weapon That Transformed Policing, Reuters Investigates (2017) (6-part interactive series).

There is considerable federal regulation of guns and gun accessories apart from the regulation of ordinary handguns, 3D-printed guns, and tasers—such as for machine guns, other types guns, silencers, and bump stocks. See, e.g., Gun Owners of Am., Inc. v. Garland, 992 F.3d 446 (6th Cir. 2021) (2–1 decision) (ATF erred in classifying bump stocks as "machine guns"). Such issues lie outside the scope of this book.

[364] See Thrush, 'Ghost Guns': Firearm Kits Bought Online Fuel Epidemic of Violence, N.Y. Times.com (Nov. 14, 2021); Jacobs, 3D-Printed Firearms and Defense Distributed: A Guide to Understanding "Ghost

a 3D printer today can merely downland its blueprints, readily available on the internet, and then "print" the files. For some years, the federal government prohibited actors from posting on the internet computer aided design (CAD) blueprint files for printing 3D guns and their components,[365] but such files once again are readily available for download to 3D printers.[366] One danger of such guns is that they are prone to explode in a user's hand, risking serious injuries to both the user and bystanders.[367] Whether the "designer" of these guns, who posts CAD blueprint files on the internet for making such guns, may be subject to liability—if such a gun proves "defective," explodes, and causes injury—is a question that may one day confront courts and legislatures.[368] Because the broader issue of liability for publishing blueprints for defective products concerns at root the liability of a publisher, it is considered in a later section on that specific topic.[369]

Drugs

In general. An important category of inherently dangerous products consists of prescription drugs,[370] ingestible products comprised of chemicals designed to alter the human body. Normally, the chemical compounds in prescription drugs are properly researched, designed, tested, produced, and labeled such that they accomplish their objectives of ameliorating human pathologies effectively and with minimal (or acceptable) harmful side effects. But drug manufacturers sometimes fail to discover or anticipate harmful side effects, and on occasion drug manufacturers may knowingly overlook or even conceal the risks of a profitable new drug.[371]

Guns" (2020); Jacobs & Haberman, 3D-Printed Firearms, Do-It-Yourself Guns, & the Second Amendment, 80 Law and Contemporary Problems 129 (2017).

365 See, e.g., Defense Distributed v. Grewal, 971 F.3d 485, 488 (5th Cir. 2020) (recounting the distribution history of the 3D-printer firearm CAD files and blueprints). Presently, California, Connecticut, the District of Columbia, Hawaii, New Jersey, New York, Rhode Island, Virginia, and Washington State have regulations that prohibit the manufacture, sale, or use of ghost guns. See Geller and Knier, 3D Printer Guns Are Threat to Public Safety, Officials Say, WUSA 9 (May 13/17, 2021).

366 See, e.g., Iovino, Ninth Circuit Lifts Ban on 3D-Printed Gun Blueprints ("but the Biden administration is expected to propose new restrictions on so-called ghost guns by May 8"), Courthouse News Service (Apr. 27, 2021); Wille, Defcad, A Website for 3D-Printed Gun Blueprints, Is Back Online (Mar. 30, 2020), www.inputmag.com/tech/defcad-a-website-netflix-for-3d-printed-guns-blueprints-is-back-online.

367 "Plastics struggle with the pressures of live ammunition, and often misfire, break, or explode in the user's hand." Just How Dangerous Are 3D Printed Guns?, www.3dsourced.com/important/3d-printed-gun-pistol/ (2020).

368 See, e.g., Bonti, Ready, Aim, Print: 3d Printing, Guns and Product Liability Cases, 38 No. 1 Trial Advoc. (FDLA) 30 (2019); Note, Showdown at High Noon: Whether a Person Injured By a "Liberator" 3d-Printed Firearm Can Recover On a Product Liability Claim Under the Third Restatement, 72 Rutgers U. L. Rev. 543 (2020).

369 See § 16.7, below.

370 Dangers in over-the-counter drugs normally are less serious but nonetheless may be substantial in individual cases. On drug litigation generally, see ch. 18, below.

371 See, e.g., Kendall v. Hoffman-La Roche, Inc., 36 A.3d 541 (N.J. 2012) (affirming over $10 million award for failing to warn of risk that acne medication could cause inflammatory bowel disease); Knipe v. SmithKline Beecham, 583 F. Supp. 2d 602, 639 (E.D. Pa. 2008) (Pa. and N.J. law) (allowing claims for compensatory and punitive damages to parents against manufacturer of anti-depressive medication for marketing drug " 'without any warnings concerning the risk of suicidal behavior despite clear, statistically significant clinical trial results showing that Paxil-treated adolescent patients engaged in suicidal behavior four times the rate that placebo treated patients did' and hid the data from the medical community"). The same is sometimes true of medical devices. See Eichenwald, Maker Admits That It Hid Problems of Artery Tool, NY Times.com (June 13, 2003). See also Conk, Punctuated Equilibrium: Why Section 402A Flourished and the Third Restatement Languished, 26 Rev. Litig. 799, 860–61 (2007) (public health scientists, government auditors, and the National Academy of Sciences all recognize "that quite little is known at time of approval about a new drug or device's toxicity and other long-term effects, and that our existing passive Adverse Event

Reports of new prescription drug side-effect problems appear with some frequency, as prominently was the case with Vioxx, a painkiller taken by about 20 million people before it was removed from the market in 2004 after an internal clinical study revealed that it doubled the risk of heart attacks and strokes in long-term users.[372] In 2007, the manufacturer settled most of the cases for nearly $5 billion.[373] The following year, the manufacturer of two other popular painkillers, Bextra and Celebrex, settled many similar claims for just under $1 billion.[374] Apart from the typical issues of warning adequacy,[375] the most significant (and provocative) inherent risk issue in drug products liability litigation is whether a manufacturer of prescription pharmaceuticals may be subject to liability for *design* defects in such products, an issue treated later from a variety of perspectives.[376]

Opioids. America is in the midst of an opioid addiction epidemic.[377] It began when Purdue Pharma first marketed OxyContin (a prescription opioid, which is a synthetic substance that mimics opiates from poppies) for pain relief in the1990s. Purdue, other manufacturers, and distributors soon began aggressively to market a variety of narcotics for pain relief to the medical community, pushing doctors to widen their use of opioids while downplaying the addictiveness of these drugs. Opioid prescriptions peaked in 2012, but opioid overdose deaths continue to mount. Nearly 70,000 Americans died from such overdoses in 2020, many from illicit and often deadly Fentanyl from China made in Mexican factory mills. More than half a million Americans have now died from opioid overdoses.

Since the mid-2010s, several thousand lawsuits have been filed against opioid manufacturers, distributors, and pharmacies, mostly by state and local governments. These claims, alleging misrepresentation, public nuisance, and violations of various statutes, seek recovery of billions of dollars for the extra police, health, and social services caused by the opioid crisis.[378] The cascading nature of such claims led Purdue

---

Reporting system clearly serves the public poorly"). On punitive damages, see Owen & Davis on Products Liability ch. 26.

[372] See Bernstein and Bernstein, An Information Prescription for Drug Regulation, 54 Buff. L. Rev. 569 (2006) (discussing phen-fen, Propulsid, and Vioxx litigation). Another major drug side-effects problem involved Zyprexa, an antipsychotic medication with allegedly inadequate warnings of the risks of weight gain and diabetes, which led to tens of thousands of claims. See Childs, When the Bell Can't Be Unrung: Document Leaks and Protective Orders in Mass Tort Litigation, 27 Rev. Litig. 565 (2008). Many other drugs could be added to the list.

[373] Claimant Enrollment in Settlement Meets 85 Percent Threshold, Merck Says, 36 Prod. Safety & Liab. Rep. (BNA) 10, at 237 (Mar. 10, 2008); Johnson, Merck to Pay $4.85B Vioxx Settlement (Nov. 9, 2007). Prior to settlement, some 60,000 personal injury Vioxx cases, together with about 265 class action petitions, had been filed against Merck. Of the cases tried, Merck had won 11 and lost five. See generally In re Vioxx Prods. Liab. Litig., 501 F. Supp. 2d 776 (E.D. La. 2007) (denying Merck's motion for summary judgment on federal preemption grounds); In re Vioxx Prods. Liab. Litig., 501 F. Supp. 2d 789 (E.D. La. 2007) (discovery order).

[374] Celebrex: Federal Court Gives Preliminary Approval to $894 Million Celebrex/Bextra Settlement, 37 Prod. Safety & Liab. Rep. (BNA) 362 (Mar. 30, 2009).

[375] See § 18.3, below.

[376] See § 10.4 (unavoidable dangers and state of the art), § 14.5 (preemption), and § 18.2 (drugs—design liability), below.

[377] See generally Stobbe, COVID-19, Overdoses Pushed US to Highest Death Total Ever, AP (Apr. 12, 2022) (provisional data suggests U.S. will have at least 105,000 overdose drug deaths in 2021, up from 93,000 in 2020); Llamas, Opioid Lawsuits, drugwatch.com/opioids/lawsuits.

[378] In 2017, the Judicial Panel on Multidistrict Litigation consolidated many of the lawsuits in the Northern District of Ohio under Judge Polster. See In re Nat'l Prescription Opiate Litigation, 290 F. Supp. 3d 1375 (U.S. Jud. Pan. Mult. Lit. 2017).

Pharma to file for bankruptcy protection in 2019, with a plan to settle all claims against the company and its owners for $10–12 billion dollars and for the company to emerge from bankruptcy as a public benefit trust corporation for the benefit of opioid victims.[379] In 2020, the bankruptcy court approved an $8.34 billion settlement between Purdue and the U.S. Justice Department,[380] and in 2021, further approved an additional contribution of $4.5 billion from the Sackler family, Purdue's owners. After a federal district court rejected the Sackler family immunity deal as impermissible under the bankruptcy code, the bankruptcy court approved the Sacklers' 2022 offer to increase their contribution to $6 billion.[381] Other defendants have also settled many claims, most notably the three largest opioid distributors and Johnson and Johnson in a $26 billion settlement in 2021.[382]

An especially important opioid case was decided in Oklahoma. Here, after a 33-day bench trial, the state of Oklahoma prevailed in a public nuisance claim against Johnson and Johnson in 2019. The judge held J & J liable under Oklahoma's public nuisance statute for using false, misleading, and dangerous marketing campaigns to sell its prescription opioids and ordered J & J to fund a $465 million opioid abatement program that included 21 state programs to combat opioid abuse.[383] In 2021, the Oklahoma Supreme Court reversed, concluding that the trial court erroneously broadened public nuisance law into an unbounded cause of action that infringed on the authority of the executive and legislative branches to use public policy to remedy public health and social problems.[384] The court compellingly reasoned that so extending public nuisance law to include the manufacture, marketing, and sale of legal products would "hold manufacturers perpetually liable for their products" and "allow consumers to 'convert almost every products liability action into a [public] nuisance claim.' "[385]

In another public nuisance case brought by two Ohio counties, a federal jury in 2021 found that three major pharmacies, Walmart, CVS, and Walgreens, had created a public

[379] Randazzo and Hopkins, Oxycontin Maker Purdue Pharma Files for Bankruptcy Protection, Wall St. J.com (Sept. 16, 2019). Some claimants opposed the settlement, and some state and municipality litigation against Purdue remained active. See, e.g., Hill, Purdue Pharma Challengers Seek to Stop Settlement Pending Appeal, Prod. Liab. & Toxics L. (Sept. 20, 2021).

[380] See, e.g., Chutchian, Purdue Pharma Judge OKs Government Deal, Pleads for Bankruptcy Exit Plan, Reuters (Nov. 18, 2020). Another opioid manufacturer, Insys, also filed for bankruptcy protection.

[381] See, e.g., Randles, Purdue Pharma's Sackler Family Approved for $6 Billion Opioid Deal With States: The agreement requires Purdue prevailing in an appeal by the Justice Department's bankruptcy division, Wall St. J.com (Mar. 9, 2022); Randles, Judge Throws Out Purdue Pharma's Deal to Shield Sacklers from Opioid Lawsuits, Wall St. J.com (Dec. 16, 2021). See also § 15.7, notes 418–420, below.

[382] See, e.g., Randazzo, States Announce $26 Billion Settlement to Resolve Opioid Lawsuits, Wall St. J.com (July 21, 2021).

[383] See, e.g., Feeley, Oklahoma to Appeal Ruling J&J Must Pay $465 Million Over Opioids, Prod. Liab. & Toxics L. (Nov. 21, 2019). Two other manufacturers, Teva and Purdue, settled before trial for $85 and $ 270 million, respectively.

[384] State ex rel. Hunter v. Johnson & Johnson, 499 P.3d 719, 731 (Okla. 2021) (5–1 decision). See Mann, Oklahoma's Supreme Court tossed out a landmark $465 million opioid ruling (NPR Nov. 9, 2021). On Nov. 1, 2021, a California Superior Court dismissed a similar public nuisance opioid case on causation grounds. Id.

[385] Id. at 730. Dissenting, Judge Edmondson argued that the public nuisance cause of action existed in the common law and that the public nuisance statute imposed liability on J & J for the time during which it deceptively marketed prescription opioids. Id. at 748. For state public nuisance claims against cigarette manufacturers, see *Cigarette litigation by states, nations, and insurers*, above. Public nuisance claims in municipal firearm litigation are addressed in notes 346–349, above, and lead paint public nuisance litigation is discussed at notes 433–443, below.

nuisance by not properly monitoring opioid prescriptions.[386] Public nuisance and other claims remain pending in a number of courts around the nation, and it is too early to know if other courts will follow the approach of the Ohio federal court, holding large retailers liable, or will instead see the logic of the Oklahoma Supreme Court in harnessing the public nuisance claim in products liability cases of this type.[387] Be that as it may, the rulings and other developments to date suggest that the trend toward settling many of the remaining opioid claims may well accelerate.[388]

Asbestos

In general. For many decades, asbestos, a mineral whose tiny, deadly fibers cause severe lung diseases, has devastated workers, suppliers, and the courts.[389] Since the 1970s, courts have been barraged with hundreds of thousands of cases involving the ravages of this mineral on people who mined and worked with it, and on their family members. Despite its highly useful insulation characteristics, asbestos has caused so much death and suffering[390] that it fairly might be viewed as inherently defective in design on a "macro-balance" of its aggregate social costs and benefits.[391] From the start of the asbestos litigation, however, asbestos has not been litigated for being defective per

---

[386] See, e.g., Feeley, Walmart, CVS, Walgreens Fueled Opioid Crisis, Jury Concludes, U.S. Law Week (Nov. 24, 2021). Now that liability has been determined, Judge Polster has scheduled a hearing on damages for May 2022.

[387] Mann, Oklahoma's Supreme Court Tossed Out a Landmark $465 Million Opioid Ruling, NPR.org (Nov. 9, 2021). On Nov. 1, 2021, a California Superior Court dismissed a similar public nuisance opioid case on causation grounds. Id.

[388] See, e.g., Banerjee, CVS Health Reaches $484 Million Opioid Settlement with Florida, Reuters (Mar. 30, 2022); Feuer, AmerisourceBergen, Cardinal Health, McKesson Agree to Opioid Settlement With 46 States, Wall St. J.com (Feb. 25, 2022) (distributors to pay $19.5 billion over 18 years); Lin, J&J Settles with State of New Mexico Over Opioid Claims, Prod. Liab. & Toxics L. (Jan. 14, 2022); Chang, J&J in $63m Pact with Nevada for Opioid-Related Claims, Prod. Liab. & Toxics L. (Jan. 4, 2022); Maher, Allergan Reaches $200 Million Opioid Settlement With New York State, Counties, Wall St. J.com (Dec. 8, 2021).

[389] On asbestos litigation generally, see, e.g., Brickman, Civil Rico: An Effective Deterrent to Fraudulent Asbestos Litigation?, 40 Cardozo L. Rev. 2301 (2019); Hare and Ryan, The More Things Change: Bankruptcy Trust Reform and the Status Quo in Asbestos Litigation, 85 Def. Couns. J. 1 (2018); Behrens, Asbestos Trust Transparency, 87 Fordham L. Rev. 107 (2018); Schwartz, A Letter to the Nation's Trial Judges: Asbestos Litigation, Major Progress Made Over the Past Decade and Hurdles You Can Vault in the Next, 36 Am. J. Trial Advoc. 1 (2012); Behrens, What's New in Asbestos Litigation, 28 Rev. Litig. 501 (2009); McGovern, The Tragedy of the Asbestos Commons, 88 Va. L. Rev. 1721 (2002); Page, Asbestos and the Dalkon Shield: Corporate America on Trial, 85 Mich. L. Rev. 1324 (1987); Am. Law Prod. Liab. ch. 122; S. Carroll, D. Hensler, et al., Asbestos Litigation (RAND 2005); P. Brodeur, Outrageous Misconduct: The Asbestos Industry on Trial (Pantheon 1986). See also note 410, below.

[390] See Hensler, Asbestos Litigation in the United States: Triumph and Failure of the Civil Justice System, 12 Conn. Ins. L.J. 255, 256–57 (2005–2006):

> Asbestos is a wonderful but harmful natural substance. It is plentiful, it has amazing fire-retardant qualities, and it can be formed into a variety of products that perform useful functions in ships, factories, and office buildings, other commercial and public facilities, and homes. Unfortunately, exposure to asbestos-containing products can also kill people. Asbestos exposure causes mesothelioma, a dreadful cancer that is always fatal. . . . Asbestos exposure also causes a variety of other cancers, including lung cancer[, and] also causes non-malignant respiratory disease, termed asbestosis. Victims of asbestosis have difficulty breathing, and severe asbestosis is fatal.

[391] See Hennegan v. Cooper/T. Smith Stevedoring Co., 837 So.2d 96, 108 (La. Ct. App. 2002) (trial court properly found that "the utility of the asbestos products is vastly outweighed by the risk of death associated with their use"); Halphen v. Johns-Manville Sales Corp., 484 So.2d 110 (La. 1986). *But see* Owens-Corning Fiberglas Corp. v. Stone, 1996 WL 397435, at *2 (Tex. App. 1996) (jury found that defendant's asbestos product "was not defective, taking into consideration 'its utility and the risk involved in its use' "); Johnstone v. American Oil Co., 7 F.3d 1217, 1223 (5th Cir. 1993) (La. law) (approving jury finding that asbestos was not defective on proof that its use as a heat insulator on Navy ships during World War II helped to win the war).

se but for failing to carry sufficient warnings to alert people coming in contact with it to the lethal dangers of inhaling asbestos dust.[392]

The seminal asbestos case was *Borel v. Fibreboard Paper Products Corp.*,[393] the first strict products liability case to uphold a verdict for an installer of asbestos insulation materials against the manufacturers of those materials. Clarence Borel was employed as an industrial insulation worker from 1936 until he was disabled in 1969 by asbestosis, a lung disease. Thereafter, he developed mesothelioma, an invariably fatal form of lung cancer, and died of that disease. Both diseases, asbestosis and mesothelioma, result from asbestos fibers lodging in the lungs of a person who inhales asbestos dust. In his employment, Borel was regularly exposed to heavy concentrations of asbestos dust generated by insulation materials. Ruling that "[a] product must not be made available to the public without disclosure of those dangers that the application of reasonable foresight would reveal,"[394] the Fifth Circuit affirmed a verdict for the plaintiff.[395]

Borel opened the proverbial floodgates for asbestos litigation, and the resulting compensatory and punitive awards, together with the enormous litigation costs of defending hundreds of thousands of cases, bankrupted virtually the entire asbestos industry.[396] The litigation swamped the dockets of many courts,[397] which have sought to find ways to manage it efficiently, as by aggregating both claimants and defendants, while attempting not to sacrifice the rights of individual victims (present and future) to reasoned judicial resolution of their claims.[398]

---

[392] Inadequate warning remains the principal theory of defectiveness in these cases. See, e.g., In re Asbestos Litig., 2021 WL 3021979, at *6 (D. Del. 2021) (dismissing plaintiffs' failure to warn claim for insufficient evidence of long-term exposure to defendant's asbestos-containing products); Fowler v. Akzo Nobel Chems., Inc., 2021 WL 2132262 (N.J. Super. Ct. App. Div. 2021) (granting defendant's motion for new trial on failure to warn claim); Whelan v. Armstrong Int'l Inc., 231 A.3d 640, 659–60 (N.J. 2020) (manufacturers and distributors "can be held strictly liable for the failure to warn of the dangers of . . . their own asbestos-containing components and a third party's replacement components"). In addition to warning claims, some cases involve design defect claims as well. See, e.g., Olson v. Brenntag N. Am., Inc., 132 N.Y.S.3d 741 (Sup. Ct. 2020) (J & J long knew and suppressed evidence that its talc powders sometimes contained dangerous levels of asbestos; remitting large compensatory and punitive damage awards on design and warning defect claims).

[393] 493 F.2d 1076 (5th Cir. 1973) (Tex. law) (Wisdom, J.).

[394] Id. at 1090.

[395] See id. at 1103.

[396] Johns-Manville, the most prominent asbestos firm, declared bankruptcy in 1983, and about 100 other firms to date have followed in its wake, filing for Chapter 11 bankruptcy protection. See generally McGovern, Filings by Companies with Asbestos Liabilities, 24 Del. Law. 18 (2006); Cupp, Asbestos Litigation and Bankruptcy: A Case Study for Ad Hoc Public Policy Limitations on Joint and Several Liability, 31 Pepp. L. Rev. 203 (2003); Stiglitz et al., The Impact of Asbestos Liabilities on Workers in Bankrupt Firms, 12 J. Bankr. L. & Prac. 51, 52 (2003).

[397] See, e.g., Harras, Asbestos Reform Summit Held on Capitol Hill; Congress, Business, Lawyers Seek Solution, 31 Prod. Safety & Liab. Rep. (BNA) 298 (Apr. 7, 2003) (noting estimates that "[a]pproximately 250,000 asbestos claims [were then] pending in courts across the country, with up to 3.1 million claims anticipated in the future," and that "the courts have adjudicated $30 billion in asbestos claims, with about $200 billion in claims [then] pending or anticipated"). Compare 2005 RAND Report, above (estimating that through 2002 at least 730,000 people had filed claims against 8,400 defendants, and that at least 50,000 claims [were then] added per year). More recently, the numbers of new asbestos filings have declined. See, e.g., Frankel, Are Asbestos Filings Another COVID-19 Casualty?, Thomson Reuters (Aug. 27, 2020) (new filings of asbestos suits declined from 5,500 in 2014 to 4,062 in 2019) (citing KCIC's Asbestos Litigation: 2019 Year in Review report).

[398] See, e.g., Ortiz v. Fibreboard Corp., 527 U.S. 815 (1999); Amchem Prods., Inc. v. Windsor, 521 U.S. 591 (1997). Another attempt to simplify this litigation was to collaterally estop defendants from continuing to litigate whether asbestos is defective, an attempt that failed. See Hardy v. Johns-Manville Sales Corp., 681 F.2d 334 (5th Cir. 1982) (Tex. law). Some courts used reverse bifurcation, where issues of medical causation

In recent years, most asbestos litigation has shifted to the bankruptcy courts, which still are struggling with how to balance competing claims of past and future injury victims of different types, to say nothing of the interests of shareholders, employees, and other creditors.[399]

Peripheral parties; the "bare metal defense." Due to the bankruptcy of almost all the asbestos manufacturers, the plaintiff's bar, in an effort to find solvent defendants, began to file claims against defendants with ever-more remote connections to injury-producing asbestos—"peripheral defendants"—such as manufacturers of respirators that became covered with asbestos dust when used by shipyard workers to protect against inhaling such dust, which endangered those who had to clean and maintain the respirators,[400] and manufacturers of valves and pumps that would need to be refurnished with asbestos gaskets made by other companies. While such valve and pump manufacturers could foresee that their products would need regular maintenance and revamping that might create a risk of harm, many courts, fearful of expanding asbestos liability too far, ruled that there is no duty to warn of dangers from products manufactured by others.[401] Other courts, however, especially more recently, have ruled against such peripheral defendants.[402]

Courts seeking to protect such peripheral asbestos defendants eagerly latched onto the so-called "bare metal defense," a catchy phrase for a doctrine which "provides that a manufacturer has no duty to warn about potential dangers from exposure to a part of its

---

and damages were tried in the first stage and issues of liability theories and product identification were tried in the second stage. See Donoughe v. Lincoln Elec. Co., 936 A.2d 52, 71–72 (Pa. Super. Ct. 2007).

[399] As of 2020, some 128 companies had declared bankruptcy at least partially due to asbestos-related liability. Crowell Moring, Chart 1: List of Asbestos Bankruptcy Cases (Oct. 7, 2020). See generally McGovern, The What And Why of Claims Resolution Facilities, 57 Stan. L. Rev. 1361 (2005); and my favorite, Owen, Against Priority, 37 Sw. U. L. Rev. 557 (2008).

[400] See, e.g., Macias v. Saberhagen Holdings, Inc., 282 P.3d 1069 (Wash. 2012) (allowing mesothelioma claim against manufacturers of respirator manufacturers for failing to warn respirator maintenance handlers of dangers from asbestos dust). See generally Calnan and Stier, Perspectives on Asbestos Litigation: Overview and Preview, 37 Sw. U. L. Rev. 459, 463 (2008); Carroll et al., Asbestos Litigation xxiii–v (RAND 2005).

[401] See, e.g., Coffman v. Armstrong Int'l, Inc., 615 S.W.3d 888, 899 (Tenn. 2021) (4–1 decision) ("manufacturers have no duty to warn with respect to products manufactured and sold by others" under the Tennessee Products Liability Act; persuasive dissent); In re Asbestos Litig., 2017 WL 2963570, at *2 (Del. Super. Ct. 2017) (Mass. law) ("Massachusetts does not hold a manufacturer liable 'for failure to warn of risks created solely in the use or misuse of the product of another manufacturer' "); O'Neil v. Crane Co., 266 P.3d 987, 998 (Cal. 2012) (surveying cases; no duty to warn of exposure to asbestos "from replacement gaskets and packing and external insulation added to defendants' products long after their installation," nor were original products defectively designed to be used with asbestos); Braaten v. Saberhagen Holdings, 198 P.3d 493, 504 (Wash. 2008) (en banc) (no duty to warn of danger from asbestos in replacement packing and gaskets manufactured by others).

Cases related to long-term use of asbestos-contaminated talc powder are discussed in the section on *Talc*, immediately below.

[402] See, e.g., Whelan v. Armstrong Int'l Inc., 231 A.3d 640, 659–60 (N.J. 2020) (manufacturers and distributors "can be found strictly liable for the failure to warn of the dangers of their products, including their own asbestos-containing components and a third party's replacement components"); Woo v. General Electric Co., 393 P.3d 869, 877 (Wash. Ct. App. 2017); In re New York City Asbestos Litig., 59 N.E.3d 458, 474–75 (N.Y. 2016) (defendant's valves required third-party asbestos-laden products to operate):

> [B]ecause the manufacturer's product is critical to the dangerous joint use of the two products, it does substantially create a defective condition insofar as both products combine to generate a defective and dangerous condition . . . . Accordingly, we recognize a manufacturer's duty to warn of the peril of a known and foreseeable joint use of its product and another product that is necessary to allow the manufacturer's product to work as intended.

product if the manufacturer did not make or distribute the part."[403] More recently, however, the judicial tide has turned, with more recent decisions understandably viewing this dubious "defense" skeptically—particularly when a defendant's "bare metal" product was designed for use and initially equipped with asbestos gaskets or other asbestos materials.[404] The United States Supreme Court has adopted this more modern trend for maritime cases, where it reasoned that the bare metal defense was too narrow a liability rule, but that a foreseeability rule imposed too broad a duty on manufacturers. It therefore ruled, but for the special maritime context alone, that a manufacturer "has a duty to warn when (i) its product requires incorporation of a part, (ii) the manufacturer knows or has reason to know that the integrated product is likely to be dangerous for its intended uses, and (iii) the manufacturer has no reason to believe that the product's users will realize that danger."[405]

In addition to peripheral defendants, some cases involve peripheral *plaintiffs*, persons other than workers with asbestos products who are affected by asbestos dust. The most common type of peripheral plaintiffs are family members, who regularly washed asbestos-covered clothing of asbestos workers, and who themselves eventually suffered asbestos diseases from repeated contact with the toxic dust. As with peripheral defendants, courts for similar reasons have split on whether to extend liability this far, some courts fearing a never-ending reach of liability,[406] while other courts finding such persons to be foreseeable victims who fully deserve compensation from asbestos defendants who failed for so long to warn of the product's lethal risks.[407] Another form

[403] Sparkman v. A.W. Chesterton Co., 2014 WL 7369494, at *5–8 (D.S.C. 2014) (reviewing cases) (later reconsidered; see note 404, below). See also Thurmon v. A.W. Chesterton Co., 61 F. Supp. 3d 1280, 1284 (N.D. Ga. 2014) ("[t]he clear thrust of the bare metal defense is that a manufacturer cannot be held liable for asbestos-containing products used in conjunction with its bare metal [product], absent evidence that the manufacturer was part of the chain of distribution for those products"); Dalton v. 3M Co., 2013 WL 4886658, at *7 (D. Del. 2013) (collecting cases; "The majority of courts embrace the principles of the bare metal defense and refuse to impose liability upon manufacturers for the dangers associated with asbestos-containing products manufactured and distributed by other entities.").

[404] See, e.g., In re Asbestos Litig., 2020 WL 5122939, at *2 (Del. Super. Ct. 2020) (R.I. law) ("Rhode Island jurisprudence . . . rejects the bare metal defense . . . and 'supports recovery against a manufacturer of a product even where the manufacturer's original product did not contain asbestos.' "); May v. Air & Liquid Sys. Corp., 129 A.3d 984, 1000 (Md. 2015), reconsideration granted in part (Feb. 19, 2016) (declining to extend a manufacturer's duty to warn to all foreseeable instances where "a defective component may be used with its product," but holding that an exception to the bare metal defense applied where "(1) [the manufacturer's] product contains asbestos components, and no safer material is available; (2) asbestos is a critical part of the pump sold by the manufacturer; (3) periodic maintenance involving handling asbestos gaskets and packing is required; and (4) the manufacturer knows or should know the risks from exposure to asbestos"); Sparkman v. Goulds Pumps, Inc., 2015 WL 727937, at *2 (D.S.C. 2015) (where defendant pump manufacturer specified use of asbestos packing and gaskets with its products, the court denied the bare metal defense, quoting a state administrative judge's characterization of the defense as "misleading and, as used here, is semantic advocacy rather than a useful doctrinal description," reconsidering its earlier approval of the defense in Sparkman v. A.W. Chesterton Co., 2014 WL 7369494, at *5–8 (D.S.C. 2014)) (reviewing cases).

[405] Air & Liquid Systems Corp. v. DeVries, 139 S. Ct. 986, 996 (2019). See also Wineland v. Air & Liquid Sys. Corp., 539 F. Supp. 3d 1149, 1156 (W.D. Wash. 2021) (maritime law) ("under maritime (or Washington) law, a manufacturer generally does not owe a duty with regards to replacement parts or ancillary products (such as insulation) manufactured and sold by third-parties unless the manufacturer in some way invites or requires the integration of the third-party product," citing *DeVries*). See generally Comment, 81 La. L. Rev. 217 (2020).

[406] See, e.g., Certainteed Corp. v. Fletcher, 794 S.E.2d 641, 645 (Ga. 2016) (no duty to warn daughter who regularly washed father's asbestos-laden work clothing); Georgia Pac., LLC v. Farrar, 69 A.3d 1028 (Md. 2013) (no duty to warn worker's granddaughter, who regularly washed grandfather's work clothes, of risks of household exposure to asbestos dust).

[407] See, e.g., Ramsey v. Georgia S. Univ. Advanced Dev. Ctr., 189 A.3d 1255, 1262 (Del. 2018) (overruling prior cases and holding "that a household member who regularly launders an employee's asbestos-covered clothing . . . may sue her spouse's employer for its failure to provide warnings and safe laundering

of peripheral plaintiffs are persons exposed to asbestos in talc powder, examined in the next following subsection on asbestos-contaminated talc.

In addition to the courts, Congress,[408] state legislatures,[409] and scholars[410] have wrestled for some time with the numerous impenetrable perplexities of fairness, ethics, doctrine, procedure, and practicality involved in resolving the myriad claims that continue to arise from this single, noxious product.

Nor is asbestos the only toxic substance that causes inhalation injuries. Apart from cigarettes, discussed earlier, other products that can cause lung, neurological, and other internal diseases and injuries include industrial sand and cement products containing silica, which may emit respirable silica that can cause silicosis;[411] manganese welding fumes, which may cause brain damage;[412] nanoparticles from the expanding number of

---

instructions"); Stegemoller v. ACandS, Inc., 767 N.E.2d 974 (Ind. 2002) (allowing claim of worker's wife who washed his clothes). Compare Boynton v. Kennecott Utah Copper, LLC, 500 P.3d 847, 867 (Utah 2021) (as a matter of first impression, job site operators "are liable to their employees' co-habitants for take-home asbestos exposure"). Family member asbestos cases are also considered in § 9.4, above.

[408] See, e.g., Hanlon, Federal Asbestos Legislation: Wrestling with the Medical Issues, 15 J.L. & Pol'y 1171 (2007). See also Reinstein and Ali, Asbestos Still Kills: Time for a Total Ban in the U.S., Prod. Liab. & Toxics L. (Oct. 22, 2021) ("Nearly 70 countries have banned asbestos to protect their residents from this harmful and often deadly toxin.").

[409] Some states enacted legislation designed to raise the proof-of-injury threshold for bringing asbestos (and, in some states, silica) claims. See, e.g., Fla. Stat. Ann. §§ 774.201 et seq. (asbestos and silica claims); Ga. Code Ann. §§ 51–14–1 et seq. (asbestos and silica claims). Georgia's statute was held unconstitutional, but the legislature reenacted it in different form. Both the Florida and Ohio statutes were held unconstitutional as applied retroactively. See Sanders, Medical Criteria Acts: State Statutory Attempts to Control the Asbestos Litigation, 37 Sw. U. L. Rev. 671 (2008).

Statutes in many states limit asbestos claims against successor corporations. See, e.g., Ariz. Rev. Stat. Ann. §§ 12–559 to –559:03; Idaho Code Ann. §§ 30–1901 to –1907. An Oregon statute limits asbestos-related claims against contractors. See Or. Rev. Stat. Ann. § 30.907(3).

Asbestos "transparency" statutes in many states require plaintiffs to identify "all existing asbestos trust claims made by or on behalf of the claimant." Ohio Rev. Code Ann. § 2307.952(A)(1)(a). See also Ariz. Rev. Stat. Ann. § 12–782; Iowa Code Ann. §§ 686A.1 et seq. See Reynolds, BNA Insight: The "George Costanza" Approach to Asbestos Transparency Litigation: Working to Prevent the "Double Dip," 41 Prod. Safety & Liab. Rep. (BNA) 657 (May 27, 2013). The statutes are compiled in Owen & Davis on Products Liability Appendix J.

[410] In addition to articles cited in note 389, above, see, e.g., Symposia, The Evolution of Asbestos Litigation, 88 Tul. L. Rev. 1153 (2014) (articles by Ableman, Bernstein, Brickman, Sanders, Sherman, Vario); Perspectives on Asbestos Litigation, 37 Sw. U. L. Rev. 459 (2008) (Behrens, Anderson, Bernstein, Freedman, Green, Hylton, McGovern, Owen, Rothstein, Sanders); Asbestos: Anatomy of a Mass Tort, 12 Conn. Ins. L.J. 281 (2005–2006) (Behrens and Goldberg, Brickman, Green, Hanlon, Stemple, and Stengel); Asbestos Litigation & Tort Law: Trends, Ethics, & Solutions, 31 Pepp. L. Rev. 1 (2003) (Bell, Bernstein, Brayton, Brickman, Chiantelli, Cramton, Cupp, Kazan, McGovern, Priest, Schwartz, Behrens, Tedesco, Silver).

[411] See, e.g., Humble Sand & Gravel, Inc. v. Gomez, 146 S.W.3d 170 (Tex. 2004) (remanded for determination of whether supplier of silica flint used in high-power blasting operation had duty to warn workers of dangers of inhaling silica dust, and of not wearing air-fed hoods to protect against inhalation, including injury and death); Liberty Mut. Ins. Co. v. Lone Star Indus., 967 A.2d 1, 11 (Conn. 2009) (dispute over terms of settlement agreement made during bankruptcy of insured, Lone Star, among various insurers and insured, over responsibility for expenses of defense and settlement of 29,000 silicosis claims arising out of inhalation injuries and sickness of workers with silica products that Lone Star manufactured, used, or sold).

[412] Macias v. Saberhagen Holdings, Inc., 282 P.3d 1069 (Wash. 2012) (allowing mesothelioma claim against respirator manufacturers for failing to warn respirator maintenance handlers of dangers from asbestos dust). See also In re Welding Fume Prods. Liab. Litig., 2010 WL 7699456 (N.D. Ohio 2009) (outline of proceedings in the 12,600 welding fume cases consolidated in multidistrict litigation).

products of nanotechnology, the inhalation of which may eventually lead to harm;[413] and various other airborne toxic substances.[414]

Asbestos-contaminated talc. A number of talcum powder companies have faced claims arising from talc powders allegedly contaminated with asbestos, with numerous recent cases involving claims against Johnson & Johnson. Plaintiffs in these cases assert claims for failure to warn, negligence, breach of warranty, civil conspiracy, concert of action, and negligent misrepresentation, among others, for damages arising from ovarian or uterine cancer, allegedly caused by contaminated talc powder used in genital areas over long periods, or mesothelioma, from inhalation of asbestos-contaminated talc dust. The contamination problem arose during mining because asbestos and talc deposits naturally occur in close proximity.[415]

A preliminary causation issue in these talc cases is whether J & J's talc powder in fact contained any asbestos at all, which the company vigorously denies. Yet some juries have disagreed, resulting in substantial damages for plaintiffs in several cases, some of which were later reversed.[416] Although J & J has successfully defended the safety of its talc products in some cases, the company's continued defense of their talc products' safety was challenged by a Reuters investigative report asserting that the company long has known of its talc asbestos contamination, dating at least to 1971.[417] As litigation

---

413 Nanoparticles might be thin enough to reach the sensitive areas of the lungs, long enough to avoid the lungs' built-in defense systems, and persistent enough to remain without dissolving for many years. See, e.g., Rogers, Clark, Tsuji, Dahlstrom, and Arndt, Labeling and Warning for Products Containing Engineered Nanomaterials: Learning from the Past or We Are Doomed to Repeat It, 39 Prod. Safety & Liab. Rep. (BNA) 1283 (Nov. 21, 2011); Report Looks at Nanoparticle Characteristics That Could Raise Asbestos-Like Concerns, Prod. Liab. Daily (BNA), Jan. 28, 2009. Whether carbon nanotube exposure may lead to asbestos-like diseases is an open question closely monitored by the Consumer Products Safety Commission. See Potential Carbon Nanotube Exposures Sorted by Regulators, Industry at CPSC Workshop, 40 Prod. Safety & Liab. Rep. (BNA) 729 (July 20, 2012). On how the law might address the unknown risks of nanoparticles, see Owen, Bending Nature, Bending Law, 62 Fla. L. Rev. 569 (2010).

414 One such product is popcorn seasoning. One day after a former popcorn factory worker died from a severe lung disease from inhaling a butter-flavoring agent ("diacetyl") at work, the trial court entered judgment on a jury verdict for him of $7.5 million in compensatory damages. See Kuiper v. Givaudan, 2009 WL 1444376 (N.D. Iowa 2009) (denying defendant's renewed motion for judgment as a matter of law). Subsequent to *Kuiper*, several hundred diacetyl and other chemical flavoring cases were filed by factory workers. See also Johnson v. Centrome, Inc., 2021 WL 4477170, at *4 (N.D. Ind. 2021) (allegations that flavoring chemicals caused popcorn worker's lung injuries were sufficiently pled to defeat defendants' motion to dismiss).

Consumers, too, have brought "popcorn lung" claims against manufacturers and distributors of microwave popcorn. See, e.g., Stults v. American Pop Corn Co., 815 F.3d 409 (8th Cir. 2016) (affirming verdict for manufacturers after 4-day trial); Watson v. Dillon Cos., 2013 WL 1461500, at *6 (D. Colo. 2013) (denying defendants' motions for JMOL or new trial after $7.2 million verdict for microwave popcorn consumer injured by inhaling diacetyl); Dulberg, The Popcorn Lung Case Study: A Recipe for Regulation?, 33 N.Y.U. Rev. L. & Soc. Change 87, 103–04 (2009).

415 See, e.g., Strobel v. Johnson & Johnson, 284 Cal. Rptr. 3d 165, 172 (Ct. App. 2021) ("asbestos is often found intergrown as an 'accessory mineral' within a talc deposit").

416 See, e.g., Lanzo v. Cyprus Amax Mins. Co., 254 A.3d 691, 715 (N.J. Super. Ct. App. Div. 2021) (reversing $117 million compensatory and punitive damages awards for long-time J & J talc user suffering from mesothelioma; trial court erred in allowing plaintiffs' experts to present unreliable theories that non-asbestiform cleavage fragments can cause an asbestos disease); Slemp v. Johnson & Johnson, 589 S.W.3d 92, 97 (Mo. Ct. App. 2019) (vacating trial court's $5.4 million compensatory and $105 million punitive damages awards to deceased whose ovarian cancer was linked to defendant's talc products; trial court erred in exercising personal jurisdiction over defendant under Bristol-Myers Squibb Co. v. Superior Ct., 137 S. Ct. 1773 (2017)).

For proof of causation in toxic substances litigation, see § 11.2, below.

417 See Girion, Powder Keg: Johnson & Johnson Knew for Decades that Asbestos Lurked in its Baby Powder, Reuters Investigates 3 (Dec. 14, 2018). See also Leavitt v. Johnson & Johnson, 2021 WL 3418410, at *3 (Cal. Ct. App. 2021) ("defendants' corporate documents and historical laboratory test reports . . . suggested

continued, the Justice Department and SEC issued subpoenas for J & J documents related to talc product safety.[418] J&J issued a limited Baby Powder recall in 2019[419] and then, in 2020, "citing a decline in customer demand amid safety concerns," Johnson & Johnson announced that it would replace talc with cornstarch in its Baby Powder sold in the U.S. and Canada.[420] In 2021, following a $2.1 billion judgment for 20 plaintiffs,[421] and reportedly facing nearly 40,000 claims, J & J filed a bankruptcy proceeding in which it sought to halt the litigation of those claims by placing its talc liabilities into a new unit and then putting that unit—but not itself—into bankruptcy (a process dubbed the "Texas two-step").[422] Approving the filing, the bankruptcy judge commented that, though controversial, this process will best serve justice "by expeditiously providing critical compensation through a court-supervised, fair, and less-costly settlement trust arrangement."[423] In addition to manufacturers of talk consumer products, bulk suppliers of mined talc also have faced asbestos-contamination claims.[424]

Lead Paint

A significant type of inherent risk litigation concerns lead poisoning.[425] For household paints, lead pigment was long a key ingredient of paint, increasing its durability and rendering it smooth and easy to wash. For many decades during the 1900s, the walls of much of the nation's residential housing were painted with coat upon coat of lead-based paint. As the century progressed, much of the housing began to deteriorate and the paint began to peel off the walls, leaving piles of lead paint chips in decaying housing around the nation. The problem is that lead, said to taste "sweet as

defendants knew, from at least the 1960's or 1970's, that their cosmetic talc (sourced from both the Korean and Vermont mines) contained trace amounts of asbestos").

[418] See Loftus, Johnson & Johnson is Subpoenaed for Talc Safety Information, Wall St. J.com (Feb. 20, 2019).

[419] See Shivdas and O'Donnell, J&J Says New Tests Show No Asbestos in Johnson's Baby Powder, Reuters (Dec. 3, 2019) ("155 tests . . . by two different third-party labs using four different testing methods on samples from the same bottle tested by the FDA's contracted lab").

[420] See Loftus, Johnson & Johnson to Stop Selling Talcum Baby Powder in U.S., Canada, Wall St. J.com (May 19, 2020).

[421] See Ingham v. Johnson & Johnson, 608 S.W.3d 663, 709 (Mo. Ct. App. 2020) (entering $2.1 billion judgment;$1.6 billion punitive damages award to 20 plaintiffs did not violate due process), cert. denied, 141 S. Ct. 2716 (2021). See also Kendall and Loftis, Supreme Court Won't Consider Johnson & Johnson Challenge to Baby Powder Judgment, Wall St. J.com (June 1, 2021).

[422] See, e.g., Feeley, J&J Offered $4 Billion to Settle Talc Months Before Bankruptcy, Prod. Liab. & Toxics L. (Oct. 21, 2021); Church, J&J Seeks Victory in Fight with Baby Powder Cancer Victims, Prod. Liab. & Toxics L. (Oct. 20, 2021); Scurria, Johnson & Johnson Places Talc Injury Claims in Bankruptcy, Wall St. J.com (Oct. 14, 2021).

[423] See Horsley, Johnson & Johnson Wins a Key Court Battle in Baby Powder Case, npr.org (Feb. 25, 2022), www.npr.org/2022/02/25/1083061992/johnson-johnson-wins-court-battle-bankruptcy-baby-powder.

[424] Imerys Talc America, Inc., which had supplied talc mined in China to Johnson & Johnson since 2003, was frequently named as a co-defendant in claims against Johnson & Johnson for asbestos-contaminated talc. After settling several claims, Imerys filed for bankruptcy. See Feeley, Fisk & Church, Imerys Talc Units File Bankruptcy as Cancer-Suit Risk Soars, Prod. Liab. & Toxics L. (Feb. 13, 2019). See also § 15.3, below.

[425] See Gifford, Impersonating the Legislature: State Attorneys General and Paren Patriae Product Litigation, 49 B.C. L. Rev. 913 (2008); Schaefer and Nykiel, Lead Paint: Mass Tort Litigation and Public Nuisance Trends in America, 74 Def. Couns. J. 153 (2007); Schwartz and Goldberg, The Law of Public Nuisance: Maintaining Rational Boundaries on a Rational Tort, 45 Washburn L.J. 541, 557–61 (2006); Smith, Turning Lead into Asbestos and Tobacco: Litigation Alchemy Gone Wrong, 71 Def. Couns. J. 119 (2004). For a thorough, scholarly examination of this topic, see D. Gifford, Suing the Tobacco and Lead Pigment Industries: Government Litigation as Public Health Prescription (U. Mich. Press 2010).

candy,"[426] is also highly toxic—particularly when ingested by toddlers ever on the lookout for things to place in their mouths. As a result, and because water pipes during the 1900s were commonly made of lead, roughly half of all American children today have detectable levels of lead in their blood.[427] Harm caused by lead in a child's blood can be severe, from speech impairment, decreased memory and intelligence, learning disabilities, brain damage, autism, kidney damage, and even death.[428] For at least a century, paint manufacturers have known of the hazards lead poses to human beings.[429] Indeed, other nations began banning the use of lead in residential paint as early as the 1920s.[430]

Beginning in the late 1980s, plaintiffs began to file products liability claims against paint manufacturers for lead poisoning in children. To date, lead poisoning victims have faced the vexing causal problem of identifying the particular manufacturers that made the particular paints and pigments in particular chips eaten by particular victims. The plaintiffs' inability to meet their conventional burden of proof on causation has typically been fatal in these cases, with most courts refusing to apply market share liability (or other theories of joint liability) to hold the industry liable as a whole.[431]

Following in the footsteps of the successful cigarette litigation, a large number of cities and the state of Rhode Island sued the lead paint industry on various grounds, seeking to recover the enormous costs of cleaning up the lead paint hazards, caring for

---

[426] See Cupp, State Medical Reimbursement Lawsuits After Tobacco: Is the Domino Effect for Lead Paint Manufacturers and Others Fair Game?, 27 Pepp. L. Rev. 685, 692 (2000).

[427] Childhood lead poisoning now appears more widespread than previously thought. Recent studies reveal that about half of all U.S. children have detectable levels of lead in their blood, and the studies confirm that high levels of this toxic metal appears in about 2% of U.S. children. Court, Lead Contamination Found in Blood of Half of Young Kids in U.S., Prod. Liab. & Toxics L. (Sept. 27, 2021); see Comment, 28 Pepp. L. Rev. 915, 915–18 (2001) (noting varying estimates).

[428] See id. at 918.

[429] See Cupp, above note 426, at 692 (one manufacturer warned of lead paint's dangers in an article published in 1904).

[430] See id. at 692–93.

[431] See, e.g., Lewis v. Lead Indus. Ass'n, Inc., 793 N.E.2d 869 (Ill. App. Ct. 2003); Brenner v. American Cyanamid Co., 732 N.Y.S.2d 799 (App. Div. 2001); Skipworth v. Lead Indus. Ass'n, 690 A.2d 169 (Pa. 1997); Santiago v. Sherwin Williams Co., 3 F.3d 546 (1st Cir. 1993) (Mass. law) (2–1 decision) (with a draft amicus brief that contained the celebrated footnote 3). See also S.F. v. Archer-Daniels-Midland Co., 2014 WL 1600414, at *5–7 (W.D.N.Y. 2014) (detailed analysis of the market share theory; "New York has not recognized market-share liability as a permissible theory of recovery outside the DES context"). *But see* Jackson v. Glidden Co., 647 N.E.2d 879 (Ohio Ct. App. 1995) (allowing claims for alternative liability and market share liability).

Wisconsin has had a long and tortured journey on whether and, if so, how, its risk-contribution theory should apply to manufacturers of white lead carbonate paint. In Burton v. American Cyanamid Co., 407 F. Supp. 3d 786, 804 (E.D. Wis. 2019), the court ruled that white lead carbonate paint was fungible as a matter of law such that plaintiffs could proceed under that state's risk contribution theory. *Burton* was reversed and remanded for a new trial in Burton v. E.I. du Pont de Nemours & Co., Inc., 994 F.3d 791 (7th Cir. 2021) (trial court erred in extending risk contribution theory to sellers or manufacturers of paint that use the white lead carbonite paint pigment produced by other manufacturers). Compare Allen v. American Cyanamid, 527 F. Supp. 3d 982, 992 (E.D. Wis. 2021) (denying defendant's motion for summary judgment on plaintiffs' risk-contribution theory).

Lead paint plaintiffs have also had difficulty proving defectiveness and proximate cause. See, e.g., Smith v. 2328 Univ. Ave. Corp., 859 N.Y.S.2d 71 (App. Div. 2008) (lead paint pigment not defective). *But see* Pollard v. Sherwin-Williams Co., 955 So.2d 764 (Miss. 2007) (allowing failure to warn claim to proceed), jury award rev'd on other grounds, 75 So.3d 41, 47 (2011).

Some time ago, recalls of toys containing dangerous levels of lead spawned class action lawsuits against their manufacturers. See, e.g., In re Mattel, Inc., 588 F. Supp. 2d 1111, 1119 (C.D. Cal. 2008) (denying defendant's motion to dismiss negligence claim); Mattel, Subsidiary to Pay Penalty to Comply with Stringent New Federal Lead Standards, 36 Prod. Safety & Liab. Rep. (BNA) 1272 (Dec. 22, 2008).

children poisoned by the lead paint, and educating the public on the hazards of lead.[432] As in the opioid lawsuits, many municipalities and states pursued public nuisance claims against the defendants, claiming that they unreasonably interfered with a right held in common by the general public. An unreasonable interference is one that affects the public's health, safety, peace, comfort, or convenience; violates a statute or ordinance prohibiting the conduct; and/or has produced a permanent effect on the public right.[433]

A couple early lead paint suits brought by Philadelphia and New Orleans ran into statute of limitations problems.[434] New York's action had more success,[435] but subsequent claims by municipalities have mostly been dismissed.[436] In Rhode Island, the jury in a second trial found that lead paint is a public nuisance requiring abatement, but this holding was reversed on appeal.[437] A Milwaukee jury declined to hold a lead paint manufacturer liable for public nuisance,[438] and at least an Ohio statute prohibits public nuisance suits seeking recovery of clean-up costs for lead paint contamination.[439]

So, by 2013, public nuisance litigation against the paint industry looked dead in the water. Late that year, however, more than a dozen years after filing suit, a coalition of California cities and counties—led by Santa Clara County and including Los Angeles—hit pay dirt when a judge unexpectedly[440] ruled in favor of the plaintiffs, ordering defendants to pay $1.15 billion to fund lead-paint cleanups in thousands of California homes.[441] In 2017 a California Court of Appeals held that "remedial abatement [was] an equitable remedy for defendants' knowing creation of a public nuisance" but reversed the judgment and ordered the trial court to "(1) recalculate the amount of the abatement fund to limit it to the amount necessary to cover the cost of remediating pre-1951 homes, and (2) hold an evidentiary hearing regarding the appointment of a suitable receiver."[442] In 2019, the lead paint defendants agreed to a $305 million settlement for lead paint abatement to be paid over six years.[443] Other than this one ruling, public-entity litigation against lead paint manufacturers for clean-up costs has been widely rejected, on one ground or another, and the future viability of such claims looks remote.

[432] See Comment, 28 Pepp. L. Rev. 915 (2001).

[433] See Rest. (2d) Torts § 821B.

[434] See City of Phila. v. Lead Indus. Ass'n, 994 F.2d 112 (3d Cir. 1993) (Pa. law) (also rejecting alternative liability and market share liability theories); Housing Auth. of New Orleans v. Standard Paint & Varnish Co., 612 So.2d 916 (La. Ct. App. 1993).

[435] See City of N.Y. v. Lead Indus. Ass'n, 644 N.Y.S.2d 919 (App. Div. 1996).

[436] See, e.g., In re Lead Paint Litig., 924 A.2d 484, 505 (N.J. 2007) ("were we to find a cause of action here, nuisance law 'would become a monster that would devour in one gulp the entire law of tort' "); City of St. Louis v. Benjamin Moore & Co., 226 S.W.3d 110 (Mo. 2007); County of Santa Clara v. Atlantic Richfield Co., 40 Cal. Rptr. 3d 313 (Ct. App. 2006).

[437] See State v. Lead Indus. Ass'n, 951 A.2d 428 (R.I. 2008).

[438] See Milwaukee Jury Finds Paint Public Nuisance, But Says Defendant Committed No Wrong, Prod. Liab. Daily, July 9, 2007, at D10. See also City of Milwaukee v. NL Indus., 762 N.W.2d 757, 784 (Wis. Ct. App. 2008) (affirming jury verdict for manufacturer).

[439] See Ohio. Rev. Code Ann. § 2307.73(C); State v. Brunner, 872 N.E.2d 912 (Ohio 2007) (upholding legislation over governor's attempted veto).

[440] See Fowler, After Flicking Away Lawsuits, Lead Industry Goes for a Final Knockout (Aug. 8, 2013), www.fairwarning.org.

[441] California v. Atlantic Richfield Co., 2014 WL 1385823 (Cal. Super. Ct. 2014).

[442] People v. Conagra Grocery Prods. Co., 227 Cal. Rptr. 3d 499, 598 (Ct. App. 2017), cert. denied sub nom. Sherwin-Williams Co. v. California, 139 S. Ct. 378 (2018).

[443] See Williams and Colvin, Paint Makers Reach $305 Million Settlement in California, Ending Marathon Lead Poisoning Lawsuit, 37 No. 12 Westlaw J. Toxic Torts (Jul. 26, 2019). See generally Lin, Dodging Public Nuisance, 11 UC Irvine L. Rev. 489, 496–97 (2020).

Fast Foods

Hot coffee—burns. Whether fast food restaurants are responsible for burns to patrons who spill coffee and other hot drinks is an issue American courts have addressed for a number of years. Except for one celebrated aberration,[444] courts almost always dismiss these claims on the ground that the hazard of such spills is obvious and widely known, and that restaurants are simply serving a type of product that consumers want.[445] This type of claim spread at least to England, where a class action of such claimants was dismissed.[446]

Fattening foods—obesity. The next type of inherent risk lawsuit is represented by a couple of putative class actions filed against fast food retailers for obesity and other health problems resulting from the plaintiffs' consumption of too much "junk food" sold by the defendants.[447] The first suit filed, *Barber v. McDonald's Corp.*,[448] sought to certify a national class action against McDonald's, Burger King, KFC, and Wendy's for intentionally and negligently selling food that is high in fat, salt, sugar, and cholesterol without properly labeling the food or warning consumers of the risks.[449] The named plaintiff, 56-year-old Caesar Barber, stood 5 feet 11 inches and weighed 285 pounds at

---

444 Liebeck v. McDonald's Rests., P.T.S., Inc., 1995 WL 360309 (D.N.M. 1994). Mrs. Liebeck, a passenger in her grandson's car, spilled the coffee when she placed it between her legs and tried to remove the plastic lid. See, e.g., Greene v. Boddie-Noell Enters., Inc., 966 F. Supp. 416, 418 n.1 (W.D. Va. 1997) (discussing *Liebeck*); Mead, Punitive Damages and the Spill Felt Round the World: A U.S. Perspective, 17 Loy. L.A. Int'l & Comp. L. Rev. 829 (1995). *Liebeck* is examined in connection with punitive damages, in Owen & Davis on Products Liability § 26:17.

445 See, e.g., Shih v. Starbucks Corp., 267 Cal. Rptr. 3d 919 (Ct. App. 2020) (hot tea); Maneri v. Starbucks Corp. Store #1527, 2019 WL 5626650, at *7 (E.D. Pa. 2019) (hot tea); Triche v. McDonald's Corp., 164 So.3d 253 (La. Ct. App. 2014) (hot coffee); Colbert v. Sonic Rests., Inc., 741 F. Supp. 2d 764 (W.D. La. 2010) (hot coffee); Kessel v. Stansfield Vending, Inc., 714 N.W.2d 206 (Wis. Ct. App. 2006) (hot chocolate); McCroy v. Coastal Mart, Inc., 207 F. Supp. 2d 1265 (D. Kan. 2002) (hot chocolate; extensive review of hot beverage cases); Immormino v. J & M Powers, Inc., 698 N.E.2d 516 (Ohio Ct. Com. Pl. 1998) (hot tea; consumers commonly aware of dangers of hot liquid spills). See also McMahon v. Bunn-O-Matic Corp., 150 F.3d 651 (7th Cir. 1998) (Ind. law) (Easterbrook, J.) (affirming dismissal of claim against manufacturer of coffee maker; because everyone knows that hot coffee will burn if spilled on skin, lack of knowledge that it can cause third-degree burns requires no warning as matter of law).

The only case to the contrary, Nadel v. Burger King Corp., 695 N.E.2d 1185 (Ohio Ct. App. 1997) (2–1 decision) (jury question as to obviousness of risk that coffee served from drive-through window of fast-food restaurant, that spilled on child, would be so hot as to cause second-degree burns), was overruled by Bouher v. Aramark Servs., Inc., 910 N.E.2d 40 (Ohio Ct. App. 2009) (no claim against manufacturer of coffee maker for burn from collapse of cup of hot water taken from defendant's coffee maker).

Of course, a restaurateur or other retail seller may be liable for negligently serving a hot beverage in a dangerous manner. See, e.g., Becton v. Starbucks Corp., 491 F. Supp. 2d 737 (S.D. Ohio 2007) (seller may have improperly attached top to cup of hot coffee).

446 See B (A Child) v. McDonald's Rests. Ltd., 2002 WL 347059 (Q.B. 2002) (people expect tea and coffee to be hot and know that, if they spill such beverages, they may be burned).

447 See generally Sugarman and Sandman, Fighting Childhood Obesity Through Performance-Based Regulation of the Food Industry, 56 Duke L.J. 1403 (2007); Cantu, Fattening Food: Should Purveyors of Fast Food Be Required to Warn? A Call for a New Tort, 2 J. Food L. & Pol'y 39 (2006); Ausness, Tell Me What You Eat and I Will Tell You Whom to Sue: Big Problems Ahead for "Big Food?," 39 Ga. L. Rev. 839 (2005); Bloche, Obesity and the Struggle Within Ourselves, 93 Geo. L.J. 1335 (2005); Epstein, What (Not) to Do About Obesity: A Moderate Aristotelian Answer, 93 Geo. J.J. 1361 (2005); Note, 54 Wm. & Mary L. Rev. 1753 (2013) (arguing against parens patriae suits by attorneys general against food industry to fight obesity). Early fast-food litigation was championed by public interest law professor John Banzhaf of George Washington University Law School. See www.banzhaf.net/obesitylinks.html.

448 No. 23145/2002 (N.Y. Sup. Ct., Bronx Cnty., filed July 24, 2002). See New York Man Files National Class Action Alleging Fast Food Chains Make People Fat, 30 Prod. Safety & Liab. Rep. 674 (Aug. 5, 2002); Fountain, Living Large; Our Just (Burp!) Desserts, N.Y. Times § 4, p.6, col.1, NY Times.com (Oct. 13, 2002).

449 See Note, 63 Ohio St. L.J. 1165 (2002) (applicability of the implied warranty of merchantability to fast-food litigation).

the time of his second heart attack after eating two or three fast food meals a day over an extended period of time. The class for which certification was sought consisted of persons who consumed the defendants' fast food and became obese or developed coronary heart disease, diabetes, high blood pressure, high cholesterol levels, or other health problems from the defendants' foods. The lawyer for the plaintiffs reportedly decided not to pursue *Barber* but to focus instead upon *Pelman v. McDonald's Corp.*,[450] another class action against McDonald's brought on behalf of obese children, including one 400-pound 15-year-old suffering from Type 2 diabetes who claimed to have eaten at McDonald's daily since he was six.[451]

Observing that its failure to act decisively "could spawn thousands of similar 'McLawsuits,' "[452] the court promptly dismissed the *Pelman* complaint, with leave to amend, ruling that fast-food restaurants have no duty to warn consumers of the open, obvious, and well-known fact that such foods contain high levels of cholesterol, fat, salt, and sugar; that the complaint failed adequately to plead proximate cause because it failed to specify how often the children ate such foods and failed to account for factors other than diet that may have contributed to the children's health problems; that it failed to specify how the fats, sugars, and other substances may have been addictive; and that it failed to allege whether the defendants purposefully included addictive elements to its fast foods.[453]

At bottom, the court correctly saw that *Pelman* raised vital questions of personal responsibility,[454] pointedly highlighted by derisive popular reactions to the filing of these lawsuits noted by the press.[455] Simply put, because the complaint failed to allege that consumers are unaware of "the potential ill health effects of eating at McDonald's, they cannot blame McDonald's if they, nonetheless, choose to satiate their appetite with a surfeit of supersized McDonald's products."[456] The plaintiffs refiled,[457] later abandoning their warning claim, and the trial court dismissed the remaining claims of deceptive

---

[450] 237 F. Supp. 2d 512 (S.D.N.Y. 2003).

[451] See Comment, Obesity Liability: A Supersized Problem or a Small Fry in the Inevitable Development of Product Liability?, 7 Chap. L. Rev. 239 (Spring 2004); Parloff, Is Fat the Next Tobacco?, Fortune Magazine (Feb. 3, 2003).

[452] 237 F. Supp. 2d at 518.

[453] See Pelman v. McDonald's Corp., 237 F. Supp. 2d 512 (S.D.N.Y. 2003) (dismissing claims); Pelman v. McDonald's Corp., 2003 WL 22052778 (S.D.N.Y. 2003) (ditto, more emphatically), vacated and remanded, 396 F.3d 508 (2d Cir. 2005).

[454] "The issue of determining the breadth of personal responsibility underlies much of the law: where should the line be drawn between an individual's own responsibility to take care of herself, and society's responsibility to ensure that others shield her?" *Pelman*, 237 F. Supp. 2d at 516.

[455] See id. at 518, quoting, among others, the following reports: Goldman, Consumer Republic: Common Sense May Not Be McDonald's Ally for Long, Adweek, Ed. 14 (Dec. 12, 2002) ("[T]he masses have expressed their incredulity at and contempt for the litigious kids—and their parents—who won't take responsibility for a lifetime of chowing down Happy Meals. With much tongue-clucking, the vox populi bemoans yet another symptom of the decline of personal responsibility and the rise of the cult of victimhood."); Shlaes, Lawyers Get Fat on McDonald's, Chi. Trib. 25 (Nov. 27, 2002) ("Every now and then America draws a cartoon of herself for the amusement of the rest of the world. Last week's fat lawsuit against McDonald's is one of those occasions."). See also Turley, Editorial, Betcha Can't Sue Just One, L.A. Times, 2002 WL 2492444 (July 24, 2002) ("Finally, there is the question of personal responsibility, which seems often ignored in these massive lawsuits. We may soon see campaigns from the industry reminding us that 'Twinkies don't kill people, people kill people.' "); Parloff, Is Fat the Next Tobacco?, N.Y. Times (Jan. 21, 2003) ("News of the lawsuit drew hoots of derision.").

[456] 237 F. Supp. 2d at 517–18. It should be recalled that, in the 1960s, the ALI included butter in § 402A's safe harbor of inherently dangerous food products commonly known to produce cholesterol and increase the risk of heart attacks. See Rest. (2d) Torts § 402A cmt. *i*.

[457] See Kaufmann, Franchising Fast Food Insanity, 229 N.Y. L.J. 3 (2003).

advertising under New York's Consumer Protection Act.[458] Ruling that the plaintiffs had indeed properly alleged claims under the deceptive trade practices act, the circuit court vacated and remanded.[459] The case continued for a while on certain claims of deceptive advertising[460] until the court finally denied class certification on those claims.[461]

The plaintiffs' bar had more success with other food claims,[462] and they reportedly decided to pursue food claims with vigor.[463] After many state legislatures limited fast food litigation,[464] plaintiffs' counsel, with varied success, turned to mislabeling claims against food manufacturers, frequently alleging violations of consumer protection statutes.[465]

Reform legislation. In 2004, the United States House of Representatives, but not the Senate, passed a "cheeseburger bill" banning obesity-related lawsuits against restaurants and other food sellers.[466] A flurry of similar "Baby McBills" were introduced in state legislatures across the nation and twenty-six states enacted such legislation.[467]

---

458 Pelman v. McDonald's Corp., 2003 WL 22052778 (S.D.N.Y. 2003).

459 Pelman v. McDonald's Corp., 396 F.3d 508 (2d Cir. 2005).

460 Pelman v. McDonald's Corp., 396 F. Supp. 2d 439 (S.D.N.Y. 2005) ((granting part of defendant's motion for more definite statement), 452 F. Supp. 2d 320, 327 (S.D.N.Y. 2006) (barring plaintiff's misrepresentation claims regarding "cholesterol-free" french fries and Mighty Kids Meals but allowing other misrepresentation claims to proceed).

461 Pelman v. McDonald's Corp., 272 F.R.D. 82, 100 (S.D.N.Y 2010) (denying class certification of deceptive marketing claims).

462 See Judge OKs McDonald's $10.5 Million Deal for Settlement of Trans Fatty Acids Suit, Prod. Liab. Daily, Sept. 21, 2007, at D9; Zernike, Lawyers Shift Focus From Big Tobacco to Big Food, NY Times.com (April 9, 2004) (reporting that McDonald's paid $12 million to settle a claim for failing to disclose that its french fries contained beef fat; that Kraft stopped using trans fats in Oreos; and that the makers of a puffy cheese snack, Pirate's Booty, paid $4 million to settle a claim that it understated fat grams). *But see* In re McDonald's French Fries Litig., 257 F.R.D. 669, 674 (N.D. Ill. 2009) (denying certification of class action alleging french fries and hash browns were not gluten-, wheat-, and dairy-free as advertised).

463 See Zernike, Lawyers Shift Focus from Big Tobacco to Big Food, NY Times.com (April 9, 2004). See also Florida Class Suits Seek Refunds, Damages, Health Monitoring for Recalled Peanut Butter, Prod. Liab. Daily, Mar. 19, 2007, at D11; Autistic Girl's Parents File Class Action Over Gluten in McDonald's French Fries, Prod. Liab. Daily, Mar. 24, 2006, at D18; Illinois, Florida Suits Against McDonald's Allege Allergens Found in French Fries, Prod. Liab. Daily, Mar. 10, 2006, at D16.

464 See note 467, below.

465 For a variety of mislabeling claims against food manufacturers, ranging from chemical additives in "natural" food, to extra ingredients in "whole wheat" products, to "slack fill" packaging, among others, see § 3.2 notes 99–104, above. See also Ramey, The Case for Plain Vanilla Gets Its Day in Court, Wall St. J.com (Feb. 7, 2021) (describing class actions alleging misrepresentation of artificial flavoring as "natural" vanilla); Note, A "Natural" Stand Off Between the Food and Drug Administration and the Courts: The Rise in Food-Labeling Litigation & the Need for Regulatory Reform, 60 B.C. L. Rev. 271 (2019) (reviewing the waves of "all natural," and "healthy" food label suits); Vogt, Food Labeling: The Next Wave of Consumer Class Actions, 41 Prod. Safety & Liab. Rep. (BNA) 565 (May 6, 2013).

466 See Burnett, Fast-Food Lawsuits and the Cheeseburger Bill: Critiquing Congress' Response to the Obesity Epidemic, 14 Va. J. Soc. Pol'y & L. 357 (2007); House Passes 'Cheeseburger Bill,' Bans Obesity-Related Suits Against Food Industry, 72 U.S. L. Week-Legal News 2547 (Mar. 16, 2004). See H.R. Rep. No. 108–432, Personal Responsibility in Food Consumption Act, H.R. 339.

467 Enacted in 2003, Louisiana's statute, perhaps the first, is typical: "Any manufacturer, distributor, or seller of a food or nonalcoholic beverage intended for human consumption shall not be subject to civil liability for personal injury or wrongful death based on an individual's consumption of food or nonalcoholic beverages in cases where liability is premised upon the individual's weight gain, obesity, or a health condition related to weight gain or obesity and resulting from his long-term consumption of a food or nonalcoholic beverage." La. Rev. Stat. Ann. § 9:2799.6. Similar statutes have been enacted in Ala., Ariz., Colo., Fla., Ga., Idaho, Ill., Ind., Kan., Ky., Me., Mich., Mo., N.C., N.D., Ohio, Okla. (held unconstitutional), Or., S.D., Tenn., Tex., Utah, Wash., Wis., Wyo. The statutes are compiled in Appendix J of Owen & Davis on Products Liability. See generally Frank, A Taxonomy of Obesity Legislation, 28 U. Ark. Little Rock L. Rev. 427, 435–37 (2006); Note, How

Reflections on Inherent Product Hazards

The extent to which manufacturers should be subject to liability for harm from inherent product hazards—such as cancer from smoking cigarettes and obesity from eating fast foods—is a fascinating chapter at the edge of products liability law.[468] It is likely that courts and (when necessary) legislatures will continue to resolve the basic principles of responsibility for such harm largely in the commonsense way they have so far—to wit, by ruling that manufacturers are required to provide warnings of foreseeable hazards that lie hidden in their products, and that they surely are to be held accountable for misrepresentations that trick consumers into thinking products are safer than they truly are.

Yet, responsibility for unavoidable dangers of which consumers generally are aware—because such dangers are commonly known, plainly visible, or warned about—typically should reside with consumers themselves, as normal risks of life. Ordinary insurance mechanisms, rather than the products liability litigation system, are preferable institutions to address the inevitable losses from widely known inherent product hazards. In this domain, courts should continue to step aside, and legislatures should continue to step up to limit the most dubious types of inherent product hazard litigation—such as responsibility for harm from obesity, from the gluttonous abuse of fast food, and from the criminal abuse of guns—to help relieve sellers, other consumers (through higher prices and reduced availability), and the courts of burdens that should remain the personal responsibility of individual consumers.

§ 10.4 State of the Art

In products liability law, "state of the art" was long an unrefined concept whose meaning and role continue to evolve.[469] The concept remains loosely and variously defined by courts and legislatures, and many courts have not yet crystallized the developing doctrine into formal rules. Nevertheless, emerging from the cases and statutes is a common meaning—that which reasonably can be known and done; and a

---

Commonsense Consumption Acts Are Preventing "Big Food" Litigation, 41 Seattle U. L. Rev. 695 (2018) (arguing for repeal of such statutes to allow for massive tobacco-like litigation).

[468] This discussion draws from Owen, Inherent Product Hazards, 93 Ky. L.J. 377, 422 (2005).

[469] On the state-of-the-art issue in products liability law, see Choi, Crashworthy Code, 94 Wash. L. Rev. 39 (2019); Kennedy, Who Knew? Refining the "Knowability" Standard for the Future of Potentially Hazardous Technologies, 9 Wash. J.L. Tech. & Arts 267 (2014); Ausness, "Fasten Your Seat Belt, Orville!": Exploring the Relationship Between State-of-the-Art, Technological and Commercial Feasibility, and the Restatement's Reasonable Alternative Design Requirement, 45 Ind. L. Rev. 669 (2012); Owen, Bending Nature, Bending Law, 62 Fla. L. Rev. 569 (2010); Stapleton, Liability for Drugs in the U.S. and EU: Rhetoric and Reality, 26 Rev. Litig. 991 (2007) (thoroughly and insightfully examining applicability of state of the art concepts under European law); Wertheimer, The Biter Bit Unknowable Dangers, the Third Restatement, and the Reinstatement of Liability Without Fault, 70 Brook. L. Rev. 889 (2005); Henderson and Twerski, A Fictional Tale of Unintended Consequences: A Response to Professor Wertheimer, 70 Brook. L. Rev. 939 (2005); Schwartz and Tedesco, The Re-Emergence of "Super Strict" Liability: Slaying the Dragon Again, 71 U. Cin. L. Rev. 917 (2003); Miller, Myth Surrenders to Reality: Design Defect Litigation in Iowa, 51 Drake L. Rev. 549, 586–95 (2003); Cupp, Rethinking Conscious Design Liability for Prescription Drugs: The Restatement (Third) Standard Versus a Negligence Approach, 63 Geo. Wash. L. Rev. 76 (1994); Vandall, State-of-the-Art, Custom, and Reasonable Alternative Design, 28 Suffolk U. L. Rev. 1193 (1994); Wertheimer, Unknowable Dangers and the Death of Strict Products Liability: The Empire Strikes Back, 60 U. Cin. L. Rev. 1183 (1992); Newdick, Risk, Uncertainty and "Knowledge" in the Development Risk Defence, 20 Anglo-Am. L. Rev. 309 (1991); Wade, On the Effect in Product Liability of Knowledge Unavailable Prior to Marketing, 58 N.Y.U. L. Rev. 734 (1983); Page, Generic Product Risks: The Case Against Comment K and for Strict Tort Liability, 58 N.Y.U. L. Rev. 853 (1983); Annot. 33 A.L.R.4th 368 (1981) (state of the art in strict liability warning cases; whether defendant must know of danger).

common theme—a reluctance to impose liability on manufacturers for dangers that were practicably unknowable, or unpreventable, at the time their products were sold. The principle that has now quite firmly emerged is a general refusal to hold producers responsible for risks they cannot control.

State-of-the-art issues conveniently may be classified according to whether an asserted defect is one of warning or design.[470] In *warning* cases, the state-of-the-art issue usually involves a manufacturer's ability to know about or reasonably foresee a product danger in order to warn consumers of its presence.[471] While manufacturers are at least generally aware of most hazards in their products before they are sold to consumers and cause harm, dangers are occasionally unknown or undiscoverable before a product is sold and put to use. Blood infected with serum hepatitis, formerly undetectable before transfusion into a person,[472] was a prime example in earlier times, as was the AIDS virus in blood products prior to the development of reliable tests during the early 1980s.[473] Pork containing trichinae parasites, causing trichinosis in people who eat such pork without proper cooking, is another example of an undiscoverable product hazard.[474] Similarly, chemicals, pharmaceutical drugs, and other substances, such as asbestos, may be discovered to have toxic effects only after such products are marketed and harm consumers, sometimes generations later.[475] If such dangers prove to have been foreseeable, discoverable with appropriate pre-market testing or analysis, and if they were avoidable by appropriate warning, processing, or redesign, then manufacturers of such products may be responsible for the harmful results of failing to discover or avoid those risks under ordinary principles of negligence, warranty, or strict liability in tort. But if the risks were in fact unknowable before consumers began to suffer harm, responsibility for failing to warn about (or otherwise address) such unforeseeable risks is far more tenuous.

The second type of state of the art case involves the feasibility of adopting curative *design* measures to reduce or eliminate a risk of which the manufacturer usually is aware. Although manufacturers are well aware of most hazards in durable products they make and sell, such hazards are often practicably unavoidable under the prevailing state of science and technology. Persons may be injured in countless ways: a person's foot may

---

[470] While the cases are split, some courts and statutes allow the defense in manufacturing defect cases. Compare Reed v. Tiffin Motor Homes, Inc., 697 F.2d 1192, 1196 (4th Cir. 1982) (S.C. law) (not available in manufacturing defect cases), Sturm, Ruger & Co. v. Day, 594 P.2d 38, 44 (Alaska 1979) (same), and Cunningham v. MacNeal Mem'l Hosp., 266 N.E.2d 897, 902 (Ill. 1970) (bad blood, same; contrary result would "emasculate" strict liability), with Indianapolis Athletic Club, Inc. v. Alco Standard Corp., 709 N.E.2d 1070 (Ind. Ct. App. 1999) (statutory state-of-the-art defense covered manufacturing defects as well as defects in warning and design), and McGuire v. Davidson Mfg. Corp., 258 F. Supp. 2d 945 (N.D. Iowa 2003) (Iowa's state-of-the-art statutory defense explicitly applies to manufacturing as well as design and warning defects), aff'd, 398 F.3d 1005 (8th Cir. 2005).

[471] These cases usually involve claims of warning rather than design defects, but the unknowable risk issue does sometimes arise in a design defect claim. See, e.g., Dean v. General Motors Corp., 301 F. Supp. 187 (E.D. La. 1969) (foreseeability of thieves breaking into cars in certain way which could have been prevented by changing lock and key design).

[472] See, e.g., Cunningham v. MacNeal Mem'l Hosp., 266 N.E.2d 897, 902 (Ill. 1970) (rejecting state-of-the-art defense). While various screening and testing approaches have substantially reduced this risk in recent years, an undiscoverable residual remains. Centers for Disease Control, www.cdc.gov.

[473] The contaminated blood issue is separately treated in § 16.9, below.

[474] See, e.g., Kircos v. Holiday Food Ctr., Inc., 477 N.W.2d 130 (Mich. Ct. App. 1991) (public knows that pork must be cooked to be sure to avoid trichinosis). See generally Frumer, Friedman, and Sklaren, Products Liability § 48.21[4][c].

[475] See § 10.5, below.

slip under a power lawnmower, a hand may be caught in a punch press or other industrial machine, a car may collide at high speed into a tree, and a kitchen stove burner may ignite a dish towel or a blouse. The science and technology of safety is constantly evolving to help reduce various risks of injury—as by the development in recent decades of guards and electrical interlocks for power lawn mowers and industrial machinery; airbags for automobiles; and flame retardant chemicals for fabrics. But hands and feet still find ways to get under mowers and into machines, bones still get broken in car accidents, and fabrics still catch fire on kitchen stoves. Other kinds of products involve dangers that are entirely unavoidable under current science and technology, not just practicably so, such as the basic health risks of cigarettes and alcohol, and various side-effects of important pharmaceutical drugs, such as penicillin and the Pasteur rabies vaccine.[476] The question in these types of cases is not whether the *risks* are known or knowable, for the hazards are well known, but whether the means of *avoiding* the risks, by designing them away, are known or reasonably knowable and feasible under the existing state of science and technology.

As science and technology evolve over time, and as new and improved methods for discovering and eliminating product hazards are developed, public attitudes toward risk and responsibility also evolve. In the twenty-first century, people expect much more safety in machine guarding, automotive crash protection, and fabric flammability than they did in 1900, or even in 1950. "A consumer would not expect a Model T to have the safety features which are incorporated in automobiles made today."[477] Whether manufacturers should be liable for failing to avert product-caused injuries that happen today, but which were unforeseeable or unpreventable (literally or practicably) at the time the products were designed and sold, raises difficult and important questions of logic, fairness, social policy, and legal doctrine.[478]

Penetrating to the heart of defectiveness and "strict" liability, the state-of-the-art issue forces courts and commentators to re-examine the goals of products liability law by raising a number of fundamental questions: Who should bear the risks and benefits of changes in science and technology that develop over time? How should the law deal with changes in public attitudes toward risk, manufacturer responsibility, individual responsibility, and products liability doctrine? Are juries capable of fairly judging products made before the jurors were born, according to the technology, standards, and values of long ago? Is the judicial system capable of resolving these problems in a principled manner, or is the legislature a preferable forum for drawing the basic liability lines? Courts, legislatures, and commentators must grapple with these perplexing questions that lie on the cutting edge of modern products liability law.

The state-of-the-art issue is treated generally in the materials that follow. Liability for the related issue of inherent dangers in products such as cigarettes, handguns, and alcoholic beverages was examined in the previous section.[479]

---

[476] See Rest. (2d) Torts § 402A cmt. *k*.

[477] Bruce v. Martin-Marietta Corp., 544 F.2d 442, 447 (10th Cir. 1976) (Md. law).

[478] See, e.g., Henderson, Coping with the Time Dimension in Products Liability, 69 Cal. L. Rev. 919 (1981), inspired by Owen, Rethinking the Policies of Strict Products Liability, 33 Vand. L. Rev. 681 (1980); Phillips, An Analysis of Proposed Reform of Products Liability Statutes of Limitations, 56 N.C. L. Rev. 663 (1978); and articles cited in note 469, above.

[479] See § 10.3, above.

Definitions

Especially as products liability law was first developing, the terms "undiscoverable," "unknowable," "unavoidable," and "state of the art" were often interchanged indiscriminately by courts and commentators attempting to describe risks that manufacturers and other sellers are unable to control. Increasingly, however, issues of this type are collected under the latter phrase—as in "state-of-the-art evidence" and the "state-of-the-art defense." Due in part to the diffuse nature of the state-of-the-art concept, which embraces such diverse aspects of manufacturer responsibility as the foreseeability of risk, the feasibility of implementing a safer design, and the proper scope of "strict" liability, courts and legislatures have yet to agree on a definition of the term.[480]

"State of the art," that is, means quite different things to different persons. To many manufacturers and some courts,[481] the phrase refers to customary practice in the industry. To many plaintiffs' counsel and some courts,[482] it means the ultimate in existing technology, including all knowledge pertinent to a problem existing at the time, regardless of its location or source, and regardless of whether possessed by or accessible from industrial, governmental, or academic institutions, or even from the defendant's competitors.[483]

Neither of these extreme views of state of the art is helpful for products liability law. To allow a manufacturer to hide behind the customary practices of an industry would create a shield stronger than that allowed by ordinary negligence law, where the *T. J. Hooper* rule[484] requires enterprises to conduct their affairs with reasonable prudence, even if the level of safety prevailing in the industry as a whole has lagged

---

480 See, e.g., Lane v. Amsted Indus., 779 S.W.2d 754, 758 n.4 (Mo. Ct. App. 1989) ("The judicial decisions and some commentary employ the term *state of the art* without distinction to mean industry practice and custom, industry capability, industry or scientific knowability, and even compliance with governmental regulations."); Potter v. Chicago Pneumatic Tool Co., 694 A.2d 1319, 1345 (Conn. 1997) ("the term 'state of the art' has been the source of substantial confusion").

481 See, e.g., Lane v. Amsted Indus., 779 S.W.2d 754, 758 (Mo. Ct. App. 1989); Smith v. Minster Mach. Co., 669 F.2d 628, 633 (10th Cir. 1982) (Okla. law) (state of the art "is understood to mean simply the custom and practice in an industry"); Sturm, Ruger & Co. v. Day, 594 P.2d 38, 44 (Alaska 1979) ("Generally speaking, 'state of the art' refers to customary practice in the industry.").

482 See, e.g., Lightfoot v. Georgia-Pac. Wood Prods., LLC, 5 F.4th 484, 489 (4th Cir. 2021) (N.C. law) (" 'the *culmination* of the relevant research' in a given field, . . . or, stated otherwise, the synthesis of the available knowledge on a certain subject *at a given time*") (emphasis in original); Wiska v. St. Stanislaus Soc. Club, Inc., 390 N.E.2d 1133, 1138 n.8 (Mass. App. Ct. 1979) ("the level of pertinent scientific and technical knowledge existing at the time"); ACandS, Inc. v. Asner, 686 A.2d 250, 254 (Md. 1996) ("all of the available knowledge on a subject at a given time, and this includes scientific, medical, engineering, and any other knowledge that may be available").

483 See Owens-Illinois, Inc. v. Zenobia, 601 A.2d 633, 644–45 (Md. 1992).

484 Named, of course, after Judge Learned Hand's celebrated decision in The T.J. Hooper v. Northern Barge Corp., 60 F.2d 737 (2d Cir. 1932) (Hand, J.). The *T. J. Hooper* rule holds that industry practice or custom, while relevant to the reasonableness of a defendant's conduct, is not generally conclusive, since the industry as a whole may have been derelict in failing to adopt precautionary measures dictated by ordinary prudence:

> [I]n most cases reasonable prudence is in fact common prudence; but strictly it is never its measure; a whole calling may have unduly lagged in the adoption of new and available devices. It never may set its own tests . . . . Courts must in the end say what is required; there are precautions so imperative that even their universal disregard will not excuse their omission.

Id. at 740. Judge Hand drew upon the wisdom of another giant, Justice Holmes, in Texas & Pac. Ry. Co. v. Behymer, 189 U.S. 468, 470 (1903): "What usually is done may be evidence of what ought to be done, but what ought to be done is fixed by a standard of reasonable prudence, whether it usually is complied with or not."

behind a standard of good behavior.[485] Thus, almost all courts properly distinguish state-of-the-art evidence from evidence of custom.[486] But to define state of the art in terms of the best science and technology in existence would go too far in the opposite direction: to require manufacturers to put new safety theories instantly into practice, when the theories may be locked away in arcane scientific journals (perhaps in another language) and are years removed from real-world application, is to ask manufacturers to perform a practical impossibility. Holding manufacturers to a standard so rigorous would in some cases force them to serve as guarantors or insurers of product safety, which for a variety of good reasons the law has never sought to do.[487]

Most statutes and judicial decisions define the state-of-the-art idea more moderately along a middle ground, lying somewhere between these two extremes. For example, Nebraska's products reform act defines state of the art as "the best technology reasonably available at the time,"[488] and Missouri's statute states that, as a defense, the phrase "means that the dangerous nature of the product was not known and could not reasonably be discovered at the time the product was placed into the stream of commerce."[489] Arizona's statute is more prolix, but similar in its spirit: " 'state of the art' means the technical, mechanical and scientific knowledge of manufacturing, designing, testing or labeling the same or similar products which was in existence and reasonably feasible for use at the time of manufacture."[490] While not defining the term, New Hampshire at least clothes it in context by formulating a defense that "the risks . . . were not discoverable under prevailing research and scientific techniques under the state of the art."[491]

Courts have variously stated that state of the art refers to "what feasibly could have been done,"[492] "the existing level of technological expertise and scientific knowledge relevant to a particular industry at the time a product is designed,"[493] "the technological feasibility of alternative safer designs in existence at the time the product was originally

---

[485] See, e.g., Hillrichs v. Avco Corp., 514 N.W.2d 94, 98 (Iowa 1994) (custom of cornpicker manufacturers not to equip them with $50 emergency stop device no bar to negligent design claim). See also §§ 2.3 (custom evidence to establish negligence) and 6.4 (evidence of custom to establish defectiveness), above.

[486] See, e.g., Kim v. Toyota Motor Corp., 424 P.3d 290, 296 (Cal. 2018) (state of the art is " 'what *can* be done' under present technological capacity" whereas industry custom and practice is "what *is* done" in the industry) (emphasis added); Bauerline v. Equity Residential Props. Mgmt. Corp., 2006 WL 3834285, at *8 (D. Ariz. 2006) (because "customs may lag behind technological development, they are not identical with state of the art"); Falada v. Trinity Indus., 642 N.W.2d 247, 250 (Iowa 2002) ("Custom refers to what was being done in the industry; state of the art refers to what feasibly could have been done."); Potter v. Chicago Pneumatic Tool Co., 694 A.2d 1319, 1347 (Conn. 1997) ("state of the art refers to what is technologically feasible, rather than merely industry custom"); ACandS, Inc. v. Asner, 686 A.2d 250, 254–55 (Md. 1996) ("Industry standards are the practices common to a given industry . . . often set forth in some type of code [or] adopted by the trade organization of a given industry. State of the art is a higher standard because scientific knowledge expands much more rapidly than industry can assimilate the knowledge and adopt it as a standard."); Carter v. Massey-Ferguson, Inc., 716 F.2d 344, 347 (5th Cir. 1983) (Tex. law) (Wisdom, J.).

[487] See §§ 5.3 and 5.4, above.

[488] Neb. Rev. Stat. § 25–21,182.

[489] Mo. Ann. Stat. § 537.764.

[490] Ariz. Rev. Stat. Ann. § 12–681(10). See Bernal v. Daewoo Motor Am., Inc., 2011 WL 2174890, at *5–6 (D. Ariz. 2011) (applying the statute).

[491] N.H. Rev. Stat. § 507:8–g.

[492] Bauerline v. Equity Residential Props. Mgmt. Corp., 2006 WL 3834285, at *8 (D. Ariz. 2006); Falada v. Trinity Indus., 642 N.W.2d 247, 250 (Iowa 2002).

[493] Crispin v. Volkswagenwerk A.G., 591 A.2d 966, 973 (N.J. Super. Ct. App. Div. 1991). See also O'Brien v. Muskin Corp., 463 A.2d 298, 305 (N.J. 1983).

manufactured,"[494] "danger . . . which [manufacturers] know or should have known on the basis of reasonably obtainable or available knowledge,"[495] whether "the particular risk was neither known nor knowable by the application of scientific knowledge available at the time of manufacture and/or distribution,"[496] "the best technology reasonably feasible at the time,"[497] whether "safety features . . . were unknown or unavailable at the time the product" was sold,[498] and "the level of relevant scientific, technological and safety knowledge existing and reasonably feasible at the time of design."[499]

Moderate definitions such as these, based on reasonableness and practicability, appear most useful in drawing the state-of-the-art line in a fair and pragmatic manner. An appropriate state-of-the-art definition protects manufacturers who strive to stay abreast of (and perhaps advance) the developing science and technology of safety in their fields, and who implement such developments when practicable to do so, while properly capturing manufacturers unwilling to make such a commitment to product safety.

In sum, the precise manner in which "state of the art" definitions are formulated varies considerably, some leaning more toward industry custom, others leaning more toward theoretical technological capability, and the best ones lying somewhere in between. Some courts[500] and legislatures[501] simply use the term without defining it, which, while it avoids misdefining the term, provides decisionmakers with little guidance. Other courts[502] and legislatures[503] use the concepts but not the "state of the art" term, which has the benefit of providing appropriate limitations on liability while avoiding ambiguities in the term itself. But the "state of the art" term, which usefully

---

[494] Lenhardt v. Ford Motor Co., 683 P.2d 1097, 1099 (Wash. 1984). See also Malen v. MTD Prods., Inc., 628 F.3d 296, 308 (7th Cir. 2010) (Ill. law) (proving a design defect requires "evidence of a practical, cost-effective alternative that was technologically feasible"). On feasible alternative designs, see § 8.5, above.

[495] Feldman v. Lederle Labs., 479 A.2d 374, 376 (N.J. 1984). Compare Salinero v. Johnson & Johnson, 2019 WL 7753438, at *9 (S.D. Fla. 2019) ("the best known and available technology").

[496] Anderson v. Owens-Corning Fiberglas Corp., 810 P.2d 549, 559 (Cal. 1991).

[497] Kaiser v. Johnson & Johnson, 947 F.3d 996, 1017 (7th Cir. 2020) (Ind. law).

[498] Owens-Corning Fiberglas Corp. v. Golightly, 976 S.W.2d 409, 411 (Ky. 1998).

[499] Potter v. Chicago Pneumatic Tool Co., 694 A.2d 1319, 1346–47 (Conn. 1997) (quoting definitions from other cases, and stating that its definition is endorsed by a majority of courts).

[500] See, e.g., Keogh v. W.R. Grasle, Inc., 816 P.2d 1343, 1349 n.10 (Alaska 1991). Compare Phillips v. Cameron Tool Corp., 950 F.2d 488 (7th Cir. 1991) (Ind. law) (because opposing lawyers defined the term differently in jury argument, trial judge's failure to define term was reversible error).

[501] Statutes in Florida, Idaho, Indiana, Iowa, Kansas, and South Dakota take this approach. See, e.g., Phillips v. Cameron Tool Corp., 950 F.2d 488 (7th Cir. 1991) (Ind. law); Montgomery Ward & Co. v. Gregg, 554 N.E.2d 1145, 1155 (Ind. Ct. App. 1990).

[502] See, e.g., Flock v. Scripto-Tokai Corp., 319 F.3d 231, 239 (5th Cir. 2003) (Tex. law) (plaintiff required to prove availability of safer alternative design that was "economically and technologically feasible at the time the product left the control of the manufacturer or seller by the application of existing or reasonably achievable scientific knowledge"); McDaniel v. Trail King Indus., 248 F. Supp. 2d 749, 757 (N.D. Ill. 2002) (alternative design must be "economical, practical and effective"); Cooper v. General Motors Corp., 702 So.2d 428, 443–44 (Miss. 1997) ("[I]mposing liability on a manufacturer for not installing an air bag in the early eighties, when air bags were new to the scene and still undergoing scientific testing, goes against the grain of public policy. The principles of law should not overlook the need for scientific development or bring manufacturers to their knees for choosing one restraint system over another, in light of what was known to them at the time of their manufacturing."). See also Artis v. Corona Corp., 703 A.2d 1214, 1217 (D.C. 1997) ("[A] safer alternative design may have been economically and technologically feasible at the time of the product's manufacture, but it may not have been commercially available. All that is required is that it be commercially feasible at the time of manufacture.").

[503] Statutes in Louisiana, Michigan, Mississippi, and Tennessee take this approach. For example, the Michigan statute provides that a manufacturer is not liable for failing to warn unless it "knew or should have known about the risk of harm based on the scientific, technical, or medical information reasonably available at the time" of manufacture. Mich. Comp. Laws Ann. § 600.2948(3).

describes a basic limitation of the law of products liability, has a commonsense ring that may help to guide both courts and juries. It would seem hard to improve upon Nebraska's simple, balanced definition of "the best technology reasonably available at the time."[504]

Applicability to Different Types of Claims

State-of-the-art evidence is highly relevant to negligence claims, which are predicated on a manufacturer's ability to foresee and reasonably prevent product accidents. As discussed above, the state-of-the-art issue usually concerns either: (1) the foreseeability of a particular risk of which the plaintiff claims the defendant failed to warn, or (2) the feasibility of modifying a design in a particular manner to eliminate a risk of which the manufacturer was aware. In the negligent *warning* context, if a risk is "unknowable," it is "unforeseeable" and so lies outside the manufacturer's duty to avoid.[505] In negligent *design* and *manufacturing* contexts, if the manufacturer has no practical ability to eliminate a danger, the burden on the manufacturer to avoid an injury outweighs virtually any risk of harm. For these reasons, perhaps all courts hold that state-of-the-art evidence is especially relevant to products liability claims brought in negligence.[506]

The relevance of the state-of-the-art issue to *strict* liability claims has been more controversial. "Strict" liability implies that liability is imposed merely for selling a product that is too dangerous, according to some standard of excessive danger, not whether the manufacturer or other seller should be faulted for selling the product. Indeed, "strict liability" is often labeled "no-fault" liability.[507] If fault indeed is irrelevant to this form of liability, the state-of-the-art issue might appear to be irrelevant to whether a manufacturer is strictly liable for selling a product that is defective. This was the position of the court in *Johnson v. Raybestos-Manhattan, Inc.*,[508] which answered a certified question in an asbestos case on whether state-of-the-art evidence on the foreseeability of the risk is relevant to a strict tort claim. The court began by noting that a strict products liability action does not require a showing of a defendant's fault, but only that the defendant was a commercial seller, that the product was defective, and that the defect caused the plaintiff's harm.[509] The court thus concluded that "in a strict products liability action, the issue of whether the seller knew or reasonably should have known of the dangers inherent in his or her product is irrelevant to the issue of liability. Although highly relevant to a negligence action, it has absolutely no bearing on the elements of a strict product liability claim." Accordingly, the court ruled that "in a strict products liability action, state-of-the-art evidence is not admissible for the purpose of establishing whether the seller knew or reasonably should have known of the dangerousness of his or her product."[510]

A small handful of other courts have reasoned similarly that state-of-the-art evidence is simply irrelevant to products liability tort claims that are "strict." Almost all

---

[504] See Neb. Rev. Stat. § 25–21,182.

[505] See § 2.2, above.

[506] See, e.g., Tucker v. Wright Med. Tech., Inc., 2013 WL 1149717, at *13 (N.D. Cal. 2013) ("A reasonable manufacturer would not be charged with knowing more than what would come to light from the prevailing scientific and medical knowledge."); Rodriguez v. Stryker Corp., 2011 WL 31462, at *8–10 (M.D. Tenn. 2011); Gourdine v. Crews, 955 A.2d 769, 781–82 (Md. 2008).

[507] See § 5.1, above.

[508] 740 P.2d 548 (Haw. 1987).

[509] See id. at 549.

[510] Id.

these cases are older decisions[511] that have been effectively overruled.[512] More recent decisions in a small number of states have reaffirmed their commitment to a truly "strict" products liability doctrine—as increasingly archaic as this view may be in design and warning cases—uncontaminated by principles of foreseeability, fault, negligence, or state of the art.[513] Yet, except for a couple instances, courts or legislatures have either entirely repudiated these more recent declarations of allegiance to pure strict liability, or at least cast them into serious doubt.[514]

From a strictly doctrinal perspective, barring state-of-the-art evidence might seem logical under a pure consumer expectations test for defectiveness because a manufacturer's knowledge of a danger or ability to eliminate it might well seem

---

[511] See, e.g., Cunningham v. MacNeal Mem'l Hosp., 266 N.E.2d 897, 902 (Ill. 1970) ("To allow a defense to strict liability on the ground that there is no way, either practical or theoretical, for a defendant to ascertain the existence of impurities in his product would be to emasculate the doctrine and in a very real sense would signal a return to a negligence theory."); Lunt v. Brady Mfg. Corp., 475 P.2d 964, 966 (Ariz. Ct. App. 1970) ("It does not matter that the seller has done 'the best he can' if the product is defective and unreasonably dangerous."); Elmore v. Owens-Illinois, Inc., 673 S.W.2d 434, 438 (Mo. 1984) ("[t]he manufacturer's standard of care is irrelevant because it relates to the reasonableness of the manufacturer's design choice; fault is an irrelevant consideration on the issue of liability in the strict liability context"); Carrecter v. Colson Equip. Co., 499 A.2d 326, 331 (Pa. Super. Ct. 1985) (state-of-the-art evidence would "inject negligence [principles] into a products liability case"); Kisor v. Johns-Manville Corp., 783 F.2d 1337 (9th Cir. 1986) (Wash. law). See also Crocker v. Winthrop Labs., 514 S.W.2d 429, 433 (Tex. 1974) (Rest. (2d) Torts § 402B: "Whatever the danger and state of medical knowledge, . . . when the drug company positively and specifically represents its product to be free and safe from all dangers of addiction, . . . the drug company is liable when the representation proves to be false and harm results.").

[512] For example, Vassallo v. Baxter Healthcare Corp., 696 N.E.2d 909 (Mass. 1998), effectively overruled Hayes v. Ariens Co., 462 N.E.2d 273 (Mass. 1984), and statutes in Arizona, Missouri, and Washington adopt some version of the state-of-the-art defense. Arizona's statute provides a general state-of-the-art defense, and Missouri's statute allows such a defense to strict tort warning claims. The Washington statute defines liability for both warning and design in terms of "negligence," specifically defines defective design partially in terms of the availability of a practical and feasible alternative design, and provides for the admissibility of evidence on custom and technological feasibility. See Ariz. Rev. Stat. Ann. § 12–683(1); Mo. Ann. Stat. § 537.764; Wash. Rev. Code Ann. §§ 7.72.030, 7.72.050.

[513] See, e.g., Wilson Sporting Goods Co. v. Hickox, 59 A.3d 1267, 1277 (D.C. 2013) (angle of throat guard on baseball umpire's mask; under consumer expectations test, design defect need not be foreseeable since plaintiff need only show "that he used the product in an intended or reasonably foreseeable fashion and the product failed to perform in that capacity as safely as expected"); Bugosh v. I.U. N. Am., Inc., 971 A.2d 1228, 1248–49 (Pa. 2009) (Saylor, J., dissenting) (criticizing Pennsylvania's "no-negligence-in-strict-liability premise," including rejection of state-of-the-art defense); Malcolm v. Evenflo Co., 217 P.3d 514, 521 (Mont. 2009), reconfirming Sternhagen v. Dow Co., 935 P.2d 1139, 1144–47 (Mont. 1997) (state-of-the-art defense rejected in strict products liability case because it raises reasonableness and foreseeability issues relevant to negligence contrary to core principles of modern products liability law: consumer protection against dangerous defects and compensation for resulting injuries, and making those who profit from sale of such products bear resulting costs, with focus on product's condition rather than manufacturer's knowledge or conduct); Townsend v. Sears, Roebuck & Co., 879 N.E.2d 893, 899 (Ill. 2007) ("inability of the defendant to know or prevent the risk" is defense to negligence but not strict liability; dictum); Golonka v. General Motors Corp., 65 P.3d 956, 963 (Ariz. Ct. App. 2003). Cf. Uxa v. Marconi, 128 S.W.3d 121, 131 (Mo. Ct. App. 2003) ("state-of-the-art" evidence, which really just shows custom, irrelevant to design defect claim); Potter v. Chicago Pneumatic Tool Co., 694 A.2d 1319, 1348–49 (Conn. 1997) (manufacturer's conformance to state-of-the-art relevant to, but not conclusive on, liability).

[514] See, e.g., Tucker v. Wright Med. Tech., Inc., 2013 WL 1149717, at *12 (N.D. Cal. 2013) (in California, warning defect recovery now requires proof "that ordinary consumers would not have recognized the potential risks," and *also* proof that the risks "were known or knowable at the time of manufacture or distribution, or sale"); Placencia v. I-Flow Corp., 2012 WL 5877624, at *3 (D. Ariz. 2012) ("In a strict liability failure to warn claim, a plaintiff must prove 'that the defendant did not adequately warn of a particular risk that was known or knowable in light of the generally recognized and prevailing best scientific and medical knowledge available at the time of manufacture and distribution.' "). As discussed below, Wisconsin's approach turned upside down when the legislature there repudiated *Green* by adopting the defect standards of the Third Restatement. See §§ 5.3 and 5.4, above.

irrelevant to the degree of safety consumers actually expect.[515] Yet, some courts allow state-of-the-art evidence even under the consumer expectations test,[516] reasoning that such evidence "helps to determine the expectation of the ordinary consumer. A consumer would not expect a Model T to have the safety features which are incorporated in automobiles made today."[517] The Wade-Keeton constructive-knowledge test of liability,[518] which imputes knowledge of all a product's dangers to the manufacturer, compels rejection of the state-of-the-art defense, at least in cases involving a failure to warn. By its nature, this test evaluates the safety of a product with the hindsight available at the time of trial and so leaves no room for evidence, much less a defense, based on the state of knowledge prevailing at the time the product was made and sold.[519]

As the risk-utility test of design defectiveness has increasingly displaced the consumer expectations standard around the nation,[520] and as the Wade-Keeton constructive-knowledge test has fallen into desuetude,[521] the relevance of state-of-the-art evidence in design cases has become increasingly clear. In balancing the costs and benefits of a design feature that would have prevented a plaintiff's injury, the risk-utility test rests on the *foreseeability* of the risk and the availability of a *feasible* alternative design.[522] Consequently, in the increasing number of jurisdictions that employ some form of risk-utility test for design defects, courts widely admit state-of-the-art evidence on that issue.[523] And at least one state holds that such evidence is relevant under both design defect liability tests.[524]

In warning cases involving "unknowable" risks of harm, state-of-the-art evidence plays a critical role, regardless of the liability test employed. Notwithstanding the approach of a few decisions (such as *Johnson*, discussed above), almost all courts allow

---

[515] See, e.g., Morton v. Owens-Corning Fiberglas Corp., 40 Cal. Rptr. 2d 22, 25 (Ct. App. 1995), based on consumer expectations prong of *Barker*'s two-pronged standard. "[E]vidence as to what the scientific community knew about the dangers of asbestos and when they knew it is not relevant to show what the ordinary consumer of OCF's product reasonably expected in terms of safety at the time of Mr. Morton's exposure. It is the knowledge and reasonable expectations of the consumer, not the scientific community, that is relevant under the consumer expectations test. The fact that the scientific community was unaware of the dangers of asbestos, if that is a fact, would not make it any less reasonable for Mr. Morton or other consumers of OCF's products to expect that they could work with or near OCF's product without getting cancer."

[516] See, e.g., *Tucker*, note 514, above; In re Wright Med. Tech. Inc., 2015 WL 6690046, at *11 (N.D. Ga. 2015) (such evidence helps show consumer expectations). *Contra* Wilson Sporting Goods Co. v. Hickox, 59 A.3d 1267, 1277 (D.C. 2013) (design defect need not be foreseeable under consumer expectations test).

[517] Bruce v. Martin-Marietta Corp., 544 F.2d 442, 447 (10th Cir. 1976) (Okla. law). See also Robinson v. Brandtjen & Kluge, Inc., 500 F.3d 691, 695 (8th Cir. 2007) (S.D. law) (design safety of press manufactured in 1940 must be measured by consumer expectations at the time); Potter v. Chicago Pneumatic Tool Co., 694 A.2d 1319, 1346–48 (Conn. 1997) (collecting cases).

[518] See § 8.7, above.

[519] The classic holding to this effect was in Beshada v. Johns-Manville Prods. Corp., 447 A.2d 539 (N.J. 1982), restricted to its facts in Feldman v. Lederle Labs., 479 A.2d 374 (N.J. 1984). Both are discussed below.

[520] See chs. 5 and 8, above.

[521] See § 8.7, above.

[522] See §§ 5.7 and 8.4–8.5, above.

[523] See, e.g., Catherine Ford v. Riina, 75 N.Y.S.3d 13, 14 (App. Div. 2018); Folsom v. Kawasaki Motors Corp. U.S.A., 509 F. Supp. 2d 1364, 1378 (M.D. Ga. 2007) ("the state of the art at the time the product is manufactured" is one factor in the risk-utility analysis); Falada v. Trinity Indus., 642 N.W.2d 247, 250 (Iowa 2002) (statutory defense); Fibreboard Corp. v. Fenton, 845 P.2d 1168, 1174 (Colo. 1993); Boatland of Houston, Inc. v. Bailey, 609 S.W.2d 743 (Tex. 1980).

[524] See Atanassova v. General Motors LLC, 2021 WL 1946504, at *4 (D.S.C. 2021) (state of the art is relevant under both risk-utility test, to show reasonableness of design, and consumer expectations test, to show such expectations).

state-of-the-art evidence in such cases to defeat strict liability claims.[525] Otherwise stated, and as examined in detail below, courts today widely refuse to impose a duty on manufacturers to warn of unknowable risks—and, hence, refuse to enforce a liability standard that is truly "strict."

Procedural Effect of State-of-the-Art Evidence

Courts and legislatures that permit state-of-the-art evidence accord it one of three procedural effects: (1) as establishing an affirmative defense; (2) as creating a rebuttable presumption of nondefectiveness or non-negligence; or (3) as merely providing relevant evidence that a product was or was not defective or that a manufacturer or other supplier was or was not negligent. Most state statutes on point shield products liability defendants from liability, directly or indirectly, if they establish that the risk that injured the plaintiff was not reasonably foreseeable, or that the science or technology did not exist to prevent it.[526]

Several state statutes explicitly provide manufacturers with an affirmative state-of-the-art defense for products liability claims, in general or limited to warning or other particular types of claims.[527] A handful of state statutes implicitly provide a state-of-the-art defense for design defects by requiring a plaintiff to prove a feasible alternative design,[528] and courts in a number of states effectively provide such a defense in failure to warn cases by requiring a plaintiff to prove that the risk was foreseeable.[529] Statutes in Colorado, Indiana, and Kentucky create rebuttable presumptions—that the product was not defective or that the defendant was not negligent—from proof that the defendant complied with the state of the art in a products liability case.[530]

Several statutes and the great majority of judicial opinions on state-of-the-art evidence take the position that this type of evidence, concerning the practical availability of safety technology at the time of manufacture and sale, is relevant and admissible on

[525] For an important decision that refused to extend Arizona's Wade-Keeton hindsight test to warning cases, in one of the few jurisdictions where this test still has a bit of life, see Powers v. Taser Int'l, Inc., 174 P.3d 777, 779–84 (Ariz. Ct. App. 2008) (declining to extend Arizona's hindsight test from design to warning defect cases, and holding by implication that the duty to warn extends only to foreseeable risks). See also Tucker v. Wright Med. Tech., Inc., 2013 WL 1149717, at *12 (N.D. Cal. 2013).

[526] "In short, the state-of-the-art defense is a complete defense." Fell v. Kewanee Farm Equip. Co., 457 N.W.2d 911, 920 (Iowa 1990) (statutory defense). See also Falada v. Trinity Indus., 642 N.W.2d 247, 250 (Iowa 2002) (same); Brown v. Philip Morris Inc., 228 F. Supp. 2d 506, 520–24 (D.N.J. 2002) (same); Fabian v. Minster Mach. Co., 609 A.2d 487, 492 (N.J. Super. Ct. App. Div. 1992) (feasible alternative design statute, referred to as a state-of-the-art statute, provides an "absolute defense" for design defect claims); Mo. Ann. Stat. § 537.764(2) ("complete defense" for failure to warn claims); N.H. Rev. Stat. Ann. § 507:8–g ("it is an affirmative defense that the risks complained of by the plaintiff were not discoverable using prevailing research and scientific techniques under the state of the art"). Statutory reform of the state-of-the art issue is treated further, below.

[527] See the statutes in Ariz., Iowa, La., Mich., Miss., Mo., Neb., N.H., N.J., and S.D. The statutes are set forth in Appendices I and J of Owen & Davis on Products Liability.

[528] Statutes in at least La., Mich., Miss., N.J., N.C., Ohio, Tex., and Wis. require proof of a feasible alternative design to establish liability for a product's design in all or most design danger cases. These are discussed below.

[529] See, e.g., Vassallo v. Baxter Healthcare Corp., 696 N.E.2d 909 (Mass. 1998); Anderson v. Owens-Corning Fiberglas Corp., 810 P.2d 549 (Cal. 1991); Brown v. Superior Ct., 751 P.2d 470 (Cal. 1988); Feldman v. Lederle Labs., 479 A.2d 374 (N.J. 1984).

[530] See Colo. Rev. Stat. Ann. § 13–21–403(1)(a); Ind. Code Ann. § 34–20–5–1; Ky. Rev. Stat. Ann. § 411.310(2), as in Boon Edam, Inc. v. Saunders, 324 S.W.3d 422, 432 (Ky. Ct. App. 2010) (affirming judgment for plaintiff; plaintiff presented "ample evidence" of defect to rebut statutory presumption).

the issues of both negligence and product defectiveness.[531] Florida's statute, for example, provides that "the finder of fact shall consider the state of the art of scientific and technical knowledge and other circumstances that existed at the time of manufacture, not at the time of loss or injury."[532] A statute in Tennessee contains a similar provision.[533] Idaho's statute prohibits evidence of changes in technological feasibility, state of the art, or the custom of the seller's industry that occurred after sale,[534] and Kansas has a similar provision.[535] Most decisions allow state-of-the-art evidence to show the foreseeability of a risk of harm,[536] the feasibility of an alternative safer design,[537] or more generally hold that such evidence is relevant to a consumer's expectations, risk-utility, or simply to the issue of defectiveness.[538]

Unknowable Dangers—Common-Law Developments

Truly unknowable risks are a rarity in products liability law. Cases involving genuinely unforeseeable hazards surely must represent less than one in a hundred products liability cases, and probably less than one in a thousand. Manufacturers of durable products virtually always can foresee the harmful consequences of their products: that a punch press may crush a hand, that a defective electrical appliance may start a fire, or that a car may crush inward or roll over in certain accidents.[539] Claims of unknowable risks occasionally do arise in cases involving deleterious substances—pharmaceutical drugs, other chemical products, and certain natural substances such as asbestos and tobacco, all of which may cause cancer or other untoward harm. Even in such toxic substance cases, however, if manufacturers have conducted proper testing and laboratory analysis, truly unforeseeable dangers are highly unusual. Not uncommonly, manufacturers of such products—such as some drugs, asbestos, and cigarettes—who persist in claiming (especially in early cases) that the risk was unforeseeable are subsequently deluged with punitive damages claims on proof that they not only could foresee the risks, but that they were well aware of, and fraudulently concealed, such

---

[531] See, e.g., Gourdine v. Crews, 955 A.2d 769, 781 (Md. 2008) (In warning defect cases under § 402A and comment *j*, "negligence concepts to some extent have been grafted onto strict liability" and most such decisions "hold that an element of knowledge or 'state of the art' evidence is directly pertinent to a cause of action under § 402A . . ., and liability is no longer entirely 'strict.' "); Potter v. Chicago Pneumatic Tool Co., 694 A.2d 1319, 1346 (Conn. 1997) (an "overwhelming majority of courts" allow state-of-the-art evidence on adequacy of a product's design).

[532] See Fla. Stat. Ann. § 768.1257.

[533] See Tenn. Code Ann. § 29–28–105(b).

[534] See Idaho Code Ann. § 6–1406.

[535] See Kan. Stat. Ann. § 60–3307(a)(1).

[536] The seminal cases on this point were Feldman v. Lederle Labs., 479 A.2d 374 (N.J. 1984), and Brown v. Superior Ct., 751 P.2d 470 (Cal. 1988), followed by Anderson v. Owens-Corning Fiberglas Corp., 810 P.2d 549 (Cal. 1991).

[537] See, e.g., Robinson v. Brandtjen & Kluge, Inc., 500 F.3d 691, 695 (8th Cir. 2007) (S.D. law) (design safety of press; consumer expectations at time of manufacture); Falada v. Trinity Indus., 642 N.W.2d 247, 251 (Iowa 2002); Boatland of Houston, Inc. v. Bailey, 609 S.W.2d 743 (Tex. 1980). See § 8.5, above.

[538] See, e.g., Potter v. Chicago Pneumatic Tool Co., 694 A.2d 1319, 1346–48 (Conn. 1997) (collecting the cases, and emphasizing that "although state-of-the-art evidence may be dispositive on the facts of a particular case," it "does not constitute an affirmative defense that, if proven, would absolve the defendant from liability" but "is merely one factor for the jury to consider" on the issue of design defectiveness); Fibreboard Corp. v. Fenton, 845 P.2d 1168, 1174 (Colo. 1993).

[539] See Brooks v. Beech Aircraft Corp., 902 P.2d 54, 63 (N.M. 1995) (referring to the "hypothetical instances in which technology known at the time of trial and technology knowable at the time of distribution differ" and musing that "outside of academic rationale we find little to suggest the existence in practice of unknowable design considerations").

risks.[540] Despite the paucity of justifiable claims that a product hazard was unknowable at the time of marketing, the issue does sometimes arise. And when it does arise, the question of whether a manufacturer has a duty to warn of unknowable dangers presents the starkest and most intriguing state-of-the-art issue of all.

In the early 1960s, before § 402A of the *Restatement (Second) of Torts* was promulgated and adopted by the courts, the few courts considering the issue generally held that a manufacturer only had to warn of risks of which "the manufacturer knew, or by the application of reasonable developed human skill and foresight should have known."[541] This was true in both negligence and implied warranty.[542] And then, in 1965, came § 402A.[543] The widespread adoption of § 402A was significant to the unknowable risk warning problem in two respects. First, § 402A defined strict liability explicitly in no-fault terms, so that the new liability standard on its face appeared to banish any possible defense based upon a manufacturer's best efforts to make its products safe. "Strict liability" seemed directly contrary to "state-of-the-art" evidence that a product risk was unforeseeable. For example, in *Wagner v. Coronet Hotel*,[544] the court rejected the manufacturer's arguments on its best efforts to make a rubber shower mat safe from the risk of slipping in a tub, which the court characterized as an irrelevant state-of-the-art argument under § 402A.[545] "Implicit in the concept of strict liability is the idea that if the manufacturer produces a defective product which causes injury, he can be held legally liable despite his best efforts to make or design a safe product."[546] The next year, the same court rejected a trial court's jury instruction limiting a manufacturer's liability

[540] **Drugs.** Compare Cudmore v. Richardson-Merrell, Inc., 398 S.W.2d 640, 644 (Tex. App. 1965) (manufacturer of MER/29 not liable in implied warranty for cataracts: makers liable "only when such results or some similar results ought reasonably to have been foreseen"), with Toole v. Richardson-Merrell Inc., 60 Cal. Rptr. 398, 404–05 (Ct. App. 1967) (upholding punitive damages verdict: in seeking FDA approval to market drug, manufacturer submitted reports that omitted information that nine of ten rats in one test developed eye opacities, as did twenty-five of thirty-six in another, and that one dog went blind).

Asbestos. In the first asbestos case, Borel v. Fibreboard Paper Prods. Corp., 493 F.2d 1076 (5th Cir. 1973) (Tex. law), the manufacturers did not appear to rely on the unforeseeability of the risk, and even defended on the ground that the plaintiff's employers knew of and had a duty to warn the plaintiffs of the hazards—and that the plaintiffs themselves knew of the hazards and assumed the risk. Within a decade, however, manufacturers had begun to rely on a state-of-the-art defense to claims that they had a duty to warn. See Beshada v. Johns-Manville Prods. Corp., 447 A.2d 539 (N.J. 1982) (rejecting the defense). Today, asbestos manufacturers continue to rely heavily on the state-of-the-art defense, even if they invariably lose on compensatory and often on punitive damages. See, e.g., Garlock, Inc. v. Gallagher, 814 A.2d 1007, 1023 (Md. Ct. Spec. App. 2003) (dangers of asbestos knowable when sold by defendant); Owens-Corning Fiberglas Corp. v. Golightly, 976 S.W.2d 409 (Ky. 1998) (upholding compensatory and punitive damages against state-of-the-art defense). On the asbestos litigation, see § 10.3, above.

Cigarettes. Although one notable decision was to the contrary, Green v. American Tobacco Co., 154 So.2d 169, 171 (Fla. 1963), cigarette manufacturers won most cases brought against them in the early and mid-1960s on the ground that the risk of cancer was unforeseeable. See, e.g., Ross v. Philip Morris & Co., 328 F.2d 3, 10 (8th Cir. 1964) (Mo. law). Beginning in the 1990s, litigation against the cigarette industry, brought by state attorneys general and private parties alike, has established without a doubt that the industry knew full well the carcinogenic and addictive effects of cigarettes, and that they fraudulently concealed this information for the last half of the twentieth century. See, e.g., Whiteley v. Philip Morris Inc., 11 Cal. Rptr. 3d 807 (Ct. App. 2004) (reversing and remanding judgment for plaintiff but ruling that substantial evidence supported finding of fraud). On the tobacco litigation, see § 10.3, above.

[541] Howard v. Avon Prods., Inc., 395 P.2d 1007, 1011 (Colo. 1964) (unforeseeable risk from cosmetic).

[542] See, e.g., id. (both claims); Ross v. Philip Morris & Co., 328 F.2d 3 (8th Cir. 1964) (Mo. law) (both claims); Cudmore v. Richardson-Merrell, Inc., 398 S.W.2d 640, 644 (Tex. App. 1965) (implied warranty).

[543] On this development, see ch. 5, above.

[544] 458 P.2d 390 (Ariz. Ct. App. 1969).

[545] See id. at 392.

[546] Id. at 392–93.

to "dangers reasonably to be foreseen,"[547] holding that it was fatally inconsistent with § 402A's black-letter injunction that the strict liability rule applies "although . . . the seller has exercised all possible care in the preparation and sale of his product."[548]

Comments j and k

But there is a second aspect to § 402A that cuts the other way with respect to the issue of whether manufacturers should have a duty to warn of unknowable risks. Notwithstanding the general "strictness" prescribed by § 402A's black-letter liability standard, two comments to that section, comments *j* and *k*, address the duty to warn in negligence terms and effectively provide that the duty to warn under § 402A is limited to foreseeable risks. Both comments describe the general parameters of the duty to warn with respect to products containing inherent, unavoidable risks, with comment *k* considering the warning obligation with respect to certain unavoidably dangerous products, particularly pharmaceutical drugs. Addressing the duty to warn consumers of the possibility of certain allergic reactions, comment *j* provides that if such a risk is significant and would be unexpected by consumers, "the seller is required to give warning against it, if he has knowledge, or by the application of reasonable, developed human skill and foresight should have knowledge, of the presence of the ingredient and the danger."[549] Comment *k* states that a seller of an unavoidably dangerous product, such as a new or experimental drug or vaccine, "is not to be held to strict liability for unfortunate consequences attending their use, merely because he has undertaken to supply the public with an apparently useful and desirable product, attended with a known but apparently reasonable risk."[550] Particularly when read with comment *j*'s limitation of the duty to warn only of foreseeable risks, and that comment's specific reference to the duty to warn of risks in dangerous drugs, comment *k* appears to immunize sellers of such unavoidably dangerous products from liability for failing to warn of unknowable product risks.

The "Wade-Keeton" Test

Because of the intuitive logic and fairness of limiting the duty to warn to foreseeable risks, comments *j* and *k* probably would have effectively squelched any notion of a duty to warn of unknowable hazards were it not for another development that first appeared in the early 1960s. In 1961, Dean Page Keeton of the University of Texas first floated a new way to view the evolving standard of a manufacturer's responsibility to consumers for harm caused by defective products.[551] In order to differentiate the developing notion of strict products liability in tort from the law of negligence, Dean Keeton, and subsequently Dean John Wade of Vanderbilt University, annunciated the idea that "strict" liability should make manufacturers liable for selling products that turned out to be defective regardless of whether a product's risks were foreseeable at the time of sale. Between 1961 and 1965, both scholars separately published their similar views that the law should base strict liability on *hindsight*, by imputing "constructive knowledge" to manufacturers of all subsequently discovered product dangers. Liability thus would

---

[547] Lunt v. Brady Mfg. Corp., 475 P.2d 964, 965 (Ariz. Ct. App. 1970).

[548] Id. at 966.

[549] Comment *j* to § 402A is examined and set forth in full in § 6.2, above.

[550] Comment *k* to § 402A is set forth and examined in § 6.2, above, and § 18.2, below. Although this comment conditions immunity from strict liability upon the provision of a "proper warning," comment *j* makes clear that proper warnings are limited to risks which are foreseeable.

[551] See Keeton, Products Liability-Current Developments, 40 Tex. L. Rev. 193, 210 (1961).

depend on whether a manufacturer would be negligent in selling a product knowing of the risks it actually possessed. From 1961 through 1980, Dean Keeton published at least a dozen articles, and, in 1965 and 1973, Dean Wade published two especially influential articles, all urging that strict liability for product defects—particularly, but not limited to, defects in design—be defined in this special manner.

In time, the similar definitional standard of the two products liability scholars was labeled the "Wade-Keeton" test.[552] The sole distinction between the Wade-Keeton test and the ordinary negligence standard was that the new "hindsight" test radically changed the conventional negligence meaning of "constructive knowledge"—knowledge that a person acting reasonably should possess, which forms the basis of foreseeability—to the very different *strict* liability notion of imputing to manufacturers full awareness of all dangers recognized today, regardless of whether those risks, at the time of a product's sale, were foreseeable or not.[553]

And so, by the late 1960s, the stage was set for courts to begin addressing the issue of whether there would be a duty in strict liability to warn of unknowable risks: comments *j* and *k* to § 402A provided that the strict liability duty, as in negligence, was limited to foreseeable risks; but the Wade-Keeton hindsight test, imputing knowledge of such risks to suppliers, required manufacturers to warn of hazards whether foreseeable or not. Cases deciding the unknowable risk issue were rare in the late 1960s, and so there was little early analysis of the unknowable risk warning problem.

At least one case during this early period, *Helene Curtis Industries, Inc. v. Pruitt*,[554] cited both Dean Wade's and Dean Keeton's articles in which they proposed their liability standard.[555] In that case the plaintiff's scalp was burned by a combination of chemical bleaching products manufactured by the defendant. Endorsing Dean Wade's formulation of the test, the court remarked that a design, to be unreasonably dangerous, "must be so dangerous that a reasonable man would not sell the product if he knew the risks involved."[556] But, like so many other courts that in time endorsed the Wade-Keeton constructive-knowledge standard, the *Helene Curtis* court seemed only to be doing so for academic purposes, for it failed to apply the test to the facts before it and instead reversed a plaintiff's judgment in part upon the unforeseeability of the risk.[557]

During the late 1960s, at least one decision addressed the applicability of comment *j* to the unknowable danger warning question. In *Oakes v. Geigy Agricultural Chemicals*,[558] the plaintiff suffered a serious skin reaction to the defendant's weed-killing chemical products. The plaintiff alleged that the manufacturer's warning of "irritation" to the skin inadequately communicated the severe nature of his particular reaction, and the defendant demurred on the ground that the plaintiff failed to allege that the defendant knew or should have known that its products could cause the

---

[552] Also known as the "prudent manufacturer" test. See § 8.7, above, citing and discussing the articles.

[553] The rise and fall of the Wade-Keeton constructive-knowledge test is examined in depth in § 8.7, above.

[554] 385 F.2d 841 (5th Cir. 1967) (Okla. law).

[555] The court cited Dean Wade's article, Strict Tort Liability of Manufacturers, 19 Sw. L.J. 5 (1965), 385 F.2d at 849–50, and Dean Keeton's article, Products Liability—The Nature and Extent of Strict Liability, 1964 U. Ill. L.F. 693, 385 F.2d at 849 n.3.

[556] *Helene Curtis*, 385 F.2d at 850. "This definition demonstrates that the only change from the traditional negligence analysis is that the maker cannot be excusably ignorant of the defect." Id.

[557] See id. at 856 (citing Lartigue v. R. J. Reynolds Tobacco Co., 317 F.2d 19 (5th Cir. 1963)).

[558] 77 Cal. Rptr. 709 (Ct. App. 1969).

plaintiff's condition. The plaintiff refused to amend his complaint in this manner, and the trial court sustained the demurrer. On appeal, the California Court of Appeal affirmed, reasoning that a manufacturer is strictly liable only for risks of which it was or should have been aware, for "[t]o exact an obligation to warn the user of unknown and unknowable allergies . . . would be for the courts to recast the manufacturer in the role of an insurer beyond any reasonable application" of the strict liability rationales.[559] The court concluded that, to establish a claim for strict liability in tort, a plaintiff had to plead and prove the defendant's actual or constructive knowledge of the danger.[560]

As products liability litigation began to spread around the nation, courts increasingly adopted the Wade-Keeton constructive-knowledge test for defining strict products liability in tort. At the same time, however, courts increasingly turned to comment *j* and, in the case of pharmaceutical drugs, to comment *k* for guidance on the scope of a manufacturer's duty to warn. The first clash of the two inconsistent standards arose with something of a whimper—in *Borel v. Fibreboard Paper Products Corp.*,[561] the first case to uphold a verdict for an installer of asbestos insulation materials against the manufacturers of those materials. The plaintiff's claim was based on strict liability for failing to warn of the dangers involved in handling asbestos. Citing Dean Wade's early article and two articles of Dean Keeton, Judge Wisdom quoted the *Helene Curtis* court's adoption of the Wade-Keeton test, which defined § 402A's "unreasonably dangerous" concept as " 'so dangerous that a reasonable man would not sell the product if he knew the risk involved.' "[562] Moreover, citing Dean Keeton's 1970 article in the Texas Law Review, which once again urged the constructive-knowledge standard, Judge Wisdom addressed the view of Dean Keeton and others that a seller should be strictly liable even if "the maker was excusably unaware of the extent of the danger."[563] But, when it came to resolving the knowability issues in the case, the *Borel* court ignored the Wade-Keeton test and applied the foreseeability-limitation principles of comment *j*.[564] On the facts of the case, the court applied these foreseeability limitations on liability, observing that the utility of asbestos insulation products should be weighed against "the known or foreseeable risk"[565] to the insulation installers, and that "[a] product must not be made available to the public without disclosure of those dangers that the application of reasonable foresight would reveal."[566] Because the jury was properly instructed,[567] the court affirmed the verdict for the plaintiff.[568]

As courts increasingly adopted and applied the foreseeability-limitation principles of comments *j* and *k*, a number of courts continued to purport to employ the Wade-Keeton constructive-knowledge test for defining product defectiveness. In 1974, one year after

---

[559] Id. at 713.

[560] Id.

[561] 493 F.2d 1076 (5th Cir. 1973) (Tex. law) (Wisdom, J.). See § 10.3, above.

[562] Id. at 1088.

[563] Id. at 1088 n.22.

[564] See id. at 1088, where Judge Wisdom observed that negligence concepts govern warning defect principles under § 402A, remarking that "[t]he requirement that the danger be reasonably foreseeable, or scientifically discoverable, is an important limitation of the seller's liability."

[565] Id. at 1089.

[566] Id. at 1090.

[567] See id. at 1090–92.

[568] See id. at 1103.

Borel, the Oregon Supreme Court decided *Phillips v. Kimwood Machine Co.*,[569] an important case in which a factory worker was injured while feeding fiberboard into a sanding machine when the machine forcibly ejected a sheet back at his abdomen. The ejection occurred because a thin sheet had become mixed into a batch of thick sheets for which the sanding machine was set, the risk of which the manufacturer had failed to warn the plaintiff's employer. In the plaintiff's action against the manufacturer, the trial court directed a verdict for the defendant, and the plaintiff appealed. Citing both *Borel* and *Helene Curtis*,[570] the *Phillips* court reversed, carefully articulating the Wade-Keeton test of defectiveness for defective warning and design:

> A dangerously defective article would be one which a reasonable person would not put into the stream of commerce *if he had knowledge of its harmful character*. The test, therefore, is whether the seller would be negligent if he sold the article *knowing of the risk involved*. Strict liability imposes what amounts to constructive knowledge of the condition of the product.[571]

Noting that the Wade-Keeton test had the advantage of preserving familiar terms and concepts, the court reasoned that the test, while appearing to judge a manufacturer's conduct in terms of negligence, ultimately addresses the quality of the product. "If the manufacturer was not acting reasonably in selling the product, knowing of the risks involved, then the product would be dangerously defective when sold and the manufacturer would be subject to liability."[572] The court also quoted comment *j*'s limitation on the duty to warn to situations where the seller "had knowledge, or by the application of reasonable, developed human skill and foresight should have knowledge" of the danger.[573] But the *Phillips* court followed precisely the opposite approach taken by *Borel*, which had referred to, but ignored, the Wade-Keeton test and applied the foreseeability limiting principles of comment *j*. Instead, the *Phillips* court quoted, and then ignored, comment *j*, and applied the Wade-Keeton test, reversing the directed verdict for the defendant because the jury could find "that a reasonably prudent manufacturer, knowing that the machine would be fed manually and having the constructive knowledge of its propensity to regurgitate thin sheets when it was set for thick ones, which the courts via strict liability have imposed upon it, would have warned plaintiff's employer . . ., and that, in the absence of such a warning, the machine was dangerously defective."[574] Although the foreseeability that the sanding machine might regurgitate thin sheets was not really a disputed issue in *Phillips*, the Wade-Keeton test's triumph over comment *j* in this important judicial opinion was a pivotal event in the evolution of the duty to warn of unknowable product risks.

*The New Jersey Experience—*Beshada *and* Feldman

Four years after the Oregon court decided *Phillips*, the New Jersey Supreme Court in 1978 adopted the Wade-Keeton standard as the test of design defectiveness in *Cepeda v. Cumberland Engineering Co.*,[575] citing *Phillips* and quoting substantially from articles

---

[569] 525 P.2d 1033 (Or. 1974).

[570] Id. at 1036 n.5.

[571] Id. at 1036 (emphasis in original).

[572] Id. at 1037.

[573] Id. at 1038.

[574] Id. at 1038–39.

[575] 386 A.2d 816 (N.J. 1978), overruled on other grounds by Suter v. San Angelo Foundry & Mach. Co., 406 A.2d 140 (N.J. 1979) .

by both Deans Wade and Keeton. Three years later, in *Freund v. Cellofilm Properties, Inc.*,[576] the New Jersey court revisited and reaffirmed the propriety of the Wade-Keeton test in the specific context of the duty to warn. Mr. Freund was burned in an industrial accident when a commercial chemical dust, nitrocellulose, suddenly ignited as it was being swept by a co-worker. In a suit against the manufacturer of the nitrocellulose, the plaintiff claimed that, in both negligence and strict liability in tort, the flammability warning was inadequate. The trial court refused to instruct on strict liability and submitted the case to the jury solely on the negligence claim. The jury found for the defendant, and the plaintiff appealed. Reversing, the New Jersey Supreme Court held that the trial court should have submitted the case to the jury on the strict liability claim. Relying on the "seminal" *Phillips* decision, and adopting the Wade-Keeton standard as the appropriate test for defining the duty to warn, the *Freund* court ruled that the trial court, even though the defendant admitted knowing the dangers of nitrocellulose, should have relieved the plaintiffs of the burden of proving the defendant's knowledge of danger by imputing it to the defendant.[577]

One year later, in 1982, the New Jersey Supreme Court had another strict liability failure to warn case, *Beshada v. Johns-Manville Products Corp.*,[578] one of the landmark cases in all products liability law. In an important way, *Beshada* was different from *Freund* and other previous cases applying the Wade-Keeton test to the duty to warn. *Beshada* was the first state high court case in the United States involving the applicability of the Wade-Keeton test, and more generally the principles of strict products liability, to a warning claim defended on the ground that the risk was unforeseeable—that is, the first such case squarely confronting the question of whether manufacturers should have a duty to warn of unknowable product risks. *Beshada* was another asbestos case brought by insulation workers who suffered asbestosis and mesothelioma from working with asbestos insulation products over many years. The workers claimed that the manufacturers had breached their strict liability duty to warn of these dangers, and the defendants responded by asserting a state-of-the-art defense, claiming that no one knew or could have known at the time that asbestos was so dangerous to insulation workers. The defendants conceded that they had known since the 1930s of the dangers of high-dose exposure of asbestos dust to workers in asbestos textile mills, but they claimed that the danger to insulation workers who were exposed to much lower doses "was not discovered until recently."[579] The trial court denied the plaintiff's motion to strike the state-of-the-art defense, the plaintiffs appealed, and the New Jersey Supreme Court reversed, holding that compliance with the state-of-the-art is not a defense to a strict liability failure to warn claim.[580]

The *Beshada* defendants claimed "that the danger of which they failed to warn was undiscovered at the time the product was marketed and that it was undiscoverable given the state of scientific knowledge at that time,"[581] and the court assumed the truth of this assertion for purposes of the appeal.[582] In response, the plaintiffs argued that the court's

---

[576] 432 A.2d 925 (N.J. 1981).

[577] "The plaintiffs were entitled to a strict liability charge that clearly and unmistakenly imputed knowledge of the dangers of the product to the defendant." Id. at 933.

[578] 447 A.2d 539 (N.J. 1982).

[579] Id. at 543.

[580] See id. at 549.

[581] Id. at 542.

[582] See id. at 543.

earlier decision in *Freund* had "disposed of the state-of-the-art issue. Since defendant's knowledge of the dangers of the product is presumed, it is irrelevant whether the existence of such dangers was scientifically discoverable."[583] Reaffirming the Wade-Keeton constructive-knowledge test it had applied in *Freund* to warning cases, the *Beshada* court examined the role of the state-of-the-art defense in the context of a strict liability duty to warn:

> As it relates to warning cases, the state-of-the-art defense asserts that distributors of products can be held liable only for injuries resulting from dangers that were scientifically discoverable at the time the product was distributed. Defendants argue that the question of whether the product can be made safer must be limited to consideration of the available technology at the time the product was distributed. Liability would be absolute, defendants argue, if it could be imposed on the basis of a subsequently discovered means to make the product safer since technology will always be developing new ways to make products safer. . . .
>
> In urging this position, defendants must somehow distinguish the *Freund* holding that knowledge of the dangers of the product is imputed to defendants as a matter of law. A state-of-the-art defense would contravene that by requiring plaintiffs to prove at least that knowledge of the dangers was scientifically available at the time of manufacture.[584]

The defendants argued that the knowledge of danger referred to in *Freund* was the knowledge existing at the time the product was manufactured and sold.[585] Conceding that *Freund* had not addressed the question of precisely what type of knowledge should be imputed to manufacturers, the *Beshada* court reasoned that state-of-the-art is essentially a negligence defense, and that the defendants essentially were arguing that, by failing to warn of an unforeseeable risk, they were not at fault. "But in strict liability cases," the court explained, "culpability is irrelevant." That the product "was unsafe because of the state of technology does not change the fact that it was unsafe. Strict liability focuses on the product, not the fault of the manufacturer."[586]

After considering the duty to warn of unforeseeable risks from a doctrinal perspective, *Beshada* turned to a policy inquiry of the compatibility of the state's goals and policies underlying its strict products liability rules with a rule imposing liability on manufacturers for failing to warn of dangers that were undiscoverable when the product was made and sold.[587] Concluding that the policies of strict products liability indeed

---

[583] Id.

[584] Id. at 545–46.

[585] *Beshada*, 447 A.2d at 546.

[586] Id. (citing Keeton, Products Liability—Inadequacy of Information, 48 Tex. L. Rev. 398, 408 (1970)). "When the defendants argue that it is unreasonable to impose a duty on them to warn of the unknowable, they misconstrue both the purpose and effect of strict liability. By imposing strict liability, we are not requiring defendants to have done something that is impossible. In this sense, the phrase 'duty to warn' is misleading. It implies negligence concepts with their attendant focus on the reasonableness of defendant's behavior. However, a major concern of strict liability—ignored by defendants—is the conclusion that if a product was in fact defective, the distributor of the product should compensate its victims for the misfortune that it inflicted on them." Id.

[587] *Beshada*, 447 A.2d at 547.

supported such a rule,[588] the court explained how liability for harm caused by undiscoverable risks is consistent with the "risk spreading" rationale:

> [S]preading the costs of injuries among all those who produce, distribute and purchase manufactured products is far preferable to imposing it on the innocent victims who suffer illnesses and disability from defective products. This basic normative premise is at the center of our strict liability rules. It is unchanged by the state of scientific knowledge at the time of manufacture.[589]

As for the deterrence or "accident avoidance" goal of strict products liability, the defendants argued that manufacturers cannot protect against risks they cannot foresee. But the court reasoned that this argument missed the point that the "state-of-the-art" at any given time is a function of the level of resources industry invests in safety research. Accordingly, although a manufacturer may never foresee all the risks of harm its products possess, its knowledge that it must eventually absorb the costs of all such harm, foreseeable or not, will spur its investment in safety research and thereby advance the state-of-the-art of product safety.[590]

Finally, the court turned to difficulties in the judiciary's ability to administer the "fact finding process" inherent in determining the scientific discoverability of particular product risks at any given time. The court saw good reason to avoid "the vast confusion" that would arise from requiring plaintiffs to prove at trial "the concept of scientific knowability" inherent in the state-of-the-art defense. Such proof—on what kind of knowledge could have been discovered with more or better research—would require costly, confusing, and time-consuming expert testimony on "the history of science and technology to speculate as to what knowledge was feasible in a given year." The court doubted that juries would "be capable of even understanding the concept of scientific knowability, much less be able to resolve such a complex issue," and it was reluctant to allow the judicial system to suffer the resulting costs.[591]

Reaching back to the traditional, overarching rationale for strict products liability in tort,[592] the court concluded that fairness required that the costs of illnesses and injuries from dangerous products such as asbestos be placed upon manufacturers who profit from their production and sale, and on society at large, rather than on the innocent victims of such harm. Barring the state-of-the-art defense would not only achieve this result, reasoned the court, but rejecting this defense should also "serve the salutary goals of increasing product safety research and simplifying tort trials."[593] For all these reasons, the Supreme Court of New Jersey in *Beshada v. Johns-Manville Products Corp.* ruled that strict liability in tort imposes a duty on manufacturers to warn consumers of all significant product hazards, knowable and unknowable alike.

The New Jersey court may have expected its unanimous decision in *Beshada* to be largely noncontroversial—after all, it merely applied the widely accepted Wade-Keeton test to a warning claim, which other courts (like the Oregon court in *Phillips*, some eight years earlier) had done before; it applied the doctrine to defendants in a singularly

---

[588] Id.

[589] Id.

[590] "By imposing on manufacturers the costs of failure to discover hazards, we create an incentive for them to invest more actively in safety research." Id. at 548.

[591] Id.

[592] See § 5.4, above.

[593] *Beshada*, 447 A.2d at 549.

unpopular industry; and it merely held that its rule of "strict" products liability was truly strict, rather than just negligence rehashed. But the opinion unleashed an immediate and powerful storm of academic protest[594] that appears to have caught the New Jersey Supreme Court by surprise, but that did not go unnoticed by the court. Commentators complained that, by adopting a duty on manufacturers to warn of unknowable dangers, the court had imposed an unfair standard that was impossible to meet; that it would lead to inefficient corporate behavior that could lead to strategic and unnecessary declarations of bankruptcy;[595] that the decision reflected an ignorance of how liability rules affect corporate behavior; and that the court had applied anachronistic strict liability rationales that had become discredited over time.

At least in part because of *Beshada*, but also because the test had "not worn well with time,"[596] Dean Wade repudiated his half of the Wade-Keeton standard in a 1983 journal article,[597] and Dean Keeton repudiated the other half in his torts treatise the following year.[598]

A scant two years after rendering *Beshada*, the New Jersey Supreme Court in 1984 had an opportunity to reconsider this now-battered decision in another products liability case, *Feldman v. Lederle Laboratories*,[599] which involved a claim against a pharmaceutical manufacturer for a possibly unforeseeable risk that a tetracycline drug could discolor an infant's teeth. In one of the most striking reversals in the history of the law of torts, a unanimous court in *Feldman* effectively overruled *Beshada*,[600] holding that "drug manufacturers have a duty to warn [only] of dangers of which they know or should have known on the basis of reasonably obtainable or available knowledge."[601] Turning *Beshada* completely on its head, the *Feldman* court not only ruled that the state of the art was a good defense to a warning claim but also largely equated strict liability and negligence in the warning context. *Feldman* endorsed comment *j*'s restriction of the warning duty to foreseeable risks and adopted the traditional negligence definition of "constructive knowledge"—what the defendant knew or should have known in view of knowledge available at the time—the same traditional definition of constructive knowledge the defendants argued and the court rejected in *Beshada*.

---

594 See, e.g., Wade, On the Effect in Product Liability of Knowledge Unavailable Prior to Marketing, 58 N.Y.U. L. Rev. 734, 754–56 (1983); Page, Generic Product Risks: The Case Against Comment K and for Strict Tort Liability, 58 N.Y.U. L. Rev. 853, 877–82 (1983); Schwartz, The Post-Sale Duty to Warn: Two Unfortunate Forks in the Road to a Reasonable Doctrine, 58 N.Y.U. L. Rev. 892, 901–05 (1983); Comments, Requiring Omniscience: The Duty to Warn of Scientifically Undiscoverable Product Defects, 71 Geo. L.J. 1635 (1983), Beshada v. Johns Manville Products Corp.: Adding Uncertainty to Injury, 35 Rutgers L. Rev. 982, 1008–15 (1983); Note, Products Liability—Strict Liability in Tort—State-of-the-Art Defense Inapplicable in Design Defect Cases, 13 Seton Hall L. Rev. 625 (1983).

595 See, e.g., A. Schwartz, Products Liability, Corporate Structure and Bankruptcy: Toxic Substances and the Remote Risk Relationship, 14 J. Legal Stud. 689, 736 (1985). Indeed, Johns-Manville declared bankruptcy the year following *Beshada*, 1983, followed by the bankruptcy of scores of additional asbestos companies in due course. See § 10.3, above.

596 See Products Liability Rest. § 2 Reporters' Note 1 to cmt. *m*.

597 Wade, On the Effect in Product Liability of Knowledge Unavailable Prior to Marketing, Postscript, 58 N.Y.U. L. Rev. 734, 761 (1983).

598 See Prosser and Keeton on Torts 697–98 n.21 (1984).

599 479 A.2d 374 (N.J. 1984).

600 The court denied that it was "overruling" *Beshada*, but it subjected the decision to house arrest, explicitly restricting it to its facts. Id. at 388.

601 Id. at 376.

Following comment *j*, *Feldman* thus held that a manufacturer's duty to warn is limited to dangers which it knows or should know at the time the product is sold, which makes the pertinent inquiry: "Did the defendant know, or should he have known, of the danger, given the scientific, technological, and other information available when the product was distributed; or, in other words, did he have actual or constructive knowledge of the danger?"[602] Restoring "constructive knowledge" to its traditional negligence meaning—directly contrary to the novel hindsight meaning the Wade-Keeton test applied to this term for strict liability—*Feldman* held that the term "embraces knowledge that should have been known based on information that was reasonably available or obtainable and should have alerted a reasonably prudent person to act."[603] The court realized that this redefinition of the knowledge for which a defendant is responsible in warning cases folds "strict liability" right back into the arms of negligence, reducing the two theories of liability essentially to one.[604]

In this way, the New Jersey Supreme Court in *Feldman* made a complete about-face on its unknowable-danger warning doctrine, holding that manufacturers have no duty to warn of risks which are unforeseeable. Reasoning that information on the knowability of risks in a particular field is more accessible to manufacturers than to plaintiffs, the court also ruled that the burden of proof should be reversed on the availability of information about the risk at the time the product is made and sold.[605]

In dramatic fashion, the *Beshada-Feldman* duo marks the rise and fall of the duty to warn of unknowable hazards—and, more broadly, of the doctrine of strict manufacturer liability for warning (and indirectly design) dangers—in American products liability law. For a time, *Beshada* had reigned supreme as the first major decision in the nation to apply a truly strict manufacturer liability rule in a warning or design context where the difference between strict liability and negligence really mattered. But *Beshada*'s moment in the sun was brief, and its fall from glory was precipitous and absolute.

The Triumph of State-of-the-Art

Four years after *Feldman*, across the continent, the California Supreme Court decided *Brown v. Superior Court*,[606] another pharmaceutical drug case, which involved the duty of manufacturers to warn of the possibly unforeseeable risks that a drug, DES, administered to pregnant women could cause certain birth defects in their unborn children. Following *Feldman* and the principles of comments *j* and *k*,[607] the California court held that manufacturers of the drug could not be held liable for failing to warn of risks "that were neither known by defendants nor scientifically knowable at the time the

[602] Id. at 386.

[603] Id.

[604] "Under this standard negligence and strict liability in warning cases may be deemed to be functional equivalents." Id.

[605] "As a matter of policy the burden of proving the status of knowledge in the field at the time of distribution is properly placed on the defendant." Id. at 388. The *Feldman* litigation saga continued for many years. See Feldman v. Lederle Labs., 625 A.2d 1066, 1070–71 (N.J. 1993) (once manufacturer learns of risk, it must warn "as soon as reasonably possible"; while manufacturer has burden of proof on state of knowledge, plaintiff must prove that any delay in warning was unreasonable).

[606] 751 P.2d 470 (Cal. 1988).

[607] The court interpreted comment *k* in the foreseeable risk terms of comment *j*: "[Comment *k*] provides that the producer of a properly manufactured prescription drug may be held liable for injuries caused by the product only if it was not accompanied by a warning of dangers that the manufacturer knew or should have known about." Id. at 475.

drug was distributed."[608] Three years later, the California Supreme Court completed the loop in an asbestos case, *Anderson v. Owens-Corning Fiberglas Corp.*,[609] by extending the holding in *Brown* beyond pharmaceutical drug products to products generally.[610] *Anderson* adopted "the requirement, as propounded by the Restatement Second of Torts and acknowledged by . . . the majority of jurisdictions, that knowledge or knowability is a component of strict liability for failure to warn."[611]

A small handful of states have continued to define strict liability in hindsight terms by imputing constructive knowledge to manufacturers of all product dangers, even risks that are entirely unknowable. In 1987, in a brief answer to a certified question in an asbestos case, the Hawaii Supreme Court ruled that "in a strict products liability action, state-of-the-art evidence is not admissible for the purpose of establishing whether the seller knew or reasonably should have known of the dangerousness of his or her product."[612] In 1995, the New Mexico Supreme Court reaffirmed the Wade-Keeton constructive-knowledge definition of design defects,[613] and a small number of other decisions have continued rotely to define strict products liability in tort in hindsight terms.[614] Each of these cases might be viewed as an aberration in the common law, which for many years has been attempting to purge itself of the Wade-Keeton liability standard and the imputed knowledge hindsight standard which it spawned, and rarely does a modern court attempt to justify the hindsight test in policy terms of whether a manufacturer should have a duty to warn of unknowable product risks.

But the appropriateness of a state-of-the-art defense based on the unforeseeability of a product risk was precisely the question raised in *Sternhagen v. Dow Co.*,[615] a 1997 Montana Supreme Court case involving an action against herbicide manufacturers for the death from cancer of a crop duster exposed to the herbicide 2,4-D from 1948 to 1950. Carefully reexamining the state's commitment to the doctrine of strict products liability in tort, the Montana court ruled that manufacturers should have a duty to warn of unknowable product risks: "[I]n a strict products liability case, knowledge of any undiscovered or undiscoverable dangers should be imputed to the manufacturer [and] state-of-the-art evidence is not admissible to establish whether the manufacturer knew or through the exercise of reasonable human foresight should have known of the danger."[616]

The *Sternhagen* court's proud reaffirmation of a pure doctrine of strict products liability is reminiscent in many respects of the New Jersey court's ill-fated opinion in *Beshada v. Johns-Manville Products Corp.* decided now so many years ago. Whether *Sternhagen* eventually will suffer as sharp a collapse as did *Beshada* is difficult to

---

608 Id. at 481. See also Carlin v. Superior Ct., 920 P.2d 1347, 1354 (Cal. 1996) ("Drug manufacturers need only warn of risks that are *actually known or reasonably scientifically knowable.*").

609 810 P.2d 549 (Cal. 1991).

610 "*Brown*'s logic and common sense are not limited to drugs." Id. at 556.

611 Id. at 557.

612 Johnson v. Raybestos-Manhattan, Inc., 740 P.2d 548, 549 (Haw. 1987).

613 See Brooks v. Beech Aircraft Corp., 902 P.2d 54, 63 (N.M. 1995): "[I]n those hypothetical instances in which technology known at the time of trial and technology knowable at the time of distribution differ—and outside of academic rationale we find little to suggest the existence in practice of unknowable design considerations—it is more fair that the manufacturers and suppliers who have profited from the sale of the product bear the risk of loss."

614 Other recent cases stating the Wade-Keeton test are cited and discussed in § 8.7, above.

615 935 P.2d 1139 (Mont. 1997).

616 Id. at 1147.

predict, but the Montana Supreme court later reaffirmed its commitment to the *Sternhagen* approach.[617] By that time, however, the tide had decisively turned against the idea of a duty to warn of unknowable product risks. In the 1990s, the high courts of at least four other states studiously affirmed or reaffirmed the necessary role of foreseeability in duty-to-warn products liability cases, two with respect to prescription pharmaceutical products[618] and two with respect to products generally,[619] all four of which repudiated any notion of a duty to warn of unknowable risks. Of these four, the experience of the Massachusetts high court is most instructive.

The evolution of the unknowable-risk warning issue in Massachusetts well illustrates the demise of a duty to warn of unknowable risks. In 1984, in *Hayes v. Ariens Co.*,[620] the Supreme Judicial Court of Massachusetts specifically addressed the role of state-of-the-art evidence in warning claim cases brought under that state's strict products liability doctrine, which rests on the implied warranty of merchantability.[621] Drawing on *Beshada*, *Phillips v. Kimwood Machine Co.*,[622] and Dean Wade's famous article on strict products liability in tort,[623] the *Hayes* court adopted the Wade-Keeton constructive knowledge test in no uncertain terms.[624] Although the Massachusetts high court reaffirmed this position in dictum in 1992,[625] it had occasion to address the matter squarely once again in 1998, whereupon it slammed the door on strict liability even harder than New Jersey had in switching from *Beshada* to *Feldman* in the 1980s.

Vassallo v. Baxter Healthcare Corp.[626] was a negligence and implied warranty of merchantability action against the manufacturer of silicone breast implants for atypical autoimmune disease suffered by a woman in whom such products had been implanted. The trial court denied the defendants' request for a jury instruction limiting its duty to warn to known or knowable risks, and the defendants appealed judgment on a verdict for the plaintiff. While upholding the plaintiff's verdict on other grounds, the *Vassallo* court took the occasion to reevaluate its strict-liability (warranty) duty-to-warn rule which "presumes that a manufacturer was fully informed of all risks associated with the product at issue, regardless of the state of the art at the time of the sale."[627] Recognizing that Massachusetts was "among a distinct minority of States that applies a hindsight analysis to the duty to warn";[628] that most states follow the foreseeability limitation of

---

[617] See Ficek v. Kolberg-Pioneer, Inc., 2011 WL 1316801, at *2 (D. Mont. 2011); Malcolm v. Evenflo Co., 217 P.3d 514, 521 (Mont. 2009).

[618] Young v. Key Pharm., Inc., 922 P.2d 59 (Wash. 1996) (4–4 decision) (brain damage from administration of theophylline for asthma without warning of drug's risks to patients suffering viral illnesses); Wagner v. Roche Labs., 671 N.E.2d 252, 256 (Ohio 1996) (pseudotumor cerebri [PTC] from combining acne drug, Accutane, with certain antibiotics such as minocycline; reaffirming prior ruling).

[619] Owens-Illinois, Inc. v. Zenobia, 601 A.2d 633, 641 n.8 (Md. 1992) (asbestos; burden of proof on knowability remains on plaintiff); Vassallo v. Baxter Healthcare Corp., 696 N.E.2d 909 (Mass. 1998) (silicone breast implants).

[620] 462 N.E.2d 273 (Mass. 1984).

[621] Massachusetts, which never did adopt the doctrine of strict liability in tort, uses the implied warranty of merchantability as its vehicle for strict products liability. See Vassallo v. Baxter Healthcare Corp., 696 N.E.2d 909, 923 (Mass. 1998). See also §§ 5.3 and 5.9, above.

[622] 525 P.2d 1033 (Or. 1974).

[623] Wade, On the Nature of Strict Tort Liability for Products, 44 Miss. L.J. 825, 834–35 (1973).

[624] 462 N.E.2d at 277–78.

[625] Simmons v. Monarch Mach. Tool Co., 596 N.E.2d 318, 320 n.3 (Mass. 1992).

[626] 696 N.E.2d 909 (Mass. 1998).

[627] Id. at 922.

[628] Id.

Restatement (Second) of Torts § 402A cmt. *j*;[629] that the *Restatement (Third) of Torts: Products Liability* § 2(c) similarly limits the duty to warn to foreseeable risks;[630] that the goal of product safety is not advanced by a rule which requires the impossible;[631] that the minority approach "has received substantial criticism in the literature";[632] and that an important basis of the Massachusetts court's original adoption of the hindsight approach, New Jersey's adoption of that approach in *Beshada*, had disappeared;[633] the *Vassallo* court decided to revise its law to state that "a defendant will not be held liable under an implied warranty of merchantability for failure to warn or provide instructions about risks that were not reasonably foreseeable at the time of sale or could not have been discovered by way of reasonable testing prior to marketing the product."[634]

The *Vassallo* court's decision to shield manufacturers from responsibility for unforeseeable product hazards appeared to signal an imminent demise of true strict products liability in American law (outside of manufacturing defect cases), but the Supreme Court of Wisconsin soon made clear that any such signal was premature. Three years after *Vassallo*, in 2001, the Wisconsin high court decided *Green v. Smith & Nephew AHP, Inc.*,[635] in which a health care worker suffered a severe reaction to allergens in latex gloves manufactured by the defendant. Although the risk that users would suffer allergic reactions to the levels of proteins in such gloves was quite high,[636] the health care industry apparently did not know of the risk at the time the plaintiff's gloves were manufactured. The plaintiff's claim did not specify a type of defect, alleging only that the gloves were defective because the danger was not contemplated by ordinary users and consumers, and the court analyzed the case as if it involved a question of design defectiveness rather than a duty to warn. Reaffirming the consumer expectations test as the proper standard for determining a defendant's responsibility for harm under the doctrine of strict products liability in tort, the court in *Green* ruled that the foreseeability of risk was relevant only to negligence, not strict liability. "[U]nder no circumstance," said the court, "must the plaintiff prove that the risk of harm presented by the product that caused his or her injury was foreseeable."[637] The court justified its refusal to endorse a state-of-the-art defense on the conventional, if by then largely abandoned, rationales for strict products liability in tort: promoting product safety, protecting justified consumer expectations, and the perceived fairness of placing the loss on the party that created and profited from the risk.[638]

While time had taken its toll on these tattered rationales for a rule of true strict liability,[639] their unabashed resurrection by the *Green* majority in Wisconsin (as by the

---

629 See id.

630 See id. at 922–23. The duty to warn under § 2(c) is defined in black-letter terms of "foreseeable risks of harm," and comment *m* provides in part: "The harms that result from unforeseeable risks—for example, in the human body's reaction to a new drug, medical device, or chemical—are not a basis of liability."

631 "The thin judicial support for a hindsight approach to the duty to warn is easily explained. The goal of the law is to induce conduct that is capable of being performed. This goal is not advanced by imposing liability for failure to warn of risks that were not capable of being known." Id. at 922–23.

632 Id. at 923.

633 Id.

634 Id.

635 629 N.W.2d 727 (Wis. 2001).

636 Stated by the court to be 5%–17%. Id. at 731.

637 Id. at 746.

638 Id. at 749–51.

639 See § 5.4, above.

Montana court in *Sternhagen*) suggested that they still then possessed at least a twitch of life. Yet, the debate in Wisconsin did not end with *Green*, but seemed only to intensify. The Wisconsin Supreme Court majority's decision to stick with true strict liability in *Green* was no accident, for that court historically had been one of the most liberal courts in products liability cases. After *Green*, a number of justices in several concurring and dissenting opinions continued a spirited debate over whether that court should continue or abandon the increasingly outmoded strict-liability approach of Restatement (Second) of Torts § 402A, or should instead switch to the *Third Restatement*.[640] Tired of the delay in modernizing products liability law, the Wisconsin legislature in 2011 put an end to the judicial wrangling by adopting the product defect definitions of the *Third Restatement*,[641] thereby effectively overturning § 402A and the Wisconsin high court's refusal to acknowledge a state-of-the-art defense.

But for a few rogue jurisdictions,[642] American products liability law, like the law of most of Europe and Japan,[643] now protectively shields manufacturers from responsibility for product risks that are unknowable and otherwise unpreventable due to the limitations of science and technology.[644] The rise and fall of the duty to warn of unforeseeable hazards, together with the rise of the state-of-the-art defense, played a decisive role in the more general rise and fall of "strict" products liability in America, a broader development examined in earlier chapters.[645] Infrequent cases involving egregiously dangerous products that never should have been marketed for widespread use, such as asbestos and thalidomide, may appear to raise troubling problems for products liability law if manufacturers are exonerated for unknowable product risks. Yet, to the extent that a product's risks are truly unforeseeable, manufacturers cannot

---

[640] See, e.g., Horst v. Deere & Co., 769 N.W.2d 536 (Wis. 2009) (Crooks, J. and Gableman, J. concurrences; Bradley, J., dissent); Godoy v. E.I. du Pont de Nemours & Co., 768 N.W.2d 674, 688–700 (Wis. 2009) (Bradley, J.; Crooks, J.; and Prosser, J. concurrences).

[641] In Wis. Stat. Ann. § 895.047(1)(a).

[642] See, e.g., Townsend v. Sears, Roebuck & Co., 879 N.E.2d 893, 898–99 (Ill. 2007); Sternhagen v. Dow Co., 935 P.2d 1139, 1144–47 (Mont. 1997); Johnson v. Raybestos-Manhattan, Inc., 740 P.2d 548, 549 (Haw. 1987). See also Brooks v. Beech Aircraft Corp., 902 P.2d 54, 63 (N.M. 1995). Consider, too, dicta in Bifolck v. Philip Morris, Inc., 152 A.3d 1183, 1199 (Conn. 2016), a design defect case: "[A]s between injured consumers who lack the ability to protect themselves physically and/or financially from the product's danger and a manufacturer who might not be able to foresee the risk of harm, Connecticut would strike the balance in favor of injured consumers."

[643] Foreign law is briefly discussed below, at note 679 et seq. and accompanying text.

[644] See, e.g., Lightfoot v. Georgia-Pac. Wood Prods., LLC, 5 F.4th 484, 494 (4th Cir. 2021) (N.C. law) (no duty to warn of risks of cancer from inhaling wood dust where "the culmination of scientific knowledge [from 1982 to 1992] did not indicate that causal connection"); Bachtel v. TASER Int'l, Inc., 2013 WL 317538, at *6 (E.D. Mo. 2013) (even under § 402A, "courts look to 'whether the defendant failed to warn of particular risks that were known or knowable in light of the generally recognized and prevailing scientific and technical knowledge *available at the time of manufacture and distribution*'") (emphasis in original); D'Agnese v. Novartis Pharms. Corp., 952 F. Supp. 2d 880 (D. Ariz. 2013) (dismissing failure to warn case where risk was unforeseeable); Georgia Pac., LLC v. Farrar, 69 A.3d 1028, 1036 (Md. 2013) (to avoid absolute liability, asbestos product manufacturer had no duty to warn of risks to family members of workers before such risks were knowable in light of "generally recognized and prevailing scientific and technical knowledge available at the time of manufacture and distribution") (emphasis omitted); Mack v. Stryker Corp., 893 F. Supp. 2d 976, 988 (D. Minn. 2012) ("The Court will not subject Stryker to liability based on speculation and hindsight."); Williams v. Wal-Mart Stores E., L.P., 99 So.3d 112, 118 n.6 (Miss. 2012) (same; "the foreseeability inquiry is not governed by hindsight"); Kaufman v. Wyeth, LLC, 2011 WL 10483576, at *6 (S.D. Fla. 2011) ("The state-of-the-art defense may be used by a manufacturer to show that its design of the product was state-of-the-art and, therefore, not defective since it complied with the best known and available technology."); Branham v. Ford Motor Co., 701 S.E.2d 5, 17 (S.C. 2010) ("The use of post-distribution evidence to evaluate a product's design through the lens of hindsight is improper.").

[645] See chapters 5, 8, and 9, above.

be faulted for placing such products on the market, nor can they be fairly or effectively encouraged by the law to guard against risks they cannot in fact foresee. While innocent victims of science and technology should not be left without any means of compensation, most courts and commentators reason that the laudable objective of spreading risks (insurance) is more fairly and efficiently administered by insurance institutions—private companies and public agencies designed to insure against and compensate for unforeseeable loss—than by the law of torts.[646] In short, modern products liability law is quite surely better off without a duty to warn or otherwise protect against unknowable product risks.

Statutory Reform

From the inception of the products liability statutory reform movement, many state legislatures have sought to afford products liability defendants with some protection from liability when a challenged product was designed, manufactured, and labeled according to the state of scientific knowledge and reasonable technological capability prevailing in the industry at the time. Colorado may have been the first state to enact such a provision, in 1977,[647] and Wisconsin so far may be the latest, in 2011.[648] At present, roughly half the states have enacted some form of statute addressing some aspect of the state-of-the-art issue, which concerns a products liability defendant's reasonable ability to prevent a particular injury based on the state of scientific knowledge and technology prevailing when the product is made and sold.

True State-of-the-Art Statutes

Many states adopted "true" state-of-the-art statutes that address this topic directly.[649] Eight states (Arizona, Iowa, Louisiana, Michigan, Mississippi, Missouri, Nebraska, and New Hampshire) have statutes that either condition liability upon the defendant's ability to conform to the state of the art, which places the burden of proof on the plaintiff, or that create a state-of-the-art affirmative defense, which places the burden of proof on the defendant.[650] Three states (Colorado, Indiana, and Kentucky) enacted rebuttable presumptions providing that products which conform to the state of the art are rebuttably presumed to be nondefective and that the manufacturers and sellers of such products are similarly presumed not negligent.[651] Moreover, a number of states (Arizona, Colorado, Florida, Idaho, Kansas, Michigan, South Dakota, Tennessee, and Washington) enacted reform statutes that address the admissibility of state-of-the-art evidence, either by providing that a defendant *may* introduce evidence of the prevailing scientific knowledge or technology at the time of manufacture or sale,[652] or

---

[646] On the importance of the foreseeability limitation on tort law, see, e.g., Owen, Bending Nature, Bending Law, 62 Fla. L. Rev. 569 (2010); Owen, Dangers in Prescription Drugs: Filling a Private Law Gap in the Healthcare Debate, 42 Conn. L. Rev. 733 (2010); Owen, Figuring Foreseeability, 44 Wake Forest L. Rev. 1277 (2009); Owen, The Moral Foundations of Products Liability Law: Toward First Principles, 68 Notre Dame L. Rev. 427 (1993).

[647] See Colo. Rev. Stat. Ann. § 13–21–403(1).

[648] See Wis. Stat. Ann. § 895.047.

[649] The statutes are set out in Appendices I and J of Owen & Davis on Products Liability.

[650] See Ariz. Rev. Stat. Ann. § 12–683; Iowa Code Ann. § 668.12; La. Rev. Stat. Ann. § 9:2800.59; Mich. Comp. Laws Ann. § 600.2948(3); Miss. Code Ann. § 11–1–63(b) and (c); Mo. Ann. Stat. § 537.764; Neb. Rev. Stat. § 25–21,182; and N.H. Rev. Stat. Ann. § 507:8–g.

[651] See Colo. Rev. Stat. Ann. § 13–21–403(1); Ind. Code Ann. § 34–20–5–1; and Ky. Rev. Stat. Ann. § 411.310(2).

[652] See Fla. Stat. Ann. § 768.1257; Mich. Comp. Laws Ann. § 600.2946(1); S.D. Codified Laws § 20–9–10.1; Tenn. Code Ann. § 29–28–105(b); Wash. Rev. Code Ann. § 7.72.050.

that a claimant may *not* introduce evidence of improved science or technology that developed thereafter.[653]

Evidentiary Provisions on Subsequent Remedial Measures

Closely related to statutory provisions that prohibit the admission of evidence on improvements in scientific knowledge and technology is Federal Rule of Evidence 407, adopted in a large majority of states, which prohibits proof of subsequent remedial measures to prove that a defendant was negligent or that a product was defective.[654] Proof of subsequent remedial measures and Rule 407 were examined earlier.[655]

Feasible Alternative Design Provisions

In proving design defects, statutes in a few states (Louisiana, Michigan, Mississippi, New Jersey, North Carolina, Ohio, Texas, Wisconsin, and maybe Washington) require proof in design cases of a feasible alternative design,[656] as previously discussed.[657] In ordinary usage, "feasible" is widely defined as "capable of being done."[658] The Idaho statute defines "technological feasibility," rather verbosely, as "the technological, mechanical and scientific knowledge relating to product safety that was reasonably feasible for use, in light of economic practicality, at the time of manufacture."[659] Mississippi's provision requires a plaintiff to prove that "[t]he product failed to function as expected and there existed a feasible design alternative that would have to a reasonable probability prevented the harm. A feasible design alternative is a design that would have . . . prevented the harm without impairing the utility, usefulness, practicality or desirability of the product to users or consumers."[660] The Texas provision on design defects requires claimants to prove that "there was a safer alternative design"[661] that "was economically and technologically feasible at the time the product left the control of the manufacturer or seller by the application of existing or reasonably achievable scientific knowledge."[662]

Miscellaneous Statutory Provisions

Finally, state reform statutes include a miscellany of other provisions, not ordinarily thought of as true "state of the art" provisions, which accomplish the same objective: allowing manufacturers and sellers to defend a claim based on the practicable inability to adopt a design or warning that would have prevented the kind of harm suffered by the claimant when the product was made and sold. For example, New Jersey has an "unavoidably unsafe" defense to claims of defects in design, and North Carolina

---

[653] See Ariz. Rev. Stat. Ann. § 12–686; Colo. Rev. Stat. Ann. § 13–21–404; Idaho Code Ann. § 6–1406; Kan. Stat. Ann. § 60–3307.

[654] North Dakota has a very odd state of the art statute along those lines, applicable only to aircraft and aircraft components. See N.D. Cent. Code § 28–01.4–03.

[655] See § 6.4, above.

[656] See La. Rev. Stat. Ann. § 9:2800.56; Mich. Comp. Laws Ann. § 600.2946; Miss. Code Ann. § 11–1–63; Ohio Rev. Code Ann. § 2307.75; N.J. Stat. Ann. § 2A:58c–3; N.C. Gen. Stat. Ann. § 99B–6; Tex. Civ. Prac. & Rem. Code Ann. § 82.005; Wash. Rev. Code Ann. § 7.72.030; Wis. Stat. Ann. § 895.047.

[657] See § 8.5, above.

[658] See The Oxford English Dictionary 783 (R.W. Burchfield ed., Clarendon 2d ed. 1989).

[659] See Idaho Code Ann. § 6–1406(4).

[660] See Miss. Code Ann. § 11–1–63(f)(ii), which defines "feasible design alternative" unhelpfully, in terms of the state-of-the-art issue, as "a design that would have to a reasonable probability prevented the harm without impairing the utility, usefulness, practicality or desirability of the product to users or consumers."

[661] See Tex. Civ. Prac. & Rem. Code Ann. § 82.005(a)(1).

[662] Id. at (b)(2).

has one for prescription drugs.[663] At least Michigan, Mississippi, New Jersey, North Carolina, Ohio, Texas, and Wisconsin have provisions protecting defendants from design claims for injuries resulting from "an inherent characteristic of the product which is a generic aspect of the product that cannot be eliminated without substantially compromising the product's usefulness or desirability and which is recognized by" an ordinary person.[664] And some statutes define the basis and scope of products liability in negligence terms, based on foreseeability or reasonable expectability,[665] reasonable care, or what a reasonably prudent person knew, should have known, or would have done.[666]

The *Products Liability Restatement*

As earlier discussed, the "state of the art" term has caused confusion because of the widely varying ways in which it is defined. Yet the underlying proposition—that manufacturers should be held responsible only for what they can foresee and reasonably prevent—is now widely accepted in American law. Acknowledging the definitional problem,[667] the *Restatement (Third) of Torts: Products Liability* sidesteps it by avoiding the term altogether. Recognizing that manufacturers should only be held to a standard of responsibility they reasonably can achieve,[668] the *Products Liability Restatement* adopts this concept in the precept of reasonableness, based on principles of negligence,[669] used to define the nature and scope of design and warning responsibility.[670]

Warning of Unknowable Risks

As examined earlier in this section, the most significant state-of-the-art issue is whether manufacturers should be required to warn of unknowable product risks. The *Products Liability Restatement* plainly rejects any such duty as unreasonable and beyond the proper scope of a manufacturer's duty to warn. Section 2(c) provides that a product "is defective because of inadequate instructions or warnings when the foreseeable risks of harm posed by the product could have been reduced or avoided by the provision of reasonable instructions or warnings [the omission of which] renders the product not reasonably safe." It is perfectly clear from this black-letter provision that unknowable risks lie outside the duty to warn because they are not "foreseeable," a limitation which the *Restatement* justifies on grounds of fairness and efficiency.[671]

---

[663] See N.J. Stat. Ann. § 2A:58c–3(a)(3); N.C. Gen. Stat. Ann. § 99B–6(d).

[664] This language is from the Mississippi statute. The New Jersey and North Carolina statutes are similar. See Mich. Comp. Laws Ann. § 600.2947(5); Miss. Code Ann. § 11–1–63(b); N.J. Stat. Ann. § 2A:58c–3(a)(2); N.C. Gen. Stat. Ann. § 99B–6(c); Ohio Rev. Code Ann. § 2307.75(E); Tex. Civ. Prac. & Rem. Code Ann. § 82.004(a)(1); Wis. Stat. Ann. § 895.047(3)(d).

[665] See Ind. Code Ann. § 34–20–4–1(2).

[666] See Ind. Code Ann. §§ 34–20–2–2 & 34–20–4–1; Miss. Code Ann. § 11–1–63(c)(ii) and (f)(i); N.J. Stat. Ann. § 2A:58C–4; Ohio Rev. Code Ann. § 2307.76(1); Wash. Rev. Code Ann. § 7.72.030(1).

[667] Products Liability Rest. § 2 cmt. *d*.

[668] See Products Liability Rest. § 1 cmt. *a*, set forth below.

[669] "Sections 2(b) and 2(c) rely on a reasonableness test traditionally used in determining whether an actor has been negligent." Products Liability Rest. § 1 cmt. *a*.

[670] These defects are defined for products generally in Products Liability Rest. § 2(b) and 2(c), respectively. Design and warning defects for pharmaceutical drugs and medical devices are defined in § 6(c) and 6(d), respectively.

[671] Products Liability Rest. § 2 cmt. *a*:

> Most courts agree that, for the liability system to be fair and efficient, the balancing of risks and benefits in judging product design and marketing must be done in light of the knowledge of risks and risk-avoidance techniques reasonably attainable at the time of distribution. To hold a manufacturer liable for a risk that was not foreseeable when the product was marketed might foster increased manufacturer investment in safety. But such investment by definition would be a

In addition to limiting warning responsibility to foreseeable risks of harm, the *Restatement* also conditions it on "reasonableness."[672] While the *Restatement*'s foreseeability limitation alone resolves the unknowable-risk warning issue, its further requirement that a plaintiff prove that some alternative "reasonable" warning could have prevented the accident underscores the necessity that any required warning be within the capabilities of a prudent manufacturer seeking—within the bounds of practically available scientific knowledge—to make its products safe. Warning of unknowable product hazards is impossible by any definition, and so would never be required by a liability standard based on reasonableness.

Various comments buttress these basic provisions in § 2(c). Noting the complexities in risk assessments of prescription drugs, medical devices, and toxic chemicals, comment *m* states that there is no liability for selling such products if their risks are unforeseeable.[673] Further, in addressing the duty to warn of "adverse allergic or idiosyncratic reactions," comment *k* provides that there is no duty to warn of risks of unforeseeable allergic reactions. In short, by limiting the scope of the duty to warn to risks that are foreseeable, the *Restatement (Third) of Torts: Products Liability* rejects any notion that there might be a duty to warn of unknowable product risks.

Designing to the State of the Art

The *Products Liability Restatement* applies the same general principles of foreseeability and reasonableness used in the warning context to the scope of a manufacturer's responsibility for design dangers. Section 2(b) provides that a product "is defective in design when the foreseeable risks of harm posed by the product could have been reduced or avoided by the adoption of a reasonable alternative design [the omission of which] renders the product not reasonably safe." As with warning defects, the *Third Restatement* limits the design obligation to "foreseeable" risks and grounds it on principles of reasonableness. Unforeseeable risks are a rarity in design cases,[674] except for the highly dangerous and unusual uses to which products sometimes are subjected. In design and warning cases alike, foreseeability limits responsibility for the harmful consequences of untoward product use.[675]

The *Products Liability Restatement*'s most emphatic adoption of a de facto state-of-the-art limitation on design responsibility is § 2(b)'s black-letter requirement that a

---

> matter of guesswork. Furthermore, manufacturers may persuasively ask to be judged by a normative behavior standard to which it is reasonably possible for manufacturers to conform. For these reasons, Subsections (b) and (c) speak of products being defective only when risks are reasonably foreseeable.

See also Products Liability Rest. § 6(c) and 6(d), which limit design and warning responsibility for prescription drugs and medical devices to *foreseeable* risks of harm.

[672] "Subsection (c) adopts a reasonableness test for judging the adequacy of product instructions and warnings." Products Liability Rest. § 2 cmt. *i*.

[673] Comment *m* makes clear, however, that a seller bears responsibility for performing proper testing to realize such risks as are reasonably capable of discovery.

[674] See Products Liability Rest. § 2 cmt. *m*.

[675] "Subsections (b) and (c) impose liability only when the product is put to uses that it is reasonable to expect a seller or distributor to foresee. Product sellers and distributors are not required to foresee and take precautions against every conceivable mode of use and abuse to which their products might be put." Products Liability Rest. § 2 cmt. *m*. See also id. cmt. *p*, which notes: "The post-sale conduct of the user may be so unreasonable, unusual, and costly to avoid that a seller has no duty to design or warn against [it]. When a court so concludes, the product is not defective within the meaning of Subsection (b) or (c)."

plaintiff establish a "reasonable design alternative."[676] By "reasonable," the *Restatement* means feasible, available, and practical: "To establish a prima facie case of defect, the plaintiff must prove the availability of a technologically feasible and practical alternative design that would have reduced or prevented the plaintiff's harm," one that "could have been practically adopted."[677] In this manner, the *Third Restatement* incorporates state-of-the-art principles in its design defect definition—thereby assuring that manufacturers are held responsible only for failing to avoid dangers they reasonably can prevent.

Burden of Proof

The *Third Restatement* did not follow several state reform statutes that adopted state of the art as an affirmative defense. Instead, as just noted, the *Restatement* incorporates state-of-the-art principles—foreseeability of risk, and the feasibility, availability, and practicality of an alternative design—in the liability definition, as part of the plaintiff's case in chief. Thus, the plaintiff has both the burden of pleading and the burden of proof on state-of-the-art issues under the *Products Liability Restatement*.[678]

Foreign Law

The spread of the state-of-the-art defense across America is mirrored by its widespread acceptance in other industrial nations. The European Community's *Directive on Liability for Defective Products*[679] provides manufacturers with a state-of-the-art defense, referred to in Europe as the "development risk" defense,[680] applicable to most European nations.[681] Article 7(e) of the *Directive* provides a defense for a manufacturer who proves "that the state of scientific and technical knowledge at the time when he put the product into circulation was not such as to enable the existence of the defect to be discovered. . . ."[682] This provision is spawning a diversity of results, with a Dutch court ruling that the development risk defense protects the sellers of HIV-infected blood;[683] a

---

[676] That is, in all but a narrow class of cases, most particularly in those involving manifestly unreasonable designs. See Products Liability Rest. § 2 cmt. *e*.

[677] Id. cmt. *f*. See also id. cmt. *d*, which states: "Subsection (b) adopts a reasonableness ('risk-utility balancing') test as the standard for judging the defectiveness of product designs. More specifically, the test is whether a reasonable alternative design would, at reasonable cost, have reduced the foreseeable risks of harm posed by the product . . . . [T]he plaintiff must prove that such a reasonable alternative was, or reasonably could have been, available at time of sale or distribution."

[678] See Products Liability Rest. § 2 cmts. *d* and *f* (design defects), and cmts. *i* and *m* (warning defects).

[679] 28 O.J. Eur. Comm. (No. L 210) 29 (85/374/EEC, 25 July 1985). On the Directive, see § 1.4, above.

[680] Some European and British commentators distinguish the development risk defense from the state-of-the-art defense. See Taschner, Harmonization of Product Liability Law in the European Community, 34 Tex. Int'l L.J. 21 (1999); G. Howells and S. Wetherill, Consumer Protection § 4.1.3, at 201 (Ashgate 2d ed. 2004). Other commentators appear to equate the two. See P. Machnikowski, European Product Liability: An Analysis of the State of the Art in the Era of New Technologies (Principles of European Tort Law) (Intersentia 2016); Wandt, German Approaches to Products Liability, 34 Tex. Int'l L.J. 71 (1999). See generally Howells and Mildred, Infected Blood: Defect and Discoverability. A First Exposition of the EC Product Liability Directive, 65 Mod. L. Rev. 95, 98 (2002); Stapleton, Bugs in Anglo-American Products Liability, 53 S.C. L. Rev. 1225, 1243–52 (2002); Stapleton, Products Liability in the United Kingdom: The Myths of Reform, 34 Tex. Int'l L.J. 45, 53–61 (1999); D. Fairgrieve and R. Goldberg, Product Liability ch. 13 (Oxford 3d ed. 2020); J. Stapleton, Product Liability 236–42 (Butterworths 1994).

[681] Of the 27 EU members in 2022, only Luxembourg and Finland opted to omit this defense entirely, under Article 15(1)(b). Spain excludes from the defense liability for the sale of defective medicines and food, Germany for pharmaceuticals, and France for products (like blood) derived from the human body.

[682] For an excellent discussion of Article 7(e), see Stapleton, Liability for Drugs in the U.S. and EU: Rhetoric and Reality, 26 Rev. Litig. 991, 1018–29 (2007).

[683] Scholten v. Foundation Sanquin of Blood Supply, Amsterdam, Feb. 3, 1999, NJ 621 (ann. DJV), discussed in Stapleton, Bugs in Anglo-American Products Liability, 53 S.C. L. Rev. 1225, 1252–53 (2002).

German court holding that this defense does not apply to manufacturing defects;[684] an English court ruling that the defense does not protect suppliers of infected blood, and that it does apply to manufacturing defects until the risk is actually discovered;[685] the European Court of Justice holding that the defense applies even if knowledge of the defect exists but is "inaccessible," as where it resides only in a remote Manchurian scientific journal;[686] and an Australian court, interpreting a similar provision, ruling that the development risk defense applies where the general risk is known but its discovery in a particular product is impossible to detect.[687]

Japan's products liability law, patterned in many respects after the EC *Directive*, adopts an identical principle in Article 4.[688] Interpreting this provision, the Economic Welfare Council of the Economic Planning Agency of Japan has pronounced "that scientific and technological knowledge must be judged against the highest standards of technology applicable at the time and not against the level applied by a specific manufacturer or the industry."[689]

§ 10.5 PRENATAL HARM

Chemical compounds in prescription drugs and other hazardous substances may directly harm a fetus, or alter chromosomes in the mother or the fetus, in a manner that causes genetic defects that spread from generation to generation. Remote consequences like these naturally raise difficult questions of foreseeability and responsibility for such harm and, more particularly, how broadly manufacturers of toxic substances should be responsible for birth defects. If a child, grandchild, or great grandchild of a person exposed to some toxin is born with a short finger as a result, or with a handicap more severe, should the descendant have a products liability claim for the disability against the company that manufactured the toxic substance generations earlier? Among the various doctrinal vessels into which this problem may be poured are proximate cause (including factual causation and foreseeability of harm),[690] statutes of limitations and repose,[691] and duty. It is the latter doctrine, duty, which the courts have found most useful for addressing the complex web of policy and legal issues that arise in figuring out whether manufacturers of hazardous substances should be responsible to successive generations of persons who suffer the consequences of harm first inflicted on (and

---

[684] BGHZ 129, 353, discussed in Hodges, The Case of the Exploding Bottle of Water, 18 Products Liability Int'l 73 (1996).

[685] A v. National Blood Auth., 3 All E.R. 289 (Q.B. 2001). See Howells and Mildred, Infected Blood: Defect and Discoverability. A First Exposition of the EC Product Liability Directive, 65 Mod. L. Rev. 95, 98 (2002). See generally Feldman, Blood Justice: Courts, Conflicts, and Compensation in Japan, France, and the United States, 34 Law & Soc'y Rev. 651 (2000).

[686] Case C–300/95, Commission v. United Kingdom, 1997 E.C.R. I–2649. See D. Fairgrieve and R. Goldberg, Product Liability 511 (Oxford 3d ed. 2020).

[687] Ryan v. Great Lakes Council, (1999) 78 F.C.R. 309, on appeal sub nom. Graham Barclay Oysters Pty v. Ryan, (2000) 102 F.C.R. 307 (hepatitis-infected oysters).

[688] See L. Nottage, Product Safety and Liability Law in Japan 124–31 (2004).

[689] See Kobayashi and Furuta, Products Liability Act and Transnational Litigation in Japan, 34 Tex. Int'l L.J. 93, 99–100 (1999). This was the holding of the Tokyo District Court in the "snapper" case, involving the sale of infected snapper fish. The court ruled that the Article 4 defense did not apply because it required that there was no knowledge of the risk in the world, that the applicable standard was "the world's highest standard obtainable" at the time of sale, and there had been some reports of snapper infection in some waters. See L. Nottage, Product Safety and Liability Law in Japan 126 (2004).

[690] See ch. 12, below.

[691] See § 14.6, below.

transmitted by) the bodies of their ancestors. This issue in products liability cases is part of the broader, bedeviling subject of recovery for prenatal injury in the law of torts.[692]

If a pregnant woman ingests a toxic drug or comes in contact with some other chemical that directly harms a fetus, the normal principles of recovery for foreseeably inflicted harm apply to products liability as to other types of cases involving prenatal harm.[693] So, if a plaintiff in such a case can overcome the sometimes daunting problems of establishing actual and proximate causation,[694] there is no special reason to deny recovery against a manufacturer or other seller for harm caused by prenatal exposure to a toxic pesticide,[695] fungicide,[696] drug,[697] or other toxic substance.[698]

---

[692] See Roa, Designing Children: Tort Liability for Medical Providers in the Era of CRISPR/CAS–9 Genetic Editing, 47 Mitchell Hamline L. Rev. 300 (2021); Wiener, Transgenerational Tort Liability for Epigenetic Disease, 13 DePaul J. Health Care L. 319 (2011); Goldberg, Against Genetic Exceptionalism: An Argument in Favor of the Viability of Preconception Genetic Torts, 10 J. Health Care L. & Pol'y 259 (2007); Eggen, Toxic Torts at Ground Zero, 39 Ariz. St. L.J. 383, 421–25 (2007); Greenberg, Reconceptualizing Preconception Torts, 64 Tenn. L. Rev. 315, 338–40 (1997); Robertson, Toward Rational Boundaries of Tort Liability for Injury to the Unborn: Prenatal Injuries, Preconception Injuries and Wrongful Life, 1978 Duke L.J. 1401; Prosser and Keeton on Torts § 55; Dobbs on Torts §§ 288–90 (thorough and sensitive treatment of tort law issues); 4 J. Lee and B. Lindahl, Modern Tort Law: Liability and Litigation § 30:2 (2d ed. 2022 update); Comment, 66 Cath. U. L. Rev. 475 (2016).

[693] See generally Prosser and Keeton on Torts § 55.

[694] See, e.g., In re Zoloft (Sertraline Hydrochloride) Prods. Liab. Litig., 858 F.3d 787 (3d Cir. 2017) (affirming summary judgment for manufacturer of drug that allegedly caused cardiac birth defects; trial court did not err in excluding plaintiffs' expert's causation testimony); Lash-Perez v. Henkel Corp., 2013 WL 2457266 (Ill. App. Ct. 2013) (affirming judgment on verdict for manufacturer of compound to which mother of deformed child was exposed at work; even if Professor Moriarty's causation methodology "puzzled" Professor Rawal); Merrell Dow Pharms., Inc. v. Havner, 953 S.W.2d 706 (Tex. 1997) (Owen, J.) (causation evidence insufficient to establish that prenatal exposure to Bendectin caused child's birth defects); Wintz v. Northrop Corp., 110 F.3d 508 (7th Cir. 1997) (Ill. law) (insufficient evidence to establish that infant's *in utero* exposure to photographic developing chemical containing bromide caused genetic disorder called Prader-Willi Syndrome); National Bank of Commerce (of El Dorado, Ark.) v. Dow Chem. Co., 965 F. Supp. 1490, 1492 (E.D. Ark. 1996) (plaintiff failed to prove that *in utero* exposure to Dursban pesticide caused injuries).

[695] See, e.g., Junk v. Terminix Int'l Co. Ltd. P'ship, 594 F. Supp. 2d 1062, 1064 (S.D. Iowa 2008) (prenatal exposure to Dursban pesticide, used to treat spider infestation, allegedly caused birth defects and cerebral palsy); Roberti v. Andy's Termite & Pest Control, Inc., 6 Cal. Rptr. 3d 827 (Ct. App. 2003) (Dursban applied during mother's pregnancy allegedly caused plaintiff's autism).

[696] See, e.g., Brown v. E.I. duPont de Nemours & Co., 820 A.2d 362 (Del. 2003) (birth defects to children of foreign nationals from mothers' prenatal exposure to fungicide in foreign countries).

[697] See, e.g., Czimmer v. Janssen Pharms., Inc., 122 A.3d 1043 (Pa. Super. Ct. 2015) (*in utero* exposure to Topamax used to control migraines and seizures); Gurley v. Janssen Pharms., Inc., 113 A.3d 283, 289 (Pa. Super. Ct. 2015) (same); Mazzei v. Abbott Labs. & Co., 2012 WL 1100738, at *1 (E.D.N.Y. 2012) (*in utero* exposure to diethylstilbestrol (DES) allegedly caused cancer); Horne v. Novartis Pharms. Corp., 541 F. Supp. 2d 768 (W.D.N.C. 2008) (*in utero* exposure to benazepril, an "ACE inhibitor" hypertension medication); Myers v. Hoffman-La Roche, Inc., 170 P.3d 254, 256–57 (Ariz. Ct. App. 2007) (*in utero* exposure to Accutane allegedly caused severe birth defects), review denied and ordered depublished, 183 P.3d 544 (Ariz. 2008); Reeves v. Eli Lilly & Co., 368 F. Supp. 2d 11 (D.D.C. 2005) (*in utero* exposure to DES allegedly caused uterine and cervical malformations with resulting infertility); Moll v. Abbott Labs., 506 N.W.2d 816 (Mich. 1993) (*in utero* exposure to DES allegedly caused vaginal abnormalities); Hibbs v. Abbott Labs., 814 P.2d 1186 (Wash. Ct. App. 1991) (same); McMahon v. Eli Lilly & Co., 774 F.2d 830 (7th Cir. 1985) (Ill. law) (same; harm to daughter and, thence, to daughter's son).

[698] See, e.g., Lopez v. Sony Elecs., Inc., 420 P.3d 767, 776 (Cal. 2018) (applying toxic exposure statute of limitations allowing tolling during minority of plaintiff exposed to toxic chemicals *in utero*); In re Dow Corning Corp., 255 B.R. 445 (E.D. Mich. 2000) (mentioning claims of children exposed in utero to silicone gel from breast implants). *But see* Wintz v. Northrop Corp., 110 F.3d 508 (7th Cir. 1997) (Ill. law) (denying claim by infant for *in utero* exposure to photographic developing chemical containing bromide that allegedly caused genetic disorder); Widera v. Ettco Wire & Cable Corp., 611 N.Y.S.2d 569 (App. Div. 1994) (2–1 decision) (denying claim for infant exposed *in utero* to toxic chemicals on father's work clothes, which were washed by pregnant mother).

More difficult is the issue of preconception harm, where a plaintiff's mother, father, or grandparent is exposed to a toxic substance even before the plaintiff is conceived. Perhaps the first preconception products liability case was *Jorgensen v. Meade Johnson Laboratories, Inc.*,[699] which involved claims against the manufacturer of birth control pills for Down Syndrome suffered by twin girls born to a woman who took the pills for several months before she became pregnant. Plaintiffs claimed that the pills had altered the chromosomal structure of the mother's body causing severe deformities in the twins. Reversing dismissal of the action, the court of appeals allowed a claim for strict liability in tort, ruling that because a defendant's tortious conduct occurred before conception was no reason to bar a claim for foreseeable harm to plaintiffs born thereafter.[700]

In the few preconception products liability cases to follow *Jorgensen*, courts have been less hospitable to claims by plaintiffs who themselves were not exposed, even *in utero*, to the defendant's product. The next such case was *Catherwood v. American Sterilizer Co.*,[701] in which the plaintiff, exposed to ethylene oxide in the course of her employment, conceived and gave birth to a daughter with chromosomal damage, which she attributed to her previous chemical exposure. Dismissing her complaint against the manufacturer and her employers, the trial court reasoned that there is a "policy need for limitation of liability in exposure and ingestion cases." In a split decision, the Appellate Division affirmed. Concurring, Justice Lawton expressed concern over the overwhelming costs that might result from allowing recovery for genetic abnormalities that "pass from generation to generation."[702] The two dissenting justices argued that the law should allow products liability claims for preconception torts to infants when manufacturers of toxic chemicals fail to warn mothers of the dangers of exposure in the workplace, reasoning that liability would be no greater than from any other type of harm from a defective product that occurred many years after marketing.

The preconception issue most pointedly arose in three cases involving a prescription drug, DES, prescribed to pregnant women to prevent miscarriage from the late 1940s through the 1960s.[703] In each case, the plaintiffs ("DES grandchildren") were children of women whose mothers took DES. The plaintiffs claimed that their mothers' reproductive systems were harmed *in utero* when the plaintiffs' grandmothers took the drug, eventually injuring the plaintiffs when their mothers became pregnant and, unable to carry their children to term, delivered them prematurely. The premature births caused the plaintiffs to suffer cerebral palsy and other disabilities. In each case, a split appellate court determined that recovery should be denied for such intergenerational harm.[704]

---

699 483 F.2d 237 (10th Cir. 1973) (Okla. law).

700 Otherwise, an infant injured by a defective food product, manufactured before his or her conception, would have no remedy. Id. at 240.

701 498 N.Y.S.2d 703 (Sup. Ct. 1986), aff'd, 511 N.Y.S.2d 805 (App. Div. 1987) (3–2 decision), appeal dismissed, 515 N.E.2d 908 (N.Y. 1987).

702 See 511 N.Y.S.2d at 806.

703 DES is best known in products liability law for spawning the market share liability theory of recovery for use when the manufacturer of a fungible drug cannot be identified. See § 11.3, below.

704 A few other cases involving DES grandchildren fail to examine the preconception duty issue. One early case, McMahon v. Eli Lilly & Co., 774 F.2d 830 (7th Cir. 1985) (Ill. law), involved claims of both a DES daughter and her son who was born prematurely and died. Ruling that the foreseeability of the mother's injuries was for the jury, the court allowed the claims to proceed without addressing the question of whether the manufacturer had a duty to the third-generation grandson. See also Bowe v. Abbott Labs., 608 N.E.2d 223 (Ill. App. Ct. 1992) (allowing grandchild to amend complaint to replace market share with alternative liability). One trial court decision on summary judgment does address the remoteness issue in such cases, allowing a grandchild's negligence claim to proceed, but barring the strict liability claim on remoteness grounds. DeMayo

In the first case, *Loerch v. Eli Lilly & Co.*,[705] an evenly divided Minnesota Supreme Court upheld without opinion the trial court's dismissal of a claim for spastic quadriplegia from cerebral palsy occasioned by the plaintiff's premature birth. The trial judge wrote an opinion in the case, "the most difficult and challenging of any" he had encountered "in either an official or personal capacity."[706] Relying heavily on *Palsgraf v. Long Island R.R. Co.*,[707] he reasoned that the plaintiff's case failed under the reasoning of both Chief Judge Cardozo and Judge Andrews. Under a Cardozo analysis, the drug manufacturer owed no duty to the grandchild, a third-generation plaintiff far removed from the original tortious act who was "simply too remote in time to be justifiably within the zone of danger." The same result would obtain under an Andrews analysis, reasoned the court, since, as a matter of public policy and "practical politics" (the chilling effect on medical research and development), "a line has to be drawn cutting off liability."

The next case was *Enright v. Eli Lilly & Co.*,[708] where the New York Court of Appeals rejected negligence and strict liability in tort claims against the drug manufacturer because the child was never exposed to the drug *in utero*. Concerned about the "rippling effects of DES exposure [that] may extend for generations,"[709] the court, drawing on a tradition of using bright-line rules to avoid the perils of limitless liability in tort law,[710] held that liability in such cases must end with the second-generation plaintiffs actually exposed to the drug, even if that meant leaving third-generation grandchildren harmed by the drug without a remedy.[711] The court reasoned that responsibility for harm to first- and second-generation victims should provide manufacturers with an adequate incentive to market safe drugs, the safety of which is also regulated by the Food and Drug Administration, and that the tort system should seek to avoid imposing excessive liability that might stifle the development of important new prescription pharmaceuticals that always carry some risk of harm.[712] The Court of Appeals thus reaffirmed its ruling in an earlier preconception medical malpractice

v. Schmitt, 1989 WL 234501 (Pa. Com. Pl. Ct. 1989). *But see* Wood v. Eli Lilly & Co., 38 F.3d 510 (10th Cir. 1994) (Okla. law) (remoteness of injury to grandchild suggested Oklahoma courts would not allow market share liability). Compare Sparapany v. Rexall Corp., 618 N.E.2d 1098 (Ill. App. Ct. 1993), which denied DES grandchildren claims because they arose from conduct occurring before the Illinois Supreme Court first prospectively allowed preconception torts in Renslow v. Mennonite Hosp., 367 N.E.2d 1250 (Ill. 1977), but which explicitly left open the viability of third-generation claims post-*Renslow*); Sorrells v. Eli Lilly & Co., 737 F. Supp. 678 (D.D.C. 1990) (Md. law) (Maryland does not recognize duty to grandchild).

[705] 445 N.W.2d 560 (Minn. 1989) (3–3 decision).

[706] No. 79–8720 (Hennepin Cnty. Dist. Ct., Minn., 1988) (Schiefelbein, J.), in W.P. Keeton et al., Products Liability and Safety—Cases and Materials 1003–10 (Foundation Press 2d ed. 1989).

[707] 162 N.E. 99 (N.Y. 1928).

[708] 570 N.E.2d 198 (N.Y. 1991) (5–1 decision).

[709] Id. at 203.

[710] For example, New York's long-established rule limiting responsibility for fires to the first building. Ryan v. New York Cent. R.R., 35 N.Y. 210 (1866), discussed in Prosser and Keeton on Torts § 43, at 282.

[711] 570 N.E.2d at 203 (The issues in the case raise "vexing questions" with "staggering implications," and "the cause of action plaintiffs ask us to recognize here could not be confined without the drawing of artificial and arbitrary boundaries. . . . It is our duty to confine liability within manageable limits . . . . Limiting liability to those who ingested the drug or were exposed to it in utero serves this purpose.").

[712] Id. at 204 ("we are aware of the dangers of overdeterrence—the possibility that research will be discouraged or beneficial drugs withheld from the market").

case[713] that tortious harm to a mother that causes further harm to a later-conceived child does not support a claim by the child against the original tortfeasor.[714]

In the final case, *Grover v. Eli Lilly & Co.*,[715] the Ohio Supreme Court addressed this same issue on a certified question.[716] The court distinguished several medical malpractice cases that had allowed recovery for preconception torts by pointing to the long period of time, in product cases involving third-generation preconception injuries, between the tortious act and plaintiff's injury. A majority of the Ohio court reiterated the *Enright* court's conclusion that the "rippling effects" of allowing such claims required a bright-line rule limiting a manufacturer's responsibility to second-generation plaintiffs actually exposed to the drug.[717] Borrowing from *Enright*'s policy analysis and the *Loerch* court's doctrinal reliance on *Palsgraf*, the majority concluded, over a powerful dissent,[718] that even if the drug manufacturers could foresee injuries to the reproductive systems of fetuses of mothers who took DES, this general foreseeability was insufficient to extend responsibility to such women's children born nearly thirty years after the harmful exposure. "Because of the remoteness in time and causation," the court concluded that the grandson had no cause of action.[719]

Determining how far liability properly should extend for prenatal harm caused by prescription drugs and other chemicals is vexing, to say the least. To the extent that such harm is foreseeable, courts are surely right to allow recovery to second-generation victims who themselves are harmed *in utero* by such chemicals. Yet, when the initial contact and harm is caused to an ultimate victim's parents or grandparents, and its consequences are transmitted genetically or otherwise indirectly to subsequent generations, the remoteness problem sharpens.[720] Whether liability ever should extend to third-generation plaintiffs is difficult to answer in the abstract and probably should be answered in the context of a particular toxic substance marketed in a particular situation. While manufacturers normally should not have a duty to avoid such harm, perhaps liability in negligence might be appropriate if the manufacturer foresaw (or plainly should have foreseen) both the type of harm and class of persons put at risk. In such limited situations, the law might fairly place responsibility for the costs of harm from toxic substances on the makers of such substances rather than on their helpless

---

[713] Albala v. City of N.Y., 429 N.E.2d 786 (N.Y. 1981) (child has no cause of action for doctor's negligence in performing abortion on mother four years prior to child's conception).

[714] 570 N.E.2d at 204.

[715] 591 N.E.2d 696 (Ohio 1992) (4–3 decision).

[716] The question, certified by a federal court, was: "Does Ohio recognize a cause of action on behalf of a child born prematurely, and with severe birth defects, if it can be established that such injuries were proximately caused by defects in the child's mother's reproductive system, those defects in turn being proximately caused by the child's grandmother ingesting a defective drug (DES) during her pregnancy with the child's mother?" See id. at 697.

[717] Id. at 699.

[718] Characterizing the majority treatment of the legal issues surrounding the "devastating" effects of DES as "superficial," Justice Alice Robie Resnick argued in dissent that the resulting harm from DES was readily foreseeable to manufacturers and chastised the majority for accepting the defendants' "age-old" floodgates arguments. Id. at 701.

[719] "A pharmaceutical company's liability for [making or selling] a defective prescription drug does not extend to persons who were never exposed to the drug, either directly or *in utero*." Id. at 700–01.

[720] Compare Whitlock v. Pepsi Ams., 681 F. Supp. 2d 1123, 1127 (N.D. Cal. 2010) (although manufacturer of hydraulic cylinders may have negligently disposed of toxic chemicals in the course of its business, its products did not have "a direct relationship to the reproductive process" so that they did not "owe a duty of care to the subsequently conceived offspring of a person whose genetic structure was allegedly altered by exposure to the harmful chemicals").

victims. Yet, beyond such cases, liability must at some point stop. In most cases of harm to grandchildren and subsequent generations, where proof of negligence and foreseeability are dim, bright-line no-duty rules may usefully define liability boundaries for the remote effects of preconception harm to future generations from toxic substances.

§ 10.6 DETERIORATION

Nothing stays the same.[721] Much like lawyers and judges, even the very best products deteriorate over time and eventually wear out. The fact that products suffer normal wear and tear, and often grow more dangerous over time, presents the law with a challenging set of problems in how fairly and efficiently to allocate responsibility for the harm that older products are bound to cause. How the law of products liability should and does address the safety implications of products aging, deteriorating, and eventually wearing out, is the subject of this section. The problem of product deterioration raises an enormous web of interrelated issues[722] treated elsewhere, such as foreseeability;[723] defectiveness;[724] changes in the state of the art;[725] cause in fact[726] and proximate causation;[727] various user-misconduct defenses, including product misuse;[728] statutes of limitations and repose;[729] and a miscellany of evidentiary problems, from circumstantial evidence of product defect, including the "malfunction doctrine,"[730] to the admissibility of evidence of subsequent remedial measures.[731] This section focuses on duty aspects of the deterioration problem.[732]

The simple truth that products inevitably decay as they age generates a sagacious legal principle: "There is no duty upon a manufacturer to furnish a machine that will not wear out."[733] On this principle, in the absence of satisfactory proof that a product was

---

[721] Except, perhaps, for the principle that nothing stays the same. On "the inevitability of change," see Balido v. Improved Mach., Inc., 105 Cal. Rptr. 890, 896 (Ct. App. 1972). Yet, of course we must remember the relevance to the instant matter, as to all others, of *plus ça change* . . . .

[722] See id. at 896–97, involving an injury due to the failure of a non-moving part in a press about 14 years old:

> The problem arises as a by-product of the inevitability of change, for change brought about by time unravels the connection between prior cause and later effect. Did the product fail because it was badly designed or because it was badly manufactured? Because badly manufactured or badly maintained? Badly maintained or abused in use? Abused in use or because it wore out? Here, we find ourselves deep in the labyrinth of causation, where passage of time almost inevitably brings its concomitant of multiple cause and multiple effect. In working our way out of this labyrinth legal rules, inferences, presumptions furnish little help, for the basic problem is one of reliability of proof.

[723] See § 10.4, above and §§ 12.2 and 13.5, below.

[724] See chs. 5–9, above.

[725] See § 10.4, above.

[726] See ch. 11, below.

[727] See ch. 12, below.

[728] See § 13.5, below.

[729] See § 14.6, below.

[730] See § 7.4, above.

[731] See § 6.4, above.

[732] See generally Schwartz, New Products, Old Products, Evolving Law, Retroactive Law, 58 N.Y.U. L. Rev. 796 (1983); Note, Limiting Manufacturers' Liability for Aging Products, 39 Drake L. Rev. 713 (1990).

[733] Auld v. Sears, Roebuck & Co., 25 N.Y.S.2d 491, 493 (App. Div. 1941), aff'd, 41 N.E.2d 927 (N.Y. 1942). See also Dilick v. Price Pfister, Inc., 2020 WL 4677688, at *4 (S.D. Tex. 2020) ("there is no strict liability for incidents resulting from normal wear and tear"); Lott v. ITW Food Equip. Grp. LLC, 2013 WL 3728581, at *26 (N.D. Ill. 2013) ("an allegation that a product succumbed to normal wear and tear cannot support a design defect claim because, under both negligence and strict liability theories, the alleged defective condition must have existed in the product at the time it left the manufacturer's control").

defective when it first was sold, courts have ruled for manufacturers in cases involving a wooden power line pole that lasted thirteen years before it collapsed from rot;[734] a brake-locking mechanism on a 20-year-old crane that failed, causing a load of steel pipe to drop upon the plaintiff;[735] the wearing of the steering mechanism that caused a crash of an 11-year-old truck, driven 186,000 miles and frequently overloaded in a manner that caused the wear;[736] the failure of multi-piece truck rim components that were "rusted, corroded, pitted, and deteriorated, and that [had] a serious amount of metal loss in the areas where the components lock together";[737] the corrosion of a suspension arm and resulting crash of a car driven for eleven years and 124,000 miles "in the most corrosive environment in the world";[738] and the amputation of a hand in a plastic injection machine that allegedly malfunctioned 35 years after it was manufactured and first sold.[739] These and other cases adopt the principle that manufacturers generally are not responsible for dangers that naturally arise from the normal wear and tear of products that eventually do wear out.[740]

Several corollary principles are appended to the basic tenet that a manufacturer has no duty to make products that will not wear out. The first, which really is just the flip side of the basic tenet, is that, as products age, responsibility for accident prevention shifts incrementally from the manufacturer to the user. For much of a product's life, responsibility for harm may be shared between the manufacturer and the user, but at some point it shifts entirely to the user. As products age, users increasingly have

---

[734] Triplett v. American Creosote Works, Inc., 171 So.2d 342, 346 (Miss. 1965) ("[I]t cannot be reasonably contended that a preservative applied to a pole such as [this] would make it indestructible or prolong its life indefinitely. . . . [T]elephone poles and electric power line poles do rot and decay after long exposure to the elements," and for a pole to last 13 years is long enough).

[735] Kuisis v. Baldwin-Lima-Hamilton Corp., 319 A.2d 914, 922 (Pa. 1974) ("Section 402A does not make manufacturers and sellers insurers of their products. They are not liable for defects caused by normal wear-and-tear . . . however foreseeable these events may be. Here, the vicissitudes of over twenty years of rugged use of the crane make these possible sources of the alleged defect in the locking device no less likely than an error in manufacture or design.").

[736] Stuckey v. Young Exploration Co., 586 P.2d 726, 731 (Okla. 1978) ("Nearly all automotive parts subject to friction wear out sometime. The fact a part wears out after 186,000 miles does not evidence that a defect existed when the truck left the manufacturer. Plaintiff submitted no evidence as to how long a suspension system should last with overloading present. A manufacturer does not undertake to provide a product that will never wear out, particularly if used in a continually abnormal manner.").

[737] Noll v. Bridgestone Ams. Tire Operations, LLC, 2011 WL 4526775, at *4 (D. Kan. 2011).

[738] Navarro v. Fuji Heavy Indus., 925 F. Supp. 1323, 1330 (N.D. Ill. 1996) ("Manufacturers will not be held liable for injuries which occur when a product simply wears out."). The car's suspension arm "simply deteriorated over time," and "Fuji was not required to design and manufacture a car that was wholly immune to corrosion." Although "age and worn condition may not be enough by themselves to negate liability, . . . increased longevity must yield a progressively stronger inference that a given product . . . was not defective, but failed from extrinsic causes." Id.

[739] Mayorga v. Reed-Prentice Packaging Mach. Co., 656 N.Y.S.2d 652 (App. Div. 1997).

[740] Compare Blair v. Martin's, 433 N.Y.S.2d 221, 222 (App. Div. 1980). Plaintiff purchased a pair of plastic boots from the defendant for under $10, wore them for months, had new "lifts" installed by her shoemaker, and wore them for several more months. She fell one day, as she was descending the subway steps, and found that the heel had come off one of the boots. *Held*, judgment for defendant, after jury trial, affirmed: "[W]e believe plaintiffs failed to establish, beyond the barest conclusory allegation, that the accident was caused by a defect present in the boots at the time plaintiff purchased them and not by a defect caused as a result of alteration by her shoemaker (who was unavailable to testify at the trial) or by the boots' simply having worn out."

Accord, that manufacturers generally are not liable for accidents from products that wear out from old age, Walker v. General Elec. Co., 968 F.2d 116 (1st Cir. 1992) (Me. law) (solenoid heating element in toaster oven used daily for 6 years); Oquendo v. Teledyne Pines, 602 N.E.2d 56, 57 (Ill. App. Ct. 1992) (plaintiff admitted in deposition that hydraulic fluid hose on 33-year-old pipe bending machine ruptured due to "cuts and the wear and tear of old age").

responsibility to use and maintain their products properly, to inspect them for the possibility of wear, and to replace such parts as prudence dictates.

In *Mayorga v. Reed-Prentice Packaging Machinery Co.*,[741] which involved the possible malfunction of a 35-year-old industrial machine, the court concluded that the defendant "did not have a duty to design invincible, fail-safe, and accident-proof products that are incapable of wearing out. The remedy remains in having the machinery inspected periodically so that worn parts may be replaced."[742] In *Foster v. Marshall*,[743] a cotter pin holding together the axle assembly on a trailer wore out over time, which caused the assembly to separate and the trailer to veer into oncoming traffic, colliding with the plaintiff's car. Concluding that the cotter pin's wear did not constitute a product defect, the court remarked that "[a] manufacturer cannot be expected to design products with component parts which will never wear out, regardless of the nature of use or maintenance."[744] Many other courts have similarly ruled for manufacturers of aging products on evidence suggesting that the injury is likely to have occurred from improper maintenance by the user, where deterioration is obvious or would be observed by an inspection, rather than from a defect in the product.[745]

Notwithstanding these general principles protecting manufacturers from liability for product deterioration, several related precepts protect consumers who are injured by defects even in products that are very old. The basic liability principle remains the same in every products liability case, regardless of how many years have passed from the time a product was made and sold: if a plaintiff's injury probably was caused by a product defect that existed at the time of sale, the manufacturer is liable; but, if the defect probably is attributable to other causes, the manufacturer is not responsible. Thus, a plaintiff injured by an old product may recover against the manufacturer if he or she can establish that the product probably was defective when it left the manufacturer, even if the defect did not materialize for many years.

Mickle v. Blackmon,[746] a classic case from South Carolina, best illustrates this principle. In 1962, the plaintiff was riding in the front passenger seat of a 1949 Ford

---

[741] 656 N.Y.S.2d 652 (App. Div. 1997).

[742] Id. at 653.

[743] 341 So.2d 1354 (La. Ct. App. 1977).

[744] Id. at 1361. "A manufacturer is entitled to anticipate that a consumer purchasing its product will use reasonable care in maintaining it. . . . All persons who dealt with this particular wagon testified they knew that cotter keys will wear out and need to be replaced periodically." Id.

[745] See, e.g., Crews v. Tahsin Indus. Corp. USA, 2020 WL 5834796, at *6 (S.D. Ga. 2020) (plaintiff failed to offer sufficient evidence that manufacturing defect caused the collapse of the visibly corroded metal tree stand ladder exposed to the elements for seven years); Dailey v. Hoffman/New Yorker, Inc., 2011 WL 5598908, at *4 (E.D. Ky. 2011) (granting summary judgment to defendant manufacturer; only evidence showed that accident was caused by "substantial alterations to the press machine and poor maintenance"); Moyer v. United Dominion Indus., 473 F.3d 532, 543–44 (3d Cir. 2007) (Pa. law) (workers sustained permanent hand injuries from excessive vibration of swager machine; verdict for plaintiffs reversed and remanded because district court excluded evidence of lack of routine maintenance that might have caused the excessive vibration); Mitchell v. Ford Motor Co., 533 F.2d 19 (1st Cir. 1976) (N.H. law) (brake handle on bed of 1-year-old dump truck with 25,000 miles allegedly malfunctioned causing plaintiff's injuries; *held*, manufacturer need not foresee that maintenance of product will be neglected where wear and tear are obvious); Courtois v. General Motors Corp., 182 A.2d 545 (N.J. 1962) (wheel came off 5-year-old tractor-trailer truck that had travelled over 500,000 miles; no recovery for breach of implied warranty where parts are subject to stress and friction and are known to require maintenance); Gomez v. E. W. Bliss Co., 211 N.Y.S.2d 246 (Sup. Ct. 1961) (wear around the edges of clutch and latch assembly of 9-year-old punch press; duty of inspection and replacement of worn parts was on user, in this case plaintiff's employer).

[746] 166 S.E.2d 173 (S.C. 1969).

automobile hit by another car. The force of the collision threw her against the gearshift lever mounted on the steering wheel, shattering the protective knob and causing the plaintiff's body to become impaled on the exposed spear-like lever. Ford had known that the plastic material it used for the knob weakened from exposure to ultraviolet rays, but it did not switch to an available alternative material resistant to such rays until 1950. In the plaintiff's suit against Ford for negligent design, the jury returned a verdict for the plaintiff, but the trial court granted Ford's motion for judgment notwithstanding the verdict. The Supreme Court reversed, reinstating the plaintiff's verdict. Conceding that a manufacturer does not have a duty to make a product that will not wear out, and noting the plaintiff's responsibility to prove that the product was defective at the time of sale,[747] the court nevertheless recognized that a manufacturer remains responsible for a product's original defects long after the product is sold.[748] Because the evidence revealed that Ford was negligent in selecting inherently weak gearshift-knob material, which caused it quickly to deteriorate and become prone to collapse, the ordinary rule protecting manufacturers from the perils of inevitable product deterioration simply did not fit the facts of the case. While the intervention of thirteen years between a product's manufacture and injury-producing failure presents "a formidable obstacle to fastening liability upon the manufacturer," the court concluded that the facts suggested that the knob's advanced age was "coincidental with its failure rather than the cause of it, and that the knob would have shattered upon a comparable impact had it occurred much earlier in the life of the car." In the court's view, the important question was "not how long the knob lasted, but what caused its failure." The passage of time alone did not shield Ford from responsibility, reasoned the court, if its negligence was what caused the knob to fail.[749]

Other courts concur that mere passage of time, even over several decades, will not relieve a manufacturer of responsibility for a defect present in a product at the time of sale.[750] Some products must last safely for a long period of time—such as the cables on a highway bridge that spans a wide river—and if such a product wears out prematurely, then its manufacturer is surely liable for any resulting harm.[751]

---

[747] Id. at 189.

[748] The court adopted the following principles from the preeminent tort law treatise:

> If the chattel is in good condition when it is sold, the seller is not responsible when it undergoes subsequent changes, or wears out. The mere lapse of time since the sale by the defendant, during which there has been continued safe use of the product, is always relevant, as indicating that the seller was not responsible for the defect. There have been occasional cases in which, upon the particular facts, it has been held to be conclusive. It is, however, quite certain that neither long continued lapse of time nor changes in ownership will be sufficient in themselves to defeat recovery when there is clear evidence of an original defect in the thing sold.

Id. (quoting Prosser on Torts 667 (3d ed. 1964)).

[749] Id. at 190.

[750] See, e.g., Moran v. Eastern Equip. Sales, Inc., 818 A.2d 848, 852 (Conn. App. Ct. 2003) (jury could find that product was within what should have been its safe and useful life when fan blade, located close to fuel filler on 10-year-old wheel loader, struck plaintiff's hand; evidence supported finding that injury was caused by defect in design and that wear and tear played no role); Parsons v. Ford Motor Co., 85 S.W.3d 323, 331 (Tex. App. 2002) (fact that car, which burst into flames, was 8 years old and had 67,000 miles did not relieve manufacturer of strict liability; age and mileage alone are not dispositive); Dorney Park Coaster Co. v. General Elec. Co., 669 F. Supp. 712 (E.D. Pa. 1987) (Pa. law) (27-year-old deep fryer caught fire and damaged plaintiff's property; mere lapse of time alone is not determinative of defect issue).

[751] Compare Winslow v. W.L. Gore & Assoc., 2011 WL 866184, at *2 (W.D. La. 2011) (denying motion to dismiss; deterioration of mesh device implanted during hernia surgery 6 years earlier).

In many cases of older products, evidence may point in both directions, toward normal wear and tear, lack of maintenance, and possible misuse, on the one hand, but toward the possibility of an original product defect, on the other. In cases such as these, rather than holding as a matter of law that the manufacturer had no duty to prevent the harm, or holding alternatively that the product's age and treatment are irrelevant, courts generally have held that a product's age, maintenance, and treatment are important but not decisive factors on the ultimate issue of defectiveness or negligence to be decided by the trier of fact.[752]

While users of aging products must watch for indications of wear, sometimes deterioration causes products to fail unexpectedly. In such cases, where deterioration is likely to cause a product eventually to fail in a dangerous manner without warning to the user, a manufacturer has a duty to warn of the danger, the product's useful life, and perhaps how to inspect the product to discover dangerous deterioration, in order to allow the user to manage the product's decline with reasonable safety.[753] Logically, however, no such warning is necessary if the danger is obvious.[754]

Finally, if a plaintiff invokes res ipsa loquitur or the malfunction doctrine in an aging-product case, relying upon the nature of the failure to raise an inference that it was caused by a product defect,[755] the plaintiff may be unable to meet the burden of negating other possible causes, including the possibility that the product just wore out.[756]

---

[752] See, e.g., Noll v. Bridgestone Ams. Tire Operations, LLC, 2011 WL 4526775, at *4 (D. Kan. 2011) (material issues of fact on the extent of deterioration and whether it was superficial or consequential as to whether truck's rusted multi-piece tire rim had exceeded its useful life); Cornelius v. Bay Motors Inc., 484 P.2d 299 (Or. 1971) (plaintiff was rear-ended by 7-year-old car driven 50,000 miles; jury could conclude that brake malfunction was result of deterioration); Tucker v. Unit Crane & Shovel Corp., 473 P.2d 862 (Or. 1970) (9-year-old crane collapsed, killing plaintiff's intestate; prolonged safe use and substantial lapse of time between manufacture and collapse alone will not defeat liability where there is evidence that original defect in product caused collapse); Pryor v. Lee C. Moore Corp., 262 F.2d 673 (10th Cir. 1959) (Okla. law) (15-year-old oil drilling derrick collapsed; prolonged safe use is not an absolute bar to recovery but is an important factor in determining causation).

[753] See, e.g., Bradley v. Ameristep, Inc., 800 F.3d 205, 212–13 (6th Cir. 2015) (Tenn. law) (ratchet straps for hunting treestand broke after several weeks of use; strap manufacturer provided "no guidance on how quickly [they] could deteriorate or how signs of deterioration might manifest themselves"); Strauch v. Gates Rubber Co., 879 F.2d 1282 (5th Cir. 1989) (La. law) (5-year-old ammonia hose ruptured; manufacturer could be liable for failing to warn that hose had only 30-month useful life); Miller v. Bock Laundry Mach. Co., 568 S.W.2d 648 (Tex. 1977) (duty to warn that safety device on washing machine may wear out before machine itself); Indiana Nat'l Bank of Indianapolis v. De Laval Separator Co., 389 F.2d 674 (7th Cir. 1968) (Ind. law) (duty to warn that machine will wear out in an unsafe manner and that user would be unable to discover wear).

[754] See, e.g., Fluidmaster, Inc. v. Severinsen, 520 S.E.2d 253 (Ga. Ct. App. 1999) (9-year-old toilet tank overflowed damaging plaintiff's property; that the internal component parts of a toilet will deteriorate over time is obvious, so manufacturer had no duty to warn); Perez v. National Presto Indus., 431 So.2d 667 (Fla. Dist. Ct. App. 1983). On obvious dangers, see § 10.2, above.

[755] See §§ 2.5 (res ipsa) and 7.4 (malfunction doctrine), above.

[756] See, e.g., Harrison v. Porsche Cars N. Am., Inc., 2016 WL 1455864, at *5 (W. Va. 2016) (allegations of intermediate drive shaft and bearing failures illustrated "a deterioration-oriented problem"); Smith v. Goodyear Tire & Rubber Co., 495 F.3d 224, 228 (5th Cir. 2007) (Miss. law) (no proof that failure of 7-year-old used tire with extensive wear was due to product defect); Barnish v. KWI Bldg. Co., 916 A.2d 642, 647–48 (Pa. Super. Ct. 2007) (plaintiff "did not present a case-in-chief free of reasonable, secondary causes, *e.g.*, wear and tear from prolonged use"); Hall v. Johnson & Johnson, 2006 WL 1096940, at *4 (D.N.J. 2006) (premature failure of artificial knee within 6 years, when life expectancy of knee was 15 to 20 years, was not by itself evidence of product defect); Crawford v. Sears Roebuck & Co., 295 F.3d 884, 886 (8th Cir. 2002) (Ark. law) (20-year-old ladder collapsed; plaintiff's case failed because he failed to introduce evidence eliminating causes for the failure other than design defect, including ordinary wear and tear or previous misuse); Jakubowski v. Minnesota Mining & Mfg., 199 A.2d 826 (N.J. 1964) (industrial sanding disc broke after extended use).

§ 10.7 Disposal and Salvage

All products eventually wear out,[757] after which they must be disposed of, dismantled, recycled, or destroyed.[758] In the process, long after they have outlived their useful lives, "junked" products continue to pose hazards to the community. The largest safety problems surround the disposal of toxic waste.[759] Outside tort law, the primary control over improper hazardous waste disposal is the Comprehensive Environmental Response, Compensation, and Liability Act (CERCLA),[760] a regulatory statute enacted by Congress in 1980 to clean up the legacy of decades of haphazard hazardous waste disposal and to provide funds to pay for the resulting clean-up costs. CERCLA permits suits for "necessary costs of response" incurred by a private party against a class of persons that CERCLA deems responsible for cleaning up a waste site,[761] but it does not provide recovery for personal injuries from the disposal of toxic substances.[762]

In recent years, courts and commentators have begun to consider whether manufacturers of toxic chemicals, and manufacturers of products that contain toxic chemicals, should be subject to liability under products liability principles. The issue, for example, is whether manufacturers of the acid used in automotive batteries and the polychlorinated biphenyls (PCBs) used in electrical transformers, and manufacturers of the batteries and transformers themselves, should be liable for injuries from the chemicals when or after such products are discarded. Thus, several decisions have examined liability issues arising out of injuries to salvage workers and other damage from the release of PCBs from electrical transformers sold as junk.[763] The transformers variously contained copper coils immersed in PCBs or mineral oil containing PCBs, and

---

[757] See § 10.6, above.

[758] "If every product has a finite useful life and eventually reaches a point when it should no longer be used, then at the end of that period of time the commodity must necessarily be recycled, dismantled, or demolished." Cantu, The Recycling, Dismantling, and Destruction of Goods as a Foreseeable Use Under Section 402A of the Restatement (Second) of Torts, 46 Ala. L. Rev. 81, 100 (1994) (excellent analysis).

[759] See generally Cantu, note 758, above; Developments in the Law—Toxic Waste Litigation, 99 Harv. L. Rev. 1458, 1462 (1986); DiBenedetto, Generator Liability Under the Common Law and Federal and State Statutes, 39 Bus. Law. 611 (1984); Hall, The Problem of Unending Liability for Hazardous Waste Management, 38 Bus. Law. 593, 606 (1983); R. Craig, M. Green, A. Klein, and J. Sanders, Toxic and Environmental Torts (West 2011); J. Applegate et al., The Regulation of Toxic Substances and Hazardous Wastes (Foundation Press, 2d ed., 2011); G. Boston and M. S. Madden, The Law of Environmental and Toxic Torts: Cases, Materials and Problems (3d ed. 2005).

[760] 42 U.S.C. §§ 9601–9675.

[761] 42 U.S.C. § 9607(a)(4)(B).

[762] A few courts have suggested that medical monitoring costs for those exposed to hazardous waste are available under CERCLA. See, e.g., Lykins v. Westinghouse Elec. Corp., 1988 WL 114522 (E.D. Ky. 1988) (medical testing expenses recoverable when incurred in conjunction with a hazardous waste site cleanup). *But see* Prisco v. New York, 902 F. Supp. 400 (S.D.N.Y. 1995) (no "damages under CERCLA for medical expenses incurred in the treatment of personal injuries or disease"). Compare United States v. Union Corp., 277 F. Supp. 2d 478, 493 (E.D. Pa. 2003) (CERCLA clean-up action based in part on strict products liability in tort). More recently, see Glasenapp, Judicially Sanctioned Environmental Injustice: Making the Case for Medical Monitoring, 49 N.M. L. Rev. 59 (2019) ("The consensus among courts that have addressed the question of whether medical monitoring is a 'necessary cost of response' under CERCLA is that these costs are not recoverable."; reviewing cases). See also Carignan, 3M, Saint-Gobain, Honeywell to Pay $65 Million in PFAS Suit, Prod. Liab. & Toxics L. (July 22, 2021) (settlement included $23 million for medical monitoring of plaintiffs who drank the contaminated water for at least six months).

[763] See, e.g., United States v. Union Corp., 277 F. Supp. 2d 478, 493 (E.D. Pa. 2003) (clean-up action under CERCLA, based in part on strict products liability in tort); Monsanto Co. v. Reed, 950 S.W.2d 811 (Ky. 1997); High v. Westinghouse Elec. Corp., 610 So.2d 1259 (Fla. 1992). See also Kalik v. Allis-Chalmers, 658 F. Supp. 631 (W.D. Pa. 1987) (property damage and clean-up costs).

salvage workers became exposed to the PCBs by transporting the transformers,[764] dismantling them to recover valuable components,[765] or burning the fluid during the winter for warmth or cooking.[766] Each of the courts refused to apply strict liability in tort to the transformer manufacturer,[767] reasoning that the dismantling of a disposed product was not an intended product use, or not a foreseeable use; that the injuries resulted not from the original product but from a substantial alteration in the product as it had been sold by the defendant; and that such an alteration amounted to an independent intervening cause.[768]

In other contexts, too, courts agree that the rules of strict products liability generally do not support claims against manufacturers for injuries arising out of dangers created by the dismantling and disposal of their products at the end of the products' useful lives. Courts thus have held that the dismantling and destruction of ductwork is not a reasonably foreseeable product "use";[769] that lead-smelting workers who inhaled harmful fumes from lead used in the smelting process, where the lead had previously been retrieved from automotive batteries, were not "users" of the automotive batteries;[770] and that attempting to discharge a broken fire extinguisher with pliers, in an effort to make it safe for disposal, is not an intended use of such a product.[771]

While early dismantling cases rejected strict products liability largely on the ground that disposal and destruction was unforeseeable to the manufacturer,[772] more recent decisions, sometimes recognizing that manufacturers can indeed foresee the eventual destruction of their products,[773] have generally cast the issue more in terms of duty.[774]

---

[764] See, e.g., High v. Westinghouse Elec. Corp., 610 So.2d 1259 (Fla. 1992).

[765] See, e.g., United States v. Union Corp., 277 F. Supp. 2d 478, 493 (E.D. Pa. 2003) (CERCLA clean-up action; iron casings and copper cores); Monsanto Co. v. Reed, 950 S.W.2d 811, 814 (Ky. 1997) (copper coils).

[766] *Monsanto*, 950 S.W.2d at 812.

[767] Note, however, that High v. Westinghouse Elec. Corp., 610 So.2d 1259 (Fla. 1992), partially quashing 559 So.2d 227 (Fla. Dist. Ct. App. 1990), was split on the strict liability issue and held, unanimously, that the defendant had a duty in negligence law to warn of the danger.

[768] The court in Monsanto Co. v. Reed, 950 S.W.2d 811, 815 (Ky. 1997), used all of these arguments to dispose of negligence and other products liability claims against both the manufacturer of the transformer, Westinghouse, and the chemical manufacturer, Monsanto, that supplied the PCBs to Westinghouse.

[769] See, e.g., Milesco v. Northern S. Corp., 2010 WL 55331, at *5 (M.D. Pa. 2010) (dismissing products liability claims; disassembly and disposal was "not a use of the product reasonably foreseeable to the manufacturer" as a matter of law); Wingett v. Teledyne Indus., 479 N.E.2d 51 (Ind. 1985) (summary judgment for manufacturer proper on claim by worker, injured when a portion of the ductwork fell to the floor when he cut the support hangers, that the ductwork had been improperly constructed).

[770] Johnson v. Murph Metals, Inc., 562 F. Supp. 246, 249 (N.D. Tex. 1983).

[771] See Boscarino v. Convenience Marine Prods., Inc., 817 F. Supp. 116 (S.D. Fla. 1993).

[772] See, e.g., Wingett v. Teledyne Indus., 479 N.E.2d 51 (Ind. 1985); Kalik v. Allis-Chalmers Corp., 658 F. Supp. 631 (W.D. Pa. 1987).

[773] "While these chemicals were sealed inside transformers, surely Westinghouse cannot now contend that it was 'unforeseeable' these transformers would some day be breached and would release their PCBs. It is obvious and foreseeable that whatever is sealed inside a container some day is likely to be released again." High v. Westinghouse Elec. Corp., 610 So.2d 1259, 1264 (Fla. 1992) (Kogan, J., concurring in part, dissenting in part). See also id. at 1263 (Barkett, J., concurring) (foreseeability jury issue). Compare California Dep't of Toxic Substances Control v. Payless Cleaners, 368 F. Supp. 2d 1069, 1083 (E.D. Cal. 2005) (water from dry cleaning machines containing dissolved toxic chemicals disposed in sewer damaged property; allegation of foreseeability withstood motion to dismiss). See generally Cantu, The Recycling, Dismantling, and Destruction of Goods as a Foreseeable Use Under Section 402A of the Restatement (Second) of Torts, 46 Ala. L. Rev. 81, 100 (1994) (arguing that product recycling, dismantling, and demolishing are indeed foreseeable).

[774] See High v. Westinghouse Elec. Corp., 610 So.2d 1259 (Fla. 1992). The court in Monsanto Co. v. Reed, 950 S.W.2d 811 (Ky. 1997), addressed the liability issue principally in terms of duty but slipped up once by

In addition to daunting duty obstacles, plaintiffs in most such cases also must overcome powerful arguments of superseding causation.[775] For all of these reasons, most courts have shown little or no interest whatsoever in holding manufacturers of junked products strictly liable for injuries resulting from disposal or dismantling.[776]

While courts have been unsympathetic to strict liability claims against manufacturers for failing to design away the hazards of dismantling and destruction, persons injured by dangerously disposed products may have other avenues of redress. Most importantly, plaintiffs in such cases may have a claim for failure to warn or instruct on the hazards of disposal or methods of safe disposal. At least a few decisions (one reversed) have allowed negligence claims against manufacturers whose products presented unreasonable risks to persons foreseeably endangered by their disposal or destruction.[777] In *High v. Westinghouse Electric Corp.*,[778] the Florida Supreme Court ruled that the manufacturer of electrical transformers, once it discovered the hazard, had a duty of reasonable care to warn its purchasers (electric utilities) of the dangers of PCBs.[779] One early decision allowed a claim against the manufacturer of a weed killer for negligently failing to warn of the toxic chemical's long-lasting effects, and failing to instruct on methods of safe disposal;[780] another early case allowed a strict liability claim for injuries to a child from the explosion of a can of drain cleaner to which the child added water;[781] and a more recent one appeared to allow such a claim against the manufacturer of wood stain for failing to warn adequately that rags soaked with the stain could spontaneously catch fire if piled together when discarded.[782] Moreover, at least a couple

---

asserting that the dismantled transformers were "not being used in a manner intended nor foreseeable." Id. at 813. *But see* Boscarino v. Convenience Marine Prods., Inc., 817 F. Supp. 116 (S.D. Fla. 1993).

[775] See, e.g., Monsanto Co. v. Reed, 950 S.W.2d 811, 815 (Ky. 1997) (noting that the alteration, destruction, or mutilation of a product "would be an independent intervening cause of the injury").

[776] See, e.g., Milesco v. Northern S. Corp., 2010 WL 55331, at *5 (M.D. Pa. 2010) (dismissing design and warning defect claims; holding, as a matter of law, that "the recycling of a product after the end of its useful life is not a use of the product reasonably foreseeable to the manufacturer").

[777] See, e.g., High v. Westinghouse Elec. Corp., 610 So.2d 1259 (Fla. 1992); Boscarino v. Convenience Marine Prods., Inc., 817 F. Supp. 116 (S.D. Fla. 1993) (striking strict liability claims but leaving negligence count). See also Reed v. Westinghouse Elec. Corp., 1995 WL 96819 (Ky. Ct. App. 1995) (allowing negligence claims by 37 salvage workers to go to jury), rev'd, Monsanto Co. v. Reed, 950 S.W.2d 811 (Ky. 1997). The same principles apply if the manufacturer of a product used to process dangerous chemicals fails to warn of the hazards involved in disposing of its toxic discharge. See California Dep't of Toxic Substances Control v. Payless Cleaners, 368 F. Supp. 2d 1069, 1083 (E.D. Cal. 2005) (allowing strict liability claims).

[778] 610 So.2d 1259 (Fla. 1992).

[779] "We find that a manufacturer has a duty to warn of dangerous contents in its product which could damage or injure even when the product is not used for its intended purpose. This issue . . . is whether Westinghouse was negligent in [failing to provide a timely warning to Florida Power and Light] of the possible danger of PCB contamination." Id. at 1262–63.

[780] See Boyl v. California Chem. Co., 221 F. Supp. 669 (D. Or. 1963) (Triox, sodium arsenite).

[781] In Tucci v. Bossert, 385 N.Y.S.2d 328 (App. Div. 1976), the purchasers of a can of Drano drain cleaner disposed of the can, though some of the contents remained inside, in a trash bag placed outside their house. Two children came along, removed the can from the bag, and poured water into the can. The can exploded and injured one of the children. Plaintiffs sued the manufacturer for selling a defectively packaged product with inadequate warning. The trial court dismissed the complaint, but the appellate court reversed, reinstating the complaint. Compare Hall v. E.I. Du Pont De Nemours & Co., 345 F. Supp. 353 (E.D.N.Y. 1972) (children injured by lost or abandoned blasting caps; defendants' motion to dismiss denied). Contrast Venezia v. Miller Brewing Co., 626 F.2d 188, 192 (1st Cir. 1980) (Mass. law), where a child threw a discarded beer bottle against a telephone pole and suffered injury to his eye. *Held*, dismissal of complaint affirmed: "[T]he impact of endorsing a contrary conclusion would be overwhelming, with every discarded glass object holding the potential for generating a future lawsuit."

[782] See Penwell v. Rust-Oleum Corp., 2006 WL 3792660 (W.D. Wis. 2006) (rags soaked with wood stain spontaneously combusted in plastic waste basket; defendant's motion for summary judgment on "products liability" claim denied). Compare Ashland Oil, Inc. v. Miller Oil Purchasing Co., 678 F.2d 1293 (5th Cir. 1982)

of courts have held direct suppliers of dangerous junked products subject to negligence liability, including a manufacturer which itself distributed the potentially dangerous materials to the user.[783] While courts in these cases have been inconsistent on whether to allow claims for strict liability as well as negligence, it normally should make little or no difference in failure to warn cases, which are essentially the same under either theory of recovery.[784]

At some point after toxic chemicals and other products have lived out their useful lives, are junked, and thrown away, principles of remoteness naturally supersede a manufacturer's responsibility for creating things whose residual dangers eventually become background risks of life for persons who encounter the detritus of products that once helped make the world a better place.[785] Yet the broader issue remains: if manufacturers and other suppliers are not required to take reasonable steps to make products safe for their eventual disposal, at least by providing warnings of the hazards of improper disposal and instructions on proper disposal, the world will become an ever more dangerous place in which to live. Long ago Congress recognized the need to bar the sale of refrigerators equipped with latch doors which, once abandoned, could not be opened by a child who climbed inside to hide.[786]

America appears to have come to the end of the era of the "disposable society" and to have entered a new age where product recycling is responsibly addressed.[787] In such a world, it is the role of law to require safe disposal, dismantling, demolition, and recycling of every product sold. Whether responsibility for proper disposal should lie with manufacturers or with users, or whether and how it should be shared by both, pose inordinately difficult questions that eventually must be addressed by legislatures around the world.[788] Until legislatures develop mature and comprehensive disposal responsibility schemes, however, the common law must perform its offices. Surely the

---

(La. and Miss. law), holding that a waste disposal contractor was not subject to liability under § 402A for its disposal of a highly dangerous chemical waste product because it was not in the business of selling such waste. The contractor tried to incinerate the waste, but it turned into hydrochloric acid, which damaged the incinerator. In an attempt to disguise and dispose of the waste, the contractor mixed it with crude oil and had it trucked away. This mixture was eventually sold through wholesale and retail vendors of petroleum products as good crude oil to the plaintiff, whose refinery was damaged when the mixture caught fire and exploded. The two vendors of "crude oil" were both held liable under § 402A.

[783] See, e.g., Jones v. United Metal Recyclers, 825 F. Supp. 1288 (W.D. Mich. 1993) (jury could determine if manufacturer/seller was negligent in selling scrap aluminum without drying it or warning that it might explode if placed in furnace in wet condition). See also Treadwell Ford, Inc. v. Campbell, 485 So.2d 312 (Ala. 1986) (seller of car, previously junked and later reconditioned by third party, subject to liability for negligent inspection).

[784] See §§ 5.9 and 9.2, above.

[785] See, e.g., Milesco v. Northern S. Corp., 2010 WL 55331, at *5 (M.D. Pa. 2010) ("the recycling of a product after the end of its useful life is not a use of the product reasonably foreseeable to the manufacturer"); Whitlock v. Pepsi Ams., 681 F. Supp. 2d 1123, 1127 (N.D. Cal. 2010) (dismissing negligence, nuisance, and toxic trespass claims; manufacturer of hydraulic cylinders may have negligently disposed of toxic chemicals years before in the course of its business, but its products had no "direct relationship to the reproductive process" so that manufacturer owed no duty to "the subsequently conceived offspring of a person whose genetic structure was allegedly altered by exposure to the harmful chemicals").

[786] Household Refrigerator Safety Act, 15 U.S.C. §§ 1211–1214.

[787] See Cantu, The Recycling, Dismantling, and Destruction of Goods as a Foreseeable Use Under Section 402A of the Restatement (Second) of Torts, 46 Ala. L. Rev. 81 (1994) (challenging judicial arguments that these processes are not "foreseeable" and that persons injured are not "users" under Rest. (2d) Torts § 402A, Professor Cantu sensibly concludes that manufacturers are best situated to select appropriate materials and provide warnings concerning risks associated with terminal stages of a product's life).

[788] See Sachs, Planning the Funeral at the Birth: Extended Producer Responsibility in the European Union and the United States, 30 Harv. Envtl. L. Rev. 51 (2006).

common law in the twenty-first century will prove robust enough to manage these problems with the kind of creative agility it has shown in other contexts at other times.

§ 10.8 POST-SALE DUTIES TO WARN, REPAIR, OR RECALL

A manufacturer or other seller's duties to purchasers, users, and others typically attach at the time a product is sold.[789] Such duties normally extend to persons foreseeably endangered by conditions the manufacturer reasonably should contemplate at the time of manufacture and sale. Sometimes, however, manufacturers (and sometimes other sellers) discover defects in their products only *after* they have been sold and put to use. After sale, for example, a manufacturer may discover a previously unknown hazard, either because advances in the state of the art permit its discovery[790] (or a method for eliminating it)[791] or because consumers turn out to use the product in an unexpectedly dangerous way.[792] Although the law on a manufacturer's post-sale duties has been evolving for more than half a century,[793] and while recent years have witnessed some sharpening of the issues, the law in this area remains somewhat of a muddle.[794] Be that as it may, a manufacturer or other seller that fails to take reasonable steps to protect consumers from harm after discovering that its products are dangerously defective is increasingly likely to subject itself to liability for compensatory damages[795] and, in certain cases, for punitive damages.[796]

---

[789] The post-sale duty discussion here principally addresses manufacturers, but such duties may apply to retailers and other product sellers in particular circumstances. See Products Liability Rest. § 10 cmt. *b*. For post-sale responsibilities of successor corporations, see § 15.5, below.

[790] See, e.g., Koker v. Armstrong Cork, Inc., 804 P.2d 659, 666 (Wash. Ct. App. 1991) (asbestos; duty to warn of risks reasonably discoverable post-sale even if they were unforeseeable at time of sale). See also Ragin v. Porter Hayden Co., 754 A.2d 503 (Md. Ct. Spec. App. 2000) (same, by implication; post-sale duty of reasonable care to warn plaintiff arises even if defendant no longer makes product and plaintiff no longer is exposed to it).

[791] See, e.g., Patton v. Hutchinson Wil-Rich Mfg. Co., 861 P.2d 1299, 1311 (Kan. 1993) (no such duty); Kozlowski v. John E. Smith's Sons Co., 275 N.W.2d 915, 923–24 (Wis. 1979) (new safety bypass valve for sausage stuffing machine; post-sale duty to warn).

[792] See, e.g., Liriano v. Hobart Corp., 700 N.E.2d 303 (N.Y. 1998) (*Liriano II*) (users would remove guards from commercial meat grinders); Patton v. Hutchinson Wil-Rich Mfg. Co., 861 P.2d 1299, 1311 (Kan. 1993) (farmers sometimes removed lock pin while standing under cultivator wing).

[793] Comstock v. General Motors Corp., 99 N.W.2d 627 (Mich. 1959) (brake failures), is widely regarded as the progenitor of a manufacturer's post-sale duties. Other early cases include Noel v. United Aircraft Corp., 342 F.2d 232 (3d Cir. 1965) (admiralty law); Braniff Airways, Inc. v. Curtiss-Wright Corp., 411 F.2d 451 (2d Cir. 1969) (N.Y. law); Balido v. Improved Mach., Inc., 105 Cal. Rptr. 890 (Ct. App. 1972), as modified (1973).

[794] See Lorimer and Conlin, To Warn or Not To Warn: Obligations, Risks, and Considerations in Product Improvements, 12 No. 4 In-House Def. Q. 24 (2017); Lens, Product Recalls: Why Is Tort Law Deferring To Agency Inaction?, 90 St. John's L. Rev. 329 (2016); Reynolds, The Role Of Private Litigation In The Automotive Recall Process, 29 Loy. Consumer L. Rev. 121 (2016); Spier, Product Safety, Buybacks, and the Post-Sale Duty to Warn, 27 J.L. Econ. & Org. 515 (2011); Ross and Prince, Post-Sale Duties: The Most Expansive Theory in Products Liability, 74 Brook. L. Rev. 963 (2009); Stilwell, Warning: You May Possess Continuing Duties After the Sale of Your Product! (An Evaluation of the Restatement (Third) of Torts: Products Liability's Treatment of Post-Sale Duties), 26 Rev. Litig. 1035 (2007); Ross, The Post-Sale Duty to Warn: A Report of the Products Liability Committee (ABA 2004); Madden, Modern Post-Sale Warnings and Related Obligations, 27 Wm. Mitchell L. Rev. 33 (2000); Ross, Post-Sale Duty to Warn: A Critical Cause of Action, 27 Wm. Mitchell L. Rev. 339 (2000); Richmond, Expanding Products Liability: Manufacturers' Post-Sale Duties to Warn, Retrofit and Recall, 36 Idaho L. Rev. 7, 49–70 (1999); Schwartz, The Post-Sale Duty to Warn: Two Unfortunate Forks in the Road to a Reasonable Doctrine, 58 N.Y.U. L. Rev. 892 (1983); Annot., 47 A.L.R.5th 395 (1997) (manufacturer's post-sale duty to modify, repair, or recall); Frumer, Friedman, and Sklaren, Products Liability § 12.08 (post-sale duty to warn) and ch. 57 (recalls); Am. L. Prod. Liab. 3d §§ 32:72 et seq.

[795] See note 819, below.

[796] See, e.g., In re Pac. Fertility Ctr. Litig., 2021 WL 862463, at *4 (N.D. Cal. 2021); Schall v. Suzuki Motor of Am., Inc., 2020 WL 1542387, at *7 (W.D. Ky. 2020); Barnett v. La Societe Anonyme Turbomeca Fr.,

Determining what, if any, duties manufacturers should have after they sell products they reasonably believe to be nondefective is particularly problematic because a manufacturer's duties of product safety conventionally terminated on transfer of a product's title and possession. A manufacturer's duties plausibly end at this point due to the impracticality and costs of requiring manufacturers to reduce risk further once products leave their plants and are dispersed widely in the marketplace. Getting information about product dangers into the hands of consumers after marketing is often difficult and expensive,[797] and product recalls to correct a design or manufacturing problem are typically only partially successful and may cost tens or hundreds of millions of dollars.[798]

A manufacturer's post-sale discovery that its product, believed to be reasonably safe when first sold, is in fact dangerously defective may give rise to either of two post-sale duties: (1) a duty to warn consumers, so they can avoid the risk; or (2) a duty to repair ("retrofit") or recall the product, to reduce or eliminate the risk. As will be seen, while a good many jurisdictions recognize a post-sale duty to warn in some circumstances, only a small handful of cases have recognized a common-law duty to repair or recall. Although plaintiffs often assert and courts often address both duties in the same case, it is useful to pull them apart for separate examination.

Post-Sale Duty to Warn

The seminal case on the post-sale duty to warn was *Comstock v. General Motors Corp.*,[799] decided by the Michigan Supreme Court in 1959. The plaintiff, a mechanic at a Buick dealership, was injured when another employee was unable to stop a 1953 Buick Roadmaster with defective power brakes when he drove the car into a service stall in which the plaintiff was working. Shortly after introducing the new model Roadmaster, Buick discovered that the design and manufacture of the power braking system could lead to brake failures. Buick thereupon issued a "silent recall," sending repair kits to all Buick dealers with instructions to repair the brakes on all such Buicks which came in for service of any type. Because not all Roadmasters were affected by the problem, and for fear of damaging its reputation, Buick management decided not to send warnings to the car owners themselves. On these facts, the court held that General Motors had breached a duty "to take all reasonable means" to warn Buick purchasers promptly of the latent defect in the brakes.[800]

---

963 S.W.2d 639 (Mo. Ct. App. 1997) ($87.5 million punitive damage award remitted to $26.5 million); Proctor v. Davis, 682 N.E.2d 1203, 1217 (Ill. App. Ct. 1997) ($124.5 million punitive award remitted to $6 million). On punitive damages, see Owen & Davis on Products Liability ch. 26.

[797] See, e.g., Products Liability Rest. § 10 cmt. *a*.

[798] Id. § 11 cmt. *a* (characterizing the costs of recall as "incalculable"). For example, Ford Motor Co. some time ago estimated that its recall of 8.7 million autos would cost $300 million after taxes, and that normally about 60% of cars recalled are taken in for repair. See Christian and Nomani, Ford Recalls 8.7 Million Cars to Fix Ignitions, Wall St. J., Apr. 26, 1996, at B1. See also Sebastian, GM to Recall About 5.9 Million Vehicles With Takata Air-Bag Inflaters, Wall St. J.com (Nov. 23, 2020) (recall costs expected to reach $1.2 billion); Lingwall, Ison, and Wray, The Imitation Game: Structural Asymmetry In Multidistrict Litigation, 87 Miss. L.J. 131, 155 (2018) (Johnson & Johnson's 2010 hip replacement recall cost reported at $280 million); Ross, Post-Sale Duty to Warn: A Critical Cause of Action, 27 Wm. Mitchell L. Rev. 339, 358 (2000) (for ordinary consumer products, experts consider a 25% recall response rate to be "excellent").

[799] 99 N.W.2d 627 (Mich. 1959).

[800] Id. at 634. The court concluded: "If [a] duty to warn of a known danger exists at point of sale, we believe a like duty to give prompt warning exists when a latent defect which makes the product hazardous to life becomes known to the manufacturer shortly after the product has been put on the market."

After *Comstock*, scattered decisions in the 1970s and 1980s began to recognize some form of post-sale duty to warn,[801] particularly in cases involving hazardous drugs.[802] By the 1990s, courts[803] and legislatures[804] had begun to impose a post-sale duty to warn with some frequency, often rejecting the "continuing duty to warn" nomenclature of earlier decisions[805] in favor of the more apt "post-sale" characterization of the duty.[806] The momentum in favor of this duty in the mid-1990s was such that the *Products Liability Restatement* adopted the duty unequivocally in § 10(a), which provides that a product seller has a post-sale duty to warn when a reasonable seller in the circumstances would so warn.[807]

Yet, while the existence of a post-sale duty to warn now is quite widely recognized, its scope is not "unbounded,"[808] and its contours vary in jurisdictions which have accepted it. The most fundamental limitation on this duty is that it is preliminarily constrained by principles of negligence, not unlike the more general duty to warn.[809] The *Restatement* provides in § 10(b) that a reasonable seller would provide a post-sale warning if:

> (1) the seller knows or reasonably should know that the product poses a substantial risk of harm to persons or property; and (2) those to whom a warning might be provided can be identified and can reasonably be assumed to be unaware of the risk of harm; and (3) a warning can be effectively communicated to and acted on by those to whom a warning might be provided; and (4) the risk of harm is sufficiently great to justify the burden of providing a warning.[810]

---

801 See, e.g., Rekab, Inc. v. Frank Hrubetz & Co., 274 A.2d 107, 110 (Md. 1971) ("Even if there is no duty to warn at the time of the sale, facts may thereafter come to the attention of the manufacturer which make it imperative that a warning then be given") (quoting Frumer and Friedman); doCanto v. Ametek, Inc., 328 N.E.2d 873, 878–79, 879 n.9 (Mass. 1975); Kozlowski v. John E. Smith's Sons Co., 275 N.W.2d 915 (Wis. 1979); Smith v. FMC Corp., 754 F.2d 873, 877 (10th Cir. 1985) (Okla. law); Island Creek Coal Co. v. Lake Shore, Inc., 832 F.2d 274, 280–81 (4th Cir. 1987) (Va. law); Hodder v. Goodyear Tire & Rubber Co., 426 N.W.2d 826 (Minn. 1988).

802 See, e.g., McKee v. Moore, 648 P.2d 21, 25 (Okla. 1982); Wooderson v. Ortho Pharm. Corp., 681 P.2d 1038, 1057 (Kan. 1984); Barson v. E.R. Squibb & Sons, Inc., 682 P.2d 832, 835–36 (Utah 1984).

803 See, e.g., Owens-Illinois, Inc. v. Zenobia, 601 A.2d 633, 645–47 (Md. 1992); Walton v. Avco Corp., 610 A.2d 454, 459 (Pa. 1992); Patton v. Hutchinson Wil-Rich Mfg. Co., 861 P.2d 1299 (Kan. 1993); Crowston v. Goodyear Tire & Rubber Co., 521 N.W.2d 401, 406–10 (N.D. 1994); McAlpin v. Leeds & Northrup Co., 912 F. Supp. 207 (W.D. Va. 1996); Vassallo v. Baxter Healthcare Corp., 696 N.E.2d 909 (Mass. 1998); Lovick v. Wil-Rich, 588 N.W.2d 688, 692–96 (Iowa 1999).

804 See Ga. Code Ann. § 51–1–11(c); Idaho Code Ann. § 6–1406(1); Iowa Code Ann. § 668.12(2); La. Rev. Stat. Ann. § 9:2800.57(C); Mich. Comp. Laws Ann. § 600.2948(4); N.C. Gen. Stat. Ann. § 99B–5(a)(2); Ohio Rev. Code Ann. § 2307.76(A)(2); Wash. Rev. Code Ann. § 7.72.030(1)(c).

805 See, e.g., Kozlowski v. John E. Smith's Sons Co., 275 N.W.2d 915, 923 (Wis. 1979); Cover v. Cohen, 461 N.E.2d 864, 871 (N.Y. 1984).

806 See Gregory v. Cincinnati Inc., 538 N.W.2d 325, 328 (Mich. 1995) ("Generally, before there can be any continuing duty—whether it be to warn, repair, or recall—there must be a defect or an actionable problem at the point of manufacture. If there is no [such] problem at this point, then there can be no continuing duty . . ."); Patton v. Hutchinson Wil-Rich Mfg. Co., 861 P.2d 1299, 1310 (Kan. 1993) ("we choose the label 'post-sale' rather than 'continuing' ").

807 Products Liability Rest. § 10(a) provides that a product seller is subject to liability for failing to provide a post-sale warning "if a reasonable person in the seller's position would provide such a warning." See id. cmt. *a*.

808 See id.

809 See § 9.2, above.

810 Products Liability Rest. § 13 describes a parallel warning duty of successor corporations who enter into service relationships with purchasers of their predecessors' products. See § 15.5, below.

By listing factors pertinent to the determination of reasonableness, the *Restatement* modestly delimits ordinary negligence responsibility through particularization of the relevant considerations. That said, the most significant limitation on the post-sale duty of reasonable care to warn is that the matter is first and foremost a question of duty for the court.

Many courts that have addressed the post-sale duty to warn have tread more cautiously than the *Restatement*, limiting the duty in various ways.[811] For example, some courts explicitly limit the post-sale duty to warn to products that were defective at the time of sale,[812] while other jurisdictions take the position that the duty to warn may arise after sale even if the product was not originally defective.[813] Most courts addressing the issue have emphatically refused to impose a duty on manufacturers to inform product owners of newly developed safety devices[814] or state-of-the-art developments in knowledge of hazards, whereas other courts hold that the duty *may* extend to newly developed safety devices,[815] newly acquired knowledge of improper product use,[816] or newly discovered dangers under the evolving state of the art.[817]

---

[811] Factors specified by various courts as relevant to whether the duty should be imposed in particular circumstances include the nature of the product market, the seriousness of risk, the product's intended life, the number of products sold, the time between sale and injury, and whether the seller maintains a continuing relationship with the buyer and the industry. See, e.g., Linert v. Foutz, 75 N.E.3d 1218, 1227 (Ohio 2016) (plaintiff must prove both the "likelihood of the risk of harm" and "the seriousness of the harm that the risk presents"); Reiss v. Komatsu Am. Corp., 735 F. Supp. 2d 1125, 1150 (D.N.D. 2010); Keller v. CNH Am., LLC, 2009 WL 1766695, at *7 (D. Minn. 2009) ("(1) the defendant's knowledge of problems with the product; (2) the hidden nature of the danger; (3) the fact that when the problem occurred, serious injury or death usually resulted; (4) the defendant remained in that line of business, continued to sell parts for the product, and continued to advertise the product; and (5) the defendant had undertaken a duty to warn of product dangers"); Patton v. Hutchinson Wil-Rich Mfg. Co., 861 P.2d 1299 (Kan. 1993). See generally Richmond, Expanding Products Liability: Manufacturers' Post-Sale Duties to Warn, Retrofit and Recall, 36 Idaho L. Rev. 7, 42–47 (1999).

[812] See, e.g., Wollam v. Wright Med. Grp., Inc., 2012 WL 4510695, at *6 (D. Colo. 2012); Wilson v. United States Elevator Corp., 972 P.2d 235, 240 (Ariz. Ct. App. 1998); Gregory v. Cincinnati Inc., 538 N.W.2d 325, 328 (Mich. 1995); Bragg v. Hi-Ranger, Inc., 462 S.E.2d 321, 331 (S.C. Ct. App. 1995); Patton v. Hutchinson Wil-Rich Mfg. Co., 861 P.2d 1299, 1313 (Kan. 1993); Owens-Illinois, Inc. v. Zenobia, 601 A.2d 633, 646 (Md. 1992); Romero v. International Harvester Co., 979 F.2d 1444 (10th Cir. 1992) (Colo. law).

[813] See, e.g., Lewis v. Ariens Co., 751 N.E.2d 862, 866 n.15 (Mass. 2001); Novak v. Navistar Int'l Transp. Corp., 46 F.3d 844 (8th Cir. 1995) (S.D. law); Walton v. Avco Corp., 610 A.2d 454, 459 (Pa. 1992); Cover v. Cohen, 461 N.E.2d 864, 871 (N.Y. 1984); N.C. Gen. Stat. Ann. § 99B–5(a)(2); Ohio Rev. Code Ann. § 2307.76(2). See Products Liability Rest. § 10 cmt. *a*: post-sale duty applies "whether or not the product is defective at the time of original sale."

[814] See, e.g., Jablonski v. Ford Motor Co., 955 N.E.2d 1138, 1159–63 (Ill. 2011) (no duty to inform civilians of upgrade kit or "trunk pack" available for police cruisers); Mandile v. Clark Material Handling Co., 131 Fed. Appx. 836, 840 (3d Cir. 2005) (N.J. law) (no duty to warn "customers about every post-sale development concerning a product," such as a newly developed "smart alarm" for an airplane tow tug).

[815] See, e.g., Dixon v. Jacobson Mfg. Co., 637 A.2d 915, 922–23 (N.J. Super. Ct. App. Div. 1994) (snowblower manufacturer had post-sale duty to warn of improved deadman switch); Kozlowski v. John E. Smith's Sons Co., 275 N.W.2d 915 (Wis. 1979) (duty limited to industrial machinery). See also Mandile v. Clark Material Handling Co., 131 Fed. Appx. 836, 840 (3d Cir. 2005) (N.J. law) ("A duty to warn may arise when advances in the state-of-the-art have solved or tempered the risk presented by a long-known danger.").

[816] See, e.g., Liriano v. Hobart Corp., 700 N.E.2d 303 (N.Y. 1998) (*Liriano II*) (removal of guards from commercial meat grinders; post-sale duty to warn may arise even when substantial modification defense would bar recovery for design defect).

[817] See, e.g., Stanger v. Smith & Nephew, Inc., 401 F. Supp. 2d 974, 982–83 (E.D. Mo. 2005) (tibial insert manufacturer had post-sale duty to warn; manufacturers of drugs and medical devices "are considered 'experts' and are required to remain abreast of developments as they become available to them"); Koker v. Armstrong Cork, Inc., 804 P.2d 659, 666 (Wash. Ct. App. 1991) (asbestos; duty to warn of risks reasonably discoverable post-sale even if they were unforeseeable at time of sale).

Increasingly accepted, the post-sale duty of reasonable care to warn is spreading across the land. While many courts still refuse to adopt this duty,[818] most states now agree with at least the general proposition of the *Third Restatement* that manufacturers (and possibly other sellers) have a post-sale duty of reasonable care to provide warnings of newly-discovered, serious hazards to those who can best avoid the danger, assuming there is a practicable and cost-effective means to distribute the information.[819] Today, the internet often provides such a portal.[820]

On the scope of the post-sale duty to warn, compare Richmond, Expanding Products Liability: Manufacturers' Post-Sale Duties to Warn, Retrofit and Recall, 36 Idaho L. Rev. 7, 80 (1999) (extending post-sale duty to warn to development of safer products is bad social policy because it discourages safety improvements), with Products Liability Rest. § 10 Reporters' Note on cmt. *a* ("If a newly discovered risk imposes risk of serious harm and safety improvements can be practically implemented, there may in certain instances be a duty to inform the buyer of the availability of such safety improvements.").

[818] See, e.g., Garner v. Goodyear Tire & Rubber Co., 2021 WL 4187832, at *7 (Ark. Ct. App. 2021); Dubas v. Clark Equip. Co., 532 F. Supp. 3d 819, 829–30 (D. Neb. 2021); Nolen v. C.R. Bard Inc., 2021 WL 2144835, at *2 (M.D. Tenn. 2021) ("Tennessee law likely does not recognize an assumed post-sale duty to warn under the present facts"); Indiana Farm Bureau Ins. v. Amazon.com, Inc., 2020 WL 9424669, at *4 (S.D. Ind. 2020) (Indiana does not recognize a post-sale duty to warn); Goodwin v. Premier Ford Lincoln Mercury, Inc., 2020 WL 3621317, at *4 n.2 (N.D. Miss. 2020) ("there is no post-sale duty to warn or recall in Mississippi"); Great N. Ins. Co. v. Amazon.com, Inc., 2019 WL 3935038, at *2 (N.D. Ill. 2019) ("there is no post-sale duty to warn under Illinois law"); Davenport v. Goodyear Dunlop Tires N. Am., Ltd., 2018 WL 1166091, at *3 (D.S.C. 2018) ("South Carolina does not recognize a post-sale duty to warn."); Jablonski v. Ford Motor Co., 955 N.E.2d 1138, 1159–63 (Ill. 2011) (declining to adopt post-sale duty to warn on facts of case). *But see* Williams v. NIBCO Inc., 2021 WL 1069044, at *11 (W.D. Tex., 2021) ("Not only are there exceptions to [the] general rule [that Texas courts generally do not recognize any post-sale duty to warn in the context of product hazards arising after sale], but that context is distinct from a negligence theory, which has its own governing legal principles, including possibilities for a post-sale duty to warn.").

[819] See, e.g., Bailey v. B. Braun Med., Inc., 2022 WL 591467, at *3 (N.D. Ga. 2022) ("the ongoing duty to warn post-sale is statutory in Georgia"); Schall v. Suzuki Motor of Am., Inc., 450 F. Supp. 3d 771, 788 (W.D. Ky. 2020); Wurster v. Plastics Grp., Inc., 917 F.3d 608, 617 (8th Cir. 2019) (Iowa law) (applying § 10; but no post-sale duty to warn where gas can manufacturer "had no way of determining who purchased the cans and who should have been warned"); Great Northern Ins. Co. v. Honeywell Int'l, Inc., 911 N.W.2d 510, 520 (Minn. 2018) (adopting § 10); Russell v. Wright, 916 F. Supp. 2d 629, 650 (W.D. Va. 2013) (post-sale duty to warn in negligence failure to warn cases); Jones v. Bowie Indus., Inc., 282 P.3d 316, 335 (Alaska 2012) (adopting § 10); Rosa v. Taser Int'l, Inc., 684 F.3d 941, 949 (9th Cir. 2012) (Cal. law) (though strict liability duty to warn applies to time of sale, manufacturer may be liable in negligence for failure to warn of a subsequently discovered risk; but no negligence on facts); In re Avandia Mktg., Sales Practices & Prods. Liab. Litig., 817 F. Supp. 2d 535, 547 (E.D. Pa. 2011) (N.Y., Pa., Tex., and Fla. law) (duty to warn is a continuing one that obligates manufacturers "to conduct research and otherwise investigate risks associated with its products, and then update warnings as appropriate"). See also Hiner v. Deere & Co., 340 F.3d 1190, 1196 (10th Cir. 2003) (Kan. law) ("even when it may be infeasible for a manufacturer to issue post-sale warnings to consumers, there may still be a duty to issue warnings to retailers"); Lewis v. Ariens Co., 751 N.E.2d 862, 867 (Mass. 2001) (adopting § 10; but no duty to second-hand purchaser of 16-year-old snow blower who was "a member of a universe too diffuse and too large for manufacturers or sellers of original equipment to identify"); Liriano v. Hobart Corp., 700 N.E.2d 303 (N.Y. 1998) (*Liriano II*).

In addition, § 13 prescribes a duty of reasonable care on a successor corporation to warn of defects in products previously sold by its predecessor if the successor enters into a service or maintenance agreement with purchasers of the predecessor's products.

[820] Increasingly, the internet provides a practical, cost-effective method for distributing warnings of newly discovered, serious product hazards. See, e.g., MedWatch: The FDA Safety Information and Adverse Event Reporting Program, which provides current drug, biologic, medical device, and dietary supplement safety and recall information. See also NHTSA's Safety Issues & Recalls website and the FDA's CFSAN Adverse Event Reporting System (CAERS) database of food, dietary supplement, and cosmetic adverse events and complaint reports. For a survey of global safety reporting requirements, see Ross, World-wide Government Safety Reporting Requirements: A Comparison. In 2012, The Organization for Economic Co-Operation and Development (OECD) developed a global recalls portal "to serve as a single window for sharing information about product recalls worldwide," available at www.oecd.org/about/impact/global-recalls-portal.htm.

Post-Sale Duty to Recall and Retrofit

Apart from providing post-sale warnings to consumers, a more aggressive (and expensive) way for a manufacturer to remedy dangerous conditions discovered in its products after sale is to remedy the danger by some form of repair, upgrade, or "retrofit." Because repairing a defective product often can be performed properly only by a manufacturer or dealer, curing a product hazard by "retrofit" often is preceded by a product "recall,"[821] a notification to consumers of a product hazard and procedures for accomplishing its repair.[822] When manufacturers of automotive vehicles[823] and other products[824] discover that their products contain a serious hazard they did not expect,

---

[821] Some courts and commentators distinguish between these terms. See, e.g., Richmond, Expanding Products Liability: Manufacturers' Post-Sale Duties to Warn, Retrofit and Recall, 36 Idaho L. Rev. 7, 49–70 (1999); Frumer, Friedman, and Sklaren, Products Liability § 57.01. Others use the term "recall" generically to describe the post-sale duty of manufacturers and other sellers to physically remedy product hazards. See, e.g., Products Liability Rest. § 11. Compare Madden, Modern Post-Sale Warnings and Related Obligations, 27 Wm. Mitchell L. Rev. 33, 57–58 (2000) (using the terms interchangeably).

[822] **Recalls generally.** See, e.g., Bernstein, Voluntary Recalls, 2013 U. Chi. Legal F. 359; Hua, Product Recall and Liability, 27 J.L. Econ. & Org. 113 (2011); Stilwell, Warning: You May Possess Continuing Duties After the Sale of Your Product! (An Evaluation of the Restatement (Third) of Torts: Products Liability's Treatment of Post-Sale Duties), 26 Rev. Litig. 1035 (2007); Annot., 47 A.L.R.5th 395 (1997).

Silent recalls. "Silent recalls" are somewhat different, but even this peculiar form of secret retrofit by dealers involves a form of recall via dealers. See, e.g., General Motors Corp. v. Johnston, 592 So.2d 1054, 1056 (Ala. 1992) (defendant denied making "silent" or "unpublished" recall by informing dealers to make repairs only on consumer complaints). See also Brewster, Johnson & Johnson and the "Phantom" Recall: Practical Advice to Prevent Risk Management and Quality Systems from Failing to Identify and Address Sentinel Events, 23 No. 6 Health Law. 1 (2011).

[823] Manufacturers of cars, trucks, and related products commonly issue recalls for a large variety of safety issues. "NHTSA sees an average of about 650 recalls involving 25 million cars annually . . . ." Miller and Green, Bugatti Recalls a Single $3 Million Chiron to Inspect Screws, Prod. Liab. & Toxics L. (Apr. 6, 2022). See, e.g., Barton, Mercedes-Benz USA Recalls 9,156 U.S. Vehicles: NHTSA, Prod. Liab. & Toxics L. (Mar. 25, 2022) (software issues); Coppola, Stellantis Recalls Plug-In Hybrid Minivans on Fire Risk, Prod. Liab. & Toxics L. (Feb. 11, 2022); Laing, Tesla's Latest U.S. Recall Is the Carmaker's Ninth Since October, Prod. Liab. & Toxics L. (Feb. 3, 2022) (various hardware and software safety issues); CPSC, Polaris Recalls Youth All-Terrain Vehicles Due to Fire Hazard (Recall Alert), cpsc.gov (Jan. 6, 2022); Sebastian, Ford Recalls Mustang Mach-E Electric SUVs Over Windshield, Roof Concerns, Wall St. J.com (Sept. 27, 2021); Ellis et al., GM Expands Chevy Bolt EV Recall for Fire Risk, Will Take $1 Billion Hit, Reuters (Aug. 20, 2021); Park, Hyundai's $900 Million Recall Shows How Costly EVs Can Be, Prod. Liab. & Toxics L. (Feb. 25, 2021) (battery cells' fire risks); Waller, Fiat Chrysler Recalls 300,000 Cars That May Roll Unexpectedly, Prod. Liab. & Toxics L. (Apr. 19, 2019).

Takata airbags, when activated, could explosively hurl metal shards at vehicle occupants causing injuries and, in some cases, death. Recalls, begun in 2008, were still in progress more than a decade later. See, e.g., Shields and Beene, NHTSA to Probe Millions More Takata Air Bags That Escaped Recall, Prod. Liab. & Toxics L. (Sept. 20, 2021); Sebastian, GM to Recall About 5.9 Million Vehicles With Takata Air-Bag Inflaters, Wall St. J.com (Nov. 23, 2020) (recall costs for GM expected to reach $1.2 billion); Krisher, Automakers Tesla, Volkswagen and More Recall 1.7 Million Cars over Takata Air Bags, USA Today (Feb. 8, 2019). Takata filed for bankruptcy protection in 2017.

[824] Recalls cover a large range of products. See, e.g., Peng, Fitbit Recalls Ionic Smartwatches Over Burn Hazard, Prod. Liab. & Toxics L. (Mar. 2, 2022); Muller and Butler, Abbott Nutrition Recalls Fourth Infant Formula Linked to Illness, Prod. Liab. & Toxics L. (Mar. 1, 2022); Barton, FDA: E25bio Recalls Covid-19 Direct Antigen Rapid Tests, Prod. Liab. & Toxics L. (Feb. 18, 2022); Edny, Coppertone Aerosol Sunscreens Recalled After Benzene Is Found, Prod. Liab. & Toxics L. (Sept. 30, 2021); Franklin, Boppy Recalls 3.3. Million Baby Pillows After the Deaths of 8 Infants, NPR (Sept. 23, 2021); Barash, Zen Magnets Recalled Over Ingestion Risk After Long Court Fight, Prod. Liab. & Toxics L. (Aug. 17, 2021); Terlep and Prang, Peloton Recalls All Treadmills as CEO Apologizes, Wall St. J.com (May 5, 2021); Misha and Balu, Allergan Recalls Textured Breast Implants Worldwide, Reuters (July 24, 2019); Steinberg, Suits Mount Over Recalled Generic Blood Pressure Drug, Prod. Liab. & Toxics L. (Oct. 12, 2018); Lavelle, JBS Hit with First Suit Amid Beef Recall, Salmonella Outbreak, Prod. Liab. & Toxics L. (Oct. 9, 2018); Sellers, Metal in SPAM, Plastic in Patties: 'Foreign Object' Recalls Surge, Prod. Liab. & Toxics L. (July 3, 2018); Barash, Half a Million Hoverboards Recalled for Fire Risk, 44 Prod. Safety & Liab. Rep. (BNA) 702 (July 6, 2016).

Guns. Guns fall through a troubling regulatory gap, since no federal agency appears to have jurisdiction over gun safety, leaving the market and lawsuits as the only incentives for gun manufacturers to produce safe

they sometimes voluntarily recall the products to remove the hazard. Quite commonly, however, manufacturers fail to recall dangerous products promptly when they should.[825]

Accordingly, Congress has empowered several product safety agencies to order recalls,[826] the violation of which may give rise to a civil penalty and perhaps liability for resulting harm.[827] As a matter of common law, however, most courts hold that there is no general duty to recall defective products. But a couple of early cases did suggest that manufacturers might have a duty to recall and repair hazardous conditions discovered after sale.[828] And several more recent decisions suggest that there may be a duty to recall and retrofit a product if it was defective when originally sold,[829] or if the manufacturer has a special continuing relationship with the buyer based on the manufacturer's post-sale undertaking to maintain or even recall the product,[830] and in various other

---

products and initiate recalls of defective guns. In one class action, plaintiffs alleged that a defective trigger mechanism in the Remington Model 700 Bolt Action rifle may allow the rifle to fire without a trigger pull, resulting in more than 140 lawsuits. See Barash, Can Class Actions Solve the Gun Defects Problem?, 44 Prod. Saf. & Liab. Rep. (BNA) 395 (April 12, 2016) (second of two-part series).

[825] For example, 37 deaths were traced to babies rolling over in inclined baby sleepers, smothering the baby or causing the bassinette to tip over and crash to the floor, as from a kitchen counter. In 2019, the manufacturers recalled these popular products. Mattel, Inc., the owner of Fisher-Price, "issued a recall for 4.7 million Rock 'n Play Sleepers, but did so only grudgingly in response to public outcry, dragging its heels for months while dozens of babies died. . . .' CPSC said. Recalls for similar products were quick to follow." Simon, Millions of Dangerous Infant Sleepers Recalled, Yet Risk of Death Remains—Who's Responsible? Health News, dailyhornet.com (Aug. 13, 2019).

[826] Among the agencies Congress has vested with recall power are the Consumer Product Safety Commission, 15 U.S.C. § 2064(a) (consumer products with "substantial product hazards"); the National Highway Traffic Safety Administration, 49 U.S.C. §§ 30117–30121 (automotive products); the Food and Drug Administration, 21 U.S.C. § 360h (drugs and medical devices); the Coast Guard, 46 U.S.C. § 4310 (recreational boats with safety defects); and Health and Human Services, 21 U.S.C. § 360*ll*(f) (electronic products emitting unsafe radiation). See, e.g., United States v. General Motors Corp., 565 F.2d 754 (D.C. Cir. 1977) (NHTSA).

This recall power provides safety agencies with a club to encourage manufacturers to initiate "voluntary" recalls in appropriate cases. See, e.g., Laing, Daimler Trucks Failed to Quickly Recall Vehicles, NHTSA Says, Prod. Liab. & Toxics L. (Dec. 31, 2020) ($30 million civil penalty for failure to conduct seven recalls in a timely manner and noncompliance with reporting requirements). See also Barash, Amazon's New Distributor Status Means Safety 'Headache' Ahead, Prod. Liab. & Toxics L. (Feb. 15, 2022) (federal agency judge ruled that Amazon was a "distributor" of third-party products sold under its Fulfillment by Amazon program; Consumer Product Safety Commission suit seeking to force Amazon to recall faulty third-party products, including carbon monoxide detectors, hair dryers, and flammable children's sleepwear).

[827] See Products Liability Rest. § 11(a)(1) (liability for negligently recalling product after government-ordered recall). See generally Lens, Product Recalls: Why Is Tort Law Deferring To Agency Inaction?, 90 St. John's L. Rev. 329 (2016); Reynolds, The Role of Private Litigation in the Automotive Recall Process, 29 Loy. Consumer L. Rev. 121 (2016). See also note 826, above.

[828] See Noel v. United Aircraft Corp., 342 F.2d 232 (3d Cir. 1965) (Del. law) (failure to provide safety device to prevent over-speeding propeller; manufacturer with continuous relationship to owner had continuing duty to provide safety device); Braniff Airways, Inc. v. Curtiss-Wright Corp., 411 F.2d 451, 453 (2d Cir. 1969) (N.Y. law) (cylinder failure from overheated aircraft engine; when manufacturer learns of dangerous design defects after product is sold, it "has a duty either to remedy these or, if complete remedy is not feasible, at least to give users adequate warnings and instructions concerning methods for minimizing the danger"). See also Downing v. Overhead Door Corp., 707 P.2d 1027, 1033 (Colo. App. 1985) (similar dictum).

[829] See, e.g., Readenour v. Marion Power Shovel, 719 P.2d 1058 (Ariz. 1986), as explained by Wilson v. United States Elevator Corp., 972 P.2d 235 (Ariz. Ct. App. 1998).

[830] See, e.g., Silver v. Bad Boy Enters. LLC, 907 F. Supp. 2d 1351, 1356–57 (M.D. Ga. 2012) (manufacturers have duty of care in conducting voluntary recalls); Couch v. Astec Indus., 53 P.3d 398 (N.M. Ct. App. 2002) (manufacturer undertook to provide continuing service); Hernandez v. Badger Constr. Equip. Co., 34 Cal. Rptr. 2d 732, 754 (Ct. App. 1994) ("failure to conduct an adequate retrofit campaign may constitute negligence apart from the issue of defective design"); Bell Helicopter Co. v. Bradshaw, 594 S.W.2d 519, 532 (Tex. App. 1979) ("[o]nce the duty [to recall and repair] was assumed, Bell had an obligation to complete the remedy by using reasonable means available to it"). See generally Schwartz, The Post-Sale Duty to Warn: Two Unfortunate Forks in the Road to a Reasonable Doctrine, 58 N.Y.U. L. Rev. 892, 897–901 (1983); Products Liability Rest. § 11(a)(2).

situations.[831] Finally, a manufacturer would seem to have a duty in negligence law to stop marketing a product once it becomes clear that it is defective and causing substantial harm.[832]

Yet a great majority of decisions, sometimes explaining that government regulatory agencies are better suited than courts to forge such complex and onerous duties that might discourage manufacturers from developing new safety technologies, emphatically refuse to impose a common-law duty on manufacturers to recall their products or retrofit them with newly developed safety devices, especially if the product was not defective when sold.[833] This is the position of the *Third Restatement*, which states categorically that there is no common-law duty to recall, even if the product was defective from the start.[834] The *Restatement* provides two exceptions to its broad no-duty-to-recall rule: one for sellers who violate recall orders of government agencies,[835] and the other for sellers who are negligent in performing a recall they voluntarily undertake.[836] The first, government-recall-order exception, is noncontroversial. The second, negligent undertaking-to-recall exception, has been accepted by some courts[837] but was rejected by

---

[831] See, e.g., M. G. v. Bodum USA, Inc., 2021 WL 718839, at *22 (N.D. Cal. 2021) ("A claim for failure to recall/retrofit sounds in negligence and requires that the following elements be established: '(1) defendant manufactured/distributed/sold the product; (2) defendant knew or reasonably should have known that the product was dangerous when used in a reasonably foreseeable manner; (3) defendant became aware of this defect after the product was sold; (4) defendant failed to recall/retrofit; (5) that a reasonable manufacturer/distributor/seller under the same or similar circumstances would have recalled/retrofitted the product; (6) plaintiff was harmed; and (7) defendant's failure to recall/retrofit was a substantial factor in causing plaintiff's harm.' "); Downing v. Overhead Door Corp., 707 P.2d 1027, 1033 (Colo. App. 1985) (dictum: "[a]fter a product involving human safety has been sold and dangerous defects in design have come to the manufacturer's attention, the manufacturer has a duty either to remedy such defects, or, if a complete remedy is not feasible, to give users adequate warnings and instructions concerning methods for minimizing danger") (citing *Braniff Airways* and *Noel*, see note 828, above). For a collection of cases both ways, see Annot., 47 A.L.R.5th 395 (1997) (manufacturer's post-sale duty to modify, repair, or recall).

[832] Lance v. Wyeth, 85 A.3d 434, 460 (Pa. 2014) ("Whatever the policy considerations may be in the recall/retrofit arena, we are convinced that a manufacturer or supplier has a duty to cease further distribution of a product at such point as it [reasonably should know] that the commodity is too dangerous to be used by anyone.").

[833] See, e.g., Skinner v. Ethicon, Inc., 2021 WL 640809, at *3 (E.D. Ky. 2021); Simien v. C. R. Bard, Inc., 2020 WL 4922331, at *2 (E.D. Tex. 2020); King v. Flinn & Dreffein Eng'g Co., 2012 WL 4459568, at *3 (W.D. Va. 2012) ("Virginia law does not recognize a post-sale duty to retrofit"); Estate of Bruess v. Blount Int'l, Inc., 2011 WL 2680760, at *19 (N.D. Iowa 2011) (no duty to retrofit); Riley v. Ford Motor Co., 2011 WL 2728142, at *4 (S.D. Miss. 2011) (no duty to recall or retrofit); Adams v. Genie Indus., 929 N.E.2d 380, 385 (N.Y. 2010) (same); Lance v. Wyeth, 4 A.3d 160, 168 (Pa. Super. Ct. 2010) (whether to impose duty to recall/withdraw a drug is up to FDA, "which is better equipped to weigh the benefits and risks associated with permitting a drug to remain on the market"), aff'd and rev'd in part on other grounds, 85 A.3d 434 (Pa. 2014); Gregory v. Cincinnati Inc., 538 N.W.2d 325 (Mich. 1995) (agencies better qualified); Patton v. Hutchinson Wil-Rich Mfg. Co., 861 P.2d 1299, 1315 (Kan. 1993) (recognizing post-sale duty to warn, but holding that "product recalls are properly the business of administrative agencies as suggested by the federal statutes").

[834] Products Liability Resta. § 11 cmt. *a*:

> If every improvement in product safety were to trigger a common-law duty to recall, manufacturers would face incalculable costs every time they sought to make their product lines better and safer. Moreover, even when a product is defective . . ., an involuntary duty to recall should be imposed on the seller only by a governmental directive issued pursuant to statute or regulation. Issues relating to product recalls are best evaluated by governmental agencies capable of gathering adequate data regarding the ramifications of such undertakings.

[835] Products Liability Rest. § 11(a)(1).

[836] Products Liability Rest. § 11(a)(2). Note that sending post-sale hazard information and even retrofit kits to dealers may not amount to an undertaking to recall or retrofit. See Ray v. Rheem Textile Sys., Inc., 2002 WL 433157 (Mich. Ct. App. 2002) (manufacturer did not voluntarily assume duty to retrofit by distributing to its dealers and distributors dealer bulletins and retrofit kits).

[837] See, e.g., Silver v. Bad Boy Enters. LLC, 907 F. Supp. 2d 1351, 1356–57 (M.D. Ga. 2012) (manufacturers have duty of care in conducting voluntary recalls). Compare Plyler v. Whirlpool Corp., 751

the Kentucky Supreme Court as unduly liberalizing the normal duty-to-rescue rule that a plaintiff must prove detrimental reliance on the negligent undertaking or show how it otherwise increased the plaintiff's risk of harm.[838]

The law on post-sale duties has long been in a muddle, but key issues are beginning to sharpen.[839] The *Third Restatement*'s endorsement in § 10 of a post-sale duty to take reasonable and practicable steps to warn users of serious hazards makes good sense, assuming that the duty remains limited to newly discovered hazards and does not expand to include a duty to provide information about evolving safety enhancements in a product's design. Yet, whether the common law should recognize (and how it should define) a post-sale duty to retrofit or recall is much more difficult to determine. The *Restatement*'s absolute denial in § 11 of any such common-law duty, even if the product originally was defective and despite what special circumstances might exist, seems unduly harsh and rigid, while its provision of a duty of due care for voluntary recalls ignores traditional tort law limitations on responsibility for voluntary undertakings. Yet the *Restatement* is not too far off the mark in describing how the law on the post-sale duty to repair or recall now stands, and much may be said for its clarity and simplicity. So, while the fog has lifted on the warning side of the post-sale duty pond, it remains swirling on the other.

F.3d 509, 513 (7th Cir. 2014) (Ill. law) (upholding judgment on verdict that manufacturer's recall of defective microwave ovens was not negligent, where recall had unusually high success rate of 75%).

[838] See, e.g., Ostendorf v. Clark Equip. Co., 122 S.W.3d 530, 537–40 (Ky. 2003) (rejecting § 11, noting that plaintiff failed to cite a single case relying on § 11 to justify imposing liability for a negligent retrofit campaign). On the duty of affirmative action (to rescue), see Rest. (3d) Torts: Liability for Physical Harm § 43; Rest. (2d) Torts § 324A (relied on by *Ostendorf*).

[839] **Subsequent remedial measures.** Evidence of product recalls often involves evidence of subsequent remedial measures and, hence, Fed. R. Evid. 407. See, e.g., Wood, Liability and Evidentiary Issues Involving Prescription Production Recalls, 74 Def. Couns. J. 64 (2007) (issues under Rule 407); J. Weinstein and M. Berger, Weinstein's Evidence Manual § 7.04 (9th student ed. 2011); Am. Law Prod. Liab. 3d §§ 14:56–14:61; Annot., 84 A.L.R.3d 1220 (1978) (admissibility of recall letter by defendant manufacturer). On evidence of subsequent remedial measures, see § 6.4, above.

Part III

CAUSATION

Chapter 11

CAUSE IN FACT

Table of Sections

§ 11.1 CAUSE IN FACT—GENERALLY

Few problems are more intriguing, and their solutions more illusive, than causation. Perhaps the most fundamental issue in the universe, and in life, is causation—the causes and effects of molecular actions, biologic activity, and human choices to act and refrain from acting in certain ways.[1] In the words of Leon Green, one of the twentieth century's great tort law scholars: "The attraction of causes is as magnetic for people as flames are for insects, and it is frequently as deadly."[2]

While philosophers, theologians, and scientists may delight in theorizing about the nature of causal agents and their consequences, courts and lawyers do not have the luxury of pure cogitation and hypothesizing.[3] Instead, as difficult as some causal problems may be, the law must resolve them one way or another. Before it assigns responsibility, the law demands commonsense proof, in a court of law, of a cause and effect relationship between a plaintiff's injuries and a defendant's misconduct or defective product.[4] Each day of every year, numerous food products go bad, numerous workers are injured in machines, numerous people contract cancer, and numerous cars crash. But most sickness is not caused by bad food, most machine injuries are not caused by defective machines, most cancers are not caused by defective chemicals, and most car crashes are not caused by defective automobiles. Thus, in products liability litigation, the manufacturer of such a product may be held responsible for such an injury only if a plaintiff satisfactorily proves that his or her injury was caused, at least in part, by the manufacturer's breach of legal duty.[5]

---

1 "The search for causes must have been an incident of the early awakening of primordial man. There is no human who hesitates to identify the cause of any calamity that touches his life. In the highest echelons of social and scientific research, the vain attempts to reduce to control the causes of war, crime, poverty, cancer, and other barriers to man's happy existence continue with unabated zeal." L. Green, Strict Liability Under Sections 402A and 402B: A Decade of Litigation, 54 Tex. L. Rev. 1185, 1208 (1976).

2 Id.

3 B. Williams, Afterword—What Has Philosophy to Learn from Tort Law?, in Philosophical Foundations of Tort Law 487 (D. Owen ed., Oxford 1995).

4 "The courts . . . often insist that the causal questions which they have to face must be determined on common-sense principles." H.L.A. Hart and T. Honoré, Causation and the Law 26 (Oxford 2d ed. 1985).

5 On factual causation in products liability, see, e.g., Twerski and Cohen, Resolving the Dilemma of Nonjusticiable Causation in Failure-To-Warn Litigation, 84 S. Cal. L. Rev. 125 (2010); Gifford, The Death of Causation: Mass Products Torts' Incomplete Incorporation of Social Welfare Principles, 41 Wake Forest L. Rev. 943 (2006); Gifford, The Challenge to the Individual Causation Requirement in Mass Products Torts, 62 Wash. & Lee L. Rev. 873 (2005); Conway-Jones, Factual Causation in Toxic-Tort Litigation: A Philosophical View of

Causation (sometimes referred to as "proximate causation") is comprised of two distinct issues: (1) cause in fact and (2) proximate cause.[6] "Cause in fact" (or "factual cause")[7] is the actual connection between a product defect or the defendant's negligence and the plaintiff's harm. Although this nexus is not controverted in most cases, a plaintiff must always establish this actual link between his or her injury or disease to a defect in a product which the defendant sold, and, in negligence cases, to the defendant's negligence.[8] "Proximate cause" refers to the closeness of whatever actual causal connection is proven to exist. Although these concepts thus are very different—the one requiring that a causal connection in fact exists, and the other requiring that the nexus be reasonably close (not "remote")—courts and commentators often confusingly interchange the terms when talking about these two separate issues.

"Causation" is sometimes used generically to describe both issues.[9] Quite frequently, courts also use the phrase "proximate causation" to refer in umbrella fashion

---

Proof and Certainty in Uncertain Disciplines, 35 U. Rich. L. Rev. 875 (2002); Henderson and Twerski, Intuition and Technology in Product Design Litigation: An Essay on Proximate Causation, 88 Geo. L.J. 659 (2000); Symposium, Liability Without Cause? Further Ruminations on Cause-In-Fact as Applied to Handgun Liability, 32 Conn. L. Rev. 1379 (2000); Berger, Eliminating General Causation: Notes Towards a New Theory of Justice and Toxic Torts, 97 Colum. L. Rev. 2117 (1997); Firak, The Developing Policy Characteristics of Cause-In-Fact: Alternative Forms of Liability, Epidemiological Proof and Trans-Scientific Issues, 63 Temp. L. Rev. 311 (1990); V. Schwartz and Mahshigian, Failure to Identify the Defendant in Tort Law: Towards a Legislative Solution, 73 Cal. L. Rev. 941 (1985); Frumer, Friedman, and Sklaren, Products Liability ch. 3; Owen & Davis on Products Liability ch. 11.

A rich literature has grown up around the general topic of causation. See, e.g., Weigand, Tort Law—The Wrongful Demise of But For Causation, 41 W. New Eng. L. Rev. 75 (2019); Dillbary, Causation Actually, 51 Ga. L. Rev. 1 (2016); Wright and Puppe, Causation: Linguistic, Philosophical, Legal and Economic, 91 Chi.-Kent L. Rev. 461 (2016); Stapleton, Factual Causation and Asbestos Cancers, 126 Law Q. Rev. 351 (2012); Brown, The Possibility of "Inference Causation": Inferring Cause-in-Fact and the Nature of Legal Fact Finding, 55 McGill L.J. 1 (2010) (Canadian law); Stapleton, The Two Explosive Proof-of-Causation Doctrines Central to Asbestos Claims, 74 Brook. L. Rev. 1011 (2009); Wright, Liability for Possible Wrongs: Causation, Statistical Probability, and the Burden of Proof, 41 Loy. L.A. L. Rev. 1295 (2008); Goldberg and Zipursky, Tort Law and Moral Luck, 92 Cornell L. Rev. 1123 (2007); Stapleton, Two Causal Fictions at the Heart of U.S. Asbestos Doctrine, 122 Law Q. Rev. 189, 191 (2006); Stapleton, Legal Cause: Cause-in-Fact and the Scope of Liability for Consequences, 54 Vand. L. Rev. 941 (2001); Wright, Once More Into the Bramble Bush: Duty, Causal Contribution, and the Extent of Legal Responsibility, 54 Vand. L. Rev. 1071 (2001); Robertson, The Common Sense of Cause in Fact, 75 Tex. L. Rev. 1765 (1997); Fischer, Causation in Fact in Omission Cases, 1992 Utah L. Rev. 1335; Wright, Causation in Tort Law, 73 Cal. L. Rev. 1735 (1985); King, Causation, Valuation, and Chance in Personal Injury Torts Involving Preexisting Conditions and Future Consequences, 90 Yale L.J. 1353 (1981); Calabresi, Concerning Cause and the Law of Torts: An Essay for Harry Kalven, Jr., 43 U. Chi. L. Rev. 69 (1975); Keeton, Dobbs, Keeton, and Owen, Prosser and Keeton on the Law of Torts § 41; Dobbs, Law of Torts ch. 9; H.L.A. Hart and T. Honoré, Causation and the Law 26 (Oxford 2d ed. 1985); J. Mackie, The Cement of the Universe: A Study of Causation (L. Cohen ed., 1974); A. Becht and F. Miller, The Test of Factual Causation in Negligence and Strict Liability Cases (1961).

[6] See, e.g., West v. Ride the Ducks Int'l, LLC, 2021 WL 2809609, at *11 (Wash. Ct. App. 2021) ("Proximate cause is composed of both cause in fact and legal cause."); Heeter v. Honeywell Int'l Inc., 706 Fed. Appx. 63, 66 (3d Cir. 2017) (Pa. law) ("Causation consists of 'two separate and essential concepts' . . .: 'cause-in-fact and legal, or proximate, cause.' "); Nye v. Bayer Cropscience, Inc., 347 S.W.3d 686, 704 (Tenn. 2011) ("Causation, an essential element of any products liability action, refers to both 'proximate cause' and 'cause in fact.' "). On the nature of these two causation concepts, how they relate to one another, and how they fit with other tort concepts, see Owen, Figuring Foreseeability, 33 Wake Forest L. Rev. 1277 (2009); Owen, The Five Elements of Negligence, 35 Hofstra L. Rev. 1672 (2007).

[7] "Factual cause" is the term employed by Res. (3d) Torts: Liability for Physical and Emotional Harm § 26.

[8] Because a product's defectiveness is an element of almost every negligence claim in products liability litigation, proof of causation in a negligence case requires proof that (1) the product was defective, (2) the defendant was negligent in allowing it to be defective, and (3) the defendant's negligence caused the plaintiff's harm. See §§ 2.1 and 5.9, above.

[9] See note 6, above.

to cause in fact and proximate cause together,[10] and sometimes also when referring to factual cause alone,[11] since it is part of the umbrella. To complicate matters further,[12] the *Restatement (Second) of Torts* uses the term "legal causation" to embrace both issues,[13] such that courts sometimes use this term to refer to factual causation,[14] but more commonly to mean proximate cause.[15] The *Third Restatement* helpfully divides these issues clearly in two, calling the one "factual causation"[16] and the other "scope of liability (proximate cause)."[17] Because of the varying terminology applied to these two issues, often in the same jurisdiction and sometimes in the same judicial opinion, a lawyer reading cases involving either of these issues—"factual cause" or "proximate cause"—must read each decision cautiously to ascertain which issue the court truly has addressed. Relying on causation terminology, in other words, is risky business.[18]

In almost every products liability case,[19] the plaintiff must establish the central element of factual causation—that the plaintiff's harm resulted, at least in part, from some defect in a product that the defendant manufactured or sold.[20] In negligence, the plaintiff's causal proof must further show that the harm resulted from some negligent act or omission by the defendant in making or selling the product in a defective condition.[21] To satisfy the burden of proof on cause in fact, a plaintiff must introduce

---

[10] See, e.g., Bates v. Tippmann Sports, LLC, 2019 WL 1532230, at *5 (W.D.N.C. 2019) ("[t]here is a two-pronged formula for proximate cause, which consists of a cause-in-fact and reasonable foreseeability"); Kovach v. Caligor Midwest, 913 N.E.2d 193, 197 (Ind. 2009) (" 'Proximate cause' has two components: causation-in-fact and scope of liability.").

[11] See, e.g., Sigler v. American Honda Motor Co., 2007 WL 1004313, at *4 (E.D. Tenn. 2007) ("Proximate cause is the familiar, negligence-based principle of 'cause-in-fact'; to succeed in a products liability action, a plaintiff must demonstrate the injury would not have occurred 'but for' the defect."), rev'd in part on other grounds, 532 F.3d 469 (6th Cir. 2008); Tuttle v. Lorillard Tobacco Co., 377 F.3d 917, 924 (8th Cir. 2004) (Minn. law) (proximate cause requires proof that "user would have acted differently had the manufacturers provided adequate warnings").

[12] As for terminological confusion, see Ford Motor Co. v. Boomer, 736 S.E.2d 724, 728 n.2 (Va. 2013) ("[T]here are inconsistencies in the national legal nomenclature as to whether cause-in-fact is considered to be a subset of proximate cause or whether cause-in-fact, in addition to proximate cause (defined as additional legal restrictions as to liability), together create legal cause. We opt for the former nomenclature as it is the more widely used terminology in Virginia as well as the terminology used by the circuit court in this case.").

[13] See Rest. (2d) Torts § 431. See, e.g., First Premier Bank v. Kolcraft Enters., Inc., 686 N.W.2d 430, 454 (S.D. 2004) ("Proximate or legal cause is a cause that produces a result in a natural and probable sequence and without which the result would not have occurred.").

[14] See, e.g., Whiteley v. Philip Morris Inc., 11 Cal. Rptr. 3d 807, 858 (Ct. App. 2004) ("A tort is a legal cause of injury only when it is a substantial factor in producing the injury.").

[15] See, e.g., City of St. Louis v. Benjamin Moore & Co., 226 S.W.3d 110, 114 (Mo. 2007) (en banc); Jamison v. Ford Motor Co., 644 S.E.2d 755, 765 (S.C. Ct. App. 2007); Moroney v. General Motors Corp., 850 A.2d 629, 634 (Pa. Super. Ct. 2004).

[16] See Rest. (3d) Torts: Liability for Physical and Emotional Harm ch. 5 and § 26.

[17] See id. at ch. 6.

[18] For further discussion of this terminological confusion, see § 12.1, below.

[19] Arguably excepting breach of express warranty, deceptive practices, and misrepresentation.

[20] See, e.g., Vodanovich v. A.P. Green Indus., 869 So.2d 930, 932 (La. Ct. App. 2004) ("A plaintiff seeking to recover under either negligence or strict liability theories must prove that the negligent act or defect complained of was a cause-in-fact of the injury."); Soldo v. Sandoz Pharms. Corp., 244 F. Supp. 2d 434, 524 (W.D. Pa. 2003) ("Proof of causation is a necessary element in a products liability action. Absent a causal relationship between the defendant's product and the plaintiff's injury the defendant cannot be held liable on a theory of negligence, strict product liability, or misrepresentation."). See also Flippo v. Mode O'Day Frock Shops, 449 S.W.2d 692, 694 (Ark. 1970) (spider bite on thigh while trying on slacks in clothing store; "the injury . . . was caused by the spider—and not the product").

[21] See § 2.2, above.

evidence that establishes, more likely than not, that the defendant's negligence, and/or a defective condition in the defendant's product, was a cause of the plaintiff's harm.[22]

This chapter first considers the tests of factual causation, notably the "but-for" and "substantial-factor" tests. Certain recurring issues of proof of causation are also reviewed, including the sufficiency of circumstantial evidence to connect a defendant to an accident product and to connect the accident to a *defect* in that product.[23] Special tests and issues applicable to toxic substance litigation are also examined, followed by a discussion of the special issues raised when a plaintiff's proofs point to two or more defendants who possibly caused the harm, including the theory of market share liability.[24] The chapter concludes with a look at some of the special issues of factual causation raised in warning cases.[25]

§ 11.2 TESTS AND PROOF OF CAUSATION

In order to establish causation, a plaintiff normally must prove two things: (1) that the defendant is the source of the challenged product—that is, that the product most likely was manufactured or sold by the defendant, not by someone else; and (2) that some defective condition in the product most likely caused the plaintiff's harm. A plaintiff's causation evidence must satisfy the but-for or substantial-factor test for factual causation.

Defendant Identification

A plaintiff's first step in establishing causation is to show that the challenged product was manufactured or sold by the defendant. Usually, establishing the identity of the manufacturer of a toaster, a punch press, an SUV, a prescription drug, or a butane lighter is a simple task, and the issue is not controverted. Yet, after a serious accident, sometimes butane lighters and other products disappear,[26] and memories fade. Many kinds of products—like dish towels, cleaning solvents, and other toxic substances—may come from sources not remembered or quite unknown.[27] And so a plaintiff must connect the defendant to the product that caused the plaintiff's harm by establishing that the subject product was manufactured or sold by the defendant.[28]

If a product is destroyed in an accident, lost, or otherwise disappears, a plaintiff may have difficulty tracing its manufacture (or retail sale) to a particular defendant. In *Moore v. Mississippi Valley Gas Co.*,[29] for example, the plaintiff was one year old when she was scalded by hot water in a bathtub. Two years later, the heater was discarded. Four years after that, the plaintiff's mother sued the manufacturer of the brand of hot

---

[22] See, e.g., Needham v. Roho Grp., 2007 WL 470551, at *8–9 (E.D. Mich. 2007); Richardson v. General Motors Corp., 223 F. Supp. 2d 753, 755–56 (M.D.N.C. 2002). See generally Conway-Jones, Factual Causation in Toxic-Tort Litigation: A Philosophical View of Proof and Certainty in Uncertain Disciplines, 35 U. Rich. L. Rev. 875, 938 (2002) ("In virtually every case, plaintiffs carry the burden of proof on the factual causation element.").

[23] See § 11.2, below.

[24] See § 11.3, below.

[25] See § 11.4, below.

[26] See, e.g., Flock v. Scripto-Tokai Corp., 319 F.3d 231 (5th Cir. 2003) (Tex. law) (utility lighter melted in fire that it might have started).

[27] For special defendant identification issues in toxic substance cases, see this section and § 11.3, below.

[28] See In re Toy Asbestos, 2021 WL 2020561, at *4 (N.D. Cal. 2021) (insufficient evidence that defendant made/supplied asbestos gaskets); Annot., 51 A.L.R.3d 1344 (1973) (product identification).

[29] 863 So.2d 43 (Miss. 2003).

water heater she believed was in her apartment complex at the time, although the landlord at the time of suit had no record identifying the manufacturer of the heater. In these circumstances, the court upheld summary judgment for the defendant manufacturer. Similarly, in *Brown v. Stone Manufacturing Co.*,[30] a child was injured when her nightgown caught fire, but its remnants were discarded at the hospital. The child and her mother remembered that it was pink, but neither could remember the name of the manufacturer. The mother had purchased the nightgown from a store that carried several similar brands. The child thought that a nightgown manufactured by the defendant, which her mother purchased at the same store one year after the accident, was "sort of like" the accident gown, but she thought that it had a different color design on the front. The washing instructions remembered by the mother differed somewhat from those on the subsequently purchased gown manufactured by the defendant. On these facts, because a jury would be required to resort to guesswork, speculation, and surmise in attempting to identify the manufacturer, the court granted summary judgment for the defendant. *Moore* and *Brown* illustrate the important point that, if a plaintiff cannot prove that the accident product was most likely produced or sold by the defendant, a jury will not be permitted to speculate on this crucial issue of identification, and the plaintiff's case usually will fail.[31]

Even if the product is lost, however, a plaintiff may be able to establish the product's identity by circumstantial evidence, provided that such evidence establishes "that it is reasonably probable, not merely possible or evenly balanced, that the defendant was the source of the offending product."[32] One especially probative method of identification is proof that the product bears the defendant's name, as by a label or decal of some sort.[33] The memory of the plaintiff or the purchaser of the product's name may sometimes suffice, although such testimony must establish the manufacturer's identity by a preponderance of evidence.[34] Another method of identification is testimony by the retailer that it had purchased the product it sold to the consumer from a particular supplier.[35] Where there is no direct identifying information, other evidence may point

---

30 660 F. Supp. 454 (S.D. Miss. 1986).

31 See, e.g., Yaw v. Air & Liquid Sys. Corp., 2019 WL 3891792, at *3 (W.D. Wash. 2019) (plaintiff failed to identify a particular product that created asbestos dust or time when decedent was on a ship where such dust was present); Martinez v. Skirmish, U.S.A., Inc., 2009 WL 1437624, at *3–4 (E.D. Pa. 2009) (plaintiff's failure to identify which paintball gun caused his injury was fatal to his claim); Waters v. NMC-Wollard, Inc., 2007 WL 2668008 (E.D. Pa. 2007) (4 companies made 2 different models of product with "Wollard" name for over two decades); Clift v. Vose Hardware, Inc., 848 A.2d 1130 (R.I. 2004) (conclusory assertions that bungee cord that blinded person was sold by one defendant and manufactured by another defendant were insufficient, without specific facts, to connect defendants to the offending bungee cord).

32 Healey v. Firestone Tire & Rubber Co., 663 N.E.2d 901, 903 (N.Y. 1996) (but no liability where plaintiff's employer failed to keep truck tire rims, identified by plaintiff's expert as the likely cause of plaintiff's injury, even after a court order requiring they be preserved; summary judgment for Firestone affirmed).

33 See, e.g., Bilenky v. Ryobi Techs., Inc., 115 F. Supp. 3d 661 (E.D. Va. 2015) (defective lawnmower; manufacturer's name on mower and in the owner's manual); Kim v. Ingersoll Rand Co., 921 F.2d 197 (8th Cir. 1990) (Minn. law) (logo on air hammer); Helm v. Pepsi-Cola Bottling Co., 723 S.W.2d 465 (Mo. Ct. App. 1986) (plaintiff's wife and lawyer both read "Mead Corporation" on bottom of defective carton subsequently lost by another lawyer); Smith v. Ariens Co., 377 N.E.2d 954 (Mass. 1978) ("Ariens" decal on defective snowmobile).

34 See, e.g., Drayton v. Jiffee Chem. Corp., 395 F. Supp. 1081 (N.D. Ohio 1975) (although circumstantial evidence tended to identify drain cleaner as "Mister Plumber," landlady firmly remembered buying "liquid-plumr" manufactured by defendant; *held*, defendant liable), modified and aff'd, 591 F.2d 352 (6th Cir. 1978).

35 See, e.g., Gassmann v. Eli Lilly & Co., 407 F. Supp. 2d 203, 212–13 (D.D.C. 2005) (pharmacy always purchased DES made by defendant); Daniels v. GNB, Inc., 629 So.2d 595 (Miss. 1993) (batteries always bought from same supplier). *But see* Buckel v. Tube Pro Inc., 2016 WL 1296079 (Ill. App. Ct. 2016) (summary judgment for snow tube manufacturer; defective snow tube involved in accident was never produced, photographed, or examined, even though most of such tubes at ski facility were manufactured by defendant).

toward the defendant, such as the product's color,[36] composition, or method of construction (like a garment's stitching) that is unique to the defendant.[37]

Tests of Cause in Fact

Once a defendant's identity is established, connecting a plaintiff's injury to a product defect involves the same kind of causal inquiries involved in other tort law contexts. In ordinary products liability litigation, as in tort law generally,[38] the standard method for establishing factual causation is the "but-for" test. By this test, a manufacturer or other defendant may be found causally responsible for a plaintiff's harm if it would not have occurred but for a defect in the product or the defendant's otherwise tortious conduct. That is, a product defect may be a cause in fact of the plaintiff's injury if the defect was a *sine qua non* of the injury—a necessary antecedent without which the injury would not have occurred.[39]

The but-for issue arises quite clearly in some cases. In *Stewart v. Von Solbrig Hospital, Inc.*,[40] a stainless steel surgical pin made by a defendant was implanted in the plaintiff's broken leg to help align and stabilize the bone, and the leg was put in a cast. When the fracture did not heal in the cast, the plaintiff's doctor removed the cast but instructed the plaintiff not to walk on the leg. The plaintiff disobeyed, and the pin broke, causing various complications. At trial, the plaintiff presented evidence that the pin had inclusions and scratches that reduced its strength by a factor of one-third. Yet he presented no evidence that this defect in the pin caused it to break. The defendant proved that even if the pin had contained no defects, it was not strong enough to support the plaintiff's weight—so that it would have broken anyway when he walked, contrary to his doctor's orders, after the cast was removed. Affirming judgments for the defendants, the court ruled that the cause of the pin's break was misuse, not any defect in the pin.

A large majority of courts apply but-for principles to exclude claims for injuries the plaintiff does not establish were a but-for result of a product defect. So, if a driver crashes into a traffic warning sign whose flashing arrow was not working, injuring the plaintiff, recovery is barred if the driver would not have seen a flashing arrow because he was asleep.[41] Similarly, if a doctor fails to read a drug manufacturer's warnings about the side effects of a prescription drug, then it is likely that a more specific warning would have made no difference, and the plaintiff's case will fail.[42] In warning cases like these,

---

[36] See, e.g., Thrasher v. B & B Chem. Co., 2 F.3d 995 (10th Cir. 1993) (Okla. law) (barrels of paint stripper); English v. Crenshaw Supply Co., 387 S.E.2d 628 (Ga. Ct. App. 1989) (brackets painted red).

[37] See, e.g., C.K.S., Inc. v. Helen Borgenicht Sportswear, Inc., 268 N.Y.S.2d 409 (App. Div. 1966) (appearance and composition of blouse).

[38] See Prosser and Keeton on Torts § 41; Dobbs, Law of Torts §§ 168–69; Rest. (3d) Torts: Liability for Physical and Emotional Harm § 26.

[39] Wolf v. Toyota Motor Corp., 2013 WL 3864305, at *3 (Del. Super. Ct. 2013) ("Under the 'but for' test, '[t]he defendant's conduct is a cause of the event if the event would not have occurred but for that conduct; conversely, the defendant's conduct is not a cause of the event, if the event would have occurred without it.' ").

[40] 321 N.E.2d 428, 432 (Ill. App. Ct. 1974).

[41] See Lear Siegler, Inc. v. Perez, 819 S.W.2d 470 (Tex. 1991).

[42] Hrymoc v. Ethicon, Inc., 249 A.3d 191, 219–20 (N.J. Super. Ct. App. Div. 2021) ("the inadequacy of a warning cannot be the proximate cause of an injury where . . . the physician either did not read the warning, or had independent knowledge of the risks"); Bayes v. Biomet, Inc., 2020 WL 5095346, at *13 (E.D. Mo. 2020) (surgeon never read hip replacement's instructions); Marie Renteria v. Ethicon, Inc., 2020 WL 7414744, at *7 (C.D. Cal. 2020) (doctor did not read manufacturer's warnings).

however, the result would be otherwise if the warning's inadequacy were its failure to be more prominent in a fashion that probably would have attracted the user's attention.[43]

Another test for factual causation is the "substantial-factor" test, which the *Second Restatement* employed in an unfortunate attempt to resolve all factual causation problems with a single, umbrella test. Section 431(a) of the *Second Restatement* defines cause in fact in terms of whether the defendant's negligent conduct "is a substantial factor in bringing about the harm." Noting that this test subsumes the but-for test, the comments to this section explain that the substantial-factor test requires a plaintiff to establish, not only that the defendant's tortious conduct was a necessary antecedent of his or her harm, but also that the conduct had a substantial effect in bringing about that harm.[44] The *Second Restatement*'s efforts to include both of these important—yet separate—notions in a single test proved quite unsuccessful, such that most courts instead have divided the causal inquiry in two, using the but-for test for ordinary cases and reserving the substantial-factor test for multiple cause situations in which some question exists as to the materiality of a defendant's contribution to the harm. In these latter situations, usually toxic substance cases, the substantial-factor test appears to work quite well,[45] although a number of courts and the *Third Restatement* reject it as an ambiguous and confusing standard.[46] Some courts do use the substantial-factor test as one, or the only, factual causation test in tort and products liability cases.[47] But most courts, even in California, properly reserve the substantial-factor test for the multiple

---

[43] See, e.g., Morris v. Harley Davidson Motor Co., 2010 WL 2723079, at *3 (M.D. Ga. 2010) (jury question whether different location, color, size print, and symbols on warning would have caused user to read the warning); Folsom v. Kawasaki Motors Corp. U.S.A., 509 F. Supp. 2d 1364, 1378–79 n.11 (M.D. Ga. 2007) (plaintiff who failed to read warning on jet ski could challenge its conspicuousness, but not its substance). See § 9.3, above, and § 11.4, below.

[44] See Rest. (2d) Torts § 431(a) and cmts. *a* and *b*. California courts acknowledge that the substantial-factor test includes the but-for test, and that the substantiality requirement is of lesser moment. See, e.g., Rutherford v. Owens-Illinois, Inc., 941 P.2d 1203, 1214 (Cal. 1997) ("Undue emphasis should not be placed on the term 'substantial.' "); Lineaweaver v. Plant Insulation Co., 37 Cal. Rptr. 2d 902, 905–06 (Ct. App. 1995).

[45] See, e.g., Leavitt v. Johnson & Johnson, 2021 WL 3418410, at *11 (Cal. Ct. App. 2021), noncitable (asbestos-contaminated talc was a substantial factor in causing plaintiff's mesothelioma); Burton v. E.I. du Pont de Nemours & Co., Inc., 994 F.3d 791, 827 (7th Cir. 2021) (Wis. law) (plaintiffs must prove childhood lead paint exposure was a substantial factor in causing lead poisoning injuries); Stephens v. Union Pac. R.R. Co., 935 F.3d 852, 855–56 (9th Cir. 2019) (Idaho law) (substantial factor test distinguished from but-for test; mesothelioma may have been caused by various exposures to different asbestos products); Cooley v. Lincoln Elec. Co., 776 F. Supp. 2d 511, 565–66 (N.D. Ohio 2011) (manganese in welding rod fumes; defendant's product was a substantial factor in causing plaintiff's injury); Summers v. Certainteed Corp., 997 A.2d 1152, 1165 (Pa. 2010) (reversing summary judgment for defendant; "reasonable minds could differ" whether asbestos was a substantial factor in plaintiffs' pleural thickening); Bockrath v. Aldrich Chem. Co., 980 P.2d 398 (Cal. 1999) (substantial-factor test permitted worker's complaint against 55 manufacturers of chemicals that allegedly caused his cancer).

[46] See, e.g., Ford Motor Co. v. Boomer, 736 S.E.2d 724 (Va. 2013) (rejecting substantial factor test in asbestos case; thorough analysis); Wagner v. Bondex Int'l, Inc., 368 S.W.3d 340, 350 (Mo. Ct. App. 2012) (rejecting the "substantial factor" test and applying the "but for" actual causation test in asbestos litigation with multiple defendants). See generally Rest. (3d) Torts: Liability for Physical and Emotional Harm § 26 cmt. *j* ("the substantial-factor rubric tends to obscure [analysis]"), and § 27 cmt. *b*; Sanders, Powers, and Green, The Insubstantiality of the "Substantial Factor" Test for Causation, 73 Mo. L. Rev. 399 (2008); Robertson, The Common Sense of Cause in Fact, 75 Tex. L. Rev. 1765, 1780 (1998) (substantial factor test is merely an intuitive device rather than a logical causal test).

[47] See, e.g., Meador v. Apple, Inc., 911 F.3d 260, 264 (5th Cir. 2018) (Tex. law) ("Cause in fact means that the defendant's act or omission was a substantial factor in bringing about the injury which would not otherwise have occurred."); Anaya v. Town Sports Int'l, Inc., 843 N.Y.S.2d 599, 601 (App. Div. 2007) ("To establish a prima facie case for strict products liability based on defective design, the plaintiff must show that 'the product was not reasonably safe and that the defective design was a substantial factor in causing plaintiff's injury' . . . ."); Stevens v. Keller Ladders, 1 Fed. Appx. 452, 460 (6th Cir. 2001) (Ky. law) (ladder collapse: "the plaintiff in a products liability action has the burden of [proving] causation under the substantial-factor test").

cause situation and apply the but-for test as the principal, usually exclusive, test for factual causation in ordinary products liability contexts involving single, durable products.[48] The *Third Restatement* takes a broadly similar approach, though without the substantial-factor notion or language, by providing a general definition of factual causation in but-for terms[49] and a separate standard for multiple causation cases.[50]

It is axiomatic that a plaintiff must establish that a product defect or the defendant's negligent conduct was *a* cause of the plaintiff's harm, not that it was *the* cause of the harm.[51] Every harmful effect has an infinite number of causes,[52] and some number of those causes often are significant. In addition to the substantial factor test, principles of concurring, multiple causation help plaintiffs establish causation in such cases.[53]

Proving Causation—in General

A recurring factual causation issue in the reported products liability decisions concerns the sufficiency of a plaintiff's proof connecting his or her damages to some defect in the defendant's product. Plaintiffs frequently lose products liability cases because they provide insufficient evidence, by experts or otherwise, establishing that a defect in the

---

[48] See, e.g., Lopez v. The Hillshire Brands Co., 254 Cal. Rptr. 3d 377, 383–84 (Ct. App. 2019) (but-for test inappropriate where plaintiff was exposed to multiple sources of asbestos; "subsumed within the substantial factor test, 'the but-for test is inappropriate in cases when two forces are actively operating and each is sufficient to bring about the harm' "). See also Xavier v. Philip Morris USA Inc., 787 F. Supp. 2d 1075, 1080 (N.D. Cal. 2011), a putative class action of heavy smokers who sought damages for medical monitoring, claiming that defendant's cigarettes increased their risk of lung cancer. Noting that "the 'substantial factor' " test subsumed the " 'but for' test," the court ruled the complaint adequately alleged causation, and remarked:

> The "substantial factor" test adopted from the 2d Restatement applies the traditional "but for" cause in most circumstances, but provides an exception for [concurrent] independent causes . . . .
>
> [C]oncurrent independent causes "are multiple forces operating at the same time and independently, each of which would have been sufficient by itself to bring about the harm."

[49] See Rest. (3d) Torts: Liability for Physical and Emotional Harm § 26 ("Conduct is a factual cause of harm when the harm would not have occurred absent the conduct."). Note that Products Liability Rest., in § 15, merely provides that "[w]hether a product defect caused harm to persons or property is determined by the prevailing rules and principles governing causation in tort." Its two illustrations speak in substantial-factor terms but rely, to a large extent, on but-for reasoning.

[50] See Rest. (3d) Torts: Liability for Harm § 27 (two or more sufficient tortious causes of harm each may be factual causes of the harm).

[51] See, e.g., Lake v. Memphis Landsmen, LLC, 405 S.W.3d 47, 67 (Tenn. 2013) ("In order to show causation in fact, '[i]t is not necessary that the defendants' act be the *sole* cause of the plaintiff's injury, only that it be *a* cause.' "); Schultz v. Akzo Nobel Paints, LLC, 721 F.3d 426, 433 (7th Cir. 2013) (Wis. law) ("In order to show that a toxin is '*a* cause' or '*a substantial factor*,' Schultz was not required to demonstrate that benzene exposure was the *sole* cause of his disease, so long as he showed that benzene contributed substantially to the disease's development or significantly increased his risk of developing AML.").

The Restatements make this clear. See Rest. (3d) Torts: Liability for Physical and Emotional Harm § 26 Reporters' Note to cmt. *c* ("That a party's tortious conduct need only be a cause of the plaintiff's harm and not the sole cause is well recognized and accepted in every jurisdiction."). See also id. § 26 cmt. *c*. ("An actor's tortious conduct need only be a factual cause of the other's harm."); id. § 27; Rest. (2d) Torts § 430 cmt. *d* ("It is not necessary that [the defendant's tortious conduct] be *the* cause, using the word 'the' as meaning the sole and even the predominant cause. The wrongful conduct of a number of third persons may also be a cause of the harm . . . concurrently with the actor."). Courts sometimes get this wrong. See, e.g., Price v. Philip Morris, Inc., 848 N.E.2d 1, 52–53 (Ill. 2005) (mistakenly referring to "the" rather than "a" cause). See also *Lake*, above, where the court ironically observed, immediately prior to the above quote, that plaintiffs' proofs must show that each claim "was *the* cause in fact" of their injuries (emphasis added).

[52] See Rest. (3d) Torts: Liability for Physical and Emotional Harm § 26 cmt. *c* ("there will always be multiple (some say, infinite) factual causes of a harm").

[53] See id. § 27.

defendant's product caused their harm.[54] A classic illustration is *Price v. Ashby's Inc.*,[55] in which the plaintiff's Star-Chief Pontiac sedan inexplicably ran off the road. Before the accident, the plaintiff noticed that the right front end of the car would settle to within three or four inches above the road after he turned the engine off. Plaintiff took the car back to Ashby's, where he had purchased it, to have the sagging problem diagnosed and repaired, but Ashby's could not discover the problem. After the accident, the plaintiff discovered a hole in a line connected to the airlift mechanism that appeared to explain the sagging problem, which established the negligence of General Motors in assembling the car and Ashby's negligence in failing to discover or repair it. But the plaintiff introduced no proof connecting this defect (or, hence, either defendant's negligence) to the car's failure to stay on the road during a turn. Without proof of this connection, the plaintiff failed to establish that the accident probably was caused by the defect (and the defendants' negligence) rather than driver error.[56] For this reason, the court upheld dismissal of the plaintiff's case.

Thus, the central, linking element that a plaintiff must prove in nearly every products liability case is the causal linkage between a product defect and the plaintiff's harm—a crucial connection without which a case normally will fail. Yet, causation need not be proved with certainty, and a plaintiff may establish causation by circumstantial evidence which demonstrates that a defect in the defendant's product most likely caused the harm.[57] The fire cases illustrate the pivotal role of causation evidence in products liability litigation.[58] Fires may be started by defective products, but they also may be

---

[54] See, e.g., Williams v. Kawasaki Motors Corp., U.S.A., 30 F.4th 66, 71 (1st Cir. 2022) (Mass. law) (no admissible expert testimony that manufacturing defect in frame weld caused motorcycle fire after crash); Roe v. FCA US LLC, 2021 WL 2640107, at *15 (W.D. Okla. 2021) (no expert proof that defects caused Jeep to self-shift into reverse); Pierre v. Intuitive Surgical, Inc., 854 Fed. Appx. 316, 319 (11th Cir. 2021) (Fla. law) (proof of "a mere possibility" that insulation defect in surgical robot caused thermal injury is not enough"); Lanzo v. Cyprus Amax Mins. Co., 254 A.3d 691, 712 (N.J. Super. Ct. App. Div. 2021) (reversing awards for long-time talc user suffering from mesothelioma; plaintiffs' experts' theories that non-asbestiform cleavage fragments can cause asbestos disease were unreliable); Meador v. Apple, Inc., 911 F.3d 260, 265 (5th Cir. 2018) (Tex. law) (no showing that courts "would recognize a person's [neurobiologically] induced responses to her phone as a substantial factor in her" car crash to hold phone's manufacturer responsible); Menz v. New Holland N. Am., Inc., 507 F.3d 1107, 1111 (8th Cir. 2007) (Mo. law) (plaintiff's own expert testified that warning of tractor's propensity to roll over would not have changed plaintiff's behavior, and jury lacked experience and knowledge to determine causation on the warning claim: "The necessity of expert testimony in a failure to warn case turns on the complexity of the subject matter."); Webster v. Pacesetter, Inc., 259 F. Supp. 2d 27 (D.D.C. 2003) (insufficient evidence that any defect in pacemaker caused injury to plaintiff's heart); Ogletree v. Navistar Int'l Transp. Corp., 535 S.E.2d 545 (Ga. Ct. App. 2000) (insufficient evidence that failure to install backup alarm on truck that backed over plaintiff caused the injury).

[55] 354 P.2d 1064 (Utah 1960).

[56] "With two or more possible causes such as an inattentive driver and a mechanical defect that would have made it harder to turn; proof that it may have been either is not proof that it was in fact either. No evidence indicated that either cause was the more probable." Id. at 1065.

[57] See, e.g., Strobel v. Johnson & Johnson, 284 Cal. Rptr. 3d 165, 191 (Ct. App. 2021) (plaintiffs' experts presented "ample circumstantial evidentiary support for the inference . . . that asbestos contamination was persistently present in [baby powder] throughout the exposure period"); O'Shea v. Zimmer Biomet Holdings, Inc., 342 F. Supp. 3d 1354, 1362 (N.D. Ga. 2018) (defendant's employee-completed complaint-handling form was an admission that plaintiff's replacement knee "malfunctioned or failed to perform as intended" in the absence of "contributing conditions"; completed form provided "evidence of a defect and evidence that the defect was the most likely cause of the [knee's] failure").

[58] **Sufficient evidence.** See Love v. Weecoo™, 774 Fed. Appx. 519, 521 (11th Cir. 2019) (Ga. law) (reversing summary judgment for Amazon.com; plaintiff's allegations of prior hoverboard fires "alleged enough facts to state plausibly that Amazon had actual or constructive knowledge that the Hoverboard posed a risk of fire at the time of Plaintiff's purchase"); Illinois Farmers Ins. Co. v. Sunbeam Prods., Inc., 2013 WL 1192388 (S.D. Ill. 2013) (sufficient evidence that electric blanket caused house fire); Johnson v. Avco Corp., 702 F. Supp. 2d 1093, 1117 (E.D. Mo. 2010) (plane engine); Allstate Ins. Co. v. Hamilton Beach/Proctor Silex, Inc., 473 F.3d 450, 463 (2d Cir. 2007) (Vt. law) (coffee maker); Speller v. Sears, Roebuck & Co., 790 N.E.2d 252 (N.Y. 2003)

started by cigarettes and other things as well. Conflicting experts often provide conflicting hypotheses about a fire's origin from burn patterns and other circumstantial evidence. Assuming the preliminary sufficiency of the plaintiff's causal evidence, the trier of fact will weigh the conflicting inferences to determine whether the evidence on balance fairly traces the fire to a defect in the defendant's product.

One such case was *Henderson v. Sunbeam Corp.*,[59] an action against the seller and manufacturer of an electric blanket which allegedly caused a fire damaging the plaintiff's property. The plaintiff's fire-origin expert traced the fire to an electrical source on or near the plaintiff's bed and concluded that a defect in the electric blanket's control unit caused the fire. The plaintiff's other expert, a specialist in electrical device malfunctions, attributed the fire to a broken connection in the blanket's heating element which ignited the mantle's fabric when it arced, but he could not identify precisely which connection in the mantle's wiring grid had failed. The defendants' experts blamed the fire on the motor in the bed's vibrator, but the motor could run for only fifteen minutes on its timer, whereas the fire was first observed nearly three hours after the plaintiff left her house the morning of the fire—a delay the defendants' experts could not explain. The jury rendered a verdict for the plaintiff, the trial court denied the defendants' post-trial motions, and the appellate court affirmed, ruling that the plaintiff had presented sufficient causation evidence, even though the plaintiff's experts had offered differing theories on the fire's origins.[60] The plaintiff's failure to pinpoint precisely which part had failed was not fatal to the plaintiff's case because the blanket had been destroyed in the fire, permitting the plaintiff to rely on circumstantial evidence which suggested that a product defect of some type probably had caused the fire.[61] Particularly in malfunction cases such as this, a plaintiff may sometimes prove causation as well as defect by circumstantial evidence.[62]

No question is more fundamental than the sufficiency of the evidence on any issue, but this procedural issue plays an especially prominent role in dividing good products liability cases from bad ones when the issue is cause in fact. The *Price* sagging-car case well illustrates how a plaintiff must provide a sufficient amount of credible evidence connecting a product defect or the supplier's negligence to the plaintiff's harm to allow a trier of fact reasonably to conclude that the defect or negligence probably caused the harm. Without such evidence, if a jury is left to speculation and conjecture on what caused a plaintiff's harm, the claim will fail. Yet, as shown by *Henderson*, determinations

---

(refrigerator); Flock v. Scripto-Tokai Corp., 319 F.3d 231, 236–38 (5th Cir. 2003) (Tex. law) (Aim'n Flame utility lighter).

Insufficient evidence. See Gopalratnam v. Hewlett-Packard Co., 877 F.3d 771, 784 (7th Cir. 2017) (plaintiff's expert's theory of defect in laptop's lithium battery cell that allegedly caused fire was contrary to generally accepted battery science); Howells v. General Elec. Co., 2013 WL 419244 (D. Nev. 2013) (insufficient proof microwave started fire); Funkhouser v. Ford Motor Co., 736 S.E.2d 309 (Va. 2013) (vehicle; other vehicle fires not similar); Presley v. Lakewood Eng'g & Mfg. Co., 553 F.3d 638, 647 (8th Cir. 2009) (Ark. law) (heater; needed expert witness); 438 Main St. v. Easy Heat, Inc., 99 P.3d 801 (Utah 2004) (deicing cable); Citizens Ins. Co. of Am. v. Sears Roebuck & Co., 203 F. Supp. 2d 837 (W.D. Mich. 2002) (barbecue gas grill burner).

[59] 46 F.3d 1151 (10th Cir. 1995) (table) (Okla. law).

[60] "A jury question is created, not negated, by disagreement among experts, . . . and the fact that plaintiff's own experts disagreed did not alter the jury's authority to resolve the issue consistently with Dr. Croenwett's view . . . ." Id. at *2.

[61] "Where, as here, an allegedly defective product has largely destroyed itself, making direct evidence of the precise operative defect unavailable, the plaintiff may prove her case with circumstantial evidence, typically including expert testimony, even though she 'is unable to point an accusing finger at a particular defective component.' " Id.

[62] On proof of defect in malfunction cases, see § 7.4, above.

of factual causation are especially fact intensive, so that the plaintiff's introduction of most any plausible evidence linking his or her harm to the defendant's negligence or defective product, even circumstantially, makes cause in fact an issue for the jury.[63]

Proving Causation—Toxic Substance Litigation

In General

Toxic substance cases typically present a number of serious causation problems,[64] and the substantial-factor test previously mentioned helps plaintiffs in only limited ways. Tracing illness and injury to particular asbestos fibers, drugs, and other kinds of chemicals presents perplexing causation problems both in science and the law. Science often does not fully understand the biological mechanisms involved in disease causation, rendering it difficult for the law to be confident of evidence that a plaintiff's cancer or other disease was caused by his or her exposure to a particular product rather than something else. While the but-for test remains at the center of the causal inquiry, courts in toxic substance cases necessarily draw from scientific notions of causation to help make legal determinations of causation. Yet causation is established very differently in science than in law, which often produces a clash between these disciplines when toxic substance causation issues arise in products liability cases. Because the causal issues in such litigation are so arcane, expert testimony is almost always necessary and sits at the center of most disputes.[65] The topic of causation in toxic substance litigation runs wide and deep,[66] and the discussion here just highlights certain causal tests and issues that recur in products liability cases of this type.

---

[63] See, e.g., Perez v. FCA USA LLC, 2021 WL 2139334, at *2 (E.D. Mich. 2021) (circumstantial evidence was sufficient that "a jury could find in plaintiffs' favor as to causation without engaging in conjecture or speculation" that child's asphyxiation resulting in quadriplegia was caused by entrapment in minivan's defective power window); Lake v. Memphis Landsmen, LLC, 405 S.W.3d 47, 67 (Tenn. 2013) ("Cause in fact is ordinarily a question for the jury, and, as with other factual questions, jurors are entitled 'to use their common sense and to rely upon their life experiences in evaluating' the issue."). See note 58, above.

[64] "Causation issues represent a major impediment to the successful resolution of claims based on injuries from hazardous substances." Brennan, Causal Chains and Statistical Links: The Role of Scientific Uncertainty in Hazardous-Substance Litigation, 73 Cornell L. Rev. 469, 532 (1988).

[65] See § 6.3, above.

[66] See, e.g., Green, The Education of the Judiciary: The Sciences Addressing Disease Causation, 49 Sw. L. Rev. 492 (2021); Smith, Goldkind, and Andrichik, Statistically Significant Association: Preventing the Misuse of the Bradford Hill Criteria to Prove Causation in Toxic Tort Cases, 86 Def. Couns. J. 1 (2019); Sulyok, Managing Uncertain Causation in Toxic Exposure Cases: Lessons for the European Court of Human Rights from U.S. Toxic Tort Litigation, 18 Vt. J. Envtl. L. 519 (2017); Gold, When Certainty Dissolves into Probability: A Legal Vision of Toxic Causation for the Post-Genomic Era, 70 Wash. & Lee. L. Rev. 237 (2013); Sanders, The Controversial Comment C: Factual Causation in Toxic-Substance and Disease Cases, 44 Wake Forest L. Rev. 1029 (2009); Stapleton, The Two Explosive Proof-of-Causation Doctrines Central to Asbestos Claims, 74 Brook. L. Rev. 1011 (2009); Rodricks, Evaluating Disease Causation in Humans Exposed to Toxic Substances, 14 J.L. & Pol'y 39 (2006); Golanski, General Causation at a Crossroads in Toxic Tort Cases, 108 Penn St. L. Rev. 479 (2003); Pierce and Sexton, Toxicogenomics: Toward the Future of Toxic Tort Causation, 5 N.C. J.L. & Tech. 33 (2003); Conway-Jones, Factual Causation in Toxic Tort Litigation: A Philosophical View of Proof and Certainty in Uncertain Disciplines, 35 U. Rich. L. Rev. 875 (2002); McGarity, Proposal for Linking Culpability and Causation to Ensure Corporate Accountability for Toxic Risks, 26 Wm. & Mary Envtl. L. & Pol'y Rev. 1 (2001); Geistfeld, Scientific Uncertainty and Causation Tort Law, 54 Vand. L. Rev. 1011 (2001); Klein, A Model for Enhanced Risk Recovery in Tort, 56 Wash. & Lee L. Rev. 1173 (1999); Fischer, Successive Causes and the Enigma of Duplicated Harm, 66 Tenn. L. Rev. 1127 (1999); Bernstein, Formed by Thalidomide: Mass Torts as a False Cure for Toxic Exposure, 97 Colum. L. Rev. 2153 (1997); Wagner, Choosing Ignorance in the Manufacture of Toxic Products, 82 Cornell L. Rev. 773 (1997); Berger, Eliminating General Causation: Notes Toward a New Theory of Justice and Toxic Torts, 97 Colum. L. Rev. 2117 (1997); Feldman, Science and Uncertainty in Mass Exposure Litigation, 74 Tex. L. Rev. 1 (1995); Sanders, From Science to Evidence: The Testimony on Causation in the Bendectin Cases, 46 Stan. L. Rev. 1 (1993); Green, Expert Witnesses and Sufficiency of Evidence in Toxic Substances Litigation: The Legacy of Agent Orange and Bendectin Litigation,

A toxic substance case typically arises when a person is diagnosed with some illness or injury, such as cancer, that his or her doctor may (or may not) believe was caused by some toxic substance, such as asbestos, silicone gel in a breast implant, a cell phone, or some drug or other chemical. The doctor may suspect that a particular agent caused the illness, yet most physicians are trained principally to diagnose and treat a disease, not to determine its etiology. For a products liability claim to lie, a person suffering from an illness or injury that may have been caused by a toxic substance will have to assemble proof that the substance probably caused the harm. Such proof, for a number of reasons, may be difficult to obtain. Much mystery still surrounds the causes of many illnesses, and much remains unknown about whether (and, if so, how) many substances are hazardous to humans. This problem is exacerbated in many toxic substance cases in which the period between exposure and the onset of symptoms of an illness (the latency period) often is many years, sometimes decades.[67] Thus, proving that any particular toxic agent caused a particular person's illness or injury can be a daunting task.

General and Specific Causation

Proof of causation in toxic substance cases always involves, at least implicitly, two separate forms of causal proof: (1) general causation and (2) specific causation.[68] To establish "general causation," a plaintiff must establish that the suspect agent is capable of causing the particular type of illness or injury suffered by the plaintiff. For example, a plaintiff who seeks to prove that a cell phone caused his brain cancer, that asbestos caused his lung disease, that a silicone-gel breast implant caused her systemic disorders, or that a drug she took during pregnancy caused birth defects in her child, first must establish that the suspect agent in fact is capable of causing the particular type of harm the plaintiff suffers. General causation is sometimes so well established, or its markers so self-evident,[69] that little or no proof of general causation is necessary.[70] Ordinarily,

---

86 Nw. U. L. Rev. 643 (1992); Brennan, Causal Chains and Statistical Links: The Role of Scientific Uncertainty in Hazardous-Substance Litigation, 73 Cornell L. Rev. 469 (1988); Note, 26 Rev. Litig. 739 (2007) (differential diagnosis for causation in toxic substance cases); Frumer, Friedman, and Sklaren, Products Liability §§ 3.02[5] ("medical causation") and 3.04[2] (asbestos cases); D. Faigman, D. Kaye, M. Saks, and J. Sanders, Science in the Law—Standards, Statistics and Research Issues (2002); Federal Judicial Center, Reference Manual on Scientific Evidence (3d ed. 2011); R. Goldberg, Using Scientific Evidence to Resolve Causation Problems in Product Liability: UK, US and French Experiences, in Perspectives on Causation (R. Goldberg ed., 2011); M. Dore, Law of Toxic Torts (West 2009) (annual updates). For a helpful overview, see J. Eggen, Toxic Torts in a Nutshell ch. 8 (6th ed. 2018). For a superb review of this problem, see the Rest. (3d) Torts: Liability for Physical and Emotional Harm § 28(a) cmt. *c*, and the Reporters' Notes thereto.

[67] For example, reproductive anomalies associated with DES are not evident until the victim, exposed to the drug *in utero*, reaches puberty. See § 11.3, below. The latency period of mesothelioma, an invariably lethal cancer caused by inhaling asbestos dust extends up to forty years. See, e.g., S. Carroll, D. Hensler, et al., Asbestos Litigation 15 (RAND 2005). Justice Helen Freedman of the New York Supreme Court, responsible for managing asbestos litigation in that state, reports a case where the latency period was 60 years. Freedman, Selected Ethical Issues in Asbestos Litigation, 37 Sw. U. L. Rev. 505 (2008).

[68] This distinction is widely employed. See, e.g., Daniels-Feasel v. Forest Pharms., Inc., 2021 WL 4037820, at *5 (S.D.N.Y. 2021) ("Causation in pharmaceutical products liability, or toxic tort, cases 'has two components, general and specific, and the plaintiff must establish both in order to prevail.' "); In re Mirena IUS Levonorgestrel-Related Prods. Liab. Litig. (No. II), 387 F. Supp. 3d 323, 340 (S.D.N.Y. 2019); Howell v. Centric Group, LLC, 508 Fed. Appx. 834, 837 (10th Cir. 2013) (Colo. law) ("General causation is whether a substance is capable of causing a particular injury or condition in the general population and specific causation is whether a substance caused a particular individual's injury."); Wells v. SmithKline Beechman Corp., 601 F.3d 375, 377–78 (5th Cir. 2010) (Tex. law) ("a plaintiff must prove both").

[69] Such as DES. See Farber, Toxic Causation, 71 Minn. L. Rev. 1219, 1251–52 (1987); Abraham and Merrill, Scientific Uncertainty in the Courts, Issues In Sci. & Tech., Winter 1986, at 93, 101.

[70] The causal connections between asbestos and asbestosis and mesothelioma are so strong that courts long have held they are established as a matter of law. See, e.g., Lowery v. Sanofi-Aventis LLC, 2021 WL 872620, at *12 n.19 (N.D. Ala. 2021) ("where 'the medical community generally recognizes the toxicity of the

however a plaintiff must affirmatively establish general causation,[71] as by controlled human studies, epidemiological studies of population groups, animal experiments, laboratory studies of the chemistry of an agent and disease, or some combination of these forms of evidence.

"General causation" is most commonly proved with epidemiological studies of human population groups exposed to the suspect agent.[72] Epidemiological studies yield calculations of the "relative risk" of acquiring a disease or injury from exposure to an agent contrasted to the background risk of contracting the illness or injury from other factors. A relative risk of 1.0 means that the risk of contracting the illness is not increased at all by exposure to the agent; a relative risk greater than 1.0 means that exposure to the agent increases the likelihood of contracting the illness; and a relative risk of 2.0 means that exposure to the agent doubles a person's risk of contracting the disease.[73] With some substances, like Bendectin[74] and silicone-gel breast implants,[75] for which numerous epidemiological studies revealed no reliable evidence of a causal relationship between exposure and suspected birth defects and systemic disorders, respectively, the insistence by many courts of convincing epidemiologic evidence of causation for a plaintiff to proceed bars recovery. For other types of products, reliable epidemiologic studies may be unavailable, particularly at the beginning of a product's life cycle,[76] and other types of causation evidence often are appropriate.[77]

---

drug or chemical at issue' [such as asbestos, which causes asbestosis and mesothelioma] the court need not engage in an extensive inquiry on general causation because it is beyond doubt that the substance in question can cause the harm alleged").

71 See, e.g., In re Incretin-Based Therapies Prods. Liab. Litig., 2022 WL 898595, at *2 (9th Cir. 2022) (warning claims failed without expert's general causation evidence linking drugs to pancreatic cancer); Davis v. McKesson Corp., 2019 WL 5535376 (D. Ariz. 2019) ("Specific causation opinions of individual doctors is not enough.").

72 Controlled human studies may be the most effective way of determining whether a substance can harm human beings, but such studies are expensive and sometimes are unethical. See McGarity, Proposal for Linking Culpability and Causation to Ensure Corporate Accountability for Toxic Risks, 26 Wm. & Mary Envtl. L. & Pol'y Rev. 1, 14–15 (2001).

73 See generally In re Bextra & Celebrex Mktg. Sales Practices & Prods. Liab. Litig., 524 F. Supp. 2d 1166, 1171–74 (N.D. Cal. 2007) (good discussion of epidemiological methodologies); Note, 56 Vand. L. Rev. 1227, 1234–35 (2003). See also Merck & Co. v. Garza, 347 S.W.3d 256, 265–68 (Tex. 2011) (plaintiffs' experts failed to meet general causation "threshold requirement of reliability . . . that the evidence demonstrate a statistically significant doubling of the risk").

74 See, e.g., Brock v. Merrell Dow Pharms., Inc., 874 F.2d 307, 313 (5th Cir. 1989) (Tex. law) (lack of strong epidemiological proof was fatal to plaintiff's claim that Bendectin caused the plaintiff's birth defects; while convincing epidemiologic proof is not required in every toxic substance case, it may be crucial when animal studies, of questionable applicability to humans, are the only other form of proof). See generally M. Green, The Road Less Well Traveled (and Seen): Contemporary Lawmaking in Products Liability, 49 DePaul L. Rev. 377 (1999); J. Sanders, Bendectin on Trial: A Study of Mass Tort Litigation 89 (1998) ("the substantial weight of the scientific evidence fails to support the conclusion that Bendectin causes birth defects").

75 See, e.g., Norris v. Baxter Healthcare Corp., 397 F.3d 878, 884–86 (10th Cir. 2005) (experts' conclusions, based on case studies and differential diagnosis, that silicone gel breast implants cause systemic disease was "flatly contrary to *all* of the available epidemiological evidence" and was properly excluded as unreliable evidence of general causation); Meister v. Med. Eng'g Corp., 267 F.3d 1123 (D.C. Cir. 2001) (overwhelming epidemiological evidence has established lack of causal connection between silicone breast implants and type of injury plaintiff suffered). See generally Walker and Monahan, Scientific Authority: The Breast Implant Litigation and Beyond, 86 Va. L. Rev. 801 (2000).

76 See, e.g., Turner v. Iowa Fire Equip. Co., 229 F.3d 1202, 1209 (8th Cir. 2000) (Okla. law) ("The first several victims of a new toxic tort should not be barred from having their day in court simply because the medical literature, which will eventually show the connection between the victims' condition and the toxic substance, has not yet been completed.").

77 A "quite substantial body of case law and commentary rejects an epidemiologic threshold for sufficient proof of general causation." Rest. (3d) Torts: Liability for Physical and Emotional Harm § 28,

"Specific causation" exists when a particular plaintiff's exposure to a particular substance caused his or her particular illness. Establishing specific causation first requires proof of exposure to the defendant's product—normally not a problem in drug litigation, but sometimes a problem in cases where the suspect agent is asbestos or some chemical. Particularly in asbestos litigation, a plaintiff may have worked for many years around asbestos products produced by many manufacturers. In such cases, proving whether any particular manufacturer's asbestos products caused (or helped cause) the plaintiff's asbestos-related disease is difficult, if not impossible.[78] To address this problem, the court in *Lohrmann v. Pittsburgh Corning Corp.*[79] crafted a variant of the substantial-factor test[80]—now known as the "frequency, regularity, and proximity test"—for this particular type of litigation.

Now widely applied in asbestos litigation,[81] this test allows the finding of a causal conclusion—linking a particular asbestos product to a plaintiff's asbestos disease—if the

Reporters' Note to cmt. *c* (citing cases). See, e.g., Rider v. Sandoz Pharms. Corp., 295 F.3d 1194, 1198 (11th Cir. 2002) ("It is well-settled that while epidemiological studies may be powerful evidence of causation, the lack thereof is not fatal to a plaintiff's case."); Hollander v. Sandoz Pharms. Corp., 289 F.3d 1193, 1211–12 (10th Cir. 2002) (plaintiffs need not always use epidemiologic studies to establish general causation). See also Gold, The "Reshapement" of the False Negative Asymmetry in Toxic Tort Causation, 37 Wm. Mitchell L. Rev. 1507 (2011).

Commentators are unfriendly to epidemiologic thresholds for causation. See, e.g., Smith-Drelich, Performative Causation, 93 S. Cal. L. Rev. 379 (2020); Cranor, Milward v. Acuity Specialty Products: Advances in General Causation Testimony in Toxic Tort Litigation, 3 Wake Forest J.L. & Pol'y 105 (2013); Jurs, Judicial Analysis of Complex & Cutting-Edge Science in the Daubert Era: Epidemiologic Risk Assessment as a Test Case for Reform Strategies, 42 Conn. L. Rev. 49 (2009); Geistfeld, Scientific Uncertainty and Causation in Tort Law, 54 Vand. L. Rev. 1011 (2001); Berger, Eliminating General Causation: Notes Towards a New Theory of Justice and Toxic Torts, 97 Colum. L. Rev. 2117 (1997); Wagner, Choosing Ignorance in the Manufacture of Toxic Products, 82 Cornell L. Rev. 773 (1997); Feldman, Science and Uncertainty in Mass Exposure Litigation, 74 Tex. L. Rev. 1, 45 (1995); Green, Expert Witnesses and Sufficiency of Evidence in Toxic Substances Litigation: The Legacy of Agent Orange and Bendectin Litigation, 86 Nw. U. L. Rev. 643 (1992); Rest. (3d) Torts: Liability for Physical and Emotional Harm § 28 cmt. *c*.

[78] See, e.g., Hailey v. Air & Liquid Sys. Corp., 2020 WL 4732141, at *12 (D. Md. 2020) (plaintiffs failed to offer sufficient proof of asbestos exposure from "any specific *Defendant's products*") (emphasis in original); Corazza v. Amchem Prods., Inc., 96 N.Y.S.3d 569, 570 (App. Div. 2019); Yaw v. Air & Liquid Sys. Corp., 2019 WL 3891792, at *3 (W.D. Wash. 2019) (plaintiff "fails to identify any particular product that created the [asbestos] dust [and] fails to identify a specific time that [decedent] was on a particular ship and exposed to a particular product that had produced or was producing asbestos dust").

[79] 782 F.2d 1156, 1162–63 (4th Cir. 1986) (Md. law).

[80] See, e.g., Hoerner v. ANCO Insulations, Inc., 812 So.2d 45 (La. Ct. App. 2002).

[81] See, e.g., Connor v. Covil Corp., 996 F.3d 143 (4th Cir. 2021) (N.C. law) (insufficient evidence of exposure to defendant's asbestos insulation products under the "frequency, regularity, and proximity" test); Dickens v. A-1 Auto Parts & Repair Inc., 2021 WL 518329, at *2 (S.D. Miss. 2021) ("[I]n asbestos litigation cases, the frequency, regularity, and proximity test is the proper standard in determining exposure and proximate cause."); Callanan v. Chesterton, 605 S.W.3d 109, 117 (Mo. Ct. App. 2020) ("The 'frequency, regularity, and proximity' test has been adopted by 'a majority of courts' to apply the 'substantial factor' test.").

Some state statutes apply a "substantial contributing factor test" in asbestos and/or silica claims. See Fla. Stat. Ann. § 774.205(1) (asbestos and silica claims), held unconstitutional as retroactively applied, American Optical Corp. v. Spiewak, 73 So.3d 120, 133–34 (Fla. 2011); Ga. Code Ann. § 51–14–3(17)(B)(ii) (asbestos claims, except for mesothelioma, require "that exposure to asbestos was a substantial contributing factor to the diagnosed cancer; and that other potential causes (such as smoking) were not the sole or most likely cause of the injury at issue"); Tenn. Code Ann. § 29–34–303(26) (silica or mixed dust claims).

In cases involving diseases caused by cumulative exposures, exposures are not treated separately and the first exposure as well as the last may constitute a harmful invasion of the plaintiff's system. Borel v. Fibreboard Paper Prods. Corp., 493 F.2d 1076, 1092 (5th Cir. 1973) (Tex. law) ("Thus both Borel's earliest exposure to asbestos dust, and his most recent exposure, occurring in 1968, could have contributed to his overall condition."). See also Gorton v. Air & Liquid Sys. Corp., 2020 WL 4193649, at *2 (M.D. Pa. 2020) ("the cumulative theory of exposure [to asbestos was] reliable based upon both the [plaintiff's] experts' testimony and the weight of authority"); Davis v. Honeywell Int'l Inc., 199 Cal. Rptr. 3d 583, 597 (Ct. App. 2016) (plaintiff "is free to further establish that his particular asbestos disease is cumulative in nature, with many separate plaintiff produces "evidence of exposure to a specific product on a regular basis over some extended period of time in proximity to where the plaintiff actually worked."[82]

Because the etiology of many diseases is uncertain, courts often turn to epidemiologic evidence to help determine specific as well as general causation. Thus, as proof of specific causation, many courts allow group studies which show at least a doubling in the incidence of a disease in exposed populations (a relative risk of 2.0 or greater); other courts *require* such proof of doubling as a threshold for establishing specific causation; and many recognize the salience of a two-fold increase, in suggesting that the agent was more likely than not a cause of the plaintiff's injuries, without raising it to threshold status.[83] Experts are necessary to establish the reliability of any such epidemiology studies, to explain how the plaintiff's exposure was similar to the study's subjects, and to exclude other possible causes of the plaintiff's malady.[84]

Other forms of proof are often useful in establishing specific causation.[85] One well-established scientific method for proving or helping prove specific causation is commonly referred to as "differential diagnosis."[86] By this approach, a physician attempts to determine the specific cause of a particular patient's malady[87] by considering the range

---

exposures each having constituted a 'substantial factor' . . . that contributed to his risk of injury"). However, cumulative exposure alone may not provide sufficient evidence of specific causation. See, e.g., Schwartz v. Honeywell Int'l, Inc., 102 N.E.3d 477, 483 (Ohio 2018) ("a theory of causation based only on cumulative exposure to various asbestos-containing products is insufficient to demonstrate that exposure to asbestos from a particular defendant's product was a 'substantial factor' "); Krik v. Exxon Mobil Corp., 870 F.3d 669, 677 (7th Cir. 2017) (Ill. and maritime law) (joining the Sixth and Ninth Circuits in holding that neither the "each and every exposure" theory nor the "cumulative exposure" theory meet the requirements of the "substantial factor" test).

For cases rejecting the theory that "any exposure" increases the risk of disease, see, e.g., Swanson v. The Marley-Wylain Co., 280 Cal. Rptr. 3d 496, 507 (Cal. Ct. App. 2021) (trial court erred in using California's "any exposure to asbestos" causation standard instead of Michigan's substantial factor test); Bostic v. Georgia-Pac. Corp., 439 S.W.3d 332, 342 (Tex. 2014) (declining to apply an "any exposure" theory of liability to prove that asbestos-contaminated joint compound caused plaintiff's mesothelioma).

[82] *Lohrman*, 782 F.2d at 1162–63.

[83] See Rest. (3d) Torts: Liability for Physical and Emotional Harm § 28, Reporters' Note to cmt. *c* (collecting cases). See generally Carruth and Goldstein, Relative Risk Greater than Two in Proof of Causation in Toxic Tort Litigation, 41 Jurimetrics J. 195 (2001).

[84] See, e.g., Barnes v. Orthofix Int'l NV, 2012 WL 1931224, at *6 (W.D. Wash. 2012); In re Allied Chem. Corp., 227 S.W.3d 652, 656 (Tex. 2007). See also Parker v. Mobil Oil Corp., 857 N.E.2d 1114, 1121–22 (N.Y. 2006) (plaintiff's expert's testimony that plaintiff "had 'far more exposure to benzene than did the refinery workers in the epidemiological studies' is plainly insufficient to establish causation" because it does not compare exposures of the study subjects and the plaintiff, "thus lacking in epidemiologic evidence to support the claim").

[85] See, e.g., Hart v. Keenan Props., Inc., 463 P.3d 824 (Cal. 2020) (worker's foreman's testimony linking asbestos-cement pipe invoices to the defendant); Coene v. 3M Co., 2017 WL 1046749, at *10 (W.D.N.Y. 2017) (toxicologist's testimony linking plaintiff's silicosis to respirable silica from laser printer, extrapolated from peer reviewed articles and other sources due to the lack of epidemiological studies for the new technology, was reliable under *Daubert* standards); Alder v. Bayer Corp., AGFA Div., 61 P.3d 1068 (Utah 2002) (hospital technicians could prove that chemicals from defendant's x-ray machine caused their chronic fatigue syndrome, fibromyalgia, and cognitive deficits by circumstantial evidence of a "temporal relationship" between prolonged exposure to chemicals followed by onset of symptoms of a type associated with exposure to such chemicals).

[86] **Differential diagnosis.** Properly, "differential *diagnosis*" refers to a method for ascertaining a patient's *illness*, whereas "differential *etiology*" describes a process for determining the *cause* of that disease. See, e.g., Note, 56 Vand. L. Rev. 1227, 1228 n.5 (2003) (citing Faigman et al., Modern Scientific Evidence: The Law and Science of Expert Testimony § 20–1.1 (2d ed. 2002)). Yet the former term is widely used by courts to mean the *ruling-out process* used to ascertain causation. Another term for describing this form of reasoning is "inference to the best explanation." See, e.g., Milward v. Acuity Specialty Products Group, Inc., 639 F.3d 11, 17 (1st Cir. 2011) (Mass. law).

[87] Thus, differential diagnosis is a method for establishing *specific* (not general) causation. See, e.g., Chapman v. Procter & Gamble Distributing, LLC, 766 F.3d 1296, 1309 (11th Cir. 2014) (affirming summary

of its plausible causes, and ruling them out, one by one, until just one remains.[88] Assuming that a physician applies this technique properly[89]—and assuming further that courts, in the process of rendering admissibility determinations under *Daubert* and Rule 702, do not intrude into the realm of factual cause determinations reserved to juries[90]—differential diagnosis can be a particularly useful tool to prove a specific causal link between a defendant's toxic substance and a plaintiff's disease or injury.[91]

§ 11.3 MULTIPLE DEFENDANTS

Most causation problems involving multiple products liability defendants concern toxic substances, and methods for establishing causation in that type of litigation were just examined.[92] Yet problems from a multiplicity of known or possible causal agencies extend beyond toxic substance litigation, so that multiple-defendant causation issues arise more generally. This section first explores the general principles of concurrent causation that apply to multiple defendant situations and then examines "market share liability" and other theories of collective responsibility designed to mitigate a plaintiff's causal difficulties in certain types of cases involving multiple defendants.

Concurrent Causation

A manufacturer or other seller may be responsible, at least in part, for causing a plaintiff's injuries no matter how many other causes may also combine to cause the harm. If a product defect (or the defendant's negligence) played a material role in causing

judgment for defendant; differential diagnosis "will not usually overcome the fundamental failure of laying a scientific groundwork for the general toxicity of the drug and that it can cause the harm a plaintiff suffered"); Johnson v. Arkema, Inc., 685 F.3d 452, 468 (5th Cir. 2012) ("an expert may not rely on a differential diagnosis to circumvent the requirement of general causation"); Kilpatrick v. Breg, Inc., 613 F.3d 1329, 1342 (11th Cir. 2010) (Fla. law) (differential diagnosis "assumes the existence of general causation, and focuses instead on specific causation").

[88] "Differential diagnosis, or differential etiology, is a standard scientific technique of identifying the cause of a medical problem by eliminating the likely causes until the most probable one is isolated." Schafersman v. Agland Coop., 631 N.W.2d 862, 871 (Neb. 2001). See generally Hopp, Goldkind, and Cummings, Differential Diagnosis and Daubert: Preventing the Misuse of Differential Etiology to Prove Causation in Toxic Tort Cases, 84 Def. Couns. J. 1 (2017); Sanders and Machal-Fulks, The Admissibility of Differential Diagnosis Testimony to Prove Causation in Toxic Tort Cases: The Interplay of Adjective and Substantive Law, 64 Law & Contemp. Probs. 107 (2001).

[89] See, e.g., In re Zimmer Nexgen Knee Implant Prods. Liab. Litig., 218 F. Supp. 3d 700, 716 (N.D. Ill. 2016) (plaintiffs' expert's "criteria for ruling in reasonable potential causes [of knee implant failures varied] considerably"), aff'd sub nom. In re Zimmer, NexGen Knee Implant Prods. Liab. Litig., 884 F.3d 746 (7th Cir. 2018); Mallozzi v. EcoSMART Techs., Inc., 2013 WL 2415677 (E.D.N.Y. 2013) (in ruling in plaintiff's brief exposure to defendant's pesticide as cause of his Laryngopharyngeal Reflux (LPR), doctor inadequately explained why he ruled out plaintiff's preexisting GERD, thus failing to meet reliability requirements of Rule 702 and *Daubert*); Blackwell v. Wyeth, 971 A.2d 235, 260 (Md. 2009) (expert "did not sufficiently consider genetics in his differential diagnosis equation" of causes of autism).

[90] See, e.g., Schultz v. Akzo Nobel Paints, LLC., 721 F.3d 426, 434 (7th Cir. 2013) (reversing summary judgment for manufacturer of benzene; plaintiff's causation expert could testify). See generally Green, Pessimism About Milward, 3 Wake Forest J. L. & Pol'y 41 (2013) (relating history of Rest. (3d) Torts § 28(a) cmt. *c*); Cranor, Milward v. Acuity Special Products: Advances in General Causation Testimony in Toxic Tort Litigation, 3 Wake Forest J. L. & Pol'y 105 (2013).

[91] See, e.g., Ingham v. Johnson & Johnson, 608 S.W.3d 663, 709–11 (Mo. Ct. App. 2020) (trial court did not abuse discretion in admitting expert's specific causation evidence consisting of individual differential diagnoses of the 22 plaintiffs diagnosed with ovarian cancer after talc product use); Schultz v. Akzo Nobel Paints, LLC, 721 F.3d 426 (7th Cir. 2013) (Wis. law) (plaintiff's oncologist sufficiently ruled out smoking and other risk factors and sufficiently ruled in benzene as a cause of worker's acute myeloid leukemia); Tingey v. Radionics, 193 Fed. Appx. 747, 765 (10th Cir. 2006) (plaintiff's experts, testifying on cause of her neurogenic bladder, properly ruled in shock from the radiofrequency lesion generator used by surgeon to isolate and destroy nerves causing her back pain, and properly ruled out other possible causes).

[92] See § 11.2, above.

the plaintiff's injuries, then the defect or conduct was a cause of the harm. This is the principle of concurrent causation, as well known to tort law generally[93] as it is to the law of products liability.[94] The substantial-factor test was devised to address just this type of multiple defendant situation,[95] as previously discussed. So, if a defendant's asbestos,[96] chemical,[97] or tobacco[98] product plays a substantial role in causing a plaintiff's disease, a defendant may be held to have caused that disease, at least in part, even if it was also caused by the asbestos, chemical, or tobacco products of other manufacturers.[99]

It often is difficult to determine which portions of a plaintiff's injuries are attributable to each of two or more responsible parties. If the trier of fact, on some reasonable basis, is able to determine which aspects of the plaintiff's harm are attributable to which defendant, then damages ordinarily should be apportioned on that basis.[100] But where no fair and practicable method for apportioning the harm is available, then, at common law, each defendant whose breach of duty was a substantial

---

[93] See Rest. (3d) Torts: Liability for Physical and Emotional Harm § 27 Multiple Sufficient Causes: "If multiple acts occur, each of which under [the but-for test of] § 26 alone would have been a factual cause of the . . . harm at the same time in the absence of the other act(s), each is regarded as a factual cause of the harm."

[94] See, e.g., AMCO Ins. Co. v. Emery & Assocs., Inc., 926 F. Supp. 2d 634, 646–47 (W.D. Pa. 2013) ("a defendant is not relieved from liability because another concurring cause is also responsible for producing injury"); Ford Motor Co. v. Boomer, 736 S.E.2d 724 (Va. 2013) (considering applicability of § 27 to asbestos mesothelioma cases and concluding "that in concurring causation cases, the 'sufficient'-to-have-caused standard . . . is the proper way to define the cause-in-fact element of proximate cause . . . whether the concurring causes are all tortious in nature or whether some are innocent"); Rest. (3d) Torts: Products Liability § 3 cmt. *d* (a "defect need not be the only cause of the incident; if the plaintiff can prove that the most likely explanation of the harm involves the causal contribution of a product defect, the fact that there may be other concurrent causes of the harm does not preclude liability").

[95] See, e.g., Bostic v. Georgia-Pacific Corp., 439 S.W.3d 332, 344 (Tex. 2014) ("in products liability cases where the plaintiff was exposed to multiple sources of asbestos, substantial factor causation is the appropriate basic standard of causation"); Vodanovich v. A.P. Green Indus., 869 So.2d 930, 932 (La. Ct. App. 2004) ("When multiple causes of injury are present, defendant's conduct is a cause in fact of plaintiff's harm if it is a substantial factor generating plaintiff's harm."). See § 11.2, above.

[96] See, e.g., Stephens v. Union Pac. R.R. Co., 935 F.3d 852, 855–56 (9th Cir. 2019) (where mesothelioma may have been caused by various exposures to different asbestos products, exposure to defendant's asbestos must be proved to have been substantial rather than fleeting); Whipkey v. Aqua-Chem, Inc., 2012 WL 759200, at *9 (Ohio Ct. App. 2012) ("ample evidence" supported finding that plaintiff's exposure to asbestos "was a substantial factor in causing his lung cancer"); Verret v. American Biltrite, Inc., 2006 WL 2507318, at *4 (Tex. App. 2006) (La. law) (asbestos; "Where there are concurrent causes of an injury, the proper inquiry is whether the conduct in question was a substantial factor in bringing about the injury."); Rutherford v. Owens-Illinois, Inc., 941 P.2d 1203 (Cal. 1997). *But see* John Crane, Inc. v. Jones, 604 S.E.2d 822, 824–25 (Ga. 2004) (confused opinion rejecting substantial-factor test as test for proximate cause).

[97] See, e.g., Wagoner v. Exxon Mobil Corp., 813 F. Supp. 2d 771, 798 (E.D. La. 2011) (defendant's benzene products caused worker's multiple myeloma; "Cause-in-fact is generally a 'but for' inquiry, which tests whether the accident would or would not have occurred but for the defendant's substandard conduct. However, where there are concurrent causes of an accident, the proper inquiry is whether the conduct in question was a substantial factor in bringing about the accident."); Bockrath v. Aldrich Chem. Co., 980 P.2d 398 (Cal. 1999) (substantial-factor test permitted worker to maintain products liability complaint against 55 manufacturers of chemicals that allegedly caused his cancer).

[98] See, e.g., Burton v. R.J. Reynolds Tobacco Co., 208 F. Supp. 2d 1187, 1213 (D. Kan. 2002) (although plaintiff smoked both Camels and Lucky Strikes, he could prevail against the manufacturer of Lucky Strikes by proving that smoking them was a substantial factor in bringing about his disease).

[99] Note, however, that the substantial-factor test may not be used to undermine comparative fault, which may make a defendant liable even for very small proportions of a plaintiff's injuries. See, e.g., Burton v. R.J. Reynolds Tobacco Co., 208 F. Supp. 2d 1187, 1213 (D. Kan. 2002). Consequently, an attempt to quantify the "size" of the substantial factor in a jury instruction may be reversible error. See Jeter v. Owens-Corning Fiberglas Corp., 716 A.2d 633, 636–37 (Pa. Super. Ct. 1997) ("considerable" and "significantly large" improperly described required connection). See generally Prosser and Keeton on Torts § 41, at 267 ("The 'substantial factor' formulation is one concerning legal significance rather than factual quantum.").

[100] Dobbs, Law of Torts § 174, at 422; Rest. (2d) Torts § 433A(1)(a) and cmt. *b*.

factor in producing the damage is held jointly and severally responsible for the total loss.[101]

In *Buehler v. Whalen*,[102] for example, the plaintiffs were injured in a fire that erupted when their car was hit by another vehicle driven by Whalen. They sued Whalen for negligent driving and the manufacturer of the car in which they were riding, Ford Motor Co., for designing an uncrashworthy automobile. Whalen argued that all damages should be apportioned to Ford, since the plaintiffs' only injuries were burns caused by the uncrashworthy design of the car's fuel system. Upholding joint and several liability against Whalen as well as Ford, the Illinois Supreme Court reasoned that Whalen's negligent driving caused the collision, which precipitated the fire. Because the injuries were indivisible, the "concurrent" tortfeasors were both jointly and severally responsible for the entire harm.[103] Another example one day may involve the liability of manufacturers of smart phones without lock-out mechanisms to prevent drivers from driving negligently due to distractions from incoming calls or texts.[104]

The doctrine of joint and several liability has been widely altered in many jurisdictions (and abolished altogether in a few states) due to the rise of comparative fault and apportionment, spurred by tort reform. While the general approach of reform statutes is to apportion damages to a defendant proportionate to that defendant's fault or responsibility in causing the plaintiff's harm, variations between the statutes are significant, and there no longer is a majority rule in this area of the law.[105] Accordingly, a lawyer is referred on these issues, first, to the statutory and other law of the applicable jurisdiction and, second, to specialized texts and the *Apportionment Restatement*.

A special difficulty exists if a plaintiff can trace his or her injuries to a single type of product manufactured by A, B, or C but is unable to identify which manufacturer produced the offending product. Under conventional principles, since the plaintiff has the burden of proof on causation, the plaintiff's case in this type of situation will fail.[106]

Multiple Defendants—Theories of Collective Liability

The law normally requires that a plaintiff identify the manufacturer of the specific product that caused his or her harm—the fundamental causal identification requirement

---

[101] See, e.g., Smith v. J.C. Penney Co., 525 P.2d 1299 (Or. 1974) (plaintiff suffered severe burns from her excessively flammable imitation fur coat that caught fire when service station operator negligently sprayed gasoline on floor heater). See Dobbs, Law of Torts § 174, at 423; Rest. (2d) Torts § 433B(3).

[102] 374 N.E.2d 460 (Ill. 1977).

[103] "We have here a classic case of concurrent tortfeasors whose separate acts combine to produce a single individual injury. Under these circumstances there is no apportionment." Id. at 465. The issue of damages apportionment in indivisible-injury crashworthiness cases is examined in § 17.4, below.

[104] **Texting.** Yet courts, at least so far, have failed to hold smart phone companies concurrently liable for failing to provide lock-out mechanisms to prevent people from texting while driving. In Meador v. Apple, Inc., 911 F.3d 260, 265 (5th Cir. 2018), a driver instinctively looked down at her iPhone to read an incoming text message, causing a collision with an oncoming car. Plaintiffs claimed that Apple was liable for failing to warn of distracted driving and failing to equip its phone with a lock-out mechanism. Upholding the district court's dismissal of the claims, the court noted that no court has ruled that a phone's triggering of a driver's "unconscious and automatic, neurobiological compulsion to engage in texting behavior" is a substantial factor, together with a driver's negligence, in causing an ensuing accident.

[105] The Rest. (3d) Torts: Apportionment of Liability (2000) identified at least five variations on the use of joint and several liability. See id. Topic 2, Liability of Multiple Tortfeasors for Indivisible Harm, Introductory note, at 98–99 (describing five separate "tracks").

[106] See, e.g., Garcia v. Joseph Vince Co., 148 Cal. Rptr. 843, 846–47 (Ct. App. 1978) ("Hamlet II"), discussed below in connection with alternative liability. The defendant identification problem is discussed in § 11.2, above.

examined earlier.[107] Plaintiffs injured by toxic substances confront a variety of multiple-defendant causation problems, some of which were examined above.[108] Even in toxic substance cases, plaintiffs sometimes can reliably trace their injuries to a specific drug, chemical, or asbestos product. Yet, if the substance has left no identifying traces, it may be impossible for a plaintiff to identify its manufacturer. When such products undoubtedly are defective—like asbestos products sold without warnings of their serious health hazards, defective generic drugs like DES, or blood products infected with the AIDS virus—plaintiffs and courts alike have sought to find an equitable way to shift the resulting losses to some or all members of the industry that profited from the sale of the defective products, while still requiring the plaintiff to prove some causal link between the defendants and the harm. The most prominent theory of this type is "market share liability," but plaintiffs have also turned to other collective liability theories, including "alternative liability," "enterprise liability" (sometimes called "industry-wide liability"), "concert of action," and "civil conspiracy." None of these theories has gained widespread endorsement, but a lawyer needs to be aware of their possible use as well as their benefits and limitations.[109]

Market Share Liability

In 1980, in *Sindell v. Abbott Laboratories*,[110] the California Supreme Court gave judicial birth to the doctrine of market share liability. *Sindell* involved class actions by various women for injuries they suffered from taking a synthetic form of the hormone estrogen, diethylstilbesterol, called DES. Manufacturers first marketed DES in the early 1940s as a form of hormone replacement for menopause and for the treatment of senile and gonorrheal vaginitis. During the late 1940s, doctors began to prescribe DES to help prevent miscarriages, and eventually the drug was manufactured generically and sold for this purpose by some 300 pharmaceutical companies.[111] In 1971, the FDA banned the drug when researchers discovered that it could cause a form of vaginal cancer (adenocarcinoma), and precancerous growths in the vagina and cervix (adenosis), in

---

[107] See § 11.2, above.

[108] See id.

[109] See generally Hastings and Williams, Market Share Liability: Lessons from New Hampshire v. Exxon Mobil, 34 J. Envtl. L. & Litig. 219 (2019); Greene, Civil Conspiracy and the Rule of Law: A Proposal for Reappraisal and Reform, 64 Ark. L. Rev. 301 (2011); Robertson, Causation in the Restatement (Third) of Torts: Three Arguable Mistakes, 44 Wake Forest L. Rev. 1007 (2009); Ausness, Conspiracy Theories: Is There a Place for Civil Conspiracy in Products Liability Litigation?, 74 Tenn. L. Rev. 383 (2007); Yong, Faure, Fenn, and Willis, Multiple Tortfeasors: An Economic Analysis, 3 Rev. L. & Econ. 111 (2007); Gifford and Pasicolan, Market Share Liability Beyond DES Cases: The Solution to the Causation Dilemma in Lead Paint Litigation?, 58 S.C. L. Rev. 115 (2006); Geistfeld, The Doctrinal Unity of Alternative Liability and Market-Share Liability, 155 U. Pa. L. Rev. 447 (2006); Rostron, Beyond Market Share Liability: A Theory of Proportional Share Liability for Nonfungible Products, 52 UCLA L. Rev. 151 (2004); Bernstein, Hymowitz v. Eli Lilly and Co.: Markets of Mothers, Torts Stories 151 (R. Rabin & S. Sugarman eds., 2003); Leach, Civil Conspiracy: What's the Use?, 54 U. Miami L. Rev. 1 (1999); Klein, Beyond DES: Rejecting The Application of Market Share Liability in Blood Products Litigation, 68 Tul. L. Rev. 883 (1994); V. Schwartz and Mahshigian, Failure to Identify the Defendant in Tort Law: Towards a Legislative Solution, 73 Cal. L. Rev. 941 (1985); Fischer, Products Liability—An Analysis of Market Share Liability, 34 Vand. L. Rev. 1623 (1981); Annot., 63 A.L.R.5th 195 (1998) (concert of activity, alternate liability, market share liability, and enterprise liability); Frumer, Friedman, and Sklaren, Products Liability § 3.06.

By prohibiting "the use of enterprise theories of liability against manufacturers in product liability claims," an Ohio statute outlaws some or all of these multiple-defendant theories of recovery. See State v. Brunner, 872 N.E.2d 912, 920 (Ohio 2007) (overturning governor's veto of bill containing this prohibition).

[110] 607 P.2d 924 (Cal. 1980).

[111] *Sindell* put the total number of manufacturers at about 200, id. at 931, but subsequent opinions put the higher figure. See, e.g., In re DES Litig., 7 F.3d 20, 21 (2d Cir. 1993) (N.Y. law).

daughters of women who took the drug during pregnancy.[112] Although DES pills came in all different shapes and colors, each pill was chemically identical, and pharmacists typically filled prescriptions from whatever stock they had on hand. Thus, most women taking the pills had no idea who manufactured them, and by the time their daughters realized they had been injured by the drug (the reproductive tract injuries did not manifest themselves until puberty), it often was impossible to identify the manufacturer. Unable to identify the manufacturer of the DES taken by her mother, the named plaintiff in *Sindell* sought recovery against ten major manufacturers of the drug. Because of her failure to identify the particular manufacturer that made the precise drug ingested by her mother, the trial court dismissed the action.

Adopting a theory of "market share liability,"[113] the California Supreme Court reversed. Because DES manufacturers chose to sell a drug generically that could cause harm long after its sale, allowing them to cover their tracks with the winds of time, the court reasoned that they each should be responsible for the share of total harm for which they statistically were responsible.[114] Expanding upon its earlier alternative-liability decision in *Summers v. Tice*,[115] the celebrated quail hunter case in which a pellet from one shotgun of two negligent hunters injured the plaintiff's eye, the *Sindell* court reasoned that the burden of proof on causation in such a case should be shifted to the defendants, provided that the plaintiff had joined the manufacturers of a "substantial share" of the DES her mother may have taken.[116] Unless a manufacturer could prove that it did not manufacture the drug taken by the plaintiff's mother,[117] each would be severally liable[118] for the share of the plaintiff's injuries represented by the share of the DES market it supplied.[119]

It is difficult to quarrel with the logic and fairness of market share liability: if manufacturers benefit from selling a generic product with unduly harmful consequences

---

[112] Subsequent cases were brought by DES sons. See, e.g., Doe v. Eli Lilly & Co., Prod. Safety & Liab. Rep. (BNA) 604–05 (D.D.C. 1985) (verdict for plaintiff). And DES grandchildren. See, e.g., Grover v. Eli Lilly, 591 N.E.2d 696 (Ohio 1992) (no cause of action). The intergenerational duty issue is examined in § 10.5, above.

[113] The court borrowed the market share idea from Comment, DES and a Proposed Theory of Enterprise Liability, 46 Fordham L. Rev. 963 (1978).

[114] "In our contemporary complex industrialized society, advances in science and technology create fungible goods which may harm consumers and which cannot be traced to any specific producer. The response of the courts can be either to adhere rigidly to prior doctrine, denying recovery to those injured by such products, or to fashion remedies to meet these changing needs." 607 P.2d at 936.

[115] 199 P.2d 1 (Cal. 1948).

[116] "If plaintiff joins . . . the manufacturers of a substantial share of the DES which her mother might have taken, the injustice of shifting the burden of proof to defendants to demonstrate that they could not have made the substance which injured plaintiff is significantly diminished." *Sindell*, 607 P.2d at 937. The plaintiff's briefs asserted that six or seven companies had manufactured about 90% of all DES, which, if true, would leave only a 10% chance "that the offending producer would escape liability." Id. The student Comment from which the court borrowed the market share idea suggested that a plaintiff join 75–80% of the manufacturers, 46 Fordham L. Rev. at 995–96, but the court rejected these percentages as too high. See 607 P.2d at 937.

[117] For example, by proof that its pills all were round and yellow, when the mother testified that all her pills were triangular and white.

[118] In Brown v. Superior Ct., 751 P.2d 470 (Cal. 1988), the court clarified *Sindell* on this point, specifying that a manufacturer's liability under the market share theory is several only, thus limiting a particular manufacturer's liability in any case to the proportion of the plaintiff's damages that corresponds to its percentage share of the pertinent market.

[119] The court reasoned that it was "reasonable in the present context to measure the likelihood that any of the defendants supplied the product which allegedly injured plaintiff by the percentage which the DES sold by each of them for the purpose of preventing miscarriage bears to the entire production of the drug sold by all for that purpose." *Sindell*, 607 P.2d at 937.

that they know cannot be traced to them, they fairly may be held responsible for the share of harm appropriately assigned to each. For this reason, variations of market share liability, sometimes under other names, were adopted by the high courts of several states in addition to California, notably Wisconsin, Michigan, Washington, New York, Florida, and Hawaii, together with a handful of lower state and federal courts.[120] Each of these decisions altered the operational specifics of *Sindell* somewhat, and each except Hawaii applied the doctrine to DES.[121]

But the market share liability theory confronted two major obstacles—one practical, the other doctrinal. The practical objection, noted but belittled by the *Sindell* court,[122] is the enormous difficulty in ascertaining appropriately sized market shares for individual manufacturers. Regardless of how one resolves the significant issue of whether to designate the "market" as the plaintiff's pharmacy (or pharmacies), neighborhood, town, city, county, state, nation, or the entire world, other difficulties in finding particularized distribution records from the various manufacturers and retail pharmacies decades after sale may be colossal, to say the least.[123] The doctrinal or policy objection to market share liability is that it simply does too much violence to the fundamental tort law element of factual causation—in particular, to the fundamental requirement that a plaintiff identify the specific product, manufactured by a specific defendant before the court, that probably caused the injuries for which recovery is sought.[124]

---

[120] See Collins v. Eli Lilly Co., 342 N.W.2d 37 (Wis. 1984) ("risk contribution theory"); Abel v. Eli Lilly & Co., 343 N.W.2d 164 (Mich. 1984) ("alternative liability"); Martin v. Abbott Labs., 689 P.2d 368 (Wash. 1984) ("market share alternate liability"); Hymowitz v. Eli Lilly & Co., 539 N.E.2d 1069 (N.Y. 1989); Conley v. Boyle Drug Co., 570 So.2d 275 (Fla. 1990) (for negligence claims); Smith v. Cutter Biological, Inc., 823 P.2d 717 (Haw. 1991) (for blood cases). See also Jackson v. Glidden Co., 647 N.E.2d 879, 883–84 (Ohio Ct. App. 1995) (lead paint); McCormack v. Abbott Labs., 617 F. Supp. 1521 (D. Mass. 1985) (DES); McElhaney v. Eli Lilly & Co., 564 F. Supp. 265 (D.S.D. 1983) (same).

[121] Wisconsin's high court subsequently applied its risk contribution theory to lead paint. Thomas v. Mallett, 701 N.W.2d 523, 548–66 (Wis. 2005). After legislation and a series of decisions on its retroactive application, Burton v. E.I. du Pont de Nemours & Co., Inc., 994 F.3d 791, 813–14 (7th Cir. 2021), held that a trial court erred in extending the theory to suppliers of paint with white lead carbonite paint pigment produced by other manufacturers. See also Allen v. American Cyanamid, 527 F. Supp. 3d 982, 992 (E.D. Wis. 2021) (denying defendant's motion for summary judgment on plaintiffs' risk-contribution theory).

[122] The *Sindell* court observed that it was "not unmindful of the practical problems involved in defining the market and determining market share," noting that the defendants asserted that there are no figures available to determine market share; that DES was used for a number of conditions other than miscarriage prevention; and it would be difficult to ascertain the proportion used for miscarriage prevention, a relevant time frame, and an area for market share. 607 P.2d 924, 938 n.29.

[123] See Fischer, Products Liability—An Analysis of Market Share Liability, 34 Vand. L. Rev. 1623 (1981).

[124] See § 11.2, above. See, e.g., Sutowski v. Eli Lilly & Co., 696 N.E.2d 187, 190 (Ohio 1998):

> The plaintiff must establish a causal connection between the defendant's actions and the plaintiff's injuries, which necessitates identification of the particular tortfeasor. . . . Under the market-share theory, the plaintiff is discharged from proving this important causal link. The defendant actually responsible for the plaintiff's injuries may not be before the court. Such a result collides with traditional tort notions of liability by virtue of responsibility, and imposes a judicially created form of industry-wide insurance upon those manufacturers subject to market-share liability. In the end, [this forces manufacturers to pay for injuries their product may not have caused, which is not the law of Ohio where] "Manufacturers are not insurers of their products."

In Ferris v. Gatke Corp., 132 Cal. Rptr. 2d 819, 829 (Ct. App. 2003), the court rejected market share liability in an asbestos case: "From *Sindell* onward courts . . . have underlined repeatedly the extraordinary departure from conventional tort law doctrine, with its Aristotelian conception of causation, such notions represent. . . . [C]ourts should employ such group liability concepts with great caution and only after being satisfied that the circumstances invoked in support of their application are truly compelling."

Largely because of these two obstacles, market share liability has been rejected by a large majority of courts.[125] A small number of decisions from market share states have allowed such claims outside of DES litigation,[126] but most courts have rejected efforts to extend it beyond DES to such contexts as lead paint,[127] asbestos,[128] breast implants, guns, blood, tire rims,[129] and a miscellany of other types of products.[130]

Other Theories of Collective Liability

In addition to market share liability, courts have fashioned a number of other collective liability theories in an attempt to provide compensation to plaintiffs unable to identify the manufacturers of the specific products that caused their injuries, sometimes (as in the asbestos context) fixing responsibility on members of an industry who still are solvent. Different courts refer to similar theories by different names, and the elements

[125] See, e.g., Thurmon v. Georgia Pac., LLC, 650 Fed. Appx. 752, 757 (11th Cir. 2016) (Ga. law) (asbestos); Sutowski v. Eli Lilly & Co., 696 N.E.2d 187 (Ohio 1998); Smith v. Eli Lilly & Co., 560 N.E.2d 324 (Ill. 1990); Shackil v. Lederle Labs., 561 A.2d 511 (N.J. 1989) (DPT vaccines for children); Mulcahy v. Eli Lilly & Co., 386 N.W.2d 67 (Iowa 1986) (en banc); Zafft v. Eli Lilly & Co., 676 S.W.2d 241 (Mo. 1984) (en banc). See also Summers v. Abbott Labs., 2013 WL 125730, at *2 (E.D.N.Y. 2013) (Quebec courts "would not permit recovery under a market share theory"); Gianvito v. Premo Pharm. Labs., 940 N.Y.S.2d 272, 274 (App. Div. 2012) (N.J. law) (no market share liability); Payton v. Abbott Labs, 437 N.E.2d 171 (Mass. 1982). Some state statutes prohibit claims under market share liability. See Ga. Code Ann. § 51–1–11(d) (manufacturers not subject to liability "on theories of market share or enterprise, or other theories of industry wide liability"); Ohio Rev. Code Ann. § 2307.73(C) (no "market share, enterprise, or industrywide liability").

[126] See, e.g., Thomas v. Mallett, 701 N.W.2d 523, 548–66 (Wis. 2005) (lead paint) (for subsequent limitation of market share liability in Wisconsin see note 121, above); Jackson v. Glidden Co., 647 N.E.2d 879 (Ohio Ct. App. 1995) (lead paint); Richie v. Bridgestone/Firestone, Inc., 27 Cal. Rptr. 2d 418 (Ct. App. 1994) (asbestos in brake products); Ray v. Cutter Labs., 754 F. Supp. 193 (M.D. Fla. 1991) (blood products); Smith v. Cutter Biological, Inc., 823 P.2d 717 (Haw. 1991) (same); Morris v. Parke, Davis & Co., 667 F. Supp. 1332 (C.D. Cal. 1987) (DPT vaccine). A Vermont statute allowed the state to pursue recovery of Medicaid tobacco-related health expenses under the market share theory. See Vt. Stat. Ann. tit. 33, § 1911(f).

[127] The landmark case was Santiago v. Sherwin Williams Co., 3 F.3d 546 (1st Cir. 1993) (2–1 decision) (Mass. law) (amicus containing inimitable footnote 3). See also City of St. Louis v. Benjamin Moore & Co., 226 S.W.3d 110 (Mo. 2007) (en banc) (4–3 decision); Lewis v. Lead Indus. Ass'n, Inc., 793 N.E.2d 869 (Ill. App. Ct. 2003); Brenner v. American Cyanamid Co., 699 N.Y.S.2d 848 (App. Div. 1999); Skipworth v. Lead Indus. Ass'n, 690 A.2d 169 (Pa. 1997). Compare Setliff v. E.I. Du Pont Nemours & Co., 38 Cal. Rptr. 2d 763 (Ct. App. 1995) (paint, solvents, strippers, and glue products).

[128] See, e.g., Ferris v. Gatke Corp., 132 Cal. Rptr. 2d 819, 826 n.3 (Ct. App. 2003) (noting the "phalanx of judicial decisions from across the nation, overwhelmingly declining to apply a *Summers/Sindell*-based burden-shifting instruction to asbestos-related personal injury tort litigation"); Black v. Abex Corp., 603 N.W.2d 182 (N.D. 1999); Leng v. Celotex Corp., 554 N.E.2d 468, 470–71 (Ill. 1990); Gaulding v. Celotex Corp., 772 S.W.2d 66, 70–71 (Tex. 1989); Goldman v. Johns-Manville Sales Corp., 514 N.E.2d 691 (Ohio 1987); Celotex Corp. v. Copeland, 471 So.2d 533, 537–39 (Fla. 1985). See also Farris v. 3M Co., 2019 WL 1904206, at *4 (N.D. Cal. 2019) (dismissing market-share asbestos exposure liability claim without prejudice to amend complaint).

[129] See, e.g., In re Dow Corning Corp., 250 B.R. 298, 363 (Bankr. E.D. Mich. 2000) ("no court has permitted a breast implant plaintiff to utilize the market-share theory to prove her claim"); District of Columbia v. Beretta U.S.A. Corp., 2002 WL 31811717 (D.C. Super. Ct. 2002) (guns), rev'd in part on other grounds, 847 A.2d 1127 (D.C. 2004); Hamilton v. Beretta U.S.A. Corp., 750 N.E.2d 1055 (N.Y. 2001) (same); Spencer v. Baxter Int'l, Inc., 163 F. Supp. 2d 74 (D. Mass. 2001); Tirey v. Firestone Tire & Rubber Co., 513 N.E.2d 825 (Ohio Ct. C.P. 1986) (tire rims); Cummins v. Firestone Tire & Rubber Co., 495 A.2d 963 (Pa. Super. Ct. 1985) (same).

[130] See, e.g., Napier v. Osmose, Inc., 399 F. Supp. 2d 811 (W.D. Mich. 2005) (arsenic pesticide; alternative liability theory without proof of causation conflicts with statutory bar of joint and several liability); Bly v. Tri-Continental Indus., 663 A.2d 1232, 1244 (D.C. 1995) (benzene); York v. Lunkes, 545 N.E.2d 478 (Ill. App. Ct. 1989) (car battery that exploded); Kinnett v. Mass Gas & Elec. Supply Co., 716 F. Supp. 695 (D.N.H. 1989) (Me. law) (heat tape that allegedly caused fire); Bixler v. Avondale Mills, 405 N.W.2d 428 (Minn. Ct. App. 1987) (cotton flannelette).

of each theory vary from jurisdiction to jurisdiction, but the contours of the theories are roughly similar.[131]

Alternative liability. *Sindell* is an outgrowth of the theory that has become known as "alternative liability," illustrated by *Summers v. Tice*,[132] which shifts the burden of proof on causation to two or more defendants when their independent, tortious actions threatened harm to a plaintiff who cannot establish which particular defendant caused the harm. The *Restatement (Second) of Torts* adopts this principle: "Where the conduct of two or more actors is tortious, and it is proved that harm has been caused to the plaintiff by only one of them, but there is uncertainty as to which one has caused it, the burden is upon each such actor to prove that he has not caused the harm."[133] The *Third Restatement* similarly shifts the burden of proof to the defendants in this type of situation.[134]

A very few courts have applied some form of alternative liability to certain multiple-defendant products liability situations.[135] But the alternative liability theory presumes that there are only two or a small number of defendants who are all before the court,[136]

---

131 See, e.g., In re Methyl Tertiary Butyl Ether ("MTBE") Prods. Liab. Litig., 739 F. Supp. 2d 576, 598 (S.D.N.Y. 2010) (discussing the judge's newly-created "commingled product theory of liability," a hybrid of market share liability and concurrent wrongdoer liability). See also State v. Exxon Mobil Corp., 406 F. Supp. 3d 420, 458 (D. Md. 2019) (denying defendants' motion to dismiss products liability MTBE gasoline water supply contamination claims for failure to plead causation; "Maryland courts would allow the State to proceed on its claims under the commingled product theory, which is 'closer to traditional causation than market share liability.' However, it applies only when: (1) the product of each defendant is present in the commingled product, and; (2) the commingled product caused the plaintiff's harm."); In re Methyl Tertiary Butyl Ether ("MTBE") Prods. Liab. Litig., 725 F.3d 65, 117 n.39 (2d Cir. 2013) (N.Y. law) (declining to review the commingled product theory on appeal because the theory was not considered by the jury during the trial of the New York City claims); In re Methyl Tertiary Butyl Ether ("MTBE") Prods. Liab. Litig., 980 F. Supp. 2d 425, 457 (S.D.N.Y. 2013) (finding that the City of Fresno could not rely on the commingled product theory in the absence of proof that "defendants' products were at the stations at issue when [MTBE] releases occurred").

132 199 P.2d 1 (Cal. 1948).

133 Rest. (2d) Torts § 433(B)(3). Illustration 9, following comment *h*, presents the *Summers* quail hunting facts.

134 See Rest. (3d) Torts: Liability for Physical and Emotional Harm § 28(b):

> When the plaintiff sues all of multiple actors and proves that each engaged in tortious conduct that exposed the plaintiff to a risk of harm and that the tortious conduct of one or more of them caused the plaintiff's harm but the plaintiff cannot reasonably be expected to prove which actor or actors caused the harm, the burden of proof, including both production and persuasion, on factual causation is shifted to the defendants.

135 See, e.g., Abel v. Eli Lilly & Co., 343 N.W.2d 164 (Mich. 1984) (DES). See also Jackson v. Glidden Co., 647 N.E.2d 879, 883 (Ohio Ct. App. 1995); Poole v. Alpha Therapeutic Corp., 696 F. Supp. 351, 355–56 (N.D. Ill. 1988) (blood products).

136 Even if there are only two defendants, both of their products must have been defective, or the doctrine does not apply. In Garcia v. Joseph Vince Co., 148 Cal. Rptr. 843, 846–47 (Ct. App. 1978) ("Hamlet II"), a college student's eye was injured during a fencing match when his opponent's saber penetrated his mask because its tip was thin and sharp instead of round. The saber was thereafter placed back in the team bag with all the other sabers and was not produced at trial because it had either been lost or "mixed up with the others in the shuffle." The coach had purchased the sabers from two manufacturers. Since there was no evidence pointing to either manufacturer in particular, plaintiff sued both under the alternative liability theory of *Summers v. Tice*. The plaintiff was nonsuited, and the judgments in favor of both defendants were affirmed. Because the evidence was evenly divided, the jury could only speculate as to which manufacturer had produced the offending saber, and *Summers v. Tice* did not apply to shift the burden of proof because only one of the defendants had acted tortiously toward the plaintiff.

See also Vincent v. C.R. Bard, Inc., 944 So.2d 1083, 1086 (Fla. Dist. Ct. App. 2006) (one of hospital's two brands of morphine pump failed; court declined to adopt alternative liability, stating that the doctrine would not apply anyway since plaintiff could not identify which pump failed). Compare Burks v. Abbott Labs., 917 F. Supp. 2d 902, 915–16 (D. Minn. 2013) (La. law) (predicting that Louisiana Supreme Court "would allow . . . alternative liability" as "a jury could reasonably find that both [defendants] breached a duty[,] all potentially and that the defendants are likely to know who among them caused the harm,[137] both of which conditions reduce the unfairness of shifting to the defendants the burden of establishing causation.[138] Because these conditions were not present in the litigation involving DES, the alternative liability theory was rejected by the California Supreme Court in *Sindell*,[139] as it has been rejected by many other courts in DES and various other contexts in products liability litigation.[140]

Enterprise liability. "Enterprise liability," also referred to as "industry-wide liability," was the first collective theory of liability devised for products liability litigation, initially proposed in 1972 by Judge Jack B. Weinstein in *Hall v. E.I. Du Pont De Nemours & Co.*[141] *Hall* and another case involved the liability of the blasting cap industry arising out of injuries to eighteen children across the nation who could not identify the manufacturers of blasting caps that injured them because the caps blew themselves to smithereens in each such incident. The defendants in *Hall* were the six blasting cap manufacturers (the entire American industry) and their trade association. Each manufacturer had acted independently, but each adhered to industry-wide safety standards, and they all delegated to their trade association certain safety responsibilities, including labeling standards and accident investigation. Liability was premised on the defendants' failure to place warnings on individual caps and to design the caps to make them more difficult for children to detonate. On motions to dismiss, Judge Weinstein ruled that each member of the industry could be held jointly liable only if the plaintiffs established that the defendants (1) were all aware of the risks, and (2) jointly controlled those risks. Recognizing that enterprise liability could not fairly be applied to industries that are large and decentralized, Judge Weinstein limited its application to small industries of five to ten producers.[142] The enterprise liability theory has not caught on, and other courts (including the California court in *Sindell*)[143] have

---

liable parties [were] before the Court[, and] the plaintiff cannot reasonably be expected to prove which actor or actors caused the harm"); Drayton v. Pilgrim's Pride Corp., 472 F. Supp. 2d 638, 646–48 (E.D. Pa. 2006) (plaintiffs' alternative liability theory survived summary judgment; all processors of tainted turkey products were named as defendants and evidence supported no other possible source of plaintiffs' illness). Compare Ruiz v. Wintzell's Huntsville, L.L.C., 2017 WL 4305004 (N.D. Ala. 2017) (80% of oysters in restaurant's inventory came from one defendant supplier).

[137] So that shifting the burden of proof onto defendants collectively might "smoke out" the guilty party.

[138] See, e.g., Snider v. Bob Thibodeau Ford, Inc., 202 N.W.2d 727, 732–33 (Mich. Ct. App. 1972), where plaintiff was injured when the defective brakes on his delivery truck failed. Since plaintiff was unable to prove whether the manufacturer or dealer had caused the defect, the trial court directed a verdict for the manufacturer. Reversing, the appellate court pointed out that courts may shift the burden of proof when fairness or policy reasons so counsel. Here, because of the technical nature of brake systems, Ford's expertise, and its close relationship with the dealer, the court shifted "the burden of negating individual responsibility for the brake failure" to the defendants.

[139] See Sindell v. Abbott Labs., 607 P.2d 924, 931 (Cal. 1980).

[140] See, e.g., Garcia v. Pfizer, Inc., 268 Fed. Appx. 270, 275–76 (5th Cir. 2008) (Tex. law) (polio vaccine); Doe v. Baxter Healthcare Corp., 380 F.3d 399 (8th Cir. 2004) (Iowa law) (blood products); Spencer v. Baxter Int'l, Inc., 163 F. Supp. 2d 74, 79 (D. Mass. 2001) (same); Burns v. Haines Equip., Inc., 726 N.Y.S.2d 516, 519–20 (App. Div. 2001) (loading machine); Rutherford v. Owens-Illinois, Inc., 941 P.2d 1203, 1220–21 (Cal. 1997) (asbestos); Setliff v. E.I. Du Pont de Nemours & Co., 38 Cal. Rptr. 2d 763, 767 (Ct. App. 1995) (chemicals, solvents, glues, strippers, and paints); City of Phila. v. Lead Indus. Ass'n, 994 F.2d 112, 127–28 (3d Cir. 1993) (Pa. law) (lead paint pigments); Gaulding v. Celotex Corp., 772 S.W.2d 66, 68–69 (Tex. 1989) (asbestos); Hymowitz v. Eli Lilly & Co., 539 N.E.2d 1069, 1074 (N.Y. 1989) (DES); Senn v. Merrell-Dow Pharms., Inc., 751 P.2d 215 (Or. 1988) (DPT vaccine); Bixler v. Avondale Mills, 405 N.W.2d 428, 430–32 (Minn. Ct. App. 1987) (flannelette in nightshirt); Mulcahy v. Eli Lilly & Co., 386 N.W.2d 67 (Iowa 1986) (DES).

[141] 345 F. Supp. 353 (E.D.N.Y. 1972).

[142] Id. at 378.

[143] Sindell v. Abbott Labs., 607 P.2d 924, 935 (Cal. 1980).

uniformly refused to apply this not illogical, but clearly radical, departure from the basic causal requirement of product identification.[144]

Concert of action. The "concert of action" theory of liability results in collective liability when, under a common plan or scheme, a party assists, participates with, or actively encourages one or more wrongdoers who tortiously harm the plaintiff.[145] The classic concert of action cases involve drag races, where one car hits the plaintiff and the driver of the other car is also held liable for tortiously helping create the risk that harms the plaintiff.[146] Thus, concert of action turns on an actor's participation in and furtherance of group activity that the actor knows to be tortious toward the plaintiff, a kind of "aiding and abetting" of another who actively and unlawfully causes the plaintiff's harm.[147] The *Second Restatement* expresses the concert of action principle in § 876,[148] a section on which courts and commentators frequently rely.

---

[144] See, e.g., Dickens v. A-1 Auto Parts & Repair, Inc., 2018 WL 5726206, at *1 (S.D. Miss. 2018) (asbestos contaminated brake pads); Vu v. Ortho-McNeil Pharm., Inc., 602 F. Supp. 2d 1151, 1155 (N.D. Cal. 2009) (children's cold medicine); Thomas v. Mallett, 701 N.W.2d 523, 566 (Wis. 2005) (lead paint); Lewis v. Lead Indus. Ass'n, Inc., 793 N.E.2d 869, 874–75 (Ill. App. Ct. 2003) (same); In re Methyl Tertiary Butyl Ether ("MTBE") Prods. Liab. Litig., 175 F. Supp. 2d 593, 622 (S.D.N.Y. 2001) (gasoline additive that polluted ground water: "To invoke the theory of enterprise liability, plaintiffs must allege that (1) the injury-causing product was manufactured by one of a small number of defendants in an industry; (2) the defendants had joint knowledge of the risks inherent in the product and possessed a joint capacity to reduce those risks; and (3) each of them failed to take steps to reduce the risk but, rather, delegated this responsibility to a trade association."); Doe v. Cutter Biological, Inc., 852 F. Supp. 909, 914 (D. Idaho 1994) (blood products); Lee v. Baxter Healthcare Corp., 721 F. Supp. 89, 94 (D. Md. 1989) (breast implants); Case v. Fibreboard Corp., 743 P.2d 1062 (Okla. 1987) (asbestos); Martin v. Abbott Labs., 689 P.2d 368, 380 (Wash. 1984) (DES); Ryan v. Eli Lilly & Co., 514 F. Supp. 1004, 1017 (D.S.C. 1981) (S.C. and N.C. law) (DES) (observing that the "expansive notion of vicarious liability represented by the enterprise concept which would render every manufacturer an insurer not only of the safety of its own products, but of all generically similar products made by others is repugnant to the most basic tenets of tort law").

[145] "The concerted action theory of liability rests upon the principle that 'those who, in pursuance of a common plan or design to commit a tortious act, actively take part in it, or further it by cooperation or request, or who lend aid or encouragement to the wrongdoer, or ratify and adopt his acts done for their benefit, are equally liable with him. Express agreement is not necessary, and all that is required is that there be a tacit understanding.' W. Prosser, Handbook of the Law of Torts, § 46 at 292 (4th ed. 1970)." Collins v. Eli Lilly Co., 342 N.W.2d 37, 46 (Wis. 1984) (rejecting concert of action theory of liability in DES case).

[146] See, e.g., Chavers v. Gatke Corp., 132 Cal. Rptr. 2d 198, 205 (Ct. App. 2003) (citing drag racing cases); Bierczynski v. Rogers, 239 A.2d 218 (Del. 1968); Ogle v. Avina, 146 N.W.2d 422 (Wis. 1966).

[147] See, e.g., In re Opioid Litig., 2018 WL 4827862, at *4–5 (N.Y. Sup. 2018) (trial order) (defendant opioid manufacturers and distributors "devised and implemented deceptive marketing campaigns designed to eliminate [stigma] of opioid use [so] the medical community and the public would embrace prescription opioid therapy for noncancer-related pain"); Shackil v. Lederle Labs., 561 A.2d 511, 515 (N.J. 1989) (citing Ryan v. Eli Lilly & Co., 514 F. Supp. 1004, 1015 (D.S.C. 1981)). Concert of action thus should be contrasted to alternative liability, which presupposes the independence of the actors.

[148] In the Rest. (2d) Torts chapter on "Contributing Tortfeasors," the general principle of joint and several liability for jointly tortious conduct is expressed in § 875:

> Each of two or more persons whose tortious conduct is a legal cause of a single and indivisible harm to the injured party is subject to liability to the injured party for the entire harm.

Section § 876, "Persons Acting in Concert," presents the strongest case for joint liability:

> [O]ne is subject to liability if he
>
> (a) does a tortious act in concert with the other or pursuant to a common design with him, or
>
> (b) knows that the other's conduct constitutes a breach of duty and gives substantial assistance or encouragement to the other so to conduct himself, or
>
> (c) gives substantial assistance to the other in accomplishing a tortious result and his own conduct, separately considered, constitutes a breach of duty to the third person.

A couple of courts, on summary judgment motions in cases where plaintiffs are unable to identify the makers of their drugs, have allowed concert of action claims, holding that "conscious parallelism" by the manufacturers to suppress warnings of side effects,[149] or to sell without warnings drugs they knew to be ineffective and dangerous,[150] might render them subject to liability to plaintiffs injured by the drugs. Further, at least a couple courts have allowed concert of action claims against manufacturers of toxic chemicals supplied to the plaintiff's employer,[151] and the court in at least one cigarette case allowed the plaintiff to proceed on such a claim.[152] But the great majority of decisions hold to the contrary,[153] agreeing with the *Sindell* court's conclusion that applying the concert of action theory to industry-wide sharing of information and techniques in most situations stretches this joint-liability theory beyond its proper scope "and would render virtually any manufacturer liable for the defective products of an entire industry, even if it could be demonstrated that the product which caused the injury was not made by the defendant."[154]

Civil conspiracy. A "civil conspiracy" is a combination of two or more persons for the purpose of accomplishing by concerted action an unlawful purpose or a lawful purpose by unlawful means.[155] A civil conspiracy is not a tort in and of itself, and a plaintiff alleging civil conspiracy must plead and prove an underlying tort (often fraud) or other unlawful act on which the conspiracy claim may rest.[156] Like concert of action,

---

See also Rest. (3d) Torts: Apportionment of Liability § 15 ("When persons are liable because they acted in concert, all persons are jointly and severally liable for the share of comparative responsibility assigned to each person engaged in concerted activity.").

[149] See Dawson v. Bristol Labs., 658 F. Supp. 1036, 1039 (W.D. Ky. 1987) (tetracyclines administered to infants eventually stained their primary teeth).

[150] See Abel v. Eli Lilly & Co., 343 N.W.2d 164 (Mich. 1984) (DES).

[151] See Eastridge v. Goodrich Corp., 2013 WL 5460868 (W.D. Ky. 2013) (vinyl chloride); Roney v. Gencorp, 431 F. Supp. 2d 622, 632–34 (S.D. W. Va. 2006) (same).

[152] See Sackman v. Liggett Grp., Inc., 965 F. Supp. 391, 396 (E.D.N.Y. 1997) (defendant conspired to repress health risks).

[153] See, e.g., Dickens v. A-1 Auto Parts & Repair, Inc., 2018 WL 5726206, at *1 (S.D. Miss. 2018) (asbestos-lined brake pads); Kennedy v. Lasting Points, 947 A.2d 503, 507 (Md. 2008) (lead paint); In re Welding Fume Prods. Liab. Litig., 2007 WL 1087605, at *12–13 (N.D. Ohio 2007) (manganese); Chavers v. Gatke Corp., 132 Cal. Rptr. 2d 198, 205 (Ct. App. 2003) (asbestos brake products); Brenner v. American Cyanamid Co., 732 N.Y.S.2d 799, 801 (App. Div. 2001) (lead pigment); Christian v. Minnesota Mining & Mfg. Co., 126 F. Supp. 2d 951 (D. Md. 2001) (breast implants); In re Kings Cnty. Tobacco Litig., 723 N.Y.S.2d 304, 306 (Sup. Ct. 2000) (tobacco); Jodway v. Kennametal, Inc., 525 N.W.2d 883, 890–91 (Mich. Ct. App. 1994) (cobalt dust); Rastelli v. Goodyear Tire & Rubber Co., 591 N.E.2d 222, 225 (N.Y. 1992) (multipiece rim); Smith v. Cutter Biological, Inc., 823 P.2d 717, 726 (Haw. 1991) (blood products); Hymowitz v. Eli Lilly & Co., 539 N.E.2d 1069, 1074–75 (N.Y. 1989) (DES; without an express or tacit agreement, substantial parallel conduct in developing and marketing product does not suffice); Shackil v. Lederle Labs., 561 A.2d 511, 515–16 (N.J. 1989) (DPT vaccine); Collins v. Eli Lilly Co., 342 N.W.2d 37, 46 (Wis. 1984) (DES); Sheffield v. Eli Lilly & Co., 192 Cal. Rptr. 870, 887–88 (Ct. App. 1983) (Salk polio vaccine).

[154] Sindell v. Abbott Labs., 607 P.2d 924, 933 (Cal. 1980).

[155] See, e.g., Lewis v. American Cyanamid Co., 2006 WL 701981, at *4 (Ill. App. Ct. 2006); Lewis v. Lead Indus. Ass'n, Inc., 793 N.E.2d 869, 878 (Ill. App. Ct. 2003); Wright v. Brooke Grp. Ltd., 652 N.W.2d 159, 172–74 (Iowa 2002); Adcock v. Brakegate, Ltd., 645 N.E.2d 888, 893–94 (Ill. 1994). See generally Greene, Civil Conspiracy and the Rule of Law: A Proposal for Reappraisal and Reform, 64 Ark. L. Rev. 301 (2011); Ausness, Conspiracy Theories: Is There a Place for Civil Conspiracy in Products Liability Litigation?, 74 Tenn. L. Rev. 383, 383–420 (2007).

[156] See, e.g., Lloyd v. General Motors Corp., 916 A.2d 257, 284–85 (Md. 2007) (facts of fraudulent concealment sufficiently pled for civil conspiracy); Tuttle v. Lorillard Tobacco Co., 377 F.3d 917, 926 (8th Cir. 2004) (Minn. law) (because fraud claim insufficient for want of reliance, "the civil conspiracy claim, which depends on a viable underlying tort, must fail as well"); Wright v. Brooke Grp. Ltd., 652 N.W.2d 159, 172 (Iowa 2002); Brown v. Philip Morris Inc., 228 F. Supp. 2d 506, 517 (D.N.J. 2002) ("[c]ivil conspiracy is not an independent cause of action, and conspiracy liability depends on the presence of an underlying [tort]").

to which it is closely related,[157] a civil conspiracy finding provides a basis for extending liability beyond an active tortfeasor to others who worked together to effectuate the unlawful result,[158] rendering each member of the conspiracy jointly liable for all consequences ensuing from the wrong.[159] Moreover, a civil conspiracy claim may avoid federal preemption in tobacco litigation.[160]

While a defendant's *participation* in unlawful conspiracy must be intentional,[161] while the underlying wrong *may* be intentional (such as fraud),[162] and while several jurisdictions *require* that the underlying tort or other wrong be intentional,[163] the better view is that the underlying wrong may simply be the sale of a product known to be defective—conduct that may rest on negligence, warranty, or strict liability in tort.[164] Although civil conspiracy claims occasionally survive motions to dismiss and for summary judgment,[165] such claims routinely are found wanting in products liability litigation.[166]

A final note is necessary on a company's participation in a trade association.[167] Such participation alone does not subject the member to conspiracy liability for damages from defective products made and sold by other members of the association. First, civil

---

[157] Courts often look to § 876 of the Second Restatement as the basis for civil conspiracy as well as concert of action claims. See, e.g., Wright v. Brooke Grp. Ltd., 652 N.W.2d 159, 172–74 (Iowa 2002).

[158] See, e.g., Wright v. Brooke Grp. Ltd., 652 N.W.2d 159, 172 (Iowa 2002) ("conspiracy is merely an avenue for imposing vicarious liability on a party for the wrongful conduct of another with whom the party has acted in concert"); Sackman v. Liggett Grp., Inc., 965 F. Supp. 391, 394–95 (E.D.N.Y. 1997) ("A claim for civil conspiracy 'is merely the string whereby the plaintiff seeks to tie together those who, acting in concert, may be held responsible in damages for an overt act or acts.' ").

[159] See, e.g., Chavers v. Gatke Corp., 132 Cal. Rptr. 2d 198, 201 (Ct. App. 2003) ("the coconspirators are liable in the same way and [extent] as the principal who actually commits the harmful or outlawed act").

[160] See, e.g., Burkhart v. R.J. Reynolds Tobacco Co., 884 F.3d 1068, 1093 (11th Cir. 2018) (Fla. law); Grills v. Philip Morris USA, Inc., 645 F. Supp. 2d 1107, 1124–26 (M.D. Fla. 2009) (conspiracy to commit fraud); Gerrity v. R.J. Reynolds Tobacco Co., 399 F. Supp. 2d 87, 94–96 (D. Conn. 2005) (same).

[161] "There is no such thing as accidental, inadvertent or negligent participation in a conspiracy." Adcock v. Brakegate, Ltd., 645 N.E.2d 888, 894 (Ill. 1994).

[162] See, e.g., Waterhouse v. R.J. Reynolds Tobacco Co., 270 F. Supp. 2d 678, 685–86 (D. Md. 2003) (fraudulent misrepresentation); Johnson v. Brown & Williamson Tobacco Corp., 122 F. Supp. 2d 194 (D. Mass. 2000) (same).

[163] See, e.g., Flanders v. Garlock, Inc., 2003 WL 22697241, at *3 (S.D. Ga. 2003) (civil conspiracy claim must be based on "underlying intentional tortious conduct"); Altman v. Fortune Brands, Inc., 701 N.Y.S.2d 615 (App. Div. 2000); Sonnenreich v. Philip Morris Inc., 929 F. Supp. 416, 419 (S.D. Fla. 1996); Triplex Commc'ns, Inc. v. Riley, 900 S.W.2d 716, 719–20 (Tex. 1995). These decisions sometimes point to the apparent illogic of conspiring to do a negligent act. See Wright v. Brooke Grp. Ltd., 652 N.W.2d 159, 172–73 (Iowa 2002).

[164] See, e.g., Wright v. Brooke Grp. Ltd., 652 N.W.2d 159, 172–73 (Iowa 2002); In re Methyl Tertiary Butyl Ether ("MTBE") Prods. Liab. Litig., 175 F. Supp. 2d 593, 633–34 (S.D.N.Y. 2001) (Cal., Fla., Ill., and N.Y. law); Adcock v. Brakegate, Ltd., 645 N.E.2d 888, 894–95 (Ill. 1994).

[165] See, e.g., R.J. Reynolds Tobacco Co. v. Rouse, 307 So.3d 89, 95 (Fla. Dist. Ct. App. 2020) (tobacco); Jones v. Pneumo Abex LLC, 160 N.E.3d 881, 891 (Ill. 2019) (remanding for appellate review of plaintiffs' civil conspiracy claims against asbestos manufacturers and distributors under "clear and convincing" standard); Lloyd v. General Motors Corp., 916 A.2d 257, 285 (Md. 2007) (conspiracy to fraudulently conceal dangers in seat backs); Lewis v. Lead Indus. Ass'n, Inc., 793 N.E.2d 869 (Ill. App. Ct. 2003) (lead paint).

[166] See, e.g., In re Nat'l Prescription Opiate Litig., 458 F. Supp. 3d 665, 679–80 (N.D. Ohio 2020) (Mich. law) (opioids; dismissing civil conspiracy claims under statutory immunity for FDA-approved drugs); Grills v. Philip Morris USA, Inc., 645 F. Supp. 2d 1107, 1124–26 (M.D. Fla. 2009) (cigarettes); In re Welding Fume Prods. Liab. Litig., 2007 WL 1087605, at *9–12 (N.D. Ohio 2007) (manganese); Thomas v. Mallett, 701 N.W.2d 523, 566 (Wis. 2005) (lead paint); Doe v. Baxter Healthcare Corp., 380 F.3d 399 (8th Cir. 2004) (Iowa law) (blood products); Tuttle v. Lorillard Tobacco Co., 377 F.3d 917, 926 (8th Cir. 2004) (Minn. law) (smokeless tobacco); Chavers v. Gatke Corp., 132 Cal. Rptr. 2d 198, 201–03 (Ct. App. 2003) (asbestos products); In re Orthopedic Bone Screw Prods. Liab. Litig., 193 F.3d 781 (3d Cir. 1999) (Pa. law) (bone screws).

[167] On the liability of trade associations and the First Amendment, see § 15.7, below.

conspiracy requires a showing that the defendant's *purpose* of participating in a group activity was to do something unlawful, whereas the educational, developmental, promotional, and lobbying activities in which trade associations normally engage can hardly be characterized as violative of law. Second, participation in such activities may be constitutionally protected under the First Amendment, particularly if they involve lobbying for governmental standards.[168] But the First Amendment is not a teflon defense in every case of civil conspiracy, for it provides no protection to manufacturers that conspire to violate the law.[169]

§ 11.4 WARNING CASES—SPECIAL CAUSATION ISSUES

As with other types of products liability claims, factual causation is a necessary element of a warning defect claim.[170] No matter how dangerous a defective warning may make a product, the plaintiff must prove that the absence of that safety information caused the plaintiff's injury. In warning cases, like most others, the plaintiff ordinarily must prove causation by the but-for test—that the accident probably would not have occurred but for the absence of adequate warnings, that it probably would have been averted had adequate warnings been provided. If the provision of an adequate warning would have made no difference, in that the plaintiff probably would have been injured anyway, then a warning claim will fail on causation grounds.[171]

The causal connection between a warning or instruction defect and the plaintiff's harm is sometimes clear. If given proper information about serious hazards under their control, people naturally seek to avoid those dangers. It thus is likely that the user of a propane heater, if warned that it might cause asphyxiation if used inside a tent, would use some other means to warm the tent;[172] that a user of a telescope, if instructed on how properly to install a sun filter, would install it with utmost care;[173] and that the user of a spermicide contraceptive, if warned that it might cause birth defects if conception does occur, would use a different form of contraception.[174] In none of these instances is

[168] See, e.g., Chavers v. Gatke Corp., 132 Cal. Rptr. 2d 198, 206–07 (Ct. App. 2003) (requiring asbestos manufacturer to stand trial for civil conspiracy or concert of action claims without proof of unlawful intent might chill defendant's First Amendment freedom of association to contribute to, attend the meetings of, and otherwise associate with trade groups engaging in public advocacy and debate); Hamilton v. Accu-tek, 935 F. Supp. 1307, 1321 (E.D.N.Y. 1996) (*Noerr-Pennington* doctrine: lobbying before federal or state authorities cannot alone support liability); In re Asbestos Sch. Litig., 46 F.3d 1284, 1294 (3d Cir. 1994) (Pa. law).

[169] See, e.g., Lewis v. Lead Indus. Ass'n, Inc., 793 N.E.2d 869 (Ill. App. Ct. 2003) (lead paint; plaintiffs' civil conspiracy claim allowed); Rogers v. R.J. Reynolds Tobacco Co., 761 S.W.2d 788 (Tex. App. 1988).

[170] See, e.g., Moore v. Ford Motor Co., 332 S.W.3d 749, 761 (Mo. 2011) ("plaintiff must show causation in fact by showing that the product for which there was no warning caused the injuries"); R & R Insulation Servs., Inc. v. Royal Indem. Co., 705 S.E.2d 223, 233 (Ga. Ct. App. 2010) ("A breach of a duty to warn [must] be the cause of the injury about which the plaintiff complains, and the plaintiff must present evidence supporting a reasonable inference that the warning provided by the defendant would prevent the injury."); Gantt v. Absolute Mach. Tools, Inc., 2007 WL 2908254, at *3 (M.D. Pa. 2007) (lack or insufficiency of warning must be a cause in fact of plaintiff's injuries); Burley v. Kytec Innovative Sports Equip., Inc., 737 N.W.2d 397, 410 (S.D. 2007); In re Norplant Contraceptive Prods. Liab. Litig., 215 F. Supp. 2d 795, 830 (E.D. Tex. 2002).

[171] See, e.g., Pedicone v. Thompson/Center Arms Co., 2022 WL 521378, at *5 (Del. Super. Ct. 2022) (injured gun owner testified that he does not read gun manuals; " '[y]ou can look at them and tell they operate the same way' "); Miaoulis v. Toyota Motor N. Am., Inc., 2021 WL 117513, at *4–5 (Ark. Ct. App. 2021) (no evidence that a different warning would have made a difference); Estate of White v. R.J. Reynolds Tobacco Co., 109 F. Supp. 2d 424, 435 (D. Md. 2000) ("An essential element of plaintiffs' failure-to-warn claims is causation—plaintiffs must show that" Mr. White would have heeded an adequate warning, but the evidence shows that Mr. White "would have kept on smoking").

[172] See Benjamin v. Wal-Mart Stores, Inc., 61 P.3d 257 (Or. Ct. App. 2002).

[173] See Midgley v. S.S. Kresge Co., 127 Cal. Rptr. 217 (Ct. App. 1976).

[174] See Wells v. Ortho Pharm. Corp., 788 F.2d 741 (11th Cir. 1986) (Ga. law).

it certain that proper warnings and instructions would have averted harm, but in all of them it is quite probable, which satisfies the but-for test.

Sometimes causation is plainly absent from a warning claim. Not infrequently, even the most complete information on product hazards and how to avoid them would not alter a user's actions or avert an accident. Many cases where no such causal link exists involve claims that a manufacturer should have warned about a risk of which the plaintiff already was aware. If a user already knows about a hidden danger, warning the user further will almost certainly do no good, for such a user is unlikely to change his or her behavior from receiving information he or she already possesses.[175] A manufacturer still has a *duty* to warn of a material hidden risk of which a particular user happens to be aware, but the absence of *causation* fatally undermines a warning claim by such a user.[176] Thus, a worker who already knows the danger of using his hand to unjam a machine without cutting off its power, cannot prove that affixing that same warning to the machine would have caused him to turn it off;[177] nor can a mother, who puts her young child in the front seat of a vehicle who already knows to seat young children in the rear because the front seat airbag could kill them, show that further warning of that very risk would have caused her to place her child in the back;[178] nor can testimony by a surgeon who already knows the dangers of a surgical cutter/stapler establish that he would have stopped using the device had he been warned about those same dangers in a package insert or "Dear Doctor" letter from the manufacturer."[179]

Causation is also clearly missing in other contexts. A driver of a car with a high center of gravity, even if warned that it might roll over if the steering wheel were sharply turned, will probably instinctively turn the wheel sharply to avoid a high-speed collision with a concrete rail, despite the driver's awareness of the risk of rolling over.[180] It is similarly likely that a user of ski bindings, even if warned that they might not release in

---

[175] See, e.g., In re Taxotere (Docetaxel) Prods. Liab. Litig., 859 Fed. Appx. 692, 694 (5th Cir. 2021) (La. law) ("a reasonable person, with all of the information [plaintiff] possessed, would not have changed her mind by reading a warning that told her what she already knew"). Consider Vallillo v. Muskin Corp., 514 A.2d 528, 530 (N.J. Super. Ct. App. Div. 1986) (if the user knows "the very danger . . . the warning would have apprised him, but chooses to disregard that conscious knowledge, then the presence or absence of the warning is irrelevant"; yet, if "the danger had been even momentarily forgotten by the user and there is some reasonable possibility that the warning would have triggered his recollection of the danger and thus changed his conduct, then the absence of a warning is a proper ingredient in a proximate cause analysis"). Thus, in certain situations of substantial, recurring danger where distractions are likely, a manufacturer may possibly have a duty to *remind*. See § 10.2, above.

[176] Because duty arises categorically, it applies to all consumers, even those who do not need protection. See Rest. (3d) Torts: Liability for Physical and Emotional Harm §§ 6 and 7. See also Burke v. Spartanics, Ltd., 252 F.3d 131, 137 (2d Cir. 2001) (N.Y. law) (Calabresi, J.) (explaining distinction between duty and causation); § 10.2, above, at notes 115–119 and 127–129 (examining duty to warn of obvious dangers).

[177] See Clarke v. LR Sys., 219 F. Supp. 2d 323 (E.D.N.Y. 2002); Zimmermann v. Baker-Perkins, Inc., 707 F. Supp. 778, 781 (E.D. Pa. 1989).

[178] See DaimlerChrysler Corp. v. Hillhouse, 161 S.W.3d 541 (Tex. App. 2004), vacated on settlement, 2006 Tex. Lexis 25 (2006).

[179] See Ethicon Endo-Surgery, Inc. v. Meyer, 249 S.W.3d 513, 518–19 (Tex. App. 2007).

[180] See Greiner v. Volkswagenwerk A.G., 429 F. Supp. 495, 497 (E.D. Pa. 1977) ("It is simply not within the bounds of human reason to suppose that, had there been a warning, Nickel would have recalled it, considered it and then intentionally crashed head-on into a concrete rail."). See also Roy v. Volkswagenwerk A.G., 600 F. Supp. 653 (C.D. Cal. 1985) (VW van rolled over when driver swerved to avoid hitting dog); Conti v. Ford Motor Co., 743 F.2d 195, 196–97 (3d Cir. 1984) (Pa. law) (driver knew not to start car in gear, without depressing clutch, while his wife was entering the car). Compare Staymates v. ITT Holub Indus., 527 A.2d 140, 147 (Pa. Super. Ct. 1987) (warning could not prevent "instinctive, knee-jerk reaction").

every situation, might use them anyway, and break a leg;[181] that a driver who falls asleep at the wheel, even if warned by a flashing arrow on a malfunctioning traffic sign to go another way, might crash into the sign;[182] and that a doctor who fails to read a drug manufacturer's warning about the side-effects of an antidepressant, even if told that it posed a risk of suicide, might still prescribe it.[183] Occasionally, the plaintiff,[184] or (more frequently) the plaintiff's doctor,[185] will simply admit that the knowledge provided by an adequate warning would not have altered his or her behavior. Sometimes it thus is very clear that warning information would have made no difference.[186] In each such case, the plaintiff has failed to prove but-for causation—that adequate warnings or instructions probably would have averted the harm. Put conversely, the absence of adequate safety information from a warning in each such case probably did not cause the plaintiff's harm. Without causation, a warning claim will fail.

Yet causation may connect a warning defect to an injury in different ways, and a user's failure to read a warning may or may not destroy causation depending on the way in which the warning was inadequate. It will be recalled that a warning may be deficient in one of two basic ways: either because it fails to provide sufficient "substantive" information about the nature or extent of a hazard, on the one hand, or because its display is hard to see, in which case the warning's inconspicuousness renders it "procedurally" inadequate.[187] A user's failure to read a *substantively* deficient warning defeats causation because even a warning with adequate information presumably would have remained unread.[188] Yet, if a warning was unread for the very reason that it failed

---

[181] See Salk v. Alpine Ski Shop, Inc., 342 A.2d 622, 626 (R.I. 1975) ("[P]laintiff did not allege that had he been warned of the inevitable dangers of skiing, he would not have skied; nor did he allege that he would have purchased other bindings and that other bindings would have prevented his injury. Quite to the contrary, . . . plaintiff has continued to ski.").

[182] See Lear Siegler, Inc. v. Perez, 819 S.W.2d 470 (Tex. 1991).

[183] See Motus v. Pfizer, Inc., 358 F.3d 659 (9th Cir. 2004) (Cal. law).

[184] See, e.g., Neilson v. Corporation of Presiding Bishop, 2002 WL 31188444, at *9 (Wash. Ct. App. 2003) (plaintiff admitted that he still would have tried double somersault on trampoline even if he had read an adequate warning about its dangers).

[185] See, e.g., Rodman v. Ethicon, Inc., 2021 WL 2434521, at *5 (W.D. Wash. 2021) (plaintiff's doctor testified that, if warned, she still would have implanted the allegedly defective mesh); Payne v. Novartis Pharms. Corp., 967 F. Supp. 2d 1223, 1233 (E.D. Tenn. 2013) (doctor admitted he still prescribes the medication "in spite of his knowledge of the risk"); Ackermann v. Wyeth Pharms., 526 F.3d 203, 209–12 (5th Cir. 2008) (Tex. law) (doctor said he still would have prescribed the drug even if the manufacturer had provided different warnings).

[186] See, e.g., Rhodes v. Bayer Healthcare Pharm. Inc., 2013 WL 1282450, at *3–4 (W.D. La. 2013) ("Because the defective aspect of the product must cause the injury, the plaintiff must show that a proper warning would have changed the decision of the treating physician; but for the inadequate warning, the treating physician would not have used or prescribed the product."; yet plaintiff's counsel never asked her doctor "whether he would have changed his decision to prescribe Avelox to Ms. Rhodes if an allegedly different warning had been given"); Jones v. Hittle Serv., Inc., 549 P.2d 1383 (Kan. 1976) (gas travelled through soil, leaked into plaintiff's basement, where it exploded; even if it should have been odorized with 9 pounds of odorant instead of only 1, too much of the odor would have leached out in the soil to be smelled by plaintiffs to alert them to the danger in time to avoid the explosion). See also Burton v. E.I. du Pont de Nemours & Co., Inc., 994 F.3d 791, 824 (7th Cir. 2021) (Wis. law) (no evidence that warning of lead poisoning from childhood exposure to lead paint would have changed consumer behavior in the early 20th century).

[187] See § 9.3, above.

[188] See, e.g., Peart v. Dorel Juvenile Group, Inc., 456 Fed. Appx. 446, 448 (5th Cir. 2012) (La. law) (since plaintiff admitted in her deposition that she did not read the existing warning labels on a step stool, the absence of an additional warning was not a but-for cause of her fall therefrom); Altman v. HO Sports Co., 821 F. Supp. 2d 1178, 1190 (E.D. Cal. 2011) (any deficiencies in warnings on boot or in owner's manual "do not matter because Altman never read them"); Smith v. Sears Roebuck & Co., 232 Fed. Appx. 780, 784 (10th Cir. 2007) (Okla. law) (plaintiff never read owner's manual); Palmer v. Volkswagen of Am., Inc., 904 So.2d 1077, 1084 (Miss. 2005) (same); Hiner v. Bridgestone/Firestone, Inc., 978 P.2d 505 (Wash. 1999) (same).

to catch the user's eye, because the warning was inconspicuous, then it may be supposed that a more prominent warning would have attracted the user's attention and thereby averted harm. Causation in this latter type of case may well exist.[189]

Special Causal Problems in Warning Claims

Warning cases present certain *special* causation problems.[190] Unlike the causal examples just provided, where causation appears quite clearly present or quite clearly absent, the causal connection between a warning defect and the plaintiff's injury is usually quite uncertain. This differs from manufacturing and design defect claims, where the factual causation issue typically is clear. A major reason for this difference, which explains why figuring causation in warning cases usually is problematic, lies in the wide gulf between Newtonian physics and Freudian psychology. In Newtonian physics, the operations of cause and effect used to prove causation in design and manufacturing defect cases are often clear. In most such cases, the defect itself often contains a plain physical linkage to the plaintiff's injury: if a machine is defectively designed because its pinch points are unguarded, then guarding the pinch points will probably keep out human limbs; if a tire is defectively designed or manufactured, causing its tread to fly off at highway speeds, then the tread probably will stay affixed to the tire carcass, avoiding an accident, if the design and manufacturing processes both are proper. Experts may dispute whether a machine is "defective" without a guard, and whether a tread separation was due to a defect or poor maintenance, but once a design or manufacturing defect is established, its causal connection to the plaintiff's injury usually is plain. Causation, in such cases, is proven (and may be controverted) by hard science.

Causation in a warning case is an entirely different kettle of fish. Proving that an adequate warning would have prevented the plaintiff's harm depends on the vagaries of human psychology, requiring speculation on whether the user would have read and followed the warning had it in fact been provided.[191] While proving causation in design

---

[189] See, e.g., Morris v. Harley Davidson Motor Co., 2010 WL 2723079, at *3 (M.D. Ga. 2010) (no summary judgment on causation where inadequate warning claim rested on manufacturer's failure "to place a warning in such position, color and size print or to use symbols which would call the user's attention to the warning or cause the user to be more likely to read the label and warning than not"); Folsom v. Kawasaki Motors Corp. U.S.A., 509 F. Supp. 2d 1364, 1378 n.11 (M.D. Ga. 2007) (because plaintiff failed to read warning on jet ski about risks of off-throttle steering loss, she could not challenge its substance, but she could challenge its conspicuousness); Penwell v. Rust-Oleum Corp., 2006 WL 3792660, at *3 (W.D. Wis. 2006) (denying summary judgment for defendant on inadequate warning claim for lack of causation because plaintiff asserted that "she did not see or read the warning because it did not stand out").

[190] See, e.g., Geistfeld, Inadequate Product Warnings and Causation, 30 U. Mich. J.L. Reform 309 (1997); Fischer, Causation in Fact in Product Liability Failure to Warn Cases, 17 J. Prod. & Toxics Liab. 271 (1995); Latin, "Good" Warnings, Bad Products, and Cognitive Limitations, 41 UCLA L. Rev. 1193, 1286 n.413 (1994); Henderson and Twerski, Doctrinal Collapse in Products Liability: The Empty Shell of Failure to Warn, 65 N.Y.U. L. Rev. 265 (1990).

[191] See General Motors Corp. v. Saenz, 873 S.W.2d 353, 357 (Tex. 1993) (emphasis omitted):

> Proving causation in a failure-to-warn case has peculiar difficulties. Proof that a collision between two cars would not have happened had defendant swerved or braked or driven within the speed limit is mostly a matter of physics. Proof that an accident would not have occurred if defendant had provided adequate warnings concerning the use of a product is more psychology and does not admit of the same degree of certainty. A plaintiff must show that adequate warnings would have made a difference in the outcome, that is, that they would have been followed. In the best case a plaintiff can offer evidence of his habitual, careful adherence to all warnings and instructions. In many cases, however, plaintiff's evidence may be little more than the self-serving assertion that whatever his usual practice may have been, in the circumstances critical to his claim for damages he would have been mindful of an adequate warning had it been given. In the worst case, where the user of the product is deceased, proof of what the decedent would or would not have done may be virtually impossible.

and manufacturing cases similarly rests on a but-for hypothetical (figuring whether elimination of the defect probably would have prevented the plaintiff's harm), the warning hypothetical turns on figuring human responses to information, not hard science. It is one thing to hypothesize that a guard of a certain configuration would have prevented a hand from entering a machine; it is quite another to posit that a teenager, who ignores extensive warnings and instructions on how to use a trampoline, will heed additional, more specific warnings of the dangers;[192] that an adult, warned that a baby left unstrapped in a high chair might get strangled in attempting to slide out, would always remember to strap the child in;[193] or that a mother, who allowed her young son to wear a T-shirt she knew could catch fire, would throw it away if warned that it was flammable.[194]

The point is not that adequate warnings in such cases would have made no difference, only that determining whether they would have averted harm rests on an uncomfortably slender reed. The most typical form of evidence used to prove causation in a warning case is the user's own testimony that he or she would have read and heeded an adequate warning or instruction if one had been provided. This forces the user in such cases into an awkward position of having to provide self-serving testimony on a hypothetical situation that requires the user to swear, as convincingly as possible, that a good warning or instruction would have caused him to change his behavior in some manner that would have averted injury. For the legal system to require plaintiffs to provide such highly speculative, self-serving testimony provides the thinnest basis for a finding of causation.

The "Heeding Presumption"

Beginning in the early 1970s, courts began adopting a "heeding presumption" to help plaintiffs surmount the inherent difficulties, just described, in proving causation in warning cases.[195] This is a legal presumption, which shifts the burden of production,[196] that a plaintiff would have read and heeded adequate warnings and instructions, had they been provided.[197] A heeding presumption relieves a plaintiff of the necessity of testifying affirmatively on this issue, which provides a vital basis for a finding of

---

[192] See Anderson v. Weslo, Inc., 906 P.2d 336, 341 (Wash. Ct. App. 1995) ("because Anderson was aware of the risks of injury, yet paid so little attention to the warnings that were given, it is unlikely that he would have changed his behavior in response to even more detailed warnings").

[193] Cf. McConnell v. Cosco, Inc., 238 F. Supp. 2d 970 (S.D. Ohio 2003) (jury question).

[194] Cf. Shouey v. Duck Head Apparel Co., 49 F. Supp. 2d 413 (M.D. Pa. 1999) (jury question).

[195] See Technical Chem. Co. v. Jacobs, 480 S.W.2d 602, 606 (Tex. 1972) (dictum).

[196] See, e.g., Sluis v. Ethicon, Inc., 529 F. Supp. 3d 1004, 1011–14 (D.S.D. 2021) (predicting that South Dakota Supreme Court would adopt the heeding presumption to shift the burden of production, but not the burden of persuasion, to the defendant; reviewing cases); Carter v. APP Pharm., LLC, 2013 WL 5532767, at *7 (D. Ariz. 2013) ("Where evidence has been introduced that satisfies the heeding presumption, the burden of production shifts to the manufacturer who must introduce evidence that would permit 'reasonable minds to conclude that the injured party would not have heeded an adequate warning.' ").

[197] See, e.g., Twerski and Cohen, Resolving the Dilemma of Nonjusticiable Causation in Failure-to-Warn Litigation, 84 S. Cal. L. Rev. 125, 132 (2010) (inspired proposal to substitute proportional recovery for causation in warning cases); Daniel, Guide to Defeating the Heeding Presumption in Failure-to-Warn Cases, 70 Def. Couns. J. 250 (2003); Henke, The Heeding Presumption in Failure to Warn Cases: Opening Pandora's Box?, 30 Seton Hall L. Rev. 174 (1999); Geistfeld, Inadequate Product Warnings and Causation, 30 U. Mich. J.L. Reform 309 (1997); Note, The Heeding Presumption and Its Application: Distinguishing No Warning from Inadequate Warning, 37 Loy. L.A. L. Rev. 461 (2003); Annot., 38 A.L.R.5th 683 (1996) (heeding presumption).

causation where a plaintiff is killed in the accident or otherwise dies before he or she is able to provide testimony in the case.[198]

The heeding presumption is rebuttable,[199] which permits a defendant to establish that a plaintiff most likely would *not* have read or heeded an adequate warning, had one been provided, on the facts and circumstances particular to the case. For example, a manufacturer may rebut the presumption by showing that "the user was blind, illiterate, intoxicated, . . . irresponsible or lax in judgment,"[200] or for some other reason probably would have ignored the warning.[201] Thus, if a plaintiff did not read other labels, warnings, instruction booklets, or other information provided with an accident product (or generally ignored safety information),[202] or was using the accident product with reckless abandon,[203] then it is quite unlikely that additional warnings would have helped protect the plaintiff from harm. But a plaintiff's failure to heed an inadequate warning fails to rebut the presumption.[204] While some states allow presumptions to remain in a case even after they have been rebutted, the better view is that once a defendant "meets its burden to come forward with evidence rebutting the presumption, the presumption disappears,"[205] like the proverbial bat in the light.

---

[198] See, e.g., Ford Motor Co. v. Boomer, 736 S.E.2d 724, 733–34 (Va. 2013) (worker who died from mesothelioma from inhaling dust from asbestos products "was never asked if his behavior would have been changed had he known that he was inhaling a potentially fatal substance," and he died before trial).

[199] See Kirkbride v. Terex USA, LLC, 798 F.3d 1343, 1351 (10th Cir. 2015) (Utah law) (by a preponderance of the evidence).

[200] Technical Chem. Co. v. Jacobs, 480 S.W.2d 602, 606 (Tex. 1972) (the presumption may be rebutted by "evidence that the user was blind, illiterate, intoxicated at the time of the use, irresponsible or lax in judgment or by some other circumstance tending to show that the improper use was or would have been made regardless of the warning"). *But see* Sharpe v. Bestop, Inc., 730 A.2d 285, 285–87 (N.J. 1999) (holding that "only evidence of a habit related to the specific situation of a seat-belt warning, not a character trait, may be offered to rebut the heeding presumption" and hesitating to endorse an approach to rebuttal evidence that considers users as possibly 'illiterate, . . . irresponsible or lax in judgment,' " because the latter two descriptions are character traits that may be inadmissible).

[201] See, e.g., Waterhouse v. R.J. Reynolds Tobacco Co., 162 Fed. Appx. 231, 234–35 (4th Cir. 2006) (Md. law) (heeding presumption "may be rebutted where there is 'evidence that the personalities or dispositions of the [plaintiffs show] that they clearly would have ignored warnings,' " as here where plaintiff admitted he knew risks of smoking); Golonka v. General Motors Corp., 65 P.3d 956, 972 (Ariz. Ct. App. 2003) (decedent never heeded owner's manual warning to set parking break, turn off ignition, and remove key).

[202] See, e.g., Kenney v. Watts Regul. Co., 512 F. Supp. 3d 565, 584–85 (E.D. Pa. 2021) (warning defect claim failed without evidence plaintiff knew about the water pressure regulating valve or its manual that contained maintenance instructions); Santos-Rodriguez v. Seastar Sols., 858 F.3d 695, 698 (1st Cir. 2017) (P.R. law) (no evidence plaintiff or mechanics maintaining the boat had read boat's steering system's manual); Kirkbride v. Terex USA, LLC, 798 F.3d 1343, 1351 (10th Cir. 2015) (Utah law) (vacating plaintiff's verdict on failure to warn claim; presumption "conclusively" rebutted: "Not only had Kirkbride not read the warning that was in the manual but he expressed a negative view of manuals." He testified: "Why would you read a manual?"); Scordill v. Louisville Ladder Grp., LLC, 2003 WL 22427981, at *8 (E.D. La. 2003) ("even if the instructions and warnings had been adequate, the accident would have still occurred because Scordill, not having read them, would have proceeded to use the ladder in the same manner in which he did").

[203] See, e.g., Hulmes v. Honda Motor Co., 960 F. Supp. 844, 854 (D.N.J. 1997) ("evidence that a plaintiff who has been warned about consuming alcohol prior to riding his ATV, and nevertheless, does so, is relevant to rebut the 'heeding presumption,' in that it portrays an individual who is unlikely to heed warnings").

[204] See, e.g., Evans v. Lorillard Tobacco Co., 990 N.E.2d 997, 1024 (Mass. 2013) ("Evidence that an addicted smoker failed to heed a warning that was given to her after she was already addicted is insufficient to rebut the presumption that, had she received adequate warning before she started smoking, she would have heeded the warning and avoided the addiction.").

[205] Tate v. Statco Eng'g & Fabricators, Inc., 2013 WL 6185476, at *8 (E.D. Okla. 2013), the "bursting bubble" approach.

Courts in more than half the states have now adopted the heeding presumption, at least where a defendant did not warn at all,[206] to help a plaintiff prove causation in warning claims.[207] However, some jurisdictions that allow the presumption as a general proposition refuse to apply it to pharmaceutical cases where, under the learned intermediary doctrine,[208] a manufacturer's only duty is to warn physicians.[209] And a few courts have simply rejected this special presumption as bad policy and contrary to established principles of causation.[210]

Apart from resolving the causal proof dilemma faced by plaintiffs in warning cases (a dilemma for which they have no blame), and apart from avoiding the need for speculative self-serving testimony,[211] two basic rationales have been offered for the heeding presumption, one doctrinal and the other policy. The doctrinal argument draws from a sentence in comment *j* to § 402A of the *Restatement (Second) of Torts* which provides that "[w]here warning is given, the seller may reasonably assume that it will

---

[206] Some jurisdictions allow the presumption if a defendant did not warn at all, but not when a substantively inadequate warning was provided. See, e.g., DaimlerChrysler Corp. v. Hillhouse, 161 S.W.3d 541 (Tex. App. 2004), vacated on settlement, 2006 Tex. Lexis 25 (2006); Note, The Heeding Presumption and Its Application: Distinguishing No Warning from Inadequate Warning, 37 Loy. L.A. L. Rev. 461 (2003).

[207] See, e.g., Williams v. Arctic Cat, Inc., 2012 WL 6086912 (N.D.N.Y. 2012) ("there it is a triable issue of fact whether Plaintiff would have heeded an on-product warning or more conspicuous warning in the manual concerning the increased likelihood of rollover by operating the Prowler on paved surfaces"); Moore v. Ford Motor Co., 332 S.W.3d 749, 763 (Mo. 2011) (reversing directed verdict for defendant; jury should weigh evidence whether plaintiff would have "heeded a warning about the risks the seats posed for persons of greater than normal weight"); Bass v. Air Prods. & Chems., Inc., 2006 WL 1419375, at *18 (N.J. Super. Ct. App. Div. 2006) ("product defect causation is often established through application of the 'heeding presumption' "); Golonka v. General Motors Corp., 65 P.3d 956, 965–72 (Ariz. Ct. App. 2003) (thorough discussion); Eagle-Picher Indus. v. Balbos, 604 A.2d 445, 468–69 (Md. 1992). *But see* Viguers v. Philip Morris USA, Inc., 837 A.2d 534 (Pa. Super. Ct. 2003) (reasons for allowing presumption in asbestos cases do not apply to tobacco cases).

[208] See § 18.3, below.

[209] See, e.g., In re Zimmer, NexGen Knee Implant Prods. Liab. Litig., 884 F.3d 746 (7th Cir. 2018) (heeding presumption not applied if surgeon did not read instructions for knee implant technique but relied on his prior training and experience); Dopson-Troutt v. Novartis Pharms. Corp., 975 F. Supp. 2d 1209, 1214 (M.D. Fla. 2013) (Pa. law) (Pennsylvania does not use the heeding presumption in pharmaceutical failure to warn cases); Solomon v. Bristol-Myers Squibb Co., 916 F. Supp. 2d 556, 563–64 (D.N.J. 2013) (Tex. law) (predicting that Texas courts would reject the heeding presumption in learned intermediary cases). *But see* Sluis v. Ethicon, Inc., 529 F. Supp. 3d 1004, 1014 (D.S.D. 2021) (questions of fact remained whether physician was adequately warned of pelvic mesh risks; "[M]ere rebuttal of the heeding presumption does not necessarily entitle the defendant to summary judgment. Instead, the defendant must show either that there is no genuine dispute of material fact on the adequacy of the warning or that an adequate warning would not have made a difference as a matter of law."); In re Prempro Prods. Liab. Litig., 586 F.3d 547, 569 (8th Cir. 2009).

[210] See, e.g., Castorina v. A.C. & S., 49 N.Y.S.3d 238 (Sup. Ct. 2017) (explaining complicated state of law on heeding presumption in NY, and concluding that its appellate courts have not adopted the presumption, and that it should not apply it in any event unless plaintiff or his family were unable to testify on reliance); Montemayor v. Sebright Prods., Inc., 2017 WL 5560180, at *3 (Minn. Ct. App. 2017); Dolby v. Ziegler Tire & Supply Co., 2017 WL 781650, at *5 (Pa. Super. Ct. 2017) (Pennsylvania courts use heeding presumption only in workplace asbestos exposure cases); Rivera v. Philip Morris, Inc., 209 P.3d 271, 277 (Nev. 2009) (declining to adopt heeding presumption; plaintiff in strict liability case has burden of proving all its elements, including causation): Tuttle v. Lorillard Tobacco Co., 377 F.3d 917, 925 (8th Cir. 2004) (Minn. law) (baseball player died of oral cancer; recognizing that "heeding presumption would be particularly beneficial," where Tuttle died before testifying he would have read and heeded warnings had smokeless tobacco manufacturers provided them, but ruling that presumption did not apply because Minnesota courts had not adopted it). Many federal courts have refused to predict that a state that had not addressed the issue would adopt this presumption. See, e.g., Robinson v. McNeil Consumer Healthcare, 671 F. Supp. 2d 975, 991 (N.D. Ill. 2009) (Va. law) (citing cases).

[211] See, e.g., Coffman v. Keene Corp., 628 A.2d 710, 720 (N.J. 1993) ("The heeding presumption accords with the manufacturer's basic duty to warn; it fairly reduces the victim's burden of proof; and it minimizes the likelihood that determinations of causation will be based on unreliable evidence."); Reyes v. Wyeth Labs., Inc., 498 F.2d 1264, 1281 (5th Cir. 1974) (Tex. law) (heeding presumption is beneficial because it avoids plaintiff's testimony that is so self-serving as to be useless).

be read and heeded." Because this provision has been viewed as creating a presumption protecting manufacturers when they *do* provide adequate warnings and instructions,[212] many courts have reasoned that this same provision must operate reciprocally as well, by protecting the plaintiff with a presumption when a manufacturer *fails* to provide a warning and the shoe is on the other foot.[213] The policy argument is that the duty to warn gives an incentive to manufacturers to provide safety information to users and consumers, and manufacturers should not be allowed a large loophole in this vital safety obligation from the causal proof conundrum in warning cases that victims of product accidents cannot avoid.[214]

While these two arguments have some appeal, they suffer from certain weaknesses. The comment *j* argument, that the heeding presumption is merely a trade-off for the reciprocal presumption afforded manufacturers, is undermined by the fact that the "presumption" comment *j* affords to manufacturers is only a straw horse. Although it is widely read more broadly, comment *j* in fact pertains only to the narrow category of unavoidably dangerous products such as alcohol, drugs, and cigarettes whose inherently hazardous nature makes warning the only way to improve their safety.[215] With such products, since there is no way to design away the dangers, providing a warning is all a manufacturer or other seller can do to reduce the risk of harm—after which, a seller has nothing else to do except to "assume [read: "hope"] that [its warning] will be read and heeded." This statement in comment *j* thus means simply that a manufacturer of an inherently hazardous product, one that is "unavoidably unsafe," avoids liability for harm by manufacturing the product properly and providing adequate warning of its inherent dangers. Thus, the "assumption" of comment *j* does not refer to a legal presumption, nor does comment *j* address normal types of products, but only those that are unavoidably unsafe.[216]

The other problem with the heeding presumption is that it is not logical—in fact, people commonly ignore most warnings and instructions, no matter how good they may be.[217] As mentioned earlier,[218] studies suggest that many warnings alter behavior very little, since few people read or heed them.[219] Many social science behavioral studies on

---

[212] See § 6.2, above.

[213] See, e.g., Technical Chem. Co. v. Jacobs, 480 S.W.2d 602, 606 (Tex. 1972) ("Such a presumption works in favor of the manufacturer when an adequate warning is present. Where there is no warning, as in this case, however, the presumption that the user would have read an adequate warning works in favor of the plaintiff user. In other words, the presumption is that Jacobs would have read an adequate warning.").

[214] See, e.g., Geistfeld, Inadequate Product Warnings and Causation, 30 U. Mich. J.L. Reform 309 (1997); Latin, "Good" Warnings, Bad Products, and Cognitive Limitations, 41 UCLA L. Rev. 1193 (1994). See also In re Diet Drug Litig., 895 A.2d 480, 484 (N.J. Super. Ct. App. Div. 2005) (examining policy rationales); Annot., 38 A.L.R.5th 683 § 2A (1996) (same).

[215] The meaning of comment *j* is explored in depth in § 6.2, above, and inherently hazardous products are examined in § 10.3, above.

[216] See Owen, The Puzzle of Comment *j*, 55 Hastings L.J. 1377 (2004).

[217] See Riley v. American Honda Motor Co., 856 P.2d 196, 200 (Mont. 1993) (rejecting heeding presumption as counterintuitive, since "warnings are everywhere in the modern world and often go unread or, where read, ignored"). Compare Coffman v. Keene Corp., 628 A.2d 710, 718 (N.J. 1993) ("Although empirical evidence may not demonstrate the soundness of a heeding presumption, an examination of the strong and consistent public policies that have shaped our laws governing strict products liability demonstrates the justification for such a presumption.").

[218] See § 9.3, above.

[219] See, e.g., Goldhaber and deTurk, Effects of Consumers' Familiarity With a Product on Attention to and Compliance With Warnings, 11 J. Prod. Liab. 29 (1988); Dorris and Purswell, Warnings and Human Behavior: Implications for the Design of Product Warnings, 1 J. Prod. Liab. 254 (1977).

the efficacy of warnings, and a guiding principle of behavioral economics, confirm the hypothesis that people regularly ignore warnings,[220] and that consumers routinely process whatever information they do receive irrationally.[221]

Much power resides in the argument that nothing in the right to adequate safety information confers on consumers the right to force manufacturers to pay for damages they did not cause. Not only would such a result clash with fundamental principles of fairness and corrective justice, but it has no parallel in design and manufacturing defect cases where the law does not hold manufacturers responsible for harm they do not cause. In short, causation is too important an element to be tossed to the wind without the most compelling reasons, for it is a vital crucible for deciding whether claims of wrongdoing and bad products are real or fancied.[222]

In the end, despite its substantial weaknesses, the heeding presumption, subject to rebuttal defeasance, appears worth the candle. First, it will be recalled that consumers fairly may assert a fundamental "right" to important safety information so they may decide how to use products safely and to choose to avoid certain dangerous products altogether.[223] Moreover, a plaintiff's causal burden can be particularly onerous in warning cases, as previously discussed, a fact that distinguishes the causal issue in this context from claims that challenge a product's manufacture or design. And it is this peculiarly unfair obstacle, present only in warning cases, which the heeding presumption seeks to address. Finally, it should be remembered that, rather than eliminating the causal requirement in warning cases, a heeding presumption merely shifts responsibility for proving the existence *vel non* of a causal link. Thus, even with a heeding presumption, the absence of causation still should bar a claim where a warning probably would have done no good.

Finally, any discussion of the heeding presumption would be incomplete without mention of an inspired, alternative proposal by Aaron Twerski and Neil Cohen in an important study of the causation problem in warning cases.[224] Because of the myriad psychological, neurological, and behavioral factors that render causation determinations in most warning cases highly speculative—and, hence, effectively "nonjusticiable"—these leading scholars argue that allowing full recovery in such cases (via the heeding presumption) over-compensates victims—who probably would have been harmed even had a good warning been provided—and that it over-deters manufacturers,[225] but that requiring plaintiffs to prove but-for causation in all its rigor in warning cases *under-*

---

[220] See Twerski and Cohen, Resolving the Dilemma of Nonjusticiable Causation in Failure-to-Warn Litigation, 84 S. Cal. L. Rev. 125, 134 (2010) (describing the literature and several empirical studies, explaining that "even the most optimistic studies have shown that well less than half of those to whom warnings are provided actually comply with them," and concluding that "a majority of injuries that occur in the absence of a warning would occur even if a warning were given").

[221] See, e.g., Symposium: Rational Actors or Rational Fools? The Implications of Psychology for Products Liability, 6 Roger Williams U. L. Rev. 1 (2000); Hanson and Kysar, Taking Behavioralism Seriously: The Problem of Market Manipulation, 74 N.Y.U. L. Rev. 630, 724 (1999); Hanson and Kysar, Taking Behavioralism Seriously: Some Evidence of Market Manipulation, 112 Harv. L. Rev. 1420, 1425 (1999); Henderson and Twerski, Doctrinal Collapse in Products Liability: The Empty Shell of Failure to Warn, 65 N.Y.U. L. Rev. 265, 307 (1992). See generally Sunstein, The Laws of Fear, 115 Harv. L. Rev. 1119, 1123 (2002) (reviewing P. Slovic, The Perception of Risk; "ordinary people often deal poorly with the topic of risk").

[222] See Henderson and Twerski, Doctrinal Collapse in Products Liability: The Empty Shell of Failure to Warn, 65 N.Y.U. L. Rev. 265, 303–08, 325 (1992) ("a presumption makes no good sense on the merits").

[223] See § 9.1, above.

[224] Twerski and Cohen, note 220, above.

[225] A problem that may lead to "warnings pollution." See § 9.3, above.

deters manufacturers and deprives most defective warning case victims of any recovery whatsoever. To avoid this causal conundrum, these scholars recommend replacing the causal proof requirement in warning cases with *proportional* recovery—based on the severity of a manufacturer's fault in failing to provide adequate warnings and the likelihood that a good warning would have prevented the harm.[226] So, unlike the all-or-nothing approach of present causation law, the Twerski-Cohen proposal would have fact finders blend fault, causation, and damages "to assess both the seriousness of the failure to warn and its possible causal implications in a single finding that will determine proportional responsibility."[227] Substituting proportional recovery for the heeding presumption's shift *vel non* in the burden of producing evidence might just be worth a try.

[226] "Under our proposal, a manufacturer who has failed to warn under circumstances in which a warning should have been given should be charged with a fraction of the harm following from that failure, with the size of the fraction to be determined by taking into account both the seriousness of the defendant's failure to warn (which necessarily incorporates both the frequency and magnitude of the harm to be avoided) and the likelihood that the warning would have effectively prevented the plaintiff's harm." Twerski and Cohen, 84 S. Cal. L. Rev. at 154.

[227] Id. at 160.

Chapter 12

PROXIMATE CAUSE

Table of Sections

§ 12.1 PROXIMATE CAUSE—GENERALLY

Proximate cause, though linked to cause in fact, is a separate element unto itself.[1] The issue usually called "proximate cause" is very different from the issue of factual causation.[2] Presupposing some factual connection between a defendant's breach of duty and the plaintiff's injury, proximate cause addresses instead the question of whether in fairness, policy, and practicality the defendant ought to be held legally accountable for the plaintiff's harm which in some manner is "remote" from the defendant's breach.[3] Proximate cause might thus be defined, if somewhat tautologically, as a reasonably close connection between a defendant's wrong and the plaintiff's injury, a connection that is not remote. More broadly, proximate cause is a doctrine that serves to limit a tortfeasor's responsibility to the consequences of risks viewed fairly as arising from the wrong.[4] Because "[i]t is always to be determined on the facts of each case upon mixed

---

[1] "[B]ut-for causation and proximate causation . . . are two quite distinct questions." In re Neurontin Mktg. & Sales Practices Litig., 712 F.3d 21, 34 (1st Cir. 2013) (federal and Cal. law); Dobbs, Law of Torts § 180, at 443 ("To prevail in a negligence action, the plaintiff must bear the burden of showing that the defendant's negligent conduct was not only a cause in fact of the plaintiff's harm, but also a proximate or legal cause."). See § 11.1, above.

[2] "Cause in fact requires a determination of cause and effect, which involves a sometimes rigorous comparison of physical, historical facts in the actual universe with those in a hypothetical universe from which the defendant's negligence is removed. Actual causation thus logically precedes and usually has little to do with the proximate cause inquiry into the array of fairness and justice considerations bearing on the propriety of imposing negligence responsibility on a person whose wrongdoing actually, though remotely, caused the plaintiff's harm." Owen, The Five Elements of Negligence, 35 Hofstra L. Rev. 1671, 1686 (2007).

[3] See Keeton, Dobbs, Keeton, and Owen, Prosser and Keeton on the Law of Torts § 42, at 264 (noting that proximate cause limits legal responsibility to "causes which are so closely connected with the result and of such significance" as to justify liability: "Some boundary must be set to liability for the consequences of any act, upon the basis of some social idea of justice or policy.").

[4] See generally Geistfeld, Proximate Cause Untangled, 80 Md. L. Rev. 420 (2021); Knobe and Shapiro, Proximate Cause Explained: An Essay in Experimental Jurisprudence, 88 U. Chi. L. Rev. 165 (2021); Gilead and M. Green, Positive Externalities and the Economics of Proximate Cause, 74 Wash. & Lee L. Rev. 1517 (2017); Owen, Figuring Foreseeability, 44 Wake Forest L. Rev. 1277 (2009); Zipursky, Foreseeability in Breach, Duty, and Proximate Cause, 44 Wake Forest L. Rev. 1247 (2009); Cardi, Purging Foreseeability: The New Vision of Duty and Judicial Power in the Proposed Restatement (Third) of Torts (pt. 1), 58 Vand. L. Rev. 739 (2005); Cardi, Reconstructing Foreseeability (pt. 2), 46 B.C. L. Rev. 921 (2005); Kelley, Restating Duty, Breach, and Proximate Cause In Negligence Law: Descriptive Theory and The Rule of Law, 54 Vand. L. Rev. 1039 (2001); Stapleton, Legal Cause: Cause-In-Fact and the Scope of Liability for Consequences, 54 Vand. L. Rev. 941 (2001); Matsuda, On Causation, 100 Colum. L. Rev. 2195 (2000); L. Green, The Causal Relation Issue in Negligence Law, 60 Mich. L. Rev. 543 (1962); Pound, Causation, 67 Yale L. Rev. 1 (1957); James and Perry, Legal Cause, 60 Yale L. Rev. 763 (1951); J. Page, Proximate Cause (2003).

considerations of logic, common sense, justice, policy and precedent,"[5] proximate cause is an "elusive butterfly"[6] that e'er evades a net of rules.[7]

Quite like duty, proximate cause provides a broad fairness cauldron into which many factual and legal issues are thrown and mixed together. Yet, while sometimes still referred to as "legal cause" (in an effort to distinguish it from factual cause), proximate cause is an issue of "fact" for resolution by a jury.[8] Whereas courts determine duty according to policy factors applicable to whole categories of actors in recurring situations, juries determine proximate cause according to fairness factors unique to every case.[9]

Proximate cause goes by a variety of names. Some courts still refer to it by the "legal cause" term just mentioned,[10] left over from the *Second Restatement*'s confusing umbrella term referring broadly to factual and proximate cause alike, as discussed below.[11] As for umbrella terms, "proximate cause" itself is commonly used to describe both causal issues, factual and proximate alike[12]—as commonly are the terms "cause" and "causation," words that more comfortably describe cause in fact alone. This terminological confusion means, of course, that a reader of judicial decisions discussing "proximate cause" (like "causation") needs to be on guard for the possibility that the court actually may be addressing the issue of cause in *fact*, not proximate cause at all.[13] In part to reduce confusion, the *Restatement (Third) of Torts* replaces the "proximate cause" appellation with "scope of liability."[14]

By whatever name, proximate cause is an elemental requirement of every products liability claim.[15] In applying proximate cause "principles," such as they may be, products

---

5 1 Street, Foundations of Legal Liability 110 (1906).

6 Accordini v. Security Cent., Inc., 320 S.E.2d 713, 714 (S.C. Ct. App. 1984) (Sanders, C.J.).

7 "Proximate cause cannot be reduced to absolute rules." Prosser and Keeton on Torts 279.

8 See, e.g., Miaoulis v. Toyota Motor N. Am., Inc., 2021 WL 117513, at *2 (Ark. Ct. App. 2021); Edwards v. Anderson Eng'g, Inc., 251 P.3d 660, 663 (Kan. Ct. App. 2011) Dobbs, Law of Torts § 182.

9 Owen, The Five Elements of Negligence, 35 Hofstra L. Rev. 1672, 1681–85 (2007).

10 See, e.g., Midland Mortg. Corp. v. Wells Fargo Bank, N.A., 926 F. Supp. 2d 780, 787 (D.S.C. 2013) ("legal cause is proved by establishing foreseeability"); Nemmers v. Ford Motor Co., 686 F.3d 486, 490 (8th Cir. 2012) (Iowa law) ("The defendant's conduct is not a legal cause if the harm that resulted from the defendant's negligence is so clearly outside the risks he assumed that it would be unjust or at least impractical to impose liability.").

11 See § 12.2, below.

12 See, e.g., Sanghvi v. DJD Med., Inc., 2022 WL 363899, at *4 (D. Mass. 2022) (for proximate cause, plaintiff "must plead 'first, that the loss was a foreseeable consequence of the defendant's negligence, second, that the defendant's negligence was a but-for cause of the loss, and third, that the defendant's negligence was a substantial factor in bringing about the loss' "); Pitts v. Genie Indus., Inc., 921 N.W.2d 597, 609 (Neb. 2019) (for proximate cause, "plaintiff must meet three basic requirements: (1) Without the defect, the injury would not have occurred, . . . the 'but for' rule or 'cause in fact'; (2) the injury was a natural and probable result of the defect; and (3) there was no efficient intervening cause"); Meneely v. S.R. Smith, Inc., 5 P.3d 49, 58 (Wash. Ct. App. 2000) (proximate cause has "two distinct elements: cause in fact and legal cause"). See also § 11.1, above.

13 See, e.g., Sigler v. American Honda Motor Co., 2007 WL 1004313, at *4 (E.D. Tenn. 2007) ("Proximate cause is the familiar, negligence-based principle of 'cause-in-fact'; to succeed in a products liability action, a plaintiff must demonstrate the injury would not have occurred 'but for' the defect."); Wilkinson v. Duff, 575 S.E.2d 335 (W. Va. 2002); Hanford v. Taco Bell Corp., 2002 WL 570918, at *2 (Wash. Ct. App. 2002) ("If an event would have occurred regardless of a defendant's conduct, that conduct is not the proximate cause of the plaintiff's injury."). See also Ohio Rev. Code § 2307.73(A)(2).

For further discussion of this terminological confusion, see § 11.1, above.

14 See Rest. (3d) Torts: Liability for Physical and Emotional Harm ch. 6, "Scope of Liability (Proximate Cause)," and § 29 cmt. *b*.

15 See, e.g., Cupp, Proximate Cause, The Proposed Basic Principles Restatement, and Products Liability, 53 S.C. L. Rev. 1085 (2002); M. Green, The Unanticipated Ripples of Comparative Negligence: Superseding Cause in Products Liability and Beyond, 53 S.C. L. Rev. 1103 (2002); Henderson and Twerski,

liability law draws from the law of negligence. In the early days of modern products liability law, in an effort to distinguish the then new doctrine of strict products liability in tort from negligence, some courts and commentators sought to eliminate the proximate cause limitations of negligence law (principally, the limitation of responsibility to foreseeable risks) from the strict tort doctrine.[16] In time, however, this effort proved futile,[17] and proximate cause (with its limiting principle of foreseeable risk) remains alive and well today as an element for negligence,[18] breach of warranty,[19] strict products liability in tort,[20] and even fraud.[21]

While proximate cause is dealt with here as a separate doctrine, the issue permeates not only duty concepts but indeed *most* of the crucial elements of a products liability case. In a typical products liability action, the ultimate issue is whether, or the degree to which, some "defective" condition of a product, the plaintiff himself, or some third party "caused" the injury. Thus, one court was not far off the mark in noting that whether it labeled the plaintiff's unreasonable encounter with a known danger "contributory negligence" or "assumption of risk" was of little consequence because "[t]he controlling factor is causation."[22] Thought of in this broader sense, this factor pervades every

---

Intuition and Technology In Product Design Litigation: An Essay On Proximate Causation, 88 Geo. L.J. 659 (2000); Haley, Paradigms of Proximate Cause, 36 Tort & Ins. L.J. 147 (2000); Zablostky, Eliminating Proximate Cause as an Element of the Prima Facie Case for Strict Products Liability, 45 Cath. U. L. Rev. 31 (1995); Fischer, Products Liability—Proximate Cause, Intervening Cause, and Duty, 52 Mo. L. Rev. 547 (1987); Gillam, Torts—Proximate Cause in Strict-Liability Cases, 50 N.C. L. Rev. 714 (1972); Frumer, Friedman, and Sklaren, Products Liability § 3.03; Owen & Davis on Products Liability ch. 12.

16 See, e.g., Eshbach v. W. T. Grant's & Co., 481 F.2d 940, 942–43 (3d Cir. 1973) (Pa. law) ("Negligence is, of course, tested in terms of foreseeability. The focus of § 402A, however, is not directed to the foreseeability of a given injury, but to whether [the product is defective]."). See also Voss v. Black & Decker Mfg. Co., 450 N.E.2d 204, 209 (N.Y. 1983) ("Proximate cause in a products liability case serves a somewhat different role than in a case sounding in negligence because that cause of action seeks to impute liability to the manufacturer not on the basis of his negligence but because the product is not reasonably safe as it was designed.").

17 See § 10.4, above.

18 See § 2.1, above.

19 See, e.g., Avery v. Cobra Enters. of Utah, Inc., 2013 WL 2352320, at *5 (N.D. Ala. 2013) (an "essential element for proving a breach of implied warranty claim is that the injury was proximately caused by the breach," citing Official Comment to § 7–2–715); Pulte Home Corp. v. Parex, Inc., 923 A.2d 971, 1013 (Md. Ct. Spec. App. 2007) ("In an action based on breach of warranty, it is necessary for the plaintiff to show the existence of the warranty, the fact that the warranty was broken and that the breach of warranty was the proximate cause of the loss sustained."), aff'd, 942 A.2d 722 (Md. 2008).

20 See, e.g., Reese v. Ford Motor Co., 499 Fed. Appx. 163, 166 (3d Cir. 2012) (Pa. law) ("under § 402A, a plaintiff must establish that . . . the defect was a proximate cause of the plaintiff's injuries"); Graham v. American Cyanamid Co., 350 F.3d 496, 513 (6th Cir. 2003) ("To establish strict liability under Ohio law, plaintiffs must produce expert testimony that the defect at issue 'proximately caused the[ir] claimed injuries.' "); Marzullo v. Crosman Corp., 289 F. Supp. 2d 1337, 1347 (M.D. Fla. 2003) (for strict liability in tort under § 402A, "a plaintiff must prove a *defective and unreasonably dangerous condition* of a product was the proximate cause of injury").

21 While proximate cause often lies buried in claims for fraud or deceit, it sometimes sits front and center. See, e.g., In re Volkswagen "Clean Diesel" Mktg., Sales Pracs., & Prods. Liab. Litig., 467 F. Supp. 3d 849, 859 (N.D. Cal. 2020) (dismissing plaintiffs' fraud claims for failure to adequately allege proximate cause); C & E Servs., Inc. v. Ashland, Inc., 498 F. Supp. 2d 242, 256–57 (D.D.C. 2007) ("in order to recover for either a fraud or negligent misrepresentation claim, a plaintiff must prove 'that the defendant's challenged conduct proximately caused [the] plaintiff's injury' "); Goldstein v. Phillip Morris, Inc., 854 A.2d 585, 590–91 (Pa. Super. Ct. 2004) ("To recover on a claim of fraud, the plaintiff must prove [that] the resulting injury was proximately caused by the reliance."); Graham v. American Cyanamid Co., 350 F.3d 496, 507 (6th Cir. 2003) (Ohio law) ("plaintiffs bear the burden of establishing that American Cyanamid's alleged misrepresentation . . . proximately caused their injuries") (citing Rest. (2d) Torts § 557A cmt. *a*, which notes that ordinary rules of legal cause govern fraudulent misrepresentation cases involving physical harm).

22 See Palmer v. Ford Motor Co., 498 F.2d 952, 953 (10th Cir. 1974) (Kan. law).

products liability action, since each such case is comprised of many issues bound together by proximate causation twine.[23]

§ 12.2 FORESEEABILITY AND OTHER "TESTS"

Because proximate cause is a swirling maelstrom of policy, practicality, and case-specific fairness considerations—rather than a meaningful set of rules or even principles—it would seem incapable of being subjected to rational "testing." Yet, lawyers, courts, and juries[24] invariably seek guidance in unraveling the mysteries of this perplexing doctrine, which has led courts and commentators on an eternal search for a proper "test" for deciding whether a plaintiff's injury in any particular case was a proximate result of the defendant's wrong. While various other tests have been tried out over the years, the concept of "foreseeability," in one formulation or another, is the predominant notion informing proximate cause.[25]

Foreseeability as the Dominant Test

The central notion of proximate cause, often loosely referred to as its "test," is that an actor's responsibility for consequences of an unlawful action is limited by principles of reasonable "foreseeability." As some courts aptly put it, foreseeability is the "touchstone"[26] or "cornerstone"[27] of proximate cause. This outer boundary of tortious responsibility seeks to protect actors from liability for consequences falling outside the scope of their wrongdoing—beyond their moral accountability. The idea here is that responsibility for consequences should be based on the quality of an actor's choices that led to the consequences. The moral fiber of such choices is gauged by consequences the actor should have contemplated as plausible eventualities at the time the choice was made. If some other, "unforeseeable," consequence eventuates from a chosen action, the fact that it lies outside the bundle of consequences the actor reasonably should have contemplated means that it probably did not inform the actor's deliberations and choice. Thus, there usually is no substantial moral connection between a person's action and its consequences that are unforeseeable. Normally, therefore, in evaluating the moral quality of an actor's choice to act in a certain way, only foreseeable consequences of the

---

[23] Leon Green may have said it best: "The issues of a 402A action lie as close together as the fingers of one hand, and one issue cannot be considered without holding the other issues in conscious suspense; for all the issues are essential to liability, and each has a part to play in the functioning of all the others. Causal connection runs as a thread through the seller's duty, the violation of its duty, and the use made of the product in its consumption that results in the consumer's injury." L. Green, Strict Liability Under Sections 402A and 402B: A Decade of Litigation, 54 Tex. L. Rev. 1185, 1208 (1976).

[24] See Pearson v. Tippmann Pneumatics, Inc., 642 S.E.2d 691, 693, 695 (Ga. 2007) (reversing judgment for defendant; after jury asked to be instructed on proximate cause in "layman's terms," the recharge "failed to accurately and completely instruct the jury on the legal principles of proximate cause and the foreseeability of intervening acts as applied to the facts of this case").

[25] See Rest. (3d) Torts: Liability for Physical and Emotional Harm § 29 cmt. *e* (increasingly moving toward a foreseeability test for scope of liability in negligence cases, now "virtually all jurisdictions" employ such a standard in negligence cases); Cardi, Reconstructing Foreseeability (pt. 2), 46 B.C. L. Rev. 921, 927 (2005) (explicitly or implicitly, foreseeability resides in most proximate cause cases).

[26] See, e.g., Wickersham v. Ford Motor Co., 853 S.E.2d 329, 390 (S.C. 2020).

[27] See, e.g., Rodgers v. AWB Indus., Inc., 762 Fed. Appx. 1015, 1023 (11th Cir. 2019) (Ala. law); Morguson v. 3M Co., 857 So.2d 796, 800 (Ala. 2003).

choice and action may fairly be considered.[28] This is a moral justification for bounding the law of torts by the foreseeable scope of risk.[29]

For these reasons, as in other tort law contexts, the safety obligations of manufacturers and other sellers are limited by principles of reasonable foreseeability. More specifically, in making design and warning choices, a manufacturer is bound to contemplate and fairly evaluate only such risks to such persons as are reasonably foreseeable. The range of risks to be foreseen includes how a product may be used and misused, and the range of persons to be foreseen includes users and others who may be endangered by the product. Just as foreseeability is an important limiting notion on the *duty* of a product manufacturer, it is the principal "test" of proximate cause, as mentioned earlier. The "foreseeability" of a product's risks—the "scope" of the product's foreseeable risks—is thus the formal standard for deciding whether responsibility for a defendant's particular breach of duty should extend to the plaintiff's particular harm. Put otherwise, the central question of proximate cause in a products liability case is whether the risks that caused the plaintiff's harm were among the foreseeable risks that made the defendant negligent or its product defective.

Other Tests

Direct Consequences; Natural and Probable Consequences

As prominent and well-entrenched as foreseeability now appropriately may be as the standard for determining proximate cause in products liability law, other tests for proximate cause that long have challenged foreseeability in the law of negligence compete in the products liability arena as well. So, courts still sometimes use the "direct consequences" test of *Polemis* fame,[30] by which proximate cause is defined as a cause which, in natural and continuous sequence, unbroken by any efficient, intervening cause, produces the plaintiff's harm.[31] A variation on this standard is the "natural and probable consequences" test, sometimes appended to the preceding formulation,[32] which also

---

[28] See Owen, Figuring Foreseeability, 44 Wake Forest L. Rev. 1277 (2009) (foreseeability of consequences is what infuses human choice and action with moral content). If a choice to act or refrain from acting is reasonable in view of its foreseeable consequences, an unforeseeable harm that results is a "background" risk of life that victims fairly should protect against and bear. See Owen, Philosophical Foundations of Fault in Tort Law, in Philosophical Foundations of Tort Law 201, 226–27 (D. Owen ed., Oxford 1994); Owen, The Moral Foundations of Products Liability Law: Toward First Principles, 68 Notre Dame L. Rev. 427, 484 (1993) (utility, freedom, and equality all argue for limiting responsibility to foreseeable risks). *But see* Owen, Bending Nature, Bending Law, 62 Fla. L. Rev. 569, 609 (2010) (explaining the "paradox of foreseeable unforeseeability").

[29] See Rest. (3d) Torts: Liability for Physical and Emotional Harm § 29 cmt. *j* (noting that a "risk standard" (meaning a foreseeable risk approach) appeals "to the intuition that it is fair for an actor's liability to be limited to those risks that constituted the basis for the wrongful conduct"). See generally Cardi, Reconstructing Foreseeability (pt. 2), 46 B.C. L. Rev. 921, 940–52 (2005) (describing Stephen Perry's explanations); Perry, Responsibility for Outcomes, Risk, and the Law of Torts, in Philosophy and the Law of Torts 72 (G. Postema ed., Cambridge Univ. Press 2007); Perry, Risk, Harm, and Responsibility, in Philosophical Foundations of Tort Law 321 (D. Owen ed., Oxford 1995).

[30] In re Polemis, 3 K.B. 560 (1921).

[31] See, e.g., Parris v. 3M Co., 2022 WL 976007, at *21 (N.D. Ga. 2022); Stahlecker v. Ford Motor Co., 667 N.W.2d 244, 253 (Neb. 2003); Pickett v. RTS Helicopter, 128 F.3d 925, 929 (5th Cir. 1997) (La. law).

[32] See, e.g., Miaoulis v. Toyota Motor N. Am., Inc., 2021 WL 117513, at *2 (Ark. Ct. App. 2021) ("Proximate cause is defined as that which in a natural and continuous sequence, unbroken by any efficient intervening cause, produces the injury, and without which the result would not have occurred."); Green Plains Otter Tail, LLC v. Pro-Env't, Inc., 953 F.3d 541, 547 (8th Cir. 2020) (Minn. law) ("a proximate-cause analysis [looks] to whether an injury 'follows in an unbroken sequence, without an intervening efficient cause, from the original negligent act' "); Vanderwerf v. SmithKlineBeecham Corp., 529 F. Supp. 2d 1294, 1311 (D. Kan. 2008) ("Proximate cause is defined as that cause which in natural and continuous sequence, unbroken by an efficient

sometimes appears in products liability decisions.[33] Yet, in the first *Wagon Mound* opinion,[34] *Polemis* was rejected for failing to employ foreseeability as the basic standard, and foreseeability is often woven in, one way or another, when courts dredge up the "natural and probable" standard for proximate cause decisionmaking.[35]

The Second Restatement

The *Restatement (Second) of Torts* did not really define proximate cause, referring to it obliquely as a set of rules "relieving the actor from liability because of the manner in which his negligence has resulted in the harm."[36] Among these "rules," the *Second Restatement* included a variety of limiting principles, some of which are defined in terms of foreseeability.[37] The *Second Restatement's* confusing umbrella definition of "legal cause," which defines factual causation in "substantial factor" terms, misled some number of courts to believe that the concept of proximate cause, viewed narrowly, should be conceived of through a substantial-factor lens. This misinterpretation of the *Second Restatement* has contributed to the confusion surrounding the meaning of and relationship between factual causation and proximate cause, and it still infects some products liability decisions.[38]

The Third Restatement

Drawing from a wealth of judicial and academic support, and rejecting "proximate cause" phraseology as too confusing,[39] the *Third Restatement* adopts a "scope of risk" ("harm-within-the-risk") test for proximate causation.[40] The doctrine is generally defined in § 29, entitled "Limitations on Liability for Tortious Conduct," which provides: "An actor's liability is limited to those harms that result from the risks that made the actor's conduct tortious."[41] Such a "risk" test is really little more, as the Reporters acknowledge,[42] than foreseeability in disguise. Yet the Reporters quite plausibly assert that the "scope of risk" formulation, more clearly than "foreseeability," reveals that liability is fairly bounded by the risks that made an actor negligent. This argument

---

intervening cause, produces the injury and without which the injury would not have occurred, the injury being the natural and probable consequence of the wrongful act.").

[33] See, e.g., Lapsley v. Xtek, Inc., 689 F.3d 802, 816 (7th Cir. 2012) (Ind. law) (proximate cause "turns largely on whether the injury 'is a natural and probable consequence, which in the light of the circumstances, should have been foreseen or anticipated' "); Stahlecker v. Ford Motor Co., 667 N.W.2d 244, 253–54 (Neb. 2003) (whether injury was "a natural and probable result of the negligence").

[34] Overseas Tankship (U.K.) Ltd. v. Morts Dock & Eng'g Co., [1961] A.C. 388 (P.C.) ("Wagon Mound I").

[35] See, e.g., Sluis v. Ethicon, Inc., 529 F. Supp. 3d 1004, 1009 (D.S.D. 2021) ("Legal cause means an immediate cause which, in the natural or probable sequence, produces the injury complained of. For legal cause to exist, the harm suffered must be a foreseeable consequence of the act complained of."); City of Gary v. Smith & Wesson Corp., 801 N.E.2d 1222, 1244 (Ind. 2003) ("liability may not be imposed on an original negligent actor who sets into motion a chain of events if the ultimate injury was not reasonably foreseeable as the natural and probable consequence of the act or omission").

[36] Rest. (2d) Torts § 431(b).

[37] See id. § 435, "Foreseeability of Harm or Manner of Its Occurrence."

[38] See, e.g., Ford Motor Co. v. Boomer, 736 S.E.2d 724, 730 (Va. 2013) (reversing and remanding; "a reasonable juror could be confused as to the quantum of evidence required to prove causation in the face of both a substantial contributing factor and a proximate cause instruction"). See also § 11.1, above.

[39] See Rest. (3d) Torts: Liability for Physical and Emotional Harm § 29 cmt. *b*, and the informative Reporters' Note thereto.

[40] The references here are to the Restatement (3d) of Torts: Liability for Physical and Emotional Harm (2010). Products Liability Rest. § 15 takes no position on issues of causation, stating that the causation rules of tort law generally apply as well to products liability.

[41] Rest. (3d) Torts: Liability for Physical and Emotional Harm § 29.

[42] See id. cmt. *k*.

would be quite compelling if the *Restatement*'s standard were enhanced by adding (rather than hiding) its single most important defining characteristic—foreseeability. By refusing to recognize the legitimacy of "proximate cause" as a label for its own elemental field, or to acknowledge the propriety of foreseeability's prominence within the proximate cause domain, the *Third Restatement* boldly rebuffs a century or so of embedded tort law conceptual language—which it characterizes as "unfortunate."[43] Instead, the *Third Restatement* buries foreseeability in the definitions of tortious wrongs, like negligence or selling a defective product. The idea here is that conduct is not tortious unless it exposes persons to a foreseeable risk of harm, and the scope of liability for a tortious wrong naturally defines the boundaries of liability for the wrong in terms of its foreseeable, and only foreseeable, consequences.

Buried though foreseeability may be, the scope of risk definition in the *Third Restatement* fairly might be understood as limiting accountability in tort to harms that fall within "the scope of *foreseeable* risks"—a formulation that nicely (with foreseeability included) captures the essential concept that courts have long embraced. Unlike the *Restatement*, however, courts have focused on this defining limitation on tort responsibility more directly, and hence more helpfully, by framing proximate cause as an independent and vital element of most torts—an element that almost universally centers on foreseeability, on whether a plaintiff's injuries were a foreseeable consequence of the tort.

The *Restatement* Reporters' decision to bury the traditional, central role of foreseeability in proximate cause within the scope of harm idea may be conceptually pure, and it may well serve to crimp a defendant's ability to take two bites from the (un)foreseeability apple (first in breach, then in proximate cause), but courts may understandably be loathe to discard the doctrine's apt "proximate cause" designation, to reject its elemental importance to responsibility in tort, or to abandon foreseeability's exalted position at the forefront of the distinctly important doctrine of proximate cause.

While the *Third Restatement* "scope of risk" test comes close to the mark, and is helpful in many ways, for many years simple "foreseeability" has been crowding out competing proximate cause "tests," most of which have a quaint appearance of times gone by. None of the traditional "tests" is especially objectionable, except that none provides much guidance to courts or juries attempting to apply whatever principles proximate cause may possess to resolve real-world disputes. No doubt courts will long continue to parrot these alternative verbalisms in the jurisdictions where they reside, for they have deep roots in the common law and are doing little in the way of positive harm. And foreseeability itself may well be faulted for providing little guidance to adjudicators attempting to decide whether a manufacturer or other seller should bear responsibility for some harmful consequence of a defective product that somehow appears remote.[44] Yet, as earlier discussed, at least foreseeability is rooted in fundamental notions of responsibility that, at some basic level, help guide decisions on whether a manufacturer or other seller fairly may be held responsible for a plaintiff's loss.

---

[43] See id. cmt. *b*.

[44] How foreseeability may be faulted as a "test" for limiting a manufacturer's responsibility is more deeply probed in the context of misuse. See § 13.5, below.

Foreseeability and Bizarre Consequences

Perhaps the most intuitively appealing type of case for applying some proximate cause limitation on the harmful consequences of a tortious action is where the consequences appear totally bizarre, even in retrospect,[45] "too cockeyed and far-fetched."[46] If a plaintiff is injured by slipping on the vomit of a friend nauseated by a defendant's smelly plate of shrimp, the consequences may simply seem too far outside the foreseeable risks of serving foul food to hold the restaurateur responsible for the plaintiff's injury.[47] And other products liability claims have been rejected on the ground that the consequences are simply too bizarre.[48]

But courts allow juries to decide the proximate cause issue in some quite extraordinary situations. In one case, for example, the plaintiff was driving at 45–50 mph when he hit a horse that suddenly appeared in front of his car. The horse was thrown into the air and onto the roof, collapsing the roof rail (called the "header") on the passenger side of the car, which instantly killed the plaintiff's wife. Rejecting the defendant car manufacturer's argument that the accident was "freak and bizarre," the court upheld a verdict for the plaintiff.[49] Another case involved a boating accident that began when an outboard motor stalled due to a defective fuel system. While the husband attempted to restart the engine, the anchor line became entangled in the propeller and, as he tried to cut the line, he was pulled into the water. While his wife tried to rescue him, an onrush of water washed her inside the boat and below deck. The boat capsized, and the wife, trapped beneath, drowned. Despite this incredible set of freak occurrences, the court ruled that foreseeability was properly for the jury.[50] And courts in other cases quite unusual allow juries to find a product defect and the plaintiff's injuries proximately connected.[51]

Foreseeability as a Veil

An uncomfortable aspect of foreseeability (even when helpfully modified as *reasonable* foreseeability) is that, like other "tests" for proximate cause, it provides so

---

[45] See Rest. (2d) Torts § 435(2) ("where after the event and looking back from the harm" to the tortious conduct they appear "highly extraordinary"). See also id. at § 442(b).

[46] See Prosser, Palsgraf Revisited, 52 Mich. L. Rev. 1, 19 (1953).

[47] See Crankshaw v. Piedmont Driving Club, 156 S.E.2d 208 (Ga. Ct. App. 1967).

[48] In Sidwell v. William Prym, Inc., 730 P.2d 996, 999–1003 (Idaho 1986), the plaintiff was wearing a dress while her mother placed a hem in it with brittle, hardened-steel dressmaker pins manufactured by the defendant. Plaintiff bumped a coffee table with her knee, driving a pin into her knee bone where it broke into three pieces. *Held*, no duty to warn of a danger that could not be foreseen. "[T]he manufacturer is asked to anticipate, not only that pins will pierce, but they will be driven into the body with such force as to strike a bone and shatter." The event was "a freak accident that probably could not be duplicated under any condition." One judge dissented: "The 'freak accident' argument might prove not in the least persuasive to a jury." See also Shih v. Starbucks Corp., 267 Cal. Rptr. 3d 919, 925 (Ct. App. 2020) (as a matter of law, alleged defects in the cup of hot tea were not the proximate cause of plaintiff's second-degree burns; plaintiff removed the cup's lid, "bent over the table, pushed out her chair, lost her balance, grabbed the table to avoid failing, and knocked her drink off the table").

[49] See Green v. Denney, 742 P.2d 639 (Or. Ct. App. 1987). Compare Collins v. Navistar, Inc., 155 Cal. Rptr. 3d 137, 155 (Ct. App. 2013) (driver injured by chunk of concrete that crashed through truck windshield when teenager threw it from overpass onto freeway below; jury could find that such an impact was a foreseeable risk, "and the source of the risk is not relevant" to that determination).

[50] See Greenfield v. Suzuki Motor Co., 776 F. Supp. 698 (E.D.N.Y. 1991).

[51] See, e.g., Yun v. Ford Motor Co., 669 A.2d 1378 (N.J. 1996), where plaintiff was killed while trying to cross a rain-slicked highway at night, in violation of state law, to retrieve a bald tire and parts of a broken tire assembly that had fallen off the back of a van because of a defect in the spare tire assembly on the back of the vehicle. Over a vigorous dissent, the majority ruled that a jury could find this reasonably foreseeable.

little guidance that a court or jury can hide behind it all sorts of biases and ideologies that have no proper place in such decisions. Foreseeability and proximate cause, that is, serve too often as veils that shield from view the motivating reasons for allowing or, more typically, disallowing recovery. In *Winnett v. Winnett*,[52] for example, a 4-year-old child was injured when she placed her hand on a moving conveyor belt on a forage wagon being operated on her grandfather's farm. She settled a suit against her grandfather and pursued a strict tort action against the manufacturer of the forage wagon, alleging that it was defectively designed because it did not have rear-view mirrors or a guard to prevent persons from coming in contact with the conveyor belt. Stating that foreseeability is "that which it is *objectively reasonable* to expect, not merely what might conceivably occur," the Illinois Supreme Court upheld a dismissal of the complaint, ruling that it could not "fairly be said that a manufacturer should reasonably foresee that a 4-year-old child will be permitted to approach an operating farm forage wagon or that the child will be permitted to place her fingers in or on the holes in its moving screen."

In *Richelman v. Kewanee Machinery & Conveyor Co.*,[53] however, a majority of the Illinois Appellate Court seemed almost oblivious to the holding in *Winnett*, by ruling that a jury could find in favor of a 3-year-old child whose foot was injured when he wandered away from the house and came in contact with a grain auger on his grandfather's farm.[54] Reading between the lines, these inconsistent decisions appear to reveal much more about the judges' respective beliefs concerning the balance between parental (and grandparental) responsibility, on the one side, and the idea that large manufacturing enterprises may be capable of spreading the costs of accidents, on the other, than they reveal about their doctrinal views on how far true foreseeability limits responsibility for harm.

Often noted (and usually decried) by scholars,[55] the malleability and opaqueness of foreseeability as the "test" for proximate cause has significant implications for lawyers litigating products liability as other tort law cases. Foreseeability becomes a vessel into which a lawyer—in arguing either to a jury or the judge—can pour any number of equitable considerations which are present in the case but which really have no doctrinal home. In this respect, the doctrine of proximate cause, defined in terms of foreseeable risk, can be an especially powerful arrow in a lawyer's quiver of legal tools.

---

52 310 N.E.2d 1 (Ill. 1974).

53 375 N.E.2d 885 (Ill. App. Ct. 1978).

54 The dissent in *Richelman* observed: "The only question can be whether this particular plaintiff's injury was reasonably foreseeable. The *Winnett* case held that it was not and we should follow it." Id. at 890.

55 Passwaters v. General Motors Corp., 454 F.2d 1270, 1276 n.5 (8th Cir. 1972) (Iowa law), was an early case extending a manufacturer's liability to include foreseeable risks to foreseeable bystanders: "The difficulty is that 'foreseeability' is a hazardous term to define in the abstract and, like so many other doctrines, must turn on the judgmental process." The court noted the following observations of a leading tort law scholar and legal realist:

> It all depends upon what factors in the evidence a court is willing to isolate and emphasize for the purpose of making this decision, which process in turn depends pretty much on what outcome the court wishes to achieve or thinks to be politic. This factor in the judgment process, in turn, is not usually a matter of conscious choice but may be a function of the judge's accumulated experience in and observations of the world he lives in.

Gregory, Proximate Cause in Negligence—A Retreat from "Rationalization," 6 U. Chi. L. Rev. 36, 50 (1938). The court further observed: "Generally, whether a duty exists is a question of law, yet when a difficult determination depends on policy values underlying the 'common affairs of life,' it is generally thought that the jury is the best d[i]viner of such values." Id.

Foreseeability of Product Use

An important limitation on the scope of a manufacturer's responsibility for product accidents lies in the foreseeability of a product's *use*.[56] While liability is no longer restricted to product uses a manufacturer *intends*, a manufacturer's accountability still is limited to consequences from product uses it reasonably can *foresee*.[57] So, a manufacturer is not liable when a defective elevator stalls six feet short of the floor and a passenger is injured in trying to jump out; a commercial pizza dough mixer start button is pressed, the clutch moved to the run position, and the timer set while a person's head and upper body are in the mixer bowl; a spare tire strap is used to attach curtain rods to the roof of a car; a fertilizer is employed by a terrorist to make a bomb used to try to blow up the World Trade Center; an intoxicated person falls asleep or passes out in a stopped, running vehicle and presses his foot on the accelerator, causing the exhaust system to overheat and ignite; or when a person attempts to commit suicide by closing herself in a car trunk without an inside release latch, changes her mind, and is trapped inside for nine days thereafter.[58]

Nor is a manufacturer liable when a doctor transplants synthetic fibers, normally used for wigs, into a patient's scalp as a treatment for baldness, causing irritation and infection; a grocery shopper, who trips, hopes that a shopping cart does not scoot away when he grabs for it to save himself from falling; the owner of a riding lawn mower attaches a wooden "dog box" into which he places a 2-year-old child who falls out and is run over by the mower; a teenage boy hangs himself with a rope on a swing set as a joke to impress the girls; a boy, riding a canister vacuum cleaner like a toy car, is injured when his penis slips through an opening into the cleaner's fan; children play with a gas can without a child-proof top; or a youth tilts or rocks a soft-drink vending machine, to dispense a can without payment, causing the machine to fall upon and kill him.[59]

---

[56] See, e.g., Wilson Sporting Goods Co. v. Hickox, 59 A.3d 1267, 1275 (D.C. 2013) (impact of foul ball striking major league catcher's mask equipped with newly designed throat guard, that angled forward instead of straight down, caused concussion and damaged joint in plaintiff's inner ear; approving instruction that "[a] design is defective if the product fails to perform as safely as an ordinary customer would expect when [the product is] used in an intended or reasonably foreseeable manner"); Parks v. AlliedSignal Inc., 113 F.3d 1327, 1333 (3d Cir. 1997) (Pa. law) ("In strict products liability, the focus is on whether the product was sold in an unreasonably dangerous condition for reasonably foreseeable uses.").

[57] See, e.g., DZE Corp. v. Vickers, 299 So.3d 538, 541–42 (Fla. Dist. Ct. App. 2020) ("Florida law does not permit a jury to consider proximate cause where a person responsible for the injury is voluntarily impaired or intentionally misuses a product."); Weaver v. PACCAR, Inc., 52 F. Supp. 3d 1342, 1350 (S.D. Ga. 2014), aff'd, 614 Fed. Appx. 991 (11th Cir. 2015) (unforeseeable that a trained operator would absentmindedly press the start button of a large truck while it was in gear, the brakes were released, and a mechanic was under the truck; manufacturers "are not charged with building commercial trucks for those who do not think, any more than cars are to be made for sleeping drivers"). Compare Diehl v. 3M Co., 2019 WL 4412976, at *4 (Minn. Ct. App. 2019) (that a driver would "snuff" the fumes of a dust remover for acute intoxication, and then crash into a sidewalk pedestrian, might be foreseeable) (2–1 decision); Morris v. Giant Four Corners, Inc., 294 F. Supp. 3d 1207, 1217–18 (D.N.M. 2018) (criminally reckless operation of a car by an intoxicated driver who crossed the center line, and killed the driver of another car in a head-on collision, did "not as a matter of law foreclose" the negligence of the gas station that sold gas to the intoxicated driver). See misuse, in § 13.5, below.

[58] See Egan v. A. J. Constr. Corp., 724 N.E.2d 366 (N.Y. 1999) (elevator); Shannon v. Hobart, 2011 WL 442119, at *8 (E.D. Pa. 2011) (pizza dough mixer); Van de Valde v. Volvo of Am. Corp., 744 P.2d 930, 933 (N.M. 1987) (tire strap); Port Auth. of N.Y. & N.J. v. Arcadian Corp., 189 F.3d 305, 318 (3d Cir. 1999) (N.J. law) (fertilizer; past fertilizer explosions do not permit a finding of objective foreseeability; "[c]onceivability is not the equivalent of foreseeability"); Griffith v. Chrysler Corp., 2003 WL 21500037 (Ohio Ct. App. 2003) (sleeping driver); Daniell v. Ford Motor Co., 581 F. Supp. 728 (D.N.M. 1984) (closing oneself in trunk of car).

[59] See Berg v. Underwood's Hair Adaption Process, Inc., 751 F.2d 136, 137 (2d Cir. 1984) (N.Y. law) (synthetic fibers); Smith v. Technibilt, Inc., 791 S.W.2d 247 (Tex. App. 1990) (shopping cart); Erkson v. Sears, Roebuck & Co., 841 S.W.2d 207 (Mo. Ct. App. 1992) ("dog box"); Smith v. Holmes, 606 N.E.2d 627 (Ill. App. Ct.

While the product uses in these cases all were deemed unforeseeable, courts in many other cases, involving various kinds of uses beyond the normally expectable, have ruled quite the other way.[60] Because of the inherent elasticity of "foreseeability," no prudent lawyer would attempt to predict how a court or jury might rule on the foreseeability of any particular product use that seems unusual.

Conventional Foreseeability Categories

Foreseeability is the controlling issue around which various categories of proximate cause cases cluster. In assessing the foreseeable scope of risk of a defendant's conduct, foreseeability is often subdivided into four distinct components for evaluating the effect of their unforeseeability on liability—the foreseeability of (1) the extent of harm, (2) the manner of its occurrence, (3) the type of harm (or, type of *risk* of harm), and (4) the type of plaintiff. The first three of these categories may be seen to reside, if roughly, in *Restatement (Second) of Torts* § 435, entitled "Foreseeability of Harm or Manner of Its Occurrence," which provides in part:

> (1) If the actor's conduct is a substantial factor in bringing about harm to another, the fact that the actor neither foresaw nor should have foreseen the extent of the harm or the manner in which it occurred does not prevent him from being liable.
>
> (2) The actor's conduct may be held not to be a legal cause of harm [if it appears] highly extraordinary that it should have brought about the harm.

These are widely applied proximate cause principles—that a manufacturer or other tort defendant remains *subject* to liability even if it cannot foresee the *extent* or *manner* of harm, but that a defendant is *shielded* from responsibility if it cannot foresee the *type* of risk (including the type of product use) that harms the plaintiff.[61]

Extent of Harm

Myrtle Poplar pricked her finger on the jagged point of a metal star adorning a cosmetic gift box she had received for Christmas. The finger became infected and had to be amputated. The manufacturer argued it should not have to foresee "so extraordinary and unpredictable a result" as an amputation "from the otherwise trivial puncturing of her skin." The court disagreed: "[I]f the plaintiff's injury is traceable to the defendant's negligence without intervention of any other independent, legally operative event—the injured person is entitled to recover for the harm actually suffered even though the precise nature and extent of those injuries, as they finally developed, were more severe than could ordinarily have been foreseen." A defendant is responsible, continued the court, "for all the harm and suffering which his negligent act brought on even though the plaintiff's injuries were aggravated by his own predisposition or weakness or by the intervening mistake or negligence of a physician who treated the original injury."[62]

1992) (rope on swing set); Larue v. National Union Elec. Corp., 571 F.2d 51 (1st Cir. 1978) (Me. law) (vacuum cleaner); Simpson v. Standard Container Co., 527 A.2d 1337 (Md. Ct. Spec. App. 1987) (label on gas can warned against storing in living area); Oden v. Pepsi Cola Bottling Co., 621 So.2d 953 (Ala. 1993) (vending machine).

[60] Keller v. Welles Dep't Store of Racine, 276 N.W.2d 319, 324 (Wis. Ct. App. 1979) (gas can—foreseeable that "incurably curious" children might taste gasoline stored in a can on the floor, or, while playing "mow the lawn" or "gas station," might pour gasoline from can). For "misuse" decisions, on whether uses were foreseeable or unforeseeable, see § 13.5, below.

[61] See Dobbs, Law of Torts §§ 187–89.

[62] See Poplar v. Bourjois, 80 N.E.2d 334, 336–37 (N.Y. 1948) (dictum).

Manner of Harm

It generally is agreed that the precise *manner* in which harm occurs need not be foreseeable.[63] So, a meat packing company that negligently applied a rubber band to bind a shank of lamb was liable even if it could not foresee that a butcher would be hit in the eye when the band flew off as he grasped the lamb to pull it forward along a conveyor rail.[64] And the seller of an improperly designed rotary power lawn mower was liable even if it could not foresee that the mower would eject a stick at high velocity through the open window of a passing police car 26 feet away, into the eye of the officer within.[65]

Type of Harm (Risk of Harm)

In contrast to the manner and extent of harm, the foreseeability *vel non* of the *type* of harm suffered by the plaintiff—or, more properly, the type of *risk* that caused the harm—figures prominently in proximate cause determinations. Indeed, the type-of-harm phraseology is the conventional formulation of the harm-within-the-risk idea of the *Third Restatement*, discussed above, which is basically just another window on the scope-of-foreseeable-risk idea that more fully describes the operative principle of proximate causation. Courts widely accept the general principle that a manufacturer is *not* subject to liability for unforeseeable *types* of risk or harm, including risks that arise from a product's *use* that is unforeseeable.[66] But the precise type of risk or harm need not be foreseeable, just the general type of risk or harm.[67]

Emotional distress. Cases involving claims for emotional distress, while sometimes resolved on duty grounds,[68] frequently turn on whether a manufacturer of a particular type of product should be expected to foresee that some consumers will become distressed, and perhaps even suffer illness as a result, if its products are defective. Thus, a manufacturer might not fairly be required to expect that a person would become so frightened as to have a heart attack from seeing rusty brown water caused by a defect in the manufacturer's water softener.[69] But it might be fair to require a manufacturer to expect that a person would become distressed if, while drinking from a bottle of Coke, he

---

[63] See, e.g., Potter v. Ford Motor Co., 213 S.W.3d 264, 275–76 (Tenn. Ct. App. 2006) ("The foreseeability requirement is not so strict as to require the tortfeasor to foresee the exact manner in which the injury takes place, provided it is determined that the tortfeasor could foresee, or through the exercise of reasonable diligence should have foreseen, the general manner in which the injury or loss occurred.").

[64] See Katz v. Swift & Co., 276 F.2d 905, 906 (2d Cir. 1960) (N.Y. law) (unnecessary for defendant to "anticipate the particular chain of events that would result in injury in order to be held liable"; "[it] was sufficient that it was foreseeable that injury might result if the rubber bands were improperly attached ").

[65] See Swearngin v. Sears Roebuck & Co., 376 F.2d 637, 642 (10th Cir. 1967) (Kan. law). See also Stazenski v. Tennant Co., 617 So.2d 344 (Fla. Dist. Ct. App. 1993) (not necessary for plaintiff to prove that manufacturer of industrial sweeper with unnecessarily sharp edges could foresee that worker on another machine would fall off that machine and cut the nerves and tendons in his wrist, only that it could foresee that a person might come into contact with and be injured by the exposed sharp edges).

[66] The *use* to which a product is put need not be *intended*, just foreseeable. See § 13.5, below ("misuse").

[67] See, e.g., Block v. Woo Young Med. Co., 937 F. Supp. 2d 1028, 1037 (D. Minn. 2013) (pain pump maker did not have to foresee that pump could cause chondrolysis, only that it posed general risk of cartilage damage); Moran v. Faberge, Inc., 332 A.2d 11 (Md. 1975) (manufacturer of Tigress cologne had duty to warn it was flammable; general risk that cologne contact with ignition source in the home (like cigarette or candle) was foreseeable, even if use by teenage girls to scent a lit candle was not).

[68] See § 5.3, above (liability for emotional distress under § 402A).

[69] See Caputzal v. Lindsay Co., 222 A.2d 513 (N.J. 1966) (plaintiff's emotional hypersensitivity was idiosyncratic and hence unforeseeable). Nor that a plaintiff, with a history of heart problems and in poor shape, will suffer a fatal heart attack while engaging in sexual intercourse with his wife after taking the defendant's drug, Viagra. See Brumley v. Pfizer, Inc., 149 F. Supp. 2d 305 (S.D. Tex. 2001) (Viagra had merely furnished the condition for the heart attack, not caused it, since it merely did its job).

suddenly finds himself sucking on a rat;[70] or, at least in the eyes of one court, that a housewife would become hysterical, and ultimately suffer traumatic neurosis, from witnessing her washing machine vibrating violently, like a "robot gone crazy."[71]

Suicide and murder. Cases on the foreseeability that a product might be used to commit suicide or murder often involve principles of superseding causation, which itself is grounded in foreseeability,[72] as well as in the simpler concept of the foreseeability of the risk of harm.[73] On one of these two grounds, or on some other,[74] courts in most cases, but not all,[75] deny recovery against manufacturers for product-related suicides and murders.[76]

Type of Plaintiff

One should recall the lesson of Chief Judge Cardozo's opinion for the majority in the *Palsgraf* case,[77] that the scope of an actor's responsibility extends only to foreseeable plaintiffs, and not to those injured by a product who stand outside the orbit of foreseeable risk.[78] Occasionally a court will rule that a particular type of user is unforeseeable as a matter of law. So, a 14-year-old operator of a meat-grinding machine may be unforeseeable when labor laws prohibit the operation of such a machine by anyone under

---

[70] See Way v. Tampa Coca Cola Bottling Co., 260 So.2d 288 (Fla. Dist. Ct. App. 1972). Other emotional distress food and drink cases are noted in § 7.5, above.

[71] See Barnette v. Dickens, 135 S.E.2d 109 (Va. 1964).

[72] See, e.g., Johnson v. Wal-Mart Stores, Inc., 588 F.3d 439 (7th Cir. 2009) (Ill. law) (suicide); see generally § 12.3, below.

[73] See, e.g., Stupak v. Hoffman-La Roche, Inc., 326 Fed. Appx. 553, 560 (11th Cir. 2009) (Fla. law) (no evidence manufacturer should have known Accutane could cause suicide without premonitory symptoms).

[74] See, e.g., Vanderwerf v. SmithKlineBeecham Corp., 529 F. Supp. 2d 1294, 1307–09 (D. Kan. 2008) (plaintiff failed to prove Paxil antidepressant caused plaintiff's suicide); Tucker v. SmithKline Beecham Corp., 2007 WL 2726259 (S.D. Ind. 2007) (claim that Paxil manufacturer failed to warn of increased risk of adult suicide conflicted with FDA's labeling requirements and so was preempted); Martin v. Hacker, 628 N.E.2d 1308 (N.Y. 1993) (warning of risk of suicide provided by manufacturer was adequate as a matter of law).

[75] Suicides may be a foreseeable risk of certain prescription drugs. See, e.g., Smith v. Pfizer, Inc., 688 F. Supp. 2d 735, 748 (M.D. Tenn. 2010) ("if a drug company negligently or intentionally fails to warn doctors that a particular drug increases the risk of suicide, it is foreseeable that some patients who take the drug will commit suicide"); Smith v. Pfizer Inc., 688 F. Supp. 2d 735 (M.D. Tenn. 2010) (prescription pain medication; jury question whether suicide was foreseeable); Hooks SuperX, Inc. v. McLaughlin, 642 N.E.2d 514 (Ind. 1994) (in action against pharmacist for refilling prescription for dangerous and addictive drug faster than prescribed, whether customer's suicide attempt constituted unforeseeable intervening cause was a jury question). See also Wickersham v. Ford Motor Co., 997 F.3d 526, 537 (4th Cir. 2021) (S.C. law) (suicide must be a foreseeable result of injury from defective airbag system in auto accident that led to substantial pain and depression).

[76] See, e.g., Williams v. Wal-Mart Stores East, L.P., 99 So.3d 112 (Miss. 2012) (murder; illegal sale of ammunition); Kleen v. Homak Mfg. Co., 749 N.E.2d 26 (Ill. App. Ct. 2001) (unforeseeable to manufacturer of allegedly defective lock on gun case that plaintiff's adult son would break into case with a screwdriver, remove the gun stored inside, and use the gun to kill himself); Watters v. TSR, Inc., 904 F.2d 378 (6th Cir. 1990) (Ky. law) (unforeseeable that Dungeons & Dragons game would cause boy to commit suicide); Moss v. Meyer, 454 N.E.2d 48 (Ill. App. Ct. 1983) (unforeseeable that child would attempt suicide by swallowing prescription capsules delivered by pharmacist to front doorstep of home); Saxton v. McDonnell Douglas Aircraft Co., 428 F. Supp. 1047 (C.D. Cal. 1977) (unforeseeable that mother of passenger killed in plane crash would commit suicide from stress of son's death and subsequent products liability trial).

See also James v. Meow Media, Inc., 300 F.3d 683, 693 (6th Cir. 2002) (Ky. law) (unforeseeable to video game manufacturers that playing game would cause student to shoot other students in school lobby: "it is simply too far a leap from shooting characters on a video screen (an activity undertaken by millions) to shooting people in a classroom"); Sanders v. Acclaim Entm't, Inc., 188 F. Supp. 2d 1264 (D. Colo. 2002) (unforeseeable that two students would shoot and kill teacher in shooting spree). On video games, see § 16.8, below.

[77] See Palsgraf v. Long Island R.R. Co., 162 N.E. 99 (N.Y. 1928).

[78] At least a couple of the third-generation DES cases, on grounds of both duty and proximate cause, have relied on *Palsgraf* for the proposition that grandchildren of the woman to whom the drug was administered, as a matter of law, are simply too remote. See § 10.5, above.

the age of sixteen.[79] Yet courts are protective of young children in the home, and the same court allowed a 2-year-old child to recover for injuries from sticking his hand into a treadmill his sister was using.[80]

One class of plaintiffs that encountered special difficulty with proximate cause included hospitals, insurance companies, other institutions, and even nations that have sued cigarette companies for the recovery of health care expenses resulting from the cigarette industry's fraudulent marketing of cigarettes over many years. Often reasoning from a Supreme Court securities law decision,[81] cigarette health care expense reimbursement claims were dismissed,[82] as were many claims by cities against the gun industry for the costs of crime caused by the defendants' "negligent marketing,"[83] on grounds (among others) that such "derivative" claims for economic losses suffered by third parties are simply too "remote."[84]

But most courts are quite lenient in finding vulnerable plaintiffs foreseeable in many situations. Where a paraplegic, with no heat sensitivity in his feet, drove a motor home (with hand controls he had installed) for six hours while his bare feet rested on the steel floorboard that reached 175° Fahrenheit, the court ruled that the plaintiff was a foreseeable consumer;[85] and, a minor biker, who avoided large slots in a drainage grate on a pedestrian-biker pathway by riding into the street, where he was struck by a car, was a foreseeable plaintiff as well.[86] Rescuers, it will be recalled,[87] are considered foreseeable plaintiffs when they provide aid to others, "if only it be not wanton,"[88] when they are themselves injured in the process.[89]

§ 12.3 Intervening and Superseding Causes

The connection between a defendant's breach of duty and a plaintiff's harm may appear tenuous or "remote" because of the intervention of some person or force other

---

[79] See Darsan v. Globe Slicing Mach. Co., 606 N.Y.S.2d 317 (App. Div. 1994).

[80] Wheeler v. Sears Roebuck & Co., 831 N.Y.S.2d 427, 429–30 (App. Div. 2007).

[81] See Holmes v. Securities Investor Prot. Corp., 503 U.S. 258 (1992) (RICO case where plaintiff's expenses, incurred to reimburse investor losses from defendant's fraudulent activity, were "too remote").

[82] See, e.g., A.O. Fox Mem'l Hosp. v. American Tobacco Co., 754 N.Y.S.2d 368, 370 (App. Div. 2003) (claims "too remote to permit recovery"); Regence Blueshield v. Philip Morris Inc., 5 Fed. Appx. 651, 653 (9th Cir. 2001) (Wash. law) (same; plaintiff's damages not proximately caused by defendants' wrongdoing but "derivative of the personal injuries of smokers afflicted by tobacco-related illnesses"); Laborers Local 17 Health & Benefit Fund v. Philip Morris, Inc., 191 F.3d 229, 236 (2d Cir. 1999) (N.Y. law) (injuries were "wholly derivative of harm to a third party; indirect and too remote, citing *Holmes*).

[83] See, e.g., Camden Cnty. Bd. of Chosen Freeholders v. Beretta U.S.A. Corp., 123 F. Supp. 2d 245, 257 (D.N.J. 2000) (a plaintiff's harm "flowing merely from the misfortunes visited upon a third person by the defendant's acts" is generally too remote), aff'd, 273 F.3d 536 (3d Cir. 2001).

[84] On these remoteness issues, see § 10.3, above. *But see* In re Neurontin Marketing and Sales Practices Litigation, 712 F.3d 21 (1st Cir. 2013) (federal and Cal. law) (successful RICO and unfair business practices claims against drug company for fraudulently pushing Neurontin to healthcare providers for off-label conditions for which the drug was ineffective).

[85] Goree v. Winnebago Indus., 958 F.2d 1537 (11th Cir. 1992) (Ala. law).

[86] See Moffat v. U.S. Foundry & Mfg. Corp., 551 So.2d 592 (Fla. Dist. Ct. App. 1989).

[87] See § 5.3, above.

[88] See Wagner v. International Ry., 133 N.E. 437, 437–38 (N.Y. 1921).

[89] See McCoy v. American Suzuki Motor Corp., 961 P.2d 952 (Wash. 1998) (motorist, struck by hit-and-run driver in attempt to aid passengers in overturned vehicle, could maintain design defect claim against manufacturer of accident vehicle although plaintiff injured two hours after accident that prompted his rescue and after police had arrived); Dillard v. Pittway Corp., 719 So.2d 188 (Ala. 1998) (rescuers, injured or killed in a boarding house fire, foreseeable to manufacturer of smoke detectors).

than the plaintiff or defendant. Some third party may use a product abusively, or may ignore its warnings or instructions, in a manner that might give rise to a defense of contributory or comparative negligence, assumption of risk, or misuse if the conduct had been that of the plaintiff. Such misconduct by third parties,[90] which combines somehow with a product defect (or its consequences) in a manner that harms the plaintiff, raises a question of how such conduct should affect the responsibility of the manufacturer or other seller for the harm, if at all. The doctrinal question in such cases is whether the third party's conduct, intervening upon a set of risks created by the defendant's sale of a defective product, distances the seller from the plaintiff's harm so much that the product defect and the seller's misconduct become legally "remote" and, hence, no longer a "proximate" cause of the plaintiff's harm. Stated another way, the issue in products liability cases of this type is whether the third party's conduct is so significant in comparison to the product defect as to trivialize the role of the defect in causing the plaintiff's harm, so that the manufacturer or other seller fairly should be relieved of all responsibility.[91]

The first question in such cases is whether some third party's conduct, which came into existence after the defendant's sale of a defective product, combined in some manner with the product's defective condition so as to be a factual cause of the plaintiff's injury. If so, the third party's actions are viewed as an "intervening" force or cause.[92] So characterizing the third party's conduct means little more than that it was a "concurring cause," together with the product defect, which may make the third party concurrently liable with the seller for the plaintiff's injury.[93] While, traditionally, concurrent tortfeasors were jointly and severally liable for a plaintiff's entire harm, they now in most jurisdictions may be responsible only for some equitable portion of the plaintiff's damages under principles of comparative fault and apportionment. Even in such apportionment regimes, however, concurrent tortfeasors normally are responsible for a proportionate share of the plaintiff's damages. Thus, a third party whose conduct joins with a product defect to cause a plaintiff's injuries is usually subject to liability to the plaintiff anyway, under joint and several liability or comparative fault principles of apportionment, which makes the "intervening cause" classification superfluous unless something else is added to the mix.

That something else is whether the intervening party's conduct is so significant that it "breaks the chain" of proximate causation, insulating the seller from *all* responsibility

---

[90] Most courts properly limit the application of principles of intervening and superseding causes to third parties and do not apply them to plaintiffs, for whom the standard misconduct defenses, including (in unusual cases) the doctrine of "sole proximate cause," should suffice. *But see* Reott v. Asia Trend, Inc., 55 A.3d 1088 (Pa. 2012) (plaintiff's highly reckless conduct may constitute sole or superseding cause as affirmative defense to strict products liability). See ch. 13, below.

[91] See, e.g., Gash, At the Intersection of Proximate Cause and Terrorism: A Contextual Analysis of the (Proposed) Restatement Third of Torts' Approach to Intervening and Superseding Causes, 91 Ky. L.J. 523 (2003); M. Green, The Unanticipated Ripples of Comparative Negligence: Superseding Cause in Products Liability and Beyond, 53 S.C. L. Rev. 1103 (2002); Notes, Dumb as a Matter of Law: The "Superseding Cause" Modification of Comparative Negligence, 79 Tex. L. Rev. 493 (2000), Why Superseding Cause Analysis Should Be Abandoned, 72 Tex. L. Rev. 161 (1993), 59 Temp. L. Rev. 239 (1986) (failure to warn as a superseding cause); Frumer, Friedman, and Sklaren, Products Liability § 3.05; Owen & Davis on Products Liability §§ 12:7 et seq.

[92] "An intervening force is one which actively operates in producing harm to another after the actor's negligent act or omission has been committed." Rest. (2d) Torts § 441(1).

[93] On concurrent causation, see § 11.3, above.

for the plaintiff's harm.[94] When an intervening cause has such significance that a product seller's responsibility is severed altogether, the intervening cause is denominated "superseding."[95] The *Second Restatement* provides: "A superseding cause is an act of a third person or other force which by its intervention prevents the actor from being liable for harm to another which his antecedent negligence is a substantial factor in bringing about."[96] An intervening cause, which arises after a defendant's tortious conduct and is sufficient in itself to cause the plaintiff's injury, may become a superseding cause if it is an independent force that operates upon, but is not triggered by nor flows from, the defendant's wrongdoing.[97] It is important to note that these common statements characterizing superseding cause merely state the legal consequence of classifying an intervening cause as "superseding." What they do not do is provide a test for determining whether an intervening cause or force should be so classified. In other words, the "superseding cause" term is just a label, not a recipe.

For a recipe, almost every case turns principally or exclusively to a single test—foreseeability. While courts and commentators sometimes elaborate upon foreseeability, explaining how it operates in varying contexts, the underlying analysis remains essentially the same. And, as with proximate cause more generally, commentators object to the vagueness prison from which foreseeability cannot escape, often arguing that courts should use a richer, scope of (foreseeable) risk approach to superseding cause determinations. But this is what courts in fact do, if often they do not say so, and there is less debate about the appropriateness of foreseeability as the test for superseding cause than there is about proximate cause more generally. The courts, at least, seem perfectly content with using foreseeability as the polestar for determining whether a third party's misconduct should sever the responsibility of a manufacturer or other seller

---

[94] See, e.g., Bice v. Cooper Tire & Rubber Co., 2016 WL 6875973, at *4 (M.D. Tenn. 2016) (after tire tread detached, pickup truck driver safely pulled off road and entered Interstate on foot to pick up debris where he was hit by a motorcycle; tire manufacturer not liable because the truck driver's actions were an intervening cause of the accident as a matter of law). *But see* Yun v. Ford Motor Co., 669 A.2d 1378 (N.J. 1996) (6–1 decision) (a jury could find it reasonably foreseeable that, when a defectively welded spare tire assembly bracket broke causing the bald spare tire to fall off the van, an elderly passenger would race across two lanes of rain-slicked highway at night to retrieve the tire and assembly parts, only to be struck by a motorist).

[95] See, e.g., Beard v. Mighty Lift, Inc., 224 F. Supp. 3d 1131, 1137 (W.D. Wash. 2016) (plaintiff's refusal to heed warning not to operate pallet jack on an incline, despite his admission "that he understood the warning, is a superseding cause that breaks the chain of legal causation").

[96] Rest. (2d) Torts § 440.

[97] See, e.g., Novak v. Cont'l Tire N. Am., 231 Cal. Rptr. 3d 324, 331–32 (Ct. App. 2018) (tire manufacturer's failure to warn that rubber degradation in old tires could cause tire blowouts led to such a blowout causing an accident that injured an elderly man, impairing his mobility, which required him to use a 3-wheel motorized scooter, subsequently leading to his death, 6 years later, when he was struck in a crosswalk by a negligently driven car he could not avoid due to his scooter's lack of maneuverability; "the second accident [was] not a normal consequence of the original injury and the negligence of a third person—the motorist who failed to yield to Novak in the crosswalk—was the superseding cause of the injury he suffered"); Phillips v. Pneumo Abex, LLC, 713 Fed. Appx 191, 195 (4th Cir. 2017) (N.C. law) (an "intervening cause" becomes a "superseding cause"—"which entirely supersedes the original [tortious] action and renders its effect in the chain of causation remote"; it is a "new and entirely independent [force that] breaks the sequence of events, and insulates" the original wrongdoer of the consequences of its tortious conduct); Dorman v. State Indus., 787 S.E.2d 132, 139 (Va. 2016) (after a defendant tortiously creates an unreasonable risk of harm to the plaintiff, if a third party's independent actions unforeseeably bring about an accident that harms the plaintiff, the third party's intervening actions shield the defendant, whose original misconduct now is viewed as "merely a circumstance of the accident"); Landis v. Hearthmark, LLC, 750 S.E.2d 280, 293 (W.Va. 2013) (7-year-old child, seeking to restart fire with fire starter gel, in order to roast marshmallows, injured when spray from gel bottle caused vapors to ignite, flash back, and explode; defendant could assert as defense that parent's conduct in leaving bottle accessible to child was an intervening cause of child's injuries); Scruggs v. Sperian Fall Arrest System, Inc., 2011 WL 4744908, at *5 (W.D. Ky. 2011) (specifying six traits of a superseding cause).

of a defective product.[98] "For an intervening force to be a superseding cause that relieves an actor from liability, the intervening cause must be a cause that could not have been reasonably foreseen or anticipated."[99] And the converse is also true: "A third party's acts of negligence do not break the causal chain if the acts are foreseeable."[100]

Some courts enrich the foreseeability inquiry in this context by focusing on intervening force perspectives that the *Second Restatement* suggests may be relevant to this inquiry, to wit:[101]

(1) whether the intervention brought about a different kind of harm from that risked by the defendant's tortious behavior;

(2) whether *after* the event the operation or consequences of the intervention appear "extraordinary";

(3) whether the intervention operated "independently" or was a "normal result" of the actor's negligence; and

(4) whether the intervening cause was a human wrongdoer and, if so, the degree of that wrongdoing.[102]

In short, for an intervening force to supersede a defendant's wrongdoing, it must be so substantial a cause of the harm as to dwarf into insignificance the role of the defendant's prior misconduct. All of the foregoing principles and perspectives, it should be noted, although originating in the law of negligence, apply equally to claims in strict products

---

[98] See, e.g., Gaines-Tabb v. ICI Explosives, USA, Inc., 160 F.3d 613, 621 (10th Cir. 1998) (Okla. law).

[99] Small v. Pioneer Mach., Inc., 494 S.E.2d 835, 844 (S.C. Ct. App. 1997). See also Gunn v. Hytrol Conveyor Co., 2013 WL 2249241, at *13 (E.D.N.Y. 2013) ("an intervening act which is 'extraordinary under the circumstances, not foreseeable in the normal course of events, or independent of or far removed from the defendant's conduct . . . may well be a superseding act which breaks the causal nexus' ").

[100] *Small*, 494 S.E.2d at 844. See also Bader Farms, Inc. v. Monsanto Co., 2020 WL 6939364, at *31 (E.D. Mo. 2020) (third-party farmers' illegal use of older modified seed herbicide that was prone to drift was foreseeable and "in fact foreseen" by defendant, was "not an intervening and superseding cause" of damage to neighboring non-modified crops); Braswell v. Cincinnati Inc., 731 F.3d 1081, 1086 (10th Cir. 2013) (Okla. law) (modification of a product by a third party, such as an employer, is not a superseding cause if it is reasonably foreseeable); Mazant v. Visioneering Inc., 250 Fed. Appx. 60, 66 (5th Cir. 2007) (La. law) ("foreseeable intervening forces are within the scope of the original risk and, therefore, will not relieve the manufacturer of liability").

[101] See, e.g., Bertrand v. Cordiner Enters., Inc., 2013 WL 6122388, at *3–4 (V.I. Super. Ct. 2013) (applying Restatement factors); Stone v. Secretary of Health & Human Servs., 676 F.3d 1373, 1380 (Fed. Cir. 2012) (gene mutations, not vaccine, was sole cause of children's injuries).

[102] Rest. (2d) Torts § 442, "Considerations Important in Determining Whether an Intervening Force is a Superseding Cause," describes the relevant factors more fully:

(a) The fact that its intervention brings about harm different in kind from that which would otherwise have resulted from the actor's negligence;

(b) the fact that its operation or the consequences thereof appear after the event to be extraordinary rather than normal in view of the circumstances existing at the time of its operation;

(c) the fact that the intervening force is operating independently of any situation created by the actor's negligence, or, on the other hand, is or is not a normal result of such a situation;

(d) the fact that the operation of the intervening force is due to a third person's act or to his failure to act;

(e) the fact that the intervening force is due to an act of a third person which is wrongful toward the other and as such subjects the third person to liability to him;

(f) the degree of culpability of a wrongful act of a third person which sets the intervening force in motion.

liability.[103] Like most other aspects of proximate cause, whether a defendant reasonably should have foreseen an intervening cause normally is a subject of varying inferences, which ordinarily presents a question for the jury.[104]

Types of Third Parties

Parents

Many, perhaps most, products liability cases in which young children are injured involve inadequate supervision on the part of a parent or other person having custody of the child at the time of the accident. This was true in the two farm accident cases involving young children, *Winnett* and *Richelman*, examined in the previous section.[105] Modern courts are reluctant to hold that a parent's negligent supervision can supersede the responsibility of a manufacturer of a defective product.[106] Yet, in a sense, this is what the court implicitly did in *Winnett*, and what the dissent in *Richelman* argued should also have been done there. Nevertheless, at least with respect to products intended for use in and around the home, juries and courts often consider parental neglect—and the resulting wandering and mischief of curious youngsters—part of the "foreseeable environment of use" of such products.[107] While courts often may require manufacturers to foresee such hazards, they normally are loathe to attach a superseding label to a parent's merely careless behavior, such as falling asleep at the wheel of a car in which a

---

[103] See, e.g., Pittway Corp. v. Collins, 973 A.2d 771 (Md. 2009); Anderson v. Dreis & Krump Mfg. Corp., 739 P.2d 1177, 1185 (Wash. Ct. App. 1987).

[104] See, e.g., Parker-Reed v. Primal Vantage Co., Inc., 2021 WL 1193081, at *7 (S.D. Ohio 2021) (if "reasonable minds might differ as to the foreseeability of a particular risk or . . . an intervening cause, the question is one for . . . the jury"); Collins v. Navistar, Inc., 155 Cal. Rptr. 3d 137, 153 (Ct. App. 2013) (whether risk that 2½ pound chunk of concrete (thrown from overpass) might strike vehicle's windshield was foreseeable to manufacturer was question of fact for jury); Dolan v. Hilo Med. Ctr., 278 P.3d 382, 399 (Haw. Ct. App. 2012) ("Whether a subsequent cause constitutes a superseding cause is a factual question that turns on foreseeability."). *But see* West v. Ride the Ducks Int'l, LLC, 2021 WL 2809609, at *12–13 (Wash. Ct. App. 2021) (as a matter of law, boat operator's failure to implement manufacturer's axle housing collar modification was not a superseding cause of plaintiff's injury); Wilson v. Sentry Ins., 993 F. Supp. 2d 662, 666 (E.D. Ky. 2014) (when facts are undisputed, superseding cause is a legal issue for a court, not a factual issue for a jury).

[105] See § 12.2, above.

[106] See, e.g., Wheeler v. Sears Roebuck & Co., 831 N.Y.S.2d 427 (App. Div. 2007) (father's negligent supervision not imputed to 2-year-old son who got finger caught in treadmill); Talkington v. Atria Reclamelucifers Fabrieken BV, 152 F.3d 254 (4th Cir. 1998) (S.C. law) (plaintiffs died in a house fire that might have been started by infant child with cigarette lighter).

[107] See, e.g., Burton v. American Cyanamid, 341 F. Supp. 3d 941, 948 (E.D. Wis. 2018) (question of fact whether it was foreseeable that unsupervised young children would eat lead paint chips as they crawled around the floors of tenements; compare Santiago v. Sherwin Williams Co., 3 F.3d 546 (1st Cir. 1993) (amicus draft adorned with celebrated footnote 3)); Eshbach v. W. T. Grant's & Co., 481 F.2d 940 (3d Cir. 1973) (Pa. law) (unbeknownst to father, 9-year-old son drove riding mower with sister riding on back); Spruill v. Boyle-Midway, Inc., 308 F.2d 79 (4th Cir. 1962) (Va. law) (unattended infant drank furniture polish that mother left on bureau beside crib). Compare McConnell v. Cosco, Inc., 238 F. Supp. 2d 970 (S.D. Ohio 2003) (baby, left by babysitter unstrapped and unattended in high chair, squiggled out); Laney v. Coleman Co., Inc., 758 F.2d 1299, 1301 (8th Cir. 1985) (parents stored gasoline in garage in Coleman fuel can, which was not equipped with flash arrestor, accessible to young children who poured it on fire, causing flashback and explosion). *But see* Wenzell v. MTD Prods., Inc., 336 N.E.2d 125, 134 (Ill. App. Ct. 1975) (unforeseeable that riding mower would be used by group of young children "virtually as a toy").

In strict tort actions, however, Pennsylvania's "intended user"/"use" doctrine trumps foreseeability (at least for now). See Hysick v. Razor USA, LLC, 2017 WL 4084054, at *3–5 (M.D. Pa. 2017) (strict liability claim failed where child was not an intended user of electric motorbike; "In Pennsylvania, strict liability is imposed only where the product is used by an intended user . . . even where foreseeable by a manufacturer."); Phillips v. Cricket Lighters, 841 A.2d 1000 (Pa. 2003) (foreseeable misuse of butane lighter by child, not its intended user, may support a negligence claim but not a strict liability claim).

child is riding,[108] or even carelessly knocking over a bottle of liquid drain cleaner onto the child.[109] Yet sometimes a parent's conduct will indeed be considered a superseding cause of a child's harm, such as where a parent places a very dangerous item within reach of a very young child[110] or gives a child massive doses of a cold medicine, in disregard of the medication's warnings and vastly in excess of its dosage instructions.[111] The results in these cases are hard to reconcile, and their results often are dependent on juries and the persuasiveness of lawyers in particular cases.

Doctors

A common failing of doctors that quite often leads to serious harm is a failure to pass along to patients drug warnings and instructions the manufacturer provided to the doctor. *Kirk v. Michael Reese Hospital & Medical Center*[112] was such a case, where a passenger was injured when the driver of a car lost control of the vehicle and crashed into a tree. Earlier in the day, when the driver was discharged from a psychiatric hospital, his doctors prescribed two drugs, Thorazine and Prolixin, but failed to warn him of the dangers of mixing alcohol with the drugs. After leaving the hospital, he consumed an alcoholic drink which may have interacted with the drugs to cause the loss of control later in the day. On these facts, the court ruled that the drug manufacturers could not reasonably have foreseen that the drugs would be dispensed without the warnings the companies had furnished to physicians.[113] Nor must a manufacturer foresee that a doctor will use a drug contrary to its express warnings,[114] nor, in general, need a drug manufacturer warn doctors of the risks of prescribing a drug for off-label use.[115] Yet, as tortfeasors generally,[116] manufacturers must foresee that persons injured by their tortious conduct may thereafter suffer negligent medical treatment.[117]

Yet, if a medical product is unsafely designed, a court may be more willing to hold manufacturers responsible for the consequences[118] of a doctor's intervening conduct that substantially aggravates the patient's condition. For example, in *Pharmaseal*

---

[108] See Rossell v. Volkswagen of Am., 709 P.2d 517 (Ariz. 1985).

[109] See Drayton v. Jiffee Chem. Corp., 395 F. Supp. 1081 (N.D. Ohio 1975), aff'd, 591 F.2d 352 (6th Cir. 1978).

[110] Landis v. Hearthmark, LLC, 750 S.E.2d 280, 293 (W.Va. 2013) (7-year-old child, seeking to restart fire to roast marshmallows with fire starter gel, injured when spray from gel bottle caused vapors to ignite, flash back, and explode; defendant could assert as defense that parent's conduct in leaving bottle accessible to child was an intervening cause of child's injuries).

[111] See Dunson v. McNeil-PPC, Inc., 2009 WL 1178651, at *6–7 (Pa. Super. Ct. 2009) (proximate cause of child's death was parents' "failure to follow the warnings and instructions" on Children's Tylenol).

[112] 513 N.E.2d 387, 394 (Ill. 1987).

[113] Compare Hrymoc v. Ethicon, Inc., 249 A.3d 191, 219–20 (N.J. Super. Ct. App. Div. 2021) ("the inadequacy of a warning cannot be the proximate cause of an injury where there is an intervening cause, that is, that the physician either did not read the warning, or had independent knowledge of the risks").

[114] See, e.g., Dyer v. Best Pharmacal, 577 P.2d 1084 (Ariz. Ct. App. 1978).

[115] See Robak v. Abbott Labs., 797 F. Supp. 475 (D. Md. 1992) (renal failure from antibiotic Omniflox prescribed for sinusitis, although drug not indicated for upper respiratory tract conditions).

[116] "It would be an undue compliment to the medical profession to say that bad surgery is no part of the risk of a broken leg." Prosser & Keeton on Torts 309 (5th ed. 1984).

[117] See, e.g., Mavity v. MTD Prods., Inc., 714 F. Supp. 2d 577, 584–85 (W.D. Va. 2010) (negligence of ER physicians in treating plaintiff injured by defective lawnmower was not a superseding cause of injuries).

[118] See, e.g., Phelps v. Wyeth, Inc., 938 F. Supp. 2d 1055, 1067–68 (D. Or. 2013) ("this court has also recently declined to find that the failure to read a warning label by a doctor precludes a finding of proximate cause where there is evidence that the doctor would have acted differently had she been warned . . . a genuine issue of material fact remains as to whether [generic drug manufacturer's] alleged failure to update its label was a proximate cause of [plaintiff's] injuries").

Laboratories, Inc. v. Goffe,[119] a doctor inserted an intestinal tube weighted with a small balloon of mercury through the plaintiff's nostril, down through his stomach, and into his intestines, in order to treat an internal obstruction. As the doctor began to remove the tube, it stuck, leading him to tug at it forcefully several times to pull it out. In the process, the balloon was broken, and the plaintiff inhaled the mercury into his lungs. The doctor thereupon placed the plaintiff head-down on a tilt table where hospital employees pounded on his back for several hours to remove the mercury—causing the plaintiff's head constantly to hit the foot of the bed, which led him to have a heart attack. Reversing a summary judgment for the manufacturer, the court refused to find that the actions of the doctor and hospital employees shielded the manufacturer from liability as a matter of law for selling a balloon of inadequate strength.

Employers

A manufacturer of an industrial product sometimes has a duty to provide warnings and instructions directly to its buyers' employees, as previously examined.[120] If a manufacturer has such a duty, and if the manufacturer provides a warning only to the employer (as by a safety information sheet or a technical data manual) and not to the employees (as by a label on the product's container or a warning plate on a machine), the employer's failure to pass along the warning to its employees will not generally supersede the manufacturer's duty to warn them directly.[121] Yet, courts quite often refuse to hold a manufacturer liable for machinery malfunctions occasioned by an employer's improper maintenance.[122]

Failing to add guards. Before the 1970s, the custom was for employers, rather than manufacturers, to install appropriate guards on industrial machinery. Starting with *Bexiga v. Havir Manufacturing Corp.*,[123] however, courts began to hold that manufacturers had a nondelegable duty to equip their machinery with sufficient safety devices. What this means in terms of superseding cause is that, if a manufacturer fails to provide adequate guards, the employer's failure to remedy the danger will not generally shield the manufacturer. This may be true even if the employer blithely ignores warning letters from the manufacturer urging the employer to cure the danger, explaining how to do so, and offering to provide the employer with the necessary devices for a fee.[124]

---

[119] 568 P.2d 589 (N.M. 1977).

[120] See §§ 9.4 and 9.5, above.

[121] See, e.g., Gordon v. Niagara Mach. & Tool Works, 574 F.2d 1182 (5th Cir. 1978) (Miss. law).

[122] "The manufacturer is not liable for lack of normal maintenance." Rogers v. Unimac Co., 565 P.2d 181, 184 (Ariz. 1977) (failure to replace worn and cracked parts in automatic car wash mechanism). See also La Plante v. American Honda Motor Co., 27 F.3d 731 (1st Cir. 1994) (R.I. law) (poor maintenance of ATV could constitute statutory defense of alteration). *But see* Green Plains Otter Tail, LLC v. Pro-Env't, Inc., 953 F.3d 541, 548 (8th Cir. 2020) (Minn. law) (reversing summary judgment for defendant on design defect claim; reasonable minds could differ whether the failure to perform recommended maintenance to recharge accumulator was a superseding cause of explosion); Montemayor v. Sebright Prods., Inc., 898 N.W.2d 623, 632 (Minn. 2017) (jury question whether it was foreseeable that injured worker's employer would fail to comply with safety regulations or maintain product, so that employer's negligence did not supersede manufacturer's liability).

[123] 290 A.2d 281 (N.J. 1972). See § 8.9, above.

[124] See Balido v. Improved Mach., Inc., 105 Cal. Rptr. 890 (Ct. App. 1972). See also Montgomery Elevator Co. v. McCullough, 676 S.W.2d 776 (Ky. 1984). *But see* Hinojo v. New Jersey Mfg. Ins. Co., 802 A.2d 551 (N.J. Super. Ct. App. Div. 2002) (employer's ignoring of several letters from manufacturer urging employer to replace safety guards on presses entitled manufacturer to instruction on superseding cause). Compare Ontario Sewing

Removing or altering guards. A recurring problem for manufacturers attempting to comply with the *Bexiga* nondelegable duty doctrine occurs when an employer removes or alters a guard provided by the manufacturer.[125] Guards are modified or removed for a variety of reasons: because they malfunction; to facilitate cleaning or maintenance of the machinery; to enhance the usefulness of the machine, as by permitting stock of a particular size or shape to enter the machine; or to speed up production. Most courts hold manufacturers accountable for injuries attributable to "foreseeable" modifications, provided that a feasible remedy—such as an electrical interlock—was reasonably available to the manufacturer at the time it designed and sold the machine.[126] But if the employer's modification is unforeseeable, the modification is considered a superseding cause that shields the manufacturer from liability.[127] In a small number of jurisdictions, even foreseeable alterations may bar recovery.[128] At least in California and Ohio, a worker injured by an employer's removal of a safety guard may have a statutory claim against the employer outside the workers' compensation system.[129]

"Substantial change." Courts often examine alteration questions in terms of whether the product was "substantially changed" after it left the manufacturer.[130] This

---

Mach. Co. v. Smith, 572 S.E.2d 533 (Ga. 2002) (unforeseeable failure to comply with recall would be sole proximate cause, but foreseeability for jury).

[125] See Braswell v. Cincinnati Inc., 731 F.3d 1081, 1086–87 (10th Cir. 2013) (Okla. law) (citing cases, and listing factors pertinent to whether guard removal is foreseeable in varying contexts). Compare Davis v. Berwind Corp., 690 A.2d 186 (Pa. 1997) (purchaser's removal of safety devices was superseding cause of employee's injury), with Anderson v. Dreis & Krump Mfg. Corp., 739 P.2d 1177, 1185 (Wash. Ct. App. 1987) (purchaser's removal of safety devices was not a superseding cause).

[126] See, e.g., Braswell v. Cincinnati Inc., 731 F.3d 1081, 1086 (10th Cir. 2013) (Okla. law) (subsequent modification; dictum); Cepeda v. Cumberland Eng'g Co., 386 A.2d 816 (N.J. 1978) (guard attached to machine with four bolts was not reattached to machine after cleaning; since interlock installation would have cost $25–$30, and frequent cleaning was necessary; *held*, foreseeability of removal was a jury question). Accord Brown v. United States Stove Co., 484 A.2d 1234, 1240 (N.J. 1984) ("a design defect inherent in a safety feature of a product that foreseeably leads to a substantial alteration and an increased risk of danger can be a basis for strict products liability").

[127] See, e.g., CNH Am., LLC v. Roebuck, 41 So.3d 41, 50 (Ala. 2009) (manufacturer could not reasonably have foreseen that person converting backhoe to foot controls "would have both: (1) failed to follow the instructions included in the kit for accomplishing that conversion and (2) failed to install a necessary part that was included in the conversion kit"); Robinson v. Brandtjen & Kluge, Inc., 2006 WL 2796252, at *5 (D.S.D. 2006) (conversion of printing press into foil-stamping press almost 60 years after purchase was unforeseeable and superseded any negligence of manufacturer); Fisher v. Walsh Parts & Serv. Co., 296 F. Supp. 2d 551 (E.D. Pa. 2003) (unforeseeable modifications by purchaser became superseding cause breaking chain of causation).

[128] See Hines v. Joy Mfg. Co., 850 F.2d 1146, 1151 (6th Cir. 1988) (interpreting Kentucky products liability statute barring recovery for injuries caused by product modifications: "we are not inclined to read the common law concept of foreseeability" into the act). Compare Robinson v. Reed-Prentice Div. of Package Mach. Co., 403 N.E.2d 440, 444 (N.Y. 1980), in which an employee was injured when he stuck his hand through a hole in the safety guard cut by his employer. *Held*, judgment for plaintiff reversed:

> The manufacturer's duty . . . does not extend to designing a product that is impossible to abuse or one whose safety features may not be circumvented. . . . Material alterations at the hands of a third party which work a substantial change in the condition in which the product was sold by destroying the functional utility of a key safety feature, however foreseeable that modification may have been, are not within the ambit of a manufacturer's responsibility.

Id. at 480–81. *But see* Lopez v. Precision Papers, Inc., 484 N.Y.S.2d 585 (App. Div. 1985) (allowing recovery for injuries preventable by interlock on forklift guard that could have prevented lift from rising above operator's head), aff'd, 492 N.E.2d 1214 (N.Y. 1986). On employers as products liability defendants, see § 15.6, below.

[129] See Broyles v. Kasper Mach. Co., 517 Fed. Appx. 345, 353 (6th Cir. 2013) (Ohio law) (rebuttable statutory presumption that employers who deliberately remove machine guards intend to injure workers harmed as a result); LeFiell Mfg. Co. v. Superior Ct., 282 P.3d 1242, 1249 (Cal. 2012).

[130] See, e.g., Dolan v. Hilo Med. Ctr., 278 P.3d 382, 397–98 (Haw. Ct. App. 2012) ("A substantial change to a product may negate causation where the alteration, and not the originally defective condition of the

derives from *Restatement (Second) of Torts* § 402A(b), which provides for liability only if the product "is expected to and does reach the user or consumer without substantial change in the condition in which it is sold."[131] While some courts shield manufacturers from liability for injuries caused by an employer's alteration of safety devices on "substantial change" grounds,[132] other courts refuse to relieve manufacturers of liability unless the change is deemed "unforeseeable."[133] In addition, courts sometimes bar recovery in alteration cases on grounds of unforeseeable misuse.[134] Courts disagree on whether there should be a duty to warn about foreseeable risks of removing safety devices, with some courts refusing to require such a warning[135] and others holding that it makes good sense.[136]

Shifting responsibility. Particularly in the industrial setting, a proximate cause sub-doctrine relied upon occasionally, expressed in § 452 of the *Second Restatement*,[137] is the notion that full responsibility for product safety may sometimes be shifted from a manufacturer to an employer after the passage of many years and the integration of the product into the employer's operations. In *Meuller v. Jeffrey Manufacturing Co.*,[138] the

product, was the proximate cause of the injury. . . . Conversely, liability still attaches if the subsequent alteration was *not* the sole or superseding cause of the injury."). See generally 28 A.L.R.7th Art. 5 (2017).

[131] See also caveat (2) and comments *p* and *q*. See, e.g., Davis v. Berwind Corp., 690 A.2d 186, 190 (Pa. 1997) (in disregard of warnings in owner's manual and affixed to machine, plaintiff's employer removed safety devices which "clearly constitutes a substantial change" in the product, thereby relieving manufacturer of liability); Glassey v. Continental Ins. Co., 500 N.W.2d 295 (Wis. 1993) (employer put non-standard replacement cap on pressurized tank).

[132] See, e.g., Robinson v. Reed-Prentice Div. of Package Mach. Co., 403 N.E.2d 440, 444 (N.Y. 1980) (employee stuck hand through hole in safety guard cut by his employer: "Material alterations at the hands of a third party which work a substantial change in the condition in which the product was sold by destroying the functional utility of a key safety feature, however foreseeable that modification may have been, are not within the ambit of a manufacturer's responsibility.").

[133] See, e.g., Tanksley v. ProSoft Automation, Inc., 982 So.2d 1046, 1056 (Ala. 2007); Brown v. United States Stove Co., 484 A.2d 1234, 1240 (N.J. 1984) ("a design defect inherent in a safety feature of a product that foreseeably leads to a substantial alteration and an increased risk of danger can be a basis for strict products liability"). Compare Sikkelee v. Precision Airmotive Corp., 907 F.3d 701, 716 (3d Cir. 2018) (Pa. law) (reversing dismissal of strict products liability and negligence claims against aircraft engine's manufacturer; "the issues of proximate causation, whether a change to the product was substantial, and whether that change was reasonably foreseeable, are generally for the jury").

[134] See, e.g., Westchem Agric. Chem., Inc. v. Ford Motor Co., 990 F.2d 426 (8th Cir. 1993) (N.D. law) (aftermarket electrical equipment, bypassing safety device, spliced into electrical system).

[135] See, e.g., Huber v. Niagara Mach. & Tool Works, 430 N.W.2d 465 (Minn. 1988) (no duty to warn of danger in removing safety devices).

[136] See, e.g., Liriano v. Hobart Corp., 700 N.E.2d 303, 307–08 (N.Y. 1998) (*Liriano II*) ("Unlike design decisions that involve the consideration of many interdependent factors, the inquiry in a duty to warn case is much more limited, focusing principally on the foreseeability of the risk and the adequacy and effectiveness of any warning. . . . Thus, although it is virtually impossible to design a product to forestall all future risk-enhancing modifications that could occur after the sale, it is neither infeasible nor onerous, in some cases, to warn of the dangers of foreseeable modifications that pose the risk of injury.").

[137] See Rest. (2d) Torts § 452, "Third Person's Failure to Prevent Harm," which provides that "(1) Except as stated in Subsection (2), the failure of a third person to act to prevent harm to another threatened by the actor's negligent conduct is not a superseding cause of such harm. (2) Where, because of lapse of time or otherwise, the duty to prevent harm to another threatened by the actor's negligent conduct is found to have shifted from the actor to a third person, the failure of the third person to prevent such harm is a superseding cause." Comment *f* provides that a court may "find that all duty and responsibility for the prevention of the harm has passed to the third person. It is apparently impossible to state any comprehensive rule as to when such a decision will be made." Relevant factors include "the degree of danger and the magnitude of the risk of harm, the character and position of the third person who is to take the responsibility, his knowledge of the danger and the likelihood that he will or will not exercise proper care, his relation to the plaintiff or to the defendant, the lapse of time, and perhaps other considerations."

[138] 494 F. Supp. 275, 278–79 (E.D. Pa. 1980).

plaintiff fell through a 3-foot square hole in a concrete floor of his employer's foundry building. The opening was part of a sand handling system consisting of a collection of conveyors, elevators, and other equipment. Plaintiff's employer had purchased the sand handling equipment and installation design plans (which prescribed the location of the hole) fifteen years earlier from the defendant, but had done the installation itself, including the construction of the slab floor and the hole. The plaintiff claimed that the system was defectively designed and that the defendant should have warned of the risk. Relying on § 452, the court granted summary judgment for the defendant. The time interval between sale and injury, the obvious nature of the danger, the ability of the employer to remedy the danger without the manufacturer, the "indisputable duty of the employer to keep the workplace safe, and the employer's sole possession and control of the equipment" had shifted the duty from the manufacturer to the employer as a matter of law.[139]

Other Employees

Employees injure one another with industrial machinery in a variety of ways. A fellow employee's misconduct may or may not supersede the manufacturer's design errors depending on the "foreseeability" of the misconduct and the availability to the manufacturer of a feasible means to prevent it.[140] In *Wieder v. Towmotor Corp.*,[141] for example, a worker left a forklift on an incline and forgot to set the hand brake. The plaintiff was injured when the forklift rolled down the incline and struck him. His theory of liability was that the forklift should have had a passive, "back-up" brake system. The jury rendered a verdict for the plaintiff, which the trial court sustained.

Other Parties

Although intervening misconduct in products liability cases usually involves parents, doctors, employers, and sometimes fellow workers, other parties are sometimes involved. In *Dugan v. Sears, Roebuck & Co.*,[142] a 5-year-old boy was sitting on the steps of his neighbor's front porch watching her mow the lawn. When the neighbor was about 10 feet from the plaintiff, the lawn mower picked up and ejected at high velocity a small piece of plastic which hit the plaintiff in the eye and blinded him. The neighbor had read the mower manual that warned users in no uncertain terms not to operate the mower if children were in the vicinity and to stop the engine if anyone came near. The plaintiff sued Sears, alleging that it should have sold a mower with a safer alternative design. Upholding a verdict for Sears, the appellate court reasoned that the jury reasonably could have concluded that the neighbor's conduct was unforeseeable and so could be a superseding cause of the plaintiff's injuries. While acknowledging that manufacturers should foresee that people occasionally will disregard their warnings, the court concluded that a reasonable jury still might conclude that the neighbor's conduct in this case was not so "probable, natural, and foreseeable" that the defendant should be held strictly liable.

While the *Dugan* court's holding might be viewed as quite conservative, other courts in superseding cause cases stretch the flexible concept of foreseeable risk the other way.

---

139 Id. at 279.

140 See, e.g., Sanders v. Lull Int'l, Inc., 411 F.3d 1266 (11th Cir. 2005) (Ga. law) (reversing summary judgment for defendant; whether it was reasonably foreseeable for workers to use forklift to transport plaintiff co-worker contrary to defendant's explicit warnings was question for jury).

141 568 F. Supp. 1058 (E.D. Pa. 1983).

142 454 N.E.2d 64 (Ill. App. Ct. 1983).

In *Bigbee v. Pacific Telephone & Telegraph Co.*,[143] the plaintiff was standing in a telephone booth 15 feet from the street when it was struck by a drunken driver. Plaintiff saw the car coming but could not flee because the door of the telephone booth jammed shut. The plaintiff sued various defendants in connection with the design, location, installation, and maintenance of the booth, and the defendants moved to dismiss, arguing that the drunk driver's conduct was a superseding cause. The trial judge dismissed the complaint, but the appellate court reversed and remanded, concluding that "the risk that a car might hit the telephone booth could be found to constitute one of the hazards to which plaintiff was exposed."[144]

Superseding cause issues are also raised by actors who use products to cause personal harm to others (or themselves) by criminal behavior. As previously noted, some criminal conduct (such as drunk driving) creates risks that a product (such as a motor vehicle) otherwise should withstand, and thus should be considered foreseeable; whereas exceptionally reprehensible behavior, such as the use of a handgun to murder another person, serves as a superseding cause of the resulting harm.[145]

Statutory Reform

Product alteration long has been a key products liability reform issue. Several state reform acts have provisions making product alteration a defense to products liability suits. Kentucky's statute,[146] for example, provides: "In any product liability action, a manufacturer shall be liable only for the personal injury, death or property damage that would have occurred if the product had been used in its original, unaltered and unmodified condition. For the purpose of this section, product alteration or modification shall include failure to observe routine care and maintenance, but shall not include ordinary wear and tear. This section shall apply to alterations or modifications made by any person or entity, except those made in accordance with specifications or instructions furnished by the manufacturer." As noted earlier, a federal court of appeals ruled that the protections of this statute are not limited to unforeseeable alterations.[147] Other reform statutes expressly limit the defense of alteration to those that are unforeseeable.[148]

Intentional and Criminal Misconduct

If an assailant uses a defective product intentionally to harm another person, or if a defective product fails to protect a person attacked by another in the way he or she has a right to expect, an important issue is whether the doctrine of superseding causation prevents the injured plaintiff from recovering against the manufacturer or seller of the defective product. A number of cases have addressed this issue, most of which have ruled that the intentionally harmful, criminal misconduct of an intervening party was unforeseeable, and that it was accordingly a superseding cause that severed the chain of proximate causation. But courts in several cases have ruled the other way, allowing such cases to proceed if the risk of harm was deemed "foreseeable." Foreseeability, or whether

---

[143] 665 P.2d 947 (Cal. 1983).

[144] Id. at 952.

[145] See § 12.2, above.

[146] See Ky. Rev. Stat. Ann. § 411.320(1), called into question by comparative fault statute. See Wilson v. Sentry Ins., 993 F. Supp. 2d 662, 670 (E.D. Ky. 2014).

[147] See Hines v. Joy Mfg. Co., 850 F.2d 1146, 1151 (6th Cir. 1988) (Ky. law) ("we are not inclined to read the common law concept of foreseeability" into the act).

[148] See, e.g., Or. Rev. Stat. Ann. § 30.915; Tenn. Code Ann. § 29–28–108.

the intervening conduct fell within the foreseeable risk that rendered the product defective, is the purported "test" of superseding cause in cases of this type.[149] But the decisions are exceedingly difficult to reconcile, and the best that can be done here is to give some examples and highlight some competing arguments.[150]

If a defect in a product designed for the particular purpose of self-protection, like a burglar alarm or mace,[151] causes the product to malfunction, allowing a criminal to steal from or assault the plaintiff, then the resulting criminal act would appear to fall quite clearly within the foreseeable risk of a product malfunction.[152] But when this envelope is stretched a bit, the foreseeable risk approach begins to waffle.[153] Thus, a locksmith was held not liable for the rape of a woman in an apartment building supposedly protected by one of his locks.[154] In another case, *Williams v. RCA Corp.*,[155] a security service guard was injured during a robbery attempt at a restaurant he was guarding. He used his transmitter-receiver manufactured by the defendant to call other security patrols in the area for backup assistance, but the transmitter malfunctioned, and he was shot by the robber while trying to make an arrest himself. Because the receiver was designed for communication, not the prevention of criminal attack, the court ruled that the criminal intervening cause was unforeseeable as a matter of law.[156]

---

[149] See, e.g., District of Columbia v. Beretta, U.S.A., Corp., 872 A.2d 633, 641 (D.C. 2005) ("Where an injury is caused by the intervening criminal act of a third party . . . liability depends upon a more heightened showing of foreseeability than would be required if the act were merely negligent.").

[150] See generally Gash, The Intersection of Proximate Cause and Terrorism: A Contextual Analysis of the (Proposed) Restatement Third of Torts' Approach to Intervening and Superseding Causes, 91 Ky. L.J. 523 (2003); Green, The Unanticipated Ripples of Comparative Negligence: Superseding Cause in Products Liability and Beyond, 53 S.C. L. Rev. 1103 (2002).

[151] See Klages v. General Ordnance Equip. Corp., 367 A.2d 304 (Pa. Super. Ct. 1976), where plaintiff suffered severe gunshot wounds when a mace weapon manufactured by defendant failed to function during a confrontation between the plaintiff and an armed robber. *Held*, because the mace was an instrument of crime prevention, the manufacturer should have foreseen the specific risk that a user would be assaulted if the product failed to function, such that the intervening criminal act was not a superseding cause that would shield the manufacturer from liability.

[152] So, because a vehicle's windshield should protect its occupants from external debris, the fact that a youth acts in a criminal manner by dropping a 2½ pound chunk of concrete from an overpass, penetrating a truck windshield and injuring the driver, does not alone make the injury unforeseeable. See Collins v. Navistar, Inc., 155 Cal. Rptr. 3d 137, 151, 153 (Ct. App. 2013) ("[T]he same standard of foreseeability for strict products liability applies to the risk of the harm, regardless of the source of the risk. . . . In the case of a rock hitting a windshield, liability for a defective design does not depend on whether the projectile falls from a rock outcropping, passing gravel truck, or the hands of a juvenile delinquent. A windshield is not any less defective because it is pierced by an intentionally, rather than an unintentionally, thrown rock.").

[153] In Heeter v. Honeywell Int'l Inc., 706 Fed. Appx. 63, 67 (3d Cir. 2017) (Pa. law), the Heeter's weekend home was broken into by Chattin, a resident of the area known to the Heeters. After disabling the alarm system, Chattin stole several heirloom guns. Several hours later, Chattin drove to the Heeters' son's apartment and shot him in the face with one of the stolen firearms, arranging the scene to appear as if the son had committed suicide. Affirming dismissal of Heeter's claims against the alarm company and alarm system manufacturer, the court ruled:

> Intervening criminal action is not per se superseding, but becomes so when, "looking retrospectively from the harm through the sequence of events by which it was produced, it is so extraordinary as not to have been reasonably foreseeable." The chain of events and ultimate harm here were not foreseeable, and the criminal action of Chattin is, therefore, a superseding cause of harm that breaks the causal chain.

[154] Einhorn v. Seeley, 525 N.Y.S.2d 212, 215 (App. Div. 1988) (locksmith not liable for failing to properly install door lock: "[T]he act complained of by plaintiff was perpetrated by an intervening person. There will ordinarily be no duty thrust on a defendant to prevent a third party from causing harm to another.").

[155] 376 N.E.2d 37 (Ill. App. Ct. 1978).

[156] On almost identical facts, but on a misrepresentation claim under § 402B of the Second Rest., a subsequent court ruled that the seller of a pager marketed to police departments could reasonably foresee such

In *Stahlecker v. Ford Motor Co.*,[157] a young woman was driving her Ford Explorer in a remote area of Nebraska when its Firestone Wilderness AT radial tires separated due to a defective condition which subsequently led to a nationwide recall of those tires. Uninjured in the accident, but stranded, she was found alone by an assailant who assaulted and murdered her. Her parents sued Ford and Firestone, alleging that they had long known of the tires' propensity to unexpectedly blow out "causing wide-ranging results that included stranding and rollovers." The Stahleckers alleged that while their daughter's particular assault and murder may not have been foreseeable, "the potential for similar dangerous situations arising as a result of a breakdown of a Ford Explorer and/or its tires resulting in danger to its consumers and users from criminal activity, adverse weather conditions, inability to communicate with others or any combination thereof, were known and/or should have been known to Defendants Ford and Firestone." Relying on *Williams*, the court affirmed summary judgment for the defendants. Yet, it might be argued that an apartment lock, a security officer's phone, and a young woman's car are similar to burglar alarms and mace in that a purpose of all five types of products is to help the user avoid dangerous situations.

If a product's design is defective because it fails to protect users against a particular type of accidental or natural danger, a court may find that a third party's deliberate misconduct that exposes the plaintiff to that same danger falls within the scope of foreseeable risk.[158] One such case is *Price v. Blaine Kern Artista, Inc.*,[159] where an entertainer at Harrah's Club in Reno who was wearing a large caricature mask of the first President George Bush ("41") was injured when a patron pushed him from behind, causing the weight of the caricature mask to strain and injure his neck as he fell to the ground. He sued the manufacturer of the mask, alleging that it was defectively designed due to the absence of a safety harness to support his head and neck under the heavy weight. The trial court ruled that the patron's push that precipitated the plaintiff's fall constituted an unforeseeable superseding cause, insulating the mask's supplier from liability, but the Supreme Court of Nevada reversed. The court acknowledged that the patron's conduct would be considered a superseding cause of the plaintiff's injuries had it been unforeseeable, yet it reasoned that a trier of fact might find such a push foreseeable if a patron were intoxicated or "politically volatile" and became "ignited by the sight of an oversized caricature of a prominent political figure" with whose position on abortion rights he might disagree.[160]

In another case, decided on principles similar to *Price*, the plaintiff's decedent and twenty-seven others perished in a hotel fire set by an arsonist. The court refused to shield from liability the manufacturer of excessively flammable acrylic fiber used in the carpeting because it could foresee the dangers if the carpet caught fire.[161] Yet, in *Bellotte*

---

a consequence if a defect in a pager caused it to malfunction. See Hollenbeck v. Selectone Corp., 476 N.E.2d 746 (Ill. App. Ct. 1985).

[157] 667 N.W.2d 244 (Neb. 2003).

[158] See also Collins v. Navistar, Inc., 155 Cal. Rptr. 3d 137, 151, 153 (Ct. App. 2013) (2½-pound chunk of concrete dropped by youth from overpass onto truck windshield on freeway below). See note 152, above.

[159] 893 P.2d 367 (Nev. 1995).

[160] The court also attempted, heroically but unsuccessfully, to distinguish the effect of superseding cause when applied to claims for strict products liability.

[161] d'Hedouville v. Pioneer Hotel Co., 552 F.2d 886, 894 (9th Cir. 1977) (Ariz. law) (the defendant manufacturer "was aware of the danger of fire, knew fires are often the result of arson, and knew that in all likelihood its carpeting would be installed in buildings without sprinkler systems, smoke sensors, or fire alarms, and in multi-story homes lacking the safety features the Pioneer Hotel also lacked").

v. Zayre Corp.,[162] a 5-year-old plaintiff suffered burns when his pajamas caught fire from a match. Believing that his 12-year-old brother had deliberately tossed the match on him, the jury returned a verdict for the defendant seller, which the appellate court affirmed. Although many clothing flammability accidents are caused by children playing with matches, "[t]he deliberate setting afire of a child's pajamas by another would not appear to fall within those acts that ought to be anticipated by a clothing supplier." The court approved the trial court's instruction that such a deliberate act constituted an "absolute defense." And many other decisions similarly hold deliberate assaults to be unforeseeable.[163]

A case arising out of the September 11, 2001, terrorist attacks on the World Trade Center places more weight on foreseeability than it fairly may be asked to bear. *In re September 11 Litigation*[164] involved a motion to dismiss the claims of about seventy plaintiffs for injuries and deaths for Boeing's failure to design the cockpit doors of two aircraft—American Flight 77 which crashed into the Pentagon, and United Flight 93 which crashed in rural Pennsylvania—strongly enough to prevent entry by the terrorist hijackers. Boeing argued that, even if the cockpit doors could be found to have been defectively designed, the acts of the terrorists constituted a superseding cause which defeated proximate cause as a matter of law. In particular, Boeing argued that "the criminal acts of the terrorists in hijacking the airplanes and using the airplanes as weapons of mass destruction constituted an 'efficient intervening cause' which broke the 'natural and continuous sequence' of events flowing from Boeing's allegedly inadequate design." The plaintiffs argued that terrorist acts, "including hijackings of airplanes, were reasonably foreseeable," "that the lives of passengers, crew and ground victims would be imminently in danger from such hijackings," and that, "[g]iven the critical nature of the cockpit area, and the inherent danger of [a] crash when a plane is in flight," a jury might find that Boeing should reasonably have foreseen "the risk flowing from an inadequately constructed cockpit door." Ruling that a jury could agree with the plaintiffs, the court denied the motion to dismiss.

The *September 11* court attempted to distinguish three other cases, *Port Authority of New York & New Jersey v. Arcadian Corp.*,[165] *Gaines-Tabb v. ICI Explosives USA, Inc.*,[166] and *Korean Air Lines Disaster of September 1, 1983*,[167] each of which had held

---

162 531 F.2d 1100 (1st Cir. 1976) (N.H. law).

163 See, e.g., Sanders v. Acclaim Entm't, Inc., 188 F. Supp. 2d 1264, 1276 (D. Colo. 2002) (unforeseeable that video game would cause shooting incident at Columbine; superseding causes relieve defendants of liability when "the harm is intentionally caused by a third person and is not within the scope of the risk created by the actor's conduct"); James v. Meow Media, Inc., 90 F. Supp. 2d 798, 807–08 (W.D. Ky. 2000) (unforeseeable that assailant who watched violent video games would shoot girls as a result), aff'd, 300 F.3d 683 (6th Cir. 2002); Briscoe v. Amazing Prods., Inc., 23 S.W.3d 228 (Ky. Ct. App. 2000) (unforeseeable that man would throw defendant's drain cleaning product at plaintiff during altercation); Horstman v. Farris, 725 N.E.2d 698, 703 (Ohio Ct. App. 1999) (unforeseeable that 16-year-old who inhaled airbrush propellant would deliberately ram plaintiff's car; conduct broke chain of causation between plaintiffs' injuries and any warning defect of the propellant); Walcott v. Total Petrol., Inc., 964 P.2d 609, 612 (Colo. App. 1998) (unforeseeable that man purchasing cup of gasoline would throw it on plaintiff and set her on fire; "whether analyzed under the rubric of duty or proximate cause, the risk that a purchaser would intentionally throw gasoline on a victim and set the victim on fire was not reasonably foreseeable"); Chapman v. Oshman's Sporting Goods, Inc., 792 S.W.2d 785 (Tex. App. 1990) (murder with handgun sold by defendant retailer). See also the cases on murder in § 12.2, above.

164 280 F. Supp. 2d 279 (S.D.N.Y. 2003) (Va. and Pa. law).

165 189 F.3d 305 (3d Cir. 1999) (N.J. law).

166 160 F.3d 613 (10th Cir. 1998) (Okla. law).

167 1985 WL 9447 (D.D.C. 1985).

that an unprovoked terrorist or military attack was an unforeseeable superseding cause as a matter of law. The first two cases involved claims of warning defects against the manufacturers of explosive grade fertilizer used to make the bombs employed in the terrorist attacks against the World Trade Center, in 1993, and in the Oklahoma City federal building bombing, in 1995. The third case was brought against Boeing on behalf of passengers killed in Korean Airlines Flight 007, which, due to an alleged defect in the plane's navigation systems, flew off course over a sensitive Russian military zone and was shot down by Russian fighter planes. The *September 11* court valiantly attempted to distinguish each case on foreseeability grounds, concluding (with little reasoning) that, unlike the September 11 attacks, the fertilizer manufacturers and aircraft manufacturer could not foresee such unprovoked attacks.

It is difficult not to notice how little decisional power "foreseeability" has in these superseding cause cases, even when the standard is enriched as the scope of *reasonably* foreseeable risk. Any of these cases might be decided either way, and courts and lawyers in cases of this type are left with no alternative but to spin foreseeability arguments that shift, and turn, and jump about like the elusive butterfly that is proximate cause.

Superseding Cause in a Comparative Fault World

Some commentators argue that superseding cause is outmoded in a comparative fault world.[168] Because the superseding cause doctrine is so blunt, allowing manufacturers and other sellers to escape liability altogether even if a product defect is partially responsible for a plaintiff's injuries, it is seen to conflict with the basic principles of equitable damages apportionment that control comparative fault. Moreover, the argument continues, the basic proximate cause principle of limiting responsibility to the scope of risks that may foreseeably be expected to arise from a tortious act, risks that make the act tortious, sufficiently embraces the concept of superseding cause without complicating proximate cause doctrine. These arguments have some power, and they have been accepted by some courts.[169]

In *Barry v. Quality Steel Products, Inc.*,[170] the jury was instructed that the negligence of the plaintiff, his employer, and his co-workers in connection with certain defective roof brackets could act as a superseding cause of his injury. Rejecting the doctrine of superseding cause, the Supreme Court of Connecticut concluded that "the doctrine of superseding cause no longer serves a useful purpose in our negligence jurisprudence" because its functions are performed by the general principles of proximate cause. "[I]t is inconsistent," further reasoned the court, "to conclude simultaneously that all negligent parties should pay in proportion to their fault, but that one negligent party does not have to pay its share because its negligence was somehow 'superseded' by a subsequent negligent act." Nor did the court believe that it should continue "to utilize doctrines that aid factfinders in making policy decisions regarding how to assign liability among various defendants and the plaintiff because those

---

168 See generally M. Green, The Unanticipated Ripples of Comparative Negligence: Superseding Cause in Products Liability and Beyond, 53 S.C. L. Rev. 1103 (2002); Cupp, Proximate Cause, the Proposed Basic Principles Restatement and Products Liability, 53 S.C. L. Rev. 1085 (2002); Notes, Dumb as a Matter of Law: The "Superseding Cause" Modification of Comparative Negligence, 79 Tex. L. Rev. 493 (2000), Why Superseding Cause Analysis Should Be Abandoned, 72 Tex. L. Rev. 161 (1993). Accord Rest. (3d) Torts: Liability for Physical and Emotional Harm § 34, and comments thereto.

169 See, e.g., Control Techniques, Inc. v. Johnson, 762 N.E.2d 104 (Ind. 2002); Torres v. El Paso Elec. Co., 987 P.2d 386 (N.M. 1999).

170 820 A.2d 258 (Conn. 2003).

decisions already are inherent in our modern scheme of comparative negligence and apportionment." Thus, under the court's approach, "the question to be answered by the factfinder is whether the various actors' allegedly negligent conduct was a cause in fact and a proximate cause of the plaintiff's injury in light of all the relevant circumstances. If found to be both, each actor will be liable for his or her proportionate share of the plaintiff's damages."[171]

That these few rumblings of discontent with the "doctrine" of superseding cause may be well founded is demonstrated by the inconsistency and lack of meaningful reasoning in the cases discussed above. Over time, other courts may also begin to rethink the role of superseding cause in a comparative fault world, a development that may prove beneficial. It is quite unlikely, however, that courts soon will stampede to abolish the intuitively compelling sub-doctrine of superseding cause in the law of proximate cause.

---

[171] Id. at 269.

Part IV

DEFENSES

Chapter 13

USER CONDUCT DEFENSES

Table of Sections

§ 13.1 USER CONDUCT DEFENSES—GENERALLY

Product accidents result more often from consumer mishandling than from defects in the products. In the estimation of a former chairman of the Consumer Product Safety Commission, "over ⅔ of all injuries related to consumer products have nothing to do with the design or the performance of the product. They relate to the misuse or abuse of the product."[1] If a product accident is caused in whole or in part by a user's behavior that is by some measure improper, or that is informed and voluntary, the manufacturer or other seller of a defective (or misrepresented) product may avoid responsibility for some or all of the resulting harm. Manufacturers are fairly responsible for injuries proximately caused by dangerously defective conditions in their products—not for injuries caused by a user's improper or deliberately risky use of a product.

It would be unfair to a manufacturer's shareholders (and to careful consumers forced to pay higher prices for the product) to require them to subsidize users injured because they choose to use products in ways they should know expose themselves to unreasonable risks of harm.[2] In such cases, the law provides manufacturers and other sellers with at least limited protection through the traditional conduct defenses, the subject of this chapter. The misuse of a product by a third party—such as an employer, doctor, parent, or stranger—that injures a plaintiff may raise an issue of superseding causation, a topic previously addressed.[3]

---

[1] Fisk, An Interview with John Byington, Trial Magazine, Feb. 1978, at 25. This observation excludes automotive vehicles, because Congress earlier entrusted their safety regulation to NHTSA. Vehicular crashes are overwhelmingly attributable to driver error, the subject of chapter 17. "Vehicle problems" were found to be "critical pre-crash events" in only 1.2% of all crashes, and "tire deficiencies" accounted for the great bulk of these. Once "view obstructions" and "lighting deficiencies" are also deducted from the vehicle problem totals, "other vehicle problems" account for just 0.23% of all crashes. See also NHTSA, National Motor Vehicle Crash Causation Survey: Report to Congress 23, 29 (2008) (critical reasons for pre-crash events). And since "vehicle problems" often result from normal wear and tear and poor maintenance, the proportion of vehicular accidents from defects for which manufacturers are responsible is miniscule.

[2] See, e.g., Owen, The Moral Foundations of Products Liability Law: Toward First Principles, 68 Notre Dame L. Rev. 427, 476 (1993); Holford, The Limits of Strict Liability for Product Design and Manufacture, 52 Tex. L. Rev. 81, 89 (1973).

[3] See § 12.3, above.

The classic conduct defenses[4] to products liability negligence claims are contributory negligence[5] and assumption of risk.[6] With the advent of the modern doctrine of strict products liability in tort during the 1960s and 1970s,[7] most jurisdictions added a new defense[8] of product "misuse."[9] While contributory negligence has remained the basic defense to products liability claims grounded in negligence, most jurisdictions in the latter part of the twentieth century renamed the doctrine "comparative negligence," or "comparative fault," and changed its effect from barring a plaintiff's claim altogether to reducing the plaintiff's damages proportionate to his or her own fault in helping cause an accident. The doctrine of comparative fault, an approach to plaintiff conduct that cuts a broad swath across the law of torts and products liability, is examined in this chapter.[10]

Comparative fault principles to a large extent now define the role of contributory negligence in most jurisdictions, assumption of risk in many jurisdictions, and product misuse in a few, as discussed below. Nevertheless, the traditional user conduct defenses still apply to products liability claims in the handful of states that continue to reject the doctrine of comparative fault.[11] Moreover, even though the traditional defenses now often operate to reduce a plaintiff's damages, rather than to bar them altogether, much of the traditional doctrine surrounding contributory negligence, assumption of risk, and product misuse has survived the conversion to comparative fault.[12]

Although courts in comparative fault jurisdictions generally apply damages-apportioning principles to a plaintiff's contributory negligence, both contributory negligence and assumption of risk remain as *total* bars to recovery in most jurisdictions if the plaintiff's fault equals or, in some states, exceeds the fault of the defendant.[13] In addition, while some courts abolished assumption of risk as a separate doctrine after the adoption of comparative fault, or merged it into the comparative fault scheme, other courts refuse to apply comparative fault principles to assumption of risk or do so only to

---

4 On such defenses generally, see Solomon, Judging Plaintiffs, 60 Vand. L. Rev. 1749 (2007).

5 See § 13.2, below.

6 See § 13.4, below.

7 See § 5.2, above.

8 In many jurisdictions, product misuse is technically not a "defense" in the sense of an affirmative defense, but its absence is instead considered part of a plaintiff's prima facie case. In such jurisdictions, the role of misuse in products liability law may be viewed more in the nature of a limitation on defectiveness than a true defense. From whatever perspective, when a user "misuses" a defective product, his or her misconduct may operate as a bar to liability similar to traditional contributory negligence and assumption of risk. For that reason, together with the fact that a number of state reform acts treat product misuse as an affirmative defense, the doctrine of misuse is covered with other conduct "defenses" in this chapter.

9 See § 13.5, below.

10 See § 13.3, below.

11 As of 2022, the comparative fault doctrine is still rejected in Alabama, Maryland, North Carolina, Virginia, and the District of Columbia. See Am. L. Prod. Liab. 3d § 40:29 (2022 update); Gifford, The Death of the Common Law: Judicial Abdication and Contributory Negligence in Maryland, 73 Md. L. Rev. Endnotes 1, at *4 (2014).

12 One example is the contributory negligence doctrine, applicable to claims for strict products liability in tort, that a plaintiff's mere failure to discover a defect or guard against the possibility of its existence does not bar recovery. See § 13.2, below. Moreover, some courts hold that a plaintiff's fault may sometimes be the sole proximate cause of his or her injury, notwithstanding the doctrine of comparative fault. See §§ 13.2 and 13.3, below.

13 See § 13.4, below.

a limited extent.[14] Finally, in the many jurisdictions that consider the absence of misuse to be an element of a plaintiff's prima facie case of strict liability in tort, a finding of misuse should be entirely unaffected by the doctrine of comparative fault. Similarly, with claims for breach of warranty[15] and misrepresentation,[16] the issues of justifiable reliance, proximate cause, and scope of warranty implicated by a user's conduct are part of a plaintiff's case in chief without which the plaintiff's claims cannot even arise. In short, most jurisdictions hold that the traditional plaintiff conduct defenses often still operate in their conventional form as a total bar to liability.

When a plaintiff acts carelessly or adventurously in a manner that causes or contributes to a product accident, the conduct may give rise to two or all three traditional conduct defenses.[17] So, if a plaintiff proceeds to ignite a pilot light, knowing of a leaking gas valve;[18] attempts to mount a tire, expressly contrary to a warning, on a wheel rim of a different size;[19] falls as a stunt 323 feet onto a cushion rated for 200 feet;[20] locks herself into a car's trunk, which has no internal release device, in an attempt to commit suicide;[21] or hurls himself at a pressurized plate-glass wall atop a skyscraper to show aspiring law clerks how very strong glass can be, without considering that its frame might not be so strong,[22] a defendant may assert and sometimes successfully defend a products liability case against the manufacturer on some combination of contributory (or comparative) negligence, assumption of risk, and product misuse. Thus, subject to applicable principles of comparative fault, a practitioner representing a defendant seller in a case involving plaintiff conduct should almost always consider the possible availability of two or all three of the traditional conduct defenses. This assumes that the complaint includes claims in both negligence and strict liability, because misuse normally is a strict liability defense,[23] and many jurisdictions hold that "simple" contributory negligence is not a defense at all to claims for strict liability in tort.[24]

---

[14] Ohio, for example, merged assumption of risk into comparative fault for negligence claims but left it as a total bar to strict liability in tort. See, e.g., Onderko v. Richmond Mfg. Co., 511 N.E.2d 388 (Ohio 1987); Bowling v. Heil Co., 511 N.E.2d 373 (Ohio 1987).

[15] See § 13.6, below.

[16] See § 13.7, below.

[17] See, e.g., Moore v. BPS Direct, LLC, 2019 WL 2931463, at *10–11 (D.S.C. 2019) (Ill. law) (denying plaintiff's summary judgment motions on defendants' assumption of risk, misuse, and contributory negligence defenses; plaintiff ignored instructions to attach the safety harness to the tree before climbing into the tree stand); Romero v. ITW Food Equip. Grp., LLC, 987 F. Supp. 2d 93, 100–01 (D.D.C. 2013) (all three; after kitchen worker removed guard from meat grinder, his foot slipped and his hand went into grinder); Automobile Ins. Co. of Hartford v. Electrolux Home Prod. Inc., 2011 WL 1434672 (W.D.N.Y. 2011) (all three; gas clothes drier caught fire because plaintiff failed to keep exhaust opening free of lint and debris per user manual instructions); Ellsworth v. Sherne Lingerie, Inc., 495 A.2d 348, 357 (Md. 1985) ("a defendant may be entitled to instructions on contributory negligence, assumption of risk, and misuse").

[18] Freislinger v. Emro Propane Co., 99 F.3d 1412 (7th Cir. 1996) (Ill. law) (contributory/comparative negligence and assumption of risk).

[19] Uniroyal Goodrich Tire Co. v. Hall, 681 So.2d 126 (Ala. 1996) (contributory negligence, assumption of risk, and misuse).

[20] Bakunas v. Life Pack, Inc., 531 F. Supp. 89 (E.D. La. 1982) (assumption of risk and misuse), aff'd, 701 F.2d 946 (5th Cir. 1983).

[21] Daniell v. Ford Motor Co., 581 F. Supp. 728 (D.N.M. 1984) (misuse, and possibly assumption of risk and comparative fault).

[22] Though he had performed this stunt several times before, this time the glass popped out, followed promptly by the performer, a "noted and respected" corporate and securities partner (and engineer) in a major Toronto law firm. See https://en.wikipedia.org/wiki/Death_of_Garry_Hoy.

[23] See § 13.5, below.

[24] See §§ 13.2 and 13.3, below.

The three plaintiff conduct defenses are fundamental mechanisms by which the law defines the boundaries of liability by allowing manufacturers to avoid responsibility for certain types of product accidents. Accordingly, trial courts have an important obligation to admit appropriate evidence, permit appropriate argument, and submit appropriate instructions to the jury on any conduct defenses that fairly may be raised in a particular case.[25]

Reform Legislation

Many states have enacted products liability reform statutes and/or comparative fault statutes that specifically address the definition, scope, and effect of various defenses based on a plaintiff's conduct. Such statutes variously reduce damages or bar recovery if a product accident is caused by a plaintiff's unreasonable behavior or contributory fault, assumption of risk, misuse of the product, or sometimes specifically designated types of plaintiff misbehavior.[26] While most general comparative fault statutes address plaintiff conduct broadly, most products liability reform statutes that address a plaintiff's conduct in products liability litigation specify the effect of particular forms of plaintiff behavior on products liability claims, often when the conduct may be classified as product misuse.[27]

For example, one statutory provision in Connecticut specifies that contributory negligence shall merely diminish damages rather than bar liability,[28] and another specifies that neither contributory nor comparative negligence shall bar liability in strict products liability in tort claims but recognizes the separate defenses of "misuse of the product" and "knowingly using the product in a defective condition."[29] Statutes in North Carolina and Arizona provide a defense for the use of products contrary to their "express and adequate instructions or warnings . . . if the user knew or with the exercise of reasonable and diligent care should have known of such instructions or warnings."[30] Kentucky enacted a contributory negligence defense to products liability actions in 1978 but superseded it with a comparative fault act in 1988.[31] A number of products liability reform statutes provide that a plaintiff's damages shall be reduced,[32] or that recovery

---

25 See, e.g., Coleman v. Ford Motor Co., 70 So.3d 223, 227–28 (Miss. Ct. App. 2011) (trial court properly admitted defendant's evidence of results of two blood-alcohol-content tests conducted on driver during his medical treatment after accident, permitting defendant to argue that he had been driving "double drunk"). See also § 17.5, below.

26 See, e.g., Thompson v. Ryobi Ltd., 2022 WL 721527, at *5 (E.D. Mich. 2022) (Mich. Comp. Laws Ann. § 600.2955a(1) intoxication defense precluded plaintiff's negligent design and warranty claims); Wash. Rev. Code Ann. § 5.40.060 (plaintiff's drug or alcohol intoxication is complete defense in some cases).

27 See, e.g., Wyo. Stat. Ann. § 1–1–109(a)(iv) (" 'Fault' includes acts or omissions, determined to be a proximate cause of death or injury to person or property, that are in any measure negligent, or that subject an actor to strict tort or strict products liability, and includes breach of warranty, assumption of risk and misuse or alteration of a product.").

28 Conn. Gen. Stat. Ann. § 52–572h(b).

29 Conn. Gen. Stat. Ann. § 52–572*l*.

30 N.C. Gen. Stat. Ann. § 99B–4(1). See also Ariz. Rev. Stat. Ann. § 12–683(3).

31 See Ky. Rev. Stat. Ann. § 411.182, superseding Ky. Rev. Stat. Ann. § 411.320(3). See Owens Corning Fiberglas Corp. v. Parrish, 58 S.W.3d 467, 474 (Ky. 2001).

32 One source lists Alaska, Arizona, Arkansas, Colorado, Idaho, Iowa, Kansas, Minnesota, Missouri, Montana, New York, North Dakota, Utah, and Washington as strict liability states which provide by statute that assumption of risk merely reduces a plaintiff's recovery rather than serving as a total bar. H. Woods and B. Deere, Comparative Fault § 6:11, at 146–47 (3d ed. 1996 & Supp. 2022). See, e.g., Idaho Code Ann. § 6–1405(2)(a) (if "the claimant knew about the product's defective condition, and voluntarily used the product or voluntarily assumed the risk of harm from the product, the claimant's damages shall be subject to reduction to the extent that the claimant did not act as an ordinary reasonably prudent person").

shall be barred altogether,[33] if a plaintiff voluntarily—sometimes voluntarily and unreasonably[34]—encounters a known (or obvious)[35] product danger. Products liability statutes in several states reduce damages[36] or bar liability[37] when a plaintiff's use of a product is abnormal or unforeseeable, generally referred to in the statutes as product "misuse."

Finally, most of the reform legislation mentioned above specifically addresses products liability litigation. In all cases, the statutes should be checked carefully for legislative provisions that generally abolish the defense of assumption of risk;[38] that broadly apply comparative fault principles to the doctrines of contributory negligence, assumption of risk, and often product misuse;[39] or that in any other manner affect the definition or role of the traditional plaintiff conduct defenses of contributory negligence, assumption of risk, and product misuse.

---

[33] See, e.g., Conn. Gen. Stat. Ann. § 52–572*l* (assumption of risk and misuse defenses apply to products liability claims based on strict liability in tort); Ind. Code Ann. § 34–20–6–3 (no liability if user or consumer "(1) knew of the defect; (2) was aware of the danger in the product; and (3) nevertheless proceeded to make use of the product and was injured").

[34] Some statutes define assumption of risk as dangerous encounters that are known, voluntary, and *unreasonable.* Mo. Ann. Stat. § 537.765(3)(3); N.C. Gen. Stat. Ann. § 99B–4(2); S.C. Code Ann. § 15–73–20.

[35] Mississippi and Montana allow a defense in cases of encounters with obvious, as well as known, risks. See Miss. Code Ann. § 11–1–63(d) (assumed risks) and (e) (risks that are "known" or "open and obvious"); Mont. Code Ann. § 27–1–719(5)(a) (allowing defense if "[t]he user or consumer discovered the defect or the defect was open and obvious and the user or consumer unreasonably made use of the product and was injured by it").

[36] See, e.g., Idaho Code Ann. § 6–1405(3) (misuse reduces claimant's damages according to comparative responsibility; "misuse" defined as "when the product user does not act in a manner that would be expected of an ordinary reasonably prudent person who is likely to use the product in the same or similar circumstances"); Mo. Ann. Stat. § 537.765(3) (for purposes of apportionment, plaintiff's "fault" includes a product use that is (1) not reasonably anticipated or (2) not intended by the manufacturer); Wis. Stat. Ann. § 895.047(3)(c) (damages "reduced by the percentage of causal responsibility for the claimant's harm attributable to the claimant's misuse, alteration, or modification of the product").

[37] At least five states have such provisions. See Ariz. Rev. Stat. Ann. § 12–683(3) (unforeseeable purpose, manner or activity, or use contrary to express and adequate instructions or warnings, if injured person knew or with reasonable care should have known of such instructions or warnings); Colo. Rev. Stat. Ann. § 13–21–402.5 (misuse bars recovery); Ind. Code Ann. § 34–20–6–4 (same, if misuse not reasonably expected by seller at time of sale); Mich. Comp. Laws Ann. § 600.2947(2) (no liability for harm caused by misuse unless "reasonably foreseeable," which is a legal issue for court); Mont. Code Ann. § 27–1–719(5)(b) (unreasonable misuse reduces damages or bars recovery); Tenn. Code Ann. § 29–28–108 (no liability for harm from "unforeseeable alteration, change, improper maintenance or abnormal use").

[38] At least Connecticut, Massachusetts, and Oregon have abolished the defense of assumption of risk legislatively. See Conn. Gen. Stat. Ann. §§ 52–572h (abolished in negligence actions only) and 52–572*l* (retained in strict products liability in tort actions); Mass. Gen. Laws Ann. ch. 231, § 85 (abolishing assumption of risk defense); Or. Rev. Stat. Ann. § 31.620(2) (same).

[39] Statutory provisions vary widely. See, e.g., Alaska Stat. Ann. § 09.17.900 ("fault" includes "misuse of a product for which the defendant otherwise would be liable"); Ark. Code Ann. § 16–64–122(c) (" 'fault' as used in this section includes any act, omission, conduct, risk assumed, breach of warranty, or breach of any legal duty which is a proximate cause of any damages sustained by any party"); Iowa Code Ann. § 668.1 (" 'fault' means one or more acts or omissions that are in any measure negligent or reckless toward the person or property of the actor or others, or that subject a person to strict tort liability" and "includes breach of warranty, unreasonable assumption of risk not constituting an enforceable express consent, misuse of a product for which the defendant otherwise would be liable, and unreasonable failure to avoid an injury or to mitigate damages").

Some statutes also allocate fault to third parties. See, e.g., Kinseth v. Weil-McLain, 913 N.W.2d 55, 74–76 (Iowa 2018) ("Iowa's comparative fault statute permits juries to attribute fault to parties other than the defendant, including 'third-party defendants and persons who have been released [where] the issue is supported by substantial evidence' "; valve manufacturer properly excluded from fault allocation).

§ 13.2 Contributory Negligence

Contributory negligence is the conventional common-law defense to negligence claims in products liability cases.[40] Though most courts considerably restrict the availability of this defense in strict liability in tort claims, as discussed below, they widely apply ordinary contributory negligence principles to products liability claims brought in negligence.[41] In this context as in others, contributory negligence is defined as conduct of a plaintiff that falls below the standard of reasonable behavior required for a person's own protection that proximately contributes, together with a defendant's negligence or other breach of duty, to cause the person harm.[42]

Contributory negligence operates in much the same manner in products liability cases as in other types of negligence cases. So, unless comparative fault principles dictate to the contrary (as they usually do),[43] a finding that a plaintiff was contributorily negligent will bar the plaintiff altogether from recovering damages from a negligent defendant.[44] Thus, a plaintiff found to have been contributorily negligent in an encounter with a dangerously defective product may not recover from the manufacturer or other seller for negligently making or supplying the product in such a condition.[45] However, if the defendant's conduct is not merely negligent but rises to the level of reckless, willful, or wanton misbehavior, a plaintiff's recovery will not be barred by his or her contributory negligence,[46] although it will be barred if the plaintiff is contributorily reckless.[47]

---

[40] Noel, Defective Products: Abnormal Use, Contributory Negligence, and Assumption of Risk, 25 Vand. L. Rev. 93 (1972); Epstein, Products Liability: Defenses Based on Plaintiff's Conduct, 1968 Utah L. Rev. 267.

[41] See, e.g., Rodgers v. AWB Indus. Inc., 2019 WL 3779908, at *5 (N.D. Ala. 2019); Russell v. Wright, 916 F. Supp. 2d 629, 658 (W.D. Va. 2013) ("contributory negligence is available as a defense to product liability cases grounded in negligence, particularly failure to warn cases"; taser victim committed violent crime, led police on pursuit, approached officers after he pulled over, refused to obey their commands, and asked "why don't you just taser me?"); Robinson v. McNeil Consumer Healthcare, 671 F. Supp. 2d 975, 978 (N.D. Ill. 2009) (adult's contributory negligence in taking repeated doses of children's Motrin after experiencing allergic reactions barred negligence claim), aff'd, 615 F.3d 861 (7th Cir. 2010); J.H.O.C. v. Volvo Trucks N. Am., Inc., 303 Fed. Appx. 828, 833–34 (11th Cir. 2008) (Ala. law) (continued driving of tractor for six months after safety recall notification of fire danger in exhaust gas recirculation system was contributory negligence as a matter of law); Rodeheaver v. CNH Am., LLC, 2007 WL 465212, at *7–8 (D. Md. 2007) (contributory negligence, in running after and trying to jump on moving tractor, barred negligence claim); Hannah v. Gregg, Bland & Berry, Inc., 840 So.2d 839 (Ala. 2002) (in wrongful death action against manufacturer of machine that crushed worker, jury could find worker responsible for his own demise for failing to insert safety pin in machine); Gillespie v. American Motors Corp., 317 S.E.2d 32 (N.C. Ct. App. 1984) (continuing to drive car for three years while knowing of noxious fumes in passenger area: contributorily negligent). See also Duke v. American Olean Tile Co., 400 N.W.2d 677 (Mich. Ct. App. 1986) (in slip-and-fall action against manufacturer of quarry tile used for flooring in fast food restaurant, jury could find that plaintiff was walking unreasonably fast).

[42] See Keeton, Dobbs, Keeton, and Owen, Prosser and Keeton on the Law of Torts § 65, at 451.

[43] See § 13.3, below.

[44] "[I]n the absence of modifying legislation or judicial action, contributory negligence of the plaintiff is a complete bar to his action for any common law negligence of the defendant." Prosser and Keeton on Torts § 65, at 451. See also W. Prosser, Handbook of The Law of Torts § 102, at 670 (4th ed. 1971) ("There is no doubt that where the plaintiff's action is founded on negligence, his contributory negligence will bar his recovery to the same extent as in any other negligence case.").

[45] See, e.g., Russell v. Wright, 916 F. Supp. 2d 629, 658 (W.D. Va. 2013); McMahon v. Yamaha Motor Corp., U.S.A., 95 So.3d 769, 773 (Ala. 2012); Nicholson v. American Safety Util. Corp., 488 S.E.2d 240, 244 (N.C. 1997) ("contributory negligence in the context of a products liability action operates as a bar to recovery in the same manner as in an ordinary negligence action").

[46] See, e.g., McMahon v. Yamaha Motor Corp., 95 So.3d 769, 773 (Ala. 2012) ("contributory negligence . . . is not a bar to a wantonness claim"). Rest. (3d) of Torts: Liability for Physical and Emotional Harm § 33 (recklessness); Rest. (2d) of Torts § 482.

[47] Compare Reott v. Asia Trend, Inc., 55 A.3d 1088, 1092 (Pa. 2012) (a plaintiff's conduct is "highly reckless," and the sole proximate cause of an accident, when a plaintiff knew or should have known that it

Contributory negligence operates as a total bar to negligence liability not only in those few jurisdictions that have not adopted comparative fault,[48] but also in many cases in most other jurisdictions as well. Except for jurisdictions that presently have a system of *pure* comparative fault,[49] most states apply the principles of comparative fault only when a plaintiff's fault was less than (or equal to) the fault of the defendant or defendants. In jurisdictions following such a modified ("50%") approach to comparative negligence, if a plaintiff's fault was greater than (or equal to) that of the defendant(s), the contributory negligence doctrine applies in its conventional form by barring recovery altogether.[50] Thus, the doctrine of contributory negligence remains an important doctrine in modern products liability litigation.

The complex interrelationships between the human brain, the human body, and myriad different products encountered daily at home and at work result in a vast universe of ways in which user carelessness may result in injury.[51] Consumers may be contributorily negligent for using products in an unreasonably dangerous manner or by using them for an unreasonably dangerous purpose, as by driving an automobile at excessive speed[52] or in an intoxicated condition;[53] reaching into a trash compactor knowing that its door cables are broken;[54] failing to release one's hold of a piece of meat when pushing it into the revolving blade of a meat slicing machine;[55] standing on a slippery substance dangerously close to the exposed moving parts of a machine;[56] operating a spray-painting machine without using an available mask;[57] failing to wear rubber gloves, contrary to label instructions, and splattering a caustic substance on one's hand;[58] failing properly to engage a car's transmission in the "park" position;[59] improperly using a condom;[60] walking too fast on a slippery floor;[61] or carelessly lighting a cigarette with a disposable lighter near one's "big hair" bouffant hairdo held in place with excessive hair spray, the fumes of which ignite.[62]

"created a high degree of risk of physical harm to himself" yet deliberately "act[s], or fail[s] to act, in conscious disregard of that risk"). See generally Rapp, The Wreckage of Recklessness, 86 Wash. U.L. Rev. 111 (2008); Owen, The Highly Blameworthy Manufacturer: Implications on Rules of Liability and Defense in Products Liability Actions, 10 Ind. L. Rev. 769, 787–88 (1977).

[48] Alabama, Maryland, North Carolina, Virginia, and the District of Columbia.

[49] See § 13.3, below.

[50] Id.

[51] See § 13.5, below.

[52] See, e.g., Hoelter v. Mohawk Serv., Inc., 365 A.2d 1064 (Conn. 1976).

[53] See, e.g., Hill v. General Motors Corp., 168 F.3d 482 (4th Cir. 1998) (N.C. law).

[54] See, Sears v. Waste Processing Equip., Inc., 695 So.2d 51 (Ala. Civ. App. 1997).

[55] See Koske v. Townsend Eng'g Co., 526 N.E.2d 985 (Ind. Ct. App. 1988), adopted in part and vacated in part on other grounds, 551 N.E.2d 437 (Ind. 1990).

[56] See, e.g., Reed v. Carlyle & Martin, Inc., 202 S.E.2d 874 (Va. 1974).

[57] See, e.g., Parris v. M.A. Bruder & Sons, Inc., 261 F. Supp. 406 (E.D. Pa. 1966).

[58] See Lee v. Crest Chem. Co., 583 F. Supp. 131 (M.D.N.C. 1984) (defendant's motion for summary judgment granted pursuant to statutory provision barring recovery for use of product contrary to instructions).

[59] See, e.g., General Motors Corp. v. Sanchez, 997 S.W.2d 584, 594 (Tex. 1999); Ray v. Ford Motor Co., 514 S.E.2d 227 (Ga. Ct. App. 1999). Cf. Ford Motor Co. v. Bartholomew, 297 S.E.2d 675 (Va. 1982) (gear shift lever, not fully engaged in park, slipped into reverse with motor running; jury's finding of no contributory negligence upheld).

[60] See J.P.M. v. Schmid Labs., Inc., 428 A.2d 515 (N.J. Super. Ct. App. Div. 1981).

[61] See Duke v. American Olean Tile Co., 400 N.W.2d 677 (Mich. Ct. App. 1986) (in slip-and-fall action against manufacturer of quarry tile used for flooring in fast-food restaurant).

[62] See McClure v. Wilkinson Sword Consumer Prods., Inc., Prod. Safety & Liab. Rep. (BNA) 394 (Apr. 14, 1995).

As with negligence claims in general, the issues of contributory negligence are peculiarly grounded in community norms of properly safe behavior in particular circumstances, so that the issue of whether a plaintiff's behavior should be classified as unreasonable is inherently a question of fact especially suited to resolution by a jury.[63] Yet, if a plaintiff's behavior is so evidently reasonable or unreasonable that no jury could reasonably find to the contrary, a court may rule on contributory negligence as a matter of law.[64]

Whereas negligence is defined as the failure to exercise due care toward others, contributory negligence is the failure to exercise due care toward oneself. In most respects, contributory negligence is the mirror image of negligence.[65] While theorists may debate whether people properly may be said to have a "duty" to act with reasonable care to protect themselves,[66] courts are in quite general agreement that the classic

[63] See, e.g., Sardis v. Overhead Door Corp., 446 F. Supp. 3d 47, 67 (E.D. Va. 2020) ("The question of whether one was contributorily negligent is one for the jury to decide unless no reasonable minds could differ on the issue."); Bates v. Tippmann Sports, LLC, 2019 WL 1532230, at *3, 6 (W.D.N.C. 2019) ("contributory negligence is almost always a jury question"); Cantrell v. Wirtgen Am., Inc., 2011 WL 915324, at *11 (D. Md. 2011) (" 'Where there is a conflict of evidence as to material facts relied on to establish contributory negligence, or more than one inference may be reasonably drawn therefrom,' the issue of contributory negligence is for the jury.").

[64] "Only where the evidence establishes the plaintiff's own negligence so clearly that no other reasonable conclusion may be reached is summary judgment to be granted." Nicholson v. American Safety Util. Corp., 488 S.E.2d 240, 244 (N.C. 1997). See, e.g., Burleson v. RSR Grp. Fla., Inc., 981 So.2d 1109, 1112 (Ala. 2007) (placing holstered revolver on gun rack with safety disengaged and chambered cartridge in line with hammer and firing pin was unreasonable as a matter of law); Rodeheaver v. CNH Am., LLC, 2007 WL 465212, at *8 (D. Md. 2007) ("no reasonable jury at trial could find it reasonable for an individual to run after a moving piece of farm equipment and try to jump on it").

[65] See Simons, Contributory Negligence: Conceptual and Normative Issues, in Philosophical Foundations of Tort Law 461, 469 (D. Owen ed., Oxford 1995) (under current legal doctrine, "the formal criteria defining plaintiff's negligence and defendant's negligence are essentially the same").

[66] Dean Prosser and other scholars have questioned whether the doctrine of contributory negligence fairly may be said to embrace the notion of a duty. See, e.g., Prosser and Keeton on Torts § 65, at 453 ("Negligence requires a duty, an obligation of conduct to another person. Contributory negligence involves no duty, unless we are to be so ingenious as to say that the plaintiff is under an obligation to protect the defendant against liability for the consequences of the plaintiff's own negligence."). Immanuel Kant believed that the supreme principle of morality (the categorical imperative) included a respect for oneself: "Act so that you treat humanity, whether in your own person or in that of another, always as an end and never as a means only." Immanuel Kant, Foundations of the Metaphysics of Morals 429 (L. Beck trans., Macmillan 1959) (1785). Yet Kant believed that one's duty to oneself transcended law: "My duty toward myself cannot be treated juridically; the law touches only our relations with other men; I have no legal obligations towards myself . . . ." Immanuel Kant, Duties to Oneself, in Lectures on Ethics 117 (L. Infield trans., 1978) (1930), quoted in J.M. Finnis, Legal Enforcement of "Duties to Oneself": Kant v. Neo-Kantians, 87 Colum. L. Rev. 433 (1987). See generally Simons, The Puzzling Doctrine of Contributory Negligence, 16 Cardozo L. Rev. 1693, 1728–33 (1995).

elements of negligence[67]—duty,[68] breach,[69] cause in fact,[70] proximate cause,[71] and damage[72]—comprise the defense of contributory negligence as well.

A plaintiff will be contributorily negligent if he or she "fails to exercise such care as an ordinarily prudent person would exercise under the circumstances in order to avoid injury"[73] or simply "fails to use reasonable care with regard to [a] product."[74] Contributory negligence in the products liability setting has been particularized to include the use of a product contrary to adequate warnings and instructions, the unreasonable use of a product known to be defective, or the use of a product in an unreasonable manner.[75] In short, persons have a duty to exercise reasonable care in using products to avoid injuring themselves.

Although courts rarely examine the notion of contributory negligence explicitly in terms of the Hand formula, by which $B < P \times L$ implies an actor's negligence, this classic "calculus of risk" approach to ascertaining negligence applies as well to contributory negligence as it does to ordinary negligence.[76] Thus, the reasonableness of a plaintiff exposing himself to a product hazard is to be ascertained by weighing the burden of

---

[67] See § 2.1, above.

[68] See, e.g., Jenkins v. Whittaker Corp., 785 F.2d 720, 728–29 (9th Cir. 1986) (Haw. law).

[69] Prosser and Keeton on Torts § 65, at 453–54:

> The plaintiff is required to conform to the same objective standard of conduct, that of the reasonable person of ordinary prudence under like circumstances. The unreasonableness of the risks which he incurs is judged by the same process of weighing the importance of the interest he is seeking to advance, and the burden of taking precautions, against the probability and probable gravity of the anticipated harm to himself.

[70] "The ordinary negligence principles of cause in fact apply with equal force to contributory negligence." Id. at 456. See also Rest. (2d) Torts § 465(2).

[71] See, e.g., *Jenkins*, 785 F.2d at 729 ("Proximate cause is lacking because the alleged [contributory] negligence . . . has no connection with the actual injury. The acts asserted, however much they may have increased the risk of injury [from another source], had absolutely no relation to the risk that actually matured . . . . The duty breached by the alleged [contributory] negligence did not encompass the hazard that actually came about, and any such negligence is therefore irrelevant to the issue of proximate cause."). See also Rest. (2d) Torts § 468.

[72] On actual damages, see § 5.3, above; Owen & Davis on Products Liability ch. 25; Frumer, Friedman, and Sklaren, Products Liability ch. 13; Am. Law Prod. Liab. 3d ch. 60.

[73] Nicholson v. American Safety Util. Corp., 488 S.E.2d 240, 244 (N.C. 1997) (quoting Newton v. New Hanover Cnty. Bd. of Educ., 467 S.E.2d 58, 65 (N.C. 1996)); Bates v. Tippmann Sports, LLC, 2019 WL 1532230, at *3 (W.D.N.C. 2019) ("A contributory negligence defense requires: (1) that the plaintiff failed to exercise due care for his own safety and (2) that failure was a proximate cause of plaintiff's injuries."); Harris v. Costco Wholesale Corp., 2012 WL 1215238, at *4 (N.D. Cal. 2012) ("contributory negligence 'is conduct on the part of the plaintiff which falls below the standard to which he should conform for his own protection, and which is a legally contributing cause cooperating with the negligence of the defendant in bringing about the plaintiff's harm' ").

[74] Uniroyal Goodrich Tire Co. v. Hall, 681 So.2d 126, 129 (Ala. 1996).

[75] See N.C. Gen. Stat. Ann. § 99B–4:

> No manufacturer or seller shall be held liable in any product liability action if:
>
> (1) The use of the product giving rise to the product liability action was contrary to any express and adequate instructions or warnings delivered with, appearing on, or attached to the product or on its original container or wrapping, if the user knew or with the exercise of reasonable and diligent care should have known of such instructions or warnings; or
>
> (2) The user knew of or discovered a defect or dangerous condition of the product that was inconsistent with the safe use of the product, and then unreasonably and voluntarily exposed himself or herself to the danger, and was injured by or caused injury with that product; or
>
> (3) The claimant failed to exercise reasonable care under the circumstances in the use of the product, and such failure was a proximate cause of the occurrence that caused the injury or damage complained of.

[76] The Hand formula is explained at § 2.2, above.

avoiding the dangerous conduct, on the one hand, against the likelihood and severity of a foreseeably harmful result, on the other. If the burden of avoiding a risk is large, as in shutting down a machine that takes hours to restart,[77] or very great, such as the possible loss of employment if a worker refuses to engage in a dangerous task as directed by a superior, then an exposure to the risk for such reasons is more likely to be reasonable under the circumstances.[78]

On the other hand, a user's act is more likely to be contributorily negligent if a significant risk may be avoided by a relatively small degree of effort or attention. Contributory negligence may be found, for example, if a plaintiff fails to avoid a substantial risk of harm by simply donning gloves[79] or a face mask[80] to avoid chemical burns or lung damage; by driving at an appropriate speed for the condition of a tire, to avoid a high speed crash;[81] by securing the parking brake and shifting the transmission into "P" before getting out of a vehicle parked on an incline, to avoid being squashed as it rolls down the hill;[82] by using a condom in an appropriate manner, to avoid pregnancy and the birth of twins;[83] or by moving cautiously over a slippery floor, to avoid injury from a fall.[84] In sum, the same cost-benefit principles of balance that define negligence define contributory negligence as well.

Other principles governing the negligence standard of care also apply to determinations of contributory negligence. One such principle is the doctrine of negligence per se for violation of a statute.[85] So, an intoxicated driver may be barred from maintaining a negligence claim against an automotive manufacturer if the intoxication violated a DUI statute and contributed to the injury.[86] Another principle is the rescue doctrine,[87] relieving a rescuer of the normal responsibilities of acting according to a standard of reasonable prudence.[88] Additional negligence principles

---

[77] Such as the printing press in Micallef v. Miehle Co., 348 N.E.2d 571 (N.Y. 1976), which took three hours to restart after shutting down and so led to dangerous "chasing the hickie," which led to the injury in that case. See § 10.2, above.

[78] See Suter v. San Angelo Foundry & Mach. Co., 406 A.2d 140, 148 (N.J. 1979), superseded by statute on other grounds, as recognized in Dewey v. R.J. Reynolds Tobacco Co., 577 A.2d 1239 (N.J. 1990).

[79] See Lee v. Crest Chem. Co., 583 F. Supp. 131 (M.D.N.C. 1984).

[80] See Parris v. M.A. Bruder & Sons, Inc., 261 F. Supp. 406 (E.D. Pa. 1966).

[81] See Noel, Defective Products: Abnormal Use, Contributory Negligence, and Assumption of Risk, 25 Vand. L. Rev. 93, 111 (1972) (mentioning high-speed driving on tire not known to be defective as example of conduct that should bar recovery).

[82] See, e.g., Jett v. Ford Motor Co., 84 P.3d 219, 222 (Or. Ct. App. 2004); General Motors Corp. v. Sanchez, 997 S.W.2d 584, 594 (Tex. 1999) ("a driver has a duty to take reasonable precautions to secure his vehicle before getting out of it").

[83] See J.P.M. v. Schmid Labs., Inc., 428 A.2d 515 (N.J. Super. Ct. App. Div. 1981).

[84] See, e.g., Duke v. American Olean Tile Co., 400 N.W.2d 677 (Mich. Ct. App. 1986); Reed v. Carlyle & Martin, Inc., 202 S.E.2d 874 (Va. 1974).

[85] See Klinke v. Mitsubishi Motors Corp., 581 N.W.2d 272, 276 (Mich. 1998) (dictum). See generally § 2.3, above; Prosser and Keeton on Torts § 36.

[86] See Hill v. General Motors Corp., 168 F.3d 482 (4th Cir. 1998) (table) (N.C. law) (by implication). See also Smith v. State, 742 N.Y.S.2d 792, 798 (Ct. Cl. 2002) (driver's vehicle hit allegedly defective guide rail; because driver's blood alcohol level of .14% violated DWI statute, amounting to negligence per se, court ruled driver 80% at fault). On whether courts have a crashworthiness duty to protect drunk drivers, see § 17.5, below.

[87] See Prosser and Keeton on Torts § 44, at 307–09.

[88] See, e.g., Dillard v. Pittway Corp., 719 So.2d 188, 193 (Ala. 1998) (person injured in fire while trying to rescue father, who boarded in burning house, even if contributorily negligent, could maintain negligence claim against manufacturer and seller of smoke detector "unless the rescuer's own conduct in attempting the rescue is wanton").

applicable to contributory negligence include the sudden emergency doctrine,[89] and the objective nature of,[90] and role of customary behavior in relation to,[91] the standard of responsibility.

Reed v. Carlyle & Martin, Inc.[92] involved negligence claims by a farm hand against the manufacturer, dealer, and repairer of a piece of farm equipment, an ensilage wagon. At the time of the accident, the plaintiff was standing upon and removing a five-foot-deep load of ensilage from the wagon. A pair of revolving beaters, comprised of metal rods with spikes, located at the front of the wagon, deposited the ensilage onto a conveyor belt, which then discharged the substance. A co-worker was throwing the ensilage with a pitchfork from the rear of the wagon, but the plaintiff, standing on top of the load, decided that the quickest and easiest way to get the ensilage out of the wagon was to throw it with his pitchfork into the beaters at the front of the wagon. After unloading the ensilage in this manner for some time, the plaintiff found himself standing on a bank of ensilage, which contained "a good bit of sap" and was "right slippery," sloping downward toward the beaters. The bank collapsed, and the plaintiff slid into the beaters.

The trial court granted the defendants' motions for summary judgment on the basis of the plaintiff's contributory negligence, and the Supreme Court of Virginia affirmed. The court applied to the contributory negligence context two of the classic principles of negligence doctrine: the objective nature of the negligence standard of care,[93] and the effect of proof of compliance with customary behavior in ascertaining the standard and its breach.[94] In reply to the plaintiff's argument that he "didn't feel any danger" from working so close to the beaters, the court observed that "the test is not whether the plaintiff *actually* knew of the danger confronting him, but whether, in the exercise of reasonable care, he *should* have known he was in a situation of peril."[95] To the plaintiff's argument that farm laborers customarily used a similar technique in unloading ensilage wagons, the court noted the longstanding negligence law principle that "the existence of a custom or usage cannot excuse conduct which is otherwise negligent."[96]

Warning Cases

Contributory negligence doctrine operates under a special limitation in cases involving products with inadequate warnings of hidden dangers or instructions on safe

---

89 See, e.g., Jones v. Ford Motor Co., 559 S.E.2d 592, 605 (Va. 2002) ("if the sudden emergency doctrine is to apply, the conditions confronting the operator must be an unexpected happening, an unforeseen occurrence or condition").

90 See, e.g., Reed v. Carlyle & Martin, Inc., 202 S.E.2d 874 (Va. 1974).

91 Compare Nicholson v. American Safety Util. Corp., 488 S.E.2d 240, 245 (N.C. 1997) (customary behavior is evidence of due care) and Uniroyal Goodrich Tire Co. v. Martinez, 977 S.W.2d 328 (Tex. 1998) (same).

92 202 S.E.2d 874 (Va. 1974).

93 See § 2.2, above.

94 See § 2.3, above.

95 *Reed*, 202 S.E.2d at 876 (emphasis added). The court ruled that all reasonable persons would conclude that the plaintiff in this case should have known of his peril: "The plaintiff, an experienced farmer, admitted that he was familiar with the operation of the type ensilage wagon in which he was working. Moreover, the revolving beaters were exposed to his plain view. The danger posed by the turning, spike-like mechanism was, therefore, open and obvious to the plaintiff. In exposing himself to this obvious danger, he failed to exercise reasonable care for his own safety." Id. at 876–77.

96 Id. at 877.

use.[97] If a warning or instruction is substantively inadequate in failing to inform users of the nature or seriousness of a hidden danger or reason for a particular instructed method of use, then a user who has not otherwise discovered the risk ordinarily will not be contributorily negligent for using the product in disregard of the danger.[98] However, to be contributorily negligent for exposing oneself to a hazard, a user generally needs only to be aware of the *general* nature and magnitude of a risk, not the particular chemical or physical attributes of the product and how they specifically may affect the user's various organs. This was the holding in *Parris v. M.A. Bruder & Sons, Inc.*,[99] where a spray painter of more than twenty years claimed that the manufacturer of an epoxy product had failed to warn him that inhaling the epoxy fumes could cause asthma. Because the plaintiff knew generally of the substantial danger of inhaling paint fumes, even if he was not aware of the specific risk of contracting asthma, the court held that the jury properly could find that he was contributorily negligent for failing to wear a mask furnished by his employer.[100]

Children

Prior to the development of comparative fault, when contributory negligence operated as a complete bar, courts frequently adapted the contributory negligence doctrine in a protective manner for especially vulnerable plaintiffs. Courts and commentators have been particularly solicitous of young children who fail to appreciate product hazards.[101] So, when a 5-year-old plaintiff fell and was injured when she attempted to climb into a grocery shopping cart manufactured by the defendant, the court held that she was too young to be contributorily negligent, and that her parents' negligence in failing to instruct or supervise their child should not be imputed to her.[102]

As children grow older, the child standard of care adjusts according to the child's age, intelligence, and experience.[103] Little Joshua was aiming his "Nerf N-Strike Maverick Blaster" dart gun given to him by his parents at his 9-year-old sister when she

---

[97] *But see* Russell v. Wright, 916 F. Supp. 2d 629, 658 (W.D. Va. 2013) ("contributory negligence is available as a defense to product liability cases grounded in negligence, particularly failure to warn cases").

[98] This important point was made by Dillard and Hart in an early article:

> Though these time-honored defenses [contributory negligence and assumption of risk] are frequently invoked to defeat recovery, they are theoretically inapplicable when the defendant's breach of duty is based on a failure to warn. To allow these defenses is to indulge in circular reasoning, since usually the plaintiff cannot be said to have assumed a risk of which he was ignorant or to have contributed to his own injury when he had no way of reasonably ascertaining that the danger of injury existed. On the other hand, if the plaintiff knew of the danger from an independent source, the manufacturer's failure to warn would not be the proximate cause of the injury. Nevertheless, many courts hold that the issue of contributory negligence is involved, and is a question for the jury.

Dillard and Hart, Product Liability: Directions for Use and the Duty to Warn, 41 Va. L. Rev. 145, 163 (1955). See, e.g., Rhodes v. Interstate Battery Sys. of Am., Inc., 722 F.2d 1517, 1519 (11th Cir. 1984) (Ga. law) ("Failure to read a warning does not bar recovery when the plaintiff is challenging the adequacy of the [warning].").

[99] 261 F. Supp. 406 (E.D. Pa. 1966).

[100] Id. at 409.

[101] See Phillips, Products Liability for Personal Injury to Minors, 56 Va. L. Rev. 1223, 1240–41 (1970) ("even the best of educational efforts cannot be expected to change the essential nature of children, and, unless we are prepared to ignore this fact, in many instances better product design presents the only realistic means available for protecting children against injuries"); Madden, Products Liability, Products for Use by Adults, and Injured Children: Back to the Future, 61 Tenn. L. Rev. 1205, 1207 (1994); Field, The Young Consumer: A Paradigm Analysis of the Roles of Public and Private Law in Preventing and Redressing Injuries, 29 Mercer L. Rev. 523 (1978).

[102] Porter v. United Steel & Wire Co., 436 F. Supp. 1376 (N.D. Iowa 1977).

[103] See Prosser and Keeton on Torts § 32, at 179, and § 65, at 454.

defensively kicked a rubber ball toward the Nurf Blaster, knocking it back into Josh's forehead and causing a gash sewn up with 38 stitches, leaving a scar. Although children under seven years of age are rebuttably presumed incapable of negligence, Josh was eight, so the court instructed the jury on comparative negligence in his suit against the manufacturer, Hasbro, informing them that finding Joshua more responsible than Hasbro would deprive him of any damages whatsoever. The jury divided responsibility 90% to Josh and 10% to Hasbro, and the appellate court affirmed the trial court's judgment for Hasbro on the verdict.[104]

Another court upheld a jury finding of contributory negligence in the case of a 13-year-old child who, while mowing her parents' lawn with a rotary power lawn mower, hit a pipe imbedded in the ground that protruded 1¾ inches above ground level.[105] The mower bounced back and over her foot, which was injured by the revolving blade. The court held that the jury properly found that the plaintiff either negligently failed to observe the pipe, or that she saw it and negligently failed to avoid it.[106]

Even when older children act very carelessly, courts are not likely to grant summary judgment to product suppliers but instead may be expected to allow juries to decide whether such behavior properly amounts to contributory negligence.[107] But once a child's actions are determined to amount to contributory negligence, the child's contributory negligence may be imputed to the child's parent who is making a claim for wrongful death, loss of services, or similar injuries.[108]

Employees

As mentioned earlier, employees are sometimes effectively forced to work with dangerous machines, on dangerous tasks, or in some dangerous manner under an implicit threat of punishment or discharge for refusing to do so. In such situations, if the employee does not have a practical means to avoid the danger without simply refusing to perform the task, his or her exposure to the risk may not be unreasonable under the circumstances. As a means of protecting a worker's rights in this context, some courts "lessen the amount of caution required of him by law in the exercise of ordinary care."[109] And if an employer discovers but fails to inform its employees of a product danger, the employer's knowledge of the danger will not be imputed to its workers for purposes of contributory negligence.[110] But workers do not have a license to act carelessly, and the

---

104 Schwartz v. Hasbro, Inc., 2012 WL 1414094, at *12 (N.J. Super. Ct. App. Div. 2012).

105 Siemer v. Midwest Mower Corp., 286 F.2d 381 (8th Cir. 1961) (N.Y. law).

106 Id. at 384.

107 See Morgan v. Cavalier Acquisition Corp., 432 S.E.2d 915 (N.C. Ct. App. 1993) (factual dispute existed on contributory negligence of 17-year-old student crushed to death when he tilted soda machine too far in an attempt to get a soft drink; summary judgment for machine manufacturer and owner reversed).

108 And a parent's (or guardian's) own negligence (or assumption of risk) will bar the parent's claim for injuries to or death of the child. See, e.g., Moss v. Crosman Corp., 136 F.3d 1169 (7th Cir. 1998) (Ind. law) (dictum; 7-year-old boy killed by cousin while playing with BB gun manufactured and sold by defendants; wrongful death claim of parents, one of whom bought gun for son, barred). See generally Rest. (3d) Torts: Apportionment of Liability § 6(a) (2000).

109 Young v. Aro Corp., 111 Cal. Rptr. 535, 537 (Ct. App. 1973) (worker knowingly operating grinding wheel at excessive speed killed when wheel exploded; quoting the trial court's jury instructions). See also Lewis v. CRC Indus., 7 A.3d 841, 847 (Pa. 2010) (N.J. law) ("workers injured on the job have no 'meaningful choice' and are protected from the doctrines of assumption of risk and contributory and comparative negligence in similar strict product liability actions").

110 See Jackson v. Coast Paint & Lacquer Co., 499 F.2d 809 (9th Cir. 1974) (Mont. law).

conduct of a person injured on the job is properly subject to the normal standard of a reasonably prudent employee in the same or similar circumstances.[111]

As a Defense to Strict Liability in Tort

While contributory negligence is the classic defense to products liability claims brought in negligence, as a total bar or damages-reducing factor under comparative fault, it is not a defense to a claim for strict products liability in tort,[112] except in a very small number of jurisdictions.[113] In cases in which the plaintiff makes claims in both negligence and strict liability in tort, therefore, classic contributory negligence (that totally bars recovery) may be available as a defense to the negligence claim but not to the strict tort claim.[114] Because of the possibility of confusion by a jury, it is best if a court clearly instructs the jury on this difference in the applicability of the contributory negligence defense to different types of claims.[115]

Comment *n* to *Restatement (Second) of Torts* § 402A provides that "simple"[116] or "ordinary"[117] contributory negligence—conduct that is merely careless and that does not also amount to a voluntary assumption of risk—does not serve as a bar to liability under § 402A for harm caused by a defective product. Comment *n* provides in full:

---

[111] See, e.g., Sears v. Waste Processing Equip., Inc., 695 So.2d 51 (Ala. Civ. App. 1997) (manager reached into trash compactor knowing that door cables were broken; summary judgment for manufacturer); Reed v. Carlyle & Martin, Inc., 202 S.E.2d 874 (Va. 1974) (worker carelessly fell into revolving parts of farm equipment; summary judgment for manufacturer). See also Stilwell v. General Ry. Servs., Inc., 605 S.E.2d 500, 503 (N.C. Ct. App. 2004) (ordered by his supervisor to "like it, lump it or quit," employee used unsafe chair for over a year; contributory negligence for jury).

[112] See, e.g., Wickersham v. Ford Motor Co., 997 F.3d 526, 540 (4th Cir. 2021) (S.C. law); Romero v. ITW Food Equip. Grp., LLC, 987 F. Supp. 2d 93, 102 (D.D.C. 2013) ("[c]ontributory negligence is not a defense to a strict liability claim"); Gramex Corp. v. Green Supply, Inc., 89 S.W.3d 432, 439 (Mo. 2002) (en banc); Boerner v. Brown & Williamson Tobacco Corp., 260 F.3d 837 (8th Cir. 2001) (Ark. law) (smoker's claim against tobacco company). See also Spowal v. ITW Food Equip. Grp., 943 F. Supp. 2d 550, 562 (W.D. Pa. 2013) ("In limited circumstances, evidence of a plaintiff's conduct is admissible in a strict liability action to disprove a claim that a product's defect caused an injury [by showing] (1) assumption of the risk; (2) misuse of the product; or (3) highly reckless or extraordinarily unforeseeable conduct. Otherwise, a plaintiff's contributory negligence is inadmissible 'either to reduce the plaintiff's recovery or as a defense to liability."). *But see* Burleson v. RSR Grp. Fla., Inc., 981 So.2d 1109, 1112 (Ala. 2007) (AEMLD claims, otherwise quite similar to strict products liability in tort, are barred by contributory negligence); Mohr v. St. Paul Fire & Marine Ins. Co., 674 N.W.2d 576, 591 (Wis. Ct. App. 2003) (contributory negligence may be defense to a strict products liability claim).

See generally McNichols, The Relevance of the Plaintiff's Misconduct in Strict Tort Products Liability, the Advent of Comparative Responsibility, and the Proposed Restatement (Third) of Torts, 47 Okla. L. Rev. 201 (1994); Noel, Defective Products: Abnormal Use, Contributory Negligence, and Assumption of Risk, 25 Vand. L. Rev. 93 (1972); D. Epstein, Products Liability: Defenses Based on Plaintiff's Conduct, 1968 Utah L. Rev. 267; Annot., 46 A.L.R.3d 240 (1972) (contributory negligence and assumption of risk as defenses to claim for strict products liability in tort).

[113] See, e.g., McMahon v. Yamaha Motor Corp., U.S.A., 95 So.3d 769, 773 (Ala. 2012).

[114] See, e.g., Bonds v. Hyundai Motor Co., 2019 WL 1246441, at *3 (M.D. Ala. 2019). This puts aside, of course, the increasingly important effect of comparative fault, examined later. See § 13.3, below.

[115] See, e.g., Ellsworth v. Sherne Lingerie, Inc., 495 A.2d 348, 357 (Md. 1985) ("When theories of negligence and strict liability in tort are being presented to a jury, and the defense of contributory negligence is properly before the jury, a trial judge may well find it helpful to specifically instruct the jury that contributory negligence is not a defense to the strict liability action.").

[116] See Williams v. Brown Mfg. Co., 261 N.E.2d 305, 309 (Ill. 1970) (characterizing "lack of due care for one's own safety as measured by the objective reasonable-man standard" as "simple contributory negligence").

[117] See *Williams*, 261 N.E.2d at 310. See also Cepeda v. Cumberland Eng'g Co., 386 A.2d 816, 832 (N.J. 1978) (following *Williams* in rejecting "ordinary" contributory negligence as defense to claims for strict products liability in tort), overruled on other grounds by Suter v. San Angelo Foundry & Mach. Co., 406 A.2d 140 (N.J. 1979).

> *n. Contributory negligence.* Since the liability with which this Section deals is not based upon negligence of the seller, but is strict liability, the rule applied to strict liability cases (see § 524) applies. Contributory negligence of the plaintiff is not a defense when such negligence consists merely in a failure to discover the defect in the product, or to guard against the possibility of its existence. On the other hand the form of contributory negligence which consists in voluntarily and unreasonably proceeding to encounter a known danger, and commonly passes under the name of assumption of risk, is a defense under this Section as in other cases of strict liability. If the user or consumer discovers the defect and is aware of the danger, and nevertheless proceeds unreasonably to make use of the product and is injured by it, he is barred from recovery.

A couple of early decisions rejected the comment *n* approach and held that contributory negligence in any form would bar liability under strict liability in tort,[118] and at least one prominent early commentator was uncertain of the soundness of abandoning conventional contributory negligence as a defense in strict liability defective product cases.[119] Such courts and commentators reasoned that strict products liability in tort is based in part upon the likelihood that product defects are attributable to a seller's negligence, which, although it usually exists, is often difficult for a plaintiff to prove; that the doctrine functions as a kind of res ipsa loquitur or negligence per se; and that the doctrine rests upon a presumption that injured plaintiffs are incapable of protecting themselves—each of which are rationales consistent with allowing a contributory negligence defense.[120]

Despite comment *n*'s thin reasoning for abandoning the conventional tort law defense of contributory negligence on the ground that it has been rejected as a defense to strict liability in tort for harm caused by ultrahazardous activities,[121] courts widely

---

[118] See Atkins v. American Motors Corp., 335 So.2d 134, 143 (Ala. 1976); Stephan v. Sears, Roebuck & Co., 266 A.2d 855 (N.H. 1970). See also Codling v. Paglia, 298 N.E.2d 622 (N.Y. 1973) (strict products liability in warranty); Dippel v. Sciano, 155 N.W.2d 55 (Wis. 1967) (comparative fault). New Jersey, which had abolished the defense of assumption of risk in Meistrich v. Casino Arena Attractions, Inc., 155 A.2d 90 (N.J. 1959), and McGrath v. American Cyanamid Co., 196 A.2d 238 (N.J. 1963), found a need to leave "contributory negligence" available as a strict products liability in tort defense to address cases involving voluntary and unreasonable encounters of product dangers; but it defined the requisite type of contributory negligence in terms of assumption of risk. See generally Cepeda v. Cumberland Eng'g Co., 386 A.2d 816, 831 (N.J. 1978). In addition, New Jersey made an exception for plaintiffs negligently encountering a known danger where the product is defective precisely because of its failure to prevent such negligent encounters. See Bexiga v. Havir Mfg. Corp., 290 A.2d 281 (N.J. 1972) (plaintiff's hand crushed in punch press), where the court concluded that "the interests of justice dictate that contributory negligence be unavailable as a defense to either the negligence or strict liability claims," reasoning as follows:

> The asserted negligence of plaintiff—placing his hand under the ram while at the same time depressing the foot pedal—was the very eventuality the safety devices were designed to guard against. It would be anomalous to hold that defendant has a duty to install safety devices but a breach of that duty results in no liability for the very injury the duty was meant to protect against.

Id. at 286. Cf. Rivera v. Westinghouse Elevator Co., 526 A.2d 705 (N.J. 1987). *Bexiga* is noted at 86 Harv. L. Rev. 923 (1973).

[119] See Noel, Defective Products: Abnormal Use, Contributory Negligence, and Assumption of Risk, 25 Vand. L. Rev. 93, 105–19, 128–30 (1972). "If the plaintiff could have discovered the defect in a dangerous product with little effort, it may be that his failure to inspect should be a defense in this new and expanding area of liability." Id. at 117.

[120] See id. at 105–19.

[121] See, e.g., McCown v. International Harvester Co., 342 A.2d 381, 382 n.5 (Pa. 1975) (Pomeroy, J., concurring). See generally Noel, Defective Products: Abnormal Use, Contributory Negligence, and Assumption of Risk, 25 Vand. L. Rev. 93, 115–17 (1972). Comment *n* does faithfully adapt the principles of Rest. (2d) Torts § 524 to the defective product context.

adopted comment *n*'s abandonment of simple contributory negligence as a bar to strict products liability in tort.[122] Courts reasoned that the doctrine of strict liability in tort discarded the concept of fault, that strict liability was premised on requiring suppliers of defective products to internalize the costs of product accidents as a means of risk administration, and that such liability was based on the buyer's reliance upon an implicit representation that the product was safe.[123] At the other end of the spectrum, a plaintiff's voluntary and negligent encounter with a risk shifts the equities firmly in favor of the innocent manufacturer who should be asked neither to absorb resulting injury costs nor to pass them on to other consumers, in the form of higher prices, who thereby are forced to subsidize the venturesome follies of those who should bear the risks themselves. For this reason, there is much to be said for comment *n*'s policy of allowing a defense for voluntary and unreasonable risk encounters and leaving the consequences of such encounters entirely on those who make such choices.[124]

The spread of comparative fault would seem to complicate the issue by raising anew the question of whether plaintiffs should still be specially protected from the consequences of their "simple" or "ordinary" contributory negligence, but courts in comparative fault regimes have declined to reduce damages on account of a plaintiff's careless failure to discover a product defect.[125] The *Products Liability Restatement* rejects the idea of exempting from damages apportionment a plaintiff's negligence in failing to discover or guard against the possibility of a defect, but, sympathetic to this type of plaintiff misbehavior, observes that a plaintiff's simple contributory negligence of this sort generally will not breach the standard of reasonable behavior.[126]

Comment *n*, as mentioned above, divides a user's negligent conduct into two categories: failing to discover or guard against the possibility of a defect, on the one hand, and conduct which amounts to a negligent assumption of risk—voluntarily and unreasonably encountering a known and appreciated danger—on the other. Yet, rather than fully occupying the total set of consumer misconduct, these two forms of negligent behavior might instead be seen to occupy only the two ends of the spectrum of consumer mistakes: the first, a type of minimally careless conduct involving a consumer's excessive trust during initial encounters with an unfamiliar product, and the second, a type of

---

[122] The leading early case on point was Williams v. Brown Mfg. Co., 261 N.E.2d 305 (Ill. 1970). Other early decisions to this effect included Ferraro v. Ford Motor Co., 223 A.2d 746 (Pa. 1966); Martinez v. Nichols Conveyor & Eng'g Co., 52 Cal. Rptr. 842 (Ct. App. 1966); Baker v. Rosemurgy, 144 N.W.2d 660 (Mich. Ct. App. 1966); Shamrock Fuel & Oil Sales Co. v. Tunks, 416 S.W.2d 779 (Tex. 1967); Ettin v. Ava Truck Leasing, Inc., 251 A.2d 278 (N.J. 1969); Perfection Paint & Color Co. v. Konduris, 258 N.E.2d 681, 689 (Ind. Ct. App. 1970).

[123] See, e.g., McCown v. International Harvester Co., 342 A.2d 381, 382 (Pa. 1975) (allowing contributory negligence defense "would contradict this normal expectation of product safety"). Following Williams v. Brown Mfg. Co., 261 N.E.2d 305 (Ill. 1970), the court in Cepeda v. Cumberland Eng'g Co., 386 A.2d 816, 832 (N.J. 1978), observed that the "acceptance of 'ordinary' contributory negligence as a defense in actions for strict liability in tort would be incompatible with the policy considerations which led to the adoption of strict tort liability in the first instance. The manufacturer's duty is imposed precisely to avert foreseeable inadvertent injury to a user of a product." See generally McNichols, The Relevance of the Plaintiff's Misconduct in Strict Tort Products Liability, the Advent of Comparative Responsibility, and the Proposed Restatement (Third) of Torts, 47 Okla. L. Rev. 201, 260 (1994); Noel, Defective Products: Abnormal Use, Contributory Negligence, and Assumption of Risk, 25 Vand. L. Rev. 93, 105–19, 128–30 (1972).

[124] See, e.g., Haglund v. Philip Morris, Inc., 847 N.E.2d 315, 323 (Mass. 2006) ("When the consumer's knowing use of a product in a dangerous and defective condition is unreasonable, the consumer's own conduct has become the proximate cause of his injuries, and he can recover nothing from the seller [the *Correia* defense].").

[125] See § 13.3, below.

[126] See Products Liability Rest. § 17 Reporters' Note to cmt. *d*, at 259, set forth in § 13.3, below.

deliberately careless decision to encounter known and appreciated hazards of a familiar product. Arguably, neither of these categories adequately describes a consumer's ordinary careless *use* of a defective product, such as operating the product in a careless manner.[127] But comment *n* is not a statute,[128] and its provision excluding contributory negligence for failing to discover or guard against the existence of a defect may be reasonably expanded to include the idea of using a product without due care that it may be defective.[129] So interpreted, comment *n*'s two categories of user misconduct may plausibly be viewed as embracing all forms of contributory negligence by product users. Under comparative fault, however, there may be good reason to exclude from damages apportionment a plaintiff's negligence in failing to discover a product's defects, narrowly defined, but to reduce a plaintiff's damages for negligently using the product in a dangerous manner.[130]

As the Sole Proximate Cause of an Accident

With the loss of the contributory negligence defense in strict liability claims, counsel for defendants lost the most cherished arrow in their quiver. In a case involving appreciable plaintiff misconduct, a plaintiff's lawyer now may style the claim as one of strict liability in tort in order to avoid argument (and possibly evidence) on the plaintiff's negligent misbehavior. But, by rejecting a plaintiff's contributory negligence as a general defense to claims for strict products liability in tort, the law did not abolish the plaintiff's obligation to establish that a defect is a proximate cause of the harm.

From an early date, commentators observed that a plaintiff's contributory negligence sometimes is such a significant factor in producing an injury that it may amount to the *sole* proximate cause of the harm.[131] Accordingly, defendants sometimes argue that a plaintiff's behavior—rather than any defect in the product—was the "sole proximate cause" of the accident or harm. When substantial consumer misconduct is overwhelmingly the predominant force in causing an accident, and when evidence of a product defect is manifestly trivial by comparison, evidence and argument that the plaintiff's conduct was the sole proximate cause of the harm is entirely appropriate and will support a judgment for the defendant in a proper case.[132] On occasion, courts speak

---

127 See, e.g., McCown v. International Harvester Co., 342 A.2d 381, 383 (Pa. 1975) (Pomeroy, J., concurring).

128 Except in South Carolina, which codified the negligent assumption of risk defense embraced in the last sentence of comment *n*. S.C. Code Ann. § 15–73–20.

129 See Noel, Defective Products: Abnormal Use, Contributory Negligence, and Assumption of Risk, 25 Vand. L. Rev. 93, 111 (1972) (high-speed driving on tire not known to be defective as example of failing to guard against the possibility of defect). Compare W. Prosser, Handbook of the Law of Torts § 102, at 670–71 (4th ed. 1971), describing the negligent driving on a tire known to be unsafe as the kind of assumption of risk conduct to be distinguished from simple negligence in failing to discover or guard against the risk that a product might be defective.

130 See General Motors Corp. v. Sanchez, 997 S.W.2d 584 (Tex. 1999) (interpreting cmt. *n* of Second Restatement narrowly, and quoting Third Rest. § 17, cmt. *d*: plaintiff's negligence in failing to discover defect should not reduce plaintiff's damages under comparative fault, but negligence in dangerously *using* product should result in such reduction).

131 See, e.g., Noel, Defective Products: Abnormal Use, Contributory Negligence, and Assumption of Risk, 25 Vand. L. Rev. 93, 105 (1972).

132 See, e.g., Sullivan v. Werner Co., 253 A.3d 730, 749 (Pa. Super. Ct. 2021) ("a defendant can admit evidence and argue that a plaintiff's ordinary negligence was the sole cause of an accident in a strict products liability case"); Hernandez v. Asoli, 97 N.Y.S.3d 227, 229 (App. Div. 2019) ("the plaintiff's own conduct of knowingly placing his hand into the hopper of the operating cheese grater without turning it off was the sole proximate cause of his injuries"; design and warnings claims against grinder dismissed); Haglund v. Philip Morris, Inc., 847 N.E.2d 315, 323 (Mass. 2006) ("When the consumer's knowing use of a product in a dangerous

loosely of a plaintiff's substantial misconduct as a "superseding" cause of an accident.[133] Yet, the concept of superseding causation refers traditionally not to plaintiffs but to unforeseeable intervening acts of God and behavior by third parties.[134] It thus is best to avoid characterizing a plaintiff's extraordinary behavior as "superseding" but to analyze it instead in sole-proximate-cause terms.

But the sole-proximate-cause doctrine can be used improperly to drag ordinary contributory negligence back into products liability cases, to operate as a total bar, in situations where a plaintiff's misconduct should reduce damages, not bar recovery altogether.[135] Whether conduct is called "contributory negligence" or something else, it can fairly be described as the *sole* proximate cause of an accident only if it overwhelmed any causal contribution by a product defect which, by comparison, was simply trivial. Without close supervision by a trial court, evidence and argument on the plaintiff's conduct as the sole proximate cause of an accident may slip easily and impermissibly into a thinly veiled revival of the contributory negligence defense.

For example, in *Sheehan v. Anthony Pools*,[136] the plaintiff was injured during a party at his new swimming pool when he fell off the side of the diving board onto the concrete coping at the edge of the pool. In his strict tort action against the pool company, the plaintiff claimed that the non-skid material on the board should have extended to and over the edges of the board and that the design of the pool's diving board coping area was unsafe. Without using the terms "careless" or "contributory negligence," defense counsel argued essentially that the injury was caused not by any problem with the design

---

and defective condition is unreasonable, the consumer's own conduct has become the proximate cause of his injuries, and he can recover nothing from the seller [the *Correia* defense].").

Compare Goulah v. Ford Motor Co., 118 F.3d 1478, 1485 (11th Cir. 1997) (Fla. law). In this design defect case involving the rollover of a Bronco II when the trailer it was towing swung around, the manufacturer argued that the "sole legal cause" of the accident was the improper use of the trailer rather than any defect in the vehicle:

> Evidence on the issues of the trailer and driving directly refutes Plaintiffs' contention that Ford's negligence caused this accident. Ford was not limited to saying, "we didn't cause this." Ford had every right to tell the jury who or what it believed made this accident happen.

Id. at 1486. Compare also Yun v. Ford Motor Co., 669 A.2d 1378 (N.J. 1996) (plaintiff struck by another vehicle while crossing highway to retrieve spare tire that fell off van; proximate cause for jury), reversing 647 A.2d 841 (N.J. Super. Ct. App. Div. 1994), which had affirmed summary judgment for manufacturer.

[133] See, e.g., DZE Corp. v. Vickers, 299 So.3d 538, 542 (Fla. Dist. Ct. App. 2020) (driver's intoxication from synthetic marijuana "was the sole superseding proximate cause of the accident that resulted in the tragic deaths of Appellees' decedents"); Reott v. Asia Trend, Inc., 55 A.3d 1088, 1100–01 n.13 (Pa. 2012) (revealing confusion between the terms and concepts of sole proximate cause and superseding cause and futilely seeking shelter behind Dan Dobbs, The Law Of Torts § 196, by asserting that the learned professor notes the confusion, yet appearing to forget that it is the courts' responsibility to clear up confusion in the common law); Griffith v. Chrysler Corp., 2003 WL 21500037, at *6 (Ohio Ct. App. 2003) (intoxicated person fell asleep or passed out in stopped, running vehicle while his foot pressed on accelerator, causing exhaust system to overheat and ignite; proper to instruct jury that vehicle occupant's conduct could be "superseding intervening cause"); Madonna v. Harley Davidson, Inc., 708 A.2d 507, 509 (Pa. Super. Ct. 1998); Wagner v. Clark Equip. Co., 700 A.2d 38, 48 (Conn. 1997).

[134] See generally Rest. (2d) Torts § 440; Prosser and Keeton on Torts § 44, at 312.

[135] Arguably inappropriate uses of the sole-proximate-cause doctrine are Stollings v. Ryobi Techs., Inc., 725 F.3d 753, 770 (7th Cir. 2013) (Ill. law) (although plaintiff removed a power saw guard against kickbacks and operated it without the safety protection, contrary to warnings on the saw, this conduct was not uncommon); Wilson v. Vermont Castings, Inc., 170 F.3d 391, 396 (3d Cir. 1999) (Pa. law) (plaintiff's dress caught fire on wood burning stove allegedly defective because of need to leave door open to keep fire going; upholding jury finding that plaintiff's conduct was sole cause of accident); Sabbatino v. Rosin & Sons Hardware & Paint, Inc., 676 N.Y.S.2d 633, 635 (App. Div. 1998) (affirming summary judgment for defendants, where plaintiff failed to heed instructions on drain cleaner to cover opening after pouring cleaner into drain).

[136] 440 A.2d 1085, 1090–92 (Md. Ct. Spec. App. 1982).

of the board or the pool, but by the manner in which the plaintiff used the board.[137] The trial judge denied the defendant's request to instruct the jury that contributory negligence *was* a defense and also denied the plaintiff's request for a charge that the plaintiff's inadvertence in using the board was *not* a defense, and the jury returned a verdict for the defendant. Reversing and remanding, the appellate court held that the trial court should have granted the plaintiff's requested instruction.[138]

Arguments by a skillful defense attorney about a plaintiff's contributions to an accident can lead a jury to conclude—sometimes improperly—that the plaintiff's negligent manner in using a product was the sole cause of his injury.[139] This suggests that courts, in addition to closely monitoring such arguments to avoid their abuse, should instruct juries carefully on the effect of consumer carelessness and on the proper, limited role of the doctrine of sole proximate cause in modern products liability litigation. Nevertheless, courts should also instruct and allow argument on sole proximate cause when the defense has made a plausible case that a product accident might fairly be attributed entirely to the plaintiff's conduct.[140]

§ 13.3 COMPARATIVE FAULT

From the 1960s through the 1990s, the doctrine of comparative fault swept across America.[141] Its rapid and widespread adoption sprang from the evident unfairness of the all-or-nothing rule of contributory negligence that barred a plaintiff from all recovery against a tortfeasor if the plaintiff was at fault in any way in connection with the accident.[142] The law on comparative fault (otherwise known as "comparative negligence," "comparative responsibility," or "apportionment"),[143] which reduces an accident victim's damages proportionate to his or her fault rather than barring recovery altogether, is now

---

137 In closing argument, defense counsel argued, over objection, as follows:

> You must find that this defect proximately caused the accident. The clear testimony here from Mr. Weiner and using your common sense is that if someone steps on the board with about an inch of their foot on it, they will fall off the side. That was the proximate cause, the way the board was used, not the design of the board. I am not willing to concede for a moment that there is anything defective about the board when you use the standards which are customary in the industry and any governmental regulations. Even if you feel there was, I ask you to find that the proximate cause was the way Mr. Sheehan used it, not the way it was designed.

Id. at 1090 (court's emphasis omitted).

138 Id. at 1092.

139 See the several questionable cases cited in note 135, above.

140 See, e.g., Stollings v. Ryobi Techs., Inc., 725 F.3d 753, 770 (7th Cir. 2013) (dubiously concluding that trial court's excellent sole proximate cause instruction "was likely to cause undue confusion where no other person's conduct was at issue and the defendant had abandoned a comparative fault defense").

141 Comparative fault is applied today in every jurisdiction except Alabama, the District of Columbia, Maryland, North Carolina, and Virginia. See Gifford, The Death of the Common Law: Judicial Abdication and Contributory Negligence in Maryland, 73 Md. L. Rev. Endnotes 1, at *4 (2014). See also note 11, above.

142 "The hardship of the doctrine of contributory negligence upon the plaintiff is readily apparent. It places upon one party the entire burden of a loss for which two are, by hypothesis, responsible." Prosser and Keeton on Torts § 67, at 468–69.

143 See, e.g., Duncan v. Cessna Aircraft Co., 665 S.W.2d 414, 427 (Tex. 1984) ("We choose comparative *causation* instead because it is conceptually accurate in cases based on strict liability and breach of warranty theories in which the defendant's 'fault,' in the traditional sense of culpability, is not at issue."); Daly v. General Motors Corp., 575 P.2d 1162, 1172 (Cal. 1978) (suggesting "equitable apportionment of loss").

so extensive that it has its own *Restatement (Third) of Torts: Apportionment*[144] and a uniform law on this topic.[145]

Comparative fault, examined elsewhere in much greater depth,[146] significantly affects modern products liability litigation[147] by providing a giant umbrella over the traditional misconduct defenses of contributory negligence,[148] in almost every state; assumption of risk,[149] in many states; and product misuse,[150] in a few states. While comparative fault most typically affects claims for negligence and strict liability in tort, its principles of apportionment may also affect claims for breach of warranty[151] and tortious misrepresentation.[152] How the spreading tentacles of comparative fault affect negligence claims was touched on earlier, and how this doctrine affects warranty and misrepresentation claims is considered in later sections on these topics.

Prior to addressing the specifics of comparative fault, it would do well to note that its widespread adoption still leaves fairly substantial room for the traditional all-or-nothing conduct defenses to operate. As mentioned earlier, traditional conduct defenses continue to govern products actions in the few states that still reject the doctrine of comparative fault.[153] In addition, some secondary rules of plaintiff conduct defenses—such as the possible irrelevance of a plaintiff's contributory negligence in failing to discover a defect, and the role of sole proximate cause—may be unaffected by

---

[144] See Rest. (3d) Torts: Apportionment (2000).

[145] See Uniform Apportionment of Tort Responsibility Act (2002, amended 2003). See comment to § 3, discussing history of comparative fault and uniform acts thereon.

[146] See, e.g., Ogden and Hylton, Incentives to Take Care Under Contributory and Comparative Fault: The Role of Strategic Complementarity, 61 Int'l Rev. L. & Econ. 1 (2020); Schwartz and Appel, Two Wrongs Do Not Make a Right: Reconsidering the Application of Comparative Fault to Punitive Damage Awards, 78 Mo. L. Rev. 133 (2013); Westerbeke, In Praise of Arbitrariness: The Proposed 83.7% Rule of Modified Comparative Fault, 59 U. Kan. L. Rev. 991 (2011); Maraist, Johnson, Galligan, and Corbett, Answering a Fool According to His Folly: Ruminations on Comparative Fault Thirty Years On, 70 La. L. Rev. 1105 (2010); Bublick, Comparative Fault to the Limits, 56 Vand. L. Rev. 977 (2003); Robertson, Love and Fury: Recent Radical Revisions to the Law of Comparative Fault, 59 La. L. Rev. 175, 198–99 (1998); Dobbs, Accountability and Comparative Fault, 47 La. L. Rev. 939 (1987); Cooter and Ulen, An Economic Case for Comparative Negligence, 61 N.Y.U. L. Rev. 1067, 1081–83 (1986); G. Schwartz, Contributory and Comparative Negligence: A Reappraisal, 87 Yale L.J. 697, 721–23 (1978); Prosser, Comparative Negligence, 51 Mich. L. Rev. 465 (1953); Prosser and Keeton on Torts § 67; Dobbs, Law of Torts § 201; V. Schwartz, Comparative Negligence (with K. Kelly 6th ed. 2020); H. Woods and B. Deere, Comparative Fault (3d ed. 1996, annual updates); Best et al., Comparative Negligence Law and Practice (Matthew Bender, rev. ed. annual updates).

[147] See, e.g., Henke, Comparative Fault in Products Liability: Comparing California and New Jersey, 19 T.M. Cooley L. Rev. 301 (2002); Davis, Individual and Institutional Responsibility: A Vision for Comparative Fault in Products Liability, 39 Vill. L. Rev. 281 (1994); McNichols, The Relevance of the Plaintiff's Misconduct in Strict Tort Products Liability, the Advent of Comparative Responsibility, and the Proposed Restatement (Third) of Torts, 47 Okla. L. Rev. 201 (1994) (reviewing early draft of Products Liability Restatement); Roszkowski and Prentice, Reconciling Comparative Negligence and Strict Liability: A Public Policy Analysis, 33 St. Louis U. L.J. 19 (1988); Westerbeke and Meltzer, Comparative Fault and Strict Products Liability in Kansas: Reflections on the Distinction Between Initial Liability and Ultimate Loss Allocation, 28 U. Kan. L. Rev. 25 (1979); Twerski, The Use and Abuse of Comparative Negligence in Products Liability, 10 Ind. L. Rev. 797 (1977); Levine, Strict Products Liability and Comparative Negligence: The Collision of Fault and No-Fault, 14 San Diego L. Rev. 337 (1977). See generally Frumer, Friedman, and Sklaren, Products Liability § 8.04[5] (as a defense to strict liability in tort) and § 10.02[3] (as a defense to negligence); Am. Law Prod. Liab. 3d ch. 40; Dobbs, Law of Torts § 369.

[148] See § 13.2, above.

[149] See § 13.4, below.

[150] See § 13.5, below.

[151] See § 13.6, below.

[152] See § 13.7, below.

[153] Alabama, the District of Columbia, Maryland, North Carolina, and Virginia.

comparative fault. Importantly, in most states, a plaintiff's misconduct remains a *total* bar to recovery if the plaintiff's fault equals (or, in some states, exceeds) that of the defendant.[154] In addition, some courts do not apply comparative fault principles to assumption of risk, or do so only to a limited extent,[155] and almost all still consider the plaintiff's unforeseeable misuse to be a total defense.[156] Finally, in claims for breach of warranty[157] and misrepresentation,[158] a buyer's or user's misconduct often goes to issues—such as scope of warranty, justifiable reliance, and proximate cause—that are part of the plaintiff's case in chief, making the absence of such misconduct essential to the plaintiff's underlying claim. What all this means, of course, is that comparative fault has not beaten the traditional conduct defenses completely into the ground. Defendants still can sometimes put traditional all-or-nothing conduct defenses effectively to use as gladiators against misbehaving plaintiffs despite the modern urge to purge clear judgments of right or wrong from legal outcomes by fixing responsibility, like Solomon, by division.[159]

Yet, while comparative fault still has competition, let no one doubt its power. This section examines how comparative fault operates in products liability litigation more generally, especially how it alters the traditional defense of contributory negligence and affects claims based on strict liability in tort. The specific effects of comparative fault on other conduct doctrines are addressed in later sections.

Types and Examples of Comparative Fault

"Pure" and "Modified"

Comparative fault systems applicable to products liability cases come in two basic forms: "pure" and "modified."[160] A comparative fault system is "pure" if a plaintiff may recover damages from a tortfeasor, reduced proportionately by those attributable to the plaintiff's fault, regardless of how great the plaintiff's proportion of the total fault may be. For example, if a plaintiff's fault is 90% and the defendant's fault is only 10%, the

---

154 See, e.g., King v. Kayak Mfg. Corp., 387 S.E.2d 511 (W. Va. 1989) (assumption of risk). See § 13.4, below.

155 Ohio, for example, merged assumption of risk into comparative fault for negligence claims but left it as a total bar to claims for strict liability in tort. See, e.g., Onderko v. Richmond Mfg. Co., 511 N.E.2d 388 (Ohio 1987); Bowling v. Heil Co., 511 N.E.2d 373 (Ohio 1987). See § 13.4, below.

156 See § 13.5, below.

157 See § 13.6, below.

158 See § 13.7, below.

159 The dominant allure of a perfect alignment of fault to damage apportionment may make it too late to hope for widespread adoption of an equal-division ("pro rata") rule of apportionment. "In addition to being easy to understand and cheap to administer, such a simple and fundamentally fair (if 'imperfect') approach to apportionment should decrease gaming and increase settlements, for it avoids asking jurors to formulate divisions that reflect the advocacy skills of counsel more than any 'true' divisions of metaphysical responsibility." Owen, Epstein's Razor, 3 J. Tort Law 2 (Westlaw, Issue 1, Oct. 2010). Fortunately, the doctrine of sole proximate cause can help knock out fault-damage apportionments between plaintiffs and defendants at both ends of the fault scale, as variously addressed in § 12.3, above, and this chapter, passim. Consider, too, the perceptive arguments for some such arbitrary approach in Westerbeke, In Praise of Arbitrariness: The Proposed 83.7% Rule of Modified Comparative Fault, 59 U. Kan. L. Rev. 991 (2011). But an empirical comparative study of the jury behaviors under pure and comparative fault may argue for a pure approach. Best and Donohue, Jury Nullification in Modified Comparative Negligence Regimes, 79 U. Chi. L. Rev. 945 (2012).

160 One state, South Dakota, still has the "slight-gross" system, under which a plaintiff may recover (diminished) damages against a defendant if the plaintiff's contributory negligence is slight, and the defendant's is gross. See S.D. Codified Laws § 20–9–2. See, e.g., Jensen v. Hy-Vee, Corp., 2011 WL 1832997, at *10 (D.S.D. 2011) (jury might conclude that plaintiff was contributorily negligent for failing to avoid being struck by automatic door). Nebraska formerly had this system but switched to a modified system in 1992.

plaintiff in a pure comparative fault jurisdiction may still recover the 10% of damages attributable to the defendant.[161] Most states that adopted comparative fault by judicial decision, together with several that adopted it legislatively, adopted the doctrine in this pure form,[162] an approach endorsed by both the National Conference of Commissioners on Uniform State Laws (NCCUSL) in 1977[163] and the American Law Institute (ALI) in 2000,[164] although NCCUSL withdrew its endorsement in 2002.[165]

A majority of states, including most that adopted the doctrine legislatively, use some "modified" version of comparative fault. Modified comparative fault systems reduce recoverable damages proportionate to a plaintiff's fault, just as under the pure approach, but they continue to bar recovery *completely* (as under traditional contributory negligence) if the plaintiff is largely at fault—under the "Georgia system,"[166] if the plaintiff's fault *equals* or exceeds the defendant's fault, or, under the "New Hampshire system,"[167] only if the plaintiff's fault *exceeds* the defendant's fault. So, under either type of modified system, a plaintiff 30% at fault may recover the 70% of damages apportioned to the defendant, but a plaintiff 60% at fault is entitled to no recovery.[168] A plaintiff who

---

[161] See, e.g., Crawford v. ITW Food Equip. Grp., LLC, 977 F.3d 1331, 1337 (11th Cir. 2020) (Fla. law) (meat cutter whose arm was amputated by commercial meat saw was 70% at fault for failing to deploy the blade guard); Thornton v. Gray Auto. Parts Co., 62 S.W.3d 575 (Mo. Ct. App. 2001) (mechanic, 95% at fault for improperly using jack that slipped out from beneath vehicle, could recover against manufacturer of jack who was 5% at fault for not equipping jack with safety feature); Uniroyal Tire Co. v. Trujillo, 711 So.2d 606 (Fla. Dist. Ct. App. 1998) (driver, 99% at fault for speeding, having tire improperly repaired, and failing to wear seatbelt, could recover against tire manufacturer who was 1% responsible), vacated, 757 So.2d 547 (Fla. Dist. Ct. App. 2000); Winston v. International Harvester Corp., 791 F.2d 430 (5th Cir. 1986) (La. law) (tractor operator 97% negligent could recover 3% of damages against tractor manufacturer).

[162] The list of "pure" jurisdictions currently includes Alaska, Arizona, California, Florida, Hawaii (applicable to claims for strict liability in tort and warranty, but not negligence), Kentucky, Louisiana, Michigan, Mississippi, Missouri, New Mexico, New York, Rhode Island, Washington, and Puerto Rico. See H. Woods and B. Deere, Comparative Fault § 1.11 (3d ed. 1996 & Supp. 2022); V. Schwartz, Comparative Negligence § 2.01[a] (with K. Kelly 6th ed. 2020); Product Liability Desk Reference—A Fifty State Compendium (M. Daller and N. Daller, eds., 2022).

[163] See Uniform Comparative Fault Act § 1. Iowa and Washington were the only states to enact the act in any form, and their versions differed from the uniform act materially.

[164] See Rest. (3d): Apportionment § 7 (2000), which provides that a plaintiff's negligence that is a legal cause of plaintiff's injury "reduces the plaintiff's recovery in proportion to the share of responsibility the factfinder assigns to the plaintiff."

[165] See Uniform Apportionment of Tort Responsibility Act § 3(b) (2002, amended 2003), and the excellent comment to § 3.

[166] See, e.g., Johns v. Suzuki Motor of Am., Inc., 850 S.E.2d 59 (Ga. 2020). This approach is also known as the (original) "Wisconsin system," but Wisconsin itself abandoned this approach for the New Hampshire system in 1971.

[167] Or, in some jurisdictions, compared to the fault of *all* defendants.

[168] See, e.g., Doran v. Yoho, 213 Fed. Appx. 335, 336 (5th Cir. 2007) (Tex. law) (defectively designed hair trigger for rifle, 10%; owner's replacement of original trigger with hair trigger, 15%; plaintiff's loading rifle in moving vehicle without gun safety on, 75%; judgment for defendant); Shotts v. Bombardier Inc., 2007 WL 3286615, at *1 (S.D. Ind. 2007) (plaintiff, paralyzed when ATV flipped over backwards on him while towing smaller ATV up steep slope from bottom of ravine, was 68% at fault for attaching tow strap to luggage rack instead of towing hitch, and manufacturer was 32% at fault for failing to warn against this use; judgment for defendant); Hernandez v. American Appliance Mfg. Corp., 827 S.W.2d 383 (Tex. App. 1992) (plaintiff, 90% at fault for using adhesive with highly flammable fumes near gas water heater with pilot light, could take nothing against 10% at-fault heater manufacturer). See also Taylor v. Square D Co., 2003 WL 23093835 (Tenn. Ct. App. 2003) (fault of electrician, electrocuted while working on partially energized circuit contrary to supervisor's direct orders, was clearly greater than any negligence of manufacturer); Horton v. American Tobacco Co., 667 So.2d 1289 (Miss. 1995) (jury found tobacco company liable for smoker's death from lung cancer, but awarded damages of $0, presumably because it found the smoker 100% at fault); Gratzle v. Sears, Roebuck & Co., 613 N.E.2d 802 (Ill. App. Ct. 1993) (60% apportionment of causation to plaintiff reversed; jury should have been instructed on effect of finding that plaintiff's conduct accounted for 50% or more of causation).

is 50% at fault may recover half of his or her damages under the New Hampshire system but nothing whatsoever under the Georgia system. To leave plaintiffs with some recovery in the occasional cases where fault is apportioned 50–50 between plaintiffs and defendants,[169] a number of states have switched to the New Hampshire system, as have two states (Illinois and Iowa) which had been pure. Only eleven states still remain in the Georgia camp,[170] whereas twenty-one states now follow the increasingly popular New Hampshire approach, which allows a 50% at-fault plaintiff to recover.[171]

Examples of Comparative Fault

Product accidents occur in myriad ways, resulting in myriad divisions of fault between manufacturers and product users. For example, when a defect in a car's steering column caused the steering to lock, after which the plaintiff neglected to apply the brakes, responsibility for the resulting crash was divided 85% to the manufacturer and 15% to the driver;[172] a manufacturer of an aluminum ladder sold without warning of the risk from hitting power lines was 2% responsible for a painter's electrocution, the company that rented the ladder to the painting crew was 3% responsible, and the painter himself, who failed to have the power lines de-energized before painting in their vicinity and failed to use a wooden or fiberglass ladder, was 95% responsible;[173] the manufacturer of a car with a defective door latch, which allowed the door to open when it collided with another car, was 75% responsible, and the plaintiff's responsibility for speeding was 25%;[174] the manufacturer of a potato chip cooker kettle was 52% responsible for a kettle shaft that popped out of place, and the injured Frito Lay employee who attempted to repair the shaft was 48% at fault for conducting the repairs while standing on a board across a kettle of hot oil, and for slipping in;[175] a pharmacy was 51% responsible for failing properly to warn a customer that an anti-depression drug could cause permanent impotency, whereas the customer was 49% at fault for failing for

---

169 Such 50–50 findings are not rare, but oddly uncommon. See, e.g., Sowers v. R.J. Reynolds Tobacco Co., 975 F.3d 1112, 1136 (11th Cir. 2020) (Fla. law) (deceased smoker 50% at fault and cigarette manufacturer 50%); Philip Morris USA, Inc. v. Hallgren, 124 So.3d 350, 352 (Fla. Dist. Ct. App. 2013) (upholding 50% to deceased smoker, 25% to Philip Morris, and 25% to R.J. Reynolds); Damian v. Bell Helicopter Textron, Inc., 352 S.W.3d 124 (Tex App. 2011) (upholding 50% to pilot who should have more aggressively evaded hawk that struck and broke the windshield of his helicopter; 50% to manufacturer for design defect); R.J. Reynolds Tobacco Co. v. Brown, 70 So.3d 707 (Fla. Dist. Ct. App. 2011) (50–50 split between smoker and cigarette company); Laudenat v. Autec, Inc., 2010 WL 1233935 (Conn. Super. Ct. 2010) (when wash machine allegedly opened plaintiff's car door, she placed her foot on sill in attempt to close the door, but machinery caught her foot and dragged it along with car; 50% plaintiff, 50% manufacturer of car wash machinery).

170 Arkansas, Colorado, Georgia, Idaho, Kansas, Maine, Nebraska, North Dakota, Tennessee, Utah, and West Virginia. See H. Woods and B. Deere, Comparative Fault § 1.11 (3d ed. 1996 & Supp. 2022); V. Schwartz, Comparative Negligence § 2.01[b] (with K. Kelly 6th ed. 2020); Product Liability Desk Reference—A Fifty State Compendium (M. Daller and N. Daller, eds., 2022).

171 Connecticut, Delaware, Hawaii (negligence claims), Illinois, Indiana, Iowa, Massachusetts, Minnesota, Montana, Nevada, New Hampshire, New Jersey, Ohio, Oklahoma, Oregon, Pennsylvania, South Carolina, Texas, Vermont, Wisconsin, and Wyoming. Comparative fault is limited to negligence claims, and does not apply at all to strict products liability actions in Oklahoma. See H. Woods and B. Deere, Comparative Fault § 1.11 (3d ed. 1996 & Supp. 2022); V. Schwartz, Comparative Negligence § 2.01[b] (with K. Kelly 6th ed. 2020); Product Liability Desk Reference—A Fifty State Compendium (M. Daller and N. Daller eds., 2022 ed.).

172 Busch v. Busch Constr., Inc., 262 N.W.2d 377 (Minn. 1977).

173 Hoeft v. Louisville Ladder Co., 904 S.W.2d 298 (Mo. Ct. App. 1995).

174 General Motors Corp. v. Castaneda, 980 S.W.2d 777 (Tex. App. 1998). *But see* Donze v. General Motors, LLC, 800 S.E.2d 479, 481 (S.C. 2017) (gas tank dangerously located outside pickup truck's frame caused fire in collision; plaintiff could recover full damages for his burns despite driver's reckless cause of accident).

175 Blaw-Knox Food & Chem. Equip. Corp. v. Holmes, 348 So.2d 604 (Fla. Dist. Ct. App. 1977).

30 hours to seek medical attention for an erection;[176] and the divisions of responsibility for product accidents go on and on.[177]

Strict Liability in Tort

Applicability of Comparative Fault

As one state after another adopted comparative negligence in the latter decades of the twentieth century, courts had to decide whether to apply this new form of damages apportionment to claims based on non-negligence theories of recovery, such as breach of warranty,[178] fraud,[179] and, most particularly, strict liability in tort.[180] The Uniform Comparative Fault Act of 1977 resolved the strict liability in tort issue by including "strict tort liability" in its definition of the "fault" to be divided,[181] but only two states adopted versions of this uniform act.[182] In most states, courts have had to interpret statutes requiring the comparison of the parties' "negligence" or "fault" without explicitly defining those terms. The courts have split on whether such statutory language covers claims for strict products liability in tort.

Courts with leeway to decide whether or not to apportion damages in strict liability actions have weighed a number of considerations. Arguments against applying

---

[176] Cottam v. CVS Pharmacy, 764 N.E.2d 814 (Mass. 2002).

[177] See, e.g., Johns v. Suzuki Motor of Am., Inc., 850 S.E.2d 59 (Ga. 2020) (defectively designed brake cylinder that caused brake fluid to leak, 51%; motorcyclist failing to change brake fluid over 8 years he owned bike, contrary to owner's manual direction to change fluid every 2 years, 49%); Ravizza v. PACCAR, Inc., 2020 WL 5415059, at *1 (Ill. App. Ct. 2020) (tow truck driver inspecting engine suffered a fractured skull and lost an eye when wind gust blew hood down on his head; driver 5% at fault, maintenance company 25% at fault, and truck manufacturer 70% at fault); McCoy v. Augusta Fiberglass Coatings, Inc., 593 F.3d 737, 743 (8th Cir. 2010) (Ark. law) (plaintiff injured while repairing leaking flange on tank holding caustic soda; 10% fault of plaintiff, 70% fault of manufacturer, and 20% fault of tank owner); Feiteira v. Clark Equip. Co., 236 S.W.3d 54, 58 (Mo. Ct. App. 2007) (Bobcat loader's failure to have a backup alarm, 73%; experienced cement worker's failure to watch and stay out of Bobcat's way, though it was clearly visible, had passed nearby several times, and was moving at only two to three miles per hour, 27%); Doran v. Yoho, 213 Fed. Appx. 335, 336 (5th Cir. 2007) (Tex. law) (defectively designed hair trigger for rifle, 10%; owner's replacement of original trigger with much-lighter-pull trigger, 15%; plaintiff's loading rifle in moving vehicle without gun safety on, 75%); Thompson v. Brown & Williamson Tobacco Corp., 207 S.W.3d 76, 88 (Mo. Ct. App. 2006) (different brands of cigarettes combined to cause throat cancer—Philip Morris, 40%; Brown and Williamson, 10%; smoker, 50%); Jett v. Ford Motor Co., 72 P.3d 71 (Or. 2003) (delivery truck transmission that could slip from park to reverse, 85%; plaintiff's failure to wait for good truck and disregard of safety protocols, including walking behind truck with engine running, 15%); Blue v. Environmental Eng'g, Inc., 803 N.E.2d 187 (Ill. App. Ct. 2003) (failing to equip trash compactor with available safety features, 33%; worker's pushing boxes into compactor by foot, 32%; employer's allowing unsafe use of compactor, 35%), aff'd, 828 N.E.2d 1128 (Ill. 2005); Lavergne v. America's Pizza Co., 838 So.2d 845 (La. Ct. App. 2003) (restaurant's negligence in serving hot pizza sauce, 70%; parent-plaintiffs' improper supervision of child burned by sauce, 30%); Miller v. Yazoo Mfg. Co., 26 F.3d 81 (8th Cir. 1994) (Mo. law) (designing riding mower with blades that stopped 4.2 seconds after clutch released, 0%; riding so close to top edge of ravine that mower tilted and fell in, 100%); Dafler v. Raymark Indus., 611 A.2d 136 (N.J. Super. Ct. App. Div. 1992) (manufacturing asbestos products, which caused asbestosis and lung cancer, 30%; smoking, 70%); West v. Caterpillar Tractor Co., 336 So.2d 80 (Fla. 1976) (road construction grading machine with poor rear visibility, no rear view mirrors, and no audible warning system for operating in reverse, 65%; failure to maintain proper lookout around such a machine, 35%).

[178] The applicability of comparative fault to warranty claims is examined in § 13.6, below.

[179] The applicability of comparative fault to tortious misrepresentation claims is examined in § 13.7, below.

[180] See V. Schwartz, Comparative Negligence ch. 11 (with K. Kelly 6th ed. 2020); Woods and Deere, Comparative Fault §§ 14:42 et seq. (3d ed. 1996 & Supp. 2022).

[181] Uniform Comparative Fault Act § 1(b) (1977). In 2002, the National Conference of Commissioners on Uniform State Laws approved a Uniform Apportionment of Tort Responsibility Act which, in § 3(a), as amended in 2003, dodges this issue entirely. See Uniform Comparative Fault Act § 3 cmt. *c* (1977 and 2008 electronic pocket part) (excellent discussion).

[182] Iowa and Washington.

comparative negligence doctrine to strict liability in tort claims have included the "apples-and-oranges" argument, which pointed to the apparent illogic of attempting to compare a plaintiff's fault with a product defect based on no-fault liability, and the "product-safety" or deterrence argument, which rested on strict liability's goal of maximizing product safety by forcing manufacturers to shoulder the costs of accidents caused by product defects. But most courts, unpersuaded by such arguments, opted for the apparent justice of making each party to an accident bear responsibility for the losses attributable to that party's breach of good behavior. To the apples-and-oranges argument, courts replied that factfinders really have no trouble apportioning responsibility between negligent plaintiffs and manufacturers subject to strict liability. To the deterrence argument, courts reasoned that manufacturers still remain responsible for all damages attributable to defects in their products and are shielded only from the portion of losses attributable to a plaintiff's breach of proper conduct for which the plaintiff alone should be responsible. In short, while some courts disagree,[183] a great majority of courts apply comparative fault to products liability claims based on strict liability in tort.[184]

Negligent Failure to Discover a Product Defect

As examined earlier, comment *n* to *Restatement (Second) of Torts* § 402A takes the position that a plaintiff's "simple" or "ordinary" contributory negligence in failing to discover a defect, or in failing to guard against the possibility of its existence, should not shield a manufacturer from responsibility for its harmful consequences.[185] But this special category of plaintiff protection arose in the 1960s, before the advent of comparative fault, when the effect of the conduct defenses was to bar a plaintiff's claim completely. Once most courts and legislatures abandoned the all-or-nothing effect of contributory negligence in the 1970s and 1980s, one might think they would have reconsidered the role of such simple contributory negligence in products liability actions and thrown it back into the pot for damages apportionment with all other types of fault.[186] A number of states avoid the matter by simply stating that all fault must be

---

[183] Refusing to apply comparative fault to strict tort actions, see, e.g., Wickersham v. Ford Motor Co., 997 F.3d 526, 540 (4th Cir. 2021) (S.C. law) (South Carolina law *generally* does not recognize the affirmative defense of comparative fault in strict liability or breach of warranty cases.) (emphasis in original); Heinrich v. Ethicon, Inc., 2020 WL 1916767, at *2 (D. Nev. 2020) ("Comparative fault is not a defense to a strict liability claim."); Johnson v. American Honda Motor Co., 2012 WL 1027588, at *17 (D. Mont. 2012); Shipler v. General Motors Corp., 710 N.W.2d 807, 830–32 (Neb. 2006); Kimco Dev. Corp. v. Michael D's Carpet Outlets, 637 A.2d 603 (Pa. 1993); Bowling v. Heil Co., 511 N.E.2d 373 (Ohio 1987). A very few states still bar recovery altogether, even in strict liability, if a plaintiff was contributorily negligent. See § 13.2 note 113, above.

[184] Applying comparative fault to strict tort actions, see, e.g., Amguard Ins. Co. v. Marley Engineered Prods., 2022 WL 356776, at *3 n.1 (D. Colo. 2022); Johns v. Suzuki Motor of Am., Inc., 850 S.E.2d 59, 67 (Ga. 2020); Webb v. Navistar Int'l Transp. Corp., 692 A.2d 343, 347 (Vt. 1997) ("The overwhelming majority of states have rejected the 'all or nothing' rule . . . and have applied principles of comparative liability in strict products liability actions."); Whitehead v. Toyota Motor Corp., 897 S.W.2d 684, 691 (Tenn. 1995) (same, citing cases from Conn., Fla., Haw., Idaho, Ill., Kan., La., Me., Mich., Minn., N.H., N.M., N.D., Or., R.I., Tex., Utah, Wash., W. Va., Wis.; and citing as *contra* cases from Colo., Ohio, Okla., S.D., and Wyo.); Thompson v. Brown & Williamson Tobacco Corp., 207 S.W.3d 76, 117–24 (Mo. Ct. App. 2006) (in-depth discussion); Daly v. General Motors Corp., 575 P.2d 1162 (Cal. 1978) (noting that more than 30 states at that time applied comparative negligence principles to strict products liability). See generally Annot., 9 A.L.R.4th 633 (1981) (applicability of comparative fault to strict products liability in tort). Compare Lewis v. CRC Indus., 7 A.3d 841, 846 (Pa. 2010) (N.J. law) (N.J. statute "prohibits a trial court from charging the jury on contributory and comparative negligence when an employee is injured on workplace machinery or equipment").

[185] See § 13.2, above.

[186] See, e.g., Gillum v. L & J Enters., 29 P.3d 266, 270 (Alaska 2001) (negligence claim against warehouse operator for injuries from defective loading dock door; "Failure to discover a hazard can constitute

compared.[187] Yet, almost every court that has considered this precise issue has chosen to shield consumers from *all* responsibility for their failure to watch for product defects by holding that a plaintiff's careless failure to discover that a product is defective lies outside the realm of damages apportionment.[188]

The *Third Restatement of Torts* takes the opposite view—that courts should not set up special categories of protected plaintiff fault exempt from damages apportionment.[189] Its position appears to be that justice is best served if all types and degrees of plaintiff and defendant fault are thrown into one giant, fault-division cauldron. The *Products Liability Restatement* states in black letter that a plaintiff's damages may be reduced on account of the plaintiff's fault,[190] noting in commentary that "[t]he majority position is that all forms of plaintiff's failure to conform to applicable standards of care are to be considered" on apportionment.[191] While somewhat true, this assertion is misleading with respect to the role of a plaintiff's negligent failure to discover a defect or guard against its existence because, as stated earlier, most courts addressing this particular issue have continued to exempt this form of plaintiff conduct from apportionment. The *Apportionment Restatement* endorses a general throw-it-all-in-the-cauldron approach, explicitly repudiating "[s]pecial ameliorative doctrines for defining plaintiff's negligence" in § 3's black letter, but it nowhere mentions the ameliorative doctrine concerning a plaintiff's negligent failure to watch for product defects.[192]

The reluctance of both *Restatements* to address this particular issue may possibly reflect the Reporters' sympathy for shielding plaintiffs from their negligence in failing to discover product defects, together with an unwillingness to explicitly "restate" the law

---

comparative negligence."). Compare Minn. Stat. Ann. § 604.01(1a) ("fault" to be apportioned includes "unreasonable failure to avoid an injury").

[187] See, e.g., Campbell Hausfeld v. Johnson, 109 N.E.3d 953, 957 (Ind. 2018) ("all fault in products liability cases must be comparatively assessed"); Smith v. Toyota Motor Corp., 105 Fed. Appx. 47 (6th Cir. 2004) (Ky. law); Byrne v. SCM Corp., 538 N.E.2d 796 (Ill. App. Ct. 1989); Kaneko v. Hilo Coast Processing, 654 P.2d 343 (Haw. 1982); Sandford v. Chevrolet Div. of Gen. Motors, 642 P.2d 624 (Or. 1982); Star Furniture Co. v. Pulaski Furniture Co., 297 S.E.2d 854 (W. Va. 1982); Mulherin v. Ingersoll-Rand Co., 628 P.2d 1301 (Utah 1981); Daly v. General Motors Corp., 575 P.2d 1162 (Cal. 1978); Butaud v. Suburban Marine & Sporting Goods, 555 P.2d 42 (Alaska 1976) (codified in Alaska Stat. §§ 09.17.080, 09.17.900).

[188] See, e.g., Purdy v. Deere & Co., 386 P.3d 2, 7 (Or. Ct. App. 2016) ("Although Oregon tort law now recognizes comparative fault . . . the principle that negligence in the form of 'incidental carelessness or failure to discover or guard against a product defect' is not a 'defense' in a products liability action remains a part of Oregon law."); Hinton v. Outboard Marine Corp., 2012 WL 260033, at *3 (D. Me. 2012) ("comparative fault 'does not apply to strict liability claims where the plaintiff's only alleged negligence is failure to discover the defect in the product or to guard against the possibility of its existence' "); Schwartz v. Hasbro, Inc., 2012 WL 1414094, at *11 (N.J. Super. Ct. App. Div. 2012); General Motors Corp. v. Sanchez, 997 S.W.2d 584, 592–95 (Tex. 1999) (but plaintiff's actions here "amounted to conduct other than a mere failure to discover or guard against a product defect"); Simpson v. General Motors Corp., 483 N.E.2d 1 (Ill. 1985) (with strong dissent against creating separate categories of plaintiff conduct exempt from comparative fault). See also Owen & Davis on Products Liability § 13:11 (citing additional cases from Fla., Minn., Neb., Ohio, Or., and W. Va.); Idaho Code Ann. § 6–1405(1)(a).

[189] See also V. Schwartz, Comparative Negligence § 11.07 (with K. Kelly 6th ed. 2020) (criticizing this special category of protected misbehavior).

[190] See Products Liability Rest. § 17(a).

[191] Id. cmt. *d*, at 259, and Reporters' Note thereto, at 262. See also id. cmt. *a*, at 256–57, which misleadingly suggests that modern courts have abandoned comment *n*.

[192] The comments to § 3, and Reporters' Notes thereto, discuss various other ameliorative doctrines but fail to discuss this particular products liability doctrine. The Reporters elsewhere specifically mention this doctrine in their notes to Rest. (3d) Torts: Apportionment § 1 cmt. *b*, at 11, where they assert that, "Most states at least hold that a plaintiff's negligence that constitutes more than a mere failure to discover or guard against the possibility of a product defect supports the factfinder's assigning a percentage of responsibility to the plaintiff."

on this point contrary to how most courts actually (and not unreasonably) were deciding cases; or it may reflect their reluctance to deviate from a simple, consistent approach to apportionment in which all types of fault are thrown into the mix. Be that as it may, the *Products Liability Restatement* does end up offering a partial back-door escape to plaintiffs in this situation, in its observation that a plaintiff's simple contributory negligence of this sort normally does not breach a standard of reasonable behavior.[193]

Sole Proximate Cause

The doctrine of "sole proximate cause"[194] normally is used to deny recovery to a plaintiff injured in an accident caused principally by his or her own misconduct. The problem with the sole-proximate-cause doctrine in states where contributory negligence is not a defense to strict liability in tort claims, previously discussed, is the risk that defense counsel will use this doctrine as an improper back-door means to sneak contributory negligence into the case.[195] In comparative fault jurisdictions, where proof and argument about a plaintiff's fault are entirely fair game, this problem would seem to vanish. If the system is a modified one, a plaintiff even 51% at fault may not recover anyway, so that there would seem to be no need for a doctrine that means, essentially, that the plaintiff should be held 100% responsible for causing injury to himself. In states where the comparative fault system is pure, the sole-proximate-cause doctrine might be viewed as infringing the fundamental premise that plaintiffs mostly responsible for accidents in which they are injured are nevertheless entitled to recover whatever small percentage of their damages that may be placed upon a defendant's doorstep.[196] For these and other reasons, some courts hold that "[s]ole proximate cause is not a defense to comparative fault."[197]

In a case where a highly reckless plaintiff seeks to recover a tiny portion of his or her damages from a slightly negligent defendant, it might be simpler to sidestep such a nebulous doctrine as sole proximate cause and simply let comparative responsibility do its work. But, just as there is no real harm in the comment *n* doctrine, discussed above, that fully protects plaintiffs from their minor fault, there likewise is no harm in a doctrine that shields defendants from their remote responsibility for injuries that

---

[193] See Products Liability Rest. § 17 cmt. *d*, at 259:

> [W]hen the defendant claims that the plaintiff failed to discover a defect, there must be evidence that the plaintiff's conduct in failing to discover a defect did, in fact, fail to meet a standard of reasonable care. In general, a plaintiff has no reason to expect that a new product contains a defect and would have little reason to be on guard to discover it. . . . In the absence of such evidence courts refuse to submit the plaintiff's conduct to the trier of fact for apportionment based on the principles of comparative responsibility.

[194] It may give too much force to the worthy notion of sole proximate cause to call it a doctrine. See Rest. (3d) Torts: Liability for Physical and Emotional Harm § 34 cmt. *f*.

[195] See § 13.2, above.

[196] See Baker v. City of Ottumwa, 560 N.W.2d 578 (Iowa 1997) (modified; sole-proximate-cause defense is incompatible with doctrine of comparative fault because defense effectively insulates defendant from liability).

[197] See, e.g., Dahlin v. Lyondell Chem. Co., 2016 WL 4690390, at *5 (S.D. Iowa 2016) ("the sole proximate cause defense 'is incompatible with the doctrine of comparative fault' "); Schmitt v. Koehring Cranes, Inc., 798 N.W.2d 491, 496 (Iowa Ct. App. 2011). See also Heath v. C.R. Bard Inc., 2021 WL 3172315 (M.D. Tenn. 2021) ("The purpose of Tennessee's comparative liability regime 'is to assess liability in proportion to fault,' not merely in proportion to causation."). Compare Reed v. Reichhold Liquidation, Inc., 2021 WL 1518413, at *8 (M.D.N.C. 2021) (Iowa law) ("this court does not find, as a matter of law, that Defendant may raise the sole proximate cause defense . . . following the Iowa Supreme Court's decision" to adopt Rest. (3d) Torts: Liability for Physical and Emotional Harm) (citing § 34 cmts. *a* and *f* thereto).

reckless plaintiffs largely bring upon themselves.[198] Indeed, protecting defendants in such situations with the sole-proximate-cause doctrine injects refreshing moral clarity to legal problem-solving, pushing aside the moral relativism of comparative fault and permitting a declaration that a plaintiff who recklessly hurts himself is properly accountable for "the whole damn thing." For reasons such as these, courts in some comparative fault jurisdictions allow proof and argument in appropriate cases that a plaintiff's substantial fault was the sole proximate cause of a product accident.[199]

§ 13.4 ASSUMPTION OF RISK

Originating as a defense to negligence claims over two centuries ago,[200] assumption of risk is a classic defense to products liability claims.[201] As a common law and statutory[202] defense in many jurisdictions—even to claims for strict products liability in tort—assumption of risk remains a total bar to liability in a good number of states, thus significantly distinguishing it from contributory negligence which now serves (via principles of comparative fault) merely to reduce damages in most cases.[203] Because situations that give rise to the assumption of risk defense are often quite normal and foreseeable, the assumption of risk defense is not restricted (as is the defense of product

---

[198] Such as when the doctrine protects the manufacturer of a boat when a drunken boater, who drowns when thrown out of his boat while driving it wildly in a flooded river without a life preserver, claims that the boat's seat is defective. See Norman v. Fisher Marine, Inc., 672 S.W.2d 414 (Tenn. Ct. App. 1984) (Miss. law).

[199] See, e.g., Reott v. Asia Trend, Inc., 55 A.3d 1088, 1101 (Pa. 2012) (a plaintiff's "highly reckless conduct" is an affirmative defense if defendant proves that it was the sole or superseding cause of an accident); Lyons v. Caterpillar, Inc., 2005 WL 3358068, at *6 (N.J. Super. Ct. App. Div. 2005) ("even in the workplace setting plaintiff's negligence may be considered when a defendant claims that the plaintiff's conduct is the sole proximate cause of the injury, as opposed to a contributing factor"); Labzda v. Purdue Pharma, L.P., 292 F. Supp. 2d 1346, 1356 (S.D. Fla. 2003) (Florida courts consistently allow "the doctrine of sole proximate cause, rather than comparative negligence, for the intentional misuse of a product, in spite of warnings of the danger"); Kroon v. Beech Aircraft Corp., 628 F.2d 891 (5th Cir. 1980) (Fla. law) (2–1 decision) (plaintiff's misconduct may serve as sole proximate cause even in comparative fault regime; pilot attempted to take off without removing gust lock pin from steering control column). See generally Hayden, Butterfield Rides Again: Plaintiff's Negligence as Superseding or Sole Proximate Cause in Systems of Pure Comparative Responsibility, 33 Loy. L.A. L. Rev. 887, 901–07 (2000); Note, 79 Tex. L. Rev. 493, 495 (2000) ("The courts use proximate cause to declare the plaintiff 'dumb as a matter of law': so foolish that his actions are legally unforeseeable.").

[200] In Cruden v. Fentham, 2 Esp. 685, 170 Eng. Rep. 496 (1799). See Prosser and Keeton on Torts § 68, at 480.

[201] See, e.g., Sawicki, Defining the Known Risk: Context-Sensitivity in Tort Law Defenses, 12 J. Tort L. 9 (2019); Lukes, The Defense of Assumption of Risk Under Montana's Product Liability Law, 58 Mont. L. Rev. 249 (1997); Davis, Individual and Institutional Responsibility: A Vision for Comparative Fault in Products Liability, 39 Vill. L. Rev. 281 (1994); McNichols, The Relevance of the Plaintiff's Misconduct in Strict Tort Products Liability, the Advent of Comparative Responsibility, and the Proposed Restatement (Third) of Torts, 47 Okla. L. Rev. 201 (1994); Twerski, Old Wine in a New Flask-Restructuring Assumption of Risk in the Products Liability Era, 60 Iowa L. Rev. 1 (1974); Noel, Defective Products: Abnormal Use, Contributory Negligence, and Assumption of Risk, 25 Vand. L. Rev. 93 (1972); D. Epstein, Products Liability: Defenses Based on Plaintiff's Conduct, 1968 Utah L. Rev. 267; W.P. Keeton, Assumption of Products Risks, 19 Sw. L.J. 61 (1965); R. Keeton, Assumption of Risk in Products Liability Cases, 22 La. L. Rev. 122 (1961); Note, 95 Harv. L. Rev. 872 (1982) (assumption of risk as defense to strict products liability); Annot., 46 A.L.R.3d 240 (1972) (contributory negligence and assumption of risk as defenses to claim for strict products liability in tort). For more theoretical explorations of the doctrine, see Simons, Reflections on Assumption of Risk, 50 UCLA L. Rev. 481 (2002); Sugarman, Assumption of Risk, 31 Val. U. L. Rev. 833 (1997); Simons, Assumption of Risk and Consent in the Law of Torts: A Theory of Full Preference, 67 B.U. L. Rev. 213 (1987).

[202] While assumption of risk is a common-law doctrine, tort and products liability legislative reform provisions in many states govern the effect of various forms of user misconduct including assumption of risk. See § 13.1, above.

[203] See § 13.2, above. Under the comparative fault reforms of the great majority of states, a plaintiff's contributory negligence, at least if less than the defendant's negligence, serves only to diminish a plaintiff's damages, not to bar the claim altogether. See § 13.3, above.

"misuse")[204] to product use situations so unusual as to be characterized as unforeseeable. For these reasons, assumption of risk may well be the most potent of all the plaintiff conduct defenses of modern products liability law. Assumption of risk is an affirmative defense that must be pleaded and proved by a defendant.[205]

Assumption of risk may be distinguished from the other "misconduct" defenses in a more fundamental way. Conduct that gives rise to an assumption of risk *may* be unreasonable; if so, it overlaps the defense of contributory (or comparative) negligence which separately may operate to bar liability (or to reduce the plaintiff's damages). But conventional assumption of risk doctrine does not *require* that a plaintiff's decision to incur a risk be unreasonable; as discussed below, a plaintiff will be barred from maintaining a negligence claim if he or she assumes a risk for reasons and in a manner reasonable in all respects.[206] Nor, as just mentioned, does the assumption of risk defense require that a plaintiff have used a product outside the boundaries of its intended and foreseeable limits of fair use, as required by the misuse defense. Thus, unlike the defenses of contributory negligence and product misuse, which arise from user conduct that may be conceived as "improper"[207]—and so fairly classified as "*mis*conduct"—conduct giving rise to the conventional assumption of risk defense does not always so comfortably fit the "misconduct" mold.

The underlying idea of the assumption of risk defense is that a user has fully consented to incur a risk which he or she fully comprehends.[208] By choosing voluntarily to incur the risk, the user thus implicitly agrees to accept responsibility for any harmful consequences that may result from the encounter and so relieves the person who created the initial risk from responsibility. In other words, *volenti non fit injuria*.[209]

Thus, a person assumes a risk of injury if he uses his hand instead of a metal stomper to push meat into a grinder;[210] fails to keep his leg inside his off-road Yamaha Rhino open-air vehicle when it rolls over, crushing his leg;[211] reaches from outside a forklift between horizontal cross bars to engage the throttle and so lowers a bar upon his arm;[212] slips while climbing playground equipment and is injured when he falls;[213] slips from the top of a tanker truck covered with oil that he knows is "real slick";[214] is run over

---

[204] See § 13.5, below.

[205] See, e.g., Sardis v. Overhead Door Corp., 446 F. Supp. 3d 47, 59 (E.D. Va. 2020); Reott v. Asia Trend, Inc., 55 A.3d 1088, 1096 (Pa. 2012); Kaiser v. ODB Co., 2011 WL 3040085, at *3 (N.D. Ohio 2011).

[206] See Rahmig v. Mosley Mach. Co., 412 N.W.2d 56, 74 (Neb. 1987); Prosser and Keeton on Torts § 68, at 481, 485.

[207] As arising from conduct which is either unreasonable (contributory negligence) or unforeseeable (misuse). See § 13.2, above, and § 13.5, below, respectively.

[208] "[A]ssumption of risk is a user's willingness or consent to use a product which the user actually knows is defective and appreciates the danger resulting from such defect." Rahmig v. Mosley Mach. Co., 412 N.W.2d 56, 74 (Neb. 1987).

[209] "[A] person is not wronged by that to which he or she consents." Black's Law Dictionary 1805 (11th ed. 2019). See Prosser and Keeton on Torts § 68, at 480.

[210] Green v. Sanitary Scale Co., 431 F.2d 371 (3d Cir. 1970) (Pa. law).

[211] Yamaha Motor Corp., U.S.A. v. McTaggart, 720 S.E.2d 217 (Ga. Ct. App. 2011).

[212] Moran v. Raymond Corp., 484 F.2d 1008 (7th Cir. 1973) (Ill. law).

[213] Kane v. Landscape Structures, Inc., 709 S.E.2d 876, 877 (Ga. Ct. App. 2011) (as he climbed to roof of Infant Maze playground equipment, 9-year-old plaintiff fell and was injured; "Like most children nine years of age, Steven appreciated the obvious risk of falling that is associated with climbing to high places, and he voluntarily chose to assume the risk.").

[214] Hedgepeth v. Fruehauf Corp., 634 F. Supp. 93, 96 (S.D. Miss. 1986) (oil tanker truck driver, who slipped while walking on rounded top of tanker, testified that he knew top was "real slick and real cruddy").

while jump-starting a tractor he knows may lurch forward when it starts,[215] or squashed by one when he leaves it running to go behind it to check on a malfunction;[216] slips and is cut by a power mower blade left spinning while he moves an obstacle in the mower's path;[217] inflates a truck tire on a multi-piece rim he fears may be improperly assembled and might explosively fly apart;[218] or entangles his pants in a moving part of a machine he knows could injure him if he gets too close.[219]

For a product user[220] to assume responsibility for a risk to the exclusion of the defendant, his or her decision must be based on an understanding of the nature of the risk, and it must be a choice that is freely made—a person cannot "consent" to what he does not know nor to what is forced upon him. For this reason, assumption of risk arises only when a user's encounter with a risk is both "informed" and "voluntary." These two basic requirements are reflected in the definition, or statement of elements, of the assumption of risk doctrine: first, a plaintiff must (know and) understand the risk; and, second, the plaintiff's choice to encounter it must be (free and) voluntary.[221]

Because each aspect of assumption of risk involves an inquiry into a particular person's state of mind—the person's knowledge of risk, appreciation of it, and the extent to which the person's choice to encounter it was free and voluntary—the assumption of risk determination is peculiarly one of fact for a jury to resolve,[222] except, of course, in "plain, palpable, and indisputable cases" where the facts all reveal a risk the plaintiff fully comprehended and freely accepted as a matter of law.[223]

---

[215] Novak v. Navistar Int'l Transp. Corp., 46 F.3d 844 (8th Cir. 1995) (S.D. law).

[216] Lee v. CNH Am., LLC, 746 S.E.2d 243, 247–48 (Ga. Ct. App. 2013) (noting that farmer left his new tractor running, walked around behind it into the "mouse trap" area between the tractor and the attached cultivator, "an obvious crush zone," that Lee had read the manual that "instructed the operator to turn off engine before attempting to adjust the height limit," that the salesman had demonstrated to Lee multiple times the proper procedure of how to turn off the engine off before adjusting the height limit, and that Lee practiced doing it many times).

[217] See Denton v. Bachtold Bros., 291 N.E.2d 229 (Ill. App. Ct. 1972).

[218] Bishop v. Firestone Tire & Rubber Co., 814 F.2d 437, 446 (7th Cir. 1987) (Ind. law) (plaintiff stated, prior to explosion of tire mounted on multi-piece rim, that he "hoped the tire would not explode").

[219] Johnson v. Mid-South Distrib., Inc., Prod. Liab. Rep. (CCH) ¶ 7984 (Tenn. Ct. App. 1977).

[220] While most products liability cases involve product users, the assumption of risk defense may also apply to claims by injured bystanders. See, e.g., Brown v. Link Belt Corp., 565 F.2d 1107 (9th Cir. 1977) (Or. law) (worker run over by crane when worker wandered into area he knew was in crane operator's blind spot); Baker v. Chrysler Corp., 127 Cal. Rptr. 745 (Ct. App. 1976) (pedestrian, hit by allegedly uncrashworthy car with protruding metal headlight protector, ran across street trying to beat oncoming car). *But see* Barr v. Rivinius, Inc., 373 N.E.2d 1063, 1068 (Ill. App. Ct. 1978) (2–1 decision) (asphalt company worker hit by unguarded road-making machine could not assume risk because he was a bystander, not the user).

[221] See, e.g., Sardis v. Overhead Door Corp., 446 F. Supp. 3d 47, 58 (E.D. Va. 2020). See also Prosser and Keeton on Torts § 68, at 486.

[222] See, e.g., Walls v. Ford Motor Co., 2022 WL 582611, at *4 (M.D.N.C. 2022); Parker-Reed v. Primal Vantage Co., Inc., 2021 WL 1193081, at *7 (S.D. Ohio 2021); Priester v. Futuramic Tool & Eng'g Co., 2017 WL 1135134, at *6 n.7 (D.S.C. 2017); Romero v. ITW Food Equip. Grp., LLC, 987 F. Supp. 2d 93, 101 (D.D.C. 2013); Sansom v. Crown Equip. Corp., 880 F. Supp. 2d 648, 666 (W.D. Pa. 2012) (the defense "is typically a question of fact that falls within the purview of the jury because it requires a factual analysis of the plaintiff's subjective understanding of the risks involved"); Heil Co. v. Grant, 534 S.W.2d 916, 921 (Tex. App. 1976) ("Whether an injured person actually knew of the danger is peculiarly within the province of the jury."). *But see* the curious case of Frey v. Harley Davidson Motor Co., 734 A.2d 1, 9 (Pa. Super. Ct. 1999) ("assumption of the risk, particularly in product liability cases, is a question of law to be determined by the court").

[223] See, e.g., Lopez v. Delair Group LLC, 881 F. Supp. 2d 268, 271 (D.R.I. 2012) (assumption of risk often determined as a matter of law on evidence of "plaintiff's actual knowledge and appreciation of the risk—such as evidence that the plaintiff knew of the dangers, was warned repeatedly, etc."); Yamaha Motor Corp., U.S.A. v. McTaggart, 720 S.E.2d 217, 219 (Ga. Ct. App. 2011) ("[a]lthough assumption of the risk is ordinarily a jury question, in plain, palpable, and indisputable cases resolution of the issue by a jury is not required").

The ideas of knowledge and appreciation go together like a horse and carriage: in order to truly "know" something, a person must understand or appreciate it; and knowledge is a *sine qua non* of appreciation, for one cannot "appreciate" what one does not know. Because knowledge and appreciation of a risk are intertwined in this manner, the defense is sometimes defined in terms of two elements: (1) knowledge and understanding, and (2) voluntariness.[224] Yet many courts and commentators subdivide the first element into its two components, and so split the defense into three separate elements: (1) knowledge, (2) appreciation, and (3) voluntariness.[225] Courts define this defense in slightly varying ways,[226] sometimes without specifically enumerating the elements but usually emphasizing the basic nature of the plaintiff's conduct as reflecting a free and voluntary encounter with a known and appreciated risk.[227]

Knowledge and Appreciation

"Knowledge," it is said, "is the watchword of assumption of risk."[228] A plaintiff's vague and general understanding that a product may be dangerous if not carefully used is neither "knowledge" nor "appreciation" of a particular risk of harm. If the plaintiff does not know just *how* a product may be hazardous, then he cannot assume the risk that he may be injured by that hazard.[229] Particularly in jurisdictions that do not separately require that the risk be "appreciated," courts often require that the plaintiff know of the *specific* risk.[230] This means the plaintiff must know more than that the

---

[224] See Prosser and Keeton on Torts § 68, at 487 ("first, the plaintiff must know that the risk is present, and he must further understand its nature; and second, his choice to incur it must be free and voluntary").

[225] See, e.g., Karst v. Shur-Co., 878 N.W.2d 604, 617 (S.D. 2016) ("the person: '(1) [has] actual or constructive knowledge of the risk; (2) appreciate[s] its character; and (3) voluntarily accept[s] the risk, with the time, knowledge, and experience to make an intelligent choice' "); Yamaha Motor Corp., U.S.A. v. McTaggart, 720 S.E.2d 217, 219 (Ga. Ct. App. 2011) ("(1) had actual knowledge of the danger; (2) understood and appreciated the risks associated with such danger; and (3) voluntarily exposed himself to those risks").

[226] See, e.g., McRunnel v. Batco Mfg., 917 F. Supp. 2d 946, 958 (D. Minn. 2013) (the defense requires "(1) the plaintiff's knowledge of the risk; (2) his appreciation of the risk; and (3) a voluntary choice to take the risk despite the opportunity to avoid the risk"); Green v. Allendale Planting Co., 954 So.2d 1032, 1043 (Miss. 2007) (elements of assumption of risk defense: (1) "knowledge on the part of the injured party of a condition inconsistent with his safety," (2) appreciation of danger, and (3) "a deliberate and voluntary choice . . . to expose his person to that danger in such a manner as to register assent to the continuance of the dangerous condition").

[227] See, e.g., Ashford v. Accuwright Indus., Inc., 2020 WL 950217, at *6 (Ariz. Ct. App. 2020) ("The assumption of risk defense is based on an individual's knowledge of a particular risk and his consent or agreement to accept that risk."); Yamaha Motor Corp., U.S.A. v. McTaggart, 720 S.E.2d 217, 219 (Ga. Ct. App. 2011) ("a plaintiff's recovery is barred by assumption of risk "if the defendant proves that the plaintiff 'without coercion of circumstances, chooses a course of action with full knowledge of its danger and while exercising a free choice as to whether to engage in the act or not' ").

[228] Prosser and Keeton on Torts § 68, at 487 (citing Cincinnati, New Orleans & Tex. Pac. Ry. Co. v. Thompson, 236 F. 1, 9 (6th Cir. 1916)). See also Jara v. Rexworks Inc., 718 A.2d 788, 795 (Pa. Super. Ct. 1998) ("Nearly all cases in this area focus on the element of the defense encompassing knowledge of the risk."); Johnson v. Mid-South Distrib., Inc., Prod. Liab. Rep. (CCH) ¶ 7984 (Tenn. Ct. App. 1977) ("Knowledge on the part of the plaintiff is the keystone of the doctrine.").

[229] "Knowledge of the general hazard involved in operating a punch-press machine will not support the assumption of risk defense." Heil Co. v. Grant, 534 S.W.2d 916, 921 (Tex. App. 1976) (citing Rhoads v. Service Mach. Co., 329 F. Supp. 367 (E.D. Ark. 1971)). See, e.g., Yamaha Motor Corp., U.S.A. v. McTaggart, 720 S.E.2d 217, 219 (Ga. Ct. App. 2011) (the knowledge element "does not refer to a plaintiff's comprehension of general, non-specific risks that might be associated with such conditions or activities").

[230] See, e.g., Thompson v. Polaris Indus. Inc., 2019 WL 2173965, at *9 (D. Ariz. 2019) ("a general knowledge of a danger is not sufficient but, rather, the plaintiff must have actual knowledge of the specific risk which injured him and appreciate its magnitude"); Romero v. ITW Food Equip. Grp., LLC, 987 F. Supp. 2d 93, 101 (D.D.C. 2013) (a "plaintiff must have 'actual knowledge of the specific defect in question and of the danger created by the defect' "); Kaiser v. ODB Co., 2011 WL 3040085, at *3 (N.D. Ohio 2011) (defendant must establish that "the plaintiff knew of the precise product defect and the risks that defect carried[—]that the plaintiff knew of the specific condition, knew that the condition was patently dangerous, and [then] voluntarily

product encountered may be dangerous.[231] The plaintiff must further understand with some particularity how the product may cause an injury, so that he or she is able to evaluate the likelihood and seriousness of potential injury and thereby make an informed decision on whether or not to engage the risk.[232]

If one were to apply the appreciation-of-specific-risk requirement quite literally, this aspect of the doctrine would swallow the rule and prevent it from ever being applied. In the first article devoted to assumption of risk in the products liability context,[233] Robert Keeton pointed out the apparent "enigma," or self-contradiction, in the "full appreciation of risk" requirement. " 'Risk' implies a degree of want of appreciation of the forces that are at work in a given factual setting, since if one knew and understood all these forces he would know that injury was certain to occur or that it was certain not to occur."[234] Rejecting the defense, one court made a similar point in a case brought by a wireman who was severely shocked when he began to clean electrical equipment that was not de-energized, due to a defect in the way the equipment was configured.[235] "To conclude that [plaintiff] was aware of the specific defect in this configuration would be tantamount to believing that he intended to commit suicide."[236] But most courts have interpreted the appreciation requirement more loosely, ruling that this element does not require that a plaintiff understand the precise nature and operation of the mechanical, chemical, or

exposed himself to the condition"); Eastman v. Stanley Works, 907 N.E.2d 768, 781 (Ohio Ct. App. 2009) (no evidence plaintiff was aware of crack in hammer); Hadar v. AVCO Corp., 886 A.2d 225, 228–31 (Pa. Super. Ct. 2005) (while plaintiff knew *general* risk of getting hand caught in corn picker's rollers, question of fact as to whether he understood *specific* risk that rollers might pull in a 3-foot corn stalk so quickly he could not release it before his hand was pulled in as well).

[231] See, e.g., Wilson Sporting Goods Co. v. Hickox, 59 A.3d 1267, 1274 (D.C. 2013) (to establish that major league umpire assumed risk of new mask design required more than that he "knew the general risks of baseball umpiring" but also that he "knew that the throat guard's acute, forward angle had a tendency to concentrate energy and increase the risk of injury"); Wangsness v. Builders Cashway, Inc., 779 N.W.2d 136, 141 (S.D. 2010) (plaintiff must know "the specific defect and risk posed rather than simple generalized knowledge that he has entered a zone of danger"); Rahmig v. Mosley Mach. Co., 412 N.W.2d 56, 74 (Neb. 1987) ("[a] user's knowledge about the general danger or hazard in using a product will not support the defense").

[232] See, e.g., Yamaha Motor Corp., U.S.A. v. McTaggart, 720 S.E.2d 217, 219 (Ga. Ct. App. 2011) (plaintiff must know the "specific, particular risk of harm" that causes the accident, not just knowledge of the "general, non-specific risks" a product may contain; here, plaintiff in fact chose a doorless Rhino, that rolled over on his leg, instead of an ATV because he liked the easy entry and egress of the design). Contrast Mussara v. Mega Funworks, Inc., 952 N.Y.S.2d 568, 573 (App. Div. 2012) (plaintiff, who exceeded the 200 lb. weight limit for Pirate's Plunge water slide at Splashdown Park in Fishkill, NY, probably appreciated that he could collide with various things and people when riding on a water slide, but not that, after exiting the slide, his tube would travel the entire length of the 50-foot splash pool, collide with the stairs at the far end of the pool, which would propel him from his tube so that he would land on the cement ground surrounding the pool); and Patch v. Hillerich & Bradsby Co., 257 P.3d 383, 390 (Mont. 2011) (assumption of risk defense would not bar claim for death of 18-year-old pitcher hit in head and killed by ball struck by aluminum bat manufactured by defendant; "there is no evidence that Brandon actually knew he would be seriously injured or killed when pitching to a batter using one of H & B's model CB-13 aluminum bats [with its] enhanced risks").

[233] R. Keeton, Assumption of Risk in Products Liability Cases, 22 La. L. Rev. 122 (1961).

[234] Id. at 124. See also Montgomery, Cognitive Biases and Heuristics in Tort Litigation: A Proposal to Limit Their Effects Without Changing the World, 85 Neb. L. Rev. 15 (2006).

[235] Campbell v. ITE Imperial Corp., 733 P.2d 969 (Wash. 1987).

[236] Id. at 976.

biological mechanisms that may result in harm[237] nor the precise manner in which a product may be legally "defective."[238]

For example, in *Heil Co. v. Grant*,[239] the plaintiff's decedent was crushed to death while he and his brother were performing repair work under a dump truck. The raised bed suddenly descended when one of the men accidentally bumped the "pullout cable" attached to the hydraulic valve that controlled the raising and lowering of the bed. Just before the accident, the decedent's brother had warned him that the bed would crash down if he hit the cable. The plaintiff sued the manufacturer, claiming that the hoist mechanism was defectively designed, and the defendant asserted assumption of risk. The trial court excluded certain testimony going to assumption of risk, and the jury found for the plaintiff. On appeal, the court reversed the judgment. To the plaintiff's argument that the decedent had general knowledge that working beneath the dump truck could be dangerous, but had no knowledge of the specific defect involved, the appeals court noted that the specific danger was that hitting the cable would cause the bed to descend, which the decedent knew.[240] To the plaintiff's contention that the requisite knowledge must pertain to a "defect," rather than a danger, the court noted that "the assumption of risk defense is premised upon knowledge of the dangerous condition of a product rather than recognition of its defectiveness."[241]

In another case, *Haugen v. Minnesota Mining & Manufacturing Co.*,[242] the plaintiff was injured when the grinding wheel he was using exploded into three pieces, one of which hit him in the eye. At the time of the accident the plaintiff was wearing glasses but not safety goggles, although two pairs of goggles were available in the shop and he knew of their importance from prior safety training. The trial court instructed the jury: "It is not enough to bar recovery by the plaintiff on the defense of assumption of risk that the plaintiff knew that there was a general danger connected with the use of the product, but rather it must be shown that the plaintiff actually knew, appreciated, and

---

[237] See, e.g., Ensor v. Hodgeson, 615 S.W.2d 519, 525 (Mo. Ct. App. 1981) ("[K]nowledge of the precise engineering explanation of the defect is not necessary. It is sufficient that the user realizes that there is a problem with the product that renders it dangerous to use."); Heil Co. v. Grant, 534 S.W.2d 916, 922 (Tex. App. 1976) ("The assumption of risk defense is based upon the injured person's awareness of the danger of injury rather than an awareness of the producing causes of the injury."). See also Bowen v. Cochran, 556 S.E.2d 530, 532 (Ga. Ct. App. 2001) (plaintiff knew that gas grill might explode if he failed to vent it sufficiently and failed to light it properly, even if he did not understand exactly where and how the unlighted gas might pool).

[238] See, e.g., Heil Co. v. Grant, 534 S.W.2d 916, 921 (Tex. App. 1976) ("the assumption of risk defense is premised upon knowledge of the dangerous condition of a product rather than recognition of its defectiveness"). *But see* Warner Fruehauf Trailer Co. v. Boston, 654 A.2d 1272, 1275 (D.C. 1995) (evidence failed to show that plaintiff "had actual knowledge of the liftgate's alleged design defect—the lack of a back-up system (e.g., a second cylinder or other safety device) to prevent the heavy liftgate from free-falling in the event of a mechanical failure"); Mackowick v. Westinghouse Elec. Corp., 541 A.2d 749, 753 (Pa. Super. Ct. 1988) (Brosky, J. dissenting):

> [U]se of the term "defect," with its mechanical and technological connotations, has caused much confusion among members of the bench and bar. Some have argued that a plaintiff is aware of a specific defect only if he understands the mechanical process which causes the item to be dangerous. This interpretation is an overly technical misstatement of the law. For assumption of the risk to apply, a plaintiff needn't understand the mechanical process, but must be subjectively aware of the nature, character, and extent of the danger posed *by the specific attribute* which is allegedly defective; this requires more than a general awareness by the plaintiff that the product is somehow dangerous.

[239] 534 S.W.2d 916 (Tex. App. 1976).

[240] Id. at 922.

[241] Id. at 921.

[242] 550 P.2d 71 (Wash. Ct. App. 1976), superseded by statute, as recognized in Van Hout v. Celotex Corp., 853 P.2d 908 (Wash. 1993).

voluntarily and unreasonably exposed himself to the specific defect and danger which caused his injuries."[243] On appeal, affirming a judgment for the plaintiff, the court held the instruction to have been proper because the plaintiff, while knowing that small wood particles might be thrown in the direction of his face, believed that his glasses would provide sufficient protection to his eyes.[244]

Whether, and the extent to which, a plaintiff was in fact aware of a particular risk involves an inquiry into the plaintiff's *subjective* state of mind.[245] Stated otherwise, the knowledge question in such cases concerns the peculiarly factual issue of what the plaintiff personally knew and understood, *not* what a reasonable or normal person would or should have known and understood in similar circumstances. Sometimes courts speak loosely and misstate the principle,[246] but it is plainly wrong for a lawyer to argue, or for a court to instruct a jury, that assumption of risk involves a question of whether the plaintiff "*should* have known" of the risk; the only proper question is what the plaintiff actually did know.[247]

Like adults, young persons may understand and decide voluntarily to encounter product hazards.[248] Thus, unlike setting a child standard of behavior for contributory negligence, a youth's age, intelligence, experience, information, and judgment have no *direct* relevance to a determination of whether a youth assumed a risk. This is because the only legitimate assumption of risk question is whether the particular plaintiff—whether child or adult—*in fact* subjectively understood and willingly encountered the particular risk that caused the injury.

---

243 *Haugen*, 550 P.2d at 74.

244 The court explained: "If plaintiff assumed any risk at all, it was the risk of having dust or small particles of wood or metal lodged in his eye during the grinding process. He was obviously not aware of the latent defect in the structural integrity of the disc itself and the danger posed by that defect. This latent defect was not and probably could not have been known by the plaintiff. Plaintiff, therefore, could not have assumed the risk engendered by the defect." Id. at 75.

245 See, e.g., Sardis v. Overhead Door Corp., 446 F. Supp. 3d 47, 58 (E.D. Va. 2020) ("a subjective test[:] whether a plaintiff fully understood the nature and extent of a known danger and voluntarily exposed himself to it"); Johnson v. American Honda Motor Co., Inc., 2012 WL 1027588, at *16 (D. Mont. 2012) ("a subjective standard that considers 'what the particular plaintiff sees, knows, understands, and appreciates' "); Yamaha Motor Corp., USA v. McTaggart, 720 S.E.2d 217, 219 (Ga. Ct. App. 2011) ("The knowledge that a plaintiff who assumes a risk must subjectively possess is that of the specific, particular risk of harm associated with the activity or condition that proximately causes injury."); Krajewski v. Enderes Tool Co., 469 F.3d 705, 709 (8th Cir. 2006) (Neb. law) ("a subjective standard, geared to the individual plaintiff and his or her actual comprehension and appreciation of the nature of the danger he or she confronts"). See also Prosser and Keeton on Torts § 68, at 487.

246 See, e.g., Wangsness v. Builders Cashway, Inc., 779 N.W.2d 136, 141 (S.D. 2010) ("A person is deemed to have appreciated the risk 'if it is the type of risk that no adult of average intelligence can deny.' "); Patterson v. Central Mills, Inc., 64 Fed. Appx. 457 (6th Cir. 2003) (Ohio law) (stating that assumption of risk standard asks whether child of similar age, education, and experience would or should have been aware of risks); Bereman v. Burdolski, 460 P.2d 567, 569 (Kan. 1969) (approving instruction that plaintiff was barred if he continued to use vehicle once he was aware of defect in brakes or "should have been aware of it"). Such assertions are all incorrect.

247 See, e.g., Heil Co. v. Grant, 534 S.W.2d 916, 921 (Tex. App. 1976) (fact that plaintiff "*should have known* of the danger will not support the assumption of risk defense").

248 See, e.g., Kane v. Landscape Structures, Inc., 709 S.E.2d 876, 879–80 (Ga. Ct. App. 2011) (9-year-old child "appreciated" the risk of falling from playground equipment); Wangsness v. Builders Cashway, Inc., 779 N.W.2d 136, 141 (S.D. 2010) (15-year-old worker "understood that failing to keep his hands away from the rotating shaft and cable mechanism on the bi-fold door could result in serious injury"); Garner v. Rite Aid Of Ga., Inc., 595 S.E.2d 582, 587 (Ga. Ct. App. 2004) (teenagers "deliberately chose a perilous course of conduct, appreciated the danger," yet voluntarily exposed themselves to risks of inhaling ('huffing') butane).

Nevertheless, the clearly subjective nature of classic assumption of risk is subject to three important caveats or qualifications. First, a jury is not required to *believe* a plaintiff's testimony as to his or her subjective state of mind, such that the jury may test the plaintiff's avowals of what he or she claims to have known and understood against what the jury believes people with similar personal characteristics—such as "age, or lack of information, experience, intelligence, or judgment"[249]—ordinarily understand when confronting a similar product hazard.[250] This means that a plaintiff's personal characteristics—such as age, intelligence, experience, etc.—may indeed be *circumstantially* relevant to what the particular plaintiff *in fact* knew and understood.[251] Yet this distinction between direct and circumstantial evidence is a fine one, and it is easy for a lawyer or court to confuse the subjective standard that properly is at issue with the kind of objective framework that may help a jury resolve the subjective issue of the plaintiff's actual state of mind. While such confusion is understandable, it may quite easily upset the outcome of a case and so should be scrupulously avoided.[252]

The second qualification to the inherent subjectivity of assumption of risk is that the principal "test" of whether a risk encounter was *voluntary* is whether the plaintiff had a free choice to encounter the risk or not to do so—to wit, whether some *reasonable*

---

[249] Rest. (2d) Torts § 496D cmt. *c*. See also id. §§ 496A cmt. *d* and 496C cmt. *e*.

[250] See Heil Co. v. Grant, 534 S.W.2d 916, 920–21 (Tex. App. 1976): "An injured person's knowledge of a dangerous condition or defect is measured subjectively; i.e., by that person's actual, conscious knowledge. The fact that the injured person *should have known* of the danger will not support the assumption of risk defense. Sometimes, however, that person may know such facts as to be charged with knowledge of the danger. This standard would be applied when it was difficult or impossible to determine the state of the injured person's mind; as it was in the instant case of a fatal injury."

[251] Thus, the cases reveal that an experienced adult, familiar with a product's characteristics, is more likely to be viewed as having assumed a risk than an inexperienced or dim-witted adult, or a child. Compare Moore v. BPS Direct, LLC, 2019 WL 2931463, at *11 (D.S.C. 2019) (question of fact whether welder who read the treestand's warnings and instructions and arguably understood "whether something constitutes an unintended welding hole" assumed the risk of climbing a treestand with a welding burn hole in foot section); Walk v. Starkey Mach., Inc., 180 F.3d 937 (8th Cir. 1999) (Minn. law) (experienced worker, nicked by machine previously, assumed risk of hand entanglement by cleaning machine while it was operating); Mackowick v. Westinghouse Elec. Corp., 541 A.2d 749 (Pa. Super. Ct. 1988) (experienced electrician stuck screwdriver into energized capacitor-box—assumption of risk); Barnes v. Harley-Davidson Motor Co., 357 S.E.2d 127 (Ga. Ct. App. 1987) (motorcyclist of nearly 20 years, who collided with stalled car at night, claimed that motorcycle should have been equipped with crash bars as standard equipment, and that head-lamp provided too little light at high-speed—assumption of risk); and Bakunas v. Life Pack, Inc., 531 F. Supp. 89 (E.D. La. 1982) (movie stuntman performed free fall from 323 feet into air-inflated cushion rated only to 200 feet—assumption of risk), with Nettles v. Electrolux Motor AB, 784 F.2d 1574 (11th Cir. 1986) (Ala. law) (experienced but dim-witted woodcutter, injured when chain saw kicked back, had been injured by kickbacks before and knew that saws were available that were less likely to cause injury from kickbacks—no assumption of risk); and Forrest City Mach. Works, Inc. v. Aderhold, 616 S.W.2d 720 (Ark. 1981) (climbing off grain cart, 8-year-old caught pants in rotating power take-off shaft attached to tractor—no assumption of risk).

[252] See, e.g., Lopez v. Delair Group LLC, 881 F. Supp. 2d 268, 271 (D.R.I. 2012) (noting that jurors must be allowed to second-guess a plaintiff's testimony on knowledge and appreciation, in order "to overcome incredible testimony," and noting the Restatement's comment that "[t]here are some risks as to which no adult will be believed if he says that he did not know or understand them"); Prosser and Keeton on Torts § 68, at 76 (Supp. 1988):

> [To] state the doctrine in terms of what the plaintiff "knew or should have known" about the danger . . . is calculated at best to confuse the jury, and it is usually seriously misleading, since the apparent question put by such a standard is whether the plaintiff ought to have perceived the danger—by some external, objective standard of proper behavior—rather than the subjective question of whether the plaintiff himself actually knew the risk was present. But this is plainly wrong, and the use of "should have known" language in such instructions to the jury should therefore be prohibited. What the courts have here been searching for is some way to let the jurors know that they do not have to take the plaintiff at his word, but that they may instead test his protestations of ignorance of the risk by some external standard based on ordinary principles of credibility and common sense. It would be much better if the courts would simply say so.

alternative course of action existed, which the plaintiff might have chosen instead. A plaintiff's decision to forego a *reasonable* alternative course of action than the one that injures him has an uncanny resemblance to an unreasonable choice, which might well be viewed ipso facto as an objectively negligent course of action.

The third caveat to the assumption of risk's subjective nature is that comment *n* to § 402A explicitly narrows the classic assumption of risk defense in strict liability cases by adding an additional element to the defense—to wit, that the chosen risk encounter was *unreasonable.* This additional element requires a defendant to prove, not only that the plaintiff subjectively appreciated and willingly chose to encounter the risk, but also that this choice was objectively *unreasonable* in view of safer alternatives available to the plaintiff. These are all important qualifications to the subjectivity of the classic assumption of risk defense, which lawyers and courts need to keep in mind.

Warning defect cases raise special problems with respect to a plaintiff's knowledge and appreciation of a product hazard. If a plaintiff does not know of or understand a risk, it is axiomatic that the assumption of risk defense will not bar his or her damages resulting from that risk, as discussed above. Accordingly, if a product is defective because the manufacturer has not warned of a hidden risk, then a plaintiff unaware of that risk cannot be barred by the doctrine of assumption of risk.[253] If a defendant denies the existence of the risk[254] or conceals it from consumers (as manufacturers of cigarettes did for several decades),[255] the assumption of risk defense might be disallowed. But a plaintiff's knowledge may come from any source, and assumption of risk may be one reason[256] to bar a claim that a manufacturer failed to provide an adequate warning of a risk the plaintiff already knows about and understands.[257]

Voluntary Encounter

The second important limitation on the assumption of risk defense is that a plaintiff's decision to encounter a risk must be "free and voluntary."[258] The notions of appreciation and voluntariness to some extent overlap, in that the notion of consent supporting assumption of risk suggests that the plaintiff makes a true and meaningful *choice* to engage a particular risk, presumably to advance an interest (even mere convenience) that the plaintiff considers more valuable than avoidance of the risk. "Choice" in this context means, first, that the plaintiff understands the nature of the risk encountered; second, that the plaintiff has available one or more alternative courses of

---

[253] For the classic statements of this principle, see McClanahan v. California-Spray Chem. Corp., 75 S.E.2d 712, 725 (Va. 1953); Wright v. Carter Prods., Inc., 244 F.2d 53, 60 (2d Cir. 1957) (Mass. law); R. Keeton, Assumption of Risk in Products Liability Cases, 22 La. L. Rev. 122, 145 (1961). See also Warner Fruehauf Trailer Co. v. Boston, 654 A.2d 1272, 1275 (D.C. 1995).

[254] See Wilks v. American Tobacco Co., 680 So.2d 839 (Miss. 1996).

[255] See generally Spain v. Brown & Williamson Tobacco Corp., 872 So.2d 101 (Ala. 2003) (leaving open possibility that general warnings might be adequate to establish plaintiff's assumption of risk due to tobacco additives); Barnes v. American Tobacco Co., 161 F.3d 127, 146–49 (3d Cir. 1998) (Pa. law) (close question).

[256] The absence of cause in fact may be another reason. See, e.g., Raimbeault v. Takeuchi Mfg., Ltd., 772 A.2d 1056, 1064 (R.I. 2001) (plaintiff who had used and demonstrated excavator equipment for five years assumed risk and would not have been aided by warning). See also Plummer v. Lederle Labs., 819 F.2d 349, 359 (2d Cir. 1987) (Cal. law) ("no harm could have been caused by failure to warn of a risk already known"). See generally ch. 11, above.

[257] See, e.g., Heil Co. v. Grant, 534 S.W.2d 916, 922–23 (Tex. App. 1976) (dump truck defective for absence of warning of pullout cable hazard under truck that decedent's brother had warned him about).

[258] Prosser and Keeton on Torts § 68, at 490.

action by which he or she may reasonably avoid the risk; and third, that the plaintiff then decides that his or her interests will best be served by encountering the danger.

If a plaintiff's only, or best, "choice" is to encounter a known risk, then the encounter is not "voluntary." As just discussed, the voluntary requirement in assumption of risk essentially means that the plaintiff has a true choice—that he or she has *reasonable* options available to avoid the risk. While defining the consensual notions of voluntariness and choice in reasonableness terms may appear to be mixing apples and oranges, it probably is the best way to give content to this requirement. There is something wrong, indeed illogical and perverse, with a doctrine based on a plaintiff's *consent* that permits a defendant to avoid responsibility for causing harm by forcing a danger upon the plaintiff—"forcing," because the plaintiff has no reasonable means to avoid it. "Where the defendant puts him to a choice of evils, there is a species of duress, which destroys the idea of freedom of election. . . . By placing him in the dilemma, the defendant has deprived him of his freedom of choice, and so cannot be heard to say that he has voluntarily assumed the risk."[259] On the other hand, if a plaintiff has a perfectly reasonable way to avoid a danger created by the defendant, yet knowingly chooses to encounter it, then he cannot complain that he was compelled to take this path, for such a choice is free and voluntary.[260]

The voluntariness aspect of assumption of risk is a chimerical concept, for it is difficult to imagine why a person who truly understands a substantial risk of harm would not avoid it if there were a reasonable way to do so. No doubt there are occasional cases where a plaintiff acts with complete abandon of dangers that he or she full well knows to lie within a product—as when a person sticks his hand into a meat grinder because it is "more convenient" than using the metal stomper that is provided;[261] continues to ride at high speed a motorcycle with a wobbly front end on a pleasure trip without "the

---

[259] Id. at 490–91. See, e.g., Jara v. Rexworks Inc., 718 A.2d 788, 795 (Pa. Super. Ct. 1998) (quoting Rest. (2d) Torts § 496E choice-between-two-evils analysis, and stating: "An employee who is required to use certain equipment in the course of his employment and who uses that equipment as directed by the employer has no choice in encountering a risk inherent in that equipment."); Wallace v. Owens-Illinois, Inc., 389 S.E.2d 155 (S.C. Ct. App. 1989) (Bell, J.) (plaintiff injured while cleaning up effects of soft drink bottle explosion):

> The plaintiff's acceptance of a risk is not voluntary if the defendant's wrongful conduct leaves him no reasonable alternative course of conduct in order to avert harm to himself or another. . . . [T]he explosion of the defective bottle left him with no reasonable alternative. He had a choice between two evils: he could leave the spill on the floor with the risk that he or others might be injured by its presence or he could undertake to remove the spill with the risk that he or another would be injured in the process of cleaning up. In other words, either choice entailed risk. In these circumstances, his choice to remove the hazard was not a voluntary assumption of risk. The Defendants had created a condition of peril which involved a risk of harm no matter which choice Wallace made. Risk was unavoidable in the circumstances.

Id. at 158–59. See also Keller v. CNH Am., LLC, 2009 WL 1766695, at *2 (D. Minn. 2009) ("Primary assumption of the risk is 'applicable only where parties have voluntarily entered a relationship in which plaintiff assumes well-known, incidental risks.' "); Rose v. Brown & Williamson Tobacco Corp., 809 N.Y.S.2d 784, 792 (Sup. Ct. 2005) (doctrine of primary assumption of risk premised on concept that plaintiff "is free to choose whether or not to" encounter risk; a claim of addiction against cigarette manufacturers "calls the voluntariness of the activity into question. By definition, one who suffers from addiction is compelled to continue an activity even though he or she knows the activity is detrimental. Therefore, even though a cigarette smoker may be made fully aware of the elevated risks, if he or she is addicted to smoking, he or she may not be making a free choice to participate in the activity of continued smoking.").

[260] Prosser and Keeton on Torts § 68, at 491 ("where there is a reasonably safe alternative open, the plaintiff's choice of the dangerous way is a free one, and may amount to assumption of risk, negligence or both").

[261] Green v. Sanitary Scale Co., 431 F.2d 371, 374 (3d Cir. 1970) (Pa. law).

slightest compulsion of business or otherwise";[262] or sticks his arm through the cross bars of a forklift to activate the control lever to lower the bars, rather than going inside the vehicle to do so, because he is "in a hurry and [decides to take] a calculated risk that he could get his hand out of the way before the forks hit him."[263] In "calculated risk" cases such as these, assuming that the plaintiff truly appreciates the specific risk, the plaintiff's risk encounter is clearly advertent and so in that sense truly voluntary.[264]

More typical, however, are cases where the plaintiff may fully understand a specific risk but momentarily forgets about it, or becomes distracted, and then encounters it inadvertently. For example, a plaintiff might appreciate with specificity that if one's foot slips under a power mower with the blade revolving it is likely to be cut, that getting clothing caught in a rotating part of machinery may well cause a limb to become entangled in the machine, that jumping off a moving treadmill could cause injury, or that hitting the pullout cable beneath a raised dump truck is likely to cause the bed to come crashing down.[265] When such a plaintiff thereafter accidentally engages such a risk, which though earlier appreciated was not in the plaintiff's mind at the time of the accidental encounter, courts often apply the assumption of risk defense on a finding that the encounter was "voluntary."[266]

While it is true that such plaintiffs have the last and sometimes best chance to prevent such injuries,[267] since risk control at the time of the risk encounter lies exclusively with them, inadvertent encounters with the product itself may more appropriately be viewed as careless mistakes than as consensual ("voluntary") decisions to incur particular risks of harm. Plaintiffs in such situations may choose to work around a risk, which they understand may cause them harm if they were accidentally to engage certain parts of the machine, and so in this manner they may be said to voluntarily encounter such risks of harm. But the "encounter" of relevance in such cases might more properly be viewed as the *specific* encounter with the unreasonably dangerous aspect of a machine at the time of the accident, rather than the encounter of a *general* risk that such a specific encounter might sometime occur.[268] If an accident results from a plaintiff's inadvertent causative behavior, as from slipping into or otherwise accidentally contacting the dangerous parts of a machine, the plaintiff's operative behavior is purely inadvertent; being inadvertent, it is by definition "involuntary."

The appeal of the assumption of risk doctrine lies in grounding responsibility for accidents in a person's choices concerning risk control. And there are at least two

---

[262] Saeter v. Harley Davidson Motor Co., 8 Cal. Rptr. 747, 753 (Ct. App. 1960).

[263] Moran v. Raymond Corp., 484 F.2d 1008, 1016 (7th Cir. 1973) (Ill. law).

[264] In workplace settings, such "advertent" encounters may not be truly voluntary if they are compelled in some manner by the employment situation, as discussed below.

[265] See Denton v. Bachtold Bros., 291 N.E.2d 229 (Ill. App. Ct. 1972); Johnson v. Mid-South Distrib., Inc., Prod. Liab. Rep. (CCH) ¶ 7984 (Tenn. Ct. App. 1977); Ingram v. Life Fitness, 33 N.Y.S.3d 71, 72 (App. Div. 2016) (gym member, well familiar with treadmills, "assumed the obvious and inherent risks attendant to their use"); Heil Co. v. Grant, 534 S.W.2d 916 (Tex. App. 1976).

[266] See, e.g., Johnson v. Mid-South Distrib., Inc., Prod. Liab. Rep. (CCH) ¶ 7984 (Tenn. Ct. App. 1977) (pants leg caught in rotating machine shaft); Heil Co. v. Grant, 534 S.W.2d 916 (Tex. App. 1976) (hitting dump truck pullout cable); Denton v. Bachtold Bros., 291 N.E.2d 229 (Ill. App. Ct. 1972) (slip under lawn mower). *But see* Johnson v. Clark Equip. Co., 547 P.2d 132 (Or. 1976) (inadvertently activating control on forklift).

[267] See Nelson v. Brunswick Corp., 503 F.2d 376, 383 (9th Cir. 1974) (Wash. law) ("when the plaintiff knows and appreciates the danger, he is in a position as good as the defendant's to avoid his injury").

[268] See, e.g., Jackson v. Harsco Corp., 673 P.2d 363, 367 (Colo. 1983) (en banc) ("no evidence that plaintiff had actual knowledge of the specific dangers arising out of the precise defect asserted, or that he voluntarily and unreasonably proceeded to encounter those dangers despite his awareness of the defect").

perspectives that help illuminate the significance of risk control choices. The first perspective concerns the *reasonableness* of a plaintiff's choice to encounter a risk, which is embedded in the concept of voluntariness that itself is defined in terms of the availability of alternative methods—which are hardly "available" alternatives unless they are "reasonable"—for avoiding the risk, as discussed above. If circumstances force a plaintiff to encounter a product defect, then the plaintiff's encounter is not voluntary because of the absence of choice, as discussed above. And because of the absence of choice resulting from the plaintiff being forced into the encounter, the plaintiff's will is removed from a causative analysis of the accident, leaving the manufacturer's sale of a defective product as the last and most proximate cause of the accident.

The second perspective on a person's risk control choices concerns the *time* when a person decides to encounter a risk. A product user may understand and voluntarily accept a general risk of harm at the time of employment or when a particular project with a product first begins. Yet, at the precise moment a potential accident victim interacts with a product in a manner that erupts into accidental injury, the victim is rarely deliberating upon the nature and degree of risk in, and the desirability of, the specific interaction. Instead, as mentioned earlier, the actual, physical interactions—the "specific" risk encounters—in most situations are inadvertent mistakes, not deliberative choices. To put the matter slightly differently, while persons often voluntarily decide to encounter future risks in a general way, they rarely encounter particular risks voluntarily at the moment of an accident.

It is only when a person's risk encounter is "voluntary" from both the reasonableness and temporal perspectives that the person fairly may be deemed to have assumed the risk. Thus, accidents caused by a plaintiff's *unreasonable* decision to take a truly calculated risk—one that consciously involves the specific physical interaction with the product that results in injury—may be the only type of case in which the assumption of risk defense provides a proper basis for barring recovery. In such situations, where a prudent person would not knowingly and voluntarily act in such a dangerous manner for such a trivial benefit, the doctrine of sole proximate cause could quite easily be substituted for assumption of risk as a mechanism for placing full responsibility upon the plaintiff.[269]

There are at least two contexts in which courts have been especially open to challenges to the voluntariness of risk encounters: rescues and workplace accidents. In the rescue situation, as with the contributory negligence defense,[270] a number of courts have held that a rescuer of a person endangered by a defective product may not be barred by the defense of assumption of risk.[271]

The second context in which courts are more skeptical of the voluntariness of a plaintiff's risk encounter is the employment setting where a worker is injured by a dangerous industrial machine or other workplace product. For example, in *Rhoads v.*

---

[269] The sole-proximate-cause doctrine, applicable to both contributory and comparative negligence, is discussed in §§ 13.2 and 13.3, above.

[270] See § 13.2, above.

[271] See, e.g., Higgins v. Intex Recreation Corp., 99 P.3d 421, 427–28 (Wash. Ct. App. 2004) ("comparative negligence and assumption of risk do not apply when the rescuer acts neither rashly nor recklessly"); McCoy v. American Suzuki Motor Corp., 961 P.2d 952, 956 (Wash. 1998) ("the rescue doctrine may be invoked in product liability actions just as it may in ordinary negligence actions"); Dillard v. Pittway Corp., 719 So.2d 188, 193–94 (Ala. 1998) (collecting the cases; neither contributory negligence nor assumption of risk available as defense unless rescuer's conduct was "manifestly rash and reckless").

Service Machine Co.,[272] the operator's arm and hand slipped into a large punch press when she lost her balance while activating the press. Upholding the jury's rejection of the assumption of risk defense, despite the plaintiff's knowledge of the unguarded nature of the machine, the court incisively remarked: "The 'voluntariness' with which a worker assigned to a dangerous machine in a factory 'assumes the risk of injury' from the machine is illusory."[273] Other courts[274] and commentators[275] have agreed that such workplace encounters often are not "voluntary." But for the workplace bar of the assumption of risk defense logically to apply, an employer may have to *require* that the employee use the product, and the employee must further be using the product according to workplace rules.[276] The Supreme Court of Ohio has abolished the assumption of risk defense in the workplace setting on the ground that workers often are effectively trapped into performing dangerous activities, a situation which destroys any voluntariness in many such job-related risk encounters.[277]

Other courts treat voluntariness in the workplace like any other encounter, often without attention to the dynamics of this context.[278] These courts sometimes reason that any compulsion comes not from the defendant manufacturer but from a third party, the employer,[279] and that even in this setting workers not infrequently make entirely deliberate (and sometimes entirely foolish) decisions exposing themselves to risks that they fully understand to be unreasonable.[280]

---

[272] 329 F. Supp. 367 (E.D. Ark. 1971).

[273] Id. at 381.

[274] See, e.g., Pasillas v. Okuma Am. Corp., 946 F. Supp. 2d 762, 765 (N.D. Ill. 2013) ("plaintiff's job required him to dismantle the machine, and a jury could [find] that plaintiff had no alternative but to proceed without a compression tool"); Lewis v. CRC Indus., 7 A.3d 841, 847 (Pa. 2010) (N.J. law) ("courts have liberally applied the principle that workers injured on the job have no 'meaningful choice' and are protected from the doctrines of assumption of risk and contributory and comparative negligence in similar strict product liability actions"); D'Angelo v. ADS Mach. Corp., 128 Fed. Appx. 253, 256 (3d Cir. 2005) (Pa. law) ("where an employee is required to use certain equipment in the course of his employment, and uses that equipment as directed by the employer, the employee cannot be said 'voluntarily' to have assumed the risk of encountering any dangers associated with the equipment"); Jara v. Rexworks Inc., 718 A.2d 788, 795 (Pa. Super. Ct. 1998) (a worker has no choice and hence "could not *voluntarily* assume the risk [if he] is required to use equipment as furnished [and directed] by the employer"); Johnson v. Clark Equip. Co., 547 P.2d 132 (Or. 1976).

[275] See Noel, Defective Products: Abnormal Use, Contributory Negligence, and Assumption of Risk, 25 Vand. L. Rev. 93, 127 (1972) ("when a manufacturer supplies a dangerous machine for use by employees, the workman injured because of the unsafe design is subject to . . . economic pressure [so] that his consent to use the dangerous machine, perhaps in order to retain his job, is . . . not free and voluntary"); Note, 95 Harv. L. Rev. 872, 889–90 n.68 (1982) (same).

[276] Sweitzer v. Oxmaster, Inc., 2010 WL 5257226, at *8–9 (E.D. Pa. 2010) (barring assumption of risk defense in work settings on grounds of involuntariness is limited to employees *required* to use a product at work and using it "as directed by" the employer).

[277] See Cremeans v. Willmar Henderson Mfg. Co., 566 N.E.2d 1203 (Ohio 1991).

[278] For example, in Hedgepeth v. Fruehauf Corp., 634 F. Supp. 93 (S.D. Miss. 1986), the driver, whose job required walking on the rounded top of a tanker truck to open and close its hatches, complained that the top was "real slick and real cruddy" with oil residue and needed to be cleaned. The supervisor ordered him to use the truck anyway, or just to leave. After a delivery, while closing a hatch on top, he slipped and fell. Although the driver surely understood the specific risk, yet his absence of reasonable alternatives—he had to use the product in its hazardous condition or not work at all—would seem to render his decision to use the truck in that condition devoid of choice and hence "involuntary." Yet the court held the driver's actions to be "voluntary."

[279] See id., 634 F. Supp. 93, 99 n.3 (relying on Rest. (2d) Torts § 496E cmt. *b*).

[280] See, e.g., Karim v. Tanabe Mach., Ltd., 322 F. Supp. 2d 578 (E.D. Pa. 2004) (machine operator grabbed control box near moving chain and sprocket, which caught his hand); Walk v. Starkey Mach., Inc., 180 F.3d 937 (8th Cir. 1999) (Minn. law) (experienced worker, who had been nicked previously by machine, assumed risk of hand entanglement by cleaning machine while it was operating); Moran v. Raymond Corp.,

As a Defense to Strict Liability in Tort

Assumption of risk as classically defined is a standard defense to products liability claims brought in negligence, and many states have continued its conventional definition and effect as a full defense to products liability claims of strict liability in tort.[281] Yet, many other jurisdictions have altered its definition, and a couple alter its availability[282] and effect,[283] for claims of strict liability in tort.[284] *Restatement (Second) of Torts* § 402A comment *n*, examined above in connection with the contributory negligence defense,[285] provides in part:

> [T]he form of contributory negligence which consists in voluntarily and unreasonably proceeding to encounter a known danger, and commonly passes under the name of assumption of risk, is a defense under this Section as in other cases of strict liability. If the user or consumer discovers the defect and is aware of the danger, and nevertheless proceeds unreasonably to make use of the product and is injured by it, he is barred from recovery.[286]

Some states, as mentioned, ignored comment *n* and continued applying the traditional elements of assumption of risk even for claims brought in strict products liability in tort.[287] Yet, especially before the widespread adoption of comparative fault,[288] many jurisdictions adopted comment *n*'s approach of applying the assumption of risk defense in strict tort cases only when a plaintiff's choice to engage a risk, in addition to

---

484 F.2d 1008, 1016 (7th Cir. 1973) (Ill. law) (worker stuck his arm through and activated moving cross bars on fork lift: "[w]orkmen often take risks which they should not take").

[281] See, e.g., Copenhaver v. Cavagna Grp. S.P.A Omeca Div., 2021 WL 3622059, at *8 (D. Mont. 2021) (assumption of risk is "a viable defense to a strict product liability claim under Mont. Code Ann. § 27–1–719(5)(a)"); Johns v. Suzuki Motor of Am., Inc., 850 S.E.2d 59, 63 n.6 (Ga. 2020) (citing cases holding assumption of risk as a defense to strict products liability claims).

Some state reform statutes include an assumption of risk defense. See, e.g., Vold v. ARPAC, LP, 2008 WL 2788727, at *2–5 (N.D. Ohio 2008) (barring negligence, warranty, and strict liability claims under Ohio's statutory defense).

[282] Assumption of risk may be abolished as a defense to tort claims generally but be retained to operate as a bar to claims for strict products liability in tort. See, e.g., Rutter v. Northeastern Beaver Cnty. Sch. Dist., 437 A.2d 1198, 1209 (Pa. 1981). Compare Bunch v. Hoffinger Indus., 20 Cal. Rptr. 3d 780, 798 (Ct. App. 2004) (primary assumption of risk is no defense to strict liability claims, even though diving into above-ground pool involves risks inherent in a sporting activity, a context where primary assumption of risk normally applies).

[283] Assumption of risk may operate only to reduce damages on a comparative fault basis, except in strict products liability in tort where it may serve as a total bar. See, e.g., Bowling v. Heil Co., 511 N.E.2d 373 (Ohio 1987); Onderko v. Richmond Mfg. Co., 511 N.E.2d 388 (Ohio 1987).

[284] See Vargo, The Defenses to Strict Liability in Tort: A New Vocabulary with an Old Meaning, 29 Mercer L. Rev. 447 (1978); Twerski, Old Wine in a New Flask-Restructuring Assumption of Risk in the Products Liability Era, 60 Iowa L. Rev. 1 (1974); Noel, Defective Products: Abnormal Use, Contributory Negligence, and Assumption of Risk, 25 Vand. L. Rev. 93 (1972); Epstein, Products Liability: Defenses Based on Plaintiff's Conduct, 1968 Utah L. Rev. 267; Annot., 46 A.L.R.3d 240 (1972) (contributory negligence and assumption of risk as defenses to claim for strict products liability in tort); 119 Am. Jur. Proof of Facts 3d 203 (2011) (assumption of risk defense to strict products liability).

[285] Comment *n* is set forth in full in § 13.2, above, at text following note 117.

[286] Rest. (2d) Torts § 402A cmt. *n*.

[287] See, e.g., Jay v. Moog Auto., Inc., 652 N.W.2d 872, 882–84 (Neb. 2002). See also Bowen v. Cochran, 556 S.E.2d 530, 532 (Ga. Ct. App. 2001); Conn. Gen. Stat. Ann. § 52–572*l* ("Nothing in this section shall be construed as barring . . . the defense of knowingly using the product in a defective condition in an action based on strict tort liability.").

[288] After the adoption of comparative fault, many (but not all) jurisdictions saw no need to distinguish between forms of plaintiff fault and so included *all* forms of plaintiff misconduct in the comparative calculus. See V. Schwartz, Comparative Negligence ch. 11 (with K. Kelly 6th ed. 2020); § 13.3, above.

being knowing and voluntary, was also *unreasonable*[289] (or "negligent").[290] In effect, such jurisdictions added an additional element—unreasonableness—to the assumption of risk defense conventionally applied in negligence cases.[291] So altered, the assumption of risk defense to claims for strict products liability in tort narrows substantially, by requiring that a plaintiff know and appreciate the risk, voluntarily encounter it, and, further, be unreasonable in deciding to encounter the risk.[292]

As previously discussed, the voluntariness of a worker's encounters with risky products in the workplace is often suspect. Similarly, some courts have ruled that workplace decisions to encounter risk may be found not to be "unreasonable" if the practical demands of a job sabotage a worker's opportunity for making truly consensual decisions about such encounters.[293] Yet, it would seem quite clear that, even in the workplace context, a person may unreasonably (and voluntarily) choose to engage a known and appreciated risk.[294]

The reasonableness issue in strict liability in tort cases concerns the plaintiff's *decision* to encounter a particular risk, or to encounter it in a particular way, not the reasonableness of the physical execution of that decision.[295] Unlike the other elements

---

[289] See, e.g., Romero v. ITW Food Equip. Grp., LLC, 987 F. Supp. 2d 93, 101 (D.D.C. 2013) (in strict liability, defendant must show plaintiff was aware of danger and "voluntarily *and unreasonably*" used product) (emphasis added); Reott v. Asia Trend, Inc., 55 A.3d 1088, 1096–97 (Pa. 2012) ("the defendant must show that the buyer knew of a defect and yet voluntarily and unreasonably proceeded to use the product"); Johnson v. American Motor Co., 2012 WL 1027588, at *15 (D. Mont. 2012) (in strict liability, "the defense of assumption of the risk 'involves *unreasonable* exposure to the danger created by the defective product' "; emphasis in original); Goyal v. Thermage, Inc., 2012 WL 3240381, at *12–13 (D. Md. 2012).

[290] See, e.g., Egelhoff v. Holt, 875 S.W.2d 543, 548–49 (Mo. 1994) (en banc) (using "negligent assumption of risk" expression, though applying it to wrong statutory provision).

[291] See, e.g., Goyal v. Thermage, Inc., 2012 WL 3240381, at *12–13 (D. Md. 2012) ("the defendant must show that the plaintiff (1) knew of and appreciated the risk of danger, (2) voluntarily confronted that risk, and (3) was unreasonable in her decision to encounter the known risk"); Johnson v. Clark Equip. Co., 547 P.2d 132, 138 (Or. 1976):

> The concept of assumption of risk in a products liability case differs somewhat from the traditional tort doctrine of assumption of risk . . . . In contrast to the more traditional defense which includes only two elements—subjective knowledge and voluntary encounter—Comment *n* sets forth three elements which must be shown before the plaintiff can be barred from recovery. The defendant must show, first, that the plaintiff *himself* actually knew and appreciated the particular risk or danger created by the defect; second, that plaintiff voluntarily encountered the risk while realizing the danger; and, third, that plaintiff's decision to voluntarily encounter the known risk was unreasonable.

[292] See note 289, above.

[293] See, e.g., Brown v. Quick Mix Co., 454 P.2d 205, 208 (Wash. 1969) ("It could never be said as a matter of law that a workman whose job requires him to expose himself to a danger, voluntarily and unreasonably encounters the same."); Johnson v. Clark Equip. Co., 547 P.2d 132, 140–41 (Or. 1976):

> [W]orking conditions and related circumstances are a particularly relevant consideration in an inquiry into the reasonableness of a decision to encounter a job-related danger. Such factors often will have a strong influence on that decision, and, in some cases, they may represent the most important motivational factors. For example, a worker might fear that a slowdown in his individual production would slow down the entire production team and thereby draw the attention of his boss. If he has a history of such slowdowns, or of causing excessive spoilage or ruining machine parts, he may have good cause to fear dismissal. The job market could be tight, and he may have little hope of being able to find a new job. Moreover, the situation may demand an immediate, hurried decision. It is certainly possible that, under such circumstances, a reasonable jury could find that his decision to encounter a known risk was not unreasonable.

[294] See, e.g., Karim v. Tanabe Mach., Ltd., 322 F. Supp. 2d 578 (E.D. Pa. 2004) (machine operator grabbed control box near moving chain and sprocket, which caught his hand).

[295] "We are not concerned with the apparent reasonableness or unreasonableness of the physical conduct through which plaintiff encountered the danger, but rather the reasonableness of his decision to do so." Johnson v. Clark Equip. Co., 547 P.2d 132, 140 (Or. 1976).

of assumption of risk, the unreasonableness element adds an *objective* determination to the assumption of risk defense—whether a prudent person, in the exercise of reasonable care for his or her own safety, would have decided to encounter the particular risk based on all the surrounding circumstances.[296]

While adding an "unreasonableness" requirement to the definition of assumption of risk for strict liability in tort claims seemingly narrows and restricts the availability of the defense, and while it may provide a plaintiff's lawyer with an additional peg on which to hang an argument, the effect of this element may be more apparent than real. No doubt it is true that the orthodox definition of assumption of risk does not explicitly require that a plaintiff's choice to incur a known risk be unreasonable, so that the conventional defense is said to arise (theoretically at least) even if an encounter is reasonable in all respects.[297] Yet, if the "voluntary" element of assumption of risk is defined conventionally as the availability of reasonable alternatives when deciding to engage a risk, as discussed above, the set of reasonable assumptions of risk cases essentially disappears.

Assume, for example, that a pregnant woman living deep in the country goes into labor, and her doctor counsels her by telephone that complications in her pregnancy threaten her life if she does not immediately begin to drive to the distant hospital. As her husband helps her into their only car, he discovers a large bubble defect on the sidewall of one of the newly purchased front tires. Being a tire salesman, he knows that the bubble may cause the tire to fail at any time. However, because there are no neighbors, nor time to call an ambulance, the husband proceeds to drive slowly and carefully to the hospital. But the tire bursts en route, causing the car to careen into a ditch, injuring the husband.[298] No doubt a jury would find that the husband's decision to incur the risk of driving on the defective tire was reasonable, and quite probably that it was informed. But the decision to incur this risk was not voluntary; it was reasonable for the very same reason that it was involuntary—the husband had no choice, no reasonable alternative to attempting the journey (cautiously) on a tire he knew to be dangerously defective.

Thus, if voluntariness rests on the presence of choice, and if choice implies the availability of reasonable alternatives, involuntariness and reasonableness may be seen to conflate, rendering the notion of a reasonable assumption of risk a contradiction in terms and a virtually empty set.[299] In the problem above, the husband would be protected from an assumption of risk defense for two reasons: not only because his choice to incur the risk was reasonable, but also because the decision was involuntary. These results would be reversed if the husband had no good reason to drive on the defective tire, that is, if a reasonable alternative *were* available. So, if the husband chose to drive to a baseball game on a tire he knew to be dangerously defective, failing to take the time to change it with an available spare in order to arrive earlier and get a better parking space,

[296] See id. at 138 n.5.

[297] See, e.g., Rahmig v. Mosley Mach. Co., 412 N.W.2d 56, 74 (Neb. 1987); Blackburn v. Dorta, 348 So.2d 287, 291 (Fla. 1977) (explaining injustice of reasonable assumption of risk by hypothetical of father injured while rescuing his infant child from burning house, yet failing to recognize that such an encounter would not be "voluntary," since he had no reasonable alternative). See also Prosser and Keeton on Torts § 68, at 481.

[298] An ambulance eventually arrives, and mother gives birth to healthy twins, Bud and Bill.

[299] Virtually empty, rather than completely so, because the risks and other costs of an alternative course of action may be equal to, rather than less than, those of the course of action encountered. In such a case, either decision would be reasonable.

then his choice to incur the risk would be voluntary, his decision would also be unreasonable (unless it were a Red Sox—Yankees game), and his assumption of risk would bar recovery. Either way, because reasonableness is bound inextricably to voluntariness, adding the unreasonableness of a decision to encounter a risk as a formal element to assumption of risk may not materially alter the scope of the defense.[300]

Reform

Assumption of risk is on the run. Plainly problematic, the doctrine may unfairly place responsibility for injuries on a victim whose only fault lay in making a choice, perhaps correctly, that was forced upon him by a tortfeasor. To the extent that a plaintiff truly is at fault in encountering a risk, the doctrines of (no) duty,[301] contributory (and comparative) negligence,[302] and (sole) proximate causation[303] would appear to cover virtually every case where assumption of risk properly bars recovery. The assumption of risk defense thus has long been roundly criticized,[304] and it is being abolished, partially[305] or completely,[306] by an increasing number of courts and legislatures.[307] And,

[300] See, e.g., Berg v. Sukup Mfg. Co., 355 N.W.2d 833 (S.D. 1984), where the court, in applying the unreasonableness element of Rest. (2d) Torts § 402A cmt. *n*, defined it in terms of the presence of a reasonable alternative—a standard more typically used to define voluntariness, as discussed above. The court remarked: "Reasonableness refers to whether the plaintiff had a reasonable opportunity to elect whether or not to subject himself to the danger," id. at 835, and further stated the issue in terms of "[w]hether or not [plaintiff] had a reasonable opportunity to avoid the risk," id. at 836.

[301] See, e.g., Bartkewich v. Billinger, 247 A.2d 603 (Pa. 1968) (manufacturer of glass-breaking machine had no duty to design machine to prevent operators from reaching their hands in machine in an attempt to release a jam).

[302] See §§ 13.2 and 13.3, above.

[303] See Horton v. American Tobacco Co., 667 So.2d 1289, 1307 (Miss. 1995) (Lee, P.J., concurring and dissenting in part) ("Under assumption of the risk theory, if a plaintiff is found to have assumed the risk of his own injury, he is, in fact, the sole proximate cause of his injury and thus, no liability lies on the defendant.").

[304] The critical scholarly literature includes Bohlen, Voluntary Assumption of Risk, 20 Harv. L. Rev. 14 (1906); Wade, The Place of Assumption of Risk in the Law of Negligence, 22 La. L. Rev. 5 (1961); James, Assumption of Risk: Unhappy Reincarnation, 78 Yale L.J. 185 (1968); Simons, Assumption of Risk and Consent in the Law of Torts: A Theory of Full Preference, 67 B.U. L. Rev. 213 (1987) (excellent theoretical inquiry). See generally Prosser and Keeton on Torts 493–95; 4 Harper, James, and Gray, Law of Torts § 21.8. For an informative debate among tort law scholars of an earlier day, see "The Battle of the Wilderness," Rest. (2d) Torts § 893, at 70 (Tent. Draft No. 9, 1963).

[305] A few jurisdictions abolished the assumption of risk defense in all cases except for claims of strict products liability in tort. See, e.g., Central Tel. Co. v. Fixtures Mfg. Corp., 738 P.2d 510, 512 (Nev. 1987) (assumption of risk absorbed into comparative fault act except in strict liability cases); Bowling v. Heil Co., 511 N.E.2d 373 (Ohio 1987) (same); Rutter v. Northeastern Beaver Cnty. Sch. Dist., 437 A.2d 1198, 1209 (Pa. 1981) (noting 19 other jurisdictions that have abolished or "seriously modified" the defense, and concluding that "the difficulties of using the term 'assumption of risk' outweigh the benefits"). In Ohio, assumption of risk now once again completely bars products liability claims against manufacturers. Ohio Rev. Code Ann. § 2307.711. At least Connecticut does so statutorily. Compare Conn. Gen. Stat. Ann. § 52–572h(*l*) (abolishing the doctrine of assumption of risk in negligence actions) with Conn. Gen. Stat. Ann. § 52–572*l* (allowing "the defense of knowingly using the product in a defective condition in an action based on strict tort liability").

[306] New Jersey was the first such state to do so. See Meistrich v. Casino Arena Attractions Inc., 155 A.2d 90 (N.J. 1959); McGrath v. American Cyanamid Co., 196 A.2d 238 (N.J. 1963). But the state thereafter struggled with how to handle aggravated user misconduct in products liability cases. So it recognized "a defense of contributory negligence to strict liability in tort based upon a voluntary and unreasonable encountering by the plaintiff of a known safety hazard of a machine where proximately contributive to the accident." Cepeda v. Cumberland Eng'g Co., 386 A.2d 816, 833 (N.J. 1978). This is now the only type of plaintiff misconduct that may be used to reduce damages under the state's system of comparative fault. See, e.g., Lewis v. American Cyanamid Co., 715 A.2d 967, 974–76 (N.J. 1998). See also Bolduc v. Crain, 181 A.2d 641 (N.H. 1962); Hornbeck v. Western States Fire Apparatus, Inc., 572 P.2d 620 (Or. 1977) (statute).

[307] See, e.g., Wyo. Stat. Ann. § 1–1–123(a)–(b) (protects sports and recreation providers from liability arising from the inherent risks of sports and recreational activities); Roberts v. Jackson Hole Mountain Resort Corp., 884 F.3d 967, 979 (10th Cir. 2018) (Wyo. law) (injuries from skiing into a pile of boulders outside resort's boundaries; "when a skier drops into an off-piste run littered with visible obstacles including trees and rocks,

with the widespread adoption of comparative fault beginning in the 1960s, other courts and legislatures have done what amounts to the same thing by "merging" assumption of risk into a broad doctrine of comparative fault.[308] In many of the remaining states that continue to apply the assumption of risk defense, courts not infrequently recognize its harshness and, refusing to apply it except where clearly mandated by facts and precedent, proclaim that it will not be extended.[309]

The principal *theoretical* benefit of the assumption of risk doctrine is that it grounds the law on choice and so ties legal responsibility, at least in part, to this important value. But a manufacturer's choices usually are relevant to product accidents as well, and a manufacturer should not escape all responsibility for accidents when it markets a defective product that may force consumers to confront difficult choices subjecting themselves to risk. If a product defect leaves a user with no choice of an effective way to avoid a risk of harm, then the manufacturer fairly should shoulder the entire loss. But if a plaintiff knowingly, affirmatively, and voluntarily exercises substantial control over a product hazard, and simply opts to take a calculated and unreasonable risk, then the plaintiff's decision and action—whether viewed as choice, fault, or as both—should usually be considered the sole proximate cause of any resulting harm. Finally, if moral responsibility for a product accident is divided between the choices and conduct of both parties, then comparative fault provides a sound system for dividing damages. Basing responsibility on choice is a two-way street, and it would seem that a system of comparative responsibility generally offers a better method for doing justice when a product user supposedly "assumes" a risk of injury.

Probably the most important *practical* benefit of the assumption of risk doctrine is to provide a basis for summary judgment when a plaintiff is shown to have knowingly engaged an unreasonable risk and so should bear full responsibility for his or her injuries. Although courts are understandably reluctant to apply comparative fault principles to grant summary judgment against faulty plaintiffs, it would seem that courts might appropriately provide a small window for granting defendants summary judgment when a plaintiff's fault can fairly be characterized as the sole proximate cause

---

it is an inherent risk that he will encounter unseen obstacles as well"); Dullmaier v. Xanterra Parks & Resorts, 883 F.3d 1278, 1293 (10th Cir. 2018) (Wyo. law) (fatal fall during guided horseback ride; "it is an unremarkable consequence of . . . inherent risks that a rider might fall from a spooked, runaway horse"). Compare Cole v. Camelback Mountain Ski Resort, 2017 WL 4621786, at *3 (M.D. Pa. 2017) (ski resort did not owe duty of care to downhill skier under Pennsylvania Skier's Responsibility Act; "The doctrine of voluntary assumption of risk as it applies to downhill skiing injuries and damages is not modified by [the Comparative Negligence Act]").

[308] See, e.g., Wurster v. Plastics Grp., Inc., 2017 WL 4582528, at *2 (S.D. Iowa 2017), aff'd, 917 F.3d 608 (8th Cir. 2019) (unreasonable assumption of risk no longer a complete defense, but only part of comparative fault); Malen v. MTD Prods., Inc., 628 F.3d 296, 313 (7th Cir. 2010) (Ill. law) (like contributory negligence and misuse, assumption of risk was merged into comparative fault and so became merely a damages-reducing factor unless plaintiff's fault was greater than 50% of the cause of his injuries, in which case it would be a total bar); Yoneda v. Tom, 133 P.3d 796, 800–01 (Haw. 2006) (discussing merger of implied assumption of risk into comparative fault); Blankenship v. CRT Tree, 2002 WL 31195215, at *7 (Ohio Ct. App. 2002) (noting the merger); Smock Materials Handling Co. v. Kerr, 719 N.E.2d 396, 402 (Ind. Ct. App. 1999) (merging assumption of risk into comparative fault for negligence actions, but maintaining it for strict liability actions); Perez v. McConkey, 872 S.W.2d 897 (Tenn. 1994) (implied assumption of risk abolished; fault aspects included in comparative fault); Blackburn v. Dorta, 348 So.2d 287, 292–93 (Fla. 1977) (because it makes no sense to deny recovery altogether to a person who reasonably assumes a risk while allowing partial recovery to a contributorily negligent person who acts unreasonably, "assumption of risk is merged into the defense of contributory negligence and the principles of comparative negligence . . . shall apply").

[309] See, e.g., Heil Co. v. Grant, 534 S.W.2d 916, 920 (Tex. App. 1976) (applying it to facts, but stating: "The doctrine of assumed risk is harsh and will not be extended.").

of an accident.[310] This often will be the case when the facts are clear that a plaintiff knowingly and unreasonably took a calculated risk that resulted in accidental harm.

In conclusion, while the assumption of risk doctrine's grounding in choice theory renders it alluring at some levels, a complete choice theory requires consideration not only of a plaintiff's choices, but of a manufacturer's choices, too. Viewed from a social welfare or economic perspective, the doctrine's mischief quite clearly seems to outweigh its benefits.[311] And, viewed on its own terms, courts and legislatures increasingly appreciate the shortcomings of the assumption of risk defense and recognize the availability of reasonable alternative doctrines that well fill the void. Now that the *Restatement of Apportionment* has taken the position that assumption of risk as a separate doctrine should be abolished,[312] the trend toward abolishing the doctrine and merging it into comparative fault appears inexorable. No doubt assumption of risk will linger on in some jurisdictions for quite some time, yet it is a doctrine that properly appears to be heading toward the trash heap of discarded tort law doctrines.

Express Assumption of Risk

The discussion above pertains to *implied* assumption of risk, in which context a plaintiff's conduct suggests or implies consent to incur a risk.[313] The issues are quite different when a defendant claims that a product user *expressly* agreed to accept full responsibility for the possibility that the use of a product would result in an injury—often by means of a written waiver, disclaimer, or release signed by the plaintiff. The principles of express assumption of risk depend on the theory of recovery: negligence, strict products liability in tort, or warranty.

In negligence, the products liability cases parallel the general tort law principles: a disclaimer is effective only if it clearly and unequivocally relieves the defendant of responsibility for harm caused by the defendant's negligence. To most courts this has meant that the word "negligence" or "fault" (rather than more general words such as "liability") must appear in the disclaimer provision in a manner that makes it entirely clear that the shift of responsibility between the parties includes a shift of liability for harm caused by a defendant's negligence.[314] The negligence disclaimer cases have mostly involved commercial parties suffering commercial losses, but the few that have involved garden-variety consumer claims against manufacturers for personal injuries caused by defective products follow similar principles of limitation.

Several courts have held that a disclaimer is void if the defendant's negligent act or omission violated a duty imposed by statute for the benefit of the public.[315] In addition,

[310] While courts in pure comparative fault jurisdictions might reasonably be more cautious in so ruling, courts in modified (50%) comparative fault jurisdictions should more often confront situations appropriate for granting summary judgment motions on assumption of risk in favor of defendants. Even in pure comparative fault states, however, a plaintiff's extraordinary misconduct may sometimes authorize summary judgment for the defendant. See § 13.3, above.

[311] See, e.g., Rutter v. Northeastern Beaver Cty. Sch. Dist., 437 A.2d 1198, 1209 (Pa. 1981) (abolishing implied assumption of risk defense, except for strict tort products liability, on grounds that "the difficulties of using the term 'assumption of risk' outweigh the benefits").

[312] See Rest. (3d) Torts: Apportionment of Liability §§ 2 cmt. *i* and 3 cmt. *c*.

[313] See Prosser and Keeton on Torts § 68.

[314] See, e.g., Johnson v. Zimmer, Inc., 2004 WL 742038 (D. Minn. 2004); Roane v. Greenwich Swim Comm., 330 F. Supp. 2d 306 (S.D.N.Y. 2004).

[315] See, e.g., Dessert Seed Co. v. Drew Farmers Supply, Inc., 454 S.W.2d 307, 311 (Ark. 1970).

as under the principles of warranty law,[316] a plaintiff must be aware of any disclaimer of negligence responsibility at the time of sale, and such a provision will be ineffective if it is buried in fine print in an owner's manual not given to the plaintiff until after sale.[317] Even if a products liability defendant effectively avoids negligence responsibility toward the user who signed a contractual disclaimer, such a provision will not bar a negligence claim by an injured third party against the manufacturer or other seller.[318]

As for strict products liability in tort, the law is clear: a seller's attempt to disclaim responsibility to consumers for physical injuries from new products is against public policy, void, and of no effect.[319] Indeed, the untoward use of disclaimers by sellers of dangerously defective consumer goods, traditionally allowable under warranty law, was a principal reason for the development of the doctrine of strict products liability in tort in the 1960s.[320] Both the *Second*[321] and *Third Restatements of Torts*[322] agree that disclaimers of responsibility for physical injuries caused by product defects violate the law and are thus invalid. Most difficult problems with disclaimers in strict tort involve their effectiveness in commercial contexts involving economic losses, a topic treated elsewhere.[323]

A typical case illustrating the prevailing tort law principles is *Diedrich v. Wright*,[324] in which the plaintiff was severely injured when her parachute failed to open fully because its lines were crossed. In her suit against the parachute center for supplying her with an unsafe parachute, the defendant asserted that the plaintiff had waived her rights by signing a release form that generally exculpated the defendant from liability for injuries from parachuting. The court held that the release could not bar a strict liability action, and that it did not bar the negligence action because it failed clearly to state that the plaintiff was relieving the defendant from liability for *negligence*.[325]

In warranty law, disclaimers are addressed by § 2–316 of the Uniform Commercial Code, which is addressed in an earlier chapter; basically, disclaimers are allowed under state law, provided they are clearly made pursuant to the requirements of Article 2, but

---

316 See §§ 4.7–4.9, above.

317 See Omni Flying Club, Inc. v. Cessna Aircraft Co., 315 N.E.2d 885 (Mass. 1974).

318 See Blanchard v. Monical Mach. Co., 269 N.W.2d 564 (Mich. Ct. App. 1978) ("as is" sale of used machine from defendant to plaintiff's employer).

319 See, e.g., Curtis v. Hoosier Racing Tire Corp., 299 F. Supp. 2d 777 (N.D. Ohio 2004).

320 See §§ 5.2 and 5.3, above.

321 "The consumer's cause of action does not depend upon the validity of his contract with the person from whom he acquires the product, and it is not affected by any disclaimer or other agreement . . . ." Rest. (2d) Torts § 402A cmt. *m*.

322 The Products Liability Rest. § 18 provides:

> Disclaimers and limitations of remedies by product sellers or other distributors, waivers by product purchasers, and other similar contractual exculpations, oral or written, do not bar or reduce otherwise valid products liability claims against sellers or other distributors of new products for harm to persons.

323 See Owen & Davis on Products Liability § 25:14. See generally McNichols, Who Says that Strict Tort Disclaimers Can Never Be Effective? The Courts Cannot Agree, 28 Okla. L. Rev. 494 (1975); Note, 10 Tulsa L.J. 612 (1975).

324 550 F. Supp. 805 (N.D. Ill. 1982).

325 Compare Westlye v. Look Sports, Inc., 22 Cal. Rptr. 2d 781 (Ct. App. 1993) (ski equipment rental disclaimer against public policy); Ghionis v. Deer Valley Resort Co., 839 F. Supp. 789 (D. Utah 1993) (notwithstanding release, skier not aware that her rented bindings would fail to release because they were incompatible with her boots); Moore v. Sitzmark Corp., 555 N.E.2d 1305 (Ind. Ct. App. 1990) (skier's signature on release simply acknowledged laws of physics and did not show she knew of defect in bindings).

their use is substantially restricted by a number of state law provisions and by federal law in most personal injury cases involving consumer goods.[326]

Fireman's Rule

One special, narrow doctrine that concerns assumption of risk in its "primary" or no-duty sense[327] is the "fireman's rule," now sometimes called the "firefighter's rule," which applies to firefighters, police officers, and other professionals trained to rescue and preserve persons and property in emergency situations.[328] Most states still hold that emergency professionals, such as a firefighter injured in fighting a fire, may not recover against a party who tortiously caused the fire or other exigency because the firefighter is deemed to have assumed the normal risks incident to the job.[329] But, the fireman's rule generally will not apply, and so will not bar recovery, if the product defect that injures the rescue professional did not also cause the fire or other emergency situation that provided the need for the plaintiff's professional skills.[330]

§ 13.5 MISUSE

A user's "misuse" of a product—using it in a plainly improper manner, or for a plainly improper purpose—often bars recovery on a products liability claim.[331] Like assumption of risk, product misuse is thus a powerful common-law conduct "defense" in products liability litigation. Although some jurisdictions have merged misuse into comparative fault, so that some or all forms of product misuse serve generally to reduce

---

[326] See ch. 4, above.

[327] See Prosser and Keeton on Torts § 68, at 481, 496–97.

[328] See Heidt, When Plaintiffs Are Premium Planners for Their Injuries: A Fresh Look at the Fireman's Rule, 82 Ind. L.J. 745 (2007); Prosser and Keeton on Torts § 61, at 429.

[329] See, e.g., Colbert v. Norcold, Inc., 726 Fed. Appx. 956 (4th Cir. 2018) (Va. law) (volunteer firefighter injured by explosion caused by fire in recreational vehicle; Virginia's fireman's rule applies to products liability claims, barring recovery); Brown v. General Elec. Corp., 648 F. Supp. 470 (M.D. Ga. 1986) (while fighting fire caused by defective coffee pot, fireman injured from jumping off roof of burning building that exploded); White v. Edmond, 971 F.2d 681 (11th Cir. 1992) (Ga. law) (firefighter injured when car's shock absorbers exploded in fire; doctrine barred recovery). Note, however, that courts continue to abolish this doctrine. See, e.g., Roma v. United States, 344 F.3d 352 (3d Cir. 2003) (N.J. law).

[330] See, e.g., Holloway v. Midland Risk Ins. Co., 832 So.2d 1004 (La. Ct. App. 2002) (firefighter injured when rescue equipment malfunctioned; doctrine not applied since injury from defective equipment not reasonably within line of duty); McKernan v. General Motors Corp., 3 P.3d 1261 (Kan. 2000) (injured while fighting car fire by explosion of gas-filled strut for hood, firefighter could maintain action against automaker; firefighter rule did not bar suit); Labrie v. Pace Membership Warehouse, Inc., 678 A.2d 867, 868 (R.I. 1996) (thorough review of rule: "we conclude that the Superior Court responded to a false alarm when it used the firefighter's rule to torch plaintiff's complaint"); Hauboldt v. Union Carbide Corp., 467 N.W.2d 508 (Wis. 1991) (defective acetylene tank exploded, directly injuring firefighter; doctrine did not apply).

[331] See Adler and Popper, The Misuse of Product Misuse: Victim Blaming at Its Worst, 10 Wm. & Mary Bus. L. Rev. 337 (2019); Calnan, A Consumer-Use Approach to Products Liability, 33 U. Mem. L. Rev. 755 (2003); King, Outlaws and Outlier Doctrines: The Serious Misconduct Bar in Tort Law, 43 Wm. & Mary L. Rev. 1011 (2002); McNichols, The Relevance of the Plaintiff's Misconduct in Strict Tort Products Liability, the Advent of Comparative Responsibility, and the Proposed Restatement (Third) of Torts, 47 Okla. L. Rev. 201 (1994) (comprehensive review and consideration of early draft of Third Restatement); Fischer, Products Liability—Applicability of Comparative Negligence to Misuse and Assumption of the Risk, 43 Mo. L. Rev. 643 (1978); Twerski, The Many Faces of Misuse: An Inquiry Into the Emerging Doctrine of Comparative Causation, 29 Mercer L. Rev. 403 (1978); Vargo, The Defenses to Strict Liability in Tort: A New Vocabulary with an Old Meaning, 29 Mercer L. Rev. 447 (1978); Noel, Defective Products: Abnormal Use, Contributory Negligence, and Assumption of Risk, 25 Vand. L. Rev. 93 (1972); Annot., 65 A.L.R.4th 263 (1988) (comprehensive treatment of misuse "defense" in products liability). On related regulatory issues, see Adler, Redesigning People Versus Redesigning Products: The Consumer Product Safety Commission Addresses Product Misuse, 11 J.L. & Pol. 79 (1995).

a plaintiff's damages rather than to bar recovery altogether, a user's[332] *unforeseeable* misuse is widely considered to be an absolute bar to recovery.[333] While product misuse developed as a common-law doctrine, products liability reform statutes in several states reduce damages[334] or bar liability[335] in cases of a plaintiff's product misuse.

The basic idea of the misuse doctrine is that products are necessarily designed to do certain limited tasks, within certain limited environments of use, and that no product can be made safe for every purpose, manner, or extent of use. Considerations of cost and practicality limit every product's range of effective and safe use, which is a fundamental fact of life that consumers readily understand. Consumers know that products may be used safely only for certain limited purposes; that they should be used properly and within the manufacturer's warnings and instructions; and that using products beyond their capabilities may cause them to break, overheat, or otherwise fail in a possibly dangerous way. If a user chooses to put a product to a type or manner of use the product cannot fairly be expected to withstand,[336] and the user is injured as a result, he or she cannot reasonably demand that the manufacturer (and, indirectly, other consumers) shoulder the economic consequences of the loss.[337] "We cannot charge the manufacturer

---

[332] This chapter addresses the role of product misuse as a *user* misconduct "defense." Misuse by a third party (including product alteration and modification) raises issues of intervening (and possibly superseding) causation and so is examined in the chapter on proximate cause. See § 12.3, above. See generally Annots., 28 A.L.R.7th Art. 5 (2017); 41 A.L.R.3d 1251 (1972).

[333] See Products Liability Rest. § 2, Reporters' Note to cmt. *p*. The Uniform Comparative Fault Act's inclusion of *foreseeable* misuse as a form of "fault" subject to comparison means that *un*foreseeable misuse remains outside the comparative system and so is a total bar to liability. See also Powers v. Lycoming Engines, 272 F.R.D. 414, 429–30 (E.D. Pa. 2011) (collecting cases).

[334] At least Idaho, Missouri, and Wisconsin have enacted such legislation, and this is the approach of the Uniform Comparative Fault Act which reduces a plaintiff's damages, however, only on account of *foreseeable* product misuse.

[335] At least Arizona, Colorado, Indiana, Michigan, Montana, and Tennessee have such statutes, cited in § 13.1, above. Mont. Code Ann. § 27–1–719(5)(b) and (6), provides sellers with an affirmative defense if "[t]he product was unreasonably misused by the user or consumer," which shall "mitigate or bar recovery [in] accordance with the principles of comparative negligence."

[336] See, e.g., Cavanagh v. F.W. Woolworth Co., 32 N.E.2d 256 (Mass. 1941), where the court suggests that the plaintiff was demanding more of a rubber bottle stopper than he fairly could expect.

[337] See, e.g., Venezia v. Miller Brewing Co., 626 F.2d 188, 190–91 (1st Cir. 1980) (Mass. law). See generally Findlay v. Copeland Lumber Co., 509 P.2d 28, 31 (Or. 1973) ("Misuse, to bar recovery, must be a use or handling so unusual that the average consumer could not reasonably expect the product to be designed and manufactured to withstand it—a use which the seller, therefore, need not anticipate and provide for."); Holford, The Limits of Strict Liability for Product Design and Manufacture, 52 Tex. L. Rev. 81, 89 (1973):

> If a consumer employs a product in some extraordinary manner, and encounters a known danger in the course of his conduct, the doctrine of product misuse will bar recovery from the manufacturer. The adventurous consumer has voluntarily placed himself in a category distinct from the normal consumer who forgoes the pleasure and convenience of using products in novel but dangerous ways. The rationale of loss distribution does not reach his case because it is unfair to force consumers who forgo these additional benefits to subsidize those individuals who voluntarily take the additional risks. [The misuse defense] fall[s] into the general category of assumption of risk.

See generally Owen, The Moral Foundations of Products Liability Law: Toward First Principles, 68 Notre Dame L. Rev. 427, 476 (1993) (consumer who puts product to "uniquely adventuresome use that he should know may exceed the product's capabilities . . . has no fair claim to compensation from the maker, diminishing the autonomy of the maker's owners and other consumers, because the accident was caused by the victim's greed in demanding greater usefulness from the product than other consumers sought and greater usefulness than was reflected in the price he paid").

of a knife when it is used as a toothpick and the user complains because the sharp edge cuts."[338]

The misuse doctrine is difficult to apply in a principled manner, as discussed below, but the general doctrine is easy to state: manufacturers and other sellers are subject to responsibility for harm from product uses that are reasonably foreseeable but not for harm from unforeseeable product use.[339]

Development of the Doctrine

The misuse doctrine runs long and deep through products liability law, having shielded manufacturers from liability for more than a century.[340] For most of the twentieth century, the role of a user's misuse of a product in a personal injury action against the supplier was unclear. Many early courts simply treated product misuse as an issue going to proximate cause,[341] and many courts addressed the problem by limiting a seller's liability to a product's "intended" uses.[342] For example, users in early cases were barred from recovery on claims that cleaning fluid was intended to be applied to inanimate objects, not splashed in the eye;[343] that the entire edge of a grinding wheel was intended to be applied against an object being ground, not just the edge of the edge;[344] and that allegedly uncrashworthy automobiles were intended for driving on the highway, not for crashing into trees.[345]

In the 1950s and 1960s, courts and commentators increasingly framed the misuse issue as whether a user had put a product to an "abnormal" use,[346] although the "intended" use formulation of the misuse concept continued to linger on in some jurisdictions.[347] Through much of the 1960s, 1970s, and even into the 1980s, as the role of product misuse evolved and began to come into focus, all three terms and concepts—

---

[338] General Motors Corp. v. Hopkins, 548 S.W.2d 344, 349 (Tex. 1977), overruled on other grounds by Turner v. General Motors Corp., 584 S.W.2d 844 (Tex. 1979), and by Duncan v. Cessna Aircraft Co., 665 S.W.2d 414 (Tex. 1984).

[339] See, e.g., Hackney v. Pendu Mfg., Inc., 146 N.E.3d 1016, 1026 (Ind. Ct. App. 2020) (plaintiff's multiple failures to follow the wood cutting machine's warnings and instructions were not reasonably foreseeable); Nelson v. Glock, Inc., 2013 WL 425082 (W.D. Okla. 2013) (by holding slide of semi-automatic revolver with hand while firing, in attempt to simulate malfunction during weapon training, state trooper unforeseeably misused revolver); Presnell v. Cottrell, Inc., 2013 WL 878679, at *3 (E.D. Mich. 2013) (statutory provision; use was unforeseeable).

[340] "It seems quite clearly established where the purchaser, actually knowing the defective nature of the article, puts it to a use for which it is unfit and unsafe, any injury received therefrom is due to his misuse and not to the act of him who created the defect." Bohlen, The Basis of Affirmative Obligations in the Law of Tort (pt. 3), 53 U. Pa. L. Rev. 337, 343 (1905).

[341] See, e.g., Waterman v. Liederman, 60 P.2d 881 (Cal. Ct. App. 1936) (wild driving on tire). See generally Prosser, The Fall of the Citadel (Strict Liability to the Consumer), 50 Minn. L. Rev. 791, 824 (1966).

[342] At least one modern court has clung to this quaint limitation on claims based on strict liability in tort. See Hysick v. Razor USA, LLC, 2017 WL 4084054, at *3 (M.D. Pa. 2017) (quoting Pennsylvania Dep't of Gen. Servs. v. U.S. Mineral Prods. Co., 898 A.2d 590, 600 (Pa. 2006) ("the general rule is that there is no strict liability in Pennsylvania relative to non-intended uses even where foreseeable by a manufacturer"). On foreseeability and "intended use," see also § 12.2, above, and § 17.3, below.

[343] Sawyer v. Pine Oil Sales Co., 155 F.2d 855 (5th Cir. 1946) (La. law). Accord Rest. (2d) Torts § 395 cmt. *j*. *Contra* Haberly v. Reardon Co., 319 S.W.2d 859 (Mo. 1958) (paint).

[344] Zesch v. Abrasive Co., 193 S.W.2d 581 (Mo. 1946).

[345] Crashworthiness is addressed in § 17.3, below.

[346] See W. Prosser, The Law of Torts § 102 (4th ed. 1971); Noel, Defective Products: Abnormal Use, Contributory Negligence, and Assumption of Risk, 25 Vand. L. Rev. 93 (1972).

[347] See, e.g., Bazerman v. Gardall Safe Corp., 609 N.Y.S.2d 610 (App. Div. 1994); Myers v. American Seating Co., 637 So.2d 771 (La. Ct. App. 1994); Allen v. Chance Mfg. Co., 494 N.E.2d 1324 (Mass. 1986); Codling v. Paglia, 298 N.E.2d 622 (N.Y. 1973); Greenman v. Yuba Power Prods., Inc., 377 P.2d 897, 901 (Cal. 1963).

intended use, abnormal use, and misuse—shared an uncomfortable coexistence.[348] By the late 1980s and 1990s, however, many courts had worked out a generally accepted definition of the "misuse" doctrine—product suppliers are *not* responsible for harm from uses that are *un*foreseeable, but they *are* subject to liability for harm from uses that *are* deemed reasonably foreseeable—a formulation that widely prevails in products liability law today.

Theory of Liability

Although the precise formulation of the product misuse doctrine remained in ferment in many jurisdictions late into the twentieth century, the correlative ideas of restricting a seller's responsibility to normal or expectable product uses, on the one hand, and making users responsible for their injuries caused by particularly unusual product uses, on the other hand, have been central pillars of products liability law for many years. The *Restatement (Second) of Torts* provided, in negligent manufacturing cases, that a manufacturer is subject to liability for harm caused by a chattel's "lawful use in a manner and for a purpose for which it is supplied";[349] in negligent warning cases, for harm from "use of the chattel in the manner for which . . . it is supplied";[350] and in negligent design cases, for harm from "probable use."[351] In warranty law, as examined later,[352] the Uniform Commercial Code built the absence of misuse into the concept of a product's "merchantability," which is defined most broadly in terms of a product's fitness for its "ordinary" purposes.[353]

In strict liability in tort, an original premise of manufacturer liability was that an injury arose from a *proper* use of the product. As Judge Traynor observed, in *Greenman v. Yuba Power Products, Inc.*:[354]

> Implicit in the machine's presence on the market . . . was a representation that it would safely do *the jobs for which it was built*. . . . To establish the manufacturer's liability it was sufficient that plaintiff proved that he was injured while using the Shopsmith *in a way it was intended to be used* as a result of a defect in design and manufacture of which plaintiff was not aware that made the Shopsmith *unsafe for its intended use*.[355]

In § 402A of the *Restatement (Second) of Torts*, the scope of strict products liability in tort is limited to injuries from proper product uses: products safe for "normal handling" are not defective, and product sellers are shielded from strict liability for injuries

---

348 See, e.g., Dosier v. Wilcox & Crittendon Co., 119 Cal. Rptr. 135 (Ct. App. 1975) (appearing to equate "intended" and "foreseeable"). See generally Noel, Defective Products: Abnormal Use, Contributory Negligence, and Assumption of Risk, 25 Vand. L. Rev. 93 (1972). Misuse concepts and nomenclature continue to remain confused in many jurisdictions. See, e.g., Hart-Albin Co. v. McLees Inc., 870 P.2d 51, 53–54 (Mont. 1994) (interpreting statutory "unreasonable misuse" phrase in terms of intended use, abnormal use, and unforeseeable use).

349 See Rest. (2d) Torts § 395.

350 See Rest. (2d) Torts § 388.

351 See Rest. (2d) Torts § 398, special application of § 395.

352 See § 13.6, below.

353 See UCC § 2–314(2)(c). See, e.g., Phillips v. Cricket Lighters, 883 A.2d 439, 444–45 (Pa. 2005) (ordinary purpose of disposable lighter "certainly was not to be a two year old child's plaything" and its tragic misuse did "not alter the ordinary purpose"). See generally § 4.3, above.

354 377 P.2d 897 (Cal. 1963).

355 Id. at 901 (emphasis added). The California court later altered this formulation of the scope of liability to include uses that are reasonably foreseeable as well as intended. See Cronin v. J.B.E. Olson Corp., 501 P.2d 1153, 1157 (Cal. 1972).

resulting from "mishandling," "over-consumption," "excessive use," and a failure to read and heed an adequate warning.[356] The *Third Restatement* succinctly limits responsibility in black-letter definitions of both design and warning defects to "the foreseeable risks of harm posed by the product,"[357] and it makes clear that courts bar recovery in design litigation for injuries that occur "[w]hen a product is put to an unforeseeable use."[358]

Whether Misuse Is a "Defense"; Burden of Pleading and Proof

One reason the doctrine of misuse is difficult to apply is that there is no agreement on just what kind of legal doctrine it really is. While many lawyers speak loosely of a product misuse "defense," the common-law principle of product misuse was traditionally—and may more accurately be viewed as—a liability-limiting principle concerning the scope of a defendant's duty, which involves the issues of negligence, product defect, scope of warranty, and proximate causation.[359] When misuse is held to be part of a plaintiff's prima facie case, as it is in many states,[360] plaintiffs properly should be required to plead and prove that the accident arose out of a reasonably foreseeable product use.[361] Yet, a fair number of jurisdictions take the position (sometimes switching from prior views) that misuse should be treated as an affirmative

---

[356] See Rest. (2d) Torts § 402A cmt. *g* (defectiveness not established by harm from "mishandling"); cmt. *h* (product not defective when safe for "normal handling"; no liability for injuries from "abnormal handling" or "abnormal consumption"); cmt. *i* (unreasonable danger not established by harm from "over-consumption"); and cmt. *j* (no duty to warn of generally known risks of excessive use; seller may assume warnings will be read and heeded, and product with adequate warning is neither defective nor unreasonably dangerous).

[357] Products Liability Rest. § 2(b) and (c), respectively. Quite obviously, for a risk to be foreseeable, it must ordinarily result from a foreseeable product *use*. See id. cmt. *m*:

> *m. Reasonably foreseeable uses and risks in design and warning claims.* Subsections (b) and (c) impose liability only when the product is put to uses that it is reasonable to expect a seller or distributor to foresee. Product sellers and distributors are not required to foresee and take precautions against every conceivable mode of use and abuse to which their products might be put.

See also id. cmt. *p*.

[358] Products Liability Rest. § 2, Reporters' Note to cmt. *p*.

[359] See, e.g., Rodeheaver v. CNH Am., LLC, 2007 WL 465212, at *7 (D. Md. 2007) ("misuse negates the element of a defect"); Jeld-Wen, Inc. v. Gamble, 501 S.E.2d 393 (Va. 1998) (duty); Jurado v. Western Gear Works, 619 A.2d 1312, 1318–19 (N.J. 1993) (duty, product defect, and proximate cause). See generally Wade, On the Nature of Strict Tort Liability for Products, 44 Miss. L.J. 825, 846 (1973) (product defect, proximate cause, and scope of risk); Prosser, The Fall of the Citadel (Strict Liability to the Consumer), 50 Minn. L. Rev. 791, 824 (1966) (product defect and proximate cause); Dobbs, Law of Torts § 370, at 1076; Products Liability Rest. § 2 cmts. *m* and *p*, and Reporters' Note to cmt. *p* (duty):

> When a product is put to an unforeseeable use and the plaintiff claims that the product should have been designed to avoid injury when put to such a use, the courts agree that liability will not attach. There is widespread understanding that misuse in this context goes to the basic duty issue.
>
> Courts and commentators have had real difficulty in ascertaining and explaining how different forms of misuse figure into the rubrics of duty, defectiveness, proximate cause, and affirmative defenses. The complexity of the issues, particularly in the context of comparative fault, is evident by the confusion in many of the decisions. See, e.g., Jimenez v. Sears, Roebuck & Co., 904 P.2d 861 (Ariz. 1995) (separate opinions by three justices); Jurado v. Western Gear Works, 619 A.2d 1312 (N.J. 1993). Confusion still abounds. See, e.g., Reott v. Asia Trend, Inc., 55 A.3d 1088, 1096–1101 (Pa. 2012); Wedgewood v. U.S. Filter/Whittier, Inc., 2011 WL 2150102 (Neb. Ct. App. 2011).

[360] See Noel, Defective Products: Abnormal Use, Contributory Negligence, and Assumption of Risk, 25 Vand. L. Rev. 93 (1972). Cf. Products Liability Rest. § 2 cmt. *m*. *But cf.* id. cmt. *p*. See note 370, below.

[361] See, e.g., Newman v. Utility Trailer & Equip. Co., 564 P.2d 674, 676–77 (Or. 1977) (en banc):

> Before a manufacturer or other seller is strictly liable for injury inflicted by a product, the product must have been put to a foreseeable use. As an example: if a shovel is used to prop open a heavy door, but, because of the way the shovel was designed, it is inadequate to the task and the door swings shut and crushes the user's hand, no responsibility for the injury results by reason of the shovel's not being designed to prop open doors since it was not reasonably foreseeable by the manufacturer or seller that it would be so used.

defense.[362] Moreover, all but one of the several states that have statutory reform provisions on misuse also treat it as an affirmative defense[363] on which the defendant has the burden of pleading and proof.[364]

Courts and commentators long have striven to work out a clear and sound doctrine of misuse, often without success. The struggle with the meaning of the doctrine is illustrated in many judicial opinions. For example, the Colorado Supreme Court concluded that "the defense of misuse . . . is a particularized defense requiring that the plaintiff's use of the product be unforeseeable and unintended as well as the cause of the injuries,"[365] and further observed that "[m]isuse . . . is a question of causation. Regardless of the defective condition, if any, of a manufacturer's product, a manufacturer will not be liable if an unforeseeable misuse of the product caused the injuries."[366] The dissent characterized misuse as an "affirmative defense."[367] By contrast, in another case, the New Jersey Supreme Court concluded that "[t]he absence of misuse is part of the plaintiff's case," that "[m]isuse is not an affirmative defense," and that "the plaintiff has the burden of showing that there was no misuse or that the misuse was objectively foreseeable."[368] In short, courts continue to disagree on the true role of plaintiff misuse in products liability litigation, and the perplexities are magnified in jurisdictions that attempt to blend misuse into a system of comparative fault.[369]

When all is said and done, there probably is no logical way to avoid treating the absence of misuse as bearing on the scope of a defendant's responsibility and, hence, as part of a plaintiff's case-in-chief.[370] Nor does there seem to be any sound reason for a court to try to work around the logic in order to convert the doctrine into an affirmative defense. While one might think at first that plaintiffs would be advantaged if misuse were treated as an affirmative defense (giving the defendant the burden of pleading and proof) rather than its absence part of the plaintiff's case, the burden allocation issue

---

[362] See, e.g., Susman v. Goodyear Tire & Rubber Co., 2019 WL 5087279, at *3 (D. Neb. 2019) ("To prove the affirmative defense of misuse, a defendant must show '(1) that the plaintiff used the product as claimed by the defendant, (2) that the defendant could not reasonably have foreseen such a use, and (3) that this misuse by the plaintiff was a proximate cause of his own injury.' "); Reott v. Asia Trend, Inc., 55 A.3d 1088, 1101 (Pa. 2012) (Pennsylvania's version of misuse, called "highly reckless conduct," is an affirmative defense on which defendant has burden of pleading and proof); Bookhamer v. Sunbeam Prods., Inc., 913 F. Supp. 2d 809, 816–17 (N.D. Cal. 2012) (burden of proof on defendants).

[363] See § 13.1, above. Compare Zablotsky, The Appropriate Role of Plaintiff Misuse in Products Liability Causes of Action, 10 Touro L. Rev. 183 (1993) (collecting cases, and stating that most courts properly hold misuse to be an affirmative defense).

[364] See, e.g., Stevenson v. Kettler Int'l, Inc., 2006 WL 2536584, at *2 (Conn. Super. Ct. 2006) (granting plaintiff's motion to strike defendants' misuse defense; defendants "failed to plead any facts to support" the allegation of misuse).

[365] Uptain v. Huntington Lab, Inc., 723 P.2d 1322, 1325 (Colo. 1986).

[366] Id.

[367] Id. at 1332.

[368] Jurado v. Western Gear Works, 619 A.2d 1312, 1317 (N.J. 1993).

[369] For one court's valiant efforts to unravel the mysteries of how the doctrine of product misuse fits into the comparative fault system, compare the different judges' opinions in Jimenez v. Sears, Roebuck & Co., 904 P.2d 861 (Ariz. 1995).

[370] See, e.g., Alsip v. Louisville Ladder, Inc., 2010 WL 2560031, at *2 (D. Md. 2010); D'Amario v. Ford Motor Co., 806 So.2d 424, 431 n.9 (Fla. 2001) (misuse pertains to causation); Jurado v. W. Gear Works, 619 A.2d 1312, 1317 (N.J. 1993) ("The absence of misuse is part of the plaintiff's case. Misuse is not an affirmative defense. Thus, the plaintiff has the burden of showing that there was no misuse or that the misuse was objectively foreseeable."); Ellsworth v. Sherne Lingerie, Inc., 495 A.2d 348 (Md. 1985); Payne v. Soft Sheen Prods., Inc., 486 A.2d 712, 725–26 (D.C. 1985); Hughes v. Magic Chef, Inc., 288 N.W.2d 542, 546 (Iowa 1980) (abandoning view that misuse is affirmative defense for view that it is part of plaintiff's burden to prove product defect and causation).

ordinarily is of little practical consequence in products liability litigation. Defendants typically treat product misuse like any other conduct defense, offering evidence and argument on the issue whether or not the plaintiff has pleaded the absence of misuse in the complaint. In a jurisdiction that requires a plaintiff to plead the absence of misuse, it is difficult to imagine a court refusing to allow a plaintiff to amend a complaint to include this aspect of the claim. More importantly, because plaintiffs rarely fail to plead proximate causation—that the defendant's negligence, breach of warranty, or a product defect proximately caused the plaintiff's harm—virtually every complaint includes at least an implicit allegation of the absence of misuse. This is because the absence of misuse is built into the concepts of negligence, breach of warranty, product defectiveness, and, especially, proximate causation. Finally, the burden of proof only infrequently provides a significant tactical advantage, and it would seem that defendants might actually prefer to have a clear-cut misuse "defense," especially one created by the legislature, to argue to a court and jury.

The Foreseeability Limitation

"The ways in which a product might be misused are, like the stars, an endless number."[371] In order to protect product sellers from liability for accidents caused by overly adventurous product uses, courts in recent years have almost universally limited responsibility to "foreseeable" product uses.[372] Yet, defining a limitation principle keyed to such a nebulous concept creates intractable problems of application, which is a major reason why the misuse defense is so much easier to state than to apply. Indeed, the innate elusiveness of "foreseeability" as the doctrine's definitional standard—its supposed constraint—endows the standard with very little content for determining the proper reach of liability in actual cases. Thus, because product misuse is defined in terms of foreseeability, and foreseeability is such an illusory notion,[373] the doctrine effectively is without a meaningful definition.[374] At the end of the day, however, as in "defining" proximate causation in terms of foreseeable risk,[375] there is at least a bit of comfort in

---

[371] Goodman v. Stalfort, Inc., 411 F. Supp. 889, 894–95 (D.N.J. 1976) (Biunno, J.) (plaintiff burned by flashback when he poured charcoal fluid on grill after enlarging can's opening with tine of garden tool to increase its flow), rev'd in part on other grounds, 564 F.2d 89 (3d Cir. 1977).

[372] The foreseeability limitation on the product misuse doctrine has long been recognized. See James, Products Liability (pt. 1), 34 Tex. L. Rev. 44, 54 (1955) (citing cases from as early as 1852).

[373] See, e.g., Venezia v. Miller Brewing Co., 626 F.2d 188, 191 (1st Cir. 1980) (Mass. law); Moran v. Faberge, Inc., 332 A.2d 11, 26 (Md. 1975) (O'Donnell, J., dissenting): "It seems to me that the majority has fallen into the pitfall, recognized by Professor Prosser, who, in undertaking to analyze the treatment by the various courts of the illusory concept of 'foreseeability' and noting the confusion resulting therefrom, states:"

> "Some 'margin of leeway' has to be left for the unusual and the unexpected. But this has opened a very wide door; and the courts have taken so much advantage of the leeway that it can scarcely be doubted that a great deal of what the ordinary man would regard as freakish, bizarre, and unpredictable has crept within the bounds of liability by the simple device of permitting the jury to foresee at least its very broad, and vague, general outlines." W. Prosser, Torts, § 43, at 269 (4th ed. 1971).

[374] Pennsylvania's strange approach does not help. See Reott v. Asia Trend, Inc., 55 A.3d 1088, 1096–97 (Pa. 2012) ("To establish misuse of the product, the defendant must show that the use was 'unforeseeable or outrageous.' Highly reckless conduct is akin to evidence of misuse and requires the defendant to prove that the use was so extraordinary and unforeseeable as to constitute a superseding cause.").

[375] See § 12.2, above.

the moral grounding[376] and practicable flexibility in defining the outer reaches of a manufacturer's responsibility in terms of foreseeability.[377]

The best the courts have been able to do, in placing at least the appearance of some halter on the foreseeability concept, is to modify it with the word "reasonable," thus limiting a manufacturer's responsibility to accidents resulting from uses that are "reasonably foreseeable."[378] Such a definition of the standard surely may be faulted for providing no further touchstone for deciding cases, but a reasonableness modification of foreseeability is plainly better than leaving it stark naked. So modifying foreseeability usefully reminds courts and juries that there are indeed reasonable limits to the kinds of uses a manufacturer fairly must consider when making design and warning decisions.

The intrinsic vagueness of the foreseeability concept in the misuse context, which diminishes its usefulness for either ascribing or predicting liability, has been lamented by the courts.[379] While some uses, especially common ones,[380] are clearly foreseeable, and others, particularly those that are especially bizarre, are clearly unforeseeable, the great majority of uses fall in the "vast middle ground of product uses about which reasonable minds could disagree as to whether they are or should be foreseeable to the manufacturer."[381] The decisions go all over the map on the foreseeability of misuse issue, and the best that can be said is that a prudent judge will almost always recognize product misuse as a question of fact for a jury to decide.[382]

---

376 See Owen, Figuring Foreseeability, 44 Wake Forest L. Rev. 1277 (2009).

377 See Twerski, The Many Faces of Misuse: An Inquiry Into the Emerging Doctrine of Comparative Causation, 29 Mercer L. Rev. 403, 426 (1978).

378 See, e.g., Wilda v. JLG Indus., Inc., 2021 WL 392705, at *164 (N.D. Ill. 2021) ("neither intended nor reasonably foreseeable"); Holbrook v. Prodomax Automation Ltd., 2021 WL 4260622, at *8 (W.D. Mich. 2021) (robot crushed assembly line worker's head when worker climbed over a wall separating robot's work zone; assembly line manufacturer could reasonably foresee workers climbing over walls between zones because it in fact foresaw and guarded against that risk); Bourne v. Marty Gilman, Inc., 452 F.3d 632, 635 (7th Cir. 2006) (Ind. law) ("not reasonably expected"); Butz v. Lynch, 762 So.2d 1214, 1215 (La. Ct. App. 2000) ("reasonably anticipated use"). Compare McGarrigle v. Mercury Marine, 838 F. Supp. 2d 282, 295 (D.N.J. 2011) ("objectively foreseeable"). See also Iliades v. Dieffenbacher N. Am. Inc., 915 N.W.2d 338, 344 (Mich. 2018) ("[F]oreseeability depends on whether a reasonable person 'could anticipate that a given event might occur under certain conditions.' When dealing with the foreseeability of a product's misuse in particular, the crucial inquiry is whether, at the time the product was manufactured, the manufacturer was aware, or should have been aware, of that misuse.").

379 See, e.g., Venezia v. Miller Brewing Co., 626 F.2d 188, 191 (1st Cir. 1980) (Mass. law) (" 'In a sense, in retrospect almost nothing is unforeseeable.' . . . One with the time and imagination and aided by hindsight no doubt can conjure up all sorts of arguably 'foreseeable' misuses of a variety of otherwise reasonable safe products."). See also Moran v. Faberge, Inc., 332 A.2d 11, 26 (Md. 1975) (O'Donnell, J., dissenting).

380 If people regularly use a product in a dangerous, unintended manner, the use likely is foreseeable. See, e.g., Tanner v. Shoupe, 596 N.W.2d 805 (Wis. Ct. App. 1999) (jury might find pounding on battery caps to be foreseeable); Lamer v. McKee Indus., 721 P.2d 611, 615 (Alaska 1986) ("a manufacturer should not be relieved of responsibility simply because it closes its eyes to the way its products are actually used by consumers"); Gootee v. Colt Indus., 712 F.2d 1057, 1065 (6th Cir. 1983) (Mich. law) (use of revolver half-cock as safety is virtually universal practice).

381 Moran v. Faberge, Inc., 332 A.2d 11, 16 (Md. 1975).

382 See, e.g., Thompson v. Polaris Indus. Inc., 2019 WL 2173965, at *3 (D. Ariz. 2019) ("Whether misuse of a product is reasonably foreseeable is generally a question of fact for the jury."); Richardson v. Whirlpool Corp., 2017 WL 2333997, at *5 (Cal. Ct. App. 2017), noncitable (question for jury whether unforeseeable that a hyperactive dog would be left alone at home with combustible dog food sitting on a stove top); Collins v. Navistar, Inc., 155 Cal. Rptr. 3d 137, 152–55 (Ct. App. 2013); Tunnell v. Ford Motor Co., 330 F. Supp. 2d 748, 756 (W.D. Va. 2004) ("The jury needs to consider all the facts relevant to how the collision happened to resolve the question of fact regarding the misuse defense."); In re Sept. 11 Litig., 280 F. Supp. 2d 279 (S.D.N.Y. 2003) (Va. law) (declining to grant summary judgment to aircraft manufacturer); Smith v. Bryco Arms, 33 P.3d 638 (N.M. Ct. App. 2001) (although shooting by "friend" is misuse of firearm, foreseeability is for jury). *Contra* Estate of Simpson v. General Motors, LLC, 2020 WL 39978, at *11 (Mich. Ct. App. 2020) (state statute provides

Accordingly, whether advising a manufacturer or other seller trying to comply with the law when designing and marketing its products, or a plaintiff contemplating a lawsuit, a lawyer can only guess how the foreseeability issue will be resolved at trial. A prudent lawyer thus will hesitate to predict whether a judge or jury would find that a manufacturer reasonably should foresee that a young boy will hurl a beer bottle against a telephone pole;[383] a teenage girl will scent a candle by pouring cologne on it below the flame;[384] a woman wearing a cotton flannelette nightgown inside out, with its pockets protruding, will lean over the burner of a stove, causing a pocket to come in contact with a flame;[385] a person will insist on buying shoes that are too small for her feet,[386] on buying automobile tires too large for his rims,[387] on sitting in a chair[388] or an exercise bicycle[389] too frail for one's weight (300 and 500 pounds, respectively), or on standing on an ordinary chair;[390] a car will be driven at 115 m.p.h., go out of control, and injure a third party;[391] a tire, designed for speeds to 85 m.p.h., equipped on a car designed for speeds over 100 m.p.h., will blow out at 100 m.p.h.;[392] a car's emergency brake will be left on undetected at highway speeds long enough to vaporize the hydraulic brake fluid, causing the brakes to fail;[393] or that the foot of an intoxicated person, who falls asleep or passes out while listening to music in his car with the engine running, will press the accelerator and cause the exhaust system to overheat and ignite.[394]

Also unpredictable will be the foreseeability that a person will attempt suicide by closing herself in a car trunk without an inside release latch, change her mind, and be trapped inside for nine days thereafter;[395] an empty Clorox container will be used to store gasoline, will tip over, and the gasoline will be ignited by a spark from the motor of an electric appliance in another room;[396] a patient will walk, against doctor's orders, on his broken leg held together with a defective surgical pin designed only to stabilize the fracture, not to support the weight of a man;[397] a machine will not be properly

that misuse and its foreseeability are legal issues for the court); Lindholm v. BMW of N. Am., LLC, 862 F.3d 648, 652 (8th Cir. 2017) (S.D. law) (plaintiff's misuse of jack was "not foreseeable as a matter of law, given the warnings that accompanied it").

383 See Venezia v. Miller Brewing Co., 626 F.2d 188 (1st Cir. 1980) (Mass. law) (*unforeseeable* as a matter of law).

384 See Moran v. Faberge, Inc., 332 A.2d 11 (Md. 1975) (*foreseeable*—jury could properly so find).

385 See Ellsworth v. Sherne Lingerie, Inc., 495 A.2d 348 (Md. 1985) (*foreseeable* as a matter of law).

386 See Rest. (2d) Torts § 395 cmt. *j* (*unforeseeable*); Dubbs v. Zak Bros. Co., 175 N.E. 626 (Ohio Ct. App. 1931) (same).

387 See McDevitt v. Standard Oil Co. of Tex., 391 F.2d 364 (5th Cir. 1968) (Tex. law) (*unforeseeable*—by implication).

388 See Horne v. Liberty Furniture Co., 452 So.2d 204 (La. Ct. App. 1984) (*foreseeable*—by implication).

389 See Dunne v. Wal-Mart Stores, Inc., 679 So.2d 1034 (La. Ct. App. 1996) (*foreseeable*).

390 See Rest. (2d) Torts § 395, cmt. *k* (*foreseeable*).

391 See Schemel v. General Motors Corp., 384 F.2d 802 (7th Cir. 1967) (Ind. law) (no duty to foresee such grossly careless misuse), overruled on other grounds by Huff v. White Motor Corp., 565 F.2d 104, 106 n.1, 109–10 (7th Cir. 1977) (Ind. law).

392 See LeBouef v. Goodyear Tire & Rubber Co., 451 F. Supp. 253 (W.D. La. 1978) (*foreseeable*).

393 See Knapp v. Hertz Corp., 375 N.E.2d 1349 (Ill. App. Ct. 1978) (*foreseeable*).

394 See Griffith v. Chrysler Corp., 2003 WL 21500037 (Ohio Ct. App. 2003) (*unforeseeable*).

395 See Daniell v. Ford Motor Co., 581 F. Supp. 728 (D.N.M. 1984) (*unforeseeable* as a matter of law).

396 See Taylor v. General Elec. Co., 505 A.2d 190 (N.J. Super. Ct. App. Div. 1986) (*foreseeable* as a matter of law).

397 See Stewart v. Von Solbrig Hosp., Inc., 321 N.E.2d 428 (Ill. App. Ct. 1974) (misuse as a matter of law).

maintained;[398] a person will pour hot Wesson Oil from the skillet back into the bottle, and then recap the bottle, causing it to explode;[399] "burning alcohol," sold only for professional dental use, will be drunk by penal farm inmate dental assistants who then go blind;[400] a screen on a second story window will not withstand the pressure of a baby boy waving good-bye to his mother;[401] a doctor will transplant synthetic fibers, normally used for wigs and hairpieces, into a patient's scalp as a treatment for baldness, causing irritation and infection;[402] a grocery shopper who trips will hope that a shopping cart does not scoot away when he grabs for it to save himself from falling;[403] the owner of a riding lawn mower will attach a wooden "dog box" to the mower and place a 2-year-old child in the box who will fall out and be run over by the mower;[404] a youth will tilt or rock a soft-drink vending machine, to dispense a can without payment, causing the machine to fall upon and kill him;[405] a teenage boy will hang himself with a rope on a swing set as a joke to impress the girls;[406] a youth, thinking the safety is on, will point a BB gun at his friend's head and pull the trigger;[407] a small child will eat a "spit devil" firework wrapped in plain red paper that looks like candy;[408] a baby will drink bright red furniture polish that looks like a soft drink;[409] an adult will stand on a closet shelf;[410] a child will open and stand on an oven door to see what is cooking on the stove, causing the stove and a pot of boiling water to topple over;[411] a boy, while riding a canister vacuum cleaner like a toy car will be injured when his penis slips through an opening into the cleaner's fan;[412] children will play with a gas can without a child-proof top;[413] an adult will be thrown over the handlebars of his bicycle when he applies the front brakes

---

398 See Wilson v. Crouse-Hinds Co., 556 F.2d 870 (8th Cir. 1977) (Iowa law) (*foreseeable*—jury could so find).

399 See Chandler v. Hunt Food & Indus., Prod. Liab. Rep. (CCH) ¶ 5969 (Tenn. 1968) (*unforeseeable*—by implication).

400 See Barnes v. Litton Indus. Prod., Inc., 555 F.2d 1184 (4th Cir. 1977) (Va. law) (*foreseeable*—jury could properly so find).

401 See Jeld-Wen, Inc. v. Gamble, 501 S.E.2d 393 (Va. 1998) (*unforeseeable*—as a matter of law).

402 See Berg v. Underwood's Hair Adaption Process, Inc., 751 F.2d 136, 137 (2d Cir. 1984) (N.Y. law) (*unforeseeable*—no duty as a matter of law).

403 See Smith v. Technibilt, Inc., 791 S.W.2d 247 (Tex. App. 1990) (*unforeseeable*—as a matter of law).

404 See Erkson v. Sears, Roebuck & Co., 841 S.W.2d 207 (Mo. Ct. App. 1992) (*unforeseeable*—as a matter of law).

405 Compare Oden v. Pepsi Cola Bottling Co., 621 So.2d 953 (Ala. 1993) (*unforeseeable*—one may not impose liability on another for consequences of one's own act of moral turpitude), with Morgan v. Cavalier Acquisition Corp., 432 S.E.2d 915 (N.C. Ct. App. 1993) (*foreseeable*—jury could so find).

406 See Smith v. Holmes, 606 N.E.2d 627 (Ill. App. Ct. 1992) (*unforeseeable*—as a matter of law).

407 See Sherk v. Daisy-Heddon, 450 A.2d 615 (Pa. 1982) (*foreseeable*—but danger was obvious and warned against).

408 See Victory Sparkler & Specialty Co. v. Latimer, 53 F.2d 3 (8th Cir. 1931) (Mo. law) (*foreseeable*—jury could properly so find).

409 See Spruill v. Boyle-Midway, Inc., 308 F.2d 79, 83–84 (4th Cir. 1962) (Va. law) (*foreseeable*—jury could properly so find).

410 See Michael v. G & M Home Builders, Inc., 2003 WL 21634428 (Mich. Ct. App. 2003) (*unforeseeable*—as a matter of law).

411 See Ritter v. Narragansett Elec. Co., 283 A.2d 255 (R.I. 1971) (*foreseeable*—jury could so find).

412 See Larue v. National Union Elec. Corp., 571 F.2d 51 (1st Cir. 1978) (Me. law) (*foreseeable*—jury could properly so find).

413 Compare Simpson v. Standard Container Co., 527 A.2d 1337 (Md. Ct. Spec. App. 1987) (*unforeseeable* as a matter of law, where label on can warned against storing in living area), with Keller v. Welles Dep't Store of Racine, 276 N.W.2d 319, 324 (Wis. Ct. App. 1979) (*foreseeable* that "incurably curious" children might taste gasoline stored in a can on the floor, or, while playing "mow the lawn" or "gas station," might pour gasoline from the can).

suddenly, contrary to explicit instructions that a rider should always apply the rear brakes first;[414] a worker will use a forklift to lift another worker,[415] forget to turn off a dental x-ray processor before leaving for the weekend and so start a fire,[416] or stick his hand into an operating machine;[417] or that terrorists would use fertilizer[418] or an airplane[419] to blow up the World Trade Center.

As difficult as it surely is to predict whether most of these hazards fairly may be classified as "foreseeable," at least the qualification that a risk must be judged *reasonably* foreseeable provides the notion with an explicit limitation, one that offers a depth and richness for embracing the equities of a particular case. An important perspective in evaluating the fairness or foreseeability of particular uses is whether a reasonable consumer might fairly *expect* the product to be able to withstand that use.[420] As one court explained, misuse may be viewed as a "use or handling so unusual that the average consumer could not reasonably expect the product to be designed and manufactured to withstand it—a use which the seller, therefore, need not anticipate and provide for."[421] Applying this principle to deny recovery to a boy whose eye was injured when he threw a discarded beer bottle against a telephone pole, shattering the glass bottle, another court concluded that a reasonable consumer could expect nothing else.[422]

While the consumer expectations test has withered considerably as a principal test of product defectiveness,[423] a consumer expectations standard in some cases provides a sound foundation for defining the limits of use for which a manufacturer fairly may be held accountable.[424] Yet the usefulness of a consumer expectation standard in the misuse context, as when ascertaining a product's defectiveness, depends on the type of product and risk at issue. Consumers have quite well-defined and reasonable expectations about the performance limits of some products, especially more simple ones, but they often have no idea of the limitations of complex products operating in complex environments, such as the extent to which an automobile is or should be able to withstand a particular type of crash.[425] Thus, in a case where the hazards from a particular type of misuse are

---

[414] See Alexander v. Sports Auth., Inc., 2007 WL 1745328, at *9–10 (D. Md. 2007) (*unforeseeable*—as a matter of law).

[415] See Sanders v. Lull Int'l, Inc., 411 F.3d 1266, 1270 (11th Cir. 2005) (Ga. law) (*foreseeable*—jury could properly so find).

[416] See Hartford Fire Ins. Co. v. Dent-X Int'l, Inc., 2007 WL 911841, at *5 (D. Conn. 2007) (*foreseeable*—jury could properly so find).

[417] See Cobbs v. Schwing Am., Inc., 2006 WL 334271, at *5 (E.D. Mich. 2006) (*unforeseeable*—as a matter of law).

[418] See Port Auth. of N.Y. & N.J. v. Arcadian Corp., 189 F.3d 305 (3d Cir. 1999) (N.J. law) (manufacturers of fertilizer products could not reasonably foresee that their products would be used in 1993 World Trade Center terrorist attack).

[419] See In re Sept. 11 Litig., 280 F. Supp. 2d 279, 307 (S.D.N.Y. 2003) (Va. law) (manufacturer of airliner might reasonably foresee that failure to design secure cockpit could facilitate hijacking that would substantially increase risk to people and buildings on ground).

[420] See note 338, above.

[421] Findlay v. Copeland Lumber Co., 509 P.2d 28, 31 (Or. 1973).

[422] "No reasonable consumer would expect anything but that a glass beer bottle . . . would fail to safely withstand the type of purposeful abuse involved here." Venezia v. Miller Brewing Co., 626 F.2d 188, 190–91 (1st Cir. 1980) (Mass. law).

[423] See § 5.6, above.

[424] See § 8.3 (*Modern Application of the Test*), above.

[425] See, e.g., Ramirez v. ITW Food Equip. Grp., LLC, 686 Fed. Appx. 435, 439 (9th Cir. 2017) (Cal. law) ("A manufacturer is liable under the consumer-expectations test for harm arising from 'misuse and abuse of his product, either by the user or by third parties' that is foreseeable."). See generally § 8.6, above.

clear, a court might fairly conclude that the use was not reasonably foreseeable if it was one that a reasonable consumer would not expect the product safely to withstand.

Whether one views the misuse issue in terms of the foreseeability of the plaintiff's use, the presence or absence of a defect, or the presence or absence of proximate cause, the result in each case depends ultimately upon the reasonable foreseeability—or just plain fairness—of the plaintiff's particular use. So, if a manufacturer or other product seller reasonably should have contemplated and guarded against a product hazard, the supplier is properly subject to liability for the harm; but if a user puts a product to a use that cannot fairly be viewed as reasonably foreseeable, the supplier is not liable.

Failure to Follow Warnings and Instructions

A user's failure to follow a manufacturer's warnings of danger or instructions on safe use provides a special form of misuse that ordinarily should bar recovery whenever the danger from noncompliance is evident, the noncompliance is a substantial cause of the plaintiff's harm, and there is no simple way or apparent reason for the manufacturer to design the danger out of the product. Despite common knowledge (and hence foreseeability) that users often ignore warnings and instructions, many courts, and a few legislatures,[426] have long had little sympathy with plaintiffs injured because they ignore warnings and instructions.[427] Comment *j* to the *Restatement (Second) of Torts* § 402A states the rule quite clearly: "Where warning is given, the seller may reasonably assume that it will be read and heeded; and a product bearing such a warning, which is safe for use if it is followed, is not in a defective condition, nor is it unreasonably dangerous." Accordingly, if there was no practical way or reason for a manufacturer to design a danger away, courts have widely ruled that a user's failure to read or heed adequate instructions for safe use, sometimes characterized as "misuse," bars recovery.[428]

---

[426] Statutes in at least Ariz., N.J., and N.C. provide blanket protection to a defendant for injuries resulting from the plaintiff's violation of a warning or instruction. See Ariz. Rev. Stat. Ann. § 12–683; N.J. Stat. Ann. § 2A:58c–4; N.C. Gen. Stat. Ann. § 99B–4(1). New Jersey's provision limits this defense to cases involving "adequate" warnings and instructions; Arizona's and North Carolina's do not, although North Carolina's is limited to warnings and instructions of which the user reasonably should have been aware. A Michigan statute's definition of misuse includes uses contrary to warnings and instructions, Mich. Comp. Laws Ann. § 600.2945(e), but it provides an immunity only for unforeseeable misuse. Id. at § 600.2947(2).

[427] See, e.g., Alsip v. Louisville Ladder, Inc., 2010 WL 2560031, at *2 (D. Md. 2010) ("Misuse includes a failure to heed a manufacturer's warning."). An early example is Fredendall v. Abraham & Straus, Inc., 18 N.E.2d 11 (N.Y. 1938).

[428] "The seller is entitled to have his warnings and instructions followed; and when they are disregarded, and injury results, he is not liable." W. Prosser, The Law of Torts § 102, at 669 (4th ed. 1971). See, e.g., Thompson v. Ryobi Ltd., 2022 WL 721527, at *7 (E.D. Mich. 2022) (plaintiff ignored warnings and instructions when he tilted a generator after removing the gas cap); Hackney v. Pendu Mfg., Inc., 146 N.E.3d 1016, 1020–21 (Ind. Ct. App. 2020) (plaintiff ignored safety training, warnings, and instructions to turn off wood cutting machine before removing scrap wood; to wear close-fitting clothing; and to keep "proper footing and balance at all times" when servicing the machine); Campbell Hausfeld v. Johnson, 109 N.E.3d 953, 955 (Ind. 2018) (piece from grinder cut-off disc injured plaintiff's face and eye after he disregarded safety instructions to use proper eyewear, attach a guard for the cut-off disc, and limit attachments to those rated minimum 25,000 rpm); Mine Safety Appliance Co. v. Holmes, 171 So.3d 442, 453–57 (Miss. 2015) (plaintiff ignored instructions to replace his respirator filter each time he noticed resistance while breathing and used the same filter over the six years he jackhammered); Perez v. VAS S.p.A, 115 Cal. Rptr. 3d 590, 603 (Ct. App. 2010) (worker's hand crushed by paper rewinding machine when, contrary to the instruction manual and safe practice, he inserted plastic wrapping and cut it with a utility knife while the machine was rotating); Lightolier, a Div. of Genlyte Thomas Grp., LLC v. Hoon, 876 A.2d 100 (Md. 2005) (house fire started by recessed light installed too close to insulation despite warnings on the fixture, in the instruction booklet, and common knowledge in insulation and construction industry); Barnard v. Saturn Corp., 790 N.E.2d 1023 (Ind. Ct. App. 2003) (motorist jacked up car on incline and crawled underneath in manner expressly warned against on jack, in manual, and on spare tire cover); Hood v. Ryobi Am. Corp., 181 F.3d 608 (4th Cir. 1999) (Md. law) (user ignored seven clear warnings

When a user knowingly ignores full and fair warnings and instructions, the user knowingly pushes the product unfairly beyond its stated safety capabilities and so deserves no recovery for resulting harm. But if a disregarded warning or instruction is itself inadequate, so that the user is not fairly informed about the danger or how to avoid it, then the user's failure to follow such deficient information is foreseeable and, generally, excusable as well. In such a case, "if the injury resulting from foreseeable misuse of a product is one which an adequate warning concerning the use of the product would likely prevent, such misuse is no defense."[429] Moreover, because of the foreseeability that warnings may be disregarded, modern courts widely hold that manufacturers have an independent duty to design away dangers if there is a reasonable way to do so.[430]

Comparative Fault

Whether, and to what extent, "product misuse" should be merged into a jurisdiction's system of comparative fault, and so treated as a damages-reducing factor rather than as a total bar, is a vexing problem that has yet to be carefully addressed by most courts and legislatures. Viewing misuse merely as another plaintiff conduct "defense," some state legislatures and courts have simply merged it into their comparative fault schemes.[431] In those states, misuse reduces but does not bar a plaintiff's recovery unless, in modified comparative fault states, the plaintiff's fault equals or exceeds that of the defendant.[432] Such a merger requires confronting the issue of whether only *foreseeable* misuse will be treated on a comparative fault basis, so that

---

against removing saw blade guards); Bell v. Montgomery Ward, 792 F. Supp. 500 (W.D. La. 1992) (person mowing lawn, who lost two toes in mower when he slipped on wet grass, ignored warnings to keep guards in place and feet away from blade, and not to wear tennis shoes or to mow on wet grass or on slopes steeper than 15 degrees); Uptain v. Huntington Lab, Inc., 723 P.2d 1322, 1326 (Colo. 1986) (housekeeper used bare hands to wring out mop used to apply bathroom cleaning solution containing 23% hydrochloric acid; label warned against skin contact to avoid chemical burns and to wash skin area well if contact occurred).

[429] Bristol-Myers Co. v. Gonzales, 548 S.W.2d 416, 422–23 (Tex. App. 1976), rev'd on other grounds 561 S.W.2d 801 (Tex. 1978). See also AlNahhas v. Robert Bosch Tool Corp., 706 Fed. Appx. 920, 938 (10th Cir. 2017) (Okla. Law) (no warning that sander disk could fracture); Lia v. Domaine Mumm, Inc., 2003 WL 21260710 (Cal. Ct. App. 2003) (admonition not to corkscrew champagne bottle did not warn of danger from prying cork fragments with knife); Harless v. Boyle-Midway Div., Am. Home Prods., 594 F.2d 1051, 1055 (5th Cir. 1979) (Fla. law) ("It seems both confusing and internally inconsistent to ask a jury who has previously concluded that the label was *inadequate* to consider the defense of failure to read an *adequate* label.").

[430] See § 6.2, above.

[431] See, e.g., Ocampo v. Paper Converting Mach. Co., 2005 WL 2007144, at *10 (N.D. Ill. 2005) (misuse as a complete bar vs. as an affirmative defense that is merely a damage-reducer); Tungate v. Bridgestone Corp., 2004 WL 771191, at *7 (S.D. Ind. 2004); Tober v. Graco Children's Prods., Inc., 2004 WL 1987239 (S.D. Ind. 2004); Jett v. Ford Motor Co., 84 P.3d 219, 221 (Or. Ct. App. 2004); Veliz v. Rental Serv. Corp. USA, Inc., 313 F. Supp. 2d 1317, 1328 (M.D. Fla. 2003) ("product misuse reduces a plaintiff's recovery in proportion to his or her own comparative fault"); Jimenez v. Sears, Roebuck & Co., 904 P.2d 861 (Ariz. 1995).

[432] See, e.g., Barnard v. Saturn Corp., 790 N.E.2d 1023 (Ind. Ct. App. 2003) (motorist jacked up car on incline and crawled underneath in manner expressly warned against on jack, in manual, and on spare tire cover; no reasonable trier of fact could have found that plaintiff was less than 50% at fault); Standard Havens Prods., Inc. v. Benitez, 648 So.2d 1192 (Fla. 1994) (negligence); Elliot v. Sears, Roebuck & Co., 642 A.2d 709 (Conn. 1994) (strict liability). See § 13.3, above.

Statutes in some states expressly include misuse as a damages-reducing factor for comparative fault. See, e.g., Idaho Code Ann. § 6–1405(3) (misuse reduces claimant's damages according to comparative responsibility; "misuse" defined as "when the product user does not act in a manner that would be expected of an ordinary reasonably prudent person who is likely to use the product in the same or similar circumstances"); Mo. Ann. Stat. § 537.765(3) (for comparative fault apportionment, plaintiff's "fault" includes product uses (1) not reasonably anticipated by the manufacturer, and (2) for purposes not intended by the manufacturer). See also Morris v. Mitsubishi Motors N. Am., Inc., 782 F. Supp. 2d 1149, 1161 (E.D. Wash. 2011); Cavallo-Snyder v. Wohl Assocs., Inc., 2011 WL 1887549, at *1–2 (Conn. Super. Ct. 2011); Malen v. MTD Prod., 628 F.3d 296, 313 (7th Cir. 2010) (Ill. law).

*un*foreseeable misuse will still serve as a total bar. At least a couple of courts have ruled mysteriously that a plaintiff's *un*foreseeable misuse is somehow subject to comparison with the defendant's conduct or a product defect, "that where an unreasonably dangerous defect of a product and the plaintiff's assumption of risk or *unforeseeable misuse* of the product are concurring proximate causes of the injury suffered, the trier of fact must compare those concurring causes to determine the respective percentages" for the apportionment of damages.[433]

It seems more logical and fair to view *unforeseeable* misuse as lying entirely outside the scope of a product supplier's responsibility and, hence, outside the ambit of comparative fault. Because a seller has no duty to guard against unforeseeable product risks, there quite simply is no seller fault or product defect in such cases to compare.[434]

To achieve a fair and otherwise sensible result in most cases, and to avoid an utterly confusing mixture of doctrines, the best approach (if not prohibited by statute) is to consider a user's *foreseeable* misuse as any other kind of comparative fault for allocation to the plaintiff. On the other hand, if a substantial cause of the plaintiff's injury was his or her *unforeseeable* misuse of a product, then the plaintiff's conduct generally should be considered the sole proximate cause of the harm and so bar any recovery whatsoever.[435] Such a bright-line rule for unforeseeable misuse in comparative fault jurisdictions might seem crude, and juries allowed to allocate responsibility between a product defect and a plaintiff's *un*foreseeable misuse might conceivably be able to do better justice in some small set of cases. But the number of cases in which a plaintiff's injury is substantially traceable to both a product defect and a user's unforeseeable misuse (which is not the sole proximate cause of an accident) is surely very small. Like counting angels on a pinhead, the very concept of such combined causation is difficult to grasp and even more difficult to put to use.[436] In a real world where the law can only hope to do substantial justice most of the time, rather than perfect justice all of the time, a simple rule that bars liability altogether if a plaintiff's unforeseeable product misuse was a substantial cause of the harm appears to be the fairest way, both within and outside of comparative fault, to resolve most cases in a commonsense and practical way.[437]

---

[433] Mauch v. Manufacturers Sales & Serv., Inc., 345 N.W.2d 338, 348 (N.D. 1984) (emphasis added) (heroic attempt to explicate and justify this nonsense).

[434] See, e.g., Campbell Hausfeld/Scott Fetzer Co. v. Johnson, 109 N.E.3d 953, 959 (Ind. 2018) ("summary judgment based on misuse is appropriate when the undisputed evidence proves that the plaintiff misused the product in an unforeseeable manner"); Cigna Ins. Co. v. Oy Saunatec, Ltd., 241 F.3d 1 (1st Cir. 2001) (Mass. law) (unforeseeable misuse totally bars recovery, whereas foreseeable misuse factors into fault and damages allocation); States v. R.D. Werner Co., 799 P.2d 427 (Colo. App. 1990) (unlike comparative negligence, which diminishes recovery, unforeseeable misuse of ladder from which plaintiff fell goes to causation and completely bars recovery, regardless of defective condition).

[435] This is the majority approach and is adopted by the Uniform Comparative Fault Act.

[436] The confusion from combining doctrines (comparative fault and misuse) and sources of law (courts and legislatures) is illustrated by Jimenez v. Sears, Roebuck & Co., 904 P.2d 861 (Ariz. 1995), though Judge Martone's concurring opinion there makes good sense: "[T]rue misuse (unforeseeable, sole cause) continues to be an all or nothing defense. . . . Foreseeable misuse (concurring cause) is really contributory negligence, and is now a comparative defense to a products case." Id. at 873.

[437] Put simply, when a user puts a defective product to an unforeseeable use, "the accident was not proximately caused by the product defect." Prosser and Keeton on Torts § 102, at 711. This principle makes it difficult to understand cases such as Klorczyk v. Sears, Roebuck & Co., 2019 WL 1433645, at *14 (D. Conn. 2019), which asserts that "a plaintiff's *unforeseen* misuse does not completely bar recovery unless the plaintiff's unforeseen misuse was the sole proximate cause of injury" (emphasis added).

§ 13.6 CONDUCT DEFENSES TO WARRANTY CLAIMS

How a plaintiff's conduct affects liability in warranty is one of the most confused issues in all of products liability law.[438] To a large extent, the confusion springs from the long, uneasy relationship between warranty law and tort. The law of warranty, one must not forget, is "a freak hybrid born of the illicit intercourse of tort and contract."[439] But that origin lies in the distant past, and most courts now view warranty law as a part of the law of contracts.[440] In the contractual warranty context, where breach of warranty is predicated upon the falsity of a seller's representation or the failure of its goods to meet a commercial norm, rather than upon the seller's fault, a defense based upon a user's contributory negligence or dangerously venturous misbehavior seems oddly out of place. Yet, particularly in cases involving personal injuries resulting from a user's unforeseeably hazardous or knowingly dangerous and unreasonable product use, the courts have shown a manifest reluctance to accept the proposition that such conduct plays no role in fixing responsibility for accidental loss simply because a warranty claim sounds in contract.

A variety of conflicting overlaps in legal categories add to the confusion. While the doctrine of strict products liability in tort (which itself developed from warranty law)[441] is largely a creature of the common law, the law of warranty is now principally enshrined, via Article 2 of the Uniform Commercial Code, in statute.[442] In addition, there are conflicts between differing definitions of the tort-based conduct defenses of the common law, on the one hand, and the conduct defenses enacted in recent products liability reform statutes, on the other. Further, user conduct is handled in a variety of ways under various systems of comparative fault, most created by legislation but some by common law. In the warranty setting, many courts compound the confusion by altering traditional tort law definitions and effects of various forms of plaintiff behavior.[443] In an attempt to avoid this quagmire, some courts in warranty cases have simply abandoned tort law terms in describing plaintiff conduct.[444]

---

[438] See Little, "It is Much Easier to Find Fault with Others, Than to Be Faultless Ourselves": Contributory Negligence as a Bar to a Claim for Breach of the Implied Warranty of Merchantability, 30 Campbell L. Rev. 81 (2007); White and Summers, UCC §§ 12:11 to 12:14; Levine, Buyer's Conduct as Affecting the Extent of Manufacturer's Liability in Warranty, 52 Minn. L. Rev. 627 (1968); Annots., 75 A.L.R.4th 538, §§ 16–20 (1989) (warranty misconduct defenses to claims of failure to provide safety devices), 4 A.L.R.3d 501 (1965) (warranty misconduct defenses in general); 1 B. Clark and C. Smith, The Law of Product Warranties § 12:10, at 12–27 (2d ed. 2002); R. Nordstrom, Law of Sales §§ 81–84 (1970).

[439] Prosser, The Assault Upon the Citadel (Strict Liability to the Consumer), 69 Yale L.J. 1099, 1126 (1960). See also Note, 42 Harv. L. Rev. 411, 414–15 (1929). See generally §§ 1.2, 4.3, and 5.2, above.

[440] See, e.g., Russell v. Wright, 916 F. Supp. 2d 629, 658 (W.D. Va. 2013) ("breach of warranty claims . . . derive from contract law"); Van Alfen v. Toyota Motor Sales, USA, Inc., 2011 WL 4633986, at *5 (C.D. Cal. 2011) (Utah law) (Selna, J.); Pritchard v. Liggett & Myers Tobacco Co., 350 F.2d 479 (3d Cir. 1965) (Pa. law).

[441] This development occurred in America during the 1950s and early 1960s. See §§ 5.2 and 5.3, above.

[442] See ch. 4, above.

[443] "Some courts maintain that contributory negligence is no defense but hold that the defendant may parade the same misconduct of the plaintiff before the jury to show a lack of proximate cause." White & Summers, UCC § 12:11 ("In an action predicated on a breach of warranty, there is no defense per se of contributory negligence, but such defense presents a jury question as to whether the injuries resulted from the breach.").

[444] See Huebert v. Federal Pac. Elec. Co., 494 P.2d 1210, 1216 (Kan. 1972) (noting that several courts have abandoned use of "contributory negligence" and "assumption of risk" terms to avoid semantic problems in implied warranty cases, and holding that such concepts "in their normal meaning are not defenses" to actions for breach of express warranty).

The issue examined here is what the effect should be on a claim for breach of express or implied warranty against a product seller if a plaintiff carelessly uses a product, ignores warnings and instructions, deliberately and unreasonably engages a product danger, or puts a product to an unforeseeably dangerous use. Stated otherwise, do the tort law conduct defenses of contributory negligence, assumption of risk, and product misuse apply to warranty claims; are there any conduct defenses unique to warranty claims; and what is the effect of comparative fault doctrine on warranty conduct defenses? While the developing warranty law on these questions in some states roughly parallels the law applied in strict products liability in tort,[445] and while eventual convergence is not unfathomable,[446] the law on warranty conduct defenses teeters on the edge of chaos. The best that can be done here is to describe the principal approaches courts have taken and to indicate which appear most logical and fair.

Contributory Negligence; Assumption of Risk

In 1966, Dean Prosser wrote that "[s]uperficially the warranty cases . . . are in a state of complete contradiction and confusion as to the defense of contributory negligence."[447] Some early cases held that contributory negligence should simply bar recovery in warranty, reasoning, for example, that "[w]arranty is not insurance, and there is nothing in this contract to indicate that either party supposed the defendant was to answer for the plaintiff's carelessness."[448] Occasional decisions still hold that a plaintiff's contributory negligence should bar recovery.[449] But many courts long have held to the contrary—that a consumer's contributory negligence should be irrelevant to warranty claims, which lie in contract or assumpsit,[450] particularly in cases involving

---

[445] See, e.g., Van Alfen v. Toyota Motor Sales, USA, Inc., 2011 WL 4633986, at *5–7 (C.D. Cal. 2011) (Utah law) (Selna, J.); Krajewski v. Enderes Tool Co., 396 F. Supp. 2d 1045, 1052 (D. Neb. 2005) ("When an implied warranty action cannot be distinguished from a strict liability action, a defense against strict liability operates as a defense to implied warranty claims, because those two theories of recovery express one basic public policy."); Duff v. Bonner Bldg. Supply, Inc., 666 P.2d 650 (Idaho 1983) (assumption of risk and misuse are defenses to breach of warranty actions, but contributory negligence is not).

[446] See H. Woods and B. Deere, Comparative Fault § 14:17, at 339 (3d ed. 1996 & Supp. 2022). Note that the Iowa Supreme Court has unified products liability claims under the Third Restatement, as do a number of state products liability reform statutes. See, e.g., Estate of Thompson v. Kawasaki Heavy Indus., 933 F. Supp. 2d 1111, 1122 (N.D. Iowa 2013) (plaintiffs did not resist summary judgment motion on their implied warranty and negligence claims because Iowa has only a single product defect claim, "pursuant to the Restatement (Third) of Torts, Product Liability, encompassing design and manufacturing defects and negligence principles"); Conn. Gen. Stat. Ann. § 52–572n(a) (products liability claims are "in lieu of all other claims against product sellers, including actions of negligence, strict liability and warranty, for harm caused by a product").

[447] Prosser, The Fall of the Citadel (Strict Liability to the Consumer), 50 Minn. L. Rev. 791, 838 (1966). On whether contributory negligence is a defense to an implied warranty action, "the authorities are hopelessly divided." Gardner v. Coca Cola Bottling Co., 127 N.W.2d 557, 562 (Minn. 1964). See also Levine, Buyer's Conduct as Affecting the Extent of Manufacturer's Liability in Warranty, 52 Minn. L. Rev. 627 (1968).

[448] Razey v. J.B. Colt Co., 94 N.Y.S. 59, 61 (App. Div. 1905) (using gas generator in room with lighted gas jet). See also Finks v. Viking Refrigerators, Inc., 147 S.W.2d 124 (Mo. Ct. App. 1940); Dallison v. Sears, Roebuck & Co., 313 F.2d 343 (10th Cir. 1962) (Colo. law) (sole proximate cause of harm to plaintiff, burned when match ignited her nightgown, was her contributory negligence in smoking and using matches in bed while in semiconscious state induced by potent sleeping pill).

[449] See, e.g., Virgin v. Fireworks of Tilton, LLC, 215 A.3d 892, 898 (N.H. 2019) ("contributory negligence is a defense to an action for breach of warranty"); Powers v. Lycoming Engines, 272 F.R.D. 414, 430 (E.D. Pa. 2011) (stating that contributory negligence is a defense to breach of implied warranty in Mass., N.H., and N.Y.); Nicholson v. American Safety Util. Corp., 488 S.E.2d 240, 244 (N.C. 1997) (products liability statute).

[450] See, e.g., Russell v. Wright, 916 F. Supp. 2d 629, 658 n.15 (W.D. Va. 2013) (contributory negligence no defense to warranty claims, "as they derive from contract law"); Pritchard v. Liggett & Myers Tobacco Co., 350 F.2d 479 (3d Cir. 1965) (Pa. law).

defective food.[451] Many of the more recent cases take the same approach, holding that simple contributory negligence,[452] or contributory negligence more generally, has no effect on a plaintiff's claim for breach of warranty.[453]

Prosser's case study revealed that courts did not bar recovery on grounds of contributory negligence if a plaintiff's only fault lay in failing to inspect or discover a danger in a product, but "if he discovers the defect, or knows the danger arising from it, and proceeds nevertheless deliberately to encounter it by making use of the product, his conduct is the kind of contributory negligence which overlaps assumption of risk; and on either theory his recovery is barred."[454] This is precisely the position taken in *Restatement (Second) of Torts* § 402A comment *n* for strict liability in tort.[455] While there is some thin authority to the contrary,[456] courts quite widely agree that a plaintiff's negligent assumption of risk—his or her unreasonable decision to encounter a known and appreciated product danger—properly bars recovery in warranty as well.[457]

---

[451] "Contributory negligence, in general, is a defense only to actions grounded on negligence." Kassouf v. Lee Bros., 26 Cal. Rptr. 276, 277–78 (Ct. App. 1962). In *Kassouf,* after she bought groceries (including a Hershey "Mr. Goodbar") at defendant's food store, plaintiff put the candy bar on a table and sat down to read the newspaper. "While reading, she reached with one hand and took the candy bar from the table. Without looking, and with one hand, she opened one end of the wrapper and slid the bar partially out from it. Using this one-handed method, she broke off pieces, one after another, and put them into her mouth. From the outset she noticed that the bar 'didn't taste just right,' but she assumed this was because she hadn't eaten all day. She had consumed about one-third of the candy bar by the time she bit into a mushy worm. When she looked at the bar, she saw that it was covered with worms and webbing; worms were crawling out of the chocolate and the webbing had little eggs 'hanging onto it.' " Sickened from ingesting the contaminated candy, plaintiff sued the grocery store for breach of warranty of merchantability, and the jury found for plaintiff. Defendant appealed the trial court's refusal to instruct the jury that plaintiff had a duty "to take reasonable precautions for her own safety in the handling, inspection, and consumption" of the candy bar. *Held,* affirmed. There is no duty to look at and feel a candy bar prior to biting into it.

Compare Coulter v. American Bakeries Co., 530 So.2d 1009 (Fla. Dist. Ct. App. 1988) (metal wire in doughnut—comparative fault generally applicable to implied warranty claims, but sucking on doughnut while sipping milk, rather than chewing the doughnut properly, was not faulty conduct that could reduce recovery).

[452] On the contributory negligence defense to products liability claims in tort, see § 13.2, above. "Simple" or "ordinary" contributory negligence—negligently failing to discover or guard against the possibility of a defect—is to be distinguished from a plaintiff's assumption of risk in voluntarily, and perhaps unreasonably, encountering a known and appreciated danger. See § 13.4, above.

[453] See, e.g., Wickersham v. Ford Motor Co., 997 F.3d 526, 540 (4th Cir. 2021) (S.C. law) (addressing comparative fault but relying on earlier contributory negligence decisions); Robinson v. McNeil Consumer Healthcare, 615 F.3d 861, 873 (7th Cir. 2010) (Va. law) ("there is no defense of contributory negligence, as such, to breach of implied warranty"); Shipler v. General Motors Corp., 710 N.W.2d 807, 826 (Neb. 2006) (contributory negligence, in failing to discover defect or guard against it, is no defense to either warranty or strict tort action); Jones v. Ford Motor Co., 559 S.E.2d 592, 605 (Va. 2002); Wallace v. Owens-Illinois, Inc., 389 S.E.2d 155 (S.C. Ct. App. 1989) (illuminating analysis by Bell, J.).

[454] Prosser, The Fall of the Citadel (Strict Liability to the Consumer), 50 Minn. L. Rev. 791, 838–40 (1966).

[455] See §§ 13.2 and 13.4, above.

[456] See, e.g., Wood v. Bass Pro Shops, Inc., 462 S.E.2d 101, 103 (Va. 1995), noting that implied warranty actions are *ex contractu,* and holding that "the tort or *ex delicto* defense of assumption of the risk is not applicable in an action for breach of an implied warranty." Yet, true to principles of warranty, the court held that liability is barred if a defect is "known, visible or obvious" to plaintiff. See §§ 4.3 and 4.7, above.

[457] Massachusetts has the most extensive jurisprudence on this point. See, e.g., Haglund v. Philip Morris, Inc., 847 N.E.2d 315, 323–24 (Mass. 2006) (implied warranty actions normally barred by knowing and unreasonable product use (the *Correia* defense), but such defense does not apply to smoking cigarettes unless smoker knows that his or her prior medical condition was exacerbated thereby). See also Powers v. Lycoming Engines, 272 F.R.D. 414, 430 (E.D. Pa. 2011) (assumption of risk bars recovery on implied warranty claims in Mich., Mo., Utah, Va., Wash., and Wyo.); Epstein v. Eastman Kodak Co., 638 N.Y.S.2d 490 (App. Div. 1996); Gillespie v. American Motors Corp., 317 S.E.2d 32 (N.C. Ct. App. 1984) (where buyers of vehicle complained of noxious fumes in passenger compartment immediately upon purchase, their contributory negligence in driving vehicle for three years thereafter, despite their doctor's advice not to ride therein, barred recovery in warranty

Misuse

Many courts have applied a misuse defense to warranty claims quite similarly to how they apply it to products liability claims based in tort.[458] Thus, early warranty cases denied recovery if the injury arose out of a product use not *intended* by the manufacturer.[459] More recently, courts have limited the scope of implied warranty of merchantability, which requires that products be "fit" for their "ordinary" purposes,[460] to uses that are reasonably *foreseeable*.[461] In other words, a seller's implied warranties may not extend to abnormal use, and plainly do not extend to unforeseeable misuse, whether by the user or another.[462]

In *Venezia v. Miller Brewing Co.*,[463] mentioned earlier, a young boy injured his eye when he threw a discarded Miller Beer bottle against a telephone pole, shattering the bottle. In his warranty claim against Miller and the bottle manufacturers for failing to make their bottles strong enough to withstand this type of use, the federal appeals court noted that the Massachusetts high court had previously found no breach of warranty of merchantability where a plaintiff was injured by breaking glass while trying to pry the cover off a glass baby food jar with a beer can type of opener.[464] While noting that "[t]he linchpin of the warranty claim . . . is thus the proper scope of the term ordinary purpose," and that "at first blush it might appear beyond dispute that throwing a glass container into a telephone pole is by no means an 'ordinary' use of that product,"[465] the court

for resulting injuries); Brackett v. Johnson, 273 A.2d 499 (Conn. Super. Ct. 1970) (plaintiff placed hand in chute of snow blower he knew to be defective). See generally 1 Crockett, Product Warranties 2d § 12.11 ("the warranty cases generally parallel the § 402A cases"); White and Summers, UCC § 12:12 ("courts agree that the more specific form of contributory misconduct called 'assumption of the risk' bars a plaintiff's recovery in either strict tort or warranty," consistent with § 402A cmt. *n*).

[458] See, e.g., Ford Motor Credit Co. v. Mendola, 48 A.3d 366, 377 (N.J. Super. Ct. App. Div. 2012) (express warranty; misuse is "a defense to a breach of warranty claim, such as when the buyer or lessee became aware of faulty performance and continued to make deliberate and unreasonable use of the product"); Powers v. Lycoming Engines, 272 F.R.D. 414, 430 (E.D. Pa. 2011) (misuse bars recovery on implied warranty claims in Idaho, Mass., Mich., N.Y., Va., Wis., and Wash., and reduces damages in Ill.).

[459] See Levine, Buyer's Conduct as Affecting the Extent of Manufacturer's Liability in Warranty, 52 Minn. L. Rev. 627 (1968).

[460] See UCC § 2–314(2)(c), discussed below.

[461] See, e.g., Shuras v. Integrated Project Servs., Inc., 190 F. Supp. 2d 194, 199 (D. Mass. 2002) ("The touchstone of a negligent design or warranty analysis is foreseeability."); Venezia v. Miller Brewing Co., 626 F.2d 188 (1st Cir. 1980) (Mass. law) (beer bottle broke when thrown against telephone pole for that purpose—unforeseeable).

[462] See, e.g., Putman v. Savage Arms, Inc., 2019 WL 1007527, at *7 (W.D. Va. 2019) (Va. law) ("using a product 'in a manner which the seller could not have reasonably foreseen' bars a claim for breach of warranty (or negligent design)"); Phillips v. Cricket Lighters, 883 A.2d 439, 444–45 (Pa. 2005) (child's misuse of disposable lighter as a toy was not its ordinary purpose); Patterson v. Central Mills, Inc., 64 Fed. Appx. 457 (6th Cir. 2003) (Ohio law) (jury could find that child wearing adult T-shirt unforeseeably misused shirt by climbing onto kitchen counter and reaching for ketchup in cupboard over lit burner on stove); Carbone v. Alagna, 658 N.Y.S.2d 48 (App. Div. 1997) (boy struck by projectile fired from friend's slingshot; no implied warranty action against suppliers of slingshot); Wheeler v. Sunbelt Tool Co., 537 N.E.2d 1332, 1342 (Ill. App. Ct. 1989) (citing UCC § 2–715, and observing that "[m]isuse . . . contest[s] proximate cause"); Watson v. Uniden Corp. of Am., 775 F.2d 1514 (11th Cir. 1985) (Ga. law) (hearing loss from loud ring of cordless phone when user forgot to switch from standby to talk, as manual instructed, before placing on ear; use of product contrary to instructions is not use of product in normal manner); Daniell v. Ford Motor Co., 581 F. Supp. 728, 731–32 (D.N.M. 1984) (after locking herself in trunk in attempt to commit suicide, buyer could not get out for nine days because of absence of internal release mechanism; use was highly extraordinary rather than "ordinary," and buyer did not think about, much less rely on, seller's skill or judgment to select automobile suitable for her "unfortunate" purpose).

[463] 626 F.2d 188 (1st Cir. 1980) (Mass. law).

[464] Id. at 190 (citing Vincent v. Nicholas E. Tsiknas Co., 151 N.E.2d 263 (Mass. 1958)).

[465] Id. at 189.

observed that the Massachusetts high court had already rejected the "ordinary use" standard as being devoid of content for deciding misuse cases.[466] Instead, the "manufacturer's warranty of product fitness for ordinary use includes a guarantee that such product will withstand, in a reasonably safe manner, *foreseeable* 'misuse' incident to or arising out of the product's intended use."[467] Applying this standard, the court concluded that "it would be stretching too far to believe that the Massachusetts courts are presently prepared to expand their definition of 'ordinary purposes' to include the deliberate misuse of an otherwise reasonably safe container in a manner totally unrelated to any normal or intended use of that item. . . . *A fortiori,* we can see no possible implied fitness warranty that an empty glass bottle discarded by unknown persons would . . . safely withstand being intentionally smashed against a solid stationary object."[468]

UCC Article 2

Since warranty law is now governed by UCC Article 2,[469] a search for the proper role of user misconduct in warranty law should begin there. But the Code's black-letter ("Official Text") references to consumer conduct are at best oblique—the scope of warranty liability is defined by whether a product is fit for its "ordinary" purposes,[470] by whether the buyer is probably aware of the product's dangerous condition,[471] and by whether a breach of warranty "proximately" results in the plaintiff's injuries.[472]

The warranty most frequently litigated in products liability cases, the implied warranty of merchantability, is principally defined in § 2–314(2)(c)'s provision that a merchantable product is "fit for the ordinary purposes for which such goods are used."[473] This provision quite obviously suggests that an implied warranty of merchantability will *not* arise under this subsection[474] if a product's performance capabilities are exceeded by a use which is not "ordinary," however that word may be interpreted. Under § 2–316(3)(b), no warranties arise with respect to defects a buyer does or should discover during a pre-sale examination of a product.[475] Finally, the remedies provision of Article 2 includes, in defining the "consequential damages" recoverable for breach of warranty in § 2–715(2)(b), "injury to person or property proximately resulting from any breach of warranty." While each of these provisions in Article 2 may be interpreted to implicate

---

466 See Back v. Wickes Corp., 378 N.E.2d 964 (Mass. 1978).

467 *Venezia*, 626 F.2d at 190 (emphasis added).

468 Id. The court concluded that "the impact of endorsing a contrary conclusion would be overwhelming, with every discarded glass object holding the potential for generating a future lawsuit." Id. at 192.

469 On warranty claims in products liability litigation, see ch. 4, above.

470 See UCC § 2–314(2)(c).

471 See UCC § 2–316(3)(b).

472 See UCC § 2–715(2)(b). See also Official Comment 13 to § 2–314.

473 See § 4.3, above.

474 Note that UCC § 2–314(2) contains a total of six subsections, so that even if a product is merchantable under one or more subsections it may be found unmerchantable under one or more of the other provisions. So, if opening a Pepsi bottle on a metal fence causing it to explode is not an "ordinary purpose" under subsection (2), the bottle might still be unmerchantable for not being "adequately contained" under subsection (5). For such facts, see Natale v. Pepsi Cola Co., 182 N.Y.S.2d 404 (App. Div. 1959).

475 See, e.g., Light v. Weldarc Co., 569 So.2d 1302 (Fla. Dist. Ct. App. 1990) (no implied warranty that safety glasses would not slip down user's nose, and so fail to protect eye from metal sliver thrown from punch press, when user inspected glasses, knew their propensity to slip, and made "conscious decision" to buy them). See § 4.7, above.

the role of a buyer's conduct in warranty litigation, none of them does so in a manner that is clear and to the point.[476]

In contrast to the obscure manner in which buyer conduct is treated in the UCC's Official Text, the Official Comments specifically address the effect of both a buyer's carelessness and behavior which implies risk acceptance, framing the issue in terms of whether a buyer's loss is "proximately caused" by a product defect or, alternatively, by the buyer's choice or conduct. Comment 13 to § 2–314 provides in part:

> In an action based on breach of warranty, it is of course necessary to show not only the existence of the warranty but the fact that the warranty was broken and that the breach of the warranty was the proximate cause of the loss sustained. In such an action an affirmative showing by the seller that the loss resulted from some action or event following his own delivery of the goods can operate as a defense. . . . Action by the buyer following an examination of the goods which ought to have indicated the defect complained of can be shown as matter bearing on whether the breach itself was the cause of the injury.

Comment 8 to § 2–316 provides that "if the buyer discovers the defect and uses the goods anyway, or if he unreasonably fails to examine the goods before he uses them, resulting injuries may be found to result from his own action rather than proximately from a breach of warranty." Comment 5 to § 2–715 provides more fully:

> Subsection (2)(b) states the usual rule as to breach of warranty, allowing recovery for injuries "proximately" resulting from the breach. Where the injury involved follows the use of goods without discovery of the defect causing the damage, the question of "proximate" cause turns on whether it was reasonable for the buyer to use the goods without such inspection as would have revealed the defects. If it was not reasonable for him to do so, or if he did in fact discover the defect prior to his use, the injury would not proximately result from the breach of warranty.

This last comment imposes the greatest burden on buyers, for it states that there is no proximate cause, and hence no damages for breach of warranty, if a buyer either (1) unreasonably fails to inspect a product for defects, or (2) uses a product after discovery of a defect, whether such use was unreasonable or not.

Erdman v. Johnson Brothers Radio & Television Co.[477] illustrates one court's attempt to harmonize the awkward fit between a plaintiff's contributory negligence and the law of warranty. From the start, the plaintiffs' television-radio-stereo console purchased from the defendant emitted crackling sounds, often accompanied by a tear in the picture, and it sometimes emitted "sparks and heavy smoke shooting out of the back of the set and the smell of burning rubber, wire, or some other substance."[478] The defendants purported to repair the problem, but sparks and smoke still emanated from the rear of the television. After one of these recurring episodes, the plaintiffs turned off (but did not unplug) the television, went to bed, and were later awakened by a fire from the set that destroyed their house. In plaintiffs' warranty and negligence action against the dealers, the trial court ruled for the defendants, finding that the plaintiffs had been contributorily negligent in continuing to use a television that was arcing, smoking, and

---

[476] See 1 Crockett, Product Warranties 2d § 12.11.

[477] 271 A.2d 744 (Md. 1970).

[478] Id. at 745.

emitting sparks and a burning odor for two hours on the night of the fire. The court concluded that the implied warranty of merchantability did not cover the continued use of a television under these conditions since such was not a "normal" use.[479]

On appeal, the Maryland high court affirmed. Pondering whether contributory negligence is a bar to an implied warranty claim under the Uniform Commercial Code, on the one hand, or falls outside the scope of the seller's implied warranty, on the other, the *Erdman* court observed that "[t]he important factor under either theory or an amalgam of them is that, although there may have been a breach of the warranty, that the breach is no longer considered 'the proximate cause of the loss.' "[480] Thus, "the defect in the set, of which the plaintiffs had knowledge, could no longer be relied upon by them as a basis for an action of breach of warranty."[481] The court concluded that "the breach of warranty, if any there was, was not the proximate cause of the fire because of the appellants' continued use of the set after the discovery of the obvious defects," remarking "that such a holding is consistent with the trial judge's characterization of the plaintiffs' conduct as contributory negligence and with the UCC's Official Comment 13 to § 2–314, and Comment 5 to § 2–715."[482]

Despite the specificity of the UCC's Official Comments on how buyer conduct affects a warranty claim, *Erdman* is one of the few decisions that analyzes these useful comments together with the vague black-letter provisions to resolve the user conduct issue in a warranty case.[483] Why most courts have failed to use Article 2's buyer conduct comments in a similarly forthright manner might be because the courts have sensed the rough manner in which the contract law scholars who drafted Article 2 incorporated the tort law concepts of contributory negligence, assumption of risk, misuse, and proximate cause into the warranty law context. Or perhaps the courts, feeling bound only by the UCC's Official Text, have largely ignored the comments to provide more flexibility in their effort to standardize the conduct defenses applicable to all products liability claims, in tort and warranty alike. Finally, beginning in the late 1960s, courts increasingly may have perceived that the all-or-nothing approach to buyer conduct in the comments is inconsistent with the comparative fault approach to damages apportionment that swept the nation in the late twentieth century.[484]

The infrequency with which courts have used the UCC's black-letter provisions to decide consumer conduct cases is more problematic. Certainly the paucity of this type of analysis is partially explained by the vague and indirect manner in which these provisions refer to buyer conduct in terms of ordinary use, discovery of defects, and proximate causation. Moreover, because this Official Text did not explicitly address the subject of buyer conduct, the enactment of the UCC did not displace prior law. Nor did it interfere with the ongoing development of supplementary law on how a buyer's conduct

---

479 Id. at 747.

480 Id. at 749 (citing UCC § 2–314, cmt. 13).

481 Id.

482 Id. at 750–51.

483 More recent decisions that explicitly consider and apply the Official Comments include Avery v. Cobra Enters. of Utah, Inc., 2013 WL 2352320, at *5–6 (N.D. Ala. 2013) (plaintiff's "conduct is a factor to be considered when determining the proximate cause of his injury; but because this is not a tort action, any negligence of which he was guilty does not automatically bar his recovery under a non-tort theory"); JCW Elecs., Inc. v. Garza, 257 S.W.3d 701, 706–07 (Tex. 2008).

484 See § 13.3, above.

should affect a warranty claim.[485] Thus, courts may have felt authorized by the UCC itself to substitute developing principles of consumer conduct from the tort law context for the rough, vague, and increasingly anachronistic provisions of Article 2.

Since warranty law claims in most products liability actions are secondary to overlapping claims of strict liability in tort and negligence, many courts and lawyers may simply view these liability claims collectively as lying essentially in tort and so may view the defenses from the same perspective. While the temptation to view tort and warranty claims as falling under a single "products liability action" umbrella for purposes of evaluating available defenses is understandable, it improperly denigrates the legislative prerogative. Until the legislatures themselves choose to unify tort and warranty claims in products liability litigation, as a couple now have done,[486] the courts should clarify how differing forms of consumer conduct affect claims and damages for breach of warranty under Article 2 of the UCC.

Express Warranty

Much of the analysis above applies to express as well as implied warranty claims.[487] But express warranties arise from *explicit* contractual representations, and so the issue of whether a representation was part of the basis of the particular bargain (or whether a plaintiff justifiably relied thereon) is an issue that cannot be ignored.[488]

One special doctrine that has developed in some of the express warranty cases is that contributory negligence is irrelevant if the plaintiff's conduct consists merely in relying on the truthfulness of the defendant's representation. *Hensley v. Sherman Car Wash Equipment Co.*[489] was an action by a car wash employee against the manufacturer of the automobile conveyor unit. On the day of the accident, the pivoting safety hood that ordinarily covered the open pit at the end of the conveyor was not operating, and the plaintiff stepped into the pit. The plaintiff's express warranty claim was based on the assertion in the defendant's information sheet that "[c]ar wash personnel are assured safe working conditions on all areas of the vehicle by the pivoted safety hood [which] eliminates all possibility of persons stepping into an open pit."[490] Holding that the plaintiff's contributory negligence was not a bar to her express warranty claim, the court reasoned that the plaintiff's faulty behavior in failing to observe where she was going was "within the scope of the risk warranted against by defendant," since the stated "purpose of the safety hood was to prevent a person from stepping into the opening at the end of the conveyor unit."[491] Accordingly, "[t]he very risk which defendant warranted

---

485 See UCC § 1–103.

486 Connecticut is one example. See Conn. Gen. Stat. Ann. § 52–572n(a). See also Mich. Comp. Laws Ann. § 600.2945. Note, however, that some states treat express warranty claims as generating special responsibilities and so exclude them from the general definition of a "product liability action." See, e.g., N.J. Stat. Ann. § 2A:58C–1(b)(3).

487 See, e.g., Trishan Air, Inc. v. Dassault Falcon Jet Corp., 532 Fed. Appx. 784, 789 (9th Cir. 2013) (Cal. law) (noting that the California Supreme Court has not yet decided the issue, and that the Courts of Appeal decisions point both ways, the court concluded that comparative fault would reduce the plaintiff's damages in his breach of express warranty claim); Ford Motor Credit Co., LLC v. Mendola, 48 A.3d 366, 377 (N.J. Super. Ct. App. Div. 2012) (express warranty; misuse is "a defense to a breach of warranty claim, such as when the buyer or lessee became aware of faulty performance and continued to make deliberate and unreasonable use of the product").

488 See § 4.2, above.

489 520 P.2d 146 (Colo. App. 1974).

490 Id. at 147.

491 Id. at 148.

not to exist was encountered by plaintiff, and her negligence or lack of due care is irrelevant."[492] Indeed, a person's "fault" in believing a manufacturer's express promise should only rarely be allowed to undercut the manufacturer's fundamental obligation to speak the truth.[493] Other courts have agreed with *Hensley* that a plaintiff's contributory negligence will not bar a breach of express warranty claim if the conduct merely "puts the warranty to the test."[494]

Comparative Fault

Only in recent decades have most American courts and legislatures realized that a plaintiff's conduct and damages need not always be treated in an all-or-nothing manner.[495] Today, whether consumer conduct should be considered a matter of comparative fault for damages apportionment on a warranty claim depends largely upon the scope of each particular jurisdiction's comparative fault system.[496] While the development of the comparative fault doctrine is generally beneficial, it has magnified the profound confusion that already existed in fashioning a proper role for user conduct in warranty litigation.

In states that have enacted "comparative *negligence*" legislation, courts understandably have been hesitant to compare a user's conduct with a defendant's breach of warranty.[497] But in states with legislation which has defined the apportionment system more broadly in terms of comparative "fault"[498] or "culpability,"[499] especially if "fault" is defined to include breach of warranty[500] or something similar,[501] or when the statute provides for apportionment in all cases involving personal injury,

[492] Id.

[493] See Owen, The Moral Foundations of Products Liability Law: Toward First Principles, 68 Notre Dame L. Rev. 427, 463–65 (1993).

[494] Hensley v. Sherman Car Wash Equip. Co., 520 P.2d 146, 148 (Colo. App. 1974). See, e.g., Imperial Die Casting Co. v. Covil Insulation Co., 216 S.E.2d 532, 534 (S.C. 1975); Brown v. Chapman, 304 F.2d 149 (9th Cir. 1962) (Haw. law); Hansen v. Firestone Tire & Rubber Co., 276 F.2d 254, 258 (6th Cir. 1960) (Mich. law) ("If the manufacturer chooses to extend the scope of his liability by certifying certain qualities as existent, the negligent acts of the buyer, bringing about the revelation that the qualities do not exist, would not defeat recovery.").

[495] An early case where a court allowed a jury to reduce a plaintiff's recovery for breach of implied warranty on account of contributory negligence, rather than to bar recovery altogether, was Chapman v. Brown, 198 F. Supp. 78 (D. Haw. 1961), aff'd, 304 F.2d 149 (9th Cir. 1962). See Levine, Buyer's Conduct as Affecting the Extent of Manufacturer's Liability in Warranty, 52 Minn. L. Rev. 627 (1968).

[496] See H. Woods and B. Deere, Comparative Fault §§ 14:16, 14:17 (3d ed. 1996 & Supp. 2022).

[497] See, e.g., Phillips v. Duro-Last Roofing, Inc., 806 P.2d 834, 837 (Wyo. 1991) (statute applies only to claims of negligence). *But see* Larsen v. Pacesetter Sys., Inc., 837 P.2d 1273, 1289–90 (Haw. 1992) ("merging" breach of implied warranty into pure apportionment products liability scheme).

[498] As in at least New Hampshire and Colorado. See, e.g., Union Mut. Fire Ins. v. Hamilton Beach/Proctor-Silex, Inc., 2006 WL 3782716, at *1 (D.N.H. 2006); Montag v. Honda Motor Co., 75 F.3d 1414, 1419 (10th Cir. 1996) (interpreting products liability apportionment statute, Colo. Rev. Stat. Ann. § 13–21–406, to permit comparison of driver's fault with automotive manufacturer's fault in designing defective seatbelt).

[499] As in at least New York. See N.Y. C.P.L.R. § 1411.

[500] As in at least Arkansas, Arizona, Iowa, North Dakota, and Wyoming. See Ark. Code Ann. § 16–64–122; Ariz. Rev. Stat. Ann. § 12–2506(F)(2); Iowa Code Ann. § 668.1(1); Wyo. Stat. Ann. § 1–1–109(a)(iv); Miller v. Stryker Instruments, 2012 WL 1718825, at *14 (D. Ariz. 2012) ("fault" includes "breach of express or implied warranty of a product"); Leno v. K & L Homes, Inc., 803 N.W.2d 543, 549 (N.D. 2011) ("the modified comparative fault provision of N.D.C.C. § 32–03.2–02 was amended so that instead of excluding products liability actions like 'breach of warranty for product defect,' such actions would be subject to modified comparative fault").

[501] As in at least Maine, where "fault" includes a "breach of statutory duty." See Me. Rev. Stat. Ann. tit. 14, § 156.

death, or damage to property,[502] then courts may or must include breach of warranty as an item to be apportioned.[503] In the two states that have adopted the Uniform Comparative Fault Act,[504] breach of warranty is explicitly included as a type of "fault" to be apportioned.[505] Some state legislatures have enacted special products liability reform statutes that do not in that context address either warranty liability or comparative fault,[506] while others explicitly provide for the comparative fault apportionment of damages in products liability actions generally, regardless of the basis of the claim.[507] Finally, in a number of jurisdictions where comparative fault apportionment is a creature of the common law, the courts have generally chosen to include breach of warranty in the apportionment system.[508] So, while some states preclude apportionment in warranty cases,[509] a substantial number of states reduce damages in warranty actions in proportion to a plaintiff's fault.[510]

A variety of secondary comparative fault issues arise in connection with warranty claims involving user conduct. In a majority of comparative fault states that have adopted a "modified" rather than "pure" system of comparative fault, a plaintiff's contributory negligence continues to bar recovery altogether, in warranty as in tort, when the plaintiff's fault equals or exceeds that of the defendant.[511] When comparative fault statutes specify apportionment for claims of personal injury and property damage, they may not apply to breach of warranty actions seeking recovery for purely economic loss.[512]

---

[502] As in at least Mississippi and Rhode Island. See Miss. Code Ann. § 11–7–15; R.I. Gen. Laws § 9–20–4; Fiske v. MacGregor, Div. of Brunswick, 464 A.2d 719 (R.I. 1983) (thorough analysis of case law).

[503] See H. Woods and B. Deere, Comparative Fault § 14:16 (3d ed. 1996 & Supp. 2022).

[504] Uniform Comparative Fault Act (1977). Only Iowa and Washington adopted the Act, and both made changes to the "uniform" provisions. The Uniform Apportionment of Tort Responsibility Act replaced the Uniform Comparative Fault Act in 2002, as amended, 2003. See § 13.3, above.

[505] Under § 1(b) of the Uniform Comparative Fault Act, "fault" is defined to include "breach of warranty." See, e.g., Morris v. Mitsubishi Motors N. Am., Inc., 782 F. Supp. 2d 1149, 1160 (E.D. Wash. 2011) (same, under Washington's comparative fault act).

[506] As in South Carolina's early 402A statute. See, e.g., Wickersham v. Ford Motor Co., 997 F.3d 526, 540 (4th Cir. 2021) (S.C. law) (while "South Carolina law generally does not recognize the affirmative defense of comparative fault in strict liability or breach of warranty cases," defendants "are of course entitled to use evidence of plaintiffs' fault in causing enhanced injuries to defeat proximate cause").

[507] As in Michigan and Texas. See Karl v. Bryant Air Conditioning Co., 705 F.2d 164 (6th Cir. 1983) (Mich. law); Tex. Civ. Prac. & Rem. Code Ann. § 82.001.

[508] See, e.g., Owens v. Truckstops of Am., 915 S.W.2d 420, 434 (Tenn. 1996); Wheeler v. Sunbelt Tool Co., 537 N.E.2d 1332 (Ill. App. Ct. 1989); Coulter v. American Bakeries Co., 530 So.2d 1009 (Fla. Dist. Ct. App. 1988); In re Certified Questions from the United States Court of Appeals for Sixth Circuit, 331 N.W.2d 456 (Mich. 1982).

[509] See, e.g., Wickersham v. Ford Motor Co., 997 F.3d 526, 540 (4th Cir. 2021) (S.C. law); Virgin v. Fireworks of Tilton, LLC, 215 A.3d 892, 900 (N.H. 2019) (damages apportionment statute does not apply to claims for personal injury alleging breach of implied warranty).

[510] See generally JCW Elecs., Inc. v. Garza, 257 S.W.3d 701, 706–07 n.6 (Tex. 2008) (comparative fault applies to warranty claims in Texas and at least, citing cases, in Ky., N.J., Wyo., Colo., Fla., Iowa, Kan., Mich., Minn., N.D., R.I., Tenn., and Utah).

[511] See, e.g., JCW Elecs., Inc. v. Garza, 257 S.W.3d 701, 707 (Tex. 2008) (inmate 60% responsible for suicide; implied warranty claim barred); Union Mut. Fire Ins. v. Hamilton Beach/Proctor-Silex, Inc., 2006 WL 3782716, at *1 (D.N.H. 2006) (summary judgment for manufacturer because consumer continued to use toaster despite knowing its fire hazard).

[512] See, e.g., Ethyl Corp. v. BP Performance Polymers, Inc., 33 F.3d 23 (8th Cir. 1994) (Iowa law); Little Rock Elec. Contractors, Inc. v. Okonite Co., 744 S.W.2d 381, 382 (Ark. 1988). See also Eastern Mountain Platform Tennis, Inc. v. Sherwin-Williams Co., 40 F.3d 492 (1st Cir. 1994) (N.H. law).

For the many reasons why damages apportionment principles are widely applied to products liability claims in tort,[513] a division of damages based on responsibility in warranty is also sound in principle. Because treating plaintiff misconduct as a basis for apportioning damages was largely nonexistent when UCC Article 2 was drafted in the 1940s and 1950s, Article 2 fails to address the topic. But Article 2's formulation of buyer conduct issues in proximate causation terms is compatible with the concept of damages apportionment, which assigns responsibility for damages to each party in proportion to the extent to which the party's breach of duty proximately caused the harm.[514]

The widening application of comparative fault principles to warranty actions has occurred mostly in the context of *implied* warranty claims, and there has been a greater reluctance to apply damages apportionment principles to claims for *express* warranty.[515] But the several comparative fault statutes that apply to injury claims generally, together with the products liability statutes that apply comparative fault provisions to all products liability claims, would seem quite clearly to embrace express warranty claims within the ambit of comparative responsibility. However, jurisdictions without these statutes generally should not reduce a plaintiff's damages on account of simple contributory fault, for such behavior usually consists in merely putting the warranty to the test. More egregious misconduct, however, particularly if it involves plaintiff conduct which is knowingly dangerous and unreasonable, or puts a product to an unforeseeable use, unfairly tests the product outside the warranty and so should continue to bar express warranty recovery altogether.

While damages apportionment for consumer conduct in implied warranty cases is sound as a principle of general application, it needs exceptions. No doubt some forms of consumer misconduct (such as knowingly dangerous unreasonable behavior, and putting products to unforeseeably dangerous use), should be left entirely outside the area of damages apportionment for all warranty claims.[516] Regardless of how user conduct is characterized, the issue of damages apportionment needs to be addressed only if the product use was within the scope of warranty. And for most products liability claims involving user conduct, in warranty no less than tort, courts should leave room for a robust doctrine of "sole proximate cause"[517]—often better treated as an issue of "scope of

---

[513] See § 13.3, above.

[514] See Levine, Buyer's Conduct as Affecting the Extent of Manufacturer's Liability in Warranty, 52 Minn. L. Rev. 627, 662–63 (1968) (arguing that comparative fault approach, "while not a panacea, can serve to substantially ameliorate the harshness of the contributory negligence doctrine while balancing the manufacturer's responsibility to society with the buyer's action in contributing to his injury").

[515] See, e.g., Coca-Cola Bottling Co. of Cape Cod v. Weston & Sampson Eng'rs, Inc., 695 N.E.2d 688, 695 (Mass. App. Ct. 1998) (comparative negligence statute does not apply to express warranty claims); Ferdig v. Melitta, Inc., 320 N.W.2d 369, 374 (Mich. Ct. App. 1982) ("Contributory negligence has never been an available defense in cases involving express warranties."). *But see* Trishan Air, Inc. v. Dassault Falcon Jet Corp., 532 Fed. Appx. 784, 789 (9th Cir. 2013) (Cal. law) (approving 70% reduction in breach of express warranty damages award based on plaintiffs' fault and concluding that, "because the contract-based claim at issue here is essentially an equivalent, alternative method of pleading the same basic theory of liability as the tort claims, the California Supreme Court would have applied comparative fault in this case").

[516] See, e.g., Union Mut. Fire Ins. v. Hamilton Beach/Proctor-Silex, Inc., 2006 WL 3782716, at *1 (D.N.H. 2006) (summary judgment for manufacturer when consumer continued to use toaster despite knowing of toaster's fire hazard). Compare Haglund v. Philip Morris, Inc., 847 N.E.2d 315, 323–24 (Mass. 2006) (implied warranty actions normally barred by knowing and unreasonable product use, but this defense does not apply to normal smoking unless smoker knows of that his or her prior medical condition was exacerbated thereby).

[517] See, e.g., Fournier Furniture, Inc. v. Waltz-Holst Blow Pipe Co., 980 F. Supp. 187, 190 (W.D. Va. 1997) (misuse of product, defined as "using it in manner which seller could not reasonably have foreseen," bars breach of warranty claims if misuse is sole proximate cause of harm).

warranty."[518] Both doctrines embrace the notion that there must be a fair limit to a seller's responsibility, such that both express and implied promises are reasonably construed to exclude responsibility for injuries resulting from the use of a product outside the scope of a warranty.

How scope of warranty fits with product abuse may be illustrated with a hypothetical. Assume that a new sport utility vehicle has a high center of gravity, a narrow track width, and a large bubble visible on the sidewall of one tire—all of which obvious characteristics a buyer is well aware. If the buyer chooses to turn the steering wheel sharply at high speed, in an effort to spin the vehicle sideways like a movie stuntman, the tire might blow out and the vehicle might roll over, injuring the driver. In such a case, although the tire is clearly defective, and while the safety of the vehicle's stability may fairly be subject to inquiry, the sole proximate cause of the driver's injuries might well be viewed as the driver's harsh driving rather than any lack of merchantability in the tire or the vehicle. Stated otherwise, the scope of the implied warranty of quality in such a case may not include safe performance when the product is put to such abusive use. The issue of comparative fault should never be reached at all in such a case because there was no proximate connection between breach of warranty and the plaintiff's harm.

§ 13.7 Conduct Defenses to Misrepresentation Claims

The basic conduct "defense" asserted in tortious misrepresentation actions is that the plaintiff's reliance, if any,[519] was not "justifiable."[520] Indeed, the justifiability of reliance, sometimes referred to as "reasonable reliance" or the "right to rely,"[521] has long

---

[518] See, e.g., Erdman v. Johnson Bros. Radio & Television Co., 271 A.2d 744 (Md. 1970). Professor Nordstrom viewed user misconduct as bearing on the nature of the agreement between the parties, addressed in Article 2 in terms of whether the goods "conformed" to the warranty. See UCC § 2–106(2). In view of his focus on the intent of the parties and the nature of their agreement, he preferred the concept of assumption of risk to the vaguer concept of proximate cause. See R. J. Nordstrom, Law of Sales § 84 (1970).

[519] A plaintiff of course must plead and prove reliance on a specific representation, as explained in ch. 3, above. See, e.g., Gray v. Abbott Labs., Inc., 2011 WL 3022274, at *5 (N.D. Ill. 2011) (fraud and negligent misrepresentation claims dismissed because plaintiff failed to allege specific representations, pertinent to the alleged harm, on which she purportedly relied).

[520] See generally 2 Harper, James, and Gray, Law of Torts §§ 7.7 and 7.8; Prosser and Keeton on Torts §§ 108 and 109; Sales, The Innocent Misrepresentation Doctrine: Strict Tort Liability Under Section 402B, 16 Hous. L. Rev. 239 (1979); Comment, 28 Cumb. L. Rev. 177 (1997–1998). Tortious misrepresentation bases of recovery, including requirements that a plaintiff justifiably rely, are examined in ch. 3, above.

[521] The dominant term is "justifiable." See, e.g., Rest. (2d) Torts §§ 402B, 537(b), 538(1), and 552. The Products Liability Restatement does not really address the issue. Compare id. § 9 cmt. *b* (adopting the principles of Rest. (2d) Torts § 402B), cmt. *c* (referring only to the issue of "contributory fault"), and id. Reporters' Notes 1 and 2 (referring to § 402B's requirement of "justifiable reliance"). But other terms—particularly "reasonable"—are used as well, sometimes interchangeably. See, e.g., Russell v. Ethicon Inc., 2020 WL 4732106, at *6 (N.D. Ala. 2020) (reasonable reliance); Boeken v. Philip Morris, Inc., 26 Cal. Rptr. 3d 638, 658 (Ct. App. 2005) (same); IFD Constr. Corp. v. Corddry Carpenter Dietz & Zack, 685 N.Y.S.2d 670, 673 (App. Div. 1999) (reliance was "neither reasonable nor justified"); G & M Farms v. Funk Irrigation Co., 808 P.2d 851, 855 (Idaho 1991) (stating eighth element of fraud claim as plaintiff's "right to rely thereon"); Rest. (2d) Torts § 310 cmt. *b* (relying on an opinion may make the person's reliance "less reasonable, and so less justified"); Fraud & Deceit, 37 Am. Jur. 2d §§ 236 et seq. (1968) (classifying issue as plaintiff's "right to rely" and, in § 236, examining basis for ascertaining whether reliance is "justifiable or excusable"). Except perhaps on the issue of whether a victim's conduct should be measured objectively or subjectively, discussed below, it matters little which term a court selects to characterize the form of misconduct which will defeat a claim for tortious misrepresentation.

been a central element of all three forms of tortious misrepresentation: fraud,[522] negligent misrepresentation,[523] and strict products liability in tort for misrepresentation under the *Restatement (Second) of Torts*[524] and the *Restatement (Third) of Torts: Products Liability*.[525]

Probably because the justifiability of a plaintiff's reliance overlaps several other elements of fraud (fact, materiality, plaintiff's ignorance of falsity, and reliance), as discussed below, it is sometimes omitted in recitations of the elements of fraudulent[526] and negligent misrepresentation.[527] This omission might be viewed as suggesting that there exists some uncertainty as to whether the justifiability of a plaintiff's reliance is truly an element of a tortious misrepresentation claim or whether instead a plaintiff's unjustified reliance should be considered an affirmative defense. But the omission is better explained by its embedded nature in the other elements, and there is no real doubt that the justifiability of a plaintiff's reliance is an essential component in a common-law[528] tortious misrepresentation claim.[529]

As an essential element of all three causes of action for tortious misrepresentation, the non-justifiability of a plaintiff's reliance cannot be characterized as an affirmative defense because the plaintiff in all such cases has the burden, as with each element of such claims, to plead and prove the justifiability of his or her reliance upon the defendant's misrepresentation.[530] If a plaintiff is unable to prove that his or her reliance

---

[522] See Rest. (2d) Torts § 537(b). Although § 537 by its terms applies only to recovery for pecuniary loss, § 557A applies the principles of liability in deceit for pecuniary loss to cases in which the deceit causes physical harm. Rest. (2d) Torts § 557A and cmt. *a*.

[523] See Rest. (2d) Torts § 552(1).

[524] Id. § 402B. See id. cmt. *j*.

[525] Section 9 of the Products Liability Restatement incorporates the doctrine of § 402B of the Second Restatement. See Products Liability Rest. § 9 cmt. *b*.

[526] See, e.g., In re Valsartan, Losartan, & Irbesartan Prods. Liab. Litig., 2021 WL 307486 (D.N.J. 2021) ("While there are certainly differences across the fifty states in terms of common law fraud claims, the basic elements are virtually the same. A plaintiff must prove: (1) defendant made a materially false representation; (2) had knowledge of its falsity, believed it to be false, or made it with reckless indifference as to its falsity; (3) with the intent to deceive; (4) plaintiff acted in reliance on the statement; and (5) plaintiff suffered damages as a result of the reliance."); Wyeth, Inc. v. Weeks, 159 So.3d 649, 656 (Ala. 2014) (stating elements of fraud as "(1) a false representation (2) concerning a material fact (3) relied upon by the plaintiff (4) who was damaged as a proximate result"); Small v. Lorillard Tobacco Co., 720 N.E.2d 892, 898 (N.Y. 1999) ("[t]o make out a prima facie case of fraud, the complaint must contain allegations of a representation of material fact, falsity, scienter, reliance and injury"); Bank of Montreal v. Signet Bank, 193 F.3d 818 (4th Cir. 1999) (Va. law). See also Frumer, Friedman, and Sklaren, Products Liability § 2.05[2][c] (characterizing element as "reliance upon the truth of the representation").

[527] See, e.g., Rest. (2d) Torts § 310.

[528] Justifiable reliance is not a required element of certain statutory claims for deceptive business practices and consumer fraud. See, e.g., Small v. Lorillard Tobacco Co., 679 N.Y.S.2d 593, 599 (App. Div. 1998), aff'd, 698 N.Y.S.2d 615 (1999); Gennari v. Weichert Co. Realtors, 691 A.2d 350 (N.J. 1997).

[529] See, e.g., City of High Point, N. C. v. Suez Treatment Sols. Inc., 2020 WL 1307017, at *11 (M.D.N.C. 2020) ("Justifiable reliance is an essential element of both fraud and negligent misrepresentation."); Aldana v. RJ Reynolds Tobacco Co., 2007 WL 3020497, at *5, 8 (D.S.C. 2007) (fraudulent and negligent misrepresentation; right to rely and justifiable reliance, respectively); Gawloski v. Miller Brewing Co., 644 N.E.2d 731 (Ohio Ct. App. 1994); Boyd v. A.O. Smith Harvestore Prods., Inc., 776 P.2d 1125, 1129 (Colo. App. 1989) ("An essential element of both fraud and negligent misrepresentation is justifiable reliance."). *But see* Klein, Comparative Fault and Fraud, 48 Ariz. L. Rev. 983, 999–1000 (2006) (arguing that a plaintiff's failure justifiably to rely on a fraudulent misrepresentation should not bar recovery but should instead reduce damages under comparative fault principles).

[530] See, e.g., American Safety Equip. Corp. v. Winkler, 640 P.2d 216, 223 (Colo. 1982) (by implication). Compare Kruse v. Bank of Am., 248 Cal. Rptr. 217 (Ct. App. 1988) (fraud pleading insufficient without allegations of justifiable reliance).

was justifiable, the tortious misrepresentation claim will fail.[531] Similar to the other conduct defenses examined in this chapter, the justifiability of a plaintiff's reliance is normally a question of fact for a jury to resolve.[532]

When Is Reliance Justifiable?

Whether a plaintiff's reliance is justifiable depends upon the nature of the representation and all of the circumstances of the particular transaction. These include the materiality of the representation;[533] the extent to which it was precise and factual, on the one hand, or vague and subjectively a matter of opinion, on the other;[534] its form and the context in which it was made, as in television advertising, face-to-face negotiations, or in the owner's manual;[535] its apparent plausibility, or its suspiciousness—suggesting that the plaintiff should have "smelled a rat";[536] the availability of other sources of information revealing the falsity of the representation;[537] and any other matter bearing on whether in the circumstances the plaintiff, or a reasonable person,[538] could properly believe and base a decision upon the representation.[539] So, a court or jury may conclude that the user can reasonably believe

---

[531] See, e.g., Baker v. Danek Med., 35 F. Supp. 2d 875 (N.D. Fla. 1998) (negligent misrepresentation and strict liability for misrepresentation); Gawloski v. Miller Brewing Co., 644 N.E.2d 731 (Ohio Ct. App. 1994) (fraudulent misrepresentation: no justifiable reliance as a matter of law).

[532] See, e.g., Whiteley v. Philip Morris Inc., 11 Cal. Rptr. 3d 807, 843 (Ct. App. 2004) ("Except in the rare case where the undisputed facts leave no room for a reasonable difference of opinion, the question of whether a plaintiff's reliance is reasonable is a question of fact.").

[533] Section 538 of the Rest. (2d) Torts provides that "[r]eliance upon a fraudulent misrepresentation is not justifiable unless the matter misrepresented is material," and it defines a matter as "material" if:

> (a) a reasonable man would attach importance to its existence or nonexistence in determining his choice of action in the transaction in question; or
>
> (b) the maker of the representation knows or has reason to know that its recipient regards or is likely to regard the matter as important in determining his choice of action, although a reasonable man would not so regard it.

[534] See Prosser and Keeton on Torts § 109, at 755.

[535] Cf. Rest. (2d) Torts § 538A cmt. *c*.

[536] Thanks to Judge Posner for this colorful metaphor. See AMPAT/Midwest, Inc. v. Illinois Tool Works Inc., 896 F.2d 1035, 1041 (7th Cir. 1990) (Ill. law). See note 557, below.

[537] See, e.g., Gawloski v. Miller Brewing Co., 644 N.E.2d 731 (Ohio Ct. App. 1994) (even if Miller beer commercials had represented that prolonged and excessive beer drinking was safe, no justifiable reliance as a matter of law because of common awareness for centuries of risks of alcoholism from prolonged and excessive consumption of alcohol):

> Our nation continues to inform its citizens of those dangers, supporting the community's common knowledge with well-documented and highly publicized scientific and statistical information that repeatedly warns of the detrimental physical, psychological, and emotional effects caused by prolonged and excessive alcohol use. Even though we acknowledge that beer advertising is pervasive in our society, we hold that, as a matter of law, a beer manufacturer's commercial images, although enticing, are not enough to neutralize or nullify the immense body of knowledge a reasonable consumer possesses about the dangers of alcohol. Therefore, a reasonable consumer could not, as a matter of law, ignore basic common knowledge about the dangers of alcohol and justifiably rely upon beer advertisements and their idyllic images to conclude that the prolonged and excessive use of alcohol is safe and acceptable.

Id. at 736. Compare Small v. Lorillard Tobacco Co., 679 N.Y.S.2d 593 (App. Div. 1998), aff'd, 698 N.Y.S.2d 615 (1999), where the court decertified a class action against the tobacco industry for fraudulently concealing the addictive nature of cigarette smoking, questioning the plausibility of plaintiff's claim of reliance because of the hundreds of articles published in New York newspapers during the 1980s and 1990s about nicotine addiction.

[538] As discussed below, the standard for establishing justifiability of reliance for fraud is tailored to the knowledge and characteristics of the specific plaintiff, in contrast to the objective reasonable person standard for negligent and innocent misrepresentation.

[539] See, e.g., Sippy v. Cristich, 609 P.2d 204, 208 (Kan. Ct. App. 1980) (various factors bear on a person's right to rely on another's representation, such as "the intelligence, education, business experience and relative

explicit assurances that a golfing practice device is "completely safe" and that the "ball will not hit player,"[540] and that a mace weapon sold for self-defense "disables as effectively as a gun" and will "subdue" an attacker "instantly."[541] However, a person, ignoring widespread publicity about the perils of drinking and smoking, may *not* justifiably base personal beer or cigarette consumption decisions on commercials that glorify drinking or smoking and that somehow convey the idea that the prolonged and excessive consumption of such products is not harmful or addictive.[542]

Reliance itself, apart from its justifiability, involves the entirely factual subjective question of whether the representee personally believed the representation and took action, at least in part, upon it.[543] In contrast, the *justifiability* of that reliance requires an evaluation of the basis for reliance to determine if it was sound or had at least some plausible explanation in reason. Because it gauges the wisdom of a plaintiff's decision to rely upon a particular representation, the justifiability of reliance is often said to be based upon an "objective" determination.[544] In cases involving the intentional tort of fraud, however, the standard differs from the normal objective standard of a reasonable prudent person, since the gullibility or other fault of a person in believing such a misrepresentation cannot, in fairness, bar a claim against an intentional deceiver who deliberately and shamelessly exploits a person's trust.[545] In such cases, "[j]ustification is a matter of the qualities and characteristics of the particular plaintiff, and the circumstances of the particular case, rather than of the application of a community standard of conduct to all cases."[546] Normally, a person *may* justifiably rely upon a fraudulent misstatement unless the falsity of the representation is so clearly based on the known or obvious facts as to place in doubt his or her own truthfulness (or possibly even sanity) in claiming to have relied upon it.[547] In reality, tailoring justifiability

---

situation of the parties;" customs in the industry; and "the opportunity for both parties to make an independent investigation . . . . [T]he test is whether the recipient has 'information which would serve as a danger signal and a red light to any normal person of his intelligence and experience.' ") (quoting from, *inter alia*, Rest. (2d) Torts § 540 and comments thereto).

[540] Hauter v. Zogarts, 534 P.2d 377, 379 (Cal. 1975).

[541] Klages v. General Ordnance Equip. Corp., 367 A.2d 304, 306 (Pa. Super. Ct. 1976).

[542] See, e.g., Bruner v. Anheuser-Busch, Inc., 153 F. Supp. 2d 1358 (S.D. Fla. 2001), aff'd, 31 Fed. Appx. 932 (11th Cir. 2002) (table); Small v. Lorillard Tobacco Co., 679 N.Y.S.2d 593 (App. Div. 1998), aff'd, 698 N.Y.S.2d 615 (1999).

[543] See § 3.2, above.

[544] See, e.g., Berarov v. Archers-Daniels-Midland Co., 2019 WL 277717, at *9 (N.D. Ill. 2019) (puffery is not a basis for a fraud or misrepresentation claim; "no reasonable consumer would rely on such an implicit assertion as the sole basis for making a purchase"); Rose v. Ford, 2003 WL 21495081, at *3 (Cal. Ct. App. 2003) (whether "a reasonable consumer would likely rely"); Gawloski v. Miller Brewing Co., 644 N.E.2d 731, 736 (Ohio Ct. App. 1994). See generally Prosser and Keeton on Torts § 108, at 750 (purpose of justifiable reliance requirement is for "providing some objective corroborations to plaintiff's claim that he did rely").

[545] "One who justifiably relies upon a fraudulent misrepresentation is not barred from recovery by his contributory negligence in doing so." Rest. (2d) Torts § 545A. "Although the plaintiff's reliance on the misrepresentation must be justifiable . . ., this does not mean that his conduct must conform to the standard of the reasonable man." Id. cmt. *b*. This is the prevailing rule, but there is authority to the contrary. See 37 Am. Jur. 2d, Fraud & Deceit § 249 (1968).

[546] Rest. (2d) Torts § 545A cmt. *b*. Not unlike the child standard of care in the law of negligence, the standard of justifiability for fraud is often said to conform to the particular attributes of the plaintiff, including his or her age, intelligence, experience, and mental and physical condition. See, e.g., Boeken v. Philip Morris, Inc., 26 Cal. Rptr. 3d 638, 658–59 (Ct. App. 2005); Cheney Bros. v. Batesville Casket Co., 47 F.3d 111, 115 (4th Cir. 1995) (S.C. law).

[547] See Prosser and Keeton on Torts § 108:

> Rather than contributory negligence, the matter seems to turn upon an individual standard of the plaintiff's own capacity and the knowledge which he has, or which may fairly be charged

criteria to a plaintiff's personal characteristics makes the standard look suspiciously subjective,[548] such that it might be best if the courts in fraud cases would abandon pounding and twisting the justifiability standard into an "objective" hole in which it does not fit.

The justifiability requirement is not designed to provide a shield behind which wicked fraudfeasors may hide in order to exploit the gullibility of trusting victims, for the law seeks the opposite result.[549] Instead, justifiability overlaps and serves as a useful check on other components of a fraud claim: whether the representation was factual, or merely opinion; whether it was material, or actually quite trivial; whether the plaintiff was ignorant of the falsity of the representation, or truly knew (or at least suspected) that it might be false; and, ultimately, whether the plaintiff in fact relied upon the representation in making a decision to buy or use the product.[550] Even in fraud cases, therefore, the justifiability requirement serves this important validation function of helping weed out claims where a plaintiff unfairly seeks to hold a defendant liable for harm caused principally by the plaintiff's bad judgment rather than any false statement the defendant may have made.[551]

In claims for merely negligent misrepresentation, the standard of conduct for the plaintiff reverts to the normal objective standard of reasonable behavior for a person exercising due regard for his or her own welfare.[552] As for strict liability claims for

> against him from the facts within his observation in the light of his individual case, and so comes closer to the rules which are associated with assumption of risk. "More succinctly stated, the rule is that one cannot be heard to say he relied upon a statement so patently ridiculous as to be unbelievable on its face, unless he happens to be that special object of the affections of a court of Equity, an idiot."

Id. at 751 (citing Obiter Dicta, 25 Ford. L. Rev. 395, 397 (1956)). Compare AMPAT/Midwest, Inc. v. Illinois Tool Works Inc., 896 F.2d 1035, 1041–42 (7th Cir. 1990) (Ill. law) (Posner, J.):

> We think it comes down to this: while the victim of an ordinary accident is required to use the ordinary care of an average person [to avoid being contributorily negligent], the victim of a deliberate fraud is barred only if he has notice of the fraud, and so he need only avoid deliberate or reckless risk-taking.

Thus, a fraud victim "cannot close his eyes to a known risk," for that would be to "ignore a manifest danger," which would be reckless. Id. at 1042.

[548] So, justifiability might be said to lie closer to assumption of risk than it does to contributory negligence. See AMPAT/Midwest, Inc. v. Illinois Tool Works Inc., 896 F.2d 1035, 1042 (7th Cir. 1990) (Ill. law) (Posner, J.) ("It differs by only a shade, if that, from . . . assumption of risk that defeats liability under the first aspect of the duty of reasonable reliance as we conceive it."); Prosser and Keeton on Torts § 108.

[549] See Prosser and Keeton on Torts § 108, at 751 (citations omitted):

> "The design of the law is to protect the weak and credulous from the wiles and stratagems of the artful and cunning, as well as those whose vigilance and security enable them to protect themselves," and "no rogue should enjoy his ill-gotten plunder for the simple reason that his victim is by chance a fool."

[550] See, e.g., *Berarov*, note 544, above; AMPAT/Midwest, Inc. v. Illinois Tool Works Inc., 896 F.2d 1035, 1042 (7th Cir. 1990) (Ill. law) (Posner, J.) ("The requirement of justifiable reliance backstops the jury's determination of actual reliance."). Compare Miller v. Pfizer Inc. (Roerig Div.), 196 F. Supp. 2d 1095 (D. Kan. 2002) (plaintiffs failed to raise genuine issue of fact as to reliance upon subtle and subliminal marketing influences, unknown even to the prescribing physician himself), aff'd, 356 F.3d 1326 (10th Cir. 2004). Justifiable reliance is conventionally used as an umbrella concept that includes the elements of materiality and fact. See Rest. (2d) Torts § 538 cmt. *b*; Prosser and Keeton on Torts §§ 108 and 109. See generally Dobbs, Law of Torts § 474, at 1360–61.

[551] See § 3.2, above.

[552] See, e.g., Mainline Tractor & Equip. Co. v. Nutrite Corp., 937 F. Supp. 1095, 1105 (D. Vt. 1996) (justifiability of reliance based on objective standard). See generally Rest. (2d) Torts § 552A, stating that "[t]he recipient of a negligent misrepresentation is barred from recovery for pecuniary loss suffered in reliance upon

misrepresentation, the case law is very sparse, but most courts would probably agree that the justifiability of a plaintiff's reliance upon a manufacturer's innocent misrepresentation "involves an objective standard" of whether a "reasonable consumer" would rely on the particular representations in dispute.[553]

Contributory and Comparative Negligence; Assumption of Risk; Misuse

If a plaintiff is justified in relying upon a tortious misrepresentation, there may well be no room for the conventional conduct defenses to operate. To put the matter another way, the defenses of contributory negligence, assumption of risk, and misuse all logically appear to be absorbed into the requirement that a plaintiff establish the justifiability of his or her reliance upon the defendant's representation.

An example may help to illustrate this point. Assume that a plaintiff purchases a "Golfing Gizmo," a golfers' training device consisting of two metal pegs, two cords (one cotton and one elastic), and a golf ball attached to the cotton cord.[554] The purpose of the device, described by the manufacturer as "completely safe—ball will not hit player," is to return the ball to the golfer, via the elastic cord connecting the in-ground pegs, after the golfer hits the ball. If the player sets up the Gizmo device ten feet in front of a brick wall and squarely hits the ball against the wall, the ball might well bounce back and hit the golfer in the head. Using the Gizmo in such an obviously dangerous manner is clearly unreasonable, hence contributorily negligent, and the golfer would appear quite plainly to have misused the product and assumed the risk. Similarly, if the golfer were to strike the ball with a sledgehammer rather than a golf club, shattering the ball which injured his eye, or if the golfer were injured by falling on the ball when the cord broke as he used it to climb a tree, such unforeseeable misuse surely would seem to bar recovery. Yet in none of these cases could the golfer's harm conceivably be viewed as having resulted from a justifiable reliance on the manufacturer's safety representation.[555] In short, the justifiable reliance element of tortious misrepresentation claims appears to embrace and so supplant the traditional forms of user conduct defenses.

Over centuries of fraud cases, courts developed a substantial body of doctrine in tortious misrepresentation cases on the conduct of the representee, largely in cases involving pecuniary loss and mostly involving the effect of a plaintiff's contributory negligence. Although many decisions have required plaintiffs engaged in business transactions to maintain a reasonable vigilance for their own protection, even from fraudulent misrepresentation,[556] the cases widely hold that "contributory negligence" as

---

it if he is negligent in so relying," but noting that comparative fault may be applicable to claims involving physical harm. Id. cmt. *b*.

[553] Gawloski v. Miller Brewing Co., 644 N.E.2d 731, 736 (Ohio Ct. App. 1994) (prison inmates sued Miller for causing their alcoholism that led to lives of crime, on ground that commercials misrepresented Miller beer as "an enhancer of the quality of life"; *held*, any reliance not justifiable as matter of law).

Comment *j* to Rest. (2d) Torts § 402B (on justifiable reliance) provides scant assistance in discerning the standard for assessing justifiability in the strict liability context. However, comment *g* (on materiality) suggests an objective standard: "[T]he fact misrepresented must be a material one, of importance to the normal purchaser, by which the ultimate buyer may justifiably be expected to be influenced in buying the chattel."

[554] This was the product in fact involved in Hauter v. Zogarts, 534 P.2d 377 (Cal. 1975), an early, prominent case decided under § 402B of the Second Torts Restatement.

[555] See Sales, The Innocent Misrepresentation Doctrine: Strict Tort Liability Under Section 402B, 16 Hous. L. Rev. 239, 271 (1979). Nor in such cases may the representation be deemed *false*, in that it fairly contains an implicit limitation that the Gizmo not be used in a manner that is patently dangerous.

[556] See, e.g., Cheney Bros. v. Batesville Casket Co., 47 F.3d 111, 115 (4th Cir. 1995) (S.C. law) (noting the established duty of recipient to safeguard his own interests).

such is no defense to fraud.[557] The rule is said to be different for claims of negligent misrepresentation, where contributory negligence is conventionally said to bar the claim.[558] Yet, here as well, these cases have mostly involved business transactions involving pecuniary loss,[559] and there is little case law on whether the contributory negligence defense is applicable to products liability misrepresentation cases involving physical harm.

For claims of strict products liability for misrepresentation, as set forth in § 402B of the *Second Restatement* and § 9 of the *Third Restatement*, the effect of a plaintiff's contributory negligence is unclear. Comment *j* to § 402B, which explicitly addresses justifiable reliance, provides scant assistance in discerning the meaning of justifiability in the strict liability context; it merely mentions that justifiability is a requirement and references the *Second Restatement* sections on justifiable reliance for fraud, "so far as they are pertinent," including the provision that contributory negligence does not bar liability.[560] There is little value in such dated, offhand treatment of an important doctrine, and the *Third Restatement* addresses the issue even less.[561] While some isolated case law involving strict liability claims suggests that contributory negligence should not serve as a defense, the authority is old and not entirely on point.[562] Thus, whether a plaintiff's contributory negligence should play some role in strict products liability claims for tortious misrepresentation, or whether contributory negligence is exclusively absorbed into the issue of the justifiability of the plaintiff's reliance, remains a problem to be solved. Surely the most appropriate resolution of this issue, as discussed above, is to view contributory negligence, in all forms of tortious misrepresentation cases, as merged entirely into the justifiability of reliance.

But contributory negligence has been resurrected in recent years in the guise of comparative fault, and so some courts may feel obligated to consider whether and, if so, how the comparative fault doctrine may affect claims for tortious misrepresentation. This issue has received little consideration from either courts or commentators.[563] In cases involving intentional misrepresentation (fraud), the comparative fault doctrine is

---

[557] "That a more cautious buyer might not have relied, might have smelled a rat, does not defeat liability. There is no defense of contributory negligence to an intentional tort, including fraud." AMPAT/Midwest, Inc. v. Illinois Tool Works Inc., 896 F.2d 1035, 1041 (7th Cir. 1990) (Ill. law) (Posner, J.). See also 37 Am. Jur. 2d, Fraud & Deceit § 247, at 329 (1968) (noting the conflicting policies of suppressing fraud, on the one hand, while not encouraging the neglect of one's own interests, on the other, and observing that the law has opted to protect not only the vigilant but also the gullible "against the machinations of the designedly wicked"); Rest. (2d) Torts § 545A. Although § 545A by its terms applies to recovery for pecuniary loss, it is incorporated by reference into the Restatement's fraud section governing liability for physical harm. See Rest. (2d) Torts § 557A cmt. *a*.

[558] See Rest. (2d) Torts § 552A.

[559] Id. The principal Restatement section on negligent misrepresentation involving risk of physical harm, § 311, addresses the plaintiff misconduct issue only in terms of the reasonableness of the plaintiff's reliance. See Rest. (2d) Torts § 311 cmt. *c*.

[560] Rest. (2d) Torts § 545A.

[561] In short, because of the brevity of explicit discussion of justifiability in either § 402B of the Second Rest. or § 9 of the Third Rest., neither Restatement provides a basis for determining whether, in addition to the justifiable reliance element, the doctrine of strict products liability in tort for misrepresentation may be barred, or damages reduced, on the ground of a plaintiff's contributory negligence.

[562] See Prosser and Keeton on Torts § 108, at 750–51 n.10.

[563] The commentary includes a couple of suggestions that comparative fault principles might be applied to negligent misrepresentation claims. See, e.g., Dobbs, Law of Torts 1359–60; Rest. (2d) Torts § 552A cmt. *b*. *Contra* Comment, 28 Cumb. L. Rev. 177 (1997–1998). But such observations probably spring from a desire to reduce the harshness of contributory negligence serving as a total bar, rather than to provide misrepresenters a second bite at the misconduct apple.

widely viewed to be inapplicable[564] for the same reasons of fairness and policy that properly preclude the use of contributory negligence as a bar to fraud recovery discussed above. In negligent misrepresentation cases involving pecuniary loss outside the realm of products liability, the few cases are split, but the better view appears to be that comparative fault should not apply here either.[565] No case has been found applying comparative fault to cases involving strict products liability for misrepresentation under § 402B of the *Second Restatement* or its *Third Restatement* counterpart. Surely comparative fault is inappropriate for strict liability claims where the very idea of a buyer's negligence in relying justifiably upon a manufacturer's product safety representations is a concept that is difficult to grasp.

Because a plaintiff must prove the justifiability of his or her reliance for any tortious misrepresentation claim, the traditional products liability conduct defenses are simply out of place. Of the few decisions that have addressed this issue, the better reasoned ones have exhibited little tolerance for attempts by defense lawyers to get two or more bites at the misconduct apple by arguing, first, that a plaintiff's reliance upon a misrepresentation was unjustified, and, second, that, even if the reliance in fact was justified, the plaintiff was negligent, assumed the risk, or misused the product.[566] These decisions persuasively conclude that the justifiability (or reasonableness) of a plaintiff's reliance encompasses all forms of plaintiff conduct addressed by the traditional conduct defenses.[567] If a statute does not compel a contrary result,[568] little would be lost, except confusion, if courts would clearly rule that none of the traditional conduct defenses apply to common-law tortious misrepresentation claims in products liability litigation.

---

[564] See, e.g., Schoeff v. R.J. Reynolds Tobacco Co., 232 So.3d 294, 297 (Fla. 2017) (comparative fault does not apply to cigarette cases if jury finds for plaintiff on an intentional tort claim unless the plaintiff waived the intentional tort exception); R.J. Reynolds Tobacco Co. v. Sury, 118 So.3d 849, 853 (Fla. Dist. Ct. App. 2013) (upholding trial court's refusal to reduce $1 million jury award for father's death from cancer, where jury found father 60% at fault and two defendant tobacco companies 20% each at fault; no apportionment because jury found defendants liable for intentional torts (fraudulent concealment and civil conspiracy to fraudulently conceal) as well as negligence); Scott v. American Tobacco Co., Inc., 949 So.2d 1266, 1280–82 (La. Ct. App. 2007) (comparative fault of smokers no defense to tobacco manufacturers' "fraudulent and conspiratorial behavior, i.e., denying the addictive nature of its products"). *But see* Klein, Comparative Fault and Fraud, 48 Ariz. L. Rev. 983, 999–1000 (2006) (arguing that a plaintiff's failure justifiably to rely on a fraudulent misrepresentation should lead to damages reduction under principles of comparative fault rather than barring recovery altogether). See generally H. Woods and B. Deere, Comparative Fault § 14:51, at 396 (3d ed. 1996 & Supp. 2022); Annot., 18 A.L.R.5th 525 (1995) (applicability of comparative negligence to intentional torts).

[565] See, e.g., Condor Enters., Inc. v. Boise Cascade Corp., 856 P.2d 713 (Wash. Ct. App. 1993); Estate of Braswell v. People's Credit Union, 602 A.2d 510 (R.I. 1992); Greycas, Inc. v. Proud, 826 F.2d 1560 (7th Cir. 1987) (Ill. law). See generally Annot., 22 A.L.R.5th 464 (1995) (applicability of comparative negligence to negligent misrepresentation actions).

[566] See, e.g., Klages v. General Ordnance Equip. Corp., 367 A.2d 304, 313 (Pa. Super. Ct. 1976) ("the lower court fully charged the jury regarding justifiable reliance, and that instruction encompassed appellant's claim of assumption of the risk"); Schwabe v. Porter, 501 N.W.2d 470 (Wis. Ct. App. 1993) (comparative fault).

[567] Not all courts and commentators agree. See Daye v. General Motors Corp., 720 So.2d 654 (La. 1998) (sole cause of accident was driver's negligent driving, not defendant's advertising); Nugent v. Utica Cutlery Co., 636 S.W.2d 805, 809–10 (Tex. App. 1982) (misuse defense allowed in defense of § 402B claim). See generally Sales, The Innocent Misrepresentation Doctrine: Strict Tort Liability Under Section 402B, 16 Hous. L. Rev. 239, 269–77 (1979) (acknowledging that the justifiability of reliance requirement fully embraces the assumption of risk defense, but arguing that misuse and comparative fault should be allowed as independent defenses).

[568] At least Connecticut has a products liability statute which provides that misrepresentation is a products liability claim, and which specifies misconduct defenses that apply generally to such claims. Conn. Gen. Stat. Ann. §§ 52–572*l*, –572m(b), and –572*o*.

Chapter 14

SPECIAL DEFENSES

Table of Sections

§ 14.1 SPECIAL DEFENSES—GENERALLY

Products liability defenses may be broadly divided into three categories: (1) user conduct defenses; (2) no-duty defenses; and (3) other, "special," defenses. The first category of defense, based on a user's conduct—contributory negligence, comparative fault, assumption of risk, product misuse, and unreasonable reliance on a misrepresentation—were addressed in the previous chapter.[1] Those are the most common and pervasive forms of defense, potentially applicable in many products liability cases.

The second category of "defense," the no-duty type, gives rise to defensive arguments that a manufacturer may assert but which may not be affirmative defenses that a defendant must plead and on which meet the burden of proof. In many states, product misuse falls into the no-duty classification; however, it is treated in the misconduct "defense" chapter because it so centrally concerns consumer conduct.[2] Another chapter addressed a series of no-duty issues, "quasi-defenses," including such matters as obvious dangers, inherent risks, and the state-of-the-art "defense."[3] Though defendants press such issues, most courts consider no-duty matters to be part of a plaintiff's prima facie case. For example, a plaintiff in most states must prove that, under the prevailing state of the art at the time a product was made and sold, the manufacturer reasonably should have foreseen and taken steps to avoid a particular risk of harm. In several states, products liability reform statutes create true affirmative defenses centered on product misuse, obvious dangers, inherent risks, and state of the art, as previously discussed. But the common law of most states views these "defenses" as limitations on the scope of a manufacturer's duty, the breach of which a plaintiff must plead and prove. Be that as it may, such no-duty "quasi-defenses" may be every bit as effective[4] in blocking liability as a plaintiff's assumption of risk.[5]

---

[1] See ch. 13, above.

[2] See § 13.5, above.

[3] See ch. 10, above.

[4] Or more so, in view of the spreading tentacles of comparative fault that may serve merely to reduce a plaintiff's damages rather than to relieve a defendant of responsibility altogether. See § 13.3, above.

[5] See § 13.4, above.

The third category, "special" defenses, is a catch-all classification that holds most remaining defenses. Some of these are scattered throughout the book in other chapters, such as the "seatbelt defense," examined in the chapter on automotive products liability litigation;[6] the "sealed-container defense," treated in the chapter on retailers;[7] and the bulk-supplier and sophisticated-user doctrines,[8] considered in the chapter on warning defects. The present chapter examines the most important remaining "special" defenses: (1) the contract specification defense;[9] (2) the government contractor defense;[10] (3) the regulatory compliance defense;[11] (4) federal preemption;[12] and (5) statutes of limitations and repose.[13] Except for the regulatory compliance defense, the other special defenses considered here are affirmative defenses, such that a products liability claim ordinarily will be dismissed entirely if a defendant establishes the applicability of such a defense to the case.

§ 14.2 Contract Specification Defense—Fabricators

A manufacturer's responsibility for design defects has always firmly rested on the fact that the manufacturer *created* the bad design, even if only by including a defectively designed component into a larger product over which it had overall design responsibility.[14] Hence, the manufacturer of a *non*defective component that an assembling manufacturer buys and combines with other components in a dangerously defective manner is not subject to liability for resulting injuries unless the component manufacturer helped the assembler design the larger, defective product.[15] A manufacturer's responsibility for injuries caused by defects in its product's design thus rests comfortably on the manufacturer's control over design decisions, and hence, design choices that are somehow flawed. Our sensibilities normally would be jarred if the law were to hold a manufacturer liable for harm for which it was in no fair way responsible.

Two important products liability defenses are based on the idea that a manufacturer, relying entirely on a purchaser's own design specifications, did not originate the design defect—a general defense, based on a manufacturer's fabrication of a product according to a buyer's contractual design specifications; and a specific one, where the buyer is the government. The crucial point in both situations is that it hardly seems fair to hold a manufacturer responsible, if it merely fabricates a product to design specifications supplied and required by the purchaser, for injuries that result if the design proves defective. This section deals with the first, general problem; and the further problem of government contractors is addressed in the following section.

The quandary facing manufacturers of products designed by others is well illustrated by a hypothetical. Assume that General Motors contracts with a punch press manufacturer to construct a press for making hub caps according to precise design specifications that GM provides to the press manufacturer. If the design specifications

---

6 See § 17.5, below.

7 See § 15.2, below.

8 See § 9.5, above.

9 See § 14.2, below.

10 See § 14.3, below.

11 See § 14.4, below.

12 See § 14.5, below.

13 See § 14.6, below.

14 See § 8.1, above.

15 See § 15.3, below.

include no guards on the press and a GM worker is injured as a result, it hardly seems fair to allow a worker injured on the press to have a claim against the press manufacturer for making and selling a defectively designed machine. Or, suppose that Wal-Mart designs a toaster with a dangerously defective heating element and contracts out production of the toaster to a small appliance manufacturer. The toaster manufacturer, it would seem, normally should not be liable for harm that results when the toaster overheats and starts a fire due to a defect in Wal-Mart's design.

Manufacturers usually are responsible for the harmful consequences of design defects in products they make and sell,[16] but this is because a manufacturer's own engineers normally develop the designs used to make those products. When a manufacturer simply follows the design requirements specified by a purchaser, the design and manufacturing functions of the product's manufacture are separated. If a manufacturer's role is reduced to merely "fabricating" a product according to design specifications mandated by the purchaser, the logic and fairness of holding the manufacturer liable for a dangerously defective design are called into question.

The contract specification defense arose to protect manufacturing "fabricators" from unfair liability for defective designs. The defense shields fabricators from liability for injuries caused by a design defect in products it manufactures pursuant to plans and specifications supplied by the purchaser, unless the design is obviously defective.[17] From an early New York case,[18] the contract specification "defense" evolved as a rule of non-liability for negligence when an independent contractor simply follows its employer's directions on how a product should be built and has no reason to know that the directions are unsafe.[19] This widely accepted principle[20] is described in the *Restatement (Second) of Torts*, which provides that an independent contractor "is not required to sit in judgment on the plans and specifications or the materials provided by his employer" and is not liable for their insufficiency unless the design or materials specified are "so obviously bad that a competent contractor would realize that there was a grave chance that his product would be dangerously unsafe."[21]

The contract specification defense rests on the fact that a contractor usually is not negligent in following design specifications provided by a purchaser ("employer") pursuant to contract.[22] Accordingly, some courts have held that the defense should not apply to products liability claims based on strict liability, reasoning that implied warranty claims are based on a product's failure to be in a merchantable condition, not on the seller's fault,[23] and that the defense is inconsistent with the doctrine and policies

---

[16] See ch. 8, above.

[17] See Comments, 33 San Diego L. Rev. 385 (1996), 9 J. Corp. L. 113 (1983).

[18] Ryan v. Feeney & Sheehan Bldg. Co., 145 N.E. 321 (N.Y. 1924).

[19] See, e.g., Dorse v. Armstrong World Indus., 513 So.2d 1265 (Fla. 1987); Bynum v. FMC Corp., 770 F.2d 556 (5th Cir. 1985) (Miss. law).

[20] Although the principle is widely accepted, not every jurisdiction recognizes it. See, e.g., Collins v. Newman Mach. Co., 380 S.E.2d 314 (Ga. Ct. App. 1989).

[21] See Rest. (2d) Torts § 404 cmt. *a*.

[22] " '[W]here a product is manufactured according to plans and specifications furnished by the buyer and the alleged defect is open and obvious, the manufacturer is protected from liability for injuries occasioned by use of the product.' " Kelter v. Wasp, Inc., 2014 WL 4639914, at *3 (W.D. Ky. 2014).

[23] See Maldonado v. Creative Woodworking Concepts, Inc., 796 N.E.2d 662 (Ill. App. Ct. 2003). *Contra* Sunbeam Constr. Co. v. Fisci, 82 Cal. Rptr. 446 (Ct. App. 1969).

of strict liability in tort.[24] A growing majority of courts have disagreed, however, holding that even in strict liability, a manufacturer who merely fabricates a product according to the purchaser's design is not responsible, in the absence of an obvious defect, if the design proves bad.[25] "To hold [a contractor] liable for defective design would amount to holding a non-designer liable for design defect. Logic forbids any such result."[26]

In recent years, the notion of truly "strict" products liability in tort has withered substantially as courts and commentators have increasingly recognized the close nexus between negligence and strict liability in cases involving defects in design.[27] As the strict liability straw man continues to unravel, courts that in the past declined to allow the contract specification defense in actions denominated as "strict" liability should be more open to recognizing the appropriateness of this defense under modern products liability principles. In short, the soundness of applying the contract specification defense to design defect claims should not depend on the underlying theory of liability, whether negligence, implied warranty, or strict liability in tort.[28]

Some products liability reform statutes, directly or indirectly, address the effect of compliance with contract specifications. Thus, at least one state statute effectively adopts a contract specification defense by shielding altogether defendants who manufacture products according to the design specifications of others;[29] a couple of statutes classify such manufacturers as "sellers," meaning retailers, and so relieve them from strict products liability entirely[30] or contingently if the designing manufacturer is insolvent or not subject to suit;[31] and a couple of others give a manufacturer a right of indemnity against a seller (perhaps a large retail chain, like Walmart) which provides plans and specifications that give rise to a products liability claim.[32]

---

[24] See, e.g., Hendricks v. Comerio Ercole, 763 F. Supp. 505 (D. Kan. 1991); Dorse v. Armstrong World Indus., 513 So.2d 1265 (Fla. 1987); Nobriga v. Raybestos-Manhattan, Inc., 683 P.2d 389 (Haw. 1984); McLaughlin v. Sikorsky Aircraft, 195 Cal. Rptr. 764 (Ct. App. 1983); Michalko v. Cooke Color & Chem. Corp., 451 A.2d 179 (N.J. 1982).

[25] See, e.g., Smith v. Holland LP, 2019 WL 1228079, at *5 (D.D.C. 2019); Hopfer v. Neenah Foundry Co., 477 S.W.3d 116, 125 (Mo. Ct. App. 2015) (contract specifications defense is available in both negligence and strict liability actions); Hatch v. Trail King Indus., 656 F.3d 59, 69 (1st Cir. 2011) (Mass. law) (most cases—whether in negligence, implied warranty, and strict liability in tort—"limit the liability for fabricators/manufacturers who build to specification"; quoting and relying on Rest. (2d) of Torts § 404 cmt. *a*); Rogers v. Budget Truck Rental, LLC, 2008 WL 4926698, at *3 (Conn. Super. Ct. 2008) (adopting the defense as a matter of first impression; "a manufacturer is not liable for a design defect that causes injury to the consumer if the product is manufactured according to the designer/buyer's specifications, unless the specifications are obviously dangerous and should not be followed"); Thompson v. Hirano Tecseed Co., 456 F.3d 805, 809–10 (8th Cir. 2006) (Minn. law) (collecting cases); Szatkowski v. Turner & Harrison, Inc., 584 N.Y.S.2d 170, 171 (App. Div. 1992); Moon v. Winger Boss Co., 287 N.W.2d 430, 434 (Neb. 1980); Hunt v. Blasius, 384 N.E.2d 368, 371 (Ill. 1978).

[26] Garrison v. Rohm & Haas Co., 492 F.2d 346, 351 (6th Cir. 1974) (Ky. law).

[27] See §§ 5.7–5.9, 8.7, and 8.8, above.

[28] See, e.g., Hannah v. Johnson & Johnson Inc., 2020 WL 3497010, at *9 (D.N.J. 2020) (Mo. law) ("a contractor's compliance with its customer's plans and specifications is, with limited exceptions . . ., a complete defense to strict liability and negligence claims based on defective design"); Thompson v. Hirano Tecseed Co., 456 F.3d 805, 809–10 (8th Cir. 2006) (Minn. law).

[29] See Wash. Rev. Code Ann. § 7.72.010(2) (such a party not a "manufacturer" for purposes of design defect liability). *But cf.* Neher v. II Morrow Inc., 145 F.3d 1339 (9th Cir. 1998) (Wash. law).

[30] See Ga. Code Ann. § 51–1–11.1.

[31] See N.J. Stat. Ann. §§ 2A:58C–8 (classifying any person who "prepares or assembles a manufacturer's product according to the manufacturer's plan, intention, design, specifications or formulations" as a "product seller") and 2A:58C–9 (product sellers contingently relieved of all strict liability claims).

[32] See Ariz. Rev. Stat. Ann. § 12–684(C); Idaho Code Ann. § 6–1407(3).

§ 14.3 GOVERNMENT CONTRACTOR DEFENSE

The government contractor defense, a close cousin to the contract specification defense, is a special doctrine that applies only to manufacturers who contract with the government to build a product according to specifications provided or approved by the government.[33] The issue here may be illustrated by considering the difficulty facing an automotive company—say, Chrysler—that contracts with the United States Army to produce a number of Jeeps according to a design provided by a federal procurement official. If a roll bar designed according to the contract specifications collapses in a rollover accident, injuring the occupants, it hardly seems fair to allow the accident victims to maintain a design defect claim against Chrysler.

While some form of government contractor defense has existed for many decades,[34] this defense gained prominence in 1988 when the Supreme Court decided *Boyle v. United Technologies Corp.*[35] Having redefined the nature and scope of the defense and clarified its elements, *Boyle* is now the starting point for determining how a products liability claim may be affected if a product was fabricated according to specifications provided or approved by a federal (and possibly by a state or local) governmental agency.[36]

The *Boyle* Case

In *Boyle v. United Technologies Corp.*,[37] the copilot of a Marine Corps helicopter was killed during a training exercise when his helicopter crashed in the ocean. Boyle survived the impact of the crash, but, as the helicopter sank in the water, he was unable to escape and drowned. Boyle's representatives sued the helicopter's manufacturer, the Sikorsky Division of United Technologies, claiming that the escape hatch was defectively designed because (1) it opened out rather than in, precluding it from opening in a submerged craft because of water pressure, and (2) the position of various instruments blocked access to the escape hatch handle.[38] Plaintiff won at trial, but the Fourth Circuit Court of Appeals reversed on the basis of that court's version of the "military contractor defense,"[39] and the Supreme Court granted certiorari.[40] The issue before the Court was whether and "when a contractor providing military equipment to the Federal Government can be held

---

[33] See, e.g., Clark, *Boyle* As Constitutional Preemption, 92 Notre Dame L. Rev. 2129 (2017); Johns, Should Blackwater and Halliburton Pay for the People They've Killed? Or Are Government Contractors Entitled to a Common-Law, Combatant-Activities Defense?, 80 Tenn. L. Rev. 347 (2013); Watts, Differences Without Distinctions: *Boyle*'s Government Contractor Defense Fails to Recognize the Critical Differences Between Civilian and Military Plaintiffs and Between Military and Non-Military Procurement, 60 Okla. L. Rev. 647 (2007); Slawotsky, The Expansion of the Government Contractor Defense, 31 Tort & Ins. L.J. 929 (1996); Davis, The Supreme Court and Our Culture of Irresponsibility, 31 Wake Forest L. Rev. 1075, 1091–1116 (1996); Cass and Gillette, The Government Contractor Defense: Contractual Allocation of Public Risk, 77 Va. L. Rev. 257 (1991); Green and Matasar, The Supreme Court and the Products Liability Crisis: Lessons from *Boyle*'s Government Contractor Defense, 63 S. Cal. L. Rev. 637 (1990). See generally Frumer, Friedman, and Sklaren, Products Liability ch. 31; Am. Law Prod. Liab. 3d ch. 45.

[34] See, e.g., Sanner v. Ford Motor Co., 381 A.2d 805, 806 (N.J. Super. Ct. App. Div. 1977) (passenger injured in army jeep accident could not maintain suit against jeep manufacturer for failing to equip vehicle with seatbelts and a roll bar "since defendant had no discretion with respect to the installation of seatbelts and since it strictly adhered to plans and specifications owned and provided by the Government").

[35] 487 U.S. 500 (1988).

[36] The history of the defense is sketched in Frumer, Friedman, and Sklaren, Products Liability § 31.01.

[37] 487 U.S. 500 (1988).

[38] Id. at 502–03.

[39] Boyle v. United Tech. Corp., 792 F.2d 413 (4th Cir. 1986). The Fourth Circuit had adopted this defense in another case, Tozer v. LTV Corp., 792 F.2d 403 (4th Cir. 1986), decided on the same day as *Boyle*.

[40] 479 U.S. 1029 (1987).

liable under state tort law for injury caused by a design defect."[41] As a matter of federal common law, a bare majority of the Court approved a government contractor defense.[42]

Writing for the majority, Justice Scalia reasoned that allowing state products liability claims against military contractors who fabricate products according to designs approved by federal officials would frustrate the purposes of the discretionary function exception to governmental liability in the Federal Tort Claims Act.[43] Because military design specifications involve a host of choices including the "tradeoff between greater safety and greater combat effectiveness,"[44] they involve discretionary decisions with which tort suits against contractors would interfere. If products liability claims challenging such choices were allowed, government contractors would raise their prices to offset this risk of liability, passing on the financial burden to the United States.[45] "It makes little sense," reasoned Justice Scalia, "to insulate the Government against financial liability for the judgment that a particular feature of military equipment is necessary when the Government produces the equipment itself, but not when it contracts for the production."[46] Thus, when these federal interests conflict with state products liability law that would allow a design defect claim against a military contractor, the state law must give way.[47]

To protect these federal interests, *Boyle* adopted a three-part test that shields military contractors from design defect liability under state products liability law—when "(1) the United States approved reasonably precise specifications, (2) the equipment conformed to those specifications, and (3) the supplier warned the United States about the dangers in the use of the equipment that were known to the supplier but not to the United States."[48]

Boyle in the Courts

"Stripped to its essentials," in the words of one court, "the government contractor defense arises when the defendant can prove that 'the government made me do it.' "[49] This may be a fair summary of *Boyle*'s underlying concept, but the case has raised a number of thorny issues. For example, while it is clear that *Boyle*'s first element, the "approval" prong, does not require that the government completely design a product by itself,[50] the Court did not specify the requisite type or extent of government involvement

---

41 *Boyle*, 487 U.S. at 502.

42 Because it was unclear whether the Fourth Circuit had decided whether a jury reasonably could have found each of the elements of the defense as formulated by the Supreme Court, the Court remanded for clarification. See id. at 514.

43 Although Congress in 28 U.S.C. § 1346(b) waived the sovereign immunity of the United States for negligent or wrongful conduct of federal employees, 28 U.S.C. § 2680(a) retains sovereign immunity for "[a]ny claim . . . based upon the exercise or performance or the failure to exercise or perform a discretionary function or duty on the part of a federal agency or an employee of the Government, whether or not the discretion involved be abused."

44 *Boyle*, 487 U.S. at 511.

45 Id. at 511–12.

46 Id. at 512.

47 Id.

48 Id.

49 Gray v. Lockheed Aeronautical Sys. Co., 125 F.3d 1371, 1377 (11th Cir. 1997), vacated, 524 U.S. 924 (1998).

50 "The design ultimately selected may well reflect a significant policy judgment by Government officials whether or not the contractor rather than those officials developed the design. In addition, it does not seem to us sound policy to penalize, and thus deter, active contractor participation in the design process . . . ." *Boyle*, 487 U.S. at 513.

in "approving" a product's design. Thus, it was early held that the defense does not apply if the government merely "rubber stamps" the contractor's design.[51] Yet the government need not participate in developing a product's design, so long as it genuinely evaluates the content of the contractor's ultimate design decisions.[52] And even if the government is significantly involved in and approves a product's design as a whole, *Boyle* requires proof that a government officer considered the particular design feature that created the hazard that caused the injury giving rise to the products liability claim.[53] *Boyle* raises a host of other issues.[54] For example, courts are split on whether the government contractor defense applies only to manufacturers of *military* equipment (military contractors);[55] some hold the defense so limited,[56] while others hold that *Boyle*'s reasoning protects manufacturers of any type of government equipment (government contractors).[57]

As for the types of defects covered by the defense, *Boyle* by its terms protects a contractor only for *design* defect claims. Yet warning claims also are covered by the

---

[51] See, e.g., Trevino v. General Dynamics Corp., 865 F.2d 1474 (5th Cir. 1989) (although Navy ultimately "approved" contractor's design of diving hangar, Navy set only general performance standards and left contractor with complete design discretion). "A rubber stamp is not a discretionary function; therefore, a rubber stamp is not 'approval' under *Boyle*." Id. at 1480. Accord Getz v. Boeing Co., 654 F.3d 852, 861 (9th Cir. 2011); Jowers v. Lincoln Elec. Co., 617 F.3d 346, 353 (5th Cir. 2010); In re Agent Orange Prod. Liab. Litig., 517 F.3d 76, 90 (2d Cir. 2008).

"Rather, approval must result from a 'continuous exchange' and 'back and forth dialogue' between the contractor and the government. When the government engages in a thorough review of the allegedly defective design and takes an active role in testing and implementing that design, *Boyle*'s first element is met." Getz v. Boeing Co., 654 F.3d 852, 861 (9th Cir. 2011).

[52] See Haltiwanger v. Unisys Corp., 949 F. Supp. 898 (D.D.C. 1996).

[53] *Boyle*, 487 U.S. at 512. See, e.g., Lofgren v. Polaris Indus., Inc., 2021 WL 2580047, at *6 (M.D. Tenn. 2021) (denying defendant's summary judgment motion; issues of fact remained whether evidence of Army's participation in design of Lightweight Tactical All-Terrain Vehicle satisfied first *Boyle* prong); Determan v. Boeing Co., 782 Fed. Appx. 657, 658 (9th Cir. 2019) (mem.) ("undisputed evidence [that] government considered and approved reasonably precise specifications for the design feature" of the EAPS system that allegedly caused fatal helicopter crash); Kase v. Metalclad Insulation Corp., 212 Cal. Rptr. 3d 198, 201 (Ct. App. 2016) (the defense extended to broker of commercially available asbestos insulation; Navy's "years of evaluating and weighing the utility of and the health hazards associated with asbestos products" and specifications requiring asbestos products satisfied *Boyle* test); Getz v. Boeing Co., 654 F.3d 852, 861 (9th Cir. 2011) (Army reviewed and approved reasonably precise specifications of helicopter that crashed in Afghanistan, including a specification explicitly stating the absence of the particular safety system complained of by plaintiffs, which "specification resulted from careful deliberation, not a 'rubber stamp' "); Lewis v. Babcock Indus., 985 F.2d 83 (2d Cir. 1993) (reordering product with knowledge of defect constitutes approval).

[54] See Annot., 53 A.L.R.5th 535 (1997).

[55] See Al-Khawaldeh v. Tackett, 2021 WL 3145669, at *8 (W.D. Tex. 2021) ("Although the government contractor defense originally was limited to product liability cases involving contractors providing defective products to the United States military, it has been applied to a broader class of cases."; reviewing cases); Stilwell v. General Ry. Servs., Inc., 605 S.E.2d 500, 504 (N.C. Ct. App. 2004) (noting split in federal circuits whether defense applies to all contractors and collecting cases).

[56] See, e.g., In re Hawaii Fed. Asbestos Cases, 960 F.2d 806, 812 (9th Cir. 1992) (asbestos insulation used in Navy ships not "manufactured with the special needs of the military in mind"); Nielsen v. George Diamond Vogel Paint Co., 892 F.2d 1450 (9th Cir. 1990) (civilian government employee injured by paint manufactured to specifications of Army Corps of Engineers).

[57] See, e.g., Silverstein v. Northrop Grumman Corp., 842 A.2d 881 (N.J. Super. Ct. App. Div. 2004) (manufacturer of postal vehicle); Wisner v. Unisys Corp., 917 F. Supp. 1501, 1509 (D. Kan. 1996) (Postal Service designed letter sorter that caused repetitive stress injuries); Haltiwanger v. Unisys Corp., 949 F. Supp. 898 (D.D.C. 1996) (same); Carley v. Wheeled Coach, 991 F.2d 1117 (3d Cir. 1993) (defense applicable to manufacturer of ambulance, with high center of gravity, manufactured to General Services Administration specifications). In Hercules, Inc. v. United States, 516 U.S. 417 (1996), the Supreme Court characterized the *Boyle* defense as the "government contractor defense" which "shields contractors from tort liability for products manufactured for the Government in accordance with Government specifications, if the contractor warned the United States about any hazards known to the contractor but not to the Government." Id. at 422.

government contractor defense,[58] protecting contractors from defective warning claims, particularly if the federal contract includes warning requirements that significantly conflict with state products liability law. Yet, here, too, the defense will be denied if a manufacturer fails to establish the three *Boyle* prongs.[59] While the second prong of the *Boyle* test strongly suggests that manufacturing defects lie outside the government contractor defense,[60] leaving manufacturers liable for such defects, the defense should apply to such defects, too, in unusual situations where the government requires or truly approves specific manufacturing standards.[61] As for causes of action, the government contractor defense logically should apply to claims for negligence, breach of warranty, and strict liability in tort alike.[62]

While the *Boyle* government contractor defense is a federal common-law rule applicable only to manufacturers supplying equipment to federal agencies, such a defense applies to products liability claims tried in state as well as federal courts.[63]

---

[58] See, e.g., In re Asbestos Litig., 2021 WL 3025842, at *4 (D. Del. 2021) (the defense "is applicable to both design defect and failure to warn claims"); Sebright v. General Elec. Co., 525 F. Supp. 3d 217, 252 (D. Mass. 2021) (defense applies in failure to warn cases when the contractor demonstrates: "(1) the government issued reasonably precise specifications governing warnings; (2) the contractor provided the warnings required by the government; and (3) the contractor warned the government about dangers in the equipment's use that were known to the contractor but not to the government").

[59] See, e.g., Spurlin v. Air & Liquid Sys. Corp., 537 F. Supp. 3d 1162, 1178–79 (S.D. Cal. 2021) (denying defendant's motion to dismiss under government contractor defense; no proof that defendants warned the US about asbestos hazards in the equipment, and question of fact whether defendant knew more about the dangers of asbestos than did the Navy); Sebright v. General Elec. Co., 525 F. Supp. 3d 217, 252 (D. Mass. 2021) (defense inapplicable; "The contractor must show 'that the government exercised its discretion in connection with the warnings in some meaningful way.' "); Graves v. 3M Co., 447 F. Supp. 3d 908, 916 (D. Minn. 2020) (defendant failed to establish government control over combat earplug instructions or warnings).

[60] See, e.g., Rodriguez v. General Dynamics Armament & Tech. Prods., Inc., 2010 WL 1507979, at *1 (D. Hawai'i 2010) (if a manufacturing defect caused explosion, the mortar shell could not have been manufactured per government specifications, and the defense would not apply); Feldman v. Kohler Co., 918 S.W.2d 615 (Tex. App. 1996); Sundstrom v. McDonnell Douglas Corp., 816 F. Supp. 587 (N.D. Cal. 1993).

[61] See, e.g., Lofgren v. Polaris Indus. Inc., 2021 WL 2580047, at *4 n.22 (M.D. Tenn. 2021) (defense applies to design or manufacturing defects); Rodriguez v. Lockheed Martin Corp., 627 F.3d 1259, 1265–66 (9th Cir. 2010) (acknowledging the possibility that government contractor defense might apply to manufacturing defects, but noting that the equipment must conform to the precise specifications, which conformity the defendant must prove); In re Hanford Nuclear Reservation Litig., 497 F.3d 1005, 1018 (9th Cir. 2007) (government contractor defense applies to manufacturing processes as well as design defects); Roll v. Tracor, Inc., 102 F. Supp. 2d 1200 (D. Nev. 2000) (recognizing that *Boyle* may apply to manufacturing defect claims but holding that manufacturer of flare failed to establish that government approved reasonably specific manufacturing specifications and that mishap could have been caused by aberrational defect that does not implicate federal interests); Bentzlin v. Hughes Aircraft Co., 833 F. Supp. 1486 (C.D. Cal. 1993) (when government involves itself in manufacturing process of sophisticated military weaponry such as Maverick missile, manufacturer of such equipment may be immunized from manufacturing defect claims).

[62] See, e.g., Lofgren v. Polaris Indus. Inc., 2021 WL 2580047, at *4 n.22 (M.D. Tenn. 2021) (government contractor defense "applies to strict liability, negligence, and breach of warranty claims arising out of design or manufacturing defects"); Kern v. Roemer Mach. & Welding Co., 820 F. Supp. 719 (S.D.N.Y. 1992) (summary judgment for defendant on all three claims), aff'd without opinion, 996 F.2d 302 (2d Cir. 1993).

The result may be different under state law versions of the government contractor defense. See, e.g., Graham v. Concord Constr., Inc., 999 P.2d 1264, 1266 (Wash. 2000) (contractor immunized from liability only if not negligent).

[63] See, e.g., Preston v. M1 Support Servs., L.P., 628 S.W.3d 300, 315 (Tex. App. 2020); Tarjani v. Metalclad Insulation Corp., 2018 WL 1870722, at *3 (Cal. Ct. App. 2018), noncitable; Stilwell v. General Ry. Servs., Inc., 605 S.E.2d 500, 504–05 (N.C. Ct. App. 2004); Silverstein v. Northrop Grumman Corp., 842 A.2d 881 (N.J. Super. Ct. App. Div. 2004); Graham v. Concord Constr., Inc., 999 P.2d 1264 (Wash. 2000); Feldman v. Kohler Co., 918 S.W.2d 615 (Tex. App. 1996) (thorough review of doctrine). While applicable in state courts, *Boyle* appears to allow defendants sued in state courts to remove the case to federal court whether or not federal claims are alleged or if there is diversity of citizenship. See, e.g., Madden v. Able Supply Co., 205 F. Supp. 2d 695 (S.D. Tex. 2002) (clothing the manufacturer of turbine generator on Navy vessel with "federal officer" status under federal officer removal statute); Miller v. Diamond Shamrock Co., 275 F.3d 414 (5th Cir.

Whether contractors who manufacture and sell products to state and local governments should receive similar protection under state law against both design and warning defect claims is an entirely separate question that the individual states must answer as a matter of their local products liability law. Most state courts thus are free, as a matter of state common law, either to apply or refuse to apply a *Boyle*-type government contractor defense to state and local government contractors.[64] Several states, however, have enacted products liability reform statutes that protect government contractors who comply with mandatory government contract specifications.[65]

§ 14.4 REGULATORY COMPLIANCE DEFENSE

Manufacturers of many types of products are subject to different forms of safety regulation—by federal (and possibly state) administrative agencies, *ex ante*, and by the judicial products liability system, *ex post*. For example, manufacturers of cars and airplanes first must meet the often detailed design safety standards of the National Highway Traffic Safety Administration or the Federal Aviation Administration only to be second-guessed by juries passing on the very same issues, years later, when a person injured in a crash complains in court. Producers of other products, such as industrial machinery, have to endure a third layer of regulation, first having to conform to safety standards of a federal agency—like the Occupational Safety and Health Administration—then to the standards of each state's occupational safety agency, and finally to a state's judicial standards of "defectiveness," if the product is involved in an accident and ends up subject to a products liability challenge in court. Thus, manufacturers fairly question the logic and fairness of having to conform to safety regulations imposed by the government's executive/administrative branch before marketing a product only to have the government's judicial branch declare the conforming product illegal thereafter.

The idea of a "regulatory compliance" (or "government standards") defense,[66] which would bar a products liability action if an accident product complied with all relevant

---

2001) (Agent Orange manufacturer protected by *Boyle* with status of a "federal officer" entitled to remove cases to federal court under 28 U.S.C. § 1442(a)(1)).

[64] Compare Showers Appraisals, LLC v. Musson Bros., 835 N.W.2d 226, 240 (Wis. 2013) (action by owner of flooded store against contractor hired by state to replace storm sewer in front of owner's building; government contractor must establish the three *Boyle* requirements and also "demonstrate that the conduct for which immunity is sought was the implementing of a governmental entity's decision made during the exercise of the entity's legislative, quasi-legislative, judicial or quasi-judicial functions" and that it does not arise from contractor's negligent performance of the work), with Conner v. Quality Coach, Inc., 750 A.2d 823, 834 (Pa. 2000) (rejecting defense, and noting "the perverse effect of permitting a government officer to minimize as a consideration in procurement decisions (at least as a matter of financial concern) external societal costs, particularly in terms of potential diminishment to public safety"). See also Nickolson v. Alabama Trailer Co., 791 So.2d 926 (Ala. 2000) (reversing summary judgment where plaintiff proved that state's design of trailer was so obviously dangerous that no competent manufacturer would follow specifications).

[65] See Ind. Code Ann. § 34–20–5–1(2) (rebuttable presumption of non-liability); Kan. Stat. Ann. § 60–3304(c) (absolute defense), limited on preemption grounds, Troutman v. Curtis, 143 P.3d 74 (Kan. Ct. App. 2006); Wash. Rev. Code Ann. § 7.72.050(2) (absolute defense).

[66] See Lens, Product Recalls: Why Is Tort Law Deferring To Agency Inaction?, 90 St. John's L. Rev. 329 (2016); Geistfeld, Tort Law in the Age of Statutes, 99 Iowa L. Rev. 957, 991–1019 (2014); Ausness et al., Providing a Safe Harbor for Those Who Play by the Rules: The Case for a Strong Regulatory Compliance Defense, 2008 Utah L. Rev. 115; Symposium, U.S. Food and Drug Regulation in Its First Century and Beyond, 93 Cornell L. Rev. 901 (2008) (articles by Grossman, Lawson, Noah, O'Reilly, Struve, Tobias, and Vladeck); V. Schwartz, Silverman, and Appel, "That's Unfair!" Says Who—The Government or the Litigant?: Consumer Protection Claims Involving Regulated Conduct, 47 Washburn L.J. 93 (2007); V. Schwartz and Goldberg, A Prescription for Drug Liability and Regulation, 58 Okla. L. Rev. 135, 174–76 (2005); Symposium, Regulatory Compliance as a Defense to Products Liability, 88 Geo. L.J. 2049 (2000) (articles by Rabin, Dinh, M. Green and

regulations of a safety agency, is a cousin of the federal preemption defense.[67] However, the two defenses are fundamentally distinct. When a manufacturer in a products liability case asserts that it complied with certain government standards of product safety, the regulatory compliance/government standards issue is whether the court, as a matter of state law, should borrow the safety standards of the regulatory agency (or statute) as the formal test of product defect. By contrast, the federal preemption defense concerns the constitutional issue, under the Supremacy Clause, of when federal law (such as safety regulations of a federal agency) overrides state products liability law (normally standards set by courts in defect adjudications) with which it may conflict.[68] While the two defenses share the common issue of whether statutory and regulatory safety standards should bar products liability actions, the government standards defense is a state law defense recognized narrowly in only a small minority of jurisdictions, whereas the federal preemption defense is a federal law defense that binds all courts when Congress so intends.

A government standards defense, which would bar a products liability action if the accident product complied with all relevant governmental safety standards at the time it was sold,[69] has a superficial appearance of fair play and common sense. However, arguments favoring the defense are in most instances more than offset by a large number of problems: statutes (and sometimes regulations) tend to be abstract, vague, limited in scope, and incapable of adequately addressing the myriad factual situations that may arise in individual cases; conversely, regulations may be so narrow and specific that they fail to capture related matters at the margins of the regulation, leaving large categories of similar matters unregulated; statutes and regulations are difficult to amend to reflect changes over time, and those dealing with science and technology may quickly become obsolete; statutes and regulations both may be shaped more by lobbyists for the regulated parties than by detached and objective decisionmakers neutrally balancing all affected interests in pursuit of optimal safety; and, unlike the inherent flexibility of the common law, the rigidity of regulatory safety standards tends to stifle creativity and

---

Schultz, Noah, and Stewart); T. Schwartz, Regulatory Standards and Products Liability: Striking the Right Balance Between the Two, 30 U. Mich. J.L. Reform 431 (1997); Ausness, The Case for a "Strong" Regulatory Compliance Defense, 55 Md. L. Rev. 1210 (1996); T. Schwartz, The Role of Federal Safety Regulations in Products Liability Actions, 41 Vand. L. Rev. 1121 (1988); Frumer, Friedman, and Sklaren, Products Liability § 18.05.

[67] See Rabin, Reassessing Regulatory Compliance, 88 Geo. L.J. 2049, 2053 (2000). Products Liability Rest. § 4(b) cmt. *e* explains the distinction between the two doctrines:

> When a court concludes that a defendant is not liable by reason of having complied with a safety . . . statute or regulation, it is deciding that the product in question is not defective as a matter of the law of that state. The safety [law] may be a federal provision, but the decision to give it determinative effect is a state-law determination. In contrast, in federal preemption, the court decides as a matter of federal law that the relevant federal [law] reflects, expressly or impliedly, the intent of Congress to displace state law, including state tort law, with the federal statute or regulation.

A closer cousin to the regulatory compliance defense is the negligence doctrine governing the effect of compliance with a safety statute or regulation. See § 2.4, above. A more distant cousin is the government contractor defense. See § 14.3, above.

[68] See, e.g., Rollins v. Bombardier Recreational Prod., Inc., 366 P.3d 33, 43 (Wash. Ct. App. 2015) (Federal Boat Safety Act; preemption savings clauses in general "do not broadly protect tort claims but, rather, prevent manufacturers from using compliance with federal regulation as a general defense to tort liability"). On federal preemption, see § 14.5, below.

[69] For a brief discussion of the effects of a manufacturer's compliance with government safety standards, see § 6.4, above.

innovation.[70] For these and other reasons, courts have rarely seen fit to allow a common-law regulatory compliance defense. As explored below, however, courts in very unusual instances have recognized a kind of government standards defense, and several states have legislated various narrow forms of the defense as part of tort reform.

Judicial Rejection of Government Standards Defense

The issue of whether there should be a government standards defense is not unique to products liability law. For many years, many types of actors, in many types of situations where conduct is subjected to governmental regulation *ex ante*, have sought to assert a government standards defense to liability in tort *ex post*. Courts[71] and commentators[72] long ago rejected the idea that the law should conclusively protect an actor from liability for harm from conduct that comports with a safety standard required by statute or administrative regulation. Courts do make an exception to the general rule in limited, infrequent situations where a defendant conformed its behavior precisely as directed by an especially well-considered government standard.[73] But it is fundamental law that governmental safety standards adopt only a minimum safety floor below which an actor may face criminal penalties but above which due care may require the actor to be more cautious.[74]

Following these fundamental tort law principles, virtually all courts reject the general idea of a regulatory compliance defense to products liability actions, whether based on negligence, warranty, or strict liability in tort.[75] Compliance with a relevant

---

70 "Common law tort courts have long provided a safer haven from the corruption that can accompany the making of statutes and regulations; among institutional actors, judges are relatively likely to treat injured persons fairly." Bernstein, Products Liability in the United States Supreme Court: A Venture in Memory of Gary Schwartz, 53 S.C. L. Rev. 1193, 1219 (2002). See T. Schwartz, The Role of Federal Safety Regulations in Products Liability Actions, 41 Vand. L. Rev. 1121 (1988).

71 See, e.g., Grand Trunk Ry. Co. of Can. v. Ives, 144 U.S. 408, 419–27 (1892). "Courts have generally not looked with favor upon the use of statutory compliance as a defense to tort liability." Ramirez v. Plough, Inc., 863 P.2d 167, 173 (Cal. 1993).

72 See, e.g., Morris, The Role of Criminal Statutes in Negligence Actions, 49 Colum. L. Rev. 21, 42 (1949).

73 See Keeton, Dobbs, Keeton, and Owen, Prosser and Keeton on the Law of Torts § 36, at 233.

74 "Such a standard is no more than a minimum, and it does not necessarily preclude a finding that the actor was negligent in failing to take additional precautions." Id. See Rest. (2d) Torts § 288C ("Compliance with a legislative enactment or an administrative regulation does not prevent a finding of negligence where a reasonable man would take additional precautions.").

75 See, e.g., Specter v. Texas Turbine Conversions, Inc., 2021 WL 243776, at *9 (D. Alaska 2021) (FAA approval of engine conversion was "not dispositive"); Evans v. Nacco Materials Handling Grp., Inc., 810 S.E.2d 462, 469 (Va. 2018) ("not dispositive"); Cruz v. Kumho Tire Co., 2015 WL 2193796, at *16 (N.D.N.Y. 2015) (compliance with regulatory testing requirements not determinative of due care); Kendall v. Hoffman-La Roche, Inc., 36 A.3d 541, 554 (N.J. 2012) (compliance with FDA regulations is "compelling" but "not absolute" proof that manufacturer satisfied its duty to warn); Red Hill Hosiery Mill, Inc. v. MagneTek, Inc., 582 S.E.2d 632 (N.C. Ct. App. 2003) (compliance not determinative of defectiveness; implied warranty); Abadie v. Metropolitan Life Ins. Co., 784 So.2d 46, 82 (La. Ct. App. 2001) (jury charge that "[c]ompliance with government standards is but one element or item of proof of whether or not the product is defective" accurately stated the law); Doyle v. Volkswagenwerk A.G., 481 S.E.2d 518 (Ga. 1997) (all three liability theories). See also Egbert v. Nissan N. Am., Inc., 167 P.3d 1058, 1060–62 (Utah 2007) (though Utah statute provides rebuttable presumption of nondefectiveness for compliance with government regulations, such a presumption is met by preponderance of evidence of defectiveness; at common law, manufacturer's compliance with regulation would be evidence of no defect to be weighed with all evidence).

The only apparent exception to this universal rule is where a plaintiff brings a design defect claim based solely on the consumer expectations test and the manufacturer has complied with governmentally mandated warnings. A few courts have held that compliance with the government's warning standards precludes a design defect claim based solely on consumer expectations because it would be "anomalous" for a consumer to expect a product to perform more safely than its government-mandated warnings indicate. This narrow exception was

governmental safety standard is some evidence of a manufacturer's non-negligence and a product's nondefectiveness, but it is not conclusive proof on those issues,[76] nor even on liability for punitive damages.[77] Compliance evidence is not unimportant,[78] particularly in helping disprove the kind of reprehensibility necessary for punitive damages,[79] but in a products liability case it serves only as "a piece of the evidentiary puzzle" rather than as "an impenetrable shield from liability."[80] This has been the rule since the early days of modern products liability law,[81] and, except for some relatively minor legislative retrenchments in several states, discussed below, the rule is as firmly entrenched today

first employed in cases alleging toxic shock syndrome from tampons but has now been applied to other products. See, e.g., Eriksen v. Mobay Corp., 41 P.3d 488 (Wash. Ct. App. 2002); Murphy v. Playtex Family Prods. Corp., 176 F. Supp. 2d 473 (D. Md. 2001), aff'd on point, 69 Fed. Appx. 140 (4th Cir. 2003); Haddix v. Playtex Family Prods. Corp., 138 F.3d 681 (7th Cir. 1998) (Ill. law); Papike v. Tambrands Inc., 107 F.3d 737 (9th Cir. 1997) (Cal. law).

[76] See, e.g., Walker v. Macy's Merch. Grp., Inc., 288 F. Supp. 3d 840, 861 (N.D. Ill. 2017) (as a matter of law, compliance with federal flammability standard was not conclusive proof that jacket was not defective); Kendall v. Hoffman-La Roche, Inc., 36 A.3d 541, 554 (N.J. 2012) (compliance with FDA regulations is not conclusive proof of warnings adequacy); Estep v. Mike Ferrell Ford Lincoln-Mercury, Inc., 672 S.E.2d 345, 356 (W. Va. 2008) (compliance with federal safety standards not conclusive that design was reasonable).

[77] Nor is compliance conclusive on liability for punitive damages where the manufacturer knows that the standard is insufficient. See, e.g., Daniel v. Wyeth Pharms., Inc., 15 A.3d 909, 932 (Pa. Super. Ct. 2011) ("compliance with industry and governmental safety standards 'does not, standing alone, automatically insulate a defendant from punitive damages' "); Morris v. Cessna Aircraft Co., 833 F. Supp. 2d 622, 643 (N.D. Tex. 2011) (though defendant conclusively proved compliance with all applicable regulations, plaintiff's other proofs of gross negligence sufficient to escape summary judgment on defendant's liability for punitive damages); Wyeth v. Rowatt, 244 P.3d 765, 779–84 (Nev. 2010) (affirming separate judgments for three women who developed breast cancer after taking defendant's hormone replacement drug, Prempro, totaling $35 million compensatory and $35 million punitive damages; company downplayed breast cancer risks, promoted unproven benefits, and claimed in its "warning" that the rate of breast cancer in its own human study did "not exceed that expected in the general population" contrary to evidence of appreciably increased risk and that it never even conducted a human study: "conduct that was fraught with reprehension and deception"); Gryc v. Dayton-Hudson Corp., 297 N.W.2d 727, 733–35 (Minn. 1980). See generally Owen & Davis on Products Liability § 26:33.

[78] See, e.g., Kendall v. Hoffman-La Roche, Inc., 36 A.3d 541, 554 (N.J. 2012) (compliance with FDA regulations); Morris v. Cessna Aircraft Co., 833 F. Supp. 2d 622, 641 (N.D. Tex. 2011) (compliance with governmental safety standards "constitutes strong and substantial evidence that a product is not defective"); Neill v. Novartis Consumer Health, Inc., 55 Cal. Rptr. 3d 551, 558 (Ct. App. 2007) (FDA standards do not "immunize a drug manufacturer from liability [but] are nevertheless entitled to 'serious consideration' on the issue of the safety"); Gable v. Gates Mills, 784 N.E.2d 739 (Ohio Ct. App. 2003) (compliance probative of what a reasonable consumer would expect when evaluating purchase but does not immunize manufacturer from liability); Wagner v. Clark Equip. Co., 700 A.2d 38, 51 (Conn. 1997) ("compliance with a federal regulation may carry more weight with a jury than compliance with an industry standard" because it "has the imprimatur of the federal government").

[79] See, e.g., Hardeman v. Monsanto Co., 997 F.3d 941, 980 (9th Cir. 2021) (Smith, J., dissenting) (Cal. law) ("Although compliance with regulations cannot 'eviscerate a claim for punitive damages,' . . . it does evidence that the harm 'was [not] the result of intentional malice, trickery, or deceit . . . .' "); Trenado v. Cooper Tire & Rubber Co., 2010 WL 9546053, at *16–17 (S.D. Tex. 2010). A number of states have statutes barring punitive damages against drug manufacturers for selling drugs that comply with applicable FDA regulations. See Owen & Davis on Products Liability § 26:33.

[80] Doyle v. Volkswagenwerk A.G., 481 S.E.2d 518, 521 (Ga. 1997).

[81] Early cases include Sherman v. M. Lowenstein & Sons, Inc., 282 N.Y.S.2d 142 (App. Div. 1967) (Flammable Fabrics Act, flammability standard); LaGorga v. Kroger Co., 275 F. Supp. 373 (W.D. Pa. 1967) (same), aff'd, 407 F.2d 671 (3d Cir. 1969); Berkebile v. Brantly Helicopter Corp., 281 A.2d 707 (Pa. Super. Ct. 1971) (FAA, airworthiness standard); Jonescue v. Jewel Home Shopping Serv., 306 N.E.2d 312 (Ill. App. Ct. 1973) (Federal Hazardous Substances Labeling Act); Stevens v. Parke, Davis & Co., 507 P.2d 653 (Cal. 1973) (FDA, drug labeling); Raymond v. Riegel Textile Corp., 484 F.2d 1025 (1st Cir. 1973) (N.H. law) (Flammable Fabrics Act, flammability standards); Hill v. Husky Briquetting, Inc., 220 N.W.2d 137 (Mich. Ct. App. 1974) (warnings on bags of charcoal for home use prescribed by state statute), aff'd, 223 N.W.2d 290 (Mich. 1974).

as ever.[82] The *Products Liability Restatement* provides quite simply that "a product's compliance with an applicable product safety statute or administrative regulation is properly considered in determining whether the product is defective with respect to the risks sought to be reduced by the statute or regulation, but such compliance does not preclude as a matter of law a finding of product defect."[83]

Occasionally a court asserts that regulatory compliance carries more weight than mere evidence of due care and a product's nondefectiveness—that compliance with government safety standards provides "strong evidence" of the manufacturer's non-liability.[84] And sometimes courts note that "where no special circumstances require extra caution, a court may find that conformity to the statutory standard amounts to due care as a matter of law."[85] While this is true, it is also tautological to say that a defendant who complies with a statutory standard is not liable for acting more safely than required by the statute if there was no reason to act more safely—which circles back to basing liability on the defendant's lack of negligence, not on the defendant's compliance with the statutory standard.[86]

Denying manufacturers a full-fledged regulatory compliance defense may appear to be unfair because it forces them to meet the safety standards of both governmental regulators and the courts, but this dual approach to product safety oversight generally makes good sense. Most product safety statutes, and most product safety regulations promulgated thereunder, are designed to prohibit (and criminalize) only the clearest and most egregious hazards. In addition to the problems with a regulatory compliance defense noted earlier, the limited resources of safety agencies generally preclude them from being effective arbiters of optimal, rather than minimal, safety. Consequently, the law allocates responsibility for product safety, first, to manufacturers, to make their products reasonably safe and so conforming to the safety obligations of both the regulators and the courts; second, to governmental regulators, to set minimum safety standards for products whose special dangers require regulatory intervention; and, finally, to the courts, to test a manufacturer's safety decisions, in the event of a product

---

[82] See, e.g., In re Bard IVC Filters Prods. Liab. Litig., 2021 WL 1616101, at *10 (D. Ariz. 2021); Evans v. Nacco Materials Handling Grp., Inc., 810 S.E.2d 462, 469 (Va. 2018) ("Governmental safety standards . . . are highly relevant on the question of whether the manufacturer's design was negligent because they permit an inference that the manufacturer exercised (or failed to exercise) ordinary prudence. . . . Governmental regulations and industry standards and practices are not dispositive, however."); Kendall v. Hoffman-La Roche, Inc., 36 A.3d 541, 554 (N.J. 2012) (compliance with FDA regulations "provides compelling, although not absolute, evidence that a manufacturer satisfied its duty to warn"); Estep v. Mike Ferrell Ford Lincoln-Mercury, Inc., 672 S.E.2d 345, 356 (W. Va. 2008); Red Hill Hosiery Mill, Inc. v. MagnaTek, Inc., 582 S.E.2d 632 (N.C. Ct. App. 2003) (implied warranty); Edwards v. Basel Pharms., 933 P.2d 298 (Okla. 1997) (strict liability in tort); Doyle v. Volkswagenwerk A.G., 481 S.E.2d 518 (Ga. 1997) (NHTSA Standard 208 on passive restraints); Wagner v. Roche Labs., 671 N.E.2d 252 (Ohio 1996) (FDA approval of package insert).

[83] Products Liability Rest. § 4(b). See cmt. *a*, noting that this principle concerns design and warning defects, but not manufacturing defects.

[84] See, e.g., Sims v. Washex Mach. Corp., 932 S.W.2d 559, 565 (Tex. App. 1995) ("Compliance with government regulations is strong evidence, although not conclusive, that a machine was not defectively designed.").

[85] Beatty v. Trailmaster Prods., Inc., 625 A.2d 1005, 1014 (Md. 1993). See also Jones v. Hittle Serv., Inc., 549 P.2d 1383, 1390 (Kan. 1976).

[86] See Rest. (2d) Torts § 288C cmt. *a*. Thus, in *Beatty*, the court, applying the statutory standard as a matter of law, ruled for the defendant because the plaintiff had failed to prove that the product, "either for negligence or strict liability purposes, was foreseeably unsafe, defective, or unreasonably dangerous." 625 A.2d at 1014.

accident, against judicial safety standards based on balance, reason, and fairness.[87] Admittedly, this multi-layered allocation of safety responsibility is somewhat complicated and burdensome on manufacturers, but it normally works quite well to minimize government intrusion into product design and labeling decisions while protecting the basic safety rights of product consumers.[88]

Litigation involving industrial machinery raises an interesting question of the admissibility of evidence that a manufacturer's industrial product complied with safety regulations of the Occupational Safety and Health Administration (OSHA), the federal agency that regulates the safety of products in the workplace.[89] Manufacturers normally are eager to introduce such evidence to show that their products met these safety standards and so are at least arguably nondefective. Moreover, such evidence helps focus the jury's attention on the employer's role in causing (or at least in not preventing) the injury, perhaps by failing to equip a machine with a safety device, and also on the possibility that the employee may have received workers' compensation. Manufacturers generally are barred from introducing evidence or argument directly on these issues,[90] and using evidence of compliance with OSHA standards may permit a manufacturer's counsel to get the jury thinking about these other factors related to the larger responsibility and compensation issues surrounding such cases. For these same reasons, plaintiffs' counsel seek to exclude evidence of an industrial machine's compliance with OSHA standards in order to keep attention focused on the manufacturer's responsibility for the injury.

But cases involving compliance with OSHA regulations are different from other types of regulatory compliance cases because OSHA standards on design and warning requirements of industrial machinery impose requirements for *employers*, not manufacturers.[91] Nevertheless, such standards do set safety minimums for industrial products, which would seem to have some relevance to the issue of product defectiveness in products liability litigation. Because such regulations may have some relevance to a manufacturer's duty,[92] to the defectiveness of its product or negligence,[93] a user's safety

---

[87] See Owen, The Moral Foundations of Products Liability Law: Toward First Principles, 68 Notre Dame L. Rev. 427 (1993).

[88] "It has long been the concern of this state to protect the health and safety of its citizens. . . . It is the widely held view that the FDA sets minimum standards for drug manufacturers as to design and warnings [but] compliance with these minimum standards does not necessarily complete the manufacturer's duty." Edwards v. Basel Pharms., 933 P.2d 298, 302 (Okla. 1997).

[89] See the Occupational Safety and Health Act of 1970, 29 U.S.C. §§ 651 et seq.

[90] Workers' compensation statutes bar employees from suing their own employers in tort for workplace injuries, of course, in exchange for guaranteed compensation under such insurance systems. See Weiler, Workers' Compensation and Product Liability: The Interaction of a Tort and a Non-Tort Regime, 50 Ohio St. L.J. 825 (1989); § 15.6, below.

[91] See, e.g., Hughes v. Lumbermens Mut. Cas. Co., 2 S.W.3d 218 (Tenn. Ct. App. 1999); Minichello v. U.S. Indus., 756 F.2d 26, 29 (6th Cir. 1985).

[92] See, e.g., Parker v. Schmeide Mach. & Tool Corp., 445 Fed. Appx. 231, 236–37 (11th Cir. 2011) (Ga. law) (proof that plaintiffs' employer, Lockheed, employed a much safer beryllium exposure standard than required by OSHA, because its studies showed OSHA standards were inadequate, relieved beryllium suppliers and manufacturers of a duty to warn under sophisticated user doctrine).

[93] See, e.g., Faulkner v. ABB, Inc., 2012 WL 2192285, at *5 (W.D. Ky. 2012) (state OSHA regulations "may establish the relevant standard of care [and] are admissible as evidence that [defendant's] alleged negligence was the proximate cause of [plaintiff's] death"); Parker v. Allentown, Inc., 891 F. Supp. 2d 773, 784 (D. Md. 2012) (state OSHA citation for accident subject to litigation probative of product's defectiveness); Doyle v. Volkswagenwerk A.G., 481 S.E.2d 518, 521 (Ga. 1997); Knitz v. Minster Mach. Co., 1987 WL 6486, at *31–33 (Ohio Ct. App. 1987).

expectations,[94] or proximate cause,[95] many courts allow evidence of a product's compliance with relevant OSHA standards in a products liability action against the manufacturer.[96] Yet, because of the limited relevance and probable prejudice of such evidence, other courts hold that OSHA safety standards are generally inadmissible in products liability litigation.[97]

Special Situations Where Compliance with Safety Standards May Be Conclusive

In certain limited situations, federal and state regulators study and regulate the safety of particular aspects of particular products especially closely. In such situations, if an agency has reasonably settled on a specific safety standard that appears optimal at the time, then much may be said for foreclosing products liability actions that demand more safety of manufacturers than the agency determined was appropriate. The Consumer Product Safety Commission (CPSC), for example, after conducting a major study of the problem of injuries to operators of power lawn mowers, adopted a regulation requiring that manufacturers design their mowers so that the blades will stop rotating within three seconds of when an operator releases the control handle.[98] Apart from the possibility of federal preemption,[99] and assuming that technology has not advanced sufficiently to resolve the problem in a clearly better way, a court might reasonably decide not to permit an operator, injured when his foot slips beneath the mower, to attempt to prove that the mower's design was defective because the blade did not stop within *two* seconds after the handle was released.

A rare situation where a court chose to adopt a regulatory standard as a matter of law was *Ramirez v. Plough, Inc.*[100] In this case, a 4-month-old child contracted Reye's Syndrome after his Spanish-speaking mother gave him some St. Joseph's Aspirin for Children to relieve his cold symptoms. The aspirin's label warned of the risk only in English, not in Spanish. Although the Food and Drug Administration (FDA) specifically permitted English-only labeling, the plaintiff claimed that the failure to warn in Spanish was inadequate. After considering the web of rules on foreign-language labeling requirements in various other contexts adopted by the California legislature; the FDA's quite specific rules governing foreign-language labeling that permitted, but did not

---

[94] See Wagner v. Clark Equip. Co., 700 A.2d 38, 50 (Conn. 1997).

[95] See Faulkner v. ABB, Inc., 2012 WL 2192285, at *5 (W.D. Ky. 2012) (whether the plaintiff's employer was the proximate cause of an accident).

[96] See, e.g., Arnoldy v. Forklift L.P., 927 A.2d 257, 263 (Pa. Super. Ct. 2007) (OSHA regulations properly admitted on negligence but not on strict liability), overruled on other grounds by Kiak v. Crown Equip. Corp., 989 A.2d 385 (Pa. Super. Ct. 2010); Couch v. Astec Indus., 53 P.3d 398 (N.M. Ct. App. 2002) (failure to comply with OSHA regulations relevant to manufacturer's negligence); Wagner v. Clark Equip. Co., 700 A.2d 38, 48–51 (Conn. 1997); Sims v. Washex Mach. Corp., 932 S.W.2d 559 (Tex. App. 1995); Vaughn v. Cannon USA, Inc., 1990 WL 369721 (W.D. Mich. 1990); Knitz v. Minster Mach. Co., 1987 WL 6486, at *27–33 (Ohio Ct. App. 1987) (OSHA and Ohio Industrial Commission standards, not conclusive of liability, but relevant to feasibility of design, availability of alternative safeguards, and other risk-benefit defect factors).

[97] See, e.g., Zickuhr v. Ericsson, Inc., 962 N.E.2d 974, 988–90 (Ill. App. Ct. 2011) (OSHA asbestos standards were relevant to employers, not to suppliers, so trial court's exclusion was not error); Hughes v. Lumbermens Mut. Cas. Co., 2 S.W.3d 218 (Tenn. Ct. App. 1999). See generally Frumer, Friedman, and Sklaren, Products Liability § 18.05[3] (citing cases both ways); R. Hogan and R. Moran, The Use of OSHA in Private Litigation, in Occupational Safety and Health Act ch. 12 (2004); Siris, OSHA Compliance: Can it be Used to Show that a Product is Safe?, 4 Prod. Liab. L.J. 156 (1993).

[98] Details of the study and regulation are examined in Southland Mower Co. v. Consumer Prod. Safety Comm'n, 619 F.2d 499 (5th Cir. 1980), which upheld the CPSC's three-second blade-stop criterion.

[99] See § 14.5, below.

[100] 863 P.2d 167 (Cal. 1993). *Ramirez* is also examined in § 9.3, above.

require, such labeling; and the multiplicity of health, social, cost, and practicability factors, the court concluded that foreign-language labeling requirements were better determined by legislatures and regulatory agencies than by the courts. For this reason, the court chose to adopt the legislative/regulatory rule permitting English-only warnings as the safety standard that properly should be applied in the case.[101]

The FDA closely reviews applications submitted by pharmaceutical manufacturers for new prescription drugs. Examining clinical data provided by the manufacturer, the agency balances the safety and efficacy of each proposed new drug and evaluates the adequacy of proposed warnings and usage information to be provided to doctors who will prescribe the drug. If a manufacturer properly performs its research and reporting obligations, and if the FDA approves a drug for sale with particular warnings and instructions, then it would seem to make little sense to let a jury reevaluate the same information and find the drug or warnings "defective."[102] On this basis, at least three states have immunized manufacturers of prescription drugs from strict liability,[103] and another has ruled that a manufacturer's compliance with FDA regulations for warnings in direct-to-consumer advertising of pharmaceuticals gives rise to a rebuttable presumption that the warnings satisfy the duty to warn.[104] When a plaintiff is harmed by an aspect of a product that met an applicable safety standard which the FDA or other regulatory agency scrupulously investigated and approved, and the perfect agency model fits the situation, then a court may properly conclude that the product's compliance with the governmentally approved safety standard conclusively establishes that the challenged aspect of the product was not defective.[105] Such cases, however, will be unusual.

Resting as it must on the ideal of a properly functioning safety agency fairly informed by the manufacturers it regulates, the notion of a regulatory compliance defense is supported by a slender reed. The model of a perfect FDA—fully informed of a

---

[101] Noting that the FDA stresses the importance of "uniformity in presentation and clarity of message," the court concluded: "To preserve that uniformity and clarity, to avoid adverse impacts upon the warning requirements mandated by the federal regulatory scheme, and in deference to the superior technical and procedural lawmaking resources of legislative and administrative bodies, we adopt the legislative/regulatory standard of care that mandates nonprescription drug package warnings in English only." Id. at 177.

[102] See Noah, Rewarding Regulatory Compliance: The Pursuit of Symmetry in Products Liability, 88 Geo. L.J. 2147 (2000).

[103] See, e.g., Berarov v. Archers-Daniels-Midland Co., 2019 WL 277717, at *8 (N.D. Ill. 2019) (Mich. law) (interpreting Mich. Comp. Law § 600.2946(4) as providing an absolute "affirmative defense" if a drug was approved by the FDA); Grundberg v. Upjohn Co., 813 P.2d 89 (Utah 1991); Brown v. Superior Ct., 751 P.2d 470 (Cal. 1988). See § 18.2, below.

[104] See Perez v. Wyeth Labs. Inc., 734 A.2d 1245, 1259 (N.J. 1999). "For all practical purposes, absent deliberate concealment or nondisclosure of after-acquired knowledge of harmful effects, compliance with FDA standards should be virtually dispositive of such claims. By definition, the advertising will have been 'fairly balanced.' " Id.

[105] See, e.g., Dentson v. Eddins & Lee Bus Sales, Inc., 491 So.2d 942, 944 (Ala. 1986) ("in this context, involving *school transportation*, an area traditionally reserved for the legislature, we find that the legislature's pronouncement is conclusive: a school bus in Alabama may not be found defective . . . because it is not equipped with passenger seat belts"). Products Liability Rest. § 4 cmt. *e* provides:

> Occasionally, after reviewing relevant circumstances, a court may properly conclude that a particular product safety standard set by statute or regulation adequately serves the objectives of tort law and therefore that the product that complies with the standard is not defective as a matter of law. Such a conclusion may be appropriate when the safety statute or regulation was promulgated recently, thus supplying currency to the standard therein established; when the specific standard addresses the very issue of product design or warning presented in the case before the court; and when the court is confident that the deliberative process by which the safety standard was established was full, fair, and thorough and reflected substantial expertise.

drug's foreseeable hazards before the drug is marketed, kept fully informed thereafter of adverse drug-reactions, fully funded by Congress, and with no political pressure to expedite the approval of new drugs—does not closely fit the real world.[106] And other safety agencies stray even further from the ideal than the FDA. This suggests that courts should base defectiveness determinations on broader considerations than a manufacturer's compliance with an administrative agency's product safety regulation—even if the safety standard applies directly to the product feature of which the plaintiff complains, and even if the agency's procedures normally are rigorous and precise—because of the probability of imperfections in the safety standard or the agency's procedures in any particular case. Thus, courts and juries should give only such weight to a product's compliance with a governmental safety standard as is warranted by the particular circumstances of each case.[107]

State Reform Legislation

About a dozen states have enacted products liability reform statutes concerning the effect of a manufacturer's compliance with a governmental safety standard. Commonly, the statutes create a rebuttable[108] presumption that a product was not defective—or not defective and that the manufacturer or seller was not negligent—if the product complied with applicable state or federal safety statutes or agency regulations.[109] For example, Michigan's statute provides that "there is a rebuttable presumption that the manufacturer or seller is not liable if . . . the aspect of the product that allegedly caused the harm was in compliance with standards relevant to the event causing the death or injury [set forth in] a federal or state statute or . . . regulations . . . ."[110] Taking a slightly

[106] See Kessler and Vladeck, A Critical Examination of the FDA's Efforts to Preempt Failure-to-Warn Claims, 96 Geo. L.J. 461 (2008); Conk, Punctuated Equilibrium: Why Section 402A Flourished and the Third Restatement Languished, 26 Rev. Litig. 799, 860–61 (2007); O'Steen, The FDA Defense: Vioxx and the Argument Against Federal Preemption of State Claims for Injuries Resulting from Defective Drugs, 48 Ariz. L. Rev. 67 (2006); Struve, The FDA and the Tort System: Postmarketing Surveillance, Compensation, and the Role of Litigation, 5 Yale J. Health Pol'y, L. & Ethics 587, 594–606 (2005); Green and Schultz, Tort Law Deference to FDA Regulation of Medical Devices, 88 Geo. L.J. 2119 (2000); Schwartz, The Role of Federal Safety Regulations in Products Liability Actions, 41 Vand. L. Rev. 1121 (1988). On the FDA, see § 18.1, below.

[107] See Rabin, Reassessing Regulatory Compliance, 88 Geo. L.J. 2049 (2000).

[108] Since the plaintiff has the burden of proof on negligence and product defect anyway, it is difficult to understand what if any additional proof a plaintiff must offer to rebut such a presumption. In Duffee v. Murray Ohio Mfg. Co., 879 F. Supp. 1078 (D. Kan. 1995), the court suggested that a plaintiff's rebuttal could consist of proof that (1) the regulatory standards were outdated, or (2) that a reasonable manufacturer would know of dangers in the product's use not contemplated by the standard. Alternatively, it would seem that rebuttal evidence could lie in the plaintiff's proofs on negligence or defectiveness in the prima facie case. Expert testimony is not necessarily required to rebut such a presumption. See, e.g., Egbert v. Nissan N. Am., Inc., 167 P.3d 1058, 1061–62 (Utah 2007) ("a preponderance of the evidence is sufficient to overcome the presumption of nondefectiveness"); BIC Pen Corp. v. Carter, 171 S.W.3d 657, 667–68 (Tex. App. 2005) (plaintiff rebutted no-defect presumption: "design specifications and test results demonstrate[d] a wide variance in the [disposable lighter's] child resistance"), rev'd on preemption grounds, 251 S.W.3d 500 (Tex. 2008); Cansler v. Mills, 765 N.E.2d 698, 706–07 (Ind. Ct. App. 2002) (airbag that met Standard 208 failed to inflate in crash; circumstantial evidence of defectiveness sufficient to overcome presumption).

[109] In Flax v. DaimlerChrysler Corp., 272 S.W.3d 521, 536 (Tenn. 2008), the court ruled that that state's rebuttable presumption does not "provide immunity from punitive damages to a manufacturer who is aware that compliance with a regulation is insufficient to protect users of the product." Compare Hughes v. Lumbermens Mut. Cas. Co., 2 S.W.3d 218 (Tenn. Ct. App. 1999) (compliance with OSHA regulations does not create a rebuttable presumption of nondefectiveness because its regulations apply to employers, not manufacturers).

[110] Mich. Comp. Laws Ann. § 600.2946(4). See also Colo. Rev. Stat. Ann. § 13–21–403(1)(b); Fla. Stat. Ann. § 768.1256(1); Ind. Code Ann. § 34–20–5–1(2); N.D. Cent. Code § 28–01.3–09; Tenn. Code Ann. § 29–28–104; Utah Code Ann. § 78B–6–703(2). See, e.g., Wade v. Terex-Telelect, Inc., 966 N.E.2d 186, 195 (Ind. Ct. App. 2012) (jury should not have been instructed on presumption of nondefectiveness and non-negligence from compliance with government standards because ANSI standard incorporated into OSHA standard did not

different approach, the Kansas statute provides that, if a product conforms to a governmental safety standard, the plaintiff must prove "that a reasonably prudent product seller could and would have taken additional precautions."[111] Three statutes restate the common law rule on regulatory compliance—that a manufacturer's compliance with government standards may be considered by the trier of fact.[112] Several statutes are directed at drugs that comport with FDA standards, one raising a rebuttable presumption that complying warnings are adequate,[113] another giving manufacturers of complying drugs complete immunity,[114] and several barring punitive damages for drugs marketed with FDA approval.[115]

§ 14.5 FEDERAL PREEMPTION

No issue in modern products liability law is more important, or more inscrutable, than the doctrine of federal preemption. The doctrine is important because the defense of federal preemption since the 1990s has grown from little more than a blip on the radar screen to one of the most powerful defenses in all of products liability law. The doctrine is inscrutable because it is a formless and elusive creature, based on ephemeral notions of federalism and the oft-obscure intent of Congress, that vacillates according to shifting political sentiments of the courts—views on federal versus states' rights, on Congress versus the courts, and on regulatory versus products liability law.[116] Despite the best efforts of courts and commentators to bring order to the chaos,[117] the law on federal

apply to particular risk complained of by plaintiff and so was irrelevant and prejudicial); Ehlis v. Shire Richwood, Inc., 233 F. Supp. 2d 1189 (D.N.D. 2002) (evidence that prescription drug Adderall was used for off-label illnesses overcame statutory presumption of no defect from compliance with FDA standards), aff'd on other grounds, 367 F.3d 1013 (8th Cir. 2004); Rogers v. Cosco, Inc., 737 N.E.2d 1158 (Ind. Ct. App. 2000) (plaintiff overcame statutory presumption of no defect from compliance with government standard for child booster seats).

[111] Kan. Stat. Ann. § 60–3304(a), limited on preemption grounds, Troutman v. Curtis, 143 P.3d 74 (Kan. Ct. App. 2006) .

[112] Ark. Code Ann. § 16–116–205(a); Ohio Rev. Code Ann. § 2307.75(B)(4); Wash. Rev. Code Ann. § 7.72.050(1).

[113] N.J. Stat. Ann. § 2A:58C–4. See also Tex. Civ. Prac. & Rem. Code Ann. § 82.007(a).

[114] Mich. Comp. Laws Ann. § 600.2946(5). This statutory immunity has survived constitutional attack. See, e.g., Taylor v. Smithkline Beecham Corp., 658 N.W.2d 127 (Mich. 2003); Garcia v. Wyeth-Ayerst Labs., 265 F. Supp. 2d 825 (E.D. Mich. 2003), aff'd, 385 F.3d 961 (6th Cir. 2004).

[115] Ariz. Rev. Stat. Ann. § 12–701, preempted, Kobar v. Novartis Corp., 378 F. Supp. 2d 1166 (D. Ariz. 2005); N.J. Stat. Ann. § 2A:58C–5(c), preempted, McDarby v. Merck & Co., 949 A.2d 223 (N.J. Super. Ct. App. Div. 2008); Ohio Rev. Code Ann. § 2307.80(C), preempted, Monroe v. Novartis Pharms. Corp., 29 F. Supp. 3d 1115 (S.D. Ohio 2014); Or. Rev. Stat. Ann. § 30.927; Utah Code Ann. § 78B–8–203, limited on preemption grounds, Grange v. Mylan Labs., 2008 WL 4813311 (D. Utah 2008). The statutes provide that protection from punitive damages is lost if the manufacturer knowingly withholds or misrepresents pertinent information.

[116] See, e.g., Nelson, Preemption, 86 Va. L. Rev. 225, 229 (2000) (noting that "the politics of preemption are complicated"); Smith and Grage, Federal Preemption of State Products Liability Actions, 27 Wm. Mitchell L. Rev. 391, 415 (2000) (predicting that "the preemption defense is almost certain to remain highly politicized"). On preemption generally, see 1 L. Tribe, American Constitutional Law §§ 6–28 et seq. (3d ed. 2000); J. Nowak and R. Rotunda, Treatise on Constitutional Law: Substance and Procedure ch. 12 (5th ed. 2020, annual updates); Spence and Murray, The Law, Economics, and Politics of Federal Preemption Jurisprudence: A Quantitative Analysis, 87 Cal. L. Rev. 1125, 1129 (1999) ("For most judges, whether liberal or conservative, these cases pit one dimension of their ideology, their principles of federalism, against another, their policy preferences or attitudes toward the particular local regulation at issue."). For a penetrating analysis of the untoward but "happy" relationship between Congress and the courts, see W. Quirk, Courts & Congress: America's Unwritten Constitution (Routledge 2008).

[117] See, e.g., V. Schwartz and Appel, Where's the Beef?: A Guide to Judges on Preemption of State Tort Litigation Involving Branded Drugs, 89 U. Cin. L. Rev. 597 (2021); Davis, Time for A Fresh Look at Strict Liability for Pharmaceuticals, 28 Cornell J.L. & Pub. Pol'y 399 (2019); Geistfeld, Tort Law in the Age of Statutes, 99 Iowa L. Rev. 957, 1004–1019 (2014); Eggen, Navigating Between Scylla and Charybdis:

preemption has obstinately refused to set anchor in enduring principles. Instead, it continues to wallow in a state of utter chaos—"ad hoc, unprincipled . . ., seemingly bereft of any consistent doctrinal basis,"[118] "a muddle,"[119] "inexplicable,"[120] "confusing and chaotic,"[121] "terrible,"[122] "indeterminate,"[123] "unruly,"[124] and "in a state of disarray"[125]—quite simply, in a "mess."[126]

Federal preemption is an affirmative defense, subject to waiver, on which the defendant has the burden of proof.[127] The federal preemption defense arises, and a

---

Preemption of Medical Device "Parallel Claims," 9 J. Health & Biomedical L. 159 (2013); Moreland, Preemption as Inverse Negligence Per Se, 88 Notre Dame L. Rev. 1249 (2013); Hylton, An Economic Perspective on Preemption, 53 B.C. L. Rev. 203 (2012); Sharkey, Inside Agency Preemption, 110 Mich. L. Rev. 521 (2012); Zipursky, Palsgraf, Punitive Damages, and Preemption, 125 Harv. L. Rev. 1757 (2012); Davis, The Case Against Preemption: Vaccines & Uncertainty, 8 Ind. Health L. Rev. 291 (2011); Kotler, Tort Reform and Implied Conflict Preemption, 44 J. Marshall L. Rev. 827 (2011); Davis, The "New" Presumption Against Preemption, 61 Hastings L.J. 1217 (2010); Schwartz and Silverman, Preemption of State Common Law by Federal Agency Action: Striking the Appropriate Balance that Protects Public Safety, 84 Tul. L. Rev. 1203 (2010); Eggen, The Mature Product Preemption Doctrine: The Unitary Standard and the Paradox of Consumer Protection, 60 Case W. Res. L. Rev. 95 (2009); Davis, On Restating Products Liability Preemption, 74 Brook. L. Rev. 759 (2009); Rabin, Territorial Claims in the Domain of Accidental Harm: Conflicting Conceptions of Tort Preemption, 74 Brook. L. Rev. 987 (2009); Sharkey, Products Liability Preemption: An Institutional Approach, 76 Geo. Wash. L. Rev. 449 (2008); Kessler and Vladeck, A Critical Examination of the FDA's Efforts to Preempt Failure-to-Warn Claims, 96 Geo. L.J. 461 (2008); Sharkey, Preemption by Preamble: Federal Agencies and the Federalization of Tort Law, 56 DePaul L. Rev. 227 (2007); Buzbee, Asymmetrical Regulation: Risk, Preemption, and the Floor/Ceiling Distinction, 82 N.Y.U. L. Rev. 1547 (2007); Curtin and Relkin, Preamble Preemption and the Challenged Role of Failure to Warn and Defective Design Pharmaceutical Cases in Revealing Scientific Fraud, Marketing Mischief, and Conflicts of Interest, 35 Hofstra L. Rev. 1773 (2007); Davis, The Battle Over Implied Preemption: Products Liability and the FDA, 48 B.C. L. Rev. 1089 (2007); Ausness, The *Welding Fume* Case and the Preemptive Effect of OSHA's HazCom Standard on Common Law Failure-to-Warn Claims, 54 Buff. L. Rev. 103 (2006); Davis, On Preemption, Congressional Intent, and Conflict of Laws, 66 U. Pitt. L. Rev. 181 (2004); Ausness, Preemption of State Tort Law by Federal Safety Statutes: Supreme Court Preemption Jurisprudence Since Cipollone, 92 Ky. L.J. 913 (2004); Owen, Federal Preemption of Products Liability Claims, 55 S.C. L. Rev. 411 (2003); Raeker-Jordan, A Study in Judicial Sleight of Hand: Did *Geier v. American Honda Motor Co.* Eradicate the Presumption Against Preemption?, 17 BYU J. Pub. L. 1 (2002); Davis, Unmasking the Presumption in Favor of Preemption, 53 S.C. L. Rev. 967 (2002); Scordato, Federal Preemption of State Tort Claims, 35 U.C. Davis L. Rev. 1 (2001); Madden, Federal Preemption of Inconsistent State Safety Obligations, 21 Pace L. Rev. 103 (2000); Nelson, Preemption, 86 Va. L. Rev. 225 (2000); Dinh, Reassessing the Law of Preemption, 88 Geo. L.J. 2085 (2000); Rabin, Reassessing Regulatory Compliance, 88 Geo. L.J. 2049 (2000); Raeker-Jordan, The Pre-Emption Presumption That Never Was: Pre-Emption Doctrine Swallows the Rule, 40 Ariz. L. Rev. 1379, 1418 (1998); Grey, Make Congress Speak Clearly: Federal Preemption of State Tort Remedies, 77 B.U. L. Rev. 559 (1997); Noah, Reconceptualizing Federal Preemption of Tort Claims as the Government Standards Defense, 37 Wm. & Mary L. Rev. 903 (1996); Ausness, Federal Preemption of State Products Liability Doctrines, 44 S.C. L. Rev. 187 (1993). See generally T. McGarity, The Preemption War (Yale 2008); Frumer, Friedman, and Sklaren, Products Liability ch. 24; Owen & Davis on Products Liability ch. 15; Am. Law Prod. Liab. §§ 2:27–:42; Prod. Liab. Rep. (CCH) ¶ 2810.

[118] Note, 75 Colum. L. Rev. 623, 624 (1975).

[119] Nelson, Preemption, 86 Va. L. Rev. 225, 232 (2000).

[120] Smith and Grage, Federal Preemption of State Products Liability Actions, 27 Wm. Mitchell L. Rev. 391, 415 (2000).

[121] Id. at 392.

[122] Ausness, Preemption of State Tort Law by Federal Safety Statutes: Supreme Court Preemption Jurisprudence Since *Cipollone*, 92 Ky. L.J. 913, 968 (2004).

[123] Dinh, Reassessing the Law of Preemption, 88 Geo. L.J. 2085, 2085 (2000).

[124] R. Epstein, Torts 161 (Aspen 1999).

[125] Scordato, Federal Preemption of State Tort Claims, 35 U.C. Davis L. Rev. 1, 7 (2001). See Raeker-Jordan, A Study in Judicial Sleight of Hand: Did *Geier v. American Honda Motor Co.* Eradicate the Presumption Against Preemption?, 17 BYU J. Pub. L. 1, 33 (2002).

[126] Dinh, note 123, above, at 2085.

[127] See, e.g., Colon v. BIC USA, Inc., 136 F. Supp. 2d 196, 199–200 (S.D.N.Y. 2000) (but a statement in the answer that the product met government standards may suffice); Hawkins v. Leslie's Pool Mart, Inc., 184 F.3d 244, 256 (3d Cir. 1999) (affirmative defense on which defendant has burden of proof). Hence, a defendant

products liability claim is foreclosed, when the claim somehow conflicts with a federal product safety statute or regulation specifying design, marketing, or manufacturing standards. When enacting product safety legislation, Congress normally vests regulatory authority over the matter in a federal administrative agency, often specifying, in a preemption clause, that state law may not interfere with safety standards or "requirements" in the statute itself or, more typically, as promulgated by the federal agency. Whether or not Congress in any particular statute expressly prohibits the states from interfering with implementation of the legislation, any state law that *in fact* interferes with the operation of a federal statute or regulation thereunder contravenes the Supremacy Clause of the United States Constitution. This clause provides that federal law "shall be the supreme Law of the Land; and the Judges in every State shall be bound thereby, any Thing in the Constitution or Laws of any State to the Contrary notwithstanding."[128]

State statutes and administrative regulations are of course governed by the Supremacy Clause, but so too are products liability actions, the requirements of which can interfere, if less directly, with the administration of a federal safety statute. "[R]egulation can be as effectively exerted through an award of damages as through some form of preventive relief. The obligation to pay compensation can be, indeed is designed to be, a potent method of governing conduct and controlling policy."[129] Thus, a products liability claim is preempted if its application is prohibited by or conflicts in some way with a federal statute or regulation.[130] In determining whether a products liability claim conflicts with federal law, courts must interpret the statute to ascertain its aims. "The purpose of Congress is the ultimate touchstone" in every preemption case.[131] Put otherwise, statutory construction is the cornerstone of preemption analysis.[132]

In general, federal courts are more willing than state courts to find preemption. State courts normally are more focused on protecting the right to compensation of their citizens harmed by the unlawful behavior of others (a right often protected by state constitutions),[133] whereas federal courts of limited jurisdiction generally are more concerned about federal supremacy.[134]

---

who fails to assert preemption in a timely manner may waive the defense. See, e.g., Violette v. Smith & Nephew Dyonics, Inc., 62 F.3d 8, 10–12 (1st Cir. 1995) (although pleaded in answer, defendant did not raise defense substantively until after adverse verdict); Gonzales v. Surgidev Corp., 899 P.2d 576, 581–83 (N.M. 1995) (waived if not raised before end of trial). *But see* Kennan v. Dow Chem. Co., 717 F. Supp. 799 (M.D. Fla. 1989) (not affirmative defense subject to waiver).

[128] U.S. Const. art. VI, cl. 2.

[129] San Diego Bldg. Trades Council v. Garmon, 359 U.S. 236, 247 (1959).

[130] Federal administrative agencies may be authorized to preempt state law by regulation. Hillsborough Cnty., Fla. v. Automated Med. Labs., Inc., 471 U.S. 707, 713 (1985) ("state laws can be pre-empted by federal regulations as well as by federal statutes"). See also Medtronic, Inc. v. Lohr, 518 U.S. 470, 503, 505 (1996) (Breyer, J., concurring).

[131] Gade v. National Solid Wastes Mgt. Ass'n, 505 U.S. 88, 96 (1992) (quoting Allis-Chalmers Corp. v. Lueck, 471 U.S. 202, 208 (1985)).

[132] See 1 L. Tribe, American Constitutional Law § 6–28, at 1176–79 (3d ed. 2000); J. Nowak and R. Rotunda, Constitutional Law § 9.1, at 393 (8th ed. 2009).

[133] See Moreland, Preemption as Inverse Negligence Per Se, 88 Notre Dame L. Rev. 1249, 1289 (2013) (critiquing "the failure to attend to the specific tort aspects of federal preemption of state tort claims and a rush to embrace constitutional and administrative law approaches to preemption at the expense of more precise, historically sound, and well-developed common law doctrines such as negligence per se").

[134] See Smith and Grage, Federal Preemption of State Products Liability Actions, 27 Wm. Mitchell L. Rev. 391, 412 (2000).

Types of Preemption

Federal preemption of state law may be "express" or "implied." That is, preemption "is compelled whether Congress' command is explicitly stated in the statute's language or implicitly contained in its structure and purpose."[135] Express preemption may helpfully be viewed as *textual*, in contrast to implied preemption which may be thought of as *contextual*. What this means is that express preemption is discernable from the explicit language of a federal statute, whereas implied preemption must be deduced from the broader purposes of a statute—whether or not it contains an express preemption clause.[136]

Express Preemption

Congress by statute may *expressly* preempt state law in a preemption clause that explicitly states the statute's preemptive scope—the extent to which it precludes state law.[137] In legislation regulating product safety, enacted mostly in the late 1960s, Congress was less concerned with common-law damage claims in products liability cases than with the possibility that state statutes or administrative regulations might somehow undermine the federal legislation.[138] Accordingly, as discussed below, preemption clauses in federal statutes typically provide that the states may not adopt conflicting "requirements" or "standards." Phrasing of this sort has raised the question of whether the words "requirements" and "standards" mean only legislative and regulatory requirements and standards, or whether Congress intended these terms more broadly to include judicial rulings on common-law damages claims. As stated earlier, the Supreme Court has ruled that these phrases in preemption clauses can indeed preclude products liability judgments,[139] as well as more obvious and direct kinds of state action through legislation and administrative regulation. Accordingly, to the extent that allowing a products liability claim would establish a form of common-law safety standard different from that imposed by federal law, an express preemption clause may preclude the claim.

Two types of clauses are particularly relevant in determining whether a statute expressly preempts a state law products liability claim: (1) *preemption clauses*, and (2) *savings clauses*. A "preemption clause" describes the extent to which a statute precludes the application of state law, and a "savings clause" provides that compliance with a statute does not exempt a party from liability under common law. These two provisions thus generally point in opposite directions: preemption clauses tend to deny, and savings clauses tend to allow, state law products liability claims. Normally, therefore, the express preemption issue should be clearer if a federal safety statute has only a

---

[135] Jones v. Rath Packing Co., 430 U.S. 519, 525 (1977). See also Medtronic, Inc. v. Lohr, 518 U.S. 470, 486 (1996) (Stevens, J.).

[136] See Madden, Federal Preemption of Inconsistent State Safety Obligations, 21 Pace L. Rev. 103, 106 (2000).

[137] State law is expressly preempted "[w]hen Congress has considered the issue of pre-emption and has included in the enacted legislation a provision explicitly addressing that issue, and when that provision provides a 'reliable indicium of congressional intent with respect to state authority . . . .' " Cipollone v. Liggett Grp., Inc., 505 U.S. 504, 517 (1992).

[138] See, e.g., Leflar and Adler, The Preemption Pentad: Federal Preemption of Products Liability Claims After *Medtronic*, 64 Tenn. L. Rev. 691, 746–48 (1997).

[139] See Riegel v. Medtronic, Inc., 552 U.S. 312, 322–24 (2008); Cipollone v. Liggett Grp., Inc., 505 U.S. 504, 521 (1992).

preemption clause,[140] or only a savings clause.[141] Preemption determinations are complicated in statutes that contain *neither* type of clause, and thus are silent on the matter,[142] and in statutes that contain *both* types of clause,[143] and so appear internally conflicted.

Implied Preemption

Even if a federal statute or regulation is silent with respect to the preemption issue, a products liability claim may be foreclosed by the doctrine of *implied* preemption. There are two forms of implied preemption, "*field* preemption" and "*conflict* preemption." Implied *field* preemption arises (a) when federal regulation of a field is so complete and "so pervasive as to make reasonable the inference that Congress left no room for the States to supplement it,"[144] or (b) when Congress legislates in a field in which "the federal interest is so dominant that the federal system [must] be assumed to preclude the enforcement of state laws on the same subject."[145] Implied *conflict* preemption may arise in one of two ways: (a) when federal and state provisions conflict directly, so that it is impossible for a person to comply with both requirements,[146] or (b) when the state law "stands as an obstacle to the accomplishment and execution of the full purposes and objectives of Congress."[147] Thus, even if a federal product safety statute or regulation does not contain a clause expressly preempting damages claims under state law, it still may impliedly preempt such claims.[148]

The Presumption Against Preemption

Principles of federalism command congressional respect for the sovereignty of the states,[149] including their authority to render damages judgments in products liability

---

[140] Such as the Federal Insecticide, Fungicide, and Rodenticide Act (FIFRA), discussed below.

[141] Such as the Occupational Safety and Health Act. As discussed below, however, a federal agency (as OSHA) may, by regulation, preempt state law with respect to particular matters.

[142] Such as the Federal Food, Drug, and Cosmetic Act, discussed below. Like OSHA, however, the FDA expressly preempts state law on certain issues. See, e.g., Soja v. Medtronic, Inc., 2019 WL 2391609 (E.D. Cal. 2019) (express preemption of injured plaintiff's claims against implanted pain pump's manufacturer under the Medical Device Amendment to the Food, Drug, and Cosmetic Act).

[143] Such as the National Traffic and Motor Vehicle Safety Act, discussed below.

[144] Rice v. Santa Fe Elevator Corp., 331 U.S. 218, 230 (1947).

[145] Id. See also Kurns v. Railroad Friction Prods. Corp., 565 U.S. 625, 637 (2012) (affirming dismissal on field preemption grounds of railroad employee's design defect and warning claims against manufacturer of asbestos brake pads and successor of manufacturer of engine valves containing asbestos; the Locomotive Inspection Act " 'occup[ied] the entire field of regulating locomotive equipment' to the exclusion of state regulation"). Even when Congress "occupies the field," state filing and other procedural rules control. See Norfolk S. Ry. Co. v. Bogle, 875 N.E.2d 919, 922, 926 (Ohio 2007) (FELA claims governed by state filing requirements for asbestos claimants).

[146] See Weinberg, The Federal-State Conflict of Laws: "Actual" Conflicts, 70 Tex. L. Rev. 1743, 1751 (1992).

[147] Hines v. Davidowitz, 312 U.S. 52, 67 (1941). See also Perez v. Campbell, 402 U.S. 637, 649 (1971). This last form of conflict preemption is often aptly termed "obstacle" or "frustration-of-purpose" preemption. In addition to the conventional divisions, implied preemption also may result from federal common law and from the "dormant" commerce clause. See Dinh, above note 123, at 2109–12.

[148] See, e.g., Buckman Co. v. Plaintiffs' Legal Comm., 531 U.S. 341, 352 (2001); Geier v. American Honda Motor Co., 529 U.S. 861, 869 (2000). See also Farina v. Nokia Inc., 625 F.3d 97, 125 (3d Cir. 2010) (affirming dismissal on preemption grounds of claim that radio frequency radiation from cell phones is dangerous without headsets; such liability would conflict with FCC regulations), cert. denied, 565 U.S. 928 (2011). *But see* Pinney v. Nokia, Inc., 402 F.3d 430, 458 (4th Cir. 2005) (allowing claims that wireless telephones emit unsafe level of radio frequency radiation; "a headset requirement would not stand as an obstacle to Congress's goal of achieving nationwide coverage"). For additional radio frequency radiation cases, see note 344, below.

[149] See Dinh, above note 123, at 2085–86.

and other litigation. In the words of the Supreme Court, "because the States are independent sovereigns in our federal system, we have long presumed that Congress does not cavalierly pre-empt state-law causes of action."[150] From this premise, the Court has relied upon an "assumption that the historic police powers of the States were not to be superseded by a Federal Act unless that was the clear and manifest purpose of Congress."[151] At bottom, this "presumption against preemption" rests on the precept that the Constitution constrains the federal government, the powers of which are limited and specifically enumerated, from trampling on the reserved powers of the states.[152] In the first two products liability preemption cases decided by the Supreme Court, the Court interpreted the federal product safety statutes against this backdrop assumption that disfavored preemption.[153]

The Court for a while appeared to be moving away from the presumption against preemption, noting its inapplicability when the matter regulated implicates federal interests[154] at least as much as matters traditionally addressed by state law. As the Supreme Court strayed from its former regard for the presumption against preemption, commentators increasingly questioned the meaning, strength, and legitimacy of any such presumption.[155] Subsequently, however, the Court again relied on this "presumption,"[156] suggesting that it might still have at least a twitch of life.

It is true, of course, that Congress should be guided by principles of federalism in enacting legislation on and regulating health and safety, subjects that traditionally have resided largely under state control. However, if Congress has authority under the Commerce Clause to enact particular legislation regulating health and safety, then the Supremacy Clause might seem to certify, automatically, the legitimacy of this federal incursion into a domain normally controlled by the states. If this view is correct, then the responsibility of courts is merely to interpret such a statute, untrammeled by any presumption for or against preemption, to determine whether, and the extent to which, Congress intended to restrict common-law claims.[157] Rather than being an independent principle of federalism, therefore, the doctrine of federal preemption might more accurately be viewed as a doctrine governing the interpretation of legislation, which

---

150 Medtronic, Inc. v. Lohr, 518 U.S. 470, 485 (1996) (Stevens, J.).

151 Rice v. Santa Fe Elevator Corp., 331 U.S. 218, 230 (1947). See 1 L. Tribe, Constitutional Law § 6–28, at 1175 (3d ed. 2000).

152 See Gade v. National Solid Wastes Mgt. Ass'n, 505 U.S. 88 (1992), a workplace safety standards case in which state standards were challenged as preempted under OSHA. Justice Kennedy concurred only in the result because he believed the plurality's broad resort to implied preemption principles contradicted "two basic principles of our pre-emption jurisprudence. First, we begin 'with the assumption that the historic police powers of the States [are] not to be superseded . . . unless that was the clear and manifest purpose of Congress.' . . . Second, '[t]he purpose of Congress is the ultimate touchstone' in all pre-emption cases." Id. at 111.

153 See Cipollone v. Liggett Grp., Inc., 505 U.S. 504, 516 (1992); Medtronic, Inc. v. Lohr, 518 U.S. 470, 485 (1996). See generally Dinh, above note 123, at 2085–86.

154 Such as regulating fraud on a federal agency, see *Buckman*, notes 285–297, below, or boat safety, traditionally the domain of the Coast Guard, see *Sprietsma*, notes 313–314, below.

155 See, e.g., Raeker-Jordan, A Study in Judicial Sleight of Hand: Did *Geier v. American Honda Motor Co.* Eradicate the Presumption Against Preemption?, 17 BYU J. Pub. L. 1 (2002); Davis, Unmasking the Presumption in Favor of Preemption, 53 S.C. L. Rev. 967 (2002); Scordato, Federal Preemption of State Tort Claims, 35 U.C. Davis L. Rev. 1, 29–32 (2001); Dinh, above note 123; Raeker-Jordon, The Pre-Emption Presumption That Never Was: Pre-Emption Doctrine Swallows the Rule, 40 Ariz. L. Rev. 1379, 1418 (1998).

156 See Bates v. Dow Agrosciences LLC, 544 U.S. 431, 449 (2005), discussed below.

157 Cf. 1 L. Tribe, American Constitutional Law § 6–28, at 1177 (3d ed. 2000) ("Perhaps, the most important point to remember is that preemption analysis is, or at least should be, a matter of precise statutory construction rather than an exercise in free-form judicial policymaking."). *But see* id. at 1195 n.74.

itself should be animated and bounded by principles of federalism lying within the Commerce Clause.[158]

Put another way, principles of federalism may help determine whether a federal statute is proper under the Commerce Clause, but, once a statute is found proper under the Commerce Clause, the statute occupies whatever space might otherwise have been occupied by state law and so is not further subject to challenge on federalism grounds. That said, however, where exactly principles of federalism may lie within the Constitution may be less important than the fact that such principles do oblige Congress, when considering legislation on matters of health and safety, to respect the traditional sovereignty of the states. So, if federal legislation on product safety does not clearly state whether products liability claims under state law are prohibited or permitted, and if such claims do not plainly conflict with federal regulation, it seems likely that Congress intended to leave unmolested the traditional state control over matters in this realm.[159] Whether or not a "presumption against preemption" is the best way to articulate this kind of backdrop deference that Congress should exhibit when it enters a field traditionally ruled by the states, the presumption idea does capture important structural truths about the republic that reside somewhere in the Constitution.

Federal Safety Legislation for Particular Products

Rooted in statutory construction, the federal preemption defense rests upon a determination that Congress in a particular statute intended to preclude particular products liability claims. The preemption issue thus is both statute-specific and claim-specific, meaning that the resolution of this issue is governed in any given case by an interpretation of the relevant provisions of the particular federal statute in relation to the particular products liability claims involved.[160] While preemption analysis in every case will therefore turn on the meaning and purposes of a specific federal statute—as revealed by its express provisions, its structure, and its legislative history[161]—the basic issue in every case remains the same: whether Congress intended, expressly or implicitly, to prohibit products liability claims of the type asserted by the plaintiff. Because preemption doctrine has thus evolved on a statute-specific basis,[162] the preemption defense in products liability litigation is helpfully informed by an examination of the doctrine's development over time as the courts have investigated the preemptive effect of particular federal statutes regulating the safety of particular types of products.

---

[158] See Dinh, above, note 123.

[159] See, e.g., Raeker-Jordan, The Pre-Emption Presumption That Never Was: Pre-Emption Doctrine Swallows the Rule, 40 Ariz. L. Rev. 1379, 1468–69 (1998).

[160] See, e.g., Dinh, above note 123, at 2085; Scordato, Federal Preemption of State Tort Claims, 35 U.C. Davis L. Rev. 1, 31 (2001).

[161] See, e.g., Gade v. National Solid Wastes Mgt. Ass'n, 505 U.S. 88, 98 (1992) (the "ultimate task in any pre-emption case is to determine whether state regulation is consistent with the structure and purpose of the statute as a whole"); Medtronic, Inc. v. Lohr, 518 U.S. 470, 486 (1996) (Stevens, J.) (courts must look to structure and purpose of statute as whole "as revealed not only in the text, but through the reviewing court's reasoned understanding of the way in which Congress intended the statute and its surrounding regulatory scheme to affect business, consumers, and the law"); Wisconsin Pub. Intervener v. Mortier, 501 U.S. 597, 617 (1991) (Scalia, J., concurring). See generally Ausness, Federal Preemption of State Products Liability Doctrines, 44 S.C. L. Rev. 187, 240–52 (1993) (model for interpreting federal regulations by evaluating text, history, and legislative policy).

[162] See, e.g., Dinh, above note 123, at 2085.

Prior to the Supreme Court's initial foray into the application of preemption doctrine to products liability law in 1992,[163] federal preemption rarely figured seriously in this type of litigation. Indeed, prior to this time, the Supreme Court had decided only a handful of preemption cases involving common-law damage claims of any type.[164] During the 1980s, as manufacturers scrambled for ways to avoid the rigors of products liability judgments, they increasingly asserted the preemption defense.[165] In part because of the Supreme Court's skeptical attitude at the time toward the preemption of state tort law claims,[166] assertions of the preemption defense during most of this decade generally fell on deaf judicial ears.[167]

Herbicides, Pesticides, and Insecticides—Early Developments

The first reported decision concerning the preemptive effect of the Federal Insecticide, Fungicide, and Rodenticide Act (FIFRA) was *Ferebee v. Chevron Chemical Co.*,[168] a prominent decision by the Court of Appeals for the District of Columbia that involved a products liability claim against the distributor of a herbicide, Paraquat, on behalf of an agricultural worker who allegedly died from breathing and contacting the herbicide.[169] In FIFRA, Congress established a comprehensive scheme for registering and labeling herbicides and other toxic products, administered by the EPA.[170] Under the Act, a manufacturer must submit proposed labels to the EPA to ensure that they are "adequate to protect health and the environment" and "likely to be read and understood."[171] FIFRA expressly prohibits the states from imposing any "requirements for labeling or packaging in addition to or different from those required" under the Act's provisions.[172] In *Ferebee*, the plaintiff claimed that the label warnings on Paraquat were inadequate and caused the decedent's death, and the jury agreed. Rejecting the defendant's federal preemption arguments, the Court of Appeals concluded that the Act did not expressly preclude state common-law actions, nor did implied field or conflict preemption apply. Although a damages award for inadequate warning might impose a dual obligation on the defendant, the court concluded that the defendant could comply with both federal and state law by using the EPA-approved warning labels while paying damages for insufficient warning as required by the state products liability judgment.[173]

---

[163] The first products liability preemption case was Cipollone v. Liggett Grp., Inc., 505 U.S. 504 (1992), discussed below.

[164] Davis, above note 155, at 969 n.9; Scordato, Federal Preemption of State Tort Claims, 35 U.C. Davis L. Rev. 1 (2001).

[165] Davis, above note 155, at 998.

[166] Notably in Silkwood v. Kerr-McGee Corp., 464 U.S. 238 (1984) (plutonium-contamination claim by worker at nuclear power plant not preempted by Atomic Energy Act). *Silkwood* is examined in Davis, above note 155, at 990–94.

[167] "[D]efendants had rarely been successful in arguing that the existence of a federal statutory standard totally preempted the plaintiff's state law based allegations of defectiveness or negligence." Davis, above note 155, at 998. See Ausness, Federal Preemption of State Products Liability Doctrines, 44 S.C. L. Rev. 187 (1993).

[168] 736 F.2d 1529 (D.C. Cir. 1984) (Md. law), cert. denied, 469 U.S. 1062 (1984).

[169] See Watnick, Federal Preemption of Tort Claims Under FIFRA: The Erosion of a Defense, 36 U. Mich. J.L. Reform 419 (2003); Madden, Federal Preemption of Inconsistent State Safety Obligations, 21 Pace L. Rev. 103, 120–28 (2000).

[170] See 7 U.S.C. §§ 136–136y.

[171] See id. §§ 136a(c)(C), 136(q)(1)(E)–(F).

[172] Id. § 136v(b).

[173] *Ferebee*, 736 F.2d at 1540.

Despite a growing minority of cases ruling against plaintiffs on the preemption issue,[174] most courts through the 1980s and early 1990s followed the *Ferebee* approach of holding that neither FIFRA[175] nor other federal safety statutes[176] preempted products liability claims. However, once the Supreme Court in 1992 energized the federal preemption defense in products liability litigation,[177] the lower courts began to rethink the role of preemption under federal statutes such as FIFRA. As the 1990s and 2000s progressed, the FIFRA decisions turned sharply in the other direction. In cases where a manufacturer complies with an EPA-required warning under FIFRA, courts eventually became nearly unanimous in holding that the Act preempts at least tort law[178] warning claims—the most common type of claim implicating FIFRA.[179] More recently, however, decisions appear to have once again swung back the other way.[180] Most courts have also

[174] See, e.g., Papas v. Upjohn Co., 926 F.2d 1019 (11th Cir. 1991) (impliedly preempted), vacated, 505 U.S. 1215 (1992), on remand, 985 F.2d 516 (11th Cir. 1993) (expressly preempted); Taylor v. General Motors Corp., 875 F.2d 816 (11th Cir. 1989) (no-airbag claim); Fitzgerald v. Mallinckrodt, Inc., 681 F. Supp. 404 (E.D. Mich. 1987) (FIFRA).

[175] See, e.g., Montana Pole & Treating Plant v. I.F. Laucks & Co., 775 F. Supp. 1339 (D. Mont. 1991); Riden v. ICI Am., Inc., 763 F. Supp. 1500 (W.D. Mo. 1991); Evenson v. Osmose Wood Preserving, Inc., 760 F. Supp. 1345 (S.D. Ind. 1990); Cox v. Velsicol Chem. Corp., 704 F. Supp. 85 (E.D. Pa. 1989); Roberts v. Dow Chem. Co., 702 F. Supp. 195 (N.D. Ill. 1988).

[176] See, e.g., Abbot v. American Cyanamid Co., 844 F.2d 1108 (4th Cir. 1988) (neurological injuries from inoculation of DTP vaccine manufactured by defendant; *held*, no express preemption by Public Health Service Act or Federal Food, Drug, and Cosmetic Act, nor any implied preemption because common-law vaccine claims do not frustrate federal statutory goals); MacDonald v. Ortho Pharm. Corp., 475 N.E.2d 65 (Mass. 1985) (compliance with FDA labeling requirements on birth control pills—no preemption).

[177] See Cipollone v. Liggett Grp., Inc., 505 U.S. 504 (1992), discussed below.

[178] Before Bates v. Dow Agrosciences LLC, 544 U.S. 431 (2005), most courts also barred warranty and tortious misrepresentation claims if based on an EPA-required warning. See, e.g., Williams v. Dow Chem. Co., 255 F. Supp. 2d 219 (S.D.N.Y. 2003); Akee v. Dow Chem. Co., 272 F. Supp. 2d 1112 (D. Haw. 2003); Grenier v. Vermont Log Bldgs., Inc., 96 F.3d 559, 563 (1st Cir. 1996), abrogated by Bates v. Dow Agrosciences LLC, 544 U.S. 431 (2005). *Contra* Arnold v. Dow Chem. Co., 110 Cal. Rptr. 2d 722, 731–32 (Ct. App. 2001) (citing cases holding that implied warranty claims are not preempted); Goeb v. Tharaldson, 615 N.W.2d 800 (Minn. 2000) (FIFRA does not preempt negligent misrepresentation or negligent testing claims).

Courts addressing claims based on off-label statements generally have held that such claims are *not* preempted if the statement differs from the label, but that such claims *are* preempted if the statements merely reiterate language on the label. See, e.g., Bourbia v. S.C. Johnson & Son, Inc., 375 F. Supp. 3d 454, 464 (S.D.N.Y. 2019) ("FIFRA does not preempt state claims for breach of express warranty, since 'a cause of action on an express warranty asks only that a manufacturer make good on the contractual commitment that it voluntarily undertook by placing that warranty on its product.' . . . This common law rule imposes no requirement on the manufacturer to make an express warranty or other rule 'for labeling or packaging.' "); Anderson v. Dow Agrosciences, 262 F. Supp. 2d 1280 (W.D. Okla. 2003); Diehl v. Polo Coop. Ass'n, 766 N.E.2d 317 (Ill. App. Ct. 2002); Dillon v. Zeneca Corp., 42 P.3d 598 (Ariz. Ct. App. 2002); Sun Valley Packing v. Consep, Inc., 114 Cal. Rptr. 2d 237 (Ct. App. 2001) (FIFRA does not preempt implied warranty of fitness for particular purpose claim based on off-label statements about matters outside scope of required label).

[179] See, e.g., Anderson v. Dow Agrosciences, 262 F. Supp. 2d 1280 (W.D. Okla. 2003); Eyl v. Ciba-Geigy Corp., 650 N.W.2d 744 (Neb. 2002) (citing cases); Lowe's Home Ctrs., Inc. v. Olin Corp., 313 F.3d 1307 (11th Cir. 2002); Netland v. Hess & Clark, Inc., 284 F.3d 895 (8th Cir. 2002), abrogated by Bates v. Dow Agrosciences LLC, 544 U.S. 431 (2005); Arnold v. Dow Chem. Co., 110 Cal. Rptr. 2d 722 (Ct. App. 2001); Etcheverry v. Tri-Ag Serv., Inc., 993 P.2d 366 (Cal. 2000) (citing cases); Lewis v. American Cyanamid Co., 715 A.2d 967, 973 (N.J. 1998); Kuiper v. American Cyanamid Co., 131 F.3d 656, 662 (7th Cir. 1997), abrogated by Bates v. Dow Agrosciences LLC, 544 U.S. 431 (2005); Greiner v. Vermont Log Bldgs., Inc., 96 F.3d 559, 563–64 (1st Cir. 1996), abrogated by Bates v. Dow Agrosciences LLC, 544 U.S. 431 (2005). *But see* Dow Chem. Co. v. Ebling, 753 N.E.2d 633 (Ind. 2001) (FIFRA does not preempt claim that pest control applicator negligently failed to convey to pesticide's ultimate user information found on required label).

[180] See, e.g., Pilliod v. Monsanto Co., 282 Cal. Rptr. 3d 679, 701 (Ct. App. 2021) (2–1 decision) (impossibility preemption cannot "be reconciled with FIFRA, which confirms that states are authorized to regulate the sale and use of pesticides and authorizes states to ban the sale of a pesticide that it finds unsafe"); Hardeman v. Monsanto Co., 997 F.3d 941, 954–58 (9th Cir. 2021) (FIFRA did not expressly or impliedly preempt plaintiffs' failure to warn claims and defendant failed to offer "clear evidence" of the impossibility of complying with federal and state law in adding a cancer warning to the Roundup label); In re Roundup Prods.

concluded that FIFRA neither expressly nor impliedly preempts claims that pertain to matters not regulated by the EPA, such as claims not based on labeling but on the defectiveness of a pesticide's design, packaging, or manufacture.[181] But courts sometimes warned that they would not be fooled by artful pleading efforts to disguise warning claims under cover of assertions of negligent testing, defective manufacture, defective design, or other claims that indirectly challenge EPA-approved labeling information, ruling that all such claims were preempted.[182] All of these developments came to a screeching halt when the Supreme Court in 2005 finally decided a FIFRA preemption case, discussed below.[183]

***Cigarettes*—Cipollone**

In *Cipollone v. Liggett Group, Inc.*,[184] the Supreme Court in 1992 for the first time applied federal preemption doctrine to a products liability case.[185] *Cipollone* was an action against three cigarette manufacturers on behalf of Rose Cipollone who died of lung cancer after smoking the defendants' cigarettes from 1942 to 1984. The products liability claims included design defectiveness; failure to provide adequate warning; negligent research, testing, and marketing; breach of express warranties in advertising; fraudulent misrepresentation of the hazards of smoking; and conspiracy to defraud by depriving the public of medical and scientific information on smoking.[186]

At issue in *Cipollone* was the preemptive effect of two cigarette labeling statutes. The preemption clause in the 1965 Cigarette Labeling and Advertising Act (the "1965 Act") provided, "No statement relating to smoking and health" other than that required

---

Liab. Litig., 364 F. Supp. 3d 1085, 1088 (N.D. Cal. 2019) (FIFRA did not expressly preempt plaintiffs' failure to warn claims or bar those claims under doctrine of impossibility preemption); Sheppard v. Monsanto Co., 2016 WL 3629074, at *7–9 (D. Haw. 2016) (failure to warn and warranty claims not preempted under FIFRA).

[181] See, e.g., Gucciardi v. Bonide Prods., Inc., 28 F. Supp. 3d 383, 394 (E.D. Pa. 2014) (consumer's claims against pesticide manufacturer for negligence, strict liability, and breach of warranty for injuries sustained from exposure to pesticide not preempted; no claims imposed additional labeling requirements); Southern States Coop. Inc. v. I.S.P. Co., 198 F. Supp. 2d 807 (N.D. W. Va. 2002) (FIFRA does not preempt claim that horse feed was adulterated with rat poison); Arnold v. Dow Chem. Co., 110 Cal. Rptr. 2d 722 (Ct. App. 2001) (true design claims not preempted; full discussion), noted in 31 Sw. U. L. Rev. 441 (2002); National Bank of Commerce v. Dow Chem. Co., 165 F.3d 602, 609 (8th Cir. 1999) ("defectively manufactured or designed products properly labeled under FIFRA may still be subject to state regulation, in the form of common law or other claims").

Courts disagree on whether FIFRA preempts claims based on a product's *efficacy*—whether a herbicide harms rather than helps a crop—that are outside the realm the EPA chooses to regulate. Compare American Cyanamid Co. v. Geye, 79 S.W.3d 21 (Tex. 2002) (no preemption), with Etcheverry v. Tri-Ag Serv., Inc., 993 P.2d 366 (Cal. 2000) (preemption).

[182] See, e.g., Dow Agrosciences LLC v. Bates, 332 F.3d 323, 332 (5th Cir. 2003) (FIFRA preempts breach of express warranty and warning claims "disguised" as defective design and negligent testing claims), vacated by Bates v. Dow Agrosciences LLC, 544 U.S. 431 (2005); Akee v. Dow Chem. Co., 272 F. Supp. 2d 1112 (D. Haw. 2003) (FIFRA preempts any claims that challenge adequacy of pesticide product's labels, directly or indirectly); Netland v. Hess & Clark, Inc., 284 F.3d 895 (8th Cir. 2002) (FIFRA preempts manufacturing defect and design defect claims that were factually premised on inadequate labeling), abrogated by Bates v. Dow Agrosciences LLC, 544 U.S. 431 (2005); Traube v. Freund, 775 N.E.2d 212 (Ill. App. Ct. 2002) (FIFRA preempts nuisance and ultrahazardous activity claims based on allegedly deficient label); Eriksen v. Mobay Corp., 41 P.3d 488 (Wash. Ct. App. 2002) (consumer expectations design defect claim was effectively a warning claim); Johnson v. Monsanto Chem. Co., 129 F. Supp. 2d 189, 195 (N.D.N.Y. 2001) ("Claims of misdesign or mismanufacture which the Court regards as thinly veiled labeling or failure to warn claims will not stand.").

[183] Bates v. Dow Agrosciences LLC, 544 U.S. 431 (2005), discussed below, notes 325–343.

[184] 505 U.S. 504 (1992).

[185] See Galligan, Products Liability—Cigarettes and *Cipollone*: What's Left? What's Gone?, 53 La. L. Rev. 713 (1993); Note, 80 Va. L. Rev. 979 (1994).

[186] 505 U.S. at 508–10.

by the Act, "shall be required" on cigarette packages or in advertising.[187] In 1969, Congress amended the 1965 Act in the Public Health Cigarette Smoking Act of 1969 (the "1969 Act") to make the labeling requirements more stringent, to ban electronic cigarette advertising, and to modify the preemption provision to read:

> No requirement or prohibition based on smoking and health shall be imposed under State law with respect to the advertising or promotion of any cigarettes the packages of which are labeled in conformity with the provisions of this chapter.[188]

Prior to *Cipollone*, the Supreme Court justices, and hence the lower courts, were badly split on the role of both express and implied preemption in barring common-law claims.[189] Even in cigarette warning cases, most pre-*Cipollone* decisions had rejected *express* preemption claims in favor of *implied* preemption.[190] Turning that approach on its head, the court in *Cipollone* ruled that, where Congress speaks expressly to the preemption issue, a largely textual express preemption analysis—not implied preemption—should control.[191]

Holding that the narrower 1965 Act did not preempt state law damages actions, the Supreme Court ruled that the broader 1969 Act—which barred "not simply 'statement[s]' but rather 'requirement[s] or prohibition[s] . . . imposed under State law' "—did bar some products liability claims because the latter statute was based on an agreement imposing stiffer warning requirements on cigarette manufacturers in exchange for explicit limitations on lawsuits.[192] Reasoning that a products liability claim is a "requirement" or "prohibition" under the Act,[193] and that the petitioner's inadequate warning claim effectively asserted that the manufacturers' "post-1969 advertising or promotions should have included additional, or more clearly stated, warnings," the Court concluded that the 1969 Act preempted the plaintiff's warning claim.[194] However, that Act did *not* preempt claims for *fraud* or *conspiracy to defraud*, which were "predicated not on a duty 'based on smoking and health,' but rather on a more general obligation—the duty not to deceive,"[195] nor those based upon *express warranty*, because "the 'requirement[s]' imposed by an express warranty claim are not 'imposed under state law,' but rather imposed by the warrantor."[196] Concurring and dissenting, Justices Blackmun, Kennedy,

---

[187] 15 U.S.C. § 5, recodified at § 1334.

[188] 15 U.S.C. § 1334(b). See 505 U.S. at 514–15.

[189] See Davis, Unmasking the Presumption in Favor of Preemption, 53 S.C. L. Rev. 967 (2002).

[190] *Cipollone*, 505 U.S. at 508 n.2.

[191] "When Congress has considered the issue of pre-emption and has included in the enacted legislation a provision explicitly addressing that issue, and when that provision provides a 'reliable indicium of congressional intent with respect to state authority, . . . there is no need to infer congressional intent to pre-empt state laws from the substantive provisions' of the legislation." Id. at 517.

[192] 505 U.S. at 520.

[193] In rejecting petitioner's argument that the 1969 Act's preemption provision did not reach common-law actions, the Court observed that "[t]he phrase '[n]o requirement or prohibition' sweeps broadly and suggests no distinction between positive enactments and common law." Id. at 521.

[194] Id. at 524. This is the conventional interpretation of *Cipollone*. See, e.g., Waterhouse v. R.J. Reynolds Tobacco Co., 270 F. Supp. 2d 678, 683 (D. Md. 2003) ("failure-to-warn allegations are quintessentially claims preempted by the Labeling Act"). *But see* Green, *Cipollone* Revisited: A Not So Little Secret About the Scope of Cigarette Preemption, 82 Iowa L. Rev. 1257, 1267 (1997) (arguing that "claims asserting inadequate warnings on cigarette packages are not preempted" under *Cipollone*).

[195] 505 U.S. at 528–29.

[196] Id. at 525. Nor does the Act preempt claims "that rely solely on respondents' testing or research practices or other actions unrelated to advertising or promotion." Id. at 524–25.

and Souter reasoned that the 1969 Act did not speak clearly enough to deny the petitioner's common-law claims,[197] while Justices Scalia and Thomas asserted that the 1965 Act preempted the warning claims and the 1969 Act barred them all.[198]

Although the justices thus were widely split, *Cipollone* appeared to put to rest most (but not all)[199] preemption issues in cigarette litigation. The preemption issue revived with the advent of common-law fraud claims brought by smokers of "light" and "lowered tar and nicotine" cigarettes.[200] Viewing such claims as attempts to impose state law prohibitions on smoking and health with respect to advertising or promotion, some courts held the claims expressly preempted by the Act and FTC oversight of labeling and advertising.[201] Other courts disagreed, concluding that the claims were based on a manufacturer's general duty not to deceive and, hence, neither expressly nor impliedly preempted.[202] The split between circuits was resolved in *Altria Group, Inc. v. Good*, where the Supreme Court held that the common-law fraud claims brought by smokers of "light" and "lowered tar and nicotine" cigarettes were neither expressly nor impliedly preempted.[203]

Motor Vehicles—Myrick *and* Geier

Anti-lock braking systems in trucks. After *Cipollone*, the next Supreme Court case to address preemption in the products liability context was *Freightliner Corp. v. Myrick*,[204] which concerned the preemptive effect of the National Traffic and Motor

---

[197] Id. at 531–44.

[198] Id. at 544–56.

[199] See, e.g., Graham v. R.J. Reynolds Tobacco Co., 857 F.3d 1169, 1186 (11th Cir. 2017) (obstacle conflict preemption did not defeat the negligence and strict liability findings upheld in Engle v. Liggett Group, Inc., 945 So.2d 1246 (Fla. 2006); "federal tobacco laws do not preempt state tort claims based on the dangerousness of all the cigarettes manufactured by the tobacco companies"); R.J. Reynolds Tobacco Co. v. Marotta, 214 So.3d 590, 600 (Fla. 2017) ("While Congress did expressly preempt state and local regulations pertaining to the labeling and advertising of cigarettes, there is no indication that Congress had a 'clear and manifest purpose' to insulate the tobacco industry from state tort liability."). Compare Liggett Grp. Inc. v. Davis, 973 So.2d 467 (Fla. Dist. Ct. App. 2007) (conflict preemption barred negligence claim for continuing to sell cigarettes after discovery of their dangers, but not strict liability in tort claim for violating consumer expectations).

[200] "The plaintiffs allege that a person smoking 'light' cigarettes . . . engages in unconscious behaviors that essentially negate the ventilation effect, such as taking more frequent, voluminous, or longer puffs, covering the air holes with the lips or the fingers, or smoking additional cigarettes," leading to the consumption of "the same quantities of tar and nicotine from light cigarettes as from full-flavored ones." Good v. Altria Grp., Inc., 501 F.3d 29, 31 (1st Cir. 2007), aff'd, 555 U.S. 70 (2008).

[201] See, e.g., Clinton v. Brown & Williamson Holdings, Inc., 498 F. Supp. 2d 639, 651 (S.D.N.Y. 2007) (fraudulent misrepresentation claim against manufacturer of "light" cigarettes expressly preempted; claim "seeks to impose a 'prohibition based on smoking and health . . . under State law with respect to the advertising or promotion' "); Brown v. Brown & Williamson Tobacco Corp., 479 F.3d 383, 391, 393 (5th Cir. 2007) (same).

[202] See, e.g., Dahl v. R.J. Reynolds Tobacco Co., 742 N.W.2d 186, 199 (Minn. Ct. App. 2007) (fraudulent misrepresentation claims against manufacturer of "light" cigarettes not preempted by FCLAA or FTC; claims were not predicated on a state duty concerning smoking and health "but rather on a broader, more general duty not to deceive"); Good v. Altria Grp., Inc., 501 F.3d 29, 58–59 (1st Cir. 2007) (same), aff'd, 555 U.S. 70 (2008); Aldana v. RJ Reynolds Tobacco Co., 2007 WL 3020497, at *9 (D.S.C. 2007) (false newspaper advertisement claim not preempted).

[203] Altria Grp., Inc. v. Good, 555 U.S. 70, 87, 90–91 (2008).

In 2009, Congress enacted the Family Smoking Prevention and Tobacco Control Act (FSPTCA), which provided the Food and Drug Administration (FDA) with regulatory authority over the design, production, marketing, and advertising of tobacco products. 21 U.S.C. § 387a. In 23–34 94th St. Grocery Corp. v. New York City Bd. of Health, 685 F.3d 174, 185–86 (2d Cir. 2012), the Second Circuit ruled that the Act preempted a New York City Health Code provision that required all tobacco retailers to display signs showing graphic images of smoking health risks.

[204] 514 U.S. 280 (1995).

Vehicle Safety Act of 1966[205] and safety standards issued by its corresponding regulatory agency, the National Highway Traffic Safety Agency (NHTSA). Congress enacted the Safety Act to regulate the safety of motor vehicles in an effort to reduce the toll of injuries and deaths from traffic accidents.[206] The Safety Act's preemption clause prohibits the states from maintaining "motor vehicle safety standard[s]" that are not "identical" to any federal standards "in effect."[207] The Act also contains a savings clause, which provides: "Compliance with any Federal motor vehicle safety standard issued under this subchapter does not exempt any person from any liability under common law."[208]

In 1970, NHTSA's predecessor agency issued Standard 121, which imposed certain stopping distances for trucks that could be achieved only if trucks were equipped with anti-lock braking systems (ABS). Various truck manufacturers challenged Standard 121, and the Ninth Circuit suspended it pending further study. *Myrick* involved design defect claims by plaintiffs who attributed their injuries to the absence of ABS in eighteen-wheel trucks. Notwithstanding the fact that Standard 121 had been previously suspended, the district court ruled that the plaintiffs' design defect claims were preempted by federal Standard 121 and the Safety Act. The Eleventh Circuit reversed, holding that the plaintiffs' claims were not expressly preempted, nor were they impliedly preempted because of "*Cipollone*'s clear instruction that when there is an express pre-emption provision we should not consider implied pre-emption."[209]

The Supreme Court affirmed.[210] Speaking for a unanimous court, Justice Thomas reasoned that express preemption could not apply because no federal safety standard was "in effect" as required by the Safety Act's preemption clause. Nor were plaintiffs' design defect claims impliedly preempted because there was no conflict with the Act. Thus, because there was no federal standard with which the plaintiffs' products liability claims could conflict, *Myrick* may be viewed as a "false preemption" case. *Myrick*'s importance lies not in its holding, but in its dictum that resurrects and applies the doctrine of *implied* preemption to federal statutes containing express preemption clauses. Rejecting the court of appeals' interpretation of *Cipollone* "that implied pre-emption cannot exist when Congress has chosen to include an express pre-emption clause in a statute,"[211] the Court inscrutably observed: "At best, *Cipollone* supports an inference that an express pre-emption clause forecloses implied pre-emption; it does not establish a rule."[212]

Airbags. Five years after *Myrick*, the Supreme Court tackled the preemption issue in another motor vehicle safety case, *Geier v. American Honda Motor Co.*,[213] which involved the preemptive effect of certain NHTSA regulations on the use of airbags in

---

205 15 U.S.C. §§ 1381 et seq., now recodified at 49 U.S.C. §§ 30101 et seq.

206 Id.

207 Id. § 1392(d), recodified at 49 U.S.C. § 30103(b)(1).

208 Id. § 1397(k), recodified and revised, 49 U.S.C. § 30103(e).

209 Myrick v. Freuhauf Corp., 13 F.3d 1516, 1522 (11th Cir. 1994).

210 Freightliner Corp. v. Myrick, 514 U.S. 280 (1995).

211 Id. at 287.

212 Id. at 289.

213 529 U.S. 861 (2000).

passenger cars.[214] *Geier* revealed the latent strength and resilience of the *implied* preemption doctrine that *Myrick* had suggested.

Geier involved the preemptive effect of Federal Motor Vehicle Safety Standard 208 (entitled "Occupant Crash Protection"), a NHTSA regulation pertaining to airbags and other passive restraints.[215] From its initial formulation in 1967, when it required only lap belts, Standard 208 evolved in fits and starts.[216] Beginning in 1975, Standard 208 began to offer manufacturers an evolving menu of passive restraint options, including airbags or various combinations of passive restraints, shoulder harnesses, lap belts, and warning systems. Beginning in the late 1980s, an increasing number of automotive products liability claims were based on the failure of manufacturers to equip their cars with airbags during the transitional period before NHTSA required such devices in all cars.[217] The courts were divided on the preemption issue: many state courts ruled that such airbag claims were not preempted,[218] while all federal circuit courts ruled that such claims were.[219]

The plaintiffs in *Geier* claimed that the driver's injuries were aggravated by a design defect in their 1987 Honda Accord because it was not equipped with a driver's-side airbag. Honda argued that such an airbag claim was preempted by Standard 208 which, during the transitional period, permitted manufacturers to choose between seatbelts and airbags. The district court granted summary judgment for Honda, ruling that the plaintiffs' no-airbag claims were *expressly* preempted, and the court of appeals affirmed on the basis that such claims were *impliedly* preempted because they conflicted with the objectives of federal Standard 208.[220]

The Supreme Court affirmed, agreeing with the court of appeals that "no-airbag" claims are impliedly preempted because they conflict with FMVSS 208.[221] The Court again was badly split, and Justice Breyer spoke for the five-judge majority which reasoned from "three subsidiary questions":

> First, does the Act's express pre-emption provision pre-empt this lawsuit? [No.] Second, do ordinary [implied] pre-emption principles nonetheless apply? [Yes.]

---

[214] See Bough and Johnson, Crossing the Center Line: Preemption in Automobile Product Liability Cases, 57 J. Mo. B. 30 (2001); Raeker-Jordan, The Pre-Emption Presumption That Never Was: Pre-Emption Doctrine Swallows the Rule, 40 Ariz. L. Rev. 1379, 1445–68 (1998); Lichtenstein and Ferrera, Airbag Products Liability Litigation: State Common Law Tort Claims Are Not Automatically Preempted by Federal Legislation, 45 Clev. St. L. Rev. 1 (1997); Nader and Page, Automobile-Design Liability and Compliance with Federal Standards, 64 Geo. Wash. L. Rev. 415 (1996).

[215] 49 C.F.R. § 571.208.

[216] "Passive restraint regulation (Standard 208) has advanced over the years along a protracted, winding, sometimes perilous course." Public Citizen v. Steed, 851 F.2d 444, 445 (D.C. Cir. 1988). Its history is chronicled in Hernandez-Gomez v. Leonardo, 884 P.2d 183 (Ariz. 1994), and Motor Vehicle Mfrs. Ass'n v. State Farm Mut. Auto. Ins. Co., 463 U.S. 29, 34–38 (1983).

[217] It was not until 1997 that NHTSA finally mandated dual front-seat airbags in all (1998 model) passenger cars (actually, those manufactured on or after September 1, 1997). 49 C.F.R. § 571.208, at S4.1.5.3.

[218] See, e.g., Drattel v. Toyota Corp., 699 N.E.2d 376 (N.Y. 1998); Minton v. Honda of Am. Mfg., Inc., 684 N.E.2d 648 (Ohio 1997); Munroe v. Galati, 938 P.2d 1114 (Ariz. 1997); Wilson v. Pleasant, 660 N.E.2d 327 (Ind. 1996); Tebbetts v. Ford Motor Co., 665 A.2d 345 (N.H. 1995).

[219] See, e.g., Harris v. Ford Motor Co., 110 F.3d 1410 (9th Cir. 1997) (express preemption); Montag v. Honda Motor Co., 75 F.3d 1414 (10th Cir. 1996) (implied preemption); Pokorny v. Ford Motor Co., 902 F.2d 1116 (3d Cir. 1990) (same); Taylor v. General Motors Corp., 875 F.2d 816 (11th Cir. 1989) (same); Wood v. General Motors Corp., 865 F.2d 395 (1st Cir. 1988) (same).

[220] 166 F.3d 1236 (D.D.C. 1999).

[221] 529 U.S. at 866.

Third, does this lawsuit actually conflict with FMVSS 208, hence with the Act itself? [Yes.][222]

The Safety Act did not expressly preempt products liability claims, the Court reasoned, because the savings clause suggests that Congress believed that there were common-law claims that needed to be saved. For this reason, the Court narrowly construed the phrase "safety standard" in the express preemption clause to exclude common-law claims.[223] But the savings clause does not reach further, thought the majority, in that it does not foreclose *implied* preemption when common-law claims actually conflict with a statute or regulation.[224] Because the plaintiffs alleged that the car was defectively designed due to the manufacturer's *failure* to equip it with an airbag, while the Safety Act *permitted* manufacturers at the time to choose between airbags and alternative passive restraints, the no-airbag claims actually conflicted with the federal standard and so were impliedly preempted.[225]

Subsequently, some courts applied *Geier* to hold that a later version of FMVSS 208—which provided manufacturers with options on which seats to equip with lap belts, shoulder harnesses, and passenger side airbags—preempted claims against manufacturers for failing to equip a seat with a particular passive restraint because of the options provided in the rule.[226] In 2011, the Supreme Court reconsidered *Geier* and the significance of optional restraint system approaches the Department of Transportation (DOT) sometimes allows in its automotive safety rules. *Williamson v. Mazda Motor of America, Inc.*[227] concerned the preemptive effect of a provision in FMVSS 208 that allowed manufacturers to choose to install either lap-and-shoulder belts or simple lap belts in a vehicle's rear inner seats. A plaintiff in *Williamson*, who only had a lap belt in such a seat, was killed when the minivan in which she was riding had a collision. The plaintiffs contended that Mazda should have equipped all the seats in the van with safer lap-and-shoulder belts, as Mazda had an option to do under rule 208. Mazda argued that the optional nature of FMVSS 208 preempted the products liability claim, as it had in *Geier*. Because of the different regulatory history of the two provisions, the Supreme Court ruled that the optional nature of the safety belt provisions in FMVSS 208 did not impliedly preempt state tort claims. The DOT allowed manufacturers a choice between airbags and other passive restraints at issue in *Geier*, the Court explained, to promote variety among such technologies in an effort to spur development of alternative restraint approaches, whereas DOT allowed the belt options at issue in

---

222 Id. at 867.

223 Id. at 867–68.

224 Id. at 869. Applying *Geier*, courts have since focused on whether the claimed defect actually conflicts with a relevant FMVSS. See, e.g., Carden v. General Motors Corp., 509 F.3d 227, 230–32 (5th Cir. 2007) (finding conflict with FMVSS 208 and preemption of lap belt design defect claims); Ysbrand v. Daimler Chrysler Corp., 81 P.3d 618 (Okla. 2003) (finding no conflict with FMVSS 208 and no preemption of claim that installed airbag was defectively designed); Volkswagen of Am., Inc. v. Gentry, 564 S.E.2d 733 (Ga. Ct. App. 2002) (finding no conflict with FMVSS 208 and no preemption of claim that seatbelt system was defectively designed by the improper placement and angle of the shoulder strap and placement of the knee bolster); Mejia v. White GMC Trucks, Inc., 784 N.E.2d 345 (Ill. App. Ct. 2002) (finding actual conflict with relevant standard and preemption of design defect claim based on design of doors and door handles of garbage truck).

225 529 U.S. at 874. "Because the rule of law for which petitioners contend would have stood 'as an obstacle to the accomplishment and execution of the important means-related federal objectives that we have just discussed, it is pre-empted." Id. at 881.

226 See Roland v. General Motors Corp., 881 N.E.2d 722, 719–30 (Ind. Ct. App. 2008) (rear inner seat lap belt); Carden v. General Motors Corp., 509 F.3d 227, 233 (5th Cir. 2007) (Tex. law) (same); Heinricher v. Volvo Car Co., 809 N.E.2d 1094, 1098 (Mass. App. Ct. 2004) (rear inner seat shoulder harness).

227 562 U.S. 323 (2011) (abrogating *Roland*, *Carden*, and *Heinricher*, note 226, above).

Williamson only because the safer lap-and-shoulder belts were more expensive to install on rear middle and aisle seats. So, as argued by the Solicitor General, tort suits against manufacturers for failing to install the safer belts not only do not conflict with the relevant federal safety objectives, but actually promote them.[228]

Drugs and Medical Devices

Drugs. The federal Food and Drug Administration (FDA) regulates the preparation and labeling of food,[229] drugs, and cosmetics under the Food, Drug, and Cosmetic Act (FDCA),[230] and medical devices under an amendment to that Act.[231] Because the FDCA does not contain a preemption clause relevant to drugs, the statute itself does not expressly preempt defective warning and other products liability claims against pharmaceutical manufacturers.[232] Nor, traditionally, have courts found that the FDCA *impliedly* preempts products liability claims against manufacturers of prescription drugs.[233] Yet the statute does delegate authority to the FDA to preempt state law,[234] and the agency by regulation may be seen as expressly preempting state law by mandating certain warnings for drugs.[235] Because preemption may so emanate from the edict of a mere administrative agency, however, a court may not find that an FDA regulation preempts state law unless the regulation clearly says so.[236]

Courts traditionally took the view, as did the FDA itself except during the Bush II administration,[237] that FDA drug labeling regulations generally impose only minimum standards—providing merely a safety floor—and that state tort law that imposes greater safety beneficially supplements federal regulatory efforts to promote drug safety.[238] In

---

[228] Applying *Williamson*, see Varela v. FCA US LLC, 505 P.3d 244, 262–63 (Ariz. 2022) (NHTSA policy encouraging, but not requiring, automatic emergency braking (AEB) technology did not impliedly preempt claim that AEB would have avoided the rear-end crash that injured plaintiff and killed her daughter).

[229] In Jones v. Rath Packing Co., 430 U.S. 519 (1977), the Supreme Court held that the Fair Packaging and Labeling Act and its regulations impliedly preempt inconsistent state food labeling regulations. See also Boulahanis v. Prevo's Family Mkt., Inc., 583 N.W.2d 509 (Mich. Ct. App. 1998) (claim for illness from E. Coli bacteria preempted by Federal Meat Inspection Act).

[230] 21 U.S.C. §§ 301 et seq.

[231] See discussion below.

[232] See Eve v. Sandoz Pharm. Corp., 2002 WL 181972, at *2 (S.D. Ind. 2002); Bell v. Lollar, 791 N.E.2d 849 (Ind. Ct. App. 2003) (failure to warn of risk of mixing acetaminophen and alcohol). On the preemption defense to claims against drug manufacturers, see Owen & Davis on Products Liability § 15:19.

[233] See, e.g., Bell v. Lollar, 791 N.E.2d 849 (Ind. Ct. App. 2003) (acetaminophen, risk of mixing with alcohol); Ohler v. Purdue Pharma, L.P., 2002 WL 88945 (E.D. La. 2002) (OxyContin); Caraker v. Sandoz Pharms. Corp., 172 F. Supp. 2d 1018 (S.D. Ill. 2001) (Parlodel); Abbot v. American Cyanamid Co., 844 F.2d 1108 (4th Cir. 1988) (DTP vaccine); MacDonald v. Ortho Pharm. Corp., 475 N.E.2d 65 (Mass. 1985) (birth control pills). Note, however, that some courts challenged the traditional view. See notes 234–235, below.

[234] See Hillsborough Cnty., Fla. v. Automated Med. Labs., Inc., 471 U.S. 707, 713, 721 (1985). Since the FDA is authorized to preempt state law, its failure explicitly to do so "should be taken as a strong sign that the state action does not threaten national policy and is not *impliedly* preempted." 1 L. Tribe, American Constitutional Law § 6–32, at 1213 n.1 (3d ed. 2000).

[235] See, e.g., Kanter v. Warner-Lambert Co., 122 Cal. Rptr. 2d 72 (Ct. App. 2002) (inadequate warning claim with respect to head lice treatment); Green v. BDI Pharm., 803 So.2d 68 (La. Ct. App. 2001) (failure to warn of addictive nature of Ephedrine in "Mini Thins"). See also Ohler v. Purdue Pharma, L.P., 2002 WL 88945, at *12–13 (E.D. La. 2002) (quoting 63 Fed. Reg. 66,383–84 (Dec. 1, 1998) (concerning direct-to-patient warnings)).

[236] See Ohler v. Purdue Pharma, L.P., 2002 WL 88945, at *13 n.34 (E.D. La. 2002).

[237] See id. (warnings on prescription pain medication, OxyContin); Caraker v. Sandoz Pharms. Corp., 172 F. Supp. 2d 1018, 1036 (S.D. Ill. 2001) (quoting FDA's recognition of tort litigation's value and desire not to impede it).

[238] See, e.g., Eve v. Sandoz Pharm. Corp., 2002 WL 181972, at *5 (S.D. Ind. 2002); Caraker v. Sandoz Pharms. Corp., 172 F. Supp. 2d 1018, 1033 (S.D. Ill. 2001) ("Because there is no evidence that either Congress

the early 2000s, however, the FDA reversed its position on the desirability of products liability litigation which by that time it viewed as frustrating, rather than beneficially complementing, the agency's goal of promoting public health.[239] A small handful of courts, reasoning that even federal agencies have a right to change their minds, and that an agency's current views on preemption are entitled to respect,[240] ruled that FDA approval of a manufacturer's design, manufacturing processes, or labeling in fact preempts products liability claims that challenge in some way the approved aspect of a drug[241] or medical device.[242] Yet drug regulations provide that manufacturers may and sometimes should strengthen warnings without prior FDA approval, and the FDA encourages manufacturers to take such initiatives on their own,[243] which has led other

or the FDA intended on scrap[p]ing state products liability claims based on a failure to warn . . ., it is reasonable to find that the FDA has imposed a minimum—as opposed to conclusive—standard of safety."); Motus v. Pfizer, Inc., 127 F. Supp. 2d 1085 (C.D. Cal. 2000) (Zoloft; manufacturer was unable to cite a single decision holding that FDA prescription drug requirements preempted state law claims), aff'd on other grounds, 358 F.3d 659 (9th Cir. 2004); Merrell Dow Pharms., Inc. v. Oxendine, 649 A.2d 825, 828 (D.C. 1994) (Bendectin).

[239] First in amicus briefs, later in a 2006 regulatory preamble and another statement published in the Federal Register. See Amicus Brief for FDA in Motus v. Pfizer, Inc., 358 F.3d 659 (9th Cir. 2004), brief at 2002 WL 32303084; Miller, "Failure to Warn"—Blocking Bad Claims, Nat'l L.J. 31 (Nov. 10, 2003) (describing FDA filings of amicus briefs in some cases arguing that FDA approval of labeling for prescription drugs preempts failure-to-warn claims against manufacturers); O'Reilly, A State of Extinction: Does Food and Drug Administration Approval of a Prescription Drug Label Extinguish State Claims for Inadequate Warning?, 58 Food & Drug. L.J. 287 (2003); 71 Fed. Reg. 3922, 3933–36 (Jan. 24, 2006) ("the Preamble"); 73 Fed. Reg. 2848, 2853 (Jan. 16, 2008). See generally Curtin and Relkin, Preamble Preemption and the Challenged Role of Failure to Warn and Defective Design Pharmaceutical Cases in Revealing Scientific Fraud, Marketing Mischief, and Conflicts of Interest, 35 Hofstra L. Rev. 1773 (2007); Davis, Unmasking the Presumption in Favor of Preemption, 53 S.C. L. Rev. 967 (2002); Sharkey, Federalism in Action: FDA Regulatory Preemption in Pharmaceutical Cases in State Versus Federal Courts, 15 J.L. & Pol'y 1013 (2007).

[240] See Chevron, U.S.A., Inc. v. Natural Res. Def. Council, Inc., 467 U.S. 837, 844 (1984) (noting that it has been "long recognized that considerable weight should be accorded to an executive department's construction of a statutory scheme it is entrusted to administer"). See also Buckman Co. v. Plaintiffs' Legal Comm., 531 U.S. 341, 353 (2001); Geier v. American Honda Motor Co., 529 U.S. 861, 883 (2000) (noting that the Court "place[s] some weight upon [a federal agency's interpretation of a regulation's] objectives and its conclusion . . . that a tort suit . . . would stan[d] as an obstacle to the accomplishment and execution of those objectives"); Medtronic, Inc. v. Lohr, 518 U.S. 470, 496 (1996) (according weight to FDA's position on preemptive effect of FDCA § 510(k) as contrasted to § 360e(b) medical device approval processes).

[241] See Sykes v. Glaxo-SmithKline, 484 F. Supp. 2d 289, 308–18 (E.D. Pa. 2007) ("additional labeling would have posed a threat to the federal regulatory objectives of the FDA"; most claims preempted); Colacicco v. Apotex, Inc., 432 F. Supp. 2d 514 (E.D. Pa. 2006) (Paxil and its generic equivalent; discussing FDA arguments for preemption in amicus briefs and in the "Preemption Preamble," 71 Fed. Reg. 3922, 3933–36 (Jan. 24, 2006), and agency's argument that regulations do not allow warning changes without FDA approval), aff'd, 521 F.3d 253 (3d Cir. 2008), vacated, 556 U.S. 1101 (2009).

[242] See, e.g., Horn v. Thoratec Corp., 376 F.3d 163, 178 (3d Cir. 2004) (2–1 decision). This decision quoted the FDA's Amicus Curiae Letter Brief which argued that the plaintiff's claims of defects in the design, manufacture, and labeling of the heart pump which met FDA requirements suggest that products liability law may require that the device be designed, manufactured, and marketed differently from the way approved by FDA. According to the FDA at the time, products liability actions "threaten the statutory framework" for regulating medical devices, particularly the agency's review and approval of a product's labeling. Rather than being based on "centralized expert evaluation of device regulatory issues," products liability actions require "lay judges and juries to second-guess the balancing of benefits and risks of a specific device to their intended patient population—the central role of FDA." The threat of large damage awards "creates pressure on manufacturers to add warnings that FDA has neither approved, nor found to be scientifically required, or withdrawal of FDA-approved products from the market in conflict with the agency's expert determination that such products are safe and effective. This situation can harm the public health by retarding research and development and by encouraging 'defensive labeling' by manufacturers to avoid state liability, resulting in scientifically unsubstantiated warnings and underutilization of beneficial treatments."

[243] And the comments of a former FDA Commissioner memorializing the prior FDA view that manufacturers may be under a state-law duty to do so.

courts[244] and commentators[245] to conclude that products liability litigation may well be allowed in the absence of clearly preemptive action by the FDA.

The Supreme Court addressed the drug warning preemption issue in *Wyeth v. Levine*,[246] where the plaintiff went to her local clinic for treatment of the pain and nausea of a migraine headache. For her nausea, the clinic first gave her an intramuscular injection of an antihistamine manufactured by the defendant. When the plaintiff returned for further treatment later in the day because her symptoms had not abated, a physician's assistant administered a second injection of the drug—by injection directly into the plaintiff's vein. But the drug entered the plaintiff's artery instead, which caused gangrene, requiring amputation of her forearm. The plaintiff sued Wyeth for failing to provide adequate warnings of the risk of attempting to inject the drug directly into a vein and instructions to clinicians to administer the drug by the much safer IV-drip method, particularly as reports of similar amputations mounted over the years—at least 20 since the 1960s. Wyeth claimed that the FDA's approval of its label warnings and instructions preempted the plaintiff's claims, but a 6–3 majority of the Supreme Court agreed with the plaintiff that the jury could find that Wyeth should have strengthened the warnings and instructions, which federal regulations permit a drug manufacturer to do on an interim basis without FDA approval. The Court reasoned that the products liability claims did not obstruct the federal regulation of drug labeling, that the FDA's position in the preamble that state tort suits interfere with its statutory mandate was entitled to "no weight," and that it was not *impossible* for Wyeth to comply with both its state and federal obligations.[247]

---

[244] See In re Vioxx Prods. Liab. Litig., 501 F. Supp. 2d 776, 788 (E.D. La. 2007) (FDA "statements on preemption in the preamble to the 2006 Final Rule lack the 'power to persuade' "); In re Zyprexa Prods. Liab. Litig., 489 F. Supp. 2d 230, 270–78 (E.D.N.Y. 2007) (same); Levine v. Wyeth, 944 A.2d 179, 193 (Vt. 2006) (the FDA's new statement "deserves no deference"), aff'd 555 U.S. 555 (2009) (discussed below); Coutu v. Tracy, 2006 WL 1314261, at *3–4 (R.I. Super. Ct. 2006) (discounting FDA's preemption preamble: "Courts have consistently held that FDA regulations regarding labels and warnings for drugs do not preempt state law."); Caraker v. Sandoz Pharms. Corp., 172 F. Supp. 2d 1018 (S.D. Ill. 2001) (extensive discussion of FDA's views on preemption and history of 1965 amendment to FDA regulations that allows supplemental warnings without prior FDA approval). See also Jackson v. Pfizer, Inc., 432 F. Supp. 2d 964, 969 (D. Neb. 2006) (noting FDA regulation allowing manufacturers to strengthen drug warnings at any time without FDA approval).

In Johnson & Johnson v. Fitch ex rel. State, 315 So.3d 1017 (Miss. 2021), cert. denied sub nom. Johnson & Johnson v. Fitch, 142 S. Ct. 732 (2021), the Mississippi Supreme Court ruled that the Food and Drug Act neither expressly nor impliedly preempted the Mississippi Attorney General's consumer protection claims against J&J for failing to provide a cancer warning on talc powder cosmetic products. Noting that courts "have a duty to accept the reading that disfavors pre-emption," the Court held that the FDA's *inaction* and failure to "follow the notice and comment rule making process," following citizen petitions to add a cancer warning to talc-based products, did not create a "requirement," but, instead, "allow[ed] the states the freedom to regulate cosmetics." Id. at 1024–25.

[245] See, e.g., Davis, The Battle Over Implied Preemption: Products Liability and the FDA, 48 B.C. L. Rev. 1089 (2007); Ausness, "After You, My Dear Alphonse!": Should the Courts Defer to the FDA's New Interpretation of § 360K(A) of the Medical Device Amendments?, 80 Tul. L. Rev. 727, 733 (2006) (noting that '[c]ertain labeling changes that enhance safety without a corresponding impact on effectiveness are eligible for implementation without prior FDA approval"); J. O'Steen and V. O'Steen, The FDA Defense: Vioxx® and the Argument Against Federal Preemption of State Claims for Injuries Resulting from Defective Drugs, 48 Ariz. L. Rev. 67 (2006); Struve, The FDA and the Tort System: Postmarketing Surveillance, Compensation, and the Role of Litigation, 5 Yale J. Health Pol'y L. & Ethics 587 (2005).

[246] 555 U.S. 555 (2009).

[247] Id. at 581. Impossibility preemption issues "arise with some regularity in litigation asserting state-law tort claims against prescription-drug manufacturers." Jankowski v. Zydus Pharms. USA, Inc., 2021 WL 2190913, at *3 (D.N.J. 2021). To prove that it would have been impossible to comply with both state and federal requirements, *Levine* held that a manufacturer must present "clear evidence" that the FDA would have rejected a label change. *Levine*, 555 U.S. at 571. In Merck Sharp & Dohme Corp. v. Albrecht, 139 S. Ct. 1668 (2019), Justice Breyer defined "clear evidence" as "evidence that shows the court that the drug manufacturer

In *PLIVA, Inc. v. Mensing*,[248] the Supreme Court addressed the viability of preemption assertions by manufacturers of *generic* drugs sued for inadequate warnings. Because a generic drug must have "the same" label as its (FDA-approved) brand-name drug,[249] and so can add stronger warnings only with the prior approval of the FDA,[250] a 5 to 4 majority of the Court concluded that it would be impossible for a generic drug maker, who chose to strengthen its drug's warnings, to comply with both state and federal drug labeling laws:

> We find impossibility here. It was not lawful under federal law for the Manufacturers to do what state law required of them. And even if they had fulfilled their federal duty to ask for FDA assistance, they would not have satisfied the requirements of state law.[251]

Although *Mensing* preempts warnings claims against generic drug manufacturers, courts have split on whether failure-to-*update* warning claims against a generic drug manufacturer—based on its failure to update a warning on its version of a brand-name drug whose warning have already been strengthened—are also preempted under *Mensing*.[252]

Most courts extended the *Mensing* preemption ruling to design defect claims against generic drug makers.[253] But the First Circuit, refusing to do so in *Bartlett v. Mutual Pharmaceutical Co., Inc.*,[254] affirmed a large award to the plaintiff, Karen Bartlett, who was prescribed Clinoril, a non-steroidal anti-inflammatory drug (NSAID), for shoulder pain. Her pharmacist filled the prescription with a generic, sulindac, manufactured by Mutual Pharmaceutical, and she soon developed an acute case of toxic epidermal

---

fully informed the FDA of the justifications for the warning required by state law and that the FDA, in turn, informed the drug manufacturer that the FDA would not approve a change to the drug's label to include that warning." Id. at 1672. Due to the complexity in deciding whether FDA actions amount to such formal determinations, *Albrecht* held that the question of whether federal and state laws "irreconcilably" conflict is a matter of law for the court. Id. at 1679.

[248] 564 U.S. 604 (2011).

[249] 21 U.S.C. § 355(j). See also 57 Fed. Reg. 17950–01.

[250] 564 U.S. at 620. "Unlike the manufacturer of the brand-name drug, a generic drug maker . . . can only request the FDA to make a change." V. Schwartz, Goldberg, and Silverman, Warning: Shifting Liability to Manufacturers of Brand-Name Medicines When the Harm Was Allegedly Caused by Generic Drugs Has Severe Side Effects, 81 Fordham L. Rev. 1835, 1853 (2013).

[251] 564 U.S. at 618.

[252] **Failure-to-update claims preempted.** See, e.g., Guarino v. Wyeth, LLC, 719 F.3d 1245, 1249 (11th Cir. 2013) (plaintiff's "attempt to elude *Mensing* by clothing her allegations as 'failure-to-communicate' claims rather than failure-to-warn claims" failed to escape preemption); Morris v. PLIVA, Inc., 713 F.3d 774, 777 (5th Cir. 2013) (*Mensing* forecloses "failure to 'communicate' " claims); Smith v. Wyeth, 657 F.3d 420, 423 (6th Cir. 2011) ("federal law preempts state laws that impose on generic-drug manufacturers the duty to change a drug's label"), cert. denied, 566 U.S. 974 (2012).

Failure-to-update claims not preempted. See, e.g., In re Fluoroquinolone Prods. Liab. Litig., 2021 WL 3047172, at *3 (D. Minn. 2021) (plaintiff's negligence and negligent misrepresentation claims alleging defendants breached their duty of care by failing to update generic's label with FDA approved language were not preempted); In re Reglan Litig., 142 A.3d 725 (N.J. 2016) (failure-to-update claims against generic manufacturer not preempted); Huck v. Wyeth, Inc., 850 N.W.2d 353, 362–67 (Iowa 2014) (same); Fulgenzi v. PLIVA, Inc., 711 F.3d 578, 586 (6th Cir. 2013) (failure-to-update generic label with FDA-mandated stronger warning label on brand-name drug); In re Fosamax Prods. Liab. Litig., 965 F. Supp. 2d 413, 420 (S.D.N.Y. 2013) (failure-to-update claim not preempted, but failure to warn and failure to communicate claims were preempted).

[253] See, e.g., Aucoin v. Amneal Pharms., LLC, 2012 WL 2990697, at *9 (E.D. La. 2012) ("this Court joins numerous other lower courts that have considered this issue and found the failure-to-warn reasoning of *Mensing* equally applicable to a design defect claim").

[254] 678 F.3d 30, 38 (1st Cir. 2012).

necrolysis, which caused 65% of her body surface to deteriorate, burn off, or turn into an open wound. This side effect, which occurred in a small number of patients, was not described on the labeling when Bartlett was prescribed the drug. Bartlett sued Mutual Pharmaceutical, asserting both failure to warn and design defect claims. The failure to warn claim was dismissed because Bartlett's physician admitted not reading the warning that did accompany the drug. But a jury awarded Bartlett $21 million based on a design defect claim. The First Circuit affirmed, concluding that the design defect claims were not preempted under *Mensing* because "the generic maker can avoid . . . design defect lawsuits by not making the drug."[255]

In *Mutual Pharmaceutical Co., Inc. v. Bartlett*,[256] the Supreme Court reversed. Because the FDCA regulations governing generic pharmaceuticals do not permit a generic manufacturer to alter the chemical composition of its drugs, the only recourse for Mutual under New Hampshire law, reasoned the Court, was to change the drug's labeling, which *Mensing* had held was impossible under federal law and thus preempted.[257] The Court rejected the First Circuit's argument that Mutual could choose not to make sulindac at all, deprecating such a " 'stop-selling' rationale" as contrary to the Court's preemption jurisprudence: "Our pre-emption cases presume that an actor seeking to satisfy both his federal- and state-law obligations is not required to cease acting altogether in order to avoid liability. Indeed, if the option of ceasing to act defeated a claim of impossibility, impossibility pre-emption would be 'all but meaningless.' "[258]

Mensing and *Bartlett* left the vast population of generic drug users in a bind, since these two decisions afford makers of such drugs preemption protection from liability for failing to warn of newly discovered dangers (or failing to design them away), until such measures are adopted by the corresponding makers of brand name drugs.[259]

A final and altogether different drug preemption issue involves the National Childhood Vaccine Injury Act (NCVIA) of 1986,[260] which established a federal no-fault program to compensate children for side-effects from DTP and other childhood vaccines. The Act substituted the compensation program for products liability litigation—the threat of which had led all but one drug manufacturer to abandon making childhood vaccines—in order to stabilize the market for such vaccines. Addressing the preemptive effect of the NCVIA, *Bruesewitz v. Wyeth LLC*[261] ruled that a plaintiffs' ordinary design defect products liability claims are preempted by the manufacturer's immunity under the Act for harm caused by unavoidable side-effects in vaccines.[262]

---

[255] Id. at 38.

[256] 570 U.S. 472 (2013).

[257] Id. at 486–87.

[258] Id. at 487, n.3. The Court "save[d] for another day" two issues: (1) "whether a true absolute-liability state law system could give rise to impossibility preemption," and (2) the viability of "state design-defect claims that parallel the federal misbranding statute." Id. at 2474 n.1, 2477, n.4. But whether a state bases its "strict" liability for design defects on consumer expectations or risk-utility makes no difference. See Drager v. Pliva USA Inc., 741 F.3d 470, 478 (4th Cir. 2014) (Md. law).

[259] The FDA's 2013 proposed rule that would have allowed generic drug makers to add new warnings as they deemed appropriate was withdrawn in 2018 in response to public comments. See Fed. Reg. 64,301 (Dec. 14, 2018) ("The concerns raised in the comments reflect significant competing interests, and FDA acknowledges that the proposed rule, if finalized, would present significant potential downsides.").

[260] 42 U.S.C. §§ 300aa–1 et seq. (1986). On the NCVIA, see § 18.1, below.

[261] 562 U.S. 223 (2011).

[262] See 42 U.S.C. § 300aa–22(b)(1).

Medical devices. Prior to the mid-1970s, the FDA possessed limited regulatory power over manufacturers of medical devices.[263] In response to a number of safety problems with various medical devices during the early 1970s—including an intrauterine device (IUD) called the Dalkon Shield, catheters, artificial heart valves, defibrillators, and pacemakers—Congress enacted the Medical Device Amendments of 1976 (the MDA) to the FDCA, directing the FDA to classify and regulate the safety and effectiveness of medical devices.[264] The FDA divides medical devices among three categories, depending on the potential health and safety implications of the device: Class I devices, such as tongue depressors and stethoscopes, contain minimal risk and are subject to minimal regulation; Class II devices, such as hearing aids and tampons, are potentially more harmful and so are subject to "special controls"; Class III devices, such as pacemakers and artificial hearts, pose considerable potential risk and thus are subject to substantial regulatory control.[265]

Prior to marketing a new Class III device, the manufacturer must submit the device to a rigorous, time-consuming, and expensive "premarket approval" (PMA) process in order to assure the FDA that the device is safe and effective and, so, proper for sale. Congress provided two exemptions to the premarket approval process: (1) a "grandfathering" exemption for devices marketed prior to the 1976 enactment of the MDA, until such time as the FDA initiates and completes the requisite PMA; and (2) an exemption for post-1976 devices that are "substantially equivalent" to pre-1976 devices, in order to prevent manufacturers of the grandfathered devices from obtaining an unfair competitive advantage over manufacturers of new devices, and to facilitate improvements to the designs of existing devices. Prior to marketing an exempted device under this second exemption, a manufacturer must submit a premarket notification to the FDA[266] to permit the agency to determine the new device's "substantial equivalence" to an existing device. Quite simple and inexpensive, the "premarket notification" (or "§ 510(k)") process usually results in prompt FDA approval of the new device.

Unlike the FDCA's non-preemptive approach to regulating prescription drugs, the MDA expressly preempts inconsistent state law, providing that the states may not enforce any requirement for a medical device that is "different from or in addition to" any federal requirement "applicable . . . to the device."[267] The FDA has interpreted this provision to mean that state requirements are preempted only if the agency has a "specific" counterpart regulation or requirement, thereby rendering any divergent state requirements "different from or in addition to" the specific FDA requirements;[268] although the agency subsequently changed its position on this point.[269]

In *Medtronic, Inc. v. Lohr*,[270] the plaintiffs alleged that the defendant's pacemaker, which the FDA had approved under the substantial equivalence § 510(k) process, failed

---

[263] See Medtronic, Inc. v. Lohr, 518 U.S. 470, 475–80 (1996) (history of medical device regulation and FDA safety controls under MDA).

[264] See 21 U.S.C. §§ 360 et seq.

[265] See Fowler v. Smith & Nephew Richards, Inc., 1999 WL 1132967 (M.D. Fla. 1999).

[266] See 21 U.S.C. § 360(k).

[267] 21 U.S.C. § 360k.

[268] 21 C.F.R. § 808.1(d).

[269] See Plaintiff, Device Maker Differ on Significance of Government's New Stand on Preemption, 32 Prod. Safety & Liab. Rep. (BNA) 23 (June 21, 2004).

[270] 518 U.S. 470 (1996).

due to a defectively designed and manufactured wire lead,[271] and that the manufacturer failed to warn of this risk despite knowing of earlier failures. The district court dismissed the action, concluding that the MDA preempted all of the plaintiffs' claims, and the court of appeals reversed in part, ruling that the design defect claims were preempted, but that the manufacturing and warning defect claims were not.

The Supreme Court reversed in part, concluding that the MDA did not preempt *any* of the plaintiffs' products liability claims. Applying an express preemption analysis, the *Lohr* Court reasoned that, for a state safety requirement to be "different from or in addition to" a corresponding FDA regulation, the federal regulation would have to be "specific" to the device, not a regulation of general applicability. With respect to the plaintiffs' design defect claims, the Court ruled that the FDA did not impose any specific design safety "requirements" by its cursory § 510(k) determination that the defendant's product was a "substantially equivalent" device.[272] As for the defective manufacturing and warning claims, the Court reasoned that both the FDA's general "Good Manufacturing Practices" regulations, as well as its general labeling regulations that required manufacturers of almost every device to provide warnings appropriate to the device, were simply too general to be either "applicable . . . to the device," as required in the preemption clause, or "specific" to a "particular device," as required by the FDA's interpretation of that clause.[273]

Consistent with *Lohr*'s holding that generalized FDA safety regulations are not preemptive, courts have ruled that state law products liability claims are indeed preempted where the FDA's regulations are exacting or specific to a particular product.[274] For example, in a case involving a pacemaker that was an investigational device,[275] a context where the FDA imposes quite exacting standards,[276] the Sixth Circuit Court of Appeals held that the FDA's specific approval of the product's design was preemptive because a state law design-defect claim "would thwart the [federal] goals of safety and innovation."[277] So, too, because the FDA labeling requirement for tampons (Class II devices) are specific to tampons, at least a couple federal circuit courts have ruled that this "device-and-disease-specific" requirement accordingly preempts a products liability claim.[278] But, no matter how specific the regulations, claims for *manufacturing* defects logically are not preempted, even if a manufacturer follows FDA-

271 The lead carries the current into the heart muscle. See Martin v. Medtronic, Inc., 254 F.3d 573 (5th Cir. 2001).

272 518 U.S. at 492–94.

273 Id. at 497–502. Nor were the plaintiffs' claims based on violation of FDA regulations preempted because the preemption clause precluded safety requirements that are "different from," not identical to, the federal standards. Id. at 494–97.

274 "Most courts of appeal have interpreted *Lohr* to mean that the MDA preempts common-law claims to the extent that they interfere or conflict with specific federal requirements." Brooks v. Howmedica, Inc., 273 F.3d 785, 795 (8th Cir. 2001) (en banc).

275 The MDA exempts investigational devices from the PMA process "to encourage, to the extent consistent with the protection of the public health and safety and with ethical standards, the discovery and development of useful devices intended for human use." 21 U.S.C. § 360j(g).

276 See, e.g., 21 C.F.R. §§ 812.20, 812.25.

277 Martin v. Telectronics Pacing Sys., Inc., 105 F.3d 1090, 1099 (6th Cir. 1997). *But see* Baird v. American Med. Optics, 713 A.2d 1019 (N.J. 1998).

278 Papike v. Tambrands Inc., 107 F.3d 737, 740 (9th Cir. 1997) (tampon caused toxic shock syndrome; failure to warn and design defect claim based on consumer expectations preempted by labeling requirements). Accord Murphy v. Playtex Family Prods. Corp., 69 Fed. Appx. 140, 143 (4th Cir. 2003) ("federal regulators considered exactly the risk that [plaintiff] was exposed to and determined how best to warn consumers of this risk through product labeling").

approved manufacturing procedures, because such claims rest on a defendant's failure to meet the very design standards approved by the FDA.[279]

Lohr did not rule on whether the doctrine of preemption exempts a medical device approved under the rigorous PMA process from products liability claims. A number of lower courts ruled that such claims are preempted,[280] while other courts ruled to the contrary.[281] The issue was resolved in *Riegel v. Medtronic, Inc.*,[282] where the Supreme Court affirmed the dismissal of products liability claims against the manufacturer of an allegedly defective balloon catheter approved under the PMA process to unblock clogged coronary arteries. Unlike the pacemaker in *Lohr*, the FDA established requirements specific to the catheter at issue in *Riegel* during the PMA process.[283] Because the FDA had mandated device-specific requirements for the catheter, together with the majority's interpretation of "requirements" as including products liability claims based on safety standards differing from those approved by the FDA,[284] Justice Scalia reasoned for the Court that the products liability claims against the catheter's manufacturer were federally preempted.

In 2001, the Supreme Court decided a quite different medical device preemption case, *Buckman Co. v. Plaintiffs' Legal Committee.*[285] In the mid-1980s, the FDA rejected a § 510(k) substantial equivalency application by the Acromed Corporation for a variable screw spinal plate fixation system for use in spinal surgery, determining that the device was a Class III device that was not substantially equivalent to any other device. Acromed hired a regulatory consultant, the Buckman Company, to refile the application, which the FDA again rejected. Acromed and Buckman then split the device in two and filed two new § 510(k) applications, one for the bone plates and one for the bone screws, and changed the intended use from the spine to the long bones of the arms and legs. Finding that the devices, when applied to these uses, met the test of substantial equivalence, the FDA approved the bone-plate and bone-screw devices for these purposes.

Once Acromed marketed the bone-plate and bone-screw devices, surgeons widely began to use the devices for spinal surgery; thousands of persons eventually were injured from the implantation of orthopedic bone screws into the pedicles of their spines. During the 1990s, thousands of suits were filed, and over 2,000 actions were consolidated for pre-trial proceedings in the District Court for the Eastern District of Pennsylvania.[286]

---

[279] See Chambers v. Osteonics Corp., 109 F.3d 1243 (7th Cir. 1997) (negligent manufacturing claim allowed, though strict liability and breach of warranty claims for manufacturing defects mistakenly ruled preempted).

[280] **Preempted.** See, e.g., Jessen v. Mentor Corp., 71 Cal. Rptr. 3d 714, 722 (Ct. App. 2008); Blunt v. Medtronic, Inc., 738 N.W.2d 143, 153 (Wis. Ct. App. 2007); Troutman v. Curtis, 143 P.3d 74, 86 (Kan. Ct. App. 2006).

[281] **Not preempted.** See, e.g., Notmeyer v. Stryker Corp., 502 F. Supp. 2d 1051, 1057–58 (N.D. Cal. 2007); Woods v. Gliatech, Inc., 218 F. Supp. 2d 802 (W.D. Va. 2002) (citing split of authority); Weiland v. Teletronics Pacing Sys., Inc., 721 N.E.2d 1149 (Ill. 1999).

[282] 552 U.S. 312 (2008).

[283] Id. at 322–26.

[284] Id. Following *Riegel*, some courts have held that manufacturing defect claims involving medical devices approved under the PMA process are preempted. See, e.g., Carrelo v. Advanced Neuromodulation Sys., Inc., 777 F. Supp. 2d 303, 314 (D.P.R. 2011); In re Medtronic, Inc. Sprint Fidelis Leads Prods. Liab. Litig., 623 F.3d 1200, 1207 (8th Cir. 2010). *But see* Bausch v. Stryker Corp., 630 F.3d 546, 558 (7th Cir. 2010) (negligence claims not preempted).

[285] 531 U.S. 341 (2001).

[286] See In re Orthopedic Bone Screw Liab. Litig., 159 F.3d 817 (3d Cir. 1998).

Many of the claims against Acromed and Buckman, styled "fraud on the FDA," alleged that the defendants fraudulently misrepresented the product's intended use to the FDA by seeking agency "approval of its VSP plates and screws for use in long bones simply as a pretext in order to market the device for its true intended use in the spine."[287] The district court dismissed the fraud-on-the-FDA claims as preempted by the MDA, but the court of appeals reversed, ruling in a split decision that the claims were not preempted.[288]

Reversing, the Supreme Court held that the plaintiffs' fraud-on-the-FDA claims were *impliedly* preempted because they conflicted with federal law.[289] There was no "presumption against the preemption" of state law claims, reasoned the Court, because "[p]olicing fraud against federal agencies is hardly 'a field which the States have traditionally occupied.' "[290] The state law claims conflicted with federal law since "the federal statutory scheme amply empowers the FDA to punish and deter fraud against the Administration, and that this authority is used by the Administration to achieve a somewhat delicate balance of statutory objectives."[291] Because the FDCA expressly approves "off-label" use of medical devices by medical practitioners, "the FDA is charged with the difficult task of regulating the [safety] of medical devices without intruding upon decisions statutorily committed to the discretion of health care professionals."[292] The Court reasoned that fraud-on-the-FDA claims would interfere with the FDA's judgment on how best to achieve a sensitive balance between policing fraud without discouraging § 510(k) applications for "devices with potentially beneficial off-label uses for fear that such use might expose the manufacturer or its associates [such as Buckman] to unpredictable civil liability."[293]

Buckman left unresolved whether the MDA impliedly preempts normal products liability claims, those grounded solely on state tort or warranty law rather than on a violation of federal law. Although the Court in its earlier *Lohr* decision had only ruled on express preemption, the Court in *Buckman* distinguished *Lohr* on the ground that the *Lohr* "claims arose from the manufacturer's alleged failure to use reasonable care in the production of the product, not solely from the violation of FDCA requirements."[294] The Court thus observed that *Lohr* might be read to shelter from implied preemption attack state law claims that parallel federal safety regulations.[295] So reasoning, several courts have held that *Buckman* should be read to allow traditional products liability

---

[287] Id. at 820.

[288] Id. at 829.

[289] The Court in *Buckman* reiterated the point it made in Geier v. American Honda Motor Co., 529 U.S. 861 (2000), that an express preemption clause in a federal statute in no way precludes the operation of implied ("ordinary") preemption principles. *Buckman*, 531 U.S. at 352.

[290] *Buckman*, 531 U.S. at 347.

[291] Id. at 348.

[292] Id. at 350.

[293] Id. See also Baker v. St. Jude Med., S.C., Inc., 178 S.W.3d 127 (Tex. App. 2005) (fraud-on-the-FDA claim preempted under *Buckman*).

[294] *Buckman*, 531 U.S. at 352.

[295] Id. at 353.

claims,[296] even fraud claims based on a manufacturer's misrepresentations to the plaintiff rather than to the FDA.[297]

Recreational Boats—Sprietsma

In an effort to stem an increasing number of boat-related injuries and fatalities, Congress enacted the Federal Boat Safety Act of 1971 (FBSA)[298] to establish "a coordinated national boating safety program."[299] The FBSA gives the Coast Guard authority to promulgate safety standards for boating equipment and recreational boats, thereby creating a uniform safety regulatory scheme to guide manufacturers in designing such equipment.[300] Before issuing a boat-safety regulation, the Coast Guard is required to consult with the National Boating Safety Advisory Council to help determine whether the regulation is appropriate.[301] A recurring safety problem in recreational boating is the risk, to swimmers and persons falling from boats, of being struck by the rapidly moving propeller blades on boat motors. Addressing this risk, the Coast Guard in 1988 decided to investigate the possibility of requiring manufacturers to install propeller guards to minimize the propeller danger to persons in the water.[302] The Coast Guard directed the Advisory Council to study the data, feasibility, advantages, and disadvantages of minimizing propeller-strike injuries with propeller guards. After studying the issue and holding public hearings, the Propeller Guard Subcommittee unanimously determined that the Coast Guard should *not* require propeller guards for reasons of safety,[303] economics, and feasibility.[304] The Advisory Committee adopted the

---

[296] **Not preempted.** See, e.g., Russell v. Johnson & Johnson, Inc., 610 S.W.3d 233, 242 (Ky. 2020) (plaintiffs' negligent manufacturing and failure to warn parallel state claims against manufacturer of defective catheter approved under the investigational device exemption were not preempted); Sullivan v. Medtronic, Inc., 498 F. Supp. 3d 1106, 1115 (E.D. Mo. 2020) (plaintiff's manufacturing defect allegations that pain pump deviated from pre-market specifications and violated specific Current Good Manufacturing Practices were parallel state claims surviving preemption); Money v. Johnson, 2016 WL 3055875, at *4–5 (N.D. Cal. 2016) (manufacturing defect parallel state claims tied to specific contact lens PMA requirements were not expressly preempted).

Preempted. See, e.g., Engle v. Medtronic, Inc., 2021 WL 1318322, at *4 (W.D. Ky. 2021) (preempting plaintiff's claims arising from doctor's off-label use of unapproved medication in pain pump); Nunn v. Mentor Worldwide, LLC, 847 Fed. Appx. 373, 376 (9th Cir. 2021) (affirming dismissal of plaintiffs' manufacturing defect claims; plaintiffs failed to sufficiently allege a parallel state law claim that could survive the "narrow gap" to escape preemption); Conklin v. Medtronic, Inc., 431 P.3d 571, 578–79 (Ariz. 2018) (plaintiff's failure to warn claim alleging that pump manufacturer failed to report post-PMA adverse events to the FDA was impliedly preempted under *Buckman*).

[297] See, e.g., In re Testosterone Replacement Therapy Prods. Liab. Litig. Coordinated Pretrial Proc., 430 F. Supp. 3d 516, 532 (N.D. Ill. 2019) (off-label promotion claims were not preempted; "a jury reasonably could conclude, independently of the FDCA, that Actavis's conduct violated Minnesota law prohibiting fraudulent misrepresentation"); Alton v. Medtronic, Inc., 970 F. Supp. 2d 1069, 1097–99, 1102–03 (D. Or. 2013) (fraudulent misrepresentation and fraud in the inducement for marketing device for off-label use); Eve v. Sandoz Pharm. Corp., 2002 WL 181972 (S.D. Ind. 2002) (citing other cases). See also Caraker v. Sandoz Pharms. Corp., 172 F. Supp. 2d 1018, 1033 (S.D. Ill. 2001) (*Buckman* did not alter wealth of authority holding that FDA regulations do not impliedly preempt products liability failure to warn claims).

[298] 46 U.S.C. §§ 4301 et seq.

[299] S. Rep. No. 92–248, at 14 (1971), as reprinted in 1971 U.S.C.C.A.N., 1333, 1335.

[300] Id. at 1333–35. Regulatory authority was delegated by the Secretary of Transportation to the Coast Guard. 49 C.F.R. § 1.46(n)(1) (1997).

[301] 46 U.S.C. § 4302(c).

[302] See Note, 68 Fordham L. Rev. 487 (1999) (preemption of propeller strike injuries).

[303] The Subcommittee found that propeller guards tend to hinder steering, increase the risk of blunt contact with persons in the water, and create a risk that a person's arm or leg could be caught between the guard and propeller blades. See, e.g., Sprietsma v. Mercury Marine, 757 N.E.2d 75, 78–79 (Ill. 2001), rev'd, 537 U.S. 51 (2002).

[304] See Sprietsma v. Mercury Marine, 537 U.S. 51, 61 (2002).

Subcommittee report and recommended to the Coast Guard that manufacturers not be required to install propeller guards, and the Coast Guard adopted the Advisory Committee recommendation in 1990.[305]

The FBSA contains both a preemption clause and a savings clause. The preemption clause prohibits state laws and regulations that are not identical to federal regulations promulgated under the Act.[306] The savings clause provides: "Compliance with this chapter or standards, regulations, or orders prescribed under this chapter does not relieve a person from liability at common law or under State law."[307]

During the 1990s and early 2000s, a number of "no-propeller-guard" claims were asserted against manufacturers of boats and motors for failing to equip boat motors with propeller guards. A large majority of courts, but not all,[308] held that the FBSA preempted such claims—most on the basis of express preemption,[309] but several, influenced by the savings clause, on implied conflict preemption grounds.[310] On both bases, many courts concluded that the Coast Guard's deliberative decision *not* to require propeller guards was preemptive of no-propeller-guard claims that effectively would require manufacturers to install such guards—a state "requirement" not "identical" to the federal requirement,[311] indeed, "in direct contravention to the Coast Guard's policy against mandating such a device in favor of affording manufacturers flexibility in the matter."[312]

In *Sprietsma v. Mercury Marine*,[313] the plaintiff's wife fell from a boat and was killed when struck by the motor's propeller blades. The plaintiff sued the manufacturer of the motor, claiming that it was unreasonably dangerous for not being equipped with a propeller guard. The trial court held that the claims were impliedly preempted by the FBSA; the appellate court affirmed on the basis of express preemption; and the Illinois Supreme Court affirmed, ruling that the plaintiff's claims conflicted with the Coast Guard's no-propeller-guard decision and so were barred on implied preemption

[305] See, e.g., Sprietsma v. Mercury Marine, 757 N.E.2d 75, 78–79 (Ill. 2001), rev'd, 537 U.S. 51 (2002).

[306] "Unless permitted by the Secretary[,] a State . . . may not establish, continue in effect, or enforce a law or regulation establishing a recreational vessel . . . safety standard . . . that is not identical to a regulation prescribed under section 4302 of this title." 46 U.S.C. § 4306.

[307] 46 U.S.C. § 4311(g).

[308] See, e.g., Ard v. Jensen, 996 S.W.2d 594 (Mo. Ct. App. 1999) (waterskier); Moore v. Brunswick Bowling & Billiards Corp., 889 S.W.2d 246 (Tex. 1994) (swimmer).

[309] See, e.g., Ryan v. Brunswick Corp., 557 N.W.2d 541 (Mich. 1997) (swimmer struck by propeller), abrogated by Sprietsma v. Mercury Marine, 537 U.S. 51 (2002); Moss v. Outboard Marine Corp., 915 F. Supp. 183, 187 (E.D. Cal. 1996) (passenger fell from boat and struck by propeller; emotional distress claim by other passenger).

[310] See, e.g., Sprietsma v. Mercury Marine, 757 N.E.2d 75, 78–79 (Ill. 2001) (fall from boat), rev'd, 537 U.S. 51 (2002); Lady v. Neal Glaser Marine, Inc., 228 F.3d 598 (5th Cir. 2000) (jet skier collided with boat), abrogated by Sprietsma v. Mercury Marine, 537 U.S. 51 (2002); Lewis v. Brunswick Corp., 107 F.3d 1494 (11th Cir. 1997) (plaintiff thrown from boat), abrogated by Sprietsma v. Mercury Marine, 537 U.S. 51 (2002).

[311] See, e.g., Cartenson v. Brunswick Corp., 49 F.3d 430, 432 (8th Cir. 1995) (express preemption), abrogated by Sprietsma v. Mercury Marine, 537 U.S. 51 (2002).

[312] See, e.g., Lady v. Neal Glaser Marine, Inc., 228 F.3d 598, 611 (5th Cir. 2000) (implied preemption), abrogated by Sprietsma v. Mercury Marine, 537 U.S. 51 (2002).

Courts have allowed as not preempted other claims against boat manufacturers for unsafe features the Coast Guard has not addressed. See, e.g., Folsom v. Kawasaki Motors Corp. U.S.A., 509 F. Supp. 2d 1364, 1374 (M.D. Ga. 2007) (operator of jet ski unable to turn craft once he turned off throttle; failure to equip with off-throttle steering); LaPlante v. Wellcraft Marine Corp., 114 Cal. Rptr. 2d 196 (Ct. App. 2001) (child thrown from boat; failure to equip boat with handrails).

[313] 537 U.S. 51 (2002).

grounds.[314] Reversing, the Supreme Court unanimously held that the Boat Safety Act neither expressly nor implicitly preempted the plaintiff's common-law products liability claims. The Court reasoned that, first, the Act's *express* preemption clause, which referred to "a" state "law or regulation," appeared to preempt only a state's positive regulatory law, not common-law compensation claims, particularly in view of the savings clause provision that compliance with the Act "does not relieve a person from liability at common law or under State law." Nor was the plaintiff's claim *impliedly* preempted by *conflict* or *field* preemption principles. The plaintiff's products liability claim did not conflict with the Coast Guard's decision not to require propeller guards, consistent with its policy of leaving state law regulations in place until the Coast Guard adopted a conflicting regulation under the Act—which it had not done. Finally, Congress's effort to promote uniformity in boat safety regulation had to yield to the Act's primary goal of boat safety, a goal served by both the Coast Guard's policy of allowing broad state regulation of boat safety and by products liability claims like those in this case.

***Herbicides, Pesticides, and Insecticides*—Bates**

As discussed above, the products liability preemption journey largely began in 1984 with *Ferebee v. Chevron Chemical Co.*,[315] which ruled that the Federal Insecticide, Fungicide, and Rodenticide Act (FIFRA) neither expressly nor impliedly precluded defective warning claims. After the Supreme Court rendered *Cipollone v. Liggett Group, Inc.*[316] in 1992, the FIFRA cases began to turn the other way, with most courts eventually ruling that the Act does indeed broadly preempt warning and misrepresentation claims. Further, some courts admonished that they would not allow claims implicating a label's warnings but masqueraded as claims of negligent testing, defective manufacture, defective design, or other claims that indirectly challenge EPA-approved labeling information.[317]

One such case was *Dow Agrosciences LLC v. Bates*[318] in which a group of Texas farmers asserted damage claims against Dow, the manufacturer of "Strongarm," a weed killer conditionally registered by the EPA under FIFRA, for damage Strongarm had caused to their peanut crops. Both the label and Strongarm salesmen initially recommended the weed killer for peanut crops whereas, in certain soil conditions, it not only failed to control weeds but also severely damaged the peanuts. The district court granted Dow's motion for summary judgment on preemption grounds to the farmers' claims for breach of express warranty, fraud, negligence, strict liability for defective manufacture and design, and breach of the state deceptive trade practices act, ruling that most of the claims were preempted by FIFRA's preemption clause that prohibits states from imposing "any requirements for labeling or packaging in addition to or different from those required" by the Act.[319]

---

314 757 N.E.2d 75, 82–88 (Ill. 2001), rev'd, 537 U.S. 51 (2002).

315 736 F.2d 1529 (D.C. Cir. 1984). See text at notes 168–183 on earlier FIFRA preemption litigation.

316 505 U.S. 504 (1992), discussed above.

317 See, e.g., Akee v. Dow Chem. Co., 272 F. Supp. 2d 1112 (D. Haw. 2003) (FIFRA preempts any claims that challenge adequacy of pesticide product's labels, directly or indirectly); Netland v. Hess & Clark, Inc., 284 F.3d 895 (8th Cir. 2002) (FIFRA preempts manufacturing defect and design defect claims that were factually premised on inadequate labeling), abrogated by Bates v. Dow Agrosciences LLC, 544 U.S. 431 (2005); Johnson v. Monsanto Chem. Co., 129 F. Supp. 2d 189, 195 (N.D.N.Y. 2001) ("Claims of misdesign or mismanufacture which the Court regards as thinly veiled labeling or failure to warn claims will not stand.").

318 205 F. Supp. 2d 623 (N.D. Tex. 2002).

319 7 U.S.C. § 136v(b).

Following a "groundswell" of other decisions favoring preemption of such claims,[320] the Court of Appeals affirmed,[321] reasoning that FIFRA preempts all such claims,[322] whether forthright warning claims or such claims "disguised" as defective design or negligent testing claims,[323] since allowing the plaintiffs to recover on such claims would provide Dow with a "strong incentive" (and so "induce" it) to change the label warning approved by the EPA.[324]

In *Bates v. Dow Agrosciences LLC*,[325] the Supreme Court reversed. Pointing to the statutory prohibition of misbranding, together with the long histories of tort litigation against pesticide manufacturers and state regulation of poisonous substances, the Court noted that the EPA had stopped evaluating pesticide efficacy for routine label approvals in 1979, leaving enforcement of pesticide efficacy to private damage suits.[326] The Court further observed that FIFRA does not prohibit states from imposing sanctions on manufacturers for violating state rules that duplicate federal requirements, such as for violating EPA labeling requirements.[327] While common-law duties may sometimes amount to preempted "requirements,"[328] the Court of Appeals was wrong to conclude that a verdict should be viewed as a "requirement" because it might "induce" a manufacturer to change its label.[329] Hence, the plaintiffs' claims for defective design, defective manufacture, and negligent testing were not preempted because they did not "require" labeling contrary to that approved by the EPA.[330] Although the express warranty claim arose from statements on the label, such a claim "asks only that a manufacturer make good on the contractual commitment that it voluntarily undertook by placing that warranty on its product."[331] Because the farmers' fraud and failure to warn claims "are premised on common-law rules that qualify as 'requirements for labeling or packaging,' " they might be preempted, but not if those claims were based on "particular common-law duties . . . equivalent to FIFRA's misbranding standards."[332]

More important to preemption jurisprudence than the technical reasoning of *Bates* was the tone of its discussion on the preemption of state tort law. Invoking once again

---

[320] This was Justice Stevens' characterization, in Bates v. Dow Agrosciences LLC, 544 U.S. 431, 441 (2005).

[321] 332 F.3d 323 (5th Cir. 2003).

[322] "For a state to create a labeling requirement by authorizing a claim linked to the specifications of a label, even where the EPA has elected not to impose such labeling requirements, would clearly be to impose a requirement 'in addition to or different from those' required under FIFRA." Id. at 331.

[323] Id. at 332–33.

[324] Id. at 331–32.

[325] 544 U.S. 431 (2005).

[326] Id. at 437–40.

[327] Id. at 442.

[328] Id. at 443.

[329] Id. "An occurrence that merely motivates an optional decision does not qualify as a requirement." Id. "A requirement is a rule of law that must be obeyed; an event, such as a jury verdict, that merely motives an optional decision is not a requirement." Id. at 445.

[330] "Rules that require manufacturers to design reasonably safe products, to use due care in conducting appropriate testing of their products, to market products free of manufacturing defects, and to honor their express warranties or other contractual commitments plainly do not qualify as requirements for 'labeling or packaging.' " Id. at 444.

[331] Id. Because a rule requiring manufacturers to stand behind their warranties does not require manufacturers to make warranties, it "does not impose a requirement 'for labeling or packaging.' " Id. at 445.

[332] 544 U.S. at 446–47.

the presumption against preemption[333]—an assumption that Congress does not intend legislation to preempt traditional areas of state law such as safety unless that intention is "clear and manifest"[334]—Justice Stevens for the majority reasoned that the recency of the federal agency's change in position on the preemptive reach of FIFRA over state tort law rendered the agency's interpretation "particularly dubious."[335] "The long history of tort litigation against manufacturers of poisonous substances"[336] suggests that Congress, had it intended "to deprive injured parties of a long available form of compensation,"[337] would have clearly expressed such intent. Because FIFRA contemplates that pesticide and insecticide labels will evolve over time, "tort suits can serve as a catalyst in this process . . . ."[338] Thus, "[p]rivate remedies that enforce federal misbranding requirements would seem to aid, rather than hinder, the functioning of FIFRA."[339]

Finally, *Bates* makes quite clear that FIFRA's express preemption of conflicting state "requirements" does not protect a defendant from liability for a particular label's false statements or inadequate warnings solely because a federal agency has approved the label's language. Because the statute itself prohibits sale of "misbranded" pesticides, a manufacturer has a "continuing obligation to adhere to" the statute's labeling requirements—a continuing duty to ensure that the label does not misbrand the pesticide.[340] Even if the agency has approved particular label language, the statute's misbranding prohibition thus bars a manufacturer from selling a pesticide under a label the manufacturer discovers to be false or inadequate, which would render a products liability verdict for such a sale entirely consistent with the statute.

Bates strongly suggests, therefore, that a regulatory agency's approval of specific label language is not in itself a "requirement." Even Justice Thomas (joined by Justice Scalia), dissenting in part, appeared to recognize this limited interpretation of "requirements" in the FIFRA preemption clause.[341] What this means is that even fraud and inadequate warning claims may survive preemption attack under FIFRA, and that jury verdicts on such claims are not preempted so long as they are "fully consistent with federal requirements," that is, with the safety and efficacy goals and provisions of the statute and its regulations.[342] *Bates* thus appears to lead the FIFRA preemption journey

---

333 "The long history of tort litigation against manufacturers of poisonous substances adds force to the basic presumption against pre-emption." Id. at 449.

334 Id.

335 Id. (noting that, just five years previously, in the prior administration, the United States had advocated the very interpretation the Court now applied in *Bates*). "Indeed, for much of this period [from the inception of FIFRA in 1947 to present,] EPA appears to have welcomed these tort suits." Id. at 452.

336 Id. at 449. "[T]ort suits alleging failure-to-warn claims were common well before" FIFRA was enacted in 1947. Id. at 451.

337 Id. at 449.

338 544 U.S. at 451.

339 Id.

340 Id. at 438–39.

341 See id. at 455–56.

342 See id. at 452–54. By contrast, in Cipollone v. Liggett Grp., Inc., 505 U.S. 504, 520 (1992), the term "requirements" in the 1969 Act barred some products liability claims because the statute there was based on a Congressional agreement with the tobacco industry that stiffer label warning requirements would be imposed in exchange for explicit limitations on private litigation.

a long way back toward where it stood in the pre-*Cipollone* days of *Ferebee*,[343] when defective warning claims and verdicts were largely immune from preemption attack.

Other Types of Products

The preemption issue has arisen in the lower courts in connection with a large number of other federal statutes that regulate the safety of many different types of products, and the diversity of approaches in the decisions reflects the failure of Congress to speak clearly to this issue together with the tangled evolution of the federal preemption doctrine in the Supreme Court.[344] The two major categories of products subject to safety regulation by federal agencies are consumer products and workplace products.

Consumer products. Consumer products are regulated by the Consumer Product Safety Commission (CPSC) under the Consumer Product Safety Act (CPSA),[345] the Federal Hazardous Substances Act (FHSA),[346] and two other statutes.[347] The CPSA

---

[343] Ferebee v. Chevron Chem. Co., 736 F.2d 1529 (D.C. Cir. 1984), discussed note 168, above. See, e.g., In re Roundup Prods. Liab. Litig., 364 F. Supp. 3d 1085, 1088 (N.D. Cal. 2019) (FIFRA does not expressly preempt plaintiffs' failure to warn claims or bar those claims under the "doctrine of impossibility preemption"); Sheppard v. Monsanto Co., 2016 WL 3629074, at *7–9 (D. Haw. 2016) (failure to warn and warranty claims not preempted under FIFRA); Peterson v. BASF Corp., 711 N.W.2d 470 (Minn. 2006) (finding no preemption, and affirming $52 million jury award to farmers, after United States Supreme Court required reconsideration in light of *Bates*). See note 180, above, for more recent cases.

[344] See, e.g., Webb v. Trader Joe's Co., 999 F.3d 1196, 1202 (9th Cir. 2021) (*poultry products*: Poultry Products Inspection Act preempted claims that poultry products sold in grocery store contained too much water); Suarez v. W.M. Barr & Company, Inc., 842 F.3d 513, 519–20 (7th Cir. 2016) (*paint remover*: Federal Hazardous Substances Act—warning claim preempted); Nemphos v. Nestle USA, Inc., 2013 WL 4501308 (D. Md. 2013) (*fluoridated bottled water and baby food*: Food, Drug, and Cosmetic Act—preemption); Harrison v. Skyline Corp., 686 S.E.2d 735, 745 (W. Va. 2009) (*formaldehyde-treated floor decking*: Manufactured Home Construction and Safety Standards Act—no preemption); In re Wireless Tel. Radio Frequency Emissions Prods. Liab. Litig., 248 F. Supp. 2d 452 (D. Md. 2003) (*cellular phones*: multi-district consolidated class action; claim that phones emitted unsafe levels of radiation impliedly preempted because suit would necessarily require judge and jury to usurp the regulatory functions that Congress entrusted to FCC under Federal Communications Act), rev'd and remanded, Pinney v. Nokia, Inc., 402 F.3d 430 (4th Cir. 2005) (2–1 decision) (Congress intended to allow such claims); Darby v. A-Best Prods. Co., 811 N.E.2d 1117 (Ohio 2004) (5–2 decision) (*asbestos in locomotive equipment*: Federal Locomotive Boiler Inspection Act (BIA) preempts tort law claims against manufacturers of locomotives for injuries from asbestos contained in locomotives); General Motors v. Kilgore, 853 So.2d 171 (Ala. 2002) (same: BIA gives rise to field preemption); Choate v. Champion Home Builders Co., 222 F.3d 788 (10th Cir. 2000) (*mobile homes*: National Manufactured Housing Construction and Safety Standards Act does not preempt design defect and warning defect claims based on lack of battery-powered backup in smoke detectors); Symens v. SmithKline Beecham Corp., 152 F.3d 1050 (8th Cir. 1998) (*animal vaccines*: USDA, cattle infections—preemption); Hall v. Fairmont Homes, Inc., 664 N.E.2d 546 (Ohio Ct. App. 1995) (*mobile homes*: NMHCSSA, level of formaldehyde emissions violated HUD regulations—no preemption); Olson v. Prosoco, Inc., 522 N.W.2d 284 (Iowa 1994) (*hydrochloric acid in mortar cleaner*: Hazardous Materials Transportation Act—no preemption); Wong v. Precision Airmotive, LLC, 2008 WL 160212 (D. Conn. 2008) (*general aviation aircraft*: FAA, defective carburetor—no preemption).

[345] 15 U.S.C. §§ 2051 et seq.

[346] Id. at §§ 1261 et seq.

[347] The Federal Flammable Fabrics Act (FFA), id. §§ 1191 et seq., and the Poison Prevention Packaging Act (PPPA), id. §§ 1471 et seq. Despite a preemption clause, the courts have ruled that the FFA does not preempt products liability claims for flammable clothing. See, e.g., O'Donnell v. Big Yank, Inc., 696 A.2d 846, 853 (Pa. Super. Ct. 1997); Wilson v. Bradlees of New England, Inc., 96 F.3d 552, 553 (1st Cir. 1996); Raymond v. Riegel Textile Corp., 484 F.2d 1025, 1028 (1st Cir. 1973).

contains both a preemption clause[348] and a savings clause.[349] The preemption defense has arisen only infrequently in consumer products liability litigation. A couple of decisions involving warning and design defect claims against power mower manufacturers have held that the plaintiffs' warning claims were preempted, because the CPSC had promulgated a specific regulation governing such warnings, but that the design claims were not,[350] and one court has ruled that the CPSA preempts all such claims.[351] In several cases involving injuries from fires caused by children playing with lighters, a couple of courts have found no preemption,[352] while a couple of others have ruled that the CPSA preempts a design defect claim but not warning or manufacturing defect claims.[353] And in a case involving injuries from the shattering of a glass shower door, the Ninth Circuit ruled that the CPSA did not preempt either the design or warning claims.[354]

Pursuant to the Federal Hazardous Substances Act (FHSA), the CPSC establishes mandatory labeling requirements for certain hazardous substances intended for household use.[355] Because the structure and purpose of the FHSA are similar to the CPSA, the CPSC applies a single preemption regulation to both acts, interpreting the preemption of state "requirements" to mean statutory and regulatory requirements, not common-law holdings by the courts.[356] Although early decisions found no preemption,[357] courts in recent years have quite uniformly found that the FHSA preempts warning claims when a manufacturer's warning complies with federal requirements,[358] but that

---

[348] The preemption clause provides that, if the CPSC has established federal safety standards for a product, the states may not adopt a safety standard or regulation "which prescribes any requirements as to the performance, composition, contents, design, finish, construction, packaging, or labeling of such product which are designed to deal with the same risk of injury associated with such consumer product, unless such requirements are identical to the requirements of the Federal standard." 15 U.S.C. § 2075(a).

[349] The savings clause provides: "Compliance with consumer product safety rules or other rules or orders under this chapter shall not relieve any person from liability at common law or under State statutory law to any other person." 15 U.S.C. § 2074(a).

[350] See Cortez v. MTD Prods., Inc., 927 F. Supp. 386 (N.D. Cal. 1996); Moe v. MTD Prod., Inc., 73 F.3d 179 (8th Cir. 1995).

[351] Frazier v. Heckingers, 96 F. Supp. 2d 486 (E.D. Pa. 2000).

[352] See, e.g., Hittle v. Scripto-Tokai Corp., 166 F. Supp. 2d 142 (M.D. Pa. 2001); Colon v. BIC USA, Inc., 136 F. Supp. 2d 196 (S.D.N.Y. 2000).

[353] See BIC Pen Corp. v. Carter, 251 S.W.3d 500, 509 (Tex. 2008) (design defect claim impliedly preempted: "we agree that, under *Riegel*, a common-law tort claim could impose duties that conflict with the federal regulatory scheme"; manufacturing claim not preempted); Ball v. BIC Corp., 2000 WL 33312192 (E.D. Mo. 2000). See also Frith v. BIC Corp., 863 So.2d 960 (Miss. 2004) (design claims preempted; warning claim not preempted).

[354] Leipart v. Guardian Indus., 234 F.3d 1063 (9th Cir. 2000).

[355] 15 U.S.C. § 1261.

[356] See Leflar and Adler, The Preemption Pentad: Federal Preemption of Products Liability Claims After Medtronic, 64 Tenn. L. Rev. 691, 745 (1997) (citing 56 Fed. Reg. 3414, 3415 (Jan. 30, 1991); preamble to 16 C.F.R. § 1061).

[357] See, e.g., Burch v. Amsterdam Corp., 366 A.2d 1079, 1084–86 (D.C. 1976) (explosive floor tile adhesive); Jonescue v. Jewel Home Shopping Serv., 306 N.E.2d 312, 316 (Ill. App. Ct. 1973) (toxic cleaning agent).

[358] See, e.g., Suarez v. W.M. Barr & Co., Inc., 842 F.3d 513, 519–20 (7th Cir. 2016) (paint remover; warning claim preempted); West v. Mattel, Inc., 246 F. Supp. 2d 640 (S.D. Tex. 2003) (child's toy; Child Safety Protection Act amendment to FHSA preempts claim for inadequate warning of choking hazard, but not design defect claims); Schrader v. Sunnyside Corp., 747 N.Y.S.2d 26 (App. Div. 2002) (warning on can of denatured alcohol); Milanese v. Rust-Oleum Corp., 244 F.3d 104, 109 (2d Cir. 2001).

the Act does not preempt design (or manufacturing defect) claims[359] or "misbranding" claims based on violation of FHSA regulations.[360]

Workplace products. The safety of workplace products is regulated by the Occupational Safety and Health Administration under the Occupational Safety and Health Act (OSHA).[361] OSHA does not contain an express preemption clause,[362] but it does contain a savings clause that seems to make clear that it does not displace state tort law claims for injuries.[363] When the savings clause is considered together with the fact that OSHA applies only to employers, not manufacturers, it is difficult to escape the conclusion that OSHA does not preempt injury claims against manufacturers of products in the workplace.[364] While a couple of cases have found conflict preemption in narrow circumstances,[365] it appears quite clear that OSHA usually has no preemptive effect on third-party products liability claims by injured workers against manufacturers of industrial products.[366]

Ruminations on Federal Preemption

The ever-shifting law of federal preemption is rife with perplexities. In attempting to unravel these perplexities, the first thing a judge or lawyer should do in any particular case is to determine if the courts have spoken definitively on the issue. If the courts have not done so, one must try to discern whether the particular products liability claims involved would contravene a particular statute's express preemption clause or goals, or

---

[359] See Smith and Grage, Federal Preemption of State Products Liability Actions, 27 Wm. Mitchell L. Rev. 391, 408–09 (2000). The Act probably does not preempt design and manufacturing defect claims that are bona fide, that is, claims that are not merely warning claims dressed in sheep's clothing in an attempt to circumvent the Act's preemption of warning claims. See generally Beadling v. William Bowman Assocs., 809 A.2d 188 (N.J. Super. Ct. App. Div. 2002) (FHSA did not preempt design defect claim alleging that government-mandated warning for methanol should have been placed on side of drum rather than top); Arnold v. Dow Chem. Co., 110 Cal. Rptr. 2d 722 (Ct. App. 2001) (full discussion of issue in FIFRA context), noted in 31 Sw. U. L. Rev. 441 (2002), and discussion of issue in FIFRA context, above.

[360] See, e.g., Pollard v. Sherwin-Williams Co., 955 So.2d 764, 774–75 (Miss. 2007) (claims based on non-compliance with FHSA not preempted); Richards v. Home Depot, Inc., 456 F.3d 76 (2d Cir. 2006) (same); Milanese v. Rust-Oleum Corp., 244 F.3d 104, 109 (2d Cir. 2001) ("a state cause of action alleging non-compliance with the FHSA would *not* be preempted by the Act"); Kirstein v. W.M. Barr & Co., 983 F. Supp. 753, 761 (N.D. Ill. 1997), aff'd, 159 F.3d 1065 (7th Cir. 1998); Canty v. Ever-Last Supply Co., 685 A.2d 1365, 1374 (N.J. Super. Ct. App. Div. 1996).

[361] 29 U.S.C. § 651(b).

[362] But the Occupational Safety and Health Administration has adopted certain preemption regulations. See 29 C.F.R. § 1910.1200(a), (f)(1).

[363] 29 U.S.C. § 653(b)(4). "There is a solid consensus that section 4(b)(4) operates to save state tort rules from preemption." Pedraza v. Shell Oil Co., 942 F.2d 48, 53 (1st Cir. 1991) (quoting Notes, 88 Colum. L. Rev. 630, 641 (1988), 101 Harv. L. Rev. 535, 543 (1987) (extent of OSHA preemption)).

[364] See, e.g., Lindsey v. Caterpillar, Inc., 480 F.3d 202 (3d Cir. 2007); In re Welding Fume Prods. Liab. Litig., 364 F. Supp. 2d 669 (N.D. Ohio 2005) (thorough analysis); Guzman y Ortos v. Estado Libre Asociado De Puerto Rico, 2002 WL 1009685, at *12 (P.R. 2002); Wickham v. American Tokyo Kasei, Inc., 927 F. Supp. 293 (N.D. Ill. 1996); York v. Union Carbide Corp., 586 N.E.2d 861, 866 (Ind. Ct. App. 1992); Pedraza v. Shell Oil Co., 942 F.2d 48, 54 n.6 (1st Cir. 1991).

[365] See Gonzalez v. Ideal Tile Importing Co., 877 A.2d 1247, 1251–53 (N.J. 2005) (6–1 opinion) (forklift; additional warning devices would conflict with OSHA decision that additional devices might create more dangers than they prevent). See also In re Welding Fume Prods. Liab. Litig., 364 F. Supp. 2d 669, 689 (N.D. Ohio 2005) ("if Congress meant to imply pre-emption of any tort claims, it meant to do so only in the narrowest of circumstances—that is, only when there is a conflict between state tort law and federal regulation that is especially 'direct, clear and substantial' ").

[366] "The structure of the OSH Act, with its savings clause and provision for state regulation, strongly suggests that it is not intended to preempt state tort claims . . . unless there was a direct and unavoidable conflict." Ausness, The *Welding Fume* Case and the Preemptive Effect of OSHA's HazCom Standard on Common Law Failure-to-Warn Claims, 54 Buff. L. Rev. 103, 155 (2006).

the regulations a federal agency has promulgated under the statute to achieve those goals. Because regulatory objectives (and the phrasing of preemption and savings clauses) differ among the various federal product safety statutes, preemption issues normally are resolved by the growing jurisprudence specific to the particular federal statute relevant to the plaintiff's particular products liability claims.

Because Congress has authorized federal regulation of product safety to quite a large extent, widening the reach of the preemption doctrine erases more and more areas of products liability law. Such a shift toward safety regulation in substitution for compensating injuries caused by defective products, similar to the European approach,[367] makes sense in terms of broad-scale social engineering, assuming that *ex ante* regulation and *ex poste* litigation are coordinated. But the achievement of some ideal level of federal regulation of product safety that appears desirable in the abstract should not be allowed to trample the state law compensatory rights of persons injured by defective products to judicial remedies[368]—remedies protected by both federal and state constitutions. In enacting most of the product safety statutes during the consumer protection period of the late 1960s and early 1970s, Congress probably intended only to preempt state regulatory law, not broadly to immunize manufacturers from their duties to consumers under state products liability law.[369] And there is in fact no reason, as a general matter, why product safety regulation and products liability litigation cannot comfortably co-exist.[370]

Congress, if it had the will, could largely clean up the current "preemption mess." That is, if Congress truly desired to leave damages actions intact for persons injured by product hazards subject to federal regulation, it could explicitly limit the preemptive reach of its product safety statutes to state legislation and regulatory agency provisions while simultaneously providing, in a savings clause, that damages actions do not conflict with (indeed, may be complementary to) congressional purpose. Or it could choose to do the opposite, and declare with clarity that private lawsuits of one type or another are incompatible with the federal regulatory scheme contemplated by the statute. While Congress fairly may be urged to speak clearly in this way, on whether particular federal statutes are intended to preempt particular state law damage claims,[371] it seems quite unrealistic to expect Congress now to amend the product safety statutes of the 1960s and 1970s to cure the problem. As a practical matter, there simply is no simple route out of the preemption thicket in which we now are largely lost. In any single case, courts and lawyers simply must do their best to ascertain whether the language of particular federal legislation or regulations bearing on a particular product safety issue in fact appears to bar particular products liability claims, and, if not, whether such claims do or do not reasonably appear to interfere substantially with the particular statute's goals. In this,

---

[367] See § 1.4, above.

[368] See Rabin, Reassessing Regulatory Compliance, 88 Geo. L.J. 2049 (2000).

[369] See Leflar and Adler, The Preemption Pentad: Federal Preemption of Products Liability Claims After Medtronic, 64 Tenn. L. Rev. 691, 746–48 (1997).

[370] See Bates v. Dow Agrosciences LLC, 544 U.S. 431, 451 (2005) (Stevens, J.) ("Private remedies that enforce federal misbranding requirements would seem to aid, rather than hinder, the functioning of FIFRA.").

[371] See, e.g., Davis, Unmasking the Presumption in Favor of Preemption, 53 S.C. L. Rev. 967, 972 (2002); Raeker-Jordan, The Pre-Emption Presumption That Never Was: Pre-Emption Doctrine Swallows the Rule, 40 Ariz. L. Rev. 1379, 1381 (1998); Grey, Make Congress Speak Clearly: Federal Preemption of State Tort Remedies, 77 B.U. L. Rev. 559, 615–18 (1997).

it is worth remembering that the key to federal preemption begins and ends with statutory interpretation—deciphering congressional intent.

§ 14.6 STATUTES OF LIMITATIONS AND REPOSE

Statutes of limitations and statutes of repose impose maximum time limits on products liability claims. Both forms of time-limitation statute cut off a plaintiff's ability to maintain a products liability claim after a particular period of time, although the period within which a plaintiff must file a claim may be extended in certain limited circumstances. If a plaintiff files a products liability claim after the statutory period has run, the time-limitation statute simply bars the claim. A statute of *limitations* is an affirmative defense that a defendant must raise in a timely manner, which ordinarily means that it must be pleaded in the answer.[372] By contrast, because a statute of *repose* cuts off the plaintiff's rights rather than just the remedy, the defendant does not waive the running of a statute of repose by failing to raise it in a timely manner.[373] Statutes of limitations and repose provide a potent defense to products liability actions that a plaintiff's lawyer must seek to avoid and a defendant's lawyer must be sure not to overlook.[374]

As creatures of state legislation (with one exception),[375] time-limitation statutes vary widely in their provisions—the time periods, what starts the clock running, what stops it running, what types of claims they affect, and many others. Moreover, courts vary in how they interpret and apply similar provisions of similar statutes. Accordingly, each state has developed its own complex set of rules, both statutory and judicial,

---

[372] See Fed. R. Civ. P. 8(c); 2 C. Corman, Limitations of Actions § 15.2.1, at 349 (1991) (noting "the uniform requirement that when the statute of limitations is used as a defense it must be set forth affirmatively in a party's responsive pleading"). But a court in its discretion may allow a defendant to amend its answer to include the defense if doing so is not unfair or prejudicial to the plaintiff. See id. § 15.3, at 355–58. See generally id. at 345.

[373] 2 C. Corman, above, § 15.2.3, at 355. If the running of a statute of repose is apparent on the face of the complaint, the defendant may raise the defense by a motion to dismiss. See, e.g., Albrecht v. General Motors Corp., 648 N.W.2d 87, 89 (Iowa 2002).

[374] On statutes of limitations and repose in products liability litigation, see Shepherd, Products Liability and Economic Activity: An Empirical Analysis of Tort Reform's Impact on Businesses, Employment, and Production, 66 Vand. L. Rev. 257, 316 (2013) (reporting author's empirical study revealing that statutes of repose, together with comparative fault and retailer protection statutes, have a statistically significant impact on economic activity—increasing the number of businesses, employment, and production in affected industries); Bruggenschmidt, Asbestos for the Rest of Us: The Continued Viability of Statutes of Repose in Product Liability, 76 Def. Couns. J. 54 (2009); La Fave, Remedying the Confusion between Statutes of Limitations and Statutes of Repose in Wisconsin—A Conceptual Guide, 88 Marq. L. Rev. 927 (2005); Green, The Paradox of Statutes of Limitations in Toxic Substances Litigation, 76 Cal. L. Rev. 965, 976–78 (1988) (limitation statutes should be abolished in toxic substance cases to promote more accurate fact finding, efficiency, and fairness); Epstein, The Temporal Dimension in Tort Law, 53 U. Chi. L. Rev. 1175 (1986); Schwartz, New Products, Old Products, Evolving Law, Retroactive Law, 59 N.Y.U. L. Rev. 796 (1983); Phillips, An Analysis of Proposed Reform of Products Liability Statutes of Limitations, 56 N.C. L. Rev. 643 (1978); Frumer, Friedman, and Sklaren, Products Liability ch. 26; Am. Law Prod. Liab. ch. 47. See generally Prosser and Keeton on Torts § 30; C. Corman, Limitations of Actions (1991) (2 vols.); 2 Prod. Liab. Rep. (CCH) ¶¶ 3100 and 3200; Annots., 4 A.L.R.3d 821, § 4 (1965) (products liability statutes of limitations), 30 A.L.R.5th 1 (1995) (products liability statutes of repose).

[375] The General Aviation Revitalization Act (GARA), 49 U.S.C. § 40101 note, examined below, is the one federal time-limitation statute applicable to products liability litigation. Congress enacted a discovery rule for personal injury and property damages actions brought under the Comprehensive Environmental Response, Compensation, and Liability Act (CERCLA). 42 U.S.C. § 9658. For a variety of reasons, courts have held that this statute does not apply in product liability actions. See, e.g., Rivas v. Safety-Kleen Corp., 119 Cal. Rptr. 2d 503 (Ct. App. 2002) (CERCLA federal discovery rule does not preempt state time limits in toxic tort claims asserted against third-party manufacturers because Congress did not have such actions in mind when drafting the relevant CERCLA provisions). The discovery rule is discussed in more detail below.

detailing the time periods within which various types of products liability claims must be filed to escape the time limitation defenses. More so than with many other issues in products liability litigation, therefore, the law on time-limitation issues in products liability cases tends to be unusually localized and twisted. Thus, outcomes in particular cases involving time-limitation statutes are controlled by the language of particular statutes as interpreted by particular judges in particular jurisdictions, according to particular common-law rules, and applied in varying fashions to the facts of particular cases. Because so many cases have been decided so many different ways on limitations issues in every jurisdiction,[376] little can be said about statutes of limitations and repose for which there is not contrary authority. For this reason, a lawyer must study the local statutory and case law especially closely in an attempt to fathom how a court might rule on a limitations issue in any particular case. Nevertheless, a general discussion of some of the recurring issues in this area of the law should be useful to a lawyer getting started on a limitations problem.

Reasons for Time Limitations

It may seem unjust for a legislature to terminate the legal responsibility of a party who has wrongfully caused harm to another person, no matter how much time has passed since the harmful event occurred. Yet the law has recognized across the ages—from early Hebrew law,[377] to late Roman law,[378] thence into early German law,[379] early English law,[380] and in the early law of this nation[381]—that there is good reason to call a halt to legal responsibility after some period of time for most wrongs. In the products liability context, a major reason for eventually calling an end to litigation about old products is the simple fact that the available proofs—of the manufacturer's alleged wrongdoing, the product's alleged defectiveness, the plaintiff's alleged harms, and the alleged causal connection between them all—diminish over time. The legal system thus operates less accurately and hence less fairly in attempting to ascertain responsibility

---

[376] "It would be a laborious and unprofitable task, to examine all the cases which have been decided, on the statute of limitations." Fries v. Boisselete, 9 Serg. & Rawle 128, 131 (Pa. 1822).

[377] See Deuteronomy 15:1 (7 years—money debts should be cancelled).

[378] See R. Sohm, The Institutes—A Textbook of the History and System of Roman Private Law § 54, at 282–85 (J. Ledlie trans., 3d ed. 1970) (temporal limitations on civil actions were "quite exceptional" prior to 424 A.D., but from that date forward most claims were barred after 30 years, some after 40 years, and some after shorter periods). See also L. Wenger, Institutes of the Roman Law of Civil Procedure § 16(7), at 170, and § 29(V), at 302–03 (O. Fisk trans., 1940).

[379] R. Sohm, above, at 378.

[380] See T. Plucknett, A Concise History of the Common Law 719 (5th ed. 1956) (after 1540, "no seisin could found a claim in a writ of right unless it was within sixty years of the date of the writ").

[381] See United States v. Kubrick, 444 U.S. 111, 117 (1979) (White, J.) (citing Bell v. Morrison, 26 U.S. (1 Pet.) 351, 360 (1828) and other cases):

> Statutes of limitations, which "are found and approved in all systems of enlightened jurisprudence," Wood v. Carpenter, 101 U.S. 135, 139 (1879), represent a pervasive legislative judgment that it is unjust to fail to put the adversary on notice to defend within a specified period of time and that "the right to be free of stale claims in time comes to prevail over the right to prosecute them." Railroad Telegraphers v. Railway Express Agency, 321 U.S. 342, 349 (1944). These enactments are statutes of repose; and although affording plaintiffs what the legislature deems a reasonable time to present their claims, they protect defendants and the courts from having to deal with cases in which the search for truth may be seriously impaired by the loss of evidence, whether by death or disappearance of witnesses, fading memories, disappearance of documents, or otherwise.

See generally 1 C. Corman, Limitations of Actions § 1.1 (1991).

for harm as the years roll by after damaging events:[382] witnesses (and the parties and their agents) forget important facts, move, grow old, and eventually die; defendant manufacturers change their personnel, merge, and otherwise become transformed in myriad ways; and physical objects pertinent to a particular case—the product, its environment of use, and documentary evidence of its creation, the accident, and the plaintiff's injuries—deteriorate, are discarded, or otherwise disappear. In addition to these practical reasons of diminishing proof for time-limitation statutes, they are substantively supported by the fact that the needs served by the justice system—deterrence, retributive justice, and even compensation—tend to lessen over time. Similarly, the economic logic of loss-shifting to manufacturers and their insurers diminishes with time, not only with respect to the goal of efficiently deterring wrongdoing but also because manufacturers and their insurers can organize their resources more efficiently if they have some reasonable basis for estimating their exposure to liability for past occurrences. Finally, the equities of providing judicial remedies to persons who have long neglected to use them—who have "sat upon their rights"—weaken as years progress. In short, after *some* period of time, in fairness to potential defendants and recognition of the limits of the judicial system, victims of possible wrongdoing who have long ignored their rights can fairly be required to accept their bygone losses as their own.[383]

Types of Time-Limitation Statutes

As further explained below, time-limitation statutes come in a variety of forms. The two basic types of time-limitation statutes are statutes of *limitations* and statutes of *repose*. While both forms of statute cut off a defendant's products liability exposure after a period of time, they operate quite differently. The time periods of statutes of limitations are shorter—from as short as 1 year to as long as 6 years, depending on the jurisdiction—than those of statutes of repose, which run from 5 or 6 years, in a few jurisdictions, to as long as 18 or 20 years, in others. But there are a number of other important differences between these two types of time-limitation statutes. For example, statutes of limitations begin to run at the time an injury occurs or is discovered (actually or constructively), whereas statutes of repose generally begin to run when a product is sold; statutes of limitations normally may be delayed ("tolled") by certain equitable circumstances, such as a plaintiff's infancy or failure to discover an injury, whereas statutes of repose ordinarily may not; and a number of other important differences distinguish the two basic forms of time-limitation statutes.[384]

---

[382] "The process of discovery and trial which results in the finding of ultimate facts for or against the plaintiff by the judge or jury is obviously more reliable if the witness or testimony in question is relatively fresh. Thus in the judgment of most legislatures and courts, there comes a point at which the delay of a plaintiff in asserting a claim is sufficiently likely either to impair the accuracy of the fact-finding process or to upset settled expectations that a substantive claim will be barred without respect to whether it is meritorious." Board of Regents v. Tomanio, 446 U.S. 478, 487 (1980).

[383] See, e.g., Freund v. Purdue Pharma Co., 2006 WL 482382, at *5 (E.D. Wis. 2006) (addiction to OxyContin; "she recognized the dangers, yet she sat on her rights for more than two years"). See generally Note, Developments in the Law—Statutes of Limitations, 63 Harv. L. Rev. 1177, 1185 (1950) (quoting Order of R.R. Telegraphers v. Railway Express Agency, Inc., 321 U.S. 342, 349 (1944)):

> The primary consideration underlying such legislation is undoubtedly one of fairness to the defendant. There comes a time when he ought to be secure in his reasonable expectation that the slate has been wiped clean of ancient obligations, and he ought not to be called on to resist a claim when "evidence has been lost, memories have faded, and witnesses have disappeared."

[384] For example, a statutes of limitations defense, being remedial, may be waived if not raised in a timely manner; but a statute of repose defense, based on the termination of a plaintiff's rights, may not.

Statutes of *limitations* come in various forms. All states have statutes of limitations applicable to personal injury torts and for wrongful death. In the absence of a more specific statute, such as a products liability statute of limitations,[385] these general statutes of limitations govern products liability claims for both negligence and strict liability in tort. In addition, most states adhere to the uniform statute of limitations for breach of warranty claims in UCC § 2–725, which is 4 years from the date of sale. An increasing number of states, now a slight majority, have special statutes of limitations specifically applicable to products liability claims.

Statutes of *repose* also come in a number of forms. The most basic form of repose statute pertains to products liability claims generally, though sometimes making exception for particular types of products, such as asbestos. A quite different form of repose statute, called a "useful-life" statute, bars a plaintiff's claim at the expiration of the product's useful life rather than after a set period of time. In addition, some states apply repose statutes governing improvements to realty to cases involving products attached to land, such as large grain silos or overhead cranes. Finally, a federal statute of repose places outer time limits on products liability claims against manufacturers of small airplanes.

Statutes of Limitations

In General

Tort law statutes. Every state has a statute of limitations governing claims for personal injuries or tortiously caused harm, with time periods ranging from 1 year (in California, Kentucky, Louisiana,[386] and Tennessee) to 6 years (in Maine and North Dakota). The most common periods are 2 and 3 years.[387] Separate statutes of limitations governing wrongful death and survival claims normally are of the same duration as the injury statutes, but they are sometimes shorter[388] and occasionally longer.[389] Although a state may have a special statute of limitations for fraud or tortious misrepresentation, the statute of limitations governing personal injuries, wrongful death, or tortious misconduct may apply when the misconduct results in personal injury or death because the defendant's misrepresentation "wrongfully" or "tortiously" produces the result.[390] And if the gist or gravamen of a products liability claim is really negligence or strict

[385] Specific statutes of limitations, such as those governing products liability actions, normally take precedence over general statutes of limitations for personal injuries or wrongful death. See, e.g., Kambury v. DaimlerChrysler Corp., 50 P.3d 1163, 1166 (Or. 2002); Harper v. Holiday Inns, Inc., 498 F. Supp. 910 (D. Tenn. 1978), aff'd, 633 F.2d 215 (6th Cir. 1980).

[386] See, e.g., In re: Taxotere (Docetaxel) Prods. Liab. Litig. v. Sanofi U.S. Servs., 860 Fed. Appx. 886, 894 (5th Cir. 2021) (La. law) (Louisiana's 1-year prescriptive limit on delictual actions barred claims against makers of chemotherapy drug that caused hair loss).

[387] See Prod. Liab. Rep. (CCH) ¶ 3210 (time periods of each state's statute for personal injuries); Annot., 91 A.L.R.3d 455 (1979) (strict tort claims).

[388] See D.C. (injuries—3 years; death—1 year); Fla. (injuries—4 years; death—2 years); Me. (injuries—6 years; death—2 years); Mo. (injuries—5 years; death—3 years); Neb. (injuries—4 years; death—2 years); N.C. (injuries—3 years; death—2 years); Utah (injuries—4 years; death—2 years); Wyo. (same); Prod. Liab. Rep. (CCH) ¶¶ 3210, 3240 (collecting statutes by state).

[389] See Minn. (injuries—2 years; death—3 years); N.H. (injuries—3 years; death—6 years); Or. (injuries—2 years; death—3 years).

[390] See, e.g., Clark v. Baxter Healthcare Corp., 100 Cal. Rptr. 2d 223, 226 n.2 (Ct. App. 2000) (allergic reaction to latex gloves; applying 1-year personal injury statute rather than 3-year fraud statute).

liability in tort for selling a defective product, a court may not allow a plaintiff to circumvent a shorter personal injury statute by alleging fraud.[391]

Traditionally, tort law claims begin to run when the claim "accrues," which is when the tort is complete because all of its elements have occurred. The last element in a tort is the plaintiff's damage—harm that is proximately caused by the defendant's breach of duty. For this reason, the traditional rule was that a tort law statute of limitations begins to run at the time the plaintiff is injured.[392] A number of limitations statutes, even special products liability statutes, still are phrased in terms of when the tort or products liability cause of action arises or accrues,[393] and some actually specify that the statutory period begins when the damage occurs.[394] However, a majority of states now have jettisoned the traditional accrual rule based on the time of injury, in favor of the discovery rule discussed below.

Warranty law statutes. State commercial law statutes contain statutes of limitations for warranty claims, based on Uniform Commercial Code § 2–725(1), Statute of Limitations in Contracts for Sale.[395] In the absence of other agreement, this section specifies a 4-year limitation period[396] for Article 2 breach of warranty claims.[397] This provision is quite specific, and it would seem that courts would be bound to apply this statutory period—which often is longer than the jurisdiction's limitation period for torts—to products liability claims brought in warranty. Duly considering themselves so bound, many courts apply the Article 2 limitations provision to products liability claims brought in warranty.[398] Yet, a number of courts, sometimes drawing on the warranty law derivations of the doctrine of strict products liability in tort, reason that modern products liability actions for personal injuries (and death) sound more properly in tort than in warranty.[399] So flouting the legislature's prerogative to define warranty statutes

---

391 See, e.g., Larkins v. Glaxo Wellcome, Inc., 1999 WL 360204, at *9 (E.D.N.Y. 1999) (side effects from drug; fraud claim incidental to negligence and strict liability claims).

392 See Prosser and Keeton on Torts § 30; Annot., 4 A.L.R.3d 821, § 4 (1965).

393 See, e.g., Colo. Rev. Stat. Ann. § 13–80–107 (products liability claims, except in warranty, 2 years after claim arises); Idaho Code Ann. § 6–1403(3) (products liability claims, 2 years after claim accrues); Ind. Code Ann. § 34–20–3–1 (products liability claims, 2 years after claim accrues); Mich. Comp. Laws Ann. § 600.5805 (products liability claims, 3 years after claim accrues).

394 See, e.g., Ala. Code § 6–5–502 (products liability actions must be brought within 1 year of time of injury, death, or property damage); Ark. Code Ann. § 16–116–203 (same—3 years); Neb. Rev. Stat. § 25–224 (products liability claims—4 years after death, injury, or other damage); Or. Rev. Stat. Ann. § 30.905 (products liability claims—2 years after injury, death, or property damage); Tenn. Code Ann. § 29–28–103 (products liability claims—6 years after injury, death, or property damage).

395 See 1 Crockett, Product Warranties ch. 11; White and Summers, UCC § 12–9; Annot., 49 A.L.R.5th 1 (1997).

396 Except in Oklahoma (5 years), Mississippi (6 years), South Carolina (6 years), Wisconsin (6 years), and Rhode Island (10 years). See Prod. Liab. Rep. (CCH) ¶ 3220 (contract limitations for each state).

397 UCC § 2–725(1) provides: "An action for breach of any contract for sale must be commenced within four years after the cause of action has accrued. By the original agreement the parties may reduce the period of limitation to not less than one year but may not extend it."

398 See, e.g., Badilla v. Wal-Mart Stores E. Inc., 357 P.3d 936, 949 (N.M. 2015) (holding 4-year statute of limitations for breach of warranty claims rather than 3-year tort statute of limitations applied to plaintiff's claims); Barban v. Rheem Textile Sys., Inc., 2005 WL 387660, at *10 (E.D.N.Y. 2005); In re Latex Gloves Prods. Liab. Litig., 152 F. Supp. 2d 667, 675 (E.D. Pa. 2001); Strange v. Keiper Recaro Seating, Inc., 117 F. Supp. 2d 408, 410 (D. Del. 2000). See generally Frumer, Friedman, and Sklaren, Products Liability § 26.03[4][a][iv] (noting that a majority of courts apply § 2–725 to all breach of warranty actions).

399 See, e.g., Jenkins v. Novartis Pharm. Corp., 2013 WL 1760762, at *5 (E.D. Tenn. 2013) (though plaintiff styled one count of her proposed amended complaint "Breach of Implied Warranty of Merchantability," she did not even cite a section of the state's UCC, such that the tort 1-year statute of limitations would apply, rather than the 4-year provision of UCC § 2–725, because the "gravamen" of the drug products liability claim

of limitations however it may choose,[400] these courts thus have held that the *tort* law statutes of limitations apply to *warranty* as well as tort claims in ordinary products liability actions.[401]

Section 2–725(2) of the Code provides that the statute of limitations on breach of warranty claims under Article 2 "accrues" when the *breach* occurs, which generally is when the product is "tendered for delivery" unless the seller has explicitly extended the warranty to future performance:

> A cause of action accrues when the breach occurs, regardless of the aggrieved party's lack of knowledge of the breach. A breach of warranty occurs when tender of delivery is made, except that where a warranty explicitly extends to future performance of the goods and discovery of the breach must await the time of such performance the cause of action accrues when the breach is or should have been discovered.[402]

This means that the 4-year statute of limitations on warranty claims normally begins to run when the seller tenders delivery to a buyer—which usually is when the buyer first takes delivery of a product[403]—whether or not the buyer or other plaintiff has reason to know at that time that the product is unmerchantable or an express warranty is false. In other words, the Code explicitly rejects the discovery rule. However, as with the 4-year time period in § 2–725(1), courts applying § 2–725(2) to personal injury cases sometimes ignore its explicit language and apply the discovery rule to warranty actions involving personal injuries.[404]

Section 2–725(2) contains some ambiguous wrinkles. First is the issue concerning a product's "shelf-life," a problem which results when a manufacturer tenders delivery of a product to a retailer who places it on a shelf for three years before selling it and tendering delivery to a buyer. If the product malfunctions and injures the buyer two years thereafter (5 years after the manufacturer tendered delivery to the retailer, but only 2 years after the retailer tendered delivery to the injured purchaser), and if the injured buyer thereupon sues the manufacturer for breach of warranty, a court will have to determine which tender of delivery started the 4-year time limitations clock ticking under § 2–725(2). On this point the courts disagree, some ruling that the period begins to run on the manufacturer's tender of delivery[405] in order to promote commercial certainty, others holding that the period begins only when delivery by somebody is

---

was tort rather than contract). Some courts that ignore the legislature in this respect struggle to find a rationale for such arguably imperious behavior, often drawing on such dubious factors as the nature of the injury (if the injuries are tort-like, then the tort law statute supposedly is appropriate) and whether the parties are in privity of contract (if not, then the tort statute may be applied). Neither of these rationales usually is sound. See 1 Crockett, Product Warranties §§ 11:15–:16.

[400] See id. § 11.17 (characterizing a court's ignoring of UCC § 2–725 as "statutory destruction"). "In all cases the court should invoke the statute of limitations applicable to the cause of action." Id.

[401] See, e.g., Fritchie v. Alumax Inc., 931 F. Supp. 662 (D. Neb. 1996); Taylor v. Ford Motor Co., 408 S.E.2d 270 (W. Va. 1991) (state's 2-year tort law statute barred plaintiff's breach of warranty claim for personal injuries brought within 4 years of product's delivery). See generally 1 Crockett, Product Warranties § 11:15 ("Unfortunately, some courts are willing to ignore the plain language of Section 2–725 when personal injury is sought under a warranty banner, thus fuzzing the line between tort and warranty.").

[402] UCC § 2–725(2). See the nonuniform variations in Alabama and Maine, where claims for personal injury accrue when the injury occurs; and in South Carolina, which substitutes the discovery rule.

[403] See, e.g., Barban v. Rheem Textile Sys., Inc., 2005 WL 387660, at *10 (E.D.N.Y. 2005).

[404] See discussion of discovery rule, below.

[405] See, e.g., Heller v. U.S. Suzuki Motor Corp., 477 N.E.2d 434 (N.Y. 1985) (4–2 decision).

tendered to the ultimate buyer[406] in order to spread the risk of loss and allow an injured plaintiff at least some chance to bring an action for breach of warranty.[407]

A second interpretative wrinkle in § 2–725(2) concerns the question of when a seller's warranty "extends to future performance," in which event the 4-year time period does not begin to run until the plaintiff does or should discover the breach of warranty (normally the time of injury). Because the discovery-rule exception applies only to warranties that "explicitly" extend to future performance, courts quite firmly hold that this exception cannot logically apply to *implied* warranties.[408] And while *express* warranties would in a sense seem *always* to extend to a product's future performance, most courts have been reluctant to rule that normal express warranties "explicitly" so extend.[409] Consequently, unless an express warranty (as distinguished from a remedy, such as repair or replacement)[410] provides that it will last for a specified period of time,[411] most courts hold that such a warranty does *not* extend to future performance, which means that the 4-year limitations period begins to run when delivery is tendered rather than when plaintiff discovers the harm.[412]

Products liability statutes. An increasing majority of states have enacted special statutes of limitations, usually as part of a larger products liability reform act, that specifically governs products liability claims.[413] Because they apply specially to products liability claims, such provisions take precedence over more general statutes of

---

[406] See, e.g., Patterson v. Her Majesty Indus., 450 F. Supp. 425 (E.D. Pa. 1978), discussed in Case Comment, 17 Am. Bus. L.J. 221 (1979).

[407] This latter approach appears correct. 1 Crockett, Product Warranties § 11:2. See Heller v. U.S. Suzuki Motor Corp., 465 N.Y.S.2d 822 (Sup. Ct. 1983) (endorsing this approach), rev'd, 475 N.Y.S.2d 146 (App. Div. 1985), aff'd, 477 N.E.2d 434 (N.Y. 1985).

[408] See 1 Crockett, above, § 11:5 ("The courts have consistently ruled that implied warranties of merchantability and fitness do not explicitly extend to future performance."). See, e.g., Shumaker v. Atrium Med. Corp., 2019 WL 3802468, at *3 (D.N.H. 2019) ("The discovery rule for future performance does not apply to implied warranties."); Selzer v. Brunsell Bros., 652 N.W.2d 806 (Wis. Ct. App. 2002) (implied warranties cannot extend to future performance); Marvin Lumber & Cedar Co. v. PPG Indus., 223 F.3d 873 (8th Cir. 2000) (Minn. law) (same).

[409] See 1 Crockett, above, § 11:5 (noting that the great bulk of cases refuse to find that warranties extend to future performance).

[410] See, e.g., Tittle v. Steel City Oldsmobile GMC Truck, Inc., 544 So.2d 883 (Ala. 1989) ("repair-or-replacement" warranty for 36,000 miles or 36 months addresses remedy, not warranty, and so does not explicitly extend to future performance). *But see* Mississippi Chem. Corp. v. Dresser-Rand Co., 287 F.3d 359 (5th Cir. 2002) (Miss. law) (limitations period based on "repair or replace" provision did not begin to run until the promise to repair or replace failed of its essential purpose); Krieger v. Nick Alexander Imps., Inc., 285 Cal. Rptr. 717 (Ct. App. 1991) (promise to repair defects that occur within 36,000 miles or 36 months explicitly extends to future performance; discovery rule applied).

[411] Such as a 2-year limited express warranty, or a limited automotive warranty for the lesser of 3 years or 36,000 miles. Compare LTL Acres Ltd. P'ship v. Butler Mfg. Co., 136 A.3d 682, 688 (Del. 2016) (10-year express limited warranty statements that cladding materials " 'will not . . . lose their bond,' 'will be fade resistant,' and 'will be water resistant' " explicitly extended the warranty to future performance); Kelleher v. Marvin Lumber & Cedar Co., 891 A.2d 477, 490 (N.H. 2005) (warranty that window preservative "permanently protects against rot and decay" satisfied the future performance exception and invoked the discovery rule).

[412] See, e.g., Forbes v. General Motors Corp., 993 So.2d 822, 826–27 (Miss. 2008) (auto owner's manual contained no explicit reference to the air bag's future performance); Sherman v. Sea Ray Boats, Inc., 649 N.W.2d 783 (Mich. Ct. App. 2002) (reference in boat manual to "years of trouble free boating" and "family fun for many years to come" did not create a warranty of future performance). *But see* Marvin Lumber & Cedar Co. v. PPG Indus., 223 F.3d 873 (8th Cir. 2000) (Minn. law) (warranty may extend to future performance even if length of coverage is imprecise; warranty that product would last as long as other manufacturers' products and longer than similar product that plaintiff already owned created jury issue on whether warranty of future performance was created).

[413] See Prod. Liab. Rep. (CCH) ¶ 3210 (collecting the statutes).

limitations covering torts, personal injuries, and wrongful death.[414] Products liability statutes of limitations typically apply to all "products liability claims," including claims for breach of warranty and wrongful death.[415] Yet, because of Article 2's special statute of limitations for warranty claims in UCC § 2–725, it is unclear whether a legislature's enactment of a statute of limitations for "products liability claims" captures warranty claims under that umbrella. Many products liability statutes cure this ambiguity by specifying the types of claims included, as by expressly including or excluding breach of warranty and possibly other types of claims, such as those for wrongful death. Colorado's products liability statute, for example, specifies that all products liability actions for personal injury or death, other than in warranty, must be brought within two years after a claim for relief arises.[416] Some special products liability statutes combine statutes of limitations with statutes of repose.[417]

Stopping the Clock

Certain conduct by a defendant, or a plaintiff's status or reasonable ignorance of an injury or a products liability claim, may "toll"—stop the running of—the statute of limitations clock. Some statutes explicitly so provide, and courts sometimes apply the doctrine of equitable tolling to achieve the same result.[418] Moreover, a statute of limitations clock may be delayed until the plaintiff's final exposure to a toxic substance; and long after the plaintiff first suffers an initial injury from such a substance, the limitations clock may begin to run anew if the plaintiff subsequently suffers another separate type of harm.

Tolling. The running of a statutory limitations period may be delayed on account of certain wrongful conduct by a defendant. If a defendant fraudulently prevents a plaintiff from learning that he or she has a products liability claim against the defendant, a court may apply the equitable doctrine of tolling to delay a statute of limitations from running until the plaintiff does, or should, discover the existence of the claim.[419] For a defendant's fraudulent concealment to be sufficient to toll a limitations statute, the defendant must act affirmatively to hide facts necessary to the plaintiff's claim and thereby prevent the plaintiff from discovering its existence.[420] Silence alone, including a

---

[414] See, e.g., Kambury v. DaimlerChrysler Corp., 50 P.3d 1163 (Or. 2002) (applying ordinary canon of statutory construction, *held,* 2-year products liability statute of limitations, being more specific, trumps 3-year wrongful death statute). *But see* Alder v. Bayer Corp., AGFA Div., 61 P.3d 1068 (Utah 2002) (4-year statute of limitations for negligence actions, and not 2-year statute of limitations for products liability actions, governed claim that manufacturer negligently installed and serviced its machine).

[415] See, e.g., Ark. Code Ann. § 16–116–203 (3 years—all products liability actions for injury, death, or damage); Neb. Rev. Stat. § 25–224 (4 years—all products liability actions for injury, death, or damage).

[416] See, e.g., Colo. Rev. Stat. Ann. § 13–80–106.

[417] See, e.g., Conn. Gen. Stat. Ann. § 52–577a(a).

[418] See 2 C. Corman, Limitations of Actions chs. 8–10 (1991); Frumer, Friedman, and Sklaren, Products Liability § 26.07.

[419] See 2 Corman, above, § 9.7.2, at 67: "Fraudulent concealment involves the use of artifice to prevent inquiry or investigation and to mislead or hinder the acquisition of information that would disclose a right of action. Postponing the accrual of the cause of action is based on the concealing party's wrongdoing and the plaintiff's blameless ignorance of the cause of action." See also Marcus, Fraudulent Concealment in Federal Court: Toward a More Disparate Standard?, 71 Geo. L.J. 829 (1983).

[420] See, e.g., Hoefs v. Sig Sauer Inc., 2022 WL 823496, at *3 (W.D. Wash. 2022) (defendant's "representation that the [inspected] pistol contained no defect whatsoever, despite the numerous incidents of discharge without trigger in the preceding 14 years" tolled statute of limitations); Dean v. Dometic Corp., 2020 WL 9454954, at *6–7 (M.D. Fla. 2020) (plaintiffs allegations of defendant's affirmative steps to conceal refrigerator's defect were sufficient to toll statute of repose); Shumaker v. Atrium Med. Corp., 2019 WL 3802468, at *3 (D.N.H. 2019) (plaintiff's allegations "that defendants concealed the defective design of the

failure to warn of a known defect, is insufficient.[421] As a predicate for tolling on the basis of fraudulent concealment, most jurisdictions require that a plaintiff prove the defendant's intent to deceive the plaintiff.[422] Even in the absence of an intent to deceive, however, a defendant whose misrepresentation is relied on by a plaintiff may be equitably estopped from relying on a statute of limitations.[423]

By statute and case law, most states toll statutes of limitations for claims by plaintiffs whose disabilities interfere with a fair opportunity to pursue a legal claim. Most states, but not all, also toll statutes of limitations for a minor's claims until he or she reaches the age of majority.[424] In addition, at least when the defendant's product causes a person to become mentally incompetent, a plaintiff's incompetency may toll the statute of limitations.[425] Further, federal law provides for the tolling of claims by persons on active duty in the armed services.[426]

Various jurisdictions toll statutes of limitations in a miscellany of other situations. Statutes in some states protect retailers and other non-manufacturing defendants from strict liability unless, among other things, the manufacturer is (or is likely to become) insolvent.[427] In a state with such a statute, if a plaintiff after diligent investigation chooses not to join a non-manufacturing defendant because the manufacturer (or its successor) reasonably appears likely to remain solvent, a court may toll the statute of limitations against the non-manufacturing seller until the plaintiff should discover the

---

[hernia repair mesh] . . . and that they misled physicians about the mesh product's likelihood of failure" were sufficient to toll the statute of limitations at that stage of litigation); In re FCA US LLC Monostable Elec. Gearshift Litig., 2018 WL 4352702, at *8 (E.D. Mich. 2018) (equitable tolling based on repeated false assertions by defendant's agents). Compare Cortez v. Cook Inc., 27 F.4th 563, 567 (7th Cir. 2022) (Ind. law) (statute of repose not tolled by fraudulent concealment, especially where passive); Hatfield v. Dyncorp., Inc., 187 F.3d 647 (9th Cir. 1999) (Ariz. law) (limitations statute not tolled where no positive act by defendant). See generally 2 Corman, above, at § 9.7.

421 See, e.g., Martin v. Arthur, 3 S.W.3d 684, 690 (Ark. 1999); Curlee v. Mock Enters., Inc., 327 S.E.2d 736, 741 (Ga. Ct. App. 1985).

422 See, e.g., Harris v. BMW of N. Am., LLC., 2020 WL 7074879, at *5 (E.D. Tex. 2020) (allegations that defendant knew cause of defect and hid this from plaintiffs raised questions of fact on fraudulent concealment tolling of warranty claims); Estate of Brice v. Toyota Motor Corp., 373 P.3d 977, 981 (N.M. 2016) (to toll a limitations period for fraudulent concealment, a "plaintiff must prove that (1) the defendant knew of the alleged wrongful act and concealed it from the plaintiff or had material information pertinent to its discovery which he failed to disclose, and (2) the plaintiff did not know, or could not have known through the exercise of reasonable diligence, of the cause of action within the statutory period"). See generally 2 Corman, above, § 9.7.1, at 61.

423 See, e.g., Northwestern Pub. Serv. v. Union Carbide Corp., 115 F. Supp. 2d 1164, 1171 (D.S.D. 2000); Anane v. Pettibone Corp., 560 N.E.2d 1088 (Ill. App. Ct. 1990).

424 See, e.g., Lopez v. Sony Elecs., Inc., 420 P.3d 767, 776 (Cal. 2018) (applying toxic exposure statute of limitations allowing tolling during minority; minor plaintiff filed while claims "were not time-barred under the previously applicable [prenatal injury] statute of limitations"); Pollard v. Sherwin-Williams Co., 955 So.2d 764, 770 (Miss. 2007); Mueller v. Parke Davis, 599 A.2d 950, 955 (N.J. App. Div. 1991) (applying N.J. or Va. law, both of which tolled statute for plaintiff's infancy, rather than that of Conn., which did not).

In contrast to a statute of limitations, a plaintiff's minority will *not* toll a statute of repose. See, e.g., Stevenson v. Ford Motor Co., 608 S.W.3d 109, 132 (Tex. App. 2020) ("the legislature did not . . . make an exception to the products-liability statute of repose . . . for reviving minor plaintiffs' products-liability claims"); Budler v. General Motors Corp., 689 N.W.2d 847 (Neb. 2004).

425 See, e.g., Abels v. Genie Indus., 202 S.W.3d 99, 106 (Tenn. 2006) (statute tolled for as long as plaintiff's mind remains "unsound"); Pardy v. United States, 548 F. Supp. 682 (S.D. Ill. 1982) (reviewing the law nationally). *Contra* for statutes of repose. See Penley v. Honda Motor Co., 31 S.W.3d 181 (Tenn. 2000) (statute of repose not tolled for plaintiff who was on nearly constant pain medication in hospital after accident and often did not know where she was).

426 See the Servicemembers Civil Relief Act (Soldiers' and Sailors' Civil Relief Act of 1940), 50 U.S.C. app. §§ 501 et seq.

427 See § 15.2, below.

manufacturer's insolvency.[428] And, while a class action is pending certification, most courts toll the statute of limitations provisionally, in case the petition fails, for the individual claims of persons who would have been class members had the class action been approved.[429]

The discovery rule. In products liability actions involving toxic substances (such as asbestos, dangerous drugs, or other toxic chemicals) and medical devices implanted in the human body, a plaintiff may have no way to know that he or she has suffered injury until long after it first occurs. For example, the incubation period for mesothelioma, a form of lung cancer resulting from inhaling asbestos dust, may be as long as 40 years.[430] If a statute of limitations begins to run on a plaintiff's claim for harm from a toxic substance at the time the plaintiff first suffers harm, the conventional accrual point for tort law claims as discussed above, then the limitations statute would bar the legal rights of many persons injured by toxic substances before they even knew that they were injured. Applying the traditional accrual rule to cases of this type, as courts used to do, snuffed out the products liability rights of many consumers and workers to recover for grievous injuries caused by the most insidious kinds of defective products.[431]

Beginning in the 1960s and 1970s,[432] several courts began to remedy this problem by extending the "discovery rule" from medical malpractice litigation, where it had been incubating,[433] to products liability litigation.[434] Under the discovery rule, a cause of

---

[428] See, e.g., Braswell v. AC & S, Inc., 105 S.W.3d 587 (Tenn. Ct. App. 2002) (statute that precluded strict liability in tort claim against seller unless manufacturer is insolvent tolled statute of limitations until manufacturer filed for bankruptcy); Crego v. Baldwin-Lima-Hamilton Corp., 1998 WL 80240 (Ohio Ct. App. 1998), and 1999 WL 1043887 (Ohio Ct. App. 1999). See generally Frumer, Friedman, and Sklaren, Products Liability § 26.07[5].

[429] See, e.g., In re Ford Motor Co. DPS6 Powershift Transmission Prods. Liab. Litig., 2021 WL 1220948, at *3 (C.D. Cal. 2021); Patrickson v. Dole Food Co., 368 P.3d 959, 968–70 (Haw. 2015) (reviewing cases in matter of first impression); In re New England Compounding Pharm., Inc. Prods. Liab. Litig., 2013 WL 4456757, at *4 (D. Mass. 2013); Stevens v. Novartis Pharms. Corp., 247 P.3d 244, 257 (Mont. 2010) (thorough discussion); In re Vioxx Prods. Liab. Litig., 478 F. Supp. 2d 897 (E.D. La. 2007) (same); American Pipe & Constr. Co. v. Utah, 414 U.S. 538, 551 (1974).

Note too that transfer between federal district courts may toll the limitations period. See Franco v. Mabe Trucking Co., 3 F.4th 788, 800–01 (5th Cir. 2021) (2–1 decision) (transfer from Eastern District of Texas to Western District of Louisiana under 28 U.S.C. § 1631 preempted Louisiana's 1-year prescriptive limitations period).

But see In re Chinese-Manufactured Drywall Prods. Liab. Litig., 854 Fed. Appx. 570, 572 (5th Cir. 2021) (plaintiffs "cannot piggyback on [earlier] class action to avoid the expiration of the statute of limitations"); Casey v. Merck & Co., 722 S.E.2d 842, 846 (Va. 2012) ("Virginia recognizes neither equitable nor statutory tolling due to the pendency of a putative class action in another jurisdiction."); Maestas v. Sofamor Danek Grp., Inc., 1999 WL 74212, at *4 (Tenn. Ct. App. 1999) (in bone screw litigation, statute not tolled for subsequent state claims filed after federal class certification denied; state does not recognize "cross-jurisdictional tolling"), aff'd, 33 S.W.3d 805 (Tenn. 2000); Jolly v. Eli Lilly & Co., 751 P.2d 923 (Cal. 1988) (refusing to toll statute during DES putative class action, where variance among individual claims made class certification very unlikely). See generally Frumer, Friedman, and Sklaren, Products Liability § 26.07[6].

[430] See Hamilton v. Asbestos Corp., 998 P.2d 403, 405–08 (Cal. 2000) (noting 30 to 40 year latency period for mesothelioma).

[431] See, e.g., Locke v. Johns-Manville Corp., 275 S.E.2d 900, 905–06 (Va. 1981).

[432] A progenitor case was Urie v. Thompson, 337 U.S. 163 (1949) (FELA compensation claim for silicosis).

[433] See Prosser and Keeton on Torts § 30.

[434] Early cases include R.J. Reynolds Tobacco Co. v. Hudson, 314 F.2d 776 (5th Cir. 1963) (La. law); Raymond v. Eli Lilly & Co., 371 A.2d 170, 174 (N.H. 1977) (Kenison, C.J.) ("we do not think the drug company can reasonably expect to be immune to suit before its customer has a fair opportunity to discover the company's tortious conduct"). See generally Annot., 4 A.L.R.3d 821 (1965).

action accrues not when the plaintiff is injured but when the plaintiff *discovers*, or in the exercise of reasonable diligence should discover, pertinent facts about the injury. Today, courts in a great majority of jurisdictions apply the discovery rule to products liability cases,[435] and some states have codified the rule, either for tort actions generally[436] or products liability actions in particular.[437] Some decisions and statutes specify that the discovery rule, or some particular version of it, applies to cases involving injuries or illnesses from toxic substances—cases where the rule is needed most.[438]

Courts and legislatures are widely split on precisely what type of facts a plaintiff must discover to trigger a limitations statute and start the clock ticking. Some jurisdictions start the clock when the plaintiff learns or should be aware that he or she is ill or injured,[439] while others hold that the clock does not begin to run until the plaintiff

---

435 See, e.g., Cutter v. Ethicon, Inc., 2021 WL 3754245, at *4 (6th Cir. 2021) (Ky. law) (reversing dismissal of strict products liability design defect claims; "applicability of the common law discovery rule turns on the character of the plaintiff's injury, not on the label for [the] cause of action"); Stark v. Johnson & Johnson, 10 F.4th 823, 837 (7th Cir. 2021) (Ill. law) (reversing dismissal of plaintiff's claims against pelvic mesh manufacturer; jury could conclude that discovery rule applied to plaintiff's claims); Zamboni v. Aladan Corp., 304 F. Supp. 2d 218 (D. Mass 2004); In re Bridgestone/Firestone, Inc., 200 F. Supp. 2d 983 (S.D. Ind. 2002) (Cal. & Ariz. law); Degussa Corp. v. Mullens, 744 N.E.2d 407 (Ind. 2001). Compare Fluke Corp. v. LeMaster, 306 S.W.3d 55, 60–61 (Ky. 2010) (reversing appellate court and reinstating summary judgment for defendant; "Despite [plaintiffs'] argument to the contrary, the discovery rule simply has no application to this case. . . . [Plaintiffs] should have reasonably suspected that the voltage meter was not working properly and investigated this possibility."). See generally Frumer, Friedman, and Sklaren, Products Liability § 26.04[2][a] ("It has become the near-unanimous rule.").

Some courts apply the discovery rule in products liability actions on a case-by-case basis while others hold that their states' various statutes of limitations do not allow a discovery rule. See Hoffman v. Orthopedic Sys., Inc., 765 N.E.2d 116 (Ill. App. Ct. 2002) (case-by-case basis); Griffith v. Blatt, 51 P.3d 1256 (Or. 2002) (discovery rule does not apply to 2-year products liability statute of limitations); Colormatch Exteriors, Inc. v. Hickey, 569 S.E.2d 495 (Ga. 2002) (discovery rule does not apply to 4-year statute for damage to realty).

436 See, e.g., S.C. Code Ann. § 15–3–535, applied to toxic substance products liability case in Grillo v. Speedrite Prods., Inc., 532 S.E.2d 1 (S.C. Ct. App. 2000); Colo. Rev. Stat. Ann. § 13–80–108(1).

437 See, e.g., Conn. Gen. Stat. Ann. § 52–577a(a); Fla. Stat. Ann. § 95.031(2)(b); Or. Rev. Stat. Ann. § 30.905(2)(a); Utah Code Ann. § 78B–6–706; Wash. Rev. Code Ann. § 7.72.060(3).

438 See, e.g., Cornett v. Johnson & Johnson, 48 A.3d 1041, 1049 (N.J. 2012) (Ky. law) (Kentucky limits discovery rule in product cases to latent injuries and illnesses); Griffin v. Unocal Corp., 990 So.2d 291 (Ala. 2008) (5–4 decision) (replacing last-exposure rule with manifest, present injury rule for cases involving injuries from toxic chemicals); Carter v. Brown & Williamson Tobacco Corp., 778 So.2d 932 (Fla. 2000) (discovery rule applies to "creeping diseases" such as lung cancer). See also Baxley v. Harley-Davidson Motor Co., 875 N.E.2d 989, 991 (Ohio Ct. App. 2007) (discovery rule normally applies only in cases of latent injury, not latent defects where causal link is obvious).

Statutes to this effect include Or. Rev. Stat. Ann. § 30.907 (claims for asbestos injuries to be brought within 2 years of when injuries were or should have been discovered, in contrast to 2 years from date of injury for normal products liability claims, Or. Rev. Stat. Ann § 30.905). Va. Code Ann. § 8.01–249(4) provides that actions for injury from asbestos exposure accrue when diagnosis of the "asbestos-related injury or disease is first communicated to the person or his agent by a physician." And under Va. Code Ann. § 8.01–230, actions to recover for injuries from other toxic materials accrue "from the date the injury is sustained." See Adams v. American Optical Corp., 979 F.3d 248, 261 (4th Cir. 2020) (Va. law) (barring plaintiff's claims for black lung disease arising from coal dust inhalation, undiagnosed for fourteen years). But Va. Code Ann. § 8.01–249(4a), enacted in 2021 to address "injuries that remain dormant or do not develop," provides that claims for latent injuries accrue "when the person knew or should have known of the injury and its causal connection to an injury-causing substance or product."

439 See, e.g., Palmer v. Walker Jamar Co., 945 N.W.2d 844, 848–50 (Minn. 2020) (wrongful death action filed more than six years after decedent learned that asbestos exposure caused his mesothelioma was time barred; rejecting plaintiff's request to adopt a discovery rule triggered "when all of the elements of the cause of action, including the identity and fault of the tortfeasor, are discoverable or reasonably discoverable by the plaintiff"); Clabo v. Johnson & Johnson Health Care Sys., Inc., 982 F.3d 989, 995 (6th Cir. 2020) (declining to extend a discovery rule to plaintiff's claims against vaginal mesh manufacturer; Tennessee's 6-year statute of limitations barred claims filed in 2013 arising from 2006 injury); Ex parte Integra LifeScis. Corp., 271 So.3d 814, 819–20 (Ala. 2018) (2-year statute of limitation expired on plaintiff's products liability claim for damages

discovers both the injury and its cause.[440] Even these latter courts cannot agree on how specific the plaintiff's discovery of "cause" must be. Some courts start the clock ticking only when a plaintiff discovers a causal connection between the injury and a particular product;[441] others start the clock only when the plaintiff discovers the identity of the party responsible for causing the injury (to wit, the defendant);[442] and some require that a plaintiff must discover the defendant's wrongdoing that gives the plaintiff a cause of action, or at least be put on notice of that reasonable possibility.[443] One reasonable way to formulate a discovery rule, capturing the essence of what many courts have ruled, is to hold a statute triggered when an injured person acquires facts reasonably suggesting that a likely cause of the injury was a particular product that plausibly may have been

from allegedly defective surgical mesh before she filed the second amended complaint naming the manufacturer; medical records in plaintiff's possession listed the "SurgiMend" product name and "a simple Internet query using the word 'SurgiMend' would have led her to . . . Integra's identity as the manufacturer of the mesh"); American Optical Corp. v. Estate of Rankin, 227 So.3d 1062, 1074 (Miss. 2017) (vacating judgment for plaintiff as time-barred; cause of action accrued on discovery of lung disease three years before plaintiff associated the disease with silica exposure); Phillips 66 Co. v. Lofton, 94 So.3d 1051, 1059 (Miss. 2012) (accrual on discovery of injury, not discovery of injury and its cause). Statutes to this effect include Conn. Gen. Stat. Ann. § 52–577a(a); Mo. Ann. Stat. § 516.100; S.D. Codified Laws § 15–2–12.2; Vt. Stat. Ann. tit. 12, § 512(4).

440 See, e.g., First American Specialty Ins. Co. v. Carmax Auto Superstores Cal., LLC, 2017 WL 5235646, at *2 (N.D. Cal. 2017) (under the discovery rule, "the question is not whether a plaintiff could have become aware of wrongdoing, but rather whether he *reasonably should have* become aware of wrongdoing") (emphasis in original); Timothy v. Boston Sci. Corp., 665 Fed. Appx. 295, 297 (4th Cir. 2016) (Utah law) ("A claim accrues when a person knows or should know all of the information necessary to state her claim for relief."); Sheppard v. Monsanto Co., 2016 WL 3629074, at *4 (D. Haw. 2016) ("a cause of action for personal injury does not accrue until a plaintiff 'discovers or should have discovered the negligent act, the damages, and the causal connection between the former and the latter' "); Cornett v. Johnson & Johnson, 48 A.3d 1041, 1049 (N.J. 2012) (Ky. law) (injury and fact that it was caused by defendant's conduct); Carter v. Brown & Williamson Tobacco Corp., 778 So.2d 932 (Fla. 2000) (statute begins to run on latent injury for "creeping disease," like lung cancer from smoking, when plaintiff is on notice of causal connection between exposure to product and injury). See generally Frumer, Friedman, and Sklaren, Products Liability § 26.04[4][f] (listing, as following this rule, Ariz., Ark., Colo., Haw., Ind., Ky., La., Mass., Md. (latent diseases), Mich., Minn., N.H., Ohio, Okla., Or., Pa., Tenn., Utah, V.I., and Wis.).

441 See, e.g., Stewart v. Philip Morris, Inc., 205 F.3d 1054 (8th Cir. 2000) (Ark. law) (connection between cigarette smoking and breathing and coughing problems); Bowen v. Eli Lilly & Co., 557 N.E.2d 739 (Mass. 1990) (connection between DES and cancer).

442 See, e.g., Michals v. Baxter Healthcare Corp., 289 F.3d 402 (6th Cir. 2002) (Ky. law) (breast implants; plaintiff must know or should have known that she has been wronged and by whom wrong has been committed). See generally Frumer, Friedman, and Sklaren, Products Liability § 26.04[4][g] (listing, as following this rule, Ariz., Kan., N.H., Or., P.R., Utah, V.I., Wash., Wis., and W. Va.).

443 See, e.g., Collin v. Securi Int'l, 322 F. Supp. 2d 170 (D. Conn. 2004); Clark v. Baxter Healthcare Corp., 100 Cal. Rptr. 2d 223, 227 (Ct. App. 2000) ("Under the discovery rule, the statute of limitations begins to run when the plaintiff suspects or should suspect that her injury was caused by wrongdoing, that someone has done something wrong to her."). See generally Frumer, Friedman, and Sklaren, Products Liability § 26.04[4][h] (listing, as following this rule, Alaska, Fla., Iowa, Mont., Nev., N.J., N.D., S.C., Tex., Vt., Wash., and W. Va.). At least South Carolina's rule is statutory. See S.C. Code Ann. § 15–3–535, applied in Brugger v. C.R. Bard, Inc., 2017 WL 3085749, at *3 (D.S.C. 2017) ("reasonable fact finder could conclude" that plaintiffs were not on notice that injuries arose from hernia repair mesh when physicians attributed injuries to complications from subsequent lap band surgery); Grillo v. Speedrite Prod., Inc., 532 S.E.2d 1, 3–6 (S.C. Ct. App. 2000) (factual question whether circumstances would have put plaintiff on notice that some claim against another party might exist).

defective.[444] Knowledge of this type should put most people on notice that they should see a lawyer to determine if they have a legal remedy.[445]

As seen above, the Uniform Commercial Code is perfectly clear in stating that claims for breach of warranty under the Code accrue on breach, defined as when tender of delivery occurs, "regardless of the aggrieved party's lack of knowledge of the breach."[446] It is hard to imagine how the Code's drafters could have been any more explicit in rejecting the discovery rule. Yet, for whatever reason,[447] some courts have ignored the clear language and applied the discovery rule to products liability claims for breach of warranty involving personal injury or death.[448]

Splitting claims—the "single action" ***vs.*** **"separate injury" rules.** A special statute of limitations issue arises when a single defective condition in a product harms a person in two or more separate ways at different times. A problematic question in such cases is when the statute of limitations should begin to run on the *second* injury—at the time the plaintiff discovered the first injury, or at the time he or she discovers the second. Normally, because each breach of duty by a defendant is thought to generate a single, indivisible cause of action, a plaintiff is required to seek all damages caused thereby at the time the complaint is filed; thereafter, the plaintiff is precluded from suing the defendant again for damages arising from the same transaction.[449] So, if the operator of

---

[444] See, e.g., In re: Zostavax (Zoster Vaccine Live) Prods. Liab. Litig., 2021 WL 3164293, at *3–4 (E.D. Pa. 2021) (jury question whether plaintiff had reason to believe, in 2007/08, that shingles vaccine caused her eye and face injuries, well before she saw 2018 television ad by her subsequent attorney linking the vaccine to shingles cases); Adams v. Zimmer US, Inc., 943 F.3d 159, 167–68 (3d Cir. 2019) (Pa. law) (jury question whether plaintiff was reasonably diligent in discovering cause of her hip pain); Levitt v. Merck & Co., 914 F.3d 1169, 1174 (8th Cir. 2019) (en banc) (Mo. law) (reports of Vioxx heart risks and Vioxx litigation in national news were "relevant to whether 'notice of a potentially actionable injury' existed, but [were] not determinative as a matter of law"); In re Mentor Corp. Obtape Transobturator Sling Prods. Liab. Litig., 748 Fed. Appx. 212, 215–17 (11th Cir. 2018) (Fla. law) (whether plaintiff's symptoms were "sufficiently distinct . . . from what might be expected after vaginal surgery to put her on notice of her cause of action" was a question for jury); Edwards v. Thomas, 2018 WL 1866712, at *6 (Ill. App. Ct. 2018) (issue of fact whether plaintiff reasonably should have known that micro-cracks in da Vinci robotic machines could cause thermal injuries to surgical patients prior to surgeon's deposition in her malpractice action); Zamudio-Soto v. Bayer Healthcare Pharms. Inc., 2017 WL 386375, at *8 (N.D. Cal. 2017) (plaintiff's untimely claims arose over 3½ years earlier when she posted on Facebook a link between her injury and IUD); Jolly v. Eli Lilly & Co., 751 P.2d 923, 928 (Cal. 1988) (DES; "[o]nce the plaintiff has a suspicion of wrongdoing, and therefore an incentive to sue, she must decide whether to file suit or sit on her rights").

[445] Demanding any greater confidence in the existence of a products liability claim might require a plaintiff to have the expertise of a meticulous reader of this book, which would be monstrously unfair even to a person with an exceptional intellect.

[446] UCC § 2–725(2).

[447] For example, some courts read § 2–725(2) as applying only to buyers rather than third parties—an approach that seems rather strained. However, in a state with a special statute of limitations for products liability claims, a court might reasonably conclude that a products liability statute of limitations trumps the Article 2 statute of limitations because the former is more specific than the latter. See Doll v. Ford Motor Co., 814 F. Supp. 2d 526, 536 (D. Md. 2011) (implied warranty claims not time barred because defendant's alleged fraudulent concealment of torque converter defect would toll the running of the statute).

[448] See 1 Crockett, Product Warranties § 11:15 ("some courts construe § 2–725 as embodying a 'discovery' rule, even though the language defies such a reading").

[449] See Henderson and Twerski, Asbestos Litigation Gone Mad: Exposure-Based Recovery for Increased Risk, Mental Distress, and Medical Monitoring, 53 S.C. L. Rev. 815, 819–20 (2002):

> In most tort cases, the law provides a plaintiff one indivisible cause of action for all damages arising from a defendant's breach of duty. This hoary rule against splitting a cause of action is designed to prevent vexatious and repetitive litigation of a single underlying claim when plaintiff's injuries eventually result in damages that are more serious than originally contemplated. [Despite the real problem of proof and risks of undercompensation facing injured plaintiffs,] the specter of

a defective punch press recovers damages for resulting injuries to his hand and arm in an action against the manufacturer, he cannot later maintain a second action against the manufacturer for injuries from the same accident that he subsequently discovers in his back. Underlying res judicata, this principle of claim preclusion is sometimes called the single-action rule, or the rule against claim-splitting.[450]

Although the claim-splitting issue can arise in traumatic injury cases, such as the punch press situation just discussed, it most frequently and acutely arises in cases involving injuries and illnesses from toxic substances like asbestos. Two decades after exposure,[451] an asbestos worker may suffer asbestosis (or pleural thickening) for which damages may be available against the asbestos supplier, perhaps for failing to warn of the risk. Another one or two decades later,[452] long after the initial asbestosis claim is resolved, the very same worker may contract a deadly form of lung cancer, mesothelioma. In this context, some courts have applied the single-action rule to bar the second claim, holding that the statute of limitations on *all* claims runs from the first injury or its discovery.[453] Yet, "[g]iven the harshness of the single-action rule, . . . the overwhelming majority of courts abandoned the single-action rule and now allow separate causes of action later, when a plaintiff actually develops asbestosis, lung cancer, or mesothelioma."[454] Thus, in place of the old single-action rule, courts in latent or "creeping" disease cases are rapidly switching to a converse doctrine—the separate-injury or two-disease rule—which starts separate limitations clocks ticking on separate and distinct diseases when each was independently discovered.[455]

---

repetitive litigation and the lack of finality to litigation present unacceptable costs to the legal system. Thus, the single-action rule is deeply embedded in the jurisprudence of this country.

450 See F. James, G. Hazard, and J. Leubsdorf, Civil Procedure §§ 11.8 et seq. (5th ed. 2001).

451 See, e.g., Hamilton v. Asbestos Corp., 998 P.2d 403, 405–08 (Cal. 2000) (noting the 20-year average latency period of asbestosis).

452 See id. (noting the 30- to 40-year average latency period of mesothelioma).

453 See, e.g., Gideon v. Johns-Manville Sales Corp., 761 F.2d 1129, 1136 (5th Cir. 1985) (Tex. law) ("a plaintiff may not split this cause of action by seeking damages for some of his injuries in one suit and for later-developing injuries in another"). Compare Kemp v. G.D. Searle & Co., 103 F.3d 405 (5th Cir. 1997) (Miss. law) (IUD caused pelvic inflammatory disease that eventually led to infertility; *held*: statute ran from discovery of PID 8 years prior to diagnosis of scarred fallopian tubes that caused plaintiff's infertility).

In smoking cases, courts have likewise applied the "first injury" rule, holding that the alleged addiction to cigarettes is the injury that triggers the statute of limitations on subsequently developed illnesses. See Spain v. Brown & Williamson Tobacco Corp., 872 So.2d 101, 114 (Ala. 2003) ("Artful pleading such as is presented here, where Spain disavows seeking a recovery for all pre-cancer injuries, should not defeat the operation of the first-injury rule."); Soliman v. Philip Morris Inc., 311 F.3d 966, 972 (9th Cir. 2002) (Cal. law) (smoker's claims accrued when he knew or should have known that smoking is addictive; "the injury he should have known about first is the one that starts the statute of limitations"). *But see* Pooshs v. Philip Morris USA, Inc., 250 P.3d 181 (Cal. 2011), note 455, below.

454 Henderson and Twerski, Asbestos Litigation Gone Mad: Exposure-Based Recovery for Increased Risk, Mental Distress, and Medical Monitoring, 53 S.C. L. Rev. 815, 821 (2002) (citing cases).

455 The fountainhead case was Wilson v. Johns-Manville Sales Corp., 684 F.2d 111, 120–21 (D.C. 1982) (diagnosis of asbestosis did not trigger limitations statute for other injuries from same exposure to asbestos). See also Potts v. Celotex Corp., 796 S.W.2d 678, 685 (Tenn. 1990) (same; good summary of rationales); Pooshs v. Philip Morris USA, Inc., 250 P.3d 181, 183 (Cal. 2011) (answering certified question from Ninth Circuit; "when a later-discovered disease [lung cancer] is separate and distinct from an earlier-discovered disease [COPD], the earlier disease does not trigger the statute of limitations for a lawsuit based on the later disease"); John Crane, Inc. v. Puller, 899 A.2d 879, 894–97 (Md. Ct. Spec. App. 2006) ("a claim based on *asbestosis* and a claim based on *mesothelioma* are not the same claim"); Hamilton v. Asbestos Corp., 998 P.2d 403, 405–08 (Cal. 2000) (use of single-action rule in asbestos cases precluded by state statute); Pustejovsky v. Rapid-Am. Corp., 35 S.W.3d 643, 648 (Tex. 2000) ("[T]he single action rule is a catch 22 for victims of multiple latent diseases [because a] plaintiff who sues for asbestosis is precluded from any recovery for a later-developing lethal mesothelioma. But the discovery rule would preclude a plaintiff with asbestosis from waiting to see if an

Statutes of Repose

In General

The discovery rule, which courts and legislatures widely adopted in products liability litigation in the 1970s and 1980s, protects injury victims from losing their claims before they know that they have been harmed or that they may have a means of legal redress. But by delaying the running of statutes of limitations, sometimes for many years past the time of injury (and long after the product was manufactured), the discovery rule undermines the central purpose of limitations statutes. It will be recalled that limitations statutes are designed to provide a point in time after which both actors and courts can avoid having to address claims for injuries allegedly caused by actors and suffered by victims many years in the past. So, while promoting fairness for injured plaintiffs, the discovery rule promotes unfairness for manufacturers and inconvenience for the courts.

In an attempt to reinstate some portion of the defendant-fairness objectives of limitations statutes in a world committed to the plaintiff-fairness objectives of the discovery rule, many state legislatures from the 1960s through the early 1980s,[456] and the European Community in 1985,[457] enacted statutes of "repose." A major pillar of the tort "reform" movement, these special limitations statutes addressed problems with long-delayed claims,[458] especially claims against three particular groups disadvantaged by the discovery rule: doctors, who wanted an eventual end to the threat of malpractice suits for medical accidents; architects, engineers, and contractors, who wanted an end to potential liability for injuries from buildings and other structures that might last for decades or even centuries;[459] and manufacturers of products, who may have to answer products liability claims for products manufactured many decades in the past.[460]

asbestosis-related cancer later develops . . . ."). Statutes include Fla. Stat. Ann. § 774.206; Iowa Code Ann. § 686B.8; Va. Code Ann. § 8.01–249(4) (2020 amendment); W. Va. Code Ann. § 55–7G–9.

[456] See, e.g., Note, 1989 Duke L.J. 1689, 1697–1702.

[457] See E.C. Product Liability Directive art. 11, discussed in § 1.4, above (10 years from date product put into circulation).

[458] Some states have general statutes of repose to address problems of old claims. At least Minnesota's wrongful death act statute, which has a 3-year statute of limitations from the date of death, requires that all such cases be brought within 6 years of the act or omission. Minn. Stat. § 573.02, subd. 1. See Lamere v. St. Jude Med., Inc., 827 N.W.2d 782, 787 (Minn. Ct. App. 2013) (barring wrongful death claim from defective heart valve implanted in 1988, where action was filed within 3 years of date of death in 2007). At least Alaska has a general 10-year statute of repose, applicable to claims for personal injury, death, or property damage, Alaska Stat. Ann. § 09.10.055, which *excludes* products liability claims. See Jones v. Bowie Indus., Inc., 282 P.3d 316, 338 (Alaska 2012). Kentucky's products liability statute of repose presumes that a product is not defective after 5 years from sale or 8 years from manufacture; however, the statute allows for rebuttal by "a preponderance of the evidence to the contrary." Ky. Rev. Stat. Ann. § 411.310(1). See, e.g., Cox v. General Motors, LLC, 2019 WL 6719486, at *2 (E.D. Ky. 2019) (denying defendant's motion for dismissal; plaintiff may rebut presumption of non-defectiveness in 2006 Hummer H3 that caught fire in 2018).

[459] "The pyramids of Egypt, the Colosseum in Rome, the Parthenon in Greece are only now, at the end of the twentieth century, starting to succumb to the ravages of time. Consequently, it would be easy to imagine ten-, twenty-, fifty- or even one-hundred-year-old buildings and other structures as potential liability problems. So too are the products that are an integral part of them, such as elevators, furnaces, heavy machinery and the like." Frumer, Friedman, and Sklaren, Products Liability § 26.05[5][a], at n.160.

[460] See generally Martin, A Statute of Repose for Product Liability Claims, 50 Fordham L. Rev. 745 (1982); McGovern, The Variety, Policy and Constitutionality of Product Liability Statutes of Repose, 30 Am. U. L. Rev. 579 (1981); Frumer, Friedman, and Sklaren, Products Liability § 26.05; Am. Law Prod. Liab. §§ 47:70–:75; Prod. Liab. Rep. (CCH) ¶ 3100; Annot., 30 A.L.R.5th 1 (1995) (products liability statutes of repose).

Distinguished from Statutes of Limitations

Like statutes of limitations, products liability and other statutes of repose terminate a plaintiff's right to bring a claim after a period of time; but statutes of repose are different in two principal respects.[461] First, statutes of repose *begin to run* at a *time certain*: products liability statutes of this type typically run from the time the manufacturer first sells the product, and realty improvement statutes normally run from when the structure is completed. This aspect of repose statutes gives manufacturers (and their insurers) much more confidence that their potential liability eventually will stop some number of years after a product has been manufactured, sold, and very possibly worn out. Second, statutes of repose have a much greater *duration* than statutes of limitations, varying in length from state to state, from 5 or 6 years to as long as 10, 12, or even 20 years. The much longer periods within which a claim may be filed under statutes of repose reflect a deference to the discovery rule's objective of providing most persons injured by most defective products with an opportunity to assert their claims once they discover their injuries. While repose statutes bar some claims, sometimes even before they are discovered or otherwise accrue,[462] such claims normally are infrequent and the defective product quite old. Moreover, as time marches on after particular products are made and sold, one must weigh the decreasing hardships of barring plaintiffs from making possibly legitimate, but aging, claims against the increasing burdens on manufacturers and courts in responding to such claims long after the fact—a balance that at some point tips in favor of terminating claims after a reasonable, but arbitrary, period of time.[463] For this reason, absent affirmative fraudulent concealment,[464] repose statutes do not normally allow for the kind of equitable tolling applied to statutes of limitations.[465]

Choice of Law

Differences between statutes of limitations and repose may affect the choice of law.[466] Limitations and repose statutes often are contrasted on the ground that statutes

---

[461] In addition to their practical differences, statutes of limitations and repose often are contrasted conceptually on the ground that a limitations statute merely limits a plaintiff's right to seek a remedy for a defendant's breach of duty, whereas a repose statute limits the duty itself. That is, the former merely limits the time for bringing a claim after it has accrued, whereas the latter extinguishes the claim after a fixed period of time. See note 467, below.

[462] See, e.g., Camacho v. Ford Motor Co., 993 F.3d 308, 315 (5th Cir. 2021) (Tex. law) ("statutes of repose 'can cut off rights of action before they accrue.' "); Hutton v. Boeing Co., 2015 WL 6577418, at *9 (Ill. App. Ct. 2015) (12-year Illinois statute of repose barred claim before plaintiff was injured by falling overhead panel); Albrecht v. General Motors Corp., 648 N.W.2d 87, 94–95 (Iowa 2002) (15-year statute of repose barred claim before car accident involving minor plaintiff). See also Folta v. Ferro Eng'g, 43 N.E.3d 108, 116–17, 120 (Ill. 2015) (holding Workers' Occupational Diseases Act § 6(c) acted as statute of repose barring wrongful death action against employer filed 41 years after asbestos exposure; claims against third-party defendants not restricted by the Act).

[463] See Schwartz, New Products, Old Products, Evolving Law, Retroactive Law, 58 N.Y.U. L. Rev. 796, 842–51 (1983).

[464] See, e.g., Herbst v. Givaudan Flavors Corp., 341 F. Supp. 3d 1006, 1013 (N.D. Iowa 2018) (plaintiff's pleadings gave "rise to inferences of concealment [for] 'fraudulent concealment' exception to the statute of repose"); Stimpson v. Ford Motor Co., 988 So.2d 1119, 1120–21 (Fla. Dist. Ct. App. 2008).

[465] See, e.g., Camacho v. Ford Motor Co., 993 F.3d 308, 315 (5th Cir. 2021) (Tex. law) (statute of limitations minority tolling provision did not apply to statute of repose); In re Bldg. Materials Corp. of Am. Asphalt Roofing Shingle Prods. Liab. Litig., 2013 WL 1827740, at *3 (D.S.C. 2013) ("Generally, statutes of repose are not subject to tolling."); Budler v. General Motors Corp., 689 N.W.2d 847, 851 (Neb. 2004) (contrary to statute of limitations, plaintiff's minority does *not* toll statute of repose).

[466] See, e.g., Frumer, Friedman, and Sklaren, Products Liability ch. 25; Am. Law Prod. Liab. 3d ch. 46; R. Felix and R. Whitten, American Conflicts Law § 66 (6th ed. 2011).

of limitations are "procedural," because they merely limit a plaintiff's right to seek a remedy for a defendant's breach of duty, whereas statutes of repose are "substantive," because they limit the duty itself. Stated otherwise, this traditional view characterizes statutes of limitation as procedural because they merely limit the time for bringing claims after they have accrued, whereas statutes of repose are characterized as substantive because, after a fixed period of time, they extinguish claims altogether.[467] This procedural/substantive distinction is important in states that adhere to traditional conflict of laws principles and that lack an applicable borrowing statute. Traditionally, a forum state applied its own "procedural" statute of limitation even if another state's law governed the parties' substantive rights.[468] Over time, many state legislatures altered this traditional rule by enacting "borrowing statutes" which typically provide that the forum state's court will borrow the statute of limitations or repose of another state where the cause of action arose or accrued, or where the defendant resided or was domiciled.[469] Courts adhering to the traditional procedural/substantive distinction which lack an applicable borrowing statute are divided on several points: whether a statute of repose is procedural or substantive;[470] whether the traditional conflict of laws rule applies to its or another state's statutes of repose;[471] and whether the forum state is bound by the other state's characterization of its statute of repose.[472]

---

[467] See, e.g., Romero v. Toyota Motor Corp., 916 F. Supp. 2d 1301, 1313 n.12 (S.D. Fla. 2013); Daidone v. Buterick Bulkheading, 924 A.2d 1193, 1198 (N.J. 2007); Albrecht v. General Motors Corp., 648 N.W.2d 87, 91 (Iowa 2002) ("a statute of limitations affects only the remedy, not the right, whereas a statute of repose affects the right itself, extinguishing existing rights or preventing rights from arising"); Martin, A Statute of Repose for Product Liability Claims, 50 Fordham L. Rev. 745, 749 (1982).

[468] See, e.g., Sun Oil Co. v. Wortman, 486 U.S. 717 (1988) (because statutes of limitation are traditionally characterized as procedural, a state may apply its own statute of limitation to a claim governed by another state's law without violating due process or the Full Faith and Credit Clause).

[469] See, e.g., Giest v. Sequoia Ventures, Inc., 99 Cal. Rptr. 2d 476 (Ct. App. 2000) (California action barred by Montana's realty statute of repose under California borrowing statute). Compare Felix v. Novelis Corp., 2021 WL 2418006, at *3–4 (S.D. Tex. 2021) (2-year Texas statute of limitations barred Utah widow's claims in Texas even if they met Utah's limitations statute, since Texas borrowing statute requires nonresident plaintiffs to satisfy limitations statutes of both states); Annot., 41 A.L.R.4th 1025 (1985) (borrowing statutes). *But see* Kornfeind v. New Werner Holding Co., Inc., 241 A.3d 1212, 1225 (Pa. Super. Ct. 2020) (as a matter of first impression, Pennsylvania's borrowing statute did not apply to statutes of repose; "Pennsylvania views statutes of limitations as procedural laws that bar a party's right to a remedy, and statutes of repose as substantive laws that 'wholly extinguish a party's cause of action upon the expiration of the time period.' ").

[470] Compare Walls v. General Motors, Inc., 906 F.2d 143 (5th Cir. 1990) (Or. law) (repose statute is substantive), with Baxter v. Sturm, Ruger & Co., 32 F.3d 48 (2d Cir. 1994) (Conn. law) (repose statute is procedural). See also Moore v. Arvin Indus., 2011 WL 6413827, at *2 (Conn. Super. Ct. 2011) (whether statutes of repose are characterized as substantive or procedural "depends on the nature of the underlying right that forms the basis of the lawsuit").

[471] See, e.g., Thornton v. Cessna Aircraft Co., 886 F.2d 85 (4th Cir. 1989) (S.C. law) (under lex loci delicti rule of forum state, substantive law of place where accident occurred applied, including its statute of repose which barred tort claim; but warranty claim could proceed according to forum state law under UCC § 1–105 "appropriate relation" test).

[472] See, e.g., Etheredge v. Genie Indus., 632 So.2d 1324 (Ala. 1994) (North Carolina products liability statute of repose is procedural and thus inapplicable in Alabama lawsuit governed by North Carolina substantive law even though North Carolina characterizes its statute of repose as substantive); Walls v. General Motors, Inc., 906 F.2d 143 (5th Cir. 1990) (Miss. law) (Oregon products liability statute of repose is substantive, and thus applicable in Mississippi lawsuit governed by Oregon substantive law, because Mississippi is bound to apply Oregon's view that its statute of repose is substantive); Boudreau v. Baughman, 368 S.E.2d 849 (N.C. 1988) (Florida's 12-year products liability statute of repose, and not North Carolina's 6-year product liability statute of repose, applied because both statutes are substantive and the North Carolina lawsuit was governed by Florida's substantive law).

The sharp split characterizing statutes of limitations as procedural and statutes of repose as substantive has begun to blur,[473] and it is less important for choice of law purposes in jurisdictions that have adopted some form of the modern "most significant relationship" or "governmental interests" tests. Under this latter approach, courts generally apply the statute of limitations or repose of the state where the injury occurred unless the place of the injury is insignificant or another state has a greater interest in applying its time bars.[474] For breach of warranty claims, the *Uniform Commercial Code* contains a choice of law provision providing that the law of the forum "applies to transactions bearing an appropriate relation to this State."[475] This provision is generally construed as employing a standard similar to the "most significant relationship" test described above, with one significant difference: the focus is on the place of contracting or manufacture rather than the place of the injury.[476]

Types of Repose Statutes

There are two basic types of products liability statutes of repose, depending on how the statute defines the period of time before repose. The most common type of statute, "time-certain" statutes, define the time period with certainty as a particular number of years after the sale or purchase of the product. Another form of statute, called a "useful-life" statute, measures the time period variously, according to whatever a court or jury determines the particular product's useful, safe life to be. Presently, seventeen states[477]

---

[473] See, e.g., Cameron v. Olin Corp., 838 F. Supp. 2d 59, 63 (D. Conn. 2012) ("Under Connecticut law, statutes of limitation are generally considered procedural; however, in cases where the cause of action did not exist at common law and the foreign statute of limitation is 'so interwoven with . . . the cause of action as to become one of the congeries of elements necessary to establish the right,' the foreign statute of limitations is considered substantive and properly applies to the case."); Vicknair v. Phelps Dodge Indus., 794 N.W.2d 746, 751 (N.D. 2011) (under the Uniform Conflict of Laws—Limitations Act adopted by North Dakota, "limitations laws are treated as substantive rather than procedural, and ordinarily courts are to apply the statute of limitations of the state whose law governs the substantive issues in the case").

[474] See, e.g., McCarrell v. Hoffmann-La Roche, Inc., 153 A.3d 207 (N.J. 2017) (adopting Rest. (2d) Conflict of Laws § 142; New Jersey has a substantial interest in drug safety and no "exceptional circumstances" called for Alabama's shorter, 2-year statute); McCann v. Foster Wheeler LLC, 225 P.3d 516, 537 (Cal. 2010) (defendant's injury-producing conduct exposing plaintiff to asbestos in Oklahoma rendered that state's interest in enforcing its statute of repose greater than California's interest in enforcing its statute of limitations due to plaintiff residing there); Brewer v. Dodson Aviation, 447 F. Supp. 2d 1166 (W.D. Wash. 2006) (under "most significant relationship" choice-of-law test of forum state, Washington, separate statutes of repose of Ohio (10 years), North Carolina (6 years), and Kansas (10 years), applied to vacuum pump manufacturer, rebuilder, and installer, respectively, rather than that of Washington (12 years)); Tune v. Philip Morris Inc., 766 So.2d 350 (Fla. Dist. Ct. App. 2000) (Florida's 4-year statute of limitations, not New Jersey's 2-year statute of limitations, applied where injury occurred in Florida and New Jersey did not have more significant relationship); Gantes v. Kason Corp., 679 A.2d 106 (N.J. 1996) (Georgia's 10-year products liability repose statute did not apply even though injury occurred in Georgia because New Jersey's interest in deterring tortious conduct by its manufacturers outweighed Georgia's interest in enforcing its statute of repose).

[475] UCC § 1–105. See, e.g., Thornton v. Cessna Aircraft Co., 886 F.2d 85, 89–90 (4th Cir. 1989) (affirming application of S.C. law to warranty claim that had an "appropriate relationship" to that state).

[476] See, e.g., Terry v. Pullman Trailmobile, 376 S.E.2d 47 (N.C. Ct. App. 1989) (North Carolina's 6-year product liability statute of repose did not apply to tort claims brought in a North Carolina lawsuit governed by New York's substantive law but did apply to the breach of warranty claims because the sale and distribution of the product occurred in North Carolina).

[477] Alaska (10 years), Arizona (12 years), Colorado (7 years, new manufacturing equipment), Connecticut (10 years), Florida (12 years), Georgia (10 years, new personal property), Indiana (10 years), Iowa (15 years), Kentucky (5 years after first consumer sale, or 8 years after manufacture), Nebraska (10 years), North Carolina (12 years), North Dakota (10 years of purchase, or 11 years of manufacture), Ohio (10 years), Oregon (10 years), Rhode Island (10 years), Tennessee (shorter of 6 years from injury and 10 years from purchase), Texas (15 years), and Wisconsin (15 years). The statutes in Connecticut, Florida, and Tennessee have some combination of time-certain and useful-life statutes of repose.

have time-certain products liability statutes of repose in effect, and seven states[478] have some form of useful-life statute of repose.[479] The most fundamental issue regarding statutes of repose concerns their constitutionality, discussed below.

Time-certain statutes. The limitations periods of most products liability statutes of repose are absolute, and a plaintiff's rights to sue are terminated after a set period of time, ranging from 6 to 15 years, but most typically 10 years after the manufacturer first sold the product.[480] For example, Indiana's statute provides that "a product liability action must be commenced: . . . within ten (10) years after the delivery of the product to the initial user or consumer." This 10-year repose provision does not apply to asbestos claims, and it may be extended up to 2 years for claims accruing after 8 years.[481] Indiana's statute is atypical of the repose statutes in that most contain more qualifications. For instance, Colorado's 10-year statute establishes a rebuttable presumption that an older product was not defective;[482] Georgia's 10-year statute does not bar negligence claims resulting in "disease or birth defect, or arising out of conduct which manifests a willful, reckless, or wanton disregard for life or property," nor does it bar actions for breach of the post-sale duty to warn;[483] Iowa's 15-year statute does not apply to asbestos, tobacco, and other specified types of products;[484] Nebraska's 10-year statute does not apply to warranty actions subject to UCC § 2–725 nor does it apply to asbestos claims;[485] Oregon's 10-year statute is extended if the state in which a product was manufactured has a longer repose period, and asbestos and silicone breast implant claims are exempted;[486] Tennessee's 10-year statute applies if it is shorter than that state's useful-life statute and does not apply to minors, nor does it apply to claims from asbestos or silicone gel breast implants which have a 25-year period;[487] and Texas's 15-year statute applies only to the sale of manufacturing equipment that has not been warranted to last longer.[488] In addition, several statutes have exceptions for the

---

[478] Connecticut, Florida, Idaho, Kansas, Minnesota, Tennessee, and Washington.

[479] One might question the characterization of useful-life statutes as statutes of repose, but that is what they are. See Frumer, Friedman, and Sklaren, Products Liability § 26.05[3][a] (distinguishing time-certain statutes, which it calls "true" statutes of repose, from useful-life statutes). While the limitation period of useful-life statutes is uncertain, these statutes do indeed put an end to (and hence place in "repose") products liability claims at some point. The useful life of a flashlight battery, for example, might be 3 to 5 years. If acid from a flashlight battery leaks and causes injury after 20 years, a useful-life statute surely would preclude a claim for such an injury.

[480] See McGovern, The Variety, Policy and Constitutionality of Product Liability Statutes of Repose, 30 Am. U. L. Rev. 579 (1981); Frumer, Friedman, and Sklaren, Products Liability § 26.05; Annot., 30 A.L.R.5th 1 (1995).

[481] See Ind. Code Ann. § 34–20–3–1(b)(2). The Indiana Supreme Court has held that its repose statute's exception for certain asbestos claims is constitutional. See AlliedSignal, Inc. v. Ott, 785 N.E.2d 1068 (Ind. 2003).

[482] See Colo. Rev. Stat. Ann. § 13–21–403(3).

[483] See Ga. Code Ann. § 51–1–11(c).

[484] See Iowa Code Ann. § 614.1(2A).

[485] See Neb. Rev. Stat. § 25–224. The statute also provides for the application of the statute of repose of the state where a product was manufactured if that state's period of repose is at least 10 years. See Farber v. Lok-N-Logs, Inc., 701 N.W.2d 368, 374 (Neb. 2005).

[486] See Or. Rev. Stat. Ann. § 30.905 (products liability claims, general repose), Or. Rev. Stat. Ann. § 30.907 (asbestos disease claims), and Or. Rev. Stat. Ann. § 12.276 (silicone breast implant claims).

[487] See Tenn. Code Ann. § 29–28–103.

[488] See Tex. Civ. Prac. & Rem. Code Ann. § 16.012.

defendant's fraudulent conduct;[489] and other statutes specify applicable causes of action, defendants, and other circumstances to which they do or do not apply.[490] One noteworthy exception to repose statutes allowed by a few courts has been for a manufacturer's breach of its post-sale duty to warn.[491] The post-sale duty to warn exception rests on the reasonable hypothesis that the purpose of repose legislation is to provide a manufacturer with eventual relief from liability for any errors it may have made at the time it designed, made, and sold its products—not for the negligent failure to observe its safety obligations that arise thereafter.

Products liability statutes of repose are drafted quite differently from state to state, and courts have ruled on a large variety of interpretative issues. For example, courts have ruled that while the discovery rule does not normally apply to statutes of repose,[492] it may apply in cases involving latent diseases such as those caused by asbestos;[493] that a repose statute is not tolled for mental incompetency[494] or infancy;[495] that it may be tolled by a continuing breach of a duty to warn;[496] that it may bar a claim by a governmental plaintiff notwithstanding a contrary rule for statutes of limitations;[497] and that it does or does not apply in a host of other situations.[498]

---

[489] See, e.g., Colo. Rev. Stat. Ann. § 13–80–107(1)(c); Conn. Gen. Stat. Ann. § 52–577a(d); Idaho Code Ann. § 6–1403(2)(b)(2); Iowa Code Ann. § 614.1(2A)(a); Kan. Stat. Ann. § 60–3303(b)(2)(B), limited on preemption grounds, Troutman v. Curtis, 143 P.3d 74 (Kan. Ct. App. 2006).

[490] See, e.g., Dominguez v. Hayward Indus., Inc., 201 So.3d 100, 103 (Fla. Dist. Ct. App. 2015) (exception to 12-year statute of repose for improvements to real property did not apply to pool filter); Woodard v. Ford Motor Co., 2007 WL 1858542 (N.D. Ga. 2007) (jury question on applicability of repose statute exception for claims arising "out of conduct which manifests a willful, reckless, or wanton disregard for life or property"; repose provision also does not apply to "products which cause a disease or birth defect" (Ga. Code Ann. § 51–1–11(c))); Nelson v. Delta Int'l Mach. Corp., 2006 WL 1283896 (D. Minn. 2006) (Colo. law) (repose exception for injury from hidden defects); Masters v. Hesston Corp., 291 F.3d 985 (7th Cir. 2002) (Ill. law) (construing repose exception for products modified after originally made and sold; *held*: hay baler was not modified within meaning of exception). See generally Frumer, Friedman, and Sklaren, Products Liability § 26.05[3][b].

[491] See Sharp v. Case Corp., 595 N.W.2d 380, 385 (Wis. 1999); Hodder v. Goodyear Tire & Rubber Co., 426 N.W.2d 826 (Minn. 1988). See also Sherwood v. Danbury Hosp., 746 A.2d 730, 737–38 (Conn. 2000) (continuing duty to warn; plaintiff not warned that blood she received in transfusion had not been tested for HIV). See generally Kulbaski, Statutes of Repose and the Post-Sale Duty to Warn: Time for a New Interpretation, 32 Conn. L. Rev. 1027 (2000) (advocating that repose statutes be construed as containing exception for post-sale duty to warn).

[492] See, e.g., Neuser v. Carrier Corp., 2007 WL 484779, at *3 (W.D. Wis. 2007); Albrecht v. General Motors Corp., 648 N.W.2d 87, 91 (Iowa 2002).

[493] See Wilder v. Amatex Corp., 336 S.E.2d 66 (N.C. 1985). Some statutes specifically address the problem of latent disease. See, e.g., Tex. Civ. Prac. & Rem. Code Ann. § 16.012(d)(3) (excepting claims for disease manifested after 15-year period expires). See also In re Asbestos Litig., 2012 WL 1995930, at *1 (Del. Super. Ct. 2012) (finding the latent disease exception applies to the real property improvement statute of repose).

[494] See Simonsen v. Ford Motor Co., 102 P.3d 710 (Or. Ct. App. 2004); Penley v. Honda Motor Co., 31 S.W.3d 181 (Tenn. 2000) (plaintiff, on constant pain medication in hospital after accident, often did not know where she was).

[495] See Budler v. General Motors Corp., 689 N.W.2d 847, 851 (Neb. 2004) (contrary to statute of limitations, plaintiff's minority does *not* toll statute of repose); Albrecht v. General Motors Corp., 648 N.W.2d 87, 91 (Iowa 2002) (same).

[496] See Sherwood v. Danbury Hosp., 746 A.2d 730, 737–38 (Conn. 2000) (plaintiff not warned that blood she received in transfusion had not been tested for HIV).

[497] See Shasta View Irrigation Dist. v. Amoco Chem. Corp., 986 P.2d 536 (Or. 1999). *But see* People v. Asbestospray Corp., 616 N.E.2d 652 (Ill. App. Ct. 1993) (holding that *nullum tempus* doctrine exempts state from both statutes of limitation and repose); Mack, Nullum Tempus: Governmental Immunity to Statutes of Limitation, Laches, and Statutes of Repose, 73 Def. Couns. J. 180 (2006).

[498] See, e.g., Estabrook v. Mazak Corp., 140 N.E.3d 830, 836–37 (Ind. 2020) (Indiana statute of repose "cannot be extended by a manufacturer's post-delivery repair, refurbishment, or reconstruction of the disputed product"); Jones v. Bowie Indus., Inc., 282 P.3d 316, 338 (Alaska 2012) (products liability exception to Alaska's

Useful-life statutes. Following an approach recommended in the late 1970s by the Commerce Department's Interagency Task Force on Products Liability,[499] several states adopted some form of "useful-life" statute,[500] which is a weak form of statute of repose. Standing between rigid statutes of repose (that conclusively terminate liability after a set number of years from a product's sale) and open-ended statutes of limitations that (in view of the discovery rule) keep a manufacturer's responsibility open indefinitely, "useful-life" statutes cut off a manufacturer's liability conclusively after a period of time, but only after a product's "useful safe life" has expired. For this reason, useful-life statutes are viewed as something of a compromise,[501] but a compromise filled with interpretative land mines and subject to criticism for being ambiguous.[502]

First enacted in Minnesota,[503] useful-life statutes have also been adopted in a handful of other states.[504] Most of the statutes provide that, at the end of its period of safe life, a product is presumed nondefective. A typical useful-life statute is Washington's, which provides: "If the harm was caused more than twelve years after the time of delivery, a presumption arises that the harm was caused after the useful safe life had expired. This presumption may only be rebutted by a preponderance of the evidence."[505] Illustrative of other differences between such statutes, Connecticut's normal 10-year period is extended if a claimant proves that the harm occurred before the product's "useful safe life" has expired;[506] it does not apply at all to claims of fraud;[507] and it is extended to 80 years for asbestos claims.[508] Tennessee, which has a one-year statute of limitations,[509] blends into its repose statute a useful-life provision with a time-

general 10-year statute of repose applies to all theories of products liability, not just negligence); Jones v. Methodist Healthcare, 83 S.W.3d 739 (Tenn. Ct. App. 2001) (human blood is "product" within meaning of products liability statute of repose even though blood is otherwise exempted from strict liability claims).

[499] See Model Uniform Product Liability Act § 110(A) (1979), 44 Fed. Reg. 62,714, 62,733 (Oct. 31, 1979). The Model Act provided that a seller would not be subject to products liability if it proved that the harm occurred "after the product's useful safe life had expired," unless it had "expressly warranted the product for a longer period." The term " 'useful safe life' begins at the time of delivery of the product and extends for the time during which the product would normally be likely to perform or stored in a safe manner." Evidence on any particular product's "useful safe life" may include: (a) the amount of its wear and tear; (b) its deterioration; (c) the types and frequency of its use, repair, renewal, and replacement; (d) any representations, warnings, or instructions about its maintenance, storage, use, or expected life; and (e) whether it was modified or altered.

[500] See Cantu, The Useful Life Defense: Embracing the Idea that All Products Eventually Grow Old and Die, 80 Neb. L. Rev. 1 (2001); Note, The Evolution of Useful Life Statutes in the Products Liability Reform Effort, 1989 Duke L.J. 1689; Frumer, Friedman, and Sklaren, Products Liability § 26.05[4].

[501] See Frumer, Friedman, and Sklaren, Products Liability § 26.05[4][a].

[502] See Hodder v. Goodyear Tire & Rubber Co., 426 N.W.2d 826, 830 (Minn. 1988) ("ambiguous"; although jury found that useful life of corroded 26-year-old multi-piece rim for truck tire had expired, court held that statute placed no limits on duty to warn); Schwartz, New Products, Old Products, Evolving Law, Retroactive Law, 58 N.Y.U. L. Rev. 796, 848 (1983) (expressing some sympathy for concept, but criticizing such statutes as drafted for being "incoherent both theoretically and operationally").

[503] Minn. Stat. Ann. § 604.03. See Nelson v. Delta Int'l Mach. Corp., 2006 WL 1283896, at *5 (D. Minn. 2006).

[504] See Conn. Gen. Stat. Ann. § 52–577a (default rule for time-certain statute of repose); Idaho Code Ann. § 6–1403; Kan. Stat. Ann. § 60–3303 (rebuttably presuming that a product has exceeded its useful life 10 years after delivery); Tenn. Code Ann. § 29–28–103; Wash. Rev. Code. Ann. § 7.72.060(1)–(2), applied in Pardo v. Olson & Sons, Inc., 40 F.3d 1063 (9th Cir. 1994) (Wash. law) (summary judgment for manufacturer of 21-year-old dump truck reversed and remanded where plaintiff's expert's affidavit asserted useful safe life was 30 years, putting matter in contention).

[505] Wash. Rev. Code. Ann. § 7.72.060(2).

[506] Conn. Gen. Stat. Ann. § 52–577a(c).

[507] Conn. Gen. Stat. Ann. § 52–577a(d).

[508] Conn. Gen. Stat. Ann. § 52–577a(e).

[509] Tenn. Code Ann. § 28–3–104.

certain provision, terminating liability at the lesser of ten years or one year after the end of a product's anticipated life.[510] The statutes in two other states, Kentucky and Colorado, while not using the "useful-life" concept, borrow the approach of creating a presumption of nondefectiveness but apply the presumption after a set period of time.[511]

Realty Improvement Statutes

Many states have another, entirely different form of statute of repose that may bar products liability claims with respect to a narrow category of old products—those attached to realty. During the 1950s and early 1960s, most state legislatures enacted real property improvement statutes of repose in an effort to stem the tide of rising liability claims confronting architects, engineers, and contractors who designed and built buildings and other structures that could last for decades, if not centuries.[512] Like time-certain products liability statutes of repose, realty improvement statutes of repose begin to run, not on the accrual of a plaintiff's cause of action, but upon the occurrence of a designated event—usually the substantial completion of the improvement—without regard to when an injury occurs or is discovered. The length of time before repose varies in these statutes from as short as 5 years in Virginia, to as long as 20 years in Maryland, with a number of statutes at 6 years and the great majority at 10 years before the repose occurs.[513]

Although some realty improvement repose statutes expressly provide that they are applicable only to the building professions, not to products,[514] most of the statutes do not provide explicitly one way or the other, leaving their application to products liability defendants to the courts. On this issue the courts have split, some construing their statutes as *not* applying to products liability defendants,[515] others holding that their statutes *do* apply to products that are part of improvements to land.[516] Several courts employ a contextual approach, applying this type of statute of repose to manufacturers who also participate in some manner in installing or otherwise constructing a real estate improvement.[517]

---

[510] Tenn. Code Ann. § 29–28–103.

[511] Ky. Rev. Stat. Ann. § 411.310(1); Colo. Rev. Stat. Ann. § 13–21–403(3).

[512] See, e.g., McGovern, The Variety, Policy and Constitutionality of Product Liability Statutes of Repose, 30 Am. U. L. Rev. 579 (1981) Comment, 18 Cath. U. L. Rev. 361 (1969); Note, 57 N.D. L. Rev. 43 (1981); Frumer, Friedman, and Sklaren, Products Liability § 26.05[5].

[513] The statutes are summarized, and annotated, at Prod. Liab. Rep. (CCH) ¶ 3100. See also Annot., 5 A.L.R.6th 497 (2005).

[514] See, e.g., D.C. Code § 12–310(b)(3); Mo. Ann. Stat. § 516.097; Wash. Rev. Code Ann. § 4.16.300. Compare Va. Code Ann. § 8.01–250 (repose statute does not apply to manufacturers or suppliers of machinery or equipment installed in real property structures).

[515] Such statutes do *not* apply to products liability defendants: Ark., Cal., Mont., Nev., N.H., N.J., N.M., N.D., and Pa. See Frumer, Friedman, and Sklaren, Products Liability § 26.05[5][a].

[516] Such statutes *do* apply to products liability defendants: Fla., Iowa, La., Md., Mass., Minn., N.C., R.I., Tenn., and Utah. See, e.g., Stearns v. Metropolitan Life Ins. Co., 117 N.E.3d 694, 702 (Mass. 2019) (realty improvement statute of repose "completely eliminates all tort claims . . . after the established [6-year] time period has run, even if the cause of action arises from a disease with an extended latency period and even if a defendant had knowing control of the instrumentality of injury at the time of exposure"; answering certified question in negligence action alleging asbestos exposure from steam generators that caused decedent's mesothelioma). See Frumer, Friedman, and Sklaren, Products Liability § 26.05[5][b].

[517] Such statutes *may* apply to products liability actions if the defendant participates in design or construction of an improvement, as in Colo., Ill., Mich., Miss., Mo., Okla., Pa., and other states. See, e.g., Phaneuf Funeral Home v. Little Giant Pump Co., 48 A.3d 912, 919 (N.H. 2012) (statute protects designer of funeral home who custom-designed and installed defective water fountain in wall of renovated area; defect started fire after renovation); Biniek v. Exxon Mobil Corp., 818 A.2d 330 (N.J. Super. Ct. Law Div. 2002)

Perhaps the central issue litigated concerning realty improvement statutes of repose is whether a particular product qualifies as an "improvement" to real property, often defined in part in terms of a permanent addition to realty that enhances its value.[518] Courts have applied these statutes and barred liability after the expiration of the period of repose in cases involving such products as a wall fountain customized to install on a funeral home wall; precast concrete used in the structural framework of a garage; an outdoor incline conveyor; a glass vestibule attached to an airport terminal building; a mounting plate for an overhead garage door in a warehouse; a larry car for shuttling coal at a coke processing plant; a custom crane; a manufactured home; an ordinary house; a home furnace; an automatic garage door opener; an in-ground swimming pool; an above-ground swimming pool surrounded by an elaborate 3-tier deck; asbestos products; a concrete block curing machine; a 27-foot grain bin structure; gas transmission lines; a sorting conveyor at a farm; an escalator; a commercial roof membrane; windows supplied for residential development; and a glass door installed in a school.[519]

Among the many types of products held *not* to be protected under various realty improvement statutes of repose are asbestos insulation and asbestos fireproofing sold as standard, not custom, products; fiberglass insulation; a standardized (rather than custom) switch installed in an electrical supply system; a steel tube mill; a rubber calender machine; a grass-seed mixer; a machine for removing doors from coke-ovens at a coke steel plant; formaldehyde-generating plywood used as a component in a home; a diving platform; a boric acid evaporator system; a sand manufacturing system; and a mass-produced "Spin Around" playground amusement ride anchored to the ground.[520]

(statute does not protect manufacturer of mass-produced underground storage tanks). See also Noll v. Harrisburg Area YMCA, 643 A.2d 81, 86–87 (Pa. 1994). Cf. Meneely v. S.R. Smith, Inc., 5 P.3d 49 (Wash. Ct. App. 2000) (statute does not protect trade association that promulgated safety standards for swimming pool).

[518] As in Wisconsin and Michigan. See, e.g., Kohn v. Darlington Cmty. Sch., 698 N.W.2d 794, 805 (Wis. 2005) (bleachers were "improvement"); Dominguez v. Lanham Mach. Co., 122 F. Supp. 2d 852 (W.D. Mich. 2000) (oven was "improvement").

[519] See Phaneuf Funeral Home v. Little Giant Pump Co., 48 A.3d 912, 919 (N.H. 2012); Two Denver Highlands Ltd. v. Stanley Structures, Inc., 12 P.3d 819, 822 (Colo. App. 2000); Anderson v. M.W. Kellogg Co., 766 P.2d 637 (Colo. 1988); Enright v. City of Colo. Springs, 716 P.2d 148 (Colo. App. 1985); Garner v. Kinnear Mfg. Co., 37 F.3d 263 (7th Cir. 1994) (Ill. law); Herriott v. Allied Signal, Inc., 998 F.2d 487 (7th Cir. 1993) (Ill. law); Bilbow v. Kochs Crane, Inc., Prod. Liab. Rep. (CCH) ¶ 13,958 (E.D. Pa. 1994) (several hundred tons, several stories high, at marine terminal); Ball v. Harnischfeger Corp., 877 P.2d 45 (Okla. 1994) (customized overhead crane); Frankenmuth Mut. Ins. Co. v. Marlette Homes, Inc., 573 N.W.2d 611 (Mich. 1998); Daidone v. Buterick Bulkheading, 924 A.2d 1193, 1198 (N.J. 2007) (house built on pilings); Jaworsky v. Frolich, 850 P.2d 1052 (Okla. 1992); Dedmon v. Stewart-Warner Corp., 950 F.2d 244 (5th Cir. 1992) (Tex. law); Ablin v. Morton Sw. Co., 802 S.W.2d 788 (Tex. App. 1990); Jackson v. Coldspring Terrace Prop. Owners Ass'n, 939 S.W.2d 762 (Tex. App. 1997); Rose v. Fox Pool Corp., 643 A.2d 906 (Md. 1994); Fleck v. KDI Sylvan Pools, Inc., 981 F.2d 107 (3d Cir. 1992) (Pa. law); Tallman v. W.R. Grace & Co., 558 N.W.2d 208 (Iowa 1997); Pendzsu v. Beazer E., Inc., 557 N.W.2d 127 (Mich. Ct. App. 1997); Freeman v. Paco Corp., 2000 WL 709481 (E.D. Pa. 2000); Theunissen v. GSI Grp., 109 F. Supp. 2d 505 (N.D. Miss. 2000); S.C. Pipeline Corp. v. Lone Star Steel Co., 546 S.E.2d 654 (S.C. 2001) (13-year statute; natural gas pipeline lay peacefully before exploding 38 years after installation); MBA Enters., Inc. v. Northern Ill. Gas Co., 717 N.E.2d 849 (Ill. 1999) (10-year statute; explosion 33 years after installation); Cross v. Ainsworth Seed Co., 557 N.E.2d 906 (Ill. App. Ct. 1990); Homrighausen v. Westinghouse Elec. Corp., 832 F. Supp. 903 (E.D. Pa. 1993); Ferrell v. River City Roofing, Inc., 912 So.2d 448 (Miss. 2005); Sutton Place of Santa Clara Cty. Owners Ass'n v. Queen, 2020 WL 500172, at *13 (Cal. Ct. App. 2020), noncitable; Mahathy v. George L. Ingram & Assoc., 584 S.W.2d 521 (Tex. App. 1979).

[520] See Krueger v. A.P. Green Refractories Co., 669 N.E.2d 947 (Ill. App. Ct. 1996) (asbestos insulation); State Farm Mut. Auto. Ins. Co. v. W.R. Grace & Co., 24 F.3d 955 (7th Cir. 1994) (Ill. law) (asbestos fireproofing); Petro Stopping Ctrs., Inc. v. Owens-Corning Fiberglas Corp., 906 S.W.2d 618 (Tex. App. 1995) (fiberglass insulation); Garrison v. Gould, Inc., 36 F.3d 588 (7th Cir. 1994) (Ill. law) (electrical switch); Ritter v. Abbey-Etna Mach. Co., 483 N.W.2d 91 (Minn. Ct. App. 1992) (steel tube mill); McIntyre v. Farrell Corp., 97 F.3d 779

Federal Repose Statute for Private Airplanes—"GARA"

More than manufacturers of most other types of products, manufacturers of general aviation aircraft were especially hard hit by the rapid expansion of products liability law during the 1980s, a time when the industry was facing a number of other serious problems. Within about fifteen years, from the late 1970s to the early 1990s, the general aviation industry was "decimated."[521] Whereas some twenty-nine manufacturers of general aviation aircraft (led by Piper, Cessna, and Beech) had manufactured more than 14,000 light piston airplanes per year in the late 1970s, by 1993, the remaining nine manufacturers produced only about 500 small planes.[522] Congress finally responded, amending the Federal Aviation Act with the General Aviation Revitalization Act of 1994 (GARA).[523] GARA provides an 18-year statute of repose, from the date of first delivery,[524] for manufacturers of "general aviation aircraft and the components, systems, subassemblies, and other parts of such aircraft."[525] This federal statute[526] makes exception for (and hence does not bar) claims for fraud,[527] breach of express warranty, and claims brought by passengers being transported for medical emergencies or by persons injured or killed on the ground.[528]

(5th Cir. 1996) (Miss. law) (calender machine); Christ v. Prater Indus., 67 F. Supp. 2d 491 (E.D. Pa. 1999) (grass-seed mixer); Vargo v. Koppers Co., 715 A.2d 423 (Pa. 1998) (door machine); Ferricks v. Ryan Homes, Inc., 578 A.2d 441 (Pa. Super. Ct. 1990) (formaldehyde-generating plywood); Noll v. Harrisburg Area YMCA, 643 A.2d 81 (Pa. 1994) (diving platform); Puente v. Resources Conservation Co. Int'l, 428 P.3d 415, 422 (Wash. Ct. App. 2018) (boric acid evaporator); Potter v. BFK, Inc., 860 S.E.2d 703, 707–08 (Va. 2021) (sand manufacturing system); Schmoyer v. Mexico Forge, Inc., 645 A.2d 811 (Pa. 1994) ("Spin Around" ride).

[521] See Ewalt, Et Resurrexit: GARA and the Trio of Cases on Collateral Review, 46 Duq. L. Rev. 177 (2008); V. Schwartz and Lorber, The General Aviation Revitalization Act: How Rational Civil Justice Reform Revitalized an Industry, 67 J. Air L. & Com. 1269 (2002); McAllister, A "Tail" of Liability Reform: General Aviation Revitalization Act of 1994 & The General Aviation Industry in the United States, 23 Transp. L.J. 301, 304–07 (1995); Comment, 34 Transp. L.J. 43 (2007); Casenote, 68 J. Air L. & Com. 631 (2003) (noting case allowing immediate appeal of trial court's refusal to allow GARA defense).

[522] See McAllister, above, at 306.

[523] 49 U.S.C. § 40101 note [hereinafter GARA]. "Congress decided that the economic health of the general aviation aircraft manufacturing industry depended on lifting the requirement that manufacturers abide the possibility of litigation for the indefinite future when they sell an airplane." Lyon v. Agusta S.P.A., 252 F.3d 1078, 1089 (9th Cir. 2001).

[524] GARA § 2(a). See, e.g., United States Aviation Underwriters, Inc. v. Nabtesco Corp., 697 F.3d 1092, 1096, 1100–01 (9th Cir. 2012) (GARA trigger date began with delivery of nose landing gear actuator to first purchaser; later installation in different airplane "did not re-start the GARA clock because the actuator was used, not new"); Estate of Kennedy v. Bell Helicopter Textron, Inc., 283 F.3d 1107 (9th Cir. 2002) (GARA clock begins to run on date of first delivery of helicopter to Navy, not when helicopter later sold as military surplus and resold as general aviation aircraft).

[525] See GARA § 3(3). A "general aviation aircraft" is defined as a plane having less than 20 passenger seats and not engaged in scheduled passenger-carrying operations at the time of the accident. Id. § 2(c).

[526] By simply placing a federal repose on certain old products liability claims, GARA neither raises a substantial federal issue, establishes a federal cause of action, nor otherwise "arises under" federal law for purposes of federal question jurisdiction. See Wright v. Bond-Air, Ltd., 930 F. Supp. 300 (E.D. Mich. 1996).

[527] See, e.g., Butler v. Bell Helicopter Textron, Inc., 135 Cal. Rptr. 2d 762 (Ct. App. 2003) (manufacturer's failure to report tail rotor yoke failure in violation of FAA's reporting requirement triggered fraud exception to GARA). *But see* Quinn v. Continental Motors, Inc., 2020 WL 1333183, at *8 (D. Del. 2020) (plaintiffs' "conclusory allegation that Continental engaged in a 'pattern of concealment and misrepresentation'" were insufficient to trigger GARA's fraud exception); Tillman v. Raytheon Co., 430 S.W.3d 698 (Ark. 2013) (insufficient evidence of knowing misrepresentation to or concealment from FAA about flat-spin characteristics of Beech Baron causally related to crash when aircraft went into spin after engine failure); Burton v. Twin Commander Aircraft LLC, 254 P.3d 778, 792 (Wash. 2011) (same; rudder system); Robinson v. Hartzell Propeller, Inc., 454 F.3d 163 (3d Cir. 2006) (question of fact whether GARA fraud exception applied; propeller).

[528] See GARA § 2(b).

For each "new component, system, subassembly, or other part" installed in an existing aircraft,[529] GARA's 18-year repose period starts anew, a provision aptly referred to as the statute's "rolling" feature.[530] The clock thus starts ticking again for manufacturers of replacement parts,[531] including a successor of the company that actually made the part,[532] at the time the part is installed in an existing plane.[533] In an important decision, the Ninth Circuit Court of Appeals ruled that each aircraft's *flight manual* is a "part" of an aircraft falling within GARA's rolling provisions,[534] although other courts disagree.[535] The Ninth Circuit reasoned that the limitations clock for each *revision* of a flight manual, if causally responsible for an accident, starts ticking on the date of the revision.[536] But a manufacturer's failure to revise its manual,[537] or revising it on unrelated points, will not stop the clock ticking on other inadequacies in the original manual, whether misrepresentations or inadequate warnings or instructions.[538] Thus, a manufacturer's post-sale or continuing failure to warn does not begin the clock anew

---

[529] See, e.g., Quinn v. Avco Corp., 2022 WL 621610, at *3 (D. Del. 2022) (rebuilder of airplane's dual magneto 11 years before crash acted in the "capacity as a manufacturer" under GARA); Specter v. Texas Turbine Conversions, Inc., 519 F. Supp. 3d 576, 587 (D. Alaska 2021) ("The STOL Kit, and especially the engine conversion, were not simply 'replac[ing] a few parts' of the plane, but squarely 'new component[s] [or] system[s]' that would trigger the new limitations period, as contemplated by GARA."); Snider v. Sterling Airways, Inc., 758 Fed. Appx. 283, 286 (3d Cir. 2018) (replacement cylinder assembly, installed 6 years before crash).

[530] See H.R. 103–525(II), 103d Cong. (2d Sess. 1994), reprinted in 1994 U.S.C.C.A.N. 1644, 1647. GARA extends the limitation period "with respect to any new component, system, subassembly, or other part which replaced another component, system, subassembly, or other part originally in, or which was added to, the aircraft, and which is alleged to have caused such death, injury, or damage." GARA § 2(a)(2). See generally Pridgen v. Parker Hannifin Corp., 905 A.2d 422, 434–37 (Pa. 2006) (explaining GARA's rolling provision and holding it not applicable to manufacturer of original engine).

[531] But the clock starts anew only for the manufacturer of the defective component, not for the manufacturer of the aircraft into which it is installed, even if the latter's name is stamped on the replacement parts together with that of the actual manufacturer of the parts. Compare Campbell v. Parker-Hannifin Corp., 82 Cal. Rptr. 2d 202, 209 (Ct. App. 1999) (twin 1975 Cessna 310R crashed due to failure of both engine-driven vacuum pumps, causing loss of supply to air-driven gyroscopic flight instruments which thereupon provided erroneous altitude and directional data; although Cessna did not manufacture replacement parts, "Cessna" name was stamped on vacuum pumps, replaced in 1984, and on gyroscopic artificial horizon, replaced in 1994); Snider v. Sterling Airways, Inc., 758 Fed. Appx. 283, 286 (3d Cir. 2018) (sufficient evidence for jury to conclude that cylinder assembly manufacturer was the "manufacturer" of the allegedly defective third-party replacement exhaust valve guide; the replacement part was marked with the cylinder assembly manufacturer's part number and was designed by, built for, and tested by the cylinder manufacturer six years before the fatal crash).

[532] See Burroughs v. Precision Airmotive Corp., 93 Cal. Rptr. 2d 124, 132–34 (Ct. App. 2000). "The central objective of GARA would be materially undermined if its protection did not apply to a successor to the manufacturer who, as part of its ongoing business, acquired a product line long after the particular product had been discontinued and years after the statute of repose had run as to the original manufacturer."

[533] See GARA § 2(a)(2). But the clock is reset only for the replaced part, not for other parts of the particular system. See Hiser v. Bell Helicopter Textron Inc., 4 Cal. Rptr. 3d 249 (Ct. App. 2003).

[534] See Caldwell v. Enstrom Helicopter Corp., 230 F.3d 1155, 1156–58 (9th Cir. 2000).

[535] See Sulak v. America Eurocopter Corp., 2012 WL 6567237, at *5 (N.D. Tex. 2012) (maintenance manuals are not component parts subject to GARA rolling provision); Scott v. MD Helicopters, Inc., 834 F. Supp. 2d 1334, 1340 (M. D. Fla. 2011) (same).

[536] See *Caldwell*, 230 F.3d at 1157.

[537] See Tillman v. Raytheon Co., 430 S.W.3d 698, 707–09 (Ark. 2013) (failing to revise manual to warn about flat-spin issue does not invoke GARA's new part provision).

[538] See, e.g., Carolina Indus. Prods., Inc. v. Learjet, Inc., 189 F. Supp. 2d 1147 (D. Kan. 2001) (manufacturer's issuance of new maintenance manual sections did not restart repose period on owner's claims of failing to warn owners of a defect in landing gear, and of failing to instruct on proper repair, since owner failed to allege that landing accident was proximately caused by any information in manual); Caldwell v. Enstrom Helicopter Corp., 230 F.3d 1155 (9th Cir. 2000). Nor are placards, service bulletins, or revisions to maintenance manuals "parts" under GARA's rolling provision. See Lunn v. Hawker Beechcraft Corp., 417 P.3d 1206, 1211 (Okla. Ct. Civ. App. 2017).

because such an interpretation of GARA could keep the limitations clock ticking forever and so undermine the basic objective of the statute.[539]

Constitutionality of Repose Statutes

By imposing an absolute cut-off to products liability claims after a set period of time, time-certain statutes of repose sometimes extinguish claims before they can be discovered, and sometimes even before injuries occur and claims exist at all. For this reason, some courts[540] and commentators have denounced statutes of repose as fundamentally illogical and unfair, sometimes invoking Judge Jerome Frank's celebrated critique of statutes of limitations for generating such an "Alice in Wonderland" effect:[541]

> Except in topsy-turvy land you can't die before you are conceived, or be divorced before ever you marry, or harvest a crop never planted, or burn down a house never built, or miss a train running on a non-existent railroad. For substantially similar reasons, it has always heretofore been accepted, as a sort of legal "axiom," that a statute of limitations does not begin to run against a cause of action before that cause of action exists, *i.e.*, before a judicial remedy is available to the plaintiff.

So reasoning, several courts have struck down products liability statutes of repose for being unconstitutional,[542] sometimes as applied to particular types of products liability claims.[543] The typical constitutional objection is that repose statutes violate the due process or equal protection clauses of the federal or a state constitution, or that they abrogate the open courts or similar provision of a state constitution.[544] Nevertheless, a

---

[539] See Lyon v. Agusta S.P.A., 252 F.3d 1078, 1088 (9th Cir. 2001), where the court rejected plaintiffs' argument "that a failure to warn about a newly perceived problem also amounts to something like replacement of a component part because it breaches an alleged continuing duty to upgrade and update [which would gut GARA] because the plaintiff could always argue that an 18-year period commenced if the manufacturer did nothing at all, while simultaneously arguing that if the manufacturer did do something that, too, would start a new 18-year period running. . . . [A] failure to warn is decidedly not the same as replacing a component part with a new one." See also Burroughs v. Precision Airmotive Corp., 93 Cal. Rptr. 2d 124 (Ct. App. 2000) (limitations clock is not tolled by post-sale or continuing duty to warn).

[540] See, e.g., Heath v. Sears, Roebuck & Co., 464 A.2d 288, 295–96 (N.H. 1983) (Douglas, J.).

[541] See Dincher v. Marlin Firearms Co., 198 F.2d 821, 823 (2d Cir. 1952) (Conn. law) (dissent).

[542] In addition to the *Heath* case in New Hampshire, see, e.g., Hazine v. Montgomery Elevator Co., 861 P.2d 625 (Ariz. 1993). See also Dickie v. Farmers Union Oil Co., 611 N.W.2d 168 (N.D. 2000) (holding unconstitutional statute of repose reenacted in 1995 after it had previously been ruled unconstitutional).

Products liability statutes of repose have been repealed in at least Florida and South Dakota.

See generally Werber, The Constitutional Dimension of a National Products Liability Statute of Repose, 40 Vill. L. Rev. 985 (1995) (arguing that statutes of repose are unconstitutional); McGovern, The Variety, Policy and Constitutionality of Product Liability Statutes of Repose, 30 Am. U. L. Rev. 579 (1981); Frumer, Friedman, and Sklaren, Products Liability § 26.05[2]; Annot., 30 A.L.R.5th 1 (1995); Note, The Constitutionality of Statutes of Repose: Federalism Reigns, 38 Vand. L. Rev. 627 (1985).

[543] See, e.g., Jurich v. Garlock, Inc., 759 N.E.2d 1066, 1077 (Ind. Ct. App. 2001) (unconstitutional as applied to asbestos claim), adopted in part, vacated in part, 785 N.E.2d 1093 (Ind. 2003). But other courts have held that a repose statute's exception for certain asbestos claims is constitutional. See, e.g., AlliedSignal, Inc. v. Ott, 785 N.E.2d 1068 (Ind. 2003). Subsequently, in Myers v. Crouse-Hinds Div. of Cooper Indus., Inc., 53 N.E.3d 1160, 1167 (Ind. 2016), the Indiana Supreme Court declined to reconsider *AlliedSignal* but held that the repose statute exception applied to claims against persons who mined and sold commercial asbestos was unconstitutional under the equal privileges and immunities clause of the Indiana Constitution, invalidating Ind. Code Ann. § 34–20–3–2 under the non-severability clause.

[544] See, e.g., Kohn v. Darlington Cmty. Sch., 698 N.W.2d 794, 805 (Wis. 2005) (rejecting right-to-remedy and equal protection challenges); Branson v. O.F. Mossberg & Sons, Inc., 221 F.3d 1064, 1065 (8th Cir. 2000) (Iowa law) (rejecting challenges on all three grounds).

growing majority of decisions uphold products liability statutes of repose against a variety of these and other constitutional challenges.[545] Similarly, while some realty improvement statutes of repose have been held unconstitutional,[546] most have withstood constitutional scrutiny.[547] To date, GARA has proved immune to successful constitutional challenge.[548]

[545] See, e.g., Brown v. Exactech, Inc., 376 F. Supp. 3d 811, 820 (E.D. Tenn. 2019) (Tex. law) (15-year products liability statute of repose did not violate Texas Constitution's Open Courts provision or "the fundamental fairness principles inherent in the Texas and U.S. Constitutions"); Lunsford v. NCH Corp., 396 P.3d 288 (Or. Ct. App. 2017) (10-year statute of repose did not violate the Oregon Constitution's remedy clause or right to jury trial); Adams v. Air Liquide Am., L.P., 2014 WL 6680693, at *6 (Tenn. Ct. App. 2014) (10-year repose statute that excepted asbestos and silicone breast implant claims, but not silica claims, did not violate Equal Protection Clause or Tennessee Class Legislation Clause); Rabatin v. Allied Glove Corp., 24 A.3d 388, 395–96 (Pa. Super. Ct. 2011) (12-year real property improvement statute of repose did not violate Pennsylvania Constitution's "open courts" provision); Godbout v. WLB Holding, Inc., 997 A.2d 92, 95–96 (Me. 2010) (3-year statute of repose barring asbestos injury claim against dissolved corporation did not violate Maine Constitution's "open courts" provision); Gorch v. General Motors Corp., 883 N.E.2d 377 (Ohio 2008).

[546] See, e.g., Brennaman v. R.M.I. Co., 639 N.E.2d 425 (Ohio 1994) (violates open courts provision of state constitution); Perkins v. Northeastern Log Homes, 808 S.W.2d 809 (Ky. 1991) (statute arbitrary and violates open courts guarantee and limits on legislative power provisions).

[547] See, e.g., Donnelly v. Anthony & Sylvan Pools Corp., 432 P.3d 741 (Nev. 2018) (table) (real property statute of repose amended after pool accident but prior to plaintiff's filing violated neither the plaintiff's access to courts nor the Equal Protection clauses of the United States or Nevada constitutions); Baugher v. Beaver Constr. Corp., 791 So.2d 932 (Ala. 2000); Craftsman Builder's Supply, Inc. v. Butler Mfg. Co., 974 P.2d 1194 (Utah 1999).

[548] See, e.g., Lyon v. Agusta S.P.A., 252 F.3d 1078, 1085–88 (9th Cir. 2001) (although GARA was not passed until after accident, it violated neither due process nor equal protection).

Part V

SPECIAL DEFENDANTS, TRANSACTIONS, AND PRODUCTS

Chapter 15

SPECIAL DEFENDANTS

Table of Sections

§ 15.1 SPECIAL DEFENDANTS—GENERALLY

In most products liability cases, the only or principal defendant is the manufacturer that designed, manufactured, and marketed the product that injured the plaintiff. For this reason, most cases and most discussion in this book concern the responsibility of manufacturing enterprises. Yet parties in the product distribution chain other than manufacturer-assemblers, notably retail sellers, often profit from moving products from factories to consumers and so may bear some responsibility when product hazards injure users and consumers. While a defendant's role in the chain of distribution often has no bearing on what liability theories may be available to persons injured by defective products, a number of variations in policy and doctrine do arise in products liability litigation when the defendant is not the primary manufacturer of the accident product.

The types of defendants considered in this chapter display a diversity of size, function, and methods of doing business. Retailers, for example, vary in size from small corner stores to major and even multi-national enterprises like Walmart and McDonald's; in function, from serving as conduits for products made by others to imposing on upstream suppliers their own design specifications and quality control programs; and, in range of services, from sale alone to sale plus substantial services.[1] The most significant new type of retailers are internet providers, like Amazon, who sell their own products on their websites and, further, make their websites available to other companies to list and sell third-party products as well. Wholesalers and distributors exhibit a variety of diversities.[2] Other defendants examined in this chapter include suppliers of raw materials and component parts, enterprises that ordinarily have no control over how their products will be put to use;[3] parent and apparent manufacturers, who may benefit from products sold by a subsidiary corporation or trademark licensee;[4] successor corporations, who benefit from the durable assets and goodwill of predecessor

---

1 See § 15.2, below.

2 See id.

3 See § 15.3, below.

4 See § 15.4, below.

enterprises that may have manufactured and sold defective products;[5] employers, who sometimes design and manufacture products for their own internal use, such as solvents, tools, and machinery that may injure their employees if dangerously defective;[6] and a miscellany of other types of non-manufacturing defendants.[7]

Sometimes the varying roles of special defendants call for liability principles differing from those applicable to principal manufacturer-assemblers, but often liability rules remain the same. The most recurring issue in all such cases is the applicability of the doctrine of strict liability in tort. Yet negligence, breach of warranty, tortious misrepresentation, and other theories of liability[8] can also be important claims in cases brought against the types of defendants examined in this chapter.

Manufacturers, retailers, and other providers of certain special types of products—such as used products, electricity, computer games, blood, automotive vehicles, and pharmaceuticals—are subject to various special rules of liability and defense, developed in a particular fashion to best fit their distinct contexts. Principles applicable to sellers of these and other special products are addressed separately in chapters 16, 17, and 18, below.

The discussion in this chapter focuses on special defendants who deal in more traditional types of products, durable and chemical, which have been the subject of the great bulk of products liability law developed over the years. The normal chain of distribution of such products begins with suppliers of raw materials, includes manufacturers of component parts, then moves to the principal manufacturer-assembler, sometimes to a wholesaler or other distributor, almost always to a retailer, and finally moves to the consuming purchaser and user. After manufacturers, retailers are the most common defendants in products liability actions, and so their liability (together with that of internet providers, wholesalers, and other distributors) is examined first.

§ 15.2 RETAILERS, INTERNET PROVIDERS, AND OTHER DISTRIBUTORS

Retail dealers and other non-manufacturing sellers of ordinary types of products are subject to liability for negligence,[9] tortious misrepresentation,[10] breach of warranty,[11] and, in most states, strict liability in tort.[12] In general, the elements of these basic products liability claims are the same whether the defendant is a manufacturer, a retailer, a wholesale distributor, or some other party in the chain of distribution. Thus, the first step in understanding the legal responsibility of a retailer, wholesaler, or other distributor of an ordinary product[13] is to examine the underlying liability principles applicable to the particular type of claim.

---

[5] See § 15.5, below.

[6] See § 15.6, below.

[7] See § 15.7, below.

[8] Such as negligent entrustment, in the case of retail dealers. See § 15.2, below.

[9] See ch. 2, above.

[10] See ch. 3, above.

[11] See ch. 4, above.

[12] See ch. 5, above.

[13] The liability of pharmacists arising out of their dispensing of prescription drugs is addressed in § 18.4, below.

Retailers—Negligence in General

Like other product suppliers, retail sellers for centuries have had a duty to exercise reasonable care, in supplying products, not to injure their customers or others.[14] Unlike manufacturers, however, who typically design, manufacture, label, package, and advertise their products, most retailers ordinarily have little or no knowledge of, or control over, whether products they sell may be dangerously defective. Also, unlike manufacturers, retailers usually have no practical way to test products to discover hidden dangers. As a result, they ordinarily have no reason to know about latent dangers and, hence, no reason to warn consumers about them. In short, a "seller who reasonably believes that the chattel he is selling is safe for use is not, in selling and delivering the chattel, doing anything which is foreseeably likely to cause harm."[15] Thus, most jurisdictions hold as a general rule that a retailer who has no reason to know that a product may be dangerous has no duty to test or inspect it before sale.[16] Many of the cases, particularly the older ones, express this rule in terms of the absence of a duty on the retail dealer to test or inspect its products for latent defects.[17] Nor, of course, does a retailer have a duty to warn consumers of hidden dangers of which it has no reason to know,[18] nor dangers that are as obvious to the consumer as to the retailer.[19] Put simply, in the absence of some reason to believe that a product may be dangerously defective, a retailer normally is not negligent in merely passing it along to a consumer.[20]

---

[14] See, e.g., Garvey v. A.I. Namm, 121 N.Y.S. 442 (App. Div. 1910) (4–1 decision) (retailer had duty to exercise "ordinary care" to find basting needle in flannel wrappers before delivery to customer). See generally Annot., 6 A.L.R.3d 12 (1966).

[15] Rest. (2d) Torts § 402 cmt. *d*.

[16] See, e.g., Lacour v. AmeriGas Propane, L.P., 2020 WL 7135794, at *3 (W.D. La. 2020) ("a non-manufacturing seller of a product is not presumed to have knowledge of a product's vices, and it is not required to inspect the product it sells prior to sale to determine the possibility of any inherent vices or defects in the product"); Johnson v. Serv. Tool Co., LLC, 2015 WL 7760480, at *5 (E.D. Mich. 2015) (seller has no duty to inspect unless it has reason to know it is defective or defect is readily ascertainable); Lind v. Beaman Dodge, Inc., 356 S.W.3d 889, 898 n.10 (Tenn. 2011) (stating the "general no-duty to inspect, test, or warn rule"); Krumpek v. Millfeld Trading Co., 709 N.Y.S.2d 265, 267 (App. Div. 2000) (vendor who buys products from reputable source may reasonably believe they are free from defects). *But see* Moore v. BPS Direct, LLC, 2019 WL 2931463, at *7 (D.S.C. 2019) (Ill. law) ("a seller has a duty to discover defects causing a product to become dangerous that can be discovered by reasonable inspection").

Rest. (2d) Torts § 402, entitled "Absence of Duty to Inspect Chattel," provides that a non-manufacturing seller "who neither knows nor has reason to know that it is, or is likely to be, dangerous, is not liable in an action for negligence for harm caused by the dangerous character or condition of the chattel because of his failure to discover the danger by an inspection or test of the chattel before selling it."

[17] See, e.g., Pan v. Sumitomo Rubber Indus., Ltd., 2018 WL 3055773, at *5 (S.D. Tex. 2018) (sellers have no duty to test or inspect products manufactured by others for latent defects); Wilcher v. Redding Swainsboro Ford Lincoln Mercury, Inc., 743 S.E.2d 27, 30 (Ga. Ct. App. 2013) (same; auto dealers); Topliff v. Wal-Mart Stores E. LP, 2007 WL 911891, at *44 (N.D.N.Y. 2007) (same; retailer not liable for failing to test or inspect flammable polyester jogging suit that injured child); Levis v. Zapolitz, 178 A.2d 44 (N.J. Super. Ct. App. Div. 1962) (weak arm of plastic slingshot that broke). See generally Annot., 6 A.L.R.3d 12 (1966).

[18] See, e.g., Gomez v. Harbor Freight Tools USA, Inc., 2018 WL 3430685, at *5 (M.D. Ga. 2018) ("Georgia law imposes a duty on a seller to warn only of dangers actually or constructively known *at the time of the sale*"; no post-sale duty to warn) (emphasis in original); Beers v. One World Techs., Inc., 769 F. Supp. 2d 15, 16 (D. Mass. 2011) (table saw designed without SawStop "flesh-detection technology"; "a retailer cannot be held liable for negligence for latent defects in a manufactured product of which it has no notice").

[19] See, e.g., Bren-Tex Tractor Co. v. Massey-Ferguson, Inc., 97 S.W.3d 155 (Tex. App. 2002) (no duty on retailer to warn customer of risk of tractor without a rollover protection system); Zamora v. Mobil Corp., 704 P.2d 584 (Wash. 1985) (distributor). See generally § 10.2, above.

[20] See, e.g., In re: Zantac (Ranitidine) Prods. Liab. Litig., 2021 WL 2685605, at *10 (S.D. Fla. 2021) (dismissing MDL plaintiffs' negligence claims against retailers and distributors that used common carriers to deliver Zantac to customers; claims "simply insufficient to 'nudge [them] from conceivable to plausible' ");

Courts long have held that this no-duty rule applies when a retailer serves merely as a conduit of a product that arrives at the retailer in a pre-packaged condition, like a can of tuna,[21] a toaster in a sealed box, a bottle of Coke,[22] a honeybun sold in a sealed cellophane package,[23] a jar of cold cream,[24] or some other product in a sealed container.[25] In such cases, consumers understand that the retailer has no way to inspect or test the product so that the only party who may be relied upon for quality of the goods is the manufacturer.[26] Some states shield retail sellers and other distributors from negligence liability for selling goods in their original, sealed containers or packages, which variously is known as the "sealed-container" or "original-package" doctrine or defense.[27]

But the general no-duty to inspect, test, or warn rule has exceptions in situations where the retail seller knows,[28] or has reason to know,[29] of a danger, in which case the seller has a duty of reasonable care to test, inspect, or warn. For example, if a retailer knows or should know that a space heater can dangerously overheat if it is used in a poorly insulated house trailer, the retailer has a duty to give warning of this fact if it learns that a purchaser intends to use it for this purpose.[30] Moreover, if a retail seller acts affirmatively to prepare, install, repair, test, or inspect a product, it no longer acts merely as a conduit, and it will have a duty to exercise reasonable care in its actions.[31] Thus, a retail tractor seller is liable in negligence for injuries caused by its failure to

---

Hester v. Human, 439 S.E.2d 50, 53 (Ga. Ct. App. 1993) (retailer not negligent since it was entitled to assume that products it bought and resold were not defective).

21 See Porrazzo v. Bumble Bee Foods, LLC, 822 F. Supp. 2d 406, 422 (S.D.N.Y. 2011) (dismissing breach of implied warranty claim against retail grocer for mercury poisoning from canned tuna that had no warning of hazard). On the doctrine's application to food and drink cases, see § 7.5, note 266, above.

22 See, e.g., Coca-Cola Bottling Co. v. Swilling, 57 S.W.2d 1029 (Ark. 1933) (bottle contained partially-decomposed centipede).

23 See Sirmons v. Derst Baking Co., 470 S.E.2d 515 (Ga. Ct. App. 1996) (plaintiff bit into honeybun containing dime; since store owner held not liable, no discussion of whether plaintiff's damage recovery would have been reduced by the 10¢ she received in bun).

24 See Bel v. Adler, 11 S.E.2d 495 (Ga. Ct. App. 1940).

25 See, e.g., Alexander v. Sports Auth., Inc., 2007 WL 1745328, at *8 (D. Md. 2007) (sealed-container defense more broadly includes unpackaged products a retailer sells in "unaltered form"); Federal Ins. Co. v. Farmer's Supply Store, 555 S.E.2d 238, 240 (Ga. Ct. App. 2001); Jones v. GMRI, Inc., 551 S.E.2d 867 (N.C. Ct. App. 2001) (plaintiff broke tooth when she bit into meatball; restaurant protected by sealed-container statute); Annot., 6 A.L.R.3d 12, § 4 (1966). *But see* Sparks v. Total Body Essential Nutrition, Inc., 27 So.3d 489, 496 (Ala. 2009) (5–4 decision) (sealed container doctrine does not protect retailer against warranty claims).

26 See, e.g., Jones v. GMRI, Inc., 551 S.E.2d 867 (N.C. Ct. App. 2001); Pierce v. Liberty Furniture Co., 233 S.E.2d 33 (Ga. Ct. App. 1977); Ross v. Spiegel, Inc., 373 N.E.2d 1288 (Ohio Ct. App. 1977).

27 See, e.g., Leonard v. Bed, Bath & Beyond, Inc., 2016 WL 1064515, at *2 (E.D.N.C. 2016) (question of fact whether sealed container defense applied to seller of gel fuel ingredient); Alexander v. Sports Auth., Inc., 2007 WL 1745328, at *8 (D. Md. 2007) (defense covers any product in any container, wrapping, housing of any nature that covers it and unpackaged products a retailer sells in "unaltered form"; to protect retailers and distributors who could not reasonably discover defects); Annot., 6 A.L.R.3d 12, § 4 (1966).

28 See, e.g., Edwards v. Hop Sin, Inc., 140 S.W.3d 13 (Ky. Ct. App. 2003) (restaurant owner failed to pass along manufacturer's warning of risk of eating raw oysters). See Rest. (2d) Torts § 399. See also Rest. (2d) Torts §§ 388–90 and 401.

29 See, e.g., Gentry v. Hershey Co., 687 F. Supp. 2d 711, 718, 721 (M.D. Tenn. 2010) (sealed-container doctrine protected distributor of peppermint patties, but question of fact whether retail seller who opened corrugated box for display had reasonable opportunity to inspect for larvae infestation); Arslanian v. Volkswagen of Am., Inc., 493 N.Y.S.2d 588 (App. Div. 1985) (brake system with defect that could be visually detected). See also Rest. (2d) Torts § 401 (liability of seller who knows chattel is or is likely to be dangerous).

30 See Frey v. Montgomery Ward & Co., 258 N.W.2d 782 (Minn. 1977).

31 See, e.g., Coulon v. Wal-Mart Stores, Inc., 734 So.2d 916 (La. Ct. App. 1999) (Wal-Mart considered manufacturer under products liability act because its employees or its independent contractor assembled bike); Annot., 6 A.L.R.3d 12, § 8 (1966).

tighten the grab handle it loosens prior to touching up the paint job on a tractor and by its failure to inspect the job after the painting is complete.[32] So, too, some courts find an exception to the no-duty rule for retail sellers of *used* goods, especially automobiles, holding that such sellers have a duty of reasonable care to test or inspect,[33] while other courts apply the normal retailer negligence rules to dealers in used products.[34]

Retailers—Negligent Entrustment

Retailers may be subject to liability for selling dangerous products to children, or other persons likely to use them dangerously, under the theory of negligent entrustment.[35] This doctrine is expressed in § 390 of *Restatement (Second) of Torts*, entitled "Chattel for Use by Person Known to be Incompetent": "One who supplies . . . a chattel for the use of another whom the supplier . . . has reason to know to be likely because of his youth, inexperience, or otherwise, to use it in a manner involving unreasonable risk of physical harm to himself and others . . . is subject to liability for physical harm resulting to them."

So, if a retail dealer sells a gun,[36] fireworks,[37] or a jet ski to a young child, an intoxicated person, or a mental incompetent; an automobile to a person known to be an unlicensed driver[38] or perhaps to an habitual drunkard; or gasoline to a very young child[39] or a clearly intoxicated driver,[40] the seller may possibly be subject to liability for

---

[32] See Schweich v. Ziegler, Inc., 463 N.W.2d 722 (Minn. 1990).

[33] See, e.g., Crothers v. Cohen, 384 N.W.2d 562 (Minn. Ct. App. 1986) (duty to discover latent defects); Realmuto v. Straub Motors, Inc., 322 A.2d 440 (N.J. 1974); Thrash v. U-Drive-It Co., 110 N.E.2d 419 (Ohio 1953). See generally Annot., 6 A.L.R.3d 12, § 4 (1966).

[34] On the duties of sellers of used products, see § 16.5, below.

[35] See Woods, Negligent Entrustment: Evaluation of a Frequently Overlooked Source of Additional Liability, 20 Ark. L. Rev. 101 (1966); Note, 1988 Duke L.J. 755.

[36] See Shirley v. Glass, 308 P.3d 1 (Kan. 2013) (upholding negligent entrustment ruling against pawn shop for selling 12-gauge shotgun to straw man, knowing that gun was intended for known felon, who used gun to murder victim); Smith v. Atlantic Gun & Tackle, Inc., 376 F. Supp. 2d 291, 293 (E.D.N.Y. 2005) (Weinstein, J.) ("a knowing straw sale by the retailer supports a finding of its liability for a killing using a gun it sold wielded by the purchaser or another"); Ireland v. Jefferson Cnty. Sheriff's Dep't, 193 F. Supp. 2d 1201, 1229 (D. Colo. 2002) (plaintiff injured in shooting spree at Columbine High School sued retailers who sold shotgun to minors through "straw man purchase"; intervening criminal acts of minors does not absolve defendant if third-party's conduct is reasonably foreseeable); Salvi v. Montgomery Ward & Co., 489 N.E.2d 394 (Ill. App. Ct. 1986) (retailer sold air gun to 14-year-old who accidentally shot younger brother in eye while cleaning gun).

The 2005 Protection of Lawful Commerce in Arms Act (PLCAA) that bars litigation against manufacturers for injuries arising out of the "criminal or unlawful misuse" of firearms or ammunition provides an exception for negligent entrustment claims. 15 U.S.C. § 7903(5)(A) and (B). See, e.g., Delana v. CED Sales, Inc., 486 S.W.3d 316, 324–26 (Mo. 2016) (en banc) (plaintiff's negligent entrustment claim allowed). Compare Soto v. Bushmaster Firearms Int'l, LLC, 202 A.3d 262, 282 (Conn. 2019) (rejecting view that mere foreseeability that entrustee might give gun to dangerous person would give rise to negligent entrustment PLCAA exception). On liability for gun sales, see § 10.3, above.

[37] See, e.g., Schmidt v. Capital Candy Co., 166 N.W. 502, 503 (Minn. 1918) (dictum).

[38] See, e.g., Beasley v. Best Car Buys, 363 P.3d 777, 779–83 (Colo. App. 2015) (reviewing cases).

[39] Jones v. Robbins, 289 So.2d 104 (La. 1974) (service station subject to liability to young child burned when she threw match into gasoline sold by defendant to another 6-year-old child). *But see* Daniels v. Dauphine, 557 So.2d 1062 (La. Ct. App. 1990) (not negligent to sell gasoline to 12-year-old boy to use to destroy ant hill, causing injury to younger child).

[40] See, e.g., Morris v. Giant Four Corners, Inc., 498 P.3d 238 (N.M. 2021) (after buying gas from defendant gas station, inebriated driver struck and killed driver of another vehicle); West v. East Tenn. Pioneer Oil Co., 172 S.W.3d 545, 553–56 (Tenn. 2005) (after refusing to sell beer to obviously intoxicated driver, convenience store sold driver gas and helped him pump it); O'Toole v. Carlsbad Shell Serv. Station, 247 Cal. Rptr. 663 (Ct. App. 1988) (after buying gas from defendant gas station, inebriated driver struck motorcycle, killing driver and passenger).

negligently supplying a chattel to a person likely to use it in an unreasonably dangerous manner. For example, in *Moning v. Alfono*[41] a retail merchant sold a slingshot to an 11-year-old boy who shot a pellet that ricocheted off a tree into his friend's eye. In a negligent entrustment action against the retailer, wholesaler, and manufacturer of a slingshot for marketing it directly to children, the Michigan Supreme Court held that a jury could find that such a sale created an unreasonable risk of harm to the injured boy.[42]

But neither *Moning*, decided in 1977 by a split court, nor the more general doctrine of negligent entrustment has been widely applied by the courts to hold retailers liable for harm caused by a " 'defective' customer,"[43] and some courts and commentators are wary of extending the negligent entrustment doctrine into the realm of product sales.[44] While courts in California[45] and a few other jurisdictions[46] have applied the negligent entrustment doctrine to retailers in certain limited situations, most courts have refused to apply, much less expand, the doctrine to the sale of products.[47] While the basic idea of allowing claims against retailers for negligent entrustment is theoretically sound, most courts, troubled by the implications of broadly allowing such claims, have held that it is not negligent for retailers simply to sell children bows and arrows,[48] CO_2 cartridges,[49]

---

41 254 N.W.2d 759 (Mich. 1977).

42 "Entrusting potentially dangerous articles to a child may pose an unreasonable risk of harm not only because the child may not appreciate the risk or may not have the skill to use the article safely but even if he does appreciate the risk and does have the requisite skill because he may recklessly ignore the risk and use the article frivolously due to immaturity of judgment, exuberance of spirit, or sheer bravado." Id. at 769. The court allowed the negligent entrustment claim against each member of the marketing chain, including the retailer, wholesaler, and manufacturer.

43 Vic Potamkin Chevrolet, Inc. v. Horne, 505 So.2d 560, 562 (Fla. Dist. Ct. App. 1987) (en banc), aff'd, 533 So.2d 261 (Fla. 1988). See Note, 1988 Duke L.J. 755, 776–79 (discussing case).

44 See, e.g., Noble v. Shawnee Gun Shop, Inc., 409 S.W.3d 476, 482 (Mo. Ct. App. 2013) (chattel sellers not subject to liability for negligent entrustment; gun store sold firearm magazines to murderer with stolen credit card—excellent policy analysis); Comment, 46 U. Cin. L. Rev. 1047, 1054 (1977) (criticizing *Moning*, arguing that the case would "have a devastating effect on the merchandisers of inexpensive toys and games. In effect, the court has banned the marketing of any such products that have even a slight propensity to cause physical injury."); Note, The Negligent Commercial Transaction Tort: Imposing Common Law Liability on Merchants for Sales and Leases to "Defective" Customers, 1988 Duke L.J. 755 (arguing against applying negligent entrustment doctrine to commercial transactions).

45 See, e.g., O'Toole v. Carlsbad Shell Serv. Station, 247 Cal. Rptr. 663 (Ct. App. 1988) (sale of gasoline to clearly inebriated driver); Dillon v. Suburban Motors, Inc., 212 Cal. Rptr. 360 (Ct. App. 1985) (unlicensed driver), dismissed as moot, 705 P.2d 1260 (Cal. 1985); Roland v. Golden Bay Chevrolet, 207 Cal. Rptr. 413 (Ct. App. 1984) (same), dismissed as moot, 704 P.2d 175 (Cal. 1985).

46 See, e.g., Morris v. Giant Four Corners, Inc., 498 P.3d 238, 253 (N.M. 2021) (under negligent entrustment doctrine, gasoline vendor owes to a third party using the roadway a duty of care to refrain from selling gasoline to a driver the vendor knows or has reason to know is intoxicated"; answering certified question from 10th Circuit); Barsness v. General Diesel & Equip. Co., 383 N.W.2d 840, 845–46 (N.D. 1986) (construction company hired inexperienced supervisor to oversee crane operations at construction site); Tosh v. Scott, 472 N.E.2d 591 (Ill. App. Ct. 1984) (suit against father for selling car to son); Killeen v. Harmon Grain Prods., Inc., 413 N.E.2d 767 (Mass. App. Ct. 1980) (jury might find retailer negligent for selling cinnamon flavored toothpicks to 10-year-old girl who fell, face down, while sucking on one while playing).

47 See, e.g., Noble v. Shawnee Gun Shop, Inc., 409 S.W.3d 476, 482 (Mo. Ct. App. 2013); Estate of Pemberton v. John's Sports Ctr., Inc., 135 P.3d 174, 188 (Kan. Ct. App. 2006) (sale of shotgun to mentally-ill young man who used it to commit suicide; Kansas has never applied the doctrine to chattel sales and noting that "other courts appear reluctant to extend" the doctrine to sales transactions).

48 See Morris v. Toy Box, 22 Cal. Rptr. 572 (Ct. App. 1962) (dismissing failure to warn claim against retailer).

49 See Warren v. K-Mart Corp., 765 So.2d 235 (Fla. Dist. Ct. App. 2000) (used in pellet gun).

ordinary darts,[50] lawn darts,[51] or (contrary to *Moning*) slingshots.[52] While the sale of a potentially dangerous implement such as a slingshot to a child who is very young, or a shotgun to a child under suspicious circumstances,[53] might fairly give rise to a negligent entrustment claim, both courts[54] and commentators[55] have emphasized that such claims will not lie unless the seller has reason to believe that the particular purchaser is likely to misuse the product dangerously.

Most courts today seem inclined toward the no-duty approach of *Vic Potamkin Chevrolet, Inc. v. Horne*,[56] which refused to apply the negligent entrustment doctrine to a claim arising out of a dealer's sale of a car to a clearly incompetent driver—for fear of creating a slippery slope of commercial uncertainty over when and how retailers might have to investigate the fitness of their customers.[57] Yet, while the slippery-slope problem is very real, courts may choose to leave their doors slightly ajar for negligent entrustment claims in extraordinary cases where retailers sell particularly dangerous products to persons whose incompetence or irresponsibility is clear and the unreasonable danger is manifest.

Retailers—Tortious Misrepresentation

A retail dealer is subject to liability for tortious misrepresentation, including fraud, negligence, and possibly strict liability in tort for misrepresentation. Thus, the tortious

---

[50] See Stanford v. Wal-Mart Stores, Inc., 600 So.2d 234 (Ala. 1992) (store sold dart game to 9-year-old child). See also Pitts v. Basile, 219 N.E.2d 472 (Ill. 1966) (claim against wholesaler).

[51] See Atkins v. Arlans Dep't Store Inc., 522 P.2d 1020 (Okla. 1974).

[52] See, e.g., Carbone v. Alagna, 658 N.Y.S.2d 48 (App. Div. 1997); Bojorquez v. House of Toys, Inc., 133 Cal. Rptr. 483 (Ct. App. 1976).

[53] See, e.g., Ireland v. Jefferson Cty. Sheriff's Dep't, 193 F. Supp. 2d 1201, 1229–30 (D. Colo. 2002) (plaintiff injured in mass shooting at Columbine High School; gun retailer had reason to know shotgun was to be used by minors accompanying 18-year-old supposed purchaser, and retailer advised minors on how to saw off gun's barrel).

[54] See, e.g., Noel v. Bayer Corp., 481 F. Supp. 3d 1111, 1125 (D. Mont. 2020) ("a person who supplies a chattel to another whom the supplier knows or has reason to know is likely to use it in a manner involving unreasonable risk of physical harm is subject to liability for the resulting physical harm"); Cook v. Shapiro, 871 N.Y.S.2d 714, 716 (App. Div. 2009) (automobile salesperson had no duty "to assess the ability or mental or physical fitness" of 80-year-old woman who two days later struck and fatally injured plaintiffs' decedent); Estate of Pemberton v. John's Sports Ctr., Inc., 135 P.3d 174, 188 (Kan. Ct. App. 2006) (retail store employees had no reason to believe that shotgun purchaser was mentally ill and would use it to kill himself); Horstman v. Farris, 725 N.E.2d 698, 708 (Ohio Ct. App. 1999) (plaintiff injured in collision with minors high from "huffing" airbrush propellant; retailer had no reason to believe boys would use airbrush propellant to get high); Carbone v. Alagna, 658 N.Y.S.2d 48, 50 (App. Div. 1997) ("[w]hile the misuse of a slingshot certainly carries with it grave potential dangers, the weight of authority supports a finding that slingshots constitute toys used by adolescents [so that] entrustment of a slingshot to an adolescent is not actionable absent further evidence" that seller knew of user's unsuitability). See also Adams v. Aircraft Spruce & Specialty, Co., 2021 WL 761811, at *7–10 (Conn. Super. Ct. 2021) (discussing the history and principles of the negligent entrustment tort).

[55] "It is essential to an entrustment case that the claiming party establish that the entrustor knew or should have known of the entrustee's condition or propensities." Woods, Negligent Entrustment: Evaluation of a Frequently Overlooked Source of Additional Liability, 20 Ark. L. Rev. 101, 106–07 (1966).

[56] 505 So.2d 560 (Fla. Dist. Ct. App. 1987) (en banc) (examined approvingly in Note, 1988 Duke L.J. 755, 776–79), aff'd, 533 So.2d 261 (Fla. 1988).

[57] See, e.g., Allen v. Walmart Stores, L.L.C., 907 F.3d 170 (5th Cir. 2018) (Tex. law) (no duty to refuse to sell abusable aerosol dust remover to impaired customer); Noble v. Shawnee Gun Shop, Inc., 409 S.W.3d 476, 482 (Mo. Ct. App. 2013) (no-duty rule applied to chattel sellers for negligent entrustment; gun store sold firearm magazines to murderer with stolen credit card). See generally Frumer, Friedman, and Sklaren, Products Liability § 6.02[4] ("It is extremely difficult for a plaintiff to succeed in such a lawsuit, however, because most courts have exonerated retailers by determining that a duty does not exist.").

misrepresentation liability principles examined previously[58] apply as readily to retailers as they do to manufacturers.

Retailers—Warranty

Retailers, of course, are as liable as manufacturers or any other seller for breach of warranty under Article 2 of the Uniform Commercial Code, a topic addressed in detail earlier.[59] Consequently, retailers are subject to liability for breach of express warranty,[60] the implied warranty of merchantability,[61] and the implied warranty of fitness for particular purpose[62]—subject to the normal limitations based on disclaimers,[63] privity,[64] notice,[65] and limitations on remedies,[66] all as previously addressed.

A retail seller is subject to liability for breaching its own express warranties, but it often is said that a retailer bears no responsibility for the failure of a *manufacturer's* express warranties. This ordinarily makes sense since retailers normally have no control over the content of such warranties and buyers normally have no reason to expect that a retail dealer is personally responsible if the manufacturer's warranty proves false. But there are a couple of exceptions to a retailer's ordinary immunity from the failure of a manufacturer's express warranty. One rather large exception is for a manufacturer's express warranties made on the container or label of a product. Uniform Commercial Code § 2–314(2)(f) provides that such warranties must be true in order for a product to be merchantable.[67] Stated otherwise, if representations on a product's container or label are false, the product is unmerchantable, and a seller is subject to liability for breach of the implied warranty of merchantability under UCC § 2–314 for selling such a mislabeled product.[68] A retail dealer will also be subject to liability for selling a product

---

58 See ch. 3, above.

59 See ch. 4, above.

60 Under UCC § 2–313. See, e.g., Rite Aid Corp. v. Levy-Gray, 894 A.2d 563, 571 (Md. 2006) (pharmacy's false statement in patient package insert); Jones v. Kellner, 451 N.E.2d 548, 549 (Ohio Ct. App. 1982) (used car sold as "mechanically A-1"). See generally § 4.2, above.

61 Under UCC § 2–314. See, e.g., Grubbs v. Wal-Mart Stores, Inc., 514 F. Supp. 3d 820, 825 (D.S.C. 2021) (plaintiff adequately alleged that gas can without flame arrestor was not merchantable at the time of sale); Hollister v. Dayton Hudson Corp., 201 F.3d 731 (6th Cir. 2000) (Mich. law) (plaintiff's shirt caught fire; failure to warn claim allowed); Patterson v. Central Mills, Inc., 112 F. Supp. 2d 681 (N.D. Ohio 2000) (child's T-shirt caught fire; design and warning defect claims allowed); Maybank v. S.S. Kresge Co., 266 S.E.2d 409 (N.C. Ct. App. 1980) (sealed flashcube, in package of flashcubes plaintiff bought at K-Mart), modified on other grounds and aff'd, 273 S.E.2d 681 (N.C. 1981). See generally § 4.3, above.

62 Under UCC § 2–315. See, e.g., Travelers Indem. Co. v. Industrial Paper & Packaging Corp., 2006 WL 2050686, at *3–4 (E.D. Tenn. 2006); Klein v. Sears Roebuck & Co., 773 F.2d 1421 (4th Cir. 1985) (Md. law) (riding mower tipped over on hilly property inspected by retail dealer who assured buyers that mower was appropriate for property); Barb v. Wallace, 412 A.2d 1314 (Md. Ct. Spec. App. 1980) (sale of used engine for go-cart). See generally § 4.4, above.

In consumer goods products liability cases, claims for breach of the implied warranty of fitness for particular purpose arise in the retail context more than any other.

63 Under UCC § 2–316. See §§ 4.7 and 4.8, above.

64 Under UCC § 2–318. See § 4.5, above.

65 Under UCC § 2–607(3). See § 4.6, above.

66 Under UCC § 2–719. See § 4.8, above.

67 "Goods to be merchantable must be at least such as . . . (f) conform to the promises or affirmations of fact made on the container or label if any." UCC § 2–314(2)(f).

68 While a comment to UCC § 2–314 suggests that this particular provision is intended to protect dealers against the risk of receiving mislabeled articles from manufacturers, see UCC § 2–314 Official Comment 10, on its face it appears as well to protect consumers against the risk of purchasing mislabeled products from retailers. So interpreted, this section to some extent serves "to overturn the 'adoption' of

accompanied by a manufacturer's express warranty which provides that both the manufacturer and the retail dealer are making and are responsible for the express warranties, in which case the retailer may be treated as a co-warrantor together with the manufacturer.[69]

An alternative method for holding a retailer responsible for a manufacturer's express warranty is to establish that the retailer "adopted" the manufacturer's warranty.[70] It is reasonable, of course, to hold a retailer liable for the failure of another party's express warranty that the retailer has undertaken to support. But "adoption" logically requires that the retailer affirmatively communicate to the purchaser the idea that the retailer stands behind the manufacturer's warranty,[71] for otherwise the purchaser has no fair claim to hold the retailer to a warranty it did not make.[72] Thus, the mere resale of a product that a manufacturer has expressly warranted does not alone constitute adoption, even if the retailer explains its terms to the buyer.[73] Nor does making repairs on behalf of the manufacturer pursuant to the terms of the latter's warranty amount to an adoption.[74] Some courts have expanded the adoption notion further than it logically should extend;[75] but such stretching misconceives the nature of the buyer's separate relationships with the manufacturer and the retail dealer, and does violence to fundamental principles of warranty and agency law.[76]

Retailers—Strict Liability in Tort

The most significant retailer issue in modern products liability litigation is whether such sellers are subject to strict liability in tort for the sale of defective products.[77] In 1964, a year after the California Supreme Court decided *Greenman v. Yuba Power Products, Inc.*[78] and only a few weeks before the American Law Institute approved § 402A of the *Restatement (Second) of Torts*, the California court rendered its landmark decision in *Vandermark v. Ford Motor Co.*[79] In *Vandermark*, the plaintiff was injured when the brakes failed on his new car, causing it to crash into a pole. In actions against both the retail dealer and the manufacturer of the automobile, the court ruled that the retail dealer was strictly liable in tort for injuries caused by a defect in the car. Writing for the court, Justice Roger Traynor reasoned that retailers are just as much engaged in the business of distributing goods to the public as manufacturers. As "an integral part

---

warranty rule which sometimes has shielded the retailer." See W. Hawkland, A Transactional Guide to the U.C.C. 69–70 (1964).

[69] See 1 Crockett, Product Warranties § 4:36.

[70] See, e.g., Scovil v. Chilcoat, 424 P.2d 87 (Okla. 1967) (new VW engine).

[71] See, e.g., Hillcrest Country Club v. N.D. Judds Co., 461 N.W.2d 55 (Neb. 1990) (distributor contracted with buyer that product would meet manufacturer's warranty).

[72] Recall, however, that a retail seller may nevertheless be liable for a manufacturer's express warranties on the container or label under UCC § 2–314(2)(f), as discussed above.

[73] See, e.g., Import Motors, Inc. v. Matthews, 557 S.W.2d 807 (Tex. App. 1977). This is especially true if the retail seller effectively disclaims all warranties. See, e.g., Frank Griffin Volkswagen, Inc. v. Smith, 610 So.2d 597 (Fla. Dist. Ct. App. 1992) (thorough discussion of adoption cases).

[74] See, e.g., Carbo Indus. v. Becker Chevrolet Inc., 491 N.Y.S.2d 786 (App. Div. 1985).

[75] See, e.g., Riley v. Ken Wilson Ford, Inc., 426 S.E.2d 717 (N.C. Ct. App. 1993) (by telling buyers about manufacturer's 12-month/12,000 mile warranty, dealer adopted warranty).

[76] See 1 Crockett, Product Warranties § 4:34.

[77] See Cavico, The Strict Tort Liability of Retailers, Wholesalers, and Distributors of Defective Products, 12 Nova L. Rev. 213 (1987).

[78] 377 P.2d 897 (Cal. 1963).

[79] 391 P.2d 168, 171–72 (Cal. 1964).

of the overall producing and marketing enterprise," and sometimes as the only member of that enterprise available to injured consumers, retailers properly should "bear the cost of injuries resulting from defective products." Because retailers sometimes can and do pressure manufacturers to ensure product safety, "the retailer's strict liability thus serves as an added incentive to safety." In sum, imposing strict liability on retailers as well as manufacturers "affords maximum protection to the injured plaintiff and works no injustice to the defendants, for they can adjust the costs of such protection between them in the course of their continuing business relationship."[80]

Vandermark's application of the doctrine of strict products liability in tort to retailers was validated by the ALI in comment *f* to § 402A of the *Restatement (Second) of Torts*, which provides that retailers are covered by the strict liability doctrine.[81] Thereafter, with little dissent,[82] courts widely applied the strict tort doctrine to retailers and other non-manufacturing distributors of defective products,[83] which courts continue widely to do.[84] Although the *Restatement (Third) of Torts: Products Liability* speaks approvingly of the statutory reform discussed below, it reaffirms, in § 1 cmt. *e*, the *Second Restatement*'s unqualified rule of strict tort liability for retailers and other non-manufacturing sellers in the chain of distribution.

Retailers—Internet Providers

In general. When Amazon and Walmart sell their own products on the internet, they are subject to liability as retailers for harm from defects just as if they were to sell defective products from their brick-and-mortar stores.[85] In addition to such direct sales to consumers, Amazon, Walmart, eBay and certain other website owners serve as "internet providers," making their websites available, for a fee, to other companies to list and sell their own products. Amazon, for example, provides this service, the "Amazon Marketplace," to more than one million third-party vendors who submit to a complex set

---

80 Id. at 171–72. See also Godoy v. Abamaster of Miami, Inc., 754 N.Y.S.2d 301, 307 (App. Div. 2003) (imposing strict liability on retailers and distributors enhances product safety; distributors and importers, closest to manufacturers, are in the best position to advance this goal).

81 "The rule stated in this Section applies to any person engaged in the business of selling products for use or consumption. It therefore applies to any manufacturer of such a product, to any wholesale or retail dealer or distributor, and to the operator of a restaurant." Rest. (2d) Torts § 402A cmt. *f*.

82 For an example of the sprinkling of dissent, see Bailey v. Montgomery Ward & Co., 431 P.2d 108, 114 (Ariz. Ct. App. 1967) (Molloy, J., dissenting): "As to the non-negligent distributor, wholesaler, and retailer, the new doctrine is heavy-handed to point of injustice. . . . The new philosophy of liability without fault will mean the difference between survival and extinction to many a small businessman." Id. at 117–18.

83 See, e.g., Webb v. Zern, 220 A.2d 853, 854–55 (Pa. 1966); McKisson v. Sales Affiliates, Inc., 416 S.W.2d 787, 793–94 (Tex. 1967); Dippel v. Sciano, 155 N.W.2d 55, 61–63 (Wis. 1967); Bailey v. Montgomery Ward & Co., 431 P.2d 108, 111 (Ariz. Ct. App. 1967); Dunham v. Vaughan & Bushnell Mfg. Co., 247 N.E.2d 401, 403–04 (Ill. 1969); Keener v. Dayton Elec. Mfg. Co., 445 S.W.2d 362, 365 (Mo. 1969); Cottom v. McGuire Funeral Serv., Inc., 262 A.2d 807, 809 (D.C. 1970).

84 See, e.g., LaScala v. QVC, 162 N.Y.S.3d 383, 388 (App. Div. 2022) (trial court erred in dismissing strict liability claim against QVC for sale of defective hoverboard); Sharma v. ARS Aleut Constr., LLC, 2021 WL 4554193, at *1 (N.D. Cal. 2021) ("products strict liability also extends to distributors, retailers, and those who play 'an integral part of the overall producing and marketing enterprise of products placed on the market' "); Bylsma v. R.C. Willey, 416 P.3d 595, 617 (Utah 2017).

85 Prior to mid-2021, Amazon's terms of service limited the resolution of customer claims to arbitration. See, e.g., Randazzo, Amazon Faced 75,000 Arbitration Demands. Now It Says: Fine, Sue Us—The retail giant is no longer steering customers away from the court system, as companies scramble to find ways to avoid lawyers who file mass-arbitration claims, Wall St. J.com (June 1, 2021); Lenkner, Amazon to Let Customers Sue After Thousands of Alexa Complaints, Prod. Liab. & Toxics L. (June 1, 2021). Class action attorneys responded to Amazon's change in terms. See, e.g., Barash, Amazon Faces New Class Claim Over Sales of Lithium-Ion Batteries, Prod. Liab. & Toxics L. (Aug. 16, 2021). As of this writing, Walmart.com's terms of service continue to limit dispute resolution to arbitration.

of rules for payment, shipping, returns, communications with customers, and other details of such transactions.[86] If a third-party vender sells a defective battery on Amazon's website, and the battery catches fire and causes harm, the third party is subject to liability, of course, just as Amazon would be if it had sold its own defective battery on its website itself. But if the third party is insolvent or a foreign company beyond the practical reach of American courts, an important question is whether Amazon itself may also be considered a "seller" of the defective third-party product and so subject to strict liability for the harm.[87]

Some courts have found Amazon liable in negligence or warranty for harm caused by defective third-party products. Negligence liability has attached to Amazon for defective third-party products when Amazon knew, or had reason to know, of defects in products sold on its website by others.[88] One court refused to dismiss an implied warranty claim against Amazon for a third-party pasta product containing an ingredient that was known to swell in the digestive system, causing choking and stomach or intestinal blockage.[89]

Most courts addressing the issue of a website provider's liability for third-party sales have strictly interpreted the notion of a "sale," ruling that Amazon[90] and other such

---

[86] Amazon allows third parties to sell their products under a complex Business Solutions Agreement (BSA) that governs the terms of the customer transaction, requires compliance with applicable laws, and indemnifies Amazon. See Loomis v. Amazon.com LLC, 277 Cal. Rptr. 3d 769, 773–74 (Ct. App. 2021). Third-party sellers operating under the BSA may also choose, under the Fulfillment by Amazon program, to store inventory in Amazon warehouses for shipment to customers by Amazon. Customers are told they are buying from an identified third-party vendor but are not informed of the resulting products liability consequences.

[87] Most commentators argue that Amazon should be subject to products liability law in such situations. See, e.g., Janger and Twerski, The Heavy Hand of Amazon: A Seller Not a Neutral Platform, 14 Brook. J. Corp. Fin. & Com. L. 259, 263–64) (2020) (in view of "Amazon's substantial control over virtually all aspects of [third-party sales,] it is absolutely ludicrous to see [it] as anything but a 'seller' for product liability purposes"); Sprague, It's A Jungle Out There: Public Policy Considerations Arising from A Liability-Free Amazon.com, 60 Santa Clara L. Rev. 253, 280 (2020) ("Amazon's control over third parties and involvement in the sales and delivery processes [and] public policy considerations [lead to the conclusion that Amazon] should be liable for defective products it places into the stream of commerce."); Zitter, Liability of Online Marketplace Operator for Defective Product, 60 A.L.R.7th Art. 3 (2021). *But see* Comment, 125 Penn St. L. Rev. 321 (2020).

[88] See, e.g., Diew v. Amazon.com Servs., LLC, 2021 WL 2435265, at *5 (N.D. Cal. 2021) (denying defendant's motion to dismiss negligence claim; plaintiffs' allegation that Amazon had notice of battery's defect satisfied Rule 8(a) pleading requirements); Brodie v. Green Spot Foods, LLC, 503 F. Supp. 3d 1, 8 (S.D.N.Y. 2020) (pasta product's labeling and "customer complaints lead to a plausible inference that Amazon knew or had reason to know of the product's potential to cause injury when consumed because it contained konjac"); Love v. Weecoo™, 774 Fed. Appx. 519, 522 (11th Cir. 2019) (Ga. law) (reversing summary judgment for Amazon.com on plaintiff's negligence and negligent failure to warn claims; "Plaintiff has alleged enough facts to state plausibly that Amazon had actual or constructive knowledge that the Hoverboard posed a risk of fire at the time of Plaintiff's purchase."); State Farm Fire & Casualty Co. v. Amazon.com, Inc., 414 F. Supp. 3d 870, 876 (N.D. Miss. 2019) (rejecting Amazon's immunity as a marketplace or internet service provider from negligence claims for sale of defective hoverboard that caused house fire; "Amazon had been notified of nine fires caused by hoverboards sold through its website yet failed to warn"). Compare State Farm Fire & Casualty Co. v. Amazon.com, Inc., 528 F. Supp. 3d 686, 698 (W.D. Ky. 2021) (granting summary judgment to defendant on negligence, strict liability, and negligent failure to warn claims where Amazon was not a "seller" of defective third-party hoverboard, but denying summary judgment on question whether Amazon assumed a duty to warn when it sent out an email about hoverboard safety); Fox v. Amazon.com, Inc., 930 F.3d 415, 425 (6th Cir. 2019) (Amazon's assumption of a duty to act by sending emails of hoverboard danger raised factual issues for plaintiffs' negligence claim).

[89] Brodie v. Green Spot Foods, LLC, 503 F. Supp. 3d 1, 9 (S.D.N.Y. 2020) (denying Amazon's motion to dismiss breach of implied warranty claim; "ordinary inspection would have revealed that Better than Pasta contained konjac, an ingredient whose dangers are 'well-known' and the subject of numerous negative reviews on Amazon.com").

[90] See, e.g., Skaggs v. Amazon.com, Inc., 334 So.3d 780, 788, 791 (La. Ct. App. 2021) (Amazon was neither a "seller" of the defective battery nor assumed a duty to warn); State Farm Fire & Casualty Co. v.

internet providers[91] are not truly "sellers" and so are not subject to strict products liability for third-party sales of defective products on their websites. For example, in *McMillan v. Amazon.com, Inc.*,[92] a child was injured from swallowing a small battery from a remote control the child's father had bought from a third-party seller on Amazon's website. Although the product was technically sold by a third party, the trial court ruled that Amazon was subject to strict products liability as a "seller" of the remote control purchased on its website and "fulfilled" by Amazon. On appeal, the Fifth Circuit asked the Texas Supreme Court by certified question whether Amazon, under that state's products liability law, is a " 'seller' of third-party products sold on Amazon's website when Amazon does not hold title to the product but controls the process of the transaction and delivery through Amazon's Fulfillment by Amazon program."[93] Answering the question in *Amazon.com, Inc. v. McMillan*,[94] the Texas Supreme Court followed conventional wisdom, ruling that Amazon, though controlling the transaction and delivery of the defective battery, was not its "seller" because it never held nor relinquished title to the product, whereupon the Fifth Circuit reversed the District Court and remanded with instructions to enter judgment for Amazon.[95]

Amazon.com, Inc., 528 F. Supp. 3d 686, 698 (W.D. Ky. 2021) (Amazon was not a "seller" of defective third-party hoverboard under Rest. (2d) of Torts § 402A or the Kansas Products Liability Act); Great Northern Ins. Co. v. Amazon.com, Inc., 524 F. Supp. 3d 852, 857–58 (N.D. Ill. 2021) (Amazon was not the "seller" of defective third-party hoverboard under Illinois strict liability law); Stiner v. Amazon.com, Inc., 120 N.E.3d 885, 895 (Ohio Ct. App. 2019) (affirming summary judgment for Amazon; "the evidence cannot support [plaintiff's] claim that Amazon was a supplier of the caffeine powder" that caused the death of an 18-year-old high school student), aff'd, 164 N.E.3d 394 (Ohio 2020); Erie Ins. Co. v. Amazon.com, Inc., 925 F.3d 135, 144 (4th Cir. 2019) (Md. law) (Amazon.com was not a "seller [of the headlamp that caused a house fire] and therefore did not have liability under Maryland law for the allegedly defective product sold on its website by [a third-party]."); Fox v. Amazon.com, Inc., 930 F.3d 415, 425–28 (6th Cir. 2019) (Tenn. law) (Amazon "exercised [in]sufficient control over [the defective hoverboard that caused a house fire] to be deemed a 'seller' of the hoverboard under the [Tennessee Product Liability Act]"; Amazon's assumption of a duty to act raised factual issues for plaintiffs' negligence claim); Carpenter v. Amazon.com, Inc., 2019 WL 1259158, at *5 (N.D. Cal. 2019) (plaintiffs' strict liability claims against Amazon failed due to insufficient evidence sustaining a marketing enterprise theory "that Amazon was integral to the hoverboard business, such that its conduct was a necessary factor in bringing the defective [hoverboard that caused the house fire] to market"); Philadelphia Indemnity Ins. Co. v. Amazon.com, Inc., 425 F. Supp. 3d 158, 163–64 (E.D. N.Y. 2019) (granting Amazon's motion for summary judgment on strict liability, negligence, and breach of warranty claims arising from defective blender that caused fire in sushi restaurant; "Amazon is better characterized as a provider of services").

In Oberdorf v. Amazon.com Inc., 818 Fed. Appx. 138, 143 (3d Cir. 2020) (en banc), the Third Circuit reheard and vacated Oberdorf v. Amazon.com Inc., 930 F.3d 136 (3d Cir. 2019), in which the panel (in a 2–1 decision) had held Amazon liable under Rest. (2d) Torts § 402A as a product seller for injuries from a defective third-party dog collar and had rejected Amazon's claims to immunity under § 230 of the Communications Decency Act (47 U.S.C. § 230), except those related to the plaintiff's failure to warn claims, which the court affirmed as dismissed. Following oral arguments, the en banc court decided to certify to the Pennsylvania Supreme Court the question of whether an e-commerce business could be held strictly liable in tort for an injury from a defective product purchased from a third party on its internet platform. The parties thereupon settled the case, leaving the question unresolved in the Third Circuit and Pennsylvania. See Barash, Amazon Seller Liability Issue Dropped at Pennsylvania High Court, Prod. Liab. & Toxics L. (Sept. 25, 2020).

[91] See, e.g., Indiana Farm Bureau Ins. Co. v. Shenzhen Anet Tech. Co., 2020 WL 7711346, at *6–7 (S.D. Ind. 2020) (under the Indiana Product Liability Act, Wal-Mart.com was not liable as a "seller" or "manufacturer" of the defective third-party 3D printer that caused a house fire; summarizing cases against Amazon arising from defective third-party products sold on its website); Inman v. Technicolor USA, Inc., 2011 WL 5829024, at *6 (W.D. Pa. 2011) (plaintiff's pleadings were insufficient to hold eBay liable as a "seller" of allegedly defective vacuum tubes).

[92] 433 F. Supp. 3d 1034, 1044 (S.D. Tex. 2020).

[93] McMillan v. Amazon.com, Inc., 983 F.3d 194, 203 (5th Cir. 2020).

[94] 625 S.W.3d 101, 112 (Tex. 2021) (5–2 decision). Two justices argued in dissent that Amazon was a "seller" "when it 'controls the process of the transaction and delivery' of a product through its ['Fulfillment by Amazon'] program, regardless of whether it ever holds title to the product." Id. at 118.

[95] McMillan v. Amazon.com, Inc., 2 F.4th 525 (5th Cir. 2021).

Troubled by the superficiality of this conventional approach, a few courts have ruled that Amazon is indeed subject to strict products liability as a "seller" of defective products sold by third parties on its website.[96] In *Bolger v. Amazon.com, LLC*,[97] a California Court of Appeal reversed a lower court's summary judgment for Amazon, holding that Amazon could be held strictly liable for burn injuries from an exploding third-party laptop battery purchased on its website. The defective battery was stored at and shipped from an Amazon warehouse under the "Fulfillment by Amazon" program. As such, the court reasoned that Amazon was "a direct link in the chain of distribution, acting as a powerful intermediary between the third-party seller and the consumer."[98] Subsequently, in *Loomis v. Amazon.com LLC*,[99] another California appellate court reversed dismissal of strict products liability and negligence claims against Amazon for the third-party sale of a defective hoverboard that caused a house fire. Unlike the defective battery in *Bolger*, Amazon never had physical possession of, nor took title to, the defective hoverboard. Yet, as in *Bolger*, the court concluded that Amazon was a "direct link in the vertical chain of distribution" and so was subject to strict products liability under the "stream-of-commerce approach." Ultimately, *Loomis* reasoned that traditional policies of strict products liability—such as promoting product safety, consumer compensation, and loss spreading[100]—supported applying strict products liability to Amazon's third-party seller business model.[101]

Communications Decency Act § 230. Claims for third-party sales of defective products on internet platforms also raise an important federal issue—whether § 230 of the Communications Decency Act of 1996 (CDA)[102] provides immunity to internet providers such as Amazon in this type of case. This section protects such providers from civil liability for the publication of information posted by others on their websites. Amazon has contended that § 230 fully shields it from liability for harm caused by defective third-party products sold on its platform. But Congress enacted this section when the web was first getting established to protect internet providers from liability for harm caused by wrongdoers who abused the web by posting damaging content on internet platforms that injured innocent people,[103] not to protect a provider for its own

---

[96] See, e.g., State Farm Fire & Cas. Co. v. Amazon.com Servs., Inc., 137 N.Y.S.3d 884, 888 (Sup. Ct. 2020) (Amazon could be held liable under strict liability as the "seller" of the defective wireless thermostat controller that caused house fire); Papataros v. Amazon.com, Inc., 2019 WL 4011502, at *17 (D.N.J. 2019) (Amazon was subject to strict liability under the New Jersey Products Liability Act as a "seller" of an allegedly defective third-party scooter that caused a child's injuries); State Farm Fire & Casualty Co. v. Amazon.com, Inc., 390 F. Supp. 3d 964, 972 (W.D. Wis. 2019) ("Amazon is an integral part of the chain of distribution, an entity well-positioned to allocate the risks of defective products to the participants in the chain").

[97] 267 Cal. Rptr. 3d 601 (Ct. App. 2020).

[98] Id. at 605.

[99] 277 Cal. Rptr. 3d 769, 779–81 (Ct. App. 2021).

[100] Despite the shortcomings we now know such policies contain. See § 5.4, above.

[101] Id. at 783–85.

[102] 47 U.S.C. § 230 (immunizes interactive computer service providers from civil liability for: (1) the publication of information posted by others on their websites, and (2) good faith actions to remove or restrict access to obscene, violent, harassing, and other such posting by others on their websites; § 230(2)). See also § 16.8, below.

[103] See, e.g., Daniel v. Armslist, LLC, 926 N.W.2d 710, 727 (Wis. 2019) (website linking firearm buyers and sellers on which semiautomatic handgun and high-capacity magazines used in a mass-casualty shooting at a salon were illegally purchased; "Section 230(c)(1) prohibits claims that treat Armslist, an interactive computer service provider, as the publisher or speaker of information posted by a third party on its website"); Seaver v. Estate of Cazes, 2019 WL 2176316, at *3 (D. Utah 2019) (§ 230 immunity applied to company providing the "dark web" Tor browser used for the sale of illicit drugs to deceased 13-year-old boy); Herrick v. Grindr, LLC, 306 F. Supp. 3d 579, 588–92 (S.D.N.Y. 2018) (plaintiff's product liability claims against internet

conduct in actively managing the harmful conduct of third-party posters. So, several courts have reasonably concluded that § 230 allows claims against internet publishers like Amazon for their own posting conduct—such as actively managing the sale by others of dangerously defective goods[104]—and that § 230 shields website owners only from liability for third-party postings that may fail to warn of such a product's dangers,[105] negligently misrepresent its safety,[106] or falsely advertise it.[107] Accordingly, in considering Amazon's role in the distribution of defective goods, several courts have refused to apply CDA § 230 to bar strict products liability claims against Amazon for defects in the design or manufacture of third-party goods.[108]

Today's "stream of commerce" has been profoundly altered by product sales on the internet. Just as traditional business models of how products are distributed and "sold" have adjusted to this modern platform, so too must the law evolve its conception of a product "seller" when internet providers move defective products through the internet. Thus, in view of Amazon's substantial control of third-party sales of products on its website, Amazon fairly may be viewed as their "seller," rendering it responsible for harm from design and manufacturing defects such products may contain.[109] Indeed, one might plausibly argue further that § 230 of the CDA should be amended—or maybe even interpreted—to allow claims against internet providers for warning defects and misrepresentations in third-party sales.[110] To protect itself financially from all defective

---

dating site for gay and bi-sexual men failed under § 230 due to provider immunity from liability for third-party content), aff'd, 765 Fed. Appx. 586 (2d Cir. 2019).

[104] *Bolger*, 267 Cal. Rptr. 3d at 605 ("Amazon is not shielded from liability by [§ 230 that] generally prevents internet service providers from being held liable as a speaker or publisher of third-party content. It does not apply here because Bolger's strict liability claims depend on Amazon's own activities, not its status as a speaker or publisher of content provided by [the third-party] for its product listing."); State Farm Fire & Casualty Co. v. Amazon.com, Inc., 390 F. Supp. 3d 964, 974 (W.D. Wis. 2019) (§ 230 does not shield Amazon from claims that it sold a defective product). See also § 16.8, notes 387–389, below.

[105] McMillan v. Amazon.com, Inc., 433 F. Supp. 3d 1034, 1045 (S.D. Tex. 2020) (§ 230 immunity barred plaintiff's failure to warn claims as they related to "Amazon's editorial control over its website"), rev'd on other grounds, 2 F.4th 525 (5th Cir. 2021); Papataros v. Amazon.com, Inc., 2019 WL 4011502, at *19 (D.N.J. 2019) (dismissing plaintiff's failure to warn claims under § 230 immunity but retaining strict liability claims against Amazon as a "seller" of the allegedly defective third-party scooter).

[106] Great N. Ins. Co. v. Amazon.com, Inc., 524 F. Supp. 3d 852, 859 (N.D. Ill. 2021) (Amazon was not the "author" of the defective hoverboard's description).

[107] Brodie v. Green Spot Foods, LLC, 503 F. Supp. 3d 1, 12 (S.D.N.Y. 2020) (no evidence that Amazon controlled or edited the product information).

[108] *Bolger*, 267 Cal. Rptr. 3d at 626 ("The content of the product listing [was] not determinative, and it need not be attributed to Amazon to support strict liability."). See also Erie Ins. Co. v. Amazon.com, Inc., 925 F.3d 135, 140 (4th Cir. 2019) (CDA protects interactive computer service providers from liability as publishers of speech, but not for selling defective products); State Farm Fire & Casualty Co. v. Amazon.com, Inc., 390 F. Supp. 3d 964, 974 (W.D. Wis. 2019) (Amazon not immune under CDA for claims it sold a defective product).

[109] Control over third-party sellers now appears to require Amazon to recall faulty third-party products sold under the Fulfillment by Amazon program. See In the Matter of Amazon.com, Inc., CPSC Docket No. 21–2 (Jan. 19, 2022) (Amazon met "the statutory definition of the term *distributor* and [did] not fall within the terms of the safe harbor for *third-party logistics providers*") (emphasis in original). See also Lee v. Amazon.com, Inc., 291 Cal. Rptr. 3d 332, 380 (Ct. App. 2022) (reversing dismissal of claims that third-party lightening face creams sold on Amazon contained mercury; § 230 immunity inapplicable to Proposition 65 violations).

[110] As of this writing, Congress has yet to consider amending § 230 to address internet marketplace provider liability for defective third-party products. See, e.g., Karalis, Section 230 Challenged by Contract, Product Claims, Prod. Liab. & Toxics L. (July 30, 2021) ("As a result of partisan division, there has not been a single floor vote on any of the numerous legislative proposals to amend Section 230 introduced in the last few years."); Tracy, Section 230: What It Is, and Why Politicians Want to Change It—The foundational U.S. internet law is under more scrutiny than at any time in its history. Here is what to know about the debate, the law and how it could be changed, Wall St. J.com (Mar. 25, 2021). See generally Dickinson, Rebooting Internet Immunity, 89 Geo. Wash. L. Rev. 347 (2021).

product claims, Amazon can ensure that its suppliers and vendors are appropriately insured to reimburse it for resulting losses, as such sellers already promise contractually to do. Such a fairly modest change in Amazon's business model might well be a sensible way to protect consumers, as well as Amazon itself, from undue financial harm from third-party internet sales of defective products.

After years of increasing customer complaints about injuries and property damage from third-party products sold on its website, Amazon announced in 2021 that it would resolve valid claims for up to $1,000 of damages.[111] While Amazon states that this new policy represents some 80% of property damage and personal injury claims, it fails to address ordinary products liability claims involving much higher damages. In view of its controlling role in sales of third-party products on its website, and because it is so well-positioned to sensibly allocate financial responsibility for harm caused by defects in such products, Amazon would do well to adopt a similar policy for substantial products liability claims arising from third-party sales on its website—before the courts or legislatures so demand.

Wholesalers and Other Distributors

The principles examined above applicable to retail dealers generally apply to wholesalers and other non-manufacturing distributors as well.[112] Thus, subject to the same limitations protecting retailers,[113] most states hold that wholesalers and other distributors ordinarily are subject to liability for negligence,[114] warranty,[115] and strict liability in tort.[116] Some states, however, offer non-manufacturing distributors common-

---

[111] See Dastin, Amazon To Pay Shoppers Hurt By Others' Products, Does Not Admit Liability, Reuters (Aug. 10, 2021).

[112] See Cavico, The Strict Tort Liability of Retailers, Wholesalers, and Distributors of Defective Products, 12 Nova L. Rev. 213 (1987).

[113] See, e.g., Wilcher v. Redding Swainsboro Ford Lincoln Mercury, Inc., 743 S.E.2d 27, 32 (Ga. Ct. App. 2013) (auto dealership wholesaler had no duty to inspect van for latent defects); Thomasson v. Rich Prods. Corp., 502 S.E.2d 289 (Ga. Ct. App. 1998) (no liability, under sealed-container doctrine, for injuries from staple baked by third-party baker into bagel); Townsend v. General Motors Corp., 642 So.2d 411, 424–25 (Ala. 1994) (no liability of mere "middleman" distributor who is unaware of defect and who has no better opportunity to inspect product than consumer); Zamora v. Mobil Corp., 704 P.2d 584 (Wash. 1985) (distributor who purchased propane gas from reputable supplier had no duty to test or inspect gas to determine if it was odorized, nor did it have duty to warn retailer of obvious risk if gas were in fact not odorized).

[114] See, e.g., McAllister-Lewis v. Goodyear Dunlop Tires N. Am., Ltd., 2017 WL 2312232, at *2 (D.S.D. 2017) (jury question whether wholesaler, in the exercise of due care, knew or should have known of latent defect in tire); Ide v. Foreign Candy Co., 2006 WL 3361525, at *3 (Mass. App. Ct. 2006) (hot gum ball importer/distributor stood in manufacturer's shoes with same duties to consumers); Kennedy v. Guess, Inc., 806 N.E.2d 776 (Ind. 2004) (umbrella distributor); Mills v. Allegiance Healthcare Corp., 178 F. Supp. 2d 1 (D. Mass. 2001); Bishop v. Farhat, 489 S.E.2d 323 (Ga. Ct. App. 1997) (distributor of gloves could be liable for failing to warn if it reasonably should have known of latex allergies); Beam v. Omark Indus., 237 S.E.2d 607 (Ga. Ct. App. 1977) (wholesaler removed product from container and failed to pass along warnings and instructions).

[115] See, e.g., Hernandez v. Apple Auto Wholesalers of Waterbury LLC, 460 F. Supp. 3d 164 (D. Conn. 2020) (structurally damaged vehicle; implied warranty); Ide v. Foreign Candy Co., 2006 WL 3361525, at *3 (Mass. App. Ct. 2006); Mills v. Allegiance Healthcare Corp., 178 F. Supp. 2d 1 (D. Mass. 2001) (latex gloves; implied warranty; failing to warn of latex allergies); Peris v. Western Reg'l Off-Track Betting Corp., 680 N.Y.S.2d 346 (App. Div. 1998); Jones v. Cranman's Sporting Goods, 237 S.E.2d 402 (Ga. Ct. App. 1977) (distributor subject to express and implied warranties for "fully guaranteed" rifle that exploded).

[116] See, e.g., Honeywell v. GADA Builders, Inc., 271 P.3d 88, 95 (Okla. Civ. App. 2011) (strict products liability is imposed on retailers and distributors for safety of consumers); Rivera v. Baby Trend, Inc., 914 So.2d 1102 (Fla. Dist. Ct. App. 2005) (notwithstanding fact that distributor never had possession of product; good policy analysis); Kennedy v. Guess, Inc., 806 N.E.2d 776 (Ind. 2004); Levey v. Yamaha Motor Corp., 825 A.2d 554 (N.J. Super. Ct. App. Div. 2003) (distributor of jet boat failed adequately to warn of risks); Fronckowiak v. King-Kong Mfg. Co., 735 N.Y.S.2d 294 (App. Div. 2001) (bicycle); Lawrence v. Brandell Prods., Inc., 619 So.2d

law protection from strict liability in tort (and, implicitly, from negligence) if they act as mere conduits of goods that they have no reason to believe may be defective.[117] Moreover, the reform statutes discussed below that conditionally protect retailers also apply to wholesalers and other non-manufacturing distributors.[118]

Statutory Reform

Apart from the issue of internet provider liability,[119] commentators and an occasional court have sometimes questioned the logic and fairness of holding retailers liable for harm from defects they neither caused nor could have known about.[120] In recent decades, legislative tort reformers have increasingly stressed the unfairness of holding retailers strictly liable for harm from design and other defects over which they have no control, such as an uncrashworthy automobile a consumer buys from a retail dealer. The result has been the enactment of statutory provisions in many states that shield retail dealers and other non-manufacturing distributors (usually conditionally) from some or all forms of strict products liability.[121] In at least a couple instances, statutory provisions exempt non-manufacturers unconditionally from strict products liability in tort.[122] A number of the statutes follow the approach of the Model Uniform Product Liability Act,[123] to a greater or lesser extent, by holding non-manufacturing sellers[124] subject to liability for negligence but relieving them of strict products liability (except for express warranty), unless the manufacturer (1) is not subject to the jurisdiction of the court;[125]

---

427 (Fla. Dist. Ct. App. 1993) (even though defective golf club warm-up weight was shipped directly from manufacturer to retailer); Promaulayko v. Johns Manville Sales Corp., 562 A.2d 202, 205 (N.J. 1989) (asbestos); Zamora v. Mobil Corp., 704 P.2d 584 (Wash. 1985); Smith v. Fiat-Roosevelt Motors, Inc., 556 F.2d 728 (5th Cir. 1977) (Fla. law) (uncrashworthy car).

[117] See, e.g., Lindholm v. BMW of N. Am., LLC, 862 F.3d 648, 653 (8th Cir. 2017) (S.D. law) (negligent design claim failed where vehicle distributor did not design or manufacture the car or the jack); Townsend v. General Motors Corp., 642 So.2d 411 (Ala. 1994); Wolfgram v. Neveln, 502 N.W.2d 617 (Wis. Ct. App. 1993) (motorcycle's distributor not liable for design defects).

[118] For the statutes, see Owen & Davis on Products Liability Appendix I. See, e.g., Makoski v. Zimmer Holdings, Inc., 538 F. Supp. 3d 757, 763–64 (N.D. Ohio 2021) (hip replacement distributors were not liable under Ohio Product Liability Act; suppliers were fraudulently joined); Kolarik v. Cory Int'l Corp., 721 N.W.2d 159, 162 (Iowa 2006) (Iowa statute gave re-packager of olives immunity from strict liability claim; re-packaging did not contribute to alleged product defect so statute's assembler exception in the statute did not apply). See also Prods. Liab. Rest. § 1, cmt. *e*.

[119] Legislation treating Amazon and other electronic marketplace providers as "retailers" under California's strict liability law passed the California State Assembly, but not the Senate, in 2020. A letter from an Amazon executive to the Assembly Judiciary Chair supported the legislation if all retailers, whether electronic or bricks-and-mortar, are held to the same standard. See Barash, Amazon Letter on Marketplace Liability Helps Case, Family Says, Prod. Liab. Toxics L. (Aug. 27, 2020). *Bolger* and *Loomis*, discussed above at notes 97–101, may have obviated further action by the California legislature.

[120] See, e.g., Baird v. Mervyn's, Inc., 2000 WL 295616 (N.D. Tex. 2000) (hypodermic needle in pocket of blue jeans bought at defendant department store). To recover under strict liability in tort (as well as negligence) for failure to warn, a plaintiff must establish "that the defendant knew or should have known that the jeans were defective so as to render them unreasonably dangerous at the time they were sold." Id. at *2.

[121] See Shepherd, Products Liability and Economic Activity: An Empirical Analysis of Tort Reform's Impact on Businesses, Employment, and Production, 66 Vand. L. Rev. 257, 316 (2013) (reporting her study revealing that retailer protection statutes have improved economic activity); Sachs, Product Liability Reform and Seller Liability: A Proposal for Change, 55 Baylor L. Rev. 1031 (2003).

[122] See Ga. Code Ann. § 51–1–11.1; Neb. Rev. Stat. § 25–21,181.

[123] See Model Uniform Product Liability Act § 105, reprinted in Appendix H of Owen & Davis on Products Liability. See generally Frumer, Friedman, and Sklaren, Products Liability § 6.01[2][c].

[124] See, e.g., Kennedy v. Guess, Inc., 806 N.E.2d 776 (Ind. 2004) (question of fact whether defendant was a "principal distributor" under statute).

[125] See, e.g., Williams v. REP Corp., 302 F.3d 660 (7th Cir. 2002) (Ind. law); Malone v. Schapun, Inc., 965 S.W.2d 177, 182–83 (Mo. Ct. App. 1997) (retailer not protected by "innocent seller statute" where plaintiff

or (2) is, or likely to become, insolvent.[126] The statutes vary in their formulations,[127] so that the particular provisions of an applicable statute must be examined carefully in every case.[128] Several states have enacted sealed-container defenses, usually with an exception for the manufacturer's insolvency and sometimes excluding claims for breach of warranty, which also shield non-manufacturing sellers from strict liability in tort.[129] A miscellany of other state statutes may also affect a retailer's liability.[130]

§ 15.3 RAW MATERIAL AND COMPONENT PART SUPPLIERS

Suppliers of raw materials and component parts stand at the top of the chain of distribution. Like retailers, these suppliers usually have little control over the safety of final products into which their items are incorporated because the design and assembly of finished products normally lie exclusively in the hands of manufacturer-assemblers. For example, an automobile manufacturer—which obtains sheet metal, plastic, screws, glass, carpeting, tires, batteries, and radios from a wide diversity of suppliers of raw materials and component parts—makes most of the design decisions and conducts most of the production and marketing operations that bear on the safety of the finished car. While cases against suppliers of raw materials (iron ore) and component parts (sheet metal) are much less common than against manufacturer-assemblers of finished products, and while the rules applicable to component suppliers were long in a state of some confusion, the law in this area has by now largely settled sensibly.[131]

---

had earlier settled with manufacturer and distributor who were thereafter voluntarily dismissed, after which court no longer had jurisdiction over them).

[126] See, e.g., Marcon v. Kmart Corp., 573 N.W.2d 728 (Minn. Ct. App. 1998) (retailer, although found 0% at fault versus manufacturer's 100% fault, liable for all damages assigned to bankrupt manufacturer). See also Cassidy v. China Vitamins, LLC, 120 N.E.3d 959, 975 (Ill. 2018) (adopting a "range of factors to determine if a particular manufacturer is 'unable to satisfy' the judgment against it" under 735 Ill. Comp. Stat. Ann. 5/2–621(b)(4) and remanding for determination of that issue).

[127] See, e.g., Ga. Code Ann. § 51–1–11.1 (non-manufacturer seller not liable for strict liability in tort); Ind. Code Ann. § 34–6–2–77 (seller who knows of defect, provides product specifications, alters product, or owns or is owned by manufacturer is liable as manufacturer); Iowa Code Ann. § 613.18 (seller not liable as manufacturer in strict tort); Kan. Stat. Ann. § 60–3306; Minn. Stat. Ann. § 544.41; Mo. Ann. Stat. § 537.762 (seller dismissed if manufacturer properly before court in same action); Neb. Rev. Stat. § 25–21,181; S.D. Codified Laws § 20–9–9; Tenn. Code Ann. § 29–28–106 (seller liable only if it substantially controlled defective aspect of product, altered it, gave express warranty, or if manufacturer not subject to service of process or declared insolvent); Tex. Civ. Prac. & Rem. Code Ann. § 82.003 (similar); Wash. Rev. Code Ann. § 7.72.040; W. Va. Code Ann. § 55–7–31 (similar); Wis. Stat. Ann. § 895.047(2).

[128] For examples of these types of statutes, see, e.g., Colo. Rev. Stat. Ann. § 13–21–402; Del. Code Ann. tit. 18, § 7001; Idaho Code Ann. § 6–1407; Iowa Code Ann. § 613.18; Kan. Stat. Ann. § 60–3306; Ky. Rev. Stat. Ann. § 411.340; Md. Code Ann., Cts. & Jud. Proc. § 5–405(c); Minn. Stat. Ann. § 544.41; Miss. Code Ann. § 11–1–63(h); Mo. Ann. Stat. § 537.762; N.J. Stat. Ann. § 2A:58C–9; Ohio Rev. Code Ann. § 2307.78; Tenn. Code Ann. § 29–28–106; Wash. Rev. Code Ann. § 7.72.040. See also Hinton v. Sportsman's Guide, Inc., 285 So.3d 142, 149 (Miss. 2019) ("the innocent-seller provision is an affirmative defense").

[129] See, e.g., Del. Code Ann. tit. 18, § 7001; Idaho Code Ann. § 6–1407; Ky. Rev. Stat. Ann. § 411.340; Md. Code Ann., Cts. & Jud. Proc. § 5–405; and Tenn. Code Ann. § 29–28–106.

[130] For example, a number of states have statutes requiring manufacturers to indemnify retailers for the amount of judgment and attorneys' fees unless the retailer provided defective specifications for the product. See, e.g., Ariz. Rev. Stat. Ann. § 12–684; Cal. Civ. Code § 1792; N.J. Stat. Ann. § 2A:58C–9; Tex. Civ. Prac. & Rem. Code Ann. § 82.002. Four states have statutes holding motor vehicle manufacturers liable for products liability damages incurred by dealers. See Del. Code Ann. tit. 6, § 4905; Idaho Code Ann. § 49–1622; Me. Rev. Stat. Ann. tit. 10, § 1175; S.C. Code Ann. § 56–15–50.

[131] See, e.g., Smith and Beard, Disassembling Assembler Liability: Are OEMs Strictly Liable for PMA Parts in Aviation Cases?, 82 J. Air L. & Com. 169 (2017); Fischer, Product Liability: A Commentary on the Liability of Suppliers of Component Parts and Raw Materials, 53 S.C. L. Rev. 1137 (2002); Kennelly, Trial of a General Aviation Aircraft Case Against Manufacturer, Component-Part Maker, and Overhaul Company—Defective 5¢ Screws Result in $660,000 Aggregate Awards for Two Deaths, 15 Tr. Law. Guide 281 (1971);

Theories of Liability

Since suppliers of raw materials and component parts are always remote from the ultimate consumer, the privity-of-contract requirement of negligence as well as warranty law precluded claims against such defendants well into the twentieth century. But with the crumbling of the privity bar in negligence law in the early to mid-1900s,[132] courts began to allow negligence claims against suppliers of dangerously defective component parts that caused consumer harm.[133] Although privity of contract in many jurisdictions still remains an important requirement of warranty law,[134] vertical privity is no longer an absolute requirement to warranty claims in most states, as discussed above.[135] Accordingly, a number of courts have allowed warranty claims by remote plaintiffs against component part suppliers.[136]

In the 1960s and 1970s, however, courts turned their principal attention to whether the new doctrine of strict products liability in tort should be allowed against manufacturers of raw materials and component parts. What courts in time came to understand is that raw materials—like pig iron, sand, gravel, or kerosene—ordinarily cannot be considered defective in design, nor can their suppliers normally be fairly required to warn their usually sophisticated purchasers of the natural hazards such materials may contain.[137] This is the position of both the *Second*[138] and *Third*[139] *Restatements of Torts*.

Comment, Apportionment Between Partmakers and Assemblers in Strict Liability, 49 U. Chi. L. Rev. 544, 547 (1982); Annot., 58 A.L.R.7th Art. 4 (2020) (component part supplier duty to warn of danger). Many issues considered here overlap those surrounding optional safety devices, examined in § 8.9, above.

[132] See § 1.2, above.

[133] See, e.g., Smith v. Peerless Glass Co., 181 N.E. 576 (N.Y. 1932); Spencer v. Madsen, 142 F.2d 820 (10th Cir. 1944) (Kan. law); Carson v. Weston Hotel Corp., 97 N.E.2d 620 (Ill. App. Ct. 1951); Maryland v. Garzell Plastics Indus., 152 F. Supp. 483 (D. Mich. 1957) (Md. law); Edison v. Lewis Mfg. Co., 336 P.2d 286 (Cal. Ct. App. 1959). More recently, see, e.g., Swanstrom v. Teledyne Cont'l Motors, Inc., 43 So.3d 564, 583–84 (Ala. 2009) (N.M. law) (allowing negligence claim against manufacturer of fuel pump in aircraft); Yu-Santos v. Ford Motor Co., 2009 WL 1392085, at *19 (E.D. Cal. 2009) (allowing negligence claim against manufacturer of allegedly defective seatbelt that supplied it to automobile assembler); Thorndike v. DaimlerChrysler Corp., 2003 WL 21212591 (D. Me. 2003) (defective bolt used to secure spare tire to van floor).

[134] See Yu-Santos v. Ford Motor Co., 2009 WL 1392085, at *20–21 (E.D. Cal. 2009) (granting summary judgment to automobile seatbelt supplier on warranty claim due to absence of vertical privity).

[135] See § 4.5, above.

[136] See, e.g., Thorndike v. DaimlerChrysler Corp., 2003 WL 21212591 (D. Me. 2003); Shaw v. General Motors Corp., 727 P.2d 387 (Colo. App. 1986); Favors v. Firestone Tire & Rubber Co., 309 So.2d 69 (Fla. Dist. Ct. App. 1975); Clark v. Bendix Corp., 345 N.Y.S.2d 662 (App. Div. 1973).

[137] See, e.g., In re: 3M Combat Arms Earplug Prods. Liab. Litig., 545 F. Supp. 3d 1239, 1245 (N.D. Fla. 2021) (reason "for absolving a supplier from liability to ultimate users of the end-product is strongest . . . when a supplier sells to a knowledgeable manufacturer raw materials in bulk, which are not themselves inherently dangerous and which are substantially changed during the manufacturing process before resale to consumers, and when the supplier has little to no role in the design of the end product.' "); Gibbs v. 84 Lumber Co., 2020 WL 5798072, at *7 (Del. Super. Ct. 2020) (S.C. law) (raw asbestos supplier "did not have a duty directly to warn the end users of its customers' finished products"); Walker v. Stauffer Chem. Corp., 96 Cal. Rptr. 803 (Ct. App. 1971) (supplier of sulfuric acid, used as ingredient in drain cleaner which exploded, not subject to strict liability).

[138] Rest. (2d) of Torts § 402A cmt. p ("a manufacturer of pig iron, which is capable of a wide variety of uses, is not so likely to be held to strict liability when it turns out to be unsuitable for the child's tricycle into which it is finally made by a remote buyer").

[139] Products Liability Restatement § 5 cmt. *c* (while sellers of raw materials are subject to liability for contamination, they are not subject to liability for design defects nor, usually, for failure to warn: "a basic raw material, such as sand, gravel, or kerosene cannot be defectively designed" because it is the fabricator that may put such raw materials to improper use).

Yet some products, like asbestos and silica in their raw form, pose such dangerous inherent hazards to workers that a supplier of such a product is required to warn of those hazards unless it has good reason to be confident that the purchasing company will provide warnings to its employees expected to work with the substance,[140] and perhaps even end users. Thus, bulk supplier liability may arise for asbestos contamination of talc during the mining process, as in cases against Johnson & Johnson and its bulk supplier, Imerys Talc America, Inc., brought by plaintiffs alleging that their ovarian cancer or mesothelioma was caused by talc powder products contaminated with asbestos fibers.[141]

Component parts are another kettle of fish. A prominent early decision held that strict products liability claims were inappropriate against component part manufacturers, at least when the manufacturer of a final integrated product is available to answer to victims of a product accident.[142] But courts in recent decades have regularly applied strict liability in tort to claims for physical harm brought against suppliers of defective component parts.[143] As in other contexts, claims against sellers of defective component parts for pure economic loss are normally barred in tort.[144]

Several state products liability reform statutes expressly provide for the liability of manufacturers of component parts.[145] Yet, a narrow federal statute protects suppliers of

---

[140] See, e.g., Webb v. Special Elec. Co., 370 P.3d 1022, 1035 (Cal. 2016) (warning the intermediary usually is necessary, but "warnings are not required if the intermediary was so sophisticated that it actually knew or reasonably should have known about the potential harm."). See also Ramos v. Brenntag Specialties, Inc., 372 P.3d 200, 204–05 (Cal 2016) (Products Liability Rest. § 5 cmt. a inapplicable to injury "allegedly caused directly by the materials themselves when used in a manner intended by the suppliers").

[141] See § 10.3 (*Asbestos-contaminated talc*), above.

[142] See Goldberg v. Kollsman Instrument Corp., 191 N.E.2d 81 (N.Y. 1963) (defective altimeter caused crash of plane). See generally Hunt, A Reporter at Large: The Case of Flight 320, The New Yorker (Apr. 30, 1960, at 119) (fascinating account of *Goldberg* crash and subsequent investigation into its cause). Although *Goldberg* played a role in the development of strict products liability in tort, see § 5.3, above, it characterized the claim in warranty terms. It did lay the basis, however, for the debate that followed over whether the new doctrine of strict liability in tort should be extended to manufacturers of component parts.

[143] See, e.g., Pertile v. General Motors, LLC, 2017 WL 4237870, at *4 (D. Colo. 2017) (seatbelt components and assembly); Swanstrom v. Teledyne Cont'l Motors, Inc., 43 So.3d 564, 583–84 (Ala. 2009) (N.M. law) (jury could find manufacturer of fuel pump and engine, as well as manufacturer of aircraft, subject to negligence and strict liability for making and selling defective products that caused Cirrus aircraft to crash); Bearint v. Johnson Controls, Inc., 2006 WL 1890186 (M.D. Fla. 2006) (automobile seats); Thorndike v. DaimlerChrysler Corp., 2003 WL 21212591 (D. Me. 2003) (defective bolt used to secure spare tire to van floor); Jimenez v. Superior Ct., 58 P.3d 450, 454 (Cal. 2002) (windows for mass-produced homes).

[144] See, e.g., CHMM, LLC v. Freeman Marine Equip., Inc., 791 F.3d 1059, 1067 (9th Cir. 2015) (admiralty law) (economic loss doctrine barred recovery for luxury yacht, but did not bar claims against manufacturer of allegedly defective weathertight door component that damaged other property added by yacht owner); Agape Flights, Inc. v. Covington Aircraft Engines, Inc., 2012 WL 2792452, at *4 (E.D. Okla. 2012) (economic loss doctrine bars recovery for damages to aircraft engine and component fuel pump, but does not bar recovery for damages to the aircraft "itself as 'other property' "). *But see* AIG Aviation Ins. v. Avco Corp., 709 F. Supp. 2d 1124, 1131 (D.N.M. 2010) (without evidence supporting parity in parties' bargaining power, economic loss rule did not preclude plaintiffs' negligence and strict liability claims against component manufacturers).

The economic loss rule may also bar claims against suppliers of raw materials. See, e.g., Petri Paint Co. v. OMG Ams., Inc., 595 F. Supp. 2d 416, 421 (D.N.J. 2008) (economic loss doctrine precluded manufacturer of polyurethane products from pursuing tort claims of negligence, strict liability, and failure to warn against supplier of chemical products and raw materials). On the economic loss doctrine, see § 5.3, above.

[145] Arizona does so by including component parts in the definition of "product." See Ariz. Rev. Stat. Ann. § 12–681(4). Other states include manufacturers of component parts in the definition of a "manufacturer." See, e.g., Ark. Code Ann. § 16–116–202(3); Colo. Rev. Stat. Ann. § 13–21–401(1); Idaho Code Ann. § 6–1402(2); Kan. Stat. Ann. § 60–3302(b).

biomaterials used by medical device manufacturers in medical implants from liability for harm caused by the implants.[146]

Liability Principles

The fulcrum on which the liability issue usually rests is whether the dangerously defective condition resides in the component itself, in which case the component supplier generally is liable for resulting harm, or whether the defect arises from the manner in which the final product's manufacturer-assembler integrates the component into the product, in which case the component supplier usually is *not* responsible for resulting harm.[147] It is clear that suppliers of component parts (including raw materials) are subject to liability for harm proximately caused by defects in the components at the time they are sold, notwithstanding the fact that the defective components are integrated into final products that ultimately cause the harm.[148] If a wheel or tire manufacturer supplies a defective wheel or tire to the assembler of a vehicle, and the defect causes the vehicle to crash, then the supplier of the defective wheel[149] or tire[150] (in addition to the manufacturer-assembler of the entire vehicle) is properly liable for the harmful consequences of the crash. Suppliers thus are subject to liability for harm that is proximately caused[151] by manufacturing defects[152] and design defects,[153] in components they provide.

---

[146] This is the Biomaterials Access Assurance Act of 1998, 21 U.S.C. §§ 1601 et seq., set forth in Appendix K of Owen & Davis on Products Liability. See, e.g., Connell v. Lima Corp., 988 F.3d 1089, 1093 (9th Cir. 2021) (as a matter of first impression, supplier of biomaterials hip implant component was immune from liability under the Biomaterials Access Assurance Act); Mattern v. Biomet, Inc., 2013 WL 1314695 (D.N.J. 2013) (pursuant to the Act, granting motion to dismiss to manufacturer of piece of cast metal, comprised of chromium and cobalt, that later became part of medical devices).

[147] See, e.g., White v. ABCO Eng'g Corp., 221 F.3d 293 (2d Cir. 2000) (N.J. law) (question turns on whether component part itself was defective).

[148] The logic of this point has been evident from the inception of modern products liability law. See Rest. (2d) Torts § 402A cmt. *q* ("where there is no change in the component part itself, but it is merely incorporated into something larger, the strict liability will be found to carry through to the ultimate user or consumer").

[149] See, e.g., City of Franklin v. Badger Ford Truck Sales, Inc., 207 N.W.2d 866 (Wis. 1973).

[150] See, e.g., Harbor City Disc. Auto Ctr., Inc. v. Firestone Tire & Rubber Co., 157 Cal. Rptr. 438 (Ct. App. 1979).

[151] So, the doctrine of proximate cause barred liability in a products liability action against the manufacturers of otherwise safe fertilizer products used by terrorists to construct the device exploded in the World Trade Center in New York City. See Port Auth. of N.Y. & N.J. v. Arcadian Corp., 189 F.3d 305, 317–19 (3d Cir. 1999) (N.Y. and N.J. law). See also Davis v. Berwind Corp., 640 A.2d 1289, 1299–1300 (Pa. Super. Ct. 1994) (removal of safety interlock from component product was unforeseeable); Temple v. Wean United, Inc., 364 N.E.2d 267, 271 (Ohio 1977) (employer's dangerous installation and use of component was "sole responsible cause" of accident).

[152] See, e.g., Thorndike v. DaimlerChrysler Corp., 2003 WL 21212591 (D. Me. 2003) (defectively manufactured bolt used to secure spare tire to van floor); Jimenez v. Superior Ct., 58 P.3d 450 (Cal. 2002) (defective windows in manufactured home); Sipes v. General Motors Corp., 946 S.W.2d 143, 159–60 (Tex. App. 1997) (automotive airbag component); Jones v. Aero-Chem Corp., 680 F. Supp. 338 (D. Mont. 1987) (tear gas canister valve); Bradford v. Bendix-Westinghouse Auto. Air Brake Co., 517 P.2d 406 (Colo. App. 1973) (truck brake pedal assembly); Burbage v. Boiler Eng'g & Supply Co., 249 A.2d 563 (Pa. 1969) (defective valve in boiler); Suvada v. White Motor Co., 210 N.E.2d 182 (Ill. 1965) (truck brake), overruled on other grounds, Dixon v. Chicago & N.W. Transp. Co., 601 N.E.2d 704, 711 (Ill. 1992).

[153] See, e.g., Stephenson v. Caterpillar Inc., 2019 WL 1066177, at *2 (E.D. Tex. 2019) (skid steer's seat heater); Bearint v. Johnson Controls, Inc., 2006 WL 1890186 (M.D. Fla. 2006) (automobile seats); White v. ABCO Eng'g Corp., 221 F.3d 293 (2d Cir. 2000) (N.J. law) (unguarded line conveyor of recycling machine); Dougherty v. Edward J. Meloney, Inc., 661 A.2d 375 (Pa. Super. Ct. 1995) (shut-off valve for boilers); Gryc v. Dayton-Hudson Corp., 297 N.W.2d 727 (Minn. 1980) (flammable cotton flannelette fabric made into children's pajamas); d'Hedouville v. Pioneer Hotel Co., 552 F.2d 886 (9th Cir. 1977) (Ariz. law) (flammable acrylic fiber made into carpeting). See also Brewer v. PACCAR, Inc., 124 N.E.3d 616 (Ind. 2019) (semi-truck, with 40' blind spot in rear, backed over supervisor; because truck had only one use, jury should decide whether component

Courts quite frequently assert that manufacturers of component parts have no duty to warn of possible dangers from another firm's integration of the component into another product unless the component supplier participates in the design of the integrated product.[154] But such assertions overstate the principle, for suppliers of raw materials and component parts surely are subject to liability for failing to adequately warn or instruct in certain situations.[155] If a component contains an inherent hidden danger of which the manufacturer-assembler of the finished product is likely to be unaware, then the component supplier quite clearly has a duty to provide a warning of the danger.[156] But if the danger is unforeseeable;[157] or if it is obvious, commonly known,[158] or otherwise likely to be known by the manufacturer-assembler of the final product;[159] or if the large variety of possible uses of a material or other component make it impractical to warn of a large and amorphous bundle of speculative risks,[160] then the supplier has no reason or obligation to provide a warning. When a supplier of raw materials or component parts does have a duty to warn of hidden dangers, most cases hold that the duty is fulfilled by providing the information to the manufacturer-assembler, such that the component supplier ordinarily has no duty to warn the end user[161]—not, at least, if the component part supplier does not participate in designing the integrated product.

---

seller of all parts of the truck reasonably should have at least offered buyer various safety features, such as a rear-view window, a backup alarm, a backup camera, or backup flashers).

[154] See, e.g., Gibbs v. 84 Lumber Co., 2020 WL 5798072, at *7 (Del. Super. Ct. 2020) (S.C. law) (component parts manufacturers "generally have no duty to warn end users of the potentially dangerous uses to which their products may be put"); Faddish v. Buffalo Pumps, 881 F. Supp. 2d 1361, 1371 (S.D. Fla. 2012) (where component is not defective and its supplier does not substantially participate in its integration into final product, supplier has no duty to warn of risks of integration, regardless of their foreseeability); Schaffer v. A.O. Smith Harvestore Prods., Inc., 74 F.3d 722, 729 (6th Cir. 1996) (Ohio law) ("a manufacturer of a non-defective component part has no duty to warn about dangers that may result when the part is integrated into another product or system, where the component manufacturer was not involved in the design or assembly of the integrated product or system").

[155] See, e.g., Fleck v. KDI Sylvan Pools, Inc., 981 F.2d 107, 118 (3d Cir. 1992) (Pa. law) (replacement pool-liner supplier had duty to provide diving warnings and depth markers—warning obligation was more logically affixed to supplier of pool liner than to manufacturer of finished pool); Gryc v. Dayton-Hudson Corp., 297 N.W.2d 727 (Minn. 1980) (flammable cotton flannelette fabric made into children's pajamas that parents could flame-retard at home).

[156] See, e.g., Hammond v. North Am. Asbestos Corp., 454 N.E.2d 210 (Ill. 1983) (strict liability in tort for sale of raw asbestos fiber, which defendant mined, milled, and packaged, without adequate warnings). See generally Products Liability Rest. § 5 cmt. *b*. *But see* id. cmt. *c* (raw material supplier has no duty to warn).

[157] Zaza v. Marquess & Nell, Inc., 675 A.2d 620 (N.J. 1996); Schaffer v. A.O. Smith Harvestore Prods., Inc., 74 F.3d 722, 731 (6th Cir. 1996) (Ohio law).

[158] See, e.g., Kurzinsky v. Petzl Am., Inc., 794 Fed. Appx. 187, 189 (3d Cir. 2019) (Pa. law) (obvious risk of dangerous speed while going downhill on a zip line's pulley); Wood v. Phillips Petroleum Co., 119 S.W.3d 870 (Tex. App. 2003) (benzene dangers commonly known in petrochemical industry); Fluidmaster, Inc. v. Severinsen, 520 S.E.2d 253 (Ga. Ct. App. 1999) (obvious that toilet-tank's flush valve seal could deteriorate over time).

[159] See, e.g., Artiglio v. General Elec. Co., 71 Cal. Rptr. 2d 817 (Ct. App. 1998) (supplier of silicone used in breast implants had no duty to warn recipients of risk; implant manufacturers were sophisticated buyers); Zaza v. Marquess & Nell, Inc., 675 A.2d 620, 633 (N.J. 1996) (manufacturer of component part, not dangerous in itself, has no duty to warn employee of immediate purchaser of component which itself is aware of need to attach safety devices). See generally § 9.4, above.

[160] See, e.g., Pomplun v. Rockwell Int'l Corp., 552 N.W.2d 632 (Wis. Ct. App. 1996) (manufacturer of foot switch did not know how manufacturer of press might integrate switch into overall design of press).

[161] See, e.g., Gibbs v. 84 Lumber Co., 2020 WL 5798072, at *7 (Del. Super. Ct. 2020) (S.C. law) (bulk supplier of raw asbestos reasonably relied on purchasing manufacturers to warn end users of dangers in finished products); Wood v. Phillips Petroleum Co., 119 S.W.3d 870 (Tex. App. 2003) (manufacturers of benzene did not have duty to warn decedent of dangers of exposure because decedent's employer knew of such dangers); Artiglio v. General Elec. Co., 71 Cal. Rptr. 2d 817 (Ct. App. 1998) (supplier of silicone to manufacturer of

In limited contexts, however, a component supplier will have a duty to go beyond the purchasing assembler and warn users directly.[162] Such a duty fairly may arise when the supplier has good reason to suspect that its purchasing intermediary will not inform users or consumers about serious latent hazards in its component product. Whether such a suspicion requires a component supplier to warn end users directly rests ultimately on whether a reasonable supplier would do so in the circumstances. The *Restatement (2d) of Torts* § 388 comment *n* provides a comprehensive list of considerations that are well summarized in § 2(c) cmt. *i* of the *Third Restatement*:

> There is no general rule whether one supplying a product for the use of others through an intermediary has a duty to warn the ultimate product user directly or may rely on the intermediary to relay warnings. The standard is one of reasonableness in the circumstances. Among the factors to be considered are [1] the gravity of the risks posed by the product, [2] the likelihood that the intermediary will convey the information to the ultimate user, and [3] the feasibility and effectiveness of giving a warning directly to the user.[163]

The spirit of this rule of reason in a comment to *Products Liability Restatement* § (2)(c)—which rests on a flexible, fact-specific balance of factors—clashes with the definitive no-duty assertions in comments to § 5. This tension, which the *Third Restatement* fails to reconcile, leaves modern courts with the decision whether to pass such warning issues along to juries or to rule on them as a matter of law.[164]

If a component material or product is not itself dangerously defective but becomes so only because of the manner in which a manufacturer-assembler incorporates it into a finished product, then the component supplier generally is not liable for harm caused by

---

defective breast implant did not have duty to warn patient-victims of dangers of using silicon in medical applications); In re TMJ Implants Prods. Liab. Litig., 872 F. Supp. 1019 (D. Minn. 1995) (manufacturer of Teflon, a product with numerous industrial uses that was utilized by a surgical-implant manufacturer as a component in jaw implants had no duty to warn consumers directly of defects in the integrated products). See generally Schwartz and Appel, Effective Communication of Warnings in the Workplace: Avoiding Injuries in Working with Industrial Materials, 73 Mo. L. Rev. 1, 2, 17–24 (2008).

[162] See, e.g., Union Carbide Corp. v. Aubin, 97 So.3d 886, 898–901 (Fla. Dist. Ct. App. 2012) (asbestos; reasonableness of warnings for jury); Tellez-Cordova v. Campbell-Hausfeld/Scott Fetzger Co., 28 Cal. Rptr. 3d 744, 748 (Cal. Ct. App. 2004) (manufacturer of power grinders designed to be used with abrasive wheels or discs had duty to warn users of inhalation risks); White v. ABCO Eng'g Corp., 221 F.3d 293 (2d Cir. 2000) (N.J. law) (defendant may have had a duty to warn foreseeable users of product hazard); Gryc v. Dayton-Hudson Corp., 297 N.W.2d 727 (Minn. 1980) (manufacturer of cotton flannelette sold for use in making young girls' pajamas had duty to warn consumers directly, as on hang-tags provided to clothing manufacturers, of the flammability risk and methods of reducing it). See also Rest. (2d) Torts § 388 cmt. *n*.

[163] Products Liability Rest. § 2(c) cmt. *i*.

[164] See the excellent decision in Union Carbide Corp. v. Aubin, 97 So.3d 886 (Fla. Dist. Ct. App. 2012), reasoning from the Second and Third Restatements of Torts and Florida law that processed asbestos was not defectively designed but that a jury should decide whether the supplier should have warned end users of its hazards. DuPont's counsel in the TMJ litigation, see note 182, below, argued that a duty to warn end users is more appropriate for component materials that are inherently dangerous or when a component is "toxic or otherwise dangerous for normal handling." Mansfield, Reflections on Current Limits on Component and Raw Material Supplier Liability and the Proposed Third Restatement, 84 Ky. L.J. 221, 229–30 (1996). See, e.g., Hunnings v. Texaco, Inc., 29 F.3d 1480 (11th Cir. 1994) (Fla. law) (manufacturers and suppliers of "inherently dangerous" mineral spirits sold in bulk, which they knew retailers were routinely repackaging and selling in milk containers without adequate warnings, were subject to negligence liability). Compare the "inherently dangerous" product exception to the normal no-duty principle applied to raw materials, note 140, above.

the defect in the integrated product.[165] In *Temple v. Wean United, Inc.*,[166] for example, the manufacturer of a dual-button operating control panel, Square D, sold a control panel to the plaintiff's employer who proceeded to install it on a power press incorrectly, with the control buttons facing upwards—which created an unreasonable risk that stock could fall upon and accidentally activate the buttons, which subsequently occurred, injuring the plaintiff. Holding Square D free of responsibility for the accident, the court observed:

> [T]he obligation that generates the duty to warn does not extend to the speculative anticipation of how manufactured components, not in and of themselves dangerous or defective, can become potentially dangerous dependent upon the nature of their integration into a unit designed and assembled by another. Because of limited contact with [the employer], there is no indication that Square D could have known that its components were to be fashioned or fabricated into the power press in the particular manner that they were.[167]

Courts widely agree that suppliers of nondefective components do not generally have a duty to police the manner in which their components are integrated into finished products and so are not liable for dangers that manufacturer-assemblers introduce into finished products containing the components.[168] As discussed below, however, this general no-duty rule is subject to an important exception where the supplier of a component participates with its buyer in designing the finished product in a manner that creates an unreasonable risk to users of the finished product.[169]

The pivotal issue in most of the cases is whether the supplier of the component product or the assembling manufacturer of the finished product was substantially responsible for creating the unreasonable risk of harm that injured the plaintiff. The

---

[165] See, e.g., Stephenson v. Caterpillar Inc., 2019 WL 1066177, at *2 (E.D. Tex. 2019) ("a component-part manufacturer that does not participate in the integration of the component into the finished product is not liable for defects in the final product if the component itself is not defective"); Flores v. Kaman Indus. Techs. Corp., 2010 WL 1888710, at *7 (Cal. Ct. App. 2010) (supplier of nondefective motor and gearbox components of conveyor belt system, who did not participate in system's design or construction of system, not liable for injury from defect in conveyor system). Compare Donner v. Alcoa Inc., 2011 WL 207972, at *4 (W.D. Mo. 2011) (manufacturer of aluminum sheets not liable for worker's pulmonary fibrosis, from inhaling dust from grinding and other processing of aluminum into forms, because it did not participate in "manipulation of the aluminum sheets into the particles" that caused plaintiff's lung damage).

[166] 364 N.E.2d 267 (Ohio 1977).

[167] Id. at 272.

[168] See, e.g., Gudmundson v. Del Ozone, 232 P.3d 1059, 1073–74 (Utah 2010) (component manufacturer did not have duty to analyze or anticipate design of product or system of which its component was part); In re Dow Corning Corp., 2008 WL 4585249, at *10–11 (E.D. Mich. 2008) (silicone raw materials supplier had no duty to analyze design and assembly of outer breast implant shell that ruptured); Jacobs v. E.I. du Pont de Nemours & Co., 67 F.3d 1219, 1241 (6th Cir. 1995) (Ohio law) (manufacturer of Teflon, integrated by medical device manufacturer into jaw implant prosthesis which disintegrated from foreign-body reaction to commercial-grade plastic being implanted in human jaws, not subject to liability for harmful results); Crossfield v. Quality Control Equip. Co., 1 F.3d 701, 704 (8th Cir. 1993) (Mo. law) (supplier of chain for machine not liable for failing to provide warning decal or interlock guard to cover chain that ripped off worker's fingers; otherwise, such suppliers would need "to hire machine design experts to scrutinize machine systems that the supplier had no role in developing," forcing them to modify and add warnings to another company's machines; "[m]ere suppliers cannot be expected to guarantee the safety of other manufacturers' machinery"); Lee v. Butcher Boy, 215 Cal. Rptr. 195, 199 (Ct. App. 1985) (motor manufacturer, which played no role in design of meat grinder into which motor was integrated, not liable for plaintiff's injuries when his hand was caught and injured in machine).

[169] See, e.g., Springmeyer v. Ford Motor Co., 71 Cal. Rptr. 2d 190, 194–97 (Ct. App. 1998) (supplier of defective fan blade used on engines in Ford trucks liable for resulting injuries because it helped Ford in design and testing of blade); Pasquale v. Speed Prods. Eng'g, 654 N.E.2d 1365 (Ill. 1995).

Restatement (Second) of Torts and many of the cases[170] address this issue in terms of whether the dangerous defect was in the component at the time it left the component supplier's control, or whether the danger was introduced into the product through "further processing or other substantial change" by the manufacturer-assembler of the finished product.[171] Indeed, § 402A declares that a seller is subject to strict products liability in tort only if the product "is expected to and does reach the user or consumer without substantial change in the condition in which it is sold."[172]

The *Third Restatement* focuses more precisely on the circumstances that may give rise to liability for suppliers of component parts. Section 5 provides that a component part supplier is subject to liability caused by a product into which the component is integrated only if (1) the component itself is defective; or (2) the seller "substantially participates" in a dangerously defective integration of the component into the design of the finished product.[173] Because § 5 clearly and faithfully distills much of the rather confused prior case law, courts have relied on this section of the *Products Liability Restatement* as an authoritative statement of applicable principles of law.[174] For

---

[170] See, e.g., Zager v. Johnson Controls, Inc., 18 N.E.3d 533, 547–59 (Ohio Ct. App. 2014) (affirming JMOL for component manufacturer; insufficient evidence that seatback was defective or that defendant substantially participated in the vehicle's design); Haase v. Badger Mining Corp., 669 N.W.2d 737 (Wis. Ct. App. 2003), aff'd on other grounds, 682 N.W.2d 389 (Wis. 2004).

[171] See Rest. (2d) Torts § 402A cmt. *p*, entitled "Further processing or substantial change" provides in part:

> [T]he mere fact that the product is to undergo processing, or other substantial change, will not in all cases relieve the seller of liability. . . . If, for example, raw coffee beans are sold to a buyer who roasts and packs them for sale to the ultimate consumer, it cannot be supposed that the seller will be relieved of all liability when the raw beans are contaminated with arsenic, or some other poison. . . . On the other hand, the manufacturer of pig iron, which is capable of a wide variety of uses, is not so likely to be held to strict liability when it turns out to be unsuitable for the child's tricycle into which it is finally made by a remote buyer.

Comment *q*, entitled "Component parts," notes that "where there is no change in the component part itself, but it is merely incorporated into something larger, the strict liability will be found to carry through to the ultimate user or consumer."

Compare, with comment *p*'s pig iron tricycle example, States S.S. Co. v. Stone Manganese Marine, Ltd., 371 F. Supp. 500 (D.N.J. 1973). This was a suit brought by a ship owner against the manufacturer of alloy ingots that were cast into propellers and installed on plaintiff's ships by a third-party shipyard. The alloy was inadequate for the job, and several of the propeller blades fractured, causing various damage. Defendant argued that casting the ingots into propellers was a "substantial change" in their condition, precluding liability under § 402A. The court thought this "too simplistic a reading of Section 402A(1)(b)," because at issue were "the qualities of the alloy, regardless of its shape." Id. at 505.

[172] Rest. (2d) Torts § 402A(1)(b).

[173] Products Liability Rest. § 5, entitled "Liability of Commercial Seller or Distributor of Product Components for Harm Caused by Products Into Which Components Are Integrated" provides in full:

> One engaged in the business of selling or otherwise distributing product components who sells or distributes a component is subject to liability for harm to persons or property caused by a product into which the component is integrated if:
>
> (a) the component is defective in itself, as defined in this Chapter, and the defect causes the harm; or
>
> (b)(1) the seller or distributor of the component substantially participates in the integration of the component into the design of the product; and
>
> (2) the integration of the component causes the product to be defective, as defined in this Chapter; and
>
> (3) the defect in the product causes the harm.

[174] See, e.g., Coffman v. Armstrong Int'l, Inc., 2019 WL 3287067, at *16–17 (Tenn. Ct. App. 2019) (citing Davis v. Komatsu Am. Indus. Corp., 42 S.W.3d 34, 43 (Tenn. 2011), which adopted Products Liability Rest. § 5), reversed in part on other grounds, 615 S.W.3d 888 (Tenn. 2021); Estate of Thompson v. Kawasaki Heavy Indus., 922 F. Supp. 2d 780, 793–96 (N.D. Iowa 2013); Smith v. Robin Am., Inc., 484 Fed. Appx. 908, 912 (5th Cir. 2012) (Tex. law); Gudmundson v. Del Ozone, 232 P.3d 1059, 1072–74 (Utah 2010); Boyle v. Ford Motor

example, in *Buonanno v. Colmar Belting Co.*,[175] a worker's arm was caught and injured in the unguarded nip point of a conveyor belt system at the point where the belt moved over the stationary "wing pulley." In a negligence and strict liability in tort action against both the manufacturer of the wing pulley and the supplier of various component parts of the conveyor system, principally for failing to shield the conveyor system's nip point, a majority of the court upheld summary judgment for the wing pulley manufacturer, ruling that the wing pulley component was not "defective in itself," under § 5(a):

> [T]he nip point is created only when the belt meets the wing pulley after the entire conveyor belt system is assembled. There was no evidence presented to suggest that a single, isolated wing pulley presents a danger. Therefore, the wing pulley is not defective "in itself" or "at the time of sale or distribution," but only creates the potential for injury when integrated into the conveyor-belt system.[176]

As for § 5(b), the court ruled that there was some evidence that the distributor of the various component parts had "substantially participated" in the conveyor system design, but no evidence that the wing pulley manufacturer had participated at all in the design of the integrated system. Hence, the court reversed the summary judgment for the distributor of the conveyor system's various component parts, remanding for a trial on the issue of whether it had substantially participated in the conveyor system's design.[177]

The *Buonanno* decision was split, however, on two issues, illustrating the difficulty of many of the cases dealing with the liability of component part manufacturers. Two of the justices thought that, in the case against the wing pulley manufacturer, the plaintiff had presented sufficient evidence that the pulley could have been designed in a safer manner that would have reduced the risk of harm, rendering the pulley defectively designed "in itself" under § 5(a).[178] And, while four of the justices thought that the wing pulley manufacturer "had no duty to warn against any injuries caused by the final integrated product since it had no involvement with the design of the entire system,"[179] one justice asserted that there was sufficient evidence to find the pulley defective in itself under § 5(a) because of the absence of a "warning on the pulley itself that would alert users to the nip-point danger."[180]

Indeed, § 5 is not entirely clear on the most difficult issue in many component part cases—the component supplier's duty to warn the manufacturer-assembler and, possibly, even ultimate users. Section 5(a) provides that a component supplier is liable for providing a component that is defective in itself, and a product may be defective under *Products Liability Restatement* § 2(c) if the supplier fails to provide adequate warnings or instructions—a point made clear in § 5 comment *b*. But comment *b* also asserts that "when a sophisticated buyer integrates a component into another product, the component seller owes no duty to warn either the immediate buyer or ultimate

---

Co., 942 A.2d 850, 853 (N.J. Super. Ct. App. Div. 2008); Godoy v. E.I. du Pont de Nemours & Co., 743 N.W.2d 159, 164–65 (Wis. Ct. App. 2007), aff'd, 768 N.W.2d 674 (2009); Gray v. Badger Mining Corp., 676 N.W.2d 268 (Minn. 2004); Jimenez v. Superior Ct., 58 P.3d 450 (Cal. 2002).

[175] 733 A.2d 712 (R.I. 1999).

[176] Id. at 717.

[177] See id. at 719–20.

[178] See id. at 717–18.

[179] Id. at 714.

[180] Id. at 721.

consumers of dangers arising because the component is unsuited for the special purpose to which the buyer puts it," even if the component supplier is aware of "the component purchaser's lack of expertise and ignorance of the risks of integrating the component into the purchaser's product."[181]

While much of the case law supports the view that component part makers have no duty to warn beyond the manufacturer-assembler,[182] reason suggests that, for warnings to be effective, they sometimes will have to be transmitted through, over, or around the manufacturer-assembler directly to end users.[183] Comment *b* to § 5 does acknowledge that such cases may be covered by the doctrine of negligent entrustment, which may ordinarily be a better vehicle for addressing this small subset of cases concerning component supplier liability. But courts may wish to define a general duty for suppliers of raw materials and component parts to warn of dangers they know are likely to injure consumers from the manner in which manufacturer-assemblers integrate the components into finished products.[184] However the law chooses to protect consumers in cases of this type, surely component suppliers should not be immunized from liability for failing to provide effective warnings of serious product hazards by permitting them to hide behind the coattails of manufacturer-assemblers in every case.[185]

In summary, a supplier of raw materials or component parts normally has no duty to warn end users of risks arising out of the incorporation of the component into a larger, finished product. On rare occasions, when a component supplier knows that a manufacturer-assembler has used or intends to use its components in a way that is likely to be unreasonably dangerous to consumers,[186] the component supplier should not be shielded by a blanket no-duty rule. Instead, a supplier of such materials should be required to take reasonable steps to protect consumers from an unreasonable risk of harm. Often these steps may involve no more than effectively notifying the manufacturer-assembler of the safety problem, how to remedy it, and the manufacturer-assembler's obligation to do so. If the danger is great enough, however, and if the component supplier knows that the manufacturer-assembler is unlikely to address the danger effectively, then logic suggests that the component supplier should have a duty to monitor the situation and, if the problem is not resolved, to take whatever steps may

---

[181] Products Liability Rest. § 5 cmt. *b*.

[182] Particularly the spate of cases shielding Du Pont from responsibility for the massive injuries resulting from the inappropriate use of Du Pont's Teflon, by a small medical device company that promptly went bankrupt, in jaw implants for treating TMJ syndrome. See, e.g., In re TMJ Implants Prods. Liab. Litig., 872 F. Supp. 1019 (D. Minn. 1995) (summary judgment in multidistrict case granted in favor of Du Pont; *held*, raw-material supplier or component-part manufacturer has no duty to warn consumers directly of defects in the integrated products, purportedly the rule in all jurisdictions), aff'd 97 F.3d 1050 (8th Cir. 1996). Compare In re Silicone Gel Breast Implants Prods. Liab. Litig., 887 F. Supp. 1463 (N.D. Ala. 1995).

[183] See, e.g., Beauchamp v. Russell, 547 F. Supp. 1191, 1197 (N.D. Ga. 1982); Gryc v. Dayton-Hudson Corp., 297 N.W.2d 727 (Minn. 1980) (brilliantly briefed); Suchomajcz v. Hummel Chem. Co., 524 F.2d 19, 25–27 (3d Cir. 1975) (Pa. law). See Rest. (2d) Torts § 388 cmt. *n*.

[184] See, e.g., Hunnings v. Texaco, Inc., 29 F.3d 1480 (11th Cir. 1994) (Fla. law) (manufacturers and suppliers of mineral spirits sold in bulk, which they knew retailers were routinely repackaging and selling in milk containers without adequate warnings, were subject to negligence liability).

[185] "[M]anufacturers do not enjoy blanket protection from liability simply because others in the chain of distribution may repackage or reformulate the product before it reaches the ultimate consumer." Id. at 1485. See also Godoy v. E.I. du Pont de Nemours & Co., 768 N.W.2d 674, 688 (Wis. 2009) (component manufacturers do not enjoy "blanket immunity from liability"; "Integration into another product does not shift responsibility from the manufacturer of a defective component to another party 'who [is] in no position to detect the hidden defect.' ").

[186] Perhaps by prior lawsuits concerning the same danger in which they both were defendants. See, e.g., Speer v. Wheelabrator Corp., 826 F. Supp. 1264, 1272–73 (D. Kan. 1993).

be reasonably necessary in the circumstances to protect consumers from unreasonable risks of harm arising from the component's use in the finished product.[187]

§ 15.4 PARENT AND APPARENT MANUFACTURERS; FRANCHISERS

Sometimes a plaintiff injured in a product accident seeks recovery beyond the manufacturer from some other, perhaps more solvent, defendant who profitably exploited another company's manufacture and sale of the accident product. Corporate parents of manufacturing subsidiaries are one such possible defendant, as are franchisers and trademark-owners who license their mark to other companies who make and sell a product. Parent corporations and trademark-owners reap the commercial benefits of products designed, manufactured, and/or marketed substantially or wholly by their subsidiaries or trademark licensees. The latter, as product manufacturers, are of course subject to the normal rules of products liability law. But sometimes subsidiaries are thinly capitalized, and trademark licensees and franchisees typically are small enterprises in comparison to their licensors or franchisers. This section briefly examines when a parent corporation, trademark-holder, or franchiser that profits from the manufacture and sale of products by a related company is insulated from liability, and when such a non-manufacturing but related enterprise may be subject to liability for product-caused harm.

Parent Corporations—Alter Ego Liability

Fundamental principles of corporate law ordinarily shield shareholders from the debts and other liabilities of the corporation. Indeed, shareholder immunity from the enterprise's liabilities is an essential pillar of the corporate form of organization,[188] and courts are properly reluctant to allow inroads into this basic tenet of corporate limited liability.[189] Thus, when a parent corporation owns most or all of the stock of a financially unstable subsidiary corporation, the fact that the two corporations have separate identities normally precludes a subsidiary's creditors—including products liability claimants—from recovering against the parent corporation.

As strong as the limited shareholder liability principle certainly is, a court may nevertheless "pierce" the "corporate veil" in certain limited situations.[190] Among the

---

[187] Sometimes reasonable care will require providing warnings directly to end users; other times it may require terminating sales to the offending manufacturer-assembler of the finished product; and on rare occasions it may require informing safety agencies or law enforcement authorities. See, e.g., Hunnings v. Texaco, Inc., 29 F.3d 1480 (11th Cir. 1994) (Fla. law); Suchomajcz v. Hummel Chem. Co., 524 F.2d 19 (3d Cir. 1975) (Pa. law).

[188] "Limited liability is a distinguishing feature of corporate law—perhaps *the* distinguishing feature." F. Easterbrook and D. Fischel, The Economic Structure of Corporate Law 40 (1991). See generally 1 W. Fletcher, Fletcher Cyclopedia of the Law of Corporations § 41.35 (Perm. ed. 2006, and annual updates) [hereinafter Fletcher, Corporations]; 1 J. Cox and T. Hazen, Corporations § 7.07 at 271 (2d ed. 2003) ("limited shareholder liability is not simply a principle of corporate law, but a cornerstone of capitalism"); H. Henn and J. Alexander, Law of Corporations and other Business Enterprises § 202, 547 (3d ed. 1983) ("limited liability of shareholders is probably the most significant attribute of the modern corporation").

[189] "Limited liability," according to Justice Douglas, "is the rule not the exception; and on that assumption large undertakings are rested, vast enterprises are launched, and huge sums of capital attracted." Anderson v. Abbott, 321 U.S. 349, 362 (1944). See Thompson, Piercing the Corporate Veil: An Empirical Study, 76 Cornell L. Rev. 1036, 1058 (1991) (courts pierce veil about 30% of time in tort cases).

[190] See Koosed, Badaracco, and Iverson, Disregarding the Corporate Form: Why Judges, Not Juries, Should Decide the Quiddits and Quillets of Veil Piercing, 13 N.Y.U. J.L. & Bus. 95 (2016); Oh, Veil-Piercing Unbound, 93 B.U. L. Rev. 89 (2013); Marcantel, Because Judges Are Not Angels Either: Limiting Judicial Discretion By Introducing Objectivity Into Piercing Doctrine, 59 U. Kan. L. Rev. 191 (2011); Cheng, Form and Substance of the Doctrine of Piercing the Corporate Veil, 80 Miss. L.J. 497 (2010); Millon, The Still-Elusive

various grounds for holding a parent corporation responsible for the defective products of its manufacturing subsidiary,[191] the principal derivative basis for responsibility is "alter ego" liability, based on the idea that the parent may so dominate its subsidiary that they are essentially a single economic entity.[192] "[W]hen a corporation is so controlled as to be the alter ego or mere instrumentality of its stockholder, the corporate form may be disregarded in the interests of justice."[193] This "disregarding" of the corporate form, allowing a subsidiary corporation's creditor to reach the parent corporation, is regularly called "piercing the corporate veil."[194]

For a plaintiff to prevail on an "alter ego" claim, many jurisdictions require that the plaintiff show *both* (1) that the parent and subsidiary acted as a single economic entity; and (2) some injustice, unfairness, or improper conduct by the defendant parent.[195] Whether a parent and subsidiary acted as a single economic entity depends on a variety of factors, including whether they had common directors and officers; whether the subsidiary was adequately capitalized for its undertaking; whether it was solvent at the relevant time; whether it paid dividends, kept corporate records, and observed other corporate formalities; whether its officers and directors operated according to regular

---

Quest to Make Sense of Veil-Piercing, 89 Tex. L. Rev. 15 (2010) (response to Oh, below); Oh, Veil-Piercing, 89 Tex. L. Rev. 81 (2010); Hansmann and Kraakman, Toward Unlimited Shareholder Liability for Corporate Torts, 100 Yale L.J. 1879 (1991); Note, 29 Rutgers L.J. 121 (1997) (silicone-gel breast implant victims' efforts to reach Dow Chemical); F. Gevurtz, Corporation Law § 1.5 (3d ed. 2021); Annot., 7 A.L.R.3d 1343 (1966) (liability of corporation for torts of subsidiary).

[191] For examples of both derivative and direct theories of recovery, see, e.g., Dow Chem. Co. v. Mahlum, 970 P.2d 98, 106 (Nev. 1998) (reversing findings on (1) fraudulent concealment of dangers in silicone breast implants, (2) concert of action, and (3) aiding and abetting, but allowing claim on negligent undertaking); Fletcher v. Atex, Inc., 68 F.3d 1451 (2d Cir. 1995) (Del. law) (affirming summary judgment for defendant on each of four theories of liability: (1) alter ego, (2) agency and apparent agency, (3) apparent manufacturer, and (4) concerted tortious action). See also In re Silicone Gel Breast Implants Prods. Liab. Litig., 887 F. Supp. 1447 (N.D. Ala. 1995) (allowing alter ego and negligent undertaking claims against Bristol-Meyers Squibb).

[192] See, e.g., Fletcher v. Atex, Inc., 68 F.3d 1451, 1456 (2d Cir. 1995) (Del. law).

[193] In re Silicone Gel Breast Implants Prods. Liab. Litig., 887 F. Supp. 1447, 1452 (N.D. Ala. 1995).

[194] See, e.g., Leonard v. General Motors L.L.C., 504 F. Supp. 3d 73, 86 (D. Conn. 2020) ("Connecticut courts generally pierce the corporate veil only under 'exceptional circumstances,' such as when 'the corporation is a mere shell, serving no legitimate purpose, and used primarily as an intermediary to perpetuate fraud or promote injustice.' "). See also Marchan v. John Miller Farms, Inc., 352 F. Supp. 3d 938, 943–49 (D.N.D. 2018) (holding that piercing the corporate veil is a question for the jury under federal law; reviewing cases).

[195] Fletcher v. Atex, Inc., 68 F.3d 1451, 1457 (2d Cir. 1995) (Del. law). "[F]raud or wrongdoing is not necessary under an alter ego theory, but the plaintiff must demonstrate an overall element of injustice or unfairness." Id. at 1458. Wehner v. Linvatech Corp., 2008 WL 495525, at *6 (D. Minn. 2008) (veil piercing requires proof of: "(1) the corporation functions as a mere instrumentality of the shareholders; and (2) injustice or fundamental unfairness would occur if the corporate veil were left intact").

> It is well settled that a parent corporation, even one that owns all the stock of a subsidiary corporation is not subject to liability for the acts of its subsidiary unless the parent so controls the operation of the subsidiary as to make it a mere adjunct, instrumentality, or alter ego of the parent corporation. However, the mere domination or control of a corporation by its stockholder cannot be enough to allow a piercing of the corporate veil; rather, there must be the added elements of misuse and harm or loss resulting from the misuse.

In re Birmingham Asbestos Litig., 619 So.2d 1360, 1362 (Ala. 1993). See also In re Johnson & Johnson Talcum Powder Cases, 2017 WL 4780572, at *7 (Cal. Super. Ct. Trial. Div. 2017) (trial order) (granting defendant's motion for new trial and reversing $417 million jury award to plaintiff suffering from ovarian cancer allegedly caused by regular exposure to subsidiary's asbestos-contaminated talc products; plaintiff failed to present evidence "suggesting that an alter ego or agency theory could be put to the jury"); Finerty v. Abex Corp., 51 N.E.3d 555, 339 (N.Y. 2016) (piercing the corporate veil required finding that Ford USA "disregarded the separate identity of Ford UK and involved itself directly in that entity's affairs"); Everkrisp Vegetables Inc. v. Tobiason Potato Co., 870 F. Supp. 2d 745, 758 (D.N.D. 2012) ("an element of injustice, inequity or fundamental unfairness must be present before a court may properly pierce the corporate veil"). See generally F. Gevurtz, Corporation Law § 1.5, at 75 (3d ed. 2021) (discussing second, "fraud, wrong or injustice," prong).

corporate form; whether the parent siphoned off the subsidiary's funds; and whether, more generally, the subsidiary corporation served merely as "a facade for the dominant shareholder."[196]

The opinions of Chief Judge Pointer in *In re Silicone Gel Breast Implants Products Liability Litigation*[197] illustrate the "substantial domination" rule in action. Arising out of injuries from the surgical implantation of silicone gel breast implants in many thousands of women over many years, *In re Breast Implants* was a consolidated multi-district action in federal court in which thousands of plaintiffs sought recovery from the implant manufacturers and related companies for systemic autoimmune diseases caused by silicone leaking from the implants into the body. The principal implant supplier, Dow Corning, was jointly owned by Dow Chemical Company and Corning Incorporated. Another implant supplier, Medical Engineering Corporation (MEC), was solely owned by Bristol-Meyers Squibb Company. Because neither Dow Corning nor MEC had sufficient assets to meet the massive damages claims of thousands of plaintiffs,[198] relief was also sought from the implant suppliers' much larger parent corporations.

Judge Pointer's treatment of the two parent-subsidiary sets in these cases is instructive in illustrating when a court may allow a plaintiff to reach a parent corporation in products liability litigation. After dismissing the derivative, alter-ego claims against both parent corporations of Dow Corning,[199] Judge Pointer allowed such a claim against MEC's parent, Bristol-Meyers Squibb[200] and also allowed the plaintiffs to maintain direct liability claims against Dow Chemical based on that parent corporation's own alleged misconduct in researching silicone toxicity.[201]

In the Dow Corning litigation, Judge Pointer found that the parent corporations did not dominate the control of their subsidiary. "Dow Corning," he wrote,

> has observed all corporate formalities, including but not limited to, maintaining its own books, filing its own tax returns; hiring its own auditor; employing its own officers, management, and workers; owning and operating its own plants in seven states and nine countries; holding its own stockholders' and directors' meetings; and, in recent years, paying regular dividends.[202]

---

196 Simeone v. Bombardier-Rotax GmbH, 360 F. Supp. 2d 665, 675–76 (E.D. Pa. 2005) (listing ten "interrelationship" factors). See also Patterson v. Home Depot, USA, Inc., 684 F. Supp. 2d 1170, 1178 (D. Ariz. 2010) (seven factors); Higley v. Cessna Aircraft Co., 2010 WL 3184516, at *2 (C.D. Cal. 2010) (eight); Estate of Thomson v. Toyota Motor Corp., 545 F.3d 357, 362–63 (6th Cir. 2008) (Ohio law) (ten); In re Silicone Gel Breast Implants Prods. Liab. Litig., 887 F. Supp. 1447, 1452 (N.D. Ala. 1995) (eleven substantial-domination factors). See also Mortimer v. McCool, 255 A.3d 261, 286 (Pa. 2021) ("Pennsylvania has resisted the temptation to formalize the inquiry with an ever-increasing number of predefined factors embodying the many considerations that might aid in determining whether the corporate form has been abused. [S]implicity is to be preferred. [T]he inquiry reduces to a two-pronged test: 'First, there must be such unity of interest and ownership that the separate personalities of the corporation and the individual no longer exist, and second, adherence to the corporate fiction under the circumstances would sanction fraud or promote injustice.' "). See generally F. Gevurtz, Corporation Law § 1.5 (3d ed. 2021) (discussing requirements).

197 837 F. Supp. 1128 (N.D. Ala. 1993); 887 F. Supp. 1447 (N.D. Ala. 1995).

198 Dow Corning petitioned for bankruptcy protection on May 15, 1995. See, e.g., Dow Chem. Co. v. Mahlum, 970 P.2d 98, 106 (Nev. 1998).

199 In re Silicone Gel Breast Implants Prods. Liab. Litig., 837 F. Supp. 1128 (N.D. Ala. 1993).

200 In re Silicone Gel Breast Implants Prods. Liab. Litig., 887 F. Supp. 1447 (N.D. Ala. 1995).

201 Id. at 1455.

202 In re Silicone Gel Breast Implants Prods. Liab. Litig., 837 F. Supp. 1128, 1133 (N.D. Ala. 1993).

Such facts, in Judge Pointer's view, "clearly demonstrate a separate corporate existence for Dow Corning, recognized and respected by it and its parent corporations."[203] Accordingly, Dow Chemical and Corning were not derivatively liable for the actions of their subsidiary.[204]

In the litigation involving MEC, owned entirely by Bristol-Meyers Squibb, the facts concerning the relationship between parent and subsidiary were quite different. Applying the substantial-domination factors listed above,[205] the evidence revealed that "two of MEC's three directors were Bristol directors; MEC was part of Bristol's Health Care group and used Bristol's legal, auditing, and communications departments; MEC and Bristol filed consolidated federal tax returns and Bristol prepared consolidated financial reports; Bristol operated as MEC's finance company . . .; Bristol effectively used MEC's resources as its own by obtaining interest on MEC's money and requiring MEC to make requests for capital appropriations to obtain its own funds; some members of MEC's board were not aware that MEC [had] a board of directors, let alone that they were members; and the senior Bristol member of MEC's board could not be out-voted by the other two directors." In short, a jury "could—and, under the laws of many states probably should—find that MEC was but the alter ego of Bristol."[206]

While it is difficult for a plaintiff injured by a subsidiary's product to prevail against the parent corporation on the alter-ego theory of liability,[207] other grounds of liability may be available. In the breast implant litigation in particular, both Judge Pointer[208] and the Nevada Supreme Court[209] allowed claims against Dow Chemical on a negligent performance of an undertaking theory, under *Restatement (Second) of Torts* § 324A, based on Dow Corning's reliance for many years on Dow Chemical's negligent toxicity testing of Dow Corning's silicones.[210] "[A] cause of action under § 324A does not involve an assertion of derivative liability but one of direct liability, since it is based on the actions of the defendant itself."[211] So, while the alter-ego theory may be the traditional derivative liability route for reaching the parent of an underfunded manufacturing subsidiary, a parent's active participation in the subsidiary's affairs can make it vulnerable on some other, direct theory of liability.[212]

---

[203] Id. at 1134.

[204] Id. at 1138.

[205] The court applied many of a list of eleven separate factors relevant to the substantial domination issue. 887 F. Supp. at 1452.

[206] Id. at 1452–53.

[207] See, e.g., Levy v. Jaguar Land Rover N. Am., LLC., 2020 WL 563637, at *5 (D.N.J. 2020) (plaintiffs' conclusory allegations of alter ego insufficient to impute subsidiary's forum contacts to parent entities for jurisdictional purposes); Nelson v. International Paint Co., 734 F.2d 1084 (5th Cir. 1984) (Tex. law) (no alter ego).

[208] In re Silicone Gel Breast Implants Prods. Liab. Litig., 887 F. Supp. 1455 (N.D. Ala. 1995).

[209] Dow Chem. Co. v. Mahlum, 970 P.2d 98 (Nev. 1998).

[210] On the negligent undertaking theory, plaintiffs alleged that Dow Chemical negligently marketed silicone-gel implants without having conducted reasonable tests and research on the toxicity, biological activity, and safety of silicones to determine their safety for use in breast implants. 887 F. Supp. at 1460.

[211] Id.

[212] Other claims in In re Silicone Gel Prods. Liab. Litig., 887 F. Supp. 1455 (N.D. Ala. 1995), which Judge Pointer did not then address, included "strict liability, corporate conspiracy, concert of action, aiding and abetting, fraud, and fraudulent concealment." Id. at 1462. See also In re Asbestos Prods. Liab. Litig. (No. VI), 2011 WL 3240827, at *4, 8 (E.D. Pa. 2011) (Ala. law) (allowing direct theory of recovery against defendant based on negligent voluntary undertaking to inspect premises).

Apparent Manufacturers

The "apparent manufacturer" theory imposes the liability of a manufacturer on a seller who holds itself out to the public as the manufacturer of a product.[213] For a statement of this theory, most courts turn to *Restatement (Second) of Torts* § 400: "One who puts out as his own product a chattel manufactured by another is subject to the same liability as though he were its manufacturer."[214] This doctrine would apply, for example, to a power drill manufactured by Black and Decker but sold by Sears under its "Craftsman" brand name.[215] If a person buys the drill thinking it to be a Sears product, and then is injured by some defect in the drill, the user can hold Sears liable as if it were Black and Decker. So, if Black and Decker were subject to liability for the defect, then Sears, derivatively, would be liable as well.[216] While some courts have held parent and other up-stream defendants liable on this basis, most of the cases involve retailers or other distributors holding themselves out as a product's manufacturer.[217]

An underlying rationale for the apparent manufacturer doctrine is that a retail seller or other defendant cannot avoid responsibility as a manufacturer if it represents itself to be the product's manufacturer, or sponsor, in order to induce consumers to buy the product. Being a species of estoppel, liability resting on a defendant's "holding out" itself as a product's manufacturer[218] is based on the idea that a "vendor who, through its labeling or advertising of a product, caused the public to believe that it was the manufacturer and to buy the product in reliance on the vendor's reputation and care in making it, was held to have assumed the obligations of a manufacturer and to be estopped to deny its identity as the manufacturer."[219]

Two ideas thus merge in this rationale: estoppel and reliance. The estoppel idea is present in the earliest cases.[220] Reliance, of course, provides a causal link between the seller's trade name representation and the buyer's harm. And so, for an apparent

---

[213] For an early statement of the doctrine, see Thornhill v. Carpenter-Morton Co., 108 N.E. 474 (Mass. 1915). See generally Franklyn, The Apparent Manufacturer Doctrine, Trademark Licensors and the Third Restatement of Torts, 49 Case W. Res. L. Rev. 671 (1999).

[214] Rest. (2d) Torts § 400.

[215] See, e.g., Sears, Roebuck & Co. v. Black, 708 S.W.2d 925, 928 (Tex. App. 1986) ("Kenmore" washing machine); Chappuis v. Sears Roebuck & Co., 358 So.2d 926, 928–29 (La. 1978) ("Craftsman" hammer).

[216] See Rest. (2d) Torts § 400 cmt. *d*:

> The actor puts out a chattel as his own product in two types of cases. The first is where the actor appears to be the manufacturer of the chattel. The second is where the chattel appears to have been made particularly for the actor. In the first type of case the actor frequently causes the chattel to be used in reliance upon his care in making it; in the second, he frequently causes the chattel to be used in reliance upon a belief that he has required it to be made properly for him and that the actor's reputation is an assurance to the user of the quality of the product.

[217] See Hebel v. Sherman Equip., 442 N.E.2d 199, 201 (Ill. 1982).

[218] " 'Holding out' cases usually involve either (a) a defendant's labeling or affixing to the product its own name, trade name, or trademark; or (b) advertising identifying the defendant as the maker of the product." Id. at 202.

[219] Id. at 201. See also id. at 201–02 ("where a defendant puts out a product as its own, the purchaser has no means of ascertaining the identity of the true manufacturer, and it is thus fair to impose liability on the party whose actions effectively conceal the true manufacturer's identity").

[220] Thornhill v. Carpenter-Morton Co., 108 N.E. 474, 596–97 (Mass. 1915) (wood stain, labeled as the defendant retailer's product, was sold without warning of its inflammability; "It is no justification that the defendant procured the stain instead of having it compounded on its own premises. The jury could find that [the seller's] representations to the purchasing public or consumer without any notice of its dangerous character that it was the manufacturer must be taken as essentially true.").

manufacturer claim to lie, the product must be labeled with a name the buyer knows to be the retailer's trade name.[221]

Courts have allowed recovery on the basis of a defendant holding itself out as the manufacturer, or sponsor, of a product in a variety of situations. For example, a retailer has been held subject to strict liability as the "ostensible manufacturer" where the retailer directs a manufacturer to place the retailer's label in garments made to order; places its private label on a product without disclosing the actual manufacturer; the retailer holds out a defective attic stairway as its own by listing the product in its catalogue, and providing its own name and model number on the product instruction sheet; where it places an assembled product on a sales rack without giving any notice that another entity assembled the product; and in other apposite situations.[222]

When the apparent manufacturer doctrine was first set forth in § 400 of the *Restatement of Torts* in 1934, it expressed a bold way to hold retail sellers strictly liable in tort for production errors made by manufacturers who were often hard to identify and who were still immunized even from negligence liability in many jurisdictions by privity of contract.[223] But with the fall of the privity defense, the spread of effective discovery techniques for uncovering both the identity and production methods of manufacturers, and, most importantly, the adoption of a general doctrine of strict products liability in tort in the 1960s and 1970s, § 400 and the apparent manufacturer doctrine became quaintly obsolete.[224] Although the principle has some lingering, secondary value as a sub-issue in the trademark-licensor and franchiser doctrines discussed below, the apparent manufacturer doctrine has little remaining independent value as a theory of liability. Thus, there seems little reason for a court to adopt the rule if it has not already

---

[221] See, e.g., Bernier v. One World Techs., Inc., 746 F. Supp. 2d 240, 243 (D. Mass. 2010) (for apparent manufacturer doctrine to apply, plaintiff must produce evidence that labeling or advertisements of chattel causes consumer to rely on retailer's reputation for product quality; doctrine did not apply because no evidence plaintiff thought "Ridgid" was Home Depot's "store brand" of table saw manufactured by another company); Stones v. Sears, Roebuck & Co., 558 N.W.2d 540, 545 (Neb. 1997) ("While 'Kenmore' may be commonly associated with Sears, there is no evidence supporting that contention in the record before us.").

[222] See, e.g., Maury v. BDF Holdings, Inc., 2016 WL 4530564, at *3 (Conn. Super. Ct. 2016) (defendant "sold the [defective] chair as its own product, such that it is subject to the same liability as though it were the chair's manufacturer"); Bilenky v. Ryobi Techs., Inc., 115 F. Supp. 3d 661 (E.D. Va. 2015) (defective lawnmower made by one manufacturer but sold by another whose name was on the mower and owner's manual), aff'd, Bilenky v. Ryobi Techs., Inc., 666 Fed. Appx. 271, 275 (4th Cir. 2016) (discussing split among courts whether the apparent manufacturer doctrine is limited to parties in the chain of distribution); Watson v. Dillon Cos., 797 F. Supp. 2d 1138, 1162 (D. Colo. 2011) (under state products liability statute, Kroger may be considered "manufacturer" of microwave popcorn, the butter flavorings of which may have caused plaintiff's lung condition, since popcorn was labeled with Kroger store brands and without disclosure of actual manufacturers); Lou v. Otis Elevator Co., 933 N.E.2d 140, 148 (Mass. App. Ct. 2010) (defendant had trademark license and detailed cooperation agreement with Chinese manufacturer of escalators; thorough analysis of history, nature, and scope of doctrine).

[223] While the apparent manufacturer doctrine may have been bold in 1934, it had a basis in common law from at least 1915. See note 213, above.

[224] See Hebel v. Sherman Equip., 442 N.E.2d 199, 202 (Ill. 1982) (the purpose of the doctrine was to provide a remedy against the retailer, who now is subject to strict liability in tort: "The function of the apparent-manufacturer doctrine has, as it were, been absorbed by the theory of sellers' strict liability in tort for injuries caused by unreasonably unsafe products.").

done so,[225] or to apply the rule if it has.[226] Perhaps because a majority of jurisdictions are said to follow the rule,[227] but acknowledging that the rule has "little practical significance,"[228] the ALI curiously readopted this harmless but now largely hollow doctrine in the *Third Restatement*.[229] And while the apparent manufacturer doctrine may find sporadic service from time to time in limited contexts,[230] one may comfortably predict that it will not appear in the *Fourth Restatement*.

Trademark Licensors; Franchisers

Cases involving trademarks and franchises are a species of apparent manufacturer cases in which a trademark or trade name leads consumers to believe that the trademark owner or franchiser is responsible for the quality of the product. Owners of trademarks and trade names license their marks and names to induce consumers to buy or use a product based on the reputation for product quality possessed by the holder of the mark or name. Consumer reliance on the owner's reputation rests on an assumption, based on an implicit representation of the owner (often a franchiser), that the owner has contributed in substantial measure to the quality of the product sold by the licensee or franchisee. If a person is injured by a product manufactured by one company, but bearing the name or logo of another, the question that arises is whether the trademark owner is subject to the responsibility of a manufacturer despite the fact that the product was manufactured by someone else. The central issue in this type of case is whether the trademark owner or franchiser should be permitted to commercially exploit the value of its reputation without a corresponding responsibility—whether such a party should be accountable for defects in products sold under its name or mark. As discussed below, a licensor is subject to liability for injuries caused by a defect in a product distributed by a licensee if the licensor exercised substantial control over the design, production, marketing, or distribution of the product.[231]

---

[225] Rejecting the doctrine, see, e.g., A.L. ex rel. Limkemann v. Jake's Fireworks, Inc., 2020 WL 4548755, at *5 (S.D. Iowa 2020) (Iowa Supreme Court would not apply the apparent manufacturer doctrine to hold a non-manufacturing seller strictly liable for a manufacturing defect under Iowa Code Ann. § 613.18(1)(a)); Bornsen v. Pragotrade, LLC, 804 N.W.2d 55, 61 (N.D. 2011) (North Dakota legislature intended to "sharply curtail liability of a 'nonmanufacturing seller[,]' leaving no room . . . to recognize—or . . . 'adopt'—the common law or the Restatement theory of 'apparent manufacturer' liability"). *But see* Rublee v. Carrier Corp., 428 P.3d 1207, 1219 (Wash. 2018) (adopting § 400 and recognizing apparent manufacturer liability for claims before state products liability statute).

[226] See, e.g., Stein v. Pfizer Inc., 137 A.3d 279, 294–99 (Md. Ct. Spec. App. 2016) (parent of company that manufactured and sold cement with asbestos was not an apparent manufacturer under objective reliance, actual reliance, or Products Liability Rest. § 14 tests); Sprague v. Pfizer, Inc., 2015 WL 144330, at *4 (W.D. Wash. 2015) (actor who allows his name or trademark to be placed on product, but does not distribute product, does not "put out" the product under § 400).

[227] Products Liability Rest. § 14 Reporters' Note.

[228] Id. § 14 cmt. *b*.

[229] Id. § 14.

[230] Such as where a state has a rule protecting retailers from a duty to warn of latent dangers. As apparently in Massachusetts. See Bernier v. One World Techs., Inc., 746 F. Supp. 2d 240, 243 (D. Mass. 2010) (but apparent manufacturer doctrine did not apply because plaintiff did not buy "Ridgid Saw" thinking that "Ridgid" was Home Depot's "store brand").

[231] See, e.g., Micjan v. Wal-Mart Stores, Inc., 2016 WL 4141085, at *9 (W.D. Pa. 2016) (Va. law) (licensor of GARANIMALS trademark involved in product testing); Lou v. Otis Elevator Co., 933 N.E.2d 140, 148 (Mass. App. Ct. 2010) ("a nonseller trademark licensor who participates substantially in the design, manufacture, or distribution of the licensee's products may be held liable . . . as an apparent manufacturer"). See generally Higgins, What's in a Name? Possibly, Strict Liability as an Apparent Manufacturer, 78 Def. Couns. J. 355, 355, 361 (2011) (discussing *Lou*); King, Limiting the Vicarious Liability of Franchisors for the Torts of Their Franchisees, 62 Wash. & Lee L. Rev. 417 (2005); Franklyn, The Apparent Manufacturer Doctrine, Trademark

Liability principles applicable to trademark licenses are illustrated in *Kosters v. Seven-Up Co.*,[232] where the plaintiff was blinded in one eye when a bottle of 7-Up slipped out of a defectively designed carton supplied by a third party to the franchisee bottling company. Seven-Up's liability as a franchiser, the court declared, depended upon a variety of factors: "(1) the risk created by approving for distribution an unsafe product likely to cause injury, (2) the franchisor's ability and opportunity to eliminate the unsafe character of the product and prevent the loss, (3) the consumer's lack of knowledge of danger, and (4) the consumer's reliance on the trade name which gives the intended impression that the franchisor is responsible and stands behind the product."[233] In sum, the court concluded that "[l]iability is based on the franchisor's control and the public's assumption, induced by the franchisor's conduct, that it does in fact control and vouch for the product."[234] Based on these principles, and because the Seven-Up Company had contractually retained control over the design of the cartons, the court held that it was subject to strict liability (in implied warranty) for the carton's design.

Courts widely agree that trademark owners and franchisers that substantially control product safety[235] may be subject to liability for injuries from defective products made and sold by their licensees.[236] The reverse is true, of course, if the trademark owner or franchise licensor does *not* substantially control a product's safety. While some courts disagree,[237] a trade name franchiser or trademark licensor is not responsible for a product defect merely because the product carries the defendant's name or logo; liability does not attach, in other words, from simply selling a name or mark to a licensee who places it on an unsafe product.[238] This is simply the flip side of the liability coin that

Licensors and the Third Restatement of Torts, 49 Case W. Res. L. Rev. 671 (1999); Products Liability Rest. § 14 cmt. *d*; Frumer, Friedman, and Sklaren, Products Liability § 5.14.

[232] 595 F.2d 347 (6th Cir. 1979) (Mich. law).

[233] Id. at 353.

[234] Id.

[235] The case for franchiser liability is enhanced, of course, if it designed the product itself. See, e.g., Cook v. Branick Mfg., Inc., 736 F.2d 1442 (11th Cir. 1984) (Ala. law). Yet franchisers are subject to vicarious liability for the tortious conduct of their franchisees only if the franchisee is an agent of the franchiser, which means that the latter exercises control of the day-to-day specifics of the operations of the franchise. See, e.g., Ruiz v. Wintzell's Huntsville, L.L.C., 2017 WL 4305004 (N.D. Ala. 2017).

[236] See, e.g., Thomas v. Borg-Warner Morse Tec LLC, 2018 WL 8733352, at *2 (E.D. Ark. 2018) (quoting Rest. (3d) § 14 cmt. *d*); Lou v. Otis Elevator Co., 933 N.E.2d 140, 148 (Mass. App. Ct. 2010) (non-seller trademark licensor who participates substantially in design, manufacture, or distribution of licensee's products may be liable as apparent manufacturer); Torres v. Goodyear Tire & Rubber Co., 786 P.2d 939 (Ariz. 1990) (Goodyear subject to strict liability in tort for defects in tires of its subsidiary, Goodyear Great Britain); Harris v. Aluminum Co. of Am., 550 F. Supp. 1024 (W.D. Va. 1982) (Coke bottle's cap flew off into plaintiff's eye; implied warranty); Connelly v. Uniroyal, Inc., 389 N.E.2d 155, 163 (Ill. 1979) ("A licensor is an integral part of the marketing enterprise, and its participation in the profits reaped by placing a defective product in the stream of commerce presents the same public policy reasons for the applicability of strict liability which supported the imposition of such liability on wholesalers, retailers and lessors."); Carter v. Joseph Bancroft & Sons Co., 360 F. Supp. 1103 (E.D. Pa. 1973) (BAN-LON trademark used on fabrics and garments, made per specifications and quality standards trademark owners prescribed and controlled; trademark owners liable as manufacturer for flammability of dress that ignited during dinner party); Kasel v. Remington Arms Co., 101 Cal. Rptr. 314, 325 (Ct. App. 1972) (Remington liable for exploding shotgun shell that bore its trademark where it had overwhelming control of design and manufacture of shells made by Mexican company).

[237] See, e.g., Kasel v. Remington Arms Co., 101 Cal. Rptr. 314, 323–24 (Ct. App. 1972) (though control over cause of defect in product is an important factor, franchisers and trademark licensors are subject to liability in strict liability in tort so long as they "can be said to be a link in the marketing enterprise which placed a defective product within the stream of commerce").

[238] See, e.g., Cruz Vasquez v. Ridge Tool Pattern Co., 131 N.Y.S.3d 488, at *6 (Sup. Ct. 2020) (table) ("A trademark licensor uninvolved in the manufacture, design, sale, distribution, or quality control of a defective product is not liable for it."); Nunez v. Bargain Supply Co., 2014 WL 5144770, at *4 (Cal. Ct. App. 2014), noncitable (use of trademark alone not sufficient; licensor must participate in "overall process" by which a

bears substantial-control-over-product-safety on its obverse side.[239] Nevertheless, a licensor or franchiser need not actually exercise control if it has the right to do so.[240]

At least one court, *Kennedy v. Guess, Inc.*,[241] has taken an interesting, comparative responsibility approach to the liability of the owners of trademarks and trade names. In *Kennedy*, the plaintiff was injured by a defective umbrella that bore a "Guess" logo, which a retailer had given to his wife as a gift when she purchased a Guess watch. The plaintiff sued Guess for his injuries. Guess defended on the ground that the umbrella had been manufactured by a Hong Kong company, and that Guess had merely sold the use of its logo to a licensee. Unwilling to allow trademark owners and licensors to escape responsibility by avoiding participation in product safety decisions, the court rejected the traditional rule that shields such parties from liability. Instead, the court adopted a principle of comparative responsibility in which a trademark licensor's damages reflect the degree it participated in the product's design, advertising, manufacturing, and distribution.[242] This comparative approach to a duty issue creatively encourages licensors to play at least a minor role in reviewing the safety of products they want the public to believe are connected with them in some respect, and, if not, it will extract from licensors a kind of safety penalty for misleading the public into thinking they knew something about products in which they pretended to have some role.

§ 15.5 SUCCESSOR CORPORATIONS

When a manufacturer goes out of business, it is obligated under the dissolution statutes of most states to make provisions for its existing creditors, including products liability judgment creditors, prior to distributing remaining assets to its shareholders.[243] Once a corporation is formally dissolved, however, its shareholders generally are immune from responsibility for the firm's liabilities, and there usually is no remaining entity subject to responsibility for injuries caused by defective products the corporation made and sold.[244] Yet, sometimes a part or all of a dissolving company (the "predecessor")

"product reaches consumers" and must have "right to control the incidents of manufacture or distribution"); Estate of Miller v. Thrifty Rent-A-Car Sys., Inc., 637 F. Supp. 2d 1029, 1041 (M.D. Fla. 2009) (franchisee's mere use of franchiser's trademarks insufficient to establish reliance prong of apparent authority); Patterson v. Central Mills, Inc., 112 F. Supp. 2d 681, 692 (N.D. Ohio 2000) ("Numerous courts have held that a trademark licensor—who does nothing more than permit the use [of] its trademark—is not liable in tort for potential defects in the final product."); Yoder v. Honeywell, Inc., 900 F. Supp. 240 (D. Colo. 1995) (without reliance by plaintiff, trademark on back of keyboard not enough to hold trademark owner liable for wrist injuries). See Products Liability Rest. § 14 cmt. *d*; Frumer, Friedman, and Sklaren, Products Liability § 5.14.

[239] In addition to control, Professor Joseph King argues that a franchiser should be protected from vicarious liability if it (1) takes "reasonable steps to require that its franchisees prominently display a notice clearly indicating that the franchised units are owned and operated by the independent franchise entity," and (2) requires its franchisees to "carry reasonable levels of liability insurance." See King, Limiting the Vicarious Liability of Franchisors for the Torts of Their Franchisees, 62 Wash. & Lee L. Rev. 417, 424 (2005).

[240] See, e.g., Automobile Ins. Co. v. Murray, Inc., 571 F. Supp. 2d 408, 422–23 (W.D.N.Y. 2008); Miller v. McDonald's Corp., 945 P.2d 1107 (Or. Ct. App. 1997) (franchiser could be liable under right-to-control test for injury from heart-shaped sapphire stone found in Big Mac).

[241] 806 N.E.2d 776 (Ind. 2004).

[242] See id. at 786 (The "law should treat trademark licensors as having responsibility for defective products . . ., but only so much of the liability for those defects as their relative role in the larger scheme of design, advertising, manufacturing, and distribution warrants. Consumers rightly expect that products bearing logos like 'Guess' have been subject to some oversight by those who put their name on the product, but those same consumers can well imagine that in modern commerce the products they buy may have actually been manufactured by someone else.").

[243] See, e.g., 16A Fletcher, Corporations § 8130.

[244] "Tort claimants who, as a result of defective products sold by a predecessor corporation, seek recovery only after transfer of assets to a successor corporation often face difficulties [in collecting on their claims,

is sold to another enterprise (the "successor") that puts some portions of the predecessor's productive assets—its plants and equipment, capital, labor force, marketing apparatus, and goodwill—to some continued use. Indeed, sometimes the successor uses the predecessor's productive assets to continue making and selling the same products to the same customers. When a company is acquired by another firm, it typically will dissolve at, or immediately after, the transfer of stock or assets to the successor firm.[245] After such a corporate transfer of ownership, if a person is injured by a product made and sold by the predecessor before the transfer, the only viable enterprise from whom the victim may seek recovery is the successor corporation.[246] Whether and when a successor company may be liable for its predecessor's defective products has generated a spate of litigation[247] and commentary.[248]

General Rule of Non-Liability with Specific Exceptions

Under general corporate law principles, when one company merely acquires the assets of another, the successor entity is generally not responsible for the obligations of the predecessor.[249] This rule of successor corporation non-liability applies generally to the predecessor's debts and other liabilities, including products liability claims and judgments from defective products made and sold by the predecessor before the

which] typically accrue after the predecessor corporation has lawfully distributed to its shareholders the proceeds from the transfer of assets and has ceased to exist. Under these circumstances, tort claimants who were not existing creditors at the time of transfer of assets ordinarily have no recourse against the predecessor's shareholders." Products Liability Rest. § 12 cmt. *a*.

[245] "Almost all of the reported decisions applying the bases of successor liability stated in this Section involve predecessors that transfer all of their assets to successors and then dissolve or otherwise cease operations. Indeed, the predecessor's termination is the circumstance that, as a practical matter, most often gives rise to the need for a post-transfer tort plaintiff to look to the successor for recovery." Products Liability Rest. § 12 cmt. *h*.

[246] See id. cmt. *a*.

[247] Among the many judicial decisions thoroughly examining this issue are Northland Indus., Inc. v. Kouba, 620 S.W.3d 411 (Tex. 2020); Nationwide Mut. Ins. Co. v. Eagle Window & Door, Inc., 818 S.E.2d 447 (S.C. 2018); Gonzalez v. Standard Tools & Equip. Co., 348 P.3d 293 (Or. Ct. App. 2015); Semenetz v. Sherling & Walden, Inc., 851 N.E.2d 1170 (N.Y. 2006); Fisher v. Allis-Chalmers Corp. Prod. Liab. Trust, 116 Cal. Rptr. 2d 310 (Ct. App. 2002); Fish v. Amsted Indus., 376 N.W.2d 820 (Wis. 1985) (4 opinions thoroughly examining pros and cons of expanding successor liability); Leannais v. Cincinnati, Inc., 565 F.2d 437 (7th Cir. 1977) (Wis. law); Ray v. Alad Corp., 560 P.2d 3 (Cal. 1977); Turner v. Bituminous Cas. Co., 244 N.W.2d 873 (Mich. 1976).

[248] See, e.g., Donenfeld, Successor Liability In the Bankruptcy Context: The Problem Or The Solution?, 39 Cardozo L. Rev. 719 (2017); Matheson, Successor Liability, 96 Minn. L. Rev. 371 (2011); Cupp and Frost, Successor Liability for Defective Products: A Redesign Ongoing, 72 Brook. L. Rev. 1173 (2007); Reilly, Making Sense of Successor Liability, 31 Hofstra L. Rev. 745 (2003); Epstein, Imperfect Liability Regimes: Individual and Corporate Issues, 53 S.C. L. Rev. 1153 (2002); Cupp, Redesigning Successor Liability, 1999 U. Ill. L. Rev. 845; Green, Successors and CERCLA: The Imperfect Analogy to Products Liability and an Alternative Proposal, 87 Nw. U. L. Rev. 897, 909 (1993); Cantu and Goldberg, Products Liability: An Argument for Product Line Liability in Texas, 19 St. Mary's L.J. 621 (1988); Green, Successor Liability: The Superiority of Statutory Reform to Protect Products Liability Claimants, 72 Cornell L. Rev. 17 (1986); Roe, Mergers, Acquisitions, and Tort: A Comment on the Problem of Successor Corporation Liability, 70 Va. L. Rev. 1559 (1984); Phillips, Product Line Continuity and Successor Corporation Liability, 58 N.Y.U. L. Rev. 906 (1983); Annots., 18 A.L.R.6th 629 (2006) (product line exception), 13 A.L.R.6th 355 (2006) (continuity of enterprise exception).

See generally 15 Fletcher, Corporations §§ 7122, 7123; Frumer, Friedman, and Sklaren, Products Liability ch. 7; Am. Law Prod. Liab. 3d §§ 7:1 et seq. The whole topic of successor corporation liability in the products liability context is exceptionally well examined in the comments and Reporters' Notes to Products Liability Rest. §§ 12 and 13. Note, however, that its conclusions differ materially from the more recent study by Professor Cupp, noted above, the results of which are discussed below.

[249] "The general rule, which is well settled, is that where one company sells or otherwise transfers all its assets to another company, the latter is not liable for the debts and liabilities of the transferor." 15 Fletcher, Corporations § 7122.

transfer.[250] "A corporate successor is not a seller and bears no blame in bringing the product and the user together. It seems patently unfair to require such a party to bear the cost of unassumed and uncontemplated products liability claims primarily because it is still in business and is perceived as a 'deep pocket.' "[251] In such cases, injury victims and other late-discovered creditors of a predecessor enterprise are sometimes prejudiced by the protective mantle thrown over successor corporations, but this result is seen as not unfair and a reasonable cost for the offsetting benefits to the economic system believed to flow from a rule providing successor enterprises security from unexpected debts following a good-faith acquisition of the assets of another enterprise.[252]

Notwithstanding the general rule of non-liability, the courts have recognized that a successor fairly should be responsible for the liabilities of a predecessor if the successor *consents* to undertake the predecessor's liabilities, if the successor and predecessor are essentially *the same entity*, or if a transfer is *fraudulently designed* to avoid liability.[253] So, where one company sells its assets to another, the purchaser is not liable for the seller's products liability obligations unless: (1) the purchaser expressly or impliedly assumes such liability;[254] (2) the transaction amounts to a consolidation or merger of the two companies;[255] (3) the purchaser is a mere continuation of the seller;[256] or (4) the transaction is a fraudulent effort to avoid such liability.[257]

While the question of whether successor liability should be limited to these four traditional exceptions is controversial,[258] all products liability decisions accept the general rule of non-liability, and roughly thirty jurisdictions subject the general rule to

---

[250] See id. § 7123.10, at 264–65.

[251] Nissen Corp. v. Miller, 594 A.2d 564, 569 (Md. 1991).

[252] See Products Liability Rest. § 12 cmts. *a* and *b*.

[253] See 15 Fletcher, Corporations § 7122; Products Liability Rest. § 12.

[254] See, e.g., Northland Indus., Inc. v. Kouba, 620 S.W.3d 411, 418 (Tex. 2020) (no recovery on implied warranty claim from fatal treadmill accident; asset purchase agreement, while expressly assuming liability for repair and replacement of defective treadmill parts, unambiguously excluded liability for implied warranties); In re Motors Liquidation Co., 943 F.3d 125, 133 (2d Cir. 2019) (punitive damages were barred against "New GM based on Old GM's conduct"; punitive damages were not an assumed liability in sale agreement that barred such damages under successor liability); American Standard, Inc. v. OakFabco, Inc., 927 N.E.2d 1056, 1058 (N.Y. 2010); Fisher v. Allis-Chalmers Corp. Prod. Liab. Trust, 116 Cal. Rptr. 2d 310 (Ct. App. 2002).

[255] See, e.g., Cooper Indus., LLC v. City of South Bend, 899 N.E.2d 1274, 1288, 1290 (Ind. 2009) (de facto merger; listing factors for determining whether de facto merger exception to successor non-liability applies); T.H.S. Northstar Assocs. v. W.R. Grace & Co., 840 F. Supp. 676, 678 (D. Minn. 1998) (transfer held merger rather than mere asset purchase; key difference between merger and asset purchase is "continuity of shareholders resulting from an exchange of stock, rather than cash, for assets"). Compare DeJesus v. Bertsch, Inc., 898 F. Supp. 2d 353, 363 (D. Mass. 2012) (no de facto merger or continuation of enterprise where predecessor did not retain control or ownership of successor).

[256] See, e.g., Nationwide Mut. Ins. Co. v. Eagle Window & Door, Inc., 818 S.E.2d 447, 453–54 (S.C. 2018) ("While commonality of ownership is a keystone of the analysis and almost always sufficient to establish mere continuation when paired with common directors and officers, we stress control is an essential consideration as well."); Pichon v. Asbestos Defendants, 52 So.3d 240, 247–48 (La. Ct. App. 2010) (same product name, production location, employees, and business operations); Arevalo v. Saginaw Mach. Sys., Inc., 782 A.2d 931, 937 (N.J. 2001) (corporation merely reorganized).

[257] See, e.g., Nichols v. Roper-Whitney Co., 843 F. Supp. 799 (D.N.H. 1994). A finding of fraud or other bad faith in these cases is highly unusual. See, e.g., Cox v. DJO, LLC, 2009 WL 3855084, at *4 (D. Or. 2009) (no evidence that defendants fraudulently manipulated corporate forms or structured transaction to avoid liability); Reina v. Gingerale Corp., 472 So.2d 530 (Fla. Dist. Ct. App. 1985) (fraud not proved). On the four exceptions, see generally 15 Fletcher Corporations, §§ 7122, 7123.

[258] See, e.g., Cupp and Frost, Successor Liability for Defective Products: A Redesign Ongoing, 72 Brook. L. Rev. 1173 (2007); Cupp, Redesigning Successor Liability, 1999 U. Ill. L. Rev. 845.

the conventional four exceptions.[259] Proclaiming that these principles of successor corporation liability are "supported by fairness and efficiency considerations,"[260] the *Restatement (Third) of Torts: Products Liability* adopted the traditional rule of non-liability with its standard four exceptions.[261]

Continuity of Enterprise and Product Line Exceptions

Due to the general rule of non-liability and narrowness of the standard four exceptions, some courts have applied one or both of two additional exceptions to the general rule of non-liability to offer broader opportunities for redress to persons injured by defective products manufactured by defunct corporations. Building on the logic and fairness of allowing liability when the successor and predecessor are essentially the same entity (the idea behind the standard merger and mere-continuation exceptions), the new nonstandard exceptions extend a successor's liability well beyond the traditional four.

In the 1976 case of *Turner v. Bituminous Casualty Co.*,[262] the Michigan Supreme Court adopted the first new exception of this type, called the "continuity of enterprise" exception, remarking:

> [I]t seems both unfair and unbelievable that a corporate combination or acquisition decision would be . . . made on the basis of cutting off the contingent right to sue of a products liability victim. . . . First, it would seem illogical that a merger or de facto merger be encumbered by liability for a products liability suit while a cash acquisition of corporate assets is free from such liability. [Second], if there are no real business reasons for choosing a cash acquisition of corporate assets and the only real reason is to avoid products liability suits, then it would seem that the machinery of corporate law is unreasonably geared up to accomplish a purpose not really intended for it or in the public interest.

A number of other courts have adopted the continuity of enterprise exception,[263] but most courts still reject it for unfairly holding one entity liable for the acts of another contrary to the traditional set of principles applied to the liability of successor corporations.[264]

---

[259] See, e.g., DeJesus v. Park Corp., 530 Fed. Appx. 3 (1st Cir. 2013) (Mass law) (but de-facto-merger and mere-continuation exceptions essentially the same and require continuity of shareholder ownership); Nationwide Mut. Ins. Co. v. Eagle Windows & Doors, Inc., 714 S.E.2d 322, 326 (S.C. 2011); Semenetz v. Sherling & Walden, Inc., 851 N.E.2d 1170 (N.Y. 2006); Welco Indus. v. Applied Cos., 617 N.E.2d 1129 (Ohio 1993). From the fourth, fraud exception, a few courts have spun out a fifth exception for transactions made in bad faith or with inadequate consideration. See, e.g., Man v. Raymark Indus., 728 F. Supp. 1461 (D. Haw. 1989); Everest v. American Transp. Corp., 685 F. Supp. 203 (D. Minn. 1988).

[260] Products Liability Rest. § 12 cmt. *b*.

[261] Section 12 of the Products Liability Restatement, entitled "Liability of Successor for Harm Caused by Defective Products Sold by Predecessor." This section is set out in § 6.5, following note 548, above. See also this section, notes 253–257, above.

[262] 244 N.W.2d 873, 880 (Mich. 1976) (3–2 decision).

[263] See, e.g., Altman v. Motion Water Sports, Inc., 722 F. Supp. 2d 234, 243–44 (D. Conn. 2010); Asher v. KCS Int'l, 659 So.2d 598 (Ala. 1995); McCaffrey v. Weaver Jack Corp., 1992 WL 266923, at *2 (E.D.N.Y. 1992); Flaugher v. Cone Automatic Mach. Co., 507 N.E.2d 331, 334 (Ohio 1987); Cyr v. B. Offen & Co., 501 F.2d 1145, 1152–54 (1st Cir. 1974) (N.H. law).

[264] See, e.g., Campbell v. Davol, Inc., 620 F.3d 887, 893–94 (8th Cir. 2010) (Ark. law) (predicting that Arkansas Supreme Court would reject non-traditional continuity of enterprise exception to successor non-liability); Tabor v. Metal Ware Corp., 168 P.3d 814, 817 (Utah 2007) (refusing to adopt continuity of enterprise exception and leaving issue to legislature); Nissen Corp. v. Miller, 594 A.2d 564, 573 (Md. 1991) (5–2 decision) ("Like the majority of our sister states, we adhere to the general rule of nonliability of successor corporations, with its four traditional exceptions, in products liability cases.").

The year after *Turner* was decided, in *Ray v. Alad Corp.*,[265] the Supreme Court of California promulgated the "product line" exception to the general rule of a successor's non-liability for defective products produced by a predecessor company: "a party which acquires a manufacturing business and continues the output of its line of products . . . assumes strict tort liability for defects in units of the same product line previously manufactured and distributed by the entity from which the business was acquired."[266] The California court provided three rationales for its new product line exception:

> (1) the virtual destruction of the plaintiff's remedies against the original manufacturer caused by the successor's acquisition of the business, (2) the successor's ability to assume the original manufacturer's risk-spreading role, and (3) the fairness of requiring the successor to assume a responsibility for [its predecessor's] defective products that was a burden necessarily attached to the original manufacturer's good will being enjoyed by the successor in the continued operation of the business.[267]

A number of courts have followed *Ray* in adopting a product line exception,[268] but most courts that have addressed the issue have rejected this new exception, too.[269] For example, in *Guzman v. MRM/Elgin*,[270] the Massachusetts high court systematically rejected each of *Ray*'s three reasons for the new exception. It criticized *Ray*'s first rationale because "the plaintiff's lack of a remedy against the original manufacturers is not a justification for imposing liability on another absent fault and causation";[271] *Ray*'s second, "risk-spreading" rationale was contrary to modern products liability theory,[272] which rests on deterrence or risk control by holding parties responsible for making and selling defective products.[273] *Ray*'s third rationale failed to recognize that a purchaser

---

[265] 560 P.2d 3 (Cal. 1977).

[266] Id. at 11.

[267] Id. at 9.

[268] See, e.g., Duran v. United Tactical Sys., LLC, 2022 WL 457878, at *8 (D.N.M. 2022) (question of fact whether plaintiffs met "the factual elements necessary to establish the product line exception"); Leren v. Kaiser Gypsum Co., 442 P.3d 273, 279 (Wash. Ct. App. 2019) (product line exception applied where successor asbestos distributor acquired predecessor's goodwill, held "itself out as akin to the predecessor by continuing to distribute similar unreasonably dangerous products, and realize[d] benefits" therefrom); Schmidt v. Boardman Co., 11 A.3d 924, 945–46 (Pa. 2011).

[269] See, e.g., Lopez v. Delta Int'l Mach. Corp., 312 F. Supp. 3d 1115, 1162 (D.N.M. 2018) (predicting that Delaware would not adopt this exception), aff'd on other grounds sub nom. Lopez v. Stanley Black & Decker, Inc., 764 Fed. Appx. 703 (10th Cir. 2019); Gonzalez v. Standard Tools & Equip. Co., 348 P.3d 293, 295 (Or. Ct. App. 2015) (declining to adopt this exception); Floyd Valley Grain, LLC v. CTB, Inc., 2013 WL 3458073, at *4 (Iowa Ct. App. 2013) (table) (declining to adopt this and continuity of enterprise exceptions); Diguillo v. Goss Int'l Corp., 906 N.E.2d 1268, 1277 (Ill. App. Ct. 2009) (refusing to apply this exception); Albini v. Osteoimplant Tech., 2008 WL 4925967, at *3 (Conn. Super. Ct. 2008) (same); Dahlke v. Cascade Acoustics, Inc., 171 P.3d 992, 998 (Or. Ct. App. 2007) (same); Tabor v. Metal Ware Corp., 168 P.3d 814, 817 (Utah 2007) (same); Semenetz v. Sherling & Walden, Inc., 851 N.E.2d 1170, 1175 (N.Y. 2006) (adopting this exception "would mark 'a radical change from existing law implicating complex economic considerations better left [for] the Legislature' "); Flaugher v. Cone Automatic Mach. Co., 507 N.E.2d 331 (Ohio 1987). See generally Am. Law of Prod. Liab. 3d § 7:27 n.8 (2008) (citing cases rejecting the doctrine from Ala., Ariz., Ark., Colo., Fla., Ill., Ind., Iowa, Ky., La., Mass., Md., Mich., Minn., Mo., Neb., N.C., N.H., N.Y., N.D., Ohio, Or., S.D., Tex., Utah, Va., Vt., and Wis.).

[270] 567 N.E.2d 929 (Mass. 1991).

[271] Id. at 931.

[272] The rise and fall of the risk-spreading rationale for strict products liability is traced in § 5.4, above.

[273] 567 N.E.2d at 932.

pays fair value for the seller's good will.[274] Finally, *Guzman* explained that the product line exception ignored the financial burden it forced on successors, who often would be unable to insure effectively against the risk, so that the threat of liability would "inhibit the free alienability of corporate assets, forcing some small businesses to liquidate rather than transferring their assets, to the detriment of the economy in general."[275]

Conventional wisdom,[276] supported by the *Products Liability Restatement*,[277] holds that the traditional four exceptions are deeply ingrained in American corporate and products liability jurisprudence and that the two upstarts ("continuity of enterprise" and "product line") were but temporary aberrations in what is otherwise an unwavering set of exceptions to the general non-liability rule for successor corporations. Into the 1990s, most courts appeared to have rejected the two new liability-expanding approaches,[278] but in the late 1990s one scholar reported that "the evolution toward loosening restrictions has fitfully continued,"[279] which he applauded,[280] a trend that continued for some years.[281] While a large majority of states so far has stuck with the traditional four exceptions,[282] it is difficult to know whether a creeping expansion in exceptions continues apace,[283] or whether it was largely halted by the *Restatement*'s unequivocal adherence to the conventional four exceptions.[284]

---

[274] Id. *Ray*'s third rationale, that a successor ought to bear the burdens along with the benefits of the predecessor's good will, is characterized as "specious" in Green, Successor Liability: The Superiority of Statutory Reform to Protect Products Liability Claimants, 72 Cornell L. Rev. 17, 29–30 (1986).

[275] 567 N.E.2d at 933.

[276] See, e.g., Green, Successors and CERCLA: The Imperfect Analogy to Products Liability and an Alternative Proposal, 87 Nw. U. L. Rev. 897, 909 (1993) (stating that the expansion of corporate successor liability "fizzled in the 1980s and 1990s"); Henderson and Eisenberg, The Quiet Revolution in Products Liability: An Empirical Study of Legal Change, 37 UCLA L. Rev. 479, 492 & n.64 (1990) (citing six state supreme court cases decided in the mid-to-late 1980s rejecting product line exception).

[277] See Products Liability Rest. § 12 cmt. *b*.

[278] See, e.g., Johnston v. Amsted Indus., 830 P.2d 1141 (Colo. App. 1992) (rejecting product line and continuity of enterprise exceptions); Lopez v. Delta Int'l Mach. Corp., 2017 WL 3142028, at *38 n.41 (D.N.M. 2017) ("the 'vast majority of jurisdictions' have rejected [product line] exception"); Gonzalez v. Standard Tools & Equip. Co., 348 P.3d 293, 295 (Or. Ct. App. 2015) (declining to adopt product line exception); Albini v. Osteoimplant Tech., 2008 WL 4925967, at *3 (Conn. Super. Ct. 2008) (rejecting product line exception and recognizing "compelling rationale" of Third Restatement). See generally Products Liability Rest. § 12 cmt. *b*.

[279] See Cupp, Redesigning Successor Liability, 1999 U. Ill. L. Rev. 845, 894.

[280] Professor Cupp concludes: "Courts should not rest from . . . redesigning of successor liability until they settle on the less restrictive approaches that both protect tortiously injured consumers, and . . . allow innocent successors to channel responsibility back to the original manufacturers." 1999 U. Ill. L. Rev. at 896.

[281] Professor Cupp's earlier study, see note 279, above, is updated in Cupp and Frost, Successor Liability for Defective Products: A Redesign Ongoing, 72 Brook. L. Rev. 1173, 1208 (2007) (recent cases reveal "the less restrictive approaches are continuing to find new jurisdictional homes, and are neither dead to growth nor the subject of overwhelming judicial rejection as asserted by the Restatement (Third)").

[282] See note 269, above.

[283] See, e.g., In re General Motors LLC Ignition Switch Litig., 2017 WL 6509256, at *4 (S.D.N.Y. 2017) (predicting Michigan would apply continuity of enterprise exception to economic loss claims); Paradise Corp. v. Amerihost Dev., Inc., 848 So.2d 177 (Miss. 2003); Huff v. Shopsmith, Inc., 786 So.2d 383, 386–88 (Miss. 2001); Savage Arms, Inc. v. Western Auto Supply Co., 18 P.3d 49 (Alaska 2001).

[284] See, e.g., Lopez v. Delta Int'l Mach. Corp., 312 F. Supp. 3d 1115, 1162 (D.N.M. 2018) (Del. law) (predicting Delaware would not adopt either exception), aff'd on other grounds sub nom. Lopez v. Stanley Black & Decker, Inc., 764 Fed. Appx. 703 (10th Cir. 2019); Winsor v. Glasswerks PHX, L.L.C., 63 P.3d 1040, 1049 (Ariz. Ct. App. 2003) (declining to adopt either new exception; "a fundamental tenet of our products liability law is that compensation for injury is tied to those who have a causal connection to placing the product into the stream of commerce [but the] product line and continuity of enterprise exceptions at issue overlook or minimize this causal link"); Pearson v. National Feeding Sys., Inc., 90 S.W.3d 46, 52 (Ky. 2002) (such broad public policy issues "are more appropriately left to legislative determination"). See also Campbell, Product Line

Successor Corporation's Duty to Warn

The issue just examined concerns the liability of a successor firm for harm caused by defective goods produced by a predecessor, solely because the successor acquired the predecessor's assets. An entirely different issue is whether a successor corporation should have an independent duty to *warn* the predecessor's consumers of the danger when it discovers that its predecessor's products are dangerously defective.[285] "[B]y virtue of succeeding to the predecessor's interests, the successor is often in a good position to learn of problems arising from use of the predecessor's product and to prevent harm to persons or property. When the relationship between the successor and pre-transfer purchasers of the predecessor's products gives rise to actual or potential economic benefit to the successor, it is both fair and efficient to require the successor to act reasonably to prevent such harm."[286] For these reasons, many courts have concluded that a successor does have an independent duty to warn such parties, dependent upon various factors, even if none of the four traditional exceptions apply.[287]

Adopting basically a negligence standard, the *Products Liability Restatement* provides that a successor corporation is subject to liability for failure to warn of risks in products sold by its predecessor in limited situations, where (1) the successor enters into a maintenance, repair, or similar product service relationship with its predecessor's customers;[288] and (2) "a reasonable person in the position of the successor would provide a warning."[289] Whether a reasonable person in such a position would provide a warning depends on a variety of factors, distilled from the cases, which the *Restatement* describes as whether (1) the successor reasonably should know that the product is dangerous; (2) the persons to whom a warning might be provided can be identified and are likely to be unaware of the risk; (3) there is an effective way to convey a warning, and the recipients can practicably act upon it; and (4) the risk is great enough to justify the burden of providing a warning.[290] Because the *Restatement*'s formulation of these commonsense

---

Liability Just Doesn't Fly, 84 Def. Couns. J. 1 (2017) (in a 50-state review, finding few courts adopted the continuity of enterprise or product line exception).

[285] See Kommer, The Successor Corporation's Continuing Duty to Warn, 23 Prod. Safety & Liab. Rep. (BNA) No. 36, p. 990 et seq. (Sept. 15, 1995).

[286] Products Liability Rest. § 13 cmt. *a*.

[287] Cases holding that successor corporations have a post-sale duty to warn if they maintain a substantial continuing relationship with their predecessor's customers include Knott v. AMFEC, Inc., 2010 WL 1528393, at *8 (D. Minn. 2010); Tabor v. Metal Ware Corp., 168 P.3d 814, 818 (Utah 2007) (adopting Third Rest. § 13); Colon v. Multi-Pak Corp., 477 F. Supp. 2d 620, 627 (S.D.N.Y. 2007); Foster v. Cone-Blanchard Mach. Co., 597 N.W.2d 506 (Mich. 1999); Flaugher v. Cone Automatic Mach. Co., 507 N.E.2d 331, 337–38 (Ohio 1987); Gee v. Tenneco, Inc., 615 F.2d 857, 866 (9th Cir. 1980) (Cal. law). See Annot., 92 A.L.R.5th 227 (2001).

[288] "For example, a successor may sell or offer to sell spare parts to the predecessor's customers for machinery sold by the predecessor when the successor knows or should know the machinery is defective." Products Liability Rest. § 13 cmt. *b*. See, e.g., Sherlock v. Quality Control Equip. Co., 79 F.3d 731 (8th Cir. 1996) (Mo. law) (upholding verdict for plaintiff against successor corporation, which sold replacement parts for machine sold by predecessor, for failing to warn of dangers successor learned about after asset transfer).

"The critical element required for the imposition of the duty is a continuing relationship between the successor and the predecessor's customers for the benefit of the successor." 15 Fletcher, Corporations § 7123.40. In deciding whether there is a sufficient continuing relationship between a successor and a predecessor's customers, courts often identify an ongoing service contract as critical. See, e.g., In re Old Carco LLC, 492 B.R. 392, 405 (Bankr. S.D.N.Y. 2013); Thornton v. M7 Aerospace LP, 903 F. Supp. 2d 654 (N.D. Ill. 2012) (insufficient ongoing relationship); Florom v. Elliott Mfg. Co., 867 F.2d 570 (10th Cir. 1989) (Colo. law). Yet, while such a service contract is one important basis for imposing a duty to warn upon a successor corporation, it should not be a *sine qua non* for the creation of such a duty. See Products Liability Rest. § 13 cmt. *b*.

[289] See Products Liability Rest. § 13(a)(2).

[290] See Products Liability Rest. § 13(b).

principles of responsibility developed by the courts seems reasonable and fair, other courts may be expected to impose a similar duty to warn on successor corporations, unless, of course, requiring such a warning would be unreasonable.[291]

Special Considerations in Asbestos Litigation

A lawyer handling an asbestos case should be aware of at least two special successor liability considerations pertinent to such cases. First, a growing number of states have enacted statutes (a couple of which have been ruled unconstitutional) limiting asbestos claims against successor corporations.[292] Second, since almost all manufacturers of asbestos are now insolvent, claims against successor asbestos firms may be preempted by federal bankruptcy laws.[293]

§ 15.6 Employers as Manufacturers

In bringing products and workers together, employers stand at the "nip point" of product safety in the industrial setting.[294] Employers have virtually exclusive control over many product safety matters, such as selecting industrial machinery and specifying guards for that machinery; allocating particular employees to operate particular machines; training workers to use dangerous chemicals and machinery; designing the production process, including the speed of the assembly line; and supervising all of these production activities. With such extensive control over product safety in the workplace, employers bear principal responsibility for most injuries to workers from industrial tools, chemicals, and machines. For this reason, Congress in 1970 enacted legislation imposing major safety responsibilities upon employers under the regulatory supervision of the Occupational Safety and Health Administration.[295]

Employers as Suppliers of Dangerous Equipment; Workers' Compensation Acts

Because of their commercial exploitation of workers, together with their tenacious hold on industrial safety, employers are properly held responsible for on-the-job injuries to workers from dangerous products supplied by the employer.[296] It was for just this reason that state legislatures enacted "workmen's compensation" acts in the early

---

[291] See, e.g., Huff v. Shopsmith, Inc., 786 So.2d 383, 389 (Miss. 2001) ("In the present case, contacting the Huffs would have been a virtual impossibility.").

[292] The statutes are collected in Appendix J of Owen & Davis on Products Liability.

[293] See, e.g., Thornton v. M7 Aerospace LP, 903 F. Supp. 2d 654, 664 (N.D. Ill. 2012) (bankruptcy court transferred assets "free and clear of any and all liens, claims, and encumbrances"); MPI Acquisition, LLC v. Northcutt, 14 So.3d 126, 130 (Ala. 2009) (federal bankruptcy court order declaring successor corporation's purchase of corporation's assets to be free and clear of liability for any claims involving products manufactured and sold by predecessor corporation preempted application of Alabama's successor liability law). See also Lyons v. Rienzi & Sons, Inc., 863 F. Supp. 2d 213, 222 (E.D.N.Y. 2012) (asset purchase agreement approved during bankruptcy proceedings "that specifically negates facts that might otherwise support successor liability is entitled to enforcement"). *But see* In Matter of Motors Liquidation Co., 829 F.3d 135, 166 (2d Cir. 2016) (bankruptcy sale order barring faulty ignition switch claims against successor violated procedural due process); In re Grumman Olson Indus., 467 B.R. 694, 711 (S.D.N.Y. 2012) (extinguishing plaintiffs' claims against successor arising after bankruptcy closed would violate due process and "the Bankruptcy Code's requirements of notice and opportunity to be heard for those affected by a bankruptcy court's rulings").

[294] See Weiler, Workers' Compensation and Product Liability: The Interaction of a Tort and a Non-Tort Regime, 50 Ohio St. L.J. 825 (1989); Annot., 9 A.L.R.4th 873 (1981).

[295] See the Occupational Safety and Health Act of 1970, 29 U.S.C. §§ 651 et seq.

[296] "The theory underlying the workers' compensation acts never has been stated better than in the old campaign slogan, 'the cost of the product should bear the blood of the workman.' " Keeton, Dobbs, Keeton, and Owen, Prosser and Keeton on the Law of Torts § 80, at 573 (quoting Bohlen, A Problem in the Drafting of Workmen's Compensation Acts, 25 Harv. L. Rev. 328, 401, 517 (1911)).

1900s.[297] Prior to such legislation, a worker injured on the job could sue his or her employer for negligence, but the difficulties of proving an employer's fault, together with the rigorous defenses of contributory negligence, assumption of risk, and the fellow servant rule, prevented recovery in "by far the greater proportion" of cases.[298] In place of protracted common-law actions which had little chance of success, the workers' compensation statutes substituted speedy, assured no-fault compensation from employers[299] for workplace accidents.[300] The legislative trade-offs for providing workers with these benefits were to restrict the amounts of compensation paid and to abolish negligence and other common-law claims against employers for workplace accidents.[301] Thus, a central feature of all workers' compensation statutes is that the modest benefits legislatively prescribed are the worker's "exclusive remedy" against the employer for injuries on the job.[302] Over time, the level of worker compensation benefits have failed to keep pace with even the basic needs of injured workers, while the size of tort recoveries for accidents outside the workplace have mushroomed. For these reasons, workers have once again looked to the common law for help in obtaining greater compensation for workplace injuries.

Since industrial and other workplace accidents usually involve some kind of hazardous product (some kind of material,[303] tool,[304] machine,[305] vehicle,[306] process,[307] or chemical[308]), and since many workplace product hazards (as many consumer product

[297] See Prosser and Keeton on Torts § 80; Beauchamp v. Dow Chem. Co., 398 N.W.2d 882, 884–85 (Mich. 1986) (tracing the background of Michigan's workers' compensation act enacted in 1912).

[298] Prosser and Keeton on Torts § 80, at 572 (citing various estimates of uncompensated industrial accident injuries from seventy to ninety-four percent). See also Comment, Bell v. Industrial Vangas: The Employer-Manufacturer and the Dilemma of Dual Capacity, 34 Hastings L.J. 461, 463–70 (1982).

[299] And, as a practical matter, from their workers' compensation insurance carriers.

[300] See Dobbs, Law of Torts §§ 392–96.

[301] "The chief benefit of the workers' compensation system for the injured employee is that it provides a much speedier and more certain recovery than a suit at law. By abolishing the requirement of proving negligence on the part of the employer, workers' compensation also makes some recovery available for injured workers in a large number of cases where employer fault would be difficult to establish. In contrast, the benefits of the system for industrial employers lie in the protection from excessive liability in tort for employee injuries. In a more general sense, workers' compensation also benefits society by providing incentives for employers to run safe operations." Comment, *Bell v. Industrial Vangas*: The Employer-Manufacturer and the Dilemma of Dual Capacity, 34 Hastings L.J. 461, 467–68 (1982).

[302] Mississippi's provision is typical: "the liability of an employer to pay compensation shall be exclusive and in place of all other liability of such employer to the employee." Miss. Code Ann. § 71–3–9. See generally Prosser and Keeton on Torts § 80, at 574; 9 A. Larson, L. Larson, and T. Robinson, Larson's Workers' Compensation Law §§ 100.01 et seq. (2022) [hereinafter Larson's Workers' Compensation Law].

[303] See, e.g., Estate of Blakely v. Asbestos Corp., 766 F. Supp. 721 (E.D. Ark. 1991) (asbestos); Franco v. United Wholesale Lumber Co., 196 Cal. Rptr. 430 (Ct. App. 1983) (wood board kicked back while being cut).

[304] See, e.g., Caraccioli v. KFC Mfg. Corp., 761 F. Supp. 119 (M.D. Fla. 1991) (automatic cooker); Toth v. Westinghouse Elevator Co., 449 N.E.2d 1005 (Ill. App. Ct. 1983) (elevator).

[305] See, e.g., Holbrook v. Prodomax Automation Ltd., 2020 WL 6498908 (W.D. Mich. 2020) (errant robot crushed worker's head); Duffy v. Liberty Mach. Co., 562 N.Y.S.2d 769 (App. Div. 1990) (tile planisher machine); Hyman v. Sipi Metals Corp., 509 N.E.2d 516 (Ill. App. Ct. 1987) (smelter exploded); Horne v. General Elec. Co., 716 F.2d 253 (4th Cir. 1982) (N.C. law) (hydraulic press).

[306] See, e.g., Coello v. Tug Mfg. Corp., 756 F. Supp. 1258 (W.D. Mo. 1991) (industrial tow tractor); Gurry v. Cumberland Farms, Inc., 550 N.E.2d 127 (Mass. 1990) (sand buggy used in farming business); Christman v. Allison Gas Turbine, 702 F. Supp. 369 (D. Mass. 1989) (helicopter).

[307] See, e.g., Estate of Coates v. Pacific Eng'g, 791 P.2d 1257 (Haw. 1990) (diver employed by engineering firm that designed powerful water sucking process for elaborate "water features" at hotel swimming pool).

[308] See, e.g., Ervin v. Great Dane Trailers, Inc., 393 S.E.2d 467 (Ga. Ct. App. 1990) (workers alleged that their cancers resulted from workplace exposure to hazardous chemicals); White v. E.I. Du Pont De Nemours

hazards) are excessive and unnecessary, workers not infrequently seek compensation from the manufacturers of those products to supplement workers' compensation benefits, which benefits are usually quite inadequate. Employers most often are not directly involved in such products liability claims by workers against manufacturers of workplace products, so such third-party actions lie largely outside the workers' compensation system. An employer,[309] however, ordinarily may recoup its workers' compensation payments and obligations from any recovery the worker might obtain from such a products liability lawsuit.[310]

Employers as Manufacturers; the "Dual Capacity" Doctrine

Not infrequently, industrial employers design and manufacture products for their own use. Often these are specialty tools used only in the employer's own business and not manufactured and sold widely to the public. Yet, some manufacturers make products not only for their own use but also for sale to the general public: a press manufacturer may use its own presses on its own assembly line to make parts for presses sold to others, and a tire manufacturer may equip the trucks it uses around its factories with tires from its normal production inventory.[311] Because such an enterprise in a real sense wears two hats, it may be said to act in a "dual capacity"—both as a manufacturer and employer.

Normally, as discussed above, if an employee is injured on the job by an unguarded punch press or a defective tire blowout, the employee may recover workers' compensation benefits from the employer and damages in a products liability action from the manufacturer. But what if the manufacturer of a workplace product that injures a worker is also his or her employer? May the injured employee maintain an ordinary products liability action against the company in its capacity as manufacturer? Or is the employee limited to workers' compensation benefits as his or her "exclusive remedy" for such injuries? This situation raises what is called the "dual capacity" (or "dual persona")[312] issue.

The dual capacity doctrine had an intriguing yet short and narrow life in products liability law. A California appellate court first recognized the doctrine in *Duprey v. Shane*,[313] a 1952 case in which the defendant chiropractor treated his nurse for an injury. The treatment aggravated the injury, and the nurse sued for malpractice. Notwithstanding the exclusive remedy rule of the workers' compensation statute, the court permitted the action because the defendant had removed the mantle of employer, and assumed the obligations of a chiropractor, when he undertook to treat his employee as a patient. A quarter of a century later, in *Mercer v. Uniroyal, Inc.*,[314] an Ohio appellate court first applied the dual capacity doctrine to a products liability case. In *Mercer*, while

& Co., 523 F. Supp. 302 (W.D. Va. 1981) (employee in Orlon-making plant alleged that his liver damage was caused by chemical made by defendant employer).

[309] Or, typically, the employer's workers' compensation insurance carrier.

[310] See 10 Larson's Workers' Compensation Law §§ 117.01 et seq.

[311] Compare Mercer v. Uniroyal, Inc., 361 N.E.2d 492 (Ohio Ct. App. 1976) (dual capacity recovery allowed), with Schump v. Firestone Tire & Rubber Co., 541 N.E.2d 1040 (Ohio 1989) (dual capacity doctrine disapproved and recovery not allowed).

[312] Most courts refer to the doctrine as the "dual capacity" doctrine in products liability cases, but the principal workers' compensation treatise argues that "dual persona" is a better name for the narrower, proper conception of the doctrine, nomenclature followed by some courts. See 10 Larson's Workers' Compensation Law §§ 113.01[2], 113.03.

[313] 249 P.2d 8 (Cal. 1952).

[314] 361 N.E.2d 492 (Ohio Ct. App. 1976).

driving a company truck equipped with Uniroyal tires, a Uniroyal employee was injured when a tire blew out. Relying on *Duprey v. Shane*[315] and other cases outside the products liability context, and reasoning that "[i]t was only a matter of circumstance that the tire on the truck in which the plaintiff was riding was a Uniroyal tire rather than a Sears, Goodyear or Goodrich,"[316] the Ohio court allowed the Uniroyal employee to maintain a products liability action against his employer.[317]

Twelve days after the Ohio court rendered *Mercer*, a California appellate court similarly extended the dual capacity doctrine to the products liability context. In *Douglas v. E. & J. Gallo Winery*,[318] the plaintiffs were injured by the collapse of scaffolding on which they were working—scaffolding that their employer also manufactured and sold to the general public. Allowing the workers to maintain a products liability suit against their own employer, the court held that the dual capacity doctrine permitted the claim in this context despite the exclusive remedy doctrine that normally precludes tort claims by workers against their employers. Noting that "[t]here is nothing ghostly or fictional about two capacities,"[319] the court explained that "[a]n employer *qua* employer enjoys the cloak of immunity waived by the Workers' Compensation Law. But when an employer engages in the dual capacity of the manufacturer of a product for sale to the public, the employer assumes all of the duties and liabilities of such manufacturer."[320] While an employee may generally surrender his or her rights to sue the employer for workplace hazards as part of the workers' compensation tradeoff, the court reasoned that the employment relationship does not require that a worker also surrender his or her rights as a product consumer.[321] Four years later, in *Bell v. Industrial Vangas, Inc.*,[322] the California Supreme Court reaffirmed the use of the dual capacity doctrine in products liability cases asserting that "there is naught to commend a rule of the law which would encourage manufacturers to do less in the area of product safety if by chance the product is to be used by their own employees."[323]

Outside of California and Ohio, the dual capacity doctrine experienced a much cooler reception. Troubled by the doctrine's obvious conflict with the exclusive remedy rule, and fearful that it would undermine the long-established balance the legislatures had struck in the workers' compensation legislation,[324] courts in other states widely

[315] 249 P.2d 8 (Cal. 1952).

[316] 361 N.E.2d at 496.

[317] See also Guy v. Arthur H. Thomas Co., 378 N.E.2d 488, 490–92 (Ohio 1978).

[318] 137 Cal. Rptr. 797, 802–03 (Ct. App. 1977).

[319] Id. at 801.

[320] Id.

[321] "When an employee is hired, he assumes all of the hazards and risks of employment which naturally flow from that employment. He does not as employee give up his rights as a user against a manufacturer." Id. The court concluded: "Failure to apply the dual capacity doctrine to the manufacturer who sells to the public would unduly restrict the injured person's remedy. There is no reason to relieve a manufacturer who sells to the public of liability *as a manufacturer* by the chance circumstance that the defendant manufacturer also happens to be an employer of the injured person." Id. at 803 (emphasis added). The *Douglas* court limited application of the doctrine "to a defendant who engaged in manufacturing for sale to the general public." Id. Other courts agreed that the dual capacity doctrine only applied to products also made available to the general public. See, e.g., Bibby v. Central Indus. Eng'g Co., 200 Cal. Rptr. 412 (Ct. App. 1984); Simpkins v. Delco Moraine Div., 444 N.E.2d 1064 (Ohio Ct. App. 1981).

[322] 637 P.2d 266 (Cal. 1981).

[323] Id. at 273.

[324] See, e.g., Vineyard v. Southwest Eng'g & Contracting Co., 570 P.2d 823, 824 (Ariz. Ct. App. 1977) ("in view of the exclusivity provisions of the [workers' compensation] statute which are 'part of the *quid pro quo* in which the sacrifices and gains of employees and employers are to some extent put in balance,' absent

rejected the doctrine. In 1980, for example, characterizing the dual capacity doctrine as "fundamentally unsound," the New York Court of Appeals explained that "[w]e would be seriously undermining the salutary social purposes underlying the existing workers' compensation scheme if we were to permit common-law recovery outside of that scheme on the basis of such illusory distinctions."[325] Following "[t]he vast majority of courts [that] have rejected the dual capacity doctrine and have held that an employer who designs, manufactures or distributes a product used by its employees cannot be held liable to an injured employee on the theory of products liability,"[326] a Mississippi federal district court in 1985 observed: "Imagine how much would remain of employer immunity if it were forfeited every time an employer adjusted or tinkered with a machine."[327]

Even in California and Ohio—the states that spawned the dual capacity doctrine in products liability cases—the doctrine quickly ran out of steam. In 1982, the year after the California Supreme Court approved the doctrine in *Bell*, the California legislature effectively abolished it,[328] and the Ohio Supreme Court restricted the doctrine substantially in the following year.[329] Thus, "[t]he dual capacity doctrine, in spite of widespread and varied attempts to invoke it as a way to defeat exclusiveness, flourished in only two states, Ohio and California, and even there for only a few years, from 1977 to 1983."[330] Recent courts have continued to reject the rule,[331] and it seems safe to proclaim that the dual capacity doctrine in products liability law essentially is dead.[332]

Post-Merger Accidents

Although the dual capacity doctrine appears now to have been put to rest, the "dual persona" doctrine, applicable to a small set of products liability cases, has properly

---

an express agreement, the workmen's compensation laws should offer the exclusive remedy"). One commentator at the time argued that the courts were more solicitous of the workers compensation system than was warranted. Note, 96 Harv. L. Rev. 1641, 1661 (1983).

325 Billy v. Consolidated Mach. Tool Corp., 412 N.E.2d 934, 939 (N.Y. 1980). The court explained:

> The Workers' Compensation Law was designed to spread the risk of industrial accidents through [insurance] coverage and, more specifically, to [provide a swift and sure source of benefits to injured employees] without regard to fault in most instances. In exchange for the security of knowing that fixed benefits will be paid without the need to resort to expensive and sometimes risky litigation, however, the employee has been asked to pay a price [by surrendering] his common-law right to sue his employer in tort and perhaps to enjoy a more substantial recovery through a jury award. The legislative implementation of this "trade-off" is embodied in section 11 of the Workers' Compensation Law, which precludes suits against the employer and limits [an employee] to the recompense afforded under the statute when he is injured in the course of his employment.
>
> We cannot sanction the circumvention of this clear legislative plan by approving a theory which would permit the employer to be sued in his capacity as property owner or manufacturer of equipment used on the job site. As we have previously observed, "an employer remains an employer in his relations with his employees as to all matters arising from and connected with their employment. He may not be treated as a dual legal personality, 'a sort of Dr. Jekyll and Mr. Hyde.' "

326 Rader v. United States Rubber Reclaiming Co., 617 F. Supp. 1045, 1046 (S.D. Miss. 1985).

327 Id.

328 See Cal. Lab. Code § 3602.

329 See Freese v. Consolidated Rail Corp., 445 N.E.2d 1110 (Ohio 1983).

330 10 Larson's Workers' Compensation Law § 113.01[4].

331 See, e.g., Evanston Ins. Co. v. Dean, 2009 WL 2972336, at *9 (N.D. Okla. 2009); Chairez v. James Hamilton Const. Co., 215 P.3d 732, 742 (N.M. Ct. App. 2009) (by modifying construction equipment, employer did not acquire separate persona as equipment manufacturer); Minton v. Ralston Purina Co., 47 P.3d 556 (Wash. 2002); Suburban Hosp. v. Kirson, 763 A.2d 185 (Md. Ct. App. 2000).

332 "It is now held with virtual unanimity that an employer, who is also the manufacturer . . . of a product used in the work, cannot be held liable in damages to his own employee on a theory of products liability." 10 Larson's Workers' Compensation Law § 113.03.

remained alive. A manufacturer may be considered a third person for purposes of the workers' compensation statutes if it possessed "a second persona so completely independent from and unrelated to its status as employer"[333] at the time an accident product was manufactured. In the merger context, a number of decisions have held that the dual persona doctrine allows a worker to maintain a products liability claim against his or her employer if the worker is injured by a defective product manufactured by a firm acquired by the employer.[334]

In such cases, courts have reasoned that the exclusive remedy rule of the workers' compensation statutes is not subverted by holding the successor corporation[335] responsible for the liability it assumed as a result of the merger. Indeed, a successor company that expressly undertakes to assume a predecessor's liabilities cannot in fairness or equity be allowed to use the merger as a tool for depriving its own employees of the very liabilities it expressly agreed to assume in the merger agreement.

Intentional Employer Misconduct

One possible escape from the exclusive remedy rule, applicable to a very small set of cases in which an employee is injured by a dangerously defective product supplied by his or her employer, is where a worker can prove that his employer *intended* to harm him. If an employer intentionally harms a worker, the worker in most states may maintain a tort action against the employer.[336] The workers' compensation statutes in some states expressly exclude intentional tort actions (or "willful misconduct") from the exclusive remedy bar.[337] In states with statutes that do not expressly exclude such misconduct from coverage, courts generally hold that the statutes do not cover an employer's intentional misconduct.[338] Typically, such courts reason persuasively that the workers' compensation laws are intended to cover only "accidental" injuries to employees in the workplace—not to shield an employer from civil litigation for injuries it intentionally inflicts on its employees.[339]

---

[333] See 10 Larson's Workers' Compensation Law § 113.01[4].

[334] The seminal case for this proposition is Billy v. Consolidated Mach. Tool Corp., 412 N.E.2d 934 (N.Y. 1980). See also Scott v. Key Energy Servs., Inc., 990 F.3d 1101, 1105–07 (8th Cir. 2021) (N.D. law) (state would not apply dual capacity doctrine against merged firm); Peterson v. Indus. Door Co., Inc., 2008 WL 131916 (Minn. Ct. App. 2008) (coupled with merger, dual persona doctrine is exception to workers' comp act's general rule of employer tort immunity); Van Doren v. Coe Press Equip. Corp., 592 F. Supp. 2d 776, 798, 804 (E.D. Pa. 2008); Gurry v. Cumberland Farms, Inc., 550 N.E.2d 127 (Mass. 1990).

[335] On the liability of successor corporations generally, see § 15.5, above.

[336] See, e.g., Caldwell v. Petersburg Stone Co., 2003 WL 21443746 (Ohio Ct. App. 2003) (discussing elements of intentional employer tort in Ohio); Laidlow v. Hariton Mach. Co., 790 A.2d 884 (N.J. 2002) (exception would apply if plaintiff could prove that employer desired or knew with substantial certainty that tying up of safety guard would injure an employee); Beauchamp v. Dow Chem. Co., 398 N.W.2d 882 (Mich. 1986). See generally 10 Larson's Workers' Compensation Law §§ 103.01 et seq. Compare Zurbriggen v. Twin Hill Acquisition Co., Inc., 338 F. Supp. 3d 875, 884 (N.D. Ill. 2018) (depending on jurisdiction, whether intentional harm exception to exclusive remedy rule applies depends on whether employer specifically intended, was certain, or was substantially certain that its conduct would injure the plaintiff).

[337] See, e.g., Ky. Rev. Stat. Ann. § 342.610; La. Rev. Stat. Ann. § 23:1032; N.J. Stat. Ann. § 34:15–8; Or. Rev. Stat. Ann. § 656.156; S.D. Codified Laws § 62–3–2; Wash. Rev. Code Ann. § 51.24.020.

At least Ohio's statute provides that a deliberate removal of safety guards or misrepresentation of hazardous substances creates a rebuttable presumption of intent to injure. See Ohio Rev. Code Ann. § 2745.01(C). See generally 9 Larson's Workers' Compensation Law § 103.04[2][b].

[338] See note 345, below.

[339] See 9 Larson's Workers' Compensation Law § 103.01.

For example, *Handley v. Unarco Industries, Inc.*[340] was an action by workers and the representatives of deceased workers at an asbestos company against their employer, alleging claims of intentional murder, fraud, and battery: the murder claim alleged that the defendant "intended to kill plaintiff and his coworkers in that it knew that exposing plaintiffs and his coworkers to huge amounts of asbestos caused a strong probability of death"; the fraud claim asserted that the defendant "fraudulently concealed the dangers of working with asbestos" from the plaintiffs and that the defendant fraudulently represented to the plaintiffs that asbestos was not harmful; and the battery claim charged that the defendant, "intend[ing] bodily harm to the plaintiffs," had a "conscious purpose . . . that asbestos would become trapped in the lungs and bodies of the workers."[341] Allowing the workers' claims, the court reasoned that no matter how clearly the state's workers' compensation act stated that compensation under the act was the exclusive remedy against an employer, "the legislature could not be presumed to have intended to permit an intentional tortfeasor to shift his liability to a fund paid for with premiums collected from innocent employers."[342] Similarly, in a carefully reasoned opinion,[343] the Michigan Supreme Court allowed a Dow Chemical Company research scientist and his wife to maintain various intentional tort claims—for intentional misrepresentation, fraudulent concealment, assault, and intentional infliction of emotional distress—against Dow for injuries from the researcher's on-the-job exposure to Agent Orange.[344]

However, fearful that a flexible intentional harm exception might cause a precipitous erosion of the exclusive remedy principle, most courts interpret this exception narrowly as allowing common-law claims only if a plaintiff is able to prove that the employer truly intended to harm the employee, at least in the sense of knowing to a substantial certainty that the employee would be injured.[345] Thus, most courts scrupulously refuse to allow the intentional injury exception to be "stretched to include accidental injuries caused by the gross, wanton, wilful, deliberate, intentional, reckless,

---

[340] 463 N.E.2d 1011 (Ill. App. Ct. 1984).

[341] Id. at 1020.

[342] Id. at 1022. See generally 9 Larson's Workers' Compensation Law §§ 103.01 et seq.

[343] For a thorough analysis and critique of *Beauchamp*, cited note 344, below, see 9 Larson's Workers' Compensation Law § 103.04[3][b].

[344] Beauchamp v. Dow Chem. Co., 398 N.W.2d 882 (Mich. 1986). See also Travis v. Dreis & Krump Mfg. Co., 551 N.W.2d 132 (Mich. 1996) (allowing action for injuries from explosion of aerosol can, even on tightened statutory standard requiring employer's knowledge that injury was certain—as opposed to substantially certain—to occur).

[345] See, e.g., Miller v. Goodyear Tire & Rubber Co., 434 F. Supp. 3d 869, 877 (D. Or. 2020) (allegations failed to support claim of employer's "deliberate intention" to harm plaintiff; no evidence employer knew of supervisors' misconduct in failing to enforce safety measures); Reinholt v. Schwan's Home Serv., Inc., 2014 WL 5801419, at *5 (E.D. Wash. 2014) (failure to show employer knew injury would result from defrosting delivery truck with propane heater); Broyles v. Kasper Mach. Co., 517 Fed. Appx. 345, 353 (6th Cir. 2013) (Ohio law) (failure to show employer removed safety guards from machine); Calle v. Hitachi Power Tools, 2009 WL 509850, at *5–6 (N.J. Super. Ct. App. Div. 2009) (same); Chairez v. James Hamilton Const. Co., 215 P.3d 732, 741 (N.M. Ct. App. 2009) (failure to show employer's conduct was intentional); Morocco v. Rex Lumber Co., 805 A.2d 168, 173 (Conn. App. Ct. 2002) (failure to show employer knew with substantial certainty that employee would be hurt).

See generally Prosser and Keeton on Torts § 80, at 576 ("The vast majority of courts have held that conduct that falls short of an intent to injure will not permit an employee to overcome the exclusivity provision."); 9 Larson's Workers' Compensation Law § 103.04. See also Doe v. United States, 797 F. Supp. 2d 78, 83–84 (D.D.C. 2011) ("Specific intent by the employer will not be found even where an employer has knowledge to a 'substantial certainty' that an injury will result from an act [and] workplace injuries caused by intentional acts of third parties demonstrate specific intent on part of an employer only where the employer and a third party conspired to injure an employee.").

culpable, or malicious negligence, breach of statute, or other misconduct of the employer short of a conscious and deliberate intent directed to the purpose of inflicting an injury."[346]

Scope of Exclusive Remedy Rule

The exclusive remedy rule has various inherent limitations, such as barring a worker's tort recovery against an employer if the worker is a "statutory employee,"[347] while allowing such a claim if he or she is not.[348] Also, the rule may not bar a spouse's claim for loss of consortium.[349] And while the rule will bar a claim against the employer-manufacturer, it may not always bar a claim against a supervisor who directly caused the harm, depending on the particular circumstances and the particular statutory provision.[350] Here, as elsewhere, claims against an employer involve the interpretation of the applicable workers' compensation statute against the backdrop of a broad scheme of workers' compensation law principles, so that a lawyer with such a case should consult authorities on that topic.[351]

§ 15.7 MISCELLANEOUS DEFENDANTS

This chapter so far has examined a variety of special types of product suppliers who often play important roles in the chain of distribution. In addition to such key parties, a number of other types of marketing participants sometimes contribute in a secondary way to the sale and distribution of products in society. This section examines the responsibility of some of these secondary parties, including certifiers and endorsers, safety inspectors, trade associations, and various other incidental marketing participants, such as auctioneers and trade representatives.

Product Certifiers and Endorsers

Some enterprises, notably Underwriters Laboratories, stimulate the demand for particular products by certifying or endorsing the safety or general quality of products that pass their inspection process. Such tools or other products (such as stepladders) may then be marketed with a "UL" seal of approval. Although Underwriters Laboratories is nominally a nonprofit testing organization, financial support for this large enterprise comes from manufacturers whose product marketing is materially enhanced by a UL certification. Because endorsements by Underwriters Laboratories

---

[346] 9 Larson's Workers' Compensation Law § 103.03. See, e.g., Sarocco v. General Elec. Co., 879 F. Supp. 156 (D. Mass. 1995) (statute barred claims for all personal injuries, even if arising from fraudulent concealment); Poyser v. Newman & Co., 522 A.2d 548 (Pa. 1987) (statute barred claim for deliberately failing to guard saw blades).

[347] See, e.g., DuBose v. Flightsafety Int'l, Inc., 824 S.W.2d 486 (Mo. Ct. App. 1992).

[348] See, e.g., Moses v. Hanna's Candle Co., 234 S.W.3d 872, 875 (Ark. 2006) (temporary worker; workers' comp. commission had exclusive jurisdiction to decide whether defendant was immune from suit); Willison v. Texaco Ref. & Mktg., Inc., 848 P.2d 1062 (Nev. 1993) (defendant might not have had requisite control over employee of wholly-owned subsidiary); Duvon v. Rockwell Int'l, 807 P.2d 876 (Wash. 1991) (former employee). See also Adams v. Owens-Corning Fiberglas Corp., 921 So.2d 972, 982 (La. Ct. App. 2005) (asbestos worker's claim against employer barred for asbestosis, a disease covered at the time by workers' comp. law, but not for colon cancer from asbestos exposure, which was not then a covered disease).

[349] See, e.g., Lynn v. Haybuster Mfg., Inc., 627 A.2d 1288 (Conn. 1993).

[350] See, e.g., Hedglin v. Stahl Specialty Co., 903 S.W.2d 922 (Mo. Ct. App. 1995) (supervisor's actions in dangling plaintiff's decedent by chain over vat of scalding water to retrieve object that had fallen in were outside scope of employment; supervisor might be personally liable). See generally 9 Larson's Workers' Compensation Law § 103.06.

[351] The classic work, of course, is Larson's Workers' Compensation Law, see note 302, above.

and other certifiers of product quality may figure materially in a consumer's purchasing decisions, and because such certifications sometimes may mislead consumers as to a particular product's safety, courts from time to time have addressed the nature and scope of a product certifier's responsibility for injuries from products it has endorsed.[352]

The most cited products liability case concerning a product endorser's liability is *Hanberry v. Hearst Corp.*[353] The plaintiff purchased a pair of shoes that were defective in manufacture and design in that they had a low co-efficient of friction on vinyl surfaces, making them slippery and unsafe, which caused the plaintiff to slip, fall, and injure herself on her kitchen floor. The shoes had been advertised in the defendant Hearst Corporation's magazine, Good Housekeeping, as meeting the "Good Housekeeping's Consumers' Guaranty Seal," which the magazine claimed was its "Consumers' Guaranty." The magazine further represented that "[w]e satisfy ourselves that products advertised in Good Housekeeping are good ones and that the advertising claims made for them in our magazine are truthful." The seal itself represented that "[i]f the product or performance is defective, Good Housekeeping guarantees replacement or refund to consumer."[354]

The plaintiff sued the Hearst Corporation for negligent misrepresentation, breach of warranty, and strict liability in tort. She alleged that she bought the shoes on the strength of the advertisement in the magazine; that the Good Housekeeping seal was affixed to the shoes and the box in which they came; that Hearst either failed to test, investigate, or even examine the type of shoes she bought or, that if it did, it did so negligently; and that "Hearst's issuance of its seal and certification as to the shoes was not warranted by the information it possessed."[355] The trial court dismissed the plaintiff's complaint on demurrer.

On appeal, the *Hanberry* court allowed the negligent misrepresentation claim, but denied the claims for breach of warranty and strict liability in tort. On the negligent misrepresentation claim, the court observed that the Good Housekeeping seal enhances the value of its advertisements "because its seal and certification tend to induce and encourage consumers to purchase products advertised in the magazine and which bear that seal and certification," which was their very purpose. "Implicit in the seal and certification is the representation respondent has taken reasonable steps to make an independent examination of the product endorsed, with some degree of expertise, and found it satisfactory."[356] In this situation, the court concluded that a negligent misrepresentation claim was proper: "Having voluntarily involved itself into the marketing process, having in effect loaned its reputation to promote and induce the sale of a given product, . . . we think respondent Hearst has placed itself in the position where public policy imposes upon it the duty to use ordinary care in the issuance of its seal and certification of quality so that members of the consuming public who rely on its

---

[352] See Baby, Liability of a Product Endorser as Certifier: A Tort Whose Time Has Come and Gone, 20 Trial 38 (April 1984); Comment, Tort Liability for Nonlibelous Negligent Statements: First Amendment Considerations, 93 Yale L.J. 744 (1984); Note, Publisher Liability for Material that Invites Reliance, 66 Tex. L. Rev. 1155 (1988); Annot., 1 A.L.R.5th 431 (1992) (products liability of endorsers, trade associations, certifiers, and similar parties).

[353] 81 Cal. Rptr. 519 (Ct. App. 1969).

[354] Id. at 521.

[355] Id.

[356] Id. at 522.

endorsement are not unreasonably exposed to the risk of harm."[357] But the claims for breach of warranty and strict liability in tort were inappropriate, in the court's view, because the seal implied merely that the defendant had approved the general type of product (presumably its design and possibly its warnings and instructions), not the particular pair of shoes purchased by the plaintiff. If the plaintiff's shoes had a manufacturing defect, the defendant's endorsement could not fairly be interpreted to cover such a defect.[358]

Although the cases are quite sparse,[359] other courts have agreed that certifiers and endorsers (and sometimes even mere standards-setting entities, like Underwriters Laboratories)[360] are subject to liability for negligent misrepresentation, but that such defendants ordinarily are not subject to liability for breach of warranty or strict liability in tort.[361] This appears to be the correct approach: a certifier should not be permitted to escape responsibility for negligent misrepresentation, and especially not for fraud, for falsely representing the safety of a product. Yet certifiers do not "sell" products nor otherwise directly participate in product sales transactions, nor can they properly spread the cost of injuries from defective products.[362] Accordingly, product certifiers generally should not be held accountable for manufacturing defects or other product dangers that lie outside the scope of a fair interpretation of their endorsements.[363] Nor, of course, are

---

[357] Id.

[358] The representation associated with the defendant's seal of approval, the court observed, does not suggest that the defendant had tested or examined the particular pair of shoes purchased by the plaintiff:

> The most that can be implied from respondent's representation is that it has examined or tested samples of the product and found the general design and materials used to be satisfactory. Application of either warranty or strict liability in tort would subject respondent to liability even if the general design and material used in making this brand of shoe were good, but the particular pair became defective through some mishap in the manufacturing process. We believe this kind of liability for individually defective items should be limited to those directly involved in the manufacturing and supplying process, and should not be extended through warranty or strict liability to a general endorser who makes no representation it has examined or tested each item marketed.

Id. at 524.

[359] See generally Annot., 1 A.L.R.5th 431 (1992).

[360] See the separate discussion of such entities, below.

[361] See, e.g., U.S. Lighting Serv., Inc. v. Llerrad Corp., 800 F. Supp. 1513 (N.D. Ohio 1992) (defective lighting equipment approved by Underwriters Laboratories, a nonprofit testing organization, which was negligent in applying its own internal testing procedures), vacated, 807 F. Supp. 439 (N.D. Ohio 1992):

> The raison d'etre of the UL mark is to show that a product has met safety standards. By offering its mark to manufacturers, UL has placed itself into the stream of commerce. . . . The UL seal does not guarantee that a manufacturer has acted with ordinary care but sound public policy requires that UL act with ordinary care in the conduct of its own business—the certification process.

800 F. Supp. at 1517. The court emphasized, however, that liability against a product endorsement service is 'limited to negligence, and that it should not extend to strict liability. Id. *But see* Bennett v. Forest Lab'ys, 99 F. Supp. 3d 1360, 1364 (M.D. Fla. 2015) (company that sponsored foreign pharmaceutical for FDA approval, wrote warning label, and marketed the product could be subject to strict products liability).

See also Hempstead v. General Fire Extinguisher Corp., 269 F. Supp. 109 (D. Del. 1967), where UL allowed use of its inspection and testing label on a manufacturer's fire extinguishers. *Held*, UL could be held liable, for injuries from the explosion of an extinguisher carrying its label, for negligent approval of its design.

[362] See, e.g., Bay Summit Cmty. Ass'n. v. Shell Oil Co., 59 Cal. Rptr. 2d 322 (Ct. App. 1996).

[363] See Kertz and Ohanian, Recent Trends in the Law of Endorsement Advertising: Infomercials, Celebrity Endorsers, and Nontraditional Defendants in Deceptive Advertising Cases, 19 Hofstra L. Rev. 603 (1991); Baby, Liability of a Product Endorser as Certified: A Tort Whose Time Has Come and Gone, 20 Trial 38 (April 1984).

publishers liable merely for advertising products that turn out to be defective, as discussed below.[364]

Safety Inspectors

Insurance companies and gas utilities having the duty to inspect products for safety—such as industrial machinery, furnaces, or service lines—may be liable for negligent inspection.[365] The courts are split on this issue, however, and many courts hold that such inspectors have no duty or liability to third parties, with whom they are not in privity of contract, for injuries arising out of negligent inspections.[366] A safety inspector's duty to third parties depends on whether a jurisdiction has expanded the tort law duties of persons contracting to perform services for others to include the prevention of risks to third parties foreseeably placed at risk by the negligent performance of an inspection undertaking.[367]

Various federal agencies have testing and inspection responsibilities, although the discretionary function exception to liability in the Federal Tort Claims Act often,[368] but not always,[369] will defeat recovery against the government.[370]

---

[364] See, e.g., Walters v. Seventeen Magazine, 241 Cal. Rptr. 101 (Ct. App. 1987) (no liability for advertising tampons that caused toxic shock syndrome); Yuhas v. Mudge, 322 A.2d 824 (N.J. Super. Ct. App. Div. 1974) (no liability for advertising fireworks in Popular Mechanics magazine). See generally § 16.7, below.

[365] See, e.g., Huggins v. Aetna Cas. & Sur. Co., 264 S.E.2d 191 (Ga. 1980) (providing there is reliance; adopting Rest. (2d) Torts § 324A); Jackson v. New Jersey Mfg. Ins. Co., 400 A.2d 81 (N.J. Super. Ct. App. Div. 1979) (insurer liable to third persons only if it has undertaken to make safety inspections upon which insured has relied); O'Laughlin v. Minnesota Natural Gas Co., 253 N.W.2d 826 (Minn. 1977) (gas furnace). See generally Weinberger, Inspection Companies as Defendants, 130 Products Liability Advisory 8 (Dec. 1999).

[366] See, e.g., Bauerlein v. Salvation Army, 905 N.Y.S.2d 215, 220 (App. Div. 2010) (holding that elevator inspector's mere failure to become an "instrument for good" by negligently failing to discover U-bolts was insufficient to impose a duty of care upon inspector who was not in privity of contract with injured building occupant); Mueller v. Daum & Dewey, Inc., 636 F. Supp. 192 (E.D.N.C. 1986); Scott v. City of Detroit, 318 N.W.2d 32 (Mich. Ct. App. 1982); Matthews v. Liberty Mut. Ins. Co., 238 N.E.2d 348 (Mass. 1968); DeJesus v. Liberty Mut. Ins. Co., 223 A.2d 849 (Pa. 1966). Compare Lacy v. State Accident Ins. Fund, Inc., 832 P.2d 1268 (Or. Ct. App. 1992) (after accident, workers' compensation insurer does not have duty to inform injured employee that he might have products liability claim against manufacturer of product involved).

[367] As such, this topic is basically a question of general tort law, to which the reader is referred. See, e.g., Comment, 66 Ky. L.J. 910 (1977–78) (insurers); Annots., 93 A.L.R.2d 598 (1964) (workmen's compensation insurance carriers), 26 A.L.R.2d 136 (1952) (gas companies). See generally Boynton and Evans, What Price Liability for Insurance Carriers Who Undertake Voluntary Safety Inspections, 43 Notre Dame L. Rev. 193 (1967); Prosser and Keeton on Torts § 56, at 381; Rest. (2d) Torts § 324A.

[368] See, e.g., Irving v. United States, 162 F.3d 154 (1st Cir. 1998) (discretionary function exception barred claim against US by injured factory worker for negligent OSHA inspection; OSHA officers had wide discretion in conducting inspections); Cassens v. St. Louis River Cruise Lines, Inc., 44 F.3d 508 (7th Cir. 1995) (Coast Guard's failure to notice missing handrail on cruise boat fell within discretionary function exception); United States v. S.A. Empresa de Viacao Aerea Rio Grandense (Varig Airlines), 467 U.S. 797 (1984) (FAA's negligence in certifying aircraft fell within discretionary function). See also In re 3M Combat Arms Earplug Prods. Liab. Litig., 474 F. Supp. 3d 1231, 1245–46, 1260 (N.D. Fla. 2020) (FTCA's discretionary function exception underlies government contractor defense; design defect claims against manufacturers of allegedly defective combat earplugs did not "implicate a uniquely federal interest"—no evidence the Army "actually participated in discretionary design decisions' ").

[369] See, e.g., Bobo v. AGCO Corp., 981 F. Supp. 2d 1130 (N.D. Ala. 2013) (in wife's mesothelioma claim from exposure to asbestos dust on clothes of husband who worked for TVA, discretionary function exception protected TVA from liability for failing to warn or train employees, but not for violating specific OSHA safety rules); In re Sabin Oral Polio Vaccine Prods. Liab. Litig., 984 F.2d 124 (4th Cir. 1993) (FDA failed to follow its own inspection procedures on lot of polio vaccine); Berkovitz v. United States, 486 U.S. 531 (1988) (same).

[370] See Am. Law Prod. Liab. 3d §§ 5:52 et seq.

Trade Associations

Trade associations are nonprofit organizations variously comprised of manufacturers, retailers, and other product suppliers (often competitors) who share a mutual interest in gathering information about, and promoting, the products that they make or sell.[371] Manufacturers and retailers often form industry-wide trade associations to perform a variety of functions, from serving merely as an information clearing house to performing a wide-ranging assortment of services, such as conducting and sponsoring product testing, research studies, workshops, and technical symposia; developing and recommending design specifications, construction techniques, and packaging and handling procedures; promoting plant safety; collecting, analyzing, and furnishing various safety and other information; and lobbying governmental entities for beneficial legislation.[372] Trade associations, as other standards-developing entities, are sometimes defendants in products liability litigation.[373]

Because trade associations do not make or sell products, they are not subject to strict liability in tort[374] nor for breach of warranty[375] for defective products sold by members of such associations.[376] Whether trade associations owe a duty of care to customers of their members, subjecting them to claims of negligence for harm to such third parties, is a more difficult question. Many of the negligence duty cases involve an interpretation of the negligent undertaking provision in the *Restatement (Second) of Torts*, § 324A, which concerns negligence that foreseeably endangers third parties. Section 324A provides that one who undertakes to render a service to another, which the actor should recognize as necessary for the protection of a third person, is subject to liability for physical harm to the third person resulting from the failure to exercise reasonable care if: (a) the negligence increases the risk of harm; (b) the actor has undertaken to perform a duty owed by the other to the third person; or (c) the third person relies on the actor's undertaking.[377]

---

[371] See Annot., 1 A.L.R.5th 431 (1992); Frumer, Friedman, and Sklaren, Products Liability § 5.15.

[372] The trade association defendants in Arnstein v. Manufacturing Chemists Ass'n, 414 F. Supp. 12 (E.D. Pa. 1976) (trade association for chemical suppliers), and Meneely v. S.R. Smith, Inc., 5 P.3d 49 (Wash. Ct. App. 2000) (trade association for swimming pool companies), were held subject to negligence liability.

[373] See generally Heidt, Damned for Their Judgment: The Tort Liability of Standards Development Organizations, 45 Wake Forest L. Rev. 1227 (2010) (proposing immunity for such organizations from negligence liability); Schotland and Rhyne, Products Liability Implications of Trade Association Activities, 7 J. Prod. Liab. 215 (1984); Comment, Trade Association and Product Liability, 16 Cap. U. L. Rev. 581 (1988); Frumer, Friedman, and Sklaren, Products Liability § 5.15; Am. Law Prods. Liab. 3d § 5:40.

[374] See, e.g., Aquarulo v. A.O. Smith Corp., 2011 WL 7095179, at *4 (Conn. Super. Ct. 2011) (trade association not a "seller" under products liability statute); Swartzbauer v. Lead Indus. Ass'n, 794 F. Supp. 142 (E.D. Pa. 1992); Evenson v. Osmose Wood Preserving, Inc., 760 F. Supp. 1345 (S.D. Ind. 1990); Harmon v. National Auto. Parts Ass'n, 720 F. Supp. 79 (N.D. Miss. 1989); Howard v. Poseidon Pools, Inc., 506 N.Y.S.2d 523 (Sup. Ct. 1986).

[375] See, e.g., Hughes v. Tobacco Inst., Inc., 278 F.3d 417, 424 (5th Cir. 2001) (Tex. law) (only sellers, not trade associations, could be liable for breach of express warranty); Evenson v. Osmose Wood Preserving, Inc., 760 F. Supp. 1345 (S.D. Ind. 1990); Harmon v. National Auto. Parts Ass'n, 720 F. Supp. 79 (N.D. Miss. 1989) (trade association not a "seller" under UCC § 2–103(1)(d)); Howard v. Poseidon Pools, Inc., 506 N.Y.S.2d 523 (Sup. Ct. 1986); Klein v. Council of Chem. Ass'n, 587 F. Supp. 213 (E.D. Pa. 1984) (neither trade association nor industry research institute placed any chemical product into stream of commerce).

[376] A trade association normally is not a "seller" under a state products liability statute. See, e.g., Jefferson v. Lead Indus. Ass'n, 930 F. Supp. 241, 247–48 (E.D. La. 1996) (trade association not subject to suit under state products liability act), aff'd, 106 F.3d 1245 (5th Cir. 1997).

[377] See, e.g., Rountree v. Ching Feng Blinds Indus., 560 F. Supp. 2d 804, 809 (D. Alaska 2008) (trade association subject to liability for undertaking under § 324A); FNS Mortg. Serv. Corp. v. Pacific Gen. Grp., Inc., 29 Cal. Rptr. 2d 916 (Ct. App. 1994); King v. National Spa & Pool Inst., Inc., 570 So.2d 612 (Ala. 1990);

All courts agree that a trade association that neither designs, tests, conducts safety research on, sets standards for, manufactures, nor sells its members' products does not owe an affirmative duty of care to protect the customers of its member companies from defects in the products that the companies make and sell.[378] Indeed, while some courts have found industry trade associations to have a duty of care to ultimate customers when they promulgate standards for use by association members,[379] most courts, reluctant to force such useful organizations to don the burdensome mantle of rule-making organizations,[380] have refused to find a duty even when the trade association plays some role in the development and promulgation of safety standards.[381]

But the greater a trade association's participation in the development and promulgation of safety standards, the more likely it is that the individual members of the association will come to rely upon and defer to the standards of the association. In such cases, a trade association may effectively undertake design and warning responsibilities for an entire industry, a circumstance that may make it reasonable to hold the association responsible for negligently failing to perform its responsibilities in a manner adequately protective of the safety of consumers of products manufactured to association specifications by members of the trade association. Thus, in *Meneely v. S.R. Smith, Inc.*,[382] the court upheld a judgment against the trade association for swimming pool suppliers for negligently failing to revise its industry-wide safety standard, which

---

Arnstein v. Manufacturing Chemists Ass'n, 414 F. Supp. 12 (E.D. Pa. 1976). *But see* Lockman v. S.R. Smith, LLC, 405 Fed. Appx. 471, 474 (11th Cir. 2010) (Ga. law) (no undertaking by trade association under § 324A). Compare Rest. Third, Torts: Liability for Physical and Emotional Harm § 41 comment i.

[378] See, e.g., Bailey v. Edward Hines Lumber Co., 719 N.E.2d 178 (Ill. App. Ct. 1999) (2–1 decision); Evenson v. Osmose Wood Preserving, Inc., 760 F. Supp. 1345 (S.D. Ind. 1990). Even King v. National Spa & Pool Inst., Inc., 570 So.2d 612, 614 (Ala. 1990), agreed with this basic tort law principle: "There is no duty imposed by judicial decision on trade associations to promulgate industry standards." Yet *King* turned on an alternative principle captured in Justice Cardozo's precept that "one who assumes to act, even though gratuitously, may thereby become subject to the duty of acting carefully." Glanzer v. Shepard, 135 N.E. 275, 276 (N.Y. 1922). Hence, once a trade association undertakes to formulate a standard, it is obligated to exercise reasonable care in doing so. *Held*, swimming pool trade association was subject to negligence liability for the construction and installation standards that it promulgated that were relied upon by manufacturer or installer of pool. *King*, 570 So.2d at 614–16.

[379] See, e.g., Rountree v. Ching Feng Blinds Indus. Co., 560 F. Supp. 2d 804, 809 (D. Alaska 2008) (by developing safety standard for window covering, trade association voluntarily undertook at least a duty to warn consumers of risks of harm associated with window coverings); Meneely v. S.R. Smith, Inc., 5 P.3d 49 (Wash. Ct. App. 2000); Weigand v. University Hosp. of N.Y. Univ. Med. Ctr., 659 N.Y.S.2d 395 (Sup. Ct. 1997); Snyder v. American Ass'n of Blood Banks, 676 A.2d 1036 (N.J. 1996); Prudential Prop. & Cas. Ins. Co. v. American Plywood Ass'n, 1994 WL 463527 (S.D. Fla. 1994) (construction standards proved far too lax by Hurricane Andrew); Arnstein v. Manufacturing Chemists Ass'n, Inc., 414 F. Supp. 12 (E.D. Pa. 1976). See also Aquarulo v. A.O. Smith Corp., 2011 WL 7095179, at *4 (Conn. Super. Ct. 2011) (question of fact whether trade association holding ceramic tile adhesive technology patents and developing adhesive formulas was "holding itself out as a manufacturer").

[380] See, e.g., Meyers v. Donnatacci, 531 A.2d 398, 405 (N.J. Super. Ct. Law Div. 1987).

[381] See, e.g., DeLong v. Am. Home Furnishings All., 464 F. Supp. 3d 727, 730–31 (E.D. Pa. 2020) (voluntary furniture standards-setting organization did not have a duty to end user); Lockman v. S.R. Smith, LLC, 405 Fed. Appx. 471, 474 (11th Cir. 2010) (Ga. law); In re Welding Fume Prods. Liab. Litig., 526 F. Supp. 2d 775, 797–99 (N.D. Ohio 2007) (American Welding Society safety assertions were "aspirational in nature" and did not amount to an undertaking; no duty); Tuttle v. Lorillard Tobacco Co., 2003 WL 1571584 (D. Minn. 2003) (absent proof Smokeless Tobacco Council manufactured, sold, or designed cigarettes, or set standards, no duty), aff'd, 377 F.3d 917 (8th Cir. 2004); Friedman v. F.E. Myers Co., 706 F. Supp. 376 (E.D. Pa. 1989) (no duty even if trade association disseminated misleading information to members about dangers of PCBs); Meyers v. Donnatacci, 531 A.2d 398 (N.J. Super. Ct. Law Div. 1987) (swimming pool trade association promulgated suggested minimum standards); Howard v. Poseidon Pools, Inc., 506 N.Y.S.2d 523 (Sup. Ct. 1986) (no duty even if trade association made design change recommendations); Klein v. Council of Chem. Ass'n, 587 F. Supp. 213 (E.D. Pa. 1984) (four trade associations and research institute; no duty).

[382] 5 P.3d 49 (Wash. Ct. App. 2000).

permitted the use of a particular type of diving board in a particular type of pool, when its own testing revealed that certain divers risked serious injury from this particular combination, and the trade association knew that pool and board manufacturers relied upon its standard.

Similarly, in view of the heavy reliance placed by blood banks, hospitals, and patients on the American Association of Blood Banks' recommended procedures for assuring the quality of blood, several courts have held this organization subject to liability for negligence in its recommended procedures.[383] Yet, strict liability in tort does not apply to nonprofit standards-setting organizations that merely establish safety standards for products and neither manufacture nor sell such products.[384] Such entities may possibly be subject to liability in negligence, however, under *Restatement (Second) of Torts* § 324A.[385]

Sometimes plaintiffs claim that trade associations are basically a front for civil conspiracies to obstruct legislation and litigation and, more generally, to frustrate the principles of products liability and safety.[386] Normally courts reject such claims, on both substantive[387] and First Amendment grounds,[388] but the claims sometimes do survive early motions for dismissal.[389]

Standards-Setting Organizations

Standards-setting entities—such as the American National Standards Institute (ANSI), the American Standards Association (ASA), the American Society for Testing and Materials (ASTM), the National Safety Council (NSC), Underwriters Laboratories (UL), and the National Fire Protection Association, previously discussed[390]—play an

[383] See, e.g., Jappell v. American Ass'n of Blood Banks, 162 F. Supp. 2d 476 (E.D. Va. 2001); Weigand v. University Hosp. of N.Y. Univ. Med. Ctr., 659 N.Y.S.2d 395 (Sup. Ct. 1997); Snyder v. American Ass'n of Blood Banks, 676 A.2d 1036 (N.J. 1996) (negligence in failing to recommend surrogate testing for AIDS virus); In re Factor VIII or IX Concentrate Blood Prods. Litig., 25 F. Supp. 2d 837 (N.D. Ill. 1998) (First Amendment no bar to negligent misrepresentation claims against nonprofit organization that provides information to hemophiliacs about blood products). *But cf.* N.N.V. v. American Ass'n of Blood Banks, 89 Cal. Rptr. 2d 885 (Ct. App. 1999) (but blood bank only liable for negligence, so not liable if it could not reasonably have known of danger).

[384] See, e.g., Wissel v. Ohio High Sch. Athletic Ass'n, 605 N.E.2d 458 (Ohio Ct. App. 1992) (nonprofit organization engaged in setting safety standards for athletic equipment, including setting minimum impact requirements for football helmets, was not a "seller" for purposes of strict liability in tort but was subject to liability in negligence under Rest. (2d) Torts § 324A).

[385] Id. See previous discussion of trade associations.

[386] Civil conspiracy claims are examined in § 11.3, above.

[387] See, e.g., James v. National Shooting Sports Found., Inc., 2003 WL 1843975 (N.J. Super. Ct. App. Div. 2003) (no proof that handgun manufacturer trade associations engaged in activities amounting to public nuisance).

[388] See, e.g., Chavers v. Gatke Corp., 132 Cal. Rptr. 2d 198 (Ct. App. 2003) (requiring asbestos manufacturer to stand trial for civil conspiracy or concert of action claims without proof of unlawful intent might chill defendant's first amendment freedom of association to contribute to, attend the meetings of, and otherwise associate with trade groups engaging in public advocacy and debate); In re Asbestos Sch. Litig., 46 F.3d 1284 (3d Cir. 1994) (2–1 decision) (membership in trade association does not support civil conspiracy and concert of action claims and is protected by first amendment).

[389] See, e.g., Remmes v. International Flavors & Fragrances, Inc., 389 F. Supp. 2d 1080, 1095–96 (N.D. Iowa 2005) (pleading of popcorn company worker, who suffered respiratory injury from inhaling volatile compounds in butter flavorings, that flavor manufacturers and their trade association conspired to fraudulently conceal hazards of flavorings was sufficient for personal jurisdiction); Lewis v. Lead Indus. Ass'n, Inc., 793 N.E.2d 869 (Ill. App. Ct. 2003) (reinstating plaintiffs' civil conspiracy claim against defendants associated with lead paint).

[390] See §§ 2.3 (negligence) and 6.4 (strict liability), above. See generally Howells, The Relationship between Product Liability and Product Safety—Understanding a Necessary Element in European Product

important role in helping manufacturers in many industries determine appropriate design standards for their products. Such nonprofit organizations serve much the same function as trade associations, but they are more narrowly focused on setting design (and warning) standards rather than more broadly promoting an industry's economic welfare. Like trade organizations, such organizations may be subject to liability in negligence under principles of *Restatement (Second) of Torts* § 324A, but the kinds of ancillary design services they provide do not render them manufacturers or sellers of products, nor "merchants," so that principles of strict products liability do not apply to harm from products designed according to standards such entities develop.[391]

Other Marketing Participants

A large miscellany of other types of defendants are sometimes involved in products liability litigation.[392] Certain important products liability defendants—manufacturers of automotive vehicles, prescription drugs, medical devices, and blood and biological products—are treated later in this work.[393] The following chapter covers many different types of transactions and products, such as product leases, bailments, and used products, and the responsibilities of those special types of defendants (lessors, bailors, and used product sellers) are treated there.[394] The remaining part of the present section summarizes principles applicable to certain miscellaneous defendants whose liability is not addressed elsewhere in this work.

Most participants in product marketing, particularly product suppliers who directly place a product in the marketing chain, are subject to liability in negligence for failing to exercise reasonable care to avoid conduct that foreseeably endangers product users.[395] However, as a party's connection to the chain of product distribution (and hence to the ultimate consumer or user) grows more remote, the likelihood that the party will owe a duty of care to accident victims attenuates and eventually disappears. Thus, secondary participants in the chain of product distribution may or may not have a duty of care to such persons, depending on the nature and degree of their control over the safety and marketing of particular injury-producing products.[396]

Many of the cases involving miscellaneous defendants involve the issue of whether the particular type of defendant is subject to strict products liability in tort or liability for breach of warranty. Because most secondary participants in product marketing do

---

Liability Through a Comparison with the U.S. Position, 39 Washburn L.J. 305, 310 (2000) (noting that, among the numerous standards-setting entities, the CPSC then worked most closely with ANSI, the ASTM, and UL).

[391] See, e.g., Wissel v. Ohio High Sch. Athletic Ass'n, 605 N.E.2d 458 (Ohio Ct. App. 1992) (nonprofit organization engaged in setting safety standards for athletic equipment, including setting minimum impact requirements for football helmets, was not a "seller" for purposes of strict liability in tort but was subject to liability in negligence under Rest. (2d) Torts § 324A).

[392] For discussions of such miscellaneous defendants, see generally Frumer, Friedman, and Sklaren, Products Liability §§ 5.06–.17; Am. Law Prods. Liab. §§ 5:22–51.

[393] See § 16.9 (Blood and Other Biologics), ch. 17 (Automotive Vehicles), and ch. 18 (Drugs and Medical Devices), below.

[394] See ch. 16, below.

[395] Negligence liability is examined generally in ch. 2, above.

[396] See, e.g., Grubb v. Do It Best Corp., 279 P.3d 626, 629 (Ariz. Ct. App. 2012) (participation of cooperative that negotiates prices for benefit of hardware stores "was too tangential to the heater's distribution to merit imposing product liability"); Inman v. Technicolor U.S.A., Inc., 2011 WL 5829024, at *6, 8 (W.D. Pa. 2011) (eBay not liable as seller). Compare Wissel v. Ohio High Sch. Athletic Ass'n, 605 N.E.2d 458 (Ohio Ct. App. 1992) (safety-standards organization subject to liability under § 324A), with Meyers v. Donnatacci, 531 A.2d 398 (N.J. Super. Ct. Law Div. 1987) (trade association not subject to liability under § 324A). Internet marketplace provider liability for defective third-party products is examined in § 15.2, above.

not design, manufacture, market, or sell products, they generally are not subject to strict liability either in tort or for breach of the implied warranty of merchantability. Such defendants ordinarily are not "engaged in the business of selling" or "otherwise distributing" such products, as required by both *Restatement (Second) of Torts* § 402A[397] and *Restatement (Third) of Torts: Products Liability* § 1.[398]

Section 402A clearly does not apply to isolated product sales by ordinary individuals,[399] such as an individual's one-time sale of a used car,[400] nor does it apply to "sales of the stock of merchants out of the usual course of business, such as execution sales, bankruptcy sales, bulk sales, and the like."[401] Nor does the Uniform Commercial Code usually apply to such secondary products liability defendants who often do not qualify as "merchant" sellers for purposes of the implied warranty of merchantability.[402] In short, the principles of strict products liability normally apply only to commercial sellers, and even then only to their regular,[403] rather than occasional, products sales.[404]

Auctioneers. Auctioneers are a good example of this type of secondary participant in product sales transactions. While they provide an integral role in moving usually second-hand products from sellers to buyers, this narrow kind of brokerage service lies outside of the kind of chain of distribution of new products whose participants properly bear responsibility for the quality of those goods. Because their limited function is moving used goods from sellers to buyers, auctioneers ordinarily sell goods "as is," and buyers understand that they take the risk that the goods may be dangerously defective.[405] Consequently, auctioneers are not strictly liable in tort for dangerous defects in the products that they auction.[406]

---

397 See Rest. (2d) Torts § 402A(1)(a) and cmt. *f*.

398 See also Products Liability Rest. § 20.

399 Section 402A does not apply to "the ordinary individual who makes the isolated sale, and he is not liable to a third person, or even to his buyer, in the absence of his negligence." Rest. (2d) Torts § 402A cmt. *f*.

400 See, e.g., Griffin Indus. v. Jones, 975 S.W.2d 100 (Ky. 1998).

401 Rest. (2d) Torts § 402A cmt. *f*. Products Liability Rest. § 1 cmt. *c* is the same.

402 Under UCC § 2–314(1), the implied warranty of merchantability applies to goods only "if the seller is a merchant with respect to goods of that kind." UCC §§ 2–313 (express warranties) and 2–315 (implied warranties of fitness for particular purpose) apply to "sellers" generally. Section 2–103(1)(d) defines "seller" as "a person who sells or contracts to sell goods."

403 For example, strict liability products liability was applied to Hewlett Packard because it regularly resold its fleet of more than 3,000 cars to used car dealers, after about one year of use. Nutting v. Ford Motor Co., 584 N.Y.S.2d 653, 656 (App. Div. 1992).

404 A seller who does not regularly deal in used good sales, even if it regularly sells off its used equipment, is not considered a "seller" of the goods. See, e.g., Garcia v. Becker Bros. Steel Co., 125 Cal. Rptr. 3d 73, 80, 83 (Ct. App. 2011) (occasional seller of used equipment not strictly liable and had no duty to warn subsequent user); Jaramillo v. Weyerhaeuser Co., 570 F.3d 487, 489–90 (2d Cir. 2009) (N.Y. law) (defendant not regular seller of used machine, so not strictly liable); Sukljian v. Charles Ross & Son Co., 503 N.E.2d 1358, 1361 (N.Y. 1986) (G.E. not strictly liable for annual auctions of two or three used machines it purchased new and used for many years because it was not regularly engaged in business of selling such equipment. *But cf.* Bylsma v. R.C. Willey, 416 P.3d 595, 617 (Utah 2017) (passive retailers are liable for strict liability in tort claims under state reform act).

405 See, e.g., New Tex. Auto Auction Servs., L.P. v. Hernandez, 249 S.W.3d 400 (Tex. 2008); Antone v. Greater Ariz. Auto Auction, 155 P.3d 1074 (Ariz. Ct. App. 2007).

406 See, e.g., New Tex. Auto Auction Servs., L.P. v. Hernandez, 249 S.W.3d 400, 402 (Tex. 2008) ("product-liability law requires those who *place* products in the stream of commerce to stand behind them; it does not require everyone who *facilitates* the stream of commerce to do the same"); Antone v. Greater Ariz. Auto Auction, 155 P.3d 1074, 1080 (Ariz. Ct. App. 2007) (auctioneer not a "seller" under products liability statute); Pelnar v. Rosen Sys., Inc., 964 F. Supp. 1277 (E.D. Wis. 1997) (machinery auctioneer); Musser v. Vilsmeier Auction Co., 562 A.2d 279, 283 (Pa. 1989) (as "an ad hoc salesman of the goods of another," auctioneer has "no relationship to the manufacturer or the goods, beyond their immediate sale"); Tauber-Arons

Nevertheless, auctioneers may be subject to liability for fraudulent misrepresentation[407] or for breach of implied warranty of merchantability if they regularly auction merchandise of a particular type and hold themselves out as being experts in the field,[408] particularly if they fail to reveal the identity of their principals.[409]

Sales representatives and brokers. The liability of sales representatives, agents, and brokers, is less clear, although normally they are not subject to strict products liability.[410] But sales representatives and agents, particularly if they serve in an exclusive capacity, may be subject to strict liability for harm from defective products if they participate directly in and profit from a sales transaction, thereby becoming an important link in the product's distribution.[411] For example, in *Brumbaugh v. CEJJ, Inc.*,[412] the plaintiff brought a strict liability action against the exclusive marketing agent of a trash compactor to recover for fatal injuries of a worker when a dumpster swung loose from the trash compactor. A New York appeals court permitted the action, explaining that imposing liability against such defendants "would provide injured consumers with a greater opportunity to commence an action against the party responsible, fix liability on one who is in a position to exert pressure on the manufacturer to improve the safety of the product, [and] ensure that the burden of accidental injuries . . . be treated as a cost of production by placing liability upon those who market them."[413]

Though *Brumbaugh* is plainly dated, it at least suggests that a marketing agent may be strictly liable for harm from defects in products that it markets—even if it never takes possession of the product, controls it, or takes title to it.

Auctioneers Co. v. Superior Ct., 161 Cal. Rptr. 789 (Ct. App. 1980) (auctioneer treated as dealer in used machinery). *But see* Duclos v. Altec Indus., Inc., 2017 WL 748951, at *3 (S.D. Ill. 2017) ("self-proclaimed 'auctioneer' " seller of aerial device was not insulated from strict products liability; "strict liability arises, not because of the defendant's legal relationship with the manufacturer or with the other entities in the manufacturing-marketing system, but because of its participatory connection, for [its] personal profit or other benefit, with the injury-producing product and with the enterprise that created consumer demand for and reliance upon the product"). See generally Annot., 83 A.L.R.4th 1188 (1991) (liability of auctioneers for strict products liability).

[407] See Werremeyer v. K.C. Auto Salvage Co., 2003 WL 21487311 (Mo. Ct. App. 2003) (car auctioneer subject to liability for fraudulent misrepresentation for car that contained stolen chassis of one car and stolen body of another), rev'd in part on other grounds, 134 S.W.3d 633 (Mo. 2004) (en banc).

[408] See, e.g., Bradford v. Northwest Ala. Livestock Ass'n, 379 So.2d 609 (Ala. Civ. App. 1980).

[409] See Alabama Powersport Auction, LLC v. Wiese, 143 So.3d 713, 723–24 (Ala. 2013) (under common-law principles of agency, an auctioneer is subject to liability under UCC § 2–314 as a "merchant-seller" if he fails to disclose the principal for whom he sells a good); Powers v. Coffeyville Livestock Sales Co., 665 F.2d 311 (10th Cir. 1981) (Kan. law).

[410] See, e.g., Dillard Dep't Stores, Inc. v. Associated Merch. Corp., 782 P.2d 1187, 1191 (Ariz. Ct. App. 1989) (broker lacked the "participatory connection" to chain of distribution to be held strictly liable); Memphis Bank & Trust Co. v. Water Serv., Inc., 758 S.W.2d 525 (Tenn. 1988) (sales representative); Alvarez v. Koby Mach. Co., 516 N.E.2d 930 (Ill. App. Ct. 1987) (sales facilitator); Lyons v. Premo Pharm. Labs, Inc., 406 A.2d 185 (N.J. Super. Ct. App. Div. 1979) (passive role of broker, who never had control over product, prevents him from being strictly liable).

[411] See, e.g., Bittler v. White & Co., 560 N.E.2d 979 (Ill. App. Ct. 1990) (manufacturer's exclusive sales rep for product could be strictly liable in tort because he had sufficient "participatory connection" with marketing product); Brumbaugh v. CEJJ, Inc., 547 N.Y.S.2d 699, 701 (App. Div. 1989) (exclusive marketing agent); Weber v. Johns-Manville Corp., 630 F. Supp. 285 (D.N.J. 1986); Hoffman v. Loos & Dilworth, Inc., 452 A.2d 1349 (Pa. Super. Ct. 1982). See also McCarty v. Johnson & Johnson, 2010 WL 2629913, at *5 (E.D. Cal. 2010) (defendant sales representative may qualify as a distributor because he worked for separate sales company and attended plaintiff's surgery to assure femoral products were "present and available").

[412] 547 N.Y.S.2d 699 (App. Div. 1989).

[413] Id. at 701.

While a broker involved in the sale of an airplane was held to be a product supplier in one case,[414] brokers generally are viewed as mere go-betweens whose only duty is to effect a sales agreement between the parties.[415] Often they do not take physical control of the products that they broker and usually do not otherwise qualify as the type of "sellers" to which strict liability appropriately attaches.[416] In a case concerning a spice broker who arranged sales of recleaned and treated peppercorns between an importer and a seller, the court found that the plaintiff could not bring a strict liability claim against such an intermediary unless the broker controlled the transaction sufficiently to be able to reduce or eliminate the risk, or to pressure the parties responsible for the defect to improve the safety of the product.[417]

Individuals: Owners, Executives, and Technical Professionals. Persons who are principals in companies subject to products liability lawsuits for injuries caused by defective products rarely are sued or subject to such liability themselves. And, of course, the whole idea of a corporation is to protect its owners from liability for the corporation's conduct that may harm others. On rare occasion, however, such individuals may be so thoroughly entwined in the creation and sale of a product that it may seem unfair to immunize them from personal responsibility.

The Sackler family, who owned Purdue Pharma LP, are a current example of such persons, some of whom for decades directly controlled the company's production and allegedly reckless marketing of its opioid, OxyContin. Some plaintiffs alleged that, because the Sackler family withdrew roughly $10 billion from Purdue between 2008 and 2017,[418] the $4.5 billion they first offered to contribute to the company's assets in bankruptcy—in exchange for personal immunity from responsibility—was far too little.[419] A federal judge agreed, striking down the bankruptcy judge's approval of the settlement.[420] Subsequently, the Sacklers increased their offer to $6 billion, which many plaintiff states and the bankruptcy court again approved.[421] How this issue will be resolved is yet to be seen, but it promises to provide intriguing developments as the Purdue opioid bankruptcy and related litigation progresses. Eventually, courts may have

---

414 See Alaskan Oil, Inc. v. Central Flying Serv., Inc., 975 F.2d 553 (8th Cir. 1992) (Ark. law).

415 See Straley v. United States, 887 F. Supp. 728 (D.N.J. 1995) (but broker may be subject to liability for taking title to product in its own name, even briefly).

416 See, e.g., Massey v. Cassens & Sons, Inc., 2007 WL 2710490, at *5 (S.D. Ill. 2007) (broker not strictly liable where it had no input into production and marketing of product, exercised no control over its design or production, and never profited from its sale); Geboy v. TRL Inc., 159 F.3d 993 (7th Cir. 1998) (Wis. law); Oscar Mayer Corp. v. Mincing Trading Corp., 744 F. Supp. 79 (D.N.J. 1990) (N.J. and N.Y. law).

417 Oscar Mayer Corp. v. Mincing Trading Corp., 744 F. Supp. 79 (D.N.J. 1990) (N.J. and N.Y. law).

418 Randles, Purdue Pharma Bankruptcy Plan Approved, Freeing Sacklers from Lawsuits, Prod. Liab. & Toxics L. (Sept. 1, 2021).

419 Chutchian, Purdue Pharma Judge Rejects Call to Halt Opioid Deal, Reuters (Oct. 13, 2021).

420 See, e.g., Randles, Judge Throws Out Purdue Pharma's Deal to Shield Sacklers from Opioid Lawsuits, Prod. Liab. & Toxics L. (Dec. 16, 2021); § 10.3, note 381, above. See also Hill, Purdue Pharma's Shock Ruling Echoes Through Retail Bankruptcy, Prod. Liab. & Toxics L. (Jan. 19, 2022):

> [T]hird-party releases, a long-controversial legal tool that can protect a bankrupt company's executives and owners from lawsuits, are coming under increased scrutiny. Federal courts are split on whether the releases are legal, and now [after the Sackler family releases in the Purdue Pharma bankruptcy settlement were struck down] once-permissive jurisdictions are increasingly questioning such maneuvers.

421 See, e.g., Randles, Purdue Pharma's Sackler Family Approved for $6 Billion Opioid Deal with States: The agreement requires Purdue prevailing in an appeal by the Justice Department's bankruptcy division, Wall St. J.com (Mar. 9, 2022); § 10.3, notes 379–381, above.

to determine whether these family members may be held personally liable to plaintiffs, very well then forcing them personally into bankruptcy.

Among rare instances where company officials figured personally in products liability cases was the Johns-Manville Corporation asbestos litigation, where the bankruptcy court stayed more than 1,000 cases seeking compensation in excess of $230 million that named past and present directors, officers, and employees as defendants.[422] In another example, a former DuPont engineer founded Vitek, Inc. to manufacture implantable temporomandibular joints from DuPont Teflon fibers purchased through a third-party distributor.[423] Although DuPont warned Vitek that Teflon was designed exclusively for industrial use, Vitek obtained FDA approval for marketing the implants in 1983.[424] By 1990, implant failures had resulted in 426 suits alleging strict liability or failure to warn against Vitek and its officers and directors,[425] forcing the company into bankruptcy. More than 2,200 claims were ultimately filed against the bankrupt company.[426] Eluding the products liability claims naming him as a defendant,[427] the Vitek founder fled to Switzerland.[428] These are just a few instances of individuals being personally involved in responsibility for harm from product accidents. And there are others.[429]

[422] In re Johns-Manville Corp., 33 B.R. 254, 260 (Bankr. S.D.N.Y. 1983). The Manville Personal Injury Settlement Trust ultimately settled cases stayed by the Bankruptcy Court. See, e.g., Smith, Resolving Asbestos Claims: The Manville Personal Injury Settlement Trust, Law & Contemp. Probs., Autumn 1990, at 31.

[423] In re TMJ Implants Prods. Liab. Litig., 872 F. Supp. 1019, 1022–23 (D. Minn. 1995).

[424] Id. at 1023.

[425] Matter of Vitek, Inc., 51 F.3d 530, 532 (5th Cir. 1995).

[426] TMJ Implants: Lessons for All of Us, Orthopedic Network News, Trauma Update, Vol. 6, No. 2 (April 1995).

[427] See, e.g., Hoyt v. Vitek, Inc., 894 P.2d 1225 (Or. Ct. App. 1995); Seifert v. Vitek, Inc., 1993 WL 765636 (D. Or. 1993) (claims also filed against the oral surgeon who first experimented with Teflon as implant material).

[428] See Militzer, Lamontagne v. E.I. Dupont De Nemours & Co.: A Pro-Defendant Stance in A Failure-to-Warn Case, 5 J. Pharmacy & L. 181, 187 (1996).

[429] See, e.g., In re Ephedra Prod. Liab. Litig., 478 F. Supp. 2d 624, 634 (S.D.N.Y. 2007) (corporate veil did not shield sole shareholder, director, and president of company that sold the product that caused plaintiff's stroke; the corporate "acts allegedly constituting products liability and fraud are attributable to Michnal individually"); In re Northern Dist. of California, Dalkon Shield IUD Prod. Liab. Litig., 693 F.2d 847 (9th Cir. 1982) (among the founders and major shareholders of Dalkon Corp., later acquired by A. H. Robbins Co., defendants in this class action included the two inventors of the Dalkon Shield). Criminal investigations into fraudulent corporate behavior may parallel products liability litigation, as in the racketeering conviction of the founder of a major opioid distributor and conspiracy charges against a drug co-operative's CEO. See Voris and Dolmetsch, Ex-Pharma CEO Aided Opioid Sales to Addicts, U.S. Says, Prod. Liab. & Toxics L. (Jan. 18, 2022). See also Barash, Gree Executives' Trial Should Delay House Fire Case, U.S. Says, Prod. Liab. & Toxics L. (Dec. 23, 2021) (defective dehumidifier); § 3.2, note 122, above.

Chapter 16

SPECIAL TRANSACTIONS AND PRODUCTS

Table of Sections

§ 16.1 SPECIAL TRANSACTIONS AND PRODUCTS—GENERALLY

Some products liability litigation involves transactions other than a typical sale of a new chattel, the paradigm around which most products liability law is centered. The principal issue involved in many of the cases examined in this chapter is whether the usual principles of products liability law, particularly the doctrine of strict products liability, should be extended beyond the new chattel sale situation to contexts where other policies and principles may predominate. In some of these situations, the differing objectives and doctrinal borderlines of products liability, premises liability, professional malpractice, environmental protection, free speech, public health, and other areas of the law are brought into sharp relief.

This chapter considers a number of special types of transactions and products that differ from the paradigm. Section 16.2 examines the major types of non-sale transactions—those involving leases, bailments, and licenses—that may implicate products liability principles. Section 16.3 addresses the extent to which traditional products liability rules may apply to transactions in which a supplier provides services together with a product. Sections 16.4 and 16.5 consider how legal principles may change if the product sold is not new—if it has been repaired, rebuilt, reconditioned, or is simply used. The remaining sections examine legal principles surrounding the provision of a variety of particular products that sometimes prove harmful, including hazardous buildings, dangerous types of publications, electronic technology (including electricity, websites, and computer programs), infected blood and other biologics, and dangerous animals, among other products.[1] Disposal and salvage transactions were examined previously in the discussion of limitations on defectiveness.[2]

---

1 See §§ 16.6–.10, below.

2 See § 10.7, above.

§ 16.2 LEASE, BAILMENT, AND LICENSE TRANSACTIONS

From its hybrid origin in tort and contract, products liability law classically involves chattel *sales*. The discussions here survey the major types of *non*-sale commercial relationships—leases, bailments, and licenses—that involve transfers of product possession and control sufficiently similar to product sales to suggest that products liability principles might plausibly be extended to embrace these analogous transactions. The primary issue pertinent to these special types of transactions often is the applicability of the doctrine of strict products liability in tort, and secondarily the availability of claims for breach of warranty. In each situation involving these particular non-sale transactions, the first question is doctrinal—whether the rules of strict liability in tort (and warranty) facially apply to these special contexts. Yet, in cases of these types, a doctrinal analysis often is unhelpful because warranty law and strict products liability in tort both are defined in terms of chattel *sales*. Thus, courts and legislatures deciding whether to broaden the applicability of strict liability principles to non-sale transactions need to proceed to examine the underlying policies advanced by strict products liability to determine whether such policies logically and fairly apply outside of true sale situations to transactions that are instead leases, bailments, or licenses.

Leases

In General

Lease transactions[3] are an increasingly common method by which consumers take possession of the products they put to daily use, such as cars, trucks, cranes, power tools, and other chattels that may be dangerous if defective.[4] Indeed, consumers and businesses to a large extent are moving away from purchase and sale transactions for many types of products, notably automotive vehicles, and shifting instead to short-term and long-term leases.[5] In general, products liability principles that presently control a supplier's *sale* of a product apply with equal force to those applicable to product *leases*. But the law has taken some time to evolve to this point, and some jurisdictions have yet to complete the process of breaking down the barriers separating principles of products liability law that govern product sales from those that govern product leases.

Theory of Liability

Negligence. Ordinary negligence principles govern the liability of lessors of defective products that injure lessees and other people. *Restatement (Second) of Torts* § 408 provides that a lessor is subject to liability to lessees and others foreseeably endangered by the lessor's failure to exercise due care to make a leased product safe for

---

[3] " 'Lease' means a transfer of the right to possession and use of goods for a term in return for consideration . . . ." UCC § 2A–103(1)(j).

[4] See, e.g., Samuel Friedland Family Enters. v. Amoroso, 630 So.2d 1067, 1070 (Fla. 1994) (court was "[m]indful of the recent growth of the commercial leasing business in recent years"); Martin v. Ryder Truck Rental, Inc., 353 A.2d 581, 587 (Del. 1976) (noting the "present-day magnitude of the motor vehicle rental business"); Price v. Shell Oil Co., 466 P.2d 722, 726 (Cal. 1970) (noting "the widespread use of the lease of personalty in today's business world"); Cintrone v. Hertz Truck Leasing & Rental Serv., 212 A.2d 769, 776 (N.J. 1965) (Francis, J.) (taking judicial notice of growth in vehicular rental business). See generally Ausness, Strict Liability for Chattel Leasing, 48 U. Pitt. L. Rev. 273 (1987); Henszey, Application of Strict Liability to the Leasing Industry, 33 Bus. Law. 631 (1978); Annot., 52 A.L.R.3d 121 (1974) (applicability of strict liability in tort to chattel lessors); Frumer, Friedman, and Sklaren, Products Liability § 5.07.

[5] See Ausness, Strict Liability for Chattel Leasing, 48 U. Pitt. L. Rev. 273, 274–76 (1987) (detailing boom in both short-term and long-term leasing in America); Lawrence's Anderson on the UCC § 2–314:64.

its probable uses and for failing to warn of any hidden dangers the product may possess.[6] The lessor's duty of care includes subjecting its products to appropriate inspections from initial purchase throughout the product's periodic use.[7] Indeed, a commercial lessor's duty of care is said to include, in the absence of an agreement to the contrary, an implied promise "that the article is leased as fit for immediate use."[8] In addition to other claims, plaintiffs commonly include allegations of negligence in products liability actions against lessors of dangerously defective products.[9]

Warranty—Article 2. By its terms, "Article 2—Sales" of the Uniform Commercial Code applies only to true sales transactions,[10] which suggests that it was not intended to apply to lease transactions in which the lessor retains title to the goods. In *Leake v. Meredith*,[11] for example, the plaintiff was injured by the collapse of an aluminum extension ladder he had rented from the defendant. In his suit against the lessor, the plaintiff alleged negligence and breach of an implied warranty of fitness. The trial court ruled for the defendant on the negligence claim but submitted the implied warranty claim to the jury, which found for the plaintiff. On appeal, the court reversed the judgment, ruling that a literal reading of the relevant sections of the Code "indicates that the implied warranty of fitness for a particular purpose . . . applies to sales only, and not to bailments or chattel lease transactions."[12] Other courts have similarly construed Article 2 strictly as not applying to lease transactions.[13]

---

[6] Rest. (2d) Torts § 408 provides in full:

> One who leases a chattel as safe for immediate use is subject to liability to those whom he should expect to use the chattel, or to be endangered by its probable use, for physical harm caused by its use in a manner for which, and by a person for whose use, it is leased, if the lessor fails to exercise reasonable care to make it safe for such use or to disclose its actual condition to those who may be expected to use it.

But to be liable for negligently failing to warn, a lessor must be shown to have had reason to know of the defect. See, e.g., Evans v. Byers Enters., Inc., 2000 WL 522469 (Ohio Ct. App. 2000) (no proof that lessor knew or had reason to know that trunk could unexpectedly fall and injure user).

[7] See Rest. (2d) Torts § 408 cmt. *a*. Compare Hernandez v. Grando's LLC, 429 P.3d 1259, 1267 (N.M. Ct. App. 2018) ("A lessor's reservation of the right to inspect a leased chattel and take remedial action does not impose on the lessor a duty of maintenance and repair owed to a third party.").

[8] Id. cmt. *b*.

[9] See, e.g., Shimmel by Shimmel v. Navistar Int'l Corp., 440 F. Supp. 3d 438, 447 (W.D. Pa. 2020) (denying motion to dismiss negligence claim against lessor for failing to equip truck with collision avoidance technology); Noveck v. Avis Rent A Car Sys., LLC, 446 Fed. Appx. 370 (2d Cir. 2011) (N.Y. law) (car; Avis not negligent for failing to order Trailblazer with side curtain air bag since it reasonably could rely on GM to design safe vehicle); Garnett v. Strike Holdings LLC, 882 N.Y.S.2d 115, 116 (App. Div. 2009) (go-kart; lessor subject to negligence liability); Bostwick v. Ballard Marine, Inc., 112 P.3d 571, 574 (Wash. Ct. App. 2005) (sublessor subject to liability in negligence); Evans v. Byers Enters., Inc., 2000 WL 522469 (Ohio Ct. App. 2000) (not liable).

[10] UCC § 2–106(1) provides that "[a] 'sale' consists in the passing of title from the seller to the buyer," and § 2–103(1)(d) provides that " 'Seller' means a person who sells or contracts to sell goods."

[11] 267 S.E.2d 93 (Va. 1980).

[12] Id. at 95.

[13] See, e.g., Bechtel v. Paul Clark, Inc., 412 N.E.2d 143 (Mass. App. Ct. 1980) (injuries from defective brakes on rental car not recoverable in claim for breach of warranty under UCC § 2–314). Although the state legislature had subsequently amended Article 2 to include lessors within its scope, the court refused to apply it retroactively to cover the plaintiff's transaction. Id. at 149–50. Cf. DiCintio v. DaimlerChrysler Corp., 97 N.Y.2d 463 (2002) (holding that Magnuson Moss Act, enacted against backdrop of UCC Article 2, does not apply to lease transactions). See generally Lawrence's Anderson on the UCC § 2–314:65.

One way or another, however, most courts have extended the principles of Article 2 to lease transactions.[14] Some courts[15] have relied on a comment to UCC § 2–313 that disclaims any effort to displace developing case law on this issue;[16] some courts have applied Article 2 to leases if a transaction partakes of a disguised sale;[17] while others have applied Article 2 by analogy, reasoning that such transactions are closely similar to sales,[18] an approach criticized by commentators for being at once too narrow and too vague.[19] Some courts, applying a policy-oriented approach, extend Article 2's warranty protections to lessees when such an approach is consistent with underlying policies of the law. For example, the Washington Supreme Court used this approach in extending Article 2's warranty provisions to a plaintiff's claim for injuries resulting when defective brakes on his rental golf cart caused the cart to overturn,[20] as did the Florida Supreme Court in an action against the lessor of a defective forklift hoist that malfunctioned while lifting a wheelchair passenger from an airplane.[21] Many other courts have similarly applied a policy-based perspective,[22] an approach applauded by the commentators.[23]

Warranty—Article 2A. The problem of whether Article 2 should be applied to lease transactions was resolved in 1987 when a new "Article 2A—Leases" was promulgated and promptly enacted into law in a number of jurisdictions. The article was amended in a number of respects in 1990,[24] and all states except Louisiana enacted this new article of the Uniform Commercial Code that explicitly applies to personal property "lease" transactions.[25] In 2002–2003, Article 2A was revised again, but industry opposed the promulgated amendments (particularly certain e-commerce amendments), state

---

[14] See, e.g., Cucchi v. Rollins Protective Servs. Co., 574 A.2d 565, 571 (Pa. 1990) (alarm system: "lessees rely upon implied and express representations of lessors as to the quality, merchantability, and fitness of goods to the same extent and in the same manner as buyers rely upon similar representations by sellers").

[15] See, e.g., Cintrone v. Hertz Truck Leasing & Rental Serv., 212 A.2d 769, 775–76 (N.J. 1965).

[16] See UCC § 2–313 cmt. 2 (observing that "the warranty sections of this Article are not designed in any way to disturb those lines of case law growth which have recognized that warranties need not be confined . . . to sales contracts [but] may arise in other appropriate circumstances such as in the case of bailments for hire, [and] the matter is left to the case law").

[17] See Lawrence's Anderson on the UCC § 2–314:65.

[18] See id. § 2–314:67.

[19] See, e.g., Ausness, Strict Liability for Chattel Leasing, 48 U. Pitt. L. Rev. 273, 293 (1987); Murray, Under the Spreading Analogy of Article 2 of the Uniform Commercial Code, 39 Fordham L. Rev. 447, 451 (1971).

[20] Baker v. City of Seattle, 484 P.2d 405 (Wash. 1971).

[21] See W.E. Johnson Equip. Co. v. United Airlines, Inc., 238 So.2d 98, 100 (Fla. 1970) ("The reasons for imposing the warranty of fitness in sales cases are often present in lease transactions. Public policy demands that in this day of expanding rental and leasing enterprises the consumer who leases be given protection equivalent to the consumer who purchases. Although a sale transfers ownership and a lease or bailment merely transfers possession and anticipates future return of the chattel to the owner, there may be as much or more reliance on the competence or expertise of the lessor than on the competence of the seller.").

[22] See, e.g., Owens v. Patent Scaffolding Co.-Div. of Harsco, 354 N.Y.S.2d 778, 784 (Sup. Ct. 1974) (Article 2 warranty provisions applied to lease transactions since there is no real difference to users "of scaffolding equipment between buying equipment and leasing it for use on a job"), rev'd on other grounds, 376 N.Y.S.2d 948 (App. Div. 1975).

[23] See, e.g., Ausness, Strict Liability for Chattel Leasing, 48 U. Pitt. L. Rev. 273, 295 (1987) (this approach "correctly focuses on the policies that underlie warranty protection instead of applying a mechanical test"); Krasnow, The Extension of Warranty Protection to Lease Transactions, 10 B.C. Ind. & Com. L. Rev. 127, 138 (1968).

[24] See UCC § 2A–101 Official Comment (History).

[25] UCC § 2A–103(j) provides: " 'Lease' means a transfer of the right to possession and use of goods for a term in return for consideration . . . ." See cmt. to id. ("a lease is created when the lessee agrees to furnish consideration for the right to the possession and use of goods over a specified period of time") (citing Mooney, Personal Property Leasing: A Challenge, 36 Bus. Law. 1605, 1607 (1981)).

legislatures ignored them, and the amendments were withdrawn in 2011.[26] Article 2A's key provisions closely mimic Article 2's provisions governing the law of sales, including similar provisions on express and implied warranties, damages, and the various bases for exclusion and limitation.[27] So, statutes adopting Article 2A provide a basis for products liability claims against chattel lessors for breach of warranty,[28] subject to the normal warranty law limitations and defenses,[29] similar to warranty actions against product sellers under Article 2.

Strict Liability in Tort. The landmark case extending strict liability in tort to lessors of motor vehicles was *Cintrone v. Hertz Truck Leasing & Rental Service*,[30] in which a passenger in a rental truck was injured when the brakes failed. The plaintiff sued the rental company, Hertz, for breach of implied warranty and negligence in failing properly to maintain the brakes. The trial court dismissed the warranty claim, and the jury found for Hertz on the negligence claim. On appeal, the New Jersey Supreme Court reversed the dismissal of the warranty claim, holding that the commercial rental of a truck included an implied warranty that the truck was fit and would remain so throughout the rental period. Writing for the majority, Judge Francis, who had authored *Henningsen v. Bloomfield Motors, Inc.*[31] five years earlier, reasoned that the policies underlying implied warranties in sales transactions applied with equal or greater force to commercial rentals of motor vehicles: rental vehicles are subjected to harder use than new vehicles offered for sale, and commercial lessors have a greater opportunity to inspect the vehicles for defects than the consuming public who necessarily rely on a lessor's expertise to discover and correct any defects prior to leasing such vehicles to the public; advertising and the nature of short-term lease transactions include a lessor's implied representation that its vehicles are fit for use and will remain so throughout the rental period; and, because defective vehicles present widespread and substantial risks to persons on the highways, the law should place maximum incentives on lessors of cars and trucks to ensure that they will be put in a safe condition before their release to the

---

[26] In 2002, the National Conference of Commissioners on Uniform State Laws (NCCUSL) approved the revision of Article 2A, as did the American Law Institute (ALI) in 2003. See 25 ALI Reporter 1 (Summer 2003). In 2010, "[r]ecognizing that the prospects for enactment of the 2003 amendments are bleak, the [UCC Permanent Editorial Board (PEB)] concluded that no purpose was served by retaining those amendments in the Official Text of the Uniform Commercial Code, which would represent the law of no state either now or in the foreseeable future. Accordingly, . . . the PEB unanimously decided to recommend amending the Official Text of the Uniform Commercial Code to revert to the prior text of Articles 2 and 2A, as amended in conjunction with the 2003 revision of Article 7 . . . ." Memorandum, UCC Permanent Editorial Board (2011). The ALI approved this recommendation at its annual meeting in May 2011. See § 4.1, above.

[27] For example, see § 2A–210 (express warranties), § 2A–212 (implied warranty of merchantability), § 2A–213 (implied warranty of fitness for particular purpose), § 2A–214 (exclusion or modification of warranties), § 2A–216 (third-party beneficiaries, including alternatives A, B, and C), § 2A–503 (modification or impairment of rights and remedies, including prima facie unconscionability of limitations on injury to the person in the case of consumer goods), § 2A–520 (lessee's incidental and consequential damages, including injury to person or property proximately resulting from breach). See, e.g., Mollins v. Nissan Motor Co., 836 N.Y.S.2d 494, at *4–5 (Sup. Ct. 2007) (table) (warranties disclaimed under § 2A–214).

[28] See, e.g., Banks v. International Rental & Leasing Corp., 680 F.3d 296, 300 (3d Cir. 2012) (V.I. law) (passengers in van rented from Budget Rent-A-Car injured when brakes failed, causing van to crash into tree, could maintain breach of warranty claim against Budget under statute that enacted UCC Article 2A).

[29] See, e.g., Cianfrani v. Kalmar-AC Handling Sys., Inc., 1995 WL 563289, at *8 (D.N.J. 1995) (Del. law) (4-year statute of limitations from tender of delivery).

[30] 212 A.2d 769 (N.J. 1965).

[31] 161 A.2d 69 (N.J. 1960). For a discussion of *Henningsen*, see § 5.2, above.

public. For all these reasons, Judge Francis concluded that commercial lessors should be subject to strict liability in tort just like sellers of new products.[32]

Although a few early decisions were reluctant to apply the doctrine of strict products liability in tort to lease transactions,[33] most courts fully embraced *Cintrone*'s application of strict liability in tort to short-term[34] commercial leases of defective products, frequently relying on the same policy rationales.[35] A noteworthy example is *Price v. Shell Oil Co.*,[36] in which a mechanic was injured when a ladder on a rental truck gave way. Relying heavily on *Cintrone*'s reasoning, supplemented by its own risk-spreading rationale,[37] the California Supreme Court extended strict products liability in tort to commercial lessors because it could discern "no substantial difference between sellers of personal property and non-sellers, such as bailors and lessors."[38] In both situations, the product supplier places a product on the market knowing that it will not be inspected for defects. In view of "the market realities and the widespread use of the lease of personalty in today's business world," the court concluded that it made good sense to impose responsibility for physical harm on lessors as well as sellers of defective products.[39] On similar reasoning, most modern courts have followed suit by routinely holding commercial lessors[40] of new and like-new[41] products subject to strict liability in tort[42] to

[32] *Cintrone*, 212 A.2d at 775–81.

[33] See, e.g., Bona v. Graefe, 285 A.2d 607 (Md. 1972); Speyer, Inc. v. Humble Oil & Ref. Co., 403 F.2d 766 (3d Cir. 1968) (Pa. law). See generally Ausness, Strict Liability for Chattel Leasing, 48 U. Pitt. L. Rev. 273, 300–02 (1987).

[34] Though most cases involve short-term leases, and the Restatement limits its provision in this regard, see Products Liability Rest. § 20 cmt. *c*, several decisions do extend strict liability to long-term leases. In addition to *Cintrone*, see, e.g., Berman v. Watergate W., Inc., 391 A.2d 1351 (D.C. 1978); Coleman v. Hertz Corp., 534 P.2d 940 (Okla. 1975); Price v. Shell Oil Co., 85 Cal. Rptr. 178 (Ct. App. 1970). See also Bainter v. Lamoine LP Gas Co., 321 N.E.2d 744 (Ill. App. Ct. 1974) (propane gas tank provided to customer). The problem with long-term leases is that maintenance responsibilities, and to this extent risk control, may lie principally with the lessee, who thus may be the better party to bear responsibility for at least certain types of dangerous defects arising during the lease. See P. Sherman, Products Liability § 8.06, at 241 (1981). "However, a distinction based solely on whether a lease is 'long-term' or 'short-term' is likely to be arbitrary and unrelated to the policies that underlie strict liability." Ausness, above note 33, at 323.

[35] Other early decisions include Bachner v. Pearson, 479 P.2d 319 (Alaska 1970) (Piper Comanche aircraft); Stewart v. Budget Rent-A-Car Corp., 470 P.2d 240 (Haw. 1970); Galluccio v. Hertz Corp., 274 N.E.2d 178 (Ill. App. Ct. 1971); Stang v. Hertz Corp., 497 P.2d 732 (N.M. 1972); Rourke v. Garza, 530 S.W.2d 794 (Tex. 1975); Martin v. Ryder Truck Rental, Inc., 353 A.2d 581 (Del. 1976) (nicely summarizing policy rationales for extending strict products liability in tort to commercial lease transactions); Francioni v. Gibsonia Truck Corp., 372 A.2d 736 (Pa. 1977) (reviewing early cases).

[36] 466 P.2d 722 (Cal. 1970).

[37] Id. at 725–26 ("the paramount policy to be promoted by the rule is the protection of otherwise defenseless victims of manufacturing defects and the spreading throughout society of the cost of compensating them").

[38] Id. at 726.

[39] Id.

[40] Most courts have limited the extension of strict products liability to commercial lessors, such that strict liability has been held not to apply to "private" lease transactions. See, e.g., Burns v. Haines Equip., Inc., 726 N.Y.S.2d 516 (App. Div. 2001) (as casual lessor, crane owner who leased crane to plaintiff's employer could not be strictly liable in tort); Brescia v. Great Rd. Realty Trust, 373 A.2d 1310, 1312 (N.H. 1977).

[41] The Restatement limits strict liability to products rented in new or like-new condition, reasoning that many of the rationales for the strict liability of sellers do not apply to the rental of older used property. See Products Liability Rest. § 8 cmt. *j* ("when the rental units are in obviously used condition, and rented under circumstances in which a reasonable person would not expect the risk of defect to be substantially the same as if the rental units were new, liability of the lessor will depend upon a showing of fault"). See also id. at § 20 cmt. *c*.

[42] See, e.g., Shimmel by Shimmel v. Navistar Int'l Corp., 440 F. Supp. 3d 438, 445 (W.D. Pa. 2020) ("Lessors can be held strictly liable if they lease defective products."); Dunning v. Dynegy Midwest Generation, Inc., 33 N.E.3d 179, 204 (Ill. App. Ct. 2015) (lessor who "repeatedly placed its cart in the stream of commerce

the same extent as manufacturers and other sellers—an approach certified by the *Products Liability Restatement*.[43]

Financial Lease Transactions

Strict liability principles do not apply to financial lease transactions except in the unusual case where the financial lessor actively participates in marketing the product.[44] In a financial lease transaction, a financial institution takes title to a chattel and leases it to the user as an alternative to loaning funds and taking a security interest in the chattel. While financial lessors technically do "lease" chattels, their role is to provide financial services to their "lessees," not to ensure the safety of the products. Despite some protestations to the contrary,[45] courts have widely refused to hold financial lessors liable for injuries caused by defects in the products they finance, reasoning that such financial institutions rarely participate directly in the chain of product distribution and have little control over product safety.[46]

Bailments

In General

Traditionally, product leases were regarded as "bailments for hire."[47] In modern practice, lease transactions often are set forth in formalized contracts, whereas product bailment transactions normally are much more casual.[48] Typical product bailment transactions include a hotel providing chairs in its rented rooms,[49] a bowling alley that

---

for over a decade and obtained profits each time the cart was leased" was subject to strict liability for resulting injuries); Lyzhoft v. Waconia Farm Supply, 2013 WL 3368832, at *3 (Minn. Ct. App. 2013) (strict liability in tort applied to commercial lessors for same reasons as commercial sellers); Banks v. International Rental & Leasing Corp., 2011 WL 6299025, at *6 n.8 (V.I. 2011) (surveying cases); Ruzzo v. LaRose Enters., 748 A.2d 261, 267 (R.I. 2000) (same policy reasons as sellers); Samuel Friedland Family Enters. v. Amoroso, 630 So.2d 1067 (Fla. 1994) (sailboat); Westlye v. Look Sports, Inc., 22 Cal. Rptr. 2d 781 (Ct. App. 1993) (ski equipment); Kemp v. Miller, 453 N.W.2d 872 (Wis. 1990) (1984 Ford Tempo). See generally Ausness, Strict Liability for Chattel Leasing, 48 U. Pitt. L. Rev. 273 (1987); Annot., 52 A.L.R.3d 121 (1974) (applicability of strict liability in tort to chattel lessors).

[43] See Products Liability Rest. § 20 cmt. *c* ("A commercial lessor of new and like-new products is generally subject to the rules governing new product sellers."). The Restatement includes "lessors, bailors, and those who provide products to others as a means of promoting either the use of or consumption of such products or some other commercial activity" as parties subject to the basic liability principles of §§ 1 and 2. Products Liability Rest. § 20(b). See also Banks v. International Rental & Leasing Corp., 2011 WL 6299025, at *7 (V.I. 2011) (adopting § 20).

[44] See Products Liability Rest. § 20 cmt. *e* and Reporters' Note to cmt. *c*. See generally Ausness, above note 42, at 347; Annot., 28 A.L.R.4th 326 (1984).

[45] See, e.g., Nath v. National Equip. Leasing Corp., 439 A.2d 633, 636–38 (Pa. 1981) (Larsen, J., dissenting, joined by Flaherty and Kauffman, JJ.); Ausness, above note 42, at 349–50; Annot., 28 A.L.R.4th 326 (1984).

[46] See, e.g., Bolger v. Amazon.com, LLC, 267 Cal. Rptr. 3d 601, 621 (Ct. App. 2020) ("a critical policy consideration behind the doctrine of strict liability, enhancing product safety, would not be satisfied by imposing liability on finance lessors"); Houston v. McNeilus Truck & Mfg., Inc., 997 N.Y.S.2d 572, 575 (App. Div. 2015); Starobin v. Niagara Mach. & Tool Works Corp., 577 N.Y.S.2d 327 (App. Div. 1991) (Owen, J.); Nath v. National Equip. Leasing Corp., 439 A.2d 633, 636 (Pa. 1981) (4–3 decision) (because a finance lessor is "in the business of circulating funds" rather than selling merchandise, buyers cannot reasonably rely on them for the safety of the merchandise).

[47] "At common law a lease of personal property is a bailment for hire." UCC § 2A–103(j) cmt. *j*. See, e.g., Cintrone v. Hertz Truck Leasing & Rental Serv., 212 A.2d 769 (N.J. 1965).

[48] On product bailment transactions, see, e.g., Ausness, above note 42, at 313–17 and 335–39; Products Liability Rest. § 20 cmt. *f* and Reporters' Note thereto; Annot., 48 A.L.R.3d 668 (1973).

[49] See, e.g., Jones v. Keetch, 200 N.W.2d 227 (Mich. 1972) (chair in motel room collapsed; subject to common-law implied warranty of fitness) (citing Schnitzer v. Nixon, 439 F.2d 940 (4th Cir. 1971) (Va. law), and 8 Am. Jur. 2d Bailments § 144 (now 8A Am. Jur. 2d Bailments § 101) (implied warranty of fitness)). *But*

provides balls for its customers to use,[50] a skating center that rents roller skates to the skaters,[51] a restaurant that provides wine glasses and other implements for its patrons' use,[52] a supplier of propane gas that supplies its customers with tanks to hold the gas,[53] and a sports complex that rents go-carts to its patrons.[54] Not only do such transactions in many ways resemble short-term leases, but they generally overlap the category of product license transactions, considered next.

Since commercial bailments place chattels in the stream of commerce, like sales and leases, courts consider such transactions subject to strict liability in tort if a defect in a commercially bailed product causes physical harm,[55] which is the position of the *Third Restatement*.[56] Since this point is now well settled, a plaintiff injured while using a product that he did not buy or lease generally will seek to establish that he was a bailee.[57] For example, in *Golt v. Sports Complex, Inc.*,[58] the renter of a go-cart at a sports complex was injured when rammed from behind by another cart. Claiming that the cart's design was uncrashworthy, the plaintiff sued the complex for negligence and strict liability in tort. The court defined a bailment as the transfer of possession, but not title, of a chattel from the bailor to the bailee to use for some purpose during which the bailee's possession is exclusive.[59] Applying these principles to the rental of the go-cart, the court concluded that the go-cart drivers had full possession and control of the go-carts during each lap around the track, subject only to certain normal restrictions. Accordingly, and consistent

---

see Ferrucci v. Atlantic City Showboat, Inc., 51 F. Supp. 2d 129 (D. Conn. 1999) (no bailment of hotel bed over which plaintiff tripped because hotel never surrendered exclusive possession and control, precluding plaintiff's recovery under state products liability statute).

[50] See, e.g., Dixon v. Four Seasons Bowling Alley, Inc., 424 A.2d 428 (N.J. Super. Ct. App. Div. 1980).

[51] See Wilson v. Dover Skating Ctr., Ltd., 566 A.2d 1020 (Del. Super. Ct. 1989).

[52] See, e.g., Shaffer v. Victoria Station, Inc., 588 P.2d 233 (Wash. 1978) (restaurant liable in both warranty and strict tort for injuries to patron from wine glass shattering in his hand).

[53] See, e.g., Bainter v. Lamoine LP Gas Co., 321 N.E.2d 744 (Ill. App. Ct. 1974). See also Fulbright v. Klamath Gas Co., 533 P.2d 316 (Or. 1975).

[54] See Golt v. Sports Complex, Inc., 644 A.2d 989, 992–93 (Del. Super. Ct. 1994). *But see* Hardy v. Kroger Co., 2019 WL 1306216, at *5 (E.D. Tex. 2019) (bailor not liable to indemnify bailee for shopper's products liability claims arising from motorized shopping cart injuries; grocery store did not charge for use of the cart and was not a "seller" of the cart under Rest. (3d) Torts § 20 cmt. *f*); Leonard v. Tractor Supply Co., 88 F. Supp. 3d 459 (W.D. Pa. 2015) (under Rest. (3d) Torts, defendant was not a "seller" of the displayed porch swing that fell, injuring customer).

[55] See Lyzhoft v. Waconia Farm Supply, 2013 WL 3368832, at *3–4 (Minn. Ct. App. 2013) ("[o]ther jurisdictions have extended strict products liability to commercial bailors, lessors, or both, due to the same policy considerations that support strict products liability for commercial sellers," and citing cases). See also Thomas v. St. Joseph Hosp., 618 S.W.2d 791, 796–98 (Tex. App. 1981) (hospital provided flammable gown to patient); Martin v. Ryder Truck Rental, Inc., 353 A.2d 581, 586–87 (Del. 1976).

[56] See Rest. (3d) Torts § 20(b) and cmt. *f*.

[57] Compare Kalumetals, Inc. v. Hitachi Magnetics Corp., 21 F. Supp. 2d 510 (W.D. Pa. 1998) (supplier of grinding swarf with retort tube that exploded was bailor and hence subject to strict liability), with Winslow v. L.B.O. Holding, Inc., 2009 WL 3739657, at *5–6 (Conn. Super. Ct. 2009) (N.H. law) (no bailment created when employee sold Alpine sled ride ticket and handed slide to plaintiff); Ferrucci v. Atlantic City Showboat, Inc., 51 F. Supp. 2d 129 (D. Conn. 1999) (no bailment of hotel bed over which plaintiff tripped because hotel never surrendered exclusive possession and control; thus, products liability statute did not apply).

[58] 644 A.2d 989 (Del. Super. Ct. 1994).

[59] Id. at 992.

with the underlying policies of risk distribution and deterrence,[60] the court ruled that the defendant was subject to strict liability in tort as a bailor of the go-cart.[61]

Because a bailment is not a sale, however, the warranties provided by UCC Article 2 have been held not to apply to such a transaction. In *Garfield v. Furniture Fair-Hanover*,[62] for example, a woman was injured by the collapse of a bed loaned to her and her husband by the defendant furniture store pending the delivery of a new bed they had purchased. The court held that since the plaintiffs had never taken title to the loaned bed, and since they were bound to return it upon delivery of the purchased bed, the transaction was a bailment rather than a sale under UCC § 2–106(1).[63]

Demonstrators, Loaners, and Giveaways

If a seller provides a user with a demonstrator,[64] a loaner,[65] or even a product giveaway[66] as part of its marketing scheme, then the product has entered the stream of commerce, and the supplier is subject to strict liability in tort. However, if a supplier provides a product for use exclusively in a commercial context, a court may find that it never enters the stream of commerce so that strict liability should not apply. *Armstrong Rubber Co. v. Urquidez*,[67] for example, held that strict liability in tort did not apply to an action brought for the death of a test driver caused by the blowout of an allegedly defective tire manufactured by the defendant, Armstrong. The defendant had supplied the tire in question to the plaintiff's employer, a tire-testing facility, as a "non-interest spare" to be used on test vehicles along with whatever tires were actually being tested at the time. Ruling that the tire had never entered the stream of commerce, the court held that strict liability in tort did not apply.[68]

---

[60] See id. at 994:

> The cost of supplying a defective go-cart should be imposed on the party profiting from the public's use of the go-cart. The owner of the go-cart can best spread the risk of injury through the prices of tickets. [The owner of a go-cart] implies a representation that the go-cart is fit to travel around the track and adequately absorb the energy created from a collision of two go-carts. Placing liability on the owner will also ensure the go-cart owner will take care in selecting responsible manufacturers who design and construct safe go-carts, resulting in general risk-reduction.

[61] "Buying an amusement ticket and using the ticket to gain control and possession of a go-cart creates a bailment. . . . Since strict liability applies to bailments, . . . strict liability applies to this transaction." Id.

[62] 274 A.2d 325 (N.J. Super. Ct. Law Div. 1971).

[63] Nor did the court think that the bailment had become integrated into the sale of the new bed so as to extend the warranties attaching to the sale to the bailment as well. See id. at 326–27.

[64] See, e.g., Nazari v. Kohler Co., 2008 WL 4542850, at *3 (5th Cir. 2008) (Tex. law) (defective shower door displayed in Home Depot store entered stream of commerce); Beattie v. Beattie, 786 A.2d 549, 551 (Del. Super. Ct. 2001) (dealership furnished "demonstrator vehicle" to customer for test drive); Robert F. Bullock, Inc. v. Thorpe, 353 S.E.2d 340 (Ga. 1987) (supplier placed deep-fat fryer in restaurant kitchen on trial basis); First Nat'l Bank of Mobile v. Cessna Aircraft Co., 365 So.2d 966, 967 (Ala. 1978) (demonstrator plane crashed); Delaney v. Towmotor Corp., 339 F.2d 4 (2d Cir. 1964) (N.Y. law) (fork-lift truck). *But see* Mason v. General Motors Corp., 490 N.E.2d 437 (Mass. 1986) (dealer who allowed customer to test drive car not subject to liability).

[65] See, e.g., Johnson v. Stanley-Bostitch, Inc., 2000 WL 709480 (E.D. Pa. 2000) (pneumatic nail gun loaner provided by manufacturer as business incentive to existing customers).

[66] "[A] commercial entity is subject to strict liability for products it distributes free of charge, since title has passed to the consumer." Products Liability Rest. § 20 Reporters' Note to cmt. *b*. See, e.g., Levondosky v. Marina Assocs., 731 F. Supp. 1210 (D.N.J. 1990) (casino served free drink in defective glass); Perfection Paint & Color Co. v. Konduris, 258 N.E.2d 681 (Ind. Ct. App. 1970) (free lacquer thinner supplied following sale of lacquer that failed to bond).

[67] 570 S.W.2d 374 (Tex. 1978).

[68] Id. at 377 ("The defective tire, although not itself the subject of the test, always remained within the industrial, testing process.").

License Transactions

In General

Two separate types of license situations arise in products liability litigation: (1) trademark or trade name licenses, by which the owner of a valuable mark or name—such as 7-Up, Goodyear, or McDonald's—sells the rights to use its mark or name to another supplier further down the chain of product distribution; and (2) product-use licenses, by which the owner of a product—such as a laundromat with washing machines and dryers, or an amusement park with rides—charges customers to use its products. Trademarks and trade-name licenses were previously addressed,[69] and the present discussion addresses the topic of licenses for product use.

Product-use licenses and commercial bailments frequently overlap and are often indistinguishable. Transactions include a laundromat providing washing machines, a hotel providing chairs and bath mats, a bowling alley providing balls, a skating center renting roller skates, a restaurant providing wine glasses and other eating implements, a supplier of propane gas supplying tanks to hold the gas, and an amusement park providing seats on rides.[70] These transactions in many respects resemble short-term product leases,[71] but true license transactions have a number of distinguishing characteristics: (1) they generally are less formal than chattel lease transactions; (2) the user often does not pay a specific fee for the product's use; (3) and the product's use is often restricted to the supplier's premises. Most of these situations are properly classified as license transactions, or possibly as bailments.[72]

When a defect in such a product injures the user, courts sometimes attempt to determine whether the transaction should be classified as a bailment or a license on the belief that the classification may have some bearing on whether the doctrine of strict liability in tort properly applies to the transaction. This was the situation in *Golt v. Sports Complex, Inc.*,[73] the go-cart case examined previously, in which the court declared that classifying the go-cart rental as a bailment (or "lease-bailment") was crucial to its application of strict liability in tort. Other courts, however, proceed in products liability cases to examine such non-sale transactions without ever attempting to classify the precise type of property transaction involved.[74]

---

69 See § 15.4, above.

70 See, e.g., Garcia v. Halsett, 82 Cal. Rptr. 420 (Ct. App. 1970); Fogge v. Tropitone Furniture Co., 2014 WL 12737624, at *3 (D. Md. 2014) (motel was not the "seller" of defective pool area lounge chair); Burnett v. Covell, 191 P.3d 985, 989 (Alaska 2008) (strict liability does not apply to owner of law office chair that collapsed under client; chair not placed into the stream of commerce); Dixon v. Four Seasons Bowling Alley, Inc., 424 A.2d 428 (N.J. Super. Ct. App. Div. 1980); Wilson v. Dover Skating Ctr., Ltd., 566 A.2d 1020 (Del. Super. Ct. 1989); Shaffer v. Victoria Station, Inc., 588 P.2d 233 (Wash. 1978) (restaurant liable in both warranty and strict liability in tort for injuries to patron from wine glass shattering in his hand); Bainter v. Lamoine LP Gas Co., 321 N.E.2d 744 (Ill. App. Ct. 1974); Wagner v. Coronet Hotel, 458 P.2d 390 (Ariz. Ct. App. 1969) (hotel not strictly liable for defective bath mat). Other examples of licenses might include a woodworking shop that charges a fee for use of its table saws and a batting practice operation that allows batters for a fee to use its pitching machines.

71 See discussion of lease transactions, above.

72 On product license and bailment transactions, see, e.g., Ausness, Strict Liability for Chattel Leasing, 48 U. Pitt. L. Rev. 273, 313–17 (1987); Products Liability Rest. § 20 cmt. *f* and Reporters' Note thereto; Annot., 48 A.L.R.3d 668 (1973). Bailments are separately examined above.

73 644 A.2d 989, 992–93 (Del. Super. Ct. 1994).

74 See, e.g., Safeway Stores, Inc. v. Nest-Kart, 579 P.2d 441 (Cal. 1978) (grocery shopping cart); Keen v. Dominick's Finer Foods, Inc., 364 N.E.2d 502 (Ill. App. Ct. 1977) (same).

While most of these transactions fairly may be characterized as bailments,[75] they often are better viewed as license transactions because such transactions do not involve a transfer of "legal" possession to the user, who typically has a limited right of possession to use the product in restricted ways on the licensor's premises.[76] While the distinction may possibly be relevant to whether Article 2A of the Uniform Commercial Code applies to a transaction,[77] courts would be better advised to avoid becoming ensnared in fine distinctions of property law in tort law cases involving personal injuries.[78]

Theory of Liability

Negligence. Licensors, of course, are subject to negligence liability for failing to submit their products to inspections reasonable under the circumstances, for failing to exercise care to repair or replace products that become damaged or worn, and for failing to exercise reasonable care to warn users of dangers in the products that they license.[79]

Warranty. Neither Article 2 nor Article 2A of the Uniform Commercial Code expressly applies to product license transactions: "Article 2—Sales" by its terms applies only to "sales" transactions,[80] and "Article 2A—Leases" by its terms is limited to product "lease" transactions.[81] Because both sales and leases ("bailments for hire")[82] involve the transfer of rights to the exclusive use and possession of a product, and because such "legal" possession by hypothesis is *not* transferred to a licensee, as mentioned earlier, a license cannot logically be considered within the scope of either a sale or lease transaction. In short, a literal construction of the terms of Articles 2 and 2A excludes license transactions from coverage.[83] Nevertheless, a court might extend Article 2, or apply it by analogy, to license transactions similar to how many courts approached lease transactions under Article 2 prior to adoption of Article 2A.[84] In addition, a court might

---

[75] See, e.g., Golt v. Sports Complex, Inc., 644 A.2d 989, 992–93 (Del. Super. Ct. 1994) (go-cart rented to plaintiff: bailment).

[76] See, e.g., Reeder v. Bally's Total Fitness Corp., 963 F. Supp. 530, 533 (E.D. Va. 1997) (health club patron injured on stomach curl machine was merely a business invitee on defendant's premises; no bailment or lease of the machine: "[W]hat plaintiff purchased with the membership agreement was a right to use the Club and its exercise equipment during business hours, provided the equipment was not being used by any other members of the Club. Plaintiff did not purchase the right to possess and use specific equipment for a specific period of time to the exclusion of all others."); Garcia v. Halsett, 82 Cal. Rptr. 420, 422 (Ct. App. 1970). See also Ausness, above note 72, at 335 ("a license differs from a chattel lease in that legal possession of the product is transferred to the lessee in a lease relationship, but remains with the licensor in a license arrangement").

[77] See, e.g., *Reeder*, above (Article 2A did not apply because health club did not bail its equipment to patrons).

[78] Because of the overlap and imprecision among classifications, this admonition applies to bailment and license transactions alike.

[79] See Rest. (2d) Torts §§ 388–93 and 405–06.

[80] UCC § 2–106(1) provides that "[a] 'sale' consists in the passing of title from the seller to the buyer," and § 2–103(d) provides that " 'Seller' means a person who sells or contracts to sell goods."

[81] UCC § 2A–103(1)(j) provides that " 'Lease' means a transfer of the right to possession and use of goods for a term in return for consideration . . . ."

[82] See UCC § 2A–103 cmt. *j*. "[A] lease is created when the lessee agrees to furnish consideration for the right to the possession and use of goods over a specified period of time." Id. (citing Mooney, Personal Property Leasing: A Challenge, 36 Bus. Law. 1605, 1607 (1981)). See also note 47, above.

[83] See Lawrence's Anderson on the UCC § 2–314:39.

[84] Note that UCC § 2–313 cmt. 2 appears to authorize courts to extend the warranty principles of Article 2 beyond sales transactions, as discussed in the lease context above.

find that a product license contains a common-law implied warranty of quality,[85] similar to the rulings of a few courts in bailment cases, as discussed above.

Strict liability in tort. The distinctions between leases, bailments, and licenses[86] are often blurred in products liability cases, as noted earlier,[87] but courts sometimes do decide to allow or deny a strict liability in tort, warranty, or other claim on the basis of its characterization of the particular transaction.[88] Most courts, however, in deciding whether strict products liability in tort applies to a non-sale transaction, ignore the niceties of property law classification distinctions. Instead, courts generally base their decisions of whether to apply strict liability in tort to such transactions on basic tort law considerations: whether the product supplier is in the business of supplying such products, whether it has placed its products into the "stream of commerce," and sometimes on the policy goals supporting strict products liability.[89] Property law technicalities, in other words, are usually subordinated in such cases to the principles and goals of higher law—the law of torts.

Yet the fact that courts in products liability cases do not dwell on the fine points of the law of chattel transactions does not mean that the doctrine of strict liability in tort is applied in every product license case. In fact, courts sometimes refuse to apply strict liability principles, and the cases are difficult to distinguish or to classify. Because product licenses generally are limited to the premises of the licensor, and because they often are provided as a service to customers, the license cases are often complicated by overlapping principles governing the liability of landowners or providers of services. In both of the latter contexts, as examined later,[90] courts have generally applied traditional negligence principles rather than the doctrine of strict liability in tort.

---

85 See, e.g., Hurley v. Larry's Water Ski Sch., 762 F.2d 925 (11th Cir. 1985) (Fla. law) (tow rope).

86 See Bobryk v. Lincoln Amusements, Inc., 1996 WL 24566, at *4 (Conn. Super. Ct. 1996):

> A lease is a contract under which the lessor, for a fee or other valuable consideration, transfers an interest or estate in real or personal property to the lessee for a stated period of time, with a reversion in the owner after the expiration of the lease. A lease is distinguishable from a license. While the former confers a right, during the term of the lease, to exercise exclusive possession of and control over the property in question, assertable even against the lessor, the latter extends but a [privilege of possession].

Further, the court defined a bailment in terms of the owner's surrender of property to another for some particular purpose for some period of time during which the bailor retains the right of control. Id. at *5. See generally Ausness, Strict Liability for Chattel Leasing, 48 U. Pitt. L. Rev. 273 (1987).

87 See, e.g., Jones v. Keetch, 200 N.W.2d 227, 229 (Mich. 1972) (noting that "it matters not that the chattel comes to the possession of the plaintiff either as lessee or bailee" and citing sources as to liability of bailors and lessors).

88 For example, in Hurley v. Larry's Water Ski Sch., 762 F.2d 925 (11th Cir. 1985) (Fla. law), plaintiff was injured while taking water skiing lessons from defendant when the wooden tow handle he was holding broke. In plaintiff's action against the ski school, the court held that since the tow rope and handle were at all times attached to the boat, plaintiff never had complete possession and control over them and so never had a bailment. Although plaintiff's strict liability in tort claim thus would not lie, his breach of warranty claim could. Implicit in the defendant's agreement to provide ski lessons to plaintiff was "an implied warranty that the equipment supplied by Larry's was fit for the purpose of teaching an individual to ski." Id. at 929.

Compare Ferrucci v. Atlantic City Showboat, Inc., 51 F. Supp. 2d 129 (D. Conn. 1999) (no bailment of hotel bed over which plaintiff tripped because hotel never surrendered exclusive possession and control; so, products liability statute did not apply); Kalumetals, Inc. v. Hitachi Magnetics Corp., 21 F. Supp. 2d 510 (W.D. Pa. 1998) (supplier of grinding swarf with retort tube that exploded was a bailor and hence subject to strict liability); Golt v. Sports Complex, Inc., 644 A.2d 989, 992–93 (Del. Super. Ct. 1994) (go-cart rented to plaintiff was a bailment, thereby allowing claim for strict liability in tort).

89 See Ausness, above note 86, at 335–39.

90 See § 16.3 (service transactions), and § 16.6 (real estate), below.

One of the first modern cases to examine a product license transaction was *Garcia v. Halsett*.[91] The 11-year-old plaintiff injured his arm while trying to remove clothes from a washing machine belonging to the defendant laundromat when a defect in the machine caused it unexpectedly to start up, entangling the boy's arm in the clothing. The trial court refused to instruct the jury on strict liability in tort, but the appellate court reversed, ruling that strict liability in tort properly applied to a license transaction of this type. Reasoning that a licensee of a product may be in a worse position than a buyer because the licensee has less opportunity or motivation to inspect the product for defects, the court concluded that such suppliers "play more than a random and accidental role in the overall marketing enterprise of the product in question."[92] Like manufacturers and lessors, argued the court, licensors "are an integral part of the overall . . . marketing enterprise that should bear the cost of injuries resulting from defective products."[93] In other cases in which a fee was charged for the use of a defective product, courts have also applied strict liability in tort, including cases involving the use of defective roller skates at a skating center[94] and the use of a defective go-cart at an amusement park.[95] But other courts have refused to apply strict liability in tort to defective amusement rides, finding that they principally involve a service.[96]

When a licensor (or bailor) provides a product as a service to its customers without charging a separate fee for the use of the product, whether strict liability in tort should apply is more difficult to determine. If the use of the licensed (or bailed) product is necessary or "integral" to the sale of some other product, then courts generally have considered the provision of the tie-in product subject to strict liability in tort. So, a defective propane gas container provided by a gas company,[97] a water glass provided by a restaurant,[98] or a ladder provided by a pick-it-yourself orchard[99] all must be provided if the defendants expect to sell their primary products. In each such case, the courts have reasoned that providers of such tie-in products are appropriately subject to strict products liability for defects in those products.[100]

However, when a product seller allows its customers to use an ancillary product without charge and merely as a convenience, courts have been more reluctant to impose strict liability in tort. For example, in *Keen v. Dominick's Finer Foods, Inc.*,[101] the plaintiff was injured while using a grocery cart in the defendant's grocery store when she grabbed the cart in an attempt to prevent it from overturning. Plaintiff sued the

---

91 82 Cal. Rptr. 420 (Ct. App. 1970).

92 Id. at 423.

93 Id. (citing Vandermark v. Ford Motor Co., 391 P.2d 168, 171 (Cal. 1964)).

94 See Wilson v. Dover Skating Ctr., 566 A.2d 1020, 1024 (Del. Super. Ct. 1989).

95 See Golt v. Sports Complex, Inc., 644 A.2d 989, 992–93 (Del. Super. Ct. 1994) (transaction classified as bailment).

96 See, e.g., Greenwood v. Busch Entm't Corp., 101 F. Supp. 2d 292 (E.D. Pa. 2000) (by providing plaintiff license to use its water slides, defendant provided service, not a product); Siciliano v. Capitol City Shows, Inc., 475 A.2d 19 (N.H. 1984) (arm of octopus ride broke off while in operation).

97 See, e.g., Bainter v. Lamoine LP Gas Co., 321 N.E.2d 744 (Ill. App. Ct. 1974). See also Fulbright v. Klamath Gas Co., 533 P.2d 316 (Or. 1975) (vine burner).

98 See, e.g., Gunning v. Small Feast Caterers, Inc., 777 N.Y.S.2d 268, 271–72 (Sup. Ct. 2004) (glass of water exploded in patron's hand; restaurant subject to liability in warranty and strict tort as "seller" of the container). See also Shaffer v. Victoria Station, Inc., 588 P.2d 233 (Wash. 1978) (restaurant liable in both warranty and strict tort for injuries to patron from wine glass shattering in his hand).

99 See Gabbard v. Stephenson's Orchard, Inc., 565 S.W.2d 753 (Mo. Ct. App. 1978).

100 See Products Liability Rest. § 20 Reporters' Note to cmt. *f*.

101 364 N.E.2d 502 (Ill. App. Ct. 1977).

grocery store for strict liability in tort and other claims, alleging that the cart was dangerously defective, and the store defended on the ground that it could not be held strictly liable since it had not placed the cart into the stream of commerce. Agreeing with the defendant, the trial court dismissed the claim for strict liability in tort. On appeal, a divided court affirmed dismissal of the plaintiff's strict liability in tort claim, reasoning that the doctrine of strict liability in tort, while not requiring an actual sales transaction, does require that the supplier be in the chain of distribution.[102] The dissent persuasively argued that the store was the final link in the chain of distribution,[103] but the majority concluded that the store, like the injured customer, was merely a user of the cart.

Distinguishing *Bainter v. Lamoine LP Gas Co.*,[104] in which strict liability in tort had been applied to the supplier of propane gas in a defective tank, the *Keen* majority reasoned that in the *Bainter* case "the fluidity of the product compelled supplying the tank as a necessary concomitant of the sale of gas," whereas a shopping cart "can be classified only as a convenient receptacle which the customer may temporarily utilize to move groceries to the checkout" or to a car.[105] "Public policy considerations," concluded the court, "do not demand that the duty of a storekeeper to keep its premises in a safe condition be elevated beyond the traditional standard of reasonable care."[106]

Most courts have agreed that, by allowing customers to use an ancillary product as a convenience, a defendant generally does not place the product into the chain of distribution sufficient to support a strict liability in tort claim, especially if the product must remain on the defendant's premises.[107]

---

[102] "One of the underlying reasons for imposing strict liability is to ensure that losses are borne by those who have created the risk and subsequently reaped the profit of marketing the allegedly defective product. Liability will not be imposed upon a defendant who is not a part of the original producing and marketing chain." Id. at 504.

[103] See id. at 505 ("the stream of commerce did not stop, as the majority views it, with the parties who distributed the cart to Dominick's, but continued until the cart reached the customers who were intended to use it [and Dominick's was] a conduit in the marketing chain which brought the carts to their ultimate users, Dominick's customers").

[104] 321 N.E.2d 744 (Ill. App. Ct. 1974).

[105] *Keen*, 364 N.E.2d at 504.

[106] The court noted that its ruling did not deny plaintiff her claim for negligence against the grocery store nor her claim for strict liability in tort against the manufacturer of the cart. Id. at 505.

[107] See, e.g., Ranalli v. Edro Motel Corp., 690 A.2d 137, 140 (N.J. Super. Ct. App. Div. 1997) (frying pan in motel room kitchenette: "to apply the broad brush of strict liability to motel owners would impose an unusual and unjust burden"); Dixon v. Four Seasons Bowling Alley, Inc., 424 A.2d 428 (N.J. Super. Ct. App. Div. 1980) (bowling alley not subject to strict liability for defective bowling ball); Gilliland v. Rothermel, 403 N.E.2d 759, 761 (Ill. App. Ct. 1980) (tire gauge loaned to customer was not a necessary incident of products defendant offered for sale nor "an integral part of defendant's marketing operation").

Compare Ferrucci v. Atlantic City Showboat, Inc., 51 F. Supp. 2d 129 (D. Conn. 1999) (no bailment of hotel bed over which plaintiff tripped because hotel never surrendered exclusive possession and control); Reeder v. Bally's Total Fitness Corp., 963 F. Supp. 530 (E.D. Va. 1997) (health club patron injured on stomach curl machine was merely business invitee on defendant's premises; no bailment or lease of machine); Wagner v. Coronet Hotel, 458 P.2d 390, 395 (Ariz. Ct. App. 1969) (plaintiff slipped on rubber shower mat provided by defendant hotel: "Of all the various policy views expressed for the theory of strict liability, none are applicable to the Coronet Hotel."). *But see* Safeway Stores, Inc. v. Nest-Kart, 579 P.2d 441 (Cal. 1978), where a supermarket shopping cart broke and fell on plaintiff's foot. The jury found the supermarket liable, in negligence and strict liability in tort, and the cart manufacturer strictly liable, apportioning 80% to the supermarket and 20% to the manufacturer. Without discussing the propriety of the strict liability claim against the supermarket, the Supreme Court affirmed.

Statutory Reform

Products liability reform statutes often address lease, bailment, and license transactions either directly or indirectly. A popular type of reform statute, considered in the previous chapter,[108] exempts non-manufacturing product suppliers from strict liability if the manufacturer is solvent and subject to the jurisdiction of the court. Such statutes have obvious applicability to product lessors who rarely manufacture the products they sell.

For example, *Saieva v. Budget Rent-A-Car of Rockford*[109] was a case involving a leased van with defective brakes, in which the court granted summary judgment for the lessor on the plaintiff's negligence claim for failing to provide evidence that the lessor reasonably should have discovered the safety defect. The court further held the lessor exempt from strict liability under the Illinois statute conditionally protecting non-manufacturing sellers from such liability. *Saieva* is a good example of the impact that statutes of this type can have in shielding lessors from liability for defects in the products that they lease.[110]

These non-manufacturing supplier shield statutes also apply to product bailment and license transactions. As with commercial lessors, to the extent that such statutes apply to bailors and licensors, such non-manufacturing defendants should be conditionally protected from the rigors of strict liability in tort. Accordingly, while courts which have reasoned that the policies of strict liability in tort apply alike to sellers, bailors, and licensors may be correct, reform statutes which relieve non-manufacturing defendants of strict liability convert the liability issue from a question of policy to one of statutory interpretation.

Non-sale transactions may affect recovery under other types of products liability statutes that apply only to qualifying sellers or suppliers. For example, *Bobryk v. Lincoln Amusements, Inc.*[111] was a claim against a carnival ride provider for injuries to a child who rode the defendant's "Flying Chairs." Since the plaintiff sought recovery under Connecticut's products liability act (as well as in ordinary negligence), the court ruled that the plaintiff was required to prove that the defendant was a "product seller" as defined in the act.[112] While holding that the statutory term included lessors and bailors of products engaged in the business of leasing or bailing goods,[113] the court ruled that the selling of rides did not amount to a bailment of the Flying Chairs because the defendant never relinquished control.[114] Thus, because the plaintiff acquired no more than a license to use a Flying Chair, the products liability statute did not apply and the plaintiff was left to the negligence claims.[115]

---

108 See § 15.2, above.

109 591 N.E.2d 507 (Ill. App. Ct. 1992).

110 Note also that Illinois' products liability statute of repose specifically provides that a product's initial lease triggers the running of the statute. See Garza v. Navistar Int'l Transp. Corp., 666 N.E.2d 1198, 1200 (Ill. 1996).

111 1996 WL 24566 (Conn. Super. Ct. 1996).

112 See Conn. Gen. Stat. Ann. § 52–572m(a).

113 *Bobryk*, 1996 WL 24566, at *2.

114 Id. at *5.

115 Id. Compare Ferrucci v. Atlantic City Showboat, Inc., 51 F. Supp. 2d 129 (D. Conn. 1999) (no bailment of hotel bed over which plaintiff tripped because hotel never surrendered exclusive possession and control; so, state products liability statute did not apply).

§ 16.3 SERVICE TRANSACTIONS

The law of "*products* liability" concerns the responsibility of manufacturing, retail, and other enterprises for harm caused by products they supply to others.[116] As examined earlier, modern products liability law is constituted by the confluence of warranty and tort law principles governing accountability for selling harmful chattels.[117] If an actor harms a person in a manner other than by supplying a dangerous chattel, more general principles of tort and contract law—not the law of products liability—define the nature and extent to which the actor may be liable for the harm. In short, it is the commercial supply of chattels that defines products liability as a discrete area of the law.[118]

General principles of tort law, principally negligence, define the responsibilities of people for harmful interactions with other people while *using* products. If a driver runs over a pedestrian with a car, this incident implicates the driver and the law of negligence, not the law of products liability. If, instead, a person buys and is injured in the crash of a new car with defective brakes, these events implicate the law of products liability. But the modern world increasingly requires specialists to help design, select, adapt, repair, and install products that consumers need and want. Architects, engineers, and building contractors create structures to house people and business firms; doctors and other health professionals select drugs, use hypodermic needles, and implant medical devices and prostheses for health care; and plumbers select and install water heaters for hot water. When such specialists make mistakes, or when they use or install defective products, negligence law (including professional malpractice) establishes their basic responsibilities for resulting harm.[119] The special question addressed in this section is whether and when architects, doctors, plumbers, and other service providers should also be subject to strict products liability.[120]

As a starting point, it is axiomatic that strict liability and other products liability principles apply to the commercial distribution of new chattels. At the other end of the spectrum, strict liability doctrine does *not* apply to the provision of pure services. In between, of course, lie a large number of sales-service hybrid transactions; in between resides the devil.[121]

---

[116] See § 1.1, above.

[117] See § 5.2, above.

[118] "A premise of strict products liability is that product injuries constitute a discrete, integral problem that merits special treatment. Otherwise, it would be inappropriate to distinguish product injuries from other personal injuries, liability for which is governed by negligence." Powers, Distinguishing Between Products and Services in Strict Liability, 62 N.C. L. Rev. 415, 418 (1984). Compare Stapleton, Bugs in Anglo-American Products Liability Law, 53 S.C. L. Rev. 1225, 1255 (2002) ("there does not seem to be any particular moral, economic, or social reason why the victims of [product] injuries should have been accorded any more special treatment than the victims of [other types of] disasters").

[119] See Keeton, Dobbs, Keeton, and Owen, Prosser and Keeton on the Law of Torts ch. 5.

[120] Often, a plaintiff's counsel desires to recover in strict liability rather than negligence and so is indifferent to whether strict liability is available in warranty or tort. While distinctions in secondary doctrine (such as privity, statutes of limitations, other defenses, and the availability of punitive damages) sometimes are important, decisions examining the sales-service issue typically do not dwell upon differences between the separate theories of strict products liability.

[121] See Chagal-Feferkorn, Am I an Algorithm or A Product? When Products Liability Should Apply to Algorithmic Decision-Makers, 30 Stan. L. & Pol'y Rev. 61 (2019); Elvy, Hybrid Transactions and the Internet of Things: Goods, Services, or Software?, 74 Wash. & Lee L. Rev. 77 (2017); Lannetti, Toward a Revised Definition of "Product" under the *Restatement (Third) of Torts: Products Liability*, 55 Bus. Law. 799 (2000); Taylor, Applicability of Strict Liability Warranty Theories to Service Transactions, 47 S.C. L. Rev. 231 (1996); Cantu, A New Look at an Old Conundrum: The Determinative Test for the Hybrid Sales/Service Transaction

The Classic Cases

Two sets of cases, all classics in this field, illuminate how courts address the basic liability issues involving service providers. The first two cases were both decided in 1954, one in California and the other in New York. *Gagne v. Bertran*[122] was an action against a test hole driller for providing incorrect information as to the depth of fill on lots purchased by the plaintiffs in reliance on his report. Writing for the majority of the California high court, Judge Traynor ruled that negligence, not strict liability, was the proper basis of liability for a specialist of this type. Strict liability was inappropriate, reasoned Judge Traynor, because the defendant had in no way assumed responsibility to guarantee that the information he provided was correct. The size of the defendant's fee, together with the fact that he charged by the hour, suggested that he was selling and the buyer was buying "service and not insurance." For these reasons, the court applied the general rule that providers of services are not subject to strict liability for providing defective services but are only required to meet the standard of reasonable care according to ordinary levels of skill and care of members of their profession.[123]

Two months later, across the continent, the New York Court of Appeals decided another service-provider case, *Perlmutter v. Beth David Hospital*,[124] involving the provision of a defective product. The plaintiff was a patient who sued the hospital for breach of warranty under the Sales Act for injuries resulting from "the transfusing of 'bad' blood, supplied by the hospital for a price as part of the customary services rendered by the hospital to its patients."[125] Holding that the hospital's provision of blood was a service rather than a sale, a majority of the New York Court of Appeals reasoned that the hospital's principal role was to promote the healing of its patients, not to sell them medicines, drugs, or blood. That title to such items may be transferred "from the hospital to the patient during the course of medical treatment does not serve to make each such transaction a sale," explained Judge Fuld, and "[i]t has long been recognized that, when service predominates, and transfer of personal property is but an incidental feature of the transaction, the transaction is not deemed a sale within the Sales Act."[126] Applying that standard to the facts before the court, Judge Fuld concluded that "the main object sought to be accomplished in this case was the care and treatment of the patient," such that the hospital's supply of blood was "entirely subordinate to its paramount function of furnishing trained personnel and specialized facilities in an endeavor to restore plaintiff's health."[127] Nor should the transaction be split in two, dividing the doctor's provision of services from the hospital's sale of blood, since what mattered was the essence of the transaction as a whole. The food warranty cases were not analogous at all because people enter restaurants to buy food in contrast to patients who enter hospitals "to obtain a course of treatment in the hope of being cured." Because sales law warranties

---

under Section 402A of the Restatement (Second) of Torts, 45 Ark. L. Rev. 913 (1993); Reynolds, Strict Liability for Commercial Service—Will Another Citadel Crumble?, 30 Okla. L. Rev. 298 (1977); Frumer, Friedman, and Sklaren, Products Liability §§ 5.10–.13; Lawrence's Anderson, UCC § 2–314:39.

122 275 P.2d 15 (Cal. 1954).

123 Id. at 20–21.

124 123 N.E.2d 792 (N.Y. 1954).

125 Id. at 793. See § 16.9, below.

126 Id.

127 "It was not for blood or iodine or bandages for which plaintiff bargained, but the wherewithal of the hospital staff and the availability of hospital facilities to provide whatever medical treatment was considered advisable. The . . . furnishing of blood was only an incidental and very secondary adjunct to the services performed by the hospital and, therefore, was not within the provisions of the Sales Act." Id. at 795.

did not apply to the hospital's provision of the contaminated blood, the plaintiff was left to his remedies under the law of negligence.[128]

The second important set of sales-service cases were decided in New Jersey during the late 1960s. In *Magrine v. Krasnica*,[129] while a dentist injected an anesthetic into a patient's gum, the syringe needle broke leaving the entire 1⅝ inch needle in plaintiff's jaw. The needle was defective, and surgery was required to remove it. The dentist could not determine from whom he had purchased the needle, and the plaintiff sued him for strict liability, breach of warranty, and breach of contract. Inspired by *Cintrone*, the New Jersey Supreme Court's earlier decision extending the doctrine of strict liability in warranty and tort beyond sales transactions to commercial lessors,[130] and apparently thinking that "the gates are wide open," the plaintiff argued that the strict liability doctrine should be extended to service cases involving the use of defective products.[131]

The plaintiff was wrong. Unlike cases against manufacturers, retailers, lessors, and other commercial distributors of products, the court thought that the dentist was in no better position than the plaintiff to discover or control the risk. Further, traditional products liability defendants are all in the business of supplying chattels to consumers whereas the essence of the defendant dentist's business was providing professional services.[132] Moreover, to the extent that risk spreading might be considered a legitimate goal of strict products liability, it is premised on the assumption that defendants are large-scale enterprises engaged in widespread product distribution as distinguished from the one-on-one nature of a dentist-patient relationship. Nor would shifting the risk of loss to a dentist's or doctor's insurers be appropriate in view of the rapidly increasing costs of medical insurance and care.[133] And it would not be fair to allow the plaintiff to use the dentist as a mere conduit to reach the manufacturer of the defective needle when the plaintiff, through discovery, had a means to identify the manufacturer, if identification were possible at all. Finally, the court reasoned that because the law of professional malpractice limits a health care provider's liability to negligence, it would be illogical to expand responsibility to strict liability for merely *using* (not selling) an instrument that happens to be defective.

Shortly after *Magrine*, the New Jersey courts were asked to decide whether a "beauty parlor" should be subject to strict liability for applying a defective permanent wave solution to a patron's hair and scalp, causing contact dermatitis and baldness. In *Newmark v. Gimbel's, Inc.*,[134] nearly a decade after penning his landmark decision in *Henningsen v. Bloomfield Motors, Inc.*,[135] Justice Francis had an opportunity to explore how far the principles of strict products liability law should extend. Holding that Gimbel's was a retailer subject to strict liability in both warranty and tort, and that Mrs.

---

[128] Id. at 795–96.

[129] 227 A.2d 539 (Hudson Cnty. Ct. 1967), aff'd sub nom. Magrine v. Spector, 241 A.2d 637 (N.J. Super. Ct. App. Div. 1968) (2–1 decision) (implicitly on the basis of Judge Lynch's opinion), aff'd, 250 A.2d 129 (N.J. 1969) (Francis, J.) (7–0 decision) (largely on same basis).

[130] See Cintrone v. Hertz Truck Leasing & Rental Serv., 212 A.2d 769 (N.J. 1965); § 16.2, above.

[131] 227 A.2d at 541.

[132] Id. at 542–43. "[T]he *essence* of the transaction between the retail seller and the consumer relates to the *article sold*. The seller is *in the business* of supplying the product to the consumer. It is that, and that alone, for which he is paid. A dentist or a physician offers, and is paid for, his professional services and skill. That is the essence of the relationship between him and his patient." Id. at 543.

[133] Id. at 545–46.

[134] 258 A.2d 697 (N.J. 1969) (Francis, J.), aff'g 246 A.2d 11 (N.J. Super. Ct. App. Div. 1968).

[135] 161 A.2d 69 (N.J. 1960). See § 5.2, above.

Newmark was a consumer of a defective product entitled to protection, Justice Francis addressed the defendants' argument that *Magrine* afforded them protection against strict liability because the same principles applied to all service providers, whether dentists, doctors, or dispensers of beauty. But the court saw vast differences between the "commercial enterprise" of a beauty parlor and the "profession" of a dentist or a doctor. While the former caters to "convenience or luxury," the latter, who cannot advertise for patients, addresses the "felt necessity" of the patient. Unlike the "mechanical or routine" nature of a beautician's services, highly trained and skilled medical care professionals must apply individualized study and judgment to the particular medical condition of each patient.[136] A doctor or dentist neither guarantees results nor sells a product in any reasonable sense of that word. Instead, the "paramount function" of such professionals, licensed after many years of study to fulfill their "special and essential role" of diagnosing and relieving ailments, must be viewed as "the furnishing of opinions and services."[137] Thus, the court concluded that negligence is the only appropriate standard of liability for doctors and dentists, professionals whose vital services are fundamentally distinguishable from beauty parlor operators.[138] The latter type of commercial enterprise, as a retailer of consumer products, is subject to strict liability, both in warranty and tort, for supplying defective products that harm their customers.[139]

General Principles

The preceding cases illustrate most of the important principles about service transactions in products liability law. The first principle, best illustrated by *Gagne*, is that pure service transactions merely involve a service provider's *conduct* and so must be judged according to the law of negligence. While a very few early courts found common-law implied warranties in the provision of pure services,[140] and while a very few early commentators argued for the expansion of strict liability to service transactions,[141] the vast majority of courts have rejected out of hand any thought of applying strict liability to such transactions.[142]

The second point, illustrated by *Perlmutter*, *Magrine*, and *Newmark*, is the way in which the courts often rely upon a blend of doctrine and policy analysis in deciding whether to apply strict liability to mixed sales-service transactions. In sales-service hybrid cases, most courts search for the "essence" of the transaction to ascertain whether the sale or service aspect predominates.[143] If the transaction predominantly involves a

---

136 258 A.2d at 702–03.

137 Id. at 703 (citing Gagne v. Bertran, 275 P.2d 15 (Cal. 1954)).

138 258 A.2d at 703.

139 Id. at 705.

140 See, e.g., Broyles v. Brown Eng'g Co., 151 So.2d 767 (Ala. 1963) (as to routine engineering survey of subdivision drainage requirements); Bloomsburg Mills, Inc. v. Sordoni Constr. Co., 164 A.2d 201 (Pa. 1960).

141 See, e.g., Schmidt, Ince, and Richbourg, Piercing the Aluminum Overcast: A Case for Strict Liability for Commercial Air Carriers, 9 Lincoln L. Rev. 37 (1974); Comment, 22 UCLA L. Rev. 401, 450 (1974) ("The extension of enterprise liability to all services would have a sound basis in economic and justice considerations.").

142 For example, doctors uniformly have been held not subject to strict liability for medical accidents arising purely from their treatment. Barton v. Owen, 139 Cal. Rptr. 494 (Ct. App. 1977); Hoven v. Kelble, 256 N.W.2d 379 (Wis. 1977).

143 For more recent examples, see, e.g., Hernandezcueva v. E.F. Brady Co., Inc., 196 Cal. Rptr 3d 594 (Ct. App. 2015) (whether service or sale aspect predominated in view of strict liability policies: "whether [defendant] was in a position to enhance product safety or exert pressure on the manufacturer to promote that end, and bear the costs of compensating for injuries"; *held*, trial court erred in granting nonsuit on plaintiff's strict liability claim against subcontractor that bought and installed asbestos-containing products and was in

product sale, then strict liability principles are appropriate; if service aspects dominate the transaction, then negligence alone should be applied. The essence-of-the-transaction or predominant-factor "test,"[144] together with the very distinction between products and services on which the test is based, have both been criticized by commentators who call for courts to abandon mechanical distinctions in favor of a policy analysis that looks to whether the principles of strict products liability are appropriate in a given case.[145] But in this respect, many courts were ahead of the commentators: in *Perlmutter v. Beth David Hospital*, Judge Fuld recognized that determining "whether the essence of a particular contract is for the rendition of services or for the sale of property, may at times be troublesome and vexatious,"[146] and a large number of decisions (including *Perlmutter* and the other early decisions considered above) have applied policy analysis (often blending it with the "essence" test) to help determine whether a case should be located in the "sale" or "service" category.[147] Indeed, one must be cautious of reposing too much confidence in "policy analysis" as a panacea; what with the numerous and diverse policies said to support modern products liability law (many of which are hotly controverted),[148] a lawyer or court may reach virtually any result desired by manipulating the panoply of theories that lie behind the righteous veil of "policy analysis."[149] In the final analysis, courts often appropriately return to boundary definitions that distinguish products liability from other types of cases—whether the defendant was instrumental in moving a harm-producing "product" through the stream of commerce[150] and whether the chain of distribution ended effectively with a defendant who was more of a product user than supplier.[151]

---

stream of commerce); Foster v. Bergson Tire Co., 2013 WL 1010776, at *3 (Conn. Super. Ct. 2013) (tire recapper, who was given a tire to retread, was not a "product seller" because recapping was essentially a service); Utah Local Gov't Trust v. Wheeler Mach. Co., 199 P.3d 949, 956 (Utah 2008) (surveying cases and adopting a "predominant purpose" test); In re Dow Corning Corp., 220 Fed. Appx. 457, 458–59 (9th Cir. 2007) (Cal. law) (California courts look to the " '*essence*' of the transaction"); Brandt v. Boston Scientific Corp., 792 N.E.2d 296 (Ill. 2003) (where hospital surgically implanted pubovaginal sling, "thrust" of transaction was provision of service, not sale of good). See also Sharufa v. Festival Fun Parks, LLC, 263 Cal. Rptr. 3d 112, 122 (Ct. App. 2020) (at summary judgment stage, record insufficient to determine whether amusement park waterslide was the provision of service or product); § 16.8 (*Computer software*) note 390, below.

[144] This approach is also referred to as the gravamen-of-the-action test. See Taylor, Applicability of Strict Liability Warranty Theories to Service Transactions, 47 S.C. L. Rev. 231, 253 (1996).

[145] See, e.g., Stapleton, note 118, above, at 1253 (noting "the artificiality of any product/service distinction in our law of obligations and the incoherence of the idea that products liability can sensibly look at the product and not the human behaviour surrounding its production and handling"); Lannetti, Toward a Revised Definition of "Product" under the *Restatement (Third) of Torts: Products Liability*, 55 Bus. Law. 799 (2000); Powers, note 118, above.

[146] 123 N.E.2d 792, 795 (N.Y. 1954).

[147] The older classics include *Gagne*, *Perlmutter*, *Magrine*, and *Newmark*, all discussed above. See also Wallace v. Gerard Med., Inc., 2003 WL 1995910 (Conn. Super. Ct. 2003); Cafazzo v. Central Med. Health Servs., Inc., 668 A.2d 521 (Pa. 1995); Porter v. Rosenberg, 650 So.2d 79 (Fla. Dist. Ct. App. 1995); Hector v. Cedars-Sinai Med. Ctr., 225 Cal. Rptr. 595, 597–601 (Ct. App. 1986).

[148] See § 5.4, above.

[149] See, e.g., Cafazzo v. Central Med. Health Servs., Inc., 668 A.2d 521, 528 (Pa. 1995) (Cappy, J., dissenting) (criticizing majority's "distorted" and "muddled" application of that state's multiple-policy test improperly to protect hospital and doctor from liability for selling and implanting a defective TMJ prosthesis).

[150] See, e.g., *Cafazzo*, above; Hector v. Cedars-Sinai Med. Ctr., 225 Cal. Rptr. 595, 597–601 (Ct. App. 1986) (pacemaker); Silverhart v. Mount Zion Hosp., 98 Cal. Rptr. 187 (Ct. App. 1971) (surgical needle).

[151] See, e.g., Bhardwaj v. 24 Hour Fitness, Inc., 2002 WL 373563 (Cal. Ct. App. 2002) (exercise equipment; chain of distribution ended not with plaintiff, but with health club, as there was no evidence that health club played role in manufacture, design, or marketing of product); Podrat v. Codman-Shurtleff, Inc., 558 A.2d 895 (Pa. Super. Ct. 1989) (pituitary forceps that broke); *Silverhart*, above (defective surgical needle).

This last issue, whether a defendant is fairly to be regarded as more of a product *user* than supplier, is another especially important perspective highlighted by the court in *Magrine*. Refusing to apply strict liability to the dentist for using a defective hypodermic needle, the court explained that a contrary holding would require it to apply strict liability "to any user of a tool, other equipment or any article which, through no fault of the user, breaks due to a latent defect and injures another. It would apply to any physician, artisan or mechanic and to any user of a defective article—even to a driver of a defective automobile." The court was aware of no rationale for intruding so deeply into the domain of negligence law.[152] This slippery-slope problem is very real, and no American court has held a driver subject to strict liability in tort merely for driving a defective car.[153] Such a holding would turn accident law entirely on its head, converting the basic liability principle from negligence to strict liability. In the field of products liability, the distinction between product "use" and product "supply" is perhaps the most fundamental divide between negligence and strict liability—since using a product implicates a person's conduct, which the law of torts judges only according to the law of negligence,[154] whereas selling or otherwise commercially supplying a product is what provides the very foundation for strict products liability.[155]

All four of the decisions discussed above, from *Gagne* through *Newmark*, resolutely refuse to impose a strict liability standard on doctors in particular, and professionals more generally. As discussed below, subsequent decisions have adhered closely to these principles, exempting doctors and other professionals from the rigors of strict products liability. Yet *Newmark*, the final case examined above, reveals a couple of related loopholes that may be available in a sales-service case to help a plaintiff injured by a specialist's use of a defective product avoid the general rule that service providers are not subject to strict liability. First, a plaintiff may be permitted to apply the principles of strict products liability to a sales-service hybrid transaction if the defendant specialist is classified as a *non*-professional, like the beautician in *Newmark*, or a plumber or electrician. This distinction has been criticized as "elitist,"[156] as it may well be, but it serves an important function that is well described in the cases discussed above.

Newmark suggests a second and related loophole for plaintiffs seeking to impose strict liability on service providers—the distinction between simple, routine, mechanical tasks, for which strict liability might arguably be appropriate, and discretionary judgments that involve complex and multi-faceted decisions, for which only negligence responsibility is proper. There is an analogy here to the protected realm of policy decisionmaking lying at the core of governmental[157] and family[158] managerial decisions which traditionally have been held off-limits to judicial oversight. But behind the

---

[152] Magrine v. Krasnica, 227 A.2d 539, 547 (Hudson Cnty. Ct. 1967).

[153] Compare Hammontree v. Jenner, 97 Cal. Rptr. 739 (Ct. App. 1971) (driver not strictly liable for driving accidents); Maloney v. Rath, 445 P.2d 513 (Cal. 1968) (Traynor, C.J.) (driver not strictly liable for bad brakes but has nondelegable duty rendering her vicariously liable for mechanic's negligence).

[154] See Prosser and Keeton on Torts ch. 5.

[155] See ch. 5, above. See also Products Liability Rest. § 20.

[156] See Murphy v. E.R. Squibb & Sons, Inc., 710 P.2d 247, 258 (Cal. 1985) (Bird, J., dissenting) (protecting pharmacists as "professionals" creates "elitist distinctions"). See also Polelle, Who's on First, and What's a Professional?, 33 U.S.F. L. Rev. 205, 227 (1999); Kotler, Utility, Autonomy and Motive: A Descriptive Model of the Developments of Tort Doctrine, 58 U. Cin. L. Rev. 1231, 1263 (1990).

[157] Policy decisions are protected in this context by the "discretionary function" exception to governmental liability. See Prosser and Keeton on Torts § 131.

[158] See id. at § 122.

governmental and parental exemptions for core decisions lies a basic rule of negligence for the misconduct of such special parties—not a rule of strict liability. And while a very occasional decision has allowed strict liability recovery for service providers,[159] most courts properly refuse to apply strict liability to providers of pure services for making even "simple" mistakes, reasoning that the normal principles of professional negligence adequately protect persons harmed by errors of this type.[160]

Professional Services

For the many reasons developed in the early decisions discussed above, and others examined below, courts have broadly refused to apply strict liability rules to doctors, dentists, hospitals, and other health care providers,[161] or to architects, engineers, and other design professionals,[162] for damages from providing professional services. *Audlane Lumber & Builders Supply, Inc. v. D.E. Britt Associates, Inc.*[163] involved the question of whether an engineering firm that prepared design specifications for a chattel could be liable for breach of implied warranty for damages to a third party for defects in the specifications. The court saw no room for implied warranty principles in cases involving professional responsibility. Engineers and other professionals normally do not "warrant" the quality of their work as sellers warrant the quality of their goods. "Rather, in the preparation of design and specifications as the basis of construction, the engineer or architect 'warrants' that he will or has exercised his skill according to a certain standard of care, that he acted reasonably and without neglect." But this is nothing more than saying that a professional who is negligent breaches his or her warranty of quality, which conflates the separate concepts of negligence and warranty and sows confusion in "an area of law where confusion abounds."[164]

A later decision, *City of Mounds View v. Walijarvi*,[165] which involved a claim for defects in a building against the firm of architects and engineers responsible for its design, explained that all professionals—including architects, doctors, engineers, and lawyers—are immune from strict liability largely because they deal in "inexact sciences" involving "random factors which are incapable of precise measurement" which require the exercise of skilled judgment by the professional.[166] The indeterminate nature of professional decisions precludes consistently perfect results: "doctors cannot promise

---

[159] See, e.g., Broyles v. Brown Eng'g Co., 151 So.2d 767 (Ala. 1963) (implied warranty of fitness for intended use as to routine engineering survey of subdivision drainage requirements). See also Bloomsburg Mills, Inc. v. Sordoni Constr. Co., 164 A.2d 201 (Pa. 1960); Hill v. Polar Pantries, 64 S.E.2d 885 (S.C. 1951).

[160] See, e.g., City of Mounds View v. Walijarvi, 263 N.W.2d 420, 424–25 (Minn. 1978) (reexamining and reaffirming majority rule holding professionals only to a negligence standard).

[161] See discussion below.

[162] See, e.g., Romine v. Johnson Controls, Inc., 169 Cal. Rptr. 3d 208, 222–23 (Ct. App. 2014) (engineering company that participated in design of vehicle seat not subject to strict liability); Lawson v. Honeywell Int'l, Inc., 75 So.3d 1024, 1029 (Miss. 2011) (seatbelt buckle designer not a "manufacturer" for purposes of strict liability under statute); Milford v. Commercial Carriers, Inc., 210 F. Supp. 2d 987 (N.D. Ill. 2002) (designer of auto trailer, with no role in manufacture, not subject to strict liability); Bruzga v. PMR Architects, P.C., 693 A.2d 401, 404–06 (N.H. 1997) (architects who designed facility not strictly liable for suicide in psychiatric cell because they provided professional service); Chubb Grp. of Ins. Cos. v. C.F. Murphy & Assocs., Inc., 656 S.W.2d 766, 780 (Mo. Ct. App. 1983) (no products liability claims against consulting structural engineers for roof collapse of arena). *But see* Burlington N. & Santa Fe Ry. Co. v. ABC-NACO, 906 N.E.2d 83, 90–91 (Ill. App. Ct. 2009) (Ariz. law) (strict liability extended to designer of defective railroad car transom).

[163] 168 So.2d 333 (Fla. Dist. Ct. App. 1964).

[164] Id. at 335.

[165] 263 N.W.2d 420 (Minn. 1978).

[166] Id. at 424.

that every operation will be successful; a lawyer can never be certain that a contract he drafts is without latent ambiguity; and an architect cannot be certain that a structural design will interact with natural forces as anticipated."[167] Clients are protected against simple, routine errors by negligence law,[168] and modern products liability law cannot be borrowed because the contexts are so different. Unlike mass producers of defective products, architects normally work one-on-one with their clients and build a single "product," and so they do not have a manufacturer's opportunity to test prototypes to discover latent defects.[169] For these reasons, the court concluded that negligence malpractice actions are sufficient protection against architectural errors, and there is no room for implied warranty or strict liability guaranteeing clients good results.[170]

Patients in a number of cases have tried to hold doctors and hospitals strictly liable for "selling" defective medical products for which the patients must pay, either directly or indirectly. With a very few exceptions,[171] courts have rejected strict products liability claims (in both tort and warranty) against doctors, hospitals, and other health care providers for providing defective pacemakers,[172] silicone breast implants,[173] jaw implants,[174] joint prostheses,[175] pharmaceutical drugs,[176] and other products surgically

---

[167] Id. "If every facet of structural design consisted of little more than the mechanical application of immutable physical principles, we could accept the rule of strict liability which the city proposes." Id.

[168] Id.

[169] Id. at 425.

[170] Id.

[171] A scattering of cases are to the contrary. See, e.g., Basso v. Boston Scientific Corp., 2008 WL 5252198, at *3 (Conn. Super. Ct. 2008); Snyder v. Davol, Inc., 2008 WL 113902, at *7 (D. Or. 2008) (remanded to state court to determine whether hospital was subject to strict liability for sale of defective hernia patch, surveying cases); Phillips v. Howmedica Osteonics Corp., 2007 WL 4441228 (S.D. Ill. 2007) (same; defective hip replacement); Garcia v. Edgewater Hosp., 613 N.E.2d 1243 (Ill. App. Ct. 1993) (hospital charged patient for defective heart valve engaged in sale subject to implied warranty liability). Several lower court decisions in Missouri formerly allowed strict products liability claims against health care providers, but the Missouri Supreme Court put a halt to that. See Budding v. SSM Healthcare Sys., 19 S.W.3d 678 (Mo. 2000) (en banc).

[172] See, e.g., St. Mary Med. Ctr., Inc. v. Casko, 639 N.E.2d 312 (Ind. Ct. App. 1994); Hector v. Cedars-Sinai Med. Ctr., 225 Cal. Rptr. 595, 597–601 (Ct. App. 1986).

[173] See, e.g., In re Breast Implant Prod. Liab. Litig., 503 S.E.2d 445 (S.C. 1998) (Toal, J.), noted in 50 S.C. L. Rev. 463, 465 (1999); Porter v. Rosenberg, 650 So.2d 79 (Fla. Dist. Ct. App. 1995). For an illuminating explanation of why certain medical professionals might properly be held subject to strict products liability for serious complications from breast implants, see Cupp, Sharing Accountability for Breast Implants: Strict Products Liability and Medical Professionals Engaged in Hybrid Sales/Service Cosmetic Products Transactions, 21 Fla. St. U. L. Rev. 873 (1994). See also Spanbauer, Breast Implants as Beauty Ritual: Woman's Sceptre and Prison, 9 Yale J.L. & Feminism 157 (1997).

[174] See, e.g., Budding v. SSM Healthcare Sys., 19 S.W.3d 678 (Mo. 2000) (en banc) (overruling earlier cases); Ayyash v. Henry Ford Health Sys., 533 N.W.2d 353 (Mich. Ct. App. 1996); Parker v. St. Vincent Hosp., 919 P.2d 1104 (N.M. Ct. App. 1996); Cafazzo v. Central Med. Health Servs., Inc., 668 A.2d 521 (Pa. 1995).

[175] See, e.g., Royer v. Catholic Med. Ctr., 741 A.2d 74 (N.H. 1999) (knee); Hoff v. Zimmer, Inc., 746 F. Supp. 872 (W.D. Wis. 1990) (hip).

[176] See, e.g., Carrozza v. CVS Pharm., Inc., 992 F.3d 44, 60–61 (1st Cir. 2021) (Mass. law) (antibiotic triggering allergic reaction—pharmacy); O'Dell v. Greenwich Healthcare Servs., Inc., 2013 WL 2278752, at *5 (Conn. Super. Ct. 2013) (neuraxial medications—hospitals); Garza v. Endo Pharms., 2012 WL 5267897, at *2 (C.D. Cal. 2012) (birth control pills—pharmacist); Kohl v. American Home Prods. Corp., 78 F. Supp. 2d 885 (W.D. Ark. 1999) ("fen-phen" diet drug—pharmacist); Coyle v. Richardson-Merrell, Inc., 584 A.2d 1383 (Pa. 1991) (Bendectin—pharmacist); Murphy v. E.R. Squibb & Sons, Inc., 710 P.2d 247 (Cal. 1985) (DES—pharmacist); Batiste v. American Home Prods. Corp., 231 S.E.2d 269, 272–73 (N.C. Ct. App. 1977) (contraceptives—doctor). On pharmacist liability in negligence for incorrectly filling drug prescriptions, see Annot., 3 A.L.R.4th 270 (1981). For a pharmacist's liability for harm from properly filling a prescription, see Annots., 44 A.L.R.5th 393 (1996), 79 A.L.R.5th 409 (2000) (liability of pharmacists for failure to warn of potential drug interactions in use of prescription drug). For pharmacist liability, see § 18.4, below.

implanted, used, prescribed, or otherwise provided by health care professionals.[177] In such cases, drawing on the principles developed above, courts reason that strict products liability is inappropriate because the defendants are predominantly providing medical services, not selling products, and because they are themselves merely product users, not suppliers.[178]

The rule against holding health care providers strictly liable for injuries to patients logically is limited, however, to injuries directly related to medical treatment of the plaintiff. Thus, a Texas court held a hospital subject to strict liability for providing a patient with a flammable gown.[179] A California court, however, properly concluded that it would stretch strict products liability too far to extend it to a patient's wife who made a products liability claim against the hospital for injuries from tripping on defective carpeting in her husband's hospital room.[180]

Non-Professionals—Product Installers

Like professionals, non-professionals are also subject to the normal rules of negligence.[181] Perhaps the two largest classes of non-professionals who routinely deal with products are those who install products and those who repair them, two different forms of service often performed by the same tradesperson. So, a plumber, electrician, or contractor may either install or repair a water heater that blows up. Product installation is treated here, and product repair is addressed in the next section, below.[182]

To a considerable extent, the product installation cases mirror the service and sales-service hybrid cases discussed above. Thus, most courts appear to search for the essence or predominant purpose of the transaction in an effort to determine whether it was more in the nature of a service transaction, involving at most an incidental sale of a defective product, or primarily a sales transaction in which the installer was in the chain of product distribution.[183] If a homeowner buys a new hot water heater from a plumbing contractor who installs it, the transaction probably will include significant aspects of

---

[177] See, e.g., Normandy v. American Med. Sys., Inc., 262 A.3d 698, 709 (Conn. 2021) (hospital not a seller of implanted pelvic mesh sling; reviewing cases); Von Downum v. Synthes, 908 F. Supp. 2d 1179, 1180 (N.D. Okla. 2012) (surveying cases; lumbar fusion with allegedly defective medical device implants); Conway v. A.I. DuPont Hosp. for Children, 2007 WL 560502 (E.D. Pa. 2007) (surgically implanted heart stent); Brandt v. Sarah Lincoln Health Ctr., 792 N.E.2d 296 (Ill. 2003) (surgically implanted pubovaginal sling); Condos v. Musculoskeletal Transplant Found., 208 F. Supp. 2d 1226 (D. Utah 2002) (bone tissue); Cobb v. Dallas Fort Worth Med. Ctr.-Grand Prairie, 48 S.W.3d 820 (Tex. App. 2001) (implantation of pedicular hardware in plaintiff's back); Silverhart v. Mount Zion Hosp., 98 Cal. Rptr. 187 (Ct. App. 1971) (surgical needle that broke and became imbedded in plaintiff's lower pelvic area during vaginal hysterectomy); Barbee v. Rogers, 425 S.W.2d 342 (Tex. 1968) (contact lens prescribed and fitted by optometrist).

[178] See Annot., 65 A.L.R.5th 357 (1999) (strict liability in tort or warranty of doctor or hospital for harm to patients from products used in treatment).

[179] See, e.g., Thomas v. St. Joseph Hosp., 618 S.W.2d 791, 796–97 (Tex. App. 1981) (smoking in bed, plaintiff died from burns when his gown caught fire).

[180] Pierson v. Sharp Mem'l Hosp., Inc., 264 Cal. Rptr. 673 (Ct. App. 1989).

[181] See, e.g., Couch v. Astec Indus., 71 F. Supp. 2d 1145 (D.N.M. 1999).

[182] See § 16.4, below.

[183] See, e.g., Okland Constr. Co. Inc. v. Zurn Indus. LLC, 2019 WL 2233298, at *4 (Ariz. Ct. App. 2019) (general contractor was in the "business of providing a service, and its provision of plumbing parts was incidental to that service"); DISA Indus., Inc. v. Bell, 272 So.3d 142, 151 (Ala. 2018) (engineering firm, as installer of foundry furnace system, was not a seller, designer, or manufacturer); Hidalgo v. Fagen, Inc., 206 F.3d 1013 (10th Cir. 2000) (Colo. law) (construction of plant's conveyor system was not sale of product but, rather, sale of contractor's services); Scordino v. Hopeman Bros., 662 So.2d 640, 645 (Miss. 1995) (subcontractor who installed asbestos paneling in ships was not a "seller" of such materials, but "merely supplied the materials to complete the service for which it was hired," and so was not subject to strict liability in tort). See generally Frumer, Friedman, and Sklaren, Products Liability § 5.13[2].

both sales and service. If the water heater explodes because of a manufacturing defect, the homeowner may seek to recover from the plumber for "selling" a defective product. Especially if the plumber separated the heater price from the plumbing services in billing for the project,[184] the transaction to a large extent will have involved the supply of a defective product, and the plumber will have played a significant role in the chain of distribution. In such a case, the plumber could not be viewed merely as a user, but should instead be considered the necessary final link in the chain of distribution to the ultimate consumer. Just as a tire dealer that sells and installs a defective tire is subject to the strict liability of a retailer,[185] so too may be a plumber, electrician, contractor, or other tradesperson for selling a defective product that it installs.[186] But if a product installer supplies a defective product only incidentally to his or her provision of services, and so cannot fairly be classified as a member of the chain of distribution, then most courts decline to apply either warranty or strict liability in tort.[187]

Many of the cases involving product installers concern the applicability of implied warranty and strict liability in tort theories to the defective installation of a *non*defective product. *State Stove Manufacturing Co. v. Hodges*[188] was an early case of this type, in which a plumber and the contractors that hired him were both held strictly liable in tort for the destruction of a home from an explosion of the water heater due to its defective installation.[189] Several other courts have similarly allowed implied warranty or strict liability in tort claims against suppliers of nondefective products who install them in a dangerously defective manner.[190] In most instances, however, courts properly refuse to apply strict products liability to claims of improper installation of a nondefective product, concluding that the service component of the transaction must be judged according to traditional principles of the law of negligence.[191]

Other Services

In many other contexts, with some exceptions,[192] courts have refused to extend strict products liability law to a large miscellany of service providers who in some respect provide "products" to their patrons. Thus, courts have refused to apply strict liability to

---

184 See Parker v. St. Vincent Hosp., 919 P.2d 1104 (N.M. Ct. App. 1996); Prod. Liab. Rest. § 20 cmt. *d*.

185 See, e.g., Barth v. B. F. Goodrich Tire Co., 71 Cal. Rptr. 306 (Ct. App. 1968).

186 See, e.g., ACandS, Inc. v. Abate, 710 A.2d 944, 999 (Md. 1998) (supplier-applier of asbestos fireproofing spray); Hinojasa v. Automatic Elevator Co., 416 N.E.2d 45 (Ill. 1980) (defective elevator). See also Prompt Air, Inc. v. Firewall Forward, Inc., 707 N.E.2d 235 (Ill. App. Ct. 1999) (aircraft engine overhauler subject to strict tort liability for forced landing caused by reconditioned turbocharger procured, paid for, and installed by, defendant). See generally Products Liability Rest, § 20(a) and (d).

187 See, e.g., Two v. Fujitec Am., Inc., 305 P.3d 132 (Or. Ct. App. 2013); Duncan v. M & M Auto Serv., Inc., 898 N.E.2d 338, 342 (Ind. Ct. App. 2008) (strict liability in tort inapplicable to installer of natural gas system in van); Warford v. Industrial Power Sys., Inc., 2008 WL 4642638, at *12 (D.N.H. 2008) (installer of boat generator not liable under § 402A); Winters v. Fru-Con Inc., 498 F.3d 734, 745 (7th Cir. 2007) (Ill. law) (installer not subject to strict liability); Monte Vista Dev. Corp. v. Superior Ct., 277 Cal. Rptr. 608 (Ct. App. 1991) (installer of defective soap dish in house); County of Chenango Ind. Dev. Agency v. Lockwood Greene Eng'rs, Inc., 494 N.Y.S.2d 832, 834 (App. Div. 1985).

188 189 So.2d 113 (Miss. 1966).

189 Id. at 123–24.

190 See, e.g., O'Laughlin v. Minnesota Natural Gas Co., 253 N.W.2d 826 (Minn. 1977) (defective installation of furnace by plumbing and heating contractor); Worrell v. Barnes, 484 P.2d 573 (Nev. 1971).

191 This principle is axiomatic. See, e.g., Winters v. Fru-Con Inc., 498 F.3d 734, 745–46 (7th Cir. 2007) (Ill. law). See also Ramos v. Silent Hoist & Crane Co., 607 A.2d 667 (N.J. Super. Ct. App. Div. 1992).

192 See Almquist v. The Finley Sch. Dist. No. 53, 57 P.3d 1191 (Wash. Ct. App. 2002) (school lunch is a "product" under Washington products liability statute, not a service).

health clubs, for providing patrons with defective exercise equipment;[193] amusement ride operators, for providing defective rides;[194] ski facilities, for providing defective equipment for transporting skiers up the mountain;[195] travel agents, for providing defective trips fraught with unexpected dangers;[196] and baseball stadiums, for providing spectators with defective protection from foul balls.[197] Such providers are liable, of course, for negligence.[198] But, because they are not commercial suppliers of products in the chain of distribution, they appropriately are immune from strict products liability.

Statutory Reform

Products liability reform statutes are playing an increasingly significant role in cases involving providers of product services. The scope of many products liability statutes is limited to product "sellers," a category from which pure service transactions, together with some sales-service hybrid transactions, generally are excluded. Some statutes more specifically exclude claims arising out of transactions that predominantly involve product services.[199] Moreover, in cases involving healthcare providers, medical malpractice reform statutes must be considered as well, and a number of cases have ruled that the statutory malpractice negligence standard, rather than that of strict products liability, governs mixed sales-service cases involving such providers.[200]

---

[193] See, e.g., Crannage v. Gold's Gym, 2019 WL 7856763, at *5 (C.D. Cal. 2019) (Nautilus Machine); Leka v. Health Quest Fitness, 2017 WL 4818886, at *3 (N.J. Super. Ct. App. Div. 2017) (hack squat machine); Grebing v. 24 Hour Fitness USA, Inc., 184 Cal. Rptr. 3d 155, 163 (Ct. App. 2015) (low row machine); Ontiveros v. 24 Hour Fitness Corp., 86 Cal. Rptr. 3d 767, 775 (Ct. App. 2008) (stair step machine); La Fata v. LA Fitness Int'l, LLC, 2008 WL 4194508, at *4 (Cal. Ct. App. 2008) (weight bench); Bhardwaj v. 24 Hour Fitness, Inc., 2002 WL 373563 (Cal. Ct. App. 2002) (hack squat machine); Reeder v. Bally's Total Fitness Corp., 963 F. Supp. 530 (E.D. Va. 1997) (stomach curl machine); Watford v. Jack LaLanne Long Island, Inc., 542 N.Y.S.2d 765, 767 (App. Div. 1989) (rowing machine). See also Lovett v. Omni Hotels Mgmt. Corp., 2016 WL 777781, at *10 (N.D. Cal. 2016) (no liability for hotel that distributed exercise equipment to guests).

But manufacturers and other sellers of defective exercise equipment to consumers for use in the home are of course subject to strict liability for resulting injuries. See, e.g., Mauer v. Icon Health & Fitness, Inc., 2020 WL 1052521, at *6 (N.D. Iowa 2020) (treadmill; but design defect claim failed without evidence of reasonable alternative design); McRee v. Dick's Sporting Goods, Inc., 2017 WL 5201525, at *4 (D.S.C. 2017) (inversion table); Chong v. STL Int'l, Inc., 152 F. Supp. 3d 1305, 1319 (D. Or. 2016) (same).

[194] See, e.g., Mussara v. Mega Funworks, Inc., 952 N.Y.S.2d 568, 572 (App. Div. 2012) ("Since Splashdown had no role in the manufacture, sale, or distribution of the injury-producing product, it cannot be held liable for breach of express or implied warranty, or strict products liability."); Wallace v. Busch Entm't Corp., 837 F. Supp. 2d 1093, 1106–07 (S.D. Cal. 2011) (bungee cord ride—dominant purpose was service); Greenwood v. Busch Entm't Corp., 101 F. Supp. 2d 292 (E.D. Pa. 2000) (water slide—service); Marsh v. Dixon, 707 N.E.2d 998, 1001–02 (Ind. Ct. App. 1999) (ride not "product").

[195] See, e.g., Bolduc v. Herbert Schneider Corp., 374 A.2d 1187, 1189–90 (N.H. 1977) (tramway); Lewis v. Big Powderhorn Mountain Ski Corp., 245 N.W.2d 81 (Mich. Ct. App. 1976) (2–1 decision) (tow rope).

[196] See, e.g., Pena v. Sita World Travel, Inc., 152 Cal. Rptr. 17, 18 (Ct. App. 1978). See also Birmingham v. Fodor's Travel Publ'ns, Inc., 833 P.2d 70 (Haw. 1992) (travel guide not "product" subjecting publisher to strict liability for failing to warn body-surfing tourist of ocean surf conditions at beach).

[197] See Romeo v. Pittsburgh Assocs., 787 A.2d 1027 (Pa. Super. Ct. 2001) (sale of ticket to baseball game is sale of service, not product, precluding strict products liability).

[198] Operators of ski resorts and are subject to liability in negligence, apart from statutes that commonly place inherent risks of skiing on skiers. See, e.g., Morgan v. State, 618 N.Y.S.2d 967 (Ct. Cl. 1994) (bobsled run); Clover v. Snowbird Ski Resort, 808 P.2d 1037 (Utah 1991) (negligent design of ski trails).

[199] See, e.g., N.J. Stat. Ann. § 2A:58C–8 ("The term 'product seller' does not include . . . A provider of professional services in any case in which the sale or use of a product is incidental to the transaction and the essence of the transaction is the furnishing of judgment, skill or services); Ohio Rev. Code Ann. § 2307.71(A)(15)(b) (same).

[200] See, e.g., Budding v. SSM Healthcare Sys., 19 S.W.3d 678 (Mo. 2000) (en banc); Huffaker v. ABC Ins. Co., 659 So.2d 544 (La. Ct. App. 1995); Porter v. Rosenberg, 650 So.2d 79 (Fla. Dist. Ct. App. 1995).

§ 16.4 REPAIRED, REBUILT, AND RECONDITIONED PRODUCTS

While all products eventually wear out, sometimes in a dangerous manner,[201] most products can be repaired or renovated in some manner along the way to substantially increase their useful lives.[202] Such processes range from simple repairs, to "refurbishing" and "reconditioning" the product, to "rebuilding" or "remanufacturing" it altogether. These descriptions are terms of art that carry special meaning: each level implies greater work by the renovator which generates a heightened expectation of reliability and safety by purchasers of such goods.[203] The type and extent of product improvement thus moves along a sliding scale, from minor repairs and basic fix-ups, at the light end of the scale, to major remakes—often accompanied by product sales and warranties—at the remanufacturing end of the scale.[204]

Repaired Products

Those who repair products are subject to liability for their negligence that causes injury.[205] A number of early cases held that the rendition of personal services included a common-law implied warranty that the services would be provided in a workmanlike manner,[206] defined simply as a duty of due care.[207] But pure repair transactions cannot give rise to implied warranties of quality under the Uniform Commercial Code because they involve pure services and do not involve the sale of goods.[208] Similarly, because the repair process is merely a service transaction not involving a product sale—nor an implied promise of perfection of the repaired product—strict liability in tort does not apply to faulty product repairs, which are governed by negligence alone.[209] Some courts

---

201 See § 10.6, above.

202 See, e.g., Malen v. MTD Prods., Inc., 628 F.3d 296, 306 (7th Cir. 2010) (Ill. law); Whitaker v. T.J. Snow Co., 953 F. Supp. 1034, 1038 (N.D. Ind. 1997).

203 "Refurbishing entails work which is less extensive than reconditioning, which in turn, entails work which is less extensive than remanufacturing. Normally, a refurbishing is 'just an upgrade' of a product, a very minimal amount of work is performed on equipment that is refurbished. In contrast, when a machine is remanufactured, its frame is completely torn down and all of the component parts are removed and inspected individually during reassembly." *Whitaker*, 953 F. Supp. at 1037.

204 See Hogan and Colonna, Products Liability Implications of Reprocessing and Reuse of Single-Use Medical Devices, 53 Food Drug L.J. 385 (1998).

205 See, e.g., Sutherland v. Thering Sales & Service, Inc., 830 N.Y.S.2d 833 (App. Div. 2007); Meadows v. Anchor Longwall & Rebuild, Inc., 2006 WL 995842, at *3 (W.D. Pa. 2006) (claims for poor repair lie in negligence, not strict liability). See generally Frumer, Friedman, and Sklaren, Products Liability § 5.13[1]; Rest. (2d) Torts § 404.

206 "In circumstances involving the rendition of personal services the duty upon the actor is to perform the services in a workmanlike manner." Hoffman v. Simplot Aviation, Inc., 539 P.2d 584, 589 (Idaho 1975), noted in 42 J. Air L. & Com. 881, 919 (1976). Accord Pepsi Cola Bottling Co. of Anchorage v. Superior Burner Serv. Co., 427 P.2d 833 (Alaska 1967).

207 See, e.g., Nationwide Prop. & Cas. Ins. Co. v. General Motors, LLC, 98 F. Supp. 3d 901, 906 (S.D. Tex. 2015) (GM dealer servicing vehicle tire had duty to run VIN check for outstanding recalls); Nationwide Agribusiness Ins. Co. v. SMA Elevator Const. Inc., 816 F. Supp. 2d 631, 665 (N.D. Iowa 2011) (a duty "to use reasonable care and competence to ensure that the chattel in question was in the safe condition in which a competent contractor would have put it," breached by "a deceptive appearance of safety"); Hoffman v. Simplot Aviation, Inc., 539 P.2d 584 (Idaho 1975); Pepsi Cola Bottling Co. of Anchorage v. Superior Burner Serv. Co., 427 P.2d 833, 840–41 (Alaska 1967) (standard of care for provider of personal services is identical for both negligence law and implied warranty of workmanlike performance).

208 See, e.g., Stafford v. International Harvester Co., 668 F.2d 142, 146–47 (2d Cir. 1981) (N.Y. law) (predominantly service contract for repairing truck, not sale of goods); Lemley v. J & B Tire Co., 426 F. Supp. 1378 (W.D. Pa. 1977) (defective brakes). See § 16.3, above.

209 See, e.g., Stephenson v. Honeywell Int'l, Inc., 703 F. Supp. 2d 1250, 1261 (D. Kan. 2010) (neither strict liability in tort nor warranty applies to airplane engine repairer); Santoyo v. Bear Lake Holdings, Inc., 2010 WL 2522745, at *2 (W.D. Mo. 2010) (no strict liability for repair of rifle unconnected to original sale);

have pointed to *Restatement (Second) of Torts* § 404's use of negligence as the standard of liability for repairers,[210] distinct from § 402A's "special rule applicable to sellers of products,"[211] as further support for the proposition that strict liability in tort does not apply to product repairers.[212]

Refurbished, Reconditioned, Rebuilt, and Remanufactured Products

As previously mentioned, after simple repairs, the extent of product renovation progresses along a scale, at the start of which is "refurbishing."[213] If a product is simply refurbished, few if any major parts are likely to be replaced or substantially altered, and the addition of any new or rebuilt parts will likely be incidental to a transaction that both parties understand to be essentially a product improvement service transaction. For this reason, simple reconditioning or refurbishing generally will give rise to negligence liability alone, and strict products liability generally will not be available with respect to products furnished with only such basic upgrades.[214]

At the other end of the spectrum lie "rebuilt" and "remanufactured" products, which frequently are sold or otherwise placed in the stream of commerce by their restorers to compete with new products. Purchasers fairly expect such products to have nearly the reliability and overall quality of new goods,[215] and rebuilders and remanufacturers have the opportunity and obligation to rebuild or remanufacture their products to demanding standards, subjecting them to whatever testing and quality control is reasonably called for in the circumstances. Buyers of rebuilt and remanufactured products thus reasonably

---

Meadows v. Anchor Longwall & Rebuild, Inc., 306 Fed. Appx. 781, 787 (3d Cir. 2009) (Pa. law) (no strict liability for repair and refurbishment of mine shield). See also Products Liability Rest. § 19 cmt. *f* ("Even when the service relates directly to a product that is commercially distributed, as in the case of installation or repair, the courts do not extend strict liability to the service provided.").

If a repairer was also the original retail *seller*, however, it may possibly be subject to strict products liability. See Winters v. Sears, Roebuck & Co., 554 S.W.2d 565, 572 (Mo. Ct. App. 1977) ("Upon completion of servicing the product, whether it is done on the seller's premises or on the premises of the purchaser, the effect is a re-delivery of the product with the same assurances and with the same obligations as the original sale."). A repairer who was also the original *manufacturer* may also be subject to strict products liability.

[210] Rest. (2d) Torts § 404, "Negligence in Making, Rebuilding, or Repairing Chattel," provides: "One who as an independent contractor negligently makes, rebuilds, or repairs a chattel for another is subject to the same liability as that imposed upon negligent manufacturers of chattels."

[211] Rest. (2d) Torts § 402A cmt. *a*. Section 402A is entitled "Special Liability of Seller of Product for Physical Harm to User or Consumer."

[212] See, e.g., Nickel v. Hyster Co., 412 N.Y.S.2d 273, 274–76 (Sup. Ct. 1978); Lemley v. J & B Tire Co., 426 F. Supp. 1378 (W.D. Pa. 1977).

[213] See note 203, above.

[214] See, e.g., Meadows v. Anchor Longwall & Rebuild, Inc., 306 Fed. Appx. 781, 787 (3d Cir. 2009) (Pa. law) (no strict liability for refurbishing of mine shield with a few new parts); Whitaker v. T.J. Snow Co., 953 F. Supp. 1034, 1038 (N.D. Ind. 1997); Rolph v. EBI Cos., 464 N.W.2d 667, 671 (Wis. 1991) (Busch "simply 'reconditioned' the machine, a process the record shows is nothing more than a very thorough cleaning and repair job that includes taking a machine apart, replacing worn parts, and reassembling the machine. Any profit Busch reaped was from reconditioning the machine, not from placing it in the stream of commerce."). See also Strasser v. Transtech Mobile Fleet Serv., Inc., 613 N.W.2d 142 (Wis. 2000) (crane reconditioner subject to negligence liability for lack of safety treads on new ladder it fabricated and installed on crane).

[215] See, e.g., Malen v. MTD Prods., Inc., 628 F.3d 296, 306 (7th Cir. 2010) (Ill. law) ("Reconditioning extends the useful life beyond what was contemplated at the point of manufacture and effectively creates a new product."); Britton v. Dallas Auto. Inc., 2010 WL 797177, at *17 (D. Idaho 2010) ("a piece of machinery that is substantially rebuilt or reconditioned becomes a 'new' product for the purpose of a products liability action"). See also Gaumer v. Rossville Truck & Tractor Co., 257 P.3d 292, 307 (Kan. 2011) (surveying states extending strict liability to remanufacturers).

expect the same performance as new production—and are entitled to the same legal protection against harm therefrom.[216]

In between simple refurbishing and complete remanufacturing lies a broad range of product upgrade services, sometimes called reconditioning, overhauling, or something else. Because of the wide scope of possible services, including a lesser or greater repair or replacement of worn parts, the cases are very fact-specific, making it difficult to generalize how the law does or should treat such transactions. It may be said, however, that courts generally use some rough form of the essence-of-the-transaction or predominant-factor test examined earlier.[217] Thus, if a particular renovation called for mostly skill and effort inputs from the product renovator, so that it is predominantly a service transaction, then it should be treated as a service transaction for which negligence, not strict products liability, principles will apply.[218] If, on the other hand, a renovator substantially transforms a product from a used one into basically a new one—as by rewiring, replacing or reconfiguring many important parts, and otherwise reconstructing key aspects of the product—then this rebuilding or remanufacturing usually should subject the supplier to strict products liability for manufacturing defects in such products.[219] The cases do not always divide nicely along these lines, but this classification is consistent with broader liability principles that subject manufacturers, but not service providers, to a rule of strict products liability for harm from defective manufacture.

Most of the cases and the discussion to this point have concerned *manufacturing* defects; design and warning defects raise questions of a different kind. Buyers understand that rebuilders and remanufacturers have no magic wand to eliminate most inherent product dangers. Consequently, some courts reasonably shield product reconditioners from any obligation, even in negligence, to correct or warn of design

---

[216] See id. See also Mesman v. Crane Pro Servs., 512 F.3d 352, 356 (7th Cir. 2008) (Ind. law) (Posner, J.) (Products Liability Act applies to rebuilt products, otherwise "there would be an inefficient incentive to rebuild an old product rather than make a new one"). Compare Lack v. Cruise Am., Inc., 2017 WL 3841863, at *3 (N.D. Cal. 2017) (statements that motorhome was "fully refurbished," "in excellent condition," and "put through a detailed checklist to make sure everything is working properly" satisfied fraud claim's pleading standard).

[217] See § 16.3, above.

[218] See, e.g., Meadows v. Anchor Longwall & Rebuild, Inc., 306 Fed. Appx. 781, 786 (3d Cir. 2009) (Pa. law) (no strict liability when any new parts were "merely incidental to servicing"); Levine v. Sears Roebuck & Co., 200 F. Supp. 2d 180 (E.D.N.Y. 2002) (repair of dishwasher door); Turbines, Inc. v. Dardis, 1 S.W.3d 726 (Tex. App. 1999) (rebuilt aircraft engine; evidence suggested pilot error); Micciche v. Eastern Elevator Co., 645 A.2d 278 (Pa. 1994) (elevator repaired and modernized by defendant misaligned with floor landing); Watts v. Rubber Tree, Inc., 848 P.2d 1210 (Or. Ct. App. 1993) (recapped tire).

[219] See, e.g., Bell v. Precision Airmotive Corp., 42 P.3d 1071 (Alaska 2002) (overhauler of engine held subject to strict products liability for selling and installing, during course of overhaul, used and defective component part that overhauler had subjected to extensive inspection, repair, and testing); R.R. Donnelley & Sons Co. v. North Tex. Steel Co., 752 N.E.2d 112 (Ind. Ct. App. 2001) (defendant created "new product," and did not merely provide service, when it transformed raw material into components that differed substantially from original raw material); Stillie v. AM Int'l, Inc., 850 F. Supp. 960, 962 (D. Kan. 1994) (purchasers of " 'like new' rebuilt" products fairly may expect safety of new products); Anderson v. Olmsted Util. Equip., Inc., 573 N.E.2d 626, 629 (Ohio 1991) ("When a product is totally remanufactured or rebuilt, it becomes, for all intent[s] and purposes, a new product."); Michalko v. Cooke Color & Chem. Corp., 451 A.2d 179 (N.J. 1982).

The Illinois courts have an unusually strong tradition of holding providers of sales-service hybrid transactions subject to strict products liability (see § 16.3, above), and the overhaul situation is no different. See Prompt Air, Inc. v. Firewall Forward, Inc., 707 N.E.2d 235 (Ill. App. Ct. 1999) (aircraft engine overhauler which procured, paid for, and installed reconditioned turbocharger that was defective and caused forced landing was subject to strict tort liability for resulting damage).

defects lurking in the machines they recondition.[220] Yet, by undertaking to rebuild or remanufacture products and then to re-introduce them into the stream of commerce, such suppliers in a true sense step into the shoes of the original manufacturer. Indeed, rebuilders and occasionally even refurbishers sometimes undertake to ensure that their reconditioned products are properly guarded and otherwise meet appropriate safety requirements.[221] Nevertheless, negligence, rather than any form of strict products liability, appears to be the preferable standard of liability in such cases.

Whether suppliers of rebuilt or remanufactured products should be liable for failing to supply warnings of inherent dangers is a difficult question. Because of the fact-specific nature of product overhauling and rebuilding,[222] courts should be prepared to rule that in certain contexts a supplier has no duty to design away a particular danger, such as an obvious inherent danger, nor any duty to warn of risks of which the reconditioner did not know or that were clearly evident to intended purchasers.[223] In cases where a reconditioner fairly should be obligated to provide a warning,[224] the duty should be limited to one of reasonable care.

Not distinguishing between different types of defects, the *Products Liability Restatement* in no uncertain terms provides that remanufactured products are subject to the normal rules of products liability applicable to sellers of new products.[225]

Statutes of limitations and repose are treated elsewhere,[226] but it may be noted here that a substantially rebuilt or remanufactured product may be treated as a "new" product that will start a statute of repose running anew from the date the product is sold in its refurbished condition.[227] Yet, such a statute will not begin to run again, of course,

---

[220] See, e.g., Rodriguez v. Riddell Sports, Inc., 242 F.3d 567 (5th Cir. 2001) (Tex. law) (reconditioner of football helmet had no obligation to upgrade helmet to safer alternative, even if it knew that helmet was unsafe at time); Rolph v. EBI Cos., 464 N.W.2d 667, 673 (Wis. 1991) ("Imposing liability on Busch for failing to correct a design defect simply because it reconditioned the machine would make all repairers who disassemble a product in order to repair it insurers against design defects created by manufacturers.").

[221] See, e.g., Whitaker v. T.J. Snow Co., 953 F. Supp. 1034 (N.D. Ind. 1997) (per agreement with regular buyer, refurbisher was to determine if guarding was needed and either bring welding machine into compliance with OSHA regulations or inform buyer).

[222] See Gentile v. MacGregor Mfg. Co., 493 A.2d 647, 652 (N.J. Super. Ct. Law Div. 1985) (service transactions not subject to strict liability "because of the individuality of the service rendered").

[223] See, e.g., Strasser v. Transtech Mobile Fleet Serv., Inc., 613 N.W.2d 142 (Wis. 2000) (no duty to warn of absence of safety treads on ladder of reconditioned crane).

[224] See, e.g., Slaid v. Evergreen Indem., Ltd., 745 So.2d 793, 798 (La. Ct. App. 1999) (bank that sold mobile home to purchaser had duty to warn of defective window after inspection).

[225] Products Liability Rest. § 8, covering the liability of suppliers of defective used products, provides that such suppliers are subject to liability for resulting harm "if the defect: . . . (c) is a defect under § 2 or § 3 in a used product remanufactured by the seller . . . ." Comment *i* to § 8 explains: "When one undertakes to remanufacture a used product and bring it to market as a product that meets current design and production standards, it is fair to subject the seller of the remanufactured product to liability for harm caused by §§ 2 and 3 defects existing at the time of sale of the remanufactured used product." See Malen v. MTD Prods., Inc., 628 F.3d 296, 306 (7th Cir. 2010) (Ill. law) (applying Products Liability Rest. § 8(c)).

[226] See § 14.6, above.

[227] See, e.g., Tipton v. CSX Transp., Inc., 2017 WL 10398182, at *7 (E.D. Tenn. 2017) (questions of fact remained "whether the 2013 requalification of the Tank Car constituted a substantial reconstruction or reconditioning of that product" that would restart 10-year period of repose); Jones v. Walker Mfg. Co., 2012 WL 1142889, at *2–3 (Ohio Ct. App. 2012) (dictum) (statutes of repose); Florian v. Gatx Rail Corp., 930 N.E.2d 1190, 1201 (Ind. Ct. App. 2010) (same); Richardson v. Gallo Equip. Co., 990 F.2d 330 (7th Cir. 1993) (Ind. law). Compare Estabrook v. Mazak Corp., 140 N.E.3d 830, 836–37 (Ind. 2020) (statute of repose not extended by manufacturer's "post-delivery repair, refurbishment, or reconstruction of the disputed product").

if the defect lay in the product's original manufacture and if the rebuilder did not have some responsibility to find or cure it.[228]

Reform Statutes

If a state products liability act limits coverage to product "sellers," a defendant who merely repairs or otherwise reconditions a product owned by another is not subject to the act's provisions.[229] However, if a statute does not expressly limit its scope to new products, a court may interpret the statute as including the sale of products that have been rebuilt or remanufactured.[230] Moreover, statutes in at least four states include "remanufacturer" or "rebuilder" in the definition of "manufacturer," subjecting such parties to the principal provisions of such statutes and to the common law.[231]

§ 16.5 USED PRODUCTS

Sellers of used products are subject to liability in negligence.[232] While early courts held that the sale of a used product did not carry an implied warranty,[233] the situation is different today. Both express warranties[234] and implied warranties[235] may arise in appropriate cases[236] under Article 2 of the Uniform Commercial Code.

---

[228] See, e.g., Divis v. Clarklift of Neb., Inc., 590 N.W.2d 696 (Neb. 1999).

[229] See, e.g., Smith v. Invacare Corp., 2004 WL 2164891 (Conn. Super. Ct. 2004) (claim for negligent repair of wheelchair not covered or barred by state's products liability statute); Watts v. Rubber Tree, Inc., 848 P.2d 1210, 1213 (Or. Ct. App. 1993) (tire recapper only affixed new tread on client's casing; strict liability statute inapplicable to service providers); Rollins v. Cherokee Warehouses, Inc., 635 F. Supp. 136, 138 (E.D. Tenn. 1986).

[230] See, e.g., Rollins v. Cherokee Warehouses, Inc., 635 F. Supp. 136, 138 (E.D. Tenn. 1986).

[231] See, e.g., Idaho Code Ann. § 6–1402(2); Kan. Stat. Ann. § 60–3302(b); Tex. Civ. Prac. & Rem. Code Ann. § 82.001(4); Wash. Rev. Code Ann. § 7.72.010(2). See Stillie v. AM Int'l, Inc., 850 F. Supp. 960, 962 (D. Kan. 1994) ("remanufacturers and sellers in the chain of distribution after remanufacture are subject to strict liability").

[232] See, e.g., Florence v. Ford Motor Co., 2020 WL 5971772, at *3 (M.D. Fla. 2020) (remanding case; negligence claim against seller of used vehicle with faulty airbag that had been recalled); Garrido v. Team Auto Sales, Inc., 913 N.W.2d 95, 103–04 (S.D. 2018) (negligence, among other claims, against seller of used vehicle; questions of fact whether muffler was missing at time of sale and whether missing muffler caused carbon monoxide exposure precluded summary judgment on causation); Whelchel v. Briggs & Stratton Corp., 850 F. Supp. 2d 926 (N.D. Ill. 2012); Meyering v. General Motors Corp., 275 Cal. Rptr. 346 (Dist. Ct. 1990).

[233] See, e.g., Bayer v. Winton Motor Car Co., 160 N.W. 642 (Mich. 1916).

[234] See, e.g., Limited Flying Club, Inc. v. Wood, 632 F.2d 51, 55–57 (8th Cir. 1980) (Iowa law) (repair and inspection history stated in log book of used airplane); Barb v. Wallace, 412 A.2d 1314, 1316–18 (Md. Ct. Spec. App. 1980) (statement that used engine sold for go-cart ran "real good"; engine promptly exploded).

[235] See, e.g., Gaston v. Bobby Johnson Equip. Co., 771 So.2d 848, 852 (La. Ct. App. 2000) ("Although this warranty does not apply as extensively as with new products, it requires that even used equipment operate reasonably well for a reasonable period of time."); Fernandes v. Union Bookbinding Co., 507 N.E.2d 728 (Mass. 1987) (implied warranty of merchantability); Hoort v. Oklahoma Truck Parts, Inc., 650 P.2d 71, 73 (Okla. Ct. App. 1981) (implied warranty of merchantability "reasonably appropriate to the particular goods sold"); Barb v. Wallace, 412 A.2d 1314 (Md. Ct. Spec. App. 1980) (implied warranty of fitness for particular purpose accompanied sale of used engine for use in go-cart); Roupp v. Acor, 384 A.2d 968 (Pa. Super. Ct. 1978) (both implied warranties accompanied sale of used truck).

But see Potts v. Ford Motor Co., 2021 WL 2014796, at *7 (S.D. Cal. 2021) (manufacturer not liable for used car implied warranty claim; "[c]ourts routinely dismiss implied warranty claims for used cars that are directed at the manufacturer"); Fuquay v. Revels Motors, Inc., 389 So.2d 1238 (Fla. Dist. Ct. App. 1980) (implied warranty not applicable if seller did not know, have reason to know, nor have superior knowledge of latent defect); Valley Datsun v. Martinez, 578 S.W.2d 485 (Tex. App. 1979) (no implied warranty of merchantability where purchaser knows goods are used).

[236] See UCC § 2–314 Official Comment 3: "A contract for the sale of second-hand goods, however, involves only such obligation as is appropriate to such goods."

The big question in modern products liability litigation is whether the seller of a used product is subject to strict liability in tort.[237] On this issue, the decisions are sharply split. Following the position taken in an early Illinois case,[238] a majority of courts hold that strict liability in tort ordinarily does *not* apply to the sale of used products unless the seller repaired or modified the product or otherwise caused the defect.[239] Courts following this majority approach often rely on an influential early case, *Tillman v. Vance Equipment Co.*,[240] which held that a dealer who sold a used crane "as is," without making any inspection or repairs, was not strictly liable for design and warning defects that had originated with the manufacturer. Of the three principal policies the court thought were served by strict liability—risk spreading, protecting a user's expectations, and risk reduction—the court concluded that only risk spreading would be served by holding used product sellers strictly liable. Buyers ordinarily do not expect new-product quality from used products, and buyers can bargain for safety assurances if they so desire. Imposing strict liability on sellers of used products would raise the price of such products and otherwise disrupt markets in those goods. Nor can a used product seller, lying entirely outside the chain of new product distribution, pressure manufacturers to improve product safety.[241] Probably reflecting these rationales, at least a couple of products liability reform statutes explicitly exclude sellers of used products from coverage.[242]

Following an early New Jersey case,[243] however, a fairly large minority of courts have held that strict liability in tort *does* apply to used product sales.[244] *Jordan v.*

---

[237] On the applicability of strict liability in tort to sellers of used products, see 33 Stan. L. Rev. 535 (1981) (strict liability should not apply to sellers of unmodified used products); Annot., 9 A.L.R.5th 1 (1993); Frumer, Friedman, and Sklaren, Products Liability § 5.06; Products Liability Rest. § 8 Reporters' Note to cmt. *b* (thorough summary and analysis of cases).

[238] Peterson v. Lou Bachrodt Chevrolet Co., 329 N.E.2d 785 (Ill. 1975) (used car dealer not subject to strict liability in tort for defects arising after car's original manufacture because such a rule would make dealer insurer for defects arising while car is under control of others). See also Bruce v. Martin-Marietta Corp., 544 F.2d 442 (10th Cir. 1976) (Okla. law).

[239] See, e.g., Loomis v. Amazon.com LLC, 277 Cal. Rptr. 3d 769, 795 (Ct. App. 2021) (Wiley, J., concurring) ("Imposing strict liability on secondhand dealers would require them 'routinely to dismantle, inspect for latent defects, and repair or recondition their products[,' and] make used goods dealers the insurers of the goods they sold."); Lidey v. Moser's Rides, SRL, 2018 WL 6308690, at *8 (M.D. Fla. 2018) (dismissing strict products liability claim against seller of used amusement park ride; "Florida plaintiffs are barred from bringing strict product liability actions against sellers of used goods"); Harber v. Altec Indus., 812 F. Supp. 954 (W.D. Mo. 1993) (same); Peterson v. Idaho First Nat'l Bank, 791 P.2d 1303, 1306 (Idaho 1990) (no strict liability on used product seller); Peterson v. Lou Bachrodt Chevrolet Co., 329 N.E.2d 785, 787 (Ill. 1975). See generally Senagore, The Benefits of Limiting Strict Liability for Used-Product Sellers, 30 N. Ill. U. L. Rev. 349 (2010); Annot., 9 A.L.R.5th 1 (1993).

[240] 596 P.2d 1299 (Or. 1979).

[241] *Tillman*, 596 P.2d at 1303–04. See also Arriaga v. CitiCapital Commercial Corp., 85 Cal. Rptr. 3d 143, 153 (Ct. App. 2008) (summarizing policies for excluding dealers in used products from strict liability).

[242] See, e.g., Idaho Code Ann. § 6–1402(1)(b) (used product seller not included in definition of "product seller"); Wash. Rev. Code Ann. § 7.72.010(1)(c) (same).

[243] Turner v. International Harvester Co., 336 A.2d 62, 69 (N.J. Super. Ct. Law Div. 1975) ("realistic expectations of quality and durability will be lower for used goods, commensurate with their age, appearance and price [but the] safety of the general public demands that when a used motor vehicle, for example, is sold for use *as a serviceable motor vehicle* (and not as junk parts), absent special circumstances, the seller [will] be responsible for safety defects whether known or unknown at time of sale").

[244] See, e.g., Gaumer v. Rossville Truck & Tractor Co., 257 P.3d 292, 308 (Kan. 2011) (surveying cases and concluding that "strict liability should be available in Kansas against a seller of a used product"); Frey v. Harley Davidson Motor Co., 734 A.2d 1, 9 (Pa. Super. Ct. 1999); Stanton v. Carlson Sales, Inc., 728 A.2d 534 (Conn. Super. Ct. 1998); Stiles v. Batavia Atomic Horseshoes, Inc., 579 N.Y.S.2d 790, 792 (App. Div. 1992), rev'd on other grounds, 597 N.Y.S.2d 666 (N.Y. 1993); Nelson v. Nelson Hardware, Inc., 467 N.W.2d 518, 524 n.6 (Wis. 1991) (used product sellers strictly liable "even though completely innocent or completely uninvolved in creating the defect").

Sunnyslope Appliance Propane & Plumbing Supplies Co.,[245] which involved an explosion of a used propane storage tank with a defective shut-off valve, outlined the rationales for applying strict liability in tort to used product sales. Pointing out that *Restatement (Second) of Torts* § 402A by its terms applies to the sale of "any" product, not merely to any *new* product, the court addressed the *Tillman* court's arguments for rejecting strict liability in tort for used product sales. The *Jordan* court first challenged the view that buyers of used products have lower safety expectations, arguing that such buyers do not expect unreasonably dangerous defects in used products that they buy. And as for risk reduction, the *Jordan* court reasoned that strict liability in tort should encourage sellers of used products to increase their maintenance and inspections of such products before offering them for sale. Sellers of used goods are very much in the chain of distribution, thought the court, because they offer their goods for sale and profit therefrom. Finally, the *Jordan* court reasoned that "[t]here is no justification for finding that used good dealers as a class cannot shift losses, distribute costs, or insure against losses."[246]

Some courts limit strict liability in the used product situation to cases where a seller reconditions or rebuilds the product prior to sale;[247] other courts limit strict liability to defects of which the seller is aware;[248] and some courts condition strict liability on *both* the seller's reconditioning of the product together with the opportunity to discover the defect prior to the product's sale.[249] Finally, even in states that hold sellers of used products subject to strict liability, such liability requires that the seller regularly deal in used good sales.[250] So, if the dealer sells used goods infrequently, it will not be considered a "seller" of such used goods.[251]

---

245 660 P.2d 1236 (Ariz. Ct. App. 1983).

246 Id. at 1242.

247 See, e.g., Arriaga v. CitiCapital Commercial Corp., 85 Cal. Rptr. 3d 143, 153 (Ct. App. 2008) (strict liability does not extend to sellers of used products "unless the seller rebuilds or reconditions the product and thus assumes a role analogous to that of a manufacturer"); Bell v. Precision Airmotive Corp., 42 P.3d 1071 (Alaska 2002) (seller of used component part strictly liable because of his extensive repair of part); Harber v. Altec Indus., 812 F. Supp. 954, 961 (W.D. Mo. 1993) (excellent review; declining to impose strict liability in tort on seller of used product); Crandell v. Larkin & Jones Appliance Co., 334 N.W.2d 31 (S.D. 1983) (dealer, who reconditioned and guaranteed used clothes dryer which caught fire, liable in strict tort, express warranty, and implied warranty of merchantability).

248 See, e.g., Stump v. Indiana Equip. Co., 601 N.E.2d 398 (Ind. Ct. App. 1992) (former owner had hot-wired starter on grader that cut off operator's legs; duty of due care to inspect and warn not breached since defect was latent); Grimes v. Axtell Ford Lincoln-Mercury, 403 N.W.2d 781 (Iowa 1987) (no strict liability for latent defects).

249 See, e.g., Wynia v. Richard-Ewing Equip. Co., 17 F.3d 1084 (8th Cir. 1993) (S.D. law).

250 See, e.g., Nutting v. Ford Motor Co., 584 N.Y.S.2d 653, 656 (App. Div. 1992), where Hewlett Packard regularly resold its fleet of more than 3,000 cars: "[O]ne who regularly purchases a substantial quantity of new cars for use by its employees and who regularly disposes of those vehicles by auction sales to used car dealers for resale to the public after the vehicles have been used for approximately one year is in the regular business of a used car dealer for the purposes of imposing strict products liability."

251 See, e.g., Garcia v. Becker Bros. Steel Co., 125 Cal. Rptr. 3d 73, 79 (Ct. App. 2011) ("an 'occasional seller' of used equipment is not a conduit for the production or distribution of that product"); Jaramillo v. Weyerhaeuser Co., 570 F.3d 487, 490 (2d Cir. 2009) (N.Y. law) (defendant was not a "regular seller [so] that it can be held strictly liable"); McCabe v. Allied Prods. Corp., 2000 WL 1805687, at *4 (D. Me. 2000) (defendant who had sold only two brake presses in two years not "engaged in the business of selling" such products); Sukljian v. Charles Ross & Son Co., 503 N.E.2d 1358, 1361 (N.Y. 1986) (G.E. each year sold at auction two or three used machines of particular type that it had purchased new and used for many years: "strict liability was inapposite because [G.E. had not] *regularly* engaged in the business of selling the equipment in issue").

The *Products Liability Restatement* basically adopts the majority approach.[252] Section 8 provides that sellers of defective used products are liable generally for negligence,[253] for manufacturing defects and product malfunctions when a seller's marketing causes buyers to expect the safety of a new product,[254] for any type of defect in a remanufactured product,[255] and for noncompliance with applicable safety statutes and regulations.[256]

§ 16.6 Real Estate

Products liability law conventionally is defined as the liability of suppliers for harm from selling chattels in a defective condition. Chattels, of course, are personal property, as distinguished from real property. Thus real estate, including any fixtures attached to it,[257] would not appear to be a proper subject of "products" liability law. Most courts thus do not apply strict products liability in tort to claims involving defects in land, houses, and other structures attached to the land.[258] Similarly, because Article 2 of the Uniform Commercial Code applies only to "goods," it does not apply to real estate transactions.[259] A number of products liability reform statutes explicitly provide that real estate is not a covered "product."[260] The *Products Liability Restatement* § 19 limits coverage of the *Third Restatement* to "tangible personal property" but includes real property in its coverage "when the context of [its] distribution and use is sufficiently analogous to the

---

[252] The Reporters' Note to § 8 cmt. *b* contains a particularly thorough and useful summary and analysis of the used product cases.

[253] Products Liability Rest. § 8(a).

[254] Id. at § 8(b). Comment *h* explains that such reasonable expectations may be influenced by a large variety of factors, such as the product's age and condition; price; representations that the product has been rebuilt, reconditioned, or repaired; any guarantees, warranties, and disclaimers and limitations thereof; and any information provided on the product's condition or prior use.

[255] See id. at § 8(c). See also § 16.4, above.

[256] Products Liability Rest. § 8(d).

[257] For an article to be a fixture, as opposed to a product, it must be annexed to realty or something appurtenant thereto; it must have been appropriated to the use or purpose of the part of the realty to which it is connected; and the party making the annexation must intend to make the article a permanent accession to the freehold. See Wireman v. Keneco Distribs., Inc., 661 N.E.2d 744, 747 (Ohio 1996) (defectively designed vapor recovery system attached to above-ground gasoline storage tank, causing explosion that killed worker, was "product" for purposes of products liability statute, not fixture, because oil company did not intend to make system a permanent addition to plant and had previously sold it along with tanks by bill of sale: "when property is sold by bill of sale, the property is presumed to be personalty"). See also Pamperin v. Interlake Cos., 634 So.2d 1137 (Fla. Dist. Ct. App. 1994) (if an improvement is not permanent, and can be disassembled and removed with ease, it is not a fixture and may be a "product" for purposes of strict liability).

[258] See, e.g., Simmons v. Rave Motion Pictures Pensacola, L.L.C., 197 So.3d 644, 648 (Fla. Dist. Ct. App. 2016) (strict products liability inapplicable to movie theater seats that were "a structural improvement" to real property); Martens v. MCL Constr. Corp., 807 N.E.2d 480, 493 (Ill. App. Ct. 2004) ("buildings and indivisible component parts of the building structure itself, such as bricks, supporting beams and railings, are not deemed products for the purpose of strict liability in tort."); Keck v. Dryvit Sys., Inc., 830 So.2d 1, 6 (Ala. 2002) (items "part of the structural integrity of the house or building" are not products for purposes of strict liability).

[259] See UCC § 2–105(1) (defining goods as movable things).

[260] Directly or indirectly. Statutes in at least Arkansas, New Jersey, and Washington explicitly exclude real estate from the definition of "product." See Ark. Code Ann. § 16–116–202(4) (defining "product" as "any tangible object or goods produced, excluding real estate and improvements located thereon"); N.J. Stat. Ann. § 2A:58C–8(1) ("The term 'product seller' does not include: (1) A seller of real property . . .); Wash. Rev. Code Ann. § 7.72.010(1)(a). And statutes in at least Georgia, Indiana, and Ohio define "product" in terms of "personal property" and "personalty," respectively. See Ga. Code Ann. § 51–1–11(b)(1) ("personal property"); Ind. Code Ann. § 34–6–2–114(a) ("personalty"); Ohio Rev. Code Ann. § 2307.71(A)(12)(a) ("tangible personal property").

distribution and use of tangible personal property that it is appropriate to apply the rules stated in this Restatement."[261]

Notwithstanding the general rule excluding real property from the strict liability principles applied to defective chattels, an early New Jersey case, *Schipper v. Levitt & Sons, Inc.*,[262] began a judicial drift toward applying products liability doctrine to various real estate transactions. Accordingly, the mere fact that a defective article is connected in some way with real estate does not in every jurisdiction preclude the application of certain products liability principles.[263]

Homes and Related Structures—Strict Liability in Tort

In *Schipper*, the landmark case, an infant was severely scalded by excessively hot water from a faucet in the bathroom sink because the developer had failed to install an inexpensive mixing valve to reduce the temperature of water drawn from the boiler.[264] The court held the developer strictly liable for the injuries, reasoning that mass-builders can better bear the risk of construction defects than consumers, that "there are no meaningful distinctions between Levitt's mass production and sale of homes and the mass production and sale of automobiles, and that pertinent overriding policy considerations are the same."[265] Following *Schipper*, a handful of courts applied strict liability in tort to builder-vendors of residential homes[266] and to manufacturers of prefabricated homes and structures.[267] A lower New Jersey court extended the *Schipper* principle to a small developer of custom homes,[268] but the New Jersey legislature subsequently excluded real estate from coverage in its products liability act.[269] Even with

---

[261] Comment *e* to this section summarizes the types of real estate cases to which courts have applied strict products liability principles.

[262] 207 A.2d 314 (N.J. 1965).

[263] See Cantu, A Continuing Whimsical Search for the True Meaning of the Term "Product" in Products Liability Litigation, 35 St. Mary's L.J. 341 (2004); Lannetti, Toward a Revised Definition of "Product" Under the *Restatement (Third) of Torts: Products Liability*, 55 Bus. Law. 799 (2000); Morgan, When the Walls Come Tumbling Down—Theories of Recovery for Defective Housing, 56 St. John's L. Rev. 670 (1982) (arguing for strict liability for defects in houses); Love, Landlord's Liability for Defective Premises: Caveat Lessee, Negligence, or Strict Liability?, 1975 Wis. L. Rev. 19 (excellent overview); Ursin, Strict Liability for Defective Business Premises—One Step Beyond Rowland and Greenman, 22 UCLA L. Rev. 820 (1975); Moscovitz, Implied Warranty of Habitability: A New Doctrine Raising New Issues, 62 Cal. L. Rev. 1444 (1974); Roberts, The Case of the Unwary Home Buyer: The Housing Merchant Did It, 52 Cornell L.Q. 835 (1967); Haskell, The Case for an Implied Warranty of Quality in Sales of Real Property, 53 Geo. L.J. 633 (1965); Annots., 75 A.L.R.5th 413 (2000) (tort liability of building contractors), 25 A.L.R.4th 351 (1983) (strict liability for defects in buildings and land); Am. Law Prod. Liab. 3d ch. 38; Products Liability Rest. § 19 cmt. *e*; Frumer, Friedman, and Sklaren, Products Liability § 5.08. See also Nolan and Ursin, Understanding Enterprise Liability (1995) (proposing rule of strict business premises liability).

[264] 207 A.2d 314 (N.J. 1965).

[265] Id. at 325. In its reform act, New Jersey overruled *Schipper*. See note 260, above.

[266] See, e.g., Bednarski v. Hideout Homes & Realty, Inc., 711 F. Supp. 823, 826–27 (M.D. Pa. 1989) (plaintiff's son died and home destroyed in fire originating in electrical outlet); Bastian v. Wausau Homes, Inc., 620 F. Supp. 947, 950 (N.D. Ill. 1985); Vincent v. Jim Walter Homes, Inc., Prod. Liab. Rep. (CCH) ¶ 8278 (Tenn. Ct. App. 1978); Kriegler v. Eichler Homes, Inc., 74 Cal. Rptr. 749 (Ct. App. 1969) (builder of mass-produced tract homes strictly liable for replacement costs of heating system made of steel tubing which corroded).

[267] See, e.g., Bastian v. Wausau Homes, Inc., 620 F. Supp. 947 (N.D. Ill. 1985) (defective baseboard heater); Kaneko v. Hilo Coast Processing, 654 P.2d 343 (Haw. 1982) (temporary weld in prefab building failed, and iron worker injured in collapse). See generally Model Uniform Product Liability Act § 102(A)(1), 44 Fed. Reg. 62,714, 62,717–19 (1979) (builder-vendor strictly liable only if mass producer and seller of standardized dwellings, including modular homes); Annot., 4 A.L.R.5th 667 (1993) (products liability and prefab buildings).

[268] See Patitucci v. Drelich, 379 A.2d 297, 298 (N.J. Super. Ct. Law Div. 1977) (defective sewage disposal system).

[269] See N.J. Stat. Ann. § 2A:58C–8(1) (definition of product seller excludes sellers of real property).

respect to mass-produced tract homes, some courts have rejected *Schipper*, reasoning that developers and building contractors generally are not as financially capable as manufacturers of mass-produced chattels to absorb and spread the costs of accidents.[270]

A few courts have extended strict liability to defects in less-standardized structures. For example, the doctrine has been applied to a defective sewage system,[271] a single family home,[272] condominiums,[273] and a residential building.[274] California courts have applied strict liability in tort to "defective" residential lots that subsided from inadequate compaction of the fill or erosion,[275] and to the defective "design" of a house for locating the hot water heater in the garage.[276]

Many courts have applied strict products liability to defective products incorporated as *fixtures* in homes or other structures on real property, including a storage rack system, an air-conditioning system, a gas floor furnace, a heat exchanger, an entire heating and air-conditioning system, a hot water heater, concrete panels, windows, a roof-covering system, driveway paint, and synthetic stucco exterior finish systems.[277] Some courts arrive at their decisions on a simple "product" *versus* "real estate" division, while others reason by policy analysis as to whether the goals of strict products liability are served by extending strict liability to the particular situation.[278]

---

[270] See, e.g., Chapman v. Lily Cache Builders, Inc., 362 N.E.2d 811 (Ill. App. Ct. 1977). See also Kojoklyan v. Lee, 2018 WL 2455677, at *3 (Cal. Ct. App. 2018), noncitable (declining to apply strict liability in tort to real estate speculator who renovated home for resale).

[271] See Patitucci v. Drelich, 379 A.2d 297, 298 (N.J. Super. Ct. Law Div. 1977) (strict liability extends to professional builder-vendor because "[t]he buyer of a home from a builder vendor can no more dig up the ground to inspect the sewage system than the buyer of an automobile can cause the car to be disassembled and tested").

[272] See Salka v. Dean Homes of Beverly Hills, Inc., 22 Cal. Rptr. 2d 902 (Ct. App. 1993), opinion superseded by 864 P.2d 1037 (Cal. 1993); Blagg v. Fred Hunt Co., 612 S.W.2d 321, 324 (Ark. 1981).

[273] See Towers Tenant Ass'n. v. Towers Ltd. P'ship, 563 F. Supp. 566 (D.D.C. 1983) (converted condominiums; strict liability in tort).

[274] See Hyman v. Gordon, 111 Cal. Rptr. 262 (Ct. App. 1973).

[275] See Avner v. Longridge Estates, 77 Cal. Rptr. 633 (Ct. App. 1969). See also Stearman v. Centex Homes, 92 Cal. Rptr. 2d 761 (Ct. App. 2000) (shifting land under house foundation deformed slab and caused extensive cracks); GEM Developers v. Hallcraft Homes of San Diego, Inc., 261 Cal. Rptr. 626, 633 (Ct. App. 1989) (soil subsidence; "a developer who mass grades land into finished lots for sale to the public for residential housing has produced a 'product' and is strictly liable to the consumer for any defects in the design or manufacture of the lots"); Del Mar Beach Club Owners Ass'n v. Imperial Contracting Co., 176 Cal. Rptr. 886 (Ct. App. 1981) (erosion of bluff on which apartment complex was situated).

[276] See Hyman v. Gordon, 111 Cal. Rptr. 262 (Ct. App. 1973).

[277] See Schueler v. Ad Art, Inc., 472 P.3d 686, 699–700 (Nev. Ct. App. 2020) (casino sign was a product; "fixtures are not exempt from the doctrine of strict liability"); Pamperin v. Interlake Cos., 634 So.2d 1137 (Fla. Dist. Ct. App. 1994) (storage rack system that can be disassembled and resold is thus product rather than permanent fixture); Berman v. Watergate W., Inc., 391 A.2d 1351 (D.C. 1978); O'Laughlin v. Minnesota Natural Gas Co., 253 N.W.2d 826 (Minn. 1977); Smith v. Fluor Corp., 514 So.2d 1227 (Miss. 1987); Trent v. Brasch Mfg. Co., 477 N.E.2d 1312 (Ill. App. Ct. 1985) (whether HVAC system is a product is based on policy analysis, not whether article is "attached" to real estate). See also Loughridge v. Goodyear Tire & Rubber Co., 207 F. Supp. 2d 1187 (D. Colo. 2002) (heating system constitutes "product" under Colorado products liability law); Nichols v. Agway, Inc., 720 N.Y.S.2d 691 (App. Div. 2001); State Stove Mfg. Co. v. Hodges, 189 So.2d 113 (Miss. 1966), superseded by statute as stated in Huff v. Shopsmith, Inc., 786 So.2d 383 (Miss. 2001); Trustees of Columbia Univ. v. Exposaic Indus., 505 N.Y.S.2d 882 (App. Div. 1986); Jimenez v. Superior Ct., 58 P.3d 450 (Cal. 2002) (in mass-produced homes); Soproni v. Polygon Apartment Partners, 971 P.2d 500 (Wash. 1999). See also Kelleher v. Marvin Lumber & Cedar Co., 891 A.2d 477 (N.H. 2005); Federal Ins. Co. v. HPG Int'l, Inc., 758 N.E.2d 261 (Ohio Ct. App. 2001); Halpryn v. Highland Ins. Co., 426 So.2d 1050 (Fla. Dist. Ct. App. 1983). Compare Fresh Coat, Inc. v. K-2, Inc., 318 S.W.3d 893, 898 (Tex. 2010) (finding EIFS is a product under the Texas products liability statute).

[278] See Menendez v. Paddock Pool Constr. Co., 836 P.2d 968 (Ariz. Ct. App. 1991) (excellent analysis; inapplicability of policies precluded application of strict liability to installer of custom swimming pool). See

Homes—Implied Warranty

While most courts have been reluctant to extend strict liability in tort to defective homes and fixtures, and while the UCC Article 2 warranties do not apply to real estate transactions, as mentioned earlier, most states have now replaced the traditional rule of *caveat emptor* in the sale of new homes with a common-law implied warranty of reasonable quality—often referred to as a warranty of "habitability."[279] Reasoning that new home sale transactions involve primarily the sale of a house rather than the conveyance of land, courts have justified this warranty on the basis of "the disparity of bargaining positions between the seller and purchaser, reliance by the purchaser on the skill of the builder, and the inability of the purchaser to inspect the house for latent defects."[280] Such a warranty has been applied to leaky pipes, and smelly floors and toilets; water with a high iron content that stained fixtures "chocolaty brown," had an offensive odor, fizzled like Alka-Seltzer, and emitted methane gas; a smelly carpet; a flooded basement; leaky and overflowing septic tanks; a fire from a defective fireplace; cracking walls; and numerous other defective conditions.[281] Warranty and other products liability principles have also been held applicable to cooperative apartments,[282] condominiums,[283] and mobile homes.[284] Courts in a few decisions have disagreed, fearing to venture into uncharted seas.[285]

---

also Schueler v. Ad Art, Inc., 472 P.3d 686, 700 (Nev. Ct. App. 2020) (MGM casino pylon sign was a "product" under § 402A; policy considerations for applying strict products liability were satisfied).

[279] Compare Davencourt at Pilgrims Landing Homeowners Ass'n v. Davencourt at Pilgrims Landing, LC, 221 P.3d 234, 249–53 (Utah 2009) (warranty of workmanlike manner and habitability); Heath v. Palmer, 915 A.2d 1290, 1293 (Vt. 2006) (warranty of habitability and good workmanship); Council of Unit Owners of Breakwater House Condo. v. Simpler, 603 A.2d 792 (Del. 1992) (warranty of good quality and workmanship; distinguishing warranty of habitability).

[280] Lane v. Trenholm Bldg. Co., 229 S.E.2d 728, 729 (S.C. 1976).

[281] See, e.g., Berish v. Bornstein, 770 N.E.2d 961 (Mass. 2002) (condominium complex contained defective sliding doors, chimneys, decks, and roofs); Hoke v. Beck, 587 N.E.2d 4 (Ill. App. Ct. 1992) (many problems); McDonald v. Mianecki, 386 A.2d 1325 (N.J. Super. Ct. App. Div. 1978) (high iron content in water), aff'd, 398 A.2d 1283 (N.J. 1979); Blagg v. Fred Hunt Co., 612 S.W.2d 321 (Ark. 1981) (smelly carpet); Hartley v. Ballou, 209 S.E.2d 776 (N.C. 1974) (flooded basement; implied warranty of freedom from major, latent structural defects); Trien v. Croasdale Constr. Co., 874 S.W.2d 478 (Mo. Ct. App. 1994) (leaky and dusty house); Rutledge v. Dodenhoff, 175 S.E.2d 792 (S.C. 1970) (overflowing septic tank).

[282] See, e.g., Berman v. Watergate W., Inc., 391 A.2d 1351 (D.C. 1978) (implied warranty).

[283] See, e.g., Lofts at Fillmore Condo. Ass'n v. Reliance Commercial Constr., Inc., 190 P.3d 733, 736 (Ariz. 2008) (warranty action allowed against contractor); Berish v. Bornstein, 878 N.E.2d 581 (Mass. App. Ct. 2007) (table) (implied warranty of habitability); Council of Unit Owners of Breakwater House Condo. v. Simpler, 603 A.2d 792 (Del. 1992) (conversion from apartments; negligence and warranty). *Contra* Association of Unit Owners of Bridgeview Condos. v. Dunning, 69 P.3d 788 (Or. Ct. App. 2003) (refusing to extend definition of "product" to include 18-unit condominiums); Messier v. Association of Apartment Owners of Mt. Terrace, 735 P.2d 939 (Haw. Ct. App. 1987).

[284] See, e.g., Gautheir v. Mayo, 258 N.W.2d 748 (Mich. Ct. App. 1977) (implied warranty).

[285] See, e.g., Bruce Farms, Inc. v. Coupe, 247 S.E.2d 400, 403–04 (Va. 1978) (cracking bricks). In *Bruce Farms*, the court reasoned that the "modern rule" would open too many questions: "Should it apply only when the seller is the builder? Should it be confined to the sale of houses under construction or those newly constructed or extended to the sale of renovated homes? Should it be limited to single-family detached dwellings or should it also reach owner-occupied condominium units or duplex houses? Should the warranty cover materials, fixtures, and other physical appurtenances?" The court also saw troubles in determining the duration of such warranties and damages for their breach. "[T]he decision . . . is one properly within the province of the General Assembly. The issue involves a multitude of competing economic, cultural, and societal values which courts are ill-equipped to balance, a fact best illustrated by the disparate conclusions reached by the several courts which have tinkered with the common law rule." Id. at 404.

Other Structures

Courts generally have refused to apply strict liability in tort to non-dwelling structures on real property. For example, an Illinois court refused to apply strict liability principles to the design of a parking garage.[286] The plaintiff's decedent was killed when he fell from an upper level of an open-air parking garage that allegedly had insufficient walking space around the vehicles and no railings to prevent such falls.[287] Similarly, a Pennsylvania court ruled that strict liability in tort is applicable only to defective components of a building, not the entire building itself.[288] And an Arizona court refused to apply strict liability principles to the installation of a custom swimming pool in the common area of a subdivision, persuasively reasoning that the policies of strict products liability do not apply to the custom construction on real estate of a single structure of this type.[289] On this basis, the Arizona court distinguished an Iowa decision that had applied strict liability in tort to the design, manufacture, and sale of a prefabricated fiberglass pool.[290] Other courts have refused to apply strict liability in tort to a crude oil refinery, a jail, an enclosed public arena, a petroleum separator facility, and many other kinds of structures on real property.[291]

Landlords

Negligence

For centuries, the rule of caveat emptor, or more precisely "caveat lessee," dominated the law of real estate leases as it did the law of real estate sales. Because of the dominant position of the landowner in medieval society, landlords were cloaked at an early date with a mantle of immunity from liability for injuries caused by defective conditions in premises that were leased. As time progressed, however, various exceptions grew up around the general rule of non-liability, so that landlords became subject to liability in negligence for: (1) hidden dangers known to the lessor but not to the lessee, (2) injuries to persons off the premises, (3) defects in premises leased for admission of the public, (4) defects in "common areas" retained under the landlord's control, (5) failure to keep the premises in good repair when the landlord had covenanted so to do, (6) negligence in making repairs, and (7) defects constituting violations of building or

---

[286] See Lowrie v. City of Evanston, 365 N.E.2d 923 (Ill. App. Ct. 1977).

[287] The court distinguished *Schipper*, above note 264, and *Kriegler*, above note 266, on the ground that they "[D]o not deal with a defect in the home *per se* but with a defect in some product installed therein. Thus, it appears to us that these builder-vendor cases apply strict liability to a contractor who sells a defective product along with the home, as distinguished from holding that a home is itself a product." Id. at 928.

[288] See Cox v. Shaffer, 302 A.2d 456 (Pa. Super. Ct. 1973) (plaintiff asphyxiated in silo from lack of ventilation).

[289] See Menendez v. Paddock Pool Constr. Co., 836 P.2d 968 (Ariz. Ct. App. 1991) (excellent analysis; collecting cases). See also Jackson v. City of Franklin, 554 N.E.2d 932 (Ohio Ct. App. 1988) (strict liability in tort inapplicable to custom-designed public swimming pool).

[290] See Duggan v. Hallmark Pool Mfg. Co., 398 N.W.2d 175 (Iowa 1986), superseded by statute on other grounds, as stated in Reed v. Chrysler Corp., 494 N.W.2d 224 (Iowa 1992).

[291] See McClanahan v. American Gilsonite Co., 494 F. Supp. 1334 (D. Colo. 1980); Easterday v. Masiello, 518 So.2d 260 (Fla. 1988) (jail); Chubb Grp. of Ins. Cos. v. C.F. Murphy & Assocs., Inc., 656 S.W.2d 766 (Mo. Ct. App. 1983); Papp v. Rocky Mountain Oil & Minerals, Inc., 769 P.2d 1249 (Mont. 1989); Brooks v. Eugene Burger Mgmt. Corp., 264 Cal. Rptr. 756 (Ct. App. 1989) (young child who wandered off unfenced grounds of apartment complex struck by car; entire complex could not be defective product). See generally Annot., 25 A.L.R.4th 351 (1983).

housing code provisions.[292] Then, in a spectacular decision in 1973, *Sargent v. Ross*,[293] the New Hampshire Supreme Court turned the general rule of non-liability on its head by holding a landlord subject to the general principles of negligence liability. A large number of other courts have followed this eminently sound approach.[294]

Warranty

On the warranty side of the matter, while a warranty of habitability had been implied into short-term leases of furnished dwellings by a few courts for some time, courts began to find a general implied warranty of habitability in leases of residential premises in the 1960s and early 1970s.[295] While most of the cases have involved essentially contractual disputes surrounding the nonpayment of rent and other economic complaints,[296] occasional cases concern products liability claims involving personal injuries.[297] For example, a Maryland decision held that a landlord was subject to liability for breach of warranty under that state's consumer protection act for injuries to a child

---

[292] See Prosser and Keeton on Torts § 63. For example, courts have allowed negligence claims for lead poisoning in children who consume lead-based paint chips that flake off in violation of city building codes. See, e.g., Brooks v. Lewin Realty III, Inc., 835 A.2d 616 (Md. 2003).

[293] 308 A.2d 528 (N.H. 1973) (Kenison, C.J.) (brilliantly conceived and penned).

[294] See, e.g., Gendell v. 42 W. 17th St. Hous. Corp., 148 N.Y.S.3d 76, 77 (App. Div. 2021) (landlord negligently failed to repair roof)); Miller v. David Grace, Inc., 212 P.3d 1223, 1229–30 (Okla. 2009); Tenney v. Atlantic Assocs., 594 N.W.2d 11 (Iowa 1999) (plaintiff raped by stranger in her own apartment; landlord negligent in not securing spare apartment keys in office); Anderson v. Sammy Redd & Assoc., 650 A.2d 376, 379 (N.J. Super. Ct. 1994); Newton v. Magill, 872 P.2d 1213 (Alaska 1994); Favreau v. Miller, 591 A.2d 68 (Vt. 1991); Turpel v. Sayles, 692 P.2d 1290 (Nev. 1985); Stephens v. Stearns, 678 P.2d 41 (Idaho 1984); Young v. Garwacki, 402 N.E.2d 1045 (Mass. 1980); Pagelsdorf v. Safeco Ins. Co. of Am., 284 N.W.2d 55 (Wis. 1979); Stephenson v. Warner, 581 P.2d 567 (Utah 1978); Brennan v. Cockrell Invs., Inc., 111 Cal. Rptr. 122 (Ct. App. 1973). See also Merrill v. Jansma, 86 P.3d 270, 276–77 (Wyo. 2004); Mansur v. Eubanks, 401 So.2d 1328 (Fla. 1981) (holding residential landlord has duty to reasonably inspect and repair in order to deliver a reasonably safe dwelling to tenant); Shroades v. Rental Homes, Inc., 427 N.E.2d 774, 777 (Ohio 1981) ("abrogation of this [landlord] immunity has been advocated by legal commentators, and the overwhelming majority of states have abolished, either in whole or in part, the traditional immunity"). *But see* Thomas v. Stewart, 60 S.W.3d 415, 420 (Ark. 2001) (noting that *Sargent* was rejected in the past, but suggesting that it might be followed in the future); Propst v. McNeill, 932 S.W.2d 766 (Ark. 1996) (plaintiff's aircraft damaged in leased hangar during windstorm; although a majority of states have done so, abandoning doctrine of caveat lessee is for legislature); Ortega v. Flaim, 902 P.2d 199 (Wyo. 1995).

[295] See, e.g., Pines v. Perssion, 111 N.W.2d 409 (Wis. 1961); Lemle v. Breeden, 462 P.2d 470 (Haw. 1969); Javins v. First Nat'l Realty Corp., 428 F.2d 1071 (D.C. Cir. 1970). See generally Comment, 33 Land & Water L. Rev. 329 (1998).

[296] See, e.g., Witherbee Court Assocs. v. Greene, 777 N.Y.S.2d 200 (App. Div. 2004); Fairchild v. Park, 109 Cal. Rptr. 2d 442 (Ct. App. 2001).

[297] See, e.g., Gerlach v. Cove Apartments, LLC, 471 P.3d 181, 191 (Wash. 2020) (guest severely injured in fall from second floor apartment when rotted balcony railing gave way; "recognizing a cause of action for tenants and their guests for personal injuries caused by a landlord's violation of the common law warranty of habitability"); Joyner v. Durant, 716 N.Y.S.2d 221 (App. Div. 2000) (plaintiff's daughter contracted lead poisoning); Richardson v. Simone, 712 N.Y.S.2d 672 (App. Div. 2000) (plaintiff injured while standing on staircase that separated from building and fell to ground); Old Town Dev. Co. v. Langford, 349 N.E.2d 744 (Ind. Ct. App. 1976) (explosion of defective furnace in apartment building), set aside without opinion, 369 N.E.2d 404 (Ind. 1977). See also Alharb v. Sayegh, 604 N.Y.S.2d 243 (App. Div. 1993) (child contracted lead poisoning from ingesting paint chips in rental housing; landlord's lack of notice of dangerous condition may be a defense, by implication); Rivera v. Selfon Home Repairs & Improvements Co., 439 A.2d 739 (Pa. Super. Ct. 1982). See also Avignone v. Valigorski, 137 N.Y.S.3d 911, 915 (N.Y. City Ct. 2020) (landlords breached implied warranty of habitability by failing to supply adequate water pressure and hot water, increasing tenant's risk of contracting pandemic virus by forcing her to use public laundromats).

who ingested lead-based paint chips in the dwelling at the inception of the lease in violation of a local housing code.[298]

Strict Liability in Tort

At the height (and close to the end) of the tort expansionary era in the mid-1980s, the California Supreme Court, in *Becker v. IRM Corp.*,[299] adopted a rule of landlord strict tort liability for injuries from defects in leased dwellings, reasoning that an apartment itself may be considered a "product" placed in the stream of commerce by the landlord.[300] Louisiana, by statute, was the only other state to have such a rule, and it was overruled by statute in 1996.[301] No court followed *Becker*, and courts and commentators widely rejected it as an excessive extension of the principles of products liability law.[302] Hawaii, for example, which has a strong tradition of protecting plaintiffs' rights, would have nothing to do with the *Becker* approach.[303] Shortly after *Becker* was decided, the composition of the California Supreme Court changed substantially, and the newly constituted court eventually found an opportunity to revisit *Becker* when asked to extend its strict liability rule to hoteliers. In *Peterson v. Superior Court*,[304] the court declared that landlords have no duty "to insure the safety of their tenants in situations in which injury is caused by a defect of which the landlord neither knew nor should have known."[305] Admitting that it had erred in *Becker*, the court ruled that strict liability in tort does *not* apply to either landlords or hoteliers for injuries to tenants or guests caused by defects in the premises.[306]

Statutes of Repose

Many states have special statutes of repose for improvements to real property.[307] These statutes protect building contractors from suits long after a structure has been completed,[308] but manufacturers of component products used in the structure may not

[298] Benik v. Hatcher, 750 A.2d 10, 26 (Md. 2000) (4–3 decision) ("the landlord who leases premises for human habitation is presumed to have knowledge of any defective condition that a reasonable inspection would have disclosed").

[299] 698 P.2d 116 (Cal. 1985).

[300] Earlier, the California court had held that a landlord negligence disclaimer violated public policy. See Henrioulle v. Marin Ventures, Inc., 573 P.2d 465 (Cal. 1978).

[301] For application of the strict liability statute, see Marcantel v. Karam, 601 So.2d 1 (La. Ct. App. 1992). In 1996, the statute was substantially altered, and a landlord's liability now requires knowledge of the defect, that the damage could have been prevented by the exercise of reasonable care, and failure to exercise such care. See also Meaux v. Wendy's Int'l, Inc., 51 So.3d 778, 787–88 (La. Ct. App. 2010).

[302] See, e.g., Leong v. Sears Roebuck & Co., 970 P.2d 972 (Haw. 1998); Ortega v. Flaim, 902 P.2d 199 (Wyo. 1995); Armstrong v. Cione, 738 P.2d 79 (Haw. 1987) (shower door made of ordinary glass); Duncavage v. Allen, 497 N.E.2d 433 (Ill. App. Ct. 1986) (broken lock on window permitted murderer to enter); Young v. Morrisey, 329 S.E.2d 426 (S.C. 1985) (electrical system), superseded by statute, as stated in Byerly v. Connor, 415 S.E.2d 796 (S.C. 1992); Livingston v. Begay, 652 P.2d 734 (N.M. 1982) (gas heater in hotel room emitted carbon monoxide); Dwyer v. Skyline Apartments, Inc., 301 A.2d 463 (N.J. Super. Ct. App. Div. 1973) (hot water faucet in bathtub), aff'd, 311 A.2d 1 (N.J. 1973).

[303] See Armstrong v. Cione, 738 P.2d 79 (Haw. 1987).

[304] 899 P.2d 905 (Cal. 1995).

[305] Id. at 912 (noting that "every other jurisdiction that has considered this issue expressly has rejected the approach followed by *Becker*").

[306] Id. at 906. Compare Serna v. New York State Urban Dev. Corp., 586 N.Y.S.2d 413 (App. Div. 1992) (plaintiff tripped when exiting elevator that stopped below floor level; strict products liability principles inapplicable to commercial lessor of building).

[307] See § 14.6, above.

[308] See, e.g., Conway v. Hi-Tech Eng'g, Inc., 381 S.W.3d 56, 65 (Ark. 2011) (N.C. law) (applying 6-year North Carolina statute to deny negligence claim related to sawmill log-stacking machine); Trust Co. Bank v.

be protected under the more narrowly drawn statutes.[309] Yet some of the statutes are drawn more broadly, thus protecting component manufacturers. In *Krull v. Thermogas Co.*,[310] a gas control valve in the furnace of the plaintiffs' home malfunctioned, causing an explosion and fire that destroyed their home. The furnace had been purchased in 1969 and the explosion occurred in 1990. Iowa's repose statute provided that "an action arising out of the unsafe or defective condition of an improvement to real property based on tort and implied warranty . . . shall not be brought more than fifteen years after" the act complained of.[311] Since "[t]he furnace—including its component control valve—was an integral part of the house," it was an "improvement" to realty, such that its manufacturer was shielded by the repose statute which barred all such claims after 1984—15 years after the purchase and sale of the furnace.[312] As in most states, the Iowa court in *Krull* held its statute constitutional.[313]

§ 16.7 PUBLICATIONS

Harmful publications have always been subject to the law of defamation,[314] as well as to the law of tortious misrepresentation[315] and breach of express warranty.[316] In recent years, however, publishers have been subjected to an additional type of claim—one based on products liability. A number of products liability claims have been brought against publishers for injuries attributable to information or thoughts communicated in books, magazine articles, films, records, and aeronautical charts. (Games, music, video games, and websites are considered below, in § 16.8.) Plaintiffs in these cases have alleged that the publishers, producers, and distributors of the materials breached a duty to persons put at risk by the information or ideas communicated in these various forms and that the law of products liability, or the broader law of torts, provides a basis for recovery.[317]

Except for cases involving defective navigational charts and publications providing contract killer information, these actions have all been rejected. In some cases, courts

---

United States Gypsum Co., 950 F.2d 1144 (5th Cir. 1992) (Miss. law) (6-year statute barred claim for asbestos abatement costs against manufacturer of materials).

[309] See, e.g., Puente v. Resources Conservation Co. Int'l, 428 P.3d 415, 422 (Wash. Ct. App. 2018) (6-year construction statute of repose inapplicable to boric acid evaporator system that was not an improvement to real property); Phaneuf Funeral Home v. Little Giant Pump Co., 48 A.3d 912, 919–20 (N.H. 2012) (statute of repose for improvements to real property did not shield manufacturer of water fountain installed in funeral home); Royal Indem. Co. v. Tyco Fire Prods., LP, 704 S.E.2d 91, 94 (Va. 2011) (statute of repose did not apply to sprinkler head equipment installed in structure); Dziewiecki v. Bakula, 824 A.2d 241, 246 (N.J. Super. Ct. App. Div. 2003) (statute of repose was intended "to protect those who contribute to the design, planning, supervision or construction of a structural improvement to real estate," not manufacturers and sellers of products used in or incorporated into improvement); Noll v. Harrisburg Area YMCA, 643 A.2d 81 (Pa. 1994).

[310] 522 N.W.2d 607 (Iowa 1994).

[311] Iowa Code Ann. § 614.1(11).

[312] *Krull*, 522 N.W.2d at 611.

[313] Id. at 614. Accord Kohn v. Darlington Cmty. Sch., 698 N.W.2d 794 (Wis. 2005); Coleman v. United Eng'rs & Constructors, Inc., 878 P.2d 996 (N.M. 1994). *Contra* Brennaman v. R.M.I. Co., 639 N.E.2d 425 (Ohio 1994) (holding Ohio's similar statute unconstitutional).

[314] See Prosser and Keeton on Torts ch. 19.

[315] See ch. 3, above.

[316] See § 4.2, above.

[317] "Plaintiffs allege that the information delivered was false and misleading, causing harm when actors relied on it. They seek to recover against publishers in strict liability in tort based on product defect, rather than on negligence or some form of misrepresentation." Products Liability Rest. § 19 cmt. *d*.

have ruled that books cannot be classified as "products," and many of the decisions are troubled at a deeper level by First Amendment implications of such potential liability.[318]

Books, Magazines, and Print Media

In products liability actions against publishers of books and other printed media, the fault is claimed to lie with the intangible information contained in the publication, not with the physical book itself.[319] For example, in *Winter v. G.P. Putnam's Sons*,[320] the plaintiff mushroom hunters suffered liver damage from eating mushrooms they thought were safe to eat based on mushroom descriptions in "The Encyclopedia of Mushrooms." The mushroom eaters sued the publisher, alleging products liability, breach of warranty, negligence, negligent misrepresentation, and false representations. The trial court granted the publisher's summary judgment motion, and the Ninth Circuit affirmed, reasoning that the materials that physically comprise the book may be a product, but the ideas expressed inside are not.[321] The court ruled that principles of products liability law, especially strict liability, may not be applied to the written word.[322] "We place a high priority on the unfettered exchange of ideas. We accept the risk that words and ideas have wings we cannot clip and which carry them we know not where. The threat of liability without fault . . . could seriously inhibit those who wish to share thoughts and theories."[323]

Other courts, with very few exceptions, have similarly refused to apply products liability principles, particularly a rule of strict liability, to the publication of dangerously false information. Decisions typically conclude that the message, as distinct from the packaging of the message, is not a "product" within the meaning of *Restatement (Second) of Torts* § 402A.[324] On this basis, courts have rejected strict liability claims against publishers of a liquid diet book, for the death of a woman from complications associated with the diet;[325] a medical textbook, for injuries to a nursing student from following a

---

[318] See, e.g., Sanders v. Acclaim Entm't, Inc., 188 F. Supp. 2d 1264 (D. Colo. 2002). See generally Gilles, "Poisonous" Publications and Other False Speech Physical Harm Cases, 37 Wake Forest L. Rev. 1073 (2002); Ausness, The Application of Product Liability Principles to Publishers of Violent or Sexually Explicit Material, 52 Fla. L. Rev. 603 (2000); Noah, Authors, Publishers, and Products Liability: Remedies for Defective Information in Books, 77 Or. L. Rev. 1195 (1998); Mince, Strict Liability for Commercial Intellect, 41 Cath. U. L. Rev. 617 (1992); Powell, Products Liability and the First Amendment: The Liability of Publishers for Failure to Warn, 9 J. Prod. Liab. 159 (1986); Am. Law Prod. Liab. 3d ch. 119.

[319] "Although a tangible medium such as a book, itself clearly a product, delivers the information, the plaintiff's grievance in such cases is with the information, not with the tangible medium." Products Liability Rest. § 19 cmt. *d*. But sometimes books themselves do carry dangerous physical defects. See Kids' Books Recalled for Choking, Cutting Risks, 41 Prod. Safety & Liab. Rep. (BNA) 1116 (Sept. 11, 2013).

[320] 938 F.2d 1033 (9th Cir. 1991) (Cal. law), noted 105 Harv. L. Rev. 1147 (1992).

[321] "A book containing Shakespeare's sonnets consists of two parts, the material and print therein, and the ideas and expression thereof. The first may be a product, but the second is not. . . . Products liability law is geared to the tangible world." 938 F.2d at 1034.

[322] "Strict liability principles even when applied to products are not without their costs. Innovation may be inhibited. We tolerate these losses. They are much less disturbing than the prospect that we might be deprived of the latest ideas and theories." Id. at 1035.

[323] Id.

[324] See, e.g., James v. Meow Media, Inc., 300 F.3d 683 (6th Cir. 2002) (Ky. law); Sanders v. Acclaim Entm't, Inc., 188 F. Supp. 2d 1264 (D. Colo. 2002); Wilson v. Midway Games, Inc., 198 F. Supp. 2d 167 (D. Conn. 2002). Compare Kercsmar v. Pen Argyl Area Sch. Dist., 1 Pa. D. & C. 3d 1 (Pa. Com. Pl. 1976) (action for injuries to secondary school student while conducting chemistry experiment described in textbook; *held*, textbook was a "good" under UCC § 2–105); Roccaforte v. Nintendo of Am., Inc., 802 So.2d 764, 766 (La. Ct. App. 2001) (by implication).

[325] See Smith v. Linn, 563 A.2d 123, 126 (Pa. Super. Ct. 1989), aff'd, 587 A.2d 309 (Pa. 1991). See also Gorran v. Atkins Nutritionals, Inc., 464 F. Supp. 2d 315, 324 (S.D.N.Y. 2006).

constipation remedy described in the textbook;[326] a travel guide, for injuries to a swimmer injured in hazardous beach conditions not mentioned in the guide;[327] a metalsmithing book, for injuries from the explosion of a caustic substance mixed according to the book's instructions;[328] and magazines and other formats, for harmful results spurred by the written word.[329] Reasoning that book merchants should not be required to evaluate the thought processes of every author of the thousands of books they sell, a court disallowed an implied warranty action against the retail seller of a cookbook which failed to warn that an ingredient was poisonous if not cooked.[330]

The one very limited situation in which courts have allowed tort claims against publishers of books and magazines is for the promotion of contract killing. Several courts have allowed claims against *Soldier of Fortune Magazine* for publishing advertisements of contract killers.[331] In one case,[332] a husband hired the person who placed such an ad in the magazine to kill his wife, and the job was done. In view of the nature of the magazine, and the fact that other ads explicitly offered criminal services, the district court allowed a negligence action for failure to investigate, reasoning that the First Amendment was not a bar because this form of commercial speech was not as stringently protected as core speech.[333] Without addressing the First Amendment issue, the court of appeals reversed, ruling that the advertisement was sufficiently ambiguous not to give rise to a duty by the defendant to refrain from publishing it.[334]

In *Rice v. Paladin Enterprises*,[335] the Fourth Circuit allowed a tort law aiding-and-abetting claim against the publisher of a "how-to" book for contract killers, including precise instructions on every gruesome detail of such projects. "[R]eadied by these instructions and steeled by these seductive adjurations from *Hit Man: A Technical Manual for Independent Contractors*, a copy of which was subsequently found in his apartment, James Perry brutally murdered Mildred Horn, her 8-year-old quadriplegic

---

326 See Jones v. J.B. Lippincott Co., 694 F. Supp. 1216 (D. Md. 1988).

327 See Birmingham v. Fodor's Travel Publ'ns, Inc., 833 P.2d 70 (Haw. 1992).

328 See Lewin v. McCreight, 655 F. Supp. 282 (E.D. Mich. 1987).

329 See, e.g., Way v. Boy Scouts of Am., 856 S.W.2d 230 (Tex. App. 1993) (Boys' Life magazine and advertising supplement for shooting sports; *held,* not "products"); Appleby v. Miller, 554 N.E.2d 773 (Ill. App. Ct. 1990) (strict liability in tort did not apply to defective standardized medical history intake forms, on which dentist relied in making diagnosis, allegedly resulting in improper treatment; forms were service, not product); Walters v. Seventeen Magazine, 241 Cal. Rptr. 101 (Ct. App. 1987) (publishers not liable for toxic shock syndrome caused by Playtex tampons advertised in Seventeen Magazine); Herceg v. Hustler Magazine, Inc., 565 F. Supp. 802, 803–04 (S.D. Tex. 1983) (boy died from trying "autoerotic asphyxiation" described in magazine article); Walter v. Bauer, 439 N.Y.S.2d 821, 822–23 (Sup. Ct. 1981) (student injured doing science project described in textbook), rev'd in part on other grounds, 451 N.Y.S.2d 533 (App. Div. 1982). *But see* Henneghan v. Crown Crafts Infant Prods., Inc., 868 F. Supp. 2d 1153, 1158 (W.D. Wash. 2012) (whether pediatrician who authored Baby Book promoting sale of defective Nojo baby sling that allegedly caused infant's death was a product seller under Washington products liability statute was for trier of fact).

330 See Cardozo v. True, 342 So.2d 1053 (Fla. Dist. Ct. App. 1977) (Dasheen plant, commonly known as "elephant's ears").

331 See Braun v. Soldier of Fortune Magazine, Inc., 968 F.2d 1110 (11th Cir. 1992) (Ga. law); Eimann v. Soldier of Fortune Magazine, Inc., 680 F. Supp. 863 (S.D. Tex. 1988), rev'd, 880 F.2d 830 (5th Cir. 1989) (2–1 decision); Norwood v. Soldier of Fortune Magazine, Inc., 651 F. Supp. 1397 (W.D. Ark. 1987).

332 Eimann v. Soldier of Fortune Magazine, Inc., 680 F. Supp. 863 (S.D. Tex. 1988).

333 Id. at 865–66.

334 Eimann v. Soldier of Fortune Magazine, Inc., 880 F.2d 830, 838 (5th Cir. 1989) (Tex. law) ("we decline to impose on publishers the obligation to reject all ambiguous advertisements for products or services that might pose a threat of harm").

335 128 F.3d 233 (4th Cir. 1997) (Md. law).

son Trevor, and Trevor's nurse."[336] Mildred Horn's ex-husband had hired Perry, the contract killer, so he could receive his son's $2 million settlement for injuries that had left him paralyzed. In conducting the murders, Perry meticulously followed numerous details from the *Hit Man* manual. Since the defendant publisher stipulated that it targeted the book to murderers and would-be murderers and that it knew and intended that the manual would be used for contract murders, the court found no difficulty in ruling that a jury could find that *Hit Man* had "little, if any, purpose beyond the unlawful one of facilitating murder," and so was unprotected by the First Amendment.[337] After the court allowed the action to proceed, the publisher settled the case for millions of dollars.[338]

Navigational Charts

One type of case in which the courts have allowed claims against a publisher involves the publication of aeronautical charts containing false information that causes a pilot, for example, to fly into a mountain not shown on the chart.[339] "[A]lthough a sheet of paper might not be dangerous, per se, it would be difficult indeed to conceive of a salable commodity with more inherent lethal potential than an aid to aircraft navigation that, contrary to its own design standards, fails to list the highest land mass immediately surrounding a landing site."[340] Noting that the total reliance pilots necessarily place on the accuracy of navigational charts can directly cause a fatal crash if the information proves false,[341] courts have distinguished navigational charts from other types of publications because the very purpose of such charts is to portray physical phenomena rather than ideas. While such cases may fit more comfortably in the law of misrepresentation and express warranty,[342] there seems little harm in allowing such claims under the conventional product defect umbrella.

Computer Aided Design (CAD) File Publication

An issue addressed earlier,[343] is whether publishers of computer aided design (CAD) files or blueprints for 3D-printed products with defects that cause harm should bear responsibility for such harm. While courts have yet to address this issue, surely they will need to do so as the availability of 3D printing technology evolves and spreads. For example, if a person publishes a design for 3D printing of a kitchen knife, and the blade's

---

[336] Id. at 239.

[337] Id. at 267. See also Wilson v. Paladin Enters., 186 F. Supp. 2d 1140, 1144 (D. Or. 2001) (similar case against publisher of Hit Man).

[338] Liability Week 6 (May 24, 1999).

[339] See, e.g., Fluor Corp. v. Jeppesen & Co., 216 Cal. Rptr. 68, 71–72 (Ct. App. 1985) (jet pilot crashed into mountain not depicted on approach chart, although lower mountain was). See also Times Mirror Co. v. Sisk, 593 P.2d 924 (Ariz. Ct. App. 1978). In Saloomey v. Jeppesen & Co., 707 F.2d 671 (2d Cir. 1983) (Colo. law), the chart showed the Martinsburg, W. Va., airport as having a full ILS instrument approach, including a glideslope (providing pilots with vertical descent information), rather than only a localizer (providing pilots only with horizontal guidance information). While attempting an approach, an off-duty commercial pilot flew his personal Beechcraft Sierra into a 1,600-foot ridge. Martinsburg airport (MRB) now has a full ILS.

[340] 216 Cal. Rptr. at 71–72.

[341] "In those cases, the charts were physically used in the operation of the aircraft at the time of the accident. The inaccurate data directly caused or was alleged to have caused the accidents in question in the same manner in which a broken compass or an inaccurate altimeter would have caused a plane to crash." Way v. Boy Scouts of Am., 856 S.W.2d 230, 238–39 (Tex. App. 1993) (distinguishing charts from magazines).

[342] See Products Liability Rest. § 19 Reporters' Note to cmt. *d*; Phillips, Information Liability: The Possible Chilling Effect of Tort Claims Against Producers of Geographic Information Systems Data, 26 Fla. St. U. L. Rev. 743 (1999).

[343] See § 10:3, *3D-printed guns*, above.

design or recommended material causes it to break and injure the user, courts will need to decide whether the publisher bears responsibility for such defective product accidents. As one practitioner observes: "While the legal, practical and societal implications associated with 3D printing are uncertain, without a doubt 3D printing will change the trajectory of traditional product liability cases in the future."[344]

Products Liability and Freedom of Expression

Whether and to what extent the law of products liability should provide recovery for persons injured by the transmission of improper information and ideas involves a host of intriguing questions, including the propriety of extending legal principles designed to provide a remedy for injuries caused by defective chattels to injuries resulting from the dissemination of thought. Once private law begins to press upon the freedom of expression, First Amendment rights are implicated.

While the menace of products liability claims to free expression is real, the threat to First Amendment interests may be overdrawn. If the challenged information is false or incites violence, then it may well fall outside the protected sphere of freedom of expression.[345] In any event, plaintiffs in such cases face a major hurdle in showing how the provision of such information might have been a proximate cause of violently inflicted harm.[346] The courts appear to have drawn a sound distinction between the expression of thoughts and ideas, which needs constitutional protection, and the communication of factual information (the accuracy of which is capable of objective determination), which needs little or no breathing space. While line drawing of this type may invite error and abuse,[347] it may sometimes be necessary in this context to accommodate the competing goals of tort law and freedom of expression.

Of the various types of injury claims arising out of publications for which plaintiffs have sought recovery under products liability law, only two are clearly deserving of protection. Claims for publishing inaccurate aeronautical charts and manuals for contract murder both deserve a private remedy, and neither form of conduct needs constitutional protection. Closely analogous claims, such as publishing false information

---

[344] Bonti, Ready, Aim, Print: 3D Printing, Guns and Product Liability Cases, 38 No. 1 Trial Advoc. (FDLA) 30 (2019). See also Beck and Jacobson, 3d Printing: What Could Happen to Products Liability When Users (and Everyone Else in Between) Become Manufacturers, 18 Minn. J.L. Sci. & Tech. 143 (2017); Pantella, Ready, Print, Fire! Regulating the 3D-Printing Revolution, 8 Case W. Reserve J.L. Tech. & Internet 1 (2017); Staed, Open Source Download Mishaps and Product Liability: Who Is to Blame and What Are the Remedies?, 36 St. Louis U. Pub. L. Rev. 169 (2017).

[345] *But see* Davidson v. Time Warner, Inc., 1997 WL 405907, at *15–22 (S.D. Tex. 1997) (thorough discussion, rejecting claim that cop-killing rap song was unprotected expression).

[346] Even if the provision of information or entertainment in some way stimulates a violent act, the violence itself nearly always supersedes any responsibility of the publisher. See, e.g., James v. Meow Media, Inc., 300 F.3d 683, 699 (6th Cir. 2002) (Ky. law) (recovery against makers and distributors of video games, violent movies, and obscene internet websites for student murders at Kentucky school precluded by superseding cause; discussing other cases); Sanders v. Acclaim Entm't, Inc., 188 F. Supp. 2d 1264 (D. Colo. 2002) (criminal acts of killers were superseding cause).

[347] In Winter v. G.P. Putnam's Sons, 938 F.2d 1033, 1035 (9th Cir. 1991) (Cal. law), the court rejected such a distinction:

> Plaintiffs suggest, however, that our fears would be groundless were strict liability rules applied only to books that give instruction on how to accomplish a physical activity and that are intended to be used as part of an activity that is inherently dangerous. We find such a limitation illusory. Ideas are often intimately linked with proposed action, and it would be difficult to draw such a bright line. While "How To" books are a special genre, we decline to attempt to draw a line that puts "How To Live A Good Life" books beyond the reach of strict liability while leaving "How To Exercise Properly" books within its reach.

about poisonous mushrooms and advertisements for contract killers, also may be proper for tort law treatment, but evaluating such claims requires considerable caution.[348] The proper basis for false safety information claims appears to lie in the law of tortious misrepresentation and breach of express warranty; and the contract killer cases fit most comfortably within tort law rules on aiding and abetting,[349] which is the essence of those claims. Thus, while the "strict" liability rules of products liability law may offer a tempting haven to plaintiffs in either type of case, other bases of recovery may be preferable to conventional theories of products liability.

§ 16.8 ELECTRONIC TECHNOLOGY

Electronic technology issues in products liability law range from harms caused by stray voltage, to misleading information posted on a website, to errant autonomous software algorithms. Beginning with a discussion of electricity, followed by games, music, video games, and websites, and concluding with computer software, liability for harm from electronic technology is the focus of this section.

Electricity

Invisible and elusive, electricity is hard to comprehend. Its mysterious character puts in question whether electricity should be considered a "product" at all, subject to the principles of products liability law.[350] "What is electricity? Simply stated, it is a force, like the wind . . . ."[351] Electricity is "a form of energy that can be made or produced by men, confined, controlled, transmitted and distributed to be used as an energy source for heat, power and light and is distributed in the stream of commerce."[352] On this reasoning, a majority of courts hold that electricity is a "product" that may subject its suppliers, electrical utility companies, to strict liability in tort[353] for selling it in a

---

[348] The court in Winter v. G.P. Putnam's Sons, id. at 1036, rejected the plaintiff's argument that the Encyclopedia of Mushrooms was analogous to an aeronautical chart because the purpose of both was to describe natural features to promote safety:

> Aeronautical charts are highly technical tools. They are graphic depictions of technical, mechanical data. The best analogy to an aeronautical chart is a compass. Both may be used to guide an individual who is engaged in an activity requiring certain knowledge of natural features. Computer software that fails to yield the result for which it was designed may be another. In contrast, *The Encyclopedia of Mushrooms* is like a book on how to *use* a compass or an aeronautical chart. The chart itself is like a physical "product" while the "How to Use" book is pure thought and expression.

Compare Schultz, Application of Strict Products Liability to Aeronautical Chart Publishers, 64 Air L. & Com. 431 (1999) (criticizing *Winter* court's analogy of chart to compass).

[349] See Rest. (2d) Torts § 876. See § 11.3, above.

[350] See Ferry, Defining Power: Electrons and the Law, 32 Envtl. L. Rep. 10038 (2002); Myers, The Sale of Electricity in a Deregulated Industry: Should Article 2 of the Uniform Commercial Code Govern?, 54 SMU L. Rev. 1051 (2001); Cantu, Twenty-Five Years of Strict Product Liability Law: The Transformation and Present Meaning of Section 402A, 25 St. Mary's L.J. 327 (1993); Cantu, The Illusive Meaning of the Term "Product" Under Section 402A of the Restatement (Second) of Torts, 44 Okla. L. Rev. 635 (1991); Comment, 26 Cap. U. L. Rev. 421 (1997); Note, 29 Suffolk U. L. Rev. 161 (1995); Annot., Products Liability: Electricity, 60 A.L.R.4th 732 (1988); Am. Law Prod. Liab. 3d ch. 117 (electricity and electrical equipment); Products Liability Rest. § 19 and cmt. *d*.

[351] Pierce v. Pacific Gas & Elec. Co., 212 Cal. Rptr. 283, 288 n.3 (Ct. App. 1985) (holding that electricity is a product under § 402A).

[352] Ransome v. Wisconsin Elec. Power Co., 275 N.W.2d 641, 643 (Wis. 1979).

[353] Or possibly to liability in warranty. See Myers, The Sale of Electricity in a Deregulated Industry: Should Article 2 of the Uniform Commercial Code Govern?, 54 SMU L. Rev. 1051 (2001) (arguing that electricity should be treated as a "good" for Article 2 purposes).

defective condition.[354] These courts, sometimes calling on policy rationales,[355] reason that once electricity passes through a customer's meter, it is a product that has been sold into the stream of commerce and so is subject to strict liability for harm if it is defective.[356] Such cases typically involve power surges, causing personal injury or property loss by the excessive flow of electricity into a building.[357] Yet a quite substantial minority of courts refuse to apply strict liability to electrical injuries, often reasoning that the provision of electricity is a service rather than the sale of a product,[358] whether the harm is caused before or after the current passes through a consumer's meter.[359]

As for electrical injuries from high-voltage transmission lines, typically incurred when the plaintiff hits a power line with some tall object,[360] courts are in general agreement that negligence alone is the proper basis of liability[361] and that neither strict

[354] See, e.g., O'Neill v. Connecticut Light & Power Co., 2020 WL 1889124 (Conn. Super. Ct. 2020) (affirming jury verdict for plaintiff on negligence and products liability claims; "electricity is a product for the purposes of The Connecticut Products Liability Law once it passes through the meter of a consumer"); Cincinnati Ins. Co. v. PPL Corp., 979 F. Supp. 2d 602 (E.D. Pa. 2013); Travelers Indem. Co. of Am. v. Connecticut Light & Power Co., 2008 WL 2447351, at *5 (Conn. Super. Ct. 2008) (house fire caused by electricity surge traced to defective component maintained by power company); Pierce v. Pacific Gas & Elec. Co., 212 Cal. Rptr. 283 (Ct. App. 1985) (plaintiff injured by surge of 7,000 volts of electricity into her home traced to defective component in utility's system). See also Bryant v. Tri-County Elec. Membership Corp., 844 F. Supp. 347 (W.D. Ky. 1994) (series of voltage spikes destroyed electrical transformer switch over time, causing it to explode, setting saw mill on fire; claims for warranty and strict liability in tort, in addition to negligence, allowed).

[355] The rationales are summarized in Am. Law Prod. Liab. 3d § 117:4.

[356] See Note, 29 Suffolk U. L. Rev. 161 (1995); Annot., Products Liability: Electricity, 60 A.L.R.4th 732 (1988). This position is endorsed by the Products Liability Rest. § 19(a) cmt. *d* ("the distinction drawn between pre- and post-delivery is reasonable"); Am. Law Prod. Liab. 3d § 117:2.

[357] See note 354, above. If the surge is caused by lightning, however, it is not placed in the stream of commerce by the utility. See Mancuso v. Southern Cal. Edison Co., 283 Cal. Rptr. 300, 308 (Ct. App. 1991).

[358] Or that even defective current may not be unreasonably dangerous. See Elgin Airport Inn, Inc. v. Commonwealth Edison Co., 432 N.E.2d 259 (Ill. 1982). See generally Nazar v. Palli, 2013 WL 1867072, at *4 (Conn. Super. Ct. 2013) (water; "companies that provide electricity, gas and/or water are considered to be service providers, and not sellers or manufacturers of products").

[359] See, e.g., Universal Underwriters Ins. Grp. v. Public Serv. Elec. & Gas Co., 103 F. Supp. 2d 744 (D.N.J. 2000) (defendant not subject to strict liability for failure to shut off electricity in response to emergency); Balke v. Central Mo. Elec. Coop., 966 S.W.2d 15 (Mo. Ct. App. 1997); Wyrulec Co. v. Schutt, 866 P.2d 756 (Wyo. 1993) (electricity is service, not product); Bowen v. Niagara Mohawk Power Corp., 590 N.Y.S.2d 628 (App. Div. 1992); Otte v. Dayton Power & Light Co., 523 N.E.2d 835 (Ohio 1988); Rodgers v. Chimney Rock Pub. Power Dist., 345 N.W.2d 12 (Neb. 1984); Wood v. Public Serv. Co. of N.H., 317 A.2d 576 (N.H. 1974). The *Otte* court, 523 N.E.2d at 838, explained its position:

> A "product" is anything made by human industry or art. Electricity appears to fall outside this definition. This is so because electricity is the flow of electrically charged particles along a conductor. [A utility] does not manufacture electrically charged particles, but rather, sets in motion the necessary elements that allow the flow of electricity. What we have here is a purported defect in the distribution system. Such a system is, in our view, a service.

[360] See, e.g., Aguirre v. Home Depot U.S.A., Inc., 2012 WL 3639078, at *1 (E.D. Cal. 2012) (pole saw extended from boom lift); Lempke v. Osmose Util. Servs., Inc., 2012 WL 94497, at *1 (W.D. Pa. 2012); Martinez v. Duke Energy Corp., 130 Fed. Appx. 629 (4th Cir. 2005) (S.C. law) (crane); Hayes v. Entergy Corp., 850 So.2d 916 (La. Ct. App. 2003) (logging shear); Smith v. Florida Power & Light Co., 857 So.2d 224 (Fla. Dist. Ct. App. 2003) (boom of crane); Monroe v. Savannah Elec. & Power Co., 471 S.E.2d 854 (Ga. 1996) (towed shrimp boat); Martinez v. Grant Cnty. Pub. Util. Dist. No. 2, 851 P.2d 1248 (Wash. Ct. App. 1993) (farmhand touched 7,620 volt wire located 27½ feet off ground with 32-foot irrigation pipe); Fuller v. Central Me. Power Co., 598 A.2d 457 (Me. 1991) (ladder); Priest v. Brown, 396 S.E.2d 638 (S.C. Ct. App. 1990) (deceased tried to move downed power line).

[361] See, e.g., Martinez v. Grant Cnty. Pub. Util. Dist. No. 2, 851 P.2d 1248, 1250 (Wash. Ct. App. 1993) (recognizing "the societal necessity of transmitting lethal amounts of electricity through uninsulated overhead power lines through rural areas; it does not impose strict liability on electrical power companies for injuries arising out of contact with those power lines," but affirming jury finding of no negligence on facts of case).

liability for an abnormally dangerous activity,[362] nor strict products liability,[363] is an appropriate basis for recovery. The courts reason that electricity in high-voltage lines is still under the ownership and control of the supplier, and that neither the high-power line nor the electricity in it have been prepared or made available for consumption or sale.[364] Thus, courts consider electricity in this form not yet to be a "product" in the "stream of commerce"[365] or reason simply that it is not "sold" until it passes through the meter of a customer.[366]

Courts are split, however, on whether an electrical utility should be liable for damage to dairy herds from naturally-occurring stray voltage from transmission lines or other sources,[367] some courts allowing strict liability and other claims for such losses,[368] other courts ruling that strict liability in tort or warranty is not appropriate.[369]

Section 19 of the *Restatement (Third) of Torts: Products Liability* applies the principles of that *Restatement* to electricity "when the context of [its] distribution and use is sufficiently analogous to the distribution and use of tangible personal property that it is appropriate to apply the rules stated in this Restatement."[370]

Finally, courts have held that the use of x-rays[371] and other forms of radiation therapy[372] for medical treatment is the provision of a service, not the sale of a product that will support a claim for strict products liability.[373] Products liability actions against

---

Although some courts have held that electric companies are under a duty to exercise the highest degree of care to prevent injury, see, e.g., Cerretti v. Flint Hills Rural Elec. Coop. Ass'n, 837 P.2d 330, 335 (Kan. 1992), the better view is that the standard of care is reasonable care under all the circumstances. See, e.g., Wyrulec Co. v. Schutt, 866 P.2d 756, 762 (Wyo. 1993). See generally Prosser and Keeton on Torts § 34.

[362] See, e.g., Wyrulec Co. v. Schutt, 866 P.2d 756, 761 (Wyo. 1993); Wirth v. Mayrath Indus., 278 N.W.2d 789 (N.D. 1979); Wertz v. Holy Cross Elec. Ass'n, 512 P.2d 286 (Colo. App. 1973). See also § 5.9, above.

[363] See cases in note 359, above.

[364] See Am. Law Prod. Liab. 3d § 117:3.

[365] See, e.g., Fuller v. Central Me. Power Co., 598 A.2d 457 (Me. 1991) (electricity in high-voltage transmission line hit by plaintiff's ladder was not "product" for purposes of state's products liability statute); Smith v. Home Light & Power Co., 734 P.2d 1051, 1055 (Colo. 1987).

[366] See, e.g., Travelers Indem. Co. of Am. v. Connecticut Light & Power Co., 2008 WL 2447351, at *4 (Conn. Super. Ct. 2008); Darling v. Central Vt. Pub. Serv. Corp., 762 A.2d 826 (Vt. 2000); Monroe v. Savannah Elec. & Power Co., 471 S.E.2d 854 (Ga. 1996) (no strict liability for death when towed boat hit high power line).

[367] See Annot., 91 A.L.R.5th 517 (2001); Products Liability Rest. § 19 Reporters' Note to cmt. *d*.

[368] See, e.g., James v. Beauregard Elec. Coop., Inc., 736 So.2d 353 (La. Ct. App. 1999); ZumBerge v. Northern States Power Co., 481 N.W.2d 103 (Minn. Ct. App. 1992) (negligence, breach of warranty, and strict liability); Public Serv. Ind., Inc. v. Nichols, 494 N.E.2d 349, 355 (Ind. Ct. App. 1986); Schriner v. Pennsylvania Power & Light Co., 501 A.2d 1128 (Pa. Super. Ct. 1985).

[369] See, e.g., Pillow v. Entergy Corp., 828 So.2d 83 (La. Ct. App. 2002); G & K Dairy v. Princeton Elec. Plant Bd., 781 F. Supp. 485 (W.D. Ky. 1991) (allowing negligence claim but denying claims for breach of warranty and strict liability in tort because stray voltage not "good" or "product" that defendant sold to plaintiff); Otte v. Dayton Power & Light Co., 523 N.E.2d 835 (Ohio 1988).

[370] Comment *d* to this section explains the contexts in which courts have applied strict liability principles to electricity.

[371] See, e.g., Dubin v. Michael Reese Hosp. & Med. Ctr., 415 N.E.2d 350, 352 (Ill. 1980) ("the true object of [the complaint] is the alleged error in professional judgment and not . . . the nature of X-radiation itself"). See also Greenberg v. Michael Reese Hosp., 415 N.E.2d 390 (Ill. 1980); Pitler v. Michael Reese Hosp., 415 N.E.2d 1255 (Ill. App. Ct. 1980).

[372] See, e.g., Nevauex v. Park Place Hosp., Inc., 656 S.W.2d 923 (Tex. App. 1983) (radiation burns from cobalt therapy).

[373] See Rest. (Third) of Torts: Products Liability § 19 cmt. *d*.

manufacturers and sellers of cell phones alleging health risks from radio-frequency emissions have been largely unsuccessful.[374]

In *Farina v. Nokia Inc.*,[375] the Third Circuit affirmed dismissal of a class action alleging breach of warranty and other claims against cell phone manufacturers and retailers, holding that conflict preemption barred the claims.[376] Allowing a jury to weigh the adequacy of regulations designed to protect the public, reasoned the court, would erect an obstacle to the accomplishment of the FCC's radio frequency emissions regulatory scheme and "the full purposes and objective of Congress."[377] But the controversy over the hazards of cell phone use continues.[378]

Games, Music, Video Games, and Websites

First Amendment protection for publications, considered in the last section, extends as well to distributors of games, recordings, movies, video games, and internet websites.[379] In an action against the publisher and manufacturer of the game "Dungeons and Dragons" for the suicide death of a player thereof, the court upheld the defendants' First Amendment defense and further ruled that the defendant-publishers had no duty to warn mentally fragile persons of the possibly dangerous consequences of playing the

---

[374] See, e.g., Stewart v. AT & T Mobility LLC, 2011 WL 3626654, at *5 (D.S.C. 2011) (plaintiff failed to produce expert witness establishing that radiation emitted during a single call from allegedly defective phone proximately caused injury). See generally Shields and Cortez, Cell Phone Radiation Tied in U.S. Study to Rare Tumor in Rats, 46 Prod. Safety & Liab. Rep. 157 (February 2, 2018); Hallam, Cortez, and Kharif, Mobile-Phone Link to Cancer Stirred Up by Rat Study, 44 Prod. Safety & Liab. Rep. (BNA) 597 (June 13, 2016); Sherman, No Implied Effect: The "Safe" FCC Cell Phone Radiation Standard and Tort Immunity by Implied Conflict Preemption, 19 Rich. J.L. & Tech. 13 (2013). *But see* FDA, Review of Published Literature Between 2008 and 2018 of Relevance to Radiofrequency Radiation and Cancer 5 (Feb. 2020) ("the available epidemiological and cancer incidence data continues to support the Agency's determination that there are no quantifiable adverse health effects in humans caused by exposures at or under the current cell phone exposure limits").

Compare Environmental Health Tr. v. Federal Commc'ns Comm'n, 9 F.4th 893, 914 (D.C. Cir. 2021) (2–1 decision) (requiring the FCC to "(i) provide a reasoned explanation for its decision to retain its testing procedures for determining whether cell phones and other portable electronic devices comply with its guidelines, (ii) address the impacts of RF [radiofrequency] radiation on children, the health implications of long-term exposure to RF radiation, the ubiquity of wireless devices, and other technological developments that have occurred since the Commission last updated its guidelines, and (iii) address the impacts of RF radiation on the environment").

[375] 625 F.3d 97, 134 (3d Cir. 2010) (Pa. law).

[376] Id. at 134.

[377] Id. The Supreme Court denied certiorari in Farina v. Nokia, Inc., 565 U.S. 928 (2011). See also Kinsey v. Virginia Elec. & Power Co., 861 S.E.2d 59, 64 (Va. 2021) (conflict preemption barred plaintiffs' claims alleging injuries from smart meter radio frequency emissions).

[378] See note 374, above. Apart from whether cell phones cause cancer, infertility, pego itch, or lower bone density, claims against cellular companies and cell phone manufacturers for car accidents and other types of harm usually are dismissed. See, e.g., Estate of Doyle v. Sprint/Nextel Corp., 248 P.3d 947, 951 (Okla. Civ. App. 2010) (collision; no duty to warn users against driving while talking); Thomas v. Kyocera Wireless Corp., 2012 WL 379481, at *1 (N.D. Miss. 2012) (hearing loss; "And the phone was like boosh. And then when it did that, I threwed [sic] it and my mother ducked. And she said, girl, what's wrong with you, why did you throw that phone? I said, don't you see that phone smoking? It was smoking."). See generally Brown, Steering the Nation's Cell Phone Laws in the Right Direction, 31 Temp. J. Sci. Tech. & Envtl. L. 31 (2012); Note, 59 Drake L. Rev. 217 (2010) ("crashes caused by cell phone use are common and often fatal").

[379] See Brown v. Entertainment Merchs. Ass'n, 564 U.S. 786, 790 (2011) (affirming unconstitutionality of 2009 California statute banning sale or rental of violent video games to minors; "video games qualify for First Amendment protection"); Interactive Digital Software Ass'n v. St. Louis Cnty., Mo., 329 F.3d 954 (8th Cir. 2003) (video games protected speech under First Amendment), reversing 200 F. Supp. 2d 1126 (E.D. Mo. 2002); Swartz and Swartz, Holding the Electronic Game Industry Accountable for the Deleterious Effects Violent Video Games Can Have on Our Children, 147 Products Advisory 1 (West, May 2001); Note, 60 Ala. L. Rev. 519, 530–36 (2009) (violent video games).

game.[380] Likewise, in an action against musician Ozzy Osbourne, his composer, and CBS Records for damages arising from the suicide of a listener, the court held that music is also entitled to First Amendment protection, that the song did not fall within the incitement exception, and that the listener's suicide was unforeseeable.[381] For similar reasons, the trial court granted summary judgment to Tupac Shakur, a rap "artist," and the record companies that produced and distributed his recording, "2Pacalypse Now," for the murder of a police officer in a manner suggested by the recording.[382]

Courts have rejected a number of claims against manufacturers of video games and other visual entertainment products, often concluding that products liability principles do not apply to them because they simply are not "products."[383] *James v. Meow Media, Inc.*[384] was a case arising out of the massacre of Kentucky high school students by a fellow student who took six guns to school and shot other students after their prayer session. In a products liability suit against makers and distributors of violent video games, a violent movie, and obscene internet websites of which the assailant was an avid consumer, the parents of the murdered students claimed that the defendants made and distributed these materials in a defective and unreasonably dangerous condition giving rise to strict liability in tort under *Restatement (Second) of Torts* § 402A.[385] Not claiming that the tangible materials themselves were defective, the parents' claim instead was that intangible and subliminal thoughts, ideas, and messages contained within the products presented a danger of which the defendants had a duty to warn. Finding that the few analogous cases and the *Products Liability Restatement* unanimously opposed extending products liability law to such materials, the court ruled that "intangible thoughts, ideas, and messages contained within games, movies, and website materials are not products for purposes of strict products liability."[386]

---

[380] See Watters v. TSR, Inc., 715 F. Supp. 819 (W.D. Kan. 1989), aff'd, 904 F.2d 378, 381 (6th Cir. 1990) (Kan. law) (courts have never extended strict liability to "words or pictures").

[381] See McCollum v. CBS, Inc., 249 Cal. Rptr. 187 (Ct. App. 1988).

[382] See Davidson v. Time Warner, Inc., 1997 WL 405907, at *15–22 (S.D. Tex. 1997) (finding all case law against a products liability claim, together with constitutional problems).

[383] See, e.g., James v. Meow Media, Inc., 300 F.3d 683 (6th Cir. 2002) (Ky. law); Sanders v. Acclaim Entm't, Inc., 188 F. Supp. 2d 1264 (D. Colo. 2002); Wilson v. Midway Games, Inc., 198 F. Supp. 2d 167 (D. Conn. 2002). Compare Roccaforte v. Nintendo of Am., Inc., 802 So.2d 764, 766 (La. Ct. App. 2001) (by implication); Kercsmar v. Pen Argyl Area Sch. Dist., 1 Pa. D. & C. 3d 1 (Pa. Com. Pl. 1976) (action for injuries to secondary school student while conducting chemistry experiment described in textbook; *held*, textbook was "good" under UCC § 2–105).

Augmented Reality/Virtual Reality. Augmented reality (AR) and virtual reality (metaverse) devices and apps can give rise to real-world dangers. For a consideration of failure to warn problems in the context of the AR Pokémon Go game, which combines GPS and smart phone cameras to help players find and control virtual creatures, see Steinberg, Can Pokémon Go and Product Liability Coexist?, Prod. Liab. & Toxics L. (Aug. 17, 2016). A public nuisance class-action against the Pokémon Go developer brought by homeowners plagued by trespassing players received tentative settlement approval. See Steinberg, Pokémon Go Trespass Settlement Gets Tentative Nod, Prod. Liab. & Toxics L. (May 3, 2019). See also Karalis, VR Injuries—A Cost of Doing Business in the Metaverse?, Prod. Liab. & Toxics L. (Mar. 3, 2022); Comment, Pokémon Go-Es Directly to Court: How Pokémon Go Illustrates the Issue of Virtual Trespass and the Need for Evolved Tort Laws, 49 Tex. Tech L. Rev. 959 (2017).

[384] 90 F. Supp. 2d 798 (W.D. Ky. 2000) (noting that plaintiffs' products liability theory was "deeply flawed"), aff'd, 300 F.3d 683, 700 (6th Cir. 2002).

[385] 90 F. Supp. 2d at 809.

[386] Id. at 810. See also Doe v. MySpace, Inc., 629 F. Supp. 2d 663, 665 (E.D. Tex. 2009) (products liability claims barred under the Communications Decency Act; insufficient evidence that MySpace.com was "an information content provider" subject to claims arising from communications between sexual predator and victim on website).

The Communications Decency Act of 1996[387] broadly immunizes interactive website providers from liability for harmful consequences of communications by third parties. *Doe v. MySpace, Inc.*,[388] involved claims against a social networking website called "MySpace." A user of the website would create a profile that included contact information and whatever additional information (on personality, interests, and the like) the user chose to provide. In addition to providing a structure for this information, MySpace provided users with a means to search for, browse, and communicate with other users as a way to meet and get to know people remotely. *Doe* was brought by the parents of a 15-year-old girl who committed suicide after being lured from her home and assaulted by a sexual predator she had "met" on the website. Rejecting the parents' claims that MySpace should have implemented safety measures to prevent such communications, the court ruled that MySpace.com, by simply providing an organized means by which users could provide information to one another, was not itself "an information content provider" and so was sheltered from such claims under the Act.[389]

Computer Software

Whether manufacturers of computer software should be subject to products liability law for personal injuries caused by defective software is a perplexing question.[390] Scholars increasingly grapple with whether and how products liability law might apply to artificial intelligence algorithms and autonomous systems in various contexts, such

[387] 47 U.S.C. § 230. See also § 15.2, notes 102–110, for a discussion of § 230 and products liability claims against internet marketplace providers for harm from sales of third-party defective products.

[388] 629 F. Supp. 2d 663 (E.D. Tex. 2009).

[389] Id. at 665. See also In re Facebook, Inc., 625 S.W.3d 80, 96 (Tex. 2021) (§ 230 immunity barred plaintiffs' products liability claims against Facebook for failing to warn of dangers from sex traffickers); Great Northern Insurance Co. v. Amazon.com, Inc., 524 F. Supp. 3d 852, 859 (N.D. Ill. 2021) (granting summary judgment to Amazon under § 230 on plaintiff's negligent misrepresentation claim); Daniel v. Armslist, LLC, 926 N.W.2d 710, 727 (Wis. 2019) (§ 230 immunity applied to website on which semiautomatic handgun and high-capacity magazines, used in mass shooting, were illegally purchased); Seaver v. Estate of Cazes, 2019 WL 2176316, at *3 (D. Utah 2019) (§ 230 immunity applied to provider on "dark web" of Tor browser used for the sale of illicit drugs to deceased 13-year-old boy); Herrick v. Grindr, LLC, 306 F. Supp. 3d 579, 588–92 (S.D.N.Y. 2018), aff'd, 765 Fed. Appx. 586 (2d Cir. 2019) (plaintiff's products liability claims against internet dating site for gay and bi-sexual men barred by § 230). *But see* Lemmon v. Snap, Inc., 995 F.3d 1085, 1094 (9th Cir. 2021) (§ 230 did not shield designer of mobile app that predictably encouraged young decedents to drive at unsafe speeds); State Farm Fire & Casualty Co. v. Amazon.com, Inc., 390 F. Supp. 3d 964, 974 (W.D. Wis. 2019) ("Amazon is not immune under the Communications Decency Act for claims that it sold a defective product"); Maynard v. Snapchat, Inc., 816 S.E.2d 77, 81 (Ga. Ct. App. 2018) (passenger injured in car accident after driver exceeded 100 mph while using Snapchat's Speed Filter mobile device app; no § 230 immunity where driver had not uploaded or posted her third-party content to Snapchat's website). See also Karalis, Section 230 Challenged by Contract, Product Claims, Prod. Liab. & Toxics L. (July 30, 2021) (discussing *Lemmon v. Snap*, above, this note).

[390] "The law of software liability seems to be strangely undeveloped, considering the size of the software industry and the infiltration of software into virtually every aspect of our lives. . . . Whether or not software is a product [or a service] has always been a matter of some controversy." 68 Am. Jur. Proof of Facts 3d 333 §§ 2, 4 (2022 update). See also Bass and Redick, Products Liability: Design and Manufacturing Defects § 2:18 (2021 update) ("Standard off-the-shelf software may ultimately be determined to be a product subject to strict liability, while 'tailor-made' software most likely will be treated as a service."); S. Elvy, A Commercial Law of Privacy and Security for the Internet of Things ch. 5 (Cambridge University Press 2021) (products liability law and the hybrid nature of internet-connected devices); Chagal-Feferkorn, Am I an Algorithm or a Product? When Products Liability Should Apply to Algorithmic Decision-Makers, 30 Stan. L. & Pol'y Rev. 61 (2019); Elvy, Hybrid Transactions and the Internet of Things: Goods, Services, or Software?, 74 Wash. & Lee L. Rev. 77 (2017).

as robotic and other medical devices,[391] and more generally.[392] A number of commentators favor the application of products liability theories in such situations,[393] and at least a couple of courts have allowed claims against Snapchat for a design that encouraged reckless driving and a design defect claim against a cell phone software provider for a 911 system that didn't work properly.[394] Other cases involve commercial claims for economic loss without physical harm;[395] and various consumer class actions for product software defects asserting breach of warranty, misrepresentation, and

---

[391] For legal issues that may arise as artificial intelligence algorithms in medical devices learn and change after their original FDA approval, see, e.g., Tschider, Medical Device Artificial Intelligence: The New Tort Frontier, 46 B.Y.U. L. Rev. 1551 (2021); Malek, Anderson, and Schmitt, Modernizing the Approach to Regulating Software as a Medical Device, Prod. Liab. & Toxics L. (June 10, 2019); Kramer, Medical Device Makers May Risk Liability Following FDA Effort, Prod. Liab. & Toxics L. (May 14, 2019); Merken, Who Is Liable for Faulty Artificial Intelligence in Health Care?, 45 Prod. Safety & Liab. Rep. (BNA) 1207 (Dec. 11, 2017); Price, Artificial Intelligence in Health Care: Applications and Legal Issues, ABA SciTech Law., Fall 2017, at 10. See also FDA, Artificial Intelligence/Machine Learning (AI/ML)-Based Software as a Medical Device (SaMD) Action Plan (Jan. 2021).

[392] See, e.g., Chagal-Feferkorn, How Can I Tell If My Algorithm Was Reasonable?, 27 Mich. Tech. L. Rev. 213 (2021); Nersessian and Mancha, From Automation To Autonomy: Legal and Ethical Responsibility Gaps In Artificial Intelligence Innovation, 27 Mich. Tech. L. Rev. 55 (2020); Rachum-Twaig, Whose Robot Is It Anyway?: Liability For Artificial-Intelligence-Based Robots, 2020 U. Ill. L. Rev. 1141 (suggesting a liability framework structured around rules, including duties to monitor and maintain automated systems, and to provide built-in fail safe mechanisms); Dahiyat, Artificial Intelligence and Law: Do We Need a Thoughtful Reconsideration?, 18 Colo. Tech. L.J. 351 (2020); Jackson, Artificial Intelligence and the Fog of Innovation: A Deep-Dive On Governance and the Liability of Autonomous Systems, 35 Santa Clara High Tech. L.J. 35 (2019); Weber, Robot, Inc.: Personhood For Autonomous Systems?, 88 Fordham L. Rev. 591 (2019); Choi, Crashworthy Code, 94 Wash. L. Rev. 39 (2019); Abbott, The Reasonable Computer: Disrupting the Paradigm of Tort Liability, 86 Geo. Wash. L. Rev. 1 (2018) (suggesting a negligence-based liability regime); Chagal-Feferkorn, The Reasonable Algorithm, 2018 U. Ill. J.L. Tech. & Pol'y 111. See also § 17.6 (*Autonomous Vehicles*), below.

[393] See Scott, Tort Liability for Vendors of Insecure Software: Has the Time Finally Come?, 67 Md. L. Rev. 425 (2008); Zollers, McMullin, Hurd, and Shears, No More Soft Landings for Software: Liability for Defects in an Industry That Has Come of Age, 21 Santa Clara Computer & High Tech. L.J. 745 (2005).

[394] See, e.g., Maynard v. Snapchat, Inc., 870 S.E.2d 739, 743 (Ga. 2022) (allowing design defect claims against designer of Speed Filter for failing to prevent driver's reckless speeding while trying to record a picture of the speedometer at 100 m.p.h. or higher using the mobile app, ending in a crash); Lemmon v. Snap, Inc., 995 F.3d 1085, 1094 (9th Cir. 2021) (reversing dismissal of negligent design claims; designer of mobile app that predictably encouraged young decedents to drive at unsafe speeds was not immune from liability under Communications Decency Act § 230). Compare Estate of Alex through Coker v. T-Mobile US, Inc., 313 F. Supp. 3d 723, 732 (N.D. Tex. 2018) (allowing plaintiffs' claim that design defects in 9-1-1 mobile device software caused injured child's death after babysitter was repeatedly put on hold dialing 9-1-1 from cellphone) (collecting cases). *But see* Modisette v. Apple Inc., 241 Cal. Rptr. 3d 209, 221–23 (Ct. App. 2018) (no duty to design mobile phone to prohibit FaceTime app video calls while driving; public policy concerns). See generally Allyn, Snapchat Ends 'Speed Filter' That Critics Say Encouraged Reckless Driving, NPR (June 17, 2021); Civil Liability Arising from Cell Phone or Smartphone Use While in Traffic, 53 A.L.R.7th Art. 4 (2020).

[395] In the commercial law context, there is case law holding mass-marketed software to be a "good" under UCC Article 2. See, e.g., Shema Kolainu-Hear Our Voices v. Providersoft, LLC, 832 F. Supp. 2d 194, 199–200 (E.D.N.Y. 2010); Advent Sys. Ltd. v. Unisys Corp., 925 F.2d 670 (3d Cir. 1991) (Pa. law); RRX Indus. v. Lab-Con, Inc., 772 F.2d 543 (9th Cir. 1985) (Cal. law). Software developed specifically for a customer, however, has been found to be a "service." See, e.g., Micro-Managers, Inc. v. Gregory, 434 N.W.2d 97 (Wis. Ct. App. 1988); Data Processing Servs., Inc. v. L.H. Smith Oil Corp., 492 N.E.2d 314 (Ind. Ct. App. 1986). *But see* Challenge Printing Co., Inc. v. Electronics for Imaging Inc., 500 F. Supp. 3d 952, 961 (N.D. Cal. 2020) (under "the predominant factor test" the "essence of the agreement" was a product sale under the UCC); Surplus.com, Inc. v. Oracle Corp., 2010 WL 5419075, at *5 (N.D. Ill. 2010) (customized software, under the predominant purpose test, was a "good" subject to Article 2 of the UCC, since labor was only incidentally involved); Analysts Int'l Corp. v. Recycled Paper Prods., Inc., 1987 WL 12917, at *3 (N.D. Ill. 1987) (custom software was a "good"). See generally Comment, The Warranty of Merchantability and Computer Software Contracts: A Square Peg Won't Fit in a Round Hole, 59 Wash. L. Rev. 511 (1984); Note, Computer Software as a Good Under the Uniform Commercial Code: Taking a Byte Out of the Intangibility Myth, 65 B.U. L. Rev. 129 (1985); Products Liability Rest. § 19 Reporters' Note to cmt. *d*.

violation of state consumer protection statutes, among other claims.[396] One major software problem that has received considerable attention is its susceptibility to hacking,[397] a problem that carries potentially serious risks for many types of products,[398] but especially for automotive vehicles[399] and medical devices.[400] Because hacking

---

[396] See, e.g., In re Subaru Battery Drain Prods. Liab. Litig., 2021 WL 1207791, at *12 (D.N.J. 2021) (software errors caused "parasitic" battery drain); In re Apple Inc. Device Performance Litigation, 386 F. Supp. 3d 1155 (N.D. Cal. 2019) (software updates slowed phone processor speeds to mask battery defects); Beyer v. Symantec Corp., 333 F. Supp. 3d 966 (N.D. Cal. 2018) (defective computer security software); In re Chrysler-Dodge-Jeep Ecodiesel Mktg., Sales Pracs., & Prods. Liab. Litig., 295 F. Supp. 3d 927, 942 (N.D. Cal. 2018) (software deactivated emission controls during "real world driving"); Granillo v. FCA US LLC, 2016 WL 9405772 (D.N.J. 2016) (faulty transmission control software caused vehicles to shudder, jerk, or hesitate prior to accelerating or stopping, and to jolt forward when engaging gears). See also In re Myford Touch Consumer Litig., 2016 WL 7734558, at *24 (N.D. Cal. 2016) (certifying class of Colorado plaintiffs' strict liability claims against Ford Motor Co. for alleged software defects in "infotainment system" controlling GPS navigation, cameras, and cruise control, among other systems, causing driver distraction and raising safety concerns).

[397] See generally Amodio, The Intersection of Product Liability Law and the Internet of Things, B.C. Intell. Prop. & Tech. F., Jan. 4, 2021, at 1 (discussing "internet of things" data breaches); Robinson, Click Here to Sue Everybody: Cutting the Gordian Knot of the Internet of Things with Class Action Litigation, 26 Rich. J.L. & Tech. 4 (2020) (discussing *Flynn*, note 399, below); Butler, Products Liability and The Internet of (Insecure) Things: Should Manufacturers Be Liable for Damage Caused by Hacked Devices?, 50 U. Mich. J.L. Reform 913 (2017); Barash, Hackable Home-Security System Suit Advances, 44 Prod. Safety & Liab. Rep. (BNA) 1150 (Oct. 31, 2016).

[398] See, e.g., In re Apple Processor Litig., 832 Fed. Appx. 507 (9th Cir. 2020) (reinstating class action alleging that Apple violated state consumer protection laws by failing to disclose their products' vulnerabilities to hacking and that security patches caused performance degradations).

[399] A 2015 article in Wired disclosed a hacking vulnerability in the Uconnect infotainment system that controlled phone, navigation, and entertainment in some 2013–2015 Chrysler vehicles. Although Chrysler issued a recall to address the vulnerability, a class action was filed alleging consumer fraud, design defect, and other claims against the manufacturers. The court held that plaintiffs lacked standing to bring claims against the manufacturers for "risk of injury or death and the fear of that injury":

> Consider the chain of events that would need to occur for a serious injury to befall [the plaintiffs]. Their automobiles would need to be hacked by a hacker proficient enough to access the vehicles by remote. The hack would need to occur despite the fact that the recall fixed some of the vulnerabilities referenced in the Wired article. The hacker would need to gain access to the critical systems of the vehicle, and then the hacker would need to hijack those systems in a way that would cause a wreck of the kind of magnitude that could injure or kill. The plaintiffs don't allege that this chain of events has ever happened to anyone, and the chain looks a lot like the kind deemed too attenuated and speculative to create standing in other cases.

Flynn v. FCA US LLC, 2016 WL 5341749, at *2 (S.D. Ill. 2016). While some class claims were certified in Flynn v. FCA US LLC, 327 F.R.D. 206, 227 (S.D. Ill. 2018) (certifying Ill., Mo., and Mich. class actions), the classes were subsequently dismissed for lack of standing by the new judge assigned to the case. Flynn v. FCA US LLC, 2020 WL 1492687, at *5 (S.D. Ill. 2020) ("Ultimately, Plaintiffs have not suffered any injury in fact. They received what they bargained for—vehicles equipped with infotainment services—and do not plausibly allege that they were financially harmed by virtue of their vehicle purchases."). See also Cahen v. Toyota Motor Co., 717 Fed. Appx. 720, 723 (9th Cir. 2017) ("Plaintiffs do not allege that any of their vehicles have actually been hacked. . . . These alleged risks and defects are speculative."); Wenzel, Not Even Remotely Liable: Smart Car Hacking Liability, 2017 U. Ill. J.L. Tech. & Pol'y 49.

[400] The FDA recognizes the risk of medical device hacking: "Anytime a medical device has software and relies on a wireless or wired connection, vigilance is required. The software behind these products . . . can become vulnerable to cyber threats, especially if the device is older and was not built with cybersecurity in mind. FDA, Medical Device Cybersecurity: What You Need to Know (Oct. 13, 2020). See also Turton, U.S. Warns Cybersecurity Flaws Could Impact Medical Devices, Prod. Liab. & Toxics L. (Oct. 1, 2019) (FDA and Department of Homeland Security issued urgent warnings of 11 vulnerabilities in operating system software of various medical devices); Alexander, Google, GE Bite on Medical AI While FDA Readies New Rules, Prod. Liab. & Toxics L. (Sept. 13, 2019); Swan, Device Makers Combating Cyber Risks to Patient Health, Prod. Liab. & Toxics L. (Aug. 27, 2018); Swann, Cardiac Devices Vulnerable to Cyberattacks, Prod. Liab. & Toxics L. (Apr. 24, 2018).

problems may be preventable, or minimized,[401] they may be expected to become subject to liability.

An early commentator[402] noted four scenarios implicating products liability claims arising hypothetically from actual cases in which computer programming issues were not developed by the parties or the courts: a program for an energy management system that failed to activate a chemistry lab fan, causing a teacher to inhale chlorine gas;[403] a defective computer-generated warning label for a prescription drug;[404] a system that failed to inform an arraignment judge of an arrestee's prior violent crimes, leading to a victim's injuries after the arrestee's release;[405] and a software program's erroneous calculation of the proper doses of radiation for radioactive seeds implanted in a prostate cancer patient.[406] Because these cases conceptually appear to fall somewhere between mushroom cookbooks and navigational charts, it is difficult to know how they should be classified. Where a defect lies in a software program design or failure to warn, rather than in a user feeding incorrect information into the program,[407] a defective software program might seem to lie closer to a defective navigational chart for which a producer might appropriately be subject to responsibility for resulting harm.[408]

§ 16.9 BLOOD AND OTHER BIOLOGICS

Nothing could be further from a typical, commercially manufactured "product" than human blood. Yet blood is "sold" to millions of American patients each year, for use in

---

401 Blockchain technology, which links encrypted transaction records across a network, may strengthen software privacy and decrease hacking vulnerability. See, e.g., Vogel and Hilliard, Blockchain Can Address Privacy Worries with Self-Driving Cars, Prod. Liab. & Toxics L. (Aug. 5, 2019); Merian, IBM Watson, FDA to explore blockchain for secure patient data exchange, Computer World.com (Jan. 11, 2017). The FDA is expected to develop blockchain technology to drive pharmaceutical and medical device reviews and recalls. See, e.g., Kuhn, Blockchain May Be Used in FDA Medical Reviews and Recalls, Coindesk.com (Aug. 23, 2019); FDA, Press Release: FDA Takes New Steps to Adopt More Modern Technologies For Improving the Security of the Drug Supply Chain Through Innovations That Improve Tracking and Tracing of Medicines (Feb. 7, 2019).

402 Wolpert, Product Liability and Software Implicated in Personal Injury, 60 Def. Couns. J. 519 (1993).

403 This scenario is based on Sparacino v. Andover Controls Corp., 592 N.E.2d 431 (Ill. App. Ct. 1992).

404 This scenario is based on Frye v. Medicare-Glaser Corp., 579 N.E.2d 1255 (Ill. App. Ct. 1991), rev'd, 605 N.E.2d 557 (Ill. 1992). See also Hardin v. PDX, Inc., 173 Cal. Rptr. 3d 397, 407 (Ct. App. 2014) (affirming denial of defendant's anti-SLAPP motion challenging customer's negligence and product liability claims; defendant software provider "intentionally modified its software to allow [pharmacy] to distribute abbreviated drug monographs that automatically omitted warnings of serious risks"). *But see* In re Sears Holdings Corp., 628 B.R. 402, 412–13 (S.D.N.Y. 2021) (dismissing plaintiff's inadequately pled design defect and negligence claims against provider of software that allegedly produced inaccurate drug information sheets).

405 This scenario is based on Akins v. District of Columbia, 526 A.2d 933 (D.C. 1987).

406 This scenario is based on Jones v. Minnesota Mining & Mfg. Co., 669 P.2d 744 (N.M. Ct. App. 1983).

407 In Lowe v. Cerner Health Services, Inc., 2020 WL 6829770 (E.D. Va. 2020), Mr. Taylor, a morbidly obese patient recovering from gallbladder surgery, was found unresponsive and in respiratory distress on the morning he was scheduled for release. The hospital had purchased a "toolkit" software system that allowed hospitals to customize templates for entering and tracking hospital workflows, such as physician orders for patient monitoring. Due to his risk of sleep apnea, Mr. Taylor's oxygen levels should have been continuously monitored after his surgery. However, the surgeon's incorrect entry on the system that delayed oxygen monitoring until the morning after surgery was not detected or questioned by hospital staff. Granting summary judgment to defendants on the products liability negligent design claim, the court held that plaintiff failed to prove that the toolkit software system was unreasonably dangerous under the consumer expectations test or that the alleged defects existed when the software system left the manufacturer. Id. at *6–7. Dismissing the plaintiff's negligent failure to warn claim, the court held that the plaintiff failed to present evidence that the software manufacturer "knew or had a reason to know that its [software] was likely to be dangerous for its intended use or that . . . a sophisticated billion-dollar hospital, would not have been capable of realizing any purported dangerous conditions at the time it received the system." Id. at *8.

408 See § 16.7, above.

blood transfusions, by hospitals, blood banks, and manufacturers of blood products.[409] Less commonly, surgeons transplant other human and animal[410] parts—bones, tendons, and organs—into human beings. Still uncommonly, but at an accelerating pace, biotechnology firms are selling and developing a wide range of products made from human cells ("allografts")—such as musculoskeletal, other bone, meniscal, and stem cell materials—often harvested from human cadavers,[411] which physicians transfuse or surgically transplant into patients.

Despite the difficulty of trying to fit such biological "products" into the normal pigeonholes of products liability law, courts and legislatures had to address the problem of legal responsibility for infected or otherwise defective blood, organs, and tissues transfused or otherwise transplanted into patients. In the few non-blood cases involving claims of infected or otherwise defective biological matter, courts have applied principles developed in the blood cases, blunt though they may be—ruling that biological materials (though chattels that are sold) are not "products," for purposes of products liability law, and that their supply principally involves a "service" rather than a sale.[412] As biotech firms develop an increasing array of new biological products to enhance human health,[413] it is inevitable that patients will sometimes suffer diseases and other untoward consequences, sometimes unforeseeable and almost always unexpected, that will call for increasingly creative solutions by products liability law.[414] So far, however, the vast

[409] Blood products include "whole blood and its component parts, such as red blood cells, platelets, and plasma, and coagulation products derived from blood plasma, such as factor concentrates." Comment, 3 J. Pharmacy & L. 129 n.5 (1994).

[410] Pigs have been the primary source of animal organs for some time, the propriety of which unfolds the more one casts a discerning eye over the body politic, mercantile and hominoid, of America today. In the 1960s, Squibb marketed a calf bone product (Boplant) for spine grafts and similar purposes, but its pre-marketing tests had been rigged and the results for many patients were disastrous. See E.R. Squibb & Sons, Inc. v. Stickney, 274 So.2d 898 (Fla. Ct. App. 1973), cert. denied 416 U.S. 961 (1974); Owen, Punitive Damages in Products Liability Litigation, 74 Mich. L. Rev. 1057, 1332–34 (1976).

[411] Often, also, from blood, and sometimes from amniotic membrane tissue from placenta, donated by a mother during childbirth. See www.mimedx.com/.

[412] See, e.g., Palermo v. LifeLink Found., Inc., 152 So.3d 1177, 1181 (Miss. Ct. App. 2014) (claims against tissue bank that supplied allograft used in surgery; "like blood made available for transfer to others, human tissue provided to others in medical procedures is not a 'product' subject to products-liability law, and the distribution of human tissue, including reasonable payments for related services, does not constitute a 'sale' for purposes of strict liability"); Miller v. Hartford Hosp., 2006 WL 2808215, at *4 (Conn. Super. Ct. 2006) (allegedly contaminated human heart valve implanted into decedent prior to death was not a "product" under products liability act); Cryolife, Inc. v. Superior Ct., 2 Cal. Rptr. 3d 396 (Ct. App. 2003) (infected cadaver tendon used in knee surgery; supply of human tissue is a service under a state statute that immunizes suppliers from strict liability); Condos v. Musculoskeletal Transplant Found., 208 F. Supp. 2d 1226 (D. Utah 2002) (dismissing claims against supplier and processor of bone tissue, infected with hepatitis C virus, implanted in plaintiff; bone tissue not a "product," and defendants not negligent). See also In re Human Tissue Prods. Liab. Litig., 2009 WL 737048 (D.N.J. 2009) (class action by recipients and unknowing donor corpses of allegedly contaminated human tissue).

Some "blood shield" statutes, discussed below, broadly include other human tissue and organs. See, e.g., Mont. Code Ann. § 50–33–102; 42 Pa. Cons. Stat. Ann. § 8333. See also Products Liability Rest. § 19(c) ("Human blood and human tissue, even when provided commercially, are not subject to the rules of this Restatement.").

[413] One leading company, RTIX, in its 2009 public offering filing, listed its allograft competitors as MTF, AlloSource, LifeCell, LifeNet, and Osteotech. Since that time, more biotech firms have entered the field of allograft (and "xenograft," from other species) transplant products, sometimes leading to harmful consequences. See, e.g., CDC, Multistate Outbreak of Tuberculosis (TB) Associated with a Suspected Contaminated Bone Allograft Material Used In Surgical Procedures (June 14, 2021).

[414] See generally Owen, Bending Nature, Bending Law, 62 Fla. L. Rev. 569 (2010); Owen, Dangers in Prescription Drugs: Filling a Private Law Gap in the Healthcare Debate, 42 Conn. L. Rev. 733 (2010).

majority of cases have involved responsibility for blood transfusions infected with serum hepatitis or AIDS, to which the discussion now will turn.

While the first reported transfusion of human blood was in 1795, the use of blood transfusions in surgery did not become reliable and common until the middle of the twentieth century.[415] The widespread medical use of blood transfusions created a market which impelled the rise of blood banks—firms that collect, store, and distribute blood products—a development considered one of the great advances in the history of medicine. If supplies of whole blood were not readily available at hospitals across the land, many important medical procedures that now are common would be impossible.[416] But with this boon came the dire risk that blood gathered from other persons may be infected with some serious, possibly deadly, disease. Especially since the early to mid-1980s, the transfusion risk of greatest concern has been the risk of HIV and AIDS. Prior thereto, the most troubling risk in transfused blood was serum hepatitis.[417]

In the 1960s, one-third of blood transfusion recipients contracted hepatitis.[418] By 2011, about 5 million patients in the United States received transfusions of about 13.8 million units of whole blood and red blood cells (20.9 million units of all blood components).[419] Studies revealed that the 20% of blood collected from paid donors in large cities at the time was ten to fifteen times more likely to be infected with hepatitis than that collected from volunteers.[420] It was then estimated that some 30,000 serious, overt hepatitis cases resulted from transfusions in the U.S. each year (some 5%–10% of which were fatal) together with 150,000 additional sub-clinical cases.[421] Nearly 25% of persons over forty who contracted the illness died.[422] To make matters worse, there was then no reliable test to determine whether blood was infected with hepatitis and, as late as 1975, hepatitis C was "unknown to the medical community."[423] Following the adoption

---

[415] See Banks, Legal and Ethical Safeguards: Protection of Society's Most Vulnerable Participants in a Commercialized Organ Transplantation System, 21 Am. J.L. & Med. 45, 48 n.20 (1995).

[416] See Annot., 24 A.L.R.4th 508, at § 2 (1983).

[417] Early writings on blood transfusion liability focused on serum hepatitis. See, e.g., Franklin, Hepatitis, Blood Transfusions, and Public Action, 21 Cath. U. L. Rev. 683 (1972); Franklin, Tort Liability for Hepatitis: An Analysis and a Proposal, 24 Stan. L. Rev. 439 (1972); Kessel, Transfused Blood, Serum Hepatitis, and the Coase Theorem, 17 J.L. & Econ. 265 (1974); Annot., 24 A.L.R.4th 508 (1983) (liability of blood suppliers for harm from blood transfusions). In the 1990s, there was a flurry of writings on the risks of contracting AIDS from the blood products of others. See, e.g., Eckert, The AIDS Blood-Transfusion Cases: A Legal and Economic Analysis of Liability, 29 San Diego L. Rev. 203 (1992); Klein, A Legislative Alternative to "No Cause" Liability in Blood Products Litigation, 12 Yale J. on Reg. 107 (1995); Trebilcock, House, and Daniels, Do Institutions Matter? A Comparative Pathology of the HIV-Infected Blood Tragedy, 82 Va. L. Rev. 1407 (1996), critiqued, Glied, Markets Matter: U.S. Responses to the HIV-Infected Blood Tragedy, 82 Va. L. Rev. 1493 (1996); Salbu, AIDS and the Blood Supply: An Analysis of Law, Regulation, and Public Policy, 74 Wash. U. L.Q. 913 (1996). The few more recent articles on liability for selling infected blood include Shu-Acquaye and Innet, Human Blood and Its Transfusion: The Twists and Turns of Legal Thinking, 9 Quinnipiac Health L.J. 33 (2005); Reser and Radnofsky, New Wave of Tainted Blood Litigation: Hepatitis C Liability Issues, 67 Def. Coun. J. 306 (2000); Feldman, Blood Justice: Courts, Conflict, and Compensation in Japan, France, and the United States, 34 L. & Soc'y Rev. 651 (2000).

[418] See Note, Strict Liability, Negligence and the Standard of Care for Transfusion-Transmitted Disease, 36 Ariz. L. Rev. 473, 474 n.2 (1996) (citing Langdale, Infectious Complications of Blood Transfusions, 6 Infectious Disease Clinics of North America 731, 732 (1992)).

[419] See U.S. Dpt. H.H.S., The 2011 National Blood Collection and Utilization Survey Rpt. (2011) (noting that the number of blood units transfused in America dropped 8% from 2008).

[420] See Franklin, Tort Liability for Hepatitis: An Analysis and a Proposal, 24 Stan. L. Rev. 439, 444 (1972).

[421] Id. at 443.

[422] Id. at 444.

[423] Bourque v. Louisiana Health Sys. Grp., 956 So.2d 60, 65 (La. Ct. App. 2007).

of improved screening and virus inactivation methods in the early 1990s, the risk of hepatitis transmission due to blood transfusion or organ transplantation was virtually eliminated.[424]

The rapid expansion of blood transfusions and blood banks in the middle of the twentieth century was coincident with the rise of modern products liability law with its strict liability doctrines for the sale of defective products.[425] In an early case, *Perlmutter v. Beth David Hospital*,[426] the plaintiff was a patient who sued a hospital for breach of implied warranty for injuries resulting from "the transfusing of 'bad' blood, supplied by the hospital for a price as part of the customary services rendered by the hospital to its patients."[427] Holding that the hospital's provision of blood to the patient was a service rather than a sale, a majority of the New York Court of Appeals reasoned in 1954 that the hospital's principal role was to promote the healing of its patients, not to sell them medicines, drugs, or blood.[428] A similar claim arose in Florida, in *Community Blood Bank v. Russell*,[429] where the Florida Supreme Court in 1967 remanded for a determination of whether it was possible for the defendant blood bank to have detected hepatitis in the blood it sold. While the court explicitly took no position on whether the detectability of hepatitis in the blood would affect the outcome, Justice Roberts strongly argued in a concurring opinion that the sale of blood by a blood bank was every bit as much of a "sale" for purposes of strict warranty liability as the sale of any other product, and that neither the fact that hepatitis might not be discoverable before the sale nor any other policy should prevent blood suppliers from being strictly liable for harm from defects in the blood they sold.[430] Relying heavily on *Russell*, and persuaded that hepatitis-infected blood was undeniably "defective," the Illinois Supreme Court in *Cunningham v. MacNeal Memorial Hospital* ruled in 1970 that the supplying hospital was strictly liable in tort regardless of the defendant's inability to detect or prevent the virus.[431]

These developments, particularly *Cunningham*, were widely criticized on the policy ground that imposing strict liability on blood suppliers who had no way to detect the hepatitis virus would deter blood banks from collecting and selling blood and undermine the market for this uniquely valuable commodity that had become so necessary to public

---

424 Centers for Disease Control and Prevention, Recommendations for Prevention and Control of Hepatitis C Virus (HCV) Infection and HCV-Related Chronic Disease (1998) (noting that the CDC hepatitis surveillance system had not detected a transfusion-related hepatitis transmission since 1994). Intravenous drug use (rather than blood products) now accounts for 60% of hepatitis C transmission in the United States. Id. See also Ly, Xing, Klevens, Jiles, Ward, and Holmberg, The Increasing Burden of Mortality from Viral Hepatitis in the United States Between 1999 and 2007, 156 Annals Internal Med. 271 (2012) (noting that by 2007, hepatitis C surpassed HIV as a cause of death in the United States).

425 See § 5.3, above.

426 123 N.E.2d 792 (N.Y. 1954).

427 Id. at 793.

428 *Perlmutter* is further examined in the sales-service context, at § 16.3, above.

429 196 So.2d 115 (Fla. 1967).

430 See id. at 118, 121 (Roberts, J. specially concurring) ("it is more consonant with right and justice to require the Blood Bank to be held absolutely and strictly answerable to the consumers of its product for defects therein, so that the burden of the losses resulting therefrom may be spread among all who benefit from the operation of the blood bank, rather than to require such losses to be borne by the innocent victims alone").

431 266 N.E.2d 897 (Ill. 1970). "To allow a defense to strict liability on the ground that there is no way, either practical or theoretical, for a defendant to ascertain the existence of impurities in his product would be to emasculate the doctrine and in a very real sense would signal a return to a negligence theory." Id. at 902. See also DeBattista v. Argonaut-Southwest Ins. Co., 403 So.2d 26 (La. 1981) (blood bank strictly liable in tort for transfusion of blood infected with hepatitis). *Cunningham* is addressed elsewhere in the context of state of the art. See § 10.4, above.

health.[432] Not only did other state courts refuse to apply strict liability in tort or warranty to the sale of blood,[433] but the Illinois legislature promptly overturned *Cunningham* by statute.[434] Other state legislatures around the nation, if they had not already done so,[435] enacted similar statutes restricting the responsibility of blood suppliers to negligence liability. Today, every state exempts blood suppliers from strict liability, in warranty or tort, for supplying infected blood. Almost all American jurisdictions[436] accomplish this exemption from strict products liability through "blood shield statutes," which prohibit strict liability actions by providing that the supply of blood is a service (rather than a sale) or by more directly stating that the supply of blood products does not give rise to liability unless the supplier was at fault.[437]

Blood shield statutes may apply broadly to all kinds of blood and human tissue products, such as various types of allografts, organs, Achilles tendon tissue, and sperm.[438] In addition, these protective statutes may protect suppliers against strict

---

[432] See, e.g., Notes, 69 Mich. L. Rev. 1172 (1971), 66 Nw. U.L. Rev. 80 (1971), 24 Vand. L. Rev. 645 (1971).

[433] See, e.g., McMichael v. American Red Cross, 532 S.W.2d 7 (Ky. 1975); Brody v. Overlook Hosp., 317 A.2d 392 (N.J. Super. Ct. App. Div. 1974), aff'd, 332 A.2d 596 (N.J. 1975). The trial court in *Brody*, reversed on appeal, examined the policy issues and allowed a claim for strict liability in tort. See 296 A.2d 668 (N.J. Super. Law Div. 1972).

[434] See 745 Ill. Comp. Stat. Ann. 40/2, enacted in 1971, discussed in Glass v. Ingalls Mem. Hosp., 336 N.E.2d 495 (Ill. App. Ct. 1975).

[435] By the time *Cunningham* was decided in 1970, half the states had already enacted blood shield statutes. See *Cunningham*, 266 N.E.2d at 902.

[436] The District of Columbia, New Jersey, and Puerto Rico appear to be the only jurisdictions without blood shield statutes, and their case law accomplishes the same result. See Fisher v. Sibley Mem'l Hosp., 403 A.2d 1130, 1134 (D.C. App. 1979) ("characterizing blood plasma as a product governed by strict tort liability is as unnatural as forcing a blood transfusion into the commercial sales mold"); Brody v. Overlook Hosp., 317 A.2d 392 (N.J. Super. Ct. App. Div. 1974) (no liability under strict liability in tort for undiscoverable defect), aff'd, 332 A.2d 596 (N.J. 1975); Nestor v. Hospital Pavia, 2005 WL 348313, at *8 (D.P.R. 2005) (rejecting application of strict liability in tort to blood suppliers).

[437] See, e.g., Cal. Health & Safety Code § 1606 (procuring and distributing blood is a service); Colo. Rev. Stat. Ann. § 13–22–104 (medical service that does not constitute a sale); Conn. Gen. Stat. Ann. § 19a–289q(c) (service); Fla. Stat. Ann. § 672.316(5) (service); Haw. Rev. Stat. § 325–91 (no implied warranty that blood is pure in absence of scientific technology to detect possible impurities); Idaho Code Ann. § 39–3702 (service, unless provider operates blood bank for profit); 745 Ill. Comp. Stat. Ann. 40/2 (service, not sale, and no warranties or strict liability in tort apply); Mich. Comp. Laws Ann. § 333.9121(2) (service, whether remuneration paid or not); Nev. Rev. Stat. Ann. § 460.010 (no liability without negligence or willful misconduct); N.M. Stat. Ann. § 24–10–5 (no implied warranties; no strict liability in tort for transmission of hepatitis or HIV); N.Y. Pub. Health Law § 580(4) (public health service); Tex. Civ. Prac. & Rem. Code. Ann. § 77.003 (no liability except for negligence, gross negligence, or intentional tort). The statutes are collected in Owen & Davis on Products Liability Appendix J, and Cantu, A Continuing Whimsical Search for the True Meaning of "Product" in Products Liability Litigation, 35 St. Mary's L.J. 341, 345 n.7 (2004).

Some courts have held that strict liability is applicable in certain situations. See, e.g., JKB v. Armour Pharm. Co., 660 N.E.2d 602, 605 (Ind. Ct. App. 1996) (statute does not protect pharmaceutical company when production is for commercial use); Rogers v. Miles Lab., Inc., 802 P.2d 1346, 1349 (Wash. 1991) (statute does not protect paid donors).

[438] See, e.g., In re Coloplast Corp. Pelvic Support Sys. Prods. Liab. Litig., 2017 WL 6417807, at *3–4 (S.D. W. Va. 2017) (Or. law) (Oregon blood shield statute barred plaintiff's strict liability claim against manufacturer/distributor of pelvic mesh allograft consisting of human collagen; reviewing cases and citing Products Liability Rest. § 19(c)) (one of a series of *In re Coloplast* opinions from MDL in which blood shield statutes of Ark., Cal, Fla., Ky, Miss., Ohio, and S.C. barred strict tort claims against the allograft manufacturer/distributor); Wamsley v. LifeNet Transplant Servs. Inc., 2011 WL 5520245, at *9 (S.D. W. Va. 2011) (statutory immunity from strict liability for company that furnished infected Achilles tendon, "human tissue" implanted in plaintiff); D.D. v. Idant Labs., 374 Fed. Appx. 319 (3d Cir. 2010). See also Palermo v. LifeLink Foundation, Inc., 152 So.3d 1177, 1181 (Miss. Ct. App. 2014) (claims against tissue bank that supplied allograft used in surgery; "like blood made available for transfer to others, human tissue provided to others in medical procedures is not a 'product' subject to products-liability law, and the distribution of human tissue, including reasonable payments for related services, does not constitute a 'sale' for purposes of strict liability").

liability for derivative products of this type, including blood products manufactured by commercial enterprises.[439]

During the quarter century following the outset of the AIDS epidemic in the late 1970s and early 1980s, about 10,000 people in the United States contracted HIV/AIDS by blood transfusion, blood components, or tissue.[440] Not until 1984 did the medical community learn that AIDS was transmitted by blood, and a reliable test for the presence of the virus in blood first became available in 1985.[441] The various collection, testing, and heat-treating procedures devised during the mid-1980s now permit virtually 100% assurance of avoiding, killing, or detecting the virus if due care is exercised.[442] Hence, most such cases today are decided on the basis of negligence, and, because of the blood shield statutes, strict liability in tort or warranty rarely is involved at all.[443] And, because of the difficulties of proof of negligence, such claims generally fail.[444]

But see Donovan v. Idant Labs., 625 F. Supp. 2d 256, 273, 276 (E.D. Pa. 2009) (under New York law, "the sale of sperm is considered a product and is subject to strict liability," but strict products liability claim for selling sperm that carried the donor's Fragile X Syndrome gene constituted non-cognizable claim of wrongful life).

Compare Norman v. Xytex Corp., 848 S.E.2d 835, 844 (Ga. 2020) (affirming dismissal of non-cognizable wrongful birth claims against sperm bank for providing sperm from donor number 9623, whose hospitalizations for mental health issues and criminal background went undiscovered while he biologically fathered child, while reversing dismissal of misrepresentation, consumer protection violations, and other claims "not predicated on life as an injury"), with Doe 1 v. Xytex Corporation, 2017 WL 1112996, at *8 (N.D. Cal. 2017) (retaining wrongful birth, negligence, false advertising, and unfair business practices claims—while dismissing strict products liability, breach of warranty, and battery claims—against sperm bank providing sperm from same donor number 9623). See generally Vagle, Putting the "Product" in Reproduction: The Viability of a Products Liability Action for Genetically Defective Sperm, 38 Pepp. L. Rev. 1175 (2011); McIntyre, The Potential for Products Liability Actions when Artificial Insemination by an Anonymous Donor Produces Children with Genetic Defects, 98 Dick. L. Rev. 519 (1994); Am. Law Prod. Liab. 3d § 37:33.

439 See, e.g., Scher v. Bayer Corp., 258 F. Supp. 2d 190 (E.D.N.Y. 2003) (strict liability in tort and warranty claims dismissed against commercial supplier of allegedly defective blood derivative product, Hyp-Rho(D), used to prevent hemolytic disease in newborn children of Rh-Negative mothers and Rh-Positive fathers; case allowed to proceed on negligence claims). See also cases, note 438, above; Products Liability Rest. § 19(c) ("Human blood and human tissue, even when provided commercially, are not subject to the rules of this Restatement."). *But see* Note, 2 Ind. Health L. Rev. 295 (2005) (arguing that tissue banks should be subject to strict liability).

440 See Campsmith et al., Cases of HIV Infection and AIDS in the United States and Dependent Areas, 2005, Table 17 (CDC 2007) (statistics through Dec. 2005). The CDC no longer reports blood transfusions as a separate category.

441 For public health responses to AIDS, see Trebilcock, House, and Daniels, Do Institutions Matter? A Comparative Pathology of the HIV-Infected Blood Tragedy, 82 Va. L. Rev. 1407 (1996), critiqued, Glied, Markets Matter: U.S. Responses to the HIV-Infected Blood Tragedy, 82 Va. L. Rev. 1493 (1996); Eckert, The AIDS Blood-Transfusion Cases: A Legal and Economic Analysis of Liability, 29 San Diego L. Rev. 203, 295–98 (1992) (chronology); Kozup v. Georgetown Univ., 663 F. Supp. 1048 (D.D.C. 1987) (chronicling developments in AIDS research), rev'd on other grounds, 851 F.2d 437 (D.C. Cir. 1988).

442 See Stramer, Glynn, Kleinman, Strong, Caglioti, Wright, Dodd, and Busch, Detection of HIV-1 and HCV Infections among Antibody-Negative Blood Donors by Nucleic Acid-Amplification Testing, 351 New Eng. J. Med. 760 (2004) (modern testing methods have reduced the risk of transfusion-transmitted HIV-1 and hepatitis C to approximately 1 in 2 million blood units).

443 See, e.g., In re Factor VIII or IX Concentrate Blood Products Liability Litigation, 595 F. Supp. 2d 855, 864 (N.D. Ill. 2009) (negligence claims barred by Taiwan's two-year statute of limitations); Christiana v. Southern Baptist Hosp., 867 So.2d 809 (La. Ct. App. 2004) (blood shield law in effect at time of transfusion protected hospital that supplied blood from patient's strict liability claim).

444 See, e.g., Johnson v. American Nat'l Red Cross, 578 S.E.2d 106 (Ga. 2003) (negligence claims against blood bank for HIV and fear of HIV failed); Advincula v. United Blood Servs., 678 N.E.2d 1009 (Ill. 1996) (blood bank's conduct should have been measured against professional standard of care according to state of the art at time of injury). *But see* Snyder v. American Ass'n of Blood Banks, 676 A.2d 1036 (N.J. 1996) (allowing claim against association of blood banks for negligently setting standards for prevention of AIDS).

A final form of biological product of enormous significance to healthcare—stem cells—deserves special mention here.[445] Such products, grown in laboratories, may be expected eventually to provide treatments for diabetes, heart disease, spinal cord injuries, Alzheimer's and Parkinson's diseases, and to grow internal organs.[446] In an important article,[447] Stephen Munzer begins an inquiry into policy issues involved in legal responsibility for harm that stem cell products may incidentally cause. At bottom, he argues convincingly for a "qualified system of strict liability for stem cell products in which patients and manufacturers contribute on a per-product basis to a compensation fund and the federal government acts as an insurer of last resort."[448] It is hard to envision what the healthcare system may look like when stem cell products become a significant reality, and their harmful results become known, but Professor Munzer's proposal offers intriguing insights on how we might consider framing an alternative compensation system to ordinary products liability law for injuries from efforts to put this type of "product" derived from fundamental human cells to ameliorative use in improving the human condition.[449]

§ 16.10 Miscellaneous Transactions and Products

Because of the attraction of not having to prove negligence, plaintiffs often attempt to stretch strict products liability doctrine beyond the paradigm case of a commercial sale of a new chattel.[450] Most recurring types of miscellaneous transactions and products have been addressed in this and the previous chapter. Already examined, for example, is the applicability of strict products liability to franchise transactions,[451] auction sales,[452] financial lease arrangements, electricity, real estate, the provision of information and entertainment, blood, and various other special types of transactions and products.[453] Four special, recurring issues remain to be briefly considered here: casual sales, cannabis-infused products, animals, and toxic contaminants.

Casual Sales

It is fundamental that strict liability in tort is applicable only to harm from products that have been commercially distributed.[454] The *Restatement (Second) of Torts* § 402A

[445] See Munzer, Risk and Reward in Stem Cell Products: A New Model for Stem Cell Product Liability, 18 B.U. J. Sci. & Tech. L. 102 (2012).

[446] See id. at 107–08.

[447] See note 445, above.

[448] Id. at 105.

[449] "[D]octors routinely use stem cells that come from bone marrow or blood in transplant procedures to treat patients with cancer and disorders of the blood and immune system"; however, the FDA warns that "unproven stem cell therapies can be particularly unsafe [and it has] increased enforcement of regulations and oversight of stem cell clinics." FDA, FDA Warns About Stem Cell Therapies (Sept. 3, 2019).

[450] See generally Cantu, A Continuing Whimsical Search for the True Meaning of the Term "Product" in Products Liability Litigation, 35 St. Mary's L.J. 341 (2004); Lannetti, Toward a Revised Definition of "Product" under the *Restatement (Third) of Torts: Products Liability*, 55 Bus. Law. 799 (2000); Cantu, Twenty-Five Years of Strict Product Liability Law: The Transformation and Present Meaning of Section 402A, 25 St. Mary's L.J. 327 (1993); Cantu, The Illusive Meaning of the Term "Product" Under Section 402A of the Restatement (Second) of Torts, 44 Okla. L. Rev. 635 (1991).

[451] See § 15.4, above.

[452] See § 15.7, above.

[453] See §§ 16.2–16.9, above.

[454] The same principle applies to claims for breach of the implied warranty of merchantability, under Article 2 of the Uniform Commercial Code, which applies to sales of goods only "if the seller is a merchant with respect to goods of that kind." UCC § 2–314(1).

applies only if "the seller is engaged in the business of selling such a product,"[455] and the *Products Liability Restatement*, which applies only to commercial transactions in the normal course of business, explicitly excludes "casual sales."[456] Accordingly, as previously mentioned,[457] courts have refused to apply strict products liability to occasional commercial sales of a used tractor, an airplane, a pool and waterslide, or machinery and products of various types.[458] There is even less reason, of course, to apply strict products liability against a private party who, on one occasion, loans an acquaintance a defective propane tank[459] or sells a neighbor a pound of sugar or his car.[460]

Cannabis-Infused Products

American sales of legal recreational and medical cannabis[461] and cannabidiol (CBD) products exceeded $37 billion in 2021.[462] However, few such products have received FDA approval as safe and effective drugs, and the FDA "continues to be concerned at the proliferation of products asserting to contain CBD that are marketed for therapeutic or medical uses although they have not been approved."[463] The FDA recently issued a non-binding draft guidance for cannabis and cannabis-derived drug product clinical

---

[455] Rest. (2d) Torts § 402A(1)(a).

[456] See Products Liability Rest. § 1 cmt. *c* (the liability rule for sales of defective products "applies only to manufacturers and other commercial sellers and distributors who are engaged in the business of selling or otherwise distributing the type of product that harmed the plaintiff"; "a commercial seller or distributor [need not] be engaged exclusively or even primarily in selling or otherwise distributing the type of product that injured the plaintiff, so long as the sale of the product is other than occasional or casual [that are] outside the regular course of the seller's business").

[457] See §§ 5.3 and 15.7, above.

[458] See, e.g., Clute v. Paquin, 631 N.Y.S.2d 463 (App. Div. 1995); Nastasi v. Hochman, 396 N.Y.S.2d 216 (App. Div. 1977) (isolated lease of plane with defective strobe light system by lingerie manufacturer that owned plane); Konold v. Superior Int'l Indus., 911 F. Supp. 2d 303, 313 (W.D. Pa. 2012) (designer who may have acted as intermediary to help sell pool and waterslide to water park was "occasional seller," not in the business of supplying such products and so not a "seller" subject to strict liability); Garcia v. Becker Bros. Steel Co., 125 Cal. Rptr. 3d 73, 80 (Ct. App. 2011) ("the occasional seller of used equipment is *not strictly* liable for its sale of a defective product"); Jaramillo v. Weyerhaeuser Co., 570 F.3d 487 (2d Cir. 2009) (N.Y. law) (folder-gluer machine). See also AMC, LLC v. Nw. Farm Food Coop., 2020 WL 485529, at *8 (D. Or. 2020) (Or. and Wash. law) (dismissing products liability claim against casual seller of euthanized hens for use in mink food).

[459] See Lyzhoft v. Waconia Farm Supply, 2013 WL 3368832, at *5 (Minn. Ct. App. 2013) (loaner of propane cylinder, not known to contain acetylene, was not subject to strict liability when cylinder exploded when filled with propane, because bailors were not in the business of supplying propane cylinders).

[460] See Rest. (2d) Torts § 402A cmt. *f*. See also Products Liability Rest. § 1 cmt. *c*.

[461] As of mid-2021, 18 states (Alaska, Ark., Cal., Colo., Conn., Ill., Me., Mass., Mich., Mont., N.J., N.M., N.Y., Nev., Or., Vt., Va., and Wash.) and the District of Columbia had legalized cannabis for recreational use, and an additional 18 states had legalized medical cannabis (Ark., Del., Fla., Haw., La., Md., Minn., Miss., Mo., N.H., N.D., Ohio, Okla., Pa., R.I., S.D., Utah, and W. Va.). Rense, Here Are All the States That Have Legalized Weed in the U.S., Esquire.com (July 1, 2021). At the federal level, legislation to legalize marijuana has been passed in the House of Representatives, but it appears unlikely that the Senate will enact such a bill. See, e.g., Furst, House Votes to Decriminalize Marijuana, Wall St. J.com (Apr. 1, 2022).

[462] U.S. Cannabis Sales Topped $37 Billion in 2021. Will Sales Decline in 2022?, 420 Intel.com (Jan. 11, 2022).

[463] FDA, FDA Regulation of Cannabis and Cannabis-Derived Products, Including Cannabidiol (CBD) (Jan. 22, 2021) (the Agriculture Improvement Act of 2018 (Pub. L. 115–334), provisions of the Food, Drug, and Cosmetic Act, and section 351 of the Public Health Service Act (21 U.S.C. § 381) provide the FDA with authority to regulate cannabis and cannabis-derived products).

research,[464] but it is quite uncertain how this controversial issue may affect products liability litigation until the FDA releases final regulations.[465]

Animals

The cases are split on whether strict liability in tort applies to animals.[466] Most courts have held that "living things do not constitute 'products' within the scope of the strict tort liability doctrine which requires that a product's nature be fixed when it leaves the manufacturer's or seller's control."[467] Thus, courts have been particularly reluctant to hold sellers subject to liability for natural proclivities in animals, such as the tendency of a "fractious" horse to expand its lungs while being saddled,[468] or a dog to bite.[469] But negligence remains a viable claim against the seller of a fractious horse,[470] and most courts have allowed recovery on some basis for the sale of animals infected with diseases transmitted to the owner, sometimes on the theory that the animal is a defective

---

[464] See FDA, Cannabis and Cannabis-Derived Compounds: Quality Considerations for Clinical Research Guidance for Industry (July 2020).

[465] See Okun, Jalandoni, and Huda, Product Liability Cases: Cannabis Products, Cannabis Law 300:200, 3 (Aug. 29, 2020) (suggesting that the present lack of FDA rules and regulations would allow manufacturers to stay products liability claims on the basis of primary jurisdiction, while future rules and regulations may provide a preemption defense). For cannabis cases stayed pending FDA regulation, see, e.g., Steinberg, Hemp Bombs Gets Pause in CBD False Ad Suit to Await FDA Rule, Prod. Liab. & Toxics L. (June 16, 2020). See also, Pippins and Mody, FDA Authority Over Cannabis Products, Cosmetics Gets Hill Attention, Prod. Liab. & Toxics L. (Sept. 21, 2021) (reviewing proposed legislation); FDA Objects to CBD as Diet Supplement, Extending Uncertainty, Prod. Liab. & Toxics L. (Aug. 11, 2021) (application to sell "full-spectrum hemp extract with CBD as a dietary supplement won't be considered because of the FDA's own prior decision to treat CBD as a drug, [illustrating the FDA's] ongoing hesitancy to regulate cannabidiol, the non-psychoactive ingredient in cannabis plants better known as CBD"). See generally Schuster and Bird, Legal Strategy During Legal Uncertainty: The Case of Cannabis Regulation, 26 Stan. J.L. Bus. & Fin. 362 (2021); Lustrin and Greenberg, A Budding Opportunity—Why the CBD Industry Requires Regulation, Prod. Liab. & Toxics L. (Jan. 15, 2020); Grossman, Life, Liberty, (and the Pursuit of Happiness): Medical Marijuana Regulation in Historical Context, 74 Food & Drug L.J. 280 (2019); Campbell and Singh, Budding Torts: Forecasting Emerging Tort Liability in the Cannabis Industry, 30 Loy. Consumer L. Rev. 338 (2018); Note, 16 Hastings Bus. L.J. 65 (2020).

[466] On animals, see Comment, 12 Animal L. 241 (2006) (arguing that sellers of defective animals should be liable for personal injury); Annot., 63 A.L.R.4th 127 (1988) (live animal as "product" for products liability).

[467] See, e.g., Zendejas v. Redman, 2017 WL 2547202, at *6 (S.D. Fla. 2017) ("as a living, breathing, sentient creature that constantly grows, learns, experiences, and changes based on both external and internal factors that often cannot be controlled by the seller, [a Grand Prix show jumping horse] will never have the sort of fixed nature at the time he enters the stream of commerce that a 'product' must have in order to impose strict liability on manufacturers and sellers"); Kaplan v. C Lazy U Ranch, 615 F. Supp. 234 (D. Colo. 1985) (horse not "product"). See also Malicki v. Koci, 700 N.E.2d 913, 915 (Ohio Ct. App. 1997) (parakeet not product whose health is not totally in defendant's control); Latham v. Wal-Mart Stores, Inc., 818 S.W.2d 673, 676 (Mo. Ct. App. 1991) (parrot not product; "due to their mutability and their tendency to be affected by the purchaser, animals should not be products under § 402A as a matter of law"); Anderson v. Farmers Hybrid Cos., 408 N.E.2d 1194 (Ill. App. Ct. 1980) (unbred female pigs not products); Whitmer v. Schneble, 331 N.E.2d 115 (Ill. App. Ct. 1975) (dog not product). *But see* Tyson Fresh Meats, Inc. v. Dykhuis Farms, Inc., 2022 WL 971111, at *3 (N.D. Ind. 2022) (contaminated hogs are "products").

[468] See Kaplan v. C Lazy U Ranch, 615 F. Supp. 234 (D. Colo. 1985).

[469] See, e.g., Blaha v. Stuard, 640 N.W.2d 85, 89 (S.D. 2002) (yellow Labrador retriever: "living creatures have no fixed nature and cannot be products as a matter of law"); Whitmer v. Schneble, 331 N.E.2d 115 (Ill. App. Ct. 1975) (after giving birth, Doberman bit child).

[470] See Kaplan v. C Lazy U Ranch, 615 F. Supp. 234 (D. Colo. 1985).

product[471] and sometimes on simple negligence principles such as the failure to warn.[472] The *Products Liability Restatement* states that "when a living animal is sold commercially in a diseased condition and causes harm to other property or to persons, the animal constitutes a product for purposes of this Restatement."[473]

Toxic Contaminants

Toxins that escape from products into the environment can seriously harm people and property. As noted in the discussion of liability for harm from the destruction and disposal of products at the end of their useful lives, a complex set of federal and state laws and regulations, including products liability law, govern liability for harm resulting when such toxins are released.[474] One such toxin is the organic chemical compound methyl tertiary butyl ether (MTBE), which petroleum refiners widely added to gasoline from 1979 to 2005. Its purpose, at first, was to replace lead as a way to enhance octane and thereby help prevent engine knock. In 1990, after Congress enacted the Clean Air Act Amendments, refiners substantially increased the amount of MTBE in some gasoline to meet certain air pollution reduction requirements in that legislation. The problem is that gasoline containing this chemical not infrequently spills and leaks from service station storage tanks, which poses an especially high risk of serious ground water contamination due to the special chemical characteristics of this particular additive.[475]

Whether strict products liability in tort should apply in such situations to claims brought against refiners by cities and water utilities, for damage this chemical causes to their water supplies, involves a host of issues, including most particularly whether relief is limited to persons injured after retail sale or an equivalent transaction. Reasoning that manufacturers are subject to strict liability once they place a defective product in the stream of commerce, and that storage in possibly faulty containers is a foreseeable use of gasoline once it is placed on the market, a California court ruled that policy reasons support holding a refiner strictly liable for failing to warn of the foreseeable risk of noxious harm to the water supply if a gas station's storage tanks allow the contaminant to leak into the ground.[476]

---

[471] See, e.g., Johnson v. William Benedict, Inc., 1993 WL 408058 (Conn. Super. Ct. 1993) (ducklings infected with salmonella bacteria passed disease to child); Worrell v. Sachs, 563 A.2d 1387 (Conn. Super. Ct. 1989) (child suffered eye damage from diseased, parasite-carrying puppy purchased from defendant's pet shop; puppy was "product" under products liability statute); Sease v. Taylor's Pets, Inc., 700 P.2d 1054 (Or. Ct. App. 1985) (pet shop skunk: "product"); Beyer v. Aquarium Supply Co., 404 N.Y.S.2d 778, 779 (Sup. Ct. 1977) (risk presented to humans by diseased animals as least as great as by defectively manufactured products). *But see* Pankey v. Petco Animal Supplies, Inc., 264 Cal. Rptr. 3d 644, 668 (Ct. App. 2020) (pet rat carrying bacteria that was harmless to rat but fatal to bitten child was "not a designed product for purposes of design defect strict products liability").

Animals may be considered "goods" under UCC Article 2. See, e.g., Blaha v. Stuard, 640 N.W.2d 85 (S.D. 2002) (dog); Flanagan v. Consolidated Nutrition, L.C., 627 N.W.2d 573 (Iowa Ct. App. 2001) (pigs); Trad Indus. v. Brogan, 805 P.2d 54 (Mont. 1991) (elk); Claxton v. Boothe, 790 P.2d 1201 (Or. Ct. App. 1990) (horse); Vince v. Broome, 443 So.2d 23 (Miss. 1983) (cattle).

[472] See, e.g., Malicki v. Koci, 700 N.E.2d 913 (Ohio Ct. App. 1997) (parrot fever caught from parakeet bought from pet store).

[473] Products Liability Rest. § 19 cmt. *b*.

[474] See § 10.7, above.

[475] Water is a "product" so that, if defective, its sale may be subject to products liability law. See Adel v. Greensprings of Vt., Inc., 363 F. Supp. 2d 692 (D. Vt. 2005) (sale of water that causes Legionnaires' disease gives rise to warranty liability and strict liability in tort).

[476] See Nelson v. Superior Ct., 50 Cal. Rptr. 3d 684 (Ct. App. 2006). In California, which never adopted § 402A, courts require only that a product be placed on the market, not sold. Id. at 688.

In 2003 and 2004, New York City and several of its agencies filed a complaint against more than fifty petroleum companies in federal court for damage from MTBE to its water supply. All defendants but Exxon settled, and the case proceeded to trial against Exxon on various claims in 2009. This particular case was selected as a bellwether trial for long-running multidistrict litigation, consolidated in the District Court, over the contamination of groundwater by MTBE. The jury found Exxon liable for negligence, trespass, public nuisance, and one products liability warning count, which the amended complaint styled as a "strict duty to warn against latent dangers resulting from foreseeable uses of [MTBE] that [d]efendants knew or should have known about."[477] The district court entered judgment against Exxon for $105 million, and the Second Circuit Court of Appeals affirmed the judgment, ruling in particular that the jury reasonably could find that Exxon failed to warn of the unusually deleterious environmental risks from spills and leaks of oil containing MTBE.[478]

Other highly toxic carcinogenic substances, particularly hazardous to young children, are polychlorinated biphenyls or PCBs, a group of manmade chemicals that formerly were used in transformers, capacitors, and other electrical equipment because of their stability rendering them resistant to extreme temperature and pressure. Cities and states have filed a number of recent cases against Monsanto, which for many decades manufactured PCBs that have been polluting waters across the nation. In *Mayor & City Council of Baltimore v. Monsanto Co.*,[479] the court ruled that it was foreseeable under the consumer expectations test that defectively designed and manufactured PCBs would contaminate the city's water systems and waterways. Moreover, ruled the court, strict liability recovery for design defects was not limited to a product's ultimate users but extended to bystanders as well. In addition, at least some individual plaintiffs have prevailed in claims against Monsanto for injuries from their exposure to PCBs.[480]

In another toxic pollution case,[481] manufacturers in upstate New York settled residents' claims that polyfluoroalkyl substances (PFOA) had contaminated their drinking water. The $65 million settlement included $23 million for medical monitoring of plaintiffs who drank the contaminated water for at least six months.[482]

A case alleging that glyphosate used in Roundup pesticide caused a plaintiff's non-Hodgkin's lymphoma ended with large punitive damages awards that were reduced on appeal.[483] Although the manufacturer pledged to withdraw glyphosate as an active

[477] In re Methyl Tertiary Butyl Ether ("MTBE") Prods. Liab. Litig., 725 F.3d 65, 82 (2d Cir. 2013) (N.Y. law). The jury ruled in favor of Exxon on the design defect claim. Id. at 79.

[478] Id. at 130. The court also upheld the jury's findings on negligence, trespass, and public nuisance. Compare In re Nassau Cnty. Consol. MTBE (Methyl Tertiary Butyl Ether) Prods. Liab. Litig., 918 N.Y.S.2d 399 (Sup. Ct. 2010) (table) (dismissing strict liability warnings claims against all defendants and design defect claims against pipeline distributors but sustaining strict liability design defect claims against retailers).

[479] 2020 WL 1529014, at *11 (D. Md. 2020).

[480] See, e.g., Burnson, Monsanto Told to Pay Teachers $185 Million Over PCB Exposure, Prod. Liab. & Toxics L. (July 27, 2021) (jury awarded $50 million compensatory and $135 million punitive damages to 3 teachers injured by exposure to PCBs in old fluorescent light ballasts).

[481] Baker v. Saint-Gobain Performance Plastics Corp., 2021 WL 2548825 (N.D.N.Y. 2021).

[482] See Steinberg, 3M, Saint-Gobain $65 Million Deal Over N.Y. Pollution Approved, Prod. Liab. & Toxics L. (Feb. 4, 2022).

[483] See, e.g., Pilliod v. Monsanto Co., 282 Cal. Rptr. 3d 679, 727 (Ct. App. 2021) (affirming remittitur of $2 billion punitive damages awards to $69 million); Hardeman v. Monsanto Co., 997 F.3d 941 (9th Cir. 2021) (Cal. law) (upholding bellwether trial court's remittitur of $75 punitive damages award to plaintiff suffering from non-Hodgkin's lymphoma to $20 million); Johnson v. Monsanto Co., 266 Cal. Rptr. 3d 111, 136 (Cal. Ct.

ingredient in the product in 2023, subject to EPA approval, and to set aside a large reserve for settlements, it is expected that Roundup litigation will continue for many years.[484]

Of all toxic products, surely asbestos, examined earlier,[485] has generated the most harm and litigation of any toxic substance so far. In the years ahead, products liability law will continue to stand ready to assess responsibility for new sources of cancer and other hazards uncovered in chemicals and other substances once thought largely beneficial to humans and society.[486]

App. 2020) (trial court's remittitur of punitive damages award to Roundup user with non-Hodgkin's lymphoma from $250 million to $39 million further reduced to $10 million).

484 Loh and Feeley, Bayer's Roundup Costs Could Top $16 Billion as Provisions Mount, Prod. Liab. & Toxics L. (July 29, 2021).

485 See § 10.3, above.

486 See, e.g., Steinberg, Procter & Gamble Benzene-in-Deodorant Suits Sent to Ohio Court, Prod. Liab. & Toxics L. (Apr. 8, 2022) (U.S. Judicial Panel on Multidistrict Litigation centralization of multiple actions); Rizzuto, FDA Food Survey Finds 'Forever Chemicals' in Tuna, Fish Sticks, Prod. Liab. & Toxics L. (Aug. 26, 2021).

Chapter 17

AUTOMOTIVE VEHICLES

Table of Sections

§ 17.1 AUTOMOTIVE LITIGATION—GENERALLY

Many products liability cases involve claims against manufacturers of cars, sport utility vehicles, vans, trucks, motorcycles, and other vehicles alleging that defective conditions in such products caused or aggravated injuries to the plaintiffs.[1] The usual victims in such accidents are drivers and passengers in the allegedly defective vehicles, but sometimes an accident vehicle (or some portion thereof) injures someone in another vehicle[2] or a pedestrian.[3] Automotive products liability cases may be divided into two major categories: (1) accidents caused by automotive defects,[4] and (2) aggravated injuries caused by a vehicle's failure to be sufficiently "crashworthy" to protect its occupants adequately from their "second collisions" with the vehicle and its environs resulting from the forces of an accident.[5]

In many respects, automotive products liability cases are no different from any other type of products liability case: a plaintiff normally must prove that some manufacturing, design, or warning defect, or some false assertion by the manufacturer or dealer, caused the plaintiff's harm. An automotive manufacturer typically defends cases of this type in conventional fashion by claiming that the accident was attributable to something other than a product defect, such as the driver's careless use. But various

---

1 Crashes attributable to vehicle defects are quite rare. See ch. 13, note 1, above. On automotive products liability generally, see, e.g., Nader and Page, Automobile-Design Liability and Compliance with Federal Standards, 64 Geo. Wash. L. Rev. 415 (1996); Sugarman, Nader's Failures?, 80 Cal. L. Rev. 289 (1992) (reviewing J. Marshaw and D. Harfst, The Struggle for Auto Safety (1990)); Nader and Page, Automobile Design and the Judicial Process, 55 Cal. L. Rev. 645 (1967); Katz, Liability of Automobile Manufacturers for Unsafe Design of Passenger Cars, 69 Harv. L. Rev. 863 (1956); Am. Law Prod. Liab. 3d ch. 95 Automobiles; Frumer, Friedman, and Sklaren, Products Liability ch. 22 Automotive Products Liability Law.

2 See, e.g., Ho v. Michelin N. Am., Inc., 520 Fed. Appx. 658 (10th Cir. 2013) (Kan. law) (pickup truck crossed median and struck plaintiff's car when its tire failed); Hajek v. Kumho Tire Co., 2010 WL 503044 (D. Neb. 2010) (pickup truck crossed interstate median and crashed into plaintiffs' vehicle when tire's tread and belt separated); Boyle v. Ford Motor Co., 942 A.2d 850, 853 (N.J. Super. Ct. App. Div. 2008) (car burrowed under frame of flatbed truck that had no rear bumper guard, injuring occupants of car).

3 See, e.g., Roe v. FCA US LLC, 2021 WL 2640107 (W.D. Okla. 2021) (Jeep allegedly self-shifted into reverse, backing over and injuring plaintiff who had exited the vehicle to close a gate); Wright v. Ford Motor Co., 508 F.3d 263 (5th Cir. 2007) (Tex. law) (truck with blind spot backed over child); Haumersen v. Ford Motor Co., 257 N.W.2d 7 (Iowa 1977) (child in school yard struck by car).

4 See § 17.2, below.

5 See § 17.3, below.

issues that may affect the outcome of automotive products liability litigation—automotive crashworthiness, apportionment of damages, and the role of plaintiff fault—involve certain special applications of, and limitations on, the general rules of products liability law. Thus, while much of the applicable doctrine in products liability cases involving automobiles is no different from that applied in other types of products liability cases, enough special issues occur in the automotive context to warrant their separate examination.

This chapter explores the recurring special issues in automotive products liability law.[6] By causing crashes, defects in tires and other automotive components may become integral to automotive products liability litigation, as illustrated by the rash of accidents involving Ford Explorers and other vehicles equipped with defective Firestone tires some time ago.[7] Since liability issues for manufacturers of tires and other automotive components are generally the same as in cases involving components of other types of products,[8] the discussion here does not address the liability of manufacturers of such components. This chapter examines special liability theories and defenses based on driver fault that recur in accident litigation against manufacturers of automotive vehicles.[9] A number of more general issues examined in other chapters, such as the malfunction (or general defect) theory of liability,[10] product recalls,[11] and federal preemption[12] often play a major role in automotive products liability litigation, and the treatment of those issues in other chapters should be referred to as appropriate.

Section 17.2 examines the kinds of automotive defects, such as defects in a vehicle's steering, brakes, acceleration system, transmission, and other design components that can cause automotive accidents. Section 17.3 considers the nature and historical development of the doctrine of automotive crashworthiness. Section 17.4 explores apportionment issues that arise when responsibility for an accident is shared by an automotive manufacturer and another party. Section 17.5 examines the role of plaintiff fault in automotive products liability litigation, including the effect of a driver's intoxication and the consequence of a plaintiff's failure to use a seatbelt or other safety device. Finally, § 17.6 provides an introduction to some of the evolving issues surrounding autonomous vehicles.

§ 17.2 DEFECTS THAT CAUSE ACCIDENTS

Numerous automotive products liability cases involve accidents that may have resulted from some defect in the vehicle. As discussed below, many of these cases allege

---

[6] Crashworthiness and other auto liability principles and defenses often apply equally to other types of vehicles, such as airplanes, tractors, and boats. See, e.g., Valente v. Textron, Inc., 931 F. Supp. 2d 409 (E.D.N.Y. 2013) (golf cart); Malen v. MTD Prods., Inc., 628 F.3d 296 (7th Cir. 2010) (Ill. Law) (riding mower); Deere & Co. v. Grose, 586 So.2d 196 (Ala. 1991) (tractor without ROPS); Rose v. Mercury Marine, 483 So.2d 1351 (Miss. 1986) (boat propeller injured swimmer); Bruce v. Martin-Marietta Corp., 544 F.2d 442 (10th Cir. 1976) (Md. law) (airplane); Frumer, Friedman, and Sklaren, Products Liability § 22.09[3] (collecting cases on crashworthiness claims for various products). See also Copeland, Electric Scooters: A New Frontier in Transportation and Products Liability, 26 Rich. J.L. & Tech. 4 (2020). Liability principles applied in cases involving these other types of vehicles normally are the same as those applied in cases involving automotive vehicles.

[7] See Yates, Tire Hysteria Veers Out of Control, Wall St. J., Aug. 14, 2000, at A18.

[8] See § 15.3, above.

[9] Liability issues involving used car dealers are examined in § 16.5, above.

[10] See § 7.4, above.

[11] See § 10.8, above.

[12] See § 14.5, above.

that the accident was caused by a manufacturing defect, some allege that the vehicle was defectively designed, and others allege that the manufacturer failed to provide adequate warnings or instructions. Although a vehicle's general design features may lead to accidents in certain situations, as by generating a propensity to roll over, most of the cases concerning defects that cause accidents involve claims of defects in one of a vehicle's essential control mechanisms or components, such as its steering, brakes, accelerator, transmission, engine, suspension system, wheels, or tires.

Manufacturing Defect Claims

Two of the most renowned products liability cases of all time, *MacPherson v. Buick Motor Co.*[13] and *Henningsen v. Bloomfield Motors, Inc.*,[14] arose out of manufacturing defects in automobiles which caused the cars to crash. *MacPherson* involved a twenty-two horsepower Buick runabout equipped with wooden wheels, one of which was made of brittle, coarse-grained hickory, which caused the wheel to break and the car to crash. The plaintiff claimed that Buick Motor Company had been negligent in failing to test or inspect the wheel sufficiently for defects, and Buick contended that its limited testing and inspection process was sufficient because of the reputation of its supplier, a wheel manufacturer, for making high quality wheels.[15] A modern analogue was Ford Motor Company's plight some years ago from having equipped its Explorer SUVs with Firestone tires with treads that had a tendency to peel off at highway speeds.[16] The other classic products liability case, *Henningsen*, involved a mechanical defect in the steering mechanism of a Plymouth Plaza 6 Club Sedan that caused the car to veer off the highway and hit a brick wall, injuring Mrs. Henningsen and destroying the car.[17]

When the sudden malfunction of a new vehicle leads to a crash, as in both *MacPherson* and *Henningsen*, the cause of the accident usually is some type of manufacturing defect, although it may be some defect in design. Especially if the vehicle is badly damaged, it may be difficult (if not impossible) to discover precisely what went wrong. In such cases, a plaintiff may be assisted by res ipsa loquitur[18] or the malfunction doctrine,[19] previously discussed. Although accident reconstructionists frequently disagree, such experts usually are able to ascertain the precise manufacturing or design defect that caused a crash. Cases involving claims that manufacturing defects caused an

---

13 111 N.E. 1050 (N.Y. 1916) (Cardozo, J.). *MacPherson* is discussed in § 1.2, above.

14 161 A.2d 69 (N.J. 1960) (Francis, J.). *Henningsen* is discussed in § 5.2, above.

15 See, e.g., D. Peck, Decision at Law 40–64 (1961).

16 States Launch Investigation of Tire Recall, Wall St. J., Sept. 26, 2000, at A3.

17 161 A.2d at 75.

18 See § 2.5, above.

19 See, e.g., Guilkey v. Com. Truck & Van Equip., Inc., 2021 WL 1093623, at *2–3 (E.D. Ky. 2021) (circumstantial evidence sufficient to establish that manufacturing defect caused truck's tailgate collapse, injuring plaintiff); see also § 7.4, above.

accident include claims of defects in a vehicle's steering,[20] brakes,[21] accelerator,[22] transmission,[23] engine,[24] suspension system,[25] electrical system,[26] and wheels or tires.[27]

Design Defect Claims

Design defects are the other principal cause of automotive accident claims in products liability litigation. Since design defects infect the entire product line, threatening the safety of thousands of persons, some have become quite notorious. Control problems in the Corvair, publicized by Ralph Nader in the 1960s in *Unsafe at Any Speed*, is one example.[28] Accelerator sticking problems in certain Audis led to claims in the 1970s;[29] as did rollover tendencies of certain Jeeps in the 1970s and

---

[20] See, e.g., Jackson v. Ford Motor Co., 842 F.3d 902, 909 (6th Cir. 2016) (Tenn. law) (alleged defects in steering system caused loss of driver's control over vehicle, resulting in accident); Smith v. Ford Motor Co., 215 F.3d 713 (7th Cir. 2000) (Ind. law) (driver lost control of Ford Econoline 150 van; design and manufacturing defects in steering gearbox); Annot., 100 A.L.R.3d 158 (1980) (defects in steering systems); Am. Law Prod. Liab. 3d §§ 95:145–95:171 (defects grouped by elements of steering system).

[21] See, e.g., McKinney v. Superior Van & Mobility, LLC, 2021 WL 1699885, at *10 (E.D. La. 2021) (Electronic Mobility Control's braking interface deviated from federal motor vehicle safety standards); Castaldi v. Land Rover N. Am., Inc., 2007 WL 4165283 (E.D.N.Y. 2007) (misaligned brake light switch deactivated brake shift interlock, causing rapid acceleration); Annot., 99 A.L.R.3d 179 (1980) (brake system defects); Am. Law Prod. Liab. 3d, §§ 95:58–95:77 (defects grouped by elements of braking system).

[22] See, e.g., Krikorian v. Ford Motor Co., 2019 WL 7042939 (S.D. Ala. 2019) (denying plaintiff's motion to remand; claims that manufacturing and design defects caused sudden acceleration, among other problems); Foster v. Craig Equip. Co., 550 So.2d 818 (La. Ct. App. 1989) (misaligned accelerator pedal on school bus could slide past stop and cause throttle to remain in open position). See generally Annot., 76 A.L.R.6th 465 (2012) (sudden or unexpected acceleration of motor vehicle); Am. Law Prod. Liab. 3d §§ 95:110–95:111 (acceleration problems).

[23] See, e.g., Milisits v. FCA US LLC, 2021 WL 3145704, at *4 (E.D. Mich. 2021) (vehicle lost all acceleration without warning and driver had to coast through traffic to pull over); Hardt v. Chrysler Grp. LLC, 2015 WL 12683965, at *5 (C.D. Cal. 2015) (same); Davis v. Ford Motor Co., 128 F.3d 631 (8th Cir. 1997) (Ark. law) (parking gear released in defective Ford transmission); Annot., 100 A.L.R.3d 471 (1980) (transmission defects); Am. Law Prod. Liab. 3d § 95:178 (gearshift mechanisms).

[24] See, e.g., Hernandez v. Avis Budget Grp., Inc., 2017 WL 6406838, at *2 (E.D. Cal. 2017); Delvecchio v. General Motors Corp., 625 N.E.2d 1022 (Ill. App. Ct. 1993) (engine stall caused by malfunction in engine throttle system).

[25] See, e.g., Wallace v. Ford Motor Co., 2013 WL 3288435 (S.D. Miss. 2013) (defective bolt in suspension system allegedly caused steering failure); Norton v. Ford Motor Co., 470 F.2d 992 (5th Cir. 1972) (Tex. law) (spindle nut on right front wheel defectively manufactured); Annot., 100 A.L.R.3d 912 (1980) (collecting cases); Am. Law of Products Liability 3d §§ 95:145–95:171 (collecting cases).

[26] See, e.g., Anderson v. Chrysler Corp., 403 S.E.2d 189 (W. Va. 1991) (electrical fire behind dashboard). See also Hull and Malick, Battery Fires Haunt the Electric Car and Clean Power Revolution, Prod. Liab. & Toxics L. (Sept. 24, 2021); Yang, GM Recalls Chevrolet Bolt EVs Again Following Battery Fires, Prod. Liab. & Toxics L. (July 23, 2021).

[27] See, e.g., Downey v. Roof Bolt Transp., Inc., 2021 WL 232592, at *5 (E.D. Ky. 2021) (issue of fact whether manufacturing defect caused truck's wheel assembly to detach); Wilcher v. Redding Swainsboro Ford Lincoln Mercury, Inc., 743 S.E.2d 27 (Ga. Ct. App. 2013) (tire on van); Wright v. Suzuki Motor Corp., 2005 WL 1594850 (Ohio Ct. App. 2005) (motorcycle); MacPherson v. Buick Motor Co., 111 N.E. 1050 (N.Y. 1916) (wheel); Annot., 81 A.L.R.3d 318 (1977) (collecting cases).

[28] See, e.g., Faust v. General Motors Corp., 377 A.2d 885 (N.H. 1977); Chart v. General Motors Corp., 258 N.W.2d 680 (Wis. 1977); Jenkins v. General Motors Corp., 446 F.2d 377 (5th Cir. 1971) (Ga. law).

[29] See, e.g., Ferro v. Volkswagen of Am., Inc., 588 A.2d 1047 (R.I. 1991); Bradofsky v. Volkswagen of Am., Inc., 17 Prod. Liab. Advisory 5 (N.D. Ohio 1988).

1980s,[30] the Suzuki Samurai,[31] the Ford Bronco II[32] and other SUVs[33] in the 1980s and 1990s,[34] the Ford Explorer in the late 1990s and early 2000s;[35] unintended acceleration claims in the 2010s;[36] and issues with autonomous vehicle accidents in the 2020s.[37] The SUV rollover problems mentioned above resulted from the relatively high center of gravity in Jeeps and many SUVs, combined with their narrow track width, high center of gravity, and sometimes light weight, which made some models quite unstable and apt to roll over in sharp steering maneuvers at highway speeds.[38]

Ford Motor Company encountered a rash of litigation during the 1970s and 1980s from the tendency of some of its transmissions to slip from park to reverse.[39] Accidents could occur when a driver tried to place the gear shift lever in park but mispositioned it on the gatepost between park and reverse. If the driver then left the car with the engine running, the vibration from the engine or the door slamming could cause the transmission to slip into reverse. Plaintiffs' experts testified that the design of the gatepost and springs made it much more likely that the Ford FMX transmission would accidentally slip into Reverse as compared to transmissions in other cars. For example, in *Ford Motor Co. v. Nowak*,[40] the plaintiff's decedent drove into her driveway, stopped the car, attempted to shift the car into park, stepped out of the car, and went behind it to close the driveway gate. The transmission slipped from park to reverse, and the car backed over the decedent.

---

30 See, e.g., Am. Law Prod. Liab. 3d § 97:31 (Jeep rollover accidents).

31 See, e.g., Rodriguez v. Suzuki Motor Corp., 936 S.W.2d 104 (Mo. 1996); Am. Law Prod. Liab. 3d § 97:32 (Suzuki Samurai).

32 See, e.g., Clay v. Ford Motor Co., 215 F.3d 663 (6th Cir. 2000) (Ohio law); Ford Motor Co. v. Ammerman, 705 N.E.2d 539 (Ind. Ct. App. 1999); Am. Law Prod. Liab. 3d § 9:27 (Ford Bronco II).

33 See, e.g., Pannu v. Land Rover N. Am., Inc., 120 Cal. Rptr. 3d 605, 610–11 (Ct. App. 2011) (Land Rover Discovery Series I); Jonas v. Isuzu Motors Ltd., 210 F. Supp. 2d 1373 (M.D. Ga. 2002) (1993 Isuzu Rodeo), aff'd, 58 Fed. Appx. 837 (11th Cir. 2003); McCathern v. Toyota Motor Corp., 23 P.3d 320, 333 (Or. 2001) (1994 Toyota 4Runner).

34 See Bradsher, Auto Industry May Ease Safety-Ratings Stance, N.Y. Times, Sept. 19, 2000, at C16 (rollovers kill 9,500 of 41,000 Americans who die each year in automobile crashes).

35 See, e.g., Ford Motor Co. v. Hall-Edwards, 971 So.2d 854 (Fla. Dist. Ct. App. 2007) ($60 million judgment on verdict reversed and remanded for evidentiary errors). Many of these mishaps resulted from blowouts of allegedly defective Firestone tires. See, e.g., Rosenthal v. Ford Motor Co., 462 F. Supp. 2d 296 (D. Conn. 2006); In re Bridgestone/Firestone, Inc., Tires Prods. Liab. Litig., 287 F. Supp. 2d 943, 943 (S.D. Ind. 2003). See also McDonald, Don't Tread on Me: Faster Than a Tire Blowout, Congress Passes Wide-Sweeping Legislation That Treads on the Thirty-Five Year Old Motor Vehicle Safety Act, 49 Buff. L. Rev. 1163 (2001); Bradsher, Ford Intends to Replace 13 Million Firestone Wilderness Tires, N.Y. Times, May 23, 2001, at C1.

36 See, e.g., Bullock v. Volkswagen Grp. of Am., 107 F. Supp. 3d 1305, 1315 (M.D. Ga. 2015) (jury question whether design defect caused unintended acceleration); In re Toyota Motor Corp. Unintended Acceleration Mktg., Sales Pracs., & Prods. Liab. Litig., 978 F. Supp. 2d 1053, 1103 (C.D. Cal. 2013) (Ga. law) (denying manufacturer's motion to dismiss design defect and failure to warn claims).

37 See, e.g., Wang v. Tesla, Inc., 2021 WL 3023088 (E.D.N.Y. 2021) (Tesla Autopilot failed to react to vehicle merging in between the Tesla and a tractor-trailer, causing Tesla driver to quickly steer and crash into two other cars). See generally Trudell and Laing, Tesla Autopilot Probed by U.S. Over Crash-Scene Collisions, Prod. Liab. & Toxics L. (Aug. 16, 2021) (listing 11 confirmed crashes involving Tesla's Autopilot system).

38 See, e.g., Oshima v. Kia Motors Corp., 2012 WL 1578397 (D. Colo. 2012) (rollover propensity of Kia Rondo); McCathern v. Toyota Motor Corp., 23 P.3d 320, 333 (Or. 2001); Clay v. Ford Motor Co., 215 F.3d 663, 671 (6th Cir. 2000) (Ohio law).

39 Transmissions in other vehicles sometimes experience similar problems. See, e.g., Roe v. FCA US LLC, 2021 WL 2640107 (W.D. Okla. 2021) (Jeep); General Motors Corp. v. Sanchez, 997 S.W.2d 584 (Tex. 1999) (1990 Chevy pickup); Klein v. BMW of N. Am., Inc., 705 So.2d 1200 (La. Ct. App. 1997).

40 638 S.W.2d 582 (Tex. App. 1982) (5–1 decision) (affirming $400,000 pecuniary damages and $4,000,000 punitive damages awards) (gatepost diagramed at 586–87).

Other cases in which design defects allegedly caused accidents include claims of defects in a vehicle's steering,[41] brakes,[42] accelerator,[43] transmission,[44] ignition,[45] engine,[46] suspension system,[47] air bags,[48] and wheels and tires.[49]

Warning and Instruction Defect Claims

Warning and instruction defect claims are less common than manufacturing and design defect claims in this context. Indeed, in automotive as well as other types of products liability litigation,[50] defective warning claims often piggyback on underlying claims of some deficiency in a vehicle's design.[51] For example, although the park-reverse litigation against Ford mentioned earlier involved an allegedly defective design of the transmission's gatepost and springs, the danger would have been reduced had drivers known that their transmissions could slip out of gear if they did not take particular caution to ensure that their shift levers were carefully secured in park before leaving their vehicles. Accordingly, in addition to allegations of design

---

[41] See, e.g., Logan v. Ford Motor Co., 293 So.3d 840 (Miss. Ct. App. 2019) (steering column design); Roman v. General Motors Corp., 727 F. Supp. 1153 (N.D. Ill. 1989) (loss of steering); Annot., 100 A.L.R.3d 158 (1980) (collecting cases).

[42] See, e.g., Bourgeois v. Garrard Chevrolet, Inc., 811 So.2d 962, 963 (La. Ct. App. 2002) (ABS malfunction); Duren v. Paccar, Inc., 549 S.E.2d 755 (Ga. Ct. App. 2001) (no anti-lock brakes on tractor-trailer). See also Laing, Tesla 'Phantom Braking' Complaints Spur Formal NHTSA Probe, Prod. Liab. & Toxics L. (Feb. 17, 2022) (unanticipated automated braking causing rapid deceleration from high speeds).

[43] See, e.g., Hill v. Kia Motors Am., Inc., 2022 WL 557823, at *13 (6th Cir. 2022) (Tenn. law) (unintended acceleration allegedly caused by electronic-throttle-control system failure); Kesse v. Ford Motor Co., 2020 WL 832363 (N.D. Ill. 2020) (same); Bolt v. Ford Motor Co., 2019 WL 1254662 (N.D. Ala. 2019) (unintended acceleration); In re Toyota Motor Corp., Unintended Acceleration Mktg., Sales Practices, & Prods. Liab. Litig., 2013 WL 3224585 (C.D. Cal. 2013); Jarvis v. Ford Motor Co., 283 F.3d 33 (2d Cir. 2002) (N.Y. law) (design defect in cruise control—sudden acceleration).

[44] See, e.g., McKinney v. Superior Van & Mobility, LLC, 2021 WL 1699885 (E.D. La. 2021) (design of Advanced Electronic Vehicle Interface Technology that allegedly caused crash of van used by partially paralyzed driver); Reis v. Volvo Cars of N. Am., 18 N.E.3d 383 (N.Y. 2014) (design and warning claims; failure to install starter interlock to prevent manual transmission car from lurching forward when started in forward gear); Annot., 100 A.L.R.3d 471 (1980) (collecting cases).

[45] See, e.g., In re General Motors LLC Ignition Switch Litig., 2019 WL 952348 (S.D.N.Y. 2019); Spector, GM Settles Ignition 'Bellwether' Cases, Wall St. J.com (Sept. 5, 2016).

[46] See, e.g., Great W. Cas. Co. v. Volvo Trucks N. Am., Inc., 2013 WL 617068 (N.D. Ill. 2013) (engine defect caused fire); Delvecchio v. General Motors Corp., 625 N.E.2d 1022 (Ill. App. Ct. 1993) (design flaw caused engine stall).

[47] See, e.g., Nelson v. American Honda Motor Co., 2021 WL 2646840 (W.D. Pa. 2021) (ATV stability and maneuverability); Rooker v. Ford Motor Co., 100 So.3d 1229 (Fla. Dist. Ct. App. 2012) (Explorer roll over); Thomasson v. A.K. Durnin Chrysler-Plymouth, Inc., 399 So.2d 1205 (La. Ct. App. 1981) (front suspension collapsed); Annot., 100 A.L.R.3d 912 (1980) (suspension cases).

[48] See, e.g., Coates v. Ford Motor Co., 2021 WL 2207367 (E.D. Mich. 2021) (airbag spontaneously exploded, causing crash that injured driver); Moore v. Toyota Motor Corp., 2019 WL 1199614 (E.D. La. 2019) (airbag spontaneously deployed, causing crash into utility pole).

[49] See, e.g., Estate of Shield v. Kumho Tire U.S.A., Inc., 2020 WL 4464508 (D.S.D. 2020) (granting plaintiffs' discovery request for accident tire's design specifications to "determine if the too-thin inner liner was a manufacturing defect (i.e. the accident tire's inner liner was less thick than the design specifications) or a design defect"); Moore v. The Goodyear Tire & Rubber Co., 2011 WL 2176175 (N.D. Tex. 2011) (absence of nylon overlay that would have helped prevent tread separation).

[50] See § 9.1, above.

[51] See, e.g., Perez v. FCA USA LLC, 2021 WL 2139334, at *2 (E.D. Mich. 2021) (failure to warn that car's power window lacked auto-reverse feature that could have protected a child's head and neck); Moore v. Ford Motor Co., 332 S.W.3d 749 (Mo. 2011) (collapse of driver's seat in rear-impact collision; design defect claim and failure to warn of risk to 300-pound drivers).

defectiveness, the transmission-slip cases typically included claims that Ford failed to provide adequate warnings and instructions to operators of these vehicles.[52]

Similarly, rollover cases often logically involve warning and instruction defect claims in addition to allegations of a vehicle's design deficiency. For example, the manufacturer's failure to warn of this risk was a central claim in *Greiner v. Volkswagenwerk A.G.*,[53] which involved the propensity of old-model Volkswagen Beetles to roll over on sharp steering maneuvers. The failure to warn of this propensity was also a principal claim in the rollover litigation involving the Bronco II,[54] discussed above, especially before prominent warnings were required by the National Highway Traffic Safety Administration.[55] Other claims of an automotive manufacturer's failure to adequately warn or instruct involve dangers in a vehicle's steering,[56] brakes,[57] accelerator,[58] transmission,[59] suspension system,[60] seat strength,[61] restraint system,[62] driver-assistance features,[63] and wheels or tires.[64]

§ 17.3 CRASHWORTHINESS

The previous section examined some of the principal ways in which automotive defects may cause vehicular accidents. Yet automotive accidents have many causes, including driver error,[65] collisions caused by other drivers, and dangerous highway conditions. An issue that cuts across nearly every type of automotive accident, regardless

---

52 See, e.g., Kallio v. Ford Motor Co., 407 N.W.2d 92, 93–94 (Minn. 1987) (adequate warnings not provided); Ford Motor Co. v. Nowak, 638 S.W.2d 582, 585 (Tex. App. 1982) (same). Compare Pavoni v. Chrysler Grp., LLC, 789 F.3d 1095, 1098–99 (9th Cir. 2015) (Cal. law) (reversing summary judgment for defendant; strict liability and negligent design and warning claims that "false park" defect caused vehicle's self-shift into reverse in garage, pinning elderly couple under car, causing their deaths).

53 540 F.2d 85 (3d Cir. 1976) (Pa. law) (passenger's failure to warn claim warranted submission to jury).

54 See, e.g., Ford Motor Co. v. Ammerman, 705 N.E.2d 539, 563 (Ind. Ct. App. 1999) (upholding punitive damages judgment of $13.8 million, remitted by trial judge from verdict of $58 million); Watkins v. Ford Motor Co., 190 F.3d 1213, 1217 (11th Cir. 1999) (Ga. law); Greco v. Ford Motor Co., 937 F. Supp. 810, 816 (S.D. Ind. 1996) (denying Ford's motion for summary judgment).

55 See Fisher v. Ford Motor Co., 224 F.3d 570 (6th Cir. 2000) (Ohio law).

56 See, e.g., Fordham v. Garrett-Schwartz Motor Co., 173 S.E.2d 450 (Ga. Ct. App. 1970) (failure to warn that steering was defective); Annot., 100 A.L.R.3d 158 (1980) (steering defects); Am. Law Prod. Liab. 3d §§ 95:155–95:171 (steering cases grouped by specific elements).

57 See, e.g., White v. Ford Motor Co., 500 F.3d 963, 970 (9th Cir. 2007) (Nev. law) (failure to warn of defective parking brake); Hasson v. Ford Motor Co., 564 P.2d 857 (Cal. 1977); Annot., 99 A.L.R.3d 179 (1980).

58 See, e.g., In re Toyota Motor Corp., Unintended Acceleration Mktg., Sales Practices, & Prods. Liab. Litig., 754 F. Supp. 2d 1208, 1220–21 (C.D. Cal. 2010) (alleged failure to warn adequately of unintended acceleration risk); Babb v. Ford Motor Co., 535 N.E.2d 676 (Ohio Ct. App. 1987); Annot., 76 A.L.R.6th 465 (2012); Am. Law Prod. Liab. 3d §§ 95:110–95:111.

59 See, e.g., Davis v. Ford Motor Co., 128 F.3d 631 (8th Cir. 1997) (Ark. law); Kallio v. Ford Motor Co., 407 N.W.2d 92 (Minn. 1987); Annot., 100 A.L.R.3d 471 (1980).

60 See, e.g., Haberkorn v. Chrysler Corp., 533 N.W.2d 373 (Mich. Ct. App. 1995); Bond v. Fruehauf Corp., Prod. Liab. Rep. (CCH) ¶ 8830 (Tenn. Ct. App. 1978); Annot., 100 A.L.R.3d 912 (1980); Am. Law Prod. Liab. 3d §§ 95:145–95.171. See also Nelson v. American Honda Motor Co., 2021 WL 2646840, at *2 (W.D. Pa. 2021) (post-sale duty to warn of ATV stability and maneuverability design flaws).

61 See, e.g., Moore v. Ford Motor Co., 332 S.W.3d 749 (Mo. 2011) (collapse of driver's seat in rear-impact collision; design defect claim and failure to warn of risk to 300-pound drivers).

62 See, e.g., Nissan Motor Co. v. Maddox, 2013 WL 4620488 (Ky. Ct. App. 2013) (restraint system spooled out four inches in frontal collision, allowing 240-pound plaintiff to submarine under seatbelt).

63 See, e.g., Wang v. Tesla, Inc., 2021 WL 3023088, at *1 (E.D.N.Y. 2021) (allegations that Tesla failed to warn of Autopilot limitations and failed to give proper instructions on its use).

64 See, e.g., Mascarenas v. Cooper Tire & Rubber Co., 643 F. Supp. 2d 1363, 1371 (S.D. Ga. 2009); Rougeau v. Hyundai Motor Am., 805 So.2d 147 (La. 2002).

65 See § 17.5, below.

of its cause, is the extent to which the design of the vehicle protects the safety or aggravates the injuries of its occupants during a vehicular accident. This is the issue of vehicular crashworthiness, one of the most important types of design defectiveness in modern American products liability law.[66]

Crashworthiness in General

Congress aptly defines automotive "crashworthiness" as "the protection a passenger motor vehicle gives its passengers against personal injury or death from a motor vehicle accident."[67] A vehicle's capacity to offer such protection is a function of its ability to withstand and absorb the physical stresses of a collision combined with its ability to prevent additional ("enhanced" or "aggravated") injuries to the occupants in a "second collision" with the vehicle's interior.[68] Thus, a vehicle's crashworthiness is improved or diminished by the extent that its body can absorb the forces of a crash without collapsing into the passenger compartment against the occupants; that its dashboard and head restraints are appropriately padded, rather than being made of solid steel; that the glass in its windows crumbles harmlessly, rather than fracturing into lethal slivers; that the steering wheel telescopes to absorb the force of a collision with the driver's chest, rather than remaining rigid as a wall; that the edges and ends of knobs, levers, and other protrusions are rounded and covered by protective material, rather than being left as sharp, pointed steel; that the fuel tank is located in a safe position and securely protected against the varying insults it may encounter in different types of collisions; that the doors and windows have sufficient latches to hold them closed in accident situations to keep the occupants contained, rather than popping open and allowing the occupants to be flung outside; that airbags protect the occupants from injury, rather than activating spontaneously or with explosive force;

---

[66] See, e.g., Hubbard and Sobocinski, Crashworthiness: The Collision of Sellers' Responsibility for Product Safety with Comparative Fault, 69 S.C. L. Rev. 741 (2018); Bublick, The Tort-Proof Plaintiff: The Drunk in the Automobile, Crashworthiness Claims, and the *Restatement (Third) of Torts*, 74 Brook. L. Rev. 707 (2009); Latin and Kasolas, Bad Designs, Lethal Profits: The Duty to Protect Other Motorists Against SUV Collision Risks, 82 B.U. L. Rev. 1161 (2002); Nader and Page, Automobile-Design Liability and Compliance with Federal Standards, 64 Geo. Wash. L. Rev. 415 (1996); Sugarman, Nader's Failures?, 80 Cal. L. Rev. 289 (1992) (reviewing J. Mashaw and D. Harfst, The Struggle for Auto Safety (1990)); Harris, Enhanced Injury Theory: An Analytic Framework, 62 N.C. L. Rev. 643 (1984); Nader and Page, Automobile Design and the Judicial Process, 55 Cal. L. Rev. 645 (1967); Katz, Liability of Automobile Manufacturers for Unsafe Design of Passenger Cars, 69 Harv. L. Rev. 863 (1956); C. Buck, Injury and Jury—Pennsylvania's "Unique" Crashworthiness Law (2008) (unpublished manuscript); Frumer, Friedman, and Sklaren, Products Liability ch. 22.09[3].

[67] 49 U.S.C. § 32301(1) (the Motor Vehicle Information and Cost Savings Act). While this definition is limited to passenger vehicles, common-law crashworthiness principles apply more broadly to other types of vehicles. See, e.g., Norman v. Textron Inc., 2018 WL 3199487 (W.D. Mo. 2018) (forklift); Malen v. MTD Prods., Inc., 628 F.3d 296, 311–13 (7th Cir. 2010) (Ill. law) (riding lawnmower); Duren v. Paccar, Inc., 549 S.E.2d 755 (Ga. Ct. App. 2001) (tractor-trailer); Schroeder v. Com., Dep't of Transp., 710 A.2d 23 (Pa. 1998) (truck); Kupetz v. Deere & Co., 644 A.2d 1213 (Pa. Super. Ct. 1994) (bulldozer). See also Miller v. Todd, 551 N.E.2d 1139, 1141 n.1 (Ind. 1990) (noting that crashworthiness doctrine has been applied to motorcycles, airplanes, snowmobiles, pleasure boats, and tractors). *But see* Confessore v. Agco Corp., 2020 WL 6703550, at *11 (N.J. Super. Ct. App. Div. 2020) ("Despite [Rest. (3d) Torts § 16, cmt. *b.*, illus. 4], our Supreme Court has yet to prescribe that a jury charge on crashworthiness is appropriate to use in a products liability case that involves a tractor . . . .").

[68] "Crashworthiness" might be viewed as broader than "second-collision" liability, in that the latter term suggests interior collision injuries to the exclusion of injuries from ejection, see, e.g., Lee v. Volkswagen of Am., Inc., 688 P.2d 1283 (Okla. 1984) (ejected occupant "collided" with street), and from burns caused by defective fuel systems, as discussed below. See also Linert v. Foutz, 75 N.E.3d 1218, 1221 n.3 (Ohio 2016) ("Crashworthiness claims, sometimes framed as 'second collision' or 'injury enhancement' claims, arise when a defect in a motor vehicle allegedly enhances or increases the injuries sustained by a driver or passenger in the vehicle.").

and that safety belts, harnesses, and head rests effectively restrain and protect the occupants rather than serving as instruments of injury or death.

The Crashworthiness Duty

Whether manufacturers have a duty to design crashworthy vehicles was a major issue of products liability law in the late 1960s and early 1970s. The controversy originated with the 1966 decision in *Evans v. General Motors Corp.*,[69] where the driver of a 1961 Chevrolet station wagon manufactured by the defendant was killed when the side of his car collapsed on him when it was struck by another vehicle. The plaintiff alleged that the car's frame was defective because it was designed in the shape of an "X" without the kind of steel perimeter railing used in other cars. But the court disagreed. While it might be desirable for manufacturers to construct automobiles to be safe in collisions, the court viewed the imposition of such a requirement to be a legislative function,[70] and "[a] manufacturer is not under a duty to make his automobile accident-proof or fool-proof."[71] Reasoning that the "intended purpose" of automobiles does not include their participation in collisions,[72] a split panel[73] of the Seventh Circuit Court of Appeals ruled that General Motors did not have a duty to equip its cars with side frames to protect the occupants from collisions, even if such events were foreseeable.

Two years later, after critical reviews of *Evans* in the law journals,[74] the Eighth Circuit joined issue in *Larsen v. General Motors Corp.*[75] The plaintiff was injured in a head-on collision, the force of which propelled the top of the steering shaft, the bottom end of which protruded 2.7 inches in front of the forward tires, back into his head. Citing *Evans*, General Motors argued once again that its design obligation was limited to making cars safe for their intended use of driving on the highways and did not extend to designing them for safety in head-on collisions. But the argument was wearing thin, and the Eighth Circuit was markedly unimpressed by the "intended use" argument, which it viewed as "much too narrow and unrealistic." Because injuries in car accidents are "readily foreseeable," the court reasoned that manufacturers should be subject to liability for injuries caused by their negligent design that causes or aggravates such harm. "The sole function of an automobile," the court remarked, "is not just to provide a means of transportation, it is to provide a means of safe transportation or as safe as is reasonably possible under the present state of the art."[76] Citing data on the high rate of serious injuries and deaths from automotive accidents,[77] including the fact that many or

---

[69] 359 F.2d 822 (7th Cir. 1966) (Ind. law).

[70] Id. at 824.

[71] Id.

[72] "The intended purpose of an automobile does not include its participation in collisions with other objects, despite the manufacturer's ability to foresee the possibility that such collisions may occur. As defendant argues, the defendant also knows that its automobiles may be driven into bodies of water, but it is not suggested that defendant has a duty to equip them with pontoons." Id. at 825. On the rise and fall of the intended use doctrine, see § 13.5, above.

[73] Judge Kiley's persuasive dissenting opinion, 359 F.2d at 825, foreshadowed (and was relied upon by) Larsen v. General Motors Corp., 391 F.2d 495, 499 (8th Cir. 1968) (Mich. law).

[74] See, e.g., Nader and Page, Automobile Design and the Judicial Process, 55 Cal. L. Rev. 645, 655 (1967); Notes, 80 Harv. L. Rev. 688 (1967), 32 Iowa L. Rev. 953 (1967), all cited at 391 F.2d at 505 n.9.

[75] 391 F.2d 495 (8th Cir. 1968) (Mich. law).

[76] Id. at 502.

[77] Including National Safety Council motor vehicle accident data revealing 49,000 deaths and 1.8 million disabling injuries in 1965, rising to 52,500 deaths and 1.9 million disabling injuries in 1966. 391 F.2d at 502 n.4. "In automobile accidents since the advent of the horseless carriage up to the end of 1965, 1.5 million people have been killed in the United States." Id.

most cars eventually are involved in at least one accident causing injury or death,[78] *Larsen* concluded that car manufacturers, as an extension of their general duty to make their products reasonably safe for normal use,[79] have a duty of due care to design their vehicles with reasonable safety for the crash environment.[80]

While a small handful of cases briefly followed the *Evans* no-duty approach,[81] an increasingly large majority in time adopted *Larsen*'s view that automotive manufacturers have a duty of reasonable care to design crashworthy vehicles. If there ever was any doubt as to the final outcome of the controversy, it was put to rest in 1977 when the Seventh Circuit abandoned its own decision in *Evans*[82] and adopted *Larsen*'s reasoning and result.[83] While the Supreme Court of Virginia purported to reject the crashworthiness doctrine in a 1995 decision involving the rollover of a truck,[84] it proceeded to apply the doctrine's principles by allowing the plaintiff's claim that the truck's cab, crushed in the rollover, was inadequately braced and padded to protect its occupants against such a risk.[85] Although the Virginia high court chose to reaffirm its formal rejection of the crashworthiness doctrine in a case involving the rollover of a convertible in 2016,[86] the court nevertheless explained, citing NHSTA's exclusion of convertibles from its ordinary roof crush standards, that it continued to adhere to "a vehicle manufacturer's duty to exercise reasonable care to design a product that is reasonably safe for the purpose for which it is intended."[87] In short, Virginia locates its crashworthiness duty within the broader negligence duty it applies to all products. Thus, it seems safe to affirm that the crashworthiness doctrine is now the law in all American jurisdiction.[88]

Ascertaining Crashworthiness

Establishing that manufacturers have a duty to design their cars to be crashworthy does not resolve the far more complex matter of deciding the extent of that design obligation. All courts start with the premise that manufacturers are not expected to make their vehicles crash-proof and able to protect occupants in accidents of every type,

---

[78] Id. (citing O'Connell, Taming the Automobile, 58 Nw. U. L. Rev. 299, 348 (1963), for proposition that "between one-fourth to two-thirds of all automobiles during their use at some time are involved in an accident producing injury or death").

[79] Id. at 504. See also Mazda Motor Corp. v. Lindahl, 706 A.2d 526, 531 (Del. 1998).

[80] "We perceive of no sound reason, either in logic or experience, nor any command in precedent, why the manufacturer should not be held to a reasonable duty of care in the design of its vehicle consonant with the state of the art to minimize the effect of accidents." 391 F.2d at 503.

[81] See, e.g., Shumard v. General Motors Corp., 270 F. Supp. 311 (S.D. Ohio 1967); Willis v. Chrysler Corp., 264 F. Supp. 1010 (S.D. Tex. 1967); Walton v. Chrysler Corp., 229 So.2d 568 (Miss. 1969).

[82] See Huff v. White Motor Corp., 565 F.2d 104, 108 (7th Cir. 1977) (Ind. law) (death by fire from rupture of fuel tank; "In light of an expanding extension of protection for consumers in products liability cases, the 'intended purpose' rationale in *Evans* as to motor vehicles is unrealistically narrow. . . . [M]anufacturers must anticipate and take precautions against reasonably foreseeable risks in the use of their products.").

[83] "There is no rational basis for limiting the manufacturer's liability to those instances where a structural defect has caused the collision and a resulting injury. . . . Since collisions [from] whatever cause are foreseeable events, the scope of liability should be commensurate with the scope of foreseeable risks." Id. at 109. Indiana itself finally adopted the crashworthiness doctrine in Miller v. Todd, 551 N.E.2d 1139 (Ind. 1990).

[84] Slone v. General Motors Corp., 457 S.E.2d 51 (Va. 1995).

[85] Id. at 52.

[86] Holiday Motor Corp. v. Walters, 790 S.E.2d 447, 455 (Va. 2016).

[87] Id.

[88] So, the crashworthiness "controversy is now [virtually] settled. . . . A manufacturer has a duty to design and manufacture its product so as reasonably to reduce the foreseeable harm that may occur in an accident brought about by causes other than a product defect." Products Liability Rest. § 16 cmt. *a*.

such as when a small car crashes head-on into an 18-wheeler truck at highway speeds.[89] Even *Larsen* recognized that "manufacturers are not insurers,"[90] that "all risks cannot be eliminated nor can a crash-proof vehicle be designed,"[91] and that the crashworthiness duty extends only to eliminating *unreasonable* risks and requires only "*reasonable* steps in design . . . to minimize the injury-producing effect of impacts."[92] All courts now agree that a manufacturer's obligation to produce a "crashworthy" vehicle is bounded by a reasonable balance of the costs and benefits of reducing various risks of injury.[93] In short, automotive crashworthiness is not an absolute concept but a matter of degree.

This important point might be better understood if courts and commentators were to rephrase an automotive manufacturer's duty in terms of an obligation to design vehicles that are "*reasonably* crashworthy" in view of the balance of costs and benefits involved in removing (or reducing) the hazard that caused (or aggravated) a particular injury. While the term "crashworthy" remains unmodified in explicit legal discourse, the concept is understood to include this silent modifier. Thus, courts and lawyers understand that a vehicle's "crashworthiness" is a function of the costs and benefits (and, to a lesser extent, of consumer expectations) of various safety features, some included and others left out. In short, "crashworthy" means reasonable—not perfect—automotive crash safety.[94]

Determining what types and severity of accidents any particular vehicle reasonably should be expected to withstand is sometimes quite easy. For example, if a low-speed collision causes a steering wheel hub cover to pop off, exposing sharp prongs that injure a passenger's face, no such car could be found reasonably safe for the crash environment.[95] As collisions increase in severity, however, the crashworthiness issue becomes increasingly more difficult. With collisions at higher speeds, it generally is not self-evident whether a vehicle should have been reasonably designed to protect its

---

[89] For early statements of this basic proposition, see, e.g., Dreisonstok v. Volkswagenwerk, A.G., 489 F.2d 1066, 1073 (4th Cir. 1974) (Va. law); Dyson v. General Motors Corp., 298 F. Supp. 1064, 1073 (E.D. Pa. 1969).

[90] 391 F.2d at 503.

[91] Id.

[92] Id. (emphasis added).

[93] See, e.g., Piltch v. Ford Motor Co., 11 F. Supp. 3d 884, 889 (N.D. Ind. 2014) (" 'Given the reality that safety technology is expensive, the operative consideration in defining a crashworthiness defect is the balance between reasonable safety and economics,' which means that in a crashworthiness case, 'a defect is "not merely the conclusion that a product failed and caused injury, but that the product failed to provide the consumer with reasonable protection under the circumstances surrounding a particular accident." ' "); Nissan Motor Co. v. Nave, 740 A.2d 102 (Md. Ct. Spec. App. 1999) (design of steering column); Soule v. General Motors Corp., 882 P.2d 298 (Cal. 1994) (design of floorboard and wheel assembly). Compare Alabama's standard jury instruction for crashworthiness cases, which requires a plaintiff to prove that:

> The utility of the alternative design outweighed the utility of the design actually used. In deciding [this issue], factors which may be considered would include the intended use of the vehicle, its styling, cost, desirability, safety aspects, the foreseeability of the particular accident, the likelihood of injury, the probable seriousness of the injury if that accident occurred, the obviousness or not of the defect, and the manufacturer's ability to eliminate the defect.

Flemister v. General Motors Corp., 723 So.2d 25, 27 (Ala. 1998). Consumer expectations may also bear on automotive crashworthiness. Cf. Bruce v. Martin-Marietta Corp., 544 F.2d 442, 447 (10th Cir. 1976) (Okla. law) (aircraft crashworthiness: "A consumer would not expect a Model T to have the safety features which are incorporated in automobiles made today.").

[94] This specific proposition rests on more general notions of the nature of a manufacturer's duty to adopt reasonably safe designs. See chs. 2, 5, and 8, above.

[95] See Horn v. General Motors Corp., 551 P.2d 398, 402 (Cal. 1976) (plaintiff, while attempting to avoid collision at speed of 25 mph, brushed hand over horncap, dislodging it and exposing prongs); Ellithorpe v. Ford Motor Co., 503 S.W.2d 516 (Tenn. 1973) (prong designed in emblem).

occupants against various injuries, and the factfinder in each such case will have to carefully evaluate the various safety-utility-cost tradeoffs to determine if the plaintiff has fairly made a case that a particular design danger rendered the vehicle uncrashworthy.[96] Cases involving moderate to severe crashes and injuries almost always require the plaintiff to show by expert testimony how the injuries were caused, how particular design enhancements would have prevented such injuries, and the costs and feasibility of such preventive measures.[97]

Dreisonstok v. Volkswagenwerk, A.G.[98] was an influential early case that helped to set the limits of the crashworthiness doctrine and to illustrate the necessary tradeoffs between safety, cost, and function inherent in all aspects of a vehicle's design. The plaintiff was injured while riding as a passenger in the front seat of a Volkswagen microbus when the vehicle collided with a telephone pole head-on at 40 mph. The plaintiff sued VW for defective design, based on the relative weakness of the vehicle's passenger compartment in front-end collisions compared to the greater ability of standard American passenger cars to withstand such collisions. The district court found for the plaintiff, concluding that the vehicle's design was defective for not having "sufficient energy-absorbing materials or devices or 'crush space' . . . so that at 40 miles an hour the integrity of the passenger compartment would not be violated."[99]

Rejecting the plaintiff's comparison, the Court of Appeals reversed, reasoning that this multipurpose van was designed to provide users with maximum space for cargo or passengers, while keeping its dimensions as small as possible for easy maneuverability and its cost as low as possible. To achieve these goals, the manufacturer brought the front seat as far forward as possible to leave as much space for cargo and passengers in the rear. While this design reduced the space between the front of the vehicle and the driver's compartment, this aspect of the design was not only evident but the very design feature that made the vehicle uniquely useful. The court noted that the usefulness of the microbus design was vouchsafed by its popularity; indeed, after the accident, the driver's father purchased another VW microbus to replace the one destroyed in the collision.

---

[96] See, e.g., Poliseno v. General Motors Corp., 744 A.2d 679, 683 (N.J. Super. Ct. App. Div. 2000) (tree protruded 20 inches through door in collision at delta-V speed of 10–23 mph); Seattle-First Nat'l Bank v. Volkswagen of Am., Inc., 525 P.2d 286 (Wash. Ct. App. 1974) (VW microbus struck rear end of flatbed truck at relative speed of 20 mph), aff'd, 542 P.2d 774 (Wash. 1975).

[97] See, e.g., White v. Ford Motor Co., 2021 WL 2826458, at *4 (N.D. Ala. 2021) (ability of Ford Taurus roof to provide adequate crush resistance in rollovers); Jones v. IC Bus, LLC, 626 S.W.3d 661, 679–80 (Ky. Ct. App. 2020) (feasibility of alternative school bus roof designs); Vogel v. Fernandes, 2013 WL 3762881, at *13–14 (N.J. Super. Ct. App. Div. 2013) (plaintiffs' expert failed to show that a reasonable alternative design would have averted injuries; jury charge correctly focused on need for jury "to evaluate the crashworthiness of the vehicle in light of the expert testimony"); Gurule v. Ford Motor Co., 2011 WL 2071701, at *5 (N.M. Ct. App. 2011) (expert could testify on cause of roof structure failure and "technological and economical feasibility of a safer design"); May v. Ford Motor Co., 2010 WL 5391605, at *4 (E.D. Ky. 2010) (plaintiffs' expert failed to present tests, statistics, or other data on enhancement of injuries caused by alleged design defect in Taurus coil spring); Gray v. General Motors Corp., 312 F.3d 240, 242 (6th Cir. 2002) (Ky. law) (plaintiff's expert unable to identify any "probable" defect in the seatbelt mechanism that caused injury); Walters v. General Motors Corp., 209 F. Supp. 2d 481, 490 (W.D. Pa. 2002) ("[p]laintiffs have had more than sufficient time to procure the use of an accident reconstruction expert, an airbag design expert or a biomechanical injury expert"); Mazda Motor Corp. v. Lindahl, 706 A.2d 526, 533 (Del. 1998) (defendant contested survivability of crash if yielding seat had not permitted decedent to be partially ejected; accident forces on decedent and corresponding injuries not evident, so jurors needed expert testimony on proximate cause); Soule v. General Motors Corp., 882 P.2d 298 (Cal. 1994) (adequacy *vel non* of floorboard and wheel assembly designs testified to by numerous experts). On expert testimony generally, see § 6.3, above.

[98] 489 F.2d 1066 (4th Cir. 1974) (Va. law).

[99] Id. at 1068–69.

Finally, the court observed that the plaintiff had offered no evidence of any practical way to improve the safety of the microbus for front-end collisions without interfering with its many uses for carrying light cargo, serving as a family camper, and as a conveyor of more passengers than could be carried by a normal car.[100]

As *Dreisonstok* illustrates, there can be no single standard for automotive crashworthiness; instead, crashworthiness determinations necessarily involve evaluations of the various trade-offs between safety and utility inherent in the design of each particular type of vehicle.[101] So, consumers may not fairly expect a convertible to be as safe in a rollover situation as a "standard four-door sedan with center posts and full-door frames."[102] And the necessary tradeoffs are not restricted to safety and utility, but extend as well to cost and price—like most goods, safety has a cost.[103] "Price is, also, a factor to be considered, for, if a change in design would appreciably add to cost, add little to safety, and take an article out of the price range of the market to which it was intended to appeal, it may be 'unreasonable' as well as 'impractical' for the Courts to require the manufacturer to adopt such change."[104] The public, thought the court, surely expects less crashworthiness in an economy car than in a Cadillac.[105] For these reasons, the court sensibly concluded that the plaintiff had failed to show that the manufacturer of the VW microbus had been negligent in its design.[106]

Because of the different ways in which accidents can occur, automotive engineers must balance a vehicle's safety in one type of crash against its safety in other types of crashes; making it safer for one type of accident often makes it more dangerous for other types of accident. It thus is axiomatic that a design which allows or enhances one type of hazard in order to prevent another, greater hazard is not defective. This important principle of design defectiveness, briefly put in doubt by *Dawson v. Chrysler Corp.*,[107] but

---

100 Id. at 1074.

101 The court noted that Congress, in the National Traffic and Motor Vehicle Safety Act of 1966, pronounced that specific automotive safety regulations must take into account what is "reasonable, practicable and appropriate for the particular type of motor vehicle." Id. at 1072, quoting § 15 U.S.C. 1392(f)(3), now recodified at 49 U.S.C. § 30111(b)(3).

102 Dyson v. General Motors Corp., 298 F. Supp. 1064, 1073 (E.D. Pa. 1969).

103 See, e.g., Whitted v. General Motors Corp., 58 F.3d 1200, 1205 (7th Cir. 1995) (Ind. law) ("within economic reason," car makers have a duty to design their cars to be crashworthy; because "safety technology is expensive, the operative consideration in defining a crashworthiness defect is the balance between reasonable safety and economics," so that "the law does not require manufacturers to follow . . . economically suffocating measures").

104 *Dreisonstok*, 489 F.2d at 1072–73.

105 Id. at 1073. Compare Products Liability Rest, § 2 cmt. *f*, illus. 9: "Given that the risks and benefits associated with relative automobile size are generally known, decisions regarding which sizes to purchase and use should be left to purchasers and users in the market."

106 *Dreisonstok*, 489 F.2d at 1073–76. Compare Seattle-First Nat'l Bank v. Volkswagen of Am., Inc., 525 P.2d 286 (Wash. Ct. App. 1974), aff'd, 542 P.2d 774 (Wash. 1975), where the court, distinguishing *Dreisonstok* on the basis of the difference in speed, held that the crashworthiness of the front end of a VW microbus which struck the rear end of a flatbed truck at a relative speed of 20 mph was a material question of fact.

107 630 F.2d 950 (3d Cir. 1980) (N.J. law). In *Dawson*, plaintiff lost control of his 1974 Dodge Monaco, which "slid off the highway, over a curb, through a small sign, and into an unyielding steel pole that was fifteen inches in diameter. The car struck the pole in a backwards direction at a forty-five degree angle on the left side of the vehicle; the point of impact was the left rear wheel well. As a result of the force of the collision, the vehicle literally wrapped itself around the pole. The pole ripped through the body of the car and crushed Dawson between the seat and the 'header' area of the roof, located just above the windshield." Id. at 954. Dawson's collision with the interior of the car ruptured his cervical vertebrae, rendering him a quadriplegic.

The plaintiffs alleged that the car was defectively designed "because it did not have a full, continuous steel frame extending through the door panels, and a cross-member running through the floor board between the posts located between the front and rear doors of the vehicle. Had the vehicle been so designed, the Dawsons

now widely accepted, receives unequivocal expression in the *Products Liability Restatement*: "When evaluating the reasonableness of a design alternative, the overall safety of the product must be considered. It is not sufficient that the alternative design would have reduced or prevented the harm suffered by the plaintiff if it would also have introduced into the product other dangers of equal or greater magnitude."[108]

Proof that a vehicle is uncrashworthy, however, is not in itself sufficient to make out a crashworthiness case. As in all products liability cases,[109] the plaintiff must connect his or her allegation of product defect with the particular injury suffered. Thus, an essential element in every crashworthiness case is that the uncrashworthy aspect of the vehicle proximately caused the plaintiff's harm.[110] What this means, at a minimum, is that a plaintiff must prove that an uncrashworthy design was a substantial factor in aggravating his or her injuries.[111]

Theories of Liability and Defect Tests

Although *Larsen* was based on negligence, courts have applied crashworthiness principles more broadly to claims based on breach of implied warranty and on strict liability in tort.[112] This follows logically from the proposition that "strict" liability is in

---

alleged, it would have 'bounced' off the pole following relatively slight penetration by the pole into the passenger space." Id. Chrysler's experts testified that the vehicle's propensity to deform was in fact a safety feature in most crashes because deformation "absorbs the impact of the crash and decreases the rate of deceleration on the occupants of the vehicle." Id. For this reason, Chrysler's experts claimed that the plaintiff's alternative design was actually *more* dangerous than the existing design for most types of automobile accidents. Nevertheless, the jury returned a verdict for the plaintiffs, a result the Court of Appeals found unfair and inefficient: "[W]hile the jury found Chrysler liable for not producing a rigid enough vehicular frame, a factfinder in another case might well hold the manufacturer liable for producing a frame that is too rigid. . . . In effect, this permits individual juries applying varying laws in different jurisdictions to set nationwide automobile safety standards and to impose on automobile manufacturers conflicting requirements." Id. at 962. Against its better instincts, however, the Court of Appeals felt compelled to affirm, ruling that the jury could find the car "not reasonably fit, suitable and safe" under then-prevailing New Jersey law. Id. at 959–60.

[108] Products Liability Rest. § 2 cmt. *f*. See also id. § 16 cmt. *b*, repeating this principle in the context of a defendant's liability for enhanced injury. The Reporters' Note to § 2 cmt. *f* observes:

> The proposition that, in order to determine that a design is not reasonably safe, the alternative must contribute to greater overall safety needs no citation; it is axiomatic. If the alternative design proffered by the plaintiff does not make the product safer, let alone if it makes it more dangerous, such an alternative is not reasonable. In such a case the fact that the alternative design would have avoided injury in a specific case is of no moment.

The Third Restatement explicitly rejects *Dawson* in § 16 cmt. *b*, illus. 5.

[109] See chs. 11 and 12, above.

[110] See, e.g., Blank v. Garff Enters. Inc., 482 P.3d 258, 267 (Utah Ct. App. 2021) (plaintiff failed to produce expert evidence that driver-side curtain airbag's nondeployment enhanced her injuries); Mazda Motor Corp. v. Hurst, 261 So.3d 167, 188 (Ala. 2017) (crashworthiness claims "focus on the alleged defect as being the proximate cause of the injury or damage"); Green v. Ford Motor Co., 942 N.E.2d 791, 793 (Ind. 2011) (crashworthiness doctrine "merely expands the proximate cause requirement to include enhanced injuries"); General Motors Corp. v. Iracheta, 161 S.W.3d 462 (Tex. 2005) (no reliable expert testimony that alleged design defect in fuel system caused post-collision fuel-fed fire in which plaintiff died).

[111] See, e.g., Green v. Ford Motor Co., 942 N.E.2d 791, 794 (Ind. 2011); Bustos v. Hyundai Motor Co., 243 P.3d 440, 446 (N.M. Ct. App. 2010) (elements of enhanced injury claim: (1) existence of an enhanced injury, and (2) degree of enhancement); Harsh v. Petroll, 887 A.2d 209, 217, 219 (Pa. 2005). Apportionment is examined in § 17.4, below.

[112] See, e.g., Vogel v. Fernandes, 2013 WL 3762881 (N.J. Super. Ct. App. Div. 2013) (strict liability appropriate for crashworthiness claim); Rooker v. Ford Motor Co., 100 So.3d 1229 (Fla. Dist. Ct. App. 2012) (same); Pannu v. Land Rover N. Am., Inc., 120 Cal. Rptr. 3d 605, 618–20 (Ct. App. 2011) (affirming judgment for plaintiff on strict liability risk-benefit test); Bustos v. Hyundai Motor Co., 243 P.3d 440, 442 (N.M. Ct. App. 2010) (negligence, strict liability, and implied warranty); Gaudio v. Ford Motor Co., 976 A.2d 524, 533–34 (Pa. Super. Ct. 2009) (same; detailed analysis); Harris v. General Motors Corp., 34 Fed. Appx. 487, 489–90 (7th Cir.

effect a lesser included offense of negligence liability, in that negligence logically means the negligent sale of a defective product.[113]

More difficult is the question of the appropriate theory of defectiveness for crashworthiness cases. The basic contest here, as elsewhere, is between the consumer expectations and risk-utility tests.[114] From the start, courts experienced difficulty in attempting to apply the consumer expectations test to questions of automotive design safety that by nature involve the kinds of trade-offs between safety, usefulness, and cost discussed above. In a very early case, *Heaton v. Ford Motor Co.*,[115] a 5- to 6-inch rock struck a wheel on the plaintiff's 4-wheel-drive pickup truck that was traveling at normal highway speed. Half an hour later, the wheel came apart, and the truck crashed, injuring the plaintiff. Although the court used the case to adopt § 402A of the *Second Restatement*, together with the consumer expectations test for assessing design defectiveness, it affirmed the trial court's refusal to submit the case to the jury, reasoning that a jury could only speculate, in the absence of "data concerning the cost or feasibility of designing and building" a stronger wheel, on what consumers in fact would expect under circumstances such as these.[116]

Heaton illustrates the courts' recognition, which has strengthened over time, that an intelligent evaluation of the complex safety-usefulness-cost tradeoffs involved in design engineering generally requires the kind of cost-benefit analysis embraced by the risk-utility test.[117] While a number of courts have attempted to apply the consumer expectations test in crashworthiness cases,[118] courts have widely turned to cost-benefit analysis to test the reasonableness of a vehicle's design for particular types of accident environments.[119]

2002) (Ill. law) (res ipsa loquitur, strict liability, negligence, and breach of warranty); Elsasser v. American Motors Corp., 265 N.W.2d 339 (Mich. Ct. App. 1978) (common-law implied warranty).

[113] See, e.g., Hayles v. General Motors Corp., 82 F. Supp. 2d 650, 658–59 (S.D. Tex. 1999); Oanes v. Westgo, Inc., 476 N.W.2d 248, 253 (N.D. 1991). See generally § 5.9, above.

[114] See chs. 5 and 8, above.

[115] 435 P.2d 806 (Or. 1967).

[116] Id. at 809.

[117] See, e.g., Bowman v. General Motors Corp., 427 F. Supp. 234, 242 (E.D. Pa. 1977) (adopting risk-utility balancing test by which jury "makes a judgment as to the social acceptability of the conscious design choice trade-off"). See § 8.4, above.

[118] See, e.g., Mills v. FCA US, LLC, 2021 WL 4079363, at *9 (D. Colo. 2021) ("An ordinary user of a motor vehicle might expect that they could suffer some degree of injury in a high-speed collision . . . . But it may be that a user would expect vehicles to be designed to protect against more severe forms of injury . . . ."); Jones v. IC Bus, LLC, 626 S.W.3d 661, 676–77 (Ky. Ct. App. 2020) ("To recover under the [crashworthiness] doctrine, . . . the plaintiff must prove that the product was unreasonably dangerous, i.e., dangerous to an extent beyond that which would be contemplated by the user with ordinary knowledge common to the community."); Sigler v. American Honda Motor Co., 532 F.3d 469, 486 (6th Cir. 2008) (Tenn. law) (consumer expectations test; alleged airbag defect). Compare Bresnahan v. Chrysler Corp., 38 Cal. Rptr. 2d 446 (Ct. App. 1995) (deployment of airbag in low-impact collision, breaking driver's elbow; ordinary consumer could form expectation of how airbag would perform in such situations, which authorized consumer expectations test), with Pruitt v. General Motors Corp., 86 Cal. Rptr. 2d 4 (Ct. App. 1999) (deployment of airbag in low-impact collision, breaking driver's weak jaw, was *not* part of everyday experience of consuming public, so trial court correctly refused to give consumer expectations instruction).

[119] See, e.g., Walker v. Ford Motor Co., 406 P.3d 845, 850 (Colo. 2017) ("risk-benefit test, not the consumer expectation test, is the proper test to use in assessing whether a product like [a] car seat . . . is unreasonably dangerous due to a design defect"); Vogel v. Fernandes, 2013 WL 3762881 (N.J. Super. Ct. App. Div. 2013) (affirming judgment on defense verdict; plaintiffs failed to prove that a reasonably safer alternative design would have prevented injuries in crash); Miranda C. v. Nissan Motor Co., 741 S.E.2d 34, 40 (S.C. Ct. App. 2013) (affirming new trial of crashworthiness claim under risk-utility test instead of consumer expectations test; "proof of a feasible alternative design was a required element"); Pannu v. Land Rover N.

Perhaps the best example of the risk-utility test's supremacy in crashworthiness cases is *Soule v. General Motors Corp.*,[120] decided by the California Supreme Court in 1994.[121] The plaintiff's ankles were fractured when the Chevrolet Camaro she was driving collided with another vehicle at a closing speed between 30 to 70 miles per hour. She sued the manufacturer, asserting that the design of her automobile was defective in allowing the left front wheel to break free, collapse rearward, and smash the toe pan and floorboard into her feet. In particular, she claimed that the configuration of the car's frame, and the bracket attaching the wheel assembly to it, were defectively designed because they did not limit the wheel's rearward travel in the event the bracket should fail. At trial, the parties disagreed on the angle and force of the impact and the extent to which the toe pan had actually deformed. To testify on design defectiveness and causation, both parties employed numerous experts on biomechanics, metallurgy, orthopedics, design engineering, crash-test simulation, and other matters. The plaintiff's experts explained, on the basis of crash tests, metallurgical analysis, and other facts, how the damage to her car would have been minimized had it been alternatively designed. In refuting these claims, defendant's experts explained how the plaintiff's ankle injuries were caused by the force of the collision and her failure to wear a seatbelt rather than any defect in the car. The jury rendered a verdict for the plaintiff, the intermediate appellate court affirmed, and General Motors appealed.

The question before the California Supreme Court was whether an "ordinary consumer expectations" instruction may be used in a case where the question of how safely the product should have performed cannot be answered by the common experience of its users. In a prior case, *Barker v. Lull Engineering Co.*,[122] the court had pronounced its celebrated two-pronged defect test which provided for a finding of design defectiveness if either the product's design failed to meet consumer expectations or if its risks outweighed its benefits.[123] While *Barker* was widely interpreted as holding that a plaintiff could recover on either prong,[124] the *Soule* court pointed to *Barker*'s admonition that "when the ultimate issue of design defect calls for a careful assessment of feasibility, practicality, risk, and benefit, the case should not be resolved simply on the basis of ordinary consumer expectations" but should turn instead upon "the balancing or weighing of competing considerations" provided in the risk-utility test.[125] On the facts of *Soule*, therefore, because consumers normally have no meaningful expectations about how the complex mechanisms of physics and mechanics may combine in violent automotive crashes,[126] the court concluded that the risk-utility test was the only appropriate standard for use in a crashworthiness case of this type.[127]

Am., Inc., 120 Cal. Rptr. 3d 605, 618–20 (Ct. App. 2011) (affirming judgment for plaintiff under risk-benefit test).

[120] 882 P.2d 298 (Cal. 1994).

[121] *Soule* is examined in detail in § 8.6, above.

[122] 573 P.2d 443 (Cal. 1978).

[123] Id. at 457–58.

[124] See § 8.6, above.

[125] 882 P.2d at 305.

[126] "[A] complex product, even when it is being used as intended, may often cause injury in a way that does not engage its ordinary consumers' reasonable minimum assumptions about safe performance. For example, the ordinary consumer of an automobile simply has 'no idea' how [safely] it should perform in [various] situations." Id. at 308.

[127] Consequently, on the facts before it, the court concluded that the jury should not have been instructed on the consumer expectations test:

Contexts

Courts have applied the crashworthiness doctrine in a large variety of contexts. Probably the most recurring type of case, including most of those discussed above, involves the structural integrity of a vehicle: *Evans* and *Dawson* involved the resistance of vehicles to impacts from the side, *Dreisonstok* and *Soule* involved the vehicles' resistance to head-on collisions, and *Heaton* concerned a side impact to a wheel. Other cases have similarly involved the integrity of a vehicle's exterior in impact situations,[128] while many others have involved the ability of a vehicle's roof,[129] liftgate latch,[130] or some other component,[131] to withstand the forces of a rollover.

Some of the most notorious crashworthiness cases have involved the ability of a vehicle's fuel system to withstand certain types of collisions. It was the vulnerability of the Ford Pinto's fuel system that formed the basis for a California jury's assessment of $125 million in punitive damages against Ford in *Grimshaw v. Ford Motor Co.*,[132]—a 1979 verdict that was eclipsed two decades later by another California jury's levy of a $4.8 *billion* punitive damage assessment against General Motors for locating the 1979 Chevrolet Malibu gas tank behind the rear axle close to the rear bumper, causing the car to burst into flames when hit at high speed from the rear.[133] Both punitive damage verdicts were substantially reduced by the trial courts, but both were partially allowed

---

> An ordinary consumer of automobiles cannot reasonably expect that a car's frame, suspension, or interior will be designed to remain intact in any and all accidents. Nor would ordinary experience and understanding inform such a consumer how safely an automobile's design should perform under the esoteric circumstances of the collision at issue here. Indeed, both parties assumed that quite complicated design considerations were at issue, and that expert testimony was necessary to illuminate these matters. Therefore, injection of ordinary consumer expectations into the design defect equation was improper.

Id. at 310. Yet, because of the "voluminous evidence on the risks and benefits of the Camaro's design," the court saw no reason to believe that the jury ignored such evidence and instead relied upon the consumer expectations test. Id. at 311. Accordingly, the court held that the trial court's error in instructing the jury on the consumer expectations prong was harmless. Id.

[128] See, e.g., Rider v. Township of Freehold, 2008 WL 2699805, at *1 (N.J. Super. Ct. App. Div. 2008) (utility pole penetrated door and intruded into passenger compartment of BMW); General Motors Corp. v. McGee, 837 So.2d 1010, 1017 (Fla. Dist. Ct. App. 2002) (fuel tank exploded in low impact collision).

[129] See, e.g., Motelson v. Ford Motor Co., 957 N.Y.S.2d 341, 345–46 (App. Div. 2012); Pannu v. Land Rover N. Am., Inc., 120 Cal. Rptr. 3d 605, 609 (Ct. App. 2011) (roof crushed during rollover); Bustos v. Hyundai Motor Co., 243 P.3d 440, 442 (N.M. Ct. App. 2010) (roof pillars crushed nearly 11" during rollover). See also Jones v. IC Bus, LLC, 626 S.W.3d 661 (Ky. Ct. App. 2020) (school bus careened off road, turned on its side, and crashed into a large tree, causing the roof to collapse to the floor in a v-shape, killing 2 preschoolers and injuring others).

[130] See, e.g., Clark v. Chrysler Corp., 310 F.3d 461 (6th Cir. 2002) (Ky. law), vacated by Chrysler Corp. v. Clark, 540 U.S. 801, on remand Clark v. Chrysler, 80 Fed. Appx. 453 (6th Cir. 2003); Jimenez v. DaimlerChrysler Corp., 269 F.3d 439, 458 (4th Cir. 2001) (S.C. law); Norwest Bank N.M., N.A. v. Chrysler Corp., 981 P.2d 1215 (N.M. Ct. App. 1999).

[131] See, e.g., Riley v. Ford Motor Co., 757 S.E.2d 422 (S.C. Ct. App. 2014) (Few, J.) (door latch design); Burns v. Ford Motor Co., 2008 WL 222711 (W.D. Ark. 2008) (side window glass on Mountaineer should have been laminated rather than glazed because of roof design and vehicle's propensity to roll over); O'Hara v. General Motors Corp., 508 F.3d 753 (5th Cir. 2007) (Tex. law) (same; Tahoe); Alami v. Volkswagen of Am., Inc., 766 N.E.2d 574 (N.Y. 2002) (defectively designed sub-frame reinforcement); Rossell v. Volkswagen of Am., 709 P.2d 517 (Ariz. 1985) (battery located inside passenger compartment of VW Beetle where it could drip acid on occupants if vehicle rolled on back).

[132] 174 Cal. Rptr. 348 (Ct. App. 1981).

[133] Anderson v. General Motors Corp., No. BC 116926 (L.A. Cnty. Super. Ct. 1999). See White, Jury Orders GM to Pay $4.9 Billion (AP), The State, Columbia, S.C., at A1 (July 10, 1999).

to stand.[134] Many other crashworthiness cases have also involved the integrity of a vehicle's fuel system.[135]

Some crashworthiness cases have involved dangerous design aspects of a vehicle's *interior*, such as a seat latch unable to withstand the forces of a collision,[136] or the presence of sharp or hard objects inside a vehicle that can aggravate injuries to occupants in a collision.[137] Other cases have involved claims challenging the safety of a vehicle's *exterior* design for presenting untoward risks to innocent bystanders who may come in contact with sharp or unyielding parts of an automotive vehicle.[138]

Safety devices in vehicles, such as head restraints, lap and shoulder belts, and airbags are all designed to protect occupants in the event of collisions—in short, to make a vehicle more crashworthy. Normally such devices do indeed improve occupant safety, but sometimes they fail or otherwise expose an occupant to an unexpected and unreasonable risk of harm. Thus, a vehicle is uncrashworthy if its roll bar collapses;[139] its headrest contains a sharp metal edge that strikes the driver's skull and kills him when the vehicle is rear-ended;[140] its lap or shoulder belts cause severe abdominal

---

[134] The trial court in *Grimshaw* reduced the punitive award to $3.5 million, which the appellate court affirmed. Grimshaw v. Ford Motor Co., 174 Cal. Rptr. 348 (Ct. App. 1981). *Anderson* was not reviewed by an appellate court, but the trial court remitted the punitive verdict to $1.09 billion.

[135] See, e.g., Mazda Motor Corp. v. Hurst, 261 So.3d 167, 171 (Ala. 2017) (punctured plastic fuel tank was ½" from sharp protruding edges of steel muffler); Harsh v. Petroll, 887 A.2d 209, 210–11 (Pa. 2005) (design defect in fuel distribution system caused fatal fire after collision); General Motors Corp. v. McGee, 837 So.2d 1010, 1017 (Fla. Dist. Ct. App. 2002) (placement of fuel tank between rear axle and bumper made tank vulnerable to puncture); Ford Motor Co. v. Stubblefield, 319 S.E.2d 470 (Ga. Ct. App. 1984) (Ford Pinto-type fuel tank used in Mustang II). *But see* Jablonski v. Ford Motor Co., 955 N.E.2d 1138, 1158–59 (Ill. 2011) (no negligent design in locating Lincoln Town Car's fuel tank behind the axel, or in failing to afix shield to prevent its puncture).

[136] See, e.g., Moore v. Ford Motor Co., 332 S.W.3d 749 (Mo. 2011) (300-pound driver; driver's seat collapsed in rear-impact collision); Carillo v. Ford Motor Co., 759 N.E.2d 99, 107 (Ill. App. Ct. 2001) (driver suffered serious back injury when her seat collapsed during rear-end collision); Sumnicht v. Toyota Motor Sales, 360 N.W.2d 2 (Wis. 1984).

[137] See, e.g., Ellithorpe v. Ford Motor Co., 503 S.W.2d 516 (Tenn. 1973) (wheel hub popped off exposing sharp prongs that injured driver's face); Mickle v. Blackmon, 166 S.E.2d 173 (S.C. 1969) (passenger impaled on gear shift lever mounted on steering column when plastic knob cover shattered in side-impact collision); Ford Motor Co. v. Zahn, 265 F.2d 729 (8th Cir. 1959) (Minn. law) (passenger's eye struck jagged burr on corner of ash tray when driver jammed on brakes to avoid collision).

[138] See, e.g., Threats v. General Motors Corp., 890 S.W.2d 327 (Mo. Ct. App. 1994) (rigid side-view mirror unreasonably dangerous to pedestrians); Knippen v. Ford Motor Co., 546 F.2d 993 (D.C. Cir. 1976); Green v. Volkswagen of Am., Inc., 485 F.2d 430 (6th Cir. 1973) (Mich. law) (finger of young girl, walking by parked van, severed by sharp side vent); Passwaters v. General Motors Corp., 454 F.2d 1270 (8th Cir. 1972) (Iowa law) (motorcycle passenger's leg injured by Ben-Hur-type wheel cover of passing motorist). Compare Boyle v. Ford Motor Co., 942 A.2d 850, 853 (N.J. Super. Ct. App. Div. 2008) (Ford not liable to prevent car burrowing under modified truck's undercarriage by installing rear bumper); Kahn v. Chrysler Corp., 221 F. Supp. 677 (S.D. Tex. 1963) (Chrysler had no duty to protect child riding bike from injury from protruding fins of 1957 Dodge); Hatch v. Ford Motor Co., 329 P.2d 605 (Cal. Ct. App. 1958) (boy walked into hood ornament which pierced his eye).

Not to be forgotten in this context is Guido Calabresi's classic discussion of a car designed without a spongy bumper. G. Calabresi, The Costs of Accidents 133–40 (1970). See also Latin and Kasolas, Bad Designs, Lethal Profits: The Duty to Protect Other Motorists Against SUV Collision Risks, 82 B.U. L. Rev. 1161 (2002).

[139] Leichtamer v. American Motors Corp., 424 N.E.2d 568 (Ohio 1981) (Jeep).

[140] See, e.g., Huddell v. Levin, 537 F.2d 726 (3d Cir. 1976) (N.J. law).

injuries, paralysis, brain damage, or death;[141] or its airbag fails to deploy, deploys too late, unnecessarily, or too forcibly, injuring or killing an unsuspecting occupant.[142]

During the 1970s, airbag technology began to become available to automotive manufacturers, at least in rudimentary form. This development led NHTSA in 1976 to promulgate Standard FMVSS 208, which provided manufacturers with the option of installing (1) lap and shoulder belts (with a belt warning system), (2) airbags, or (3) both.[143] Amending Standard 208 in 1984, NHTSA conditionally mandated a gradual phase-in of passive restraints, including airbags, in passenger automobiles. The deadline, originally set at 1989, was subsequently extended.[144] By 1989, only a few manufacturers[145] had begun to equip some of their models with airbags as standard equipment, but most manufacturers began to install airbags over the next several years. By the mid-1990s Volvo, Ford, and several other manufacturers had begun to develop airbags for side impacts; and airbag technology and the extent of airbag protection still continues to improve. As manufacturers gradually installed airbags in more and more automotive vehicles during the 1980s and 1990s, courts increasingly were confronted with the vexing question whether a particular model vehicle could be held uncrashworthy if it had not been equipped with an airbag.[146]

During Standard 208's phase-in period, particularly during the 1990s, persons injured in cars not equipped with airbags increasingly brought "no-airbag" claims against manufacturers alleging that the absence of airbags in their cars unreasonably aggravated their injuries in accidents, thereby rendering the vehicles defective in design. Many state courts allowed such claims,[147] but most federal courts denied the no-airbag claims on grounds of federal preemption.[148] When the Supreme Court finally took up the

---

[141] See, e.g., Nissan Motor Co. v. Maddox, 2013 WL 4620488 (Ky. Ct. App. 2013) (restraint system spooled out four inches in frontal collision, allowing 240-pound plaintiff to submarine under seatbelt); Babcock v. General Motors Corp., 299 F.3d 60 (1st Cir. 2002) (N.H. law) (seatbelt failed to latch properly); Nelson v. Ford Motor Co., 761 N.E.2d 1099 (Ohio Ct. App. 2001) (seatbelt designed with comfort feature that allowed for slack in shoulder-belt portion of three-point system; passenger suffered severe and permanent spinal cord injury). Hundreds of cases were brought some time ago on whether the standard rear-seat lap belt used on older cars, as opposed to the three-point shoulder belt used in the front, renders a vehicle uncrashworthy. See Sakayan, Holtz, and Kelley, More Than a Case About a Car—An Analysis of Garrett v. Ford Motor Company, 25 Trial Mag. 34 (Feb. 1989); E. Swartz, F. Swartz, and Cantor, Seat-Belt Injury Litigation, 24 Trial Mag. 47 (Nov. 1988).

[142] See, e.g., Bensenberg v. FCA US LLC, 31 F.4th 529 (7th Cir. 2022) (Ill. law) (front airbag failed to deploy during crash); Finegold v. General Motors Co., 2021 WL 2810091 (D.N.J. 2021) (front passenger was killed when airbag failed to deploy when sideswiped car crashed into tree); Coates v. Ford Motor Co., 2021 WL 2207367 (E.D. Mich. 2021) (airbag spontaneously exploded, causing crash that severely injured driver); Morris v. Mitsubishi Motors N. Am., Inc., 782 F. Supp. 2d 1149, 1152 (E.D. Wash. 2011) (airbag deployment into 5' 4" plaintiff's head and neck severed her spinal cord).

[143] 49 C.F.R. § 571.208.

[144] "Passive restraint regulation (Standard 208) has advanced over the years along a protracted, winding, sometimes perilous course." Public Citizen v. Steed, 851 F.2d 444, 445 (D.C. Cir. 1988). The history of FMVSS 208 is chronicled in Hernandez-Gomez v. Leonardo, 884 P.2d 183 (Ariz. 1994), cert. granted, judgment vacated, 514 U.S. 1094 (1995), and Motor Vehicle Mfrs. Ass'n v. State Farm Mut. Auto. Ins. Co., 463 U.S. 29, 34–38 (1983).

[145] Notably Mercedes Benz, Honda (Acura), and BMW.

[146] On airbag litigation, see Raeker-Jordan, The Pre-Emption Presumption That Never Was: Pre-Emption Doctrine Swallows the Rule, 40 Ariz. L. Rev. 1379 (1998); Chadwell, Automobile Passive Restraint Claims Post-Cipollone: An End to the Federal Preemption Defense, 46 Baylor L. Rev. 141 (1994); § 14.5, above.

[147] See, e.g., Tebbetts v. Ford Motor Co., 665 A.2d 345 (N.H. 1995), abrogated by Geier v. American Honda Motor Co., 529 U.S. 861 (2000) . *But see* Cooper v. General Motors Corp., 702 So.2d 428 (Miss. 1997) (6–3 decision).

[148] See, e.g., Harris v. Ford Motor Co., 110 F.3d 1410, 1413–15 (9th Cir. 1997) (express preemption).

issue in *Geier v. American Honda Motor Co.*,[149] it ruled that the National Traffic and Motor Vehicle Safety Act of 1966, and FMVSS 208 promulgated thereunder, impliedly preempted state common-law no-airbag actions, since NHTSA had decided that automotive safety would best be served at that time by the options it provided manufacturers in Standard 208. As a result, no-airbag claims became prohibited under the federal preemption doctrine.[150]

§ 17.4 INDIVISIBLE HARM AND DAMAGES APPORTIONMENT

Damages apportionment broadly concerns how damages should be divided between plaintiffs, defendants, and any third parties. General principles of damages apportionment applicable to products liability litigation are examined elsewhere in treatments of the extent to which a plaintiff's fault or other form of conduct may bar or reduce the plaintiff's damages[151] and the extent to which defendants may share responsibility for damages with other defendants.[152] In many respects, the damages apportionment principles normally applicable to products liability cases apply as well to automotive products cases. Yet, a number of special apportionment issues have arisen in the automotive context that require separate examination. This section considers the question of who has the burden of proving apportionment in crashworthiness cases—the plaintiff or defendant.[153] The next section considers the role of plaintiff fault in crashworthiness and other automotive products liability cases.

As examined in the preceding section, the crashworthiness doctrine maintains that vehicular manufacturers have a duty to afford as much protection as reasonably possible against the risks of "second collisions" between a vehicle's occupants and its interior.[154] More generally, the duty is one of affording reasonable protection to occupants against defects in design[155] that may aggravate injuries in a collision or other accident situation.

---

[149] 529 U.S. 861 (2000).

[150] *Geier* and federal preemption are examined in depth in § 14.5, above. Claims for the absence of *side* airbags may possibly be another matter. Although at least one court has held no-side-airbag claims to be preempted, Ellison v. Ford Motor Co., 650 F. Supp. 2d 1298, 1305 (N.D. Ga. 2009), at least two courts have ruled that such claims are *not* preempted. See, e.g., Durham v. County of Maui, 696 F. Supp. 2d 1150, 1162 (D. Hawai'i 2010) (plaintiff's side-airbag claims not preempted); Noveck v. PV Holdings Corp., 742 F. Supp. 2d 284, 295 (E.D.N.Y. 2010) (same), aff'd sub nom. Noveck v. Avis Rent A Car Sys., LLC, 446 Fed. Appx. 370, 373 (2d Cir. 2011) (dismissing Avis' appeal of no-preemption ruling for lack of standing).

[151] See ch. 13, above.

[152] See Owen & Davis on Products Liability ch. 23 (*Multiple Defendants—Joint and Several Liability, Contribution, Indemnity, and Apportionment*).

[153] See Hubbard and Sobocinski, Crashworthiness: The Collision of Sellers' Responsibility for Product Safety with Comparative Fault, 69 S.C. L. Rev. 741 (2018); Bublick, The Tort-Proof Plaintiff: The Drunk in the Automobile, Crashworthiness Claims, and the *Restatement (Third) of Torts*, 74 Brook. L. Rev. 707 (2009); O'Donnell, Public Policy and the Burden of Proof in Enhanced Injury Litigation: A Case Study in the Dangers of Trends and Easy Assumptions, 17 W. St. U. L. Rev. 325 (1990); Tietz, Bushman, and Podraza, Crashworthiness and *Erie*: Determining State Law Regarding the Burden of Proving and Apportioning Damages, 62 Temp. L. Rev. 587 (1989); Clark, Second Collision Liability: A Critique of Two Approaches to Plaintiff's Burden of Proof, 68 Iowa L. Rev. 811 (1983). Annot., 9 A.L.R.4th 494 (1981) (sufficiency of proof of injuries in second collision cases); Frumer, Friedman, and Sklaren, Products Liability § 22.09[3][e].

The Products Liability Rest. § 16, including its comments and Reporters' Notes, contains one of the best treatments of this entire issue.

[154] See § 17.3, above.

[155] While the vast majority of crashworthiness cases are grounded in design defects, they usually raise tag-along warning defect claims and even sometimes manufacturing defect and misrepresentation claims. See, e.g., Jones v. IC Bus, LLC, 626 S.W.3d 661, 680–82 (Ky. Ct. App. 2020) (trial court erred in granting defendant a directed verdict on plaintiffs' crashworthiness and failure to warn claims); Lloyd v. General Motors Corp., 916 A.2d 257, 285 (Md. 2007) (tortious misrepresentation and civil conspiracy claims against manufacturer of

If a manufacturer breaches this duty, it is axiomatic that it will be responsible for any resulting harm, that is, any harm proximately resulting from the uncrashworthy design of the vehicle.[156] But liability for such additional ("aggravated" or "enhanced") harm does not render the manufacturer responsible for other injuries—those resulting from the collision but not from any "uncrashworthy" aspect of the vehicle's design.

Some examples might help illustrate these points. If a defect in the steering of a car causes it to leave the highway and crash into a tree, the manufacturer of course is subject to liability for all injuries to the occupants proximately resulting from the accident. Assume, however, that the car leaves the highway for some reason *other* than an automotive defect, such as driver error or dangerous highway conditions, in which case responsibility becomes more complex. In such a case, if the car's design engineers failed to provide reasonable protection to occupants against foreseeable collision risks (as by failing to design shoulder and lap belts with sufficient strength to restrain occupants in ordinary crashes), the car would *not* be reasonably crashworthy and the manufacturer *would* be responsible for injuries that occur from failures of the passenger restraints. If, on the other hand, the vehicle's design was crashworthy in all respects (including its passenger restraints, which provided reasonable protection to occupants in ordinary collisions), the manufacturer of the car would *not* be responsible for any injuries from the car smashing into the tree. Car accidents are dangerous by nature, and manufacturers are responsible (even under strict liability) only for failing to prevent injuries they can and reasonably should prevent, not for failing to prevent *all* injuries from whatever cause.

These fundamental principles of causal responsibility were first enunciated in *Larsen v. General Motors Corp.*,[157] the case which first imposed the crashworthiness duty on manufacturers of automotive vehicles.[158] "Any design defect not causing the accident would not subject the manufacturer to liability for the entire damage, but the manufacturer should be liable for that portion of the damage or injury caused by the defective design *over and above* the damage or injury that probably would have occurred as a result of the impact or collision absent the defective design."[159] This basic apportionment principle is simple, logical, and fair: a manufacturer should pay for damage caused by defects in its vehicles, but not for damage caused by something else.

When this kind of division of injuries is feasible, the division clearly must be made. Each actor, therefore, will be responsible for the specific harm it caused; and it is not responsible for the plaintiff's remaining harm attributable to the driving plaintiff or another actor. This will be the case, of course, only when injuries attributable to a

---

uncrashworthy front seats that could collapse rearward in rear-impact collisions); Gable v. Village of Gates Mills, 816 N.E.2d 1049, 1051 (Ohio 2004) (failure to provide adequate warnings of "lethal potential" of airbags); Chandler v. Gene Messer Ford, Inc., 81 S.W.3d 493, 503–04 (Tex. App. 2002) (failure to warn of possible risks from airbag deployment to child riding in front passenger seat); Carlson v. Hyundai Motor Co., 164 F.3d 1160 (8th Cir. 1999) (Minn. law) (defectively manufactured seatbelt system and door welds); Jimenez v. Chrysler Corp., 74 F. Supp. 2d 548 (D.S.C. 1999) (manufacturer negligently misrepresented that minivans equipped with flimsy liftgate latch were safe), rev'd sub nom. Jimenez v. DaimlerChrysler Corp., 269 F.3d 439 (4th Cir. 2001).

[156] Products Liability Rest. § 16, "Increased Harm Due to Product Defect," provides in part: "(a) When a product is defective at the time of commercial sale or other distribution and the defect is a substantial factor in increasing the plaintiff's harm beyond that which would have resulted from other causes, the product seller is subject to liability for the increased harm."

[157] 391 F.2d 495 (8th Cir. 1968) (Minn. law).

[158] See § 17.3, above.

[159] *Larsen*, 391 F.2d at 503 (emphasis added).

vehicle's uncrashworthy design can be reasonably separated from those the collision would have caused anyway, even if the design had been reasonably crashworthy. In such a case, the plaintiff's injuries are said to be "divisible," and a manufacturer's responsibility is limited to those damages caused by the vehicle's uncrashworthy characteristic.

Consider an accident where both types of injuries result—some attributable to a car's uncrashworthy design, some not. If a truck is driven through a red light and smashes into the passenger door of a car entering the intersection, the force of the collision may break the arm of a passenger in the car and may also cause the car to roll over, injuring the passenger's head when the roof collapses. Assuming that a properly designed roof structure would not have collapsed, the passenger, in a crashworthiness action against the manufacturer of the car, may recover for his head injuries caused by the uncrashworthy roof. But the manufacturer would not be subject to liability for the broken arm, assuming, of course, that the passenger's door was designed with reasonable attention to crash safety. Probably all courts would agree with this commonsense result, which is also embraced by the *Products Liability Restatement*.[160]

Much more difficult are accident situations—often involving severe injuries, such as paralysis, brain damage, and death—where ascertaining whether an injury was caused by the first collision or only by the second collision is often difficult or impossible.[161] If, in addition to some crashworthiness shortcoming in the vehicle (say, a roof that collapses too greatly in a roll-over), the injury (say, brain damage) is attributable to careless driving by the plaintiff or the operator of another vehicle, then two causes—a defective roof design and driver error—both will be proximate causes fairly linked to the plaintiff's harm. Unlike the separate injuries reasonably divisible in the door-crash roof-crush hypothetical above, brain damage, death, paralysis, and many other types of harm are single, "indivisible" forms of damage that are not in these joint-cause situations separately allocable to a single responsible cause. In such indivisible-injury joint-cause crashworthiness cases, therefore, deciding who has the *burden of proof* on damages apportionment—who has the burden to establish which damages were caused by the vehicle's uncrashworthy feature—often effectively determines whether recovery is allowable or not. The burden of proof, in other words, becomes outcome determinative.[162]

The first case expressly to address the apportionment burden-of-proof problem in crashworthiness cases was *Huddell v. Levin*,[163] decided in 1976 by the Third Circuit

---

[160] Products Liability Rest. § 16(b) provides: "If proof supports a determination of the harm that would have resulted from other causes in the absence of the product defect, the product seller's liability is limited to the increased harm attributable solely to the product defect."

[161] See Note, Apportionment of Damages in the "Second Collision" Case, 63 Va. L. Rev. 475, 476 (1977) ("Courts will hold the manufacturer liable for the plaintiff's loss in the second collision only if defective design of the automobile caused or exacerbated the plaintiff's injury. Yet, if a court finds that defective automobile design did cause some injury, determining where one defendant's liability ends and another's begins may be virtually impossible. Both those injuries for which the manufacturer should be liable and those attributable to other causes, such as another driver's negligence, occurred during the very brief time span of the second collision.").

[162] See Green and Powers, Conceptual Clarity and Necessary Muddles, 90 Tex. L. Rev. See also 41, 44 (2011) ("Of course, the allocation of the burden of proof when evidence is unavailable is outcome dispositive . . . .").

[163] 537 F.2d 726 (3d Cir. 1976) (N.J. law).

Court of Appeals. Plaintiff Huddell was killed when his Chevrolet Nova, which had run out of gas, was hit from behind at 50 to 60 miles per hour by another car. The plaintiff died from brain injuries caused by the impact of his head against the head restraint, which contained "a relatively sharp, unyielding metal edge, covered by two inches of soft, foam-like material."[164] In an action against General Motors, the manufacturer of the Nova, the plaintiff contended that the head restraint was defective "because its relatively sharp edge of unyielding metal allowed for excessive concentration of forces against the rear of the skull," and that it "was designed much like an airplane wing, with the front 'ax-like' portion aimed directly at the rear of the head."[165] The jury decided in favor of the plaintiff. In General Motors' appeal, the Third Circuit reversed, ruling that plaintiffs in design defect crashworthiness cases must prove three things: (1) the existence of a feasible, alternative, safer design; (2) the injuries that would have resulted from such an alternative design; and (3) "the extent of enhanced injuries attributable to the defective design."[166] Because the plaintiff's expert had only testified that a properly designed head restraint would have been "survivable," and because the plaintiff offered no proof of the probable extent of injury had such a restraint been used,[167] a majority of the court[168] ruled that the plaintiff had failed to carry his burden of proof showing the extent to which the design defect had caused his damages.[169]

One year after *Huddell*, in 1977, the federal circuits began to split. In *Smith v. Fiat-Roosevelt Motors, Inc.*,[170] the plaintiff was injured when the Fiat he was driving was rear-ended, causing his seat to collapse. In a crashworthiness action against the supplier of the car, the district court granted the defendant's summary judgment motion because the plaintiff's doctor admitted his inability to apportion the injuries between those caused by the initial rear-ending and those caused by the collapse of the plaintiff's seat. Reversing, the Fifth Circuit ruled that the plaintiff's inability to apportion the damages was not fatal to his crashworthiness case, because "[i]n Florida, where an injury is indivisible and apportionment is impossible, plaintiff may recover his entire damages from either tortfeasor."[171]

During the next year, 1978, the split among the circuits widened. *Fox v. Ford Motor Co.*[172] involved the deaths of two rear-seat passengers who were killed in a 1970 Ford Thunderbird when they were thrown forward in a head-on collision. Both plaintiffs suffered fractured spines and fatal abdominal injuries caused by the

---

[164] Huddell v. Levin, 395 F. Supp. 64, 68 (D.N.J. 1975).

[165] 537 F.2d at 735.

[166] Id. at 738.

[167] "It was not established whether the hypothetical victim of the survivable crash would have sustained no injuries, temporary injuries, permanent but insignificant injuries, extensive and permanent injuries, or, possibly, paraplegia or quadriplegia." Id.

[168] Over Judge Rosenn's persuasive concurring opinion arguing that the burden of proof should have been shifted to the defendant. See id. at 744.

[169] "Without proof to establish what injuries would have resulted from a non-defective head restraint, the plaintiff could not and did not establish what injuries resulted from the alleged defect in the head restraint." Id. at 738.

[170] 556 F.2d 728 (5th Cir. 1977) (Fla. law).

[171] Id. at 729. The year before, the Fifth Circuit had ruled ambiguously on the apportionment issue in Higginbotham v. Ford Motor Co., 540 F.2d 762, 772–74 (5th Cir. 1976) (Ga. law).

[172] 575 F.2d 774 (10th Cir. 1978) (Wyo. law) (Doyle, J.).

seatbelts they were wearing.[173] Their case alleged that Ford had designed the car in an uncrashworthy condition by failing to install shoulder harnesses in the rear passenger compartment, setting the seatbelts at the wrong angle, and failing to provide adequate padding on the backs of the front seats.[174] The trial court refused Ford's requested jury instruction that it was liable only for that portion of the damage caused by the defective design over and above the injury attributable to the initial impact. Rejecting the defendant's argument from *Huddell* that the plaintiffs should have been required to prove with specificity the injuries caused by the alleged design defects, and reasoning that the "duty to prove so-called enhanced damages is simply a part of the plaintiff's responsibility to prove proximate cause,"[175] a split panel of the Tenth Circuit ruled that the trial court had sufficiently instructed the jury that the plaintiffs only had to prove that the alleged defects proximately contributed to the deaths.[176]

Over the next few years, the split among the circuits widened even further. In 1981, a divided panel of the Second Circuit followed *Huddell* in a thinly reasoned decision, *Caiazzo v. Volkswagenwerk A.G.*[177] The following year, in *Mitchell v. Volkswagenwerk, A.G.*,[178] the Eighth Circuit followed the *Fox* approach, lucidly explaining how automotive manufacturers and other defendants may properly be held jointly and severally liable for indivisible injuries (such as paraplegia and death) in crash cases where there is no reasonable basis for determining causation between them.[179] Thereafter, the number of jurisdictions following the *Huddell* approach of burdening plaintiffs with apportionment[180] dwindled; a few states followed their own apportionment paths;[181] and a growing majority of courts—including an intermediate appellate court in New Jersey, the state whose law was predicted in *Huddell*—now follow the *Fox-Mitchell* approach of holding manufacturers of uncrashworthy vehicles responsible for indivisible injuries.[182]

---

173 Id. at 777–78. The head of one plaintiff hit an unpadded portion of the front seat, which broke her neck.

174 Id. at 783.

175 Id. at 787.

176 See id. at 788.

177 647 F.2d 241 (2d Cir. 1981) (N.Y. law).

178 669 F.2d 1199 (8th Cir. 1982) (Minn. law).

179 See id. at 1206:

> [T]he plaintiffs' burden of proof should be deemed satisfied against the manufacturer if it is shown that the design defect was a substantial factor in producing damages over and above those which were probably caused as a result of the original impact or collision. [T]he extent of the manufacturer's liability depends upon whether or not the injuries involved are divisible such that the injuries can be clearly separated and attributed either to the manufacturer or the original tortfeasor. If the manufacturer's negligence is found to be a substantial factor in causing an indivisible injury such as paraplegia, death, etc., then absent a reasonable basis to determine which wrongdoer actually caused the harm, the defendants should be treated as joint and several tortfeasors.

180 See, e.g., Campbell v. Fawber, 975 F. Supp. 2d 485, 496 (M.D. Pa. 2013) (to prevail on a crashworthiness claim, a plaintiff must prove by expert testimony: (1) that the vehicle design was defective in that a safer, practicable, alternative design was available; (2) what injuries he would have received had the safer design been used; and (3) what injuries the defect caused); Sumner v. General Motors Corp., 538 N.W.2d 112 (Mich. Ct. App. 1995), overruled on other grounds by Lopez v. General Motors Corp., 569 N.W.2d 861 (Mich. Ct. App. 1997); Chretien v. General Motors Corp., 959 F.2d 231 (4th Cir. 1992) (Va. law).

181 See, e.g., Egbert v. Nissan Motor Co., 228 P.3d 737, 747 (Utah 2010) (rejecting both *Huddell* and *Fox-Mitchell*, and collecting cases; holding that, when a plaintiff proves that a defect enhanced his injuries, the jury shall "apportion fault between the defendant original tortfeasor and the defendant product seller").

182 See, e.g., Jahn v. Hyundai Motor Co., 773 N.W.2d 550, 559 (Iowa 2009) (aligning itself with Products Liability Rest. § 16, note 185, below); Boryszewski v. Burke, 882 A.2d 410, 419 (N.J. Super. Ct. App. Div. 2005); Trull v. Volkswagen of Am., Inc., 761 A.2d 477 (N.H. 2000); Tracy v. Cottrell, 524 S.E.2d 879 (W. Va. 1999);

Proponents of the *Fox-Mitchell* method of shifting the burden of apportionment to defendant manufacturers often point to the established common-law principle that two or more tortfeasors whose actions combine to cause a single injury are jointly and severally liable for the harm unless they can prove a basis for apportionment.[183] Indeed, the *Restatement (Second) of Torts* shifts the burden of proof to defendants in such cases,[184] and the *Third Restatement* follows essentially this same approach.[185]

Similar to the *Second Restatement*,[186] the *Third Restatement* explains that "[t]he defendant, a wrongdoer who in fact has caused harm to the plaintiff, should not escape liability because the nature of the harm makes such a determination impossible."[187] Adopting the position of *Fox-Mitchell* and most other judicial decisions,[188] the *Third Restatement* provides that if a plaintiff establishes that an uncrashworthy feature of a vehicle was a substantial factor in aggravating his or her injuries, the defendant bears responsibility for all such injuries which are incapable of apportionment.[189]

In short, a large and growing majority of courts, most objective scholars,[190] and the *Second* and *Third Restatements of Torts*, all maintain that the *Huddell* approach provides an unfair escape for wrongdoing manufacturers when the extent of harm they

---

General Motors Corp. v. Farnsworth, 965 P.2d 1209 (Alaska 1998); Polston v. Boomershine Pontiac-GMC Truck, Inc., 423 S.E.2d 659 (Ga. 1992); Blankenship v. General Motors Corp., 406 S.E.2d 781 (W. Va. 1991); Doupnik v. General Motors Corp., 275 Cal. Rptr. 715 (Ct. App. 1990); Shipp v. General Motors Corp., 750 F.2d 418 (5th Cir. 1985) (Tex. law); Sumnicht v. Toyota Motor Sales, U.S.A., Inc., 360 N.W.2d 2 (Wis. 1984); McLeod v. American Motors Corp., 723 F.2d 830 (11th Cir. 1984) (Fla. law).

183 "[W]here wrongdoers each play a substantial role in creating an indivisible harm, they are treated as joint and several tortfeasors." Mitchell v. Volkswagenwerk, A.G., 669 F.2d 1199, 1207 (8th Cir. 1982) (Minn. law). See Products Liability Rest. § 16 Reporters' Note to cmt. *d*; Keeton, Dobbs, Keeton, and Owen, Prosser and Keeton on the Law of Torts § 52; Dobbs, Law of Torts § 174.

184 Rest. (2d) Torts § 433B(2) provides: "Where the tortious conduct of two or more actors has combined to bring about harm to the plaintiff, and one or more of the actors seeks to limit his liability on the ground that the harm is capable of apportionment among them, the burden of proof as to the apportionment is upon each such actor."

185 Products Liability Restatement § 16(c) provides: "If proof does not support a determination under Subsection (b) of the harm that would have resulted in the absence of the product defect, the product seller is liable for all of the plaintiff's harm attributable to the defect and other causes." The Reporters assert that subsection (c) does not formally shift the burden of proof to the defendant. See Reporters' Note to cmt. *d*.

186 See Rest. (2d) Torts § 433B cmt. *d*, justifying "the exceptional rule placing the burden of proof as to apportionment upon the defendant or defendants," rather than upon the innocent plaintiff, by pointing to "the injustice of allowing a proved wrongdoer who has in fact caused harm to the plaintiff to escape liability merely because the harm which he has inflicted has combined with similar harm inflicted by other wrongdoers," rendering causal attribution impossible. See also Products Liability Rest. § 16 Reporters' Note to cmt. *d*.

187 Products Liability Rest. § 16 cmt. *d*.

188 *But see* Chadwick, "Causing" Enhanced Injuries in Crashworthiness Cases, 48 Syracuse L. Rev. 1223, 1258–61 (1998) (criticizing the Third Restatement for adopting a confusing position lying somewhere between *Huddell* and *Fox-Mitchell*).

189 In addition to a defect, "[t]he plaintiff must also establish that the defect was a substantial factor in increasing the plaintiff's harm beyond the harm that would have occurred from other causes," and "when proof does not support a determination of increased harm, the product seller is liable for all harm suffered by the victim." Products Liability Rest. § 16 cmt. *b*.

Cases involving multiple defendants are governed by the applicable apportionment rules of joint and several liability. See Products Liability Rest. § 16(d) ("A seller of a defective product . . . is jointly and severally liable or severally liable with other parties who bear legal responsibility for causing the harm, determined by applicable rules of joint and several liability.").

190 Much scholarship on this topic, sometimes cogently argued, was authored by defense counsel.

have caused to innocent plaintiffs[191] is by nature impossible to ascertain.[192] Thus, subject to a weakening minority to the contrary, the courts now widely hold that automotive manufacturers are responsible for both the divisible and indivisible harm caused by uncrashworthy features of their vehicles. A plaintiff must establish that such a feature was a substantial factor in aggravating his or her injuries, after which the manufacturer is liable for all such injuries that it is unable to prove were not caused by the vehicle's uncrashworthy design.

§ 17.5 PLAINTIFF FAULT

The vast majority of automotive accidents are caused by driver fault, evidence of which defendant manufacturers routinely seek to introduce in automotive products liability litigation.[193] Whether the evidence concerns a driver's intoxication, speeding, cell phone use, erratic driving, failing to wear an available seatbelt, falling asleep, overloading the vehicle, failing to keep the tires inflated or otherwise to maintain the accident vehicle, or any other form of misbehavior, the manufacturer of the vehicle will often seek to strengthen its own case, and weaken the plaintiff's, with evidence that the plaintiff used the vehicle improperly. Such evidence may undercut a plaintiff's prima facie case on cause in fact and proximate causation, establish affirmative defenses, and diminish the plaintiff's damages. Moreover, evidence of a plaintiff's misbehavior may intangibly diminish his or her standing in the jury's eyes and thus tip the balance of the scales of justice toward the manufacturer.

The general role of plaintiff conduct in products liability litigation, including its affect on the defenses of contributory negligence, assumption of risk, product misuse, and comparative fault, was considered earlier.[194] But courts and legislatures have confronted a number of special issues involving the fault of drivers and other plaintiffs

---

[191] If the plaintiff affirmatively causes an accident by his or her own fault, as by driving recklessly while intoxicated, it seems more reasonable to require him or her to apportion damages. But a plaintiff's merely passive failure to wear a seatbelt does not in any respect diminish his or her fairness claim to have the defendant apportion damages. See § 17.5, below. For a contrary view, see Caiazzo v. Volkswagenwerk A.G., 647 F.2d 241, 253 (2d Cir. 1981) (N.Y. law) (Mansfield, J., concurring).

[192] See, e.g., Stecher v. Ford Motor Co., 779 A.2d 491, 497–98 (Pa. Super. Ct. 2001); Williams v. Ford Motor Co., 1986 WL 110681, at *2 (W.D. Tenn. 1986); Lee v. Volkswagen of Am., Inc., 688 P.2d 1283, 1288 (Okla. 1984); Tietz, Bushman, and Podraza, Crashworthiness and Erie: Determining State Law Regarding the Burden of Proving and Apportioning Damages, 62 Temp. L. Rev. 587, 620 (1989). See generally Products Liability Rest. § 16 Reporters' Note to cmt. *d* (collecting authorities).

[193] A 2015 study of light vehicle crashes between 2005 and 2007 concluded that 94% of the crashes were attributable to driver fault. U.S. Dep't of Transp. and NHTSA, Traffic Safety Facts Crash Stats: Critical Reasons for Crashes Investigated in the National Motor Vehicle Crash Causation Survey (Feb. 2015). See generally Bublick, The Tort-Proof Plaintiff: The Drunk in the Automobile, Crashworthiness Claims, and the *Restatement (Third) of Torts*, 74 Brook. L. Rev. 707 (2009); Davis, Individual and Institutional Responsibility: A Vision for Comparative Fault in Products Liability, 39 Vill. L. Rev. 281 (1994); DeDominicis, No Duty at Any Speed?: Determining the Responsibility of the Automobile Manufacturer in Speed-Related Accidents, 14 Hofstra L. Rev. 403 (1986). See also ch. 13, note 1, above.

Driver Distraction. In 2021, NHTSA reported: (1) 9% of fatal crashes and 15% of all crashes involving injury in 2019 were caused by distracted driving, (2) distracted drivers aged 15 to 20 years of age were more likely to be involved in a fatal crash than older drivers, and (3) 7% of distracted driving crashes involving injury were attributed to cell phone use. U.S. Dep't of Transp. and NHTSA, Traffic Safety Facts Research Note: Distracted Driving 2019 (April 2021). For cases alleging negligence against mobile app providers that distracted drivers, see § 16.8, note 394, above. See generally Annot., 53 A.L.R.7th Art. 4 (2020) (liability for cell phone use in traffic). There were more than 20,000 traffic fatalities during the first half of 2021—an 18.4% increase over 2020 and the most since 2006—from more speeding and lower seatbelt use than before the pandemic. NHTSA, USDOT Releases New Data Showing That Road Fatalities Spiked in First Half of 2021 (Oct. 28, 2021).

[194] See ch. 13, above.

in automotive products liability cases. General aspects of plaintiff fault in automotive products liability litigation are examined first, followed by a consideration of the role of a driver's intoxication and the effect of a plaintiff's failure to wear a seatbelt or other safety devices.

Accident Causation

Evidence of a driver's conduct is relevant in a products liability action if, but only if, it contributed in some way to cause the accident or the plaintiff's injuries. Assume, for example, that a drunken driver is injured while driving erratically and at excessive speed when one of his tires blows out. If the evidence reveals that the tire failed solely because it was manufactured in a defective condition, and that neither the speed nor erratic driving caused by his intoxication contributed in any way to the tire's failure or to a subsequent crash, then the driver's conduct simply has no bearing on any issue in the case. Surely the driver's behavior has no relevance to the defectiveness of the tire, nor to the manufacturer's negligence in making and selling it in such a condition. Nor, assuming that the defect was latent, does it have any relevance to assumption of risk (which requires that a plaintiff appreciate the specific risk), to contributory or comparative negligence, or to product misuse, all of which defenses require a showing that the conduct was a contributing cause of the plaintiff's harm. In a case like this, a court should exclude all such evidence of the driver's conduct simply because it has no bearing on accident causation. Stated simply, evidence of a plaintiff's bad behavior must be excluded if it was not a cause in fact of the accident or resulting injuries.

To help avoid the defense of contributory negligence, a negligent driver typically will base a products liability claim on strict liability in tort. As previously discussed, many courts hold that a plaintiff's simple contributory negligence is not a bar to a claim for strict products liability in tort.[195] Thus, if a drunken driver, injured when his fast and erratic driving causes his sport utility vehicle to roll over, asserts that the SUV was too susceptible to rolling over, he normally should limit his claim to strict liability in tort and ask the court to exclude evidence of his intoxication, speed, and erratic driving.

However, a court may decide to allow some or all of this misconduct evidence for at least three reasons. First, in replacing the absolute bar of contributory negligence with the damages-reducing feature of comparative fault,[196] most states now reasonably allow evidence of a plaintiff's contributory fault in automotive products liability cases, even those based on claims of strict products liability in tort.[197] A second, related reason for admitting such misconduct evidence in the SUV hypothetical is that, unlike the defective tire situation, such evidence may well be relevant to the defenses of misuse and assumption of risk. The third reason this kind of evidence may properly be admissible is that the SUV in this example may have rolled over because the forces placed on it were too great for any SUV, not because of any defect in its design. While the mere fact of the driver's intoxication may have no direct bearing on the vehicle's rollover propensities, certainly both the driver's speed and erratic maneuvering caused by the intoxication are highly relevant to how and why the rollover occurred and, so, to proximate causation, and possibly to the defectiveness of the vehicle's design. Thus, the SUV driver's misconduct probably will not bar liability on grounds of contributory negligence, but it

---

[195] See § 13.2, above.

[196] See § 13.3, above.

[197] See Annot., 9 A.L.R.4th 633 (1981) (applicability of comparative fault to strict liability in tort).

likely will be relevant to comparative fault, misuse, assumption of risk, proximate causation, and product defectiveness.

A driver's conduct implicates two principal causation issues—cause in fact and proximate cause. Sometimes the actual cause of an accident is hotly in dispute, with the plaintiff typically claiming that the accident was caused by some defect in the vehicle and the manufacturer asserting that the failed component in the vehicle was caused by the violence of the accident which itself was caused by the driver's misbehavior. In *Hardy v. General Motors Corp.*,[198] for example, the driver of a Corvette was injured when he lost control of his car and struck a tree while attempting to negotiate a curve at between 104 and 111 miles per hour. The plaintiff's expert testified that the loss of control resulted when a tie rod broke due to a fatigue fracture, while the defendant's engineers testified that the tie rod broke when the vehicle hit the tree. Affirming a directed verdict for the defendant, the court determined that the evidence clearly established that the loss of control was caused by the driver's dangerous driving, not by any defect in the car. Other courts similarly have allowed evidence of the driver's speeding and erratic driving,[199] or recklessly jamming on the brakes in a high-speed turn,[200] to support the defendant's theory of accident causation, but not to prove the plaintiff's contributory fault.

The other principal causation issue to which driver fault is relevant is *proximate* causation, as distinguished from factual causation. If a driver's misconduct is clearly the dominant cause of the injuries, and any defect in the vehicle is trivial by comparison, the driver's claim may be barred on grounds that his or her misconduct was the sole proximate cause of the accident.[201] Often characterized merely as a "sole cause" or "proximate cause" issue, courts sometimes admit evidence of a driver's grossly careless driving to bar the claim on some such basis. On this ground, for example, courts have allowed evidence of a driver's speeding while intoxicated,[202] or speeding at 110 to 120 miles per hour on underinflated tires.[203]

Relevance in Crashworthiness Cases

Most cases involving a driver's conduct discussed above involve defects alleged to have caused the initial accident. A difficult issue that has sharply split the courts[204] is whether the conduct of the driver or other occupant in causing an accident may be considered, as a matter of proximate cause or comparative fault, in apportioning damages for enhanced injuries in crashworthiness cases.[205] Some courts take the

---

198 710 N.E.2d 764 (Ohio Ct. App. 1998).

199 See, e.g., Reidelberger v. Highland Body Shop, Inc., 416 N.E.2d 268 (Ill. 1981).

200 See Daye v. General Motors Corp., 720 So.2d 654, 660 (La. 1998) ("In reality, plaintiff's vigorous application of the brakes while driving through a blind curve on a substandard two-lane country road at a breakneck speed—and not his reliance on the promotional information—was the cause of the accident.").

201 See ch. 13, above.

202 See, e.g., Mazda Motor Corp. v. Lindahl, 706 A.2d 526 (Del. 1998) (driver killed when car failed to negotiate curve and plunged down embankment, tumbling end over end through air, and striking ground several times before it came to rest; claim for defective design of seats denied).

203 Hegwood v. General Motors Corp., 286 N.W.2d 29 (Iowa 1979) (tire blowout; jury properly could find that no failure of manufacturer was proximate cause of accident).

204 See Products Liability Rest. § 16 Reporters' Note to cmt. *f* (characterizing driver fault as "more difficult" and noting that courts are "sharply split").

205 See Annot., 69 A.L.R.5th 625 (1999) (collecting cases on driver's comparative fault as defense to second collision claims). More generally, most courts now reduce a plaintiff's damages on account of his or her comparative fault. See ch. 13, above.

position that evidence of the plaintiff's conduct in causing the first collision is simply irrelevant to a manufacturer's duty to protect occupants against statistically inevitable second collisions.[206] Other courts disagree, reasoning that the role of plaintiff conduct in crashworthiness cases logically is no different than in other contexts.[207]

A closely divided 1992 decision, *Reed v. Chrysler Corp.*,[208] illustrates the two perspectives. The plaintiff, riding as a passenger, injured his arm in the rollover of a Jeep CJ-7. The plaintiff's claim against Jeep's manufacturer was that the vehicle was uncrashworthy because its top was made of brittle fiberglass rather than the much stronger steel used by other manufacturers. Both the driver and plaintiff were intoxicated at the time of the collision, evidence that Chrysler introduced at trial. Ruling that the intoxication evidence should have been excluded, a five-judge majority of the Iowa Supreme Court, overruling an earlier decision to the contrary, reasoned that a driver's misconduct in causing an accident is "beside the point" because the role of the crashworthiness duty is to reduce damages in "accidents precipitated for myriad reasons."[209] The four judges in dissent thought that the majority entirely missed the point: "Because under settled principles of proximate cause a claimant's fault that produces an injury-producing occurrence will also be a proximate cause of the enhanced injuries sustained, the usual rules for fault comparison should apply to the enhanced injury portion of the claim."[210] In 2009, in *Jahn v. Hyundai Motor Co.*,[211] the Iowa Supreme Court overruled *Reed*, applying comparative fault analysis to enhanced injury cases and aligning Iowa law with the *Restatement (Third)* and most other courts.[212]

This issue is a close and difficult one, as illustrated not only by the sharp division of the court in *Reed*, but also by the number of decisions that go both ways. It is sometimes said that a majority of courts allow evidence of a driver's comparative fault to be considered in crashworthiness enhanced injury cases.[213] While the decisions were quite evenly divided when the first edition of this book was researched on point in the early 2000s,[214] courts since then have turned decidedly toward *Jahn* and the *Third Restatement*'s position that favors the application of comparative fault to a driver's conduct that causes an accident. Many of the cases, particularly older ones, fail to focus

---

206 Early cases included Pree v. Brunswick Corp., 983 F.2d 863, 866 n.3 (8th Cir. 1993) (Mo. law) ("evidence of intoxication is irrelevant in a strict tort liability action for enhancement of injury"); Reed v. Chrysler Corp., 494 N.W.2d 224 (Iowa 1992); Ford Motor Co. v. Hill, 404 So.2d 1049 (Fla. 1981). For more recent cases, see note 213, below.

207 Early cases included Harvey v. General Motors Corp., 873 F.2d 1343 (10th Cir. 1989) (Wyo. law) (drinking and reckless driving); Keltner v. Ford Motor Co., 748 F.2d 1265 (8th Cir. 1984) (Ark. law) (intoxication); Daly v. General Motors Corp., 575 P.2d 1162, 1174 (Cal. 1978) (intoxication). For more recent cases, see note 216, below.

208 494 N.W.2d 224 (Iowa 1992).

209 Id. at 230.

210 Id. at 231.

211 773 N.W.2d 550 (Iowa 2009).

212 Id. at 559–60.

213 See, e.g., id; Green v. Ford Motor Co., 942 N.E.2d 791, 795 (Ind. 2011); Davis v. Daimler Chrysler Corp., 2009 WL 323428, at *3 (Conn. Super. Ct. 2009); Whitehead v. Toyota Motor Corp., 897 S.W.2d 684, 693 (Tenn. 1995); Products Liability Rest. § 16 Reporters' Note to cmt. *f*; 2 Prod. Liab. Rep. (CCH) ¶ 3030, at 6903 (1997).

214 See Annot., 69 A.L.R.5th 625 (1999) (collecting cases on driver's comparative fault as defense to second collision claims).

on the precise issue,[215] and many of the more recent ones allow evidence of driver fault in cases of this type.[216] A simple head count of decisions may make little sense because it diverts attention from the difficult issues of policy and fairness that need attention.

The commentators are also markedly divided on this issue, some viewing driver fault as irrelevant to claims for enhanced injuries,[217] others viewing such conduct as no different from other types of plaintiff (or third party) fault.[218] The *Third Restatement* addresses this issue ambiguously. The Reporters favored a rule excluding evidence of driver fault in crashworthiness cases, cogently explained in an early draft comment[219]

---

[215] See Meekins v. Ford Motor Co., 699 A.2d 339, 343 (Del. Super. Ct. 1997) (correctly noting that "[m]any of the decisions on both sides of the issue reach a conclusion but fail to analyze the issue in depth").

[216] Over the last couple of decades, the cases have continued to split, but most recent decisions that explicitly examine the issue rule that evidence of driver negligence should be allowed in apportioning responsibility for enhanced injuries in crashworthiness cases. Frumer, Friedman, and Sklaren, Products Liability § 22.09[3][e] (2021 Supp.) classifies the cases into: (1) the *majority view*, which applies comparative fault in crashworthiness/enhanced injury cases (Alaska, Ark., Cal., Colo., Conn., Del., Fla. (by statute), Ind., Iowa, Ken., La., Miss., N.H., N.J., N.C., N.D., Ore., P.R., Tenn., and Tex.); and (2) the *minority view*, which bars comparative fault in crashworthiness cases (Ariz., Ill., Mo., Neb., Nev., and S.C.).

Allowing evidence of driver fault in crashworthiness cases. E.g., Norman v. Textron Inc., 2018 WL 3199487, at *2 (W.D. Mo. 2018) (seatbelt evidence); Nemmers v. Ford Motor Co., 686 F.3d 486, 490 (8th Cir. 2012) (Iowa law) (driver intoxication); Graham v. Hamilton, 872 F. Supp. 2d 529, 539 (W.D. La. 2012) (marijuana use); Green v. Ford Motor Co., 942 N.E.2d 791, 795 (Ind. 2011); Morris v. Mitsubishi Motors N. Am., 782 F. Supp. 2d 1149, 1161 (E.D. Wash. 2011) (inattention and sitting out of position, possibly after retrieving something from floor); Meekins v. Ford Motor Co., 699 A.2d 339 (Del. Super. Ct. 1997) (balanced presentation of both positions); Montag v. Honda Motor Co., 75 F.3d 1414 (10th Cir. 1996) (Colo. law) (driving car equipped with defective seatbelt into path of train).

Disallowing evidence of driver fault. E.g., Wickersham v. Ford Motor Co., 853 S.E.2d 329, 334 (S.C. 2020); Gaudio v. Ford Motor Co., 976 A.2d 524, 542 (Pa. Super. Ct. 2009); Giannini v. Ford Motor Co., 616 F. Supp. 2d 219 (D. Conn. 2007) (good analysis, but materially misquoting Restatement); Gable v. Gates Mills, 784 N.E.2d 739, 741 (Ohio Ct. App. 2003), rev'd, 816 N.E.2d 1049 (Ohio 2004); D'Amario v. Ford Motor Co., 806 So.2d 424, 426 (Fla. 2001), overturned by legislature in 2011, Fla. Sess. Law Serv. Ch. 2011–215, § 2; Gerow v. Mitch Crawford Holiday Motors, 987 S.W.2d 359 (Mo. Ct. App. 1999) (falling asleep); Norwest Bank N.M., N.A. v. Chrysler Corp., 981 P.2d 1215 (N.M. Ct. App. 1999); Binakonsky v. Ford Motor Co., 133 F.3d 281, 287 (4th Cir. 1998) (Md. law) (intoxication); Green v. General Motors Corp., 709 A.2d 205, 210–11 (N.J. Super. Ct. App. Div. 1998) (speeding irrelevant to crashworthiness claims but allowed on proximate cause); Kritzberg v. Chrysler Corp., No. 1:97 CV 03579, Tr. at 17 (N.D. Ill. May 15, 1997) (Posner, J.).

[217] See, e.g., Hubbard and Sobocinski, Crashworthiness: The Collision of Sellers' Responsibility for Product Safety with Comparative Fault, 69 S.C. L. Rev. 741, 824 (2018) ("[U]sing comparative fault to impose accident costs on humans is a relatively ineffective way to reduce accident costs. Instead, because corporations are better at assessing risks, imposing liability for inefficient safety decisions on sellers is a better way to reduce accidents efficiently."); Hogan, The Crashworthiness Doctrine, 18 Am. J. Trial Advoc. 37, 52–53 (1994) ("The crashworthiness doctrine, by taking driver actions out of the case, can also restrict available defenses. The logic seems unassailable that where the plaintiff makes no claim that the accident was caused by the defendant, the defendant should not have a defense based on the cause of the accident."); Harris, Enhanced Injury Theory: An Analytic Framework, 62 N.C. L. Rev. 643, 673–74 (1984) ("[i]n enhanced injury cases, unlike ordinary products liability cases, a claimant's fault in causing the accident is not a basis for reducing his recovery [because] a manufacturer's duty is that of minimizing the injurious effects of contact however caused [and a] negligent operator is entitled to the same protection against unnecessary injury as the careful user").

[218] See, e.g., Vickles and Oldham, Enhanced Injury Should Not Equal Enhanced Liability, 36 S. Tex. L. Rev. 417 (1995) (plaintiff's conduct affecting severity of accident affects severity of injuries and thus constitutes proximate cause of enhanced injuries which should be considered in damages apportionment); Thomas, Comparative Fault in Crashworthiness or "Second Collision" Cases, 22 Prod. Safety & Liab. Rep. (BNA) No. 20, 520 (April 29, 1994) (plaintiff's fault should be considered in enhanced injury cases); V. Schwartz, Comparative Negligence § 4.06 (with K. Kelly 6th ed. 2020).

[219] Their discussion remains the most considered analysis of this issue. After explaining that the black-letter general rule "provides that all forms of plaintiff fault are to be considered by the trier of fact for the purposes of apportioning liability between the plaintiff and the product seller" without exempting, for example,

that the ALI Council tentatively approved and presented to the general membership for consideration in 1994.[220] But the defense bar membership had been forewarned, and a polished brief was presented to the Institute advocating the other way.[221] Despite an impassioned explanation by the Reporters of the logic of their view,[222] a slight majority of the membership voted to deny the Reporters' exemption of driver fault from apportionment of enhanced injuries in crashworthiness cases.[223] Dutifully deleting this enhanced injury exception from the comments to the apportionment rule,[224] together with the relevant portion of their persuasive Reporters' Note,[225] the Reporters artfully redrafted the pertinent comment to leave wiggle room for courts in appropriate cases to apportion enhanced injuries *in toto* to manufacturers of uncrashworthy vehicles.[226]

---

a plaintiff's failure to discover a product defect, they summarized the case for excepting driver fault from apportionment in enhanced injury cases:

> Cases of increased harm require a different rule. The requirement that an automobile be reasonably crashworthy, for example, aims to protect the plaintiff from increased harm arising from harm-causing uses of the product that defendant should have foreseen and protected against. An automobile, not otherwise defective, does not become defective because it fails to protect a plaintiff against harm-causing conduct where the risks exceed those that defendant could reasonably have protected against. However, if the risks created by plaintiff's conduct are within the range that justifies crashworthiness protection, plaintiff's conduct creates the very situation in which the plaintiff has a legitimate right to expect the automobile to provide reasonable protection. This is so regardless of the nature of the plaintiff's conduct. Accordingly, plaintiff's fault should not be taken into account in determining the defendant's liability for the defect-caused increase in harm.
>
> Ignoring the role of plaintiff's fault in connection with increased harm in cases where the proof supports causal apportionment has troubled many courts who find it objectionable that drunken drivers or drug abusers be allowed full recovery for increased harm when the initial accident was brought about by such egregious conduct. The issue is admittedly a difficult one. On balance, however, the theoretical justification for requiring a defendant to provide reasonable protection against increased harm when a plaintiff is fully dependent on the product to mitigate harm makes it difficult to distinguish between the forms of conduct that brought the plaintiff to the state of dependency.

Products Liability Rest. § 6 cmt. *f*, "Plaintiff's fault in cases of increased harm" (Tent. Draft No. 1, 1994). See also the Reporters' Note to comment *f*, note 225, below, which further explicated their position.

[220] See Products Liability Rest. § 6 cmt. *f* (Tent. Draft No. 1, 1994).

[221] By a memorandum and oral presentation, both exceptionally well crafted, presented to the ALI membership by a defense attorney member of the Institute. See 71 ALI Proc. 207–08 (1994).

[222] See id. at 208–14.

[223] See id. at 214.

[224] See Products Liability Rest. § 11 cmt. *f* (Tent. Draft No. 2, 1995).

[225] Products Liability Rest. § 6 Reporters' Note to cmt. *f* (Tent. Draft No. 1, 1994) provided in part:

> [Assume that] a plaintiff who was injured when either a seatbelt or an air bag failed because it was either defectively manufactured or defectively designed. [N]egligent conduct, on the part of the plaintiff in causing the first collision, [should not] be taken into account to reduce the plaintiff's recovery [because the] purpose of the seatbelt or air bag is to function when the plaintiff is involved in an accident and to offer protection when the plaintiff can no longer do anything in self protection. The seatbelt or air bag is designed to protect the plaintiff in a crash situation. How the plaintiff got into the situation is of little relevance. No manufacturer would say that its seatbelts or air bags are there only for the protection of the non-negligent. A crashworthiness claim is very much like a defective seatbelt or defective air bag claim. [If an auto is found to be uncrashworthy,] it should not lie in the mouth of the auto manufacturer to claim that the plaintiff put [himself in a position where he] had to make use of the very aspect of the product that made it non-crashworthy. . . .

[226] In their redraft of comment *f*, the Reporters excluded an explicit exemption of driver fault from apportionment of enhanced injuries and stated that "the nature of the product defect [is] relevant in allocating the appropriate percentages between the plaintiff and the product seller, but should not serve automatically to absolve the plaintiff from fault." The comment further provided that: "[T]he contributory fault of the plaintiff in causing the accident that resulted in defect-related increased harm is relevant in apportioning damages between or among the parties, according to applicable apportionment law. In apportioning damages in these cases, it may be important that requiring a product to be designed reasonably to prevent increased harm aims

The *Restatement* Reporters are not the only conservative scholars who believe that driver fault should be immune from enhanced injury apportionment in crashworthiness cases. No less a judicial scholar than Judge (and professor) Richard Posner, not generally viewed as a mindless advocate for plaintiff interests, ruled (without much analysis) that evidence of driver fault should be excluded in a crashworthiness case because a contrary conclusion "wouldn't make any sense."[227] Indeed, if one accepts NHTSA's findings that 93% of crashes are attributable to driver fault,[228] it might be said that allowing a driver's fault to reduce his or her damages goes a long way to "emasculate second collision liability."[229] But the siren call of comparative fault, which has beguiled many intelligent people into surrendering to juries the responsibility for resolving difficult issues of responsibility, continues its seductive draw of tort law issues into the clutches of its greedy grasp.[230]

Advocates on both sides of the driver-fault crashworthiness debate assert that logic supports only their position. Yet neither logic nor fairness leads ineluctably to an evident, true resolution of the problem whether a driver's fault in causing an accident should be included in a comparative fault calculus applicable to crashworthiness claims. My own view has changed since the second edition of this book. Although for many years I thought that a plaintiff's conduct in causing a collision was entirely unrelated to a manufacturer's prior responsibility to adopt reasonable design precautions against that eventuality, I now believe that both auto makers and auto drivers have roughly equivalent responsibilities to take reasonable steps to avoid and minimize injuries in automotive collisions—at bottom, quite like the duty of care all actors owe to one another when they interact in the world. Tort law, that is, broadly and fairly requires people to act with reasonable care to protect the interests of those who may be expected to be affected by their conduct.

Outside products liability law, drivers are obligated to avoid intoxication, maintain a proper lookout, observe traffic signals, drive at an appropriate speed, and adopt other reasonable measures to protect foreseeable victims on and near the highway—certainly other people, but also themselves. If two drivers collide, of course, we allow fact finders to apportion responsibility between both actors—both of whom were duty-bound to act carefully to protect one another and themselves—on the basis of comparative fault.[231] Inside products liability law, regardless of the type of product, it now is axiomatic that

---

to protect the plaintiff from harm when the plaintiff is in a position where self-protection is no longer possible." Products Liability Rest. § 11 cmt. *f* (Tent. Draft No. 2, 1995). The final version, approved by the ALI in 1997 and published in 1998, is nearly identical. See Products Liability Rest. § 16 cmt. *f*. See also Bublick, The Tort-Proof Plaintiff: The Drunk in the Automobile, Crashworthiness Claims, and the *Restatement (Third) of Torts*, 74 Brook. L. Rev. 707 (2009).

[227] Kritzberg v. Chrysler Corp., No. 97 C 3579, Tr. at 17 (N.D. Ill. Dec. 1, 1999, Hr'g). Temporarily assigned (by himself) as a district judge, Judge Posner reasoned: "[I]f you have an accident, no matter how much it's your fault, [the manufacturer's duty to build a crashworthy vehicle is] going to minimize the consequence of it. So I can't see as a matter of basic tort theory how the [plaintiff's] negligence in falling asleep [while driving] has anything to do with the case." Id. at 15. See also Haugh v. Jones & Laughlin Steel Corp., 949 F.2d 914, 920–21 (7th Cir. 1991) (Ind. law) (Posner, J.) (discussing policy reasons for not requiring plaintiffs to anticipate negligence of others).

[228] See note 193, above.

[229] Comment, 43 Mont. L. Rev. 109 (1982).

[230] See Prosser and Keeton on Torts § 67, at 479 (observing that "[c]ourts need to be cautious not to become caught up by the sheer momentum of the [comparative fault] movement, and with the facile simplicity of the doctrine, but instead should apply deliberate thought to each new call for its further extension").

[231] This author is grateful to John Thomas, who long served as counsel for an automotive company, for taking the time to help guide him toward the light.

manufacturers must employ designs with reasonable attention to the kinds of mistakes foreseeably made from time to time by users and consumers—persons who are sometimes distracted, sometimes careless, and sometimes intoxicated. And basic principles of comparative fault and equity also hold that drivers, who are bound to act prudently to avoid harm, have no fair claim on that portion of their damages attributable to their own misconduct in causing a vehicular accident—whether the other party was another driver or the manufacturer of the plaintiff's vehicle.

In the end, a vehicle manufacturer's duty to design its products to be reasonably safe for a user's mistakes is nothing special in the law of tort, as it should be nothing special in the field of products liability. For this reason, principles of comparative fault logically should be held to apply to crashworthiness cases no less than to any other type of case involving responsibility for product accidents.

Plaintiff Intoxication

In General

In products liability claims against manufacturers and other sellers of automotive vehicles, evidence that the plaintiff driver[232] was intoxicated is often relevant and admissible.[233] Because intoxication obviously reduces the skill and judgment a driver needs to operate a vehicle safely, and because driving under the influence of intoxicants is widely criminalized for just this reason,[234] intoxication evidence logically bears on a driver's failure to exercise reasonable care for his or her own safety. Thus, a driver's intoxication (but not necessarily the mere fact that he or she had been drinking)[235] generally is proof of a driver's contributory negligence[236] that may bar recovery, or of comparative fault that may reduce the driver's damages proportionate to his or her fault.[237] Indeed, in the majority of jurisdictions that have adopted modified (as opposed

---

232 While normally it is the driver's intoxication that is relevant in a products liability action, sometimes a passenger's intoxication is relevant to his own products liability claim. See, e.g., Truchan v. Nissan Motor Corp., 720 A.2d 981 (N.J. Super. Ct. App. Div. 1998) (rear-seat passenger allegedly lay down in seatbelt and was too drunk to heed warnings about seatbelt system); Rodriguez v. Suzuki Motor Corp., 936 S.W.2d 104, 109 (Mo. 1996) (passenger's alcohol consumption relevant to her comparative fault in deciding to enter and remain in vehicle operated by intoxicated driver); Harvey v. General Motors Corp., 873 F.2d 1343 (10th Cir. 1989) (Wyo. law) (passenger's drinking relevant to lack of care for his own safety and to whether he had negligently encouraged driver's misconduct).

233 See Am. Law Prod. Liab. 3d § 40:20. See Bublick, The Tort-Proof Plaintiff: The Drunk in the Automobile, Crashworthiness Claims, and the *Restatement (Third) of Torts*, 74 Brook. L. Rev. 707 (2009).

234 Hence, operating an automotive vehicle in violation of a state's prohibitions against driving under the influence may be (contributory) negligence per se. See, e.g., Hinkamp v. American Motors Corp., 735 F. Supp. 176, 177–78 (E.D.N.C. 1989), aff'd, 900 F.2d 252 (4th Cir. 1990).

235 The facts of ultimate relevance in civil litigation ordinarily are intoxication and impairment, not any particular level of blood alcohol. See, e.g., In re: General Motors LLC Ignition Switch Litig., 2016 WL 4077117, at *3 (S.D.N.Y. 2016) (Va. law) ("Evidence of intoxication is admissible if the intoxicants 'impair [the driver's] capacity to perceive the dangers with the clarity, make the decisions with the prudence, and operate the vehicle with the skill and caution required by law.' "); Miles v. General Motors Corp., 262 F.3d 720, 723 (8th Cir. 2001) (Ark. law); Hunter v. General Motors Corp., 729 So.2d 1264 (Miss. 1999) (proper to admit evidence of driver's intoxication even if below statutory level of legal intoxication); Surowiec v. General Motors Corp., 672 A.2d 333, 336 (Pa. Super. Ct. 1996) ("where recklessness or carelessness is at issue, proof of intoxication is relevant, but the mere fact of consuming alcohol is inadmissible as unfairly prejudicial unless it reasonably establishes intoxication").

236 See, e.g., Shores v. Dupps Co., Inc., 2020 WL 6302362, at *7 (C.D. Ill. 2020); Hinkamp v. American Motors Corp., 735 F. Supp. 176 (E.D.N.C. 1989), aff'd, 900 F.2d 252 (4th Cir. 1990); Jarrell v. Ford Motor Co., 327 F.2d 233 (4th Cir. 1964) (W. Va. law). On contributory negligence generally, see § 13.2, above.

237 See, e.g., Dalrymple v. United States Postal Serv., 2021 WL 926721, at *10 (E.D. La. 2021) ("Louisiana courts look to a driver's potential intoxication when assessing comparative fault."); Nemmers v. Ford Motor Co., 686 F.3d 486, 490 (8th Cir. 2012) (Iowa law) (Iowa Comparative Fault Act; evidence of driver

to "pure") comparative fault, a driver's intoxication will bar recovery altogether if it exceeds the responsibility of the manufacturer.[238] Moreover, under any form of comparative fault, a driver's intoxication operates as a total bar to recovery if it is determined to have been the sole cause of an accident.[239]

A driver's intoxication also may possibly help establish the defense of assumption of risk.[240] If an intoxicated driver is aware of and understands the risks of a particular defect in a vehicle, his or her decision to operate the vehicle, or to use it in a particular manner, may bar (or reduce)[241] recovery because of the driver's voluntary decision to encounter the risk.[242] But if a driver does not know about nor voluntarily encounters a particular danger, the assumption of risk defense will fail.[243]

Evidence of a driver's intoxication also has been held admissible for the purpose of establishing a driver's misuse of an automotive vehicle.[244] However, driving under the influence is such a common problem that it fairly must be viewed as a foreseeable risk against which a manufacturer is duty-bound to guard.[245] Put otherwise, a driver's intoxication cannot *ipso facto* bar a products liability action under the common-law misuse doctrine. Yet comparative fault, which commonly requires throwing all forms of misconduct into the fault pot, naturally includes driving under the influence, whether called misuse, contributory negligence, or something else.

In addition to its relevance to the conduct defenses, evidence of a driver's intoxication may be admissible on "proximate causation," including both cause in fact and proximate or legal cause. Thus, intoxication may bear on whether a driver's dangerous driving maneuvers (brought about by the intoxication), rather than some problem in the vehicle (such as a defective axle), proximately caused an accident.[246] Such

---

intoxication was properly submitted to allow jury to determine if it was a proximate cause of plaintiff's injuries); Rodriguez v. Suzuki Motor Corp., 936 S.W.2d 104, 107 (Mo. 1996) ("Since the apportionment of fault and damages is factual by nature, a jury should be as fully informed as possible in order to determine relative fault of the parties, [and a] comparative fault system can better accommodate alcohol evidence than a contributory negligence system."). See also Daly v. General Motors Corp., 575 P.2d 1162, 1173–74 (Cal. 1978) (by implication). On comparative fault generally, see § 13.3, above.

[238] See § 13.3, above.

[239] See, e.g., Wallace v. Ford Motor Co., 723 A.2d 1226 (N.J. Super. Ct. App. Div. 1999).

[240] On assumption of risk generally, see § 13.4, above.

[241] A plaintiff's recovery will be reduced rather than barred, at least if the plaintiff's fault is less than the manufacturer's, in jurisdictions which have merged assumption of risk into their general systems of comparative fault. See id.

[242] See, e.g., Davis v. Brooks Transp. Co., 186 F. Supp. 366, 371 (D. Del. 1960).

[243] See, e.g., Mercurio v. Nissan Motor Corp., 81 F. Supp. 2d 859, 861–62 (N.D. Ohio 2000) (no evidence that intoxicated driver knew that vehicle's subfloor posed unreasonable risk of buckling, nor that he voluntarily exposed himself to vehicle's uncrashworthy condition); LeBouef v. Goodyear Tire & Rubber Co., 623 F.2d 985 (5th Cir. 1980) (La. law) (insufficient evidence that intoxicated driver killed in accident caused by tread separation knew that tire could not be used safely at speeds in excess of 100 mph).

[244] See, e.g., Tunnell v. Ford Motor Co., 330 F. Supp. 2d 748 (W.D. Va. 2004); Kirkland v. General Motors Corp., 521 P.2d 1353, 1367 (Okla. 1974) (driving under intoxication is "an abnormal use or misuse of the product and is a complete defense to strict liability theory"). On misuse generally, see § 13.5, above.

[245] See, e.g., Mercurio v. Nissan Motor Corp., 81 F. Supp. 2d 859 (N.D. Ohio 2000).

[246] See, e.g., Wallace v. Ford Motor Co., 723 A.2d 1226 (N.J. Super. Ct. App. Div. 1999) (intoxication evidence relevant to "proximate cause" or comparative fault, to establish that cause of vehicle's rollover was bad driving rather than defect in axle); Swajian v. General Motors Corp., 916 F.2d 31, 34 (1st Cir. 1990) (R.I. law) (intoxication evidence relevant to causation):

> Armed with this evidence, the jury could have concluded that driver error contributed significantly to, if not caused, decedent's accident. As it was, the jury was presented with the following factual scenario: the two month old vehicle was travelling down a straight, flat road in good weather when

evidence is especially relevant if the plaintiff proceeds under the "malfunction theory" of liability,[247] since that theory requires a plaintiff to negate reasonable secondary causes of the accident.[248] In addition, if a driver's severe intoxication results in an accident, the drunk driving, rather than some defect in the vehicle, may be found to be the sole proximate cause of the resulting injuries.[249]

Finally, it is important to remember that some courts hold that evidence of a driver's fault is irrelevant to an enhanced injury claim based on some uncrashworthy aspect of an automotive vehicle. Although many courts disagree,[250] as previously discussed, some courts view the manufacturer's duty broadly to require that vehicles be designed and manufactured in a manner that reasonably protects all its occupants from second collision injuries regardless of the cause of the initial accident, whether from the driver's intoxication or something else.[251]

Statutes

Many states have driving-under-the-influence statutes that specifically address the role of a driver's intoxication in civil litigation. Several statutes provide broadly that the results of breath tests are admissible evidence in any civil action,[252] and others provide that such evidence is admissible in civil (or criminal) actions arising out of

---

> it swayed and went out of control for no apparent reason. The only explanation proffered was that there was a defect in one of the axles. Without the evidence of intoxication the jury was left with no reason for the loss of control other than [plaintiff's] allegations.

See also Truchan v. Nissan Motor Corp., 720 A.2d 981, 989 (N.J. Super. Ct. App. Div. 1998) (rear-seat passenger claimed to be sitting upright when injured by seatbelt in collision: "evidence of plaintiff's intoxication may be admitted both to prove that she was in a 'slumped' position at the time of impact and to show that she would not have heeded warnings pertaining to the dangers posed by the seatbelt system had they been given").

[247] See § 7.4, above. See also § 2.5 (res ipsa loquitur), above.

[248] See, e.g., Surowiec v. General Motors Corp., 672 A.2d 333, 336–37 (Pa. Super. Ct. 1996).

[249] See, e.g., Timmons v. Ford Motor Co., 982 F. Supp. 1475, 1479 (S.D. Ga. 1997) ("when the circumstances of the crash itself rise to such an extreme level of violence that manufacturers cannot reasonably and cost-effectively protect consumers," the consequences of such a high-speed collision are unforeseeable and driver's drunk driving is sole proximate cause of deaths in collision), aff'd, 161 F.3d 22 (11th Cir. 1998); Goodman v. General Motors Corp., 652 N.Y.S.2d 626 (App. Div. 1997) (proximate causes of accident were driver's intoxication and plaintiff's standing in dark roadway—not design of plaintiff's delivery van whose rear lights were blocked by van's open doors).

[250] Some courts allow intoxication evidence in crashworthiness cases without appearing to recognize the issue. See, e.g., Ake v. General Motors Corp., 942 F. Supp. 869 (W.D.N.Y. 1996) (intoxication evidence admitted, without discussion of appropriateness in this context, in claim of uncrashworthy fuel system design).

[251] See, e.g., Donze v. General Motors, LLC, 800 S.E.2d 479, 485 (S.C. 2017) ("the doctrine of crashworthiness itself divides and allocates fault to a manufacturer for damages it alone caused, so it would be incongruous to allow comparative negligence to apply to further reduce the manufacturer's liability or shift that responsibility to another party"; driver smoked synthetic marijuana); Reed v. Chrysler Corp., 494 N.W.2d 224, 230 (Iowa 1992) ("The theory, which presupposes the occurrence of accidents precipitated for myriad reasons, focuses alone on the enhancement of resulting injuries [so that] any participation by the plaintiff in bringing the accident about is quite beside the point."), overruled, Jahn v. Hyundai Motor Co., 773 N.W.2d 550 (Iowa 2009); Andrews v. Harley Davidson, Inc., 796 P.2d 1092, 1095 (Nev. 1990) ("[a] major policy [reason] behind holding manufacturers strictly liable for failing to produce crashworthy vehicles is to encourage them to do all they reasonably can do to design a vehicle which will protect a driver in an accident," and manufacturers can foresee that intoxicated drivers will drive negligently and cause accidents); Mercurio v. Nissan Motor Corp., 81 F. Supp. 2d 859, 861 (N.D. Ohio 2000):

> The fact that a collision may have been caused by the driver's intoxication, as opposed to another form of negligence, does not reduce the manufacturer's duty to provide a reasonably safe vehicle. The Court is reminded of the old adage that "[a] drunken man is as much entitled to a safe street as a sober one, and much more in need of it." Robinson v. Pioche, Bayerque & Co., 5 Cal. 460, 461 (1855).

[252] See, e.g., Ariz. Rev. Stat. Ann. § 28–1323; Okla. Stat. Ann. tit. 47, § 752(H); Or. Rev. Stat. Ann. § 813.320.

driving under the influence.[253] An Alaska statute provides that a driver's *refusal* to submit to the prescribed DUI chemical test is admissible evidence in an action arising out of an accident allegedly resulting from his or her driving while intoxicated.[254] Statutes in at least Michigan and Washington provide an absolute defense to claims for injury or death in accidents in which the plaintiff's intoxication was at least,[255] or more than,[256] 50% responsible for the accident.

Failure to Use Seatbelts and Other Safety Devices

One of the easiest and most effective ways to increase one's life expectancy, and to improve the general level of automotive safety,[257] is to buckle up one's seatbelt.[258] Put another way, occupants of automotive vehicles who fail to use their seatbelts double their risk of being seriously injured or killed in motor vehicle accidents.[259] Although the enormous value of seatbelts and shoulder harnesses was not fully appreciated at the time, automotive manufacturers began equipping some vehicles with seatbelts in the 1950s, state legislatures began requiring manufacturers to install seatbelts in automobiles in the early 1960s,[260] and, by 1966, the automotive industry began equipping the entire fleet of automobiles with seatbelts.[261]

But equipping cars with seatbelts did not mean that people would use them. As late as the mid-1980s, a pathetically low 13% of Americans voluntarily wore their seatbelts.[262] To hasten seatbelt usage, NHTSA in 1984 issued a rule requiring that all new cars be equipped with automatic seatbelts or airbags by 1990, unless by 1989 states comprising two-thirds of the nation's population enacted qualifying mandatory seatbelt use laws.[263] One qualifying criterion was the jurisdiction's adoption of the seatbelt defense—reducing damages in civil actions for seatbelt nonuse.[264] From 1984 through 1987, thirty-one states enacted mandatory seatbelt use laws, and seatbelt usage correspondingly increased from 14% to 42%.[265] By 1998, seatbelt usage had increased to 62% in states with secondary enforcement laws and 79% in states with primary

[253] See, e.g., N.M. Stat. Ann. § 66–8–110(A). Similar statutes include: Fla. Stat. Ann. § 316.1934(2); Ga. Code Ann. § 40–6–392(a); 625 Ill. Comp. Stat. Ann. 5/11–501.2(a); Minn. Stat. Ann. § 169A.41 subd. 2(2).

[254] Alaska Stat. § 28.35.032(e).

[255] Mich. Comp. Laws. Ann. § 600.2955a.

[256] Wash. Rev. Code Ann. § 5.40.060.

[257] Using automotive seatbelts is one of the most effective ways to improve one's life expectancy. In 2017, seatbelts saved the lives of nearly 15,000 people and reduced the risk of fatal injury during a crash by 45%. NHTSA, Seat Belts, www.nhtsa.gov/risky-driving/seat-belts (last visited Apr. 18, 2022).

[258] See, e.g., McAlonan v. Tracy, 2011 WL 6125, at *9 (N.J. Super. Ct. App. Div. 2011) ("Courts recognize that the use of seatbelts reduces death and injury in automobile accidents."); Waterson v. General Motors Corp., 544 A.2d 357, 373 (N.J. 1988) (like other courts, taking judicial notice of "the effectiveness of seat belts in reducing death and injury from automobile accidents"); Spier v. Barker, 323 N.E.2d 164, 168 (N.Y. 1974) ("[t]he seat belt, properly installed [a]nd properly worn, still offers the single best protection [to auto occupants] exposed to an impact").

[259] See note 257, above.

[260] New York was the first state to require seatbelts in 1962. See Comment, 36 Hous. L. Rev. 1371, 1377 n.34 (1999).

[261] See id. at 1377.

[262] See Note, 64 N.C. L. Rev. 1127, 1132 (1986).

[263] See Federal Motor Vehicle Safety Standard; Occupant Crash Protection, 49 Fed. Reg. 28,962–63 (1984), codified at 49 C.F.R. § 571.208.

[264] 49 C.F.R. § 571.208 (1984), at S4.1.5.2(c)(2)(d)(c)(2).

[265] Comment, 36 Hous. L. Rev. 1371, 1378 n.43 (1999).

enforcement laws.[266] By 2021, all states except New Hampshire[267] had adopted mandatory seatbelt use statutes applicable to adults,[268] and the national seatbelt usage rate had risen to 90%.[269]

Seatbelt Defense; Common-Law Development

From the time seatbelts first began to be widely available in the 1960s, defendants in car accident litigation have sought to introduce evidence that the plaintiff failed to use an available seatbelt.[270] In defending a vehicular accident case, the "seatbelt defense" is used to try to establish that the plaintiff, rather than the defendant, is responsible for those injuries which a seatbelt would have prevented.[271]

Depending on the underlying claim and the nature of the particular collision and injuries,[272] a defendant may seek to introduce evidence of seatbelt nonuse on any number of legal issues, including a plaintiff's contributory or comparative fault,[273] assumption of risk,[274] or failure to mitigate damages;[275] the proximate cause of an accident[276] or of the injuries;[277] or, in a products liability case, the crashworthy

---

[266] See NCSA Fact Sheet: Traffic Safety Facts 1998—Occupant Protection, at 1.

[267] New Hampshire's motto is "Live Free or Die."

[268] All 50 states, including New Hampshire, have mandatory child restraint use laws. Seatbelt use in New Hampshire was estimated at 71% in 2020. CDC, Buckle Up: Restraint Use in New Hampshire (July 2020).

[269] NHTSA, Seat Belts, www.nhtsa.gov/risky-driving/seat-belts (last visited Apr. 2022).

[270] The first use of the seatbelt defense may have been in a 1964 Wisconsin case where a jury reduced the plaintiff's damages by 10% for failing to use an available seatbelt. See Westenberg, Buckle Up or Pay: The Emerging Safety Belt Defense, 20 Suffolk U. L. Rev. 867, 869 n.4 (1986).

[271] See, e.g., Mobley, Revisiting Alabama's Seat Belt Defense: Is the Failure to Buckle Up a Defense in AEMLD Claims?, 53 Ala. L. Rev. 963 (2002); Bomer, The Seatbelt Defense: A Doctrine Based in Common Sense, 38 Tulsa L. Rev. 405 (2002); Nielsen, Tort Litigation—The New Case for the "Seat Belt Defense"—Norwest Bank, New Mexico N.A. v. Chrysler Corporation, 30 N.M. L. Rev. 403 (2000); LeBel, Reducing the Recovery of Avoidable "Seat-Belt Damages": A Cure for the Defects of Waterson v. General Motors Corporation, 22 Seton Hall L. Rev. 4 (1991); Schwartz, The SeatBelt Defense and Mandatory SeatBelt Usage: Law, Ethics, and Economics, 24 Idaho L. Rev. 275 (1988); Annot., Nonuse of Seatbelt as Reducing Amount of Damages Recoverable, 62 A.L.R.5th 537 (1998); Frumer, Friedman, and Sklaren, Products Liability § 22.07 (excellent overview).

[272] And depending, of course, on the jurisdiction, since many jurisdictions preclude use of the defense entirely or for certain purposes. See Annot., 62 A.L.R.5th 537 (1998).

[273] See, e.g., Nabors Well Servs., Ltd. v. Romero, 456 S.W.3d 553 (Tex. 2015) (use or nonuse of seat belts is admissible for apportioning responsibility); Waterson v. General Motors Corp., 544 A.2d 357 (N.J. 1988); Dahl v. Bayerische Motoren Werke (BMW), 748 P.2d 77 (Or. 1987).

[274] See, e.g., Walsh v. Emergency One, Inc., 1992 WL 180134 (N.D. Ill. 1992), aff'd, 26 F.3d 1417 (7th Cir. 1994). See also MacDonald v. General Motors Corp., 784 F. Supp. 486 (M.D. Tenn. 1992). See generally Ackerman, The Seat Belt Defense Reconsidered: A Return to Accountability in Tort Law?, 16 N.M. L. Rev. 221, 227 (1986) (application of assumption of risk defense to seatbelt nonuse is "quite plausible" because of "the well-known dangers of the highway"). Yet, to establish assumption of risk, many courts require a defendant to establish that the plaintiff was aware of the particular risk that caused injury, which renders it difficult to apply this defense to the seatbelt nonuse situation. Compare Swajian v. General Motors Corp., 559 A.2d 1041, 1046–47 (R.I. 1989) ("the failure to buckle up does not constitute a self-willed and knowing exposure to the specific risk of sustaining enhanced injuries originally set in motion by another person's negligence or undetectable product defect").

[275] See, e.g., Hutchins v. Schwartz, 724 P.2d 1194 (Alaska 1986); Spier v. Barker, 323 N.E.2d 164 (N.Y. 1974).

[276] See, e.g., Jimenez v. DaimlerChrysler Corp., 269 F.3d 439, 458 (4th Cir. 2001) (S.C. law); Floyd v. General Motors Corp., 960 P.2d 763 (Kan. Ct. App. 1998) (plaintiff claimed that broken steering mechanism caused accident, but defendant contended that mechanism was broken in driver-caused accident by force of unbelted driver thrown against steering wheel; nonuse evidence not allowable to show comparative fault or mitigation of damages, but could be used for causation).

[277] See, e.g., Hodges v. Mack Trucks Inc., 474 F.3d 188, 202 (5th Cir. 2006) (Tex. law) (admissible on causation); General Motors Corp. v. Wolhar, 686 A.2d 170 (Del. 1996). *But see* Gaudio v. Ford Motor Co., 976

nature[278] or the plaintiff's misuse[279] of the vehicle. The law concerning the seatbelt defense is fragmented and ever-shifting,[280] and the best that can be done here is to highlight some of its central features.

In early attempts to invoke the seatbelt defense, most courts were hostile to the concept in any form. Rejecting the defense, many courts reasoned that tort law does not impose a pre-accident duty on plaintiffs to take protective measures to minimize damages to themselves that might result if other people are negligent; that a plaintiff's failure to wear a seatbelt does not meet the requirements of any of the traditional tort law defenses or other tort law doctrine; that, at the time, most people did not in fact use seatbelts, so that the failure to do so did not deviate from the norm of a person of ordinary prudence; that the efficacy of seatbelts was questionable; that allowing the defense would raise substantial administrative problems, including the difficulty of connecting seatbelt nonuse with actual damages; and that the matter was better left for legislative determination.[281]

Notwithstanding these arguments, a small number of courts did adopt some version of the seatbelt defense during the 1960s and early 1970s.[282] In the products liability context, an important decision was *Daly v. General Motors Corp.*,[283] decided by the California Supreme Court in 1978. In *Daly*, an attorney was driving his Opel on a Los Angeles freeway in the early hours of the morning when his car struck a metal divider fence, causing the latch button on the exterior door handle of the driver's door to depress. The collision with the fence spun the car out of control, throwing the driver's door open and hurling him from the car, resulting in fatal injuries to his head. In a products liability action brought by his representative against the manufacturer of the vehicle,[284] the defendant introduced evidence that the plaintiff was intoxicated, that he had failed to lock the door or use his seatbelt-shoulder harness, and that use of the seatbelt-shoulder harness would have saved his life.[285] Appealing a judgment on a verdict for General Motors, the plaintiff challenged the admissibility of the seatbelt nonuse evidence. Extending the comparative fault doctrine to claims based on strict liability in tort, the court reversed, ruling that the jury may have believed that the

---

A.2d 524, 542 (Pa. Super. Ct. 2009) (inadmissible); Shipler v. General Motors Corp., 710 N.W.2d 807, 833 (Neb. 2006) (inadmissible).

278 See, e.g., Gable v. Village of Gates Mills, 816 N.E.2d 1049 (Ohio 2004); Daly v. General Motors Corp., 575 P.2d 1162, 1174–75 (Cal. 1978).

279 See, e.g., Morgen v. Ford Motor Co., 797 N.E.2d 1146, 1148–50 (Ind. 2003); Melia v. Ford Motor Co., 534 F.2d 795, 799 (8th Cir. 1976) (Neb. law). *But see* MacCuish v. Volkswagenwerk A.G., 494 N.E.2d 390, 395 (Mass. App. Ct. 1986); Daly v. General Motors Corp., 575 P.2d 1162, 1174 (Cal. 1978).

280 See, e.g., LaHue v. General Motors Corp., 716 F. Supp. 407, 410 (W.D. Mo. 1989) (noting that the law on the seatbelt defense is "split, fragmented and changing [and] varies in time, place, rationale, effect and implementation").

281 Compare Swajian v. General Motors Corp., 559 A.2d 1041 (R.I. 1989) (refusing to allow the defense), with Waterson v. General Motors Corp., 544 A.2d 357, 367–68 (N.J. 1988) (allowing the defense). See also Cochran, New Seat Belt Defense Issues: The Impact of Air Bags and Mandatory Seat Belt Use Statutes on the Seat Belt Defense, and the Basis of Damage Reduction under the Seat Belt Defense, 73 Minn. L. Rev. 1369 (1989).

282 See, e.g., Sams v. Sams, 148 S.E.2d 154 (S.C. 1966); Bentzler v. Braun, 149 N.W.2d 626 (Wis. 1967); Mount v. McClellan, 234 N.E.2d 329 (Ill. App. Ct. 1968); Tiemeyer v. McIntosh, 176 N.W.2d 819 (Iowa 1970); Spier v. Barker, 323 N.E.2d 164 (N.Y. 1974); Horn v. General Motors Corp., 551 P.2d 398 (Cal. 1976). The spread of the seatbelt defense ground to a halt in the mid-1970s, and no appellate court decision adopted the defense from 1975 to 1984. See Westenberg, Buckle Up or Pay: The Emerging Safety-Belt Defense, 20 Suffolk U. L. Rev. 867, 875 (1986).

283 575 P.2d 1162 (Cal. 1978).

284 The plaintiff claimed that the vehicle's door latch was defectively designed. Id. at 1164.

285 Id. at 1164–65.

plaintiff's drunken failure to use his seatbelt constituted contributory negligence that barred recovery altogether.[286]

Another issue in *Daly* was the propriety of the trial court's instruction that "[i]n determining whether or not the vehicle was defective you should consider all of the equipment on the vehicle including any features intended for the safety of the driver."[287] The plaintiff challenged this instruction, arguing that the jury could only consider the defectiveness of the challenged design feature that allegedly had malfunctioned—the latch on the driver's door.[288] Concluding that the defectiveness of a vehicle's design "is to be determined with respect to the product as a whole,"[289] the *Daly* court reasoned that a "jury could properly determine whether the Opel's overall design, including safety features provided in the vehicle, made it 'crashworthy,' thus rendering the vehicle nondefective. . . . [A] product's components are not developed in isolation, but as part of an integrated and interrelated whole."[290]

While plaintiffs in defective design cases ordinarily must assert some deficiency in a particular feature of a product's design,[291] manufacturers logically should be permitted to defend the safety of their products viewed as a whole; it is difficult to deny that "safety belts are an essential part of the total safety package provided by the manufacturer."[292] Thus, the availability of seatbelt-shoulder harnesses of a particular design is surely relevant to the overall crashworthiness of a particular vehicle, as other courts have held.[293] Yet the appropriateness of evidence of seatbelt *nonuse* (as opposed to availability) raises difficult issues apart from the defectiveness *vel non* of a vehicle's design, and the propriety of such evidence is not so clear.

During the 1980s, two important developments served to reinvigorate the seatbelt defense and propel it forward in the courts.[294] The first development was the increasingly rapid spread of the doctrine of comparative fault.[295] One of the biggest conceptual hurdles to the adoption of a seatbelt defense had been tort law's all-or-nothing approach to liability and damages, resulting in the courts' reluctance to shift an entire loss from a negligent tortfeasor to a plaintiff who had merely failed before an accident to reduce potential harm to himself. Because the emerging comparative fault doctrine rested upon the pillar of damages apportionment, it much more easily accommodated the damages-reduction aspect of the seatbelt defense.

The second development affecting the adoption of the seatbelt defense was NHTSA's prodding of the states to enact mandatory seatbelt use laws. By the late 1980s, most states had enacted mandatory seatbelt use laws, some containing a seatbelt nonuse defense providing for the reduction of damages in civil actions. As discussed below,

---

[286] Id. at 1174.

[287] Id.

[288] See id.

[289] Id.

[290] Id. at 1175.

[291] See Owen, Toward a Proper Test for Design Defectiveness: "Micro-Balancing" Costs and Benefits, 75 Tex. L. Rev. 1661 (1997).

[292] Westenberg, Buckle Up or Pay: The Emerging Safety-Belt Defense, 20 Suffolk U. L. Rev. 867, 878 (1986).

[293] See, e.g., General Motors Corp. v. Wolhar, 686 A.2d 170 (Del. 1996); Lowe v. Estate Motors Ltd., 410 N.W.2d 706, 707–08 (Mich. 1987).

[294] See Westenberg, above, at 20 Suffolk U. L. Rev. 867, 875–85.

[295] See § 13.3, above.

however, many of the statutes explicitly *prohibited* use of seatbelt nonuse evidence in civil actions, and several limited the amount of damages reduction to five percent. Nevertheless, in states where legislation did not prohibit evidence of seatbelt nonuse, the seatbelt laws facilitated the adoption of the seatbelt defense by undercutting some of the traditional arguments against adopting it. That is, mandatory use laws imposed a duty on occupants of self-protection before an accident and so converted seatbelt use into the practice of a reasonable person.

Thus spurred by the spread of comparative fault and the adoption of mandatory seatbelt legislation around the nation, a number of courts in the late 1980s and 1990s adopted some form of seatbelt defense,[296] including some in products liability cases against vehicle manufacturers.[297] Today, much of the litigation on seatbelt nonuse has shifted to questions of statutory interpretation, which requires that the applicable statutes be examined.

Seatbelt Use Statutes

As mentioned earlier, all states except New Hampshire, which does not require adult use, eventually enacted some form of legislation requiring the use of seatbelts.[298] The statutes may usefully be classified into four categories: those that prohibit using seatbelt nonuse evidence in civil litigation to reduce ("mitigate") a plaintiff's damages; those that permit such evidence to reduce a plaintiff's damages; those that permit such evidence to reduce a plaintiff's damages, but cap the reduction; and those that leave the matter to the courts.[299]

Seatbelt use statutes in most states provide that the "[f]ailure to wear a seat safety belt shall not be considered as contributory negligence nor shall such failure be admissible evidence in any civil action"[300] or words to similar effect.[301] But the statutes differ in various significant respects, and it is difficult to generalize on whether or how such statutes may be specifically applicable to automotive products liability crashworthiness litigation.[302]

---

[296] See, e.g., Insurance Co. of N. Am. v. Pasakarnis, 451 So.2d 447 (Fla. 1984); Hutchins v. Schwartz, 724 P.2d 1194 (Alaska 1986); Wemyss v. Coleman, 729 S.W.2d 174 (Ky. 1987); Law v. Superior Ct., 755 P.2d 1135 (Ariz. 1988).

[297] See, e.g., Jordan v. General Motors Corp., 624 F. Supp. 72 (E.D. La. 1985); Dahl v. Bayerische Motoren Werke (BMW), 748 P.2d 77 (Or. 1987); Waterson v. General Motors Corp., 544 A.2d 357 (N.J. 1988); McElyea v. Navistar Int'l Transp. Corp., 788 F. Supp. 1366 (E.D. Pa. 1991); Barron v. Ford Motor Co. of Can., Ltd., 965 F.2d 195 (7th Cir. 1992) (N.C. law); Gardner v. Chrysler Corp., 89 F.3d 729 (10th Cir. 1996) (Kan. law); General Motors Corp. v. Wolhar, 686 A.2d 170 (Del. 1996).

[298] The statutes are collected and updated in Owen & Davis on Products Liability Appendix J.

[299] This is the classification used in Products Liability Rest. § 16 Reporters' Note to cmt. *f*. This Restatement does not take a position on the seatbelt defense issue, but notes that the Rest. (3d) of Torts: Apportionment, in § 3 (illus. 3) approves of the defense as part of its broad approach to apportionment in general.

[300] Conn. Gen. Stat. Ann. § 14–100a(c)(3).

[301] Similar statutes are in Ala., Del., D.C., Ga., Idaho, Ill., Kan., Ky., La., Me., Md., Mass., Minn., Miss., Mont., Nev., N.M., N.C., Okla., Pa., R.I., S.C., Vt., Va., Wash., W. Va., and Wyo. Texas repealed a statute to this effect. Seatbelt statutes are collected and updated in Owen & Davis on Products Liability Appendix J.

[302] Contrast Connecticut's terse provision, above, with the one in Georgia: "The failure of an occupant of a motor vehicle to wear a seat safety belt in any seat of a motor vehicle which has a seat safety belt or belts shall not be considered evidence of negligence or causation, shall not otherwise be considered by the finder of fact on any question of liability of any person, corporation, or insurer, shall not be any basis for cancellation of coverage or increase in insurance rates, and shall not be evidence used to diminish any recovery for damages arising out of the ownership, maintenance, occupancy, or operation of a motor vehicle." Ga. Code Ann. § 40–8–76.1(d).

Some statutes *allow* evidence of a person's failure to wear a seatbelt in mitigation of damages in any civil action,[303] and a few states limit the admissibility of such evidence to products liability actions.[304] Several states allow the reduction of a plaintiff's damages at a small percentage of the plaintiff's total damages.[305] Statutes in at least a couple of states appear to leave the matter to the courts.[306]

One recurring issue of statutory interpretation is whether statutes that prohibit evidence of seatbelt nonuse (or cap damages reduction) apply to crashworthiness claims against automotive manufacturers.[307] For example, the Michigan Supreme Court has ruled that the legislature's capping of mitigated damages does *not* apply to products liability claims because the statute by its terms applies only to cases "arising out of the ownership, maintenance, or operation of a motor vehicle."[308] But other courts disagree, holding that the plain language of similar statutes, prohibiting evidence of seatbelt nonuse as proof of contributory negligence or "as evidence in a trial of any civil action,"[309] requires their application to crashworthiness actions like any others.[310] Statutes and judicial interpretations split on whether such provisions also bar manufacturers from using nonuse evidence to argue other defensive issues such as proximate cause and design defectiveness in addition to comparative fault, with some courts precluding nonuse evidence on all issues in crashworthiness as other litigation,[311] while other courts allow nonuse evidence on these other issues.[312]

---

[303] Statutes of this type include Cal. Veh. Code § 27315(i); Colo. Rev. Stat. Ann. § 42–4–237(7); N.Y. Veh. & Traf. Law § 1229–c(8); and Ohio Rev. Code Ann. § 4513.263(F)(1).

[304] Statutes of this type include Ark. Code Ann. § 27–37–703, held unconstitutional by Mendoza v. WIS Int'l, Inc., 490 S.W.3d 298 (Ark. 2016); Ind. Code Ann. § 9–19–10–7(c); and Tenn. Code Ann. § 55–9–604. For a routine application of the Tenn. statute, see England v. Suzuki Motor Corp., 521 F. Supp. 2d 707, 710 (E.D. Tenn. 2007) (evidence of violation of statute requiring safety belt use in vehicles driven forward on the highway is inadmissible in civil actions, except products liability cases where compliance would have reduced injuries; but no violation when allegedly defective vehicle rolled backwards down driveway and up embankment, causing vehicle to roll over).

[305] Statutes of this type include Mo. Ann. Stat. § 307.178(4)(2) (1%); Mich. Comp. Laws Ann. § 257.710e(8) (5%) (*but see Klinke*, discussed in note 308, below); Neb. Rev. Stat. § 60–6,273 (5%); Wis. Stat. Ann. § 347.48(2m)(g) (15%); and Iowa Code Ann. § 321.445(4)(b)(2) (25%).

[306] Statutes of this type include N.J. Stat. Ann. § 39:3–76.2h and Haw. Rev. Stat. § 291–11.6(d). See also Fla. Stat. Ann. § 316.614(10) (nonuse can be evidence of comparative negligence).

[307] At least Oregon's statute explicitly excludes products liability cases from operation of its 5% reduction provision. See Or. Rev. Stat. Ann. § 31.760 (5%).

[308] See Klinke v. Mitsubishi Motors Corp., 581 N.W.2d 272 (Mich. 1998) (jury found that decedent was 90% at fault for wearing her lap belt but not her shoulder harness; *held*, damages reduced by 90%). Accord LaHue v. General Motors Corp., 716 F. Supp. 407, 410, 412 (W.D. Mo. 1989).

[309] MacDonald v. General Motors Corp., 784 F. Supp. 486, 490 (M.D. Tenn. 1992) (so, nonuse of seatbelts by rear passengers could not be used to show contributory negligence, nor that passengers failed to mitigate damages, nor that they had assumed the risk of additional harm, but defendant could argue that it constituted the proximate cause of their injuries).

[310] See, e.g., Milbrand v. DaimlerChrysler Corp., 105 F. Supp. 2d 601, 608 (E.D. Tex. 2000); Newman v. Ford Motor Co., 975 S.W.2d 147 (Mo. 1998). One court taking this approach reasoned that carving out a crashworthiness exception to the seatbelt nonuse law would frustrate the statutory policy of encouraging manufacturers "to design cars in a crashworthy manner in spite of the fact that drivers and passengers often fail to wear their seatbelts." Estate of Hunter v. General Motors Corp., 729 So.2d 1264, 1270 (Miss. 1999).

[311] See, e.g., Gaudio v. Ford Motor Co., 976 A.2d 524, 536 (Pa. Super. Ct. 2009) (construing provision as "a blanket exclusion of evidence of seat belt usage in civil actions for any purpose, including to prove not only contributory negligence but also defect, causation and/or damages"); Ulm v. Ford Motor Co., 750 A.2d 981 (Vt. 2000).

[312] See, e.g., MacDonald v. General Motors Corp., 784 F. Supp. 486, 490 (M.D. Tenn. 1992) (while nonuse evidence inadmissible to show contributory negligence, failure to mitigate damages, and assumption of risk, defendant could argue that it was proximate cause of injuries).

Another interpretation issue on which courts have split is whether a statutory prohibition of seatbelt use evidence applies in an action against the manufacturer of an allegedly defective seatbelt that malfunctions. At least a couple of cases have ruled that Minnesota's seatbelt "gag rule" prohibits plaintiffs from making crashworthiness claims based on defective seatbelts because the plaintiff's seatbelt use was necessary to the claim.[313] But the Minnesota seatbelt law has now been amended to allow such claims,[314] and other courts have interpreted their statutes more sensibly to allow this type of action.[315] Other seatbelt statutory interpretation issues abound,[316] providing grist galore for future litigation.

Other Safety Devices

While the discussion to this point has concerned an occupant's failure to wear a seatbelt, a person's failure to use other kinds of safety devices may raise similar issues in products liability litigation. Thus, a parent's failure to buckle up a child in a child-restraint seat logically may bar or reduce the parent's claim for medical expenses and other derivative damages arising out of injury to the child to the same extent as if the parent had failed to use his or her own seatbelt. Yet, the child's own claim for injuries should not, of course, be affected by the parent's failure to perform his or her parental duties.[317] But many of the state seatbelt use laws that prohibit the use of seatbelt nonuse evidence are broad enough to include a parent's failure to use child restraints,[318] and many others specifically provide that evidence of the nonuse of child restraints is not admissible in civil actions.[319]

Motorcycle helmets are another safety device mandated in many, but not all, jurisdictions,[320] and the failure of a motorcycle rider to wear a helmet logically raises issues similar to those applicable to the seatbelt nonuse situation.[321]

§ 17.6 AUTONOMOUS VEHICLES

Automotive companies and others long have been conceiving, researching, and developing various types of vehicles that to a lesser or greater extent steer, accelerate,

---

[313] See, e.g., Carlson v. Hyundai Motor Co., 164 F.3d 1160 (8th Cir. 1999) (Minn. law); Olson v. Ford Motor Co., 558 N.W.2d 491, 494 (Minn. 1997).

[314] See Minn. Stat. Ann. § 169.685 Subd. 4(b).

[315] See, e.g., Milbrand v. DaimlerChrysler Corp., 105 F. Supp. 2d 601, 608 (E.D. Tex. 2000) (allegation that seatbelt is defective creates only exception to statutory prohibition on seatbelt evidence); Chapman v. Mazda Motor of Am., Inc., 7 F. Supp. 2d 1123 (D. Mont. 1998) (plaintiff may not use seatbelt usage to prove the absence of contributory fault, but may use such evidence to prove seatbelt defective); Bridgestone/Firestone, Inc. v. Glyn-Jones, 878 S.W.2d 132 (Tex. 1994).

[316] For simply one example, see Hopper v. Carey, 716 N.E.2d 566 (Ind. Ct. App. 1999) (ruling that fire truck was not "passenger motor vehicle" for purposes of mandatory seatbelt statute).

[317] A contrary result would indirectly resurrect the "hideous" doctrine of imputed contributory negligence from parent to child. See Prosser and Keeton on Torts § 74, at 531–32.

[318] See, e.g., Ky. Rev. Stat. Ann. § 189.125(5); Me. Rev. Stat. Ann. tit. 29–A, § 2081(5); N.M. Stat. Ann. § 66–7–373(A); 75 Pa. Cons. Stat. Ann. § 4581(e); R.I. Gen. Laws § 31–22–22(h).

[319] See, e.g., Ky. Rev. Stat. Ann. § 189.125(5); Me. Rev. Stat. Ann. tit. 29–A, § 2081(5); N.J. Stat. Ann. § 39:3–76.2a(e); N.M. Stat. Ann. § 66–7–373(A); R.I. Gen. Laws § 31–22–22(h).

[320] See, e.g., N.J. Stat. Ann. § 39:3–76.7(a). See also N.J. Stat. Ann. §§ 39:3–76.8 to 39:3–76.9 (riders of motorcycles without wind screens required to wear goggles or face shields).

[321] Compare Rogers v. Frush, 262 A.2d 549 (Md. 1970) (rejecting motorcycle helmet defense on analogy to seatbelt defense), with Halvorson v. Voeller, 336 N.W.2d 118, 121 (N.D. 1983) (allowing mitigation of motorcyclist's damages based on helmet nonuse). Cf. Thurel v. Varghese, 621 N.Y.S.2d 633 (App. Div. 1995). See Annot., 85 A.L.R.4th 365 (1991) (failure of motorcyclist to wear helmet as contributory negligence, assumption of risk, or failure to avoid consequences of accident).

brake, navigate, and park themselves, with greater or lesser input from drivers—"autonomous vehicles."[322] Today, many vehicles include some self-driving components, and sometime soon vehicles will be able to largely drive themselves. In taking driver error out of the equation, it is likely that autonomous vehicles in time will reduce substantially the toll of serious automotive accidents.[323] Yet mixing humans and machines effectively can be tricky, and robotic vehicular controls themselves cannot completely anticipate and safely address all collision risks and resulting driver inputs, such that vehicle accidents undoubtedly will continue to occur, sometimes caused at least in part by defects in the autonomous systems themselves. And so the law of products liability has already begun to address various claims that an accident was caused at least in part by some flaw in an autonomous system in an automotive vehicle.

To standardize "autonomous vehicle" definitions, NHTSA adopted the 6-tiered model of autonomous systems promulgated by the Society of Automotive Engineers (SAE): no automation at level 0, driver assistance at level 1, automated driver assistance at level 2, conditional automation at level 3, high automation at level 4, and full automation at level 5.[324] Standard cruise control acceleration systems represent level 1, while adaptive cruise control systems keeping a vehicle at a pre-set distance behind a car or truck ahead, requiring the autonomous system to brake or accelerate in response to varying speeds of the vehicle ahead while keeping the vehicle in its lane, with driver monitoring, represent level 2. Such systems presumably can malfunction, requiring prompt action by the driver, and possibly contributing to cause an accident.[325] Vehicles that have been designed to change lanes by themselves followed by centering in the new lane, with an alert driver ready to take control if needed, represent level 3. Level 4 vehicles are fully autonomous under certain conditions,[326] while level 5 vehicles are fully autonomous under all conditions without the need for driver interaction.

The federal government formally began to address this topic in 2016, when NHTSA and the U.S. Department of Transportation issued a Federal Automated Vehicles Policy, which "set a proactive approach to providing safety assurance and facilitating innovation."[327] Following public comments and Congressional hearings, NHTSA issued an updated guidance in 2017 that described a non-regulatory "flexible framework" for

---

[322] Cruise control is an autonomous feature that has been available for several decades. Car manufacturers have contemplated fully autonomous vehicles since at least 1956. See the General Motors video, A Future Vision of Driverless Cars, created for the 1956 Motorama Auto Show, available at www.youtube.com/watch?v=F2iRDYnzwtk (posted by CBS Sunday Morning).

[323] See, e.g., Rahwan and Shariff, Self-Driving Cars Could Save Many Lives. But Mental Roadblocks Stand in the Way, Wall St. J.com (Apr. 6, 2021) ("AVs promise extraordinary safety benefits. A 90% reduction in traffic fatalities . . . is the most frequently repeated figure."); Ludlow, Alphabet's Waymo Says Its Tech Would Avoid Fatal Human Crashes, Prod. Liab. & Toxics L. (Mar. 8, 2021).

[324] U.S. Dep't of Transp. and NHTSA, Automated Driving Systems 2.0: A Vision for Safety 4 (Sept. 2017).

[325] See, e.g., Wang v. Tesla, Inc., 2021 WL 3023088 (E.D.N.Y. 2021) (Tesla Autopilot failed to react to vehicle merging in between the Tesla and a tractor-trailer, causing Tesla driver to quickly steer into two other cars; dismissing plaintiffs' fraud claim); Umeda v. Tesla Inc., 2020 WL 5653496 (N.D. Cal. 2020) (Tesla in Japan with active Autopilot and drowsy driver hit and killed person standing in far-right lane directing traffic around an accident; dismissed on forum non conveniens); Trudell and Laing, Tesla Autopilot Probed by U.S. Over Crash-Scene Collisions, Prod. Liab. & Toxics L. (Aug. 16, 2021) (listing 11 confirmed crashes involving Tesla's Autopilot that is a "driver-assistance system that maintains vehicles' speed and keeps them centered in lanes when engaged, though the driver is supposed to supervise at all times").

[326] See, e.g., Boudway, Waymo Begins Fully Driverless Rides for All Arizona Customers, Prod. Liab. & Toxics L. (Oct. 8, 2020) (50-square-mile service area); Korosec, Waymo's Robotaxi Pilot Surpassed 6,200 Riders in Its First Month in California, Techcrunch.com (Sept. 16, 2019) (rides limited to geofenced property).

[327] U.S. Dep't of Transp. and NHTSA, Automated Vehicles for Safety (Sept. 2016).

industry to address twelve priority safety design elements, including "vehicle cybersecurity, human machine interface, crashworthiness, consumer education and training, and post-crash" behavior.[328] A third guidance, issued in 2018, expanded the framework for safely integrating automation "across passenger vehicles, commercial vehicles, on-road transit, and the roadways on which they operate."[329]

In 2018, a pedestrian fatality involving an Uber test vehicle raised new questions about design safety and federal control of autonomous vehicles.[330] However, federal legislation, first introduced in Congress in 2018, continues to stall.[331] In the states, regulatory frameworks for autonomous vehicles vary widely.[332] And innumerable roadblocks—regulatory, technological, political, and judicial—seem never ending.[333]

---

[328] U.S. Dep't of Transp. and NHTSA, Automated Driving Systems 2.0: A Vision for Safety ii (Sept. 2017).

[329] U.S. Dep't of Transp., Preparing for the Future of Transportation: Automated Vehicles 3.0 (AV 3.0) viii (2018). In 2019, NHTSA issued an advance notice of proposed rulemaking to remove AV regulatory barriers and requested public comments on the "challenges of testing and verifying compliance with existing crash avoidance" standards for autonomous vehicles. 84 Fed. Reg. 24433 (May 28, 2019).

[330] Stone, Regulators are Asleep at the Wheel on Self-Driving Cars, 46 Prod. Safety & Liab. Rep. (BNA) 323 (April 2, 2018) ("The technology, which promises to save millions of lives, confounds the old regulatory model, where federal agencies are responsible for carmakers and DMVs oversee drivers."). In 2021, to speed identification of emerging safety issues, NHTSA began requiring manufacturers to report all crashes in vehicles with automated driver assistance and automated driving systems. NHTSA, NHTSA Orders Crash Reporting for Vehicles Equipped with Advanced Driver Assistance Systems and Automated Driving Systems (June 29, 2021).

[331] See, e.g., Laing, Self-Driving Cars Pose Crucial Question: Who to Blame in a Crash, Prod. Safety & Toxics L. (May 20, 2021) (describing debate over federal legislation proposals); Laing, Self-Driving Car Bill Reintroduced in House Minus Biggest Backer, Prod. Safety & Toxics L. (Sept. 23, 2020); Courtney, Driverless Cars Stall in Congress as Trial Lawyers Drop Support, Prod. Liab. & Toxics L. (Dec. 7, 2018).

[332] See Hocksted and Fisher, Automated Unity: Evaluating the Uniform Law Commission's Autonomous Vehicle Act, 61 Washburn L.J. 275, 294 (2022) ("[T]hirty-eight states and the District of Columbia have enacted legislation or issued executive orders that pertain to autonomous vehicles. The differences in how state governments have chosen to regulate automated vehicles are profound . . . .). The statutes are reproduced in Owen & Davis on Products Liability Appendix J. The Uniform Automated Operation of Vehicles Act "is intended to explicitly accommodate and specifically regulate the automated operation of automated vehicles." National Conference of Commissioners on Uniform State Laws, Uniform Automated Operation of Vehicles Act 1 (July 2019). As of early 2022, no state has adopted the Act.

[333] See, e.g., Mims, For Self-Driving Cars, the Hot New Technology Is . . . Radar, Wall St. J.com (Sept. 25, 2021); Coppola and Bergen, Waymo is 99% of the Way to Self-Driving Cars: The Last 1% is the Hardest, Bloomberg Businessweek (Aug. 17, 2021); Somerville and Smith, For Robot Trucks, Navigating Highways Is Just One Bump in the Road, Wall St. J.com (Aug. 18, 2021); Mims, Self-Driving Cars Could Be Decades Away, No Matter What Elon Musk Said, Wall St. J.com (June 5, 2021); Higgins, Driverless Cars Tap the Brakes After Years of Hype: Developers Take a More Cautious, Low-Key Approach in Testing and Talking about Autonomous Vehicles after Uber Crash, Wall St. J.com (Jan. 17, 2019); Higgins, Moriarty, and Zhang, The Bumps Ahead for Autonomous Vehicles: How Soda Cans, Bad Weather and Snakes Present Challenges to the Latest Technology, Wall St. J.com (Nov. 15, 2018); Coppola, Can Neuroscience Teach Robot Cars To Be Less Annoying?, Prod. Liab. & Toxics L. (Oct. 9, 2018) ("driverless vehicles now undergoing testing on public roads are overly cautious, maddeningly slow, and prone to abrupt halts or bizarre paralysis caused by bikers, joggers, crosswalks or anything else that doesn't fit within the neat confines of binary robot brains"); Stock, Self-Driving Cars Still Can't Handle Bad Weather, Prod. Liab. & Toxics L. (Sept. 17, 2018) ("At the moment, autonomous cars rely on a patchwork of sensors: GPS, traditional cameras, radar, and lidar technology that bounces lasers off nearby cars and pedestrians. Mother Nature essentially sidelines two of those four applications: Cameras are useless in fog and heavy snow, and lidar lasers careen wildly off raindrops and snowflakes. The remaining systems also have major deficiencies. GPS connections can be slow and spotty, and radar is lousy at distinguishing obstacles—is that a pedestrian or a seagull?"); Castro, Self-driving Cars Are Headed Toward an AI Roadblock: Skeptics Say Full Autonomy Could Be Farther Away Than the Industry Admits, The Verge (Jul. 3, 2018) ("[N]early every car accident involves some sort of unforeseen circumstance, and without the power to generalize, self-driving cars will have to confront each of these scenarios as if for the first time.").

Nonetheless, autonomous vehicle technology and commercial development continue to accelerate inexorably toward eventual fruition.[334]

Many commentators have speculated on how products liability law should apply to accidents in which autonomous vehicles are involved.[335] At this undeveloped stage of vehicular autonomy, and because the nature and domain of federal and state regulation has still to be worked out, little useful can be said about the extent to which federal law may preempt state products liability law is an important yet nascent issue.[336] Yet, regardless of the eventual regulatory framework, and regardless of how a particular accident vehicle may be autonomous, the basic principles of current products liability law may be expected to continue to govern responsibility for vehicular accidents for many years. That is, manufacturers of such vehicles (and of any such components) will surely continue to be responsible for defects in manufacture, design, warnings, and instructions in autonomous systems that play a role in causing accidents, and drivers will continue to bear responsibility for failing properly to monitor and control vehicles to the extent they are expected to do so. In the many cases where responsibility for causing accidents may lie with one or more manufacturers and one or more drivers, principles of comparative fault should continue to apply.

---

[334] See, e.g., Laing, Robot Trucks Get U.S. Tests, Raising Self-Driving Safety Stakes, Prod. Liab. & Toxics L. (Jan. 9, 2022); Welsh, Cruise, Waymo Get Permits for Autonomous Services in California, Prod. Liab. & Toxics L. (Sept. 20, 2021); Ludlow and Black, FedEx Partners with Self-Driving Car Startup Aurora in Texas, Prod. Liab. & Toxics L. (Sept. 22, 2021); Naughton, Ford, Lyft and Argo Team Up to Deploy Robo-Taxis This Year, Prod. Liab. & Toxics L. (July 21, 2021); Smith and Somerville, Autonomous-Truck Developer TuSimple Plans Driverless Road Test This Year, Wall St. J.com (Apr. 15, 2021); Gurman and Welch, Apple More Than Doubled Autonomous-Car Road Tests in 2020, Prod. Liab. & Toxics L. (Feb. 9, 2021); Vartabedian, Auto Makers Bet on Augmented Reality Startup, Wall St. J.com (Oct. 7, 2020) (capital investment in development of hologram technology for autonomous vehicles); Boston and Colias, VW to Invest Nearly $2 Billion in Ford Self-Driving Car Venture, Wall St. J.com (Feb. 26, 2019); Naughton, Ford's Autonomous Cars Will Whisk Walmart Deliveries to Doorsteps, Prod. Liab. & Toxics L. (Nov. 14, 2018).

[335] For commentary on liability for accidents involving autonomous vehicles, see, e.g., Wansley, The End of Accidents, 55 U.C. Davis L. Rev. 269 (2021); Johnson, Overhyping Mass Torts for Autonomous Vehicles: Why Preempting Civil Tort Liability Is Unwarranted, 21 J. High Tech. L. 321 (2021); Marchant and Bazzi, Autonomous Vehicles And Liability: What Will Juries Do?, 26 B.U. J. Sci. & Tech. L. 67 (2020); Pearl, Hands Off the Wheel: The Role of Law In the Coming Extinction of Human-Driven Vehicles, 33 Harv. J.L. & Tech. 427 (2020); Shavell, On the Redesign of Accident Liability for the World of Autonomous Vehicles, 49 J. Legal Stud. 243 (2020); Abraham and Rabin, Automated Vehicles and Manufacturer Responsibility for Accidents: A New Legal Regime for a New Era, 105 Va. L. Rev. 127 (2019); Lemann, Autonomous Vehicles, Technological Progress, and the Scope Problem in Products Liability, 12 J. Tort L. 157 (2019); Gifford, Technological Triggers to Tort Revolutions: Steam Locomotives, Autonomous Vehicles, and Accident Compensation, 11 J. Tort L. 71 (2018); Duplechin, The Emerging Intersection of Products Liability, Cybersecurity, and Autonomous Vehicles, 85 Tenn. L. Rev. 803 (2018); Geistfeld, A Roadmap for Autonomous Vehicles: State Tort Liability, Automobile Insurance, and Federal Safety Regulation, 105 Cal. L. Rev. 1611 (2017); Gurney, Sue My Car Not Me: Products Liability and Accidents Involving Autonomous Vehicles, 2013 U. Ill. J.L. Tech. & Pol'y 247 (Fall 2013).

[336] See, e.g., Varela v. FCA US LLC, 505 P.3d 244, 262–63 (Ariz. 2022) (plaintiff's claim that automatic emergency braking technology, available as an option in the vehicle that caused the crash, would have avoided her injuries and her daughter's death was not impliedly preempted). See generally Johnson, Overhyping Mass Torts for Autonomous Vehicles: Why Preempting Civil Tort Liability Is Unwarranted, 21 J. High Tech. L. 321 (2021).

Chapter 18

DRUGS AND MEDICAL DEVICES

Table of Sections

§ 18.1 PRESCRIPTION DRUGS—GENERALLY

Many have been bewitched, bedazzled, and bewildered in trying to discern just how products liability principles should be applied to prescription drugs[1] and, to a lesser extent, medical devices.[2] Medical products pose a number of special problems for products liability law. Whether and how pharmaceuticals should be treated differently from other types of products has consumed more time and effort, and resulted in the

[1] See, e.g., Beck, Off-Label Use in the Twenty-First Century: Most Myths and Misconceptions Mitigated, 54 UIC J. Marshall L. Rev. 1 (2021); Bernstein, (Almost) No Bad Drugs: Near-Total Products Liability Immunity for Pharmaceuticals Explained, 77 Wash. & Lee L. Rev. 3 (2020); Davis, Time for a Fresh Look at Strict Liability for Pharmaceuticals, 28 Cornell J. L. & Pub. Pol'y 399 (2019); Janssen, *Iqbal* "Plausibility" in Pharmaceutical and Medical Device Litigation, 71 La. L. Rev. 541 (2011); Owen, Dangers in Prescription Drugs: Filling a Private Law Gap in the Healthcare Debate, 42 Conn. L. Rev. 733 (2010); Noah, This Is Your Products Liability Restatement on Drugs, 74 Brook. L. Rev. 839 (2009); Gilhooley, Addressing Potential Drug Risks: The Limits of Testing, Risk Signals, Preemption, and the Drug Reform Legislation, 59 S.C. L. Rev. 347 (2008); Bernstein, Enhancing Drug Effectiveness and Efficacy Through Personal Injury Litigation, 15 J.L. Pol'y 1051 (2007); Stapleton, Liability for Drugs in the U.S. and EU: Rhetoric and Reality, 26 Rev. Litig. 991 (2007); V. Schwartz and Goldberg, A Prescription for Drug Liability and Regulation, 58 Okla. L. Rev. 135 (2005); Green, Prescription Drugs, Alternative Designs, and The Restatement (Third): Preliminary Reflections, 30 Seton Hall L. Rev. 207, 209 (1999); Gilhooley, When Drugs Are Safe for Some But Not Others: The FDA Experience and Alternatives for Products Liability, 36 Hous. L. Rev. 927 (1999); T. Schwartz, Prescription Products and the Proposed Restatement (Third), 61 Tenn. L. Rev. 1357 (1994); Ausness, Unavoidably Unsafe Products and Strict Products Liability: What Liability Rule Should be Applied to the Sellers of Pharmaceutical Products?, 78 Ky. L.J. 705 (1989–1990); Merrill, Compensation for Prescription Drug Injuries, 59 Va. L. Rev. 1 (1973); Frumer, Friedman, and Sklaren, Products Liability § 8.07 and ch. 50; Am. Law Prod. Liability §§ 28:11, 89.3–89:6.

Much of the most important commentary in this field focuses on liability for dangerous drug designs, federal preemption, the learned intermediary doctrine, and other more specific topics addressed below, where such scholarship is noted in context.

[2] Medical devices involve fewer special issues than prescription drugs, and so they are touched on lightly in this chapter. See, e.g., Dagne, Governance of 3d-Printing Applications in Health: Between Regulated and Unregulated Innovation, 21 Colum. Sci. & Tech. L. Rev. 281 (2020); Shapiro et. al., Nothing Generic About It: Promoting Therapeutic Access by Overcoming Regulatory and Legal Barriers to A Robust Generic Medical Device Market, 98 N.C. L. Rev. 595 (2020); Corbin, When "Things" Go Wrong: Redefining Liability for the Internet of Medical Things, 71 S.C. L. Rev. 1 (2019); Jacxsens, Deskins, and Jessee, Beyond the Basics: Expanding Theories of Liability and Defenses for Claims Involving Medical Device Sales Representatives, 39 Wm. Mitchell L. Rev. 1087 (2013); Patsner, Direct-to-Consumer Advertising of Restricted, Surgically Implanted Medical Devices: What Does the Advertising Arena Look Like, and Whose Regulatory Problem Is It?, 39 Wm. Mitchell L. Rev. 1207 (2013); Janssen, *Iqbal* "Plausibility" in Pharmaceutical and Medical Device Litigation, 71 La. L. Rev. 541 (2011); Green and Schultz, Tort Law Deference to FDA Regulation of Medical Devices, 88 Geo. L.J. 2119 (2000); Comment, 80 Tenn. L. Rev. 477 (2013) (transvaginal mesh litigation); Frumer, Friedman, and Sklaren, Products Liability ch. 53 (liability for medical devices). See also Owen & Davis on Products Liability ch. 20.

gnashing of more teeth, than any other particularized issue in all of products liability law. In addition to featuring two prominent *Restatement* provisions—comment *k* to § 402A of the *Restatement (Second) of Torts* and § 6 of the *Restatement (Third) of Torts: Products Liability*—the special story of how products liability law applies to prescription drugs wends through two of the most prominent cases in modern products liability law history: *Feldman v. Lederle Laboratories*[3] and *Brown v. Superior Court*.[4] The special issues are numerous and complex, involving the learned intermediary doctrine,[5] inherent dangers (product category liability),[6] state of the art,[7] the battle for supremacy between the consumer expectations and risk-utility liability tests for design defects,[8] the never-ending struggle between negligence and strict liability, how design and warning defect notions fit together,[9] and the vexing doctrine of federal preemption.[10]

At bottom, the question that has tortured courts, lawyers, and commentators for so long has been whether pharmaceuticals in particular are sufficiently different from other types of chattels to deserve separate treatment by products liability law. Yet, of all the many insights into this nearly impenetrable thicket of separate yet intertwined forays into distinct doctrinal quagmires, the discovery that transcends the rest in clarity and brilliance is this: that, for drugs, "the liability game is with the warnings candle, not with design."[11] Appreciating this important truth requires burrowing into the drug design defect problem,[12] then exploring various imbroglios surrounding warning duties for drug and device dangers,[13] and finally examining the duties of pharmacists to consumers of prescription drugs.[14] First, however, a lawyer travelling in this peculiar terrain needs a map of the broader, medical product landscape.

The Perplexing Problem of Dangerous Drugs

Pharmaceuticals are paradoxical: as one of the greatest triumphs of the twentieth century, their powerful chemicals and biologics regularly save millions of humans from suffering and death; yet, these same substances also cause great suffering and death.[15] Put simply, prescription drugs in particular possess substantial costs as well as abundant benefits. This is because most drug hazards are inherent and unavoidable.[16] Normally, the dangers residing in drugs cannot be removed without destroying the drug: the same chemical properties in drugs that can cause great harm are usually the very properties that are therapeutic. Put another way, if a drug's chemical structure were altered to avoid some adverse health effect, that change would often reduce or eliminate

---

3 479 A.2d 374, 382–83 (N.J. 1984).

4 751 P.2d 470 (Cal. 1988).

5 See § 18.3, below.

6 See § 10.3 (*Drugs*), above.

7 See § 10.4, above.

8 See §§ 8.3–8.8, above.

9 See § 6.2, above.

10 Federal preemption, a major issue in both pharmaceutical and medical device litigation, is addressed in § 14.5, above. For articles on federal preemption in the drug and medical device context, see note 27, below.

11 Green, Prescription Drugs, Alternative Designs, and the Restatement (Third): Preliminary Reflections, 30 Seton Hall L. Rev. 207, 209 (1999).

12 See § 18.2, below.

13 See § 18.3, below.

14 See § 18.4, below.

15 "[A]ll drugs do harm." Bernstein and Bernstein, An Information Prescription for Drug Regulation, 54 Buff. L. Rev. 569, 570 (2006).

16 On inherent hazards in drugs and other products, see §§ 6.2 and 10.3 (*Drugs*), above.

the drug's beneficial health effects as well.[17] In general, that is, the "design" of pharmaceuticals cannot be changed.

Penicillin may be the classic example of a drug that, while highly beneficial to most people, can be hazardous, indeed lethal, to others.[18] But other examples abound. Accutane is another example of a drug that combines great benefits with great risks of harm: it is highly effective in treating the most severe cases of acne; yet, it is a virulent teratogen that can cause birth defects when given to pregnant women.[19] Surely the most impelling example is thalidomide, another teratogen, prescribed widely as a sedative and for morning sickness throughout much of the world (but not the U.S.) during the 1950s and 1960s.[20] Despite the enormous suffering from birth defects this drug then wreaked around the globe, the federal Food and Drug Administration (FDA) approved thalidomide in 1998 for fighting leprosy.[21] These are only three examples, and the list of unavoidably unsafe drugs goes on and on.[22]

Outside tort law, America's medico-legal systems address this conundrum—the bad-comes-with-the-good aspect of pharmaceuticals—in two basic ways. First, prior to being allowed onto the market, prescription drugs must be developed and subjected to rigorous analysis, laboratory testing, and clinical trials, the results of which are quite closely reviewed by the FDA, to help ensure both the safety and efficacy of all new drugs—the developmental costs of which are enormous.[23] Under the Food, Drug, and

---

17 "Normally," because the hazard in some drugs may be reduced or eliminated by changing the prescribed dosage, the active ingredients in combination drugs, or the inert ingredients used in a drug. See Green, Prescription Drugs, Alternative Designs, and the Restatement (Third): Preliminary Reflections, 30 Seton Hall L. Rev. 207 (1999).

18 See W. Prosser, Handbook of the Law of Torts § 99, at 661 (4th ed. 1971).

19 See, e.g., Myers v. Hoffman-La Roche, Inc., 170 P.3d 254, 256 (Ariz. Ct. App. 2007).

20 Thalidomide caused severe limb deformities in children born to women who took the drug while pregnant. The FDA's protracted review of the drug barely saved most Americans from this terrible tragedy. See Sanders, The Bendectin Litigation: A Case Study in the Life Cycle of Mass Torts, 43 Hastings L.J. 301, 313–14 (1992) (characterizing thalidomide as "one of the most potent human teratogens ever found"). See also Berstein, Formed by Thalidomide: Mass Torts as a False Cure for Toxic Exposure, 97 Colum. L. Rev. 2153 (1997).

21 "Thalidomide, the sedative that produced thousands of babies with flipperlike limbs and other gross deformities, was approved today for use in the United States for the first time, nearly four decades after it was stripped from pharmacy shelves around the world." Stolberg, Thalidomide Approved to Treat Leprosy, with Other Uses Seen, N.Y. Times, July 17, 1998, at A1.

22 "The whole pharmacopeia is full of drugs which are not safe, and at present cannot be made safe." W. Prosser, Handbook of the Law of Torts § 99, at 661 (4th ed. 1971).

23 **New drug development costs.** In 2020, a study of 63 of the 355 new drugs and biologics approved by the FDA between 2009 and 2018 concluded that the mean capitalized research and development costs for a single pharmaceutical was $1.3 billion. Wouters, McKee, and Luyten, Estimated Research and Development Investment Needed to Bring a New Medicine to Market, 2009–2018. 323 J. Am. Med. Ass'n 844 (2020). An earlier study of 106 randomly selected drugs developed by ten large firms estimated the research and development costs of a single product at $2.5 billion. See DiMasi, Grabowski, and Hansen, Innovation in the Pharmaceutical Industry: New Estimates of R&D Costs, 47 J. Health Econ. 20 (2016). See also Ohly and Patel, The Hatch-Waxman Act: Prescriptions for Innovative and Inexpensive Medicines, 19 U. Balt. Intell. Prop. L.J. 107, 128–130 (2011) (explaining that about half such estimates are opportunity costs). Another commentator states: "The capitalized cost of developing a new drug that makes it to market is roughly $1.9 billion, including preclinical testing and FDA-monitored clinical trials. Still, many of the drugs that are eventually approved by the FDA fail to return the investment costs of development. In fact, only about 20% of FDA-approved drugs actually earn back the substantial initial investment required for development." Ingram, Eliminating Innovation, 32 J. Legal Med. 115, 124 (2011) (further reporting that, in 2007, 2,742 new drugs were in development, and only 16 new drugs were approved that year; and that, of the few hundred that enter pre-clinical testing each year, only five enter FDA-monitored clinical testing, only one in five of these are approved by the FDA and go onto the market, and, therefore, that drug companies "must recoup the investment costs of the failures through the success of their other drugs"). See also John, Informed Consent: Requiring Doctors to

Cosmetic Act of 1938, as amended,[24] Congress has vested more regulatory power in the FDA to regulate drug safety than it has vested in other agencies to regulate the safety of other products, mirroring the special role of prescription drugs in preserving health and life together with the special dangers they pose to health and life. The principal function of the FDA is to help assure that only drugs that are safe and effective reach and stay on the market.[25]

The second relevant feature of America's medico-legal system is that it positions experts in diagnosis and drug therapy—doctors and nurse practitioners—between beneficial yet dangerous prescription drugs, on the one hand, and the lay public who need drug therapy, on the other. The role of such health care professionals—such "learned intermediaries"—is to connect individual drugs with individual patients, to select from the panoply of available prescription drugs the one with the highest benefit-risk ratio for each particular patient's needs and wants. Thus, the very purpose of a doctor in drug therapy is to ensure that the right prescription medicine, in view of its particular benefits and risks, is assigned to the right patient, in view of that patient's special needs.[26]

The Role of Products Liability Law

The question of interest here is what role, if any, does the American medico-legal system leave for the law of torts and products liability? Because the system just described breaks down in many ways in practice, revealing many weaknesses, the answer to the question must be that products liability law—putting aside for now the

---

Disclose Off-Label Prescriptions and Conflicts of Interest, 58 Hastings L.J. 967, 973–74 (2007) ("The FDA approval process takes six to fifteen years and costs between $100 million and $880 million per drug.").

[24] 21 U.S.C. §§ 301–392. The Act's key provisions are § 331(a), prohibiting the sale of "any food, drug, device, or cosmetic that is adulterated or misbranded," and § 355, requiring FDA approval prior to the marketing of any new drug. The FDCA and the FDA are addressed more fully in the warnings context in § 18.3, notes 107–119 and accompanying text, below.

[25] On drug regulation by the FDA, see, e.g., Zettler, The FDA's Power over Non-Therapeutic Uses of Drugs and Devices, 78 Wash. & Lee L. Rev. 379 (2021); Hagie et al., Reducing New Medical Device Regulatory Risks Utilizing FDA's Designation Pathways and Requests for Information Pathway, 46/47 Lincoln L. Rev. 1 (2020); Lietzan, Access Before Evidence and the Price of the FDA's New Drug Authorities, 53 U. Rich. L. Rev. 1243 (2019); Cooper, The Food and Drug Community, 68 Food & Drug L.J. 225 (2013); Avery and Liu, Bringing Smart Pills to Market: FDA Regulation of Drug/Device Combination Products, 66 Food & Drug L.J. 329 (2011); Gilhooley, Addressing Potential Drug Risks: The Limits of Testing, Risk Signals, Preemption, and the Drug Reform Legislation, 59 S.C. L. Rev. 347 (2008); O'Reilly, Losing Deference in the FDA's Second Century: Judicial Review, Politics, and a Diminished Legacy of Expertise, 93 Cornell L. Rev. 939 (2008); Cahoy, Medical Product Information Incentives and the Transparency Paradox, 82 Ind. L.J. 623 (2007); Bernstein and Bernstein, An Information Prescription for Drug Regulation, 54 Buff. L. Rev. 569 (2006); Shulman and Kuettel, Drug Development and the Public Health Mission: Collaborative Challenges at the FDA, NIH, and Academic Medical Centers, 53 Buff. L. Rev. 663 (2005); Epstein, Regulatory Paternalism in the Market for Drugs: Lessons from Vioxx and Celebrex, 5 Yale J. Health Pol'y L. & Ethics 741 (2005); Struve, The FDA and the Tort System: Postmarketing Surveillance, Compensation, and the Role of Litigation, 5 Yale J. Health Pol'y L. & Ethics 587 (2005); V. Schwartz and Goldberg, A Prescription for Drug Liability and Regulation, 58 Okla. L. Rev. 135 (2005); Gilhooley, When Drugs Are Safe for Some But Not Others: The FDA Experience and Alternatives for Products Liability, 36 Hous. L. Rev. 927 (1999); Green, Safety as an Element of Pharmaceutical Quality: The Respective Roles of Regulation and Tort Law, 42 St. Louis U. L.J. 163 (1998); T. Schwartz, Regulatory Standards and Products Liability: Striking the Right Balance Between the Two, 30 U. Mich. J.L. Reform 431 (1997); Merrill, The Architecture of Government Regulation of Medical Products, 82 Va. L. Rev. 1753 (1996). See generally Termini, Food and Drug Law: Federal Regulation of Drugs, Biologics, Medical Devices, Foods, Dietary Supplements, Personal Care, Veterinary and Tobacco Products (10th ed. 2018).

[26] The "learned intermediary doctrine" is examined in § 18.3, below.

substantial constraints of federal preemption[27]—has a vital role to play in compensating persons harmed unnecessarily by defective drugs, and some role (if a lesser one) in deterring their sale and promoting drug safety. The model of a perfect FDA, unfortunately, does not fit the real world closely. Legislative, budgetary, and political constraints mar the ideal of a perfect regulatory body that optimally protects the public from exposure to defective drugs.[28] Nor, as most people painfully well know, do doctors typically match prescription drugs to patients in a manner that approaches optimality.[29] Because of these and other shortcomings in the medico-legal structure for the production and distribution of prescription drugs, products liability law needs to play a significant role in compensating, and hopefully in helping protect, consumers of defective prescription drugs.[30]

Because the answer to the question posed above was that products liability law indeed plays a crucial role when people are harmed by defects in pharmaceuticals and medical devices, we must ask whether the ordinary rules of products liability law should be applied in drug and device cases, as they are in other contexts, or whether instead the

---

[27] On federal preemption of drug and device claims, see, e.g., Beck, Off-Label Use in the Twenty-First Century: Most Myths and Misconceptions Mitigated, 54 UIC J. Marshall L. Rev. 1, 60–83 (2021); Davis, Time for A Fresh Look at Strict Liability for Pharmaceuticals, 28 Cornell J.L. & Pub. Pol'y 399 (2019); Smith, A Shift in the Preemption Landscape?, 87 Tenn. L. Rev. 213 (2019); Prince, The Puzzle of Parallel Claims, Preemption, and Pleading the Particulars, 39 Wm. Mitchell L. Rev. 1034 (2013); Smirniotopoulos, Bad Medicine: Prescription Drugs, Preemption, and the Potential for a No-Fault Fix, 35 N.Y.U. Rev. L. & Soc. Change 793 (2011); Davis, The Case Against Preemption: Vaccines & Uncertainty, 8 Ind. Health L. Rev. 291 (2010–2011); Ausness, The Impact of *Wyeth v. Levine* on FDA Regulation of Prescription Drugs, 65 Food & Drug L.J. 247 (2010); Cupp, Preemption's Rise (and Bit of a Fall) as Products Liability Reform: *Wyeth, Riegel, Altria*, and the *Restatement (Third)*'s Prescription Product Design Defect Standard, 74 Brook. L. Rev. 727 (2009); Kessler and Vladeck, A Critical Examination of The FDA's Efforts To Preempt Failure-To-Warn Claims, 96 Geo. L.J. 461 (2008); Davis, The Battle over Implied Preemption: Products Liability and The FDA, 48 B.C. L. Rev. 1089 (2007); O'Steen and O'Steen, The FDA Defense: Vioxx® and the Argument Against Federal Preemption of State Claims for Injuries Resulting from Defective Drugs, 48 Ariz. L. Rev. 67 (2006); Dorfman, Quinn, and Brophy, Presumption of Innocence: FDA's Authority To Regulate the Specifics of Prescription Drug Labeling and the Preemption Debate 61 Food & Drug L.J. 585 (2006). On federal preemption generally, see § 14.5, above.

[28] On weaknesses in the perfect FDA model, see, e.g., Duranske, Reforming Regenerative Medicine Regulation, 34 Ga. St. U. L. Rev. 631 (2018); Kapczynski, Dangerous Times: The FDA's Role in Information Production, Past and Future, 102 Minn. L. Rev. 2357 (2018); Chirba and Garfield, FDA Oversight of Autologous Stem Cell Therapies: Legitimate Regulation of Drugs and Devices or Groundless Interference with the Practice of Medicine?, 7 J. Health & Biomedical L. 233 (2011); Gilhooley, Vioxx's History and the Need for Better Procedures and Better Testing, 37 Seton Hall L. Rev. 941 (2007); Conk, Punctuated Equilibrium: Why Section 402A Flourished and the *Third Restatement* Languished, 26 Rev. Litig. 799, 860–61 (2007); Rabin, Reassessing Regulatory Compliance, 88 Geo. L.J. 2049 (2000); T. Schwartz, The Role of Federal Safety Regulations in Products Liability Actions, 41 Vand. L. Rev. 1121 (1988).

Congress addressed some of the weaknesses in The Food and Drug Administration Amendments Act of 2007, Pub. L. No. 110–85, 121 Stat. 823, which expands agency oversight of drug safety and provides the agency with additional resources. See President Bush Signs FDA Legislation Expanding Drug Safety, Drug, Device Fees, Prod. Liab. Daily, Sept. 28, 2007, at D7. See also § 16.10 (*Cannabis-Infused Products*), above, for a discussion of the FDA's role in regulating these products.

[29] Apart from the increasingly limited time many doctors are able to devote to treating each patient, doctors typically receive woefully limited education—from one to three semesters—on pharmaceuticals. See § 18.4 notes 223 and 224, below. See generally Green, Prescription Drugs, Alternative Designs, and The Restatement (Third): Preliminary Reflections, 30 Seton Hall L. Rev. 207, 229 n.67 (1999) (explaining how the "idealized role of the physician is not borne out in practice").

[30] See, e.g., Owen, Dangers in Prescription Drugs: Filling a Private Law Gap in the Healthcare Debate, 42 Conn. L. Rev. 733 (2010); Noah, This Is Your Products Liability Restatement on Drugs, 74 Brook. L. Rev. 839 (2009); Bernstein, Enhancing Drug Effectiveness and Efficacy Through Personal Injury Litigation, 15 J.L. Pol'y 1051 (2007); Stapleton, Liability for Drugs in the U.S. and EU: Rhetoric and Reality, 26 Rev. Litig. 991 (2007); Gilhooley, Innovative Drugs, Products Liability, Regulatory Compliance and Patient Choice, 24 Seton Hall L. Rev. 1481 (1994); Merrill, Compensation for Prescription Drug Injuries, 59 Va. L. Rev. 1 (1973). See also articles cited notes 1, 25, and 27, above, and elsewhere throughout this chapter.

legal principles need to be adjusted to fit the context of these special types of product. While some courts and scholars believe that consumer protection requires application of the full array of conventional products liability principles to medical products, the law has long and broadly recognized that many pharmaceuticals and other medical products are indeed fundamentally different from other types of product, a distinction that requires a variety of nuanced adjustments in ordinary legal principles. Drugs, in short, are different.[31]

The next two sections of this chapter address the responsibility of manufacturers for design defects and warning defects in products liability litigation involving prescription drugs and, to a lesser extent, medical devices. What the inquiry reveals is that most courts, commentators, and the *Torts Restatements* agree that the principles of products liability law should be crafted to help assure that doctors and (often indirectly) patients receive adequate warnings of drug dangers, and instructions on how to avoid them, and that judicial reevaluations of prescription drug designs should be limited. The following discussions explore how these general propositions have evolved doctrinally in judicial decisions and in the *Restatements of Torts.* The final section examines special principles applicable to pharmacists in their dispensing of drugs.

Other issues bearing particularly on prescription drug and medical device litigation treated elsewhere include the responsibility of drug manufacturers for side effects that are unavoidable[32] or unforeseeable under the prevailing state of the art;[33] the scope of a drug company's liability for prenatal harm;[34] the limitations on litigation of this type

---

[31] See Henderson and Twerski, Drug Designs Are Different, 111 Yale L.J. 151 (2001); Note, 27 Vt. L. Rev. 1017, 1049 (2003) ("Drugs are different."); Madden, The Enduring Paradox of Products Liability Law Relating to Prescription Pharmaceuticals, 21 Pace L. Rev. 313, 361–62 (2001) ("Pharmaceutical products liability law departs from all other dimensions of products liability. [This is because these products, if defective,] can create the highest degree of risk of death or serious bodily injury. At the same time, [they] are not simply products, but also medicines [that] have the highest importance in matters of private and public health."). Professor Madden concludes: "No other realm of accident law has required the reconciliation of accident law policy for products importing the highest levels of risk, but produced by manufacturers needing the highest degree of liability solicitude." Id.

In Green, Prescription Drugs, Alternative Designs, and the Restatement (Third): Preliminary Reflections, 30 Seton Hall L. Rev. 207, 232 (1999), Michael Green helpfully explains the variety of ways in which drugs are different:

> (1) "they cannot be manipulated physically to provide marginally greater safety";
>
> (2) they are harmful for some people while beneficial for others;
>
> (3) their adverse effects frequently are not discoverable through research and testing, such that these harmful effects are not revealed until they injure drug consumers;
>
> (4) they are subject to especially heavy regulatory oversight, much of it pre-market, by the FDA;
>
> (5) they are especially beneficial to mankind, sometimes even necessary to the preservation of health and life;
>
> (6) learned intermediaries, doctors, stand between drug products and consumers, matching particular drugs to particular people.

To these six claims of difference specified by Professor Green, one might add:

> (7) that they are extremely costly to develop and bring to market—new brand-name prescription drugs that now average over $1 billion for research, development, laboratory testing, clinical testing, FDA submission work, and production.

See note 23, above. For the contrary view, that drugs should be treated the same as other products, see notes 88–90 and accompanying text, below.

[32] See § 10.3 (*Drugs*), above.

[33] See § 10.4, above.

[34] See § 10.5, above.

occasioned by a manufacturer's compliance with FDA regulations under the common law[35] and, especially, by the federal preemption doctrine;[36] and the liability of suppliers of human blood, organs, and tissue.[37]

Compensation Programs for Certain Vaccine and Drug Injuries

Before considering how state law addresses pharmaceutical injury claims, however, we should note two small but important federal drug-injury compensation programs that affect products liability drug litigation in certain cases. In 1986, Congress addressed an important class of prescription drug injuries, those from childhood vaccines. In the National Childhood Vaccine Injury Act,[38] Congress created a no-fault compensation program to facilitate compensation to persons suffering adverse reactions to childhood vaccinations required by public health statutes.[39] The Act sought to restore balance to a vaccine market destabilized by products liability litigation and awards that had disrupted liability insurance markets, driving most drug manufacturers from the childhood vaccine market, which in turn led to a sudden and drastic decrease in the availability of such vaccines and a commensurate increase in their cost.[40]

The compensation program under the Vaccine Act lies largely outside products liability law, and hence outside the scope of this book, but its provisions are important to attorneys helping victims of vaccine injuries. Under the Act, claims for adverse reactions to vaccines regularly administered to children, even if the victim is an adult,[41] must be made in the Court of Claims against the Secretary of Health and Human Services, including claims for economic losses, pain and suffering (limited to $250,000),

---

[35] See § 14.4, above.

[36] See § 14.5, above.

[37] See § 16.9, above.

[38] See National Childhood Vaccine Injury Act of 1986, 42 U.S.C. §§ 300aa–1 et seq.

[39] See, e.g., Levine and Davey, The National Vaccine Injury Compensation Program and Maternal Immunizations, 11 J. Health & Life Sci. L. 32 (2017); Haertlein, Causation in Law and Science Immunizing Against Bad Science: The Vaccine Court and The Autism Test Cases, 75 Law & Contemp. Probs. 211 (2012); Holland, Compulsory Vaccination, The Constitution, and The Hepatitis B Mandate For Infants And Young Children, 12 Yale J. Health Pol'y, L. & Ethics 39 (2012); Crawford and Axelrad, Legislative Modifications to Tort Liability: The Unintended Consequence of Public Health and Bioterrorism Threats, 45 Creighton L. Rev. 337 (2012); Grey, The Plague of Causation in The National Childhood Vaccine Injury Act, 48 Harv. J. on Legis. 343 (2011); Meyers, Fixing The Flaws in The Federal Vaccine Injury Compensation Program, 63 Admin. L. Rev. 785 (2011); Davis, The Case Against Preemption: Vaccines & Uncertainty, 8 Ind. Health L. Rev. 291 (2010–2011); Waldenberg and Wallace, When Science is Silent: Examining Compensation of Vaccine-Related Injuries When Scientific Evidence of Causation is Inconclusive, 42 Wake Forest L. Rev. 303 (2007); Calandrillo, Vanishing Vaccinations: Why Are So Many Americans Opting Out of Vaccinating Their Children?, 37 U. Mich. J.L. Reform 353 (2004); Noah, Triage in the Nation's Medicine Cabinet: The Puzzling Scarcity of Vaccines and Other Drugs, 54 S.C. L. Rev. 741 (2002); Rabin, Some Thoughts on the Efficacy of a Mass Toxics Administrative Compensation Scheme, 52 Md. L. Rev. 951, 958 (1993); V. Schwartz and Mahshigian, National Childhood Vaccine Injury Act of 1986: An Ad Hoc Remedy or a Window for the Future?, 48 Ohio St. L.J. 387 (1987); Annot., 129 A.L.R. Fed. 1 (1996); 5 Harper, James, and Gray, Law of Torts § 28.8A, at 226–27 (2013–1 Supp.); Dobbs, Law of Torts § 399, at 1112–13.

[40] See generally Bruesewitz v. Wyeth LLC, 562 U.S. 223, 227–28 (2011).

[41] To minimize litigation costs on makers of childhood vaccines, the Act applies to all recipients of childhood vaccines, even adults. See Case Comment, 8 J. Health & Biomedical L. 315, 331 (2012). So, the Act covers reactions to vaccines against tetanus, which are commonly administered to children (but also to adults), but not vaccines against typhoid or the flu. See Charette v. Secretary of Dep't of Health and Human Services, 33 Fed. Cl. 488 (Fed. Cl. 1995). The 21st Century Cures Act (Cures Act) (Pub. L. No. 114–255), enacted in 2016, amended the Vaccine Act injury table to include "vaccines recommended by the Centers for Disease Control and Prevention for routine administration in pregnant women," 42 U.S.C. § 300aa–14(3). The Cures Act also amended Vaccine Act compensation petitions to cover "both a woman who received a covered vaccine while pregnant and any child who was in utero at the time such woman received the vaccine." 42 U.S.C. § 300aa–11(f).

and death (limited to $250,000). If a claimant rejects the court's award, the claimant may then (and only then) initiate a products liability action against the manufacturer. The Act importantly bars recovery in such actions for "side effects that were unavoidable even though the vaccine was properly prepared and was accompanied by proper directions and warnings."[42] In *Bruesewitz v. Wyeth LLC*,[43] the Supreme Court ruled that the National Childhood Injury Act "pre-empts all design-defect claims against vaccine manufacturers brought by plaintiffs who seek compensation for injury or death caused by vaccine side effects."

Another, less substantial compensation program for injuries from certain pandemic and epidemic vaccines and other medical treatments is administered by the Countermeasures Injury Compensation Program (CICP),[44] authorized by the Public Readiness and Emergency Preparedness Act (PREP Act).[45] Addressing injuries from such medical products, including COVID-19[46] and H1N1 swine flu vaccines, the CICP compensates persons who directly sustain serious physical injuries from a drug, vaccine, or other medical treatment[47] (called "countermeasures") covered by a PREP Act "declaration."[48] Correspondingly, manufacturers and providers are insulated from liability for manufacturing or administering covered drugs and other treatments.[49]

§ 18.2 DESIGN DEFECTS

An understanding of how the notion of a design defect fits together with prescription drugs ideally should begin with a study of the biology, chemistry, manufacturing, marketing, and therapeutic applications of this peculiar type of product. Yet, because time and space require that such deep explorations be left to specialized texts on drugs,[50] and journal articles on law and pharmaceuticals,[51] the best place to begin the inquiry here is by looking at the special provisions on prescription drugs in the *Restatements (Second)* and *(Third) of Torts*, as reflecting (and affecting) the special treatment of these products in the courts.

The *Second Restatement*—Comment *k*

Undoubtedly, the special treatment the law accords pharmaceuticals was most emphatically set forth at an early date in comment *k*, a controversial comment to § 402A

---

[42] 42 U.S.C. § 300aa–22.

[43] 562 U.S. 223, 243 (2011).

[44] The CICP is administered by HRSA, within the Department of Health and Human Services.

[45] 42 U.S.C. §§ 247d–6d–6e.

[46] See, e.g., CRS, The PREP Act and COVID-19: Limiting Liability for Medical Countermeasures (Mar. 19, 2021).

[47] Claims must be filed, accompanied by proper medical records, within one year of treatment. See 42 C.F.R. § 110.50 (required medical records) and § 110.42 (filing deadline); HRSA, Filing for Benefits (Jan. 2021), www.hrsa.gov/cicp/filing-benefits.

[48] The Secretary of HHS declared COVID-19 a covered disease in 2020. "As of April 1, 2022, the CICP has not compensated any COVID-19 countermeasures claims. Thirteen COVID-19 countermeasure claims have been denied compensation because the standard of proof for causation was not met and/or a covered injury was not sustained. One COVID-19 countermeasure claim, a COVID-19 vaccine claim due to an anaphylactic reaction, has been determined eligible for compensation and is pending a review of eligible expenses." HRSA, Countermeasures Injury Compensation Program (CICP) Data Aggregate Data as of April 1, 2022, www.hrsa.gov/cicp/cicp-data#table-1.

[49] 42 U.S.C. § 247d–6d(a)(2)(B).

[50] See, e.g., 1 M. Dixon and F. Woodside, Drug Product Liability ch. 3 (2000) (principles of pharmacology). See also Frumer, Friedman, and Sklaren, Products Liability ch. 50 (drug litigation).

[51] See § 18.1, note 1, above.

of the *Restatement (Second) of Torts*.[52] Part of a triumvirate of comments addressing the general topic of inherent product hazards, comment *k* in a nutshell[53] provides that manufacturers are not subject to strict liability in tort for harm caused by certain "unavoidably unsafe" but useful products, notably prescription drugs, solely on the basis of their inherent hazards that cannot feasibly be designed away.[54] The Reporter for the *Second Restatement* who drafted comment *k*, William Prosser, justified this exemption in a famous quote:

> The argument that industries producing potentially dangerous products should make good the harm, distribute it by liability insurance, and add the cost to the price of the product, encounters reason for pause, when we consider that two of the greatest medical boons to the human race, penicillin and cortisone, both have their dangerous side effects, and that drug companies might well have been deterred from producing and selling them.[55]

Drugs, that is, are distinctive types of products that need distinctive treatment by products liability law.[56] As a result, most courts and commentators have come to understand that comment *k* properly exempts useful prescription drugs that are unavoidably unsafe from strict products liability,[57] assuming always that they were

---

[52] See Cupp, Rethinking Conscious Design Liability for Prescription Drugs: The *Restatement (Third)* Standard Versus a Negligence Approach, 63 Geo. Wash. L. Rev. 76, 78 n.6 (1994) (asserting that comment *k* is "the most frequently debated comment to 402A").

[53] See D. Owen, Products Liability in a Nutshell §§ 6.2 and 10.4, and ch. 18 (10th ed. 2023).

[54] This is the theme of three companion comments to § 402A, comments *i*, *j*, and *k*, which are examined in § 6.2, above. In full, comment *k* provides:

> *k. Unavoidably unsafe products.* There are some products which, in the present state of human knowledge, are quite incapable of being made safe for their intended and ordinary use. These are especially common in the field of drugs. An outstanding example is the vaccine for the Pasteur treatment of rabies, which not uncommonly leads to very serious and damaging consequences when it is injected. Since the disease itself invariably leads to a dreadful death, both the marketing and the use of the vaccine are fully justified, notwithstanding the unavoidable high degree of risk which they involve. Such a product, properly prepared, and accompanied by proper directions and warning, is not defective, nor is it *unreasonably* dangerous. The same is true of many other drugs, vaccines, and the like, many of which for this very reason cannot legally be sold except to physicians, or under the prescription of a physician. It is also true in particular of many new or experimental drugs as to which, because of lack of time and opportunity for sufficient medical experience, there can be no assurance of safety, or perhaps even of purity of ingredients, but such experience as there is justifies the marketing and use of the drug notwithstanding a medically recognizable risk. The seller of such products, again with the qualification that they are properly prepared and marketed, and proper warning is given, where the situation calls for it, is not to be held to strict liability for unfortunate consequences attending their use, merely because he has undertaken to supply the public with an apparently useful and desirable product, attended with a known but apparently reasonable risk.

[55] W. Prosser, Handbook of the Law of Torts § 99, at 661 (4th ed. 1971).

[56] On how drugs are different, see § 18.1 note 31, above.

[57] See, e.g., V. Schwartz, Unavoidably Unsafe Products: Clarifying the Meaning and Policy Behind Comment k, 42 Wash. & Lee L. Rev. 1139 (1985); Page, Generic Product Risks: The Case Against Comment k and for Strict Tort Liability, 58 N.Y.U. L. Rev. 853 (1983); Willig, The Comment k Character: A Conceptual Barrier to Strict Liability, 29 Mercer L. Rev. 545 (1978); Note, 16 Rev. Litig. 413 (1997) (AIDS vaccine; comment *k* and the Third Restatement). See generally Frumer, Friedman, and Sklaren, Products Liability § 8.07[3] (citing cases from 32 states and the District of Columbia applying comment *k*).

A small number of courts have explicitly *rejected* comment *k*. See, e.g., Allison v. Merck & Co., 878 P.2d 948, 954 (Nev. 1994); Collins v. Eli Lilly Co., 342 N.W.2d 37, 52 (Wis. 1984), now effectively superseded by statute. See also Shanks v. Upjohn Co., 835 P.2d 1189 (Alaska 1992) (refusing to adopt comment *k* but agreeing with its basic policy).

properly prepared and carried adequate warnings.[58] And while design hazards in medical devices often can be designed away,[59] some courts have extended comment *k*'s strict liability design defect immunity from prescription drugs to prescription medical devices as well.[60] This makes good sense when a device's risks are inherent in its design and so are unavoidable, but not necessarily so when such risks may reasonably be designed away, as discussed below.

In addition to questioning comment *k*'s very premise, that prescription drug manufacturers should be protected from the rigors of strict liability, courts and commentators disagree on a number of other important aspects of comment *k*, including: (1) whether it should be confined to a limited class of drugs properly characterized as "unavoidably unsafe" on a case-by-case basis, or whether it broadly applies to *all* prescription drugs as a blanket matter; and (2) whether the exemption it affords from strict liability in tort should apply as well to negligence.

On the first question, the New Jersey Supreme Court in 1984 ruled in *Feldman v. Lederle Laboratories*[61] that only certain drugs qualify for comment *k*'s exemption from design defect liability—those proven on a case-by-case basis to be highly useful and unavoidably unsafe.[62] The year after *Feldman*, a California intermediate appellate court

---

[58] This important proviso, which leaves room for claims of defects in manufacture, warning, and instruction, is from comment *k* itself.

[59] See note 71, below.

[60] See, e.g., Bostic v. Ethicon Inc., 2022 WL 952129, at *9 (E.D. Pa. 2022) (pelvic mesh); Gunter v. Bos. Sci. Corp., 2021 WL 1921891, at *4 (Del. Super. Ct. 2021) (same); In re Wright Med. Tech. Inc., Conserve Hip Implant Prods. Liab. Litig., 178 F. Supp. 3d 1321, 1349 (N.D. Ga. 2016) (Utah law); Payne v. Paugh, 360 P.3d 39, 50 (Wash. Ct. App. 2015) (cmt. *k* "establishes an exception to strict liability for 'unavoidably unsafe products' such as prescription drugs and medical devices"); Prather v. Abbott Labs., 960 F. Supp. 2d 700, 707 (W.D. Ky. 2013) (no meaningful difference between a prescription pain control infusion pump and a prescription drug); Tucker v. Wright Med. Tech., Inc., 2013 WL 1149717, 6 (N.D. Cal. 2013) (hip implant; blanket immunity of medical devices from strict liability); Creazzo v. Medtronic, Inc., 903 A.2d 24, 31 (Pa. Super. Ct. 2006) (finding "no reason why the same rational[e] applicable to prescription drugs may not be applied to medical devices," court applied comment *k* to implanted electrical pulse generator for relieving chronic pain); Transue v. Aesthetech Corp., 341 F.3d 911 (9th Cir. 2003) (Wash. law) (all medical devices, including breast implants, receive blanket exemption from strict liability for design defects under comment *k*); Tansy v. Dacomed Corp., 890 P.2d 881 (Okla. 1994) (penile implant); Terhune v. A.H. Robins Co., 577 P.2d 975 (Wash. 1978) (Dalkon Shield IUD).

Some courts, however, do not grant blanket immunity to all medical devices under comment *k*. See, e.g., Nolen v. C.R. Bard Inc., 533 F. Supp. 3d 584, 592 (M.D. Tenn. 2021) (" 'Jurisdictions are split on whether' medical devices automatically qualify as unavoidably unsafe for the purposes of Comment k, 'with the majority of courts favoring [a] case-by-case methodology' that looks at the details of the particular device."); Burningham v. Wright Med. Tech., Inc., 448 P.3d 1283, 1292–93 (Utah 2019) (a defendant may raise cmt. *k* as an affirmative defense on a case-by-case basis where a medical device was marketed under the FDA's "substantially equivalent" approval process; devices marketed through the premarket approval process are exempt from design defect claims under federal preemption); Williamson v. Stryker Corp., 2013 WL 3833081 (S.D.N.Y. 2013) (not all medical devices, if any, are subject to immunity from design defect claims under comment *k*); Wollam v. Wright Med. Grp., Inc., 2012 WL 4510695, at *5 (D. Colo. 2012) (hip system; no blanket immunity, and manufacturer failed to establish elements of comment *k* defense); Creech v. Stryker Corp., 2012 WL 33360, at *5 n.6 (D. Utah 2012) (pain pump; in Utah, comment *k* applies only to prescription drugs, not medical devices).

[61] 479 A.2d 374, 382–83 (N.J. 1984).

[62] "Comment *k* immunizes from strict liability the manufacturers of some products, including certain drugs, that are unavoidably unsafe. However, we see no reason to hold as a matter of law and policy that all prescription drugs that are unsafe are unavoidably so. Drugs, like any other products, may contain defects that could have been avoided by better manufacturing or design. Whether a drug is unavoidably unsafe should be decided on a case-by-case basis; we perceive no justification [in policy or under comment *k* for immunizing prescription drug manufacturers from their safe manufacturing, warning, and risk-utility design obligations under strict liability in tort.]" Id. at 383.

decided *Kearl v. Lederle Laboratories*,[63] in which it adopted and elaborated upon the *Feldman* approach, prescribing a detailed "mini-trial" necessary for a judge to decide whether a drug qualifies for exemption from strict liability under comment *k*.[64]

Soon thereafter, however, the California Supreme Court rejected the *Feldman-Kearl* approach in *Brown v. Superior Court*,[65] interpreting comment *k* as embracing *all* prescription drugs within its unavoidably-unsafe safe harbor. The *Brown* court reasoned that forcing drug manufacturers to litigate whether the design of their drugs deserves an exemption from strict liability in every case would emasculate comment *k*'s objective of shielding prescription drug manufacturers *ex ante* from the risks of design defect litigation *ex post* in order to reduce the perils of over-deterrence, including higher drug prices and fewer drugs. A number of courts have followed *Brown*'s general exemption of all prescription drugs from design defect liability,[66] while others, probably a fairly large majority, take the *Feldman-Kearl* case-by-case approach, reluctant to surrender judicial oversight of a drug manufacturer's responsibility for design safety.[67]

Many good reasons support *Brown*'s blanket exemption of prescription drugs from strict liability design defect claims as quite surely the better rule: the unavoidable nature of most drug designs, whose chemical formulations innately include detrimental (as well as therapeutic) properties on which warnings normally can and should be provided; the substantial FDA oversight of prescription drugs; the sufficiency of negligence claims to

---

[63] 218 Cal. Rptr. 453 (Ct. App. 1985).

[64] In this phase of a trial without a jury, the judge would determine: "(1) whether, when distributed, the product was intended to confer an exceptionally important benefit that made its availability highly desirable; (2) whether the then-existing risk posed by the product both was 'substantial' and 'unavoidable'; and (3) whether the interest in availability (again measured as of the time of distribution) outweighs the interest in promoting enhanced accountability through strict liability design defect review." Id. at 464. See also Freeman v. Hoffman-La Roche, Inc., 618 N.W.2d 827, 840–41 (Neb. 2000) (exemption applies if: (1) product is properly manufactured and adequate warnings are provided; (2) its benefits exceed its risks; and (3) it was incapable of being made safer).

[65] 751 P.2d 470 (Cal. 1988).

[66] See, e.g., Moncibaiz v. Pfizer Inc., 532 F. Supp. 3d 452, 460 (S.D. Tex. 2021) ("Texas expressly applies comment k in the prescription-drug context."); Burningham v. Wright Med. Tech., Inc., 448 P.3d 1283, 1287, 1290 (Utah 2019) (cmt. *k* "immunize[s] all prescription drugs from strict liability design defect claims," but does not extend that immunity to all medical devices); Bergstresser v. Bristol-Myers Squibb Co., 2013 WL 1760525 (M.D. Pa. 2013) (thorough discussion of application of comment *k* in Pennsylvania); Young for Young v. Key Pharms., Inc., 922 P.2d 59, 62–65 (Wash. 1996) (drug for child's asthma caused severe brain damage); Martin v. Hacker, 628 N.E.2d 1308, 1311 (N.Y. 1993); Terhune v. A. H. Robins Co., 577 P.2d 975 (Wash. 1978) (Dalkon Shield IUD). See also Gensler v. Sanolfi-Aventis, 2009 WL 857991, at *6 (E.D.N.Y. 2009) (begrudgingly acknowledging *Martin*).

[67] See, e.g., In re Testosterone Replacement Therapy Prods. Liab. Litig. Coordinated Pretrial Proc., 2020 WL 6487327, at *3 (N.D. Ill. 2020) (Fla. law) ("Florida courts have rejected a 'blanket approach' that applies comment k to all prescription drugs and instead have held 'that comment k is an affirmative defense to a strict liability claim.' "); Prather v. Abbott Labs., 960 F. Supp. 2d 700, 707 (W.D. Ky. 2013); Moss v. Wyeth Inc., 872 F. Supp. 2d 162, 167 (D. Conn. 2012) ("[C]ourts are split on whether comment k applies categorically to all prescription drugs or whether comment k should only be applied as an affirmative defense on a case-by-case basis. The majority of courts take the latter approach, holding that comment k does not provide all prescription drugs with blanket immunity from strict liability design defect claims. These courts apply comment k on a case-specific basis and as an affirmative defense to be proven by the defendant."); Glassman v. Wyeth Labs., Inc., 606 N.E.2d 338, 342 (Ill. App. Ct. 1992) ("not all prescription drugs *per se* fall under comment k, and comment k's applicability must be decided on a case by case basis"); White v. Wyeth Labs., Inc., 533 N.E.2d 748 (Ohio 1988); Castrignano v. E.R. Squibb & Sons, Inc., 546 A.2d 775, 781 (R.I. 1988); Toner v. Lederle Labs., 732 P.2d 297 (Idaho 1987). Compare Hanrahan v. Wyeth, Inc., 2012 WL 2395881 (E.D. Mo. 2012) (breast cancer from estrogen replacement drugs; refusing defendant's comment *k* motion for summary judgment because defendant offered only conclusory assertions that drug was highly beneficial and its risks unavoidable).

provide judicial oversight of drug manufacturers;[68] the perverse effects on drug costs and prices (and, sometimes, drug availability) of repetitive litigation; and the commensurate advantages of a clear common law rule. Ironically, New Jersey (in *Feldman*) was correct in effectively returning warnings law to negligence, where negligence claims *always* are decided on a case-by-case basis, yet California (in *Brown*) was right in providing manufacturers of prescription drugs with a blanket exemption from strict liability in *all* design defect claims in pharmaceutical drugs. In short, the so-called majority view, rejecting blanket immunity for pharmaceutical drugs in favor of case-by-case analysis, is bad policy and simply wrong.[69]

Prescription medical devices, however, are another kettle of fish. A court may reasonably decide *not* to extend blanket immunity from strict liability to such devices under comment *k* because there may be any number of alternative designs for these devices—which are durable products in contrast to chemically formulated drugs—that do not diminish their effectiveness.[70] And now that cost-benefit analysis (in both negligence and "strict" liability) has become widely recognized as the proper basis for most design defect determinations, as discussed in previous chapters, case-by-case application of ordinary cost-benefit principles (whether in negligence or "strict" liability) to medical device cases should provide an effective and appropriate remedy for design mistakes in such products.[71] Thus, while it should not matter much if courts accord prescription medical devices a blanket exemption from strict liability, the simplest approach may be to do so, leaving negligence in such cases as the principal remedy.[72]

Another aspect of comment *k* engendering some debate is whether comment *k*, assuming (as almost all courts do) that it exempts manufacturers of at least some drugs

---

[68] See *Brown*, 751 P.2d at 483 n.12 (noting oversight of drug manufacturers by the "general principles of negligence").

[69] In Pennsylvania, the law on this point is unclear, and the federal district courts have split. To resolve the uncertainty, the Third Circuit certified the following question to the Pennsylvania Supreme Court: "are prescription implantable medical devices categorically subject to strict liability, categorically immune from strict liability, or immune from strict liability on a case-by-case basis? If they are immune on a case-by-case basis, what test should a court apply to determine whether a particular device is immune?" Ebert v. C.R. Bard, Inc., 2021 WL 2656690, at *6 (3d Cir. 2021), certified question accepted, 260 A.3d 81 (Pa. 2021). Subsequently, the case was closed without further opinion.

[70] See, e.g., Heath v. C.R. Bard Inc., 2021 WL 3172315, at *9 (M.D. Tenn. 2021) (IVC filter; "a case-by-case approach is appropriate, to determine not only whether the relevant broad product category is unavoidably unsafe, but also whether the risks of the particular product at issue were unavoidable or whether, instead, the product suffers from an additional, avoidable level of risk"); Baccaro v. Coloplast Corp., 2021 WL 3089202, at *15–16 (N.D.N.Y. 2021) (vaginal mesh; "[T]here is no clear test to determine whether the unavoidably unsafe [cmt. *k*] defense should apply in a particular [medical device] case. . . . The purpose of the unavoidably unsafe product doctrine of ensuring that manufacturers are not disincentivized from producing life-saving goods due to their inherent risks is just too poor a fit for these facts."); Burningham v. Wright Med. Tech., Inc., 448 P.3d 1283, 1290 (Utah 2019) (although some implanted medical devices have unavoidable risks, this will not always be the case as a matter of law; thus courts should treat the unavoidable risk exception to strict liability as "an affirmative defense to be determined by the factfinder on a case-by-case basis"; answering certified question).

[71] See, e.g., Baccaro v. Coloplast Corp., 2021 WL 3089202, at *13, 17 (N.D.N.Y. 2021) ("The ultimate inquiry for a design defect claim is whether, 'if the design defect were known at the time of manufacture, a reasonable person would conclude that the utility of the product did not outweigh the risk inherent' in marketing it."; plaintiffs' expert offered evidence "that every design flaw Altis possesses is cured by an alternative product, which makes this alternative design safer[, and the alternative] product is also available on the market, demonstrating that it is both economically and technically feasible"). While this case applied New York's archaic strict liability rule, the expert's risk-benefit analysis is standard negligence theory.

[72] Note that the Third Restatement presents a very narrow version of cost-benefit analysis, one that makes good sense, as discussed below. Whether courts will see fit to apply this curious (if logical) standard is another question.

from strict liability in tort, should exempt them also from liability in *negligence* for defects in design.[73] The language of comment *k*, of course, should not be parsed as if it were a statute,[74] but it should be noted that comment *k* does not address the question of a drug manufacturer's liability in *negligence* for defects in design. After all, this provision is a comment to § 402A, which addresses a seller's *strict* liability in tort—not negligence, which is a different topic the *Restatement* separately addresses in another section.[75] Apart from this quite obvious fact, the debate may be resolved quite simply:[76] if the design of a drug is not defective for purposes of strict liability in tort, it cannot be negligent to sell it in that nondefective condition.[77] While this kind of doctrinal, set-theory reasoning normally is sound, it falters somewhat here. Comment *k* exempts *all* prescription drugs from strict liability in tort, not because they all are truly nondefective, but because (1) *most* drugs indeed are not defective (due to market competition and oversight by the FDA) and, (2) a protective umbrella shielding all prescription drugs (including the defective ones) from strict liability avoids discouraging manufacturers from developing important new drugs (most of which *will* be nondefective) and from setting high drug prices. Thus, some prescription drugs surely are "defective" in design, in some way or another, notwithstanding the comment *k* exemption, and the manufacturers of some of those defective drugs may well have been negligent in their development and sale.

Even if strict liability were allowed for design defects in prescription drugs, its usefulness to consumers appears quite limited. Because the doctor is the "consumer" in prescription drug cases under the learned intermediary rule,[78] the consumer expectations test provides no relief to patients suffering foreseeable drug injuries if the manufacturer adequately warns doctors of the risk that such injuries might result. And

---

[73] Perhaps most courts hold that negligence liability applies to the design of drugs. See, e.g., Atkinson v. Luitpold Pharms., Inc., 2020 WL 4518022, at *6 (E.D. Pa. 2020) (Tex. law) ("Comment k makes no mention of negligence. Thus, the 'immunity provided by Comment k' to pharmaceutical manufacturers does not apply to design defect claims based in negligence."); In re Testosterone Replacement Therapy Prods. Liab. Litig. Coordinated Pretrial Proc., 2020 WL 6487327, at *9 (N.D. Ill. 2020) ("For design defect cases . . . the Minnesota Supreme Court has adopted a 'negligence-like "reasonable care" standard' that 'implicitly acknowledges' the policy considerations reflected in comment k"); Crockett v. Luitpold Pharms., Inc., 2020 WL 433367, at *10 (E.D. Pa. 2020) (considering *Lance v. Wyeth*, below, in the context of an FDA pre-approved drug and finding plaintiff's negligent design defect claims were cognizable); Mahnke v. Bayer Corp., 2019 WL 8621437, at *5 (C.D. Cal. 2019) ("Under California law, a drug manufacturer may be held liable for an alleged design defect only when the plaintiff establishes that the manufacturer was negligent in designing the drug."; negligent design defect claim failed under impossibility preemption); Lance v. Wyeth, 4 A.3d 160, 165–66 (Pa. Super. Ct. 2010); Toner v. Lederle Labs., 732 P.2d 297, 310 (Idaho 1987); Johnson v. American Cyanamid Co., 718 P.2d 1318, 1324–25 (Kan. 1986). This means that all such cases are tried on a case-by-case basis.

[74] Except, perhaps, in Oregon and South Carolina, both of which adopted the comments to § 402A by statute. See § 5.3, above.

[75] The Second Restatement addresses negligent design in § 395, which makes no reference to liability for the sale of dangerous drugs.

[76] Dean Prosser appears to have believed that the answer to whether negligence claims should lie against drug manufacturers for selling drugs that are harmful as well as beneficial usually is simple: they should not. "Where only negligence liability is in question, the answer as to such products [inherently hazardous drugs] is usually a simple one. The utility and social value of the thing sold normally outweighs the known, and all the more so the unknown risk, and there is no negligence in selling it, provided always that proper warning and directions are given." W. Prosser, Handbook of the Law of Torts § 99, at 661 (4th ed. 1971). It is possible, however, that Dean Prosser only meant that because drugs normally are not defectively designed, it normally is not negligent for a manufacturer to sell them; not that, because drugs normally are not defective, courts should not inquire into whether a particular drug was defective, and, if so, whether its manufacturer was negligent in marketing it in that condition.

[77] See §§ 2.1 and 5.9, above.

[78] See § 18.3, below.

if the drug contains foreseeable dangers that doctors do not expect, failure-to-warn claims protect persons injured by such drugs. Finally, because almost every jurisdiction now shields manufacturers from liability for dangers that are unforeseeable under the prevailing state of the art,[79] a patient injured by an unforeseeable drug risk in most jurisdictions has no claim on any theory of recovery.

Under a risk-utility test, whether it be called "negligence," "strict liability," or simply "design defectiveness,"[80] a manufacturer is subject to liability for failing to adopt an alternative design feature that would have prevented the plaintiff's harm if the safety benefits of the design feature were greater than its costs.[81] But this suggests that a drug can be re-engineered to eliminate a particular design danger without sacrificing its therapeutic benefits, which normally is untrue since the hazards in most drugs, as mentioned earlier, are inherent and unavoidable. This leaves only one narrow version of risk-benefit analysis available for properly assessing the defectiveness of a drug's design, the approach adopted by the *Third Restatement*.

The Third Restatement

In 1998, the American Law Institute promulgated a liability standard for defective drug designs that is unusual, to say the least.[82] Section 6(c) of the *Products Liability Restatement* provides:

> (c) A prescription drug or medical device is not reasonably safe due to defective design if the foreseeable risks of harm posed by the drug or medical device are sufficiently great in relation to its foreseeable therapeutic benefits that reasonable health-care providers, knowing of such foreseeable risks and therapeutic benefits, would not prescribe the drug or medical device for any class of patients.

The most important thing to note about this novel liability standard is that it leaves a very small window for design defect claims for prescription drugs, a window so tiny that almost no drug claim could fit through it. Even thalidomide would not be captured by the *Third Restatement* design defect test because of its value in treating leprosy. But thalidomide may prove the virtue of this test, rather than its folly, for lepers should not be deprived of beneficial drug therapy because some doctors improperly prescribe the drug for child-bearing women. In such a case, the defect, it seems, would lie in the doctor rather than the drug. While not minimizing the tragedy of a child born deformed to a woman who was prescribed the drug improperly, perhaps tort (and possibly criminal) remedies against the prescribing doctor would be a better way to address the problem, rather than forcing the manufacturer and lepers to suffer from an untoward misuse of a pharmaceutical that is highly beneficial to this one (especially needy) class of patients.

In a world in which the medico-legal scheme described earlier were to operate with perfection—where manufacturers carefully engage in good-faith drug-safety investigations, where a fully-funded and politically neutral FDA keeps drugs with

---

[79] On the state of the art, see § 10.4, above.

[80] See §§ 2.2 (negligence), 5.7 (strict liability in tort), and 8.4 (design defect), above.

[81] See, e.g., R.S.B. v. Merck & Co., 2021 WL 1842280, at *2–3 (E.D. Wis. 2021) (denying dismissal of plaintiffs' strict liability design defect claims; proposed alternative designs included a version "similar to an inhaled corticosteroid" and tablets or granules at lower doses). See also §§ 8.4, 8.5, and 8.8, above.

[82] For scholarly commentary on the Third Restatement's approach to prescription drug and medical device liability, see § 18.1, note 1, above.

foreseeable excess dangers from being sold, and where doctors perfectly match individual drugs to individual patients—the § 6(c) formulation of design defectiveness for drugs would appear ideal. The problem, of course, is that the models of an ideal FDA and of ideal prescribing doctors are quite unrealistic.[83] But the solution to imperfections in the medico-legal framework is not to allow juries to engage in risk-utility comparisons of different drugs used to treat the same condition.

For example, assume that three drugs, *A*, *B*, and *C*, each are used to fight lung infections, and that drug *A* causes drowsiness in some persons, drug *B* causes birth defects when given to some women, and drug *C* causes acne in some teenage boys. A doctor presumably would prescribe drug *B* or possibly *C* to an adult male truck driver, drug *A* or *B* to a teenage boy, and drug *A* or *C* to a woman capable of bearing children. Surely products liability law should not force substantial economic costs on manufacturers of any of these drugs because a prescribing doctor matches one drug to the wrong patient. Nor should these manufacturers have to litigate such "design defect" cases of misprescription, over and over again in courtrooms around the nation—assuming, of course, that they fully and properly performed their investigation and reporting duties to the FDA, and that they provide adequate warnings to doctors. Nor should consumers be deprived of one or two of these drugs because the litigation costs (including occasional lost verdicts) prove too much for the manufacturers of the drugs, particularly when juries begin to classify one drug of the three as causing the least net harm to all these patient groups, considered as a whole.

This latter example reveals the virtue of § 6(c), and the perils of using a global, macro-balance approach to risk-utility analysis.[84] Notwithstanding the frailties of doctors and the FDA, a drug's design should not be characterized as defective on the ground that its total harm to all users exceeds its total benefits to all users, assuming that the drug provides net benefits to any class of patients, and assuming further that the drug's dangers are adequately warned about, and that any excessive harm it may cause results from its improper use by doctors.[85] Applying such a global macro-balance test to declare drug designs defective in such cases would be both "unfair and inefficient," in the words of the *Restatement* Reporters, because it "would require courts to deny classes of patients access to a particular drug that provides them unique benefits in order to protect other patients from the risks of misprescription by negligent physicians."[86]

---

[83] See § 18.1 note 29, above.

[84] For a discussion of "macro-" and "micro-balancing," see §§ 8.4 and 8.5, above.

[85] This assumes that a manufacturer's sales reps do not promote the drug for such improper use, in which case the manufacturer should be subject to liability. On the prevalence of off-label use, see Beck, Off-Label Use In The Twenty-First Century: Most Myths And Misconceptions Mitigated, 54 UIC J. Marshall L. Rev. 1 (2021); Ausness, "There's Danger Here, Cherie!": Liability for the Promotion and Marketing of Drugs and Medical Devices for Off-Label Users, 73 Brook. L. Rev. 1253 (2008); Noah, Constraints on the Off-Label Uses of Prescription Drug Products, 16 J. Prod. & Toxic Liab. 139 (1994).

[86] See Henderson and Twerski, Drug Designs Are Different, 111 Yale L.J. 151, 180–81 (2001); Henderson, Prescription Drug Design Liability Under the Proposed Restatement (Third) of Torts: A Reporter's Perspective, 48 Rutgers L. Rev. 471 (1996). For agreement that § 6(c) basically is sound, if in need of some adjustment, see, e.g., Owen, Dangers in Prescription Drugs: Filling a Private Law Gap in the Healthcare Debate, 42 Conn. L. Rev. 733, 747–50 (2010); Bernstein, Enhancing Drug Effectiveness and Efficacy Through Personal Injury Litigation, 15 J.L. & Pol'y 1051, 1088–94 (2007) (suggesting how courts may "modify the radicalism of § 6(c)"); Green, Prescription Drugs, Alternative Designs, and the Restatement (Third): Preliminary Reflections, 30 Seton Hall L. Rev. 207 (1999); Dreier, Manufacturers' Liability for Drugs and Medical Devices Under the Restatement (Third) of Torts: Products Liability, 30 Seton Hall L. Rev. 258 (1999).

Because of the fundamental logic of so recognizing the interests of various minorities of patients, a number of courts have seen the wisdom of applying this provision.[87]

Pointing to the weaknesses in the FDA and health care delivery systems, the natural profit motivations of drug manufacturers to scrimp on research and design,[88] a patent system that artificially protects manufacturers from competition, and the industry's temptation to over-promote its products, some commentators[89] and some courts[90] object to the *Third Restatement*'s narrow definition of design defectiveness for drugs. The argument for rejecting § 6(c) is the belief that drug designs should be subject to judicial challenge on some basis or another—either by means of a normal risk-utility test (on proof of a safer alternative design) or a macro-balance test (on proof that a drug causes patients as a whole more harm than good). Yet neither approach works well in most drug cases, as previously discussed. The first test simply does not work—most drugs cannot be redesigned because their hazards are inherent. As for the second test, it is true that any product that causes more harm than good is truly bad ("defective") from a utilitarian point of view. And, if there were an effective way to identify such products, their manufacturers might fairly be required to pay for all the harm they cause, and the products normally should be banned.[91] Yet, as discussed above, particular classes of patients (like lepers) deserve therapy from drugs, even if doctors sometimes do misuse those drugs on other classes of patients. Moreover, there is a devil residing in the

---

[87] See, e.g., Drescher v. Bracco Diagnostics Inc., 2020 WL 1466296, at *6 (D. Ariz. 2020) (§ 6(c) applied to "foreseeable risks of harm"); D'Agnese v. Novartis Pharms. Corp., 952 F. Supp. 2d 880, 889 n.7 (D. Ariz. 2013); Madsen v. American Home Prods. Corp., 477 F. Supp. 2d 1025, 1037 (E.D. Mo. 2007) (Iowa law) (diet drugs; defendant's expert testified that "risks of obesity for some patients are greater than the risks of those medications"); Gebhardt v. Mentor Corp., 191 F.R.D. 180, 185 (D. Ariz. 1999) (plaintiff failed to prove that a reasonable health-care provider would not have prescribed Angelchik for any class of patients), aff'd, 15 Fed. Appx. 540 (9th Cir. 2001); Sita v. Danek Med., Inc., 43 F. Supp. 2d 245, 256 (E.D.N.Y. 1999) (applying § 6(c) at plaintiff's request, and dismissing design defect claim thereunder). See also Ebert v. C.R. Bard, Inc., 2021 WL 2656690, at *2–3, 6 (3d Cir. 2021) (discussing § 6(c) and asking the Pennsylvania Supreme Court to determine whether "a plaintiff bringing a negligent design claim against a prescription medical device manufacturer [must] prove that the device was too harmful to be used by anyone, or may the plaintiff also prevail on other theories of liability where appropriate?"), certified question accepted, 260 A.3d 81 (Pa. 2021). The case was later closed without further opinion.

[88] See, e.g., Note, 82 Cornell L. Rev. 644, 692 (1997) ("in light of the enormous amounts of money at stake in the global pharmaceutical industry, manufacturers are inevitably tempted to market products that are clearly less effective and more dangerous than others").

[89] See, e.g., Cupp, Preemption's Rise (and Bit of a Fall) as Product Liability Reform: *Wyeth*, *Riegel*, *Altria*, and the *Restatement (Third)*'s Prescription Product Design Defect Standard, 74 Brook. L. Rev. 727 (2009); Conk, The True Test: Alternative Safer Designs for Drugs and Medical Devices in a Patent-Constrained Market, 49 UCLA L. Rev. 737 (2002); Conk, Is There a Design Defect in the *Restatement (Third) of Torts: Products Liability*?, 109 Yale L.J. 1087 (2000); Cupp, The Continuing Search for Proper Perspective: Whose Reasonableness Should Be at Issue in a Prescription Product Design Defect Analysis?, 30 Seton Hall L. Rev. 233 (1999); T. Schwartz, Regulatory Standards and Products Liability: Striking the Right Balance Between the Two, 30 U. Mich. J.L. Reform 431, 459 (1997); Vandall, Constructing a Roof Before the Foundation Is Prepared: The *Restatement (Third) of Torts: Products Liability* Section 2(b) Design Defect, 30 U. Mich. J.L. Reform 261, 270 (1997); Phillips, The Unreasonably Unsafe Product and Strict Liability, 72 Chi.-Kent L. Rev. 129, 130 (1996); Cupp, Rethinking Conscious Design Liability for Prescription Drugs: The *Restatement (Third)* Standard Versus a Negligence Approach, 63 Geo. Wash. L. Rev. 76 (1994); Schwartz, Prescription Products and the Proposed Restatement (Third), 61 Tenn. L. Rev. 1357, 1378–85 (1994).

[90] See, e.g., Noorchashm v. Muto, 2021 WL 3612425, at *4 n.5 (Mass. Super. 2021) ("Massachusetts courts have not adopted § 6(c)"); Mele v. Howmedica, Inc., 808 N.E.2d 1026, 1039 (Ill. App. Ct. 2004) ("Adoption of section 6(c) would change basic principles applicable to product liability suits. Such a fundamental shift should come from the legislature and not this court."); Bryant v. Hoffmann-La Roche, Inc., 585 S.E.2d 723, 727, 731 (Ga. Ct. App. 2003); Freeman v. Hoffman-La Roche, Inc., 618 N.W.2d 827, 840 (Neb. 2000) (refusing to adopt § 6(c), which it viewed "as too strict of a rule, under which recovery would be nearly impossible"). See also McBroom v. Ethicon, Inc., 2022 WL 675813, at *4 (D. Ariz. 2022) (refusing to adopt § 6(c); medical device).

[91] See § 10.3, above.

process of distinguishing which drugs, on balance, have net value from those that produce net harm—the threat of repeated litigation over the ultimate social value of any type of drug that causes someone harm, because it did not suit that patient.

So the *Third Restatement*'s test for defective drug designs, though very narrow, and arguably incomplete in failing to identify certain exceptions,[92] seems basically correct, at least when applied to prescription drugs. That is, by putting most drugs beyond the reach of design defect litigation (under any liability theory), the *Third Restatement* properly pours most litigation concerning hazardous drugs into the defectiveness *vel non* of their warnings and instructions.[93] However, § 6(c)'s unusual and narrow formulation applies awkwardly in medical device cases, for reasons earlier expressed, where, normally, the ordinary risk-utility principles of § 2(b) more naturally and comfortably apply.[94]

Resolving the Dilemma: Empowering Warning Claims

For the various reasons discussed above, design defectiveness has never been a favored theory of recovery for drug injuries. While strict liability in tort generally got off the ground in the 1960s, and while design defect claims for most types of products became prevalent in the 1970s, courts did not even begin imposing design defect liability on drug manufacturers until the 1980s and 1990s.[95] And even to the present, most courts have been chary in allowing such claims, properly directing drug litigation away from design defect claims to warning claims. While many courts do allow broad risk-utility challenges to a drug's design, as discussed above, this approach appears mistaken because of the availability of a far preferable basis of recovery in most cases for injuries from harmful drugs.

Most prescription drug litigation properly is based on the adequacy of warnings and instructions provided to the doctor about the drug,[96] because the best place to locate a drug manufacturer's responsibility is in the information it provides to doctors and other health care professionals—information that must be clear, complete, and properly conveyed.[97] And in the great majority of deserving cases, a challenge to a drug's design can easily be reformulated as a defect in a warning or instruction, that is, the manufacturer's failure to warn of some material danger in the drug. If a drug's adverse effects are not reasonably foreseeable, of course, the manufacturer should not be responsible for its untoward effects for reasons examined elsewhere.[98] But if the problem in fact is reasonably discoverable by a manufacturer properly performing its research and development obligations, then it will have a duty to provide adequate warnings to

---

[92] For discussions of some exceptions, see Green, Prescription Drugs, Alternative Designs, Products Liability, 30 Seton Hall L. Rev. 258 (1999).

[93] While § 6(c) might seemingly be improved by including a proviso that allows claims for a manufacturer's failure to meet its research and reporting responsibilities to the FDA, a robust warning approach appears a better way for products liability law to perform its oversight of those responsibilities.

[94] See notes 70–71, above.

[95] Brochu v. Ortho Pharm. Corp., 642 F.2d 652 (1st Cir. 1981) (N.H. law), is widely thought to be the first prescription drug case in which a defective drug design claim figured prominently. A small number of earlier cases also involved challenges to drug designs. See, e.g., Tinnerholm v. Parke Davis & Co., 285 F. Supp. 432 (S.D.N.Y. 1968), aff'd as modified, 411 F.2d 48 (2d Cir. 1969); Stromsodt v. Parke-Davis & Co., 257 F. Supp. 991 (D.N.D. 1966), aff'd, 411 F.2d 1390 (8th Cir. 1969). For the most part, however, drug design defect cases did not even get off the ground until the 1980s.

[96] See § 18.3, below.

[97] See id.

[98] See § 10.4, above.

the FDA and doctors of those effects. And if a doctor fails to provide this information to his or her patients (fails to give them a basis for informed consent to drug therapy), then a medical malpractice claim would seem the proper remedy—not a claim against the manufacturer for a supposed defect in the drug's design. As a final backstop to physician failures of this sort, courts might consider abandoning the learned intermediary doctrine and requiring that information about all prescription hazards be provided not only to physicians but also directly to the patients who will take the drugs.[99]

Prescription drugs, it may be said again, are a special type of "product." Because their safety is subjected to close technical review by the FDA, and because of the problem of over-deterrence of regular judicial oversight, drug designs should remain exempt from scrutiny in courtrooms in all but special situations.[100] But as a counterweight to relieving manufacturers from judicial scrutiny of their drug designs, courts should insist that judicial review of drug warnings and instructions be robust. As one prominent tort scholar concludes, litigation over injuries from prescription drugs lies properly in the sufficiency of their warnings and instructions, not in the sufficiency of their designs.[101]

§ 18.3 WARNINGS

Warning issues in cases involving prescription drugs and medical devices in many ways parallel warning issues involving other types of products. Yet, as seen in connection with design defects,[102] prescription drugs and medical devices raise a variety of special issues for products liability law. While design defectiveness is the most prevalent claim in products liability cases involving most types of products,[103] warning claims properly dominate prescription drug and medical device law and litigation.[104]

Several important warning issues recur in cases involving drugs and medical devices. The first concerns the regulatory backdrop to this area of the law, provided by the FDA, previously discussed. As in every products liability case, another preliminary matter involves the identification of appropriate theories of liability for claims of this type. The principal question in most warning cases, of course, is whether a warning or instruction for the product (here, a drug or medical device) was "adequate." A further recurring issue in drug and device warning cases is whom a manufacturer of such products should warn—the patient or the doctor. A final who-should-be-warned question,[105] quite narrow and quite recent, is whether manufacturers of brand-name products do and should have a duty to warn users of generic drugs. A wealth of information is available on each of these important issues,[106] and each is briefly considered here.

[99] See Gilhooley, When Drugs Are Safe for Some but Not Others: The FDA Experience and Alternatives for Products Liability, 36 Hous. L. Rev. 927 (1999). See also § 18.3, below.

[100] Such as where a manufacturer's failure to comply with requirements for FDA approval, or its misrepresentations, cause the plaintiff's harm; and, possibly, where practicable drug engineering plainly would have foreseeably eliminated a drug's adverse effects while leaving its beneficial effects unchanged.

[101] See M. Green, Prescription Drugs, Alternative Designs, and the Restatement (Third): Preliminary Reflections, 30 Seton Hall L. Rev. 207, 209 (1999).

[102] See § 18.2, above.

[103] See § 1.3, above.

[104] "Failure to warn or instruct is the major basis of liability for manufacturers of prescription drugs and medical devices." Products Liability Rest. § 6 cmt. *d*.

[105] Whether pharmacists should have a duty to warn patients about prescription drug risks at all, and, if so, what the scope of that duty should be, is addressed in § 18.4, below.

[106] See sources cited in § 18.1, above.

Regulation by the FDA

Drug and device warning litigation must be considered against the backdrop of the fairly strict regulation provided by the FDA,[107] which ascertains the safety and efficacy of drugs and certain medical devices before allowing them on the market.[108] As part of this process, the FDA must approve all information a manufacturer plans to provide physicians on a drug's recommended uses (benefits), contraindications, risks, and side effects. Underlying the regulatory scheme are two assumptions reflecting the special types of dangers that inhere in drugs classified as prescription pharmaceuticals. First is the belief that the risks in many drugs are so complex and dangerous that the FDA must determine their safety and effectiveness before they can be marketed at all. The second premise is that the potential risks of many drugs are so substantial as to require professional medical judgment and supervision by doctors and other health care professionals, rendering such products available to consumers only through prescriptions written by such health experts.

The principal federal statute regulating the quality of drugs is the Federal Food, Drug, and Cosmetic Act,[109] originally enacted by Congress in 1938. The Act's key provisions prohibit the sale of "any food, drug, device, or cosmetic that is adulterated or misbranded"[110] and require FDA approval of all new drugs prior to marketing.[111] The Act addresses warnings and instructions through its requirement that drug labels not be "misbranded."[112] Accordingly, manufacturers must provide information on the purpose, proper dosage, and possible dangers to consumers, for over-the-counter (OTC) drugs,[113] and appropriate information to medical professionals, for prescription drugs. A prescription drug is one which, "because of its toxicity or other potentiality for harmful effect, or the method of its use, or the collateral measures necessary to its use," is safe only when prescribed and used under the supervision of a licensed medical practitioner,[114] and such drugs must be labeled accordingly.[115] Labels for over-the-counter drugs must state the drug's active ingredients and "established name"[116] and must contain information on dosages, duration of use, directions for use, and warnings.[117] Advertisements for prescription drugs, including by radio and television,

---

[107] Despite the FDA's regulatory weaknesses, its pre-marketing approval process for prescription drugs is rigorous, time-consuming, and expensive. See § 18.1, text at notes 23–25, above.

[108] "Drugs" over which the FDA has authority are defined in 21 U.S.C. § 321(g)(1) as "articles (other than food) intended to affect the structure or any function of the body." A "device" subject to regulation is defined in § 321(h) as "an instrument, apparatus, implement, machine, contrivance, . . . or other similar or related article [that is] intended to affect the structure or any function of the body."

[109] 21 U.S.C. §§ 301–392.

[110] Id. § 331(a).

[111] Id. § 355(a). This requirement applies to "any new drug," including over-the-counter drugs. See id. § 321(g)(1).

[112] Id. §§ 352 and 353.

[113] Over-the-counter (OTC) drugs are addressed in 21 C.F.R. § 330.10, which details the process for assessing a drug's safety and effectiveness based on a benefit-to-risk ratio. See id. § 330.10(a)(4)(iii). See also 21 C.F.R. 330.10(a)(4)(vi) ("A drug shall be permitted for OTC sale and use by the laity unless, because of its toxicity or other potential for harmful effect or because of the [collateral] measures necessary to its use, it may safely be sold and used only under the supervision of a practitioner licensed by law to administer such drugs.").

[114] 21 U.S.C. § 353(b)(1)(B).

[115] Prescription drugs must provide any special directions for use and cautionary statements contained in the prescription. Id. § 353(b)(2).

[116] Id. § 352(e).

[117] Id. § 352(f).

must provide information on the drug's established name, effectiveness, side effects, and contraindications.[118]

This significant regulatory backdrop by the FDA raises a host of federal preemption issues in drug and device warning cases, just as in the design context—issues that may be critical to the viability of warning defect claims.[119]

Theory of Liability

Settling on a proper theory of liability for inadequate warnings and instructions has been of greater interest in cases involving prescription drugs and medical devices than any other type of product. Courts widely apply all three conventional theories of liability to cases of this type—negligence, breach of the implied warranty of merchantability, and strict liability in tort,[120] and they apply any special liability provisions on drugs in state products liability statutes.[121] As earlier discussed, courts have been drawn to negligence principles in warning cases more than in cases involving other types of defects.[122] This has been especially true where prescription drugs and medical devices are involved. Except for cases of contamination, drugs were largely exempted from strict liability in tort from the very start of modern products liability law in § 402A of the *Restatement (Second) of Torts*,[123] as previously discussed, and many courts have continued to apply negligence principles—and to reject true strict liability principles—in prescription drug and medical device cases over the years.[124]

The reasons for preferring negligence principles to true strict liability in drug warning cases run broad and deep,[125] but they are worth summarizing here. First,

---

118 Id. § 352(n). The FDA Amendments Act of 2007 amended this section to require that television and radio ads state the name of the prescription drug and present its conditions of use, side effects, and contraindications "in a clear, conspicuous, and neutral manner." Id. See also 21 C.F.R. § 202.1. An FDA study of the effects of distractions on consumer perceptions of the risks and benefits of prescription drugs presented in television and radio advertisements revealed that simultaneous audio and textual presentations of risk information improved risk comprehension without reducing benefit comprehension. See FDA Experimental Evaluation of the Impact of Distraction on Consumer Understanding of the Risk and Benefit Information in Direct-to-Consumer Prescription Drug Television Advertisements (2011).

119 See § 18.1, note 27, above. On federal preemption generally, see § 14.5, above.

120 See, e.g., Taupier v. Davol, Inc., 490 F. Supp. 3d 430 (D. Mass. 2020) (implanted mesh hernia patch; breach of express and implied warranties, negligence, and strict liability failure to warn); Casey v. Merck & Co., 722 S.E.2d 842, 844 (Va. 2012) (prescription drug: strict liability, failure to warn, breach of express and implied warranty, negligence); Larkin v. Pfizer, Inc., 153 S.W.3d 758 (Ky. 2004) (prescription drug; negligence, breach of warranty, and "strict liability").

121 See, e.g., Graham v. American Cyanamid Co., 350 F.3d 496 (6th Cir. 2003) (Ohio law) (vaccine; statute defines duty to warn in negligence terms); Perez v. Wyeth Labs. Inc., 734 A.2d 1245 (N.J. 1999) (drug). Compare Marks v. Ohmeda, Inc., 871 So.2d 1148 (La. Ct. App. 2004) (anesthesia machine). The statutes are collected in Owen & Davis on Products Liability Appendix I.

122 See § 9.2, above.

123 See Rest. (2d) of Torts § 402A cmts. *j* and *k*. See generally Madden, The Enduring Paradox of Products Liability Law Relating to Prescription Pharmaceuticals, 21 Pace L. Rev. 313 (2001).

124 See, e.g., Rouviere v. DePuy Orthopaedics, Inc., 2021 WL 4255042, at *12 (S.D.N.Y. 2021) (hip replacement component; "failure to warn [claims] can be 'framed in terms of strict liability or negligence,' but the two causes of action are 'functionally equivalent' "); Lopez v. Ethicon Inc., 2020 WL 5569770, at *3–6 (E.D. Pa. 2020) (pelvic mesh); Feldman v. Lederle Labs., 479 A.2d 374, 386 (N.J. 1984) (prescription drug; in warning cases, negligence and strict liability are "functional equivalents"); Brown v. Superior Ct., 751 P.2d 470 (Cal. 1988) (prescription drug); Vassallo v. Baxter Healthcare Corp., 696 N.E.2d 909 (Mass. 1998) (breast implants). *But see* Carlin v. Superior Ct., 920 P.2d 1347, 1350–51 (Cal. 1996) (while "strict liability is to some extent a hybrid of traditional strict liability and negligence doctrine," because a manufacturer's "strict liability" duty to warn embraces only risks "known to the scientific community at the time" of manufacture, strict liability in tort and warranty nevertheless remain viable claims in drug warning cases).

125 See generally § 6.2 and § 10.3, above.

banning foreseeability from the liability calculus—the principal way in which strict liability distinguished itself from negligence—does violence to basic principles of justice and fair play.[126] Another reason for preferring negligence principles in this context has been the belief that the extra deterrent effect of strict liability is less necessary for products whose warnings must be specifically approved prior to marketing by a federal agency, the FDA,[127] as just discussed. Indeed, as shown by the sudden decrease in childhood vaccines some years back,[128] the fear of truly strict liability[129] may result in too *much* deterrence, discouraging pharmaceutical manufacturers from investing in new prescription drugs and medical devices, already extremely expensive to develop and bring to market,[130] for fear of financial ruin if the new product possesses unexpected problems. For these and other reasons, while many courts in this context continue ostensibly to apply "strict" liability by name to warning cases, the principles that they in fact apply are nothing more than negligence. The *Third Restatement* follows this approach in limiting a manufacturer's warning responsibility in prescription drug and medical device cases to a duty to provide "reasonable instructions or warnings regarding foreseeable risks of harm."[131]

Adequacy of Warnings

Prescription Drugs

At the heart of the duty to warn (and instruct) lies the fundamental issue of the *adequacy* of the danger information conveyed to those who need it. Most of the general principles of adequacy applicable to warnings generally, discussed earlier,[132] apply to prescription drugs as well, adapted to this special context. For warnings and instructions in this context to be adequate, drug manufacturers must convey all material information about known and knowable risks to doctors, with some specificity, comprehensible to the general practitioner as well as to the specialist—or to consumers, comprehensible to them, as special circumstances may infrequently warrant.[133] For a drug warning to be truly "adequate," it must describe the danger; the effects of misuse, including the failure to follow instructions; and the physical aspects of the warning, and broader method of

---

[126] See, e.g., Owen, Figuring Foreseeability, 44 Wake Forest L. Rev. 1277 (2009); Owen, The Moral Foundations of Products Liability Law: Toward First Principles, 68 Notre Dame L. Rev. 427 (1993).

[127] See, e.g., Brown v. Superior Ct., 751 P.2d 470 (Cal. 1988).

[128] See § 18.1 note 40, above.

[129] See V. Schwartz, The Death of "Super Strict Liability": Common Sense Returns to Tort Law, 27 Gonz. L. Rev. 179 (1991). The threat of "super strict" liability may have diminished appreciably since the childhood vaccine scare in the 1980s, but drug manufacturers continue periodically to suffer enormous costs of drug and device consequences that, whether technically foreseeable or not, they certainly did not contemplate. See Owen, Dangers in Prescription Drugs: Filling a Private Law Gap in the Healthcare Debate, 42 Conn. L. Rev. 733, 737 (2010) (reporting costs in 2004 by Wyeth of $3.75 billion to settle the Phen-fen litigation, and in 2007 by Merck of nearly $5 billion to settle the Vioxx litigation).

[130] See § 18.1 note 23, above.

[131] See Products Liability Rest. § 6(d). See generally T. Schwartz, Prescription Products and the Proposed Restatement (Third), 61 Tenn. L. Rev. 1357 (1994).

[132] See § 9.3, above.

[133] See, e.g., In re Accutane Prods. Liab., 2012 WL 3194954, at *5 (M.D. Fla. 2012) (summary judgment for defendant on warning claim; Physician Package Insert, Medication Guide, and patient brochures "plainly and prominently identified" risk of "*permanent damage to the bowels*" with "direct, unequivocal and sufficiently forceful" warnings); Perez v. Wyeth Labs. Inc., 734 A.2d 1245, 1257 (N.J. 1999) (warning must include all material risks, meaning those to which a reasonable patient would attach significance in deciding whether to take the drug); Wagner v. Roche Labs., 671 N.E.2d 252, 256 (Ohio 1996) (drug warnings were inadequate, meaning there was not a reasonable disclosure of "all risks inherent in the use of the drug of which the manufacturer, being held to the standards of an expert in the field, knew or should have known to exist").

conveyance, must be calculated to alert recipients to the danger.[134] Other aspects of a warning's adequacy previously addressed often apply as well to drugs, including whether warnings should be made in foreign languages,[135] and the effect of "overpromotion."[136]

An example of the adequacy issue in a drug case is *Martin v. Hacker*,[137] in which a doctor treated the decedent, Mr. Martin, for hypertension (high blood pressure) with two drugs manufactured by the defendant, including reserpine. Mr. Martin became severely depressed and fatally shot himself in the head, allegedly because of the reserpine. The issue was whether the information provided by the manufacturer to physicians about the drug's risks was adequate as a matter of law. The package insert specified among the drug's CONTRAINDICATIONS, "mental depression (especially with suicidal tendencies)"; and, among its WARNINGS, the package insert stated: "Extreme caution should be exercised in treating patients with a history of mental depression. Discontinue the drug at first sign of despondency, early morning insomnia, loss of appetite, impotence, or self-deprecation. Drug-induced depression may persist for several months after drug withdrawal and may be severe enough to result in suicide."

Carefully applying a full list of adequacy factors, the court concluded that the warning was adequate: it was commensurate with the risk, including possible adverse

---

[134] See, e.g., In re Fluoroquinolone Prods. Liab. Litig., 517 F. Supp. 3d 806, 823 (D. Minn. 2021) (Ill. law) (plaintiff adequately pled that label failed to warn of drug's neuropathy side effects); B.F. v. Abbott Labs., 2016 WL 1258582 (E.D. Mo. 2016) (label on drug for bipolar disorder may have failed adequately to warn doctors of drug's risks of birth defects; that the drug should only be used as a "last line" treatment in women of childbearing potential; and the importance of contraceptive use); Madsen v. American Home Prods. Corp., 477 F. Supp. 2d 1025, 1035 (E.D. Mo. 2007) (drug warnings must effectively alert reasonably prudent practitioners of a danger's scope and seriousness); Thom v. Bristol-Myers Squibb Co., 353 F.3d 848, 853 (10th Cir. 2003) (Wyo. law) (jury question whether manufacturer of Serzone antidepressant adequately warned of seriousness of risk of priapism, a persistent and painful erection of the penis). Compare Myers v. Hoffman-La Roche, Inc., 170 P.3d 254, 262–65 (Ariz. Ct. App. 2007) (refusing to hold Accutane warnings adequate as a matter of law under learned intermediary doctrine on motion to dismiss), with Gerber v. Hoffman-La Roche, Inc., 392 F. Supp. 2d 907, 917–19 (S.D. Tex. 2005) (Accutane label stating that drug is contraindicated for pregnant patients adequately warned of danger of birth defects).

[135] See, e.g., Maciejewski, The Dilemma Over Foreign-Language Labeling of Over-the-Counter Drugs, 15 J. Legal Med. 129 (1994).

[136] As with other types of products, risks in pharmaceuticals and medical devices must not be unduly downplayed, nor safety "overpromoted"; instead, a manufacturer's communications to doctors must present a reasonably balanced portrayal of the effectiveness and dangers of a drug. See Motus v. Pfizer Inc., 196 F. Supp. 2d 984, 998 (C.D. Cal. 2001) ("An overpromotion theory is one way that a plaintiff in a failure-to-warn case can overcome the manufacturer's argument either (1) that it provided adequate warnings or (2) that the doctor's decision to prescribe a drug despite his awareness of its dangers was an intervening cause sufficient to vitiate the manufacturer's liability."), aff'd, 358 F.3d 659 (9th Cir. 2004). Compare Lempa v. Eon Labs, Inc., 2019 WL 1426011, at *4 (N.D. Ill. 2019) (preemption did not bar claim that negligent promotion of amiodarone's off-label use to treat non-life-threatening atrial fibrillation caused patient's death); Stevens v. Parke, Davis & Co., 507 P.2d 653 (Cal. 1973) (overpromotion of Chloromycetin, a broad-spectrum antibiotic, downplaying risk of fatal aplastic anemia), with Spinden v. Johnson & Johnson, 427 A.2d 597 (N.J. Super. Ct. App. Div. 1981) (AMA Journal ads did not amount to overpromotion). See generally Madden, The Enduring Paradox of Products Liability Law Relating to Prescription Pharmaceuticals, 21 Pace L. Rev. 313, 330 (2001) ("An otherwise suitable warning may be vitiated by the conduct of the manufacturer or those acting at [its direction] if they promote the product in such a fashion as to obscure or lessen the cautionary impact of the seller's warnings."); Annot., 94 A.L.R.3d 1080 (1997) (effect of manufacturer's promotional efforts aimed at doctors).

Public nuisance suits arising from the overpromotion of opioids by manufacturers and distributors are discussed in § 10.3 (*Opioids*), above.

At least two states have enacted legislation allowing pharmaceutical manufacturers and their representatives to "engage in truthful promotion" of off-label uses. See Ariz. Rev. Stat. Ann. § 32–1997 (2017); Tenn. Code Ann. § 53–10–113 (2018). The statutes are reproduced in Appendix J10 of Owen & Davis on Products Liability. See also Adams and Crudele, The Eroding Off-Label Drug Use Promotion Prohibition, 12 J. Health & Life Sci. L. 1 (2019).

[137] 628 N.E.2d 1308 (N.Y. 1993).

consequences of use (death from suicide was specifically mentioned); the insert's language was accurate, clear, direct, unequivocal, sufficiently forceful, complete, consistent, devoid of contradiction, and the information was current;[138] and, when read as a whole, the meaning conveyed about the possible consequences of taking the drug was unmistakable. The court thus determined that the warnings were adequate as a matter of law. Yet, in this context as in others, adequacy is usually a matter for the jury.[139]

Medical Devices

Medical devices involve many of the same adequacy issues as warnings.[140] For example, in *Phillips v. Baxter Healthcare Corp.*,[141] the plaintiff underwent breast augmentation surgery in which prostheses filled with silicone gel were implanted in her breasts. Several years later, when her doctor performed a closed capsulotomy, applying force to the breast to break up scar tissue that had formed around the implants, the implants broke. The implants were surgically removed and replaced, and the plaintiff sued the original implant manufacturer on various theories including the failure to provide adequate warnings. The warning accompanying the implants stated:

> The silicone elastomer envelope of these products has a low tear strength and is thin to achieve desired prosthesis softness and mobility. For these reasons, the envelope may be easily cut by a scalpel or rupture by excessive stresses . . . . Care must be exercised during handling to prevent such events.

In addition, the warning specifically provided that the manufacturer could not "guarantee the structural integrity of its implant should the surgeon elect to treat capsule firmness by forceful external stress."[142] The jury found that these warnings were adequate, a finding the court ruled was supported by the evidence.

By contrast, in *Hufft v. Horowitz*,[143] the plaintiff's penile implant malfunctioned, resulting in an almost constant erection with persistent pain and emotional distress, which required the plaintiff to have the implant surgically removed. The implant, which the plaintiff's surgeon viewed to be the "Cadillac of the industry," came with warnings of possible complications, such as malfunction of the pumping mechanism or cylinder, tubing kinks, and leakage of fluids, which might require removal. The court concluded that a jury might find this warning inadequate because it failed to warn that the implant

---

[138] To be adequate, a warning must be *timely*. A long series of cases involving Aralen, a drug used in the treatment of rheumatoid arthritis and eventually linked to irreversible eye damage in some users, established certain principles. To be timely, a warning of side effects must be made promptly upon discovery of the coexistence of the side effect and use of the drug, even though a causal relationship has not been clearly proved. See Basko v. Sterling Drug, Inc., 416 F.2d 417 (2d Cir. 1969) (Mo. law). The warning is required as soon as the side effect is documented even in only a very small percentage of users. See Sterling Drug, Inc. v. Cornish, 370 F.2d 82 (8th Cir. 1966) (Kan. law). Since the drug company is held to have the knowledge of an expert, a warning to be timely must be given as soon as the risks are pointed out in reputable scientific journals. See Schenebeck v. Sterling Drug, Inc., 423 F.2d 919 (8th Cir. 1970) (Ark. law).

[139] See, e.g., Madsen v. American Home Prods. Corp., 477 F. Supp. 2d 1025, 1035 (E.D. Mo. 2007); McNeil v. Wyeth, 462 F.3d 364, 368 (5th Cir. 2006) (Tex. law).

[140] See, e.g., Hix v. Zimmer Biomet Holdings, Inc., 2022 WL 946914, at *6 (D. Nev. 2022) (jury question whether hip replacement warnings were adequate); Cates v. Zeltiq Aesthetics, Inc., 535 F. Supp. 3d 1222, 1229 (M.D. Fla. 2021) (CoolSculpting medical device side effect warnings were adequate as a matter of law); Bravman v. Baxter Healthcare Corp., 984 F.2d 71 (2d Cir. 1993) (N.Y. law) (jury question on whether manufacturer should have warned that heart valve might be noisy).

[141] 1993 WL 524688 (Cal. Ct. App. 1993).

[142] Id. at *1 n.2.

[143] 5 Cal. Rptr. 2d 377 (Ct. App. 1992).

was inappropriate for patients with well-muscled abdomens; that it could cause a continual and painful erection; and that scar tissue might encapsulate its reservoir, preventing it from functioning properly.

Method of Conveyance

There are several standard avenues of communication between drug companies and physicians for transmitting information about drugs, and a manufacturer must select the best methods reasonably available to convey important new information on drug dangers to doctors who need the information. The Physician's Desk Reference (PDR), updated periodically, contains copies of package inserts for many prescription drugs. Other sources of information that are more complete than the PDR are Facts and Comparisons (updated monthly), the United States Pharmacopeial Drug Information (USPDI) for the Health Care Professional (vol. I), and Advice for the Patient—Drug Information in Lay Language (vol. II). Information on warnings and contraindications is readily available to physicians from these reference works, and the warnings in package inserts and the PDR ordinarily are adequate to alert physicians to drug hazards.

New developments, however, may render information in the PDR obsolete, and a manufacturer's failure promptly to update the medical profession may subject it to liability. If information is critical, the manufacturer may need to send "Dear Doctor" letters advising physicians individually of the new information.[144] However, the typically busy doctor may not regularly consult the PDR or even routinely read "Dear Doctor" letters. If the need to warn is compelling enough, reasonable care may require a drug company to use its salespersons who regularly call on doctors ("drug reps," formerly called "detail men"), to warn them personally of a particular risk.[145]

The Products Liability Restatement

Unlike the controversial provision on design defects in prescription drugs and medical devices,[146] the *Third Restatement* defines a manufacturer's responsibility for warning defects in drugs and medical devices in conventional negligence terms that give no cause for cavil. In § 6(d), the *Third Restatement* provides that "[a] prescription drug or medical device is not reasonably safe due to inadequate instructions or warnings if reasonable instructions or warnings regarding foreseeable risks of harm are not provided to" health-care providers or patients, depending on the applicability of the learned intermediary doctrine,[147] as discussed above and below. Principles of adequacy are embraced by the requirement that warnings and instructions be "reasonable," and the limitation on responsibility to "foreseeable" risks reflects the now well-established principle, discussed above, that the law should not hold manufacturers of drugs, medical

---

[144] As to the standards of adequacy for such letters, see, e.g., Lawson v. G.D. Searle & Co., 356 N.E.2d 779 (Ill. 1976).

[145] An early, leading case that examines factors bearing on whether a company must warn doctors in this manner is Sterling Drug, Inc. v. Yarrow, 408 F.2d 978 (8th Cir. 1969) (S.D. law) (Aralen; failure to use detail men to alert doctors of possible eye damage was unreasonable in light of the fact that the PDR and letters might not warn fast enough).

The FDA now publishes and regularly updates comprehensive drug, biologic, medical device, and dietary supplement safety information on its MedWatch Safety Information and Adverse Event Reporting website, available at www.fda.gov/safety/medwatch-fda-safety-information-and-adverse-event-reporting-program. See Scheve and Costa, The Learned Intermediary Doctrine After FDA's Drug Watch and PHRMA's Clinical Study Results Database, 73 Def. Couns. J. 12 (2006).

[146] See § 18.2, above.

[147] Products Liability Rest. § 6(d).

devices, or any other type of product responsible for harm that is unforeseeable or otherwise unavoidable under the prevailing state of the art, an important aspect of products liability law previously explored.[148]

The Learned Intermediary Doctrine—Warning Doctors, Not Patients

After obtaining the FDA's pre-market approval of a prescription drug's proposed warnings and instructions,[149] a manufacturer must provide such information to doctors and other health professionals, rather than directly to patients. Such "learned intermediaries" stand between the drug manufacturers and patients, dispensing medications and information they deem best in the circumstances. Thus, like the sophisticated user and bulk supplier doctrines previously examined,[150] the learned intermediary doctrine is an exception to the general rule that manufacturers must provide warnings directly to a product's ultimate user or consumer.[151] That is, under the "learned intermediary doctrine," a prescription drug manufacturer's duty to inform consumers normally runs only indirectly to physicians and other health care providers, rather than directly to consumers.[152]

The basic rationale for the learned intermediary doctrine is quite powerful: medical professionals, and only medical professionals, have the requisite knowledge, training, and judgment to properly match particular drugs containing distinctive benefits and dangers to particular patients with distinctive medical conditions and constitutions, and to properly monitor the results thereafter.[153] If manufacturers fulfill their obligations to provide full and fair information to health care professionals, the thought is that those professionals should be able to make intelligent, safe, and effective treatment decisions.[154] In turn, a prescribing doctor should, and is obliged under the law of torts to,

---

148 See § 10.4, above.

149 See notes 107–119, above, and accompanying text.

150 See § 9.5, above.

151 See Vitanza v. Upjohn Co., 778 A.2d 829, 836 (Conn. 2001).

152 See Poser, Unlabeled Drug Samples and the Learned Intermediary: The Case for Drug Company Liability Without Preemption, 62 Food & Drug L.J. 653 (2007); Kemp and Alleman, The Bulk Supplier, Sophisticated User, and Learned Intermediary Doctrines Since the Adoption of the Restatement (Third) of Torts, 26 Rev. Litig. 927 (2007); Ausness, Will More Aggressive Marketing Practices Lead to Greater Tort Liability for Prescription Drug Manufacturers?, 37 Wake Forest L. Rev. 97 (2002); Lear, The Learned Intermediary Doctrine in the Age of Direct Consumer Advertising, 65 Mo. L. Rev. 1101 (2000); Plant, The Learned Intermediary Doctrine: Some New Medicine for an Old Ailment, 81 Iowa L. Rev. 1007 (1996); Ausness, Learned Intermediaries and Sophisticated Users: Encouraging the Use of Intermediaries to Transmit Product Safety Information, 46 Syracuse L. Rev. 1185 (1996); Walsh, Rowland, and Dorfman, The Learned Intermediary Doctrine: The Correct Prescription for Drug Labeling, 48 Rutgers L. Rev. 821 (1996); Ferguson, Liability for Pharmaceutical Products: A Critique of the Learned Intermediary Rule, 12 Oxford J. Legal Stud. 59 (1992); Notes, 51 Stan. L. Rev. 1543 (2001) (learned intermediary doctrine and patient package inserts), 75 N.Y.U. L. Rev. 1452 (2000) (failure to warn liability for online prescriptions); Owen & Davis on Products Liability ch. 19.

153 Judge Wisdom provided one of the best descriptions of the rationale in Reyes v. Wyeth Labs., Inc., 498 F.2d 1264, 1276 (5th Cir. 1974) (Tex. law):

> Prescription drugs are likely to be complex medicines, esoteric in formula and varied in effect. As a medical expert, the prescribing physician can take into account the propensities of the drug, as well as the susceptibilities of his patient. His is the task of weighing the benefits of any medication against its potential dangers. The choice he makes is an informed one, an individualized medical judgment bottomed on a knowledge of both patient and palliative. Pharmaceutical companies then, who must warn ultimate purchasers of dangers inherent in patent drugs sold over the counter, in selling prescription drugs are required to warn only the prescribing physician, who acts as a "learned intermediary" between manufacturer and consumer.

See also Larkin v. Pfizer, Inc., 153 S.W.3d 758, 763–64 (Ky. 2004).

154 For a good summary of the doctrine's rationales, see Larkin v. Pfizer, Inc., 153 S.W.3d 758 (Ky. 2004).

inform the patient of a drug's benefits and risks (as well as the benefits and risks of alternative treatments, and none at all), and to monitor how the drug affects the patient.[155]

Sprouting in the 1960s,[156] and spreading widely in the early 1970s,[157] the learned intermediary doctrine is an established fixture in American products liability law, adopted now in a large majority of states.[158] In addition to prescription drugs, the learned intermediary doctrine has been applied to a wide variety of medical products—a cardiac pacemaker;[159] an implanted neurological electrical pulse generator;[160] an intrauterine device;[161] a spinal fixation device;[162] a herniated disk plate;[163] a heart catheter;[164] spinal pedicle screws;[165] an artificial knee;[166] a morphine pump;[167] an x-ray machine;[168] an electroconvulsive therapy machine;[169] an anesthesia machine;[170] nicotine chewing

---

155 See Smith, The Vagueness of Informed Consent, 1 Ind. Health L. Rev. 109 (2004); Keeton, Dobbs, Keeton, and Owen, Prosser and Keeton on the Law of Torts § 32, at 189–93; Dobbs, Law of Torts § 250.

156 See, e.g., Stottlemire v. Cawood, 213 F. Supp. 897, 899 (D.D.C. 1963); Sterling Drug, Inc. v. Cornish, 370 F.2d 82, 85 (8th Cir. 1966) (Mo. law) (With prescription drugs, "the purchaser's doctor is a learned intermediary between the purchaser and the manufacturer. If the doctor is properly warned of the possibility of a side effect in some patients, and is advised of the symptoms normally accompanying the side effect, there is an excellent chance that injury to the patient can be avoided."); Davis v. Wyeth Labs., Inc., 399 F.2d 121, 130 (9th Cir. 1968) (Idaho law). See also Magee v. Wyeth Labs., Inc., 29 Cal. Rptr. 322, 327–28 (Ct. App. 1963).

157 See, e.g., Incollingo v. Ewing, 282 A.2d 206, 220 (Pa. 1971); Hoffman v. Sterling Drug, Inc., 485 F.2d 132 (3d Cir. 1973) (Pa. law); Gravis v. Parke-Davis & Co., 502 S.W.2d 863, 870 (Tex. App. 1973) ("The entire system of drug distribution in America is set up so as to place the responsibility of distribution and use upon professional people. The laws and regulations prevent prescription type drugs from being purchased by individuals without the advice, guidance and consent of licensed physicians and pharmacists. These professionals are in the best position to evaluate the warnings put out by the drug industry."). See generally Merrill, Compensation for Prescription Drug Injuries, 59 Va. L. Rev. 1, 91 (1973).

158 See, e.g., Leavitt v. Ethicon, Inc., 524 F. Supp. 3d 360, 368 (D. Vt. 2021) ("forty-eight states have adopted, or a federal court has predicted the state's highest court would adopt, the learned intermediary doctrine"); In re Zimmer, NexGen Knee Implant Prods. Liab. Litig., 884 F.3d 746, 751–52 (7th Cir. 2018) (predicting the Wisconsin Supreme Court would adopt the learned intermediary doctrine; " 'at least thirty-five states have adopted some form of the learned intermediary doctrine within the prescription drug products-liability context or cited favorably to its application within this context' [and] the intermediate appellate courts in another 13 states have applied the learned-intermediary doctrine or have predicted that their supreme courts would do so" (citations omitted)); Centocor, Inc. v. Hamilton, 372 S.W.3d 140, 164 (Tex. 2012) (thorough review of doctrine); Meridia Prods. Liab. Litig. v. Abbott Labs., 447 F.3d 861, 867 (6th Cir. 2006) (N.J. law) ("the vast majority of jurisdictions—45 out of 50 states—apply the . . . doctrine to product liability claims"); Ehlis v. Shire Richwood, Inc., 367 F.3d 1013, 1017 (8th Cir. 2004) (N.D. law) (the doctrine "either applies or is recognized . . . in 48 states, the District of Columbia, and Puerto Rico"). A few states adopted the doctrine by statute. See Miss. Code Ann. § 11–1–63(c)(ii); N.J. Stat. Ann. § 2A:58C–4; N.C. Gen. Stat. Ann. § 99B–5(c); W. Va. Code Ann. § 55–7–30.

159 See Hurley v. Heart Physicians, P.C., 898 A.2d 777, 784 (Conn. 2006); Brooks v. Medtronic, Inc., 750 F.2d 1227 (4th Cir. 1984) (S.C. law).

160 See Creazzo v. Medtronic, Inc., 903 A.2d 24, 31–32 (Pa. Super. Ct. 2006).

161 See McKee v. Moore, 648 P.2d 21 (Okla. 1982).

162 See Vaccariello v. Smith & Nephew Richards, Inc., 763 N.E.2d 160 (Ohio 2002). See also Emody v. Medtronic, Inc., 238 F. Supp. 2d 1291 (N.D. Ala. 2003) (spinal fusion device).

163 See McCombs v. Synthes, 553 S.E.2d 17 (Ga. Ct. App. 2001).

164 See Phelps v. Sherwood Med. Indus., 836 F.2d 296 (7th Cir. 1987) (Me. law).

165 See King v. Danek Med., Inc., 37 S.W.3d 429 (Tenn. Ct. App. 2000).

166 See, e.g., Wegryn v. Smith & Nephew, Inc., 2008 WL 803405, at *3 (Conn. Super. Ct. 2008); Yanovich v. Zimmer Austin, Inc., 255 Fed. Appx. 957 (6th Cir. 2007) (Ohio law).

167 See Ellis v. C.R. Bard, Inc., 311 F.3d 1272 (11th Cir. 2002) (Ga. law).

168 See Kirsch v. Picker Int'l, Inc., 753 F.2d 670 (8th Cir. 1985) (Mo. law).

169 See Andre v. Mecta Corp., 587 N.Y.S.2d 334 (App. Div. 1992).

170 See Marks v. Ohmeda, Inc., 871 So.2d 1148 (La. Ct. App. 2004).

gum;[171] an elbow fixator device;[172] physical therapy resistance bands;[173] an inferior vena cava filter;[174] a urethral sling or pelvic mesh;[175] and a biological product used to repair injured cartilage.[176] The New York Supreme Court seems to have drawn the line at extended-wear contact lenses fitted by an optometrist.[177] While efforts to apply the doctrine outside the medical field have largely failed;[178] some courts, misled by the generality of the doctrine's name,[179] have used the "learned intermediary" label when applying principles of the "sophisticated user doctrine" to other types of products.[180]

It may be that the foundations of the learned intermediary rule are weakening somewhat,[181] but the rule was explicitly endorsed by the *Third Restatement* and appears

---

171 See Tracy v. Merrell Dow Pharms., Inc., 569 N.E.2d 875 (Ohio 1991). See also Jack v. Glaxo Wellcome, Inc., 239 F. Supp. 2d 1308 (N.D. Ga. 2002) (Zyban, a smoking suppressant drug containing bupropion, an antidepressant).

172 See O'Connell v. Biomet, Inc., 250 P.3d 1278, 1281–82 (Colo. App. 2010) (a surgically implanted medical device available only to physicians and obtained by prescription).

173 See Seifried v. Hygenic Corp., 410 S.W.3d 427, 433 (Tex. App. 2013) (duty to warn of risks of using bands extended only to the hospital, not the ultimate user).

174 See McClarty v. C.R. Bard, Inc., 2020 WL 6075520, at *10 (E.D. Mich. 2020) (an inferior vena cava filter is a surgically implanted medical device).

175 See Leavitt v. Ethicon, Inc., 524 F. Supp. 3d 360, 369 (D. Vt. 2021) (predicting that the Vermont Supreme Court would apply the learned intermediary doctrine to claims against the manufacturer of vaginal tape used for stress urinary incontinence); Wilichowski v. Boston Sci. Corp., 2021 WL 798869, at *4 (W.D. Ark. 2021) (issues of fact existed whether the mid-urethral sling manufacturer adequately warned the physician of the risks of Marlex polypropylene); Sluis v. Ethicon, Inc., 529 F. Supp. 3d 1004, 1010, 1018 (D.S.D. 2021) (predicting that the Supreme Court of South Dakota would apply the learned intermediary doctrine in a case involving the designer and manufacturer of pelvic mesh; a question of fact existed whether the physician had "substantially the same knowledge as an adequate warning from the manufacturer should have communicated").

176 See Rounds v. Genzyme Corp., 440 Fed. Appx. 753, 754 (11th Cir. 2011) (Fla. law) (product used plaintiff's cultured cells to regenerate knee articular cartilage).

177 See Bukowski v. CooperVision Inc., 592 N.Y.S.2d 807 (App. Div. 1993) (lenses caused corneal ulcers; no evidence that optometrist has ability to assimilate manufacturer's technical information to fulfill learned intermediary role).

The learned intermediary doctrine most certainly does not apply to over-the-counter medications, nor does it protect a retailer of such medicines from liability for selling such a product with defective warnings or instructions. See, e.g., Morales v. American Home Prods. Corp., 214 F. Supp. 2d 723 (S.D. Tex. 2002) (Alka-Selzer Plus).

178 See, e.g., Nye v. Bayer Cropscience, Inc., 347 S.W.3d 686, 703 (Tenn. 2011) (doctrine does not apply to workplace products liability claims); Gray v. Badger Mining Corp., 676 N.W.2d 268, 275–76 (Minn. 2004) (silica sand; learned intermediary defense is properly limited to pharmaceutical products and so refusing to extend it to the employer/employee relationship); Vitanza v. Upjohn Co., 778 A.2d 829, 845–46 (Conn. 2001) (learned intermediary and sophisticated user doctrines are dissimilar because learned intermediary doctrine applies only to medical field); Hall v. Ashland Oil Co., 625 F. Supp. 1515 (D. Conn. 1986) (differences between doctor-patient relationship and employer-employee relationship precluded application of learned intermediary doctrine to chemical manufacturer who warned decedent's employer but not decedent himself).

179 And perhaps these courts have felt the tug of the doctrine's historical roots in the more general principle that those who supply products to expert purchasers normally should be able to rely on them to pass along warnings to any employees or sub-vendees threatened by a product hazard. See, e.g., Magee v. Wyeth Labs., Inc., 29 Cal. Rptr. 322, 327–28 (Ct. App. 1963). See generally § 9.5, above.

180 See, e.g., Union Carbide Corp. v. Kavanaugh, 879 So.2d 42, 44–45 (Fla. Dist. Ct. App. 2004) (sanding compound that contained asbestos); Coleman v. Cintas Sales Corp., 40 S.W.3d 544 (Tex. App. 2001) (flammable uniform); Burke v. Dow Chem. Co., 797 F. Supp. 1128, 1133 (E.D.N.Y. 1992) (supplier of toxic chemical in "Rid-A-Bug" household insecticide that may have caused brain damage to children of pregnant women).

181 See, e.g., Castagnera and Gerner, The Gradual Enfeeblement of the Learned Intermediary Rule and the Argument in Favor of Abandoning It Entirely, 36 Tort & Ins. L.J. 119, 120 (2000) (describing a weakening of the rule due to "(1) the rise in consumer awareness, (2) the complexity of pharmaceutical products, (3) the development of clinical pharmacies that bring their own special expertise to bear on consumer and patient choices, and (4) the reduced time spent by patients in doctors' offices").

quite firmly entrenched for now.[182] Because the doctrine defines the scope of a pharmaceutical manufacturer's duty to warn, application of the rule involves a question of law for a court, not a factual question of adequacy for a jury.[183]

Exceptions to the Learned Intermediary Doctrine

If a manufacturer sells a prescription drug under circumstances where health professionals are unlikely to render the type of individualized balancing of risks and benefits contemplated by the learned intermediary doctrine, the manufacturer may need to provide warnings directly to patients. That is, when the rationale for the learned intermediary doctrine falls away, the general rule requiring manufacturers to warn consumers directly logically should return. This commonsense principle has spawned a number of supposed exceptions (often said to be three),[184] only the first of which has much support.

Mass Immunization Programs

The most established exception to the learned intermediary rule is for mass immunization programs where no health professional mediates information about drug risks for the benefit of the patient.[185] Most courts confronted with the issue have thus refused to apply the learned intermediary rule to situations where patients are vaccinated in assembly-line fashion, often by persons other than physicians, with no opportunity for individualized medical assessments. When people line up like lemmings to receive a flu, coronavirus, or other vaccination at a facility for mass distribution of a vaccine, the manufacturer must have taken all reasonable steps to ensure that each patient is directly provided warnings and instructions on risks the manufacturer should know the drug contains.[186] As an exception to the learned intermediary rule, which itself is an exception to the manufacturer's general obligation to warn consumers directly, the mass immunization doctrine restores the manufacturer's duty to provide warnings (by leaflets or posters) directly to all recipients of the vaccine. This true exception was

---

[182] See Products Liability Rest. § 6(d).

[183] See, e.g., Vitanza v. Upjohn Co., 778 A.2d 829 (Conn. 2001) (claim that manufacturer, which did provide adequate warnings of Ansaid's risks to doctors, should have placed warnings on drug samples could not be converted into a factual question of adequacy for a jury).

[184] Plaintiffs' lawyers and commentators sometimes argue for additional exceptions, and courts occasionally suggest, in dictum, the existence of one or more. See, e.g., *Vitanza*, 778 A.2d at 846–47 (listing six supposed exceptions, including "overpromoted drugs" and "drugs withdrawn from the market," but rejecting plaintiff's request for a prescription drug sample exception); In re Zyprexa Prods. Liab. Litig., 2009 WL 2004540, at *14 (E.D.N.Y. 2009) (Weinstein, J.) (citing dubious authority for the existence of an overpromotion exception in "unusual cases"); Poser, Unlabeled Drug Samples and the Learned Intermediary: The Case for Drug Company Liability Without Preemption, 62 Food & Drug L.J. 653 (2007) (arguing for drug sample exception); Woodside & Maggio, The Learned Intermediary Doctrine: Is It Eroding?, 52 Fed. Law. 28, 31 (Nov./Dec. 2005) (noting that plaintiffs sometimes argue that overpromotion by detail reps undermines "the physician's ability to act as an intermediary and insist that, in this context, drug manufacturers have a duty to warn consumers directly"). To date, however, no courts appear to have formally adopted any exceptions other than the three discussed here.

[185] See Franklin and Mais, Tort Law and Mass Immunization Programs: Lessons from the Polio and Flu Episodes, 65 Cal. L. Rev. 754 (1977).

[186] See Petty v. United States, 740 F.2d 1428, 1433–34 n.3 (8th Cir. 1984) (Iowa law) (quoting the warning provided to patients regarding the Swine Flu vaccine, which noted possible side effects, including "fever, chills, headache, or muscle aches" and special precautions to be taken by those interested in receiving the vaccine, namely, "[c]hildren under a certain age should not routinely receive flu vaccine").

applied in early cases to the polio vaccine,[187] and later to the Swine Flu vaccine.[188] Although a court has wavered here or there,[189] there is every reason to believe that courts will continue the beneficial practice of requiring that some financially responsible provider of mass immunization drugs—often the manufacturer—provides warnings by leaflet or other means directly to consumers in this context.

Birth Control Pills and Patches

In *MacDonald v. Ortho Pharmaceutical Corp.*,[190] the plaintiff suffered a stroke leaving her partially paralyzed after taking the defendant's birth control pills for an extended period of time, during which she had seen her physician once each year. The manufacturer provided information to consumers via a package insert that included a warning of the risks of blood clots but that did not specifically mention the possibility of strokes. After suffering a stroke, the plaintiff claimed that the manufacturer had a duty to provide full and adequate warnings directly to her, the patient, and not just to doctors. Although all but one of the fifteen prior reported judicial opinions had applied the learned intermediary doctrine to birth control pills, like other prescription drugs, a majority of the Massachusetts Supreme Judicial Court reinstated a jury verdict for the plaintiff, reasoning that oral contraceptives "stand apart" from other types of prescription medications because of the "heightened participation of patients in decisions relating to use of 'the pill'; the substantial risks affiliated with the product's use; the feasibility of direct warnings by the manufacturer to the user; the limited participation of the physician (annual prescriptions); and the possibility that oral communications between physicians and consumers may be insufficient or too scanty standing alone to apprise consumers fully of the product's dangers at the time the initial selection of a contraceptive method is made and at subsequent points when alternative methods may be considered."[191]

For these reasons, the *MacDonald* majority concluded that the learned intermediary doctrine should not apply to birth control pill manufacturers who, therefore, must provide warnings directly to ultimate users on the nature, gravity, and likelihood of foreseeable side effects, and who must advise consumers to ask their doctors about any other matters of concern. The dissenting justice, observing that manufacturers of prescription pharmaceuticals have a duty to provide full information on all material risks to prescribing physicians who, in turn, have a duty (under the informed consent doctrine, redressable in a malpractice action) to provide full information on all material

---

[187] See, e.g., Davis v. Wyeth Labs., Inc., 399 F.2d 121, 131 (9th Cir. 1968) (Idaho law); Reyes v. Wyeth Labs., 498 F.2d 1264, 1276 (5th Cir. 1974) (Tex. law) ("the manufacturer of a prescription drug who knows or has reason to know that it will not be dispensed as such a drug must provide the consumer with adequate information so that he can balance the risks and benefits of a given medication himself"); Givens v. Lederle, 556 F.2d 1341 (5th Cir. 1977) (Fla. law).

[188] See Brazzell v. United States, 788 F.2d 1352 (8th Cir. 1986) (Iowa law); Petty v. United States, 740 F.2d 1428 (8th Cir. 1984) (Iowa law).

[189] Compare Mazur v. Merck & Co., 964 F.2d 1348 (3d Cir. 1992) (Pa. law) (oral rubella vaccine maker satisfied duty by providing information to U.S. Center for Disease Control), with Allison v. Merck & Co., 878 P.2d 948, 959 (Nev. 1994) (measles, mumps, and rubella vaccine manufacturer could *not* delegate its duty to warn to CDC, whose information sheet made no mention of risks of blindness, deafness, and brain damage).

[190] 475 N.E.2d 65 (Mass. 1985).

[191] Id. at 70.

risks to patients for whom they prescribe the drug, argued that this traditional division of responsibility best allocates risks and responsibilities among the parties.[192]

While *MacDonald* frequently is cited as creating a new common-law exception to the learned intermediary rule for birth control pills, only a couple of federal judges followed it.[193] Other courts uniformly reject this exception and continue to apply the learned intermediary doctrine to birth control pills as other types of prescription pharmaceuticals.[194] A public health factor of possible relevance is that the *MacDonald* exception arguably creates an "over-warning" problem for birth control pills, since a manufacturer's warning, in addition to a doctor's, may frighten women away from using a drug that is beneficial to their health.[195] And this common-law birth control exception is now theoretically moot, because the FDA promulgated a regulation some time ago that requires manufacturers of birth control pills and other drugs containing estrogen to provide warnings in lay language directly to users via patient package inserts.[196]

Three decades after *MacDonald*, another Massachusetts court decided a case involving a 17-year-old college student, Duffy, who used an Ortho Evra birth-control patch her doctor prescribed because she wanted an easy and simple method of birth control other than pills:

> The patch prevents pregnancy by transferring synthetic forms of the hormones estrogen and progestin through the skin. Unlike oral birth control pills, which

---

[192] "The rules place on drug manufacturers the duty to gather, compile, and provide to doctors data regarding the use of their drugs, tasks for which the manufacturers are best suited, and the rules place on doctors the burden of conveying those data to their patients in a useful and understandable manner, a task for which doctors are best suited. Doctors, unlike printed warnings, can tailor to the needs and abilities of an individual patient the information that that patient needs in order to make an informed decision whether to use a particular drug. Manufacturers are not in position to give adequate advice directly to those consumers whose medical histories and physical conditions, perhaps unknown to the consumers, make them peculiarly susceptible to risk. Prescription drugs—including oral contraceptives—differ from other products because their dangers vary widely depending on characteristics of individual consumers." Id. at 74.

[193] See also Edwards v. Basel Pharms., 933 P.2d 298 (Okla. 1997) (dictum).

[194] See, e.g., Ideus v. Teva Pharms. USA, Inc., 986 F.3d 1098, 1102 (8th Cir. 2021) (following the "overwhelming majority rule" in cases where doctors have been adequately warned, the court refused to require a direct-to-consumer warning for an IUD that may break too easily on removal); In re Norplant Contraceptive Prods. Liab. Litig., 955 F. Supp. 700, 704 (E.D. Tex. 1997) ("Only a single jurisdiction, Massachusetts, recognizes an exception to the doctrine for prescription contraceptives."). See also Hanhan v. Johnson & Johnson, 2013 WL 5939720 (N.D. Ohio 2013) (Cal. law) (California law does not recognize birth control exception to learned intermediary doctrine; claim for blood clots from contraceptive patches barred where directing physician and health educator at birth control clinic both knew that drug doubled the risk of clots).

[195] A Gallup poll in 1985 showed that "Americans greatly overestimate the risks and understate the effectiveness of birth control methods, particularly the pill, leaving them vulnerable to unintended pregnancies." According to the American College of Obstetricians and Gynecologists, unwanted pregnancies and more than a million abortions each year needlessly threaten women's lives. Three quarters of the women surveyed thought that the pill presents substantial health risks, despite the fact that the risk of death from taking the pill is about half the mother's risk of death from childbirth. Pill Poll—National Survey Finds Many Have Bad Information, The State (Columbia, S.C.), Mar. 6, 1985, at 2A, col. 2.

[196] See 21 CFR § 310.501 (eff. Mar. 26, 2009) (patient package inserts required for oral contraceptives); 21 CFR § 310.515 (eff. Mar. 26, 2009) (requiring manufacturers to warn patients directly, by package insert, of benefits and risks of drugs containing estrogen). These "*MacDonald*" regulations reasonably suggest the availability of negligence per se actions against manufacturers who fail to comply. See Lukaszewicz v. Ortho Pharm. Corp., 510 F. Supp. 961, amended 532 F. Supp. 211 (E.D. Wis. 1981). But courts have been oddly unreceptive to such an approach. See, e.g., Hanhan v. Johnson & Johnson, 2013 WL 5939720 (N.D. Ohio 2013) (Cal. law) (notwithstanding FDA regulation, learned intermediary doctrine barred warning claim for blood clots by woman prescribed contraceptive patches). See also Martin v. Ortho Pharm., Corp., 661 N.E.2d 352 (Ill. 1996) (explicitly rejecting violation-of-warning regulation claim with respect to risk of birth limb reductions from pills used in first trimester of pregnancy).

must be taken at the same time each day, the patch is applied to the skin once per week for three weeks, followed by a fourth patch-free week.[197]

A package insert prepared by the manufacturer (J & J), a leaflet prepared by the pharmacy where Duffy bought the patches, and her prescribing doctor all explained the patch's risks, including stroke, heart attack, and blood clots. Three months after she began using the patch, Duffy died from a massive bilateral pulmonary embolus. Her mother sued J & J, claiming that its warnings were inadequate because they did not specify that the patch was twice as likely as birth control pills to cause deadly blood clots. The trial court granted summary judgment for J & J, and the intermediate appellate court affirmed:

> [The risk of blood clots in the lungs is] expressly set forth in the insert, where it is described in no less than four places. The greater dose of estrogen, and the corresponding increased risk of adverse events, such as blood clots, also is clearly stated in plain language. The insert also cautions that it is not a replacement for careful discussion between the patient and her healthcare professional and that these discussions should take place when the patient first uses the patch and during the patient's revisits. As a matter of law, the insert adequately warned both [her mother] and Duffy of the increased risk of developing blood clots that could result in death, as compared to the risks associated with the birth control pill, in terms understandable to a lay person.

Direct-to-Consumer Advertising

The learned intermediary doctrine may well be out of touch with how modern medicine is practiced and in a world where prescription drug manufacturers jump over health professionals to consumers via TV and other mass advertising and the internet.[198] In *Perez v. Wyeth Laboratories*,[199] the plaintiff experienced problems after being implanted with the Norplant contraceptive device. The plaintiff sued Wyeth (which had properly warned her doctor of possible complications) for failing to provide warnings directly to the plaintiff patient. The trial court granted summary judgment for the manufacturer, based on the learned intermediary doctrine as incorporated in a New Jersey statute, and the appellate division affirmed. In an important decision, the New Jersey Supreme Court reversed, ruling that the learned intermediary doctrine should no longer insulate prescription drug manufacturers from their duty to warn consumers directly when they seek to influence a patient's choice of drugs through mass-marketing.

---

[197] Niedner v. Ortho-McNeil Pharm., Inc., 58 N.E.3d 1080, 1083, 1086 (Mass. App. Ct. 2016).

[198] See, e.g., V. Schwartz, Silverman, Hulka, and Appel, Marketing Pharmaceutical Products in the Twenty-First Century: An Analysis of the Continued Viability of Traditional Principles of Law in the Age of Direct-To-Consumer Advertising, 32 Harv. J.L. & Pub. Pol'y 333 (2009); Hall, Regulating Direct-To-Consumer Advertising With Tort Law: Is the Law Finally Catching Up With the Market?, 31 W. New Eng. L. Rev. 333 (2009); Ausness, Will More Aggressive Marketing Practices Lead to Greater Tort Liability for Prescription Drug Manufacturers, 37 Wake Forest L. Rev. 97 (2002); Noah, Advertising Prescription Drugs to Consumers: Assessing the Regulatory and Liability Issues, 32 Ga. L. Rev. 141 (1997); T. Schwartz, Consumer-Directed Prescription Drug Advertising and the Learned Intermediary Rule, 46 Food Drug Cosm. L.J. 829 (1991); Comment, 41 Am. J. Trial Advoc. 563 (2018) (direct-to-consumer pharmaceutical advertising). See also Patsner, Direct-to-Consumer Advertising of Restricted, Surgically Implanted Medical Devices: What Does the Advertising Arena Look Like, and Whose Regulatory Problem Is It?, 39 Wm. Mitchell L. Rev. 1207 (2013).

For FDA regulation of direct-to-consumer advertisements of prescription drugs subsequent to the FDA Amendments Act of 2007, see note 118, above.

[199] 734 A.2d 1245 (N.J. 1999).

Perez reasoned that the learned intermediary doctrine is based on outmoded images of health care from a time when doctors gave medical advice in their offices, made house calls on request, charged only small sums for their advice, and prescribed medicines compounded by a neighborhood pharmacist—all at a time when "the prevailing attitude of law and medicine was that the 'doctor knows best.' "[200] Sadly, this picture is radically different from the health care world of today. Now, managed health care organizations are mammoth businesses, dispensing medical care and prescriptions impersonally; and medicines are manufactured in distant places, sold over the internet and in supermarket pharmacy departments, and often paid for by third-party providers. Against this backdrop, modern manufacturers of prescription drugs mass-market their wares directly to consumers by radio, television, the internet, billboards on public transportation, and in magazines.[201] The court observed that the problems in these advertising practices are manifest, permitting manufacturers and advertisers to manipulate information on safety and effectiveness which, at best, presents a diluted picture of a product's risks.[202]

Since *Perez*, several other courts have reconsidered the learned intermediary doctrine in light of direct-to-consumer advertising, sales of prescription pharmaceuticals over the internet from abroad, and the general depersonalization of health care delivery in the modern world. For eight years, all courts considering the issue rejected *Perez* and continued to apply the learned intermediary doctrine.[203] But in 2007, the West Virginia Supreme Court of Appeals, ruling on a matter of first impression, refused to adopt the learned intermediary doctrine in *State ex rel. Johnson & Johnson Corp. v. Karl*.[204] While acknowledging that most states have adopted the doctrine, and that many lower court decisions have applied it, the majority opinion listed twenty-one states whose high courts had *not* adopted this special drug exception to the ordinary duty of manufacturers to provide warnings directly to consumers.[205]

Agreeing with *Perez* that the learned intermediary doctrine is outmoded in the modern medical world, the *Karl* majority held that "manufacturers of prescription drugs are subject to the same duty to warn consumers about the risks of their products as other manufacturers."[206] Concurring, Justice Maynard observed that "[p]atients can read the labels, instructions and warnings, and if the manufacturer makes them clear enough, then patients can be proactive in working with their doctors to receive the best care."[207]

Despite the plausibility of *Karl*'s logic, the West Virginia legislature subsequently rejected the Supreme Court's approach and adopted the learned intermediary doctrine in prescription drug and medical device products liability claims for inadequate

---

200 Id. at 1247.

201 Id. at 1246–47.

202 Id. at 1252–53 (citing Hanson and Kysar, Taking Behavioralism Seriously: Some Evidence of Market Manipulation, 112 Harv. L. Rev. 1420 (1999)).

203 See, e.g., Beale v. Biomet, Inc., 492 F. Supp. 2d 1360, 1375–77 (S.D. Fla. 2007) (declining to follow *Perez*); In re Meridia Prods. Liab. Litig., 328 F. Supp. 2d 791, 812 n.19 (N.D. Ohio 2004) (same), aff'd 447 F.3d 861 (6th Cir. 2006); In re Norplant Contraceptive Prods. Liab. Litig., 165 F.3d 374 (5th Cir. 1999) (Ill. law) (learned intermediary doctrine shields Norplant manufacturer from having to warn patients of product's risks).

204 647 S.E.2d 899 (W. Va. 2007).

205 The court lists Arizona, Colorado, Idaho, Indiana, Iowa, Louisiana, Maine, Maryland, Michigan, Minnesota, Nevada, New Hampshire, New Mexico, North Dakota, Rhode Island, South Carolina, South Dakota, Vermont, West Virginia, Wisconsin, and Wyoming. Id. at 905.

206 *Karl*, 647 S.E.2d at 914.

207 Id. at 917, 919.

warnings and instructions.[208] Moreover, at least two state supreme courts, overturning intermediate court rulings, have adopted the learned intermediary doctrine and refused to engraft upon it an exception for direct-to-consumer advertising.[209]

Now that *Perez* is once again the sole surviving high court decision to reject the learned intermediary rule in cases of direct-to-consumer advertising, it appears doubtful that other jurisdictions will any time soon rethink the logic of this entrenched (if archaic) doctrine. Yet, why the law (or the FDA) should not require drug companies in the modern world to provide patients with important information (in lay language) about significant risks in dangerous drugs understandably eludes many who consider this problem.[210]

Status of Learned Intermediary Doctrine and Its Exceptions

In the 1990s, the *Products Liability Restatement* adopted the learned intermediary rule, provided a general exception wide enough to accommodate all three exceptions,[211] and specifically left open the question whether a new exception should be created for drugs that are mass-marketed directly to consumers.[212] In the end, however, one is left to wonder whether the exceptions matter much at all, since Congress and the FDA have adopted two of the three. As noted earlier, the FDA promulgated a "*MacDonald*" rule some time ago, requiring birth control manufacturers to provide warnings directly to users.[213]

And in 2007, Congress amended the Food, Drug, and Cosmetic Act to require that prescription drug advertisements on television and radio carry objective warnings of risks and contraindications.[214] Moreover, only one of the three exceptions—mass immunization programs—was ever accepted by more than a very small number of courts, and even the mass immunization exception has been applied infrequently.[215] What all this means, of course, is that the judicial learned intermediary doctrine today still stands tall and strong, and it displays very few "exception" holes.

---

[208] See W. Va. Code Ann. § 55–7–30 (2016).

[209] See Watts v. Medicis Pharm. Corp., 365 P.3d 944 (Ariz. 2016) (also adopting Products Liability Rest. § 6(b)); Centocor, Inc. v. Hamilton, 372 S.W.3d 140 (Tex. 2012). See also Dearinger v. Eli Lilly & Co., 2021 WL 2805328, at *2 (W.D. Wash. 2021), certifying the following question to the Washington Supreme Court: "Is a manufacturer, that promotes a prescription drug through 'direct-to-consumer' marketing, still exempt from warning the consumer of that drug's dangerous side effects under the 'Learned Intermediary Doctrine' adopted by the State of Washington in Terhune v. A.H. Robins Co., 577 P.2d 975 (Wash. 1978)?" Answering in the negative, the Washington Supreme Court rejected a "direct-to-consumer" exception to the learned intermediary doctrine. Dearinger v. Eli Lilly & Co., 2022 WL 1788992, at *8 (Wash. 2022).

[210] See, e.g., Lance v. Wyeth, 85 A.3d 434, 457 (Pa. 2014) (dictum; "[S]ome of the underpinnings of the [learned intermediary] principle have come into question in light of changed practices in the prescription drug industry. These include the emergence of direct-to-consumer advertising and the evolution of the health-care delivery system encompassing new forms of managed care.").

[211] Products Liability Rest. § 6(d) provides that a prescription drug or medical device is defective if the manufacturer fails to provide reasonable warnings of foreseeable risks to: (1) the doctor or other health-care provider, or (2) the patient, if the manufacturer should know that health-care providers are "not in a position to reduce the risks of harm in accordance with the instructions or warnings."

[212] Id. cmt. *e*.

[213] See note 196, above, and accompanying text.

[214] See note 118, above.

[215] See Mazur v. Merck & Co., 742 F. Supp. 239, 253 (E.D. Pa. 1990) ("All of the vaccine cases recognize the theoretical validity of the 'mass immunization exception' to the learned intermediary rule, but very few have found situations where its application is warranted.").

Duty of Brand-Name Drug Companies to Generic Drug Users

When a brand-name drug manufacturer wrongly fails to provide important information on risks to the FDA before a new drug is marketed, or drags its feet in adding post-sale warnings thereafter, generic drug producers are barred from improving their warnings until the brand-name maker does so, as previously discussed.[216] What this means is that users of a generic drug are unable to receive such warnings, even if the dangers have become well known in the drug industry, until the brand-name company eventually chooses to provide warnings to users of its own brand-name drugs. In such cases, the brand-name company's failure to issue appropriate warnings in a timely manner may well result in harm to numerous generic drug users whose doctors may fail to get this information to pass along to their patients. Since such failures of brand-name drug companies to provide adequate warnings to physicians foreseeably endangers users of generic drugs as well as users of the brand-name drug, an important question is whether brand-name companies have a duty toward these foreseeable victims.

This vexing duty question—exacerbated by the underlying preemption issue[217]—raises a host of problems[218] that have split the courts. Numerous courts have followed an early case, *Foster v. American Home Products Corp.*,[219] in holding that one company cannot be responsible for defects in the products of another.[220] While several other courts have ruled that the duty of care of makers of name-brand drugs does indeed extend to patients who foreseeably use generic versions of the drug,[221] it appears likely that most courts will continue to be drawn by the strong pull of *Foster*'s no-duty position.

---

[216] See § 14.5, at notes 248–259, above.

[217] See § 3.3, at note 149, and § 14.5, above. In 2013, the FDA proposed a rule that would have allowed generic drug makers to add new warnings they deemed appropriate. The generic drug makers were vehemently opposed to the proposed rule change, which they asserted "would be nothing short of catastrophic." See Savage, Generic Drug Makers Fight Rule on Health Risk Warnings, latimes.com (Feb. 16, 2014). The agency eventually withdrew its proposal in 2018, citing concerns raised in the public comments. See Fed. Reg. 64,301 (Dec. 14, 2018) (noting concerns about "significant competing interests" and acknowledging that the rule had "significant potential downsides").

[218] See generally V. Schwartz, Goldberg, and Silverman, Warning: Shifting Liability to Manufacturers of Brand-Name Medicines when the Harm was Allegedly Caused by Generic Drugs has Severe Side Effects, 81 Fordham L. Rev. 1835 (2013); Rostron, Prescription for Fairness: A New Approach to Tort Liability of Brand-Name and Generic Drug Manufacturers, 60 Duke L.J. 1123 (2011).

[219] 29 F.3d 165 (4th Cir. 1994) (Md. law).

[220] See, e.g., Johnson v. Novartis Pharm. Corp., 2020 WL 2300139, at *3 (W.D. Tex. 2020) (dismissing generic drug user's claims against brand named defendants); Trower v. Janssen Pharmaceuticals, Inc., 2019 WL 1571834, at *4 (D. Del. 2019); McNair v. Johnson & Johnson, 818 S.E.2d 852, 863 (W. Va. 2018) ("there is no cause of action [for failing to warn or] negligent misrepresentation against a brand-name drug manufacturer when the drug ingested was produced by a generic drug manufacturer"); In re Zofran (Ondansetron) Products Liability Litigation, 261 F. Supp. 3d 62, 71 (D. Mass. 2017) (an "overwhelming majority of courts" so hold); Coleson v. Janssen Pharm., Inc., 251 F. Supp. 3d 716, 720–22 (S.D.N.Y. 2017); Guarino v. Wyeth, LLC, 719 F.3d 1245, 1252 (11th Cir. 2013) ("the overwhelming national consensus . . . is that a brand-name manufacturer cannot be liable for injuries caused by the ingestion of the generic form of a product"); Schrock v. Wyeth, Inc., 727 F.3d 1273, 1285–86 (10th Cir. 2013) (Okla. law); Strayhorn v. Wyeth Pharms., Inc., 737 F.3d 378, 405 (6th Cir. 2013) (Tenn. law).

[221] See, e.g., In re Fluoroquinolone Prods. Liab. Litig., 517 F. Supp. 3d 806, 821 (D. Minn. 2021) (Ill. law) (brand name manufacturer had duty to generic user, limited to the brand name defendant's creation of the warning label upon which the generic user foreseeably relied); T.H. v. Novartis Pharms. Corp., 407 P.3d 18, 29 (Cal. 2017) ("a brand-name drug manufacturer has the duty . . . to warn of the risks about which it knew or reasonably should have known, regardless of whether the consumer is prescribed the brand-name drug or its generic 'bioequivalent' "); Kellogg v. Wyeth, 762 F. Supp. 2d 694, 706 (D. Vt. 2010) (brand name manufacturer owes duty of care to avoid causing injury to consumers of generic bioequivalents of its drug). Compare Rafferty v. Merck & Co., 92 N.E.3d 1205, 1219 (Mass. 2018) (brand-name manufacturer did not owe a duty to warn

§ 18.4 PHARMACISTS

Pharmacists dispense millions of prescriptions for drugs in America each day.[222] While doctors prescribe pharmaceutical drugs, they typically know much less about such drugs, which they normally study for one to three semesters, than pharmacists, who study all aspects of drug therapy for five to seven years.[223] For whatever reasons, doctors quite often prescribe inappropriate prescription drugs for their patients, causing numerous patients to suffer adverse drug reactions—many of which could be easily prevented if patients received adequate drug warnings, which often they do not. Studies show that a large proportion of drug prescriptions contain errors that result in adverse drug events,[224] and that most persons are inadequately warned, either by their doctors or pharmacists, of drug interactions and other hazards of prescription drugs.[225] These facts suggest that pharmacists, perhaps, should have a duty of reasonable care to warn patients of hazards in prescription drugs.[226]

Because pharmacists are more in the nature of service providers (like doctors) than retail merchants (like hatters), they are subject to liability for selling prescription drugs only in negligence, not strict liability.[227] In filling prescriptions, pharmacists are held to the highest standard of care, such that a pharmacist who makes a mistake in filling a

generic user under common-law negligence; but the court would impose a duty to warn generic users where a brand-name manufacturer recklessly disregarded users' safety).

For negligent misrepresentation claims by generic drug users against brand-name manufacturers, see § 3.3, above, and for claims against generic drug manufacturers in the preemption context, see § 14.5, above.

[222] See Huang, The Omnibus Reconciliation Act of 1990: Redefining Pharmacists' Legal Responsibilities, 24 Am. J.L. & Med. 417, 418 (1998).

[223] See id.

[224] See, e.g., Hornish, Just What the Doctor Ordered—Or Was It?: Missouri Pharmacists' Duty of Care In the 21st Century, 65 Mo. L. Rev. 1075, 1076 (2000) (noting that "courts have begun to recognize that pharmacists are the last chance that the system has to correct itself, and that pharmacists are experts in pharmaceutical science and should be treated as professionals").

[225] See Huang, above note 222, at 419.

[226] See Karwaki, Establishing A Patient-Pharmacist Relationship: Clarifying Duties and Improving Patient Care, 72 Baylor L. Rev. 507 (2020); Williams et. al., The Role of the Pharmacist in Addressing the Opioid Crisis, 11 Alb. Gov't L. Rev. 174 (2018); Myhra, The Pharmacist's Duty to Warn in Texas Reconsidered within a National Framework, 27 Rev. Litig. 607 (2008); Smearman, Drawing the Line: The Legal, Ethical and Public Policy Implications of Refusal Clauses for Pharmacists, 48 Ariz. L. Rev. 469 (2006); Fentiman, Internet Pharmacies and the Need for a New Federalism: Protecting Consumers While Increasing Access to Prescription Drugs, 56 Rutgers L. Rev. 119 (2003); Hornish, above note 224; Huang, above note 222; Termini, The Pharmacist Duty To Warn Revisited: The Changing Role of Pharmacy In Health Care and the Resultant Impact On the Obligation Of a Pharmacist To Warn, 24 Ohio N.U. L. Rev. 551 (1998); Brushwood, The Pharmacist's Duty Under OBRA-90 Standards, 18 J. Legal Med. 475 (1997); Furrow, Enterprise Liability for Bad Outcomes from Drug Therapy: The Doctor, the Hospital, the Pharmacy, and the Drug Firm, 44 Drake L. Rev. 377 (1996); Cacciatore, Computers, OBRA 90 and the Pharmacist's Duty to Warn, 5 J. Pharmacy & L. 103 (1996); Annots., 79 A.L.R.5th 409 (2000) (pharmacist liability for failure to warn of potential drug interactions), 44 A.L.R.5th 393 (1996) (liability for harm caused by accurate prescriptions), Annot., 3 A.L.R.4th 270 (1981) (liability in negligence for incorrectly filling drug prescriptions). See also National Association of Boards of Pharmacy, Survey of Pharmacy Law (annual survey, at https://nabp.pharmacy/resources/publications/survey-of-pharmacy-law/, of drug laws, licensing, census data, etc. from all U.S. jurisdictions).

[227] See, e.g., Madison v. American Home Prods. Corp., 595 S.E.2d 493 (S.C. 2004) (pharmacy not subject to strict liability for properly filling prescription in accordance with doctor's orders); Schaerrer v. Stewart's Plaza Pharmacy, Inc., 79 P.3d 922 (Utah 2003); Coyle v. Richardson-Merrell, Inc., 584 A.2d 1383 (Pa. 1991); Murphy v. E.R. Squibb & Sons, Inc., 710 P.2d 247 (Cal. 1985); Annot., 3 A.L.R.4th 270 (1981); Products Liability Rest. § 6(e) (pharmacists liable only for filling prescriptions incorrectly and for negligence; no strict liability for selling prescription drugs or medical devices with design or warning defects). *Contra* Griffith v. Blatt, 51 P.3d 1256 (Or. 2002) (pharmacist who sold prescription lotion was "seller" under § 402A and, hence, subject to strict liability in tort for failing to warn); Heredia v. Johnson, 827 F. Supp. 1522 (D. Nev. 1993).

prescription is almost certainly responsible for any resulting harm.[228] But pharmacists long have been held to have no duty, apart from not misrepresenting facts about a drug,[229] other than to dispense drugs accurately according to the terms of a valid prescription.[230]

In particular, pharmacists widely are held to have no general duty to warn patients—not even to pass along package inserts (intended for physicians) containing detailed warnings—of hazards or side effects in prescription drugs that they dispense.[231] The pharmacist's immunity from a general duty to warn patients has been justified on a number of grounds, including the learned intermediary doctrine's placement of warning responsibilities solely on doctors, nurse practitioners, and similar health care professionals who theoretically are aware of a patient's particular constitution and treatment needs, as well as the benefits and dangers of particular prescription drugs; the burdens on pharmacists of having to second-guess decisions of prescribing doctors; the confusion of patients receiving conflicting information from their doctors and pharmacists; and an assumption that doctors are simply better skilled than pharmacists at evaluating the possible consequences of prescription medications.[232]

---

[228] See, e.g., Troppi v. Scarf, 187 N.W.2d 511, 513 (Mich. Ct. App. 1971) (negligence in filling prescription for birth control pills resulting in unwanted child); Burke v. Bean, 363 S.W.2d 366, 368 (Tex. App. 1962) (sale of Oxsoralen capsules when Oxacholin tablets prescribed).

[229] See, e.g., Rite Aid Corp. v. Levy-Gray, 894 A.2d 563, 579 (Md. 2006) (learned intermediary doctrine does not protect pharmacy from breach of express warranty claim for incorrectly stating that drug could be taken with food or milk if it upset the client's stomach). Compare Carrozza v. CVS Pharm., Inc., 992 F.3d 44, 60–61 (1st Cir. 2021) (Mass. law) (dismissing breach of implied warranty claim; "a pharmacist's dispensation of prescribed medication is predominately the provision of services, and not the sale of goods").

[230] See, e.g., Kampe v. Howard Stark Prof'l Pharmacy, Inc., 841 S.W.2d 223 (Mo. Ct. App. 1992) (properly filling legal prescription fulfills pharmacist's duty), abrogated by Homer v. Spalitto, 1 S.W.3d 519, 524 (Mo. Ct. App. 1999) (rejecting idea that the only function "a pharmacist must perform to fulfill his duty is to dispense drugs according to a physician's prescription"). See generally Huang, above note 222.

[231] See, e.g., Aldrich v. Ohm Specialty Pharmacy, LLC, 2018 WL 5276416, at *5 (Mich. Ct. App. 2018) (no duty to warn patients or third parties of fentanyl side effects or to monitor prescribed use; reviewing cases); Hernandez v. Walgreen Co., 49 N.E.3d 453, 465 (Ill. App. Ct. 2015) (pharmacies did not have a duty to monitor decedent's methadone prescription history, "determine whether such use was 'excessive,' or to communicate a corresponding warning to the prescribing physician or the decedent"); Baymiller v. Ranbaxy Pharms., Inc., 2012 WL 2727874, at *5 (D. Nev. 2012) (after taking anti-depressants, patient attacked and killed husband, and then committed suicide; pharmacies had no duty to warn customer of "generalized risks inherent" in prescriptions); Kowalski v. Rose Drugs of Dardanelle, Inc., 378 S.W.3d 109 (Ark. 2011) (3–2 decision); Deed v. Walgreen Co., 927 A.2d 1001, 1003–04 (Conn. Super. Ct. 2007) (pharmacy customer died from acute toxicity resulting from 149 prescriptions filled according to physician directions in the year prior to her death; pharmacy had no duty to warn); Schaerrer v. Stewart's Plaza Pharmacy, Inc., 79 P.3d 922 (Utah 2003) (pharmacist compounded and sold phen-fen without warning of risks); Moore v. Memorial Hosp. of Gulfport, 825 So.2d 658 (Miss. 2002) (pharmacist did not warn pregnant woman that Diovan was contraindicated for pregnancy, and child suffered kidney failure as a result); In re Rezulin Prods. Liab. Litig., 133 F. Supp. 2d 272 (S.D.N.Y. 2001) (16 actions from several states on diabetes medication; no general duty to warn in Alabama, Mississippi, Louisiana, Texas, or West Virginia); Frye v. Medicare-Glaser Corp., 605 N.E.2d 557 (Ill. 1992) (no duty to warn); Laws v. Johnson, 799 S.W.2d 249, 251–55 (Tenn. Ct. App. 1990) (no liability for removing package insert that warned of risk of heart attack); McKee v. American Home Prods. Corp., 782 P.2d 1045 (Wash. 1989) (5–4 decision) (pharmacists refilled potentially addictive amphetamine, prescribed as an appetite suppressant, for 10 years without warning of addiction risk or passing on drug insert that warned about it); Stebbins v. Concord Wrigley Drugs, Inc., 416 N.W.2d 381 (Mich. Ct. App. 1987) (no duty to warn of drowsiness that caused car accident); Pysz v. Henry's Drug Store, 457 So.2d 561 (Fla. Dist. Ct. App. 1984) (doctor's responsibility, not pharmacist's, to warn plaintiff of addiction risk of Quaaludes dispensed for more than 9 years).

[232] See, e.g., Flores v. Merck & Co., 2022 WL 798374, at *5 (D. Nev. 2022) (under the learned intermediary doctrine "pharmacists do not have a 'duty to warn of a prescribed medication's generalized risks'"); Carista v. Valuck, 394 P.3d 253, 259 (Okla. Civ. App. 2016) (pharmacy's duty "is limited by [principles of] and exceptions to the learned intermediary doctrine"); Chamblin v. K-Mart Corp., 612 S.E.2d 25, 27 (Ga. Ct. App. 2005) (learned intermediary rule shields pharmacists from duty to warn of drug side effects);

Yet, cracks are beginning to appear in the pharmacist's general immunity from a duty to warn, reflecting legislative requirements that pharmacists monitor and counsel their clients about prescription drugs, a development that has stimulated increased education and professionalism in this field.[233] In a number of cases, courts have held that pharmacists may have a duty of reasonable care to warn in certain circumstances. First, pharmacists are subject to liability in negligence for failing to recognize a clear and obvious error present on the face of a prescription. So, if a prescription fails to state a medication's maximum dosage, it is patently defective on its face, and a pharmacist may be subject to liability in negligence for failing to check with the prescribing physician or inform the patient of this important dosage problem.[234] Or if a drug has been withdrawn from the market, even if prescribed, the pharmacist may have a duty to check with the doctor or warn the patient.[235] Further, a pharmacist may have a duty to warn a customer or contact the physician if the pharmacist knows a drug is contraindicated for the particular customer, as when a pharmacist knows a customer is an alcoholic,[236] has an allergy,[237] or is taking another, incompatible drug.[238] In addition, if a pharmacist undertakes to collect data on client allergies,[239] to monitor client prescriptions for drug interactions,[240] or, perhaps, to warn of side effects,[241] the pharmacist normally is bound to perform the undertaking with reasonable care.[242] In these and other situations where a pharmacist has special knowledge of a risk to a particular client, courts have

---

Schaerrer v. Stewart's Plaza Pharmacy, Inc., 79 P.3d 922 (Utah 2003) (information may confuse consumers); Moore v. Memorial Hosp. of Gulfport, 825 So.2d 658 (Miss. 2002) (learned intermediary doctrine protects pharmacists); Moore v. Wyeth-Ayerst Labs., 236 F. Supp. 2d 509, 512–13 (D. Md. 2002) ("it is unwise to impose liability on a pharmacist for filling a prescription signed by the physician, because the physician is in a better position to evaluate the patient's medical needs"); Morgan v. Wal-Mart Stores, Inc., 30 S.W.3d 455, 467 (Tex. App. 2000) (thorough review of a pharmacist's duty to warn, and retaining general no-duty rule).

233 See Huang, above note 222.

234 See Horner v. Spalitto, 1 S.W.3d 519 (Mo. Ct. App. 1999); Riff v. Morgan Pharmacy, 508 A.2d 1247 (Pa. Super. Ct. 1986). See also Nail v. Publix Super Markets, Inc., 72 So.3d 608, 616 (Ala. 2011) (pharmacy failed to inform patient that Coumadin dosage was increased from 1 to 5 milligrams).

235 See Downing v. Hyland Pharmacy, 194 P.3d 944, 949 (Utah 2008) (reversing summary judgment for defendant).

236 See Hand v. Krakowski, 453 N.Y.S.2d 121 (App. Div. 1982).

237 See Klasch v. Walgreen Co., 264 P.3d 1155 (Nev. 2011) (pharmacist knew of patient's sulfa allergy); Happel v. Wal-Mart Stores, Inc., 766 N.E.2d 1118 (Ill. 2002) (because pharmacy undertook to compile plaintiff's allergies, it had superior knowledge and a duty to exercise reasonable care to warn of foreseeable risk).

238 See Brienze v. Casserly, 2003 WL 23018810 (Mass. Super. Ct. 2003) (pharmacist has duty to warn particular customer of potentially adverse interaction of two drugs that pharmacist knows customer is taking). Compare Powers v. Thobhani, 903 So.2d 275, 278–79 (Fla. Dist. Ct. App. 2005) (reversing summary judgment for pharmacy in case where patient died from an overdose of OxyCodone and many other prescription narcotics for neck and back pain that pharmacy repeatedly filled too closely in time).

239 See Klasch v. Walgreen Co., 264 P.3d 1155, 1160–61 (Nev. 2011) (sulfa allergy); Happel v. Wal-Mart Stores, Inc., 766 N.E.2d 1118, 1124 (Ill. 2002) (pharmacy undertook to compile plaintiff's allergies, giving it superior knowledge and a duty to exercise reasonable care to warn of this foreseeable risk).

240 See Allen v. Kroger Co., 2018 WL 6729646, at *4 (M.D. Ga. 2018) (under Ga. Code Ann. § 26–4–84, defendant had a duty to monitor decedent's "prescription record, identify potential drug-drug interactions, and take 'appropriate steps' to mitigate the risk of those interactions"); Baker v. Arbor Drugs, Inc., 544 N.W.2d 727, 731 (Mich. Ct. App. 1996) (client died from adverse interaction of two drugs; "defendant voluntarily assumed a duty of care when it implemented the Arbortech Plus system and then advertised that this system would detect harmful drug interactions for its customers").

241 See, e.g., In re Propulsid Prods. Liab. Litig., 2002 WL 1446714 (E.D. La. 2002); Cottam v. CVS Pharmacy, 764 N.E.2d 814 (Mass. 2002) (by providing partial list of side effects, reasonable care might require including impotency). *Contra* Kasin v. Osco Drug, Inc., 728 N.E.2d 77 (Ill. App. Ct. 2000) (by listing some side effects, pharmacy did not have duty to list them all).

242 See Rest. (3d) of Torts: Liability for Physical and Emotional Harm § 43 (liability for negligent undertakings, if risk increased or plaintiff relies on undertaking).

sometimes broken through the traditional immunity and held pharmacists to a duty of reasonable care to warn of the risk of addiction,[243] potential drug interactions,[244] and other adverse effects of prescription drugs.[245]

How far these cracks in the pharmacist's no-duty-to-warn wall eventually may propagate is impossible to say. There clearly is no stampede to break down the pharmacist's virtual immunity from a warning obligation.[246] Yet some courts are beginning to recognize that the pharmacy profession is changing in ways suggesting that these strategically positioned experts in prescription pharmaceuticals might properly bear more responsibility for protecting patients from the hazards of such medications.[247]

---

[243] Hooks SuperX, Inc. v. McLaughlin, 642 N.E.2d 514 (Ind. 1994); Lasley v. Shrake's Country Club Pharmacy, Inc., 880 P.2d 1129 (Ariz. Ct. App. 1994).

[244] See Baker v. Arbor Drugs, 544 N.W.2d 727 (Mich. Ct. App. 1996) (pharmacist assumed a duty to warn by advertising that its computerized drug detection system identified and prevented drug interactions); Dooley v. Everett, 805 S.W.2d 380 (Tenn. Ct. App. 1990) (antibiotic and asthma medication).

[245] See, e.g., Oleckna v. Daytona Disc. Pharmacy, 162 So.3d 178, 183 (Fla. Dist. Ct. App. 2015) (controlled substance prescription quantity, frequency, dosage, or combination such that "reasonable pharmacist would either have checked with the prescribing doctor or warned the patient"); Guillory v. Dr. X, 679 So.2d 1004, 1010 (La. Ct. App. 1996). See also Pittman v. Upjohn Co., 890 S.W.2d 425, 435 (Tenn. 1994) (but duty did not extend to patient's grandson).

[246] See, e.g., Morgan v. Wal-Mart Stores, Inc., 30 S.W.3d 455, 467 (Tex. App. 2000) (thorough review of a pharmacist's duty to warn, concluding that general no-duty rule should be retained).

[247] For example, in Correa v. Schoeck, 98 N.E.3d 191, 198 (Mass. 2018), an epilepsy patient suffered a fatal seizure after her insurer denied coverage on refills submitted without physician-approved authorization and the family was unable to pay $399.99 for the seizure medication. In this situation, the court ruled:

> In light of the evolving nature of the pharmacist-patient relationship, Walgreens's specific knowledge regarding the need for prior authorization, the industry-wide customs and practices of pharmacies handling prior authorization requests, and the foreseeability of the harm to [the deceased], we conclude that Walgreens owed a limited duty to take reasonable steps to notify both [the deceased] and [the physician] of the need for prior authorization each time [the deceased] tried to fill her prescription.

See also Downing v. Hyland Pharmacy, 194 P.3d 944, 947 (Utah 2008) (surveying cases):

> [Most recent decisions addressing pharmacists and the learned intermediary rule recognize] limits or exceptions to its scope in the negligence context, concluding that its protections extend only to warnings about general side effects of the drugs in question, but not to specific problems known to the pharmacist such as prescriptions for excessively dangerous amounts of the drug or for drugs contraindicated by information about a patient. These holdings attempt to account for the nature of modern pharmacy practice and to apply traditional common law negligence rules to that practice.

Table of Cases

Index

References are to Pages

PROPELLER GUARDS

PROXIMATE CAUSE